Oxford Dictionary of
National Biography

Volume 30

Oxford Dictionary of National Biography

IN ASSOCIATION WITH
The British Academy

From the earliest times to the year 2000

Edited by
H. C. G. Matthew
and
Brian Harrison

Volume 30
Jenner–Keayne

OXFORD
UNIVERSITY PRESS

OXFORD
UNIVERSITY PRESS

Great Clarendon Street, Oxford OX2 6DP

Oxford University Press is a department of the University of Oxford.
It furthers the University's objective of excellence in research, scholarship,
and education by publishing worldwide in

Oxford New York

Auckland Bangkok Buenos Aires Cape Town
Chennai Dar es Salaam Delhi Hong Kong Istanbul Karachi
Kolkata Kuala Lumpur Madrid Melbourne Mexico City Mumbai Nairobi
São Paulo Shanghai Taipei Tokyo Toronto

Oxford is a registered trade mark of Oxford University Press
in the UK and in certain other countries

Published in the United States
by Oxford University Press Inc., New York

British Library Cataloguing in Publication Data
Data available

Library of Congress Cataloging in Publication Data
Data available: for details see volume 1, p. iv

ISBN 0-19-861380-6 (this volume)
ISBN 0-19-861411-X (set of sixty volumes)

Text captured by Alliance Phototypesetters, Pondicherry
Illustrations reproduced and archived by
Alliance Graphics Ltd, UK
Typeset in OUP Swift by Interactive Sciences Limited, Gloucester
Printed in Great Britain on acid-free paper by
Butler and Tanner Ltd,
Frome, Somerset

LIST OF ABBREVIATIONS

1 General abbreviations

AB	bachelor of arts
ABC	Australian Broadcasting Corporation
ABC TV	ABC Television
act.	active
A$	Australian dollar
AD	*anno domini*
AFC	Air Force Cross
AIDS	acquired immune deficiency syndrome
AK	Alaska
AL	Alabama
A level	advanced level [examination]
ALS	associate of the Linnean Society
AM	master of arts
AMICE	associate member of the Institution of Civil Engineers
ANZAC	Australian and New Zealand Army Corps
appx *pl.* appxs	appendix(es)
AR	Arkansas
ARA	associate of the Royal Academy
ARCA	associate of the Royal College of Art
ARCM	associate of the Royal College of Music
ARCO	associate of the Royal College of Organists
ARIBA	associate of the Royal Institute of British Architects
ARP	air-raid precautions
ARRC	associate of the Royal Red Cross
ARSA	associate of the Royal Scottish Academy
art.	article / item
ASC	Army Service Corps
Asch	Austrian Schilling
ASDIC	Antisubmarine Detection Investigation Committee
ATS	Auxiliary Territorial Service
ATV	Associated Television
Aug	August
AZ	Arizona
b.	born
BA	bachelor of arts
BA (Admin.)	bachelor of arts (administration)
BAFTA	British Academy of Film and Television Arts
BAO	bachelor of arts in obstetrics
bap.	baptized
BBC	British Broadcasting Corporation / Company
BC	before Christ
BCE	before the common (*or* Christian) era
BCE	bachelor of civil engineering
BCG	bacillus of Calmette and Guérin [inoculation against tuberculosis]
BCh	bachelor of surgery
BChir	bachelor of surgery
BCL	bachelor of civil law

BCnL	bachelor of canon law
BCom	bachelor of commerce
BD	bachelor of divinity
BEd	bachelor of education
BEng	bachelor of engineering
bk *pl.* bks	book(s)
BL	bachelor of law / letters / literature
BLitt	bachelor of letters
BM	bachelor of medicine
BMus	bachelor of music
BP	before present
BP	British Petroleum
Bros.	Brothers
BS	(1) bachelor of science; (2) bachelor of surgery; (3) British standard
BSc	bachelor of science
BSc (Econ.)	bachelor of science (economics)
BSc (Eng.)	bachelor of science (engineering)
bt	baronet
BTh	bachelor of theology
bur.	buried
C.	command [identifier for published parliamentary papers]
c.	*circa*
c.	*capitulum pl. capitula*: chapter(s)
CA	California
Cantab.	Cantabrigiensis
cap.	*capitulum pl. capitula*: chapter(s)
CB	companion of the Bath
CBE	commander of the Order of the British Empire
CBS	Columbia Broadcasting System
cc	cubic centimetres
C$	Canadian dollar
CD	compact disc
Cd	command [identifier for published parliamentary papers]
CE	Common (*or* Christian) Era
cent.	century
cf.	compare
CH	Companion of Honour
chap.	chapter
ChB	bachelor of surgery
CI	Imperial Order of the Crown of India
CIA	Central Intelligence Agency
CID	Criminal Investigation Department
CIE	companion of the Order of the Indian Empire
Cie	Compagnie
CLit	companion of literature
CM	master of surgery
cm	centimetre(s)

Cmd	command [identifier for published parliamentary papers]	edn	edition
CMG	companion of the Order of St Michael and St George	EEC	European Economic Community
		EFTA	European Free Trade Association
Cmnd	command [identifier for published parliamentary papers]	EICS	East India Company Service
		EMI	Electrical and Musical Industries (Ltd)
CO	Colorado	Eng.	English
Co.	company	enl.	enlarged
co.	county	ENSA	Entertainments National Service Association
col. *pl.* cols.	column(s)	ep. *pl.* epp.	*epistola(e)*
Corp.	corporation	ESP	extra-sensory perception
CSE	certificate of secondary education	esp.	especially
CSI	companion of the Order of the Star of India	esq.	esquire
CT	Connecticut	est.	estimate / estimated
CVO	commander of the Royal Victorian Order	EU	European Union
cwt	hundredweight	ex	sold by (*lit.* out of)
$	(American) dollar	excl.	excludes / excluding
d.	(1) penny (pence); (2) died	exh.	exhibited
DBE	dame commander of the Order of the British Empire	exh. cat.	exhibition catalogue
		f. *pl.* ff.	following [pages]
DCH	diploma in child health	FA	Football Association
DCh	doctor of surgery	FACP	fellow of the American College of Physicians
DCL	doctor of civil law	facs.	facsimile
DCnL	doctor of canon law	FANY	First Aid Nursing Yeomanry
DCVO	dame commander of the Royal Victorian Order	FBA	fellow of the British Academy
DD	doctor of divinity	FBI	Federation of British Industries
DE	Delaware	FCS	fellow of the Chemical Society
Dec	December	Feb	February
dem.	demolished	FEng	fellow of the Fellowship of Engineering
DEng	doctor of engineering	FFCM	fellow of the Faculty of Community Medicine
des.	destroyed	FGS	fellow of the Geological Society
DFC	Distinguished Flying Cross	fig.	figure
DipEd	diploma in education	FIMechE	fellow of the Institution of Mechanical Engineers
DipPsych	diploma in psychiatry		
diss.	dissertation	FL	Florida
DL	deputy lieutenant	*fl.*	*floruit*
DLitt	doctor of letters	FLS	fellow of the Linnean Society
DLittCelt	doctor of Celtic letters	FM	frequency modulation
DM	(1) Deutschmark; (2) doctor of medicine; (3) doctor of musical arts	fol. *pl.* fols.	folio(s)
		Fr	French francs
DMus	doctor of music	Fr.	French
DNA	dioxyribonucleic acid	FRAeS	fellow of the Royal Aeronautical Society
doc.	document	FRAI	fellow of the Royal Anthropological Institute
DOL	doctor of oriental learning	FRAM	fellow of the Royal Academy of Music
DPH	diploma in public health	FRAS	(1) fellow of the Royal Asiatic Society; (2) fellow of the Royal Astronomical Society
DPhil	doctor of philosophy		
DPM	diploma in psychological medicine	FRCM	fellow of the Royal College of Music
DSC	Distinguished Service Cross	FRCO	fellow of the Royal College of Organists
DSc	doctor of science	FRCOG	fellow of the Royal College of Obstetricians and Gynaecologists
DSc (Econ.)	doctor of science (economics)		
DSc (Eng.)	doctor of science (engineering)	FRCP(C)	fellow of the Royal College of Physicians of Canada
DSM	Distinguished Service Medal		
DSO	companion of the Distinguished Service Order	FRCP (Edin.)	fellow of the Royal College of Physicians of Edinburgh
DSocSc	doctor of social science		
DTech	doctor of technology	FRCP (Lond.)	fellow of the Royal College of Physicians of London
DTh	doctor of theology		
DTM	diploma in tropical medicine	FRCPath	fellow of the Royal College of Pathologists
DTMH	diploma in tropical medicine and hygiene	FRCPsych	fellow of the Royal College of Psychiatrists
DU	doctor of the university	FRCS	fellow of the Royal College of Surgeons
DUniv	doctor of the university	FRGS	fellow of the Royal Geographical Society
dwt	pennyweight	FRIBA	fellow of the Royal Institute of British Architects
EC	European Community	FRICS	fellow of the Royal Institute of Chartered Surveyors
ed. *pl.* eds.	edited / edited by / editor(s)		
Edin.	Edinburgh	FRS	fellow of the Royal Society
		FRSA	fellow of the Royal Society of Arts

FRSCM	fellow of the Royal School of Church Music
FRSE	fellow of the Royal Society of Edinburgh
FRSL	fellow of the Royal Society of Literature
FSA	fellow of the Society of Antiquaries
ft	foot *pl.* feet
FTCL	fellow of Trinity College of Music, London
ft-lb per min.	foot-pounds per minute [unit of horsepower]
FZS	fellow of the Zoological Society
GA	Georgia
GBE	knight or dame grand cross of the Order of the British Empire
GCB	knight grand cross of the Order of the Bath
GCE	general certificate of education
GCH	knight grand cross of the Royal Guelphic Order
GCHQ	government communications headquarters
GCIE	knight grand commander of the Order of the Indian Empire
GCMG	knight or dame grand cross of the Order of St Michael and St George
GCSE	general certificate of secondary education
GCSI	knight grand commander of the Order of the Star of India
GCStJ	bailiff or dame grand cross of the order of St John of Jerusalem
GCVO	knight or dame grand cross of the Royal Victorian Order
GEC	General Electric Company
Ger.	German
GI	government (*or* general) issue
GMT	Greenwich mean time
GP	general practitioner
GPU	[Soviet special police unit]
GSO	general staff officer
Heb.	Hebrew
HEICS	Honourable East India Company Service
HI	Hawaii
HIV	human immunodeficiency virus
HK$	Hong Kong dollar
HM	his / her majesty('s)
HMAS	his / her majesty's Australian ship
HMNZS	his / her majesty's New Zealand ship
HMS	his / her majesty's ship
HMSO	His / Her Majesty's Stationery Office
HMV	His Master's Voice
Hon.	Honourable
hp	horsepower
hr	hour(s)
HRH	his / her royal highness
HTV	Harlech Television
IA	Iowa
ibid.	*ibidem*: in the same place
ICI	Imperial Chemical Industries (Ltd)
ID	Idaho
IL	Illinois
illus.	illustration
illustr.	illustrated
IN	Indiana
in.	inch(es)
Inc.	Incorporated
incl.	includes / including
IOU	I owe you
IQ	intelligence quotient
Ir£	Irish pound
IRA	Irish Republican Army
ISO	companion of the Imperial Service Order
It.	Italian
ITA	Independent Television Authority
ITV	Independent Television
Jan	January
JP	justice of the peace
jun.	junior
KB	knight of the Order of the Bath
KBE	knight commander of the Order of the British Empire
KC	king's counsel
kcal	kilocalorie
KCB	knight commander of the Order of the Bath
KCH	knight commander of the Royal Guelphic Order
KCIE	knight commander of the Order of the Indian Empire
KCMG	knight commander of the Order of St Michael and St George
KCSI	knight commander of the Order of the Star of India
KCVO	knight commander of the Royal Victorian Order
keV	kilo-electron-volt
KG	knight of the Order of the Garter
KGB	[Soviet committee of state security]
KH	knight of the Royal Guelphic Order
KLM	Koninklijke Luchtvaart Maatschappij (Royal Dutch Air Lines)
km	kilometre(s)
KP	knight of the Order of St Patrick
KS	Kansas
KT	knight of the Order of the Thistle
kt	knight
KY	Kentucky
£	pound(s) sterling
£E	Egyptian pound
L	lira *pl.* lire
l. *pl.* ll.	line(s)
LA	Lousiana
LAA	light anti-aircraft
LAH	licentiate of the Apothecaries' Hall, Dublin
Lat.	Latin
lb	pound(s), unit of weight
LDS	licence in dental surgery
lit.	literally
LittB	bachelor of letters
LittD	doctor of letters
LKQCPI	licentiate of the King and Queen's College of Physicians, Ireland
LLA	lady literate in arts
LLB	bachelor of laws
LLD	doctor of laws
LLM	master of laws
LM	licentiate in midwifery
LP	long-playing record
LRAM	licentiate of the Royal Academy of Music
LRCP	licentiate of the Royal College of Physicians
LRCPS (Glasgow)	licentiate of the Royal College of Physicians and Surgeons of Glasgow
LRCS	licentiate of the Royal College of Surgeons
LSA	licentiate of the Society of Apothecaries
LSD	lysergic acid diethylamide
LVO	lieutenant of the Royal Victorian Order
M. *pl.* MM.	Monsieur *pl.* Messieurs
m	metre(s)

m. *pl.* mm.	membrane(s)
MA	(1) Massachusetts; (2) master of arts
MAI	master of engineering
MB	bachelor of medicine
MBA	master of business administration
MBE	member of the Order of the British Empire
MC	Military Cross
MCC	Marylebone Cricket Club
MCh	master of surgery
MChir	master of surgery
MCom	master of commerce
MD	(1) doctor of medicine; (2) Maryland
MDMA	methylenedioxymethamphetamine
ME	Maine
MEd	master of education
MEng	master of engineering
MEP	member of the European parliament
MG	Morris Garages
MGM	Metro-Goldwyn-Mayer
Mgr	Monsignor
MI	(1) Michigan; (2) military intelligence
MI1c	[secret intelligence department]
MI5	[military intelligence department]
MI6	[secret intelligence department]
MI9	[secret escape service]
MICE	member of the Institution of Civil Engineers
MIEE	member of the Institution of Electrical Engineers
min.	minute(s)
Mk	mark
ML	(1) licentiate of medicine; (2) master of laws
MLitt	master of letters
Mlle	Mademoiselle
mm	millimetre(s)
Mme	Madame
MN	Minnesota
MO	Missouri
MOH	medical officer of health
MP	member of parliament
m.p.h.	miles per hour
MPhil	master of philosophy
MRCP	member of the Royal College of Physicians
MRCS	member of the Royal College of Surgeons
MRCVS	member of the Royal College of Veterinary Surgeons
MRIA	member of the Royal Irish Academy
MS	(1) master of science; (2) Mississippi
MS *pl.* MSS	manuscript(s)
MSc	master of science
MSc (Econ.)	master of science (economics)
MT	Montana
MusB	bachelor of music
MusBac	bachelor of music
MusD	doctor of music
MV	motor vessel
MVO	member of the Royal Victorian Order
n. *pl.* nn.	note(s)
NAAFI	Navy, Army, and Air Force Institutes
NASA	National Aeronautics and Space Administration
NATO	North Atlantic Treaty Organization
NBC	National Broadcasting Corporation
NC	North Carolina
NCO	non-commissioned officer
ND	North Dakota
n.d.	no date
NE	Nebraska
nem. con.	*nemine contradicente*: unanimously
new ser.	new series
NH	New Hampshire
NHS	National Health Service
NJ	New Jersey
NKVD	[Soviet people's commissariat for internal affairs]
NM	New Mexico
nm	nanometre(s)
no. *pl.* nos.	number(s)
Nov	November
n.p.	no place [of publication]
NS	new style
NV	Nevada
NY	New York
NZBS	New Zealand Broadcasting Service
OBE	officer of the Order of the British Empire
obit.	obituary
Oct	October
OCTU	officer cadets training unit
OECD	Organization for Economic Co-operation and Development
OEEC	Organization for European Economic Co-operation
OFM	order of Friars Minor [Franciscans]
OFMCap	Ordine Frati Minori Cappucini: member of the Capuchin order
OH	Ohio
OK	Oklahoma
O level	ordinary level [examination]
OM	Order of Merit
OP	order of Preachers [Dominicans]
op. *pl.* opp.	opus *pl.* opera
OPEC	Organization of Petroleum Exporting Countries
OR	Oregon
orig.	original
OS	old style
OSB	Order of St Benedict
OTC	Officers' Training Corps
OWS	Old Watercolour Society
Oxon.	Oxoniensis
p. *pl.* pp.	page(s)
PA	Pennsylvania
p.a.	per annum
para.	paragraph
PAYE	pay as you earn
pbk *pl.* pbks	paperback(s)
per.	[during the] period
PhD	doctor of philosophy
pl.	(1) plate(s); (2) plural
priv. coll.	private collection
pt *pl.* pts	part(s)
pubd	published
PVC	polyvinyl chloride
q. *pl.* qq.	(1) question(s); (2) quire(s)
QC	queen's counsel
R	rand
R.	Rex / Regina
r	recto
r.	reigned / ruled
RA	Royal Academy / Royal Academician

RAC	Royal Automobile Club
RAF	Royal Air Force
RAFVR	Royal Air Force Volunteer Reserve
RAM	[member of the] Royal Academy of Music
RAMC	Royal Army Medical Corps
RCA	Royal College of Art
RCNC	Royal Corps of Naval Constructors
RCOG	Royal College of Obstetricians and Gynaecologists
RDI	royal designer for industry
RE	Royal Engineers
repr. *pl.* reprs.	reprint(s) / reprinted
repro.	reproduced
rev.	revised / revised by / reviser / revision
Revd	Reverend
RHA	Royal Hibernian Academy
RI	(1) Rhode Island; (2) Royal Institute of Painters in Water-Colours
RIBA	Royal Institute of British Architects
RIN	Royal Indian Navy
RM	Reichsmark
RMS	Royal Mail steamer
RN	Royal Navy
RNA	ribonucleic acid
RNAS	Royal Naval Air Service
RNR	Royal Naval Reserve
RNVR	Royal Naval Volunteer Reserve
RO	Record Office
r.p.m.	revolutions per minute
RRS	royal research ship
Rs	rupees
RSA	(1) Royal Scottish Academician; (2) Royal Society of Arts
RSPCA	Royal Society for the Prevention of Cruelty to Animals
Rt Hon.	Right Honourable
Rt Revd	Right Reverend
RUC	Royal Ulster Constabulary
Russ.	Russian
RWS	Royal Watercolour Society
S4C	Sianel Pedwar Cymru
s.	shilling(s)
s.a.	*sub anno*: under the year
SABC	South African Broadcasting Corporation
SAS	Special Air Service
SC	South Carolina
ScD	doctor of science
S$	Singapore dollar
SD	South Dakota
sec.	second(s)
sel.	selected
sen.	senior
Sept	September
ser.	series
SHAPE	supreme headquarters allied powers, Europe
SIDRO	Société Internationale d'Énergie Hydro-Électrique
sig. *pl.* sigs.	signature(s)
sing.	singular
SIS	Secret Intelligence Service
SJ	Society of Jesus

Skr	Swedish krona
Span.	Spanish
SPCK	Society for Promoting Christian Knowledge
SS	(1) Santissimi; (2) Schutzstaffel; (3) steam ship
STB	bachelor of theology
STD	doctor of theology
STM	master of theology
STP	doctor of theology
supp.	supposedly
suppl. *pl.* suppls.	supplement(s)
s.v.	*sub verbo* / *sub voce*: under the word / heading
SY	steam yacht
TA	Territorial Army
TASS	[Soviet news agency]
TB	tuberculosis (*lit.* tubercle bacillus)
TD	(1) *teachtaí dála* (member of the Dáil); (2) territorial decoration
TN	Tennessee
TNT	trinitrotoluene
trans.	translated / translated by / translation / translator
TT	tourist trophy
TUC	Trades Union Congress
TX	Texas
U-boat	*Unterseeboot*: submarine
Ufa	Universum-Film AG
UMIST	University of Manchester Institute of Science and Technology
UN	United Nations
UNESCO	United Nations Educational, Scientific, and Cultural Organization
UNICEF	United Nations International Children's Emergency Fund
unpubd	unpublished
USS	United States ship
UT	Utah
v	verso
v.	versus
VA	Virginia
VAD	Voluntary Aid Detachment
VC	Victoria Cross
VE-day	victory in Europe day
Ven.	Venerable
VJ-day	victory over Japan day
vol. *pl.* vols.	volume(s)
VT	Vermont
WA	Washington [state]
WAAC	Women's Auxiliary Army Corps
WAAF	Women's Auxiliary Air Force
WEA	Workers' Educational Association
WHO	World Health Organization
WI	Wisconsin
WRAF	Women's Royal Air Force
WRNS	Women's Royal Naval Service
WV	West Virginia
WVS	Women's Voluntary Service
WY	Wyoming
¥	yen
YMCA	Young Men's Christian Association
YWCA	Young Women's Christian Association

2 *Institution abbreviations*

All Souls Oxf.	All Souls College, Oxford
AM Oxf.	Ashmolean Museum, Oxford
Balliol Oxf.	Balliol College, Oxford
BBC WAC	BBC Written Archives Centre, Reading
Beds. & Luton ARS	Bedfordshire and Luton Archives and Record Service, Bedford
Berks. RO	Berkshire Record Office, Reading
BFI	British Film Institute, London
BFI NFTVA	British Film Institute, London, National Film and Television Archive
BGS	British Geological Survey, Keyworth, Nottingham
Birm. CA	Birmingham Central Library, Birmingham City Archives
Birm. CL	Birmingham Central Library
BL	British Library, London
BL NSA	British Library, London, National Sound Archive
BL OIOC	British Library, London, Oriental and India Office Collections
BLPES	London School of Economics and Political Science, British Library of Political and Economic Science
BM	British Museum, London
Bodl. Oxf.	Bodleian Library, Oxford
Bodl. RH	Bodleian Library of Commonwealth and African Studies at Rhodes House, Oxford
Borth. Inst.	Borthwick Institute of Historical Research, University of York
Boston PL	Boston Public Library, Massachusetts
Bristol RO	Bristol Record Office
Bucks. RLSS	Buckinghamshire Records and Local Studies Service, Aylesbury
CAC Cam.	Churchill College, Cambridge, Churchill Archives Centre
Cambs. AS	Cambridgeshire Archive Service
CCC Cam.	Corpus Christi College, Cambridge
CCC Oxf.	Corpus Christi College, Oxford
Ches. & Chester ALSS	Cheshire and Chester Archives and Local Studies Service
Christ Church Oxf.	Christ Church, Oxford
Christies	Christies, London
City Westm. AC	City of Westminster Archives Centre, London
CKS	Centre for Kentish Studies, Maidstone
CLRO	Corporation of London Records Office
Coll. Arms	College of Arms, London
Col. U.	Columbia University, New York
Cornwall RO	Cornwall Record Office, Truro
Courtauld Inst.	Courtauld Institute of Art, London
CUL	Cambridge University Library
Cumbria AS	Cumbria Archive Service
Derbys. RO	Derbyshire Record Office, Matlock
Devon RO	Devon Record Office, Exeter
Dorset RO	Dorset Record Office, Dorchester
Duke U.	Duke University, Durham, North Carolina
Duke U., Perkins L.	Duke University, Durham, North Carolina, William R. Perkins Library
Durham Cath. CL	Durham Cathedral, chapter library
Durham RO	Durham Record Office
DWL	Dr Williams's Library, London
Essex RO	Essex Record Office
E. Sussex RO	East Sussex Record Office, Lewes
Eton	Eton College, Berkshire
FM Cam.	Fitzwilliam Museum, Cambridge
Folger	Folger Shakespeare Library, Washington, DC
Garr. Club	Garrick Club, London
Girton Cam.	Girton College, Cambridge
GL	Guildhall Library, London
Glos. RO	Gloucestershire Record Office, Gloucester
Gon. & Caius Cam.	Gonville and Caius College, Cambridge
Gov. Art Coll.	Government Art Collection
GS Lond.	Geological Society of London
Hants. RO	Hampshire Record Office, Winchester
Harris Man. Oxf.	Harris Manchester College, Oxford
Harvard TC	Harvard Theatre Collection, Harvard University, Cambridge, Massachusetts, Nathan Marsh Pusey Library
Harvard U.	Harvard University, Cambridge, Massachusetts
Harvard U., Houghton L.	Harvard University, Cambridge, Massachusetts, Houghton Library
Herefs. RO	Herefordshire Record Office, Hereford
Herts. ALS	Hertfordshire Archives and Local Studies, Hertford
Hist. Soc. Penn.	Historical Society of Pennsylvania, Philadelphia
HLRO	House of Lords Record Office, London
Hult. Arch.	Hulton Archive, London and New York
Hunt. L.	Huntington Library, San Marino, California
ICL	Imperial College, London
Inst. CE	Institution of Civil Engineers, London
Inst. EE	Institution of Electrical Engineers, London
IWM	Imperial War Museum, London
IWM FVA	Imperial War Museum, London, Film and Video Archive
IWM SA	Imperial War Museum, London, Sound Archive
JRL	John Rylands University Library of Manchester
King's AC Cam.	King's College Archives Centre, Cambridge
King's Cam.	King's College, Cambridge
King's Lond.	King's College, London
King's Lond., Liddell Hart C.	King's College, London, Liddell Hart Centre for Military Archives
Lancs. RO	Lancashire Record Office, Preston
L. Cong.	Library of Congress, Washington, DC
Leics. RO	Leicestershire, Leicester, and Rutland Record Office, Leicester
Lincs. Arch.	Lincolnshire Archives, Lincoln
Linn. Soc.	Linnean Society of London
LMA	London Metropolitan Archives
LPL	Lambeth Palace, London
Lpool RO	Liverpool Record Office and Local Studies Service
LUL	London University Library
Magd. Cam.	Magdalene College, Cambridge
Magd. Oxf.	Magdalen College, Oxford
Man. City Gall.	Manchester City Galleries
Man. CL	Manchester Central Library
Mass. Hist. Soc.	Massachusetts Historical Society, Boston
Merton Oxf.	Merton College, Oxford
MHS Oxf.	Museum of the History of Science, Oxford
Mitchell L., Glas.	Mitchell Library, Glasgow
Mitchell L., NSW	State Library of New South Wales, Sydney, Mitchell Library
Morgan L.	Pierpont Morgan Library, New York
NA Canada	National Archives of Canada, Ottawa
NA Ire.	National Archives of Ireland, Dublin
NAM	National Army Museum, London
NA Scot.	National Archives of Scotland, Edinburgh
News Int. RO	News International Record Office, London
NG Ire.	National Gallery of Ireland, Dublin

NG Scot.	National Gallery of Scotland, Edinburgh	Suffolk RO	Suffolk Record Office
NHM	Natural History Museum, London	Surrey HC	Surrey History Centre, Woking
NL Aus.	National Library of Australia, Canberra	TCD	Trinity College, Dublin
NL Ire.	National Library of Ireland, Dublin	Trinity Cam.	Trinity College, Cambridge
NL NZ	National Library of New Zealand, Wellington	U. Aberdeen	University of Aberdeen
NL NZ, Turnbull L.	National Library of New Zealand, Wellington, Alexander Turnbull Library	U. Birm.	University of Birmingham
		U. Birm. L.	University of Birmingham Library
NL Scot.	National Library of Scotland, Edinburgh	U. Cal.	University of California
NL Wales	National Library of Wales, Aberystwyth	U. Cam.	University of Cambridge
NMG Wales	National Museum and Gallery of Wales, Cardiff	UCL	University College, London
NMM	National Maritime Museum, London	U. Durham	University of Durham
Norfolk RO	Norfolk Record Office, Norwich	U. Durham L.	University of Durham Library
Northants. RO	Northamptonshire Record Office, Northampton	U. Edin.	University of Edinburgh
		U. Edin., New Coll.	University of Edinburgh, New College
Northumbd RO	Northumberland Record Office	U. Edin., New Coll. L.	University of Edinburgh, New College Library
Notts. Arch.	Nottinghamshire Archives, Nottingham		
NPG	National Portrait Gallery, London	U. Edin. L.	University of Edinburgh Library
NRA	National Archives, London, Historical Manuscripts Commission, National Register of Archives	U. Glas.	University of Glasgow
		U. Glas. L.	University of Glasgow Library
		U. Hull	University of Hull
Nuffield Oxf.	Nuffield College, Oxford	U. Hull, Brynmor Jones L.	University of Hull, Brynmor Jones Library
N. Yorks. CRO	North Yorkshire County Record Office, Northallerton		
		U. Leeds	University of Leeds
NYPL	New York Public Library	U. Leeds, Brotherton L.	University of Leeds, Brotherton Library
Oxf. UA	Oxford University Archives		
Oxf. U. Mus. NH	Oxford University Museum of Natural History	U. Lond.	University of London
Oxon. RO	Oxfordshire Record Office, Oxford	U. Lpool	University of Liverpool
Pembroke Cam.	Pembroke College, Cambridge	U. Lpool L.	University of Liverpool Library
PRO	National Archives, London, Public Record Office	U. Mich.	University of Michigan, Ann Arbor
		U. Mich., Clements L.	University of Michigan, Ann Arbor, William L. Clements Library
PRO NIre.	Public Record Office for Northern Ireland, Belfast		
		U. Newcastle	University of Newcastle upon Tyne
Pusey Oxf.	Pusey House, Oxford	U. Newcastle, Robinson L.	University of Newcastle upon Tyne, Robinson Library
RA	Royal Academy of Arts, London		
Ransom HRC	Harry Ransom Humanities Research Center, University of Texas, Austin	U. Nott.	University of Nottingham
		U. Nott. L.	University of Nottingham Library
RAS	Royal Astronomical Society, London	U. Oxf.	University of Oxford
RBG Kew	Royal Botanic Gardens, Kew, London	U. Reading	University of Reading
RCP Lond.	Royal College of Physicians of London	U. Reading L.	University of Reading Library
RCS Eng.	Royal College of Surgeons of England, London	U. St Andr.	University of St Andrews
RGS	Royal Geographical Society, London	U. St Andr. L.	University of St Andrews Library
RIBA	Royal Institute of British Architects, London	U. Southampton	University of Southampton
RIBA BAL	Royal Institute of British Architects, London, British Architectural Library	U. Southampton L.	University of Southampton Library
		U. Sussex	University of Sussex, Brighton
Royal Arch.	Royal Archives, Windsor Castle, Berkshire [by gracious permission of her majesty the queen]	U. Texas	University of Texas, Austin
		U. Wales	University of Wales
Royal Irish Acad.	Royal Irish Academy, Dublin	U. Warwick Mod. RC	University of Warwick, Coventry, Modern Records Centre
Royal Scot. Acad.	Royal Scottish Academy, Edinburgh		
RS	Royal Society, London	V&A	Victoria and Albert Museum, London
RSA	Royal Society of Arts, London	V&A NAL	Victoria and Albert Museum, London, National Art Library
RS Friends, Lond.	Religious Society of Friends, London		
St Ant. Oxf.	St Antony's College, Oxford	Warks. CRO	Warwickshire County Record Office, Warwick
St John Cam.	St John's College, Cambridge	Wellcome L.	Wellcome Library for the History and Understanding of Medicine, London
S. Antiquaries, Lond.	Society of Antiquaries of London		
		Westm. DA	Westminster Diocesan Archives, London
Sci. Mus.	Science Museum, London	Wilts. & Swindon RO	Wiltshire and Swindon Record Office, Trowbridge
Scot. NPG	Scottish National Portrait Gallery, Edinburgh		
Scott Polar RI	University of Cambridge, Scott Polar Research Institute	Worcs. RO	Worcestershire Record Office, Worcester
		W. Sussex RO	West Sussex Record Office, Chichester
Sheff. Arch.	Sheffield Archives	W. Yorks. AS	West Yorkshire Archive Service
Shrops. RRC	Shropshire Records and Research Centre, Shrewsbury	Yale U.	Yale University, New Haven, Connecticut
		Yale U., Beinecke L.	Yale University, New Haven, Connecticut, Beinecke Rare Book and Manuscript Library
SOAS	School of Oriental and African Studies, London		
Som. ARS	Somerset Archive and Record Service, Taunton	Yale U. CBA	Yale University, New Haven, Connecticut, Yale Center for British Art
Staffs. RO	Staffordshire Record Office, Stafford		

3 Bibliographic abbreviations

Adams, *Drama*
W. D. Adams, *A dictionary of the drama*, 1: *A–G* (1904); 2: *H–Z* (1956) [vol. 2 microfilm only]

AFM
J O'Donovan, ed. and trans., *Annala rioghachta Eireann | Annals of the kingdom of Ireland by the four masters*, 7 vols. (1848–51); 2nd edn (1856); 3rd edn (1990)

Allibone, *Dict.*
S. A. Allibone, *A critical dictionary of English literature and British and American authors*, 3 vols. (1859–71); suppl. by J. F. Kirk, 2 vols. (1891)

ANB
J. A. Garraty and M. C. Carnes, eds., *American national biography*, 24 vols. (1999)

Anderson, *Scot. nat.*
W. Anderson, *The Scottish nation, or, The surnames, families, literature, honours, and biographical history of the people of Scotland*, 3 vols. (1859–63)

Ann. mon.
H. R. Luard, ed., *Annales monastici*, 5 vols., Rolls Series, 36 (1864–9)

Ann. Ulster
S. Mac Airt and G. Mac Niocaill, eds., *Annals of Ulster (to AD 1131)* (1983)

APC
Acts of the privy council of England, new ser., 46 vols. (1890–1964)

APS
The acts of the parliaments of Scotland, 12 vols. in 13 (1814–75)

Arber, *Regs. Stationers*
F. Arber, ed., *A transcript of the registers of the Company of Stationers of London, 1554–1640 AD*, 5 vols. (1875–94)

ArchR
Architectural Review

ASC
D. Whitelock, D. C. Douglas, and S. I. Tucker, ed. and trans., *The Anglo-Saxon Chronicle: a revised translation* (1961)

AS chart.
P. H. Sawyer, *Anglo-Saxon charters: an annotated list and bibliography*, Royal Historical Society Guides and Handbooks (1968)

AusDB
D. Pike and others, eds., *Australian dictionary of biography*, 16 vols. (1966–2002)

Baker, *Serjeants*
J. H. Baker, *The order of serjeants at law*, SeldS, suppl. ser., 5 (1984)

Bale, *Cat.*
J. Bale, *Scriptorum illustrium Maioris Brytannie, quam nunc Angliam et Scotiam vocant: catalogus*, 2 vols. in 1 (Basel, 1557–9); facs. edn (1971)

Bale, *Index*
J. Bale, *Index Britanniae scriptorum*, ed. R. L. Poole and M. Bateson (1902); facs. edn (1990)

BBCS
Bulletin of the Board of Celtic Studies

BDMBR
J. O. Baylen and N. J. Gossman, eds., *Biographical dictionary of modern British radicals*, 3 vols. in 4 (1979–88)

Bede, *Hist. eccl.*
Bede's Ecclesiastical history of the English people, ed. and trans. B. Colgrave and R. A. B. Mynors, OMT (1969); repr. (1991)

Bénézit, *Dict.*
E. Bénézit, *Dictionnaire critique et documentaire des peintres, sculpteurs, dessinateurs et graveurs*, 3 vols. (Paris, 1911–23); new edn, 8 vols. (1948–66), repr. (1966); 3rd edn, rev. and enl., 10 vols. (1976); 4th edn, 14 vols. (1999)

BIHR
Bulletin of the Institute of Historical Research

Birch, *Seals*
W. de Birch, *Catalogue of seals in the department of manuscripts in the British Museum*, 6 vols. (1887–1900)

Bishop Burnet's History
Bishop Burnet's History of his own time, ed. M. J. Routh, 2nd edn, 6 vols. (1833)

Blackwood
Blackwood's [Edinburgh] Magazine, 328 vols. (1817–1980)

Blain, Clements & Grundy, *Feminist comp.*
V. Blain, P. Clements, and I. Grundy, eds., *The feminist companion to literature in English* (1990)

BL cat.
The British Library general catalogue of printed books [in 360 vols. with suppls., also CD-ROM and online]

BMJ
British Medical Journal

Boase & Courtney, *Bibl. Corn.*
G. C. Boase and W. P. Courtney, *Bibliotheca Cornubiensis: a catalogue of the writings … of Cornishmen*, 3 vols. (1874–82)

Boase, *Mod. Eng. biog.*
F. Boase, *Modern English biography: containing many thousand concise memoirs of persons who have died since the year 1850*, 6 vols. (privately printed, Truro, 1892–1921); repr. (1965)

Boswell, *Life*
Boswell's Life of Johnson: together with Journal of a tour to the Hebrides and Johnson's Diary of a journey into north Wales, ed. G. B. Hill, enl. edn, rev. L. F. Powell, 6 vols. (1934–50); 2nd edn (1964); repr. (1971)

Brown & Stratton, *Brit. mus.*
J. D. Brown and S. S. Stratton, *British musical biography* (1897)

Bryan, *Painters*
M. Bryan, *A biographical and critical dictionary of painters and engravers*, 2 vols. (1816); new edn, ed. G. Stanley (1849); new edn, ed. R. E. Graves and W. Armstrong, 2 vols. (1886–9); [4th edn], ed. G. C. Williamson, 5 vols. (1903–5) [various reprs.]

Burke, *Gen. GB*
J. Burke, *A genealogical and heraldic history of the commoners of Great Britain and Ireland*, 4 vols. (1833–8); new edn as *A genealogical and heraldic dictionary of the landed gentry of Great Britain and Ireland*, 3 vols. [1843–9] [many later edns]

Burke, *Gen. Ire.*
J. B. Burke, *A genealogical and heraldic history of the landed gentry of Ireland* (1899); 2nd edn (1904); 3rd edn (1912); 4th edn (1958); 5th edn as *Burke's Irish family records* (1976)

Burke, *Peerage*
J. Burke, *A general [later edns A genealogical] and heraldic dictionary of the peerage and baronetage of the United Kingdom* [later edns *the British empire*] (1829–)

Burney, *Hist. mus.*
C. Burney, *A general history of music, from the earliest ages to the present period*, 4 vols. (1776–89)

Burtchaell & Sadleir, *Alum. Dubl.*
G. D. Burtchaell and T. U. Sadleir, *Alumni Dublinenses: a register of the students, graduates, and provosts of Trinity College* (1924); [2nd edn], with suppl., in 2 pts (1935)

Calamy rev.
A. G. Matthews, *Calamy revised* (1934); repr. (1988)

CCI
Calendar of confirmations and inventories granted and given up in the several commissariots of Scotland (1876–)

CClR
Calendar of the close rolls preserved in the Public Record Office, 47 vols. (1892–1963)

CDS
J. Bain, ed., *Calendar of documents relating to Scotland*, 4 vols., PRO (1881–8); suppl. vol. 5, ed. G. G. Simpson and J. D. Galbraith [1986]

CEPR letters
W. H. Bliss, C. Johnson, and J. Twemlow, eds., *Calendar of entries in the papal registers relating to Great Britain and Ireland: papal letters* (1893–)

CGPLA
Calendars of the grants of probate and letters of administration [in 4 ser.: England & Wales, Northern Ireland, Ireland, and Éire]

Chambers, *Scots.*
R. Chambers, ed., *A biographical dictionary of eminent Scotsmen*, 4 vols. (1832–5)

Chancery records
chancery records pubd by the PRO

Chancery records (RC)
chancery records pubd by the Record Commissions

CIPM — *Calendar of inquisitions post mortem*, [20 vols.], PRO (1904–); also *Henry VII*, 3 vols. (1898–1955)

Clarendon, *Hist. rebellion* — E. Hyde, earl of Clarendon, *The history of the rebellion and civil wars in England*, 6 vols. (1888); repr. (1958) and (1992)

Cobbett, *Parl. hist.* — W. Cobbett and J. Wright, eds., *Cobbett's Parliamentary history of England*, 36 vols. (1806–1820)

Colvin, *Archs.* — H. Colvin, *A biographical dictionary of British architects, 1600–1840*, 3rd edn (1995)

Cooper, *Ath. Cantab.* — C. H. Cooper and T. Cooper, *Athenae Cantabrigienses*, 3 vols. (1858–1913); repr. (1967)

CPR — *Calendar of the patent rolls preserved in the Public Record Office* (1891–)

Crockford — *Crockford's Clerical Directory*

CS — Camden Society

CSP — *Calendar of state papers* [in 11 ser.: *domestic, Scotland, Scottish series, Ireland, colonial, Commonwealth, foreign, Spain* [at Simancas], *Rome, Milan,* and *Venice*]

CYS — Canterbury and York Society

DAB — *Dictionary of American biography*, 21 vols. (1928–36), repr. in 11 vols. (1964); 10 suppls. (1944–96)

DBB — D. J. Jeremy, ed., *Dictionary of business biography*, 5 vols. (1984–6)

DCB — G. W. Brown and others, *Dictionary of Canadian biography*, [14 vols.] (1966–)

Debrett's Peerage — *Debrett's Peerage* (1803–) [sometimes *Debrett's Illustrated peerage*]

Desmond, *Botanists* — R. Desmond, *Dictionary of British and Irish botanists and horticulturists* (1977); rev. edn (1994)

Dir. Brit. archs. — A. Felstead, J. Franklin, and L. Pinfield, eds., *Directory of British architects, 1834–1900* (1993); 2nd edn, ed. A. Brodie and others, 2 vols. (2001)

DLB — J. M. Bellamy and J. Saville, eds., *Dictionary of labour biography*, [10 vols.] (1972–)

DLitB — Dictionary of Literary Biography

DNB — *Dictionary of national biography*, 63 vols. (1885–1900), suppl., 3 vols. (1901); repr. in 22 vols. (1908–9); 10 further suppls. (1912–96); *Missing persons* (1993)

DNZB — W. H. Oliver and C. Orange, eds., *The dictionary of New Zealand biography*, 5 vols. (1990–2000)

DSAB — W. J. de Kock and others, eds., *Dictionary of South African biography*, 5 vols. (1968–87)

DSB — C. C. Gillispie and F. L. Holmes, eds., *Dictionary of scientific biography*, 16 vols. (1970–80); repr. in 8 vols. (1981); 2 vol. suppl. (1990)

DSBB — A. Slaven and S. Checkland, eds., *Dictionary of Scottish business biography, 1860–1960*, 2 vols. (1986–90)

DSCHT — N. M. de S. Cameron and others, eds., *Dictionary of Scottish church history and theology* (1993)

Dugdale, *Monasticon* — W. Dugdale, *Monasticon Anglicanum*, 3 vols. (1655–72); 2nd edn, 3 vols. (1661–82); new edn, ed. J. Caley, J. Ellis, and B. Bandinel, 6 vols. in 8 pts (1817–30); repr. (1846) and (1970)

DWB — J. E. Lloyd and others, eds., *Dictionary of Welsh biography down to 1940* (1959) [Eng. trans. of *Y bywgraffiadur Cymreig hyd 1940*, 2nd edn (1954)]

EdinR — *Edinburgh Review, or, Critical Journal*

EETS — Early English Text Society

Emden, *Cam.* — A. B. Emden, *A biographical register of the University of Cambridge to 1500* (1963)

Emden, *Oxf.* — A. B. Emden, *A biographical register of the University of Oxford to AD 1500*, 3 vols. (1957–9); also *A biographical register of the University of Oxford, AD 1501 to 1540* (1974)

EngHR — *English Historical Review*

Engraved Brit. ports. — F. M. O'Donoghue and H. M. Hake, *Catalogue of engraved British portraits preserved in the department of prints and drawings in the British Museum*, 6 vols. (1908–25)

ER — *The English Reports*, 178 vols. (1900–32)

ESTC — *English short title catalogue, 1475–1800* [CD-ROM and online]

Evelyn, *Diary* — *The diary of John Evelyn*, ed. E. S. De Beer, 6 vols. (1955); repr. (2000)

Farington, *Diary* — *The diary of Joseph Farington*, ed. K. Garlick and others, 17 vols. (1978–98)

Fasti Angl. (Hardy) — J. Le Neve, *Fasti ecclesiae Anglicanae*, ed. T. D. Hardy, 3 vols. (1854)

Fasti Angl., 1066–1300 — [J. Le Neve], *Fasti ecclesiae Anglicanae, 1066–1300*, ed. D. E. Greenway and J. S. Barrow, [8 vols.] (1968–)

Fasti Angl., 1300–1541 — [J. Le Neve], *Fasti ecclesiae Anglicanae, 1300–1541*, 12 vols. (1962–7)

Fasti Angl., 1541–1857 — [J. Le Neve], *Fasti ecclesiae Anglicanae, 1541–1857*, ed. J. M. Horn, D. M. Smith, and D. S. Bailey, [9 vols.] (1969–)

Fasti Scot. — H. Scott, *Fasti ecclesiae Scoticanae*, 3 vols. in 6 (1871); new edn, [11 vols.] (1915–)

FO List — *Foreign Office List*

Fortescue, *Brit. army* — J. W. Fortescue, *A history of the British army*, 13 vols. (1899–1930)

Foss, *Judges* — E. Foss, *The judges of England*, 9 vols. (1848–64); repr. (1966)

Foster, *Alum. Oxon.* — J. Foster, ed., *Alumni Oxonienses: the members of the University of Oxford, 1715–1886*, 4 vols. (1887–8); later edn (1891); also *Alumni Oxonienses … 1500–1714*, 4 vols. (1891–2); 8 vol. repr. (1968) and (2000)

Fuller, *Worthies* — T. Fuller, *The history of the worthies of England*, 4 pts (1662); new edn, 2 vols., ed. J. Nichols (1811); new edn, 3 vols., ed. P. A. Nuttall (1840); repr. (1965)

GEC, *Baronetage* — G. E. Cokayne, *Complete baronetage*, 6 vols. (1900–09); repr. (1983) [microprint]

GEC, *Peerage* — G. E. C. [G. E. Cokayne], *The complete peerage of England, Scotland, Ireland, Great Britain, and the United Kingdom*, 8 vols. (1887–98); new edn, ed. V. Gibbs and others, 14 vols. in 15 (1910–98); microprint repr. (1982) and (1987)

Genest, *Eng. stage* — J. Genest, *Some account of the English stage from the Restoration in 1660 to 1830*, 10 vols. (1832); repr. [New York, 1965]

Gillow, *Lit. biog. hist.* — J. Gillow, *A literary and biographical history or bibliographical dictionary of the English Catholics, from the breach with Rome, in 1534, to the present time*, 5 vols. [1885–1902]; repr. (1961); repr. with preface by C. Gillow (1999)

Gir. Camb. opera — *Giraldi Cambrensis opera*, ed. J. S. Brewer, J. F. Dimock, and G. F. Warner, 8 vols., Rolls Series, 21 (1861–91)

GJ — *Geographical Journal*

Gladstone, *Diaries* — *The Gladstone diaries: with cabinet minutes and prime-ministerial correspondence*, ed. M. R. D. Foot and H. C. G. Matthew, 14 vols. (1968–94)

GM — *Gentleman's Magazine*

Graves, *Artists* — A. Graves, ed., *A dictionary of artists who have exhibited works in the principal London exhibitions of oil paintings from 1760 to 1880* (1884); new edn (1895); 3rd edn (1901); facs. edn (1969); repr. [1970], (1973), and (1984)

Graves, *Brit. Inst.* — A. Graves, *The British Institution, 1806–1867: a complete dictionary of contributors and their work from the foundation of the institution* (1875); facs. edn (1908); repr. (1969)

Graves, *RA exhibitors* — A. Graves, *The Royal Academy of Arts: a complete dictionary of contributors and their work from its foundation in 1769 to 1904*, 8 vols. (1905–6); repr. in 4 vols. (1970) and (1972)

Graves, *Soc. Artists* — A. Graves, *The Society of Artists of Great Britain, 1760–1791, the Free Society of Artists, 1761–1783: a complete dictionary* (1907); facs. edn (1969)

Greaves & Zaller, *BDBR* — R. L. Greaves and R. Zaller, eds., *Biographical dictionary of British radicals in the seventeenth century*, 3 vols. (1982–4)

Grove, *Dict. mus.* — G. Grove, ed., *A dictionary of music and musicians*, 5 vols. (1878–90); 2nd edn, ed. J. A. Fuller Maitland (1904–10); 3rd edn, ed. H. C. Colles (1927); 4th edn with suppl. (1940); 5th edn, ed. E. Blom, 9 vols. (1954); suppl. (1961) [see also *New Grove*]

Hall, *Dramatic ports.* — L. A. Hall, *Catalogue of dramatic portraits in the theatre collection of the Harvard College library*, 4 vols. (1930–34)

Hansard — *Hansard's parliamentary debates*, ser. 1–5 (1803–)

Highfill, Burnim & Langhans, *BDA* — P. H. Highfill, K. A. Burnim, and E. A. Langhans, *A biographical dictionary of actors, actresses, musicians, dancers, managers, and other stage personnel in London, 1660–1800*, 16 vols. (1973–93)

Hist. U. Oxf. — T. H. Aston, ed., *The history of the University of Oxford*, 8 vols. (1984–2000) [1: *The early Oxford schools*, ed. J. I. Catto (1984); 2: *Late medieval Oxford*, ed. J. I. Catto and R. Evans (1992); 3: *The collegiate university*, ed. J. McConica (1986); 4: *Seventeenth-century Oxford*, ed. N. Tyacke (1997); 5: *The eighteenth century*, ed. L. S. Sutherland and L. G. Mitchell (1986); 6–7: *Nineteenth-century Oxford*, ed. M. G. Brock and M. C. Curthoys (1997–2000); 8: *The twentieth century*, ed. B. Harrison (2000)]

HJ — *Historical Journal*

HMC — Historical Manuscripts Commission

Holdsworth, *Eng. law* — W. S. Holdsworth, *A history of English law*, ed. A. L. Goodhart and H. L. Hanbury, 17 vols. (1903–72)

HoP, *Commons* — *The history of parliament: the House of Commons* [*1386–1421*, ed. J. S. Roskell, L. Clark, and C. Rawcliffe, 4 vols. (1992); *1509–1558*, ed. S. T. Bindoff, 3 vols. (1982); *1558–1603*, ed. P. W. Hasler, 3 vols. (1981); *1660–1690*, ed. B. D. Henning, 3 vols. (1983); *1690–1715*, ed. D. W. Hayton, E. Cruickshanks, and S. Handley, 5 vols. (2002); *1715–1754*, ed. R. Sedgwick, 2 vols. (1970); *1754–1790*, ed. L. Namier and J. Brooke, 3 vols. (1964), repr. (1985); *1790–1820*, ed. R. G. Thorne, 5 vols. (1986); in draft (used with permission): *1422–1504, 1604–1629, 1640–1660*, and *1820–1832*]

IGI — *International Genealogical Index*, Church of Jesus Christ of the Latterday Saints

ILN — *Illustrated London News*

IMC — Irish Manuscripts Commission

Irving, *Scots.* — J. Irving, ed., *The book of Scotsmen eminent for achievements in arms and arts, church and state, law, legislation and literature, commerce, science, travel and philanthropy* (1881)

JCS — *Journal of the Chemical Society*

JHC — *Journals of the House of Commons*

JHL — *Journals of the House of Lords*

John of Worcester, *Chron.* — *The chronicle of John of Worcester*, ed. R. R. Darlington and P. McGurk, trans. J. Bray and P. McGurk, 3 vols., OMT (1995–) [vol. 1 forthcoming]

Keeler, *Long Parliament* — M. F. Keeler, *The Long Parliament, 1640–1641: a biographical study of its members* (1954)

Kelly, *Handbk* — *The upper ten thousand: an alphabetical list of all members of noble families*, 3 vols. (1875–7); continued as *Kelly's handbook of the upper ten thousand for 1878* [1879], 2 vols. (1878–9); continued as *Kelly's handbook to the titled, landed and official classes*, 94 vols. (1880–1973)

LondG — *London Gazette*

LP Henry VIII — J. S. Brewer, J. Gairdner, and R. H. Brodie, eds., *Letters and papers, foreign and domestic, of the reign of Henry VIII*, 23 vols. in 38 (1862–1932); repr. (1965)

Mallalieu, *Watercolour artists* — H. L. Mallalieu, *The dictionary of British watercolour artists up to 1820*, 3 vols. (1976–90); vol. 1, 2nd edn (1986)

Memoirs FRS — *Biographical Memoirs of Fellows of the Royal Society*

MGH — Monumenta Germaniae Historica

MT — *Musical Times*

Munk, *Roll* — W. Munk, *The roll of the Royal College of Physicians of London*, 2 vols. (1861); 2nd edn, 3 vols. (1878)

N&Q — *Notes and Queries*

New Grove — S. Sadie, ed., *The new Grove dictionary of music and musicians*, 20 vols. (1980); 2nd edn, 29 vols. (2001) [also online edn; see also Grove, *Dict. mus.*]

Nichols, *Illustrations* — J. Nichols and J. B. Nichols, *Illustrations of the literary history of the eighteenth century*, 8 vols. (1817–58)

Nichols, *Lit. anecdotes* — J. Nichols, *Literary anecdotes of the eighteenth century*, 9 vols. (1812–16); facs. edn (1966)

Obits. FRS — *Obituary Notices of Fellows of the Royal Society*

O'Byrne, *Naval biog. dict.* — W. R. O'Byrne, *A naval biographical dictionary* (1849); repr. (1990); [2nd edn], 2 vols. (1861)

OHS — Oxford Historical Society

Old Westminsters — *The record of Old Westminsters*, 1–2, ed. G. F. R. Barker and A. H. Stenning (1928); suppl. 1, ed. J. B. Whitmore and G. R. Y. Radcliffe [1938]; 3, ed. J. B. Whitmore, G. R. Y. Radcliffe, and D. C. Simpson (1963); suppl. 2, ed. F. E. Pagan (1978); 4, ed. F. E. Pagan and H. E. Pagan (1992)

OMT — Oxford Medieval Texts

Ordericus Vitalis, *Eccl. hist.* — *The ecclesiastical history of Orderic Vitalis*, ed. and trans. M. Chibnall, 6 vols., OMT (1969–80); repr. (1990)

Paris, *Chron.* — *Matthaei Parisiensis, monachi sancti Albani, chronica majora*, ed. H. R. Luard, Rolls Series, 7 vols. (1872–83)

Parl. papers — *Parliamentary papers* (1801–)

PBA — *Proceedings of the British Academy*

Pepys, *Diary*	*The diary of Samuel Pepys*, ed. R. Latham and W. Matthews, 11 vols. (1970–83); repr. (1995) and (2000)
Pevsner	N. Pevsner and others, Buildings of England series
PICE	*Proceedings of the Institution of Civil Engineers*
Pipe rolls	*The great roll of the pipe for . . .*, PRSoc. (1884–)
PRO	Public Record Office
PRS	*Proceedings of the Royal Society of London*
PRSoc.	Pipe Roll Society
PTRS	*Philosophical Transactions of the Royal Society*
QR	*Quarterly Review*
RC	Record Commissions
Redgrave, *Artists*	S. Redgrave, *A dictionary of artists of the English school* (1874); rev. edn (1878); repr. (1970)
Reg. Oxf.	C. W. Boase and A. Clark, eds., *Register of the University of Oxford*, 5 vols., OHS, 1, 10–12, 14 (1885–9)
Reg. PCS	J. H. Burton and others, eds., *The register of the privy council of Scotland*, 1st ser., 14 vols. (1877–98); 2nd ser., 8 vols. (1899–1908); 3rd ser., [16 vols.] (1908–70)
Reg. RAN	H. W. C. Davis and others, eds., *Regesta regum Anglo-Normannorum, 1066–1154*, 4 vols. (1913–69)
RIBA Journal	*Journal of the Royal Institute of British Architects* [later *RIBA Journal*]
RotP	J. Strachey, ed., *Rotuli parliamentorum ut et petitiones, et placita in parliamento*, 6 vols. (1767–77)
RotS	D. Macpherson, J. Caley, and W. Illingworth, eds., *Rotuli Scotiae in Turri Londinensi et in domo capitulari Westmonasteriensi asservati*, 2 vols., RC, 14 (1814–19)
RS	Record(s) Society
Rymer, *Foedera*	T. Rymer and R. Sanderson, eds., *Foedera, conventiones, literae et cuiuscunque generis acta publica inter reges Angliae et alios quosvis imperatores, reges, pontifices, principes, vel communitates*, 20 vols. (1704–35); 2nd edn, 20 vols. (1726–35); 3rd edn, 10 vols. (1739–45), facs. edn (1967); new edn, ed. A. Clarke, J. Caley, and F. Holbrooke, 4 vols., RC, 50 (1816–30)
Sainty, *Judges*	J. Sainty, ed., *The judges of England, 1272–1990*, SeldS, suppl. ser., 10 (1993)
Sainty, *King's counsel*	J. Sainty, ed., *A list of English law officers and king's counsel*, SeldS, suppl. ser., 7 (1987)
SCH	Studies in Church History
Scots peerage	J. B. Paul, ed. *The Scots peerage, founded on Wood's edition of Sir Robert Douglas's Peerage of Scotland, containing an historical and genealogical account of the nobility of that kingdom*, 9 vols. (1904–14)
SeldS	Selden Society
SHR	*Scottish Historical Review*
State trials	T. B. Howell and T. J. Howell, eds., *Cobbett's Complete collection of state trials*, 34 vols. (1809–28)
STC, 1475–1640	A. W. Pollard, G. R. Redgrave, and others, eds., *A short-title catalogue of . . . English books . . . 1475–1640* (1926); 2nd edn, ed. W. A. Jackson, F. S. Ferguson, and K. F. Pantzer, 3 vols. (1976–91) [see also Wing, *STC*]
STS	Scottish Text Society
SurtS	Surtees Society
Symeon of Durham, *Opera*	*Symeonis monachi opera omnia*, ed. T. Arnold, 2 vols., Rolls Series, 75 (1882–5); repr. (1965)
Tanner, *Bibl. Brit.-Hib.*	T. Tanner, *Bibliotheca Britannico-Hibernica*, ed. D. Wilkins (1748); repr. (1963)
Thieme & Becker, *Allgemeines Lexikon*	U. Thieme, F. Becker, and H. Vollmer, eds., *Allgemeines Lexikon der bildenden Künstler von der Antike bis zur Gegenwart*, 37 vols. (Leipzig, 1907–50); repr. (1961–5), (1983), and (1992)
Thurloe, *State papers*	*A collection of the state papers of John Thurloe*, ed. T. Birch, 7 vols. (1742)
TLS	*Times Literary Supplement*
Tout, *Admin. hist.*	T. F. Tout, *Chapters in the administrative history of mediaeval England: the wardrobe, the chamber, and the small seals*, 6 vols. (1920–33); repr. (1967)
TRHS	*Transactions of the Royal Historical Society*
VCH	H. A. Doubleday and others, eds., *The Victoria history of the counties of England*, [88 vols.] (1900–)
Venn, *Alum. Cant.*	J. Venn and J. A. Venn, *Alumni Cantabrigienses: a biographical list of all known students, graduates, and holders of office at the University of Cambridge, from the earliest times to 1900*, 10 vols. (1922–54); repr. in 2 vols. (1974–8)
Vertue, *Note books*	[G. Vertue], *Note books*, ed. K. Esdaile, earl of Ilchester, and H. M. Hake, 6 vols., Walpole Society, 18, 20, 22, 24, 26, 30 (1930–55)
VF	*Vanity Fair*
Walford, *County families*	E. Walford, *The county families of the United Kingdom, or, Royal manual of the titled and untitled aristocracy of Great Britain and Ireland* (1860)
Walker rev.	A. G. Matthews, *Walker revised: being a revision of John Walker's Sufferings of the clergy during the grand rebellion, 1642–60* (1948); repr. (1988)
Walpole, *Corr.*	*The Yale edition of Horace Walpole's correspondence*, ed. W. S. Lewis, 48 vols. (1937–83)
Ward, *Men of the reign*	T. H. Ward, ed., *Men of the reign: a biographical dictionary of eminent persons of British and colonial birth who have died during the reign of Queen Victoria* (1885); repr. (Graz, 1968)
Waterhouse, *18c painters*	E. Waterhouse, *The dictionary of 18th century painters in oils and crayons* (1981); repr. as *British 18th century painters in oils and crayons* (1991), vol. 2 of *Dictionary of British art*
Watt, *Bibl. Brit.*	R. Watt, *Bibliotheca Britannica, or, A general index to British and foreign literature*, 4 vols. (1824) [many reprs.]
Wellesley index	W. E. Houghton, ed., *The Wellesley index to Victorian periodicals, 1824–1900*, 5 vols. (1966–89); new edn (1999) [CD-ROM]
Wing, *STC*	D. Wing, ed., *Short-title catalogue of . . . English books . . . 1641–1700*, 3 vols. (1945–51); 2nd edn (1972–88); rev. and enl. edn, ed. J. J. Morrison, C. W. Nelson, and M. Seccombe, 4 vols. (1994–8) [see also *STC, 1475–1640*]
Wisden	*John Wisden's Cricketer's Almanack*
Wood, *Ath. Oxon.*	A. Wood, *Athenae Oxonienses . . . to which are added the Fasti*, 2 vols. (1691–2); 2nd edn (1721); new edn, 4 vols., ed. P. Bliss (1813–20); repr. (1967) and (1969)
Wood, *Vic. painters*	C. Wood, *Dictionary of Victorian painters* (1971); 2nd edn (1978); 3rd edn as *Victorian painters*, 2 vols. (1995), vol. 4 of *Dictionary of British art*
WW	*Who's who* (1849–)
WWBMP	M. Stenton and S. Lees, eds., *Who's who of British members of parliament*, 4 vols. (1976–81)
WWW	*Who was who* (1929–)

Jenner, Caryl [*real name* Pamela Penelope Ripman] (1917–1973), theatre director and manager, was born on 19 May 1917 at 45 Ladbroke Grove, London, the daughter of Walter Ripman (1869–1947), an inspector of schools and author of many school textbooks in French and German, and his wife, Constance Brockwill Grier. She was educated at Norland Place School and at St Paul's Girls' School. She studied for the theatre at the Central School of Speech Training and Dramatic Art in London, gaining the Central School and London University diplomas in dramatic art in 1935.

Caryl Jenner, to use the name she adopted, began her professional career as an actress and assistant stage manager at the Gate Theatre, London. From 1936 to 1938 she worked as a stage manager for various companies in London and the provinces. In December 1938 she became director of the Amersham Repertory Company, where until its closure in March 1949 she worked with the actress Sally Latimer on over 200 productions. During this time she showed a particular gift for creating theatre for young people, in 1948 becoming co-director of the Amersham Playhouse Schools Mobile Unit.

In November 1949 Caryl Jenner launched her first independent theatrical enterprise, Mobile Theatre Ltd, which was committed to bringing live performance to towns and villages otherwise denied the chance to see theatre. This proved so successful that by 1960 she was managing five touring companies, four of which, jointly named the English Theatre for Children, were exclusively devoted to children's theatre. She ran summer theatre seasons in Seaford, Southwold, Cornwall, and Ayr and toured tirelessly: she visited schools for over fifty education authorities in Britain, extending her tours to include Northern Ireland (January 1960) and Malta (May 1960). She also directed children's plays at various major venues: Sam Wanamaker's New Shakespeare Theatre, Liverpool; the Lyric, Hammersmith; the Yvonne Arnaud, Guildford; the Coventry, Belgrade; and the Toynbee, Questors, and Garrick in London.

Caryl Jenner's performances for children were distinguished by an appeal to the imagination (e.g. using a simple stepladder for a mountain). They did not involve any physical participation by the children nor post-show discussion, for she believed that this was the task of the teacher. She never avoided confronting difficult topics: one of her productions of this period, *The Tingalary Bird* by Mary Mellwood, was an absurdist piece, in which an old couple argue their lives away. Many adults thought it too advanced for a child audience, yet it was watched attentively by the children themselves.

In October 1962 Caryl Jenner renamed her organization Caryl Jenner Productions Ltd, and launched the Unicorn Theatre Club for Young People. It is for her pioneering work with the Unicorn Theatre that she is now best remembered. In October 1964 the Unicorn became a permanent London company of some eight to ten actors, but it almost failed two years later when it ran into serious financial difficulties. It was saved by support from the Gulbenkian Foundation, the Leche Trust, and members of the Unicorn itself. Most importantly, it began to receive grants from the Arts Council, establishing for the first time the principle of subsidizing children's theatre in Britain. The improved financial situation allowed her in July 1967 to take a six-year lease on the Arts Theatre in London. She would present plays and run workshops for children during the day, and let out the theatre for adult performances in the evening. By now she had abandoned touring and could rely on audiences' coming to her: from 1970 to 1973 her audiences at the Arts Theatre averaged 93 per cent, coming from 100 of London's 114 postal districts and from 308 towns outside London. In 1973 the annual audience was over 56,000, with 14,000 children from the inner London education authority attending forty term-time performances a year. In addition to her own productions she invited into the theatre puppet shows, dance pieces, films, and chamber music concerts.

From 1967 to 1969 Jenner served on the young people's theatre panel of the Arts Council, and in 1970 she became chairman of the young people's theatre executive of the Council of Repertory Theatres. She was also the British representative for the Association Internationale du Théâtre pour l'Enfance et la Jeunesse, attending its five-week assembly in Canada and the United States shortly before her death. Gaunt and mannish in appearance, a chain-smoker and extremely active to the point of being domineering, she died, unmarried, of lung cancer at the Middlesex Hospital, London, on 29 January 1973.

MICHAEL PATTERSON

Sources J. Parker, ed., *Who's who in the theatre*, 15th edn (1972) · *The Times* (30 Jan 1973) · private information (2004) · E. Smythe, 'Anniversary time', *Plays and Players* (Oct 1996), 24 · M. Ford and D. Wooder, 'Is it in colour, miss?': the first fifty years of the Unicorn Theatre for children (1997) · WWW [Walter Ripman] · b. cert. · d. cert. · *CGPLA Eng. & Wales* (1973)
Likenesses C. Harris, photograph, 1950, repro. in Ford and Wooder, 'Is it in colour, miss?' · J. Vickers, photograph, 1960, repro. in Ford and Wooder, 'Is it in colour, miss?'
Wealth at death £29,573: probate, 24 Sept 1973, *CGPLA Eng. & Wales*

Jenner, Charles (*bap.* 1736, *d.* 1774), writer and poet, the eldest son of Charles Jenner (1707–1770) and Mary, daughter of John Sawyer of Heywood, Berkshire, was baptized at St Clement Danes, London, on 1 May 1736. His father, a grandson of Sir Thomas Jenner, baron of the exchequer, was a graduate of Brasenose College, Oxford, and became rector of Buckworth, Huntingdonshire, in 1740. Subsequently he became chaplain to George II in 1746, prebendary of Lincoln in 1753, and archdeacon of Bedford in 1756 and of Huntingdon in 1757. Finances were always a problem, the fault being largely the archdeacon's own, it seems, since he 'ran into debt with everyone; … and, at last … was forced to leave England' (Nichols, *Lit. anecdotes*, 810).

Charles Jenner was admitted as a pensioner at Pembroke College, Cambridge, on 14 April 1753, graduating BA in 1757 and MA in 1760; he subsequently migrated to Sidney Sussex College on 19 December 1763. In 1764 Jenner married Rebecca, daughter of William Thomson; they had no children. In 1769 Jenner was instituted to the living of Claybrook in Leicestershire, which he obtained a dispensation to hold with that of Craneford St John in Northamptonshire. His father's financial imprudence, Cole suggests, 'much hurt him' and he himself 'was of an opposite turn' (Nichols, *Lit. anecdotes*, 810). If he was cautious with money, Jenner was an enthusiast for music and had a reputation as a good singer and performer at concerts, as well as for being 'humane and benevolent', with manners 'soft and gentle, affable and condescending' (ibid., 564).

Jenner's first published work was a volume of poems in 1766. He won the Seatonian prize at Cambridge for poems on sacred subjects in 1767 and 1768, but also turned his attention to prose narrative at about this time with *Letters from Altamont* (1767) and *Letters from Lothario* (1769). *The Placid Man* (1770) is Jenner's one piece of sustained fictional narrative, and in this he departed from the epistolary technique and followed Henry Fielding, to whom he clearly states his allegiance early on in the proceedings, in telling his story from the viewpoint of an omniscient narrator who not only recounts the incidents but also takes time to air his views on a variety of related subjects, especially in the introductory chapter to each book of the novel. As J. M. S. Tompkins points out, however, while 'Fielding's is certainly the sovereign influence', Jenner's methods and storylines owe significant debts to other writers:

> The education of the hero by his father, the musical baronet, and his uncle, the retired West Indian governor, is after Sterne; the placid man himself, with his benevolence and his sentiments, would have been a welcome guest at Sir Charles Grandison's table. (Tompkins, 42)

The Placid Man is, then, a novel that takes much from the conventions of contemporary sentimental fiction, in both form and content. Interpolated narratives turn up at irregular intervals, causing one contemporary critic to complain that 'the digressions are too numerous', although he conceded that 'many of them are instructive and entertaining' (*Critical Review*). The hero, Charles Beville, himself suffers the familiar agonies of the man of feeling, being 'just as attentive to the interests of others, as he was negligent of his own, and … if there was anything he hardly knew how to bear, it was the misfortunes of another which he could not relieve' (*Placid Man*, 1.38). Falling in love is tied in with this strong sensitivity to the sufferings of others. As Charles tells Miss Clayton the history of an unfortunate man he has been able to help, the narrator exclaims: 'how absolutely void of sensibility must that man be, who could see, unmoved, the tear of compassion stealing down the cheek of beauty! Mr. Beville was not that man' (ibid., 1.103). While drawing freely on the language and conventions of sensibility, however, Jenner steers clear of the tragic turn so often taken in novels of the genre, concluding the narrative in happy-ever-after style.

The Placid Man was successful enough for a second edition in 1773 and was received, if not exactly with enthusiasm, at least with courtesy by the critics of the day. The *Monthly Review* felt Jenner proved himself 'acquainted with the world, and conversant in literature' and asserted:

'we need not scruple to pronounce that his style is lively and agreeable' (*Monthly Review*, 43). The *Critical Review* was more lukewarm in its appraisal, finding 'strokes of good sense and good writing in the introduction' but opining that the principal figures of Charles Beville and Miss Clayton 'are not very strongly marked: they are, indeed, amiable, but too uniformly so to be striking'. Jenner's novel has received very little attention in recent years, despite the revival of interest in less well-known fiction of the period and in sensibility in particular, but it does not deserve to be so entirely overlooked. Tompkins even suggests that there is 'one note that is peculiarly his': 'It is the note that is missing in all four of the great novelists, the lyric quickening of prose, no more than a hint as yet, but pregnant with promise' (Tompkins, 42–3). Jenner was, of course, a poet before he was a novelist and lyricism would not be out of keeping. After *The Placid Man* his most interesting work was in verse once more, especially in *Town Eclogues* (1772) and *Louisa: a Tale* (1773).

Jenner died at Claybrook on 11 May 1774. Cole recounts that 'he had been at London, and at Vauxhall, and, being of a consumptive constitution, caught cold, and went home ill' (Nichols, *Lit. anecdotes*, 810). A monument was erected to his memory in Claybrook church by Lady Craven, with commemorative verses of her own.

GILLIAN SKINNER

Sources Nichols, *Lit. anecdotes* · DNB · GM, 1st ser., 44 (1774), 239 · J. M. S. Tompkins, *The popular novel in England, 1770–1800* (1932) · *Critical Review*, 29 (1770), 43 · *Monthly Review* (1779), 42–3 · Venn, *Alum. Cant.* · IGI

Jenner, Charles (1810–1893), department store owner and botanist, was born on 1 September 1810 in Chatham, Kent, one of at least four sons of John Jenner (1768/9–1852), an innkeeper, and Elizabeth Terry. Much of Jenner's childhood was spent in Rochester, where he was apprenticed at the age of thirteen to a local draper. He moved to Edinburgh in 1829, to continue his training with the firm of W. and R. Spence, a leading firm of drapers. There he was to meet his future business partner, Charles Kennington, with whom he founded the firm of Kennington and Jenner in May 1838. Reputedly the venture into business took place after the friends had been dismissed by their employer for taking time off to attend the local races.

From the outset Kennington and Jenner, of Princes Street in Edinburgh, proved to be a pioneering firm, both in the range and quality of its stock and in its methods of business. Advertised in *The Scotsman* as retailers of 'British and Parisian fashion in silks, shawls, fancy dresses, ribbons, lace, hosiery and every description of linen drapery and haberdashery' (*DSBB*, 1.370), the firm from the outset imitated the new system of retailing that was coming into existence in London and Paris, based on departments within a large-scale warehouse emporium, relying on rapid turnover to maintain competitive prices and largely with the middle-class female customer in mind. As the business expanded, absorbing adjacent premises in Princes Street, the number of departments increased to include household commodities such as furniture, carpets, and curtains as well as tearooms and other genteel leisure facilities. From 1874, following the death of Kennington, the firm was known as Charles Jenner & Co. Jenner himself retired from active management in 1881. Although Jenner was twice married, he had no surviving children, and the firm passed into the hands of a junior partner who had risen through the firm, James Kennedy, the son of an old friend of Jenner. The Kennedy family remained owner–managers of the firm throughout the twentieth century.

Jenner's influence over the firm he had founded did not cease with his retirement. The premises in Princes Street were rebuilt following a major fire in 1892 and, though by then an elderly man, Jenner was instrumental both in choosing the architect and in instructing the design to reflect the dignity and nature of the store. The new building, designed by W. Hamilton Beattie, was broadly modelled on the Bodleian Library at Oxford and was intended to be both worthy of the principal street of Edinburgh and a fitting memorial to Jenner as a powerful and pioneering merchant. In recognition of the fact that the success of Charles Jenner & Co. was founded on its appeal to the female consumer, Jenner instructed that female figures or caryatids supporting classical columns should form the principal decorative motif on the exterior of the building, to show symbolically that women were the support of the house as well as his business.

A man of great energy as well as business acumen, Jenner was well known to contemporaries as a man of science, an accomplished amateur botanist and geologist, and a patron of the arts. From 1851 he was a member of the Botanical Society of Edinburgh and in 1865 he was elected to the élite Botanical Society Club. A previously unknown alpine moss, discovered by Jenner in 1867 while on one of his many scientific tours in Europe, was officially named *Didymodon jennerii* in his honour. The focus of his botanical interest was an extraordinary and world-renowned private botanical garden of 8 acres—boasting 4000 plant species, scientifically arranged—which he created at his home at Easter Duddingston Lodge in Portobello near Edinburgh. The garden was destroyed by building developments in the early twentieth century.

Jenner was a founder of the Edinburgh Philosophical Institution in 1864. In 1865 he was elected a fellow of the Royal Society of Edinburgh and two years later he was elected a fellow of the Geological Society of Scotland. In addition to his scientific interests, Jenner had a great interest in contemporary art and literature and was a personal friend of Alfred, Lord Tennyson. Jenner gave the bust of the poet that was placed in Poets' Corner in Westminster Abbey following Tennyson's death.

Jenner was the older brother of Sir William *Jenner, personal physician to Queen Victoria. Interests formed through the connection with his brother—and possibly also reflecting the early deaths of all of his own children—influenced his charitable activity. Notably, Charles Jenner was the first director of the Royal Hospital for Sick Children in Edinburgh, founded in 1860, which was modelled on the similar institution in London with which William

Jenner was associated. Jenner also made major contributions to the ragged school movement in Edinburgh. He died at his Portobello home on 27 October 1893.

STANA NENADIC

Sources A. Slaven, 'Jenner, Charles', *DSBB* · A. K. Gibbons, *Charles Jenner, 1810–1893, man of science* (1988) · S. McNamara, *Jenners of Edinburgh: a short history, 1838–1988* [n.d.] · Boase, *Mod. Eng. biog.* · *CCI* (1894)
Wealth at death £55,583 9s. 1d.: confirmation, 18 Jan 1894, *CCI*

Jenner, David (d. 1693), Church of England clergyman, came from Northumberland. He was admitted sizar at Trinity College, Cambridge, on 22 December 1653, matriculated in 1657, and graduated BA in 1658. He then became a fellow of Sidney Sussex College, proceeding MA in 1662 and BD in 1668, both by royal mandate. From 1663 he was vicar of St Sepulchre, Cambridge, and on 30 June 1675 he took out a licence to marry Mary Sann, the daughter of a Cambridge gentleman. He was installed in the prebend of Netherbury in the cathedral church of Salisbury on 28 June 1676. On 15 October 1678 he was instituted to the rectory of Great Warley, Essex, which he resigned in 1687. He was also chaplain to the king. He retained his prebend, and when he made his will on 7 August 1691 he was also rector of Compton Bassett, Wiltshire.

Jenner published two sermons, *The Life and Death of S. Luke* (1676) and *Cain's Mark and Murder: K. Charles I. his Martyrdom* (1681), which compared the execution of Charles I to the murder of Abel. In 1683 he published *Beaufrons, or, A new-discovery of treason under the fair-face and mask of religion, and of liberty of conscience.* This was a reply to Dr Daniel Whitby's *Protestant Reconciler* (1683), an Anglican clergyman's plea for concessions to dissenters which, according to Wood, had given 'great offence to the orthodox clergy and others' (Wood, *Ath. Oxon.*, 4.675). Wood notes that Jenner's reply 'saith that the author of the Protestant Reconcilor designs nothing but to prove anarchy and confusion in church and state' (ibid., 676). Jenner also argued that 'the author is guilty of treason … a giver out unto the people that the King and governors were and are betrayers of their liberties, and therefore deserves death' (ibid.).

Jenner also published *The prerogative of primogeniture: shewing that the right of succession, to an hereditary crown, depends not upon grace, religion, & c. but onely upon birth-right and primogeniture* (1683). This was dedicated to James, duke of York, and described the previous whig attempts to pass a bill of exclusion to prevent James's succession as 'Unchristian and Unnatural' (p. 4). Jenner was buried at his old Essex parish of Great Warley, whose advowson he had acquired, on 14 March 1693. Apart from a shilling each to his brother and nephew, he left all his goods to his wife, Mary, by whom his will was proved on 16 March.

SARAH CARR

Sources Venn, *Alum. Cant.* · Wood, *Ath. Oxon.*, new edn, vol. 4 · *Fasti Angl., 1541–1857*, [Salisbury] · will, PRO, PROB 11/414, sig. 54 · J. L. Chester and J. Foster, eds., *London marriage licences, 1521–1869* (1887), 758
Wealth at death see will, PRO, PROB 11/414, sig. 54

Jenner, Edward (1749–1823), surgeon and pioneer of smallpox vaccination, was born on 17 May 1749 at the vicarage, Berkeley, Gloucestershire, the fourth son and eighth of nine children of the Revd Stephen Jenner (1702–1754), vicar of Berkeley, and his wife, Sarah (1709–1754), daughter of the Revd Henry Head and his wife, Mary, of Berkeley.

Education, marriage, and medical practice in Gloucestershire
Only five of Edward's siblings survived childhood, and he was named after a brother who died in April 1749 aged five. Jenner's parents both died in 1754 and, although his education was probably planned by his elder brother Stephen, it is likely that the necessary home environment was provided by his aunt, Deborah Hooper, of Clapton Farm near Berkeley.

In 1757 Jenner attended the Revd Clissold's school at nearby Wotton under Edge, but he soon transferred to the Revd Dr Washbourn's school, Cirencester. His education was directed towards medicine from 1763, when he began training with Daniel Ludlow, an apothecary in Chipping Sodbury, and in August 1764 he was apprenticed to George Hardwicke of Sodbury. The greatest influence on Jenner's career was John Hunter (1728–1793), with whom he trained as a private pupil and as a student at St George's Hospital, London, between 1770 and 1772. Here, in addition to receiving invaluable training, Jenner made important contacts such as Joseph Banks, later president of the Royal Society, and Everard Home and Henry Cline, both later presidents of the Royal College of Surgeons. Hunter, a stern taskmaster, evidently thought well of Jenner and recommended that he should help to arrange and catalogue the specimens brought back by Banks from Captain Cook's first Pacific voyage. It was planned that Jenner should accompany Banks on the second voyage, but in the event neither went.

On his return to Berkeley in 1772 Jenner set up in general practice, living at first with his brother Stephen. He continued in Berkeley despite the offer by Hunter of a partnership in 1775; however, the two men maintained a lively correspondence, in which Jenner was encouraged in a variety of anatomical and physiological experiments, until Hunter's death in 1793. In 1785 Jenner bought Chauntry Cottage (The Chantry), Berkeley, and on 6 March 1788 he married Catherine Kingscote (1760/61–1815) of Kingscote near Berkeley. They had three children: Edward (1789–1810), Catherine (1794–1833), and Robert Fitzharding (1797–1854). Their family life was happy, marred only by the death of young Edward from tuberculosis, and the chronic ill health of Jenner's wife, caused by the same disease. Edward Gardner of Frampton-on-Severn described Jenner in early middle age as being:

> under the middle size … robust but active … dressed in a blue coat and yellow buttons, buckskins, well-polished jockey boots with handsome silver spurs … and a smart whip with a silver handle. His hair, after the fashion … was done up in a club, and he wore a broad-brimmed hat. (Baron, 1.15–16)

Jenner's practice, which required him to make visits on horseback in all weathers, covered some 400 square miles

Edward Jenner (1749–1823), by James Northcote, 1803 [completed 1823]

and involved climbs of 700–800 feet. Social visits included regular rides to Stroud, Frampton, Sodbury, Bath, and particularly Cheltenham. A visit to Kingscote during a severe frost in 1786 caused him to suffer hypothermia, of which he left a detailed account.

Jenner kept a good table and fancied himself a musician and poet, his 'Address to a Robin' perhaps being his best-known work. He belonged to two local medical societies: the 'medico-convivial' society, which he co-founded in 1788 and which met at The Fleece inn, Rodborough; and the 'convivio-medical' society, which met at The Ship inn, Alveston. These names, by which Jenner referred to them, indicated the order of priorities.

It is inappropriate to regard Jenner, as some have done, as simply a country doctor. He had a modest private income and belonged to the minor landed gentry. His contacts through Lord Berkeley and the Kingscote family ensured his social position in the immediate neighbourhood, and Hunter and Banks also provided contacts in London and Cheltenham. Jenner's qualifications and status ensured he had a good clientele among the gentry and aristocracy. He fitted well into fashionable Cheltenham life and was founder and first president of the Cheltenham Literary and Philosophical Society.

Jenner and vaccination Most individuals in populous areas of Britain in the eighteenth century could expect to catch smallpox, which killed 20 per cent or more of those infected. Before Jenner introduced vaccination, smallpox could be prevented by variolation—the deliberate inoculation of matter from smallpox pustules into the skin in the hope that a mild but protective infection would result. This was introduced into British society in 1721 by Lady

Mary Wortley Montagu, who had seen it used in Constantinople. Variolation had an overall mortality of about 0.5 per cent, but occasional disasters occurred and there was also the risk that those in contact with variolated individuals would contract fully virulent smallpox.

Jenner, an experienced variolator, had unpleasant memories of his own variolation when he was eight years old, and with his background and training it was perhaps not surprising that he became interested in safer alternatives. Common in rural areas then was the idea that those who recovered from cowpox, a mild, localized disease traditionally acquired when milking infected cows, were thus rendered immune to natural and inoculated smallpox. Jenner probably knew of this before he went to London and certainly discussed it with Hunter and members of the Medico-convivial Society, and by the late 1770s he was collecting data to test this hypothesis. Some of the cases of cowpox had occurred many years before and could not have been seen by Jenner, but he did see some cases from 1782 onwards. Information about immunity to smallpox was gradually collected during routine variolations done after 1792 by Jenner and his nephew Henry. Data were collected on twenty-eight individuals in all, and represented cases where cowpox had occurred recently or many years before, where it had been acquired directly from a cow or a horse, and where immunity to smallpox was assessed by natural exposure and/or variolation. Jenner appreciated the value of working in a rural area where smallpox was uncommon, and of ensuring as best he could that any immunity was due to cowpox and not to previous smallpox or variolation.

In 1789 Jenner and another doctor, John Hickes, inoculated some individuals, including the infant Edward Jenner, with material from a disease variously described as swinepox, pigpox, and cowpox. This confused some later analysts, but there is no record of the use of any animal disease here. Jenner and Hickes clearly regarded the material as coming from a variety of smallpox, and the topic was not pursued.

In 1792, with twenty years' experience of general practice and surgery, Jenner obtained the degree of MD from St Andrews. This simply required recommendations from two reputable doctors, and his colleagues Caleb Parry and John Hickes acted for him. Now able to style himself physician and surgeon, Jenner left most general practice matters to his nephew and assistant, Henry Jenner, and took on the role of consultant. From 1795 he established a second home in Cheltenham where well-to-do patients of his London colleagues could consult him when they visited the fashionable spa.

Jenner performed the first documented cowpox inoculation on 14 May 1796. This was probably not the first ever vaccination, but others, by people such as Benjamin Jesty, a Dorset farmer, came to light only after Jenner's work became known. As such any earlier vaccinations had no impact on medicine. Just before his forty-seventh birthday, however, Jenner inoculated eight-year-old James Phipps with cowpox material taken from a dairymaid, Sarah Nelmes. The boy recovered uneventfully, and six weeks later he successfully resisted variolation. Jenner was tempted to publish his data at this stage, but he was advised informally by the Royal Society that it would harm his reputation to publish such slender evidence. He collected more epidemiological information, conducted more vaccinations in March–April 1798, and published his results privately in his famous *Inquiry into the causes and effects of the variolae vaccine a disease … known by the name of the cow-pox* (1798). The extra vaccinations were the important addition, but their total is not known; Jenner named only ten, though more were performed at that time. Jenner showed that cowpox could be transferred serially by arm-to-arm inoculation, and that the first and last in the series resisted variolation, though as with Phipps this challenge was made after only a few weeks.

Jenner's conclusions were that cowpox, which could be maintained by arm-to-arm transfer, was a safe alternative to variolation and produced lifelong immunity to smallpox. He also believed that cowpox originated from an equine disease called 'grease', which could be passed to cows by the hands of milkmen who had also tended infected horses, but that the vaccine needed to come from the cow in order to give consistent results. He provided preliminary information that there were different types of cowpox: 'true' cowpox, which gave the expected result, and 'spurious' cowpox, which did not protect and/or produced unacceptably severe lesions. At first 'cowpox inoculation' and 'vaccine inoculation' (from *vacca*, 'cow') were used to describe the process, but 'vaccination' was soon the generally accepted term. The information Jenner had been collecting was already known to some, and the first detailed analysis of the *Inquiry* of 1798, by George Pearson, was published in November that year. The *Inquiry* reached the United States in January 1799, and by 1801 it had been translated into Latin, German, French, Italian, Dutch, and Spanish.

Inevitably the *Inquiry* received a mixed reception. There was strong criticism from some variolators who saw the loss of a lucrative monopoly. There was also some religious opposition to inoculating humans with animal material, and caricatures showing humans with bovine characteristics appeared. There was general scepticism about the origins of cowpox in 'grease', about the idea of 'spurious' cowpox, and of the claims that vaccination gave lifelong immunity; the last could only be tested by the passage of time after the first two issues had been clarified. However, there was considerable support for the basic idea that inoculated cowpox would protect against smallpox, though everyone, including Jenner, appreciated the need for more work.

In his second monograph, *Further Observations on the Variolae vaccinae* (1799), Jenner provided more information on 'true' and 'spurious' cowpox, in particular defining four categories of the latter: 'spurious' cowpox resulted from (a) other bovine diseases infectious to humans; (b) improperly stored, or (c) old material in both of which the cowpox virus had been inactivated and which in modern terms contained pathogenic bacteria; and (d) material obtained directly from horse grease. However, 'spurious' cowpox was at times used to explain away the failures of genuine vaccine to protect completely.

There was some initial confusion over the appearance of the lesions of inoculated smallpox and cowpox, and early attempts by William Woodville to confirm Jenner's conclusions were compromised by the use of cowpox material contaminated with smallpox virus. In fact Jenner had contributed to this confusion by ambiguities in the *Inquiry*, but he helped to resolve the problem in his third monograph, entitled *A Continuation of Facts and Observations Relative to the Variolae vaccinae or Cowpox* (1800).

Jenner's seminal contribution to vaccination is contained in the three monographs discussed above. He continued to vaccinate using his own and other vaccines, but his claim, that smallpox could be prevented by use of an animal virus, was confirmed and extended by others. By 1801 vaccines were established from horsepox. So, though Jenner erred in using the term 'grease', there was some truth in this part of his hypothesis. However, after initial criticism, after 1799 Jenner quickly dropped all public mention of this idea. Nevertheless, it is clear from then unpublished sources that he made extensive use of horsepox vaccines after this date. It is also evident that some of Jenner's views were formed early and held consistently. Two manuscripts of the *Inquiry* exist, written in 1797, in which reports of the arm-to-arm vaccinations of 1798 were obviously absent. However, these early drafts included all the other ideas, particularly the basic distinction between 'true' and 'spurious' cowpox, even if expressed in a less clear form than later. In the case of vaccination, diaries and letters indicate that Jenner was well aware of the need for routine revaccination; he even revaccinated his own family, though his published work emphasized that vaccination, properly done, would provide lifelong protection.

Jenner continued to publish short pamphlets: he defended his priority for the introduction of vaccination in *On the Origin of the Vaccine Inoculation* (1801); he offered advice on vaccination procedure in *Instructions for Vaccine Inoculation* (1802); and he insisted that vaccination properly done would induce lifelong protection in *Varieties and Modifications of the Vaccine Pustule* (1804), in *Facts … Respecting Variolous Contagion* (1808), and in his *Circular Letter* (1821). Letters on the same general topics written for publication, usually in the *Medical and Physical Journal*, have been listed by Baron and LeFanu.

With some private income, a rich social life, and varied interests in science and medicine, Jenner perhaps led the dilettante life of a country gentleman restricted only by his medical practice. There is no evidence that he initially spent as much time investigating cowpox as his supporters later claimed. However, from 1798 his life was dominated by vaccination. He maintained a house in London, at considerable expense, but only spent short periods there. In the course of his vaccination crusade he corresponded with and was received by George III and Queen Charlotte, and by the prince of Wales. He was received in London by the tsar and the king of Prussia, and he corresponded with Napoleon. These contacts no doubt helped to make Jenner famous, as did the spread of the use of vaccine. It was adopted by the army and navy (Jenner was awarded a gold medal on the behalf of British naval officers in 1801), and was quickly taken up in many countries throughout the world. Jenner himself dealt with correspondence from all over the world, and William Wilberforce remarked that there was 'no man who is so much inquired after, by Foreigners when they arrive in this country' (Fisher, 112). Jenner also gained support from London's medical élite: in 1800 John Ring, a staunch defender of vaccination, organized a testimonial signed by a number of eminent physicians and surgeons supporting vaccination after attacks had been made on Jenner's work. Similar declarations of support were made in York, Leeds, Chester, Durham, and Oxford. Ring continued to be the most loyal of Jenner's defenders and received encouragement in his task from Jenner himself. In December 1801 Jenner attended a party given in London by Lord and Lady Spencer where he met, among others, Lord Lucan, Lord Macartney, and Lord Campden, possibly in an attempt to smooth the path of his application to parliament for a grant.

Jenner could evidently be awkward, but at the age of forty-nine vaccination had totally changed his life. He wrote petulant letters about insufficiently supportive colleagues, and fought acrimonious battles with supporters of variolation. He and George Pearson quarrelled over the allocation of credit, and Pearson opposed Jenner's parliamentary petition. The Royal Jennerian Society, later the National Vaccine Establishment, was founded in 1803 with Jenner as president of its medical council, but he eventually withdrew after disagreement about his role.

Jenner's other medical and scientific work From childhood Jenner had shown an interest in natural history and had collected fossils and nests. Later his fossil specimen of a plesiosaurus was the first to be identified in Britain, and he was made an honorary member of the Geological Society in 1809. About 1812–14 Jenner was also a member of the Barrow Hill Club, a group of friends interested in geology. Other members included Edward Gardner and John Baron, later Jenner's official biographer. He also undertook other minor projects on topics as diverse as manures, distemper in dogs, and tuberculosis, and his general interests in natural history were acknowledged in 1798 by his election to fellowship of the Linnean Society. In 1784, soon after both the Montgolfiers' pioneering flight and the first flight in Britain, Jenner was involved in the flight of an unmanned balloon. He also made various observations on anatomy and physiology which were incorporated into John Hunter's papers. In 1783 he published an improved method for preparing pure emetic tartar (potassium antimony tartrate) by recrystallization, and in 1799 Caleb Parry acknowledged Jenner as the first to associate the clinical features of angina pectoris with its underlying anatomical changes.

Jenner's interest in ornithology merits special mention. It had been long known that female cuckoos laid eggs in the nests of other birds. However, it was not known how the nestlings of the foster parents were disposed of. In the original manuscript of the paper on cuckoos read before the Royal Society on 29 March 1787, Jenner concluded that the cuckoos' foster parents ejected their own nestlings. Jenner could not have seen this—he may have heard the explanation from his nephew—and he had to withdraw the paper before publication in the *Philosophical Transactions* when he saw what really happened: ejection by the newly hatched cuckoo. Jenner went on to describe the transient anatomical modification to the young cuckoo's back which facilitates this action. He also reasoned that the behaviour of the mother cuckoo was determined by the fact that she did not stay long enough in Britain to rear her young. Jenner published his revised observations in the *Philosophical Transactions* for 1788, and the following year he was elected to fellowship of the Royal Society. His published account was not universally accepted until confirmed by photography. That he eventually observed what really happened rather than guessed is proved by his recognition of the transient anatomical modification.

At about the same time as his election to the Royal Society, Jenner started the work on bird migration which was completed just before his death. At a period when some still believed that birds hibernated, he helped to confirm that they did migrate. He also showed, by dissection, that this behaviour was connected to changes in the reproductive system and not due to climatic changes or to food shortage. The results of his work were published posthumously in the *Philosophical Transactions* for 1824.

Rewards Despite some scepticism, vaccination was accepted quickly, particularly so given the uncertainty about the duration of immunity, which could only be resolved by the passage of time. Jenner's role was also generally acknowledged by individuals and by official commissions set up in Britain and overseas. Parliamentary grants of £10,000 in 1802 and £20,000 in 1807 helped to compensate for the fact that he made his findings freely available.

Already received by British and foreign royalty, during the wars with France letters from Jenner to Napoleon secured the release of English prisoners. Jenner also received honours, testimonials, and diplomas from all over the world. These are listed by Baron in the second volume of his *Life of Edward Jenner* (1838, pp. 449–56), and include fellowships of colleges and societies in America, France, Italy, Russia, Spain, and Sweden; freedom of the cities of London, Edinburgh, Glasgow, and Dublin; and honorary doctorates from Oxford and Harvard universities. Although he accepted the fellowship of the Royal College of Physicians of Edinburgh, he declined to be put forward for fellowship of the Royal College of Physicians of London because it involved sitting a Latin examination.

Shortly before his seventy-second birthday Jenner was made physician-extraordinary to George IV, a purely honorary title. However he did not receive a knighthood. This may have been due to his allegiance to Queen Caroline, whose daughter he attended in 1808, and for whom he apparently had some sympathy in her dispute with the king.

Later years and death Jenner did not enjoy good health after middle age. He had serious attacks of typhus, or more likely typhoid, in 1794 and 1811, and suffered bouts of depression particularly following his son Edward's death in 1810. He served terms as mayor of Berkeley and commissioner of Cheltenham, and as magistrate in both places. Despite having close family associations with the Church of England, Jenner apparently showed no more than routine interest in religious matters, though he was vice-president of Cheltenham Auxiliary Bible Society. He was a freemason by 1804 and served some official role in a Berkeley lodge in 1811. His mobility and perhaps enjoyment of his new-found fame was marred by increasing concern over his wife's illness. Catherine Jenner died from tuberculosis on 13 September 1815 and Jenner, increasingly depressed, spent his remaining years in Berkeley. He had a minor stroke in 1821 but still continued to see patients occasionally, until just before his death. He died from a stroke on 26 January 1823 at his home, The Chantry, Berkeley (now the Jenner Museum), and was buried in Berkeley parish church on 3 February.

At his death Jenner's household and personal effects, including more than 800 books, 648 bottles of port, and 200 gallons of ale, were officially valued at £2477 19s. 0d. His executor and nephew William Davies estimated the total estate as less than £35,000, though Jenner had settled £13,333 on his daughter the year before. Jenner's papers were left for his executors to dispose of by publication or destruction as they thought fit. Although very few were published at the time, many survived and have since been published and analysed.

Reputation Jenner's reputation has suffered from over-enthusiastic supporters as well as critics. Of the former, John Baron and later Saunders depicted Jenner as a genius, whereas many popular accounts describe him as the simple country doctor fascinated by milkmaids' tales. However, all his critics claim that he was lazy and evasive, and to Creighton he was a charlatan whose cuckoo and vaccination studies were a hoax (Creighton, 49). In fact Jenner, though no genius, was a well-trained physician and surgeon, competent at formulating and testing hypotheses. Some, particularly Creighton, Crookshank, and more recently Razzell, have argued that, although Jenner conducted some preliminary work with cowpox, the bulk of nineteenth-century vaccine was established—by others—from modified smallpox virus. If so, this would severely dent Jenner's reputation. However, many vaccines were established from cowpox and horsepox, and modern studies discount the role of smallpox virus in the origin of smallpox vaccine.

Jenner's claims, based on few vaccinations (not all of which were tested by variolation and then after a very short interval), and his original cuckoo observations, show that he was inclined to make conclusions based on incomplete or dubious evidence. However, even when this is taken into account it has to be accepted that Jenner's use of an animal virus to induce immunity to smallpox marks a distinct break with previous practice. This, together with his analysis of 'true' and 'spurious' cowpox, without which vaccination could not have been developed, justifies the credit he has been given. Jenner's major error was not to acknowledge publicly that vaccination did not provide lifelong protection. However, vaccination and revaccination, properly carried out, continued to reduce the impact of smallpox, and culminated in the final eradication of this disease—an outcome forecast by Jenner in 1801.   DERRICK BAXBY

Sources J. Baron, *The life of Edward Jenner*, 2 vols. (1827–38) · W. R. LeFanu, *Bibliography of Edward Jenner*, rev. 2nd edn (1985) · E. M. Crookshank, *History and pathology of vaccination*, 2 vols. (1889) · D. Baxby, *Jenner's smallpox vaccine: the riddle of vaccinia virus and its origin* (1981) · R. Palmer, 'Edward Jenner (1749–1823)', *Wellcome Institute for the History of Medicine Western Manuscripts Handlist*, no. 6 (1986) · D. Baxby, 'The genesis of Edward Jenner's *Inquiry* of 1798: a comparison of the two unpublished manuscripts and the published version', *Medical History*, 29 (1985), 193–9 · P. Saunders, *Edward Jenner: the Cheltenham years, 1795–1823* (1982) · R. B. Fisher, *Edward Jenner* (1991) · D. Baxby, 'Edward Jenner's Inquiry: a bicentenary analysis', *Vaccine*, 17 (1999), 301–7 · C. Creighton, *Jenner and vaccination* (1889) · P. E. Razzell, *Edward Jenner's cowpox vaccine: the history of a medical myth*, 2nd edn (1980) · I. Bailey, 'Edward Jenner (1749–1823): naturalist, scientist, country doctor, benefactor to mankind', *Journal of Medical Biography*, 4 (1996), 63–70 · *BMJ* (23 May 1896), 1245–302 [Jenner centenary number] · J. Kirkup, 'Edward Jenner's accompt-book for the pocket or desk', *Medical History*, 40 (1996), 487–98 · E. Gethyn-Jones, 'Edward Jenner's family background', *Transactions of the Bristol and Gloucestershire Archaeological Society*, 109 (1991), 195–8 · J. H. Hunt, 'An inventory and evaluation of all the household furniture ... and all other effects the property of Dr Edward Jenner decd.', 1823, Wellcome L., MS 3028 · C. D. Hellman, ed., 'An unpublished diary of Edward Jenner (1810–1812)', *Annals of the History of Medicine*, n.s. 3 (1931), 412–38 · F. D. Drewitt, ed., *The notebook of Edward Jenner in the possession of the Royal College of Physicians of London* (1931) · G. Miller, ed., *Letters of Edward Jenner* (1983) · L. Crummer, ed., 'Copy of Jenner notebook', *Annals of Medical History*, new ser., 1 (1929), 403–28 · D. Baxby, 'Edward Jenner's unpublished cowpox inquiry and the Royal Society: Everard Home's report to Sir Joseph Banks', *Medical History*, 43 (1999), 108–10 · parish register, Berkeley, Gloucestershire, 22 May 1749 [baptism]
Archives Duke U., medical library, papers · Glos. RO, corresp., diary, and papers · Jenner Museum, Berkeley, Gloucestershire, letters · Johns Hopkins University, Baltimore, Milton S. Eisenhower Library, letters · McGill University, Montreal, Osler Library of the History of Medicine, papers · RCP Lond., diary and papers · RCS Eng., corresp. and papers · RS, observations on the cuckoo · U. Mich., Clements L., corresp. and papers [transcripts] · Wellcome L., corresp. and MSS | Glos. RO, letters to T. G. B. Estcourt · Royal Society of Medicine, London, letters to A. J. C. Marcet
Likenesses J. R. Smith, pastels, 1800, Wellcome L. · S. Medley, oils, c.1802, Medical Society of London · J. Northcote, oils, 1802, Plymouth Medical Society · J. Northcote, oils, 1803 (completed 1823), NPG [*see illus.*] · P. Anderloni, engraving, 1809 (after line engraving by J. R. Smith, 1800), Wellcome L. · T. Lawrence, oils, c.1809, RCP Lond. · attrib. H. Edridge, pencil drawing, c.1821, Wellcome L. · W. Hobday, oils, 1821, Royal Society of Medicine, London · R. W. Sievier, memorial statue, 1825, Gloucester Cathedral · H. Wyatt, oils, 1828, Wellcome L. · W. C. Calder Marshall, bronze statue, 1858, Kensington Gardens, London · E. Paul, iron statue, 1865, Boulogne, France · G. Monteverde, marble statue, 1878, Genoa; bronze copy, Wellcome L. · J. R. Smith, engraving (after pastel portrait), Wellcome L. · Yonehara Unkai, bronze statue, Tokyo, Japan · oils (after J. R. Smith, 1800), Johns Hopkins University Library, Baltimore, Maryland
Wealth at death £2477 19s. 0d. personal possessions and household effects: Hunt, 'Inventory', Wellcome L., MS 3028 · under £35,000 est. total estate: Fisher, *Edward Jenner*, 283; William Davies, Jenner's nephew and executor

Jenner, Edward (1803–1872), botanist, who was born on 13 March 1803, was for forty-seven years traveller to the printing house of Baxter of Lewes, publishers of the *Sussex Express*. Although quite ignorant of Latin, he worked hard at entomology and botany, securing a close and critical knowledge of the freshwater algae. He was elected an associate of the Linnean Society in 1838. The cryptogamic portion of his admirable little *Flora of Tunbridge Wells* (1845) gives it a distinctive character. He provided the illustrations for John Ralfs's *The British Desmidieae* (1848). He was married, and his wife predeceased him; her name is not known. They had a son, Edward, a grocer in Lewes. Jenner died suddenly at Lewes, on 13 March 1872, his sixty-ninth birthday.   B. D. JACKSON, *rev.* ALEXANDER GOLDBLOOM

Sources Desmond, *Botanists*, rev. edn, 383 · *Proceedings of the Linnean Society of London* (1871–2), 67 · *Gardeners' Chronicle* (23 March 1872), 398
Archives NHM, Broome corresp., illustrations, and letters
Likenesses portrait, Hunt Botanical Library, Pittsburgh, Pennsylvania
Wealth at death under £100: administration, 18 April 1872, CGPLA Eng. & Wales

Jenner, Thomas (b. 1606/7). *See under* Jenner, Thomas (d. 1673).

Jenner, Thomas (d. 1673), printseller and writer, of whose early life nothing is known, kept a noted print shop in London from 1618 until his death. His place of business was in Cornhill, initially at the sign of the White Bear, and then from 1624, for the remainder of his long career, at the Royal Exchange. Jenner became pre-eminent among London print publishers. Many of the engravings sold by Jenner suggest that he catered for customers of puritan inclination and, with the advent of civil war, for those who espoused the parliamentary cause. Jenner gave his own support by publishing a number of political pamphlets with illustrations, such as *A Copy of the Letter from ... Cromwell* (1656). Jenner's stock was eventually devoted substantially to portraits. In 1662 a catalogue of the books printed and sold by him (found at the end of the anonymous *A Book of the Names of All Parishes*) contains some 170 items, of which well over a third are engraved portraits. In addition to a substantial holding of maps, Jenner offered almanacs, art manuals, broadsides, newsbooks, and polemics.

Among the engravers whose work Jenner published were Renold Elstrack, John Goddard, Wenceslaus Hollar, William Marshall, Simon De Passe, and his brother Willem (to whom Jenner may have been related by marriage). Jenner's professional association with Willem De Passe was happily productive, and three of his early publications of De Passe's engravings are among his best: *Frederick of Bohemia and his Family* (1621), *James I and Charles as Prince of Wales* (1621), and a striking dynastic portrait, *The Family of James I* (1622). Other productions of Jenner's earlier career which, in a different way, are also remarkable are the collections of prints depicting allegorical figures such as *The Seven Deadly Sins* (c.1630), *The Five Senses* (c.1630), and, later, *The Four Elements* (*c*.1640) (engraved, respectively, by Goddard, Barra, and Marshall).

As an author Jenner was not distinguished. But his first work, *Souls Solace* (1626), together with his *Ages of Sin* (1655) and *Path of Life* (1656), shorter books of a similar nature, occupy a significant place in emblem literature. *Souls Solace* has thirty engraved plates which Jenner interprets in verse. It was reprinted with an additional plate in 1631 and 1639, and yet again as *Divine Mysteries that cannot be Seene, Made Plain by that which may be Seene* in 1651. The influence of the work of Gabriel Rollenhagen has been detected in the plates. Jenner's last work in this idiom, *A Work for none but Angels and Men* (1653), is derived from Sir John Davies's *Nosce teipsum* (1599) and lacks some of the common features of the emblem book.

Not all Jenner's books were devotional, and with *London's Blame if not its Shame* (1651) he revealed both patriotism and business acumen. The work is a plea for developing the fishing of English coastal waters which, Jenner argues, if efficiently exploited would not only provide a vital source of food but also give employment 'for a thousand Ships, and at least twenty thousand Fishermen and Mariners at Sea, and consequently as for as many Tradesmen and Labourers at Land' (*London's Blame*, 10).

Walpole remarked that Jenner 'attempted the art [of engraving] himself with no bad success' (Walpole, 18n.), but his work does not appear to have been extensive. Only an etched likeness of Cromwell (signed 'Tho: Jenner fecit') is noticed by Hind (Hind, 3.252) as Jenner's work. A portrait of Sir William Waad, lieutenant of the Tower, is attributed to him by Walpole, who owned a print of it. In 1653 Jenner etched a reversed copy of the marvellously detailed *The Sovereign of the Seas* (1638). This engraving, on two plates, is by far the largest of its kind to survive from the first half of the century. The engraved plates of Jenner's three emblem books have commonly been accepted as his work. Jenner died in 1673.

This Thomas Jenner must be distinguished from **Thomas Jenner** (*b*. 1606/7), Independent minister, who was born in Fordham, Essex, the son of Thomas Jenner, a farmer. After attending the school of Mr Cone in Fordham, Jenner was admitted sizar at Christ's College, Cambridge, in February 1624, aged seventeen. In 1635 he emigrated to New England with his father, and settled in Roxbury, Massachusetts. He served as minister in Weymouth from 1636 to 1640, then at Saco, Maine, in 1640, and moved to Charlestown where he was from 1646 to 1649.

Jenner returned to England in 1650. By the following year he was in Ireland, ministering to the combined Independent-Presbyterian congregation at Drogheda. From 1652 to 1658 he was minister at Coltishall, Norfolk, returning in 1658 to Ireland, this time to Carlow. In 1670 he published *Quakerism Anatomiz'd and Confuted*, a work published in response to the growing numbers of Quaker converts in Ireland. Jenner's will is dated 26 May 1676, in Dublin.   JOHN HORDEN

Sources A. Griffiths and R. A. Gerard, *The print in Stuart Britain, 1603–1689* (1998) [exhibition catalogue, BM, 8 May – 20 Sept 1998] · L. Rostenberg, *English publishers in the graphic arts, 1599–1700* (1963) · J. Horden, review of Rostenberg, *English publishers*, *The Library*, 5th ser., 19 (1964), 304–7 · A. M. Hind, *Engraving in England in the sixteenth and seventeenth centuries*, ed. M. Corbett and M. Norton, 3 vols. (1952–64) · STC, 1475–1640 · Wing, STC · M. Praz, *Studies in seventeenth-century imagery*, 2nd edn (1964) · H. Walpole, *A catalogue of engravers, who have been born, or resided in England* (1763) · *A book of the names of all parishes* (1662) [incl. catalogue, 'Books printed and sold by Thomas Jenner, at the South Entrance of the Royal Exchange, London'] · Venn, *Alum. Cant.* · R. L. Greaves, *God's other children: protestant nonconformists and the emergence of denominational churches in Ireland* (1997)

Jenner, Sir Thomas (1638–1707), judge, was born in Mayfield, Sussex, the son of Thomas Jenner and his wife, Dorothy, daughter of Jeffrey Glyde of Dallington, Sussex. The elder Jenner, probably from a yeoman family, must have achieved some measure of success. He was a captain of militia, and in 1655 he was named one of the Sussex commissioners to advise and assist William Goffe, Cromwell's major-general for the region. In 1672 he was chosen master of the Worshipful Company of Skinners. The association with the Skinners is evident in the son's enrolment in Tonbridge School in 1654. Jenner remained at Tonbridge only one year, matriculating as a pensioner from Queens' College, Cambridge, at Easter 1655. In 1659 he left the university without a degree for the Inner Temple. He was called to the bar in 1663 and made a bencher of the inn in 1683. On 1 January 1661 Jenner had married Anne (*d*. 1698), daughter of James Poe of Kirkby Overblow, Yorkshire, and granddaughter of Leonard Poe, a physician who had attended Queen Elizabeth, James I, and Charles I. The marriage produced thirteen children, including two sons who followed their father at the bar.

While establishing himself as a practising lawyer Jenner associated with some prominent figures including Sir John Bramston and the Catholic Lord Powis. In the 1670s he progressed from fairly impecunious circumstances to a successful professional life. In 1672 he was given (with Charles Whitaker) the office of steward of honours and lands of Windsor Castle, a position he surrendered the next year. In 1680 he entered 173 appearances in the equity side of the exchequer court—more than any lawyer but one.

Jenner received his first major official appointment on 3 October 1683 when, upon the surrender of the London charter after Charles II's *quo warranto*, he was named recorder of London. He was knighted the same day. At the opening of the next term of court he was made a serjeant-at-law. Jenner's appointment was perceived to be less a tribute to his legal talent than to his loyal and compliant nature. He appeared to meet these expectations, agreeing among other things to the prosecution of desertion as a capital felony, a policy at which a successor, Sir John Holt, baulked—costing him the recordership. At the same time Jenner represented the crown in several political cases, including the seditious libel trial of Samuel Barnardiston and the treason trial of Lord Delamere after Monmouth's rebellion.

Jenner's fortunes prospered on the accession of James II. He sat for Rye in the 1685 parliament. In 1686 he was appointed a baron of the exchequer, replacing William

Gregory, who had expressed doubts about the king's dispensing power. In this respect Jenner obliged the king by acquiescing in the judgment in *Godden* v. *Hales*.

In October 1687 Jenner, along with Thomas Cartwright, bishop of Chester, and Robert Wright, the lord chief justice, was added to the ecclesiastical commission for the purpose of dealing with the defiant fellows of Magdalen College, Oxford, in connection with the choice of their president. These three were instructed to visit the college, where they installed the king's nominee, the bishop of Oxford, and expelled twenty-five fellows who refused to submit. The next month Jenner was in the minority when the full ecclesiastical commission decided by a single vote to declare the expelled fellows permanently incapable of any clerical appointment. Jenner depicted himself as having had a distinctly passive role in these proceedings, leaving the direction of affairs to Cartwright. After the revolution he wrote a note declaring himself a most reluctant participant, 'too submissive, and something overawed by the King requiring it at my hands ... well knowing at the best it would be an invidious errand' (Jenner, fol. 44). Jenner's lack of enthusiasm was noticed and it was rumoured he would be discharged. Instead, in July 1688 he was promoted to the common pleas, which appointment he held in the few months until the revolution.

The revolution held a particular danger for Jenner. Prominent among the events leading to it were the London *quo warranto*, the establishment of the ecclesiastical commission, the affair at Magdalen College, and the approval of the dispensing power. Jenner was involved in all of them. As William of Orange's army entered London in December Jenner attempted to flee with James, but was captured with the king by sailors at Faversham. Jenner was arrested and held at Canterbury until January, when he was committed to the Tower. There is evidence of his notoriety at the time in the fact that on 18 December his effigy was hanged and burned along with that of Lord Chancellor Jeffreys by a London mob. In October 1689 he successfully sued out a writ of habeas corpus in the king's bench but was returned to custody the same day on order of the House of Commons. The house denied his pleas for release the next week when one member protested that 'no man was more forward in the Maudlin College business' (Morrice, 2.646). He remained a prisoner until January, when the house was prorogued. Later that year, when the Act of Grace was passed Jenner was one of seven of James II's judges excepted. But he was not prosecuted until November 1692, shortly after his son had been arrested for distributing seditious material. In this case Jenner was one of several of the former judges charged with having levied fines on dissenters without accounting for the proceeds. When the case came to trial in February 1693 he successfully pleaded a pardon secured from King James in the last desperate days of his reign. Thereafter he returned to his law practice, in which he appears to have been active as late as 1702.

Jenner was regarded by his contemporaries as a man of modest talents and accomplishments. He was disparaged and ridiculed sometimes even as he sat on the bench. He was under no illusions as to his abilities. In his diary he expressed himself '[a]lways doubtful of my own sufficiency to acquit myself in great matters' (Jenner, fol. 42*b*). That he frankly followed what he saw as his own interest is illustrated by an incident reported in June 1688. He sued a debtor, one Curthopp, a commissioner in the alienation office, for £200. When Curthopp responded by committing suicide Jenner promptly 'applied himself to his majesty and begged to have the defunct's place for his son' (Dover, 1.378–9). Attempting to excuse his activities before the Commons after the revolution he explained that 'his temptations were great, he had a wife and ten children and but a small estate' (Morrice, 2.634).

Jenner died at Petersham on 1 January 1707 and was buried in Petersham church. His will, executed in 1703, reveals an estate of various kinds of interests in scattered parcels of property, almost all apparently held for investment. These were carefully distributed among his surviving descendants. An elaborate memorial tablet was erected by his daughter in Petersham church.

RICHARD S. KAY

Sources T. Jenner, diary, 1686–9, Magd. Oxf., MS 429 · J. R. Bloxam, ed., *Magdalen College and James II, 1686–1688: a series of documents*, OHS, 6 (1886) · O. Manning and W. Bray, *The history and antiquities of the county of Surrey*, 1 (1804), 442 · N. Luttrell, *A brief historical relation of state affairs from September 1678 to April 1714*, 6 vols. (1857), vol. 1, pp. 283, 372, 424, 449, 469, 482, 486, 493, 554, 594–5; vol. 2, pp. 10, 612; vol. 3, pp. 37; vol. 6, p. 123 · W. G. Hart, ed., *The register of Tonbridge School from 1553 to 1820* (1935), 31, 133 · G. W. Keeton, *Lord Chancellor Jeffreys and the Stuart cause* (1965), 224, 335–6, 410, 427–31 · HoP, *Commons, 1660–90* · R. Morrice, 'Entring book', DWL, Morrice MS 31, P, Q, 1. 376–7; 2. 175, 218, 411–12, 634, 646, 649 · G. Dover, ed., *Letters written during the years 1686, 1687, 1688 and addressed to John Ellis, esq.*, 1 (1831), 378–9 · *Report on the manuscripts of the marquis of Downshire*, 6 vols. in 7, HMC, 75 (1924–95), vol. 1, p. 321 · Venn, *Alum. Cant.*
Wealth at death see will, PRO, PROB 11/494, fols. 342r–343v

Jenner, Sir William, first baronet (1815–1898), physician, was born on 30 January 1815 in Chatham, Kent, the fourth son of John Jenner, innkeeper, afterwards of Rochester, and his wife, Elizabeth, daughter of George Terry. Little is known of his early life before he arrived in London as one of the early students at University College and its hospital. At sixteen he was apprenticed to an apothecary practising in nearby Marylebone, and on qualifying as a licentiate of the Society of Apothecaries in 1835 he immediately began practice in the same area.

Jenner possessed seemingly limitless energy and ambition. He became a member of the Royal College of Surgeons in 1837 and was soon appointed surgeon-accoucheur to the Royal Maternity Charity, Finsbury Square, London. In 1844 he graduated MD at London University and ceased general practice to concentrate on pathology at University College Hospital. In 1847 he began studying continued fevers at the London Fever Hospital. At this time, while physicians in France had distinguished between typhoid and typhus, in Britain the identity of these fevers was still in dispute. To some they were all varieties of a single species, while to others two or more diseases were involved. Over the next two years Jenner made

Sir William Jenner, first baronet (1815–1898), by unknown photographer

notes on nearly one thousand cases and in 1849 he published his results on the pathological examination of 66 fatal cases in the *Monthly Journal of Medical Sciences*; these were also published as a monograph, *On the Identity or non-Identity of Typhoid and Typhus Fevers* (1850).

Many British physicians were convinced by Jenner's results, as were some in the United States. Most importantly, his work established the distinction in terms that were important in Britain. This major new achievement brought a number of appointments: in 1849 as professor of pathological anatomy to University College, and soon thereafter as assistant physician to the hospital (he became full physician in 1854); in 1852 as the first physician to the Hospital for Sick Children, Great Ormond Street—his classical accounts of rickets and of the treatment of diphtheria were based on his observations there; and as assistant physician to the London Fever Hospital in 1853. On 30 July 1858 Jenner married Adela Lucy, daughter of Stephen Adey; they had five sons and a daughter.

Jenner's reputation and the demands on his time grew throughout the 1850s. He relinquished his appointment to the Fever Hospital in 1861 and the Hospital for Sick Children in 1862, and in the latter year he was appointed physician-extraordinary to Queen Victoria. The queen stood sponsor to Jenner's second son, Albert Victor (1862–

1954), later third baronet. Jenner attended Prince Albert before he died from typhoid fever in 1861. In 1871 he attended the prince of Wales when he was suffering the same illness. His service to the queen was highly valued: the court circular of 12 December 1898, following Jenner's death, referred to him as not only a most able physician but a true and devoted friend of the queen.

Jenner had acted as professor of clinical medicine at University College while the incumbent, E. A. Parkes, was at the Crimean War. When Parkes resigned to take up another appointment Jenner was confirmed in the chair. In 1862 he was appointed professor of the principles and practice of medicine at University College Hospital. This he resigned in 1867 because of the increasing demands of his private practice, though he continued to attend the hospital and to teach until 1878. By general agreement he was regarded as the leading consultant of his day and as an unforgettable clinical teacher. His pre-eminence as a physician was founded on his wide experience of disease in adults and children, for which he had remarkable recall. Some of this is distilled in his publications which, though few in number, were of marked originality. Towards the end of his life he gathered together what he regarded as his most important contributions in two volumes. They were: *Lectures and Essays on Fevers and Diphtheria, 1849–1879* (1893) and *Clinical Lectures and Essays on Rickets, Tuberculosis, Abdominal Tumours, and other Subjects* (1895).

As a teacher Jenner's method was Socratic, his style direct and aphoristic, and his exposition logical and concise. Sir William Gowers (himself a great clinical teacher) described Jenner's approach: 'Pathological observation, scrupulously precise and thorough, was applied to the elucidation of symptoms, and the results were expressed in concise, terse, emphatic words, which fixed themselves in the memory of those who heard him'. Gowers tells the story of W. Stebbing FRS, the elderly but active chaplain to University College Hospital, who often stopped on the wards to listen to Jenner teaching at the bedside. On one occasion he rushed up when Jenner had finished, and grasping his hand said, 'Dr Jenner, I should like to send you to Oxford, sir, and make you Professor of Logic and Moral Philosophy' (*BMJ*).

An important element in Jenner's influence as a teacher was his belief in the importance of the service which a physician could render to the patient. He stated his position in an address to the British Medical Association (BMA) in Leeds in 1869: 'so far as concerns the non-professional public, the aims and objects of medicine ought to be: to prevent disease, to cure disease, to prolong life, and to alleviate physical suffering'. In matters of treatment, at a time when therapeutic nihilism was fashionable, he struck a balance between undue scepticism and undue credulity.

From 1866 Jenner held a succession of important positions in the profession. He was president of the Epidemiological Society (1866–8), the Pathological Society of London (1873), and the Clinical Society of London (1875). In 1881 and for the following six years he was elected president of the Royal College of Physicians. During this period the college, through Jenner, played an influential part in preparing the profoundly important Medical Act of 1886. Reflecting his constant emphasis on the preventive aspects of medicine, the diploma of public health was initiated under his auspices.

Jenner was a strong chairman. He formed opinions rapidly and held them tenaciously. In matters which particularly concerned him he at times seemed to argue more from prejudice than from his customary logic. In March 1878 he threatened to resign if women were admitted to the BMA. Jenner was also intolerant of opposition and inclined to personalize differences of opinion. Nevertheless, his transparent honesty and forthrightness were deeply respected, and, as the *British Medical Journal* observed, 'his failings were the excess of qualities which were of the highest value to his time and generation'. He received many honours, both professional and public. He was elected FRS in 1864, created a baronet in 1868, and appointed KCB in 1872 and GCB in 1889; he was a commander of the order of Leopold of Belgium; and he was awarded the honorary degrees of DCL by Oxford and LLD by Cambridge and Edinburgh.

Jenner died on 11 December 1898 at Greenwood, Bishop's Waltham, Hampshire, in the house where he had lived since his retirement, and was buried nearby, at Durley, six days later. His wife survived him, and his eldest son, Major Walter Kentish William Jenner (1860–1948), succeeded him as second baronet. W. I. MCDONALD

Sources BMJ (17 Dec 1898), 1849–53 · The Lancet (17 Dec 1898), 1674–6 · Munk, Roll · PRS, 75 (1905), 28–9 · Edinburgh Medical Journal, new ser., 5 (1899), 99 · Medico-Chirurgical Transactions, 82 (1899) · private information (1901) · M. Pelling, Cholera, fever and English medicine, 1825–1865 (1978) · On the causes of fevers (1839) by William Budd, ed. D. C. Smith (1984) · CGPLA Eng. & Wales (1899) · m. cert. · d. cert.
Archives UCL, lecture notes | BL, corresp. with W. E. Gladstone, Add. MSS 44419–44482, passim · Bodl. Oxf., letters to H. W. Acland · UCL, letters to C. J. Hare · Wellcome L., letters to Thomas Barlow · Wellcome L., corresp. with Thomas Longmore
Likenesses V. Prinsep, oils (after F. Hall, 1888), RCP Lond. · Spy [L. Ward], chromolithograph, caricature, NPG; repro. in VF (26 April 1873) · R. Taylor, wood-engraving, NPG; repro. in ILN (23 Dec 1871) · photograph, NPG [see illus.]
Wealth at death £385,083 18s. 5d.: probate, 5 April 1899, CGPLA Eng. & Wales

Jennings, David (1691–1762), Independent minister and tutor, was born on 18 May 1691 at Kibworth, Leicestershire, the younger son of John Jennings (1634–1701), ejected clergyman and dissenting minister, and his wife, Mary (1645/6–1721). He was educated at Kibworth grammar school and in 1709 entered Moorfields Academy in London, where he was prepared for the ministry, first by Isaac Chauncy and then by Thomas Ridgley and John Eames. He preached his first sermon at Battersea in May 1714, and was chosen as one of the evening lecturers at Rotherhithe in March 1715. In June 1716 he became assistant to John Foxon at Girdlers' Hall, Basinghall Street, in the City of London, and in May 1718 he was appointed pastor of the Independent congregation at Wapping New

Stairs. Ordained in July 1718, he remained the minister at Wapping until his death. In 1719 he married Elizabeth Cox, who died in childbirth the following year, and on 19 May 1724 he married Sarah Collins, daughter of John Collins of Hackney, who outlived him; they had two sons.

As a preacher Jennings was considered clear and lucid, and 'gloried in being the immediate descendent of a confessor for liberty of conscience' (Toulmin, 82). In theology he was orthodox, and was not tempted towards the anti-Trinitarian position: 'his sentiments came nearest to Calvinism' (Savage, 33–7). He spent many hours in his study, but was also convivial:

> his natural temper was easy and cheerful, and at the same time warm and sanguine ... he greatly relieved the fatigue ... by intervals of daily exercise and amusement, at the turner's wheel, and with the carpenter's plane; in the use of which, he was ingenious, neat and active. (Toulmin, 123, 86)

His other chief form of relaxation was music.

Jennings was chosen by William Coward to become one of his lecturers at Bury Street in the City of London in 1733. In the same year Coward decided to open his own academy, and asked Jennings to approach Philip Doddridge to become its first professor of divinity; Doddridge declined. In 1743 Jennings became both a Coward trustee and a lecturer at Little Helen's. However, the career for which he is chiefly known started in 1744, when on Eames's death he opened a theological academy at Wellclose Square, Wapping, taking over not only the students but also the equipment and library from Moorfields Academy. The venture was on his own initiative but had the support of the Coward Trust. 'I enter upon my new Work with a deep Sense of my unfitness for it, after I had laid aside academical Studies for near 30 Years' (letter to Doddridge, 8 Sept 1744, Calendar, ed. Nuttall, 205).

Jennings ran his academy successfully, in association with his deputy Samuel Morton Savage, until his death eighteen years later. He was attracted to the physical sciences, particularly astronomy, and encouraged its study among his students, who numbered eighty-six in total. Despite his orthodoxy, strict teaching methods, and adherence to the Westminster confession, his most celebrated students, Philip Furneaux, Joshua Toulmin, Eliezer Cogan, and Abraham Rees, were heterodox. The terms of Coward's will encouraged Jennings to curb any form of difference from him on grounds of doctrine. Some like John and Thomas Wright, who later became radical dissenting ministers in Bristol, were forced to leave the academy to complete their training elsewhere. Despite his lifelong advocacy of the right of individual judgement—'I disallow the authority of popes and councils, and of all the men in the world, to make one article of a creed for me; for Christ Jesus is the only Lord of faith and conscience' (Toulmin, 125)—he was criticized for his inconsistency, or even hypocrisy. According to Toulmin, on the treatment of these students, 'the conduct of Dr Jennings was not truly liberal' (ibid., 88).

Jennings prepared numerous students for the Presbyterian ministry. It is from John Barker's letter to their mutual

friend Philip Doddridge of 5 June 1750 that the importance of the academy's contribution can be assessed.

> Yours and Dr Jennings Academys are Fountains I highly prize
> and rejoyce in … Had not you supplyd our Presbyterian
> Churches for many years past what would have become of
> Us—nay—It is certain that what is called the Presbyterian
> Interest in England has been supported by Independent
> Tutors. (*Calendar*, ed. Nuttall, 331)

Jennings's published output was mainly of sermons,
including those for his friends Isaac Watts, Daniel Neal,
and Timothy Jollie. However, he did venture into unusual
fields for a dissenting minister, and wrote on the use of
globes as well as a work on medals that Alexander Gordon
concluded was 'a poor book' (*DNB*). His main work, which
continued to be reprinted into the next century, was *Jewish
Antiquities* (1766); a later edition was edited by Philip Furneaux. The University of St Andrews made him a DD in
May 1749 on the strength of his published vindications of
orthodox theological positions, though he thought little
of the honour: 'it will save me from being called old Mr
Jennings, in distinction from my Son, who is looking
towards matrimony' (*Calendar*, ed. Nuttall, 304).

Jennings died on 16 September 1762, of an epileptic fit,
at Wapping, strong in the defence of Independency to the
last, as he expressed in his letter to Doddridge of 27 June
1743: 'I am persuaded the principles of true independency, which are surely the true principles of Christian liberty, will be the wisest and safest to act upon' (*Calendar*, ed.
Nuttall, 181).   ALAN RUSTON

Sources S. M. Savage, *Good men dismiss'd in peace: a sermon, occasioned by the death of D. Jennings* (1762), 33–7 · J. H. Thompson, *A history of the Coward Trust: the first two hundred and fifty years, 1738–1988*
(1998), 14, 16–17, 20, 22, 23 · J. Toulmin, *Protestant Dissenter's Magazine*, 5 (1798), 81–9, 121–7 · *Calendar of the correspondence of Philip Doddridge*, ed. G. F. Nuttall, HMC, JP 26 (1979), 297 ·
J. Hunter, *Familiae minorum gentium*, ed. J. W. Clay, 1, Harleian Society, 37 (1894), 180 · J. H. Colligan, *Eighteenth century nonconformity*
(1915), 41–2 · H. McLachlan, *English education under the Test Acts: being
the history of the nonconformist academies, 1662–1820* (1931), 120–21 ·
W. D. Jeremy, *The Presbyterian Fund and Dr Daniel Williams's Trust*
(1885), 41, 51 · A. P. Davis, *Isaac Watts: his life and works* (1948), 51, 71,
105 · *GM*, 1st ser., 32 (1762), 448 · *DNB*
Archives DWL, corresp. and papers | DWL, corresp. with Philip
Doddridge
Likenesses J. Macardell, mezzotint (after W. Jones), BM, NPG ·
engraving, repro. in Toulmin, *Protestant Dissenter's Magazine*, facing
p. 81 · portrait, Tower Hamlets Local History Library, London;
repro. in Thompson, *History of the Coward Trust*, following p. 30

Jennings, Hargrave (1817?–1890), writer and occultist,
began to publish early when, at the age of fifteen, he contributed several anonymous sea-sketches to the *Metropolitan Magazine*, near the end of Frederik Marryat's term as
editor. These were followed by his first collection of similar sketches, *My Marine Memorandum Book* (3 vols., 1845),
and *The Ship of Glass, or, The Mysterious Island: a Romance*,
together with *Atcherley*, a novel (3 vols., 1846). He then
served for several years as secretary to the English impresario James Mapleson, who had a colourful career as manager of the Italian Opera first in London and then on tour
in the USA. Some of his experiences Jennings incorporated into *The Opera, or, Views before and Peeps behind the Curtain* (1847).

Not long afterwards Jennings began to research and
write his best-known book, on the subject of the Rosicrucians, a task which occupied him for the next twenty
years. His growing interest in religious and occult themes
was shown in *The Indian Religions, or, Results of the Mysterious
Buddhism, by an Indian Missionary*, published anonymously
in 1858, and by 1868 he was well enough known to provide
the basis for the character of Ezra Jennings in Wilkie Collins's novel *The Moonstone*. Ezra is there described as a doctor addicted to opium (neither of which applied to Hargrave), and as a man of Gypsy complexion, gaunt, ageless,
cleverly imaginative, and rather mysterious, which are
certainly appropriate.

In 1870 Jennings published *The Rosicrucians, their rites and
mysteries; with chapters on the ancient fire- and serpent-
worshippers*. This was followed by a further five editions,
the last being printed in 1921. It was also translated
into German (1912). It contains a number of illustrations, reproduced without acknowledgement from an
expanded work by Georg van Welling, *Opus mago-
cabalisticum et theologicum* (1719). Jennings sent a copy to
Edward Bulwer-Lytton, then Lord Lytton, who had established himself as an expert on Rosicrucianism through his
novel *Zanoni*. With the presentation Jennings sent a begging letter, asking Lytton if he could find him 'some moderate position or place … as secretary or librarian, or as
some such lettered officer'. Lytton replied in polite, but
vague, terms. The revised third edition of *Rosicrucians*
(1887) was savagely reviewed by A. E. Waite in *Walford's
Antiquarian Magazine*, but Waite's motives were not
unmixed, as he himself published his *Real History of the
Rosicrucians* that same year, deliberately echoing both the
title and cover design of Jennings's earlier work. Jennings
was furious, and when he next met the publisher, Redway,
shrieked, 'Et tu, Brute!' in vociferous reproach. Nevertheless, Jennings survived Waite's scorn and came to be
regarded as an authority on the subject, being cited as
such as recently as 1970 by the *Encyclopaedia Britannica*.
Even Aleister Crowley mentioned him without disparage-
ment as a seeker after truth in the occult traditions.

Jennings was also a long-standing acquaintance of Peter
Davidson (1837–1915), probably through membership of
the Hermetic Brotherhood of Luxor, an occult order
which formally announced its existence in 1884 through
an edition of *The Divine Pymander*, to which Jennings contributed the preface. Davidson became the order's provincial grand master of the north, and was part author of several teaching documents which plundered ideas from
Jennings and Blavatsky, in addition to others from earlier
sources. Certain pieces, indeed, such as the *Wheel of Eze-
chiel*, were borrowed directly from Jennings's *Rosicrucians*.

Whether Jennings ever became grand master of the
order, as was claimed by Paschal Randolph, however, is
somewhat unlikely. Randolph was a doctor and an occultist particularly interested in sexual magic—he founded
the Brotherhood of Eulis to promulgate his ideas, and
according to René Guénon this order was the origin or
antecedent of the Hermetic Brotherhood of Luxor—and
although Jennings had touched on phallic worship in his

book on the Rosicrucians, it may be no accident that the year of the Hermetic Brotherhood's formal emergence saw Jennings begin to publish a series of books on phallicism. First came *Phallicism, celestial and terrestrial, heathen and Christian: its connection with the Rosicrucians and the gnostics, and its foundation in Buddhism; with an essay on magic anatomy* (2 vols., 1884). This had a second edition in 1892. It was followed by *Phallism: a description of the worship of lingam-yoni in various parts of the world and in different ages, With an account of ancient and modern crosses and other symbols concerned with the mysteries of sex worship* (1889), which also went into a second edition in 1892; *Phallic objects, monuments and remains: illustrations of the rise and development of the phallic idea (sex worship) and its embodiment in works of nature and art* (1889); *Fishes, flowers and fire as elements and deities in the phallic faiths and worship of the ancient religions of Greece, Babylon, Rome, India, etc. with illustrative myths and legends* (1890); *Nature worship: an account of phallic faiths and practices, ancient and modern, including the adoration of the male and female powers in various nations and the sancti puji of Indian gnosticism* (1891; 2nd edn, 1929); and *Phallic miscellanies: facts and phases of ancient and modern sex worship, as illustrated chiefly in the religions of India; an appendix of additional and explanatory matter to the volumes 'Phallism' and 'Nature worship'* (1891?).

The rest of Jennings's œuvre consists of novels and essays, and a pre-phallic study of ancient monuments, *The Obelisk: Notices of the Origin, Purpose, and History of Obelisks* (1877). He was working on his reminiscences just before his death, which occurred after a short illness at the house of his brother, F. W. Jennings, in Ambassador's Court, St James's Palace, London, on Tuesday 11 March 1890.

PETER MAXWELL-STUART

Sources *The Athenaeum* (15 March 1890), 342 · *The Athenaeum* (22 March 1890), 374 · *The Times* (13 March 1890) · *The Times* (14 March 1890) · A. Crowley, *Confessions* (1929) · C. McIntosh, *The Rosicrucians*, rev. edn (1987) · R. A. Gilbert, *A. E. Waite: magician of many parts* (1987) · J. Godwin, C. Chanel, and J. P. Deveney, *The Hermetic Brotherhood of Luxor* (1995)

Jennings [later Nowell], **Henry Constantine** (1731–1819), collector, the son of Henry Jennings (*bap.* 1700, *d.* 1739) and his wife, Susannah Kent (1723–1791), was baptized on 15 August 1731 at Shiplake, Oxfordshire, where his father owned the estate. After graduation from Westminster School and three years as an ensign in the 1st foot guards, he resigned his commission in 1752. He is said to have spent eight years in Italy (*c.*1756–1763), three in Rome; it was there that he purchased marbles from the restorer and art dealer, Bartolomeo Cavaceppi. Jennings's fame principally rests on his acquisition of an ancient masterpiece of an over-life-sized, crouching dog. He claimed to have uncovered the marble from amid the rubbish of a statuary's (Cavaceppi's) workshop and bought it on the spot; its cost and transportation charges totalled £80. The work made a remarkable impact in England, especially after Horace Walpole pronounced it to be among the finest animal statues in classical art (*Description of Strawberry Hill*). The canine earned its owner the nickname 'Dog Jennings', and his reported boast that 'A fine dog it was,

and a lucky dog was I to purchase it' (*Annual Biography*) added to its aura. Although the animal was not tailless, he called it 'the dog of Alcibiades' in an effort to enhance its distinction by association with the celebrated Athenian.

After returning to his Shiplake estate, Jennings married, on 19 July 1766, Juliana Atkinson (*d.* 1769), who survived only three years; they had one son, James Henry. In 1777 he married Elizabeth Katherine Nowell (1760–1831), and took her surname in order to share in her inheritance. They had three children, of whom only one, Elizabeth, survived; she married William, son of the collector William Lock of Norbury Park. A passion for acquiring artefacts and poor judgement of horseflesh (two lifelong weaknesses) resulted in his bankruptcy and imprisonment in 1778, and his collection, including the famous dog, came under the hammer of the auctioneer Christie in 1778 and 1779. The imminent sale of the hound provoked a discussion of its merits by Samuel Johnson and Edmund Burke at the Literary Club on 3 April 1778. Increasing public interest was attested by the amount, £1000, paid for the figure by Charles Duncombe, who installed it in Duncombe Park, Helmsley, Yorkshire.

On release from debtors' prison Jennings eventually moved to Havering atte Bower, Essex, where he formed a second collection of objects of virtu, but financial embarrassments again led to his confinement, in Chelmsford gaol *c.*1785, and most of his assemblage was sold. In the early 1800s Jennings settled in London at Lindsey Row, Chelsea, and there indulged himself once more in creating a museum. His resources once again exhausted, he was remanded in 1816 to prison on debt charges, and his collection was sold by Phillips of Bond Street between 1816 and 1819.

Jennings was remarkable for both his fluctuating fortunes and his many personal idiosyncrasies. At bedtime and upon rising he exercised with his 'broadsword', a long, ponderous wooden instrument, capped with lead; then, mounting his leather chaise-horse, which was inflated like a pair of bellows, he took 'exactly one thousand gallops'. Abstemious by nature, he spurned all luxuries and entertainments, declaring that 'a feast was the conversion of gold into excrement [*sic*]' (*Annual Biography*). His published essays on theology, education, art, the benefits of hill-built as opposed to valley-built dwellings, and a translation into blank verse of the fifth canto of Dante's *Inferno* indicate the scope and versatility of his mind. Contemporary portraits show him to have been lean with strong features and in old age much bent.

The *Annual Biography* offers an entertaining, firsthand account of Jennings during his later years. A visitor, after encountering a stuffed polar bear in the entrance hall, might find his host reclining on his 'Roman triclinium', amid heaps of ancient and modern rubbish, apparently lost in the contemplation of his riches. He forbade any cleaning of his rooms, living by preference in complete squalor. At one time his regular dinner companion was his most prized treasure, a bronze bust of a goddess, set at the head of his table. One of his more bizarre collections was that of shoes, which he obtained from every woman of his acquaintance. Jennings's omnivorous tastes and collecting mania were legendary—his various residences overflowed with thousands of items of art objects, as well as natural history specimens and scientific instruments—but the low prices these objects fetched at the sales (apart from his valuable and rare shell collection) reveal that his discernment was generally poor. The 'dog of Alcibiades' alone continued to inspire scholarly and national interest by virtue of its quality and uniqueness. Though its ownership has changed, its history, its fanciful epithet, and the colourful life of its finder, together with the numerous casts of the piece (from a mould that Pietro Angelo Sarti possessed) which have continued to decorate countless country houses and parks, ensure Jennings's renown, long after his death at his lodgings in Belvedere Place, St George's Fields, London, on 17 February 1819. He was buried on 24 February at St Margaret's, Westminster.

E. ANGELICOUSSIS

Sources *Annual Biography and Obituary*, 4 (1820), 326ff. • E. Climenson, *The history of Shiplake Oxon with allusions to contemporary events in the neighbourhood* (1894), 335ff. • G. Jackson-Stops, ed., *The treasure houses of Britain: five hundred years of private patronage and art collecting* (1985), 318f., no. 243 [C. Picon] [exhibition catalogue, National Gallery of Art, Washington, DC, 3 Nov 1985 – 16 March 1986] • sale catalogues (1778) [Christies, 3–4 April 1778] • sale catalogue (1778) [Christies, 15 April 1778] • sales catalogues (1779) [Christies, 26 Feb – 1 March 1779] • Phillips of Bond Street sales catalogues, 8–15 May 1816 • Phillips of Bond Street sales catalogues, 11–17 July 1816 • S. P. Dance, *A history of shell collecting*, rev. edn (1986), 101ff. • H. Wilson, *Wonderful characters*, 2 (1821), 350–1 • J. Ingamells, ed., *A dictionary of British and Irish travellers in Italy, 1701–1800* (1997), 557 • J. Boswell, *Life of Johnson*, ed. R. W. Chapman, rev. J. D. Fleeman, new edn (1970); repr. with introduction by P. Rogers (1980), 900f. • J. T. Smith, *Nollekens and his times*, 1 (1828), 292n • B. Cavaceppi, *Raccolta d'antiche statue*, 1 (1768), pls. 6–9 • *Description of the villa of Mr. Horace Walpole at Strawberry Hill* (1774), 67 • *IGI* • parish registers, Shiplake, Oxon. RO [baptism; burials, mother, first wife] • *Old Westminsters*, 1.514 • prison records, PRO, PRIS 4/6, 216 and 4/28, 419 • *GM*, 1st ser., 89/1 (1819), 189 • catalogue of Anglican parish records, City Westm. AC, 96.1972 [burial] • PRO, WO 25/22, fol. 251; WO 25/136, fol. 206; WO 64/9, fol. 28

Archives priv. coll., family papers, notes, and records

Likenesses E. Dorrell, etching, pubd 1815, BM, NPG • R. Cooper, engraving (after E. Dorrell), repro. in Wilson, *Wonderful characters* • R. Cooper, stipple, BM; repro. in R. Cooper and R. Page, *Fifty wonderful portraits* (1824) • T. Lawrence, chalk, NPG • group portrait, etching (*Portraits from sketches made at rare print sales*), BM; repro. in R. Cooper and R. Page, *Fifty wonderful portraits* (1824)

Wealth at death bankrupt, dying within the rules of the king's bench; still in possession of property in Jamaica: *GM*; Climenson, *History*, 348f.

Jennings, (Frank) Humphrey Sinkler

Jennings, (Frank) Humphrey Sinkler (1907–1950), film maker, painter, and writer, was born at The Gazebo, Walberswick, Suffolk, on 19 August 1907, the elder of two sons of Frank Jennings (1877–c.1950), an architect, and of his wife, Mildred Jessie Hall (1881–c.1950), a painter and shopkeeper. In 1916 he went to the Perse School, Cambridge, at that time a progressive institution where the classicist Dr W. H. D. Rouse was headmaster and Caldwell Cook, author of *The Play Way*, was an inspiring teacher of English and drama. Jennings soon excelled both at work and at games

(Frank) Humphrey Sinkler Jennings (1907–1950), by Lee Miller, 1942

and showed promise as an actor, set designer, and poet. In 1926 he won a scholarship from Pembroke College, Cambridge, to read for the English tripos, which was still in its early days. His undergraduate years were busy and set the pattern for a varied working life. He painted a great deal, designed sets for many theatrical productions, including the first British performances of Stravinsky's *The Soldier's Tale* and Honneger's *King David*, and, with his fellow undergraduates Jacob Bronowski and William Empson, founded and wrote for *Experiment*, a student magazine of unusual distinction. Despite these and many other distractions he studied assiduously, particularly in sixteenth-century literature and art, and managed to take a first in part one of the tripos (1928) and a first with distinction in part two (1929).

On 19 October 1929, after a brief courtship, Jennings married Cicely Cooper (*b*. 1908), the daughter of Richard Synge Cooper, a civil engineer; their first daughter, Mary-Lou, was born in September 1933 and their second, Charlotte, in August 1935. Under the direction of I. A. Richards, then an influential English don, Jennings began work on a doctoral thesis about the poetry of Thomas Gray, a former student of Pembroke. This was never completed though Richards thought his research 'a very remarkable combination of elaborate erudition with speculative daring' (private information) and T. S. Eliot offered to publish a shortened version of one chapter in the *Criterion*. The only tangible evidence of Jennings's postgraduate labours was his edition of the 1593 quarto of Shakespeare's *Venus and Adonis*, published in a small edition by the Experiment Press in 1930. Chronically short of money Jennings was often forced to interrupt his studies to take short-term employment and worked as a schoolteacher in Salisbury, as a textile designer in Paris, and as a set designer at the

Festival Theatre in Cambridge. Finally, in 1934, he joined the General Post Office film unit (later renamed the Crown Film Unit), which gave him his first training as an editor and director.

For the next five years Jennings earned his living making short documentaries, both for the Post Office and for independent production companies, where he was able to experiment with the new colour processes Gasparcolor and Dufaycolor. The greater part of his always restless energies, however, was given to his usual extra-curricular activities of painting, writing (including an angry essay on theatre for *The Arts Today*, edited by Geoffrey Grigson), and various forms of private research. For a short period he became a leading figure of the British surrealist movement, and, with Roland Penrose, Herbert Read, and others, organized the famous International Surrealist Exhibition of June 1936, at which his collage *Minotaur*, an unflattering portrait of Lord Kitchener, proved to be one of the most notorious exhibits. With David Gascoyne he translated a collection of poems by the French surrealist Benjamin Peret, *Remove your Hat* (1936). Though brief Jennings's spell as a surrealist had lasting consequences. His many years of work on *Pandaemonium*, an epic anthology of texts illuminating the industrial revolution as seen by contemporary witnesses, began with a short article for the surrealist journal *London Bulletin* in 1938, while his contributions to Mass-Observation, the pioneering project in domestic anthropology which he founded early in 1937 with Tom Harrisson and Charles Madge, also showed marked surrealist tendencies. His principal publication while involved in the movement was *May the Twelfth: Mass-Observation Day Surveys 1937*, a collage account of George VI's coronation, co-edited with Madge for Faber and Faber.

Jennings's first distinctive film, *Spare Time* (1939), has sometimes been mistakenly identified as a product of Mass-Observation. In fact it marked Jennings's full-time return to the General Post Office film unit, where he remained until after the war, but the misattribution is understandable since the film—a rapid series of vignettes, cut to the music of brass bands, kazoos, and other amateur performances, and almost wordless, save for a terse commentary by Laurie Lee—depicted the leisure activities of working-class men, women, and children in much the same spirit as a Mass-Observation day report: deadpan, inquisitive, alert to idiosyncrasy and humour. Some of Jennings's colleagues found it condescending though it now appears far less so than many documentaries of the period and can stand comparison with certain essays of George Orwell as a remarkably sympathetic enquiry into popular culture. Like Orwell, too, Jennings was an unconventional member of the non-communist left and once defined his politics as 'those of William Cobbett' (Jackson, 232).

In collaboration with his gifted if cantankerous editor Stewart McAllister, whose contribution tended to be unjustly overlooked before Dai Vaughan's biography of McAllister, *Portrait of an Invisible Man* (1983), redressed the balance, Jennings developed the techniques of *Spare Time* in the films he made during the Second World War. In these documentaries Jennings drew on his several vocations as painter, poet, historian, and sociologist and brought each skill to a new pitch of refinement and passion. Though their fascination as a record of the home front and their efficacy as propaganda can hardly be overstated (they were among the films which helped bring the United States into the war), they are also works of outstanding eloquence, complexity, and emotional force; in brief, works of art. At least three of them—*Listen to Britain* (1942), *Fires were Started* (1943), and *A Diary for Timothy* (1945)—are now agreed to be masterpieces. Several contributors to *Sight and Sound*'s international poll of directors and critics in 1992 nominated one of these titles in their list of the ten best films ever made.

Critics have been less kind to the four films Jennings made after the war—*A Defeated People* (1945), *The Cumberland Story* (1947), *The Dim Little Island* (1949), and *Family Portrait* (1950)—finding them at best unimaginative, at worst complacent, and animated by a sentimental patriotism that is almost a caricature of the ardent love of his native country which fired Jennings's greatest efforts. Such at least was the limiting judgement of the film director Lindsay Anderson, whose otherwise admiring essay of 1954, 'Only connect', did much to keep Jennings's reputation alive through periods of neglect. Anderson called Jennings 'the only real poet the British cinema has yet produced' and few have seriously challenged the verdict (Jennings, 53). Yet there is little biographical evidence to support the view that Jennings was a spent force. He continued to work tirelessly at accumulating texts on science and industry for *Pandaemonium* (some of which bore fruit in *Family Portrait*), he completed dozens of paintings, and he wrote erudite, searching articles for the *Times Literary Supplement* and other publications. He seems to have been particularly stimulated by a visit in 1947 to Burma, where he went to look into the possibilities of a feature based on a novel by H. E. Bates, *The Purple Plain* (1947). Neither this nor any of the other features he prepared for his main post-war employer, Wessex Films, ever went into production. It is possible, as some sceptics have suggested, that he would never have thrived in the world of features although certain sequences in his dramatized documentaries *The Silent Village* (1943) and *Fires were Started* show that he was quite as comfortable with the prose of fictional narrative as with the more associative poetry of his personal form of documentary. The critic David Thomson, one of Jennings's most articulate advocates, suggests that Jennings had it in him to grow into Britain's Buñuel.

Though he is still not widely known outside specialist circles Jennings's reputation has grown with the years and his work has been brought back to a broader public on several occasions, notably by Robert Vas's *Omnibus* documentary for BBC television in 1970, by a well-received exhibition of paintings and films at London's Riverside Studios in 1982, and by the publication in 1985 of an abbreviated version of *Pandaemonium*, edited by Mary-Lou

Jennings and Charles Madge, which was greeted by surprised and enthusiastic reviews on both sides of the Atlantic. His wartime films are regularly screened and discovered by new generations, at the National Film Theatre.

Jennings was appointed OBE, in 1946, for his contributions to sustaining morale at home and for publicizing the British cause abroad; he was promptly 'excommunicated' by one of the surviving surrealist factions. He died, on 24 September 1950, on the Greek island of Poros, after falling from a cliff while scouting locations for a film about health services in Europe. He was buried in the protestant cemetery in Athens.   KEVIN JACKSON

Sources M.-L. Jennings, ed., *Humphrey Jennings: film-maker, painter, poet* (1983) · A. W. Hodgkinson and R. E. Sheratsky, *Humphrey Jennings: more than a maker of films* (1982) · K. Jackson, ed., *The Humphrey Jennings film reader* (1993) · D. Vaughan, *Portrait of an invisible man: the working life of Stewart McAllister, film editor* (1983) · M.-L. Jennings and C. Madge, eds., *Pandaemonium, 1660–1886: the coming of the machine as seen by contemporary observers* (1985) · D. Thomson, *A biographical dictionary of film*, 3rd edn (1994) · H. Jennings, ed., *Venus and Adonis: the quarto of 1593* (1930); repr. with new introduction (1993) · b. cert. · b. cert. [Cicely Cooper] · m. cert. · private information (2004) [M.-L. Legg]

Archives BFI, papers · priv. coll., MSS | FILM BFI NFTVA, 'Humphrey Jennings—the man who listened to Britain', Channel 4, 23 Dec 2000 · BFI NFTVA, performance footage | SOUND BL NSA, performance recording

Likenesses L. Miller, photograph, 1942, NPG [*see illus.*] · L. Miller, photographs, *c.*1944, Vogue archives · Beiney, photograph, *c.*1946, repr. in Jackson, ed., *Humphrey Jennings film reader*, back cover

Jennings, Sir (William) Ivor (1903–1965), jurist, was born in Bristol on 16 May 1903, the son of William Jennings, carpenter and joiner, and his wife, Eleanor Jane Thomas. He was educated at Queen Elizabeth's Hospital, Bristol grammar school, and St Catharine's College, Cambridge. He obtained first classes in part one of the mathematical tripos (1923) and both parts of the law tripos (1924–5), was Whewell scholar in 1925, and was clearly destined for a university career. He was appointed Holt scholar of Gray's Inn in 1925 and Barstow scholar in 1926 and was called to the bar in 1928. He married Helena Emily, daughter of Albert Konsalik, of London in 1928; they had two daughters.

Jennings's first appointment was as lecturer in law in Leeds University from 1925 to 1929. From there he went to the London School of Economics and Political Science, first as lecturer, then in 1930 as reader in English law. He remained there as a teacher of public law until 1940, and this period saw the production of his most original and creative work. The mutual stimulus of colleagues such as Harold Laski, Hersch Lauterpacht, and William Robson, with whom he was in close contact, undoubtedly acted as a ferment on them all.

In these eleven years he produced eleven substantial books. Some of these were legal treatises intended for the practitioner, the official, or the student. They included treatises on the poor-law code, the law of housing, the law of public health, the law of town and country planning, and a vast tome on the law relating to local authorities,

Sir (William) Ivor Jennings (1903–1965), by Walter Bird, 1962

published soon after the great consolidating Local Government Act, 1933. These works were produced at extraordinary speed, but they were scholarly and accurate. Although mainly of vocational interest, they displayed the author's remarkable gift of lucid and succinct exposition.

The books which represent his greatest intellectual achievement were also written during these vital years. The most distinguished of them is *Cabinet Government*, first published in 1936. This was instantly recognized as a masterly analysis of the principal characteristics of the cabinet system. It is immeasurably superior to anything which had preceded it. To obtain the information on which it was based, Jennings had read widely and deeply in the memoirs and biographies of statesmen past and present; and he presented the material in a clear and systematic manner. The book long held its place as a standard work on the subject. Other literary incursions into the sphere of politics during this period consisted of a large work entitled *Parliament* (1939) which again displayed the author's extraordinary power of exposition; a provocative and highly original book entitled *The Law and the Constitution* (1933); a short study entitled *Parliamentary Reform* (1934); and a work entitled *A Federation for Western Europe* which appeared in 1940.

In that year Jennings was appointed principal of University College, Ceylon. Two years later the college became a university and Jennings its first vice-chancellor. His energy, skill, and foresight resulted in a vast expansion on a new site; and the standards he laid down were high.

Jennings's services as constitutional adviser were in

considerable demand after the war, not only in Ceylon, where he was a member of the commission on the Ceylon constitution, but in other countries which were becoming independent states—for example, he was the constitutional adviser and chief draughtsman to Pakistan in 1954–5 and a member of the Malayan constitutional commission in 1956–7.

The concluding phase of Jennings's career began when he returned to England in 1954 as master of Trinity Hall, Cambridge. From 1961 to 1963 he was vice-chancellor of the university and, while holding that office, in 1962 he was appointed to the Downing professorship in the laws of England in succession to E. C. S. Wade. From 1955 to 1958 he was chairman of the royal commission on common land.

Jennings's interest in the Commonwealth was shown in 1938 when he produced in collaboration with C. M. Young a casebook entitled *The Constitutional Laws of the British Empire*. In 1949 he delivered the Waynflete lectures at Magdalen College, Oxford, on the Commonwealth in Asia, and in 1956 he published *The Approach to Self-Government*. He delivered a course of lectures entitled 'Problems of the New Commonwealth' in 1958 at the Commonwealth Studies Center at Duke University. His final literary contribution in this field was on democracy in Africa. Jennings believed in the new Commonwealth; he saw the problems confronting its political leaders without illusions; but he did not foresee the forces which later caused repeated wars between India and Pakistan, the exclusion of South Africa, and the disappearance of parliamentary government on the Westminster model throughout Africa.

Towards the end of his life Jennings resumed the study of British government and politics; but his long absence led to a loss of the freshness and originality which had marked his earlier work. It was a mistake to complete and publish (1960–62) a long study of *Party Politics* in three volumes which he had begun before leaving England in 1940.

Jennings was knighted in 1948, and appointed QC in 1949 and KBE in 1955. He was elected FBA in 1955, became a bencher of Gray's Inn in 1958, and received honorary degrees in law from the universities of Bristol, Southampton, Ceylon, Leeds, Belfast, Hong Kong, Manchester, and Paris.

Jennings's outstanding characteristic was his extraordinary capacity for both intellectual and practical work. Every task which he undertook he accomplished rapidly, efficiently, and in an apparently effortless manner. In politics he was left of centre; but his work was not politically tendentious though sometimes controversial and was generally marked by good judgement and common sense. He had no known recreations apart from an occasional walk with his dog and an insatiable interest in books. He never gave offence, but it was difficult for even close colleagues to penetrate the aloofness which made it difficult to know him well. He died in Addenbrooke's Hospital, Cambridge, on 19 December 1965.

W. A. ROBSON, *rev.*

Sources *The Times* (20 Dec 1965) · *The Guardian* (20 Dec 1965) · personal knowledge (1981) · *WWW* · *CGPLA Eng. & Wales* (1966)
Archives PRO, corresp., BW 90 · U. Lond., Institute of Commonwealth Studies, corresp. and papers | JRL, letters to the *Manchester Guardian*
Likenesses W. Bird, photograph, 1962, NPG [*see illus.*] · I. M. Noakes, drawing, Trinity Cam.
Wealth at death £35,213: probate, 2 Feb 1966, *CGPLA Eng. & Wales*

Jennings, James (1772–1833), writer, was born in Huntspill, Somerset, on 1 December 1772, the second son of John Jennings (1736–1805), who kept the village shop, and his wife, Elizabeth, *née* Fear (1741?–1806). He attended Mary Ramsey's village school and then North Petherton School near Bridgwater until 1785. In 1786 he was apprenticed to a Bristol apothecary, and in the course of the next few years came to know some of the radical authors who settled in that city, notably the poets Samuel Taylor Coleridge and Robert Southey. He had poems published in the *European Magazine*, and in 1794 wrote a satire, *The Times*, which was conspicuously unsuccessful. In 1795 he married Charlotte Sawier, and shortly afterwards moved to work in London. Conditions there affected their health; Charlotte's first child was born prematurely, and she herself was so ill that she never fully recovered. In 1801 they returned to Huntspill and the family business. Charlotte was particularly active in helping the poor of the parish, and when she died, in April 1807, Jennings wrote an eloquent account of her good works which was published in the *Monthly Magazine*, to which thereafter he was a fairly frequent contributor.

In December 1807 Jennings married Sarah Rouquet (*d.* 1830). His philanthropic concerns continued, and in 1813 he and the local rector established a village school conducted on the monitorial system popularized by Joseph Lancaster and Andrew Bell. But soon afterwards, the onset of the British economic depression at the end of the Napoleonic wars forced him to abandon his shop, and in the summer of 1817 he settled in London. He supported himself as a professional writer, with some patronage from a wealthy banker, Sir William Paxton, to whom he seems to have been introduced by the republican artist George Cumberland. In 1821 Jennings published *The Family Cyclopaedia*. It placed a special emphasis on recent inventions and improvements, and he was always an enthusiastic champion of the 'march of intellect'. When the Surrey Institution, scene of lectures by Coleridge and Hazlitt, had to close in 1823, he set up a successor, the Metropolitan Literary Institution. It did not succeed, however, and Jennings's last years were confined to authorship. He was something of an ornithologist, and published a verse treatise on the subject in 1828. His most successful venture was *Observations on some of the Dialects of the West of England* (1825), which included some pleasant poems illustrating the speech patterns of his own part of Somerset. He died in Greenwich on 8 October 1833.   GEOFFREY CARNALL

Sources G. D. Carnall, 'The life and works of James Jennings', BLitt diss., U. Oxf., 1952 · J. Jennings, *Poems, consisting of the mysteries of Mendip, the magic ball* (1810) · [J. Watkins and F. Shoberl], *A biographical dictionary of the living authors of Great Britain and Ireland*

(1816) • *Public characters*, 2 (1823) • *Metropolitan Literary Journal* (1824) • Huntspill parish registers • *GM*, 1st ser., 103/2 (1833)
Archives BL, letters to George Cumberland, Add. MSS 36504–36505 • DWL, H. Crabb Robinson, MS diary

Jennings, Sir John (1664–1743), naval officer, was the fifteenth child of Philip Jennings (d. 1697) of Dudleston Hall, Shropshire, and Christina Eyton, daughter of Gerard Eyton of Eyton, Shropshire. Having passed the Navy Board examination on 15 February 1687 he was appointed lieutenant, successively, of the *Pearl* on 12 May 1687, the *St David* on 27 August 1688, and the *Swallow* by Lord Dartmouth on 22 December 1688. He was promoted captain on 16 November 1689, and commanded the *St Paul* fireship, for several weeks, before a two and a half year period as captain of the frigate *Experiment*. After cruising with some success on the coast of Ireland he went on to North America. While there he gained some notoriety among the colonists, when in May 1681, with six seamen, he invaded the court house in Lower Norfolk, Virginia, in the midst of a trial, and inexplicably took away the defendant, John Porter. After leaving the *Experiment* in June 1692 he commanded the *Chester* for three months, and the *Winchester* and the *Mary*, each for five months. Then, after commanding the *Crowne* for only three weeks, he settled in for a two year and ten month period in command of the *Mary*, one of the fleet which went with Admiral Edward Russell (later earl of Orford) to the Mediterranean. In September 1695 he was moved for a year into the *Chichester* (80 guns), and in January 1696 he was placed in command of the *Plymouth*, in which he was employed actively cruising in the channel until the peace of 1697. While in this ship he captured the *St Malo* privateer, and the *Concorde* (14 guns); and with the aid of the *Rye* he captured the *Noveau Cherbourge* (36 guns) and the *Dauphin* (28 guns). During 1698, still in the *Plymouth*, he was commander-in-chief in the Medway, and in May 1699 he was moved to the *Orford* for four months. In February 1701 he was appointed to the *Kent* (70 guns), which in 1702 was one of the fleet under Sir George Rooke at Cadiz. In May 1703 Jennings was appointed to the *St George*, in which he accompanied Sir Cloudesley Shovell to the Mediterranean. He was with Rooke again in 1704, at the capture of Gibraltar and the battle of Malaga; he was one of the seconds of the commander-in-chief and his ship was heavily damaged while fighting singly for some hours with the French flagship.

On 24 October 1704, after his return to England, Jennings was knighted, and on 20 January 1705 he was advanced to rear-admiral of the blue. In the general election of 1705 he was returned as a whig MP for Queenborough, Kent, a seat which he held until 1710. In May 1705 he hoisted his flag on board the *Royal Anne*, as commander in the third post of the fleet going out to the Mediterranean. Because the enemy's force in Brest remained a threat in home waters Jennings was ordered to shift his flag to the *Mary* and remain cruising in the Soundings and off Ushant, under the orders of Sir George Byng. When Byng became ill in August 1705 Jennings temporarily succeeded to his command. In 1706 he was sent to the Mediterranean, with Byng, to reinforce Sir John Leake, and took part

in the relief of Barcelona and the operations on the coast of Spain. On the surrender of Cartagena Jennings was left with a small squadron to maintain peace and order. In August 1706 he went to Alicante and rejoined Leake, who appointed Jennings a general to command the 1900 fleet seamen and marines ashore. After the capture of Alicante he refitted at Lisbon and proceeded to the West Indies. Leaving Lisbon on 15 October he passed Tenerife and attempted unsuccessfully to cut out enemy shipping at Santa Cruz. He later landed a supply of arms for the defence of Barbados and the Leeward Islands. While there he sent a letter to the Spanish governor of Cartagena, recounting for him the recent allied successes in Spain in the hope of inducing the Spanish settlements to declare in favour of King Charles. The governor of Cartagena, however, refused to accede to his proposals. After resupplying at Jamaica Jennings returned to England, arriving at Spithead on 22 April 1707. Later that year he commanded a convoy for the duke of Marlborough, and on 10 December he was promoted to rear-admiral of the white. One month later, on 9 January 1708, he was promoted to vice-admiral of the red; this was one in the series of promotions to fill the vacancies left by the deaths of Shovell and Sir Thomas Dilkes. In March, on intelligence of plans for the French-led invasion of Scotland, he was appointed commander-in-chief in the Thames and Medway. Responsible for the defence of south-east England, Jennings oversaw the fitting out of all available ships to meet the threat, commanding from his flagship in the Downs. He sailed as second in command to Byng and was with the fleet off Dunkirk and later continued to the east coast of Scotland. Towards the end of the year he was ordered to the Mediterranean, again under Byng, but was left at Lisbon to keep watch on the Strait of Gibraltar. In April 1708 Byng and Jennings were offered places on the lord high admiral's council, but as loyal supporters of Orford and the whig junto they both declined. Lord Godolphin thought this 'a wrong step' (*Byng Papers*, 2.189) because it implied a personal criticism of Prince George of Denmark as lord high admiral and earned the queen's resentment. Even after Orford returned as first lord of the Admiralty, the queen refused to allow Jennings to be an Admiralty commissioner during the remainder of her reign. He remained in the Mediterranean and on the coast of Portugal until the end of 1710, when he returned to England. He was advanced to the rank of admiral of the blue on 17 December 1708, and to admiral of the white on 14 November 1709. In the 1710 election he was defeated in his old seat at Queenborough, but was returned for Portsmouth; he was, however, unseated by petition in February 1711.

On 3 November 1710 Jennings was appointed commander-in-chief in the Mediterranean; he sailed from St Helens on 8 January, with his flag on board the *Blenheim* and in company with transports carrying troops to relieve the garrison at Gibraltar and three Dutch ships under Vice-Admiral Anthony Pieterson. Having collected the trade at Lisbon, he convoyed it through the straits, and on 20 March arrived at Barcelona; he remained there, occasionally going for provisions to Port Mahon where on his own initiative he ordered construction of the navy's first purpose-built hospital. The French were powerless in the presence of the fleet and the work of the British was limited to protecting trade and providing for the safety of transports or store ships. After the death of the emperor Joseph I Jennings escorted King Charles to Genoa in September, *en route* to his election as Emperor Charles VI. In March 1713 he escorted Charles's empress from Barcelona to Genoa, and she presented Jennings with a ring and her picture set in diamonds. He afterwards assisted in conveying some 30,000 allied troops to Italy, and conducted the duke of Savoy to Sicily. Having obtained permission to resign his command, Jennings returned home through France, stopping for a few days in Paris; he reached England at the end of November and was placed on half pay from 1 December 1713. He continued on half pay until 14 October 1714, when, under the new king, George I, Orford became first lord of the Admiralty and Jennings was finally appointed one of the lords commissioners of the Admiralty. He remained a member of the Admiralty board until 16 April 1717, and was a member again from 19 March 1718 until 1 June 1727. For a short time he took active command of the squadron on the coast of Scotland in February 1716, just as the Pretender succeeded in making good his escape.

Jennings was appointed ranger of Greenwich park and governor of Greenwich Hospital on 28 August 1720. At about this time he purchased the manor of Newsells, near Barkway, Hertfordshire. He married Alice Breton, daughter of Francis Breton of Wallington, Hertfordshire. They had one son, George, who died in 1790. Remaining governor for twenty-three years, he supervised completion of Wren's plans for the hospital and oversaw Sir James Thornhill's work in the painted hall, personally donating Rysbrack's statue of George II for the centre of the main quadrangle. In the 1715 general election he had been returned as MP for Rochester on the Admiralty's interest; he held that seat until 1734.

In 1726 Jennings again hoisted his flag, this time in command of a small squadron sent to the coast of Spain. One of his goals was to ascertain the truth of reports of warlike preparations at Santander; he was further instructed to cruise between Cape St Vincent and Cadiz, in order to attempt to intercept any Spanish treasure-ships which had evaded Vice-Admiral Hosier in the West Indies. Jennings returned to England in October, leaving the squadron off Cape St Vincent, under the command of Rear-Admiral Edward Hopson. This was his last service afloat, and on the death of George I he ceased to be a lord of the Admiralty. Following Lord Torrington's death on 17 January 1733 he was appointed rear-admiral of Great Britain. He finally 'quit his flag' on 26 February 1734 after the appointment of Sir John Norris as admiral of the fleet. He died at Greenwich on 23 December 1743.

J. K. LAUGHTON, *rev.* JOHN B. HATTENDORF

Sources list of captains, 1688–1715, NMM, Sergison MS SER/136 · commissions and warrants, PRO, AOM 6 · deposition concerning Jennings, 1691, PRO, CO 5/1306, fols. 108–13 · J. S. Kepler, 'Sir John Jennings and the preparation for the naval expedition to the Mediterranean, 1711–13', *Mariner's Mirror*, 59 (1973), 13–33 · J. Charnock, ed., *Biographia navalis*, 2 (1795), 261–77 · *The Byng papers: selected from the letters and papers of Admiral Sir George Byng, first Viscount Torrington, and of his son, Admiral the Hon. John Byng*, ed. B. Tunstall, 3 vols., Navy RS, 67–8, 70 (1930–32) · J. H. Owen, *War at sea under Queen Anne, 1702–1708* (1938) · *The Marlborough–Godolphin correspondence*, ed. H. L. Snyder, 3 vols. (1975) · J. Coad, *The royal dockyards* (1989) · HoP, *Commons* · PRO, PROB 11/730, fols. 224–6

Archives BL, letterbook, Add. MSS 42839–42840 · University of Kansas, Lawrence, Kenneth Spencer Research Library, journal, letterbook, and orderbook, MS G15 | NMM, letters to John Baker · TCD, letters to John Baker

Likenesses G. Kneller, oils, *c.*1708–1709, NMM · J. Richardson, oils, *c.*1720, NMM · J. M. Rysbrack, bust on monument, 1743, parish church, Barkway, Hertfordshire · J. Thornhill, group portrait, drawing (*Sir J. Jennings showing the prince of Wales the plans for Greenwich Hospital*), repro. in P. Newell, *Greenwich Hospital* (1984)

Wealth at death entire estate left to son: will, PRO, PROB 11/730, fols. 224–6

Jennings, John (1687/8–1723), Independent minister and tutor, was the eldest son of John Jennings (1634–1701), ejected minister, and his wife, Mary (1645/6–1721), of Kibworth Harcourt, Leicestershire. He was educated for the nonconformist ministry at Timothy Jolly's academy at Attercliffe with the assistance of the Congregational Fund from 1703. In 1709, at the age of twenty-one, he took charge of his father's former congregation at Kibworth Harcourt. He also preached at Glen Magna, to a lecture maintained by the Congregational Fund, and to a small meeting at Church Langton, both neighbouring parishes. According to John Evans's list of dissenting congregations in 1715 the three meetings totalled 320 hearers, with 41 voters in parliamentary elections for county; Jennings was the Leicestershire correspondent for the survey, on which the list was based.

From 1715 until his death Jennings conducted an academy preparing students for the nonconformist ministry. The names of twenty-four students are known, mostly those who entered the nonconformist ministry, but many of his students conformed. The academy itself has gained some fame because of the detailed account of Jennings's teaching preserved by his most celebrated student, Philip Doddridge. Jennings's influence upon him, as Doddridge himself readily acknowledged, can hardly be exaggerated, and Doddridge later used many of the same methods and even lectures in his own academy at Northampton (1729–51), the most celebrated nonconformist academy of the period.

The four-year course was divided into eight half-year periods and covered logic, philosophy, ethics, divinity, ecclesiastical history, languages (French as well as Hebrew, Greek, and Latin), physics (using texts by Le Clerc and Rohault), mathematics, and mechanics. Jennings was a teacher of some originality. His *Miscellanea in usum juventutis academicae*, which he published in 1721, gives details of the studies of his academy. He devised his own system of logic, 'a great deal of which was taken from Mr Locke', though 'we first skimmed over Burgersdicius in about six lectures' (Doddridge to Saunders, 16 Nov 1725, DWL, MS 24.179.4). The recommended textbooks included

John Locke's *Essay Concerning Human Understanding* and Joshua Oldfield's *Essay towards the Improvement of Reason* (which embodied Locke's ideas), Newton's *Principia*, and the Newtonian Le Clerc's *Logica*. His lectures, published as *Logica in usum juventutis academicae* in 1721, were admired by Isaac Watts. His *Two Discourses* (1723; 6th edn, 1793), academic exercises in preaching, were published posthumously with a preface by Watts. Highly regarded, they were translated into German and were even recommended by two bishops during their visitations. More unusually Jennings used illustrations from drama when teaching, drawing upon accounts of comedies and plays often from the *Tatler*. Doddridge played the part of the emperor in Nicholas Rowe's *Tamerlane* at a performance given by the students in 1722.

On matters of doctrine and controversy Jennings encouraged his students to form their own judgement after reading the different authorities for themselves. According to Doddridge, Jennings always allowed 'the greatest freedom of inquiry' and 'inculcates it as a law, that the scriptures are the only genuine standard of faith'. As a result Jennings did not follow 'the doctrines or phrases of any particular party; but is sometimes a Calvinist, sometimes an Arminian, and sometimes a Baxterian, as truth and evidence determine him' (*Correspondence and Diary*, 1.152). His system of instruction was, however, eccentric. Based on a mathematical method of proposition, demonstration, and proof, while effective for scientific subjects it was unsuited to moral philosophy and similar disciplines.

Nothing is known of Jennings's first wife. He married secondly Anna Letitia, daughter of Sir Francis Wingate and his wife, Anne, daughter of Arthur Annesley, first earl of Anglesey. They had four children. John (*d.* 1775), the second son, was educated by Doddridge and served as minister of St Ives, Huntingdon, from 1742 until 1756, when he was forced by the loss of his voice to enter business. Jane, the youngest daughter, married John *Aikin (1713–1780) and was the mother of Anna Letitia *Barbauld.

In May 1722 Jennings became the minister of the Presbyterian congregation at Hinckley, 'one of the best congregations in Leicestershire', where he moved with his academy (*Correspondence and Diary*, 1.59). By July his new congregation was building a meeting-house: 'it will be a pretty large place, … for we have a congregation of five hundred people' (ibid., 1.152). It was opened on 25 November. The following year Jennings caught smallpox and died at Hinckley on 8 July 1723. His death, involving the closure of his academy, was a serious blow to the dissenting interest in the midlands. Doddridge acquired some of his books, which are now in the New College collection at Dr Williams's Library. Jennings was abler and had a more original mind than his younger brother the strictly orthodox David *Jennings (1691–1762), tutor at Hoxton Academy. DAVID L. WYKES

Sources The correspondence and diary of Philip Doddridge, ed. J. D. Humphreys, 1 (1829), 26–254 • Calendar of the correspondence of Philip Doddridge, ed. G. F. Nuttall, HMC, JP 26 (1979) • P. Doddridge, letter to Thomas Saunders, 16 Nov 1725, DWL, MS 24.179.4 • Philip Doddridge, 1702–51: his contribution to English religion, ed. G. F. Nuttall (1951), 13, 104–6, 120 • 'An account of the dissenting academies from the Restoration of Charles the Second', DWL, MS 24.59, p. 37 • documents and memoranda relating to early nonconformist academies collected by the late Joshua Wilson, Esq, of Tunbridge Wells, DWL, New College collection, L54/1/19–20, L54/3/20–29 • H. McLachlan, English education under the Test Acts: being the history of the nonconformist academies, 1662–1820 (1931), 134–42, 291–3, 298, 309–10 • G. F. Nuttall, New College, London and its library: two lectures (1977), 33–4 • J. Nichols, The history and antiquities of the county of Leicester, 2/2 (1798), 642–3, 652–3; 4/2 (1811), 695 • Congregational Fund board, minutes, DWL, OD402 [vol. 2], 4 Oct 1703, 7 Feb 1703/4 • J. Hunter, Familiae minorum gentium, ed. J. W. Clay, 1, Harleian Society, 37 (1894), 180 • Calamy rev., 297 • DNB

Archives DWL, Blackmore MSS, 'An account of John Jennings's method of education', MS 12.40 (122) • DWL, Philip Doddridge's interleaved copy of his lectures in Latin, 'Theologia sive pneumatologia & ethica', part 2, MS 28.117 • DWL, Isaac Watts's remarks on Philip Doddridge's letter to Thomas Saunders describing his educational system, MS 24.180 (3)

Jennings, Louis John (1836–1893), journalist and politician, son of John Jennings, a member of an old Norfolk family, was born in London on 12 May 1836. Before he was twenty-five he became connected with *The Times*, for which journal he was sent to India as special correspondent in 1863; for some time he was editor of the *Times of India*. In 1865 he was sent to be *The Times*'s correspondent in New York, a new broom in the American office, for the paper's reputation had suffered from its support for the Confederacy. In 1867 he published *Eighty Years of Republican Government in the United States* and in the same year he married Madeleine Louise, daughter of David Henriques of New York; they had at least two children. Jennings was briefly (and unsuccessfully) a leader writer on *The Times* in 1867–8; he then settled in New York and became the editor of the *New York Times*. He was a crusading campaigner against Tammany Hall and 'Boss' Tweed and played a part in exposing corruption in New York; he was thanked by a testimonial from the New York establishment. It was probably at this time that he acquired the hostility to the Irish that so marked his later life.

Jennings returned to London in 1876 to devote himself to literature, founded and edited *The Week*, a newspaper that did not meet with much success, and became a contributor to the *Quarterly Review*, for the publisher of which, John Murray, he acted as reader. In 1877 he had charge of the City article in the *World*. He was an active walker, and published *Field Paths and Green Lanes: being Country Walks, Chiefly in Surrey and Sussex* (1877), followed by *Rambles among the Hills in the Peak of Derbyshire and the South Downs* (1880), with some charming woodcuts after sketches by A. H. Hallam Murray. In 1882–3 he wrote a novel, *The Millionaire*, said to depict the American businessman Jay Gould, which appeared in *Blackwood's Magazine* and was afterwards published anonymously (3 vols., 1883). His most important literary undertaking was to edit—to a good standard, given the conventions of the day—*The Croker Papers: the Correspondence and Diaries of the Late Rt Hon John Wilson Croker* (3 vols., 1884; revised edn, 1885).

In November 1885 Jennings was elected MP for Stockport as a Conservative; he was re-elected in 1886 and 1892.

His toryism was evidenced in *Mr Gladstone: a Study* (1887). He was a close follower of Lord Randolph Churchill, acting as his researcher, but they disagreed about fair trade (Jennings being a pronounced fair-trader), and about the appointment of the Parnell commission in 1888; Churchill's attack on the commission and on a motion by Jennings caused a sharp row in the Commons, and an immediate and permanent estrangement. His last substantial literary work—just before the row—was to edit Lord Randolph Churchill's *Speeches, with Notes and Introduction* (2 vols., 1889), though he sometimes wrote for the *New York Herald* as its London correspondent. Winston Churchill recorded that he suffered from 'an internal malady' (Churchill, 2.432).

After two years of illness Jennings died on 9 February 1893, at his home, 73 Elm Park Gardens, London, aged fifty-six; his wife survived him.   H. C. G. MATTHEW

Sources *The Times* (10 Feb 1893) • *The Times* (11 Feb 1893) • *The Athenaeum* (18 Feb 1893), 221 • *Men and women of the time* (1891) • W. S. Churchill, *Lord Randolph Churchill*, 2 vols. (1906)
Archives CAC Cam., corresp. with Randolph Churchill
Wealth at death £6454 2s. 9d.: probate, 22 Feb 1893, *CGPLA Eng. & Wales*

Jennings, Mary (*bap.* 1649?). *See under* Speke, George (1623–1689).

Jennings, Sir **Patrick Alfred** (1831–1897), pastoralist, and politician in Australia, was born at Newry, co. Down, Ireland, on 20 March 1831, the son of Francis Jennings, a linen merchant, and his wife, Mary O'Neil. Both parents traced direct descent from families who had forfeited local estates for religious reasons under Charles I. He was educated in Newry and Exeter, where he sought training for a business career since his family could not afford a preferred education for the bar. He emigrated to the goldfields of Victoria in 1852, and was followed by his family after the death of his father in 1857. In 1855 he settled at St Arnaud, and engaged very successfully in storekeeping and quartz crushing. He was the driving force in converting a mining settlement into a prosperous, law-abiding town. He was made a magistrate in 1857 and elected chairman of the first St Arnaud municipal council in 1861.

Together with a fellow Irish migrant, Martin Shanahan, a wealthy Wimmera squatter, he invested in pastoral properties in New South Wales, including Warbreccan in the Riverina district, which Jennings made his home in 1863. In February 1864 he married Shanahan's eldest daughter, Mary Anne (*d.* 1889). They had one daughter and two sons, who were educated in Sydney but returned to sheep-breeding careers in the country. Another of Shanahan's daughters married a brother of the Roman Catholic archbishop of Sydney, Roger Vaughan. Shanahan's eldest son, John, married a daughter of a former Victorian premier, Sir John O'Shannassy, another Irish migrant with property in the Riverina. After Shanahan's death in 1882 John carried on the Jennings–Shanahan partnership, which extended into Queensland with the 1874 acquisition of Westbrook, near Toowoomba. This property of more than 85,000 acres, which pastured 69,000 sheep before the 1890s drought, became Jennings's home after Warbreccan was sold in 1885.

Jennings's political career began in Victoria, without much success, but his move into the Riverina coincided with agitation for creation of a separate colony. In 1865 he was asked to help take the district's grievances direct to London, but he opposed this, believing the matter should be settled locally. In 1867 he accepted the conciliatory offer made by the New South Wales premier James Martin of a legislative council seat. In 1870 he transferred to the more robust politics of the assembly. He represented the Murray in 1870–72, was defeated at Mudgee in 1874, and was three times elected for the Bogan (1880–87).

During the 1870s Jennings received, but did not pursue, three invitations to join governments. He did accept appointment to represent the colony at the Melbourne exhibition of 1875 and to be commissioner for New South Wales, Queensland, and Tasmania at the Philadelphia exhibition in 1876. Knowledge of agricultural and commercial matters, administrative capacity, and an equable temperament made him the ideal choice for executive commissioner of Australasia's first international exhibition, held in Sydney in 1879. His achievement was recognized by appointment as KCMG in 1880.

After returning to the assembly Jennings held office in the governments of Alexander Stuart and George Dibbs. He contributed, especially, to debate on the dominant land issue, trying to harmonize the interests of squatters and settlers. Strongly conservative, his British model was Disraeli rather than Gladstone. Although he was proud of his Irish heritage, he believed in an overriding, 'providential' British world mission and supported, and contributed to, the 1884 Sudan expedition. He represented his colony at the 1887 conference and supported the formation of an imperial fleet for local defence. He was genial, urbane, tactful, conciliatory, and perceived as a compromise leader for difficult times. Budgets were unbalanced by loss of land sale revenue; old factions were breaking up; and former premier Sir Henry Parkes was particularly difficult. Jennings finally succeeded in forming a government on 26 February 1886. He met the fiscal crisis with a minor tariff, which seemed to conflict with his free-trade principles. Legislation was passed only by extraordinary expedients and all-night sittings. During one chaotic night Parkes advanced on him, shouting, 'You damned bugger, you Fenian'. The gentlemanly, now ailing Jennings wearied of this turmoil. He gave up the uncongenial job on 19 January 1887, and left the assembly. As an elder statesman, he accepted appointment to the legislative council in 1890 and selection as a delegate to the 1891 federal convention where, characteristically, he advocated compromise to advance a cause he had supported since the 1860s.

A friend said politics had been 'an accidental diversion' from Jennings's more worthwhile activities. He was vice-president of the (Royal) Agricultural Society of New South Wales (1876–87), and helped it secure its Sydney showground; a trustee of the art gallery (1885–97); and a fellow of the University of Sydney senate (1883–91), and the donor of an organ for its great hall. He was the most generous patron of musical activity in late colonial Sydney, supporting the Liedertafel (with which he sang), the Philharmonic Society, and the Amateur Orchestral Society. He had a keen interest in Wagner and 'the music of the future'. Between 1878 and 1897 he made the largest individual contributions to Roman Catholic building appeals, especially for the new Sydney Cathedral, to which he presented a window in memory of his wife, who died in 1889. His 'princely liberality' provided a library for St John's (Roman Catholic) University College, of which he was a fellow (1868–72, 1874–91). He received papal awards in 1874 and 1877 and was made a Roman marquess in 1887.

In the 1890s serious health problems combined with colonial financial crises and droughts to greatly reduce Jennings's pastoral wealth and his capacity to respond to new circumstances. By 1893 he held only Westbrook, part of which was sold for closer settlement. He died at his home, Ormiston, Gregory Terrace, Brisbane on 11 July 1897 and was buried in Sydney in the family vault in Waverley cemetery on 14 July.   A. E. CAHILL

Sources *Sydney Morning Herald* (12 July 1897) • *Sydney Morning Herald* (15 July 1897) • *Freeman's Journal* [Dublin] (17 July 1897) • *Town and Country Journal* [Sydney] (17 July 1897) • *The Bulletin* [Sydney, NSW] (24 July 1897) • *The Bulletin* [Sydney, NSW] (31 July 1897) • *St Arnaud Mercury* (14 July 1897) • *Sydney Morning Herald* (1864–97) • New South Wales parliamentary debates, 1867–97 • *Freeman's Journal* [Dublin] (1864–97) • *The Bulletin* [Sydney, NSW] (1880–97) • *The Express* [Sydney] (1880–86) • *Maryborough & Donolly Advertiser* (1859–63) • A. E. Cahill, 'Jennings, Sir Patrick Alfred', *AusDB*, vol. 4 • A. W. Martin, *Henry Parkes: a biography* (1980) • Y. S. Palmer, *Track of the years: the story of St Arnaud* (1967) • R. B. Ronald, *The Riverina: people and properties* (1960) • P. Mennell, 'Jennings, Sir Patrick', *The dictionary of Australasian biography* (1892) • d. cert.
Archives Mitchell L., NSW • New South Wales State Archives • University of Sydney | Mitchell L., NSW, Parkes MSS • Sydney Catholic Archdiocesan Archives, Moran MSS
Likenesses A. Clint, watercolour, 1879?, Mitchell L., NSW • photograph, 1885?, Sydney Catholic Archdiocesan Archives; repro. in P. O'Farrell, *The Irish in Australia* (1987) • oils, New South Wales Parliament House, Sydney
Wealth at death £4407—New South Wales estate: probate, New South Wales registrar-general's office

Jennings, Paul Francis (1918–1989), humorist, was born in Leamington Spa, Warwickshire, on 20 June 1918, the only son and second of the three children of William Benedict Jennings, musician, and his wife, Mary Gertrude Hewitt, the daughter of a watchmaker. They soon moved to a Coventry Roman Catholic parish, where Paul's father was organist and choirmaster, and Paul became the city's boy soprano, performing solo at the Hippodrome. Music was an absorbing interest from Paul's youth, as was his religion. He won a scholarship to the King Henry VIII School at Coventry, but went on to Douai in France, his parents thinking he might have a vocation for the priesthood. He loved Douai and its admirable headmaster, Father Ignatius Rice, but decided he was not cut out for the priesthood. His grounding in the classics fed his literary imagination and his loving, lifelong, obsessive play with words.

Jennings's humour was innate, or at least formed very early. He joined the Royal Corps of Signals in the Second World War and, when he was a subaltern in India in 1943, *Lilliput* published a characteristic piece of his, beginning: 'Have you ever watched a soldier marching, and wondered what he was thinking about? If he's a Young Soldier, I can tell you! He is thinking about a little booklet excitingly titled "Army Form B51"'. *Punch* took an army piece in 1945. Jennings worked at the central office of information (1946–7) and in advertising (1947–9). His celebrated parody of Jean-Paul Sartre appeared in *The Spectator* in 1948: 'Resistentialism is a philosophy of tragic grandeur … deriving its name from the thesis that Things resist Men … *Les choses sont contre nous*'. Resistentialism's leading luminary was Pierre-Marie Ventre, who built on the work of his nineteenth-century predecessors, Friedegg and Heidansiecker. Jennings imagined the seminal play 'Puits clos' about three old men endlessly stumbling over bricks in the bottom of a well. (It was used by *Time* magazine as a news story.) In 1949 he joined the staff of *The Observer*, with a regular column, 'Oddly Enough', which continued for seventeen years. His method was to start with something very familiar and then spin illogical and fantastic speculations around it, creating a brilliant and often subversive parody.

The *Observer* years, which lasted until 1966, were years of fulfilment, establishing Jennings, as *The Times* obituarist adjudged, as 'the most consistently original English comic writer of our century' (29 Dec 1989). In the year he joined *The Observer* so did Eric *Blom, as its music critic, and Jennings met his daughter, Celia. They married in 1952 and later had three sons and three daughters; the marriage was a happy one and ended only with his death. Jennings knew a great deal about music; he sang madrigals with the Oriana Society and enjoyed singing—as far afield as Istanbul—with the Philharmonia Chorus and the London Philharmonic Choir. As he noted, 'For members of choirs, there's harmony beyond the heard harmony of music'.

The family moved from Hampstead to East Bergholt in Suffolk, and Jennings's pieces in *The Observer* began to reflect his deep love of that county. His wife became involved in the work of the Suffolk Preservation Society. To celebrate its sixtieth anniversary in 1989, she edited a book to which her husband contributed inimitably—not only the title, *Suffolk for Ever*, but the last word. This was a clever discussion, disguised as a Platonic dialogue, of the complexities and the pitfalls confronting everyone moved to action by the erosions of our environs. In *The English Difference* (1974)—the wide-ranging book Jennings edited, and mostly wrote—he illustrated his speculative inclination:

> You can see on the face of a child, deep in a game, the kind of total absorption observable in the figure of Pythagoras, *Thinking*, carved on a portal at Chartres. … Though children the world over play games, it is the English who, perhaps sensing the Death of God, once did unconsciously try to preserve religion in their untranslatable phrase *playing the game*.

After 1966 Jennings wrote freelance, and from this period

emerged his compilation, *The Book of Nonsense* (1977). He mourned the loss of anything old-fashioned: steam trains, red telephone kiosks, the Fahrenheit classification of temperature. His prejudices were conservative and patriotic.

Jennings's *Observer* (and other) essays were collected and published with such titles as *Even Oddlier* (1952), *Next to Oddliness* (1955), *Golden Oddlies* (1983), and *The Paul Jennings Reader* (1990). *The Living Village* (1968) was a picture of the women's institutes of Britain. He also wrote two children's books. He was a fellow of the Royal Society of Literature.

Jennings suffered serious illnesses—including tuberculosis and a heart attack—all belied by the laughter of his high, quick, musical voice and by lively, wide-open, grey eyes. He and his wife moved to Orford, on the Suffolk coast, where he died of liver cancer at his home, 25 High Street, on 26 December 1989.   NORMAN SCARFE, *rev.*

Sources *The Times* (29 Dec 1989) · personal knowledge (1996) · private information (1996) · *CGPLA Eng. & Wales* (1990)

Wealth at death under £100,000: probate, 4 April 1990, *CGPLA Eng. & Wales*

Jenour, John (1465/6–1542), legal official, was the son of William Jenour of Stonham Aspal, Suffolk, and Katherine Whiting. He and his brother Robert Jenour (*d.* 1536) both became officers of the common pleas, John being mentioned as an attorney in the rolls of the common pleas for 1491. In 1503 he became filazer of the common pleas for Devon, Dorset, and Somerset, and in 1513 was promoted to be second prothonotary. From 1510 he was clerk of assize on the midland circuit. He had been a member of the Middle Temple before 1501, and served as treasurer in 1517–20. As a prothonotary he was one of the officials responsible for settling the forms of pleading and entries, and he is mentioned several times in the law reports. A fair copy of his great book of entries, which was an acknowledged authority and sometimes cited in court, is now in the Library of Congress, Washington (Phillipps MS 26752). It includes some earlier cases taken from the collections of William Copley, chief prothonotary from 1468 to 1490. Though never printed, it had some influence on the anonymous *Intrationum liber* of 1546.

A number of Jenour's pupils or under-clerks can be identified, thanks to an obituary note written by Chief Justice Catlin, and the list shows what a remarkable influence he had on the judiciary of the next generation. His pupils, all Middle Templars, included four future chief justices—Sir Robert Catlin himself, Sir Robert Brooke, Sir Anthony Browne, and Sir James Dyer—and two puisne judges, Corbet and Freville. According to the *Visitations of Essex* Jenour married in 1500 Anne, daughter of John Fincham of Outwell, Norfolk; however, his widow was called Alice (*d.* 1549). Jenour died, aged seventy-six, on 17 September 1542, and was probably buried according to his testamentary instructions in the chancel of Temple Church. There was formerly a monumental inscription at Great Dunmow, Essex. Besides his property in Essex he left a house and garden in St Bride's, Fleet Street, leased from the bishop of Salisbury. His eldest son, Richard (1511–1548), to

whom he left his book of entries, was a member of parliament and clerk of the court of surveyors. To his second son, Robert, he left the manor of Rendham Hall, Suffolk, 'so that he contynue his study and lernyng in the Temple'. His nephew Richard Lone (*d.* 1581) was third prothonotary of the common pleas.   J. H. BAKER

Sources *The reports of Sir John Spelman*, ed. J. H. Baker, 2, SeldS, 94 (1978), 2.101, 103, 130, 377 · W. C. Metcalfe, ed., *The visitations of Essex*, 1, Harleian Society, 13 (1878), 221–2 · will, PRO, PROB 11/29, fol. 81 · J. H. Baker and J. S. Ringrose, *A catalogue of English legal manuscripts in Cambridge University Library* (1996), 378–9 · J. H. Baker, *English legal manuscripts in the United States of America: a descriptive list*, 1 (1985), no. 29, p. 11 · N. Salmon, *The history and antiquities of Essex* (1740), 210 · inquisition post mortem, PRO, C142/65/70 · PRO, CP 40 · C. H. Hopwood, ed., *Middle Temple records*, 1: *1501–1603* (1904) · HoP, *Commons, 1509–58*, 2.442–3

Jenour, Joshua (1755–1853), printer and writer, was born on 31 July 1755 at Serjeants' Inn, Fleet Street, the eldest son of Joshua Jenour (*bap.* 1715, *d.* 1774), master of the Stationers' Company in 1772, co-proprietor and manager of the *Daily Advertiser*, and his wife, Ann. After an apprenticeship with the Stationers' Company, Jenour was called to the livery on 6 August 1776. On his death in 1786 Joshua's uncle Matthew Jenour left him an inheritance (including his interest in the *Advertiser*). Jenour followed the trade of printer at 33 Fleet Street from 1774 until 1797, shortly before the *Daily Advertiser* stopped publication. He married Harriet Andrews (*bap.* 1758), third daughter of Robert Andrews of Essex, by 1801.

An obituary in the *Gentleman's Magazine* described Jenour as 'a voluminous though obscure author' (*GM*, 39.325). His entry in the *Dictionary of National Biography* has ensured his nominal survival, but of approximately twenty publications (mostly anonymous and published at his own expense), only two survive in the British Library: a poem entitled *Horns for Ever! or, A Procession to Blackheath* (1813), dedicated to R. B. Sheridan, and a moral tale, *The Weight of a Feather, and the Value of Five Minutes* (1820). By 1820 Jenour was making the first of many applications to the Royal Literary Fund for a grant (he was awarded £5 on this occasion). He appeared to believe that society owed him a living as a writer: his constant requests include mention of unpaid printers' bills, loss from piracy, arrears of rent, and a wife and five children to support (there were eleven children from his marriage to Harriet Andrews). On 8 October 1824 he married Amelia Stacy (*b.* 1788) in St Pancras. Subsequent appeals to the fund described a disastrous accident in 1835, in which he was struck by a galloping horse and his left eye severely damaged, and when a few weeks later he lost a daughter, he used this fact to add a twist of pathos to his appeal for further funds.

In his eighties, when living in Gravesend, Jenour recorded that his income was principally from letting a large portion of his small house. Clearly his writing was financially unprofitable. He ranged in verse and prose over various forms and subjects, with a particular liking for pamphlets of a political or social bent: his list of works includes *Observations on the Taxation of Property* (1795) which apparently went through several printings (presumably his most successful work); *A Plan for Meliorating the Condition of the Labouring Poor*; *Thoughts on Indecorum at Theatres*; *A Plan for the Reform of Parliament*; *Hints for the Recovery and Preservation of Health* (1829). He also wrote translations of Boileau's satires and produced guidebooks to Gravesend and nearby Greenhithe. He contributed pieces to *John Bull* and the local *Rochester Gazette*. Jenour lived to the age of ninety-seven, dying in Gravesend on 23 January 1853. His widow made a further application to the Royal Literary Fund in April of the same year.   ROSEMARY SCOTT

Sources GM, 2nd ser., 39 (1853), 325 • GM, 2nd ser., 40 (1853), 434 • letters from Joshua Jenour to Royal Literary Fund, BL, loan no. 96, folder 410 • I. Maxted, *The London book trades, 1775–1800: a topographical guide* (privately printed, Exeter, 1980) • D. F. McKenzie, ed., *Stationers' Company apprentices, [3]: 1701–1800* (1978) • Boase, *Mod. Eng. biog.* • J. Jenour, letters to Royal Society of Arts, RSA, 47/J1 and A/RSA/2/B/42 • IGI

Archives BL, letters to Royal Literary Fund, loan 96

Jenye [Janney], **Thomas** (*fl.* 1565–1583), rebel and poet, probably came from Yorkshire, although his exact origins and details about his parentage are unknown. He was possibly related to William Jennings (*d.* 1573) of Clifford's Inn in the West Riding of Yorkshire. He may have been from Arskey in the West Riding.

Nothing is known about Jenye's early life; the first extant source dates from 31 December 1565, when he was named as a servant of the English ambassador in Scotland, Thomas Randolph. While in Edinburgh he wrote a fifty-nine stanza poem, the 'Epistle Dedicatorie' entitled 'Maister Randolphe's Phantasey', giving an account of the chaseabout raid, a farcical rebellion by James Stewart, earl of Moray, against Mary, queen of Scots, in which no pitched battle was ever fought. The poem recounts how Mary ruled over a 'mysordered comonweale' through a coterie of flatterers of 'slipperie renowne', while Moray was praised as springing from a noble and 'aincyent race'. Randolph was portrayed in the poem searching in his library for support on how to counter tyranny and concluding that 'bloodye feicty doth aske vengeance'. As Jenye lifted from Horace, Richard Tottell's 'Miscellany' (1557), and other sources, the Victorian editor James Cranstoun disdainfully referred to him as a 'literary cockroach stealing the sweets stored by the industry of others' (Cranstoun, 1.121–162). However, the work is significant as an eyewitness account of this important period in Mary's personal rule and caused great annoyance to the Scottish queen, who, despite his denials over the authorship, banished Randolph from court in February 1566. Elizabeth I wrote to Mary in June, disturbed at the treatment of her ambassador but vowing to inflict punishment on the true author should he be found.

Jenye was in the service of the English ambassador to France, Sir Henry Norris, during the late 1560s. Writing to Sir William Cecil, principal secretary, from Dieppe on 13 July 1567 Jenye related his attempt to secure a safe passage to England for Moray, who wanted to escape from France. Norris was in the Low Countries in 1568 and Jenye dedicated his translation of a work by Pierre de Ronsard to him. Jenye appears to have been his secretary. A letter of

1567 suggests he was married, but his wife's name is not known.

Jenye was in England in 1569 and became involved in the rising of the northern earls. His writing skills were put to good use in the proclamation issued by Henry Percy, eighth earl of Northumberland, and Charles Neville, sixth earl of Westmorland, on 15 November, which challenged 'the diverse newe set upp nobles' about Elizabeth and demanded ancient customs be restored to the church (Alford, 207). According to a copy of his confession of April 1570, Jenye was forced to write this at Westmorland's command. However, this confession is vague and focused on reducing his own responsibility, claiming he was 'not privy to the enterprise' and that he even attempted to persuade Northumberland to refrain from resisting the queen when he met him nine days before the rising. Jenye claimed that he did not know the rebels intended to take up arms, that he held no office in the company because he was regarded with suspicion for his religious beliefs, and that he was distrusted as a possible spy sent by Thomas Radcliffe, third earl of Sussex, lord president of the queen's council of the north (Sharp, 171).

Jenye's confession was most probably extracted at Fast Castle, situated about 30 miles over the border from Berwick, as his old master Randolph revealed in a letter to Cecil on 27 February 1570 that he was being held there. At some point after this Jenye escaped. Henry Carey, first Baron Hunsdon, wrote to Cecil in March and explained that he believed Jenye, Egremont Radcliffe, and others had a ship ready to pass to Flanders, which he hoped to intercept off the Farne Islands. This plan evidently did not work because by 27 June Jenye was in Brussels writing to Sir William Maitland of Lethington that 'all things are here in quiet' and wishing him to forward letters to Katherine Percy, countess of Northumberland, and 'his dear friend' Radcliffe. Cecil was still on his tail however. The spy William Herle wrote to Cecil on 27 April 1571, telling him that he had pretended to be a friend of the exiles and spoke to a potential informant. He was especially desirous to know how 'a companion of mine—Thomas Janney' and the countess of Northumberland fared, but failed to glean any further information (CSP Scot., 1569–71).

Jenye's intrigues did not wane. In May 1572 he was among English exiles in receipt of a Spanish pension in reward for spying. Cecil listed Jenye as among a 'rabble of rebels' around Don John of Austria in February 1577 (CSP for., 1575–7). He is also known to have travelled to Milan, secured contacts in Cologne, and to have been involved in the Throckmorton plot of 1583. Thereafter he vanishes from the scene with the same suddenness with which he entered it; his death cannot be traced. Much about his life and motivations is an intriguing mystery.

Jenye's correspondence and exile along with major rebels and traitors, his writing of the proclamation of November 1569, and the fact he was exempt from pardon imply that he was more involved in the northern uprising than his confession would suggest. The queen herself wrote to Randolph that she 'misliked much' Jenye's escape, particularly because it was an embarrassment to her regime (*CSP Scot.*, 1569–71). However, his true motivation for turning from crown servant in Scotland to rebel remains elusive. Perhaps all that can be concluded is that he had an opportunistic nature and an apparent delight in intrigue and adventure. SARAH CLAYTON

Sources CSP Scot., 1563–71 · CSP dom., 1547–80 · CSP for., 1569–71; 1575–7 · J. Cranstoun, ed., *Satirical poems of the time of the Reformation*, 2 vols. in 4 pts, STS, 20, 24, 28, 30 (1891–3) · C. Sharp, ed., *Memorials of the rebellion of 1569* (1840); repr. with foreword by R. Wood as *The rising in the north: the 1569 rebellion* (1975) · A. Fletcher and D. MacCulloch, *Tudor rebellions*, 4th edn (1997), 94–153 · *Calendar of the manuscripts of the most hon. the marquis of Salisbury*, 1–2, HMC, 9 (1883–8) · *DNB* · S. Alford, *The early Elizabethan polity: William Cecil and the British succession crisis, 1558–1569* (1998) · M. Lynch, *Scotland: a new history* (1991) · [J. W. Clay], ed., *North country wills*, 2 vols., SurtS, 116, 121 (1908–12)
Archives BL, Proclamation of the earls, 1569, Harley MS 6990, fol. 44

Jenynges, Edward (*fl.* 1565–1590), writer, is unknown apart from his works. He was the author of a verse adaptation of Boccaccio's *Titus and Gesippus* (itself based on the story of Orestes and Pylades) entitled *The Notable Hystory of Two Faithfull Lovers Named Alfagus and Archelaus*, which is prefaced by a 'definytion of freyndshyppe', in the form of a poem to the reader.

Although Thomas Colwell obtained a licence to print this work in 1565, he refrained from doing so until 1574, the reasons for which are unclear. Jenynges also wrote *A briefe discovery of the damages that happen to this realme by disordered and unlawfull diet, the benefites and commodities that otherwise might ensue, with a persuasion of the people for a better maintenance to the navie*, printed by R. Ward in 1590 (and again in 1593). The work is dedicated to Charles Howard, lord high admiral, and afterwards earl of Nottingham. Jenynges argues for the economic and strategic benefits of maintaining a fast day for eating fish only—a practice which Jenynges is keen to stress should not be associated with 'papistry', but rather offers the means of sustaining a strong maritime force. The topic is also addressed by Jenynges in a treatise dedicated to William Cecil, Lord Burghley, the lord treasurer, entitled 'On the utility to the realm by observing days for eating fish only' (BL, Lansdowne MS 101). CATHY SHRANK

Sources T. Corser, *Collectanea Anglo-poetica, or, A … catalogue of a … collection of early English poetry*, 8, Chetham Society, 102 (1878) · W. C. Hazlitt, *Hand-book to the popular, poetical and dramatic literature of Great Britain* (1867) · W. C. Hazlitt, *Collections and notes, 1867–1876* (1876) · J. Ritson, *Bibliographia poetica* (1802) · Arber, *Regs. Stationers* · *DNB*

Jenyns, Frances. *See* Talbot, Frances, duchess of Tyrconnell (1648–1731).

Jenyns, Leonard. *See* Blomefield, Leonard (1800–1893).

Jenyns, Sarah. *See* Churchill, Sarah, duchess of Marlborough (1660–1744).

Jenyns, Soame (1704–1787), author and politician, was born on 1 January 1704 in Great Ormond Street, London, the only child of Sir Roger Jenyns (1663–1740), receiver of the Bedford Level Corporation in London, and his second wife, Lady Elizabeth Jenyns (1666–1728), daughter of Sir

Peter Soame, bt, of Hayden, Essex. He was raised at Bottisham Hall, on the family estate in Cambridgeshire, and received his education from private tutors until the age of seventeen. He entered St John's College, Cambridge, as a fellow commoner in 1722 and matriculated in 1724, but left the following year without taking a degree. After dissipating his time in Bottisham and London, on 5 May 1726 he married at Burwell, Cambridgeshire, the heiress Mary Soame (d. 1753), illegitimate daughter of Colonel Edmund Soame of Dereham Grange, Norfolk, with the encouragement of his father, and he succeeded his father as the squire of Bottisham in 1740. Mary Jenyns deserted her husband in 1742 and died on 30 July 1753; they had no children. On 26 February 1754 Jenyns married his cousin, Elizabeth Gray, daughter of Henry Gray of Hackney, who remained his devoted companion for the rest of his life.

From his university years Jenyns had displayed a gift for amatory and satiric verse in the post-Restoration style. He published the mock-heroic poem *The Art of Dancing* in 1729 and in 1730 produced a manuscript volume of songs and love poems dedicated to Lady Margaret Cavendish Harley. When Robert Dodsley brought out a large segment of it in his *Collection of Poems. By Several Hands* (1748) Jenyns began to receive recognition as a wit and satirist. A personal collection, *Poems. By * * * ** (1752), was followed by two subsequent collections: *Miscellaneous Pieces, in Two Volumes* (1761) and *Miscellaneous Pieces, in Verse and Prose* (1770). By then, however, he was publishing only occasional verse and *jeux d'esprit*, preferring to devote his attention to the essay and to political, philosophical, and economic writings.

Jenyns possessed a graceful prose style reminiscent of Addison and admirably suited to the personal essay. He published five essays in the *World* in 1755, and there followed a series of eminently readable tracts and political pamphlets, which were reformulations of current thinking on the problem of evil, the evidences of Christianity, the taxation of the American colonies, the national debt, parliamentary reform, and other controversial matters, but they received a mixed reception. In *A Free Inquiry into the Nature and Origin of Evil* (1757), a rationalist theodicy typical of eighteenth-century optimism, Jenyns seemed to dismiss social ills too easily, embracing the hierarchical theory of the Great Chain of Being adopted by Alexander Pope in *The Essay on Man* (1732–4). The ills we suffer owe their existence to necessity, he argued. What we perceive as evils are elements of a grand plan we can glimpse only in part. For this, Samuel Johnson ridiculed the *Free Inquiry* so severely in the *Literary Magazine* that he virtually put an end to optimistic theorizing. Then, in *A View of the Internal Evidence of the Christian Religion* (1776), an unsystematic defence of Christianity aimed at deists and freethinkers, Jenyns accentuated the ethical qualities of Christianity favoured by innovating apologists of the later eighteenth century rather than the standard defensive arguments from prophecy and miracle. The book was widely read and applauded for its clarity and ease (it was also translated into French, Polish, and Greek), but readers familiar with his characteristic irony questioned his sincerity. 'He is undoubtedly a fine writer', wrote John Wesley, 'but whether he is a Christian, Deist, or Atheist, I cannot tell' (*Works*, 4.82). His miscellaneous political and economic pamphlets were conditioned by long parliamentary experience. Being a typical government placeman and a conservative whig landowner he was wary of reforming ideas about equality, personal liberty, and resistance to authority, and tended to support the position of the government of the day on issues of policy.

For some time Jenyns lived at ease at Bottisham Hall, a place he half-mockingly described in his *Epistle to Lord Lovelace* (1735) as

A house, where quiet guards the door,
No rural wits smoke, drink, and roar,
Choice books, safe horses, wholesome liquor,
Clean girls, backgammon, and the vicar.
(Jenyns, *Works*, 1.49)

But his life of rural comfort changed when he was elected to represent Cambridgeshire in 1741 as the preferred candidate of Lord Chancellor Hardwicke; and he was returned in 1747 as part of the whig electoral machine dominated by the duke of Newcastle. When Lord Granby, Hardwicke's whig opponent, decided to stand in the county himself in 1753, Jenyns was removed, then compensated with £600 and provided with a safe seat purchased for him in the rotten borough of Dunwich. He continued to receive this payment until 1755, when he was appointed one of the lords commissioners of trade and plantations, the *ad hoc* committee of parliament which advised government about proposals from abroad. Though the members of this body normally came and went with some frequency, he retained his place for twenty-five years, during which time he was re-elected to parliament five more times, but for the town of Cambridge.

Although decidedly unattractive physically, Jenyns maintained a dandyish mode of dress and cultivated a vein of entertaining conversation and good humour that endeared him to friends and colleagues. Richard Cumberland wrote of him in later life,

… as nature had cast him in the exact mould of an ill-made pair of stiff stays, he followed her so close in the fashion of his coat, that it was doubted if he did not wear them: because he had a protuberant wen just under his pole, he wore a wig, that did not cover half his head. His eyes were protruded like the eyes of a lobster, who wears them at the end of his feelers, and yet there was room between one of these and his nose for another wen that added nothing to his beauty; yet I heard this good man very innocently remark, when Gibbon published his history, that he wondered any body so ugly could write a book. (Cumberland, 247–8)

Thus, in 1757, when he sat for Sir Joshua Reynolds, the resulting portrait was considered flattering. 'It is proof of Sir Joshua's art', observed Horace Walpole, 'who could give a strong resemblance of so uncouth a countenance without leaving it disagreeable' (Walpole, 2.58).

Jenyns enlivened evening assemblies with his amusing conceits, which he delivered through his broken teeth.

Unfortunately, his style of wit was not suited to public oratory. He endeavoured to speak in the House of Commons at least twice, and as Edmond Malone remembered, 'every one was prepared with a half-grin before he uttered a word; but he failed miserably. He had a most inharmonious voice, and a laugh scarcely human' (Prior, 375–6). Instead he shone at committee meetings, sittings of the Board of Trade, and evening parties, and tossed off provocative satires to arouse the political and the literary world. The most celebrated of these was his 'Epitaph on Johnson', written in 1783 for private amusement but given surreptitiously to the *Gentleman's Magazine*. When Johnson died and biographies by James Boswell and Hester Thrale appeared, he added these lines:

Would you know all his wisdom and his folly,
His actions, sayings, mirth and melancholy,
Boswell and Thrale, retailers of his wit,
Will tell you how he wrote and talk'd and cough'd and s—t!
(*GM*, 56.428)

Mindful of the damage inflicted on Jenyns by Johnson's review in 1757, Boswell wrote, 'It was an unbecoming indulgence of puny resentment, at a time when he himself was at a very advanced age, and had a near prospect of descending to the grave' (Boswell, *Life*, 1.316 n.2).

During his last parliamentary session Jenyns sparkled at the 'bluestocking' evenings presided over by Mrs Elizabeth Montague, with their blend of rank, enterprise, and literary accomplishment, but he had lost his taste for public exchange. In 1780 Burke introduced into parliament a scheme to abolish sinecure places and to refloat the civil list, singling Jenyns out for his long tenure at the Board of Trade, and shortly thereafter he withdrew from public affairs. He died of a fever in London on 18 December 1787 and was buried at the church of the Holy Trinity, Bottisham, on 27 December.   RONALD ROMPKEY

Sources S. Jenyns, *The works of Soame Jenyns, esq., in four volumes*, ed. C. N. Cole, 4 vols. (1790) • R. Rompkey, *Soame Jenyns* (1984) • R. Rompkey, 'Some uncollected authors XLIX: Soame Jenyns', *Book Collector*, 25 (1976), 210–24 [descriptive bibliography] • E. Hailstone, *The history and antiquities of the parish of Bottisham* (1873) • S. Wells, *The history of the draining of the great level of the Fens, called Bedford level* (1830) • D. Cook, 'The representative history of the county, town and university of Cambridge', PhD diss., U. Lond., 1935 • A. H. Basye, *The lords commissioners of trade and plantations* (1925) • Walpole, *Corr.* • R. Cumberland, *Memoirs of Richard Cumberland written by himself* (1806) • J. Prior, *Life of Edmond Malone, editor of Shakespeare* (1860) • Boswell, *Life* • *The works of … John Wesley*, 14 vols. (1872) • S. Jenyns, 'Poems on several occasions', BL, Loan MS 29/326 • S. Johnson, 'Review of *A free inquiry into the nature and origin of evil*', *Literary Magazine*, 2 (1757), 171–5, 251–3, 301–6 • HoP, *Commons* • IGI • *GM*, 1st ser., 56 (1786), 428 • parish register, St Giles-in-the-Fields, London • J. E. B. Mayor and R. F. Scott, eds., *Admissions to the College of St John the Evangelist in the University of Cambridge*, 3 vols. in 4 pts (1882–1931) • *Morning Chronicle* (31 Dec 1787) • parish register, Church of the Holy Trinity, Bottisham, Cambs., Cambs. AS

Archives Bottisham Hall, Bottisham, Cambridgeshire, family MSS | BL, Cole MSS • BL, letters to Lord Hardwicke, Add. MS 35631 • BL, Newcastle MSS

Likenesses J. Reynolds, oils, 1757, Bottisham Hall, Cambridgeshire • W. Dickinson, mezzotint, 1776 (after J. Reynolds), BM, NPG • J. Barry, group portrait, oils, *c*.1783 (*The distribution of premiums in the*

Society of Arts), RSA • J. Bacon, monument, Church of the Holy Trinity, Bottisham, Cambridgeshire
Wealth at death manor of Allingtons and Vauxes, near Bottisham (140 acres)

Jenyns, Sir Stephen (c.1450–1523), administrator, was born at Wolverhampton, Staffordshire, the son of William Jenyns. Settling in London, he was probably apprenticed to a merchant taylor and upon completing the period of servitude entered the company and prospered. He rose through the ranks to the office of master in 1489 and instituted financial reforms in the guild. Jenyns married Margaret, née Kyrton, the widow of merchant taylor William Buk, after 1490; the Jenynses' only offspring, Catherine, married John Nichols, another merchant taylor, and died childless.

By 1495 Jenyns had a shop and residence in the parish of All Saints-the-Great which he leased for over two decades from Edward Stafford, duke of Buckingham. Jenyns became sheriff in 1498; for the shrievalty, the company advanced him over £26 for his expenses. During the following year he was chosen an alderman from Castle Baynard ward; in 1505 he removed to Dowgate, and in May 1508 to Lime Street. Elected lord mayor for 1508–9, the first merchant taylor to attain that honour, Jenyns was present in his civic capacity at the funeral of Henry VII and was knighted in 1509 at the coronation ceremonies of Henry VIII.

Jenyns's philanthropy was remarkable. He bought land at Wolverhampton in 1508 and the nearby Rushocke estate shortly thereafter, obtaining a licence on 22 September 1512 to found Wolverhampton grammar school. Jenyns used the Rushocke estate to finance the school's maintenance, and placed it under control of the Merchant Taylors' Company. The school remained under the company's jurisdiction until 1766 and a charitable focus for the guild to the present. As was the custom following office-holding in the civic guilds, Jenyns and his wife in 1512 donated generously to the decoration of the company's chapel and hall, providing luxurious cloth adorned with the emblem of St John, the Merchant Taylors' patron saint. With Sir William Fitzwilliam, Jenyns also financed a substantial portion of the reconstruction in Gothic style, in 1520–32, of the church of St Andrew Undershaft. The chronicler John Stow, himself a merchant taylor, reported that 'Stephen Gennings' paid for the rebuilding of the north side of the great middle aisle, including the choir, roofed and sealed the north aisle, and glazed the south side of the church. The pews and windows in the south chapel are proof of his substantial expenditure, and his coat of arms still adorns the north aisle ceiling. Stow is buried there.

Jenyns died in London in 1523 and was interred in Greyfriars Church; all tombs in Greyfriars were destroyed in 1547. Through a derivative will dated 30 June 1522, used to ensure the legal transfer of land, Jenyns bequeathed a large estate to the Merchant Taylors' Company by the devising of his fellow guildsman John Bennett, a citizen by birth or patrimony.   ELIZABETH LANE FURDELL

Sources DNB • C. M. Clode, *The early history of the Guild of Merchant Taylors of the fraternity of St John the Baptist, London*, 2 vols. (1888) • J. Stow, *The survey of London* (1912) [with introduction by H. B. Wheatley] • PRO, PROB 11/21, sig. 8 • A. B. Beaven, ed., *The aldermen of the City of London, temp. Henry III–[1912]*, 2 vols. (1908–13) • B. Weinreb and C. Hibbert, eds., *The London encyclopaedia* (1983) • *CClR, 1485–509* • *CPR, 1485–509* • *LP Henry VIII* • G. S. Fry and S. J. Madge, eds., *Abstract of inquisitiones post mortem relating to the City of London*, 3 vols., British RS, 15, 26, 36 (1896–1908)
Wealth at death Rushocke estate near Wolverhampton; grammar school: will, PRO, PROB 11/21, sig. 8

Jephcott, Sir Harry, first baronet (1891–1978), pharmaceutical industrialist, was born on 15 January 1891 at Tardebigge, near Redditch, Worcestershire, youngest of the five children and three sons of John Josiah Jephcott (1853–1929), train driver and former miner, and his wife, Helen (1849–1930), daughter of Charles Matthews. He was educated at King Edward Grammar School, Camp Hill, Birmingham, and was apprenticed in 1907 to a pharmacist at Redditch. He joined customs and excise in 1912 and was seconded to the department of the government chemist in 1914. Meanwhile he studied part-time at West Ham Technical College and in 1915 graduated as a bachelor of science with first-class honours in chemistry at the University of London. He gained the diploma of pharmaceutical chemist in 1916, took his master's degree in 1918 with a thesis on tobacco, and was elected fellow of the Royal Institute of Chemistry in 1920. Jephcott married on 19 April 1919 Doris (1893–1985), daughter of Henry Gregory, a builder. She was a pharmaceutical chemist of distinction before her marriage, and a woman of many qualities. They had two sons.

In 1919 Jephcott was recruited by Alec *Nathan to the family business of Joseph Nathan & Co., which sold dried milk powder imported from New Zealand under the trade name of Glaxo. Jephcott's task was to impose scientific quality controls, but he soon undertook experiments to test the antiscorbutic value of dried milk, and in 1923 visited the USA to meet scientists working on accessory food factors. He obtained a licence to fortify Glaxo powder with antirachitic vitamin D, using Theodore Zucker's new process for the extraction of the vitamin from fish-liver oil, and thus secured an immense commercial advantage over competitors. In 1924, at his instigation, Glaxo began production of its first pharmaceutical product, Ostelin, the earliest vitamin concentrate made commercially in Britain.

Jephcott was never a narrow or specialized 'boffin'. He was receptive to all new scientific ideas, keenly interested in sales of pharmaceutical products, and an astute business strategist who understood every aspect of company administration. His appreciation of the importance of patent law in pharmaceuticals led him to read for the bar and to be called to the Middle Temple in 1925. His qualities were recognized by the Nathans. He was made general manager of the Glaxo department in 1925, a director of Joseph Nathan in 1929, managing director of the newly formed Glaxo Laboratories (GL) in 1935, and of the parent

Sir Harry Jephcott, first baronet (1891–1978), by Elliott & Fry, 1956

company in 1939. He was by this date convinced that GL must concentrate on the science-based production of therapeutic substances.

The Second World War provided Jephcott's chance. He was adviser on manufactured foods to the Ministry of Food (1941–3) and chairman of the Therapeutic Research Corporation in 1943. He visited the USA on behalf of the Ministry of Supply in 1944 to report on penicillin production, and seized the opportunity for Glaxo Laboratories to build factories for penicillin production by deep fermentation under licence from two American companies, Merck and Squibb. This established his company at the forefront of the British pharmaceutical sector, and positioned it to become the largest pharmaceutical group in the world by 1995.

In 1947 Jephcott arranged the public flotation of Glaxo Laboratories and the divestiture of Nathan's non-pharmaceutical interests. Simultaneously he began establishing or extending local production in overseas markets, particularly in Commonwealth countries, Italy, and South America. In 1948 vitamin B12, the factor which combats pernicious anaemia, was isolated by Glaxo scientists. In 1950 Glaxo marketed the first commercial cortisone produced in Britain. The company collaborated in the 1950s with the National Research Development Corporation in developing cephalosporin antibiotics. Its research interests and product lines became increasingly ambitious and diversified. Jephcott retired as managing

director in 1956, but as non-executive chairman was largely responsible when his company took control of other pharmaceutical businesses, most notably Allen and Hanbury in 1958. From 1963 he was honorary life president.

Jephcott's great gifts were much in demand. He was a member of the government's Advisory Council on Scientific Policy in 1953–6 and chairman of the Council for Scientific and Industrial Research in 1956–61. He was a director of the Metal Box Company (1950–64). He was successively chairman and president of the Association of British Chemical Manufacturers (1947–55), chairman of a government committee on synthetic detergents (1953–5), president of the Royal Institute of Chemistry (1953–5), and a governor of the London School of Economics (1952–68). A generous, humane, and constructive man, he endowed several charitable trusts, most notably the Triangle Trust, and donated 35 acres of coastline to the National Trust.

'He was a formidable person, most business-like in negotiation,' according to Sir Frank Hartley, writing in *Pharmaceutical Journal*, 'with a fantastic intuitive sense of what was possible in our industry … He could divine the right course to take and rationalise his decision afterwards.' Almost 6½ feet tall, with an imposing and intellectual appearance, Jephcott brought zest to everything he did, and relished doing a job well. A shrewd judge of character, he had an exceptional capacity for inspiring others with zeal, and was passionately admired by many of his staff. Although a perfectionist, he was never cantankerous or unreasonably demanding. In financial policy he was cautious. He was an indefatigable overseas traveller from 1920 until his death, and an inveterate walker, who took an evening constitutional of at least 5 miles whenever possible. He was at different times a keen photographer, cabinet-maker, gardener, and radio ham. On a visit to Chicago in 1936 he bought a Hammond electric organ, which appealed both to his scientific mind and to musical tastes nurtured in youth by the Three Choirs festival and midlands church music. He lived from 1928 until his death at Westwood, 1 Cheney Street, Pinner, Middlesex, although he later bought farms at East Portlemouth in Devon.

Jephcott was knighted in 1946 and created a baronet in 1962. He died of heart failure on 29 May 1978, at Northwick Park Hospital, Harrow, and was cremated. His estate was valued at over £2 million.

RICHARD DAVENPORT-HINES

Sources private information (2004) · R. P. T. Davenport-Hines and J. Slinn, *Glaxo: a history to 1962* (1992) · F. Hartley, 'Sir Harry Jephcott', *Pharmaceutical Journal*, 221 (1978), 458–9 · R. P. T. Davenport-Hines, 'Glaxo as a multinational before 1963', *British multinationals: origins, management and performance*, ed. G. Jones (1986), 137–63 · b. cert. · d. cert.

Archives Glaxo Archives, Greenford, Middlesex | Verona, Italy, correspondence with Glaxo overseas subsidiaries held at foreign headquarters · Palmerston North, New Zealand, correspondence with Glaxo overseas subsidiaries held at foreign headquarters · Melbourne, Australia, correspondence with Glaxo overseas subsidiaries held at foreign headquarters | FILM private movie films taken in 1930s by subject, held by son Sir A. Jephcott

Likenesses photographs, 1945–53, repro. in Davenport-Hines, 'Glaxo as a multinational', 141, 149 • photographs, 1953–5, repro. in Davenport-Hines and Slinn, *Glaxo*, 326, 345 • Elliott & Fry, photograph, 1956, NPG [*see illus.*] • G. Kelly, oils, 1956, Glaxo Library, Greenfield, Middlesex; repro. in Davenport-Hines and Slinn, *Glaxo*, 211 • bust, priv. coll. • photographs, Glaxo Library, Greenfield, Middlesex • photographs, priv. coll.

Wealth at death £2,011,589: probate, 2 Aug 1978, *CGPLA Eng. & Wales*

Jephcott, (Agnes) Pearl (1900–1980), social researcher, was born on 1 May 1900 at Church Street, Alcester, Warwickshire, the youngest of the four children of Edward Arthur Jephcott, auctioneer, and his wife, Agnes Amelia, *née* Boobbyer. She attended Alcester grammar school and then the University of Wales, Aberystwyth, where in 1922 she graduated BA in history. She was awarded an MA degree by publication in 1946. After trying various careers (teaching, secretarial work, and fund-raising for Dr Barnardo's homes) Jephcott turned to the girls' club movement and in 1927 was appointed as the organizing secretary of the Birmingham Union of Girls' Clubs. She was a highly effective organizer and in 1935 was appointed as a temporary county organizer for the National Association of Girls' Clubs to develop youth work in the 'special areas' of high unemployment in co. Durham.

The war saw Jephcott moving to London as a national organizer for the association, working on developing service cadet companies, to provide opportunities for training and voluntary service for girls. Later she became publications secretary and editor of the association's newsletter, *Club News*. She was then granted leave of absence to complete her first major publication, *Girls Growing Up* (1942). This was an investigation into the home conditions, work, leisure, and personal relationships of 153 English and Welsh fourteen- to eighteen-year-olds. The following year her textbook for club leaders, *Clubs for Girls* (1943), was published. *Girls Growing Up* was greeted enthusiastically by professionals and the general public alike, and for the remainder of her life Jephcott pursued a career in social research. The award of a Barnett fellowship enabled her to follow up the girls in her first study, and *Rising Twenty* was published in 1948. The two studies indicate the concerns and style of much of Jephcott's subsequent research. All presented vivid, detailed, and at times passionate pictures of little researched aspects of the lives of working-class people, particularly of girls and young women. They involved detailed ethnographic research using participant observation, interviews, and autobiographical accounts, and offered practical recommendations to improve the quality of life of their subjects.

Jephcott worked briefly for Political and Economic Planning, co-authoring three of its broadsheets, and for the northern industrial group, before joining (in 1950) the University of Nottingham, where she managed two projects. The first examined the social origins of delinquency, and the second investigated the membership of youth organizations. The latter resulted in the publication of *Some Young People* (1954). In 1954 she was appointed as a senior research assistant at the London School of Economics (LSE) to work in Richard Titmuss's social administration department with Nancy Seear and John Smith, investigating the impact of married women in employment at the large Peek Frean's factory in Bermondsey. While her colleagues undertook the industrial side of the study, Jephcott investigated domestic conditions. The research involved sustained contact with the local community, and characteristically Jephcott lived in, and participated fully in the life of, the local area. The project had a troubled passage, but in 1962 *Married Women Working* was published. It joined the growing body of research that tempered popular hysteria against working wives and mothers. Her contributions while at the LSE went beyond her sociological research work. Her extensive youth work experience prompted invitations to sit on two government committees of inquiry: in 1957–8 she was a member of the Central Advisory Council for Education (England) and a contributor to its report, *15–18* (1959–60), and in 1958 she joined the Albermarle committee, which laid the foundations for the modern youth service in England and Wales. In addition, she undertook two commissions for the Home Office reporting on the needs of young people in the coastal areas of British Guiana and in the West Indies.

By the early 1960s Jephcott was keen to pursue her own research interests and turned again to the subjects of her early research, who by then were women in their twenties and thirties. She completed a third research project on the women, 'The uncertain years', but the work was never published. After leaving the LSE reluctantly, her next project was the North Kensington family study, in which she investigated housing conditions and race relations in London's Notting Hill area. Her forthright report, *A Troubled Area: Notes on Notting Hill* (1964), highlighted how scarce were the resources and support available to 'some of the most troubled of London's citizens'. She was next invited to Glasgow University to study the leisure interests of young people in Scotland. The fruits of her research were published in 1967 as *Time of One's Own*; by this time she had moved to her next project: studying high-rise living in two Glasgow tower blocks. When published as *Homes in High Flats* (1971), the work confirmed popular misgivings about multi-storey homes, especially that they were 'nae use for the bairns'. In 1970 she left Glasgow, but this was only semi-retirement. She travelled to Australia and continued to research and write, for example undertaking a study for the United Nations International Children's Emergency Fund (UNICEF) on the situation of children and youth in Hong Kong. In 1973 she gained funding for a two-year, half-time post to research the needs of families living in high-rise flats in Birmingham, and persuaded the local authority to let her live in a council flat. The work resulted in the appointment of a social development fieldworker to work with young families in high flats.

All Jephcott's work was suffused with concern for humanity and particularly for working-class people. From her early work as a youth leader, through her various research posts, she explored their lives with enormous sympathy and no sentimentality. On spring bank holiday

1980 she suffered a stroke. She died, unmarried, at the War Memorial Hospital, Chipping Norton, Oxfordshire, on 9 November 1980. After her funeral service at St Mary's Church, Oxford, on 13 November she was cremated in Oxford.   ANNMARIE TURNBULL

Sources personal MSS, priv. coll. [June Jephcott] · personal knowledge (2004) · private information (2004) · b. cert. · d. cert.
Archives priv. coll.
Likenesses portrait, priv. coll.
Wealth at death £50,003: probate, 29 Dec 1980, *CGPLA Eng. & Wales*

Jephson, Arthur Jermy Mounteney (1858–1908), traveller in Africa, born at Hutton rectory, Brentwood, Essex, on 8 October 1858, was the tenth of the twelve children of John Mounteney Jephson, vicar of Childerditch, Essex, and Ellen, daughter of Isaac *Jermy, the recorder of Norwich, of Stanfield Hill, Norfolk. He was educated at Tonbridge School (1869–74) and followed his eldest brother on to the training ship, HMS *Worcester* (1874–6), and thence into the merchant navy. In 1880 he joined the Antrim regiment of the Royal Irish Rifles, but resigned his commission in 1884. For two years he lived a life of ease, under the patronage of Helene, comtesse de Noailles, at her homes in Eastbourne and Hyères, in the south of France. In 1886 the comtesse's donation of £1000 to support the Emin Pasha relief expedition secured him a place on its staff, under Henry Morton Stanley. Leaving Europe in January 1887, the expedition travelled up the Congo River, with Jephson being given special responsibility for the transport of a steel boat, *The Advance*. Having left the ill-fated rear column at Yambuya on 28 June, Jephson accompanied Stanley and William Stairs on the difficult journey eastwards through dense forest, a march so arduous that, according to his diary, he felt at times as if he were 'drinking in malaria'; they finally reached Lake Albert in December. Jephson was the first officer to meet Emin and, at Stanley's instruction, undertook a tour with the pasha through his equatorial provinces, seeking to encourage Emin's soldiers to return with the expedition to Egypt, via Zanzibar. However, Emin's authority over his garrisons was much weaker than had been supposed, and both Jephson and Emin were temporarily imprisoned by rebel officers at Dufilé in August 1888. It was only with the renewed threat from Mahdist forces in the north that Emin recovered his position. Eventually Jephson succeeded in evacuating Emin and his party to Kavalli, where they rejoined Stanley in February 1889. Jephson returned to England in 1890 and published an account of his part in the expedition, which was translated into both German and French, and he was subsequently engaged in lecture tours in Britain and the United States. The recriminations which accompanied the publication of conflicting accounts of the expedition by or on behalf of its officers were concerned more with the conduct of its leader and the fate of the rear column than with the part played by Jephson himself, and his public reputation was if anything enhanced by the ensuing controversy. He was

Arthur Jermy Mounteney Jephson (1858–1908), by unknown photographer

awarded a medal by the Royal Geographical Society and a diploma by the Brussels Geographical Society in 1890, and was appointed a queen's messenger in 1895.

Jephson's expedition diaries, which were published in 1969, confirm in graphic detail the extent of the violence and suffering that accompanied the Emin Pasha relief expedition. As he had no previous experience of either tropical travel or warfare, his very survival was something of an accomplishment. His friendship with Stanley, whom he accompanied on the latter's honeymoon in Switzerland in 1890, lasted until Stanley's death in 1904. Jephson was married in the same year on 8 June to Anna, daughter of Addison Head of San Francisco, after an association of more than twelve years; they had one son. Jephson died on 22 October 1908 at Sandridge House, Sunninghill, Ascot, and he was buried at Sunninghill.

FELIX DRIVER

Sources *GJ*, 32 (1908), 630 · M. D. Jephson, *An Anglo-Irish miscellany: some records of the Jephsons of Mallow* (1964) · *The diary of A. J. Mounteney Jephson: Emin Pasha relief expedition, 1887–1889*, ed. D. Middleton, Hakluyt Society, extra ser., 40 (1969) · A. M. Jephson, *Emin Pasha and the rebellion at the equator* (1890) · I. R. Smith, *The Emin Pasha relief expedition, 1886–1890* (1972)
Archives priv. coll., Mallow Castle, co. Cork, Éire | RGS, Stanley MSS · SOAS, Mackinnon MSS · U. Nott., Willoughby MSS
Likenesses photograph, NPG [*see illus.*] · photographs, repro. in Jephson, *Anglo-Irish miscellany* · photographs, RGS · photographs, repro. in Jephson, *Emin Pasha and the rebellion* · photographs, repro. in Middleton, ed., *The diary of A. J. Mounteney Jephson* (1969)

Jephson, Robert (1736/7–1803), playwright, was born in Dublin, the son of Archdeacon John Jephson. He was educated at Ryder's grammar school and at the Reverend

Roger Ford's school in Molesworth Street, where he met Edmond Malone, a lifelong friend, and took part in amateur productions of Shakespeare. Jephson entered Trinity College, Dublin, on 25 June 1751, aged fourteen, but left without a degree and entered the army, having obtained a commission in the 73rd regiment of foot on the Irish establishment. He served at Bellisle but was 'unable to face the climate of the West Indies' (Prior, 77) and returned to Ireland on half pay. In the early 1760s he moved to Hampton Court as a guest of William Gerard Hamilton, with whom he lived 'in the greatest and most unreserved intimacy' (Chalmers). When Edmund Burke and Hamilton quarrelled over a pension of £300 in 1765, the money was transferred, somewhat circuitously, to Jephson. In the same year David Garrick lent Jephson £400, somewhat straining their friendship. In January 1766 Lady Hertford told Walpole that Jephson 'has not a hundred a year in the world, and is gone to England to marry a Miss Barry, who is ten or twelve years older than him, and who has no fortune' (Walpole, *Corr.*, 39.50). This was Jane Barry (*b. c.*1725), daughter of the Dublin physician Sir Edward Barry. The marriage took place on 24 August 1766. Jephson decamped to Boulogne in October that year to avoid creditors. However, he had ingratiated himself with Charles Townshend by mimicking politicians, and, when Viscount Townshend became lord lieutenant of Ireland in 1767, he made Jephson master of the horse, a position worth about £200; a pension of £300 was apparently granted to Mrs Jephson before 1775. Jephson's convivial 'felicity in ludicrous composition' (*GM*) found an outlet in a series of papers published in the government newspaper *The Mercury* under the serial title 'The Bachelor'. Jephson continued the attack on Townshend's adversaries in *An Epistle to Gorges Edmund Howard* (1771), supposedly by the printer George Faulkner, whose style the pamphlet parodies. When Townshend's administration ended, Jephson, in poor health as a result of excessive drinking, was forced to canvass support to ensure the continuance of his post, which in the event he retained under many successive lord lieutenants. In 1774 Lord Harcourt secured Jephson's election to the Irish parliament for the borough of Johnstown; he was later returned for Old Leighlin. On 11 February 1774 Jephson made a speech on behalf of Roman Catholics, which was published. The earl of Morningtown declared that Jephson was 'very well heard as a speaker in the House of Commons' (*Fortescue MSS*, 1.163). A parliamentary record for 1775, however, notes that Jephson's efforts had often misfired, and Samuel Foote portrayed Jephson's self-importance in parliament in ludicrous terms.

Jephson's first play, *Braganza*, on the subject of Portuguese resistance to Spanish tyranny, was performed, after protracted negotiations with Garrick, at Drury Lane on 17 February 1775. The prologue, by Arthur Murphy, describes the author as 'warm from Shakespeare's school', and the epilogue was by Horace Walpole. The play was extensively read in bluestocking circles before it was performed, and the audience 'clapped, shouted, huzzaed, cried bravo, and

thundered out applause' (Walpole, *Corr.*, 28.176). Walpole wrote to Jephson to commend him as a 'master poet'; with two further letters this formed an essay, 'Thoughts on tragedy' (ibid., 41.286–98). The play ran for fifteen performances in its first season, earning Jephson £474 and enabling him to repay his debt to Garrick, but it was not acted after 1785. Jephson offered Garrick a further tragedy, *Vitellia*, in the summer of 1775, but Garrick rejected it very firmly. Jephson performed the title role of *Macbeth* in January 1777 at the Phoenix Park theatre, Dublin, but returned to writing with *The Law of Lombardy*. Based on an episode in Ariosto, but taking a central dramatic device from *Much Ado about Nothing*, it ran at Drury Lane for ten nights from 8 February 1779. Mrs Siddons chose it for a benefit in 1789, but it was not thereafter performed. Jephson next composed *The Count of Narbonne*, based on Walpole's *Castle of Otranto* but using names and ideas from Walpole's own *Mysterious Mother*. Walpole commended him for making 'so rational a play out of my wild tale' (ibid., 41.409), and soothed Harris, the manager of Covent Garden, over its production, which was nearly derailed by Malone's alternative plans. Walpole attended rehearsals, and lent a suit of armour. The play was premiered on 17 November 1781 to great acclaim. Jephson, however, was displeased with Walpole over the placing of a statue, and Walpole commented with irritation 'he shall act his next play himself' (ibid., 29.167). The play was performed thirty-seven times on the London stage up to 1798, making it Jephson's greatest commercial success.

Jephson's three-act opera *The Campaign* was performed in Dublin in 1784 and at Covent Garden in 1785. It was reduced by John O'Keefe to the two-act farce *Love and War* (1787), and enjoyed greater success. On 14 April 1787 *Julia*, a tragedy of murder, lust, and revenge, was produced at Drury Lane with Siddons and Kemble in the leading roles. It ran for nine performances, but was never revived. A two-act farce, *Two Strings to your Bow*, was acted as an afterpiece on 16 February 1791 at Covent Garden: identical with the earlier *The Hotel, or, The Servant with Two Masters*, performed in Dublin in 1783, it was based on a play by Goldoni, via Thomas Vaughan's *The Hotel* (1776), and became a stock afterpiece, achieving thirty-four performances by 1800. At Drury Lane, on 15 November 1796, *The Conspiracy*, a version of the rejected *Vitellia*, was premiered: based on Metastasio's *Clemenza di Tito*, it was performed only twice, despite the efforts of Kemble and Siddons.

Some 'Extempore Ludicrous Miltonic Verses' by Jephson appeared in the *Annual Register* for 1788. His prose *Confessions of James Baptiste Couteau* (1794) was a satirical parody of revolutionary politics. In the same year Jephson published *Roman Portraits*, a didactic poem celebrating Roman history to the era of Augustus. Malone thought it would gain Jephson 'a great deal of credit'; Charlemont hoped that it would repair the losses of his 'last unfortunate publication', presumably the *Confessions* (*Charlemont MSS*, 2.237–41). It was very warmly reviewed for its educational potential, but was not reprinted.

Jephson died of paralysis at his home, Blackrock, near

Dublin, on 31 May 1803. He was Anna Seward's favourite dramatist, and several of his plays were included in nineteenth-century editions of the standard repertory.

PAUL BAINES

Sources M. Severin Peterson, *Robert Jephson (1736–1803): a study of his life and works* (1930) · Walpole, *Corr.* · *The letters of David Garrick*, ed. D. M. Little and G. M. Kahrl, 3 vols. (1963) · *The private correspondence of David Garrick*, ed. J. Boaden, 2 vols. (1831–2) · *The manuscripts and correspondence of James, first earl of Charlemont*, 2 vols., HMC, 28 (1891–4) · G. W. Stone and C. B. Hogan, eds., *The London stage, 1660–1800*, pts 4–5 (1962–8) · A. Chalmers, ed., *The general biographical dictionary*, new edn, 32 vols. (1812–17) · D. E. Baker, *Biographia dramatica, or, A companion to the playhouse*, rev. I. Reed, new edn, rev. S. Jones, 3 vols. in 4 (1812) · J. Prior, *Life of Edmond Malone, editor of Shakespeare* (1860) · *The correspondence of Edmund Burke*, ed. T. W. Copeland and others, 10 vols. (1958–78) · *The Irish parliament, 1775: from an official and contemporary manuscript*, ed. W. Hunt (1907) · Burtchaell & Sadlier, *Alum. Dubl.* · Nichols, *Illustrations*, 5.547, 7.3, 8.429 · *The manuscripts of J. B. Fortescue*, 10 vols., HMC, 30 (1892–1927), vol. 1 · *GM*, 1st ser., 73 (1803), 600 · IGI
Archives BL, Add. MSS 37873, 37877, 37880, 37915, 34417 · Bodl. Oxf., Western MSS · V&A, Forster collection · V&A NAL, corresp. with David Garrick · Yale U., Farmington, Lewis Walpole Library, MSS and letter to Lord Macartney
Likenesses J. Singleton, stipple, 1794 (after Stoker), BM, NPG; repro. in R. Jephson, *Roman portraits, a poem in heroick verse* (1794), frontispiece

Jephson, William (1609/10–1658), politician and soldier, was the son and heir of Sir John Jephson (d. 1638) of Froyle, Hampshire, and Elizabeth Norreys, daughter and heir of Sir Thomas Norreys of Mallow Castle, co. Cork. Raised in Hampshire, but with estates in co. Cork, Jephson was admitted to Brasenose College, Oxford, in 1624, aged fourteen, and graduated BA on 29 June 1627. He enjoyed influential contacts on both sides of the Irish sea: in England he was related to John Pym, Viscount Saye and Sele, and through his wife, Alice Denham (d. 1658), whom he married on 25 August 1636, to a number of Buckinghamshire families; and in Ireland his friends included Sir Philip Perceval, Sir William Fenton, and Sir William St Leger.

Jephson's political career began in the Short and Long parliaments, when he sat for Stockbridge in Hampshire. He was inactive in the early months of the Long Parliament, and played no part in the trial of the earl of Strafford, but by the late summer of 1641 he was working with John Pym and other critics of the crown. Jephson travelled to Ireland, in August 1641, and was in Munster at the outbreak of the Irish uprising in October. Sir William St Leger, the lord president of Munster, sent him back to London in December, where he presented the plight of the province to the Commons, and was commissioned sergeant-major of St Leger's regiment of horse. In February 1642 Jephson returned to Ireland, where he undertook the defence of Mallow Castle, which, he boasted, he would hold 'as long as he had life' (Coates, Young, and Snow, 3.174). With the death of St Leger in June 1642, Jephson became closely associated with Lord Inchiquin, and his relations with the rival Boyle party deteriorated as a result. In April 1643 Jephson returned to England as Inchiquin's agent, and attended Charles I at Oxford, in a last attempt to secure a bipartisan agreement between king and parliament on Ireland. Failure in this, and his

suspicions that the king had encouraged the insurgents, prompted Jephson to side openly with parliament. In September 1643 he was sent back to Ireland to encourage Inchiquin to defect to parliament. This scheme bore fruit in the summer of 1644 when, at Jephson's instigation, Inchiquin abandoned the king, while his brother, Henry O'Brien, surrendered Wareham in Dorset to parliament (Bodl. Oxf., MS Carte 11, fol. 538).

Jephson served as lieutenant-governor of Portsmouth from May 1644, but lost his command under the self-denying ordinance of 1645, and thereafter turned his attentions to Ireland. He was a conscientious member of the committee of Irish affairs founded in July 1645 and sat on the Derby House committee, supporting the presbyterian party. He continued to vindicate Lord Inchiquin, and this stance brought him into conflict with the Independent faction, whose influence over Irish affairs had grown since the appointment of Viscount Lisle as lord lieutenant in January 1646. When Sir Arthur Loftus and Lord Broghill (Roger Boyle) denounced Inchiquin in April and May 1647, they were challenged by Jephson, who promised to 'engage upon his life that the Lord Inchiquin would approve himself faithful to the Parliament' (*Diary of John Harington*, ed. M. F. Steig, Somerset RS, 74, 1977, 51). Despite his connections with the presbyterian party, Jephson distanced himself from the factional struggles of the summer of 1647, withdrawing to Oxfordshire. He was back in Westminster from September 1647, but confined his activities to Irish affairs. The defection of Inchiquin to the king's cause in the spring of 1648 tested Jephson's political allegiances. In April 1648 he was sent to Ireland as commissioner for Munster, but he failed to persuade Inchiquin to reconsider his position, and returned to England in May. He was secluded from parliament at Pride's Purge in December 1648.

Jephson's relationship with the Commonwealth has caused some confusion. One 'young Jephson' served under Inchiquin in November 1649, but this was almost certainly not the 39-year-old William, who was rewarded by parliament between April 1649 and March 1650, and whose son was baptized in London in December 1649. Indeed throughout the early 1650s Jephson was probably in retirement in England, returning to Ireland only in 1653. Under the protectorate he was rehabilitated by Henry Cromwell, who secured the payment of Jephson's arrears, and prevented his estates being allocated to English soldiers. Other important patrons included his former enemy Lord Broghill, under whose influence Jephson was elected for co. Cork and Youghal in the parliaments of 1654 and 1656, and his cousin Nathaniel Fiennes, who was a prominent Cromwellian courtier. In the 1656 parliament Jephson supported Broghill in the militia debates, and he was the first MP who 'moved in the house that Cromwell might be made king' (*The Memoirs of Edmund Ludlow*, ed. C. H. Firth, 2 vols., 1894, 2.20–21). During March and April Jephson worked with the kinglings, including Broghill and Fiennes, and his bitterness at the failure of the proposals can be seen in his suggestion to parliament on 27 May, that the letters 'k-i-n-g' be removed from the alphabet if they caused such offence (*Diary of Thomas Burton*, 2.140).

Jephson's activities in parliament encouraged Cromwell to appoint him envoy to Karl X of Sweden, whose war with Denmark threatened English trade. Jephson spent a year from August 1657 trying to encourage the two powers to make peace, and to unite the protestant leaders (including the elector of Brandenburg) against the Habsburgs, but with little success. Exhausted, and nearly bankrupt, Jephson returned to England in August 1658. He died at Boarstall in Buckinghamshire, on 11 December. The Jephson family remained at Mallow Castle until 1911.

PATRICK LITTLE

Sources HoP, *Commons* [draft] · M. D. Jephson, *An Anglo-Irish miscellany: some records of the Jephsons of Mallow* (1964) · BL, Lansdowne MSS, 821–823 · Bodl. Oxf., MSS Carte 2–20, fol. 103 · *JHC*, 2–7 (1640–59) · *CSP dom.*, 1644–58 · *Report on the manuscripts of the earl of Egmont*, 2 vols. in 3, HMC, 63 (1905–9) · *Tenth report*, HMC (1885); repr. (1906) · *CSP Venice*, 1657–9 · Thurloe, *State papers* · *Diary of Thomas Burton*, ed. J. T. Rutt, 4 vols. (1828) · M. A. E. Green, ed., *Calendar of the proceedings of the committee for advance of money, 1642–1656*, 3 vols., PRO (1888) · *CSP Ire.*, 1630–60 · W. H. Coates, A. Steele Young, and V. F. Snow, eds., *The private journals of the Long Parliament*, 3 vols. (1982–92) · [C. B. Heberden], ed., *Brasenose College register, 1509–1909*, 1, OHS, 55 (1909), 148
Archives BL, letters to Henry Cromwell, Lansdowne MSS 821–823 · BL, corresp. with Sir Philip Perceval, Add. MSS 46929–46931
Likenesses oils, repro. in Jephson, *Anglo-Irish miscellany*, facing p. 48

Jerdan, William (1782–1869), journalist and antiquary, was born on 16 April 1782 in Kelso, Roxburghshire, to John Jerdan (d. 1795) and Agnes Stuart (d. 1820). He was the third son and he had one sister. The primary source of William Jerdan's life is his *Autobiography* (1852–3), which is generally reliable, if selective about personal details. A sickly child, Jerdan first attended the Kelso parochial school, and later became a private student of William Rutherford DD at Maxwellheugh. In 1801 Jerdan assumed a clerk's post with Samuel, Samuel and Turner, London merchants, which he held intermittently due to illness until 1805. During this period he was also employed in the office of a writer to the signet in Edinburgh and it is possible that he is the William Jerdan who married Margaret Olridge in Edinburgh on 5 September 1806, although he had finally settled in London in spring 1806. He had been writing verse since childhood and he published his first poem in a Portsmouth paper in February 1806. Jerdan began his career in journalism as a reporter for an innkeepers' commercial newspaper, *Aurora*, in 1806. When *Aurora* failed in 1807 Jerdan, who had become its editor, moved on to *The Pilot*, an evening newspaper begun in 1807. In 1808 he also wrote editorials for the *Morning Post* and summaries of sessions of parliament for the *British Press*. Writing in his *Autobiography*, Jerdan said the three factors which motivated his careers as reporter, editor, and as a proprietor and projector of newspapers were literary labour, desire for pleasure, and the need to support himself.

In 1813 Jerdan spent time abroad sending in foreign correspondent's reports on Napoleon, and in 1814, back in London, he edited *A Voyage to the Isle of Elba: Translated from the French of Arsenne Thiebault de Berneaud* for the London publishers Longman, Hurst, Rees, Orme, and Brown. In five chapters the book gives a general overview of the island, its demography and political history, its geology and topography. Jerdan dedicated the translation to Charles Long, a key tory politician.

Before turning to his career's work as editor of the *Literary Gazette* in 1818, Jerdan edited a political newspaper, *The Sun*, which showed allegiance to high tory policies. In the spring of 1817 Jerdan ended a protracted legal battle with John Taylor over the editorial practices and ownership of *The Sun*. Jerdan received a settlement of £800 and sold his one-tenth share in the paper for £300. With an established reputation among booksellers, who were frequently financial projectors of newspapers, Jerdan assumed editorship of the *Literary Gazette* for Henry Colburn. This paper was begun on 25 January 1817 and Jerdan, who started with issue 25, would remain as its literary head until 1850. Within a few years, because of the *Literary Gazette*'s success, Thomas Longman also became a partner, and Colburn, Jerdan, and Longman were the operating shareholders.

Initially the *Literary Gazette*, which would grow under Jerdan, showed only marginal success, forcing its editor to earn supplemental income by writing weekly articles for such provincial papers as the *North Staffordshire Pottery Gazette* and quarterly essays for the *Chelmsford Chronicle*, among others. He also prepared two editions of travel books for John Murray, a leading London literary publisher known for his line of travel publications. In 1818 Jerdan edited G. A. F. Fitzclarence's *Journey from India to England*, and in 1819 Hippesley's *Voyage to the Orinoko*. As the popularity of the weekly *Literary Gazette* grew Jerdan met, among other noted figures, Samuel Taylor Coleridge, Thomas Frognall Dibdin, and Felicia Dorothea Hemans. From his position as editor, Jerdan was able to discover popular writers, including the poet Letitia Elizabeth *Landon (1802–1838), author of more than thirteen books of verse and with whom, it has recently been claimed, he had three children during the 1820s. He also discovered Bryan Waller Proctor, who wrote eight books of poetry, essays, and biographies under the pseudonym Barry Cornwall; William Maginn of Cork, who began his career as a poet in the pages of the *Literary Gazette*; and Marguerite, countess of Blessington, whose *Keepsakes* were a popular success, had her début in 1822 in Jerdan's paper. Letitia Landon received the first *Literary Gazette* poetry prize on 6 June 1821.

In addition Jerdan promoted the Royal Society of Literature, begun on 30 November 1820, of which he was a member, detailing its six founding meetings in volume 3 of his *Autobiography*. In 1820 he moved from Gloucester Lodge, Old Brompton, where he had resided from 1818, to Grove House, where he would remain until 1834. In 1821 Jerdan was among the first members of the Literary Fund, which supported writers, and in 1826 he was elected to membership of the Society of Antiquarians. His *Autobiography*, volume 4, notes the death of an infant daughter (1825–1826) and of his son, John Stuart Jerdan, a stipendiary magistrate in Jamaica, in 1839 at the age of thirty-nine; otherwise, Jerdan is silent on details of his two marriages and his surviving children. Evidence has recently been brought to light indicating that, between 1822 and about 1834, Jerdan had a liaison with Letitia Landon, which produced three children (C. Lawford, *London Review of Books*, September 2001, 36–7).

In 1828 Jerdan helped to form the Zoological Society, and he used the *Literary Gazette* to create interest in and support for the Royal Geographical Society, which led to its formation in 1830. Noting that he would write for nearly any publication that sought him, Jerdan briefly edited the *Foreign Literary Gazette*, published by Longman for thirteen numbers from January 1830 until it ceased for lack of profit. Jerdan estimated that he and a fellow investor lost about £1300 on the failed paper. During the last years of the 1820s Jerdan was among the first to join the Garrick Club, an association of patrons and actors as well as shareholders in theatres and plays. He had a woodcut made of David Garrick, the celebrated eighteenth-century actor and theatre manager of Drury Lane, for the *Literary Gazette*, which he used for six months to head columns he wrote to promote the club. He was an active member of the British Association until 1850.

Between 1830 and 1834 Jerdan wrote memoirs of living popular personalities which were published as *Fisher's National Portrait Gallery of Illustrious and Eminent Personages of the Nineteenth Century*, an illustrated book, which Jerdan dedicated to George IV. In the *Literary Gazette* of the early 1830s Jerdan was publishing the poets Mary Anne Browne and Elizabeth Cook, of whom he thought enough to preserve specimens of their verse in his *Autobiography*. Bringing Robert Mongomery into print enabled this poet, according to Jerdan, to enjoy sales of his books in America and England. In 1831 Jerdan ran as a tory for Weymouth and lost. The same year he contributed a romance tale, 'The Sleepless Woman', to *The Club-Book: being Original Tales by James, Picken, Galt, Power, Jerdan and Others*, edited by Andrew Picken. In 1834 Jerdan disastrously co-signed several bills on which he lost Grove House, his household goods, and about £4000. He took lodging in Westminster Bridge, but was still able to buy out Longman's and Colburn's shares in the *Literary Gazette* in 1842 and was sole proprietor until 1850. He maintained that Longman had lost interest in promoting the paper.

In 1838 Jerdan was a member of the Camden Society, for which he edited *The Rutland Papers. Original documents illustrative of the courts and times of Henry VII and Henry VIII. Selected from the private archives of his grace, the duke of Rutland* (1842). Jerdan wrote the prefatory materials for the five selections and included a date for the last piece, a household personnel inventory and an expense account in Latin for King Henry VIII, considering it to have been taken between 1513 and 1522. Other documents included in this 133-page edition are a description of the 1520 meeting of Henry VIII and the emperor Charles V at Gravelines, stating how the meeting was conducted, how the rooms

were furnished, and who attended from nobles to cooks, and the 1514 list of provisions drawn up by Sir Thomas Wriothesley for the marriage of Mary, daughter of Henry VII, to Louis XII of France. In addition to transcriptions, Jerdan provided some notes. In 1845, as a member of the Percy Society, founded for the preservation of English antiquarian writings, Jerdan assisted James Henry Dixon in selecting and verifying the authenticity of poems, ballads, and songs for the publication of *Scottish Traditional Versions of Ancient Ballads*.

Jerdan left the *Literary Gazette* in 1850 for reasons unknown, but his writing career was not over. After his departure, some friends proposed him for a pension in July 1850, which was granted in 1852 at 100 guineas. In the autumn of 1850 a testimonial dinner netted him £900. If he had lost the support of his publisher, he had not lost the friendship of some of his readers. In 1852–3 he published his four-volume *Autobiography of William Jerdan: with his literary, political, and social reminiscences and correspondence during the last fifty years*. In 1856 he moved to Bushey Heath, Hertfordshire, where he continued to contribute materials to the London periodicals *Fraser's Magazine*, the *Gentleman's Magazine*, and *Notes and Queries* (with which he had a longstanding relationship). Of equal interest is Jerdan's 1866 memoir, *Men I Have Known*, which he said was modelled after the style of Horace Walpole's prose correspondence, and which contains fifty-three profiles and a brief postscript providing Jerdan's aims and rationale for such a book: 'Few men … have lived through so long a period of such mixed and busy life in the metropolis as I have done, and been influenced by their peculiar pursuits to be equally observant and reflective' (Jerdan, 487). Among those profiled are the authors William Lisle Bowles, William Wordsworth, Sir Walter Scott, James Hogg, Samuel Taylor Coleridge, and Richard Brinsley Sheridan; the journalist William Gifford; publishers Samuel Rogers, Charles Dibdin, and Richard Martin of Galway; numerous politicians; clergymen; and Francis Douce, antiquarian and keeper of manuscripts in the British Museum. Among others, Jerdan also profiles more passionately John Galt, the novelist whom he labelled 'the Scottish Dickens', whose *Lawrie Todd* 'is a striking example of Dickensian qualities and powers' (ibid., 235); David Roberts, a Scottish painter; Edward Forbes, a Manx naturalist and founder of the Red Lion Speaking Society; and James Holman, a blind traveller who journeyed around the world. The eclecticism of *Men I Have Known* provides further insights into Jerdan's circle and his personality. The sketches consistently include what he found to be unique or representative about the subject, with a specimen autograph, quotations from the subject's own writing or comments about him made by significant others, and Jerdan's own opinions as an addendum to each essay. Throughout the *Autobiography* complimentary information about Jerdan's friends and associates, both male and female, may be found, with chapter 17 of volume 4 yielding 'an imperfect roll call' (ibid., 328) of women writers whose careers he launched or helped to establish through the *Literary Gazette*—a roster which includes Agnes Strickland, Lady Charlotte Bury, Anna Jameson, Mary Wollstonecraft Shelley, Jane Porter, Lucy Aikin, Hannah More, and Anna Eliza Bray, among others.

William Jerdan died in Bushey Heath on 11 July 1869 at the age of eighty-eight and was buried in Bushey churchyard, where a monument was erected in 1874 by members of one of the many clubs to which he belonged in London. He had a large family, and he was attended by John Jerdan at his death, most probably a son. The *Literary Gazette* was incorporated into *The Parthenon* in 1862, and it ended when the joint papers failed on 30 May 1863.

BEVERLY E. SCHNELLER

Sources W. Jerdan, *The autobiography of William Jerdan: with his literary, political, and social reminiscences and correspondence during the last fifty years*, 4 vols. (1852–3) · R. H. Stoddard, ed., *Personal reminiscences by Moore and Jerdan* (1875) · W. J. Graham, *English literary periodicals* (1930) · A. Andrews, *The history of British journalism*, 2 vols. (1859) · S. Smiles, *A publisher and his friends: memoir and correspondence of the late John Murray*, 2 vols. (1891) · *DNB* · parish register (births and baptisms), 1782, Kelso, Roxburghshire · parish register (marriages), Temple, Edinburgh, 5 Sept 1806 · d. cert. · *London Review of Books* (21 Sept 2000), 36–7
Archives Bodl. Oxf. · Hunt. L. · U. Texas | Herts. ALS, letters to Lord Lytton · Kensington and Chelsea Central Library, letters to Thomas Crofton Croker · NL Scot., corresp. with Blackwoods · U. Aberdeen L., letters to Peter Buchan · U. Edin. L., letters to James Halliwell-Phillipps
Likenesses D. Maclise, watercolour drawing, 1830, BM, NPG; repro. in *Fraser's Magazine* (1830) · T. Woolnoth, stipple, pubd 1830 (after J. Moore), NPG · R. J. Lane, lithograph (after Count D'Orsay, 1839), NPG · H. Robinson, stipple (after G. H. Harlow, 1815), NPG; repro. in W. Jerdan, *Autobiography* (1852)

Jerdon, Thomas Caverhill (1811–1872), army medical officer and zoologist, was born at Biddick House, co. Durham, on 12 October 1811, eldest son of Archibald Jerdon (*d.* 1842) of Bonjedward, Scotland, and Elizabeth Sarah Milner (*d.* 1842). He had one brother, the botanist Archibald Edward (1819–1874), and at least two sisters, Caroline Ann (*b. c.*1822) and Frances Eliza (*b. c.*1824). He was educated in Yorkshire and although he initially entered Edinburgh University as a student of literature, he completed his medical studies in London. He joined the East India Company as an assistant surgeon in 1835, arriving in Madras, India, in February 1836. On 15 July 1841 he married Flora Alexanderna Matilda (*b.* 1821), daughter of Major Alexander Macleod of Madras and his wife, Eliza. Flora drew a number of plates for Robert Wight's *Icones planatarum Indiae orientalis* (1840–53).

Jerdon's first publication appeared in 1839. His main interest was ornithology, but he wrote also on mammals, fish, reptiles, and ants. In 1862 Lord Canning gave him special leave to complete his major works, *The Birds of India* (1862–4) and *The Mammals of India* (1867), and to visit what little of India remained unknown to him. He reached the rank of major, having spent four years as civil surgeon at Tellicherry. He returned to England in 1870, suffering from an illness contracted in Assam after he had resigned from the government's service in 1868. His work, although valued for its keen observations, was marred by over-reliance on memory and unmethodical unrecording of

detail; a similar lack of attention in domestic matters led to constant debt. He died at his home in St Aubyn's Road, Upper Norwood, Surrey, on 12 June 1872, and was survived by his wife.

CHRISTINE BRANDON-JONES

Sources W. Elliot, 'Memoir of Dr. T. C. Jerdon', *History of the Berwickshire Naturalists' Club*, 7 (1873), 143–51 · W. Elliot, 'Biographical notice of A. Jerdon', *History of the Berwickshire Naturalists' Club*, 7 (1874), 338–44 · *CGPLA Eng. & Wales* (1872) · *The Times* (June 1872) · *IGI* · d. cert. · baptisms, 1824, Archdeaconry of Madras, vol. 9, p. 61 · chaplain's marriages, 1841, Archdeaconry of Madras, vol. 20, pp. 298–9
Likenesses photograph, 1908, repro. in 'Contributor to the first series of *The Ibis*', *Ibis* [jubilee supplement], 9th ser., 11 (1908), facing p. 193
Wealth at death under £600: resworn administration, June 1875, *CGPLA Eng. & Wales* (1872)

Jeremie, James Amiraux (1802–1872), dean of Lincoln, son of James Jeremie, merchant, and his wife, Margaret Amiraux, descendant of an old Huguenot family long settled in the Channel Islands, was born at St Peter Port, Guernsey, on 12 April 1802. He received his early education at Elizabeth College, Guernsey, and Blundell's Grammar School, Tiverton. He matriculated from Trinity College, Cambridge, on 13 November 1820, became a scholar in 1823, and graduated BA in 1824, MA in 1827, and BD and DD in 1850. There he showed the early promise which carried him through the rest of his career. He won the members' essay prize in 1823, the Norrisian essay prize in 1823 and 1825, and the Hulsean essay prize in 1824. He was a fellow of Trinity 1826–50.

Jeremie was ordained deacon and then priest in 1830, became examining chaplain to his patron and friend, Bishop Kaye of Lincoln, and was appointed by Kaye to the prebendal stall of Sanctae Crucis in Lincoln Cathedral on 20 December 1834, and to the subdeanery on 1 July 1848. He also held the rectory of Winwick, Northamptonshire, in the bishop of Lincoln's patronage, from 9 March 1843 to 1848. On 7 April 1830 he was appointed by the board of directors to the professorship of classical and general literature at the East India Company's college at Haileybury. From 1838 until 1850 he was also dean there. Jeremie's students included Monier Monier-Williams, Bartle Frere, and A. P. Forbes of Brechin. He was peculiarly successful as a lecturer, although he was weak as a disciplinarian. His sermons at Haileybury encouraged, in the view of the *Dictionary of National Biography*, 'that high character in the members of the East Indian civil service which was signally displayed in repressing the mutiny of 1857'.

In 1833 Jeremie was also appointed Christian advocate at Cambridge, and in 1850 he succeeded Alfred Ollivant as regius professor of divinity, and resigned his position at Haileybury. His Cambridge lectures were 'those of a sound and well-read theologian, and of a refined and elegant scholar, but they were lacking in vigour and originality' (*DNB*). In 1862 he was created DCL by the University of Oxford. In August 1864 he was raised by Lord Palmerston from the subdeanery to the deanery of Lincoln, but was persuaded to retain his regius chair for six years, 'to the sacrifice of his own comfort and to the injury of both his cathedral and his university' (*DNB*). He at last resigned the chair in 1870, that year giving £1000 to the university for the foundation of two prizes for the study of the Septuagint. In the 1850s Jeremie wrote for the *Encyclopaedia metropolitana*, republishing his contributions as *History of the Christian Church in the Second and Third Centuries*, his only substantial work, though he published many sermons. As regius professor he was an assiduous author, but what the *Dictionary of National Biography* called 'an excessive fastidiousness and a nervous sensitiveness to criticism' prevented publication; his tenure of the chair thus contributed little to the Church of England or to scholarship.

After a long illness Jeremie died suddenly at Lincoln on 11 June 1872, and was buried in Guernsey. He was unmarried; his brother, F. J. Jeremie, and his sister were his chief beneficiaries. He intended to leave his excellent library to an institution, but his habitual indecision prevented him deciding which, and on his death it was sold.

H. C. G. MATTHEW

Sources DNB · Crockford (1870) · *Clergy List* (1848) · *Clergy List* (1850) · *Clergy List* (1863) · *Clergy List* (1868) · *The Guardian* (June 1872) · Venn, *Alum. Cant.*
Archives Durham Cath. CL, letters to J. B. Lightfoot
Likenesses E. Richardson, marble relief on monument, exh. RA 1855, St Peter's Church, Guernsey · R. E. Taylor, wood-engraving, NPG; repro. in *ILN* (29 June 1872)
Wealth at death under £50,000: resworn probate, Oct 1872, *CGPLA Eng. & Wales*

Jeremie, Sir John (1795–1841), colonial judge and governor, was born on 19 August 1795 in Guernsey, the son of John Jeremie (d. 1810), an advocate. He attended Blundell's School in Tiverton, Devon, but left after his father's death. After studying law at Dijon, he returned to Guernsey to practise as an advocate in the royal court. In 1815 he gave evidence to the royal commission appointed to reform the laws of Guernsey, and published, with a preface and appendix of his own, *Traité sur la saisie mobilière*, a legal work by his father.

Jeremie's training in French law recommended him to the Colonial Office as a judge in territories taken during the Napoleonic wars. He was appointed first president, or chief justice, of the West Indies crown colony of St Lucia in October 1824. Jeremie was aware that part of his task would be to draw up a new slave code for the colony, according to the order in council of 1823 regulating the treatment of slaves. Before departing for the West Indies he attended a meeting of the Anti-Slavery Society but was not convinced of the cruelties of slavery. Once in St Lucia, though, he became as deeply involved in the slavery question as in reforming the colony's commercial law.

Jeremie came to regard the power of the colonial élite, in St Lucia and elsewhere, as tending to corrupt government in the colonies. In 1829 a controversy arose over his charge against two brothers, Daniel and Robert Gordon, for abuse of power in their official posts as magistrate and harbourmaster. Jeremie's method of proceeding against the brothers was based in French law, and his opponents complained that he subjected Britons to an alien legal code. Antagonisms grew, and the evening of 30 November was the occasion of violent scenes in Castries, the capital.

Towards eleven o'clock, a group of men gathered outside Jeremie's house; to the accompaniment of bagpipes, they stoned the house and shouted insults at the occupants. When the assault had ended Jeremie rushed out in his nightshirt to the home of Duncan Ferguson, where St Andrew's day was being celebrated, and accused Ferguson of sheltering his tormentors.

Provisions of the order in council for a protector of slaves and the admission of slaves' evidence in courts brought to light cases of cruelty. Jeremie himself was visited by a slave wearing an iron collar with protruding spikes, designed to prevent him from running away; he gave this collar to the Anti-Slavery Society in Britain, where it was displayed as an example of the barbarities of the slave system. He accused slave holders in St Lucia of murder and brutality, but failed to bring any formal prosecutions, and the protests of Governor Stewart that official business had become impossible resulted in Jeremie's recall to Britain in 1831. There he wrote *Four Essays on Colonial Slavery* (1831). The argument and the style of this work accorded with moderate emancipationist feeling in Britain at the time: the instances of cruelty which formed his body of evidence were seen to have come to his notice in the course of his official duty, and the solution he favoured was a plan of gradual emancipation.

In February 1832 Jeremie was appointed *procureur-général*, or public prosecutor, of Mauritius. The local white population was hardly reconciled to British rule, and plantation owners resenting British anti-slavery laws were further alarmed by the appointment of Jeremie. His arrival off Port Louis on 2 June provoked protests which prevented his landing for two days. His installation had been fixed for 22 June but was delayed by the intentional absence of the judges. On 20 July he was attacked in the streets. At the insistence of Governor Charles Colville he left for England on 29 July, but on arrival there at the end of October he gladly accepted an order to return to Mauritius, where he arrived for the second time on 29 April 1833. Jeremie continued in a controversial vein, censuring local judges for tolerating sedition and for failing to uphold the laws against slave trading. The new governor, William Nicolay, demanded his departure, and Jeremie resigned and left the island on 28 October. His frustration was expressed in the pamphlet *Recent Events in Mauritius* (1833).

His tribulations in Mauritius gained Jeremie popular notice as a crusader against slavery, but patience was running thin at the Colonial Office, where his cause was kept alive by the intercession of the anti-slavery leader Thomas Fowell Buxton. While awaiting another post, Jeremie prepared to testify before a parliamentary committee investigating apprenticeship, the regime which regulated the labour of ex-slaves after passage of the Emancipation Act in 1833. He deplored colonial measures such as the Jamaica Vagrancy Act, which limited freedom of movement and employment for ex-slaves. In 1836 he was honoured with silver plate from the Anti-Slavery Society, and in the same year was appointed a puisne judge of the supreme court in Ceylon. Jeremie arrived there in 1837 and served without dramatic incident, failing to gain promotion to the chief justiceship in 1838.

After West Indian emancipation, the attention of the anti-slavery movement had turned to the prospects for peaceful trade and free labour in Africa and the West Indian colonies, discussed by Jeremie in the *Letter to Thomas Fowell Buxton on Negro Emancipation* (1840). Buxton had begun to formulate a plan for a commercial and agricultural venture in Africa, which resulted in the Niger expedition of 1841. Jeremie contributed a proposal for the management of land, and Buxton suggested that he might become the 'Governor-General of Africa' if this experiment succeeded. In the event, Jeremie accepted the governorship of Sierra Leone on 15 October 1840. He was knighted on 5 November and arrived at Freetown in December.

Jeremie was pleased with his new post; his son, John Robert Jeremie, educated at Trinity College, Cambridge, served as his secretary and continued in this capacity under Jeremie's successor until his own death in 1843. Also in Sierra Leone, Jeremie's daughter married Captain Richard Taylor of the 3rd West India regiment. As governor, Jeremie was in a position to carry out Britain's policy of suppressing the foreign slave trade while advancing legitimate trade with the African interior. He proposed to make alliances with African rulers in territories surrounding Sierra Leone on terms of equality but also wished to regulate more strictly the activities of British subjects, even outside the colony's borders. Jeremie survived in this post less than five months, succumbing, as a Colonial Office note callously put it, to 'the common fate of Sierra Leone Governors'—namely, fever (probably malaria)—on 23 April 1841. His wife was granted a pension of £200 in August of that year and retired to Guernsey.

Jeremie's career rode on his education and his commitment to the anti-slavery cause. He enjoyed legal work but found society in slave colonies uncongenial; in return he earned a character in Colonial Office files as 'violent and intemperate' (PRO, CO 235/32). The testimonial of the Anti-Slavery Society in 1836 was also just; an 'inflexible adherence to right principles' gained him admirers and enemies.   ALEXANDRA FRANKLIN

Sources PRO, CO 253/32, CO 267/136 · Bodl. RH, Buxton MSS · PRO, WO 25/646 · 'Select committee on negro apprenticeship in the colonies: minutes of evidence', *Parl. papers* (1836), vol. 15, no. 560
Archives Bodl. RH, corresp. with Thomas Buxton
Likenesses E. H. Baily, bust, 1846, Sierra Leone Cathedral · B. R. Haydon, group portrait, oils (*The Anti-Slavery Society convention, 1840*), NPG

Jerman, Edward (*c.*1605–1668), carpenter and architect, was the eldest of the three sons of Anthony Jerman (*d.* 1650), master of the Carpenters' Company in 1633–4, and his wife, Mary Bennett. He belonged to at least the third generation of a family prominent as carpenters in the City of London; however, his surname (also given as Germain and Jarman) suggests that the family may have arrived there as persecuted protestants from the Low Countries. As early as 1633 he was appointed City carpenter jointly

with his father; he continued to hold the post until 1657. He succeeded his father in 1650 as one of the City viewers, and in March 1654 was appointed one of the two surveyors of City works at a salary of £60 per annum, but resigned in 1657. At the same time he was acquiring surveyorships to City livery companies, notably in 1650 to the Goldsmiths and in 1654 the Fishmongers. Whether he was already engaged in architectural design at that period is not known. Only once is he heard of acting outside the orbit of City institutions, during the period 1666–8, when he was paid by the office of the king's works for surveying at Windsor Castle. With his wife, Rose, he had one daughter and three sons.

The great fire of London in September 1666 revolutionized Jerman's life, giving him a series of major architectural commissions. That he was determined to seize these opportunities for design is suggested by the fact that—although named in October 1666 as one of the City's three surveyors for post-fire rebuilding—he resigned the following March, when the time-consuming work of surveying property in the devastated area began. In the same month he was appointed architect for the rebuilding of Mercers' Hall, and also manoeuvred so that the Gresham committee appointed him sole architect for rebuilding the Royal Exchange. During the following twenty months he supervised repairs to Goldsmiths' Hall and the Company of Barber–Surgeons' anatomy theatre, and made designs for rebuilding the halls of the Fishmongers (June 1667), Weavers (July 1667), Haberdashers (September 1667), Barber–Surgeons, Waxchandlers, and Drapers, and designed a new elevation for St Paul's School.

Although none of the buildings designed by Jerman has survived, all the most important ones are well depicted in contemporary engravings or later watercolour drawings, so that it is possible to make an aesthetic judgement on his work. In general he had a taste for dramatic grouping and florid detail, employing some of Inigo Jones's vocabulary while ignoring his harmony of proportions. Goldsmiths' Hall, designed by Nicholas Stone with Jones's advice, was his most important source of ideas; but he is likely to have been familiar with such compendia of classical designs as Sebastiano Serlio's *Architettura* and Alessandro Francini's *Livre d'architecture* (1631).

The Royal Exchange, Jerman's major work, copied the general design of the quadrangle from its Elizabethan predecessor, but its two principal external elevations showed him striking out on his own. The entrance front was a powerful if dislocated composition, poising a three-stage timber tower over a yawning central carriage arch and setting the flanking pedestrian entrances in enormously overscaled Corinthian aedicules as high as the two-storey frontages on either side. By contrast, the north front was an ingenious exercise in mannerist ambiguity, based on a motif at Goldsmiths' Hall. The façade he designed for St Paul's School exhibited extraordinary disparities in scale, the single-storey schoolroom set between twin masters' houses, five storeys in height.

The Mercers' Company built a row of houses on Cheapside to Jerman's design, which became an important prototype for post-fire brick frontages on major City thoroughfares. The fantastic façade of the entry to Mercers' Hall, which interrupted the row, doubtless owed its conception to Jerman, but as built (and as largely surviving, re-erected at Swanage town hall, Dorset) it is the work of his successor, John Oliver. For Fishmongers' Hall a plan on vellum, almost certainly Jerman's, survives. This shows that he conceived the idea of setting the hall block at the back of the site, overlooking the River Thames; but the hipped-roofed range erected there in 1669–71 almost certainly owed its elegance and fine proportions to other minds than his.

Jerman was a typical craftsman–architect of his day, bold but unscholarly. It is clear that, for the buildings which were under construction during his lifetime, he acted as architect in the fullest sense, selecting materials and master workmen and directing works on site as well as providing designs. However, he was unable to bring any of his commissions to completion. By October 1668 he was ill, he made his will on 9 November, and was buried in the church of St Giles Cripplegate on the 26th of that month.

Jerman's reputation quickly withered after his death. Colen Campbell, illustrating the plan and elevation of the Royal Exchange in volume 2 of *Vitruvius Britannicus* (1717), omitted to mention the architect's name; George Vertue recorded nothing about him. Only when Victorian antiquaries began to publish the histories of City institutions did he re-emerge as a significant figure.

JOHN NEWMAN

Sources Colvin, *Archs.* · M. Pinhorn, 'The Jerman family', *Blackmansbury*, 1/5–6 (1964), 3–9 · A. Saunders, 'The second exchange', *The Royal Exchange*, ed. A. Saunders (1997), 121–35 · H. Colvin, 'The north front of the Royal Exchange', *The Royal Exchange*, ed. A. Saunders (1997), 136–7 · J. Imray, *The Mercers' Hall* (1991) · P. Metcalf, *The halls of the Fishmongers' Company* (1977) · M. McDonnell, *The annals of St Paul's School* (privately printed, Cambridge, 1959) · J. Newman, 'Nicholas Stone's Goldsmiths' Hall', *Architectural History*, 14 (1971), 30–39 · J. Dobson and R. M. Walker, *Barbers and barber–surgeons of London* (1979) · A. H. Johnson, *The history of the Worshipful Company of the Drapers of London*, 5 vols. (1914–22), vol. 3 · Haberdashers' Company court of assistants minutes book, GL, MS 15842, 139, 141, 143 · H. Collins [forthcoming]

Wealth at death freehold messuage, The Hen and Chickens, Whitechapel: will, 9 Nov 1668, abstracted in Pinhorn, 'Jerman family'

Jerment, George (1759–1819), minister of the Secession church, was born on 9 October 1759 at Peebles, the son of Richard Jerment (1720/21–1787), minister of the Anti-Burgher Secession (General Associate Synod) church in Peebles. After attending the local grammar school and Edinburgh University (1773–6) he studied at the General Associate Divinity Hall, at Alloa (1777–80), under the synod's divinity professor, William Moncrieff. Jerment's first appointment was to assist David Wilson in the synod's congregation in Great St Thomas Apostle's, Bow Lane, Cheapside, London. He proved highly acceptable and was ordained in September 1782 as Wilson's colleague and successor. Wilson's *The Gospel Minister Encouraged and*

Instructed (1783) was his ordination sermon. Following Wilson's death in 1784 Jerment edited some of his sermons and added a biographical memoir. When its lease expired in 1807 the church removed to a chapel in Oxendon Street, Haymarket (built in 1676 for Richard Baxter by his wife Margaret). Jerment raised £1000 towards its refurbishment. He remained in the charge for the rest of his life, with the assistance of William Broadfoot of Kirkwall from June 1817. In 1789 Jerment married Agnes (d. 1795), daughter of his former teacher William Moncrieff; the couple had five children, one son, who died in 1812, and four daughters. After Agnes's death Jerment married, on 19 August 1797, Elizabeth (1760–1848), daughter of Matthew Moncrieff of Abernethy. Another daughter was born. Jerment's wives were both granddaughters (by different grandmothers) of Alexander Moncrieff of Culfargie, one of the founders of the Secession church in Scotland.

Jerment's style as a preacher and writer has been described as 'nervous, classical and generally elegant' (Button, 116). Among the founders of the London Missionary Society, Jerment preached to the society (4 July 1796) the sermon 'Peace to the heathen'; this was published in *Religion: a Monitor to the Middle-Aged and the Glory of Old Men* (1796), which also included sermons given in November 1794 'soon after the first meeting of the few Ministers who were honoured to lay the foundation of the *Missionary Society*' (iii). He maintained his support in the face of criticism of its interdenominational platform. *Parental Duty* (1791) and *Early Piety* (1793)—six discourses on Ecclesiasticus 12:1 dedicated to the Bow Lane youth—formed a trilogy with *Religion*. The first two were published together in Philadelphia as early as 1794. Jerment actively supported the *Theological Magazine and Review* (1801–7, latterly *Theological and Biblical Magazine*) for most of its short life. In 1804 he slightly abridged Thomas Gibbons's *Memoirs of Eminently Pious Women* (1777), adding a second volume including nine Scots and several lives of his own composition. In the fifth volume of a six-volume edition of Robert Leighton's works (1805–8) Jerment contributed an appreciative life of the archbishop. He recalled how, before he was seventeen, he had encountered a book of Leighton's sermons in a gardener's cottage. The gardener, ignorant of the author's identity, spoke of the volume's spiritual benefit to him. When Jerment discerned Leighton's 'crowning excellence' as 'the rich and deep vein of experimental religion', learning without pedantry, and 'solemnity without stiffness' (*The Whole Works of Robert Leighton*, new edn, 1820, 4 vols., 1.lxx–lxxii) he could almost have been speaking of himself. He worked eagerly for the union of General Associate and Associate synods in the United Secession church, but died at his home in Richard Street, Islington, London, on 26 May 1819, one year before the union was achieved. He was buried on 2 June 1819 at Bunhill Fields cemetery, London.

D. F. WRIGHT

Sources S. J. Button, 'George Jermont, DD: Scotch seceder', *Bunhill memorials*, ed. J. A. Jones (1849), 112–16 · R. Small, *History of the congregations of the United Presbyterian church from 1733 to 1900*, 2 vols. (1904) · W. Mackelvie, *Annals and statistics of the United Presbyterian church*, ed. W. Blair and D. Young (1873), 494–5, 657 · J. M'Kerrow,

History of the Secession church, rev. edn (1841), 874–6 • J. Morison, *The fathers and founders of the London Missionary Society*, new edn [1844], 506–12 • R. Lovett, *The history of the London Missionary Society, 1795–1895*, 1 (1899), 14–16 • *Evangelical Magazine and Missionary Chronicle*, 27 (1819), 324–5 • *Christian Magazine or Evangelical Repository*, new ser., 13 (1819), 340–44 • F. Moncreiff and W. Moncreiffe, *The Moncreiffs and the Moncreiffes*, 2 vols. (1929)
Likenesses etching, repro. in Morison, *Fathers and founders*, facing p. 551

Jermin [German], **Michael** (*bap.* 1590, *d.* 1659), Church of England clergyman, was baptized on 1 November 1590 at Knowstone, Devon, the son of Alexander Jermin, or German, merchant and sheriff of Exeter. His grandfather had twice been elected mayor of the city. He matriculated from Exeter College, Oxford, on 20 June 1606 and became a scholar of Corpus Christi in 1608. He graduated BA in October 1611 and proceeded MA in January 1615. He became a fellow of Corpus Christi in 1615 and was incorporated at Cambridge in 1617. He then went abroad as chaplain to Elizabeth, electress palatine, and received a doctorate in divinity from Leiden University in 1624. He was made a DD at Oxford in July 1624 and was appointed chaplain to Charles I in the same year.

In 1626 Jermin was made rector of St Martin Ludgate, London, and Edburton, Sussex. He obtained a licence on 31 October 1627 to marry a widow named Frances Armstrong, from Corby, Kesteven, Lincolnshire; they had two children, Rebecca and Katherine. In March 1633 Jermin was admitted to Gray's Inn. Both his *Paraphrasticall Meditations ... upon the Proverbs of Salomon* (1638), dedicated to the king, and his *Commentary upon the Whole Booke of Ecclesiastes* (1639), dedicated to his former patron, Elizabeth, are close textual analyses written in a dense, academic style with frequent reference to Hebrew, classical, and Christian sources. In 1640 he became president of Sion College.

In July 1643 Jermin paid £100, levied on him by the committee for the advance of money. In that October the vestry of St Martin's supported his expulsion from the parish, and he was replaced by the puritan Thomas Jacombe. Jermin was subsequently sequestrated and forced to live on the charity of other royalists. However, in November 1646 the committee for plundered ministers allowed him to keep the Edburton living on the grounds that he had behaved inoffensively since his sequestration. In April 1651 the council of state issued a pass which allowed Rebecca Jermin and her daughter Henrietta to go to France in the company of five servants. According to Anthony Wood, Jermin retired to the home of his son-in-law (presumably the husband of his other daughter Katherine) at Kemsley, near Sevenoaks, about 1652. He was in negotiations during the 1650s with the committee for compounding about his sequestrated land. In 1655 he was ejected from the parish of Edburton as part of a crack down on royalists, but in June 1658 the council of state gave him leave to resume preaching. Wood mistakenly attributes to him Francis Osborne's *The Father's Instructions to his Child* published that year; his attribution to Jermin of *The Exemplary Life and Death of Mr Jourdaine* is also highly suspect. Jermin died suddenly on 14 August 1659 on his way back to Kemsley after preaching in Sevenoaks. He was buried north of the altar at Kemsley where a black marble monument was erected over his grave. His will, dated 27 April 1658, made bequests to the poor of St Martin Ludgate and Edburton, and left £250 to Exeter corporation.

JASON MᶜELLIGOTT

Sources Foster, *Alum. Oxon.* • Venn, *Alum. Cant.* • Wood, *Ath. Oxon.*, new edn • *CSP dom.*, 1625–60 • M. A. E. Green, ed., *Calendar of the proceedings of the committee for compounding ... 1643–1660*, 5 vols., PRO (1889–92) • Wood, *Ath. Oxon.: Fasti* (1815) • *IGI* • will, PRO, PROB 11/297, fols. 366v–367r • Wing, *STC* • Walker rev.
Wealth at death under £300: will, PRO, PROB 11/297, fols. 366v–367r

Jermy [*formerly* Preston], **Isaac** (1789–1848), judge and murder victim, was born on 23 September 1789 as Isaac Preston, the eldest son of George Preston, rector of Beeston St Lawrence, Norfolk. He was educated as a town boy at Westminster School, where his brother George was afterwards usher and second master. After leaving school in 1807, he matriculated at Christ Church, Oxford, on 28 January 1808, and graduated BA on 8 February 1812. Having been admitted to Lincoln's Inn on 11 May 1809, he was called to the bar on 20 May 1814, and joined the Norfolk circuit. In 1819 he married Mary Anne, daughter of Sir Thomas Beevor, third baronet (1753–1820), and his wife, Anne (both of Norfolk); they had two children, Isaac Jermy [*see below*] and Ellen, before she died in 1823. In 1826 Preston became steward and in 1831 recorder of Norwich. He was also a commissioner of bankrupts for Norwich. In 1832 he married Fanny, daughter of the Revd Prebendary Jephson of Armagh; she died in 1835, leaving a daughter, Isabella.

George Preston had inherited the estate of Stanfield Hall, near Wymondham, Norfolk; this estate had passed into his family through the complex will of William Jermy (1715–1752), which left it, after various provisos, to male relatives of the name of Jermy. However, in 1754 Isaac Preston, brother of William Jermy's wife Frances, had bought out claims on the estate from his Jermy relatives, and it had passed down his family contrary to the requirements of the will. On the death of George Preston, Isaac Preston changed his surname by royal licence, dated 6 September 1838, to Isaac Jermy, and occupied the property. His right of possession was, however, disputed by many claimants. In September 1838 John Larner and Thomas Jermy, accompanied by a London attorney named Wingfield and other claimants, mostly tradesmen and labourers, took possession of the house, but were expelled. Many were charged, but were released after trial in April 1839 on relinquishing their claims; Larner and Wingfield were imprisoned for three months each.

Isaac Jermy's bailiff and one of his tenant farmers was **James Blomfield Rush** (*d.* 1849), who assisted in ejecting the claimants in April 1838. Rush may subsequently have read the violated will, for on the evening of 28 November 1848 he shot Jermy dead on the porch of Stanfield Hall. He then entered the house and shot dead Jermy's son, Isaac Jermy Jermy, and subsequently wounded the son's wife, Sophia Jane, and Eliza Chastney, the chambermaid. Father and son were buried in Wymondham churchyard on 5 December. Sophia Jermy recovered, and later married, on 10 December 1850, Sir Thomas Beevor, fourth baronet; she died on 22 February 1890.

Isaac Jermy Jermy (1821–1848), who was murdered with his father, was educated at Westminster School and Trinity College, Cambridge, where he graduated BA in 1844 and MA in 1848. He married Sophia Jane, daughter of Clement Chevalier, rector of Badingham, Suffolk, with whom he had one surviving child, Sophia Henrietta, who inherited the Jermy property and married Captain Reginald Thorsby Gwyn, 4th King's Own Royals. Their son, Reginald Preston Jermy Gwyn, sold the Stanfield Hall estates in 1920.

Rush's trial before Baron Rolfe at the Shire Hall, Norwich, began on 29 March 1849 and lasted six days. He defended himself, which added to the excitement of a trial which engaged the nation's attention. The Norwich newspapers were published daily and sent by the sackful for national distribution. Rush was convicted and hanged before Norwich Castle on 14 April 1849 in one of the last public executions outside London. Many of the crowd travelled to Norwich by special excursion trains. Staffordshire figures of Rush, of Stanfield Hall, and of Potash Farm (Rush's residence) were quite common, and testified to a trial in which property, deception, and passion were engagingly mingled.   H. C. G. MATTHEW

Sources J. B. Rush, *An introductory narrative and revised report of the trial and execution of J. B. Rush* (1849) • W. T. Shore, ed., *Trial of James Blomfield Rush* (1928) • S. Valdar, *A brief history of the Jermy family of Norfolk and Suffolk* (privately printed, London, 1960) • *N&Q*, 4th ser., 3 (1869), 170 • P. Burke, *Celebrated trials connected with the upper classes of society* (1851) • *GM*, 2nd ser., 31 (1849), 97–8, 532 • *ILN* (2 Dec 1848) • *ILN* (9 Dec 1848) • *ILN* (16 Dec 1848) • *ILN* (31 March 1849) • Venn, *Alum. Cant.*

Likenesses figurines on Staffordshire pottery (James B. Rush), repro. in A. Scott and C. Scott, *Staffordshire figurines* (1993)

Jermy, Isaac Jermy (1821–1848). *See under* Jermy, Isaac (1789–1848).

Jermy [*née* Withers], **Louise Jane** [Louisa] (1877–1952), domestic servant and autobiographer, was born on 30 January 1877 at Howe Lane, Romsey, Hampshire, on the Broadlands estate where her maternal grandmother, Sarah Medley, was laundress to the 'great house'. Her mother, Selina (c.1844–1879), died when Louise was eighteen months old. Her elder sister Amy lived with their paternal grandparents in Romsey, while Louise was brought up by Sarah Medley in Kents almshouse in Romsey. Widowed at twenty-three, their father, St John Withers (c.1856–c.1923), a labourer twelve years younger than his first wife, remarried and went with his second wife, Mary, to London, where he worked in a variety of small businesses.

Louise Withers was taken out of school at eleven to help in her stepmother's home-based laundry business. The heavy labour, as well as severe physical abuse from her stepmother, caused Louise to be partially disabled when she was thirteen. She was sent in 1890 to her stepmother's aunt and uncle in Radwinter, Essex, to recuperate; in January 1891 she was sent back to Broadlands to live with her

widowed paternal grandfather in Ashfield. There she knitted socks which were sold by a Romsey shop. She returned to London in September 1891. Not fit enough for laundry work, she opted for dress making. She was also expected to help look after two stepbrothers, and was again beaten by her stepmother. She was hospitalized after regular fainting fits and the onset of severe headaches, and then sent back to her paternal grandfather for four months' recuperation. Though unable to complete her two-year apprenticeship, Louise had become a proficient dress maker by 1893. By then she was attending Sunday school, where she confided in and was supported by the teacher. She also wrote verse, in which she expressed her bitterness about the ill treatment she suffered from her stepmother. At sixteen she confronted her stepmother when the stepmother tried to prevent her from reading the Bible. On her seventeenth birthday her father presented her with her own Bible, his first birthday present to her. She was forced from her first dress making job (1893–4) by her stepmother, who thought she was not earning enough.

Louise decided, despite her disability, to go into service. Though she found more freedom in domestic service, her stepmother again prevailed upon her to leave her first position with a Roman Catholic brother and sister in Kensington because of low wages (£7 a year, with board and lodging). In her second position her health suffered. Her next position (1895) led to a move to Birmingham in 1897. She was encouraged by her employer, a suffragist, to improve her education. Recurring problems with her hip led her to leave that position, and after a series of live-in jobs she returned in 1901 to London, where she found work as a cook with a Jewish family called Klein from 1903.

She moved with the Klein family about 1910 to Wroxham, Norfolk, and there met her future husband, John Jermy (1862/1863–c.1922), a farm labourer, the son of John Jermy, a gardener. Her father objected that John earned too little (13s. a week) and had poor health, but her stepmother, with whom she was now reconciled, supported her choice of marriage partner. They married at Wroxham parish church on 25 February 1911, and their first son was born on Christmas eve 1911. A second son was born in 1916. John Jermy died about 1922. Louise then worked on the land, and when that work gave out she worked as her maternal grandmother had done, as a laundry worker for the lady of the manor. Her father died about 1923, leaving everything to his third wife and their son.

Louise Jermy was unusual for a working-class woman in writing an autobiography, *The Memories of a Working Woman*, published in Norwich in 1934 with a foreword by Ralph Hale Mottram, who commented that it was 'said to be the first autobiography written by a Women's Institute member', though the Women's Institute is not mentioned in the memoir itself. Her branch at Hoveton held an official reception on the book's publication, at which she read a letter of congratulations from the queen, who had purchased a copy. Structured around a conventional working-class chronology (birth, childhood, family, work, illness, death, though precise dates are often lacking), the memoir is descriptive not just of events but of emotions. It is a powerful story of a life of struggle and suffering, from which domestic service offered not only an escape but also opportunities to improve her education (through a reading class and piano lessons). The memoir shows how strong the ties of family were, even for someone removed through work and marriage from the parental home. Louise Jermy died at her home, 23 Hoveton St John, Hoveton, Norfolk, on 28 October 1952. JANE MCDERMID

Sources L. Jermy, *The memories of a working woman* (1934) [with foreword by R. H. Mottram] · 'Women's Institute activities', *Eastern Daily Press* (9 Nov 1934), 8 · *Home and Country*, 16/2 (Feb 1934), 80 · B. P. Kanner, *Women in context: two hundred years of British women autobiographers: a reference guide and reader* (New York, 1997), 470–71 · b. cert. · m. cert. · d. cert.
Wealth at death £277 6s. 11d.: administration, 12 Jan 1953, CGPLA Eng. & Wales

Jermy, Robert (1600–1677), politician, was the son of John Jermy (1555–1630), lawyer, of Gunton, Norfolk, and his wife, Helen (*née* Jermy). John Jermy was master of the Middle Temple and chancellor of Norwich. Jermy was educated at Christ's College, Cambridge, entered the Middle Temple in 1621, and was called to the bar in 1629. He married Christian Cock (or Cooke). The details of his career may have been obscured by his descendants, squires of Bayfield, who may have sought to distance themselves from the civil war parliamentarianism of Jermy and his brother Francis.

From 1643 Jermy was a member of several Norfolk committees and commissions, including those for raising money for the parliamentarian cause, for sequestering the estates of delinquents, and for removal of scandalous clergy, and was a militia commissioner in 1648 and 1659. In 1648 he was probably the Major Jermy sent to suppress royalist stirrings at Great Yarmouth. In 1650 the royalist 'winter rising' saw a gathering on Easton Heath, mainly of tradesmen, husbandmen, and artisans, intending to march upon Norwich. It was dispersed without bloodshed or violence, being a smaller and less powerful affair than expected, but the Commonwealth authorities wished to make much of it. Jermy was instrumental in the setting up of a high court of justice to deal with the royalists concerned, and was a member of this court. Thirty-four people were sentenced to death, including the Revd Thomas Cooper, an usher at Gresham's School, Holt, and William Hobart, son of the lord of the manor at Holt.

Jermy acted as a justice of the peace and in 1656 was one of those named to maintain the security of the lord protector, as well as serving as captain of the Norfolk militia. His son-in-law, Thomas Toll, recorder of King's Lynn and husband of his daughter Eleanor, also served on local committees. Jermy was chosen by the army council to represent Norfolk in the Barebones Parliament of 1653; in 1659 he was involved in the disputed parliamentary election for Castle Rising, but was admitted a member under a new writ in 1660 after the first election had been declared void. In March 1659 passes were issued for Jermy and Toll to travel 'beyond the seas', that is, to visit New England.

By now local hostility to Jermy was emerging. An anonymous 'loyal song' attacked him for being 'a pitiful soldier', 'a cruel man', 'a rascal', and 'a coward', and accused him of corrupting the burghers of Castle Rising and having fled to New England. About the same time one John Armiger issued a proclamation addressed to the commissioners of the great seal, dealing with matters proved to a jury at Guildhall on 21 June 1656. This accused Jermy of showing preferential leniency to various people charged before him, of issuing violent prosecutions against Katherine Foxe, a widow whom he had helped materially but who refused to surrender her virtue to him, and of bringing an action against Armiger for saying 'You sit upon the Bench … to maintain roguery and villainy', which statement had been found to be justified by a jury sitting for the lord chief justice. Then, on 14 July 1660, Armiger petitioned the House of Lords for wrongs by Colonel Jermy who, after the previous jury had found for Armiger, had had him arrested on a trumped-up charge and sent as a slave to Jamaica, from whence he had escaped. Taking advantage of the restoration of Charles II, Armiger now sought reparation.

By 1661, however, Jermy had returned from abroad and taken up his manor of Bayfield, as seen by his presentations to the livings of Bayfield, Calthorp, and Letheringsett. In 1663, by command of Charles II, a letter was drafted for conferring a baronetcy on him, but the bill was never signed. His will, dated 4 April 1677, provides for his wife and several children but not for one of his sons, Revd John Jermy, from whom he was estranged for political reasons; Robert Jermy died in 1677. Coming from a privileged background, Jermy had been ambitious, seeking the powers of office. These he obtained under Cromwell, but he used his position unwisely, some of his actions being indiscreet and others even more questionable.

KENNETH E. JERMY

Sources S. Valdar, *A brief history of the Jermy family of Norfolk and Suffolk* (privately printed, London, 1960) · K. E. Jermy, 'Colonel Robert Jermy, MP', *Norfolk Ancestor*, 6 (1993), 329–34 · Venn, *Alum. Cant.* · C. H. Firth and R. S. Rait, eds., *Acts and ordinances of the interregnum, 1642–1660*, 3 vols. (1911) · *The parliamentary or constitutional history of England*, 2nd edn, 24 vols. (1751–62), vol. 10 · H. A. Glass, *The Barbone Parliament* (1899) · R. W. Ketton-Cremer, 'The winter rising, I, II', *Forty Norfolk essays* (1961) · R. H. Mason, *History of Norfolk* (1884) · *CSP dom.*, 1659–60 · *A collection of loyal songs written against the Rump Parliament between the years 1639 and 1661*, 2 vols. (1731) · J. Armiger, *An hypocrite unmasked, or, The inside of Colonel Robert Jermye discovered* (c.1660) · PRO, SP 29/84 1101 · F. Blomefield and C. Parkin, *An essay towards a topographical history of the county of Norfolk*, [2nd edn], 11 vols. (1805–10), vol. 9 · R. W. Ketton-Cremer, *Norfolk in the civil war: a portrait of a society in conflict* (1969) · Norwich Library, Norris MSS · W. Rye, *Norfolk families*, 2 (1913)

Jermy, Seth (1656–1724), naval officer, was the son of William Jermy, merchant, of London and Katherine Blackhurst, and grandson of Francis Jermy of Wighton, Norfolk, of the landed visitation family of Jermy of Norfolk and Suffolk. On 6 November 1692 he married Mary Piggot (*née* Martin), widow of a former shipmate, at St Mary Woolnoth, London. He was a lieutenant of the *Northumberland* at the battle of Barfleur in May 1692. On 15 January 1696 he was promoted to commander of the brigantine *Spy*, and in

December 1702 was appointed to the *Nightingale*, a frigate employed in convoy service in the North Sea. For the next five years she was employed to escort colliers and cornships between the rivers Forth, Tyne, Humber, and Thames. On the evening of 24 August 1707, while off the mouth of the Thames with a large convoy, she was met by a squadron of six French galleys under the command of the Chevalier de Langeron. Two of the galleys attacked the frigate; the other four gave chase to the convoy. But the *Nightingale* made such a stout defence that de Langeron was obliged to recall his whole force to his assistance. Even then Jermy, by shrewd deployment of the ship's company and by personal bravery, continued to fight against overwhelming odds, and yielded only when he saw that all his convoy had safely reached the Thames. When Jermy proffered his sword in surrender de Langeron returned it, complimenting Jermy on his courage. His wife secured an audience with Queen Anne for his exchange, and in 1708 Jermy was returned to England. A routine court martial honourably acquitted him of losing his ship, and he was appointed to command the *Swallow's Prize*. In 1710 he was promoted captain, in command of the *Antelope*, and two years later he was superannuated. He died in London on 3 August 1724.

J. K. LAUGHTON, rev. KENNETH E. JERMY

Sources J. Marteilhe, *Mémoires d'un protestant condamné aux galères de France pour cause de religion* (Rotterdam, 1757); Eng. trans. as *Galley slave: the autobiography of Jean Marteilhe*, ed. K. Fenwick (1957) • S. Valdar, *A brief history of the Jermy family of Norfolk and Suffolk* (privately printed, London, 1960) • J. Millman, 'The Norfolk roots of Capt. Seth and Capt. John Jermy', *Norfolk Ancestor*, 4 (1987), 125–8 • W. Rye, ed., *The visitacion of Norffolk ... 1563 ... 1613*, Harleian Society, 32 (1891) • D. B. Smith and Royal Navy College, eds., *The commissioned sea officers of the Royal Navy, 1660–1815*, 3 vols. [n.d., c.1954] • *Admiralty Records, 1690–1707* • G. J. Armytage, ed., *Allegations for marriage licences issued by the vicar-general of the archbishop of Canterbury, July 1687 to June 1694*, Harleian Society, 31 (1890) • N&Q (1867–8) • J. K. Laughton, 'The captains of the "Nightingale"', *EngHR*, 4 (1889), 65–80 • K. E. Jermy, 'Captain Seth Jermy RN', *Norfolk Ancestor*, 4 (1987), 106–8
Likenesses double portrait, oils? (with his wife), NMM; repro. in *Norfolk Ancestor* (June 1987), cover • double portrait, oils? (with his wife); formerly at Minehead vicarage, Somerset, 1963
Wealth at death see will, proved 8 Sept 1724, cited Smith and Royal Navy College, eds., *Commissioned sea officers*

Jermyn, George Bitton (1789–1857), antiquary, born on 2 November 1789, was the eldest son of Peter Jermyn, the younger (1767–1797), solicitor, of Halesworth, Suffolk, and Sarah, second daughter and coheir of George Bitton of Uggeshall in the same county. He was educated at Ipswich grammar school and at Dr Foster's school, Norwich, and entered Caius College, Cambridge, in February 1808. During 1811 and 1812 he travelled on the continent, chiefly for the purpose of conducting heraldic researches; he returned to Cambridge in 1813, moving to Trinity Hall. He was ordained deacon in June 1813 and graduated LLB on 14 July 1814, and LLD in July 1826. He held curacies in Hawkedon, Suffolk, and Littleport, Isle of Ely; ordained priest in 1817, he became curate of Swaffham Prior, near Newmarket, in July 1820. He married first, on 29 March 1815,

Catherine (1792–1828), daughter of Hugh Rowland of Middle Scotland Yard, London, with whom he had three sons and four daughters, the eldest of whom was the art patron and critic Paulina Jermyn *Trevelyan (Catherine died in labour on 20 January 1828); and second, on 11 December 1828, Anne Maria, second daughter of Henry Fly DD, subdean of St Paul's and confessor to the royal household, with whom he had a daughter, who died in infancy. He died on the island of Maddelena, in the kingdom of Sardinia, on 2 March 1857, and was buried on a small neighbouring island.

Jermyn, like his uncle, Henry *Jermyn (1767–1820), made voluminous collections for a genealogical history of Suffolk, including drawings of heraldic insignia, which are preserved in the Bury St Edmunds Museum. His topographical collections for Suffolk were well known in his lifetime. He also compiled an elaborate history of his own family, a folio volume of more than 700 pages.

GORDON GOODWIN, rev. MYFANWY LLOYD

Sources *Herald and Genealogist*, 5 (1870), 435–43 • Boase, *Mod. Eng. biog.* • Venn, *Alum. Cant.*
Archives JRL, heraldic papers • S. Antiquaries, Lond., notes and transcripts relating to Loches and Anjou • Suffolk RO, Bury St Edmunds, heraldic collections made with his wife

Jermyn [Germain], **Henry, earl of St Albans** (*bap.* 1605, *d.* 1684), courtier and government official, was baptized at St Margaret Lothbury, London, on 29 March 1605, the fourth but second surviving son of Sir Thomas *Jermyn (*bap.* 1573, *d.* 1644/5), politician and courtier of Rushbrook, Suffolk, and his wife, Catherine (*d.* before 1642), daughter of Sir William Killigrew of Hanworth, Middlesex.

Jermyn followed his father, a long-serving court official who eventually became vice-chamberlain of the household to Charles I and governor of Jersey, into royal service. He attended Lord Bristol's embassy to Madrid in 1622–3, and Lord Kensington's mission to Paris to negotiate the marriage of Charles I and Henrietta Maria of France, in 1624–5. He then became an MP, sitting for Bodmin in 1625 and 1626, Liverpool in 1628, and Corfe Castle in the Short Parliament of 1640, but was far less active in the Commons than his father. His real talents were as a courtier and he joined Henrietta Maria's household as a gentleman usher in 1627. In 1633 he displeased Charles I by refusing to marry the pregnant Eleanor Villiers, a maid of honour and niece of the duke of Buckingham, on the grounds that she had slept with two men besides himself. Charles banished him to France. Through the queen's intervention he was eventually allowed to return and was back at court by February 1636. His close relationship and increasing influence with Henrietta Maria caused gossip as early as the 1630s and William Davenant may have intended an ironic allusion to the pair in his play *The Platonic Lovers* (1636). Davenant also depicted Jermyn as Arigo in his poem 'Madagascar' (1638). Jermyn was promoted to the post of master of the horse to the queen in 1639.

In spring 1641 Jermyn supported the marquess of Hamilton in a scheme to broaden the government by bringing peers such as the duke of Bedford into office, and he was one of the leading conspirators in the plot to bring the king's army down from the north to frighten parliament. One commentator, reporting on his involvement in the conspiracy, identified him as 'The Queen's great favourite, a man looked upon by the whole Court, and every thing approved being done by him' (Phillips, 30). On parliament's discovery of the plot Jermyn fled to France at the begining of May 1641.

After joining Henrietta Maria at The Hague in 1642 Jermyn assisted her in pawning crown jewels, raising loans, and ciphering her correspondence. He landed with the queen at Bridlington, Yorkshire, in 1643 with arms, munitions, and French officers who formed the queen's lifeguards, of which he became colonel. They captured Burton upon Trent and joined the king at Oxford. On 8 September 1643 at the queen's behest, Charles I created him Baron Jermyn of St Edmundsbury. He was wounded at the battle of Aldbourne Chase ten days later. On 22 January 1644 Jermyn became the queen's lord chamberlain, subsequently also acting as her treasurer. He succeeded his father as governor of Jersey in 1645.

In April 1644 Jermyn and Henrietta Maria left Oxford for France, where they lived at the Louvre and St Germain-en-Laye. The majority of their subsequent policies arose from decisions made together. Jermyn was assisted greatly by his first cousin Sir John Berkeley; Lord Crofts; Davenant, who became one of his messengers (and spies); and the poet Abraham Cowley, whom he employed as his secretary and whose *Complete Works* was dedicated to Jermyn. Jermyn continued to help the queen raise money for the royalist armies and Charles I granted him authority to negotiate with the continental powers for military support. He dealt in person with the French government and worked closely with the Catholic priest Stephen Goffe to try and secure help from the prince of Orange and the duke of Lorraine, although he failed to persuade Lorraine to send his army into England. His efforts frequently brought him into conflict with the pro-Spanish royal counsellors, such as Lord Digby, who challenged him to a duel in 1647, and Sir Edward Hyde, whom he overruled by bringing the prince of Wales from Jersey to Paris in June 1646.

Perceiving that Charles I's salvation lay in an alliance with Scottish presbyterians Jermyn tried to persuade the obstinate king to bow to Scottish demands and allow the establishment of presbyterianism in England, but the king delayed too long in signing the engagement with the Scots and although he escaped from Holdenby House that November he was soon incarcerated on the Isle of Wight.

Jermyn broke the news of Charles I's execution to Henrietta Maria on 8 February 1649. Rumours that he subsequently married her are unfounded. He was, however, her closest confidant and adviser and, to the annoyance of Hyde's faction, he also continued to advise Charles II. In 1650–51 he was one of those who supported the alliance of Charles II with the Scottish presbyterians. Despite the ultimate failure of the alliance Jermyn was appointed to the king's privy council in 1652. The same year he, Lord Wilmot, and Charles II, attempting to further the royalist cause with the French, acted as mediators between the

French and the rebel duke of Lorraine, negotiating the withdrawal of Lorraine's army from the outskirts of Paris. In 1653 Edward Nicholas complained to Hyde that although the king rather disliked Jermyn, 'he is not only employed and trusted as premier ministre [first minister] in the management of his majesty's greatest and most secret affairs, but overbears his majesty even against his own judgement' (Warner, 2.31).

From 1654 Jermyn lived, with the rest of the queen's household, at the Palais Royal and from 1658 at her château of Colombe. In 1654 his power declined due to his failure to remove Hyde from office, and due to Charles II's departure from Paris. His influence further plummeted when Charles II blamed him for not informing him of Henrietta Maria's plans to convert Prince Henry to Catholicism in 1654. However, his intimate knowledge of the French court made him indispensable again after Cromwell's death in 1658. In 1659 he journeyed to the Pyrenees to help Charles II solicit Franco-Spanish backing for a projected royalist invasion of England.

At Colombe in December 1659 Charles II created Jermyn earl of St Albans. Despite his renewed favour with the king he was excluded, through Hyde's influence, from the Restoration government. Instead, he became ambassador to France in 1661, negotiating and signing the renewal of the Anglo-French treaty, the marriage treaty of Princess Henriette Anne and Philippe, duke of Orléans, and promoting the marriage of Charles II and Catherine of Braganza, all being part of the grand strategy he shared with Henrietta Maria to bring England and France into closer union.

St Albans had raised 647,416 livres tournois (about £20–25 million in modern terms) and had incurred vast debts in the royalist cause. To repay him Charles II confirmed him as co-proprietor of the Northern Neck of Virginia and granted him leases of Byfleet, Oatlands, and Weybridge, Surrey, and St James's, Westminster. In 1661–2 St Albans encouraged the development of St James's, where wide streets, including Jermyn Street, were laid out, lined with brick-built houses constructed specifically 'for the conveniency of the Nobility and Gentry who were to attend upon his Majestie's Person, and in Parliament' (PRO, SP 29/75, no. 27). The centrepiece was St James's Square, based on the principles of classical architecture advocated by Inigo Jones, whom St Albans had known well. Justly called '"the Founder" of London's West End' (Sheppard, 1), St Albans also commissioned Sir Christopher Wren—whose career he had furthered by introducing him to the best builders in Paris in 1665—to design St James's Church (Wren, 261, 312). As steward of Greenwich, 1660–76, he supported the restoration and extension of the Queen's House, the redevelopment of Greenwich Palace, and, in 1662, brought André Le Nôtre over from France to design the park. Although it is hotly disputed, the assertion of the eighteenth-century historian J. Anderson that St Albans was patron, or grand master, of the English Freemasons, 1660–66 is probably correct.

St Albans's intrigues with Henry Bennet, the future earl of Arlington, and the king's mistress Lady Castlemaine in the winter of 1662–3 resulted in the removal of Nicholas from office but failed to displace Hyde, now earl of Clarendon, or the lord treasurer, Southampton. He returned to France with Henrietta Maria in 1665 and opposed the Second Anglo-Dutch War of 1665–7 because France was obliged, by treaty, to side with the Dutch. As ambassador extraordinary in Paris, 1665–7, he negotiated with the French government to bring about the treaty of Breda, which ended the war. Andrew Marvell's great satire on the conduct of the war, 'Last Instructions to a Painter', attacked St Albans's alleged lack of ability, his appearance, and his overindulgence in the pleasures of the court:

> Paint then St Albans full of soup and gold,
> The new court's pattern, stallion of the old.
> Him neither wit nor courage did exalt,
> But Fortune chose him for her pleasure salt.
> Paint him with drayman's shoulders, butcher's mien,
> Member'd like mules, with elephantine chine.
> Well he the title of St Alban's bore,
> For Bacon never studied nature more
> But age, allaying now that youthful heat,
> Fits him in France to play at cards and treat.
> (G. de F. Lord and others, eds., *Poems on Affairs of State*, 1, 1963, 100)

After Clarendon was exiled in 1667 St Albans played some part in the scheme to overcome Arlington's Francophobia and guide Charles II into closer friendship with Louis XIV, which culminated in the signing of the secret treaty of Dover in June 1670, for which purpose he escorted Henriette Anne over from France.

St Albans was present at Henrietta Maria's death at Colombe on 31 August 1669 and was an executor to her will. He returned to England, settled in London, and was lord chamberlain to Charles II, 1672–4, being invested as a knight of the Garter on 30 June 1672, which date is stated clearly on his monument at Rushbrook church.

St Albans retired several times during the 1670s to Rushbrook but was coaxed back by letters from the philosopher Saint-Evremond, begging him to return to the gaming tables and salons of London, where his talents and urbanity would be best appreciated. He never abandoned his aim of uniting the political interests of Charles II and Louis XIV. In 1678 and 1681, though virtually blind, and crippled with gout, he was employed by Charles II for some of the unofficial negotiations with French ambassador Barillon for secret French subsidies. He died, unmarried, at his house in St James's Square on 2 January 1684 and was buried at Rushbrook eight days later. His leases and offices had brought him an enormous income but his finances never recovered from the civil war period and he died some £60,000 in debt. His earldom became extinct but his barony went to his nephews Thomas Jermyn (1633–1703) and then Henry *Jermyn, earl of Dover.

A thorough courtier, it is almost impossible to separate St Albans from Henrietta Maria and her interests, although his consistent advocacy of religious toleration and alliance with France may also represent his own views. His favour with the queen and the policies they pursued together placed him in opposition to such men as Clarendon and Nicholas, whose enmity and unrelenting vilification of him have unfairly dominated subsequent assessments of both his political influence and his character.   ANTHONY R. J. S. ADOLPH

Sources *Calendar of the Clarendon state papers preserved in the Bodleian Library*, ed. O. Ogle and others, 5 vols. (1869–1970) · S. H. A. Hervey, ed., *Rushbrook parish registers, 1567 to 1850: with Jermyn and Davers annals* (1903) · *Letters of Henrietta Maria including her private correspondence with Charles the First*, ed. M. A. E. Green (1857) · Clarendon, *Hist. rebellion* · *The life of Edward, earl of Clarendon … written by himself*, 3 vols. (1759) · F. Sheppard, ed., 'The parish of St James's, Westminster', *Survey of London*, vol. 29, pt 1 (1960) · *The letters of Saint-Evremond*, ed. J. Hayward (1930) · *The dramatic works of Sir William D'Avenant*, ed. W. H. Logan and J. Maidment (1872) · W. D'Avenant, 'Madagascar' and other poems (1638) · *The memoirs of James II: his campaigns as duke of York, 1652–1660*, trans. A. L. Sells (1962) · parish register, London, St Margaret Lothbury, 29 March 1605, GL [baptism] · R. Lockyer, *Buckingham: the life and political career of George Villiers, first duke of Buckingham, 1592–1628* (1981) · [T. Birch and R. F. Williams], eds., *The court and times of Charles the First*, 2 vols. (1848) · W. Phillips, ed., 'The Ottley papers relating to the civil war', *Transactions of the Shropshire Archaeological Society*, 2nd ser., 6 (1894), 27–78 · GEC, *Peerage*, 3.85 · A. Cowley, 'The civil war', *The complete works in verse and prose of Abraham Cowley*, ed. A. B. Grosart, Chertsey Worthies' Library (1881), repr. (New York, 1967) · *The diary of Samuel Pepys*, ed. H. B. Wheatley, 8 vols. (1904–18) · T. H. Lister, *The life and administration of Edward earl of Clarendon, with original correspondence and authentic papers never before published*, 3 vols. (1837–8) · correspondance politique, Angleterre, Archives du Ministère des Affaires Étrangères, Paris · J. Anderson, *The new book of constitutions of the Antient and Honourable Fraternity of Free and Accepted Masons* (1738), repr., Quator Coronati Reprints, 7 (1978) · C. Wren, *Parentalia, or, Memoirs of the family of the Wrens* (1750), repr. (1965) · J. Dalrymple, *Memoirs of Great Britain and Ireland*, 3 vols. (1771–8) · *CSP dom.*, 1625–85 · *CSP Venice*, 1625–75 · *The manuscripts of the Earl Cowper*, 3 vols., HMC, 23 (1888–9) · *Report on the manuscripts of Lord De L'Isle and Dudley*, 6, HMC, 77 (1966) · *Fourth report*, HMC, 3 (1874) [Earl De La Warr MSS] · *The Lismore papers, second series: selections from the private and public … correspondence of Sir Richard Boyle*, ed. A. B. Grosart, 5 vols. (1887–8), vol. 4 · *The Nicholas papers*, ed. G. F. Warner, 1–2, CS, new ser., 40, 50 (1886–92) · PRO, C 10/224/29 · J. L. Chester, ed., *The marriage, baptismal, and burial registers of the collegiate church or abbey of St Peter, Westminster*, Harleian Society, 10 (1876), 214 · J. Bruce, ed., *Verney papers: notes of proceedings in the Long Parliament*, CS, 31 (1845), 88

Archives BL, corresp. and papers | BL, Add. MSS · BL, letters to William Coventry · BL, Egerton MSS · BL, Harley MSS [esp. MS 7379] · BL, Sloane MSS · BL, Stowe MSS · Bodl. Oxf., Clarendon state papers · Bodl. Oxf., John Mordaunt's letter-books · Bodl. Oxf., Thurloe state papers · HLRO · Longleat House, Warminster, Coventry MSS · Magd. Cam., Pepys MSS · NL Ire., Carte MSS · PRO, SP domestic and French

Likenesses P. Lely, oils, c.1672, Cirencester Park, Gloucestershire · P. Lely, oils, c.1672, Ickworth House, Suffolk · Schiavonetti, engraving, 1792 (after drawing by S. Harding; after portrait by A. Van Dyck, c.1627–1641), repro. in *Memoirs of the Comte de Gramont* (1792) · W. H. Gardner, engraving (after drawing by S. Harding; after portrait by A. Van Dyck, c.1627–1641), repro. in Hervey, *Rushbrook parish registers* · R. Godfrey, stipple (after P. Lely), BM, NPG; repro. in Harding, *Biographical mirrour* (1793) · Walker & Boutall Ph.Sc., engraving (after drawing by S. Harding; after portrait by A. Van Dyck, c.1627–1641), repro. in A. E. Dasent, *The history of St James's Square* (1895) · portrait, Ickworth

Wealth at death vast; estate incl. leasehold of entire Bailiwick of St James's, Westminster; heir was thought to be worth £15,000 p.a.; was co-patentee of Northern Neck of Virginia; held various Suffolk manors; received quit rents from vast estates of marquis of Antrim in Ireland; debts were assessed after death at about £60,000: PRO, C 10/224/29; Luttrell, *Diary*

Jermyn, Henry, third Baron Jermyn and Jacobite earl of Dover (*bap.* 1636, *d.* 1708), courtier and army officer, second son of Thomas Jermyn (*d.* 1659) of Rushbrooke, Suffolk, and his wife, Rebecca Rodway (*b.* 1612/13), daughter of William Rodway, merchant of London, was baptized at Rushbrooke on 29 November 1636. His grandfather Thomas *Jermyn and his father were both royalists and members of parliament, as was his elder brother, Thomas. Henry became a Roman Catholic and spent much of the 1650s at the court of Queen Henrietta Maria in France, along with his uncle, also Henry Jermyn (and also a Catholic), who was created Baron Jermyn of St Edmundsbury in 1643 and earl of St Albans in 1660. By 1656 Jermyn had become a member of the household of James, duke of York, who remained in France after his brother, Charles II, left the country; by 1659 he was James's master of the horse. He remained in that post after the Restoration, with a salary of £400 per annum. When he was forced to resign, after the passing of the Test Act of 1673, he was given a pension of £500 per annum.

Jermyn and his uncle were one of a group of James's servants, which also included John Lord Berkeley and his nephew, Charles Berkeley, later earl of Falmouth, who were seen as having a pernicious influence on their master. In 1659 they encouraged him to assert his independence of his brother, and after the Restoration they urged James to establish a large and expensive household on the French model. They were also fully in tune with the prevailing moral tone of Charles II's court. In 1660 Jermyn was one of those who attempted to persuade James to renounce his marriage to Anne Hyde, claiming that she had given him 'long and favourable audiences' (Hamilton, 163, 165). He was renowned for his gambling, swearing, and above all his womanizing. According to Anthony Hamilton, he acquired a reputation as a lover which led a succession of women to pursue him as 'a moving trophy', although his performance was said not to match his reputation. His alleged prowess owed little to his appearance.

> He was little; his head was large and his legs small; his features were not disagreeable, but he was affected in his character and behaviour. All his wit consisted in expressions learnt by rote, which he occasionally employed either in raillery or in love. (ibid., 108)

His conquests included Charles II's sister, Mary, princess of Orange, and his mistress Barbara *Palmer, countess of Castlemaine (*bap.* 1640, *d.* 1709). In 1667 Pepys wrote that the king was jealous of Jermyn because Castlemaine was in love with him, and she was furious with Jermyn because he was allegedly planning to marry Lady Falmouth. In 1662 he was seriously wounded in a duel by one of his rivals for the favours of the countess of Shrewsbury. On 17 April 1675, having sowed his wild oats, he married Judith Pooley (*d.* 1726), daughter of Sir Edmund Pooley (or Poley), of Badley, Suffolk, 'a silly country girl' (ibid., 320); they had no children. Having lost his post at court, he lived quietly in the country, at Cheveley, near Newmarket, where he constructed a Catholic chapel.

Jermyn's fortunes changed with the accession to the throne of his former master as James II. He was raised to

the peerage as Baron Dover on 13 May 1685 and made colonel of a regiment of horse. In August 1686 he was one of a group of Catholics appointed privy councillors; soon afterwards he was the first Catholic to be appointed a lord lieutenant, for Cambridgeshire. On 30 December 1686 he was one of two Catholics appointed to the Treasury commission, along with three much more experienced protestants. In late November 1688 James showed his trust in Dover by making him governor of Portsmouth, the port from which he was about to send his wife and infant son to France. The following month a crowd pulled down the chapel at Cheveley and were with some difficulty persuaded to spare the house. Dover followed James into France and then to Ireland, which he declared was a thousand times worse than he had ever imagined it. In July 1689 (the same month that he created him earl of Dover) James made him a commissioner of the Irish Treasury and sent him to press Louis XIV for additional military aid. The French war minister, Louvois, complained of the poor management of the war effort in Ireland and explained that he could send no men or arms until the end of the campaigning season. Dover became angry and assured Louvois that the war effort would be better directed in future as he would now be in charge of it. The French eventually agreed to send more men and supplies and acceded to James's request to send the comte de Lauzun to command his army, despite warnings that he was arrogant and quarrelsome.

Lauzun wasted little time before he was blaming Dover for the lack of carts, provisions, and other resources. Ireland had been devastated by war, and fleeing protestants had taken much of the country's coin with them. The war effort the previous year had been badly mismanaged by the king's chief minister, John Drummond, earl of Melfort, whom the king had been persuaded to dismiss. There were serious divisions about priorities—the king's primary concern was to regain England—and bitter feuds between English and Irish, English and French, and among the Irish. The leading Irish commander, Richard Talbot, duke of Tyrconnell, thought Dover had done his best and was unused to Irish conditions. Lauzun accused him of hostility to the French and of profiteering. Dover was modest about his capabilities. 'I have something else to say to you', he wrote, 'but if my life were at stake I can't think of it. 'Tis a great wonder such a head as mine should have thought of so many different things as I have done since my being here' (Dover to Tyrconnell, 23 March 1690, NL Ire., MS 37). In June he resigned, claiming that the French clearly did not wish to help James, and that James should make his peace with William and join the alliance against France. He asked both Tyrconnell and the Williamite general Percy Kirk to procure him a passport out of Ireland, but neither would agree, so he made his way to Waterford. This makes it improbable that he fought at the Boyne, as some accounts suggest. During the Williamite siege of Waterford he continued to plead for a passport, which was finally granted in September. He went to Flanders, but returned to England in September 1691 and received a royal pardon in November, but his troubles were not over. Under an act of June 1689 he had been attainted for adhering to King William's enemies. Despite the best efforts of his elder brother, Thomas, who had succeeded to St Albans's title of Baron Jermyn in 1684, he remained legally an outlaw: in 1698 the king granted him a special licence to remain in England. In practice, he lived out his remaining years quietly and comfortably, at Cheveley or in London. He had inherited part of St Albans's fortune in 1684; the remainder came to him (with the barony) when Thomas died in 1703. He died at Cheveley on 6 April 1708 and was buried at the Carmelite friary at Bruges. His peerage became extinct.   JOHN MILLER

Sources A. Hamilton, *Memoirs of the court of Charles II* (1846) · Pepys, *Diary* · Evelyn, *Diary* · *Négociations de M. le Comte d'Avaux en Irlande, 1689-90*, ed. J. Hogan, 2 vols., IMC (1934-58) · 'Letter-book of Richard Talbot', ed. L. Tate, *Analecta Hibernica*, 4 (1932), 99-138 · L. von Ranke, *A history of England, principally in the seventeeth century*, 6 vols. (1875) · J. Miller, *James II* (1978) · *CSP dom.*, 1685-9 · J. Macpherson, ed., *Original papers: containing the secret history of Great Britain*, 2 vols. (1775) · *London Courant*, no. 4 (18-22 Dec 1688) · *Calendar of the Clarendon state papers preserved in the Bodleian Library*, 4: 1657-1660, ed. F. J. Routledge (1932); 5: 1660-1726, ed. F. J. Routledge (1970) · W. D. Cooper, ed., *Savile correspondence: letters to and from H. Savile*, CS, 71 (1858) · PRO, PROB 11/501, fols. 353r-356v [will of Henry Jermyn, Baron Dover] · NL Ire., MS 37 · IGI · HoP, *Commons, 1660-90* · GEC, *Peerage*
Archives BL, accounts and rent roll, Add. MSS 22062-22063 | Bibliothèque Nationale, Paris, MS français NA 9392 · Bodl. Oxf., Carte MS 181 · NL Ire., MS 37
Likenesses portrait, 1670-1679?, University of North Carolina, Chapel Hill, Ackland Art Museum · oils, Ickworth House, Park and Garden, Suffolk

Jermyn, Henry (1767-1820), antiquary, was born at Halesworth, Suffolk, on 11 February 1767 and baptized at the parish church the following 3 April. He was the second son of Peter Jermyn (1737-1810), solicitor, and Elizabeth, daughter and coheir of Dr Samuel Rye, surgeon, all of the same town. After schooling in Norwich and, like his associate D. E. Davy, under Samuel Forster at Yoxford, he went up to St John's College, Cambridge, but left without graduating for Lincoln's Inn in 1785. He was called to the bar but practised only a little from his home, Sibton Abbey. In May 1791 he married Harriott, *née* Lucke, of Sussex, widow of Thomas Douglas; they had two daughters. Jermyn, with the rank of major, was in 1804 appointed Davy's second-in-command in the Blything Hundred Volunteers. From 1815 to 1820 he was high steward of Southwold.

From 1805 until shortly before his death antiquarian pursuits filled Jermyn's time. Together with Davy, he toured Suffolk collecting materials for an intended published history; the two men kept duplicate copies of their findings. Jointly they sent printed queries to suitable people in every parish, and collated the replies. According to a near-contemporary profile,

> Jermyn's habits were too indolent for the constant research necessary to so laborious an undertaking [publishing a history of Suffolk]. His progress was slow; he had neither the piercing stimulus of pecuniary want, nor the ardent enthusiasm and industry of a true born natural Antiquary— the undertaking lingered during his life, and died with his death. (Miller, 75)

Jermyn died on 27 November 1820 at Sibton Abbey, and was buried at the church there on 1 December. At the four-day auction of his library of over 2000 books, his Suffolk notes in over fifty volumes, as good as Davy's as far as they went but less legible, were at the latter's request not offered. Hudson Gurney, the Norwich banker and antiquary, bought most of them later for presentation to the British Museum in 1830.

James Jermyn of Reydon, Henry's cousin, married the latter's daughter Emily in 1821, much against the wishes of her widowed mother. In a pamphlet of the 1820s James argued that Davy had defrauded him and his father-in-law, and in another of the 1840s that banks had deprived him of part of his expected inheritance through marriage. In the light of James's controversial career as high steward of Southwold (he was dismissed three times and reinstated twice), and his bankruptcy in 1849, Davy's defence written on a copy of the earlier tract in the British Library is credible. James Jermyn presented another four of his cousin's manuscripts to the British Museum in 1849.

J. M. BLATCHLY

Sources D. E. Davy, *A journal of excursions through the county of Suffolk, 1823-1844*, ed. J. Blatchly, Sussex RS, 24 (1982) · A. F. Bottomley and M. Chadd, *Senescali Sudwoldienses: 1505-1989* (1989) · J. Jermyn, 'A statement respecting the affairs of H. Jermyn', 1827, BL [printed pamphlet without title] · J. Jermyn, *Appeal to common sense* (c.1845) · W. Miller, *Biographical sketches*, 1 (1826), 75 · parish register (baptism), Halesworth, Suffolk, 3 April 1767 · *DNB* · parish register (burial), Sibton, Suffolk, 1 Dec 1820
Archives BL, Suffolk collections; Suffolk pedigrees and parish collections, Add. MSS 8168-8218; Add. MSS 17097-17100
Likenesses J. Godby, stipple (after Mrs Pulham), BM · pen-and-ink and wash, NPG · pen-and-ink line drawing, Suffolk RO, Ipswich, HD 480/7, fol. 49 · stipple, Suffolk RO, Ipswich, Godby Sculps HD 480/7, fol. 60

Jermyn, James (d. 1852), anthologist, was probably born in the late 1770s at Halesworth, the third son of Robert Jermyn (1733-1813), captain of a ship, but afterwards collector of the customs at Southwold, Suffolk, and Mary (1736/7-1801), daughter and coheir of Dr Samuel Rye of Halesworth in the same county. Henry *Jermyn (1767-1820) was his cousin. James Jermyn was called to the bar, but since he had a private fortune did not practise. After living for a time at Brighton he settled at Southwold, where he was appointed collector of the pier dues. On 17 May 1822 in Reydon, Suffolk, Jermyn married Emily Harriet Jermyn (1793-1824), the only surviving child of his cousin Henry. They had three daughters, one of whom survived Jermyn.

James Jermyn published the *Halesworth Review* from 14 September to 14 October 1808. It refers to various contemporary pamphlets, published at Halesworth, dealing with plays, especially those of the Revd John Dennant (1767-1851), and includes *The Halesworth Dunciad, a Satire on Pedantry Addressed to the Censor of the Stage* (that is, Dennant himself). His other publications include five anthologies of epithets or phrases, all anonymous, and some privately printed, beginning with *Opus epithetorum* (London, 1815?), and ending with a *Book of English Epithets, Literal and Figurative, with Elementary Remarks and Minute References to Authorities* (1849). In this latter, which may have been prompted by some suggestion in the works of Edmund Burke, the author acknowledges the encouragement and hospitality, over nearly half a century, of Sir Thomas Sherlock Gooch MP. Jermyn also published a *Prospectus and Specimen of an English Gradus and Dictionary of Ideas* (London, 1848).

Earlier Jermyn entered the political arena with two addresses on the subject of poor-law assessment—*To the Hundred of Blything* (Southwold?, 1821?), and *Pro & Con, or, A Hundred Arguments for a New Act and Against it* (Southwold, 1821). Jermyn left many manuscript volumes which were acquired by William Aldis Wright. He died at Reydon, Southwold, on 29 July 1852.   JOHN D. HAIGH

Sources *Herald and Genealogist*, 5 (1870), 435–9 · *N&Q*, 7th ser., 2 (1886), 368, 475 · *N&Q*, 7th ser., 3 (1887), 55 · *IGI*

Jermyn, Paulina. *See* Trevelyan, Paulina Jermyn, Lady Trevelyan (1816–1866).

Jermyn, Sir Robert (1538/9–1614), gentleman and patron of puritans, was the third but eldest surviving son of Sir Ambrose Jermyn (c.1510–1577) and Anne (d. 1568), daughter and coheir of George Heveningham. His early years are obscure. He may have matriculated at Corpus Christi College, Cambridge, and was admitted to the Middle Temple in 1560–61. Most probably in 1570 or 1571 he married Judith (d. 1614), the daughter of Sir George and Dorothy Blagg of Little Horringer, Suffolk, and their union produced at least two sons, including Sir Thomas *Jermyn, and five daughters. He succeeded to his father's Suffolk estates and seat at Rushbrooke in April 1577, aged thirty-eight, at which time he was brought onto the commission of the peace; he quickly established himself as an active and leading magistrate in west Suffolk in close communication with members of the privy council. Jermyn was the personification of the Elizabethan godly magistrate. A zealous protestant, he presented to at least ten livings in west Suffolk and had close associations to many godly clergy, perhaps most notably John Knewstub. His stance and activities, together with those of his like-minded colleagues, Sir John Heigham and Sir Edward Lewkenor, gave rise to the famous comment by Queen Elizabeth on her progress through East Anglia in 1578 that she had 'learned why my county of Suffolk is so well governed, it is, because the magistrates and ministers go together' (MacCulloch, *Suffolk*, 116). Jermyn was knighted in 1578 as the queen went on progress and he entertained the French ambassadors at Rushbrooke.

Royal favour, however, was not to last. During the episcopate of Edmund Freake, bishop of Norwich, the religious divisions within Bury St Edmunds and neighbouring parishes became acute and in the resultant and volatile mixture of nonconforming preachers, radical separatists, and powerful conservatives Jermyn's zeal for further reformation of the church was taken by Freake as an arbitrary and unwelcome intrusion into ecclesiastical matters and tacit, if not active, support for the separatists. The assize court judges acted swiftly and severely against the separatists as well as many nonconforming ministers at the Lent assizes in 1583 and made Jermyn and Heigham the scapegoats of the recent disorders by removing them

from the commission of the peace. Jermyn in particular was singled out for humiliation, being forced to serve on a common jury in a case of *nisi prius*. Such was the queen's disfavour that he was not restored to the commission of the peace until 1593. In spite of this enforced decade of absence from the bench, these years saw him solidify his position as the leading gentleman within west Suffolk. His standing was such that he sat as the junior knight in the parliament of 1584 and as the senior knight in 1586. In both parliaments he proved an extremely active member of committees and was appointed to no fewer than eighteen. From 1585 until about 1608 he served as a deputy lieutenant of the shire.

When Elizabeth sent troops to the Netherlands in December 1585 under the earl of Leicester, Jermyn accompanied his patron, although his health was not suited to the rigours of campaigning and he returned to England less than a year after his departure. In 1589 he had to go outside Suffolk for a seat in parliament and his return as a member for the Cornish town of East Looe was most probably the result of his connection with Burghley or Walsingham. Shortly before departing for the Low Countries with Leicester, Jermyn had written to Burghley not 'for fasshon or for feare, but in a true and dutifull manner', explaining that he blessed God every day:

> for the comfortes which I enjoye both in Church and common wealthe the same falling to mi parte, by your speciall wisdome, care and travaile: I can not but reverence your Lordship as Patrem Patrie and do feare that when the Lord foer our synns shall take you from us, we shall to late thoughe to trulye crye out, the horsemen and chariot of England.   (BL, Lansdowne 46, fol. 53r)

Burghley was more than willing to support such loyalty and patriotism, shot through as it was with godly and biblical zeal, and when Jermyn was restored to the commission of the peace he succeeded Henry, Lord Wentworth, as *custos rotulorum*.

Jermyn maintained his active standing in the county community until his death between 12 and 23 April 1614. On his death he bequeathed gold rings to his close friends and fellow magistrates Sir Nicholas Bacon, Sir John Heigham, and Sir Robert Gardiner, reminding them that as they had lived in 'sweet and christian societie' and by their unity had 'much furthered the peace and profitt of our countrye in the administracion of justice and other publicke dutyes', his last request was that they might 'maynteyne the same to the uttermost of theire power' (will, PRO, PROB 11/123). Whether in the donation of books to the parish library of St James in Bury St Edmunds (1595) or in the annuity he gave to Emmanuel College, Cambridge (and where he sent his two sons), his efforts were motivated by a desire to establish a godly ministry. Jermyn's will (dated 12 April 1614) made provision for the poor of ten Suffolk parishes, reaffirmed legacies made to three Cambridge colleges, disposed of his extensive properties, and included a full and reformed confession of his faith. He was buried on 23 April 1614 in the parish church of Rushbrooke. His widow was buried on 30 October the same year.   JOHN CRAIG

Sources BL, Lansdowne 46, fol. 53*r* · BL, Lansdowne 57, fol. 108*r* · BL, Lansdowne 64, fol. 114*r* · BL, Lansdowne 75, fol. 148*r* · P. Collinson, 'The puritan classical movement in the reign of Elizabeth I', 2 vols., PhD diss., U. Lond., 1957 · J. Craig, *Reformation, politics and polemics: the growth of protestantism in East Anglian market towns, 1500–1610* (2001), chap. 4 · HoP, *Commons, 1558–1603*, 2.376–7 · S. H. A. Hervey, ed., *Rushbrook parish registers, 1567 to 1850: with Jermyn and Davers annals* (1903) · C. H. Hopwood, ed., *Middle Temple records*, 4 vols. (1904–5) · D. MacCulloch, 'Catholic and puritan in Elizabethan Suffolk', *Archiv für Reformationsgeschichte*, 72 (1981), 232–89 · D. MacCulloch, *Suffolk and the Tudors: politics and religion in an English county, 1500–1600* (1986) · J. J. Muskett, *Suffolk manorial families*, 3 vols. (1910) · will, PRO, PROB 11/123, sig. 56

Likenesses portrait; formerly in possession of Hugh Jermyn, 1903

Jermyn, Sir Thomas (*bap.* **1573**, *d.* **1644/5**), soldier and courtier, was baptized on 12 February 1573 at Rushbrooke, Suffolk, the eldest son of Sir Robert *Jermyn (1538/9–1614) of Rushbrooke Hall, a leading puritan and administrator in the county, and his wife, Judith (*d.* 1614), daughter of Sir George Blagg. Admitted a fellow-commoner at Emmanuel College, Cambridge, in 1585, he should not be confused with his cousin Thomas Jermyn (*d.* 1617) of Depden, MP for Sudbury in 1589.

In 1585 Jermyn's father joined the expedition to the Low Countries of Robert Dudley, earl of Leicester, and Jermyn himself became a military follower of Leicester's stepson Robert Devereux, second earl of Essex. In September 1591 he was one of twenty-four young men whom Essex knighted in the Rouen expedition. He was with Essex in his Cadiz expedition in 1596, in Ireland in early 1597, and around the Azores in the summer and autumn of 1597. In January 1599 he raised levies in Suffolk for Ireland, and he was in Connaught by April. Early in 1600 he married Catherine, daughter of Henry Killegrew of Hanworth, Middlesex, with whom he had one daughter and four sons, including Thomas Jermyn and Henry *Jermyn (later first earl of St Albans). After his marriage Sir Thomas lived in Hanworth, but the tragic accidental death of his daughter, Elizabeth, from eating a piece of bread baited with rat poison may have impelled his move from Hanworth after 1605.

Jermyn avoided involvement in Essex's abortive 1601 rising. In March 1604 he was returned MP for Andover; in 1614 he succeeded to Rushbrooke Hall and, with this new dignity, was elected MP for Suffolk. From January 1621 until the Long Parliament he was repeatedly returned MP for Bury St Edmunds. In 1616 he presented William Bedell as rector of Horringer, Suffolk, probably having known him as preacher of St Mary's, Bury St Edmunds; later he was the means of Bedell's promotion to an Irish bishopric. Court service now replaced his military career. In July 1616, on the embassy of James, Lord Hay (later first earl of Carlisle), in marriage negotiations between Princess Christina and Prince Charles, he suffered a serious accidental fall which left him in France for some months after the embassy. In 1623 he was deputy lieutenant in Cambridgeshire, and in 1625, a colonel of the Suffolk regiments defending the coasts. In July 1628 he became vice-chamberlain to Queen Henrietta Maria, and on 30 March 1629 he was unsuccessfully seeking the comptrollership of the household. On 22 December 1631 he became non-resident governor of Jersey, and through the 1630s he sat on several administrative commissions. In January 1639 he finally achieved his comptrollership of the king's household. His busyness in seeking profitable office suggests little sympathy for the austere ideals of 'thorough': a privy councillor throughout the decade, he had no scruples in gathering a clutch of reversions for his young sons Thomas and Henry, which inhibited the king's freedom of appointment in legal, financial, and administrative offices. The younger Thomas rose through various appointments to become in 1638 groom of the bedchamber to Prince Charles, and Henry became the queen's master of the horse.

The death of the lord lieutenant of Suffolk, Theophilus Howard, second earl of Suffolk, on 3 June 1640 brought Jermyn joint appointment as lord lieutenant with James Howard, the third earl; he succeeded in quelling troop unrest at Beccles and Bungay in July 1640, and during the summer was also appointed deputy lieutenant in Cornwall. In 1640 he surrendered his comptrollership to Sir Peter Wyche, reportedly for £2000 compensation. He was returned to the Long Parliament for Bury with his son Thomas; however, in 1642 the younger Thomas openly joined the king at Oxford while Henry fled abroad.

Jermyn showed his alarm at parliament's proceedings by retiring home, pleading ill health. Political anxieties may have been reinforced by domestic concerns. Following the death of his first wife, he had recently married again, on 17 March 1642; his second wife was Mary (*d.* 1679), daughter of Edmund Barber of Bury St Edmunds, Suffolk, and widow of Thomas Newton of Edgefield, Norfolk, with whom he was to have a son and a daughter. The House of Commons summoned him to attend in August, and in October Rushbrooke was searched for arms; in mid-November he was again summoned, accused of sending the king money and discouraging the Bury townsmen from contributing on the 'propositions' (making a notionally voluntary loan to parliament). After offering 100 marks on the propositions he was allowed to return home, but soon disabled from sitting. In January 1644, assessed at £1000, he pleaded for a mitigation; his lack of money may have been due to personal extravagance at court as much as to political troubles.

Jermyn, at home both on the battlefield and at court, may be seen as a curiously neat transitional figure between his austere and deeply religious father and his extrovertly cavalier sons; his friendship with Bedell suggests a mainstream protestant piety unaffected by the Laudian theological revolution.

Jermyn died, presumably at Rushbrooke, about the beginning of 1645; he was buried in Rushbrooke (where his monument remains) on 7 January 1645.

DIARMAID MACCULLOCH

Sources S. H. A. Hervey, ed., *Rushbrook parish registers, 1567 to 1850: with Jermyn and Davers annals* (1903) · J. J. Muskett, *Suffolk manorial families*, 3 vols. (1900–11), 2.243–58 · G. E. Aylmer, *The king's servants:*

the civil service of Charles I, 1625–1642 (1961) • HoP, *Commons, 1558–1603*

Jerne, Niels Kaj (1911–1994), immunologist, was born on 23 December 1911 at Brownswood Park Road, Stoke Newington, London, the fourth of five children of Hans Jessen Jerne (1877–1950), industrialist, and his wife, Else Marie, *née* Lindberg (1874–1956). His parents were Danish but had moved to London a year before his birth to start a celluloid factory. In 1914 they moved to the Netherlands where his father acquired a refrigerated storehouse in Rotterdam and later became reasonably wealthy.

After leaving Hoogere Burgerschool in 1928 with average grades Jerne (who remained a British subject throughout his life) was employed as a clerk in Elders and Fyffes banana company. The photographs and correspondence of his late adolescent years portray a medium built, good-looking and arrogant young man who immersed himself in romantic and modernist literature and was drawn to élitist ideas. From 1931 to 1933 he studied chemistry at the University of Leiden, but he failed to concentrate on the academic work.

In 1934 his father supported a renewed attempt at university education, now in medicine at Copenhagen. In May 1935, soon after his arrival in Denmark, Jerne married a Czech painter, Ilse Elisabeth Ernestine (Tjek) Wahl (1910–1945), and dropped out of university again. He did not resume his medical studies until 1939. In order to support his growing family (their two sons were born in 1936 and 1941) Jerne took a part-time position as a secretary in the department of standardization at Statens Seruminstitut in Copenhagen, one of the world's leading institutions for serology and vaccinology. There he discovered his aptitude for statistical analysis and mathematical thinking.

Tjek's suicide in the autumn of 1945 was a turning point in Jerne's life. He eventually succeeded in finishing his medical degree in 1947, married his former mistress, Adda Sundsig-Hansen the following year, and decided, after internship, to go into research. Using the reaction between diphtheria toxin and antitoxin in a rabbit skin assay system, Jerne made a quantitative measure of antibody avidity (binding strength); the dissertation was received by serologists as a masterpiece of conceptual clarity, statistical treatment, and experimental skill.

Stimulated by bacteriophage geneticists James D. Watson and Gunther Stent's visit in 1951–2, Jerne adopted a sensitive bacteriophage–antiphage system to study how antibody avidity increases during the early stages of immunization. After a couple of years of inconclusive experimentation, interrupted by an inspection tour for the World Health Organization (WHO) in Asia, he was struck, in the summer of 1954, by an experiment that apparently demonstrated the existence of preformed antibodies. Their existence was a highly disputed fact in serology, but Jerne was convinced; drawing on his self-understanding, that he had a repertory of states of mind which could be mobilized in interactions with other people, he formulated a new theory of the formation of antibodies in opposition to the instruction theories then

dominant. The natural selection theory of antibody formation could explain both the avidity increase and a number of other serological and immunological phenomena.

As a research fellow at the California Institute of Technology in 1954–5, Jerne worked out the details of the new theory. It was positively received by the Darwinistically inclined molecular biologists, but the immunologists were more lukewarm, and Jerne felt discouraged; he left his family and a permanent research position in Copenhagen in 1956 to work as head of biological standards at the WHO.

In Geneva, Jerne drew up international guidelines for the production of vaccines and sera, and in 1960 he was assigned the responsibility for organizing the WHO's immunology programme. In the meantime the selection theory had won the attention of a growing number of immunologists after Sir Frank Macfarlane Burnet formulated a cellular version of it (the clonal selection theory) in 1957. Jerne began to consider making a scientific comeback. The opportunity came in 1962 when the medical faculty at the University of Pittsburgh asked him to become professor and chairman of the department of microbiology.

Shortly after his arrival in Pittsburgh, Jerne utilized his bacteriophage research experiences to construct, with Albert Nordin, an innovative, simple, and powerful plaque assay for the quantification of antibody producing cells *in vitro*. Throughout the 1960s the selection theory acquired the status of a central dogma, and the plaque assay became one of the most frequently used methods in cellular immunology. Those were also the years when immunology was established internationally as an independent scientific discipline with its own departments and chairs; the number of immunological journals, textbooks, and societies proliferated. Jerne's star rose and his reputation as the leading theoretician in immunology was cemented at the Cold Spring Harbor symposium in 1967 where his final report, 'Waiting for the end', was regarded as a brilliant summary of the state of the discipline.

Jerne received offers from Harvard and Copenhagen, but chose—partly for financial, partly for nostalgic reasons—to take up a position as director of the venerable Paul Ehrlich Institut in Frankfurt am Main in 1966. His goal was to build up a European counterpart to the strong American domination in the field, but he was increasingly frustrated by German bureaucracy; so when the multinational pharmaceutical company Hoffman-La Roche asked him in 1968 to become director of a new institute for immunological research in Basel, Switzerland, he quickly accepted. His ideal was to build a non-hierarchical institute based on the idea of a communicative network.

During the planning period Jerne was constantly working on the problem of the generation of antibody diversity, and in the summer of 1969 he came up with a possible solution (the somatic generation theory) which assigned the thymus a central role both as a breeder of mutant, specific lymphocytes and as a generator of self-tolerance. The theory was contested by many immunologists but partly confirmed by Susumu Tonegawa in the mid-1970s.

Basel Institut für Immunologie was opened in 1971 with a staff of 150. Jerne had a knack of selecting talented young immunologists and, in the course of the 1970s, it became the leading immunological research institute in the world, housing, among others, three future Nobel laureates (Jerne, Tonegawa, and Georges Köhler). Jerne spent most of his time in perpetual discussions and allegedly never visited the laboratories, because, as he once said, 'the reality would confuse me' (Söderqvist, 269). His own theoretical work centred around the problem of the regulation of the immune system; in 1973 he came up with a theory of the immune system in which all anti-bodies and lymphocyte receptors were conceived as mutually independent parts of a steady state system. The idiotypic network theory is still a matter of dispute among immunologists.

After his retirement in 1980 Jerne withdrew to his country home near Castillon-du-Gard, Languedoc, France, together with his third wife, Ursula (Alexandra) Kohl (b. 1936), whom he had married in 1964. He continued to develop his ideas about the immune system as a cybernetic network; he became increasingly fascinated by semiotics and the analogies between linguistics and immunology. He received a multitude of honorary degrees and prizes, including the Nobel prize for physiology or medicine in 1984. He had been elected a fellow of the Royal Society in 1980.

Jerne loved to fashion himself as a European bohemian intellectual; he frequented shabby bars and expensive restaurants and engaged in conversations about language, art, and philosophy, particularly about Kierkegaard. He never felt exclusive ties to any single nation, and often described himself as a citizen of the North Sea: Denmark provided his family roots, Dutch was the language in which he was most fluent, and England represented his cultural preferences and political sympathies. He remained an Anglophile throughout his life, and returned to England as often as he could. (At one point he intended to buy a *pied-à-terre* in Soho, but he was put off by the discovery that his British birth would render him liable for UK income tax.) He could be friendly and listen for hours, but he was also extremely precise in his remarks: Burnet called Jerne 'one of the most intelligent biologists of this century' (Söderqvist, xvi). Despite a lifetime of heavy smoking and an increasing alcohol consumption, he was not afflicted by any serious illness until the very last years. He died on 7 October 1994 in his country home, the Château de Bellevue, and was buried three days later in nearby Castillon-du-Gard.   THOMAS SÖDERQVIST

Sources T. Söderqvist, *Science as autobiography: the troubled life of Niels Jerne* (2003) • Kongelige Bibliotek, Copenhagen, Jerne MSS, Utilg 811, 1992/84 • B. A. Askonas and J. G. Howard, *Memoirs FRS*, 43 (1997), 237–49 • *The Times* (10 Nov 1994) • *The Independent* (3 Nov 1994) • WWW • m. cert. [I. Wahl] • private information (2004) • personal knowledge (2004)
Archives Kongelige Bibliotek, Copenhagen, MSS, Utilg 811, 1992/84 | SOUND priv. coll., interview recordings [Thomas Söderqvist, Copenhagen]

Likenesses photograph, repro. in *The Times* • photograph, repro. in *The Independent* • photographs, repro. in Askonas and Howard, *Memoirs FRS* • portraits, repro. in Söderqvist, *Science as autobiography*

Jerningham, Edward (1737–1812), poet and playwright, was born at Costessey Hall, Norfolk, the third and youngest son of Sir George Jerningham, fifth baronet (1680–1774), and his wife, Mary (d. 1785), daughter of Francis Plowden, of Plowden, Shropshire, who had been comptroller of the household of James II. The Jerninghams, long-established Norfolk Catholic gentry with a history of church and army service, enjoyed access to royal circles in both England and France. During the French Revolutionary period they welcomed exiled aristocrats to Norwich and London, supported their favourite order of Blue Nuns, and were active in subsequent campaigns for Catholic emancipation.

Jerningham stayed with his parents until the age of ten, living at Costessey and at Cambrai in northern France. He was educated in theology and the humanities at Douai College, arriving on 14 July 1748 and remaining there until 1755. He completed his education as a boarder at St Gregory's College in Paris until October 1757. Strict religious training and European culture had formative if ambiguous results: 'the French and Italian languages [and literatures] ... were nearly as familiar to him as that of his native country' (GM, 1813, 283). But Jerningham reacted against his devout background by becoming a youthful enthusiast for Voltaire and Rousseau, an artistic dilettante and profligate man of fashion, and in the 1790s converted to Anglicanism, much to his family's distress. Nevertheless, he lived with or nearby his family and was financially supported by them throughout his life. His father died in his nineties on 21 January 1774, and Jerningham then looked after his mother in London until her death on 23 September 1785. Thereafter he lived in a modest house at 26 Green Street, off Grosvenor Square, described in 1809 by his niece Lady Charlotte Bedingfield (1771–1854) as 'dirty, but well-filled with Books, & [it] contains some interesting pictures & drawings' (*Jerningham Letters*, 1.340).

Jerningham began as an exquisitely affected poet, who also played the harp, sang, and took part in amateur dramatics at the country or town houses of his friends. These included many among the fashionable whig aristocracy: the Harcourts of Nuneham Courtenay, Oxfordshire; Lord and Lady Mount Edgcumbe; the Jerseys of Middleton Park; and in particular 'his Maecenas', Frederick Howard, fifth Lord Carlisle, of Castle Howard. The latter relationship was noted by the young Byron in an amusing postscript to 'English bards and Scotch reviewers' (1809); he recalled Jerningham's personal kindness to him: 'whatever he may say or do, "pour on, I will endure"' (Lord Byron, *The Complete Poetical Works*, ed. J. J. McGann, 1980, 1.264). Jerningham was in his element at genteel literary gatherings: the London salons of Mrs Montagu, Mrs Vesey, and later Samuel Rogers's house. He also frequented Lady Miller's circle at Bath Easton Villa, where he met admirers such as Anna Seward, Hannah More, and Robert Merry ('Della

Crusca'). The more sceptical novelist Fanny Burney, in Bath during April 1780, observed him, even in middle age, as 'a mighty delicate gentleman; looks to be painted, and [he] is all daintification in manner, speech, and dress … (whom Lord Mulgrave calls a pink-and-white poet, for not only his cheeks but his coat is pink)' (Bettany, 8). His gossiping high-flown wit made him a much sought-after theatre companion for dowager socialites as well as, from the late 1780s onwards, the prince of Wales. Jerningham was especially appreciative of the opera: 'it is everyday company, the place of Intelligence and the best Assembly in Town. The Prince continues to favour me with his Ticket which saves me a good many half-guineas!' (letter to Lady Bedingfield, 18 June 1806, *Jerningham Letters*, 1.275).

As an habitué of the London theatre world and observer of the political theatre of parliament, Jerningham was well acquainted with R. B. Sheridan. Indeed, the foppish poet Sir Benjamin Backbite in *The School for Scandal* (1777), caricaturing the Devonshire House set, is likely to have been based on Jerningham, just as scheming Lady Sneerwell was modelled on his friend Frances Villiers, Lady Jersey. She later became the prince's favourite mistress during the mid-1790s; Jerningham had also known the Catholic Mrs Fitzherbert, as well as the actress and poet Mary (Perdita) Robinson. Lady Jersey's correspondence with Jerningham shows that he was used as their go-between, especially when his royal patron wished to end the relationship (Bettany, 229–55). Jerningham's own plays were 'historical interludes', short-lived and unsuccessful with critics and audiences alike. *Margaret of Anjou*, a tragedy, with Elizabeth Younge (Mrs Pope) in the title role, ran in tandem with Sheridan's comedy *The Rivals* at Drury Lane from 11 March 1777. His *The Siege of Berwick* ran at Covent Garden for five nights from 13 November 1793 before the illness of its star, Mrs Pope, closed the play. It was chiefly remarkable because 'on the first night the heroine died, but on the succeeding representations her life was spared' (*DNB*). Lord Harcourt urged Jerningham to try comedy, 'for … with your knowledge of character, and a fund of humour as inexhaustible as it is peculiar and original, you should … write such a play as would delight the town, [and] fill your purse with gold' (Bettany, 98). *The Welch Heiress* lasted for only one night, 17 April 1795, even with the leading comic actress Mrs Jordan in the role of Miss Plinlimmon. He also wrote *The Peckham Frolic: or Nell Gwyn* (1799), a comedy in three acts, never performed professionally.

As a poet Jerningham's role models were the early romantics Thomas Gray, William Mason, and especially Horace Walpole whom he first met in Paris during late 1765, a lifelong mentor. His initial works were, however, far more flimsy and sentimentally effusive, their typical subjects being mistreated women, suicidal lovers, and doomed passion within cloisters, as in 'The Nunnery: in Imitation of Mr Gray's Elegy' (1762) and 'The Funeral of Arabert, Monk of La Trappe' (1771). The first collected edition, *Poems by Mr Jerningham* (1774), while formally derivative and portentously high-flown, also exhibited his range from the 'occasional' ode to gothic horror and humour: 'Il

latte', for instance, exhorted fashionable ladies to consider the patriotic benefits of breastfeeding their child, 'unblam'd inebriate at that healthful spring' (*Poems by Jerningham*, 55). Yet even his friends tended to patronize him. Mason, on receiving the lachrymose 'Faldoni and Teresa' (1773), sent a sarcastic *jeu d'esprit* to Lord Harcourt (E. W. Harcourt, ed., *The Harcourt Papers*, 1890, 7.43–5), and Walpole praised 'The rise and progress of Scandinavian poetry' (1784) as 'not like his uniform turtle-ditties' (Walpole, *Corr.*, 29.331). Walpole's personal affection for 'the charming man' was undoubted, while admitting to Mary Berry that 'in truth he has no genius: there is no novelty … in his poetry, though many of the lines are pretty' (26 February 1791, ibid., 11.211).

However much he was satirized by hostile poet-critics such as William Gifford (in 'The Baviad', 1791) and T. J. Mathias (in 'The pursuits of literature', 1794), Jerningham was not without influence or contemporary admirers of his works. His feverishly sentimental style certainly encouraged the 'Della Cruscans', the last flowering before authentic Romantic poetry. He contributed poems to *The World* newspaper during 1788 and, as 'The Bard' to their anthologies, notably the *British Album* (1790). Among his later poems are 'The Ancient English Wake', in which a cross-dressing female crusader returns to her home village; 'The Shakspeare Gallery' (1791), celebrating John Boydell's enterprise, and 'Peace, Ignominy and Destruction' (1796), ironically dedicated to Charles James Fox. Its reviewer, John Aiken, commented: 'The burden of the song is the sacrilegious barbarity of France. The picture which the poet draws is darkened with every shade of horror that fancy, aided by passion, could paint' (*Monthly Review*, 22, 1797, 343–4). His final poem, 'The Old Bard's Farewell' (1811), reflected with tranquil melancholy upon his life, and his conversion to the established church, ending by urging the bishops 'to perfect with a gradual hand' the Reformation and efface 'Each ling'ring semblance of the elder style' (*GM*, 1811, 256). He bequeathed unpublished manuscripts to William Clarke, his bookseller of New Bond Street, but his works have been out of print and largely forgotten since his death.

Jerningham was a link from the artistic generation of Gray, Mason, and Walpole to that of Sheridan, Coleridge, and Byron. He also knew, and shrewdly described in his highly entertaining correspondence, a myriad of the political and high society figures of his day. Indeed, his best poetic conceits and flights of fancy went into his 'chit-chat gazettes' rather than his poetry and dramas, much of which must be regarded as delightful nonsense. And, by a nice irony, his activities as a trusted go-between for the prince of Wales and his mistresses continued the Jerningham tradition of royal service. Jerningham was unmarried, despite habitual flirtations with young actresses, and died at home in London after months of illness on 17 November 1812.   JULES SMITH

Sources *Poems and plays by Mr Jerningham*, 4 vols. (1806) · L. Bettany, ed., *Edward Jerningham and his friends: a series of eighteenth century letters* (1919) · *The Jerningham letters, 1780–1843*, ed. E. Castle, 2 vols. (1896) · P. R. Harris, ed., *Douai College documents, 1639–1794*,

Catholic RS, 63 (1972) · *GM*, 1st ser., 83/1 (1813), 283 · Walpole, *Corr.*, vols. 11–12, 29 · *The British album: poems of Della Crusca*, 3rd edn (1790) · *Poems by Jerningham* (1774) · *The diary of Mrs Hester Lynch Thrale, 1776–1809, Thaliana*, ed. K. C. Balderston, vol. 1 (1942) · W. N. Hargreaves-Mawdsley, *The English Della Cruscans and their time, 1783–1828* (The Hague, 1967) · *Letters of Anna Seward: written between the years 1784 and 1807*, ed. A. Constable, 4 (1811) · P. W. Clayden, *The early life of Samuel Rogers* (1887) · *GM*, 1st ser., 81/1 (1811), 256

Archives Hunt. L., corresp. · Norfolk RO, journal of a tour, MS 365 · Staffs. RO, letters, notes, verses, D. 641/3/P/3/9/17–19, 72–97 | Bodl. Oxf., MS Montagu, d. 3, fols. 14–27 · Staffs. RO, letters to Frances, Lady Stafford · U. Birm. L., letters, mainly to Charlotte Jerningham

Likenesses attrib. A. Plimer, miniature, V&A · W. Ridley, stipple (after S. Drummond), BM, NPG; repro. in *Monthly Mirror* (1800) · P. Thomson, line engraving (after M. A. Shee), BM, NPG; repro. in *European Magazine*, 25 (Jan–June 1794), 411–12 · portrait, repro. in H. E. H. Jerningham, ed., *The siege of Berwick* (1882) · portraits, NPG; repro. in Bettany, ed., *Edward Jerningham*, frontispiece, 28

Wealth at death from wealthy family; house 'well filled with books and contains some interesting pictures and drawings': *Jerningham letters*, ed. Castle, journal, 1809

Jerningham [Jernegan], **Sir Henry** (1509/10–1572), courtier and administrator, was the son of Edward Jernegan of Somerleyton, Suffolk, and his wife, Mary, the daughter of Richard Scrope. Both his parents served in Katherine of Aragon's household, and his mother's second marriage, to Sir William Kingston, which took place before 1534 ensured Jerningham's career at court. About 1528 he entered the service of Princess Mary as a sewer, while by 1536 Kingston had arranged his stepson's marriage to his own granddaughter Frances, daughter of Sir George Baynham of Clearwell, Gloucestershire. As a gentleman pensioner after 1540 he was present at the major state occasions and participated in Henry VIII's French campaign of 1544. In 1547 he obtained the Norfolk manor of Costessey. Little is known about his activities during Edward VI's reign other than his continued connection with Mary's household, but that he became her trusted adviser is demonstrated by the critical role he played during the 1553 succession crisis. He helped to plot her escape to the East Anglian coast, obtained the surrender of five government ships laden with men and arms, and raised troops in the Yarmouth area.

Described by Wingfield as 'a vigorous, modest and noble man' (MacCulloch, 252), by 20 July 1553 Jerningham had been selected by Mary for positions of greater responsibility as a privy counsellor, vice-chamberlain, and captain of the guard, while his wife served as one of the queen's gentlewomen. At the coronation he was made a knight of the Bath. Mary further rewarded the Jerninghams with substantial grants of land. As captain of the guard Jerningham saw action during Thomas Wyatt's rebellion; he had to retreat from Rochester, but his later successful engagement with Wyatt's forces at Charing Cross contributed to the collapse of the rebellion. He later sat on the jury that condemned Wyatt, and in 1556 he served on the commission to investigate Dudley's conspiracy. He was knight of the shire for Suffolk in Mary's first four parliaments and for Gloucestershire in her last. An active member of the council, at first he sided with the more conservative members led by Stephen Gardiner, but in the later years of the

reign his political alignments were less predictable. Nevertheless in December 1557 Mary made Jerningham master of the horse with an annuity of £300. As a member of the 1558 'council of war' he was actively engaged in the conflict with France; he expressed concern about England's defences, and in the summer of 1558 prepared Kent for invasion. By that time he had emerged as one of the queen's most influential advisers. The Spanish king's agent Feria considered Jerningham one of the councillors best suited to consult about plans to recapture Calais, and when Mary made arrangements for the use of her signet in October 1558, he was one of the councillors who had to be present when documents were stamped. She also appointed him one of the six assistant executors of her will.

Elizabeth I dismissed Jerningham from office at her accession, and his name disappears from official records after 1559, when he received a general pardon. He retired to Costessey, where in spite of their persistent recusancy his descendants flourished for centuries, in 1824 succeeding to the barony of Stafford. Sir Henry died at Costessey on 6 September 1572, aged sixty-three, and was buried on the 30th in the parish church. As well as containing bequests to members of his family, his will provided for London prisoners and for almshouses founded from his lands in Herringfleet. Among the supervisors were two kinsmen who had been fellow councillors to Queen Mary, Sir Henry Bedingfeld, and Sir Thomas Cornwallis.

ANN WEIKEL

Sources D. MacCulloch, 'The *Vita Mariae Angliae Reginae* of Robert Wingfield of Brantham', *Camden miscellany, XXVIII*, CS, 4th ser., 29 (1984), 181–301 · D. E. Hoak, 'Two revolutions in Tudor government: the formation and organization of Mary I's privy council', *Revolution reassessed: revisions in the history of Tudor government and administration*, ed. C. Coleman and D. Starkey (1986) · J. D. Alsop, 'A regime at sea: the navy and the 1553 succession crisis', *Albion*, 24 (1992), 577–90 · HoP, *Commons, 1509–58*, 2.443–4 · M. St C. Byrne, ed., *The Lisle letters*, 6 vols. (1981), vol. 2, p. 56; vol. 4, pp. 111–12, 119–20; vol. 5, pp. 716–17 · D. M. Loades, *Two Tudor conspiracies* (1965), 59, 61–2, 176 · *LP Henry VIII*, 14/2, no. 783; 15, no. 14(5); also vols. 13, 16, 18–21 · D. Loades, *Mary Tudor: a life* (1989), 41, 177–8, 190–2, 206, 355, 379 · *CSP Spain, 1553–8* · *CPR, 1547–58* · *DNB* · D. Loades, *The reign of Mary Tudor: politics, government and religion in England, 1553–58*, 2nd edn (1991), 208, 319, 324, 332, 388 · PRO, prerogative court of Canterbury, wills, PROB 11/55, fols. 134–136v · BL, Royal App. MS 89 · BL, Harley MS 897

Archives BL, Harley MS 897, fol. 48; 6949, fol. 39 · Norfolk RO, 55x1 12090/38–44; 55x2; T176 A–C/13 · PRO, SP11/2

Jerningham, Sir Richard (d. 1525), soldier and diplomat, was the second son of Sir John Jerningham (d. 1503) of Somerleyton, Suffolk, and Isabel, daughter and heir of Sir Gervase Clifton. The family was certainly of ancient lineage and its genealogy can be traced back to the beginning of the thirteenth century to a Suffolk knight, Robert fitz Jernegan.

Jerningham's service to Henry VIII began in October 1509, when he was chosen to be a gentleman of the king's chamber with an annuity of £20. In January 1511 he undertook the first of a series of missions, intended to acquire large quantities of armour from Germany and Italy. Over the next two years his travels took him to Milan, Brussels, Innsbruck, and Venice, where he was granted audiences with Massimiliano Sforza, Charles, archduke of Burgundy, and Maximilian, king of the Romans. By July 1513 he was back in England and ready to accompany the king on his expedition against France. Although nothing is known of his actions in this first war he presumably acquitted himself with honour, since he was one of those knighted by Henry in Tournai Cathedral on 25 September 1513.

For much of the next five years Jerningham remained in Tournai. In February 1515 he was appointed marshal, and two months later was promoted to treasurer. Finally, in January 1517, he replaced William Blount, Lord Mountjoy, as the city's deputy. In November 1518 Henry agreed to return Tournai to the French and three months later, on 8 February 1519, Jerningham surrendered the city's keys to Marshal Châtillon and returned to England. Shortly afterwards he was chosen by Wolsey to be one of the 'foure sad and auncient knightes' (*Hall's Chronicle*, 576) who composed the newly reorganized and far more prestigious privy chamber established in October 1518. No doubt partly a reward for their services to the king, the appointment of Jerningham and his colleagues to the privy chamber may also have represented a desire on Wolsey's part to distance Henry VIII from the influence of the younger courtiers who had previously served as his personal attendants. It was as a gentleman of the privy chamber that Jerningham attended Henry at the Field of Cloth of Gold and at Gravelines in July 1520.

The remaining five years of Jerningham's life were dominated by war and diplomacy. Altogether he performed four embassies, and in all of them drew upon the experience provided by the various facets of his earlier career. Between August 1520 and February 1521 he served as resident ambassador at the French court, to which he returned three months later as a special envoy, remaining there until July. The main aim of his first embassy was to convince François I that Henry VIII had not abandoned either his position of neutrality or his friendship for France. The object of his second mission was to persuade the French king to accept Henry's mediation in his escalating struggle with the emperor. On both occasions Jerningham's status as a gentleman of Henry's privy chamber made his task considerably easier. In deference to his office François invited the ambassador to his own privy chamber morning and night, and often included him in his frequent hunting trips.

Jerningham's ambassadorial duties were interrupted when hostilities between England and France broke out again in May 1522. Appointed treasurer of the wars beyond the sea, he also took an active part in the earl of Surrey's invasion of Picardy and was present at the abortive siege of Hesdin. But in June 1523 he was once more sent on embassy, this time to Spain, where, in tandem with Henry's resident envoy, Richard Sampson, he represented the king at the imperial court until May 1524. The object of this embassy was military, to observe Charles V's preparations for war against France, and if necessary to urge him on to greater efforts. It was with this mission in mind that he accompanied the imperial army on its invasion of Guyenne in December 1523. Finally, in August 1524, Jerningham performed a brief embassy to the Low Countries, again concerned with observing Habsburg preparations for an attack on France later that year. In November he returned to England, and died there in February or March of the following year. LUKE MACMAHON

Sources LP Henry VIII, vols. 1–4 • A. I. Suckling, *The history and antiquities of the county of Suffolk*, 2 vols. (1846–8) • *Hall's chronicle*, ed. H. Ellis (1809) • C. G. Cruickshank, *The English occupation of Tournai* (1971) • W. Bradford, ed., *Correspondence of the emperor Charles V* (1850) • J. G. Nichols, ed., *The chronicle of Calais*, CS, 35 (1846) • J. G. Russell, *Peacemaking in the Renaissance* (1986) • CSP Spain, 1509–25 • D. Starkey, *The reign of Henry VIII: personalities and politics* (1985)

Jerome, Jerome Klapka (1859–1927), novelist and playwright, was born on 2 May 1859 at Bradford Street, Walsall, Staffordshire, the fourth child and younger son of Jerome Clapp Jerome (1807–1872), nonconformist lay preacher and Staffordshire coalmine owner, and Marguerite Jones (d. 1874), daughter of a Swansea solicitor. His father was of puritan background and had trained as an architect; his mother came from a nonconformist family and had some financial assets. After the failure of the colliery the family followed Jerome senior to London, where he became an ironmonger. Jerome's first school was the Philological School (later Marylebone grammar school). After his father's death Jerome, aged fourteen, left school and worked as a clerk with the London and North Western Railway. His mother died two years later. Jerome joined an acting company part-time, then full-time. He then turned to journalism, teaching, and secretarial work before finally settling on a literary career.

Jerome's experiences as an actor led to his first book, *On the Stage—and Off* (1885), humorous sketches of theatrical life; *Barbara*, the first of many plays, was produced in June 1886. This was quickly followed by a collection of essays entitled *The Idle Thoughts of an Idle Fellow* (1886). Jerome's reputation as a humorist was firmly established with the publication of the classic *Three Men in a Boat* (1889), subtitled (*to say nothing of the dog*), which depicts a series of comic episodes on a riverboat trip up the Thames. It has been translated into many languages and filmed three times, with a television production in 1979. Its combination of light-hearted satire, sharp dialogue, and slapstick has made it perennially popular, and it is the book for which Jerome is remembered.

Jerome married Georgina Elizabeth Henrietta Stanley Marris (1859–1938), daughter of George Nesza, on 21 June 1888, nine days after her divorce from her first husband. She had a five-year-old daughter, Georgina, known as Elsie (d. 1921). A daughter, Rowena, was born in 1897.

Jerome co-edited *The Idler*, an illustrated monthly founded by Robert Barr in 1892. As editor he published, among others, Mark Twain, R. L. Stevenson, Marie Corelli,

Jerome Klapka Jerome (1859–1927), by Solomon Joseph Solomon, c.1889

Arthur Conan Doyle, and Rudyard Kipling, as well as new writers such as Eden Phillpotts and W. W. Jacobs. After a disagreement with Barr, Jerome became sole editor from August 1895 to November 1897. In 1893 he founded the weekly *To-Day* and added to his contributors the writers Richard Le Gallienne and George Gissing, and the illustrators Aubrey Beardsley and Phil May. His forthright journalism led to a libel action in 1897 which he lost with costs of £9000, and this forced him to sell his interest in both magazines.

A two-year stay in Germany in 1898–9 resulted in *Three Men on the Bummel* (1900), an unsuccessful sequel to *Three Men in a Boat*, in which the same characters, minus the dog, go on a cycling tour through the Black Forest. In 1902 he published the autobiographical novel *Paul Kelver*, which he considered his best work. Jerome visited Germany, Norway, and Russia and made a successful lecture tour of America, where his books had been well received, in 1908, followed by a second visit in 1914. Despite his work in comic genres Jerome wished to be considered as a serious writer and in his play *The Passing of the Third Floor Back* (1908), adapted from one of his short stories, he adopted a moral tone which initially alienated the public, although the play went on to become a success.

During the First World War Jerome served as ambulance driver in the French army (being too old for the British army), and recorded his experiences in his autobiography *My Life and Times* (1926), a book which shows him at his idiosyncratic best. His works reveal that, although in private life he had a melancholy outlook, he could see and appreciate the humour of life. Jerome was made a freeman of Walsall on 17 February 1927, and died on 14 June 1927 in Northampton General Hospital after a series of strokes. He was cremated at Golders Green, Middlesex, on 17 June and buried at St Mary's Church, Ewelme, Oxfordshire. His wife died on 29 October 1938, aged seventy-eight, and was buried beside him.

DAMIAN ATKINSON

Sources J. Connolly, *Jerome K. Jerome: a critical biography* (1982) · J. K. Jerome, *My life and times* (1992) · R. M. Faurot, *Jerome K. Jerome* (1974) · R. M. Faurot, 'Jerome K. Jerome', *Modern British dramatists, 1900–1945*, ed. S. Weintraub, DLitB, 10 (1982); T. F. Stanley, *British novelists, 1890–1929: traditionalists*, DLitB, 34 (1985) · L. Baker, 'Jerome K. Jerome', *British short-fiction writers, 1880–1914: the realist tradition*, ed. W. B. Thesing, DLitB, 135 (1994) · A. Moss, *Jerome K. Jerome: his life and work* (1928) · C. Markgraf, 'Jerome K. Jerome: annotated bibliography of writing about him', *English Literature in Transition, 1880–1920*, 26 (1983), 83–132 · C. Markgraf, 'Jerome K. Jerome: update of an annotated bibliography of writings about him', *English Literature in Transition, 1880–1920*, 30 (1987), 180–211 · C. Markgraf and R. Wiebe, 'Jerome K. Jerome: update of an annotated bibliography of writings about him [pt 2]', *English Literature in Transition, 1880–1920*, 31 (1988), 64–76 · E. Kilmurray, *Dictionary of British portraiture*, 3 (1981) · J. Shattock, ed., *The Cambridge bibliography of English literature*, 3rd edn, 4 (1999) · m. cert. · d. cert. [Georgina Henrietta Elizabeth Stanley Jerome] · DNB · *The Times* (15 June 1927), 18

Archives Birm. CL, letters · BL, corresp. with Society of Authors, Add. MS 56733 · Jerome K. Jerome Birthplace Museum, Walsall · Walsall Central Library | HLRO, letters to H. L. Samuel · Richmond Local Studies Library, London, corresp. with Douglas Sladen · U. Leeds, Brotherton L., Clodd MSS · U. Leeds, Brotherton L., letters to Clement Shorter · U. Leeds, Brotherton L., letters mainly to Bram Stoker

Likenesses S. J. Solomon, oils, c.1889, NPG [*see illus.*] · W. & D. Downey, woodburytype, 1893, NPG; repro. in *The cabinet portrait gallery*, 4 (1893) · Bassano, photographs, 1897, NPG · P. A. de Laszlo, oils, 1921, NPG · J. Russell & Sons, photograph, NPG · H. Wrightson, photograph, NPG · photograph, NPG · photographs, repro. in Jerome, *My life and times* · photographs, repro. in DLitB, vols. 10 (1982), 34 (1985), 135 (1994)

Wealth at death £5478 16s. 11d.: probate, 27 Aug 1927, CGPLA Eng. & Wales

Jerome [Hierome]**, Stephen** (*fl.* 1604–1650), writer and Church of England clergyman, was of unknown parentage, but may have come from Yorkshire. He was educated at St John's College, Cambridge, where he had graduated BA by 1604 and proceeded MA in 1607. He was ordained deacon at York, and priest in 1609. By 1612 he was a lecturer in St Bride's Church, Fleet Street, London, writing a number of popular devotional works which went into several editions. In 1619, after a brief appointment to the parish of Hutton Buscell in Yorkshire, he moved to Newcastle, where he was lecturer at St Nicholas's until 1622, by which time he had married Katherine (*d.* 1627). His theological views and his association with godly clergy marked him out as a rising young puritan preacher, but his career was interrupted in 1622 by a scandal which forced him to leave in disgrace. Caught *in flagrante* with the wife of one of his parishioners—being 'deprehended by her husband and by another with his points uncuffed etc. and ready for the wicked act, in her house'—he then frustrated efforts to hush up the scandal by returning to try to seduce the woman another four or five times, 'besides', as the local puritan minister, Robert Jenison, put it, 'shrewd presumptions of fouler matters with his own maid-servants' (Jenison, 29 March 1622).

Like many other errant English clerics Jerome fled to Ireland, arriving with Thomas, first Viscount Beaumont of Swords when he came to celebrate the wedding of his son to the earl of Cork's daughter in 1622. Jerome attached himself to the earl of Cork, first as tutor to one of his sons, and then as his chaplain, before being made minister of the parish of Tallow in co. Waterford. It was to the 'sovereign' (mayor) of Tallow that he dedicated his most original work, *Ireland's Jubilee* (1624), a godly celebration of the failure of Prince Charles's Spanish marriage plans, which also gives a rare insight into the religious and racial outlook of an early seventeenth-century English settler in Ireland. He sees the 'Britannical Hibernians' as Israelites in a heathen land, a conceit he then uses to attack both their lukewarmness and backsliding, and the antichristian popery of the native population.

In 1625 Jerome left Ireland and tried his luck once more in England, being established as minister at Nantwich in Cheshire by 1626, where his wife Katherine died. There again he was the subject of further, and all too believable, allegations of sexual harassment and attempted rape by his maidservant, Margaret Knowsley. But faced with her 'bare affirming against Mr Jerome's denying', the differences in gender and social class of the two main figures, and complex local religious and political cross-currents, the authorities opted to uphold Jerome's version, and had Knowsley publicly whipped for slander (Hindle, 399).

Again Jerome sought refuge in Ireland, turning to the earl of Cork for help in 'muzzling that infernal Cerberus malice' and protecting him from 'the envenomed fangs of envious detraction which ... haunt ... me in both kingdoms', and launching a public attack in 1628 upon those reprobates who slander godly preachers as puritans and 'vile hypocrites' (Jerome, *Haughty*, sig. A2). Again he secured preferment, preaching before the lords justices in Dublin in 1631 and being appointed minister of St Brigid's in Dublin. At the outbreak of the 1641 rising he was minister at Athy, co. Kildare, writing a vivid account of the cruelties of the Irish rebels, *Treason in Ireland* (1641). Though captured by the Catholic forces he found shelter in Dublin, where he instructed parishioners and soldiers in St Patrick's Cathedral. But he was soon in trouble, this time for a strongly anti-royalist sermon preached at Christ Church, Dublin, on 13 November 1642. Jerome claimed that King Charles was 'blinded by lust' through his marriage to a Catholic 'Jezebel's daughter'. He further displayed his parliamentarian credentials by claiming that the 'roaring Cavaliers of England' and the Catholic Irish rebels were 'birds of a feather', and warning that kings who broke their covenants with the people would be punished (Bodl. Oxf., MS Carte fols. 60r–64r). Not surprisingly the king complained about the seditious sermons of the mischievous brood of factious preachers in Ireland. No record of whether Jerome was punished survives.

No details of the death of this paradoxical puritan have been discovered: the last sighting of Jerome is at Greenwich in 1650, when he published (under the surname Hierome) *A Minister's Mite*, a pedagogical work explaining how to improve and stock one's memory. Here he mixes high-minded lists of books—his recommended reading in divinity (Calvin, Polanus, Zanchius, and Perkin's and 'Ussher's' catechisms) amply confirms his double predestinarian Calvinism—with more practical advice on mental hygiene, such as 'the speedy expulsion of all excrements from the brain by the nose' and the avoiding of 'cold and moist cucumbers' (Jerome, *Minister's* 21, 24).

THOMAS SECCOMBE, *rev.* ALAN FORD

Sources S. Jerome, *Ireland's jubilee* (1624) · S. Jerome, *The haughty heart humbled* (1628) · S. Hindle, 'The shaming of Margaret Knowsley: gossip, gender and the experience of authority in early modern England', *Continuity and Change*, 9 (1994), 391–419 · A. Ford, *The protestant Reformation in Ireland, 1590–1641*, 2nd edn (1997), 168–78 · S. Hierome [S. Jerome], *A minister's mite* (1650) · S. Jerome, *Treason in Ireland* (1641) · R. Jenison, letter to S. Ward, 29 March 1622, Bodl. Oxf., MS Tanner 73, fol. 136 · Bodl. Oxf., MS Carte, fols. 37r, 40r, 44r, 50r, 52r, 60r–64r, 85r, 114r, 118r · S. Jerome, *A serious fore-warning to avoid the vengence to come ... together with S. Bernard's holy meditations* (1613) · S. Jerome, *Moses his sight of Canaan* (1613) · S. Jerome, *The soul's sentinel ringing an alarm against impietie and impenitency* (1631) · S. Jerome, *Seven helps to heaven* (1614) · S. Jerome, *The arraignment of the whole creature* (1631) · S. Jerome, *Origen's repentance* (1619) · Venn, *Alum. Cant.*

Jerram, Charles (1770–1853), Church of England clergyman, born on 17 January 1770 in the parish of Blidworth in Sherwood Forest, Nottinghamshire, was the second of five sons of Charles Jerram (c.1732–1807), a member of an old but impoverished Derbyshire family, who farmed his own freehold land. His mother, Mary (c.1747–1812), a devout woman from a Presbyterian family, was the daughter of William Knutton, a farmer of the same parish. From his childhood she planned that Charles should enter the ministry. He was educated by the Revd Thomas Cursham, the curate of Blidworth, a man of strong evangelical views, whom he accompanied in his successive moves, first as pupil and subsequently as assistant teacher. About 1790 Jerram became assistant at a Unitarian school at Highgate, Middlesex. From Dr Alexander Crombie, one of the principals there, Jerram received much assistance in his classical studies, but his attendance at the sermons of the Revd Richard Cecil prevented him from adopting Crombie's religious opinions. Cursham recommended him to the Elland Society, established in Yorkshire to fund needy candidates for holy orders. He was thus enabled in 1793 to enter Magdalene College, Cambridge, where he attended the ministry of the Revd Charles Simeon, the great evangelical leader, and helped to form various evangelical undergraduate societies. He won the Norrisian prize in 1796, graduated BA in 1797 as last wrangler, and proceeded MA in 1800.

In 1797 Jerram took holy orders and served his first curacy in Long Sutton, Lincolnshire. Just over a year after his arrival he married in April 1798 Mary Anne, the younger daughter of James Stanger, a yeoman of Tydd St Mary. The parish of Long Sutton had suffered from a succession of non-resident vicars and ineffective curates, but Jerram's energetic ministry revitalized it. The neighbouring clergy included the Revd John Pugh, vicar of Rauceby, at whose house Jerram took part in the discussion which led to the foundation of the Church Missionary Society in 1799. In

October 1805 ill health led Jerram to transfer to Chobham in Surrey, where Cecil was vicar and also rector of Bisley. Jerram acted as Cecil's curate until the latter's death in 1810, when he succeeded to the benefice. At Chobham, as at Long Sutton, he continued to prepare private pupils for the universities until 1822, and he gained a high reputation as a tutor. The initial prejudice which his evangelical opinions excited against him at Chobham soon disappeared. He was placed on the commission of the peace and devoted much attention to abuses in the administration of the poor laws, which, he felt, tended to reduce the labouring class to pauperism. Four of Jerram's eight children had already died in infancy, and in May 1823 his daughter died and sixteen months later his eldest son was taken; these events may explain his departure from Chobham in 1824 for the chapelry of St John's, Bedford Row, though he still retained the former benefice. However, a town charge dependent on pew-rents proved uncongenial, and he resigned it at the end of two years, returning to Chobham in 1826.

Bishop C. R. Sumner, a fellow evangelical, on succeeding to the see of Winchester in 1827 made Jerram a rural dean, and in April 1834 presented him to the lucrative rectory of Witney in Oxfordshire, which he held until his death, his elder son succeeding him at Chobham. His predecessor at Witney had been non-resident, and the parish had become a stronghold of dissent. During Jerram's incumbency the parish church was restored, district churches and schools were built in two hamlets, Sunday trading was suppressed, and the parish was divided into districts for systematic visitation. In addition to various earlier works on subjects such as the atonement (1804) and infant baptism (1819) he wrote in 1836 a pamphlet in response to some recent secessions of evangelical clergymen to nonconformity; he also combated what he called 'the Tractarian heresy'. Jerram's health began to fail in 1844, and on Good Friday 1848 he preached his last sermon in Witney church. He died at the rectory on 20 June 1853, and was buried at Witney. Jerram may be regarded as a representative figure from the second generation of Anglican evangelicals. His two surviving sons, James and Samuel, were also in holy orders; James, rector of Fleet, Lincolnshire, became his biographer.

EDMUND VENABLES, *rev.* TIMOTHY C. F. STUNT

Sources J. Jerram, ed., *The memoirs and a selection from the letters of the late Rev. Charles Jerram* (1855) · J. Pratt, *Remains of the Rev. Richard Cecil … to which is prefixed a memoir of his life*, 14th edn (1854) · J. Bateman, *The life of the Right Rev. Daniel Wilson*, 2 vols. (1860) · Venn, *Alum. Cant.*

Jerram, Charles Frederic (1882–1969), Royal Marines officer, was born on 13 November 1882 at Frith Hill Cottage, Godalming, Surrey, the son of Charles Samuel Jerram, schoolmaster, and his wife, Maria Florence Knight. He was educated at a number of schools including Clifton House, Eastbourne, and was commissioned in the Royal Marine light infantry in September 1901. He received his initial training at the Royal Naval College, Greenwich. By 1914 his career had followed the traditional marines pattern: he had served on twelve ships, his duty at sea interspersed with periods at his home barracks in Plymouth. He became a proficient military maritime officer, and while on the China station between 1907 and 1910 he received a commendation from the Admiralty for his intelligence work. On 15 August 1912 he married Sybil Victoria Greys O'Neill (d. 1952), daughter of Dr A. G. O'Neill of Auckland, New Zealand. They had two sons (one of whom was killed in action in Normandy in June 1944) and two daughters.

When war broke out in 1914 Jerram was stationed on HMS *Euryalus*, flagship of an obsolete four-sister-ship squadron (the 'live-bait' squadron), patrolling the Heligoland Bight. His ship was in port on 22 September 1914 when the other three were sunk by the U-9. In December 1914 Jerram became staff captain of the Royal Marine brigade of the Royal Naval division, dispatched to the Dardanelles for the Gallipoli campaign. He first landed at Kum Kale in February 1915, participating in a raid on Turkish forts there. Later he served ashore, initially at Anzac Cove and then at Cape Helles, from which he was evacuated with the last troops in January 1916. He had, he wrote, 'been ashore from first to last, without having my foot off [the peninsula], and must have been one of the only persons who did' (unpublished memoir, Royal Marines Museum). In May 1916 he went with his division to the western front, where he served with distinction until June 1917. He was awarded the DSO in January 1917 for his actions during the battle of the Ancre (1916). He was then seconded to the army, serving on the staffs of the 31st division and 13th corps. In July 1918 he joined the 46th (North Midland) division as its chief of staff. His naval background helped 46th division storm across the water-filled St Quentin Canal at Bellenglise as part of the key offensive by the Fourth Army on the Hindenberg and Beaurevoir lines in September 1918: the success of this exploit won Jerram the Croix de Guerre, and in 1919 the CMG.

In December 1919 Jerram graduated from the first post-war course of the Army Staff College, Camberley. In 1921 he commanded the marines on the new cruiser HMS *Raleigh*, until she sank, having struck rocks in the St Lawrence River. He was subsequently based primarily at the Plymouth barracks. In 1924 he submitted a paper to the Madden committee assessing the role of the corps after the 1923 amalgamation of the Royal Marine light infantry and the Royal Marine Artillery. He proposed a standing and trained amphibious force, a conceptual precursor to the eventual formation of the Royal Marine commandos. Although prescient, Jerram's paper was not well received, and he retired as a major in January 1929; in 1931 he was advanced to lieutenant-colonel on the retired list.

Jerram was recalled to active service in 1940 to train young officers. He later claimed that his most lasting contributions were preserving horses and the nucleus of the corps library for the Royal Marines, but his superiors praised his training of probationary officers. Major-General Dallas Brooks wrote in 1945, 'no-one could have brought along our probationary officers as efficiently, as firmly and objectively as you have done' (Brooks to Jerram, 26 March 1945, Royal Marines Museum, archives

9/2/J). Jerram returned to the retired list in July 1945, but his concern for the marines continued: in 1966 he wrote to his corps journal, attacking the use of the phrase 'if possible' in any military order. He stressed that such wording 'had been the cause of great disasters', including that at Suvla Bay at Gallipoli (Globe and Laurel, 74/3, June 1966, 189). Jerram, who was suffering from heart disease, took his own life on the shore near Chapel Point, Helford, Cornwall, at the age of eighty-six, on 12 January 1969. The coroner recorded a verdict of suicide while the balance of his mind was disturbed.

Jerram had high standards: Dallas Brooks had commented approvingly that '"nothing but the best" is still the Military Instructor's slogan' (Globe and Laurel, 74/3, June 1966, 189). His own professionalism, courage, and abilities enabled him to function well not only in the marines, but working alongside the army and navy as well. He personified the best traditions of Britain's armed forces.

DONALD F. BITTNER

Sources official record of service, PRO, ADM 196/63, pp. 155 and 146 with attachments · C. F. Jerram, 'The life of Charles Frederic Jerram, companion of the most noble order of Saint Michael and Saint George, companion of the distinguished order, and holder of the croix de guerre of France', unpublished memoir, Royal Marines Museum, Eastney barracks, Southsea, Hampshire, archives 11/13/024 · Jerram MSS, Royal Marines Museum, Eastney barracks, Southsea, Hampshire · 'Par mare, par terram—a soldier gone to sea: the life of Charles Frederic Jerram, CMG, DSO, royal marines', ed. D. Bittner, Royal Marines Museum, Eastney barracks, Southsea, Hampshire [copy; orig. in private hands] · Globe and Laurel, 29/6 (June 1922), 87, 89 · Globe and Laurel, 29/9 (Sept 1922), 139–40 · Globe and Laurel, 29/10 (Oct 1922), 154–5 · Globe and Laurel, 73/2 (April 1965), 85, 92–4 · Globe and Laurel, 74/3 (June 1966), 189 · Globe and Laurel, 74/10 (Dec 1966), 384 · Globe and Laurel, 76/3 (June 1968), 140–41 · Globe and Laurel, 76/4 (Aug 1968), 222 · Globe and Laurel, 76/2 (April 1969) [obituary and old comrades], 130 · WWW, 1961–70 · D. Jerrold, The royal naval division (1923) · R. E. Priestly, Breaking the Hindenburg Line: the story of the 46th (north midland) division (1919) · H. E. Blumberg, Britain's sea soldiers: a record of the royal marines during the war, 1914–1919 (1927) · C. Field, Britain's sea soldiers: a history of the royal marines and their predecessors and of their services in action, ashore, and afloat, and upon sundry other occasions of moment (1924) · J. Thompson, The royal marines: from sea soldiers to a special force (2000) · J. D. Ladd, The royal marines, 1919–1980 (1980) · E. Fraser and L. G. Carr-Laughton, The royal marine artillery, 1804–1923, 2 (1930) · b. cert. · d. cert.
Archives Royal Marines Museum, Eastney barracks, Southsea, Hampshire, personal papers | priv. coll., corresp., incl. with J. L. Moulton on Gallipoli
Likenesses photographs, Royal Marines Museum, Eastney barracks, Southsea, Hampshire, photograph albums, photograph 13/11/89 · portraits, Royal Marines Museum, Eastney barracks, Southsea, Hampshire, archives 11/14/5
Wealth at death £2031: probate, 11 March 1969, CGPLA Eng. & Wales

Jerram, Sir (Thomas Henry) Martyn (1858–1933), naval officer, was born at Chobham, Surrey, on 6 September 1858, the second son of Samuel John Jerram, vicar of Chobham, and his wife, Grace, daughter of Thomas Hunt, of Hermitage, co. Waterford. He was a grandson of Charles *Jerram. Martyn's early education was at Woodcote House, Windlesham, Surrey, and in 1871 he entered the navigating branch of the Royal Navy through the naval training school on HMS Britannia. After service as

navigating cadet and midshipman in the Channel Fleet he was promoted navigating sub-lieutenant in 1877; two years later he transferred to the executive branch and joined the sailing-sloop Seaflower, employed in the training of boys. He was promoted lieutenant in 1881 and after a year in the Iron Duke, flagship on the China station, he returned to the Seaflower as first lieutenant for another year. In 1884 he was given command, for the passage to Australia, of the torpedo boat Childers (65 tons), just completed by Sir J. I. Thornycroft for the government of Victoria. Although the Childers's complement was only twelve all told, and her coal capacity but 10 tons, she made the long voyage with complete success; Jerram received the appreciation of the Admiralty and a special letter of thanks from the Victorian minister of defence.

Jerram then became first lieutenant of the sloop Reindeer on the North American station for three and a half years and later, in 1889, of the cruiser Conquest on the China station. The Conquest was transferred the next year to the East India station and was in the squadron commanded by Vice-Admiral Sir Edmund Fremantle from which a naval brigade, in which Jerram commanded a battalion, was landed for the punitive expedition against the sultan of Vitu in east Africa. In 1891, while in command of the Pigeon, he was landed for a time at Beira, Mozambique, to act as British vice-consul. He returned home in 1892 and became first lieutenant of the Ruby, in the training squadron, thereby resuming the close association with the training service which was to last for many years more. That year he married Clara Isabel Parsons (d. 1926), second daughter of Joseph Parsons of Ennox, Somerset. They had two sons.

Jerram was promoted commander in 1894, and was for two years executive officer of the masted training ship Northampton, employed in the training of youths; he was then given command of the masted sloop Curaçao, tender to the Northampton, which he held until promoted captain in 1899. During the next three years he commanded the training ship Boscawen at Portland, combining this with his appointment as assistant to the inspecting captain of boys' training ships.

In 1902 Jerram returned to the China station for eighteen months in the battleship Albion, as flag captain to the second in command, Rear-Admiral Harry Tremenheere Grenfell, and to the Channel Fleet in May 1904 in command of the battleship Russell. In December 1905 he came ashore to command the Royal Naval Engineering College at Keyham, Devonport, until his promotion to flag rank in 1908. After a year as chief of staff to Sir George Neville in the reserve divisions of the Home Fleet, he was appointed in 1910 second in command in the Mediterranean, with his flag in the Duncan, until 1912, in which year he was appointed CB. In 1913 he became commander-in-chief on the China station, as acting vice-admiral with his flag in the armoured cruiser Minotaur; he was promoted vice-admiral in June 1913 and created KCB in 1914. His chief preoccupation on the outbreak of war in 1914 was the powerful German squadron under Vice-Admiral Graf von

Spee, which had been based in Tsingtao (Qingdao) but of which the whereabouts was at first unknown. He might have intercepted the German cruiser *Emden*, which subsequently caused much damage to British shipping, had he been permitted to follow his original plans to concentrate off the mouth of the Yangtze (Yangzi) River. Unfortunately the Admiralty, in an ill-advised attempt at distant control, ordered him over 900 miles south to Hong Kong, leaving a clear field for the *Emden* to escape. Jerram subsequently pursued a variety of missions and soon had under his command Russian, French, and Japanese ships as well as his own. German radio stations in the Caroline Islands and elsewhere were destroyed by bombardment, and measures were taken to cope with commerce raiding by the *Emden* and to protect troop convoys from Australia. The flagship *Minotaur* being needed for these duties, Jerram first shifted his flag to the armed merchant cruiser *Empress of Japan* but later found it necessary to remain ashore at Singapore in order adequately to control his composite and scattered forces.

In 1915 Jerram returned home to command the second battle squadron of the Grand Fleet. Since his squadron formed the port wing of the fleet, it fell to him, in the *King George V*, to lead the battle line in the battle of Jutland; and although in his official dispatch Admiral Sir John Jellicoe paid a tribute to Jerram's qualities as a squadron commander, he became the target for a certain amount of criticism. The dispute centred on an apparent lack of initiative in failing to support Vice-Admiral Sir David Beatty's battle cruisers in keeping contact with the Germans as darkness fell. Beatty reportedly believed Jerram had let him down. Jerram also stopped a torpedo attack on German battleships which had been sighted, in the belief they were actually British. Some, if not the majority, of this criticism may have been based on a misconception of what it actually would have been practical for Jerram to have done. Nevertheless the controversy was probably enough to end his chances for higher command. For his services in the battle he was created KCMG in 1916; but when Beatty, who was his junior, succeeded to the command of the Grand Fleet at the end of 1916, Jerram left the fleet and was appointed to the Admiralty for special service. He was promoted admiral in April 1917 and retired at his own request a few months later. He was raised to GCMG in 1919.

In September 1918, when the inadequacy of the current pay scales for officers and men became an urgent matter, Jerram was appointed president of a committee to investigate this; the rates recommended by his committee, somewhat reduced by official parsimony, became the basis of the new scales then introduced. He was also president of a permanent welfare committee set up in 1919. After his retirement he lived at Alverstoke, Hampshire, where he died, at his home, 7 The Crescent, on 19 March 1933. His funeral was held on the 23rd at the church in Harpsden, near Henley-on-Thames, Oxfordshire.

Jerram was twice commended for jumping overboard and saving life at sea. While not, perhaps, an outstanding leader of men, he was one in whose sympathy, fairness, and understanding of their needs in the difficult matters of their pay and conditions of service the men of the navy had full confidence.

H. G. THURSFIELD, rev. PAUL G. HALPERN

Sources *The Times* (21–4 March 1933) · personal knowledge (1949) · private information (1949) · I. H. Nish, 'Admiral Jerram and the German Pacific fleet, 1913–15', *Mariner's Mirror*, 56 (1970), 411–21 · A. J. Marder, *From the Dreadnought to Scapa Flow: the Royal Navy in the Fisher era, 1904–1919*, 2nd edn, 3 (1978) · S. W. Roskill, *Admiral of the fleet Earl Beatty: the last naval hero, an intimate biography* (1980) · *The eastern squadrons, 1914*, Naval Staff, Training and Staff Duties Division (1922) · S. W. Roskill, *The period of Anglo-American antagonism, 1919–1929* (1968), vol. 1 of *Naval policy between the wars* · A. Gordon, *The rules of the game: Jutland and British naval command* (1996) · *The Jellicoe papers*, ed. A. T. Patterson, 2 vols., Navy RS, 108, 111 (1966–8) · N. J. M. Campbell, *Jutland: an analysis of the fighting* (1986) · G. Bennett, *Naval battles of the First World War*, rev. edn (1974) · *WWW, 1929–40* · *CGPLA Eng. & Wales* (1933)

Archives NMM, corresp. and papers

Likenesses W. Stoneman, photograph, 1917, NPG; repro. in Marder, *From the Dreadnought to Scapa Flow* · N. Lytton, oils, 1920, IWM

Wealth at death £8030 18s. 3d.: English probate resworn in Singapore, 5 Oct 1933, *CGPLA Eng. & Wales*

Jerrard, George Birch (1804–1863), mathematician, was born in Cornwall, the son of Joseph Jerrard (*d.* 1858), who later became a major-general. He entered Trinity College, Dublin, in 1821, graduating in 1827, and is known for his work in the theory of equations. He published two treatises: *Mathematical Researches* (3 vols., 1832–5) and *An Essay on the Resolution of Equations* (2 vols., 1858), and about a dozen mathematical articles, almost all in the *Philosophical Magazine*, between 1835 and 1863.

Much of Jerrard's work related to his attempt to solve one of the most famous unsolved problems in mathematics, the question of a formula solution to equations of the fifth degree. What was sought was a formula analogous to that for second degree (quadratic) equations familiar to generations of schoolchildren, a solution 'by radicals' in mathematical parlance. Such formulae existed for equations of the third and fourth degrees as well, but the quintic, so called, remained elusive until the 1824 proof by the Norwegian Niels Henrik Abel (1802–1829) that no such formula for quintics existed. In *Mathematical Researches* Jerrard believed he had shown that a solution by radicals for the quintic did exist. Sir William Rowan Hamilton published a rebuttal of this in 1837. Nevertheless, to the end of his life, Jerrard refused to accept Abel's result. His scepticism was shared, in various degrees, by others, notably by James Cockle, though Cockle's opinion was 'not proven' rather than outright disbelief in Abel's result. A long exegesis of Abel by Hamilton in 1839 did nothing to shake Jerrard, and nothing immediately to shake Cockle. Finally, however, in 1862, Cockle published a guarded surrender to Abel and Hamilton which must have been a blow to Jerrard: Cockle had been the best he had had by way of a mathematical supporter. Moreover, by the 1860s, Cockle was being forced to point out in print mistakes of Jerrard, and in this he was joined by Arthur Cayley. The exchange ended unpleasantly, with a good deal of asperity on either side. Jerrard's last rejoinder is a very brief note, in the

October 1863 number of the *Philosophical Magazine*, terminating his part in the correspondence: his exasperation is evident.

Jerrard was not alone in claiming the existence of solutions by radicals for the quintic equation, but he was the most persistent, in the face of the objections of Cayley, Cockle, and Hamilton over more than twenty-five years. The method he proposed in *Mathematical Researches* was valid up to a point. He showed that the question of solubility or insolubility by radicals could be decided by considering a very specific quintic equation. Using this result the Frenchman Charles Hermite (1802–1901) was able to effect a formula solution of the quintic, but he used functions not encompassed within the meaning of the term 'by radicals'. It is, however, this reduction of the problem to manageable form which is Jerrard's main claim to fame. It is somehow typical of the life of this mathematically tragic figure that his method of reduction had, unknown to him, been discovered in 1786 by the Swede E. S. Bring (1736–1798), though its first publication in England was in 1864, well after Jerrard's *Mathematical Researches* had appeared.

Jerrard died on 23 November 1863 at the rectory in Long Stratton, Norfolk, the home of his brother, Frederick William Hill Jerrard, the rector, who also had mathematical training: he had attended Gonville and Caius College, Cambridge, and was eighth wrangler in 1833.

R. A. BRYCE

Sources J. D. North, 'Jerrard, George Birch', *DSB* • W. R. Hamilton, 'Inquiry into the validity of a method recently proposed by George B. Jerrard esq.', *Report of the British Association for the Advancement of Science* (1837), 295–348 • J. Cockle, 'Concluding remarks on a recent mathematical controversy', *London, Edinburgh, and Dublin Philosophical Magazine*, 4th ser., 26 (1863), 223–4 • N. H. Abel, *Mémoire sur les équations algébriques* (Christiania, 1824) • *Catalogue of scientific papers*, Royal Society, 3 (1869), 547–8 • *Catalogue of scientific papers*, Royal Society, 8 (1879), 25 • *DNB* • Boase, *Mod. Eng. biog.* • *GM*, 3rd ser., 16 (1864), 130 • D. Bank and A. Esposito, eds., *British biographical index*, 4 vols. (1990) • Crockford (1859) • C. B. Boyer, *A history of mathematics* (1968) • *CGPLA Eng. & Wales* (1863)

Wealth at death under £3000: administration, 30 Dec 1863, *CGPLA Eng. & Wales*

Jerrold, (William) Blanchard (1826–1884), journalist and playwright, was born on 22 December 1826 in Little Queen Street, London, the second of the seven children of Douglas William *Jerrold (1803–1857), also a journalist and playwright, and Mary Anne Swann (d. 1859). His godfather was his father's close and much-loved friend, the poet and journalist Samuel Laman Blanchard, after whom he was named. Jerrold was educated at Brompton grammar school, London, and a private school run by a Monsieur Bonnefoy in Boulogne, and he became a student at the Royal Academy Life School in London. He was, however, prevented by defective eyesight from following an artistic career, and so turned to journalism.

Jerrold was appointed to the reporting staff of the newly established morning paper the *Daily News* and wrote for it a series of articles, 'The literature of the poor' (1846). He wrote also for the *Illustrated London News*, *The Athenaeum*, and his father's journal, *Douglas Jerrold's Weekly Newspaper*, to which he contributed a series on emigration entitled

'The old woman who lived in a shoe'. In 1848 he published his first novel, *A Disgrace to the Family: a Story of Social Distinction*, which appeared in monthly parts in 1847–8, illustrated by H. K. Browne (Phiz), and met with some success; a number of other novels, set in London or Paris, featured among his voluminous literary output in later years. Although entries in earlier works of biographical reference, including one proof-corrected by Jerrold himself, give the year of his marriage as 1849, it was in fact on 26 June 1847 he married his godfather's daughter, Lavinia Lillie Blanchard (1825–1899), with whom he had three children, the youngest of whom became the father of the author and right-wing polemicist Douglas Francis Jerrold (1893–1964). From 1850 to 1859 he wrote regularly for Dickens's weekly journal *Household Words* and for its successor *All the Year Round*. Jerrold's first play was a one-act farce, *Cool as a Cucumber*, which was successfully produced at the Lyceum Theatre in London on 24 March 1851 and provided the younger Charles Mathews with one of his best roles; its 'inventive' conclusion is praised by Michael Booth (*English Plays of the Nineteenth Century*, 4, 1973, 18). In the same year Jerrold published, in four parts, a guide to the Great Exhibition, followed in 1852 by a similar one to the British Museum. In 1852 he also visited Norway and Sweden and in the following year published *A Brage Beaker with the Swedes, or, Notes from the North in 1852*, illustrated with his sketches (repr. as *Travels … in Sweden and Norway*, 1854).

In London Jerrold belonged to a set of young bohemian journalists, miscellaneous writers, and general bons viveurs, including George Augustus Sala, Peter Cunningham, and two of Dickens's younger brothers, that met to dine 'three or four nights a week at certain favourite restaurants' (G. A. Sala, *Life and Adventures*, 1, 1895, 441). From about 1853 or 1854 Jerrold began to spend much time in Paris and wrote a series of articles on that city for *Household Words* (repr. in his *Imperial Paris*, 1855). He covered the Paris Universal Exhibition (1855) for the *Daily News* and other journals and published an official guide to it. Guides such as this seem to have become rather a speciality of his, for in 1857 he published yet another one, this time to the Art Treasures Exhibition in Manchester. From the mid-1850s onwards Jerrold lived a great deal in Paris and produced numerous books and articles on various aspects of French culture, politics, and history. These included the major literary undertaking of his career, his sustained apologia for the Second Empire, the four-volume *Life of Napoleon III: derived from state records, from unpublished family correspondence, and from personal testimony* (1874–82), for which he was given every assistance by the imperial family; Napoleon III's character, he comments in his preface, has been 'not a little misunderstood by Englishmen' (*Life of Napoleon III*, 1, 1874, v).

On the death of his father in 1857, Jerrold succeeded him as editor of *Lloyd's Weekly Newspaper*, a post which he held until his death, vigorously maintaining the paper's strong Liberal stance; in 1868 he reprinted several of his father's leaders in *Other Times, being Liberal Leaders Contributed to 'Lloyd's Weekly Newspaper'*. His deeply filial *Life and Remains of Douglas Jerrold* was published in 1859, followed in the same year by a supplementary volume, *The Wit and Opinions of Douglas Jerrold*; and a collection of his father's early writings entitled *The Brownrigg Papers* appeared in 1861. He also acquired a reputation as a gourmet and under the pen-name Fin-Bec published several books on gastronomy, such as *The Epicure's Year-Book* (1867) and *The Dinner Bell* (1878), and edited a periodical, *The Knife and Fork* (1871–2), which began as a monthly and became a twopenny weekly. In all these publications Jerrold (as Fin-Bec) lays great emphasis on the avoidance of waste and what is called in the first number of *The Knife and Fork* 'the art of eating healthily, with refinement, and with economy'.

In 1855 Jerrold began a friendship with the French artist Gustave Doré which led eventually to their collaboration on *London: a Pilgrimage*, published first in monthly parts and then as a volume (1872). Doré's magnificent engravings have made this one of the classic works on Victorian London, but Jerrold's amiably discursive letterpress, notably devoid of social criticism, hardly matches up to the illustrations. A similar collaborative work on Paris was projected but never accomplished. Doré died in 1883 and Jerrold began work on a biography of him which was nearly completed when he himself died; it was published posthumously in 1891. Jerrold's other biographical work includes the popular series *The Best of All Good Company* (1871–3), in which each of the six instalments describes, with illustrations, an imaginary day spent in the company of, respectively, Dickens, Scott, Bulwer-Lytton, Disraeli, Thackeray, and Douglas Jerrold; and a *Life of George Cruikshank: in Two Epochs* (1882). He wrote also several works on Egypt, including *Egypt under Ismail Pacha* (1879) and *The Belgium of the East* (1882).

Jerrold was founder and president of the English branch of the international Société des Gens de Lettres, dedicated to the assimilation of copyright laws; it was on account of this work that he was awarded the palmes académiques by the French government, together with the rank of officier de l'instruction publique, and also made a knight of the order of Christ by the Portuguese government. Blanchard Jerrold died, after a short illness, at his home,

27 Victoria Street, Westminster, London, on 10 March 1884 and was buried on the 13th in the family grave at Norwood cemetery, London.   MICHAEL SLATER

Sources M. Slater, *Douglas Jerrold: 1803–1857* (2002) · C. Kent, *Illustrated Review* (13 March 1873) · *The Graphic* (19 April 1884) · *The Times* (11 March 1884) · W. Jerrold, *Douglas Jerrold, dramatist and wit*, 2 vols. [1914] · m. cert. · d. cert. · burial register, 1884, West Norwood cemetery, London
Archives *Punch Library* | BL, letters to Royal Literary Fund, Loan 96 · Bodl. Oxf., letters to Disraeli · UCL, letters to Lord Brougham · V&A NAL, letters to John Forster about life of his father
Likenesses W. B. Gardner, woodcut (after Elliott & Fry), NPG; repro. in *Illustrated Review* [see illus.] · engraving, repro. in *The Graphic* · wood-engraving, NPG; repro. in *ILN* (22 March 1884)
Wealth at death £2047 16s. 2d.: administration, 24 April 1884, CGPLA Eng. & Wales

Jerrold, Douglas Francis (1893–1964), publisher and author, was born on 3 August 1893 at Westwood Priory, Westwood Road, Scarborough, Yorkshire, the only son of Sidney Dominic Jerrold, a district auditor for the Local Government Board, and his wife, Maud Frances Goodrich. He grew up in Lichfield and London, so steeped in the writings of his grandfather Blanchard Jerrold and great-grandfather Douglas W. Jerrold as to feel detached from contemporary culture. After attending a private school in South Kensington, Jerrold went to Westminster School (1906–12) and won a scholarship to read modern history at New College, Oxford, where he involved himself in student journalism and politics as a Liberal. Eager to fight, he abandoned his studies in 1914 and saw action with the Royal Naval division at Gallipoli and in France until severely wounded at Beaumont Hamel in November 1916. A shattered left arm caused him great pain ever after, yet by early 1918 he was fit enough to command the officer school at Aldershot and then become director, rationing and distribution, at the Ministry of Food. He married Eleanor Arnold Arnold (*b*. 1886) on 31 December 1919; they had no children. Four years as a civil servant in the Treasury (1919–23) left him convinced of the moral bankruptcy of post-war politics and fearful of the bureaucratization of British life.

Jerrold then made his career in publishing, working with Victor Gollancz for Benn Brothers (1923–8) before becoming a director of Eyre and Spottiswoode (1929–59). There, controlling its non-fiction list, he gave priority to authors whose political and religious views approximated to his own. Colleagues often found him troublesome. Sharp-tongued and argumentative, vehement yet changeable, Jerrold was always asserting his rights; he excelled at making mountains out of molehills. When he was not invigorated by conflict, his manner conveyed immense gloom. 'No good book can sell', he insisted—a maxim possibly self-consolatory. His own literary output began with factual accounts of the war, such as *The Royal Naval Division* (1923). Then he essayed polemical fiction: *Storm over Europe* (1930) concerned Ruritanian royalists and liberals. His subsequent books, whether current affairs, history, or autobiography, were all essentially syntheses of politics and religion—original and challenging at best, sometimes merely cantankerous, and usually hard to read,

Douglas Francis Jerrold (1893–1964), by Howard Coster, 1934

since he strove after epigram and paradox. Although *The Necessity of Freedom* (1938) comprised their fullest exposition, his opinions were mainly propagated through the monthly *English Review*, which he edited from 1931 to 1936 as an organ of 'real toryism'—as distinct from the toryism of the current Conservative Party. Contributors included Sir Charles Petrie, Francis Yeats-Brown, Arnold Lunn, and Lord Lymington.

Central to Jerrold's philosophy was staunch Roman Catholicism. The world war, he believed, had revealed the rottenness of a society based on Enlightenment ideals and industrialism. Unfortunately, liberal intellectuals were now turning to socialism in reaction—when the communist state was actually the ultimate form of monopoly capitalism. Europe required a counter-revolution to banish the false gods of 1789 and restore a Christian social order, which would reassert human values over economics and rescue mankind from capitalist exploitation and communist tyranny. Drawing on Hilaire Belloc's 'distributism', Jerrold advocated wider ownership of property and the replacement of party politics by the corporate state. He praised Mussolini and defended the British Union of Fascists.

Jerrold wanted to be a Conservative MP; the party did not want him. He made the *English Review* a platform for tories who dreamed of ousting Baldwin in favour of Lord Lloyd, but lack of readers led Eyre and Spottiswoode to sell it in 1936. His next political outlet was a group called the Friends of Nationalist Spain. Having helped charter a British aeroplane to fly Franco secretly to Morocco in July 1936 to launch his revolt, Jerrold passionately promoted his cause during the Spanish Civil War: the generalissimo, a probable saint, was creating the finest regime on earth. Hitler did not inspire comparable enthusiasm; Jerrold eschewed racial theories and extreme nationalism while judging Nazis highly preferable to communists. An appeaser until 1939, he then conceded the case for war.

In 1945 Jerrold became chairman of Eyre and Spottiswoode and re-launched his journal as the *New English Review Magazine*. Part of a coterie of Roman Catholic men

of letters, he collaborated with Graham Greene in publishing and Hugh Kingsmill in editing. Daily life revolved around his flat at 2 Whitehall Court, an office in Bedford Street, the Lamb and Flag pub in Covent Garden, and many London clubs. He was a member of the Athenaeum, Carlton, Garrick, Pratt's, and Hurlingham, and a stalwart of the Author's Club, whose turn-of-the-century atmosphere especially suited him. A very large man with a small head, Jerrold wore an old-fashioned black coat, striped trousers, and stiff collar. Though scarcely popular, he played bridge and croquet and amused acquaintances with his diatribes. His review editorship ended in 1950, but he attracted attention in 1954 by denouncing the historian Arnold Toynbee as a traitor to Christian civilization. The union of western Europe was now his political goal. He resented never receiving an official honour.

Douglas Jerrold retired in 1959 and died at his home, 130 Marsham Court, Marsham Street, London on 21 July 1964 after a lengthy illness. He was buried at Kensal Green cemetery, London, on 24 July 1964. He was survived by his wife. JASON TOMES

Sources D. Jerrold, *Georgian adventure* (1937) · *The Times* (23 July 1964) · D. Jerrold, *The necessity of freedom* (1938) · R. Griffiths, *Fellow travellers of the right: British enthusiasts for Nazi Germany, 1933–9* (1980) · A. Powell, *Faces in my time* (1980) · G. Webber, *The ideology of the British right, 1918–1939* (1986) · J. Keane, *Fighting for Franco* (2001) · D. Jerrold, *England: past, present, and future* (1950) · M. Muggeridge, *The infernal grove* (1973) · D. Jerrold, *Britain and Europe, 1900–1940* (1941) · *WW* · m. cert. · d. cert.
Archives U. Reading L., corresp. | Bodl. Oxf., corresp. with H. A. L. Fisher · Bodl. Oxf., corresp. with E. J. Thompson
Likenesses H. Coster, photographs, 1931–9, NPG [*see illus.*]
Wealth at death £29,933: probate, 9 Nov 1964, *CGPLA Eng. & Wales*

Jerrold, Douglas William (1803–1857), playwright and journalist, was born on 3 January 1803 in Greek Street, London, the third of the four children of Samuel Jerrold (1749–1820), provincial actor and theatre manager, and his second wife, Mary, *née* Reid (1775–1851), actress. Jerrold passed his earliest years in Kent, Samuel's strolling company being based at Cranbrook. In 1807 Samuel leased the theatre at Sheerness, a profitable venture because of the many sailors and marines stationed there, and later leased the Southend theatre also. When a play required children he used his family, and the infant Douglas was once carried on in *Rolla* by Edmund Kean during the latter's brief membership of the Sheerness troupe. Jerrold received some rudimentary education from another actor in his father's company, J. P. Wilkinson, and later (1809–13) attended schools in Sheerness and Southend. He became a passionate reader and his fervent devotion to literature, above all to Shakespeare, dates from this time.

Naval career and early plays In 1813 he entered the navy as a 'volunteer of the first class' under the patronage of Captain Charles Austen, brother to Jane, and served first on a Nore guard-ship, the *Namur*, on which he, together with the press-ganged Clarkson Stanfield, organized some private theatricals. In 1815 he was transferred to the brig *Ernest*, which was used to ferry back to England soldiers wounded at Waterloo. The terrible injuries and suffering

Douglas William Jerrold (1803–1857), by Herbert? Watkins, 1857

the young Jerrold saw affected him deeply and this accounts for the hatred of the cult of military glory omnipresent in his later writings. He was appalled also by the extreme brutality of naval discipline (he had once to witness the barbaric punishment of flogging through the fleet) and later lost no opportunity to raise public awareness of it, notably in his drama *The Mutiny at the Nore* (1830).

Jerrold's naval career was cut short by the need to return home and help the family. His father was age-stricken and the Sheerness theatre audience had dwindled following the peace. In January 1816 the family moved to Broad Court, Covent Garden, near the major London theatres. His mother and elder sister sought work on the stage and he himself became a printer's apprentice (not, apparently, formally indentured), and may at times have been the family's chief breadwinner. He later wrote, 'I began the world at an age when, as a general rule, boys have not laid down their primers … the cockpit of a man of war was at thirteen exchanged for the struggle of London' (*The Writings of Douglas Jerrold*, 1, 1851, iii–iv). He continued to read voraciously despite unpropitious circumstances, studying French, Italian, and Latin; he also became involved, along with his fellow apprentice Samuel Phelps, in the world of private theatres—more, it seems, as supplier of scripts than as actor. Despite the strong radical sympathies for which he was to become so celebrated he seems not to have participated directly in the intense political activity of the day.

A two-act farce submitted to the English Opera House in 1818 remained unacted, but three years later Wilkinson, by now a popular comedian, arranged for its production,

with himself in the lead, at Sadler's Wells. It was called *More Frightened than Hurt* and audiences relished its sprightly dialogue and well-contrived traditional farce situations. Between 1821 and 1824 Jerrold provided five further dramatic pieces for this theatre, including another successful farce, *The Smoked Miser* (1823), and three melodramas adapted respectively from works by 'Ossian', Scott, and Byron, all relying greatly on the spectacular aquatic effects for which this theatre was famous. Jerrold also began his journalistic career at this time, contributing dramatic criticism to the Liberal *Sunday Monitor* and (from 1825) to the *Weekly Times*. During 1823–4 he wrote a lively series of sketches of minor theatre actors for the *Mirror of the Stage* and contributed both verse and prose to other obscure periodicals. He formed a very close and lasting friendship with Samuel Laman Blanchard and the two young men encouraged each other in their literary ambitions; they also shared a few moments of enthusiastic determination to follow Byron to Greece and help in the struggle for Greek independence.

Despite his precarious financial situation, Jerrold married his childhood sweetheart, Mary Anne Swann (1808?–1859) on 15 August 1824. It seems to have been a happy and successful marriage, though Mary Anne apparently took very little part in her husband's public life or, generally, in his very active social life. This latter was characteristic of the contemporary literary and artistic community in that it centred on the numerous (naturally all-male) clubs that met in various taverns to drink, smoke, gossip, and exchange 'chaff' or banter, often of a startlingly personal kind. Jerrold, who founded several such clubs and belonged to still more, soon acquired a formidable reputation as a master of witty repartee, to be later much exercised at the bibulous weekly dinner parties of the *Punch* coterie; 'his intimates gained reflected glory by repeating "Jerrold's latest"' (*The Times*, 9 June 1857). Typical 'Jerroldisms' were his much-quoted remark about having to feed his family out of his inkwell; his prompt comment when told that someone was trying to convert Thackeray to Romanism: 'They had better begin with his nose'; and another, equally prompt, when told Macready was 'eating his heart out': 'What an appetite he must have!' Mrs Jerrold entertained her husband's friends and colleagues at home, but her main concerns seem to have been maternal and domestic, and in this respect at least she may be reflected in his most famous creation, Mrs Caudle. In addition to their eldest son, (William) Blanchard *Jerrold, who became a noted journalist and miscellaneous writer, the Jerrolds' children were: Jane Matilda (b. 1825), who married Henry Mayhew; Douglas Edmund (b. 1828); Mary Anne (b. 1831), who remained unmarried; and Thomas Serle (b. 1833). Two others died in infancy.

Sketch-writing and *Black-Eyed Susan* In 1826 Jerrold wrote some dramatic pieces for George Bolwell Davidge at the Coburg Theatre and began contributing sketches of occupational types and other essays to the *Monthly Magazine*. He also prepared his first book, a series of linked essays entitled *Facts and Fancies*, but the publishers went bankrupt before the book could be issued (the British Library has a set of bound-up proofs). In autumn 1828 he became the Coburg's house dramatist, supplying six farces and melodramas in three months, but Davidge's ungenerous treatment caused him to transfer his services to Robert William Elliston at the rival Surrey Theatre. Jerrold's fourth piece for Elliston was *Black-Eyed Susan*, a nautical melodrama suggested by John Gay's ballad and written as a vehicle for the sailor-actor T. P. Cooke. It proved a sensational success. First produced on 8 June 1829, it ran for a phenomenal 300 nights, was quickly pirated by other theatres in London and throughout the country, and remained a favourite with audiences for the rest of the century. For Elliston and Cooke it proved a goldmine, but Jerrold himself earned only £60 by it. Despite such embittering experiences, he was still ardent to revive the national drama and make it worthy of its Shakespearian heritage. He was determined to write only original English dramas and fiercely attacked the wholesale pirating of French plays so common at this time. His first attempt at establishing himself as a 'legitimate' (patent theatre) dramatist was a historical drama (*The Witchfinder*, Drury Lane, 1829). This failed but *The Rent Day* (Drury Lane, 1832), inspired by David Wilkie's genre paintings, with a contemporary domestic setting and its strong social message, was a great success. Jerrold indeed came to be seen as the father of that most popular Victorian genre the 'domestic drama', which he referred to as 'a poor thing but mine own'. For the next two decades he continued writing plays, now mainly for the patent theatres and mainly five-act comedies stuffed with elaborately 'witty' dialogue which reads a bit like bowdlerized Congreve or imitation Sheridan. Some of these, such as *Bubbles of the Day* (Covent Garden, 1842) and *Time Works Wonders* (Haymarket, 1845), enjoyed a brief *succès d'estime*, but Jerrold's fatal weaknesses as a dramatist, his inability to structure a full-length play or to create characters of any complexity (his witty one-liners and elaborate conceits are mostly put in the mouths of cardboard stereotypes with names such as Lord Skindeep or Mrs Quarto), mean that this whole aspect of his literary output is now of interest only to theatre and cultural historians. *Black-Eyed Susan* alone of all his more than seventy dramas is still sometimes effectively staged as a Christmas entertainment or by community theatre groups.

Parallel with his playwriting, from which, as was the case with nearly all British dramatists before the 1860s, his earnings were very meagre, Jerrold continued to write copiously for the periodical press. He wrote dramatic criticism for the *Sunday Monitor*, the *Weekly Times*, the *Morning Herald*, and Thomas Wakely's *The Ballot*. His other periodical writings mainly took the form of satirical sketches of occupational or social types, anecdotes exemplifying particular human follies and vanities, and moral fables and comic-satiric tales about the theatre, such as the still very entertaining 'Bajazet Gag, or, The Manager in Search of a Star' (*New Monthly Magazine*, 1841–2). These appeared in various journals including *The Athenaeum*, *The Examiner*, the *Freemason's Quarterly*, *Blackwood's*, and, most regularly of all, the *New Monthly*. Several of his contributions to the last-named journal appeared under the pen-name Henry Brownrigg, a grimly joking reference to his harsh apprenticeship to literature (the midwife Elizabeth Brownrigg was hanged in 1767 for savagely murdering a female apprentice). During an enforced retreat to Paris in 1835 to avoid his creditors Jerrold developed friendships with his future son-in-law, Henry Mayhew, and with Thackeray, and later worked with the latter on a short-lived 'ultra-liberal' daily, *The Constitutional* (1836–7), largely funded by Thackeray's stepfather. Thackeray also illustrated, anonymously, a collection of Jerrold's *Blackwood's* pieces, *Men of Character* (3 vols., 1838). In 1836 he first met Dickens, with whom he became very good friends (the closeness of their social and political views made their one quarrel, over capital punishment, all the more notable); he acted in Dickens's amateur theatricals, but the only time the two writers were professionally associated was when Jerrold wrote leaders for the *Daily News* during Dickens's brief editorship of the new paper (1846). A two-volume collection of Jerrold's *New Monthly* contributions, *Cakes and Ale*, appeared in 1842 with illustrations by Cruikshank.

Writing for *Punch* With the launching of *Punch* (1841) Jerrold found the ideal vehicle for his particular brand of satirical journalism and contributed regularly from the second number until his death. His position as a salaried member of the *Punch* staff greatly eased his financial situation, enabling him in 1844 to move his family out to a suburban villa, West Lodge, on Putney Common. His so-called 'Q papers' (1841–5, always signed with the letter Q) were like a series of editorials for the new magazine. Commenting with biting satire, and from a sturdily radical perspective, on events of the day (the lords, both temporal and spiritual, judges, and magistrates were particular targets), they were an important element in the establishment of *Punch*'s popularity and the definition of its character. Later Jerrold series, such as his Chesterfield parody, *Punch's Letters to his Son*, and *The Story of a Feather*, a serialized novel about a beautiful young girl retaining her goodness and her virtue amid desperate London poverty ('a wise and beautiful book' Dickens called it), were also well received. But most popular of all his *Punch* writings, somewhat to his chagrin, was the purely domestic comedy of 'Mrs. Caudle's Curtain Lectures' (1845). 'Almost all the events and perplexities of Cockney domestic economy pass before her', wrote Thackeray of Mrs Caudle, 'and … a student in the twentieth century may get out of her lectures as accurate pictures of London life as we can get out of the pictures of Hogarth' (W. M. Thackeray, *Contributions to the 'Morning Chronicle'*, ed. G. N. Ray, 1955, 94). Until his death Jerrold continued to be a prolific contributor to *Punch* (christening the Crystal Palace in one 1851 piece), but none of his other writings approached the Caudle lectures in popularity, while his fiery radicalism was increasingly countered by the 'gentlemanly' liberalism of Thackeray, who on one occasion wondered if he ought to 'pull any longer in the same boat as such a savage little Robespierre' (*Letters and Private Papers*, 2.681).

Jerrold's efforts to establish a periodical of his own were hampered by his lack of business sense and injudicious generosity towards contributors. His first journal, financed by Herbert Ingram, was a monthly, the *Illuminated Magazine* (1843–4), for which he wrote, among much else, a quasi-Rabelaisian utopian fantasy, 'The Chronicles of Clovernook'. This was succeeded by another monthly, *Douglas Jerrold's Shilling Magazine* (1845–8), in which he serialized 'St. Giles and St. James', a melodramatic treatment of the extremes of poverty and wealth in contemporary London, and wrote much else besides, including a regular feature, 'The Hedgehog Letters', containing satiric comment on topics of the day. From 1846 to 1848 he edited *Douglas Jerrold's Weekly Newspaper*, for which he wrote a similar regular feature entitled 'The barber's chair' and vigorously promoted his pet project, the establishment of a club for city clerks named the Whittington Club. In 1849 he published his only monthly-part novel, *A Man Made of Money*, illustrated by John Leech, a satiric fantasy modelled upon Balzac's *Peau de chagrin*. It was not until 1852 and his appointment by Edward Lloyd, at an annual salary of £1000, to the editorship of *Lloyd's Weekly Newspaper* (a post he retained until his death and in which he was succeeded by his eldest son) that he finally achieved real financial security. A collection by his son of his leading articles entitled *Other Times; being Liberal Leaders Contributed to 'Lloyd's Weekly Newspaper'* appeared in 1868. In 1853 Jerrold moved back into London, first to Circus Road, St John's Wood, and then in 1856 to Greville Place, Kilburn Priory. Throughout most of his adult life he suffered greatly from severe attacks of rheumatism, having often to work while in great pain and with much impaired eyesight. But his unexpected death at Kilburn Priory on 8 June 1857, after a short but agonizing illness (the cause of death was recorded as 'pulmonary and renal congestion'), created a sensation, and the funeral at Norwood cemetery on the 15th was attended by thousands of mourners. Dickens and Thackeray were among the pallbearers and, notwithstanding William Blanchard Jerrold's public denial that his father had left his affairs in a poor state, Dickens afterwards organized a series of theatrical performances, public readings, and lectures to raise a fund for Mrs Jerrold and her unmarried daughter which realized £2000.

His reliance on melodramatic devices and stereotypes and his ornate prose style, full of conceits, elaborate similes, and erudite allusions, and consciously modelled on Jeremy Taylor, Fuller, and other masters of seventeenth-century English, makes Jerrold's work largely unsympathetic to present-day taste, although it contains many passages of striking realism, especially when he is dealing with life among the poor or conditions in the contemporary theatre. The intense topicality of his best *Punch* work (apart, of course, from 'Mrs. Caudle's Curtain Lectures', which were still being reprinted as late as 1974) creates a further difficulty for the modern reader. No one today would group him as a great comic writer to be ranked alongside Dickens and Thackeray, as David Masson and many other contemporary critics did, but he remains a

remarkable voice providing, especially in his *Punch* writings, a unique perspective on the first twenty years of the Victorian age.   MICHAEL SLATER

Sources M. Slater, *Douglas Jerrold: 1803–1857* (2002) • W. Jerrold, *Douglas Jerrold, dramatist and wit*, 2 vols. [1914] • W. B. Jerrold, *The life and remains of Douglas Jerrold* (1859) • W. Jerrold, *Douglas Jerrold and Punch* (1910) • J. Hannay, 'Douglas Jerrold', *Atlantic Monthly*, 1 (1857), 1–12 • *The letters and private papers of William Makepeace Thackeray*, ed. G. N. Ray, 4 vols. (1945–6) • R. M. Kelly, *Douglas Jerrold* (1972) • *The Times* (9 June 1857) • parish register (baptism), St Anne's Church, Soho, 23 Sept 1807 • *The Lancet* (13 June 1857)

Archives BL, letters to Royal Literary Fund, loan 96 • Hunt. L., letters | BL, letters to Thomas James Serle, Add. MS 52476 • Morgan L., G. N. Ray collection • New York University, De Coursey Fales collection • NYPL, Berg collection, corresp. with R. H. Horne • U. Leeds, Brotherton L., corresp. with Charles Cowden Clarke and Mary Cowden Clarke • V&A NAL, library MSS, corresp. with John Forster, and papers

Likenesses watercolour, *c*.1830, New York University, New York, Fales Collection • portraits, *c*.1835–1847, repro. in Jerrold, *Douglas Jerrold*, frontispiece • photographs, *c*.1850–1867, NPG • E. H. Baily, marble bust, 1853, NPG • D. Macnee, oils, 1853, NPG • H. W. Diamond, photographs, 1857, repro. in *The Bookman* [New York] (1910–11), 32.568 • H.? Watkins, photograph, 1857, NPG [*see illus.*] • R. Doyle, group portrait, pen-and-ink, BM • H. Furniss, pen-and-ink, NPG • D. Maclise, group portrait, pencil (*Dickens reading 'The chimes' to his friends, 1844*), V&A • T. A. Prior, line engraving (after photograph by Beard), NPG • J. Sartain, mezzotint (after photograph by R. Beard), NPG • W. M. Thackeray, caricature (with Thackeray), repro. in *Punch* (1848) • woodcut (after photograph by London Stereoscopic Company), NPG; repro. in *Illustrated Review* (15 May 1872) • woodcuts (some after photographs), BM, NPG

Jersey. For this title name *see* Villiers, Edward, first earl of Jersey (1655?–1711); Villiers, William, second earl of Jersey (*c*.1682–1721) [*see under* Villiers, Edward, first earl of Jersey (1655?–1711)]; Villiers, George Bussy, fourth earl of Jersey (1735–1805); Villiers, Frances, countess of Jersey (1753–1821); Villiers, Sarah Sophia Child-, countess of Jersey (1785–1867); Villiers, Victor Albert George Child-, seventh earl of Jersey (1845–1915); Villiers, Margaret Elizabeth Child-, countess of Jersey (1849–1945).

Jervais, Thomas (*d.* 1799), glass painter, was born in Dublin. 'The only son of a distinguished cleric' (La Roche, 195), Jervais abandoned his early theological training to experiment with the reputedly 'lost art' of enamel glass painting, having first made a tour of the Netherlands to look at stained-glass windows there. Jervais produced a number of works for Irish patrons before going to England about 1770 and rapidly established his reputation with small-scale, finely detailed panels—generally copies of Italian, Dutch, and Flemish masters—for the expanding domestic market: he specialized in scenes lit by moon and fire which fully exploited the transparency of the medium. He held a number of popular exhibitions of his work in London in the 1770s and 1780s. In 1777 Jervais won the commission for which he is best remembered: the great west window of the ante-chapel of New College, Oxford, to designs provided by Sir Joshua Reynolds: a large Correggio-inspired *Nativity* over standing figures of the cardinal virtues and Christian graces. This work, completed in 1787, though now much deteriorated, remains a high point of naturalistic enamel glass painting in the late eighteenth century. While contemporary opinion on the window's aesthetic merit was divided, Reynolds's elegant figures were frequently copied by other glass painters. In the upper portion of the window, Reynolds introduced his own portrait and that of Jervais as shepherds. About 1786 Jervais was commissioned by George III to execute a huge *Resurrection* for the east window of St George's Chapel, Windsor. The design (provided by Benjamin West) drew heavily on seventeenth-century Italian paintings. The inauguration service for the window was mentioned by Fanny Burney in her diary. As at New College, portions of the medieval window tracery were removed to accommodate the new glass. The *Resurrection* was replaced in the 1860s and is now lost. Jervais was forced through ill health to retire about 1790, remaining in Windsor until his death at Peascod Street on 29 August 1799. He left property and money to his widow, Margaret (d. 1810), his sister, Elizabeth Knowles, to nieces, a nephew, and a friend and co-executor, John Foster. His only known pupil—his successor at St George's Chapel—was Charles Forrest (d. c.1807).

L. H. CUST, rev. SARAH BAYLIS

Sources M. Wynne, 'Irish stained and painted glass in the eighteenth century', *Crown in glory: a celebration of craftsmanship*, ed. P. Moore (1982), 58–68 · *Court and private life in the time of Queen Charlotte, being the journals of Mrs Papendiek*, ed. V. D. Broughton, 1 (1887), 277–8; 2 (1887), 38–40, 98 · S. van La Roche, *Sophie in London, 1786*, trans. C. Williams (1933), 193–5, 202 · W. G. Strickland, *A dictionary of Irish artists*, 1 (1913), 534–5 · Redgrave, *Artists*, 229 · J. Dallaway, *Observations on English architecture, military, ecclesiastical and civil, compared with similar buildings on the continent* (1806), 284 · *GM*, 1st ser., 69 (1799), 819 · W. Warrington, *The history of stained glass from the earliest period of the art to the present time* (1848), 15 · PRO, PROB 11/1337, sig. 118, fols. 179r–180r

Likenesses T. Jervais, self-portrait, enamel painted glass, c.1778, New College, Oxford

Wealth at death property and money left to widow and other family members: will, PRO, PROB 11/1337, sig. 118

Jervas [Jarvis], **Charles** (1675–1739), portrait painter and translator, was born in Clonliske, Shinrone, King's county, Ireland, the son of John Jervas (d. 1697) and Elizabeth Baldwin. According to George Vertue, by the mid-1690s Jervas was living in London, where he stayed and studied with Sir Godfrey Kneller for about a year. In early 1698 his copies of the newly hung Raphael cartoons at Hampton Court were bought by the politician and virtuoso Dr George Clarke, who also lent him £50 to travel. He set off immediately for Paris and by May 1698 was studying in the Louvre. He then proceeded to Italy, reaching Rome by 28 November 1699. There he set about copying antique statues and the works of, among others, Raphael, Guido Reni, and Titian. He also acted as an agent for collectors in England, buying considerable numbers of paintings, prints, and sketches. His most significant purchase, a cartoon for Raphael's *Transfiguration of Christ*, was, however, blocked for export by the pope—despite Jervas's repeated threats to petition for English ships to blow up Civita vecchia the principal port for Rome.

On his return to England in 1708, Jervas entered the literary circle of Addison, Pope, and Swift, setting up his home and studio in London in Cleveland Court, Westminster. He was hailed by Richard Steele in *The Tatler* of 16 April 1709 as 'the last great painter Italy has sent us'. His stylized portraits of society ladies, typically in the guise of milkmaids or shepherdesses, became fashionable—his reputation enhanced 'by his talk and boasting manner' (Vertue, 3.17). Examples of his best works include portraits of Alexander Pope's friends Martha and Theresa Blount (c.1715, Mapledurham House, Oxfordshire) and Anne, countess of Sunderland (date unknown, priv. coll.), both of which display his accomplished handling of colour and his taste for rather elongated figures with tiny waists. Among his other major works are portraits of Jonathan Swift (c.1718, National Portrait Gallery, London) and *The Family of Charles, Second Viscount Townshend* (1720–25, priv. coll.). Frequent trips to Ireland, where he held considerable land, also resulted in several fine portraits, including a full-length portrait of Jane Seymour Conway reclining (c.1732, National Gallery of Ireland, Dublin).

As well as literary friends, Jervas also had an influential patron in the prime minister, Sir Robert Walpole. Jervas played an important role in acquiring works of art for Walpole's ever-expanding collection, as well as contributing his own portraits. In November 1723 it was Walpole and his allies who engineered Jervas's appointment as king's painter—a post he held for the rest of his life. Among the works known to have been produced by Jervas in this capacity are portraits of the young prince William, duke of Cumberland (1728, National Portrait Gallery, London) and coronation portraits of George II and Queen Caroline (1728, Guildhall Art Gallery, London).

Jervas had literary ambitions and with his friend Alexander Pope (whose painting instructor he had been for about six months in 1713) he edited (1716) a version of Charles-Alphonse Du Fresnoy's *De arte grafica*. This was followed about 1719 by the publication of his own translation of Machiavelli's *Novella di Belfagor*. However, his major literary undertaking was an English translation of Cervantes' *Don Quixote*. Published posthumously in 1742 and frequently reprinted, it is generally acknowledged as being close in spirit to the original.

Jervas's reputation as a painter appears to have declined during the 1730s. His marriage on 14 January 1726 at St Benet Paul's Wharf, Thames Street, London, to Penelope Hume (d. 1746), a widow with a fortune of £20,000, secured his future financially, and he was able to maintain a second home, in Hampton, Middlesex. By late 1738 his health was fading and a brief sojourn collecting paintings in Italy was followed by his death from a wasting condition, on 2 November 1739 at his home in Cleveland Court, Westminster, London. He was survived by his wife. The sale of his huge art collection conducted by Christopher Cock ran from 11 March until 1 May 1740. Several decades after Jervas's death Horace Walpole dismissed his style as 'a light, flimsy kind of fan painting as large as the life' (Walpole, 653–7). More recently he has been recognized as an accomplished portrait painter and a translator of considerable ability.

EDWARD BOTTOMS

Sources Vertue, *Note books* · *The correspondence of Alexander Pope*, ed. G. Sherburn, 5 vols. (1956) · letters to J. Ellis, BL, Add. MS 28,882, fols. 292, 333 · E. Bottoms, 'Charles Jervas, Sir Robert Walpole and the Norfolk whigs', *Apollo*, 145 (Feb 1997), 44–8 · *The correspondence of Jonathan Swift*, ed. H. Williams, 5 vols. (1963–5) · letter to G. Clarke, 1699, Worcester College, Oxford, MS 181 · letter to Bishop Hough, Bodl. Oxf., MS Eng. lett c. 275(20) · M. K. Talley, 'Extracts from Charles Jervas's "sale catalogues"', *Burlington Magazine*, 120 (1978), 6–9 · W. G. Strickland, *A dictionary of Irish artists*, 2 vols. (1913); repr. with introduction by T. J. Snoddy (1989) · H. Walpole, *Anecdotes of painting in England: with some account of the principal artists*, ed. R. N. Wornum, new edn, 3 vols. (1849); repr. (1862) · *IGI* · *The Tatler* (16 April 1709)

Archives BL, Add. MS 28882, fols. 292, 333 · BM, MS C. 119.h.3, nos. 14 and 15 · Worcester College, Oxford, MS 181 | BL, Blenheim MSS, 61365, fol. 9 · CUL, Cholmondeley (Houghton) MSS, vouchers, 1725 · Raynham Hall archives, Raynham, Norfolk, 1733 account · Wolterton Hall archives, Wolterton, Norfolk

Likenesses G. Vandergucht, engraving, 1739, BM, NPG; repro. in *A catalogue of the most valuable collection of pictures, prints, and drawings late of Charles Jarvis* (1740), frontispiece [sale catalogue, London 11 March 1740] · G. Vandergucht, line engraving, pubd 1740 (after G. Vandergucht), NPG · C. Jervas, self-portrait, NPG · G. Vandergucht, etching (after T. Priscott), NPG

Wealth at death land in Ireland; two houses in England; several large monetary bequests

Jervis, John, earl of St Vincent (1735–1823), naval officer, the second of four children of Swynfen Jervis (1700–1771) of Meaford in Stone, Staffordshire, barrister at law, and Elizabeth (*fl.* 1700–1770), daughter of George Parker of Park Hall, Staffordshire, was born at Meaford on 20 January 1735 and baptized at Stone on 26 January. His uncle was Sir Thomas *Parker, chief baron of the exchequer. John was educated at Burton upon Trent grammar school, and at the Revd Samuel Swinden's academy in Greenwich from 1747, a year in which his father was appointed counsel to the Admiralty (5 June), auditor of Greenwich Hospital (1 July), and one of its directors (4 November), possibly through the influence of Admiral George Anson, a distant relative of Swynfen Jervis's wife.

Early naval career Although he was intended for the law, Jervis ran away to Woolwich to join the navy in 1748. He was discovered and returned home. Undeterred by family remonstrances, and through the combined influence of Lady Archibald Hamilton, wife of the governor of the hospital, Lady Burlington, and Lady Gower, he gained in December an introduction to the Hon. George Townshend, lately appointed commodore and commander-in-chief on the Jamaica station. As a result on 4 January 1749 he was entered as an able seaman on the *Gloucester* (50 guns, Captain John Storr) at Portsmouth. Bearing Townshend's broad pennant from 17 March, the ship was bound for Jamaica with a small squadron whose task was to protect the British West Indian trade from Spanish privateers and *guarda costas*. Jervis volunteered for these duties whenever he could, cruising off the Mosquito Coast in the sloop *Ferret* between October 1750 and February 1751. When in June 1752 Townshend went home for his health, he discharged Jervis into the *Severn* (50 guns), the flagship of his successor, Thomas Cotes, on 26 June. Here Jervis was rated midshipman by Captain Henry Dennis, until 5 August. But there were few opportunities for action and by his own account, he spent his time in 'reading, studying navigation, and perusing my old letters' (Mackay, 61).

On 31 July 1754 Jervis was entered as midshipman in the

John Jervis, earl of St Vincent (1735–1823), by Sir William Beechey, *c.*1792–3

Sphinx (24 guns) going home for major repairs, which arrived at Spithead on 3 October and was paid off on 7 November. In that year Charles Saunders, one of Anson's protégés, became treasurer of Greenwich Hospital. His acquaintance with the Jervis family was to have a major impact on Jervis's career. Nominal service for the month of December 1754 in the newly launched *Seaford* (20 guns) and from 27 December to 2 February 1755 in the yacht *Mary*, moored at Greenwich under Captain John Campbell, another Anson protégé, completed Jervis's necessary six years, and he passed his examination for lieutenant on 22 January 1755. On 19 February he was promoted sixth lieutenant of the *Royal George* (90 guns) and on 11 March he was moved as third lieutenant to the *Nottingham* (60 guns). She formed one of Edward Boscawen's fleet trying, unsuccessfully, to prevent French reinforcements reaching Canada. On 31 March 1756 he moved, still as third lieutenant, to the *Devonshire* (80 guns) and on 22 June he was made fourth lieutenant in the *Prince* (90 guns), Saunders's flagship in the Mediterranean. He rose to third (3 October) and second lieutenant (27 October) in the flagship before moving with the admiral to the *Culloden* (74 guns), again as second lieutenant, on 29 November 1756.

Jervis had entered the navy during peace. His career, supported by influence, had been unspectacular but he had been continually employed and steadily promoted, gaining experience and knowledge of his profession under notable commanders. Anson's influence had been ever present, chiefly through his protégés; that of Saunders, now in command in the Mediterranean, was to be decisive in placing Jervis in a position and giving him the opportunity to reach post rank. In January 1757 Jervis was lent to the *Experiment* (20 guns) during her captain's illness, and he commanded her on 16 March in a severe but indecisive engagement with a large French privateer off Cape Gata. He returned to the *Culloden* a few days later and on 1 June followed Saunders to the *St George* (90 guns), Vice-Admiral Henry Osborn having assumed command. When Saunders was superseded in May, Jervis was appointed to the *Foudroyant* (80 guns), captured in a chase on 28 February 1758 off Cartagena. He returned home in her and on 15 January 1759, as her first lieutenant, joined the *Neptune* in which Saunders went to North America as commander-in-chief. Jervis was promoted commander on 15 May and on 4 July he was made acting commander of the sloop *Porcupine*, an appointment confirmed by the Admiralty. It was here he met and impressed General James Wolfe with his decision and promptness. With the frigate *Halifax*, the *Porcupine* led the ships in charge of transports past Quebec to take part in the capture of that fortress. The story that Wolfe sent his last message and her miniature to Lady Katherine Lowther, to whom he was engaged, by Jervis may be true. But Jervis did not deliver them in person.

Promoted to the command of the *Scorpion* (10 guns) on 15 May upon the death of her commander, Jervis was sent home with dispatches on 25 September, but he returned immediately on 13 January 1760 in the *Albany*, with important dispatches for General Jeffrey Amherst. After his return to England in May Jervis was attached for a short time to the channel squadron under Rear-Admiral George Rodney before being promoted to post rank on 13 October 1760 and placed in command of the *Gosport* (44 guns). In her he served first in the North Sea, and in April 1762 he was charged with convoying the Virginia and Maryland trade to America. In company with the East and West India trade, under the escort of Captain Joshua Rowley in the *Superb*, on 11 May, they encountered and repelled the French squadron under Ternay on its way to capture Newfoundland. Having joined Lord Colvill, commander-in-chief in North America, in August 1762, Jervis took part in the recovery of Newfoundland in September, and returned in the *Gosport* to England in the spring of 1763.

Peace brought the customary unemployment but in February 1769 Jervis was appointed to the frigate *Alarm* (32 guns), the first coppered warship, delivering bullion to English merchants in Genoa. Here between 9 and 15 September he protested at the insult to the British flag occasioned by the forcible removal from the *Alarm*'s boat of two Turkish slaves who had escaped from a Genoese galley. His protests and threats of retaliatory force against the doge and senate of Genoa produced the slaves and the arrest of their detainers. Jervis himself felt it had given him 'an opportunity of carrying the dignity of the British flag as high as a Blake' (Jervis to father, 21 Jan 1770, Parker–Jervis MSS, 49/44, bundle 91/1). On 30 March 1770 his prompt seamanship saved the *Alarm* when she was driven on the rocks during a severe gale at Marseilles and seemed a total loss. With the help of the French officials and his crew's exertions she was repaired and ready for service by mid-May. 'A glorious action in the midst of a war could not be more applauded than the gallantry of the officers and crew', he wrote to his father on 11 May (ibid.). Both these actions were approved by the Admiralty publicly and privately. Ordered home in 1771, the *Alarm* arrived at Spithead in the middle of May and in August sailed for the Mediterranean with the king's brother, the duke of Gloucester; he was to winter in Italy and lived on board the *Alarm* until May 1772 when she returned to England to be paid off. Jervis's professional expertise and courtly manners seem to have been the reasons why he was chosen, but influence also played a part. Jervis had dined with the duke in 1769 and in describing this to his father commented that Sir Charles Saunders had 'been so flattering to say to Colonel Barré that he had the greatest affection and regard for me and … added there is no better Officer in the King's Naval Service' (ibid., 16 Feb 1769). On this Mediterranean cruise he learned a good deal about the area which was to prove useful when he commanded there in 1795–6.

European travels and political career Jervis used his leisure to further his professional knowledge. In October 1772 he went to France to learn the language, studying so hard that he endangered his health. Then he toured the country, condemning the French for their folly and dissipation, but equally blaming the English travellers he saw 'post-haste after the bubble Pleasure' (Anson, 36). In November 1773 he returned to England. The following summer, with his friend Captain Samuel Barrington, he visited Russia. During the month he spent at St Petersburg he saw the admiralty, went on the yacht designed by Sir Charles Knowles, inspected the arsenal and dockyards at Kronstadt, and visited the most notable British merchants and shipbuilders. He kept a journal of all he saw, particularly noting safe anchorages and harbours in the Baltic and correcting his charts. On his way back he did the same at the ports of Sweden, Denmark, and north Germany, from Lübeck to Hamburg, and came home via the Netherlands with a mass of naval information. In 1775 he and Barrington made a yachting cruise off the west coast of France. They visited Brest, where Jervis paid particular attention to the approaches to the roadstead. This was to stand him in good stead when he blockaded that port in 1800–1801. They then moved on to Lorient, Rochefort, and Bordeaux.

In June 1775 Jervis was appointed to the *Kent* but as she was found to be defective he was, on 1 September, appointed to the command of the *Foudroyant*, the French prize he had brought home from the Mediterranean in 1758 and which was still the largest two-decked ship in the Royal Navy. She served chiefly as a guardship until 1778 when she became part of Admiral Augustus Keppel's Channel Fleet and took part in the battle of Ushant on 27 July 1778. In November 1778 Lord Sandwich had listed Jervis as 'a good officer, but turbulent and busy, and violent as a politician attached to Mr. Keppel' (*Correspondence of George III*, ed. J. Fortescue, 1927, no. 2460) and at the subsequent court martial of Keppel in January 1779 Jervis's evidence was strongly in Keppel's favour and helped secure the admiral's honourable acquittal. The *Foudroyant* remained with the Channel Fleet during 1779, when a Franco-Spanish invasion force appeared in the channel and Jervis was mortified to retreat before them. But on 19 April 1782 off Brest, Barrington's squadron, of which he was part, fell in with a French convoy which had just left that port. The French scattered and the *Foudroyant* gave chase to the largest of the ships of war, the *Pegase* (74 guns), came up with her just after midnight, and took her after a close engagement of nearly an hour. The *Pegase*, newly commissioned and poorly manned, suffered considerable damage. The *Foudroyant*, which Jervis had made notable for her perfect discipline and efficiency, had only five men slightly wounded, one of them Jervis himself.

Jervis was made a knight of the Bath on 28 May 1782 as a reward for this action which made his name more widely known outside the navy. He was at all three reliefs of Gibraltar, the first by Rodney in January 1780, again in March 1781 by Darby, and finally by Lord Howe in October 1782, taking part in the skirmish off Cape Spartel on 20 October. The *Foudroyant* was paid off on 31 December 1782 but Jervis had already been appointed commander of a squadron on a particular service on 26 December 1782, and on 3 January 1783 he was directed to go to the West Indies, with a broad pennant in the *Salisbury* (50 guns). However, as the peace preliminaries were signed in that month, he was ordered to strike his flag on 14 January 1783. On 5 June 1783 he married his first cousin Martha (1741–1816), first daughter of Sir Thomas Parker and his second wife, Martha; the couple had no children.

Peace had brought Jervis the opportunity to enter parliament and at the end of January he was returned as MP for Launceston, a pocket borough in the duke of Northumberland's interest. This was at the request of the earl of Shelburne, a friend of Jervis who shared his interest in reform. Jervis voted for Pitt's early proposals for parliamentary reform on 7 May 1783 and against Fox's East India Bill (27 November 1783) and was classed as a Pittite in the lists drawn up before the April election of 1784. On a platform of support for Pitt and reform he stood, with Henry Beaufoy, for Great Yarmouth—an independent borough with approximately 800 voters, many of whom were merchants, seamen, and dissenters—and he was successfully returned. In the succeeding years Jervis again voted for Pitt's unsuccessful motion for parliamentary reform. He opposed the duke of Richmond's fortification plans, as a member of the commission of inquiry, but supported Pitt in the regency crisis of 1788/89. Jervis was promoted rear-admiral of the blue on 24 September 1787 and hoisted his flag in the *Carnatic* (74 guns) during the weeks of the Dutch crisis and in the *Prince* (90 guns) in the dispute with Spain in 1790, being promoted rear-admiral of the white on 21 September 1790. But he did not support Pitt's bellicose policies and, perhaps as a consequence of these political differences, he left his seat at Yarmouth and in 1790 was returned for Chipping/High Wycombe through the interest of Shelburne, now marquess of Lansdowne, who controlled the borough. He remained its member for three years but he spoke rarely in the Commons, and then usually on naval matters. In March 1786 he had deplored

the inefficient maintenance of the navy and expressed his desire 'to root up and totally prevent the growth of evils so enormous and alarming' (Drummond, 2.682).

In December 1792 Jervis introduced a scheme, supported by government, to relieve distressed superannuated seamen. On 4 February 1793 he drew attention to the hardship newly commissioned officers suffered from delayed payments of subsistence money. He continued to support the government in its unsuccessful attempt to repeal the Test Act in 1791, and voted for the opposition's motion for parliamentary reform in May 1793, but he opposed further proceedings against Warren Hastings that year and the government's warlike attitude over the Ochakov crisis of 1791–2. He did not attend the debates of February 1793 on the outbreak of war with France, after consulting Lansdowne, and because he believed the attitudes of Pitt's government were compelling the French to declare war. But his patriotism was unquestioned; he was ready to serve, and in the autumn of 1793 he was appointed to command the expedition to the West Indies. He later declared that he had not been influenced politically by Lansdowne, but to avoid further prejudice he resigned his seat in January 1794. He declined to stand for Yarmouth in 1796, where he was popular with the dissenting interest, and did not again enter the House of Commons.

Service in the West Indies and Mediterranean, 1793–1796
Jervis's appointment as naval commander of the 1793 expedition to the West Indies may have surprised some contemporaries, but he had served in the West Indies, had experience of combined operations, and his professional abilities were undoubted. Moreover Dundas had offered Sir Charles Grey the military command on 18 August, and Jervis and Grey were friends and shared some political sympathies. The expedition left England on 26 November 1793. Jervis, who had been promoted vice-admiral of the blue on 1 February 1793, flew his flag in the *Boyne* (98 guns), whose flag-captain was Sir Charles Grey's son, George. At first the expedition went well. There was warm co-operation between the naval and military forces, and the French were outnumbered and politically divided. Martinique, Guadeloupe, and St Lucia were swiftly captured between March and April 1794. Jervis had been promoted vice-admiral of the white on 12 April 1794 and was on the point of returning to England, for health reasons, when French reinforcements landed at Guadeloupe on 2 June 1794. As soon as the news reached him at St Kitts, on 5 June, Jervis sailed for Guadeloupe to repulse this force. But the English troops, suffering from fever, were themselves repulsed and besieged and the previous success was turned to defeat and failure. In November 1794 Vice-Admiral Benjamin Caldwell came out to relieve Jervis who arrived in England in February 1795.

The original expedition has been described as 'a superbly conducted military operation and also a well-organized and thoroughly executed plundering enterprise' (M. Duffy, *Soldiers, Sugar and Seapower*, 1987, 109). It led to disputes with neutrals, chiefly the Americans, over the regulation of maritime neutral trade and alienated French colonial opinion, making it easier for republican forces to reconquer the islands. Grey and Jervis, quoting past precedents, warmly defended the system of prize money, which for naval officers was an important part of their professional rewards and an additional spur to enterprise. Jervis had been involved in a dispute with his superior, Lord Colvill, in 1764 over prize money, and between 1799 and 1801 he was disputing issues of prize money with both Nelson and Lord Keith. Both Grey and Jervis faced a vote of censure in the Commons in May 1795, which was defeated by the unusual combination of the opposition and Dundas. It cost both commanders the peerages they should have gained though Jervis was promoted admiral of the blue on 1 June 1795, in anticipation of his appointment to command the Mediterranean Fleet in succession to Lord Hood. But on 1 May his flagship, the *Boyne*, caught fire at Spithead and blew up, and Jervis lost everything in her. His appointment to the Mediterranean had been discussed in May when Lord Hugh Seymour, a member of the Board of Admiralty, suggested his name to Lord Spencer, the first lord. On 28 June he again pressed Jervis's claims, despite the recent censure motion, as 'an officer of rare merit' who would do 'honour to the minister who avails himself of his talents afloat' (Anson, 111). Spencer agreed, and Jervis left England in November in the frigate *Lively* (32 guns) accompanied by George Grey as his flag-captain and Robert Calder as captain of the fleet. They arrived at Gibraltar on 23 November and joined the fleet at San Fiorenzo Bay, Corsica, on 29 November where Jervis moved to the *Victory* (100 guns) on 4 December and gave the signal to unmoor on the 13th. The admiral quickly recognized the quality of many of his captains—Nelson, Collingwood, Troubridge—and by a more vigorous prosecution of the war in the Mediterranean gave them their opportunities. A close blockade of Toulon was begun; Jervis co-operated closely with Sir Gilbert Elliot, the viceroy of Corsica, while a squadron under Nelson supported allied Austrian troops on the Italian coast, and unsuccessful attempts were made to prevent French troops, under Bonaparte, penetrating Italy via the republic of Genoa. Jervis exercised his ships constantly in cruising and working them up to a high pitch of discipline and efficiency. Because the dockyard at Gibraltar was woefully short of stores he had his ships caulked and repaired at sea, a considerable feat. At the same time he bombarded the navy's civil departments for much needed supplies of food, clothing, ammunition, and stores. The situation worsened. In July 1796 Spain made peace with France. Bonaparte had occupied Leghorn on 27 June and threatened the British position in Corsica. Jervis attempted to concentrate his forces, recalling Admiral Mann from the blockade of Cadiz in July. This allowed the Spanish admiral, Langara, to sail for Toulon with seventeen ships of the line, chasing Mann into Gibraltar *en route* and creating a Franco-Spanish force which quite outnumbered Jervis's fleet. Nelson commented:

They at home do not know what this fleet is capable of performing; anything and everything … of all the fleets I ever saw, I never saw one, in point of officers and men equal to Sir John Jervis's, who is a commander able to lead them to glory. (*Dispatches and Letters*, 2.229)

His words accurately reflect the efficiency and high morale of the fleet, but Jervis's position was rapidly becoming untenable. He was desperately short of all supplies with no base nearer than Gibraltar, itself under threat. To continue to hold Corsica was impossible and he received orders on 25 September to evacuate the island and withdraw from the Mediterranean. He left San Fiorenzo on 2 November and reached Gibraltar on 1 December, having been delayed by storms and head winds, and having become seriously short of rations. A few days later a hurricane hit his weakened ships, wrecking one and badly damaging two others. Gibraltar offered few facilities or supplies and by the end of the month Jervis had withdrawn to Lisbon. It was an undoubted reverse, but Jervis's resource, patience, and nerve had never failed.

The battle of Cape St Vincent, 1797 Spain had declared war against Britain in October and France lost little time in using the naval resources of her reluctant ally. The combined Franco-Spanish fleet left Toulon in December 1796. The French sailed through the straits for Lorient but the Spanish fleet put into Cartagena to refit. Undermanned, lacking experienced seamen, and short of supplies, it sailed on 1 February 1797, its task to escort four ships, carrying mercury for refining silver, to Cadiz. Blown by strong winds through the straits and further into the Atlantic than intended, the Spanish admiral, Córdoba, worked his way back towards Cadiz. Jervis had left Lisbon on 18 January with a Portuguese convoy for Brazil and was patrolling off Cape St Vincent, having been joined by five ships under Admiral Sir William Parker on 6 February. Various sightings and news of the Spanish fleet in the days before the battle were confirmed on 13 February when the frigate *Minerve* joined the fleet. The British were confident that they would win the imminent engagement. The final toast at dinner in the *Victory* on the eve of the battle was 'Victory over the Dons in the battle from which they cannot escape to-morrow!'. At dawn on 14 February in mist and light winds the British fleet of fifteen sail of the line was sailing in admirable close order. It was not until 10.30 a.m. that the number of Spanish ships confronting Jervis became apparent. When the reported total reached twenty-seven Calder remarked on the disparity of forces. 'Enough sir', replied Jervis. 'The die is cast and if there are fifty sail I will go through them!'. In the heightened enthusiasm of the moment Captain Benjamin Hallowell, a passenger in the *Victory*, clapped the admiral on the back, declaring 'That's right Sir John, that's right. By God, we shall give them a damned good licking!' (Tucker, 1.255).

As the morning mist parted the Spanish ships were revealed, trying to form their line and cover the mercury convoy. As they did so a gap opened, separating the convoy and escort, under Admiral Moreno, from the main body of the fleet. Jervis signalled his ships to pass through the gap. The *Culloden* (Captain Troubridge) reached it before the Spaniards could close the space, and this enabled the rest of the British ships to make their way through, effectively separating the Spanish force into two parts. Just after midday Jervis ordered his ships to tack in succession towards the larger of the Spanish divisions. The smaller Spanish leeward division under Admiral Moreno attempted to prevent this, close range fighting took place, and the Spanish attacks were beaten off. But a gap had now opened in the British line, and a shift in the wind increased this. The five ships of Jervis's van were heading north by west into the enemy. Jervis therefore altered course to north-west, possibly to enable the ships in his centre division to double the Spanish line, catching the Spanish ships between them and his van. He ordered his rearmost ships, among them Nelson in the *Captain*, to take up a suitable station and get into action as soon as possible.

Naval signals were not sufficiently precise for Jervis to explain exactly what he intended and some of his rearmost ships did not respond. But Nelson had noticed the leading Spanish ships moving as though to attack the British rear. He saw that the British van had still to engage, that Jervis could not see what was going on, and that time would be lost while the British rear obeyed the admiral's signals. He therefore wore out of the line and set off to join the *Culloden* and the British van as they attacked the Spanish centre. This risky manoeuvre was approved by Jervis when he saw it. The Spaniards abandoned their move towards the British rear and headed north-west, their line disintegrating as they went. By 2 p.m. a mêlée had developed as the British ships overtook and engaged the Spaniards. Nelson boarded and took the *San Nicolas* and the *San Josef*, while others captured the *Salvador del Mundo* and *San Ysidro*. At 4.22 p.m. Jervis gave the signal to break off the action. The Spaniards had lost four ships, four others were badly damaged, and it was impossible for them to renew the action on 15 February. The British fleet, guarding its prizes, made first for Lagos on 16 February for immediate repairs, and then for Lisbon where they arrived on 24 February.

News of the victory, which reached London on 3 March, was greeted with delighted relief. The preceding months had been filled with bad news and there was then a general fear of invasion. It was known that the fleet had abandoned the Mediterranean; the unsuccessful French attempt to invade Ireland in the previous December had been thwarted not by the Channel Fleet but by bad weather, and public confidence in the navy was at its lowest. Jervis's remark, just before the battle began, that 'a victory is very essential to England at this moment' (Anson, 157) had been correct and the rewards were correspondingly great. Jervis had been nominated for a peerage in 1796 as a reward for earlier services. He was now created Baron Jervis of Meaford and earl of St Vincent on 23 June 1797 with a life annuity of £3000. The City of London presented him with its freedom and a splendid sword. The thanks of both houses of parliament, on 3 and 9 March 1797, were followed by thanks and addresses from the major ports and a gold medal from the king. Jervis, 'wishing to avoid an appearance of arrogance in naming the action as my title' (Jervis to W. Jervis, 16 July 1797, Parker–Jervis MSS, 49/44, bundle 91/2), had suggested his earldom should bear the title Yarmouth, because of his attachment to the borough, and when that was rejected he put forward that of Orford, the title given to Edward Russell after

La Hogue, as originally belonging to the navy, but he left the final choice to the king, who chose St Vincent.

Once repairs were completed the fleet put to sea. St Vincent had received orders to blockade the Spanish fleet, which had taken refuge in Cadiz. A close blockade was begun, with an inshore squadron of ten ships, the main body of the fleet lying at Rota. St Vincent hoped, in vain, the Spaniards would come out for a decisive action. In July, writing to his brother, he claimed the consequences of 14 February were more important than the battle itself, since the Spanish fleet had 'been palsied from that hour to this' and that he had 'been riding triumphant one hundred and seven days in the entrance to the Port' (16 July 1797, Parker–Jervis MSS, 49/44, bundle 91/2). But the task was made more difficult as the effects of the general fleet mutinies at Spithead and the Nore began to spread to the Mediterranean ships.

Service in the Mediterranean and the channel, 1797–1800 St Vincent suppressed every manifestation of mutiny with unbending severity. Ships' companies were kept occupied and Cadiz was regularly bombarded. Nelson and a squadron of seven ships were sent to attack Santa Cruz in Tenerife in July 1797 to carry the war to Spain and divert men with opportunities for prize money. The speaking of Irish was forbidden, to discourage the seditious activity of United Irishmen in the fleet. The marines in each ship were berthed separately and marine officers were ordered to visit their men and call the roll regularly. Ship visiting was forbidden with ships newly arrived from England and greatly curtailed elsewhere. Yet a suggestion that mutinous letters and appeals from the Nore, arriving from England in the *Alcmene*, should be withheld was firmly rejected. 'Certainly not, sir', the admiral declared, 'let every letter be immediately delivered: I dare to say the commander in chief will know how to support his own authority' (Tucker, 1.300–2). When necessary one of Jervis's own captains trained in his discipline was transferred to a newly arrived and mutinous ship, to bring it back to good order. Above all, discipline and the rules of the service were constantly maintained for all ranks, and punishments quickly followed breaches of the rules. When two sailors, convicted of mutiny on Saturday, were hanged on Sunday, Vice-Admiral Thompson protested at 'a profanation of the Sabbath', for which, St Vincent wrote, 'I have insisted on his being removed from this fleet immediately, or that I shall be called home' (*DNB*). The danger came to a head in May 1798 when ships, under Sir Roger Curtis, from the channel and the Irish stations, many seriously infected with mutiny, joined the Mediterranean Fleet. The case of the *Marlborough* was typical. One of the ringleaders on her was court martialled and sentenced to death, the sentence to be carried out by the crew of that ship. Protests from the captain and declarations by the men that the sentence would not be carried out were equally useless. Extraordinary precautions were taken to prevent an open outbreak. The ship was surrounded by launches, armed with carronades, with orders on any appearance of mutiny, to fire into the *Marlborough* until all resistance ceased, sinking the ship if necessary. The man was hanged the following morning. 'Discipline has been preserved' was St Vincent's comment (Tucker, 1.303). St Vincent refused to appear afraid or overwhelmed by the serious situation. 'Responsibility', he once declared, 'is the test of a man's courage.'

Meanwhile French preparations at Toulon, from the end of 1797, indicated the formation of a large force; this was Bonaparte's expedition to Egypt. It was essential for British forces to re-enter the Mediterranean to discover the object of the enterprise. Lord Spencer, writing to St Vincent in April 1798, had suggested sending a squadron under Sir Horatio Nelson for this purpose. St Vincent had already decided that Nelson, though a junior flag-officer, was best qualified for this task. But those officers passed over hardly saw the appointment in that light: Rear-Admiral Sir John Orde in particular was furiously angry. Never patient with critical subordinates, St Vincent ordered Orde home, ignoring his protests. He was censured by the Admiralty for not having shown proper attention and support to subordinate flag-officers, a censure he protested against. Orde retained his grudge, and when St Vincent returned to England in 1799 he challenged the admiral to a duel. At sixty-five and in indifferent health St Vincent was hardly fit to respond, but it was only the direct command of George III which prevented his accepting the challenge.

Nelson's Mediterranean squadron, detached on 24 May, was formed from the ten best ships in St Vincent's fleet. They were replaced the same day by Curtis's mutinous reinforcements. Once this force had been disciplined and formed into an effective unit the admiral planned to capture Minorca as a vital base for the protection and safety of the fleet. He arrived at Gibraltar in October, and put Commodore John Thomas Duckworth in command of the naval forces of the expedition which finally took Minorca on 15 November 1798. St Vincent's energies had also been directed to improving the limited facilities of Gibraltar. In February 1799 he suggested the resiting and expansion of the victualling yard. Freshwater tanks were built to conserve winter rainwater and a beginning made on an underground reservoir. He was particularly proud of repairing the defects of those ships, damaged at the battle of the Nile, which came to Gibraltar with their prizes. Great exertions were required, for officers always wanted to go home 'to recount their feats after a glorious Victory; and the officers of the dockyards shrink from work of so much labour' (Jervis to W. Jervis, 13 Dec 1798, Parker–Jervis MSS, 49/44, bundle 91/2), but St Vincent's vigorous presence overcame all these obstacles and he thought the ships better fitted than if they had gone to England.

The strain of these events and responsibilities told on his health. Ministers were unwilling for him to be relieved and 'had put it on a footing so honourable to me that I am determined to die in harness' (Jervis to W. Jervis, 6 July 1798, Parker–Jervis MSS, 49/44, bundle 91/2), and on 14 February 1799 he was created admiral of the white. In December 1798 Admiral Lord Keith came out to command the blockading squadron off Cadiz under St Vincent's orders, and when in April 1799 Admiral Bruix escaped from Brest

and entered the Mediterranean it was Keith, not St Vincent, who pursued him. Reluctant to resign, St Vincent still thought himself the only officer capable of handling the important operations he was charged with. He was in very weak health at Gibraltar when Bruix went through the straits on 6 May. He summoned Keith to join him there and together they sailed for Minorca, which St Vincent thought the object of Bruix's expedition, arriving on 19 May. Here news that Bruix was heading north led St Vincent to attempt, unsuccessfully, to intercept him by sailing in the direction of Cape Creus on 22 May. Already ill when he sailed, St Vincent was forced to return to Minorca on 1 June, leaving Keith to continue to Toulon where Bruix had temporarily taken refuge. For the next few weeks St Vincent tried to retain command. He supported Keith in his attempts to find and defeat Bruix before he defeated the smaller British squadrons scattered about the Mediterranean, but he was anxious about the safety of Minorca. By 17 June he was forced to relinquish command, and he left for England in early July.

Throughout the winter, which he spent at his Essex property of Rochetts, St Vincent was ill with a combination of rheumatism and dropsy but with the spring he improved. The Admiralty had been urging him to take command of the Channel Fleet, still plagued with the remains of mutiny, and he suddenly decided to do so. 'The king and the government require it,' he said, 'and the discipline of the British navy demands it. It is of no consequence to me whether I die afloat or ashore' (DNB). He hoisted his flag on the Namur (100 guns) on 26 April 1800 and sailed for Brest, where he transferred to the Ville de Paris (100 guns), with Sir Thomas Troubridge as his captain of the fleet.

The news was most unwelcome to the Channel Fleet itself. The reputed toast given at Lord Bridport's table, 'May the discipline of the Mediterranean never be introduced into the Channel Fleet' expressed an unavailing hope. As soon as he was appointed St Vincent proceeded to issue all the orders which had made the Mediterranean Fleet a pattern of discipline and efficiency. Most officers resented the order which forbade them to go more than 3 miles from the landing place or to sleep ashore and the consequent separation from their wives. The wives resented it too, and one lady reputedly gave as a toast 'May his next glass of wine choke the wretch' (Tucker, 2.37n). Leave was only granted from sunrise to sunset, no boats were to remain ashore after sunset, and captains were to take their turn at watering duties to prevent desertions and the bringing of liquor into ships.

St Vincent was determined on so close and effective a blockade of Brest that the inshore squadron would not be driven off without provoking a general action, and that the main body of the fleet, based at Ushant, would be near enough to support them. Thus between twenty-four and thirty of his forty ships were constantly employed. Ushant not Torbay now became the accepted rendezvous for the Channel Fleet, while the inshore squadron cruised off the entrance to the Goulet (between the Black Rocks and the Parquette shoal), a station strewn with reefs and shoals, with hazardous currents and exposed to the full force of south-westerly winds. With grim humour St Vincent called this station 'the Elysian Lake' but it needed an officer of uncommon fortitude to command there and those who did so needed regular relief. Whenever possible, repairs were to be done at sea. Ships were forbidden to go to Spithead except in an emergency or for some major work which could not be done at sea, at Torbay, or Cawsand Bay. Nor were ships to remain even there for more than a week. On 16 and 17 May 1800, only a few weeks after he took command, a violent gale caused much damage to his ships and forced most of them to take shelter in Torbay, but in a few days the repaired squadron regained its station off Ushant where it remained for four months. St Vincent restored the pattern of close blockading Lord Hawke had initiated in the Seven Years' War. His familiarity with these waters, owing to the peacetime cruise of 1775, now stood him in good stead. His presence with the fleet was not only an example to all officers but enabled him to see how the fleet performed. The constant manoeuvring to take advantage of the tides and winds necessitated good seamanship at all times of the day and night. St Vincent had ordered that captains must be on deck when such evolutions were performed and made a point of seeing himself that these orders were obeyed.

Close blockading for such a long time would have been impossible without well-fed and healthy crews, and St Vincent ensured that there were regular, adequate supplies of food and clothing from England. The medical services were transformed through the work of his private physician, Andrew Baird, who acted informally as physician of the fleet. Regular supplies of lemon juice, fresh meat, and vegetables kept scurvy at bay; better ventilation and dry scrubbing rather than washing the lower decks helped to make the atmosphere less damp; those men who wished could be vaccinated against smallpox; and regular, isolated sick bays were introduced into all ships. As a result health improved and the hospital ship which normally accompanied the fleet was not required. The fleet is reported to have kept its watch on Brest without a break for 121 days, from May to September 1800, and to have had on board only sixteen hospital cases when it returned to Torbay in November. St Vincent later declared, with some truth, that the preservation of health in the fleets was his greatest achievement. But winter and illness forced the admiral to live ashore, at Torre Abbey, overlooking Torbay. From here he co-ordinated the fleet's movements and kept up the pressure on Brest, and this policy was successfully followed by his successor, Admiral William Cornwallis.

First lord of the Admiralty, 1801–1804 In 1801 William Pitt resigned and George III called on Henry Addington to form a government. St Vincent accepted the post of first lord of the Admiralty in Addington's cabinet on 19 February, though not without some hesitation. A long-time supporter of Catholic emancipation he had applauded Pitt's attempt to pass such a measure and stated his opinions to the king. George III honoured his opinions and motives

but urged him to accept, and St Vincent formally took office with the rest of the cabinet on 17 July 1801.

With the war still ongoing St Vincent's first task was the equipment of the fleet sent to the Baltic to break the combination of those states against Britain. The workers in the royal dockyards took this opportunity to strike for a permanent doubling of their pay. Treating them as though they were mutinous seamen, St Vincent ordered the delegates out of the yards, sent an investigating committee to each yard, and offered an additional allowance while the price of bread remained high. When this was rejected he dismissed every man who had taken a leading part in the strike. The remainder returned to work but an ominous foretaste of St Vincent's methods with the navy's civil departments had been given. The victory at Copenhagen in 1801 and the death of the tsar broke up the northern coalition. St Vincent was next occupied with a threatened invasion by a flotilla at Boulogne, but the peace of Amiens was signed on 27 March 1802 and he was now able to give his full attention to the reform of the civil administration of the navy. The desire to root out abuses, apparent when he was an MP, and the passion for order and discipline which marked his career were now given full rein.

St Vincent had already determined on a wholesale elimination of the corruption and waste he believed were weakening the navy and causing the high taxes which were ruining the country. Moreover the tide of opinion was moving in his direction. Since the late 1780s an increasing concern for government efficiency and economy had favoured reform. The recommendations of the commission on fees, and the reports of the select committee on finance in the 1790s, though resisted by the civil administration of the navy and held up by the war, had begun to be implemented. Before he left office in 1801 Lord Spencer had approved reforms based on some of these recommendations which were carried into effect by an order in council of 21 May 1801. The movement for reform was thus already established when St Vincent came to the Admiralty in February 1801 and reflected his own determination. Aware of support for change in parliament and the navy, he was willing to use politics to effect it, to exert the Admiralty's authority over the Navy Board to its utmost, and ignore or discard that board's authority and expertise. His experiences at Gibraltar in 1798–9 had given him an interest in dockyard improvements. His belief in the inherent abuses in the civil administrative system and the necessity of a wholesale purge of them was supported by his two naval colleagues at the Admiralty, Sir Thomas Troubridge and Captain John Markham.

As soon as peace preliminaries were signed on 1 October 1801 St Vincent therefore began investigations which, by February 1802, convinced him that a thorough inquiry into the dockyards was necessary. In July the Board of Admiralty began a series of yard visitations, starting with Plymouth. Here, he told Addington, he had found a multitude of abuses that made the establishment of a commission of inquiry a necessity. Visitation of the other yards confirmed the impression. An act appointing commissioners to inquire into abuses and frauds was introduced and passed at the end of 1802. This commission was St Vincent's. He was its prime mover and nominated the commissioners. He appears to have wanted either to force the members of the civilian naval boards to resign or to abolish them altogether. William Marsden, second secretary to the Admiralty, thought the frauds detected in the yards were only a pretext for crushing these subordinate boards. St Vincent had hoped that the commission would be given powers to examine witnesses under oath but there was much opposition to this and witnesses were allowed the right to refuse to answer questions lest they incriminate themselves. Had the commissioners been able to examine witnesses on oath they would have got evidence for legal proceedings against many officials in the civil departments, who were appointed by letters patent under the great seal, could not be summarily dismissed, and chose not to resign. But if they had been prosecuted for fraud or malfeasance St Vincent would have been able to replace them with his nominees and reshape naval administration as he wished. He certainly believed the Navy Board had failed in its duty to the service and the public.

After the visitations the board was censured by the Admiralty for permitting the public to be defrauded and allowing abuses to go unpunished. There was inevitably some fraud and corruption in the civil departments of the navy, and carelessness and lack of financial supervision in offices frequently overburdened with work. Equally St Vincent failed to recognize the many practical difficulties the Navy Board grappled with and its experience and expertise in handling them, and he refused to credit the board with an equal, though different, professionalism to his own. As a result relations between the two boards became strained and then broke down. On the publication of the first report of the commission of naval inquiry, the Navy Board tried to present a memorial to the House of Commons, defending itself. St Vincent refused to permit them to do so. But the comptroller of the Navy Board, Sir Andrew Hamond, was also an MP and in June 1803 declared in the house that since St Vincent took office 'there has been so strong a prejudice' that it was 'impossible to go on' as things now stood (Morriss, 187). Morale in the civil departments slumped, and St Vincent's policies also alienated timber and shipbuilding contractors. The problems of a naval administrative system, traditionally divided between the Board of Admiralty and the Navy Board and its subordinates, were thus starkly revealed.

It was impossible to exclude politics from these events which provided Pitt with a weapon to attack Addington and regain power. Thus from 1803 St Vincent's naval administration was attacked in press and parliament. The renewal of the war in that year encouraged accusations that the effect of his economies had been to slow naval mobilization. He had cancelled contracts with private shipbuilders, thinking the work could be done more cheaply in the reformed dockyards. He had also checked the prices the navy offered for ship timber, which resulted in a drying up of supplies from the private timber contractors. He quarrelled with old friends and former political allies; Lord Spencer headed a 'new opposition' group against his policies and in January 1804 Evan Nepean, secretary to the Admiralty and a former protégé, resigned after increasing difficulties with the commission of naval inquiry. St Vincent's administration proved an increasing source of weakness for Addington's government. On 15 March 1804, in moving for a comparative return of ships built, Pitt attacked St Vincent's policies and declared him 'less brilliant and less able in a civil capacity than in a warlike one' (Morriss, 197–8). Increasingly some naval officers, notably Nelson, agreed. Addington's government resigned on 10 May and St Vincent left office on 15 May 1804. The commission was replaced by one for revising the civil affairs of the navy. Within a year the political repercussions from publication of the commission of inquiry's reports led to the resignation and impeachment of Lord Melville, St Vincent's successor at the Admiralty. The attacks on St Vincent were continued through 1805 by John Jeffrey, MP for Poole, who repeatedly moved for papers to prove the admiral's incompetence. On 14 May 1806 he moved for a committee of the whole house to consider these matters, in a rambling and ineffective speech. But the whigs were now in government. The tide of opinion had changed in favour of St Vincent in a post-Trafalgar world. The first lord, Lord Howick, son of St Vincent's old friend Sir Charles Grey, with several members of the Admiralty board and Charles James Fox, repudiated Jeffrey's allegations and the motion was negatived without a division. Fox moved a vote of thanks to St Vincent for his administration which had 'added lustre to his exalted character, and is entitled to the approbation of this house' (DNB), and this was agreed without a division.

Final years and reputation In the summer of 1805 St Vincent had been asked, through Addington, now Lord Sidmouth, to command the Channel Fleet. He had indignantly refused 'unless Mr Pitt should unsay all he had said in the House of Commons' on 15 March 1804 (Tucker, 2.268). He sought an interview with George III on 23 June to explain his position, declaring that he was the guardian of his own honour and that after Pitt's treatment of him, he could not entrust that honour to the prime minister. After Pitt's death, however, when Lord Grenville repeated the request, St Vincent agreed on 1 February 1806. He had been created admiral of the red on 9 November 1805 and on 7 March 1806 hoisted his flag in the *Hibernia* (110 guns). He was now seventy-one and in indifferent health, but resumed his old station off Ushant and the strenuous work of blockade. He was one of the commissioners to Lisbon between August and October 1806 when, on the threat of a French invasion of Portugal, it was proposed to secure the Portuguese fleet and transport the king of Portugal to Brazil. But these measures were postponed by both sides and St Vincent returned to command of the Channel Fleet until the end of October when it returned to Cawsand Bay for the winter. His health was poor and the Admiralty gave him leave to live ashore in the neighbourhood. On 18 March 1807 the whig ministry resigned. St

Vincent did not wish to serve under its tory successors and on 24 April 1807 he hauled down his flag for the last time.

In retirement he spent most of his time at Rochetts. Until 1810 he occasionally attended the House of Lords, speaking chiefly on naval issues; in 1808 he spoke strongly against the expedition to Copenhagen and the capture of the Danish fleet as dishonourable. He long retained a keen interest in both national and local politics. His mind remained alert though physically he was plagued by rheumatism, a tendency to dropsy, and a troublesome cough; a visit to the south of France in the winter of 1818–19 did not alleviate these complaints. St Vincent's wife, Martha, had died on 8 February 1816 after suffering for some years from nervous illness and confusion.

In these last years honours fell thick upon St Vincent. He was made an elder brother of Trinity House in 1806. On 26 August 1800 he had been made lieutenant-general of marines and on 11 May 1814 he was promoted general. On 7 May 1814 he became acting admiral of the fleet and commander-in-chief in the channel and on 2 January 1815 he was made GCB. On the coronation of George IV he was promoted admiral of the fleet, and on 19 July 1821 the king personally sent him the gold mounted baton which symbolized the office. This was an honour all the more marked as, by custom, there could be only one officer of that rank, already held by the duke of Clarence. St Vincent's health was now much broken, but at eighty-seven he was still able to attend the king on the royal yacht at Greenwich on 11 August 1822. Here he met and talked to four pensioners, former seamen who had served under him and remarked 'We were all smart fellows in our day' (Anson, 337). He died on 13 March 1823 at Rochetts and was buried at St Michael's, Stone, as he desired, simply and without ostentation. A monument by Francis Chantrey was erected to him in the church in 1825 and another, condemned as tasteless, in St Paul's Cathedral in 1823. Since he had no children, on his death the earldom of St Vincent and the barony of Jervis of Meaford became extinct. On 27 April 1801 the admiral had been created Viscount St Vincent of Meaford, with a special remainder to his nephew, Captain William Henry Ricketts, who was drowned off Ushant on 26 January 1805. The title therefore passed to the latter's younger brother, Edward Jervis Ricketts, who took the name Jervis in lieu of Ricketts on 7 May 1823.

St Vincent's life and career were marked by self-sufficiency. Whether this was the result of his father's refusal to honour a bill for £20 at the beginning of the young Jervis's career, and his subsequent hardships, it is now difficult to determine. Possibly his memory in old age magnified those youthful hardships he described to Edward Pelham Brenton, his biographer. But his early career, revealed in letters to his sister, makes it plain that he devoted himself to learning his seamanship from the warrant officers with whom he served, which, enriched by his later experience, earned him an unsurpassed professional reputation. By the time he was appointed to command his character was fixed. It was marked by devotion to the navy, which he believed superior to other services, though his admiration for the marines was heartfelt. His belief in

efficiency and discipline was absolute, his hatred of slackness and inefficiency vigorously expressed, and his suppression of mutiny, though essential, was often marked by extreme harshness. At a critical period his resolution and courage did not falter; yet his authoritarian temper could not tolerate criticism. Careless of wounded feelings when convinced he was right, he could be both stubborn and impetuous, inflexible and quick tempered. He possessed a grim humour, not always appreciated by its recipients. But he was ungrudging to zeal, skill, and courage, promoting those who showed such qualities, particularly the sons of old officers who lacked influence. In private life he was kind and generous, always ready to help anyone he believed had any claim on him.

St Vincent was not a great tactician. The battle of St Vincent, the only major battle in which he commanded, though temporarily deflecting a projected Franco-Spanish invasion, was not decisive and gained its fame largely through the nation's relief at the news of a victory during a gloomy period of the war. His importance lies in his being the organizer of victories; the creator of well-equipped, highly efficient fleets; and in training a school of officers as professional, energetic, and devoted to the service as himself. His mind was firm, clear, and decisive. Although his workload was exhausting, no significant detail escaped him and he excelled in the introduction of major improvements in naval health and hygiene. As a reforming administrator St Vincent was well-intentioned but tactless. Dauntless and persevering in his crusade against what he saw as institutionalized corruption in the royal dockyards and civil offices, he impatiently rejected traditional working methods and office practice, and condemned unheard a system often corrupt yet effective, which he did not fully understand. In the short term he alienated the existing naval administration and his reforms resulted in disruption when war was renewed. But St Vincent's term of office at the Admiralty produced important results. By providing a mass of information on working practices in the commission reports, by reducing abuses and promoting greater honesty and efficiency, and by clearing away outdated customs of work and rewards, St Vincent ensured that the navy was better prepared to meet the challenges of the nineteenth century.

P. K. CRIMMIN

Sources J. S. Tucker, *Memoirs of Admiral the Rt Hon. the earl of St Vincent*, 2 vols. (1844) · E. P. Brenton, *Life of Lord St Vincent* (1838) · R. F. Mackay, 'Lord St Vincent's early years, 1735–55', *Mariner's Mirror*, 76 (1990), 51–65 · C. White, *The battle of Cape St Vincent* (1997) · M. M. Drummond, 'Jervis, John', HoP, *Commons, 1754–90* · D. R. Fisher, 'Jervis, John', HoP, *Commons, 1790–1820* · GEC, *Peerage*, new edn, vol. 11 · W. V. Anson, *The life of John Jervis, Admiral Lord St Vincent* (1913) · William Salt Library, Stafford, Parker–Jervis MSS, 49/44, bundles 49, 81A, 88/1, 89, 90, 91/1–9 · survey of estates, 1800, 1808, D1798/663/39, 40; will and codicils, 1823, D1798/663/200; fuller account of estates, will, etc., 1825, Staffs. RO, Hand Morgan collection, Parker–Jervis of Meaford papers, D1798/663/204 · NMM, Jervis MSS [letters 1794–1804 from Nelson; lieutenant's promotion book 1801; letterbook 1806–7] · J. Jervis, earl of St Vincent, letters to Andrew Baird, 1799–1823, NMM, Parker MSS, PAR/166/4, 167/a–c [approx. 280 letters] · NMM, Baird MSS, BAI/1/1–53 [letters from St Vincent] · W. Boxall, letter to Andrew Baird, 4 March 1823, NMM,

Baird MSS, BAI/2 [about St Vincent's last illness] · J. Jervis, earl of St Vincent, letters, 1793–1803, NMM, Nepean MSS, NEP/4–7 · *Letters of … the earl of St Vincent, whilst the first lord of the admiralty, 1801–1804*, ed. D. B. Smith, 2 vols., Navy RS, 55, 61 (1922–7) · *Private papers of George, second Earl Spencer*, ed. J. S. Corbett and H. W. Richmond, 4 vols., Navy RS, 46, 48, 58–9 (1913–24) · *The dispatches and letters of Vice-Admiral Lord Viscount Nelson*, ed. N. H. Nicolas, 7 vols. (1844–6) · R. Morriss, *The royal dockyards during the revolutionary and Napoleonic wars* (1983) · C. Lloyd, *St Vincent and Camperdown* (1967) · J. J. Keevil, J. L. S. Coulter, and C. Lloyd, *Medicine and the navy, 1200–1900*, 3: 1714–1815 (1961) · D. Syrett and R. L. DiNardo, *The commissioned sea officers of the Royal Navy, 1660–1815*, rev. edn, Occasional Publications of the Navy RS, 1 (1994) · D. Lyon, *The sailing navy list: all the ships of the Royal Navy, built, purchased and captured, 1688–1860* (1993) · E. Berckman, *Nelson's dear lord. A portrait of St Vincent* (1962) · D. Mathew, *The naval heritage* (1944)

Archives BL, corresp. and papers, Add. MSS 29910–29920, 30001–30013, 31181, 34902–34940, 31159–31167, 31175–31179, 31186–31187 · Duke U., Perkins L., papers · NMM, naval corresp., letter-book, and papers · Staffs. RO, Hand Morgan collection · William Salt Library, Stafford, corresp. | BL, corresp. with Lord Nelson, Add. MSS 34902–34940 *passim* · BL, letters to Evan Nepean, Add. MS 36708 · BL, letters to Charles Rainsford, Add. MSS 23669–23670 · Bodl. Oxf., MSS Shelburne 22, 29, 59 [microfilm] · Devon RO, corresp. with first Viscount Sidmouth · Harrowby Manuscript Trust, Sandon Hill, Staffordshire, letters to earl of Harrowby · Hunt. L., Stowe MSS · Hunt. L., letters to Grenville family · NMM, letters to Andrew Baird · NMM, letters to Richard Bowen · NMM, letters to Sir Thomas Foley · NMM, corresp. with Sir William Hamilton · NMM, letters to Sir Richard Keats · NMM, letters to Lord Keith · NMM, corresp. with Lord Minto · NMM, letters to Lord Nelson · NMM, letters to Sir Evan Nepean · NMM, Orde MSS · NMM, corresp. with Lord Shelburne · NRA, priv. coll., letters to Lord Lansdowne · Royal Arch., letters to George III · Som. ARS, Waldegrave MSS · U. Durham L., letters to second Earl Grey · Yale U., Beinecke L., letters to Sir John Duckworth

Likenesses F. Cotes, oils, 1769, NPG · G. Stuart, oils, 1782–7, NMM · W. Beechey, oils, c.1792–1793, NMM [*see illus.*] · J. De Vaere, Wedgwood medallion, 1798, BM · D. Pellegrini, oils, 1806, NMM · J. Hoppner, oils, 1809, Royal Collection · W. Beechey, oils, c.1810, NMM · J. Hoppner, oils, c.1810, St James's Palace, London; repro. in Anson, *Life of John Jervis*, 312 · J. Hoppner, oils, c.1810, City of London Corporation · oils, c.1822–1823, NMM · L. F. Abbott, oils, NPG · W. Beechey, oils, Guildhall Art Gallery, London · W. Beechey, oils, NPG · J. Bouch, pencil drawing, NPG · F. Chantrey, bust, AM Oxf. · F. Chantrey, bust on monument, St Michael's Church, Stone, Staffordshire · H. Robinson, engraving (after J. Hoppner) · oils (after J. Hoppner), NMM

Wealth at death approx. £29,700 land in Staffordshire, Essex, London, and Bristol (leasehold); English and Irish pension; balances in three banks; plate, etc. to value of over £5000; stock in public funds: 1823, Staffs. RO, Hand Morgan collection, Parker-Jervis MSS, D1798/663/200; abstract of contents of will of Earl St Vincent

Jervis, John (1752–1820). *See under* Jervis, Thomas (1748–1833).

Jervis, Sir John (1802–1856), judge, was born on 12 January 1802 in London, the third and youngest son of Thomas Jervis (1770–1838), MP, barrister, and judge, and Mary Ann, daughter of Oliver Dixon of Red Hill, Old Swinford, Worcestershire. His family name, often wrongly pronounced as Jarvis, derived from a noble ancestor named Gervasius de Stanton, who lived before the time of Edward III. Jervis's father was a leading king's counsel of the Oxford circuit and the last holder of the office of second justice of Chester up to the abolition of the Welsh courts in 1830. Jervis's elder brother was also named John, as was his second cousin, John Jervis, the earl of St Vincent.

Early life and political career Jervis was educated at Westminster School, entering on 18 September 1815. He was enrolled at Middle Temple on 12 January 1819 and matriculated at Trinity College, Cambridge, in the same year (his brother John attended Trinity Hall, confusing some biographers). After two years Jervis left the university without a degree to take a commission as a carabinier in the army, but he seems to have stayed only two years before returning to the study of law. On 3 November 1823 he married Catherine Jane (c.1804–1862), daughter of Alexander Mundell of Great George Street, Westminster. They had three sons and two daughters; the two eldest sons emulated their father by joining the bar and the army respectively.

Following his call to the bar on 6 February 1824 Jervis joined the Oxford circuit where his father had worked, but quickly moved to the Chester and north Wales circuit, where he established a formidable reputation. He became a leading barrister at a young age, with a lucrative practice at Westminster and Guildhall. He became a postman at the court of exchequer, and received an offer of silk in 1837, which he refused, taking instead a patent of precedence. He was elected member for Chester at the general election of December 1832, and remained the Liberal representative for that city until he became a judge. He was an unswerving Liberal, and voted with his party on all major divisions, except over the Jamaica Constitution Bill promoted by Lord Melbourne's ministry in 1839, when he voted against the government, along with the radicals Grote, Hume, and Molesworth (*Hansard 3*, 47.970–72). It was said uncharitably that his failure to support the administration in that year on a number of lesser issues was driven by his resentment at being passed over for an Indian judgeship. However, there is no compelling evidence to suggest that Jervis's political behaviour was governed other than by principle. He seems to have belonged to neither the Benthamite nor the whig tendency of his party, but to have judged each issue on its merits. He was not an especially popular politician, and the *Chester Chronicle*, a Liberal paper, criticized him for lacking any real interest in his constituency, citing his failure to support the River Dee Bill, and later, his attempts to promote his son as his successor in the seat in 1850. As a parliamentarian he was more concerned with national legal issues than his electors' interests.

Jervis was appointed solicitor-general by Lord John Russell in 1846, though within three days he was moved to the post of attorney-general on the promotion of Thomas Wilde to the common pleas. Jervis served as attorney-general during the civil turmoils of 1848. He was responsible for the prosecutions of the Chartist insurgents, and this episode may fairly be regarded as the climactic moment of his life. By winning all the many prosecutions that he conducted with cool professionalism and lack of rancour, Jervis achieved acclaim and respect in higher society and was soon rewarded with high judicial responsibility. The cost to him was overwork, which undermined his health. When Lord Denman retired, Jervis sought to succeed him as lord chief justice, claiming that the attorney-general had precedence for that post by usage, but Russell determined that he could only rightly claim to head the common pleas. Lord Campbell became lord chief justice presiding over king's bench, and Jervis was instead offered a new post comprising the political duties of the lord chancellorship, including the speakership of the House of Lords. The scheme for the new post fell through, however, and Wilde became lord chancellor instead as Lord Truro, leaving the common pleas. Jervis was duly appointed chief justice of common pleas on 16 July 1850, and was knighted and admitted to the privy council. He died in that office after six years of judicial service.

Publications and legislative achievements Jervis was one of the most able lawyers of his age, making notable contributions as a writer and legislator, especially in criminal law and legal procedure. As a young barrister he showed great facility in legal writing, co-producing a notable series of law reports with Younge (1826–30) and then Crompton (1832–3), and concurrently preparing treatises on civil and criminal procedure that quickly became authoritative. Jervis's *Office and Duties of Coroners* (1829) went into nine editions and remained in print for 120 years. Jervis's definition of suicide therein was adopted by the House of Lords a century later (*Beresford* v. *Royal Assurance Co.* (1938) per Lord Atkin). His next book was a major rewriting of Archbold's *Pleading and Evidence in Criminal Cases* (1831). This, the fourth edition, was a huge success and went into five further editions under Jervis's editorship; it remains one of the leading sources on the subject today. Jervis was one of the founders of *The Jurist* in 1837, and for over a decade he authored many of the unsigned notes and articles of that important journal. In 1832 he published perhaps his most innovative text, a commentary on *All the Rules of the Courts of King's Bench and Common Pleas and Exchequer.* The work was sufficiently popular for a second edition to be printed that year; and with the introduction of the radical new pleading rules of Hilary term 1834 a third edition was made. Jervis issued a fourth edition in 1839, and such was his authority in this field that he was appointed chairman of the commission on the practice and procedure of the common law courts in 1850, a panel which included such major jurists as James Shaw Willes and George William Bramwell. Jervis signed the two reports of the commission (*Parl. papers*, 1851, 22; 1852–3, 40), and these laid the foundation for the Common Law Procedure Acts 1852–4, some of the most important legislation in the history of the common law. The acts addressed many thorny problems in the operation of the adversarial pleading system, the application of the forms or writs of action, and the relationship of rights to remedies within the bifurcated system of law and equity. As a fundamental reform of the common-law system, the Common Law Procedure Acts are second in importance only to the Judicature Acts of 1873–5; and Jervis must be accorded much credit for this most successful phase of Victorian law reform.

Jervis's greatest achievements as a law reformer were three bills for the reform of local justice, passed in 1848 and known thereafter as the Jervis Acts (11 & 12 Vict. cc. 42–44). He was indeed the sponsor and chief draftsman of these acts, conceiving and executing the policy and details of the legislation more or less single-handedly. The acts codified the powers of justices of the peace to administer criminal and civil law in local jurisdictions, using the deft technique of providing model precedents rather than mandatory rules. These precedents were swiftly adopted and won normative force. The policy of the Jervis Acts was not so much Benthamite utilitarian reform, but rather a modernized restatement of the ancient magistracy system, designed to instil best practice uniformly across the country. Without these reforms the system of local justices may have fallen eventually into terminal decline. The first act dealt with indictable offences, defined in terms of the severity of penalty and the need for jury trial. The second act dealt with the lesser summary offences. The entire mesne process of information, complaint, summons, and warrant, and the procedures for adjudication, witnesses, and administration of remedies including imprisonment, fine, execution, and accountability for money judgments, were spelt out with full precedents. One of the advances of this legislation was the reduction of barriers to co-operation between magistrates in different locales; for example writs of arrest and summons could now be issued where the events in question had occurred in another county. The third act provided for immunity from suit for bona fide actions of the magistracy, thus professionalizing their function and bringing them within the apparatus of a nascent technocratic state. This last act was said at the time to be 'the keystone of the arch which now so gracefully spans the stream of administrative justice' (Freestone and Richardson, 15). Other commentators were less generous, with Justice Coleridge remarking in 1850 that the legislation was 'exceedingly ill-worded' and verbose (*Barton* v. *Bricknell*, 1850), and indeed many judges were called upon to give meaning to its vague provisions, including Jervis himself in the case of *Ratt* v. *Parkinson* (1851). But despite occasional problems, Jervis's achievements as a law reformer were said to be second only to Sir Robert Peel's in his time. He seems to have been motivated by a desire for pragmatic improvement and a dislike for the uncodified and untrammelled powers of the traditional magistracy—good liberal promptings rather than doctrinaire zeal.

Judgments Jervis the advocate and politician became a good judge, well able to lead and even dominate his court; but reservations were expressed about whether he was entirely suited to high judicial office. It was said that he was too political, dexterous, and even unscrupulous an advocate to make a profound judge, and though he quickly dispelled any impression that he was merely a political appointment, he seems to have conformed only partially to the reserved and dignified style expected of the higher judiciary. He gained a reputation among counsel as a rude and abrasive head of court, still in some part a querulous barrister-politician. He was perceived to be prejudiced, tending to make up his mind on the merits of a case quickly at the outset, and then guiding the litigation from the bench so as to confirm his early intuitions. Pragmatism and an urge to resolve situations rapidly seemed stronger in him than any lofty principles, or fidelity to established legal rules. He never made a serious adjudicative error and was rarely successfully appealed, and this was no small matter in the notoriously hazardous jurisdiction of criminal law. However, as chief justice of the common pleas, Jervis's achievements were less remarkable than those accomplished as attorney-general. He was, unsurprisingly, especially fine in criminal cases, and was an acknowledged expert on fraud. In one case he worked out the cheating system of a gang of card sharps in the midst of the trial. In the important case of *R. v. Bird* (1851), Jervis in the minority held that if a defendant was acquitted on a major charge such as murder, then evidence could not later be brought to launch a new indictment on a lesser charge such as assault, an expansive reading of the doctrine of *autrefois acquit*. The reason for this holding was that the jury dealing with the larger indictment was entitled to find the lesser charge proved without a separate indictment at that stage. This minority view was later instated by legislation (14 & 15 Vict. c. 100). In *R. v. Powell* (1852), Jervis held that a burglar could not be indicted for intent to steal 'goods and chattels' when he was really trying to steal a mortgage deed, which until paid was not a chattel but a chose in action or abstract record of an obligation. There are many other instances of legalism being used to protect defendants in criminal cases and so uphold the rule of law. Similar tendencies were exhibited in Jervis's civil judgments. For example, in *Helsham v. Blackwood* (1851), he ruled that a man who killed for honour in a duel was at law a murderer and could be called such without libel; but that for another to state publicly that the killer had practised all night with a pistol and had premeditatedly planned to kill could be a libel as an imputation on honour. The case demonstrated the perversity of both the duellists' code of honour and of the English law of libel. More sensible was *Wenman v. Ash* (1856), where defamatory statements communicated to a man's wife were held to be actionable public statements. In *Arden v. Goodacre* (1852), it was held that the tortious compensation against a sheriff who allowed a debtor to escape from debtors' prison was not to be discounted by any amount the creditor could possibly have recovered against the debtor after the escape. In *Greg v. Cotterell* (1855) it was held that the sheriff was strictly liable even when a debtor's escape or other mishap in the mesne process was caused by his agents or through honest mistake. The stringency of the sheriff's liability may have helped undermine the legal system's commitment to debtors' prisons in the longer term. Jervis developed the important principle that a menacing action could be an assault even without physical contact (*Read v. Coker*, 1853). He ruled that non-resident aliens could not enjoy English copyright protection (*Jeffreys v. Boosey*, 1854); and that only a full assignment of copyright by an author could transfer a registrable copyright to another (*Ex parte Bastow*, 1854). Jervis also gave judgments establishing the following doctrines:

that contract damages for late delivery should be limited to immediate loss rather than lost business, thus foreshadowing the modern doctrine of proximity (*Peterson v. Ayre*, 1853); that the remedy for breach of contractual warranty was confined to damages (*Dawson v. Collins*, 1851); that valid foreign contracts lacking necessary formalities in England were non-enforceable (*Leroux v. Brown*, 1852); that banknotes taken bona fide from a thief were fully negotiable and usable for exchange (*Raphael v. Bank of England*, 1855); and that railway companies were entitled to promote monopolist freight charges (*Parker v. Great Western Railway Co.*, 1851); though as protected monopolists the railway companies could be subjected to duties to complete lines and to provide a decent service (*York and North Midland Railway Co. v. R.*, 1853). Jervis narrowed the doctrine of *negotiorum gestio* so that men needed only directly pay for the necessary debts of wives, not of children (*Sheldon v. Springett*, 1851). Finally, in *Taylor v. Best* (1854), Jervis extended and refined the law of diplomatic immunity. These samples of his judicial work demonstrate the solidity of his achievements, though he cannot be put in the very first rank of judges with contemporaries such as Parke and Bramwell.

Jervis died suddenly at his home in Eaton Square on 1 November 1856, a little short of the age of fifty-five, probably from lung cancer. He was buried at Shipbourne. His early death genuinely shocked and upset his brother judges and the entire legal profession. Though his flaws as a judge and politician were remembered, there was a sense that a great figure of the early era of Victorian law reform had passed away.   JOSHUA S. GETZLER

Sources D. Freestone and J. C. Richardson, 'The making of English criminal law (7): Sir John Jervis and his acts', *Criminal Law Review* (1980), 5–16 · E. Manson, *Builders of our law during the reign of Queen Victoria*, 2nd edn (1904), 50–57 · *Law Magazine*, new ser., 2 (1856–7), 302–7 · Holdsworth, *Eng. law*, vol. 15 · ER, vols. 118–19, 138–9, 148, 169 · *Law Times* (8 Nov 1856), 85–6 · Foss, *Judges*, 9.216–18 · *The Jurist*, new ser., 2/2 (1856), 458 · A. H. Manchester, 'Jervis, John', *Biographical dictionary of the common law*, ed. A. W. B. Simpson (1984), 279–80 · R. W. Kostal, *Law and English railway capitalism, 1825–1875* (1994) · J. H. Baker, *An introduction to legal history*, 4th edn (2002) · Venn, *Alum. Cant.* · R. G. Thorne, 'Jervis, Sir Thomas', HoP, *Commons, 1790–1820*

Jervis, Sir John Jervis White (1766–1830), writer, was born on 10 June 1766, the eldest son of John Jervis-White, of Bally Ellis, co. Wexford, a barrister. Jervis was educated at Dublin University, graduating BA as a fellow-commissioner before becoming a barrister and LLD. Jervis was deeply committed to the British cause in Ireland during the wars with revolutionary France. His services were rewarded by a special royal licence, which enabled him to assume the additional surname of Jervis and by a baronetcy on 10 November 1797 for raising and equipping at his own cost a corps of volunteers, a feat of loyalty he later repeated in Somerset in 1803. On 1 June 1789 he married Jane, daughter of Henry Nisbett of Ashmore, co. Longford. Their first son died young, but they went on to have three more: Henry Meredyth, Humphrey, and Thomas.

Jervis also wrote various propagandist works which

were published in Ireland and England. In 1811 he published a brief work defending British policy against various French calumnies, followed in 1813 by *A Brief View of the Past and Present State of Ireland*. In the same year Jervis also published *A Brief Statement of the Rise, Progress, and Decline of the Ancient Christian Church*.

After the death of his first wife, in 1828 Jervis married Mary (*d*. 1879), the daughter of Thomas Bradford of Sandbach, Cheshire. Jervis died in 1830. His commitment to the British cause was, however, continued by his eldest surviving son, Sir Henry Meredyth Jervis White Jervis (1793–1869), who was a commander in the Royal Navy. Jervis's young widow, Mary, later married his nephew, John Jervis LLD of Ferns, a barrister.　　　　JASON EDWARDS

Sources J. Foster, *The peerage, baronetage, and knightage of the British empire for 1882*, 2 [1882], 656 · Burke, *Peerage* (1890), 759 · W. B. S. Taylor, *History of the University of Dublin* (1845), 469 · Burke, *Peerage* (1907), 916

Jervis, Thomas (1748–1833), Unitarian minister and author, born at Ipswich on 13 January 1748, was the son of William Jervis (*d*. 1792), minister of the Presbyterian congregation in St Nicholas Street, Ipswich. He was educated for the ministry in London at Wellclose Square Academy under David Jennings, and afterwards at Hoxton Academy under Samuel Morton Savage, Andrew Kippis, and David Rees. In 1770 he became classical and mathematical tutor at the Exeter Academy, and at about the same time he also took charge of a Presbyterian congregation at Lympstone, Devon. During 1771–2 he shared with James Perry Bartlett the charge of congregations at Lympstone and Topsham, Devon. In October 1772 he resigned his charge in Devon to become tutor to the earl of Shelburne's two sons at Bowood, Wiltshire, a position he retained for the next eleven years. Here he associated with Joseph Priestley, who was Shelburne's librarian until 1780. In 1773 he was succeeded at Lympstone by his younger brother **John Jervis** (1752–1820), who was ordained in 1779 and continued minister of Lympstone until his death on 27 October 1820.

Thomas Jervis, who was ordained in 1779 in a service conducted by Priestley and Kippis, moved to London in 1783 to succeed Rees as minister of the Presbyterian congregation in St Thomas Street, Southwark. He was elected a trustee of Dr Williams's foundation in 1786, a position he retained until 1808. He was also a member of the Presbyterian board from 1783 to 1808. On the death of Kippis in 1796 he was elected his successor at Princes Street, Westminster. Up to this time his views were low Arian and it is doubtful if they underwent any further development. As a preacher he was described as not eloquent but possessing 'a plain, interesting delivery', while his devotional services were 'particularly good' (Murch, 358). In the summer of 1808 he succeeded William Wood as minister of the Unitarian congregation at Mill Hill, Leeds. He resigned this charge, and left the active ministry in 1818. On his return to London he was re-elected to Dr Williams's Trust in 1823.

Jervis was the author of numerous religious works. A manuscript written by Walter Wilson lists twenty separate sermons and funeral orations. Some of these are reprinted in a volume published in 1811 entitled *Sermons on Various Subjects*. He also collaborated with Kippis, Rees, and Thomas Morgan in the compilation of *A Collection of Hymns and Psalms for Public Worship*, designed for anti-Trinitarian congregations. In addition he wrote numerous contributions to the *Gentleman's Magazine* and the *Monthly Repository*.

Jervis was married to Frances Mary Disney, the daughter of John Disney and Frances Cartwright. His closing years were spent in literary leisure. He died at Brompton Grove, London, on 31 August 1833 and was buried in the church of Fryerning, Essex. His wife survived him.

ALEXANDER GORDON, *rev.* M. J. MERCER

Sources W. Wilson, 'Various dissenting congregations in England', DWL, Wilson MS A 11 · C. Surman, index, DWL · J. Murch, *A history of the Presbyterian and General Baptist churches in the west of England* (1835) · W. Wilson, *The history and antiquities of the dissenting churches and meeting houses in London, Westminster and Southwark*, 4 vols. (1808–14), vol. 4 · G. E. Evans, *Vestiges of protestant dissent* (1897) · E. F. Hatfield, *The poets of the church: a series of biographical sketches of hymn writers* (1884) · R. V. Taylor, ed., *Supplement of the Biographia Leodiensis, or, Biographical sketches of the worthies of Leeds* (1867) · W. D. Jeremy, *The Presbyterian Fund and Dr Daniel Williams's Trust* (1885) · will, PRO, PROB 11/1825, fols. 104v–105v
Archives DWL, Wilson MS A 11 · N. Yorks. CRO, corresp. with Christopher Wyvill
Likenesses P. MacDowell, plaster bust, DWL

Jervis, William Henley Pearson- (1813–1883), ecclesiastical historian, second son of Hugh Nicholas *Pearson (1776–1856), dean of Salisbury from 1823 to 1846, and his wife, Sarah Maria Elliott (1781–1858), was born on 29 June 1813 at Oxford. He was brother of Henry Hugo *Pierson, Charles Buchanan *Pearson [*see under* Pearson, Hugh Nicholas], and Hugh *Pearson [*see under* Pearson, Hugh Nicholas]. In 1824 he was sent to a preparatory school at Mitcham, Surrey, whence he was removed two years later to Harrow School. He distinguished himself at Harrow, but, unfortunately, at the sacrifice of his health. In 1831 he entered Christ Church, Oxford, but a severe illness from a spinal complaint threw him back a year in his course of study. He spent his enforced leisure cultivating a strong natural taste for music and singing. In June 1835 he graduated BA (MA 1838); in July of the following year he was ordained deacon, and in 1837 was instituted to the rectory of St Nicholas, Guildford. He was appointed by his father, then dean of Salisbury, a prebendary of the collegiate church of Heytesbury, Wiltshire. In 1848 he married Martha Jervis (*d*. 1888), daughter of Osborne Markham and granddaughter of William Markham, archbishop of York. His wife's mother was a great-niece of John Jervis, the earl of St Vincent, and on her death in 1865 Pearson assumed the surname of Jervis.

Owing to the delicate state of his health, Jervis and his wife lived abroad for six years (November 1856 to July 1862), chiefly in the south of France and in Paris. Here he studied, in the archives of Pau, Bayonne, and other places, as well as in the Bibliothèque Nationale at Paris, the memoirs and documents illustrating the ecclesiastical history of France. The fruit of these labours appeared in 1872 as *A History of the Church of France from the Concordat of Bologna to the Revolution* (2 vols.). Ten years later he published a sequel, *The Gallican Church and the French Revolution*. He also published *The Student's History of France* (1862) and other works. Jervis's books on church history were subsequently presented by his widow to the London Library. He never quite rallied from the loss of his brother, Hugh Pearson (1817–1882), vicar of Sonning, Berkshire, and canon of Windsor, and died on 27 January 1883 at his home, 28 Holland Park, London. He was buried in Sonning churchyard, near his brother. His widow died on 8 March 1888.

ROBERT HARRISON, *rev.* H. C. G. MATTHEW

Sources *Guardian* (31 Jan 1883), 168 · *Annual Register* (1883), pt 2, p. 124 · private information (1891) · *CGPLA Eng. & Wales* (1884)

Wealth at death £15,379 1s. 7d.: resworn probate, March 1884, *CGPLA Eng. & Wales* (1883)

Jervise, Andrew (1820–1878), antiquary, was born on 28 July 1820 at Brechin, Forfarshire, the son of Jean Chalmers (d. 1878), a nurseryman's daughter, with whom he lived all his life. In his short school career he began to develop antiquarian tastes, which were fostered by the legendary stories of a widowed aunt who settled with his mother. Leaving school at the age of eleven, Jervise soon became a compositor, and formed the acquaintance of Alexander Laing, 'the Brechin poet'. Finishing his apprenticeship in 1837, he oscillated until 1841 between Brechin and Edinburgh, nominally a compositor, but affecting poetry and painting. Laing, in his letters, dissuaded him from poetry; and after taking lessons in design and colour under Sir William Allan and Thomas Duncan between 1842 and 1846, Jervise settled in Brechin as a teacher of drawing, selling a number of pictures locally. In 1847 he delivered there three lectures on the popular history of painting and its principles.

In 1856 two patrons—Lord Panmure, whose birthday he had celebrated in verse (1847), and Mr Chalmers of Aldbar, Forfarshire, whose library he had catalogued—secured for Jervise the examinership of registers, with a salary of £200 p.a., which enabled him to travel widely in eastern Scotland. This gave him opportunities for research of which he took substantial advantage. He published in various antiquarian societies' transactions, and collected for a series of newspaper articles inscriptions from the churchyards within his range. He began publishing specimens of churchyard poetry in the *Montrose Standard* in 1848 (republished in two volumes, 1875–9), an important and extensive collection. He was the 'Old Mortality' of his counties, and as a genial correspondent in the newspapers supplied antiquarian information of the most diverse kinds. His varied tastes and experience gave him curious stores of knowledge, and he amassed a valuable library, specially rich in broadsides and ballads. He published several books, including *Sketches of the History and Traditions of Glenesk* (1852), dedicated to Lord Panmure, *History and Traditions of the Land of the Lindsays* (1853), and *Memorials of*

Angus and the Mearns (1861), almost exclusively of antiquarian interest. Jervise died at Dundee on 12 April 1878, four months before his mother.

T. W. BAYNE, *rev.* H. C. G. MATTHEW

Sources W. Alexander and J. G. Michie, memoir, in A. Jervise, *Epitaphs and inscriptions from burial grounds and old buildings in the north-east of Scotland*, 2 (1879) · Irving, *Scots.* · Boase, *Mod. Eng. biog.* · *CCI* (1878)

Archives Montrose Library, Montrose, Angus Archives, MSS and papers · Museum of Scotland, Edinburgh, genealogical collections relating to north-east Scotland | U. Edin. L., letters to David Laing

Wealth at death £5046 19s. 1d.: confirmation, 1878, *CCI*

Jerviswoode. For this title name *see* Baillie, Charles, Lord Jerviswoode (1804–1879).

Jervois, Sir William Francis Drummond (1821–1897), army officer, was born in Cowes on 10 September 1821, the eldest son of General William Jervois (1782–1862), Peninsular War veteran and governor of Hong Kong, from an Anglo-Irish family, and his wife, Elizabeth (d. 1865), daughter of William Maitland of Montreal. He attended Dr Burney's academy, Gosport, then went to Mr Barry's school, Woolwich, to prepare for entry to the Royal Military Academy, Woolwich, which he attended from 1837 to 1839. From an early age he excelled at drawing, and after he was commissioned second lieutenant in the Royal Engineers on 19 March 1839 his survey sheets were used as an example for the others at Chatham. In 1841 he was sent to the Cape of Good Hope to carry out survey work on the eastern ('Kaffir') border. In October 1841 he was promoted lieutenant. He made the drawings for the Fish River Bridge at Fort Brown. In 1845 he was made adjutant of the Royal Sappers and Miners and accompanied Colonel Piper to Natal, making a survey of his return journey via Colesberg to Cape Town in small notebooks (which still survive).

In 1847 Jervois went with General Sir George Berkeley to Kaffirland, where he made a series of military sketches of about 2000 square miles from Keiskamma to the Kei River and from Fort Hare to the sea; his survey was used by Lord Chelmsford thirty years later, and was subsequently published by Arrowsmith of London. He was promoted captain in December 1847. His service in the Cape was noted by General Smith who reported to Lord Raglan in 1848 that Jervois was 'one of the most able, energetic and zealous officers I have ever exacted more than his share of duty from' (*The Times*).

Jervois was already working very hard. On 19 March 1850 he married Lucy, daughter of William Norsworthy, a London builder from Devon; they had two sons and three daughters. At this time he was undergoing a religious experience and his diary is full of notes on his Bible reading. For his honeymoon in Torquay, Jervois packed Henry Venn's *Duty of Man* and Martin Tupper's *Proverbial Philosophy*. In 1847 the prince de Joinville, a senior French naval officer, published *Note sur l'état des forces navales de la France*, which was translated into English. This suggested that paddle warships could attack British merchant ships and

Sir William Francis Drummond Jervois (1821–1897), by D. J. Pound (after John & Charles Watkins)

raid the British coast. He stated that it would need to be a future plan as the French fleet was then inferior to the British. However, Joinville was put in command of the fleet in the Mediterranean where France was at war with Morocco, and some feared he might attempt an attack when at sea. In England the duke of Wellington wrote a letter which his friends leaked to the press, stating his concern to the government that only 5000 troops could be gathered in any one place to stop a French invasion that could well consist of 40,000 troops. Lord Palmerston agreed, and spoke in the House of Commons of a 'steam bridge' being thrown over the channel by invading forces. He claimed the British fleet was far too busy policing the empire and protecting trade to stop an invasion. Forts were required to protect British ports: France was fortifying Cherbourg.

Jervois was sent to Alderney in 1852, where there was under construction a 'harbour of refuge': so called for political reasons, it was a crucial forward naval base from which to attack Cherbourg. At first he was not keen to go there, and it was not until he read a report by Sir John Burgoyne that Alderney was as important as Gibraltar that he became enthusiastic. For the next three years Jervois was responsible for the design and construction of all the fifteen forts in Alderney, except Grosnez. A barracks and arsenal were also constructed. Jervois was visited by the queen and Prince Albert, who was taken round Fort Tourgie and expressed it 'very strong'. Later it was renamed Fort Albert. In late 1853 Jervois volunteered for the Crimea, but was turned down as his duties at Alderney were

considered more important, even though France was an ally against Russia.

Promoted major in September 1854 Jervois became in January 1855 commanding royal engineer, London district, and in the same year a member of the barracks (construction) committee. From 7 April 1856 to 4 September 1862 he was assistant inspector-general of fortifications. The director, Lieutenant-Colonel Owen, gave Jervois a free hand. There must have been considerable communication problems as the office was divided between Harrington House, 13A Abingdon Street, and 109 Victoria Street, as well as a house in Great George Street.

From 1859 to 1875, in addition to his other duties, Jervois was secretary to the defence committee presided over by the duke of Cambridge. Once Prince Albert had indicated his approval of Jervois and his Alderney forts, doors opened to him. The Orsini plot to assassinate Napoleon III worsened Anglo-French relations and led to a war scare in Britain. General Jonathan Peel, secretary of state for war, used Jervois for making secret plans for fighting an invading enemy south of London, and both Croydon and Chislehurst were areas considered. From 1859 to 1860 Jervois was secretary to the royal commission on the defences of the United Kingdom. The commission looked at Plymouth, Portsmouth (including Spithead and the Isle of Wight), Pembroke, Dover, Chatham, Medway, Haulbowline (Cork), and at first Woolwich, though this was later omitted. The commission proposed a complex system of government loans and annuities with an estimated cost of nearly £12 million for the forts, some of which, notably in Plymouth and Portsmouth, had been started before the commission was set up. Gladstone, then chancellor of the exchequer, was opposed to forts, especially their cost, but Palmerston overruled him. Jervois worked night and day to finish the report, which was presented to parliament in 1860. After the defence committee had nearly thrown it out, Jervois drew up a memorandum showing the inconsistency of the committee's report, and the commission's report was adopted by a majority in the House of Commons, but they reduced the £12 million to £7,460,000.

Promoted lieutenant-colonel in February 1861, Jervois was deputy director of works at the War Office from September 1862 to March 1875. A new fortifications committee was set up to examine the implementation of the works, and Jervois (for once) had to delegate much of the fort building, as there was need of a firm control in London. There were great improvements in ordnance, projectiles, and armour at this time, and Jervois attended experiments with new weapons. There was some criticism by the 'blue water' school, who thought the navy could defend more effectively than the proposed forts, especially those built inland at Plymouth and Portsmouth. Both Palmerston and Jervois thought that an enemy force could land away from the ports, circle inland, and attack them from the rear, hence the design of forts like Crownhill at Plymouth.

Jervois travelled the empire inspecting fortifications. In 1863 he went to British North America, and reported on the defences of Canada, Nova Scotia, New Brunswick, and

Bermuda. During the American Civil War Jervois twice visited the United States to examine its defences, visiting the principal forts of the eastern seaboard. Disguised as an artist, he sketched the harbour defences of Portland and Boston from rowing boats. In November 1863 he was made a CB, civil division, and in 1865 he went to Canada to study the fortifications of Toronto, but the money that was voted for his scheme, over £1 million, was spent on railways. Promoted colonel in 1867, in 1869 he went to Halifax and Bermuda to inspect the defence works, and then to Gibraltar and Malta. In 1871–2 he was sent by the Indian government to inspect the defences of Aden, Perim, Bombay, and the Hooghly, also going to Rangoon and Moulmein. In February 1872 at Port Blair in the Andaman Islands he was with the viceroy, Lord Mayo, when the latter was assassinated by a convict. There was considerable opposition to some of Jervois's schemes, and he was always ready to lecture on the subject. Thus in 1868 he spoke at the Royal United Service Institution on the 'Application of iron to fortifications in special reference to Plymouth Breakwater Fort'. In May 1874 he was made a KCMG for his service to Canada.

From April 1875 to July 1877 Jervois was governor of the Straits Settlements (later part of Malaya), arriving at Singapore in May 1875. The situation in Perak was unstable, and Jervois decided it should be annexed—a policy Lord Carnarvon, the colonial secretary, did not want. Following Jervois's initial moves, in November James Birch, the British resident in Perak, was assassinated, and a revolt spread. With troops from India and Hong Kong, the 1875 Perak expedition crushed the revolt. However Disraeli and Carnarvon, who believed himself insulted by Jervois, enforced a political settlement which reversed Jervois's policy: annexation was forbidden. Jervois had been rash and insubordinate, and he had to back down. According to W. D. McIntyre, 'the Perak War is a classic example of the man on the spot embarrassing the home government' (McIntyre, 315–16). At Singapore Jervois drew up a report on the defences needed there, which was used some years later though it did not, with hindsight, go far enough. He distrusted and despised Malays, preferring the Singapore Chinese. His intervention on the Malay mainland committed Britain to continued presence there.

In 1877 Jervois visited Australia and advised the colonies on defence. While in Australia, on 6 July 1877 he was appointed governor of South Australia (because Lord Carnarvon disliked his active intervention on the Malay mainland) retaining the duty of defence adviser to the other Australian colonies. In October 1877 he was promoted major-general. He also visited Tasmania and New Zealand to report on defences. In his reports Jervois stressed that the colonies should keep cruisers in their ports, with a small force available to deter an enemy from landing. He thought that as long as Britain had command of the seas a fleet could be sent in pursuit of an enemy. The danger was that, with the Australian coastline being so long, a small expedition could easily land undetected. The Australian and New Zealand governments wanted defence expenses to be paid by the mother country, but Jervois persuaded them to agree to colonial contributions. In South Australia forts were built at Glanville and Largs Bay, with a lightly armed vessel, *Protector*, as guard ship. The 1882 royal commission on the defence of British possessions and commerce abroad considered that Jervois's plans were sufficient. A popular governor, he supported local religious and philanthropic organizations and also encouraged horse-racing and Turkish bathing in Adelaide.

From 1882 to November 1888 Jervois was governor of New Zealand, retiring (with the rank of lieutenant-general) from military service on 7 April 1882. In 1885 there was a war scare over Russia. With the help of Admiral Tryon he arranged for the immediate defence of the harbours at Wellington, Auckland, Lyttelton, and Port Chalmers, where strong forts were built. There was a crisis over Samoa, which wanted British protection to avoid annexation by Germany or the USA. Jervois telegraphed London and was told that there was a treaty with both Russia and Germany and that neither power could annex Samoa, which Britain recognized as an independent kingdom.

Jervois differed from majority opinion in New Zealand and Australia on the question of Chinese immigration. The colonies dreaded being overrun by Chinese; Jervois thought the Chinese hardworking and useful immigrants who could work in the tropical areas of Australasia, and argued that they would be consumers as well as workers. He failed to convince the Australians or New Zealanders. Jervois left New Zealand in March 1889 having reportedly won the esteem of all classes. The *Sydney Morning Herald* claimed he was, 'beyond measure the best and most popular governor that New Zealand has ever had' (*The Times*).

Back in England Jervois sat on the 1889 Stanhope committee on coastal defence. He advocated, in the press and by lectures, handing over coastal defence to the navy. In 1893 he was made a colonel-commandant of the Royal Engineers. Jervois was a talented artist. He published in the Royal Engineers' *Professional Papers* and elsewhere on fortification, coast defence, and colonial defence. On 18 March 1895 his wife died, and two months later his second son, John, a major in the Royal Engineers, also died. In 1897 he was staying with his daughter-in-law in Southampton when, on 16 August, he was driving at Bitterne in an open carriage, sitting on the kerb side with the coachman behind. A lady friend took the reins and the horse shied at a piece of paper in the road. Jervois was flung out when the horse bolted. He suffered cerebral haemorrhage, and on 17 August died at 4 Victoria Road, Woolston, near Southampton. He was buried at Christ Church, Virginia Water, Surrey.   JOHN S. KINROSS

Sources *Royal Engineers Journal*, 27 (1897), 244–6 • *Royal Engineers Journal*, 28 (1898) • *DNB* • *The Times* (18 Aug 1897) • Burke, *Gen. Ire.* • *Army and Navy Illustrated* (11 Feb 1899) • J. S. Kinross, 'Jervois and the defence of Britain, 1860', *The Historian* [London], 47 (1995), 26–8 • C. Partridge and T. Davenport, *The fortifications of Alderney* (1993) • *Hart's Army List* • J. S. Kinross, 'The Palmerston forts in the SW: why were they built?', MA diss., University of Exeter, 1994 • Boase, *Mod.*

Eng. biog. · *AusDB* · W. D. McIntyre, *The imperial frontier in the tropics, 1865–75* (1967) · d. cert.

Archives NAM · NRA, priv. coll., corresp. and papers · Royal Engineers, Brompton barracks, Chatham, Kent, Canadian diary · Royal United Services Institute, London · State Library of South Australia, Adelaide, addresses, corresp., and papers | Wilts. & Swindon RO, corresp. with Sydney Herbert

Likenesses W. Fisher, group portrait, 1851 (with family) · W. Fisher, group portrait (with family) · D. J. Pound, line engraving (after photograph by John & Charles Watkins), NPG [*see illus.*] · bust, Adelaide Club, Australia · photograph, repro. in *Army and Navy Illustrated* · wood-engraving (after photograph by Elliott & Fry), NPG; repro. in *ILN* (10 April 1875)

Wealth at death £141 10s. 5d.: probate, 11 Sept 1897, *CGPLA Eng. & Wales*

Jesse, Edward (1780–1868), writer on natural history, was born at Hutton Cranswick, near Driffield, Yorkshire, on 14 January 1780, the third son of the Revd William Jesse (1738–1814), vicar of Hutton Cranswick. His father was descended from a branch of the Languedoc barons de Jessé Lévas, who emigrated to England after the revocation of the edict of Nantes in 1685.

Privately educated, in 1798 Jesse was appointed clerk in the government's Santo Domingo office, and about 1802 became private secretary to Lord Dartmouth, president of the Board of Control. In 1806 he received the sinecure post of gentleman of the ewry, and later a clerkship in the Office of Woods and Forests, and a commissionership of hackney coaches (c.1814–c.1830). He lived for some years in Richmond Park, where he developed his taste for natural history. Jesse was deputy surveyor of the royal parks and palaces, probably from about 1822 to 1830/31, when he retired from public life with a pension.

For some years, Jesse rented a cottage at Bushey Park, where he perfected a plan for removing honey from beehives without killing the bees. Here he was on very familiar terms with the duke of Clarence who later became William IV. Jesse lived next at Molesey, Surrey, where he formed a close friendship with the Revd John Mitford, editor of the *Gentleman's Magazine*, who took a great interest in royal park improvements planned by Jesse. Jesse then lived for some years at Hampton, where he was greatly involved with the restoration of Hampton Court Palace. In 1807 Jesse married Matilda, third daughter of Sir John Morris bt, of Glamorgan. The couple had one son, John Heneage *Jesse, and two daughters, including Matilda Charlotte *Houstoun, author. His first wife died and, in 1852, he married Jane Caroline, daughter of J. G. Meymott of Richmond, Surrey, who survived him.

Jesse was a sincere lover of animals. Always surrounded by pets, he could not believe that quadrupeds at least could be denied immortality. His lack of scientific training is reflected in his writings which though colourful are often anecdotal rather than systematic. Besides contributions to the *Gentleman's Magazine*, *Bentley's Miscellany*, *Once a Week*, and *The Times*, Jesse wrote a number of works describing the countryside around Hampton Court, Windsor, and Eton. His interests in natural history and angling are reflected in his *An Angler's Rambles* (1836) and

Edward Jesse (1780–1868), by Daniel Macdonald, 1844

Anecdotes of Dogs (1846). Jesse died on 28 March 1868, aged eighty-eight, at his home in Belgrave Place, Brighton, where he had lived since 1862.

G. T. BETTANY, *rev.* ALEXANDER GOLDBLOOM

Sources *The Times* (31 March 1868) · *GM*, 4th ser., 5 (1868), 682 · Mrs Houstoun, *A woman's memoirs of world-known men*, 2 vols. (1883) · M. C. Houstoun, *Sylvanus Redivius, the Rev. John Mitford, with a memoir of Edward Jesse* (1889) · F. Ross, *Celebrities of the Yorkshire wolds* (1878) · Boase, *Mod. Eng. biog.* · C. Knight, ed., *The English cyclopaedia: biography*, 3 (1856) · Ward, *Men of the reign* · *CGPLA Eng. & Wales* (1868)

Archives Hunt. L., letters to Annie Fields and James Thomas

Likenesses D. Macdonald, chalk and wash drawing, 1844, NPG [*see illus.*] · B. Leighton, lithograph (aged seventy-one), BM · marble bust, Brighton Art Gallery

Wealth at death under £3000: probate, 24 April 1868, *CGPLA Eng. & Wales*

Jesse, John Heneage (bap. 1809, d. 1874), historical writer, was baptized at West Bromwich, Staffordshire, on 15 March 1809, the only son of Edward *Jesse (1780–1868), a placeholder and writer on natural history, and his first wife, Matilda, née Morris. The family (there were also two daughters) lived at Richmond, Bushey Park, and finally West Molesey, Surrey. Edward Jesse's many influential friends included William, duke of Clarence (later William IV), John Wilson Croker, and the Revd John Mitford, editor of the *Gentleman's Magazine*. The children were introduced at home to literary and political discussion. The younger Jesse attended Eton College on the foundation; he seems to have been best known there for his wild pranks. One of these caused him to flee to Norway for several months with his friend Lord Waterford, thereby effectively ending his formal education. In 1835, through the influence of

William IV, Jesse obtained a clerkship at the Admiralty. He remained in this position for many years, before retiring with a comfortable pension. As an adult he was a dedicated Londoner, and seldom ventured away from the metropolitan area. He never married and was estranged from his family. He maintained a small circle of devoted friends and was a frequenter of the Garrick Club and Lady Blessington's salon.

Jesse early cherished literary ambitions. In 1829 he published 'Mary Queen of Scots' and other Poems; in the dedication to Sir Walter Scott he called this work 'my first step in literary life'. The long biographical poem about Mary and the several shorter verses are entirely conventional in form and diction, and of little lasting value. The title poem is accompanied by 'historical notes' which, along with the author's exalted view of the queen, suggest the direction and content of his future works. The first of his historical volumes, Memoirs of the Court of England during the Reigns of the Stuarts (4 vols.), appeared in 1840. It was followed by volumes which covered English history from 1688 until the death of George III. In addition Jesse published works on London and on Richard III. Memoirs of Celebrated Etonians (2 vols., 1875) did not appear until after his death. Jesse never lost his dream of making a mark in literary circles. His Memoirs of King Richard the Third (1862) originated with his intention to write a play about the battle of Bosworth. As he explained in the preface, he felt it necessary to do research on 'the characters and motives of action of the different historical personages'. Thus he acquired the material which he published in addition to his historical drama. However, the play (in blank verse) adds nothing to his reputation.

Jesse's works are largely uncritical and routine retellings of well-known facts and stories. His narratives focus on court anecdotes and the public characters of his protagonists. He cited and quoted from all the available printed memoirs, letters, and journals. The principal exception is George Selwyn and his Contemporaries (4 vols., 1843), in which he printed for the first time a number of letters to Selwyn. His Memoirs of the Life and Reign of King George the Third (3 vols., 1867) also included some previously unprinted letters. These volumes were for many years the only published source for this material. Jesse's style is not remarkable but is easily comprehensible, which probably accounted for his apparent popularity. His sister Matilda Charlotte *Houstoun, who led a much more adventurous and interesting life than he, said 'He was entirely free from any gifts, either of fancy or imagination', which explained 'the somewhat dry tone of his works'. She did, however, acknowledge the validity of the critics who always mentioned his 'conscientiousness' (Houstoun, 230–31).

Jesse wrote about royalty, courts, and romantic, often lost, causes. In an age when history was highly regarded and widely read, he found a particular niche. He should be regarded more as a popular early to mid-Victorian writer than as a historian. Jesse died in his long-tenanted rooms at 7 Albany Court Yard, Piccadilly, London, on 7 July 1874.

BARBARA BRANDON SCHNORRENBERG

Sources DNB · Mrs Houstoun, A woman's memoirs of world-known men, 2 vols. (1883) · Annual Register (1874) · IGI
Likenesses Count D'Orsay, pencil and chalk drawing, NPG
Wealth at death under £1500: administration with will, 24 Oct 1874, CGPLA Eng. & Wales

Jesse, Lucy. See Townsend, Lucy (1781–1847).

Jesse [married name Harwood], **Wynifried Margaret** [Fryniwyd; pseud. F. Tennyson Jesse] (**1888–1958**), writer and criminologist, was born Wynifried Margaret Jesse on 1 March 1888 at Holly Bowers, Chislehurst, Kent, second of three daughters of the Revd Eustace Tennyson d'Eyncourt Jesse (1853–1927), a high Anglican clergyman, and his wife, Edith Louisa James (1866–1941), second child of a self-made Cornishman. Jesse's paternal grandmother, a sister of Alfred *Tennyson, had been engaged to A. H. Hallam (the subject of Tennyson's In Memoriam) at the time of his tragic death. With no settled career, her father often went abroad, sometimes taking the family, and she early imbibed the love of travel. Her mother seemed to cherish ill health and became increasingly erratic and bad-tempered. Jesse recalled an 'infinite succession' of lodgings as a dreary feature of her childhood. Her formal education was mostly at various day schools, but from an early age she showed both an aptitude for art and the gift of independent thought. In her nineteenth year she went to study art under Stanhope and Elizabeth Forbes at the Newlyn School in Cornwall, where she acquired the name Fryniwyd, edited the colony's short-lived magazine, and exhibited a few pictures.

Realizing that her métier lay more in writing than in art, Jesse descended on London in 1911 and was soon contributing to leading dailies under her gender-neutral nom de plume F. Tennyson Jesse. In 1912 her short story 'The Mask' was published to acclaim in the influential English Review. It attracted the attention of the successful playwright Harold Marsh (Tottie) *Harwood (1874–1959), who wanted to dramatize it (and who on 9 September 1918 married her), and of William Heinemann, who offered to publish her first novel. She later described The Milky Way (1913) as a light-hearted affair and a 'very bad book', but in a contemporary review in the Daily News and Leader Rebecca West said the author had shown herself 'a master of descriptive prose'.

Jesse had been launched on a literary career that would span nearly forty-five years. Her œuvre, of an uncommon range, was to include nine novels, three books of short stories, two of poems, and four volumes of belles-lettres, three plays (and another six—including Billeted, 1917—with Harwood), a history of Burma, and eight books on criminology.

Long wanting to fly, Jesse went up in a pusher-type aircraft over Lake Windermere. Unaware of any danger, she waved to people below and put her right hand into the invisibly spinning propeller just behind her. Seven unsuccessful operations to save her fingers followed, and to enable her to bear the pain she was prescribed morphia, to which she became addicted. She was fitted with a mechanical device, which she called her 'pandy', and courageously resumed her travels. In 1914 she persuaded the Daily

Mail to send her to the Belgian front as a war correspondent, one of the few women then to achieve that status. Visits to France followed and the Ministry of Information asked her to write about the women's army; *The Sword of Deborah* (1919) was the vividly written result.

The twenties and thirties were decades of wide travel and of intense literary activity, with diversity the keynote. A success in one genre was followed by a move into another. 'That is why I have never been a best seller,' Jesse once explained (J. Colenbrander, 'Introduction' to F. T. Jesse, *The Lacquer Lady*, 1984 reprint). In the highly respected *Murder and its Motives* (1924, rev. edn 1952), in which she illustrated the six motives with celebrated cases, she coined the word 'murderee' to describe those who laid themselves out to be murdered. Francis Camps, an expert in forensic medicine, described her as one of England's greatest criminologists. Harry Hodge, publisher of the renowned Notable British Trials, recruited her as his first woman editor, and she produced six in the series, starting with Madeleine Smith in 1927 and including Rattenbury and Stoner (1935) and finally Evans and Christie in 1957. She attended trials and went to crime venues to soak up atmosphere.

A chance meeting in Burma, which led to Jesse hearing at first hand the story behind the British annexation of Upper Burma in 1885, gave rise to her most critically acclaimed novel. *The Lacquer Lady* (1929) is a remarkable vision of life at the royal palace with its splendours and its horrors seen through the eyes of a young woman who becomes the favourite of the Burmese queen. It was the Book Society's choice for January 1930 and the book Jesse felt she should live by.

Jesse's other well-known novel, *A Pin to See the Peepshow* (1934), was based on the Thompson–Bywaters case. The hanging of Edith Jessie *Thompson outraged her, as did injustice wherever it was found. She assiduously espoused the cause of women, firmly believing that women should hold any post of which they were capable. However, as early as 1919 she asserted: 'I am not, and never have been a feminist … never having been able to divide humanity into two different classes labelled "men" and "women"' (F. T. Jesse, *Sword of Deborah*, 1919, 7). In 1948 she and Harwood wrote a dramatized version of her novel, which led to a row with the lord chamberlain.

In 1939 Jesse and Harwood began a correspondence with friends in America in which they reported on the political events and their personal experiences during the first two years of the Second World War. The letters were published as *London Front* (1940) and *While London Burns* (1942). Another war book was *The Saga of the 'San Demetrio'* (1942), a classic and moving account of a tanker set ablaze by a German raider and then reboarded and salvaged by some of her crew. It was later filmed.

There is compassion in Jesse's writing, even though she made so many of her fictional characters die. Her prose style is direct and engaging and her descriptive passages reveal a painter's eye. Her imagination was that of a poet, but always under control. She was very much a down-to-earth romantic.

Jesse was delicately built with golden hair when young, had large grey-green eyes, and was renowned for an aura which captivated men and women alike. She personally deprecated her looks—'It was the beauty of youth and it did not last long' (Colenbrander, 65)—but Rebecca West said she had never seen a lovelier girl and claimed her to be one of the three great beauties of the time, the only flaw her voice—West called it hideous, others stentorian, though it improved as Jesse grew older (ibid., 78). She loved good conversation and regarded letter writing as a natural function, and her sense of humour illuminated both. She was generous with her time for her friends, but periodically crippling depression brought despair, distrust, the inability to work, and uncharacteristic unkindness, and even attempts at suicide. Three miscarriages and the strain of keeping her marriage a secret for several years—her husband feared that he would lose access to his son should his married mistress hear of it—also cast shadows over a relationship which nevertheless endured until Jesse's death. Jesse died of a heart attack on 6 August 1958 at her home, Pear Tree Cottage, 11 Melina Place, St John's Wood, London, and was cremated at Golders Green.   RAYMOND CORDERO

Sources J. Colenbrander, *A portrait of Fryn* (1984) • *Manchester Guardian* (7 Aug 1958) • *The Times* (7 Aug 1958) • F. E. Camps, *Camps on crime* (1973)
Archives JRL, letters to the *Manchester Guardian* • Lincoln Central Library, corresp. and literary papers
Likenesses E. S. Forbes, watercolour; formerly in possession of J. Colenbrander • Lenare, photograph, W. Heinemann Ltd, Tadworth, Surrey
Wealth at death £36,653 6s. 5d.: probate, 1 Oct 1958, CGPLA Eng. & Wales

Jessel, Sir George (1824–1883), judge, was born in Savile Row, London, on 13 February 1824, the youngest of the four surviving children of Zadok Aaron Jessel, a wealthy London merchant, and his wife, Mary, daughter of Henry Harris of Coventry. He was educated at Mr Neumegen's School for Jews at Kew, before matriculating in 1840 at University College, London, where he took his BA with honours in mathematics, natural philosophy, vegetable physiology, and structural botany, and his MA in 1844, winning a gold medal in mathematics and natural philosophy. In 1846 he was elected a fellow of University College, London. In 1842 he was admitted a student of Lincoln's Inn and five years later was called to the bar.

At the bar Jessel read with the eminent conveyancer Peter Bellinger Brodie, and then became the pupil of Edward John Lloyd (later QC) and Sir Barnes Peacock. His practice grew rapidly both as a conveyancer and in the rolls court. He owed his success not to any Jewish solicitors (there was at that time no Jewish firm which could have briefed him), but to the firm of Budd and Hayes, to whom he was introduced by his fellow pupil (in Stone Buildings) and later chief secretary, George Thomas Jenkins. While young he visited both Turkey and America.

On 20 August 1856 Jessel married Amelia, the eldest daughter of Joseph Moses, a City of London merchant and

Sir George Jessel (1824–1883), by Richard Josey (after John Collier)

his wife (*née* Königswarter), an heiress of Vienna. After their marriage the couple lived in Cleveland Square, Hyde Park, but on Jessel's elevation to the bench they moved to 10 Hyde Park Gardens. Jessel acquired a country seat at Ladham House, Goudhurst, Kent.

After his initial success, Jessel's practice remained static for several years. His seniors thought him too self-reliant, and certainly Jessel did not go out of his way to conciliate them. He was becoming discouraged when a chance appearance in court demonstrated that his real talent was for advocacy rather than conveyancing. Thereafter his reputation grew and he soon became the leading junior in the rolls court, with a practice so large that in 1861 he applied for silk. This was refused by the lord chancellor, Lord Westbury; old prejudices may have died hard. It was not until four years later that he became a QC and a bencher of Lincoln's Inn.

Solicitor-general In December 1868 Jessel was elected Liberal MP for Dover. As with many lawyers, his precise and dogmatic style of oratory did not make him a popular speaker in the house; he did not conceal his contempt for weaker minds. None the less, his speech on the Bankruptcy Bill (1869) so impressed W. E. Gladstone that in November 1871 he offered Jessel the post of solicitor-general which he accepted (in a memorial, after Jessel's death, Gladstone said that his legal speeches were 'the object of [his] warm though unintelligent admiration'). Jessel combined this office, as was customary, with a lucrative private practice. His duties were unusually onerous because of the Geneva arbitration, but he never failed to give the cabinet valuable advice expressed with clarity and precision.

Master of the rolls In August 1873 Jessel succeeded Lord Romilly as master of the rolls, J. D. Coleridge having refused the office. Romilly had resigned the previous April but Jessel's technical expertise was needed in the House of Commons to carry through the judicature bills. Jessel had found his métier. His judicial career was rivalled by few equity judges. This was a view which he himself warmly endorsed. For he considered himself third in the pecking order of great English equity judges, after two lord chancellors, the towering Lord Hardwicke and Lord Cairns, whom he was inclined to place second.

The years 1873–5 were, for lawyers, ones of great change. They saw the enactment of the Judicature Acts of 1873–5, bringing the fusion of the administration of law and equity. These statutes also created a new court of appeal, consisting of lords justices of appeal. Jessel, being third in the judicial hierarchy (only the lord chancellor and the lord chief justice took precedence over him), was an *ex officio* member. But between 1873 and 1881 he sat exclusively as a judge of first instance in the rolls court. His son, Sir Charles Jessel, recalled that it was entirely owing to Jessel that the master of the rolls became a permanent judge of the Court of Appeal. After the death of Lord Justice James in 1881 there was no one of sufficient weight in the Court of Appeal to hear appeals from a man of Jessel's standing. By a special act of parliament (the Judicature Act of 1881) the master of the rolls ceased, to Jessel's regret, to be a judge of the first instance.

Jessel's output in the rolls court was prodigious. A remarkable memory combined with mastery of the subject matter enabled him never to reserve a judgment in the rolls courts and only very occasionally in the Court of Appeal, and then only at the instigation of his brethren. Not even in the Epping Forest case in 1874—when the arguments based on statutes extending from the time of King John lasted twenty-three days, with 100 witnesses called, and the evidence filled several folio volumes—did he pause to reflect. He was not like Lord Eldon, whom he unkindly dismissed as the 'dubitative Chancellor'. It was unusual for an appeal to be filed, and even more unusual for the Court of Appeal to reverse his decisions.

An unpublished index to Jessel's decisions, dicta, judgments, and observations between 1873 and 1883, in the library of Lincoln's Inn, is a testament to him; 126 reported cases appear under the letter 'A' alone, while the index, if published, would fill a book. Only a judge with a remarkably acute and logical mind could have achieved what he did. It is not surprising to learn that he made up his mind quickly; it has been said that it moved so quickly that could read both sides of a sheet of paper at once. He was, and was seen to be, no doubting Thomas. Lawyers dined out on the story that he told Sir John Duke Coleridge, then attorney-general, that 'I may be wrong, and often am, but I never doubt.' Lord James later asked him if the story were true. Jessel replied: 'Very likely, but Coleridge, with his constitutional inaccuracy, has told it wrong. I can never have said "OFTEN WRONG"' (Jessel, 51). Senior counsel of standing were often much put out by his dogmatic per-emptoriness, sensing that he had decided the case almost before they had opened it. In an acerbic exchange with Jessel, Farrer Herschell retorted that 'important as it was that people should get justice, it was even more important that they should be made to feel and see that they were getting it' (Atlay, 2.460).

Characteristics as a lawyer Jessel could not have achieved what he did if his practice at the bar had not endowed him with a formidable knowledge of the diverse technicalities of English equity. But he was no insular lawyer; like so many of his remarkable Victorian contemporaries, he studied in private, not in any university, the general principles of Roman law and chosen continental codes. So, in language faintly redolent of Edward Gibbon, he said in the debate on the Bankruptcy Bill of 1869: 'we had used the Roman law as the Turks used the remains of the splendid temples of antiquity. We had pulled out the stones and used them in constructing buildings which we called our own' (*Hansard 3*, 195, 1869, 143). And he urged the house to remodel English bankruptcy law upon the Roman *cessio bonorum* as exemplified in the continental codes, an invitation which parliament wisely declined.

The cast of Jessel's mind was, however, essentially practical. He was a pragmatist, a man of business, whose clarity of mind was only rivalled by his intuition. This is reflected in the style of his prose; the written reports simply reproduce the spoken words. Short crisp sentences, never ponderous, need never be reread. The heavy diet of equity fare was lightened by such phrases as, '"counsel searching for authority for lack of argument", "a man is allowed by law to be a fool if he likes", and "vultures feeding upon expiring copyrights"' (Goodhart, 22) which enliven the often grey pages of the chancery reports.

Posterity will not say of a judge that he was a great judge unless he was an innovator, although innovation necessarily has to be cautious. Jessel could be impatient of inherited precedent if he deemed it to be the foundation of anomaly: 'I have no hesitation in making a precedent.' Such a precedent was *Re Hallett's Estate* in 1880. He refused to conclude that in equity 'money had no earmark', and that consequently beneficiaries of a trust could not 'identify' their money which their trustee had improperly deposited with his own money in his personal bank account. This was an important break with the past. *Re Hallett's Estate* is a decision which continued in the late twentieth century to be cited as authoritative by counsel and judge in every common-law jurisdiction. As his obituarist in *The Times* said: 'There is little likelihood that we shall see again that combination of contradictory qualities which made the Master of the Rolls a tower among his brethren and regarded by many suitors as the ideal of a judge.'

Other activities and death Jessel's energies were not confined to the courts. He was a leading member of the committee empowered to make rules for the then recently established (1875) Supreme Court of Judicature, establishing thereby a complete code of civil procedure. In this work, and in his judgments in the rolls court, he contributed as much to the fusion of law and equity as the 1873–5 acts themselves.

Jessel's loyalty to University College, London, reflected itself in active work in the management of the University of London, of which he was vice-chancellor from 1881 until his death. He never lost his scientific interests. He was an *ex officio* commissioner of patents, his duties including the superintendence of the registration of trade marks; in addition he was the working head of the Patent Office for ten years, from 1873. He was a member of the Brown Institute's committee which reported on the diseases and injuries of animals, and of the royal commission whose report formed the nucleus of the Medical Act of 1886. Among his many honours were the treasurership of Lincoln's Inn (1883), and his election as a fellow of the Royal Society (1880).

Jessel was of middle height, and in later life inclined to corpulence. 'He had dark hair, grey eyes, a fresh complexion, a straight nose and a somewhat large mouth. His face in repose had a rather heavy look, but became wonderfully animated in argument' (*DNB*). On 22 February 1878 he survived an attempt on his life when a deranged clergyman Henry John Dodwell, with a grievance against the law, shot at him when he was entering the rolls court. He died at his London home, 10 Hyde Park Gardens, on 21 March 1883, five days after his last day in the Court of Appeal, having presided over that court for barely two years. He was interred in the cemetery of the United Synagogue at Willesden on 23 March. It was said that he was a lax observer of Jewish religious rites. But he was no apostate; he was a good Hebrew scholar and was aware of the many critical controversies relating to the Old Testament. At the same time he could find an apt quotation from the New Testament. His mind was free from cant. Jessel was the first Jew to be solicitor-general, a regular member of the privy council, and to achieve high judicial office.

Jessel left two sons and three daughters: Emma, who married Ludwig Nathan Hardy; Constance, who married Sir Edward Stern; and Lucy, who was unmarried. Jessel had received a knighthood in 1873. A baronetcy was conferred upon his heir, Charles James (1860–1928), on 25 May 1883, a posthumous tribute to his father; his younger son, Herbert Merton (1866–1950) who was a Liberal Unionist MP, was created a baron in 1924. Both sons married daughters of Sir Julian Goldsmid bt.   GARETH H. JONES

Sources C. J. Jessel, 'An eminent Victorian lawyer', *Blackwood*, 219 (1926), 47–55 · A. L. Goodhart, *Five Jewish lawyers of the common law* (1949) · *The Times* (22 March 1883) · *Solicitors' Journal*, 27 (1882–3), 342–4 · [W. D. I. Foulkes], *A generation of judges* (1886) · J. B. Atlay, *The Victorian chancellors*, 2 (1908), 460 · Hallett's estate, re Cotterell v. Hallett (1880), 13 Ch. D. 696 · A. P. Peter, *Analyses and digest of the decisions of Sir George Jessel* (1883) · private information (2004)
Likenesses M. Ayout, oils, Lincoln's Inn, London · W. R. Ingram, marble bust, Royal Courts of Justice, London · R. Josey, mezzotint (after J. Collier), NPG [*see illus.*]
Wealth at death £225,802 2s. 1d.: resworn probate, May 1884, *CGPLA Eng. & Wales* (1883)

Jessey [Jacie], **Henry** (1601–1663), nonconformist minister, was born on 3 September 1601 at West Rounton, near

Henry Jessey (1601–1663), by unknown engraver

Northallerton, in the North Riding of Yorkshire; his father, David Jessey (d. 1623) had been rector of Rounton since 1574. He matriculated at Easter 1619 as a pensioner at St John's College, Cambridge, where, as Jacie, he was admitted as a 'Constable's scholar' on 6 November 1622. That September he had been converted to puritan principles, resolving then to become a minister. In 1623 he graduated BA, and despite acute financial difficulties following his father's death he resolved to remain at university, concentrating on the study of Hebrew and the reading of rabbinical literature. Although in November 1624 he left Cambridge to become tutor in the family of Brampton Gurdon (d. 1649), at Assington, Suffolk, he was able to proceed MA in 1626. Ordained priest in the diocese of Llandaff in June that year he was licensed to preach by the bishop of Norwich the following January; he is listed as curate of Assington also in 1627. In this period, it seems, Jessey also began the study of medicine, and applied in 1627 for incorporation at Oxford. In 1633, in circumstances which are unclear, he became curate at Aughton, in the East Riding of Yorkshire, where the vicar, William Alder, had been deprived for nonconformity. The following year Jessey himself was ejected for removing a crucifix and refusing to practise ceremonies demanded by the prayer book.

Jessey took refuge as chaplain in the home of Sir Matthew Boynton of Barmston, near Bridlington, Yorkshire, and also preached publicly in the area. In 1635 Boynton travelled to London, taking up residence at Hedgeley House, near Uxbridge, the following year. Jessey accompanied him, but in 1637 was invited to become pastor of a semi-separatist congregation founded by Henry Jacob in 1616, and later led by John Lathrop. On 18 August 1637 Jessey wrote to John Winthrop that, while convinced of the principles of the gathered congregation, he had been unable to accept the pastorate, since he was already sounding out the possibility of emigration to New England. It may be that Jessey was acting here on behalf of his patron; if so, Boynton abandoned the plan and on 14 August 1638 'by virtue of a special warrant granted unto him by his majesty did with his lady and family pass over into Holland' (Bodl. Oxf., Tanner MS 433, 84v).

The Southwark church of which Jessey now became pastor had been founded on congregational, non-separatist principles, but especially after the rise to pre-eminent power of William Laud some of its members came to stand for a more rigorous rejection of the established church. Separatist and Baptist groups began to split off, even before the emigration of John Lathrop in 1634. In June 1638, soon after Jessey's arrival, six people seceded and then joined the church of believers' Baptists led by John Spilsbury. But such losses were more than balanced by the influx of radical puritans alarmed by the trend towards the enforcement of conformity and the suspension and deprivation of lecturers and ministers, but unwilling to commit themselves to a decisive separation. Jessey's congregation itself was much harassed, as is evident from his own account. On 21 February 1638 the congregation was meeting at Queenhithe when surprised by the bishop's pursuivants; all were arrested, and despite finding a new meeting place, in an effort to keep ahead of the authorities, the church was raided again in May. In September 1639 Samuel Eaton, a former member and latterly the pastor of what was probably a mixed group of Baptists and separatists, died in prison. It seems that many of his members then returned to Jessey's church, which had become more tolerant of full separatism. In November 1639 Jessey was sent by the church on a visit to Wales, to assist Walter Cradock and William Wroth in constituting an Independent congregation at Llanvaches, Monmouthshire. His own congregation soon grew too large for effective concealment, and on 18 May 1640 it divided into two, half under the leadership of Praisegod Barbon.

Among those members remaining with Jessey the validity of their baptism in the Church of England soon became an issue. Some began to argue in the same way as the seceders to Spilsbury that baptism was for professed believers only, and it seems that about this time a related discussion was under way over the question of the mode of baptism. Jessey remained unconvinced of the merits of believers' baptism but came to believe that sprinkling or pouring was a mere modern invention, and that the proper form was immersion. For many months he baptized infants by this means.

In this period, before the outbreak of the civil war, Jessey and his congregation were still experiencing hard times, but hoping for better. On 21 April 1640, during a prayer meeting with others at 'Tower Hill at Mrs Wilsons', they were subjected to another raid. Soon afterwards, on 19 May, Jessey and others appeared at the Middlesex sessions, where he was described as a yeoman of the liberty of the Tower of London. But opinion was beginning to turn against the hardliners in church and state, and they were not pursued further, 'the prosecutors thinking it not advisable to bring in any Bill of Indictment against them, as the face of affairs then stood'. On 21 August 1641 four members were arrested at the house of a member, Peter Golding, in the parish of St Thomas the Apostle. The following day their meeting place was raided and Jessey and two others imprisoned in the Wood Street counter, but on appeal to parliament 'they were speedily set at liberty' (Whiston, 10–11).

After this Jessey and his friends were left alone, as the power of the bishops and their lay supporters waned. Continuing debate within the congregation seems to have been conducted in a reasonable and tolerant spirit. It came to a head in spring 1644, when many members were convinced of believers' baptism. Following consultation with prominent Independents such as Thomas Goodwin most of these left to join William Kiffin or Hanserd Knollys. Jessey himself recalled his own uncertainty, his desire to be sure before committing himself, and his need to confer with Christians of differing opinions 'about what is requisite to restoring of ordinances, if lost; especially in what is essential in a baptiser? Thus I did forbear and inquired above a year's space' (Jessey, 80). He was baptized by Knollys in June 1645. However, Jessey refused to impose rebaptism as a condition of communion, and a few of those who seceded, and who agreed with him on the point, returned. Jessey retained his broad, open communion convictions until his death. The closed membership Particular Baptist pastors had signed a joint confession of faith in October 1644 and a revised version in January 1646, but it should not be thought that the issue was a source of rancour between Jessey and themselves. Later that year he was reported to have attended with Hanserd Knollys a meeting 'for the restoring of an old blind woman to her sight, by anointing her with oyle in the name of the Lord' (Edwards, 3.19). Jessey's record made it hard for presbyterians to attack him and it was probably important in building respect for the Baptists among those who remembered affectionately the days of unity against the bishops, before the atmosphere was soured by factional resentment. In 1647 an elder of the first classis was persuaded to grant the use of a room at London House, 'for the accommodation of Mr Jessey, Mr Kiffin, and others, whom I conceive to be truly godly, (but dissenting in the point of baptizing infants, and I suppose in the manner of church government, and it may be in some others)' (*Reasons Humbly Offered in Justification of the Action of Letting a Room*, c.1647?)! It is clear that this caused a major row in the classis. Meanwhile in his *The Exceeding Riches of Grace Advanced* (1647) Jessey, in millenarian prophecies

which employed the vocabulary of the 'fifth monarchy', looked forward to when God 'will shortly bring down every high thing' (Capp, 39).

By 1650, when he signed *A Storehouse of Provision* (itself a useful source of information on the author and his friends), Jessey's church was in Swan Alley, Coleman Street, a famous centre of radicals and of many conventicles. Here Jessey preached on Sunday afternoons with George Barrett as his assistant, but he was also from 1651 a weekday lecturer at All Hallows-the-Great, Thames Street. In 1650 Jessey visited other open membership Independent churches in the north-east, taking time on this occasion to visit his aged mother at York. He was in touch with churches in the west of England which had been influenced by another open membership Baptist, John Tombes, and through them, in October 1653, with Thomas Tillam and the church at Hexham, near Newcastle. It was probably through his friends of Llanvaches that Jessey became acquainted with the open membership church at Broadmead in Bristol. He seems to have baptized its pastor, Thomas Erwin, and its ruling elder Robert Purnell in 1654, and helped to steady them during the offensive of the Quakers in the city which followed shortly afterwards. In 1655, on the suggestion of the Bristol church, he visited Wells, Cirencester, Somerton, Chard, Taunton, Honiton, Exeter, Dartmouth, Plymouth, Lyme, Weymouth, Dorchester, Southampton, and Chichester.

It is evident that Jessey was concerned with building up a broader communion of churches throughout the country. His activism stemmed both from his belief in the imminence of the second coming of Christ and also because of his desire, borne of practical experience, not to allow political forces opposed to reformation to reimpose their rule. It should not be supposed that he was lacking in ordinary patriotism. In the course of a tour of thirty-six congregations in Essex, Suffolk, and Norfolk with John Simpson, fellow lecturer at All Hallows-the-Great, on 25 August 1653 Jessey conducted a public thanksgiving for the English victories over the Dutch fleet, on board *The General*, off the coast of Suffolk, 'with great attention of the seamen' (*CSP dom.*, 1653–4, 104). Jessey became an approver and an ejector, under the ordinances of 20 March and 28 August 1654. There were points of contact between himself and the governments of the Commonwealth and protectorate. In 1652, with John Owen and John Row, professor of Hebrew at Aberdeen, he had been officially commissioned to work on a new translation of the Bible. This project was apparently almost completed by 1659 but was never published. In 1651 Jessey had predicted, in the preface to Mary Cary's *The Little Horns Doom*, that the conversion of the Jews might take place before 1658; Oliver Cromwell himself was sympathetic to the readmission of the Jews to England, a prospect which fitted well with the millenarian element of Jessey's thinking. He was for a time in touch with Menasseh bin Israel in Amsterdam. In December 1655 he was one of the London preachers who discussed proposals for the Jews' return and was almost certainly the author of *A Narrative of the Late Proceed's at Whitehall* (1656), which treated the idea sympathetically. Jessey was in favour of granting to the Jews rights of citizenship and permission to trade. He also collected large amounts of money for the relief of distressed Jews in Jerusalem, hoping in this way to advance their conversion.

Jessey was involved from February 1654 with the Fifth Monarchists, and was one of the leading signatories of *A Declaration of Several Churches of Christ and Godly People*, which included violent denunciations of tithes and triers. Jessey was a moderate in the movement: he never urged the use of violence to accelerate the second coming. But there was often tension between his broad acceptance of the Cromwellian establishment and his millenarian ideas. As Marchamont Nedham reported of the All Hallows gatherings in February 1654, 'the congregation is crowded, the humours boiling' (*CSP dom.*, 1653–4, 393). In October 1655 Jerome Sankey reported that Simpson, Jessey, and others were highly dissatisfied with the drift of policy in the protectorate and had been granted a meeting with Cromwell to discuss their grievances. Excitement was particularly high in 1656 when the return of Christ was widely believed to be imminent, and Jessey may have shared this optimism. In April 1657 he was a signatory to the petition which urged Cromwell against accepting the crown but the following year he was one of the leaders urging moderation against those calling for further political purges. He was enthusiastic at the return of the Rump Parliament in 1659 and in September was a signatory to *Essay towards a Settlement on a Sure Foundation*, which demanded that government be placed in the hands of godly men. In 1660 he published *The Lords Loud Call to England*, a call to national repentance and a warning of the record, and the prospect, of divine justice, and on 28 December he found himself under arrest.

Jessey's confinement appears not to have been lengthy, however; in 1661 he was still a lecturer at St George's, and in September it was reported that he preached twice a week at All Hallows; he officiated there with Hanserd Knollys and John Simpson on 24 August, and seems also to have been involved at the time in meetings at Anchor Lane. His millenarian ideas and connections, notably with Christopher Feake and Henry Danvers, together with his 'habit of collecting notes of remarkable events' brought suspicion upon him (*CSP dom.*, 1661–2, 173). On 27 November 1661 a warrant was issued for his arrest; on 8 December he was examined by the privy council over the almanac *Annus mirabilis*, to which he had contributed. This suggested the possibility of God making known his displeasure at Charles II, and Jessey was imprisoned at Lamb Inn in the parish of St Clement Dane. He was released after about three weeks because of increasing ill health. In August 1662 he informed the authorities that there were plans for a rising in London, but this resulted, after a short delay, in his own arrest on 30 August. Jessey was not released until 20 February 1663. In the summer he contracted a fever, and on 4 September he died. Four or five thousand people attended his funeral on 7 September at Woodmongers Hall in Duke's Place, London. A government spy reported that 'His dying words were that the

Lord would destroy the powers in being, and he encouraged the people to help the great work' (*CSP dom.*, 1663–4, 278). This probably relies heavily on imagination, not only because his *Life* contradicts it, but because it conflicts with Jessey's own longstanding rejection of such an approach. His death was lamented in a broadsheet elegy, 'A Pillar Erected to … Henry Jesse'. A nuncupative will named his brother Thomas Jessey and sister Sarah Thompson.

STEPHEN WRIGHT

Sources [E. Whiston], *The life and death of Henry Jessey* (1671) • B. R. White, 'Henry Jessey in the great rebellion', *Reformation, conformity, and dissent*, ed. R. B. Knox (1977), 132–53 • B. R. White, 'Henry Jessey: a pastor in politics', *Baptist Quarterly*, 25 (1973), 98–110 • H. Jessey, *A storehouse of provision* (1650) • *CSP dom.*, 1653–4, 1661–2, 1663–4 • T. Edwards, *Gangraena* (1646) • J. Jeaffreson, ed., *Middlesex county records*, 3 (1886) • E. G. van der Wall, 'A Philo-semitic millenarian on the reconciliation of Jews and Christians: Henry Jessey and his "The glory and salvation of Judah and Israel"', *Sceptics, millenarians and Jews*, ed. D. S. Katz and J. I. Israel (1990), 161–84 • *The Winthrop papers*, ed. W. C. Ford and others, 3 (1943), 484–8 • 'A pillar erected to … Henry Jesse', BL, Luttrell I, 74 • probate acts, GL, MS 9168/20, fols. 93v–95r • K. Lindley, *Popular politics and religion in civil war London* (1997) • B. S. Capp, *The Fifth Monarchy Men: a study in seventeenth-century English millenarianism* (1972) • M. Tolmie, *The triumph of the saints: the separate churches of London, 1616–1649* (1977) • Venn, *Alum. Cant.*
Likenesses J. Caldwell, line engraving, BM, NPG; repro. in S. Palmer, *Nonconformist memorial* (1802), vol. 1, p. 129 • line engraving, BM, NPG [*see illus.*]

Jessop [*née* Wilde], **Ann** (*bap.* 1782, *d.* 1864), cabinet-maker, was baptized at the church of St Peter and St Paul, Sheffield, on 9 May 1782, the daughter of Adam Wilde and his wife, Elizabeth. Nothing is known of her early life except that she was twice married: first at Sheffield on 21 June 1805 to Charles Turner; second at Rotherham parish church on 8 November 1818 to a widower, Edward Bardwell, an auctioneer and appraiser. Both marriage certificates were witnessed with a cross, indicating that she lacked education.

Around 1814 Edward Bardwell established a cabinet-making business in the centre of Sheffield at 92 Fargate. He was listed in trade directories of 1817 as an auctioneer and furniture broker, together with John Bardwell jun. (presumably a son or brother), auctioneer and appraiser, and Bardwell & Son, auctioneers and appraisers, in nearby Marketplace. By 1821 Edward had died and despite the presence of several male relatives, Ann Bardwell was listed as trading alone as a cabinet-maker, upholsterer, and furniture broker from slightly smaller premises at 95 Fargate. The business continued in her name until 14 May 1828 when she married her third husband, James Jessop, another widower. Both signed the register with their names, Ann presumably having acquired literacy and numeracy while helping her second husband run his business. Between 1828 and 1832 the firm was known as James Jessop, cabinet-maker, but the 1833 Sheffield trade directory listed Mrs Ann Jessop, cabinet-maker, upholsterer, china, glass, and earthenware dealer, as trading from 95 Fargate alone.

In the same year Ann Jessop was one of nine local cabinet-makers approached by the Company of Cutlers in

Hallamshire to tender designs and prices for the manufacture of 250 mahogany dining chairs and three large mahogany dining tables. Although she was unsuccessful in this commission, the fact that she was invited to tender for it indicates that she was one of the foremost cabinetmakers in the town. By 1839 the firm had moved to larger, rented premises at 26 Fargate, consisting of a house, shop, and warehouse. A surviving yew wood Windsor chair sold from there still bears a printed label inscribed, 'From A. Jessop's cabinet, picture frame, and looking glass manufactory'. In the 1851 census Ann Jessop was listed as a widow aged sixty-eight. She was described as upholsterer, cabinet-maker, carver, and gilder, employing a total of eighteen men.

The firm continued under the name of Mrs Jessop until 1854 when, in her seventy-first year and after thirty-four years in business, she announced her retirement in favour of her nephew, F. J. Mercer, who had managed the firm for fourteen years. Ann Jessop retired with her niece to Springfield Place, 323 Glossop Road, then part of the affluent western suburbs of Sheffield. Unfortunately, the business ceased trading around 1870 and three years later F. J. Mercer committed suicide.

Ann Jessop died from gastroenteritis on 23 September 1864 aged eighty-two at her home, 264 Western Bank, Sheffield. She had the distinction, despite losing three husbands, of successfully running one of the leading cabinet-making, upholstery, carving, and gilding businesses in Sheffield in the mid-nineteenth century.

JULIE BANHAM

Sources Sheffield and Rotherham Independent (15 April 1854) · Liber Minut Societat Cutler in Hallamshire in Com: Ebor., 27 Feb–11 March 1833, F 7/4/8, C9/4 · 'Suicide of former cabinet maker', Sheffield and Rotherham Independent (31 May 1873) · census returns for Sheffield, 1841, vol. 1338 ED 16, fol. 29b; 1851, vol. 2338, fol. 146b · register, Sheffield Cathedral Church of Sts Peter and Paul, P.R. 138/11 [baptism] · register, Sheffield Cathedral Church of Sts Peter and Paul, P.R. 138/11 [burial] · register, Sheffield Cathedral Church of Sts Peter and Paul, P.R. 138/108, 122 [marriage] · parish register, Rotherham parish church, P.R. 87/26 [marriage] · d. cert. · Sheffield rate books, 1851, R.B. 281, p.174 · G. Beard and C. Gilbert, eds., Dictionary of English furniture makers, 1660–1840 (1986) · Sheffield General Directory (1817) · Pigot & Co.'s National Commercial Directory of Sheffield (1834) · trade directories, Sheffield · CGPLA Eng. & Wales (1865)
Wealth at death under £3000: probate, 14 Jan 1865, CGPLA Eng. & Wales

Jessop, Constantine (1601/2–1658), Church of England clergyman, was the son of John Jessop, minister at Pembroke. In 1624 at the age of twenty-two he entered Jesus College, Oxford. From there he went to Trinity College, Dublin, where he graduated BA. He was incorporated BA at Oxford on 30 June 1631, and graduated MA on 8 May 1632.

Little is certain about Jessop's life or whereabouts in the years following his departure from Oxford, except that his son Constantine was born in 1639 or 1640. On 11 May 1643, he was appointed to officiate for six months at Fyfield, Essex, with half the profits of the rectory, which was sequestered from Alexander Reade. That same year he took the covenant and on 3 November 1643 received the rectory of Fyfield by order of the House of Commons. In 1644 he presented the Westminster assembly of divines with his arguments for the biblical validity of presbyterian church government. His arguments appeared in print later that year under the title The angel of the Church of Ephesus no bishop of Ephesus, distinguished in order from, and superior in power to a presbyter, which was dedicated to William Twisse as well as to the other divines of the assembly. Jessop said his position on this matter stemmed initially from his father's harsh treatment at the hands of prelates, and later from his reaction to the writings of Bishop Joseph Hall and of supporters of the divine right of bishops. His name appears in the sixth or Ongar classis of the presbyterial arrangements for Essex, sanctioned by an ordinance of 31 January 1648, but he had left Fyfield in August 1647 for the sequestered vicarage of St Nicholas, Bristol.

On 23 November 1650 complaints that Jessop had preached against the government were brought before the council of state. While he protested, he did not deny all of the charges. On 14 December he was allowed to remain in the ministry on the conditions that he take the engagement and not return to Bristol. On 24 January 1651 he was interdicted from going within 10 miles of Bristol after 20 March. He may have ministered at Coggeshall, Essex, after John Owen left it for Oxford in 1651, but he did not obtain the vicarage. On 19 February 1652 he was allowed to visit Bristol for two months, 'but not to increase former factions'. On 7 September he was allowed to visit the city again for the purpose of removing his goods, provided he did not stay for more than fourteen days.

By 23 March 1654 Jessop had the rectory of Wimborne Minster, Dorset. In April the interdict respecting Bristol was removed. In Dorset he was an assistant commissioner to the 'expurgators' for removing scandalous and inefficient ministers. In 1654 he published The nature of the covenant of grace, wherein is a discovery of the judgment of Dr. Twisse in the point of justification, clearing him from antinomianism therein, as a preface to A Modest Vindication by John Grayle.

Jessop died at Wimborne on 16 April 1658 and was buried there; administration of his estate was granted to his widow, Elizabeth, of whom nothing else is known. His son Constantine, a DD of Oxford (4 July 1685), was rector of Brington, Northamptonshire, and prebendary of Durham, and died on 11 March 1695, aged fifty-five.

ALEXANDER GORDON, rev. MARK ROBERT BELL

Sources T. W. Davids, Annals of evangelical nonconformity in Essex (1863), 275–6, 467–8 · CSP dom., 1650–54 · Wood, Ath. Oxon., new edn, 3.540–41 · Foster, Alum. Oxon. · Wood, Ath. Oxon.: Fasti (1815), 461, 465; (1820), 397 · B. Brook, The lives of the puritans, 3 (1813), 375–6 · Walker rev., 162, 176, 178 · The division of the county of Essex into severall classes: together with the names of the ministers and orders fit to be of each classis (1648) · PRO, PROB 6/34, fol. 185r · tombstone, Wimborne Minster, Dorset
Archives BL · Bodl. Oxf.

Jessop, Gilbert Laird (1874–1955), cricketer, was born on 19 May 1874 at 30 Cambray, Cheltenham, the eleventh child of Henry Edward Jessop, surgeon, and his wife,

Gilbert Laird Jessop (1874–1955), by Albert Chevallier Tayler, 1905

Susannah Radford Hughes. He went to the local grammar school in Cheltenham, where he won a place in the first eleven at the age of thirteen. A year later he was a valuable all-rounder in the team while also gaining experience in club cricket. His father's sudden death in 1890 meant that he had to leave school. For the next six years he earned a precarious living assisting with supervision and games in various schools in return for little more than his board. He made successful appearances in club cricket in Suffolk, Oxfordshire, and Essex (where he made his first century in 1892) as well as having a prolific season (1895) for Beccles College in Suffolk.

In 1894 Jessop made his first-class début for Gloucestershire, when 'a capital cricketer was discovered' (Wisden, 1895, 153). For Gloucestershire he at once established a reputation for rapid scoring and monopolizing the play while at the wicket. This was sustained throughout his career, and may be illustrated by a few examples: 63 out of 65 against Yorkshire (1895); 171 out of a total of 246 against Yorkshire (1899); 66 out of 66 against Sussex (1901); 286 out of 355 in three hours against Sussex (1903); 50 in twelve minutes against Somerset (1904). In the Hastings festival in 1907 he scored 191 out of a total of 234 for the Gentlemen of the South against the Players of the South. In 1900, for Gloucestershire against the first West Indies team to tour England, he made 157 in an hour in a match which was not first-class.

Jessop had gone up to Christ's College, Cambridge, in 1896, at an older age than was usual, with little academic background but with ordination in mind. He won his blue (1896–9) and was captain of the university eleven in his last year, but went down without a degree and abandoned his ecclesiastical ambitions. In 1897 he made his first century in first-class cricket—140 for the university against the touring Philadelphians—and, with his cricket for Gloucestershire as well, completed the 'double' of 1000 runs and 100 wickets besides being picked for the Gentlemen against the Players at Lord's: 'his terrific hitting aroused the spectators to the highest pitch' (Wisden, 1898, 294). In 1897 and 1899 he was a member of touring teams to Philadelphia, USA.

From 1899 Jessop earned his living as the director of a tobacco firm and as a feature writer on cricket. An association began with the Daily Mail, which was his main source of income until 1909, when he succeeded E. M. Grace as Gloucestershire secretary, at a salary of £200 a year. He had succeeded W. G. Grace as captain in 1900 and, in the post-Grace era, scoured the county to find talent. In 1902 he married Millicent Osborne (d. 1953) of New South Wales, whom he had met on board ship while returning from touring Australia with A. C. MacLaren's side in 1901–2. Jessop declined later invitations to tour Australia because of financial circumstances and because he had experienced seasickness.

Jessop made the first of eighteen test appearances (1899–1912) for England at Lord's against Australia in 1899, having been selected as an opening fast bowler; his late-order batting brought him a half-century. Three years later, against Australia at the Oval in 1902, he went in when England were 48 for five, needing a further 225 for victory. In scoring a century in 75 minutes, 'he did what would have been scarcely possible under the same circumstances to any other living batsman', Wisden rapturously reported (Wisden, 1903, 283). Against the South Africans at Lord's in 1907 he scored 93, against their googly attack, in sixty-three balls. Although briefly an automatic selection for England, these were spectacular but isolated performances and he was often below his best at that level, making only 569 runs (average 21.88) and taking ten wickets. In 1911 he was an England selector. For the Gentlemen against the Players he made twenty-five appearances, that in 1913 being the most unusual. He filled a vacancy at the last minute, scoring a half-century in borrowed kit which was too tight and playing 'strokes of the weirdest description' (The Times, 15 July 1913). Ten years earlier he had declined an invitation to play in the same fixture, at Lord's because he had already promised a friend he would play in a village match.

Jessop's short stature (5 feet 7 inches) and his huddled posture at the wicket earned him the nickname the Croucher. He was immensely strong; H. S. Altham believed the secret of his success as a hitter 'lay in his speed, of eye, of foot and of hand [with] a bewildering variety of strokes' (Altham, 241). Once in form, a bowler's length meant little to him as he drove, swept, cut, and improvised.

In his earlier years Jessop achieved some pace as a

bowler and his second 'double' came in 1900, the year in which he took eight for 29 for Gloucestershire against Essex at Cheltenham and virtually 'pulled the side through' (*Wisden*, 1901, 137) in many matches. Thereafter injury reduced his performances as a bowler but did not inhibit his outstanding contribution as a fielder at cover or mid-off, with a devastatingly accurate throw to the wicket. Jessop, simply by being present at a match, diminished the hopes of his opponents; they were reluctant to declare too soon if they knew he had to bat, and reluctant to run if they played the ball near him in the field. As captain of Gloucestershire for thirteen years (1900–12) he did his best, if only by example, with a side always weak in bowling. He scored his last century—116 in 138 minutes—in the Scarborough festival of 1913, and played his last innings in first-class cricket on 31 July 1914 against Yorkshire: five days later the First World War broke out. It ended a career in which he had made 26,698 runs (average 32.63), scored fifty-three centuries, taken 873 wickets (average 22.79), and secured 463 catches.

Although aged forty when the First World War broke out, Jessop at once enlisted in the 14th Manchester regiment and spoke at numerous public gatherings to encourage recruitment. While undergoing heat treatment for lumbago, an accident led to his suffering severe heart damage and he was invalided out in 1917. His recovery was slow, but gradually in the 1920s he resumed his work as a journalist. In 1922 he published *A Cricketer's Log*, an interesting commentary on what was the 'golden age' of cricket—which his own career exactly paralleled—but with too brief a mention of his own contribution to it. Two novels for schoolboys, *Arthur Peck's Sacrifice* (1920) and *Cresley of Cressingham* (1924), together with a manual, *Cricket and How to Play It* (1925), completed his achievements as an author. While continuing as a journalist he also earned a reasonably substantial salary of £250 a year as secretary (1924–36) of Edgware golf club and he was honorary secretary of the Cricketers' Golfing Society. He was a scratch golfer besides having been close to blues for both hockey and association football when at Cambridge. Later, he was a rugby wing three-quarter for Gloucester.

Jessop's son Gilbert Laird Osborne (1906–1990) briefly appeared in first-class cricket (1929–33) and enjoyed a long career with Dorset (1939–54), where he was a country clergyman. It was at his son's vicarage, St George's, Fordington, near Dorchester—where he had lived since 1936—that Jessop died on 11 May 1955. He was a man whom 'the muse of History leaves on record' (*The Times*, 12 May 1955) and who was, in character, modest, shy, generous in nature, and unassuming.   GERALD M. D. HOWAT

Sources Venn, *Alum. Cant.* · G. Brodribb, *The croucher: a biography of Gilbert Jessop* (1974) · C. J. Britton, *G. L. Jessop* (1935) · *Wisden* (1895) · H. S. Altham, *A history of cricket* (1926) · *DNB*
Likenesses A. C. Tayler, drawing, 1905, Cheltenham Art Gallery and Museum [*see illus.*] · G. W. Beldam, lithograph (after photograph by A. C. Tayler), NPG · Spy [L. Ward], chromolithograph, caricature, NPG; repro. in *VF* (25 July 1901)
Wealth at death £2044 5*s*. 6*d*.: probate, 6 July 1955, *CGPLA Eng. & Wales*

Jessop, William (*bap.* 1603, *d.* 1675), government official and politician, was baptized in Stafford on 22 September 1603, the son of Thomas Jessoppe, and his wife, Margery. He moved to London, becoming a law clerk and then confidential man of business to Robert Rich, second earl of Warwick. Jessop served as secretary or chief clerk to the Providence Island Company from 1631 to 1641, and to the Saybrook plantation trustees; his command of shorthand (then known as secret writing) must have been a valuable qualification. In 1640 he was on familiar terms with John Pym, his colleague as treasurer of the Providence Island Company. With the outbreak of civil war in 1642 he moved into both military and naval administration. When his patron ceased to be parliament's lord admiral, with the passage of the self-denying ordinance in 1645, Jessop stayed on as secretary to the admiralty commissioners, holding this post until the demise of the Rump Parliament in 1653. Through his service under the war treasurers in 1642, Jessop had also become man of business to Robert Devereux, third earl of Essex, and served conscientiously as an executor of the former lord general's encumbered estate after his death in 1646.

Jessop had considerable scruples about taking the engagement, the oath of loyalty to the republic; the abolition of the House of Lords seems to have upset him more than the 1649 regicide and abolition of the monarchy. He may have found service under the protectorate more congenial than that of the Commonwealth; in 1653–4 he moved from the navy to the central executive, becoming assistant secretary and then clerk of Oliver Cromwell's council and treasurer of the protector's contingencies. He also served on numerous other committees and commissions. In the 1659 parliament he sat for his old home town; in one of his two recorded speeches he had to justify having arrested a leading Fifth Monarchy man on the orders of the late lord protector. His Cromwellian sympathies were no doubt strengthened by the marriage of the protector's younger daughter to the earl of Warwick's grandson early in 1658, and not surprisingly he left public life altogether with the restoration of the Commonwealth in 1659. This and his aristocratic connections served him well at the Restoration. He was assistant clerk of the parliaments in the Convention of 1660, a witness against the regicides, and briefly employed under the navy commissioners. Due either to age or to lack of an appropriate patron, he held no central office again until 1668–9, when he was secretary to the public accounts committee, the body charged with investigating whether financial malpractice had contributed to the naval disaster at the end of the Second Anglo-Dutch War. Jessop held two offices in the duchy of Lancaster without a break, from the 1650s until his death.

Jessop married first Margaret Edwin, and second Mary Cox, widow and sister-in-law of a politically moderate parliamentarian colonel. His daughter by his first wife, and only child, married into the Hulton family of Lancashire, which accounts for the survival of his papers in the county record office at Preston and in the British Library. He died in London, at his house in Holborn, in March 1675. His efficiency and discretion are as evident from the record as is his dislike of political extremism.   G. E. AYLMER

Sources G. E. Aylmer, *The state's servants: the civil service of the English republic, 1649–1660* (1973) · *Diary of Thomas Burton*, ed. J. T. Rutt, 4 vols. (1828) · Pepys, *Diary* · R. Somerville, *Office-holders in the duchy and county palatine of Lancaster from 1603* (1972) · BL, Add. MSS 63854A, 63854B
Archives BL, papers, Add. MS 46188 · BL, papers, Add. charters 71765–71797 · Lancs. RO, corresp. and MSS

Jessop, William (1746–1814), civil engineer, was the son of Josias Jessop, quartermaster at the naval dockyard, Devonport, and his wife, Elizabeth Foot. The eldest of three sons and one daughter, he was born at the Foots' home in Plymouth Dock on 23 January 1746. In 1756 his father was engaged to assist John Smeaton (1724–1792) in the reconstruction of the lighthouse on Eddystone Rock, some 15 miles off Plymouth, the previous structure having burnt down at the end of 1755. Smeaton came to rely heavily on Jessop senior, who took charge of the yard at Millbay where the masonry for the new lighthouse was assembled and shaped. The work was completed in 1759, and in that year Smeaton took on the young Jessop as an apprentice, to serve a 'clerkship' with a view to becoming his draughtsman and assistant.

Jessop had been educated at Devonport, where he had shown a talent for French and mathematics, as well as some progress in the classics and mechanical ability. However, when he joined Smeaton he moved to Austhorpe Lodge, the Smeaton family home near Leeds, from where the engineer directed his rapidly expanding engineering practice. Smeaton did more than anybody to lay the foundations of the British engineering profession, so it was of considerable significance for Jessop that he spent his formative years in the service of this pioneer, first as an apprentice, until 1767, and then as his assistant, until 1772. In these capacities he obtained wide experience in engineering work on river navigations, canals, harbour works, and land drainage projects, which enabled him to become, on Smeaton's retirement from active engineering, the outstanding man in his profession. At the time of the 'canal mania' in the 1790s, it was rightly said of him that with his experience and abilities he was looked upon as 'the first engineer of the kingdom' (Hadfield and Skempton, preface).

Jessop was a resourceful but cautious engineer, with a pragmatic approach to problems for which he preferred simple affordable solutions, so that he tended to avoid costly spectacular constructions such as aqueducts and long tunnels. These qualities put him in great demand by canal promoters in the 1790s. He was among the first engineers to appreciate the value of cast iron as a constructional material, recommending its use in the monumental Pontcysyllte aqueduct on the Ellesmere Canal, completed in 1805, and he acquired an interest as a founding partner in the Butterley Ironworks Company, Derbyshire. He also pioneered the use of iron railways in situations where canals were uneconomic, building the Surrey iron railway which opened in 1803. In the last part of his career, Jessop became much involved in harbour improvement projects, including the West India docks in London—one of the first systems of enclosed docks—and the Bristol docks, where his imaginative scheme for redirecting the tidal waters of the River Avon enabled the old river course through the city centre to be enclosed as the 'Floating Harbour'. Soon after setting up in business on his own in 1772 Jessop was enrolled by Smeaton in the Institution of Civil Engineers which was the first professional institution of engineers, and he came to take a prominent role in its activities.

Jessop married Sarah (d. 1816), the daughter of John Sawyer of Haddlesey, on 3 February 1777, and a few years later—certainly by March 1784—the couple were persuaded to make their home at Newark, convenient for work with the Trent Navigation, and for the Great North Road to London. Jessop was soon elected an alderman of Newark and served twice as mayor, in 1790–91 and 1803–4. Jessop and his wife had seven sons, four of whom followed him into the engineering profession, and one daughter. He was a man of simple tastes, ready to encourage younger engineers without becoming jealous of their success or that of colleagues, and he always showed concern for the safety of workmen on his projects. In 1805 the family moved to Butterley Hall in Derbyshire. Jessop died there on 18 November 1814, of paralysis after several years of declining health; he was buried in Pentrich churchyard, Derbyshire, on the 22nd.   R. ANGUS BUCHANAN

Sources C. Hadfield and A. W. Skempton, *William Jessop, engineer* (1979) · D. Brewster and others, eds., *The Edinburgh encyclopaedia*, 18 vols. (1808–30), vol. 11, pp. 735–7 · S. Hughes, 'Memoir of Wm Jessop', *Weale's Quarterly Papers on Engineering*, 1/2 (1844)
Likenesses G. Dance, pencil, 1796, NPG · oils, c.1805, priv. coll. · E. Williams, portrait, c.1845, Inst. CE · Walker, group portrait, engraving, pubd 1862 (*Distinguished men of science in Great Britain*)
Wealth at death see will, Hadfield and Skempton, *William Jessop*, 269

Jessopp, Augustus (1823–1914), schoolmaster and historical writer, was born at Cheshunt, Hertfordshire, on 20 December 1823, the third son and youngest of the ten children of John Sympson Jessopp (d. 1851), JP, of Cheshunt, and his wife, Elizabeth, daughter of Bridger Goodrich, of Bermuda. The family moved to Belgium about 1832, and Augustus Jessopp received a roving education at schools abroad and later at Clapham under the Revd H. A. Plow. He was a studious boy and, much to his relief, was sent in 1844 to St John's College, Cambridge, after three irksome years in a merchant's office in Liverpool. In 1848 he took a pass degree, and was ordained to a curacy at Papworth St Agnes, Cambridgeshire. In the same year he married Mary Ann Margaret, daughter of Charles Cotesworth RN, of Liverpool. They had no children. In 1855 he returned to Cambridge, but shortly afterwards moved to Helston, Cornwall, as master of the local grammar school, which had fallen on evil days and had hardly any pupils left. Jessopp soon restored its fortunes, leaving in 1859 to become headmaster of King Edward VI's School, Norwich, where a bigger task awaited him.

Norwich School was at a low ebb: it had few day-boys

and only one boarder; discipline was bad, the buildings dilapidated. During Jessopp's twenty-year rule it was transformed into a modern public school, with buildings enlarged, teaching and equipment improved, and with a good record at the universities. Jessopp was an imposing, if unconventional, headmaster; not a great scholar, but a teacher of originality and enthusiasm. He set the boys new standards in work, in discipline, in games; was admired by them for his vigour, fine presence, and noble voice; beloved for his kindliness and magnificent moments of indiscretion and frivolity. The publication of his school sermons (1864) and his manual of Greek accidence (1865) confirmed his credentials as a headmaster; he was one of the earliest members of the Headmasters' Conference, founded in 1869. His efforts to turn Norwich School into a boarding-school, though successful during his headship, were subsequently undermined by an insufficient endowment and the effects of agricultural depression, and it later thrived as a city day school.

Jessopp retired from Norwich in 1879 and was presented by Henry Evans-Lombe to the rectory of Scarning, Norfolk. There he found leisure to pursue the antiquarian researches which had become his chief interest, and which he did much to popularize. As early as 1855 he had published an edition of Donne's *Essays in Divinity*, and since 1866 he had been at work upon the records of the Walpole family. His *One Generation of a Norfolk House*—perhaps the best of his works—appeared in 1878, and the next year the Camden Society issued his edition of a seventeenth-century text, *The Oeconomy of the Fleete* (the prison).

At Scarning Jessopp lived the life of a well-to-do country parson of wide accomplishments, active in his poor parish, well known in East Anglia as a learned antiquary, and outside it as an attractive writer on medieval England, and a vigorous critic of the conditions of village and clerical life of his own day. His racy, provocative articles were readily taken by James Knowles for the newly founded *Nineteenth Century* magazine; many were later reissued by Jessopp in his volumes, *Arcady, for Better for Worse* (1887) and *Trials of a Country Parson* (1890). They remain a valuable source for historians of the late Victorian rural church, but their outspokenness probably ensured that their author received no high ecclesiastical preferment.

Of Jessopp's historical articles—many of them also written for the *Nineteenth Century*—the best collections were *The Coming of the Friars* (1889), a well-known book, *Studies by a Recluse* (1893), and *Before the Great Pillage* (1901); they gave popular, sympathetic accounts of parish life in the middle ages. Of more lasting value were Jessopp's edition of the *Visitations of the Diocese of Norwich, 1492–1532* (Camden Society, 1888)—the first English monastic visitations to be printed—his text of the *Life of St. William of Norwich* (with Dr M. R. James, 1896), and his reports on MSS of the bishop and chapter of Ely, at Shadwell Court, and at Holkham House, for the Historical Manuscripts Commission (1891, 1903, 1907). He also wrote biographies of Donne (1897) and Lord Burghley (1904), of Queen Elizabeth and others for the *Dictionary of National Biography*.

Jessopp's work and record brought him popular repute, eminent friends—especially George Meredith—and, in time, academic recognition. He incorporated at Oxford (from Worcester College) and took the degree of DD in 1870; he was select preacher there in 1890. In 1895 his Oxford and Cambridge colleges elected him honorary fellow on the same day. In that year also he was made honorary canon in Norwich Cathedral, and in 1902 a chaplain in ordinary to the king. After the death of his wife (1905) his circumstances were much reduced, and he was granted a civil-list pension. Later, his mind became affected and, having sold his library and offered his sermons to young clergymen—over 1000 of whom made application for them—he resigned his living in 1911, retiring to Norwich. He died at Virginia Water, Surrey, on 12 February 1914.

Jessopp disclaimed the title of historian, calling himself 'a smatterer and a fumbler', but he had some of the gifts and equipment of the best historians. Had his powers been directed to more solid historical work it would at least have redeemed his 'exile' at Scarning from the futility which he was wont to deplore; 'I was burning my boats in taking a country living', he used to say. Yet his achievement was not without merit. He called attention to much unworked material for English parochial and monastic history, and encouraged the sympathetic study of those subjects; while by many who never read his books he was remembered as one of the most stimulating headmasters of his time.   J. R. H. WEAVER, rev. M. C. CURTHOYS

Sources *The Times* (13 Feb 1914) · *Norvicensian* [Norwich School magazine] (1914) · *Letters of George Meredith*, ed. [W. M. Meredith], 2 vols. (1912) · *Cornhill Magazine*, [3rd] ser., 51 (1921) · E. Gaskell, *Norfolk leaders* (1910) · *Men and women of the time* (1899) · Venn, *Alum. Cant.* · R. Harries, P. Cattermole, and P. Mackintosh, *A history of Norwich School* (1991) · O. Chadwick, *The Victorian church*, 2 (1970) · *Wellesley index*
Archives Norfolk RO, papers relating to the history of Norwich diocese, library catalogue · Norfolk RO, calendar of Rougham charters and some genealogical notes · NRA priv. coll., historical and antiquarian corresp. · PRO, corresp. as HMC inspector, HMC 1 | BL, letters to Philip Bliss, Add. MS 34582 · Duke U., Perkins L., corresp. with William Stubbs · LPL, corresp. with Randall Thomas Davidson · Norfolk RO, corresp. with Walter Rye · U. Leeds, Brotherton L., letters to Edmund Gosse · University of British Columbia Library, letters to H. R. Haweis
Likenesses P. Naumann & R. Taylor & Co., wood-engraving, BM; repro. in *ILN* (14 May 1892) · photograph, repro. in A. Jessopp, *Arcady* (1887), frontispiece · photograph, repro. in A. Jessopp, *Random roaming* (1894), frontispiece
Wealth at death £11,863 8s. 6d.: probate, 10 March 1914, CGPLA Eng. & Wales

Jesty, Benjamin (*bap.* 1736, *d.* 1816), farmer and vaccinator, was born in Yetminster, Dorset, and baptized there on 19 August 1736, the youngest of at least four sons of Robert Jesty, butcher. Little else is known of his early life. In March 1770 he married Elizabeth Notley (1740–1824) in Longburton, 4 miles north-east of Yetminster. The marital home was established at Upbury Farm, adjoining Yetminster churchyard, and the couple had four sons and three daughters.

It was known in the dairy-farming areas of south-west England that milkmaids, and others who contracted the relatively mild and non-infectious disease of cowpox through handling udders of infected cows, obtained immunity from smallpox, and in 1765 the Medical Society of London received from a Dr Fewster (possibly John Fewster) a paper entitled 'Cow pox and its ability to prevent smallpox'. In 1774 smallpox was widespread throughout England, with epidemics in countless towns and villages, including Yetminster. Jesty's servants Ann Notley and Mary Reade, who, like him, had been infected with cowpox, had nursed smallpox patients without themselves catching the disease. Worried for his family's safety in the epidemic, Jesty resolved to provide immunity by giving his wife and two elder sons cowpox. Finding a suitable cow in neighbouring Chetnole, he used a needle to transfer the pox matter and, copying the technique used by inoculators, infected his wife and sons by scratching their arms. The boys had local reactions and quickly recovered but his wife's arm became very inflamed and for a time her condition gave cause for concern. Thus took place the earliest known vaccinations, though the treatment was thought of as inoculation with cowpox until the term vaccination (from the Latin *vacca* for cow) was coined in 1802.

Jesty's experiment was met by hostility in the neighbourhood; he was labelled inhuman, and 'hooted at, reviled and pelted whenever he attended markets in the neighbourhood'. The introduction of an animal disease into a human body was thought disgusting and some even 'feared their metamorphosis into horned beasts'. But the treatment's efficacy was several times demonstrated in the years which followed, when Jesty's two elder sons, exposed to smallpox, failed to catch the disease.

Interest in the prophylactic powers of cowpox virus grew and in May 1796 Edward Jenner began his series of vaccination experiments. About 1797 Jesty became tenant at Downshay Manor Farm in Worth Matravers where, encouraged by Andrew Bell, rector of neighbouring Swanage from 1801, he conducted more vaccinations. Following Jenner's reward of £10,000 from the House of Commons in June 1802 for discovering and promoting vaccination, Bell took up Jesty's cause and in August 1803 wrote to George Pearson, founder of the Vaccine Pock Institute, describing in detail the 1774 vaccinations. In 1805 Jesty gave his evidence in London at the institute's invitation, when he was presented with a long testimonial and pair of gold mounted lancets. The institute also commissioned his portrait from Michael William Sharp.

Jesty died in Worth Matravers on 16 April 1816 and was buried in the parish churchyard. His widow, Elizabeth, died on 8 January 1824 and was buried alongside him.

J. R. SMITH, rev.

Sources E. M. Crookshank, *History and pathology of vaccination*, 1 (1889) · C. W. Dixon, *Smallpox* (1962) · C. Creighton, *A history of epidemics in Britain*, 2 (1894) · J. R. Smith, *The speckled monster* (1987) · E. M. Wallace, *The first vaccinator* (1981) · parish registers, Dorset RO [Longburton, Yetminster, Worth Matravers]

Likenesses M. W. Sharp, portrait, priv. coll. · portrait, repro. in Wallace, *First vaccinator*

Wealth at death over £1200; also land at Yetminster; other goods: Wallace, *First vaccinator*

Jeune, Francis (1806–1868), college head and bishop of Peterborough, was born on 22 May 1806 at St Aubin, Jersey, in the parish of St Brelade, the eldest of the five children of François Jeune (1781–1836), miller, and Elizabeth (1783–1851), *née* Le Capelain. He had two brothers and two sisters. Jeune's early education was at the college of St Servan at Rennes and a Huguenot theological college at Saumur. However, coming to the notice of Sir John de Veulle, bailiff of Jersey, he was encouraged to go to Pembroke College, Oxford, where he matriculated on 21 October 1822, was soon elected into a scholarship, and took a first class in *literae humaniores* in 1827. He graduated BA in 1827, MA in 1830, and BCL and DCL in 1834; he held an Ossulston fellowship at Pembroke from 1830 to 1837, was tutor for several years, and was a public examiner in 1834. For approximately a year in 1832–3 he was in Canada as tutor to the sons of Sir John Colborne (Lord Seaton), the lieutenant-governor of Upper Canada. In 1834 he became chief master of King Edward's School, Birmingham, then in an ailing condition, which in four years he did much to revitalize and remodel so that it could cater properly for 'the wants of a great commercial community'. On 15 December 1836, Jeune married Margaret Dyne (1818–1891), only child of Henry Symons of Axbridge, Somerset, and niece of Benjamin Symons, warden of Wadham College, Oxford.

It may have been while at King Edward's that Jeune came to the attention of the whig politician, Lord John Russell, for it was on his recommendation that, early in 1838, Jeune was appointed dean of Jersey ('with quasi-episcopal powers') and rector of St Helier. Although he worked in Jersey for nearly six years with energy and success, and later contributed greatly to the foundation of Victoria College (1852), he had inherited the handling of a grave scandal concerning a clergyman, and Jeune suffered from the political divisions (and public vilification) which resulted. However, on the death of G. W. Hall in late 1843, Jeune was offered the mastership of Pembroke College, and, after the delicate question of his eligibility had at last been settled in his favour, took up his appointment in 1844; a canonry at Gloucester Cathedral was attached *ex officio*. He also held (1844–64) the rectorship of Taynton, Gloucestershire.

It was now that Jeune's combination of energy and Victorian liberalism were seen at their most effective. Important new buildings, especially the hall (1848), transformed the appearance of Pembroke College, where matriculations increased very markedly. He played a decisive role in the discussions which led to the complete revision of Oxford's examination statutes in 1850, (*inter alia*) introducing law and modern history to the syllabus. Most important of all, his recommendation to Lord John Russell was instrumental in leading to the setting up of the royal commission on Oxford University in 1850, of which he became a highly active member, thereby incurring the odium (with social consequences) of his fellow heads of house, all of whom were deeply opposed to the commission. His contribution to the famous report of 1852, especially on matters concerning the colleges, was

Francis Jeune (1806–1868), by unknown engraver, pubd 1863
(after William Menzies Tweedie)

considerable. Before the Oxford Act of 1854 was passed, Jeune corresponded ceaselessly with Gladstone, with the main objective of freeing Pembroke from the severe restrictions placed upon it in elections to fellowships and scholarships by the closeness of its ties to Abingdon School. By early 1857 the college had new, and much less restrictive statutes.

Jeune's energy on the hebdomadal board (council from 1854) was manifested in many ways, perhaps most enduringly in his successful advocacy of a professorship of Latin, to which the first appointment was made in 1854. From 1858 to 1862 he was vice-chancellor of the university, when the residence of the prince of Wales, later Edward VII, occupied much of his time. Of greater moment was the University Elections Act of 1861, which introduced the postal vote; Jeune unsuccessfully opposed this, rightly fearing that it might cost Gladstone his university seat.

Evangelical in his religious views, and a long-standing and determined opponent of 'Newmanism' (the Oxford Movement), Jeune had passed through the various stages of qualifying for the priesthood by 1833, and by the mid-1850s at the latest his interest in securing a bishopric was surfacing. Certain difficulties, partly of his own making, had to be surmounted before his nomination to the deanship of Lincoln in early 1864 and his subsequent rapid elevation to the see of Peterborough (consecrated 27 June 1864). His episcopacy was one of considerable vigour, as is evidenced by his lengthy *primary charge* of 1867; but

on doctrinal grounds he refused to attend the first Lambeth conference of that year.

Jeune was a handsome man, with very strong features; he was probably the ablest man of business of his era at Oxford (*DNB*), a fact recognized by Gladstone; and his work both for the university and for Pembroke College has proved to be of great and enduring significance. Other than his *Primary Charge*, he published little, but his 1845 Act Sermon on *The Studies of Oxford Vindicated* has retained some interest in the context of the (by then declining) Oxford Movement. Jeune died, almost certainly of coronary thrombosis, at Whitby on 21 August 1868, and was buried in the cathedral yard at Peterborough. His widow died in 1891, aged seventy-three, and of their six children (four sons and two daughters) the second son did not survive his first year and the eldest son was Francis Henry *Jeune.

J. H. C. LEACH

Sources J. H. C. Leach, *Sparks of reform: the career of Francis Jeune, 1806–68* (1994) · D. Macleane, *A history of Pembroke College, Oxford*, OHS, 33 (1897) · A. Trott, *No place for fop or idler* (1992) · G. R. Balleine, *A biographical dictionary of Jersey*, [1] [1948] · W. R. Ward, *Victorian Oxford* (1965) · E. G. W. Bill, *University reform in nineteenth-century Oxford: a study of Henry Halford Vaughan, 1811–1885* (1973) · D. J. Cottrill, *Victoria College, Jersey, 1852–1972* (1977) · A. M. G. Stephenson, *The first Lambeth conference, 1867* (1967) · M. J. Gifford, *Pages from the diary of an Oxford lady, 1843–1862* (1932) · DNB

Archives Pembroke College, Oxford, corresp. and papers | BL, corresp. with W. E. Gladstone, Add. MS 44221 · Bodl. Oxf., MSS Symons · Bodl. Oxf., corresp. with Sir T. Phillipps · LPL, letters to Charles Golightly · LPL, C. T. Longley MSS · LPL, A. C. Tait MSS · Lpool RO, Derby MSS · Pusey Oxf., letters to Pusey · U. Southampton L., letters to first duke of Wellington

Likenesses portrait, 1850, Victoria College, Jersey · W. M. Tweedie, oils, c.1863, Pembroke College, Oxford · engraving, pubd 1863 (after W. M. Tweedie), AM Oxf. [*see illus.*] · portrait, 1880, Victoria College, Jersey · W. Walker & Sons, carte-de-visite, NPG · wood-engraving (after photograph by John & Charles Watkins), NPG; repro. in *ILN* (28 May 1864)

Wealth at death under £35,000: probate, 12 Sept 1868, *CGPLA Eng. & Wales*

Jeune, Francis Henry, Baron St Helier (1843–1905), judge, was born on 17 March 1843 at St Helier, the eldest son of Francis *Jeune (1806–1868), then rector of St Helier and dean of Jersey, and later bishop of Peterborough, and his wife, Margaret Dyne Symons (1818–1891) of Axbridge, Somerset. He was educated at Penrose's school at Exmouth, and then sent to Harrow School (1856–61), where he obtained a scholarship and won many prizes. As a boy he was particularly talented at English and his oratory was described by Lord Brougham (who visited Harrow on a speech day) as 'perfect'.

In 1861 he obtained a scholarship to Balliol College, Oxford, where he graduated BA with a first class in classics in 1865, having also achieved distinction in moderations in 1863. In 1863 he also won the Stanhope prize for an essay entitled *The Influence of the Feudal System on Character*, and in 1867 the Arnold prize for one entitled *The Mohammedan Power in India*. He was president of the Oxford Union in 1864. He took his MA in 1874 and the same year was made one of the original members of Hertford College on its establishment as a full college of Oxford University.

Jeune was called to the bar by the Inner Temple on 17

November 1868. Before his call he gained considerable legal experience working for a well-known firm of solicitors of the day, Messrs Baxter, Rose, and Norton, and in 1869 was sent by them to Australia to gather evidence for the celebrated case in which Arthur Orton claimed to be the long-lost 'Sir' Roger Tichborne. After he was called to the bar and on his return from Australia he was counsel for the plaintiff in the *Tichborne* v. *Lushington* case. The case was tried for a record 103 days, after which the plaintiff was committed for trial for perjury.

Jeune's involvement in such a *cause célèbre* as the Tichborne case helped to win him the reputation of a promising young advocate who was thought to be exceptionally able and industrious, while his family background made him well acquainted with ecclesiastical law and theological disputes. A large proportion of his growing practice was in ecclesiastical courts, or before the judicial committee of the privy council. He often acted on the evangelical side, notably in the Mackonochie case, *Green* v. *Lord Penzance*, the Dale case, the Enraght case, *Julius* v. *Bishop of Oxford*, and *Cox* v. *Hake*. He also served on the royal commission on ecclesiastical patronage in 1874, and on the royal commission on ecclesiastical courts in 1881. Before his appointment to the bench he also served as chancellor of the dioceses of St Albans, Durham, Peterborough, Gloucester, and Bristol, and St Asaph, Bangor, and St David's.

In 1880 Jeune stood as Conservative candidate for Colchester, and was defeated by two votes by William (afterwards Judge) Willis QC. After this election he sat with Messrs Holl QC and Turner as a commissioner to inquire into the corruption alleged at Sandwich. The report of the existence of flagrant corruption meant that the borough was consequently disfranchised, until by the Redistribution Act of 1885 it became part of one of the divisions of Kent. In 1881 Jeune married Susan Elizabeth Mary Constantine Stanley (1849–1931), daughter of the Hon. Keith Stewart Mackenzie and widow of the Hon. John Constantine Stanley. Their marriage appears to have been a happy one and brought them one son, Christian Francis Seaforth, who served in the Grenadier Guards as aide-de-camp to Lord Lamington and sadly died at Poona in 1905 of enteric fever. Lady St Helier was well known for her entertaining and her acts in service of the poor.

In 1888 Jeune was appointed a queen's counsel, and in June 1891 was elected a bencher of the Inner Temple. The last case of great importance in which he appeared at the bar was for the defendant in the prosecution before the archbishop of Canterbury (Benson), with assessors, of Edward King, bishop of Lincoln, for alleged unlawful ritual, in which some of the practices impugned were held to be unlawful, winning a victory for the evangelical party within the Church of England.

In 1890 it was suggested to Jeune that he should again stand for parliament, with a view to his appointment as solicitor-general should an expected vacancy in that office arise, but he declined the proposal on the ground that his health would be unequal to the strain of parliamentary and official work. In 1891 Sir James Hannen was created a

lord of appeal and Sir Charles Parker Butt succeeded him; so Jeune accepted the office of judge of the Probate, Divorce, and Admiralty Division in place of Butt. Jeune was knighted in 1881. The work of the division fell principally on his shoulders for the following year and a half, owing to Butt's illness and subsequent death in May 1892. An act was passed creating a definite office of the Probate, Divorce, and Admiralty Division, with the judicial rank of one of the lords justices of appeal. This meant that the president would always be a privy councillor. Jeune became the first holder of this office and his tenure, which lasted thirteen years, was successful. Jeune was regarded as a sound lawyer and a polite and courteous judge. With the assistance of his colleague, Mr Justice Gorell Barnes (later Lord Gorell), he greatly increased the efficiency of the Probate, Divorce, and Admiralty Division. The lists were increasingly full at the beginning of each year, and arrears were practically unknown. In each of the three classes of work Jeune was an efficient and capable judge. Of Admiralty work he had little or no special knowledge at the time of his appointment as a judge but read up on the subject and acquired the necessary technical knowledge. He came to be best known by the general public for his decisions in divorce cases, but inspired the confidence of his colleagues in all three branches of the law.

When the Liberal government came into office in 1892 a difficulty arose as to the payment of the judge-advocate-general. Gladstone, acting on the precedent of the appointment to that office of Sir Robert Joseph Phillimore when judge of the court of Admiralty, eventually asked Jeune to take on the duties of that post, which he accepted and continued to discharge until 1904. Although he received no salary, his services were rewarded by his creation as KCB in 1897 and as GCB at the close of the Second South African War in 1902. During these ten years, as previously, the daily work of the office was performed by two deputies, one legal and the other military. However, the finding of every 'general court-martial' had to be confirmed or quashed by the judge-advocate-general himself, who was also required to advise the sovereign personally in many cases. As a result it was necessary that the office should be held by a privy councillor. Jeune was the last holder, as the post was effectively abolished by statute in 1904, the title and some of the duties being transferred to a legal official of the War Office.

In 1898 Jeune acted as chairman of a committee on the load line regulations for winter north Atlantic freeboard, and in 1902 on a committee on the effect of employment of lascars and other foreigners on the reserve of British seamen available for naval purposes. In 1904 he was a member of Sir Michael Hicks Beach's commission on ecclesiastical discipline.

In January 1905, on medical advice, he resigned the presidency of the Probate, Divorce, and Admiralty Division, and was created a peer with the title of Baron St Helier. Grief at the death of his son speeded the decline in his health and he died at his house, 79 Harley Street, London, on 9 April 1905. He was buried in the churchyard at

Chieveley, Berkshire. In appearance, Jeune was tall and distinguished; he was one of the first judges to wear a full beard and moustache.

HERBERT STEPHEN, rev. SINÉAD AGNEW

Sources WWW, 1897–1915 · L. G. Pine, *The new extinct peerage, 1884–1971: containing extinct, abeyant, dormant, and suspended peerages with genealogies and arms* (1972), 244 · J. Foster, *Men-at-the-bar: a biographical hand-list of the members of the various inns of court*, 2nd edn (1885), 244 · A. T. C. Pratt, ed., *People of the period: being a collection of the biographies of upwards of six thousand living celebrities*, 2 (1897), 18–19 · *Leading men of London: a collection of biographical sketches* (1895), 7 · *Men and women of the time* (1899), 573 · Lady St Helier [S. M. E. Jeune], *Memories of fifty years* (1909) · *Annual Register* (1905), 124 · *The Times* (11 April 1905) · E. Kilmurray, *Dictionary of British portraiture*, 3 (1981), 183 · private information (2004) · J. D. Woodruff, *The Tichborne claimant: a Victorian mystery* (1957), 171
Archives BL, corresp. with Lord Carnarvon, Add. MS 60822 · Bodl. Oxf., Harcourt MSS, corresp. mainly with Sir William Harcourt
Likenesses H. von Herkomer, oils, 1895, Inner Temple, London · E. Fuchs, marble bust, Gov. Art Coll. · Stuff [Wright], chromolithograph caricature, NPG; repro. in *VF* (11 April 1891) · photograph, repro. in *ILN*, 98 (1891), 167
Wealth at death £229,588: probate, 29 June 1905, *CGPLA Eng. & Wales*

Jevon, Rachel (*bap.* 1627), poet, was baptized on 23 January 1627 in Broom, Worcester, the daughter of Daniell Jevon (*d.* 1654), rector of Broom, and his wife, Elizabeth. In his will dated 1649 Daniell Jevon named his wife, Elizabeth, their daughter Elizabeth and her husband, Robert Cooper, a brother, Thomas Jevon of Stowbridge, and a cousin, Thomas Scott of the Overhouse in Barre. He declared other (unnamed) children as heirs with his wife. Beyond the parish record of Rachel's baptism, only four other known documents witness her name and life. The main two are her poems, one Latin and one English, congratulating Charles II on his restoration (*Exultationis carmen* and *Carmen thriambeutikon*, each printed in 1660). The other two are petitions to the king dated May(?) 1662, one for 'the place of one of the meanest servants about the Queen' and the other for 'the place of Rocker to the Queen'. The first petition informs that her father, 'a loyal clergyman in the diocese of Worcester, though threatened and imprisoned, contrived to preserve his flock, so that not one took arms against His Majesty, but could only give his children education, without maintenance'.

The more concise Latin poem (138 hexameter lines) probably preceded Jevon's more expansive English version (190 lines of iambic pentameter couplets). Both 'exultation' poems have much the same order of contents: humble presentation of the poem to Charles; his royal lineage; his providential escape after defeat at Worcester and travels on the continent; his triumphal return to England; celebration of Charles, the king, as a spirit of peace and spring, wearing five crowns and figured as bridegroom, royal lion, royal oak, King David, and star (sun). Both poems exhibit considerable education (unusual for a woman then), in verbal and versifying skills, rhetorical devices, and allusions to biblical and classical literature. Both express enthusiastic loyalty to the monarchy and Charles. Congruence between Jevon's

(English) congratulatory poem and the petitions two years later led Elaine Hobby to conclude that the poem 'was not the naïve outpouring that it might at first appear'. It seemed rather 'a planned strategy of publicizing her learning, loyalism and humility', in order to win a position (Hobby, 19). Rachel's petitions for a position in service to the queen came with Charles's marriage to Catherine of Braganza in May 1662. Whether she received such a position is not known.

JOSEPH P. CROWLEY

Sources E. Hobby, *Virtue of necessity: English women's writing, 1649–1688* (1988), 18–19, 210 · M. Bell, G. Parfitt, and S. Shepherd, *A biographical dictionary of English women writers, 1580–1720* (1990), 115 · *CSP dom.*, 1661–2 [petitions 45–6] · Daniell Jevon, will, PRO, PROB 11/239, sig. 333, fols. 241v–242r · parish register, Broom, Worcester, 23 Jan 1627 [baptism]

Jevon, Thomas (1651/2–1688), actor and playwright, is described as having been 'as vilely born, so careless bred' in Robert Gould's poem 'The Play-House: a Satyr' (the second redaction, of 1697, of his 'Satyr on the Players').

Initially a dancing-master, Jevon evidently became an actor in the Duke's Company at the Dorset Garden Theatre in the 1673–4 season, playing Osric in *Hamlet* in that year. From early on in his career an anecdote preserved by the prompter John Downes records an occasion when Jevon's sense of frolic got the better of him. In Elkanah Settle's tragedy *The Conquest of China*, first performed on 28 May 1675:

> [He] was Acting a *Chinese* Prince and Commander … and being in the Battle, Vanquisht by the *Tartars*; he was by his Part to fall upon the point of his Sword and Kill himself, rather than be a Prisoner by the *Tartars*: Mr. *Jevon* instead of falling upon the point of his Sword, laid it in the Scabbard at length upon the Ground and fell upon't, saying now I am Dead; which put the Author into such a Fret, it made him speak Treble, instead of Double. *Jevons* answer was; did you not bid me fall upon my Sword.   (Downes, 75)

Jevon's forte was evidently in low-comic roles, and especially in those involving singing or dancing, such as Harlequin both in Aphra Behn's farce *The Emperor of the Moon* (1686) and in William Mountfort's *Dr Faustus* (1688). None the less he also appeared in cast-lists in a number of minor to middle-sized roles in tragedies and comedies for the Duke's Company between 1675 and 1682, and thereafter for the United Company, up to the year of his death. By March 1682, when he spoke the epilogue for Aphra Behn's comedy *Like Father, Like Son* (a play for which only the prologue and epilogue were published), he was becoming a popular speaker of prologues and epilogues, especially of those containing snatches of singing, dancing, or comic by-play.

Several other anecdotes about Jevon have been preserved, all of uncertain authenticity. A biography of 1701 of the comic actor Joe Haines recounts an episode in which Haines, impersonating an obstreperous Frenchman, staged a furious argument in a London street with Jevon, who was pretending to be an English country gentleman. Drawing after them a swelling mob, who were expecting to witness a fight to the death, they rejected one site for a duel after another, until at last they came to

Hampstead and jumped into a saw-pit. When they then revealed that the whole affair was an April fools' day hoax, the crowd became enraged, pelted them with sticks and stones, and drove them before them, all the way back (Browne, 48–51).

In *The Egotist* (1743) Colley Cibber's brand of modesty is said to be 'rather like that of *Jevon* the Comedian, who coming into a Club of his Acquaintance with dirty Shoes, contentedly took a clean Napkin from the Table to wipe them; when the Waiter desiring him to stay till he could fetch him a coarse Cloth, *Jevon* gently replied, No! no! Thank you, my good Lad; this will serve me well enough' (p. 44).

Robert Gould's earliest reference to Jevon in his 'Satyr on the Players' (*c*.1684) focuses on Jevon's debasing poverty: 'He'l turn procurer for a Dish of meat' (Highfill, Burnim & Langhans, *BDA*, 8.159); but in the more extended 'A Satyr Against the Play-House', published in 1689, Gould's survey of the actors records that:

A *third*, a punning, drolling, Bantr'ing Ass,
Cocks up and fain wou'd for an *Author* pass.
His Face for *Farce* nature at first design'd,
And matcht it too with as Burlesque a Mind,
Made him pert, vain, a Maggot, vile, ill-bred,
And gave him *heels of Cork*, and *brains of Lead*.
(Gould, 184)

The second line refers to Jevon's single play, a farce, *The Devil of a Wife, or, A Comical Transformation* (first acted on 4 March 1686), and probably to a contemporary perception that he was not wholly its author, but had written it in collaboration with Thomas Shadwell (Whincop, 199). It has unmistakable echoes of and parallels with *The Lancashire Witches* (1681) and other plays by Shadwell, whose recalcitrant whiggism meant he could not get plays overtly his own staged at that time.

This farce, in which a rural cobbler's wife and a country-house great lady are magically exchanged, underwent multiple transformations. In its original form it was reasonably popular, with the published text going through eight editions by 1735. In 1731 its dialogue was reworked by Charles Coffey and John Mottley, and heavily cut to one-act length by Theophilus Cibber, with new songs added. In this new guise, as *The Devil to Pay, or, The Wives Metamorphosed*, variously described as a 'ballad farce', 'opera', or 'operatical farce', it became one of the most popular of theatrical afterpieces, and was frequently published, both in Britain and in the United States, right through to the 1860s.

In 1743 this redaction was translated into German by the Prussian ambassador Caspar Wilhelm von Borcke as *Der Teufel ist los*, with settings by a Mr Sydow, and this did much to initiate the rise of north German *Singspiel*. A new version, *Die verwandelten Weiber*, appeared in 1752, translated by Christian Felix Weisse, with a setting by Johann Standfuss, and in 1764, with a setting by Johann Adam Hiller. The farce was also translated into French by Claude Pierre Patu, in a text published in 1756, and further adapted by Michel Jean Sedaine as a French comic opera, *Le diable à quatre* (1757). In 1845 Sedaine's adaptation was set as a ballet, with music by Adolphe Adams. There were also several Italian operatic versions.

Jevon is said to have become the brother-in-law of the playwright Thomas Shadwell (Whincop, 199); he may therefore have married the actress who was listed in Duke's Company cast-lists from December 1672 to May 1678 as 'Mrs. Gibbs', probably a younger sister of Shadwell's wife, Anne, *née* Gibbs, the daughter of Thomas Gibbs, attorney and notary public of Norwich, and Anne, *née* Keepes. An infant called Thomas Jevon, possibly their son, was buried on 13 September 1684 in Hampstead churchyard, Middlesex. Jevon died on 20 December 1688 aged thirty-six, and was buried in Hampstead churchyard four days later.   JOHN C. ROSS

Sources D. E. Baker, *Biographia dramatica, or, A companion to the playhouse*, rev. I. Reed, new edn, 2 vols. (1782) · T. Banman, *North German opera in the age of Goethe* (1985), 21–34 · [T. Browne], *The life of the late famous comedian, Jo Hayns* (1701) · P. Danchin, ed., *The prologues and epilogues of the Restoration, 1660–1700*, 7 vols. (1981–8), vol. 1 · J. Downes, *Roscius Anglicanus*, ed. J. Milhous and R. D. Hume, new edn (1987) · *The egotist, or, Colley upon Cibber* (1743) · Genest, *Eng. stage* · R. Gould, *Poems chiefly consisting of satyrs and satyrical epistles* (1689), 2nd edn (1697) · Highfill, Burnim & Langhans, *BDA* · L. Hughes and A. H. Scouten, *Ten English farces* (Austin, Texas, 1948) · G. Langbaine, *An account of the English dramatick poets* (1691) · W. Van Lennep and others, eds., *The London stage, 1660–1800*, 5 pts in 11 vols. (1960–68) · D. Lysons, *The environs of London: being an historical account of the towns, villages, and hamlets, within twelve miles of that capital: interspersed with biographical anecdotes*, 4 vols. (1792–1811) · M. Summers, *The Restoration theatre* (1934) · W. R. Tate, 'Burials in Hampstead churchyard', *N&Q*, 7th ser., 9 (1890), 484 · T. Whincop, *Scanderbeg, or, Love and liberty: a tragedy* (1747)

Jevons [*née* Roscoe], **Mary Anne** (1795–1845), poet, was born in Liverpool on 5 August 1795, the eldest daughter of William *Roscoe (1753–1831), historian, writer, and politician, and Jane Griffies (1757–1824). She was brought up in a cultured, literary environment, and was encouraged from an early age in her writing and reading. She was much influenced by her father, both in the range of her reading, some of which is recorded in a manuscript literary journal, and in her enthusiasm for writing verse, as well as in her Unitarian faith. Her manuscript literary journal (1817–19) bears the motto 'Nulla dies sine libra', and she determines, in her introduction, to 'devote my attention principally to Mathematics and Natural Philosophy and in the second place to History, Languages, Logic and Polite Literature' (Roscoe, literary diary, introduction). This regime, she acknowledged, would leave her with 'not quite as much leisure as I would wish for literary purposes' (ibid., 1). However, she collected materials from her family and edited *Poems for Youth, by a Family Circle* (2 pts, 1820–21), to which her father contributed his celebrated 'The Butterfly's Ball'. This volume also contained the work of her sister, Jane Elizabeth, which was separately published as *Poems* (1820).

Mary Anne's journals reflect a self-disciplined life, of committed Unitarian faith. She attended chapel regularly and taught in the Sunday school, and also helped in the local school. She was upset by the loss of the family home,

Allerton Hall, when her father encountered financial difficulties. However, her faith gave her strength and kept the
family together through 'scenes of perplexity and woe', as
she described them in her journal (Roscoe, literary diary,
2). On 23 November 1825 she married Thomas Jevons
(1791–1855), an ironmaster and a fellow Unitarian. The
economist William Stanley *Jevons (1835–1882) was one
of their eleven children, several of whom died in childhood.

Mary Anne Jevons's main literary endeavour during this
time was *The Sacred Offering: a Poetical Annual*, which she
edited and to which she contributed during the 1830s.
Other poets whose work she published included Anna
Letitia Barbauld, Mary Anne Brown, Harriet Martineau,
and Lydia Sigourney. Her other main individual publication was *Sonnets and other Poems, Chiefly Devotional* (1845),
dedicated to her brother Richard. Her principal subjects
may be considered typical of female writers of the time:
religion and family, with an understandable emphasis on
death and loss. However, she also includes work with a
political slant, particularly emphasizing her 'patriot
hopes', seeing 'reform' as England's 'brightening day-star'
(M. A. Jevons, *Sonnets and other Poems*). Soon after the
appearance of this volume she became ill, and she went to
London to stay with her brother, who was a doctor. She
died in London on 13 November 1845, at 37 Alfred Place,
Bloomsbury. She was survived by her husband.

ROSEMARY SCOTT

Sources *Letters and journals of W. S. J.*, ed. [H. A. Jevons] (1886) · M. A.
Roscoe, literary diary, 1817–19, Liverpool Central Library, Roscoe
MS, 920 Ros 5827 (i) · M. A. Roscoe, journal, 5 Aug 1822–31 Dec 1824,
Liverpool Central Library, Roscoe MS, 920 Ros 5827 (ii) · *DNB* ·
H. Roscoe, *Life of William Roscoe* (1833) · memorial inscriptions, Uni-
tarian Chapel, Renshaw Street, Liverpool · d. cert.
Archives Lpool RO, letters; literary journal

Jevons, William Stanley (1835–1882), economist and
   philosopher of science, was born on 1 September 1835 at
   14 Alfred Street, Liverpool, the ninth of the eleven children (of whom only six survived beyond infancy) of
   Thomas Jevons (1791–1855), iron merchant and inventor,
   and his wife, Mary Anne *Jevons (1795–1845), daughter of
   William *Roscoe of Liverpool and his wife, Jane Griffies.
   His parents were both Unitarians and had many connections in the nonconformist community of the north of
   England, which played so large a part in the economic and
   social development and the intellectual life of Victorian
   Britain.

Boyhood and youth in Liverpool and London, 1835–1853
Jevons had the advantage of being born into a family that
at the time was happy, cultured, and well-to-do. Thomas
Jevons was then a partner in the firm of Jevons & Son, iron
merchants, which his father, William Jevons, had
founded soon after coming to Liverpool from Staffordshire, where the Jevons family originated, in 1798. His
business provided Thomas Jevons with the means to keep
his family in comfort, but he also found time to exercise
his talents as an inventor (he built the first iron boat to sail

William Stanley Jevons (1835–1882), by Maull & Co., 1870s

on salt water) and as an author of pamphlets on such
diverse topics as the criminal law and the corn laws.
Jevons learned much from his example, and also from
that of his mother, who was not only a talented poet, but
also much more widely learned than most women of her
time. His formal education was entrusted to a governess
until he reached the age of ten. Then in January 1846 he
was sent to the Liverpool Mechanics' Institute High
School, but in 1847 his father moved him to a private
school, Mr Beckwith's. It was from here that Jevons went
to University College School, London, in the autumn of
1850.

Before this, there had been serious changes in the circumstances of Jevons's immediate family. His mother
died in 1845 and her death seems to have contributed
towards unbalancing the mind of his elder brother Roscoe
(1829–1869), who suffered a nervous breakdown in 1847
and spent the rest of his life in mental hospitals. Roscoe
Jevons had shown much promise at school and Jevons
greatly looked up to him; in a sense the intensity with
which he worked during his own lifetime may be
regarded as an attempt to take Roscoe's place, to compensate for what he might have achieved.

Soon after these sorrows troubles of another kind came
to Jevons's family. In January 1848, after the railway construction boom had ended in the commercial crisis of
1847, the firm of Jevons & Son went into bankruptcy.
Thomas Jevons was forced to sell the family home and
take a post as manager of the Liverpool branch of another
firm of iron merchants; he did not retrieve his fortune

before his death in 1855 and his family were left in strait-ened circumstances.

Nevertheless, Jevons was able to go to London as planned. He first attended University College School in 1850–51, then moved to University College itself for the following two academic years. In these he studied mathematics under Augustus de Morgan and chemistry under A. W. Williamson and Thomas Graham. In his spare time long walks through the commercial and manufacturing districts of London and visits to the Great Exhibition aroused an interest, which never left him, in what he termed 'the industrial mechanism of society'. Yet at this time experimental science was his prime concern, and seemed likely to remain so. In October 1851 he had gone to live with his aunt Mrs Henry Roscoe in Camden Town; her son Henry Enfield (Harry) Roscoe had already decided to make chemistry his career and was acting as lecture assistant to Williamson. When Jevons won the silver medal for chemistry in 1852 and the gold medal in 1853, Harry Roscoe came to expect that his cousin would follow him in making his scientific career in chemistry. At this stage Jevons had no intention of staying on even to complete his degree in 1853–4, but he did intend to look for a place in some manufacturing firm using chemical processes in Liverpool and to carry on his scientific and literary studies in his spare time.

In the summer term of 1853 Williamson and Graham unexpectedly offered to recommend Jevons for the post of assayer at the first branch of the Royal Mint, which was about to be opened in Sydney, Australia. Not yet eighteen, Jevons was at first inclined to refuse, thinking himself unequal to such a responsible position; but, for financial reasons, his father urged him to take it. So Jevons accepted and began to train as an assayer, first under Thomas Graham and later at the Paris mint. He had also to plan his own assay office, purchase the equipment for it, and engage an assistant before finally sailing for Sydney, where he arrived on 6 October 1854.

In Australia, 1854–1859 At first, Jevons had difficulty in finding a place to live and work; the new mint building was not ready until June 1855, and there were problems about the terms of his remuneration. In time all these problems were overcome and after April 1856, when the first rush of coining at the mint was over, Jevons found himself settled in a well-paid post with easy duties, which gave him ample leisure to explore his new surroundings and follow his own interests. His study of things Australian came to include the country's botany, geology, geography, and social and economic organization; but first and foremost came meteorology. As early as January 1855 Jevons had begun to take regular meteorological observations twice daily in Sydney and from September 1856 his meteorological reports were published weekly in *The Empire* newspaper. Ultimately he incorporated the mass of data he had accumulated into a major study—'Some data concerning the climate of Australia and New Zealand', published in *Waugh's Australian Almanac* (1859).

While Jevons continued to devote much of his time to meteorology and geology throughout his years in Australia, in 1856 and 1857 he began to take an interest in philosophy and political economy. He read a variety of economic works in these years—Smith, Malthus, Mill, and Whately among others—and in his private journal accounts of his excursions around New South Wales came to be interspersed with reflections on aspects of moral philosophy. At the same time the interest that he had displayed in London in the 'industrial mechanism of society' was kindled afresh by observation of the problems arising in Sydney and throughout the colony as a result of the gold discoveries and the flood of immigrants they had produced. He sought to develop his observations of Sydney into a social survey, classifying inhabitants by social class and businesses by their products, and also contributed to contemporary debates about railway construction and operation, and official policy on the sale of public lands. So in the middle years of his time in Australia his interests shifted, gradually but fundamentally, from the study of nature to the study of man, which by 1859 he saw as 'surely a work worth a lifetime, and one not excelled in usefulness or interest by any other' (*Papers*, 2.362).

Jevons had been in Australia only three months when he wrote in his private journal that he was 'perfectly decided … to be at home again in from 5 to 10 years' (*Papers*, 1.110). He enjoyed Australian life and left vivid records of it in his journals, letters, and photographs; but once he had realized clearly what he wanted to do with his life he was equally clear that to do it he must sacrifice the comfortable circumstances which he had, return to London, and live frugally on the savings he had accumulated while he laid the foundations for his future career by acquiring further knowledge and at least completing the degree course which he had left unfinished in 1853. Hence when, in December 1858, he was offered a partnership in an assaying business in Melbourne which might have paid twice as much as his substantial salary from the Sydney mint, Jevons refused it. He resigned his position at the mint and left Sydney in March 1859. After taking time to see as much of the world as he could on his way home, he arrived back in Liverpool on 17 September 1859.

A London student again, 1859–1863 Jevons's family doubted the wisdom of his decision to abandon a lucrative position and prospects and come home with no settled plan beyond completing his university studies—not surprisingly, for his father's death in 1855 left the responsibility of supporting his brothers and sisters mainly on Jevons's shoulders. Already he had supplied the funds to allow his younger brother Tom (1841–1917) to finish his own degree at University College, London. Now in October 1859 Jevons himself re-enrolled there, and Tom and his two sisters Lucy (1830–1910) and Henrietta (1839–1909) came to live with him in lodgings in Paddington. The next three years were a time of financial anxiety for Jevons, but also a time of great academic achievement. At first he felt himself to be working 'against such great odds in mathematics, Latin and Greek' (*Papers*, 2.406) that he had no time to devote to other parts of the final year course. Nevertheless, in October 1860 he passed the BA degree examinations in the first division and decided to go on to take courses for the MA degree in mental philosophy and political economy. This involved two further years of intense study at higher levels, but in June 1862 he was awarded the degree with a gold medal in his chosen subjects. Yet he did much more in these three years than amply satisfy the requirements for a primary and a higher degree; he also began to develop significant new ideas of his own, first in political economy and later in logic. The mental discipline of college courses seemed to enable him to develop and bring to fruition the ideas that he had begun to form in Australia. In June 1860 he wrote to his brother Herbert that 'in the last few months I have fortunately struck out what I have no doubt is the *true theory of Economy*' (ibid., 2.410) but he postponed any attempt to publish this until 1862.

In 1860–61 Jevons again found time and energy to do independent research, now in applied economics, on a problem that had perennial fascination for him—the movement of time series and the causes of periodic fluctuations in them. He devoted immense labour to collecting data on movements of prices and other variables over time and presenting them in diagrams. His first plan was to publish a 'statistical atlas' of some thirty diagrams, but no publisher would undertake the risk and he had eventually to confine himself to having two diagrams published in June 1862 at his own expense—he could afford no more. To section F of the British Association, meeting at Cambridge in September 1862, he sent two papers which summarized and commented on his work of the past two years. One was a 'Notice of a general mathematical theory of political economy' in which he set out in formal terms his 'true theory of Economy' begun in 1860. In this shape, with its emphasis on 'the springs of human action—the feelings of pleasure and pain' and the fact that 'consumption of successive equal increments [of a good] does not usually produce equal increments of pleasure, but the *ratio of utility* on the last increment usually decreases as some function of the whole quantity consumed'—it owed much to what Jevons had learned about Bentham's utilitarianism in his philosophy courses and about the infinitesimal calculus in his mathematics courses. The other was 'On the study of periodic commercial fluctuations', in which he urged that 'all commercial fluctuations should be investigated according to the same scientific methods with which we are familiar in other complicated sciences' and drew attention to some of the information about such fluctuations that could be derived from his published diagrams. The papers made no stir and Jevons was particularly disappointed by the lack of interest in his new mathematical theory of economy. He put it aside for the moment and went on with his statistical research and with studies in logic. In this latter field he was now developing his own system and beginning to think 'that in the principle of *sameness* I have found that which will reduce the whole theory of reasoning to one consistent lucid process' (*Papers*, 1.186). In his statistical studies Jevons had been struck, when compiling tables of prices since 1844, by their almost universal increase since 1853. There was much debate at the time as to whether the increased gold

supplies since 1849 had or had not led to a change in its value in terms of other commodities, and Jevons now decided to tackle this problem by quantitative methods. He published the results in April 1863 in a 73-page pamphlet, *A Serious Fall in the Value of Gold Ascertained*. It was destined to become a classic, a model for future applied economic research, but it sold only seventy-four copies and its author had no regular source of income.

Jevons had now to face up to a dilemma. He could either give up time-consuming original research and devote himself to writing 'light, easy pieces' for the London literary reviews, for which he had little enthusiasm or talent, or devote himself to the research for which he had both talent and enthusiasm—if there was some way of combining it with other work that would give him a regular income. University teaching was the obvious answer, but in the England of 1863 university posts were not numerous and most of them were at Oxford or Cambridge, where assent to the doctrines of the established church was still a requirement for those appointed. Apart from University College itself, the only academic institution at which a nonconformist could be appointed was Owens College, Manchester. 'Cousin Harry' Roscoe had indeed been appointed to its chair of chemistry in 1857; at Christmas 1862 he had mentioned to Jevons that a junior tutorship was available there and suggested that he apply for it. Jevons had not done so because he thought then that he might still make a living from literary work of some sort in London, but in April 1863 he changed his mind and after a visit to Manchester to discuss the matter with the principal of Owens College, J. G. Greenwood, he decided to take the post.

In Manchester, 1863–1876 Owens College was to provide Jevons with the secure base from which he could build a national and international reputation in his chosen fields; but initially his position as tutor offered onerous duties, poor pay, and doubtful prospects. His work involved teaching day students in groups of six or eight for two or three hours each day, as well as giving 'general assistance' in all the subjects offered by the college. Although he also taught four evening classes to earn more money, his income in his first year in post was less than £100. With this hard year's work over, Jevons returned to London, to the reading-room of the British Museum, to spend the summer 'often writing for 5 or 6 hours at a stretch' (*Papers*, 1.200), compiling material on 'the question of the exhaustion of Coal, which I look upon as the coming question' (ibid., 3.58).

Before going to Manchester the previous autumn Jevons had completed his first book on formal logic—*Pure Logic, or, The Logic of Quality apart from Quantity*—which he described as 'the same as Boole's in some ways but free from all his false mathematical dress' (*Papers*, 3.13). Published in December 1863, its compilation had given Jevons great intellectual satisfaction, but by August 1864 it had sold only four copies. Still without secure or well-paid employment, he was now determined to produce a work that would establish him as a nationally recognized author. In the book which resulted, *The Coal Question*, Jevons's main argument was not that Britain's coal reserves would soon be exhausted, but that the rapid expansion of her population and industry in the nineteenth century had produced an increase of coal consumption at a rate of some 3.5 per cent per annum—a rate that, if long maintained, must compel the extension of mining to either poorer or deeper seams and hence greatly increase the cost of coal. In so far as Britain's industrial position and progress were based on cheap coal they were bound to be seriously affected within about fifty years. Even thus carefully stated the thesis was challenging enough, yet when it appeared in April 1865 *The Coal Question* was not an immediate success. Jevons continued his tutoring at Owens and in May 1865 was appointed to what he called 'a small Professorship' of political economy and logic at Queen's College, Liverpool. Despite the impressive title, this was really a part-time evening lectureship, which he held for only one year, 1865/6. In that same year Jevons was asked to act as substitute lecturer in political economy in place of R. C. Christie and took over the logic and philosophy class on the illness of A. J. Scott, having resigned his tutorship in order to do so.

Scott's death in January 1866 precipitated a reorganization of posts in Owens College, and a new chair of logic, mental and moral philosophy, and political economy was created. When it was advertised Jevons became doubtful of gaining the appointment, although he was obviously a strong candidate for it. He became increasingly fearful that all the work and sacrifice which, since 1859, he had put into equipping himself to be a social scientist might prove to have been in vain. Then in April 1866 John Stuart Mill commended *The Coal Question* to his fellow MPs in a speech in the House of Commons, and endorsed Jevons's own suggestion for 'compensating posterity for our present lavish use of cheap coal' by reduction of the national debt. W. E. Gladstone, then chancellor of the exchequer, followed up this suggestion in his budget speech in May and subsequently called Jevons to Downing Street to discuss it. Soon some of the newspapers were reporting a 'coal panic' and the last copies of the first edition of Jevons's book were selling out. By 31 May he had not only achieved his ambition to become a nationally known writer; he could also record in his journal that he had been 'finally and positively appointed' to the new chair at Owens College.

With his position thus secured Jevons, for the first time since leaving Australia, was assured of sufficient earnings to allow him to contemplate marriage. On 19 December 1867 he married Harriet Ann Taylor (1838–1910), third daughter of John Edward *Taylor, founder of the *Manchester Guardian*; they had three children, one son and two daughters. He took a house at 36 Parsonage Road, Withington, Manchester, where their family life proved happy and Jevons found relaxation in gardening in summer, skating in winter, and music at all times. As an established professor, his work at Owens College became 'more easy, familiar and congenial' but, although his students thought highly of his courses, he himself never liked lecturing.

Jevons gave both day and evening classes in logic and political economy, but as courses at Owens College were then related specifically to the examinations of the University of London, he did not have the opportunity either to enlarge the scope of teaching as he would have wished or to develop the abilities of his better pupils and introduce them to more advanced work. As regards research, the changes that the years 1866–7 brought in his professional and domestic circumstances made no difference to Jevons; he continued to work as hard as ever and in this his wife supported and helped him.

At the end of 1866 Jevons had begun 'thinking about logic again seriously' and considered grafting some developments on to the modified version of Boole's system that he had published in 1863. In the next two months the idea that 'the great and universal principle of all reasoning' was the substitution of similars became central to his thinking. With this in mind he decided to 'produce a work which will not only embody a new and luminous system but will be readable and read by many' (*Papers*, 1.209–10). In 1868 he planned out the work and chose its title, *The Principles of Science*. It proved a massive undertaking, one to which, as he had foreseen, the best years of his life were given; it was not published until 1874. Meanwhile in 1869 he published *The Substitution of Similars*, a short work presenting the essence of his system of logic as he now saw it 'to the judgement of those interested in logical science'. In *The Principles of Science* that system was set in the wider context of the philosophy of science, or, as it was then called, the philosophy of inductive investigation. Jevons argued that the processes of induction were necessarily founded in formal logic, which, unlike Boole, he saw as more fundamental than mathematics. He contended that 'there is no such thing as a distinct method of induction as contrasted with deduction … induction is simply an inverse employment of deduction' (*Principles of Science*, 1874, viii). Hence he sided with his precursor William Whewell against J. S. Mill in advocating what has come to be called the 'hypothetico-deductive' method. But he followed David Hume in holding that no inductive inference could be certain; it is only possible to use the theory of probability to assign probabilities to particular hypotheses and provisionally accept the most probable. For its time *The Principles of Science* was a remarkable achievement, anticipating the approach of more recent works on the philosophy of science and showing Jevons's ability not only to think through the principles of reasoning, but to illustrate their application in a wide range of natural sciences, with which he displayed impressive familiarity.

It is not surprising that it should have taken Jevons six years to construct and complete a work involving such depth of analysis and such breadth of subject matter. What is remarkable is that in all but one of these six years he was publishing numerous articles and books—on other aspects of logic, on economics, and on problems in other sciences as varied as chemistry and astronomy. From his thinking on the processes of logical inference he developed the idea that these might be performed mechanically. As early as 1865 he was trying to build a 'reasoning machine, or logical abacus' (*Papers*, 4.69), which evolved through several stages into a 'logical piano' or logical machine which he demonstrated before the Royal Society in January 1870. He thought it 'quite as likely to be laughed at as admired' (*Letters and Journal*, 250), but it was later to be recognized as one of the forerunners of twentieth-century computers, and is preserved in the History of Science Museum at Oxford.

In 1870 also Fleeming Jenkin, then professor of engineering at University College, London, had published an article on 'The graphic representation of the laws of supply and demand' in *Recess Studies*. It contained no reference to Jevons's 'Brief account of a general mathematical theory of political economy' of 1866, although Jevons had earlier sent Jenkin a copy. This seems to have been the deciding factor in leading Jevons to turn aside from his work on logic and philosophy of science to spend the winter of 1870–71 in writing up a full version of the theory which he had published in summary in 1862 and 1866 in a form that would compel attention. The result was *The Theory of Political Economy* (1871), the book that was to ensure for Jevons a prominent place in the history of economic thought. Comparatively short and lucidly written, it sharply attacked the classical theory of value of the 'Ricardo–Mill school', and offered in its place the challenging view that 'value depends entirely upon utility', asserting boldly that 'Economy, if it is to be a science at all must be a mathematical science' (*Theory of Political Economy*, 1871, 2–3). English economists received the book with little interest at first, but in continental Europe it attracted more attention and from it Jevons gained international recognition as an economic theorist.

The years of intense effort that Jevons put into the production of his two most original and famous works had other and more dangerous results for him personally. By Christmas 1871 he was already having symptoms of nervous exhaustion and at Easter 1872 his doctor prescribed a complete rest from work. In the academic year 1872/3 the college allowed him to employ a deputy to give his evening lectures, but he was still not sufficiently recovered to resume all his classes in 1873/4 and offered to resign his post. The council of Owens College was very reluctant to accept his resignation and agreed to give him leave of absence. From 1873 to 1876 Jevons went through a period of hesitation and doubt as to whether he should leave Manchester. He felt a strong sense of obligation to Owens College, which had made his career possible, but while he continued research and publication in both economics and logic he found teaching a growing burden. He was attracted again by the idea of living 'quietly and economically in or near London', using the resources of London libraries and attending the meetings of the Royal Society, which had elected him to its fellowship in 1872, and the Political Economy Club, of which he had become an honorary member in 1874. The balance shifted in favour of London in 1875, when the authorities of University College made it clear to Jevons that he could have first refusal of the chair of political economy there, left vacant by the death of J. E. Cairnes. Although the salary attached to the London post was considerably less than Jevons was paid at Manchester, it also involved much lighter teaching duties. So Jevons finally decided formally to apply for it, was appointed in December 1875, and began teaching there in October 1876.

A London professor and 'literary man', 1876–1882 The University College chair was not the only one that Jevons might have taken in 1875. At the time when his appointment to it had just been finalized W. B. Hodgson, professor of political economy in the University of Edinburgh, suggested privately that Jevons might become his successor there 'in a little time'. It was a tempting suggestion, for the Edinburgh chair carried twice the salary of that at Owens, and when Jevons went to Edinburgh to receive an honorary LLD in April 1876 he was impressed by the 'nice position' that Scottish professors enjoyed. Yet he did not seriously think of changing his decision, for it still seemed to him that in trying to accomplish what he had set out to do 'one labours under disadvantages in not living, like most of the political economists and literary men, in London' (*Papers*, 4.134). So in October 1876 he and his family left Parsonage Road, Withington, for Branch Hill, Hampstead. What Jevons was seeking was time and freedom to write and publish, which London and the University College post seemed to offer, but he certainly did not treat it as a sinecure. In the first year in which he held it he doubled the number of lectures from that previously offered and attracted a much increased number of students to his class. In the following year he reverted to the former practice of lecturing once a week, but even so it was not long before he felt the old tension between the demands of teaching and those of writing beginning to recur. In the spring of 1878 his health was again threatened by overwork; he did not reduce his commitments to write, but found lecturing and examining an increasing burden. In October 1880 he decided to resign his professorship, and appointed a substitute for the rest of the academic year. Explaining his decision to Robert Harley, he wrote 'you will perhaps feel it difficult to understand what a millstone upon my health and spirits the work of lecturing has been … I find that the pressure of literary work leaves me no spare energy whatever' (*Papers*, 5.116). So Jevons became what he had originally intended to be in his graduate student days—a London-based economist and logician who wrote as a freelance, a 'literary man'.

Last years, death, and reputation In fact the breakdown in his health in 1872–4, whatever its other consequences, had never stemmed the flow of Jevons's research and writing. In economics and logic he continued to develop the ideas that he had already published; a new edition of *The Principles of Science* was called for in 1877 and of *The Theory of Political Economy* in 1879. While he made no fundamental changes in either, Jevons revised each book thoroughly and discussed criticisms of them in new prefaces. New ideas were not lacking either; from 1875 onwards he was concerned with a new hypothesis to explain those 'great commercial fluctuations, completing their course in some ten years' which he had already remarked upon in *A Serious Fall in the Value of Gold* in 1863. Fascinated, as always, by periodicity, it seemed to him that the relation between these and the decennial sunspot cycle must be more than coincidental and he devoted much thought to seeking to explain the linking mechanism that he felt must exist between them. He was convinced of the validity of his hypothesis, but subsequent research has not confirmed it. This was by no means his only concern during these London years; he contributed to the debate on the then vexed question of bimetallism and also wrote on a variety of aspects of social and economic policy. His last book, *The State in Relation to Labour* (1882), displayed his continuing adherence to Benthamite utilitarianism as a touchstone in such questions.

In logic, Jevons had long planned to produce a book detailing his criticisms of J. S. Mill's approach to the subject, but in 1877 he decided instead to publish these in the form of a series of articles in the *Contemporary Review* (1877–9). Much of his time was also taken up in writing textbooks for students, mainly in logic but also in economics. His dislike of lecturing was not due to any lack of teaching ability: he had a talent for writing clear elementary outlines of his specialities, exemplified by his *Primer of Logic* (1876) and *Primer of Political Economy* (1878), which were used by many generations of students in many countries.

Even after he had divested himself of all other commitments, Jevons's constant problem was still to find time and strength for all the projects he wished to carry out. He planned a *Principles of Economics* to supplement his *Theory of Political Economy*; significantly, he gave it the subtitle 'A treatise on the industrial mechanism of society'. By 1882 he had sketched out its contents and drafted a number of chapters, but was still preoccupied with the completion of papers more urgently required—such as one for that year's social science congress, on the employment of married women in factories—and still trying to do more than his weakened health would allow. August 1882 found him taking a holiday with his wife and children at Bulverhythe, near Hastings. On 13 August he unwisely decided to go swimming, apparently suffered a heart attack brought on by the shock of the unusually cold sea, and drowned. He was buried five days later in Hampstead cemetery.

It was left to his widow and his friends to collect the published and unpublished papers Jevons had left behind and to issue them in a series of volumes: *Methods of Social Reform* (1883), *Investigations in Currency and Finance* (1884), *Pure Logic and other Minor Works* (1890), and *The Principles of Economics* (1905).

From the time of his graduation as a master of arts of London University until his death Jevons's career lasted just over twenty years. In that time he had achieved what he had planned to do before he left Australia; he had devoted his lifetime to social science and his efforts had earned him a place in its pantheon. Even in his own day Jevons was remarkable as a polymath, but with the passage of time it has become increasingly clear that the true

historical significance of his work lies not so much in its scope and depth as in his ability to generate ideas of continuing interest and to raise questions that still stimulate others to further research. As J. M. Keynes remarked, Jevons chiselled in stone where Marshall knitted in wool.

On Jevons's personal qualities, it seems appropriate that the last word should still come from someone who knew him well, Sir Adolphus William Ward, his sometime colleague at Owens College, who thus concluded his account of Jevons's life and work in the *Dictionary of National Biography*:

> Jevons was distinguished by a noble simplicity of disposition. In accordance with this, the keynote to his character, he was pious in the broadest sense of the word, tender-hearted, readily interested in whatever had a real human significance, and, notwithstanding a constitutional tendency to depression, very easily pleased and amused. Both intellectually and morally self-centred, he was entirely free from sordid ambition, and from the mere love of applause. No more honest man ever achieved fame while living laborious days, and striving from his boyhood upward to become 'a powerful good in the world'.

R. D. COLLISON BLACK

Sources *Papers and correspondence of William Stanley Jevons*, ed. R. D. Collison Black and R. Könekamp, 7 vols. (1972–81) [with biographical introduction by R. Könekamp] • H. A. Jevons, *Letters and journal of W. Stanley Jevons* (1886) • J. M. Keynes, 'William Stanley Jevons, 1835–1882: a centenary allocution', *Journal of the Royal Statistical Society*, 99 (1936); repr. in *The collected writings of John Maynard Keynes*, 10: *Essays in biography* (1972), 109–60 • L. C. Robbins, 'The place of Jevons in economic thought', *The Manchester School*, 50 (1982) • D. Laidler, 'Jevons on money', *The Manchester School*, 50 (1982) • S. M. Stigler, 'Jevons as statistician', *The Manchester School*, 50 (1982) • T. W. Hutchison, 'The politics and philosophy in Jevons's political economy', *The Manchester School*, 50 (1982) • M. Schabas, *A world ruled by number* (1990) • R. D. C. Black, 'W. S. Jevons, 1835–82', *Pioneers of modern economics*, ed. D. O'Brien and J. R. Presley (1981), 1–35 • T. Inoue and M. V. White, 'Bibliography of the published works of W. S. Jevons', *Journal of the History of Economic Thought*, 15 (1993), 122–47 • *The Times* (16 Aug 1882) • *The Times* (19 Aug 1882)

Archives JRL, corresp. and papers • Mitchell L., NSW, cash books • Royal Statistical Society, London, statistical papers • U. Glas. L., lecture notes | Bibliothèque Cantonale, Lausanne, Fonds Walras • BL, corresp. with Macmillans, Add. MS 55173 • King's AC Cam., letters to Sir Robert Palgrave • priv. coll., Foxwell MSS • RS, corresp. with Sir John Herschel • UCL, letters to C. G. Robinson

Likenesses photographs, c.1851–1858, repro. in R. Könekamp, *Papers and correspondence of William Stanley Jevons*, ed. R. D. Collinson Black, 7 vols. (1972–81), vol. 2, frontispiece • print, 1858, NPG • Maull & Co., photograph, 1870–79, NPG [*see illus.*] • photograph, c.1878–1880, Hult. Arch. • bust, University of Manchester • engraving, JRL • photograph, JRL

Wealth at death £6989 10s.: probate, 2 Oct 1882, *CGPLA Eng. & Wales*

Jewel, Jimmy [*real name* James Arthur Thomas Marsh] (1909–1995), comedian and actor, was born on 4 December 1909 at 52 Andover Street, Pittsmoor, Sheffield, the younger child of James Arthur Thomas Marsh (1881–1936), music-hall artist (under the name James A. Jewel) and designer and builder of stage scenery, and his wife, Gertrude, *née* Driver (1881–1956), also a music-hall performer.

Jimmy Jewel
(1909–1995), by
Wolfgang
Suschitzky, 1981

Jewel was involved in the theatrical world from childhood, making an albeit brief début in a Barnsley pantomime—he injured his shoulder making his first entrance—aged five. His schooling was largely peripatetic, including two unenjoyable spells at boarding-schools in Derbyshire and in south London, and ineffective. He made his début in a walk-on role in the family revue *Explosions* in 1925 and then, under the name Marsh Jewel, he developed a song-and-dance routine that involved impersonations of Maurice Chevalier and Jack Buchanan. As well as touring with the family show in the 1930s he also worked for periods with Willie Lancet's Midget Troupe and as a solo act in cinema variety spots. His career was reshaped by accident in May 1934 when he and his cousin, black-face act Ben Warriss [*see below*], were asked to form an impromptu double act to cover for the non-appearance of another duo. Their performance was successful enough for the two to link permanently from the autumn of that year and, by 1938, they were good enough to make their West End début at the Holborn Empire under Max Miller. **Ben Holden Driver Warriss** (1909–1993) had been born in the same bed as his cousin at 52 Andover Street, Sheffield, five months earlier than Jewel, on 29 May 1909, the son of Benjamin Holden Joseph Warriss, insurance company's inspector, and his wife, Mary Ann, née Driver, Jewel's mother's sister.

For much of the 1940s and 1950s, Jewel and Warriss were Britain's leading comedy double act. They appeared at the highly prestigious Palladium for the first time in 1942 in *Gangway* and they returned with *High Time* in 1946, a year that also saw them top the bill in the royal variety performance. Although they were arguably always most effective as stage performers, their BBC radio series *Up the Pole*—which ran from 1947 to 1952—was extremely successful and it brought them to an even wider audience: they were even the lead strip in the comic *Radio Fun* for a period. They did only a limited amount of film work, beginning with *Rhythm Serenade* (1943), starring Vera Lynn, but were more successful in television, becoming the stars

of *Turn it up*, the first regular television comedy series, in 1951. They were a major pantomime attraction and they regularly toured the leading provincial variety theatres. Their stage act was essentially a mixture of the fast-paced, increasingly American-influenced, cross-talk acts popular from the 1930s, and a repertory of visual gags that often made use of sophisticated props and scenery: the influence of Jewel's father was clear here. Jewel, with a slightly unconvincing toupee, a remarkably mobile and expressive face, and a broad Sheffield accent, was invariably the gullible victim of the suave Warriss's somewhat malicious humour. When, for example, a character in *Up the Pole* asked Jimmy, 'Where did you learn to kiss like that?', Warriss replied for him, 'Syphoning petrol!' (Foster and Furst, 100). Warriss regularly received letters asking him to stop bullying his partner. Their comic legacy was fairly limited, as they embodied a skilfully honed version of an old tradition, and by the 1960s their style seemed dated and less appealing to audiences who were increasingly attuned to more subtle and more intimate forms of humour. In 1966, with the variety circuit dead and the disillusioned pair reduced to working the pub and club circuit, Warriss ended the partnership.

Warriss ran a restaurant near Bath before returning to the stage to chair music-hall revivals at Blackpool, to perform in pantomime, and even to take straight acting roles in productions of Jean-Claude Grumberg's *Dreyfus* and John Osborne's *The Entertainer*. He finally retired only when his health broke down a year before his death. He was married three times. His first wife, whom he married on 22 September 1934, was Grace Mary Skinner (b. 1910/11), a dancer and teacher of dancing and daughter of Henry Arthur James Skinner, master mariner. This marriage had ended by about 1940 and two years later Warriss married the entertainer Meggie Easton. Little is known of his third marriage, which took place about 1960, other than that his third wife was named Virginia. Warriss was a prominent member of the show-business charity the Grand Order of Water Rats, and he was King Rat for the years 1953, 1961, and 1962. He died at a home run by the Entertainment Artists' Benevolent Fund, Brinsworth House, Staines Road, Twickenham, of lung cancer, on 14 January 1993.

Jewel was initially deeply upset by the break with Warriss—Warriss informed him by letter rather than in person—but he gradually forged a new career as a television and stage character actor that won him greater critical acclaim than his earlier work had ever done. In 1968 the BBC head of comedy, Frank Muir, persuaded him to play the part of a militant shop steward in the television play *A Spanner in the Works*, and this relaunched his career. From 1968 to 1972 he played opposite Hylda Baker in the successful television series, *Nearest and Dearest*, and much more television work appeared, culminating in his final series, *Funny Man* (1981), which he wrote himself and which was based on his experiences in the family troupe in the 1920s and 1930s. In 1975, aged sixty-one, his serious theatrical career commenced when he starred as the comic Eddie Walters in Trevor Griffiths's *The Comedians* at the Nottingham Playhouse, and later at the National Theatre, and as Willie Clark in Neil Simon's *Sunshine Boys* in the West End. He continued to work in television and theatre into the 1980s and he made a film appearance in *American Friends* as late as 1991. His varied and lengthy career marked him out as one of the most flexible and professional of twentieth-century comic talents. He married the Australian entertainer Isabel (Belle) Bluett (1911/12–1985) on 31 August 1939. She was the daughter of Frederick George Bluett, theatrical artist, and the sister of Kitty Bluett, the comedian. They had a son, Kerry, in 1946 and adopted a daughter, Piper, in 1955. Jewel's autobiography, *Three Times Lucky* (1982), gave evidence of few hobbies beyond golf and his family. He died at his home, 96 Troy Court, Kensington High Street, London, of respiratory failure, on 3 December 1995. He was survived by his son and adopted daughter.

DAVE RUSSELL

Sources J. Jewel, *Three times lucky: an autobiography* (1982) · *The Guardian* (4 Dec 1995) · *The Guardian* (6 Dec 1995) · *The Times* (5 Dec 1995) · *The Independent* (5 Dec 1995) · *The Times* (18 Jan 1993) [Ben Holden Driver Warriss] · *The Independent* (18 Jan 1993) [Ben Holden Driver Warriss] · *The Guardian* (19 Jan 1993) [Ben Holden Driver Warriss] · A. Foster and S. Furst, *Radio comedy, 1938–1968* (1996) · b. cert. [Ben Holden Driver Warriss] · m. cert. · d. cert. · *CGPLA Eng. & Wales* (1996)
Likenesses group portrait, photograph, 1953, Hult. Arch. · group portrait, photograph, 1976, Hult. Arch. · W. Suschitzky, bromide print, 1981, NPG [*see illus.*] · photograph, repro. in *The Guardian* (4 Dec 1995) · photograph (with B. Warriss), repro. in *The Times* (5 Dec 1995) · photograph (with B. Warriss), repro. in *The Independent* (5 Dec 1995) · photograph (with B. Warriss), repro. in *The Times* (18 Jan 1993) · photographs, repro. in Jewel, *Three times lucky*
Wealth at death £671,838: probate, 1996, *CGPLA Eng. & Wales*

Jewel, John (1522–1571), bishop of Salisbury, was born on 24 May 1522, one of ten children of John Jewel of Bowden in the parish of Berrynarbor on the north Devon coast, and grew up in a substantial farmhouse. At the age of seven he moved to Hampton, where he was taught by his mother's brother, John Bellamy, rector of the parish. Whether from his mother or uncle, the Bellamy influence was important and remembered by Jewel when he incorporated the name into a personal stamp that he placed in a number of books in his substantial library, the so-called 'Bel-Ami' volumes. He was later taught by different teachers at schools in Bampton, South Molton, and perhaps most notably by Walter Bowen at Barnstaple.

Oxford, 1535–1553 In July 1535, at thirteen, he matriculated from Merton College, Oxford, where he was first placed briefly with Peter Burry, who assigned him in turn to a younger fellow, John Parkhurst. Oxford gave Jewel two crucial friendships. The first of these was with Parkhurst who, some time prior to moving to Merton, had embraced humanism and whose influence on Jewel proved fundamental. Whether in the close comparison of the new and competing English translations of the New Testament by Tyndale and Coverdale, or in his examination of the writings of the church fathers in the newly published editions by Erasmus, Parkhurst took Jewel to the well of humanism where he drank deep. It was not long before the student surpassed his mentor. With Parkhurst's help Jewel

John Jewel (1522–1571), by unknown artist

left Merton for Corpus Christi College, where he was elected scholar on 19 August 1539. He graduated BA on 20 August 1540, was elected fellow of Corpus Christi on 18 March 1542, and proceeded MA on 28 January 1545, with Parkhurst, who was now a chaplain to Queen Katherine Parr, defraying part of the expense.

Throughout Jewel's time at Oxford he applied himself to his studies with a single-minded zeal that gained him his reputation and a number of enemies. It is not surprising that there were those who felt threatened by this self-disciplined, serious minded young humanist who reputedly rose at four and was occupied with his books until ten at night. Possessed of a remarkably acute memory he was known to practise his rhetorical skills declaiming aloud in the nearby woods of Shotover. The onset of what appears to have been rheumatoid arthritis at this time left him lame in one leg.

Following his election in 1548 to the post of reader in humanity and rhetoric, Jewel's lectures were popular occasions to which, as his biographer and friend, Laurence Humphrey, remarked, 'many came from divers colledges to behold Rhetorik so richly set forth, with her owne costlie apparel, and furniture, by the dexteritie of his wit and learning' (Southgate, 7). Yet these occasions were not simply studies in eloquence. A profound moral purpose lay at the heart of Jewel's learning. Little survives from Jewel's activities at Oxford in the late 1540s, yet the two extant addresses, one a commemorative address on Richard Fox, late bishop of Winchester and founder of Corpus Christi College, Oxford, and the other his *Oratio contra rhetoricam*, were Erasmian exhortations to take up the study of letters and live virtuous lives.

At the same time that Jewel's academic star was in the ascendant he forged a second and more crucial friendship with the Italian theologian turned reformer, Pietro Martire Vermigli, known in England as Peter Martyr, that shaped his thought and career. Having accepted Archbishop Thomas Cranmer's invitation in 1547 to become regius professor of divinity at Oxford, Vermigli gathered a small circle of devotees around himself in this largely unreformed university. Jewel, in particular, proved an assiduous attender of Vermigli's lectures and served as his notary at the famous disputation on the eucharist held in 1549. The surviving correspondence between the two men attests to the strength and closeness of the relationship established in the years that Vermigli spent in Oxford. Vermigli was Jewel's 'father and most esteemed master in Christ', his 'pride and the better half of my own soul' (*Works*, ed. Ayre, 4.1232, 1213). Long after the two men were separated, with Vermigli in Zürich and Jewel in England, a constant theme of Jewel's letters was the longing he had to engage once again in their conversations. It is not known when Jewel was ordained but he was granted a preaching licence in December 1551. It was perhaps about this time that he became vicar of Sunningwell, near Abingdon. He reportedly regularly walked from Oxford to Sunningwell in order to preach. In 1552 he proceeded BD. Although Humphrey relates that Jewel was identified as a 'Zuinglian' and 'Lutheran' well before Vermigli arrived at Oxford, it seems hard to deny the importance of the Edwardian reformation and the personal relationship with Vermigli in the formation of Jewel the reformer.

Expulsion and exile The chronology of Jewel's changed fortunes after the confused period that followed the death of Edward VI, the unsuccessful attempt to divert the succession to Lady Jane Grey, and Queen Mary's accession to the throne in July 1553 is far from clear. He was probably appointed public orator of the university prior to Mary's accession and in this capacity penned a letter of congratulation to the new queen in which he hoped that as her reign had begun without the effusion of blood it might continue in like manner. Congratulatory sentiments could not secure Jewel's place in Oxford, however. Charged with having been a diligent hearer of Vermigli, of having preached heretical doctrine, of not having been ordained according to the traditional rites, and of having refused to attend mass, Jewel was expelled from Corpus; he marked his departure with an emotional and public farewell. Although other Oxford protestants had fled and Vermigli had returned to Strasbourg, Jewel remained at the university, taking up a place at Broadgates Hall (later Pembroke College), presided over by his friend Thomas Randolph. In Vermigli's absence Jewel unsuccessfully sought advice from his old friend Parkhurst by letter and afterwards trudged in wintry weather to his living at Cleeve, only to discover that Parkhurst too had fled to the continent. Jewel returned to Oxford and served as notary to Cranmer and Bishop Nicholas Ridley in their public disputation held in April 1554. Perhaps shortly after this disputation or possibly at the time of the general visitation of Oxford in October 1554, Jewel, to his shame, subscribed to Catholic articles of faith. This proved too little too late and perhaps within weeks of his recantation, realizing that his attempt to remain a quiet scholar at Oxford had failed and that his only hope of escaping arrest and martyrdom lay in flight, he left Oxford on foot and managed through the aid of Hugh Latimer's faithful servant, Augustine Bernher, to find refuge in the house of one Mistress Warcup, who then conveyed him into various lodgings in London. Sir Nicholas Throckmorton and other London protestants enabled Jewel to flee to the continent and, probably bearing Cranmer's last letter to Vermigli, he appears to have made his way first to him in Strasbourg.

Jewel played an important if minor role in the troubles in the English church at Frankfurt. It is known that he appeared in the city on 13 March 1555 together with Richard Cox, the exiled dean of Christ Church. The latter appears to have been sent by the English exiles in Strasbourg to confront the dominant party in the church in Frankfurt led by John Knox and William Whittingham, who advocated use of the Genevan service. Matters came to a head in the Frankfurt church over the next two weeks as the advocates of the prayer book succeeded in having the English rite reinstated and Knox removed, events in which Jewel appears to have been an active participant, exchanging sharp words with William Whittingham and Christopher Goodman. Perhaps two years later Jewel wrote to both men from Zürich, anxious that the 'unhappy circumstance of the Frankfort contention' should not diminish their 'mutual friendship and union'; if he had injured either man with his words, 'carried away with zeal and the heat of contention', he asked their forgiveness (*Works*, ed. Ayre, 4.1193). It was in the midst of the Frankfurt troubles, no doubt as a way of disarming any opposition, that Jewel made an open confession of his Oxford recantation. He later wrote of it as 'openly and unrequired in the midst of the congregation' (*Works*, ed. Ayre, 1.61), and it seems to have affected the audience deeply.

Jewel did not remain long in Frankfurt, accepting an invitation from Vermigli to join him in Strasbourg. Returning to his scholarly pursuits Jewel acted as Vermigli's notary and aided the classical and biblical endeavours of the Italian reformer as he lectured on Aristotle's *Ethics* and carefully exegeted the book of Judges. Strasbourg gave Jewel contact with a wide and influential body of exiles, both clerical and lay, which included Edwin Sandys, Edmund Grindal, John Cheke, Anthony Cooke, and others who were destined to play an important role in the establishment of the Elizabethan church and who came to know and respect the Oxford scholar. In July 1556, when Vermigli accepted Heinrich Bullinger's invitation to Zürich to become professor in Hebrew, Jewel accompanied his mentor. Here Jewel flourished, reunited with his old friend and tutor Parkhurst and making important new friendships with the men of Zürich: Bullinger, Josiah Simler, the printer Froschover and others. Although it is possible that he paid a visit to Padua during this period, there is no evidence that he ever studied at the university.

Reformer and bishop of Salisbury, 1560–1571 The news of Queen Mary's death reached Zürich on 1 December 1558 and some six weeks later Jewel set out for England, arriving in London on 18 March 1559 after a journey of fifty-seven days. He spent his first six months back in England lodged in the home of the godly London merchant Nicholas Culverwell. Although Jewel complained bitterly in private to Vermigli of the slowness of the pace of reform, he publicly proved a ready supporter of the reformed church that was coming into being. During this time the new regime moved quickly to harness his abilities. Within days of his return he was appointed a disputant at the Westminster conference with the Marian bishops which began on 31 March and ended farcically a few days later (a 'useless conference', reported Jewel (*Works*, ed. Ayre, 4.1204). On 15 June he was chosen to preach at Paul's Cross and on 19 July was appointed a commissioner for the western counties in the royal visitation that took place in late summer 1559. Before he set out he was nominated bishop of Salisbury and probably took with him the letters of *congé d'élire*, dated 27 July, which were delivered to the chancellor of the diocese in Salisbury on 10 August. Returning from the visitation on 1 November, Jewel was consecrated bishop at Lambeth on 21 January 1560.

Jewel proved an exemplary bishop. As bishop-elect, on 2 November 1559 he wrote to his Zürich friend Simler mocking pre-Reformation bishops as so many 'oily, shaven, portly hypocrites' and stating that 'we require our bishops to be pastors, labourers and watchmen' (*Works*, ed. Ayre, 4.1221). This was an apt description of Jewel's eleven years in the diocese of Salisbury. Central to this work was preaching, or what he called the 'gathering of the nations' (ibid., 4.1242). One of the two portraits of Jewel in the bishop's palace at Salisbury was inscribed with the biblical phrase, 'Ve mihi si non evangelizavero' ('woe to me if I do not evangelize'; Holgate, 190–91), and there are numerous references to his sermons throughout his diocese, at Paul's Cross, and at court. Jewel was in the pulpit in Salisbury Cathedral on 11 June 1570 discussing the papal bull excommunicating Elizabeth and promised to 'read yt and expounde the same' on the following Sunday (Jackson, 21). Preaching in the early 1560s before Queen Elizabeth he was blunt in his call for a learned ministry:

> Your grace hath alreadie redressed the doctrine: now cast your eyes towardes the Ministrie, give courage and countenance unto learning, that God's house may be served: so shall you leave a Church of God, and a testimonie that the zeale of the Lords house hath eaten you up. (Booty, 'The bishop', 221)

It was during an episcopal visitation of his diocese while Jewel was riding to Lacock to preach that he was laid low with his final illness. When challenged that it was better the people should lack one sermon than lose their preacher Jewel reportedly replied: 'it becometh best a bishop to die preaching in the pulpit' (*Works*, ed. Ayre, 4.xxi). This devotion, not simply to preaching but to the spiritual cure of souls in his diocese, appears to have been profoundly earnest. It was not beneath him to perform the office of parish priest. On 29 October 1570 he baptized John Goddard, infant son of Anthony Goddard, and recorded the event in his own hand in the parish register. Jewel's determination that the work of a bishop was the work of a pastor was reflected even in the design of his episcopal seal, which depicted Christ as the Good Shepherd.

Jewel proved a careful and conscientious administrator who led by example and insisted on strict conformity to the discipline of the church (a fact concealed in Humphrey's *Vita*). He conducted visitations of his diocese in 1560, 1565, and 1571 which disclosed the usual crop of offences among both parishioners and clergy, yet, strikingly, by 1565 there is surviving evidence of only one parish that still had an altar standing. Although his most notable opponent, Thomas Harding, accused Jewel of making ministers of 'tag and rag' (Whiteman, 33), Jewel in fact took great care to ordain only worthy men and in spite of his personal views about vestments—he once called them 'the relics of the Amorites' (*Works*, ed. Ayre, 4.1223)—refused to admit his friend Humphrey to a living in the diocese unless he would fully conform. A similar policy of conscientious reform was applied to the cathedral chapter, for whom Jewel drew up new statutes. These sought to enforce standards of residency and hospitality among canons as well as their individual responsibility for the repair of their houses in the close. Jewel introduced a preaching rota for the cathedral clergy and made a serious effort to repair the fabric. During his rule windows were reglazed, the marble pillars in the cloisters renewed, and the pavement in the cathedral repaired. The bishop's relationship with the townspeople of Salisbury, potentially a prickly issue, proved harmonious in the main, although Jewel was not prepared to concede any of his authority and irritated some townsmen who 'herd the Bishop of Sarum say that the Mayor of Sarum was his Mayor and the people of Sarum his subjectes'. The resultant squabble required the judicious arbitration of the lord keeper, Sir Nicholas Bacon, who told Jewel to 'contente himselfe with the profits and lett the Mayor alone with the government' (Street, 324).

There was more than a touch of the ascetic about Jewel. Unmarried, lean in body and face with a thin beard, probably arthritic, prone to sickness, and personally abstemious, in a previous age he might have made a superb monk. His devotion to the church, his studies, and his willingness to be spent in the cause of reform often left him exhausted and no doubt contributed to his early demise. And yet he was no misanthrope. He cultivated and maintained a variety of contacts and friendships in Salisbury and London, within his diocese and beyond. On 19 March 1563 he wrote from London to his friend Edward Nicholas of Salisbury, 'I thanke yow for your fyshe, I made mery wythe it and wel refreasshed mi selfe after my sicknes, god stoare yowr pondes that sutche fyshe maye never faile yow' (BL, Egerton MS 2533, fol. 6r). His letters to his friends in Zürich and elsewhere are marked by an engaging style and lively cheer and his patronage of promising students, most notably the young Richard Hooker, is well known. Amid all his administrative and literary activities he was attentive to the running of his household and proved a careful steward who amassed a tidy fortune of £600 that he bequeathed to his brothers, sisters, friends, servants, and others. When the Swiss protestant Herman Folkerzheimer visited Jewel at Salisbury in summer 1562 he was delighted with the bishop's palace and gardens. Jewel arranged that his guest be taken hunting and later 'rode into the country with a large retinue' in order to view Stonehenge, which Jewel believed to be of Roman origin, 'the very disposition of the stones bears some resemblance to a yoke' (Robinson, 2.86–9). This too was the life of a Tudor bishop.

Challenge controversy, *Apologie*, and debate with Harding When he came to draw up his will on 22 September 1571, among various bequests and recollections of debts owing, Jewel made reference to certain sums of money in 'the first tyll of the great boxe wherupon I was wont to wryte' (PRO, PROB 11/53, 309v). By 1571 much ink had flowed from Jewel's pen, a remarkable achievement when one considers that before 1560 he was able to say that 'I never set abroad in print twenty lines'. Coinciding with the onset of his episcopal duties came the fruition of the years of study at Oxford and of his association with Vermigli. The production of an immense body of apologetic and controversial writing that this entailed absorbed much of his energies. Although he later complained of the burden of engaging with his opponents, Jewel was the first to throw down the gauntlet in public debate. As bishop-elect of Salisbury, Jewel preached his famous 'Challenge sermon' on three separate occasions. Not unlike a seminar paper doing the rounds it was preached at Paul's Cross on 26 November 1559, at court on 17 March 1560, and again at Paul's Cross on 31 March. The challenge he put forward was: 'if any learned man of our adversaries be able to bring any one sufficient sentence out of any old doctor or father, or out of any general council, or out of the holy Scripture, or any one example out of the primitive church for the space of six hundred years after Christ' (*DNB*) in support of what grew to be twenty-seven points detailing current practices and teachings of the Roman church (primarily concerned with the mass), then 'I would give over and subscribe to him' (Southgate, 50). This was a clever reversal of the traditional roles played by Rome and her critics; the burden of proof was now made to rest on Rome's shoulders. The challenge proved a sensation and was first taken up by the Marian dean of St Paul's, Henry Cole, who sought unsuccessfully to shift Jewel from his chosen ground. Both Jewel's sermon and the correspondence that passed between Jewel and Cole were printed as *The true copies of the letters betwene the reverend father in God, John bisshop of Sarum and D. Cole* (1560).

The next twelve months saw Jewel preoccupied with a more substantial publication. This was an official defence of the newly established church, co-ordinated by secretary of state William Cecil and both aided and approved by Archbishop Matthew Parker in the face of the rumours circulating on the continent about the new church and its clergy. Largely completed by mid-April 1561 the *Apologia pro Ecclesia Anglicana* appeared early in 1562. On 7 February Jewel wrote modestly to Vermigli that he was dispatching 'an Apology for the change of religion among us, and our departure from the church of Rome' although 'it is hardly worth sending to such a distance' and he complained of the inaccuracies wrought by the printers (*Works*, ed. Ayre, 4.1247). By early August a copy had reached Zürich, and Vermigli wrote back enthusiastically to Jewel in praise of the work. Intended for circulation on the continent, the *Apologia* was a brief Latin treatise in which Jewel defended the Church of England against the charge of heresy and systematically set forth the grounds of its doctrine and practice against the church of Rome. An English translation of the work which first appeared in 1562 was superseded by the more famous translation made by Ann, Lady Bacon, published in 1564 as an *Apologie or Answere in Defence of the Churche of Englande*, with a preface by Parker.

The backdrop to the *Apologie* was the bull issued by Pope Pius IV in November 1560 which summoned a third session of the Council of Trent beginning on 5 April 1561 (although it did not actually meet until January 1562). As any active participation in the council's meetings was limited to those who accepted papal authority and in light of the variety of charges and claims made about the English church, the *Apologie* explained that 'we thought good to yield up an account of our faith in writing and truly and openly to make answer to those things wherewith we have been charged' (*Apology*, 16). Claiming to deal 'herein neither bitterly nor brabbingly' (clamorously), the larger part of the work consists of a stout refutation of the charges laid against the English church and a sharp attack on papal practice. Divided into six parts, following an initial discussion of the reasons for composing the work the second part very briefly summarizes the reformed doctrine of the English church: Christ as the sole mediator, the two sacraments of baptism and eucharist, a married clergy, and the rejection of the Bishop of Rome as 'Lucifer' and a man who 'has forsaken the faith and is the forerunner of Antichrist' (ibid., 26). The following three parts of the text seek to refute systematically the various charges that had been made against the English church: that she had disintegrated into 'sundry sects', a clear sign of heresy; that the Reformation encouraged immorality; that the protestants would destroy all civil authority and obedience to the magistrate, and that the English had departed from the true church, breaking its unity. Jewel ridiculed the divisions both present and past among his Catholic opponents, depicted Rome as a city swarming with harlots and full of 'beastly sensuality', skewered the popes for their political machinations, and argued that far from leaving the true church, the English had left a corrupt church 'wherein we could neither have the word of God sincerely taught, nor the sacraments rightly administered' and had come instead 'to that church wherein … all things be governed purely and reverently, and, as much as we possibly could, very near to the order used in the old time' (ibid., 100–01). The final part of the work defended the way in which the Reformation had proceeded in England. The matter could not be decided by a general council for 'the truth of the Gospel of Jesus Christ dependeth not upon councils' (ibid., 125) nor was the 'Trent council' (ibid., 135) to be trusted. Having thrown off 'the yoke and tyranny of the Bishop of Rome' with his 'barbarous Persian-like pride' (ibid., 74), the English church had 'returned again unto the primitive church of the ancient fathers and apostles' having 'searched out of the Holy Bible, which we are sure cannot deceive, one sure form of religion' (ibid., 135). The English edition of 1564 included a brief account of the administration of the Church of England and the universities of Oxford and Cambridge. As Mandell Creighton noted a century ago, here was 'the first methodical statement of the position of the Church of England against the Church of Rome, and the groundwork of all subsequent controversy' (DNB).

The work was widely distributed. By 24 January 1562, a copy of the Apologia was in the hands of Nicholas Throckmorton, the English ambassador in Paris, who expressed pleasure that the 'papists were very well answeryd' but regretted that the Calvinists were not addressed and wished the language were toned down (Booty, John Jewel, 50). Richard Cox, bishop of Ely, had perused a copy a week earlier and 'gave god harty thankes for it', convinced that 'it will do muche good, not only in confirming and comfourting the trew Christians in all places of Europe, but also in stoppyng of the mowthes of the adversaryes' (ibid., 52). By August 1562 John Parkhurst, now bishop of Norwich, somewhat belatedly wrote to Bullinger in Zürich informing him of the publication of the Apologia 'in which it is shewn, why we have gone over from the pope to Christ, and why we refuse to acknowledge the council of Trent' (ibid.). Five years later Jewel claimed that the Apologia had been 'imprinted in Latine at Parise' and had been translated into:

[the] Frenche, the Italian, the Duche, and the Spanishe tongues and hathe beene sente, and borne abroade in France, Flaunders, Germanie, Spaine, Poole, Hungarie, Denmarke, Sveveland, Scotland, Italie, Naples and Rome it selfe to the judgments and trial of the whole Churche of God. (ibid., 56)

Jewel's efforts stung his opponents into action. The English recusant community living in exile in Louvain picked up the gauntlet and between 1564 and 1568 produced no fewer than forty-one works seeking to refute the arguments of Jewel and his colleagues. In 1564 Thomas Harding entered the lists with An Answere to Maister Juelles Chalenge, a refutation of Jewel's challenge sermon. A few years older than Jewel, Harding had followed a remarkably similar path from grammar school in Devon to Oxford, where he became a fellow of New College and was for a time regius professor of Hebrew in the university and stood with the reformers during the reign of Edward VI. Retracting his protestantism under Mary, Harding was

made a prebendary of Salisbury but lost this office when he refused to take the oath of supremacy on Elizabeth's accession. He fled to Louvain and until his death in 1572 engaged in a literary and theological battle with Jewel, motivated partly by zeal and partly by pique. Jewel responded to Harding's Answere with A replie (1565), to which Harding penned two rejoinders in 1566 and 1567. In the meantime Harding set his sights on the Apologie. His massive Confutation of a booke intituled 'An apologie of the Church of England' (1565) caused Jewel to exclaim that he knew not 'by what fatality to be always battling with these monsters' (Works, ed. Ayre, 4.1268) and to answer with an equally massive work, A defence of the 'Apologie of the Churche of England' (1567). This was only part of a lengthy debate often referred to as 'the Great Controversy' that occupied reformers like Edward Dering, Alexander Nowell, Thomas Dorman, and John Rastell and conservatives like Nicholas Sander, Thomas Stapleton, John Martiall, and Richard Shacklock. The most notable titles were those produced by Jewel and Harding in which they sought to overwhelm paragraph by paragraph and line by line each other's arguments, patristic citations, and scriptural references, with charges and counter-charges of lying, distortion, and misconstruction. Although it has often been claimed that Jewel had an advantage over Harding in maintaining a degree of civility in the debate, the civility was but paper thin and while Jewel avoided crudities he proved ever ready to employ wounding sarcasm. Where Harding concluded one section with 'As I cannot well take a hair from your lying beard, so wish I that I could pluck malice from your blasphemous heart', Jewel retorted in the margin, 'O profound divinity' (Works, ed. Ayre, 4.947) and in his preface to Harding of the Defence of the 'Apologie' wrote, 'where you say you and your fellows have espied a thousand foul great lies in my writings; had not one of you been a great father of lies, ye could never have hit so readily upon the number' (ibid., 4.1087).

The controversy with Harding made Jewel the champion of, and for a time the most famous bishop in, the English reformed church. In May 1565 he was awarded the degree of DD by special decree of the University of Oxford and in August he accompanied Queen Elizabeth on her visit to the university. As his reputation grew, so did the authoritative status of the Apologie and the Defence of the 'Apologie'. As early as 1563 Archbishop Parker had hoped to have convocation assembled to join articles of religion to a revised edition of the Apologie with the hope that this work would become a set text for the 'youth in the universities and grammar schools throughout the realm' (Booty, introduction to An Apology, xlii). Although the crown refrained from insisting that ministers and parish churches purchase copies of the Apologie or the Defence of the 'Apologie', strong lay interest as well as episcopal initiatives resulted in the widespread dissemination and ownership of these texts. In 1577 Bishop Richard Barnes required all parish churches in the diocese of Durham to purchase a copy of the Apologie and five years earlier Archbishop Parker was urging Bishop Parkhurst of Norwich to require all parishes in his diocese to purchase copies of the *Defence of the 'Apologie'*.

Last weeks and legacy In spite of his privately voiced personal dislike for conservative clerical garb Jewel had no sympathy for the rising tide of nonconformity within the church and in 1571, while parliament was still in session, together with bishops Richard Cox and Robert Horne, preached against the puritans, arguing that those who enjoyed the grain of the wheat should not contend about the chaff. His part in this controversy was curtailed. Following his sermon at Lacock, Jewel succumbed to an illness and rode with difficulty to the episcopal manor house of Monkton Fairleigh, where, having lingered for a week, and some months short of his fiftieth year, he died on 23 September 1571. On the previous day he had drawn up a will with a warmly evangelical preamble, which made reference to 'my werye bodie broken and consumed in his werye laboures'. Bequests to his brothers and sisters, friends, servants in his household, scholars at Christ Church, Oxford, 100 marks to the poor of Salisbury, his 'walkinge staffe trymed with silver' to Bishop Berkeley of Bath and Wells, 'all my notes and papers of sermondes' to Mr Richard Garbrond, and many others itemized attested both to his excellent memory and the range of his contacts. Jewel was buried in Salisbury Cathedral in the middle of the choir opposite the bishop's throne. In 1684, when the choir was paved with marble, his simple stone with its epitaph composed by Laurence Humphrey was removed to the north-east transept.

Part of Jewel's library was purchased by Magdalen College, Oxford. Humphrey's life, *Joannis Juelli Angli, episcopi Sarisburiensis, vita et mors*, was published in 1573. A condensed version by Daniel Featley appeared in the memoir that accompanied the publication of Jewel's works in 1609 under the direction of Richard Bancroft; the archbishop sought to ensure that every parish church purchased a copy. By this time Jewel was regarded as the model for the evangelical episcopate of the Jacobean church and his writings as laying essential foundations both for the English church in the generations immediately after his own, and for the theological position that was later called Anglicanism.　　　　　JOHN CRAIG

Sources *The works of John Jewel, bishop of Salisbury*, ed. J. Ayre, 4 vols. (1845–50) · J. Jewel, *An apology of the Church of England*, ed. J. E. Booty (Ithaca, 1963) · J. E. Booty, introduction, *An apology of the Church of England*, ed. J. E. Booty (Ithaca, 1963) · J. E. Booty, 'The bishop confronts the queen: John Jewel and the failure of the English Reformation', *Continuity and discontinuity in church history*, ed. F. F. Church and T. George (Leiden, 1979), 215–31 · J. E. Booty, *John Jewel as apologist of the Church of England* (1963) · G. W. Bromiley, *John Jewel, 1522–1571, the apologist of the Church of England* · S. Brown, *Sumptuous and richly adorn'd: the decorations of Salisbury Cathedral* (1999) · P. Collinson, *The Elizabethan puritan movement* (1967) · P. Collinson, 'If Constantine, then also Theodosius: St Ambrose and the integrity of the Elizabethan Ecclesia Anglicana', *Godly people: essays on English protestantism and puritanism* (1983) · C. M. Dent, *Protestant reformers in Elizabethan Oxford* (1983) · C. B. Dobson, 'The "Bel-ami" volumes in John Jewel's library in Magdalen College, Oxford', *Bodleian Library Record*, 16 (1998), 225–32 · R. H. Fritze, 'Root or link? Luther's position in the historical debate over the legitimacy of the Church of England, 1558–1625', *Journal of Ecclesiastical History*, 37 (1986), 288–302 · C. H. Garrett, *The Marian exiles: a study in the origins of Elizabethan puritanism* (1938) · C. W. Holgate, 'List of portraits in the palace', *Wiltshire Magazine*, 25 (1890), 190–91 · *The letter book of John Parkhurst, bishop of Norwich*, ed. R. A. Houlbrooke, Norfolk RS, 43 (1974–5) · L. Humphrey, *Joannis Juelli Angli, episcopi Sarisburiensis, vita et mors* (1573) · J. E. Jackson, 'Longleat papers no. 3', *Wiltshire Magazine*, 18 (1879), 9–48 · *The workes of the very learned and reverend father in God John Jewell, not long since bishop of Sarisburie. Newly set forth with some amendment of divers quotations: and a briefe discourse of his life* (1609) · will, PRO, PROB 11/53, fols. 309v–310r · N. Ker, 'The library of John Jewel', *Bodleian Library Record*, 9 (1977), 256–65 · C. W. Le Bas, *The life of Bishop Jewel* (1835) · J. K. Luoma, 'Who owns the fathers? Hooker and Cartwright on the authority of the primitive church', *Sixteenth Century Journal*, 8 (1997), 45–59 · A. R. Malden, 'The burial places of the bishops of Salisbury', *Wiltshire Magazine*, 37 (1911–12), 339–52 · P. Milward, *Religious controversies of the Elizabethan age* (1977) · H. Robinson, ed. and trans., *The Zurich letters, comprising the correspondence of several English bishops and others with some of the Helvetian reformers, during the early part of the reign of Queen Elizabeth*, 2 vols., Parker Society, 7–8 (1842–5) · W. M. Southgate, *John Jewel and the problem of doctrinal authority* (Cambridge, Mass., 1962) · F. Street, 'The relations of the bishops and citizens of Salisbury (New Sarum) between 1225 and 1612', *Wiltshire Magazine*, 39 (1915–17), 185–257, 319–67 · J. A. Vage, 'Two lists of prospective bishops, 1559', *Journal of the Society of Archivists*, 8 (1987), 192–8 · C. Van der Woude, 'John Jewel, apologeet van het Anglicanisme', *Nederlands Archief voor Kerkgeschiedenis* [Leiden], 48 (1968), 213–31 · H. Vanhulst, 'Thomas Harding, Joannes Bogardus et "An answere to maister Juelles chalenge": le contrat de 1563', *Quaerendo*, 22 (1991), 20–27 · D. K. Weiser, *The prose style of John Jewel* (Salzburg, 1973) · A. Whiteman, 'The Church of England, 1542–1837', *VCH Wiltshire*, vol. 2

Archives BL, cache of letters to steward in Salisbury diocese, Egerton MS 2533

Likenesses Passe, line engraving (after oil painting), BM, NPG; repro. in H. Holland, *Herōologia* (1620) · oil on wood panel, Bishop's palace, Salisbury · oils, Bishop's palace, Salisbury · oils (after type of, *c.*1560–1570), NPG · portrait, Merton Oxf. · portrait, CCC. Oxf. [see illus.]

Wealth at death reasonable; bequeathed over £690 plus rings; no land: will, PRO, PROB 11/53, fols. 309v–310r

Jewett, Randolph (1602/3–1675), organist and composer, was born in Chester, the son of Randle Jewett, merchant, of Chester, who died on 22 May 1619 (and was buried the following day in the cathedral there), and a grandson of William Jewett, mayor of Chester in 1578 and 'one of the Queenes Ma[jes]tes Chappell; reputed for an excellent synging man in his youthe, a martchant of great adventures, and a lover of gentlemanlye disportes and exercises'. Presumably William was the 'clerke conducte' of that name who appears in the cathedral records between 1541 and 1547. Which of his two sons, Randle and William, was the 'Mr Juett of West Chester' who was a gentleman of the Chapel Royal between 1569 and 1591 is not clear, though it was said that Randle had been 'a singer in the Kinges [sic] Chappell'.

Randolph was a chorister at Chester Cathedral between 1612 and 1615 and a scholar of the King's School. He was probably still in Chester in 1628, but soon afterwards may have followed a cousin, John, to Dublin, where from 1630 until 1643 Jewett was organist and master of the choristers at both Christ Church and St Patrick's cathedrals. (The matter is not quite so straightforward, however, since among other complications he seems to have relinquished the organ of Christ Church in favour of Benjamin

Rogers in 1638.) In fact, he had perhaps taken up similar appointments at Chester by 1643, but the civil war in England encouraged him to return to Dublin. Thus the duke of Ormond wrote to the dean and chapter of Christ Church in 1646:

Having understood how much … Randall Jewet hath suffered for his good affection to his Majesties Service, and how ably he is qualified in his p[ro]fession, and for the Quire; We … recommend into your favour for the conferring of the Vicar Chorallis place, now voide in that Cathedral upon him. (Boydell, 78)

Jewett seems to have again drawn stipends from both cathedrals until about January 1650.

By 1651 Jewett was in London, where his name appears among a number of teachers 'For the Organ and Virginall' in John Playford's *Musicall Banquet*. At the Restoration he became one of the minor canons (junior cardinal) of St Paul's Cathedral, almoner, and master of the choristers. (Indeed, Jewett seems already to have been regarded as one of the inferior officers of the cathedral by the award of grants from the trustees for the maintenance of ministers in 1655 and 1657, but how and why is not at all clear.) After the fire in 1666 he took up the same posts at Winchester Cathedral, without relinquishing his place at St Paul's. Jewett died at Winchester on 3 July 1675, aged seventy-two, and was buried in the north transept of the cathedral. One of his daughters, Sarah Woodall, signed for his St Paul's salary on several occasions, and his will (dated 20 November 1674) mentions his wife, Ann, children Benjamin and Deborah, and grandchildren John, Elizabeth, and Mary.

John Hawkins described Jewett as a pupil of Orlando Gibbons, which may or may not have been the case. References to him as 'Batchelor in Musick' in contemporary documents suggest that he may have been awarded the degree by Trinity College, Dublin. Comparatively little music by him survives; a short evening verse service and six verse anthems are known, but only the anthem 'I heard a voice from heaven' (which dates from before the civil war) is in score. IAN SPINK

Sources J. C. Bridge, 'The organists of Chester Cathedral, 1541–1644 [pt 1]', *Journal of the Architectural, Archaeological and Historical Society for the County and City of Chester, and North Wales*, new ser., 19 (1913), 63–90 • H. W. Shaw, *The succession of organists of the Chapel Royal and the cathedrals of England and Wales from c.1538* (1991), 417–18 • B. Boydell, ed., *Music at Christ Church before 1800: documents and select anthems* (Dublin, 1999) • *Walker rev.*, 11

Jewitt, Arthur (1772–1852), topographer, eldest son of Arthur Jewitt and Mary, daughter of Jonathan Priestley of Dronfield, Sheffield, was born at Dronfield on 7 March 1772. At the age of fourteen he was bound apprentice to his father, a cutler. At the expiry of his apprenticeship on his twenty-first birthday, on 7 March 1793, he married Martha (d. 1835), daughter of Thomas Sheldon of Crookes Moor, Sheffield. He now opened a private school, and in 1794 he became master of a school at Chesterfield. He was subsequently master of Kimberworth School from 1814 to 1818, after which he retired to Duffield, near Derby, where his wife died in 1835. He remained there until 1838, when

he joined members of his family at Headington, near Oxford. He died at Headington on 7 March 1852.

Jewitt was well known for his topographical works *The History of Lincolnshire* (1810) and *The History of Buxton* (1811), and was the publisher of a number of short-lived topographical journals and popular volumes, of which *The Matlock Companion* (1835) is the best-known. He also wrote mathematical papers for non-specialist journals and had two handbooks—one on perspective (1840) and one on geometry (1842)—adopted by the committee of council on education. Two of his seven sons, Llewellynn Frederick William *Jewitt (bap. 1816, d. 1886) and (Thomas) Orlando Sheldon *Jewitt (1799–1869), shared his antiquarian interests. G. C. BOASE, rev. WILLIAM JOSEPH SHEILS

Sources GM, 2nd ser., 37 (1852), 524 • M. O'Sullivan, 'Derbyshire', *English county histories: a guide*, ed. C. R. J. Currie and C. P. Lewis (1994), 107–14
Archives Derbys. RO, autobiography and diary • Derbys. RO, sketchbook of local views
Likenesses portrait, repro. in W. Smith, *Old Yorkshire* (1883)

Jewitt, Llewellynn Frederick William (bap. 1816, d. 1886), antiquary, baptized at Kimberworth, near Rotherham, Yorkshire, on 24 November 1816, was the youngest of the seventeen children of Arthur *Jewitt (1772–1852), topographer, and his wife, Martha, (d. 1835), daughter of Thomas Sheldon. He was the brother of (Thomas) Orlando Sheldon *Jewitt, wood-engraver. From 1818 he lived at Duffield, Derbyshire, where he was taught by his father. Before he was twenty-one he had learned wood-engraving. In 1835 he made the acquaintance of F. W. Fairholt, engraver and antiquary, and in 1838 he went to London to join him in the work of illustrating various publications—chiefly Charles Knight's—by drawing and engraving under Stephen Sly. He made almost all of the drawings for *London Interiors* (though his name was not mentioned), and contributed to the *Pictorial Times*, the *Illustrated London News*, and other periodicals. He married at Derby, on 25 December 1838, Elizabeth, daughter of Isaac Sage of Bath and Derby. She died on 4 March 1886. They had several children. Edwin A. G. Jewitt was the only son who survived his father. About 1846 Jewitt was at Headington Hall, near Oxford, working with his brother Orlando on the illustrations for Parker's *Glossary of Architecture* and *Domestic Architecture*. He afterwards returned to London, and for a time managed the illustrations of *Punch*.

From 13 July 1849 until 29 September 1853 Jewitt was chief librarian of the Plymouth Public Library. During his librarianship the building was enlarged, the library rearranged, the collection of William Cotton FSA, was acquired, and manuscripts were donated by James Halliwell-Phillipps. In 1853 Jewitt moved to Derby, where he started the *Derby Telegraph*, which was first issued monthly, but became weekly after the abolition of the stamp duty. He remained editor until 1868. Jewitt was vice-president of the Derbyshire Archaeological Society, and acted as honorary curator of the town and county museum at Derby. He was a promoter and one of the earliest officers of the Derby rifle volunteers and published a volume on rifle volunteer corps in 1860. Also in 1860 he established a pioneering local antiquarian quarterly journal, *The Reliquary*. He continued its editor and a chief contributor until his death. About 1868 Jewitt moved to Winster Hall, High Peak, Derbyshire. In 1871 he took a leading part in bringing pure water in pipes to Winster from a distance of 3 miles, to eradicate 'Derbyshire neck', a goitre produced by water from the local limestone. In 1880 he moved to The Hollies, Duffield. A civil-list pension was granted him in July 1885.

Jewitt was a member of the British Archaeological Association and a fellow of the Society of Antiquaries (elected 27 January 1853). He was an industrious writer on English antiquities and topography, and had practical experience in opening barrows, chiefly in Derbyshire. His best-known work was *The Ceramic Art of Great Britain*, based on twenty years' research and fieldwork. Jewitt formed a collection of ceramics, part of which was sold in London in 1871. He had a wide circle of friends, which included Thomas Bateman, archaeologist, the antiquarians Joseph Mayer and Charles Roach Smith, and the literary journalist S. C. Hall, to whose *Art Journal* he long contributed. Jewitt, like his father, was a prolific author of guidebooks and topographical works, especially on Derbyshire, from the 1850s to the 1870s. He also wrote biographies of Josiah Wedgwood, the antiquarian William Hutton, and Jacob Thompson, landscape painter. He died at his home in Duffield after a month's illness, on 5 June 1886. He was buried on 9 June at Winster.   W. W. WROTH, *rev.* MARGARET O'SULLIVAN

Sources W. H. Goss, *The life and death of Llewellyn Jewitt* (1889) • *The Reliquary*, new ser., 1 (1887) • R. B. Brown, 'Llewellynn Jewitt, art historian and archaeologist, 1816–1886', *Derbyshire Miscellany*, 9 (1980), 13–18 • parish register (baptism), Kimberworth, 24 Nov 1816 • parish register (marriage), Winster and Derby, 25 Dec 1838 • *The Reliquary*, 27 (1886), 240
Archives U. Edin. L., letters to James Halliwell-Phillipps
Likenesses photograph (after bust), repro. in W. H. Goss, *Life and death of Llewellynn Jewitt*, vol. 1
Wealth at death £706 13s. 7d.: resworn probate, March 1887, CGPLA Eng. & Wales (1886)

Jewitt, (Thomas) Orlando Sheldon (1799–1869), engraver, was born in Attercliffe, Sheffield, on 26 July 1799, the second surviving son of the seventeen children of Arthur *Jewitt (1772–1852) and his wife, Martha, née Sheldon (d. 1835). Jewitt was one of the earliest to make a lifetime career and livelihood from commercial engraving on wood. He served no apprenticeship in the regular manner of wood-engravers during the nineteenth century, but was self-educated in the skills of drawing and engraving. He became technically proficient in the rendering of architectural, ecclesiastical, and topographical illustrations, many of which he had drawn, and was recognized and admired by the Victorians for this work. However, his largely indifferent efforts in purely imaginative or pictorial subjects show the limitations of his skills as both draughtsman and engraver. He trained and employed others, including his brothers, in engraving on wood, and an undisclosed number of the illustrations signed with his name, initials, or cipher, entwining these initials, would have been engraved by them.

Jewitt's father possessed an aspiration to create an all-embracing family publishing, printing, illustration, and engraving concern. Arthur Jewitt had been apprenticed as a cutler in Sheffield, but left the trade having once served his time and became in turn a schoolmaster and an officer of excise before attempting his publishing venture. At the age of fifteen Orlando Jewitt engraved the illustrations to *Wanderings of Memory, or, Buxton and the Peak* (1815), some poems by his elder brother, Arthur George Jewitt, edited and published by their father. In 1817 he contributed not only illustrations and engravings to his father's short-lived magazine the *Northern Star*, but also an anonymous series of articles on Derbyshire and on botanical subjects.

After a peripatetic life around the West Riding of Yorkshire, Derbyshire, and Staffordshire, the Jewitt family, headed by Arthur Jewitt, settled in 1818 in Duffield, near Derby, where their publishing activities were pursued. While there Orlando Jewitt drew and engraved a miscellaneous range of illustrations, including those for chapbooks and moral and religious tracts, but from 1824 he found his niche drawing and engraving antiquarian, architectural, and topographical subjects. His contribution in 1829 of illustrations and engravings to the popular *Principles of Gothic Architecture* by Mathew Bloxam (he added further engraved illustrations to later editions) established his reputation as an engraver on wood. Also while at Duffield, on 27 September 1829 he married Phoebe Stanley (1798–1883). They had five children, four of whom, Susanna Martha, Ada Elizabeth, Arthur Stanley, and Phoebe Jane, were born in Duffield. Their last child, Walter Sheldon, was born in Oxfordshire.

In 1838 Jewitt moved to Headington, near Oxford, where he continued to work for Bloxam but also for the university printer, Thomas Coombe, and, most importantly, for the bookseller and publisher John Henry Parker. An early commission from Parker, to engrave the illustrations to the Revd James Ingram's *Memorials of Oxford* (1832–6), is considered one of Jewitt's happiest exercises in wood-engraving. It was, however, the vast amount of drawings and engravings which he contributed to works of antiquarianism, archaeology, and architecture that secured his reputation with his contemporaries. In the right place at the right time, and with an interest in the subject, he was able to publish his engravings in works by the leading practitioners of the Gothic revival—A. W. N. Pugin, Sir Gilbert Scott, and G. E. Street. He also became wood-engraver to the Oxford Society for Promoting the Study of Gothic Architecture.

In 1856 Jewitt moved his family, together with some of his assistants, to London, where he set up both home and workshop at 20 Clifton Villas, Camden Square. He had been working for London publishers while engaged by Parker in Oxford, and these connections, together with the fact that by the middle of the century London was the centre of a burgeoning wood-engraving profession, are likely to have encouraged his decision to move. He continued to engrave ecclesiastical, archaeological, and architectural subjects (significantly his work appeared regularly, from 1857, in the *Building News*) and also contributed occasional articles on archaeological and architectural subjects. He died in his seventieth year on Sunday 30 May 1869 at his home in Camden Square, probably having suffered a stroke, and was buried in Paddington old cemetery. He was survived by his wife, who died, aged eighty-five, on 11 March 1883.

A photographic portrait of Jewitt in his fifties shows a slight, alert man with an intense look. He was described as a man 'of the most retiring and exemplary habits' (*Art Journal*, 31, 1869, 251), and this taciturnity of nature is endorsed by an entry in the journal of his brother Llewellynn *Jewitt (*bap.* 1816, *d.* 1886), on an occasion when Orlando's unexpected talkativeness is recorded as a singular and unusual event.   LEO JOHN DE FREITAS

Sources F. Broomhead, *The book illustrations of Orlando Jewitt* (1995) • H. Carter, *Orlando Jewitt* (1962) • W. H. Goss, *The life and death of Llewellyn Jewitt* (1889) • *The Builder*, 27 (1869), 461 • *Art Journal*, 31 (1869), 251–2 • F. Broomhead, 'Orlando Jewitt: wood engraver to the Oxford Society for Promoting the Study of Gothic Architecture', *Oxoniensia*, 61 (1996), 369–78
Archives Bodl. Oxf., letters to Alfred Beesley • Bodl. Oxf., John Johnson collection
Likenesses Stanesbury, photograph, after 1851, repro. in Broomhead, *Book illustrations*

Jewkes, John (1902–1988), economist, was born in Barrow in Furness on 29 June 1902, the eldest of three children and only son of John Jewkes, sheet-metal worker and foreman in Vickers Armstrong's shipbuilding yard, and his wife, Fanny Cope. After attending Barrow grammar school, he took a BCom degree at the University of Manchester in 1923, with distinction in economics, and an MCom by thesis in 1924. He then spent two years as assistant secretary of the Manchester chamber of commerce before being appointed to a lectureship at the University of Manchester in 1926. His early work was on the cotton industry and in 1935 he published with E. M. Gray a study entitled *Wages and Labour in the Lancashire Cotton Spinning Industry*. In 1930 he was appointed director of a new economic research section at Manchester University and concentrated on problems of industry and labour. With Alan Winterbottom he produced for the government in 1933 *An Industrial Survey of Cumberland and Furness* (one of a series for the 'development areas'), and in the same year with the same collaborator he published a study of juvenile employment—a subject to which he returned in 1938 with his wife in *The Juvenile Labour Market*. In 1936 his university appointed him to a chair in social economics, which he held until 1946.

In December 1939, after the outbreak of the Second World War, Jewkes was recruited, along with others, to provide economic advice to the war cabinet secretariat. In 1941 he became director of its newly formed economic section, which was a prime source of economic advice to the government. Jewkes had a boyish enthusiasm, a salty humour, and above all a grasp of the practical and the significant that fitted him for the job of feeding economic ideas into the administrative machine. Within a few months he was invited to review the need for some form of planning in the Ministry of Aircraft Production. He recommended in favour of this and was promptly invited

to undertake the job. Lent initially for three months to that ministry, he stayed for nearly three years, exercising as powerful an influence there as he had done in the cabinet office and recruiting a staff made up exclusively of economists. He proved himself a skilled planner in face of confusion and discouragement, his appointment as director-general of statistics and programmes coming only in 1943 after a struggle. Early in 1944 he moved on again, this time to the Ministry of Reconstruction. One of his main contributions there was to the drafting of the white paper on employment policy, a document which he defended in later years, emphasizing the limits of the commitments assumed. In wartime Whitehall he was an effective and capable head of a team, bold in his proposals and adroit in obtaining support for them.

After the war Jewkes never found the scope for his talents that the war had provided. For two years he returned to Manchester as Stanley Jevons professor of political economy, but in 1948 he moved to Oxford to a new chair in economic organization and a fellowship at Merton College. He was devoted to his college and as garden master did much to enhance the beauty of the garden. As an economist, however, he was swimming against the tide. He was not interested in pure theory, his views on policy were unfashionable with younger economists, and he missed the company of kindred spirits. But he remained in Oxford for the rest of his life, having, after his retirement in 1969, little contact with other members of the university.

In the early post-war years Jewkes played a leading part on the first of Sir Stafford Cripps's working parties, on the cotton industry, and on the royal commission on betting, lotteries, and gaming (1949). He came to public attention with the publication in 1948 of his *Ordeal by Planning*. This established him as a leading critic of government intervention and control. He spent much of his time in the 1950s collecting material, with the help of two assistants, for his *magnum opus*, *The Sources of Invention*, which appeared in 1958. This studied the origin of over one hundred of the more important industrial inventions of the twentieth century. The results were in keeping with Jewkes's philosophy, derived from the American philosopher William James, of 'small is preferable'. He argued consistently against large organizations, pointing to the limits of economies of scale, the advantages of competition, the greater flexibility and inventiveness of small units, and the dangers of bureaucracy and monopoly. In 1957–60 Jewkes also served on the royal commission on doctors' and dentists' remuneration and developed a new interest in the economics of health care.

In 1978 Jewkes published his last work, *A Return to Free Market Economics?*, a symposium drawn from earlier writings. He was too extravagant in his attack on post-war controls, too sure that control of industry was not passing into fewer hands, and played down too much the advantages of large-scale research and development. He was more at home on issues of organization and microeconomics than on the major dilemmas of policy in post-war

Britain, especially those associated with international balance. But he was a much underrated critic of government economic policy. The book contains a *résumé* of his work as director from 1969 to 1974 of the Industrial Policy Group, consisting of a score of top businessmen. This appointment arose out of his long association with Guinness as an economic adviser. He was appointed CBE in 1943 and awarded a DSc by Hull University in 1973.

In appearance Jewkes was short and stocky with a broad, cheerful, bespectacled face and a soft, attractive voice. He was a man of many enthusiasms, a keen gardener and a house agent *manqué*. Although combative in his views, he was mild in manner, entertaining in conversation, full of humour, and a lover of paradox. In 1929 he married (Frances) Sylvia, daughter of Harry Clementi Butterworth, a Manchester cotton merchant. She collaborated in much of his work and shared his views. They had one daughter. Jewkes died in Oxford on 18 August 1988 and his wife died soon afterwards.

ALEC CAIRNCROSS, *rev.*

Sources WW · *The Times* (23 Aug 1988) · *The Independent* (23 Aug 1988) · private information (1996) · personal knowledge (1996)

Jewsbury, Geraldine Endsor (1812–1880), novelist and journalist, was born at Measham, near the Derbyshire - Leicestershire border on 22 August 1812, the fourth child and younger daughter of Thomas Jewsbury (d. 1840), a cotton manufacturer, and his wife, Maria, *née* Smith (d. 1819), a cultivated woman of artistic tastes. In 1818 the family moved to Manchester where Thomas became an insurance agent; Maria died the following year. Consequently the eldest child, Maria Jane *Jewsbury (1800–1833), became responsible for running the household and superintending her sister's education. Geraldine spent several years at the Misses Darbys' boarding-school at Alder Mills, near Tamworth, and then in 1830–31 continued her studies in French, Italian, and drawing in London. Maria Jane had intended her for a governess, but her own marriage in 1832 meant that Geraldine in turn took charge of the Jewsbury household. Maria Jane, who had become a successful writer, died in 1833, leaving her sister powerful but ambivalent memories: deeply religious herself, she had urged Geraldine to eschew any worldly ambitions and to adhere devoutly to her duty—but she had also given her Shelley's iconoclastic *Prometheus Unbound*, and had discussed her own literary achievements. Through her late teens and twenties, Geraldine read widely in metaphysics and science, and became increasingly disenchanted with what she saw as the narrow and desiccated Calvinism of her milieu. In April 1840, in a state of severe depression aggravated by an unhappy love affair and her father's mortal illness, she wrote to Thomas Carlyle. She had lost her faith in God and lacked any sense of purpose, and so asked him to elaborate on the solutions to such dilemmas which she had found adumbrated in his works. The correspondence led to lifelong friendships with both Thomas and Jane Carlyle: despite many vicissitudes in their relationship, Jewsbury became Jane Carlyle's closest friend.

After her father died in 1840, Jewsbury kept house for her youngest brother, Frank, in Green Heys and later Ardwick, on the outskirts of Manchester. Her spiritual difficulties persisted, partly because she found life as a woman particularly devoid of meaning: she believed that middle-class women's upbringing had no vocational or moral dimension, but was geared simply to securing husbands and ensuring decorous behaviour. From the early 1840s she worked on a novel which, as *Zoe: the History of Two Lives*, was accepted by John Forster for Chapman and Hall and published in 1845. It explores the passionate but unconsummated love between a woman who marries for lack of other options and a Roman Catholic priest assailed by religious doubts; the novel's interlinking of sexual feeling and spiritual anguish owes much to George Sand. Jewsbury told Jane Carlyle that *Zoe* demands 'What are we sent into this world at all for? What ought we to do with our life?' (*Selections from the Letters*, 150)—and admitted that she had no answers. Jane Carlyle was, like many contemporary readers, shocked by the novel's outspokenness, but confessed that it revealed Jewsbury as 'a far more profound and daring speculator' than she had thought (*Collected Letters*, 15.250). Jewsbury's next novel, *The Half Sisters* (1848), which she considered her best, challenged conventional assumptions about women by contrasting the dreary and unsatisfying existence of a businessman's wife with the active and purposeful life of her actress half-sister; its focus on the performer's life owes something to Madame de Staël's *Corinne* and Sand's *Consuelo*, and something too to Jewsbury's friendship with the prominent American actress Charlotte Cushman. *Marian Withers* (1851) again examines the emptiness of middle-class women's lives, but also shows Jewsbury's familiarity with the growth of manufacturing and its implications for labour relations.

Jewsbury continued to publish fiction, albeit of less interest, until 1859: for adults she produced *Constance Herbert* (1855), reviewed lukewarmly by George Eliot in the *Westminster Review* (July 1855), *The Sorrows of Gentility* (1856) and *Right or Wrong* (1859), and for children, *The History of an Adopted Child* (1852) and *Angelo, or, The Pine Forest in the Alps* (1855). Invited by Dickens to contribute to *Household Words*, she published seventeen tales there (1850–59). Jewsbury wrote for several periodicals: notable are her translations of Mazzini's articles on Carlyle and Dante, and her own 'Religious faith and modern scepticism' (*Westminster Review*, 52, January 1850), in which she presents spiritual problems as 'the beginning of a wider and deeper insight—a larger faith and increased knowledge'. She was most prolific, however, as a writer for the weekly *The Athenaeum*, a career which lasted from 1849 to her death, and involved reviewing about two thousand books, mainly fiction.

Jewsbury also became an influential publisher's reader, particularly of novels—for Hurst and Blackett, and, from 1858 to her death, for Bentley. She recommended that Bentley accept Ellen Wood's *East Lynne* (1861), which became a best-seller, but her advice lost for the firm the later popular authors Rhoda Broughton, M. E. Braddon, and Ouida—partly because Jewsbury had become more conservative about the representation of sexual feeling in fiction.

Jewsbury's literary prominence gave her an entrée to intellectual circles. A small and lively redhead, whose behaviour—such as smoking—could startle, she was an excellent conversationalist, and attracted many notable people to her home in Manchester. In 1854, after her brother Frank married, she moved to Chelsea to be near Jane Carlyle. Her friends included the Huxley, Kingsley, Rossetti, and Browning families, as well as W. E. Forster, John Tyndall, Frances Cobbe, Samuel Bamford, John Bright, A. H. Clough, John Ruskin, G. H. Lewes, and Helena Faucit Martin. She also helped the elderly Lady Morgan with her memoirs (1862), writing much of the narrative after the latter's death. Jewsbury had a succession of abortive emotional entanglements with men, even proposing by letter to the French socialist turned Muslim Charles Lambert in 1847. Her most serious entanglement was the last, in the late 1850s, with New Zealand settler Walter Mantell, whose quest to achieve justice for the indigenous Maori she supported. After abandoning her marital hopes when he returned to New Zealand in 1859, she continued to correspond with him for the rest of her life. None the less, as Virginia Woolf put it, 'though the prey to so many emotions, she was also oddly detached and speculative' (Woolf, 149). Jewsbury was conscious of being a self-made woman of letters, and predicted that women of later generations would feel less pressure to depend on men for their sense of identity (*Selections from the Letters*, 347–9).

On Jane Carlyle's death in 1866, Jewsbury moved to Sevenoaks in Kent. In her last years, her writing was hampered by deteriorating eyesight, but she received a civil-list pension of £40 in 1874. She died of cancer on 23 September 1880, at a private hospital, 3 Burwood Place, Edgware Road, London, and was buried at Brompton cemetery in Lady Morgan's vault. Jewsbury's posthumous reputation was damaged by the furore over Froude's writings on the Carlyles, which had drawn on her comments about their unhappy marriage; she was also trivialized by Annie Ireland's over-emphasis on her emotional volatility in her edition of Jewsbury's letters to Jane Carlyle. None the less recent scholarship has found much of interest and value in Jewsbury's achievements.

JOANNE WILKES

Sources S. Howe, *Geraldine Jewsbury: her life and errors* (1935) · N. Clarke, *Ambitious heights: writing, friendship, love* (1990) · *Selections from the letters of Geraldine Endsor Jewsbury to Jane Welsh Carlyle*, ed. A. Ireland (1892) · G. E. Jewsbury, letters to Walter Mantell, NL NZ, Turnbull L., W. B. D. Mantell MSS, MS Papers 83 · G. E. Jewsbury, letters to Thomas Carlyle, NL NZ, Turnbull L., Geraldine Jewsbury MSS, MS Papers 544 · Maria Jane Jewsbury's letters to GEJ, JRL, Jewsbury MSS · J. R. Fahnestock, 'Geraldine Jewsbury: the power of the publisher's reader', *Nineteenth-Century Fiction*, 28 (1973), 253–72 · *The collected letters of Thomas and Jane Welsh Carlyle*, 13–24, ed. C. de L. Ryals and K. J. Fielding (1987–95) · [V. Woolf], 'Geraldine and Jane', *TLS* (28 Feb 1929), 149–50 · M. C. Fryckstedt, *Geraldine Jewsbury's Athenaeum reviews* (1986) · E. Gillett, 'Memoir', in *Maria Jane Jewsbury: occasional papers* (1932) · BL cat. · CGPLA Eng. & Wales (1880)

Archives BL, letters to Royal Literary Fund, loan 96 · NL NZ · NL Wales, letters | BL, letters and reports to R. and G. Bentley, Add. MSS 46653–46660 · NL NZ, Turnbull L., corresp. with Carlyles · NL NZ, Turnbull L., W. B. D. Mantell MSS, MS papers 83 · NL Wales, letters to Johnes family · U. Cal., Los Angeles, department of special collections, letters to W. Hepworth Dixon

Likenesses photograph, April 1855, Col. U., Rare Book and Manuscript Collection · photograph, Birmingham Reference Library

Wealth at death under £3000: probate, 17 Dec 1880, *CGPLA Eng. & Wales*

Jewsbury [married name Fletcher], **Maria Jane** (1800–1833), writer and literary reviewer, was born at Measham, near the Derbyshire and Leicestershire border, on 25 October 1800, the eldest of the six surviving children of Thomas Jewsbury (*d.* 1840), a cotton manufacturer, and his wife, Maria, *née* Smith (*d.* 1819), an educated woman of artistic tastes. She was sent to Miss Adams's school in Shenstone, Staffordshire, but bad health forced her to leave at fourteen; she continued with a governess at home, and read Shakespeare and German writers. Ambitious from the age of nine to be an author, she wrote poems, fiction, and a fragment of a play during her adolescence, and had poetry published in the *Coventry Herald* in 1818.

In that year, however, Thomas Jewsbury's business failed, and the family moved to Manchester, where he became an insurance agent. In 1819 her mother died in childbirth, so Maria Jane became responsible for the care of her siblings, and for running a large household on a small income. At this time, she recalled, her life 'became so painfully, laboriously domestic that it was an absolute duty to crush intellectual tastes'; she later decided she needed further education as a writer, and at twenty-one began a course of systematic reading (Gillett, xviii). She began to contribute to the *Manchester Gazette* in 1821, and attracted the attention of Alaric Watts; as a result, she published in his annual, the *Literary Souvenir*, and his friend Robert Sulivan's *Album*. Throughout her career she continued to produce short prose pieces and generally sentimental poetry for the annuals—more than seventy contributions in all, primarily for *Forget-me-Not*, *Literary Souvenir*, *The Amulet*, *Winter's Wreath*, *Juvenile Forget-me-Not*, *Ackermann's Juvenile Forget-me-Not*, and *New Year's Gift*.

Watts also saw through the press a collection of Jewsbury's poetry and prose, *Phantasmagoria* (2 vols., 1825), which she both dedicated and sent to her favourite poet, William Wordsworth, so as to express her gratitude for his works and to cultivate his patronage. Dorothy Wordsworth found her a 'young woman of extraordinary talents', being particularly impressed by the way she had pursued her writing while running the household. William praised her literary criticism and satirical pieces on social affectations (*Letters of William and Dorothy Wordsworth*, 343, 405). Although *Phantasmagoria* adopts varied tones and styles, most interesting are Jewsbury's prose pieces, which focus on literature, from parodies of authors' and critics' pretensions, to more serious considerations of contemporary religious fiction, poetry, and ballad-writing. She expresses great admiration for contemporary writers such as Wordsworth, Sir Walter Scott, and Felicia Hemans, but also regrets what she sees as a

Maria Jane Jewsbury (1800–1833), by John Cochran, pubd 1847 (after G. Freeman)

devaluing of their eighteenth-century predecessors. Jewsbury's outspokenness was also facilitated by her publishing the collection as by M. J. J., and implying a male authorship.

Jewsbury was invited to stay with the Wordsworths at Kent's Bank, Lancashire, in July 1825, and produced a manuscript account of the holiday in a parody of *Morning Post*-style social news, the 'Kent's Bank Mercury'. Her appearance in a 'Noctes ambrosianae' tribute to 'genius' in *Blackwood's* for March 1829 emphasized her admiration for the poet. Jewsbury remained in contact with the family, and three of Wordsworth's poems, 'The Stuffed Owl', 'Gold and Silver Fishes in a Vase', and 'Liberty', record their friendship. She became particularly close to Wordsworth's daughter Dora, with whom she often corresponded.

In May 1826, however, Jewsbury collapsed into a protracted state of illness, aggravated by a spiritual crisis. She was afflicted with guilt over her literary ambitions, partly because they had come to represent for her worldliness—a turning away from the Christian's proper focus on eternal destiny—and partly because she had internalized her society's disapproval of female ambition in particular. Her next publication, *Letters to the Young* (1828), exhorts its youthful audience to eschew worldly desires and to concentrate on a humble life of duty, aimed at attaining eventual immortality. But its rhetoric sometimes comes across as self-castigation, as if bearing witness to Jewsbury's inner conflicts. The work is based on Maria Jane's actual letters to her sister Geraldine *Jewsbury (1812–1880),

twelve years younger, who was away at school undergoing an education for which their father had evidently delegated responsibility to his older daughter. Although these also emphasize the dangers of ambition and the need for a devout spirit, they contain much news of Maria Jane's own literary activities, and so convey a very mixed message; Geraldine later became a novelist and critic herself.

Another important friendship was with Felicia Hemans, with whom Jewsbury stayed at Rhyllon in Wales for the summer of 1828, and to whom she dedicated her poetry collection *Lays of Leisure Hours* (1829). Hemans felt that Jewsbury completely understood and appreciated her, and characterized her influence as the 'spell of *mind on mind*' (Hughes, 1.226); Jewsbury, however, also registered the increasing loneliness Hemans endured despite her literary renown. The possible emotional cost of the famous woman writer's life is expressed through the experiences of Julia Osborne, the protagonist of Jewsbury's novella 'The History of an Enthusiast', who achieves celebrity but comes to feel enervated, as well as distraught at failing to gain the man she loves. This story, which is one of many nineteenth-century texts indebted to Madame de Staël's novel *Corinne* (1807), treats sympathetically Julia's struggles to gain an education and to write in the face of family and social prejudice, but seems to portray her ambitions as ultimately misguided. The disjunctions in the text show how Jewsbury's experience of Hemans, her reading of *Corinne*, and her partial internalization of her culture's attitudes to women writers, are in conflict with her own persisting ambitions and her belief in women's intellectual capacities. The story was published in Jewsbury's collection *The Three Histories* (1830): another novella, 'The History of a Nonchalant', confronts, and then backs away from, its protagonist's struggle with religious doubt.

In 1830 Jewsbury became part of the new talent introduced by Charles Wentworth Dilke when he took over the editorship of *The Athenaeum*, for which she wrote many articles and reviews over the next two years. The then conventional anonymity of the reviewer enabled Jewsbury to be more outspoken and sardonic than was normally acceptable in women writers, while also protecting her from accusations, including self-accusations, of female ambition. She writes forcibly in several articles about the prejudices damaging women's upbringing, declaring that women's lives are so much governed by men's expectations and assumptions, that girls are cultivated 'to the highest pitch that can make them fascinating, with a careful abstinence from that which would make them wise' (*Athenaeum*, 11 Feb 1832, 95).

Jewsbury's *Athenaeum* articles also discuss early nineteenth-century women writers—including Joanna Baillie, Felicia Hemans, Anna Jameson, Letitia Landon, and Jane Austen—and in them she deals in different ways with contemporary assumptions about female authorship. In the first publication on Austen identifiable as by a woman, Jewsbury argues that the novelist got away with portraying 'folly, selfishness and absurdity' in her fiction, because in daily life she 'had too much wit to lay herself open to the charge of being too witty; and discriminated too well to attract notice to her discrimination' (*Athenaeum*, 27 Aug 1831, 553). Male writers are reviewed too: another article defends P. B. Shelley from charges of religious infidelity and poetical obscurity.

Jewsbury planned to revise Mary Wollstonecraft's controversial *Vindication of the Rights of Woman* for a contemporary audience. She enjoyed too the months she spent in London literary circles in 1830. But her life underwent a major change when in March 1831 she accepted the proposal of a persistent suitor, the Revd William Kew Fletcher (d. 1867). Months of unhappiness followed, as she combated her father's opposition, and probably her own doubts as well. One appeal of the proposal was the prospect of foreign travel, as Fletcher was chaplain to the East India Company. The pair were finally married by Felicia Hemans's brother-in-law at Penegoes, Montgomeryshire, on 1 August 1832, and embarked for India at the end of September. Jewsbury continued writing on the voyage out and during her travels in India, producing her best poetry, as well as a journal which traced her gradual recognition that she should cease to hanker after things English and appreciate India for itself. Both poems and journal extracts were published in *The Athenaeum* in 1832–3. But she contracted cholera, and died at Poona on 4 October 1833; she was buried there the same day.

Back in England, Jewsbury was lamented for her wit, brilliant conversation, and intellectual vitality, and for the literary potential left unfulfilled. Her sister and others hoped to compile a memorial volume of the anonymous publications she had taken with her to India, but Fletcher's refusal to communicate with the family made this impossible. Jewsbury was, however, praised in Elizabeth Barrett's letters to Mary Russell Mitford in the 1840s, and commemorated in Francis Espinasse's *Lancashire Worthies* (1877). Since the 1980s, her life and works have attracted renewed attention, particularly from feminist critics.

JOANNE WILKES

Sources N. Clarke, *Ambitious heights: writing, friendship, love* (1990) • Wordsworth Trust, Dove Cottage, Grasmere, letters to Wordsworth family, WLMS A • JRL, Jewsbury MSS • M. C. Fryckstedt, 'The hidden rill: the life and career of Maria Jane Jewsbury [pt 1]', *Bulletin of the John Rylands University Library*, 66 (1983–4), 177–203 • M. C. Fryckstedt, 'The hidden rill: the life and career of Maria Jane Jewsbury [pt 2]', *Bulletin of the John Rylands University Library*, 67 (1984–5), 450–73 • A. Boyle, *An index to the annuals*, 1 (1967), 152–4 • E. Gillett, 'Memoir', in *Maria Jane Jewsbury: occasional papers* (1932) • F. Espinasse, *Lancashire worthies*, 2 (1877), 323–9 • S. Howe, *Geraldine Jewsbury: her life and errors* (1935) • *The letters of William and Dorothy Wordsworth*, ed. E. De Selincourt, 2nd edn, rev. C. L. Shaver, M. Moorman, and A. G. Hill, 8 vols. (1967–93), vol. 4 • A. A. Watts, *Alaric Watts: a narrative of his life*, 2 vols. (1884); repr. (New York, 1974), 178–88 • H. Hughes, 'Memoir', *Works of Mrs Hemans*, 1 (1839) • *The letters of Elizabeth Barrett Browning to Mary Russell Mitford, 1836–1854*, ed. M. B. Raymond and M. R. Sullivan, 3 (1983)

Archives JRL, papers • Wordsworth Trust, Dove Cottage, Grasmere, MSS, WLMS A | JRL, letters to her family

Likenesses J. Cochran, stipple, pubd 1847 (after G. Freeman), NPG [*see illus.*]

Jewson, Dorothea [Dorothy] (1884–1964), feminist and politician, was born on 17 August 1884 at Thorpe Hamlet, Norwich, one of two children of Alderman George Jewson

JP, a coal and timber merchant, and his wife, Mary Jane Jarrold. The family firm Jewson & Son was established in 1836 and owned sawmills in Norwich, Yarmouth, Lowestoft, and Lincoln. Dorothy Jewson, as she was known, attended Norwich high school and Cheltenham Ladies' College. She completed the classical tripos at Girton College, Cambridge, in 1907, and it was there that she first showed an interest in socialism, joining both the university Fabian Society and the Independent Labour Party. In 1908 she gained a teacher's certificate from Cambridge Training College and then worked as an assistant mistress at West Heath, Richmond, Surrey, between 1908 and 1911.

On her return to Norwich to teach in a local school Dorothy Jewson became more actively involved in politics. She joined the militant wing of the suffrage movement and the Women's Social and Political Union, and in 1912 she stood unsuccessfully as a Labour candidate for the board of guardians. She carried out an enquiry with her brother into poverty and poor relief in Norwich, which was published as *The Destitute of Norwich and how they Live: a Report into the Administration of out Relief* (1912). During the First World War she helped to run a training centre for unemployed girls under the age of seventeen. In 1916 Dorothy Jewson was invited by the trade union leader Mary Macarthur to become an organizer for the National Federation of Women Workers in London, where she worked closely with the assistant secretary, Margaret Bondfield. When the federation merged in 1921 with the National Union of General and Municipal Workers (NUGMW), Dorothy became head of the section responsible for organization until she left in 1922 and returned to Norwich.

This marked the beginning of a very active period for Dorothy Jewson in Labour politics at both a national and a local level. She was elected as Labour MP for Norwich in 1923, but was defeated in 1924 and on two subsequent occasions in 1929 and 1931. She was more successful in her attempt to enter local politics and served on the Norwich county council from 1929 to 1936. She also took a prominent role within the Independent Labour Party (ILP) and between 1925 and 1935 represented the eastern division on the national administrative council. She served on numerous internal committees; as a member of the women's advisory committee, for example, she sought to persuade women to join the ILP, encouraged the formation of women's groups, and edited the *Monthly Bulletin* which aimed to keep local groups in contact with each other. As a former trade union organizer Dorothy Jewson retained an interest in women's employment conditions and in the 1920s she was one of two ILP delegates to the standing joint committee of women's industrial organizations. In the many controversies over protective legislation she argued that existing sex-specific legislation should be retained for the protection of the female worker, but that in the future legislation should apply to the nature of the work rather than to the sex of the worker performing it.

Dorothy Jewson combined her socialist politics with strong feminist attitudes and was one of a small group of women who worked hard in the 1920s and 1930s to persuade the Labour Party to take more interest in the needs of working-class women. Her maiden speech as an MP was on the subject of extending voting rights to young women and she sought more influence for Labour women within their own party's structures. As a delegate from the ILP to Labour women's conferences and Labour Party annual conferences in the late 1920s she used all her influence to try to gain support for controversial policies such as family allowances and easier access to birth control which, she argued, were important from a class as well as a feminist perspective. Dorothy Jewson was a leader, along with Dora Russell, of the Workers' Birth Control Group and, as an unmarried woman, was particularly courageous in taking a public stand on the issue.

Dorothy Jewson's Baptist upbringing and her membership of the ILP ensured that she had a lifelong commitment to the cause of peace. She was a pacifist in both world wars and in the 1920s was an active member of the No More War Committee. In August 1925 she was one of the British delegates to the International Conference of Labour and Socialist Women in Marseilles. Dorothy also attended meetings of the Labour and Socialist International (LSI) and in 1928 represented the ILP on the international women's advisory council of the LSI. Her pacifism drew her to the Society of Friends during the Second World War and she was formally admitted as a member of Croydon and Southwark monthly meeting in 1958.

Dorothy Jewson was described by contemporaries as retaining her youthful enthusiasm throughout her life. Photographs show a woman of middling height with a mass of dark, wavy hair parted at the side. Lively dark eyes shine from a heart shaped face and there is always a faint smile upon her lips. She was closely associated with the socialism of the ILP during the inter-war years and remained as a member after the organization's disaffiliation from the Labour Party in 1932. Her political activism was much reduced, however, after her first marriage in 1936 to Richard Tanner-Smith (1869/70–1939), a tea merchant. In 1945 she married her second husband, Campbell Stephen, MP for Camlachie and a well-known personality in the ILP. He died in 1947. Dorothy moved to Orpington, but in 1963 returned to Norwich to live in a cottage in the grounds of her brother's home at Hellesdon. She died there, on 29 February 1964, at Riverdene Cottage, 49 Low Road, Lower Hellesdon. Her funeral service was held at the Friends' meeting-house, Norwich, and she was cremated at nearby St Faith's crematorium. JUNE HANNAM

Sources A. Holt and J. Saville, 'Jewson, Dorothea (Dorothy)', *DLB*, vol. 5 · BLPES, Francis Johnson MSS, Independent Labour Party Archive · *Labour Woman* (April 1924) · *Labour Woman* (May 1929) · S. Rowbotham, *A new world for women: Stella Browne, socialist feminist* (1977) · WWW · D. Jewson and W. H. Jewson, *The destitute of Norwich and how they live: a report into the administration of out relief* (1912) · D. Jewson, *Socialists and the family: a plea for family endowment* (1926) · m. cert.

Likenesses photograph, repro. in *Labour Woman* (April 1924) · photograph, repro. in *Labour Woman* (May 1929) · photograph, People's History Museum, Manchester · photograph, London School of Economics, Frances Johnson coll. [souvenir of ILP annual conference, Norwich 1928]

Jeyes, John (*bap.* 1817, *d.* 1892), chemical manufacturer, was baptized on 10 June 1817 at Wootton, near Northampton, the second son and third child of Philadelphus Jeyes (1780–1828), a retail pharmacist, and his wife, Elizabeth, *née* Ward, daughter of a local landowner. On his father's death, the family business in Northampton was taken over by John's elder brother, also Philadelphus, who had been educated at a school in Moulton, his mother's village, before being apprenticed to a local pharmacist. It seems likely that John's own upbringing followed a similar course, although it is not known to whom he was apprenticed or to what extent he received formal training in chemistry. Unlike Philadelphus, however, he did not become a member of the Pharmaceutical Society.

Evidence suggests that Jeyes abandoned a course in pharmacy to pursue an interest in botany, which brought him a partnership with James Atkins, a local nurseryman. Philadelphus also became financially involved, so that by 1845 the joint business as seedsmen and florists, originally styled Atkins and Jeyes, had become Jeyes & Co. Little is known about Jeyes's years as a nurseryman, but it was during this period, on 10 March 1846, that he married Sarah Frances Weldon (*d.* 1888), the daughter of a 'subdistributor of stamps'. The marriage took place at St Mary's Church in her home town of Stamford, Lincolnshire. They had nine children: Oliver Weldon, Jeanne Frances, Edith, Mary Alice, Samuel Henry, Walter, Gertrude, Charles, and Robert, the last dying in infancy.

The family initially lived at Holly Lodge, Northampton, a house built by the younger Philadelphus. Following the birth of Walter in 1859, Jeyes and his family moved to London. The reason for the move is uncertain. It may simply have been to broaden his business interests, since after the birth of Charles in 1863, when the family was living in Finsbury, Jeyes's occupation is entered in local trade directories as 'hearth rug manufacturer, boot and shoe factor, importer and purifier of bed feathers, horse hair, wool, etc.' In 1871, in Plaistow, Essex, Jeyes, now styling himself as a manufacturing chemist, set up his first major business venture, the Jeyesine Oil and Paint Company Ltd. The enterprise was a failure and closed in 1873.

Meanwhile, Jeyes had become increasingly interested in the 'sanitary debate' then current among the medical and allied professions. Sanitary conditions in towns and cities at that time were often rudimentary, especially in the poorer quarters, and there was a constant threat of disease. There was an active medical and commercial concern to develop a product that would effectively combat the widespread filth and pollution. Until then it had traditionally been the practice to treat any disagreeable stench or insanitary conditions by using deodorizers or antiseptics. Jeyes saw that this was not enough. The deodorizer might replace an unpleasant smell by a sweeter one, and the antiseptic prevent decomposition or the breeding of germs, but what was also needed was a disinfectant, to kill bacteria; this could be achieved by means of a carbolic-based solution. On 7 December 1877 Jeyes patented Jeyes' Fluid, a preparation that was chemically a saponified solution of phenols, with added resins and other compounds. Although Jeyes' Fluid was not the only disinfectant, and had rivals in such products as Izal and Condy's Fluid, it had the edge over them in many respects. It was less caustic and generally safer than neat carbolic acid, had a pleasanter yet distinctive smell, and was marketed at a price that suited the public. Jeyes's popular advertising stressed the fact that his fluid was not simply a deodorizer but also an effective disinfectant and antiseptic.

In 1879 Jeyes and his son Walter established Jeyes' Sanitary Compounds Company Ltd, and built a factory to manufacture the fluid in the grounds of Richmond House, Plaistow, his home since 1874. Although initial sales were good, Jeyes was a poor businessman, and rising debts resulting from fraud and mismanagement obliged the firm to go into voluntary liquidation in 1884. Its assets were sold in 1885 to a successor company, of the same name but with a new board of directors. Although Jeyes remained an employee of the reconstituted company that bore his name, he was poorly treated by its directors, to whom he had signed away all his rights. A financial statement of 1888, the year of his wife's death, describes him simply as 'works manager' and gives his annual salary as £260, as compared to the £300 received by the company secretary.

On 12 January 1892, at his home, 5 Windsor Road, Forest Gate, West Ham, Essex, John Jeyes died of 'senile decay' at the age of seventy-five. He was buried in the same grave as his wife in the East London cemetery, Plaistow. He left only £585, as against the £24,000 in the will of his brother, Philadelphus, who died in 1893, and the £12,000 left by his son, Oliver, who died in the same year and whose business (paint manufacturing in Birmingham) was nothing like the size of his father's.

John Jeyes was a large, amiable, and kindly man, who became a household name more through his inventive mind and sound chemical knowledge than from any business acumen or entrepreneurial shrewdness.

ADRIAN ROOM

Sources D. Palfreyman, *John Jeyes … the making of a household name* (1977) · parish register, Wootton, Northamptonshire · d. cert.
Archives Jeyes, Thetford, Norfolk
Likenesses photograph, *c.*1890, repro. in Palfreyman, *John Jeyes*
Wealth at death £585 17*s.* 10*d.*: probate, 17 May 1892, CGPLA Eng. & Wales

Jezreel, James Jershom (1848×51–1885), founder of the Jezreelites, enlisted in the army on 27 July 1875, at Westminster, as James Rowland White, aged twenty-four, the son of a warehouse superintendent. Six days later he joined the 2nd battalion of the 16th regiment of foot at Chatham. He was secretive about his earlier life, cultivating the role of the 'mysterious stranger', but there were some suggestions in his speech and spelling that he might have been born in the United States. He referred once to earlier employment in an American bank and to having worked his passage as a ship's stoker. On 15 October 1875 he joined a small Southcottian congregation, the New House of Israel, in Chatham. He soon disturbed the calm of the group by claiming to be the sixth of the seven trumpeters in Revelation 7:2, the successor to the prophets Joanna Southcott and John Wroe. On 26 December he was expelled from the sect but set up his own New and Latter House of Israel, taking with him seventeen of the congregation, to whom he began reading his *Flying Roll*—a special 'revelation' to him from God (cf. Zechariah 5: 1).

The Js of the name that Jezreel now adopted reflect the first names of his prophetic predecessors, Joanna and John, and of himself, while Jershom and Jezreel are variants of the Hebrew for 'stranger' and 'Israel' (Exodus 2: 22; Hosea 1: 11). He established such a hold on his followers during the next six weeks that they remained loyal to him even when in February 1876 he was posted to India for five years. From there he sent them further 'revelations', some of which were published in 1879 and 1881 as *Extracts from the 'Flying roll' … compiled for the gentile churches of all sects and denominations, and addressed to the lost tribes of the house of Israel*. On obtaining his release on 4 November 1881 Jezreel sailed home from Calicut. On 17 December 1881 (claiming to be thirty-two years old) he married the daughter of Edward and Elizabeth Ann Rogers, Clarissa Esther (1860–1888), a follower who earlier that year had travelled to New York and had convinced Noah Drew, a Wroeite farmer in Michigan, of Jezreel's prophetic claims. In 1882–3 the newly-weds not only visited Southcottian groups in England and Scotland but also returned to America, gaining followers in Howell, Brighton, and Detroit, Michigan.

Jezreelites, as they came to be known, had to transfer their property to a fund over which their leader had total control, and with the consequent enhancement of both the numbers and funds of the sect Jezreel established in October 1883 a meeting-hall in Gillingham and a 20 acre centre for the community, which included Israel's International College (founded March 1884), as well as houses and shops—their carts, marked with the name of Jezreel, became familiar sights in the streets of Chatham. He also bought a fine house for himself at The Woodlands, Gillingham, which became his headquarters and from which Clarissa, who had assumed the title Esther, queen of Israel, administered the community's affairs while Jezreel went preaching in Australia. On his return in late 1884 he announced plans for the construction of a magnificent sanctuary, the site for which was purchased in early 1885. Its 125 feet cubical tower on Chatham Hill, Gillingham, was designed to house printing presses, a vast assembly hall, and the community's commercial offices.

Jezreel was impressively tall and broad in the shoulders and 'had a genius for showmanship' (Rogers, 29). When he proclaimed the imminent return of Christ many of his followers, responding to his charismatic summons, came to live in the Gillingham area. However, unexpectedly, he suffered from two burst blood vessels and died at The Woodlands on 1 March 1885. He was buried in Grange Road cemetery, Gillingham, on 5 March. His widow succeeded to the leadership, living in great style, but there were increasing tensions in the community and her treatment of Noah Drew was particularly harsh. When on 30

June 1888 she died of peritonitis the community began to disintegrate and the building of 'Jezreel's tower' was suspended. It was destroyed in 1959.

TIMOTHY C. F. STUNT

Sources P. G. Rogers, *The sixth trumpeter: the story of Jezreel and his tower* (1963) · R. A. Baldwin, *The Jezreelites: the rise and fall of a remarkable prophetic movement* (1962)
Wealth at death £41 10s. 0d.: administration, 25 April 1885, *CGPLA Eng. & Wales*

Jhones, Basset (*b.* 1613/14), physician, chemist, and grammarian, was the son of Richard Jones (*c.*1581–1658) of Michaelston-super-Ely, Glamorgan, and Jane, daughter of Thomas Basset, of Miskin, Glamorgan. His father was the son of John ap George (*d.* 1631) of Llantryddyd and Ann (*d.* 1613), daughter of John ap William Bassett. Basset Jhones is said to have become a student at Oxford University in 1634, 'having then his lodging' in Jesus College. Afterwards he travelled on the continent, studying 'physic and cheymistry' (Wood, *Ath. Oxon.*, 3.491). Jhones's peregrinations took him to Paris, where he became acquainted with the 'thrice learned' Dominican exile Thomasso Campanella (1568–1639), and the 'damp'd mudd' of the United Provinces (Jhones, *Herm'aelogium*, 7, 37). On 27 March 1638, aged twenty-four, Basset Jhones, gentleman, matriculated at Leiden University to study medicine. Less than two months later, on 9 May 1638, Jhones matriculated at Franeker University in Friesland, again as a medical student. Jhones later styled himself 'Dr', though there is no record of either university's conferring a higher degree upon him.

After his return to the British Isles, Jhones published *Lapis chymicus philosophorum examini subjectus* (1648). Jhones's coat of arms, argent, three chevronells gules, a canton ermine, and his motto, *Duw ar fy rhan*, are displayed on the title-page. A 'paraphrastically Englished' version 'by the sayd Author' written in verse and entitled 'Lithocymicus, or, A discourse of a chymic stone' survives in manuscript (BL, Sloane MS 315). The work indicates Jhones's familiarity with Plato's *Timaeus* and the *Tabula smaragdina* attributed to Hermes Trismegistus, as well as writings by Henry Cornelius Agrippa, Paracelsus, Jakob Boehme, and Campanella. A French translation of the manuscript was to be printed at Rouen, though this has not been traced. A transcript of the printed edition, however, probably made in the United Provinces towards the end of the eighteenth century, is now in the Beinecke Library. Another example of Jhones's versifying is his undated petition to 'that moderne text' of astrology, William Lilly. Here Jhones implores his 'friend' to use his skill to 'ayde … Love reciprocall' (Bodl. Oxf., MS Ashmole, fol. 146*r*).

Writing from his lodging 'by Jame's fields' on 7 March 1651, Dr Basset Jhones addressed a 'Letter of queries' to TheaurauJohn Tany, self-proclaimed prophet, self-appointed high priest of Aaron's order, and 'the accounted mad-man of the times'. In this epistle Jhones expresses his dissatisfaction with 'the Books of the Learned' and enquires of Tany 'who can speak somwhat experimentally thereof':

1 Whether the Soul be a created substance, distinct from the Body; and consequently departeth from the Body, in the moment of death …
2 But if you finde that the Soul is traduced with the Body, Then when is its separation …
3 Whether the whole man doth not rest in the grave until the last Trump?
4 And lastly, In what part or principle of the Creature doth this German of knowledge reside?
5 And after the dissolution of the compound, by what Organs actuated?

Jhones conceded that it would be impertinent to enquire more of his 'friend', 'since you resolv'd me that at other times you cannot reason those discoveries that are revealed to you in your transportations'. He concluded with a precept derived from the 'Alkoran' of Mohammed (perhaps he had seen a copy of the recently printed English translation). Tany replied to Jhones with an epistle entitled '*Theaurau John* his Salvat-ori, or the true knowledge in light' (*Theous ori apokolipikal*, 1651, 1–2, 3).

In October 1651 Basset Jhones, together with his brother Edward, was named as a party in a property transaction by his father. At his death Richard Jones held lands in the parish of St Fagan, Glamorgan. He had also purchased 10 acres of land in Michaelston-super-Ely of Colonel Philip Jones (1618–1674). Philip Jones was appointed governor of the garrison at Swansea in November 1645 and created a colonel the following year. A company of his soldiers reinforced Colonel Horton at the battle of St Fagans in May 1648, when the parliamentary army defeated a royalist insurrection. Horton's brigade was rewarded with several manors in the Vale of Glamorgan that had formed part of the estates forfeited by the earl of Worcester. In February 1652 Colonel Jones and others bought these manors, including that of Wrinston and Michaelston, on behalf of Horton's brigade. Richard Jones had been granted a lease dated 22 October 1625 for ninety-nine years ('if three lives should last so long') 'of a Messuage and certain Lands within the manor of *Wrinston* and *Michaelston*', and his decision to employ an agent to purchase 'by way of preemption' the state's interest in his leaseholding brought him into conflict with Colonel Jones (Jhones, *Copy of a Petition*, 6, 11). In defence of his 'aged and distressed Father' Basset petitioned Cromwell for justice alleging 'unparalell'd' oppression on the part of Colonel Jones, 'a person so grac'd by your Highness' (ibid., 8, 1, 24). Basset Jhones published 'the whole Process and Course of the Frauds, Injuries & Oppressions used by the said Colonel' in a pamphlet of 1654 (ibid., 8).

In his ephemeris for January 1655 Samuel Hartlib noted a 'very choice and rare Booke discovering the whole Philosophical Mystery'. The title of this treatise was *Lapis chymicus philosophorum*. Hartlib had been informed by Frederick Clod or Clodius, a widely travelled German alchemist, that the book was 'mighty scarce being presently bought up' and that Dr Jhones himself could 'get no more copies of it'. It was said, moreover, that: 'The Dr hath laboured all his life in that Worke and though he bee gone further than many hundred … yet hee knows it not' (Sheffield University, Hartlib papers, 'Ephemerides', January 1655, 29/5/11A). On 15 February 1655 Jhones visited Clodius for the first time and told him of his 'Philosophical medecin', claiming it could cure all fevers. Clodius remarked that if it 'proove not the elixir itself, yet it will proove infallibly a universal medecin' (Sheffield University, Hartlib papers, 29/5/12A–B). In the meantime Jhones used a Helmontian medicine to cure himself of 'the stone' (Sheffield University, Hartlib papers, 29/5/13B).

In March 1655 Robert Boyle told Clodius that Jhones was now 'trying that golden Experiment' which George Starkey had 'imparted' to Boyle 'about Antimony and gold'. It was said that Jhones promised to make 'a full trial' which he hoped to have finished within three weeks. Soon after it was reported that Jhones was going to Ireland to buy land there for £1000, though he intended to conclude his experiment before his departure (Sheffield University, Hartlib papers, 29/5/18B, 20B).

Richard Jones died on 21 April 1658 and was commemorated by an englyn carved on a mural monument in the church of Michaelston-super-Ely. To his son Basset he bequeathed the 'bedding and furniture within the white chamber and the lit[t]le chamber over the hall of my now dwelling howse' (will of Richard Jones of Michaelston-super-Ely, Glamorgan, probate 20 Aug 1658, PRO, PROB 11/280, fol. 59v). His will also named Basset's two children: Thomas (by Marie Hughes) and Marye (by Katherin Miles). In January 1659 one Theodoret Basset was presented to the rectory of Michaelston-super-Ely by its patron Philip Herbert, fifth earl of Pembroke. Like Basset Jhones, the earl of Pembroke had a passion for alchemy, having bought the first copy of Elias Ashmole's *Theatrum chemicum Britannicum* (1652). Though Jhones nowhere mentions Herbert in his writings, he does cite with approval a treatise by 'my most worthily honoured friend' Sir Kenelm Digby—another eminent figure with alchemical interests (Jhones, *Herm'aelogium*, 71).

In March 1659 Basset Jhones completed a book on grammar entitled *Herm'aelogium, or, An Essay at the Rationality of the Art of Speaking*. The work appears to have been prompted by a discussion between Jhones and his 'select companions … relating to the Grammatical part' of Francis Bacon's *The Advancement of Learning* (Jhones, *Herm'aelogium*, sig. A4). It was dedicated to the master and professors of the University of Franeker and published in London by Thomas Basset. William Dugard, headmaster of the Merchant Taylors' School, approved it for publication, finding 'much rationality in it' (ibid., leaf appended to the beginning or end of the work). On 20 November 1659 Hartlib wrote to Boyle informing him that 'Dr. *Jones's* work is going on again, and he is filled afresh with very great expectations' (Thomas Birch, ed., *The Works of the Honourable Robert Boyle*, 6 vols., 1772, 6.136). Nothing else is known with certainty about Basset Jhones. An unpublished 'History of Brecon and Glamorgan' records that a 'Basset Jones' purchased the lordship of part of the manor of Pencelli, Brecknockshire, though this seems to refer to 'one of the Joneses of Buckland' (BL, Harley MS 6108 n.d., fol. 27r).

According to the pedigrees in the 'Golden grove book' Basset Jhones, doctor of physic, married Catherine, daughter of William Lloyd. This union produced no known offspring.   ARIEL HESSAYON

Sources B. Jhones, *Lapis chymicus philosophorum examini subjectus* (1648) · B. Jhones, *The copy of a petition to his highness the lord protector* (1654) · B. Jhones, *Herm'aelogium* (1659) · B. Jhones, 'Lapis chymicus', Yale U., Beinecke L., MS 137 · A. Hessayon, 'Gold tried in the fire': the prophet Theaurau John Tany and the puritan revolution [forthcoming] · Wood, *Ath. Oxon.* · T. Jones, *A history of the county of Brecknock*, 2 (1809), 592 · [Hugh Thomas?], 'The golden grove books of pedigrees', 4 vols., Carmarthenshire RO · D. Jones, 'On a seventeenth century Welsh inscription at Michaelston-super-Ely', *Archaeologia Cantabriensis*, 5th ser., 6 (1889), 198–213 · R. S. Wilkinson, 'The Hartlib papers and seventeenth-century chemistry: part II', *Ambix*, 17 (1970), 104–5 · Sheffield University, Hartlib papers

Archives BL, Sloane MS 315 · Bodl. Oxf., Ashmole MS, fol. 146r

Jind Kaur (1817–1863), maharani and regent of Lahore, was born in 1817 in the village of Chhahar, Sialkot district, Punjab (now in Pakistan), the eldest child of the three daughters and two sons of Manna Singh Aulakh, a Sikh of the Jat caste. Her father moved to Lahore, where he became the royal kennel keeper in the service of Ranjit Singh (1780–1839), the maharaja of Punjab and sovereign of the Sikhs. The maharaja was said to have been pestered day and night by Manna Singh, who told him that his daughter was the most beautiful creature in the world, whom he would give to the maharaja as his wife, and that she would make the old maharaja young again. The maharaja married Jind Kaur in 1835, by the ceremony of *karewa*. In 1838 she gave birth to a son, Duleep *Singh (1838–1893), who became the maharaja in 1844 after Ranjit Singh's death in 1839 and the deaths of three successive monarchs after him. Jind Kaur was appointed the regent.

During this period of internal politics and unrest the maharani's illicit affairs and flirtations with her ministers came to light. As her power began to slip, the Sikh army became increasingly powerful and out of control. In November 1845 she sent the army to confront the British, who were camped provocatively by the River Sutlej on her southern border. Unknown to her, however, her two generals had treacherously sold themselves to the British. Two hard-fought wars, the First Anglo-Sikh War (1845–6) and the Second Anglo-Sikh War (1848–9), followed. The British then annexed the Punjab and dethroned Duleep Singh in 1849. He became a British ward under the care of John Login, and was exiled to England five years later.

After the First Anglo-Sikh War Jind Kaur had lost power, as a council of regency was set up under the British resident, Henry Lawrence. He found her attitude rebellious and threatening to British rule, and ordered her to the Summan Tower of the Lahore Fort. Jind Kaur called for an inquiry and appealed, among other things, against her separation from her nine-year-old son Duleep Singh, and the non-payment of her allowance of 1½ lakhs of rupees as laid down in the treaty of Bhyrowal (1846). The resident could not tolerate her pressure in Lahore. On 19 August 1847 Duleep Singh was sent away from the palace, on the same night that the maharani was removed from Lahore and incarcerated in the fort of Sheikhapura. She was transferred to Ferozepur on 15 May 1848 and her income was reduced to 1000 rupees a month. In 1849, after the annexation of the Punjab, she was moved to Fort Chunar but on 18 April that year she escaped, disguised as a slave girl, and arrived ten days later at Katmandu, where she received the protection of the Nepalese government. Lady Login described her as a 'practical prisoner in Nepal, under Jung Bahadur, who grudged her of her every penny of the pension he said he allowed her' (Login, *Recollections*, 206).

In 1860 Jind Kaur's son, now an English aristocrat, sought to contact his mother through the resident at Katmandu, Colonel Ramsay, who remarked that 'The Rani had much changed, was blind and lost much of the energy which formerly characterised her, taking apparently but little interest in what was going on' (Login, *Sir John Login*, 450). Jind Kaur and her son met at Spence's Hotel, Calcutta, on 16 January 1861, after some thirteen and a half years apart. She was granted permission to go to England, and took up residence at 1 (now 23) Lancaster Gate, London. Lady Login remarked on meeting her in 1861:

> Jinda Kour was truly an object of commiseration when one contrasted her present with her former state … Health broken, eye sight dimmed, her once famed beauty vanished, it was hard to understand the power she had wielded through her charms. It was only when she grew interested and excited in conversation, that one caught glimpses, beneath that air of indifference and the torpor of advancing age, of that shrewd and plotting brain which had distinguished the famous 'Messalina of the Punjab'. (Login, *Sir John Login*, 458)

After a short spell at Mulgrave Castle, Jind Kaur was placed in the charge of an English lady at Abingdon House, Kensington, London. On the morning of 1 August 1863 Maharani Jind Kaur died peacefully at Abingdon House, her estate on her death valued at a mere £12,000 (probate registry). Her body was kept temporarily at Kensal Green cemetery, London, and in the spring of 1864 Duleep Singh left for India and arranged for the cremation of her body there. She was cremated at Nasik in Bombay on the Panchvati side of the River Godavari where, on the left bank, a small *samadh* (memorial stone) was erected. The Kapurthala state authorities maintained the memorial until 1924, when her remains were exhumed and taken to Lahore by her granddaughter Princess Bamba Sutherland (the eldest daughter of Duleep Singh) and deposited at the *samadh* of Maharaja Ranjit Singh on 17 March 1924.

BHUPINDER SINGH BANCE

Sources E. Dalhousie Login, *Lady Login's recollections* (1916) · *Duleep Singh correspondence*, ed. G. Singh (1977) · Lady Login [L. C. Login], *Sir John Login and Duleep Singh* (1890) · B. Saggar, *Who's who in the history of the Punjab* (1993) · S. L. Suri, *Umdat-ut-Twarikh* (1885–9) · K. Singh, *Maharajah Ranjit Singh* (1962) · A. Gardner, *Soldier and traveller* (1898) · G. Carmichael Smyth, *A history of the reigning family of Lahore* (1847) · J. D. Cunningham, *History of the Sikhs* (1849) · T. Singh, *Maharani Jindan* (1959) · L. Griffin, *The Punjab chiefs* (1865) · *ILN* (30 June 1849)

Archives BL OIOC | Ancient House Museum, Thetford, Norfolk · Lahore Fort Museum, Pakistan, Princess Bamba collection · Punjab State Archives, Patiala, India · Punjabi University, India, Ganda Singh collection, private corresp.

Likenesses G. Richmond, oils, priv. coll.

Wealth at death £12,000: administration, 6 Nov 1863

Jinnah, Mohamed Ali (1876–1948), creator of Pakistan, was born on 25 December 1876 at Wazir Mansions, Newnham Road, Karachi, the first of the seven children of Jinnahbhai Poonja (*c.*1857–*c.*1901), a successful merchant, and his wife, Mithibai (*d. c.*1894). He had two brothers and four sisters, of whom Fatima (1883–1967) was to be his companion for much of his life. He was a member of the Shi'i Khoja trading community, whose origins reach back to the twelfth to the fifteenth centuries in the Sind and Kathiawar provinces of the subcontinent. Jinnah married, first, in 1892, Emibai, who died shortly afterwards, while he was a student in England, and secondly, in 1918, Ratanbai (Ruttie; *d.* 1929), the only daughter of the wealthy Parsi mill owner Sir Dinshaw Petit. They had one daughter, Dina, born in 1919.

Education and early career Jinnah was educated first in Bombay and then, from 1887, at the Sind Madrassa and the Christian Mission High School, Karachi. He was not outstanding at either school, being more interested in riding his father's Arab horses and dictating his own pattern of learning. In 1892 he was apprenticed to the London office of a business associate of his father's, Douglas Graham & Co., and changed his name from Jinnahbhai to Jinnah. Two months after arriving in England, he resigned from his apprenticeship to read for the bar at Lincoln's Inn, qualifying as a barrister in 1896. He developed an interest in politics, attending debates in the House of Commons and assisting in the 1892 election campaign of the Bombay Parsi Dadabhai Naoroji, first Indian member of parliament. He showed himself capable of high jinks on boat race night, leading to brushes with the law. He also developed a taste for the theatre, harbouring an ambition to play Shakespeare's Romeo, and displaying enough talent to be given a contract.

Little is known of Jinnah's early career at the Bombay bar, which began in August 1896. But by 1900 he was given the unusual accolade of being taken into the chambers of Bombay's acting advocate-general, John Macpherson. Soon afterwards he was appointed temporary third presidency magistrate, but in 1901 refused a permanent place on the bench at the handsome salary of Rs1500 per month, saying, 'I will soon be able to earn that much in a single day' (Wolpert, 7).

The nationalist, 1904–1920 Jinnah's early political career was one of proud Indian nationalism. He first attended the Indian National Congress in 1904 at Bombay, where he met his political hero the Maharashtrian statesman and constitutionalist G. K. Gokhale. In 1906 he attended the Calcutta sessions as secretary to Dadabhai Naoroji, now Congress president, and had a hand in writing his address, which emphasized the theme of national unity. The Indian poet Sarojini Naidu, who was present at Calcutta, warmed to Jinnah's 'virile patriotism' and 'rare and complex temperament', describing him as 'tall and stately, but thin to the point of emaciation, languid and luxurious of

Mohamed Ali Jinnah (1876–1948), by unknown photographer, c.1945

habit, Mohammad Ali Jinnah's attenuated form is a deceptive sheath of a spirit of exceptional vitality and endurance' (Wolpert, 27).

The years from 1909 saw Jinnah carrying his nationalist credo to the forefront of Indian politics. In 1909 he was elected to the reserved Muslim seat for Bombay on the legislative council. He quickly made a strong impression in this arena, which was well suited to his sharp mind and forensic gifts. In 1911 and 1912 he succeeded in piloting through the council his Wakf Validating Bill, which permitted Muslims once more to make tax-free endowments to their families that could ultimately become religious charities. In 1913 he travelled to London with Gokhale for discussions with the chairman of the royal commission on public services. In 1914 he chaired the Congress deputation to London which lobbied parliament over the proposed Council of India Bill.

Jinnah's especial achievement in these years was to play a leading role in bringing the All-India Muslim League, which had been founded to win special privileges for Muslims, into harmony of purpose with the Congress. In London in 1913 he accepted the request of a radical faction to join the League with the qualification that this should 'at no time imply even the shadow of disloyalty to the larger national cause to which his life was dedicated' (Wolpert, 34). In January 1916 he succeeded in persuading a troubled

session of the League at Bombay that together with Congress it should formulate a scheme of reforms for the Indian legislative councils which would allow them to make a common demand 'in the name of United India' (Pirzada, 1.354). The following December at the Congress and League meetings in Lucknow he played a key role in creating the so-called Lucknow pact. By reaching agreement over the percentage of reserved seats for Muslims there should be in each council, this enabled the Congress and League to support a joint scheme of constitutional reform for India. As president of the Muslim League session he praised the new spirit of 'national self-consciousness ... which has brought Hindus and Muslims together involving brotherly service for the common cause' (Wolpert, 47–8). At this moment he was an acknowledged leader of Indian politics and, as Gokhale had once described him, 'the best ambassador of Hindu–Muslim Unity' (ibid., 35).

Over the following two years Jinnah was to the fore in maintaining pressure for constitutional reform. In June 1917 he became president of the Bombay Home Rule League. He greatly impressed the secretary of state, Edwin Montagu, when he visited India later in the year: a 'very clever man', Montagu described him; 'it is, of course, an outrage that such a man should have no chance of running the affairs of his own country' (Montagu, 58). In the Delhi war conference of 1918 Jinnah took the lead in trying to bargain acknowledgement of India's constitutional demands against support for the war effort; his pitch was queered by M. K. Gandhi, newly prominent in Indian political life, who offered unconditional support. He also served on the Congress–League committee which gave qualified approval to the constitutional proposals made in the Montagu–Chelmsford report. In the second half of the year Jinnah found himself in increasing conflict with officialdom, in particular the governor of Bombay, Lord Willingdon, who did not appear to have the respect for Indian views that was consonant with political advance. This culminated in Jinnah, with several hundred followers, disrupting a meeting in Bombay town hall to honour Willingdon on his departure. The citizens of Bombay then subscribed Rs65,000 to honour Jinnah instead by building the People's Jinnah Memorial Hall.

The year 1919 saw Jinnah's star beginning to wane; 1920 saw its total eclipse by the rise of Gandhi. In March 1919 he resigned from the legislative council in protest against the Rowlatt Act, which extended into peacetime the wartime powers of government to suspend civil liberties. From May to November he led an unsuccessful Muslim delegation to persuade the prime minister, Lloyd George, to appoint a Muslim delegate to the Versailles peace conference. For the year 1920 he was elected president of the Muslim League but found himself fighting an increasingly desperate action against Gandhi's determination to win Indians to his policy of non-co-operation with government. In September Gandhi, with the help of large numbers of Muslims, persuaded a special meeting of Congress to adopt his policy. In October he persuaded the Home Rule League to adopt the goal of 'complete Swaraj for

India according to the wishes of the Indian people' (Wolpert, 69) against Jinnah's preference for self-government within the British Commonwealth by constitutional means. Jinnah resigned as president of the Home Rule League. When in December 1920 he attempted to oppose a similar resolution from Gandhi at the Nagpur Congress session, he was howled down. Jinnah, who had never been so badly humiliated, left Nagpur immediately and resigned from the Congress.

The barren years, 1921–1937 The political circumstances of the years 1921–37 did not favour Jinnah. His gifts flourished at the topmost levels of politics. The Montagu–Chelmsford reforms, however, had diverted the focus of action to the provinces; there were limited opportunities for him to shine. He gave more attention to his legal practice. Nevertheless, he remained a formidable power in the politics of the Muslim League, being elected several times from 1924 as its permanent president for three years. He also took those opportunities which came to perform at the all-India level.

The first came in September 1923, when he was elected to his old seat as Muslim member for Bombay in what was now called the central legislative assembly. He quickly demonstrated his gifts as a parliamentarian, organizing the independent Indian members to work as a bloc with the Swaraj Party and using the majority thus achieved to press forward India's demands for full responsible government. Such was the level of his activity on subjects ranging from the economy to civil liberties, and so highly was it valued, that he was offered a knighthood by Lord Reading on his departure as viceroy. Jinnah responded: 'I prefer to be plain Mr. Jinnah' (Wolpert, 87).

The next came in 1927 with the appointment of the Simon commission. This brought the prospect of further constitutional reform, and provincial politicians had once more to take note of India's political centre. Jinnah aimed to use this possibility to re-create the common front between League and Congress. He had to win the support of the Muslim provinces and various Congress factions. His failure was demonstrated by the uncompromising Nehru report of August 1928 and its almost total rejection by Muslims. Jinnah found that he had to respect the strength of provincial views, in particular those of the Punjabi Muslims, and his 'fourteen points' on constitutional advance of March 1929 reflected this fact. In the same year Jinnah's personal friendship with the prime minister, Ramsay MacDonald, helped to shift discussion of constitutional reforms to London. Jinnah managed to play a role in the abortive first round-table conference of November–December 1930, although it was provincial Muslim views which prevailed. By this time, however, he had decided that his future lay in Britain. He transferred his practice to London, concentrating on appeals to the privy council. He bought a house in Hampstead, set in 8 acres, and tried unsuccessfully to become first a Labour and then a Conservative parliamentary candidate.

Jinnah, although he was elected to the legislative assembly from Bombay in 1934, did not finally return to India until the following year. He saw a new opportunity for himself at the centre in the general elections to be fought under the 1935 Government of India Act. Like the Congress he was strongly opposed to the way in which the reforms left the British in control of the centre. He aimed to fashion the Muslim League into an effective ally of the Congress; they would together attack the centre. In 1936 he was authorized to form the League's central parliamentary board to co-ordinate the process, and the League's political platform was in almost every respect brought into harmony with that of Congress. However, the massive defeat of the League, which won a mere 21 per cent of the Muslim seats in the 1937 elections, and the triumph of the Congress, which formed governments in six out of eleven provinces, saw Jinnah's strategy in shreds. He had no significant political base.

The creation of Pakistan, 1937–1948 The years following the disaster of the 1937 elections saw Jinnah trying to make the best of a weak position. He sacrificed the interests of the League in the Punjab and Bengal to provincial parties for the right to be able to represent the Muslims of these Muslim majority provinces at the centre. On the other hand, he was able to strengthen the League's position in the minority provinces as Muslims became alarmed by the overbearing policies of their Congress governments. After the outbreak of war in September 1939 Jinnah's position improved as the British developed new interest in him as the Muslim leader at the centre, who could counter Congress demands and whose co-religionists formed half of the Indian army. In response to British encouragement to formulate a 'constructive policy' towards constitutional advance, he presided over the League sessions at Lahore which on 24 March 1940 resolved that areas in which Muslims were in a majority in the north-west and the north-east of India should be grouped to constitute 'independent states'. In April 1942 he led the Muslim League in rejecting the offer by Stafford Cripps of what the League had demanded in 1940; the offer, he claimed, did not meet the full Muslim demand for national self-determination. During the years from 1937 Jinnah had increasingly come to be called Quaid-i-Azam, or Great Leader.

From 1942 Jinnah set out to strengthen the League's position in the Muslim majority provinces. He was helped by the absence, after the Quit India movement, of a large number of the Congress leaders, who were in gaol. His policies, moreover, were articulated with increasing effect, and Muslim fears of Hindu domination were expressed with increasing force, by the League's English-language newspaper, *Dawn*, which he had founded in 1941. While he failed to achieve a position of any kind in the Punjab, League governments over which he had some hold were formed in Sind in 1942, and in Bengal and the North-West Frontier Province in 1943. In summer 1944 he rejected Rajagopalachari's formula, which offered a 'Pakistan' created by a partition of the Punjab and Bengal, and proposed to Congress instead the formation of a united nationalist front against the British in return for a Muslim share of power at the centre. In September 1944 in talks with Gandhi he demanded sovereign Muslim states based on the existing provincial boundaries, but his old opponent rejected the proposal. In June 1945 he wrecked the Simla conference, which had been called by the viceroy to bring Congress and League together in an interim government, by insisting that all Muslims in this government had to be Muslim Leaguers.

Up to this point Jinnah, by brokering deals which allowed provincial politicians a free hand in their localities while he represented Muslim interests at the centre and by refusing to come to terms with his opponents, had kept his political fortunes and those of the League alive. This situation, however, was transformed by the results of the 1945–6 general elections. The League won all thirty of the Muslim seats in the central legislative assembly with 87 per cent of the Muslim vote and 439 out of 494 Muslim seats in the provincial assemblies with 75 per cent of the Muslim vote. On the eve of the transfer of power to the citizens of south Asia Jinnah had gained a clear mandate to speak for its Muslims.

From mid-1946 to mid-1947 Jinnah's efforts were focused on achieving the best possible realization of the idea of Pakistan from the endgame of empire. On 6 June 1946 the Muslim League council, acting on his advice, accepted the cabinet mission plan by which power at independence was to be transferred to a three-tier structure in which strong Pakistan and Hindustan groupings of Muslim and Hindu majority provinces, with princely states, would be formed under a relatively weak Indian union government whose powers would be limited to defence, foreign affairs, and communications. He also sought parity for the League in any interim government formed with the Congress. But, after the Congress rejected the idea of parity, Jinnah withdrew his acceptance of the plan and declared that the League would seek an 'independent and fully sovereign state' of Pakistan by direct action. This was followed by the killing of thousands in Calcutta on 16–20 August and a steady increase in other outbreaks of communal violence. On 26 October the weakness of Jinnah's position was emphasized when he permitted the League to enter the interim government formed by the Congress on 2 September without the demand for parity being recognized. He continued, however, to use stonewalling tactics by forbidding the League to enter the constituent assembly which was to meet from December. Soon after Prime Minister Attlee's announcement of 20 February 1947 that the British would leave India by June 1948, it was clear that there was no future for the cabinet mission's solution. Both Congress and the British concluded that Jinnah must be given Pakistan, but it was a state which could only contain the Muslim majority districts of the Punjab and Bengal. Jinnah resisted this partition when it was put to him in May by the viceroy, Mountbatten. On 3 June, however, he accepted the Mountbatten plan to transfer power to two separate states. Jinnah gave his assent to this outcome with no more than a nod; it was, he declared, a 'mutilated and moth-eaten Pakistan' (statement, 30 April 1947; Zaidi, *Jinnah Papers*, vol. 1, pt 1, p. 681).

Having been given Pakistan, Jinnah now needed to defend it. On 2 July he told Mountbatten that he intended to be Pakistan's governor-general; he needed to be sure that he had complete authority over Pakistan's territory. On 7 August he flew to the capital of his new country, Karachi. On 11 August he presided over the first meeting of the Pakistan constituent assembly, emphasizing in his address, given extempore, that Pakistanis of all creeds were equal citizens of the state, and that religion was a private matter. On 14 August he was installed in the presence of the viceroy as governor-general of the British dominion of Pakistan. In the months which followed Jinnah had to restore order after the hideous communal slaughter in the Punjab, to succour over 7 million refugees, to set up the administration of his new state, to establish its policies, and to steer it through its first war with India over Kashmir. The physical toll was immense and it was borne by a body weakened since the late 1930s by lung disease, which had developed into chronic tuberculosis. On 21 March 1948 he gave his last major public address in Dacca, East Pakistan. On 11 September, after several weeks spent in the Baluchistan resorts of Quetta and Ziarat, he died at home in Karachi, where he was buried the following day. In the late 1950s a mausoleum in pink stone was raised over his grave.

Reputation and assessment Jinnah was a man of great integrity and personal authority. To some he seemed arrogant and, in particular to those who negotiated with him, cold. He was, however, a sensitive man who controlled his emotions. That his affections were strong is revealed in his relationships with his family: the love affair with Ruttie, less than half his age, who eloped to marry him, his sadness at the breakdown of their relationship, and his grief at her early death; the strong bond between him and his sister Fatima, who called him Jin, while he called her Fati; and the utter certainty of a father's love revealed in the gossipy letters from his daughter, Dina. He inspired, moreover, in those who worked close to him and in the millions who followed him, devotion and admiration.

Jinnah was renowned for his sartorial elegance, wearing two-tone shoes, a new silk tie each day, and suits, of which he had more than 200 at his death, tailored in Savile Row. To this Western garb he added, as he became a mass leader in the 1940s, the Muslim clothes of *sherwani* and Afghan hat. His accent was English upper class, as were his tastes: Craven A cigarettes, of which he smoked fifty a day, Havana cigars, billiards, whisky, roast beef, and apple tart. He paid constant attention to his financial affairs, even at the most hectic political moments, buying and selling shares and property. His standard legal fee in the late 1930s was Rs1500 per day, the highest in India, while his portfolio of shares realized dividends of over Rs40,000. Among the properties he owned were his palatial main residence on 15,000 square yards of land on top of Bombay's Malabar Hill and 10 Aurangzeb Road in New Delhi, designed by Lutyens. After legacies to various family members, Dina, and several Muslim educational institutions, he left the greater part of his fortune to his sister Fatima.

'Of all the statesmen I have known in my life—Clemenceau, Lloyd George, Churchill, Curzon, Mussolini,

Mahatma Gandhi', declared the Aga Khan, 'Jinnah is the most remarkable' (Aga Khan, 292). Through time, although Indian views tend to be derogatory, there has been general appreciation of Jinnah's qualities of vision, will, courage, and intellect. There has, however, been a reassessment of his objectives and his success. All are agreed that up to the late 1930s Jinnah aimed to resolve India's Muslim problem within the constitutional framework of a united India. From the Lahore resolution of 24 March 1940 the traditional view sees him working for a separate state of Pakistan and fighting his way to triumph at partition in 1947. More recent interpretation, which is based on much fresh evidence and has come to win the support of many historians, sees no change in Jinnah's long-term objective in 1940 and only a shift in strategy. The Lahore resolution was a bargaining card to gain recognition of Indian Muslim nationhood and the right to equal treatment at India's political centre. This makes sense of Jinnah's rejection of the Cripps offer, which meant partition, and his acceptance of the cabinet mission plan, which avoided it. Nehru's rejection of this plan and the determination of Congress high command that independent India should have a strong political centre meant that the Indian nationalists were willing to force through partition to achieve this end. In the thirteen months leading to independence Jinnah worked to minimize the consequences of his defeat. The Pakistan which emerged in August 1947 was not the Pakistan he had set out to create.

FRANCIS ROBINSON

Sources S. Wolpert, *Jinnah of Pakistan* (1984) · A. Jalal, *The sole spokesman: Jinnah, the Muslim League and the demand for Pakistan* (1985) · F. Jinnah, 'A sister's recollections', *Pakistan: past and present*, ed. H. Jalal and others (1977) · A. Roy, 'The high politics of India's partition: the revisionist perspective', *Modern Asian Studies*, 24 (1990), 385–415 · S. al Mujahid, *Founder of Pakistan: Quaid-i-Azam Mohammed Ali Jinnah, 1876–1948* (1976) · S. al Mujahid, *Quaid-i-Azam Jinnah: studies in interpretation* (1978) · Z. H. Zaidi, ed., *Quaid-i-Azam Mohammed Ali Jinnah papers*, 1st ser., vol. 1, pts 1 and 2 (1993) · Z. H. Zaidi, ed., *Quaid-i-Azam Mohammed Ali Jinnah papers*, 1st ser., vol. 2 (1994) · Z. Ahmad, ed., *Mohammed Ali Jinnah: founder of Pakistan* (1970) · Z. H. Zaidi, ed., *M. A. Jinnah: Ispahan: correspondence, 1936–1948* (1976) · *Memories of Jinnah: K. H. Khurshid*, ed. K. Hasan (1990) · S. S. Pirzada, ed., *Foundations of Pakistan: All-India Muslim League documents, 1906–1947*, 1: *1906–24* (1969) · S. S. Pirzada, ed., *Foundations of Pakistan: All-India Muslim League documents, 1906–1947*, 2: *1924–27* (1969) · E. S. Montagu, *An Indian diary*, ed. V. Montagu (1930) · Aga Khan, *The memoirs of Aga Khan: world enough and time* (1954)
Archives National Archives of Pakistan, Islamabad · University of Karachi, archives of the Freedom Movement | Bodl. Oxf., corresp. with Lord Monckton · priv. coll., Syed Shamsul Hasan collection · PRO, corresp. with Sir Stafford Cripps, CAB 127/136 | FILM Archive Films, London · BFI NFTVA, news footage · British Movietone News, London · British Pathé News, London · IWM FVA, 'The dominions of India and Pakistan', August 1947, MGH 1394 · IWM FVA, actuality footage · IWM FVA, documentary footage · IWM FVA, news footage · MacDonald and Associates, Chicago · Ministry of information and broadcasting, Bombay, films division · National Archives of Pakistan, Islamabad, Quaid-i-Azam archives · National Film Archive of Pakistan, c/o The Ismaili Centre, London · National Film Archives, Bombay · Omar Khan archives, San Francisco · Reuters, London · U. Cam., Centre of South Asian Studies · UCLA Film and TV Archive, Hollywood, California · San Francisco, Shah collection | SOUND BL NSA, news recordings · National Archives of Pakistan, Islamabad, Quaid-i-Azam archives
Likenesses photograph, *c*.1945, Hult. Arch. [*see illus.*] · J. Harley, painting, 1948, government of Pakistan, department of archaeology and museums · M. Bourke-White and W. Vandivart, photographs, repro. in *Life Magazine* · photographs, National Archives of Pakistan, Islamabad, Quaid-i-Azam MSS · photographs, priv. coll.

Jinner, Sarah (*fl.* **1658–1664**), compiler of almanacs and medical practitioner, has left no trace of her family or background and is known only through the pioneering series of almanacs she published from 1658 to 1664, aimed mainly at women. Her woodcut portrait depicts an elegantly dressed figure, and her style indicates that she was well educated and aiming at a respectable audience. The almanacs are distinctive for their spirited assertion of women's abilities, their frank treatment of female medical problems, and their combative observations on contemporary politics. Acknowledging in her first edition that readers 'may wonder to see one of our Sex in print, especially in the Celestial Sciences' (Jinner, 1658, sig. B), she insisted that women were the equals of men in judgement and memory, 'although it is the policy of men, to keep us from education and schooling, wherein we might give testimony of our parts by improvement' (ibid.). She ridiculed conventional medical wisdom on sexual differences, scorning as 'witty Coxcombs' those who spoke of women 'as if we were but imperfect pieces, and that Nature intending a man, when the feminine conception proves weak there issues a woman' (ibid.). As proofs of female ability she cited the political achievements of Queen Elizabeth (remarking tartly that 'all your Princes now a-dayes are like Dunces in comparison of her' (ibid.)), the poetry of the countess of Newcastle and Katherine Philips, and the medical and philosophical learning of the countess of Kent. Jinner's advocacy did not overstep accepted bounds, however, and she explained that she wrote 'not to animate our sex, to assume or usurp the breeches', but to make men more appreciative of their wives (ibid., sig. Bv).

The almanac sections of Jinner's publications, supplying astronomical and astrological tables, were standard in form and probably supplied by the Company of Stationers, as in many series. Her own contribution came in the prognostication sections, which supplied general observations and medical information, especially on reproductive problems. She advised on infertility in women and men, and how to trigger or stop menstruation, and gave tips for parents on how they might, 'by Art, get a Boy or a Girl, which they desire most' (Jinner, 1659, sig. B). She offered advice too on hernias, ruptures, and male genital problems. 'It is not fit the world should be deprived of such helps to Nature', she observed, 'for the want of which, many, by their Modesty, suffer much', being too bashful to speak openly to their physicians (ibid.). Jinner urged readers to keep these medical recipes for future reference, and recommended *The Woman's Counsellor*, possibly *De morbis foemineis, the Woman's Counsellor* (1657), translated from the Latin of Alexander Massaria by Robert Turner, and *The Secret Miracles of Nature* (1658), by the sixteenth-century Flemish physician and astrologer Levinus Lemnius, for further information.

Jinner's early editions also included remarkably frank comments on contemporary political affairs. In her almanac for 1659 she deplored the 'Arbitrary commands' of oppressive rulers (Jinner, 1659, sig. B2v). 'The best Title is power,' she remarked cynically. 'Other claims are void' (ibid., sig. C2). But she prophesied that the people, hitherto stupidly passive, would soon find champions to assert their liberties, anticipated popular uprisings, and predicted that the people would also demand a new parliament, observing that though parliaments were 'bad food, yet they are good Physick' (ibid., sig. C2v). The almanacs also included sharp attacks on greedy lawyers and worldly clerics. Jinner acknowledged that she worded her political predictions very carefully, 'lest I should be taken as a Trumpet to precede Rebellion: however, at a venture I will say, that a people are not bound to obey well, when Governors do not govern well' (ibid., sig. C3). Her thinly veiled attacks on the Cromwellian regime were open to both republican and cavalier readings, perhaps deliberately. Her publisher, John Streater, a former army officer, was a known republican sympathizer. But several features would appear to hint at royalist associations, such as her praise of the poetry of Newcastle and her early awareness of Katherine Philips, her scathing contempt for the soldiery ('the scum of Mankind'; ibid., sig. B3), and her fierce attacks on the 'impudent and audacious publike bablings' of sectaries, visionaries, and 'Lay Pulpetiers' (ibid., sig. C2). Her prediction that 'Ancient sports and pastimes (heretofore suppressed) grow again in fashion' may also suggest royalist sympathies (Jinner, 1658, sig. C2v). On foreign affairs, Jinner hinted at defeat in the war with Spain unless there was an early peace. This did not indicate any sympathy for Catholicism, for she condemned the papacy, and assured readers that the Roman Catholic church would fail to suppress the French Jansenists. Her aversion to the war lay in its disastrous effect on English commerce, and she paid grudging tribute to the Dutch for pursuing commercial advantage while their neighbours indulged in crippling wars. While the English government failed to protect commerce, she complained, the Dutch 'account it their principal strength to enrich the people' (Jinner, 1659, sig. C2v). Jinner's last known edition, for 1664, contained no sensitive remarks on political or religious matters, which may indicate a more positive attitude towards the Restoration regime. She confined herself instead to medical matters, including herbal recipes to take away sexual desire in both women and men, and echoed her earlier interest in witchcraft by offering remedies for sufferers convinced they had been made impotent by witchcraft.

Jinner may have been a woman of independent means, publishing simply for personal satisfaction, but was more probably a medical practitioner. Though most almanac compilers received only a pittance for their copy, such publications were a very effective means of publicizing their professional services. Jinner reported that her first edition had been very well received, a claim reinforced in 1659 by the appearance of *The Womans Almanack, or, Prognostication for Ever*, by 'Sarah Ginnor, student in physick'. This was an attempt to capitalize on Jinner's success by plagiarizing her text and adding popular and voyeuristic lore, spiced with crude humour. It did not in fact contain an almanac, and was more akin to traditional perpetual prognostications such as *Erra pater*. Nothing further is known of Jinner herself after her 1664 edition, which had a substantial print run of 8000 copies. A casual reference in 1673 by the professional soldier Captain Henry Herbert, linking Jinner with the famous astrologer Richard Saunders (1613–1675), shows that her name remained well known and may indicate that she was still alive at that date.   BERNARD CAPP

Sources S. Jinner, *An almanack and prognostication for … 1659* [1659] · B. S. Capp, *Astrology and the popular press: English almanacs, 1500–1800* (1979) · E. Hobby, *Virtue of necessity: English women's writing, 1649–1688* (1988) · C. Blagden, 'The distribution of almanacks in the second half of the seventeenth century', *Studies in Bibliography*, 11 (1958), 107–16 · 'Captain Henry Herbert's narrative of his journey through France with his regiment, 1671–3', ed. J. Childs, *Camden miscellany, XXX*, CS, 4th ser., 39 (1990), 271–369
Likenesses woodcut, repro. in Jinner, *Almanack and prognostication*, title-page

Jix. *See* Hicks, William Joynson-, first Viscount Brentford (1865–1932).

Joachim, Harold Henry (1868–1938), philosopher, was born in London on 28 May 1868, the second child and only son of Henry Joachim, a London wool merchant, who as a boy had come to England from Kitsee in Hungary, and his wife, Ellen Margaret, daughter of the organist and composer Henry Thomas Smart. He was educated at Harrow School and at Balliol College, Oxford, where he won the senior classical scholarship in 1886. He was awarded a first class in classical moderations (1888) and in *literae humaniores* (1890), and in the latter year was elected to a prize fellowship at Merton College. He lectured on moral philosophy at St Andrews University from 1892 to 1894, when he returned to Balliol as lecturer in philosophy under J. A. Smith. In 1897 he succeeded William Wallace as fellow and tutor in philosophy at Merton. In 1919 he was appointed to the Wykeham professorship of logic at Oxford in succession to J. Cook Wilson, and held the chair until his retirement in 1935.

Joachim's main publications were *A Study of the Ethics of Spinoza* (1901); *The Nature of Truth* (1906); and translations of Aristotle's *De lineis insecabilibus* and *De generatione et corruptione* (published respectively in vol. 6, 1908, and vol. 2, 1922, of the Oxford translation of the *Works of Aristotle*); the translation of the *De generatione* was followed in the same year by a revised text with introduction and commentary. His almost completed commentary on Spinoza's *Tractatus de intellectus emendatione* was published posthumously in 1940. His lectures on logic were also published posthumously as *Logical Studies* (1948) as was his *Descartes's Rules for the Direction of the Mind* (1957).

All these publications were mostly critical and expository. None of Joachim's contemporaries ranked higher than he either as a Spinozist or as a textual critic and interpreter of Aristotle. All were written in a close but luminous style, to which his undergraduate pupil T. S. Eliot acknowledged a great debt, commenting that 'to his criticism of my papers I owe an appreciation of the fact that good writing is impossible without clear and distinct ideas' (letter in *The Times*, 4 Aug 1938).

But to study minutely and scrupulously the meaning of the great thinkers was always for Joachim a means to solving his own philosophical questions. A pupil of R. L. Nettleship and, at Merton, a colleague of F. H. Bradley, he shared in general the idealist views which then dominated Oxford philosophy. In his most original work, *The Nature of Truth*, he criticizes the correspondence theory of truth as propounded by Bertrand Russell and G. E. Moore, and presents a coherence theory which Russell regarded as the best statement of an idealist theory of truth. Joachim proceeds by examining doctrines of Aristotle, Descartes, Spinoza, and Bradley. Although influenced by the latter, he confesses himself in the main inspired by Hegel; he regarded Bradley as still tinged with the empiricism of his opponents and too much affected by Lotze's reaction from Hegel. But although he conceived himself as working in Hegel's shadow, he was always loath to attempt exposition of Hegel's system, and he offers his conclusions with none of Hegel's untroubled confidence. Very certain of his own way of thinking, he pursued it without compromise; but he was most cautious in estimating the distance which he had travelled. Despite his lifelong deference to the views of J. A. Smith, who in his later years acknowledged Benedetto Croce as his master, Joachim did not fully share Smith's enthusiasm for the Italian idealists. He would praise them for going straight to the point, but he did not regard their contribution to philosophy as fundamental.

The part which Joachim played in the life and affairs of the university was restricted by his intense devotion to philosophy. His pupils at Merton found him an exacting but infinitely patient teacher, though he thought himself a failure in that regard. As a lecturer he was much praised and respected. Lord Franks remembered him giving 'the most marvellous performance—polished, learned, acute, at times witty' (interview). His acquaintance with undergraduates studying other subjects was small, but at Merton and subsequently as Wykeham professor at New College his acumen both as advocate and as critic made him a most influential member of the governing body.

In 1907 Joachim married his first cousin Elisabeth Anna Marie Charlotte, daughter of Joseph Joachim, the violinist. A son and two daughters were born of this extremely happy marriage. His admiration for his uncle was a deep influence on his life. He was himself a considerable musician and a violinist of great talent (though, characteristically, he for long gave up playing because he could not find time to practise sufficiently), and he did much to help Oxford music. It came naturally to him to illustrate the notion of a coherent whole in terms of a musical composition, and all his philosophic activity, his writings, his phrasing and diction when he lectured or discussed,

showed something akin to the exact and delicate technique of the classical violinist.

The keenness of Joachim's mind, the quiet candour of his conversation, and that sense of the greatness of his subject which he always succeeded in conveying, gained him the devotion and high respect of all his friends, but of none more than of those who asked, and always obtained, his help. The generosity with which he would read and criticize, unsparingly but constructively, work presented for his advice was never stinted even in the last years of his life, when he had become almost blind from cataract.

Joachim was elected a fellow of the British Academy in 1922 and an honorary fellow of Merton in 1919 and of New College in 1936; he received the honorary degree of LLD from St Andrews University in 1923. He died at Croyde, Devon, on 30 July 1938.

G. R. G. MURE, *rev.* MARK J. SCHOFIELD

Sources *The Times* (2 Aug 1938) · H. W. B. Jones, 'Harold Henry Joachim, 1868–1938', *PBA*, 24 (1938) · personal knowledge (1949) · interview with Lord Franks by Brian Harrison, NI5445T · 'Harold Henry Joachim', *Oxford*, 5/2 (winter 1938), 17–18 · R. Mason, 'Joachim, Harold Henry', *Biographical dictionary of twentieth-century philosophers*, ed. S. Brown, D. Collinson, and R. Wilkinson (1996) · *CGPLA Eng. & Wales* (1938)
Archives Bodl. Oxf., lecture notes · Magd. Oxf., archives (?) · New College, Oxford, papers
Likenesses W. Stoneman, two photographs, 1922–32, NPG
Wealth at death £41,771 18s. 9d.: probate, 29 Sept 1938, *CGPLA Eng. & Wales*

Joachim, Joseph (1831–1907), violinist, born in Kitsee, near Pressburg, on 28 June 1831, was the seventh of the eight children of Julius Joachim, a wool merchant, and his wife, Fanny. After the family moved to Pest in 1833 he began violin lessons with Stanislaw Serwaczyński, and he made his first public appearance in 1839, playing a double concerto by Friedrich Eck with his teacher. He then studied in Vienna with Hauser, George Hellmesberger, and Joseph Boehm, and from 1843 in Leipzig, where Mendelssohn's direct involvement in his progress profoundly influenced his musical and intellectual development.

Joachim began his long and fruitful relationship with England in 1844. Mendelssohn's letter of recommendation referred to 'his promise of a noble service to art'. After two insignificant public appearances, Joachim made his real London début, under Mendelssohn's conductorship, at the Philharmonic concert of 27 May in the then rarely performed Beethoven violin concerto (playing his own cadenzas). The review in the *Illustrated London News* described him as

a little boy of thirteen, who perhaps is the first violin player, not only of his age, but of his *siècle*. ... His tone is of the purest *cantabile* character; his execution is most marvellous, and at the same time unembarrassed; his style is chaste, but deeply impassioned at moments; and his deportment is that of a conscious, but modest genius! (Fuller Maitland, 8)

Joachim visited England twice more (1847 and 1849) before assuming the leadership of Liszt's orchestra in Weimar in 1849; but, disillusioned with the so-called New German School, he served as Konzertmeister in Hanover

Joseph Joachim (1831–1907), by Julia Margaret Cameron, 1868

from 1853 to 1866. About 1854 he converted from Judaism to Christianity. In 1863 he married the contralto Amalie Weiss (Schneeweiss; 1839–1899), from whom he separated in 1884. The great success of his visits to England in 1852, 1858, and 1859 led him, from 1862, to make them an annual event. By this time Joachim's unchallengeable pre-eminence among modern violinists was beginning to be widely acknowledged in England. Haweis, for instance, observed in *Music and Morals* in 1871:

> M. Joachim is the greatest living violinist; no man is so nearly to the execution of music what Beethoven was to its composition. There is something massive, complete and unerring about M. Joachim that lifts him out of the list of great players, and places him on a pedestal apart. Other men have their specialities; he has none. Others rise above or fall below themselves; he is always himself, neither less nor more. He wields the sceptre of his bow with the easy royalty of one born to reign; he plays Beethoven's concerto with the rapt infallible power of a seer delivering his oracle, and he takes his seat at a quartet very much like Apollo entering his chariot to drive the horses of the sun.   (Haweis, 504)

It seemed possible in the late 1860s that Joachim might make his permanent home in England. However, his assumption of the directorship of the newly established Hochschule für Ausübende Tonkunst in 1868 established him in Berlin, where he soon founded the Joachim Quartet. In London, Joachim led another regular quartet (with Louis Ries, Ludwig Strauss, and Alfredo Piatti) for many years at the Popular Concerts. Cambridge University awarded him an honorary doctorate in music in 1877, on which occasion he conducted Brahms's first symphony. He later received doctorates from Oxford and Glasgow. In 1904 a special concert was given at the Queen's Hall to celebrate the sixtieth anniversary of his appearance in

England, which included his overture *Henry IV*, and in which he played the Beethoven concerto. As a composer he made little impact, but as a musician his influence on British musical life was profound. He provided an authoritative example of 'purity of style without pedantry; fidelity of interpretation combined with a powerful individuality' (Grove, *Dict. mus.*). From 1900 he visited London annually with his Berlin Quartet, and in 1906 they gave a series of Brahms's complete chamber music at the Queen's Hall. A planned visit the following year was prevented by Joachim's illness, and he died in Berlin on 15 August 1907. He was buried in the cemetery of the Kaiser Wilhelm Gedächtnisskirche, Charlottenburg, Berlin, on 19 August.   CLIVE BROWN

Sources A. Moser, *Joseph Joachim*, trans. L. Durham (1901) · J. A. Fuller Maitland, *Joseph Joachim* (1905) · J. Joachim and A. Moser, eds., *Letters from and to Joseph Joachim*, ed. and trans. N. Bickley (1914) · H. R. Haweis, *Music and morals* (1871) · P. David, 'Joachim, Joseph', Grove, *Dict. mus.* (1904–10) · [F. G. Edwards], 'Portrait of Joseph Joachim', *MT*, 39 (1898), 225–30 · F. G. E. [F. G. Edwards], *MT*, 48 (1907), 577–83
Archives BL, family corresp., Add. MS 42718 | BL, letters to Sir George Grove, Egerton MS 3095
Likenesses R. Lehmann, drawing, 1851, BM · J. M. Cameron, photograph, 1868, priv. coll. [*see illus.*] · E. J. F. Berdermann, oils, 1870, Royal College of Music, London · J. Archer, oils, 1876, Corporation of London · A. E. Donkin, pencil drawing, 1880, Royal College of Music, London · H. von Herkomer, oils, 1882, Trinity Cam. · F. Heyser, oils, 1888, Berlin Museum, Germany · W. & D. Downey, photograph, NPG; repro. in W. Downey and D. Downey, *The cabinet portrait gallery* (1890) · Kingsbury & Notcutt, cabinet photograph, NPG · L. Lowestam, group portrait, etching (*The Quartett*; after Bruck-Lajos), BM · C. Reutlinger, carte-de-visite, NPG · Spy [L. Ward], caricature, watercolour study, NPG; repro. in *VF* (5 Jan 1905) · G. F. Watts, oils, Watts Gallery, Compton, Surrey · bronze bust, Corporation of London · photograph, NPG

Joad, Cyril Edwin Mitchinson (1891–1953), philosopher, was born on 12 August 1891 in Durham, the only child of Edwin Joad, university lecturer, and his wife, Mary Smith. His father became a school inspector and moved the family to Southampton. Cyril attended the Dragon School, Oxford, and Blundell's School, Tiverton, before entering Balliol College, Oxford, in 1910. There he developed most of the opinions that he expounded, essentially unamended, for at least the next thirty years.

Greek philosophy fascinated Joad, whose enthusiasm for Plato and Aristotle led not only to a first in *literae humaniores* (1914) but also to a contemporary brand of radical positivism. On his arrival in Oxford he had been a believer in the literal truth of the Bible. Henceforth rationalism would be his creed: humanity was not evil; it was stupid. Intelligent men had a duty to spread enlightenment and rebuild the world on a logical basis. The socialism of G. D. H. Cole, H. G. Wells, and G. B. Shaw appealed to him and, after toying with syndicalism, he joined the Fabian Society in 1912. In patent imitation of Shaw, Joad took to expressing his ideas in startling and provocative ways, leavening intellectual arrogance with witty epigrams (usually prepared in advance). His Fabianism was sincere, though: despite being the John Locke scholar in mental

Cyril Edwin Mitchinson Joad (1891–1953), by Howard Coster, 1940s

philosophy (1914), he decided to join the labour exchanges department of the Board of Trade (later part of the Ministry of Labour) in the hope of infusing the civil service with a socialist ethos. He married Mary White in 1915 and they set up home in West Humble, near Dorking. Quite soon they had a son and two daughters.

As a senior civil servant Joad did not have to face the dilemma that conscription presented to other pacifists. Far from shaking his beliefs, the First World War indicated to him how sorely the human race needed more rationality. His daily work bored him, so he channelled his energy into writing, contributing book reviews and articles to left-wing journals, such as the *Daily Herald* and *New Statesman and Nation*, in disregard of civil service rules on political impartiality. Then came the first of a stream of books on philosophy, with which he hoped to make his name and contrive a return to academia. It was the outspoken agnosticism of *Common Sense Ethics* (1921) and *Common Sense Theology* (1922) that gained most attention: Joad declared Christianity moribund and rejoiced that clergymen would be extinct by 1960. Unreason in every shape was his foe: superstition, romanticism, psychoanalysis, and also outmoded social convention. He hated 'Victorianism' and loved to shock. What reforms did reason require? Easier divorce and birth control, legalized abortion and sodomy, an end to Sunday trading laws and performing animals,

sterilization of the feeble-minded, total disarmament, and less frequent baths.

Joad defied moral orthodoxy in deed just as in word. He left his wife in 1921 and moved to Hampstead in London with a student teacher named Marjorie Thomson, who turned out to be the first of many live-in lovers. He introduced them all as 'Mrs Joad' and counted himself a polygamist (though actually married only once). Sexual desire, he opined, resembled a buzzing bluebottle that needed to be swatted promptly before it distracted a man of intellect from higher things. (Personal experience later led him to recommend nudism as an anaphrodisiac.) Female minds lacked objectivity; he had no interest in talking to women who would not go to bed with him. A surprising number would—notwithstanding his increasingly gnome-like appearance. Joad was short and rotund, with bright little eyes, round, rosy cheeks, and a stiff, bristly beard. He dressed in old tweeds of great shabbiness as a test: anyone who sneered at his clothing was too petty to merit acquaintance.

Notoriety and flippancy counted against Joad at job interviews. Not until 1930 was he able to leave the civil service on gaining the post of head of philosophy at Birkbeck College, University of London. It was a small department, with two other lecturers, but Joad made the most of it. He had a real gift for teaching: eager and compelling, he so excelled at explaining great thinkers to novices that his open lectures attracted all sorts of people. When other philosophers refused to take him seriously, Joad implied that they resented a blackleg who admitted outsiders to professional mysteries. With his *Guide to Modern Thought* (1933) and *Guide to Philosophy* (1936), he established himself as the subject's foremost popularizer. The university gave him a DLitt degree in 1936 and promoted him to reader in 1945.

C. E. M. Joad's original contributions to philosophy were rooted in Plato and Aristotle (and influenced by Shaw, Samuel Butler, Bergson, and Russell). He upheld traditional metaphysics, with a dogged emphasis on objectivity in ethics and aesthetics. The four ultimate values, he argued, were truth, beauty, goodness, and happiness. The task of the philosopher was to derive moral precepts consonant with the pursuit of them, so men might know how best to live. This bore little relation to the fashionable currents of contemporary thought, but Joad feared that logical positivists and existentialists were sapping the foundations of civilization with subjectivism and relativism.

Though Marxists scorned 'goodness, truth, and beauty' as so much bourgeois escapism, Joad shared their desire for the destruction of the capitalist system. The Fabian Society had expelled him in 1925, however, for sexual misbehaviour at its summer school (and he did not rejoin until 1943). Disenchanted with Labour in office, he became director of propaganda for the New Party in February 1931, but altercations with Oswald Mosley drove him to resign, along with John Strachey, five months later. Nazism horrified Joad, who continued to think that the best way to preserve peace was to encourage individuals to refuse military service. On 9 February 1933 he persuaded the Oxford Union to resolve by 275 votes to 153 'That this house will under no circumstances fight for its King and Country'. Pressure groups enjoying his especial support included the National Peace Council, No More War, the National Civil Liberties Union, the Next Five Years Group, and the Federation of Progressive Societies and Individuals.

Joad also involved himself in psychical research with the aim of demystifying the allegedly supernatural. Critics asked if it was quite necessary to go to the Harz Mountains and recite spells in Latin in order to prove that the 'Blocksberg tryst' did not turn a goat into a beauteous youth. More serious was his long crusade to preserve the English countryside from industrial exploitation, ribbon development, overhead cables, and destructive tourism. He wrote angrily of the desecration of the rural landscape, viewing it as one manifestation of a transcendent threat: technology was advancing so much faster than human wisdom that scientists might have to submit to a moratorium on new inventions. Leaving London most weekends, he led organized rambling parties and recklessly rode to hounds. Hunting was his only guilty passion; generally, Joad seemed to imagine that, by gleefully confessing his moral weaknesses in print, he escaped any obligation to curb them.

Terrified of finding himself alone and unoccupied, Joad averaged nine lectures per week and two books per year. He played as hard as he worked, and always to win, his conduct on the tennis court inspiring the humorist Stephen Potter's concept of 'gamesmanship'. Bridge, chess, and hockey on Hampstead Heath filled spare hours, as did the pianola (on which he performed no music more recent than Beethoven). His home was modest, but his hospitality was lavish. He liked dining with the distinguished and with bright young people. Good conversation exhilarated him, although he described himself as psychologically obtuse to the point of insensitiveness. Many could cite examples of his egotism. 'Do you mind changing beds with me?' he asked a hotel room-mate: 'I think these sheets are rather damp' (Martin, 137). Yet even those who considered him a humbug could find his company stimulating in small doses—and that was all he cared to give them, for he soon wanted a fresh audience.

Late in 1939 Joad still maintained that the sacrifice of liberty was preferable to men being gored by bayonets. By May 1940 he had changed his mind: civilization itself was at stake. He begged the Ministry of Information to make use of his services. On 1 January 1941, BBC radio launched a new weekly programme: The Brains Trust invited a panel of thinkers to answer listeners' questions, which ranged from 'How does a fly land upside-down on the ceiling?' to 'What is the meaning of life?' The regular panellists were Julian Huxley, A. B. Campbell, and C. E. M. Joad. With his mental agility, flair for controversy, fund of anecdotes, and high piping voice, Joad emerged as the star of a show that was heard by more people than any other spoken broadcast save the news. His opening line, 'It all depends what you mean by—', became a prevalent catch-phrase.

Conservatives complained about political bias, but the general public took 'Professor' Joad for Britain's leading philosopher. (Bertrand Russell detested him.)

Joad gave after-dinner speeches, opened bazaars, advertised tea, and sold more books than ever. In 1946 he purchased a farm near Hawksley in Hampshire. The Labour Party welcomed him back, though he withdrew as a candidate in 1945 and lost a by-election for the Scottish Universities in 1946. Joad's ebullience hid anxiety. His pacifism had not survived the war; his agnosticism was crumbling: Auschwitz testified to the reality of evil. Even socialism proved unsatisfying under a Labour government. Desiring eminence, he had won celebrity.

In April 1948 Joad was convicted of riding on a Waterloo–Exeter train without a ticket. A habitual fare-dodger, he offered weak excuses. The £2 fine was nothing to the loss of his (well-founded) hopes of a peerage. The BBC dropped him from The Brains Trust. Then a thrombosis confined him to bed. Estranged from his children, he tried to distract himself with tutorial teaching and writing, blaming the USA squarely for the cold war and announcing his discovery of humility. In The Recovery of Belief (1952), Joad endorsed Christianity and the Anglican church. He died of cancer at his home, 4 East Heath Road, Hampstead, London, on 9 April 1953.

Cyril Joad was an outstanding educator, a tireless proponent of 'progressive' causes, and one of the best-known broadcasters of the 1940s. His religious conversion alienated radical agnostics who might otherwise have kept his reputation alive.   JASON TOMES

Sources G. Thomas, *Cyril Joad* (1992) · J. V. Crangle, 'Joad, Cyril Edwin Mitchinson', *BDMBR*, vol. 3, pt 1 · C. E. M. Joad, *The book of Joad* (1935) · K. Martin, *Editor* (1968) · H. Nicolson, *Diaries and letters*, ed. N. Nicolson, 3 vols. (1966–8) · *The Times* (10 April 1953) · J. B. Coates, *Ten modern prophets* (1944) · R. Wilkinson, 'Cyril Edwin Mitchinson Joad', *Biographical dictionary of twentieth-century philosophers*, ed. S. Brown, D. Collinson, and R. Wilkinson (1996), 381–2 · H. Thomas, *With an independent air* (1977) · D. Matless, *Landscape and Englishness* (1998) · A. J. Ayer, *Part of my life* (1977) · *DNB*
Archives Georgetown University, Washington, DC, Lauinger Library, corresp. with Sir Arnold Lunn · King's Lond., Liddell Hart C., corresp. with Sir B. H. Liddell Hart · U. Sussex, corresp. with *New Statesman* magazine
Likenesses H. Coster, photographs, 1935, NPG · H. Coster, photograph, 1940–49, NPG [*see illus.*] · M. Gordon, oils, 1942, NPG · P. Angadi, priv. coll. · K. Pollak, photograph, NPG · photographs, Hult. Arch.
Wealth at death £36,953 16s. 7d.: probate, 13 Aug 1953, *CGPLA Eng. & Wales*

Joan. *See* Joanna, countess of Toulouse (1165–1199).

Joan [Siwan] (d. 1237), princess of Gwynedd, wife of Llywelyn ab Iorwerth, was the illegitimate daughter of *John, king of England, and an unknown mother. A charge for a ship 'to carry the king's daughter and the king's accoutrements to England' from Normandy in 1203 (*Magni rotuli*, 2.569) probably refers to her. She seems to have been betrothed to *Llywelyn ab Iorwerth, prince of Gwynedd, before 15 October 1204 and to have married him in the spring of 1205, though the Chester annalist dates the marriage to 1204 and the Worcester annalist to 1206. Part of her dowry, the castle and manor of Ellesmere, was granted to Llywelyn on 16 April 1205.

Joan frequently acted as an intermediary between her husband and her father. In 1211, when John had conducted a successful campaign in north Wales, 'Llywelyn, being unable to suffer the king's rage, sent his wife, the king's daughter, to him, by the counsel of his leading men, to seek to make peace with the king on whatever terms he could' (*Brut y tywysogyon*, s.a.). Llywelyn was obliged to hand over hostages, pay a heavy tribute of cattle, and cede the four cantrefs of north-east Wales to John. In September 1212, when John was preparing another attack on Wales, Joan sent him a warning of treason among his barons, which, coupled with like warnings from other quarters, induced him to disband his host. In 1214 she interceded for some Welsh hostages in England, whose release she obtained the next year.

Joan continued her work of mediation after the accession of Henry III; a letter is extant in which she pleads earnestly with him for a good understanding between him and Llywelyn. In September 1224 she met Henry in person at Worcester, and in 1225 he granted her the manor of Rothley in Leicestershire, to be followed the next year by that of Condover in Shropshire. In 1226 Pope Honorius III declared her to be of legitimate birth. Early in 1228 the king took back the two manors, probably as a result of rising tension between Llywelyn and Hubert de Burgh, but Joan met Henry at Shrewsbury that summer and arranged a truce, and the manors were restored to her in November. Her son *Dafydd did homage to the king as Llywelyn's heir at Michaelmas 1229.

Dafydd, who in 1240 succeeded his father as prince of north Wales, was Joan's only son; but she also had a daughter, Elen, married first, in 1222, to John the Scot, earl of Chester, and second, in 1237 or 1238, to Robert de Quincy. Joan was probably also the mother of Llywelyn's daughters Gwladus and Margaret, and there is a reference to another daughter, Susanna. Gwladus's first husband was Reginald de Briouze; her stepson, William (V) de Briouze, was hanged by Llywelyn, probably at Crogen near Bala, on 2 May 1230, having been 'caught in Llywelyn's chamber with the king of England's daughter, Llywelyn's wife' (*Brut y tywysogyon*, s.a.). The affair may have begun two years earlier when William was Llywelyn's prisoner; he had returned to the prince's court to make arrangements for the marriage of his daughter Isabella to Dafydd. The suggestion by Kate Norgate in the *Dictionary of National Biography* that this episode was the result of a plot by Llywelyn, abetted by Joan, to avenge himself on William is unlikely; Joan was imprisoned by her husband and not released until 1231. By 1232 she and Llywelyn seem to have been reconciled since she was one of a delegation given safe conduct by Henry to meet him at Shrewsbury.

Joan died on 2 February 1237 at Aber near Bangor. At the place of her burial, Llan-faes in Anglesey, Llywelyn founded a Franciscan friary in her memory. Her stone coffin, removed at the dissolution of the friary, was rescued from use as a horse-trough early in the nineteenth century. It is now in the porch of Beaumaris church. On the slab that formed its cover is sculpted an effigy of the princess.   KATE NORGATE, *rev.* A. D. CARR

Sources J. E. Lloyd, *A history of Wales from the earliest times to the Edwardian conquest*, 3rd edn, 2 vols. (1939) · T. Jones, ed. and trans., *Brut y tywysogyon, or, The chronicle of the princes: Peniarth MS 20* (1952) · W. W. Shirley, ed., *Royal and other historical letters illustrative of the reign of Henry III*, 2 vols., Rolls Series, 27 (1862–6) · T. Stapleton, ed., *Magni rotuli scaccarii Normanniae sub regibus Angliae*, 2 vols., Society of Antiquaries of London Occasional Papers (1840–44) · T. Jones, ed. and trans., *Brut y tywysogyon, or, The chronicle of the princes: Red Book of Hergest* (1955)

Likenesses effigy on coffin lid, Beaumaris church, Anglesey

Joan (1210–1238), queen of Scots, consort of Alexander II, was the eldest daughter and third of five children of *John (1167–1216), king of England, and his second wife, *Isabella of Angoulême (*c.*1188–1246); her elder brothers were King *Henry III and *Richard, earl of Cornwall and king of Germany. *Eleanor, countess of Pembroke and Leicester, and *Isabella, consort of Frederick II, were her sisters. Although English chronicles supply different dates, the Melrose chronicle is almost certainly correct in giving 19 June 1221 for her marriage to *Alexander II, king of Scots (1198–1249), which was solemnized in York Minster. Born on 22 July 1210, she may have been discussed as Alexander's intended bride in 1212, when King John secured the right to arrange his marriage. In the event John used her not to stabilize Anglo-Scottish relations but as a pawn in continental politics. Rebuffing overtures from Philip II of France, who saw Joan as a potential daughter-in-law, he employed her as a peace-offering to his old enemies, the Lusignans of Poitou. Betrothed in 1214 to Hugues (*d.* 1248), future lord of Lusignan and count of La Marche (whose father had been John's rival for Isabella of Angoulême's hand in 1200), she passed into his custody with Saintes, Saintonge, and the Isle of Oléron as pledges for her dowry. After Hugues had failed in his bid to win an outright grant of these properties he rejected Joan, and wedded early in 1220 her widowed mother, Queen Isabella.

On 22 May of that year the English government asked for Joan's surrender at La Rochelle, clearly so that she might marry Alexander. Hugues, however, detained her as a hostage to ensure his continued seisin of Saintes, Saintonge, and Oléron and to gain Isabella's dower, withheld by the English crown against the restoration of the former territories. On 15 June 1220, in conference with Henry III at York, Alexander agreed to marry Henry's second sister, Isabella, if Joan remained unavailable; but after intervention by the pope, and assurances about Queen Isabella's dower, Hugues finally returned her the following autumn. On 18 June 1221 Alexander assigned Joan dower estates worth £1000 yearly, most notably Jedburgh, Crail, and Kinghorn. Matthew Paris has a plausible but uncorroborated story that Alexander later pressed Henry III for Northumberland on the grounds that John had promised it to him as a marriage gift with Joan. She accompanied Alexander on his negotiations with King Henry at Newcastle (September 1236) and at York (September 1237). Some correspondence between her and Henry survives; and one of her letters, written in 1224, presumably on behalf of Alexander's constable, Alan of Galloway, warned him of intelligence that Haakon IV of Norway intended to aid Hugh de Lacy in Ireland.

Joan evidently found Scottish society uncongenial, and her political influence was negligible. Her youth (she was only ten at her wedding), the dominating presence of her mother-in-law, Queen *Ermengarde (d. 1233), and her inability to bear children inevitably denied her a more prominent role. Nor was her position eased by periodic tensions between Alexander and Henry III. Matthew Paris hints that she ultimately became estranged from Alexander, and it was presumably her wish to spend more time at the English court that led Henry to provide her by 1236 with the manors of Driffield, Yorkshire, and Fen Stanton, Huntingdonshire, as convenient ports of call. In September 1237, probably aware that she was seriously ill, Joan left York to undertake a pilgrimage to Canterbury. She died at Havering, Essex, on 4 March 1238 in the arms of Henry and Richard of Cornwall, her younger brother, and was buried according to her wishes at the Cistercian nunnery of Tarrant (now Tarrant Keynston), Dorset, which subsequently benefited notably from the almsgiving of Henry, whose demonstrative concern for the salvation of his sister's soul suggests that he had been devoted to her. The tomb erected over her body was made on Henry's instructions in the Salisbury workshop of Elias of Dereham, and Henry later had an effigy of her carved in marble and placed beside it. These memorials no longer survive.

KEITH STRINGER

Sources A. O. Anderson and M. O. Anderson, eds., *The chronicle of Melrose* (1936) • Paris, *Chron.*, vols. 2–3 • A. O. Anderson, ed., *Scottish annals from English chroniclers, AD 500 to 1286* (1908); repr. (1991) • *CDS*, vol. 1 • D. A. Carpenter, *The minority of Henry III* (1990) • P. Chaplais, ed., *Diplomatic documents preserved in the Public Record Office*, 1 (1964) • A. O. Anderson, ed. and trans., *Early sources of Scottish history, AD 500 to 1286*, 2 (1922); repr. with corrections (1990)

Joan [Joan of Acre], **countess of Hertford and Gloucester** (1272–1307), princess, the second surviving daughter of *Edward I (1239–1307) and *Eleanor of Castile (1241–1290), was born at Acre early in 1272 during her father's crusade. The future *Edward II was her brother, and *Mary (1278–c.1332) was her sister. She was brought up in Ponthieu by her grandmother Jeanne de Dammartin, widow of Ferdinand III of Castile, until 1278 when Stephen of Penecester and his wife were sent by Edward I to bring her to England.

Edward I had begun negotiations the year before with Rudolf of Habsburg, king of the Romans, for Joan's marriage to his eldest son, Hartman; Rudolf promised to try to secure Hartman's election as king of the Romans and of Arles. Although plans were made for the celebration of the marriage in 1278, it was in fact put off, and Hartman was drowned in an accident on the ice in 1282. The agreement for Joan's marriage to Gilbert de *Clare, earl of Hertford and Gloucester, was made in 1283. Gilbert and his first wife, Alice de la Marche, had had only two daughters; this

marriage was dissolved in 1285, and a papal dispensation for the marriage to Joan was obtained four years later. Gilbert surrendered all his lands to the king, and they were settled jointly on Gilbert and Joan for their lives, and were then to pass to their children; if however the marriage was childless, the lands were to pass to Joan's children by any later marriage. The wedding took place at Westminster on 30 April 1290. Shortly afterwards both Gilbert and Joan took the cross, but neither went on crusade. They had one son, Gilbert de *Clare, who was born in May 1291, to the great joy of both parents, and three daughters, among them Elizabeth de *Clare and Margaret de *Clare. In 1294 Gilbert and Joan and their children were driven out of the Clare lordship of Glamorgan by the Welsh rebellion, and Gilbert died on 7 December 1295.

Because of the joint enfeoffment of Gilbert and Joan, the widowed countess remained in charge of the estates, performing homage to her father on 20 January 1296. The estates included lands in Ireland and Wales as well as the honours of Clare and Gloucester and other manors in England, and produced a yearly income of about £6000 in the early fourteenth century. Edward I planned for Joan to marry Amadeus V of Savoy, and the betrothal document was dated 16 March 1297. However by then Joan had secretly married a squire of Earl Gilbert's household, Ralph de *Monthermer, whom she had persuaded her father to knight. She is reputed to have said, 'It is not ignominious or shameful for a great and powerful earl to marry a poor and weak woman; in the reverse case it is neither reprehensible or difficult for a countess to promote a vigorous young man' (Trokelowe and Blaneforde, 27). Monthermer was imprisoned for a short time in Bristol Castle, but performed homage on 2 August 1297, and the Clare estates were restored to him and Joan (although Tonbridge and Portland were not restored until 1301). Monthermer enjoyed the title of earl of Hertford and Gloucester during his wife's lifetime. He and Joan had two sons and a daughter. Joan died at Clare, Suffolk, on 23 April 1307, and was buried in the church of the Augustinian friars there; she had made benefactions to the priory and built the Chapel of St Vincent.

JENNIFER C. WARD

Sources Rymer, *Foedera*, vol. 1 • *Ann. mon.* • A. Gransden, ed. and trans., *The chronicle of Bury St Edmunds, 1212–1301* [1964] • *Bartholomaei de Cotton … Historia Anglicana*, ed. H. R. Luard, Rolls Series, 16 (1859) • *The chronicle of Walter of Guisborough*, ed. H. Rothwell, CS, 3rd ser., 89 (1957) • H. R. Luard, ed., *Flores historiarum*, 3 vols., Rolls Series, 95 (1890) • [W. Rishanger], *The chronicle of William de Rishanger, of the barons' wars*, ed. J. O. Halliwell, CS, 15 (1840) • *Chronica Johannis de Oxenedes*, ed. H. Ellis, Rolls Series, 13 (1859) • *Johannis de Trokelowe et Henrici de Blaneforde … chronica et annales*, ed. H. T. Riley, pt 3 of *Chronica monasterii S. Albani*, Rolls Series, 28 (1866) • M. Altschul, *A baronial family in medieval England: the Clares, 1217–1314* (1965) • M. A. E. Green, *Lives of the princesses of England*, 2 (1849) • J. C. Parsons, ed., *The court and household of Eleanor of Castile in 1290*, Pontifical Institute of Medieval Studies: Texts and Studies, 37 (1977)
Archives BL • PRO

Joan [Joan of the Tower] (1321–1362), queen of Scots, consort of David II, was born in the Tower of London on 5 July 1321. She was the second daughter of *Edward II (1284–

1327), king of England, and *Isabella (1295–1358), daughter of Philippe IV, king of France. The future *Edward III was her elder brother, nearly nine years her senior. By the time she was four, despite her youth, she was already being proposed as a possible bride, first for the son and heir of the king of Aragon and then for Philippe, count of Valois (soon to be Philippe VI of France), but neither of these diplomatic moves came to anything.

Matters were different, though, when in 1327–8 Queen Isabella and Roger Mortimer, the effective rulers of England following the deposition of Edward II, tried to arrange a peace with the elderly Robert I of Scotland. No agreement was possible that did not recognize Robert's position as king of Scots—something which Edward II had consistently refused to do—and did not also surrender all claims to superiority over Scotland. To make this concession, which abandoned a position kings of England had maintained since 1291, required a guarantee of Scottish friendship, and this, it was hoped, was to be provided by a marriage between Joan, by now in her seventh year, and Robert's heir, David, the future *David II (1324–1371), who was aged four. On these terms, the treaty and the marriage were agreed in Edinburgh on 17 March 1328. The parties were too young to contract a valid marriage (David was not old enough to do so canonically until 1338), and this was covered by a provision that if the marriage had not been completed within two months of David's reaching the canonical age of fourteen, all concessions made in the treaty would be invalid. Formally, however, the pair were married on 17 July 1328 at Berwick, in the presence of Isabella, but not of either Edward III, whose absence is unexplained, or Robert I, who claimed to be too ill to attend. Even without the two kings it was a splendid occasion, on which King Robert spent over £2500. Joan then took up residence in Scotland with her infant husband, and became queen of Scots on his accession to the throne in 1329.

There is very little personal information about the rest of Joan's life. In 1334, after six years in Scotland of which we know nothing, she was taken from Dumbarton Castle to France with David, to find a safe refuge while Edward Balliol attempted to establish himself as king of Scotland, subject to the overlordship of Edward III. To further this attempt Balliol had already in 1332 proposed to Edward III that he might marry Joan, assuming that the as yet incomplete marriage to David were annulled. At this point Balliol was probably in his fifties, and nothing came of the suggestion. Until 1341 Joan remained at Château Gaillard in Normandy, where the couple and a number of their Scottish attendants were given accommodation by Philippe VI of France.

The return of the king and queen to Scotland on 2 June 1341 was greeted with widespread rejoicings; but on 17 October 1346 David was captured at the disastrous battle of Nevilles Cross, and he spent much of the next eleven years as a prisoner in England, apart from a brief stay in his kingdom in 1351–2. A safe conduct was issued for Joan to visit her husband while he was attending the St George's day festivities at Windsor in 1348, though so far as we know she did not take advantage of it. We must presume that during the years of David's captivity she resided somewhere in Scotland, perhaps in some sense as a hostage for his safety. There does not appear to be any reference to her in the few documents that have survived from the negotiations for David's release.

David's homecoming provoked a crisis in their relations. While in England, he had formed a liaison with Katherine Mortimer, whose origin is unknown. According to Walter Bower, writing in the fifteenth century, 'The king loved her more than all other women, and on her account his queen was entirely neglected while he embraced his mistress' (Bower, 7.321). Whether for that reason or for some other Joan was given two safe conducts from Edward III to travel to England, one at Christmas 1357 'on business touching us and David' and another in May 1358 'by our licence for certain causes' unspecified (RotS, 1.817, 822). In fact, she had left David and spent the rest of her life in England, where she received a regular pension of £200 a year from her brother. By 1362 payments of this pension were running in advance, which may suggest that it was hardly adequate. She was able to visit her mother before Isabella's death in August 1358. Whatever Joan's relations with her husband, she does appear on occasion to have acted on his behalf: in a document of February 1359 concerning the respite of payments for his ransom David acknowledges that this was granted by Edward III 'at the great and diligent request and instance of our dear companion the lady Joan his sister' (Regesta regum Scottorum, vol. 6, ed. B. Webster, 1982, 237). This, however, is probably simply a diplomatic formula.

Few comments on Joan's character have survived. One, written by the chronicler Andrew Wyntoun about the turn of the fourteenth century into the fifteenth, is in conventional terms: 'she was sweet and debonair, courteous, homely, pleasant and fair' (Andrew of Wyntoun, 2.502). She died on 7 September 1362 at the age of forty-one and was buried in the church of the Greyfriars, London.

BRUCE WEBSTER

Sources Johannis de Fordun Chronica gentis Scotorum / John of Fordun's Chronicle of the Scottish nation, ed. W. F. Skene, trans. F. J. H. Skene, 1 (1871), 353, 365, 380 • Andrew of Wyntoun, The orygynale cronykil of Scotland, [rev. edn], 3, ed. D. Laing (1879), 374, 466, 502 • W. Bower, Scotichronicon, ed. D. E. R. Watt and others, new edn, 9 vols. (1987–98), vol. 7, pp. 42–3, 150–51, 320–21 • CDS, 4.10, 16, 22 • RotS, 1.815, 817, 822, 848 • Scalacronica: the reigns of Edward I, Edward II and Edward III as recorded by Sir Thomas Gray, trans. H. Maxwell (1907), 128 • R. Nicholson, Scotland: the later middle ages (1974), vol. 2 of The Edinburgh history of Scotland, ed. G. Donaldson (1965–75); repr. (1989), 120–21, 167 • E. B. Fryde and others, eds., Handbook of British chronology, 3rd edn, Royal Historical Society Guides and Handbooks, 2 (1986), 39

Joan, *suo jure* **countess of Kent, and princess of Wales and of Aquitaine** [called the Fair Maid of Kent] (c.1328–1385), known (perhaps sarcastically) to her contemporaries as 'the Virgin of Kent', and to later generations as 'the Fair

Maid of Kent', was the daughter of *Edmund of Wood-stock, first earl of Kent (d. 1330), the half-brother of Edward II, and Margaret (d. 1349), sister and eventual heir of Thomas, Lord Wake. Her father was executed for treason when she was two, and Joan was subsequently adopted by the queen, *Philippa of Hainault, spending much of her childhood in the royal household. In 1337, Joan may have gone with the rest of the royal family to Flanders. By the time they returned to England Joan was twelve, and already seems to have had a reputation for beauty and gaiety. She had attracted the attention of Sir Thomas *Holland, a knight of the royal household, who persuaded her to marry him in the spring of 1340. The marriage was a clandestine one, per verba de praesenti; but although such unions were punishable by excommunication, the church none the less recognized them as valid contracts provided there were no impediments of relationship or previous marriage. So even though there was no publication of banns or blessing by a priest, the match was lawful and was duly consummated. Holland was with the English army all summer, and set out for Prussia in late 1340, remaining there until the middle of the following year. In the meanwhile, Joan's marriage seems either to have remained a secret or to have been regarded as invalid, because her mother arranged for her to wed William *Montagu, the son of the earl of Salisbury. It is also possible that Sir Thomas Holland was believed to have died. She was married to Montagu, this time with due ecclesiastical ceremony, in the winter of 1340–41, and remained with her new husband even after Sir Thomas Holland's return in 1341. The latter became steward to the young couple shortly after the younger Montagu succeeded to the earldom in 1344. However, Holland's real career was as a soldier, and he was abroad on the Crécy campaign in 1346–7; in the course of the fighting he was fortunate enough to capture one of the leaders of the French army, the count of Eu: Edward III paid him 80,000 florins for his prisoner.

It was possibly lack of funds, and perhaps also his financial dependence on Salisbury as his steward, that had prevented Holland from reclaiming his wife until now. Within a few months of the king's grant of the purchase money in June 1347, he began proceedings at Avignon for the return of Joan, declaring that he and Joan had been lawfully wedded and that the marriage had been consummated. Later, 'not daring to contradict the wishes of her relatives and friends', she had been married to the earl 'by their arrangement' in Holland's absence (Wentersdorf, 220). The earl, aided and abetted by Joan's mother, refused to acknowledge Sir Thomas's claim, who had therefore brought the present case. However, the papal envoys were unable to get the earl to plead before the court, and Holland, in a subsequent petition, alleged that the earl and his accomplices were holding Joan against her will and in seclusion. The pope intervened on Joan's behalf in May 1348, but a further eighteen months elapsed, largely through the delaying tactics of the earl and his attorney, before a papal bull, dated 13 November 1349, declared

Joan's marriage to Salisbury void, and ordered that her marriage to Holland be properly celebrated in facie ecclesie.

Joan and Holland had five children in the next few years; the eldest, Thomas *Holland, was born in 1350. In 1352 Joan's younger brother, John, died, and she became countess of Kent in her own right. The following year Sir Thomas was appointed lieutenant of the king in Brittany, and he later became governor of the Channel Islands and captain-general of all English lands in France and Normandy in 1359. Joan's movements during these years are unknown, but it is possible that she spent some time in France with her husband. Sir Thomas died unexpectedly in Normandy on 28 December 1360; Joan's widowhood was, however, brief. At some time in the spring or early summer of 1361, *Edward, prince of Wales (the Black Prince), asked for her hand in marriage. The betrothal seems to have been an entirely private affair, and both in view of Joan's previous marital history and her status, this was a surprising turn of events. In addition, the pair were related within the prohibited degrees—they were cousins, and the prince was godfather to Joan's eldest son. The match has given rise to much speculation. At the time of his betrothal to Joan there were plans for the prince to marry Margaret of Flanders. French chroniclers produced a fanciful romance telling of the unspoken love of Joan for the prince, and of the prince for Joan, and of the king's subsequent fury. In fact it seems unlikely that the king was outraged, since *Edward III, as well as his son, petitioned for a papal dispensation, which was granted on 7 September 1361.

On 6 October Joan publicly plighted her troth to the prince in the presence of the archbishop of Canterbury, and four days later, in the presence of most, if not all, of the royal family, including the king, and a large congregation, the wedding was celebrated at Windsor. Joan and the prince spent Christmas at Berkhamsted, one of the prince's favourite residences, where the king and queen visited them. Joan's style of living, which had once been restricted by her lack of income, had improved when she became countess of Kent and also inherited the lands of her uncle, Lord Wake; now it seems to have become positively extravagant. The prince, already renowned for his lavish gifts, spent large sums of money on clothes and jewellery for her early in 1362. She brought to his household her two sons and two daughters, one child having died in infancy. When the prince set sail for Aquitaine from Plymouth on 9 June 1362, the whole family accompanied him.

During the nine years that the prince spent in Aquitaine he and Joan had two sons. The eldest, Edward, was born in 1365, but died five years later. His younger brother, the future *Richard II, was born in January 1367. Relatively little is known about Joan's life in Aquitaine; she seems to have spent most of the time at Angoulême or Bordeaux. It was at Angoulême in April 1365 that the prince held the most magnificent tournament of his time in France, to celebrate Joan's churching after the birth of their eldest son, and the scale of the festivities gave rise to stories about the princess's love of luxury and the latest fashions.

As early as 1363 French visitors to the prince's court had reported that the princess and her ladies wore furred gowns with slit coats and great fringes; in the French view, these were copied from the mistresses of English free-booters, and were unsuitable for courtly society. The prince's affection for Joan is evident in his letter to her after the battle of Nájera; and on his return from Spain she met him at the cathedral at Bordeaux with his eldest son: he dismounted, and 'they walked together holding hands' to the bishop's palace, where they were staying (Chandos herald, 11.3771–2).

After the prince's return to England Joan seems some-times to have acted as his representative during his ill-ness: she wrote to thank the city of London for a gift of plate made to him in 1371, and went without him to Queen Philippa's anniversary service in August that year. On his death in 1376 Joan became guardian of the person of the young Richard II, and received his allowance, while one-third of the revenues of Wales were reserved to her once he became prince. Apart from administering the estates that had once belonged to her husband, she seems to have had considerable influence with the king: a large number of pardons and grants in the years 1377–85 are recorded as being 'at the request of the king's mother', far more than appear in similar periods in Edward III's reign at the prince of Wales's request. In 1378 she was effectively granted the balance of the revenues of her husband's lands for four years, to compensate for 'her great charges on the king's behalf after his father's death' (CPR, 1377–81, 180). Royal accounts permit some glimpses of her private life: the manors of Bushey and North Weald were repaired at her expense in 1377–8, and in May 1381 a new barge was ordered for her use.

In January 1379 Joan was with Richard and John of Gaunt, duke of Lancaster, when the citizens of London put on an entertainment for the prince at his palace at Kennington. This was a festive occasion, but less than a month later Gaunt had to seek refuge with the princess at Kennington, after he had aroused the Londoners' enmity. The princess sent three of her knights to ask the citizens to make peace with the duke for her sake, and she and Gaunt seem to have remained friendly, despite the ten-sions between the latter and Richard II once he passed from her control on becoming king in 1377. Gaunt had made grants to her sons by Sir Thomas Holland, and John, the younger, had married Gaunt's daughter Elizabeth. Joan appears to have favoured the Lollard knights rather more than Gaunt, and it was at her instigation that the proceedings against Wyclif were suspended in 1378. Her entourage certainly included leading figures in the Lol-lard movement, notably Sir Richard Stury and Sir Lewis Clifford (d. 1404).

Joan remained a popular figure, and when the mob invaded the Tower of London during the peasants' revolt in 1381 she escaped unharmed, though the ringleaders 'invited the king's mother to kiss them' (Chronicon Angliae, 291). Four years later, despite ill health which had caused her to grow so fat that she could scarcely stand up, she travelled between the court and Gaunt in order to make peace between the king and his uncle; Richard had tried to arrest him, and there was a danger of civil war. Her efforts led to a formal reconciliation, but did not resolve the cri-sis. Before Richard departed for Scotland in June 1385, he appointed thirteen knights, including Clifford and Stury, to act as her bodyguard. But within two months, on 14 August, she died, probably at Wallingford Castle, almost certainly as a result of her illness. The St Albans chronic-ler, however, believed that it was out of grief because her second son, John *Holland, earl of Huntingdon and later duke of Exeter (d. 1400), had murdered Ralph Stafford in cold blood in the course of a feud, and Richard, swearing to see that justice was done, had refused to listen to his mother's pleas for mercy. She asked to be buried, not with Prince Edward at Canterbury, but near the monument of Sir Thomas Holland in the Minorite church at Stamford; the burial was delayed until 27 January 1386, when the king returned from Scotland. She left to the king her new bed, decorated with golden leopards and with the silver ostrich feather badge of his father.   RICHARD BARBER

Sources K. P. Wentersdorf, 'The clandestine marriages of the Fair Maid of Kent', *Journal of Medieval History*, 5 (1979), 203–32 • A. Good-man, *John of Gaunt: the exercise of princely power in fourteenth-century Europe* (1992) • R. Barber, *Edward, prince of Wales and Aquitaine: a biog-raphy of the Black Prince* (1978) • M. le Colonel Babinet, 'Jeanne de Kent, princesse de Galles et d'Aquitaine', *Bulletin de la Société des Antiquaires de l'Ouest*, 6 (1894), 438– • *Chroniques de J. Froissart*, ed. S. Luce and others, 15 vols. (Paris, 1869–1975) • [T. Walsingham], *Chronicon Angliae, ab anno Domini 1328 usque ad annum 1388*, ed. E. M. Thompson, Rolls Series, 64 (1874) • Chandos herald, *Life of the Black Prince by the herald of Sir John Chandos*, ed. M. K. Pope and E. C. Lodge (1910) • *CPR, 1377–85* • *CIPM*, 16 • N. H. Nicolas, ed., *Testamenta vetusta: being illustrations from wills*, 1 (1826), 13–14 • M. C. B. Dawes, ed., *Register of Edward, the Black Prince*, 4 vols., PRO (1930–33) • Scrope vs. Grosvenor papers
Likenesses portrait, *c*.1380, BL, Cotton Nero D. vii, fol. 7*v*
Wealth at death see *CIPM*; Nicolas, *Testamenta*

Joan (*fl.* 1386–1389?). *See under* Women medical practi-tioners in England (*act. c*.1200–*c*.1475).

Joan [Joan of Navarre] (**1368–1437**), queen of England, sec-ond consort of Henry IV, was the second daughter of Charles II (Charles the Bad), king of Navarre (*d.* 1387), and Jeanne de Valois, daughter of Jean II, king of France. She was probably born at Évreux in Normandy, though by April 1369 the monastery of Santa Clara at Estella in Nav-arre was receiving a florin a day for her upbringing. Other-wise little is known about her childhood. Her mother died in 1373; royal accounts refer to medicine bought for her in 1379. During these years, however, her father was one of the most active and devious of European statesmen and, like all medieval rulers, he used his own children as diplo-matic pawns. Thus by 1380 Joan was betrothed to Juan, heir to the kingdom of Castile, and when nothing came of this Charles entered into lengthy negotiations for his daughter's marriage to John de *Montfort, duke of Brit-tany (*d.* 1399), a ruler who, after two marriages, still lacked an heir. The issue was complicated both by diplomatic considerations and by the need for a papal dispensation, and it was not until June 1386 that Breton envoys could be sent to collect their duke's bride. On 25 August the contract was finally concluded at Pamplona and on 2 September, in the cathedral of Bayonne, the marriage was celebrated in the presence of a ducal proctor. Joan and her entourage then journeyed by sea to Brittany where a second ceremony was held at Saillé near Guérande on 11 September with both parties present.

Despite a wide age difference it seems to have been a very successful union, with genuine affection on both sides. Generous terms for Joan's dower in the duchy were issued in February 1387 and she amply fulfilled her primary role. Although their eldest daughter, Jeanne, died as an infant, John's succession was ensured by the couple's other seven children, of whom the oldest was Pierre, born in 1389, renamed Jean, who ruled as duke from 1399 to 1442. Preoccupied with so many pregnancies, Joan inevitably played only a minor role in Breton politics, though there are hints of a talent for reconciliation which remained one of her most conspicuous traits. She thus saved some French ambassadors from her husband's wrath in 1391, and also attempted to mediate between him and his great domestic rival, Olivier, lord of Clisson, constable of France, with whom he conducted a bitter feud for almost thirty years. She also maintained close links with Navarre and took a full part in court ceremonial, accompanying John to England in April 1398, when he was issued with Garter robes; this was one of several opportunities she had to meet her future husband, Henry, earl of Derby (1367–1413) [*see* Henry IV].

With the death of John in November 1399 Joan assumed powers of regency; she finally restored relations with Clisson and attempted to resolve other disputes. Her recognition of the importance of visual symbolism for enhancing government is evident in the impressive funerary ceremonies she held for her husband in March 1400 and the equally magnificent coronation of John (V) at Rennes a year later. In her personal life, too, Joan kept abreast of aristocratic fashion; she enjoyed luxuries like rich clothes, expensive foodstuffs, spices, and wine, and kept exotic animals and birds. A finely illuminated psalter which she owned still survives.

Although Joan had known Henry IV, her senior by three years, before his accession, their marriage surprised many contemporaries, not least because of the speed with which it was concluded. On 14 March 1402 Joan appointed Anthony Rys, a Welshman in Breton service, as her proctor to open negotiations. On 20 March the Avignonese pope Benedict XIII granted her a dispensation to marry within the fourth degree. They were married by proxy at Eltham on 2 April 1402—using the form of words, recorded here in English for perhaps the first time, 'thereto I plight thee my troth'—though it was July before she had a further papal licence to live 'among schismatics', and another six months before she arrived, diverted unexpectedly to Falmouth, after a very rough sea passage from Camaret. Henry rushed to meet her at Exeter and the

marriage, followed by a sumptuous banquet, was solemnized at Winchester on 7 February 1403. At Westminster on 26 February Joan was crowned queen, and Richard Beauchamp, earl of Warwick (d. 1439), fought as her champion in a celebratory tournament. Who took the lead in arranging the match remains unclear, but a strong mutual attraction is evident, and Henry remained faithful and indulgent. Initially there was little enthusiasm in England and considerable opposition in Brittany, where Joan was compelled to relinquish the guardianship of John (V) to Philippe, duke of Burgundy, and also to leave her younger sons behind, although her two youngest daughters accompanied her to England. Few political or financial advantages followed; indeed the costs and size of the new queen's household became a matter of bitter political argument between 1404 and 1406 and she had to dismiss most of her (politically unimportant) Breton servants.

Joan was granted a dower of 10,000 marks p.a., the largest sum received by an English queen up to that time, but she experienced great difficulty in obtaining control of the manors on which it was assigned, many of them confiscated from rebels (and later returned to their heirs), or coming from the possessions of the late Queen Anne (d. 1394) and Katherine Swynford (d. 1403). Thus, among other properties, she held Havering atte Bower, Odiham, Nottingham, Woodstock, and Leeds in Kent, and spent some time at Cirencester, Sonning, and Devizes. She was also given a new tower near the gate to Westminster Hall for custody of her muniments. Some modern commentators have seen in her determination to exact her dower rights in full a greedy, acquisitive streak, especially since Joan contributed nothing financially to her second marriage despite her apparent wealth as a widowed duchess. But much of this was illusory: on 18 November 1404 she released to John (V) claims to 70,000 livres still allegedly due from her first marriage as well as an annual rent of 6000 livres on lands in Normandy. Payments of revenue collected on lands in the county of Nantes, which were rightfully hers, were infrequent. However, she maintained close ties with Brittany; her younger sons visited her—Arthur in 1404, and Gilles in 1409 and again in 1412, when he died in England. She was active in arranging the marriages of her daughters, though Marguerite died shortly after marrying Alain, heir to the vicomte de Rohan, in 1407. In 1408 she had a fine alabaster tomb, made in England for John (IV), transported to Nantes Cathedral, while a sumptuously bejewelled reliquary made in London as a present for John (V) survives in the Louvre.

Despite her initial unpopularity and parliamentary pressure to reduce her expenses Joan established and maintained good relations with her step-family in England. At her request in 1405 Henry IV released Breton prisoners captured after a raid on Devon, and she was instrumental in arranging an Anglo-Breton truce in 1407, while in 1411–12 she advised against English intervention in the Armagnac–Burgundy feud, though if anything she sided with Prince Henry against the Armagnacs. After Henry IV's death the new king continued to treat his stepmother with great respect and she showed no desire to return to

Brittany. Taking leave of her for France in 1415, Henry allowed Joan to reside during his absence at Windsor, Wallingford, Berkhamsted, or Hertford (this last later exchanged for Kings Langley). His victory at Agincourt must have caused mixed emotions, since her son Arthur was seriously wounded and captured, while her son-in-law, Jean, duke of Alençon, was killed. But a letter written by her to John, duke of Bedford (d. 1435), from Langley on 10 November 1415 makes no mention of recent events, and she accompanied Henry on his triumphal entry into London a fortnight later. In 1416 she received Garter robes; in November 1417 another Anglo-Breton truce was arranged through her good offices and as late as July 1418 she was still receiving favours from Henry.

A strange volte-face in relations between Joan and the king then occurred. Because of the financial demands of the war with France and plans for his own marriage, the king began to cast envious eyes on Joan's dower. In August 1419 the goods of her confessor, Father John Randolph, were seized; in fact it is clear, from the inventories made of them, that they were Joan's—they included 'a woman's night cap, red after the Breton fashion' (Myers, 98). Next month Randolph sensationally accused the queen of compassing Henry's death by sorcery and witchcraft. Although the case never came to trial, she was arrested and her other possessions confiscated. On 1 October she was taken under guard from Havering to Rotherhithe and, with Sir John Pelham as her keeper, later moved to other locations, including Pevensey (from 15 December 1419 to 8 March 1420) and Leeds Castle, where she remained more or less permanently from March 1420 until Henry V's death, though he relented and ordered Joan's release and restitution six weeks before he died.

There is no doubt that the allegations were entirely bogus and that the king's motives were mercenary—to reduce the queen's expenses and pocket the surplus (some £8000 between June 1421 and August 1422 alone). Surviving accounts show, however, that Joan's confinement was far from arduous, since she retained personal servants and lived in considerable comfort. She even entertained on some scale since she was frequently visited at Leeds by important figures like her stepson Humphrey, duke of Gloucester (d. 1447), Henry Beaufort, bishop of Winchester (d. 1447), and Thomas, Lord Camoys (d. 1421), who stayed for nearly ten months (from 12 April 1420 to 31 January 1421). After her release her goods were gradually restored, but as late as 1428–9 she was still trying to get satisfaction for Breton arrears. Some household accounts from this period show her again living in style, while among her annuitants was the celebrated composer John Dunstaple (d. 1453). In 1429 she delivered her chapel and its furnishings to Eleanor Cobham, duchess of Gloucester (d. 1452), and subsequently lived in semi-retirement on a reduced pension (500 marks p.a. in 1433). A domestic crisis was the burning of her house at Langley in March 1431. Her grandson Gilles of Brittany stayed with the young Henry VI from 1432 to 1434, and she remained in contact with John (V) to the end of her life. She died at Havering in

early July 1437 and was buried alongside Henry IV at Canterbury Cathedral in a ceremony attended by many dignitaries on 11 August. Her flattering effigy was later added to the magnificent tomb which she had erected for Henry. When the tomb was opened on 21 August 1832 her remains were left unexamined, but onlookers saw Henry's quickly turn to dust.   MICHAEL JONES

Sources PRIMARY PRINTED SOURCES J. R. Castro, ed., *Catálogo de la seccion de comptos, Catálogo del archivo general de Navarra*, 7–25 (1954–60) · R. Blanchard, ed., *Lettres et mandements de Jean V, duc de Bretagne*, 5 vols. (1889–95) · P. H. Morice, *Mémoires pour servir de preuves à l'histoire ecclésiastique et civile de Bretagne*, 3 vols. (Paris, 1742–6) · A. R. Myers, 'The captivity of a royal witch: the household accounts of Queen Joan of Navarre, 1419–21', *Crown, household, and parliament in fifteenth century England*, ed. C. H. Clough (1985), 93–134 · M. Jones, ed., *Recueil des actes de Jean IV, duc de Bretagne*, 1–2 (Paris, 1980–83) · *Pageant of the birth, life and death of Richard Beauchamp, earl of Warwick*, ed. Viscount Dillon and W. H. St John Hope (1914) · *Calendar of the fine rolls*, PRO, 16 (1936), 301 · N. H. Nicolas, ed., *Proceedings and ordinances of the privy council of England*, 7 vols., RC, 26 (1834–7) · *RotP*, vol. 4 · Rymer, *Foedera* · M. A. E. Wood, *Letters of royal and illustrious ladies of Great Britain*, 3 vols. (1846)
SECONDARY SOURCES C. Allmand, *Henry V* (1992) · W. Paley Baildon, 'Three inventories: (1) The earl of Huntingdon, 1377; (2) Brother John Randolf, 1419; (3) Sir John de Boys, 1426', *Archaeologia*, 61 (1908–9), 163–76 · J. Carrasco, 'Le royaume de Navarre et le duché de Bretagne au cours du dernier tiers du XIVe siècle: politique matrimoniale et circulation monétaire', *1491. La Bretagne, terre d'Europe*, ed. J. Kerhervé and T. Daniel (1992), 205–21 · GEC, *Peerage*, new edn, 10.824 · *Les fastes du gothique* · *Le siècle de Charles V* · R. A. Griffiths, *The reign of King Henry VI: the exercise of royal authority, 1422–1461* (1981) · M. Jones, *Ducal Brittany, 1364–1399* (1970) · M. Jones, 'Le voyage de Pierre de Lesnerac en Navarre, 1386', *Mémoires de la Société d'Histoire et d'Archéologie de Bretagne*, 61 (1984), 83–104 · M. Jones, '"En son habit royal": le duc de Bretagne et son image vers la fin du moyen âge', *Représentation, royauté et pouvoir à la fin du moyen âge*, ed. J. Blanchard (1995), 253–78 · M. Jones, 'Entre la France et l'Angleterre: Jeanne de Navarre, duchesse de Bretagne et reine d'Angleterre (1368–1437)', *Autour de Marguerite d'Écosse: reines, princesses et dames du XVe siècle*, ed. G. Contamine and P. Contamine (Paris, 1999), 45–72 · M. Jones, 'Between France and England: Jeanne de Navarre, duchess of Brittany and queen of England (1368–1437)', *Between France and England: essays on society and politics in later medieval Brittany* [forthcoming] · J. L. Kirby, *Henry IV of England* (1970) · G. A. Knowlson, *Jean V, duc de Bretagne et l'Angleterre: 1399–1442* (1964) · B-A. Poquet du Haut-Jussé, *Les papes et les ducs de Bretagne*, 2 vols. (1928) · B. A. Poquet du Haut-Jussé, 'Les séjours de Philippe le Hardi, duc de Bourgogne en Bretagne (1372, 1394 et 1402)', *Mémoires de la Société d'Histoire et d'Archéologie de Bretagne*, 16 (1935), 1–62 · P. E. Russell, *The English intervention in Spain and Portugal in the time of Edward III and Richard II* (1955) · A. Strickland and [E. Strickland], *Lives of the queens of England*, new edn, 2 (1851), 42–105 · J. H. Wylie, *History of England under Henry the Fourth*, 4 vols. (1884–98) · J. H. Wylie and W. T. Waugh, eds., *The reign of Henry the Fifth*, 3 vols. (1914–29) · J. Zunzunegui, 'El matrimonio de la Infanta Juana con el duque de Bretaña', *Príncipe de Viana*, 10 (1943), 51–68
MANUSCRIPTS Accounts of Thomas Lilbourne, 8 March–21 July 1422, Leeds Castle, Kent · exchequer, accounts various, PRO, esp. E101, *passim* · MS Latin, JRL, 22 · série E, Archives départementales de la Loire-Atlantique, Nantes · MSS fonds Bizeul, Médiathèque, Nantes · série E, Archives départementales des Pyrénées-Atlantiques, Pau · accounts of John Bugge, 1427–8, S. Antiquaries, Lond., MS 216 [receiver and treasurer to Joan]
Archives Archives départementales de la Loire-Atlantique, Nantes, série E · Archivo Real y General de Navarra, Pamplona · Leeds Castle, Kent, 1422, wardrobe book · PRO, exchequer, various accounts, London, esp. E101, *passim*

Likenesses tomb effigy, Canterbury Cathedral; electrotype, NPG

Joan, duchess of York (*d.* 1434). *See under* Willoughby family (*per. c.*1300–1523).

Joan (*fl.* 1407–1409). *See under* Women medical practitioners in England (*act. c.*1200–*c.*1475).

Joan [*née* Joan Beaufort] (*d.* 1445), queen of Scots, consort of James I (1394–1437), was the daughter of John Beaufort, marquess of Dorset and of Somerset (*d.* 1410), son of *John of Gaunt, and Margaret, daughter of Thomas Holland, earl of Kent, who married Thomas, duke of Clarence, brother of Henry V, after the death of Somerset; Joan's brother was John *Beaufort, duke of Somerset. Joan was thus brought up in the highest circles of the Lancastrian regime, almost certainly in the household of her mother. Her marriage to *James I, king of Scots, was part of the Beaufort family's promotion under the auspices of her uncle Henry Beaufort, cardinal-bishop of Winchester. Although a prisoner, James enjoyed relative freedom in the entourages of Henry V and Henry VI and knew Joan from at least 1420. There may have been a degree of personal preference in their marriage (later to find expression in James's *Kingis Quair*), which took place at St Mary Overie Church in Southwark on 12 February 1424, but its principal purpose was political. James I's release had been agreed the previous year, and his Beaufort marriage was intended to perpetuate his links with the English government, separating his kingdom from its French alliance. The Scottish king's family connections in England were used on several occasions to seek diplomatic advantage. By 1440, however, the cardinal's enemy Humphrey, duke of Gloucester, characterized the marriage as the sacrifice of Henry VI's interests to those of the Beauforts.

In the opening years of her husband's reign Joan seems to have played a minor role. The arrival of an English queen, particularly one whose stepfather had been killed and two of whose brothers had been captured fighting Scottish forces in France, may have been a source of disquiet for some of James's subjects. Unlike other Scottish queens, Joan was given no landed settlement at her coronation, though she clearly had some rights of patronage, enabling her to grant her chaplain the hospital at Linlithgow in 1426. Between late 1424 and 1430 four of the royal couple's six daughters were born, the eldest of whom was *Margaret of Scotland. In 1430 the birth of twin sons, the survivor being the future *James II, provided James I with a male heir and released Joan to play a political role as more than the recipient of conventional requests for royal clemency.

This process had begun in 1428, when the king had made all magnates take an oath to Joan on succeeding to their lands, and she had jointly ratified that year's French alliance. Later in 1428 she accompanied James to Inverness for his initial attack on the lord of the Isles. From 1431 she appears as his active ally in Scottish politics. She received an annuity of at least £360 Scots and was increasingly assigned lands by the king. These included a number

of major lordships in Perthshire. Joan may well have resided in Perth separately from her husband during this period and employed her own household and local agents in her new lands. She continued to be closely associated with James's policies, however, and in 1435 he ordered the estates to give her their letters of 'retinence and fidelity'. This suggests the promotion of the queen as the regent for her son in the event of the king's death and indicates her prominence in the politics of the kingdom.

Joan's influence was a factor in the crisis surrounding her husband's murder. Her ambitions in Perthshire may have heightened the fears of Walter Stewart, earl of Atholl, and she was a target of the assassins who killed James I in Perth on 21 February 1437. In the aftermath Joan, in spite of being wounded, quickly took command of the king's supporters and, according to all contemporary accounts, directed the subsequent civil war against Atholl. Although she was completely successful in the defeat of James's killers, Joan was forced to relinquish control of the government within three months of her victory. Her sex and nationality may have counted against her, but Joan was also too closely associated with the dead king's policies. Even councillors of James, such as William Crichton and James Douglas of Balvenie, saw the fifth earl of Douglas as a more acceptable lieutenant (as a grandson of Robert III he had a strong claim to this position anyway), and, while she remained in charge of her son, she was no longer politically important.

Joan's reaction was to seek to strengthen her local position. In the summer of 1439 (probably at the end of July) she married Sir James Stewart (*d.* 1451), younger brother of the lord of Lorne, from a family with lands and influence in Perthshire. Any major plans, however, were forestalled by her arrest by the Livingstons in August. To obtain her release she was forced to abandon her custody of the king. Despite this second reverse Joan retained the support of the core of James I's following and Stewart's kin. In early 1440 she was at Falkland, which she may have held as part of her jointure, and was the focus for a group which included Bishop James Kennedy and James Douglas, third earl of Angus. Her obstruction of the council led by the Livingstons and the Black Douglases led to a final clash in 1445. Her adherents were attacked, Stewart was forfeited, and she was placed under siege in Dunbar Castle. She died there on 15 July 1445 and was buried in the Carthusian priory in Perth. The last elements of James I's regime surrendered. Her husband went into English exile, taking their children with him: James *Stewart, earl of Buchan, John *Stewart, earl of Atholl, and Andrew Stewart, bishop of Moray. Joan was the first of a series of foreign queens in Scotland, all of whom wielded influence in the kingdom.

M. H. BROWN

Sources M. Brown, *James I* (1994) · E. W. M. Balfour-Melville, *James I, King of Scots, 1406–1437* (1936) · G. L. Harriss, *Cardinal Beaufort: a study of Lancastrian ascendancy and decline* (1988) · R. A. Griffiths, *The reign of King Henry VI: the exercise of royal authority, 1422–1461* (1981) · C. McGladdery, *James II* (1990) · A. I. Dunlop, *The life and times of James Kennedy, bishop of St Andrews*, St Andrews University Publications, 46 (1950) · J. Stevenson, ed., *Letters and papers illustrative of the* wars of the English in France during the reign of Henry VI, king of England, 2 vols. in 3 pts, Rolls Series, 22 (1861–4) · N. Beckett, 'The Perth charterhouse before 1500', Analecta Cartusiana, 127 (1988), 1–74

Joan of Acre. See Joan, countess of Hertford and Gloucester (1272–1307).

Joanna [Joan, Joanna of England], **countess of Toulouse** (1165–1199), queen of Sicily, consort of William II, was the third daughter and seventh child of *Henry II of England (1133–1189) and *Eleanor of Aquitaine (c.1122–1204). She was born at Angers and brought up at Fontevrault. Henry's attempts in 1168 to arrange for her an Aragonese or Navarrese marriage make sense in view of his ambitions in Pyrenean France, ambitions later fulfilled when Joanna married the count of Toulouse in 1196. However, more puzzling was the agreement to marry her to William II, king of Sicily, for at first the Sicilians had other plans, hoping to end the long-standing conflict with Constantinople by marrying William instead to Maria Porphyrogenita, daughter of Emperor Manuel I Komnenos. E. M. Jamison examines the tie between England and Sicily in the context of Pope Alexander III's attempt to create an anti-Hohenstaufen axis as a preliminary to the peace of Venice (1177). Thus in May 1176, with papal support, a Sicilian embassy was sent to England to ask for Joanna's hand; on visiting her at Winchester (where the bishop and city appear to have borne the expenses of the embassy), the ambassadors were very impressed by the young princess's beauty, and on 20 May the king gave his assent. The match also made a considerable impression on contemporary English chroniclers, who devote much space to it.

The route Joanna took to Sicily passed from Southampton through the Angevin territories in northern France and through Aquitaine (ruled by Joanna's brother Richard) to St Gilles, where in November they found twenty-five Sicilian galleys awaiting them. The journey to Sicily was interrupted by the princess's illness, and the ships had to stop at Naples before arriving in Palermo in January 1177. On 13 February William and Joanna were married in the Palatine Chapel at Palermo, and the king of Sicily invested her with the honour of Monte Sant'Angelo. Despite rumours that she had given birth to a young prince named Bohemond, Joanna produced no surviving heir, and she found herself entangled in the tumultuous politics of Sicily when William II died in November 1189 and was succeeded by his bastard cousin Tancred, who refused to concede to her the lands given to her by William; there were good strategic reasons for this, since the honour of Monte Sant'Angelo lay astride the route taken by the invading forces of Heinrich VI of Germany.

In September 1190 Joanna's brother *Richard I of England reached Messina on his way to the Holy Land, demanding her release and the restoration of her dowry. Richard also insisted on the return of precious gifts which, Joanna said, had been bequeathed both to her and to him by William II. Tancred released Joanna, sending her to Messina, but failed to give back the property. Richard's presence caused severe riots among the Greek population, and the English king occupied the city. Philip Augustus of France visited Joanna in the hospitaller convent in Messina, where she was staying, and was thought to have plans to marry her himself. On 1 October she moved across to Calabria, remaining on the mainland while the Sicilian and English kings continued to argue their rights; in November Tancred compromised by offering money instead of the lands and other property she claimed. The offer was accepted, and on 10 April 1191 Joanna joined the English crusader fleet, in the company of Berengaria of Navarre, Richard's future wife.

In October that year Richard involved Joanna in a bizarre, and perhaps not very serious, plan to make peace with Saladin by offering her hand to Saladin's brother Saphadin, or Malik al-Adil, in the hope, Richard is said to have asserted, that Saphadin would convert to Christianity; Joanna was furious at the suggestion that she might marry a Muslim, and the Muslims do not appear to have taken the proposal any too seriously. Joanna did, however, have crypto-Muslims from Sicily in her own entourage, two of whom took advantage of the queen's visit to the Holy Land to defect to Saladin's army. Saladin kept Richard waiting for six weeks before replying and then stipulated that the marriage must take place immediately. This was surely an attempt to call Richard's bluff. Richard replied that he could not move so quickly, since only the pope could provide a dispensation for the second marriage of a king's widow. Since this would take six months to obtain, he wondered whether Saphadin might not prefer *Eleanor of Brittany instead. Saladin consequently broke off negotiations. Joanna then remained in Berengaria's entourage for about four years, until a marriage was arranged with Raymond (VI), count of Toulouse, whose territorial ambitions had long been a cause of concern to Richard, as lord of Aquitaine. Raymond married Joanna, his fourth wife, at Rouen in October 1196. In July 1197 she gave birth to a son, the future Count Raymond (VII) of Toulouse. She and Raymond (VI) spent Easter 1198 at Le Mans with Richard, and in the spring of 1199 Joanna was on her way to Richard's court when news came of his death; she went at once to visit his grave at Fontevrault. Clearly she was closely attached to Richard, unlike the other Angevin siblings, and she was eventually to be buried in a nun's habit by his side at Fontevrault.

From Fontevrault Joanna travelled to Normandy, appealing to Richard's successor, *John, for support; John promised her 100 marks a year to use charitably in whatever way she chose; but he seems to have done nothing else for her or her husband, and a few weeks later, in September 1199, she died in childbirth at Rouen. The Winchester annalist calls Joanna 'a woman whose masculine spirit overcame the weakness of her sex' (Ann. mon., 2.64). She demonstrated as much in 1197, when, very shortly after the birth of her son, and while Raymond was away, she led an attack upon a rebel castle, and only abandoned the siege when her own camp was set ablaze. The story is also told that, to avenge Richard's death, she caused the man who killed him to be blinded and then flayed alive.

(Roger of Howden, however, lays the blame for this deed on Richard's general, Mercadier.) Joanna's second marriage proved that she was capable of child bearing; but the failure of her first marriage to produce an heir brought conflict and conquest to the Norman kingdom of Sicily.

D. S. H. ABULAFIA

Sources *Chronica magistri Rogeri de Hovedene*, ed. W. Stubbs, 4 vols., Rolls Series, 51 (1868–71), vol. 2, pp. 94–7; vol. 3, pp. 55–61 • *Radulfi de Diceto ... opera historica*, ed. W. Stubbs, 2 vols., Rolls Series, 68 (1876) • H. E. Mayer, ed., *Das Itinerarium peregrinorum*, MGH Schriften, 18 (Stuttgart, 1962) • *Romualdi Salernitani chronicon*, ed. C. A. Garufi, 1 (Città di Castello, 1914) • R. Howlett, ed., *Chronicles of the reigns of Stephen, Henry II, and Richard I*, 4, Rolls Series, 82 (1889), 226, 271, 278, 303 • *Recueil des historiens des Croisades: historiens orientaux*, Académie des Inscriptions et Belles-Lettres, 5 vols. (Paris, 1872–1906), vol. 3, pp. 277–9 • *Ann. mon.*, 1–4 • C. De Vic and J. Vaissète, *Histoire générale du Languedoc*, 16 vols. (1879), vol. 6 • E. M. Jamison, 'The Sicilian kingdom in the minds of Anglo-Norman contemporaries', *PBA*, 24 (1938), 237–85 • W. L. Warren, *Henry II* (1973)

Joannes de Sancta Cruce. *See* Moor, John (1629?–1689).

Joass, John James (1868–1952), architect, was born on 12 August 1868 in the High Street, Dingwall, Ross-shire, the eldest of three sons of William Cunningham Joass, an architect, and his wife, (Jane) Helen, *née* McGregor. He received his early architectural education and experience in Scotland, working first in his father's small office before being articled to the leading Glasgow architect John Burnet, while he studied part-time at the Glasgow School of Art. He then worked in the office of R. Rowand Anderson of Edinburgh. He was awarded the Pugin studentship in 1892, and travelled to Italy. After arriving in London late in 1893, he demonstrated the extent of his ambition by working in quick succession for Ernest George and John Belcher, who were considered to be two of the four best London practitioners of the time.

Joass joined Belcher in 1897, just as his remarkable assistant Arthur Beresford Pite was leaving to set up on his own account. A scheme by Belcher and Joass was preferred to Pite's in the competition of that year for Colchester town hall. However, Joass illustrated some of Pite's early solo efforts in the St Marylebone area of London, the panache of his watercolour technique perfectly complementing the baroque flourishes of these designs. He himself later contributed some buildings to the area, notably Mowbray's bookshop in Margaret Street (1907–8), and a particularly severe house in Weymouth Street (*c*.1910).

Joass's proficiency in draughtsmanship and classical design secured him a lasting place in Belcher's office, and he was encouraged by the principal—as Pite had been—to introduce and develop new ideas. Over the next two decades Belcher's practice, already successful by the 1890s, became, under Joass's expert management, one of the most successful in Britain. Joass became a partner in 1905, and effectively ran the firm himself after 1909, when Belcher became too ill to continue work (he died in 1913). The finest building on which they collaborated was the Ashton memorial in Lancaster (1904). Joass's period at the helm of the firm coincided with a time of expansion for London, when many new stone-clad buildings were constructed, providing an opportunity for a number of technical and formal innovations. Belcher and Joass led the field in marrying the technology of the steel frame to expressive architectural details deriving from Italian mannerism and the baroque. The buildings for which Joass was responsible were, nevertheless, characterized by a dryness and spareness which marked them off from many other examples of the genre, a quality which has been attributed to the hard granite he had had to contend with in the earlier part of his career. It was a quality which increased in his later work.

The buildings for which Joass is best remembered are in London, and include: the dazzling Mappin and Webb store on Oxford Street (1906–8), with its delicious tension between the transparency of glass and the apparent weight of stone; the Royal Insurance building on the corner of St James's Street and Piccadilly (1907–9), its deep, sculptural quality enlivened by swags and putti; and the imposing classical edifice he designed in 1910–12 to house the new department store for William Whiteley (the 'Universal Provider') in Bayswater. Elongated classical devices, stone medallions, and pendant wreaths, characteristic Joass features of this time, can be seen in his Royal Society of Medicine building on Henrietta Street (1910–12), while in a rare sacred work of the same time, Holy Trinity Church, Kingsway, he adopted a much more flamboyant baroque manner.

Joass was responsible for a number of projects at the zoological gardens in Regent's Park, London, beginning with offices for the Zoological Society in 1910–12, followed by the pioneering artificial landscape of the Mappin terraces of 1913, the aquarium of 1925, and a restaurant of 1929. The Royal London offices on Finsbury Square, in the City of London, begun with Belcher in 1904–5, were given a crowning centrepiece by Joass in 1928–30. The mixture of scale and severity evident here can also be seen in the contemporary Abbey National tower on Baker Street (1930–32)—aptly dubbed 'the tomb of the unknown borrower'—and could be seen as an attempt by Joass to exorcize the rare expression of flamboyance he had allowed himself during his pre-war mannerist phase. After the war he was also involved with Reginald Blomfield in the redevelopment of Regent Street, designing a store for Swan and Edgar in 1917–20 behind Blomfield's façade.

Yet for all his dynamism and fluency as an architect, and the testimony to his private 'wit', Joass lacked an effective public persona, which led to his virtual exclusion from public positions. One of the few such roles he did perform was as a member of the council of the Royal Institute of British Architects, but it was said that, during his tenure, he failed to utter a single word. However, this exclusion meant Joass could focus undisturbed upon his central concerns as an architect, a fact which enabled him to undertake an unusually large amount of work during his life. When he retired, it was to indulge his passion for sailing: his cruiser and occasional racer *Macnab*, which he partly designed, was anchored at Poole Harbour in Dorset. Only a year before his death Joass won first prize in A division, class II, of the Cowes to Dinard race. During his final illness Joass appears still to have been finishing drawings for his office. He died on 10 May 1952 at 5 Girton House, Manor Fields, Putney, the home he had shared with his second wife, Hilda Sant David.   BRIAN HANSON

Sources A. Service, 'Belcher and Joass', *ArchR*, 148 (1970), 282–90 · *The Builder*, 192 (16 May 1952), 748 · L. K. Watson and I. MacAlister, *RIBA Journal*, 59 (1951–2), 386 · *The Times* (14 May 1952) · nomination papers for associateship and fellowship, RIBA BAL · b. cert. · d. cert. · *CGPLA Eng. & Wales* (1952)
Archives RIBA, drawings and MSS
Likenesses photograph, repro. in Service, 'Belcher and Joass'
Wealth at death £41,086 11s. 4d.: probate, 16 July 1952, *CGPLA Eng. & Wales*

Jobson, Sir Francis (b. in or before **1509**, d. **1573**), administrator, came of a Colchester family which may have originated in Yorkshire. His father was probably William Jobson. Possibly with a recommendation from another Colchester worthy, Sir Richard Rich, he was employed at the office of augmentations, where from 24 April 1536 to 1 January 1547 he worked as a receiver at the court of augmentations and, together with his colleague Thomas (or Walter) Mildmay, held jurisdictions over Bedfordshire, Essex, Hertfordshire, and Hampshire collecting king's rents and profits. The receivership brought Jobson a salary of £20 plus profits and later a pension of £83 6s. 8d. a year. He also appears to have obtained a position in the royal household. On 8 August 1538 he paid for the delivery of lead from Dunmow Priory to the king's plumbers at Charing Cross; in the bill for the related expenses Jobson was described as 'gentleman'. He seems to have been a conscientious officer who was commended by Lord Chancellor Sir Thomas Audley in 1539. His receivership was important enough to exempt him from attending the king at Boulogne during Henry's war with France in 1544. His marriage, probably before March 1543, to Elizabeth Plantagenet, third daughter and coheir of Arthur, Viscount Lisle, and his first wife, Elizabeth, widow of Edmund Dudley, brought him the patronage of prominent men in government, above all of John Dudley, Viscount Lisle.

Jobson was knighted in 1549 or 1550, and in the latter year was appointed surveyor of the woods of the northern region; he also became master of the jewel house for a few months in 1553. His Dudley connection led to his collaborating with John Dudley, now duke of Northumberland (he was Lady Jobson's half-brother) in his attempted coup against Princess Mary in July 1553. Jobson was regarded as a key supporter of the duke, and as such was the target for the Thames valley loyalists who rose in Mary's support. He is said to have held Westminster Palace for Queen Jane after Northumberland had left for Cambridge on 13 July on his way to confront Mary's East Anglian forces. Jobson was arrested early in August but he never faced trial and received a pardon on 22 December, even though his indictment records him as present in Cambridge during 16–17

July. He was soon restored to favour. Even when on 18 April 1554 parliament passed a bill restoring the bishopric of Durham, Jobson, who had earlier profited from its dissolution, was recommended for favourable treatment by the restored bishop. Jobson was one of Colchester's two MPs in the last parliament of Edward VI's reign and two of those of Mary's; under Elizabeth he was returned in 1559 and 1563. He retained his surveyorship of the woods (with a fee of £100) until 20 August 1564 when, following the sudden death of Sir Richard Blount, the queen appointed him lieutenant of the Tower of London, a post he maintained with diligence, especially during the northern uprising of 1569–70, and retained until his death.

Jobson acquired considerable monastic property in and around Colchester. He had begun his career with a modest patrimony worth £45, but his employment at the augmentations 'rendered him considerable, and procured him great estates, chiefly from the spoils of the Monasteries' in Essex and Yorkshire (Morant, *Essex*, 2.186 n. p). After his marriage he sold his inheritance to John Dudley who promised him a Staffordshire manor owned by Lord Windsor. Unable to keep his promise, Dudley nevertheless borrowed £600 from Jobson, who spent further for the 'bord of his children' (ibid.). Dudley finally repaid his brother-in-law by securing for him the grant of the lordship of West Donyland, south of Colchester, comprising Monkwick (which became his family seat), Middlewick, and Upperwick. In Colchester itself he obtained the massive estates of the Greyfriars and of St John's Abbey, though he soon sold the latter. He also acquired substantial property in Yorkshire. It has been estimated that Jobson acquired seventeen crown manors during the reign of Edward VI. Rising status seems to have been accompanied by a dubious reputation, however. Jobson was twice involved in lawsuits during which he was said to have tried to obtain property grants from men imprisoned for debt, in return for loans made to secure their release. A different sort of entrepreneurship can be seen in his seeking government support for his collaboration with Armigill Wadd (or Wade), paymaster at Rye, Sussex, in sponsoring the 'alchemical operations' of Cornelius de Vos, a mining expert.

Jobson died at Monkwick on 4 June 1573, and was buried in St Giles, Colchester. He was succeeded by his second son, Edward (d. 1590), who married Mary, daughter of John Bode of Rocheford; their surviving daughter and heir, Mary (b. 1587), married George Brooke of Aspall Hall, Suffolk, in 1610. The Jobson line became extinct when Alice, daughter of Mary and George and wife of Nicolas Marshall, died without children.   NARASINGHA P. SIL

Sources P. Morant, *The history and antiquities of the county of Essex*, 2 vols. (1760–68) · P. Morant, *The history and antiquities of the most ancient town and borough of Colchester in the county of Essex* (1748) · HoP, *Commons, 1509–58*, 2.444–6 · *DNB* · *LP Henry VIII* · *Calendar of the manuscripts of the marquis of Bath preserved at Longleat, Wiltshire*, 5 vols., HMC, 58 (1904–80) [1533–1659] · *CSP Spain, 1558–79* · *CPR, 1553–8* · W. C. Richardson, *History of the court of augmentations, 1536–1554* (1961) · *Collectanea Topographica et Genealogica*, 8 (1843) · *CSP dom., 1547–80, with addenda, 1566–1579* · C. Sharp, ed., *Memorials of* *the rebellion of 1569* (1840); repr. with foreword by R. Wood as *The rising in the north: the 1569 rebellion* (1975)

Wealth at death enormous landed possessions: grants, licences, *Letters & papers of Henry VIII, Calendar of the patent rolls* (Edward VI through Elizabeth I); will, PRO, PROB 11/55, fols. 185r–187r

Jobson, Frederick James (1812–1881), Wesleyan Methodist minister, son of John Jobson (1786/7–1875), was born at Northwich, Cheshire, on 6 July 1812, and served an apprenticeship to Edward J. Willson, architect, at Lincoln. After his conversion in 1829 he became a local preacher in the Lincoln circuit and entered the itinerant ministry in 1834, in which year he married Elizabeth Caborn of Bemersley, Staffordshire. His evangelistic fervour soon secured him a reputation as a preacher. His first appointment was at Patrington, Yorkshire, and in 1835 he went to Manchester. In 1837 he became assistant at the City Road Chapel, London, where he subsequently served three terms. Between these appointments he served at Leeds, Manchester (1843–9), Bradford, and Huddersfield (1855–61). Jobson's knowledge of architecture proved useful in the erection of the teacher training college at Westminster, the New Kingswood School in Bath, and Richmond College. His book *Chapel and School Architecture* (1850), was an important contribution to the development of the Gothic style in Methodist buildings.

In May 1856, with John Hannah, Jobson was sent as one of the representatives of the British conference to the Methodist Episcopal church conference at Indianapolis. On his return he published an influential book, *America and American Methodism* (1857). He attended the Australian conference at Sydney in January 1861, and on his return published an account of his journey entitled *Australia, with Notes by the Way of Egypt, Ceylon, Bombay, and the Holy Land* (1862). In 1864 he was chosen book steward, and under his sound financial management the Wesleyan Methodist publishing department greatly expanded. He superintended the *Methodist Magazine* for twelve years. He was elected president of the Wesleyan Methodist conference on 5 August 1869 and served his church as general treasurer of the missionary society and on committees of the theological institution, chapel department, and Methodist Preachers' Annuitant Society. Jobson died at his home, 21 Highbury Place, Highbury, London, on 4 January 1881, and was buried in Highgate cemetery on 8 January.

G. C. BOASE, *rev.* TIM MACQUIBAN

Sources B. Gregory, *The life of F. J. Jobson* (1884) · W. B. Pope, *Death and life in Christ: a funeral sermon for … F. J. Jobson* (1881) · *Wesleyan Methodist Magazine*, 67 (1844), 518–22 · *Wesleyan Methodist Magazine*, 94 (1871), facing p. 481 · *Wesleyan Methodist Magazine*, 104 (1881), 150–57, 176–85, 285–94, 397 · *The Times* (5 Jan 1881), 9 · *ILN* (14 Aug 1869), 165 · W. Hill, *An alphabetical arrangement of all the Wesleyan-Methodist ministers, missionaries, and preachers*, rev. J. P. Haswell, 9th edn (1862) · *Minutes of the Methodist conference* · N. B. Harmon, ed., *The encyclopedia of world Methodism*, 2 vols. (1974)

Archives JRL, corresp., notes · Wesley's Chapel, London, letters

Likenesses portrait, repro. in Gregory, *Life of F. J. Jobson* · portrait, repro. in *Wesleyan Methodist Magazine* (Sept 1844) · portrait, repro. in *Wesleyan Methodist Magazine* (June 1871) · wood-engraving (after photograph by John Watkins), NPG; repro. in *ILN*

Wealth at death under £12,000: probate, 13 Jan 1881, *CGPLA Eng. & Wales*

Jobson, Richard (*fl.* 1620–1623), merchant and travel writer, described himself as a gentleman, but nothing is known of his family or youth beyond references in his book to experience in Ireland. In 1620 he was sent as one of the supercargoes on the third of a series of expeditions up the Gambia River undertaken by a group of London entrepreneurs who had in 1619 been granted a crown patent to trade in west Africa. Although the area was already frequented by English traders, the first two expeditions to tap the age-old trans-Saharan gold trade, still known in Europe only from its terminus in the Moorish states of north Africa, had failed. Jobson and his companions reached the Gambia in November 1620, established a base near the mouth, and then sailed some 200 miles up the river until it became too shallow to continue. Jobson, with nine of the crew and some African guides, then went on in an open rowing boat to Tenda (in modern Senegal), where, he had been told, he would find an itinerant gold trader, Buckor Sano. Sano was delighted to meet him. He had no gold then available but promised that if they returned he could easily supply it in exchange for imported trade goods. After ten days Jobson and his party returned, rejoined the ship, and left the Gambia in June 1621.

On his return Jobson published an account of the expedition, hoping to persuade the 'gentlemen adventurers' to send out another. But none was sent. His book, however, entitled *The Golden Trade, or, A Discovery of the River Gambra, and the Golden Trade of the Aethiopians* (1623; reprinted 1904), the first account of the area in English, attracted interest. It is a garrulous, disorganized production, but full of detailed accounts of the country—the geography, the customs he observed among the inhabitants, and the flora and fauna. A more lucid, much abbreviated version was published, with his assistance, by Samuel Purchas in his *Hakluytus Posthumus, or, Purchas his Pilgrimes* (1625). No further details of Jobson's life or death are known.

CHRISTOPHER FYFE

Sources R. Jobson, *The golden trade* (1623) · S. Purchas, *Hakluytus posthumus, or, Purchas his pilgrimes*, bks 6, 9 (1625); repr. Hakluyt Society, extra ser., 19, 22 (1905) · J. M. Gray, *A history of the Gambia* (1940)

Jocelin. *See* Furness, Jocelin of (*fl.* 1199–1214).

Jocelin (*d.* 1199), abbot of Melrose and bishop of Glasgow, came of a family with rights in the church at Dunsyre, Lanarkshire, probably with land there. He became a monk at Melrose Abbey on 29 March 1157, when Waldef was abbot, and was elected prior under Abbot William, who seems to have resented the growing cult associated with the tomb of Waldef at Melrose, resigning over this on 22 April 1170 (he died at Rievaulx in 1185). The election of Jocelin as abbot on the same day represented the victory of the supporters of the sainthood of Waldef, whose tomb was opened on 22 May 1171. It was provided, at Jocelin's instigation, with a new marble cover, possibly on the model of the tomb of Thomas Becket. Jocelin was elected to the see of Glasgow (which had had two recent monastic bishops) under royal influence at Perth on 23 May 1174, during a truce in the war of King William the Lion against Henry II.

Still abbot, Jocelin went to Clairvaux to seek leave of the Cistercian general chapter to accept the bishopric, and was there for the dedication of the church and translation of the relics of St Bernard and St Malachy (whom he probably knew) in October 1174. By then the Scottish king was a prisoner, soon (8 December 1174) to concede to Henry II lordship of his kingdom and to the English church that of the Scottish church. Jocelin remained at Clairvaux, to be consecrated bishop by the archbishop of Lund there by leave of the pope, probably in January 1175. He also secured from Pope Alexander III a confirmation of the possessions of the church of Glasgow, probably datable to 30 April 1175, in common form save that it described the church as 'special daughter of the Roman church, no-one in between' (Somerville, no. 76). Jocelin joined the other Scottish prelates and magnates in swearing fealty to Henry II at York on 10 August 1175, but when Henry sought to exact obedience from the Scottish church to the 'English church' at Northampton on 25 January 1176, Jocelin used this grant to upset the claims of York to metropolitan jurisdiction. The intervention of the archbishop of Canterbury, quite possibly encouraged by Jocelin, ended the council in confusion, and shortly afterwards, in the bull *Super anxietatibus*, the pope denied York authority over the Scottish bishops.

Jocelin's reward from the king was the grant of a burgh at Glasgow, with a weekly market, and from this time he devoted much energy to development at Glasgow. In 1181 he was said to have 'extended [*dilatavit*] the episcopal seat and gloriously magnified the church of St Kentigern' (Anderson, *Early Sources*, 2.304), or, in another version, 'he enlarged his church, pretty exiguous at his appointment' (Forbes, 311). A royal charter of between 1189 and 1195 shows that he had established a fraternity (the only one known in Scotland) for rebuilding the cathedral after a fire which presumably occurred about 1180. The only fragment of his church to survive above ground is a column and capital, but excavation has revealed the foundations of a short nave whose walls reused masonry from a yet earlier church. Probably to encourage devotion and donations, Jocelin dedicated a still-incomplete church on 6 July 1197, perhaps implying the consecration of an altar incorporating relics of St Kentigern. The royal grant of an annual fair at the burgh, to last for a week from 6 July, the day when the dedication was commemorated each year at the cathedral, was not a coincidence, and may be dated to 1197.

Jocelin has left no fewer than twenty-eight *acta* as bishop, many of them granting the ecclesiastical interest in a secular donation (for example, the appropriation of a kirk), or showing him acting as judge in a case involving churchmen. Tofts in the burgh of Glasgow are the only lands he is known to have granted, and these to Cistercian abbeys, which should have rejected such secular concerns. In one act early in his episcopate (between 1175 and 1178) he agreed, 'with common counsel of the chapter of the church of Glasgow' (Innes, vol. 1, no. 47) that each

canon might devise his prebend by will for one year after his death, a concession which suggests some weakness in dealing with the canons' vested interest. The chapter was still small, with seven prebends, to which Jocelin seems to have added only one, Carnwath; unable to prevent absenteeism, he was able to insist that canons appoint vicarschoral. In the 1190s the chapter was possessed of a common seal, clear evidence of greater corporate independence. The most likely explanation of that is the cash flow and responsibility involved in managing a cult whose importance the bishop promoted very actively.

To this end Jocelin commissioned from Jocelin of Furness a new life of Kentigern, probably after 1180. The author's inept handling of location belies his claim to have walked the streets of Glasgow, just as his confession that he could find no miracles performed after the saint's death is contradicted by a passage celebrating those miracles, but specifying only one—the cow stolen from Glasgow, found alive, bound to the foot of the dead thief. The bishop was clearly working with recalcitrant materials, and perhaps sought a remedy by a link with the new cult of St Thomas the Martyr. Jocelin was involved with chapels dedicated to him in the diocese at Dumfries and Maxwell, and a similar Glasgow chapel was probably founded by him. It was Jocelin who dedicated the king's new abbey of St Thomas at Arbroath in 1178, when the see of St Andrews was vacant. Glasgow Cathedral later treasured linked relics of Kentigern and Thomas (their combs and shirts), attributable to Jocelin's devotion to both saints and to his travels through England. But although he kept a monk as his chaplain, he lost interest in the cult of Waldef, for which he was criticized in Jocelin of Furness's life of Waldef, written after Bishop Jocelin's death.

In 1178 the canons of St Andrews elected a new bishop, John (John the Scot), without the consent of King William the Lion, who tried to force his chaplain, Hugh, upon them. The resulting crisis in relations with the papacy led to the excommunication of the king and the laying of an interdict upon Scotland in 1181. The king sent Jocelin to Rome at the head of an embassy which was successful in securing the lifting of the interdict on 15 March 1182, the gift of the golden rose to William (the first secular non-Italian ruler to receive it), and the appointment of legates to resolve the St Andrews dispute. At the legates' synod that summer, a fruitless compromise implied that Jocelin would go to St Andrews, but the case was again appealed to Rome, and settled in Hugh's favour by 1183. It was reopened in 1186, when Hugh failed to appear at Rome and incurred suspension and excommunication by Jocelin, who was later instructed by Clement III to remove him from office in favour of John. When Hugh died in 1188, Jocelin was not translated to St Andrews. Jocelin was King William's tactful ally in this difficult matter, so circumspect that he was able to obtain papal confirmations of the privileges of his see in 1179, 1182, and 1186.

By 1186 Jocelin was clearly an important royal counsellor, accompanying the Scottish king thrice to England in that year: in May to arrange William's marriage, in September to attend it and bless the marriage bed. At Carlisle in August, when the king persuaded Henry II to accept the restoration of Roland of Galloway, Jocelin swore 'on the word of truth and the relics of saints' (Anderson, *Scottish Annals*, 290) that he would hold Roland to his undertakings under pain of excommunication. Jocelin was not named as present at Canterbury in December 1189, when the submission of Falaise (1174) was cancelled, but in 1194 he accompanied William to the court of Richard I, in unsuccessful pursuit of the earldom of Northumberland.

In August 1198, at Haddington, William's queen at last bore a son, the future Alexander II. It seems that some credit was claimed for Kentigern, for the king granted a money rent for a chaplain in the cathedral, while the baptism of the heir was carried out by Bishop Jocelin. He died in monastic habit at Melrose on 17 March 1199, and, although the chronicle of the house ignores the fact, was buried there in the choir of monks. Within three years Ralph, abbot of Melrose, wrote an encomium of Jocelin which is rich in rhetoric but light on facts. Jocelin clearly retained a devotion to the house where he took his monastic vows, but as a late monastic bishop, his career shows the strength of other influences, especially the cult of the saints and their relics. He honoured the Roman church, and used it to good effect, but he served his king even under the ban of the church, with no hesitation, and to equally remarkable effect.

A. A. M. DUNCAN

Sources J. Dowden, *The bishops of Scotland … prior to the Reformation*, ed. J. M. Thomson (1912), 298–300 • D. E. R. Watt, *Ecclesia Scoticana* (Stuttgart, 1991), 60–63 • N. F. Shead, 'Origins of the medieval diocese of Glasgow', *SHR*, 48 (1969), 220–25 • N. F. Shead, 'The administration of the diocese of Glasgow in the twelfth and thirteenth centuries', *SHR*, 55 (1976), 127–50 • G. W. S. Barrow, ed., *Regesta regum Scottorum*, 2 (1971) • A. P. Forbes, ed., *Lives of S. Ninian and S. Kentigern* (1874) • A. O. Anderson, ed., *Scottish annals from English chroniclers, AD 500 to 1286* (1908), 249–321 • A. O. Anderson, ed. and trans., *Early sources of Scottish history, AD 500 to 1286*, 2 (1922), 268–351 • A. O. Anderson and M. O. Anderson, eds., *The chronicle of Melrose* (1936) • R. Somerville, ed., *Scotia pontificia: papal letters to Scotland before the pontificate of Innocent III* (1982) • C. Innes, ed., *Registrum episcopatus Glasguensis*, 2 vols., Bannatyne Club, 75 (1843); also pubd as 2 vols., Maitland Club, 61 (1843)

Likenesses seal (on Melrose charter), NA Scot.?

Jocelin de Brakelond. *See* Brakelond, Jocelin of (*fl.* 1173–*c*.1215).

Jocelin of Wells. *See* Wells, Jocelin of (*d.* 1242).

Jocelin [*née* Brooke], **Elizabeth** (1596–1622), author, was the only child of Sir Richard Brooke (*d.* 1632) and Elizabeth Chaderton. Her parents separated, as Sir Peter Leycester put it, 'through some dislike after Marriage' (Leycester, 327), and her mother died when she was only six, so Jocelin was raised and educated by her maternal grandfather, Bishop William *Chaderton of Lincoln, probably in his house at Southoe, near Buckden. It was 'by and under' him that 'shee was from her tender yeeres carefully nurtured', studying languages (including Latin), history, and 'some' of the liberal arts (traditionally these were grammar, logic, rhetoric, arithmetic, geometry, music, and astronomy), but principally 'studies of piety' (Goad, sig. a1v). Her grandfather died when she was eleven or twelve, in 1608, and Jocelin may have spent the next eight years with her father, who was from 1607 in possession of the family seat at Norton, Cheshire.

In 1616, as an heiress in possession, as Leycester also reports, of 'all her Mothers Lands', Elizabeth married Taurell (Torrell) Jocelin (1592/3–1656), son and heir of Sir Thomas Josselyn of Willingale, Essex. In the 1620s Taurell Jocelin held an estate called Crowlands in Oakington, near Cambridge, and it may have been here that Elizabeth continued her studies in 'morality and history', aided both by her knowledge of foreign languages and by her 'taste and faculty in Poetry' (Goad, sig. a3r–v). She wrote some poetry herself, which seems not to have survived. She soon, however, gave up all studies except 'divinity', and when she found herself pregnant after six years of marriage she responded by composing a tract of religious instruction for her unborn child. In this 'mother's legacy' Jocelin makes clear that she was impelled not only by a sense of religious duty but by the premonitory fear that she would die in childbirth: as soon as she felt the child quicken she ordered her winding sheet, and simultaneously began to write. The legacy begins with an epistle to 'her truly louinge and most Dearly loued husband' in which she expresses the hope that he will dedicate the child, if a son, to the ministry (BL, Add. MS 27467, fol. 1r). For a daughter she advises a conventional female education (unlike her own) of learning the Bible, good housewifery, writing, and embroidery, with her stepsisters at Norton. The legacy itself addresses the unborn child as if from the grave: 'it may peradventure … appear strange to thee to receyue theas lines from a mother that dyed when thou weart born' (ibid., fol. 10r). Although written to her child, its concerns are broadly those of moderate puritans in the Jacobean church: an effective preaching ministry, strict sabbatarianism, and the cultivation of a sense of personal sinfulness and of repentance through prayer. Jocelin explicitly recommends morning and evening prayers by the puritan minister Henry Smith, but she may have been primarily influenced by the posthumously printed legacy of another woman, also puritan in her sympathies, Dorothy Leigh.

Jocelin did not finish her legacy, prevented either by a miscalculation of the time of her delivery or by some unspecified 'troubles' a month before her death. On 12 October 1622 she gave birth to a daughter, baptized Theodora after her husband's mother. After the baptism Jocelin called for the winding-sheet she had ordered to be laid on her. Nine days later she died, probably of puerperal fever; she was buried in St Andrew's Church, Oakington, on 26 October. The details of Jocelin's death, as of her education, are given by Thomas Goad, who reports that the unfinished manuscript was found in her desk after her death. As chaplain to the archbishop of Canterbury, Goad licensed her text and also supervised its publication in 1624, writing a prefatory 'Approbation' and apparently editing the text. *The Mothers Legacie to her Unborne Childe* appeared in seven further editions in the seventeenth century alone.

SYLVIA BROWN

Sources T. Goad, 'The approbation', in E. Jocelin, *The mothers legacie, to her unborne childe* (1624), 1–16 • E. Jocelin's mother's legacy,

BL, Add. MS 27467 • S. Brown, 'The approbation of Elizabeth Joce-lin', *English Manuscript Studies, 1100–1700*, 9 (2000) • S. Brown, ed., *Women's writing in Stuart England: the mothers' legacies of Dorothy Leigh, Elizabeth Joscelin and Elizabeth Richardson* (1999) • P. Leycester, *Historical antiquities in two books* (1673) • *DNB* • Venn, *Alum. Cant.* • R. Stewart-Brown, ed., *Cheshire inquisitions post mortem: Stuart period, 1608–1660*, 1, Lancashire and Cheshire RS, 84 (1934), 85–6 • J. P. Rylands, ed., *Cheshire and Lancashire funeral certificates, AD 1600 to 1678*, Lancashire and Cheshire RS, 6 (1882), 43 • J. L. Chester and J. Foster, eds., *London marriage licences, 1521–1869* (1887) • 'Particular extracts from the register of Hokinton', BL, Add. MS 5849, fol. 93r
Archives BL, Add. MS 27467

Jocelyn, Percy (1764–1843), bishop of Clogher, was the third son of Robert *Jocelyn, first earl of Roden (1720/21–1797), and Anne, daughter of James, earl of Clanbrassil. He was born in Dublin on 29 November 1764; he entered Trinity College, Dublin, in October 1781, and graduated BA in 1785. After being ordained he became rector of Tamlaght, in the diocese of Armagh, and in 1787 treasurer of Cork Cathedral. Subsequently he received the following appointments in succession: the archdeaconry of Ross (1788–90), the treasurership of Armagh (1790–1809), and a prebend of Lismore (1796–1809). In 1809 he was appointed bishop of Ferns and Leighlin, and in 1820 bishop of Clogher.

Two years later he was deprived of his see by an ecclesiastical court consisting of four Irish bishops, held at Armagh. This was as a result of his being caught in a homosexual act with a guardsman in a London public house on 19 July 1822. He appeared in court the next day and was let out on bail of £1000. The incident sparked extensive newspaper attention especially in the 'gutter' press. A mass of tracts and graphic cartoons were soon published about the affair and further exposés of clerical vice and crime quickly followed. Jocelyn was never convicted, however, and was allowed to escape without trial, although his notoriety seriously embarrassed the government and shocked the Church of Ireland. After the scandal he moved to Scotland and worked as a butler under the assumed name of Thomas Wilson. He died in Edinburgh on 3 September 1843 and was buried on the same day in the new cemetery in the city.   DAVID HUDDLESTON

Sources *N&Q*, 214 (1969), 421–30 • H. Cotton, *Fasti ecclesiae Hibernicae*, 2 (1848), 344 • H. Cotton, *Fasti ecclesiae Hibernicae*, 3 (1849), 43, 83–4 • J. B. Leslie, *Armagh clergy and parishes* (1911), 44 • I. McCalman, *Radical underworld: prophets, revolutionaries, and pornographers in London, 1795–1840* (1988), 206–7, 287 • D. Bowen, *The protestant crusade in Ireland, 1800–70* (1978), 44 • *Annual Register* (1822), 126, 138 • *Annual Register* (1843), 330 • Burke, *Peerage* (1970) • [J. H. Todd], ed., *A catalogue of graduates who have proceeded to degrees in the University of Dublin, from the earliest recorded commencements to … December 16, 1868* (1869), 302 • Burtchaell & Sadleir, *Alum. Dubl.* • private information (2004)
Archives NRA, priv. coll. • PRO NIre. • TCD

Jocelyn, Robert, first Viscount Jocelyn (1687/8–1756), lord chancellor of Ireland, was the only son of Thomas Jocelyn and his wife, Anne, daughter of Thomas Bray of Westminster; his grandfather was Sir Robert Jocelyn, bt, of Hyde Hall, Hertfordshire. He was the pupil of an attorney named Salkeld in Brooke Street, Holborn, London, where he made the acquaintance of Philip Yorke, afterwards Lord Hardwicke.

Admitted a student of Gray's Inn in 1709, Jocelyn was called to the Irish bar on 27 January 1719, and at a by-election in September 1725 he was returned, through the influence of his brother-in-law the bishop of Kilmore, to the Irish House of Commons for Granard, co. Longford. He was appointed third serjeant on 28 March 1726, and at the general election in 1727 he was elected for Newtownards, co. Down. On 4 May 1727 he became solicitor-general. On the accession of George II, Jocelyn was confirmed in his office, and on 22 October 1730 he was promoted to the post of attorney-general in the place of Thomas Marlay, who was appointed lord chief baron. On the unexpected resignation of Thomas, Lord Wyndham, Jocelyn, through the influence of his old friend Lord Hardwicke, was appointed lord chancellor (7 September 1739) and took his seat as speaker of the Irish House of Lords at the opening of parliament on 9 October 1739.

When the appointment was made Lord Lieutenant Devonshire pointed out that Jocelyn had not been the first choice among the king's servants in Ireland, and, having asked Hardwicke to request Jocelyn to be especially careful to keep 'up that harmony in the government which his Majesty's service requires' and throughout his tenure of office, Jocelyn was always careful to do so (Burns). Nevertheless in 1746 Archbishop Stone, then bishop of Derry, wrote to the new chief secretary, Edward Weston:

> my Lord Chancellor will be found always ready to bring his assistance without difficulty upon terms and conditions. There is a jealousy subsisting between these two Princes [speaker and chancellor], which some of their respective friends are constantly endeavouring to cure and others to inflame … It may possibly give you some little amusement but no real trouble.   (Walton)

In the inter-parliamentary absences of the lord lieutenant, the primate, the speaker, and the chancellor were usually appointed lords justices, and Jocelyn held this office nine times.

Jocelyn was created Baron Newport of Newport in the county of Tipperary, by letters patent dated 29 November 1743, and on 3 February 1744 he presided as lord high steward at the trial of Nicholas, fifth Viscount Netterville, who was indicted for the murder of Michael Walsh and was honourably acquitted. Described by Lord Chesterfield as 'a man of great worth' (Harris, 2.15), Newport possessed an amiable character, and literary and antiquarian tastes; he was president of the Dublin Physico-Historical Society.

Newport was a central if reluctant figure in the money bill dispute of the early 1750s. On 14 January 1754 Primate Stone wrote to the duke of Newcastle that 'the Chancellor has always before his eyes, change of times, fluctuation of power and retaliation' ('The correspondence of Archbishop Stone and the duke of Newcastle', 735). A few months earlier, in October 1753, the chief secretary, Lord George Sackville, had written: 'I cannot say enough of the support that my Lord Chancellor has given us on this occasion' (*Stopford-Sackville MSS*, 200); at the conclusion of the crisis Newport was created Viscount Jocelyn in the peerage of Ireland, by letters patent dated 6 December 1755. An interesting letter, written by Newport (from Dublin, 2 November 1754) to the duke of Newcastle, calls the duke's attention to 'the very extraordinary height to which the disputes and animosities here have been unhappily carried' (BL, Add. MS 32737, fol. 245).

Jocelyn married, first, in 1720, Charlotte, daughter and coheir of Charles Anderson of Worcester; their only son, Robert *Jocelyn (1720/21–1797), succeeded his father as second viscount and was created earl of Roden, of High Roding in the county of Tipperary, on 1 December 1771. Charlotte died on 23 February 1747, and on 15 November 1754 Jocelyn married, as his second wife, Frances (d. 1772), daughter of Thomas Claxton of Dublin and widow of Richard Parsons, first earl of Rosse. In September 1756 the great seal was put in commission during Jocelyn's absence from Ireland for the recovery of his health. He never returned, however, and died in London on 3 December 1756, aged sixty-eight, survived by his wife. He was buried in the church at Sawbridgeworth, Hertfordshire; a marble bust by Bacon was erected in Sawbridgeworth church by his son.   G. F. R. BARKER, rev. E. M. JOHNSTON-LIIK

Sources E. M. Johnston-Liik, *History of the Irish parliament, 1692–1800*, 6 vols. (2002) · C. L. Falkiner, ed., 'The correspondence of Archbishop Stone and the duke of Newcastle', *EngHR*, 20 (1905), 735–63 · R. E. Burns, *Irish parliamentary politics in the eighteenth century*, 2 (1990), 43–4 · *The king's business: letters on the administration of Ireland, 1740–1761, from the papers of Sir Robert Wilmot*, ed. J. Walton (1996), p. 6, no. 8 · D. O. Donovan, 'The money bill dispute', *Penal era and golden age: essays in Irish history, 1690–1800*, ed. T. Bartlett and D. W. Hayton (1979), 55–87 · E. M. Johnston, *Ireland in the eighteenth century* (1974), 125 · *Report on the manuscripts of Mrs Stopford-Sackville*, 2 vols., HMC, 49 (1904–10) · G. Harris, *The life of Lord Chancellor Hardwicke*, 3 vols. (1847) · J. R. O'Flanagan, *The lives of the lord chancellors and keepers of the great seal of Ireland*, 2 vols. (1870) · O. J. Burke, *The history of the lord chancellors of Ireland from AD 1186 to AD 1874* (1879) · private information (2004) [A. P. W. Malcolmson] · BL, Add. MS 32737 **Archives** Derbys. RO, corresp. relating to Ireland · NRA, priv. coll., corresp. · PRO, state papers, SP 63/360–419 · PRO NIre., corresp. | BL, corresp. with Lord Hardwicke, Add. MSS 35585–35594, *passim* · BL, corresp. with duke of Newcastle, Add. MSS 32726, 32737 · PRO NIre., Wilmot MSS, T 3019/823 **Likenesses** J. Brooks, mezzotint, 1744 (after mezzotint by R. Walpole, *c.*1740), NG Ire. · A. Miller, mezzotint, 1747 (after J. Pope-Stevens), NG Ire. · Bacon, memorial bust, Sawbridgeworth parish church, Hertfordshire · two portraits, priv. coll. **Wealth at death** Irish estates; property in Donny Brook to son in 1746: private information

Jocelyn, Robert, first earl of Roden (1720/21–1797), landowner and politician, was the son of Robert *Jocelyn, first Viscount Jocelyn (1687/8–1756), and his first wife, Charlotte (d. 1747), daughter of Charles Anderson of Worcester. The date of his baptism is usually given as 31 July 1731 but this may be an error for 1721. He matriculated at Exeter College, Oxford, on 17 October 1740 'aged 19' (Foster, *Alum. Oxon.*). He went on to study law at Lincoln's Inn. When he returned to Ireland he entered parliament as MP for Old Leighlin which he represented between 1743 and 1756. In 1750 he was appointed to the office of auditor-general for

Ireland, and he held this post until his death. Jocelyn married on 11 December 1752 Anne (1730–1802), daughter of James Hamilton, second earl of Clanbrassil, with whom he had four sons and six daughters.

Jocelyn succeeded to his father's title on 3 December 1756, and became an Irish privy councillor in 1758. On 1 December 1771 he was created earl of Roden, of High Roding, co. Tipperary, a title named after the old family seat in Essex. On 24 May 1778 he succeeded to his cousin Sir Conyers Jocelyn's baronetcy, and to the family's Hertfordshire estates. However, the lands that he inherited from his father were located in co. Tipperary, and it was here and in Dublin that he spent the rest of his life.

Throughout his political career Roden was an unswerving servant of the Dublin Castle administration, and though he returned few MPs his loyalty enabled him to secure a number of valuable offices and sinecures for himself and his adherents. His only brief flirtation with opposition politics came during the spread of volunteering in the late 1770s, when he personally led one of the more conservative local corps.

Though Tipperary politics and society were dominated by the Mathew family, Roden was still an influential figure, and did not restrict himself to tending to his estates. He was involved in a number of linen manufacturing schemes in Newport and was instrumental in the establishment of a charter school in that village, which ultimately failed to instigate any conversions *en masse*. He died at York Street, Dublin, on 22 June 1797, and was succeeded by his son Robert.   MARTYN J. POWELL

Sources DNB · 'Roden', GEC, *Peerage*, new edn · Foster, *Alum. Oxon.* · T. P. Power, *Land, politics, and society in eighteenth-century Tipperary* (1993) · A. P. W. Malcomson, *John Foster: the politics of the Anglo-Irish ascendancy* (1978) · W. P. Baildon, ed., *The records of the Honorable Society of Lincoln's Inn: admissions*, 2 vols. (1896) **Archives** PRO NIre. **Likenesses** J. Heath, stipple, pubd 1815 (after J. Oldham), NPG

Jocelyn, Robert, third earl of Roden (1788–1870), politician and religious leader, was born at Brockley Park, Queen's county, Ireland, on 27 October 1788, the eldest son of Robert Jocelyn, second earl of Roden (d. 1820), and his wife, Frances Theodosia, eldest daughter of Robert Bligh, dean of Elphin. He was educated at Harrow School between 1801 and 1805. In 1806 he was returned as MP for co. Louth. He was still a minor, however, and in the event the seat was taken over by his uncle until 1810, at which date Viscount Jocelyn, as he was styled during his father's lifetime, took the seat in the Commons and served there until his father's death in 1820 elevated him to the peerage as third earl of Roden. He showed strong tory views, and regularly voted against Roman Catholic relief.

Jocelyn married on 9 January 1813 Maria Frances Catherine Stapleton (1794–1861), second daughter of Thomas Stapleton, Lord le Despencer; they were to have three sons and three daughters. Both he and his wife became staunch adherents of the evangelical movement in the Church of Ireland, and their home at Tollymore Park, co. Down, was run on strongly spiritual lines, with the earl himself regularly leading services in his private chapel and teaching in

Sunday schools on his estates. Tollymore became something of a haven for Roden's co-religionists, while its owner took a prominent role in the network of societies which promoted the 'second Reformation' in Ireland. He saw his devotional and religious life as the mainspring of his political endeavours. His faith was also reflected in his conscientiousness as a landlord, which inspired affection among his Roman Catholic as well as his protestant tenants. He was a vigorous critic of absentee Irish proprietors.

In the meantime Roden held several appointments in the royal household, as treasurer in 1812, vice-chamberlain from 1812 to 1821, and a lord of the bedchamber from 1828 to 1831. Despite his piety, he got on well with George IV, who at his coronation in 1821 created him Baron Clanbrassill in the peerage of the United Kingdom, thereby giving him an automatic seat in the House of Lords. Roden was auditor-general of the exchequer in Ireland from 1820 to 1822, when the office was abolished, leaving him with a handsome pension for life. He was *custos rotulorum* for co. Louth from 1820 to 1849, and a member of both the English and Irish privy councils.

In the Lords, Roden became a leader of the Irish tory peers, a position which was confirmed by his election in 1831 as president of the Irish Protestant Conservative Society. During the 1830s he played a central role in mobilizing protestant opinion on both sides of the Irish Sea to defend the Church of Ireland, notably through great public meetings in 1834 and 1837, and was instrumental in the Conservative leadership's maintenance of a robustly anti-Catholic stance. In 1834 Peel offered him the post of lord steward of the household, but he turned it down in order to preserve his independence of action.

After their accession to power in 1841 Peel and Wellington found it less necessary to cultivate the Irish protestant lobby, and Roden's influence waned. In 1849 he was accused of partiality in dealing with an Orange procession at Dolly's Brae in co. Down, which led to an affray with Roman Catholics and consequent fatalities. Roden firmly defended the integrity of his conduct, but the whig government nevertheless dismissed him from the commission of the peace. Despite this indignity, Roden's commitment to the protestant cause remained intense. He took a strong interest in the conditions of protestants on the continent, having visited Piedmont in 1844. He led a delegation to Florence in 1852 to urge the release of Francesco and Rosa Madiai, imprisoned by the Tuscan government for holding a protestant religious meeting in their home. In Ireland he was grand master of the Orange order, and was a steadfast opponent of the disestablishment of the Church of Ireland.

Lady Roden died in 1861, and on 16 August 1862 Roden married Clementine Janet (*d.* 1903), daughter of Thomas Andrewes of Greenknowes, Dumfriesshire, and widow of Captain Robert Lushington Reilly of Scarvagh, co. Down; there were no children from this marriage. Roden became very infirm at the end of his life, died in Edinburgh on 20 March 1870, and was interred on 29 March in the family vault at Bryansford, co. Down.

Roden was well over 6 feet tall, and in his prime had a commanding and energetic presence with a fluent oratorical style. He was especially effective in addressing Irish protestant audiences, for he well knew 'how to call to his aid every feeling and recollection dear to their inmost souls' (*Random Recollections of Exeter Hall*, 31–6). Although by the time of his death the political and religious creed he espoused could be dismissed as 'somewhat narrow and antiquated' (*The Times*), he was nevertheless an effective ambassador for his beliefs, with a fearless consistency which commanded respect even from his opponents.

JOHN WOLFFE

Sources The Times (22 March 1870) • PRO NIre., Roden MSS • U. Southampton L., Wellington MSS • J. Wolffe, The protestant crusade in Great Britain, 1829–1860 (1991) • D. Bowen, The protestant crusade in Ireland, 1800–70 (1978) • The Record (21 March 1870) • The Record (25 March 1870) • Random recollections of Exeter Hall in 1834–1837, by one of the protestant party (1838) • DNB • GEC, Peerage **Archives** priv. coll., corresp. | BL, corresp. with Sir Robert Peel, Add. MSS 40226–40597, passim • Durham RO, letters to Lord Londonderry • U. Southampton L., letters to duke of Wellington **Likenesses** J. Doyle, black chalk caricature, 1839, BM • J. Kirkwood, etching, pubd 1840, NPG • C. Silvy, carte-de-visite, 1860, NPG • T. Lupton, mezzotint (after F. R. Say), NPG **Wealth at death** under £30,000: probate, 14 April 1870, CGPLA Ire. • under £3000 in England: Irish probate sealed in England, 14 April 1870, CGPLA Eng. & Wales

Jodrell, Sir Paul (1746–1803), physician, was born in London on 12 November 1746, the second son of Paul Jodrell (*d.* 1751) of Duffield, Derbyshire, and Elizabeth, daughter of Richard Warner of North Elmham, Norfolk. His father was solicitor-general to Frederick, prince of Wales, and his elder brother was the playwright Richard Paul *Jodrell (1745–1831), whose works have sometimes been wrongly attributed to his brother. Paul Jodrell was educated at St John's College, Cambridge. In 1769 he graduated BA as eleventh wrangler; he was elected fellow and he proceeded MA in 1772 and MD in 1786. He was elected a fellow of the Royal Society in 1781. On 30 September 1786 he was admitted to the Royal College of Physicians, and on 1 October 1787 he was elected a fellow. He was knighted on 25 October.

In December 1786 Jodrell was appointed physician to the London Hospital. He resigned in November 1787, and travelled to India to become physician to the nawab of Arcot, who had asked George III to find him a physician. This appointment was not wholly successful. The payment of Jodrell's salary was erratic, and he frequently had to appeal to the Madras council to urge the nawab for payment. In 1790 Jodrell brought a libel action against the *Calcutta Gazette*, and was awarded Re500 in damages.

Jodrell married Jane, daughter of Sir Robert Bewicke of Close House, Northumberland; they had a daughter. Jodrell died on 6 August 1803, at his house on Chaultry plain, Madras.

GORDON GOODWIN, rev. CLAIRE E. J. HERRICK

Sources D. G. Crawford, A history of the Indian medical service, 1600–1913, 1 (1914), 15 • Munk, Roll • Venn, Alum. Cant. • Nichols, Lit. anecdotes, 9.2 • Burke, Peerage (1889) • IGI **Archives** U. Cam., Centre of South Asian Studies, papers • Wilts. & Swindon RO, letters

Jodrell, Richard Paul (1745–1831), classical scholar and playwright, was born on 13 November 1745, the eldest of three sons of Paul Jodrell (1715?–1751), of St Andrew's parish, Holborn, and Duffield, Derbyshire, who was solicitor-general to Frederick, prince of Wales, and his wife, Elizabeth, daughter of Richard Warner, of North Elmham, and Elizabeth Lombe. His younger brothers were Sir Paul *Jodrell (1746–1803), physician, and Henry Jodrell (1750?–1814), barrister and MP. He was educated at Eton College from 1756 to 1763 and published some of his early verses in the *Musae Etonenses*. He matriculated from Hertford College, Oxford, on 28 June 1764 and entered Lincoln's Inn in the same year; he was called to the bar in 1771. He married, on 19 May 1772, his second cousin Vertue (d. 1806), the eldest daughter and coheir of Edward Hase, of Salle, Norfolk; they had three sons and two daughters.

Having succeeded to his father's estates at Lewknor, in Oxfordshire, Jodrell was further enriched by the terms of his marriage settlement and was able to settle on a literary rather than a legal career. He contributed to the supplementary notes to Robert Potter's edition of Aeschylus, printed in 1778, and published two volumes of commentaries on three plays by Euripedes. He wrote a series of plays that enjoyed mixed fortunes on the London stage, the first of which, *A Widow and No Widow*, was acted at the Haymarket on 17 July 1779. His 'dramatic proverb', *Seeing is Believing*, was well received at the same theatre on 22 August 1783. He failed to persuade the managers of Drury Lane and Covent Garden to perform his tragedy *The Persian Heroine*, based on Herodotus, but, once printed, it went to several editions and was translated into Italian. In 1787 he published anonymously a collection of farces and comedies that had been performed in provincial or private theatres; among the titles were *Who's Afraid* and *The Boarding School Miss*. An edition of his poetical works appeared in 1814 and a treatise, *Philology of the English Language*, in 1820. Jodrell was a friend of Samuel Johnson and became a member of the Essex Head Club in December 1783. He was elected FRS in 1772, FSA in 1773, and was created DCL of Oxford on 4 July 1793.

At the general election in 1790 Jodrell was elected to parliament as the Treasury candidate for Seaford. Though unseated on a petition in 1792 he regained his seat and held it until 1796, when he fell out with Pitt over the Curates' Maintenance Bill. He had been a reasonably steady government supporter in the House of Commons but switched allegiance after 1796. He was struck off the Lincoln's Inn register in 1816 for failing to settle debts on a bond. He suffered from mental illness in the last ten years of his life and died in Portland Place, London, on 26 January 1831.

Jodrell's eldest son, **Sir Richard Paul Jodrell**, second baronet (1781–1861), was educated at Eton College and at Magdalen College, Oxford, whence he graduated BA (1804) and MA (1806). He was called to the bar from Lincoln's Inn in 1803 but, like his father, pursued his literary interests. A selection of the Greek and Latin verses that he wrote at Eton were privately printed in 1810, and a couple of other poems were published in the 1840s. He married, on 12 December 1814, Amelia Caroline King (d. 1860), the illegitimate daughter of Robert King, second earl of Kingston; they had three sons and one daughter. Jodrell succeeded his maternal great-uncle Sir John Lombe (formerly Hase) as second baronet on 27 May 1817. He died in Portland Place, London, on 14 January 1861, leaving a fortune of £250,000.   GORDON GOODWIN, rev. S. J. SKEDD

Sources GM, 1st ser., 60 (1790), 547; 101/1 (1831), 271–3; 3rd ser., 10 (1861), 234 • Foster, *Alum. Oxon.* • Nichols, *Lit. anecdotes*, 8.77, 102, 155; 9.2–3, 68, 724 • Burke, *Peerage* (1857) • R. S. Lea, 'Jodrell, Paul', HoP, *Commons, 1715–54* • B. Murphy, 'Jodrell, Richard Paul', HoP, *Commons, 1790–1820* • will, PRO, PROB 11/1783, fols. 48v–55r [Sir Richard Paul Jodrell]
Archives Bodl. Oxf., commonplace book • Norfolk RO, memorandum book | Norfolk RO, corresp. with Lord Dalling and Bulwer • Surrey HC, letters to Reynier Tiler
Likenesses C. Heath, engraving (after M. Brown)
Wealth at death £250,000—Sir Richard Paul Jodrell: will, PRO, PROB 11/1783, fols. 48v–55r

Jodrell, Sir Richard Paul, second baronet (1781–1861). See under Jodrell, Richard Paul (1745–1831).

Joel, Betty [née Mary Stewart Lockhart] (1894–1985), furniture and interior designer, was born on 7 June 1894 in Hong Kong, the daughter of Sir James Haldane Stewart *Lockhart KCMG, LLD (1858–1937), colonial secretary and dedicated collector of Chinese art, and his wife, Edith Louise Rider, née Hancock (1870–1950), daughter of a bullion broker. She attended Miss Weisse's school, Northlands, Englefield Green, Surrey, between the ages of nine and sixteen and her education was completed with a governess. In 1918 Mary Stewart Lockhart married David Joel (1890–1973), a naval lieutenant (later commander) in Ceylon and they returned to England. She stated (Patmore, 276) that she began designing furniture for her own modern house, then began accepting commissions from friends. She and her husband set up a small furniture making business, Betty Joel Ltd, at Hayling Island, Hampshire, in 1921. She had been calling herself Betty since 1907 and this name was adopted for the firm as it was thought to convey a modern feeling and to appeal to female customers.

Neither Betty nor David Joel had received any training in design and, early on, she assumed responsibility for design while he administered the business. Betty Joel had a confident and assertive personality but was happy to take advice from the craftsmen they employed. Their employees often had a background in boatbuilding and fitting, reflected in the simplified arts and crafts style of the early furniture. This range was named Token furniture, after the two woods, teak and oak, which were predominantly used in its manufacture. It was retailed through a showroom at 177 Sloane Street in London, which, as the business developed, was moved to 25 Knightsbridge, also the Joels' home. This property included an art gallery where they exhibited both abstract paintings and modern carpets, some of which were designed by Betty Joel and manufactured in China. The factory was moved to larger premises in Portsmouth in 1929. The solidity and simplicity of the early furniture was replaced by greater sophistication as Betty Joel drew inspiration from a range of sources, including Chinese furniture, European modernism, and French art deco. The hallmarks of Joel furniture through the 1930s were extensive use of exotic woods and curvilinear shapes.

Individual clients of Betty Joel Ltd included Sir Winston Churchill, Lord Mountbatten, and the duchess of York, but the firm also produced a more moderately priced furniture range and worked for corporate bodies such as the Savoy and Claridges hotels, Fortnum and Mason, and Metro-Goldwyn-Mayer and Gaumont cinemas. She ventured into product design in the 1930s, designing an Esse stove for Smith and Wellstood Ltd of Bonnybridge and radio cabinets for K-B (Kolster-Brandes) Radio Company. Such a range indicates Betty Joel's popular success, but her work was often criticized by the modernists of the architectural press for indulging her taste for exotic materials and not being sufficiently concerned with function. Her prizewinning circular bed, designed for the British Art in Industry exhibition at the Royal Academy in 1935, was described by Herbert Read as having been 'twisted and contorted into a shape which I can only compare to a dislocated hip-bath' (Read, 48). Joel's spirited defence of her designs formed part of her extensive writings in the design press. Her support of modern architecture was demonstrated by commissioning H. S. Goodhart-Rendel to design a new factory at Kingston upon Thames in 1935.

Between 1937 and 1939 the Joels' marriage failed and the factory was briefly transferred to David Joel. It closed down during the Second World War. Betty Joel retired to Scotland and resumed her maiden name. Her retirement in her mid-forties and later reluctance to talk about her career have resulted in the neglect of her achievements by design historians, if not collectors. In her former husband's books on modern furniture design the only image of her is of a portrait head. Betty Joel's final years were spent at Fotheringay, a bungalow in Berkshire which she designed. She died in a nursing home, Millway House, near Andover, Hampshire, on 21 January 1985. Some examples of her furniture and carpets are in the Victoria and Albert Museum, London.   JILL SEDDON

Sources private information (2004) · *The Times* (1 Feb 1985) · C. Wilk, 'Who was Betty Joel?', *Apollo*, 142 (July 1995), 7–11 · R. Foulk, *Betty Joel: Celtic spirit from the Orient* (1996) · I. Anscombe, *A woman's touch* (1984), 169–72 · J. Hawkins and M. Hollis, eds., Thirties: British art and design before the war (1979) [exhibition catalogue, Hayward Gallery, London, 25 Oct 1979 – 13 Jan 1980] · D. Patmore, 'British interior architects of today', *The Studio*, 104 (1932), 276–7 · G. Boumphrey, 'The designers: 5 Betty Joel', *ArchR*, 78 (1935), 205–6 · D. Joel, *The adventure of British furniture* (1953) · D. Joel, *Furniture design set free* (1969) · H. Read, 'Novelism at the Royal Academy', *ArchR*, 77 (1935), 48 · CGPLA Eng. & Wales (1985) · d. cert.

Likenesses Miller, photograph, 1935, Hult. Arch. · T. Tennant, head, repro. in Joel, *Adventure* · photograph, repro. in Wilk, 'Who was Betty Joel?' · photographs, repro. in Foulk, *Betty Joel*

Wealth at death £372,462: probate, 17 April 1985, CGPLA Eng. & Wales

Joel, Isaac Barnato (1862–1940). *See under* Joel, Solomon Barnato (1865–1931).

Joel, Solomon Barnato (1865–1931), financier, was born on 21 December 1865, at 8 Sandys Row, Spitalfields, in the East End of London, the youngest of three sons of Joel Joel (*d.* 1893), cigar manufacturer and publican, and his wife, Catherine, daughter of Isaac Isaacs. Her brother Barnett Isaacs, known as Barney Barnato [*see* Barnato, Barnett Isaacs], played a major role in his nephews' lives and Solly (as Solomon was familiarly known) was his favourite. His formal education was limited to a brief spell at the Jews' Free School in Spitalfields, to which he and his brother Jack [*see below*] later donated a new wing.

Joel went to Kimberley in the 1880s, a penniless young man, to join his uncle Barney and his brother Woolf Joel in the diamond business of Barnato Brothers: 'His [Solly's] stepping-stone to fortune was the diamond. Diamonds made him ... one of the richest men in the world ... a towering figure in finance, sport and society' (Joel, 9–10). Throughout his long career Joel retained his fascination with diamonds. When the pessimists predicted that the diamond had had its day, he observed astutely that 'Women are born every minute—as long as women are born, diamonds will be worn' (Joel, 68). In 1917, when the diamond trade was seriously threatened by the communist government in Russia which was selling off, at a fraction of their value, huge quantities of stones looted from the aristocracy, he bought £390,000 worth of Russian jewels to support the market.

Joel was a director of Barnato Brothers as well as of De Beers Consolidated Diamond Mines from 1901 until his death in 1931. As the largest individual shareholder in De Beers, New Jagersfontein Mining Company, and Premier Diamond Mining Company, his personal support gave Ernest Oppenheimer the balance of power in 1928 when he was making a play for the chairmanship of De Beers. In 1930 they formed the Diamond Corporation from the syndicate which Joel had established in 1894 to control the world's diamond output. Nevertheless, he was arrested as a member of the Reform Committee (the members of which were deemed to be responsible for the Jameson raid) in January 1896, and sentenced to two years' imprisonment, commuted to a fine when Barney Barnato interceded with President Kruger.

The growing importance of the Witwatersrand goldfields prompted Barnato Brothers to form Johannesburg Consolidated Investment Company Limited, known as Johnnies. After Barney Barnato's suicide at sea on 14 June 1897, witnessed by Solly, Woolf Joel became chairman of the board, residing in London while Solly remained in Johannesburg. However, on a visit to the Rand in 1898, Woolf was shot dead on 14 March by Ferdinand Karl Ludwig von Veltheim, who had been blackmailing Solly. At his trial for the murder von Veltheim alleged that he had entered into an agreement with Barney Barnato and the Joel brothers to kidnap President S. J. P. Kruger, but the Joels had backed out and that was his reason for demanding money from them. He was acquitted on the grounds of self-defence and deported, but in 1907 resumed his blackmailing. He was apprehended and sentenced in a sensational trial in London in 1908 to twenty years in prison.

Solomon Barnato Joel (1865–1931), by Bassano, 1914

The firm's interests were expanded and consolidated during Joel's chairmanship. His most important business coup was on the Far East Rand, where the system of government mining leases had been introduced. Johannesburg Consolidated Investment Corporation not only successfully tendered for the Government Gold Mining Areas (Modderfontein) Limited, which came into production in 1914, but subsequently also outmanoeuvred its rivals in bidding for other government leases. When cash for further exploration and development was running out, Joel personally invested £1 million, thus ensuring the future of the Far East Rand. Johnnies controlled the new state areas, Van Ryn Deep, and acquired the Randfontein Estates group from J. B. Robinson in 1916. His many directorships and business interests included Horrockses and various London underground railway companies. He served as president of the Johannesburg stock exchange in 1896 and was a patron and member of the Witwatersrand Agricultural Society, the Rand Club, the Wanderers Club, and the Johannesburg Turf Club. He donated his uncle Barney's mansion at Barnato Park, Berea, to the Johannesburg Girls' High School, which used part of it as a boarding-school called Joel House.

Although a devout Jew, Joel's first marriage (at some point in the 1880s), was to a gentile, Ellen Ridley (d. 1919), a Lancashire actress whom he had met in Kimberley. She converted to Judaism and they had three sons and two daughters; the couple separated about 1913. After Ellen's death on 14 August 1919 Joel married a former child actress, Mrs Phoebe Benjuta, née Carlow, on 25 November 1919. Joel's three passions were described as 'the stage,

horses and smart clothes' (Gutsche, 27). He had a private box at each of the many London theatres in which he had a financial interest. He and his brother Jack shared a love of the theatre and racing and competed with each other. Between the two of them their horses won practically every classic event: the Oaks, the Two Thousand Guineas, the Derby, the St Leger, and the Ascot Gold Cup. The last named, won by Bachelor's Button in 1906, was Joel's first big success on the turf. By 1921 he headed the list of winning owners. His fine racing stables at Maiden Erlegh, near Reading, Moulton Paddocks, near Newmarket, and Sefton Lodge rivalled those of the Aga Khan, Lord Astor, and Lord Derby. Altogether his horses earned him more than £350,000 in stake money alone (Joel, 10).

A born gambler, Joel won enormous sums of money but hated to lose. He liked to sail in his yacht *Eileen* to the Riviera and do the annual circuit of the playgrounds of Europe—casinos, racecourses, winter sports, and watering places. His hospitality was legendary. The Joels entertained lavishly at their country estates and at their Great Stanhope Street mansion that housed famous works of art as well as the rarest collection of Chippendale furniture under one roof. His cellars were filled with vintage wines and his libraries with beautifully bound literary classics, which he never read. He was witty and gregarious, with catholic tastes and interests. He was a benefactor of the National Playing Fields Association and endowed the chair of physics at the Middlesex Hospital. Joel died at Moulton Paddocks, near Newmarket, on 22 May 1931, and was buried at Willesden cemetery, London, near his uncles Barney and Woolf.

Isaac Barnato [Jack] **Joel** (1862–1940), financier, second son of Joel Joel and his wife, Catherine Isaacs, was born on 29 September 1862, also at 8 Sandys Row, Spitalfields. His business career was very similar to that of the younger and more flamboyant Solly, but his sojourn in Kimberley was cut short after four years when he was arrested for illicit diamond buying, under the Diamond Trade Act of 1882. He jumped bail of £4000 and surreptitiously returned to England, where he joined his uncle Harry in the London business of Barnato Brothers. He became the head of Johnnies in London and chairman in 1931 after Solly's death. Jack's son Jim (Harry Joel Joel) succeeded him as chairman until his retirement which ended the family's direct involvement in the business. Years later the accusation of illicit diamond buying would come back to haunt Jack when Robert (Bob) Siever launched a scurrilous attack in his newspaper the *Winning Post*, referring to him as 'Joel, the notorious dealer in illicit diamonds' (Wheatcroft, 231–4). Jack had Siever arrested on a trumped-up charge of blackmail; Siever, triumphant, was acquitted and Joel humiliated.

Jack married Mrs Olive Coulson, née Sopwith, and they had a son and a daughter. Like Solly, Jack loved horseracing and built up his stud at Childwick Bury near St Albans, where he bred Humorist, who won the 1921 Derby. This was Jack's second Derby and his greatest triumph on the turf in over forty years. He headed the list of racehorse owners on many occasions. He died on 13 November 1940 at Childwick Bury and was buried in the Joel allotment at Willesden cemetery, London.   MARYNA FRASER

Sources S. Joel, *Ace of diamonds: the story of Solomon Barnato Joel* (1958) · E. Jessup, *Ernest Oppenheimer: a study in power* (1979) · *DSAB* · R. Lewinsohn, *Barney Barnato: from Whitechapel clown to diamond king* (1937) · P. H. Emden, *Randlords* (1935) · G. Wheatcroft, *The Randlords* (1985) · M. Fraser and A. Jeeves, *All that glittered* (1977) · D. Jacobson, *Fifty golden years of the Rand, 1886–1936* (1936) · M. Kaplan, *Jewish roots in the South African economy* (1986) · T. Gutsche, *A very smart medal* (1970) · b. cert. · m. cert. · d. cert. · *CGPLA Eng. & Wales* (1931) · d. cert. [Isaac Barnato Joel] · *DNB*
Likenesses Bassano, photograph, 1914, NPG [*see illus.*] · H. Amshewitz, oils, 1917, Museum Africa, Johannesburg · photograph, 1917–18, repro. in *South African Who's Who* (1917–18) · H. C. O., caricature, Hentschel-colourtype, NPG; repro. in *VF* (20 Jan 1910) · photograph (after unknown portrait), repro. in Joel, *Ace of diamonds*, frontispiece
Wealth at death £1,000,000: probate, 13 July 1931, *CGPLA Eng. & Wales* · £3,634,496—Isaac Barnato Joel

Jofroi of Waterford. *See* Waterford, Jofroi of (*fl.* late 13th cent.).

Johannes (*fl. c.*1400–*c.*1420), manuscript artist, identifies himself in the words *Magister Johannes me fecit* ('Master John made me') written on the hem of the robe of the Great Khan, as he is shown enthroned in a miniature on folio 220 of a manuscript of Marco Polo, *Li livres du Graunt Chaam* (Bodl. Oxf., MS Bodley 264), datable on stylistic grounds to *c.*1400. Nothing is otherwise known of Johannes (at least seven illuminators with the first name John are documented in the period), but it is generally accepted on stylistic grounds that he is also the main illuminator in the book of hours of *c.*1420 which later belonged to Elizabeth (*d.* 1503), queen consort of Henry VII (BL, Add. MS 50001), as well as of other manuscripts of less importance. He probably worked in London, being slightly younger than John Siferwas and a contemporary of, perhaps collaborator with, Hermann Scheerre, an illuminator from Cologne or the Low Countries, who similarly inserted his name in one of his miniatures. Johannes's miniatures, especially in the *Graunt Chaam*, are typical examples of the courtly international Gothic style. His compositions include numerous figures in elegant poses and wearing ornate costumes and extravagant headgear, and he uses a subtle palette of mainly pastel colours. The hours of Queen Elizabeth established a model for many later English books of hours, with its rich borders, its *mise-en-page*, and the iconography of its passion scenes. Important illuminators influenced by Johannes include the Cornwall Master and William Abell (*d.* 1474).   J. J. G. ALEXANDER

Sources R. Marks and N. Morgan, *The golden age of English manuscript painting, 1200–1500* (1981), 26–7, pl. 35–6 · N. Rogers, 'The artist of Trinity B.11.7 and his patrons', *England in the fifteenth century* [Harlaxton 1992], ed. N. Rogers (1994), 170–86, esp. 177–8, 182 · K. L. Scott, *Later Gothic manuscripts, 1390–1490*, 2 vols. (1996)
Archives BL, Add. MS 50001 · Bodl. Oxf., Marco Polo, MS Bodley 264, fol. 220

John. *See* Salisbury, John of (late 1110s–1180); Cornwall, John of (*d.* in or after 1198); Hexham, John of (*d.* before 1209); Schipton, John of (*d.* 1256); St Giles, John of (*d.* 1259/60); London, John of (*fl. c.*1260); Gervase, John (*d.* 1268); Peterborough, John of (*supp. fl.* 1369); Glastonbury, John of (*fl. c.*1400).

John (*d.* 1147), bishop of Glasgow, is of uncertain origins but may have been French and a monk of Tiron. First recorded *c.*1114 as chaplain of Earl David, ruler of 'the Cumbrian region' (that is, Strathclyde), he was appointed to the see of Glasgow between 1114 and 1117, probably by David. In an inquest (*c.*1115–1124) into the possessions of his see, John is described as 'a religious man', whence it has been surmised that he had been a monk of Tiron and was active in achieving the foundation of a Tironensian house by Earl David at Selkirk, about 1120. He secured consecration as bishop from Pope Paschal II because the see of York was vacant, and after the appointment of Archbishop Thurstan in October 1119 John refused to promise obedience to him. In 1122 he went to Rome to fight his case against York, and finding no sympathy, visited Jerusalem (where he is said to have helped the patriarch during Baldwin II's captivity) before returning to Scotland under papal pressure in 1123, but still refusing obedience to York.

King from 1124, David I now inherited also the dispute about York's claims over Robert, elect of St Andrews; the papal legate charged with the matter went to Rome late in 1125 with John, who returned in 1126 with a summons to all Scottish bishops to go there the following year. This was postponed and forgotten when Henry I and David I brokered a deal over St Andrews; John simply ignored papal commands to obey York in 1128 and 1131, presumably with David's support.

John's career in the 1130s is beset with problems. It seems that David I gave obedience to the antipope Anacletus II after 1134, perhaps in response to Innocent II's support of King Stephen against the empress. John was reputed a schismatic at Rome on 22 April 1136, but this may have been a malicious lie planted by York, for it is also reported that John was disenchanted with King David because in 1133 he had allowed Henry I to set up the diocese of Carlisle, where John is said to have acted as bishop. John perhaps differed from his king over the schism, and certainly about this time he retired to the abbey of Tiron. It took the combined urgings of a papal legate and King David (no longer schismatic) to bring him back to his see in 1138; and after York fell vacant in 1140 no archbishop troubled him. Between 1126 and his death he witnessed thirty-one charters of David I or Earl Henry, many issued outside his diocese, and probably acted as court chaplain-bishop.

John persuaded David to move the Tironensians from Selkirk to Kelso in 1127 and was probably involved in the king's bringing Cistercians to Melrose, in his diocese, in 1136. He was certainly responsible with David for the foundation of Jedburgh Abbey in 1139 and of Lesmahagow Priory, a cell of Tironensian Kelso, in 1144. But he also built up the resources of his cathedral, and before 1124 began building work there, leading to a rededication in 1136; David I was present and gave Govan to the see, though the dedication date of 7 July is a chronicler's error, borrowed from the dedication of 1197. Excavation in 1992 revealed re-used round columns probably taken from John's church, which some fifty years later was described as 'mean and narrow' (Innes, vol. 1, no. 76). By 1127 John had appointed an archdeacon for the eastern half of his diocese and he created prebends for canons at the cathedral. None the less, the 'chapter' to which he referred was more probably a diocesan synod than a cathedral *collegium*.

John died in 1147, soon after 3 May (his successor was consecrated in France in August), and was buried in Jedburgh Abbey (Kelso or Glasgow might have been expected). He served David I well in bringing to Scotland the monastic orders, and in reviving episcopal order; he also defended the independence of his see and the Scottish church from York. But he probably drew the line at collusion in schism.   A. A. M. DUNCAN

Sources J. Dowden, *The bishops of Scotland … prior to the Reformation*, ed. J. M. Thomson (1912), 295–6 · D. E. R. Watt, *Ecclesia Scoticana* (Stuttgart, 1991), 55–8 · N. F. Shead, 'Origins of the medieval diocese of Glasgow', *SHR*, 48 (1969), 220–25 · N. F. Shead, 'The administration of the diocese of Glasgow in the twelfth and thirteenth centuries', *SHR*, 55 (1976), 127–50 · G. W. S. Barrow, *The kingdom of the Scots: government, church and society from the eleventh to the fourteenth century* (1973), 199–204 · C. Innes, ed., *Registrum episcopatus Glasguensis*, 2 vols., Bannatyne Club, 75 (1843); also pubd as 2 vols., Maitland Club, 61 (1843) · G. W. S. Barrow, ed., *The charters of King David I: the written acts of David I king of Scots, 1124–53, and of his son Henry earl of Northumberland, 1139–52* (1999)

John (*d.* 1190), soldier and landowner, was the son of Richard fitz Eustace (*d.* 1163) and Albreda (or Aubrey) de Lisours (*d.* 1194). Albreda was a daughter and heir of Robert de Lacy (*d.* 1193). Although the two families' interests intertwined, it is inaccurate to use the Lacy surname of John: as a frequent and prominent witness to the charters of the earls of Chester he appears consistently as 'John the constable of Chester'. John served in this capacity—the chief official of the earls of Chester—from 1163, first under Earl Hugh (*d.* 1181), and then under Earl Ranulf (III) (*d.* 1232). He was preceded in this position first by his grandfather *Eustace fitz John, lord of Knaresborough and Halton (who was killed in July 1157 in a Welsh ambush at Counsylth near Basingwerk, Flintshire, during Henry II's campaign against Owain Gwynedd), and then by his father. John married Alice, daughter of Robert of Essex and his wife, Alice. His younger brother Robert fitz Richard became prior of the hospitallers in England.

In 1166 John paid a fine of 1000 marks to have his mother's estates. Some time after 1172 he founded the Cistercian abbey of Stanlaw in Cheshire and the hospital at Castle Donington. Earl Hugh granted him lands in Antrobus in Cheshire and *c.*1178 confirmed John's grant of Stanney to Stanlaw Abbey. Soon thereafter the earl freed the monks of Stanlaw from paying tolls in Chester. During the rebellion against Henry II in 1173 John was a firm supporter of the king. In early May 1181, when Hugh de Lacy lost royal favour and was recalled from his post as justiciar in Ireland, John and Richard Peche, the bishop of Coventry, and an itinerant justice, were sent to command Dublin in his stead. However, before Hugh departed they joined him in building numerous castles in Leinster. John

and Richard were recalled to England during the following winter when Hugh de Lacy returned. John was present at the coronation of King Richard on 3 September 1189 and departed England in March 1190 to participate in the third crusade. His death later that year at the siege of Acre probably occurred on 11 October.

After his death John was succeeded as constable by his eldest son, Roger de *Lacy (*d.* 1211), who adopted the surname Lacy when he inherited his grandmother Albreda's estates at Clitheroe and Pontefract after her death in 1194. John's other children included Richard of Chester, who contracted leprosy and was buried at Norton Priory; a son Geoffrey; and another son Eustace of Chester, who may have been illegitimate. John the constable's descendants became earls of Lincoln in the thirteenth century.

FREDERICK SUPPE

Sources G. Barraclough, ed., *The charters of the Anglo-Norman earls of Chester, c.1071–1237*, Lancashire and Cheshire RS, 126 (1988) · *Journal of the Chester Archaeological Society*, 71 (1991) [G. Barraclough issue, *The earldom of Chester and its charters*, ed. A. T. Thacker] · W. Farrer, 'Feudal baronage', *VCH Lancashire*, 1.291–375 · W. E. Wightman, *The Lacy family in England and Normandy, 1066–1194* (1966) · Giraldus Cambrensis, *Expugnatio Hibernica / The conquest of Ireland*, ed. and trans. A. B. Scott and F. X. Martin (1978) · R. W. Eyton, *Court, household, and itinerary of King Henry II* (1878) · L. Landon, *The itinerary of King Richard I*, PRSoc., new ser., 13 (1935) · A. J. Otway-Ruthven, *A history of medieval Ireland* (1968) · G. Ormerod, *The history of the county palatine and city of Chester*, 3 vols. (1819) · I. J. Sanders, *English baronies: a study of their origin and descent, 1086–1327* (1960) · F. M. Stenton, *The first century of English feudalism, 1066–1166* (1932)

John [*called* John the Scot] (*d.* 1203), bishop of St Andrews and of Dunkeld, was probably identical with John, nephew of Robert (*d.* 1159), bishop of St Andrews, and was certainly the nephew of Matthew of Kinninmonth, archdeacon of St Andrews and bishop of Aberdeen (1172–99). If he was Robert's nephew, his early career was passed in the *familia* of that bishop; he was absent during the episcopate of Arnald (1160–62), perhaps in the schools of Oxford or Paris, but returned under Richard (1165–78), when his father or uncle, Odo, was steward to the bishop and the priory of St Andrews.

The uncertainties end in 1178, when, speedily after the death of Bishop Richard, John was elected bishop by the canons of the priory, to the fury of the king, William the Lion, who secured the election of his chaplain Hugh (probably by the 'Culdee' chapter). John, evidently in Scotland, appealed to the curia, and after the consecration of Hugh at St Andrews, went to Rome where Alexander III quashed the election of Hugh and removed him from administration of the see. But Hugh had been consecrated bishop, and John had not. To sort matters out a legate, Alexius, held a synod under the protection of Henry II's garrison in Edinburgh Castle, negotiated with King William (who was unyielding), deposed Hugh, and on 15 June 1180 had John consecrated in Holyrood Abbey by, among others, his uncle Matthew and Hugh, bishop of Durham.

It is uncertain how long they remained in Edinburgh, but Alexius certainly laid the diocese of St Andrews under interdict, while William roughed up John's supporters and burned the property of Bishop Matthew, who fled, along with others. As this party crossed to Normandy to seek help from Henry II, who sent for William, Hugh went to Rome with an appeal. In the second quarter of 1181 Henry II, John, and William met, probably fruitlessly, for the settlement said to have been reached was the chronicler's anticipation of that proposed in 1182. Hugh, meanwhile, was unsuccessful with the pope, who appointed the archbishop of York as legate in Scotland, ordering him to secure St Andrews for John, if necessary by interdict of the kingdom and excommunication of the king, who at the same time was warned that the pope's exclusion of York's authority from Scotland by the bull *Super anxietatibus* in 1176 could be reversed if William persisted in his 'violence'.

Unaware of these papal moves, the king returned through England, meeting again with John and Bishop Hugh of Durham at Redden on the Border. That they quarrelled bitterly over admitting John to Scotland is evidence that there had been no settlement in Normandy; John excommunicated some of William's household, and when the bishop of Durham summoned the clergy of St Andrews, and Archbishop Roger of York the bishops of Scotland, to come to John and profess obedience to him, King William seized the goods of, and exiled, those who responded. The archbishop, a sick man, now pronounced the excommunication of the king and an interdict on the kingdom, but without validity if after the death of Alexander III on 30 August 1181; Roger himself died in November 1181. The way was open for 'compromise'.

In the winter of 1181–2 King William the Lion sent an embassy headed by Bishop Jocelin of Glasgow to the curia, where their and Hugh's persistence (he had been at the curia for two years) persuaded Pope Lucius III to lift the sentences on 17 March 1182, send the golden rose to King William as a mark of favour, and appoint two legates, once again to sort matters out and, if a mistake had been made, to restore Hugh. It is not known where the legates met the king, nor in what circumstances, but it may be relevant that Hugh had returned to Scotland, while John, exiled since 1180, could go no further north than Roxburgh and its English garrison. The settlement agreed between the legates and king in the summer of 1182 was that both John and Hugh should resign St Andrews, that John should have the see of Dunkeld, the king's chancellorship, 40 merks from the revenues of St Andrews, and restoration of his personal income; if this was not enough, Hugh was to resign St Andrews and receive Glasgow, a proviso which suggests that Bishop Jocelin of Glasgow was intended for St Andrews, and that he had brokered the deal.

It was not to be. John accepted, and King William reneged, asking that Hugh should keep St Andrews; but the legates refused to dishonour the deal. King William then asked John to come to talk to him, but even when offered sureties for his safety 'he would never come to the king unless first [the prelates and nobles] would swear that the king would observe all those things which had been offered to him by [the legates]' (Anderson, *Scottish Annals*, 285). Hugh, aware how weak his position was, now appealed to Rome, and the two were told to appear there on 1 October 1182. By June 1183 the settlement wanted by the king had been achieved at the curia. Both men were induced to resign the see, which the pope conferred upon Hugh, while Dunkeld and some revenues were given to John. Sold short, John could do no more; with Hugh he returned to take up office, and for three years blessed peace descended.

But John was not made chancellor (this was not in the pope's gift, and why should William pay his stake after he had won the game?), and somehow, back in Italy with Hugh by mid-1186, with his friends in Scotland under attack, John persuaded Urban III to allow the case of St Andrews to be reopened in July. He and Hugh went back to Scotland to collect evidence, but only John returned to Rome in 1187, securing the removal of Hugh from office probably in early January 1188. But having gone back to Scotland with bulls which recognized him and ordered his restoration as bishop of St Andrews, John's persistence then collapsed; Roger Howden offers only Proverbs 17:1, 'better is a morsel of bread with joy than a house full of sacrifices with strife' (Anderson, *Scottish Annals*, 298n.), as explanation of his throwing in his hand—for that is what he did. In return for the king's 'mercy' he gave up St Andrews and received Dunkeld again with his revenues but without the chancellorship. Hugh went to Rome to obtain absolution and restoration and to die in a Roman plague in 1188. In the following year John stood by while the king secured the election of Roger of Leicester to the see of St Andrews.

John now served for some fourteen years as bishop of Dunkeld, and may have acted also in his old diocese: Roger was not consecrated bishop until 1198, so John led at the consecration of Reginald, bishop of Ross, at St Andrews on 10 September 1195 and his family remained well dug in at St Andrews. His most striking act as bishop, however, was to renounce the western part of his diocese, because he did not understand the language of its people, who knew only their (presumably) Gaelic mother tongue; his chaplain Harald, it was said, became first bishop of Argyll. Argyll certainly appears as a diocese by c.1220, but there is a certain improbability about the suggested motives, which do not fit with John's devotion to his own rights. It may be that a secular lord of Argyll (perhaps Reginald, son of Somerled) secured the new diocese from the pope.

John died in 1203, supposedly at Newbattle Abbey where he was buried, having taken the Cistercian habit there. The doubt arises because this statement, along with the claim that he was born at Podoth, now Little Budworth in Cheshire, and his renunciation of Argyll, comes from Bower's *Scotichronicon*, which may have used a life, now lost, of John written by William of Binning, prior of Newbattle and later abbot of Coupar Angus. How far Binning confused John with John of Leicester, bishop of Dunkeld (1211–14), cannot now be discovered, but Bower makes John the Scot archdeacon of St Andrews, in error for John of Leicester. John remains an enigmatic figure, a valiant pigmy in the time of the giant Pope Alexander III; until the compromise of 1183 he stood sensibly for ecclesiastical liberty against royal interference in the church, anxious as much to exclude Hugh as to install himself. The failure of that compromise by 1186 makes his surrender in 1188 the more remarkable—but it might be better understood were William the Lion's version of events known. Certainly John was not of the stuff of martyrs, but was willing to put his family and supporters through many difficulties for the sake of his canonical rights.   A. A. M. DUNCAN

Sources O. Engels and others, eds., *Series episcoporum ecclesiae Catholicae occidentalis*, 6th ser., 1, ed. D. E. R. Watt (1991), 46–7, 87–9 · J. Dowden, *The bishops of Scotland … prior to the Reformation*, ed. J. M. Thomson (1912), 8–10, 51 · G. W. S. Barrow, 'The early charters of the family of Kinninmonth of that Ilk', *The study of medieval records: essays in honour of Kathleen Major*, ed. D. A. Bulloch and R. L. Storey (1971), 107–31 · A. O. Anderson, ed., *Scottish annals from English chroniclers, AD 500 to 1286* (1908), 271–304 · A. O. Anderson, ed. and trans., *Early sources of Scottish history, AD 500 to 1286*, 2 (1922), 157, 299–306, 343 · A. A. M. Duncan, *Scotland: the making of the kingdom* (1975), vol. 1 of *The Edinburgh history of Scotland*, ed. G. Donaldson (1965–75), 270–77 · W. Bower, *Scotichronicon*, ed. D. E. R. Watt and others, new edn, 9 vols. (1987–98), vol. 4

Likenesses seal, Darnaway Castle, Morayshire, Moray charters, box 32, divn V, bundle II, no.42

John (1167–1216), king of England, and lord of Ireland, duke of Normandy and of Aquitaine, and count of Anjou, was the youngest son of *Henry II (1133–1189) and *Eleanor of Aquitaine (*c*.1122–1204), and was born at Oxford on 24 December 1167.

The king's son, 1167–1189 Virtually nothing is known of John's childhood and early education, though he clearly acquired a taste for books and, as king, possessed a library of both French and Latin works. Ranulf de Glanville was his *magister* by 1183, and may have encouraged an interest in the law.

By the early 1180s John was known as Lackland, a name contemporaries believed to have been bestowed upon

him by his father. The wish to provide for his youngest son had already led Henry II to take steps that left behind a trail of resentments. John's eldest brother, *Henry, had been provoked to rebel in 1173 by the decision to bestow Chinon, Loudun, and Mirebeau upon John, when the latter was betrothed in that year to the heiress to Maurienne. On 30 September 1174, after the suppression of that revolt, John was granted annual revenues to the value of £1000 from England and 1000 livres each from Normandy and Anjou. In 1175, after the death of Reginald, earl of Cornwall, Henry II reserved the earl's estates to John's use; this disinherited the earl's daughters and their husbands, including the vicomte of Limoges, who then rebelled. In 1176, after the death of William, earl of Gloucester, John was betrothed to *Isabella of Gloucester (*c*.1160–1217) on terms that involved the disinheritance of her sisters and their husbands. In May 1177 Henry designated John as king of Ireland, and asked Pope Alexander III to provide him with a crown. All these grants were formalities. John remained subject to his father's authority; in charters his normal style was *filius regis*—'the king's son'.

In August 1184 John embarked on his first political action. Henry II wanted *Richard, now his eldest surviving son, to transfer Aquitaine to John, and when Richard refused, John—with his father's blessing and helped by his brother *Geoffrey—attacked Richard's duchy. The attack failed. In December all three brothers were summoned to court by Henry; Richard kept Aquitaine. By this time Henry was becoming worried by the degree of independence enjoyed by Hugh de Lacy in Ireland and, despite John's own request that he be sent to help the beleaguered kingdom of Jerusalem, it was probably to curb Lacy that Henry dispatched him to Ireland. He knighted him in March 1185 and gave him a well-equipped and substantial force. It arrived at Waterford on 25 April. Some Irish rulers submitted at once, but when he made huge land grants to

John (1167–1216), tomb effigy

his own followers and friends in disregard of existing Irish rights, the kings of Thomond, Desmond, and Connacht took up arms against him—and they were, it seems, encouraged in this by Hugh de Lacy. John suffered several defeats and returned home in September, complaining to his father about Lacy. By far the most detailed account of the Irish expedition, a catalogue of acts of arrogant mismanagement by John and his advisers, is given by Gerald of Wales, one of the royal clerks who accompanied the expedition. Although he had ends of his own to serve, Gerald's version is confirmed by Roger of Howden's laconic comment that John's avarice and reluctance to pay his troops led to their deserting to the Irish. Roger of Howden and Gerald, both writing soon after the event, provide the earliest judgements made upon John's capacities.

The death of Hugh de Lacy in 1186, and the arrival of a crown sent by Pope Urban III, encouraged Henry II to plan another Irish expedition for John. However, the death of Geoffrey of Brittany in August 1186 raised the possibility of a far-reaching rearrangement of the family possessions. The Irish expedition was shelved, and the crown never used. John remained 'lord of Ireland'—as did all subsequent kings of England until Henry VIII. The widely held belief that Henry loved his youngest son best led to rumours, quite likely fanned by Philip Augustus, king of France, that the Old King planned to disinherit Richard in favour of John. Some of Henry's actions gave colour to this gossip. After the fall of Jerusalem in 1187, Richard, Henry, and Philip all took the cross but Henry would not allow John to do so. In November 1188 Henry's public refusal to recognize Richard as his heir pushed Richard into revolt and an alliance with the French king which won widespread aristocratic support. In 1189 Henry II's position crumbled rapidly. The loss of Le Mans on 12 June seems to have convinced John that his father's cause was hopeless, and that he had better join the winning side. When the Old King conceded defeat he was informed that John had gone over to his enemies. In the judgement of many contemporaries this news precipitated Henry's death, betrayed, as they saw it, by the son he had most loved.

The king's brother, 1189–1192 John remained lord of Ireland, and Richard I rapidly put him in possession of the other estates promised to him by their father: in southwest Normandy the county of Mortain; in England the honours of Peverel, Lancaster, Marlborough, and Ludgershall (with castles), Tickhill, Wallingford, and the counties of Derby and Nottingham (without castles). On 29 August 1189 John married Isabella of Gloucester in defiance of the archbishop of Canterbury's prohibition of the marriage on grounds of consanguinity. John appealed to Rome, and a papal legate recognized the marriage as lawful pending the outcome of the appeal. However, since John did not pursue this, his marriage remained conveniently both lawful and voidable. His Gloucester estates included Bristol and the marcher lordships of Glamorgan and Newport, so Richard gave him command of an army and sent him to the relief of Carmarthen which was besieged by Rhys ap Gruffudd. He came to terms with the Lord Rhys, but Richard presumably thought them unsatisfactory, for

when John brought the Welsh ruler to Oxford in October, Richard refused to meet him. In December 1189 Richard gave John four more counties: Cornwall, Devon, Somerset, and Dorset, perhaps to bring his English revenues up to £4000. From 1189 until 1194 John as count of Mortain ran these counties and honours with a well-developed administration centred on Marlborough. But in William of Newburgh's opinion Richard's affection for John had led him into an imprudent generosity which only whetted his brother's appetite.

In March 1190 at Nonancourt, Richard may have recognized John as heir to the duchy of Normandy, but the fact that he made him swear to stay out of England for three years suggests that he was uneasy about what his brother might do while he was on crusade. He later modified the arrangement, giving the justiciar, his trusted Norman-born minister, William de Longchamp, authority to release John from the oath if and when he saw fit. It is unlikely that Longchamp did so, but within a year John was back in England and at odds with the justiciar. The new arrangement, made at Queen Eleanor's request, had been bound to cause tension between the two men, but it was almost certainly Longchamp's readiness to accept *Arthur of Brittany, Geoffrey's son, as heir to the kingdom in the event of Richard's dying on crusade—as envisaged in the treaty of Messina (October 1190)—which precipitated the crisis. When the sheriff of Lincolnshire, Gerard de Camville, did homage to John as heir presumptive (midsummer 1191), Longchamp laid siege to Lincoln Castle; while he was occupied there, the royal castles of Nottingham and Tickhill were handed over to John. From now until 1194 these great castles were to be the linchpins of John's bid for power. Longchamp called off his siege and agreed to meet John at Winchester in July. According to Richard of Devizes both men turned up to the conference with massive followings of Welsh troops. A settlement was mediated by the archbishop of Rouen, Walter de Coutances, whom Richard had dispatched from Sicily with authority to restore peace. John was required to restore the castles he had taken, but Longchamp withdrew his support for Arthur, recognizing John as heir presumptive and agreeing that in the event of Richard's death he should be given possession of these and other key castles. Any hopes Longchamp may have had of keeping him to the terms of the settlement were soon dashed when John took advantage of the scandal caused by the arrest of Geoffrey, archbishop of York, at Dover on 18 September 1191 to organize a coalition against the 'foreign' justiciar, and to present himself as the champion of English law and liberties. Although Geoffrey also had sworn to stay out of England for three years, public opinion, fuelled by John's populist campaign, forced Longchamp to set him free.

John summoned the justiciar and the leading men to a meeting at Loddon Bridge (between Reading and Windsor) on 5 October 'to consider certain great and difficult matters concerning the lord king and the realm' (*Diceto … opera historica*, 2.98). Longchamp refused to attend, asserting that John planned to usurp the throne. Archbishop

Geoffrey's account of his arrest further inflamed feeling. Walter de Coutances urged John to take the lead in removing the justiciar from office. On 7 October John and his supporters set out towards Windsor (where Longchamp was staying) and London. The justiciar at once made for London himself and a skirmish took place when their households clashed on the road. Longchamp returned to the Tower of London, but by now his opponents had the more powerful friends in the city. That night a torchlight procession welcomed John into London, and he repaid the favour by granting the citizens a commune. Next day at St Paul's, John was again recognized as heir presumptive. According to Richard of Devizes, he was declared supreme governor of the realm and authorized to appoint keepers of all except three royal castles. At this point, according to Gerald of Wales (writing in 1193), John was tempted by Longchamp's offer of a bribe to change sides, but was persuaded by Geoffrey of York and Bishop Hugh of Coventry not to desert his friends. On 10 October Longchamp resigned as justiciar and was replaced by Walter de Coutances. Although, according to Devizes, the appointment was made by John, it is plain that if he had hoped for untrammelled authority once Longchamp was unseated, then he was disappointed and was compelled to act in consort with the new justiciar.

Enticing new prospects were opened up when Philip Augustus returned from crusade burning with anger against Richard. Philip offered to help John become ruler of the Angevin lands on the continent if he would marry his sister Alix (whom Richard had rejected). John was preparing to go to France in February 1192 when his mother arrived, and prevailed upon him to stay on pain of losing all his lands and castles, though it apparently took four meetings of ministers and magnates before he would accept the force of the argument. He then caused further embarrassment by tricking the keepers of Windsor and Wallingford castles into handing them over to men of his own, and being much amused—according to Richard of Devizes, who calls him 'a flighty youth' (*Chronicon*, ed. Appleby, 60)—by the somewhat ineffectual attempts of queen and ministers to counter this latest manoeuvre. Perhaps he had already been cheered by Longchamp's renewed attempt to bribe him. Roger of Howden thought that at a meeting at London in March 1192 John did his best to persuade Eleanor and the ministers to restore Longchamp to his former status. According to other accounts he informed them that Longchamp had offered him 1500 marks, but let it be known that he could be flexible; as soon as he had received 2000 marks (£500 according to Devizes) from the royal treasury, he joined them in ordering Longchamp to leave the country.

Rebellion and reconciliation, 1193–1199 Early the next year came the news that Richard was a prisoner in Germany. Philip Augustus renewed his offer to John, who believed that his moment had come and threw caution to the winds. In January 1193 at Paris he sealed a treaty ceding the Norman Vexin to Philip, and he agreed to marry Alix. While Philip took Gisors, the great fortress of the Vexin, and assembled an invasion fleet at Wissant, John returned

to England, seeking allies among those who traditionally took advantage of times when the English crown was in difficulties. However, the king of Scots rejected his overtures; the best John could do was to hire some Welsh mercenaries with whom he garrisoned Windsor and Wallingford. According to Howden, Richard commented 'my brother John is not the man to win lands by force if there is anyone at all to oppose him' (*Chronica ... Hovedene*, 3.198). Very few joined a rebellion against a crusader king, an enterprise widely perceived as treacherous. Telling the king's ministers that their lord was dead, John demanded their allegiance. The lie did not convince. They laid siege to John's castles, and the preparations they made to defend England led to Philip's calling off his invasion. On 20 April Hubert Walter returned from Germany, having spoken with Richard and knowing the ransom terms. On his advice John was offered a truce; he surrendered Windsor, Wallingford, and the Peak, but was left in possession of Nottingham and Tickhill castles. Throughout these years those who opposed John had none the less constantly to bear in mind that he might be their next ruler.

Soon afterwards John received a message from Philip: 'the Devil is loosed' (*Chronica ... Hovedene*, 3.216–17). Assuming that Richard was about to be released, and that he would soon be facing a charge of treason, he fled to France. In the treaty of July 1193 negotiated between Richard's agents and Philip, it was agreed that if John acknowledged his obligation to contribute to the king's ransom, he could keep his lands. Accordingly he returned to his fealty to Richard and was given a royal writ restoring his castles, only to find that in Normandy their keepers refused to hand them over to him. Frustrated, he went back to Philip and was given possession of Arques, Drincourt, and Évreux. In January 1194 he ceded Philip the whole of Normandy east of the Seine except for Rouen. He and Philip then launched a new invasion of Normandy, and tried to bribe Heinrich VI either to keep Richard in prison for longer or to sell him to them. Allegedly John's contribution was to be 50,000 marks. In England, Hubert Walter and the council excommunicated and formally disseised him, and reinstated the sieges of his castles. Most surrendered at once, though Tickhill and Nottingham held out until after Richard's return in March 1194. At the Council of Nottingham (May 1194) all John's lands, including the lordship of Ireland, were declared forfeit. When Richard sailed to Normandy, John abandoned Philip, sought Richard out at Lisieux, and fell at his feet. He was forgiven and sent to recover possession of Évreux before the Capetian garrison there knew that he had changed sides. His record of treachery between 1189 and 1194 was such as to move the judicious William of Newburgh to call him 'nature's enemy' (William of Newburgh, *Historia rerum Anglicarum*, ed. R. Howlett, Rolls Series, 1884, 402).

For the next five years John stayed prudently in the background, gradually regaining his brother's trust, and so also possession of the lordship of Ireland and the counties of Mortain and Gloucester. He was given subordinate military commands which occasionally led to successes that came to Howden's attention, as in 1196 when he retook Gamaches, and in 1198 when he captured eighteen French knights. Newburgh commented that John now fought hard and loyally for Richard against Philip. His prospects certainly improved after Arthur of Brittany went over to the French court in 1196. By 1197 he was recognized as heir presumptive, and, despite rumours of new tensions between the brothers in early 1199, Richard named John as his successor shortly before he died (6 April 1199).

Securing the succession, 1199–1202 Until John fled from Normandy to England in December 1203 he spent more than three-quarters of his time on the continent. From the moment of his accession his overriding concern was with the security of his continental dominions, and with good reason. Philip invaded Normandy and occupied the county of Évreux as soon as he heard the news of Richard's death. The barons of Anjou, Maine, and Touraine, led by Guillaume des Roches, declared for the young duke of Brittany, and persuaded Angers to open its gates to Arthur and his mother, Constance. In Aquitaine, Philip's old allies the count of Angoulême and the vicomte of Limoges continued to resist ducal authority. Leaving Aquitanian affairs in his mother's capable hands, and perhaps calculating that his reputation there would never allow him to recover the Evrécin, John made Anjou his first priority. On 14 April he took possession of the castle and treasury at Chinon. A few days later he was very nearly trapped at Le Mans when Philip, Arthur, and des Roches met there on 20 April. After this narrow escape John proceeded to Rouen, and on 25 April was invested as duke of Normandy, before returning to Le Mans and sacking it to punish its citizens for their support for Arthur and Philip. Leaving his mother and the leading magnates of Poitou, Aimery de Thouars (whom he appointed seneschal of Anjou in opposition to Guillaume des Roches) and the Lusignans, to pursue the struggle against Arthur, he paid a brief visit to England to be crowned king at Westminster on 27 May 1199. Less than a month later he was back in Normandy with a large army. He forced Philip to raise the siege of Lavardin, but otherwise concentrated on making truces and negotiating peace.

In September 1199 John used some high-handed behaviour on Philip's part to persuade Guillaume des Roches to change sides. Des Roches brought Constance and Arthur to John at Le Mans. But that same day, according to Howden, Arthur was warned that he was in danger of being made John's prisoner, and the next night he and his mother fled for the safety of Philip's court. Aimery de Thouars (whom John had just deprived of the seneschalcy of Anjou) and Aimery's brother Gui (who married Constance) went with them. What could have been a decisive advantage had slipped out of John's hands. He was already paying a high price for the distrust with which he was regarded.

However, Philip too faced both diplomatic difficulties and resentment at the heavy burden of war taxation and was willing to negotiate. Terms were agreed in January 1200, and the treaty of Le Goulet was formally concluded on 22 May. In return for abandoning his allies, for a relief of 20,000 marks, and for territorial concessions which included the county of Évreux, the whole Norman Vexin except Les Andelys, and the lordships of Issoudun, Graçay, and Bourges in Berry, John did homage to Philip for his continental possessions. In addition, though he remained with Philip, Arthur was made to do homage to John for Brittany. Modern historians have felt—as presumably did John—that since Philip's gains since April 1199 meant that he already held virtually all the territories conceded, John had done well to get Philip to recognize him as Richard's sole heir, and hence to resolve the disputed succession. Some contemporaries, however, clearly felt that he had paid too high a price. Above all the abandonment of the diplomatic system that Richard had built up, especially the alliances with Otto IV (duke of Saxony and claimant to the imperial throne) and the counts of Flanders and Boulogne, meant that for peace John was now more than ever dependent upon the trustworthiness of the king of France.

Two of the best-informed contemporary historians (Howden and Coggeshall) report that it was on Philip's advice that John took his next step, his marriage on 24 August 1200 to *Isabella (c.1188–1246), daughter of Audemar, count of Angoulême. Soon after his accession he had found bishops willing to terminate his always voidable marriage to Isabella of Gloucester, and he had then sent envoys to Portugal to negotiate for the hand of a Portuguese princess, so the choice of Isabella came as a surprise to many—and above all to Isabella's betrothed, Hugues de Lusignan. In view of Angoulême's strategic importance there was much to be said, from John's point of view, in favour of a marriage to Count Audemar's heir. But in the first twelve months of his reign he had owed much to the powerful Lusignan family—recognized in January 1200 when he granted La Marche to Hugues—and it was foolish to insult them now. Had he compensated them suitably they might have acquiesced, but he made no effort to do so. In the spring of 1201 he added injury to insult by ordering the confiscation of La Marche (granting it to his new father-in-law) and of the Norman estates (the county of Eu) of Lusignan's brother, Raoul d'Exoudun. His treatment of the Lusignans' pleas for justice led to their appealing to the court of France. John refused to attend Philip's court, so in April 1202 the king of France pronounced the confiscation of all his fiefs and accepted Arthur's homage for all except Normandy.

The loss of Anjou and Normandy, 1202–1205 Philip and the count of Boulogne invaded eastern Normandy; unimpeded by John they captured some key castles. The defence of Anjou remained in the hands of his mother—she had already achieved the near impossible in reconciling Guillaume des Roches and Aimery de Thouars—but in July 1202 she was trapped at Mirebeau by Arthur and the Lusignans. John was at Le Mans when he heard the news on 30 July 1202. With the help of Thouars and des Roches and covering over 80 miles in forty-eight hours, John turned the tables. Arthur and more than 200 barons and knights were captured. Soon afterwards the vicomte of Limoges was also taken prisoner. By thinking and acting faster than his enemies had imagined possible John had achieved a stunning success, and he was naturally exultant. In blatant disregard of local interests he denied Thouars and des Roches any say in deciding the fate of the prisoners, many of them their neighbours and kinsmen. According to the *Histoire de Guillaume le Maréchal*, 'he kept his prisoners so vilely and in such evil distress that it seemed shameful and ugly to all those who were with him and who saw this cruelty' (vv. 12508–12). In September des Roches and Thouars turned against John; in October, with Breton support, they captured Angers itself. John remained in Anjou until December 1202, but he was unable to reverse this defeat and retreated to Normandy. His remarkable talent for driving families as powerful as Thouars, Lusignan, and des Roches into rebellion meant that Anjou, Maine, Touraine, and northern Poitou—the heartlands of the Angevin empire—had fallen into Philip's lap.

By spring 1203 John's reputation was being further damaged by rumours of Arthur's fate—unknown, but he had almost certainly been murdered on John's orders. Indeed the Margam annals, a source close to the Briouze family, asserted that John himself carried out the murder when drunk. In the early summer of 1203 Philip again invaded Normandy. In June 1203 Vaudreuil, guarding the western approaches to Rouen, surrendered without a fight. John announced that this had been done on his orders. In August Philip began the siege of Château Gaillard. John organized an attempt to break the siege employing both land and water-borne troops, but when this failed, he gave no more active help. On 5 December he sailed to England. On 6 March 1204 the castle surrendered. Its fall had a profound effect on morale. Throughout Normandy towns and castles opened their gates to Philip, Rouen doing so on 24 June 1204. By this date much of Poitou had also welcomed Philip. Eleanor's death on 1 April 1204 was followed by a scramble of Poitevin towns and lords to do homage to the king of France. In August 1204 Philip entered Poitiers in triumph. Further south Eleanor's death had been the signal for Alfonso VIII of Castile to invade Gascony, claiming that Henry II had promised his daughter Eleanor (Alfonso's wife) would have it as her dowry when her mother died. By the end of the year little was left of John's continental empire except the ports of the west coast of France from Bayonne to La Rochelle, and the isolated inland fortresses of Chinon and Loches.

In 1205 John suffered further setbacks. He made strenuous efforts to muster a large fleet and army at Portsmouth in May 1205, but the reluctance of the English magnates to follow him led to the expedition's being cancelled in humiliating circumstances. Loches and Chinon surrendered. The main Gascon towns held out, however; the Channel Islands were recovered, and in Poitou Savaric de Mauléon regained Niort. In June 1206 John disembarked at La Rochelle. Philip had moved to defend Normandy as soon as he heard John was preparing to sail, and this gave John a free hand to recover the Saintonge, to consolidate his hold on his wife's county of Angoulême (her father had died in 1202), and to drive the last Castilian garrison out of Gascony. In September he marched north into Anjou, but retreated as soon as he heard that Philip was approaching with an army. In October 1206 the two kings agreed on a two-year truce. Philip's lack of interest in Gascony and south-western Poitou (Angoulême, Aunis, and the Saintonge) allowed John to save something from the wreckage of his empire; but there was no gainsaying that wherever and whenever he and Philip met, John had been defeated.

Contemporaries explained these defeats in personal terms. By contrast in recent years many historians have been attracted to the theory that John was beaten by a richer king. John certainly had money worries. In November 1204 and January 1205 he initiated a reform of the English coinage. However, Philip also had financial problems, and there are too many gaps in the evidence for the question to be reduced to a matter of resources. What is certain is that in 1200 John was persuaded to abandon his allies, and that between 1202 and 1205 he lost a war that in the late 1190s his brother had been winning. The judgement of the Barnwell chronicler was that once John had been deserted by his own men he bowed to the inevitable. Some English annalists thought the loss of Normandy was due to Norman treachery, but most blamed John for the conduct which led to these desertions, conduct which justified his sobriquet Softsword.

The government of England After the Poitou campaign of 1206 a new determination is evident in John's government of England. Hitherto it had continued much as it had been under Richard. Although a new record source, the chancery rolls, meant that from 1199 onwards day-to-day business was much better recorded than ever before, those responsible for raising men and money in England for Richard now did much the same in the same way for John. Hubert Walter became chancellor, holding the office until his death in 1205. Geoffrey fitz Peter was made earl of Essex and continued to hold office as justiciar until he died in 1213. The treasurer, William of Ely, and the chief forester, Hugh de Neville, both stayed in office until they rebelled in 1215. One novelty, the writ of attaint, to investigate the verdicts of local juries, was designed in the king's court in Normandy and sent to England in the usual way in the summer of 1201. The first real changes came after December 1203, when John stayed almost continuously in England, and brought over with him those Frenchmen, such as Peter des Roches, Peter de Maulay, Falkes de Bréauté, and Girard d'Athée, who threw in their lot with John after their own homes had been overrun by Philip. From 1204 onward the channel was in the front line of defence; the king's fleet of galleys had to be transferred from Norman to English and Irish ports, and further strengthened. After an invasion scare in January 1205 all males over the age of twelve were required to take a loyalty oath; in each shire chief constables were appointed to appoint local constables responsible for defence and peace-keeping. But until the autumn of 1206 the recovery of his continental possessions remained John's immediate goal.

For five years after 1206 John concentrated on the British Isles, and on raising and hoarding money. Not until

1212 did he announce a new expedition to the continent. In 1207 he levied a thirteenth, a tax at the rate of 1*s*. on each mark. This alone brought in £57,425, more than two years' ordinary revenue. Although he did not repeat this lucrative experiment, his government became distinctly more aggressive after 1207. Traditional ties between crown and baron had been based upon a mutual understanding that although an ambitious baron might incur very large debts when making agreements to pay for reliefs, wardships, and marriages, the king would not press hard for repayment. John, however, began to do so, and in an arbitrary fashion. In 1207 the earl of Leicester was deprived of his lands for non-payment of debt. In 1208 John ordered Girard d'Athée to occupy the estates of William (III) de Briouze, hitherto high in royal favour. Briouze and his family were pursued to Ireland and then either driven into exile or imprisoned; it was generally believed that John had Matilda de Briouze and her eldest son starved to death. According to John's own account, this action was initiated for non-payment of debt 'in accordance with the custom of our kingdom and the law of the exchequer' (Rymer, *Foedera*, 1.107–8)—hardly reassuring words for other landowners.

Other sources of income were also more intensively exploited. A series of heavy tallages on Jews culminated in a tallage of 66,000 marks in 1210. Brutal measures were employed to enforce payment; this tallage became unpopular even outside the Jewish community since John, in his determination to collect, put pressure on those who owed debts to the Jews. Towns also fared badly from the tallage of 1210, the heaviest in the history of this tax. Revenue from forest eyres was increased, and so too, especially from 1209 onwards, were the profits of justice. All this had a dramatic effect on royal income. Whereas in the years before 1207 revenues audited at the exchequer only once exceeded £30,000 (in 1205 when they reached £31,541), the equivalent figures (that is, excluding interdict and Jewish revenues) for 1210, 1211, and 1212 were £51,913, £83,291, and £56,612. It has been estimated that by 1212 John had 200,000 marks in coin stored in castle treasuries at Bristol, Corfe, Gloucester, and elsewhere. He was now an astonishingly wealthy king, but by taking so much coin out of circulation he made it hard for his subjects to meet his demands. In the Barnwell chronicler's opinion, he had become the plunderer of his subjects.

John and Pope Innocent III, 1198–1211 Like most rulers John wanted to control ecclesiastical appointments, and this at times led to quarrels with both local churchmen and the pope. As lord of Ireland he angered Innocent III by driving the archbishop of Dublin into exile in 1198 and again in 1202; as duke of Aquitaine he upset him by his treatment of the bishops of Limoges and Poitiers. In 1203 Innocent threatened to impose an interdict on Normandy when John objected to his confirmation of a bishop of Sées; in view of the military situation, John backed down. In England, however, the traditional authority of king over church was greater, and John was determined to uphold it. In September 1205 his hand seemed to stretch even to Rome, where a delegation of Winchester monks elected Peter des Roches—the king's candidate—as their bishop. This alarmed Innocent. In March 1206 he took the opportunity to annul as uncanonical the election of John de Gray, bishop of Norwich, John's candidate to succeed Hubert Walter at Canterbury. He then persuaded the Canterbury monks to elect Stephen Langton and consecrated him in June 1207. But Langton's long residence at Paris had made him unacceptable to John; the king seized the Canterbury estates and exiled the monks. Earlier that year he had confiscated the temporalities of York when Archbishop Geoffrey protested against the thirteenth and went abroad. Innocent responded by proclaiming an interdict in March 1208. In retaliation John confiscated all clerical property, and ordered the arrest of priests' and clerks' mistresses, though he soon allowed them to purchase their freedom; favoured churchmen even recovered their property. King and pope negotiated, but John was concerned that Langton's appointment should not become a precedent, and he refused to admit liability to pay compensation. In November 1209 Innocent excommunicated him. Thereupon all the bishops of the English church went into exile, with the exception of Peter des Roches, who stayed in England, and John de Gray, who became justiciar of Ireland. Negotiations continued in a desultory fashion; when they were broken off in 1211 rumours spread that Innocent had declared John deposed. By this stage, with no fewer than seven bishoprics and seventeen abbacies vacant, John's profits from the English church were so great that he preferred being excommunicated, as were his allies Otto IV and Count Raymond (VI) of Toulouse, to reaching a settlement.

Lord of Ireland, 1185–1216 No king of England, either predecessor or successor, ever came to the throne with a stake in Ireland matching John's. From 1185 onwards his instinct remained constant: to encourage the advance of English conquerors and settlers at the expense of the Irish. After the death of Domnall Mor Ó Briain in 1194 and the capture of Limerick, William de Burgh dismembered the kingdom of Thomond and was encouraged to take the English conquest over the Shannon by being given a speculative grant of the whole of Connacht. In 1201, however, John put a brake on William de Burgh's alarmingly successful advance by granting Limerick to William de Briouze; by 1203 he was even ready, though for a price, to support the new king of Connacht, Cathal Croibhdhearg Conchobair. In a similar policy of cutting a conqueror down to size, he connived at the attacks launched by Hugh de Lacy against John de Courcy in Ulster. Courcy was forced to take refuge with Ó Néill in Tyrone, and in May 1205 Hugh was made earl of Ulster. However, after the arrival of William (I) Marshal in Ireland in 1207, John's policy of setting one baron against another was markedly less successful. A Marshal–Lacy coalition defeated one justiciar in a winter war in 1207–8, and then flouted the orders of the new justiciar, John de Gray, by sheltering William de Briouze in 1208–9. Faced with this defiance John decided on a second expedition to Ireland.

Once the massive scale of his preparations—an armada of 700 ships—was plain, William Marshal prudently crossed to Pembroke, submitted, and gave more hostages. John landed at Crook on 20 June 1210. In a whirlwind nine-week campaign he drove Walter and Hugh de Lacy out of Meath and Ulster, and captured Matilda de Briouze and her elder sons. Not surprisingly in view of its devastating impact on the English lords in Ireland, John's expedition of 1210 made a big impact on English writers. Wendover was to claim that more than twenty Irish chiefs submitted at Dublin, and that John introduced English law and currency into Ireland. Unquestionably the process of transferring English governmental and legal institutions *en bloc* to a conquered country gathered pace during his reign. In 1204 he instructed the justiciar to found towns and assess rents. The counties of Desmond (Waterford and Cork) and Munster were created, and royal lands were augmented by the forfeiture of Meath, Limerick, and Ulster. In November 1210 a register of writs was sent to Ireland. Englishmen were appointed to bishoprics within areas subject to English control.

By contrast the Irish themselves remained marginal to John's concerns, and, with the exception of Donnchad Ó Briain of Thomond who was knighted by John, they were much less impressed. The expedition ended with John on very tense terms with the two most enterprising Irish kings, Cathal Croibhdhearg and Aodh Ó Néill; the latter's refusal to hand over hostages was applauded by the Inisfallen annalist, who commented, 'The king of England came to Ireland and accomplished little' (Mac Airt, *Annals of Inisfallen*, 339). None the less John's presence there, after a twenty-five-year interval, had been a forcible reminder of the power of the English crown. After his departure John de Gray built the castle and bridge at Athlone, controlling the key passage across the Shannon between Meath and Connacht, and then launched a joint English–Ó Briain invasion of Connacht which forced Cathal to hand over a son as hostage. In the north, however, Gray's forward policy in 1211 and 1212 signally failed to reduce Ó Néill to obedience, and there are signs that he was still at war in 1215–16. Cathal Croibhdhearg tried to exploit John's difficulties by more peaceful means. In September 1215 he secured a charter granting him and his son Aodh the whole of Connacht except Athlone for 300 marks a year 'for as long as they faithfully served' (*Rotuli chartarum*, 219). On the same day John made a—presumably secret—grant of the identical territory to Richard de Burgh. This manner of dealing with Irish kings, together with the restoration of Walter de Lacy to all his lands, sufficed to keep the English lords of Ireland uniquely loyal to the crown during the civil war of 1215–16.

Relations with Wales and Scotland, 1189–1211 As lord of Glamorgan since 1189 John came to the throne knowing Wales better than any king since 1066, but at the end of his reign the English crown was weaker there than for over a century. Until 1208 he continued traditional policy, content with the crown's overlordship over marcher lords and Welsh rulers, while exploiting any opportunities that the fissile nature of Welsh politics sent his way, for example obtaining Cardigan in 1199 as the price for his support for Maelgwyn ap Rhys in the latter's feuds with

his kin. In 1199 he recognized William Marshal as earl of Pembroke, and in June 1200 he licensed William de Briouze to conquer all he could from his Welsh enemies. He acknowledged the rising star of Wales, *Llywelyn ab Iorwerth of Gwynedd, even recognizing him as prince of all north Wales by treaty in 1201, and giving him his illegitimate daughter, *Joan (Siwan; *d.* 1237), in marriage in 1205.

In 1208 he adopted a much more aggressive policy. He first sent in his mercenary captains to break his old favourite William de Briouze. Then on 8 October he summoned Gwenwynwyn, prince of Powys, to Shrewsbury, arrested him, and released him only after utterly humiliating him. These two actions unleashed a chain of events that in the short run brought John great gains but were ultimately to bring him down. Llywelyn took advantage of Gwenwynwyn's downfall to annex southern Powys and Ceredigion. Alarmed by the growing number of Llywelyn's clients, John launched two invasions of Gwynedd in 1211; the second was devastatingly successful, penetrating further into Gwynedd than any previous royal expedition. Llywelyn was forced to surrender the whole of Gwynedd east of Conwy 'for ever', and agree that if he died without issue by Joan all his lands would revert to the king. By the end of the year John was in a much stronger position in Wales than any previous king.

In November 1200 William, king of Scots, came to Lincoln and did homage to John for the lands that he held of him in England. This put an end to a period of tension between them when William, in the hope of recovering Northumbria, had toyed with the idea of an alliance with Philip of France. Thereafter relations between the two kings were restrained; William lost no opportunity to ask for Northumbria, but took no action when John prevaricated. Then, in the summer of 1209, John suddenly marched north from Newcastle intent on invading Scotland—a kingdom of which he had hitherto taken little notice. It seems likely that he had learned of discussions about a marriage alliance between one of William's daughters and the king of France, and that in his newly belligerent style he immediately decided to take advantage of the fact that William was ill. William desperately needed to buy time; he acquiesced in the humiliating treaty of Norham (August 1209), promising to pay 15,000 marks in return for John's 'good will', and handing over thirteen hostages as well as his two daughters for John to arrange their marriages. The ailing Scottish king's dependence on John's goodwill was further increased in 1211 when he found himself in difficulties against a rival for the throne, Guthred Macwilliam. In these circumstances John agreed to assist in the succession of William's twelve-year-old son, Alexander. In 1212 he knighted Alexander at London and provided him with a contingent of Brabançons, with which he defeated and killed Macwilliam.

Crisis, 1212–1214 By this time there was, in the judgement of the Barnwell chronicler, 'no one in Ireland, Scotland and Wales who did not obey his nod—something which, as is well-known, none of his predecessors had achieved'

(*Memoriale fratris Walteri de Coventria*, 2.203). Full of optimism, John turned to the recovery of his continental possessions. With the active support of Rainauld, count of Boulogne, and galvanized by the return of Emperor Otto IV to Germany in March 1212, he set about rebuilding the coalition he had sacrificed in 1200. In the Rhineland sterling once again abounded. By July preparations were well in hand for a return in force to the continent, when his plans were overtaken by events that showed his mastery of the British Isles to be more apparent than real.

It began with a Welsh revolt. The oppressive programme of castle building with which John had followed up his victorious campaign of 1211 provoked the Welsh into uniting behind Llywelyn ab Iorwerth. To counter this John ordered the land and naval forces that had been assembling at Portsmouth to muster at Chester. On 14 August he hanged twenty-eight Welsh hostages at Nottingham. There he learned of a plot against his life. Two magnates, Robert Fitzwalter and Eustace de Vescy, fled abroad. An exchequer official, Geoffrey of Norwich, was arrested and died in prison. From now on, wrote the Barnwell chronicler, John suspected everyone; he would go nowhere without an armed bodyguard. On 16 August he ordered his army to disband, allowing the Welsh to recover the lands east of Conwy. From those whom he suspected he took further guarantees of loyalty in the form of hostages and castles: this policy was applied with particular thoroughness to barons and knights of the northern counties. A popular preacher, Peter of Wakefield, prophesied the imminent end of his reign. In a bid for support from wider social groups John promised to reform abuses of power by sheriffs and forest officials, again especially in the north. His decision to reopen negotiations with Innocent III in November 1212 also indicated a new willingness to compromise. But he continued to treat English landowners with his usual capricious mix of bribery and coercion, and he pressed ahead with plans for a new continental expedition in 1213.

Philip forestalled him, announcing an invasion of England in April 1213. While he was negotiating with Aragon and Toulouse in the hope of opening a southern front against Philip, John stationed a large army in Kent from 21 April onwards. Thus virtually the entire baronage witnessed his surrender of the kingdom to the papacy on May 15 at Ewell near Dover and his promise to pay an annual tribute of 1000 marks. Although the Barnwell chronicler noted that many people saw this as a humiliating servitude, he felt that John's position was now so precarious that he had little choice. Indeed, the manoeuvre has often been praised as a master stroke of diplomacy. Although negotiations over payment of compensation meant that not until July 1214 was the interdict finally lifted, it none the less immediately converted Innocent into his most ardent defender and so—much to Langton's disquiet—John was able to promote his own clerks to vacant bishoprics. On the other hand the return of the exiles meant that his most determined enemies, including, at Innocent's insistence, Fitzwalter, Vescy, and a son of William de Briouze, namely Bishop Giles of Hereford, were now back

in England. At least John was still on the throne on the anniversary of his coronation, 27 May, and he celebrated by having Peter of Wakefield and his son hanged. However, for those who believed the prophet, John's reign had ended on 15 May 1213.

John may have hoped that Philip would obey Innocent and cancel the invasion of England. None the less when the king's illegitimate half-brother, William (I) *Longespée, earl of Salisbury, saw an opportunity to destroy the French fleet in harbour at Damme on 30 May, it was gleefully taken. In June John ordered his army to sail with him to Poitou. But, as in 1205, the magnates refused to go. Some northern barons, led by Eustace de Vescy, claimed that the terms of their tenure did not require them to serve in Poitou. This group, increasingly prominent in the opposition, came to be known as 'the northerners'. John wanted to punish them but was thwarted by Langton; in November he promised to restore their ancient liberties. However, appointing Peter des Roches as justiciar after the death of Geoffrey fitz Peter in October 1213 was a provocative act, and the political situation, particularly in the north, was far from being settled when he pressed on with a new expedition to Poitou. This time most magnates either served in person or sent proxies, but among those who did neither were Fitzwalter, Vescy, William de Mowbray, and Geoffrey de Mandeville (who had just agreed to pay 20,000 marks for the hand of Isabella of Gloucester). In these months John's tactics had created a community of interest between Langton and the future rebels.

In February 1214 John landed at La Rochelle, while his half-brother William Longespée took an army to Flanders, where he was joined by Otto IV, Count Ferrand of Flanders, and Rainauld of Boulogne. A combination of John's subsidies and Philip's attacks on Flanders had revived the old coalition. A two-pronged attack from west and northeast was to force Philip to divide his forces. By the end of May John had persuaded the Lusignans to join him, in return for the grant of Saintes and Oléron and a marriage between his daughter *Joan and Hugues de Lusignan's son. He advanced on Nantes, but Pierre, duke of Brittany, was unmoved by the offer of the honour of Richmond. On 17 June John entered Angers unopposed and then laid siege to Roche-au-Moine. However, he was unable to persuade the Poitevins to fight when Prince Louis of France advanced to its relief, and, on 2 July, he beat a hasty retreat. But by keeping an army intact he had at least prevented the Capetians from reuniting their forces. On 27 July his allies brought Philip to battle at Bouvines and suffered the overwhelming defeat that sealed John's fate. Otto IV escaped, but William Longespée and the counts of Boulogne and Flanders were captured and taken to Paris. Philip was now free to rejoin his son and to confront John in Poitou. On 18 September the two kings agreed on a five-years truce; on 13 October John landed at Dartmouth. Coggeshall reported rumours that the truce cost John 60,000 marks. There is, at any rate, no doubt that the enormous costs of the disastrous diplomatic and military campaign of 1214 had emptied John's coffers. Moreover the policy of reform of 1212–13 resulted in a huge reduction in royal revenue, which in 1214 amounted to less than half the total in 1212. John's days as a wealthy king were over; he would no longer be able to browbeat his subjects.

Magna Carta The general refusal to pay scutage, which John had set at the high rate of 3 marks on the knight's fee, showed that individual grievances were turning into a co-ordinated movement. In January 1215 the king met his opponents at London—they came armed—and it was agreed that there should be another meeting at Northampton on 26 April, when he would reply to their demands for reform and for confirmation of the coronation charter of Henry I. But both sides pursued preparations for civil war. John borrowed from the templars to pay mercenaries brought over from Poitou and Flanders, and he relied increasingly on 'aliens'. On 4 March he took the cross. The Barnwell chronicler regarded this as a cynical manoeuvre, but it led Innocent to describe those who opposed John as 'worse than Saracens' (Cheney and Semple, 208). He did not go to Northampton, and on 5 May his opponents formally renounced their fealty. Over the next few weeks they won a landslide of support. On 9 May John granted London the right to elect their mayor, but on 17 May the city opened its gates to the rebels. In Wales the alliance of Llywelyn ab Iorwerth and the Briouzes achieved some dramatic successes; even Shrewsbury fell to the Welsh. Although John retained the loyalty of a few magnates such as William Marshal and Earl Warenne, he realized he would have to make—or appear to make—substantial concessions if he wanted to buy time to build up his armed strength. On 10 June he agreed to accept the articles of the barons as a basis for further negotiations. On 15 June terms were settled and John went to Runnymede where he confirmed the final draft of the charter. Four days later peace was proclaimed, and most of the rebel barons renewed their homages.

This long document—its length led to its being called Magna Carta ('the great charter')—was drawn up as a means of winning support in a crisis. Hence it was granted 'to all the freemen of the realm and their heirs for ever' and framed so as to contain something for virtually everyone. In these circumstances its sixty-three chapters came to include much that applied to English royal government in general, to John's father and brother as much as to John himself, beginning with the conventional assurance 'that the English church shall be free' (Holt, 448–73, chap. 1) and including promises as vague as 'To no one will we sell, to no one will we deny or delay right or justice' (ibid., chap. 40), or as precise as the promise (ibid., chap. 33) to remove fish-weirs from the rivers of England. But Magna Carta was also, and this is particularly true of the most crucial clauses, a commentary on John's rule. His habit of pressing hard for the repayment of debts owed by tenants-in-chief and of turning dispossession, or the threat of it, into a regular instrument of policy resulted in the bulk of the early chapters' relating to the inheritance and property rights of the king's tenants (ibid., chaps. 2–11). His practice of taking hostages from his English subjects, as well as from the Welsh and Scots, is reflected in chapters 49, 58, and 59. His oppressive taxation led to chapter 12's stating

that, except in three closely defined cases, 'the common counsel of the realm' had to be obtained before a scutage or aid could be levied; chapter 14 set out how that counsel was to be obtained. His employment of foreigners as castellans and troops led to the promises that they would be dismissed and expelled (ibid., chaps. 50–51).

Some of Magna Carta's chapters—those on taxation and chapter 2, which set levels of reliefs—were to be reissued and have a profound effect on subsequent government practice. But the charter of 1215 also contained chapters which guaranteed that, as a peace treaty, it would have a very short life. Anticipating that John would wriggle out of any commitments made at Runnymede, the rebels set up mechanisms designed to prevent this. John had to agree that:

> if anyone has been disseised or deprived by us without lawful judgement of his peers of lands, castles, liberties or his rights, we will restore them to him at once; and if any disagreement arises on this let it be settled by the judgement of the Twenty-Five barons referred to in the security clause. (Holt, 448–73, chap. 52)

The security clause authorized the barons to:

> choose any twenty-five barons of the realm they wish … so that if we transgress any of the articles … then those twenty-five with the commune of all the land shall distress and distrain us in every way they can, namely by seizing our lands, castles and possessions. (ibid., chap. 61)

Chapters 52 and 61 did not so much reform the realm as destroy the sovereignty of the crown. More than anything else they reveal the depths of distrust in which this king was held. In spite of the proclamation of peace on 19 June the inclusion of chapters 52 and 61 ensured that the renewal of war would come sooner rather than later.

Civil war and French invasion, 1215–1216 By mid-July John had written to Innocent asking him to annul the charter. For a few weeks more he continued with a façade of compliance with its terms, but early in September the arrival of papal letters excommunicating rebels, including the Londoners and nine barons, encouraged him to throw off the mask. His troops laid siege to Rochester Castle while the rebels asked for help from France, offering the throne to Prince Louis. Louis accepted but not until December did an advance guard of French troops arrive in London. By then Rochester had already surrendered (on 30 November after a seven-week siege). But while John was detained in Kent until 10 December, his enemies enjoyed a free hand elsewhere. In October Alexander II, king of Scots, having been awarded Northumberland, Cumberland, and Westmorland by a judgment of the twenty-five barons, received the homage of the northerners. No fewer than eleven Welsh rulers joined Llywelyn in the triumphal progress that established him as the *de facto* prince of Wales; in three weeks they captured seven castles, including the traditional strongholds of the English crown at Cardigan and Carmarthen.

In December John took his army north, harrying as he went. The Yorkshire rebels retreated before him into Scotland, so John invaded Alexander's kingdom. On 13 January 1216 he captured Berwick, Scotland's richest town. He raided the Scottish lowlands and then fired Berwick before heading south again. In March 1216 he marched into rebel-held East Anglia, capturing Colchester. During these months he held the military initiative and brought some rebels to submit, but not one of their leaders was won over. Nor, though he badly needed a decisive success before Louis landed, did he try to recapture London. In April 1216 John found himself once again mustering land and naval forces in Kent to meet a French invasion. However, when Louis defied papal prohibitions and disembarked at Sandwich on 22 May, John withdrew westwards without a fight. He stayed in the west throughout June, July, and August while Louis visited London, captured Winchester, and laid siege to Dover, Windsor, and Lincoln castles, control of which would have completed his hold on the eastern counties south of the Tees. The earls of Arundel and Warenne, and even Salisbury (William Longespée) submitted to Louis. Alexander II met Louis at Canterbury, and did homage for the lands he held of the English crown. In September John moved north-east to reinforce his garrison at Lincoln, and perhaps also in the hope of intercepting Alexander on his way home. Although Louis's French troops were beginning to cause patriotic resentments, two-thirds of the most powerful barons had abandoned John, as had one-third of his household knights and a number of the most experienced crown servants such as Warin fitz Gerold, William of Wrotham, Hugh de Neville, and Reginald of Cornhill. By mid-October 1216 the key castle of Dover was on the verge of falling to the French.

Death and burial At Lynn, John suffered an attack of dysentery on the night of 9–10 October 1216. According to Coggeshall it was brought on by gluttony. On 10 October he made a grant to Margaret, daughter of William de Brouze, for the sake of the souls of her parents and brother. Over the next few days his health deteriorated and he lost part of his baggage train in the Wash. He struggled on as far as Newark, where he died during the night of 18–19 October 1216. As he had requested, his body was taken to Worcester Cathedral (still safely in loyalist hands). He was buried wearing on his head the cowl-like coif of unction he had worn at his coronation. Monastic authors such as Coggeshall and Wendover believed that he went to hell. Matthew Paris disapproved of, but repeated, the acerbic comment that 'Foul as it is, Hell itself is made fouler by the presence of John' (Paris, *Chron.*, 2.669).

Appearance and character The effigy at Worcester cannot be treated as reliable evidence for John's features; it was probably made when his body was transferred to a new sarcophagus in 1232. Gerald of Wales described John in his early twenties as of average height (or a little below it) and of quite handsome appearance. Measurements taken when his tomb was opened in 1797 indicate that he was 5 feet 6½ inches tall. Coggeshall said he was a slave to his appetite and that in later life he ran to fat. In the last fifty years historians have been sceptical of the views of monastic authors soured by their experience of the interdict, and have turned instead to the evidence of records.

The earliest extant fragments of royal household accounts date from John's reign, so it is in some respects possible to know his appetites and tastes better than those of any earlier king. In this case the accounts show that he frequently failed to observe the dietary restrictions of the church on Fridays and religious festivals—his favourite oath was 'God's teeth'—and that as a penance he gave alms to paupers. He performed similar penances whenever he went hawking on holy days.

Such routine penitential acts reveal little about his religious views. Tales of a king ready to abandon Christianity for political advantage are late and lack substance. John's wish to be buried at Worcester suggests he venerated St Wulfstan. He helped to carry Hugh of Lincoln's coffin, and he may well have shared the general admiration for the saintly bishop; it was in the atmosphere of public grief at Hugh's death in 1200 that Hubert Walter persuaded John to remit his anger against the Cistercians and to promise to found a Cistercian abbey, which he did at Beaulieu in 1204. On the other hand Hugh's biographer, Adam of Eynsham, portrayed John as a superstitious man who indulged in hypocritical displays of humility.

From the household accounts it is possible to trace debts John owed as a result of losses when playing 'tables' against Brian de Lisle; in 1209/10 the king's ewerer was paid for providing twenty-three baths in sixteen months; in 1214 John sent one of his mistresses a chaplet of roses taken from Geoffrey fitz Peter's garden at Ditton. He had an unknown number of mistresses and at least seven illegitimate children—all of these seven were born before 1200 while he was still married to Isabella of Gloucester, with whom he had no children. After divorcing her in 1200 he retained her lands until 1214. According to Coggeshall, Isabella of Angoulême looked about twelve years old when she was crowned queen in 1200. Not until October 1207 did she bear her first child, Henry [see Henry III]. Over the next eight years she had another son, *Richard, first earl of Cornwall, and three daughters, Joan, *Isabella (1214–1241), and *Eleanor, countess of Pembroke and Leicester (1215?–1275). Stories such as that while Normandy was being lost John stayed in bed with Isabella, or that she took lovers whom he had throttled on her bed, are first recorded by Wendover and Paris. Until 1207 the queen and John's first wife often stayed together, and both received gifts from him. But he never gave Isabella of Angoulême the landed endowment that a queen expected. In consequence she played no political role in England.

It was not just monastic authors who had a low opinion of John. According to the *Histoire des ducs de Normandie et des rois d'Angleterre*, written *c.*1220 by an author in the entourage of Robert de Béthune, one of John's leading commanders in the civil war, the king 'was a very bad man [*molt mal homme*], cruel and lecherous' (*Histoire des ducs de Normandie*, 105). By the standards of his own milieu his treatment of Arthur of Brittany, of the Brouze family, and perhaps also of Geoffrey of Norwich, justify the charge of cruelty. By these standards the number of his mistresses is irrelevant, but accusations such as Robert Fitzwalter's widely aired complaint, that John tried to take his daughter by force, are not. Indeed if there is any substance to the charge that he subjected wives and daughters of his barons to sexual harassment, then it would indicate political stupidity as well as lechery. The *Histoire de Guillaume le Maréchal* portrays an obsessively suspicious king. There may be nothing unusual in the fact that the members of John's household promised to report anything they heard against him. More revealing are entries in the chancery rolls which show that the king devised an elaborate system of countersigns enabling him to issue orders which he intended should not be obeyed. He instructed keepers of castles and prisoners not to hand over their charges when they received written orders to do so, unless those orders were accompanied by a prearranged sign—though he sometimes forgot what the sign was. So devious a man was inevitably distrusted, even at the start of his reign—as when Arthur fled his court in 1199. Men such as William the Lion and Stephen Langton had no confidence in his safe conducts, unless they were supported by an imposing array of prelates and barons. According to Bertran de Born the younger:

No man may ever trust him
For his heart is soft and cowardly
(*Thomas Wright's Political Songs*, 6)

Although sporadically capable of effective military action, a king believed to be soft, cowardly, and untrustworthy was incapable of winning a war.

The quality of John's kingship The record evidence demonstrates that John was a busy king. He was, for example, a tireless and rapid traveller. This restless movement around the country has sometimes led historians to conclude that no king has ever known England better. Undoubtedly the loss of his continental lands meant that after 1203 he was able to give an unprecedented degree of attention to the north. He went to York seventeen times and was the first king to visit Newcastle since 1158. But whether he knew the people of England as well as he knew its roads is another question, and one which record evidence alone cannot answer. Record evidence demonstrates that John took a deep interest in the administration of justice and that during his reign the common law continued to develop: procedures in civil actions were being made more readily available to people from a wider social range. Was the latter a consequence of the former? At times, perhaps—although in 1209 he closed down the regular courts and for three years insisted that all cases be heard in the court *coram rege* (in the king's presence). During those three years John's busyness was, at best, a nuisance. Moreover, although on the whole under-tenants benefited from increased access to a relatively inexpensive and predictable judicial system, tenants-in-chief continued to be subjected to John's dangerously expensive and arbitrary personal justice. It seemed to the author of the *Histoire des ducs de Normandie* that his policy towards tenants-in-chief was to stir up mutual hatreds between them.

Fiscal records detail how much he collected, and how;

they also throw light on how much he spent and on what. But whether he was generous or miserly was a matter of opinion. According to the Barnwell chronicle:

he was generous and liberal to aliens but he plundered his own people; he ignored those who were rightfully his men and placed his trust in strangers; before his end his people deserted him, and at his end few mourned for him. (*Memoriale fratris Walteri de Coventria*, 2.232)

In fact record evidence demonstrates that there were many Englishmen among his loyal supporters, magnates such as the earls of Chester and Derby as well as 'new men' (whose promotion often disturbed local élites) such as Robert de Vieuxpont, Brian de Lisle, Philip of Oldcotes, and Hubert de Burgh. But the chronicles voice a strongly held opinion which moved men to rebel.

The earliest description of John's character, written by Gerald of Wales in the late 1180s, emphasized John's youthful follies, his impatience with critics, his preference for pleasure rather than policy. Gerald's picture of the young prince and his courtiers in 1185, amusing themselves at Irish expense, is corroborated by the number of later writers—Devizes, Coggeshall, and the authors of the *Histoire des ducs de Normandie*, the *Histoire de Guillaume le Maréchal*, and a fragmentary Canterbury chronicle—who describe John and his courtiers sniggering at the discomfiture of others. Gerald attributed John's failure in 1185 to the fact that he followed bad advice, and expressed the hope that when he had matured he would follow wiser counsels. But fifteen years later King John's dealings with his brother Geoffrey of York and the English magnates were, in Howden's view, 'ill-advised' (*Chronica ... Hovedene*, 4.92, 161). According to Diceto, before the end of 1200 John had been imprudent, had acted on the advice of evil men, and had behaved in a manner unworthy of the royal majesty. These criticisms were voiced by men who knew government circles well and who were dead by 1202; written without hindsight they are all the more telling. They explain why he failed so badly in the crises of 1203–5 and 1214–16. The unanimity of surviving contemporary opinion is itself a significant political fact. Everyone disliked John. In the end, even though there was no rival member of John's family who could lead would-be rebels and give them a legitimate cause for which to fight, their dislike and discontent were so great that they invented a new kind of focus for revolt, a programme of reform, Magna Carta. Although John is the most common of English forenames, King John is the only king of England whose name requires no numerical qualification: he was the first and last King John.

Historiography Two authors writing in the 1220s, the Barnwell chronicler and Roger of Wendover, were to be very influential. Historians who have taken a relatively positive view of John have turned for support to the Barnwell chronicler's judgement that 'though he enjoyed no great success and, like Marius, met with both kinds of luck, he was certainly a great prince' (*Memoriale fratris Walteri de Coventria*, 2.232). Historians who have taken a hostile view of John have preferred Roger of Wendover's account, particularly when enlivened by some of Matthew Paris's additions. With a few exceptions such as the relatively neutral Ranulf Higden (though even he blamed John for the death of Arthur of Brittany and for the loss of his dominions), historians writing before the Reformation tended to follow the views of Wendover and Paris. Then Henry VIII's quarrel with the papacy led to a new perception of John as an 'illustrious predecessor' of the protestant Tudors. In John Bale's play *Kynge Johan* (*c*.1540) Verity complains of the untruths told by historians. Hence John Speed's verdict (1611), that had his story not fallen into 'the hands of exasperated writers, he had appeared a King of as great renown as misfortunes' (Speed, 572). However, as is clear from Shakespeare's *King John*, where John's conduct weakens national unity (not only does he submit to the pope but his involvement in Arthur's death provides moral justification for potential rebels), it was not easy to see this king as a heroic patriot. With the revival of the cult of Magna Carta in the seventeenth century John's reputation sank again. For Hume, he was 'mean and odious, ruinous to himself and destructive to his people' (Hume, 1.313). For Stubbs, 'he made no plans and grasped at no opportunities. He was persistent only in petty spite and greedy of easy vengeance' (*Memoriale fratris Walteri de Coventria*, 2.lxxix).

The publication of judicial and financial records in the nineteenth and twentieth centuries and the increasing reliance of historians on this type of evidence led to a tendency to rehabilitate John. The notion that he was the founder of the Royal Navy can be traced back to 1847, and the publication of the chancery rolls in the 1830s and 1840s. J. R. Green, writing in the early 1870s, remained convinced of John's 'supreme wickedness', but also asserted that he was 'no weak and indolent voluptuary but the ablest and most ruthless of the Angevins' (Green, 114–15). Twentieth-century historians—with the notable exception of Sellar and Yeatman, for whom John was 'the first memorable wicked uncle' (W. C. Sellar and R. J. Yeatman, *1066 and All That*, 1930, 25)—were to emphasize the ability and downplay the wickedness; indeed psycho-history has been invoked to suggest that he may have suffered from a sense of insecurity as a result of being scarred by his upbringing. Studies of the finances of Philip Augustus, and of prices and wages in England, led to John's failures being minimized on the grounds that the growing wealth of the French crown and high inflation in England made it virtually impossible to avoid both defeat abroad and fiscal oppression at home. D. M. Stenton, a prime mover in the publication of records, returned to John Speed's verdict: 'No king of England was ever so unlucky as John' (Stenton, 44). Work published in the early 1960s by J. E. A. Jolliffe, W. L. Warren, and, above all, J. C. Holt, established this orthodoxy for much of the rest of the twentieth century. However, work on French and English financial records undertaken in the late 1990s suggests that he was not facing insuperable odds in France, and that in England the period of steep price increases was over as early as *c*.1204.

Hence judgements on John's record as king are increasingly returning to contemporary opinion as voiced in both English and non-English narrative sources.

JOHN GILLINGHAM

Sources CHRONICLE SOURCES *Ann. mon.* · *Chronica magistri Rogeri de Hovedene*, ed. W. Stubbs, 4 vols., Rolls Series, 51 (1868–71) · W. Stubbs, ed., *Gesta regis Henrici secundi Benedicti abbatis: the chronicle of the reigns of Henry II and Richard I, AD 1169–1192*, 2 vols., Rolls Series, 49 (1867) · Paris, *Chron.*, vol. 2 · R. Howlett, ed., *Chronicles of the reigns of Stephen, Henry II, and Richard I*, 4 vols., Rolls Series, 82 (1884–9), vols. 1–2 · A. O. Anderson and M. O. Anderson, eds., *The chronicle of Melrose* (1936) · *Chronicon Richardi Divisensis / The Chronicle of Richard of Devizes*, ed. J. T. Appleby (1963) · Giraldus Cambrensis, *Expugnatio Hibernica / The conquest of Ireland*, ed. and trans. A. B. Scott and F. X. Martin (1978) · A. Holden, S. Gregory, and D. Crouch, eds., *The history of William Marshal*, 3 vols., Anglo-Norman Texts [forthcoming] · *Gir. Camb. opera* · P. Meyer, ed., *L'histoire de Guillaume le Maréchal*, 3 vols. (Paris, 1891–1901) · F. Michel, ed., *Histoire des ducs de Normandie et des rois d'Angleterre* (Paris, 1840) · *The historical works of Gervase of Canterbury*, ed. W. Stubbs, 2 vols., Rolls Series, 73 (1879–80) · Adam of Eynsham, *Magna vita sancti Hugonis / The life of Saint Hugh of Lincoln*, ed. D. L. Douie and D. H. Farmer, OMT, 1 (1961) · *Memoriale fratris Walteri de Coventria / The historical collections of Walter of Coventry*, ed. W. Stubbs, 2 vols., Rolls Series, 58 (1872–3) [incl. Barnwell Chronicle] · *Œuvres de Rigord et de Guillaume le Breton, historiens de Philippe-Auguste*, ed. H. F. Delaborde, 2 vols. (Paris, 1882–5), 210, 224 · *Radulphi de Coggeshall chronicon Anglicanum*, ed. J. Stevenson, Rolls Series, 66 (1875) · *Radulfi de Diceto ... opera historica*, ed. W. Stubbs, 2 vols., Rolls Series, 68 (1876) · S. Mac Airt, ed. and trans., *The annals of Inisfallen* (1951) · T. Jones, ed. and trans., *Brut y tywysogyon, or, The chronicle of the princes: Red Book of Hergest* (1955) · S. Ó hInnse, ed. and trans., *Miscellaneous Irish annals, AD 1114–1437* (1947) · D. Murphy, ed., *The annals of Clonmacnoise*, trans. C. Mageoghagan (1896)

RECORD SOURCES L. Deslisle, ed., *Catalogue des actes de Philippe-Auguste* (Paris, 1856) · *Curia regis rolls preserved in the Public Record Office* (1922–), vols. 1–7 · H. F. Cole, ed., *Documents illustrative of English history in the thirteenth and fourteenth centuries*, RC (1844) · *Pipe rolls*, 1–14 John · A. Teulet and others, eds., *Layettes du trésor des chartes*, 5 vols. (Paris, 1863–1909) · T. Stapleton, ed., *Magni rotuli scaccarii Normanniae sub regibus Angliae*, 1, Society of Antiquaries of London Occasional Papers (1840) · D. M. Stenton, ed., *Pleas before the king or his justices*, 4 vols., SeldS, 67–8, 83–4 (1952–67) · T. D. Hardy, ed., *Rotuli chartarum in Turri Londinensi asservati*, RC, 36 (1837) · T. D. Hardy, ed., *Rotuli de liberate ac de misis et praestitis, regnante Johanne*, RC (1844) · T. D. Hardy, ed., *Rotuli de oblatis et finibus*, RC (1835) · T. D. Hardy, ed., *Rotuli litterarum clausarum*, 2 vols., RC (1833–4) · T. D. Hardy, ed., *Rotuli litterarum patentium*, RC (1835) · T. D. Hardy, ed., *Rotuli Normanniae*, RC (1835) · *The letters of Pope Innocent III (1198–1216) concerning England and Wales*, ed. C. R. Cheney and M. G. Cheney (1967) · Rymer, *Foedera*, vol. 1 · *Selected letters of Pope Innocent III concerning England, 1198–1216*, ed. C. R. Cheney and W. H. Semple (1953) · Thomas Wright's *political songs of England*, ed. P. Coss (1996) · J. C. Holt, *Magna Carta*, 2nd edn (1992), 448–73

SECONDARY SOURCES J. Bale, *Kynge Johan: a play in two parts*, ed. J. P. Collier, CS, 2 (1838) · J. Speed, *The historie of Great Britaine*, 3rd edn (1632) · D. Hume, *The history of England from the invasion of Julius Caesar to the revolution in 1688*, new edn, 8 vols. (1786) · J. R. Green, *Short history of the English people* (1915) · K. Norgate, *John Lackland* (1902) · F. M. Powicke, *The loss of Normandy, 1189–1204: studies in the history of the Angevin empire*, 2nd edn (1961) · S. Painter, *The reign of King John* (1949) · W. L. Warren, *King John* (1961) · J. C. Holt, *The northerners: a study in the reign of King John* (1961) · J. C. Holt, *King John* (1963) · J. C. Holt, *Magna Carta and medieval government* (1985) · J. E. A. Jolliffe, *Angevin kingship*, 2nd edn (1963) · C. R. Cheney, *Innocent III and England* (1976) · R. V. Turner, *King John* (1994) · N. Vincent, *Peter des Roches: an alien in English politics, 1205–38*, Cambridge Studies in Medieval Life and Thought, 4th ser., 31 (1996) · S. D. Church, ed.,

King John: new interpretations (1999) • D. M. Stenton, *English society in the early middle ages* (1951)

Likenesses coins • manuscripts, BL • seals • tomb effigy, Worcester Cathedral [*see illus.*]

John [John de Balliol] (*c*.1248×50–1314), king of Scots, was the fourth and youngest son of John de *Balliol (*d*. 1268), lord of Barnard Castle, and his wife, Dervorguilla de *Balliol, lady of Galloway (*d*. 1290). His successful claim to the Scottish throne in 1291–2 was based on the fact that his mother was the second daughter of Margaret, eldest daughter of David, earl of Huntingdon (*d*. 1219), the younger brother of William (the Lion), king of Scots (*d*. 1214).

Early life and career Information on John's early life and career is slight. Born between about 1248 and 1250, possibly in Picardy, he succeeded to the Balliol family estates in 1278, following the deaths of his father, in 1268, and of his three elder brothers, Hugh (1271), Alan (date not known), and Alexander (1278). It was a much reduced patrimony, centred mainly upon Barnard Castle, in co. Durham, to which he succeeded. Other Balliol estates had been extensively used as dowers for his mother and two high-ranking sisters-in-law, Agnes de Valence and Aliénor de Genoure, widows respectively of Hugh and Alexander; his mother also retained possession of her own inheritance.

Upon his succession to the Balliol estates, homage was demanded of John by both King Edward I and Robert Stichill, bishop of Durham. Despite official acknowledgement of John's rights as heir, almost a year elapsed between Alexander's death and John's succession. During that period, Balliol lands in Northumberland were taken into royal custody, and a contemporary chronicler, Thomas Wykes, recorded that John himself was also in royal custody at about this time. According to Wykes, Balliol needed Edward's consent for his proposed marriage to Isabel, second daughter of John de *Warenne, earl of Surrey (*d*. 1304); he describes John as a youth, *adolescens*, and Isabel, a young girl, *adolescentula*. In fact, at the date of their marriage, which probably took place in February 1281, John was about thirty years of age and Isabel was at least in her mid-twenties. Clearly, Edward could not have been exercising rights of wardship in a minority but the true reasons for his heavy-handed intervention are not clear.

Like two of his elder brothers, John de Balliol did not marry until he had attained headship of the family. But unlike his brothers, he had not already been pursuing a career in English royal service—military, crusading, or diplomatic. As the youngest son of an especially devout mother, he may well have been destined for a monastic career. According to an account by the Durham chronicler Robert Greystones, in September 1290 there was a dispute between Ranulf de Neville, lord of Raby, and the prior of Durham concerning custom and protocol to be observed within Durham Cathedral priory at the feast of St Cuthbert. Balliol was evidently present at this dispute, since he rebutted Neville's claims for precedence and privileges, declaring that he had for a long time attended the schools of Durham but had not heard of the privileges which the

lord of Raby claimed. This may well have been the novices' school, which, as described in the later rites of Durham, provided education for intending monks, though it is also possible that he was taught in the Durham almonry school. The benefits of an education were certainly manifest in Balliol's case; a record of 1294, for example, testifies to his ability to read out a written petition in public (*ore proprio publice fecit*), a level of literacy that may have been fairly widespread but is actually attestable among relatively few contemporary members of the secular nobility.

John's wife and two sisters-in-law were of English comital families or closely associated with the English royal court, and one of his four sisters married into the celebrated de Burgh family. Another sister, Ada, married into the Anglo-Scottish baronage, her husband, William de Lindsay, being heir to the lordships of Kendal and Lamberton (Berwickshire). The only member of his generation to effect a significant Scottish connection was his sister Eleanor, who married John *Comyn (*d*. *c*.1302), lord of Badenoch, justiciar of Galloway, and one of the guardians of Scotland between 1286 and 1292.

In fact, before the sudden death of Alexander III, king of Scots, in March 1286, Scotland played little part in Balliol's business affairs. However, he does appear to have begun negotiations with King Alexander concerning the release from imprisonment in Barnard Castle of his mother's half-brother, Thomas of Galloway. Upon Alexander's death, the issue was dropped and it was not until after John's abdication in 1296 that old Thomas was finally released from over sixty years' imprisonment. In contrast, John appears to have been much more active in the management of family interests in northern France. For parts of 1283, 1284, and 1289—and possibly also 1282 and 1285—he was evidently resident on his Picard estates.

Succession to the Scottish throne, 1286–1292 Within a month of Alexander III's death, according to Walter Bower, 'bitter pleading' between Robert (V) de Brus (*d*. 1295) and John de Balliol is alleged to have broken out in a *colloquium* or parliament. John otherwise remained comparatively uninvolved in Scottish affairs during this phase of the guardianship, but in the uncertain atmosphere surrounding the Scottish royal succession the lineage of John's mother is likely to have become a matter of common knowledge.

Upon the death of the aged Dervorguilla in January 1290, Balliol gained a rich inheritance in both England and Scotland. By early March he had been granted seisin of her considerable English lands; details of his succession to her equally extensive Scottish lands and his assumption of the title of lord of Galloway are not recorded, but three years later Edward I 'pardoned' him £3000 of the £3289 14s. 1½d. allegedly due as relief payment. John was now wealthy, and thus, like his father before him, an object of intense royal cupidity. It is no coincidence that in May 1291, on the eve of the Great Cause, Edward I issued writs of distraint against John's goods and chattels for alleged debts of over £1235. A small amount was levied and then the matter was suspended, only to be raised again, with an equally nice sense of timing, two years later.

Politically, too, 1290 marked a watershed in Balliol's career. In September, the death of Alexander's recognized heir, his granddaughter, Margaret, the young 'Maid of Norway', made Balliol a leading claimant for the vacant Scottish throne, and drew him more actively into the process of faction forming. The possibility that he might seek an audience with the king of England was referred to in a letter to Edward I from Bishop William Fraser of St Andrews, but the so-called 'appeal of the seven earls', which is ascribable to late 1290 or early 1291, warned against any action on John's part which might lead 'to the prejudice and injury of the right and liberty of the seven earls of Scotland' (Stones, *Anglo-Scottish Relations*, 45). In a document issued in November 1290 in favour of Antony (I) Bek, bishop of Durham, Balliol even went so far as to style himself 'heir of the kingdom of Scotland' (Fraser, 22–3), a presumption that was probably as much a reflection of the ambition of the beneficiary, as of his own.

By common consent a court was set up by King Edward I of England to determine the Scottish succession, the proceedings of which later became known as the 'Great Cause'. After an adjournment, on 2 June Edward first demanded acceptance of his lordship. Having evidently mistaken the day, Balliol arrived on the following day, and a notary was careful to record John's personal acknowledgement of Edward's lordship and jurisdiction. In early June also auditors were appointed to hear the adjudication. It was politically significant that John Comyn of Badenoch and John de Balliol together agreed to supply forty (out of 104) nominees, their list of lay sponsors bearing a distinctively Comyn 'party' appearance. Comyn's own petition also specifically sought to avoid prejudicing Balliol's claim, which was presented to the court on 3 August 1291.

The records of the closing stages of the proceedings in October–November 1292 reflected the opposed legal viewpoints of seniority (Balliol) as against nearness of degree (Brus) in the transmission of the Scottish kingdom. The fact that Balliol's maternal grandmother was an eldest daughter was adjudged to give him a stronger right to the kingship over his mother's cousin, Robert (V) de Brus, son of their grandmother Margaret's second sister, Isabel. The court's award of the sasine of the kingdom in favour of Balliol was confirmed by Edward I, who finally awarded that kingdom to him on 17 November 1292. During these final sessions John de Balliol reached agreement—possibly involving money payments—with at least three of his fellow claimants, William de Ros (d. 1317), William de Vescy (d. 1297), and Florence (V), count of Holland (d. 1296).

King of Scots, 1292–1296 On 30 November 1292, when he was about forty-two or forty-four years of age, John was enthroned as king of Scots in an inauguration ceremony at Scone. His first written act as king was sealed with his personal seal, on the grounds that he had not as yet had one made bearing his regal style, an omission that was made good shortly afterwards. Throughout his reign, in fact, private family issues merged with public matters of state. The parliament of August 1293, for example, acknowledged his rights of inheritance to his uncle's lands in Berwickshire. But, although as king of Scots he had authority over episcopal appointments, and as lord of Galloway he had special authority over the see of Whithorn, in 1294 he was forced to accept a Brus nominee, Master Thomas of Dalton, as bishop of Galloway, an indication of lingering hostility and defiance from the Brus camp.

During his reign, Balliol family links with Picardy emerged particularly clearly. In 1293, for example, he issued a letter of protection in favour of the merchants of Amiens coming to or staying in Scotland, almost certainly promoting their lucrative trade in woad-dye. In Scotland they obviously took advantage of the exalted position of someone they could regard as a compatriot. As recently as June 1289, John had been in Amiens itself, confirming a sale of tithes by Gauthier de Grandsart to the college of Amiens. Also, by the terms of the Franco-Scottish treaty of 1295–6, part of the money for the dower of the infant Isabeau de Valois, to be married to John's elder son, Edward, was to be raised from Balliol's own private estates in Picardy.

John's royal councillors and officials included many trusted associates of the Balliols. Drawn mainly from the Comyn group that had formed the joint body of auditors, his councillors included two former guardians, Bishop Fraser and John Comyn of Badenoch, who, like Gilbert and Ingram de Umfraville, was related to Balliol by marriage. Royal officials included kinsmen such as Alexander de *Balliol of Cavers (d. 1310), chamberlain or associate chamberlain since 1287, and his cousin, Hugh de Eure, or Iver, executor of his father's will, who served as royal envoy. Master Thomas of Hunsingore, a Yorkshireman with Balliol connections, became chancellor in 1294, and other minor royal officials who had been associated with the Balliol family included Walter of Cambo, sheriff of Northumberland, and William of Silksworth, the king's sergeant. Similar associations are observable at a more modest level in persons such as Walter of Darlington, a clerk whom Balliol presented to the church of Parton. Antony Bek, bishop of Durham, and John de Lisle, a tenant of the Balliols at East Newton in Northumberland, also took advantage of John's exalted position to press claims in Scotland.

Administratively, John's reign was distinguished. It is likely, for example, that the authoritative treatise on the government of the kingdom, known as *The King's Household*, was prepared for his benefit and guidance about 1292. His reign also saw a significant assertion of royal authority through parliament, no less than four sessions of which were held between February 1293 and May 1294. In one unprecedented session, 'everyone with a complaint [was summoned before king and council] ... to show the injuries and trespass done to them by whatsoever ill-doers' (Duncan, 43). Equally constructive was the ordinance of early 1293 creating three sheriffdoms in the west highlands: Skye under William, earl of Ross (d. 1323),

Lorn under Alexander MacDougall, lord of Argyll (d. 1310), and Kintyre under James Stewart (d. 1309). MacDougall, a loyal supporter of King John and the Comyns—like Balliol, he was a brother-in-law of John Comyn of Badenoch—appears to have been granted wider powers over all three sheriffdoms. King John had clearly grasped the crucial importance of establishing royal authority in the west, and conducting government through royal agents at strategic regional centres, presaging later Stewart policy.

Politically, however, John's reign was dominated by a series of appeals from Scottish courts to those of Edward I of England. The eleven known cases involved nine separate appellants, of whom three were English subjects and three were clearly political malcontents. Of the remaining appeals, that of Master Roger Bartholomew of Berwick was used by Edward I as a test case inherited from the period of the guardianship, while Macduff of Fife, who claimed he had not been allowed to succeed to lands in northern Fife and had been imprisoned by Balliol, was a man with questionable grievances.

Initially defying Edward, King John in the autumn of 1293 eventually appeared before the English parliament, protesting against the alleged right to hear appeals. Under threat, he withdrew his protest and renewed his submission and homage to the English king. The episode revealed Balliol's personal weakness when confronted, not for the first time in his career, with Edward I's uncompromising attitude. In the words of Professor Barrow, Balliol found himself:

> ground between the upper and nether millstones of an overlord who demanded humble obedience and a community of the realm whose leaders insisted that he stand up manfully for their independence. A contemporary English writer [the Rishanger chronicler], conflating Saint Luke and Isaiah, compared him to a lamb among the wolves, who dared not open his mouth. (Barrow, 86–7)

A further step towards the break with England—and the end of John's reign—was taken when the king of Scots and twenty-six of his magnates tacitly defied Edward I's summons, issued in June 1294, to undertake personal military overseas service against the king of France. Indeed, by May 1295, Philippe IV, king of France (r. 1285–1314), was able to view the Scots 'not as enemies but rather as our friends' (Stevenson, vol. 2, no. 335), and at a parliament in Stirling in early July four Scots commissioners were appointed to negotiate a French treaty. Drawn up in October and ratified by the Scottish king and parliament on 23 February 1296, this treaty set out the terms of a military alliance between the two kingdoms; it also made provision for the marriage of John's elder son, Edward, 'future king of Scotland', to King Philippe's niece. So, although the council of twelve guardians elected at the Stirling parliament may have taken the direction of Scottish government out of John's hands, either because of his unfitness or untrustworthiness, they remained firmly committed to the maintenance of the Balliol dynasty.

Abdication, imprisonment, and exile, 1296–1314 War with England, which had long been threatening, finally broke out when the Scots, fortified by their military alliance with France, refused Edward's demand that certain Scottish towns and castles be granted as sureties for the answering of appeals. The war itself began on the eastern border at the end of March 1296, and the first and last decisive battle of this campaign, at Dunbar on 27 April, resulted in a clear victory for the English under King John's father-in-law, John de Warenne, earl of Surrey. Balliol himself retreated northwards through Angus, and in late June sent envoys to Edward, then at Perth, seeking peace.

At first Edward, probably having newly discovered the terms of the Franco-Scottish treaty, was prepared to offer Balliol favourable terms of surrender, including possibly the offer of an English earldom, in return for a voluntary submission. But in the event Edward's plenipotentiary, Antony Bek, bishop of Durham, required John to surrender the kingdom, formally break the seal, and submit himself unconditionally to the king of England's will. The formal surrender proceedings are recorded in three documents: at Kincardine on 2 July Balliol confessed his rebellion; at Stracathro on 7 July he renounced the French treaty; and at Brechin Castle on 10 July he resigned his kingdom and royal dignity. Chronicle accounts also record that John was taken to Montrose Castle where he appears to have been publicly cashiered, possibly even paraded as a penitent, the removal of the royal blazon from his surcoat or tabard giving rise to his undying nickname of Toom Tabard, meaning 'empty surcoat'.

Escorted by the sons of Edmund, earl of Lancaster (d. 1296), John de Balliol was taken from Montrose to Canterbury. From early August he was detained at the Tower of London, Hertford, and elsewhere, remaining at Hertford, where he was allowed hunting privileges, until August 1297. Thereafter, until July 1299 he was kept at the Tower of London, although on one occasion at least, on 1 April 1298, he was in the lodging of the bishop of Durham 'outside London' where, in the presence of the bishop, he denounced his former subjects, alleging that they had tried to poison him; whether that denunciation of the Scots was authentic and unforced remains unclear.

In accordance with the terms of an Anglo-French truce concluded in June 1299, Edward accepted French and papal demands for John's transfer into papal custody. Transported from Dover, Balliol found himself at Wissant-sur-Mer on 18 July where, in the presence of the papal legate, the bishop of Vicenza, and the envoys of the king of France, he swore to keep residence where the bishop or other papal mandatory consigned him. Four days later he was handed over to the representatives of the bishop of Cambrai and was later transferred to the abbot of Cluny's castle of Gevrey-Chambertin. News that the officers of the king of France had removed Balliol from the place assigned by the pope and had established him at 'his castle of Bailleul in Picardy' reached English officials in early October 1301. The letter containing this news also referred to a rumour that Philippe IV might be preparing to send John de Balliol back to Scotland 'with great strength' (Stones, 'Submission', 132–4).

Ever since his enforced abdication in 1296, Scots leaders had continued to treat John as their lawful king. With his transfer to papal custody and a strong affirmation of French and papal support, a realistic prospect of his restoration, or the succession of his elder son, Edward, began to grow, and diplomatic efforts to restore him to his throne were intensified. Indeed, Scottish royal acts began to be issued again in his name, not just on his behalf, and in 1301 he may have had a direct hand in the appointment of John Soulis (d. 1318) as sole guardian. By early 1302 even Edward I was contemplating the possibility that Balliol might return, though he was not prepared to accept him as king.

All expectations of French support for such a scheme, however, were dashed by the devastating defeat of the French army by the Flemings at Courtrai in Flanders in July 1302. An Anglo-French truce was followed in May 1303 by a peace treaty which, despite strenuous efforts by Scottish ambassadors, excluded Scottish interests. Balliol himself may well have compromised the effective representation of Scottish interests in this crucial treaty. In a letter from Bailleul in November 1302, he had authorized Philippe IV to undertake and conclude negotiations on his behalf against the king of England. He probably had little choice, either as king of Scots or lord of Bailleul. The 1303 treaty permitted Edward to concentrate his efforts against Scotland, where by 1304 he appeared to have secured almost total military and political domination. Although John de Balliol's claim to the Scottish throne was never relinquished in his lifetime, any realistic prospect of his restoration—and hence his political significance—was greatly reduced after 1304.

The county of Ponthieu, where John's ancestral home and his continental exile now lay, had been inherited by Edward I's wife, Eleanor, in 1279, at about the time that Balliol himself inherited his family estates there. Subject to French overlordship, Ponthieu had been confiscated on the outbreak of Anglo-French hostilities in 1294, but had been restored to Edward by the terms of the same 1299 truce that had involved Balliol's transfer into papal custody. Once again, Balliol was in no position to escape the controlling hand of the English king; as he later acknowledged to Edward II in his last recorded act (dated March 1314), 'we hold our land of Helicourt and its appurtenances in Vimeu in fee of our excellent prince, Edward by the grace of God, king of England and count of Ponthieu' (Belleval, 102–4).

To the end, John retained the style of 'king of Scots', although to Robert I he was merely John de Balliol. His death occurred shortly before 4 January 1315, when Louis X of France (r. 1314–16) was notified of the fact and was asked to accept the fealty of Edward, John's elder son, for the Balliol estates in Picardy. John lived long enough to have learned of the outcome of the battle of Bannockburn in June 1314, and possibly even of the Cambuskenneth parliament in the following November. Of his two sons, Edward *Balliol survived until early 1364, while Henry was killed at Annan in 1332; both died childless.

Assessment Issues and events surrounding John's short reign as king of Scots were catalysts of the first importance in converting Anglo-Scottish relations to a centuries-long course of conflict and in the firm re-establishment of Scotland as an independent kingdom. However, outside the relative limelight of his short reign, John de Balliol himself has remained among the least known kings in Britain of the high and later middle ages. Historical judgements on him have focused mainly on his handling of the appeals to Edward I and on the circumstances of his abdication. When John Stewart, earl of Carrick, succeeded to the Scottish throne in 1390, he had himself crowned as Robert III, largely in order to avoid association with the failure and shame brought upon his baptismal name by the reign of the Scottish King John. Posterity's general conclusion, which cannot easily be gainsaid, is that John's personal qualities were insufficient to cope with a difficult political situation and with an exceptionally difficult English king; there was little in the discredited figure of Toom Tabard to overcome the taint of Englishness and to endear him to later generations of Scots.   G. P. STELL

Sources *A history of Northumberland*, Northumberland County History Committee, 15 vols. (1893–1940), vol. 6, pp. 16–73, esp. 52–68 • G. P. Stell, 'The Balliol family and the Great Cause of 1291–2', *Essays on the nobility of medieval Scotland*, ed. K. J. Stringer (1985), 150–65 • G. W. S. Barrow, *Robert Bruce and the community of the realm of Scotland*, 2nd edn (1976) • E. L. G. Stones and G. G. Simpson, eds., *Edward I and the throne of Scotland, 1290–1296*, 2 vols. (1978) • R. de Belleval, *Jean de Bailleul, roi d'Écosse et sire de Bailleul-en-Vimeu* (1866) • G. G. Simpson, *Handlist of the acts of Alexander III, the Guardians, and John, 1249–1296* (1960) • J. Stevenson, ed., *Documents illustrative of the history of Scotland*, 2 vols. (1870) • M. Bateson, ed., 'The Scottish king's household and other fragments from a fourteenth-century manuscript', *Miscellany … II*, Scottish History Society, 44 (1904), 3–43 • *CDS*, vol. 2 • P. Chaplais, ed., *Treaty rolls preserved in the Public Record Office*, 1 (1955) • 'Registrum palatinum Dunelmense': the register of Richard de Kellawe, lord palatine and bishop of Durham, ed. T. D. Hardy, 4 vols., Rolls Series, 62 (1873–8) • *Records of Antony Bek … 1283–1311*, ed. C. M. Fraser, SurtS, 162 (1953) • E. L. G. Stones, 'The submission of Robert Bruce to Edward I, c.1301–2', *SHR*, 34 (1955), 122–34 • E. L. G. Stones, ed. and trans., *Anglo-Scottish relations, 1174–1328: some selected documents*, OMT (1965) • *Ann. mon.*, vol. 4 • *Historiae Dunelmensis scriptores tres: Gaufridus de Coldingham, Robertus de Graystanes, et Willielmus de Chambre*, ed. J. Raine, SurtS, 9 (1839) • N. Orme, *English schools in the middle ages* (1973) • S. I. Boardman, *The early Stewart kings: Robert II and Robert III, 1371–1406* (1996) • W. Bower, *Scotichronicon*, ed. D. E. R. Watt and others, new edn, 9 vols. (1987–98), vol. 6 • A. A. M. Duncan, 'The early parliaments of Scotland', *SHR*, 45 (1966), 36–58
Likenesses seal, repro. in H. Laing, *Descriptive catalogue of impressions from ancient Scottish seals*, Bannatyne Club, 91 (1850), 6 (nos. 19–20)
Wealth at death English holdings forfeited in 1306: Hardy, ed., *Registrum*, vol. 2, pp. 795–802 • forfeitures in 1296: *CDS*, vol. 2, p. 736

John [John of Eltham], **earl of Cornwall** (1316–1336), prince, was the second son of *Edward II (1284–1327) and Queen *Isabella (1295–1358), daughter of Philippe IV, king of France, and Jeanne de Navarre. John was born at Eltham, Kent, on 14 August 1316 and thus took his name from his birthplace. John lived his life in the shadow of his elder brother, *Edward III, and died before he came of age, so that his public career was brief, though active.

As a young child John was entrusted to the care of a nurse, Matilda Pyrie, within his brother's household. He was given lands to defray the costs of his upbringing, and in 1320 was transferred to his mother's household. In 1325 he was given a household of his own. At the age of nine John was caught up in the frenzied violence that broke out in London in the autumn of 1326, when his mother and Roger Mortimer, earl of March, invaded England and overthrew Edward II. John was in the Tower of London with other royal officials. The London crowd broke in, removed them, named John keeper of the Tower and city of London, and placed him in charge of the officials. After his brother ascended to the throne John was often in Edward's company and was frequently a witness to royal charters until his death. In 1328 he was made earl of Cornwall, and in 1333 Edward III promised him £200 per annum, until he received lands worth that amount.

Edward's other task in these years was to find John a suitable wife, a search that ranged far and wide. Initially Edward proposed to marry John to a daughter of the king of France, as part of a proposed peace agreement between the kings in 1329. Marriages with daughters of the count of Blois, the lord of Coucy, Gui, brother of the duke of Brittany, and other lords were also explored between 1330 and 1335. A match between John and Maria, daughter of Fernando IV, king of Castile, progressed as far as a papal dispensation in 1334, because the couple was related in the third and fourth degrees, but there is no evidence that John ever married.

Edward named John keeper of the realm when he travelled to France to perform homage in 1329, but since John was only thirteen at the time the archbishop of Canterbury along with other bishops, Henry of Lancaster, and the mayor of London were appointed to assist him. In 1330 John travelled with Edward to Gascony, and the following year Edward again made him keeper of the realm while he was overseas. During the last years of his life John served closely with his brother in the war in Scotland. He was present at the English victory at Halidon Hill in 1333, and was one of six earls who served in the royal army on the Roxburgh campaign in 1334, when he was eighteen. He defeated a force of Scots invading Redesdale in January 1335, with the help of Henry Percy and Ralph Neville. Edward seems to have been sufficiently impressed with the mettle his brother had shown on these campaigns to name him warden of the march of Scotland on 2 February 1335. He was supported by Percy and Neville, as well as by a large force of men-at-arms and archers. Conditions on the march were turbulent, however, and John withdrew on 19 March. Eight days later he was summoned to Newcastle to serve with the king with 135 men-at-arms.

In June 1336 John was one of several lords appointed by Edward to serve in his place at a meeting of the royal council at Northampton. He returned to Scotland, however, and died on 13 September at Perth. An elaborate funeral procession was held in London, culminating in a ceremony conducted by the archbishop of Canterbury at Westminster Abbey on Monday 13 January 1337, attended by the king and many great lords. His monument, with a fine alabaster effigy, survives. SCOTT L. WAUGH

Sources GEC, *Peerage* · F. Palgrave, ed., *The parliamentary writs and writs of military summons*, 2 vols. in 4 (1827–34) · *RotP* · *Chancery records* · Rymer, *Foedera*, new edn · I. J. Sanders, *English baronies: a study of their origin and descent, 1086–1327* (1960), 10, 91, 149 · Tout, *Admin. hist.*, 4.74–5, 78 · R. Nicholson, *Edward III and the Scots: the formative years of a military career, 1327–1335* (1965), 128, 176, 178, 188–90, 201, 218, 246, 248 · W. Stubbs, ed., *Chronicles of the reigns of Edward I and Edward II*, 2 vols., Rolls Series, 76 (1882–3) · *Adae Murimuth continuatio chronicarum. Robertus de Avesbury de gestis mirabilibus regis Edwardi tertii*, ed. E. M. Thompson, Rolls Series, 93 (1889) · J. Stevenson, ed., *Chronicon de Lanercost, 1201–1346*, Bannatyne Club, 65 (1839) · *Chronicon Henrici Knighton, vel Cnitthon, monachi Leycestrensis*, ed. J. R. Lumby, 2 vols., Rolls Series, 92 (1889–95), vol. 2 · *Chronicon Galfridi le Baker de Swynebroke*, ed. E. M. Thompson (1889) · *Calendar of the fine rolls*, PRO, 4 (1913), 494
Likenesses tomb effigy, Westminster Abbey, London [*see illus.*]

John [John of Gaunt], **duke of Aquitaine and duke of Lancaster, styled king of Castile and León (1340–1399)**, prince and steward of England, was the fourth son of *Edward III (1312–1377) and his wife, *Philippa of Hainault (1310?–1369).

John [of Eltham], **earl of Cornwall (1316–1336)**, tomb effigy

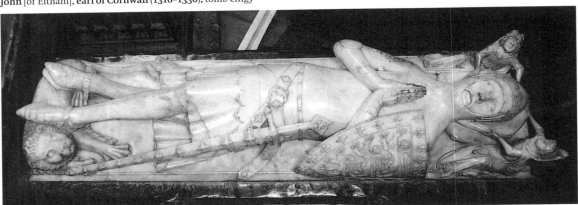

The king's son, 1340–1369 Gaunt was born at St Bavo's Abbey, Ghent, in March 1340. His godfather, from whom he took his forename, was John, duke of Brabant, one of Edward's current allies in the Low Countries. The infant John was granted the first of his many titles in September 1342 when he was invested with the earldom and honour of Richmond, traditionally valued at 2000 marks p.a.; this estate was later augmented by grants of the honour of Liddel, Cumberland, in 1357 and the castle of Hertford in 1360. The young earl of Richmond grew up in the household of his elder brother, *Edward, prince of Wales, and was soon initiated into the strenuous military traditions of the Plantagenet family. He was in the prince's ship during the bitter Anglo-Castilian sea battle off Winchelsea in August 1350 and was knighted at the start of the abortive Norman campaign in July 1355. He joined his father in the brief flurry of raids launched from Calais that November and followed him northwards to the relief of Berwick, captured by the Scots in a surprise attack, and on the 'burnt Candlemas' campaign of 1356. John of Gaunt played a more prominent role in the great *chevauchée* Edward III launched in October 1359, commanding his own retinue for the first time and taking an active part in the sieges and skirmishes of the long winter campaign until its conclusion in May 1360. In the autumn of the same year he returned to France in order to witness his father's ratification of the treaty of Brétigny at Calais. It was in recognition of these early signs of military prowess, as well as of his princely blood, that Gaunt was invested as a knight of the Garter in April 1361.

From his earliest years, the young earl of Richmond's marriage had been the subject of diplomatic exchanges but, despite suggestions that he should marry a daughter of Alfonso IV of Portugal (in 1345) or Marguerite, daughter and sole heir of Louis, count of Flanders (in 1351), it was to an English noblewoman, **Blanche of Lancaster** (1346?–1368), younger daughter and coheir of the king's most trusted captain, *Henry, first duke of Lancaster, and his wife, Isabella Beaumont, that John of Gaunt was eventually betrothed. The marriage took place amid great festivity at Reading in May 1359 and the considerable financial prospects it opened up were realized within two years, following Henry of Lancaster's death in March 1361. Gaunt was immediately given temporary custody of all the duke's lands and the death of Blanche's sister and coheir, Maude, duchess of Zeeland, a year later in April 1362 cleared the way for a further grant to him of the whole Lancastrian inheritance, together with the titles of duke of Lancaster, and earl of Derby, of Lincoln, and of Leicester, in the following November. At the age of twenty-two the new duke was suddenly the richest nobleman in England—a status he was to retain throughout his life. At their greatest extent, the duchy of Lancaster estates yielded *c.* £12,000 p.a. gross (£10,000 p.a. net), an income at least double the amount enjoyed by any contemporary English magnate.

Such wealth, together with the absence of his elder brothers, Edward and *Lionel, in Aquitaine and Ireland respectively, quickly enabled Lancaster to assume a prominent place in his father's plans and counsels. Between the autumn of 1362 and his own departure for Aquitaine, Gaunt was the most frequent witness of royal charters among the lay magnates, while he led diplomatic missions intended to secure the marriage of the daughter of the count of Flanders for his younger brother, *Edmund of Langley, to Calais in September 1364 and to Bruges in October 1365. Grandiose schemes for his own future were also in the air. In March 1364 the Scottish parliament discussed, only to reject, a proposal that the duke should succeed the childless David II as king of Scotland and in 1366 the long-dormant Lancastrian claim to the county of Provence was briefly revived on his behalf. More practically,

John [of Gaunt], duke of **Aquitaine and duke of Lancaster, styled king of Castile and León** (1340–1399), manuscript painting [seated at left end of the table]

Gaunt was dispatched to Aquitaine in January 1367 with reinforcements for the prince of Wales, who was preparing an expedition against Castile in aid of the legitimate but exiled king, Pedro I. The campaign that followed established Gaunt's military reputation. Entrusted with the task of leading the English forces over the pass of Roncesvalles, Gaunt drove off the attacks of the army of Enrique da Trastamara in early skirmishing around Vitoria and, when the two sides met in pitched battle at Nájera (April 1367), his command of the English vanguard was credited with an important part in the Black Prince's crushing victory.

The king's lieutenant, 1369–1376 New and more onerous responsibilities followed on Lancaster's return to England in October 1367. The death of Lionel, duke of Clarence, and the increasing ill health of both the king and the prince of Wales meant that, after the resumption of Anglo-French hostilities in March 1369, the task of commanding English armies overseas was chiefly entrusted to John of Gaunt. During the next five years of strenuous campaigning the duke spent almost half his time abroad and raised nearly 5000 men-at-arms and archers for the king's service from the resources of his own estates. In June 1369 he was appointed the king's captain and lieutenant in the realm of France and sent to Picardy in order to forestall the threat of a French invasion along the south coast. After some minor successes around the Calais pale the English forces encountered a French army, commanded by the duke of Burgundy, at Tournhem on 23 August 1369 and entrenched themselves in a strong defensive position. Neither side proved willing to risk a decisive encounter and, after a fortnight, Burgundy withdrew, leaving Gaunt free to pillage the Pays de Caux and to mount an unsuccessful assault on Harfleur, before returning to Calais at the end of October. Although the duke's reluctance to bring the French to battle incurred some contemporary criticism, he was entrusted with another important command in the following year, when he was sent with a retinue of 800 men to bolster the defences of Aquitaine. Gaunt was present at the siege and sack of Limoges on 19 September 1370, where he supervised the successful mining operations against the town, and was formally constituted the prince of Wales's lieutenant in Aquitaine in October, when ill health finally forced the prince back to England. He maintained a vigorous defence of the principality throughout the early months of 1371, recapturing the town of Montpont in February and strengthening several more border fortresses, before an acute shortage of money to pay his troops forced him to resign the lieutenancy in July.

Before he sailed for England, however, the duke of Lancaster, a widower since September 1368, contracted a second marriage, in September 1371, to Constanza (1354–1394), the exiled elder daughter of the murdered Pedro I of Castile. She was, at least in the eyes of her legitimist followers, the true heir to the crown of Castile and the duke showed himself, from the first, anxious to make good the rights his marriage to Constanza bestowed. Not only did

he maintain a skeleton Castilian chancery to issue documents in his name as king of Castile and León, but his persistent attempts to give substance to the title over the next fifteen years also influenced, and eventually dominated, his attitude towards all the central issues of domestic English politics and diplomacy. Behind the marriage there lay more than private ambition, however. Trastamaran Castile was firmly in alliance with Charles V of France by 1371 and the powerful Castilian galley fleet posed a real threat to English command of the seas. Since Nájera the prince of Wales had intermittently entertained plans to counteract this danger by an Anglo-Aragonese invasion, and eventual partition, of Castile. Gaunt's marriage was an attempt to adapt his brother's ambitious plan to changing circumstances and enjoyed the full approval of Edward III and his advisers. The duke was formally authorized to use the Castilian royal titles on 30 January 1372 and, six months later, Plantagenet ambitions in Castile were further confirmed by the marriage of Edmund of Langley to Constanza's younger sister, Isabella.

Gaunt seems to have intended to attempt to put his new claims into immediate effect, for in the spring of 1372 he was planning a campaign that would take him first to Aquitaine and then to Portugal. The defeat and capture of the earl of Pembroke off La Rochelle by the Castilian galley fleet in June 1372 forced a reappraisal of this ambitious strategy and the duke was directed, instead, to join his father in a naval expedition intended to bring relief to the principality of Aquitaine. In the event, contrary winds prevented the fleet from leaving port and nothing was achieved before the expedition was abandoned in October. English strategic priorities were, in any case, already shifting and the *voie d'Espaigne* ('way of Spain') receded in importance as the possibility of a permanent alliance with John de Montfort, duke of Brittany, came increasingly to the fore. In June 1372 Gaunt was required to surrender his honour of Richmond to the king in order to allow it to be regranted to the duke of Brittany, as part of the price of his adherence to the Plantagenet cause. He was granted extensive royal estates in compensation, including the honours of Tickhill, Yorkshire, Knaresborough, Yorkshire, and the High Peak, Derbyshire, in an exchange that gave him a still greater concentration of landed authority across Yorkshire and the northern midlands.

In the following year Lancaster was once again given command of an English army abroad. Although this force was initially intended to bring aid to John de Montfort in his struggle to retain control of Brittany, Duke John's flight to England in April 1373 required a late change of strategy. When Lancaster's army of 6000 men departed from Dover in July his intention seems to have been to conduct a destructive *chevauchée* from Calais to Paris and then to strike westwards towards Brittany. Stiff French resistance kept the English forces away from the Paris basin, however, and forced the duke to march eastwards, to Rheims and Troyes, and then southwards through the Auvergne to Aquitaine, which the duke and his army reached in December. Despite the severe losses his troops had suffered on this long march through difficult country, Lancaster remained in the principality until April 1374, seeking to strengthen its defences against the threatened invasion of the duke of Anjou and attempting to draw the count of Foix and Pedro III, king of Aragon, into an effective anti-Castilian alliance.

Although Edward III and his advisers did not immediately abandon their aggressive intentions after Gaunt's return to England, the failure of his expedition to yield a decisive victory inclined them to consider the possibility of a final peace with France more seriously. Desultory negotiations towards a peace, sponsored by Pope Gregory XI, had been in train since February 1372 and the changing fortunes of war now persuaded the English government to assign to them a greatly increased priority. A powerful delegation, led by the duke of Lancaster, was dispatched to the peace conference that began at Bruges in March 1375 and continued, with one substantial intermission, until March 1376. The discussions at Bruges attempted initially to resolve the central question of sovereignty over Aquitaine. One early proposal of the papal mediators, rejected by the English, was that Gaunt should give up his English estates and become the ruler of an independent duchy of Aquitaine, to be held as a fief of the French crown. Once the issue of sovereignty proved insoluble, however, attention shifted to negotiations for a forty-year truce on the basis of the existing territorial *status quo*. Here, too, agreement proved impossible to reach and the only concrete result of the talks was the conclusion of two short truces, lasting until April 1377. The leading role the duke played in these negotiations attracted some contemporary criticism, in part because the conclusion of the first of the truces in June 1375 deprived an English army led by Edmund Mortimer, earl of March, of a rare success at the siege of Quimperlé, and partly because so little had apparently resulted from such long and lavishly funded discussions. It was from Bruges, too, that the damaging rumour circulating among the diplomats, that Gaunt was using his dominant position in the negotiations to mobilize support for his plan to secure the succession to the English throne on the death of Edward III, spread to England and began to gain a wider currency.

The political crisis of 1376–1377 Such criticisms and suspicions were only a particular expression of the general frustration induced by the heavy incidence of taxation and the consistent lack of military success the English had experienced since 1369. This frustration was forcibly expressed in the Good Parliament (April–July 1376), when the parliamentary Commons, with tacit encouragement from some members of the nobility, successfully demanded the prosecution of several royal councillors for financial corruption and secured the establishment of a council of nine lords to advise the king. As the 'lieutenant of the king to hold the parliament' (*Anonimalle Chronicle*, 83), in the absence of his father and his dying elder brother, responsibility for managing this volatile assembly devolved on John of Gaunt. He adopted a generally conciliatory attitude towards the demands of the Commons and was aggrieved not to be named among the nine lords chosen to be the king's councillors when the parliament ended. Once the parliament was dissolved, however, political initiative passed rapidly back to the court, with the result that, for the first time in his career, the duke of Lancaster was required to play a leading part in domestic politics. One chronicler, Thomas Walsingham, says that the king 'now wholly laid down the government of the Kingdom and put it into the hands of the duke, allowing him to do all that he wanted' (*Chronicon Angliae*, 102).

Lancaster's response was to initiate a vigorous and aggressive policy designed to discipline those groups and individuals who had appeared to question royal authority, while rallying the lay nobility and gentry to the court by an appeal to their common interests. The courtiers and financiers impeached in the Good Parliament were rapidly pardoned and punitive measures taken against those most closely associated with that parliament's defiance; latent anti-clerical sentiment was mobilized by the sermons of John Wyclif, who preached in London against the temporal endowments of the church during the autumn of 1376; the privileges of the city of London were threatened by the efforts of Henry, Lord Percy, an ally of the duke, to extend the jurisdiction of his office as marshal of England over the city; and the burden of taxation was shifted further down the social scale by the introduction of a flat-rate poll tax in the parliament of Hilary 1377. Such vigorous policies inevitably generated tensions, which came to a head in February 1377 when William Courtenay, bishop of London, summoned Wyclif to be examined on the content of his sermons. Gaunt and Percy arrived at St Paul's in order to support their protégé and, in the altercation with Courtenay that followed, Gaunt offered to drag the bishop from his throne by the hair. This threat of violence, added to the Londoners' resentment at the attack on their judicial liberties, sparked off riots in the city against the duke. His policies were, nevertheless, generally successful in quashing criticism of the king's ministers and his own pre-eminent position within the English nobility was further emphasized by the grant to him on 28 February 1377 of palatinate rights within the duchy of Lancaster.

The king's uncle, 1377–1386 The animosity that John of Gaunt's policies created during his brief dominance, together with the lingering popular suspicion that he intended to claim the throne for himself, meant that the duke was not called upon to act as regent of the kingdom on Edward III's death (21 June 1377) and the accession of his eleven-year-old grandson, Richard II. In other respects, however, these altered circumstances relieved many of the political tensions generated in the previous year. Reconciliation with the Londoners in June was followed, in October, by a public vindication of Gaunt's conduct from the parliamentary Commons. The duke protested his loyalty in full parliament and challenged anyone who still suspected him of treason to come forward and make good their accusations. The Commons hastily accepted his avowals, nominated him as a member of the peers' intercommuning committee, and announced that they had chosen Lancaster to be 'their principal aid, strength and governor' (*RotP*, 3.5). This was to prove an accurate description of the position the duke occupied in English political life between Richard II's accession and his own departure for Castile in 1386. The precedence his royal blood demanded was enforced and underwritten by his great wealth, which allowed him both to maintain an exceptionally large indentured retinue of about 170 knights and esquires and to emphasize his princely status by an extensive programme of building work at Hertford, Dunstanburgh, Kenilworth, and several of his other residences.

Although Lancaster was not a member of any of the nominated councils that had formal responsibility for government from October 1377 to January 1380, his status as the king's uncle assured him an honourable prominence in affairs of state, as well as considerable informal influence with Richard himself throughout these years. In October 1377, for instance, Lancaster and his two brothers, Edmund of Langley and *Thomas of Woodstock, were commissioned to investigate any allegations of corruption that might arise against the king's nominated councillors, while in November 1381 the duke was named at the head of a committee to investigate the costs and personnel of the royal household. When the king clashed angrily with the earl of Arundel in open parliament at Salisbury in April 1384, only Gaunt possessed sufficient personal authority to intervene and compose their quarrel. If any magnate sought to question this pre-eminence, as Henry Percy, earl of Northumberland, did in October 1381, he was forced into a humiliating public submission to the duke. Equally, once serious negotiations for a permanent peace with France were resumed, Lancaster acted as the chief English spokesman, attending inconclusive conferences at Calais in September 1383 and at Leulinghem between July and October 1384.

This pervasive political influence had its price, for it became clear during the peasants' revolt of 1381 that it was John of Gaunt whom the common people chiefly blamed, despite his lack of formal office, for the military failings and financial exactions of government. The duke's name headed the list of traitors about the king whose arrest and execution the rebel army at Blackheath demanded, while the general distrust of Gaunt's motives among the rebels was articulated by the Kentishmen, who declared that they would have no king named John. Popular hostility towards the duke was further expressed by widespread attacks on the Lancastrian estates in East Anglia and upon several of his servants, while his great palace of the Savoy was burnt to the ground by the London rebels. Gaunt himself, conducting truce negotiations on the Scottish march when the rising began, was forced to take refuge in Scotland for ten days in order to escape the fate of the chancellor and treasurer, Simon Sudbury and Robert Hales, who were both summarily executed by the rebels. Even the duke's relatively lenient response to the rebellion, both on his own estates and as the leading commissioner to punish rebels in Yorkshire, did not entirely dispel the distrust his person and policies aroused. In February 1382 the citizens of London pointedly requested that they should have only one king and be ruled by him alone.

In reality, John of Gaunt's lively ambition to rule as a king in his own right remained fixed on the Castilian crown he could claim in the right of his wife. Throughout these years the duke tirelessly advocated the large-scale English intervention on the Iberian peninsula that would allow him to vindicate his claim to the Castilian throne. Success in realizing this objective proved for a long while elusive, since it required the favourable alignment of two unrelated and unpredictable sets of circumstances: the diplomatic situation within the Iberian peninsula itself and the strategic preferences of the English parliament, on whose financial support for his scheme the duke of Lancaster was ultimately reliant. One important obstacle to parliamentary approval of the *voie d'Espaigne* was the fear, forcibly expressed in January 1382, that the prolonged absence from the kingdom of a large army commanded by the duke would unacceptably imperil domestic security. A central object of Gaunt's policy during these years was consequently to allay this fear, as far as he was able, both by his active participation in expeditions designed to improve the realm's defences against French attack and by his efforts to maintain peace along the Anglo-Scottish border. Preparations for a naval expedition, in which Gaunt was to be one of the retinue leaders, had been well advanced in July 1377, when the death of Edward III forced the campaign's cancellation. Between July and September 1378, however, the duke patrolled the channel with a naval force of 1000 men and then, in pursuit of the council's strategy of securing a series of defensive barbicans along the northern coast of France, launched an unsuccessful attempt to capture St Malo. He was required to array his troops again in August 1383, stationing them in the Isle of Thanet in readiness to go to the aid of Bishop Despenser's beleaguered army in west Flanders.

John of Gaunt's participation in the traditional theatre of Anglo-French conflict was nevertheless overshadowed during these years by the responsibility he assumed for English efforts to maintain the peace with Scotland. Anglo-Scottish relations were regulated by a fifteen-year truce concluded in 1369 but conditions on the march had begun to deteriorate by 1376, as hostilities between the Percy and Douglas families escalated sharply. The duke of Lancaster's presence in the region, as one of the few magnates possessed of sufficient authority to impose an agreed settlement, was soon requested by both sides. John of Gaunt attended his first march day, at which infractions of the truce were redressed, in January 1378 and was appointed the king's lieutenant of the marches towards Scotland in the following year; he retained the supervisory powers of this lieutenancy until April 1384. The duke led a large force, intended for a military campaign against the Scots, to the march in October 1380 but eventually negotiated a reaffirmation of the existing truce, which was extended for a further three years at a second march day in June 1381. An already difficult situation in the region was further complicated when Gaunt's quarrel with the earl of Northumberland, which had its origin in the earl's failure to offer him shelter at either Alnwick or Bamburgh during the rising of 1381, led the duke to seek the wholesale exclusion of the Percys from marcher office. This proved detrimental to the maintenance of good order and a further march day conducted by Gaunt, in June 1383, secured a continuation of the existing truce only with difficulty. The Scots were quick to take advantage of its formal expiration, launching a successful assault on the English outpost of Lochmaben in February 1384. Gaunt retaliated with a large-scale raid in April, marching unopposed through the Lothians and ransoming Edinburgh. Further hostilities followed in July 1385 and the duke, at the head of a company of 3000 men, commanded the vanguard of the royal army that briefly ravaged the lowlands.

The renewal of hostilities against Scotland, coupled with the real possibility of a French invasion of southern England in 1385, appeared to render the possibility of Gaunt's gaining parliamentary consent and financial support for his projected Castilian expedition ever more distant. His attempt to engineer a favourable diplomatic alliance among the powers of the Iberian peninsula enjoyed, for many years, no more success. Negotiations for an alliance between England and the kingdoms of Aragon and Navarre were initiated in 1377, when Gaunt's was the guiding hand behind English strategy, but this diplomatic offensive was overtaken by the Castilian invasion of Navarre in June 1378 and parliament's preference for the more orthodox tactic of an invasion of northern France. By July 1380, however, persistent diplomatic efforts on the part of the duke's advisers had secured a renewal of the treaty of alliance between England and Portugal, which provided for an English force of 2000 men to be sent to Portugal under the command of Gaunt's brother, Edmund of Langley, earl of Cambridge. This was to be the advance party for a larger Lancastrian army, led by the duke himself, which would invade Castile from the duchy of Aquitaine. Finance remained the stumbling-block, however. Gaunt's proffer to lead an army of 4000 men to Castile, financed by a crown loan of £60,000, repayable within three years, met with little enthusiasm in the parliament of January 1382, while the failure of Edmund's expedition meant that the duke's hopes of an imminent Castilian campaign came to seem badly misplaced.

It was not until 1385 that circumstances began to favour Lancaster's ambitions once again. Portuguese rebellion against the imposition of direct rule from Castile, culminating in the devastating victory of Aljubarotta in August 1385, held out the prospect of a reliable Iberian ally for the Lancastrian pretender at precisely the time that increasing tension between John of Gaunt and Richard II was serving to persuade the king's advisers that the cost of a Castilian campaign might be a worthwhile price to pay for the greater political freedom the duke's absence from England would bestow on the king. Trouble between Richard and his uncle had been brewing for more than a year,

fomented by a group of young nobles and chamber knights, led by the earls of Oxford and Nottingham, who sought to undermine Gaunt's influence with the king by promoting a series of accusations against him. These first surfaced at the Salisbury parliament of April 1384, when a Carmelite friar accused the duke of treachery, to such good effect that Richard allegedly gave orders, hastily countermanded, for John of Gaunt's summary arrest and execution. Tension flared again in 1385, when rumours of another plot to arrest and execute the duke began to spread, following his criticism in council of Richard's irresolute defensive plans. Despite the assurances Gaunt was given on this occasion, obtained only after he had taken a body of men-at-arms to confront the king at Sheen, Richard's mistrust of his uncle was forcibly expressed again during the subsequent Scottish campaign, when he accused the duke of treachery for advising that the royal army should advance northwards beyond the Firth of Forth. The willingness of the parliament that met in October 1385 to allow part of the subsidy it granted to be devoted to a Lancastrian invasion of Castile consequently offered a welcome resolution to a threatening political impasse. Richard was even prepared to speed Gaunt on his way by advancing a loan of 20,000 marks to defray the costs of the expedition.

King of Castile and León, 1386–1389 Accordingly, Lancaster spent the early months of 1386 making careful financial and military plans for his long-anticipated invasion. The fleet carrying his army, which probably numbered about 5000 men, set sail from Plymouth in July and made a brief landfall at Brest, where the Lancastrian forces temporarily raised the siege of the English garrison, before landing at La Coruña in Galicia at the end of the month. In the short campaigning season that was left to them Gaunt and his troops brought the rest of Galicia under their control before establishing themselves at Orense for the winter. Despite this initial success, the heavy fatalities the Lancastrian army suffered from disease during the autumn and winter rendered further unaided advance from this bridgehead into the rest of Castile impractical. This difficulty was resolved by the alliance the duke concluded with João I of Portugal at Ponte de Mouro in November 1386: João undertook to bring a Portuguese force of 5000 men to the aid of the Lancastrian war effort in return for the promise of marriage to Gaunt's eldest daughter, *Philippa of Lancaster, and the cession to him of some Castilian territory. A joint Anglo-Portuguese army accordingly invaded León in March 1387 but the shortage of forage and the effective defensive tactics adopted by the Castilians caused the allies to abandon their campaign within six weeks. Negotiations for a settlement of the outstanding differences between the duke and Juan I of Castile began almost immediately and terms were agreed at Trancoso in July 1387. These were fully ratified, with only minor modifications, a year later at Bayonne.

It is likely that such an agreement represented Lancaster's preferred outcome, for his approach to the Castilian war had, from the first, been as flexible and pragmatic as Edward III's pursuit of the crown of France. The duke had been prepared to consider the possibility of a final peace settlement even before his expedition set sail. As his campaign unfolded, it became clear that his strategy was to use the well-tried English device of the destructive *chevauchée* in order to harass his opponent into an advantageous settlement rather than to attempt the near impossibility of an outright conquest of Castile. The terms he obtained were certainly generous. In return for his undertaking to renounce his claim to the Castilian throne and abandon occupied Galicia, John of Gaunt was offered a marriage alliance between his daughter, *Katherine of Lancaster, and Don Enrique, the Trastamaran heir to Castile, together with an indemnity for his renunciation of 600,000 francs and a further annual pension of 40,000 francs. It was a settlement that both satisfied his dynastic aspirations and further strengthened his domestic political position, for successive instalments of the Castilian pension over the next decade provided the duke with the resources to expand his following still further and to subsidize the ambitions of his children.

Lancaster left Portugal for Aquitaine in September 1387 and, once established in the duchy, began to work towards the general European peace that would, coincidentally, ensure the permanence of his Iberian family settlement. Appointed the king's lieutenant in Aquitaine in May 1388, the duke resisted the attempts of the appellant regime to involve him in an ambitious campaign against the French and negotiated, instead, a local truce covering all territories south of the Loire. Although his plans for a summit meeting of the Iberian powers to consider his proposals for a definitive Anglo-Castilian peace proved abortive, the conclusion of a general Anglo-French truce in July 1389 went some way towards securing his objectives. Gaunt did not, however, neglect the duties of his lieutenancy. The duke's efforts to build up support for the English allegiance among the Gascon nobility meant that, when he returned to England at Richard II's request in November 1389, he left the volatile duchy of Aquitaine in an unusually stable condition.

Duke of Aquitaine, 1390–1395 On his arrival in England Lancaster found the political atmosphere, and especially the king's attitude towards himself, transformed during his three-year absence. The reconciliation between Richard and the former lords appellant—one of whom was Lancaster's eldest son and heir, Henry Bolingbroke—was already showing signs of fragility by the autumn of 1389 and the duke's proven ability to maintain the political peace was consequently welcomed by both sides. At a royal council held at Reading in December 1389 he enjoined harmony on the nobility and, as an example to them, resolved his own long-standing quarrel with the earl of Northumberland. In return, the king confirmed Gaunt's pre-eminent political position by a series of grants and concessions: it was agreed that no royal grant with financial implications should be valid without the assent of the duke or his brothers; in the parliament of January 1390 the palatinate of Lancaster, which the duke held for life, was entailed on the heirs male of his body; and, most significantly, Gaunt was also created duke of

Aquitaine for life, holding the duchy of Richard and his heirs in their capacity as kings of France and reserving to the king direct sovereignty and resort. Despite these reservations, the grant of Aquitaine to Gaunt marked a significant change in the status of a duchy that had previously been held only by the king himself or by his eldest son. It conferred on John of Gaunt a status superior to the rest of the royal dukes and promised him a principality that he could govern in partial independence of the crown. It meant, too, that the duke of Aquitaine acquired a vested interest in promoting a permanent peace with France, in order to guarantee the territorial security of his new duchy. It was to these two, closely-related, ends that much of John of Gaunt's attention was directed over the next five years.

Following preliminary discussions between Lancaster and the French negotiators at Calais in May 1391, the parliamentary Commons approved the king's suggestion that the duke should be entrusted with the principal role in Anglo-French peace negotiations 'because he is the most sufficient person in the realm' (*RotP*, 3.286). Gaunt accordingly led an English delegation to Amiens in March 1392 where, in two months of diplomatic exchanges that taxed to the full the duke's talent for conspicuous display, the French submitted proposals that sought to break the deadlock surrounding the issue of English sovereignty over Aquitaine by suggesting that the duke and his heirs should hold an enlarged duchy as vassals of the king of France. Although this proposal created alarm among the Gascons themselves and attracted some domestic criticism in England, the renewed negotiations that Gaunt undertook at Leulinghem (March–June 1393) yielded a draft treaty in which the English conceded the central point that Richard II should himself perform liege homage for Aquitaine; this was to be in return for substantial territorial concessions and subject to a final resolution of the question of the duchy's feudal status by a panel of legal experts. So fundamental a concession proved unacceptable to parliament, however, and once Lancaster and his fellow negotiators had failed to find a way out of this impasse at a further conference at Leulinghem (March–May 1394), both sides were forced to abandon the search for a final peace.

While these prolonged negotiations provided Lancaster with a prominent and congenial international role, the considerable latitude the duke was allowed in defining the English terms began to revive domestic suspicion, epitomized in the Monk of Westminster's complaint that 'the duke of Lancaster does what he likes without check' (*Westminster Chronicle*, 518), that he was prepared to sacrifice the wider national interest to the pursuit of his own ambitions in Aquitaine. This mistrust was first publicly manifested by an armed protest in Lancashire and Cheshire in May 1393 against the apparently imminent conclusion of a final peace and, specifically, against the part played by the dukes of Lancaster and Gloucester in negotiating it. Although Gaunt was able to pacify this disturbance during the following autumn, taking many of the local gentry implicated in the rising into his own service,

Richard (III) Fitzalan, earl of Arundel, sought to make political capital out of the continuing unease that surrounded the progress of the peace negotiations by launching a bitter personal attack on the duke in the parliament of January 1394, criticizing him for his excessive influence over the king and over the formulation of royal policy. Gaunt was easily able to outface this attack, extracting from Arundel a humiliating public apology, but his conduct was once more beginning to be questioned by those about the king. The duke was forced to write to Richard in August 1394, denying the rumours of his disloyalty that were said to be circulating at court.

Fortunately, a developing crisis in Aquitaine required Lancaster's presence there. He set sail for the duchy in November 1394 with an army of approximately 1500 men. The purpose of this expedition was to stabilize the borders of the duchy and to enforce the still disputed recognition of Gaunt's authority there. Gascon resistance to the duke's authority had its origins in their objection to the separation of Aquitaine from the English crown that the original grant to Gaunt entailed and it had been further exacerbated in the last two years by the insensitive actions of ducal officials. Opposition to Gaunt's rule in Aquitaine had mounted to such a point that, in April 1394, the three estates of the duchy swore an oath of union by which they refused to accept his authority as duke. Faced with so delicate a situation, Gaunt acted circumspectly on his arrival and, by skilful conciliation, eventually succeeded in negotiating an acceptable compromise. In March 1395 the estates agreed to recognize Gaunt's authority as duke in return for a guarantee of their existing liberties and agreed restrictions on the scope of his officials' actions. With his principal objective obtained, Gaunt spent the summer working with his French counterparts to regulate infractions of the truce along the border of the duchy before travelling overland back to England in November 1395. He broke his journey in Brittany in order to make a treaty of mutual alliance with Duke John de Montfort and to arrange a marriage between his grandson, Henry of Monmouth (the future *Henry V), and the duke of Brittany's daughter. Although nothing finally came of this agreement, it indicates the ambitious scale on which John of Gaunt was still continuing to plan: if successful, the marriage alliance would have created a sphere of English, and specifically Lancastrian, influence along the entire western seaboard of the French kingdom.

Last years, 1396–1399 On his return to England Lancaster was received by the king, some said, 'with honour but without love' (*Thomae Walsingham … historia Anglicana*, 2.219). This lukewarm reception marked the beginnings of a retreat in the duke's influence. The conclusion of a twenty-eight-year truce with France at Leulinghem in March 1396 meant that Richard II was no longer so dependent upon Gaunt's natural authority among the peers to carry through a potentially unpopular policy, while the emergence of a new group of noble courtiers, closer to Richard's own age than to Gaunt's, reduced the duke's influence over the formulation and direction of royal policy. Gaunt himself, now afflicted by bouts of ill

health, seemed happy to acquiesce in this development and, while still assigned a conspicuous and honourable role at important state occasions, such as the festivities that accompanied the king's marriage to Isabella, the daughter of Charles VI of France, in November 1396, increasingly concentrated his attention on promoting the interests of his children and securing for them the safe transmission of the heritage of Lancaster. The priority the duke of Lancaster assigned to this task was signalled in February 1396 by his decision to marry his long-standing mistress and companion, Katherine Swynford (1350?–1403), widow of Sir Hugh Swynford (d. 1371), the former governess of his children [see Katherine, duchess of Lancaster]—a social mismatch that astonished contemporaries but formed the essential preliminary to the formal legitimation of their Beaufort children by papal bull, in September 1396, and by royal patent approved in the parliament of February 1397. Further royal favour towards the duke's plans was shown by the creation of John *Beaufort as earl of Somerset in the same parliament and by the provision of Henry *Beaufort to the see of Lincoln in February 1398.

The greatest threat to the security of the Lancastrian inheritance lay, however, in the person of Gaunt's son and heir, Henry Bolingbroke. By participating in the appellant rising of 1387–8, Bolingbroke had put himself permanently at risk from the king's revenge. His actions consequently tied his father to acquiescence in the royalist counter-coup launched by Richard in the summer of 1397. In his capacity as steward of England, John of Gaunt presided at the parliamentary trials of the earls of Arundel and Warwick and passed sentence upon them. He was rewarded for this public endorsement of Richard's policies by the creation of Henry Bolingbroke as duke of Hereford and John Beaufort as marquess of Somerset during the parliament of September 1397. The political future of the house of Lancaster nevertheless remained under threat. Soon after the Westminster session of parliament ended, rumours began to spread that four of Richard's most favoured courtiers were plotting the death and disinheritance of John of Gaunt and his family. In a related incident, Thomas (I) Mowbray, duke of Norfolk, attempted to ambush the duke as he travelled to Shrewsbury in January 1398. Lancaster sought to counter these threats by a rapid expansion of his indentured retinue, while Bolingbroke's delation of Mowbray to the king for treasonable conversation, made on his father's advice, appeared to confront successfully the rumoured plot against the Lancastrian family. The duke was named as one of the small committee nominated to terminate all unfinished business at the end of the Shrewsbury session of parliament and in March 1398 he undertook a final diplomatic mission, concluding a further extension of the Anglo-Scottish truce with the earl of Carrick. Another mark of royal favour followed in August, when Gaunt was created hereditary constable of Richard's new principality of Chester. The outcome of the judicial duel between Hereford and Norfolk held at Coventry in September 1398, when the king unexpectedly exiled Lancaster's son from the kingdom for six years, was consequently all the more shocking. It seems to have precipitated the final decline in John of Gaunt's health: overtaken by a 'suddane langure' (Wyntoun, 3.68), the duke retired to Leicester Castle, where he died on 3 February 1399.

In his will Gaunt established perpetual chantries for himself and Blanche of Lancaster at St Paul's, and for Duchess Constanza at St Mary Newarke, Leicester; he also expressed his desire that the king should receive one-third of all outstanding arrears of the Castilian pension and ordered his executors to discharge all his debts, always excepting those arising from the expedition of Edmund of Cambridge to Portugal, for which he would accept no responsibility. By a further provision he required that his body should lie unburied and unembalmed for forty days after his death. He was eventually buried at St Paul's Cathedral on 16 March 1399, beside his first wife.

Family John of Gaunt and his first wife, Blanche of Lancaster, made a glamorous and wealthy couple and Blanche's early death on 12 September 1368 was widely mourned. Gaunt's provision in his will that he should be buried beside Blanche may suggest that she retained a special place in his affections. Their tomb in St Paul's, of which a seventeenth-century engraving still survives, was at least partly the work of the great architect Henry Yevele. Surmounted by their alabaster effigies, it was of appropriate magnificence. Blanche's early death was lamented by both Froissart and Chaucer, whose *Boke of the Duchesse* was probably written for Gaunt. The commemoration of her death became a principal event in the Lancastrian liturgical calendar. There were three surviving children of the marriage, besides two sons, John and Edward, who died in infancy: Philippa, who married João I, king of Portugal, in 1387; *Elizabeth of Lancaster, who married John Hastings, earl of Pembroke, in 1380 and, after this marriage was dissolved at her insistence, John Holland, created earl of Huntingdon in 1388, in 1386; and his only surviving son, Henry Bolingbroke, earl of Derby and duke of Hereford, the future *Henry IV, who married Mary, younger daughter and coheir of Humphrey (IX) de Bohun, earl of Hereford, before February 1381. Constanza, Gaunt's second wife, was a valuable source of advice to him on Iberian affairs, accompanying him to Castile in 1386, but the duke seems to have preferred the company of his mistress, Katherine Swynford, in most other respects. His liaison with Swynford was openly acknowledged and, after Gaunt's renunciation of his Castilian claims, Constanza appeared only rarely in the Lancastrian household, maintaining a separate establishment at Tutbury, Staffordshire. Besides a son, John, who died in infancy, the surviving child of this marriage was Katherine, who married Enrique, prince of Asturias, later Enrique III of Castile, in 1387. Following Constanza's death in March 1394 Lancaster married, as his third wife, Katherine Swynford, with whom he already had four children, born between 1372 and 1377. They were given the dynastic name of Beaufort, a lost French lordship of the duke's: John Beaufort, earl of Somerset, who married Margaret Holland; Henry Beaufort, bishop of Lincoln and Winchester; Thomas *Beaufort, who married Margaret, daughter of Thomas Neville of Hornby; and Joan *Beaufort, wife of Sir Robert Ferrers of Overseley and, second, Ralph Neville, earl of Westmorland. The duke had one other illegitimate child, Blanche, who married Sir Thomas Morieux in March 1381; her mother was Marie de St Hilaire, a Hainaulter lady-in-waiting of Queen Philippa.

Assessment Among his contemporaries John of Gaunt generated strong but very diverse reactions. To Thomas Walsingham, he appeared at times to be a traitor to the realm, abandoning those he commanded in war and betraying those he should protect in peace (*Chronicon Angliae*, 75). The priority the rebels of 1381 attached to the duke's capture and execution makes it plain that such views were widely shared. To Henry Knighton, however, Gaunt was the 'pious duke', a lover of peace and concord who had been unjustly defamed by his enemies (*Knighton's Chronicle*, 234). Even those enemies were forced to acknowledge that the duke of Lancaster was a powerful and able politician. The Monk of Westminster, who generally distrusted the duke's motives, commented that the other magnates feared him 'because of his great power, his admirable judgement and his brilliant mind' (*Westminster Chronicle*, 112) and his opinion seems confirmed by the earl of Arundel's complaint in 1394 that Gaunt often used such 'harsh and bitter words' in council and parliament that the earl and others did not dare to state their true views (*RotP*, 3.313). In reality the duke's political influence, though considerable, was never all-pervasive. Although his preference for aristocratic self-regulation rather than legislation as the solution to the problem of illegal maintenance, expressed at Salisbury in 1384, exercised considerable influence over the formulation of royal policy on the issue, for instance, his intermittent sponsorship of John Northampton's faction within the city of London failed to alter the balance of power in London politics decisively.

John of Gaunt's most characteristic political position was an unwavering defence of the crown and its prerogatives, even in the face of the considerable provocation offered by Richard II in 1384–5 or the threat to the security of the Lancastrian inheritance posed by the exile of Henry Bolingbroke. Popular suspicions about his loyalty arose partly from the duke's great wealth and influence and partly from hostility to the strategic options he advocated: Gaunt's decision to offer financial concessions to the papacy in 1375, his opposition to full-scale intervention in the Low Countries in the early 1380s, and his advocacy of a negotiated peace with France a decade later were all unpopular policies. In each case, much of the hostility was created by the suspicion that, in the conflict of interests generated by the duke's ambitions in Castile and Aquitaine, he was too ready to sacrifice national security to his private advantage. The policies he argued for nevertheless had much to recommend them. He was quicker than most of his contemporaries to appreciate that the revival of the Valois monarchy required a new strategy of negotiation and containment, while his persistent pursuit of the *voie d'Espaigne* kept open a second front that eventually proved vital in preventing the concentration of French forces for an invasion of England planned by Charles VI.

As a military commander in the Anglo-French conflict Gaunt lacked the audacity of his father and elder brother but his record compares favourably with that of other English captains after the resumption of hostilities in 1369. He was outwitted once, in 1373, but he kept his army together in difficult circumstances. He made a reliable second in command to the Black Prince, fought some effective defensive campaigns in the marches of Aquitaine, and, once arrived in Castile, successfully allied military force to dynastic diplomacy in exemplary fashion. Indeed, it was in such negotiations that the duke's greatest talents lay. He was seen to best advantage in the courtly world of international diplomacy, where his wealth allowed him to display a ceremonial magnificence at least equal to that of his French counterparts and he appeared to observers as fluent in speech, self-controlled, and good-humoured—qualities that were not always on display in domestic politics, where Gaunt had a tendency to use his wealth and royal blood to brush aside criticism.

This was not the only contradiction in John of Gaunt's character. In his religious attitudes he seems to have combined some sympathy towards reformist criticisms of the institutional church with a practical reluctance to abandon the material benefits his control of ecclesiastical resources provided. Although he was prepared to mobilize popular anti-clericalism for political ends, as he did in 1376–7, he could also manifest a sincere devotional piety. The duke chose his confessors from among the Carmelites, the most ascetic of the mendicant orders, while the insistence in his will that his body lie unburied for forty days aligns him with a movement of penitential spirituality prevalent at Richard II's court. Equally, although John Wyclif first attracted Gaunt's attention by the virulence of his anti-episcopal rhetoric, the duke showed some sympathy for the broader criticism of ecclesiastical corruption that Wyclif and his Oxford disciples developed: 'he believed them to be holy men of God, because of their pleasing words and manner' (*Knighton's Chronicle*, 312) and it was only in May 1382 that his disapproval of Wyclif's eucharistic teaching finally caused him to sever his ties with the movement.

Despite these inconsistencies the characteristic features of John of Gaunt's life and career seem clear. What distinguishes him from other English magnates of the period is the fact that his domestic policies can only be properly understood in the light of his ambitions abroad. In his wealth and his liking for display, as well as in the breadth of his strategic interests, Gaunt bears comparison with the greatest of European princes and, among them, only the dukes of Burgundy could rival his successful pursuit of dynastic advantage.   SIMON WALKER

Sources PRO, DL 29/728/11980–11985 · *Chancery records* · RotP · Rymer, *Foedera* · S. Armitage-Smith, *John of Gaunt* (1904) · A. Goodman, *John of Gaunt: the exercise of princely power in fourteenth-century Europe* (1992) · P. E. Russell, *The English intervention in Spain and Portugal in the time of Edward III and Richard II* (1955) · R. Somerville, *History of the duchy of Lancaster, 1265–1603* (1953) · [T. Walsingham], *Chronicon Angliae, ab anno Domini 1328 usque ad annum 1388*, ed. E. M. Thompson, Rolls Series, 64 (1874) · *Knighton's chronicle, 1337–1396*, ed. and trans. G. H. Martin, OMT (1995) [Lat. orig., *Chronica de eventibus Angliae a tempore regis Edgari usque mortem regis Ricardi Secundi*, with parallel Eng. text] · L. C. Hector and B. F. Harvey, eds. and trans., *The Westminster chronicle, 1381–1394*, OMT (1982) · *Thomae Walsingham, quondam monachi S. Albani, historia Anglicana*, ed. H. T. Riley, 2 vols., pt 1 of *Chronica monasterii S. Albani*, Rolls Series, 28 (1863–4) · *John of Gaunt's register*, ed. S. Armitage-Smith, 2 vols., CS, 3rd ser., 20–21 (1911) · *John of Gaunt's register, 1379–1383*, ed. E. C. Lodge and R. Somerville, 2 vols., CS, 3rd ser., 56–7 (1937) · E. Perroy, ed., 'The Anglo-French negotiations at Bruges, 1374–7', *Camden miscellany, XIX*, CS, 3rd ser., 80 (1952) · A. Tuck, *Richard II and the English nobility* (1973) · G. Holmes, *The Good Parliament* (1975) · S. Walker, *The Lancastrian affinity, 1361–1399* (1990) · J. J. N. Palmer, *England, France and Christendom, 1377–99* (1972) · R. Delachenal, *Histoire de Charles V*, 5 vols. (Paris, 1909–31) · [T. Netter], *Fasciculi zizaniorum magistri Johannis Wyclif cum tritico*, ed. W. W. Shirley, Rolls Series, 5 (1858) · V. H. Galbraith, ed., *The Anonimalle chronicle, 1333 to 1381* (1927) · *Œuvres de Froissart: chroniques*, ed. K. de Lettenhove, 25 vols. (Brussels, 1867–77) · F. Lopes, *The English in Portugal, 1367–1387: extracts from the chronicle of Dom Fernando and Dom Joao*, ed. and trans. D. W. Lomax and R. J. Oakley (1988) · J. J. N. Palmer and B. Powell, eds., *The treaty of Bayonne (1388) with preliminary treaty of Trancoso (1387)* (1988) · Andrew of Wyntoun, *The orygynale cronykil of Scotland*, [rev. edn], ed. D. Laing, 3 vols. (1872–9) · Chandos herald, *Life of the Black Prince by the herald of Sir John Chandos*, ed. M. K. Pope and E. C. Lodge (1910) · R. L. Storey, 'The wardens of the marches of England towards Scotland, 1377–1489', *EngHR*, 72 (1957), 593–615 · J. W. Sherborne, 'Edward III's retinue and the French campaign of 1369', *Kings and nobles in the later middle ages*, ed. R. A. Griffiths and J. W. Sherborne (1986), 41–61 · C. Given-Wilson, 'Richard II, Edward II and the Lancastrian inheritance', *EngHR*, 109 (1994), 553–71 · GEC, *Peerage*, new edn · M. C. B. Dawes, ed., *Register of Edward, the Black Prince*, 4 vols., PRO (1930–33) · *Adami Murimuthensis chronica*, ed. T. Hog, EHS, 8 (1846) · J. B. Post, 'The obsequies of John of Gaunt', *Guildhall Studies in London History*, 5 (1981), 1–12 · T. Gascoigne, *Loci e libro veritatum*, ed. J. E. Thorold Rogers (1881)

Archives E. Sussex RO, household records, GLY 3469 | PRO, duchy of Lancaster, DL 28, 29, 42

Likenesses alabaster effigies, 1360–99 (with his first wife), repro. in W. Dugdale, *History of St Paul's*, ed. H. Ellis (1818); formerly in St Paul's Cathedral, London [now destroyed] · stained-glass window, 15th cent., York Minster · stained-glass window, 15th cent., All Souls Oxf.; repro. in F. E. Hutchinson, *Medieval glass at All Souls College* (1949), pl. 24 · A. Strayler, miniature, BL, *Liber benefactorum* of St Albans Abbey, Nero D.vii fol. 7r · manuscript painting, BL, Royal MS 14 E.iv, fol. 245 [*see illus.*]

Wealth at death approx. £12,000 p.a. gross: auditors' value of ducal estates for 1393–5, PRO, DL 29/728/11980–11985 · £10,500 p.a. net: auditors' value of ducal estates for 1393–5, PRO, DL 29/728/11980–11985

John [John of Lancaster], **duke of Bedford** (1389–1435), regent of France and prince, was born on 20 June 1389. He was the third son of Henry Bolingbroke, afterwards *Henry IV (1366–1413), and of Mary de Bohun (1369/70?–1394), coheir of the earls of Hereford, who died in childbirth in 1394.

Family and youth Like his brothers Henry, afterwards *Henry V (1386/7–1422), *Thomas, afterwards duke of Clarence (1387–1421), and *Humphrey, afterwards duke of Gloucester (1390–1447), John was 'wel boked' (*English*

John [of Lancaster], **duke of Bedford (1389–1435)**, manuscript painting, *c*.1423

Works of John Gower, 2.422). He began to study Latin grammar when he was eight and read and wrote English and French. From 1394 he lived in the household of his grandmother Joan, countess of Hereford. By 1397 he was in the household of Margaret Brotherton, countess marshal; a French page was among his attendants. John grew up surrounded by rich possessions. Besides cloth, silks, shoes, furs, and goldsmiths' work ordered from London merchants, he was allocated valuables taken from Richard II and his companions, and others seized from the rebels of Henry IV's reign. By 1400 he had his own small household and household chapel. The chapel soon developed into a fully-fledged institution with a staff of priests and musicians under a dean; it followed John to war.

From Henry IV's accession John of Lancaster began to accumulate the lands and offices in England that laid the foundations of his later wealth. He was knighted on 12 October 1399, on the eve of his father's coronation, and was a knight of the Garter by 1402. Between 1403 and 1405 grants of the forfeited Percy lands and of the alien priory of Ogbourne, Wiltshire, considerably increased his income. Appointed master of the mews and falcons on 21 August 1402, he succeeded to two former Percy offices: constable of England (10 September 1403) and warden of the east march (1403–14). His first military experience was in border warfare, guided by his kinsman Ralph *Neville, earl of Westmorland (*d*. 1425). In 1405 John was present at the capture of Archbishop Richard Scrope at Shipton

Moor, and wrote to York Minster to condemn demonstrations at the tomb following Scrope's execution for treason. John's letters to the king and council record his financial straits as warden. He pawned and melted down jewels and plate to pay his soldiers. By 1411/12 he claimed arrears of £13,000.

Duke of Bedford and lieutenant of Henry V Henry V recognized his brother's abilities, giving him a greater role in warfare, politics, and diplomacy, and increased his status and income. On 16 May 1414, John was created duke of Bedford and earl of Kendal, and on 24 November, earl of Richmond, with the reversion of the valuable honour of Richmond. At the restoration of the Percy lands in 1415, Bedford was awarded a pension of £2000 p.a. By 1418, in negotiations over one of a series of marriage proposals, his annual income was estimated at 7000 or 8000 marks, which placed him among the wealthiest magnates in the kingdom. However, proposals in 1419 from Queen Joanna of Sicily to adopt Bedford as her heir had foundered by 1420.

When Henry invaded France in 1415 for the campaign that led to Agincourt, Bedford remained in England as lieutenant. In 1416 Bedford took part in the ceremonies surrounding the emperor's visit, sitting at Sigismund's left hand at the Garter feast in May. On 15 August (the feast of the Assumption) Bedford commanded the fleet that won an important victory, ending the Franco-Genoese blockade of Harfleur. During Henry's conquest of Normandy and the *pays de conquête* in 1417–19, Bedford again remained in England as lieutenant. He repulsed the Scots in 1417, presided over the parliament that sentenced the Lollard Sir John Oldcastle, and was present at Oldcastle's execution. Many other issues affecting church and state in England and abroad came to Bedford's attention as lieutenant, preparing him for his future role as regent of France. In May 1420 Bedford crossed to France to campaign with his brothers Henry and Clarence.

Political rivalry between the Armagnacs and the Burgundians had fed civil war in France during the reign of the insane king, Charles VI (1380–1422). In 1419 the murder of John the Fearless, duke of Burgundy, on the bridge at Montereau, in the presence of the dauphin, drove Philip the Good, the new duke, to support Henry V's claims to the French crown. Bedford was with Henry when the treaty of Troyes or 'final peace' was signed, on 21 May 1420. This important treaty was the basis of the 'dual monarchy', the Lancastrian claim to rule France as well as England. Henry married *Catherine, daughter of Charles VI, became regent of France, and was named heir to Charles in place of the dauphin (afterwards Charles VII). Circumstances dictated that Bedford would spend the rest of his life defending the claims of his brother and his nephew, *Henry VI, to the French crown.

From June 1420 Bedford campaigned in France. He joined Henry V and his Burgundian allies at the siege of Sens in June, and brought reinforcements from Normandy to the siege of Melun (July–November). On 1

December he rode with Clarence behind the kings of England and France on their formal entry into Paris, remaining with Henry at the Louvre for Christmas. On 10 December Bedford was present when the three estates ratified the treaty of Troyes, and again on 23 December when a *lit de justice* was held to condemn the murderers of John the Fearless. In the new year he returned to England with Henry by way of Rouen, where the Norman estates ratified the treaty of Troyes, and he was present at Catherine's coronation at Westminster on 23 February 1421.

The death of Clarence in an ill-considered raid at Baugé (Maine-et-Loire) on 22 March 1421 altered Bedford's position in an important respect. He became heir to the crown of England, and after 1422 to the English claims to France. From June 1421 to May 1422 he again served as lieutenant of England, while Henry campaigned in France. In December 1421 he stood godfather with his uncle, Henry *Beaufort, bishop of Winchester, to the future Henry VI. In the same month he gave the spiritualities of Ogbourne to the Garter chapel, St George's Chapel, Windsor, one of many gifts of rents or goods that Bedford made to religious institutions in England and France. The following May Bedford escorted Queen Catherine to France, leaving Gloucester as lieutenant of England. He then assumed command in place of Henry in northern Burgundy, at Vézelay and Avallon (Yonne), and at Cosne (Nièvre), but did not see action. Bedford was at his brother's deathbed at the Bois de Vincennes, on 31 August 1422, and followed the funeral cortège to St Denis, Rouen, and Calais, but then returned to Rouen as governor of Normandy.

Regent of France Henry V seems to have intended Bedford to become regent of France only if Philip the Good refused the office, while Henry's last will assigned his youngest brother, Gloucester, the *tutela* or guardianship of the infant Henry VI's inheritance, and not, as Gloucester claimed, the government of England. In the event, Bedford became regent of France and Gloucester protector and leader of the council in England during Bedford's absence. This reversal of their previous roles, since Bedford had been mainly employed in England, whereas Gloucester had campaigned regularly in France, was essentially the result of the death of Clarence, who at the time of his death had been Henry V's principal lieutenant in Normandy. As it was, this new arrangement promoted rivalry between the brothers, and led to conflicting policies in the government of England and France.

Charles VI died on 21 October 1422. Bedford, not yet regent, wrote to the London citizens on 26 October to assert his right by birth to be protector in England. He returned to Paris from Rouen on 5 November, no doubt after Philip of Burgundy had refused the regency of France. Bedford was the only prince present at the funeral of Charles VI (9–11 November). As the procession returned to Paris from St Denis, Bedford caused the sword of state to be carried before him. Although this symbol of English claims provoked a hostile reaction, Bedford set about winning acceptance for English rule through political measures and through sustained propaganda in picture and poem. On 19 November he presided over an assembly of the Paris *parlement*. The chancellor expounded Bedford's pledge to pursue Henry V's policies; those present swore fidelity to Henry VI, the regent, and the treaty of Troyes. Except for Henry's coronation expedition to France (1430–32), when the council withdrew the style of regent, Bedford remained regent of France to his death in 1435.

The 'dual monarchy' depended above all on the Anglo-Burgundian alliance. Bedford's first marriage, to Anne of Burgundy, sister of Philip the Good, in 1423 was crucial. Philip's support for the English was bolstered by Burgundian dynastic ambitions. Bedford's childless marriage, and the death of Anne of Burgundy in November 1432, were major factors in the collapse in 1435 of an already weakened alliance. Negotiations for the marriage had begun by October 1422; the treaty was sealed at Vernon on 12 December. On 17 April 1423 at Amiens, Bedford and the dukes of Burgundy and Brittany signed a treaty of mutual support. The treaty of Amiens, or 'triple alliance', was intended to safeguard Normandy. Bedford's policies were later undermined by both dukes, but in the short term they endorsed Henry VI's claims to the crown and accepted Bedford's regency. The marriage was celebrated at Troyes on 13 May. Anne of Burgundy brought a dowry of 50,000 écus, 10,000 in cash at Bedford's entire disposal. She also brought plate, jewels, and vestments, although few details of what these were are known.

During the first six years of the regency, to the siege of Orléans in 1428–9, Bedford won tolerance of his rule. He understood the need to govern through Frenchmen (many of whom were Burgundian supporters), and through French institutions, notably the *grand conseil*. He introduced important administrative and military reforms, and popular measures to control brigandage. The influential ecclesiastics of the University of Paris lent Bedford their support, in spite of differences over collation to benefices and clerical taxes, and over the foundation of the University of Caen, mooted in 1424, enacted in 1432, but only active from about 1439. The presence of the English court in Paris meant welcome patronage of the luxury trades. English victories improved the economic climate, especially in Rouen and Normandy. In these years the English under Bedford defended Henry V's conquests and extended them to much of France north of the Loire. From 1423 victories in Champagne, at Cravant on the Yonne, and the capture (1 March 1424) of Le Crotoy in Picardy, prepared the ground for conquest. Bedford's greatest victory against the dauphin and his Scottish allies, won at Verneuil on the southern border of Normandy on 17 August 1424, was a rare instance when the regent took the field in person. The chronicler, Waurin, gives an eyewitness account of the battle; the victory was second only to Agincourt in the eyes of English contemporaries. Jean (II), duke of Alençon, the nephew of Jean (V) of Brittany (*d.* 1442), was the most important of many prisoners captured. The first instalments of Jean (II)'s huge ransom, fixed at 200,000 écus d'or, were paid to Bedford in jewels, plate, and vestments. The bed of Alençon, a set of state hangings, which Bedford valued at 'gret pris' (Stratford,

Bedford Inventories, C 90), was still prized by Henry VIII. When Bedford and Anne of Burgundy entered Paris in triumph on 8 September, the citizens made them a lavish present of plate.

The victory at Verneuil secured Normandy and Paris and opened the way for the conquest of Maine. The county of Maine and the duchy of Anjou, then under dauphinist control, were the first lands granted to Bedford in France (20 June 1424). If conquered, they would create a great apanage. Bedford's captains initiated a successful expedition into Maine in the autumn of 1424. Le Mans had been taken by August 1425; later a few places in Anjou came under English control. Besides operations on the Loire commanded by the earls of Suffolk and Salisbury, other captains attached to Bedford's household laid siege to Mont-St Michel and defeated the Bretons, who had transferred their loyalty to the dauphin.

Bedford in England, 1425–1427 From late December 1425 to March 1427, a period of minor action in the French war, Bedford was in England. He was summoned to intervene between his brother, Gloucester, and his uncle, Beaufort, in the quarrel that had originated in Gloucester's claim to the protectorship. Bedford's sympathies lay with Beaufort, whose political skills and financial resources were essential for the successful prosecution of the French war, whereas Gloucester had endangered the Anglo-Burgundian alliance by invading Hainault in 1424 and 1425. Bedford prevented a duel between Gloucester and Philip, and warned Duke Philip of Gloucester's disastrous second invasion. Peace in London was threatened by Gloucester's warmongering and encouragement of an anti-Flemish reaction. An armed confrontation between Beaufort and Gloucester took place at London Bridge on 30 October 1425, the climax of a struggle to wrest from Beaufort the power he had obtained as chancellor during Gloucester's absence.

Bedford left Paris on 2 December. He escaped an ambush near Amiens and arrived in England on 20 December, entering London on 10 January 1426. Gregory's chronicle records his displeasure with the citizens for their part in the disorders; he received their gift of a pair of silver-gilt basins and 1000 marks coldly. As laid down in 1422, Gloucester had to relinquish the protectorate and its salary to his elder brother, who was not only still heir apparent to the throne, with interests of his own to safeguard, but also enjoyed the confidence of the council. Bedford presided at the Leicester parliament, where in March the antagonists were reconciled. Beaufort resigned as chancellor and prepared to leave England. Before parliament dispersed in June, Bedford knighted the five-year-old Henry VI. In January 1427, less than two months before Bedford left for France, he swore on the gospels before the council to support conciliar government, forcing Gloucester to follow his lead. In early February 1427 he laid the first foundation stone of the new site for the Bridgettine abbey at Syon, originally Henry V's foundation, endowing the house with £20, two service books, and a legendary, and giving a ring to each nun of the first profession.

Bedford's offices, lands, and income, 1425–1435 The years 1425–9 saw a substantial increase in Bedford's income. Besides the Alençon ransom, he obtained offices, lands, and perquisites on both sides of the channel. Following the earl of Westmorland's death (25 October 1425), the honour of Richmond, nominally worth £2000 p.a., came to him. Bedford secured the profitable office of admiral of England (26 July 1426). In January 1427 he obtained the wardship and lands of Lord Grey of Codnor. Grants of the gold and silver mines of Devon and Cornwall, and the wardship of the de Vere lands (in exchange for an unreliable exchequer pension), were enrolled on 24 February, shortly before Bedford left for France. To the annoyance of the earl of Warwick, Bedford replaced him as captain of Calais (March 1427). This key appointment carried power and prestige, but also heavy costs.

Bedford held great estates in France. From Verneuil to about 1427 he styled himself duke of Anjou and of Alençon, count of Maine, of Mortain, and of Beaumont, and lord of Mantes and other *seigneuries* in the *pays de conquête*. Anjou remained unconquered, but from January 1425 Bedford administered the lands he held from his personal *chambre des comptes* in Mantes. The receipts of the former Orléans lands in Normandy also went to Mantes. Bedford's motives seem to have been disinterested (at least in the short term): to secure revenues for the war outside Paris, not to grasp personal profits. The receipts of Maine went to the defence of Maine, those of Alençon and the *pays de conquête* to the expenses of the regent's household—in effect the royal household—with its heavy burden of costs for the war and for administration; the revenue from the Orléans lands went to Normandy.

Bedford could not sustain his claims to all these lands. Mortain was granted to Edmund Beaufort on his arrival to campaign in France (22 April 1427). In 1430 the English council in France removed the duchy of Alençon, the lordships of the *pays de conquête*, and the Orléans lands, from Bedford's control and reunited them with the royal demesne. In early September 1430 Bedford obtained confirmation only of Anjou and Maine and of the *vicomté* of Beaumont-le-Roger. He had also to agree to the possible future resumption of Anjou and Maine. Council minutes suggest that at their greatest extent this group of French lands was deemed to be worth some 40,000 livres tournois annually.

Other lands acquired by Bedford in Normandy from about 1425 included the confiscated Estouteville lands, granted to Anne of Burgundy by September 1425. In May 1427 Bedford obtained the county of Harcourt. He enlarged it with neighbouring lordships after the earl of Salisbury's death in November 1428. In 1431 Bedford bought the county of Dreux, the lordship of Hambye, and the Hôtel d'Aligré in Paris from the earl of Suffolk.

Many of Bedford's French lands were held in right of Anne of Burgundy, but the regent enjoyed the revenues. It is impossible to assess their total value. A valor for 1433/4 recorded by William Worcester is incomplete, and Bedford acquired new lands in France up to the year he died.

As well as six houses in Paris and others in Rouen and Harfleur, Bedford held at his death in tail male the duchy of Anjou, the counties of Maine, Harcourt, and Dreux, the vicomté of Beaumont, the former Salisbury lordships and those of Torcy, Charlemesnil, La Haye-du-Puits, Hambye, and other lesser lordships. While private ambition was not the mainspring of Bedford's French policy, he had a huge financial stake in the English conquest in France. The scale of his French as well as his English income is directly relevant to the building works he commissioned, and to his purchasing power as a patron of luxury goods.

Bedford in France, 1427–1433 Bedford crossed to France in March 1427, accompanied by Bishop Beaufort. On 25 March in Calais, Bedford invested Beaufort as cardinal. Soon afterwards the war entered a disastrous phase, marked by the siege of Orléans. The death on 3 November 1428 of the English commander, the earl of Salisbury, as the result of a gunshot wound, was followed in the following May by the relief of Orléans by Jeanne d'Arc, and then by a series of French victories, culminating in the coronation of Charles VII at Rheims on 17 July. But the French were repulsed from outside Paris on 8 September by an Anglo-Burgundian army, reinforced by troops raised by Cardinal Beaufort for the Hussite crusade, and once more lost the initiative in the war. In 1434 Bedford openly criticized the decision to besiege Orléans, 'takyn in hand God knoweth by what avys' (*Proceedings … of the Privy Council*, 4.223). His plan, endorsed in May 1428 by the *grand conseil* and in September by the Norman estates, had been to attack Angers and Mont-St Michel. Yet Bedford contributed large sums to the siege of Orléans, and raised further money on Anne of Burgundy's jewels. In the continuing crisis of 1429 he pledged jewels and plate worth nearly 10,000 livres tournois to pay Beaufort's soldiers and 20,000 to pay Burgundy's.

Bedford understood the vital need to repair the Anglo-Burgundian alliance in 1429. His first will, sealed on 14 June 1429 (between the French victories at Jargeau and Patay), named Anne of Burgundy as his heir in France. Since Anne was childless, Philip stood to inherit after his sister's death. Bedford sent Anne to join Philip between July and September; she also attended his marriage to Isabella of Portugal in Bruges in January 1430. Bedford resigned the captaincy of Paris in Philip's favour in October 1429 and supported the crown's grant to him of Champagne and Brie in March 1430. These and other concessions repurchased Philip's co-operation. The Burgundians captured Jeanne d'Arc in Compiègne in May. She was transferred to the English for 10,000 crowns, tried, and executed as a relapsed heretic at Rouen on 30 May 1431. Bedford took no part in her trial, conducted by the church, although political motives determined the outcome, nor was he present when she was burnt at the stake in the market place at Rouen. In speaking of Jeanne in 1434 as 'a disciple and leme of the fend' (*Proceedings … of the Privy Council*, 4.223), that is, a witch, Bedford, whose orthodoxy was a marked part of his personality, was in agreement with the religious establishment of his day.

From October 1429 the English administration was centred on Rouen and Normandy, although it was not yet excluded from the rest of France. Bedford moved many of the valuables he had acquired from the French royal collections to Rouen. He enlarged Joyeux Repos, his principal house in Rouen, and improved the domestic apartments of the castle to accommodate his chapel, library, and wardrobe. Bedford lived mainly in Rouen from October 1429 to December 1430, and participated in its secular and spiritual life, most conspicuously on 23 October 1430, when he was admitted a canon of the cathedral.

Bedford had emphasized the need for Henry VI to be crowned in France as well as England. Henry arrived in Calais in April 1430. He landed on St George's day, reaching Rouen in July, and remaining there until November 1431. On 30 January 1431, in a populist but necessary gesture, Bedford, accompanied by Anne of Burgundy, arrived by water in Paris with boatloads of victuals. Prayers and processions in Rouen and Paris had been held for this dangerous journey. The recapture of Louviers in late October secured the route to Paris. Henry's entry into Paris took place on 2 December. Among the tableaux were figures of the dukes of Bedford and Burgundy, flanking the boy king. The procession ended at Bedford's principal Paris residence, the Hôtel des Tournelles. The coronation in Notre-Dame (16 December), conducted by Beaufort, rather than the bishop of Paris, antagonized the Parisians, whom it was intended to conciliate.

A quarrel seems to have erupted at the time of the coronation between Bedford and Beaufort, who appears to have been determined to assert his own primacy in the council, in France as well as in England. Central to the dispute was the commission Bedford was forced to accept as regent. Formerly he had claimed to rule by right of birth, as heir to the English claim to France, as well as to the English throne itself. From the time Henry landed in France until he left again for England in January 1432, Bedford ceased to be styled regent. The council, dominated by Beaufort, curbed Bedford's military powers and his powers of patronage. Indentures were issued in the king's name rather than (as before) in Bedford's; garrison captains from the royal household replaced some of Bedford's men. In September 1430 Bedford was appointed to the captaincy of garrisons he had already held, emphasizing that his powers derived from the king and council. There is other evidence of the council's intention to limit Bedford's powers in 1430: the removal of lands from his control, and the new grants he was compelled to obtain for the lands he kept. On 12 October 1431 Bedford's authority to rule France in the king's absence was redefined in a formal commission, and his powers of patronage restored. This forced him to acknowledge, probably at Beaufort's instigation, that he held office in France by appointment, not by right of birth. There can be no doubt that he resented what he saw as a threat to his position as regent.

By 1432 the war was turning against the regent. In February the donjon of Rouen Castle was seized; in April Chartres fell to a trick; there were losses in Maine. In August Bedford took the field in person for the first time since

Verneuil, but failed to retake Lagny, east of Paris, under English siege since the beginning of May. Paris was now vulnerable to attack from three directions. Bedford's prestige as regent was in jeopardy.

The death of Anne of Burgundy on 14 November 1432 had serious consequences for the Anglo-Burgundian alliance. Her illness and death caused Bedford intense grief. The relics of St Germain were carried in procession to intercede for Anne's recovery; Bedford endowed the Celestine church in Paris, where Anne was buried, with rich vestments. He probably made gifts in kind to Rouen Cathedral, and to the other churches where he had founded masses for himself and the duchess.

Five months later, on 20 April 1433, Bedford remarried. His bride, Jacquetta of Luxembourg (1415/16–1472), was the seventeen-year-old niece of Louis de Luxembourg, bishop of Thérouanne and chancellor of France for the English, who had come to dominate the English administration. Bedford travelled to Thérouanne by way of Calais, where he suppressed a mutiny of the soldiers and executed the ringleaders. They had seized the staplers' wool to enforce their claim to arrears of pay. Bedford's captaincy was no exception to the rule that the expenses of Calais far exceeded the treasurer's receipts. Some of his valuables were handed over in 1433 and 1434 to the treasurer of Calais and the lieutenant of Calais Castle, no doubt to guarantee arrears.

Bedford's second marriage, intended to form a useful alliance, brought about a rupture between Philip of Burgundy and Bedford, although the political consequences may have been exaggerated. Philip was offended by the remarriage and by the pretensions of a vassal house. In May Beaufort tried to reconcile Bedford and Philip at St Omer. Out of pride neither prince would make the first move and they never met again. An estrangement from Bedford may have suited Philip. By 1433 he had fulfilled his ambitions in the Low Countries, and could dispense with English support in the north. He was beginning to respond favourably to overtures of peace from France and from the church.

Before returning to England at midsummer 1433, Bedford spent about a month in Calais with Gloucester, Beaufort, and some of the English council, discussing proposals for peace made by Cardinal Albergati, the papal mediator, and by the Council of Basel.

Bedford's final years, 1433–1435 Bedford crossed to England on 18 June 1433. He had returned to seek money and soldiers for France, and to defend himself successfully, even brilliantly, from accusations of mismanagement of the war, no doubt originating from Gloucester. Bedford's speeches to parliament and the council, written in the first person, carry conviction in their words of devotion to the service of Henry VI in France and in England. On 13 July Bedford challenged his detractors under the law of arms. The chancellor, Bishop John Stafford, expressed confidence in Bedford and disarmed opposition to his war policy. In November the Commons petitioned Bedford to remain in England. Bedford seemed to stand above faction, whereas animosity between Gloucester and Beaufort

had erupted in 1428 and 1432 and there had been other violent confrontations between magnates. By December parliament had agreed to Bedford's conditions for remaining in England. He was to be chief councillor with control over the council, parliament, and patronage. These concessions reversed policy since 1422, whereby the council had limited the powers of both Bedford and Gloucester. In consideration of the burden of debt at the exchequer, Bedford proposed a cut in his annual salary as chief councillor from 5000 marks to £1000; Gloucester was obliged to follow suit. Bedford reserved the right to payments of £500 for expenses each time he crossed the channel, demonstrating that he envisaged the necessity of returning to France.

The parliament of 1433 confirmed grants beneficial to Bedford. His creations for life as duke of Bedford and earl of Kendal were altered to hereditary peerages (8 July 1433), perhaps in hopes of an heir. Five west-country manors and reversions granted on the same day remedied a shortfall in Bedford's income from the honour of Richmond. But he failed to secure adequate taxation from parliament or from convocation in 1433 to support the war, though the military situation was deteriorating and money had to be found. On 10 May 1434 Beaufort lent 10,000 marks towards the expeditions of the earl of Arundel and other captains serving under Bedford. On 20 June he advanced another £2000 for Bedford's own return to France. While Arundel's expedition was being prepared, Gloucester mounted an attack on war policy in the great council (April–May 1434). Bedford construed Gloucester's words as an insult to his honour; Bedford's reply was similarly construed by Gloucester. The quarrel was settled before the king, but Gloucester's ambitions to lead an expedition on the scale of Agincourt were shown to be impossible.

The regent crossed the channel for the last time in mid-July 1434, travelling to Rouen in early August via Calais and Thérouanne, and visiting Paris, again for the last time, over Christmas and new year 1435. By 1435 Bedford's failing health, English reverses in the war, and the preparations for the Congress of Arras, marked the gradual decline in English fortunes.

Death and reputation Bedford died in Rouen Castle on 14 September 1435 at a critical moment in the war, a week after the English left the Congress of Arras unsatisfied in their demands, and a week before the conclusion of peace between France and Burgundy. On 13 April 1436 Paris was reconquered and English possessions, including Bedford's, were confiscated for the crime of *lèse-majesté*. Normandy was lost by 1450 and by 1453 all France except Calais.

In accordance with the provisions of Bedford's nuncupative will, he was buried 'magnificently' on 30 September in Rouen Cathedral, on the north side of the choir near the high altar, near the other royal tombs. His effigy was destroyed by Calvinists in 1562, but a funerary plaque bearing his arms, heraldic insignia, and Garter collar survived to the eighteenth century, and is recorded in drawings by Dugdale (reproduced by Francis Sandford) and in the Gaignières collection (Paris, Bibliothèque Nationale,

MS Français 20077, fol. 7). The burial was excavated in 1860. A large-framed skeleton was reportedly uncovered, fitting with Waurin's description of Bedford at Verneuil as a man of great physical strength with powerful limbs. Bedford's beaked nose is depicted in his portrait in the Bedford Hours, the source of several engravings (BL, Add. MS 18850, fol. 256v), and in the smaller portraits in the Salisbury breviary (Paris, Bibliothèque Nationale, MS Lat. 17294). He left no legitimate children, but two bastards, Richard and Mary, apparently conceived before the regency. Their mother is unknown. His widow, Jacquetta of Luxembourg, married secretly in 1436 Richard Woodville, son of Bedford's chamberlain. Their daughter, Elizabeth, became the wife of Edward IV.

Bedford was a notable collector and patron of the arts. There was an important political context for his activities in this respect, even though as a great prince he no doubt also wished to be surrounded by magnificent possessions in his household and chapel. The dukes of Burgundy and Brittany had been appointed with Bedford to be executors of Charles VI in 1422. As allies they acquiesced when he obtained jewels and plate, tapestries, vestments, and books from the French royal collections, thereby adding to his prestige as regent. Bedford took one of the finest chapel sets from the royal collection to Caen at Christmas 1423, when he presided over a meeting of the Norman estates. The costs of some of these valuables were offset against Bedford's personal expenditure on the war. Bedford paid in cash for others, but his total expenditure is unknown. His outlay of 2323 livres tournois for the great Louvre Library of Charles V and Charles VI, which at this date contained 843 books, is often cited as especially meagre, but this was part payment only. The royal gold cup (now in the British Museum) and about 100 books from the Louvre library are known to survive from this treasure. Much more about Bedford's commissions and acquisitions is known from written records, notably the Bedford inventories drawn up for Bedford's executors in England. In addition twelve manuscripts written and illuminated or adapted for Bedford and Anne of Burgundy or with dedications to them are known. Besides the Bedford psalter (BL, Add. MS 42131), commissioned in England before the regency, the most important are the liturgical books written and decorated in Paris by the illuminators known as the Bedford workshop—the Bedford Hours, the Salisbury breviary, and the very large benedictional, known as the pontifical of Poitiers, which was burnt in the Hôtel de Ville during the Paris commune in 1871. These manuscripts display Bedford's arms and heraldic insignia with which many of his lost possessions were also decorated. His badge was the *racine* or root. It was also the badge of the heraldic order that Bedford founded. His motto was *Pour souffrir*, although another motto, *A vous entier*, was associated specifically with his first marriage. The benedictional was ordered for Bedford's household chapel, an important institution, with which the names of the musicians John Farley, John Dunstaple, and Thomas Hoppinel have been plausibly, but not conclusively, associated.

Bedford's reputation survived the reconquest of France and Normandy. His familia and former captains, such as Sir John Fastolf, are recorded in William Worcester's *Boke of Noblesse* as lamenting the passing of the regent and what he stood for. In his own century many English and French (especially pro-Burgundian) chroniclers eulogized Bedford; Thomas Basin described him as 'wise, humane and just' (Basin, bk 2, cap. 2). Lively pen portraits of Bedford and Anne of Burgundy are sketched by the Norman chronicler Pierre Cochon and by the anonymous Parisian, the Bourgeois de Paris, who wrote approvingly of Bedford's propensity to build (*maçonner*) wherever he was. His hot temper emerges in a few episodes, as does his religious orthodoxy. Shakespeare underlines his valour and loyalty in his two *Henry IV* plays; chronology and events are confused in *Henry V* and *Henry VI*. Criticism of Bedford and the regency has been strongest from nationalistic historians of Normandy and partisans of Jeanne d'Arc, in line with the historiography of the Hundred Years' War as it developed in the nineteenth century. Most historians have emphasized his devotion to duty, to his dead brother's intentions, and to the service of his nephew Henry VI. Bedford was a mighty prince, a brave soldier, and a considerable patron and collector. His court and its ceremonies fulfilled a crucial political role in giving an illusion of permanence and stability to the Lancastrian presence in France.

JENNY STRATFORD

Sources J. Stratford, *The Bedford inventories: the worldly goods of John, duke of Bedford, regent of France (1389–1435)*, Society of Antiquaries of London (1993) [incl. bibliography] · T. Basin, *Histoire de Charles VII*, ed. C. Samaran, 2 vols. (Paris, 1933–44) · *Chronique normande de Pierre Cochon*, ed. C. de Robillard de Beaurepaire (Rouen, 1870) · J. Gairdner, ed., *The historical collections of a citizen of London in the fifteenth century*, CS, new ser., 17 (1876) · A. H. Thomas and I. D. Thornley, eds., *The great chronicle of London* (1938) · A. Tuetey, ed., *Journal d'un bourgeois de Paris, 1405–1449* (Paris, 1881) · *Journal de Clément de Fauquembergue, greffier du parlement de Paris, 1417–1435*, ed. A. Tuetey, 3 vols. (Paris, 1903–15) · *La chronique d'Enguerran de Monstrelet*, ed. L. Douët-d'Arcq, 6 vols. (Paris, 1857–62) · *Recueil des croniques … par Jehan de Waurin*, ed. W. Hardy and E. L. C. P. Hardy, 5 vols., Rolls Series, 39 (1864–91) · B. J. H. Rowe, 'The *grand conseil* under the duke of Bedford', *Essays in medieval history presented to H. E. Salter*, ed. F. M. Powicke (1934), 207–34 · B. J. H. Rowe, 'King Henry VI's claim to France in picture and poem', *The Library*, 4th ser., 13 (1932–3), 77–88 · A. R. Myers, 'A vous entier: John of Lancaster, duke of Bedford, 1389–1435', *History Today*, 10 (1960), 460–68 · C. T. Allmand, *Lancastrian Normandy, 1415–1450: the history of a medieval occupation* (1983) · G. L. Harriss, *Cardinal Beaufort: a study of Lancastrian ascendancy and decline* (1988) · R. Vaughan, *Philip the Good: the apogee of Burgundy* (1970) · J. Stratford, 'John, duke of Bedford as patron in Lancastrian Rouen', *Medieval art, architecture and archaeology at Rouen*, ed. J. Stratford, British Archaeological Association Conference Transactions [1986], 12 (1993), 98–108 · D. Starkey, ed., *The inventory of King Henry VIII: the transcript* (1998) · F. Sandford, *A genealogical history of the kings and queens of England* (1707) · J. G. Nichols, ed., *The boke of noblesse: addressed to King Edward the Fourth on his invasion of France in 1475*, Roxburghe Club (1860) · *The English works of John Gower*, ed. G. C. Macaulay, 2 vols., EETS, extra ser., 81–2 (1900–01) · *RotP*, vols. 3–4 · N. H. Nicolas, ed., *Proceedings and ordinances of the privy council of England*, 7 vols., RC, 26 (1834–7), vols. 1–4 · R. Somerville, *History of the duchy of Lancaster, 1265–1603* (1953)

Likenesses manuscript painting, c.1423, BL, Add. MS 18850, fol. 256v [see illus.] · tomb effigy, Rouen Cathedral; destroyed, 1562

Wealth at death very great; income, incl. lands, etc., in England, est. 7000–8000 marks p.a. in 1418; lands, etc., in France, never est. and fluctuating, but by 1430 provision for compensation of annual rents of *c*.40,000 *livres tournois* for part only; est. of known fraction of treasure valued in Bedford inventories in England over £6432 sterling; other treasure in France and Normandy: Stratford, *Bedford inventories*

John, Prince (1905–1919), was born at Sandringham, Norfolk, on 12 July 1905, the fifth son and sixth child of the prince and princess of Wales who in 1910 became King *George V (1865–1936) and Queen *Mary (1867–1953). He was given the names John Charles Francis, despite a centuries-old royal prejudice against the name John. He spent most of his early childhood at Sandringham under the care of a nanny, Mrs Lalla Bill, with his older brothers and sister, and shared family holidays at Balmoral. At four he was found to be epileptic. It has been suggested that he also had a learning disability, possibly autism. This discovery appears to have had little impact on his early years, except perhaps to make his notoriously aloof mother more demonstratively affectionate towards him than she had been to his siblings. As he grew older the epileptic seizures became stronger and more frequent, and early in 1917, when he was eleven, a separate establishment was formed for him at Wood Farm, Wolferton, near Sandringham. He lived there with Lalla Bill and a manservant, separate from his family. After a severe fit on 18 January 1919, he died in his sleep in the late afternoon, and was buried in the graveyard at Sandringham church on 21 January. He was thirteen.

Prince John disappeared from the historical record in 1917 when he was taken to Wood Farm: he no longer appeared in family photographs and his death was marked by only a very private ceremony. At the time of the abdication, attempts were made to discredit the future *George VI by suggesting that he was subject to 'falling fits' like his brother and was hence unfit to rule, but otherwise almost nothing was heard of Prince John again until 1998, when the discovery of two volumes of photographs of the royal family at Balmoral between 1912 and 1915, taken by his eldest brother, the prince of Wales, later *Edward VIII, brought him to public attention. The timing of the discovery—in the aftermath of the death of Diana, princess of Wales, and at the nadir of the royal family's popularity in the twentieth century—coloured the interpretation given to Prince John's short life.

The story of Prince John has subsequently been brought forward as evidence for the inhumanity of the royal family, and the linking of his treatment with that meted out to other relations suffering from conditions affecting mental health has been used to construct a pathology of behaviour in the royal family. Prince John's removal to Wood Farm was portrayed as an example of the heartlessness of the house of Windsor, and exaggerated claims were made about his abandonment by his parents. But in 1909, when Prince John first showed the symptoms of epilepsy, there was no treatment for the condition, and any kind of mental disorder was considered a sign of eugenic unfitness and a source of shame and distress. It says as much for

George V and Queen Mary that they kept their son with their other children between 1909 and 1917 as it tells against them that thereafter they made different arrangements for him. Moreover, with the war raging and the other children away at school or in the services, some kind of separate provision for the prince was both unavoidable and desirable.

Prince John's family was undoubtedly frightened and ashamed of his illness, and viewed his early death as a blessing for the child and also for themselves. Queen Mary wrote that 'The news gave me a great shock, tho' for the poor little boy's restless soul, death came as a great release' (Hennessy, 511), and she told a friend that 'he just slept quietly into his heavenly home, no pain, no struggle, just peace for his poor little troubled spirit which had been a great anxiety to us for many years' (ibid.). A more callous view was expressed by the prince of Wales, who had been sent away to the Royal Naval College when his youngest brother was only two. 'No-one has ever seen him except the family & then only once or twice a year & his death is the greatest relief imaginable and what we've always silently prayed for' (McLeod, 60), he wrote. A television drama about the prince, *The Lost Prince*, by Stephen Poliakoff, was made for the BBC in 2002, and broadcast in 2003.   K. D. REYNOLDS

Sources J. Pope-Hennessy, *Queen Mary* (1959) · K. McLeod, *Battle royal: Edward VIII and George VI, brother against brother* (1999) · *Daily Mail* (20 May 2002) · *Sunday Herald* (7 April 2002) · *The Observer* (23 July 2000) · K. Rose, *King George V* (1983) · B. R. Lewis, 'Prince John', www.britannia.com/history/biographies/princejohn.html, 14 Nov 2002 · K. Rose, *Kings, queens and courtiers: intimate portraits of the royal house of Windsor from its foundations to the present day* (1985)
Likenesses V. Temple, photograph, 1909, NPG · photographs, Harewood House, Yorkshire

John ap John (*c*.1625–1697), Quaker leader, possibly the son of John ap John, was born at Pen-y-cefn in Coed Cristionydd township, Ruabon, Denbighshire. Upon his marriage in 1663 to Catherine Edwards (d. 1695), the widow of David ab Edward, John ap John moved to Plas Efa, Trefor, near Llangollen. A yeoman farmer, he also held other freehold properties at Trefor and Rhuddallt.

It is possible that John ap John was educated at a school at Wrexham and may well have been influenced by the puritan preacher Walter Cradock, who was the curate of the parish in 1635. Puritan influence on him was reinforced during the civil war, and it is likely that he was a chaplain to the parliamentary garrison stationed near Beaumaris during the late 1640s. John was also a member of Morgan Llwyd's congregationalists at Wrexham. In 1653 Llwyd sent John and another member of the congregation to Swarthmoor Hall in Furness, Lancashire, to meet George Fox and investigate the Quaker movement. As a result of this meeting John and his companion were convinced of the Quaker message. After this event John ap John became a notable Quaker preacher throughout Wales, whose ministry was 'very effectuall to the Convincemt. of Many' (Penney, 323).

After he established his first Quaker congregation at Pen-y-cefn, John ap John proceeded in 1654 to preach throughout south Wales and the borders. As a consequence of this missionary work he was imprisoned in Cardiff and Usk in Monmouthshire during his first year of missionary work. In their accounts of the persecution suffered by Welsh Friends, members recorded that in 1655 at Usk in Monmouthshire John ap John was the first Friend to be imprisoned for disturbing a minister in the county. He was nevertheless eventually released with the assistance of the Quaker magistrate Walter Jenkins. At Swansea in October 1655 John ap John, after disputing with Morris Bidwell, the Independent minister of St Mary's Church, was seized by the collar and confined to 'a close dark prison' before being brought before the magistrates who were intent on having 'him whipt, that the Devil might come out of him' (Besse, 1.735). On 8 October 1655 a mittimus was sent to the keeper of the common gaol at Cardiff stating that 'John ap John of Denbighshire hath misbehaved himself contrary to the Laws' (ibid., 1.736). He was kept in this prison for at least three months.

During June and July 1657 John ap John accompanied George Fox on his missionary tour around Wales. He was, however, arrested and briefly imprisoned at Tenby, and at 'a great market town' (Norris and Penney, 8), presumably referring to Carmarthen. The two men also visited Dolgellau, Caernarfon, and Beaumaris in north Wales, where John carried the main burden of preaching and bore the brunt of official hostility and popular abuse. It has been conjectured that the imprisonment of John ap John stemmed less from the 'desire on the part of the magistrates to imprison vindictively, than to imprison and send away for the purpose of preserving the peace' (ibid.). Like many other Friends John ap John was in 1658 threatened with physical force when he refused to pay tithes. He was again detained in Swansea in 1658 and imprisoned for twenty weeks in Cardiff for preaching against Evan Griffith, the minister of Oxwich in Gower, who pulled John's hair while he was also 'struck and pulled by the nose' (Great Book of Sufferings, 2, fol. 3) by Morris Bidwell. John was also briefly imprisoned in 1660, along with several other Welsh Friends, in Cardiff after conducting a Quaker meeting. In 1663, 1668, and again in 1670 he was fined by the magistrates at Wrexham and Ruthin for holding Quaker meetings. In spite of these hardships John ap John remained committed to the Society of Friends and secured notable conversions, including William Bevan, a prosperous Swansea merchant, the Lloyd family of Dolobran, and Richard Davies, a felt maker from Cloddiau Cochion near Welshpool. In 1668 John ap John again travelled as itinerant preacher when Fox returned to Wales and he similarly accompanied Richard Davies and John Burnyeat, another Quaker missionary, in their travels throughout Wales in 1669 and 1675. Davies wrote in his *Journal* that 'We declared the word of the Lord both in Welsh and English. My Friend John ap John was very sound and intelligible in the Welsh language' (*Account of the Convincement*, 165).

In August 1673 John ap John reflected upon his life as a Quaker missionary and wrote 'I have received much and done but little' (Norris and Penney, 6), yet from 1667 he

was instrumental in establishing further meetings throughout Wales. He helped to develop the organizational apparatus of Welsh monthly, quarterly, and yearly meetings which enabled the society to survive and prosper, especially in times of persecution or when many Friends in the country sought refuge in America. On 15 September 1681 John ap John and Thomas Wynne, the Quaker barber–surgeon of Caerwys, purchased 5000 acres in Pennsylvania for an initial sum of £100 with the intention of assisting Friends who were prepared to emigrate. He was, therefore, 'the father of the "Welsh Tract" in Pennsylvania' who first spoke to William Penn about buying some of his land in America. John may have been in Penn's confidence and, having early notice of the royal grant, suggested to the Welsh to secure the best lands (Bebb, 188). In 1683 John published *Tystiolaeth o gariad ac ewyllys da*—a translation of John Songhurst's *Testimony of Love and Good will* (1680) and a call to Friends to be loyal to truth and the light. He also attended many of the Welsh yearly meetings and held the 1693 yearly meeting at his own home.

On 9 February 1695 Catherine, his wife, died at Rhuddallt and was buried at Trefor. Before his death John ap John went to live with his daughter Phoebe, the wife of John Mellor of Whitehough Manor, Ipstones parish, Staffordshire, where he died on 16 November 1697. He was later buried nearby at Basford.   RICHARD C. ALLEN

Sources John ap John, *Tystiolaeth o gariad ac ewyllys da* (1683) [copy housed at NL Wales] · J. ap John, autographs, RS Friends, Lond., Gibson MS 2 [incl. signed statement regarding his testamony], vol. 335, fol. 33 · Great Book of Sufferings, 2 (Wales), RS Friends, Lond., fols. 3–4 · T. Holme, letter to M. Fell, 10 Dec 1655, RS Friends, Lond., Swarthmore MS 1.194 · J. Nayler, letter to G. Fox, 1653, RS Friends, Lond., Swarthmore MS 3.60 · F. Gawler and J. Gawler, letter to G. Fox, 1661, RS Friends, Lond., Swarthmore MS 4.221 · T. Holme, letter to G. Fox, 27 Feb 1656, RS Friends, Lond., Swarthmore MS 4.247 · T. A. Glenn, 'Early meetings of Quakers in Wales', NL Wales, MS 1116D, 116–19 · 'Dictionary of Quaker biography', RS Friends, Lond. [card index] · *DWB*, 439–40 · F. Gawler, *A record of some persecutions … in south Wales* (1659), 5 · J. Besse, *A collection of the sufferings of the people called Quakers*, 1 (1753), 735–62 · A. N. Palmer, *A history of the town and parish of Wrexham*, 3: *A history of the older nonconformity of Wrexham* [1888], 122–30 · W. G. Norris and N. Penney, eds., *John ap John and the early records of Friends in Wales* (1907) · *The journal of George Fox*, rev. edn, ed. J. L. Nickalls (1952), 289–307 · T. M. Rees, *A history of the Quakers in Wales* (1925), 17–24, 27, 34, 36, 39–41, 43–5, 47–8, 52, 57–8 · N. Penney, ed., 'The first publishers of truth': *being early records, now first printed, of the introduction of Quakerism into the counties of England and Wales* (1907), 121, 321–3 · T. Shankland, 'Pwy oedd John ap John a Chatrin ei briod?', *Cymru*, 56 (1919), 177–83 · *An account of the convincement, exercises, services, and travels of … Richard Davies* (1710), 165 · M. F. Williams, 'The Society of Friends in Glamorgan, 1654–1900', MA diss., U. Wales, Aberystwyth, 1950, chap. 1 · G. H. Jenkins, *Protestant dissenters in Wales* (1992), 35–7, 56, 100 · R. Jones, *Crynwyr Bore Cymru, 1653–1699* (1931), 13, 21, 24–5, 27–9, 35–6, 46, 61–2, 66, 69, 71, 84–5, 89, 95, 104, 126, 130 · W. A. Bebb, 'John ap John, apostol y Crynwyr yng Nghymru', *Cymru*, 62 (1922), 187–8 · R. C. Allen, 'The Society of Friends in Wales: the case of Monmouthshire, c.1654–1836', PhD diss., U. Wales, Aberystwyth, 1999, chaps. 1, 4 · G. H. Jenkins, 'Quaker and anti-Quaker literature in Wales from the Restoration to Methodism', *Welsh History Review/Cylchgrawn Hanes Cymru*, 7 (1974–5), 403–26 · G. H. Jenkins, 'From Ysgeifiog to Pennsylvania: the rise of Thomas Wynne, Quaker barber-surgeon', *Flintshire Historical Society Journal*, 28 (1977–8), 39–

61 · G. H. Jenkins, *Literature, religion and society in Wales, 1660–1730* (1978), 183, 208, 211

Archives Hist. Soc. Penn., Penn papers, deeds dated 15 Sept 1681 · Hist. Soc. Penn., Charles Morton Smith MSS, deed dated 14 Feb 1682, vol. 3, no. 1

John de Lovetot. *See* Lovetot, Sir John de (*b*. in or before 1236, *d*. 1294).

John fitz Geoffrey (*c*.1206–1258), justiciar of Ireland and baronial leader, was the son of *Geoffrey fitz Peter, fourth earl of Essex, justiciar of England (*d*. 1213), and his second wife, Aveline, daughter of Roger de Clare, earl of Hertford, and widow of William de Munchensi. In 1227 John fitz Geoffrey gave the king 300 marks to have seisin of the lands that had descended to him by right of inheritance from his father. Geoffrey fitz Peter had intended these to be extensive, for King John had granted to him and his heirs from his marriage with Aveline the castle and honour of Berkhamsted. This grant, however, never came to fruition, and Berkhamsted, after Geoffrey's death, remained in the hands of the king. Thus, with the earldom of Essex passing to the descendants of Geoffrey's first marriage, John had to make do with such manors as Aylesbury and Steeple Claydon in Buckinghamshire, Exning in Suffolk, and Cherhill and Winterslow in Wiltshire, the last the only part of the honour of Berkhamsted that he obtained. John was a substantial magnate but, in terms of land held in hereditary right, not one of the first rank. Probably this situation, and the example of his father, who had risen in the king's service from humble origins to the earldom of Essex, was the spur to his long career in the royal administration.

John began that career as sheriff of Yorkshire between 1234 and 1236. Then, in 1237, at the request of a parliament that conceded the king taxation, he was added to the king's council along with William (IV) de Warenne, earl of Surrey, and William de Ferrers, earl of Derby. If this elevation to the highest level reflected John's standing with his fellow magnates, in the ensuing years he gained and retained the confidence of the king. From 1237 until 1245 he seems to have acted as one of the stewards of the king's household, a post that he combined with the sheriffdom of Gloucestershire (1238–46) and more briefly with the office of chief justice of the southern forests (1241–2) and the seneschalship of Gascony (1243). He was thus well fitted for his long period in office as justiciar of Ireland (1245–56), where he had private interests through the dower of his wife, Isabel (daughter of Hugh Bigod, earl of Norfolk, who was the widow of Gilbert de Lacy of co. Meath. In 1254 Ireland was made part of the endowment of Edward, the king's son, and John fitz Geoffrey, between 1254 and 1258, became the prince's leading councillor. He also retained his place on the council of the king. His rewards from the latter, over his long career, had included the manors of Whaddon, Buckinghamshire, and Ringwood, Hampshire, the wardship of the land and heirs of Theobald Butler in Ireland (for which he paid 3000 marks), and 'for his immense and laudable service' the whole cantred of the Isles in Thomond.

In the political crisis of 1258, however, John fitz Geoffrey was one of the king's chief opponents. Indeed, a later chronicle, the Westminster *Flores historiarum*, named him and Simon de Montfort as the ringleaders of the revolution. Certainly he was one of the seven magnates whose confederation in April 1258 began the process of reform. He was then one of the twelve chosen by the barons to reform the realm, and one of the council of fifteen imposed on the king by the provisions of Oxford. On 23 July 1258 he went with Roger (III) Bigod, earl of Norfolk, and Simon de Montfort to demand that the Londoners accept 'whatever the barons should provide for the utility and foundation of the realm' (*Cronica maiorum et vicecomitum Londiniarum*, 38–9). John's sudden death on 23 November 1258 thus deprived the new regime of one of its bastions. The Westminster *Flores* ascribed John's conduct to resentment at being removed from the justiciarship of Ireland. Like other leading magnates he was also provoked by the behaviour of the king's Poitevin half-brothers. His place in Edward's councils was threatened by their growing influence over the prince. In addition, he was engaged in a fierce dispute over the advowson of one of his manors—Shere in Surrey—with the youngest of the brothers, Aymer de Valence, earl of Pembroke and bishop-elect of Winchester. This reached a climax on 1 April 1258 when Valence's men attacked John's at Shere and killed one of them. When John demanded justice, the king refused to hear him. This episode helped spur the revolutionary action taken against the king at the Westminster parliament which opened a week later. Indignation at John's treatment spread the more easily because his brothers-in-law were Roger Bigod, earl of Norfolk, and Hugh Bigod, who was later appointed justiciar by the provisions of Oxford. Both were his colleagues among the seven original confederate magnates.

John fitz Geoffrey was evidently a man of considerable parts, respected both by his fellow magnates and by the king. Indeed, despite his role in the revolution of 1258, when Henry III heard of John's death he ordered a solemn mass to be celebrated for his soul and donated a cloth of gold to cover his coffin. John was succeeded by his son, *John fitz John, who became a leading supporter of Simon de Montfort. D. A. CARPENTER, *rev*.

Sources *Calendar of the charter rolls*, 6 vols., PRO (1903–27) · CPR · CCIR · *Calendar of the fine rolls*, 22 vols., PRO (1911–62) · *Calendar of the liberate rolls*, 6 vols., PRO (1916–64) · PRO, Just 1/1187, m. 1 · Paris, *Chron.* · H. R. Luard, ed., *Flores historiarum*, 3 vols., Rolls Series, 95 (1890) · T. Stapleton, ed., *De antiquis legibus liber: cronica majorum et vicecomitum Londiniarum*, CS, 34 (1846) · R. F. Treharne and I. J. Sanders, eds., *Documents of the baronial movement of reform and rebellion, 1258–1267* (1973) · H. W. Ridgeway, 'Oxford (1258)', *Thirteenth century England*, ed. P. R. Coss and S. D. Lloyd, 1 (1986)

John, Sir, fitz John (*c*.1240–1275), baronial leader, was the son of *John fitz Geoffrey (*c*.1206–1258), justiciar of Ireland, and his wife, Isabel, the daughter of Hugh Bigod, third earl of Norfolk, and the widow of Gilbert de Lacy of Meath. John fitz Geoffrey was a prime instigator, with Simon de Montfort, of the political revolution of 1258. In February 1259 John fitz John undertook to pay £300 for seisin of his father's lands while still under age. He thus acquired a substantial magnate inheritance centred upon Buckinghamshire, where he was lord of Aylesbury, Whaddon, and Steeple Claydon.

In 1261 John fitz John, as part of the abortive attempt to prevent the overthrow of the provisions of Oxford, the revolutionary programme imposed in 1258, became sheriff of Bedfordshire and Buckinghamshire in opposition to the sheriff appointed by the king. Two years later he joined Simon de Montfort when the latter returned to England and reimposed the provisions. While others deserted, John fitz John remained with Montfort to the end, bringing with him several Buckinghamshire and Northamptonshire knights. In July 1263 John's local influence was acknowledged and increased when Montfort's government made him keeper of the peace in Bedfordshire and Buckinghamshire; in December, with the other Montfortians, he accepted Louis IX's offer to arbitrate on their quarrel with the king. When Louis's verdict condemned the provisions of Oxford outright, the Montfortians refused to accept the verdict and prepared for war. In March 1264 John was involved in the seizure of Gloucester. Next month he led the pillage of the Jews in London. He killed the most famous, Kok son of Abraham, with his own hands and was less than pleased when Montfort made him share part of the spoils. John then took part in the siege of Rochester (17 April) before being knighted in London (4 May), just before Montfort marched out of the city to bring the king's army to battle. However, according to the Dunstable annals, John fitz John had been knighted earlier at Gloucester.

At the battle of Lewes (14 May 1264) John fitz John commanded the 2nd division of Montfort's army with Gilbert de Clare, earl of Gloucester, and William de Munchensi. 'He fought strenuously in the battle', the annals of Worcester recorded, 'smashing steel helmets and taking many of his adversaries prisoner' (Ann. mon., 4.452). In Montfort's subsequent regime, although involved in negotiations with the marcher barons and with the increasingly disaffected Gilbert de Clare, John's role was in the provinces rather than at court, perhaps in part because of his comparative youth. As castellan of Windsor (from June 1264) he dragooned the local population into providing a garrison and munitions for the castle. In addition, when his brother-in-law Robert de Vieuxpont died in June 1264, he became custodian of Vieuxpont's lordship of Westmorland. After the desertion of Gilbert de Clare and the escape of Edward, the king's son, from captivity, John fitz John was with Montfort on his final campaign and was captured at the battle of Evesham (4 August 1265), being saved from death by the royalist Roger de Clifford, who had married his niece.

Roger de Clifford was not the only royalist to whom John fitz John was related, for he himself had married a daughter of the king's justiciar, Sir Philip *Basset. Basset's eldest daughter, however, had married Hugh Despenser, one of Montfort's closest associates, and perhaps that tie, together with the role of his father in 1258, influenced John's political sympathies. He was also one of a group of young and warlike men (Robert de Vieuxpont and William de Munchensi were others), called contemptuously 'the junior boys of England' (Ann. mon., 4.133) by the chronicler Thomas Wykes, who were attracted to Montfort's side, quite probably by the glamour of his military reputation.

John fitz John's career after Evesham provides a good example of how former Montfortians could be rehabilitated. In July 1266 he was pardoned by the king for his past trespasses. Some of his lands had meanwhile been occupied and doubtless protected by royalist kinsmen—by Roger de Clifford and by William de Beauchamp of Elmley, who had married one of John's sisters. The bulk of his lands had been given to Gilbert de Clare and, under the terms of the dictum of Kenilworth, had to be repurchased by John at five times their annual value. Perhaps the financial strain is reflected in John's sale of Ringwood Manor, Hampshire, for 2250 marks; but he was on good terms with Clare, and appeared as a member of his entourage in and after 1267. Later John gained the favour of Edward I and, in 1274, he represented the king at a great council at Lyons. His death (childless) in November 1275 caused grief to both king and court.

John fitz John had given vigorous military support to the cause of Simon de Montfort. His career permits a glimpse of both the virtues and the vices of the medieval *miles strenuus*.　　　　　　　　　　　　D. A. CARPENTER, rev.

Sources Chancery records · CIPM, vol.1 · Calendar of inquisitions miscellaneous (chancery), PRO, 1 (1916) · Ann. mon., vol. 4 · The historical works of Gervase of Canterbury, ed. W. Stubbs, 2 vols., Rolls Series, 73 (1879–80) · E. F. Jacob, Studies in the period of baronial reform and rebellion (1925)

John of Beverley [St John of Beverley] (d. **721**), bishop of York, was posthumously the focus of a major pilgrimage cult. He was known personally to Bede, who preserved almost all the contemporary evidence for John's life and work; many of the traditions about him are not recorded until after his canonization in 1037, and some are certainly unreliable.

John came first to notice, in Bede's account, as one of five future bishops trained at St Hild's monastery of Streanaeshalch (probably Whitby): his aristocratic ancestry, his birth at Harpham (East Riding of Yorkshire), and his early education under Archbishop Theodore are traditions recorded later. John was appointed bishop of Hexham, a position created after Bishop Wilfrid was first expelled from Northumbria, in August 687, and held that see until 706; it was during that period that he ordained Bede both as deacon (c.692) and as priest (c.703). It was chiefly John's miracles that Bede recorded, four of them related to him by St Berhthun, originally John's deacon, and a fifth by Herebald, who had been one of his clerks. One of Berhthun's accounts tells of a miraculous cure by John at an oratory near Hexham, where he often retreated, especially during Lent. Since Herebald later became abbot of Tynemouth, his story may also relate to John's Hexham episcopate; it reveals that when John travelled, he rode with an entourage of young men, laymen as well as clergy. In 706 John was translated to York (and his predecessor Wilfrid restored to the bishopric of Hexham), and he remained there until old age prevented him from administering his see, when he consecrated his priest, another Wilfrid, as his successor, and retired to his monastery called Inderawuda, almost certainly to be identified with Beverley. His resignation of York, not dated by Bede, is traditionally fixed at 718, but around 714 seems more likely. Certainly two, and by implication three, of Berhthun's stories relate to healing miracles performed by John while he was bishop of York. One took place while he was visiting a nunnery at Wetadun (probably Watton, north of Beverley), and two when he went to dedicate churches which had been built by local landholders (*comites* or *gesiths*). One of the churches was described by Berhthun as lying less than 2 miles from Inderawuda, and it is interesting that later tradition identified both with local estates granted to Beverley, at Bishop Burton and Cherry Burton. After his resignation, John remained at Inderawuda until his death on 7 May 721; he was buried, according to Bede, in the *porticus* of St Peter there.

Hereabald described John's way of life as 'worthy of a bishop in every particular', and his miracles were clearly of great importance to Bede, demonstrating that a bishop could still possess supernatural powers. His identification with the bishop John whose death was recorded before 754 in a necrology of Bavarian provenance with strong Northumbrian connections may indicate the speed with which his fame spread. His cult was promoted by Alcuin, who put Bede's account into verse, and added praise of his learning which led later writers to view him as a scholar and teacher. The little that is known of the early history of Beverley Minster suggests that it was the successor to John's monastery of Inderawuda, and that it owed its importance (and the town of Beverley its very existence) to the cult of John. Certainly he was described as of Beuerlic in a liturgical calendar datable not later than 892. Later tradition made King Æthelstan visit John's tomb before the battle of 'Brunanburh', and show his gratitude afterwards by endowing the church generously. The last pre-conquest archbishops of York certainly rebuilt and reorganized Beverley Minster, and promoted John's cult: Ælfric secured his canonization in 1037, and the translation of his relics to a new shrine; and Ealdred, probably shortly before 1066, commissioned Folcard first to write responsories in John's honour, and then to write a life of the saint. Pilgrims were attracted to John's tomb from great distances; twelfth-century miracle collections include cures of visitors to the tomb from Hexham, Lincolnshire, Norfolk, Scotland, and Ireland. When the minster was badly damaged by fire in 1188, there was a search for John's tomb and reliquary; they were located in 1197, and the relics translated once more. The cult was also promoted by belief in the military efficacy of St John's banner, which was used by Archbishop Thurstan's army at the battle of the Standard in 1138. By 1266 it was accepted custom that when Yorkshire levies were summoned to the royal army, Beverley Minster sent one man with the banner. The banner was lent to Edward I, Edward II, Edward III, and Henry IV for military campaigns; Edward I showed his gratitude by establishing a chantry in John's honour in the minster. When Henry V won Agincourt on the feast of John's translation (25 October), John was made one of the patrons of the royal dynasty, and Archbishop Chichele ordered national observance of both of John's feasts (7 May as well as 25 October). Henry V visited the shrine in 1420 and Henry VI apparently did so in 1448. In or about 1541, however, the shrine was destroyed on Henry VIII's orders and in 1548 the collegiate church was suppressed.

D. M. PALLISER

Sources Bede, *Hist. eccl.*, 4.23; 5.2–6, 24 • J. Raine, ed., *The historians of the church of York and its archbishops*, 3 vols., Rolls Series, 71 (1879–94) • *Acta sanctorum: Maius*, 2 (Antwerp, 1680), 165–92 • Alcuin, *The bishops, kings, and saints of York*, ed. and trans. P. Godman, OMT (1982) • A. F. Leach, ed., *Memorials of Beverley Minster*, 1, SurtS, 98 (1898), vol. 1 • J. Gerchow, *Die Gedenküberlieferung der Angelsachsen: mit einem Katalog der libri vitae und Necrologien* (Berlin, 1988) • E. F. Jacob, ed., *The register of Henry Chichele, archbishop of Canterbury, 1414–1443*, 3, CYS, 46 (1945) • W. Dugdale, *The visitation of the county of Yorke*, ed. R. Davies and G. J. Armytage, SurtS, 36 (1859) • C. Wilson, ed., *Medieval art and architecture in the East Riding of Yorkshire*, British Archaeological Association Conference Transactions [1983], 9 (1989) • *VCH Yorkshire East Riding*, vol. 6 • W. H. Dixon, *Fasti Eboracenses: lives of the archbishops of York*, ed. J. Raine (1863) • E. B. Fryde and others, eds., *Handbook of British chronology*, 3rd edn, Royal Historical Society Guides and Handbooks, 2 (1986), 217, 224 • H. R. Loyn, 'Gesiths and thegns in Anglo-Saxon England from the 7th to the 10th century', *EngHR*, 70 (1955), 529–49 • J. Blair, 'Beverley, Inderauda and St John: a neglected reference', *Northern History*, 38 (2001), 315–16

John of Bridlington [St John of Bridlington, John Thwing] (*c*.1320–1379), prior of Bridlington, was born in the Yorkshire village of Thwing in the Wolds, some 9 miles west of Bridlington, to a distinguished family with extensive landholdings in the East Riding. He showed signs of deep devotion to the church early in life, and took a vow of chastity at the age of twelve. Between the years 1336 and 1339 he studied at Oxford, returning to Yorkshire as tutor in a prominent family. He entered the convent of Augustinian canons at Bridlington in 1340, where he distinguished himself as cellarer and then as prior, the position he held from *c*.1362 until his death, perhaps of the plague, on 10 October 1379.

The holiness of John of Bridlington, who was also known as John Thwing, was widely recognized during his own lifetime. A canon named Hugh, who may himself have been a member of the Bridlington community, wrote the first biography of John between 1379 and 1401. A Middle English verse life in the northern dialect by one who claimed to have witnessed Thwing's deeds appeared about the same time. Reports of miracles occurring at his tomb prompted Alexander Neville, archbishop of York, to delegate Robert Dalton, his vicar-general, to interview witnesses to these miracles in 1386. In 1388, 'out of regard for John de Thweng, late Prior', Richard II gave permission to the Bridlington Priory to crenellate its buildings. According to Walsingham, reports of miracles at Thwing's tomb had spread all over England by 1389. Henry Bolingbroke made an offering at Bridlington in 1391 upon returning from a campaign in Prussia and, as King Henry IV, he sent John Guisburn, a canon of Bridlington, to Rome

John of Bridlington [St John of Bridlington] (c.1320–1379),
manuscript painting

some copies with an elaborate prose commentary that
pretended to untangle the dense symbolism of the prophecy. The commentary (c.1364) was dedicated to Humphrey
(IX) de Bohun, seventh earl of Hereford and twelfth earl of
Essex, who assumed his titles in 1361 and died in 1373.
Bohun family members were patrons of the Augustinian
friars.

M. R. James demonstrated that the commentary was
composed by **John Ergome** (*fl.* 1385–1386), Augustinian
friar, who became both master regent and prior of the
York convent in 1385. Ergome came from a prominent
family in the East Riding, studied at Oxford, and was probably the Johannes de Anglia who was admitted to the faculty of theology in Bologna in 1380. He became master of
the studium of the Roman curia in 1386, and in the same
year served as *magister antiquus* ('senior master') in the
Naples convent. The date of his death is unknown.
Ergome's library, which numbered over 220 books, was
one of the largest personal collections in England during
the middle ages, and included a wide range of classical
and medieval authors. It was a collection, unique in size,
of mathematical, astronomical, alchemical, and astrological treatises, and prophecies, both secular and religious, some of which were accompanied by commentaries. He also possessed a number of histories, as well as
books on civil and canon law and medicine. Two copies of
the Bridlington prophecies and an explanation of them
(possibly the same as his commentary dedicated to Humphrey de Bohun) were also among Ergome's books. It
seems doubtful whether John Thwing had a hand in the
composition of these obscure prophecies, although they
are attributed to him in some manuscripts. Whether they
were composed by Ergome himself has been a topic of
debate. Ergome says simply that they were penned by a
'canon regular, according to the common opinion of folk'.
A number of the prophecies were cited by the Bridlington
chronicler in his *Gesta Edwardi de Carnarvon* of about 1377,
but without identifying the prophet; and about 1370–76
the Kirkstall chronicler cites the prophecies, attributing
them simply to 'Bridlington'.   MICHAEL J. CURLEY

in 1400 to secure Thwing's canonization. In a bull of Boniface IX, dated 24 September 1401, John Thwing was officially canonized. With the aid of a grant from Henry IV, a
shrine for his remains was constructed adjacent to the
Bridlington Priory. In 1404 Archbishop Scrope and the
bishops of Lincoln and Carlisle officiated at the translation of Thwing's body. Henry IV placed his son Prince
Henry under the patronage of St John of Bridlington, and
the prince made an offering of 5 marks at the shrine in
1407 in fulfilment of a previous vow. The hagiographer
John Capgrave's edition of the life of St John of Bridlington added new accounts of miracles to those mentioned
in the first biography by Hugh.

Personally, John of Bridlington impressed his contemporaries with his generosity, compassion, humility, and
zeal for the contemplative life. He supported poor students from the monastery's resources, and as prior he
slept in the dormitory along with the other members of
the community rather than in the prior's more comfortable quarters. The Middle English life mentions his hospitality towards minstrels. Tradition also attributed to John
of Bridlington the composition of certain Latin prophetic
verses, couched in highly obscure symbolism, and concerned principally with English affairs during the reigns
of Edward II and Edward III. These verses circulated in

Sources P. Grosjean, 'De S. Iohanne Bridlingtoniensi
collectanea', *Analecta Bollandiana*, 53 (1935), 101–29 · *Acta sanctorum:
October*, 5 (Brussels, 1786), 137–44 · C. Horstman, ed., *Nova legenda
Anglie, as collected by John of Tynemouth, J. Capgrave, and others*, 2 (1901),
64–78 · M. Amassian, 'A verse life of John of Bridlington',
Neuphilologische Mitteilungen, 71 (1970), 136–45 · J. S. Purvis, 'St John
of Bridlington', *Journal of the Bridlington Augustinian Society*, 2 (1924),
1–50 · *Thomae Walsingham, quondam monachi S. Albani, historia
Anglicana*, ed. H. T. Riley, 2 vols., pt 1 of *Chronica monasterii S. Albani*,
Rolls Series, 28 (1863–4) · *CPR, 1385–9*, 439; *1401–5*, 248 · Rymer,
Foedera, 1st edn, 3.190–91 · Canon of Bridlington, 'Gesta Edwardi
de Carnarvon', *Chronicles of the reigns of Edward I and Edward II*, ed.
W. Stubbs, 2, Rolls Series, 76 (1883), 25–151 · *The Kirstall Abbey chronicles*, ed. J. Taylor, Thoresby Society, 42 (1952) · T. Wright, ed., *Political poems and songs relating to English history*, 1, Rolls Series, 14 (1859),
123–215 · J. A. Twemlow, 'St John of Bridlington', *A miscellany presented to J.M. MacKay* (1914), 128–31 · J. A. Twemlow, 'The liturgical
credentials of a forgotten English saint', *Mélanges d'histoire offerts à
M. Charles Bémont* (1913), 365–71 · M. J. Curley, 'The cloak of anonymity and the prophecy of John of Bridlington', *Modern Philology*,
77 (1979–80), 361–9 · A. G. Rigg, 'John of Bridlington's prophecy: a

new look', *Speculum*, 63 (1988), 596–613 • M. R. James, ed., 'The catalogue of the library of the Augustinian friars at York', *Fasciculus Joanni Willis Clark dicatus* (1909), 2–96 • F. X. Roth, *The English Austin friars, 1249–1538*, 2 (1966), 408–13, 535–7 [John Ergome] • Emden, *Oxf.* [John Ergome] • P. Meyvaert, 'John Ergome and the *Vaticinium Roberti Bridlington*', *Speculum*, 41 (1966), 656–65
Likenesses window image, 1400–1500, Morley parish church, Derbyshire • window image, 1400–1500, Ludlow parish church, Shropshire • window image, 1400–1500, Beauchamp chapel, Warwick • sculpture, *c*.1440–1470, St Andrew's Church, Hempstead-by-Eccles, Norwich • illumination, York Minster, Bolton Hours, 5 Add. MS 2, fol. 46 • manuscript painting, BL, MS Royal 2 A.xviii, fol. 7*v* [*see illus.*]
Wealth at death personal library; John Ergome: James, 'Catalogue of the library'

John of Eltham. *See* John, earl of Cornwall (1316–1336).

John of Fordham. *See* Fordham, John (*c*.1340–1425).

John of Gaunt. *See* John, duke of Aquitaine and duke of Lancaster, styled king of Castile and León (1340–1399).

John of Lancaster. *See* John, duke of Bedford (1389–1435).

John of Mettingham. *See* Mettingham, John of (*d*. 1301).

John of Pontoise. *See* Pontoise, John de (*c*.1240–1304).

John O'Groats (*supp. fl.* **1496/1523**), supposed ferryman, who gave his name to what is popularly believed to be the most northerly inhabited place in Scotland, is likely to be either identical with or related to the John Groat who in 1496 received a grant of land in Duncansby from William Sinclair, second earl of Caithness, or to the John O'Grot of Duncansby who in 1523 was recorded as the earl of Caithness's bailie in those parts. There is no contemporary evidence to support later legends that this John was a Dutchman originally named Jan Groot, who was appointed by James IV to run a ferry between Scotland and the Orkney Islands, but the story of the ferry is given at least some substance by a deed of November 1549, by which Earl George ordered that John Groat, son of Findlay Groat, should be infeft 'in the ferry-house and ferry and 20 feet round about the said house' (Calder, 285). The Groat family remained in the north of Caithness for some two centuries afterwards. At least four generations are commemorated by tombstones in the churchyard at Canisbay. A ferryman named John Groat is recorded in 1656, and the ferry remained in the hands of his presumed descendants until 1741, when they fell on hard times and had to dispose of land, the meal mill, the ferry house, and boats.

Legends abound concerning the Groat family and the place name John o' Groats. For instance, it is told that the Groats held an annual feast to celebrate their arrival in Scotland from Holland, gatherings that became increasingly disputatious as a result of conflicting claims to the right to sit at the head of the table. The original John Groat is therefore said to have built a symmetrical eight-sided house, with eight doors and an octagonal table, so that none of his kinsmen could justly claim any position of seniority at future meetings. The diplomatic John's name became attached to his house and to the local community, and a late nineteenth-century hotel (built in 1876) added

an eight-sided room to perpetuate the story, which, however, is first recorded only in Sir John Sinclair's *Statistical Account of Scotland* of 1793. Nevertheless, the late nineteenth-century antiquary John Nicolson is reported to have claimed to have found the old foundation of a house with eight sides close to the hotel. Another story associated with John O'Groats relates that the ancestor of the Groats was a ferryman plying between Caithness and Orkney who charged 1 groat (4*d*.) for the journey. The ferryman became John o' the Groat, and gave his name to the district. Since the fare for crossing the Pentland Firth in the seventeenth century was £4, this tale can be dismissed. The unreliability of such stories notwithstanding, its picturesque name and geographical location serve to keep John o' Groats in the public eye, above all as the starting or the finishing point for innumerable extended walks, many of them undertaken for charitable purposes.   DONALD OMAND

Sources J. T. Calder, *History of Caithness* (1887) • J. Sinclair, *Statistical account of Scotland, 1791–1799*, [new edn], ed. J. Withrington and I. R. Grant, 20 vols. (1977–83), vol. 8 • *Murray's handbook for travellers in Scotland*, 6th edn (1894), 418; repr. (1971)

John Scottus [called John Eriugena, John Scottus Eriugena] (*fl. c*.845–*c*.870), theologian, who was born in Ireland and died probably in Francia, was the outstanding philosopher of the ninth century.

Origins John Scottus—as he is called in contemporary sources—was an Irishman: *scottus* meant 'Irishman' in this period, and Eriugena, a description John made up for himself and used only in the title of his translation of Pseudo-Dionysius, means 'born in Ireland'. (The form John Scottus Eriugena is of more recent use.) Prudentius of Troyes, writing in 851, says John was born in Ireland. Exactly where or when is unknown. He probably studied there in a monastic school, but it is uncertain how much of the wide reading he shows even in his early works was undertaken before he went to the continent. If, as is probable, a series of biblical glosses attributed to IO or IOH are his, then the Old Irish words he uses there appear to indicate not only that he grew up in Ireland, but that he was well educated there, not just in Latin but in areas such as Irish law. The viking raids are often given as the reason for his leaving Ireland. On this conjecture, his departure would probably have been at some time after 836, when the attacks became intensive. A detail about John's family may be provided by a note in a tenth-century manuscript, Paris, Bibliothèque Nationale, MS Lat. 12949, which attributes a computistical table to 'Aldelmus, frater Iohannis Scotti'. The manuscript, linked to the grammarian Israel Scottus (*fl.* 947), contains much material which shows the influence of John Scottus, but this fact does not assure the reliability of the note especially since Aldelmus is the Old English name Aldhelm.

Career at the Carolingian court John first enters the historical record in connection with the dispute over predestination. Gottschalk (805–868), a monk of Fulda, then Corbie, then Orbais, began teaching the doctrine of dual predestination (that God has predestined the good to bliss and the wicked to damnation) in the late 830s. He was attacked by Hrabanus Maurus and by Hincmar, archbishop of Rheims, and, in 849, the Synod of Quierzy condemned him to imprisonment in the monastery of Hautvillers. None the less, Gottschalk continued to propound his views and obtained the support of a number of leading thinkers. At this point Hincmar asked John Scottus to write against Gottschalk, and in 850 or 851 John accordingly wrote his *De divina praedestinatione*. Writing about the affair in 851 or 852, Pardulus, bishop of Laon, talks of their having told John 'the Irishman who is in the king's [Charles the Bald's] palace' (Brennan, 'Materials', no. 6) to write the treatise. John was therefore working at the palace of the Carolingian West Frankish king, Charles the Bald (*r.* 840–77). He had probably been there for some time. Prudentius, bishop of Troyes, attacking John's *De divina praedestinatione*, says that he had previously treated him as a friend and been particularly affectionate to him. Prudentius had been at the palace until 845 or 846 and was presumably John's colleague (or, less likely, his teacher) there. Prudentius also says that John was 'distinguished by no degree of ecclesiastical rank'. The comment could be interpreted as saying just that John's ecclesiastical rank was not high, but in context the more probable meaning is that he was a layman.

Two pieces of evidence may add a little more detail to this picture of John's early career. First, in Laon, Bibliothèque Municipale, MS 24, there is a letter addressed to Winibert, probably the abbot of Schüttern, in the diocese of Strasbourg. The writer asks Winibert to send him his copy of Martianus Capella and promises that he will emend those parts of it which were left aside when they were together. The letter is written by the Irish hand i[1] which many scholars think is John's (see below). If these scholars are right, the letter is presumably John's and it may indicate that he spent time in the Rhine valley when he first arrived on the continent. Second, a royal diploma dated 1 October 845 mentions, in a list which also includes Pardulus, a 'Iohannes medicus'. There is a medical recipe attributed to Iohannes on the flyleaf of a ninth-century manuscript and another ninth-century medical recipe mentions that both Pardulus and Iohannes made use of it. There is also some evidence of unusual medical knowledge in works certainly by John Scottus. All this suggests that John may well have been a medical expert, perhaps the court doctor.

The reaction to John's *De divina praedestinatione* was universally hostile. Archbishop Hincmar disowned it; various scholars wrote against it at length; and it was condemned, first at the Council of Valence, 8 January 855, and then by the synod of Lotharingian bishops held at Langres in May 859. Yet John seems to have benefited from royal protection. One of his fiercest antagonists, Florus of Lyons, noted in 852 that he had neither been punished nor even forced to keep silent, but rather given praise and greater honours. None the less, there is little evidence of how John was occupied between 850 and 860–62, when he completed his translation of Pseudo-Dionysius; perhaps (see below) the translation took a number of years. During the 860s he was busy with writing, including the composition of his masterpiece, the *Periphyseon*. The date of John's death is not certain. It has been argued that his poem 'Aula sidereae' was written for the dedication of the church of Notre Dame at Compiègne, which took place on 5 May 877. But a strong case has been made more recently that, although the poem celebrates the construction of the church at Compiègne, the occasion it commemorates is Christmas 869, when Charles attended mass at Aachen. John may, then, not have lived beyond 870.

Where did John live? Between *c.*845 and 850 he was linked to the royal palace and, as his poetry—much of it about Charles the Bald—indicates, his connections with the royal court remained close, while his links with the king himself appear to have become especially strong in the 860s. But Charles's court was itinerant, moving between Compiègne, Quierzy, St Denis, and other monasteries and palaces. Only after about 865 does it seem likely that there was a fixed palace school at Compiègne. Some scholars have suggested that, at some stage, the palace school may have been at Laon and John may have lived there. The schoolmaster at Laon, Martin Scottus, certainly knew John's work, but all the evidence suggests that Martin's school there was distinct from any palace school. Another centre with which John had connections was Soissons, where Wulfad, his friend since 850, was abbot, until he became archbishop of Bourges in 866. It was to Wulfad that John dedicated the *Periphyseon* and Wulfad's library shows his close interest in John's work. Perhaps, as Schrimpf has suggested, John lived at Soissons for some time (from the early 850s until 866 or later), under the protection of Wulfad, who was himself a trusted protégé of Charles the Bald.

Legend To these meagre details of John's life there may be added his legend, which is almost entirely the invention of the monk and historian William of Malmesbury (*d.* 1143). William gives his version of John's life, in differing forms, in his *De gestis regum Anglorum*, *De gestis pontificum Anglorum*, and (the latest of these accounts) a letter to Peter (perhaps Pierre Moraunt, a monk of Cluny), with which he prefaces the edition he prepared of the *Periphyseon*. In the letter, William suggests that the name Heruligena (the form which he read, or pretended to have read, in the inscription to John's translation of Pseudo-Dionysius) shows that, despite being called Scottus, John belonged to the race of the Heruli (a Germanic people found both on the Rhine and in the Black Sea region from the third to the sixth centuries). In all three versions of his account William gives the same version of John's later career and death, in which he is identified both with the subject of an epitaph the historian found at Malmesbury, a certain 'sophista [sage] Iohannes', who died a martyr's death, and with 'John, a priest and monk, sharp in mind and very learned in all types of literature' (Brennan, 'Materials', no. 14) who, according to Asser's life of Alfred, was invited by King Alfred to come from France to teach in England. According to William of Malmesbury, then, John left France late in life, attracted by Alfred's generosity, and settled at the monastery of Malmesbury, where he taught the boys, until one day they turned on him and stabbed him with their quills, making him, some considered, a martyr. This fantastical account in William's two *Gesta* was widely copied by chroniclers and encyclopaedists, including Helinand of Froidmont in his *Chronicon* (early 13th century) and Vincent of Beauvais in his *Speculum historiale* (13th century).

Early works John's writings fall into three main groups: the works he produced early in his career, before his contact with the tradition of Greek Christian Platonism; his translations of Greek writers; and the works he wrote after he had absorbed the ideas in these Greek texts.

The earliest, precisely datable, of John's works is, as mentioned above, the *De divina praedestinatione* which he wrote in 850 or 851 at Hincmar of Rheims's request against Gottschalk. Condemned shortly after it was written, it survives in just one manuscript, Paris, Bibliothèque Nationale, MS Lat. 13386 (edited by G. Madec in 1978). Two works of his, however, may date from earlier. One of the most studied textbooks for scholars of the mid-ninth century onwards was the prosimetrum by Martianus Capella, *De nuptiis Philologiae et Mercurii*, which consists of two introductory books, telling of the allegorical marriage of Mercury and Philology (wisdom and eloquence), and seven books each devoted to an introductory survey of one of the liberal arts. In Remigius of Auxerre's commentary on *De nuptiis*, written shortly after 900, a number of comments in books 1–3 are said to be taken from John Scottus. These are found in a commentary on the whole of the *De nuptiis* in Paris, Bibliothèque Nationale, MS Lat. 12960 (referred to hereafter as 'Par.'; ed. C. Lutz, 1939). Another manuscript, Oxford, Bodleian, MS Auct. T.2.19 (referred to below as 'Oxf.'; ed. E. Jeauneau, *Quatre thèmes*, 91–166), contains much the same text as in Par. for books 2–9, but a sometimes different version of book 1, which on occasion corresponds more closely to the comments reported by Remigius as John's. Although at one stage scholars suggested that the differences between the commentary on book 1 in Par. and Oxf. could be the result of authorial revision, closer study has indicated that they are more plausibly explained as representing different selections from the same stock of material. It cannot even be said with certainty that the texts in Par. and Oxf. are abbreviations of a commentary by John, different for book 1, largely the same for books 2–9. Remigius's commentary shows merely that some, very possibly most, of the commentary to books 1, 2, and 3 in Par. and Oxf. derives from John's teaching. The same is probably true of the comments on books 4, 6, and 9: in Bern, Burgerbibliothek, MS 363, John's name is placed by passages in the text of Servius which correspond to comments on books 4 and 6 of the *De nuptiis* in Par. and Oxf., and glosses in Leiden, Bibliotheek der Rijksuniversiteit, MS BPL 88, to book 9 in an Irish hand, i², closely associated with John (see below) are very close to those in Par. and Oxf. There is good reason to place John's activity as a commentator on *De nuptiis* early in his career. Prudentius of Troyes, attacking John's *De divina praedestinatione* shortly after its composition, complains

that he has been led away from Christian truth by Martianus Capella. Yet John may also have occupied himself with glossing the Bible. Four manuscripts (Vatican City, Biblioteca Apostolica Vaticana, MS Reg. Lat. 215; Paris, Bibliothèque Nationale, MS Lat. 1977 and MS Lat. 4883a; Bern, Burgerbibliothek, MS 258) contain biblical glosses, written no later than 877, some of which are marked as being by IO or IOH and contain Old Irish words. There is a reasonable probability that the IO(H) in question is John Scottus, especially since there are some correspondences between remarks here and comments on Martianus found in Par. and Oxf. If John is their author, the rudimentary knowledge of Greek and unambitious nature of the glosses strongly suggest that he wrote them early in his career.

Translations of Greek works John's intellectual universe was transformed by his encounter with a series of Greek texts which he translated. His preface makes it clear that the first of these translations were the works of Pseudo-Dionysius (ed. H. J. Floss, *Patrologia Latina*, 122; principal manuscripts listed in Cappuyns, *Jean Scot Erigène*, 161), the fifth-century theologian who issued his writings as if their author were Dionysius, the Areopagite converted by St Paul. This deception was not uncovered until the Renaissance and, since Dionysius the Areopagite was also considered to be the same as the Dionysius who converted the Franks and who is buried at St Denis, his four treatises, *The Celestial Hierarchy*, *The Ecclesiastical Hierarchy*, *The Mystical Theology*, and *On the Divine Names*, were objects of special interest and reverence for the Carolingians. In 827 the Byzantine emperor, Michael II, sent a Greek manuscript of these treatises (now Paris, Bibliothèque Nationale, MS Grec 437) as a gift to Louis the Pious. It was kept at St Denis and translated into Latin by the abbot of St Denis, Hilduin. Charles the Bald was an enthusiast for all things Greek and imitated the Byzantines in various aspects of his ceremonial. It is not surprising that he should have wished for a new translation of Pseudo-Dionysius. He turned to John Scottus to carry out the commission; but where had the Irishman learnt the Greek necessary for the task? The evidence suggests that, to a large extent, he learned it on the job. His earlier works show a predilection for Greek (which he may have owed to his Irish background), but a very limited knowledge of the language. In his preface to the translation, John describes himself as a beginner in the language, a description which is substantiated by linguistic errors which betray the lack of a thorough grounding. Given that John finished his *Periphyseon* in 866, and that he had completed the translation of Pseudo-Dionysius and of some other Greek works before he began his masterpiece, the latest plausible date for his completion of his first commission is *c.*862; the earliest date is provided by Hincmar of Rheims's *De praedestinatione*, finished early in 860, which uses Hilduin's translation, since it seems most improbable that Hincmar, who addressed his work to King Charles, would not have used the new translation executed by royal command had it been available. John may well, however, have begun his translation a number of years earlier; if he was learning as he translated, the process might have been a lengthy one.

After translating Pseudo-Dionysius, John proceeded (c.861–2) to translate the *Ambigua* (ed. E. Jeauneau, 1988) of Maximus the Confessor (d. 662), again at the command of the king, who insisted that he do the work more hastily than he would have chosen. John believed that Maximus helped to elucidate Pseudo-Dionysius's thought. There are two early manuscripts of the translation, Paris, Bibliothèque Mazarine, MS 561, and Paris, Bibliothèque de l'Arsenal, MS 237, which is copied from it. The Mazarine manuscript has been extensively corrected but, while some of the changes may well be authorial, others distort the sense of the translation. The manuscript also contains three short biblical glosses (ed. E. Jeauneau, *Études érigéniennes*, 437–87), which are probably by John. John also translated another work by Maximus, his *Quaestiones ad Thalassium*, called by him the *Scoliae* (ed. C. Laga and C. Steel, 2 vols., 1980–90); it is preserved in Monte Cassino, Biblioteca Casinense, MS 333, and Troyes, Bibliothèque Municipale, MS 1234, along with explanatory notes, some translated from the Greek, some his own. John quotes from the *Quaestiones* in books 4 and 5 of the *Periphyseon*, but not books 1–3, a fact which suggests that he made the translation during the time he was writing his masterpiece (c.862–6). A little earlier, John had translated Gregory of Nyssa's *De hominis opificio*, which he called the *Sermo de imagine* (ed. M. Cappuyns, 1965), which survives only in Bamberg, Staatliche Bibliothek, MS B IV 13. He probably made the translation for his own use, since it lacks a prefatory letter; he may have been led to the work by Maximus, because he frequently confused Gregory of Nyssa and Gregory Nazianzen, and Gregory Nazianzen is one of Maximus's favoured authorities. Another Greek Christian text which John may have put into Latin is Epiphanius's *De fide*, since he quotes from him at length in the *Periphyseon* and no other translation available to John is known; and perhaps also Basil's *Hexaemeron*, for which he uses a translation different from the commonly available one by Eustathius.

All these translations are of works by Greek Christian thinkers. There are also grounds for attributing to John the translation of the *Solutiones ad Chosroem* written by Priscianus Lydus, one of the pagan philosophers exiled by Justinian in 529 when he closed the school of Athens. The *Solutiones* survive only in the Latin translation (ed. I. Bywater, 1886), two early manuscripts are Paris, Bibliothèque Nationale, MSS Lat. 2684 and 13386 (in a section independent from that containing the *De divina praedestinatione*). The work is a compilation of Neoplatonic material on the soul and material from Aristotle, Theophrastus, and others on natural science and medicine. The translation is from the ninth century and not unlike John's other translations in style; the two manuscripts belong to the time and region when he was working, and there are two other strong links with John: a verbal parallel with his commentary on *The Celestial Hierarchy* and the fact that two of the glosses in the early manuscripts are close to wording found in John's works. John does not, however, refer anywhere to Priscianus by name, and he does not use the *Solutiones* in the *Periphyseon*; perhaps he

made the translation only after he had completed this work.

Periphyseon John's study of the Greeks shapes his five-book masterpiece which, according both to his own cross-reference (in his commentary on *The Celestial Hierarchy*) and to many of the early manuscripts and mentions, is called the *Periphyseon*. In the earliest manuscript, however—Rheims, Bibliothèque Municipale, MS 875—the work is called *Peri physeōs merismou*, and the colophon, now missing, seems also to have given a Latin version of this phrase: *de naturae divisione*. This title, usually in the form *De divisione naturae*, proved influential, and until recently has been the work's usual name. The *Periphyseon* (books 1, 2, and 3 ed. I. P. Sheldon-Williams, 1968, 1972, and 1981; books 4 and 5 ed. E. Jeauneau, 1995 and 1996) was revised a number of times; the early manuscripts allow the different recensions to be distinguished, most fully for books 1–3. The text in Rheims (which includes books 1–3 and almost all of 4) has been corrected and revised, by changes over erasures, interlinear additions, and, most extensively, by often lengthy marginalia. These revisions and additions are written in the two Irish hands, called by scholars i[1] and i[2], as well as in Caroline hands. Four recensions can be reconstructed for books 1–3 of the *Periphyseon*, though erasures in the earliest manuscript (Rheims 875) make the very first recension, that is, the unrevised text, irrecoverable at some points. The second recension, which was made shortly after the first, survives in Bamberg, Staatliche Bibliothek, MS Phil. 2/1. It represents a substantial revision of the first, and can only have been made by John himself. Corrections and marginalia were then added to this text in the hand i[2]. This revised text, which constitutes the third recension, makes only minor changes to the second, but adds some helpful lemmata; again, it appears to be John's work. The fourth recension, preserved in Paris, Bibliothèque Nationale, MS Lat. 12964, also a contemporary manuscript, incorporates the corrections and additions made to the third, together with some extra material. These additions sometimes have an important bearing on the argument, but there is no good reason to suppose that they were John's own, and they sometimes betray a misunderstanding of his ideas. In the analysis of books 4 and 5, scholars are able to make use of part of the first recension, but are principally dependent on the second and fourth.

Ever since the Rheims manuscript was discovered, scholars have wondered whether the additions and corrections in Irish script may not provide an example of John's autograph. Originally, all the writing in Irish script was thought to be in a single hand, but it has since been recognized as the work of two distinct hands, i[1], and i[2], which are also found in a number of other manuscripts. Scholars are now agreed that if either is John's hand, it is i[1]. This hand also makes a single correction to a Greek word in Hilduin's *Passio sancti Dionysii* in Paris, Bibliothèque Nationale, MS Lat. 13345, notes Greek words in the margin of Leiden, Bibliotheek der Rijksuniversiteit, MS BPL 67 (a copy of Priscian's *Institutiones grammaticae*), writes the letter to Winibert about glossing Martianus

Capella mentioned above in Laon, Bibliothèque Municipale, MS 24, and makes some biblical glosses (which contain language and ideas characteristic of John) in Laon, Bibliothèque Municipale, MS 55 (ed. E. Jeauneau and B. Bischoff, 1977). If i[1] is John's hand, then these notes all help to round out the picture of John's intellectual interests and activities. Yet no conclusive evidence has yet been produced to show that either i[1] or i[2] is John's; i[1] might well be, as i[2] almost certainly is, the hand of a close pupil of John's, sometimes working under his master's direction, sometimes independently.

Given the dating of his translations, it does not seem that John began work on the *Periphyseon* before c.862. In his dedication of the work to Wulfad, at the end of book 5, he speaks of his friend as having been closely involved in the composition of the work from beginning to end, and he addresses him simply as 'brother in Christ'. Both these points make it most unlikely that the work was not completed before the end of 866, when Wulfad became archbishop of Bourges.

After he had written the *Periphyseon*, John went on to write three substantial works. He produced a commentary on Pseudo-Dionysius's *Celestial Hierarchy* (ed. J. Barbet, 1975; the only complete manuscript is Douai, Bibliothèque Municipale, MS 202) where, besides giving literal exegesis of the text and providing grammatical and philological discussion, he explains Pseudo-Dionysius's thoughts in the light of the ideas he had developed in the *Periphyseon*, to which he refers. He also took the chance to revise and improve his translation of the Greek text, which appears as lemmata. H. J. Floss, the nineteenth-century editor of the volume of John's works which appeared as *Patrologia Latina*, volume 122, also attributed to him a commentary on *The Mystical Theology* and the prologue of a commentary on *The Ecclesiastical Hierarchy*, both of which more recent research has shown to be inauthentic. The second of his genuine late works is a short homily on the prologue to the gospel of John (ed. E. Jeauneau, 1969), written in poetic prose and summarizing many of the main themes of the *Periphyseon*. This homily is found in over fifty manuscripts, in most cases attributed to authors other than John Scottus, such as John Chrysostom and (most commonly) Origen. The vocabulary, style, ideas, and manner of the piece leave no doubt, however, that it is John's work. Finally, John began a commentary on the gospel of John (ed. E. Jeauneau, 1972), which again shows the characteristic themes and ways of thought of the *Periphyseon*, adapted to the explanation of the biblical text. The commentary, which runs only as far as John 6: 14, survives in just one manuscript, Laon, Bibliothèque Municipale, MS 81. There are three large lacunae in the text, almost certainly due to the loss of gatherings. Among those missing is the very first, with the result that the text is anonymous. The stylistic and doctrinal evidence for attributing it to John is, however, overwhelming; moreover, the manuscript contains corrections and additions in i[1]. Most probably the work was broken off because of John's death. The sudden end of the text cannot be

explained by the loss of gatherings, and the final gathering, unlike those which precede, has the appearance of a hasty first draft, with many more corrections by i[1] than elsewhere. John therefore probably wrote this commentary about 870.

Poetry As well as being a writer of philosophical and theological prose, John was a poet, fond of using Greek words and phrases and, occasionally, composing entirely in Greek (see the edition by M. W. Herren, 1993). Some of the poems, such as those written to preface the translations of Pseudo-Dionysius and of Maximus's *Ambigua*, take up the themes of his philosophical work. Others are more clearly the work of a court poet, designed to flatter Charles the Bald, often in terms which make an appeal to theological doctrine and to his predilection for Greek ways and language. A number of the poems are clearly entitled as John's, but in other cases attribution is more problematic. Many of the surviving poems come from a lost manuscript collection, made in 869 or 870, which can be reconstructed from Laon, Bibliothèque Municipale, MS 444, and Vatican City, Biblioteca Apostolica Vaticana, MSS Reg. Lat. 1587 and 1625. What is not clear is whether all the poems in this collection were by John.

Are these surviving works all that John wrote? Jean Mabillon (1632–1707) reports seeing a manuscript in the library of Clairmarais, near St Omer, which contained a *Tractatus Iohannis Scotti de visione Dei*. The question of how God would be visible to the blessed was one debated in John's time, and the incipit which Mabillon gives for this work is found almost word for word in the *Periphyseon*. The *Tractatus* might, then, be a lost work of John's, but it is more probable that it is simply an extract (or florilegium) from the *Periphyseon*. And it is almost certain that another work attributed to John—the 'opus de egressu et regressu animae ad Deum', noted in the sixteenth century as being in the library of Trier Cathedral—is merely the *Periphyseon* under another name. Various attempts to assign commentaries on Boethius's *De consolatione philosophiae* to John have not proved convincing. There is perhaps more chance that another work by Boethius may have been glossed by John. In Paris, Bibliothèque Nationale, MS Lat. 13908, Boethius's *De musica* is glossed by a number of hands, including i[2]. Many of the glosses are technical, but some of them have been claimed to be similar in thought or manner to John's work.

Themes and character of his thought No clear view of John's distinctive ideas emerges from his early activity as a glossator of Martianus Capella: the glosses are closely tied to the text and, besides, it is hard to be completely sure of any given individual gloss that it is John's. None the less, there is no doubting John's elevated view of the seven liberal arts, nor his enthusiasm for scientific knowledge, which he uncovers behind Martianus's allegory. His contribution to the controversy on predestination shows that, well before his contact with Greek writers, he was an unusual and bold thinker. The controversy had been (and after John's *De divina praedestinatione* continued to be) conducted largely in terms of authorities: writers on each side claimed that their case had the support of the church fathers, which they quoted at length. Although John too is keen to show that Augustine and other fathers support his views, his main intent is to develop a set of convincing arguments to undermine Gottschalk's determinist position. John shared with the other opponents of dual predestination the view that, whereas God foresees both the salvation of the good and the damnation of the wicked, his predestination is single: of the good to bliss, but not of the wicked to damnation. John backed up this position by pointing out that to admit dual predestination would compromise the absolute unity of God. Like all parties to the dispute, John accepted Augustine's teaching that fallen human beings cannot by themselves act well enough to deserve salvation, but need divine grace both to begin acting well and to persevere in good behaviour. This position seemed to imply a determinism in practice no less total than Gottschalk's, since God, though not predestining to damnation, ensures damnation to whomever he does not grant the grace necessary for salvation. John responded to the problem with a startlingly original idea—though one which, while freeing God from the imputation that he punishes unjustly, does not resolve the problem of the arbitrariness of his grace. God, he argued, does not judge and punish sinners, he merely frames just laws which are inescapable. When sinners infringe these laws, they bring about the punishment of their own evil wills, although the nature of man, which is what God created, is not subject to punishment. John denies that hell is a distinct place, although he does not entirely reject the idea of eternal, physical punishment for sinners, suggesting that they will be tortured by the same fire which will glorify the blessed. He concentrates, however, on more spiritual forms of punishment. The desire of sinners for evil is, he explains, a desire to move away from the source of being and so to cease to be. God's laws prevent them from realizing this wish for annihilation and sinners are thus tormented by the frustration of their wishes.

When he came to compose the *Periphyseon*, John chose to put his Greek-inspired thinking into an external framework based on three traditions strong in the Latin culture of his own time. Like many early medieval didactic treatises, the work is a dialogue between a master (*Nutritor*) and pupil (*Alumnus*). Book 1 is mainly devoted to examining the relationship between God and Aristotle's ten categories—a subject already prominent in the work of Alcuin and his circle at the turn of the ninth century. Books 2–5 are based around the exegesis of the opening of Genesis, a form (an extended hexameron) which had its precedents both in the writings of Augustine and Ambrose and in their adaptations by earlier Carolingian scholars. Augustine and Ambrose are also important influences on the content of the *Periphyseon*, although they carry less weight for the author than Pseudo-Dionysius, Maximus, and Gregory of Nyssa. John is, however, willing to go beyond any of his sources, basing his arguments on reason alone. Reason, he claims, is 'prior by nature' to authority, whereas authority is 'prior in time', and what is prior by nature is the more excellent (*Patrologia Latina*,

122.513B). None the less, John does quote at length from his authorities, especially the Greeks; and he regards scripture not as a mere authority, but a direct source of wisdom, repository of an infinite variety of meanings.

The 'division of nature' to which the title *Periphyseon* refers is an original reworking by John of the triad, permanence–procession–return, which structures the Neoplatonic universe. Universal nature is divided into that which is not created and creates, that which is created and creates, that which is created and does not create, and that which is not created and does not create. The first division is God, seen as creator of all things. It is the subject of book 1, where John argues that none of Aristotle's *Categories*, not even that of essence, applies to God: the divine more-than-being, claims John, following Pseudo-Dionysius, is the being of all things. The second division, treated in book 2 (along with a discussion of the Trinity), consists of what John calls 'primordial causes', created intermediaries through which God creates all other things. They are at once like Platonic ideas, conceived (following patristic tradition) as being in the second person of the Trinity, the mind of God, and also like the 'seminal reasons' which Augustine had invoked in his account of creation in *De Genesi ad litteram*. The third division consists of the created universe. John treats the creation of non-human nature in book 3 and devotes book 4 to a study of man. Although man can be regarded as just one part of the created universe, John also claims that all other things are created in man and that man's essence is of greater dignity than everything else which exists. The fourth division, like the first, is God, now regarded not as creator but as the end to which all things, having proceeded from him and through the primordial causes, return. John treats the return in book 5, attaching it to his exegesis of Genesis by a tendentious interpretation of a verse (3: 24) which is taken to mean that the descendants of Adam will eventually eat the fruit of the tree of life and live eternally. One of John's tasks in this final book is to overcome the tension between the claim that all things will return to God and the Christian doctrine of hell, where sinners will be eternally punished. He goes back to ideas he had considered in *De divina praedestinatione*, refining and adapting them. He does not, however, clearly decide between a view which divides people at the end of time into three groups (those who will be deified, those who will be saved but not deified, and those who will be damned, although the integrity of their human nature will be restored) and a more unorthodox view, according to which no one will be condemned to any punishment worse than exclusion from full participation in the divine light.

As well as his fourfold division of nature, at the very beginning of the *Periphyseon* John also explains another, even more fundamental distinction: between that which is and that which is not. The distinction, he says, can be understood in five different ways, but he places especial emphasis on the first way: everything which can be perceived by the senses or the intellect is said to be; what 'eludes every sense, reason and intellect because of the excellence of its nature' (*Patrologia Latina*, 122.443BC) is said not to be. Much of the most original thinking in the *Periphyseon* develops this idea. God's more-than-being is linked to the fact that neither any created thing, nor even God himself, can know what God is. To know is to circumscribe and limit, reducing to existence what is above existence. God is limitless and so directly unknowable. He is known only indirectly, through what John calls 'theophanies'. With this notion, John tries both to safeguard divine transcendence—God is utterly beyond all appearances—and to show how the divine is immanent in creation, all of which is a theophany.

The influence of John's thought and its place in the history of philosophy In the range and daring of his thought, as well his familiarity with the ideas of Greek Christian Platonism, John was unique in his time. Yet various aspects of his work had an important influence on his contemporaries. He had some close followers, who could imitate his characteristic language and turns of thought, although without any evidently profound grasp of his ideas: i² (who was more than merely a scribe), i¹ (if this hand is not John's own), and Heiric of Auxerre. Two early florilegia from the *Periphyseon* show that contemporaries tried to study John's masterpiece. Especially through Remigius of Auxerre, John's work as a glossator of Martianus Capella affected the way in which future generations of medieval scholars approached this widely read text. John also influenced students of logic: among the earliest glosses to the principal ninth- and tenth-century textbook of logic, the *Categoriae decem* then misattributed to Augustine, there are a number which are very clearly inspired by John's thinking.

Although the *De divina praedestinatione* had been condemned by two church councils, John's reputation in his own time seems not to have been that of a dangerous or unorthodox thinker. In the course of the middle ages, however, two events occurred to place John's orthodoxy in doubt. The first was purely a matter of mistaken identity. When in the eleventh century Berengar of Tours advanced a symbolic interpretation of the eucharist, he claimed the work of John Scottus as his authority. Berengar's views were attacked as heterodox and John was implicated in the criticism. But, in fact, it was not a work of John's at all, but Ratramnus of Corbie's *De corpore et sanguine domini* which Berengar had used, mistakenly thinking it a work of John's. Despite this, the *Periphyseon* continued to be read and used in the eleventh and, especially, the twelfth centuries. For example, Honorius Augustodunensis's *Clavis physicae* is part adapted abbreviation, part transcript of the work. The *Sententie divine pagine* (a record of theological teaching in mid-twelfth-century Paris) uses the *Periphyseon*, while early in the thirteenth century the anonymous author of *De causis primis et secundis* combined themes from John's masterpiece with ideas taken from the Persian philosopher Ibn Sina (Avicenna).

The second event which cast John's orthodoxy into doubt seems at first sight, like the first, to have involved mistaken identity. Writing in 1271, Henry of Susa linked the *Periphyseon* to the pantheist heresy perpetrated by Amaury de Bène early in the century; at much the same time Martin of Trappau wrote similarly in his *Chronicon*. Their accounts influenced the way in which John was regarded for centuries and, until very recently, scholars have imagined that the *Periphyseon* was condemned because it was supposedly used by the pantheist Amaury. The *Periphyseon* was indeed condemned—according to the *Summa fratris Alexandri*, at a synod at Sens, probably in 1223 or 1224; and, in 1225, Pope Honorius III ordered all copies of the work to be burned. But this condemnation seems to have had nothing to do with Amaury. It arose because exception was taken to some of the doctrines in the *Periphyseon* itself, especially the idea of primordial causes. The link between Amaury, the *Periphyseon*, and pantheism seems to have been invented later in the century, when theologians of an Aristotelian cast were anxious to dissociate Amaury's heresy from Aristotle.

Pope Honorius's condemnation (echoed in early modern times when, on 5 September 1684, the *Periphyseon* was placed on the Vatican's list of prohibited books) did not put a complete end to John's medieval influence. Passages from the *Periphyseon* were written as glosses to the text of Pseudo-Dionysius used at the University of Paris and the *Clavis physicae* remained available. John's thought thus reached thinkers such as Meister Eckhart, Berthold of Moosburg, and Nikolaus von Kues. His work was not forgotten in early modern times: the *Periphyseon* was published in 1681, in an edition by Thomas Gale. But it was not until the period of German Idealism that it once more had a philosophical influence. W. F. Hegel saw in some of John's ideas the anticipation of his own philosophy. Other nineteenth-century thinkers welcomed what they saw as John's independence from the mainstream of scholastic thought and his championing of reason over authority.

Four main approaches characterize modern work on John Scottus. Some scholars see him especially in the context of Carolingian thought and culture: they wish to challenge the view of him which predominated in the nineteenth century as an isolated giant. Others concentrate on the many links, already evident to Hegel, between *Periphyseon* and late antique Neoplatonism. Parts of John's work have also been examined from the perspective of analytical philosophy, with sometimes disappointing results. Others have attempted to continue the approach developed by the nineteenth-century Idealists, either qualifying and sophisticating it through a keener awareness of historical distance, or extending it so as to link the *Periphyseon* not only with Hegel, but also with Heidegger and contemporary exponents of deconstruction.

JOHN MARENBON

Sources M. Brennan, *Guide des études érigéniennes/A guide to Eriugenian studies* (1989) [annotated bibliography, 1930–87] · M. Cappuyns, *Jean Scot Érigène: sa vie, son œuvre, sa pensée* (1933) · E. Jeauneau, *Études érigéniennes* (1987) · M. Brennan, 'Materials for the biography of John Scottus Eriugena', *Studi Medievali*, 3rd ser., 27 (1986), 413–60 · J. J. Contreni, *The cathedral school of Laon from 850 to 930: its manuscripts and masters* (1978) · J. Marenbon, *From the circle of Alcuin to the school of Auxerre: logic, theology, and philosophy in the early middle ages*, Cambridge Studies in Medieval Life and Thought (1981) · D. Moran, *The philosophy of John Scottus Eriugena: a study of idealism in the middle ages* (1989) · P. Lucentini, 'L'eresia di Amalrico',

Eriugena Redivivus: zur Wirkungsgeschichte seines Denkens im Mittelalter und im Übergang zur Neuzeit, ed. W. Beierwaltes, Abhandlung der Heidelberger Akademie der Wissenschaften, Philosophisch-historische Klasse (1987), 174–91 • M. W. Herren, 'Eriugena's *Aula sidereae*, the *Codex aureus*, and the palatine church of St Mary at Compiègne', *Studi Medievali*, 3rd ser., 28 (1987), 593–608 • M.-T. d'Alverny, 'Les *Solutiones ad Chosroem* de Priscianus Lydus et Jean Scot', *Jean Scot Erigène et l'histoire de la philosophie* [Laon 1975] (1977), 145–60 • G. Schrimpf, 'Johannes Scottus Eriugena', *Theologische Realenzyklopädie*, ed. G. Krause, G. Müller, and S. Schwertner, 17 (Berlin, 1988), 156–72 • D. Ganz, 'The debate on predestination', *Charles the Bald: court and kingdom*, ed. M. T. Gibson and J. L. Nelson, 2nd edn (1990), 283–302 • R. McKitterick, 'The palace school of Charles the Bald', *Charles the Bald: court and kingdom*, ed. M. T. Gibson and J. L. Nelson, 2nd edn (1990), 326–39 • J. J. Contreni, 'Masters and medicine in northern France during the reign of Charles the Bald', *Charles the Bald: court and kingdom*, ed. M. T. Gibson and J. L. Nelson, 2nd edn (1990), 267–82 • P. E. Dutton, 'Eriugena, the royal poet', *Jean Scot écrivain* [Montreal 1983], ed. G.-H. Allard (1986), 51–80 • P. P. Ó Néill, 'The Old-Irish words in Eriugena's biblical glosses', *Jean Scot écrivain* [Montreal 1983], ed. G.-H. Allard (1986), 287–97 • J. J. Contreni, 'The biblical glosses of Haimo of Auxerre and John Scottus Eriugena', *Speculum*, 51 (1976), 411–34 • C. Lutz, *Iohannis Scotti annotationes in Marcianum* (1939) • E. Jeauneau, *Quatre thèmes érigéniens* (1978) • 'Joannes Scotus Erigena: opera omnia', *Patrologia Latina*, 122 (1854), 1023–194 • Maximus the Confessor, *Ambigua ad Iohannem*, ed. E. Jeauneau, Corpus Christianorum Series Graeca, 18 (1988) • Maximus the Confessor, *Quaestiones ad Thalassium; una cum Latina interpretatione Ioannis Scotti Eriugenae iuxta posita*, ed. C. Laga and C. Steel, 2 vols., Corpus Christianorum Series Graeca, 7, 22 (1980–90) • M. Cappuyns, 'Le *De imagine* de Grégoire de Nysse traduit par Jean Scot Erigène', *Recherches de Théologie Ancienne et Médiévale*, 32 (1965), 205–62 • Priscianus Lydus, *Solutiones ad Chosroem*, ed. I. Bywater, *Supplementum Aristotelicum*, 1/2 (1886), 40–104 • E. Jeauneau and B. Bischoff, 'Ein neuer Text aus der Gedankenwelt des Johannes Scottus', *Jean Scot Erigène et l'histoire de la philosophie* [Laon 1975] (1977), 109–16 • *Iohannis Scoti Eriugenae expositiones in Ieraerchiam coelestem*, ed. J. Barbet (1975) • Eriugena, *Commentaire sur l'évangile de Jean*, ed. E. Jeauneau, Sources Chrétiennes, 180 (1972) • Eriugena, *Vox spiritualis aquilae: homélie sur le prologue de Jean*, ed. E. Jeauneau, Sources Chrétiennes, 151 (1969) • Eriugena, *Iohannis Scotti Eriugenae carmina*, ed. M. W. Herren (1993) • *Iohannis Scotti De divina praedestinatione liber*, ed. G. Madec (Turnhout, 1978) • G. Schrimpf, *Das Werk des Iohannes Scottus Eriugena im Rahmen des Wissenschaftsverständnisses seiner Zeit: eine Hinführung zu 'Periphyseon'* (1982) • S. Gersh, *From Iamblichus to Eriugena* (1978) • J. J. Gracia, *Introduction to the problem of individuation in the early middle ages* (1984) • W. Beierwaltes, *Eriugena: Grundzüge seines Denkens* (1994)

Archives Biblioteca Apostolica Vaticana, Vatican City, MSS Reg. Lat. 215, 1587, 1625 • Biblioteca Casinense, Monte Cassino, MS 333 • Bibliothèque de l'Arsenal, Paris, MS 237 • Bibliothèque Mazarine, Paris, MS 561 • Bibliothèque Municipale, Troyes, MS 1234 • Bibliothèque Municipale, Rheims, MS 875 • Bibliothèque Municipale, Douai, MS 202 • Bibliothèque Municipale, Laon, MSS 24, 55, 81, 444 • Bibliothèque Nationale, Paris, MSS Lat. 2684, 13386 • Bibliothèque Nationale, Paris, MSS Lat. 1977, 4883a, 12964 • Bibliothèque Nationale, Paris, MS Lat. 12960 • Bibliotheek der Rijksuniversiteit, Leiden, MS BPL 88 • Bodl. Oxf., MS Auct. T.2.19 • Burgerbibliothek, Bern, MSS 258, 363 • Staatliche Bibliothek, Bamberg, MS B IV 13, MS Phil. 2/1 | Bibliothèque Nationale, Paris, MSS Lat. 13345, 13908 • Bibliotheek der Rijksuniversiteit, Leiden, MS BPL 67

John the Canon [Juan Marbres] (*fl.* **15th cent.**), schoolman, is a historical riddle. His citations of positions held by Francesco da Marchia, Thomas the Englishman, Gerard Odon, and Pierre Aureole, and especially his close doctrinal attachment to John Duns Scotus, have enticed many historians, particularly Luke Wadding and Johann Tritheim (and also Pierre Duhem and Anneliese Maier in more recent times), into regarding him as a contemporary or early follower of Scotus. Recent research has challenged this assumption and the result is an accumulation of the most contradictory data. He has in turn been identified with Johann of Cologne, Johannes de Magistris, and Ioannes Marbres; and he has been assigned a life in the early fourteenth century as well as in the early, mid-, and late fifteenth century.

In reality, John the Canon was Juan Marbres; and he was not an English Franciscan who went to Oxford (as Bale claimed), but rather a Catalan canon of Tortosa who taught at Toulouse. The 1505 Venice edition of Marbres's Aristotelian commentary *Quaestiones super octo libros Physicorum*, his sole surviving work, affirms the first of these facts in question 1 of book 3, when he mentions his native Catalonia, and in question 1 of book 2, where he speaks of a moving body going from its present location in Toulouse to Paris. The colophon of the earlier 1475 edition of the work at Padua makes it all explicit: 'This is the end of the question, and thus of the whole work of the *Questions on the Physics* compiled by dom. John Marbres, master of the arts faculty at Toulouse, canon of Tortosa, who is by birth Catalonian.' The lengthy list of manuscripts of his *Physics* commentary likewise confirms him to be a fifteenth-century author, since all of them date from that century and most of them from the latter part of it. Further evidence for his living in the fifteenth century can be found in question 4 of book 1, where he refers to Wyclif's teaching on the eucharist, which was condemned at Rome in 1413 by Pope John XXIII.

The grounds for associating Juan Marbres with Duns Scotus's teaching are solid. Although he employs fifteenth-century expressions, such as 'conclusio scotistica' and 'propositio famosa apud scotizantes', he is such a close and faithful follower of the Subtle Doctor that it is easy to see why many succumbed to the temptation to place him in the time of Scotus himself. His Scotistic link is evident from his defence of Scotus's doctrine of the univocal concept of being, which he describes as a 'metaphysical univocation'. Like Scotus, he rejects the real distinction between the essence and existence of created beings and defends the formal distinction in this case and in many other instances; and he also defends the plurality of forms. Marbres's *Quaestiones super octo libros Physicorum* was a well-respected work that was printed first at Padua in 1475 (based on Florence, Biblioteca Laurenziana, MS lxxxiii, cod. xx), at St Albans in 1481, and then five more times in Venice between 1481 and 1520.　　　S. F. BROWN

Sources E. Longpré, 'La philosophie du bienheureux Duns Scot', *Études Franciscaines*, 36 (1924), 365–7 • A. Maier, 'Verschollene Aristoteleskommentare des 14. Jahrhunderts', *Autour d'Aristote* (1955), 515–41 • L. Baudry, 'En lisant Jean le Chanoine', *Archives d'Histoire Doctrinale et Littéraire du Moyen Âge*, 9 (1934), 175–97 • Emden, *Oxf.*, 1.346–7 • L. Thorndyke, 'Concerning John Canonicus', *Isis*, 40 (1949), 347–9 • J. Weisheipl, 'John Canonicus (Marbres)', *New Catholic encyclopedia* (1967–89) • C. H. Lohr, 'Medieval Latin Aristotle commentaries', *Traditio*, 26 (1970), 135–216, esp. 183–4 • R. Schönberger and B. Kible, *Repertorium edierter Texte des Mittelalters* (Berlin,

1994), nn. 14430–31 · K. Lluch, *Documents per l'historia de la cultura Catalona Mig-eval* (1921) · J. Kraus, 'Joannes Canonicus, *Super octo libros Physicorum quaestiones*: I, q. 6, a. 3, p. 3—*De universalibus*', *Opuscula et Textus*, series scholastica, 18 (1937), 57–63
Archives Biblioteca Laurenziana, Florence, MS lxxxiii, cod. xx

John the Old Saxon (*fl. c.*885–904), scholar and abbot of Athelney, was invited to England by King Alfred and contributed to Alfred's revival of English learning. In his life of Alfred, the Welshman Asser reports that John 'was a man of most acute intelligence, immensely learned in all fields of literary endeavour, and extremely ingenious in many other forms of expression' (*Life of Alfred*, chap. 78); he further states that John was in origin an 'Old' Saxon (as opposed to an 'Anglo'-Saxon or Englishman), that is, from somewhere in Saxony, east of the Rhine. It is not known precisely where John originated; as a monk, he might have been raised in one of the Saxon monasteries such as Korvey or Gandersheim, but equally he could have come to England from western Francia, as did Grimbald, who came to Alfred from Rheims at approximately the same time as John, in the mid-880s. Asser's comment (chap. 97), that John had some experience in the martial arts, implies that he had a secular upbringing.

In one of his earliest translations from the Latin, that of Gregory's *Regula pastoralis*, King Alfred acknowledged *inter alia* the help of 'John my mass-priest'. John witnessed one of Alfred's charters (*AS chart.*, S 348, a grant to Ealdorman Æthelhelm, dated 892), and presumably took a part in formulating Alfred's ecclesiastical policy. When Alfred founded the monastery of Athelney (precise date unknown), John was appointed abbot, with unfortunate consequences. As Asser relates, the newly established monks of Athelney included some who were of 'Gallic', or West Frankish, origin. Two of these plotted to kill John by paying two (Frankish) assassins to hide in the church until he entered to pray in private. One night they attacked John and wounded him severely, but his outcry caused them to flee and John was rescued by his supporters. He evidently survived, for he witnessed several charters of King Edward the Elder (*AS chart.*, S 364, 372, 373, 374), the latest of which are dated 904. It may be significant that he witnessed as 'priest' rather than as 'abbot', so implying that he had by then relinquished the abbacy of Athelney; but since none of the charters is witnessed by anyone described as an abbot, the implication is vague.

The date of John's death is unknown. William of Malmesbury preserves the epitaph of a 'Iohannes Sophista', buried at Malmesbury, but whose identity cannot be established (he cannot have been John Scottus Eriugena, who had died in Francia probably between *c.*870 and 877). John the Old Saxon is not known to have had any connection with Malmesbury, but, on the other hand, it is difficult to think of another scholar named John who lived and died in England before the time of William of Malmesbury. So, maybe, Iohannes Sophista was John the Old Saxon.

A small group of Latin acrostic poems may be attributed with some confidence to John the Old Saxon. The first is an eight-line hexameter poem, probably copied in English script during the 930s into a manuscript of continental (north Frankish) origin which later moved to England, and having the legend ADALSTAN as its acrostich, and IOHANNES as its telestich. The date of the writing, in combination with the spelling Adalstan (compare Old English Æþelstan, an apparent representation of an English name by a Germanic (probably Saxon) speaker, suggests that the author, Iohannes, is John the Old Saxon. The poem describes Adalstan as a prince, and is best understood as an encomium to King Alfred's young grandson Æthelstan, then aged no more than five, but subsequently king from 924 to 939. The diction of the poem is embellished with Greek words and archaisms, and so is a harbinger of the stylistic affectation which was to become dominant in tenth-century Anglo-Latin literature. Given the rarity of the acrostic form at this time, two further acrostics (preserved as early tenth-century additions to a late ninth-century manuscript, which has various links with Alfred) dedicated to King Alfred are possibly also the work of John the Old Saxon, and are thus evidence of the ingenuity which Asser recognized in him. MICHAEL LAPIDGE

Sources *Asser's Life of King Alfred: together with the 'Annals of Saint Neots' erroneously ascribed to Asser*, ed. W. H. Stevenson (1904) · *Alfred the Great: Asser's Life of King Alfred and other contemporary sources*, ed. and trans. S. Keynes and M. Lapidge (1983) · M. Lapidge, 'Some Latin poems as evidence for the reign of King Athelstan', *Anglo-Saxon England*, 9 (1981), 61–98 · *AS chart.*, S 348, 364, 372, 373, 374 · *Willelmi Malmesbiriensis monachi de gestis pontificum Anglorum libri quinque*, ed. N. E. S. A. Hamilton, Rolls Series, 52 (1870)

John the Painter. See Aitken, James (1752–1777).

John Trevor [Siôn Trefor] (*d.* 1410/1412), bishop of St Asaph, was a native of Powys. He was educated at Oxford, becoming BCL in 1381 and doctor of civil and canon law by 1389. Between 1382 and 1391 he accumulated canonries and prebends in the dioceses of St Asaph, St David's, Wells, Hereford, and Lincoln, often by papal provision. In the meantime, on a vacancy's occurring (December 1389) in the see of St Asaph, John was elected by the chapter and obtained a royal licence (2 March 1390) to go to Rome to secure the pope's confirmation of their choice. But Urban VI had, as he feared, already appointed Alexander Bach to the post. He settled at Rome as auditor of causes and papal chaplain, and was more fortunate when St Asaph again fell vacant in August 1394; the chapter once more elected him, and Boniface IX issued a provision in his favour. He was consecrated at Rome on 17 April 1395. As bishop he was known for his sumptuous court and table and for his patronage of Welsh poetry. The greatest contemporary Welsh poet, Iolo Goch, addressed two odes (*cywyddau*) to him.

Richard II employed John in negotiations with Scotland in 1397–9, and in discussions about the schism. But the bishop was one of the first to desert him, thereby obtaining from Henry Bolingbroke the post of chamberlain of Chester and Flint (16 August 1399) even before Richard was actually a prisoner. The captive king handed John the seals at Lichfield on 24 August 'in the presence of Henry, duke of Lancaster', who, after his accession, confirmed him in the post (1 November 1399), which he retained until 1404.

John was a member of the parliamentary commission which pronounced sentence of deposition on Richard in September 1399, and he read the sentence in full parliament before Henry took his seat on the vacant throne. After a mission to Spain to announce Henry's accession to his brother-in-law, Enrique III of Castile, John accompanied the English army into Scotland in August 1400. In February 1401 he allegedly warned parliament of the danger of driving Glyn Dŵr and the Welsh to extremes, but his comments were treated dismissively. His protest was no doubt sharpened by the exposed position of his diocese. His revenues, impaired by the rebellion, had to be made up a few months later by a licence to hold *in commendam* the church of Meifod with the chapels of Welshpool and Guilsfield. He acted as the prince of Wales's deputy in north Wales in the early months of 1402, and on 22 April 1403 the prince made him his lieutenant for Chester and Flint. He came to the prince's muster before Shrewsbury at the head of ten esquires and forty archers, and probably fought on the winning side in that battle on 23 July 1403. But his loyalty was shaken when the Welsh burnt his cathedral, palace, and three of his manor houses. Reduced to poverty, he was aggrieved that the king did nothing for him directly, and, refusing to be dependent on the bounty of the archbishop of Canterbury, he stole away in the summer of 1404 and joined Glyn Dŵr. His goods were seized and the chamberlainship was granted to Thomas Barneby. He was deprived of the temporalities of his see by royal command on 27 August 1405; but the proposal to transfer him to the see of St Andrews was aborted. He was granted the revenues of up to four benefices in the diocese of Rheims in July 1410 to make good the loss of income from his diocese.

On joining Glyn Dŵr's cause, John became one of the rebel leader's most active and influential supporters. He was sent to co-ordinate policies with Henry Percy, earl of Northumberland, in July 1405 and subsequently fled with the earl to Scotland. According to Adam of Usk, he was dispatched twice to France to raise military support for the Welsh cause. Given his international standing and diplomatic experience, he may well have played a key part in drafting the most ambitious political and ecclesiastical policies of Owain Glyn Dŵr in 1405–6, including the Tripartite Indenture and the switch of allegiance to the Avignon papacy.

According to Adam of Usk John died in Rome on 5 October 1412; but some historians have suggested that the epitaph to 'John bishop of Hereford [*sic*] in Wales' in the infirmary chapel of the abbey of St Victor in Paris commemorates John Trevor's death there in April 1410. It has been claimed that John Trevor was the author of a treatise on heraldry, which he also translated into Welsh, and of the life of St Martin, as well as of other historical works; but there is no conclusive evidence that this was so. He is not infrequently confused with his namesake, John Trevor or Trefor, who preceded him as bishop of St Asaph, 1346–57.   JAMES TAIT, *rev.* R. R. DAVIES

Sources *Chronicon Adae de Usk*, ed. and trans. E. M. Thompson, 2nd edn (1904) · 'Annales Ricardi secundi et Henrici quarti, regum Angliae', *Johannis de Trokelowe et Henrici de Blaneforde … chronica et annales*, ed. H. T. Riley, pt 3 of *Chronica monasterii S. Albani*, Rolls Series, 28 (1866), 155–420 · *RotP* · *CPR* · *CEPR letters* · *Gwaith Iolo Goch*, ed. D. R. Johnston (1988) · Emden, *Oxf.* · J. E. Lloyd, *Owen Glendower* (1931) · G. Williams, *The Welsh church from conquest to Reformation*, rev. edn (1976) · E. J. Jones, 'Bishop John Trevor (II)', *Journal of the Historical Society of the Church in Wales*, 18 (1968), 36–46 · R. R. Davies, *The revolt of Owain Glyn Dŵr* (1995)

John, Augustus Edwin (1878–1961), artist, was born on 4 January 1878 at 50 Rope Walk Field, Tenby, Pembrokeshire, the third of the four children of Edwin William John (1847–1938), solicitor, and his wife, Augusta (1848–1884), daughter of Thomas Smith, plumber, of Brighton and his second wife, Mary. His father was Welsh and his mother, who was an amateur artist, English; they lived at Haverfordwest, Pembrokeshire, until Augusta's death from rheumatic gout when she was aged thirty-five and Augustus six. At the end of that year Edwin John moved his family to Victoria House, 32 Victoria Street, off the South Sands Esplanade at Tenby.

Childhood and education Queen Victoria had gone into perpetual mourning after Prince Albert's death in 1861, and Edwin, who never remarried and who in his late thirties retired from practising as a solicitor, seems to have felt it proper to follow her example within the dark interior of Victoria House. The atmosphere in which his two sons and two daughters grew up was loveless and claustrophobic. As adolescents they appeared to be more at home swimming far out in the waters of Carmarthen Bay; and as adults they would all leave Wales to inhabit different countries: Thornton (*b.* 1875), the elder son, in Canada; Gwen *John (1876–1939), the elder daughter, in France; Augustus in England; and his younger sister, Winifred (*b.* 1879), in the United States. Edwin had cautioned his children never to go out on market days in case they were captured by the Gypsies. Augustus, who longed to be kidnapped and led away to an open-air life, was to make the Gypsies one of his artistic subjects and later improved his mother's maiden name of Smith to Petulengro, which, meaning 'blacksmith', might be taken as its Romani equivalent. 'We are the sort of people', he remarked to another Tenby-born artist, Nina Hamnett, 'our fathers warned us against!' (Holroyd, 58).

John's education was haphazard. As a child he received some tuition from a governess who was optimistically described as 'Swiss'. Later he became a mutinous pupil at Greenhill School in Tenby, and then a lonely adolescent at a boarding-school near Clifton (not the college), Bristol, before attending St Catherine's, another school in Tenby. He was also given some drawing lessons by the Royal Academician E. J. Head, who persuaded Edwin John to send Augustus to the Slade School of Fine Art in London in 1894, where his sister Gwen also went the following year.

Art school and marriage John was a shy, neat, painstaking student noticeable mainly for his close studying of the old masters at the National Gallery. All this was to change following an accident in the summer of 1895 when, diving

Augustus Edwin John (1878–1961), self-portrait, 1913 [*Portrait of the Artist in a Painter's Smock*]

from Giltar Point outside Tenby, he smashed his head on a submerged rock and emerged from the waves, so legend insists, a 'bloody genius'. It has been argued that perhaps the long convalescence at Victoria House lent him the extra impatience with which to outpace his uncertainties. Whatever the cause, he returned to the Slade as a wild, bearded, anarchical figure, his appearance well illustrated by a self-portrait etching of about 1899 called *Tête farouche* (National Museum and Gallery of Wales, Cardiff; Fitzwilliam Museum, Cambridge), and he was later described by Wyndham Lewis as 'a great man of action into whose hands the fairies had stuck a brush instead of a sword' (Holroyd, 44).

John lived and worked with feverish speed, and his drawings, remarkable for their fluent, lyrical line and their vigour and spontaneity, were passed from hand to hand with mounting excitement by his fellow students who included William Orpen and Albert Rothenstein (afterwards Rutherston). The best of these drawings were, in the opinion of the American painter John Singer Sargent, beyond anything which had been seen since the Italian Renaissance. Having won certificates for advanced antique drawing, and for head and figure paintings, John chose as his subject Poussin's *Moses and the Brazen Serpent* for the Slade summer composition of 1898. This bravura composition (Slade School of Fine Art, University College, London), 5 feet by 7, was a *tour de force* of eclecticism, done in competition style to illustrate his debt to the artists he had been studying, from Michelangelo and Tintoretto to Raphael and Rembrandt. This 'Holy Moses treat' (Holroyd, 56), as he called it, easily won the prize. On 24 January 1901 he married Ida Margaret (1877–1907), also a Slade student

and the daughter of the animal painter John Trivett *Nettleship and his wife, Ada, a dressmaker. For the first eighteen months of their marriage they lived in Liverpool, where John had taken a post in an art school affiliated to University College. Here he pursued his work as an etcher and made a lifelong friend of John Sampson, Gypsy scholar and adventurer. In 1902 the couple had their first son, David Anthony Nettleship, who later became a musician and postman.

John and his family then moved to London, where he founded, with William Orpen as co-principal, the Chelsea Art School (1903–7) in Rossetti Mansions round the corner from the Chenil Galleries in the King's Road, at which many of his early exhibitions were held. In 1903 he was elected to the New English Art Club—founded in 1886 as a salon des refusés in opposition to the Royal Academy—which included Philip Wilson Steer and Walter Sickert among its members. Also in that year his second son, Sir Caspar *John (1903–1984), a 'roaring boy' (Holroyd, 123) who later became first sea lord, was born; and he met the legendary Dorelia. She became his *femme inspiratrice* and the subject of many of his best-known pictures, most particularly the large painting called *The Smiling Woman* (1908–9), a monumental and provocative Gioconda, which established his reputation as an oil painter in the great tradition. This was to be the first picture bought by the Contemporary Arts Society which in 1917 presented it to the Tate Gallery, making it also the first of his pictures to enter a national collection. Few people seeing this emphatic and unbuttoned model, whose enigmatic smile was likened by critics to that of Leonardo da Vinci's *Mona Lisa*, would have guessed that she was a simple person of humble origins. Dorothy McNeill (1881–1969), who had been working as a junior secretary, was one of seven children of William George McNeill, a mercantile clerk, and his wife, Kate, daughter of a dairy farmer. In his pictures John re-created her in a similar way as the Pre-Raphaelites had re-created their models. He lifted her out of her class, changed her identity, and made her extraordinary as a symbol of nature and creativity, a mistress and a mother.

Between 1903 and 1907 John's life became a complex emotional tale of two cities, London and Paris, and two women, the remarkable Ida and the mythical Dorelia. With Ida he had three more sons: Robin (*b*. 1904), linguist, Edwin (*b*. 1905), boxer and watercolourist, and Henry (*b*. 1907), religious philosopher. With Dorelia he had Pyramus (*b*. 1905), who died of meningitis at the age of seven in 1912, the same year as their daughter Poppet was born; Romilly (*b*. 1906), poet and detective-story writer; and Vivien (*b*. 1915), painter.

After Ida's death from puerperal fever in Paris in 1907, Dorelia took charge of all the children (except the infant Henry who was brought up by the Nettleships) and made homes for them first in a castellated bungalow called Alderney Manor, near Parkstone in Dorset (1911–27), and from 1927 onwards at Fryern Court, near Fordingbridge in Hampshire, while John pursued his roving career.

Early works: the First World War 'The age of Augustus John was dawning', Virginia Woolf wrote of the year 1908

(Q. Bell, *Virginia Woolf: a Biography*, 1, 1972, 124). This brief period before the outbreak of war was distinguished by a series of small, simplified, open-air oil sketches. Some of these were painted in Wales in company with the Welsh artist J. D. Innes, others in France, England, and Ireland. These panels frequently show Dorelia planted in a landscape and seen against the sky or the waters of a lake or the sea, sometimes in company with the children (often at approximately the age John had been when his mother died) who are also the subjects of single portrait busts recalling Tuscan work of the late fifteenth century. These rapid, jewel-like impressions, sometimes drawn on wood in pencil and redefined over a thin skin of pigment, made the British palette brilliant with blues, greens, and crushed-strawberry pinks before Spencer Gore and Harold Gilman began similar experiments as part of the *Camden Town Group.

'This is going to be bad for art', John remarked to David Bomberg at the Café Royal in London the day war was declared (Holroyd, 401). Although this was not an accurate prediction for many contemporary artists, from John's protégé Henry Lamb to admirers such as H. W. R. Nevinson and Paul Nash, who used the war to advance their painting, it remained true for John himself who felt increasingly distanced from the art movements of the twentieth century and cut off from life itself by his growing deafness and melancholia. In 1917 the Canadian war records office granted him a commission in the overseas military forces of Canada, and, attired as a major with an alarming likeness to George V, he patrolled the Somme and Vimy Ridge making accurately observed drawings of soldiers but never bringing them together beyond the cartoon stage (cartoon, Beaverbrook Art Gallery, Fredericton, New Brunswick, Canada) for a large decoration he planned called *The Pageant of War*. His most appealing war picture, *Fraternity* (Imperial War Museum, London), showing one soldier giving another a light for his cigarette, was in fact a studio painting taken from a mass-circulation postcard.

Major works; portraits Throughout his career John drew and painted numerous portraits. But he never became a fashionable portrait painter and his formal studies of soldiers and statesmen were often dull and even incompetent. He excelled, however, at penetrating portraits of his fellow artists such as Jacob Epstein (National Portrait Gallery, London), William Nicholson (Fitzwilliam Museum, Cambridge), and Wyndham Lewis (British Museum, London); of writers he admired, including Thomas Hardy and Bernard Shaw (both Fitzwilliam Museum, Cambridge), Dylan Thomas (National Museum and Gallery of Wales, Cardiff), and W. B. Yeats (Manchester City Galleries); and at women who excited and amused him such as the hypnotic, witchlike Alick Schepeler (Fitzwilliam Museum, Cambridge) and the fantastical Lady Ottoline Morrell (National Portrait Gallery, London), her head raised under a flamboyant topsail of a hat and her strings of pearls hung like rigging—altogether a splendid galleon which provoked much furore when it was first exhibited in 1920.

John's work between the wars was dominated by portraits, among which were two supreme 'eyefuls'. The first of these (of which there are two versions) was *The Marchesa Casati* (1919, version in Art Gallery of Ontario, Toronto, Canada), a masterly blending of irony and romance which shows a vampiric figure in pyjamas, with dramatically applied mascara, poised before a veiled view of Mount Vesuvius. The second, a swagger portrait in profile of the celebrated cellist Guilherminia Suggia (1920–23, Tate collection), was a spectacular essay in painterly rhetoric which occupied painter and sitter over some eighty sittings and which won first prize at the Pittsburgh International Exhibition of 1924.

Decline From the late 1920s onwards John's talent went into a decline which, despite a number of journeys he made through Europe, Jamaica, and the United States seeking to revive it, was accelerated by his heavy drinking. The rebel artist had now moved from the roadside into London's West End where his work was irregularly exhibited from 1929 to 1961 at Dudley Tooth's gallery in Bruton Street. He was elected to the Royal Academy in 1928 (resigning in 1938 over the academy's rejection of Wyndham Lewis's portrait of T. S. Eliot (Durban Art Gallery), then rejoining in 1940) and awarded the Order of Merit in 1942. 'Everyone is agreed on the fact that Augustus John was born with a quite exceptional talent—some even use the word genius', wrote the art critic Anthony Blunt in reviewing an exhibition of his latest paintings, including Jamaican pictures, at Tooth's Gallery in 1938, '—and almost everyone is agreed that he has in some way wasted it' ('Art: Augustus John', *The Spectator*, 27 May 1938, 96). In his monograph *Augustus John* (1979), Richard Shone explained this wasting away of talent by likening his career to those of Thomas Lawrence, David Wilkie, and John Everett Millais. John's talent, Shone argued, was predominantly lyrical, and 'this lyric mode belongs essentially to youth' (Shone, 3).

But John was also misdirected as to the nature of his talent by a number of contemporary artists and critics, from Charles Conder, who believed that large decoration was his forte, to Roger Fry, who wrote that, like G. F. Watts, John was 'a great monumental designer' (*Burlington Magazine*, 15/73, 1909, 17). In fact, John's large-scale compositions, which often appear as artificial essays in the manner of Puvis de Chavannes awkwardly juxtaposed with some aspects of modernity, reveal his difficulties in organizing groups of people who do nothing in particular on a large scale. During the last fifteen years of his life he wrestled with a huge triptych celebrating the pilgrim mystery of the Gypsies. He was attempting to reassemble a fabulous past, but concluded at the end of his life that it was beyond his powers.

On Sunday 17 September 1961, in his eighty-fourth year, John went up to London to take part in a demonstration against nuclear weapons. He had been seriously ill and, unwilling to parade his infirmities, hid in the National Gallery until the demonstration began, when he walked into Trafalgar Square to join it. 'No one knew of his plan to do so, and few recognized him', wrote Bertrand Russell. 'I learned of his action much later, but I record it with admiration' (*The Autobiography of Bertrand Russell: 1944–67*, 3, 1969, 118).

Death and posthumous reputation Six weeks later, on 31 October 1961, John died of heart failure at Fryern Court and was buried at Fordingbridge. His death was treated by the newspapers as a landmark signifying the end of an era in which he had personified what Osbert Lancaster called 'a form of life-enhancing exhibitionism which grew up and flourished before the Age of Anxiety' ('Last of the great unbeats', *Daily Express*, 1 Nov 1961). John's bohemian reputation, which depended upon a powerful physical personality and the large quantity of sexual escapades with women which he enjoyed throughout his adult life, enriched many fictional characters in early twentieth-century literature, from the exuberant artist John Bidlake in Aldous Huxley's *Point Counter Point* and the unlikely Judy Johncock in Ronald Firbank's *Caprice*, to Struthers, the ill-mannered painter in D. H. Lawrence's *Aaron's Rod* and Gulley Jimson, the artist also partly based on Stanley Spencer, in Joyce Carey's *The Horse's Mouth*.

Despite successful retrospective exhibitions at the National Gallery in 1940 and the Royal Academy in 1954, John's reputation as an artist was insecure during the last twenty-five years of his life, and it deteriorated after his death when much inferior work came on to the market. The art criticism of the late twentieth century, which dealt primarily with movements, had little place for such an isolated individualist, and he was placed further in the shade by the necessary revival of his sister Gwen John's reputation which, because it seemed to have been for so long eclipsed by his newsworthy career, was partly conducted at his expense. 'Gwen and I were not opposites but much the same really', John wrote, 'but we took a different attitude' (J. Rothenstein, *Autobiography*, 3.21). He was always an admirer of her work and, after almost half a century since his death, when the practice of demonizing him and victimizing her has abated, it is possible to see more clearly what he meant. Both of them worked in strong opposition to the melodramatic and sentimental story-telling in paint which dominated the art world during the late Victorian period. Their pictures tell no story. From Gwen's interiors showing empty rooms, or women alone in rooms, we come away with the image of a story ended. From Augustus's open-air scenes showing groups of women and children poised like ballet dancers in rehearsal before the curtain goes up, we are presented with the dramatis personae of a story which has not yet begun.

To judge by the critical response to a touring exhibition, 'Themes and variations: the drawings of Augustus John, 1901–1931', mounted by the National Museums and Galleries of Wales in 1996, Augustus John's artistic fortunes had risen in the late twentieth century. His standing rested on three genres of pictures: his virtuoso draughtsmanship in the late 1890s and early years of the twentieth century; the small, brilliant oil studies of his extended family, painted

between 1909 and 1914; and the bravura portraits of men and women which, with sudden 'fits of seeing', he produced spasmodically throughout his career.

MICHAEL HOLROYD

Sources M. Holroyd, *Augustus John: the new biography* (1996) · A. John, *Autobiography* (1975) · W. Rothenstein, *Men and memories: recollections of William Rothenstein*, 2 vols. (1931–2) · J. Rothenstein, *Autobiography*, 3 vols. (1965–70) · J. Rothenstein, *Modern English painters*, rev. edn, 1: *Sickert to Smith* (1976) · R. John, *The seventh child* (1975) · M. Holroyd, M. Evans, and R. John, *Themes and variations: the drawings of Augustus John, 1901–1931* (1996) [exhibition catalogue, Cardiff, London, and Conwy, 20 July – 1 Dec 1996] · M. Easton and M. Holroyd, *The art of Augustus John* (1974) · C. Dodgson, *A catalogue of etchings by Augustus John, 1901–1914* (1920) · R. Shone, *Augustus John* (1979) · A. D. Fraser Jenkins, *Augustus John: studies for compositions* (1978) · M. L. Evans, *Portraits by Augustus John: family, friends and the famous* (1988) · CGPLA Eng. & Wales (1961) · NL Wales, Augustus John papers

Archives Lpool RO, letters · NL Wales, corresp. and papers; letters; letters and sketches · Ransom HRC · Tate collection, London | BL, letters to lady Abergavenny, Add. MS 52556 · BL, letters to Lord D'Abernon, Add. MS 48934 · BL, letters to George Bernard Shaw, Add. MS 50539 · BL, corresp. with Marie Stopes · Cornell University, Ithaca, New York, Wyndham Lewis MSS · Harvard U., Houghton L., letters to Sir William Rothenstein · Hunt. L., letters to Alexandra Schepeler · King's AC Cam., letters to John Maynard Keynes · Lpool RO, corresp. with H. C. Dowdall and his wife · McMaster University, Hamilton, Ontario, corresp. with Bertrand Russell · NL Wales, corresp. with Gwen John; papers incl. letters from Ida Nettleship; letters to George Bilankin and Sean O'Casey · RA, letters to Royal Academy · U. Glas. L., letters to D. S. MacColl · U. Leeds, Brotherton L., letters to H. J. Francis · U. Lpool L., letters to Gypsy Lore Society, etc.

Likenesses W. Rothenstein, chalk drawing, c.1896–1897, BM · W. Rothenstein, double portrait, oils, 1899 (with his wife), Tate collection · A. E. John, self-portrait, etching, c.1899–1900, FM Cam. · W. Orpen, oils, 1900, NPG · W. Rothenstein, oils, c.1900, Walker Art Gallery, Liverpool · A. E. John, self-portrait, chalk drawing, c.1901, NPG · G. C. Beresford, photographs, 1902, NPG · W. Rothenstein, chalk drawing, 1903, Bradford City Art Gallery · D. S. MacColl, oils, 1907, Man. City Gall. · M. Beerbohm, caricature drawing, 1909, National Gallery of Victoria, Melbourne, Australia · W. Orpen, group portrait, oils, 1911–12, Musée d'Art Moderne, Paris; copy, Café Royal, London · A. E. John, self-portrait, oils, 1913, NMG Wales [*see illus.*] · A. L. Coburn, photogravure photographs, 1914, NPG · J. Epstein, bronze head, 1916, NPG · A. E. John, self-portrait, etching, 1920, BM · E. Kapp, drawing, 1920, Barber Institute of Fine Arts, Birmingham · J. Hope-Johnstone, three photographs, c.1922, NPG · M. Beerbohm, pencil and watercolour drawing, 1924, AM Oxf. · W. Rothenstein, chalk drawing, 1924, NPG · D. Low, pencil drawing, c.1926, NPG · A. M. Daintrey, oils, before 1928, Man. City Gall. · A. E. John, self-portrait, oils, c.1935–1945, Metropolitan Museum of Art, New York · H. Coster, photographs, 1937, NPG · B. Seale, bronze head, c.1937, NMG Wales · A. E. John, self-portrait, oils, c.1940, National Gallery of Canada, Ottawa · T. C. Dugdale, oils, 1943, NMG Wales · H. Rayner, drypoint etching, 1943, NPG · M. Smith, oils, 1944, Montreal Museum of Fine Art, Canada · B. Brandt, photograph, before 1946, NPG · A. Wysard, watercolour drawing, 1949, NPG; repro. in *The Strand Magazine* (1949) · Y. Karsh, photographs, 1954, NPG · E. S. Lumsden, etching (in middle age), NMG Wales · J. Melgrave, drypoint etching (after J. Melgrave), NPG · B. Partridge, pen and ink, and watercolour caricature, NPG; repro. in *Punch's Almanack* (1922) · A. P. F. Ritchie, print on cigarette card, NPG · I. Roberts-Jones (in middle age), NMG Wales · A. R. Thomson, pen-and-ink drawing, Athenaeum, London · F. D. Wood, bronze bust, RA · portraits, repro. in Holroyd, *Augustus John*

Wealth at death £90,788 3s. 1d.: probate, 14 Feb 1962, CGPLA Eng. & Wales

John, Sir Caspar (1903–1984), naval officer, was born at his parents' home, 18 Fitzroy Street, London, on 22 March 1903, the second of the five sons (there were no daughters) of the artist Augustus Edwin *John (1878–1961) and his first wife, also a painter, Ida (d. 1907), daughter of John Trivett *Nettleship, animal painter. Augustus John also had two other sons and four daughters. Caspar John's mother died when he was almost four. Owing to his father's love of Gypsies and itinerant lifestyle during the years preceding the First World War, John was not subjected to any form of systematic schooling until the age of nine, when he was sent with his brothers to Dane Court preparatory school in Parkstone, Dorset. There he won the prize for the best gentleman in the school and a copy of *Jane's Fighting Ships*, and it was this, together with a wish to seek a more orderly existence, that inspired him to join the Royal Navy. In 1916 he entered the Royal Naval College, Osborne, on the Isle of Wight, at the age of thirteen. He transferred to the Royal Naval College, Dartmouth, in 1917 and passed out eighty-third of a hundred in 1920. He became a good long-distance runner and rackets champion: physical fitness being of paramount importance in naval training, he developed a lifelong love of athletics.

John's midshipman years were spent aboard the flagship of the Mediterranean Fleet, the *Iron Duke*, against a background of Graeco-Turkish disturbances and the problem of Russian refugees caused by the revolution of 1917. It was at this time (1922–3) that the future of naval aviation was being debated. The issue caught his imagination, and, heeding advice he had previously had from Admiral of the Fleet Lord Fisher to 'Look forward, not backward' (John, 70), he decided that this was to be his future. 'I was the angry young man of the day' (ibid., 66), he later wrote, and questioned the need to clutter up the navy with outdated battleships. He envisaged the role of the aeroplane as broadening the naval horizon, and during his qualifying exams for lieutenant in 1925 (he gained first class certificates in gunnery and torpedo), he applied to train as a pilot in the Fleet Air Arm, then under the dual administration of the navy and Royal Air Force. His request was not welcomed and was considered a grave risk to his promotion prospects. However, after gaining his wings in 1926, he became passionate about flying, and thenceforth devoted his naval career to building up the strength of the Fleet Air Arm, of which he was one of the founding fathers.

In the aircraft-carrier *Hermes* John spent the years 1927–9 in the China station during the warring between the communists and Chaing Kai-shek's nationalist armies. On returning from China he bought his own aeroplane, an open cockpit Avro Avian, and had many flying adventures in France and England.

A loner by nature, John became known for his zeal, clear-headedness, loyalty, and resilience. He had few interests other than the affairs of the navy: his work was his life. Throughout the 1930s he devoted his time to all aspects of naval flying—deck landing, demonstrating, surveying, testing new designs, and night flying—and gradually became involved in the design and production of naval aircraft.

Sir Caspar John (1903–1984), by Augustus John

Promotion to lieutenant-commander and commander came in 1933 and 1936 respectively, and, as a result of Italy's war with Abyssinia, John spent 1936 based in the western desert outside Alexandria, attached to the carrier *Courageous*. He spent much time practising carrier night flying which was then an innovation. In 1937 he was appointed to the Admiralty's naval air division, where he worked ceaselessly to free the Fleet Air Arm (FAA) from what he described as 'the folly' of dual control between the navy and Royal Air Force. The air force's hold on the FAA was ended with the Inskip award in July 1937.

During the Second World War, John spent eighteen months as second in command of the cruiser *York*, patrolling the North Sea, participating in the Norwegian campaign, and transporting arms around the coast of Africa to Egypt for the campaign in the western desert. Subsequently he had eighteen months at the Ministry of Aircraft Production (he was promoted to captain in 1941), and in 1943–4 he was in the USA as naval air representative in the British Admiralty delegation in Washington, and naval air attaché at the British embassy. His main task, and one which he considered of supreme importance, was to procure American naval aircraft for the under-equipped FAA and to set up the organization and training of British pilots in Canada and the USA. His meeting with the Russian aircraft designer Igor Sikorski was in large part responsible for the introduction of the helicopter into its first practical military use by the navy after the war.

John spent the last year of the war in home waters in command of two aircraft-carriers, *Pretoria Castle*, and, until 1946, *Ocean*, a brand-new light carrier. As captain of

Ocean, his main concerns were to boost the morale of his men (with the war ended, many longed to return home), and to maintain strict discipline in all flying activities. He married in 1944 Mary, daughter of Stuart Vanderpump, of New Zealand. They had two daughters and one son.

In 1947 John attended the Imperial Defence College, London, for a course in world affairs and in 1948 he was given the command of the large and complex naval air station, Lossiemouth. He then returned to the Admiralty, first as deputy chief of naval air equipment and then as director of air organization and training. Although it was not his personal ambition, he excelled at administrative work, and his promotion to rear-admiral in 1951 ushered in his last year at sea, in command of the heavy squadron. In 1952 he was appointed CB. Two years (1952–4) at the Ministry of Supply updating naval aircraft preceded the important administrative post of flag officer (air) home at Lee-on-Solent, the Clapham Junction of all naval air stations. He was promoted vice-admiral in 1954, was appointed KCB in 1956, and was made a full admiral in 1957, the year he became vice-chief of naval staff to Earl Mountbatten of Burma. This was a period of great uncertainty for the navy, and ranked as one of the most demanding periods of concentrated activity experienced by a naval officer in modern times.

John crowned his career by becoming first sea lord (1960–63), the first ever naval aviator to have done so, and was appointed GCB in 1960. The major issues he dealt with while in office were characteristic of those facing any first sea lord as professional head of the navy but particularly those concerned with plans for the building of a new generation of large aircraft-carriers. In 1962 he was promoted admiral of the fleet but later declined a peerage offered to him by Sir Alec Douglas-Home.

He embraced a number of widely differing jobs throughout the 1960s and 1970s: member of the Government Security Commission (1964–73), chairman of the Housing Corporation (1964–6), member of the Plowden committee and of the Templer committee (1965), chairman of the Star and Garter Home for disabled servicemen, chairman of the Back Pain Association, and chairman of the tri-service Milocarian Club (athletics). He was made an honorary liveryman of the Fruiterers' Company.

John inherited his parents' good looks. He was tall and slim, with brown eyes and dark bushy eyebrows. His penetrating look and brusque speech, alarming to some, belied a sensitive, moody nature. He loved children, the works of Thomas Hardy, and the music of Claudio Monteverdi. He had the ability to go straight to the point in argument, had a quick wit, and excelled at speech-making. His father painted several oil portraits of him as a child and young man, and there are a number of superb line drawings of him as a child.

In 1978 John had both his legs amputated because of vascular trouble. His extraordinary courage and his determination to regain some degree of independence gave him the spirit to face life in a wheelchair for six years. His wife was a great support during this difficult time, and together they made their home in the Cornish village of Mousehole, where John became a much loved and familiar figure on the quayside and in The Ship inn. He died on 11 July 1984 at Hayle, Cornwall.   DAVID WILLIAMS, *rev.*

Sources *The Times* (13 July 1984) · *WWW* · R. John, *Caspar John* (1987) · private information (1990) · M. Holroyd, *Augustus John: a biography*, 2 vols. (1974–5) · *CGPLA Eng. & Wales* (1985)
Archives FILM BFI NFTVA, performance footage
Likenesses A. John, drawing (as a child) · A. John, oils (as a child) · A. John, oils (as a young man) · A. John, portrait, Bradford City Art Gallery [*see illus.*]
Wealth at death £19,666: probate, 16 Jan 1985, *CGPLA Eng. & Wales*

John, Constance Agatha Cummings- (1918–2000), educationist and politician, was born at Four Roads, Freetown, Sierra Leone, on 7 January 1918, the daughter of Johnnie William Horton (*d.* 1919), city treasurer of Freetown, and his wife, Regina Elizabeth Awoonor-Wilson. Educated at Freetown Secondary School for Girls and at Achimota College in the Gold Coast, she trained as a teacher in London, at Whitelands College, Putney, and was sponsored by the Colonial Office with a loan to go to the United States to study vocational education. Shocked by the vicious, overt, racial discrimination, she returned to London with her political consciousness raised, and became involved with the International African Service Bureau run by the Sierra Leone radical I. T. A. Wallace-Johnson. On 27 July 1937 she married Ethnan Alphonso Cummings-John (*c.*1895–1977), a law student, who was later to practise at the Freetown bar. They had two sons.

Back in Freetown, Constance Cummings-John was appointed principal of the African Methodist Episcopal Girls' Industrial School. When Wallace-Johnson returned, she joined him in inaugurating the revolutionary West African Youth League. She became a youth league activist and in 1938, aged only twenty, was elected with a triumphant majority to the Freetown municipal council, where she championed the Freetown market women. When the Second World War broke out Wallace-Johnson was interned and all political activity faded away. Without giving up her school duties, Cummings-John started a quarrying business and, after being cheated or let down by male managers, ran it profitably herself.

After the war Cummings-John moved to the United States, where her half-brother Asadata Dafora Horton was a pioneer in introducing African dance techniques into African-American dance. She worked in a New York hospital and associated with radical black political movements. On her return home in 1951 she founded the Eleanor Roosevelt Preparatory School for Girls with money saved and raised in the United States, and was again elected to the city council. After organizing the market women in a mass protest against raised market fees, she went on to found the Sierra Leone Women's Movement (SLWM), a national organization with branches all over the country. Within two years there were 5000 paid-up members, the majority outside Freetown. Its activities included a women's trading co-operative, educational and welfare projects, and running its own newspaper.

Cummings-John now turned to national politics. Colonial rule in Sierra Leone was based on the 'divide and rule' principle of rigidly separating the coastal colony, with its small Krio (originally called Creole) population, from the rest of the country, which was administered as a protectorate. Decolonization began slowly, and in 1948 a new constitution was introduced, which gave legislative power to the protectorate majority. Krio politicians formed their own party to protect their interests, but some of the younger Krio intellectuals, in the interest of national unity, joined the protectorate politicians' Sierra Leone People's Party (SLPP). Having already made the SLWM a national movement, Cummings-John joined the SLPP, and organized a women's section. This 'betrayal', as it was presented, of her own Krio people, roused passionate resentment among her fellow Krios, who abused her publicly with great violence. When, at the 1957 general election, she was elected to the house of representatives, they hounded her with rancorous accusations of malpractice, and even brought a court action in which she was given a prison sentence (quashed on appeal). Rather than face further humiliation, she resigned her seat.

As independence approached, Cummings-John insisted that women be represented at the final constitutional conference in London, and was grudgingly appointed one of two women delegates. After independence in 1961 she became a victim of faction-fighting within the SLPP. Having associated herself with the losing faction, when she stood at the 1962 election she was defeated by a rival SLPP candidate. She then abandoned national politics. In 1966 she became mayor of Freetown, the first African woman to be mayor of a capital city. As mayor she organized social welfare projects and saw to the founding of a municipal secondary school.

In 1967 a military regime seized power in Sierra Leone, the city council was dissolved, and Cummings-John was accused of having misappropriated public money. She was in Canada attending a conference, and decided to remain abroad rather than return and again face vindictive enemies. She settled in Tooting, London, and became active in local Labour politics. In 1976 she returned to Sierra Leone and successfully revived the fading SLWM. But eventually, as conditions of daily life deteriorated, she went back to London. Saddened but not embittered by her experiences, in collaboration with an American historian, LaRay Denzer, she wrote her memoirs, published as *Memoirs of a Krio Leader* in 1995. Of her achievements as a pioneer for African women's rights and as an educationist, she could feel justly proud. Of her political career, she wrote that her major fault was her naïvety in being unwisely ready to ascribe her own sense of loyalty and civil courage to her male associates—the politicians whose vicious rapacity was eventually to bring her country to ruin. She died, after a stroke, at St George's Hospital, Tooting, London, on 21 February 2000. She was survived by her two sons, her husband having predeceased her.   CHRISTOPHER FYFE

Sources C. A. Cummings-John and L. Denzer, *Memoirs of a Krio leader* (1995) • *The Guardian* (2 March 2000) • d. cert.

Likenesses photographs, repro. in Cummings-John and Denzer, *Memoirs*

John, Edward Thomas (1857–1931), ironmaster and Welsh nationalist, was born at Pontypridd on 14 March 1857, the son of John John, an anchor smith, and his wife, Margaret Morgan. He attended the local Wesleyan day school. But early in life he moved to Middlesbrough where, along with many other Welshmen at the time, he worked in the iron and steel industry. His progress was dramatic: he rose from junior clerk in the firm of Bolckow Vaughan, ironmasters, a firm originally founded by a Welshman, William Edwards, to become a director; eventually he became director also of several mining concerns, and managing director of a local iron and steel company. In 1881 he married Margaret Rees of Pendeulwyn, Glamorgan; their eldest son was Idris Owen John.

A Welsh speaking Calvinistic Methodist, John became a leading figure in the religious and cultural life of the Teesside Welsh, notably in the Cleveland and Durham Welsh National Society, and a patron of their chapels. He also developed strong political interests while in Middlesbrough, notably in education and church issues. Thus in January 1910, in his early fifties, he retired from industry to begin a totally different career, becoming Liberal MP for East Denbighshire.

During the summer of 1910, with the country immersed in the conflict between the Liberal government and the House of Lords over Lloyd George's 1909 budget, he arose from obscurity to promote the issue of Welsh home rule, dormant since the collapse of Lloyd George's Cymru Fydd (Young Wales) league in 1896. John wrote an important letter to the *Manchester Guardian* on 5 August 1910 pressing the case for federal home rule as a solution to the Irish question; he also established links with the Scottish National Committee and had private meetings with Lloyd George himself in an attempt to get him to involve himself again in the movement for Welsh self-government. He was also prominent in the Welsh National League, formed early in 1911. John now embarked on a lengthy campaign of pamphleteering and speaking in favour of home rule, and in February 1914 introduced a government of Wales bill in the House of Commons. However, the issue of separatism attracted scant interest in Wales at the time, where church disestablishment was in any case the dominant theme of the day, while John himself was a dull and uncharismatic speaker. The issue made no further headway.

During the First World War, John emerged as one of the critics of the government and was one of four Welsh Liberals to oppose military conscription early in 1916. In any case, he was now drifting from Liberalism towards Labour. As the cause of Welsh home rule and of federalism showed signs of a revival in the last year of the war, John urged the foundation of a Welsh labour nationalist party, and also used Thomas Jones's influential monthly *Welsh Outlook* to argue the political, constitutional, legal, and economic case for Welsh home rule. He joined the Labour Party in the autumn of 1918 since that party was apparently sympathetic to devolution, while John also greatly admired its internationalism and backing for a League of Nations. However, his Labour candidature for Denbigh in the 1918 'coupon election' was inevitably doomed and he was heavily defeated by the Coalition Liberal.

In the post-war years John continued to campaign strongly for federal home rule; he was convinced that the success of the nationalist struggle in Ireland and the recognition of the principle of nationality in the treaty of Versailles made Welsh self-government more likely. Along with the journalist Beriah Gwynfe Evans, he lent support to the various initiatives from 1919 onwards—the Speaker's Conference, which considered a federal Britain; Sir Robert Thomas's abortive government of Wales bill of 1922; and a large number of conferences held at Llandrindod Wells to promote the nationalist cause. But all failed ignominiously: Wales was simply not Ireland. John's own Labour candidatures for Brecon and Radnor (1922), Anglesey (a by-election in 1923), and Brecon and Radnor again (1924) were all totally unsuccessful. Thereafter he devoted himself to a variety of nationalist bodies such as the Union of Welsh Societies (of which he was president) and the Celtic Congress, while he was also president of the Peace Society from 1924 to 1927. He also wrote extensively in the Welsh- and English-language press. He lived at Llanidan Hall, Llanfair Pwllgwyngyll, Anglesey, and latterly at Pickhurst Mead, Hayes, Kent. He committed suicide 'by hanging himself whilst of unsound mind' (d. cert.) at Red Gables, Bletchingley, Surrey, on 16 February 1931.

At the time John's career seemed a total failure, and he himself lacked the personality or the talents to make Welsh home rule a priority. On the other hand, as a forerunner his career is of much interest. He tried to generate an enthusiasm for federal home rule within the existing political culture, whereas Plaid Cymru, formed in 1925 in his last years, dismissed this strategy and in any case focused almost entirely on cultural objectives concerned with the language. He did spell out in detail the constitutional, legal, and financial issues opened up by the notion of federal home rule. At the time his efforts got nowhere, with the lack of interest in separatism in Wales and the centralizing ethos dominating the Labour Party. But with the revival of the idea for devolution from the 1970s and the eventual achievement of a Welsh assembly in 1999, John's career deserves far more serious attention than simply being regarded as a footnote in history. Dull and uncharismatic he may have been, but in his quiet way he was also a pioneer.   KENNETH O. MORGAN

Sources NL Wales, E. T. John papers · NL Wales, Ellis W. Davies papers · NL Wales, T. E. Ellis papers · NL Wales, David Lloyd George papers · NL Wales, William George papers · NL Wales, J. H. Lewis papers · R. Lewis and D. Ward, 'Politics, culture and assimilation: the Welsh on Teesside, c.1850–1940', *Welsh History Review / Cylchgrawn Hanes Cymru*, 17 (1994–5) · J. G. Jones, 'E. T. John and Welsh home rule, 1910–1914', *Welsh History Review / Cylchgrawn Hanes Cymru*, 13 (1987), 453–67 · J. G. Jones, 'E. T. John, devolution and democracy, 1917–1924', *Welsh History Review / Cylchgrawn Hanes Cymru*, 14 (1988–9), 439–69 · K. O. Morgan, *Wales in British politics, 1868–1922* (1992) · K. O. Morgan, *Rebirth of a nation: Wales, 1880–1980* (1981) · A. Mee, ed., *Who's who in Wales* (1921) · *DWB* · *Middlesbrough Yearbook and Almanac* · *Welsh Outlook* (1914–) · b. cert. · d. cert.
Archives NL Wales, corresp. and papers · NL Wales, papers · U. Wales, Bangor, papers, incl. records of Peace Society | NL Wales, letters to Ellis W. Davies · NL Wales, letters to T. E. Ellis · NL Wales, letters to William George · NL Wales, letters to J. H. Lewis · NL Wales, letters to David Lloyd George
Wealth at death £36,899: probate, 21 March 1931, *CGPLA Eng. & Wales*

John, Errol (1924–1988), playwright and actor, was born on 20 December 1924 in Port of Spain, Trinidad, the son of a professional cricketer, George John, who had toured England in 1923 as a fast bowler with the West Indian team. After leaving school he found work locally as a journalist and commercial artist. But his real passion was theatre, which guaranteed a measure of frustration in Trinidad in the 1940s, since there was virtually no professional theatre on the island. However, John rapidly found his way to an enthusiastic amateur dramatic group, the Whitehall Players, where he was able to act, design, and direct. The problem which then came up was an almost complete lack of suitable repertoire, let alone anything which made a vital connection with Trinidadian life and experience. Though he had thought of himself originally as an actor he felt impelled to try to fill this gap himself, and to that end produced his first dramatic writing in the shape of three one-act plays.

Irked by the constraints on being a man of the theatre in Trinidad, John moved to England in 1950, leaving his wife and three children behind in Trinidad, where they continued to live, visited occasionally by John on return journeys to his roots. Settled in London he continued to regard himself as an actor, and claimed to be driven to write his first full-length play and major success, *Moon on a Rainbow Shawl*, out of sheer necessity and irritation at the invisibility of black actors in the British theatre. As an actor John himself had done quite well, though he resented the feeling that this was more through rarity value than anything else. It was certainly true that he found himself roped in whenever a vaguely dark-skinned actor was required, whatever the ethnic background of the character: when he was moved to write *Moon on a Rainbow Shawl* he was in fact playing a Moroccan in the Arts Theatre production of Julien Green's *South*.

It was one thing to write the play, which was set in Trinidad and called for a completely black cast, and quite another to get it staged. At first all seemed set fair: the play, written in 1955, was submitted in 1957 to the *Observer* new playwrights' competition, and won first prize. But this, it turned out, did not guarantee that the play would be produced immediately, or indeed ever. Finally the enthusiasm of Kenneth Tynan for John's work had its effect, and the play reached the stage in Manchester at the end of October 1958, on its way to the Royal Court in London. The cast, assembled with some difficulty, included four Trinidadians, two Jamaicans, two Americans, one South African, and one Iranian—one of the Trinidadians being Jacqueline Chan, who was three parts Chinese and one part Russian, though, as John himself pointed out, she thereby exemplified Trinidad's ethnic diversity.

Throughout his life John remained, perhaps understandably, prickly on the ethnic question. He refused absolutely the term West Indian, insisting on African Caribbean as the acceptable alternative. But while he remained fiercely critical of British attitudes, in and out of the theatre, to immigrants from the Caribbean, he was by no means uncritical of how things stood back in Trinidad, especially of his country's complete refusal to take theatre seriously. He did not even see any hope of amelioration emerging from Africa: *Exiles*, his follow-up to *Moon on a Rainbow Shawl*, written for BBC television in 1959, concerned three young Caribbeans in England—a successful woman artist, her university lecturer brother, and their cousin, on a sentimental journey to England from his American home—all of whom felt a sense of alienation from their native Trinidad, the England they settled in, and the Africa which remained a fantasy and impossible dream to them.

This sense of being the world's rejected guest, and an exile wherever he might be, made John an angry and discontented man. As an actor he reached the apex of his career in 1958, when he was the first black person to play Othello at the National Theatre, but he had a busy career playing supporting roles (whenever he did not consider the circumstances degrading) in films such as *The African Queen*, *The Nun's Story*, *The Sins of Rachel Cade*, and *Guns at Batasi*. His last significant film role was in *Assault on the Queen* in 1966.

John was also a familiar face on television in the 1960s, breaking down at least one taboo when, in the BBC drama serial *Rainbow City*, he was seen in bed with the white actress playing his wife. In his later years he worked less and less, and became embittered, sometimes almost to the point of despair. His later plays *Caliban*, set in Trinidad at carnival time, and *Easter and I'll Come to you*, which concerned the gloomy, life-rejecting rituals of a Mexican Easter, received only very marginal fringe productions and virtually no wider notice, while he found that the only way to circulate his later screenplays was to publish them himself.

Yet *Moon on a Rainbow Shawl* survived. Essentially an atmospheric piece with heavy (initially too heavy) poetical overtones, it was revised after its first production and quite frequently staged by amateurs in Britain and professionals abroad, as well as being adapted for television. Shortly before John's death it returned to the professional stage, in two different productions, one at Stratford East by John himself, and one at the Almeida, directed by Maya Angelou, which characteristically he did not like and virtually disowned, despite its (finally) enthusiastic reception. He died at his home, 26 Well Walk, Camden, London, on 10 July 1988, of heart failure.

JOHN RUSSELL TAYLOR

Sources *The Guardian* (15 July 1988) · *Daily Telegraph* (16 July 1988) · *The Times* (16 July 1988) · 'Prize-winning play's long journey to the stage', *Manchester Guardian* (28 Oct 1958) · personal knowledge (2004) · d. cert. · S. Bourne, *Black in the British frame: black people in British film and television, 1896–1996* (1998)
Wealth at death under £70,000: probate, 4 Jan 1989, *CGPLA Eng. & Wales*

John, Griffith (1831–1912), missionary, was born on 14 December 1831 at Swansea in Wales, youngest of the four children and the only son of Griffith John and Ann, *née* Davies. His parents were deeply religious Welsh Congregationalists; his mother died before his first birthday. Having joined Ebenezer Chapel (Congregational) when he was only eight years old, what formal education John enjoyed was primarily church-related, and his precocity enabled him to memorize and often dramatically to recite large portions of scripture. At twelve years old he entered the employ of John Williams—pious owner of extensive iron and coal mines and smelting furnaces—as a clerk in the general store in Onllwyn. It was here that John, aged fourteen, preached his first sermon, successfully surmounting doubts concerning his youth; he was known throughout south Wales as the Boy Preacher by the time he was sixteen.

Determined to enrol in college John returned in 1848 to Swansea, where he was privately tutored in preparation for entry to Memorial College, Brecon, in September 1850. He graduated with his credentials for the Congregational ministry in 1854. He was deeply influenced by Henry Griffiths, then principal of the college, and offered himself to the London Missionary Society (LMS) in 1853 for missionary service in Madagascar, the land in which David and Mary Griffiths (parents of his future wife) had served with distinction from 1821 to 1834. Madagascar being at the time closed to missionaries, he was persuaded by LMS directors to accept an appointment in China instead.

John's brief attendance at Bedford Academy for missionaries in 1854 was followed by his ordination at Ebenezer Chapel in Swansea on 13 April 1855, and by his marriage to Margaret Jane Griffiths on 13 April 1855. The Johns set sail for China on 21 May 1855 and arrived at Shanghai on 24 September 1855. Margaret John was constantly plagued by ill health and died on 24 March 1873 on a voyage to England. On 23 October 1874 John married Jeannette Jenkins, widow of Dr Benjamin Jenkins, a missionary of the American Methodist Episcopal church; she was much admired and widely emulated for her work among foreign sailors. She died at Hangchow (Hangzhou) in China, on 29 December 1885. John's two sons, Griffith and David, were both born in China, as was his daughter, Mary Beatrice Louisa (*b.* 1863); she later became the wife of the LMS missionary Charles George Sparham.

John manifested a lifelong penchant for adventure. An inveterate traveller, he became well-known for his extensive missionary journeys into the Chinese interior, journeys which sometimes stretched to distances of 3000 miles or more. In July 1861 he moved to Hangchow, which remained his base until his final departure from China in 1912. It was here that John—fluent in both spoken and written Chinese—was to make his major contribution to the Chinese church as an author, translator, and preacher. A powerful and eloquent speaker, he was immensely popular with the Chinese, who would gather in great numbers to hear him preach, and he was notably successful in training and mentoring numerous Chinese evangelists.

Griffith John (1831–1912), by Edward Smith

John was a prolific pamphleteer, writing numerous tracts and serving for many years as chairman of the Central China Tract Society. He was founder of the first protestant church in inland central China (in Wei-kya-wan), and is credited with a Mandarin translation of the New Testament, Psalms, and Proverbs, as well as a Wenli New Testament, published in 1885. Nominated as chair of the Congregational Union of England and Wales for 1889, he declined the honour, electing to remain in Hangchow. It was also in 1889 that the University of Edinburgh conferred on him the degree of DD. John was instrumental in establishing the London Missionary Society's theological college in Hangchow (formally opened on 18 April 1904) for the theological and medical training of Chinese preachers, evangelists, and pastors.

Highly influential within the larger missionary community, initially because of his linguistic and oratorical skills, and later because of his seniority, John took an intense and outspoken interest in the Chinese political affairs of his day. Throughout his lengthy tenure as chaplain to the English community in Hangchow, he was deeply, though not uncritically, sympathetic to British interests in China. He was not averse to calling upon European gunboats for protection on occasion, and he was highly partisan in his sympathy for the 'Christian uprising', better known as the Taiping uprising. He played an active role in advocating the payment of indemnities to missions whose properties were damaged or destroyed in the uprising. Though critical of the opium trade and of other manifestations of unscrupulous commercial exploitation of the Chinese by Europeans, to his dying day

John held firmly to the twin convictions that most of China's problems were directly attributable to the ineptitude and self-serving intransigence of its leaders, and that the Chinese masses yearned for freedom from what they perceived as the tyranny and oppression of their rulers.

During a missionary career spanning sixty years, John left China only three times (1870–73, 1880–82, and 1906–7). He finally returned to England in January 1912, and died in London six months later, on 25 July; he was interred in Wales four days later, in Swansea cemetery.

JONATHAN J. BONK

Sources Griffith John obit., SOAS, Archives of the Council for World Mission (incorporating the London Missionary Society) · J. J. Bonk, *The theory and practice of missionary identification, 1860–1920* (1989) · A. Bonsey, 'The passing of Griffith John', *The Chronicle*, 77 (Sept 1912), 199–204 · G. John, *A voice from China* (1907) · G. John, *China: her claims and call* (1882) · G. John, *Hope for China! or, Be not weary in well-doing* (1872) · G. John, *Plain questions and straight answers about the opium trade* (1882) · W. Robson, *Griffith John: founder of the Hankow mission* (1901) · R. Lovett, *The history of the London Missionary Society, 1795–1895*, 2 vols. (1899) · J. Sibree, *London Missionary Society: a register of missionaries, deputations, etc. from 1796–1923*, 4th edn (1923) · R. W. Thompson, *Griffith John: the story of fifty years in China* (1906)
Archives NL Wales, MSS and papers relating to his career; letters and papers relating to him
Likenesses E. Smith, photograph, NPG [*see illus.*]

John, Gwendolen Mary [Gwen] (1876–1939), painter, was born on 22 June 1876 at 7 Victoria Place, Haverfordwest, Pembrokeshire, the elder daughter and the second of the four children of Edwin William John (1847–1938), solicitor, and his wife, Augusta Smith (1848–1884), an amateur artist and daughter of Thomas Smith, plumber, of Brighton and his wife, Mary. The artist Augustus *John (1878–1961) was her younger brother.

Early years Gwen's early childhood was spent at Haverfordwest, and after her mother's death when Gwen was eight, the family moved to the small resort town of Tenby, Pembrokeshire, where they lived at 32 Victoria Street. She was educated first at home by governesses and subsequently at Miss Wilson's academy in Tenby and Miss Philpott's educational establishment in London. The household in Tenby was a sombre one, and all four John children escaped its repressions at their earliest opportunity, Gwen John in 1895 by going to London to attend the Slade School of Fine Art, then the most progressive art school in Britain. She studied there for three years with Frederick Brown and Henry Tonks, winning a certificate for figure drawing (1896–7) and the Melvill Nettleship prize for figure composition (1897–8). Among her fellow students were Ambrose McEvoy, Ursula Tyrwhitt, Ida Nettleship (who later became Augustus John's wife), Gwen Salmond (later Mrs Matthew Smith), and, most gifted of all, her brother Augustus who, though younger, had preceded her to the Slade. Her lifelong tendency to form intense and smothering sentimental attachments to both men and women, by their very nature doomed to failure, became apparent at this time. Seemingly meek and self-effacing,

Gwendolen Mary John (1876–1939), self-portrait, c.1900

she was in fact strong-willed and fiercely passionate. In appearance she was slight and pale, her brown hair carefully restrained, her dark eyes solemn and watchful; however (as may be seen in her self-portraits of about 1900 in the National Portrait Gallery and c.1900–03 in the Tate collection), the firm set of her slightly receding chin hinted at her intransigent nature.

On leaving the Slade, Gwen John went to Paris in September 1898 and studied for several months at the Académie Carmen with James McNeill Whistler, who admired her 'fine sense of tone' (A. John, *Chiaroscuro: Fragments of Autobiography: First Series*, 1952, 66). And it was there, Augustus thought, that she 'acquired that methodicity which she was to develop to a point of elaboration undreamt of by her master' (ibid., 250). In January 1899 she returned to London where, for the next four years, she lived what she later called a 'subterranean' existence in various dismal rooms in Bloomsbury and Bayswater. She commented at that time: 'People are like shadows to me & I am like a shadow'; 'as to being happy … when a picture is done whatever it is it might as well not be as far as the artist is concerned—& all the time he has taken to do it it has only given him a few seconds pleasure' (John to Michael Salaman, n.d., 1902, Aberystwyth, NL Wales). During this

period she had an unhappy love affair with the painter (Arthur) Ambrose *McEvoy (1878–1927).

Gwen John exhibited for the first time in the spring of 1900 at the New English Art Club, an organization with strong connections to the Slade, and she continued to show there twice yearly until 1903. In March 1903 she and Augustus had a joint exhibition at Carfax & Co., London; she had already acquired a reputation for working extremely slowly, and contributed only three pictures to her brother's forty-five. Her early art reflects her training at the Slade. The paintings are usually faintly Victorian genre scenes of women in interiors; executed in sombre earth colors, they are small and highly finished, for example, *Interior with Figures* (1898–9, National Gallery of Victoria, Melbourne) and *Portrait of Mrs Atkinson* (probably c.1897–1898, Metropolitan Museum of Art, New York). Her drawings of that time are mostly assured, slightly restrained studies of women, for example, *Winifred John in a Large Hat* (c.1895–1898, National Museum and Gallery of Wales, Cardiff)—not unlike Augustus's work.

Move to France   In the autumn of 1903 Gwen John made a walking tour through France with Dorelia McNeill, later Augustus's lifelong companion. After stopping for several months in Toulouse, they arrived in Paris in February 1904; Gwen was never to leave. From this time she consciously distanced herself from her family and background, declaring England 'quite a foreign country'. For the next decade she lived in a series of modest residences in Montparnasse, several of them the subjects of her paintings, as in *A Corner of the Artist's Room in Paris* (1907–9, Sheffield City Art Galleries). She had a small number of friends, usually women, though one was the German poet Rainer Maria Rilke. Her requirements were few, and she earned a meagre living as an artist's model, most notably for Auguste Rodin (1840–1917), whom she met in 1904 and for whose unfinished monument to Whistler she posed. Although an unhappy liaison with Rodin consumed much of her attention during the next several years—'*Everything interests me more than painting. I am quite frightened at my coldness towards painting which gets worse & worse*', she wrote (John to Tyrwhitt, 4 Feb 1910?, Aberystwyth, NL Wales)—she did finish at least a dozen paintings, among them several of her best-known works, such as *Girl Reading at the Window* (1911, Museum of Modern Art, New York), and many drawings, including the famous series of her tortoiseshell cat (c.1905–1908) and the eloquent wash drawings of Chloe Boughton-Leigh (for example, *Bust of a Woman*, c.1910, Albright–Knox Art Gallery, Buffalo, New York) and of 'a lady' (for example, *Portrait of a Lady*, c.1910, the Swindon collection of twentieth-century art, Swindon borough council). She also continued to exhibit at the New English Art Club (1908–11).

As her love affair with Rodin drew to a close, Gwen John focused increasingly on her art, and the next decade was a highly productive one. Her brother Augustus introduced John Quinn, the distinguished American lawyer and collector, to her work and from 1911 Quinn provided her with a stipend and purchased any picture she offered. He ultimately acquired about a dozen paintings and scores of drawings. Equally valuable was Quinn's emotional support, which he provided from the start, though the two did not actually meet until 1921. He encouraged her to view exhibitions and enlarged her acquaintanceship by introducing her to his friends, including Picasso, Braque, Matisse, André Dunoyer de Segonzac, Constantin Brancusi, Maud Gonne, Henri-Pierre Roche, and Augusta, Lady Gregory. Jeanne Robert Foster, Quinn's companion, became a close friend. Her relationship with Quinn lasted until his death in 1924 and coincided with her period of greatest artistic productivity, for which he was surely at least in part responsible.

In January 1911 Gwen John took rooms at 29 rue Terre Neuve in Meudon, the Paris suburb in which Rodin lived. There she began instruction in Roman Catholicism and was received into that church, probably early in 1913. She was commissioned by the nuns of the local chapter of the Sœurs de Charité Dominicaines de la Présentation de la Sainte Vierge de Tours to paint a series of portraits of their founder, Mère Marie Poussepin, six of which are now known (mid-1910s, one in the National Museum and Gallery of Wales, Cardiff). She executed hundreds of watercolours of church interiors, often populated by those nuns and their charges, the little girls of the Orphelinat St Joseph, all typically viewed from the rear. As she wrote, 'I am in love with the atmosphere of Meudon Church and the people who go to church here have a charm for me (especially when I don't speak to them)' (John to Jeanne Robert Foster, 22 Feb 1925, priv. coll.). She remained in Paris during the First World War, though she made frequent trips to the coast of Brittany, where she did a series of spontaneously executed and profoundly moving drawings of local children, including *Study of a Child* (late 1910s, Tate collection). Because of war restrictions, she ceased exhibiting in London, but showed in New York at the Armory show (1913) and at the Penguin Club (1918).

Apart from a few still lifes, interiors, and landscapes, the paintings of Gwen John's artistic maturity are all female portraits, most often of a model known only as 'the convalescent', usually of a monumental figure isolated or before an uncomplicated background, as in, for example, *Young Woman Holding a Black Cat* (late 1910s, early 1920s, Tate collection). The artist viewed the impassive sitter not as an individual but as 'an affair of volumes' (John to Tyrwhitt, n.d., 1936, Aberystwyth, NL Wales). These pictures are relatively small (the largest no more than about 35 by 26 in.), their compositions rigorously simplified. The surfaces are fresco-like, the pigment dry and chalky, and the palette severely restricted. Multiple versions of each subject were painted, often with only minor variations.

The early 1920s were years of achievement and satisfaction for Gwen John. 'I am quite in my work now', she told Quinn, '& think of nothing else. I paint till it is dark ... and then I have supper and then I read about an hour and think of my painting. ... I like this life very much' (John to Quinn, 17 March 1922, New York Public Library). She displayed strong confidence in her work: 'I was very pleased and proud of my "Mère Poussepin". I thought it the best picture there, but I liked the Seurat landscape' (ibid., 9 May 1922); and, discussing an exhibition of Cézanne's watercolours, she observed: 'These are very good, but I prefer my own' (*Gwen John Memorial Exhibition*, 3). She exhibited in the Paris salons of 1919 to 1925 and at the Sculptors' Gallery in New York in 1922. In 1920 she met the poet Arthur Symons, of whom she made drawings. John Quinn's death in 1924 closed this happy period and brought genuine financial insecurity. She painted less and, without Quinn's encouragement, was less eager to exhibit. However, in 1926 she had the largest show of her lifetime, at the New Chenil Galleries in London, and received considerable public attention. By 1930 she was represented in various public collections, including the Tate Gallery in London, the Manchester City Art Gallery, the Hugh Lane Municipal Gallery of Modern Art in Dublin, the Albright–Knox Art Gallery in Buffalo, and the Art Institute of Chicago. In her later years Gwen John became increasingly solitary. She did maintain certain old friendships, and she formed one last obsessive attachment, to Véra Oumançoff, sister-in-law of the eminent neo-Thomist philosopher Jacques Maritain, and her neighbour in Meudon. This attachment was entirely one-sided and was ended by Véra about 1930, when she could no longer tolerate the painter's immoderate attentions.

Later years By about 1930 Gwen John had ceased painting, though for several more years she made small, colourful, increasingly abstract watercolours; there is no evidence that she did anything at all after about 1933. She occasionally exhibited earlier work (at the Carnegie Institute, Pittsburgh, in 1930; the Deffett Francis Art Gallery, Swansea, in 1935; and at the national eisteddfod in Fishguard, Pembrokeshire, in 1936). She purchased a derelict shack and a patch of ground at 8 rue Babie, Meudon, to which she moved in 1932; there she lived surrounded by her cats, often sleeping in her garden. Her last years are somewhat mysterious. She became increasingly withdrawn and displayed total disregard for her own well-being; Maynard Walker, who visited John in 1937, described her as living 'like a feminine St Gerome' (Walker to Edwin John, 6 May 1946, Aberystwyth, NL Wales). Her reclusiveness was intentional, for she considered her weaknesses to be:

1. sitting before people listening to them in an idiotic way. 2. undergoing their influence—being what they expect—demande. 3. by fear flattering them. 4. being too much touched—valuing too much their signs of friendship, or rather responding too thoughtlessly. 5. Thinking too often of people. (MS note, 26 April [1932], Gwen John MSS, Aberystwyth, NL Wales)

She still made occasional trips to Brittany; on the last of these, she fell ill and died, unmarried, in Dieppe on 18 September 1939 in the Hospice de Dieppe; her certificate does not specify a cause of death.

Posthumous reputation Since the first major retrospective exhibition after her death, which was held at Matthiesen Ltd in London in 1946, Gwen John's reputation has steadily grown, and she has become one of the most deeply loved of British artists; her following is large and passionately devoted to her art. Much of her work has now entered the public domain: more than one-third of her paintings are now in public collections; over a thousand of her drawings belong to the National Museum and Gallery of Wales in Cardiff; and most of her letters and papers are preserved in various public collections. There are substantial holdings, both public and private, in the United States as well as in Britain. John Quinn's collection was dispersed after his death in a famous auction of 1927; most of the works by Gwen John which he owned remained in America. Many more were acquired by American collectors at the Matthiesen retrospective. There have been numerous exhibitions of her work on both sides of the Atlantic.

For many years Gwen John was chiefly identified as Augustus John's sister. He once wrote: 'Fifty years after my death I shall be remembered as Gwen John's brother' (M. Holroyd, *Augustus John: a Biography*, 1974, 61). Although his prediction has not come to pass, her stature as an artist is now most certainly greater than his. She has become, in particular, a feminist heroine. However, in truth she was far less constrained by her gender than most women of her time or, in fact, later. As a girl, she was kept at home while her younger brother was permitted to attend an art school in Tenby but from the time she went to London to enter the Slade she lived as independently as she wished. Because of her unhappy love affair with Rodin, she is often viewed as a victim, but she was in reality obdurately self-willed. She once said: 'I think if we are to do beautiful pictures we ought to be free from family conventions & ties. ... I think the family has had its day. We don't go to Heaven in families now but one by one' (John to Tyrwhitt, n.d., *c*.1910, Aberystwyth, NL Wales), and she lived by that conviction.

Gwen John's art is consistently described as 'private', 'quiet', 'reticent'. She herself said: 'As to whether I have anything worth expressing ... I may never have anything to express except this desire for a more interior life' (John to Tyrwhitt, 4 Sept 1912?, Aberystwyth, NL Wales). Her art, apparently modest and unassuming, evokes from the viewer a powerful emotional response out of all proportion to its reticence. Augustus John said that her pictures were 'almost painfully charged with feeling' (perceptively adding that his own were 'painfully empty of it' (W. Rothenstein, *Men and Memories: Recollections of William Rothenstein: 1900–1922*, 1934, 65). It would be a mistake to exaggerate her importance as an artist. She was not a major historical force who influenced those after her. Although perhaps a minor master, she was surely an enduring one, possessed of genius. Gwen John herself was confident of her place. She described it, typically, with both self-deprecation and serene assurance: 'As to me, I cannot imagine why my vision will have some value in the world—and yet I know it will—I think I will count because I am patient and recueillé' (John to Tyrwhitt, n.d., Aberystwyth, NL Wales).   CECILY LANGDALE

Sources C. Langdale, *Gwen John: with a catalogue raisonné of the paintings and a selection of the drawings* (1987) · NL Wales, Gwen John papers · letters to Auguste Rodin, Musée Rodin, Paris · NYPL, Humanities and Social Sciences Library, John Quinn memorial collection, manuscripts and archives division · letters to Ursula Tyrwhitt, NL Wales · priv. coll., Augustus John MSS [USA] · *Paintings and drawings by Gwen John* (1926) [exhibition catalogue, New Chenil Galleries, London] · *Paintings and sculpture: the renowned collection of modern and ultra-modern art formed by the late John Quinn* (1927) [sale catalogue, American Art Galleries, New York, 9–12 Feb 1927] · *Catalogue of the Gwen John memorial exhibition* (1946) [exhibition catalogue, Matthiesen Fine Art Ltd, London, 19 Sept – 12 Oct 1946] · *Gwen John: a retrospective exhibition* (1968) [exhibition catalogue, London, Sheffield, and Cardiff, 26 Jan – 4 May 1968] · *Gwen John: a retrospective exhibition* (1975) [exhibition catalogue, Davis and Long Company, New York, 14 Oct – 1 Nov 1975] · C. Langdale and D. F. Jenkins, *Gwen John: an interior life* (1985) [exhibition catalogue, London, Manchester, and New Haven, Sept 1985 – April 1986] · CGPLA Eng. & Wales (1940) · d. cert.

Archives NL Wales, corresp. and papers | Musée Rodin, Paris, letters to Auguste Rodin · NL Wales, letters to Ursula Tyrwhitt · NRA, priv. coll., Augustus John MSS · NYPL, letters to John Quinn · Tate collection, letters to John Quinn [photocopies]

Likenesses G. John, self-portrait, *c*.1899–1900, Tate collection · A. John, chalk drawing, *c*.1900, Man. City Gall. · G. John, self-portrait, oils, *c*.1900, NPG [*see illus.*] · G. John, self-portrait, oils, *c*.1900–1903, Tate collection · G. John, oils, *c*.1910/11, Tate collection · G. John, oils, 1911, Museum of Modern Art, New York · A. John, pencil drawing, Man. City Gall.

Wealth at death £438 10s. 8d.: administration with will, 2 May 1940, CGPLA Eng. & Wales

John, Nicholas Andrew (1952–1996), operatic editor and dramaturge, was born at 4 Lyall Street, London, on 18 August 1952, the son of Leslie Francis John (*b.* 1919/20), a director of the Mobil oil company, and his wife, Constance Margaret Dowler (*b.* 1920/21), for many years chairman of the governors of Epsom School of Art and Design. His love of the theatre in all its forms was evident from an early age: his mother recalls that:

> He loved to act and soon had a home made puppet theatre for which he composed plays and made the scenery. At prep school [Downsend, Leatherhead] he acted in and directed plays for which he roped in his friends on summer afternoons on a neighbour's open-air stage. He had a talent for drawing and painting, so programme illustrations and design were no problem, and he played the piano with gusto. (private information)

Years later, in a book introducing schoolchildren to the delights of opera, he would advise, from experience, that 'With a bit of luck you will be able to persuade your friends to perform your opera' (N. John, *Opera*, 64).

After Westminster School (where he was a queen's scholar, and where he was handily placed for sorties to Covent Garden and the West End) and a solo expedition to Japan and Russia in his gap year, he went up to University College, Oxford, to read law in 1970. While there, although he did not neglect his studies, he pursued with great enthusiasm the theatrical interests of his childhood: 'Members of every college would regularly find him knocking on their doors with some pressing call—soliciting support for a cartoon festival, or seeking help in the manufacture of masks for a theatrical production' (Studer, 1).

Following a short—not entirely successful—period articled to the City law firm Allen and Overy, in which he nevertheless qualified as a solicitor, John joined English

National Opera in 1976 as its publications manager, also using his legal training as company secretary to the New Opera Company. He immediately set about the 'reinvention' (Cronk) of English National Opera's programme book, gradually transforming it from a relatively straightforward guide to the evening's opera into something much more unpredictable and enlightening. In keeping with his constant insistence on the primacy of drama in opera, he gave the composer and librettist equal billing on the programme's cover, and—working closely with highly skilled graphic designers, who were hand-picked for each new piece—replaced the standard succession of essays, illustrations, and biographies with assemblages of quotations and images, which often, in themselves, seemed to bear little relation to the opera to which they were linked. When juxtaposed with the piece and with each other, however, they conveyed the nature not only of the work itself but also, and perhaps more importantly, of the production and the ideas which lay behind it.

As such, they raised the humble programme to a position of importance within the production equal to that of the costumes and sets: the *TLS* review characterized Keith Warner's 1986 production of Rossini's *Moses* with a description of the programme's mixture of 'quotations from Menachem Begin … [and] photographs of recent events in El Salvador, Nigeria, Northern Ireland and South Africa' (Osborne). This technique—a sort of collage—was not always accepted by all opera-goers: one of his obituaries complained that '[t]hese publications occasionally verged on the pretentious; the reader could be left pondering the connections between the pictures or literary quotations and the opera concerned' (Kennedy), but their unprecedented ability to synthesize a conceptual understanding of both opera and staging with an exceptionally strong visual sense proved extremely stimulating to the majority of opera-goers and has had a lasting influence on many of his successors at English National Opera and elsewhere.

In addition, they often—most unusually for a piece of ephemera—contained much illuminating literary and musicological research. As John's first assistant recalls:

> Gounod's rarely performed *Mireille* provoked an investigation of the Provençal language and the group of poets led by Frédéric Mistral, author of *Mireio*, on which the opera was based. When preparing material on Puccini's *Madama Butterfly* he uncovered and translated source material by Pierre Loti that had probably not emerged from the London Library's restricted section since first placed there. (private information, H. Bredin)

Such original work was not confined to the nightly programmes: in 1980 John edited the first in the long-running series of ENO Opera Guides, published by John Calder. These slim, inexpensive volumes—'intended to be companions to opera in performance' (John, preface, *ENO Opera Guide 1*)—contained 'articles and illustrations relevant to each production and not only those mounted by English National Opera' (ibid.), and so fulfilled a function distinct from that of his programmes. They included learned essays on the background, music, and production history of many prominent works in the repertory, the

full libretto with an English translation—generally one tested many times on the English National Opera stage—and, most originally, a checklist of the opera's main musical motifs. The latter were linked, by numbers, to their place (and often places) in the text—an immensely helpful innovation, and one of especial use in the leitmotif-driven music dramas of Wagner. These were brilliantly—and entertainingly—edited:

> After being provided with a generous Sunday lunch, one person would be seated with a bundle of proofs, and another equipped with the definitive text, a spoon and a plate or some other kitchen implement. There ensued a *viva voce* rendition of the text with noises off being provided in the manner of a Victor Borge school of proof correction—bang for an accent, crash for an umlaut, depending on the language. (Studer, 5)

It is a measure of John's standing in the operatic world at this time, only four years after he had joined English National Opera, that the first batch of guides—which deal with *La Cenerentola*, *Aida*, *The Magic Flute*, and *Fidelio*—contain essays specially written by critics and scholars of the highest calibre, among them Philip Gossett, William Mann, David Cairns, and Roger Parker. By the time of his death, the series—'his greatest and most enthusiastic hobby' (private information, Sir Peter Jonas)—numbered forty-eight volumes covering sixty works, and had moved from the centre of the repertory to encompass the stage works of composers such as Bartok, Monteverdi, and Tippett. The elegance of their thought and structure—'We hope', John says in one of his later prefaces, 'that, as companions to the opera should be, they are well-informed, witty and attractive' (John, *ENO Opera Guide 33*)—was mirrored in the two collections of essays he edited for Faber and Faber, *The Don Giovanni Book* (1990, jointly with Jonathan Miller) and *Violetta and her Sisters* (1994). The latter, 'a book which looked at every aspect of Verdi's *La Traviata*' (Bredin, 'Light on the opera'), brought together in frequently provocative conjunctions—like one of his programmes on a grand scale—source material tracing the development and reception of both the opera and the Dumas novel it drew on, and contributions from, among others, Barbara Cartland, the television sex therapist Dr Ruth, and a representative of the Ridiculous Theatre Company of New York.

This 'wealth of knowledge on every aspect of Opera' (private information, Lord Harewood), which he was constantly increasing—Lord Harewood remembers him 'engag[ing] to hear Operas by Alessandro Scarlatti in, say, Switzerland, something by Jommelli in Venice, or a Marschner rarity in an obscure house in Germany' (ibid.)—led to his appointment in 1985 as English National Opera's first dramaturge, and, indeed, the first holder of such a post in any British opera company. In the same year he met Nicholas Cronk, an Oxford academic, and they remained partners until his death. His position as dramaturge 'enabled him to work more closely with conductors, directors and designers in the early stages of devising a production' (Bredin, 'Nicholas John') and to give 'advice on authentic texts, performance practice and the performance history of an opera' (Kennedy). In the second half of the 1980s and the early 1990s English National Opera, under its music director Mark Elder and director of productions David Pountney, enjoyed a period of high-profile, albeit controversial, success, and it was during this period that John produced perhaps his best work. He was a passionate believer in opera as music drama performed in the vernacular, and in involving the audience to the full—even issuing them with masks for a 1991 production of *Die Fledermaus*—and he made a significant contribution to the success of those years, which was celebrated in the book *Power House*, which he compiled and edited. Dennis Marks later wrote that 'Nick developed the art of operatic dramaturgy in this country virtually single-handed' (Marks).

John's death, in a hill-walking accident in Lichtenstein on 25 June 1996 while leading a group to the Schubertiade festival, came at a time when his work seemed to be moving beyond the relatively narrow confines of the London Coliseum. He had worked as dramaturge on productions of Janáček's *From the House of the Dead* in Strasbourg (in which he also made his début as a director, on the sudden departure of his predecessor) and *Cav* and *Pag* at the Berlin Staatsoper, was working on the *Blue Guide to Operatic Europe*, and was about to embark, with the collaboration of Lord Harewood, on a wholesale revision of *Kobbé's Complete Opera Book*. His sudden death robbed European opera of one of its most creative and knowledgeable figures.

STEPHEN FOLLOWS

Sources private information (2004) [Henrietta Bredin; earl of Harewood; Margaret John; Sir Peter Jonas] • H. Bredin, 'Light on the opera', *The Guardian* (27 June 1996) • [H. Bredin], 'Nicholas John', *The Times* (4 July 1996) • N. Cronk, 'Nicholas John', *Georgian Group News* (Sept 1996), 2–3 • S. Follows, 'Restaged in print: how do Nicholas John's English National Opera programmes address their audience?', MA diss., Oxford Brookes University, 2001 • N. John, preface, *ENO opera guide 1: La Cenerentola*, ed. N. John (1980) • N. John, ed., *ENO opera guide 2: Aida* (1980) • N. John, ed., *ENO opera guide 3: The magic flute* (1980) • N. John, ed., *ENO opera guide 4: Fidelio* (1980) • N. John, ed., *ENO opera guide 33: Jenufa/Katya Kabanova* (1985) • N. John, *Opera*, Oxford Topics in Music (1984) • N. John, ed., *Violetta and her sisters* (1994) • P. Jonas and others, *Power house: the English National Opera experience*, ed. N. John (1992) • [M. Kennedy], 'Nicholas John', *Daily Telegraph* (17 July 1996) • D. Marks, 'Nicholas John' (1996) [English National Opera programme insert] • J. Miller and N. John, eds., *The Don Giovanni book* (1990) • R. Osborne, 'Postlapsarian lapses', *TLS* (14 Feb 1986) • M. Studer, 'Nicholas John: an affectionate remembrance', priv. coll. [unpublished memorial service address, 1996] • b. cert. • m. cert. [Leslie John and Margaret Dowler] • CGPLA Eng. & Wales (1996)
Wealth at death £243,424: probate, 18 Sept 1996, CGPLA Eng. & Wales

John, Rosamund [*real name* Nora Rosamund Jones] (1913–1998), actress, was born on 19 October 1913 at 7 Bruce Castle Road, Tottenham, London, the daughter of Frederick Henry Jones, wine merchant's clerk, and his wife, Edith Elizabeth Elliott. She was educated at Tottenham high school and studied at the Embassy School of Acting. At nineteen she was introduced to actor–director Milton Rosmer, who cast her in several minor stage roles and, as

Rosamund Jones, as a Scottish girl (Maggie) in his film *The Secret of the Loch* (1934). She had a walk-on part at Stratford in *Antony and Cleopatra* (1935) and was one of C. B. Cochran's 'young ladies' in the A. P. Herbert revue *Home and Beauty* at the Adelphi before further walk-ons and understudied roles at Stratford. Robert Donat noticed her and cast her as an understudy in *Red Night* (1936) at the Queen's. In love with John, Donat cast her as Judith, the wife of Dick Dudgeon (himself), in Shaw's *The Devil's Disciple* (1940) at the Piccadilly. Although her notices were good for the pre-London tour, the capital's critics were harsh; Donat took the blame, admitting she lacked the technique to sustain the part nightly. He failed to have her cast as his love interest in the film *The Young Mr Pitt* (1941), but she fortuitously won a screen test for, and subsequently the part of, the supportive though long-suffering wife in *The First of the Few* (1942) opposite Leslie Howard as Spitfire designer R. J. Mitchell. She 'projected an extremely English combination of reticence, loyalty and gentle determination' (*The Independent*, 2 Nov 1998), and it was very successful.

In late 1942 John's relationship with Donat ended; in the following year (on 31 August 1943) she married Hugh Russell Lloyd (*b*. 1915/16), a film editor then in the Royal Navy. They had a son but divorced in 1949. In 1943 she made *The Gentle Sex*, as one of seven girls from varied backgrounds who join the ATS—Howard co-produced, co-directed, and narrated; and she impressed in *The Lamp Still Burns*, produced by Howard, as an architect who in the war gives up both her love and her profession for nursing. During the film's production Howard's plane was shot down returning from Lisbon; John gave him fulsome credit for what he had taught her. She was a nurse again in Bernard Miles's *Tawny Pipit* (1944). Gently mocking a typical Cotswold village's idiosyncrasies (a threatened breeding pair of rare pipits represented wartime England), it was a small film but very popular, especially in America. With grey eyes, red-blonde hair, and ladylike poise, John was a natural to play typically English heroines at this time. In 1944 she was second only to Margaret Lockwood as Britain's favourite female star and, more than most, could express 'a cooler sensuousness, and, when required, a quivering stiff upper lip' (*The Guardian*, 3 Nov 1998), nowhere more evident than in her best-known film, *The Way to the Stars* (1945), directed by Anthony Asquith. The film pivoted around her stoical and dignified portrayal of Toddy, manageress of a small hotel near a bomber station. First losing her husband (Michael Redgrave), a veteran flyer, then an American flyer (Douglass Montgomery) who befriends her, she advises another flyer (John Mills), reluctant to marry, to do so despite the uncertainty of the times; it was a great success. As the murderess in the delightful comedy thriller *Green for Danger* (1946) she displayed a fine neuroticism, and in *Fame is the Spur* (1947) was the idealistic wife of a radical MP (Redgrave again) who fails to live up to his ideals; her death scene was particularly touching.

John's subsequent films were largely disappointing. The best, *The Upturned Glass* (1947), a taut psychological thriller, was stolen by co-star James Mason; her last, *Operation Murder* (1957), was a dull drama. John, however, always interested in politics, had become in 1950 an Equity representative on the National Film Production Council, later serving on committees aiming to protect the rights of film and television industry workers. During the 1950 election campaign she met John Ernest *Silkin (1923–1987), former naval officer, now a solicitor and active Labour Party member. They married on 21 April 1950 and had a son. Although Silkin did not enter parliament until 1963, John began to put her husband's career before her own; she did, however, play Bella Massingham in *Gaslight* (1950) at the Vaudeville. Her few subsequent stage appearances included *Dragon's Mouth* (1952), and *Murder on Arrival* (1959) at the Westminster, her last West End role.

Silkin became chief whip in 1966, was a government minister (1969–70 and 1974–9), and, in opposition, shadow leader of the House of Commons. John shared his views on unilateralism, the Vietnam War and British non-membership of the EEC. Silkin died in April 1987. John's strong continued commitment to the party matched her public service: she had been a magistrate for many years in Kent, where she and her husband lived. She died in Collingwood Court Nursing Home, Nelson's Row, London, on 27 October 1998. ROBERT SHARP

Sources *The Times* (3 Nov 1998) · *The Independent* (2 Nov 1998) · *Daily Telegraph* (3 Nov 1998) · *The Guardian* (3 Nov 1998) · www.uk. imdb.com, 26 Oct 2001 · J. C. Trewin, *Robert Donat: a biography* (1968) · *Who was who in the theatre, 1912–1976*, 4 vols. (1978) · Burke, *Peerage* (1999) · m. cert. · d. cert.
Archives JRL, corresp. with Robert Donat
Likenesses photograph, c.1938, repro. in *The Independent* · photograph, c.1942–1943, repro. in *The Guardian* · photograph, 1947, repro. in *Daily Telegraph* · photographs, Hult. Arch. · still (from 1945 film), repro. in *The Guardian*

John, Sir William Goscombe (1860–1952), sculptor and medallist, was born at 3 Union Street, Canton, near Cardiff, on 21 March 1860, the elder son of Thomas John (1834–1893) and his wife, Elizabeth, née Smith. As a young man he assumed the name Goscombe from a Gloucestershire village near his mother's old home. His father was a woodcarver employed in the workshops set up by Lord Bute for the restoration of Cardiff Castle. He was trained in Cardiff, and later in London with Thomas Nicholls (1881–6) and Charles Bell Birch (1886–7), at the City and Guilds Kennington School of Art (1881–4) and, from 1884, at the Royal Academy Schools. With the help of money subscribed by supporters in Cardiff, he was able to visit Italy and France in 1888, and Greece, Constantinople, and Cairo in 1889. The award in 1889 of the Royal Academy's gold medal and travelling scholarship, for *Parting*, a group cast in bronze for Lawrence Alma-Tadema, enabled him to extend his travels the following year to Sicily, north Africa, and Spain, and to take a studio in Paris for a year. On 23 August 1890 he married Anna Marthe (1862/3–1923), daughter of Paul Weiss, engraver, and his wife, Clara, of Neuchâtel, Switzerland. Their only child, Muriel Goscombe, married Frederick Luke Val Fildes, the son of the painter Sir Luke Fildes.

Goscombe John returned to London in 1890 and settled in 1892 in St John's Wood, where he remained for the rest of his life. When living in Paris he had watched Rodin at work, and his nude *Morpheus*, which received an honourable mention in the Salon of 1892, shows clearly the influence of Rodin's *The Age of Bronze*. In England John's teachers and contemporaries included Lord Leighton, Sir Thomas Brock, and Sir Alfred Gilbert, the leading figure of the 'New Sculpture' movement. Gilbert's brilliance, as revealed in his psychological depth, particularly impressed Goscombe John. *Morpheus* was followed, during the next ten years, by other academic nudes: *Girl Binding her Hair* (1893); *St John the Baptist* (1894), a half-clothed figure cast in block tin for Lord Bute; *Boy at Play* (1895); *The Elf* (1898), Goscombe John's diploma work; and *Joyance* (1899). These are all characterized by complete anatomical mastery and suave rhythm, and all convey mood, which in the *St John* owes something to the work of Edward Burne-Jones. *Boy at Play* was purchased in 1896 by the Chantrey trustees, while *St John the Baptist* was awarded a gold medal at the Paris Universal Exhibition of 1900. In 1916 Goscombe John contributed a marble figure, *St David Blessing the People*, to a group of ten figures commissioned by Lord Rhondda for Cardiff city hall.

Goscombe John's numerous public statues included those of the seventh duke of Devonshire, at Eastbourne (awarded a gold medal in the Paris Salon of 1901); equestrian statues of Edward VII (Cape Town, 1904), Lord Tredegar (Cardiff, 1909), Lord Minto (Calcutta, 1913), and Sir Stanley Maude (Baghdad, 1921); the Salisbury tomb (1908) in Westminster Abbey (1908); and a Salisbury monument in St Etheldreda's Church, Hatfield, Hertfordshire. His first major public memorial was the King's regiment memorial (1905) in the centre of Liverpool, incorporating soldiers from various periods of the regiment's history, including on the reverse the famous *Drummer Boy* which was also issued as a small bronze and became his best-known work. (A monumental cast is in the National Museum and Gallery of Wales, Cardiff.) His pyramidal *Engine-Room Heroes Memorial* (1916) at the Pier Head in Liverpool, flanked by worker figures, owed a little to Jules Dalou's unrealized 'Monument to Workers: Project in the Form of a Cylindrical Pylon' (1897–8; clay models, Musée du Petit Palais, Paris). However his narrative groups and reliefs on the Port Sunlight war memorial (1921) are original, lucid depictions of war service and the defence of the home. The sense of drama in the memorial was further developed in the crowd scene for *The Response* (1923), in Newcastle upon Tyne, commemorating the Northumberland Fusiliers. The vivid depictions of contemporary life in the Port Sunlight and Newcastle pieces, hailed in 1991 as two of the finest sculptural ensembles on any British monuments (Borg, 78), were followed in 1924 by a combination of present-day and historical figures for memorials at Wrexham and Llandaff. His portrait busts include men of such diverse eminence as Andrew Carnegie, Edmund Gosse, and Lord Kitchener. He designed the regalia used at the investiture of the prince of Wales at Caernarfon in 1911 (and in the same year, at Bangor, was knighted), and the commemorative medal, the jubilee medal of George V (1935), and the great seal of Edward VIII (1936). He also modelled medals for a number of Welsh institutions.

Goscombe John's art may be described as a compound of realism and romanticism. His style underwent little change throughout his long life, apart from a broadening in the treatment of portrait busts and war memorials. Most of these were in bronze, but in bronze and marble alike he was a convincing portrayer of character and showed notable ability in rendering the soft surfaces of skin and hair.

An academic sculptor first and last, Goscombe John was quite out of sympathy with what he termed the 'Easter Island' style of modern sculpture, which appeared when he was in his prime. As a younger generation member of the 'New Sculpture' movement, critical opinion consequently left him behind. Official honours, however, were not lacking, in France and Belgium as well as at home, and in 1942 he was awarded the gold medal of the Royal Society of British Sculptors. Having first shown at the Royal Academy in 1886, he continued to exhibit there annually until 1948, a period of sixty-two years. (He had been elected an associate in 1899 and an academician in 1909.) He was a courteous and affable man, proud of his Welsh nationality and of his own success, but somewhat reserved. Goscombe John died on 15 December 1952 at his home since about 1905, 24 Greville Road, St John's Wood, London, and was buried in Kensal Green cemetery in the tomb which he had sculpted for his wife. There is a large collection of his work, including a self-portrait (1942), in the National Museum and Gallery of Wales, described in special catalogues issued by the museum in 1948 and 1979.   R. L. CHARLES, rev. FIONA PEARSON

Sources F. Pearson, *Goscombe John at the National Museum of Wales* (1979) [exhibition catalogue, NMG Wales] · A. Borg, *War memorials from antiquity to the present* (1991) · D. Pickup, 'Sir William Goscombe John: "imbued with the artistic spirit"', *The Medal*, 31 (1997), 68–72 · *CGPLA Eng. & Wales* (1953) · b. cert. · m. cert. · d. cert. · personal knowledge (1971) · artist's files, NMG Wales · H. Meller, *London cemeteries: an illustrated guide and gazetteer*, 3rd edn (1994), 147
Archives Cardiff Central Reference Library · NL Scot. · NL Wales, corresp. and papers · NMG Wales · RA
Likenesses A. G. Walker, oils, 1885–6, NMG Wales · S. H. Vedder, oils, 1901, NMG Wales · G. Roilos, oils, 1903, NMG Wales · Elliott & Fry, photograph, 1912, NPG · J. Russell & Sons, photograph, c.1915, NPG · S. L. Fildes, oils, 1924, NMG Wales · W. Stoneman, photograph, 1937, NPG · W. G. John, self-portrait, bronze bust, 1942, NMG Wales · E. Wolfsfeld, lithograph, 1944, NMG Wales · E. Wolfsfeld, oils, c.1951, NPG
Wealth at death £35,150 10s. 5d.: probate, 6 March 1953, *CGPLA Eng. & Wales*

Johnes, Arthur James [*pseud.* Maelog] (**1809–1871**), judge, was born on 4 February 1809, the only son of Edward Johnes of Garthmyl, near Montgomery, and his wife Mary, daughter of Thomas Davies of Llifior. He was educated at Oswestry grammar school, and at the University of London (now University College, London) when it opened in 1828. Called to the bar at Lincoln's Inn on 30 January 1835, he practised as an equity draughtsman and conveyancer.

When county courts were established in 1847, Johnes became judge of the district comprising all north west Wales and part of south Wales. He held this office until December 1870. A disciple of Benthamite utilitarianism and penal reform, Johnes wrote many pamphlets between 1834 and 1869 advocating various law reforms. An enthusiast for the Welsh language and its literature, he also supported the *Cambrian Quarterly Magazine* (1830–3), contributing articles under the name Maelog, the name under which in 1834 he also published English translations of poems by Dafydd ap Gwilym. In 1831 the Cymmrodorion Society published his prize essay entitled *Causes of Dissent in Wales*.

Although a member of the Church of England, Johnes was critical of many aspects of church establishment and attempted to reform what he saw as its vices. In 1838 he successfully resisted Lord John Russell's proposed union of the sees of Bangor and St Asaph, and the appropriation of the income of one to the new see of Manchester. In 1841 his *Claims of the Welsh dioceses to the funds of the ecclesiastical commissioners, in a letter to Lord John Russell* was published in London, and in 1843 he also published *Philological Proofs of the Original Unity and Recent Origin of the Human Race* (London, 1843; 2nd edn, 1846). He does not appear to have married, and died on 23 July 1871 at Garthmyl; he was buried at Aberriw, near Montgomery.

D. L. THOMAS, rev. HUGH MOONEY

Sources 'Montgomery worthies', *Montgomeryshire Collections*, 41–6 · W. P. Baildon, ed., *The records of the Honorable Society of Lincoln's Inn: admissions*, 2 (1896), 136 · catalogue [BM] · D. R. Thomas, *Esgobaeth Llanelwy: the history of the diocese of St Asaph*, rev. edn, 3 vols. (1908–13), 152–4
Wealth at death under £2000: probate, 10 Aug 1871, *CGPLA Eng. & Wales*

Johnes, Sir James Hills- (**1833–1919**). *See under* Hills, Sir John (1834–1902).

Johnes, Thomas (**1748–1816**), agriculturist and translator, was born at Ludlow, Shropshire, on 1 September 1748, the eldest son of Thomas Johnes (1727–1780) of Llanfair Clydogau and Croft Castle, Herefordshire, member of parliament for Radnorshire, and his wife, Elizabeth (d. 1813), daughter of Richard Knight of Croft Castle. Johnes was educated at a dame-school in Ludlow, at the free grammar school at Shrewsbury, at Eton College (1760–65), and from 1766 to 1768 at the University of Edinburgh, where he made friends with many of the leading literary figures of the day. After an extended tour of Europe in the company of Robert Liston, he was elected in 1774 member of parliament for the borough of Cardigan. He was subsequently elected for three terms in Radnorshire, and for five terms in Cardiganshire. Although a supporter of both Catholic emancipation and political reform, he largely eschewed active political involvement, and appears never to have spoken in the house. Johnes was also lord lieutenant of Cardiganshire, colonel of the Cardigan militia, and auditor for life of the land revenue in Wales. He was elected a fellow of the Royal Society in 1800.

Johnes married Maria, daughter of the Revd Henry Burgh, of Park Lettice, Monmouthshire, on 26 August 1779, but she died childless in 1782. In 1783 he married his cousin Jane (d. 1833), daughter of John Johnes of Dolau

Cothi, Carmarthenshire, and in that same year they went to live at his estate of Hafoduchtryd, Cardiganshire. Under the influence of his cousin Richard Payne *Knight, Johnes proceeded to embellish his barren patrimony according to 'picturesque' principles. This involved extensive rationalization of the agricultural sector of the estate, a massive programme of land improvement, and the planting of some five million trees between 1784 and 1811. Concerned to improve the lot of the impoverished farming population, Johnes rebuilt many farms on the estate, initiated a local society for the improvement of agriculture, and actively encouraged 'improving' farmers from East Lothian in Scotland to settle in the area. Meanwhile he published *A Cardiganshire Landlord's Advice to his Tenants*, printed on his own press in 1800, and translated into verse by William Owen Pughe.

The mansion of Hafod was built in 1785 by Johnes from the designs of Thomas Baldwin of Bath. Although Johnes had originally conceived a full-blown Gothic edifice as a complement to the romantic qualities of the setting, and one which would provide an appropriate 'literary' atmosphere for his burrowings among the medieval French chronicles, Baldwin presented a symmetrical classical house, which accommodated the celebrated octagonal library of John Nash, who also undertook various landscape works on the estate. The house, with its valuable library and irreplaceable collections of Welsh manuscripts, was accidentally destroyed by fire on 13 March 1807; although insurance coverage proved inadequate, Johnes employed Baldwin to rebuild, and reoccupied Hafod in 1810. Meanwhile he continued to indulge his thirst for collecting books and works of art, and to extend the development of the Hafod landscape, besides undertaking a variety of philanthropic projects.

In 1802 Johnes set up a printing press at Pwllpeiran, some distance from the main house. Encouraged by his many literary friends, including George Cumberland, Robert Anderson, and Lord Chancellor Thurlow, he embarked on a prolific career as a translator of the medieval French chronicles. His early translation of Sainte-Palaye's *Vie de Froissart* was printed by Nichols of Fleet Street in 1801. Subsequent works, including the four-volume translation of Froissart's *Chronicles* (1803–5), appeared from the Hafod Press. Among other Hafod Press works were the *Memoirs of John, Lord de Joinville* (1807), *The Travels of Bertrandon de la Brocquière* (1807), and the massive four-volume *Chronicles of Monstrelet* (1809). Despite Johnes's rather tame (and in Walter Scott's words, 'over-genteel') style, he remains the only man to have undertaken the formidable task of translating Froissart's *Chronicles* in their entirety, and the appearance of subsequent editions until 1906 testifies to their worth.

In 1811 Johnes's only child, Mariamne, to whom he was deeply devoted, died unmarried. As early as 1800 Johnes had begun to encounter serious financial difficulties consequent on family pressures and the profligacy of his own expenditure. He was accordingly forced to dispose of Croft Castle and his other English properties, together with extensive tracts of inherited land in Wales. Progressive mortgaging of the 13,000-acre Hafod estate compounded his financial plight and in 1813, after a period of illness, he retired with his wife to Langstone Cliff Cottage, near Dawlish, Devon, where he died of heart failure on 23 April 1816. He was buried at Eglwys Newydd, the church at Hafod which he had built in 1803 to a design by James Wyatt. The Hafod estate, which remained in chancery for many years, was ultimately sold in 1833 to the fourth duke of Newcastle for £62,038.   R. J. MOORE-COLYER

Sources R. J. Moore-Colyer, ed., *A land of pure delight: selections from the letters of Thomas Johnes of Hafod, 1748–1816* (1992) • E. Inglis-Jones, *Peacocks in paradise: the story of a house, its owners, and the Elysium they established there* (1950) • R. J. Moore-Colyer, 'The Hafod estate under Thomas Johnes and the fourth duke of Newcastle', *Welsh History Review / Cylchgrawn Hanes Cymru*, 8 (1976–7), 257–84 • R. J. Moore-Colyer, 'Thomas Johnes of Hafod: translator and bibliophile', *Welsh History Review / Cylchgrawn Hanes Cymru*, 15 (1990–91), 399–416 • J. A. Dearden, 'Thomas Johnes and the Hafod Press, 1803–10', *Book Collector*, 22 (1973), 315–36 • J. Thomas, 'The architectural development of Hafod', *Ceredigion* [Cardiganshire Antiquarian Society], 7/2 (1973) • J. Thomas, 'The architectural development of Hafod', *Ceredigion* [Cardiganshire Antiquarian Society], 7/3–4 (1974–5) • C. Kirkham, 'Paradise lost', *Journal of Garden History*, 11 (1991) • G. Cumberland, *An attempt to describe Hafod* (1796) • J. E. Smith, *A tour of Hafod* (1810) • W. Linnard, 'Thomas Johnes of Hafod: pioneer of upland afforestation in Wales', *Ceredigion* [Cardiganshire Antiquarian Society], 6 (1970) • G. Walters, 'A catalogue of the late Pesaro Library in Venice, now forming part of the Hafod Library', *Trivium*, 22 (1987) • J. Piper, 'Decrepit glory: a tour of Hafod', *ArchR*, 87 (1940), 207–10

Archives NL Wales, corresp. and papers | BL, letters to G. Cumberland, Add. MSS 36497–36516 • Linn. Soc., letters to Sir James Smith • Liverpool Central Library, Roscoe MSS • NL Scot., corresp. with Robert Liston • NL Wales, Dolaucothi and Crosswood MSS • U. Nott. L., Newcastle MSS

Likenesses F. Engleheart, line engraving, pubd 1810, BM, NPG • F. Chantrey, bust, c.1812, AM Oxf. • F. Engleheart, engraving, NL Wales • W. N. Gardiner, stipple, BM • T. Stothard, engraving, NL Wales • W. H. Worthington, line engraving (after T. Stothard), BM

Wealth at death over £35,000—probably absorbed by mortgage commitments: U. Nott. L., MS NeD 4479

John-Mackie. For this title name *see* Mackie, John, Baron John-Mackie (1909–1994).

Johns, Ambrose Bowden (1776–1858), landscape painter, was born at Plymouth, Devon. Of his parents nothing is known. He was apprenticed to a printer and publisher, the father of Benjamin R. Haydon, but he soon devoted himself to landscape painting. He was much encouraged by his circle of artist friends including James Northcote, Haydon, and Charles Eastlake. He was acquainted with J. M. W. Turner, who used to sketch with him and stayed at his cottage, North Hill, near Plymouth, about 1813. Johns made Turner a small portable painting box and accompanied him on sketching exhibitions around Devon. In gratitude, Turner sent him a small oil sketch after returning to London. Johns painted somewhat in the style of Turner. A picture by Johns in the collection of Samuel Carter Hall was engraved by J. Cousen in one of the annuals, when it was ascribed to Turner. Johns wrote to the publisher, who put a corrective notice in the London newspapers. This incident is said to have given rise to a coolness between the two artists. The same picture was subsequently put up for sale at Christies as an example of Turner, and on two other occasions Johns's work passed as that of Turner.

Johns was very successful in his own county and belonged to the Plymouth Society of Artists and Amateurs. He occasionally exhibited in London at the Royal Academy, British Institution, and Society of British Artists. There were good examples of his work in the collections of Dr Yonge at Plymouth and of the earl of Morley at Saltram House, of which *Plym Bridge Near Borringdon Woods* remains *in situ*. A work of rather different character from his usual paintings, *A Boy Blowing Bubbles*, was in the collection of Sir Massey Lopes at Maristow, Devon. A fine example, *Okehampton Castle*, was in the collection of the earl of Darnley at Cobham Hall, Kent. Through an overuse of asphaltum many of his pictures have blackened with age. With his wife, Rebekah, he had five children, four of whom—Sarah and Mary Anne (*bap.* 23 Sept 1808), Jane and Thomas Bowers (*bap.* 16 Nov 1827)—were baptized at the Norley Street Presbyterian Chapel, near Bilbury Street, Plymouth. The fifth child, John *Johns, became a clergyman and worked as a missionary in Liverpool.

Johns died at his home, North Hill Cottage, near Plymouth, on 10 December 1858 and was buried in the family vault on 17 December at Norley Street Presbyterian Chapel, Plymouth. His obituarist in the *Plymouth Herald* recorded that 'his amiable character secured him numerous friends; he was kind-hearted, liberal, generous, and simple-minded in his tastes and habits' (*The Inquirer*). His work drew praise from the German connoisseur Waagen, from Northcote, and from Severn. 'Those most capable of viewing nature in her truest character, poetically pourtrayed, and not in the manner of a map, esteemed his works most' (ibid.). Examples of his work are held in Plymouth Art Gallery and Museum.

L. H. CUST, rev. L. R. HOULISTON

Sources G. Pycroft, *Art in Devonshire* (1882) · *The Inquirer* (18 Dec 1858), 825 · *Art Journal*, 21 (1859) · H. Ottley, *A biographical and critical dictionary of recent and living painters and engravers* (1866) · Thieme & Becker, *Allgemeines Lexikon* · M. H. Grant, *A dictionary of British landscape painters, from the 16th century to the early 20th century* (1952) · T. Fawcett, *The rise of English provincial art: artist, patron and institution outside London, 1800–1830* (1974) · Redgrave, *Artists* · M. Butlin and E. Joll, *The paintings of J. M. W. Turner*, 2 vols. (1977) · Bryan, *Painters* (1903–5) · J. Johnson, ed., *Works exhibited at the Royal Society of British Artists, 1824–1893, and the New English Art Club, 1888–1917*, 2 vols. (1975) · CGPLA Eng. & Wales (1859) · IGI · private information (2004) [Saltram House, Devon; Plymouth Art Gallery and Museum]
Wealth at death under £4000: probate, 13 Jan 1859, CGPLA Eng. & Wales

Johns, Charles Alexander (1811–1874), writer on natural history, was born at Plymouth on 31 December 1811, the son of Henry Incledon Johns and grandson of Tremenheere Johns, a solicitor, of Helston, Cornwall. In 1831 he was second master at Helston grammar school, under the Revd Derwent Coleridge (1800–1883). Charles Kingsley (1819–1875) was a pupil at the school from 1831 to 1836, and Johns encouraged in Kingsley a passion for botany. In 1841 Johns graduated BA at Trinity College, Dublin, and in

the same year he was ordained deacon. From June 1843 to December 1847 he was headmaster of the school at Helston, and the following year he was ordained priest; he acted as curate of Yarnscombe, Devon, for two years. After 1863, until which time he was still living at Helston, he opened a private school for boys at Winton House, Winchester. He died there on 28 June 1874, leaving his wife, Ellen Julia, and at least one child.

Johns became a fellow of the Linnean Society in 1836. He was also a member of the Botanical Society of London, and a founding member and president of the Winchester Literary and Scientific Society. He was the author of many popular books on natural history, some scientific papers, and a few separately printed sermons. Of his works, *Flowers of the Field*, first published in 1853, proved the most successful, reaching its twenty-ninth edition by 1899.

G. S. BOULGER, rev. GILES HUDSON

Sources *Journal of Botany, British and Foreign*, 12 (1874), 256 · D. E. Coombe, 'The editions of *A week at the Lizard* by the Revd Charles Alexander Johns', *Journal of the Society of the Bibliography of Natural History*, 5 (1968–71), 259–69 · Desmond, *Botanists*, rev. edn · CGPLA Eng. & Wales (1874)
Archives Cornwall RO, diary · RBG Kew, botanial specimens · RBG Kew, letters | Suffolk RO, Ipswich, letters to R. H. White
Wealth at death under £7,000: probate, 12 Aug 1874, CGPLA Eng. & Wales

Johns, Claude Hermann Walter (1857–1920), Assyriologist and Church of England clergyman, was born at Banwell, Somerset, on 4 February 1857, the eldest son of the Revd Walter Pascoe Johns, a Wesleyan minister, of a yeoman family settled for generations at Wendron, Cornwall, and his wife, Eleanor, daughter of Charles Gilbert, of Mutford Hall, Suffolk. Educated at Queen Elizabeth's Grammar School, Faversham, Kent, Johns won an exhibition at Queens' College, Cambridge (1875). At Queens' he was elected to a minor scholarship, a foundation scholarship, and to a Goldsmiths' exhibition; and in 1880, while a master at the Leys School, Cambridge, he graduated as twenty-seventh wrangler, an accident having prevented him from taking the tripos examination earlier (BA 1880, MA 1885, LittD 1909, DD 1915). His health, never very good, led him to decide to go to Tasmania, where he became second master at Horton College (1880–83), but he returned to England for family reasons in 1883 and, after a short period as a master at Paston grammar school, North Walsham, Norfolk (1883–6), was ordained deacon in 1887 (priest 1888), and was appointed tutor at Peterborough Training College (1887–91). He also served curacies at Helpston, Northamptonshire (1887–8), and at St John the Baptist, Peterborough (1888–92). He returned to Queens' College as assistant chaplain in 1892, and was presented by his college to the rectory of St Botolph's, Cambridge (1892–1909).

Johns had been interested in Assyriology since 1875. The expedition to Nineveh undertaken in 1873 by George Smith of the British Museum resulted in the further discovery of deluge tablet fragments, and the discussion on these roused Johns's interest. Urged by the orientalist Sandford Arthur Strong, he took up the study of cuneiform to such good purpose that he was made lecturer in

Claude Hermann Walter Johns (1857–1920), by Elliott & Fry, 1909

Assyriology at Queens' College in 1895, and in 1904 lecturer in Assyrian at King's College, London. In 1903 he was elected to the Edwardes fellowship at Queens', and in 1909 proceeded to the degree of LittD, Jesus College making him a research fellow. A few months later he was elected to the mastership of St Catharine's College, with its accompanying canonry at Norwich, which, while it conferred well-deserved recognition on Johns's capacity, unfortunately for Assyriology, absorbed the greater part of his time. Yet he did not lose touch with his Assyrian studies, for in 1910 he visited America and delivered in Philadelphia the Bohlen lectures on the religious significance of Semitic proper names, and in 1912 he gave the Schweich lectures at the British Academy on the relations between the laws of Babylonia and the laws of the Hebrew peoples.

In 1910 he married Agnes Sophia, daughter of the Revd John Griffith, principal of Brighton College and later vicar of Sandridge, Hertfordshire; they had no children.

In 1904 Johns published *Babylonian and Assyrian Laws, Contracts, and Letters*, a collection of documents illustrated by full, ingenious, often brilliant discussions of the problems raised. His *magnum opus* was a corpus of 1100 contract tablets, in four volumes (one issued posthumously in 1923 by his wife), *Assyrian Deeds and Documents* (1898–1923). An *Assyrian Domesday Book* (1901) dealt with cuneiform records

of plantations and their proprietors round the city of Harran in what is now Turkey. His vast collection of Assyrian proper names was embodied in K. L. Tallqvist's *Assyrian Personal Names*. His short volumes, *Ancient Assyria* (1912) and *Ancient Babylonia* (1913), both contain much original work addressed to a popular audience. In addition to numerous papers in scientific journals, Johns also wrote *The Oldest Code of Laws in the World* (1903), which was the first English language translation of the legal sections of the Code of Hammurabi, discovered in 1902. The work was reprinted four times in 1903 alone, and a further three times until 1926. His other works include *Ur-Engur* (1908), *A List of the Year Names of the First Dynasty of Babylon* (1911), and *A Survey of Recent Assyriology* (1914–15). A drawback to his work was that he never travelled in the Near East.

By his energy and attractive personality Johns raised St Catharine's College from comparative obscurity. The number of its undergraduates greatly increased, and Johns reorganized its management and finances. Johns's obituary in *The Times* noted, 'A genial and kindly scholar, devoid of pettiness, he was always accessible to students of the Old Testament who wanted to consult him for Assyriological illustrations'. In his balanced introduction to the 1903 English translation of Friedrich Delitzsch's controversial *Babel and Bible* Johns maintained:

> There is no need to swallow everything whole, nor to toss the Bible on the shelf as antiquated rubbish … Much has been made of the pain which comes to those who see old beliefs perish. But that is salutary pain.

Johns called for theologians to study Assyriology to see exactly what that science contributes to the understanding of the Bible—a standard practice nowadays.

Johns advanced the understanding of the details of ancient life, especially in the study of personal names, law, and economic and social history, and addressed a broad public interested in the Bible. His work has since been redone with additional texts, but it remains basic to the understanding of some of the texts he studied.

Unhappily the stress of his labours proved too much for Johns. His devotion to his work not only in Assyriology but also in raising the status of St Catharine's caused a breakdown in his health, and he resigned his mastership and canonry in 1919. He died at his home, Rathmines, Barnes Close, Winchester, on 20 August 1920, and was buried on 24 August at Twyford, Hampshire. He was survived by his wife who in 1935 financed in his name a building now used as an undergraduate residence.

R. C. THOMPSON, *rev.* DANIEL C. SNELL

Sources E. A. W. Budge, *The rise and progress of Assyriology* (1925), 187–91 • *The Times* (23 Aug 1920), 13c • *The Times* (27 Aug 1920), 13c • *The Times* (27 Nov 1920), 13e • R. C. Thompson, notice in posthumous volume, *Assyrian deeds and documents*, ed. C. H. W. Johns and A. S. Johns, 4 (1923), ix–xx • W. H. S. Jones [W. H. Samuel], *A history of St Catharine's College, once Catharine Hall, Cambridge* (1936) • E. E. Rich, 'The nineteenth century', *St Catharine's College, Cambridge, 1473–1973: a volume of essays to commemorate the quincentenary of the foundation of the college*, ed. E. E. Rich (1973), 164–247, esp. 238–247, and 271 • C. H. W. Johns, 'Introduction', in F. Delitzsch, *Babel and Bible* (1903), xxvi–xxvii • Venn, *Alum. Cant.*

Archives St Catharine's College, Cambridge, account book, letters, and papers
Likenesses Elliott & Fry, photograph, 1909, NPG [*see illus.*] · K. Greene, oils, 1932, St Catharine's College, Cambridge · engraving, St Botolph's Church, Cambridge · photograph, repro. in Budge, *Rise and progress*, 189
Wealth at death £5384 1*s*. 5*d*.: probate, 8 Nov 1920, *CGPLA Eng. & Wales*

Johns [Jones]**, David** (*fl.* 1572–1598), literary antiquary, was the son of John ap Hugh, and appears to have been a native of the Dyfi valley, Merioneth, according to one of his notes in his manuscript collection of poems (BL, Add. MS 14866), where he apologizes for giving prominence to the work of Ieuan Dyfi, 'since he is a man from my own country'. He notes Hywel ap Siencyn of Ynysmaengwyn, Tywyn, Merioneth, the subject of an elegy by the fifteenth-century poet Tudur Aled, as his great-grandfather, and this is confirmed by the genealogy he supplied for Lewys Dwnn (*Heraldic Visitations*, ed. S. R. Meyrick, 1846, 2.348). Nothing is known of Johns's education but he was inducted vicar of Llanfair Dyffryn Clwyd, Denbighshire, in 1573 (and again in 1586); his uncle Sir Arthur ap Huw, a patron of the professional poets, held the living before him (1563–70). John Williams was presented to the vicarage in 1598 (or 1603) but the reason for the vacancy is not noted.

The Vale of Clwyd and the neighbouring area were home to a remarkable number of manuscript collectors, copyists, and literary antiquaries throughout the fifteenth and sixteenth centuries, and even later. Johns was friendly with, and shared in the work of, many of these scholars and antiquaries. He compiled a very large collection of fourteenth- to sixteenth-century *cywydd* poetry (BL, Add. MS 14866, 9–545) in 1587, which he prefaced with an introductory dedication to John Williams, perhaps his successor at Llanfair. The preface is similar in tone to other prefaces written at this time in its regard for the Welsh literary tradition and the need to ensure the publication of Welsh books. The corpus of poetry, categorized in five thematic groups, is annotated (one note is a description of Dafydd ap Gwilym given to Johns in 1572 by an old woman 'who had seen another who had conversed with Dafydd ap Gwilym' and reveals Johns's knowledge of the manuscript and oral traditions of *cywydd* poetry. He translated into 'Latin Sapphic verse' one of the best-known poems of the pseudo-Taliesin, 'Ef a wnaeth Panthon Ar lawr Ebron', but he is better known as a translator into Welsh of at least two psalms and of St Bernard's *Cur mundus militat?* in *cywydd* metre, and in prose an 'edited' protestant version of a prayer by St Augustine (1585), and 'Dengran gwahaniaeth kristhogion y byd'. In a letter to David Salysbury in 1587 (preserved in BL, Add. MS 9817), he includes two religious, and protestant, *cywyddau* he claims were his first poetic efforts.   BRYNLEY F. ROBERTS

Sources G. H. Hughes, 'Cyfieithiad Dafydd Johns, Llanfair Dyffryn Clwyd, o "Weddi Sant Augustin"', *National Library of Wales Journal*, 6 (1949–50), 295–8 · G. J. Williams, *Llythyrau at Ddafydd Jones o Drefriw* (1943), 28 · *Report on manuscripts in the Welsh language*, 2 vols. in 7, HMC, 48 (1898–1910), vol. 2, pp. 1022–38 · G. J. Williams, 'Traddodiad llenyddol dyffryn Clwyd a'r cyffiniau', *Transactions of the Denbighshire Historical Society*, 1 (1952), 20–52 · NL Wales, MS 1626, 285 · A. I. Pryce, *The diocese of Bangor in the sixteenth century* (1923) · C. Fychan, 'Y canu i wŷr eglwysig gorllewin Sir Ddinbych', *Transactions of the Denbighshire Historical Society*, 28 (1979), 115–82
Archives BL, Add. MSS 14866, 14896, 9817 | Bodl. Oxf., Jesus College MS 15 · NL Wales, MS, Peniarth 159 · NL Wales, 3029B, Mostyn 110

Johns [*formerly* Jones]**, David** (1794–1843), missionary in Madagascar, was the son of J. Jones (or Johns) of Llain, Llan-arth Fawr, Monmouthshire. He was a member of a church congregation at Penrhiwgaled, and was educated to become a missionary to Madagascar first at Neuaddlwyd, and afterwards at Newtown and Gosport. He was ordained at Penrhiwgaled on 14 February 1826.

In 1826 Jones married Mary, the daughter of W. Thomas, an independent minister at Bala. He was then sent by the London Missionary Society to Madagascar, where he was to join fellow missionaries David Jones and David Griffiths. In order to avoid confusion with his namesake he changed his surname from Jones to Johns. Having set sail from England on 11 May 1826, he arrived at Madagascar on 11 September, bringing with him a printing press and two artisans. By the end of 1827 Johns and his colleagues, with the help of local people, had not only prepared but had also printed and distributed to thirty-seven missionary schools a catechism and hymnbook, some school books, and translations of the scriptures in the Malagasy language. These projects were largely made possible by the support of Radama, the king of Madagascar, who, although not a Christian, was an enthusiastic patron of education.

King Radama's successor, Queen Ranavalona (who took power after his death in July 1828), was more ambivalent towards the missionaries and her ministers were fiercely opposed to the new religious group. Amid increasing tension in 1830 and 1831 Johns and Griffiths built new chapels and conducted baptisms, and Griffiths constituted his group into a church. By 1832 the queen's ministers were openly hostile; Johns, the other missionaries, and the London Missionary Society saw Griffiths' zeal as partly to blame for the breakdown in friendly relations between the missionaries and converts and local non-Christians.

In 1835 Ranavalona prohibited all Christian worship, teaching, and baptism among the Madagascans. By March confessions were demanded, Christians were persecuted, and in April and June all the missionaries except for Johns and Baker, who stayed to complete translations of the scriptures and *Pilgrim's Progress*, left the country, publishing Johns's eight-volume *Dictionary of the Malagasy Language* from a London press. Eventually Johns and Baker, having printed, distributed, and buried a few copies of their scriptures and *Pilgrim's Progress* for safe keeping, decided to leave Madagascar also, since they 'could no longer remain in [their] missionary capacity' (Lovett, 699). In the absence of any instructions from the London Missionary Society, they went to Mauritius in July 1836, which they used as a base from which to help Christians who were being persecuted in Madagascar.

In 1839 Johns went with some refugees to a meeting in

England at Exeter Hall in order to draw attention to the plight of both slaves and Christians in Madagascar; in 1840 his *Narrative of the Persecution of the Christians in Madagascar*, written with J. J. Freeman, was published, and he returned to Mauritius to make furtive visits to Madagascar in order to help its fugitives to escape to safety. Johns died of cholera on 6 August 1843, on the island of Nossi Bé, off the north-west coast of Madagascar, where he was trying to establish refugee settlements for Christians in the French part of Madagascar. He asked to be buried at Tafondro, from where Madagascar could be seen. He once said 'If I had a thousand lives, I would willingly lay down every one for Madagascar' (Hardyman, 18).   LYNN MILNE

Sources R. Lovett, *The history of the London Missionary Society, 1795–1895*, 1 (1899) · J. T. Jones, *Geiriadur bywgraffyddol o enwogion Cymru*, 2 vols. (1867–70) · B. Williams [Gwynionydd], *Enwogion Ceredigion* (1869) · G. Jones, *Enwogion Sir Aberteifi* (1868) · J. T. Hardyman, *Madagascar on the move* (1950) · *DNB*

Johns, John (1801–1847), Unitarian minister and missionary, was born on 17 March 1801 at Northills, Plymouth, the youngest of the five children of Ambrose Bowden *Johns (1776–1858), landscape painter, an artist who painted in the style of Turner, and his wife, Rebekah. Johns attended Plymouth grammar school and Edinburgh University, presumably because of its Presbyterian connection. In 1826 he was appointed minister to the congregation of English Presbyterians of Crediton, Devon, at a salary of £30 p.a. Though he dreamed of becoming a poet in the lakeland tradition he nevertheless devoted himself to the active promotion of schemes for popular improvement. He married Caroline Reynell (*d.* 1861), daughter of Henry Reynell of Newton Abbot, on 6 September 1833. They subsequently had eight children, of whom six survived.

In 1836 Johns was appointed minister to the poor at the Domestic Mission in Liverpool. There he lived in Nile Street (now demolished, but then newly built accommodation for the rising middle class) adjacent to St James's Mount, where the Anglican cathedral now stands. Liverpool was at that time a boom city, the decline of the slave trade having been offset by the rapid development of American and colonial commerce. The demand for labour attracted an influx of poor migrants from neighbouring countries, particularly Ireland, who crowded into slums notorious for lacking any civilized amenity. Poverty of both mind and body on such a scale constituted an enormous problem. Inspired by Tuckerman and Channing, the celebrated American ministers who had pioneered the campaign for a mission to the poor, the Unitarians in Liverpool (as the local Presbyterians were by then denominated) set up the Domestic Mission Society in 1836. If the poor refused to come to the gospel, the gospel must be brought to the poor. This would be no task for the charitable amateur; a man of exceptional commitment and skill would be required.

The appointment of Johns was a surprising but perceptive choice. He was variously described as a dreamer of dreams, as if he had no skin, and as a practical mystic. He came with no other purpose than to demonstrate the validity of his own conviction that all men were equal and

that none was beyond redemption, points of view then the subject of dissension in both religious and political circles. Confronted by people living lives that struck him as barely human, he undertook conventional missionary work, offering such spiritual and material comfort as was at his command. He made a modest contribution to civic affairs, for which he was respected. The poor regarded him with affection.

Johns achieved no spectacular results. Nevertheless he emerges as a figure of considerable significance. A frustrated poet and an indifferent preacher, he found an alternative outlet in his annual reports to his committee. His skill in the use of words and the sensibility of his powers of observation endow these detailed records with a rare quality of compassion. Issued every year throughout his period of service, the reports constitute a unique running commentary on one man's exploration of the relationship between an urban community and its members, at a point in time when this was undergoing major stress. Johns also published a number of sermons, tracts, and poems.

Johns's testimony inspired the ongoing programme of environmental reforms on which the nonconformist community focused throughout the following years and on which the tradition of 'Liverpool firsts' is founded (that is, pioneering social policies such as first medical officer of health, and first slum clearance legislation). This was his legacy to those who had sponsored his mission.

The aftermath of the potato famine in Ireland brought about conditions in Liverpool such as even Johns had never seen before. His faith sorely tried, he toiled on until struck down by typhus while tending the body of a victim whom nobody else—other than a Catholic priest—would touch. He died on 23 June 1847 at 147 Mill Street, Toxteth Park, Liverpool, and was buried at St James's cemetery, Liverpool, two days later. He was survived by his wife, who died on 7 March 1861 in Hobart, Tasmania.

      MARGARET SIMEY

Sources *Liverpool Domestic Mission Annual Report* (1837–47) · A. Holt, *A ministry to the poor* (1936) · H. V. Davis, *A minister of God* (1901) · [M. Simey], *Charitable effort in Liverpool in the nineteenth century* (1951); rev. edn as *Charity rediscovered: a study of philanthropic effort in nineteenth-century Liverpool* (1992) · *The Inquirer* (26 June 1847), 402 · J. R. W., *Christian Reformer, or, Unitarian Magazine and Review*, new ser., 4 (1848), 188–91 · *The Inquirer* (1861), 374 · *Christian Reformer, or, Unitarian Magazine and Review*, new ser., 17 (1861), 384 [death notice of Caroline Johns] · d. cert.
Archives Lpool RO, Domestic Mission archives

Johns, William (1771–1845), Unitarian minister and author, was born in the parish of Killymaenllwyd in Pembrokeshire, the son of a tenant farmer. Conflicts in accounts of his early life are probably irresolvable. That he worked with his father is an easy assumption; that he spoke no English until the age of sixteen seems improbable if he was introduced to Latin and Greek at the village school or, as the *Dictionary of Welsh Biography* suggests, at the school of John Griffiths (1731–1811) at Glandŵr; it seems certain, however, that he spent a year at the Oswestry Academy under Edward Williams (1750–1813) in 1787–8. In 1788 he entered Northampton Academy—a more likely date than the usual 1790, as the normal course was five years—where the liberal opinions of John Horsey (1754–1827), minister of the Independent church at Castle Hill, Northampton (which had been the congregation of Philip Doddridge), and principal of the academy, led him to abandon his strict Calvinism for Unitarianism.

In 1793 Johns went to the congregation in Gloucester, probably assisting Joshua Dickenson, who had been minister there since 1751. The following year he moved to Totnes in Devon, where he married; two daughters were born, one of them surviving her father. In 1799 he became classical tutor in Manchester Academy, resigning the next year. After a few months as master of a small free school at Wrexham, he became minister of the Presbyterian (Unitarian) church at Nantwich in Cheshire, where he also opened a school and proved himself a very able teacher. In 1804 he moved his school to Faulkner Street, Manchester, where he ran it with notable success for nearly thirty years. The *City News Notes and Queries* for 3 July 1880 contains a fascinating, detailed recollection of the teaching at the school in the second decade of the century.

In the autumn of 1804, apparently following a chance encounter with Mrs Johns, John Dalton (1766–1844), who had taught mathematics and natural philosophy at Manchester Academy, came to live with the Johns family, remaining with them until 1830. Johns was elected a member of the Manchester Literary and Philosophical Society. For many years he was joint secretary with Dalton and subsequently vice-president of the society; the prominence of the two men reflected the singular role played in the 'Lit. and Phil.' by Unitarians and Quakers. The numerous papers he read before the society show wide and accurate knowledge of both literary and scientific subjects. On arriving in Manchester he also preached for a short time to a congregation at Partington, Cheshire, and in 1805 accepted the ministry of the congregation at Cross Street, another Cheshire village, which he held until shortly before his death.

Johns published some Latin exercises (1805), a textbook on practical botany (1826), and several religious essays. With John Relly Beard (1800–1876) he edited the *Christian Teacher* from 1832 to 1843. He also contributed many articles to the *Monthly Repository* and the *Christian Reformer*. He died at Eaglesfield House, Higher Broughton, Manchester, on 27 November 1845.   R. K. WEBB

Sources DWB · *Christian Reformer, or, Unitarian Magazine and Review*, new ser., 2 (1846), 109–19 · *City News Notes and Queries*, 3 (1880), 133 · H. McLachlan, *English education under the Test Acts: being the history of the nonconformist academies, 1662–1820* (1931) · A. Thackray, 'Natural knowledge in cultural context: the Manchester model', *American Historical Review*, 79 (1974), 672–709 · G. E. Evans, *Vestiges of protestant dissent* (1897) · *The life and experiences of Sir Henry Enfield Roscoe … written by himself* (1906), 402–3 · J. Raymond and J. V. Pickstone, 'The natural sciences and the learning of the English Unitarians', *Truth, liberty, religion: essays celebrating two hundred years of Manchester College*, ed. B. Smith (1986), 127–64 · G. M. Ditchfield, 'Manchester College and anti-slavery', *Truth, liberty, religion: essays celebrating two hundred years of Manchester College*, ed. B. Smith (1986), 191–4 · d. cert.

Johns, William Earl (1893–1968), children's writer and journalist, was born on 5 February 1893 at Bengeo, Hertfordshire, the eldest son of Richard William Eastman Johns, a tailor, and his wife, Elizabeth Earl. He was educated at Bengeo School and Hertford grammar school, also attending evening classes at the local art school. After leaving school he completed indentures with a firm of surveyors. Taking a job in Norfolk, he fulfilled an ambition to become a soldier by enlisting as a part-time private with the Norfolk yeomanry. He was called up for active service on the outbreak of the First World War. On 6 October 1914 he married Maude Penelope (1888–1961), the daughter of the Revd John Hunt, a Norfolk clergyman, and their only son, William Earl Carmichael, was born in March 1916.

Johns served with the yeomanry at Gallipoli and then with the machine-gun corps in the Salonika campaign, transferring to the Royal Flying Corps in 1917. He was commissioned as second lieutenant on 26 September, training as a pilot. After several postings as a flying instructor, he joined no. 55 squadron at Azelot, France, in August 1918, flying DH4 bombers on long-range raids into the Rhineland.

On 16 September the squadron raided Mannheim. Johns's aircraft was damaged by anti-aircraft fire and, as he returned to base, he found himself fighting a battle with Fokker DVIIs of Ernst Udet's famous *Jagdstaffel*. Johns's observer was killed and Johns, wounded, crashed and was captured. At Strasbourg he was tried and condemned to death for war crimes, accused of indiscriminate bombing of civilian targets, but saved by the possibility of an armistice. He spent the rest of the war in prisoner-of-war camps, attempting two escapes.

Johns remained in the Royal Air Force until 1927, being promoted to flying officer in 1920. He flew in air force displays and was on the organizing committee of the Hendon air display. In 1923 it was Johns who, as recruiting officer, admitted T. E. Lawrence into the Royal Air Force under the name Ross; he wanted to reject him for giving a name that was obviously false, but accepted him under orders. Later Johns exploded the myth that Lawrence's identity in the Royal Air Force was ever a secret; from the first day, one officer warned another that 'aircraftman second class Ross' dined with cabinet ministers.

By 1923 Johns had left his wife and met Doris May (1900–1969), daughter of Alfred Broughton Leigh. In 1924 they set up home in Newcastle. Although he never divorced Maude Hunt, Doris Leigh was known as Mrs Johns until her death. On leaving the RAF Johns became an aviation illustrator (sharing a studio with the illustrator Howard Leigh, Doris Leigh's brother) and then tried his hand at journalism. In 1932 he became founder editor of the monthly *Popular Flying*. It was in this magazine that he first introduced Biggles, the archetypal Royal Flying Corps pilot. The first collection of these stories appeared as *The Camels are Coming* (1932). By the time of his death Johns had written 102 Biggles books and his airman had been consecutively a First World War 'ace', a freelance adventurer, a Second World War squadron leader, and, finally, an 'air-detective' at Scotland Yard.

William Earl Johns (1893–1968), by unknown photographer, 1960

Johns's output was prodigious. In the 1930s he wrote regularly for the *Modern Boy*, *Pearson's Magazine*, and *My Garden*, as well as editing *Popular Flying*. In April 1938 he also edited a weekly, *Flying*. In 1939, owing to his criticism of government air defence policy, he was dismissed from his editorships. At the outbreak of war he lectured to the Air Training Corps (in whose foundation he had been involved) and wrote for the *ATC Gazette*. He also wrote specialized aviation books for the Air Ministry and Ministry of Information. Johns's Biggles stories had an immense impact on recruitment to the Royal Air Force. Worrals of the WAAF, the female counterpart of Biggles, was created by Johns at the request of the Air Ministry to promote the Women's Auxiliary Air Force, and a similar demand from the War Office for a soldier hero was met by the creation of Gimlet—a commando.

After ten years in Scotland, where Johns indulged in his favourite pastimes of shooting and fishing, he and Doris Johns moved to Park House, Hampton Court, in 1953. At the time of his death, he had published 169 titles: 102 about Biggles, 11 about Worrals, 10 about Gimlet, 10 science-fiction adventures, 6 Steeley novels, 8 miscellaneous juvenile titles, 11 adult thrillers, 3 anthologies, and 8 non-fiction titles. His works were translated into fourteen languages, issued in braille, serialized in newspapers and magazines in Britain, Australia, and Europe, broadcast on radio in Britain, Australia, and South Africa, televised by Granada TV, turned into strip cartoons, and issued as cassette recordings. After Enid Blyton, Johns was the most prolific and popular children's writer of the time.

In his later years, and after his death, Johns came under attack from children's librarians and others who accused him of racism, outmoded concepts, and stereotyped characters. Although some of his books reflect the prejudices of his times, a reading of his works reveals his tremendous, almost puckish, sense of humour, and his habit of making fun of his own supposed prejudices. The critic Stanley Reynolds summed up the secret of Johns's success: 'The appeal is that "Biggles" is a flier and Captain Johns writes wondrously about flying ... The writing is so vivid that it sticks in your mind and years after you remember it'.

Popular in service circles and the book world, Johns, with his short, bulky figure and his well-groomed grey hair and ready smile, was greeted enthusiastically by his wide range of friends. A craftsman, he always delivered his work on time and to the exact length required. He died at Park House on 21 June 1968, and was buried at Hampton Court.

PETER BERRESFORD ELLIS and PIERS WILLIAMS, *rev.*
PETER BERRESFORD ELLIS

Sources P. B. Ellis and P. Williams, *By Jove, Biggles! The life of Captain W. E. Johns* (1981); new edn by P. N. Ellis and J. Schofield, *Biggles! The life story of Capt. W. E. Johns* (1993) · Record of Service, RAF Officers' Records Department, Gloucester · RFC/RAF Records, PRO, PRO/Air 1/480/15/312/241–245; 1/1750/204/139/4–9 · *Popular Flying* (June 1933) · *Popular Flying* (June 1935) · *Popular Flying* (June 1936) · Bayerisches Hauptstaatsarchiv, Munich, Germany, Kriegsarchiv · A. Morris, *First of many: the story of the independent force, RAF* (1968) · *The Times* (22 June 1968) · S. Reynolds, *The Guardian* (6 Jan 1979) · d. cert.

Archives Royal Air Force Museum, Hendon, papers and literary MSS

Likenesses V. Drees, photograph, 1960, Hult. Arch. · photograph, 1960, Sci. Mus. [*see illus.*]

Wealth at death £27,602: probate, 30 Aug 1968, *CGPLA Eng. & Wales*

Johnson. *See also* Jonson.

Johnson [*formerly* Janssen] **family** (*per. c.*1570–*c.*1630), sculptors, were of Dutch origin but worked in London. **Garat Johnson the elder** (*d.* 1611) was born in Amsterdam and appears to have moved east to Gelderland before arriving in England *c.*1567, probably as a protestant refugee. It seems that in 1568 he became an English citizen and presumably he Anglicized his name from Janssen. He settled in Southwark where he is recorded in 1582–3 and at intervals thereafter; by 1593 he and his wife, Mary (or Marie), had a family of five sons and a daughter, all English-born. His household at this time also included four journeymen, two apprentices, and an English assistant. Evidently he ran an important workshop and, together with the Cure family, he seems to have led the so-called Southwark school of sculpture which dominated the London market in the last quarter of the sixteenth century and sent its products to many parts of England.

In a period of sculpture where the evidence is thin on who did what, Johnson stands out as the only artist working in Elizabethan London for whom we have a substantial body of fully authenticated work. In his will he describes himself as a 'tombemaker' from which it may be inferred that his business was mainly in this field, at least in later years, and while he is also known to have made garden sculpture and a chimneypiece, it is only the tombs that survive. Those of Edward and John Manners, the third and fourth earls of Rutland, erected in 1591 at Bottesford, Leicestershire, were commissioned as a pair: detailed financial accounts survive which give a vivid picture of the laborious process by which they were transported from London and erected. An unusual design was employed by the workshop for the memorial at Titchfield, Hampshire, to Thomas and Henry Wriothesley, the first and second earls of Southampton, and Jane, wife of the first earl (c.1594). The effigy of the countess is raised above the other two on a central podium and tall obelisks stand at the corners of the main tomb chest. For the Gage family Johnson made three monuments in 1595 which stand at West Firle, Sussex. Two of them, commemorating Sir Edward Gage and his wife and John Gage and his two wives, have effigies in the form of brasses and these have provided a basis for numerous attributions to the Johnson workshop of memorials in this genre. Garat died in 1611 and was buried on 30 July at St Saviour's, Southwark.

Nicholas Johnson (d. 1624) was a son and the co-executor of Garat Johnson the elder. He probably trained with his father and lived and shared a workshop with him; certainly he lived in Southwark after the older man died. Nicholas collaborated with Garat on the Southampton memorial at Titchfield and he is known to have shared commissions for major tombs with other leading sculptors in London: that of Thomas Sutton at the Charterhouse with Nicholas Stone the elder in 1615 and that of Bishop Montague in Bath Abbey with William Cure the younger in 1618–19. The only work he is known to have done independently is to have made a third tomb in the Rutland series at Bottesford, commemorating Roger Manners, the fifth earl, and his wife (1618–19). He died in 1624 and was buried on 16 November at St Saviour's, Southwark.

Garrat Johnson the younger (fl. c.1612) was the son of Garat Johnson the elder and brother of Nicholas. The only other thing known about him for certain is that in May 1612 he was paid for making part of a fountain for the east garden at Hatfield House, Hertfordshire. The herald and antiquary William Dugdale noted in his diary for 1653 that the monuments to William Shakespeare (d. 1616) and John Combe (d. 1614) at Holy Trinity Church, Stratford upon Avon, were by 'one Gerard Johnson' (Life … of Sir William Dugdale, 99). To judge by the dates of death, it is likely to have been the son and not the father that Dugdale had in mind. He is not an entirely reliable source. The younger Garrat's date and place of death are not known.

Bernard Janssen (fl. 1616–1627) may or may not have been related to the Johnsons of Southwark. He is listed as a ratepayer in the parish of St Martin-in-the-Fields, Westminster, from 1616/17 to 1626/7. Nicholas Stone the elder lived near by, with whom Janssen collaborated c.1616 on the memorial to Sir Nicholas Bacon, bt, and his wife at Redgrave, Suffolk. Janssen also made the monument to

Marcelis Bax which was executed in London in 1617–20 and erected in the Grote Kerk at Bergen op Zoom in the Netherlands (des.). He may be identical with the Bernard Janssen who designed the temporary triumphal arch erected by the members of the Dutch church, Austin Friars, for the abortive ceremonial entry of Charles I into the City of London in 1626. The eighteenth-century antiquary George Vertue credits this person with having designed and constructed many buildings, including old Northumberland House, near Charing Cross in London (begun c.1608), and the mansion of Audley End, Essex (c.1608–16). Bernard the tomb sculptor was married to Alice with whom he had at least three children. The date and place of his death are not known. ADAM WHITE

Sources A. White, 'A biographical dictionary of London tomb sculptors, c.1560–c.1660', Walpole Society, 61 (1999), 1–162, esp. 63–74 · V. Manners, 'The Rutland monuments in Bottesford church', Art Journal, new ser., 23 (1903), 289–95, 335–9 · F. W. Steer, 'The Gage tombs at Firle', Sussex County Magazine, 30/2–3 (Feb–March 1956), 58–65, 114–18 · M. Whinney, Sculpture in Britain, 1530 to 1830, rev. J. Physick, 2nd edn (1988), 47–51, 70 · The life, diary, and correspondence of Sir William Dugdale, ed. W. Hamper (1827) · parish register, Southwark, St Saviour's, 30 July 1611 [burial: Garat Johnson the elder] · parish register, Southwark, St Saviour's, 16 Nov 1624 [burial: Nicholas Johnson]

Johnson, Begum. See Johnson, Frances (1728–1812).

Johnson, Captain (1771/2–1839), smuggler and pilot, was in 1798 captured in an affray with revenue officers on the Sussex coast and imprisoned in the new gaol in the Borough in London, from which he made his escape 'in a most daring way' (GM, 1802). A reward of £500 was offered for his recapture, but nothing was heard of him until, in the following year, he offered himself as pilot to the military expedition to The Helder to engage Napoleon's troops. His offer was accepted; he received a free pardon, and performed the duty to the great satisfaction of the officers in command, especially, it is said, of Sir Ralph Abercromby. He is described as then launching out into an extravagant way of living and contracting debts to the amount of £11,000; in 1802 he was imprisoned for debt in the Fleet Prison. Having resumed smuggling, and fearing to stand trial for this capital offence, he effected his escape, and succeeded in reaching the coast and in getting a passage to Calais; from there he went to Flushing, where he seems to have remained an outlaw, until in 1809 he again offered his services to pilot the Walcheren expedition. For the second time he received a free pardon, and after the satisfactory performance of the duty he was granted a pension of £100 a year, conditional on his abstaining from smuggling. He died in Vauxhall Bridge Road, London, in March 1839, aged sixty-seven.

J. K. LAUGHTON, rev. J. GILLILAND

Sources GM, 1st ser., 72 (1802), 1156–7 · GM, 2nd ser., 11 (1839), 553 · Ward, Men of the reign

Johnson, Dr. See Johnson, Samuel (1709–1784).

Johnson, Mr. See Forster, Sir Richard, first baronet (1585?–1661).

Johnson, Alan Woodworth (1917–1982), organic chemist, was born at South Shields on 29 September 1917, the eldest in the family of three sons and a daughter of James William Johnson and his wife, Jean Woodworth. His father worked as a nautical optician and had a lifelong connection with the National Adult School Union, of which he became president in 1936.

Johnson won a scholarship to Morpeth grammar school, but his family was not wealthy enough to support him through a university education and so, on leaving school, he entered industry. He worked for a year as a laboratory assistant at Swan Hunter and then as an analyst at Thomas Hedley & Co., while studying part-time at Rutherford Technical College. A scholarship and some additional help from a local benefactor got him to Imperial College, London, where he became a royal scholar the following year. A first-class BSc (1938) was followed by a university research studentship and a PhD (1940).

Johnson went to work for ICI as a research assistant with Ian Heilbron and Ewart R. H. Jones on acetylene chemistry and the synthesis of vitamin A. In spite of wartime hardships this was a very fruitful time for the development of Johnson's scientific and cultural interests, the latter in close association with the neighbouring Royal College of Music. Johnson married in 1941, Lucy Ida Celia, daughter of William Lionel Gaulton Bennett, who was of independent means. They had a daughter and a son.

In 1942 Johnson moved to Manchester to work in the ICI dyestuffs division. Here he benefited from contact with a number of talented chemists and worked with J. D. Rose on acetylene chemistry in the new exploratory research section. He burned much midnight oil writing his two-volume *The Chemistry of the Acetylenic Compounds* (1946 and 1950), timely works in a newly developing area of organic chemistry.

In 1946 Johnson went to Cambridge as one of the first ICI fellows and later became an assistant director of research (1948) and a fellow of Christ's College (1951). There A. R. Todd introduced him to the chemistry of natural products with studies on insect pigments. Over the following years Johnson applied many novel techniques to a range of problems. Microbial metabolites, from *Penicillium* species, led to studies on aromaticity, while actinomycins gave him experience in polypeptide research. His great opportunity came with vitamin B12, at that time perceived as a terrifyingly large and complex molecule. Degradation fragments isolated at Cambridge were vital in elucidating the vitamin's complete structure; most importantly, these researches brought to his notice fundamental problems of corrin and porphyrin synthesis which occupied Johnson for the rest of his career in chairs at Nottingham (1955–68) and Sussex (1968–82) universities. As head of the chemistry department at Nottingham he was involved in the design of a new building, and at Brighton he was also honorary director of the Agricultural Research Council Institute of Invertebrate Chemistry and Physiology.

Johnson was active in the Chemical Society (later the Royal Society of Chemistry). More than two-thirds of his publications appeared in its journal, and he was its honorary secretary (1958–65), vice-president (1965–8), and finally president (1977–8). He gave four of the society's named lectures and received the Meldola medal (1946) and its award for synthetic organic chemistry (1972). Elected FRS in 1965, he served three times on the Royal Society's council, and was a vice-president (1981–2) and Davy medallist (1980). His industrial connections were continuous, and he became a member of the National Research Development Corporation in 1976 and the National Enterprise Board from 1981.

Johnson was remarkably and perennially youthful in appearance and spirit and those who came into contact with him were affected by the enthusiasm he radiated and his deep love for chemistry. He was considered by contemporaries a grand social ice-breaker but behind his cheerful and informal approach there was a dedicated and hard-working scientist. Johnson died at his home, Highfields, Mays Corner, Selmeston, Sussex, on 5 December 1982, two months after his retirement.

E. R. H. JONES, rev.

Sources E. Jones and R. Bonnett, *Memoirs FRS*, 30 (1984), 319–48 · personal knowledge (1990) · CGPLA Eng. & Wales (1983)
Likenesses photograph, c.1967, RS · G. Argent, photograph, 1977, RS, 77 Jers 7959-19
Wealth at death £35,609: administration, 9 Sept 1983, CGPLA Eng. & Wales

Johnson, Alexander (*bap.* 1716, *d.* 1799), physician and advocate of resuscitation, was baptized on 13 September 1716 in the English church at The Hague, in the Netherlands, the sixth and youngest child of Thomas Johnson (1676/7–1735), publisher, and his wife, Jane Weems or Wemyss (1685/6–1756). His parents were British, residing in Holland. The family moved to Rotterdam in 1728 and after his father's death Alexander assisted his mother in the business. On 6 June 1740 Johnson married Mary Pellins or Pillans, of London, in the English Presbyterian Church, Rotterdam. Their third son was the collector Richard *Johnson. In 1741 he established himself at The Hague, where he encountered legal and financial difficulties, which came to a head in 1745. After a brief visit to England, he abandoned publishing and became a notary, advocate, and agent for the Scots brigade in the Netherlands, a post in which he was succeeded by his son Alexander. On 30 June 1769 he graduated MD at King's College, Aberdeen. By 1773 Johnson and his family were living in London.

Like other contemporary medical men, Johnson was inspired by the example of the Amsterdam Society, founded in 1767, for the resuscitation of the apparently drowned. In 1773 he published *An Account of some Societies at Amsterdam and Hamburgh for the Recovery of Drowned Persons*, which contained numerous accounts of successful resuscitations, many of them performed by people without medical training. He also published his *Proposals*, which set out his ideas for founding a similar society in England to disseminate knowledge of resuscitation procedures among the general population and to reward attempts to put them into practice. Later that year, Thomas Cogan, while acknowledging Johnson's priority, published his own translation of the Amsterdam Society's proceedings. Johnson's correspondence with the Amsterdam Society in 1774 indicated that his plans were far advanced, but on 18 April Cogan and William Hawes founded the institution that later became the Royal Humane Society. The preface to the *Gentleman's Magazine* (1774) welcomed this initiative but regretted the loss of an earlier opportunity when 'a gentleman who studied and practised physic abroad' (presumably Johnson) had proposed a similar plan. Despite the neglect of his scheme, Johnson continued to publish on resuscitation, often distributing instructions at his own expense. He claimed that the Humane Society's instructions for the general public were confusing, self-contradictory, and dangerous, its organization cumbersome and extravagant, and its reliance on professional men excessive. In *Relief from Accidental Death* (1785) he observed, 'it is a sad apology for the loss of a human life, to say the *medical assistant* came too late' (A. Johnson, *Relief from Accidental Death*, 1785, 7). The Humane Society ignored him; the fact that there is no mention of Johnson in their early publications, which display interest in all other aspects of resuscitation, appears to be the result of deliberate policy. Nevertheless, Johnson enjoyed international respect, exchanging courtesies with the Amsterdam Society and becoming FRSE in 1792. He was also a founding member of the Literary Fund for Distressed Authors. He died at his home in 10 Charlotte Street, Portland Place, London, and was buried in the cemetery of St Marylebone Church, on 15 September 1799.

CAROLYN D. WILLIAMS

Sources E. F. Kossmann, *De boekhandel te 's-Gravenhage tot het eind van de 18 de Eeuw* (1937) · *GM*, 1st ser., 69 (1799), 820 · *Resuscitation: an historical perspective* (1976) · J. A. Kool, *Geschiedkundige beschouwing van de matschappij tot Redding van Drenkelingen, te Amsterdam* (1854) · preface, *GM*, 1st ser., 44 (1774) [on 'the recovery of drowned persons'] · Letter to Sir Robert M. Keith, 28 May 1773, BL, MS Add. 35505, fol. 280 · Letter to Sir Robert M. Keith, 18 Aug 1778, BL, MS Add. 35514, fol. 251 · Letter to Dr Wride, 15 March 1784, BL, MS Add. 48707, fol. 8 · P. J. Anderson, ed., *Officers and graduates of University and King's College, Aberdeen, MVD–MDCCCLX*, New Spalding Club, 11 (1893) · burial register, Marylebone, London, 15 Sept 1799, LMA, 15 Sept 1799 · IGI · Marylebone parish rate books

Archives BL, Add. MSS 35505, fol. 280; 35514, fol. 251; 48707, fol. 8

Johnson, Alfred Edward Webb-, Baron Webb-Johnson (1880–1958), surgeon, was born at Stoke-on-Trent on 4 September 1880, the second son and third of eight children of Samuel Johnson, medical officer of health for the town, and his wife, Julia Ann, daughter of James Webb, army agent. He added his mother's surname to his own in 1915. Educated at Newcastle under Lyme high school and Owens College, Manchester, he graduated MB, ChB, with honours, in 1903, and won the Dumville surgical prize and the Tom Jones scholarship in surgery. He was a surgical registrar at the Manchester Royal Infirmary, became FRCS in 1906, and successfully applied for the post of resident medical officer at the Middlesex Hospital, London, in

1908. Only three years later he was elected assistant surgeon. He developed his lifelong interest in urological surgery at St Peter's Hospital, London. On 23 November 1911 he married Cecilia Flora MacRae (1889/90–1968), daughter of Douglas Gordon MacRae, founder of the *Financial Times*; they had no children.

In 1914 Johnson was called up for service in the Royal Army Medical Corps, and he became colonel, Army Medical Services, and consulting surgeon to the expeditionary force. He was appointed DSO (1916), thrice mentioned in dispatches, and appointed CBE (1919). Later he became consultant surgeon to the Queen Alexandra Military Hospital and to the Royal Hospital, Chelsea, and he was chairman of the army medical advisory board from 1946 to 1957.

In 1919 Webb-Johnson was made dean of the Middlesex Hospital medical school and at once, with the help of wealthy benefactors, established university chairs of physics, chemistry, anatomy, physiology, pathology, and biochemistry. He also saw the advantage of having properly developed special departments in a general hospital and started the urological clinic at the Middlesex. He ended his term of office as dean in 1925, the year in which serious defects were discovered in the foundations of the old hospital. He became chairman of the planning committee: with the slogan 'The Middlesex Hospital is falling down' he helped to raise most of the £1.25 million needed. On the completion of the building in 1935 the board took the unprecedented step of naming his own ward after him while he was still on the active staff. In 1946 he retired and was appointed consulting surgeon and vice-president.

At the Royal College of Surgeons of England, Webb-Johnson was a member of the court of examiners (1926–36) and of the council (1932–50). In 1941 he was elected president, a position which he held for a record period of eight years. The college had been severely damaged in an air raid, and in planning the rebuilding Webb-Johnson reorganized and expanded the college as a centre of postgraduate education and research. The primary examination for the fellowship was reorganized and reciprocity with other colleges established. Then specialist associations were provided with a secretariat and representatives of the major surgical specialities and of general practice were co-opted to serve on the council. Faculties were established for dental surgery (1947) and for anaesthetists (1948); specialist examinations were designed for the fellowship in ophthalmology and in otolaryngology (1947); appointments of professors were made in physiology, pathology, and anatomy; and the Nuffield College of Surgical Sciences was built, to provide residential accommodation for the increased number of postgraduate students coming from overseas. All these bore witness to his vision and tireless efforts. Overseas ties were strengthened by the endowment of the Sims travelling professorships in 1946 and by the foundation in 1947 of the college's own monthly *Annals*. However, his ambition to establish an academy of medicine on the south side of Lincoln's Inn Fields was never realized. This was owing in part to the mutual dislike that existed between Webb-Johnson and Lord Moran, president of the Royal College of Physicians, the latter being driven to exclaim 'what an oaf the fellow is' after a particularly frustrating meeting (Lovell, 255).

During the delicate period just prior to the introduction of the National Health Service in 1948, Webb-Johnson mediated between Aneurin Bevan, minister of health, and the British Medical Association (BMA) over negotiations between the two sides concerning the regulations under which the service would operate. Lord Moran's biographer concedes that Moran 'would have liked to be seen as the prime mover but Webb-Johnson at this stage was no less enterprising as a conciliator' (Lovell, 301).

From 1950 to 1952 Webb-Johnson was president of the Royal Society of Medicine and, inevitably perhaps, he was the chairman of the building committee when funds were forthcoming from the Wellcome trustees for an enlargement of the society's premises; this was completed in 1953.

Webb-Johnson's achievements as an administrator and organizer and, as a contemporary once said, 'one of the most successful beggars one could imagine' (private information), have tended to divert attention from the fact that he was first and foremost a surgeon. His judgement was sound and his technique faultless; his opinion was frequently sought by his colleagues and he excelled in the management of a difficult case. His ready wit, imperturbability, and unfailing good humour and sympathy made him loved by his patients. His lectures and ward rounds were always popular.

From 1936 to 1953 Webb-Johnson was surgeon to Queen Mary. He was knighted in 1936; appointed KCVO in 1942 and GCVO in 1954; and created a baronet in 1945 and a baron in 1948. He delivered the Syme oration to the Royal Australasian College of Surgeons in 1939. He received the honorary fellowship of that college, and of the corresponding colleges in America, Edinburgh, Glasgow, Ireland, and Canada, and of the faculties of dental surgery and of anaesthetists in England. He was made an honorary LLD of Liverpool and of Toronto, was awarded the honorary medal of the Royal College of Surgeons in 1950, and in 1956 was one of the first members of its newly formed court of patrons. After leaving the council of the college he became a trustee of the Hunterian Collection. His other interests led him to become president of the Royal Medical Benevolent Fund and in 1951 of Epsom College (for which he organized a successful appeal). He played a prominent part in the activities of the order of St John, becoming hospitaller (1946–54) and receiving the grand cross of the order in 1955.

Webb-Johnson was a man of great charm, slow to anger but ready to give a reprimand when needed. He was always immaculate in dress and his cartoon in the hospital journal bore the title of 'The Groomy Dean'. At one time a director of the Savoy Theatre, and a frequent visitor to Covent Garden, he was a recognized authority on the silver treasures of the Royal College of Surgeons. He had a deep knowledge of the Bible and of Shakespeare, and loved Kipling. Webb-Johnson died at his home, 70 Portland Place, London, on 28 May 1958, survived by his wife. As there were no children the peerage became extinct.

ERIC RICHES, *rev.* MICHAEL HOBSLEY

Sources Z. Cope, *The Royal College of Surgeons of England: a history* (1959) • R. H. O. B. Robinson and W. R. Le Fanu, *Lives of the fellows of the Royal College of Surgeons of England, 1952–1964* (1970) • D. Ranger, *The Middlesex Hospital medical school, 1935–1985* (1985) • H. Campbell-Thompson, *The story of the Middlesex Hospital medical school, 1835–1935* (1935) • M. Davidson, *The Royal Society of Medicine* (1955) • *The Times* (29 May 1958) • *The Lancet* (7 June 1958) • *BMJ* (7 June 1958), 1357–9 • private information (1971, 1996) • personal knowledge (1971) • R. Lovell, *Churchill's doctor: a biography of Lord Moran* (1992) • *CGPLA Eng. & Wales* (1958) • m. cert.

Archives Middlesex Hospital, archives • UCL, department of medicine, Middlesex Hospital medical school | RCS Eng., corresp. with Sir Edward Mellanby

Likenesses F. Hodge, oils, 1943, RCS Eng. • T. C. Dugdale, oils, 1952, Royal Society of Medicine, London • F. Hodge, oils, *c.*1954, Middlesex Hospital, London • Miss Howson, stained-glass window, 1964, Middlesex Hospital, London

Wealth at death £28,341 15*s.* 0*d.*: probate, 31 July 1958, *CGPLA Eng. & Wales*

Johnson [*married name* Mollison], **Amy** (1903–1941), aviator, was born on 1 July 1903 at 154 St George's Road, Kingston upon Hull, Yorkshire, the eldest of three daughters of John William Johnson (*d.* in or after 1941), a well-to-do herring importer, and his wife, Amy Hodge. She attended the Boulevard secondary school in Hull, and then, having graduated from Sheffield University in 1925, she worked in a solicitor's office. By then she had been smitten by the romance of flying. She joined the technical school of the De Havilland (DH) aircraft company at Stag Lane, London, and in 1927 she received the first licensed engineer's certificate awarded by the Air Ministry to a woman. This 'slip of a girl' from Yorkshire was just what Geoffrey de Havilland needed to assure the public that anyone, not just Sir Alan Cobham, could safely fly the reliable Moths that his company was producing. While at the DH-owned London Aeroplane Club at Stag Lane, she met the enthusiastic director of civil aviation, Sir Sefton Brancker, and Sir Charles Wakefield of Castrol, who, along with the Royal Dutch-Shell Oil Company, backed her attempt to break the light aeroplane record in a solo flight to Australia.

On 5 May 1930, after less than 100 hours' solo flying, Amy Johnson set out from Croydon in her two-year-old Gipsy Moth light biplane, *Jason*, to try to break Squadron Leader Bert Hinkler's 1928 England-to-Australia record of fifteen and a half days. She was two days ahead of Hinkler's time when she arrived at Karachi, India, on 10 May after flying through bad weather that forced her to land for two hours in the desert. She safely reached Calcutta and then hoped to fly non-stop to Rangoon and on to Singapore but was delayed at Rangoon and then again in Java by bad weather, shortages of fuel, and damage. Finally, having landed at Port Darwin, Australia, after nineteen and a half days, Johnnie was given a tumultuous reception. A private person, she found that adulation was not only embarrassing but also, between one leg of her journey and another, deprived her of time for vital sleep on these physically demanding flights. Her flight aroused

Amy Johnson (1903–1941), by John Capstack, c.1933–5

widespread enthusiasm: congratulations came from George V, she was appointed CBE that same year, and the *Daily Mail* made her a gift of £10,000. Later she crashed her plane at Brisbane, and James Allan *Mollison (1905–1959), another record-breaking aviator, flew her to Sydney; she subsequently married Mollison on 29 July 1932. On her return to England she was met by Lord Thomson, secretary of state for air.

Despite her success it is clear that Amy Johnson never acquired solid navigational skills. These were in short supply—even the RAF had only fourteen professional navigators—and her flying was either track or coastline flying, admittedly over difficult terrain. Nevertheless her very striking first feat was the forerunner of other remarkable long-distance flights. On 26 July 1931, accompanied by C. S. Humphreys as mechanic in *Jason II*, she departed for Tokyo via the Soviet Union and arrived on 6 August in 78 hours and 50 minutes' flying time. On 14 November 1932 she set out from Lympne, in Kent, for Cape Town by the shorter west African route and covered the 6200 miles in her Puss Moth in 4 days, 6 hours, and 54 minutes, thus beating her husband's record by 10 hours. She returned up the Imperial east coast route between 11 and 18 December.

On 22 July 1933 the Mollisons left Pendine (Pen-tywyn) Sands, Carmarthenshire, in an attempt to fly a heavily loaded ten-seat DH Dragon, *Seafarer*, to New York. Unfortunately, 39 hours later, having run out of petrol, they were forced to land at Bridgeport, Connecticut, and flipped

over in a swamp. Although the very tired pair did not reach New York they had set a record as the first husband and wife team to cross the Atlantic westbound as well as making the first direct UK–USA flight by plane, achieving five other firsts. Meanwhile the accident scotched their hopes of flying non-stop from New York to Baghdad.

During the later 1930s Amy and her husband continued to pursue other records, at a time when there were still only sixty women among 2000 amateur pilots in the UK. In late October 1934 they entered their own twin-engined DH Comet (which had cost them £5000) in the MacRobertson Mildenhall-to-Melbourne 22,000 mile race. First off and the leader to India, their navigation failed them, as it had over Nova Scotia in 1933. They landed *Black Magic* at Allahabad, where they had to withdraw from the race owing to engine failure.

By late 1934 Amy's marriage had broken down. Her husband was a playboy flyer, who had used her to build his fame, but was unfaithful. They both craved success and all that went with it, and Mollison drank heavily. The Bridgeport crash was the beginning of a rift that led Amy to seek a divorce. A *decree nisi* was granted on 7 February 1938 on grounds of her husband's adultery; Amy subsequently reverted to her maiden name. In 1936 she entered the king's cup race in a new British Aircraft Eagle monoplane but was not among the leading finishers. At the same time her 1930 Australian record was beaten by Jean Batten. She made another flight to Cape Town between 4 and 7 May 1936 in a Percival Gull. She arrived in Cape Town in 3 days, 6 hours, and 11 minutes (or 6400 miles outbound in 54 hours, 57 minutes), her round trip beating the outbound, homebound, and double-flight records. In 1939 she was the author of *Skyroads of the World*; nevertheless by this time she was beginning to move out of the limelight.

During her remarkable flying career Amy Johnson received many honours. These included the president's gold medal of the Society of Engineers (1931), the Egyptian gold medal for valour (1930), the women's trophy of the International League of Aviators (1930), the Segrave trophy (1933), the gold medal of honour of the League of Youth (1933), and the gold medal of the Royal Aero Club (1936). A Women's Engineering Society (WES) scholarship for women in aeronautics was established in her name in February 1941, following her death.

One of the founders of the WES in 1927 Johnson served as its president from 1934 to 1937. In May 1938, as the prospect of war loomed, she was appointed national leader of the Women's Air Reserve and undertook many training flights. However it was not until March 1940 that her friend Pauline Gower asked her to join the select Air Transport Auxiliary (ATA). In this role she shuttled planes back and forth from Hatfield, near the ATA base at White Waltham, to Prestwick.

Her last flight was on 5 January 1941, in an ATA Airspeed Oxford. She was warned by flying control at Squire's Gate, Blackpool, about the adverse weather conditions but, as the pilot, she chose to ignore that. Unfortunately the cloud and fog did not clear and she lost her way. Forced to bale out, unfortunately over the Thames estuary, where a pilot could not expect to survive for long, she would have drowned or died of hypothermia. Her body was never found. A memorial service for her was held at St Martin-in-the-Fields nine days later.

Amy Johnson was a heroine of the romantic age of aviation. Her image was one of a petite, photogenic pilot and mechanic, a pioneer feminist and sportswoman; she had a veneer of success in an age needing stars. With hindsight, however, a more complex figure has been revealed. According to a fellow ATA pilot, Lettice Curtis, Johnson was often insecure and unhappy. More seriously her skills as a mechanic and pilot were hands-on; she was neither a fine pilot nor a sound navigator. Amy Johnson took risks, and in the end this killed her. Nevertheless because of the indomitable record-breaking and the mystery surrounding her death she became and remains, a legendary figure.   ROBIN HIGHAM

Sources The Times (8 Jan 1941) · The Aeroplane (1930–41) · G. Dorman, Fifty years fly past: from Wright brothers to Comet (1950) · A. Johnson, Skyroads of the world (1939) · J. A. Mollison, Playboy of the air (1937) · G. de Havilland, Sky fever: the autobiography of Sir Geoffrey de Havilland (1961) · C. M. Sharp, DH: an outline of De Havilland history (1960) · Journal of the Royal Aeronautical Society, 70 (1966) · A. J. Jackson, De Havilland aircraft since 1909 (1978) · C. Babington-Smith, Amy Johnson (1967) · L. Curtis, The forgotten pilots: a story of the Air Transport Auxiliary, 1939–45 (1971) · CGPLA Eng. & Wales (1944) · b. cert. · DNB · D. Luff, Mollison: the flying Scotsman, new edn, 2000 (1993)

Archives Inst. EE, Women's Engineering Society, papers · Royal Air Force Museum, Hendon, logbooks, corresp., and papers · Sowerby Hall Park, trophies · Hull, trophies · Bridlington, trophies | Royal Air Force Museum, Hendon, corresp. and papers relating to Constance Babington Smith's biography of her

Likenesses photographs, 1930–41, Hult. Arch. · group portrait, photograph, 1933 (Injured aviatrix), Hult. Arch. · J. Capstack, photograph, c.1933–1935, NPG [see illus.] · J. A. A. Berrie, oils, priv. coll. · photograph, repro. in The Aeroplane (14 May 1930) · photograph, repro. in The Aeroplane (26 July 1933) · photograph, repro. in The Aeroplane (8 July 1936)

Wealth at death £4313 17s. 2d.: probate, 5 April 1944, CGPLA Eng. & Wales

Johnson, Benjamin (1664/5–1742), actor, was probably born in London, although as no details of his parentage are known it is impossible to be certain; he was said to be seventy-seven when he died. He was 'bred a Painter, where his Employment led him to paint, under his Master, the Scenes for the Stage' (Chetwood, 174). This gave him a taste for the theatre, and he may have joined a touring company. No evidence of his performances has been found until, soon after the departure of Thomas Betterton and others to Lincoln's Inn Fields, he is listed as taking the role of Sir Simon Barter in Thomas Scott's The Mock Marriage at Drury Lane in September 1695. The range of parts he played suggests that he was already an experienced actor before he joined Christopher Rich's company. In the same season he was the original Captain Driver in Thomas Southerne's Oroonoko and Sir William Wisewood in Colley Cibber's Love's Last Shift. In December 1696 he was the first Coupler in John Vanbrugh's The Relapse, and in the next few years he initiated parts in other new plays, above all

those by George Farquhar: Lyric in Love and a Bottle, Smuggler in The Constant Couple, Fireball in Sir Harry Wildair, and Balderdash and Alderman in The Twin Rivals.

The publication of Jeremy Collier's Short View of the Immorality and Profaneness of the English Stage in 1698 drew attention to James I's statute against blasphemy, and led to charges against 'Betterton, Bracegirdle, Ben Johnson and others' (Genest, Eng. stage, 3.124) for performing obscene and profane plays. Johnson, alone of the three, was acquitted. He continued to perform at Drury Lane, adding to his repertory roles that included Gardiner in Henry VIII and the Anabaptist Ananias in Ben Jonson's The Alchemist. The actor appears to have enjoyed parts written by his namesake, as he was also praised for his Morose in Epicene and Corbaccio in Volpone. Gildon put into the mouth of Betterton: 'I once saw Mr Benjamin Johnson (our present Roscius) act Numphs [Humphry Wasp in Bartholomew Fair] with such an Engagement in the Part, that I could not persuade myself, that it was acting but the Reality' (Gildon, 38–9).

On 11 April 1709 Johnson signed a contract with Owen Swiny to act at the Queen's Theatre for the next five years for £100 per year, with a vacation from June to September and an annual benefit. Following management changes he was back at Drury Lane in November 1710. Among the roles he created in the ensuing decade was Fossile in Three Hours after Marriage, by Alexander Pope, John Gay, and John Arbuthnot. In 1735 Johnson and some others considered renting the Drury Lane theatre from Charles Fleetwood. It did not come about, but was probably the motive for his signature on a petition against the Licensing Act at that time.

Johnson was celebrated for his 'excellent voice, great majesty in his deportment, and a very fine figure, but enormously large' (Hill, The Actor, 1755, 150) and 'large speaking blue eyes' (Highfill, Burnim & Langhans, BDA). A tradition grew up, by the time that Thomas Davies wrote his Dramatic Miscellanies, that he had been of a generous and easy-going nature, and was thus easily exploited by Cibber, Thomas Doggett, and Robert Wilks, who tended to drop plays in which he had success and squeeze him out of desirable parts. However, it is disputed whether this was actually the case, and the snide remark in A Comparison between the Two Stages that Johnson had 'the vice of all actors, he is too fond of his own merit' might suggest that those who sought to reduce the roles that Johnson played were dealing with a prickly character.

Very little is known of Johnson's personal life. Though he valued the associations of the name, it is unlikely that he was related to the playwright. On 4 January 1702 Richard, the son of Benjamin and Mary Johnson, was baptized at St Paul's, Covent Garden, but there is no record that Johnson was married, so the name (a common one) is probably a coincidence. Johnson died at Kensington Wells, London, on 31 July 1742. In his will he left a small bequest to his sister and her husband and the rest of his estate to his goddaughter, Margaret Callow, a spinster. She may have been the 'Johnson's daughter' for whom a benefit was held at Drury Lane on 15 December 1742.

Commentators remembered Johnson as a performer who 'never seemed to know that he was before an audience; he drew his character as the poet designed it' (Davies, *Memoirs*, 1.30). Hill's comment 'He never appeared upon the stage, without being the greatest player on it' (Hill, *The Actor*, 1750, 86) is perhaps excessive for a man whose career began in the days of Betterton and ended on the cusp of the age of Garrick, but it indicated great quality and consistency. It may, also, be another reference to Johnson's being 'enormously large'.   F. H. MARES

Sources Highfill, Burnim & Langhans, *BDA*, vol. 8 · W. Van Lennep and others, eds., *The London stage, 1660–1800*, pt 1: 1660–1700 (1965) · E. L. Avery, ed., *The London stage, 1660–1800*, pt 2: 1700–1729 (1960) · C. Gildon, *The life of Mr Thomas Betterton* (1710) · Genest, *Eng. stage*, vol. 3 · J. Downes, *Roscius Anglicanus*, ed. J. Milhous and R. D. Hume, new edn (1987) · C. Cibber, *An apology for the life of Mr Colley Cibber*, new edn, ed. E. Bellchambers (1822) · T. Davies, *Memoirs of the life of David Garrick*, 2 vols. (1808) · [J. Hill], *The actor: a treatise on the art of playing* (1750) · [J. Hill], *The actor, or, A treatise on the art of playing* (1755) · T. Davies, *Dramatic miscellanies*, 3 vols. (1784) · W. R. Chetwood, *A general history of the stage, from its origin in Greece to the present time* (1749) · *A comparison between the two stages* (1702)
Likenesses L. Laguerre, print, 1733 · P. van Bleeck, double portrait, oils, *c*.1738 (with B. Griffin), Garr. Club · P. van Bleeck, mezzotint, 1748, BM, NPG
Wealth at death see will, 20 April 1742, Highfill, Burnim & Langhans, *BDA*

Johnson [*née* Todd], **Bertha Jane** (1846–1927), promoter of women's higher education, was born at 3 New Street, Charing Cross, London, on 20 January 1846, the third of four children of the Irish physician Robert Bentley *Todd FRS (1809–1860), professor of physiology at King's College, London, and his wife, Elizabeth Hart. Dr Todd was a pioneering advocate of nursing education and it was a home 'where there was very much the tradition of equal advantages and opportunities for girls and boys, men and women' (*The Ship*, December 1921, 35). The two elder girls were the first pupils at Elizabeth Sewell's school on the Isle of Wight, but Bertha was educated at home, sharing a tutor and drill lessons with her younger brother James before he went to Eton College. Her own talents were in the arts. Taught by a musical aunt, she became an accomplished pianist. She was among the early women students at the Slade School of Art and several of her paintings were exhibited at the Royal Academy.

On 16 April 1873 Bertha Todd married an Eton contemporary of James's, the Revd Arthur Henry Johnson (1845–1927), the second son of Captain George John Johnson of the Grenadier Guards. Johnson, now chaplain of All Souls College and, over the years, lecturer in modern history at several Oxford colleges, was a keen sportsman, naturalist, and gardener—once described as a 'country gentleman in Holy Orders' (Goldman, 33). He shared with Bertha qualities of vitality and charm and a gift for friendship and hospitality that gave them a prominent place in university society.

The introduction of women students into an ancient residential university, already pioneered at Cambridge by Henry Sidgwick and Emily Davies, was a challenge that appealed to the 'young married Oxford' of the 1870s. The birth of the Johnsons' two sons, Robert Arthur and George

Wilfrid, did not prevent Bertha from serving on the committees that ran lecture courses for ladies from 1874, setting up the more ambitious Association for Promoting the Higher Education of Women in Oxford (AEW) in 1878, and founding the Anglican hostel Lady Margaret Hall, which opened, together with the undenominational Somerville Hall, in 1879. The success of these women's societies, not formally recognized by the university until 1910, depended on voluntary support from dons and their wives. Assisted by her husband, who delivered the first lecture in the series of 1874 and tutored women students until 1922, Bertha Johnson made it her life's work. She was secretary to Lady Margaret Hall from 1880 to 1914, and at first in effect domestic bursar, overseeing the economical running of the household. As lady secretary to the AEW (1883–94) she organized tuition for rapidly growing numbers of women students, and supervised those who were not attached to a hall but lived at home or with 'hostesses' in the city. Her encouragement also played a part in the success of two further Anglican women's halls, St Hugh's, opened in 1886 by Elizabeth Wordsworth, and St Hilda's, founded in 1893 by Dorothea Beale. But the welfare of 'home students', as they were known after 1889, became her particular concern. In 1894 she was appointed by the AEW as their principal. In 1910, when a delegacy for women students was set up and home students came under the control of the university, she became as principal of the Society of Oxford Home-Students (SOHS) the first woman with a senior university appointment. She held this post—always, at her own insistence, without payment—until she retired at seventy-five in 1921. In 1920, when women were admitted to membership of the university, she was the first of the five women principals to receive the MA by decree.

Mrs Johnson came to be regarded as a conservative figure in the movement for women's education even by many Oxford friends and admirers. A unionist in her politics and a lifelong devotee of the fashions of the 1870s— Liberty gowns and William Morris wallpapers—she could be tenacious in resisting changes to the regime adopted in the early days for women students. She attached importance to careful chaperonage, and to the AEW's role in arranging the teaching of women by men dons; she thought women should follow courses specially devised for the individual rather than the curriculum of the male undergraduates. Her resignation as the AEW's lady secretary in 1894 was the outcome of a clash with the council and principal of Somerville, who challenged her control of tuition arrangements as the hall developed into a college with its own staff of women tutors. With her husband she became in 1895–6 an influential opponent of a bid to secure the admission of women to the Oxford BA degree. In this debate there were arguments that appealed to other supporters of the AEW (and to Henry and Eleanor Sidgwick at Cambridge) against subjecting women to the rigid requirements of the degree course, including compulsory Latin and Greek. But in 1897 Mrs Johnson was the only woman educationist to support a proposal—made by opponents of degrees for women at Oxford and Cambridge and viewed with dismay by the established women's societies—for a separate degree-awarding university for women. Speaking as the mother of two undergraduate sons (Robert was president of the Oxford Union in 1897), she defended this scheme above all on the grounds that even well-wishers of women's higher education opposed the idea of co-education.

> University men are not willing that women should share fully in the life of the Universities. ... It may be right or it may be wrong, but the fact remains that we are no more liked now than when we began ... [To] bring highly educated girls into disfavour with the majority of highly educated young men, may be found to be a dangerous thing for our nation. (*University Degrees for Women: Report of a Conference Convened by the Governors of Royal Holloway College*, 4 Dec 1897, 52–3, Bertha Johnson MSS)

Bertha Johnson was not among the Oxford women who followed Mrs Humphry Ward in opposing women's suffrage—in 1894 she chaired a drawing-room meeting in support of a suffrage petition—and family pressures evidently helped to shape her views on the place of women in Oxford. But she was no egalitarian—'The imitation of men by women has always seemed to me to be a poor thing' (speech to women students' debating society, 1 Dec 1895, Bertha Johnson MSS). Nor was she much moved by the argument that an Oxford degree would be valuable to the professional woman. Her own career exemplified instead the opportunities that opened within the voluntary sector to upper-middle-class women of her generation. She became Headington's first woman poor-law guardian, president of the Oxford Working Women's Provident Society, and vice-president of the Oxford Charity Organization Society committee, and was an active and sympathetic workhouse and district visitor until the end of her life. She also served (1903–22) as a co-opted member of Oxfordshire county council's education committee. The SOHS was run from the Johnsons' comfortable and attractive home—first at 8 Merton Street, then at 5 South Parks Road—and her defence of the home student was always based on the conviction that there were 'considerations that make home life, even when the home is not our own, better for young women than College life' (*The Ship*, December 1921, 19).

By the early twentieth century, the SOHS was a diverse and growing society which included mature students, Roman Catholics based in a hostel run by nuns at Cherwell Edge, and increasing numbers of foreigners. The home students—seen by some critics as a threat to the university's policy of discouraging social contacts between male undergraduates and women, and by others as missing out on the college experience—gained some protection from Bertha Johnson's quietly autocratic regime, and appreciated her warm interest in individual students, past and present. The SOHS acquired its own common room in Ship Street (bought and presented by Arthur Johnson), and adopted as its motto that of Mrs Johnson's family, *Faire sans dire*. Twenty-five years after her death the society became Oxford's fifth women's college: St Anne's.

Despite Arthur Johnson's loyal support for her work, it cannot be assumed that there were no family tensions. Annie Rogers, the AEW's lady secretary from 1894, commented privately, 'If Mrs Johnson had been only a gentle and amiable person, I don't think she could ever have held her own against Mr. Johnson who was not very sympathetic with women's education' (Rogers to Butler, 27 Aug 1927, Rogers MSS). This fair, bespectacled woman with striking features and presence, fought her battles in middle life with 'a bit of temper' (ibid.), and remained formidable to the last. 'Her direct look, the power in her voice, the calm of her manner, her stately erect bearing were but the outward signs of a character of unnatural strength and self control' (*Oxford Chronicle*, 6 May 1927, 3). 'With all her simplicity and friendliness', wrote her obituarist in the *Oxford Magazine*, she had yet something of the 'great lady' (12 May 1927, 475). There were grandchildren, and her sons achieved professional success: Robert was knighted as deputy master of the Royal Mint and George became headmaster of Alleyne's School, Stevenage. But an obituarist claimed that in old age 'nothing gave her more pleasure than reminiscences of the old students' (*Oxford Chronicle*, 6 May 1927, 3). Bertha Johnson died of influenza at home in South Parks Road, Oxford, on 24 April 1927, less than three months after the death of her husband on 31 January, and was buried on 27 April with him in Holywell cemetery.   JANET HOWARTH

Sources R. F. Butler and M. H. Prichard, eds., *The Society of Oxford Home-Students: retrospects and recollections (1879–1921)* (1930) • G. Bailey, ed., *Lady Margaret Hall* (1923) • A. M. A. H. Rogers, *Degrees by degrees* (1938) • *The Ship* [St Anne's College, Oxford] (1911–27) • St Anne's College, Oxford, Bertha Johnson papers • *Oxford Chronicle and Berks and Bucks Gazette* (4 Feb 1927) [obit. of A. H. Johnson] • *Oxford Chronicle and Berks and Bucks Gazette* (29 April 1927) • 'The women's colleges: Mr. Arthur Johnson', *Oxford Chronicle and Berks and Bucks Gazette* (6 May 1927) • *The Times* (25 April 1927) • 'Mr Arthur Johnson', *Oxford Magazine* (12 May 1927) • St Anne's College, Annie Rogers papers • L. Goldman, *Dons and workers: Oxford and adult education since 1850* (1995) • *Hist. U. Oxf.* 7: *19th-cent. Oxf. pt 2* • b. cert. • m. cert. • d. cert.
Archives St Anne's College, Oxford | Lady Margaret Hall, Oxford, Elizabeth Wordsworth papers • St Anne's College, Oxford, Annie Rogers papers
Likenesses photograph, c.1880, repro. in Butler and Prichard, eds., *Society of Oxford Home-Students* • photograph, c.1890, St Anne's College, Oxford • A. L. Hodson, group portrait, 1909, repro. in Bailey, ed., *Lady Margaret Hall* • M. A. Egerton, pencil drawing, c.1920, St Anne's College, Oxford • J. de Glehn, coloured chalk drawings, 1921, St Anne's College, Oxford • photograph, 1921, St Anne's College, Oxford
Wealth at death £6140 13s.: probate, 15 July 1927, *CGPLA Eng. & Wales*

Johnson, Bryan Stanley William (1933–1973), writer, was born on 5 February 1933 in Queen Charlotte's Hospital, Goldhawk Road, Hammersmith, London, the only child of Stanley Wilfred Johnson (1908–1973), a bookseller's stock-keeper, and Emily Jane Lambird (1908–1971), a waitress, between-maid, and barmaid. Apart from a spell as a wartime evacuee in High Wycombe, which was to contribute to his emotional insecurity, and a later sojourn in Wales as the first Gregynog arts fellow at the University of Wales, Johnson lived in London all his life. He attended

Bryan Stanley William Johnson (1933–1973), by Ian Yeomans

lying, while his work tried to achieve what he simply called 'truth'. The introduction to his collection of short prose pieces, *Aren't you Rather Young to be Writing your Memoirs?* (1973) is something of a manifesto and contains his own account of his work. In it he writes that 'telling stories really is telling lies' and that:

> The two terms *novel* and *fiction* are not, incidentally, synonymous … the novel is a form in the same way that the sonnet is a form; within that form, one may write truth or fiction. I choose to write truth in the form of a novel.

In practice this meant an intrusive narrator, anti-illusionistic direct addresses to the reader, and an extreme self-reflexivity which constantly acknowledged its own artifice. He was much influenced by Sterne and Joyce, and by the prose of Samuel Beckett, with whom he corresponded.

'I object to the word experimental being applied to my own work', Johnson wrote in *Aren't you Rather Young to be Writing your Memoirs?* 'Certainly I make experiments but the unsuccessful ones are quietly hidden away'. Despite that, he was the best-known experimental writer of an avant-garde generation that included Ann Quin, Eva Figes, and Alan Burns, and was also involved with film, theatre, and television work as well as novels and poetry. He was disappointed that fame did not open up more journalistic opportunities, and chronic shortage of money forced him to work as a supply teacher: he even considered selling his letters from Beckett in 1971, but when he asked Beckett for permission, Beckett sent him money instead. Nevertheless his career was gradually consolidating, and after living in flats in Claremont Square and Myddelton Square, Finsbury, he bought a house in Dagmar Terrace, Islington, where he lived until his death.

Johnson was by his own description fat, and made a film entitled *Fat Man on a Beach*. He had a depressive streak, and remained resolutely working-class. He was aggressive in debate, brooking no dissent, and could be boorish to those he considered privileged. Even librarians attracted his resentment: 'And bollocks to librarians too', he wrote in a 1967 letter quoted by Zulfikhar Ghose; 'of all the ponces who feast off the dead body of literature … pay us fuckall and go out to lunch every day of the working week … the bleeding (though they have no lifeblood) librarians are the worst' (Ghose). Generalized resentment forms the basis of his very funny novel *Christie Malry's Own Double Entry* (1973).

Johnson's last major work, *See the Old Lady Decently* (published in 1975), was an experimental biography of his mother, who died of cancer in 1971. It was to be the first volume of the 'Matrix Trilogy', with its titles—*See the Old Lady Decently, Buried although, Amongst those Left are You*—to be read across the spines. It combines an account of a working-class life with the decline of the mother country and a meditation on archetypal motherhood. Although he was a staunch atheist, Johnson had a quasi-mystical feeling for the mother goddess, which was influenced by the work of Robert Graves and Erich Neumann. Women in Johnson's work are associated with a needed stability, but also with the threat of betrayal. Not long after completing

Flora Gardens primary school but having failed his eleven-plus examinations, he was sent to a technical secondary school until the age of sixteen. After a series of clerking jobs and a brush with national service he was inducted into the Royal Air Force but found unfit because of an ear problem. He educated himself to university level and at the age of twenty-three began reading English at King's College, London. From 1959, when he completed his degree, Johnson worked as a schoolteacher and sports journalist, reporting on football for *The Observer*. He married Virginia Ann Kimpton (*b.* 1938), a teaching machine programmer, the daughter of Arthur Ernest Kimpton, banker, on 31 March 1964; she figures as Ginnie in his novel *Trawl*. They had two children, Steven and Kate.

Johnson won the 1963 Gregory award with his first novel, *Travelling People*, which uses eight separate styles including interior monologue, epistolary, and film script, as well as grey and black pages to indicate unconsciousness and death. *Albert Angelo* (1964) used a special type-character to draw attention to physical descriptions, juxtaposed the thoughts of a teacher on one side of the page with his pupils' speech on the other, and revealed a future event, a stabbing, by means of a section cut through the intervening pages so that it could be read in advance. In 1967 he won the Somerset Maugham Award for *Trawl*. With the prize money, he and his family spent four months in France, mainly in Paris, where he met Samuel Beckett. His short film *You're Human Like the Rest of Them* won the 1968 grand prix of the Tours International Short Film Festival and the Melbourne International Short Film Festival. *The Unfortunates* (1969) is perhaps Johnson's most celebrated work, presenting the thoughts of a football reporter named B. S. Johnson as he remembers a friend who has died from cancer. To convey the randomness of the material and the chaotic nature of existence, Johnson composed the book of unbound sections in a box, to be read in any order.

Johnson maintained that conventional fiction was

See the Old Lady Decently, alone at the weekend, Johnson committed suicide on 13 November 1973 by cutting his wrists in the bath at home. He was cremated at Islington crematorium.   PHIL BAKER

Sources M. Bakewell, 'Introduction', in B. S. Johnson, *See the old lady decently* (1975) · B. S. Johnson, *Aren't you rather young to be writing your memoirs?* (1973) · private information (2004) [Bernard McGinley and Jonathan Coe] · Z. Ghose, 'B. S. Johnson', *Review of Contemporary Fiction*, 5 (1985) · M. P. Levitt, 'B. S. Johnson', *British novelists since 1960*, ed. J. L. Halio, DLitB, 14/1 (1983) · G. Gordon, *Aren't we due a royalty statement?* (1993) · *The Times* (15 Nov 1973) · m. cert. · P. Tew, *B. S. Johnson: a critical reading* (2001)
Archives King's Lond., corresp. and papers | FILM BBC WAC | SOUND BBC WAC [mainly plays written/adapted for radio]
Likenesses I. Yeomans, photograph, unknown collection; copyprint, NPG [*see illus.*]
Wealth at death £9621: administration, 23 Jan 1974, *CGPLA Eng. & Wales*

Johnson [*married name* Fleming], **Dame Celia Elizabeth** (1908–1982), actress, was born on 18 December 1908 at Richmond, Surrey, the younger daughter and second of three children of John Robert Johnson, physician, of Richmond, and his wife, Ethel, *née* Griffiths. She was educated at Miss Richmond's private school and then at St Paul's Girls' School, Hammersmith, London. Having obtained a GCE first-year award to the Royal Academy of Dramatic Art in London, she won, during her training there, a special prize as well as a French prize.

In 1928 Celia Johnson played her first professional part, Sarah in G. B. Shaw's *Major Barbara*, at the Theatre Royal in Huddersfield. The following year she went to London to take over from Angela Baddeley as Currita in *A Hundred Years Old*, at the Lyric Theatre, Hammersmith. In *Cynara* (1930) she stole the show from the two stars, Sir Gerald Du Maurier and Gladys Cooper. In 1931 she made her first trip to the United States to play Ophelia in *Hamlet*. Back in London the following year, she acted in *The Wind and the Rain*, a play set in a Scottish university. From that date she became a star, admired by all and unscarred by adverse criticism.

On 10 December 1935 Celia Johnson married (Robert) Peter *Fleming (1907–1971), journalist and travel writer, and the brother of the writer Ian *Fleming; both men were the sons of Major Valentine Fleming, a merchant banker and MP. She and her husband had one son and two daughters. With a young child to bring up during the war, and Fleming being overseas on active service, Celia Johnson faced difficulties. Typically, she solved them neatly. After playing Mrs de Winter in *Rebecca* in 1940 and then taking over from Vivien Leigh in *The Doctor's Dilemma* in 1942, she retired from the stage for five years, returning in 1947 to play the title role in *Saint Joan* with the Old Vic Company at the New Theatre. During the war she was an auxiliary policewoman. She starred in every kind of play, from Shakespeare to *Ten Minute Alibi* (1933), from Chekhov to *Flowering Cherry* (1957) by Robert Bolt. She also starred in four successful plays written by William Douglas-Home: *The Reluctant Debutante* (1955), *Lloyd George Knew my Father* (1972), *The Dame of Sark* (1974), and *The Kingfisher* (1977). She was, to put it in a single phrase, a playwright's dream.

Dame Celia Elizabeth Johnson (1908–1982), by John Springer, 1940s

As a film star Celia Johnson was equally successful as the captain's wife in *In which we Serve* (1942) and as the housewife in *Brief Encounter* (1945), in which, playing with Trevor Howard, she memorably caught the suppressed sexuality of English suburbia. Her other films included *A Kid for Two Farthings* (1955), *The Good Companions* (1956), and *The Prime of Miss Jean Brodie* (1969). She made over twenty appearances on television, giving excellent performances in *Mrs Palfrey at the Claremont* (1973), *The Dame of Sark* (1976), and *Staying on* (by Paul Scott, 1980), in which she appeared with Trevor Howard, her co-star in *Brief Encounter*. Although Celia Johnson's dedication to her calling was immediately apparent to her public in the theatre, it rested on her shoulders lightly in her private life, which was devoted to her family, who lived at Merrimoles House, Nettlebed, Oxfordshire. She would often come out of a play before the end of its run in order to be with them. She seldom talked about the theatre and, when she did, approached the subject with a gay irreverence. She was a person of outstanding charm, with wide eyes, a *retroussé* nose, and a remarkable voice. Extremely short-sighted, she wore thick lenses, though when she acted she never wore spectacles. To her amused delight she was appointed CBE in 1958 and, to her great surprise, DBE in 1981. She died on 25 April 1982, at Merrimoles House, while playing bridge one weekend, during a pre-London run, in harness to the end. A memorial service was held at St Martin-in-the-Fields, London, on 1 July 1982.   WILLIAM DOUGLAS-HOME, rev.

Sources personal knowledge (1990) · *The Times* (27 April 1982) · *The Times* (2 July 1982) · I. Herbert, ed., *Who's who in the theatre*, 16th edn (1977) · *WWW* · *CGPLA Eng. & Wales* (1982) · m. cert. · private information (2004)

Archives FILM BFI NFTVA, performance footage | SOUND BL NSA, performance recordings

Likenesses photographs, 1929–74, Hult. Arch. · J. Springer, photograph, 1940–49, Corbis [*see illus.*]

Wealth at death £150,557: probate, 16 Nov 1982, *CGPLA Eng. & Wales*

Johnson, Charles (1679?–1748), playwright and poet, about whose parents nothing is known, claimed to have been trained in law (Johnson, preface, *The Successful Pyrate*, 1713, sig. A2r). He was lodging in, or adjacent to, Gray's Inn when he published the first of two long poems, *Marlborough: on the Late Glorious Victory Near Hochstet in Germany*, in 1704; his second, *The Queen: a Pindaric Ode*, followed in 1705. There is no evidence that Johnson was a member of the inn. He signed his first published play, a tragedy entitled *Love and Liberty* (1709), which remained unacted, from the Middle Temple on 25 November 1708, less than three weeks before the records of Gray's Inn chapel reveal that 'Charles Johnson of the parish of St Anne Westminster & Mary Bradbury of the same parish' married on 14 December 1708 (Gray's Inn archives). The privilege allowing a non-member to marry in the chapel might be explained if Mary was related to one Francis Bradbury who was admitted to Gray's Inn in February 1660. It was perhaps about the time of Johnson's marriage that he became intimate with Robert Wilks, actor and theatrical manager, whose influence ensured that the majority of Johnson's subsequent dramatic output was performed in the Theatre Royal, Drury Lane.

Johnson's first stage success came with his comedy *The Wife's Relief, or, The Husband's Cure*, first performed at Drury Lane on 12 November 1711 with a cast including Colley Cibber, Robert Wilks, Thomas Doggett, and Anne Oldfield. The play was based on James Shirley's *The Gamester*. Henry Cromwell wrote to Alexander Pope that the play 'held seven nights, and got [Johnson] three hundred pounds' (*Works of Alexander Pope*, 6.128). It was still being printed and maybe played in 1736. On 7 November 1712 Johnson's tragicomedy *The Successful Pyrate* opened at Drury Lane. The critic John Dennis complained to the master of the revels that the play's valorization of the notorious pirate Henry Avery was causing public dismay; 'Never, say they, was the Stage prostituted to so vile a degree before. It has more than once been accus'd of promoting Vice, but was never so tax'd till now with encouraging Villany' (*The Critical Works of John Dennis*, ed. E. N. Hooker, 1939–43, 2.398).

Johnson's best and most successful comedy was *The Country Lasses*, first performed at Drury Lane on 4 February 1715. It held the stage for almost a century, its last recorded performance being on 7 December 1813 at Bath. Between 1715 and 1779 it was published in six printed editions, adapted by William Kenrick in *The Lady of the Manor* (1778), and by John Philip Kemble in *The Farm House* (1789). Johnson's play is permeated with sentimentalism which is in contrast to the hardened cynicism which characterizes earlier Restoration comedy. The play is also remarkable for the fact that when the managers of the Drury Lane theatre refused to submit to the censorship of the master of the revels, after receipt of Richard Steele's patent in January 1715, *The Country Lasses* was the play over which they made a stand, presenting it without licence (Milhous and Hume, 'Killigrew's petition', 74–9). His next play, *The Cobler of Preston* (1716), was about the Jacobite rising, and went through nine editions. Of all Johnson's plays, it is the one most frequently encountered in contemporary sources.

In the preface to his tragedy *The Sultaness*, first performed at Drury Lane on 25 February 1717, Johnson sniped at the collaboration of John Gay, Alexander Pope, and John Arbuthnot in *Three Hours after Marriage* which had opened on 16 January. Johnson's condemnation of the farce as 'Long-labour'd Nonsense' rendered him the target of a couplet which Pope incorporated in *A Fragment of a Satire* (1727):

> J[ohnso]n, who now to Sense, now Nonsense leaning,
> Means not, but blunders round about a Meaning
> (*The Poems of Alexander Pope*, Twickenham edition, 1954, 6.283–6)

Pope later recycled these lines in the *Epistle to Dr. Arbuthnot* (1735), dropping Johnson's name. Johnson also had the dubious distinction of being awarded a place in the first edition of the *Dunciad* (1728):

> A past, vamp'd, future, old, reviv'd, new piece,
> 'Twixt *Plautus*, *Fletcher*, *Congreve*, and *Corneille*,
> Can make a C[ibbe]r, J[ohnson], or O[ze]ll.
> (*Dunciad*, I.38–40)

Johnson's riposte finally came in the lengthy preface to his tragedy *Medea*, performed in Drury Lane on 11 December 1730, and published in 1731. With commendable courage, Johnson acknowledged Pope's superiority as a poet while roundly condemning his brutality towards his enemies.

Johnson's last theatrical production, *Caelia, or, The Perjur'd Lover*, a tragedy, was performed at Drury Lane on 11 December 1732. The play was an unmitigated disaster and its speedy removal deprived Johnson of his benefit. Barton Booth sold the publication rights to the printer John Watts who published the play in 1733 with an epilogue by Henry Fielding. After abandoning his career as a playwright Johnson seems to have run a tavern in Bow Street, Covent Garden. The circumstances surrounding his death on 11 March 1748 are unknown, but he was buried at Hendon on 18 March. His will, dated 19 January 1743, left everything to his wife, Mary, his sole executrix, who proved it on 20 April 1748. Johnson's widow may have pursued a modest career on the stage in the years following her husband's death.

Although Johnson reviled critics, claiming to eschew convention, he was in fact circumspect and responsive to shifts in theatrical taste. He was, for example, instinctively aware that theatrical success depended much on the approval of female theatregoers. The pathetic plight of a wronged wife or a cast mistress is Johnson's warmest theme. He was no innovator, preferring to adapt successful sources, including Shakespeare, Racine, and Cervantes, in composing drama. The actor, playwright, and historian of the theatre Benjamin Victor who knew Johnson described him as 'a modest, sensible Man, very comely in his Person, but rather too corpulent'. Victor maintains that Johnson was greatly hurt at finding himself introduced in the *Dunciad* but 'it seems he was too large an object to be miss'd; the Poet gave him a Cut with his Pen as he passed' (Victor, 2.112–13).   JAMES WILLIAM KELLY

Sources Gray's Inn archives, London, register of marriages, 1695–1754, 1975, 1978, CPL/1/1 · will, PRO, PROB 11/761, sig. 119 · W. Van Lennep and others, eds., *The London stage, 1660–1800*, 5 pts in 11 vols. (1960–68) · D. E. Baker, *Biographia dramatica, or, A companion to the playhouse*, rev. I. Reed, new edn, rev. S. Jones, 3 vols. in 4 (1812), 2.400–02 · C. Cibber, *An apology for the life of Colley Cibber: comedian, and late patentee of the Theatre-Royal: with an historical view of the stage during his own time*, 2 vols. (1756) · Corinna, 'Critical remarks on the Four Taking Plays of this Season' (1719) · *The works of Alexander Pope*, ed. W. Elwin and W. J. Courthope, 10 vols. (1871–89), vol. 6, p. 128 · M. Dias, 'A satire on John Dennis, 1711', *Review of English Studies*, 19/74 (1943), 213–14 · Highfill, Burnim & Langhans, *BDA* · E. N. Hooker, 'The force of friendship and love in a chest: a note on tragi-comedy and licensing in 1710', *Studies in Philology*, 34/3 (1937), 404–11 · Genest, *Eng. stage* · J. Milhous and R. D. Hume, eds., *A register of English theatrical documents, 1660–1737*, 2 vols. (1991) · J. Milhous and R. D. Hume, 'Charles Killigrew's petition about the master of the revels' power as censor (1715)', *Theatre Notebook*, 41 (1987), 74–9 · A. Nicholl, *A history of early eighteenth century drama, 1700–1750* (1925) · M. M. Shudofsky, 'Charles Johnson and eighteenth-century drama', *Journal of English Literary History*, 10/2 (1943), 131–58 · M. M. Shudofsky, 'A dunce objects to Pope's dictatorship', *Huntington Library Quarterly*, 14 (1950–51), 203–7 · B. Victor, *The history of the theatres of London and Dublin*, 2 vols. (1761)
Wealth at death see will, PRO, PROB 11/761, sig. 119

Johnson, Charles (*fl.* **1724–1734**), author, is known only for publishing *A General History of the Robberies and Murders of the most Notorious Pyrates*, which first appeared in London on 14 May 1724. A second edition was published later that year, a third in 1725, and a fourth, with additional lives and an appendix, in 1726. The writer, whose name is probably an assumed one, states in the preface that 'those facts which he himself was not an eye-witness of he had from the authentick relations of the persons concerned in taking the pyrates, as well as from the mouths of the pyrates themselves, after they were taken'. The book deals exclusively with British figures, including Avery, Kidd, Bartholomew Roberts, and Teach (Blackbeard). In addition it offered biographies of two female pirates, Mary Read (*d.* 1721) and Anne Bonny (1698–1782), who had recently been tried and acquitted of piracy in the Caribbean. A French translation, which appeared in 1726 as an appendix to an edition of Exquemelin's classic *Histoire des aventuriers*, was followed by Dutch and German versions (1727 and 1728).

In 1734 Johnson published his *General history of the lives and adventures of the most famous highwaymen, murderers, street robbers, &c*, which appeared in seventy-two weekly twopenny numbers. However, the *History* was merely a reprint of Alexander Smith's *A Complete History of the Lives and Robberies of the most Notorious Highwaymen* (1714) to which Johnson added his earlier pirates' biographies. Nothing is known for certain about the life of Captain

Johnson and there has been much speculation about his identity. In 1932 the American scholar John Robert Moore announced that the real author of the *History of the Pyrates* was none other than Daniel Defoe but subsequent research has cast serious doubt on this theory. Johnson's evident familiarity with seamen's language suggests that he spent time at sea and he may well have been a sea captain. He is certainly not to be confused with Charles Johnson (1679?–1748), the London playwright.

H. R. TEDDER, *rev.* DAVID CORDINGLY

Sources D. Defoe, *A general history of the pyrates*, ed. M. Schonhorn (1972) · C. Johnson, *A general history of the robberies and murders of the most notorious pyrates*, ed. P. Gosse, 1 (1925) · D. Cordingly, introduction, in C. Johnson, *A general history of the robberies and murders of the most notorious pyrates* (1998) · P. N. Furbank and W. R. Owens, *The canonisation of Daniel Defoe* (1988) · J. R. Moore, *Daniel Defoe: citizen of the modern world* (1958) · D. Cordingly, *Life among the pirates: the romance and the reality* (1995)

Johnson, Charles (1791–1880), botanist, was born in London on 5 October 1791. Little is known of his background and education. Apparently his father wanted him to become an assayer, but his bent for natural history proved too strong. He began to lecture on botany in 1819, and from then on devoted himself entirely to that science. On the founding of Guy's Hospital medical school in 1830 he was appointed lecturer in botany; he delivered forty-four courses of lectures, resigning his post in 1873. He also lectured to the Medico-Botanical Society. He is said to have been the first to introduce into his teaching living specimens, which came mostly from his own garden.

Johnson was married; his wife's name was Charlotte. He was a fellow of the Linnean Society and a member of the Botanical Society of London. In 1832 he edited an abridged version of Sowerby and Smith's *English Botany*. This appeared in twelve volumes (1832–46) and is generally known as the 'second edition' of Sowerby and Smith. Johnson also collaborated with Sowerby's grandson John Edward Sowerby, in the production of *Ferns of Great Britain* (1855, supplement 1856), *British Poisonous Plants* (1856), and *Grasses of Great Britain* (1861), for all of which he supplied the text and Sowerby the illustrations. He retained his faculties to the last, giving a course of botanical lectures in 1878, at the age of eighty-seven. He died at his home, 141 Cold Harbour Lane, Lambeth, London, on 21 September 1880. His wife survived him.

B. D. JACKSON, *rev.* ALEXANDER GOLDBLOOM

Sources Desmond, *Botanists*, rev. edn · *Journal of Botany, British and Foreign*, 18 (1880), 351–2 · *CGPLA Eng. & Wales* (1880)
Wealth at death under £100: probate, 24 Nov 1880, *CGPLA Eng. & Wales*

Johnson, Charles (1870–1961), archivist and historian, was born at Newcastle upon Tyne on 2 May 1870, the only child of Edmund White Johnson, timber merchant, and his wife, Elizabeth Hannah, daughter of his senior partner, John Herring. He was educated at Giggleswick School and at Trinity College, Oxford, which he entered as a classical scholar in 1888. After obtaining a first class in *literae humaniores* (1892) he entered the Public Record Office in

1893 and, except for a brief period on loan to the army contracts directorate of the War Office in 1918, he remained there until his retirement in 1930. After the outbreak of war in 1939 he was recalled to take charge of the records stored for safe-keeping in Culham College and finally retired in 1946.

For much of his official career Johnson was engaged in the arrangement and reclassification of the ancient miscellanea and files of the Chancery brought together from the Tower and Rolls Chapel. He also contributed substantially to various texts and calendars published by the PRO. He was secretary of the advisory committee on publications appointed by the master of the rolls in 1912, and a member of the inspecting officers and manorial records committees.

Extra-officially Johnson collaborated with two of his colleagues, C. G. Crump (whose notice he contributed to the *Dictionary of National Biography*) and Arthur Hughes, in producing the standard edition of *Dialogus de Scaccario* (1902), and he was largely responsible for the Domesday section of the *Victoria History of the County of Norfolk* (1906). With his colleague C. H. Jenkinson he produced *English Court Hand* (1915), which became a standard work for the student of the handwritings of medieval records. He was a general editor of the series of Helps for Students of History published by the Society for the Promotion of Christian Knowledge between 1918 and 1924 and himself contributed three handbooks to the series: *The Public Record Office* (1918), *The Care of Documents and Management of Archives* (1919), and *The Mechanical Processes of the Historian* (1922).

In 1913 Johnson became interested in proposals for a dictionary of medieval Latin and when, in 1924, the British Academy, in furtherance of a plan for an international dictionary of medieval Latin sponsored by the International Academic Union, set up two committees to collect materials from British and Irish sources he was appointed secretary of the committee concerned with the post-conquest period. The committees united in 1931 and in 1934 the *Medieval Latin Word-List from British and Irish Sources*, edited by the joint secretaries, was published by Oxford University Press. The next stage of the project, the revision and amplification of the materials leading to the publication of the *Revised Word-List* (1965), was carried through and plans prepared for the final stage of the full-scale dictionary with Johnson as principal initiator and guide.

After his retirement in 1930 much of Johnson's time was devoted to the editing of some of the basic texts of English medieval history. He accepted the invitation of Oxford University Press to continue the *Regesta regum Anglo-Normannorum* begun by H. W. C. Davis and with the assistance of H. A. Cronne completed the second volume, covering the reign of Henry I, which was published in 1956. His translations of *Dialogus de Scaccario*, Nicholas Oresme's *De moneta* with a selection of *English Mint Documents*, and Hugh the Chanter's *History of the Church of York, 1066–1127*, were published in Nelson's series of Medieval Classics in 1950, 1956, and 1961 respectively, and his edition of the *Register of Hamo de Hethe, Bishop of Rochester, 1316–52* was issued by the Canterbury and York Society over the years

1914 to 1948. He made frequent contributions of articles and reviews on historical topics to learned journals and served on the councils of several learned societies. He was a fellow of the Royal Historical Society and of the Society of Antiquaries and a vice-president of both, a founder-member of the Canterbury and York Society, its joint secretary for many years and later a vice-president, a member of the council of the Pipe Roll Society, and a member of the committee of the Institute of Historical Research from 1933 to 1945 and of the management committee of the Victoria History of the Counties of England from its formation in 1933 until 1955. His services to scholarship were recognized by his election as a fellow of the British Academy in 1934 and his appointment as CBE in 1951.

Johnson's career spanned a period of transformation in historical studies in England resulting in part from the development of new expertise in the use and interpretation of records, to which he himself greatly contributed. His influence was particularly felt in medieval history, where he helped to promote a new understanding of the interrelation between records and administration and to encourage a scientific rather than an antiquarian approach to the interpretation of documents. His meticulous scholarship and exhaustive knowledge of the records, supported by a grasp of the intricacies of administration and finance, earned for him a unique authority among his colleagues and the many scholars throughout the world who sought his advice.

Johnson was of shy and modest disposition, laconic in speech, and disposed to overestimate his hearer's knowledge, but most rewarding when drawn out in question and answer. He had great serenity of spirit and generosity of heart, never bitter in controversy and never wounding in criticism. His loyalty to his friends was absolute. As a young man he took pleasure in walking, cycling, and rowing and, though never of a robust appearance, he had a toughness of physique which carried him through some serious illnesses in later life. A few years after his fiftieth birthday he began to wear a beard, largely in consequence of a serious and disfiguring accident.

Johnson married twice: first, in 1907, his cousin Mabel Catherine Rudd, who died in 1947; second, in 1950, Violet Margaret, eldest daughter of Arthur Mutrie Shepherd, of Boars Hill, Oxford. There were no children of either marriage. He died suddenly at his home, 13A Downshire Hill, Hampstead, London, on 5 November 1961. His wife survived him.   H. C. JOHNSON, *rev.*

Sources H. C. Johnson, *PBA*, 51 (1965), 403–16 · *The Times* (7 Nov 1961) · personal knowledge (1981) · private information (1981) · *CGPLA Eng. & Wales* (1962)
Likenesses L. Binyon, pencil sketch, *c*.1892, Athenaeum Club, London; copy, PRO
Wealth at death £36,250 13s. 0d.: probate, 1 Jan 1962, *CGPLA Eng. & Wales*

Johnson, Christopher (*c*.1536–1597), Latin poet and schoolmaster, was born at Kedleston (or Kyddesley) in Derbyshire; he was a scholar at Winchester College (1549) and studied at New College, Oxford (fellow, 1555). He graduated BA on 23 February 1557, MA on 23 January 1562,

BM on 14 December 1570, and DM on 23 June 1571. Johnson was headmaster of Winchester College from 1560 to 1571, having been appointed by Archbishop Parker on the recommendation of Francis Hastings, second earl of Huntingdon. He wrote a Latin verse life of his founder, William of Wykeham (1564), and gained a reputation as an elegant Latin poet. Johnson also proved to be one of the most influential schoolmasters of the age. His older pupils were introduced to 'the full-scale study of poetry and rhetoric' (Fowler, 4), and he set them stimulating exercises in literary criticism, such as 'what effect has the poetic chorus upon you?' (ibid.). Among these pupils were Henry Dethick and Richard Wills, who both later wrote on the art of poetry; they both dedicated their work to Lord Burghley, and included liminary verses by their old teacher, Johnson.

Another of Johnson's pupils was Richard White of Basingstoke, author of *Historiarum Britanniae libri XI*, the most exhaustive treatment of the 'Brutus' legends, who eventually became a Roman Catholic exile and rector of Douai. Johnson sponsored White's two early treatises: before White's *Orationes Duae* (1566), delivered at Louvain, there is an important dedicatory letter by Johnson, describing White's progress from Winchester, via Oxford, to Louvain and Padua. White's uncle, a merchant of Southampton, is congratulated for supporting him: no merchandise is so valuable as learning. In sponsoring the edition Johnson hopes that White's uncle, and others, will learn how good this investment has proved, and that British youth, having relied previously on such models as Cicero, 'domesticis fortasse ac familiaribus exemplis melius excitari' ('could perhaps be better excited by native and familiar models'). Johnson recalls his own youth:

> certe ego quum puer essem, et grammatices praeceptis operam darem, ut alia non aspernabar, ita si quando in Thomae Mori aut Epigrammata, aut Utopiam, aut Declamationes ex Luciano conversas incidissem, nescio quo modo, praeter omnem modum ac rationem delectabar, studioque legendi vehementer efferebar.
>
> (For sure I myself, when as a boy I was studying grammar, though I did not scorn other texts, yet whenever I came across the works of Thomas More, either his epigrams or *Utopia* or translations from Lucian, I was excessively pleased, and carried onwards by a violent desire to read him.)

Because Thomas More was an Englishman, one could hope to emulate him. This eloquent explanation of the power of contemporary British Latin suggests that Johnson was a humanist educator of remarkable insight.

Johnson practised medicine while still headmaster; after resigning from Winchester, and obtaining his doctorate of medicine, he moved to London, where he practised successfully in the parish of St Dunstan-in-the-West. He published a medical work in English, *A Counsel Against the Plague, or any other Infectious Disease* (1577). He was admitted FRCP about 1580, and held various offices in the college of physicians. His medical career gave him a substantial fortune. He did not, however, abandon literature: probably his most important work appeared in 1580,

when he describes himself as 'Medico Londinensi' ('London physician'): this is his Latin verse rendering of the *Batrachomyomachia* ('Battle of the Frogs and Mice') attributed to Homer. His short preface defends his borrowings from Virgil; he takes a motto from Horace (*Ars poetica*, 133–4) on avoiding over-literal translation, though in fact he remains fairly close to his original (Binns, 229–30). The 'Battle of the Frogs and Mice' was a popular text in the Renaissance, the ancestor of the mock-heroic genre—hence of such vernacular works as Alexander Pope's *Rape of the Lock* or Jonathan Swift's *Battle of the Books*, and neo-Latin satires such as Joseph Addison's *Pygmaeogeranomachia* ('Battle of Pygmies and Cranes') or Edward Holdsworth's *Muscipula* ('Mousetrap'), also known as *Cambromyomachia* ('Battle of the Welsh and Mice'). Johnson's Latin translation can be interestingly compared to that of Huntington Plumptre (1629); an English version by W. Fowldes appeared in 1603. In attempting the humorous mock-heroic, Johnson as a mature physician was recalling the poetic excitements of his youth. Johnson married (his wife's name is unknown), fathered several children, and died in London in July 1597.

D. K. MONEY

Sources J. W. Binns, *Intellectual culture in Elizabethan and Jacobean England: the Latin writings of the age* (1990) · R. White, *Orationes Duae* (1566) · C. Johnson, *Batrachomyomachia* (1580) · Foster, *Alum. Oxon.* · *DNB* · *STC, 1475–1640* · R. Wills, *De re poetica*, ed. A. D. S. Fowler (1958)
Archives BL, Winchester themes and declamations, Add. MS 4379
Wealth at death 'a considerable fortune': *DNB*

Johnson, Claude Goodman (1864–1926), motor vehicle manufacturer, was born at Datchet, Buckinghamshire, on 24 October 1864, the sixth child and fourth son of William Goodman Johnson and his wife, Sophia Fanny Adams. His father worked in the Department of Science and Art of the South Kensington Museum and arranged the Wallace Collection when it was exhibited at Bethnal Green Museum in 1872–5. Claude Johnson absorbed his love of music and art. Educated at St Paul's School (1878–82), he enrolled at the Royal College of Art, but left at the age of nineteen, explaining that he lacked ability. As a clerk in the Imperial Institute, South Kensington, he proved a highly effective organizer of its exhibitions. His ability was recognized by the early motor propagandist, Frederick Simms, when the institute arranged the first exhibition of motor cars in London in 1896. Simms appointed him secretary of the newly formed Automobile Club (later the RAC). His sure management piloted the club through early difficulties. With characteristic public relations flair he promoted the motor vehicle through exhibitions and contests, culminating in the Thousand Miles Trial of 1900, when competitors drove from London to Edinburgh and back via cities selected for maximum publicity. The event, as one participant put it, convinced the public 'that motor vehicles were a thoroughly practical form of road locomotion' (Edge, 92). 'To him is owed the fact of the club's existence today,' stated the RAC's *Jubilee Book* (Noble, 25).

Johnson left the RAC in 1903 for an abortive project to

manufacture electric carriages, and instead joined Charles Rolls's motor agency. Rolls and Johnson sought out high quality vehicles for Rolls's society friends until, in 1904, Rolls travelled to Manchester to inspect Henry Royce's works, and told Johnson: 'I have found the greatest engineer in the world' (Oldham, 63). An exclusive deal entailed Royce supplying chassis while Rolls provided bodywork. Johnson promoted their cars at rallies which set off Rolls's driving skills. Johnson bet on the results and coined names like the Silver Ghost, while friendship with the newspaper owner Alfred Harmsworth, later Lord Northcliffe, ensured more publicity.

In 1906, Johnson became managing director of Rolls-Royce Ltd. Although he nicknamed himself 'the hyphen', he was the business entrepreneur who kept the company alive when Rolls died in an aircraft accident in 1911 and then the increasingly temperamental Royce became seriously ill. Johnson moved him to a villa next to his own in the south of France, ensuring that he continued to design but no longer interfered in the factory. Royce wrote: 'The great success would never have been achieved but for your influence' (Oldham, 149).

CJ, as Johnson was known, was a large, broad-shouldered extrovert who loved house parties at his cliff-top house overlooking the English Channel. His artistic enthusiasm brought permanent seats for Rolls-Royce workers at the Theatre Royal in Derby, and on one occasion he hired the Albert Hall for a protégé French organist. His key business decision, which marked him out from other British manufacturers in 1906, was to insist that Royce concentrate on a single model. The result was the celebrated 40/50 Silver Ghost, constructed at a new works at Derby after Johnson had bargained with various cities over incentives to transfer production.

The First World War enhanced Rolls-Royce's reputation as it produced sought-after armoured cars and Royce designed its first aero-engine, the Eagle. The company became the world's largest producer of aero-engines by 1918. Less happy was the decision to build an ill-fated US car factory whose problems remained even when it opened in 1921. Post-war the company prospered. Profits reached £200,000 in 1920 on a turnover of £3.4 million, rising to £5.6 million by 1926.

However, Johnson's remorseless schedule caught up with him. He contracted pneumonia, insisted on attending a niece's wedding, and died at Adelphi Terrace House, London, on 11 April 1926. He was cremated at Golders Green. He left two daughters. As a young man he had eloped with, and married on 4 November 1891, Fanny May Morrieson, but of their six children only one survived infancy. From a later marriage he had one daughter.

MARTIN ADENEY

Sources W. J. Oldham, *The hyphen in Rolls-Royce* (1967) · I. Lloyd, *Rolls-Royce, 1: The growth of a firm* (1978) · I. Lloyd, *Rolls-Royce, 2: The years of endeavour* (1978) · H. Nockolds, *The magic of a name* (1938) · D. Noble, ed., *RAC jubilee book, 1897–1947* (1947), 25 · C. Johnson and Lord Montagu, *Roads made easy by picture and pen* (1907) · C. Johnson, *The works of Ambrose McEvoy*, 2 vols. (1917) · S. F. Edge, *My motoring reminiscences* (1934), 92 · d. cert. · m. cert. (first marriage, 4 Nov 1891)

Archives Rolls-Royce Enthusiasts Club, Derby, corresp. [photocopies] · Rolls-Royce Heritage Trust, Derby, corresp. and notebooks | Veteran Car Club of Great Britain, corresp. with F. R. Simms

Likenesses portrait, Rolls-Royce Motor Cars, Crewe · portrait, Rolls Royce Ltd, London

Wealth at death £42,972 14s. 1d.: resworn probate, 18 June 1926, CGPLA Eng. & Wales

Johnson, Cornelius [Cornelius Jansen, Janssen, or Jonson van Ceulen] (*bap.* **1593**, *d.* **1661**), painter, was baptized in London on 14 October 1593 at the Dutch church, Austin Friars, the son of Johanna le Grand and Cornelius Johnson (*d.* in or before 1605), an exile from Antwerp whose own grandfather, Peter Jansen, had originated in Cologne. The family sometimes used the name Jonson or Jansen van Ceulen. After his baptism no documentary reference to Johnson is found before 1619, when he witnessed the baptism of his nephew Nicasius in London. According to the antiquarian and engraver George Vertue, who knew Johnson's great-nephew Anthony Russell, the painter had come to England from Amsterdam the previous year (although Vertue was incorrect in stating that he had been born in that city; Vertue, *Note books*, 2.23, 5.90). From his style it is possible that Johnson did receive at least part of his training in the Netherlands in this interim period.

Johnson's earliest portraits depict the sitters at head and shoulders within a feigned stone oval, for example *An Unknown Elderly Lady* (1619; priv. coll.). From the outset Johnson signed and dated his works—generally, with the monogram 'C.J.'—making his *œuvre* comparatively easy to establish. Later, following his emigration to the Netherlands, he was to sign his works 'Cornelius Jonson van Ceulen', an allusion to his family's origins in Cologne. On 16 July 1622, Johnson married Elizabeth Beck or Beke (*d.* after 1661), of Colchester, at the Dutch church in London, by which date he had settled beside the River Thames in the Blackfriars area, where their son James (who presumably died young) was baptized on 30 September 1623 at St Anne's Church. Another son, Cornelius (later also a painter), was baptized there in 1634.

Throughout the 1620s Johnson produced numerous portraits of gentry, professional, and court sitters, to a consistently high technical standard. Perhaps his most assiduous patron was Thomas, first Baron Coventry, who was appointed lord keeper by Charles I, and who evidently sat to Johnson on various occasions. Signed portraits of him survive of varying dates: a three-quarter-length of 1623, another of 1627 with a signed replica of 1629 and, possibly the finest, the one dated 1631 (priv. coll.); there is another half-length of 1634 and a final image of 1639. In January 1625 the artist took on an apprentice called John Evoms. His nephew Theodore Russell is also said to have trained with him. Johnson may also have worked in collaboration with the Dutch-born royal portraitist Daniel Mytens, for in 1631 he signed a version of Mytens's full-length official portrait *Charles I* (priv. coll.). In 1632 Johnson was himself appointed 'his Majesty's servant in the quality of Picture drawer'. In the same year, however, Sir Anthony Van Dyck arrived at the English court and soon monopolized the top portrait commissions. This may have been one reason why Johnson moved to Kent during the mid-1630s, where he is said to have taken up residence at Bridge near Canterbury, with a wealthy merchant of Flemish descent, Sir Arnold Braems. His clients included many sitters from Kentish families, including the Campions of Combwell, the Filmers of East Sutton, and the Oxindens of Deane. In 1638 Sir Thomas Pelham of Halland House, Sussex, paid £4 for his portrait by Johnson (accounts book, Pelham family papers, BL, Add. MS 33145, fol. 107). Johnson was himself portrayed, as a prosperous family man with his wife and son Cornelius, about 1637 by the Dutch painter Adrian Hanneman (Rijksmuseum Twenthe, Enschede). At this period Hanneman was working in Britain, and indeed, according to Vertue, unsuccessfully courted Johnson's niece.

In 1637 Johnson painted a small full-length *Charles I*, again based on a Mytens pattern, included in a perspective setting painted by Hendrick van Steenwick (now in the Staatliche Kunst Sammlungen Dresden, Gemäldegalerie Alte Meister), and collaborated with Gerard Houckgeest on a similar small full-length *Queen Henrietta Maria* (priv. coll.); as these two works entered the king's collection, they were presumably commissioned by him. In 1639 Johnson produced three small individual full-length portraits on panel of Charles I's eldest children (NPG). He was still listed among the servants of Charles I in 1641.

Alongside his head-and-shoulders, half-length, three-quarter-length, full-length, and large group portraits, on panel or canvas, Johnson produced portrait miniatures, painted in oil on metal. This was not a combination of medium and support that miniaturists working in England had previously generally used; they worked in water-based media on vellum over card. Johnson may have learned this technique overseas. He did not always sign these miniatures, but his handling of them is extremely characteristic. A pair of about 1637 depict a London-based couple of Netherlandish descent, *Peter Vandeput* and *Sarah Hoste* (priv. coll.), indicating that Johnson also had clients among his own immigrant community.

Johnson was one of the artists questioned in London by the Swiss-born physician Dr Theodore Turquet de Mayerne, who included Johnson's comments on how to use the poisonous yellow pigment orpiment in his manuscript 'Pictoria sculptoria et quae subalternarum artium' (BL, Sloane MS 2052). Technical advice from Johnson on methods of painting draperies also cropped up in an English manuscript compiled in the 1650s by a minor graphic artist, Daniel King.

According to Vertue, at the time of the civil war it was at the persuasion of his wife that Johnson left England for the Netherlands late in 1643, taking with him 'such pictures and colours, bedding, household stuff, pewter and brass as belonged to himself' (Finberg, 'Chronological list', 6). In October 1644 Johnson and his wife were recorded in Middelburg, in which city he became a member of the guild of St Luke. In 1646 he was in Amsterdam, and the following year painted the large group *Magistrates of The Hague* (Oude Stadhuis, The Hague). In 1650 he portrayed members of the St Sebastian guild—the archers'

guild—of Middelburg, a composition of seventeen figures (Middelburg town hall), and was recorded in that city again in 1652. In November 1652 he was also in Utrecht where, at his house in Heerenstraat, he made a will (private information). In 1657 he painted *William of Orange* (the future William III of England) as a boy (various versions; a signed and dated one is at Knole, Kent).

Johnson is thought to have died in Utrecht on 5 August 1661. His son Cornelius also practised as a painter in the Netherlands, and was recorded in Utrecht as late as 1700.

KAREN HEARN

Sources R. Ekkart, 'Jonson van Ceulen, Cornelis', *The dictionary of art*, ed. J. Turner (1996) · E. Waterhouse, *Painting in Britain, 1530–1790*, 5th edn (1994), 60–62 · D. Foskett, 'Cornelius Johnson: miniaturist', *Antique Collector*, 60 (1989), 61–5 · M. Edmond, 'Limners and picturemakers', *Walpole Society*, 47 (1978–80), 60–242 · K. Hearns, 'The English career of Cornelius Jonson van Ceulen', *Leids Kunsthistorisch Jaarboek* (2002) · O. Millar, *The age of Charles I: painting in England, 1620–1649* (1972), 30–35 [exhibition catalogue, Tate Gallery, London, 15 Nov 1972 – 14 Jan 1973] · E. Croft-Murray and P. H. Hulton, eds., *Catalogue of British drawings*, 1 (1960), 371–2 · M. Whinney and O. Millar, *English art, 1625–1714* (1957), 64–8 · O. Millar, 'An attribution to Cornelius Johnson reinstated', *Burlington Magazine*, 90 (1948), 322 · K. E. Maison, 'Portraits by Cornelius Johnson in Scotland', *Burlington Magazine*, 74 (1939), 86–7 · R. Edwards, 'Oil miniatures by Cornelius Johnson', *Burlington Magazine*, 61 (1932), 131–2 · H. Schneider and J. D. Milner, 'The portraits of Cornelius Janssen van Ceulen', *Burlington Magazine*, 45 (1924), 295–7 · A. J. Finberg, 'A chronological list of portraits by Cornelius Johnson, or Jonson', *Walpole Society*, 10 (1921–2), 1–37, see also pl. I–LXXX · A. J. Finberg, 'Two anonymous portraits by Cornelius Johnson', *Walpole Society*, 6 (1917–18), 1–13 · L. Cust, 'Notes on various works of art: Cornelius Janssen van Ceulen', *Burlington Magazine*, 16 (1910), 280–81 · F. D. O. Obreen, ed., *Archief voor Nederlandsche kunstgeschiedenis*, 7 vols. (Rotterdam, 1877–90), 171 · *The visitation of London, anno Domini 1633, 1634, and 1635, made by Sir Henry St George*, 2, ed. J. J. Howard, Harleian Society, 17 (1883), 15 · H. Walpole, *Anecdotes of painting in England: with some account of the principal artists*, ed. R. N. Wornum, new edn, 3 vols. (1888), vol. 1, pp. 211–15 · Vertue, *Note books*, 1.54, 2.123, 5.90 · J. Sandrart, *Academia nobilissimae artis pictoriae* (1683), 1.314 · D. King, 'Secrets in the noble arte of miniature or limning', c.1653–7, BL, Add. MS 12461; transcribed in M. K. Talley, *Portrait painting in England* (1981), 223–4 · *Pictoria sculptoria & quae subalternarum artium, 1620: le manuscrit de Turquet de Mayerne*, ed. and trans. M. Faidutti and C. Versini (Lyons, [n.d.]), 148–9 · private information (2004) [Marten Jan Bok]
Archives BL, Add. MS 12461 · BL, Sloane MS 2052
Likenesses A. Hanneman, group portrait, oils, c.1637, Rijksmuseum Twenthe, Enschede, Netherlands · T. Chambars, engraving, pubd 1762 (after A. Hanneman), repro. in Walpole, *Anecdotes* · C. de Bie, engraving (after self-portrait by C. Johnson), repro. in *Het gulden cabinet* (1661) [previously engraved by C. Waumans in *Image de divers hommes d'esprit sublime* (1649)] · W. H. Worthington, line engraving (after self-portrait by C. Johnson), BM, NPG; repro. in Walpole, *Anecdotes*

Johnson, Cuthbert William (1799–1878), writer on agriculture, was born at Widmore House, Bromley, Kent, on 28 September 1799, the eldest surviving son of William Johnson of Liverpool and Widmore House. His father was proprietor of several chemistry-based businesses. Johnson was admitted a member of Gray's Inn on 6 January 1832, called to the bar on 8 June 1836, and practised as a barrister on the western circuit. Though his main profession was the law, it was his agricultural expertise for which he was best known. He became a leading and trusted authority on the use of agricultural fertilizers.

Johnson's interest in this subject developed at an early age while he was employed with his brother George William *Johnson (later the editor of the *Journal of Horticulture*) on his father's salt works at Heybridge in Essex. In the year 1820 he was a prize essayist for the 'old' board of agriculture on the subject of the use of salt as a manure and this encouraged him to investigate other fertilizing substances that were then gaining attention. The more notable of his many agricultural works included *The Use of Crushed Bones as Manure* (1836), *On Fertilisers* (1839), *The Farmers' Encyclopaedia and Dictionary of Rural Affairs* (1842), and *Agricultural Chemistry for Young Farmers* (1843). With his close associate William Shaw in 1832 he helped to found the *Mark Lane Express and Agricultural Journal*, which became one of the leading nineteenth-century farming newspapers, and he also collaborated with Shaw in the production of *Johnson and Shaw's Farmer's Almanac*, which they started in 1841; three years later they published a translation from the German of Thaer's *System der Landwirtschaft*. Johnson made numerous contributions to a range of agricultural periodicals including the *Quarterly Journal of Agriculture*, *Journal of the Royal Agricultural Society of England*, the *Farmer's Magazine*, and the *Journal of the Bath and West of England Society*.

Johnson was twice appointed a commissioner of metropolitan sewers and he campaigned for the legislation which resulted in the 1848 Public Health Acts; he produced an annotated edition of the acts in 1852. He resided at Waldronhurst, Croydon, where for nearly thirty years he was associated with the local board of health, which pioneered a number of sanitary improvements under his chairmanship. His knowledge of law was very valuable to the local board, which was involved in extensive legal actions over matters of water rights and river pollution during its early years. His public service was marked by a presentation of silver plate on his retirement, because of failing health, from the local board in March 1877. He was elected FRS on 10 March 1842, and was a director of the Royal Farmers' Insurance Company and chairman of the Tithe and Rent Guarantee Company. He died at Waldronhurst on 8 March 1878 and was buried three days later at St Peter's Church, Croydon, near his wife, Mary Ann (1803/4–1861), about whom no other details are known.

NICHOLAS GODDARD

Sources 'Noteworthy agriculturists: Mr Cuthbert W. Johnson', *Agricultural Gazette* (29 May 1875) · 'Death of Mr C. W. Johnson', *Journal of Horticulture, Cottage Gardener and Country Gentleman*, 34 (1878), 215 · *Croydon Guardian and Surrey County Gazette* (16 March 1878) · d. cert.
Archives Central Library, Croydon
Likenesses engraving (after photograph), repro. in 'Noteworthy agriculturists: Mr Cuthbert W. Johnson'
Wealth at death under £30,000: probate, 8 May 1878, *CGPLA Eng. & Wales*

Johnson, Daniel (1766/7–1835), surgeon and author, was appointed assistant surgeon in the Bengal medical service on 22 January 1789. He conducted experiments on snakebite, and later communicated his findings to his fellow Bengal surgeon James Johnson. He was promoted to surgeon on 11 March 1805, and retired from the service in 1809. He settled at Great Torrington, Devon, and in 1822 printed, with the aid of a daughter of the local bookseller, 'not more than eight and a half years old', his *Sketches of Indian Field-Sports*. The book was dedicated to the court of directors of the Hon. East India Company. In 1827 he issued a second edition, to which he added a chapter on 'Hunting the wild boar'. In 1823 he published, also at Great Torrington, *Observations on Colds, Fevers, and other Disorders*, accompanied by prescriptions. Johnson died at Torrington on 12 September 1835, aged sixty-eight.

M. G. WATKINS, rev. JULIAN LOCK

Sources *GM*, 2nd ser., 4 (1835), 556 · Dodwell [E. Dodwell] and Miles [J. S. Miles], eds., *Alphabetical list of the Honourable East India Company's Bengal civil servants, from the year 1780 to the year 1838* (1839)

Johnson, Denis (1759/60–1833), manufacturer of velocipedes and coachbuilder, is of unknown parentage. There is no record of his life until his marriage to Mary Newman, by licence of the archbishop of Canterbury at St Anne's Church, Soho, on 17 February 1792; the couple, who lived in Soho during the 1790s, had two daughters, Mary and Ann, born in 1795 and 1798 respectively. His wife predeceased him.

In March 1818 Johnson took occupation of 75 Long Acre in the City of Westminster, which was to remain his workshop and home for the rest of his life. It was at about this time that the two-wheel velocipede, invented by the German nobleman Karl von Drais, was becoming known in France. Johnson obtained one of these wooden machines and set about making some significant alterations, in particular improving the steering and replacing some wooden parts with metal. His professional skills as a coachmaker enabled him to produce an elegant machine which was in a number of respects superior to the German original. Johnson applied for an English patent for his 'pedestrian curricle', acknowledging its foreign origin, and this was granted on 22 December 1818 (no. 4321); the detailed specification was filed six months later. He then set about making the machines, which were probably first marketed in February 1819, and also opened a school which taught how to ride them. There was enormous public interest throughout the country in his novel product, which soon became popularly known as the hobby-horse, or more respectfully (after the French word) as the 'velocipede'.

Regency dandies seem to have been the principal purchasers of the machine (alternatively known as the 'dandy horse'). Nobility and even royalty succumbed to the craze, the prince regent himself arranging for four Johnson velocipedes to be transported to his Brighton home. More than 300 were made by Johnson and sold during the first half of 1819, and during the same period many prints depicting (and in most cases satirizing) the hobby-horse were on sale in London. One print purports to show Johnson himself with his machine—he appears to have been a man of only modest stature. Another depicts his son, described as 'the first rider on the pedestrian hobby-horse'.

The pedestrian hobby-horse era lasted for no more than three years. After it was over Johnson continued working as a coachmaker on his own account until about 1825, by which date he had entered into partnership with another coachmaker, John Allen, who also became his son-in-law by marrying Johnson's elder daughter. The partnership between the two men continued until Johnson's death, at home from an unspecified illness, at the age of seventy-three, on 25 December 1833. He was buried at St Martin's Chapel, Camden Town, on 2 January 1834. The firm he had started was in existence for some ninety years until the early years of the twentieth century.

Johnson's will shows him to have been a methodical individual, giving precise instructions as to how his wishes were to be effected. He was also a kindly man, making thoughtful provision for his elderly sister and younger daughter. He was clearly proud of the business he had built up over the years: 'whatever I am possessed of has been gained by sheer industry and labour'—industry and labour which had at one time provided Britain with the forerunner of the bicycle, one of the most important inventions of the nineteenth century.

ROGER STREET

Sources J. Fairburn, *An accurate, whimsical, and satirical description of the new pedestrian carriage, or walking accelerator* (1819) • 'Newly invented carriage', *The Courier* (11 Dec 1818) • R. T. C. Street, *The pedestrian hobby-horse* (1998) • parish register, Westminster, St Anne [marriage, baptisms] • parish register, Westminster, St Martin-in-the-Fields, 2 Jan 1834 [burial] • PRO, PROB 11/1829, fols. 41r–43v • trade directories, London, 1790–1908

Likenesses G. Cruikshank, lithograph, 1819, BM

Wealth at death £943 9s. 4d.: PRO, death duty registers, IR 26/1355, no. 1101; will, PRO, PROB 11/1829, fols. 41r–43v

Johnson, Don [real name James Macdonald John] (1911–1994), singer and actor, was born on 3 February 1911 at 2 Thomas Terrace, Working Street, Cardiff, the second son in the family of four sons and two daughters of Elvin John (c.1872–1924), a corn merchant's labourer, and his wife, Maria, née Thomas (1886–1938). His father was from the Caribbean, probably from Barbuda or Antigua; his mother, from Swansea, was Welsh. He grew up in Grangetown, Cardiff, where his father had moved the family in order to escape the accent and culture of Butetown's docks area (known, derisively, to outsiders as Tiger Bay) and was educated at Grangetown National School. The family, which included an elder half-brother, lived at 17 Hewel Street, but following his father's death, John began to frequent forbidden territory. He became part of the docklands community of itinerant musicians of Caribbean and African descent and at seventeen was playing mandolin with the guitarist brothers Frank and Joe Deniz and others. Determined to avoid going to sea, he earned his living selling newspapers and started boxing. As 'Newsboy John', he had several successful bouts in the Welsh valleys before deciding that life in the ring was too rugged. He would, however, retain the capacity to avert trouble through his stance—and the short step of the boxer—for the rest of his life.

About 1932 John teamed up with guitarist Victor Parker to entertain in Butetown cafés; they were joined by another guitarist, George Glossop, for school dances and parties. In 1935 he appeared in an all-black touring show in Newport before travelling to London with Joe Deniz, who was working at a clip-joint with a Hawaiian trio; he sang with them, but when the club was wrecked by thugs, returned to Cardiff. Another London venture with a group of his hometown associates also failed, and he recommenced his association with Parker. Despite having an attractive tenor voice, he remained ambivalent about following a career in music, but, encouraged by a local bandleader who recognized his musicality, he found work singing and playing guitar with local dance bands. John had adopted Don Johnson as his performing name in the 1930s, and when the Guyanese dancer Ken 'Snake Hips' Johnson brought his band to Cardiff his namesake's future was changed. Don Johnson introduced himself to the leader and, following an audition, was hired on the spot. He left Wales in August 1937, separating from his wife, Edith Evelyn (Edie) Carter (b. 1914/15), a dancer, whom he had married on 8 February 1934; their son Laurence (1935–6) lived for eighteen months.

In London Johnson took lessons from John Payne at Ken Johnson's instigation. Payne helped iron out the imperfections of an amateur singer, and through observation and social interaction Johnson familiarized himself with the techniques and cultural aesthetic of visiting African-American performers such as the dance–comedy teams of Brookins and Van and the Four Flash Devils. Without copying the black American style, he incorporated his informal studies with his intrinsic ability, to present himself as a well-rounded performer. As a permanent member of Ken Johnson's West Indian Dance Orchestra (1937–40), he was the band's main featured vocalist. For dance music fans who listened to the band's regular BBC broadcasts he became a household name, and was featured on five of the orchestra's recordings, including *A Small Café by Nôtre Dame*. In December 1940 he was called up for war service, ending a steady relationship with his partner Kay, with whom he had lived since soon after joining the orchestra. He joined the City of London regiment, then moved to the Royal Fusiliers, where he helped organize a dance band, ending up as its drummer and occasional vocalist while learning to play the trumpet. He also worked in Stars in Battledress productions.

Following his demobilization Johnson worked with Latin American and Hawaiian bands and entertained at parties in society circles, singing and playing guitar. He formed a relationship with Bella, with whom he lived for several years, and in 1951 joined Lauderic Caton and the former Ken Johnson saxophonist Louis Stephenson in a vocal trio. He then devoted most of his time to the stage, taking musical and acting roles in West End theatrical productions including *Annie Get your Gun*, *South Pacific*, and *Cat on a Hot Tin Roof*. He joined the American Negro Theatre Guild (1953–4) for *The Square Ring* and *Anna Lucasta*, and was also in the London production of Langston Hughes's play *Simply Heavenly* (1958).

Johnson's radio appearances brought an African Welsh voice to prominence several years before Shirley Bassey made her début. His work with Ken Johnson had made him a well-known radio singer, and he continued to play a significant role in broadcasting throughout the 1950s as a member of the pool of African Caribbean talent used by the BBC for radio and television plays with a 'black' theme that were increasingly part of the service's domestic output. He continued to act in more general radio productions and to broadcast as an instrumentalist on the popular *Guitar Club*, where he sang and played Josh White material. On retiring from music, he spent five years in a Welsh steelworks; there he suffered superficial injuries to his hands that made him reluctant to play guitar again. He returned to London, and in 1970 began a relationship with Lillian (Lil) Carey. In his final decade he participated in recording several oral histories. He died from cancer of the prostate on 4 February 1994 at St Joseph's Hospice, Hackney, London. Lil Carey predeceased him.

VAL WILMER

Sources J. Green, 'Joe Deniz: a guitarist from Cardiff', *Keskidee*, 1 (autumn 1986), 13–17 · '*Lucasta* star "under arrest"', *Jet* (18 March 1954), 59 · D. Johnson and V. Wilmer, interview, BL NSA · personal knowledge (2004) · private knowledge (2004) · b. cert. · m. cert. · d. cert.
Archives SOUND BL NSA, oral history
Likenesses A. McBean, photograph, 1946–9, priv. coll. · A. Armstrong-Jones, photograph, 1954, priv. coll. · V. Wilmer, photographs, 1986–90, priv. coll.

Johnson [*née* Garrat; *other married name* King], **Dorothea** (**1732–1817**), Methodist leader, was born on 4 December 1732 in Dublin, the only daughter of John Garrat (*d.* 1765), a Dutchman who had settled in Ireland in 1707 and established a business in Dublin. Nothing is known of her mother but Dorothea was partly brought up by her paternal grandmother, whose piety contrasted with her father's irreligion. Her early education was reportedly scanty: she taught herself to write in adulthood and 'carefully cultivated her mind by the diligent study of useful books' (Crookshank, *Memorable Women*, 56). In appearance, she was 'very beautiful, a little above the average height' with a 'fair complexion' and a 'sweet placid smile' (ibid., 55).

When Dorothea was about sixteen her father's business failed. In order to save him from imprisonment she agreed to marry one of his creditors, a man named King. The couple had two children, a daughter, and a son who died in childhood, but the marriage was unhappy and after some years Dorothea left her husband and returned to live with her father.

On 15 December 1757 Dorothea was converted to Methodism by the Revd George Whitefield. Shortly afterwards her father followed her into the society. She soon became a prominent figure in the local congregation, taking charge of classes and bands, and achieving a reputation for charity, humility, and holiness. According to Crookshank, 'many women occupied a more prominent position in the Society, and displayed talents of a higher order, but none lived closer to God' (Crookshank, *Memorable Women*, 56). John Wesley, visiting Dublin in 1762, witnessed her entry into the state known by Methodists as 'sanctification': 'She had been seeking it for some time; but her convictions and desires grew stronger and stronger, as the hour approached … On the Lord's day, she felt an entire change … She now walks in sweet peace and rejoices evermore' (Smith, 47–8). In 1771 she began a journal, primarily as a record of her spiritual development, which she kept intermittently for the rest of her life.

Dorothea's first husband died in 1774, and in 1784 she married John Johnson, a Methodist preacher, and moved with him to Lisburn, co. Antrim. Adam Averell, visiting the Johnsons there some years later, saw them as a pattern of married life: 'This couple have never had a dispute, nor the slightest difference to settle. O religion! What a treasure! … If all our friends possessed the invaluable secret of living as they do, what a heaven it would bring upon earth' (Stewart and Revington, 185). In Lisburn Dorothea worked alongside her husband to promote Methodism, taking particular responsibility for female members of the society. Her efforts were instrumental in the expansion of Methodism in the district: in 1785 John Wesley noted the liveliness of the society in Lisburn, 'owing chiefly to the good providence of God in bringing Mrs Johnson hither' (Crookshank, *History of Methodism*, 1.402).

John Johnson died in 1803 but Dorothea maintained her involvement in the affairs of the Lisburn congregation, leading groups in study and worship and corresponding with believers on spiritual matters. The final entry in her journal, dated 19 January 1817, is a catalogue of blessings received and a reiteration of faith:

> He gives me peace in my family, protection from the wicked, a great measure of health, a competency of this world's treasure, and … a constant witness of His indwelling spirit, that I am His child. I feel no inward corruption, and I have strong confidence that He will, through the blood and righteousness of my Redeemer, bring me where He is, His hand graciously holding me up in death. (Johnson, 78)

Dorothea Johnson died of typhus fever in Lisburn on 23 July 1817. Her *Memoirs*, including extracts from her journal and correspondence, and a number of short poems on religious themes, were edited by the Revd Adam Averell and published in 1818.

ROSEMARY RAUGHTER

Sources D. Johnson, *Memoirs*, ed. A. Averell (1818) · C. H. Crookshank, *Memorable women of Irish Methodism in the last century* (1882) · D. Hempton and M. Hill, 'Born to serve: women and evangelical religion', *Evangelical protestantism in Ulster society* (1992), 129–42 · D. Hempton, 'Methodism in Irish society, 1770–1830', *TRHS*, 5th ser., 36 (1986), 117–42 · C. H. Crookshank, *History of Methodism in Ireland*, 1 (1885) · A. Stewart and G. Revington, *Memoir of the life and labours of the Rev Adam Averell* (1848) · W. Smith, *A consecutive history of the rise, progress and present state of Wesleyan Methodism in Ireland* (1830) · R. L. Cole, *A history of Methodism in Dublin* (1932)

Johnson, Edward (*b. c.*1549, *d.* in or after **1602**), composer, was born about 1549, according to a 1601 deposition in which he gave his age as about fifty-two; nothing is known of Johnson's parentage or musical training. Between 1572 and 1575 he appears in account books of Sir Thomas Kytson of Hengrave Hall, Suffolk, as receiving 'rewards' as well as regular wages. In July 1575 he was reimbursed for waiting on the earl of Leicester at Kenilworth, where he took part in the lavish entertainment of Queen Elizabeth. He was still at Hengrave in 1587, and an indenture of 1588 granted him and his wife, Rose, *née* Springwell, whom he married at Hengrave parish church on 28 September 1579, a house and land nearby for twenty-one years, in return for providing strings for the instruments.

Johnson's contemporary reputation was high, despite confusion with the lutenist John Johnson (possibly related). Anthony Munday's *Banquet of Daintie Conceits* (1588) specifies 'Johnson's Medley' for one of the 'ditties', which seems to fit a keyboard 'Medley' by Edward Johnson, although there are medleys ascribed to John Johnson in lute sources. The famous pavan-galliard 'Delight' may be by either composer. Several writers on music from 1585 praise 'Johnson', but Francis Meres, in *Palladis tamia* (1598), mentions 'M[aster] Edward Iohnson' in a list of English musicians equalling those of ancient Greece.

When the earl of Hertford entertained the queen at Elvetham in 1591, with pageantry reminiscent of Kenilworth, Johnson's music was again in demand. Two of his songs survive, in five-part settings, for voice(s) and instruments. One was originally 'a Song of six parts, with the musicke of an exquisite consort, wherein was the lute, bandora, base-violl, citterne, treble-violl, and flute'. This important 'English consort' may have originated at Hengrave under Johnson in the 1570s.

In 1594 Johnson supplicated for the MusB degree from Gonville and Caius College, Cambridge, citing his many years of study and practice in music, and requesting Dr John Bull and Dr Thomas Dallis as examiners for his choral composition. The surviving Latin text of his *Hymnus comitialis* is literally the 'hymn sheet' for his degree exercise.

Thomas East's 1592 psalter included three settings by Johnson, his first published music. 'A Galliard Made by Ed. I.' for the wire-strung orpharion (tuned like a lute) in William Barley's *New Booke of Tabliture* (1596) is his only known lute solo. The two Elvetham songs and one for three voices all survive in manuscript. The text of his madrigal in Morley's *The Triumphes of Oriana*, 'Come, blessed bird', is somewhat enigmatic.

Too little of Edward Johnson's music survives for his importance as a composer to be assessed. There are some pavans of his for strings in north German sources from the early 1600s which may represent a body of lost music on which his contemporary reputation was based.

In the 1601 deposition, which is in a lawsuit concerning John Dowland's *Second Booke* (1600), both Johnson and John Wilbye, his successor at Hengrave from about 1598, were described as of Clerkenwell, Middlesex. Both men were provided with mourning cloth for Sir Thomas Kytson's funeral on 23 February 1602, but nothing is known of Johnson's own later life and death.   IAN HARWOOD

Sources M. Ross, 'The Kytsons of Hengrave: a study in musical patronage', MMus diss., King's Lond., 1989 · *New Grove* · I. Harwood, *Sweet broken music: the Elizabethan and Jacobean consort lesson*

[forthcoming] · M. Dowling, 'The printing of John Dowland's *Second booke of songs or ayres*', *The Library*, 4th ser., 12 (1931–2), 365–80 · P. Holman, *Four and twenty fiddlers: the violin at the English court, 1540–1690*, new edn (1993), 126, 133–5, 164

Johnson, Edward (*bap.* **1598**, *d.* **1672**), historian, was born at Canterbury, Kent, and baptized at St George's Church there on 16 September 1598, the eldest son of William Johnson (1559–1637) and his wife, Susan Porredge (1566–1604). Like his father, he was brought up to the trade of joiner, though later in New England he apparently also surveyed land and farmed. About 1620 he married Susan Munnter (*c.*1598–1690), with whom he eventually had eight children. He was admitted freeman of the city by birth in 1623.

It was once thought that Johnson emigrated to New England in 1630 with John Winthrop on board the *Arbella*, but it now seems that he went, with his wife and children, in 1637. He lived in the Boston area until 1642, at which time he helped to found the church at, and lay out, the new town of Woburn, Massachusetts. He held the town clerkship from 1642 until his death, and was also captain of the local militia company. He served for many years as the town's representative to the colony's general court.

Johnson was author of a valuable *History of New England from the English Planting in 1628 untill 1652*, published anonymously in London in 1653, which is more generally known and is reprinted as *Wonder-Working Providence of Zion's Saviour in New England*. Johnson's intense commitment to nonconforming congregationalism as it developed both as a theological system and as a social reality in New England is apparent on every page of his prose history, as well as in the poems with which the history is interspersed. Still important for its factual content, the narrative has come to be highly regarded by literary critics for its imaginative reconstruction of early New England history.

Johnson died at Woburn on 23 April 1672, leaving a sizeable personal estate and property in England. He was survived by his wife, who died on 7 March 1690.

STEPHEN CARL ARCH

Sources E. F. Johnson, 'Captain Edward Johnson, of Woburn, Mass., and some of his descendants', *New England Historical and Genealogical Register*, 59 (1905), 79–86 · E. French, 'Genealogical research in England: Johnson and Porredge', *New England Historical and Genealogical Register*, 67 (1913), 169–80 · A. Johnson, 'One line of descent from Capt. Edward Johnson of Woburn, Mass.', *New England Historical and Genealogical Register*, 68 (1914), 142–5 · J. Savage, 'Gleanings for New England history', *Collections of the Massachusetts Historical Society*, 3rd ser., 8 (1843), 243–348 · J. Farmer, *A genealogical register of the first settlers of New England*, ed. S. G. Drake (1964), 162 · R. C. Anderson, ed., *The great migration begins: immigrants to New England, 1620–1633*, 2 (Boston, MA, 1995), 1098
Wealth at death £1297—in inventory, homestead, rents due, property in England: Johnson, 'Captain Edward Johnson'

Johnson, Sir Edwin Beaumont (1825–1893), army officer, fourth son of Sir Henry Allen Johnson, baronet (*d.* 27 June 1860), and of his wife, Charlotte Elizabeth (*d.* 21 Feb 1883), daughter of Frederick Philipse of Philipsburg, New York, was born at Bath on 4 July 1825. His father, a student of Christ Church, Oxford, was tutor there to the prince of

Orange, and, having received a commission in the 81st regiment, accompanied him as aide-de-camp to the Peninsula, where he served under Wellington.

Edwin Beaumont entered Addiscombe College on 7 August 1840, received a commission as second-lieutenant in the Bengal artillery on 10 June 1842, and arrived in India on 12 December of that year. He was promoted lieutenant in July 1845 and served with the 5th troop of the 1st brigade of the Bengal horse artillery in the Sutlej campaign of the First Anglo-Sikh War. He took part in the battles of Ferozeshahr on 21 and 22 December 1845, and of Sobraon on 10 February 1846. From 5 August 1848 to 17 November 1850 he was deputy judge-advocate-general of the Bengal army. In the Punjab campaign of the Second Anglo-Sikh War in 1848–9 he served on the divisional staff of Major-General William Sampson Whish, and was present at the action of the passage of the Chenab River at Ramnagar on 22 November 1848; at the battle of Chilianwala on 13 January 1849; at the battle of Gujrat on 21 February, on Sir Walter Gilbert's staff; in the subsequent pursuit of the Sikhs and Afghans to Peshawar; and at the surrender of the Sikh army on 14 March 1849. He was mentioned in dispatches and noted for a brevet majority on attaining the rank of captain.

From 12 March 1855 Johnson was aide-de-camp to the commander-in-chief in India, Sir William Maynard Gomm, and on 21 December was appointed assistant adjutant-general of artillery in the Oudh division. He was at Meerut when the mutiny broke out in May 1857, and accompanied the column of Brigadier-General Archdale Wilson on its march to join that of the commander-in-chief from Ambala. He took part in the actions on the Hindan River at Ghazi-ud-din-nagar on 30 and 31 May, when he was slightly wounded, and in the action of Badli-ki-sarai on 8 June and the subsequent occupation of the ridge before Delhi. He was promoted brevet captain on 10 June, captain on 25 June, and brevet major on 5 July. He served throughout the siege as assistant adjutant-general. At the assault of 14 September he resumed his place on Wilson's staff. He was mentioned in dispatches and in January 1858 received a brevet lieutenant-colonelcy.

Johnson accompanied Wilson, who commanded the artillery, to the siege of Lucknow as assistant adjutant-general, and on its capture in March 1858 was honourably mentioned for his services. He was made CB, military division, on 26 July. After the mutiny was suppressed he resumed his duties as assistant adjutant-general of the Oudh division, and held the appointment until January 1862, when, after officiating for a time as adjutant-general of the army, he went to England on furlough. He was promoted brevet colonel in January 1863, and regimental lieutenant-colonel in March 1865. On 10 July 1865 he was appointed assistant military secretary for Indian affairs at the headquarters of the army in London, and on 4 August of the following year was nominated an extra aide-de-camp to the duke of Cambridge. He held both appointments until 1 August 1872, when he returned to India, having been promoted major-general in March 1868. On 8 July 1873 he became quartermaster-general in India, but eight months later was summoned home to take his seat as a member of council of the secretary of state for India in October 1874. He was promoted KCB, military division, on 29 May 1875. He again returned to India in 1877, having been appointed military member of the council there on 19 March, and held the office until 13 September 1880. He was promoted lieutenant-general and general in October 1877, and was made CIE in January 1878. He was director-general of military education at the War Office from 10 December 1884 to 31 December 1886. He was made GCB in June 1887 and promoted colonel-commandant, Royal Artillery, in December 1890. Johnson retired from the active list on 31 January 1891, and died at his home, 53 Victoria Road, Kensington, London, on 18 June 1893. He was buried at Hanwell.   R. H. VETCH, rev. JAMES FALKNER

Sources BL OIOC · *Army List* · *The Times* (21 June 1893) · F. W. Stubbs, *History of the Bengal artillery* (1895) · *LondG* (April 1849) · *LondG* (Dec 1857) · *LondG* (May 1858) · *CGPLA Eng. & Wales* (1893)
Likenesses C. Tayler, oils, *c.*1843; Christies, 1990
Wealth at death £9241 6s. 3d.: resworn probate, Jan 1894, *CGPLA Eng. & Wales* (1893)

Johnson, Elizabeth (*fl.* 1779–1798), printer, ran her printing business from the old state lottery offices between 4 and 5 Ludgate Hill in London. Her husband, Edward (*d.* 1789), also a printer, operated from the same premises. Although female printers were not uncommon, Johnson is noteworthy for setting up two papers which were published under her name. The more significant, the *British Gazette and Sunday Monitor*, was the first Sunday newspaper, and was produced in contravention of sabbatarian legislation banning printing on Sundays. Although this venture was a success, when Johnson launched another newspaper in 1788, the *Evening Star*, only a few numbers were printed before the paper appears to have folded. After her husband died on 7 March 1789 Elizabeth seems to have carried on both businesses. In 1798, possibly the year of her own death, she was succeeded by Samuel John Johnson, who was probably her son.

HANNAH BARKER

Sources I. Maxted, *The London book trades, 1775–1800: a preliminary checklist of members* (1977) · A. Aspinall, 'Statistical accounts of the London newspapers in the eighteenth century', *EngHR*, 63 (1948), 201–32 · S. Morison, *The English newspaper* (1932)
Archives JRL, Methodist Archives and Research Centre, letters to Sarah Ryan and Mary Fletcher

Johnson, Esther [Stella] (1681–1728), friend of Jonathan Swift, was born on 13 March 1681 and baptized as Hester on 20 March in the parish church of Richmond, Surrey, the eldest child of Edward Johnson and his wife, Bridget, waiting woman to Sir William Temple's sister Lady Giffard. Stella's father was perhaps a merchant and master of a trading sloop running between England and Holland, where he died at a date unknown. On 25 October 1711 her mother married her second husband, Ralph Mose, who had been Temple's steward. The marriage took place six months after the death of the first Mrs Mose, the cook whom Temple had had replaced by Jonathan Swift's sister Jane Fenton in September 1711. In 1721 Bridget was left £20 in Lady Giffard's will. Stella's sister Anne was baptized on

12 April 1683 and married a Mr Filby; her brother Edward was baptized on 8 July 1688 and died overseas.

An alternative genealogy (though not one that has found many supporters), developed to justify Stella's privileged position as a well-educated gentlewoman at Moor Park, her financial comfort after Temple's death, her alleged physical resemblance to Temple, and the fact that Swift could have been attracted only to a 'superior' kind of woman, is that she was the natural daughter of Sir William Temple and Bridget.

Stella first encountered Jonathan *Swift (1667–1745) in her eighth year, at Temple's houses at Sheen and Moor Park, where Swift was her tutor (it was he who gave her the name Stella). Their relationship was lifelong and largely hidden from the public gaze. Swift's memorial 'On the Death of Mrs. Johnson' was begun on the evening of her death and depicts an idealized woman without sexual status, an intellectual and companionable partner. As Swift's star pupil, she exemplifies her master's pedagogic skills and requirements in a woman: 'well versed' in Greek and Roman history, French and English history, she had read the 'best books of travels' and understood 'the Platonic and [the defects of] Epicurean philosophy ... the nature of government', and had some grasp of physic and anatomy. Poor health dominated Stella's life until her fifteenth year, and in adulthood she was plagued by asthma, eye problems, headaches, and neuritis.

Stella remained at Moor Park or Farnham for about two years after Temple's death on 27 January 1699. He bequeathed her a lease on lands in Morristown, co. Wicklow, worth about £1000—an income later augmented with Swift's assistance—and there was an annuity paid to her from £400 held for her by Lady Giffard. She was in London with Lady Giffard at the Temples' Pall Mall house for winter and spring 1698, and Swift describes her as 'one of the most beautiful, graceful, and agreeable young women in London, only a little too fat' (*Prose Writings of Jonathan Swift*, 5.227). Her companion Rebecca Dingley (c.1665–1743) was daughter of the second son of Sir John Dingley of the Isle of Wight, who had married Jane Hammond, elder sister of Mary Hammond, Sir William Temple's mother. In summer or autumn 1701 the two women moved to Dublin at Swift's urging. Apart from one extended visit to England (from about December 1707 to the end of October 1708), and probably at Lord Berkeley of Stratton's expense (Le Brocquy, *Friend*, 65), she spent her life in Dublin, mostly in lodgings at Mary Street, close to the Liffey. Swift's account book for November 1702 records an annual allowance paid to Stella and Dingley by or through him.

Swift and Stella were hardly ever alone in each other's presence, yet close friends (Thomas Swift and Archbishop King) expected a marriage. She shared his friends, Thomas Sheridan, Charles Ford, and St George Ashe, but also established her own circle, including Dean Stearne, Archdeacon Walls, Dillon Ashe, Primate Lindsay, and bishops Lloyd, Brown, and Pulleyn. In 1703 the thirty-five-year-old Revd William Tisdall, fellow of Trinity College, Dublin, unsuccessfully proposed marriage to Stella. Writing as adviser rather than rival, Swift confessed to Tisdall: 'if my fortunes and humour served me to think of that state, I should certainly, among all persons on earth, make your choice; because I never saw that person whose conversation I entirely valued but hers' (20 April 1704, *Correspondence of Jonathan Swift*, 1, no. 25).

Sixty-five extant letters written by Swift between 1710 and 1713, collectively one side of a 'conversation' between him and MD (Stella and Dingley) about his political and social career in Queen Anne's London, were first brought together as a group in Thomas Sheridan's edition of Swift's *Works* (1784), misleadingly but forever after titled *Dr. Swift's Journal to Stella*. Two additional letters from Swift to Stella survive (c.January 1698 and 30 April 1721, *Correspondence of Jonathan Swift*, 1, no. 12, 2, no. 536). There is a weakening in Swift's 'spontaneity and unaffected naturalness' from the end of 1711, and from 9 February 1712 'his greetings are ... more stereotyped and perfunctory' (Swift, *Journal*, xxxix). The first extant letter is Swift's from Chester, 2 September 1710, the last from the same place, 6 June 1713. For eighteen months before March 1712 he was a daytime and evening guest of the Van Homrighs in their London lodgings, where he had a room reserved for his use. Vanessa Van Homrigh is mentioned by name only three times in the *Journal*. Stella may not have known of Vanessa's deep emotional claim on Swift, but it is only in letters to Stella that Swift uses his 'little language', a lightly coded form of intimate address.

Mrs Whiteway, Swift's cousin and close friend, asserted that there had been a secret marriage between Stella and Swift 'two or three years after he was Dean', that is, between 30 July and 4 October 1716, performed by Bishop St George Ashe (c.1658–1718) in the bishop's garden at Clogher. Biographers who knew Swift accepted the marriage as a fact—Dr Evans (bishop of Meath, writing to Archbishop Wake, 27 July 1723), Orrery (1752, using Mrs Whiteway's letters transcribed in Orrery's own copy of *Remarks*, now at Harvard University Library), Laetitia Pilkington (1748–1754), Delany (1754). Deane Swift dismisses the idea in an undated letter to Orrery written during Swift's lifetime, but then asserted it as a fact in his *Essay* of 1755. Dr Johnson believed the marriage combined 'the expectation of all the pleasures of perfect friendship, without the uneasiness of conjugal restraint' ('Life of Swift', in *Lives of the Poets*, 1779–81). Maxwell Gold presents arguments for and against, and supports the probability of a marriage. Ehrenpreis avoids taking up the issue. All agree that it effected no change in their respective domestic arrangements—in Johnson's words (using information from Dr Madden), 'they lived in different houses, as before; nor did she ever lodge in the deanery, but when Swift was seized with a fit of giddiness' (ibid.)—and it may have been a 'sacramental occasion, and not a civil ceremony', since it took place in a garden and not a consecrated building (Byrn, 7).

The sobriquet Stella first appears in 'On Stella's Birthday' (1719) and thereafter until 1727 in annual birthday verses. Stella copied out Swift's poems and some of *Gulliver's Travels* at Sheridan's Quilca in autumn 1725.

Stella spent her last eighteen months at Arbourhill, on the site of the barracks, Phoenix Park, home of the widowed Lady Clotilda Eustace, whose daughter married Thomas Tickell in 1726. Signing her will 'Esther Johnson: Spinster' on 30 December 1727, she endowed a chaplaincy in Dr Steevens' Hospital, Dublin. Swift was not an executor, but received her strong box and papers. For the apprenticeship of an adopted child named Bryan M'Loghlin 'whom I keep on charity' she left £25. Le Brocquy proposes that Bryan was the natural son of the dean and Vanessa, and not Stella's own child by Swift (Le Brocquy, *Friend*, 52). *Bon mots de Stella*, compiled by Swift, appeared in 1745. For a portrait, from an original drawing by Thomas Parnell, see *Journal to Stella*, ed. H. Williams, 160. Stella died at Arbourhill on Sunday 28 January 1728. She was buried at St Patrick's Cathedral two days later; Swift did not attend the funeral.   CLIVE PROBYN

Sources 'On the death of Mrs. Johnson', *Prose writings of Jonathan Swift*, ed. H. Davis and others, 16 vols. (1939–74), 5.227–36 • J. Swift, *Journal to Stella*, ed. H. Williams, 2 vols. (1948); repr. (1963) • [F. E. Ball], 'Stella and her history', in *The correspondence of Jonathan Swift*, 4 (1913), 449–63, appx 1, 449–62 • R. F. M. Byrn, 'Jonathan Swift's locket for Stella Swift: a sacramental marriage "certificate"?', *Swift Studies*, 3 (1988), 2–8 • H. Davis, *Stella: a gentlewoman of the eighteenth century* (1942) • I. Ehrenpreis, *Swift: the man, his works and the age*, 3 vols. (1962–83) • M. B. Gold, *Swift's marriage to Stella, together with unprinted and misprinted letters* (1937) • S. Le Brocquy, *Swift's most valuable friend* (1968) • S. Le Brocquy, *Cadenus: a reassessment in the light of new evidence of the relationships between Swift, Stella, and Vanessa* (1962) • H. Mangan, 'Portraits of Stella and Vanessa', in J. Swift, *Journal to Stella*, ed. H. Williams, 2 (1948); repr. (1963), 687–703 • Lord Orrery, *Remarks on the life and writings of Dr. Jonathan Swift* (1752) • D. Swift, *An essay upon the life, writings and character of Dr. Jonathan Swift* (1765) • *The correspondence of Jonathan Swift*, ed. D. Woolley, 4 vols. (1999–2004)
Archives V&A NAL, Forster Library
Likenesses Dr T. Parnell, drawing, before 1718, repro. in Swift, *Journal to Stella* • attrib. J. Latham, oils, NG Ire. • line engraving, BM • oils, NG Ire.
Wealth at death provided stipend for chaplain at Dr Steevens' Hospital, Dublin: will, W. R. Wilde, *The closing years of Dean Swift's life*, 2nd edn (1849), 97–101

Johnson, Folorunṣo [Ginger] **(1916–1975)**, percussionist and band leader, was born in Ijebu, Nigeria, on 2 May 1916, the son of a Muslim priest whose name he later gave as George Johnson. His parents were Ijebu-Yoruba from Nigeria. He was orphaned as a child and grew up in Lagos, where he was brought up by his sister, Yetunde. He learned to make his own drums and picked up basic drumming techniques through playing with his brother's band, and began to travel at an early age by joining the merchant navy. He reached the United States before arriving in England in 1939 or 1940. As George Johnson he lived in Liverpool and in Manchester, where he worked in a munitions factory, before moving to London about 1943 and continuing his war work, apprenticed as a fitter–mechanic.

In London Johnson started playing bongos and began a close association with the main figures in the emerging local modern jazz movement. At the historically important Club Eleven he played with guitarist Dave Goldberg and with Ronnie Scott's Boptet, with which he recorded (1949), and he was a regular participant at the popular swing sessions held at Feldman's in Oxford Street on Sundays. He also recorded with the clarinettist Harry Parry (1949), playing conga drums in addition to bongos. In 1949 he began a long association with the band leader Edmundo Ros. Featured with Ros's rumba band on radio, television, and recordings, he developed a reputation as an expert in Latin-American percussion and was often called upon to deputize and record with other Mayfair band leaders. Ros recognized Johnson's capabilities and remained his champion: 'Unless a man is able to think rhythm he is unable to play rhythm. Ginger does just that … I consider myself fortunate' (Ros, 36).

While earning his living through work in exclusive nightclubs, Johnson remained grounded in vernacular improvisation. At west African clubs such as the Abalabi, where he played with the Nigerian guitarists Ambrose Campbell and Brewster Hughes, he continued to interact with British modern jazz musicians who went there for rhythmic and social inspiration. The drummer Phil Seamen was one of these, and Johnson was one of several African percussionists in a band Seamen organized for occasional dances. He also played in the Afro-Cuban band of the saxophonist Kenny Graham, with whom he recorded (1951), and in 1954 he played with the bi-racial big band led by the exuberant percussionist and vocalist Leon Roy.

In the late 1940s Johnson formed a relationship with Vera Tomlinson; their son Norris Assikuru Johnson (b. 1949) became a London-based drummer and teacher. In the early 1950s he met Christine Eleanor Jenour (1933/4–1998); they married on 26 July 1960. Their children were Rupi Toro (b. 1955), Abegail Rosemary (b. 1957), Dennis Abas (b. 1960), Ricky Fela (b. 1962), and Amos Olanubi Alakambi Tekabu (b. 1965).

In 1954 Johnson began his band-leading career. At Le Club Contemporain in Mayfair his Afro-Cubans featured the Vincentian trumpeter Shake Keane; he also played mambos and recorded, but he returned frequently to Edmundo Ros, who regarded him as the 'cornerstone' of his orchestra. At his home at 6 Churton Street, Victoria, he opened the Folorunṣo Sun Rhythm School, where he offered 'Authentic instruction in Bongoes, Conga Drum and all Afro-Cuban Rhythms' (advertisement, *Melody Maker*, 1957) from tutors including the Nigerian Bob Caxton. By 1960, 150 students were enrolled in the institution, which acted also as a casting agency by providing percussionists and singers for films. Johnson's own film appearances included *The Captain's Paradise* (1953).

Johnson was a cultural ambassador. By the 1960s he was the leading percussionist figure in the new artistic 'underground' as well as in African circles, and was responsible for influencing other musicians and poets such as those associated with the 'New Departures' movement. A slight, energetic man, with a freckled complexion and the light brown skin colouring and hair that gave him his nickname (he explained this by claiming some Scottish or Portuguese ancestry—although such colouring does occur in parts of the Nigerian hinterland), he was a familiar figure at dances and festivals. There he wore Yoruba dress made from handwoven cloth (*aao-oke*), and, through example, guided audiences to recognize the African antecedents of much popular music. He continued to lead a working band in Soho nightclubs while playing for serious theatrical productions, and provided many African and Caribbean musicians with their first opportunity to play to a general audience. His own visibility increased when he appeared at the free concert given by the Rolling Stones in Hyde Park; his African Drummers were recorded in the video *Stones in the Park* (1969).

In 1970 Johnson opened the Iroko Club in Belsize Park, north London. This became an important black cultural centre while also attracting white music lovers who went there to experience its 'African' atmosphere. In 1975 he returned to Nigeria to settle. He planned to build a club and campsite where he and his musicians could live together and had purchased land for this purpose, but he was taken ill in Lagos shortly after his arrival. Rumours persisted that he had been poisoned, but his family rejected Western medical treatment and he was taken to Ijebu, where he died from a heart attack on 15 July 1975. He was buried at Ijebu.   VAL WILMER

Sources E. Borneman, *Contemporary moods from the Club Contemporain, Mayfair, London* [disc notes, Melodisc MLP 508] · E. Ros, 'Introduces Ginger Johnson', *Beat*, 1/1 (Dec 1956), 36 · 'Sun Rhythm School', *Beat*, 1/2 (Jan 1957), 34–5 · B. Okonedo, 'Ginger brings Africa to Hampstead', *Melody Maker* (13 May 1972), 36 · S. Hopkins, *Time Out* (8–14 Aug 1975), 46 · personal knowledge (2004) · private information (2004) · m. cert.
Likenesses V. Wilmer, photographs, 1960–69, priv. coll.

Johnson [*née* Croke]**, Frances** [*called* Begum Johnson] (1728–1812), hostess, was celebrated not only for her remarkable longevity in India, where few Britons outlived two monsoon seasons, but also for her four marriages and her influential circle of friends. She was born on 10 April 1728 at Fort St David, on the Coromandel coast. Her father was an East India Company official, Edward Croke (1690–1769), and her mother, Isabella Beizor (*d.* 1780), of Portuguese descent. Frances was sent to Calcutta in 1743 to marry Perry Purpell Templer, merchant, with whom she had two children, both of whom died in infancy. Templer died on 25 January 1748 and that November she married another merchant, James Altham, who died ten days later of smallpox. Her third marriage, in 1749, to William Watts, company agent at Cossimbazar, was the most long-lasting and successful.

Eighteenth-century India saw a power struggle between France and Britain for mastery, especially in the Carnatic and Bengal, led by heroic figures like General J.-F. Dupleix and Robert Clive. In 1756 Cossimbazar was besieged by Siraj ud-daula, nawab of Bengal, who was misinformed about the reputed wealth of its British inhabitants. The Watts now had three children and Frances was pregnant with the fourth. William Watts surrendered the fort without resistance, but Frances was allowed to remain there unharmed, until ordered to neighbouring Murshidabad. A former acquaintanceship with the nawab's mother, Amina Begam, meant Frances and her children were protected there until they could be safely (and fortunately)

Frances Johnson (1728–1812), attrib. Thomas Hickey, c.1784

moved to Chandernagore, thereby escaping the sack of Calcutta in June of that year. (In later life it was Frances Johnson's constant affectionate references to Amina Begam that led to her being styled Begam Johnson herself, by her friends, though she is more commonly known to later generations as Begum Johnson.) After Calcutta's recapture by Clive, Frances rejoined her husband there, and William was sent to negotiate with the nawab, who was defeated at the battle of Plassey in 1757. Two years later William, now a rich man, took his wife and children to England, but Frances could not settle in this cold, foreign country. William died in 1764, the children grew up, and she returned to Calcutta in 1769, buying a house at 10 Clive Street, where she lived for the rest of her life, mixing in the highest circles of company officials.

In 1774, aged forty-six, Frances made a fourth, unfortunate, marriage, this time to the Revd William Johnson (*b.* c.1744), chaplain of St John's Church, Calcutta, nicknamed the Revd Tally-Ho, and sixteen years her junior. He treated her unkindly, and she eventually paid him to leave India in 1788, to the relief of her many friends. She blossomed into a society hostess, and Warren and Marian Hastings, Lord Cornwallis, Arthur Wellesley (later the duke of Wellington), and his brother Richard, Lord Mornington, all visited her at Clive Street. The remarkable absence of elderly Britons in India (for many died young and others returned home after service) meant she became a unique institution, especially as she kept up the old habits of dining at four in the afternoon and entertaining until the early hours. She kept nine slave girls, not unusual at the time, when Africans were imported and Bengali children captured or sold by their parents. Four of her five grandsons came to serve in India, including Mordaunt Ricketts, later the resident at Lucknow. Another grandson, Lord Liverpool, later British prime minister, sent her boxes of millinery every year. Her portrait, by Thomas Hickey, shows an elderly, though still handsome, woman, draped in lace ruffles, ribbons, and bows.

Begum Johnson died at her home on 3 February 1812 after a series of 'spasms' (probably strokes) and abscesses, aged eighty-three. She was buried two days later in St John's churchyard, at a spot she had chosen, next to the tomb of Job Charnock, the founder of Calcutta; her funeral was attended by the governor-general, the chief justice, and other notables. Her elaborate tomb bears a long, somewhat inaccurate inscription, taken verbatim when her memory had begun to fail.

ROSIE LLEWELLYN-JONES

Sources I. Edwards-Stuart, *The Calcutta of Begum Johnson* (1990) • H. E. A. Cotton, *Calcutta old and new: a historical and descriptive handbook to the city*, rev. edn, ed. N. R. Ray (1980)
Archives BL, Lord Liverpool MSS, Add. MSS 38469–38475
Likenesses attrib. T. Hickey, portrait, c.1784, Gov. Art Coll. [*see illus.*] • T. Hickey, portrait, BL OIOC

Johnson, Francis (*bap.* 1562, *d.* 1617), separatist minister and religious controversialist, was born at Richmond, Yorkshire, and baptized there on 27 March 1562, the elder son of John Johnson, woollen draper and sometime town alderman or bailiff, and elder brother of George *Johnson (*bap.* 1563, *d. c.*1605). In April 1579 he matriculated as a pensioner at Christ's College, Cambridge, graduating BA in 1582 and proceeding MA in 1585. He was elected fellow of the college by 29 September 1584, having been ordained deacon in London on 16 April 1584 and priest on 28 April.

While at Cambridge Johnson espoused Thomas Cartwright's presbyterian views on church polity and discipline. He expressed these opinions in a university sermon delivered on 6 January 1589 at Great St Mary's, Cambridge. Preaching on 1 Peter 5: 1–4 he declared that an eldership founded on the New Testament model was the only lawful form of church polity. Moreover, he contended that the lack of proper discipline was the cause of many problems in church and state. Word of the sermon reached the queen's ecclesiastical commissioners, who demanded punishment. Vice-chancellor Thomas Nevile tried to administer the *ex officio mero* oath to Johnson, and imprisoned him when he declined to take it. On 13 September Johnson was released on bail. Nevile now asked that he deny that there was only one God-given pattern of ecclesiastical government and affirm that her majesty could regulate the governance of the church and state; Johnson refused. He was expelled from the university, and left before Easter 1590.

Disillusioned, Johnson travelled to Middelburg in the Netherlands, where he became minister of the English Merchant Adventurers Church. In spring 1591, on learning that a volume containing Henry Barrow's *A Plaine Refutation* and John Greenwood's *A Briefe Refutation* was awaiting secret shipment to England, he notified Sir Robert Sidney, the English governor of Flushing. Sidney seized these separatist books and had them burnt. However, Johnson

kept a copy, and it influenced him to adopt separatist beliefs. By October he was insisting that members of his congregation subscribe to a set of articles that would pledge them to join together:

> to live as the churche of Christe, watching one over another, and submittinge our selves unto them, to whom the Lorde Jesus committeth the oversight of his churche, guidinge and censuringe us according to the rule of the Worde of God. ('Francis Johnson his articles', fol. 169*r*)

These articles would have put the church on a covenantal basis similar to that used in separatist churches.

Controversies ensued and by April 1592 Johnson had left the pulpit. Soon thereafter he went to London, where he conferred with Barrow and Greenwood. These conversations completed his conversion and led to his election as the pastor of the newly organized London separatist church the following September.

In October the authorities arrested and gaoled Johnson, but he was later released. He was rearrested on the night of 5/6 December at the home of Edward Boyes, a well-to-do separatist haberdasher. He was sent to the Fleet prison, where he spent more than four years. During his captivity he remained true to separatist principles, as shown in his 5 April 1593 examination and several defiant petitions.

In 1595 Johnson defended separatist positions in *A Treatise of the Ministery of the Church of England*. Here he responded to the puritan Arthur Hildersam's defence of the established church's ministers by declaring that they held their positions by virtue of an unscriptural, and therefore antichristian, office, power, and calling. This book was subversive and was probably printed abroad, as were subsequent editions of his works until the civil war years. His most important accomplishment during his imprisonment was his formulation of *A True Confession of the Faith* (1596). It defined the church's beliefs, doctrine, polity, and discipline. It also included attacks on the Church of England, a summons to separate, and instructions for organizing a gathered, covenanted separatist congregation—one where scriptural church officers were elected, discipline was dispensed according to Matthew 18: 15–17, and final authority resided in the congregation. Two years later this *Confession* was translated into Latin with a new preface addressed to scholars at protestant universities, asking them for their opinions and requesting scriptural proofs refuting any errors they might find. The Dutch professor Francis Junius replied, and the correspondence was later published under the title of *Certayne Letters* (1602).

While Johnson engaged external adversaries, he became embroiled in controversies with members of the church. The first of these arguments sprang from his marriage to Tomison, *née* Leigh (*bap.* 1570), widow of Edward Boyes, in late 1594 or early 1595. Francis's brother George disapproved of the match, 'she being much noted for pride, which would give great offence' (G. Johnson, 94). Although Tomison promised to reform herself, her dress, speech, and deportment still caused criticism. Francis claimed that George was overzealous and mentally unbalanced. The disputes continued intermittently after the brothers were released from prison in April 1597, during their abortive colonization voyage to the Magdalen Islands in the Gulf of St Lawrence that summer, and following their mid-September arrival in Amsterdam. There they joined the bulk of the congregation who had been exiled earlier under the provisions of the statute 35 Elizabeth c. 1. The united group became known as the 'Ancient' Separatist church of Amsterdam, and it set out to serve 'as a light upon an hil' for godly people in England (ibid., 156).

Despite the church's lofty aspirations, dissensions multiplied. Some time before March 1599 Francis, 'in his fury and rage', pronounced George's excommunication (G. Johnson, 76). Ultimately Tomison acknowledged that her apparel had violated scriptural rules and reformed, but Francis continued to defend George's expulsion. These quarrels, together with other allegations of injustice and ill dealing, were narrated in George's *Discourse* (1603). Thomas White, a separatist minister who had fled to Amsterdam, made additional accusations in his *Discoverie of Brownisme* (1605), while Francis rebutted White in *An Inquirie and Answer* (1606). In the meantime other disputes arose. The most serious concerned the lawfulness of attending corrupt Dutch Reformed church services and changing church practice to allow reformed apostates to hold office. The latter resulted in the excommunication of John Johnson, who had journeyed to Amsterdam to reconcile his sons. During this turmoil, Johnson wrote *An Answer to Maister H[Enry] Jacob* (1600). In it he argued that the persecuted protestant congregations of Queen Mary's reign were closer to the separatists' conception of the church than they were to that of the puritans.

After James I's accession in 1603 Johnson and others travelled to England, where they presented petitions requesting toleration and urging a conference with the bishops. James rebuffed them, and when Oxford doctors attacked them in print the separatists published *An Apology or Defence* (1604). Johnson again denounced the English church in 1608, when he produced *Certayne reasons and arguments proving that it is not lawfull to heare or have any spirituall communion with the present ministerie of the Church of England*. In this work he recapitulated separatist thinking and presented it in the form of seven syllogistic positions. Later he conducted a correspondence with the Anglican cleric John Carpenter where he attacked the use of read liturgical prayers. Their letters were published in *Quaestio de precibus et leiturgiis* (1610).

Johnson's reputation among English radical protestants was now at its height. In fact, one critic sarcastically labelled him the Bishop of Brownisme (Clapham, sig. I2v). Nevertheless, succeeding years brought decline and disintegration. The most important cause was the arrival of a new separatist group led by Johnson's former pupil John Smyth in 1607. By late 1608 Smyth had concluded that, since all other churches were guilty of apostasy, he must revive the true church himself. Accordingly he rebaptized himself and his brethren, and declared that the church's ministry must be firmly subordinated to the congregation. Later, he sought union with Dutch Mennonites.

Smyth's defection to Anabaptism deeply affected Johnson. First it caused him to change his polemical priorities. In 1609 he published *A Brief Treatise … Against Two Errours of the Anabaptists*, in which he denounced Smyth's 'schisms and heresies' and stated that the infant baptism of apostolic churches, including Rome, was 'not to be renounced' (*Treatise* 3, 16). Second, because of his belief that Smyth's errors could be traced to a misperception about where ultimate power in the church should reside, and because of his own authoritarian tendencies, he declared that henceforth final authority would rest with the elders rather than with the congregation. Johnson's abandonment of congregational supremacy moved the church's teacher, Henry Ainsworth, to assume leadership of an opposition faction. After a year of strife, the Ainsworthians seceded on the night of 15/16 December 1610. The parting was bitter, and both sides wrote books to justify their positions. Johnson's new teacher, Richard Clyfton, went first, publishing his *Advertisement* (1612). Ainsworth replied in *An Animadversion* (1613). In addition a lawsuit developed over ownership of the congregation's meeting-house. The Ainsworthians triumphed, and the Johnsonians moved to Emden in Germany about 1613. They returned to Amsterdam in 1617, where Johnson published *A Christian Plea* (1617). In it he continued his criticism of Anabaptism and reiterated that Rome was a true but deeply apostate church.

Johnson died at Amsterdam; he was buried there on 10 January 1618 NS (31 December 1617 OS). He may have had a daughter, Perseverance, but conclusive evidence is lacking. He had a controversial character: he was a brave man, a learned polemicist, and an effective debater, but his shifting opinions, intellectual pride, and choleric temperament made him an overbearing colleague, a difficult family member, and a divisive pastor.

MICHAEL E. MOODY

Sources G. Johnson, *A discourse of some troubles and excommunications in the banished English church at Amsterdam* (1603) · M. Moody, 'A critical edition of George Johnson's *Discourse* (1603)', PhD diss., Claremont Graduate School, 1979 · parish register, Richmond, St Mary, 27 March 1562, N. Yorks. CRO, PR/RM 1/1 pt 1 [baptism] · B. R. White, *The English separatist tradition* (1971) · K. L. Sprunger, *Dutch puritanism: a history of English and Scottish churches of the Netherlands in the sixteenth and seventeenth centuries* (1982) · 'Francis Johnson his articles which he urged to be underwritten by the Englishe mearchants in Middleboroughe in October 1591', BL, Add. MS 28571, fol. 169r · *The writings of Henry Barrow, 1590–1591*, ed. L. H. Carlson (1966) · *The writings of John Greenwood and Henry Barrow, 1591–1593*, ed. L. H. Carlson (1970) · W. Nijenhuis, ed., *Matthew Slade, 1569–1628* (1986), 73 · P. Lake, 'The dilemma of the establishment puritan: the Cambridge heads and the case of Francis Johnson and Cuthbert Bainbrigg', *Journal of Ecclesiastical History*, 29 (1978), 25–35 · H. Clapham, *A chronological discourse* (1609) · T. White, *A discoverie of Brownisme* (1605) · H. M. Dexter and M. Dexter, *The England and Holland of the pilgrims* (1905) · R. Clyfton, *An advertisement* (1612) · F. Du Jon the Elder [F. Junius] and others, *Certayne letters, translated into English [by R. G.]* (1602) · J. Peile, *Biographical register of Christ's College, 1505–1905, and of the earlier foundation, God's House, 1448–1505*, ed. [J. A. Venn], 1 (1910), 150–51 · H. Dexter, *Congregationalism of the past 300 years, as seen in its literature* (1880), 16 · P. Milward, *Religious controversies of the Jacobean age* (1978)

Johnson, Francis (1795/6–1876), orientalist, spent much time in his youth in Italy, where he studied oriental languages, and learned Arabic from an Arab. In March 1818 he left Rome with Charles Barry, Charles Lock Eastlake, and Kinnaird, an architect, for Athens. After studying antiquities there until June, Johnson and Barry travelled overland to Constantinople, but they parted in August, Johnson returning to Italy, while Barry pursued his travels in Egypt. In 1824 Johnson was appointed to the chair of Sanskrit, Bengali, and Telugu at the East India College at Haileybury. He resigned his chair in 1855, was married in 1857, and died at Railway Place, St John, Hertford, on 29 January 1876.

The great work of Johnson's life was his *Persian Dictionary*. On its first publication in 1829 it was described as the third edition of John Richardson's *Dictionary of Persian, Arabic, and English*. It contained, however, much original matter, especially as regards the Arabic element in Persian. In 1852 Johnson published a revised and much extended edition under his own name alone. This work was regarded as an extremely significant contribution to Persian lexicography. A revised and extended edition was published by F. J. Steingasse, in 1892. Johnson also edited the *Gulistan* of Sa'di (1863). His translations from Sanskrit of the *Meghadūta* (1867), *Hitopadeśa* (1840), and *Mahabhrata* (1842), were very useful to English beginners in the study of Sanskrit, during the rest of the century.

CECIL BENDALL, rev. PARVIN LOLOI

Sources *Hertfordshire Mercury* (12 Feb 1876) · *Journal of the Royal Asiatic Society of Great Britain and Ireland*, new ser., 8 (1876) · Boase, *Mod. Eng. biog.* · Allibone, *Dict.* · C. E. Buckland, *Dictionary of Indian biography* (1906) · d. cert.

Johnson, Sir Frank William Frederick (1866–1943), entrepreneur and army officer, was born at Watlington, near Downham Market, Norfolk, on 21 June 1866, the son of Frederick William Johnson (*bap.* 1819, *d.* 1879) MRCS LSA, general practitioner of Watlington—the son of William Johnson, apothecary and medical practitioner of Watlington—and his wife, Elizabeth Mary (Lizzie), *née* Swain. F. W. Johnson died when his son was fourteen. Educated at King's Lynn grammar school from May 1876 to April 1881, first as a day-boy and later as a boarder, the young Johnson was intended for a medical career, but in August 1882 he left his widowed mother and emigrated to Cape Colony in southern Africa.

Johnson had been promised employment at the Cape Commercial Bank but on arrival he found it had failed. He became a clerk at the Table Bay Harbour Board and also, for free accommodation, a volunteer fireman. He joined the duke of Edinburgh's own rifles, a local volunteer unit, and was soon promoted corporal, and he won prizes for swimming. In September 1884 he attended a meeting in Cape Town addressed by the Revd John Mackenzie, the Scottish missionary, on the Boer threat to Bechuanaland. By his own account inspired by this, Johnson enlisted in the 2nd mounted rifles (Carrington's Horse), recruited by Colonel (later Sir) Frederick Carrington, in which he was soon promoted quartermaster sergeant, in the 1884–5

Warren expedition—see Sir Charles *Warren (1840–1927)—to Bechuanaland which without bloodshed expelled the Boer freebooters and established the British protectorate. In 1885 he transferred to the new paramilitary Bechuanaland border police. By Johnson's own account, at Shoshong, then the Ngwato capital, a Danish hunter showed him gold dust he said was from the Mazoe valley in Zambesia.

Thickset, broad-shouldered, dark-eyed, bullet-headed, and with a 'voice like a foghorn' (Blake, 67), Johnson was tough, ambitious, dynamic, self-confident, optimistic, unscrupulous, and determined to enrich himself in Africa. Major Arthur Glyn Leonard of the chartered company's police described Johnson in 1890 as 'short and stout with a jovial face and manner, full of push and energy, but he does not give me the impression of being either clever or deep' and noted his 'aggressive nature', 'bounce', and 'gift of the gab' (Leonard, 34, 188). Lured by gold, Johnson, Maurice Heany, and Edward Burnett resigned from the police and in 1887, with Cape Town businessmen persuaded by Johnson to finance it, formed a prospecting syndicate, the Great Northern Gold Fields Exploration Company, 'this petty enterprise with the impressive title' (Galbraith, 49). In March 1887 Johnson, Heany, and others left Mafeking to seek a concession and prospect in Matabeleland. *En route*, in Bechuanaland, they obtained a concession from Khama III of the Ngwato. At the Ndebele (Matabele) capital Bulawayo, after frustrating delays, they obtained from the king, Lobengula, a limited prospecting concession. Johnson found alluvial gold, but when he returned to the capital to claim the concession he was tried on charges including poisoning and espionage and was fined £100, gunpowder, and blankets. Aggrieved, Johnson wanted revenge. He and his associates were also involved in the Bechuanaland Trading Association. Johnson's Cape Town backers sold Khama's concession, and it was later acquired by the new London-based Bechuanaland Exploration Company, registered in April 1888, headed by Lord Gifford and George Cawston and backed by influential London financiers. Johnson was appointed the company's manager in southern Africa and had grandiose hopes of it, as possibly an African counterpart to the East India Company. Gifford and Cawston also formed the Exploring Company to seek a concession from Lobengula. The Gifford–Cawston group was a rival to Cecil Rhodes's group but in 1889 merged with it, Gifford and Cawston receiving lucrative directorships in Rhodes's new British South Africa Company. Johnson's relations with the two Gifford–Cawston companies are unclear, but he claimed he had been tricked by Gifford and Cawston and he remained bitter against them.

Johnson married at Cape Town, on 12 June 1888, Jane, daughter of Captain J. H. Day of Cowes, and they had three sons and two daughters; she survived her husband. Their youngest son, Derrick Sivewright, born in December 1896, was killed in December 1916 serving with the Royal Flying Corps, and two of their grandsons were killed in the Second World War serving with the Royal Air Force.

In summer 1888 Johnson went to Lisbon to obtain a concession: he later claimed in his memoirs that he attempted to buy Portuguese East Africa south of the Zambezi for £4 million. In August he obtained a Mazoe valley concession from the Mozambique Company. In early 1889, with his Cape Town backers (apparently members of the Gold Fields Exploration Company) and Frederick Courtney Selous (1851–1917), the famous hunter and explorer, he formed the Selous Exploration Syndicate. For it Selous obtained from local chiefs, in September 1889, a Mazoe concession (to replace Johnson's which the Portuguese had cancelled) on which the syndicate negotiated with Rhodes. Selous accepted Rhodes's payment, but Johnson and others refused his offer. In late 1889 Rhodes wanted to occupy southern Zambesia and was considering various options. Johnson refused to join the chartered company service while Gifford and Cawston were among its directors, but was willing to work for Rhodes. Wanting both revenge on Lobengula and profit, Johnson proposed that he and Heany raise a force and, without declaration of war, launch a surprise attack on the Ndebele strongholds and kill Lobengula or take him hostage. In December a contract was drafted whereby they would raise a force of some 500 Europeans to 'break up the power of the Amandebele' (Keppel-Jones, 154); and if their assault was successful the contractors would receive £150,000 and 50,000 *morgen* of land. Historians have differed on whether the contract was signed; the original is apparently no longer extant. However, apparently because Selous advised against it and proposed a better alternative, Rhodes rejected Johnson's plan. It was 'hare-brained' (Gann, 89), indicative of Johnson's foolhardiness and unscrupulousness: his force might well have ended as did the Shangani patrol in 1893.

Rhodes decided to adopt Selous's proposal of a peaceful occupation of Mashonaland, bypassing Matabeleland, and to use Johnson for this. At Cape Town on 1 January 1890 Johnson signed an agreement as 'contractor' to raise and equip a force of pioneers, construct a road, and occupy Mashonaland, handing it over to the chartered company by 30 September. He was to be paid £87,500 and land and gold claims. He and his associates raised and prepared the pioneer corps, some 190 strong, and Rhodes added an armed police force of about 500 men. Johnson wanted to command the entire pioneer column but an imperial officer, Lieutenant-Colonel Edward Pennefather, was appointed. Selous, whom Johnson resented, was intelligence officer and guide. Johnson, with the rank of major, commanded the pioneer corps. Some of them disliked him—one wrote of Johnson's 'great want of consideration for his men' (Cary, *Charter Royal*, 88)—and his swaggering air was such that they called him 'Napoleon Buonaparte Johnson' (Ransford, 201). Dr Leander Starr Jameson, Rhodes's crony, also accompanied the column. The pioneer column—with ox-wagons, Africans, artillery, Maxims, and a steam-powered searchlight, but no women—left Bechuanaland in June and reached its Mashonaland destination in September and established Fort Salisbury, the nucleus of the city of Salisbury, on the upper Hunyani. The pioneer corps was disbanded and its members dispersed to their claims.

Rhodes believed the eastern route to the sea—to replace the long, expensive overland route from the Cape—through Portuguese-claimed Mozambique, essential to his company's sphere. Johnson saw in development of the route a lucrative opportunity for himself. He planned that after the pioneer column ended he would explore the route, and so took a collapsible boat. Jameson insisted on accompanying him and they left Fort Salisbury, with two others, on 5 October. At a village on the Pungwe, Jameson knocked over a candle, starting a fire which destroyed most of the party's property, though their boat survived. They travelled down the Pungwe, suffered much hardship, narrowly escaped death, and were finally picked up, as arranged, at the mouth of the Pungwe (near where the Portuguese later built Beira) by the steamer chartered by Johnson's Cape Town backers.

Confident in the future of Mashonaland and European immigration there, Johnson established a company 'to exploit whatever was exploitable in Mashonaland' (Galbraith, 256): his interests included mining, transport, and land. A. G. Leonard wrote of Johnson in early 1891, 'as he is representing a great many syndicates and people, as well as holding contracts of all kinds for every conceivable thing, his stake is very considerable' (Leonard, 180). Johnson—over-optimistic and confident there would be a rush into Mashonaland via Beira—through Frank Johnson & Co., backed by Rhodes, attempted to operate the east coast route with stagecoaches and wagons from the Pungwe. Through tsetse fly and incompetence the venture failed: the animals died and Johnson's company reportedly lost 2500 cattle and £25,000. He acquired huge land claims by grant and by purchase from departing pioneers, not for farming but for absentee speculation. In March 1893 his Rhodesia Lands Ltd acquired title to nearly 55,000 acres in the Marandellas alone. His cavalier attitude was expressed in his naming his three Marandellas farms Ta-ra-ra, Boom, and De-ay.

In 1891, at Rhodes's request, Johnson accompanied the visiting Lord Randolph Churchill in Mashonaland and found him cantankerous, interfering, and most difficult to get on with. In 1893 Johnson quarrelled with chartered company officials and left Rhodesia. According to Johnson, in July 1895 at Cape Town he was told by Rhodes of his plot to overthrow Kruger's government and was offered command of Rhodes's invasion force. Johnson claimed he approved of Rhodes's aim but not his plan, and offered an alternative whereby Rhodes's force was gradually infiltrated into the Transvaal and there was no invasion, but Rhodes rejected this so Johnson declined his offer. After the Jameson raid Johnson publicly condemned it and so, he claimed, lost the Mafeking parliamentary election. He continued to be interested in military matters, and in 1896 published articles in the *South African Volunteer Gazette* condemning the Cape volunteer system and advocating a compulsory militia. The Cape government appointed a defence commission, with Johnson a member, which recommended reforms. In 1897 Johnson was chief staff officer of the Cape colonial force which suppressed the Bechuanaland rebellion in the Landberg mountains of British Bechuanaland, since 1895 incorporated into Cape Colony.

Johnson returned from Bechuanaland to the Cape, then resided in Salisbury, Southern Rhodesia. During the Second South African War the Rhodesian mines were short of African labour, and in May 1900 Johnson, at the Salisbury chamber of mines, proposed the importation of Chinese labour. Though advocated for several years by mining interests this was controversial and was not implemented. Johnson moved back to England to run his business from London. He became involved in more ventures, mainly mining, in several countries, and by early August 1914 was chairman of 'some seventeen different companies, all housed in my own offices' (Johnson, 250). Having experienced protection in South Africa, he became an active tariff reformer, chairman of the south London federation of the Tariff Reform League, then on the league central executive, and speaking frequently at league meetings throughout Britain. 'Fanatically opposed' (ibid., 252) to the voluntary system, against which he had worked in South Africa, he refused to support or join the Territorial Force.

At the beginning of the First World War Johnson served as a major with the 6th (cyclist) battalion, Royal Sussex regiment, a territorial unit from Brighton, on coast defence. Ordered to raise another battalion, he recruited the 2/6th, initially a cyclist unit, partly from colonials and members of the Cyclists' Union. He commanded the 2/6th, as lieutenant-colonel (23 December 1915), and served with it in India from 1916, including on the 1917 Waziristan campaign against the Mahsuds. In June 1918 he was officially notified he had been made a CMG, but subsequently was told this was an error and he had been made a DSO for the Waziristan campaign. In 1919, during the Punjab disturbances, he commanded the Lahore (civil) area. He enforced martial law, threatening reprisals for the killing of troops or police and fixing prices of necessities, and maintained law and order. He was thanked by the lieutenant-governor, Sir Michael O'Dwyer, and later exonerated by the Hunter commission. He served with his battalion in the Third Anglo-Afghan War (1919).

Johnson then returned to his business interests, which included Burmese oilfields. In 1924 he returned to Southern Rhodesia and in 1927 stood as an opposition candidate in Salisbury South, a constituency with many white working-class voters. A flamboyant right-wing radical and an effective if inaccurate speaker, he denounced the chartered company and the railways and advocated a 'whiter Rhodesia' with white smallholders and a 'Greater Rhodesia' with a western outlet at Walvis Bay. He was elected to the legislative assembly and with other opposition members formed the Progressive Party, but in the 1928 general election was defeated at Salisbury North by Godfrey Huggins. In 1930 the Progressive and Country parties merged as the Reform Party, with Johnson one of its vice-presidents and at first acting as its real leader.

In 1930 Johnson returned to England, where he continued his business interests. He lived at Brundall, Norfolk, and in 1940 moved to Jersey. He continued a committed imperialist, was anti-socialist, and 'enjoyed a reputation as a raconteur' (*Lynn Advertiser*, 10 Sept 1943). In 1940 he published his unreliable memoirs, *Great Days: the Autobiography of an Empire Pioneer*, its content, particularly on Selous, belying his claim 'I do not bear grudges' (Johnson, 243). Its inaccuracies were later exposed by Robert Cary in *Charter Royal* (1970). Johnson fled from Jersey in June 1940 shortly before the German occupation. He corresponded with Godfrey Huggins, prime minister of Southern Rhodesia from 1933 to 1953. Huggins, offered a knighthood, made it a condition of acceptance that Johnson receive one, and in 1941 Johnson was made a KBE. In 1942, shaken by the British defeats in Asia, Johnson urged Huggins to introduce limited African representation. Johnson died on 6 September 1943 at Douglas, Isle of Man, 'the last of those who played a prominent part in assisting Cecil Rhodes in his great Imperial schemes' (Huggins, xiii).

ROGER T. STEARN

Sources F. Johnson, *Great days* (1940) • *DSAB* • R. Cary, *The pioneer corps* (1975) • L. H. Gann, *A history of Southern Rhodesia: early days to 1934* (1965) • A. Keppel-Jones, *Rhodes and Rhodesia: the white conquest of Zimbabwe, 1884–1902* (1983) • A. G. Leonard, *How we made Rhodesia* (1896) [1973 repr.] • R. Cary, *Charter royal* (1970) • R. Blake, *A history of Rhodesia* (1977) • *WWW, 1941–50* • Kelly, *Handbk* (1939) • *London and Provincial Medical Directory* (1867) • O. Ransford, *The rulers of Rhodesia: from earliest times to the referendum* (1968) • R. Hodder-Williams, *White farmers in Rhodesia, 1890–1965: a history of the Marandellas district* (1983) • L. H. Gann and M. Gelfand, *Huggins of Rhodesia: the man and his country* (1964) • *Lynn Advertiser* (10 Sept 1943) • J. S. Galbraith, *Crown and charter: the early years of the British South Africa Company* (1974) • *A short history of the royal Sussex regiment (35th–107th foot), 1701–1926* (1927) • O'M. Creagh and E. M. Humphris, *The V.C. and D.S.O.*, 3 [1924] • J. R. D. Cobbing, 'Lobengula, Jameson and the occupation of Mashonaland, 1890', *Rhodesian History*, 4 (1973), 39–56 • *Royal Sussex Herald: the Journal of the 2/6th Battalion, Royal Sussex Regiment*, 4 (15 June–5 Oct 1918), 29, 171 • private information (2004) [D. Cook, M. J. Walker] • G. M. Huggins, 'Preface', in F. Johnson, *Great days* (1940) • *CGPLA Eng. & Wales* (1943)

Archives Derbys. RO, Derby, papers relating to British South Africa Company • National Archives of Zimbabwe, Harare, corresp., journal, and typescript of *Great days* • National Archives of Zimbabwe, Harare, corresp. and papers

Likenesses photograph, 1890, repro. in Johnson, *Great days*, facing p. 120 • Lafayette, photograph, 1938, repro. in Johnson, *Great days*, frontispiece

Wealth at death £70 18s. 3d.: probate, 20 Dec 1943, *CGPLA Eng. & Wales*

Johnson, Garat, the elder (d. 1611). *See under* Johnson family (*per. c.*1570–*c.*1630).

Johnson, Garrat, the younger (*fl. c.*1612). *See under* Johnson family (*per. c.*1570–*c.*1630).

Johnson, George (*bap.* 1563, *d. c.*1605), separatist leader, was baptized on 3 October 1563 at Richmond, Yorkshire, the younger son of John Johnson, a woollen draper and sometime town alderman or bailiff, and the younger brother of Francis *Johnson (*bap.* 1562, *d.* 1617). In 1580 he matriculated as a pensioner at Christ's College, Cambridge, graduating BA in 1585 and proceeding MA in 1588.

Upon leaving the university he travelled to London, where he became a schoolmaster in St Nicholas Lane.

Some time before February 1593, Johnson forsook the Church of England and became a separatist. When later asked why, he replied that he had been 'drawen therto' by the word of God and the sermons of Stephen Egerton, a popular puritan preacher at St Ann Blackfriars (Carlson, 320). After his conversion, Johnson joined a recently organized London separatist church where his brother, Francis, was serving as pastor. He soon became an influential member of this church and presided at services after the pastor and John Greenwood, the teacher, were imprisoned on 6 December 1592.

Johnson was soon in trouble for these activities. On 4 March 1593 he was apprehended while leading worship at one Cunstable's house in Islington Wood. The court of high commission committed him to the Fleet prison, where he was examined on 7 March and 2 April. Although not indicted, he remained in prison for the next four years, living part of that time in 'the most dankish and unholesome rooms of the prison' and enduring both ill treatment and solitary confinement (Lansdowne MS 77, fol. 66r).

While both brothers were imprisoned, the first of several contentions that were to divide both them and the church began. Francis wanted to marry Tomison Boyes, the widow of a well-to-do London separatist haberdasher. George objected to the match on the grounds that her dress, deportment, and speech were unsuitable for the wife of the leading separatist pastor, 'she being much noted for pride' (Johnson, 94). Among other things, George complained about Tomison's protruding busks and whalebones, her wearing of three or four gold rings at once, and her low-cut gowns. He even noted that she had been compared with the bishop of London's fashionable wife, while many of the congregation who had been banished to the Netherlands were living in great poverty. When Francis married Tomison secretly, a bitter quarrel ensued. George remained in prison until March 1597, when he, Francis, and two other separatists were released on condition that they sail for Newfoundland, found a colony there, and never return to England. This venture proved abortive.

Both brothers secretly returned to London in September. Shortly thereafter, they fled to Amsterdam, where they were reunited with the rest of the congregation. There, arguments about Tomison soon broke out afresh. Then, on 15 January 1598, Henry Ainsworth, the church's teacher, got the majority of the congregation to agree with the elders' condemnation of George Johnson for being overzealous and bearing false witness. However, the quarrels were not over. The officers' attempts to appoint repentant apostates to church office, Tomison's purchase of a new velvet hood, and debates over whether or not members of the congregation could attend Dutch Reformed church services followed. Finally, sometime between October 1598 and March 1599, a fuming Francis stood before a silent congregation and personally excommunicated George. Even though Tomison eventually repented and reformed, Francis still refused to reinstate him. Then, in 1602, when John Johnson appeared to reconcile his two sons, he too was cast out.

Cut off from his brethren, George Johnson gathered a group of adherents and became their preacher. On 26 June 1603 NS he and his followers asked about joining the Dutch Reformed church, but this enquiry apparently came to nothing. Meanwhile, he began writing his *Discourse of some Troubles and Excommunications in the Banished English Church at Amsterdam*, a detailed apologia for his conduct in the disputes, replete with many letters and documents, and published, unfinished, in 1603. Some time in late 1603 or 1604 George Johnson and his father returned to England. Still a separatist, George went to Durham, where the bishop imprisoned him for proselytizing. While in gaol he finished the *Discourse*, sickened, and died about 1605.

After Johnson's death Henry Ainsworth, John Robinson, and later William Bradford denounced his character in the course of polemical debate. However, contemporary evidence shows that George was a man of integrity and conscience, who sought to live by the letter of the scriptures as he understood them in the light of his conscience.

MICHAEL E. MOODY

Sources G. Johnson, *A discourse of some troubles and excommunications in the banished English church at Amsterdam* (1603) • M. Moody, 'A critical edition of George Johnson's *Discourse* (1603)', PhD diss., Claremont Graduate School, 1979 • parish records of St Mary's, Richmond, N. Yorks. CRO, PR/RM 1/1, pt. 1, 13 Oct 1563 [baptism] • John Johnson's petition to Lord Burghley, 1 July 1594, BL, Lansdowne MS 77, fol. 66r–v • Matthew Slade to Sir Dudley Carleton, 17 Jan 1618, PRO, SP 84/82, fol. 34v • Examination of John Johnson, 7 Dec 1594, PRO, STAC 5/H37/3 • Protocollen van den bijzonderen kerkeraad, Gemeete Archief, Amsterdam, no. 376, vol. 3, fol. 98r • *The writings of John Greenwood and Henry Barrow, 1591–1593*, ed. L. H. Carlson (1970) • D. B. Quinn, 'The first pilgrims', *William and Mary Quarterly*, 23 (1966), 359–90 • J. Peile, *Biographical register of Christ's College, 1505–1905, and of the earlier foundation, God's House, 1448–1505*, ed. [J. A. Venn], 1 (1910), 160 • H. Broughton, *Certayne questions* (1605) • R. Clyfton, *An advertisement* (1612) • H. Ainsworth, *Counterpoyson* (1608) • J. Robinson, *A justification of separation* (1610) • W. Bradford, 'A dialogue, or, The sume of a conference between som younge men borne in New England and sundery ancient men that came out of Holland and old England anno domini 1648', *Publications of the Colonial Society of Massachusetts*, 22 (1920), 115–41

Johnson, Sir George (1818–1896), physician, was born on 29 November 1818 at Goudhurst, Kent, the eldest son of George Johnson, yeoman, and Mercy, second daughter of William Corke, timber merchant, of Edenbridge in the same county. In 1837 he was apprenticed to his uncle, a general practitioner at Cranbrook in Kent, and in October 1839 he entered the medical school of King's College, London. While a student Johnson was awarded many prizes and obtained the senior medical scholarship; he was also beginning original work, and was awarded the prize of the King's College Medical Society for his essay 'On auscultation and percussion'. In 1841 he passed the first MB London, in the first class, and in 1842 at the MB examination he received the scholarship and gold medal in physiology and comparative anatomy. In 1844 he graduated MD. He became a member of the Royal College of Physicians in 1846 and a fellow in 1850; he was an examiner in medicine in 1872–3, censor in 1865, 1866, and 1875, councillor in 1865, 1874, 1881, 1882, and 1883, Goulstonian lecturer in 1852, materia medica lecturer in 1853, Lumleian lecturer in 1877, Harveian orator in 1882, and vice-president of the college in 1887.

At the end of his medical course Johnson held in succession the offices of house physician and house surgeon to King's College Hospital. He was an associate of King's College and in 1843 became resident medical tutor; four years later he was appointed assistant physician to the hospital. In 1850 he was made an honorary fellow of King's College, and in that year he married Charlotte Elizabeth (d. 1855), youngest daughter of the late Lieutenant William White of Addington, Surrey. Five years later, however, he was left a widower with five children.

In 1856 Johnson became physician to King's College Hospital, and in 1857 he succeeded Dr Royle as professor of materia medica and therapeutics, an office which he continued to hold until 1863, when, on the resignation of Dr George Budd, he succeeded to the chair of medicine and also became senior physician to the hospital. He was professor of medicine at King's College for thirteen years. In 1876 he was appointed professor of clinical medicine and consulting physician to King's College Hospital, and in 1883 the prince of Wales appointed him consulting physician to the Royal College of Music.

In 1862 Johnson was nominated by convocation and elected a member of the senate of the University of London. In 1872 he was elected fellow of the Royal Society; in 1884 president of the Royal Medical and Chirurgical Society; and in 1889 physician-extraordinary to the queen. In 1892 he was knighted. He was a member of the British Medical Association and a frequent contributor to the pages of the *British Medical Journal*. In 1871, at the annual meeting of the association at Plymouth, he delivered the address in medicine, taking for his topic 'Nature and art in the cure of disease'.

Johnson was a physician who proceeded logically in his thought and work and who formed strong opinions, occasionally prompting dissent from equally eminent colleagues. He was frequently involved in controversy in the medical press and expressed his views in language which, one of his contemporaries observed, was at times stronger than the occasion seemed to demand. Yet he was not combative by nature, and was a voice of moderation in the affairs of his own medical school. He was careful to avoid controversy in his undergraduate teaching. On one occasion a distinguished American confrère, in a somewhat free and easy way, introduced him as 'Sir George Johnson, commonly called "Kidney Johnson"'. 'If I am to have a sobriquet', said Johnson, 'pray call me "Cholera Johnson", not "Kidney Johnson"'. He was sometimes referred to as 'Castor Oil Johnson' (Lyle, 206). The cholera and the castor oil referred to the most anxious period of Johnson's life, during the cholera epidemic of 1854, castor oil being his preferred treatment.

Johnson's contributions to medical literature were extremely numerous and dealt chiefly with the pathology and treatment of kidney disease. He reintroduced the picric acid test for albumen and the picric acid and potash test for sugar. He at once recognized the great use of the ophthalmoscope in renal pathology, and assisted Sir Thomas Watson in revising the last edition of his famous *Lectures on the Principles and Practice of Medicine*. Johnson was an ardent exponent of the views of Richard Bright, and extended Bright's observations in many directions. His discovery of the hypertrophy of the small arteries in Bright's disease, and his 'stop-cock' explanatory theory, led to what was known as the 'hyaline-fibroid degeneration' controversy with Sir William Gull and Dr Sutton: the practical outcome was that attention was directed to the high tension pulse of chronic kidney disease, together with its importance in connection with other symptoms, and this opened up a new field of treatment. In 1852 he published *Diseases of the Kidney, their Pathology, Diagnosis, and Treatment*, and in 1873 *Lectures on Bright's Disease*. His last publication was *The Pathology of the Contracted Granular Kidney* (1896).

Johnson died from cerebral haemorrhage at his residence, 11 Savile Row, on Wednesday, 3 June 1896, and was buried on 8 June at St Mary's Church, Addington. In 1897 an ophthalmological theatre at King's College Hospital was built and equipped in his memory. His portrait, by Frank Holl, subscribed for by the staff and students of King's College Hospital, was presented to Johnson in 1888 by Sir Joseph Lister.

W. W. WEBB, *rev.* W. I. MCDONALD

Sources H. W. Lyle, *King's and some King's men* (1935) · Munk, *Roll*, 4.60–61 · *The Lancet* (13 June 1896), 1654, 1663–4 · *BMJ* (13 June 1896), 1477–9 · *Churchill's Medical Directory* · *King's College Hospital Reports* (1897) · *The Times* (4 June 1896), 6e · *The Times* (9 June 1896), 12b · *Provincial Medical Journal*, 7 (1888), 49
Likenesses F. Holl, oils, 1888, RCP Lond.
Wealth at death £14,007 18s. 1d.: probate, 26 June 1896, CGPLA Eng. & Wales

Johnson, George Henry Sacheverell (1808–1881), dean of Wells, was born at Keswick, Cumberland, the third son of Revd Henry Johnson. He matriculated at Queen's College, Oxford, on 13 May 1825, aged seventeen, and was elected to a college scholarship in 1826. In 1827 he became the third holder of the university scholarship for classical learning founded in 1825 by Dean Ireland, and in 1831 was the first to win the university mathematical scholarship. Taking first classes in both classics and mathematics in 1828, he graduated BA in 1829 and MA in 1833. Ordained in 1834, he was a fellow of his college from 1829 to 1855, tutor in 1844, bursar in 1844, and dean in 1848. One of the leading Oxford tutors of his day, he had among his private pupils A. C. Tait, A. P. Stanley, and Roundell Palmer. He was university mathematical examiner on five occasions between 1834 and 1852. His election in 1839 as Savilian professor of astronomy was controversial, since the Radcliffe Trust, which objected to the appointment of a mathematician with no practical knowledge of astronomy, made its own appointment (Manuel Johnson) to the position of Radcliffe Observer, thus severing the professorship from the observatory. From 1842 to 1845 he held the White professorship of moral philosophy. Both elections took place at the height of the Tractarian movement, and Johnson's known antipathy to it may have influenced his appointment. On 13 January 1838 he was elected a fellow of the Royal Society.

With his pupil William Thomson, Johnson was the chief advocate within Queen's College for opening to competition college positions hitherto restricted to natives of Cumberland and Westmorland. It was a particular blow when the fellows declined, in 1849, to elect an outsider, Goldwin Smith. Johnson became an ally of A. P. Stanley and Benjamin Jowett in their pressure for the appointment of a royal commission to inquire into the university and colleges, and was a member of the commission appointed by Lord John Russell in 1850, reporting in April 1852. Johnson believed that his decision to serve on the commission, which was unpopular in the university, cost him the headship of Queen's College, which became vacant in 1855. He was, however, one of the university reformers whom the clerical party found least objectionable, and on this account he was made one of the executive commissioners under the 1854 Oxford University Act to revise the statutes of the university and colleges.

Johnson, who was one of the Whitehall preachers from 1852 to 1854, was rewarded for his services on the earlier commission by his appointment on 27 March 1854 to the deanery of Wells. Shortly afterwards, on 20 April 1854, at Romsey, he married Lucy, youngest daughter of Rear-Admiral Robert O'Brien. As dean he was one of the assessors in G. A. Denison's case in 1856. In 1881 he raised money to reopen the Wells Cathedral school. But his period of office was clouded by a controversy over his incumbency of the living of St Cuthbert's, Wells, which he had held in plurality since 1855 to supplement the comparatively modest stipend attached to the deanery. He resigned from St Cuthbert's in 1870, following threats of prosecution, and was absent from Wells for a period thereafter. After his death the *Church Times* commented unfavourably on his tenure at Wells (Colchester, 188). Among his publications were *Optical Investigations* (1835), *Sermons Preached in Wells Cathedral* (1857), and *Science and Natural Religion: a Sermon* (2nd edn, 1875). With F. C. Cook and C. J. Ellicott he edited the book of Psalms for the Speaker's Commentary (1880). Johnson died at 1 Royal Terrace, Weston-super-Mare, on 5 November 1881, leaving a widow, and was buried in the Palm churchyard, Wells Cathedral, on 10 November.   M. C. CURTHOYS

Sources The Times (7 Nov 1881), 9 · Guardian (9 Nov 1881), 1592 · L. S. Colchester, ed., *Wells Cathedral: a history* (1982) · *The historical register of the University of Oxford … to the end of Trinity term 1900* (1900) · J. R. Magrath, *The Queen's College*, 2 vols. (1921) · W. R. Ward, *Victorian Oxford* (1965) · E. G. W. Bill, *University reform in nineteenth-century Oxford: a study of Henry Halford Vaughan, 1811–1885* (1973) · I. Guest, *Dr John Radcliffe and his trust* (1991) · Foster, *Alum. Oxon.* · *CGPLA Eng. & Wales* (1882) · *Hist. U. Oxf. 6: 19th-cent. Oxf.*
Archives LPL, corresp. with A. C. Tait

Likenesses B. Johnson, oils (after G. Richmond, *c*.1861), Queen's College, Oxford
Wealth at death £4237 1s. 3d.: probate, 30 March 1882, *CGPLA Eng. & Wales*

Johnson, George William (1802–1886), writer on gardening, was born on 4 November 1802 at Blackheath, Kent, the younger of the two sons of William Johnson, businessman and owner of the Vauxhall distillery, who then founded the Coalbrookdale china works, and later the salt works at Heybridge in Essex. Johnson and his elder brother, Cuthbert William *Johnson, worked at Heybridge and carried out experiments on the use of salt as manure, which they described in *An Essay on the Uses of Salt for Agriculture* (2nd edn 1821). They discovered a method of separating sulphate of magnesia, or Epsom salts, from sea water.

From 1826 Johnson sent articles to J. C. Loudon's *Gardener's Magazine*, including a series of papers on the application of chemistry to horticulture. His first book was *A History of English Gardening* (1829). At Great Totham, where he lived, he conducted experiments in gardening, especially in the manufacture of manures, and he published a *History of the Parish of Great Totham* (1834). In 1835 he published *Memoirs of John Selden*. With his brother he edited an edition of William Paley's works in 1839, taking responsibility for *Evidences of Christianity* himself.

Johnson, a student of Gray's Inn since 1832, was called to the bar on 8 June 1836. In 1839 he was appointed professor of moral and political economy at the Hindoo College in Calcutta, and he became one of the editors of the *Englishman* newspaper there and also edited the government *Gazette* for the governor-general, Lord Auckland. On his return to England from India in 1842, he wrote *The Stranger in India, or, Three Years in Calcutta* (1843).

Johnson settled in Winchester, and turned his attention to gardening pursuits. He edited the *Gardeners' Almanack* for the Stationers' Company from 1844 to 1866. In 1845 he published *The Principles of Practical Gardening*, which was later enlarged and reissued as *The Science and Practice of Gardening* (1862). A *Dictionary of Modern Gardening* (1846) was reprinted as *Johnson's Gardening Dictionary* many times until 1917. In 1847 Johnson began issuing *The Gardener's Monthly Volume*, and wrote the first issue himself, on the potato. Twelve volumes appeared, each on a different plant.

On 5 October 1848 the first issue of the *Cottage Gardener* appeared, a weekly journal edited by Johnson. In 1851 Dr Robert Hogg became joint editor, and in 1861 the title was changed to the *Journal of Horticulture and Cottage Gardener*. Johnson retired from the editorship in 1881, and it continued to appear until 1915.

Among his many publications were *The Potato Murrain and its Remedy* (1846), *The British Ferns Popularly Described* (2nd edn 1857), *The Wild Flowers of Great Britain* (with R. Hogg, in eleven volumes, 1863–80), and a translation of *A Selection of the Eatable Funguses of Great Britain* by M. Plues (1866).

By 1848 Johnson was married to the daughter of Newington Hughes, a banker in Maidstone, Kent; they had at
least one son. On Hughes's death, Johnson inherited his
property, including the Fairfax manuscripts, which he
published as *The Fairfax Correspondence* in four volumes
(1848–9), editing the first two himself. Johnson died at his
home, Waldronhurst, Croydon, Surrey, on 29 October
1886, and was buried at St Peter's Church, Croydon.

G. C. BOASE, rev. ANNE PIMLOTT BAKER

Sources G. E. Fussell, 'George William Johnson, 1802–1886', *Gar-
deners' Chronicle*, 3rd ser., 127 (1950), 106–7 · *Journal of Horticulture* (4
Nov 1886) · *Gardeners' Chronicle*, new ser., 26 (1886), 592 · *The Times* (5
Nov 1886) · Desmond, *Botanists* · Boase, *Mod. Eng. biog.* · d. cert.
Archives UCL, letter to Society for the Diffusion of Useful Know-
ledge
Likenesses portrait, repro. in *Journal of Horticulture*, pp. 401–4
Wealth at death £10,265 10s. 10d.: administration with will, 13
Dec 1886, CGPLA Eng. & Wales

Johnson, Guy (*c.*1740–1788), colonial official, was born in
Ireland, probably in Smithtown, near Dunshoughlin, co.
Meath, said to be the son of John Johnson and nephew of
Sir William *Johnson. By April 1756 he found his way to
Boston and by June of that year was in the Mohawk valley
of present-day New York, at the home of Sir William,
recently appointed British superintendent of Indian
affairs for the northern department.

Guy Johnson almost immediately became Sir William's
secretary and served with him in the victorious British
and allied American Indian campaign against Niagara in
1759. In 1762 Sir William appointed him a deputy agent. In
that position he not only kept meticulous records of
treaty conferences, but used his talents as a draughtsman
to produce important maps of the continental interior. He
married William Johnson's daughter Mary (1744–1775) in
March 1763 and took up residence at Guy Park, a tract near
present-day Amsterdam, New York, that was a wedding
present from his father-in-law. The couple had two daughters. Continuing his Indian affairs duties, Guy Johnson
began to build his own public career, becoming a militia
colonel in 1768, a judge of the Tryon county court of common pleas in 1772, and a member of the provincial
assembly in 1773.

Johnson's comfortable country-squire life was soon disrupted. On 11 July 1774, in the midst of Dunmore's War, a
major crisis in British-Indian relations, William Johnson
collapsed and died during a treaty with the Six Nations Iroquois, leaving Guy Johnson to assume the superintendent's post. The challenges of that position became infinitely greater within the next few months, as a revolutionary committee of safety challenged royal authority. Guy
Johnson used his court to condemn the continental congress and, along with his brother-in-law John Johnson,
raised a loyalist militia that briefly seized control of Tryon
county. In July 1775, however, he was forced to evacuate to
Fort Oswego, where his wife died in childbirth. At Oswego
and Montreal, Johnson began organizing Native Americans to fight for the crown, but, having found his status as
Indian superintendent questioned by other officials, in
November he left to seek clarification in England. He
returned to North America the next summer, but inexplicably remained in British-occupied New York city until
1779, when he went to Niagara to direct Indian and loyalist
raiders and provide for the thousands of Native American
refugees settled there. Implicated, justly or not, in a scandal involving padded accounts for the refugees' provisions, he turned over his superintendency to Sir William's
son John Johnson in 1782, and went to England seeking
restitution of his New York estates, which had been confiscated by the revolutionaries. He died at Haymarket,
London, on 5 March 1788.   DANIEL K. RICHTER

Sources J. G. Rossie, 'Johnson, Guy', *DCB*, vol. 4 · W. Burch, 'John-
son, Guy', *ANB* · M. W. Hamilton, *Sir William Johnson: colonial
American, 1715–1763* (1976) · C. G. Calloway, *The American Revolution in
Indian country: crisis and diversity in Native American communities*
(1995), 129–57 · H. J. Gibb, 'Colonel Guy Johnson, superintendent
general of Indian affairs, 1774–82', *Papers of the Michigan Academy of
Science, Arts and Letters*, 27 (1941), 595–613 · *DNB* · *The papers of Sir
William Johnson*, ed. J. Sullivan and others, 14 vols. (1921–65) · E. B.
O'Callaghan and B. Fernow, eds. and trans., *Documents relative to the
colonial history of the state of New York*, 15 vols. (1853–87), vol. 8 ·
B. Graymont, *The Iroquois in the American Revolution* (1972) · I. T.
Kelsay, *Joseph Brant, 1743–1807: man of two worlds* (1984)
Archives BL, papers relating to Indian affairs · PRO, corresp.,
PRO 30/55 | BL, corresp. with Frederick Haldimand, Add. MSS
21670, 21736, 21766–21768 · NA Canada, Claus MSS · U. Mich.,
Clements L., corresp. with Thomas Gage
Likenesses B. West, portrait, 1776, National Gallery of Art, Wash-
ington, DC; repro. in Sullivan, Flick, and Hamilton, eds., *Papers of
William Johnson*, vol. 10, frontispiece · portrait, New York State His-
torical Association Museum, Cooperstown, New York; repro. in
Sullivan, Flick, and Hamilton, eds., *Papers of William Johnson*, vol. 13,
facing p. 635

Johnson [Finlay-Johnson; *married name* Weller], **Harriet**
(**1871–1956**), schoolteacher and educationist, was born at
9 Elizabeth Terrace, Hampstead, London, on 12 March
1871, the daughter of Thomas Conolly Johnson, house
painter, and his wife, Jane Anne Fitz Patrick. She and her
sister Emily entered teaching, possibly owing to financial
pressure following the accidental death of her father. She
qualified as a teacher through private study rather than
through apprenticeship or college training, passed her
certificate examinations in 1892, and received her certificate in 1894. She was employed for eight years at St Mary's
School, Willesden, and then briefly by the Tottenham
school board. In 1897 she became headmistress at Sompting, Sussex, her sister Emily being appointed in charge of
the infants' class. Sompting School had approximately
120 pupils, and Finlay-Johnson (as she was generally
known, for reasons that remain obscure) taught single-
handed fifty children of all ages from eight to fourteen.

The Sompting School logbook for 1897–9 records the
adoption of kindergarten methods, reflecting a growing
Froebelian trend in infant education, and for the older
scholars under Finlay-Johnson's charge there are signs of
more notable curricular initiatives from 1900. In that year
she arranged for an exchange of letters between her
scholars and Canadian children accompanied by a
lantern-slide lecture on Canada for older children and
adult villagers. The Second South African War became a
study topic, with one child writing to Lord Roberts, pupil

discussion of the war's progress, and an address from a former pupil who had fought in South Africa. A large library was assembled in the school and was freely accessible to the pupils.

Finlay-Johnson publicized her school's activities, sending pupils' work and news concerning her ventures to local newspapers. In summer 1900 older scholars visited a local fig garden and grape houses, and subsequent project work included letters from children to the press. Nature study and observational drawing became subjects in which Sompting children excelled, and the quality of their work was endorsed by the chief inspector of drawing at the Board of Education, who commented that the teaching at this school reached the highest educational level he had ever met (Holmes, *In Defence of what Might Be*, 342–3). Out-of-classroom activities became an established feature of the curriculum: nature walks and rambles in the surrounding country and on the local seashore, beekeeping, gardening, and cooking. In 1903 she was appointed to an advisory committee of West Sussex county council, and the following year she lectured on nature study to a conference of local teachers and managers.

Finlay-Johnson's work was strongly supported by the local inspector of schools Edward Burrows. He first visited the school in 1904 and aroused interest among other inspectors. In 1906 the chief inspector, Edmond Holmes, visited, and it was his response that in due course elevated Finlay-Johnson to a position of national significance in pedagogical development. It was above all her innovation in the educational use of drama that attracted widespread attention. She placed emphasis on drama and acting as a pretext and channel for the acquisition of knowledge: motivation, research, problem-solving. But she also believed in dramatic creations as the children's own invention, anticipating Franz Cizek, who later revolutionized educational approaches to the visual arts: '… instead of letting the teacher originate or conduct the play, I demanded that, just as the individual himself must study Nature and not have it studied for him, the play must be the child's own' (Finlay-Johnson, 19). It has been claimed that Finlay-Johnson was the first teacher to apply the term 'dramatization' to education (Bolton, 24).

As parents, former scholars, and others became involved in theatrical work centred on the school, Finlay-Johnson's initiatives modelled a new relationship between school and community. *Julius Caesar* was produced and performed by men of the village, and played at the Theatre Royal, Worthing, to an 'enthusiastic, overflowing audience' and to critics from the London dailies (Finlay-Johnson, 254). A mothers' band was formed, and 'the school thus became really a centre of light and learning' (ibid., 255). Through this community activity, Finlay-Johnson met George William Weller (*b.* 1887/8), village wheelwright and carpenter (who became a funeral director), the son of William Weller, also a wheelwright. In 1910 she resigned her post in order to marry (6 April 1910).

Following her retirement, Finlay-Johnson's book *The Dramatic Method of Teaching* (1911), written at Holmes's persuasion, was published in Nisbet's series Self-Help. It was a practical account at a time when much of the literature of progressive education was written in a more abstract philosophical vein. Though freely adapting Froebel's kindergarten methods, her 'dramatic method' was based more on common-sense pragmatism than on theory. It appeared at a period of national revival in dramatic culture and corresponds with Caldwell Cook's more celebrated 'play way' which he developed at the Perse School from 1911 onwards.

Highly innovative in its own right, Finlay-Johnson's book attracted widespread attention and even notoriety, because Edmond Holmes's *What is and What Might Be* had appeared a few months earlier. Holmes had recently retired amid controversy, and his book took the educational world by storm; it has been called 'the manifesto of the English progressives' (W. H. G. Armytage, *Four Hundred Years of English Education*, 1964, 227). Though he championed her pseudonymously as a paragon of progressive teaching, the true identity of 'Egeria' and her 'Utopia' became quite widely known, arousing some resentment and hostility among teacher organizations deeply suspicious of the former chief inspector. For Holmes, 'self-realization' was the highest aim of education, and despite his contacts with philosophical idealism and with Buddhism, by his own admission these made little difference to his life's work until his eyes were opened by Egeria: 'I thought it might be well if I were to describe her school and her work, and try to interpret her philosophy of education' (Holmes, *In Defence of what Might Be*, 2). Holmes described how Egeria's school gradually transformed and vitalized the whole community, especially through interest in drama and Shakespeare. Parents became deeply interested in the school life of their children.

In her management of large and complex groupings of children, Finlay-Johnson was representative of most elementary school teachers of her time. However, for the traditional relationships of teacher and scholar she substituted that of 'fellow-workers, friends and playmates' (Finlay-Johnson, 20–22). Holmes described her as 'the very symbol and embodiment of love, the centre whence all happy, harmonious, life-giving, peace-diffusing influences radiate' (Holmes, *What is and What Might Be*, 210), but defending himself against the argument that Egeria was in some way exceptional, he added: '… there are thousands of teachers who are endowed with these qualities; and if they could and would but cultivate them, there is no reason why they should not do as well in their respective schools as Egeria did in hers' (Holmes, *In Defence of what Might Be*, 322). In relation to the world of educational reform, Finlay-Johnson situated herself through her opening words:

> Go forth, little book, from my halting pen, into the world of men and women of learning, knowledge, culture, and research! Tell them of the little school on the Sussex Downs where children and teachers lived for a space in the world of romance and happiness. Preach the gospel of happiness in childhood. (Finlay-Johnson, 13)

Following her retirement Finlay-Johnson helped her husband in his family business, and after his death remained in Sompting. She died at Southlands Hospital, Shoreham by Sea, Sussex, on 29 February 1956.

PETER CUNNINGHAM

Sources H. Finlay-Johnson, *The dramatic method of teaching* (1911) · E. Holmes, *What is and what might be* (1911) · E. Holmes, *In defence of what might be* (1914) · M. H. Hyndman, 'Utopia reconsidered: Edmond Holmes, Harriet Johnson and the school at Sompting', *Sussex Archaeological Collections*, 118 (1980), 351–7 · G. Bolton, *Acting in classroom drama* (1998), 1–26 · R. J. W. Selleck, *English primary education and the progressives, 1914–1939* (1972) · J. Liebschner, *Foundations of progressive education* (1991), 2–3 · C. Shute, *Edmond Holmes and 'The tragedy of education'* (1998), 35–40 · b. cert. · m. cert. · *CGPLA Eng. & Wales* (1956) · d. cert.

Archives FILM BFI NFTVA, documentary footage

Likenesses photographs (with her class), repro. in Finlay-Johnson, *Dramatic method*

Wealth at death £6,697 11s. 3d.: probate, 28 May 1956, *CGPLA Eng. & Wales*

Johnson, Harry Gordon (1923–1977), economist, was born on 26 May 1923 in Toronto, Canada, the elder son of two children of Henry Herbert Johnson, newspaperman and later secretary of the Liberal Party of Ontario, and his wife, Frances Lily Muat, lecturer in child psychology at the Institute of Child Study of the University of Toronto. He was educated at the University of Toronto schools and then obtained scholarships to the University of Toronto. After considering law, favoured by his father, he entered the honours course in political science and economics. He developed an interest in the history of thought, and was much influenced by Harold Innes's lectures and ideas on Canadian and general economic history. He later wrote that they remained an integral part of his intellectual equipment ever since. He graduated in 1943 and then, at the age of twenty, became, for one year, acting professor and sole member of the economics staff at St Francis Xavier University in Antigonish, Nova Scotia.

Cambridge, Toronto, Harvard, and Manchester In 1944 Johnson volunteered for active service in the Canadian armed forces and, after training, was sent to England in 1945, eventually doing clerical work in Canada House. Demobilized in Britain, he was able to go to Cambridge, became an affiliated student of Jesus College, and took another bachelor's degree, obtaining the top first class in the economics tripos. Maurice Dobb was his supervisor. He became a member of the Political Economy Club, and at his first meeting heard J. M. Keynes present a paper.

Johnson then returned to Toronto, where he took the degree of MA while teaching for a year. By now, pure economics had become his central interest. In 1947 he enrolled as a graduate student in economics at Harvard, where he quickly made a mark on a generation of remarkable fellow students. He was particularly impressed by the breadth and the ideas of Joseph Schumpeter, which greatly influenced his writings in later years. He completed the course work requirements for the doctorate in three terms. In 1948 he married Elizabeth Scott, daughter of Harold Victor Serson, civil engineer. She later became one of the editors of the collected writings of Keynes. They had one son and one daughter.

On the invitation of Dennis Robertson, Johnson returned to Cambridge, England, in 1949 as assistant lecturer and in 1950 became a lecturer and was also elected to a fellowship at King's College, then at the height of the fame to which it had been raised by J. M. Keynes and A. C. Pigou. In 1956 he was appointed to a professorship in economic theory at the University of Manchester.

At Cambridge, Johnson flourished with teaching and, above all, embarking on his incredible research and writing career. But he was getting intellectual stimulation only from his students and from American visitors. The seven years at Cambridge began his alienation from British economics. As he saw it—and wrote about it in later years—his colleagues were stuck in dead monetary controversies, they were parochial and amateur, and the dominant Keynesian establishment was motivated in its economic analysis by political bias. In addition, the Cambridge economics faculty was a battleground, fierce verbal battles being fought over issues of questionable importance.

Johnson was much happier with his colleagues at Manchester. He tried to build up a serious programme of graduate education and took on a big teaching programme himself. But the principal problem was lack of finance—the need for 'penny-pinching' in British provincial universities, about which he later frequently complained.

While at Cambridge and later in Manchester, Johnson started his career as an international trade theorist and quickly became one of the world's leaders in this field. He produced a number of path breaking articles, in particular pioneering the formal theory of trade and growth. These articles were published in the first of his many volumes of collected articles, *International Trade and Economic Growth* (1958). In later years he made similarly pioneering and influential contributions to the theory of tariffs, published in *Aspects of the Theory of Tariffs* (1971).

Chicago, the London School of Economics, and Geneva In 1959 Johnson left Britain and accepted a professorship of economics at the University of Chicago. He remained at the Chicago economics department until his death, becoming the Charles F. Grey distinguished service professor of economics in 1974. He found Chicago tremendously stimulating intellectually. Some adjustment was needed to powerful personalities, but he was in sympathy with the approach to graduate training, the dedication to economics, and the outstanding and committed faculty.

Once Johnson settled in Chicago he visited numerous Canadian universities and maintained close contact with Canada. In 1962 he became an important member of the staff of the Porter royal commission on banking and finance. He published a book of collected articles, *The Canadian Quandary*, in 1963. Later, in 1972, he was one of three commissioned to survey the graduate economics departments of Ontario universities—and was heavily critical. He had a complicated love–hate relationship with Canada. He acted like a resident when he was within Canada, freely criticizing everything within sight without the detachment of the visitor. He vigorously opposed Canadian protectionism and nationalism. He criticized Canadian economists for lack of professionalism and for pontification. But he went to great trouble to advise Canadian university economics departments and assist them with recruitment. He was generous in help to Canadian students and faculty struggling to get on abroad. He was offered many positions in Canada and obtained many honours.

In 1966 Johnson joined to his chair at Chicago a professorship at the London School of Economics (LSE), spending two quarters of each year in London and half in Chicago. He was recruited to build up a postgraduate school in economics on US lines, and in fact wanted to convert the economics department into a purely graduate school. But eventually he concluded that there was neither money nor enthusiasm for his project. Changes in UK tax laws, as well as a severe stroke suffered in the autumn of 1973, also played a role in his decision to give up his LSE position in 1974.

The stroke caused physical incapacity from which Johnson never fully recovered, but he did not reduce the extraordinary amount of work which he undertook. In 1976 he became professor of international economics at the Graduate Institute of International Studies of the University of Geneva, while continuing to perform his regular duties at Chicago.

Monetary theorist Johnson published about 500 academic papers and 15 books, tackling an incredible variety of theoretical and current policy topics. His writings on social questions, economics and universities, income distribution and poverty, the Keynesian revolution, and other topics, were collected in *On Economics and Society* (1976). His writings were full of original insights, though these were not always developed in depth.

Apart from trade theory and policy, Johnson's great interest was in monetary theory, stimulated by his Chicago environment. He was not a monetarist in the Milton Friedman sense, but in Britain he played a key role in bringing monetary factors back into theory and policy discussion. In the 1960s he wrote several extremely influential surveys of monetary economics. These were brilliantly synthetic, with remarkable historical perspective. His most famous paper in this field was 'The Keynesian revolution and the monetarist counter-revolution' (1971). All these, and many other papers on macro- and monetary economics, were reprinted in *Essays in Monetary Economics* (1967) and *Further Essays in Monetary Economics* (1972). In his last years he became a prolific writer on, and enthusiastic advocate of, the monetary approach to the balance of payments. Here he departed from the more judicious and sceptical approach to various theories of his earlier years.

Johnson was indeed 'a master of creative synthesis' (Tobin, 446). A widely read book was *Economic Policies towards Less Developed Countries* (1967). Here, characteristically, magpie-like, he picked up bits and pieces of the latest relevant research and adapted and fitted it all into a coherent framework. His many surveys in trade theory, monetary economics, and, to a lesser extent, other fields were highly influential in guiding the development of academic economics for more than twenty years. No student reading list was complete without Johnson surveys. In a sense, apart from his original contributions, he was a historian of current and very recent economic thought.

Professional economist Harry—as Johnson was universally known—was an inveterate conference-goer. In addition he visited innumerable universities, especially in Canada and in Asia. He 'circled the globe like a planet' (Scott, 80). This travelling style began in the fifties when he was teaching refresher courses for economists in Karachi and Singapore. His travelling and ubiquitousness became legendary.

Among Johnson's many activities his role as editor took much of his energy. At Cambridge, Manchester, and the LSE he edited or jointly edited journals, but his most important role was the editorship of Chicago's *Journal of Political Economy*, which he edited from 1960 to 1966 and jointly from 1969 until his death, and which he turned into the best edited academic economics journal in the world.

Johnson interacted with a vast number of economists, and his contributions to economics, especially international economics, go well beyond the work published under his name. He must be given some credit for numerous important articles published over a period of more than twenty years, mostly in the journals which he edited. He had the remarkable ability to guide numerous authors in fruitful directions. He was able to see a contribution—however apparently narrow in the perspective of the whole field—in the light of the scientific development (as he would put it) of the subject. He played a key communication role in the field of international economics in particular, ensuring that the paper that one potential author had been drafting took into account the unpublished ideas of another in a faraway place. This was an important by-product of his travelling and conference-going. The greatest crime in his eyes was to fail to acknowledge adequately. He was thus: a 'builder of intellectual bridges … a broker of ideas' (Courchene, S12). He acted as a one-man employment agency for young economists. His circle was worldwide and in no sense institution-bound. In this respect, as in his writings, he was the complete internationalist.

Johnson had a concept of the economics profession using a scientific approach, steadily advancing knowledge, each little contribution building on the professional heritage. Indeed, 'professional' was a key word in his vocabulary. He wanted economics to be a science cumulative in knowledge. He was a complex character, both fierce in debate and kind in personal relationships. He was forthright in criticisms and intolerant—perhaps unduly so in the views of some—of what he believed to be error, pretentiousness, or pomposity, or an unscholarly failure to take into account previous work on a subject. But he had a highly developed conscience, and was almost puritan in his sense of responsibility to 'the profession', and especially its younger members. He was a missionary. He believed in the rightness of his task—to improve economics and spread its light.

In his early and very creative years Johnson was certainly a builder of theoretical models. In his later years he became impatient with what he regarded as the pursuit of arcane analytical problems, and felt that the trend to mathematical theorizing was discrediting international trade theory in particular.

Johnson was a fellow of the British Academy (1969), the Econometric Society (1972), and the Royal Society of Canada (1976), and a member of theAmerican Academy of Arts and Sciences. In 1976 he was named an officer of the order of Canada. He was awarded an honorary DSc by Manchester (1972) and an honorary DLitt by Sheffield (1969). He also was honorary LLD of St Francis Xavier, Windsor, Queen's, Carleton, and Western Ontario universities in Canada. He served as president of the Canadian Political Science Association, section F of the British Association, and the Eastern Economic Association, as vice-president of the American Economic Association, and as chairman of the Association of University Teachers of Economics in Britain. He was awarded the Innis-Gerin medal by the Royal Society of Canada, and the Bernhard Harms prize by the University of Kiel.

While Johnson clearly had a powerful and surely lasting influence on his contemporaries and, above all, on students worldwide, much of his writing was not of the kind that would be read or cited a great deal many years later. This applied inevitably to numerous surveys and synthetic or expository papers, and to critical essays on the views and writings of his contemporaries and analyses of current issues. Thus there is a contrast between his extraordinary impact, as measured by scholarly citations, during his lifetime, and the impact a quarter of a century later. His lasting influence in the field of macroeconomics rests on his pioneering paper 'Towards a general theory of the balance of payments', published in 1958, and otherwise primarily on his contributions to the pure theory of trade and the theory of tariffs collected in *International Trade and Economic Growth* and *Aspects of the Theory of Tariffs*. As a contributor to pure trade theory and the theory of trade policy he must be regarded as having had a very important place. His articles on trade and growth and on tariffs and 'optimal intervention' have become classics.

Physically Johnson was a large man, overweight or at least stout, with piercing dark brown eyes. But he was far from sluggish, and gave an impression of intense and disciplined intellectual and physical energy. He was often loudly and informally dressed. His energy was kept under control by his continuous carving of wooden statuettes, of which he made thousands in many different artistic styles. He carved at seminars and in his room, throughout the most concentrated discussions of intricate economic problems.

The enormous admiration and affection for Johnson was reflected in the numerous obituaries by members of the economics profession that appeared in 1977. 'For the economics profession throughout the world, the third quarter of this century was an Age of Johnson' (Tobin, 443). 'He bestrode our discipline like a Colossus', 'He was an institution' (ibid.). 'Canada lost one of its greatest sons'. He was 'larger than life' (the most common remark). 'The one and only Harry' (*The Economist*, 14 May 1977, 121). Harry Johnson died of a stroke in Geneva on 9 May 1977; he was survived by his wife.   W. MAX CORDEN

Sources personal knowledge (2004) · H. G. Johnson, 'Autobiographical notes', June 1969, University of Chicago, Department of Special Collections [mimeo] · *DNB* · J. Tobin, 'Harry Gordon Johnson, 1923–77', *PBA*, 63 (1977), 443–58 · G. Reuber and A. Scott, 'In memoriam: Harry Gordon Johnson, 1923–77', *Canadian Journal of Economics*, 10 (1977), 670–77 · *University of Chicago Record* (1978), 156–61 · *Canadian Journal of Economics*, 11 (1978) [supplement] · *Journal of Political Economy*, 92 (1984), 565–711 · J. N. Bhagwati and J. A. Frenkel, 'Harry G. Johnson', *International encyclopedia of the social sciences*, ed. D. L. Sills, 18: *Biographical supplement* (1968–91), 351–8 · A. Scott, 'Harry Gordon Johnson, 1923–77', *Proceedings and Transactions of the Royal Society of Canada*, 4th ser., 15 (1977), 79–82 · T. J. Courchene, 'Harry Johnson: macroeconomist', *Canadian Journal of Economics*, 11 (1978), S11–S33 [supplement]
Archives University of Chicago Library, MSS
Likenesses photograph, repro. in *Journal of Political Economy*, 565

Johnson, Henry (1698/9–1760), traveller, was the eldest son of William Johnson (d. 1718), captain-general of the Royal African Company at Cape Coast Castle, and his wife, Agneta. His grandfather was Sir Henry Johnson (d. 1683), the wealthy proprietor of the dockyard at Blackwall and a member of parliament for Aldborough; both his father and uncle subsequently represented the same borough in parliament. Henry Johnson himself is known as a traveller and translator. He was elected as a fellow of the Society of Antiquaries on 31 August 1720. He subsequently made a journey to South America on behalf of the South Sea Company, which at that time was the subject of a parliamentary inquiry into corruption and fraud among its officials. He travelled to various parts of South America, including Carthagena, Puerto Bello, Lima, and Buenos Aires, and returned to England with a large fortune. In 1724 he published *Romulus*, a translation from the French of La Motte's tragedy of the same name. In 1730 he communicated to the Society of Antiquaries an extraordinary account of the remains of a pygmy accompanied by a fortune which had been discovered in Peru. In 1733 he went on a tour to Spain, visiting Gibraltar, Granada, Cadiz, and Madrid. He returned to London a year later, and took a house in Richmond Buildings, Dean Street, Soho. At this time he seems to have considered standing for election to parliament as the representative of Aldborough. In the mid-1730s he married Laetitia (1714–1784), daughter of John Dowling of St Andrew's, Holborn, and they had three daughters: Laetitia, who became the second wife of Sir William Beauchamp Proctor, bt; Agneta, who became the second wife of Charles *Yorke (1722–1770), the lord chancellor; and Henrietta. Johnson finally settled on a residence at Berkhamsted St Peter, Hertfordshire, where he devoted much time to translations of historical and political works from the Spanish. He published *A true and particular relation of the dreadful earthquake which happen'd at Lima … and the port of Callao on the 28th October, 1746* (1748), translated from an anonymous Spanish original attributed to Pedro Lozana. Johnson augmented the translation with an account of the kingdom of Peru, its manners and customs, and its natural history, as well as an enquiry into the cause of earthquakes, a map of Lima and its surroundings, plans of Callao and Lima, and drawings of their inhabitants. He also translated selections from the works of the Spanish Benedictine monk Feyjoo, including 'A defence of women' which appeared in several numbers of the *Lady's Magazine* throughout 1760. Henry Johnson died after a long and painful illness on 12 May 1760, aged sixty-one, and he was buried in the north transept of the chapel of St John in the church at Berkhamsted St Peter.

LUCIANA DE LIMA MARTINS

Sources R. Clutterbuck, ed., *The history and antiquities of the county of Hertford*, 1 (1815) · *DNB* · D. Lysons, *The environs of London*, 3 (1795) · H. Johnson, letters to the earl of Strafford, 1722, 1733, 1734, BL, Add. MS 22221, fols. 504–10 · J. Duncombe, *Letters by several eminent persons deceased … with notes explanatory and historical*, 2nd edn, 3 (1773) · monument, church of Berkhamsted St Peter
Archives BL, Strafford MSS, Add. MS 22221

Johnson, Sir Henry, first baronet (1748–1835), army officer, was born on 1 January 1748, the second son of Allen Johnson (*d.* 1747) of Kilternan, co. Dublin, and his wife, Olivia, the daughter of John Walsh of Ballykilcavan, Queen's county. His military career began in 1761, when he was appointed ensign in the 28th foot. Promoted captain in 1763 and major in 1775, he served in America during the War of Independence, first as a commander of battalion of light infantry and, from 17 October 1778, as lieutenant-colonel of the 17th foot. In 1779 he was captured with his garrison at Stony Point. After being exchanged, he was court-martialled at his own request and acquitted of blame. In 1781 he was captured again, at Yorktown, and returned to England. On 17 January 1782 he married Rebecca (*d.* 1823), the daughter of David Franks of Philadelphia. The same year he was made colonel (brevet) of the 81st foot. Following service in Nova Scotia and Newfoundland he was promoted major-general in 1793.

Johnson served in Ireland from 1793 as major-general of recruiting for the English establishment. As a member of the viceroy's 'cabinet' of Irish advisers, he favoured the severe counter-insurgency methods first advocated by General Gerard Lake against the United Irishmen in Ulster. Following the outbreak of the 1798 uprising he was posted first to Waterford, then to New Ross, co. Wexford, where, on 5 June 1798, with a garrison of around 1400 troops, mainly militia, yeomanry, and fencibles, he repulsed a rebel force of between 10,000 and 15,000, which, according to an experienced witness, 'made as severe an attack as is possible for any troops with such arms' (Colonel Crauford to General Lake, 6 June 1798, Home Office, 100/77/fols. 76–7). During the battle Johnson had several horses shot from under him, and his force withdrew twice before he counter-attacked and drove the assailants from the town. This victory was the turning point in the Wexford rebellion and was achieved largely through Johnson's intelligent redeployments as well as his personal courage in leading the counter-attack at the

head of his troops. Johnson's loss totalled ninety, while the rebel casualties were at least 1500. He was subsequently lionized as 'the saviour of the south' and was made colonel of the 81st foot on 18 June 1798. However, Cornwallis considered Johnson 'a wrong-headed blockhead' (*Correspondence of … Cornwallis*, 3.116), presumably because of his standing among Irish loyalists, who criticized Cornwallis's lenient policy towards the defeated rebels. Johnson was promoted lieutenant-general in 1799 and became a full general in 1808. He was made a baronet on 1 December 1818 and in 1819 colonel of the 5th foot. The following year he was nominated a GCB.

Johnson and his wife had two sons: Henry Allen, who became aide-de-camp to the prince of Orange, and George Pigot, a captain in the 81st regiment, who was killed in Portugal in 1812. Johnson himself died on 18 March 1835 at his house in Catharine Place, Bath; he has a monument in Bath Abbey. His surviving son inherited the baronetcy.

H. M. CHICHESTER, *rev.* A. F. BLACKSTOCK

Sources PRO, Home Office 100 ser., vol. 77, fols. 72–82 · PRO NIre., Shannon MSS, D 2707/A3/3/80 · Lake to Pelham, 27 Jan 1798, BL, Pelham MSS, Add. MS 33105, fol. 337 · *Correspondence of Charles, first Marquis Cornwallis*, ed. C. Ross, 3 vols. (1859), vol. 3, p. 116 · *GM*, 2nd ser., 4 (1835), 659 · D. Gahan, *The people's rising: Wexford, 1798* (1995) · Burke, *Peerage* (1953) · M. M. Boatner, *Cassell's biographical dictionary of the American War of Independence, 1763–1783* (1973) · J. Philippart, ed., *The royal military calendar*, 3rd edn, 1 (1820), 346–7 · *The American rebellion: Sir Henry Clinton's narrative of his campaigns, 1775–1782*, ed. W. B. Willcox (1954) · W. A. Shaw, *The knights of England*, 2 vols. (1906)
Archives PRO NIre., Dublin army letters, MIC 67 [microfilm copies]
Likenesses R. Dunkarton, mezzotint (after R. Woodburn), BM, NPG · C. Jagger, portrait (after miniature), NG Ire. · S. Sangster, line engraving (after C. Jagger), BM

Johnson, Sir Henry Cecil (1906–1988), businessman, was born on 11 September 1906 in Lavendon, Buckinghamshire, the third of three sons and the fifth of six children of William Longland Johnson, farmer and butcher, of Lavendon, and his wife, Alice Mary Osborne. He was educated at Bedford modern school.

Johnson joined London and North Eastern Railway (LNER) as a traffic apprentice in 1923, the usual first step towards a career in railway management, and in 1926 became an assistant yard manager near Ely, entitled to wear a bowler hat, the symbol of a railway manager. In 1932 he married Evelyn Mary (Maisie), daughter of Thomas Morton, corn merchant; they had two daughters.

After various posts in the operating department of LNER Johnson was appointed assistant superintendent of southern area, LNER, in 1942. In 1955 he became chief operating superintendent of the eastern region, one of the six regions formed when the railways were nationalized in 1948. He was promoted to the position of assistant general manager of the eastern region at the end of 1955, becoming general manager in 1958. While at the eastern region he introduced the successful line management concept—an assistant general manager (traffic) co-ordinating the work of the line managers.

In 1962 Johnson became general manager of the London

midland region, the most important of the British Railways regions, and he was also chairman in 1963–7. He took charge of the electrification of the Euston to Manchester and Liverpool line, the first main-line electrification, completed in 1966, which had been part of the modernization plan of 1955, and the new Euston Station was opened in 1968. Johnson became vice-chairman of the British Railways board in 1967. Following the forced resignation of the chairman, Sir Stanley Raymond, at the end of 1967, after disagreements with the minister of transport, Barbara Castle, Johnson was appointed chairman, a post he held from 1968 until 1971.

The finances of British Railways improved under Johnson, largely as a result of the 1968 Transport Act, in which the government promised specific grants to make unprofitable passenger services financially viable where they were providing a public service, in contrast to the recommendations of Richard Beeching (chairman in 1963–5), who wanted to make the railways profitable by closing uneconomic lines. Although Richard Marsh, Johnson's successor, estimated in 1972 that the government invested five times as much each year in new motorways and trunk roads as in the railways, modernization continued: InterCity, started in 1966 as a new operation of high-speed trains linking major cities, expanded, and in 1968 the last steam engines were taken out of service. In 1969 work began at the research centre in Derby on the advanced passenger train, a high-speed train running on existing tracks, but it was withdrawn two weeks after it entered regular passenger service in 1981. Johnson took a particular interest in the commercial development of surplus railway land, and established and became chairman of the British Rail property board in 1970. In the 1970s British Railways earned £20 million a year from land sales.

Although there were large reductions in railway staff following modernization and the closure of uneconomic lines, there was some progress during the Johnson years towards improving industrial relations. The rail unions objected to pay being linked to productivity at a time when this was not the case in other industries, and Johnson had to steer British Railways through periods of 'work-to-rule', with the unions demanding large pay increases while British Railways proposals for price increases were being held back by the National Board for Prices and Incomes.

Johnson was not an innovator, and most of the changes which took place under his chairmanship had been put in motion by his predecessors. While he did not capture the public imagination in the way of Beeching, he was extremely popular with the railway employees, who admired him as the only railwayman to have started at the bottom and worked his way up through the ranks to become chairman of British Railways. He was fortunate to become chairman when the 1968 Transport Act had paved the way towards improving the financial situation, and he left British Railways with a surplus of £9.7 million. Johnson was appointed CBE in 1962, knighted in 1968, and became KBE in 1972. In 1981 a locomotive was named after him.

After his retirement Johnson started a new career in the City, as chairman of Metropolitan Estate and Property Corporation, a post he held from 1971 to 1976. He later held positions on the boards of Lloyds Bank, the Trident Life Assurance Company, and Imperial Life of Canada.

Always known as Bill Johnson, he had a friendly and relaxed manner, but he was shrewd, a good listener, and expert at delegating. Sir Peter Parker, a later chairman, admired his honesty and courage, describing him as 'straight as a gun barrel'. He had an open, distinguished face, with silver-grey hair and large bushy eyebrows. In his younger days he was a keen rugby player and a cricketer, and he also enjoyed golf. He was a member of the Marylebone Cricket Club and the Royal and Ancient Golf Club. He died on 13 March 1988 in Great Missenden, Buckinghamshire.   ANNE PIMLOTT BAKER, rev.

Sources *The Times* (15 March 1988) · T. R. Gourvish, *British Railways, 1948–73: a business history* (1986) [research by N. Blake and others] · M. Bonavia, *British Rail: the first 25 years* (1981) · P. Parker, *For starters: the business of life* (1989) · private information (1996) · *CGPLA Eng. & Wales* (1988)
Likenesses group portrait, photograph, 1969, repro. in Gourvish, *British Railways*, pl. 37
Wealth at death £138,636: probate, 6 May 1988, *CGPLA Eng. & Wales*

Johnson, Henry John [Harry] (1826–1884), watercolour painter, was born in Birmingham on 10 April 1826, the son of Benjamin Johnson. Named Henry at birth he was later known as Harry, possibly to avoid confusion with the Henry Johnson who was exhibiting figure subjects in the 1840s. He is said to have had some lessons from the Birmingham landscape painter Samuel Lines before going to London in the winter of 1842–3 to work as a pupil in the studio of William James Müller. The position was evidently paid for and arranged by Johnson's father, a patron of Müller, and soon Benjamin Johnson gave permission for his son to travel to Turkey in 1843 with Müller, as companion and pupil, to join the third and final excavations by Sir Charles Fellows in Lycia. They were away for nearly eight months, and Harry Johnson's later description of the expedition and of Müller's working practices, written for Müller's biographer N. N. Solly, provides a vivid background to Müller's remarkable Lycian watercolours. After his return in 1844 Johnson continued as Müller's pupil into 1845 and probably until ill health forced Müller to retreat to Bristol in May of that year.

In June and July 1844, while Müller was in Bristol and Devon, Johnson travelled in north Wales as companion to the landscape painter David Cox. They stayed for some weeks at Betws-y-coed, the first of the important series of annual visits that Cox was to make to that village. On 1 April 1845 Müller wrote to his pupil's anxious father reporting that his son had just been elected a subscriber to the small Clipstone Street Society in London (a fairly informal society of artists who drew from the model), where he probably continued his studies after Müller's death in September. Müller's last letter, written four days before he died, was to Benjamin Johnson, concerning his patron's recent purchase, and stated that his son had again been at Betws-y-coed.

Johnson first exhibited at the Royal Academy in 1845, and showed there intermittently until 1880; he exhibited annually at the British Institution from 1846 to 1867. His earliest exhibits at both institutions were Turkish subjects, but scenes in Italy, France, Switzerland, Britain, and (from 1862) Greece followed. All commentators have agreed on the superiority of his watercolours over his exhibition oils, which are very seldom seen. Johnson was elected an associate of the Institute of Painters in Water Colours in 1868 and a full member in 1870. He is said to have been popular among fellow artists but to have suffered for many years from increasing deafness. He lived in London from 1843, residing from 1857 at 10 Loudoun Road, St John's Wood, and from 1877 at The Holt, 12 Loudoun Road. There he died on 31 December 1884, leaving a widow, Fanny Elizabeth Hervet, and a daughter, Melicent. A representative selection of his watercolours is in the Victoria and Albert Museum, some of which reflect the vitality and confidence of Müller's best work—an inspiration and a shadow from which Johnson never really escaped.   FRANCIS GREENACRE

Sources DNB · N. N. Solly, *Memoir of the life of William James Müller* (1875) · N. N. Solly, *Memoir of the life of David Cox* (1875) · M. Hardie, *Water-colour painting in Britain*, ed. D. Snelgrove, J. Mayne, and B. Taylor, 2: *The Romantic period* (1967) · S. Wildman, ed., *David Cox, 1783–1859* [exhibition catalogue, Birmingham Museums and Art Gallery, 26 July – 14 Oct 1983, and V&A, 9 Nov 1983 – 8 Jan 1984] · Graves, *RA exhibitors* · Graves, *Brit. Inst.* · Bryan, *Painters* · S. Wildman, *The Birmingham school* (1990) · d. cert.

Wealth at death £7670 1s. 11d.: resworn administration, April 1885, CGPLA Eng. & Wales

Johnson, Hewlett (1874–1966), dean of Canterbury, was born on 25 January 1874 in Kersal, Manchester, the fifth child and third son of Charles Johnson, a wire manufacturer, and his wife, Rosa, daughter of the Revd Alfred Hewlett. His early childhood was spent in and around Manchester. He was educated at Macclesfield grammar school and from 1890 to 1894 he studied at Owens College where he took a BSc in civil engineering in 1894.

Intending to offer himself for missionary service overseas, Johnson entered training as an engineer at the Ashbury carriage works in Manchester, where he was first introduced to socialist ideas by two workmates. With a view to joining the Church Missionary Society, he spent a year on the ordination course at Wycliffe Hall, Oxford, at his father's expense. He later read theology at Wadham College, Oxford (1902–5), and graduated with second-class honours. In 1903, while still at Oxford, he married Mary, daughter of Frederick Taylor, a merchant, of Broughton Park, Manchester. Much influenced by radical theology, he was rejected by the board of the Church Missionary Society because of his liberal churchmanship. Johnson was nevertheless ordained deacon by Bishop Jayne of Chester in 1905 and became curate at St Margaret's, Altrincham. He was ordained a priest in 1906, and in 1908 he was made vicar of the same parish. In Altrincham Johnson and his wife ran holiday camps for the young people of the

Hewlett Johnson (1874–1966), by Howard Coster, 1944

parish and Johnson campaigned extensively for the improvement of housing conditions for the poor, which became a lifelong interest. In 1913 he was appointed examining chaplain to the bishop of Chester.

In 1905 Johnson began the monthly (later quarterly) journal *The Interpreter* which he published and edited for twenty years. The aim of the journal was to communicate the ideas of recent biblical scholarship and archaeology as part of the pursuit of the truth of Christianity: 'Our ultimate aim is construction, not destruction, and we know no means to attain this end but fidelity to truth' (*The Interpreter*, 1/1, 1905, 1). Johnson regarded engagement with biblical criticism as a fundamental responsibility of the ministers of the established church:

> To forbid the leaders of Christian communities to apply the scientific standards which a man of science or a man of business now uses in every thought or transaction, will be to put them in a position where they will speedily earn the distrust of their people.   (*The Interpreter*, 1/1, 1905, 3)

During the years of its publication (1905–24), many leading theologians and scholars contributed to the journal.

The Russian Revolution in 1917, together with his experiences of capitalism in the wealthy parish of Altrincham, laid the foundations for Johnson's growing socialist convictions, which he saw as the natural consequence of his commitment to Christian morality. During the First World War he and his wife organized a hospital for the returning wounded in his parish. He was also chaplain to a

German prisoner-of-war camp. This and the impact of the war on both England and Germany, which he visited shortly after the war, fed his pacifist convictions. Johnson had continued his studies, and in 1917 he was awarded a bachelor of divinity degree in Oxford, followed by a DD in 1924 for his work on the Acts of the Apostles. In 1919 he was made an honorary canon of Chester Cathedral, and in 1922 he became rural dean of Bowden and proctor of convocation.

In 1924, when Ramsay MacDonald was prime minister, Johnson was appointed dean of Manchester Cathedral, a broader platform for his campaigning on behalf of the poor of the north-west. He opened the cathedral particularly to children. He ordered a new altar for the Jesus chapel and inner doors with glass panels for the west end of the cathedral to enable passers-by to get a view of the nave and the choir. In January 1931 his first wife Mary died of cancer. In that year, on the recommendation of archbishops Cosmo Gordon Lang and William Temple, who were impressed by his work in Manchester, Johnson was appointed dean of Canterbury, an office he held until his retirement in 1963. In the 1930s Johnson was interested in the industrial conditions of the working classes and the social credit movement propounded by C. H. Douglas. In 1935 he visited Alberta, Canada, to learn more about Douglas's ideas. His favourite theme in his well-attended sermons was the gospel in its social implications. He also became a member and later chairman of the board of the *Daily Worker*. At Canterbury he continued his interest in international politics and the development of socialism in countries such as the Soviet Union and China. At the suggestion of C. F. Andrews, Johnson visited China in 1932 to investigate the damage done by the floods of 1931 and to organize relief for the starving population. Back at home in Canterbury, he sought to assist the large numbers suffering from unemployment and destitution by establishing the Canterbury Pilgrimage to raise aid for those in need.

In 1937 Johnson visited Spain and witnessed the bombing of Durango by members of the German condor legion. He subsequently spoke out against fascist claims that the republican government had set out to bomb Durango in order to destroy churches. His experience of the Spanish Civil War as a dress rehearsal for the war against Nazism enhanced and shaped Johnson's view of communism as the only possible salvation for humanity. Through contacts that included his friendship with the Soviet ambassador to London and his vice-presidency of the Society for Cultural Relations with the USSR (from 1935), Johnson's interest in Soviet developments grew; he first visited the Soviet Union in 1937. Unaware, like many contemporary travellers to Russia, of the show trials and the activities of Stalin's persecution machine, Johnson saw Soviet Russia as on the way to becoming the perfect society, in which socialist principles were being realized for the good of all. In the autumn of 1938, Johnson married Nowell Mary Edwards, an old friend and the daughter of his cousin the Revd George Edwards. In 1940 their first daughter, Mary Kezia, was born, followed by a second, Helene Keren, in

1942. During his time in office as dean of Canterbury, Johnson travelled extensively in the eastern bloc, especially in the Soviet Union and China. He also became a much sought-after speaker on issues relating to Soviet Russia and communism, both in Britain and internationally.

Communism, for Johnson, was not an anti-Christian force, but rather a natural result and practical outworking of the Christian gospel. In *Christians and Communism* (1936) he articulated the 'certainty' that the Soviet Union and communism

> are going along with the trend of the world, coupled with a passion for living which they conceive of as a cosmic demand, which gives not only an élan in work but a certain peace and settlement of mind within … And it is out of that content that I find many points of contact with the spirit and intention of the founder of Christianity. (*Christians and Communism*, 11)

In *The Socialist Sixth of the World* (1939), which enjoyed enormous sales, Johnson wrote that 'The communist puts the Christian to shame in the thoroughness of his quest for a harmonious society. Here he proves himself to be the heir of the Christian intention' (*The Socialist Sixth of the World*, 367).

Johnson's openly pro-communist and pro-Soviet stance earned him the nickname the Red Dean and caused significant friction between himself and other clergy in the Church of England—not least among his colleagues at Canterbury Cathedral, who proposed his removal on several occasions. But Johnson never joined the Communist Party, his understanding of socialism and communism being based less on agreement with their ideology than on the fact that he saw the outworking of Christian moral and social teaching realized in countries such as the Soviet Union and China. Yet his extensive writings on Soviet Russia reflected a naïve and romantic perspective on the transformations after the 1917 revolution. Until the end of his life he ignored the realities of mass persecution and the extermination of political opponents, as well as the anti-religious aspects of Marxism and Stalinism. 'Other Communists deserted over Khrushchov's speech at the 20th Congress or over the invasion of Hungary', Alan Wilkinson has written, 'but Johnson's faith remained unshaken. His romantic hyperbole effortlessly soared over disagreeable facts into a cloud of utopian rhetoric' (Wilkinson, 174). 'Having decided that Soviet Communism was helping the cause of human betterment, he refused to criticize' (*DNB*).

After the war, Johnson travelled extensively in eastern Europe and was among the first foreign witnesses to the extensive destruction there, including the village of Lidice where a massacre of the local population by German SS officers had taken place, and also to the recently liberated concentration camp of Auschwitz. He met high-ranking politicians such as Stalin, Mao Zedong, and Fidel Castro, and in 1952 he was awarded the Stalin peace prize. Johnson wrote and published extensively, describing his experiences of Soviet Russia and China as models for the rebuilding of a socialist society. His writings include *The*

Socialist Sixth of the World (1939), which was translated into many languages, and *Christians and Communism* (1936).

Having retired as dean in 1963, Johnson died at the age of ninety-two on 22 October 1966 at the Kent and Canterbury Hospital and was buried in the cloister garth in Canterbury Cathedral. NATALIE K. WATSON

Sources R. Hughes, *The Red Dean* (1987) · H. Johnson, *Searching for light* (1966) · *The Times* (23 Oct 1966) · *WWW* · A. Wilkinson, *Christian socialism* (1998) · *DNB* · L. Lang-Sims, *A time to be born: volume one of an autobiography* (1971) · *CGPLA Eng. & Wales* (1967)

Archives University of Kent, Canterbury, papers and corresp. | BL, corresp. with Albert Mansbridge, Add. MSS 65255A–B | FILM BFI NFTVA, documentary footage · BFI NFTVA, news footage | SOUND BL NSA, oral history interview

Likenesses N. Johnson, oils, *c.*1932, Canterbury Cathedral, deanery · F. Man, double portrait, photograph, *c.*1940 (with Jacob Epstein), NPG · H. Coster, two photographs, 1944, NPG [*see illus.*] · V. Mukhina, metal bust, 1945, NPG

Wealth at death £24,187: probate, 13 Feb 1967, *CGPLA Eng. & Wales*

Johnson, Humphrey (*fl.* **1710–1713**), writing-master and mathematician, is known to have been apprenticed to the celebrated writing-master George Shelley but nothing else is recorded regarding his early life or training. At the time of the first edition of his *New Treatise of Practical Arithmetic* (1710) he was a writing-master teaching penmanship, merchant accounts, and arithmetic at his own day school in Old Bedlam Court near Bishopsgate, London. This practical maths primer was aimed at teaching youths the necessary skills for a merchant career. At the same time this work reveals Johnson's interest in promoting standardized forms of accounts within the ever-increasing merchant population. The same desire underpinned his next publication, a modest fifteen-plate copybook entitled *Youth's Recreation* (1711) which was engraved by J. Nutting and sold by Henry Overton for 6*d*. Although Johnson was best known as a mathematician, in this copybook he promoted the 'free running hand' (*Youth's Recreation*) as the most clear and precise style of penmanship for business transactions and accounts. The success of these works can be gauged from the appearance of second editions of both in 1719 and 1713, respectively. Towards the end of his life Johnson moved to rural Hornsey, Middlesex, where he kept a boarding-school. The date of his death is unknown. LUCY PELTZ

Sources A. Heal, *The English writing-masters and their copy-books, 1570–1800* (1931) · W. Massey, *The origin and progress of letters: an essay in two parts* (1763) · *A biographical history of England, from the revolution to the end of George I's reign: being a continuation of the Rev. J. Granger's work*, ed. M. Noble, 3 vols. (1806) · Thieme & Becker, *Allgemeines Lexikon*

Likenesses engraving, repro. in H. Johnson, *Youth's recreation* (1711) · engraving, repro. in H. Johnson, *Common arithmetic* (1710) · line engraving, NPG

Johnson, Isaac (*bap.* **1601, *d.* 1630**), colonist in America, was baptized at St John's, Stamford, Lincolnshire, the eldest son of Abraham Johnson (1577–1649), gentleman, of South Luffenham, Rutland, and Anne (*née* Meadows) (*c.*1583–*c.*1602). He was grandson of Robert *Johnson (1540/41–1625), archdeacon of Leicester, and step-

grandson of Laurence Chaderton, first master of Emmanuel College, Cambridge, where he matriculated in 1614. Having graduated BA in 1618 and MA in 1621, he was ordained at Peterborough, deacon in 1620, and priest in 1621, but entered Gray's Inn in 1621. In 1623, while resident at Sempringham, despite paternal prohibition, he married Lady Arbella Clinton (or Fiennes; 1601–1630), daughter of the third earl of Lincoln. Two years later he inherited some £20,000 from his paternal grandfather. He first contemplated emigration in 1627, became an assistant of the Massachusetts Bay Company on 13 May 1629, and sent servants ahead. He spent over £5000 on the *Arbella* expedition of 1630 and arrived at Salem on 12 June. At the invitation of Emmanuel contemporary and old planter William Blackstone, he led the settlement of Boston. His wife died at Salem in August, and he, in poor health for some time, died at his home in Boston, between Court Street and School Street, on 30 September 1630. There were no heirs. Johnson had vindicated his vow 'to spend and be spent' on the great migration; he was remembered as 'the chiefest stud in the land' (Canavan, 272, 285). ROGER THOMPSON

Sources M. J. Canavan, 'Isaac Johnson, esquire, founder of Boston', *Publications of the Colonial Society of Massachusetts*, 27 (1932), 272–85 · R. C. Anderson, ed., *The great migration begins: immigrants to New England, 1620–1633*, 2 (Boston, MA, 1995), 1104–5 · P. Thompson, 'The Johnson family', *New England Historical and Genealogical Register*, 8 (1855), 359–62 · Venn, *Alum. Cant.* · John Winthrop's journal: 'History of New England', 1630–1649, ed. J. K. Hosmer, 2 vols. (1908)

Wealth at death inherited £20,000 from grandfather in 1625: Thompson, 'The Johnson family', 361

Johnson, Isaac (**1754–1835**), topographical artist and land surveyor, was born at Pettistree Lodge, near Wickham Market, Suffolk, and baptized in Pettistree church on 27 January 1754, the second of three artistic sons of John Johnson (*c.*1722–1780), land surveyor and farm bailiff, and Mary, *née* Nichols (*bap.* 1715, *d.* 1800). His father and his grandfather, also Isaac Johnson, were farmers of Debach, near Woodbridge. When Isaac was six the family moved to Alderton, where all three sons helped and learned from their father, for whose surveys they drew the ornaments. Three books of exercises dated March 1770 in Isaac's hand were probably written at the navigation school then on Woodbridge quayside. He first signed and dated surveys in 1777 and watercolours in 1780, and was a tireless and prolific worker to the end of his life. He married, at St Peter Permountergate Church in Norwich on 20 April 1786, Elizabeth (*bap.* 1761, *d.* 1813), daughter of Thomas Maxwell, a worsted weaver there; they had twelve children at their house in Cumberland Street, Woodbridge, six of whom were baptized at the Quay Presbyterian Meeting-House. In his 'Miscellaneous Pieces in Prose and Verse' collected and continued from 1810, Johnson poured out his pious sorrow at the loss in 1780 of both his father and his elder brother John, a schoolmaster and artist, of his son Benjamin in 1812, and of his wife on 17 January 1813. The death in 1797 of his younger brother, William, portraitist and teacher of perspective, seems not to have affected him so deeply. After four and a half years as a widower,

Isaac Johnson (1754–1835), self-portrait

Isaac married again, on 17 October 1817 in St Mary's Church, Woodbridge (by licence as a nonconformist), Mary Fisher (b. 1791, d. in or after 1841), milliner and dressmaker. She was thirty-seven years his junior, but there were no more children. Mary, disapproved of by at least one stepdaughter, carried on her business from their home on Market Hill.

A fragment of Johnson's account book covering the years 1791–6 shows how varied were the commissions he received, and that in those five years he earned £1069 from surveying and charged £108 for drawings of churches and other antiquities for collectors, who were grangerizing topographical works. His patrons included the Suffolk nobility, clergy, and gentry, and more particularly the London author and publisher John Nichols, and through him the antiquaries Sir John Cullum, Richard Gough, and Craven Ord, all of whom were eager to have illustrations for their Suffolk collections and published works. Some of Johnson's largest and finest wash-drawings, of Letheringham church and its remarkable series of monuments destroyed in the drastic restoration of 1789, are in Ord's elephant folio Suffolk volumes in the British Library. Nichols had some of Johnson's drawings engraved for the *Gentleman's Magazine* and others for his *History and Antiquities of Leicestershire*. Gough's *Sepulchral Monuments* has several plates engraved by Basire 'after drawings by an ingenious and modest artist of Woodbridge' (R. Gough, *Sepulchral Monuments*, 2, 1796, pt 2)— Johnson, of course.

Between 1799 and 1816 Johnson drew the south view of every church in Suffolk, keeping the pen-and-ink originals for reference in order to make neat copies of all 514 churches in bound volumes to order. He charged 7s. 6d. per page for albums of drawings, titling them so immaculately that his hand has often been mistaken for printing. Collections were given such titles as 'Architectural and monumental remains', 'Ancient remains of art', and 'Excursions on the sea coast of Suffolk'. Three volumes produced speculatively were left unsold at his death. Many of the reference drawings and surveys passed at Johnson's death to his successor, but not partner, in business, Benjamin Moulton; the former are now in the J. S. Earle collection at the Society of Antiquaries and the latter at Suffolk Record Office in Ipswich. The most elaborate surveys (for example, of Felixstowe, Walton, and the Trimleys, 1784, and of Great Saxham, 1801) include books with finished drawings of all the estate properties. Johnson painted a series of remarkable trees in Norfolk and Suffolk, some hollow, and a few inhabited. For portraits, and a conversation piece including a self-portrait with his family in 1803, he worked in oils; for still-life and flower painting he used gouache.

Johnson died while on a working trip to Aldeburgh. On Friday, 24 July 1835, after having ordered tea and a bed at The Mill inn, he went out for a walk. Probably attacked by apoplexy, he fell from the river wall, and was unable to move. Not found for a whole day, he was carried indoors, but died on the following Monday, 27 July, and was buried in the churchyard of St Mary's, Woodbridge, three days later without any memorial. His widow subsequently married a Mr Salmon and died in or after 1841.

J. M. BLATCHLY

Sources priv. coll. · J. Blatchly and P. Eden, *Isaac Johnson of Woodbridge, 1754–1835* (1979) · I. Johnson, account book fragment, 1791–6, Suffolk RO, Ipswich, HD 11:432 · I. Johnson, MS commonplace book, priv. coll. · corresp. Percy Rushen, priv. coll. · *Ipswich Journal* (23 Jan 1813) · *Ipswich Journal* (25 Oct 1817)
Archives BL, corresp., Add. MSS 11802, 23958, 26108, 31981 · Bodl. Oxf., corresp. · priv. coll., pieces in prose and verse · Suffolk RO, Ipswich, account book fragment · Suffolk RO, Ipswich, estate surveys | BL, Craven Ord's Suffolk collections, Add. MSS 8986, 8987 · S. Antiquaries, Lond., Joseph Sim Earle collection · Suffolk RO, Ipswich, Fitch Suffolk illustrations, HD 480/1-31 · Suffolk RO, Ipswich, Gillingwater's *History of Lowestoft*, HD 373/2 · Suffolk RO, Ipswich, Loder's extra-illustrated *Suffolk traveller*, HD 487/1-5
Likenesses I. Johnson, oils, repro. in Blatchly and Eden, *Isaac Johnson of Woodbridge*; priv. coll. · I. Johnson, self-portrait, wash drawing, priv. coll. [see illus.]

Johnson, Isaac Theophilus Akuna Wallace-

Johnson, Isaac Theophilus Akuna Wallace- (1894–1965), politician, was born on 6 February 1894 in Wilberforce Village outside Freetown, Sierra Leone, to poor Krio parents, his father a farmer named Johnson (c.1836–1924) and his mother a fish seller named Wallace (c.1850–1938). Educated at Methodist schools, he left early and worked in clerical jobs and as a lay preacher. In 1914 he enlisted as an army clerk in the West African regiment, serving in the Cameroons campaign, and then with the carrier corps in east Africa and in the Middle East. Demobilized in 1920, he returned to clerical employment in Freetown until 1926, when he was dismissed from a city council post for inciting his colleagues to demand better pay and conditions.

The details of Wallace-Johnson's subsequent life-history, dramatized in histrionic reminiscences or deliberately mystified for political reasons, are uncertain. He went to sea as a purser's clerk, but by 1930 was a journalist in Lagos where he helped found the African Workers' Union of Nigeria. Under the name E. Richards he went to Hamburg, attended the first International Trade Union Conference of Negro Workers, and contributed to its journal, the *Negro Worker*, writing articles and satirical poems under the pseudonym Wal. Daniels. He toured Europe and attended a conference in Moscow, where he remained for a few months and may have attended university.

In 1933 Wallace-Johnson returned to Lagos, edited the *Daily Telegraph*, and was active in trade union affairs. Investigated by the colonial authorities, he moved to Accra, worked as a journalist, and helped trade unions and individuals with grievances to present their cases publicly, sometimes getting them raised in parliament through left-wing contacts in London. In 1935 with Nnamdi Azikiwe, editor of the Accra *African Morning Post* (and later a leading figure in Nigeria), he founded the West African Youth League (WAYL), to organize protests against colonial rule. The Italian invasion of Ethiopia gave him a dramatic public platform coupling local issues with violent denunciations of white imperialism worldwide.

Wallace-Johnson's provocative, outspoken oratory and journalism brought a new mass dimension to Gold Coast politics. WAYL branches opened in the main towns. The government found a pretext to silence him when he published an article declaring that Europeans believe in a God whose law is: 'Ye "civilized Europeans", you must "civilize" the Africans with machine guns. Ye Christian Europeans, You must "Christianize" the pagan Africans with bombs, poison gases etc' (Spitzer and Denzer, 414). He was tried for sedition, fined £50, and left for London. There he joined the Afro-Caribbean radical George Padmore, who had recently broken with the Communist Party to found the International African Service Bureau, a non-political pan-African organization operating in London. As general secretary he contributed to its journal, the *African Sentinel*, until dismissed for misappropriating funds.

In April 1938 Wallace-Johnson returned to Freetown where political activity had hitherto been confined to a small, wealthy Krio élite, customarily ignored by the government. This he now changed dramatically. He founded a Sierra Leone branch of the WAYL, and addressed packed public meetings, winning mass appeal with flamboyant, inflammatory speeches. He organized eight trade unions and published a journal, the *African Standard*, which included anti-imperialist articles by British left-wingers. But his message, though inflammatory, was non-violent and non-revolutionary. Beyond the address 'comrade', there was little identifiable as communist. Instead he concentrated on local grievances, thus winning over the Freetown non-élite middle class as well as the workers. At the municipal election in November 1938 the WAYL won all the electable seats. Wallace-Johnson also appealed to the

Freetown Muslims and, for the first time, took politics into the Sierra Leone protectorate. The horrified colonial authorities were determined to muzzle him. Arrested in September 1939 and charged with criminal libel, he was detained under wartime defence regulations, then tried and sentenced to a year's imprisonment. After his release he was sent to detention in Bonthe, a small town south of Freetown, until 1944.

In England in 1945 Wallace-Johnson attended the inaugural conference of the World Federation of Trade Unions and the Manchester Pan-African Congress. But, back in Freetown, he was unable to revive the WAYL as a national force. The political alignments of the 1950s left him stranded, moving from one party to another, even joining up briefly with the old Krio élite he had once derided. He was among the opposition politicians imprisoned in 1961 lest they disrupt the independence day celebrations. Then he faded out of politics, but from 1963 published a typescript newsletter including (as Professor W. Daniels) his customary verse. On 9 May 1965, while attending the Afro-Asian solidarity conference in Ghana, he was killed in a car accident on Winnebah Road, Accra. He was buried at the Wilberforce Village cemetery on 16 May. He was survived by his second wife, Enith, and his first wife, Eudora, his first marriage having ended in divorce.

Wallace-Johnson was a loner. Adored by supporters, he antagonized colleagues who distrusted his irresponsible, devious ways, and believed he misappropriated funds—though he never enriched himself, and lived and died poor. But if his career ended in disappointment, his sudden, spectacular agitation in the 1930s changed the course of west African politics irrevocably.

CHRISTOPHER FYFE

Sources L. Spitzer and L. Denzer, 'I. T. A. Wallace-Johnson and the West African Youth League', *International Journal of African Historical Studies*, 6 (1973), 413–52, 565–601 • L. Denzer, 'Wallace-Johnson and the Sierra Leone labor crisis of 1939', *African Studies Review*, 25 (1982), 159–83 • S. K. B. Asante, *Pan-African protest: west Africa and the Italo-Ethiopian crisis, 1934–41* (1977) • J. R. Cartwright, *Politics in Sierra Leone, 1947–67* (1970) • A. J. G. Wyse, *H. C. Bankole-Bright and politics in colonial Sierra Leone, 1919–58* (1990) • I. T. A. Wallace-Johnson, SALNB publications, 1963–5 • I. T. A. Wallace-Johnson, *Prison in the muse* (1945) • L. H. Ofosu-Appiah, ed., *The encyclopaedia Africana dictionary of African biography*, 2: *Sierra Leone, Zaire* (1979), 159–61
Archives PRO, CO 267/665, 666, 670, 671, 677
Likenesses bust, city council building, Freetown, Sierra Leone • photograph, repro. in Ofosu-Appiah, ed., *Encyclopædia Africana dictionary*, 159

Johnson, James (*bap.* 1705, *d.* 1774), bishop of Worcester, was baptized on 20 September 1705 at Long Melford, Suffolk, the son of James Johnson, rector of that parish, and his wife, Anne. He attended Westminster School from 1718 (king's scholar, 1719) and matriculated at Christ Church, Oxford, in 1724. He was admitted to the degrees of BA (1728), MA (1731), and BD and DD (1742). He was undermaster of Westminster from 1733 to 1748 and held the livings of Turweston, Buckinghamshire (1741–4), Mixbury, Oxfordshire (1744–59), and Watford, Hertfordshire (1744–59). Johnson was made chaplain-in-ordinary to George II in 1744 and accompanied the king to Hanover at least twice. In 1748 he was appointed to a residentiaryship of St Paul's and prebend of Consumpta-per-Mare in St Paul's Cathedral. In 1752 he was appointed bishop of Gloucester; he was translated to the see of Worcester in 1759 and held it until his death in 1774.

Johnson owed his advancement to the help of Andrew Stone and the patronage of the duke of Newcastle. The duke wanted Johnson's appointment to the see of Gloucester despite Archbishop Herring's reluctance, and, respecting his translation to Worcester, maintained: 'My friendship to him has long made me determined to do it, if I could … I have always put poor Johnson with regard to myself upon a different footing from everybody' (Sykes, 'The duke of Newcastle', 70). But politics also brought Johnson trouble. Edmund Pyle observed in November 1752: '[h]e has been a pretty high Tory, & is devilishly belied if he has not a deal of the old leaven in him yet' (Pyle, 181). Herring, in 1752, recalled tales that Johnson had 'been once a Jacobite, of the first order' (BL, Add. MS 35599, fols. 57–8) and believed: 'there is on political accounts a greater abhorrence of the man among the whigs, the great whigs, than ever I met with of any man' (Sykes, 'The duke of Newcastle', 66). Certainly the whigs violently and successfully opposed Johnson's suggested promotion to the position of preceptor to George, prince of Wales.

Shortly after Johnson's elevation to Gloucester a scandal raged. The recorder of Newcastle, one Fawcett, declared that Johnson had once been a Jacobite, along with Stone and William Murray (both Old Westminsters). Fawcett subsequently retracted, exonerating Johnson, then zig-zagged about the other charges. The matter was discussed in the cabinet council in February 1753. It was debated in the House of Lords in March; Johnson defended himself and the issue was allowed to drop. None the less memories of the affair persisted. When Johnson was to be nominated to Worcester, Newcastle felt obliged to assure the earl of Coventry that he would comply with whatever would further the whig interest in the locality.

As a bishop Johnson discharged his duties conscientiously. He ordained regularly. He held his primary visitation as bishop of Gloucester in 1754 and a triennial visitation in 1757. As bishop of Worcester his primary visitation was held in 1761 and he conducted triennial visitations in 1764, 1767, 1770, and 1773. He published three sermons—that delivered before the Lords in 1759 examined the role of providence in wartime, and particularly in the context of the *annus mirabilis*. He improved the residences of the bishops of Worcester in the city and at Hartlebury Castle.

Johnson died, unmarried, in Bath on 26 November 1774, having fallen from his horse. He was buried on 4 December at Lacock in Wiltshire; there is a monument to him, by J. Nollekens, in Worcester Cathedral. George Butt, who delivered his memorial address at Bath, spoke of his 'Temper equally social, gentle, and obliging', of 'his humble Manners', and of his piety, unclouded 'by any Mixture of gloomy Superstition'; he saw him as 'honest, and honourable, and benevolent' (Butt, 18, 20). Others regarded him differently. Pyle wrote in 1752 of his 'pride & disdain' (Pyle, 181). Similarly when describing Johnson's denial of Jacobitism in the Lords, Horace Walpole wrote of 'the Bishop of Gloucester's pedantic scorn' and of his insolence (Walpole, 1.220). His portrait at Hartlebury Castle shows a fat, shrewd face; the bust on his monument at Worcester is more agreeable.

COLIN HAYDON

Sources parish register, Long Melford, Suffolk, 1705, Suffolk RO, Ipswich [baptism] · bishop's register, Lincs. Arch., Lincoln diocesan archives, register 38 · bishop's register, diocese of London, 1733–62, GL, MS 9531/20, pt 2 · Gloucester diocesan records, Glos. RO, GDR C3/18, 20 · Worcester (St Helen's) RO, Worcester diocesan MSS, Ref. b. 802, BA 2610; Ref. 778.7322, BA 2448 · note, Bodl. Oxf., Vet. A5 d.197(1) · BL, Add. MS 35599 · G. Butt, *A sermon preached at the Octagon Chapel, in the city of Bath, on the day the late bishop of Worcester was buried* (1775) · *JHL*, 28 (1753–6) · *St James's Chronicle* (29 Nov–1 Dec 1774) · E. Pyle, *Memoirs of a royal chaplain, 1729–1763*, ed. A. Hartshorne (1905) · *The political journal of George Bubb Dodington*, ed. J. Carswell and L. A. Dralle (1965) · H. Walpole, *Memoirs of King George II*, ed. J. Brooke, 1 (1985) · J. Johnson, *A sermon preached before the right honourable the lords spiritual and temporal in parliament assembled … on … November 29, 1759* (1759) · *GM*, 1st ser., 44 (1774) · monument, Worcester Cathedral · *Letters from George III to Lord Bute, 1756–1766*, ed. R. Sedgwick (1939) · N. Sykes, *Church and state in England in the XVIII century* (1934) · N. Sykes, 'The duke of Newcastle as ecclesiastical minister', *EngHR*, 57 (1942), 59–84 · Foster, *Alum. Oxon.* · E. B. Fryde and others, eds., *Handbook of British chronology*, 3rd edn, Royal Historical Society Guides and Handbooks, 2 (1986); repr. (1996) · G. Hennessy, *Novum repertorium ecclesiasticum parochiale Londinense, or, London diocesan clergy succession from the earliest time to the year 1898* (1898) · W. J. Oldfield, 'Index to the clergy whose ordination, institution, resignation, licence or death is recorded in the diocesan registers of the diocese of Oxford … 1542–1908', 1915, Bodl. Oxf., MS Top. Oxon. c. 250 · *Old Westminsters*

Archives BL, corresp. with Thomas Hurdis and duke of Newcastle, Add. MSS 32731–33072, *passim* · Glos. RO, Gloucester diocesan MSS · Worcester Cathedral Library, corresp. with his dean and chapter · Worcs. RO, Worcester diocesan MSS

Likenesses J. Nollekens, bust, 1774, Worcester Cathedral · T. Hudson, portrait, Hartlebury Castle, Worcestershire · portrait, Bishop's House, Gloucester

Johnson, James (*bap.* 1753, *d.* 1811), engraver and publisher, was baptized on 6 May 1753 at Shorthope, Ettrick, Selkirkshire, the third of the four children of James Johnstan, herdsman, and his wife, Bessie Bleck. In spite of his humble rural beginnings, his native aptitude saw him successfully complete training as an engraver, and by 1786 he had become a burgess of Edinburgh. On 2 July 1791 he married Charlotte Grant, daughter of Lauchlan Grant, writer. They had a son, James, baptized on 13 September 1792, who appears not to have survived to his majority.

Johnson is first identified in Williamson's *Directory* as an engraver operating from a High Street luckenbooth in 1783; his place in history is entirely due to his pivotal role in conceiving of, printing, and publishing the six-volume *Scots Musical Museum* between April 1787 and June 1803. Composed of six hundred songs, it remains the most substantive, valuable, and comprehensive collection of Scots song ever published. Although it became a work of enduring quality primarily through the contributions of Robert

Burns, credit for devising the base for this seminal collection must go to Johnson. That he was on the point of publishing part one of his proposed two-volume book on Scots, English, and Irish song when he met Burns, and was happy to see his proposal evolve and develop its exclusively Scottish theme, reflects favourably on both his good taste and his commercial sense. His role has been sadly overlooked, as the collection resulted from his instant recognition and encouragement of Burns, combined with his wisdom in allowing his most important contributor a free hand in identifying, writing, selecting, and editing songs such as 'Auld Lang Syne' and 'Killiecrankie'.

Unfortunately, the undoubted importance of the *Scots Musical Museum* did not bring Johnson financial security, and even the novelty and economy of his pewter rather than copperplate printing of music did not raise his fortunes. He died at his home in Lawnmarket, Edinburgh, on 26 February 1811; numerous reprints, the sale of the original printing plates, and the high regard in which the *Scots Musical Museum* was held were not enough to save his widow from penury. She was the subject of a public appeal in March 1819, and died shortly afterwards.

The most significant and illuminating descriptions of James Johnson come from Robert Burns. Although in a letter to Alexander Cunningham the opinionated John Syme referred to James Johnson as a 'W(astre)L' and 'the wretch', the poet himself in a letter of May 1787 stated: 'I have met with few people whose company and conversation gave me so much pleasure, because I have met with few whose sentiments are so congenial to my own' (*Letters*, 1.98). Some nine years later, in one of Burns's last letters, he remarked, 'my dear friend … you are a good, worthy, honest fellow' (*Letters*, 2.381–2), showing that their friendship was warm, genuine, and, as the numerous reprints of their elegant and substantial collaboration amply testify, hugely significant to Scottish song.

RICHARD IAN HUNTER

Sources *The letters of Robert Burns*, ed. J. de Lancey Ferguson, 2nd edn, ed. G. Ross Roy, 2 vols. (1985), vol. 1, p. 98; vol. 2, pp. 381–2 · *The life and works of Robert Burns*, ed. R. Chambers, rev. W. Wallace, [new edn], 4 vols. (1896) · *Edinburgh Star* (15 March 1811), 3 · *Scots Magazine and Edinburgh Literary Miscellany*, 73 (1811), 318 · *Book of the Old Edinburgh Club*, 3 (1910), 163–5 · Ettrick parish register, 774 A/B, 118, frame 74 (6/5/1753) [microfiche] · Edinburgh parish register, 2/7/1791 · Williamson's *Directory*, Edinburgh and Leith, 1773–1812 · Denovan's *Directory*, Edinburgh and Leith, 1773–1812 · *Post Office annual directory of Edinburgh and Leith* (1773–1812) · DNB · M. Lindsay, *The Burns encyclopedia*, 3rd edn (1980), 190–91 · Edinburgh City Archives, accession 543, item 1/9

Johnson [Johnstone], **James** (1777–1845), physician and surgeon, the youngest son of an Irish farmer, was born at Ballinderry, co. Londonderry, in February 1777. His family, whose name was originally spelt Johnstone, had migrated from Scotland, and had come to own a small farm, on which his father lived. He lost his parents early, received a rudimentary education at a school in Ballinderry, and at the age of fifteen was apprenticed to Mr Young, a surgeon apothecary at Port Glenone, co. Antrim. Here he stayed for two years; he spent two more in Belfast with a Mr Bankhead, before moving to London, where he arrived without money or friends, in order to finish his medical education. While supporting himself as an apothecary's assistant he passed a creditable examination at Surgeons' Hall in 1798.

Johnson was immediately appointed surgeon's mate in the navy, and sailed to Newfoundland and Nova Scotia, visiting the naval hospitals whenever his ship was in harbour. In January 1800 he passed his second examination, and in February he was made full surgeon and was appointed to the sloop-of-war *Cynthia*. He accompanied the expedition to Egypt, but was invalided and forced to return to London. He spent the winter studying anatomy at the theatre in Great Windmill Street, and in June 1801 he obtained an appointment on the warship HMS *Driver*, in which he served in the North Sea. At the peace of 1802 he was again unemployed for a time; but in May of the following year he sailed for the East, and did not return to England until January 1806. In the autumn of that year he married Charlotte Wolfenden of Lambeg, co. Antrim, who survived him, along with their six children, two of whom followed their father into the medical profession.

In 1807 Johnson published an account of his voyage to the East with the title, *The oriental voyager, or, Descriptive sketches and cursory remarks on a voyage to India and China in his majesty's ship Caroline, performed in the years 1803–4–5–6*. In 1808 he was appointed to HMS *Valiant*, in which he served for nearly five years. He attended the disastrous expedition to Walcheren in 1809, where he contracted ague. In 1812 he published *The Influence of Tropical Climates on European Constitutions*, as the result of his own observations in the East. It reached a sixth edition in 1841, under the supervision of Sir James R. Martin, who made additions.

Johnson's *Influence* was very much the repository of the age, encapsulating the growing pessimism among Europeans about their ability to colonize India and to adapt to its climate. It was also typical of contemporary medical opinion in that it was receptive to Indian culture, some aspects of which—such as diet and dress—were recommended to Europeans inhabiting hot climates. Johnson's measured respect for Indian culture was characteristic of the great emphasis he placed on observation and practical experience, and his firsthand experience of India (though relatively brief) led him to challenge prevailing opinions regarding the nature of cholera and other diseases. His expertise in cholera, especially, led to his being called upon to advise the emergency board of health during the cholera epidemic which swept Great Britain in 1831–2.

At the conclusion of war with France in 1814 Johnson served in the *Impregnable*, in which the duke of Clarence (afterwards William IV) brought the emperor of Russia and the king of Prussia to Great Britain. Johnson attended the duke for a slight attack of fever, and as a result was appointed his surgeon-in-ordinary. He became a good friend of the duke and, after the latter's accession to the throne in 1830, became physician-extraordinary to the king.

In 1814, after the end of the French wars, Johnson was

placed on half pay, and settled in general practice at Portsmouth. There he commenced in 1816 his well-known *Medico-Chirurgical Review*. Originally undertaken in conjunction with Shirley Palmer and William Shearman, it was called at first the *Medico-Chirurgical Journal*, and appeared in monthly numbers. But in 1818 Johnson moved to London, where he published the *Review* at his own expense, and was its sole editor. The contents, almost all of which were written by Johnson himself, were mainly analytical. Although a libel in the *Review* against Thomas Wakely (1795–1862) did cost him £100 in 1826, the journal enjoyed a wide readership and was for several years reprinted in America. Johnson is said to have graduated MD at Aberdeen in 1813, and on 3 June 1821 he also proceeded MD at St Andrews; on 25 June of the same year he was admitted a licentiate of the Royal College of Physicians.

In January 1836 Sir John Forbes began the publication of his *British and Foreign Medical Review*, which affected to some extent the circulation of Johnson's periodical. Johnson consequently modified his plans, and in later volumes of the *Review* his son, Henry James Johnson, became joint editor. Johnson himself retired from the editorship in October 1844. The last 'new series' (6 vols., 1845–7) was published chiefly under the editorship of Gavin Milroy, though his name does not appear on the title-page. An index to the first ten volumes was published in 1834. In 1848 Johnson's and Forbes's rival reviews were amalgamated under the title, *British and Foreign Medico-Chirurgical Review*.

Since 1818 Johnson had gradually built a large practice in London before his health began to fail. He died while on a visit to Brighton, on 10 October 1845, and was buried at Kensal Green cemetery.

In appearance Johnson was 'rather under than above the middle height, spare, though of an active make, with a ruddy complexion, remarkably large and intelligent eyes, bushy eyebrows, square and copious forehead, and an expression in which unmistakeable benevolence was shaded with a cast of care or melancholy' (Munk, 240). He was also a man of great ability, industry, and religious feeling. Despite being a keen phrenologist and an exponent of 'rational medicine', Johnson continually stressed that he was not a materialist, and that 'mind' was infinitely more powerful than 'matter'.

In addition to those publications already mentioned, Johnson was the author of several popular works on subjects relating to health spas, rheumatism, gout (from which he suffered), and indigestion. But his most interesting work is, perhaps, his *Economy of health, or, The stream of human life with reflections on the septennial phases of human existence* (1836). The work betrays a uniquely Anglo-Indian blending of ancient Greek and Indian conceptions of health, and how best to preserve it at different stages of life. One of Johnson's principal concerns was diet, an area in which he claimed to have learned much from the dietary practices of Hindus and from the Greek mathematician Pythagoras. Though no vegetarian himself, Johnson

maintained that the British generally ate far too much, more meat than was conducive to health either in India or 'at home'.   W. A. GREENHILL, *rev.* MARK HARRISON

Sources Munk, *Roll* · *Medico-Chirurgical Review*, new ser., 3 (1845–6), 1–48 · M. Harrison, *Public health in British India: Anglo-Indian preventive medicine, 1859–1914* (1994)
Likenesses J. Smart, pencil, 1799, NPG · J. Wood, oils, *c.*1833, RCP Lond. · G. H. Phillips, mezzotint, 1835 (after J. Wood), Wellcome L. · T. Bridgford, lithograph, Wellcome L. · W. Holl, stipple (after J. Wood), Wellcome L. · lithograph (after T. Bridgford), NPG

Johnson [*née* Russell], **Jane** (1706–1759), writer, was the daughter of Richard Russell, esquire, of Warwick, and his wife, Lucy Rainsford. She and her sister Lucy inherited their father's estate, which they sold in 1727. They lived for a time in London, and it was probably there that Jane met Woolsey Johnson (*bap.* 1696, *d.* 1756), a graduate of Clare College, Cambridge, who was curate of St Andrew's, Holborn, from 1724 to 1727. A man of private means, he inherited an estate at Witham on the Hill, in Lincolnshire, built the manor house there, and enclosed the park in 1752. In 1735 he became vicar of Olney, in Buckinghamshire, where in December he and Jane were married. They had four children: Barbara (1738–1825), George William (1740–1814), Robert Augustus (1745–1799), and Charles Woolsey (1748–1828). Before the sons went to Rugby School Jane taught them and her daughter at home. The illustrated cards that she used as teaching aids, the fairy story that she wrote for them ('A very pretty story to tell children when they are about five or six years of age'), and a small collection of her letters together provide rare evidence of a mother's role in educating her young children in the mid-eighteenth century.

The 'very pretty story', written in 1744 and published in facsimile in 2001 by the Bodleian Library, where the manuscript survives (MS Don. d. 198), is one of the earliest extant pieces of continuous narrative written for very young children, and the first to include a magical, fairy episode. It is remarkable in having as two of its main characters the children, Barbara and George, for whom it was written, and includes many details of daily life to which they could readily relate. Its strong moral lesson, that good behaviour is rewarded and evil punished, recurs throughout the collection of alphabets and cards that Jane made to teach her children to read (Elizabeth Ball collection, Lilly Library, Indiana University). Over 400 items, illustrated with elaborate cut-outs from sheets available through London booksellers, contain rhymes, maxims, and stories that reveal their author as an affectionate mother with a lively sense of humour as well as strong religious convictions.

These same characteristics are evident in the letters that Jane Johnson wrote to her children and to relatives and friends (Bodl. Oxf., MS Don. c. 190), while her wide reading and Christian faith are reflected in her commonplace book and religious verse. She died suddenly at Witham Manor on 9 February 1759, and was buried at Witham on the Hill.   MARY CLAPINSON

Sources M. Hilton, M. Styles, and V. Watson, eds., *Opening the nursery door* (1997) · J. Johnson, *A very pretty story* (2001) [introduction by

G. Avery] • N. Rothstein, ed., *Barbara Johnson's album of fashions and fabrics* (1987) • M. Clapinson, 'Notable accessions', *Bodleian Library Record*, 16/2 (Oct 1997), 165–8
Archives Bodl. Oxf., family corresp. | Indiana University, Bloomington, Lilly Library, Elizabeth Ball collection, nursery library
Likenesses portrait?, priv. coll.

Johnson, John (*fl.* 1641), writer and poet, was the author of *The Academy of Love, Describing ye Folly of Younge Men and ye Fallacy of Women*, a work of 102 pages dedicated to Richard Compton and published for H. Blunden in London in 1641. It presents a humorous view of the ways men are deceived by women. Of particular interest is the reference in 'Love's Library' to the popularity of Shakespeare with 'young sparkish girles' (p. 99).

It is difficult to determine John Johnson's life story. He may have been John, son of John Johnson of Oddington, Gloucestershire, who entered New Inn, Oxford, in 1639. Alternatively, he may have been the son of Gilbert Johnson of Burfield, Berkshire, who matriculated from New College, Oxford, on 15 November 1622 aged eighteen. This John Johnson was a demy of Magdalen College from 1625 to 1629, and graduated BA on 7 December 1626 and MA on 20 June 1629. He was a fellow of Magdalen College from 1629 to 1641, proceeding BD on 14 July 1638, before becoming vicar of Old Shoreham, Sussex, an office he held from 1641 until his death in 1663.   F. D. A. BURNS

Sources *DNB* • Wood, *Ath. Oxon.: Fasti* (1820), 162 • Foster, *Alum. Oxon., 1500–1714*, 2.814 • J. Johnson, *The academy of love* (1641)

Johnson, John (1662–1725), theologian, was born on 30 December 1662, at Frindsbury in Kent. He was the son of Thomas Johnson (*fl.* 1637–1664), vicar of Frindsbury, and Mary, daughter of Francis Drayton, rector of Little Chart, Kent. His father died about four years after his marriage, and his mother moved to Canterbury with her two children, a son and a daughter. John attended the King's School at Canterbury before matriculating at Magdalene College, Cambridge, in March 1678. He graduated BA in 1682. Nominated to a scholarship at Corpus Christi College by the dean and chapter of Canterbury, he proceeded MA in 1685.

Johnson received holy orders on 19 December 1686 and served the curacy of Hardres, near Canterbury. In 1687 he was collated by Archbishop William Sancroft to the vicarage of Boughton under the Blean and the neighbouring vicarage of Hernhill, which was under sequestration. He married Margaret Jenkin, daughter of Thomas Jenkin, on 24 October 1689 in Canterbury Cathedral. They had five children. In 1697 Archbishop Thomas Tenison appointed him vicar of St John's, Margate. As the salary was small he also received the vicarage of Appledore, on the borders of Romney Marsh, on 1 May 1697. He took in two or three boarders to teach with his sons; but having become absorbed in his teaching, he resigned from Margate and settled at Appledore in 1703. After finding that the air at Appledore did not agree with him, he obtained the living of Cranbrook, Kent, on 21 April 1707 where he remained until his death in 1725. He wrote most of his books there,

and became known as 'Johnson of Cranbrook'. He was chosen in 1710 and 1713 by the clergy of the diocese of Canterbury to be one of their proctors in convocation. A diligent parish priest, he always had daily service in his church.

Although Johnson remained within the established church he was sympathetic to nonjuror principles. The nonjuror bishop George Hickes was a close friend, who claimed that 'Johnson deserved thanks from the whole Church of God' for his writings (Broxap, 5). He also corresponded with nonjurors Robert Nelson and Thomas Brett. He was an able theological writer and published many works, mostly anonymously. His first was a paraphrase, with notes, of the book of Psalms, entitled *Holy David and his Old English Translation Cleared* (1706). His next work, *The Clergyman's Vade Mecum* (1708), described the rights and duties of the clergy. Part two appeared in 1709 and contained 'the canonical codes of the primitive, universal, eastern, and western church to the year 787'.

Johnson's eucharistic works have been described by W. Jardine Grisbrooke as the climax of the Laudian theological tradition. In these works, Johnson 'set out clearly and at considerable length the eucharistic doctrines of mature high Anglicanism' (Grisbrooke, 71). His *The Propitiatory Oblation in the Holy Eucharist* (1710), which included a reply to remarks by Charles Trimnell, bishop of Norwich, on the second part of the *Vade mecum*, offered a direct challenge to latitudinarianism and thus alienated Thomas Tenison and provoked many replies. In 1714 he gave further expression to his views on the eucharist in his best known work, *The Unbloody Sacrifice and Altar Unvail'd and Supported* (part two appeared in 1717), which was reissued in 1847 in the Anglo-Catholic Library. These works, which argued for a real sacrifice in the eucharist, influenced the liturgical developments among the nonjurors. Although Johnson remained convinced that he could reconcile his doctrines with the existing liturgy, Thomas Brett and Thomas Deacon revised the English liturgy in 1718 in accordance with his teachings, thereby provoking the 'usages' controversy, which divided the nonjuror movement over the necessity of amending the existing liturgy. Johnson's eldest son, John, graduated BA from Corpus Christi College, Cambridge, in 1709, proceeded MA in 1712, and received the BD from St John's College in 1719; he served several parishes, but died on 9 January 1724, while rector of Standish, Lancashire. Johnson never recovered from this blow, and died in Cranbrook on 15 December 1725; he was buried in Cranbrook churchyard. His wife survived him. Thomas Brett wrote *The Life of the Late Reverend John Johnson* which was published with three posthumous tracts in 1748.   ROBERT D. CORNWALL

Sources Venn, *Alum. Cant.* • W. J. Grisbrooke, *Anglican liturgies of the seventeenth and eighteenth centuries* (1958) • H. Broxap, *The later nonjurors* (1924) • T. Brett, *The life of the late Reverend John Johnson, A.M., vicar of Cranbrook* (1748) • J. McClintock and J. Strong, *Cyclopaedia of biblical, theological, and ecclesiastical literature*, 12 vols. (1894–5) • Allibone, *Dict.* • T. Secker, *The speculum of archbishop Thomas Secker*, ed. J. Gregory (1995) • *IGI*
Archives Bodl. Oxf., sermons and discourses

Johnson, John (1705/6–1791), Baptist minister, was born at Lostock Gralam, in the parish of Great Budworth, in Cheshire, the son of humble and pious parents. He was baptized in March 1720, joining a General Baptist congregation and then the Calvinist church at Warrington. When he was twenty years old the church members recognized him as a preacher, although from 1728 until his move to Liverpool he was an itinerant preacher, and not attached to any particular congregation. About 1741 he was appointed pastor of the Byrom Street Baptist Church, Liverpool, but left about 1747–8 because of serious disagreement over doctrine with a section of his congregation. His supporters built a new chapel in Stanley Street, opened in 1750, and he remained with this congregation until his death. He married about 1740, and he and his wife had three children, born between 1741 and 1744.

A vigorous pastor and preacher, with an originality of mind, unafraid of controversy, Johnson was of medium height and short-sighted. His manner in the pulpit was solemn and majestic, but he used plain language. He attacked Anglicans, Methodists, and other Baptists in print, entering into dispute with John Brine, Richard Smith of Wainsgate, and Alvery Jackson. Adopting a singular fusion of elements of the Arminian and Calvinist systems, he was accused by his opponents of being both a Sabellian and a modalist because of his unorthodox views on the Trinity, charges he strenuously denied. He was very active in evangelism in the north-west, and won over Samuel Fisher of Norwich to his way of thinking. His friends included Christopher Hall and James Rutherford, the latter's church in Dublin providing a base to publicize Johnson's views in Ireland. In 1757 Johnson was the architect of a short-lived association of high-Calvinist churches in the north, and his influence was such that his circle was often dubbed Johnsonian Baptists.

Johnson produced many sermons and works of theology, of which the most popular was *The Advantages and Disadvantages of the Married State* (1760), which had five editions. Several of his works were published in Dublin and a few were translated into Welsh. Johnson died in Liverpool on 20 March 1791, aged eighty-five, and was survived by his wife. Samuel Fisher preached the funeral sermon and wrote an account of his life, appended to the two volumes of Johnson's *Original Letters* published in Norwich in 1796 and 1800. Johnson's influence depended mainly on his personality, and after his death the churches associated with him declined. His Liverpool church, then meeting in Comus Street, closed its doors in 1850.   S. L. COPSON

Sources *Original letters written by the late Mr. John Johnson of Liverpool*, ed. S. Fisher, 2 vols. (1796–1800) · R. Dawbarn, 'The Johnsonian Baptists', *Transactions of the Baptist Historical Society*, 3 (1912–13), 54–61 · D. Thom, *Liverpool churches and chapels: their destruction, removal or alteration* (1854) · DNB
Archives Regent's Park College, Oxford, Angus Library, late eighteenth-century transcripts of original letters

Johnson, John (1732–1814), architect, was born on 22 April 1732 in Southgate Street, Leicester, the elder son of John Johnson (1707–1780), joiner, and Frances (1708–1776),

John Johnson (1732–1814), by John Russell, 1786

daughter of Thomas Knight. Nothing is known of his early life or education. Johnson was admitted a freeman of Leicester in 1754, but had left for London, 'possessing little more than strong natural abilities' (*GM*, 296), before 1760. He began his career as a speculative builder, working on the Berners estate in St Marylebone from 1766 and moving into 32 Berners Street in 1767; he ran his business from this address for the rest of his life. From 1769 Johnson built up a country house practice, mainly in Essex, Northamptonshire, Devon, Suffolk, and Glamorgan. His surviving country houses include Terling Place (1772–8), Bradwell Lodge (1781–6), and Hatfield Place (1791–5), all in Essex, Woolverstone Hall (1776) in Suffolk, Sadborow (1773–5) in Dorset, Holcombe House (c.1775–8) in Middlesex, and Kingsthorpe Hall (1773–5) in Northamptonshire. He was exhibiting designs, including town houses (61 and 63 New Cavendish Street), at the Society of Artists between 1775 and 1783.

In 1775 Johnson patented an oil-based composition for covering and ornamenting houses, claiming to have improved on John Liardet's patent stucco, which had been developed commercially in association with the Adam brothers. In the resulting case of *Liardet v. Johnson* (1778) judgment was twice given for the plaintiff. Johnson's appointment as county surveyor of Essex in 1782 may have owed something to those clients, such as John Strutt of Terling Place, who were on the bench; he held the post until 1812. His principal works as county surveyor were at Chelmsford, where he rebuilt Moulsham Bridge in stone in 1787. He designed the shire hall, erected between 1789 and 1791, and published the designs in 1808; after its completion under budget, he was presented with a testimonial and a silver cup by quarter sessions. County Hall, Lewes, was erected to an almost identical design between 1808 and 1812. After the collapse of the nave of St Mary's Church, Chelmsford (now the cathedral), in January 1800, Johnson was responsible for a major restoration, reconstructing the fifteenth-century columns in Coade stone. Johnson also designed buildings in Leicester, including the county rooms (1799–1800) and the 'Consanguinitarium', a charitable foundation he had endowed in 1795 to provide accommodation for his poor relatives, behind houses he had erected in Southgate Street on the site of his birthplace.

Johnson was a competent and successful architect, who made use of a limited neo-classical vocabulary. He had a 'special fondness for Coade stone' (Kelly, 81) and excelled as a designer of staircases. The list of his works given in John Nichols's *History of Leicestershire* was probably supplied by the architect himself. He was married to Elizabeth, and their eldest son, John (1761–1813), a surveyor, assisted his father, but is not known to have designed any buildings. Johnson amassed considerable wealth, apparently from speculative building, but was declared bankrupt on 5 May 1803 as a result of the failure of the banking firm Dorset, Johnson, Wilkinson, Berners, and Tilson, in which he had been a partner since 1785, originally with Sir Herbert Mackworth, one of his earliest patrons. After Johnson's retirement as county surveyor at Michaelmas 1812, he moved back to Leicester. During 1813 the Essex magistrates raised subscriptions for him, amounting to over £300. Johnson died in Southgate Street on 27 August 1814; he was buried on 3 September in St Martin's Church (now Leicester Cathedral), where he is commemorated on the base of the monument which he had designed for his parents. His portrait by John Russell shows a strong face with well-defined features and blue-grey eyes. Johnson's second son, the Revd Charles Johnson (1768–1841), was the ancestor of the later Brooke Rajahs of Sarawak.

NANCY BRIGGS

Sources N. Briggs, *John Johnson, 1732–1814: Georgian architect and county surveyor of Essex* (1991) · Colvin, *Archs.* · J. Nichols, *The history and antiquities of the county of Leicester*, 1/2 (1815), 528 · *Chelmsford Chronicle* (23 Sept 1814) · *GM*, 1st ser., 84/2 (1814), 296 · *Leicester Journal* (16 Sept 1814) · J. Simmons, 'A Leicester architect', *Parish and empire* (1952), 128–45, 242–5 · N. Briggs, 'John Johnson and the Wyatts in Portman Square', *Westminster History Review*, 1 (1997), 19–21 · A. Kelly, 'Coade stone in Georgian architecture', *Architectural History*, 28 (1985), 71–102
Archives City Westm. AC, design for 10 (later 13) Portman Square · Essex RO, Chelmsford, quarter sessions records · Essex RO, Chelmsford, unexecuted design for refronting Thorpe Hall, Thorpe-le-Soken
Likenesses J. Russell, pastel, 1786, Chelmsford Museum [*see illus.*] · portrait (identical to that by J. Russell), Yale U. CBA; priv. coll.

Johnson, John (d. *c.*1797). *See under* Johnson, Robert (1770–1796).

Johnson, Sir John, second baronet (1742–1830). *See under* Johnson, Sir William, first baronet (1715?–1774).

Johnson, John (1760–1833). *See under* Johnson, John (1769–1833).

Johnson, John (*c.*1763–1804), minister of the Countess of Huntingdon's Connexion, was born near Norwich. Details of his parentage and education are not known. He was converted about 1776 by a sermon of John Clayton at the Norwich Tabernacle, one of Selina, countess of Huntingdon's chapels. In April 1780 he entered the countess's college at Trefeca, near Brecon, and stayed for three years. Unlike some other students who spent little time at the college he was sent to preach only in its vicinity, and so acquired a sound academic training. On 9 March 1783 he was ordained at the countess's chapel at Spa Fields, Clerkenwell, London—one of the first six students to be ordained in the Countess of Huntingdon's Connexion. He was sent to her congregation at Wigan and preached regularly in the surrounding area despite strong opposition. This led to the establishment of a new congregation at Tyldesley, west of Manchester, about 1785, where he erected a new chapel in 1790.

Later that year Johnson was chosen by Lady Huntingdon to go to Bethesda, Savannah, Georgia, to replace the previous minister, David Phillips, who had managed by his behaviour to alienate her supporters there. Bethesda orphan house had been bequeathed to Lady Huntingdon by George Whitefield, and she had hoped to convert it into a college. She had recovered the estate after the American War of Independence and tried to make progress to make it both a college and a mission to the local Native Americans. Johnson had the misfortune to arrive at Bethesda shortly before Lady Huntingdon died. By her will she bequeathed the estate to a group of English evangelicals headed by Lord Dartmouth. However the state assembly argued that she had only a life interest in Bethesda and proceeded to pass an act to vest it in thirteen trustees to make it a county academy. Johnson's attempts to prevent this by legal action and publicity in local newspapers were frustrated by the refusal of everyone concerned to co-operate. After a brief siege Johnson and his wife, of whom further details are unknown, were evicted and imprisoned temporarily, and they fled to Charleston, South Carolina. There he published a poetical account of the incident in *The Rape of Bethesda, or, The Georgia Orphan House Destroyed* and also compiled a report for the English trustees. His fears for the future of Bethesda were confirmed when the property was allowed to become derelict.

On his return to England, Johnson was again sent to Tyldesley by Lady Ann Erskine, Lady Huntingdon's successor, and had the misfortune to be imprisoned for the debts incurred in building the chapel. In 1798 he left Tyldesley for St George's Church in Manchester. This was one of the private unconsecrated Anglican chapels of ease erected in expanding urban areas. Johnson converted it to a connexion chapel using the revised Book of Common Prayer.

While there he included the local Jewish community in his mission work, preaching to them in Hebrew. He died at Manchester on 22 September 1804.

EDWIN WELCH

Sources 'Biographical memoir of the late Rev. John Johnson', *Evangelical Review* (1835), 128–34, 209–14 · J. Johnson, *The rape of Bethesda, or, The Georgia orphan house destroyed* (Charleston, S.C., 1792) · *Digest of the laws of the state of Georgia* (1802) · *An authentic narrative of the primary ordination held in the countess of Huntingdon's chapel, at Spa-Field, London, on Sunday the 9th day of March 1783, upon the plan of secession* (1784) · G. F. Nuttall, 'The students of Trevecca College, 1768–1791', *Transactions of the Honourable Society of Cymmrodorion* (1967), 249–77 · R. Halley, *Lancashire: its puritanism and nonconformity*, 2 vols. (1869) · W. E. A. Axon, ed., *The annals of Manchester: a chronological record from the earliest times to the end of 1885* (1886) · W. Roby, *Funeral sermon for the Rev. John Johnson* (1804) · E. Welch, ed., *Two Calvinistic Methodist chapels*, London RS, 11 (1975) · *The chronicle of St Paul's* (1977) [St Paul's, Wigan] · Southern Methodist University, Dallas, Center for Methodist Studies
Archives Georgia Historical Society, Savannah, official journal; letter-book, coll. 430, 1; coll. 430, 2 | Georgia Archives, Atlanta, typescript copy of state trustees' minutes · Southern Methodist University, Dallas, Center for Methodist Studies, letter of Lady Huntingdon to Thomas Haweis, 7 Aug 1790, Hunt 127 · Westminster College, Cambridge, Cheshunt Foundation, letter to Lady Huntingdon, 12 July 1790, F1/2139

Johnson, John (1769–1833), writer, was the son of John Johnson, a tanner from Ludham, Norfolk, and Anne Donne (*b.* 1748). He was related to Cowper through his mother, who was the daughter of Harriot and Roger Donne, rector of Catfield, Norfolk, and brother of Cowper's mother. He was educated at Bungay School before being admitted in 1787 to Gonville and Caius College, Cambridge, where he graduated LLB in 1794 and LLD in 1803. He was ordained a deacon and priest at Norwich in 1793. He became chaplain to the earl of Peterborough, and on 1 January 1800 was presented to the rectory of Yaxham with Welborne, Norfolk, which he held until his death. In 1808 he married Maria, the daughter of George Livius, who was at the head of the commissariat in India. They had three sons: William Cowper Johnson (1813–1893), John Barham Johnson (1818–1894), and Henry Robert Vaughan Johnson (1820–1899?).

For twenty-seven years Cowper had no contact with his maternal relatives, and did not know whether they were living or dead. When he was a student at Cambridge, however, Johnson introduced himself to the poet during a Christmas vacation. Cowper conceived an affection for 'the wild but bashful boy', which was amply requited. Cowper, who used to call Johnson 'Johnny of Norfolk', was deeply indebted to his kinsman for the care he took of him during the latter years of his life. Cowper died in Johnson's house in the market place of East Dereham on 25 April 1800.

Johnson wrote *The Tale of the Lute, or, The Beauties of Audley End*, a pastoral poem, which Cowper advised him not to publish. He edited volume 3 of Cowper's *Poems* (1815); *The Letters of William Cowper* (3 vols., 1817); *Memoirs of William Hayley* (2 vols., 1823); and *The private correspondence of William Cowper with several of his most intimate friends, now first published from the originals in the possession of* [and edited by]

John Johnson (2 vols., 1824). Johnson died at Yaxham on 29 September 1833.

Another **John Johnson** (1760–1833) was born on 30 March 1760 in Holborn, London, the son of John and Elizabeth Johnson. He was educated at the Charterhouse, and was admitted in 1776 to Oriel College, Oxford, where he graduated BA in 1779 and MA in 1782. In March 1784 he married Eliza, only child of John Waters of Bath, and in October of that same year he became rector of Great Parndon, Essex, and on 26 November 1790 vicar of North Mimms, Hertfordshire until his death. He published two fast day sermons, *A Fast Sermon* in 1794 and *A Sermon for the Fast* in 1795. He also produced a translation from French entitled *Observations on the military establishment and discipline of his majesty the king of Prussia; with an account of the private life of that celebrated monarch ...* (1780) and published *Trifles in Verse*, in 1796. He died on 11 September 1833.

THOMPSON COOPER, *rev.* REBECCA MILLS

Sources IGI · Venn, *Alum. Cant.*, 2/3.580 · T. S. Grimshawe, ed., *The life and works of William Cowper* (1835), vol. 8., frontispiece · J. Romilly, ed., *Graduati Cantabrigienses* (1856), 289 [for the years 1760–1856] · *N&Q*, 3rd ser., 4 (1863), 409 · Watt, *Bibl. Brit.*, 2.549 · GM, 1st ser., 103/2 (1833), 379 · Foster, *Alum. Oxon.* · *A catalogue of all graduates ... in the University of Oxford, between ... 1659 and ... 1850* (1851), 367
Archives CUL, record of Cowper's dreams | Bodl. Oxf., letters to William Hayley · FM Cam., letters and verses to William Hayley
Likenesses Abbott, portrait, 1793 · E. Finden, engraving (after Lady Palgrave) · Lady Palgrave, sketch (after Jackson), repro. in Grimshawe, ed., *Life and works*, frontispiece · H. Robinson, engraving (after Abbott)

Johnson, John (1777–1848), printer, was probably born in Chester, was brought up as a compositor, and was for some time in the printing office of Thomas Bensley. Through Bensley, Johnson and a press man, John Warwick, met Sir Samuel Egerton Brydges in 1813 who allowed them to establish a private press at Lee Priory, near Canterbury, Kent (Brydges, 2.191–2). Johnson and Warwick took all pecuniary liabilities and sold the books, and Brydges supplied the copy. A large number of books, pamphlets, and leaflets were printed, all in small editions, including the *Poems* and *Autobiography* of Margaret Cavendish, duchess of Newcastle, Walter Ralegh's *Poems*, and Brooks's life of Sir Philip Sidney (see lists in J. Martin, *Books Privately Printed*, 1834, 379–404; Lowndes, 6.218–25). In 1817 Johnson ceased his connection with the press under difficult circumstances. Brydges said he was financially inconvenienced by the arrangement and J. Martin suggests that Johnson and Warwick, who produced only a small number of books, were 'tippling' on Kentish hop (Martin, 380). In 1824 Johnson himself complained of 'cruel and unjust treatment', adding that chancery proceedings were still lingering (Johnson, preface, p. viii). He circulated, in July 1818, the prospectus of a work on printing, which he said he was induced to undertake following his exit from Lee Priory. With the financial support of Edward Walmsley, Johnson printed in 1824 at his London office, the Apollo Press, Brooke Street, Holborn, in two volumes, *Typographia, or, The printer's instructor, including an account of the origin of printing, with biographical notices of the printers of*

England from Caxton to the close of the sixteenth century, a series of ancient and modern alphabets and Domesday characters; together with an elucidation of every subject connected with the art (Richard Thomson, librarian of the London Institution, helped in the historical part). The book appeared in four sizes and, as Bigmore and Wyman document, was a product of the bibliomania which was rife a few years previously, but by 1824 was on the wane. Consequently Johnson suffered financially. It was unfavourably reviewed in the *Gentleman's Magazine*, where it was remarked that 'in his attempts to surpass all his predecessors in ornamental typography, he has filled the book with useless matter and suffered the most glaring errors to escape his notice' (1824, 538). But Bigmore and Wyman judge that 'whatever its defects and shortcomings it has long since become, and deservedly, a printer's classic' with its 'originality, humour, and freshness' (Bigmore and Wyman, 371–2). An abridgement, with an appendix, was printed in 1828. Johnson describes an improved composing case introduced by him (Johnson, *Typographia*, 2.108–17), and advertises a 'typographic specimen' (ibid., preface). It was executed with brass rules and flowers which differed from that commonly in use. He was a printer of the 'old school' and was opposed to stereotype and machine presses. In his characteristic style of ornamental printing Johnson later printed Thomson's *History of Magna Charta* and his *Chronicles of London Bridge*. Johnson died in Brooke Street, Holborn, London, on 17 February 1848.

H. R. Tedder, *rev.* Clare L. Taylor

Sources E. Brydges, *The autobiography, times, opinions, and contemporaries of Sir Egerton Brydges*, 2 (1834) · J. Johnson, *Typographia, or, The printer's instructor*, 2 vols. (1824) · *Book-lore*, 2 (1885), 30–32 · E. C. Bigmore and C. W. H. Wyman, eds., *A bibliography of printing* (1945), vol. 1 · *GM*, 1st ser. 94/2 (1824); 2nd ser., 30 (1848), 667 · J. Martin, *A bibliographical catalogue of books privately printed* (1834) · W. T. Lowndes, *The bibliographer's manual of English literature*, ed. H. G. Bohn, [new edn], 6 vols. (1864), vol. 6, pp. 218–25
Likenesses H. Robinson, stipple, pubd 1836 (after L. F. Abbott), NPG · W. Harvey, wood-engraving (aged forty-six), repro. in Johnson, *Typographia*, vol. 2

Johnson, John de Monins (1882–1956), printer, ephemerist, and classical scholar, was born on 17 May 1882 at Kirmington, Lincolnshire, the second son and third child of the vicar, the Revd John Henry Johnson (1841–1938), and his wife, Anna Braithwaite, *née* Savory (1846–1928). He was educated at Magdalen College School, Oxford, and in 1900 won an open scholarship at Exeter College. He obtained a first class in classical moderations (1902) and a second class in *literae humaniores* (1904), remaining in residence for an extra year reading Arabic in preparation for the Egyptian civil service, which he entered in 1905 and left in 1907.

From 1909 to 1912 Johnson was a senior demy of Magdalen College and during this period and later, while a pupil of A. S. Hunt, he edited papyri: Johnson was chiefly responsible for volume 2 of the *Catalogue of the Greek Papyri in the John Rylands Library*, which was published in 1915. In 1911, and again in 1913–14, he was in Egypt conducting explorations on behalf of the Graeco-Roman branch of

John de Monins Johnson (1882–1956), by Hubert Andrew Freeth, 1956

the Egypt Exploration Society. During his second expedition he found at Antinoë the earliest known manuscript of Theocritus. It was edited by Hunt and Johnson together, but publication (*Two Theocritus papyri*) was delayed until 1930 when Johnson's name, unusually duplicated, appeared both on the title-page and in the printer's colophon at the end.

In 1915 (unfit for active service) Johnson was appointed acting assistant secretary to the delegates of Oxford University Press, and later assistant secretary. He was discerning in choosing manuscripts, enterprising and persuasive in seeking authors, and, when there was opportunity, a brilliant innovator in illustration. Inspired by his work as a papyrologist, Johnson was the originator of the use of contemporary documentation in the illustration of school history books.

On 31 July 1918 Johnson married (Margaret) Dorothea (1892–1981), daughter of Charles Cannan, secretary to the delegates. They had one son, Charles Cannan Johnson (who became manager of the Canadian branch of the press but who died in 1963), and one daughter, Paulla Bolingbroke.

In 1925 the delegates appointed Johnson printer to the university—a daring choice, for he had no practical knowledge of either printing or factory management. Nevertheless he possessed other significant qualifications: he was in his prime, his capacity proved; he was on terms with the delegates and apprised of policy; and he was known to the university and familiar with its governmental machinery. He was immediately plunged into the less agreeable excitement of industrial management, for within a year he experienced, successively, a sectional strike, and the general strike of 1926, events which made a deep impression on him. He then faced the necessary unpleasantness of disturbing some members of his well-entrenched staff, and the introduction of replacements. In the factory he found on the one hand a modern bindery and on the other a department in which 100 compositors still worked by candlelight. As he moved among other publishers and printers, he learned that the reputation of Oxford printing had fallen very low. The urgent need for planned re-equipment and development was recognized and the delegates gave Johnson a free hand in his spending.

For the next few years Johnson devoted those resources, and all his time, to the restoration of Oxford printing; but the slump of the early thirties arrested expansion, and the outbreak of war in 1939 ended it. Eventually 90 per cent of the press's output was employed by the government in the war effort. Johnson was appointed CBE in 1945 in recognition of his special services during the war, and retired in the following year. He had been elected an honorary fellow of Exeter College in 1936.

Many great and beautiful books were produced under the direction of Johnson, who was in the vanguard of those responsible for the renaissance of book printing in the twenties. In 1928 he completed the printing of the *Oxford English Dictionary* and received from the university the honorary degree of DLitt. Other works were the lectern Bible designed by Bruce Rogers and completed in 1935; the handsome *Survey of Persian Art* (1938–9) in six folio volumes; and the two-volume *Old Spain* (1936), printed for Macmillan with illustrations by Muirhead Bone in colour collotype.

Johnson was quick to appreciate the importance of, and assiduous in adding to, the unique collection of printing material preserved at the press where the typographical museum illustrates the history of Oxford printing. With his friend Strickland Gibson, Johnson edited *The First Minute Book of the Delegates of the Oxford University Press* (1943) and together they wrote *Print and Privilege at Oxford to the Year 1700* (1946). Other works by John Johnson include: *The Oxford University Press, 1468–1926* (1926), *The printer: his customers and his men* (1933), and *Oxford and industrial education considered as a foundation of the Beveridge plan* (1943).

Johnson's most notable monument, however, may prove to be his vast collection of ephemeral printing. In this collection Johnson broke new ground. Previous collectors of what is now termed 'printed ephemera' had generally confined themselves to one area of collecting. Johnson's collection encompassed them all, embracing both printing and social history.

> It was to be [he wrote] the museum of what is commonly thrown away … all the ordinary printed paraphernalia of our day-to-day lives in size from the large broadside to the humble calling card, and varying in splendour from the magnificent invitations to coronations of Kings to the humblest piece of street literature sold for a penny or less. (Bodl. Oxf., MS Johnson c.18, fol. 53)

A discriminating collector, Johnson amassed over a million items which he grouped under about 700 headings. With a few exceptions, Johnson chose to collect retrospectively, his collection mainly spanning the years 1508 to 1939. The collection, often referred to as the Sanctuary of Printing, was formed for the University of Oxford and housed at Oxford University Press in rooms informally termed 'the cabin'. During Johnson's lifetime the collection was called the Constance Meade memorial collection of ephemeral printing, after one of its principal benefactors. In 1968 it was transferred to the Bodleian Library and renamed the John Johnson collection of printed ephemera. It is considered to be the most important single collection of printed ephemera in Britain, and possibly in the world.

Johnson was a tall man and well proportioned, slow and deliberate in his movements. His nose, large and well-chiselled, was his most striking feature: his hair, fine and combed over his brow, completed an arresting head. He turned a stern countenance to the world, and showed an explosive temper to those who displeased him; but he was a delightful conversationalist and a brilliant and voluminous correspondent. He was a busy controversialist, but was always ready to champion the weak and many were warmed by his kindness or helped by his charity. He devoted much time, energy, and enthusiasm to committees and public work. In his later years he withdrew from all these activities save the Oxford Preservation Trust, spending most of his time in his collection at the press.

Johnson died at the Radcliffe Infirmary, Oxford, on 15 September 1956, and was buried at Headington cemetery, Oxford. CHARLES BATEY, *rev.* JULIE ANNE LAMBERT

Sources *The Times* (17 Sept 1956) · *Oxford Magazine* (8 Nov 1956) · *Bodleian Library Record* (Oct 1957) · H. Jackson, 'A sanctuary of printing', *Signature*, 1 (Nov 1935) · Bodl. Oxf., MSS Johnson c.16–37, d.14–15, e.21–22 · M. W. Cannan, *Grey ghosts and voices* (1976) · *The John Johnson collection: catalogue of an exhibition* (1971) [exhibition catalogue, Bodl. Oxf., 1971] · A. B. How, *Register of Exeter College, Oxford, 1891–1921* (1928) · P. Sutcliffe, *The Oxford University Press: an informal history* (1978) · *Kelly's Oxford directory* (1905–32) · Crockford (1882–1938) · Venn, *Alum. Cant.*, 2/3.581 · *The Ephemerist*, 53 (June 1986) · *The Ephemerist*, 59 (Dec 1987) · *The Ephemerist*, 72 (March 1991) · *The Ephemerist*, 73 (June 1991) · *The Ephemerist*, 74 (Sept 1991) · *The Ephemerist*, 77 (June 1992) · H. J. Foss, 'John Johnson, printer to the University of Oxford, 1925–1946', *The Periodical* (Nov 1946) · personal knowledge (1971) · private information (1971, 2004)

Archives Bodl. Oxf., corresp. and papers · Bodl. Oxf., collection, MSS, printed ephemera, books, maps, music · Oxford University Press, business letter-books; research corresp. | BL, Add. MSS 42771, fols. 155–8; 44919, fol. 103; 45680, fols. 50–52; 45687, fol. 37 · BL, corresp. with Idris Bell, Add. MS 59513 · Bodl. Oxf., letters to O. G. S. Crawford · Bodl. Oxf., corresp. with L. G. Curtis · Bodl. Oxf., MS Eng. hist. b.224 · Bodl. Oxf., MSS Eng. hist. c.776–877 · Bodl. Oxf., corresp. with Auriol Stein | FILM BFI, London, *Cover to cover*, produced by Paul Rotha in collaboration with the National Book Council, 1936

Likenesses H. Coster, photographs, 1930, NPG · E. Plachte, drawing, 1938, Bodl. Oxf., John Johnson collection · W. Rothenstein, drawing, 1940, Oxford University Press · H. Whistler, drawing, 1945, Bodl. Oxf., John Johnson collection · H. A. Freeth, drawing, 1956, Bodl. Oxf., John Johnson collection [*see illus.*] · H. Coster, photograph, Bodl. Oxf., John Johnson collection · photographs,

Bodl. Oxf., Johnson MS c.36 • photographs, Bodl. Oxf., John Johnson collection
Wealth at death £25,582 9s. 1d.: probate, 1956, *CGPLA Eng. & Wales*

Johnson, John Mordaunt (1780?–1815), diplomatist, was a native of Dublin. He was probably the John Johnson who was the son of Thomas Johnson, solicitor in Dublin, and who matriculated at Trinity College, Dublin, on 2 November 1795, aged fifteen, but appears not to have taken a degree. His father died in spring 1798 and Johnson was gazetted an ensign in the 51st regiment of foot on 20 September 1798. In January 1799 he purchased a lieutenancy in the same regiment but, becoming disgusted with the monotony of barrack life, he sold out in the autumn of the following year. It was probably at this time that he added Mordaunt to his name.

Johnson then went to the continent, where he became acquainted with the duke of Brunswick, and 'made himself perfect master of almost all the modern languages' ('Memoir', *Bibliothecae Johnsonianae*, iii). In the spring of 1803 he returned to England and subsequently went to Dublin, where he remained until the autumn of 1804. Going once more abroad he spent three years 'chiefly in Germany, cultivating the valuable connections which he had formed on his first excursion to the continent, and acquiring information on all subjects of continental policy' (ibid.).

In the hope of obtaining an official appointment Johnson returned again to England, and was soon in financial difficulties. Subsequently Spencer Perceval's attention was drawn to his abilities by the manuscript of 'A memoir on the political state of Europe', which Johnson had written with a view to publication. After an interview with the prime minister Johnson obtained employment in the Foreign Office, and was frequently used for confidential missions to the continent. After the peace of Paris of 1814 he was appointed British chargé d'affaires in Brussels, and, upon the reunification of Holland with the rest of the Netherlands, was promoted to the post of British consul in Genoa. He died, unmarried, in Florence, where he had gone for reasons of health, on 10 September 1815, said to be aged thirty-nine, and was buried in the cemetery attached to the British factory, near Leghorn, on the following day. He was an excellent linguist and collected a large library, part of which was sold after his death by Evans of Pall Mall in June 1817.

G. F. R. BARKER, rev. H. C. G. MATTHEW

Sources *Bibliothecae Johnsonianae, pars prima: a catalogue of … the library of John Mordaunt Johnson* (1817) [sale catalogue, London, 2–3 June 1817] • *GM*, 1st ser., 85/2 (1815), 377 • *GM*, 1st ser., 87/1 (1817), 521–6 • *Army List* (1780) • *Army List* (1799) • TCD
Archives PRO, entry books of corresp., PRO 30/26/70 • PRO NIre., corresp. and papers [copies] • Yale U., Beinecke L., journal of mission to British fleet in Adriatic | PRO NIre., corresp. with Lord Castlereagh • U. Nott. L., letters to Lord William Bentinck

Johnson, John Noble (1787–1823), physician, son of John Johnson, physician, of Aylesbury, was educated in Lincolnshire before entering Magdalen Hall, Oxford, on 23 May 1803, aged sixteen. He graduated BA (1807), MA (1810), BM (1811), and DM (1814). He became a fellow of the Royal College of Physicians in 1815, and was Goulstonian lecturer at the college in 1816. In 1818 he was elected physician to the Westminster Hospital, London, but resigned his office in 1822 and died on 6 October 1823 at the Albany, London. Before his death he had completed an admirable *Life of Thomas Linacre*, founder of the Royal College of Physicians, with memoirs of his contemporaries; it was published in 1835, edited by the barrister Robert Graves.

G. T. BETTANY, rev. MICHAEL BEVAN

Sources Foster, *Alum. Oxon.* • Munk, *Roll* • *GM*, 2nd ser., 3 (1835), 633

Johnson, Joseph (1738–1809), bookseller, was born on 15 November 1738 at Everton, near Liverpool, the second of two sons of John Johnson, a Baptist landowner and businessman who came to Everton from Cheshire in 1733. Johnson left for London in 1752, where two years later on 12 February 1754 he was apprenticed to George Keith, a member of the Musicians' Company and a publisher of religious tracts based at the Bible and Crown in Church Street. Freed in May 1761, Johnson at once set up his own shop, moving premises three times—from the Golden Anchor in Fenchurch Street, to Lombard Street, and finally settling at the sign of Mead's Head at 12 or 14 Fish Hill Street—within the same year. In 1765 he moved to 8 Paternoster Row, forming partnerships first with Benjamin Davenport until June 1767, and from 1768 with John Payne, until a fire completely destroyed their shop on 8 January 1770. Johnson relocated to 72 St Paul's Churchyard, where he was to live and work for the rest of his life.

Johnson's early publications were dissenting religious tracts, medical texts, and writings connected with the intellectual life of Liverpool. From the mid-1760s Johnson began a close association and friendship with the theologian and scientist Joseph Priestley, for whose works Johnson was to become the exclusive publisher. Under Priestley's influence Johnson began to embrace Unitarianism, publishing the works of a number of other members of the dissenting academy in Warrington, such as Johan Reinhold Forster, Anna Letitia Aiken Barbauld, John Aiken, William Enfield, Thomas Robert Malthus, and Gilbert Wakefield. According to Thomas Rees the Unitarian minister, as London's main publisher of Unitarian tracts, sermons, and liturgical writings, Johnson 'held the same position among the dissenters that [the bookselling dynasty] the Rivingtons did with members of the Church of England' (Hall, 160). In 1774 Johnson helped Theophilus Lindsey establish London's first Unitarian chapel, which opened in April that year.

Johnson's support for Unitarian causes led to a lifelong association with the leading political and religious radicals in late eighteenth-century London, many of whose works he published, including William Godwin, Mary Wollstonecraft, Thomas Paine, Henry Fuseli, as well as Priestley. The 'Johnson circle' met for regular dinners at

Joseph Johnson (1738–1809), by William Sharp (after Moses Haughton)

Johnson's premises in St Paul's Churchyard. In May 1788 Johnson established the *Analytical Review*, which he published in collaboration with a young Scotsman, Thomas Christie, intended as a kind of clearing-house for current political and philosophical debate. Alongside advertisements for Johnson's own publications, it contained book reviews, essays, news from abroad, and articles in areas as diverse as medicine, music, natural sciences, travel, and commerce. Critical of the British government and generally supportive of the revolutionary ideas in America and France, the periodical had a reputation for radicalism resting on its political and religious articles rather than its rather more conventional literary reviews.

The Swiss exile Fuseli, in particular, was a close friend of Johnson. First introduced to Johnson and the bookseller Andrew Millar in 1764, Fuseli lived with Johnson until 1770 and they collaborated on a number of projects, including an ill-fated attempt in the 1790s to publish a grand new edition of Milton, edited by William Cowper; Johnson hoped to supplement the work with engravings based on a gallery of paintings illustrating the life and works of Milton produced by Fuseli. However, Cowper's increasing infirmity led Johnson to abandon the project. Johnson was also very supportive of Wollstonecraft. He helped her find a suitable home following her return from Ireland in 1787 and provided an advance for the writing of her first pamphlet, *Thoughts on the Education of Daughters*, and first novel, *Mary*. She was a regular contributor to the *Analytical Review*, and he urged her to write her famous work *A Vindication of the Rights of Woman*, which he published in 1792. Godwin met Wollstonecraft, whom he later

married, at one of Johnson's famous three o'clock dinners, and he described Johnson's relationship with her as 'in many respects that of a father' (Godwin, 228).

Johnson had evident sympathies for the revolutionaries in America and France. During the 1770s he published a number of works critical of British actions against the colonists; and in 1779 he published the first English edition of Benjamin Franklin's writings. The *Analytical Review* supported the French Revolution following its outbreak in 1789 and Johnson published most of the key responses to Edmund Burke's *Reflections on the Revolution in France* (1790). He was also the prime mover behind the publication of Thomas Paine's *Rights of Man*, although, pragmatically, he persuaded another London bookseller to appear as its publisher on the book's imprint and he was not among the publishers charged at Paine's trial in 1792. However, his activities as a leading liberal publisher during the 1790s eventually led to a successful prosecution for sedition in early 1798 for publishing a pamphlet by the radical theologian Gilbert Wakefield. The *Analytical Review*, already depleted through the death in 1796 of Christie and the effective retirement of a number of the other editorial staff, and under fierce attack from the conservative *Anti-Jacobin Review*, was suspended in 1798. On 11 February 1799 Johnson was sentenced to six months' imprisonment, although he does not seem to have suffered much privation, as he was able to rent a house next to the marshal of the prison and continued to host weekly dinners.

Alongside these radical publications, Johnson was also an important literary publisher. He held shares in the works of many earlier writers, most notably works by Addison, Steele, Pope, and Dr Johnson, as well as the Malone and Steevens's edition of Shakespeare. As a part of a consortium of major publishers, the Friends of Literature, Johnson was involved in the publication of new editions of Milton's *Paradise Lost*, James Thomson's *The Seasons*, and Daniel Defoe's *Robinson Crusoe*. He also supported contemporary literary figures. From 1781 he acted as agent, editor, and adviser to the poet William Cowper until the poet's death in 1800. In exchange for Cowper's copyright, Johnson agreed to publish his *Poems* at his own risk, which proved highly profitable for Johnson, who retained these copyrights until his own death in 1809. He also published Cowper's well-received *Task* in 1785, which was later republished as the second volume of *Poems*; the inexpensive two-volume set proved very popular and Johnson generously granted the poet the entire profits from the fifth edition. Cowper's translations of the *Iliad* and *Odyssey* were also published by Johnson; and in 1803 he published William Hayley's biography of Cowper in an elegant quarto edition illustrated with engravings by Blake. Blake, who was probably introduced to Johnson by Fuseli, supplied engravings for Johnson publications for over two decades; these included several of Wollstonecraft's books, Erasmus Darwin's poem *The Botanic Garden*, and particularly fine engravings of Fuseli's illustrations for a translation of Wieland's *Oberon*. However, the only connection between Blake's poetry and Johnson is the survival of proofs for the first seven books of Blake's 'The

French Revolution' from 1791. Johnson also published early works by Wordsworth and Coleridge.

Johnson also published medical, educational and juvenile literature. Among the medical works were writings by prominent physicians such as George Fordyce, John Hunter, Samuel Foart Simmons, and Humphrey Davy. Johnson was the proprietor of England's first medical periodical, *Medical Facts and Observations*, published between 1791 and 1800. He published the non-medical works of the physicians John Aiken the younger and Erasmus Darwin. Johnson's publication of juvenile literature played an important role in the expansion of that market: moral guides for children by Wollstonecraft, Sarah Trimmer, and Anna Letitia Barbauld were issued in many inexpensive editions. When Godwin and his second wife established the Juvenile Library in 1805, Johnson was both a source of texts and encouragement, and a link to other booksellers and publishers in the juvenile book trade. Johnson also produced a wide variety of textbooks, such as John Bonnycastle's *An Introduction to Mensuration and Practical Mathematics* and other pedagogical texts on English grammar, elocution, and history. In June 1797, he accepted a proposal by Anthony Robinson for 'a British Biog[raph]y' that would provide accounts of 'the important events of life, the character of mind & at least an enumeration of the labours of each individual', but nothing further seems to have come of this venture (Tomalin, 15).

His body wasted by chronic respiratory disease, Johnson died at his house in St Paul's Churchyard on 20 December 1809. He was buried in the churchyard at Fulham (where he had rented Acacia Cottage from Lord Dungannon as a retreat since 1804) on 29 December; Fuseli delivered the eulogy. Unmarried and with no direct heirs, Johnson left his business and shares in publishing consortia to his great-nephews Roland Hunter and John Miles. In addition, a legacy of approximately £60,000 was shared among friends and relatives. Priestley's son was remembered with a bequest of £100 and a portrait of Priestley by Opie to be 'presented to an American College or Institution for promoting knowledge' (PRO, PROB 11/1513, sig. 376, fol. 179r); and Wollstonecraft's daughter by Gilbert Imlay, Fanny, was granted an annuity of £200. Aiken wrote an obituary in which he bestowed the title 'Father of the booktrade' on his friend, describing him as one who held himself above party animosity and as a man who had friends of varied and opposite opinions in religion and politics (Nichols, 383). On Johnson's gravestone are the words of Fuseli, who described him as

> beneficent without ostentation, ever ready to produce merit and to relieve distress; unassuming in prosperity, not appalled by misfortune; inexorable to his own, indulgent to the wants of others; resigned and cheerful under the torture and malady which he saw gradually destroy his life.

CAROL HALL

Sources G. Tyson, *Joseph Johnson: an eighteenth-century bookseller* (1979) · C. Hall, 'Joseph Johnson (London 1761–1809)', *The British literary book trade, 1700–1820*, ed. J. K. Bracken and J. Silver, DLitB, 154 (1995), 159–68 · L. Chard, 'Bookseller to publisher: Joseph Johnson and the English book trade, 1760–1810', *The Library*, 5th ser., 32 (1977), 138–54 · L. Chard, 'Joseph Johnson: father of the book trade', *Bulletin of the New York Public Library*, 78 (1975), 51–82 · J. Aiken, 'Biographical account of the late Mr Joseph Johnson', *GM*, 1st ser., 79 (1809), 1167–8 · A. A. Engstrom, 'Joseph Johnson's circle and the *Analytical Review*: a study of English radicals in the late eighteenth century', PhD diss., University of Southern California, 1986 · P. Mann, 'Death of a London bookseller', *Keats Shelley Memorial Bulletin*, 15 (1964), 8–12 · J. W. Symser, 'The trial and imprisonment of Joseph Johnson, bookseller', *Bulletin of the New York Public Library*, 77 (1974), 418–35 · G. E. Bentley, *Blake records* (1969) · A. Gilchrist, *Life of William Blake, 'Pictor ignotus'*, 2 vols. (1863) · R. M. Wardle, 'Mary Wollstonecraft, analytical reviewer', *Proceedings of the Modern Language Association of America*, 62 (1947), 1000–09 · P. M. Zall, 'The cool world of Samuel Taylor Coleridge: Joseph Johnson, or, The perils of publishing', *Wordsworth Circle*, 3 (winter 1972), 25–30 · J. Knowles, *The life and writings of Henry Fuseli*, 3 vols. (1831) · G. Schiff, *Johann Heinrich Füssli, 1741–1825: Text and Oeuvrekatalog*, 1 (1973) · J. H. Füssli, *Briefe*, ed. W. Muschg (1942) · W. Godwin, *Memoirs of the author of the 'Vindication of the rights of woman'* (1798) · J. Nichols, *Minor lives: a collection of biographies by John Nichols*, ed. E. L. Hart (1971) · W. Hayley, *The life and posthumous writings of William Cowper, esqr.* (1804) · *The letters and prose writings of William Cowper*, ed. J. King and C. Ryskamp, 5 vols. (1979–86) · M. Butler, *Maria Edgeworth: a literary biography* (1972) · C. H. Timperley, *Encyclopaedia of literary and typographical anecdote*, 2nd edn (1842); repr. (1977) · *The Farington diary*, ed. J. Greig, 2 (1923) · H. R. Plomer and others, *A dictionary of the printers and booksellers who were at work in England, Scotland, and Ireland from 1726 to 1775* (1932) · F. A. Mumby, *Publishing and bookselling: a history from the earliest times to the present day* (1930), 243–7 · G. P. Tyson, 'Johnson, Joseph', BDMBR, vol. 1 · will, PRO, PROB 11/1513, sig. 376 · C. Tomalin, 'Publisher in prison: Joseph Johnson and the book trade', *TLS* (2 Dec 1994), 15–16

Archives DWL, corresp. · Morgan L., letter-book

Likenesses M. Haughton, line engraving, Hunt. L.; Providence Public Library · W. Sharp, engraving (after M. Haughton), BM, NPG [*see illus.*]

Wealth at death approx. £60,000; incl. £30,000 in direct gifts; also properties, leases, and shares: will, PRO, PROB 11/1513, sig. 376; Mann, 'Death of a London bookseller'

Johnson, Joshua (1742–1802), merchant, was born in Maryland, America, on 25 June 1742, the son of Thomas Johnson (1702–1777) and his wife, Dorcas Sedgwick (1705–1770). His family originally came from Great Yarmouth in Norfolk, but his father resided principally in Calvert county on the Patuxent River, in the heart of the Maryland tobacco country. Joshua's eldest brother, Thomas (1732–1819), became a prosperous lawyer in Annapolis, acquired land thereabouts and to the west, and was from 1762 regularly elected to the provincial assembly from Anne Arundel county; he was also a leader of the independence movement in Maryland, becoming in time a delegate to the Continental Congress, revolutionary governor of the state (1777–9), and associate justice of the United States supreme court (1791–3). Of four other brothers who settled in the western parts of Maryland, two, James and Robert, became pioneers in the new iron industry there. Joshua remained in the older part of the colony, in Annapolis, as a small merchant trading to the West Indies and London.

Dissatisfied with the slow progress of his business, in 1770 Johnson joined John Davidson (1738–1794), another Annapolis merchant, and Charles Wallace (1727–1812), also of Annapolis, a wealthy landowner, businessman, and public figure, to form the firm of Wallace, Davidson, and Johnson. Davidson was left in charge of the Annapolis end, while Johnson settled in London in 1771 as purchasing agent for the firm. In such activity he made the fullest possible use of the long-term credit available to the export trades, and thus alleviated the burden on his partners in Maryland who had to remit bills of exchange to pay for the goods he purchased. The firm was badly pressed by the crisis of 1772, provoked by the failure of Alexander Fordyce, during which it became very difficult in London to get bills discounted or credits extended. However, his partners in Maryland were in the end able to remit enough to keep him in business in London. As the crisis abated he persuaded them to let him expand his operations by adding the functions of a commission merchant, selling tobacco and performing other services for American correspondents. In 1774–5 this business brought him 4283 hogsheads of tobacco, primarily Maryland leaf, most often sold to firms exporting to the Netherlands and Germany.

As the political relations between the colonies and the London government deteriorated, Johnson's family and partners were definitely on the 'patriot' or rebel side. Johnson considered himself one of the few American merchants in London who consistently defended the colonists' interest. He kept his partners informed of traders there planning to send tea to America, and thus helped provoke the burning of the *Peggy Stewart* at Annapolis (in which his partner Wallace took a leading part), the Maryland equivalent of the Boston Tea Party. Even after the outbreak of fighting in America, Johnson remained active in London until Wallace, Davidson, and Johnson was wound up in 1777. The next year he withdrew to France, where he settled in Nantes as consul for the Continental Congress and Maryland commercial agent, while continuing substantial private trade. In 1781 he re-established his Maryland connections through the new firm of Wallace, Johnson, and Muir. After the recognition of American independence Johnson returned to London to represent his new firm, soon involved in transactions much more substantial but even more debt-encumbered than its pre-war predecessor. In August 1789 he was named the first United States consul in London.

On 22 August 1785 Johnson married Catherine Newth or Nuth at the church of St Anne, Soho, London. All their eight children appear as legitimate in church records, though four were born before the aforementioned marriage date. This suggests that there may have been an earlier marriage outside the Church of England. Little about Catherine's family has as yet been established. She had a reputation for extreme extravagance and has been blamed in part for her husband's financial difficulties in the 1790s. He was in such straitened circumstances in 1797 that he could not immediately find the cash to pay the modest £500 dowry promised when his daughter Louisa married John Quincy Adams, the future president. That same year he and the rest of his family returned to America, where he settled in the District of Columbia. He was on familiar terms with the Washingtons and other leading personalities thereabouts, but his financial situation remained straitened. His last years were troubled with lawsuits with his former partners concerning his accounts, finally settled by arbitration in 1798. President Adams tried to help by naming him superintendent of stamps in 1800, a position he lost when Jefferson entered office in 1801. Johnson suffered severely from 'the gravel' (kidney stones), and he died on 21 April 1802 at the home of his brother Baker Johnson in Fredericktown, Maryland. He left his widow almost destitute.

Johnson was later described by a nephew as 'a weak, vain man, fond of great people, and impoverished by an ambitious and extravagant wife' (Delaplaine, 351). From the marriage of his daughter Louisa to John Quincy Adams were descended many notable members of that distinguished family, including their son, Charles Francis, and grandsons Henry and Brooks Adams.

JACOB M. PRICE

Sources J. R. Challinor, 'The mis-education of Louisa-Catherine Johnson', *Proceedings of the Massachusetts Historical Society*, 98 (1986), 20–48 · P. C. Nagel, *The Adams women: Abigail and Louisa Adams, their sisters and daughters* (1987) · E. C. Papenfuse, *In pursuit of profit: the Annapolis merchants in the era of the American revolution, 1763–1805* (1975) · J. M. Price, 'Joshua Johnson in London, 1771–5: credit and commercial organization in the British Chesapeake trade', *Statesmen, scholars and merchants: essays in eighteenth-century history presented to Dame Lucy Sutherland*, ed. A. Whiteman, J. S. Bromley, and P. G. M. Dickson (1973), 153–80 · *Joshua Johnson's letterbook, 1771–1774: letters from a merchant in London to his partners in Maryland*, ed. J. M. Price, London RS, 15 (1979) · J. Shepherd, *Cannibals of the heart: a personal biography of Louisa Catherine and John Quincy Adams* (1980) · IGI · E. S. Delaplaine, *The life of Thomas Johnson* (1927) · admon, PRO, PROB 6/181, fol. 113r
Archives Maryland Hall of Records, Annapolis, Wallace, Davidson, and Johnson MSS
Likenesses portraits (of family), repro. in A. Oliver, *Portraits of John Quincy Adams and his wife* (1970), 24

Johnson, Kenrick Reginald Hijmans [Ken; *called* Ken Snakehips Johnson] (1914–1941), dancer and band leader, was born on 10 September 1914 at 193 Wellington Street, Georgetown, British Guiana, the first of two surviving sons and eldest of six children of Dr Reginald Fitzherbert Johnson, a private medical practitioner and government medical officer of health, and his wife, Anna Delphina Louisa (Annie), *née* Hijmans, a professional nurse. His father was from British Guiana, his mother from Dutch Guiana (Surinam). He played violin as a child but an early interest in dancing was discouraged by his father, who wanted his son to follow him into the medical profession, and after early education at Queen's College, Georgetown, he was sent to England to complete his secondary schooling. He attended Sir William Borlase School in Marlow, Buckinghamshire (1929–31), where he played the violin in the school chapel and continued to dance for his friends.

On leaving school Johnson began studying law instead of medicine but shortly abandoned this in favour of a show-business career. He found work as a dancer with touring revues and sought professional tuition from several teachers, but his main influence was the African American instructor Clarence 'Buddy' Bradley who had a dance school in London's West End, and for whom he subsequently worked as an assistant. Taking his nickname from the American dancer Earl 'Snake Hips' Tucker, he

Kenrick Reginald Hijmans Johnson (1914–1941), by unknown photographer, c.1940

began establishing himself as a dancer and producer of dance acts, and after appearing in the film *Oh Daddy!* (1934), embarked on a year of travelling. In British Guiana he created a sensation when he danced on stage with local musicians, and he appeared also in Trinidad before travelling to the United States early in 1935 with a contract to make film shorts. In New York he lived in Harlem, where he took the opportunity to study African American vernacular dancers. He improved on his tap-dancing technique and learnt to wind his hips in the suggestive manner that his nickname implied. He also met and was encouraged by the band leader Fletcher Henderson and claimed to have conducted his band. He returned to Guiana for further stage appearances there and in Trinidad where he was accompanied by instrumentalists including Carl Barriteau and Dave Wilkins, who would later join him in London.

Inspired by his American experiences, his meeting with Henderson, and his Caribbean reception, Johnson decided to form his own band. British dance bands, sometimes augmented by imported white Americans, were technically proficient but generally lacked the ability then to 'swing' like African Americans. However, an interest in 'hot' jazz and authenticity of expression was growing. The idea of all-black ensembles attracted promoters, but it was Johnson and his Jamaican colleague Leslie Thompson who were able to realize this with their Jamaican Aristocrats (or Emperors) of Jazz, formed in 1936. Thompson recruited musicians from the small community of black British professionals and Caribbean settlers such as Jamaican saxophonists Joe Appleton and Louis Stephenson and trumpeter Leslie Hutchinson, all of whom had, like Thompson, learnt their trade in the West India regiment band. They toured in variety, with Johnson, aged twenty-one and dressed in white tie and tails, conducting enthusiastically between his featured dance spots. They entered fashionable London circles with a residency at Mayfair's Florida Club, but in February 1937 the venture ended in acrimony and disintegration when Johnson renewed his contract unilaterally, excluding Thompson. For a new band at the Florida, he sent for four of the musicians he had met on his travels, and re-formed as the Emperors of Swing.

In March 1938 Johnson's band appeared in an early British television production. Now known as the West Indian Dance Orchestra, they continued to tour between London residencies with Johnson himself, well over 6 feet tall and handsome, the main attraction. His lithe dancing and physical energy were impressive, especially when he tapped up a set of glass steps, an act popularized by the American dancer Bill 'Bojangles' Robinson. For the general public, the sight of twelve disciplined men of African descent, dressed smartly in white band jackets, was exciting and memorable.

In October 1939 the West Indian Dance Orchestra began an engagement at the Café de Paris in Coventry Street, London. This nightclub, a byword for sophistication, became more egalitarian with the onset of war and Johnson's presence there echoed the changes. He continued to play for dancers but his desire to emulate Americans such as Count Basie remained. 'I determined to play swing at the Café or die—and boy, I nearly died!', he told a *Melody Maker* reporter, yet between the dance tunes and inevitable commercial dross, he still featured jazz. He also continued to broadcast, with Cardiff-born Don Johnson his main vocalist, and became one of the country's best-known bandleaders. He was killed in the bombing of the Café de Paris, London, on 8 March 1941. He was cremated and his ashes were subsequently placed in the Borlase School chapel. He was unmarried.

Whatever their function as entertainers, Johnson and his musicians played a wider and more complex role in British society. Setting out to copy the style of the bands he had seen in Harlem, he encouraged his musicians to fraternize with visiting Americans. At after-hours 'jam sessions', they became popular with local jazz players who sought them out for their spontaneity and fire. They attracted the teenage element, too, and when they began broadcasting regularly, were recipients of fan mail. Most importantly, critics and musicians alike acknowledged them as the first British band really to 'swing'. Johnson's was neither the first black British band nor the first all-black ensemble to appear in Britain. He played some excellent musical arrangements, but as these owed strict allegiance to prevailing American principles and style, his significance in maintaining the first established black British band was social as much as musical. But the individual band members were capable jazz musicians at a time when many of their white equivalents had limited improvisational ability, and had an important influence on British jazz that continued beyond Johnson's death. Furthermore, Johnson's achievements provided a template for other black musicians to follow. Frank Deniz, who played briefly with Johnson's band as a second guitarist, said 'He elevated the colour question—people thought something of him … It made me think and that's why I tried to model my band on his' (private information).

VAL WILMER

Sources V. Wilmer, 'The first sultan of swing', *Independent on Sunday* (24 Feb 1991) · *Melody Maker* (15 March 1941) · L. Thompson, *An autobiography* (1985), 89–99 · private information (2004) · *Daily Chronicle* [Georgetown, British Guiana] (1914) · F. Deniz and V. Wilmer, interview, 24 Jan 2003
Archives SOUND BL NSA
Likenesses photographs, 1935, priv. coll. · Roye [H. Narbeth], photographs, *c*.1936, priv. coll. · A. McBean, photographs, *c*.1940, priv. coll. · photograph, *c*.1940, priv. coll. [*see illus.*]
Wealth at death £382

Johnson, Laurence (*fl.* 1603), engraver, was one of the earliest native print makers practising in England. In 1603 he engraved a title-page and twenty-six portraits to Richard Knolles's *The Generall Historie of the Turkes*, printed by Adam Islip. With the exception of that of Tamerlane, the portraits are copied from those engraved by Theodor de Bry for J. J. Boissard's *Vitae et icones sultanorum Turcicorum*, published in Frankfurt am Main in 1596. Johnson also engraved in the same year a half-length portrait of James I, which is of extreme rarity; copies are held in the National Maritime Museum, Greenwich, the Ashmolean Museum in Oxford, and the Museum of Fine Arts in Boston. Besides these works, nothing by or about Johnson is known.

L. H. CUST, *rev.* ANTONY GRIFFITHS

Sources A. M. Hind, *Engraving in England in the sixteenth and seventeenth centuries*, 2 (1955), 35–8

Johnson, Leonard Benker [Len] (1902–1974), boxer and political activist, was born at 12 Barnabas Street, Clayton, Manchester, on 22 October 1902, the first of three sons and a daughter of William Benker Johnson, mechanical engineer and booth boxer, and his wife, Margaret Maher. Early in his life Johnson moved to Leeds, where his father worked as a waiter. Here he attended both St Silas and Park Lane elementary schools in Hunslet before returning in 1914 to Manchester, where he was employed in a local gas engine makers. His first professional boxing contest was in Manchester in 1921. After two wins and two losses in his first four fights, he joined a travelling boxing booth, but this only lasted six months. With nine contests (seven wins and two losses) in 1922, a period when he combined his work on the boxing booth with his professional career, he established himself as a capable if inexperienced boxer. However, by the end of 1923—a year in which he had his first fight abroad (in Copenhagen) and his first fight in London—he was good enough to be ranked among Britain's top six middleweights.

Fourteen wins and a draw out of twenty-four fights followed in 1924. In the following year Johnson firmly established himself as one of the country's, and the continent's, leading boxers. In February and September 1925 he

defeated Roland Todd, the reigning British middleweight champion: both fights took place in Manchester. Owing to the colour bar in operation in Britain at the time, however, black boxers could not contest British titles, and despite his achievements Johnson was not allowed to fight for the championship, even though Todd was willing to meet him a third time with the title at stake. As a result of his victories over Todd, opposition to the ban surfaced in the dedicated boxing press for the first time. In June 1925 Johnson also outpointed Herman Van't Hof of the Netherlands, who became European champion in 1926.

Like most top boxers of the time, Johnson then travelled to Australia for a six-month tour, although in his case the disenchantment he felt at the lack of championship opportunities probably forced the trip. After eight contests (six victories) he returned to Manchester, where in his first contest he defeated George West, who had just lost to Tommy Milligan for the British title. When Johnson also won their rematch six weeks later, calls were again made in the national boxing press for Johnson to be allowed to fight for the title. However, the boxing authorities did not lift the ban until 1947 and Johnson, despite his undoubted skill, was destined never to fight for the British title. Over the next seven years he met most of the top British and European boxers, including two meetings with Len Harvey. Johnson outpointed Harvey in London in January 1927 but lost a rematch—which many thought of as an 'unofficial' title match—in May 1932, by which time Harvey was British champion.

After retiring from the ring in 1933 Johnson ran a travelling boxing booth for a number of years, until he was forced to sell it in 1939 as the Second World War approached. After the war, during which he served in civil defence, Johnson drove buses and lorries for a living and he continued in this employment until 1972. He married on 17 November 1926 Annie Forshaw, a bookbinder. About 1945, however, their marriage broke down and Johnson settled with Marie Reid (who had three children of her own, and later adopted her sister's three children), with whom he remained until his death.

Near the end of the Second World War, Johnson joined the Communist Party of Great Britain, of which he remained a member until his death. Along with C. L. R. James, George Padmore, and other black radicals such as Jomo Kenyatta, he was heavily involved in the Pan-African Congress held in Manchester in July 1945. Involvement here also led Johnson to establish the New International Society with Wilf Charles and Syd Booth. He also stood as a Communist Party member in the Manchester council elections in 1947, 1949 (when he spoke at various left-wing meetings with Paul Robeson), 1950, 1955, 1956, and 1962. During the 1950s he visited Russia.

Although Johnson's communist affiliations make him almost unique among British sportsmen, it is his boxing career for which he is most famous. He was one of only a handful of highly talented black British boxers active before the Second World War, and was probably the most skilful black British boxer until the emergence of Randolph (Randy) Turpin in the early 1950s. He met all the leading British and European boxers of his day, and defeated most of them. However, owing to the colour bar in British boxing, which was lifted by the time Turpin came to the fore, he was unable to contest a British title, even though many contemporaries, including boxing journalists, rated him as the best middleweight in Europe about 1925–8. Johnson died in Oldham General Hospital on 28 September 1974 and was cremated at Manchester crematorium a few days later.   GARY SHAW

Sources M. Herbert, *Never counted out: the story of Len Johnson, Manchester's black boxing hero and communist* (1992) • G. Shaw, 'The rise and fall of the colour bar in British boxing, 1911–1947', *2000 British Society of Sports History conference* [Liverpool 2000] [2000] • G. Odd, *The Hamlyn encyclopaedia of boxing* (1989) • D. Fleming, *The Manchester fighters* (1986) • S. Shipley, 'Boxing', *The history of sport in Britain*, ed. T. Mason (1988) • b. cert. • m. cert. [Annie Forshaw] • d. cert.

Johnson, Lionel Pigot (1867–1902), poet and literary scholar, was born on 15 March 1867 at Broadstairs, Kent, the sixth child and third son of Captain William Victor Johnson (1822–1891), captain of the 90th light infantry, and Catharine Delicia Walters (d. 1903), only daughter of Robert Walters, barrister. Never physically developing beyond his sixteenth year and only 2 or 3 inches over 5 feet tall, he was not fashioned to follow his father and brothers into the army. Instead he set about creating himself as a literary man.

Privately educated at Mr Wilkinson's school at Clifton Downs, near Bristol, Johnson entered his beloved Winchester College on a scholarship in 1880. There he transformed the school paper, *The Wykehamist*, into a literary periodical, wrote the letters of religious exploration and serious thought which were subsequently collected in *Some Winchester Letters of Lionel Johnson* (1919), and composed a large number of poems, including the successful prize-poems *Sir Walter Raleigh in the Tower* (1885) and *Julian at Eleusis* (1886).

In 1886 Johnson won a Winchester scholarship to New College, Oxford, where he was tutored and strongly influenced by Walter Pater and became president of the New College Essay Society. Oxford reinforced his love of tradition, and, although one finds him beginning to associate not so much with the living as with those who enliven the literary gathering of his imagination, he was not yet the recluse of his later years. His health was undermined at Oxford and the chance recommendation of alcohol to help him sleep may have initiated the habit of drinking which was to hasten his death. He also began, perhaps through insomnia, the pattern of working or walking through the night and sleeping late into the day. However, he gave papers to the Essay Society, corresponded with the publisher Charles Kegan Paul, and was introduced by Arthur Galton to the members of the Century Guild.

When he graduated with a first in *literae humaniores* in 1890, Johnson went to join Herbert Horne, Selwyn Image, and Arthur Mackmurdo, members of the guild, in their house at 20 Fitzroy Street in London. Two significant moments occurred in late June 1891. On St Alban's day (22 June) 1891 he was received into the Roman Catholic faith at St Etheldreda's, Ely Place, London, by Father William

Lockhart, a step in his search for some priestly function which is adumbrated in the Winchester letters. He was for a time in great demand as a Catholic lecturer. Later that month he introduced Oscar Wilde to his fellow Wykehamist and close friend from Oxford, Lord Alfred Douglas. His own homosexuality, always strictly repressed, may well have added to his sense of isolation and consciousness of 'the Dark Angel'.

Johnson threw himself into the task of writing and reviewing, both to establish himself as an author and to pay off the debts he had incurred at Oxford. He was involved in the Rhymers' Club, formed in the summer of 1890, and published in both its books in 1892 and 1894. Yeats describes how Johnson and Horne 'imposed their personalities upon us' (Yeats, 166–7), but Johnson's close friendship with Ernest Dowson and his familiarity with Arthur Symons and Yeats indicate that he was at the centre of 1890s poetic movements. Yeats, who remembered Johnson in the early 1890s as 'always at my side' (ibid., 312), thought of him as 'our critic, and above all our theologian' (ibid., 221) and, impressed and influenced by Johnson's erudition, encouraged his attempts to transform himself into an Irishman. This was another attempt to place himself within an order which could give his life meaning, though the love of things Celtic had been there right from the early days. He visited Ireland several times between 1891 and 1898 to give lectures on Irish writers to the National Literary Society. He became a regular contributor of essays and reviews to *The Academy*, the *Anti-Jacobin*, and the *Daily Chronicle*, and wrote occasionally for journals such as *The Pageant*, *The Savoy*, *The Speaker*, and *The Spectator*. He even acted as co-editor with Eleanor Hull of the Irish Literary Society's *Irish Home Reading Magazine*, which ran for two issues in 1894. His ambition was to be a poet, but he earned his living by his prose and his first book, *The Art of Thomas Hardy* (1894), was the first seriously to consider the writing of novels as an art. His reputation was confirmed by the publication of his *Poems* in 1895, which marks the high point in his career.

In 1895 Johnson's drunken behaviour forced Mackmurdo to ask him to leave the Fitzroy house, and he left for Gray's Inn Square, whose cloistral and academic mood suited his increasingly solitary lifestyle. Although his life was breaking down, his writing kept its clarity and scholarship. *Ireland, with Other Poems* (1897) explores his triad of passions, Catholicism, classicism, and Celticism and, although the book predominantly contains poems rejected from the first volume, the effect is by no means of the second-rate. Their literary topics, religious anxiety, and classical decorousness give his poems a distinctive flavour, and there is always a power of subdued passion, deep wells of brooding covered by fastidious grace, his anguish exacerbated by his strong religious belief and his homosexuality. His may not be the poems first remembered from the 1890s, but they remain among the most powerful.

Johnson became more and more solitary as the decade progressed, closeting himself with his books and his drink, though still producing his scholarly and incisive reviews and involving himself in the Irish movement. He retreated into paranoia and alcoholism; at the inquest his laundress said that he was drinking 2 pints of whisky every twenty-four hours. The manner of his death has often been mythologized; by Ezra Pound, for example, who has Victor Plarr telling him:

> how Johnson (Lionel) died
> By falling from a high stool in a pub
> (E. Pound, 'Hugh Selwyn Mauberley', *Personae: Collected Shorter Poems*, 1952, 202)

Johnson fell quite often, both symbolically and physically. In his poem 'Mystic and Cavalier' he warns: 'Go from me: I am one of those, who fall' (L. P. Johnson, *Complete Poems*, ed. I. Fletcher, 1953, 29), the most powerful of several poems expressing an unspecified but deeply felt and memorably stated sense of moral failure. But he also fell physically, often from too much drink, and in the end from a series of strokes. The last of these strokes caused a fall and a skull fracture in the Green Dragon in Fleet Street. Johnson was taken to St Bartholomew's Hospital, where he died on 4 October 1902. He was buried in Kensal Green Roman Catholic cemetery, London.

R. K. R. THORNTON

Sources D. H. Millar, 'Lionel Johnson', PhD diss., The Queen's University, Belfast, 1947 · R. Roseliep, 'Some letters of Lionel Johnson', PhD diss., University of Notre Dame, Indiana, 1954 · *DNB* · G. A. Cevasco, *Three decadent poets: Ernest Dowson, John Gray and Lionel Johnson, an annotated bibliography* (1990) · W. B. Yeats, *Autobiographies* (1955) · L. P. Johnson, *The complete poems of Lionel Johnson*, ed. I. Fletcher (1953)

Archives NL Scot. | BL, corresp. with Campbell Dodgson, Add. MS 46363 · BL, letters to Edmund Gosse, Ashley MS 931, A.3412, B.658 · BL, letter to his cousin Marjorie, Add. MS 42576, fol. 94 · BL, letter to Ernest Rhys, Eg. 3247, fol. 41 · BL, note from Oscar Wilde, Add. MS 42577, fol. 316 · BL OIOC, letter to Alfred Perceval Graves, Eur. MS E. 267/70 · Bodl. Oxf., letters to E. K. Chambers, MS Autogr.e.11, fols. 7–12 · CUL, letter to Arthur Christopher Benson, Add. 7339/20 · JRL, letters to Katharine Tynan and her family · King's Cam., letter to Roger Fry · L. Cong., letters to Louise Imogen Guiney · NL Ire., letters to John O'Leary, MS 8001 · NL Scot., letter to John Purves, Acc. 7175 · U. Leeds, Brotherton L., letters to Edmund Gosse · U. Reading, letters to Charles Elkin Mathews, MS 392/1/1 · U. Reading, letters to John Todhunter, MS 202/1/1

Likenesses portrait, 1883, repro. in [I. Fletcher], ed., *W. B. Yeats: images of a poet* (1961), 50 [exhibition catalogue, Manchester and Dublin, 3 May – 1 July 1961] · photograph, 1885, repro. in *Poetical works of Lionel Johnson* (1915) · photograph, 1889, repro. in *Poetical works of Lionel Johnson* (1915), facing p. 1 · photograph, repro. in T. Wright, *The life of Walter Pater*, 2 (1907), 157

Wealth at death £9525 8s. 5d.: administration, 13 Nov 1902, CGPLA Eng. & Wales

Johnson, Manuel John (1805–1859), astronomer, was the only son of John William Johnson of Macau (Macao), China, where he was born on 23 May 1805. He was educated at Addiscombe College, entered the St Helena artillery with the rank of lieutenant in 1821, and became aide-de-camp to General Alexander Walker, who encouraged his taste for astronomy and induced the East India Company to establish an observatory on the island. Johnson made two trips to the Cape of Good Hope, in 1825 and 1828, to consult with the astronomer there, the Revd Fearon Fallows, as to its construction, and he began observing in November 1829 with a transit instrument of 3.8 inches aperture and a mural circle 4 feet in diameter. By 1833 he had the data for *A Catalogue of 606 Principal Fixed Stars in the Southern Hemisphere* (1835), for which he received the Royal Astronomical Society's gold medal. The importance of the catalogue was that, with the Madras catalogues, it was the source for exact places of those stars largely invisible from European observatories. Johnson also observed from St Helena the solar eclipse of 27 July 1832 and the opposition of Mars from October to December 1832.

When the East India Company handed control of St Helena to the British government the artillery corps was disbanded. Johnson was retired on a pension, and after some months of continental travel he matriculated at Magdalen Hall, Oxford, on 15 December 1835 (BA 1839, MA 1842). After being appointed to succeed Professor Stephen Peter Rigaud in charge of the Radcliffe Observatory, Oxford, he conformed to the main concern of academic astronomy, namely the measurement of star positions. With one assistant, he embarked on the redetermination of Stephen Groombridge's catalogue of circumpolar stars (observed between 1806 and 1817), reducing by day the observations made by night, and publishing at regular intervals a total of eighteen volumes of *Radcliffe Observations*. Johnson was to reobserve these stars some forty years later, so that he could ascertain the exact motion of individual stars during that period.

Supported by Sir Robert Peel, one of the Radcliffe trustees, Johnson set about re-equipping the observatory, the original instruments being nearly seventy years old and by then obsolete. New apparatus was vital if further serious research was to be undertaken. A 6 foot mural circle by Thomas Jones was delivered in 1836, a transit circle by Simms in 1843, and a heliometer by Repsold of Hamburg in October 1849. This heliometer, with an object glass 7.5 inches in diameter, was the largest of its kind in existence, and was fully described by Johnson in the eleventh volume of the *Observations*. In 1850 he observed with it twenty-six important double stars, and in 1852–3 measured the chief stars of the Pleiades cluster and the annual parallaxes of the stars 61 Cygni, 1830 Groombridge, and α Lyrae. Similar series for the stars Castor, Arcturus, and α Lyrae were obtained in 1854–5, after which he effectively ceased to use the heliometer.

In 1850 Johnson married Caroline, the daughter of James Adey Ogle, regius professor of medicine at Oxford. She and several of their children survived him. He acquired Norman Pogson as a second assistant in 1851, when he proposed to revise Giuseppe Piazzi's catalogue of 1814, but substituted the plan (which his death frustrated) of forming a catalogue of nearly 1500 stars remarkable for their physical or systematic peculiarities.

Johnson greatly expanded the range of meteorological observations at the observatory. He adopted photographic recording of some of these instruments in 1854, and installed an electrical recorder on his transit circle in 1858. He was elected a fellow of the Royal Society in 1856, and served as president of the Royal Astronomical Society in 1857–8.

Johnson was a popular figure in the university, and the observatory became in his time a chief resort of the Oxford leaders of the high-church party, among them John Henry Newman. In his *Apologia* (1864), part 4, Newman records that, having resigned his Anglican orders and all his university offices prior to being admitted into the Roman Catholic church, he spent his last night in Oxford as Johnson's guest at the Radcliffe Observatory. It is possible that Johnson's own high-churchmanship could have played a part in the university's refusal to appoint him to the Savilian professorship of astronomy, a post which had been attached to the Radcliffe Observatory since the late 1760s.

Johnson's artistic tastes led him to form a fine collection of engravings, some of which were shown at the Manchester exhibition in 1857. He died suddenly of heart disease at the observatory on 28 February 1859. His catalogue of 6317 circumpolar stars, then with the printer, was published under the editorship of his successor, Robert Main, and proved to be a valuable record. Main also reduced and published two additional volumes of his observations. A prize, instituted in Johnson's memory, was offered at Oxford once every four years for an essay on an astronomical or meteorological subject.

A. M. CLERKE, rev. ALLAN CHAPMAN

Sources J. H. Newman, *Apologia pro vita sua* (1864); repr. with introduction by J. Gamble (1913), pt 6, p. 97 • C. L. F. André, *L'astronomie pratique et les observatoires en Europe et en Amérique*, 1: *Angleterre* (Paris, 1874), 57–60 • Foster, *Alum. Oxon.* • T. Mozley, *Reminiscences, chiefly of Oriel College and the Oxford Movement*, 1 (1882), 189 • *The Times* (4 March 1859), 5a • *Monthly Notices of the Royal Astronomical Society*, 19 (1858–9), 169–70 • *Monthly Notices of the Royal Astronomical Society*, 20 (1859–60), 123–31 • PRS, 10 (1859–60), xxi–xxiv • CGPLA Eng. & Wales (1859)
Archives Bodl. Oxf., corresp. • MHS Oxf., papers • RAS, letters and papers | CUL, corresp. with Sir George Airy • Inst. EE, archives, corresp. with Sir Francis Ronalds
Likenesses chalk and pencil drawing, c.1850 (after G. Richmond), Radcliffe Observatory, Oxford
Wealth at death under £1500: administration, 27 May 1859, CGPLA Eng. & Wales

Johnson, Martin (d. c.1686), seal engraver and landscape painter, probably lived and worked in London, but almost nothing is known of his origins and career. He was a noted engraver of seals and medals and a rival, as George Vertue recorded from contemporary witnesses, of the more famous Thomas Simon (1623–1665) (BL, Add. MS 23070, fol. 79, quoted by Farquhar). Johnson apparently despised Simon's technique because of his reliance on the punch, which Johnson never used, rather than the graver. Johnson was also a landscape painter of some repute, admired for his 'judgement, freedom and warmth of colouring' (Walpole, 2.47). He died in London about 1686, and within a few years of his death his paintings were reported to be very scarce, although a few were known to be still in private hands. None of his works, either engraved or painted, can now be identified. CHRISTOPHER MARSDEN

Sources [B. Buckeridge], 'An essay towards an English school of painters', in R. de Piles, *The art of painting, and the lives of the painters* (1706), 398–480 • H. Farquhar, 'Portraiture of our Stuart monarchs on their coins and medals, part 1', *British Numismatic Journal*, 5

(1908), 219n. • H. Walpole, *Anecdotes of painting in England: with some account of the principal artists*, ed. R. N. Wornum, new edn, 3 vols. (1888), vol. 2, pp. 46–7 • M. H. Grant, *A dictionary of British landscape painters, from the 16th century to the early 20th century* (1952), 105 • C. F. Bell, ed., *Evelyn's 'Sculptura' with the unpublished second part* (1906), 99

Johnson, Maurice (1688–1755), antiquary and barrister, was born in Spalding, Lincolnshire, on 19 June 1688, the eldest surviving son (a boy had been stillborn on 20 August 1685) of the seven children of Maurice Johnson (1661–1747), landowner, and his wife, Jane, née Johnson (1666–1703), of Ayscoughfee Hall, Spalding. The Johnsons had been a substantial family in the region and, according to John Nichols, the poet and playwright Ben Jonson was a lineal ancestor. Maurice Johnson was educated at Spalding Free Grammar School and possibly subsequently at Eton College: in a letter to the duke of Buccleuch of 26 July 1738 he excused himself for 'talking like a School Fellow a liberty I find every Man thinks he has a Right to take to the end of his Days & wch makes Eaton ever Remembred [sic] by me wth much more pleasure' (Spalding Gentlemen's Society MSS). He also learned French from Huguenot refugees resident at Thorney, Cambridgeshire. He trained in the law at London: he was admitted a member of the Society of the Inner Temple on 26 May 1705, and was called to the bar on 26 June 1710.

From 1710 Johnson lived at Ayscoughfee Hall, though he visited London regularly during the law terms. He held various legal positions in the region around Spalding, where the family owned considerable property: he was deputy recorder of Stamford in 1721, chairman of the South Holland quarter sessions, a justice of the peace, and steward of the manor of Spalding for the duke of Buccleuch, of Kirton and Croyland for the earl of Exeter, and of Hitchin for James Bogdani. On 5 January 1710 he married Elizabeth Ambler (bap. 1690, d. 1754), daughter of William Ambler of Kirton, Lincolnshire. They had twenty-six children, of whom six girls and five boys reached adulthood; seven of his children survived him. The eldest son, Maurice Johnson (1714–1793), became a lieutenant-colonel in HRH the duke of Cumberland's regiment of foot guards, was Cumberland's aide-de-camp, and served at the battles of Dettingen and Culloden.

While living in London, Johnson had met William Stukeley and was, along with the brothers Roger and Samuel Gale, Browne Willis, and other gentlemen, part of a club that met at a coffee house near the Temple to discuss the ancient history of Britain. These meetings were the genesis of the future refounding of the Society of Antiquaries in 1717, in which Johnson took a leading role, and he was provisionally appointed their librarian. When in London he also associated with the literary circle that included Joseph Addison, John Gay, Alexander Pope, and Richard Steele which met at Button's Coffee House, Covent Garden, from 1712. On returning to Spalding in 1710 Johnson established a small literary society which met at Mr Younger's Coffee House in the town, where they read *The Tatler* and, when it came out in 1711, *The Spectator*. These

Maurice Johnson (1688–1755), by George Vertue, 1731

meetings were formalized in November 1712 with proposals issued for establishing 'a Society of Gentlemen, for the supporting of a mutual benevolence, and their improvement in the liberal science and in polite learning' (Moore, 3–4). A president was appointed, and Johnson took on the role of secretary. The interests of the Gentlemen's Society of Spalding were antiquarian as well as literary, and the arts and sciences were also subjects of discussion. In a letter of 1746 Johnson explained that 'We deal, in all arts and sciences, and exclude nothing from our conversation but politics' (Nichols, *Lit. anecdotes*, 6.6–7).

As the society grew it established a substantial library, a museum, and a physic garden, but its survival depended very much on the energetic efforts of Johnson. He encouraged his friends to correspond with the society and to send material for its meetings. Honorary members included John Gay, Alexander Pope, Sir Hans Sloane, Sir Isaac Newton—whom Johnson met in 1720—and Sir Andrew Michael Ramsay, whom he met in London in 1729. Johnson wrote numerous dissertations (none of which was published) for presentation to the society on a wide range of subjects from legal history and numismatics, to gardening, heraldry, and fossils. Nichols, however, records Johnson's complaint some ten years before his death of

> the difficulty of keeping up such an institution in the corner of the country where he had established it, and of inducing the members to give their own thoughts on any subject, either in the way of their own profession, or their more relaxed studies.　(Nichols, *Lit. anecdotes*, 6.20)

Johnson was a close friend of the Revd Samuel Wesley (father of the Methodists Samuel and John Wesley), who was also a member of the society, and assisted him in the legal aspects of his *Dissertationes in librum Jobi* (1735). He appears to have been a friendly, amiable man, and Nichols recorded that 'Mr. Johnson acquired general esteem from the frankness and benevolence of his character' (ibid., 6.22).

From 1748 to 1755 Johnson was the society's president: the secretarial duties were taken over by his son-in-law Dr John Green, a move that possibly reflected increasing ill health. According to Nichols, Johnson 'was in the latter part of his life attacked with a vertiginous disorder in his head, which frequently interrupted his studies and at last put a period to his life' (Nichols, *Lit. anecdotes*, 6.21). In June 1754 Green wrote to Emanuel da Costa informing him that Johnson 'Declines apace; we keep up the spirit of the Society as yet, but I doubt when we lose him, we lose our main support' (Green to Costa, 8 June 1754, BL, Add. MS 28537, fol. 371). According to the treasurer's accounts book Johnson died on 8 February 1755 and not, as Stukeley wrote, on the 6th ('Treasurers accounts of the Spalding Gentlemen's Society', 3.27, Spalding Gentlemen's Society MSS). In his eulogium for his deceased friend Stukeley described Johnson as 'a fluent orator' and 'a great lover of gardening' who possessed 'a fine collection of plants, and excellent cabinet of medals. … In general the antiquities of the great mitred priory of Spalding, and of this part of Lincolnshire, are for ever obliged to the care and diligence of Maurice Johnson, who has rescued them from oblivion' (Nichols, *Lit. anecdotes*, 6.23). Johnson was buried in the church of the Blessed Virgin and St Nicholas, Spalding, on 11 February. Although the society went into decline after his death, and although various such gentlemanly clubs were established in provincial centres around England in the eighteenth century, Johnson's foundation is the oldest still surviving to this date.　　　DAVID BOYD HAYCOCK

Sources Nichols, *Lit. anecdotes*, 6.1–162; 7.201–2 · Spalding Gentlemen's Society, miscellaneous MSS · W. Moore, *The Gentlemen's Society at Spalding: its origin and progress* (1851) · BL, Add. MS 28537, fol. 371 · *DNB*
Archives BL, printed works annotated by him [copies] · BL, collections relating to Isle of Ely and Cambridgeshire fens, Add. MS 35171 · Northants. RO, corresp. and papers, incl. formulary of legal documents relating to south Lincolnshire · Spalding Gentlemen's Society Museum, Lincolnshire, antiquarian corresp., collections, and papers | BL, letters to Thomas Birch, Add. MS 4310 · Bodl. Oxf., his annotated copy of Stukeley's *Itinerarium curiosum* and MS copy of *Foresta* · Bodl. Oxf., letters to William Stukeley
Likenesses oils, 18th cent. (Maurice Johnson?), Spalding Gentlemen's Society Museum, Broad Street, Spalding, Lincolnshire · G. Vertue, miniature, 1731, NPG [*see illus.*] · M. Vandergucht, pen-and-ink drawing, Bodl. Oxf., Eng. misc. MS e. 136
Wealth at death wealthy: will, 1752, Spalding Gentlemen's Society, miscellaneous MSS

Johnson, Sir Nelson King (1892–1954), meteorologist, was born on 11 March 1892 at Barton Mill House, Canterbury, the second son of John Gilbert Johnson, master miller, and his wife, Emily Alice Williams. From the Simon Langton School, Canterbury, he obtained a scholarship to the Royal College of Science, South Kensington, where in 1913 he took his BSc, was admitted as an associate, and became an assistant demonstrator in spectroscopy. A year later he began the life of a professional astronomer by joining Sir Norman Lockyer at Sidmouth observatory, but this career was terminated by the war and in 1915 he joined the Royal Flying Corps. His experiences as a pilot undoubtedly influenced his decision to join the Meteorological Office in 1919. In 1927 he married (Mary) Margaret Lofthouse, daughter of J. Taylor, of Blackburn; they had one son and one daughter.

In 1921 Johnson was put in charge of the meteorological section of the Chemical Warfare Experimental Station at

Porton, Wiltshire, a post he held until 1928. During these seven years he did the scientific work for which he is best remembered. He was charged with investigating the physics of the atmosphere very close to the ground, especially in relation to diffusion, a subject later known as micrometeorology. When he began relatively little was known about these matters and few reliable systematic observations were available. Within a remarkably short space of time he and his team had devised apparatus for the routine recording of the surface temperature and wind fields and their variations with height to an accuracy hitherto unapproached. They also laid the foundations, both experimental and theoretical, of the study of the diffusion of gases and suspended matter by the turbulence of the natural wind. For reasons of national security much of this work was withheld from open publication until after the Second World War but the claim may be fairly advanced that Johnson truly laid the foundations of micrometeorology; his contributions were recognized by the award of the degree of DSc by the University of London in 1939.

Johnson became director of experiments at Porton in 1928 and afterwards chief superintendent of the chemical defence research department at the War Office. In 1938 he succeeded Sir George Simpson as director of the Meteorological Office. Within a year he was faced with the reorganization of the service for war, when the staff rose from fewer than 1000 to more than 6000. During this period he undoubtedly overworked, and damaged his health. Apart from the successful organization of the wartime service he also, during this period, began organized research within the office and founded the meteorological research committee. In 1943 he was knighted.

After the war Johnson turned his attention to recreating international links and in 1946 became president of the International Meteorological Organization. In this capacity he did much to bring into being the World Meteorological Organization, acting as president for the first congress of the Organization in 1951. He retired from the Meteorological Office in 1953.

Johnson was a far-seeing but not particularly forceful administrator and was naturally modest with a tendency to self-effacement. As an individual scientist his gifts inclined more to the experimental than the theoretical side and his work in atmospheric turbulence was distinguished chiefly by the excellence of the basic measurements which he made with simple but usually ingenious instruments. But for the intervention of the war he would undoubtedly have turned the Meteorological Office into a very effective research institution as well as a public service; but this had to wait for more favourable circumstances.

Johnson was a keen mountaineer, but during his later years contracted Parkinson's disease; this may have played a part in hastening his death, by his own hand, at Charing Cross Hospital, London, on 23 March 1954. He was survived by his wife.

O. G. SUTTON, rev. ISOBEL FALCONER

Sources *The Times* (24 March 1954) · *Quarterly Journal of the Royal Meteorological Society*, 80 (1954) · *Journal of Atmospheric and Terrestrial Physics*, 5 (1954) · private information (1971) · personal knowledge (1971) · CGPLA Eng. & Wales (1954)
Likenesses W. Stoneman, photograph, 1943, NPG · oils (after photograph), World Meteorological Organization
Wealth at death £7859 0s. 8d.: probate, 22 May 1954, CGPLA Eng. & Wales

Johnson, Nicholas (d. 1624). *See under* Johnson family (*per. c.*1570–*c.*1630).

Johnson, Pamela Helen Hansford [married name Pamela Helen Hansford Snow, Lady Snow] (1912–1981), writer and playwright, was born on 29 May 1912 in London, the elder child (the younger daughter died as a baby) of Reginald Kenneth Johnson (1874–1923?), a colonial administrator in west Africa, and his wife, Amy Clotilda, daughter of C. E. Howson, actor and treasurer to Sir Henry Irving for twenty-five years. She was educated at Clapham county secondary school, leaving at the age of sixteen to learn shorthand and typing. Her father had died five years earlier leaving only debts and there was no money for further education. She never regretted this deprivation, claiming that 'a course in Eng. Lit. has rotted many a promising writer' and finding in *Texts and Pretexts* (1933) by Aldous Huxley the key to her own 'higher education' in both English and French literature.

For five years Pamela Hansford Johnson worked in a bank, writing (and occasionally publishing) verse, essays, and short stories in her spare time. In 1934 she won the *Sunday Referee*'s annual poetry prize—a subsidy for a book of her poems. She met and fell in love with Dylan Marlais *Thomas (1914–1953), who won the prize the following year. They contemplated marriage but decided amicably to go their separate ways. Her diaries for the two years of their friendship and his letters to her are now in the library of the University of New York at Buffalo.

Pamela Hansford Johnson had an immediate success, both critical and commercial, with her first novel, *This Bed thy Centre* (1935), but she was quite unprepared for the ordeal of having achieved unintentionally a *succès de scandale*. The novel is the love story of a teenaged couple forced by the unforgiving conventions of the time to endure a lengthy engagement. The plot was in no way autobiographical but she was given to understand that she had disgraced herself and the entire area of Clapham Common. For a while she was disowned by her late father's family and was subjected to a shoal of anonymous letters.

However, reassured and encouraged by Cyril Connolly and others, Pamela Hansford Johnson abandoned the bank in favour of full-time writing. She went on to publish thirty-one novels; seven plays; a book of memoirs, *Important to Me* (1974); an appraisal of contemporary 'permissiveness' in the light of the infamous moors murders case, *On Iniquity* (1967); and *Six Proust Reconstructions* (1958), the radio plays in which she placed Proust's characters in different settings and situations. These were commissioned by the BBC Third Programme and were repeated frequently during the 1950s. The tapes have been erased.

Pamela Helen Hansford Johnson (1912–1981), by Jorge Lewinski, 1966

After the great promise of Pamela Hansford Johnson's first novel it seemed that she had lost both her way and her touch. She wrote five undistinguished novels in four years and it was not until 1940 that she regained her true form with *Too Dear for my Possessing*. She was invited to review regularly for the *Sunday Times* and became well known as a demanding but generous-minded and constructive critic.

On 15 December 1936 Pamela Hansford Johnson married Gordon Neil Stewart (*b.* 1911/12), an Australian journalist, and they had a son, Andrew, in 1941, and a daughter, Lindsay, in 1944. The marriage came to an end in 1949. On 14 July 1950 she married the writer Charles Percy (later Lord) *Snow (1905–1980), and they had a son, Philip (*b.* 1952). Their considerable talents were complementary, their tastes and interests largely coincided, and they made a formidable and influential literary partnership. They travelled widely in the United States and in the Soviet Union and her books were published with success in both countries, leading to translations in many European languages.

Pamela Hansford Johnson wrote ten of her best and best-known novels between 1950 and 1978, including *Catherine Carter* (1952), her only novel with a theatrical setting; *The Unspeakable Skipton* (1959), a satirical comedy based on the character of Frederic Rolfe, Baron Corvo, and generally accepted as her masterpiece; *The Humbler Creation* (1959), about an unfashionable London parish; and *The Honours Board* (1970), set in the enclosed world of the teaching staff of a boys' preparatory school. Her last

novel, *A Bonfire* (1981), was published two months before her death.

Pamela Hansford Johnson's work was popular in the best sense: she had a large library following and attracted the respect and admiration of the literary pundits of the day. She was generous with help to young writers and was a warm-hearted and entertaining friend and companion. She was a fellow of the Royal Society of Literature and was appointed CBE in 1975. She had four American honorary degrees. A sufferer for thirty years from migraine, she helped to found the Migraine Trust in 1969. Pamela Hansford Johnson died on 18 June 1981 in the London Clinic, Devonshire Place, after a series of strokes.

ALAN MACLEAN

Sources P. H. Johnson, *Important to me* (1974) · I. Quigly, *Pamela Hansford Johnson*, Writers and their Work Series, 203 (1968) · personal knowledge (2004) · *CGPLA Eng. & Wales* (1982)
Archives State University of New York, Buffalo | CUL, corresp. with W. A. Gerhardie · Eton, corresp. with Susan Hill · Royal Society of Literature, London, letters to Royal Society of Literature
Likenesses J. Lewinski, photograph, 1966, NPG [*see illus.*]
Wealth at death £64,082: probate, 27 Jan 1982, *CGPLA Eng. & Wales*

Johnson, Percival Norton (1792–1866), metallurgist, was born on 29 September 1792 at 6–7 Maiden Lane, in the City of London, the third of the ten children of John Johnson (1765–1831), assayer of ores and metals, and his wife, Mary (*née* Wight) (1766–1863). Percival was Johnson's only Christian name in the baptismal register and it is not known when he acquired the additional name of Norton. Furthermore, nothing is known of his early life and education. He was apprenticed to his father in the Worshipful Company of Goldsmiths, obtaining the freedom of the company on 2 March 1814 and becoming a liveryman on 24 April 1816. On 1 January 1817 he married Elizabeth Lydia Smith (1794–1857), fourth daughter of Thomas Smith, receiver-general to the dean and chapter of St Paul's Cathedral; they were to have no children.

At about the same time as his marriage, Johnson set up on his own, first in the City and from 1822 in Hatton Garden, Holborn. His friend and brother-in-law, Thomas Cock, who had evolved a process for making platinum malleable, assisted in the early development of the business, which included assaying and refining, and the preparation of colours for the decoration of pottery and glass. In time Johnson perfected a number of pottery colours, including a much sought-after rose pink, and a range of yellows and oranges based on uranium oxide. Following a visit to Germany, Johnson commenced production of an alloy containing nickel, copper, and zinc, which was known by various names including nickel silver, German silver and British plate. During preparation of this alloy, used largely for the manufacture of spoons, forks, and candlesticks, he refined nickel for the first time in England.

The first of many publications by Percival appeared in the *Philosophical Magazine* in July 1812 and concerned the parting of platinum from gold. A footnote initialled by both him and his father reported an original observation, that Brazilian gold could be discoloured by the presence of palladium. Some twenty years later Percival successfully refined crude gold from the Gongo Soco mines in Brazil, which had defeated other refiners because of the presence of palladium and tellurium. Rapid expansion of his firm followed, funded in part by Captain W. R. B. Sellon (formerly Smith) another brother-in-law. Johnson was elected a fellow of the Royal Society in 1846.

In 1838 Johnson implemented an agreement with John Matthey, a stockbroker, whereby, in return for the injection of new capital, the latter's sons, George and Edward, should enter the business. The company became Johnson and Matthey in September 1851 when George Matthey was taken into full partnership. By persistent scientific endeavour and acute business sense, Matthey was to transform the refining and fabrication of platinum from a laboratory activity into a successful industrial operation, making platinum available for use throughout the world. The firm's assaying expertise was recognized in 1852 when the company was appointed assayers to the Bank of England.

Johnson's scientific work brought him into contact with numerous mining enterprises, especially in Devon and Cornwall, though he also advised governments and mining companies in many parts of the world. This led him to become involved, in a managerial capacity and financially, in both mining and smelting. As a result, from 1854 he lived mainly in Devon. In addition to introducing many pioneering technical practices, he worked to improve the social conditions of the miners and their families. For instance, at great expense to himself he had schools erected in the neighbourhood of the mines, and he took an active part in their supervision. In this he was supported by his wife, Elizabeth, who did much charitable work. She was also the prime mover in the formation of the London Society for Teaching the Blind to Read (later the Royal London Society for the Blind).

Elizabeth Johnson died on 8 September 1857; fourteen months later, on 25 November 1858, Percival Johnson married Georgina Elizabeth Ellis, daughter of George Stevenson Ellis, formerly head of the bullion office at the Bank of England. Since 1852 Johnson had gradually withdrawn from his mining activities; he retired from Johnson and Matthey on 31 March 1860 and died of a stroke at his home, Stoke House, Stoke Fleming, Devon, on 1 June 1866, at the age of seventy-three. He was buried in a vault under the chancel of St Peter's Church, Stoke Fleming, where a stained-glass memorial window was later placed by his widow (in this the year of his birth was given incorrectly as 1793). The business that Johnson founded was eventually to become Johnson Matthey plc, a world leader in the refining, marketing, and fabrication of precious metals and raw materials. IAN E. COTTINGTON

Sources D. McDonald, *Percival Norton Johnson* (1951) · D. McDonald, *The Johnsons of Maiden Lane* (1964) · E. Matthey, private memoirs (unpublished), Johnson Matthey plc, Cockspur Street, London

Archives V&A, silver snuff-box with platinum lid [made by Johnson in 1850 from largest platinum ingot yet produced by him] Likenesses G. J. Robertson, oils, 1829, Johnson Matthey plc, Cockspur Street, London · M. Backhouse, oils, 1880 (after G. J. Robertson), Johnson Matthey plc, Cockspur Street, London

Johnson, Ralph (*bap.* 1629, *d.* 1695), naturalist, was born at Earby near Newsham, Richmondshire, North Riding of Yorkshire, and baptized on 15 November 1629. He was one of four sons of William Johnson (1600?–1677?), husbandman. In 1652 he married Anne (1623–1695), daughter of Henry Pinkney of East Hope; they had five children, of whom the three sons died young. Johnson attended Sedbergh School, and then St John's College, Cambridge, from 1648 to 1652. From 1652 until 1656 he was master of Darlington grammar school. He was presented to the vicarage of Brignall, very near his birth place, on 6 December 1656, and ordained on 8 August 1661. He remained the resident incumbent for the rest of his life. He was styled MA in his lifetime but it is not known if he was ever given this degree.

In his younger days Johnson had an ideal botanical mentor in Walter Stonehouse, rector of Darfield in south Yorkshire. Stonehouse had helped with the production of the first British flora, Thomas Johnson's *Mercurius botanicus* (1634 and 1641). He also knew both John Tradescants, elder and younger, and many of the plants in his herbarium came from the Tradescants' famous garden in south Lambeth, Surrey.

John Ray who was a 'great friend' of Johnson's (Ray, *Synopsis*, preface), described him as 'a Person of singular skill in Zoology, especially the History of Birds, who communicated to us [at my request] his Method of Birds … his judgement concurring with ours in the divisions and characteristic notes of the Genera' (Willughby and Ray, *Ornithology*, preface). Johnson made a significant contribution to *Ornithology* by Willughby and Ray, which marks the start of scientific ornithology. Ray also described Johnson as 'a man most expert … in all branches of Natural History' (Willughby and Ray, *Piscium*, preface).

Johnson suggested to Ray that in the next edition of his *Catalogus plantarum Angliae* (1670) he should arrange the plants in natural rather than alphabetical order (Ray, *Synopsis*, preface). Ray taught Johnson scientific botany, at Brignall, and Johnson became the pioneer botanist of upper Teesdale. Johnson died on 7 May 1695 at Brignall, probably of gout; he had survived his wife by only eighteen days. He was buried two days later in the graveyard of his church, St Mary's, which is now in ruins.

F. HORSMAN

Sources 'Ralph Johnson vicar of Brignall, 1656–1695', *Teesdale Record Society*, 15 (1945), 9–32 · F. Horsman, 'Ralph Johnson's notebook', *Archives of Natural History*, 22 (1995), 147–67 · John Ray Correspondence, NHM, botany library · J. Ray, *Synopsis methodica stirpium Britannicarum* (1690) · F. Willughby and J. Ray, *The ornithology* (1678) · F. Willughby and J. Ray, *Historia piscium* (1686) · York restoration exhibit book, 1662 · J. Brownhill, ed., *List of clergymen … in the diocese of Chester, 1691* (1915) · parish register (baptism), Barningham, Yorkshire, 15 Nov 1629 · parish register (burial), Brignall, Yorkshire, St Mary's, 9 May 1695 · F. Horsman, 'Ralph Johnson', www.nhm.ac.uk/botany/cuttings/ [*Plant Cuttings*, Natural History

Museum, department of Botany on-line newsletter, 4 (July 2000), 2]

Archives Durham Cath. CL | NHM, corresp. with John Ray, Sloane herbarium, vol. 27

Wealth at death £409 7s. 6d.: will

Johnson, Richard (*fl.* 1592–1622), writer, is an obscure figure. No record has yet been found of his birth or death. J. P. Collier referred to a baptismal record dated 24 May 1573, which is chronologically plausible, but he neither located that record nor explained how he identified it as relating to the writer rather than any other Richard Johnson. Thomas Seccombe, in his 1891 *Dictionary of National Biography* article, located the unseen baptismal record in London. A Richard Johnson, son of Richard Johnson of 'litelworthe' (perhaps Lutterworth), Leicestershire, was bound prentice to Richard Hancockes, merchant taylor, in 1584 and transferred in 1585 to Philip Dye (Merchant Taylors' Company, apprentice binding books, vol. 1, fols. 23a, 41a); and a Richard Johnson was made free of the Merchant Taylors by Peter Peerson on 17 May 1593 (ibid., court minute books, vol. 2, fol. 275b). On 24 February 1618 Peter Johnson, son of Richard, citizen and merchant taylor, was bound prentice to John Emerton, tiler and bricklayer 'for seven years as he is a freeman's son and has served a year of his time' (Webb, 43). These dates would fit the writer; but his name is too common to make the identification at all safe.

Sparse personal references in Johnson's books tell what little is known of him. In 1592 he was 'a poore prentice'; by 1603 'a poore freeman' of the city of London, though he never names his company. On 22 November 1608 and 22 May 1616 he dated reprints of *The Seaven Champions of Christendome* (at the end of part 1) 'from my house at London'. He dedicated his other popular romance *Tom a Lincolne* (part 1, 1599, part 2, 1607, surviving in the sixth edition of 1631) to Simon Wortedge of 'Okenberrie' (Alconbury), Huntingdonshire, signing himself 'Your worships devoted, and Poore Country-man', R. I., and speaking of the 'great friendship' shown by Wortedge's 'renowned' father to his own parents. On 9 June 1612 he was present on the occasion of the funeral at Hatfield of Robert Cecil, earl of Salisbury, which he describes in *A Remembrance of the Honours Due … to Robert, Earl of Salisbury* (1612).

Johnson's writings fall into three groups: prose narratives; collections of ballads and jests of which he was as much compiler as author; and elegies and topical pamphlets. His claim to celebrity is based on the first and, in some measure, the second of these groups. His earliest known publication is *The Nine Worthies of London* (1592), dedicated to Sir William Webbe, lord mayor of London. The work eulogizes nine famous mayors of London in the manner of *The Mirror for Magistrates* and sets a pattern of celebration of the city and dedication to the current lord mayor that Johnson would repeat. His opening epistle claims that he was mocked by more learned writers for his literary ambitions. Will Kemp's ridicule, in the final pages of *Kemps Nine Daies Wonder* (1600), of a ballad maker whose name was evoked by the name 'Jansonius' and whose subjects include 'the red crosse knight' may be directed at Johnson.

The Seaven Champions of Christendome was published in two parts in 1596 and 1597 respectively. This vastly popular romance purports to tell the stories of the seven patron saints of England, Scotland, Wales, Ireland, France, Italy, and Spain. Like the later *Tom a Lincolne*, it is based on 'a varied stock' of narrative materials from which Johnson made 'an original and interesting synthesis of his own' (Hirsch, *Tom a Lincolne*, xix). The 1596 dedication of part 1 to Lord Thomas Howard was never reprinted, though that of part 2 to his brother, Lord William, appears in most seventeenth-century reprints. Johnson never published the further sequel promised at the end of part 2, though the third edition in 1616 advertised seven added chapters which briefly describe the deaths of the seven saintly heroes as 'by the first Author'. A third part, first published in 1686, was added later, after the Restoration, by 'W. W.' (plausibly identified by Plett as William Winstanley). The popular success that was to keep *The Seaven Champions* in print, in a wide variety of forms, abridgements, and adaptations, until 1932, may be explained by its patriotic emphasis on St George, whose adventures predominate, and by its being, as Arthur Burrell expressed it in his 1916 school edition, 'one of the few books that the uneducated as we call them have taken to their hearts'. It contains a heady mix of romance, adventure, Christian crusading high-mindedness, and misogynist, vindictive, and racially directed violence.

The two parts of *The Most Pleasant History of Tom a Lincolne, Bastard Son of King Arthur*, were entered in the Stationers' register in 1599 and 1607 respectively: the second part shows knowledge of Shakespeare's *Titus Andronicus* and *Hamlet*, both in print by 1607. Like *The Seaven Champions*, this romance was much reprinted in the seventeenth and eighteenth centuries, in both complete and abridged forms. A prose version of *Tom Thumbe* by R. I. (identified on sufficient grounds as Richard Johnson) survives in a single copy of its first part, dated 1621, though the 'First and 2. parte of Tom Thombe' are named in the Stationers' register on 13 December 1620 (Arber, *Regs. Stationers*, 4.44). Light-hearted dramatizations of *The Seaven Champions*, printed in 1638 as by John Kirke, and of *Tom a Lincolne*, subscribed by 'Morganus Evans' of Gray's Inn, which survives incomplete in manuscript, appear to date from the second decade of the seventeenth century and reveal the ease with which such romances could become butts of good-natured ridicule. Thomas Heywood has been proposed as one of the collaborating authors of both plays.

The Pleasant Conceites of Old Hobson the Merry Londoner (1607), 'Colected together by, R. IOHNSON' and dedicated to Sir Robert Stone, mercer to the queen, contains thirty-five anecdotes, mostly well known from earlier jest-books but here loosely attached to the figure of William Hobson, haberdasher, who died in 1581. The description of Hobson comes, as do three of the best jests, from Thomas Heywood's play, *If you Know not me you Know Nobody*, part 2 (1605), in which Hobson is a leading character. An enlarged edition appeared in 1610. Johnson's two successful collections of ballads, many on royal subjects, *A Crowne Garland of Golden Roses* (1612, revised 1631) and *The Golden Garland of Princely Pleasures* (1620), 'The third time imprinted, enlarged and corrected by Rich. Iohnson', doubtless contain some pieces of his own composition but they also include ballads and songs by others, among them Thomas Deloney and George Wither. *The Golden Garland* is the earliest source for ballads on Titus Andronicus and King Lear that appear to derive from knowledge of Shakespeare's plays, perhaps in performance (though both were in print long before 1620). Eight of the fourteen poems in the second part of *The Golden Garland* come from earlier printed songbooks by Richard Alison, Nicholas Breton, John Dowland, Thomas Ford, and Robert Jones.

Johnson's later pamphlets are topical and ephemeral: they are also heavily plagiaristic. *Anglorum lacrimae* (1603), his elegy on Queen Elizabeth, dedicated to Robert Lee, lord mayor, owes 130 of its 180 lines to the *Celestiall Elegies of the Goddesses and the Muses* (1598) by Thomas Rogers of Bryanston. *A Lanterne-Light for Loyall Subjects*, dedicated to Lord Thomas Howard, is a mosaic recycling of George Whetstone's *Censure of a Loyal Subject* (1587), which contains no more than three or four paragraphs of Johnson's own composition. Whetstone's subject was the Babington plot against Queen Elizabeth: Johnson's occasion the treason trial of Sir Walter Ralegh in November 1603, before a commission headed by Robert Cecil and Thomas Howard. *The Pleasant Walkes of Moore-Fieldes* (1607), which celebrates local improvements and city history, was entered in the Stationers' register on 11 June (the day after Prince Henry was made free of the Merchant Taylors' Company, an event alluded to in *A Crowne Garland*). It is dedicated to the knights and aldermen of London. Substantial sections are derived verbatim from John Stow's *Survey of London* (1598). For his last pamphlet, *Look on me London* (1613), the 'poore Freeman' of London drew heavily on George Whetstone's *A Mirrour for Magistrates of Cities and a Touchstone of the Time* (1584), extending Whetstone's address from the 'yong Gentlemen, of the Innes of Court' to all 'the yong Men of London, as well Gentlemen as others', and dedicating his book to Sir Thomas Middleton, lord mayor. He makes Whetstone's work his own mainly by drastic abbreviation and by excision of all classical allusions and particular reference. Doubtless Johnson compiled his pamphlets in haste to feed the press, but the extent of his plagiarism is remarkable, even by Jacobean standards.

Collier, echoed by Seccombe, thought it unlikely, though not impossible, that Johnson might have lived to prepare the 1659 revision of his *Crowne Garland of Golden Roses* (1612). That the revised version was in fact first printed in 1631 might make Johnson's participation likelier, but the revision is such as any publisher could have undertaken and there is no mention, as there is with supplements to two of his other works (*Seaven Champions* in 1616 and *Tom a Lincolne* in 1607), of 'the first author' as the source of new material. Johnson's name makes its final appearance in the Stationers' register in an entry, on 31

January 1622, of 'Johnsons hearb-John. by Richard Johnson' (Arber, *Regs. Stationers*, 4.64). It must be presumed that near this date he either died or abandoned the attempt to make his living, or supplement his income, by his pen.

Richard Johnson was in every sense a derivative writer: his romances synthesize a mass of traditional materials along with some more sophisticated modern texts, *The Faerie Queene* among them; he retails familiar ballads, songs, and jests under a light disguise of novelty; and his secondhand pamphlets are aimed at the prides and prejudices of a readership of London citizens and their families. His career is a paradigm of popular commercial writing for the press in his time; he achieved lasting fame only with his two prose romances, *The Seaven Champions* and *Tom a Lincolne*.   RICHARD PROUDFOOT

Sources *The new Cambridge bibliography of English literature*, [2nd edn], 1, ed. G. Watson (1974) · *DNB* · Arber, *Regs. Stationers*, vols. 3–4 · Merchant Taylors' Company, apprentice binding books, GL, vol. 1, fols. 23a, 41a · court minute books, GL, vol. 2, fol. 275b · H. W. Willkomm, *Über Richard Johnson's 'Seven champions of Christendom'* (Berlin, 1911) · C. Webb, ed., *London livery company apprenticeship registers*, 2: *Tylers' and Bricklayers' Company, 1612–1644, 1668–1800* (1996), 43 · R. Johnson, *The most pleasant history of Tom a Lincolne*, ed. R. S. M. Hirsch (1978) · R. S. M. Hirsch, 'The source of Richard Johnson's *Look on me London*', *English Language Notes*, 13 (1974–5), 107–13 · H. F. Plett, 'An Elizabethan best seller: Richard Johnson's *The seven champions of Christendom* (1596)', *Modes of narrative*, ed. R. M. Nischik and B. Korte (Würzburg, 1990), 234–51 · S. Clark, *The Elizabethan pamphleteers* (1983) · F. B. Williams, 'Richard Johnson's borrowed tears', *Studies in Philology*, 34 (1937), 186–90 · *The pleasant walkes of Moore-fieldes*, *Illustrations of early English popular literature*, ed. J. P. Collier, 2 (1864) [1607], item 11 · W. Kemp, *Nine daies wonder*, ed. G. B. Harrison (1923) · *The pleasant conceites of Old Hobson the merry Londoner* (1607), *Shakespeare jest-books*, ed. W. C. Hazlitt, 3 (1864) · H. E. Rollins, *An analytical index to the ballad-entries in the registers of the Company of Stationers of London* (1924) · G. R. Proudfoot, ed., *Tom a Lincoln* (1992), from BL Add. MS 61745 · N. C. Liebler, 'Elizabethan pulp fiction: the example of Richard Johnson', *Critical Survey*, 12/2 (2000) · *STC, 1475–1640*

Johnson, Richard (1656/7–1721), schoolmaster and grammarian, was born at Market Harborough, Leicestershire, the son of Robert Johnson. Having been educated at the grammar school there, he was admitted as a sizar at the age of eighteen at St John's College, Cambridge, on 15 September 1675. He was a fellow student of the classical scholar Richard Bentley, and both graduated BA in 1679. Although he later described himself as MA in his publications, he does not seem to have proceeded to that degree. He was second master at King's School in Canterbury from 1681, and became headmaster in 1684. He also served as the perpetual curate of Nackington, Kent, for 1684–5. Following the accession of William and Mary, he refused to take the oath of allegiance in 1689 and was dismissed from the headmastership. At some point afterwards he ran a private school in Kensington, probably until at least 1707, as a publication of his from that year describes him as a schoolmaster there.

In 1703 Johnson published *A Treatise of the Genders of Latin Nouns*, a specimen for a proposed Latin grammar intended to rival Lily's grammar, which had been the standard school grammar since the sixteenth century; the resulting grammar appeared in 1706 as *Grammatical commentaries:*

being an apparatus to a new national grammar: by way of anim-adversion upon the falsities, obscurities, redundancies, and defects of Lilly's system now in use. A lengthy preface included a justification for the continued teaching of Latin if only to prevent French from gaining pre-eminence as a universal language. Anat Biletzki, in a study of Johnson's comments on grammatical mood, described the work as 'the most detailed and copious theoretical discussion of all elements of grammar' of its period (Biletzki, 284). Proof sheets were circulated prior to publication, prompting a series of testimonials from leading schoolmasters that were printed with the volume; they also prompted two published defences of Lily by schoolmasters Edward Leeds and William Symes, to each of whom Johnson published responses. The work was reissued with a new title-page in 1718.

In 1707, upon the recommendation of the archbishop of York, John Sharpe, Johnson was appointed headmaster of the free school in Nottingham; his appointment coincided with a period of expansion for the school. In 1709 he published a fifteen-page Latin poem on the Nottingham races, *Cursus equestris Nottinghamiensis*. Over the next decade he produced two further works, both printed in the city. The first, a treatise criticizing the syntax of Lily's grammar, *Noctes Nottinghamicae* (1714), was reissued in 1718 with a dedication to William Dawes, archbishop of York, in which Johnson described the standard grammar as 'utterly incompetent … false, obscure, defective, and yet in some things superfluous' (sig. 3*2r). In 1717 Johnson issued an abusive attack in Latin on the translation of Horace by Bentley, *Aristarchus Anti-Bentleianus* (1717), which was described later in the century by the Nottingham-born biblical scholar Gilbert Wakefield as 'replete with accuracy of erudition and sprightliness of wit'. However, Johnson's venom may have implied personal problems. In June 1718, claiming that Johnson had been mentally ill for over three months and hence 'unfit to hold office', the town council appointed a successor to the headmastership. Johnson's protests led to an action of ejectment against him in which the corporation cited Festus's verdict on Saint Paul: 'Much learning hath made thee mad' (*VCH Nottinghamshire*, 2.234). Despite producing a testimonial from the very council that sought to dismiss him, Johnson agreed to resign the post in December 1719, and received £60 as compensation. Johnson committed suicide two years later, drowning himself in a local stream known as Tinker's Leen in October 1721. He was buried in St Nicholas's parish, Nottingham, on 26 October. The administration of the estate of a Richard Johnson of St Mary's parish in Nottingham was granted to a son, Jacob Johnson, on 21 July 1722.

THOMPSON COOPER, *rev.* I. GADD

Sources VCH Nottinghamshire, 2.233–4 · VCH Leicestershire, 5.149 · Venn, *Alum. Cant.* · administration, PRO, PROB 6/98, fol. 154r. · A. Biletzki, 'Richard Johnson: a case of eighteenth-century pragmatics', *Historiographia Linguistica*, 18/2–3 (1991), 281–99 · R. Johnson, *Grammatical commentaries* (1706) [repr. 1969]

Johnson, Richard (1753–1807), East India Company servant and collector of oriental art and manuscripts, was born on 16 November 1753, the third son of Alexander *Johnson MD (*bap.* 1716, *d.* 1799), lawyer, and of his wife, Mary Pellins (*b.* 1720, *d.* in or after 1800). Johnson's family had lived for at least two generations in the Netherlands and he was born and brought up at The Hague. His father held the office of agent for the estates of East Friesland and the town of Emden.

Appointed a writer on the Bengal establishment of the East India Company's service on 5 October 1769, he arrived at Calcutta on 25 September 1770. His letters home suggest that he felt himself under a strong compulsion to advance his career in India as rapidly as possible in order to make money to pay off family debts. His early service was spent in the company's central administration at Calcutta, where he was able to impress his superiors by his intelligence and capacity for business. Through his appointment in the personal office of the governor, he began a sometimes uneasy relationship with Warren Hastings. It was rumoured that he had been instrumental in negotiating the divorce that left Hastings free to marry his second wife. In addition to his official duties, Johnson ran a private agency business in partnership with Richard Croftes, his superior in the company's accountant-general's office. The firm managed the affairs of clients and specialized in arranging remittances to Britain. Johnson also looked after his younger brother Alexander, who had joined him in India, obtaining a valuable contract for him.

Johnson manoeuvred with some dexterity, even deviousness, among the bitter rivalries on the company's Bengal council. He cultivated Hastings's opponent General John Clavering and later the new commander-in-chief Sir Eyre Coote, through whom, it would seem, he obtained in 1780 the extremely lucrative appointment of deputy to the company's resident at the court of the wazir of Oudh at Lucknow. Johnson certainly took the opportunity of making money at Lucknow with both hands, but he took other opportunities as well. He was a fine linguist, reputed to have a good knowledge of Persian and Arabic as well as of Urdu, and he clearly found the culture of the court at Lucknow much to his liking. Since the downfall of the Mughal emperors at Delhi, Lucknow had become the major centre of artistic patronage in north India. Johnson himself became the patron of poets, he had a taste for Indian music, and he acquired both a large number of Sanskrit and Persian manuscripts and a most important collection of miniatures. An Indian artist's portrayal of Johnson shows him as a short, sharp-featured man.

The company residents at Lucknow were required to implement Warren Hastings's policies of extracting resources from the wazir to settle his debts to the company. This involved them in highly contentious measures such as the attempted confiscation of some of the assets of the wazir's mother and grandmother, the begums of Oudh. Johnson was notably ruthless in pursuing such measures, later attracting the unfavourable notice of Edmund Burke, who called him 'the outrageous Mr Johnson' (*Correspondence*, 8.202). Although Johnson confidently expected to succeed to the post of resident, he had, however, lost the governor's confidence and in 1782 he was recalled, ostensibly for preventing the transfer from Oudh of a sum of money promised personally to Hastings by the wazir.

Johnson's fortune evidently suffered severely from his recall. He told his mother that although he was commonly thought to be worth £150,000, he had 'dissipated in folly the best part of what fortune threw within my reach' and in a series of penitential letters blamed himself for 'avarice, ambition and licentiousness' as well as 'vanity and self-conceit' (letters of 16 Nov 1783 and 30 Aug 1784, JRL, Eng. MS 191, nos. 27 and 34). His problems were exacerbated by the failure of the business of Croftes and Johnson, which was dissolved in 1785, leaving Johnson with heavy obligations when Croftes died insolvent in the following year.

Johnson was, however, able to restore his reputation if not his fortune. With assurances of goodwill from Hastings, he was appointed to the prestigious but not very lucrative residency with the nizam of Hyderabad in 1784. There at least he could add Deccani paintings to his collection. Recalled from Hyderabad in 1785, he again served in the company's revenue administration at Calcutta and launched proposals for a public bank. He was highly regarded by discriminating men. William Jones learned 'Indian Mythology' from him (Cannon, 316) and called him 'one of the most distinguished of the Company's servants' (Jones, 2.854). Lord Cornwallis's government commended him as a 'very able, Zealous and deserving Servant of the Company' (*Fort William–India House Correspondence*, 322).

In 1788 Johnson sent ahead of him to Britain part of what he called his 'live lumber', two girls, presumably the daughters of an Indian mother, whom he wished to be educated with the 'moderate expectations' that would fit them for 'decent husbands'. A boy and a girl were to follow and there were two little girls still too young to travel (letter to his mother, 9 Nov 1788, JRL, Eng. MS 191, no. 43). Forced to leave India by illness, Johnson himself took his passage in February 1790.

Johnson settled in London. He married Sophia, daughter of John *Courtenay MP, on 1 March 1792. They had four daughters and a son. To supplement his limited resources, Johnson hoped for a new career in public life, entering parliament in 1791 as member for Milborne Port; he retained his seat until 1794. In 1792, however, he turned again to banking with various partners, including Nathaniel Middleton, the resident to whom he had acted as deputy at Lucknow. Warren Hastings and his wife were among the clients of the business situated at Stratford Place, off Oxford Street. Johnson was 'the president and acting manager' until 1803, when he was deposed (note, JRL, Eng. MS 179a, fol. 46). By that time he was in serious financial difficulties. He had to leave his house, sell his collection of books and paintings, and prepare to go back to India. He died insolvent at Brighton on 19 August 1807.

P. J. MARSHALL

Sources T. Falk and M. Archer, *Indian miniatures in the India Office Library* (1981), 14–29 · JRL, MSS Eng. 177–97 · Johnson calendars, SOAS, MSS 12235 ff. · HoP, *Commons, 1790–1820*, 4.311–12 · O. Schutte, ed., *Repertorium der buitenlandse vertegenwoordigers residerende in Nederland, 1584–1810* (The Hague, 1983), 283–4 · BL, Warren Hastings MSS, Add. MSS 29154, 29155 · BL OIOC, Home misc., 435 · K. K. Datta and others, eds., *Fort William–India House correspondence*, 11 (1959) · *The letters of Sir William Jones*, ed. G. Cannon, 2 vols. (1970) · *The works of Edmund Burke*, 8 vols. (1854–89), vol. 8 · memorandum relative to the services of Mr Richard Johnson, BL OIOC, O/6/1, 87–92 · S. Banerjee, *Calcutta, 200 years: a Tolleygunge Club perspective*, ed. N. K. Nayak (1981) · H. E. Busteed, *Echoes from old Calcutta*, 4th edn (1908) · G. Cannon, 'British orientalists' cooperation: a new letter from Sir William Jones', *Bulletin of the School of Oriental and African Studies*, 55 (1992), 316–18

Archives BL OIOC, corresp. relating to India, Home misc. series 435 · JRL, corresp. and papers relating to India · SOAS, calendars, MSS 12235ff. | BL, corresp. with Warren Hastings, Add. MSS 29144–29193

Likenesses portrait, BL, MS Or 6633, fol. 680

Wealth at death evidently insolvent: HoP, *Commons, 1790–1820*

Johnson, Richard (*bap.* 1755, *d.* 1827), Church of England clergyman and colonial chaplain, was the son of John Johnson of Welton, Yorkshire, where he was baptized in March 1755. He was educated at the Kingston upon Hull grammar school and engaged in farming and teaching until he went up to Magdalene College, Cambridge, in January 1780. He gained his BA there in 1784. Made deacon by the bishop of Winchester on 21 December 1783, he was ordained priest by the bishop of Oxford on 31 October 1784. From 1784 to 1785 Johnson was curate of Bere, Hampshire. On 24 October 1786 he was appointed as 'chaplain to the settlement' at New South Wales. His appointment was influenced by the Eclectic Society, of which John Newton and William Wilberforce were members.

An evangelical of great piety and a man of gentle character and inflexible integrity, Johnson was charged with a mission beyond the powers of most, because he was to be custodian of the morals of the infant settlement but he had also to conform to the pragmatism of Arthur Phillip, the first governor of New South Wales. Phillip's yardstick was survival. To the degree that religion and morality assisted that end he tolerated the role of Johnson.

Accompanied by his wife, whom he had married shortly before sailing, Johnson arrived with the first fleet and celebrated the first Anglican service under 'a great tree' at Sydney Cove on 3 February 1788. He took as his text 'What shall I render unto the Lord for all His benefits toward me' (Psalm 116:12), which probably aroused a chill response in his convict hearers.

Johnson threw himself unsparingly into his daily tasks, whether celebrating divine service, catechizing, marrying, baptizing, burying, or attending frequent executions. To and fro, from Sydney to Parramatta he devoted himself to the spiritual and physical welfare of the convicts. He went down into the foetid holds of the 'sick ships' of the Second Fleet, where hundreds lay dying or ill.

Francis Grose, the successor to Phillip, regarded Johnson as 'one of the people called Methodists … a very troublesome, discontented character' (Cable, 2.18) and obstructed his work in all possible ways. Grose was unable to prevent him erecting a pleasing but modest church in

1793, which Johnson paid for in rum. The church was burnt down in 1798. Johnson was the first to extend his apostolate to the Aboriginal people: he took an Aborigine into his own home and gave the first of his two children, a daughter born in 1790, the Aboriginal name Milbah. A son was born in 1792. His ecumenical spirit was such that when two Spanish vessels visited Sydney in 1793 he 'outdid himself in his sociable gestures, particularly toward our chaplain fathers approaching them with a kindness and humility and a simplicity that was truly evangelical' (*The Spanish at Port Jackson*, 30–32). His main relief was farming, which he engaged in with considerable proficiency.

Johnson returned to Britain in 1800, leaving 'as a mere skeleton', said his successor Samuel Marsden. He served firstly as a curate in Essex and then as rector of the combined parishes of St Antholin and St John the Baptist in London. He was also the perpetual curate of Ingham, Norfolk, from 1817. His *An Address to the Inhabitants of the Colonies Established at New South Wales and Norfolk Island*, published in London in 1794, was an early item of Australian literature. He died in London on 13 March 1827, and was survived by his wife.   JOHN N. MOLONY, *rev.*

Sources F. M. Bladen, ed., *Historical records of New South Wales*, 1–4 (1892–6) [repr. (1978–9)] · [F. Watson], ed., *Historical records of Australia*, 1st ser., 1–5 (1914–15) · J. Bonwick, *Australia's first preacher* (1898) · W. H. Rainey, *The real Richard Johnson* (1947) · G. Mackaness, ed., *Some letters of Rev. Richard Johnson* (1954) · K. J. Cable, 'Johnson, Richard', *AusDB* [and corrigenda (1969)], vol. 2 · *The Spanish at Port Jackson*, Australian Documentary Facsimile Society (1967) · Venn, *Alum. Cant.* · *GM*, 1st ser., 97/1 (1827), 473

Archives LPL, diaries, letters, and papers

Johnson, Robert (*d.* after 1549), priest and composer, was born in Duns, Berwickshire. According to an annotation in the partbooks that Thomas Wode, vicar of St Andrews, copied (*c.*1562–92), Johnson fled to England after being 'deletit', that is, delated, or summoned before an ecclesiastical court, on charges of heresy. During the reign of Henry VIII protestant heretics were no safer in England than in Scotland, so Johnson's flight is unlikely to predate 1547. Wode also states that 'Thomas hutsons fayther now wyth the king kend him' (BL, Add. MS 33933). The Hudson family of musicians, who entered service at the Scottish court in 1565, was originally from York, and it is conceivable that Johnson passed through the city on his way south. His song 'Ty the Mare Tomboy' may date from this period, for it survives only as a single part in Harley MS 7578 (BL), a manuscript with close links to York. There may be some truth in John Baldwin's assertion that Johnson was a minor canon of St George's Chapel, Windsor, since Baldwin was himself a singing-man there. Although no records confirm his presence at Windsor, Johnson could have held a position there at any time between 1548 and 1553, or between 1559 and 1562, without leaving a trace in the surviving archives. His domicile in London or its vicinity by the late 1540s is also suggested by the inclusion of a number of his anthems in John Day's *Certaine Notes* (1565), a retrospective collection of vernacular church music by composers active in and around the capital during Edward

VI's reign. It is remotely possible that he may be identified with the Robert Johnson who, according to returns generated by the 1548 chantries legislation, was rector of the parish church of St Margaret Moyses, London. No will has been traced, and the date of his death is speculative. A tradition that Johnson was once chaplain to Anne Boleyn cannot be substantiated, and probably stems from the fact that his 'Defiled is my name' is a setting of the 'complaint' she allegedly wrote during her imprisonment in the Tower.

Johnson's output comprises music for both the Latin and vernacular rites, as well as songs and instrumental pieces. His settings of Marian texts, such as the large-scale votive antiphon *Ave Dei patris filia*, presumably predate his conversion to the reformed faith. Wode's marginalia provide more precise chronological information about Johnson's *Domine, in virtute tua* and *Deus misereatur nostri*. Both were composed in England, the latter 'ten or xii yeiris before reformation', and the former 'in tyme of papistry ix or x yeiris before reformation' (Edinburgh University Library, MS La.III.483). This would appear to identify them as examples of devotional pieces to Latin texts composed for domestic use during the reign of Edward VI. Both settings are examples of the psalm-motet, a continental genre that reached its first flowering during the early decades of the sixteenth century in the works of Josquin Desprez and his generation. This type of composition consisted of the polyphonic treatment of a complete or nearly complete Vulgate psalm (or a formal section of the extended Psalm 118), and in Britain (where it flourished *c.*1540–80) Johnson was one of its earliest exponents. His influence can be detected in the psalms of later composers such as Sheppard and White, particularly in his structural procedures, some of which derive from continental models.

Johnson was also one of the first composers to write for the English liturgy of the 1549 Book of Common Prayer. His morning, communion, and evening service (consisting of Te Deum, Jubilate, Benedictus, creed, Magnificat, and Nunc dimittis) is in the severe chordal style advocated by certain leading figures of the Edwardian Reformation, as is the anthem 'O eternal God'; on the other hand, his setting of 'I give you a new commandment' is somewhat more imitative in character. Owing to a shortage of music for the new protestant services, existing Latin pieces were sometimes adapted to English words: thus Johnson's 'O Lord with all my heart' and 'Relieve us, O Lord' are *contrafacta* of *Benedicam domino* and *Deus misereatur* respectively. Johnson's instrumental consorts include a work entitled 'A Knell'—essentially a set of variations on a short descending bell-like scale—and an In nomine which, like some of his vocal settings, survives in both four- and five-part versions.   DAVID MATEER

Sources K. Elliott and H. M. Shire, eds., *Music of Scotland, 1500–1700*, 3rd edn, Musica Britannica, 15 (1975) · K. Elliott, 'Robert Johnson (i)', *New Grove* · K. Elliott, 'Music in Scotland, 1500–1700', PhD diss., U. Cam., 1960 · P. Le Huray, *Music and the Reformation in England, 1549–1660* (1967); repr. with corrections (1978) · J. Caldwell, *From the beginnings to c.1715* (1991), vol. 1 of *The Oxford history of English music* · J. Kerman, 'The Elizabethan motet: a study of texts for music', *Studies in the Renaissance*, 9 (1962), 273–308 · F. L. Harrison, *Music in medieval Britain*, 4th edn (Buren, Netherlands, 1980) · H. G. Farmer, *A history of music in Scotland* (1947) · F. Kisby, 'British Library, Harley MS 7578: its codicological characteristics and musical content', MMus diss., King's Lond., 1991 · C. J. Kitching, ed., *London and Middlesex chantry certificate, 1548*, London RS, 16 (1980) · H. S. P. Hutchison, 'The St Andrews psalter: transcription and critical study of Thomas Wode's psalter', DMus diss., U. Edin., 1957

Archives BL, Thomas Wode's part-books, Add. MS 33933 · TCD, Thomas Wode's part-books, MS F.5.13 · U. Edin., Thomas Wode's part-books, MS La.III.483 · U. Edin., Thomas Wode's part-books, MSS Dk.5.14–15 [duplicates]

Johnson, Robert (*d.* 1559), religious controversialist, was educated at Cambridge University where he became a bachelor of civil law in 1531. He was appointed canon of Rochester by the king in its foundation charter of 1541, but probably resigned this benefice upon being made canon of Worcester on 10 July 1544. This appointment followed the death of Thomas Baggard, whom he also succeeded as chancellor of the diocese. He had the prebend of Putston Major in Hereford Cathedral on 9 September 1551, and was the same year incorporated BCL at Oxford. He was made rector of Clun in Shropshire on 10 April 1553, then prebendary of Stillington in York Minster on 22 February 1556. In July 1558 he was collated to the rectory of Bolton Percy in Yorkshire and on 7 September he was made prebendary of Norwell Overhall in the collegiate church of St Mary, Southwell.

Johnson is known chiefly for participating in a major controversy with John Hooper, bishop of Gloucester. In 1552 Johnson, with another canon of Worcester named Henry Joliffe, refused to subscribe to the articles compiled by Bishop Hooper for the diocese of Worcester. These nineteen articles were based on an early draft of what were to become the forty-two articles, and had been specially devised by Hooper as a test for the conservative canons of Worcester. The refusal led to a public disputation. After this encounter between Joliffe and Johnson on the one hand, and Hooper on the other, the written texts of both parties were sent to Bishop Gardiner, then imprisoned for his opposition to Edwardian religious policies. He wrote his own answer to Hooper, according to Joliffe, with incredible diligence. The incident meanwhile prompted Hooper to write an indignant letter to William Cecil, also enclosing copies of the disputation, and lamenting 'Ah! Mr Secretarye, that there were goodd men in the Cathedral churches!' (Strype, 2.873). In 1559 the combined texts of the 'protestatio' by Johnson and Joliffe, the 'confutatio' by Hooper, and the additional 'confutatio' by Gardiner, were all published together in Antwerp by Joliffe in a single work, entitled *Responsio venerabilium sacerdotum, Henrici Joliffi et Roberti Jonson, sub protestatione facta, ad illos articulos Joannis Hoperi* (1564). It was dedicated to Philip II, and a preface by Joliffe explained the events of 1552. The major part of the work is, however, by Gardiner, including discussions of the sacrament, purgatory, justification, the invocation of saints, and clerical celibacy. Johnson was dead before the publication of this work; he died in 1559.   L. E. C. Wooding

Sources *Fasti Angl., 1541–1857*, [Canterbury], 63 · *Fasti Angl., 1541–1857*, [York], 54 · *Fasti Angl., 1541–1857*, [Ely], 115 · BL, Lansdowne MS 980, fol. 308r–v · J. Strype, *Memorials of the most reverend father in God Thomas Cranmer*, new edn, 2 vols. (1812), vol. 2, pp. 873–4 · Cooper, *Ath. Cantab.*, 1.203 · A. F. Allison and D. M. Rogers, eds., *The contemporary printed literature of the English Counter-Reformation between 1558 and 1640*, 1 (1989), 95 · L. Voet, ed., *The Plantin Press (1555–1589): a bibliography of the works printed and published by Christopher Plantin at Antwerp and Leiden*, 6 vols. (Amsterdam, 1980–83); vol. 3, no. 1472 · *Miscellaneous writings and letters of Thomas Cranmer*, ed. J. E. Cox, Parker Society, [18] (1846), 492 · J. A. Muller, *Stephen Gardiner and the Tudor reaction* (1926), 314–15 · D. MacCulloch, *Thomas Cranmer: a life* (1996), 504 · D. MacCulloch, *Tudor church militant: Edward VI and the protestant Reformation* (1999), 118–19, 244 · H. Joliffe, *Responsio venerabilium sacerdotum, Henrici Joliffi et Roberti Jonson, sub protestatione facta, ad illos articulos Joannis Hoperi* (1564)

Johnson, Robert (*d.* 1574), Church of England clergyman, is not always easy to distinguish from Robert Johnson (1540/41–1625), founder of Oakham and Uppingham schools, who in spite of an impressive portfolio of livings held in plurality shared the puritan credentials of this Robert Johnson. The latter is not known to have had any university career, and at his trial in February 1574 he was described as 'unlearned'. All the little that is known of Johnson relates to the last two years of his life. In 1572 he was one of those who visited in prison the authors of the *Admonition to the Parliament*, John Field and Thomas Wilcox, when he was identified as 'Mr Johnson dwelling in Middlesex near to Mr Gresham' (Petyt MS 538/47, fol. 481). He seems to have been a preacher at St Clement Danes when in 1573 he was put on trial at Middlesex assizes for baptizing without using the sign of the cross and marrying without the ring. On 21 December 1573 Wilcox reported to Anthony Gilby that Johnson was 'laid in the Gatehouse at Westminster' and 'others with him' (CUL, MS Mm.1.43, p. 441).

Several documents relating to what followed were printed in 1593 in *A Parte of a Register*. These may (or may not) compound the problem of identity, since they are given the running headline: 'The articles, letters, and examina. of Mai. Ro. Jonson, of late Preacher at Northampton'. Moreover, the first of these documents consists of Johnson's answer to articles objected against him by the bishop of Lincoln, containing references to 'us in Saint Martines' (*A Parte of a Register*, 95) and to an alleged threat of the bishop to come to Leicester to preach against him. This may concern the other Robert Johnson, although Northampton is not in the diocese of Lincoln, and neither Johnson is known to have been beneficed at St Martin's Leicester.

A Parte of a Register prints Johnson's own account of his trial in Westminster Hall, which he says took place seven weeks after his imprisonment, on 20 February 1574. Here may be more confusion, since the trial is said to have been conducted before the ecclesiastical commissioners, yet a jury is also mentioned as being empanelled and charged. Johnson was again indicted for neglect of the sign of the cross in baptism and the ring in marriage, but most time was spent on a third, almost technical, offence: failure to repeat the words of consecration when fresh supplies of wine were called for at communion. Johnson was a dextrous barrack-room lawyer, and both Bishop Edwin Sandys of London—whom Johnson accused of being 'the chief of my trouble' (*A Parte of a Register*, 118)—and the lord chief justice remarked on his stubborn and arrogant nature. Johnson was sentenced to a year's imprisonment, but died in the Westminster Gatehouse no later than April 1574.

Johnson wrote prison letters to Sandys—'superintendent of popish corruptions in the diocese of London' (*A Parte of a Register*, 101)—and Gabriel Goodman, dean of Westminster, in which he exercised a sharply satirical tongue. Commenting on Goodman's Lenten and Easter sermons as essentially popish, he asked 'as for Schism, who is a greater schismatic than you? … And as for Puritanism, who is a greater Puritan than you?' (ibid., 115). Johnson's pointed wit may support the unprovable theory that he was the father of 'Ben Jonson of Westminster' [*see* Jonson, Benjamin (1572–1637)], who is known to have been the son of a minister, born posthumously and quite possibly in 1574.   PATRICK COLLINSON

Sources *A parte of a register* [1593] · A. Peel, ed., *The seconde parte of a register*, 1 (1915), 124 · Inner Temple Library, London, Petyt MS 538/47, fol. 481 · CUL, MS Mm.1.43, p. 441 · P. Collinson, 'Ben Jonson's *Bartholomew Fair*: the theatre constructs puritanism', *The theatrical city: culture, theatre and politics in London, 1576–1649*, ed. D. L. Smith, R. Strier, and D. Bevington (1995), 157–69

Johnson, Robert (1540/41–1625), Church of England clergyman and school founder, was second and youngest son of Maurice Johnson, dyer, of Stamford and Jane, daughter of Henry Lacy. Johnson senior and Lacy were among the town's leading citizens, both several times serving as alderman (chief magistrate) and MP. In the 1523 parliament Maurice Johnson's fellow burgess was David Cecil, grandfather of Sir William. These associations with the local merchant oligarchy and the larger world of court and government gave support to Robert Johnson's career as a radical preacher and educationist. Maurice Johnson died in 1551 and Robert, who by the custom of borough English (ultimogeniture) inherited his father's town property, was brought up by an uncle, Robert Smith of Stanground. He was sent to the King's School, Peterborough, and thence to Clare College, Cambridge, where he matriculated sizar on 18 March 1558. He migrated to Trinity College, where he was admitted junior fellow on 10 October 1563 and senior on 3 May 1564. He graduated BA in 1560/61, MA in 1564, and DTh in 1570. He had also studied in Paris and elsewhere in France, having (according to Johnson's son) received the queen's licence to be absent three years for this purpose.

On 27 June 1568 Johnson was ordained deacon at Peterborough, receiving the priesthood from Bishop Jewel of Salisbury, acting for the bishop of London, on 23 December following. In 1569 he preached before the University of Cambridge, and was appointed chaplain to the lord keeper, Sir Nicholas Bacon. This key position involved examining candidates for livings in the lord keeper's extensive patronage and offered opportunity for his own advancement. From Bacon's house at Gorhambury, Hertfordshire, Johnson participated in the clergy 'exercise' organized by Archdeacon David Kempe of St Albans, and it was at Johnson's suggestion that these meetings were opened to the laity in 1572.

Johnson had meanwhile (23 June 1569) been nominated by the lord keeper to a canonry at Rochester, and in February 1570 to another at Norwich, where he was installed on 26 July. On 27 June 1571 he was named an original fellow of Jesus College, Oxford. Some time between July 1571 and September 1573 he acquired a canonry of Peterborough (vacated by September 1582). His association with various 'exercises' or 'prophesyings' prompted investigation of his opinions. On 4 July 1571 he was summoned before Archbishop Parker and two other bishops at Lambeth. On his refusal to sign articles in support of the prayer book he was suspended from ministry; but on 14 August, writing from Gorhambury, he submitted with only minor reservations, promising in future to observe the prescribed liturgy and the articles of religion. He offered to resign his Norwich stall, though this was not vacated until 1575. He was further advanced, on 25 July 1572, to a canonry of Windsor, which he retained for life (a record fifty-three-year tenure in St George's Chapel). On 17 December he was presented by the lord keeper, probably at the instance of Sir Walter Mildmay, to the rectory of North Luffenham, Rutland, to which he was instituted on 14 April 1574 and where he thereafter mainly lived. On 28 March 1575, in the church of St Magnus the Martyr, London, he married Susanna Davers, who died within a year. On 20 June 1576, in the Huguenot church in London, he married Mary Herd (d. 1598), who bore him his only child, Abraham, in 1577. He was occasionally resident at his other benefices; at Rochester he was elected subdean on 25 November 1579, and his Oxford fellowship intermittently received his attention. But his simultaneous occupation of four canonries drew adverse comment from both wings of the church; Parker objected to his 'cocking abroad … against statute and his oath' (canonries within the new foundations were not supposed to be held in plurality), while Grindal thought it offensive that Johnson and others took church livings 'and yet affirm it to be no church' (Bruce and Perowne, 450; Nicholson, 348).

As a puritan Johnson would have regarded cathedrals and their services as ridiculous, and he doubtless had no scruples about redirecting their revenues to purposes he considered more edifying. But he preferred to remain within the system while bending it as much as he could. Well connected as he was, he was politically acute enough to keep his nonconformity non-political. Bishop Parkhurst of Norwich licensed him to study the *Admonition to Parliament* or Cartwright's *Replye* to Whitgift's response; in May 1573 Johnson and others were brought before the privy council for disseminating views expressed in these works, but although Parker had wanted other matters discussed, the council did not pursue the investigation.

Johnson continued to promote his brand of religion in

the east midlands, where in 1576 he was delated for non-conformity. In June 1580 he was the leading figure in a controversial fast at Stamford; following an earthquake Bishop Cooper of Lincoln had given conditional approval for a public act of penitence, but Johnson broke the arrangements by swamping the event with preachers of his own persuasion brought in from the diocese of Peterborough. Johnson incurred Burghley's censure, and the Catholic polemicist Robert Persons seized on the chance to castigate the puritans for disaffection to public authority. At Rochester in 1587 Johnson was reported for still refusing to wear the surplice. He resigned (or was perhaps deprived of) his canonry there on 21 November, but was reappointed on 22 November 1588, with a grant of the next vacant stall. Also in November 1587 he was presented by his Rutland churchwardens for preaching when he had been suspended by the bishop. In 1589 he engaged the semi-separatist Giles Wiggington, possibly a writer of the Marprelate tracts, to preach in his church, and in 1590 Johnson and other local clergy were in trouble for permitting unlicensed preaching at Oakham. Johnson adopted an irregular practice of celebrating communion after the manner of an ordinary meal. Although according to his son's pious recollection he was a careful and regular preacher, he was repeatedly accused of neglecting to repair his chancel and its windows. No doubt the friendship of William Cecil, Lord Burghley, kept Johnson out of trouble. Indeed, despite his maverick career he was on 19 April 1591 collated to the archdeaconry of Leicester, the duties of which he appears to have performed in person. About this time he petitioned the queen for a grant of £50 in recompense for his foundations; Burghley noted that his benefactions had been 'rare in this age' (*Salisbury MSS*, 4.107), and the queen consented. On 29 June 1591 Johnson was licensed to be absent from his canonries. At Windsor this was confirmed by chapter order of 19 January 1593, allowing him his stipend of £51 1s. 10d. despite non-residence; but this was restricted to five years, and an extension was refused in 1598. On 23 March 1593 he was granted arms. Early in 1598 his second wife died; she was buried at North Luffenham on 20 February. On 14 May 1599 Johnson took as his third wife Margaret Wheeler, *née* Lilley; she died in 1616, being buried at North Luffenham on 25 November.

Johnson's enduring achievement was in founding the schools at Oakham and Uppingham, the two towns of Rutland. For these he provided land and erected buildings in 1584. Each foundation originally also included a hospital for twenty-four paupers. Although the schools may well have functioned as soon as the buildings were completed, it was not until 14 October 1587 that letters patent were issued authorizing the foundation and endowment. At Oakham, Johnson's school absorbed an earlier one maintained by the dean and chapter of Westminster, but neither this, nor the uncertain extent to which Johnson augmented his personal benefaction with funds badgered from others, need detract from the credit due to him as originator and accomplisher of the project. Johnson also refounded William Dalby's hospital at Oakham in 1597.

On 7 June 1625 he drew up statutes for the school and hospital foundations.

In his latter years Johnson continued to add to his family land holdings, from which his various foundations were funded. He died on 23 July 1625 and was buried next day at North Luffenham, where a memorial details his liberality. In his will he further provided for scholarships at St John's, Sidney Sussex, Clare, and Emmanuel colleges in Cambridge for boys from his schools. He made many other charitable bequests from a personal estate reckoned at £20,000. But he effectively disinherited his son, Abraham, who himself became a patron of radical preaching and in 1637 compiled an account of his father's life and his own.

C. S. KNIGHTON

Sources C. R. Bingham, *Our founder: some account of Archdeacon Johnson* (1884) • A. Hawley, ed., *A translation of a graunte from hir Matie to Robert Johnson* (1929) • B. Matthews, *By God's grace …: a history of Uppingham School* (1984), 1–15 • J. L. Barber, *The story of Oakham School* (1983), 18–39 • VCH Rutland, 1.148–9, 162, 260–67; 2.7, 25, 26, 42, 104, 196, 199, 202, 203 • CPR, 1569–72, 166, 450; 1585–7 (draft), 158 • *Correspondence of Matthew Parker*, ed. J. Bruce and T. T. Perowne, Parker Society, 42 (1853), 450 • W. Nicholson, ed., *The remains of Edmund Grindal*, Parker Society, 9 (1843), 348 • *Fasti Angl., 1541–1857, [Canterbury]*, 64 • *Fasti Angl., 1541–1857, [Ely]*, 59 • *Fasti Angl., 1541–1857, [Bristol]*, 134 • HoP, *Commons, 1509–58*, 2.448–9 • P. Collinson, *The Elizabethan puritan movement* (1967), 148, 171–2 • R. Tittler, *Nicholas Bacon: the making of a Tudor statesman* (1976), 61, 158, 169–70 • W. J. Sheils, *The puritans in the diocese of Peterborough, 1558–1610*, Northamptonshire RS, 30 (1979), 3, 34, 38–9, 45–6, 62, 99 • Fuller, *Worthies* (1811), 2.23–4 • *The letter book of John Parkhurst, bishop of Norwich*, ed. R. A. Houlbrooke, Norfolk RS, 43 (1974–5), 41, 60 • C. S. Knighton, 'The reformed chapter, 1540–1660', *Faith and fabric: a history of Rochester Cathedral, 604–1994* (1996), 63–4, 70, 72 • S. L. Ollard, *Fasti Wyndesorienses: the deans and canons of Windsor* (privately printed, Windsor, 1950), 54 • GL, MS 9535/1, fol. 140v • S. Bond, ed., *The chapter acts of the dean and canons of Windsor: 1430, 1523–1672* (1966), 23–4, 32 • B. Matthews, 'Archdeacon Robert Johnson: puritan divine', *Rutland Record*, 2 (1981), 53–7 • MS of Abraham Johnson, 1637, Uppingham School Archives • BL, Lansdowne MS 443, fols. 176r, 207r • S. E. Lehmberg, 'Archbishop Grindal and the prophesyings', *Historical Magazine of the Protestant Episcopal Church*, 34 (1965), 87–145, esp. 101 • *Calendar of the manuscripts of the most hon. the marquis of Salisbury*, 4, HMC, 9 (1892)

Wealth at death household goods £5900; incl. £522 16s. 2d. cash: will, PRO, PROB 11/145, fols. 489–489v • £20,000—incl. £1000 p.a.: Bingham, *Our founder*, 15

Johnson, Robert (*c*.1583–1633), composer and lutenist, was probably born in the parish of St Botolph, Aldgate, London, to John Johnson (*d*. 1594), lutenist to Queen Elizabeth, and his wife, Alice (*née* Skelton), who were married on 3 February 1575 at St Margaret's, Westminster. From 29 March 1596 until 1603 Johnson was indentured to Sir George Carey, lord chamberlain (Berkeley Castle, select charter 822). At midsummer 1604 he was appointed as lutenist to James I at 20d. a day, with £16 2s. 8d. a year for livery, and he held the post—formerly occupied by his father—until his death, his name occurring annually in the Audit Office declared accounts up to 1633. In the years 1610 to 1612 he enjoyed a second appointment among the musicians to Prince Henry, with a salary of £40 a year. Henry died in 1612, but the position was revived for Johnson during the years 1617–25 as musician to Prince Charles. This second royal appointment was transferred, after 1625 (when Charles became king), to the new group called the 'lutes, viols and voices' and was also held by Johnson until his death.

Johnson was included along with John Daniel among the musicians who accompanied the earl of Hertford's embassy to Albert, archduke of Austria, in 1605; he was paid arrears for three years in 1607, indicating that he was abroad for this period. In 1620 he was among those musicians invited to provide music for the proposed amphitheatre in London, a clear mark of distinction. When Thomas Lupo died towards the end of 1627, Johnson petitioned for his place as composer for the 'lutes and voices' but was unsuccessful, the post going to Theophilus Lupo. Johnson had responsibilities for distributing money for resources among the king's lutes, and was regularly given payments (normally £20 p.a.) for strings from 1609. On 5 June 1611 £10 was paid to him for a lute; and from 1617 Johnson had general responsibility for maintaining Charles's lutes, a job that seems to have been transferred to John Coggeshall in 1629. Johnson played in the consort of lutes that was maintained at the Jacobean court. In this he may have well played the bass lute, as he is mentioned in one account for 10 January 1611 as 'musicon for the base Lute' (Ashbee, 4.87). Johnson was a most successful musician, and among Jacobean lutenists only Daniel Batcheler, as a groom to Queen Anne, received better payment, though Johnson's success was far more conspicuous.

The lord chamberlain, Sir George Carey, was both Johnson's patron and patron of the King's Men, who performed masques and plays at the Globe and Blackfriars theatres. Probably through this connection Johnson began to be associated with the theatre from 1607 onwards. The compositions for which he is best known are the many songs he wrote for theatre productions, including Shakespeare's *Cymbeline* (c.1609), *A Winter's Tale* (c.1611), and *The Tempest* (1611), Middleton's *The Witch* (1609), Webster's *The Duchess of Malfi* (c.1613), Jonson's *The Gypsies Metamorphosed* (1621), and five plays by Beaumont and Fletcher, *The Captain* (c.1612), *Valentinian* (c.1614), *The Mad Lover* (c.1616), *The Chances* (c.1617), and *The Lover's Progress* (1623).

Johnson was closely connected with Ben Jonson and others in the composition, arrangement, and performance of the music for a number of court masques. The accounts for Ben Jonson's *Oberon* (1611) record a payment of £20 made to Johnson for composing dances which were then set for violins by Thomas Lupo, and a further £40 for '20 lutes p[ro]vided ... for the Princes Dance' (Ashbee, 4.33). Accounts for *Love Freed from Ignorance and Folly* (1611) included £5 for songs by Alfonso Ferrabosco (d. 1628) set to the lutes by Johnson. Among other notable works in which he collaborated were George Chapman's *Masque of the Middle Temple and Lincoln's Inn* (1612–13) and Thomas Campion's *Lord's Masque* (1613).

Johnson's songs, which are early examples of the declamatory English ayre, exhibit a style probably prompted by dramatic context and by influences from Italian monody. They are historically important as the earliest settings for some of the most celebrated Jacobean play songs. They are characterful miniatures that combine the tunefulness of the English ayre with the freedom and drama of the new continuo song. Source evidence suggests that his surviving lute music, some twenty pieces from over seventeen different sources, with several unattributed but likely additions, was written during the period 1600–15, although the masque pieces are probably arrangements and may not have been made by Johnson. Johnson was the last of the English lute composers to flourish before the adoption of the new tunings in England during the 1630s. In 1676 Thomas Mace in his *Musick's Monument* paired Johnson and Dowland as the most remarkable of the old school.

Johnson's will was proved on 28 November 1633 (PRO, PROB 11/164, quire 97). It indicates that he had a wife, Anne, but no surviving children, and lived in Acton, where he had lands and tenements.

MATTHEW SPRING

Sources A. Ashbee, ed., *Records of English court music*, 9 vols. (1986–96) · Berkeley Castle, Gloucestershire, select charter 822 · will, PRO, PROB 11/164, sig. 97 · M. Spring, *The lute in Britain: a history of the instrument and its music* (2000) · P. Holman, 'New sources of lute music by Robert Johnson', *Lute Society Journal*, 20 (1978), 43–52 · P. Walls, *Music in the English courtly masque, 1604–1640* (1996) · J. P. Cutts, 'Robert Johnson: king's musician in his majesty's public entertainment', *Music and Letters*, 36 (1955), 110–25 · J. P. Cutts, 'Robert Johnson and the court masque', *Music and Letters*, 41 (1960), 111–26 · B. Jeffrey, 'The lute music of Robert Johnson', *Early Music*, 2 (1974), 105–9 · J. P. Cutts, *La musique de scène de la troupe de Shakespeare* (Paris, 1959) · A. Ashbee and D. Lasocki, eds., *A biographical dictionary of English court musicians, 1485–1714*, 2 vols. (1998) · New Grove

Archives Berkeley Castle, select charter 822 · Bodl. Oxf., MS Tanner 89

Wealth at death lands and tenements in Acton and Ealing to wife, Anne; 20s. to Mrs Elizabeth Hynd, Mrs Jane Levermore, and Thomas Bell; 20s. to poor of Acton; 40s. to Roger Cox; rest of estate to wife, Anne: will, PRO, PROB 11/164, sig. 97

Johnson, Robert (1676?–1735), colonial governor, was born in England, the eldest child of Sir Nathaniel Johnson (1644–1713), politician, and Joanna, daughter of Robert Overton and Anne Gardiner. Nathaniel Johnson was a member of parliament and mayor of Newcastle upon Tyne. Knighted in 1680, he was governor of the Leeward Islands from 1686 until 1689 when he moved to South Carolina and settled a plantation on the Cooper River called Silk Hope. He was proprietary governor of South Carolina from 1702 to 1709. He maintained his family at home in England and his son, Robert, acted as family agent. After his term of office he retired to Silk Hope, and died in 1713. In 1717 the lords proprietors of Carolina appointed Robert Johnson governor.

Nathaniel Johnson's governorship had been stormy. A strong supporter of the Church of England, he had clashed with nonconformist political leaders over the establishment of the Church of England in the colony and had paid little heed to the political aspirations of colonial leaders. His son's tenure was even more troubled. Robert

Johnson arrived in Carolina in October 1717, at a time when the war with the Yemassee and their allies was ending. The conflict had been violent in the first year and skirmishes persisted until the end of the decade. By the time Johnson arrived to take up his office, settlers were angry with the proprietors for failing to support the war effort adequately. They grew more disenchanted as Johnson revealed his plans for the colony's future. Before embarking for Carolina, Johnson had received strict instructions from the lords proprietors to regain control of the colonial government and economy from local leaders. He reasserted proprietary authority by wrangling with the Commons house of assembly and grand council and by announcing the proprietors' disallowances of colonial laws relating to elections, finances, and American Indian policies.

In December 1719 disaffected colonial leaders formed a convention of the people and declared themselves independent of proprietary rule. The rebels invited Johnson to join them and to govern by royal authority. He refused their offer and was dismissed from office. James Moore jun., one of the revolutionary leaders, took office as interim governor and during his tenure the British crown assumed control of South Carolina's government. Johnson retired to his plantation, Silk Hope, but continued to oppose the revolutionary regime. The 1721 appointment of Sir Francis Nicholson to be governor of Carolina precipitated a short-lived attempt at counter-revolution. On 9 May 1721 Johnson, allied with Nicholas Trott and William Rhett, led an armed force of 120 men to demand the revolutionaries' surrender. James Moore refused to hand over the government to Johnson and he backed down. In 1723 Johnson returned to England where, despite his failed coup attempt, he served as an agent for the Carolina government and took part in the crown's 1729 purchase from the lords proprietors of the Carolina colonial charter.

Soon after the charter purchase Johnson was appointed the first royal governor of the province. He arrived at Charles Town on 15 December 1730 and reassumed the office he had been forced to abandon in 1719. His tenure as royal governor was successful. He mediated in disputes between Carolina's planter élite and Charles Town's urban merchant class, and restored stability to a badly divided colony.

Governor Johnson's chief success was his township settlement plan. Combining promotional campaigns and land grants, he encouraged European immigrants to settle strategic townships on the South Carolina frontier. Swiss Protestants founded Purrysburg; Palatine Germans settled Orangeburg and Amelia; and French Huguenots established Hillsborough. Johnson's townships settled the backcountry and brought white settlers to the colony to counterbalance the flood of African slaves imported to the colony prior to the American War of Independence.

Johnson married Margaret Bonner (d. 1732) and they were the parents of six children. He died in office in Charles Town on 3 May 1735 and was buried in a vault near the altar of St Philip's Episcopal Church, Charles Town. In his will he bequeathed 12,000 acres of land and six working low-country Carolina plantations to his children and in-laws. He also made gifts of real estate in England and £1500 sterling to his daughters. ALEXANDER MOORE

Sources P. Sherman, Robert Johnson: proprietary and royal governor of South Carolina (1966) · A. D. Watson, 'Johnson, Robert', ANB · A. Moore, 'Johnson, Nathaniel', ANB · R. L. Meriwether, The expansion of South Carolina, 1729–1765 (1940) · J. A. Moore, 'Royalizing South Carolina: the revolution of 1719 and the evolution of early South Carolina government', PhD diss., University of South Carolina, 1991 · South Carolina Gazette (24 May 1735) · M. L. Webber, 'Sir Nathaniel Johnson and his son Robert, governors of South Carolina', South Carolina Historical and Genealogical Magazine, 38 (1937), 109–15
Wealth at death more than 12,000 acres of land in South Carolina; land and moneys in Great Britain: will, Charleston county wills, inventories, and miscellaneous records, South Carolina Archives and History Center, Columbia, vol. 66 (1737), 293–304

Johnson, Robert (1770–1796), draughtsman and engraver, was born at Shotley, near Consett, co. Durham, the son of Thomas Johnson (c.1743–1805), joiner and cabinet-maker, and Mary Maffen (or Maughan), a house servant. They shortly afterwards moved to Ovingham, Northumberland, where Johnson was baptized on 9 September 1771 in the parish church, and later to Gateshead, co. Durham. Through the influence of his mother, who knew Thomas Bewick, Johnson was apprenticed in 1787 to Ralph Beilby and Bewick in Newcastle upon Tyne to learn copperplate-engraving. He executed some unimportant engravings during his apprenticeship but with encouragement and tuition from Bewick, mainly devoted himself to sketching from nature in watercolour. He also prepared drawings for a number of book illustrations engraved by the workshop, notably for William Bulmer's editions of Oliver Goldsmith's and Thomas Parnell's poems, published in 1795. His most outstanding work was his drawing of St Nicholas's Church, Newcastle (c.1792), later engraved in wood by a fellow apprentice and friend Charlton Nesbit [see also Bewick, Thomas, apprentices].

When his apprenticeship ended in 1794, Johnson commenced business as a copperplate-engraver in Newcastle with some success. He continued to employ his skills as a draughtsman, however, and in the summer of 1796 was recommended to Messrs Morison of Perth to copy the portraits by George Jamesone at Taymouth Castle, Kenmore, Perthshire, seat of the earl of Breadalbane, for reproduction in John Pinkerton's Gallery of Scottish Portraits (1797). He had completed fifteen of the twenty copies commissioned when he caught a chill, and he died at Kenmore on 26 October 1796. He was buried there, and a tablet in his memory was later erected in Ovingham churchyard by his friends. Johnson's reputation as a draughtsman rests on the small number of mainly topographical drawings and watercolours which he produced during his apprenticeship and immediately after, some of which have been compared to those of Thomas Girtin. His works are in the collections of the Laing Art Gallery and the Central Library, Newcastle, and the Scottish National Portrait Gallery, Edinburgh.

Robert Johnson's cousin **John Johnson** (d. c.1797),

wood-engraver, was born at Stanhope, co. Durham, and was apprenticed in 1782 to Ralph Beilby and Thomas Bewick in Newcastle upon Tyne. He is credited by Chatto and Jackson with the cutting of some of the tailpieces to Bewick's *British Birds* (1797) but is mainly remembered for his drawing for 'The Hermit' in William Bulmer's edition (1795) of Thomas Parnell's *Poems*. Johnson died at Newcastle about 1797, very soon after he had finished his apprenticeship.   L. H. CUST, rev. MARSHALL HALL

Sources *A memoir of Thomas Bewick, written by himself*, ed. I. Bain (1975) · I. Bain, *The watercolours of Thomas Bewick and his workshop apprentices* (1981) · M. Hall, *The artists of Northumbria*, 2nd edn (1982) · R. Welford, *Men of mark 'twixt Tyne and Tweed*, 3 vols. (1895) · P. M. Horsley, *Eighteenth-century Newcastle* (1971) · E. Mackenzie, *A descriptive and historical account of the town and county of Newcastle upon Tyne*, 2 vols. (1827) · R. Robinson, *Thomas Bewick: his life and times* (1887) · W. Chatto and J. Jackson, *A treatise on wood engraving* (1839) [J. Johnson] · registers (baptisms, vol. 1, 1679–1812); marriages and burials, Ovingham parish church, Newcastle upon Tyne Central Library · memorial tablet, churchyard, Ovingham, Northumberland

Johnson, Samuel (1649–1703), Church of England clergyman and pamphleteer, was born in Warwickshire. He was educated at St Paul's School, London, and was admitted as a sizar at Trinity College, Cambridge, on 6 June 1666. He matriculated in 1666–7 and received his BA in 1669–70. He was ordained a priest at Holborn on 27 February 1670 and became the rector of Corringham, Essex, two days later. Although the living was worth only £80, Johnson provided a curate and went to reside in London. There he became the domestic chaplain of William, Lord Russell, who valued Johnson for his knowledge of the 'constitution and laws of this country and for speaking his mind freely' ('Some memorials').

On 13 April 1679 Johnson preached an anti-papist sermon before the lord mayor at Guildhall Chapel. But his fame came in the summer of 1682 when he published a political treatise, *Julian the Apostate*. It was an overnight sensation. As George Hickes (whose 1681 sermon apparently prompted Johnson's tract) observed, 'On the very morning it was available at the bookstores, two or three gentlemen' claimed that 'it is an unanswerable piece, it hath undone all your pleas for succession, your passive obedience, and it is written by a Church divine and we thank God that there is one among them who is not enslaving the people' (Hickes, 1–2). The tract drew an elaborate parallel between the fourth-century apostate emperor, Julian, and the Catholic successor to the crown, James, duke of York. The moral of the story was that, as the primitive Christians of the fourth century had openly resisted their pagan emperor, so the English might oppose a popish prince. The tract justified both the efforts of whigs to exclude the duke of York from the throne as well as active resistance to him. Julian Johnson, as Johnson soon became known, was praised and celebrated by fellow whigs. He became the 'oracle of the cause', and his tract 'the pocket-book of all the party, carried to coffee-houses in triumph' (ibid., 3).

During 1682 two tory responses to *Julian the Apostate* were rushed to the press, and in 1683 five more appeared.

Johnson himself was preparing a detailed reply to his critics in the summer of 1683. But once the trials connected with the Rye House plot began, including that of Johnson's patron, Lord Russell, he prudently suppressed the printed copies. None the less, Johnson was examined before the privy council three times in July 1683 but he refused to tell the council the location of the hidden copies. At one point he was fined, committed to Gatehouse prison, and soon afterwards bailed. Then on 21 July Lord Russell was executed; his dying speech was highly offensive to the court and many suspected that Johnson was its true author. Once again, Johnson was hauled before the privy council. Finally, in November 1683 he was charged with seditious libel for *Julian the Apostate*. Chief Justice George Jeffreys presided over his subsequent trial. Johnson was fined 500 marks and his tract was burnt by the common hangman. Unable to pay his fine, Johnson spent the next four years in London gaols.

While a resident of king's bench prison in 1684, Johnson met Hugh Speke, a whig agitator who was able to have Johnson's writings printed and distributed. In March 1686 Johnson and Speke decided to arouse the consciences of the protestant soldiers serving in James II's army. Johnson's *A Humble and Hearty Address to All English Protestants in this Present Army* exhorted the soldiers to come to the defence of their religion rather than assist their Catholic officers in erecting a 'popish-kingdom of darkness and desolation' (Johnson, *Works*, 160). Speke later claimed that he had 20,000 copies of Johnson's address distributed. Authorities were quick to suspect Johnson; he was convicted of high misdemeanour, sentenced to pay 500 marks, to stand in the pillory for three days, and to be flogged from Newgate to Tyburn. Johnson was also degraded from the priesthood. His degradation and whipping made a profound impression on contemporaries. He was rarely mentioned after 1686 without reference to his public flogging and suffering for the protestant cause.

Following the accession of William and Mary, Johnson was released from prison in the spring of 1689. On 11 June the House of Commons resolved that the sentence passed against him in 1686 should be deemed 'cruel and illegal' ('Some memorials', x). Johnson's degradation was also reversed, and he was reinstated as the rector of Corringham. His tracts were republished, including *Julian the Apostate*, which was reissued in the crucial month of December 1688. In January 1689 the formerly suppressed *Julian's Arts to Undermine and Extirpate the Christian Religion* appeared in print for the first time, and in the same year Richard Baldwin brought out a collection of Johnson's works, *A Second Five Year's Struggle Against Popery and Tyranny* (1689), mostly written during his imprisonment and dedicated to William III.

Johnson expected to be rewarded by the new regime. The earl of Sunderland reported that the new king was 'well inclined' towards the whig divine (*Downshire MSS*, 1.535). At one point, there was talk of sending Johnson to an Irish bishopric in order to 'stop many mouths as well as his' (*Letters of Lady Rachel Russell*, 153). However, in 1695

Johnson was simply pensioned off, given £1000 in 'ready money' and £300 per year for his life and his son's (Luttrell, 3.559).

In the early 1690s, despite his exclusion from favour, Johnson continued to be a public figure. He wrote numerous tracts, instructing the new government on the genius of England's ancient constitution. In 1692 Johnson published what he hoped would be recognized as the quintessential interpretation of the events of 1688. His pamphlet, *An argument proving that the abrogation of King James by the people of England … was according to the constitution of the English government*, went into five editions in 1693 alone, and was translated into Dutch. Even Johnson's enemies recognized that this latest 'pamphlet of renown filled as has fill'd every tongue in town' (*Canonical Statesman's Grand Argument Discussed*, 3). Johnson declared that the Convention's abdication/vacancy masked the simple fact that the people had dethroned James II for his violation of the nation's established laws and promoted William and Mary in his place. Johnson wished to expose the conventioneers' efforts to sustain the myth of public non-resistance to James. The abdication/vacancy formula was created 'to cover the doctrine of passive obedience and to keep it safe and sound notwithstanding the Prince and the whole nation engaged in resisting oppression and defending their rights' (Johnson, *Works*, 262). On 27 November 1692 seven men broke into Johnson's house near Piccadilly; he was beaten with clubs and cut with swords. One of his assailants shouted: 'Pistol him, kill him; kill him for the book he wrote' (*A True and Faithful Relation*, 2).

In Johnson's eyes the whole nation had resisted James because he had violated England's ancient constitution, and during the 1690s Johnson's numerous tracts glorified England's 'ancient and approved laws' which had 'passed through all the British, Roman, Danish, Saxon and Norman times with little nor no alternation in the main'. Magna Carta was no 'invention or innovation', for it affirmed ancient liberties and, though born in 1215, had 'a grey beard' (Johnson, *Works*, 340–41). Johnson also believed that the coronation oath represented that contract between king and people, calling the oath a 'fundament contract', the 'covenant of the kingdom', and a 'downright English bargain' (ibid., 238–9). Should the king dispense with or violate the law, the crown reverted to 'the people of England, who had always had the disposal of it until they invest a new king with it' (ibid., 337). William III 'is the rightfullest king that ever sat on the English throne. For he is set up by the same hands which made the first king, and which have always unmade all tyrants as fast as they could' (ibid., 237).

Although Johnson accumulated numerous enemies, including John Dryden, who vilified him in 'Absalom and Achitophel', he also had many politically like-minded admirers, including Lady Rachel Russell, Sir Robert Howard, John Hampden the younger, Archbishop John Tillotson, and Bishop Edward Fowler. John Hampden, who spent time with Johnson in king's bench prison, later stated that he 'never knew a man of greater sense, of a more innocent life, nor of greater virtue'. Hampden published an open letter to Johnson in 1692, calling his '*Julian* the next best book to the Bible' (Hampden, 2).

Johnson was married and had a son and daughter. He died in London in May 1703. Johnson was the only whig propagandist of the 1680s and 1690s to have his writings published together in a single volume. His complete works were first published in 1710; a second edition was issued in 1713. The 1710 edition was prefaced by a hagiographic memorial to the whig divine.

MELINDA ZOOK

Sources M. S. Zook, *Radical whigs and conspiratorial politics in late Stuart England* (1999), esp. chaps. 2, 6 • M. Zook, 'Early whig ideology, ancient constitutionalism, and the Reverend Samuel Johnson', *Journal of British Studies*, 32 (1993), 139–65 • 'Some memorials', *The works of … Samuel Johnson*, 2nd edn (1713), iii–xiii • G. Hickes, *Jovian, or, An answer to Julian the apostate* (1683) • *Report on the manuscripts of the marquis of Downshire*, 6 vols. in 7, HMC, 75 (1924–95), vol. 1, pt 1, p. 535 • *The letters of Lady Rachel Russell* (1854) • N. Luttrell, *A brief historical relation of state affairs from September 1678 to April 1714*, 3 (1857), 559 • *JHC*, 10 (1688–93), 177, 193–4 • *The canonical statesman's grand argument discussed* (1693) • *A true and faithful relation of the horrid and barbarous attempt to assassinate the Reverend Mr Samuel Johnson* (1692) • J. Hampden, *A letter to Mr Samuel Johnson* (1692) • Venn, *Alum. Cant.* • M. Goldie, 'The roots of true whiggism, 1688–94', *History of Political Thought*, 1 (1980), 195–236

Johnson, Samuel (1690/91–1773), dancing-master and playwright, was a native of Cheshire, but the exact place and date of his birth are unknown: as, too, are the names of his parents and other relations. (He had a brother who was a gaoler in Manchester in 1730.) The earliest traced references to Johnson are in October 1722 when he gave a ball in Manchester and recited his opera to John Byrom (1692–1763) and other friends. The opera was presumably *Hurlothrumbo*, first mentioned by name in March 1724 when Johnson was in London hoping to have it staged; he was in London again on the same errand in December 1725. At some time earlier he acted in a work of his own composition before Francis Gastrell (1662–1725), bishop of Chester. He may be the Samuel Johnson who was imprisoned for debt in the Fleet prison in 1728.

Hurlothrumbo, or, News from terra Australis incognita, with the whimsical flights of my Lord Flame eventually opened at the Haymarket Theatre on 29 March 1729. With both words and music by Johnson, this heroic drama mostly in bombastic prose is so absurd that it could be a deliberate parody. Byrom, who wrote an epilogue for the second night, thought it was a joke on all stage plays (*Private Journal*, 1.349; 2 April 1729) and it was later claimed that the second duke of Montagu, deviser of the 'bottle conjuror' hoax, engaged Johnson to write the work in order to ridicule the credulity of the age (*Monthly Magazine*, 5, 1798, 415). Whatever the author's intention, it proved popular and enjoyed a first run of twenty-nine performances. Johnson himself played the mad lover Lord Flame, 'speaking sometimes in one key, sometimes in another, sometimes fiddling, sometimes dancing, and sometimes walking on high stilts' (Baker and Reed, 2.315). *Hurlothrumbo*, now subtitled *The Supernatural*, was published by subscription in 1729 with a dedication to Rhoda, Lady Delves (d.

Samuel Johnson (1690/91–1773), by unknown engraver, pubd 1732 [as Lord Wildfire playing the violin, with Eliza Haywood as Lady Flame on the balcony, in a scene from *The Blazing Comet: the Mad Lovers, or, The Beauties of the Poets* by Johnson]

1772), of Cheshire, the county from which came the bulk of subscriptions. A second edition in the same year was dedicated to Horatio Walpole, the prime minister's brother, who had subscribed for thirty copies. Johnson's play was much ridiculed, for instance in James Miller's *Harlequin Horace* (1729) and Henry Fielding's *The Author's Farce* (1730), but it caught the fancy of Londoners for a while: it is even said that a Hurlothrumbo Society was formed.

Johnson could not be persuaded to stage *Hurlothrumbo* in Manchester when he returned there in June 1729, but it had eight more performances at the Haymarket in the 1729–30 season. He tried to repeat its success with two more plays at the Haymarket: 'The Chester Comics, or, The Amours of Lord Flame' (February 1730) and *The Blazing Comet: The Mad Lovers, or, The Beauties of the Poets* (March 1732). The first had only four performances and was never printed; the second achieved six nights; it was printed (with a dedication to the duchess of Richmond) and was the subject of a well-known satirical print which shows Johnson, in the character of the lunatic lover Lord Wildfire, upon stilts shaped like legs and playing his fiddle. He

signed himself 'Hurlothrumbo Johnson … from my apartment in Moorfields Palace' in a published letter, *Harmony in an Uproar* (1733), where he implies that he is second only to Handel as a composer for the theatre.

By 1737 Johnson was back in Manchester as a dancing-master and was conceited enough to lodge an affidavit against a postmaster who failed to deliver promptly a letter addressed to 'Lord Flame, Manchester'. Perhaps he was justified: his obituarist said that Johnson had a high reputation in Cheshire and the adjoining counties 'as an excellent Comedian, a famous Dancing Master, a masterly player on the Violin, an extraordinary Singer' (*Manchester Mercury*, 25 May 1773). He tried his luck on the London stage again with the comedies 'All Alive and Merry' (January 1737, seven nights), 'The Mad Lovers' (August 1738, acted once, perhaps a rehash of *The Blazing Comet*), and the 'operatical comedy', 'A Fool Made Wise', and its afterpiece 'Sir John Falstaff in Masquerade', a farce, acted three times by 'the Hurlothrumbo Company of Comedians' at the Haymarket in April 1741. The last two survive in the Larpent collection of MSS of plays submitted for licensing (Hunt.); none of these was printed. His farrago, *A Vision of Heaven* (1738), was published by subscription and received little notice. *Hurlothrumbo* had only three performances after 1730: the last, on 15 May 1741, was Johnson's own farewell appearance on the stage as Lord Flame.

After this Johnson retired to Cheshire where, as a man of wit and humour, 'his acquaintance was sought by most of the gentlemen of fortune in that country, at whose houses he used to reside alternately for a considerable time' (Baker and Reed, 1.403). He lived mainly in Gawsworth New Hall, near Macclesfield, by courtesy of two successive earls of Harrington, the second of whom, William Stanhope (1719–79), was himself an eccentric who rejoiced in the nickname Peter Shambles. Johnson continued to be known as Lord Flame, also as Maggoty (i.e. whimsical) Johnson and Fiddler Johnson. His only publication during retirement was *Court and Country* (April 1759), a discussion of *Paradise Lost* in the form of a 'conversation play' dedicated to Philip Egerton of Oulton, Staffordshire.

Johnson was said to be eighty-two years old when he died at Gawsworth New Hall on 3 May 1773; he was buried two days later, first in Gawsworth churchyard and then, at his own request, on a hilltop in a coppice near Gawsworth. His gravestone has an elegant, though self-congratulatory and misogynistic, inscription, probably of his own composition; an adjacent gravestone, set up by Lady Harrington in 1851, carries 'an inscription of a reproachfully pious cast' (*DNB*). He left in manuscript three dramatic works now lost: one was a tragedy, 'Pompey the Great', another was an opera which Johnson believed, at the age of about eighty, was his best work. The word 'Hurlothrumbo' remained current as a synonym for confusion long after Johnson's death. Johnson's self-portrait as a young man and his violin are preserved at Gawsworth Old Hall. The first dedication of *Hurlothrumbo* (1729) mentions an 'Amante Sposa', but no other trace of Johnson's wife has been found: the style of his life in old age suggests that he was then wifeless.   JAMES SAMBROOK

Sources *The private journal and literary remains of John Byrom*, ed. R. Parkinson, 2 vols. in 4 pts, Chetham Society, 32, 34, 40, 44 (1854–7), 1.46–7, 73, 84, 89, 91, 98, 349–50; 2.127, 174–5 • D. E. Baker, *Biographia dramatica, or, A companion to the playhouse*, rev. I. Reed, new edn, rev. S. Jones, 1 (1812), 402–6; 2 (1812), 315 • *Manchester Mercury* (25 May 1773) • Highfill, Burnim & Langhans, *BDA*, 8.181–4 • 'Memoir of the author of *Hurlothrumbo*', *Monthly Magazine*, 5 (1798), 415–18 • W. Van Lennep and others, eds., *The London stage, 1660–1800*, 5 pts in 11 vols. (1960–68) • F. G. Stephens and M. D. George, eds., *Catalogue of prints and drawings in the British Museum, division 1: political and personal satires*, 2 (1873), 768–70 • J. E. Bailey, 'John Byrom's journal, letters, etc.', *Palatine Note-Book*, 2 (1882), 89–96; pubd separately (1882) • *The poems of John Byrom*, ed. A. W. Ward, 1/1, Chetham Society, new ser., 29 (1894), 138–47 • R. Richards, *The manor of Gawsworth* (1957), chap. 6 • *N&Q*, 5 (1852), 596–7 • *N&Q*, 3rd ser., 1 (1862), 456–7 • *N&Q*, 6th ser., 1 (1880), 338–9 • *N&Q*, 6th ser., 5 (1882), 157–8 • *N&Q*, 6th ser., 6 (1882), 257 • J. P. Earwaker, *East Cheshire: past and present, or, A history of the hundred of Macclesfield*, 2 (1880), 570–71

Likenesses caricature, c.1732, repro. in Highfill, Burnim & Langhans, *BDA* • engraving, 1732, BM; repro. in S. Johnson, *The blazing comet* (1732) [*see illus.*] • S. Johnson, self-portrait, oils, repro. in Highfill, Burnim & Langhans, *BDA*; priv. coll.

Johnson, Samuel (1696–1772), Church of England clergyman and teacher in America, was born on 14 October 1696 in Guilford, Connecticut, the second child of Samuel Johnson (d. c.1728), a farmer and proprietor of a fulling mill, and his wife, Mary Sage (d. c.1728). Early in Samuel Johnson's life he demonstrated scholarly tendencies. He could read and write at four, and was studying Hebrew at five. Because of a scarcity of funds for public schools in Guilford, Johnson was not able to begin his formal education in the local grammar school until he was eleven. The traditional curriculum of Latin and Greek prepared him for admission in 1710 to the collegiate school at Saybrook. There he continued to study classical languages and Hebrew, but added logic, natural philosophy, mathematics, metaphysics, and theology. The schedule included morning and evening prayers in Latin, lectures, recitations, formal debates, and Sunday worship at Saybrook's Congregational church. Even before he graduated in 1714, Johnson taught briefly in Guilford's public school. In 1716 he became a tutor in the collegiate school, which moved in that year to New Haven where it later became Yale College and then University. In the following year he received the degree of master of arts.

Having been granted a licence to preach by Connecticut's Congregational Association, Johnson was ordained and installed in 1720 as the minister of the church in West Haven. Proximity to the college's library, and the small size of his congregation, enabled him to continue to read philosophy, theology, and church history. His studies and conversations with the college's rector, Timothy Cutler, fellow tutor Daniel Browne, Church of England missionary George Pigot, and others caused him to doubt the validity of his ordination. By whose authority he was ordained was the issue that troubled Johnson and his circle of clerical friends. They feared that they had broken the connection with the leaders of the early church through their failure to be ordained in apostolic succession. They expressed their concerns at the college's commencement exercises in 1722. Despite the

Samuel Johnson (1696–1772), by unknown artist

intense opposition of Congregational colleagues, Johnson, Cutler, Browne, and James Wetmore, another Congregational minister, renounced their Congregational ordination and sailed to Great Britain, where they were ordained by the bishop of Norwich as priests of the Church of England. Johnson became a missionary of the Church of England Society for the Propagation of the Gospel (SPG), and was assigned to the colony of Connecticut and the parish of Stratford. Beginning on Christmas day 1724, he conducted services according to the Book of Common Prayer in the first Church of England building in the colony, and he continued to preach and administer the church's rites and sacraments in his parish for the next thirty years. In 1725 he married Charity Floyd Nicoll (d. 1756), a New York widow who had two sons and a daughter, and with whom he had two sons. His marriage gave him entrée to prominent New York families. Some sent their children to the rectory school that he opened in 1725. He encouraged and prepared promising students for the Anglican priesthood, and advised SPG officials on their placement in Connecticut. In 1727 he organized a convention of Church of England clergy in the northern colonies. Recognizing the lack of bishops to confirm the laity and ordain the clergy, he became an early advocate of an American episcopate. He continued a copious correspondence with English churchmen about this and other matters almost until the end of his life. He also published explanations of Church of England liturgy, polity, and doctrines. Largely because of his efforts the church's presence increased in Connecticut. By the early 1790s there were forty-three congregations served by sixteen priests, many of whom Johnson had trained.

Throughout Johnson's ministry he expanded the scholarly activity that he had begun as a child and deepened at the collegiate school. One of his major interests was encyclopaedics, the organization of knowledge. It proceeded from his early training in the methods of the scholastic Peter Ramus (1515–1572), who was popular among puritan educators. In 1714, Johnson's last year in college, he applied the Ramist method in the preparation of his first treatise, 'Technologia ceu technometica'. Shortly afterward he read the works of Francis Bacon and probably John Locke, and became a convert to the 'new learning', later known as the Enlightenment. Johnson's *Republic of Letters* (1731) reflects their broader and more complex schemes. Also modifying Johnson's puritan heritage was philosopher and mathematician George Berkeley, later bishop of Cloyne, who lived in Newport, Rhode Island, between 1729 and 1731. After discussions and correspondence with Berkeley, Johnson became one of the few colonial Americans who advocated Berkeley's philosophical idealism. Berkeley's influence enabled Johnson to reconcile revealed religion with Enlightenment thought. The climax of Johnson's study of encyclopaedics was his enlarged *Introduction to Philosophy* (1743). His purpose in this work was to give students an overview of what they should learn and the relationship of the branches of knowledge to one another. In the 1752 edition he specified a schedule that suggested at what age students should study which particular subjects. Because both contained Johnson's interpretation of philosophical idealism, neither sold well in the increasingly materialistic culture of the mid-eighteenth century.

Nevertheless, Johnson's publications earned for him an honorary doctor of divinity degree from Oxford University in 1744 and offers of two college presidencies. In 1750 Benjamin Franklin invited him to lead the new College of Philadelphia (later the University of Pennsylvania). Johnson declined, citing his poor health. That did not curtail his interest in the emerging college in New York. The city's wealthy Anglicans wanted a college that would counter the Congregationalists' Harvard, the Congregationalists' Yale, and the Presbyterians' College of New Jersey. When the college's trustees made the offer in 1754, Johnson accepted the presidency of King's College, which became Columbia University after the American War of Independence.

Despite the Church of England influence, Johnson envisioned a college that would be non-sectarian, except for its Church of England religious services. Dissenting students were permitted to worship elsewhere, however. Students of all denominations were to be admitted if they were qualified academically. Although religious and political controversies over the charter and finances afflicted the young institution, Johnson implemented an unusually broad curriculum that ran the gamut from traditional classics to vocational training. He required that students be in residence for four years, and that senior examinations be administered six weeks prior to graduation. In contrast to other colleges, he forbade tutors to stay with a class for all four years. Instead, he assigned tutors to teach specific subjects. He taught five classes, lectured on the importance of piety, conducted morning and evening prayers, and established strict rules of behaviour. Early classes were held in Trinity Church's school building. At Johnson's urging, the trustees authorized the construction of college buildings in 1757. For Johnson and other eighteenth-century intellectuals the most significant aspect of the system of learning was 'moral philosophy'. Although Johnson's writings and classes demonstrated the influence of the Enlightenment, he retained the belief of his puritan ancestors in the ultimate sovereignty of God, as well as in human depravity. Johnson believed that religion and education were different methods of developing 'Christian virtue'. In his view education was all that stood between people and their sinful nature.

Although Johnson was in full charge during the college's early years, he gradually lost his influence. When smallpox epidemics broke out in 1756 and 1759, he left the city. As the college drifted in his absence, the trustees assumed control. They refused to establish a preparatory school, rejected his request for additional buildings, disputed his salary, and began to look for his successor. After the deaths between 1756 and 1763 of his wife, son, grandson, and second wife, Sarah Beach (d. 1763), whom he had married about 1761, he resigned the presidency and returned to Stratford to live with his remaining son and his family. There he became again the rector of its Anglican parish, and wrote on English and Hebrew grammar. His last intellectual exercise was the composition of his selective autobiography, which he completed late in 1771. He died quietly in Stratford on 6 January 1772. His son William Samuel *Johnson survived him.

Johnson's contemporaries did not value his accomplishments. Many of the New England clergy disapproved of his attempt to spread Church of England doctrines among them. His campaign to secure a bishop failed. His philosophical idealism was ahead of its time, and was more appreciated later than in his day. His publications were required reading at King's College, but were not widely read elsewhere. He is best remembered as the first president of King's College, now Columbia University.

JOHN B. FRANTZ

Sources H. Schneider and C. Schneider, eds., *Samuel Johnson, president of King's College: his career and writings*, 4 vols. (New York, 1929) · J. S. Ellis, *The New England mind in transition: Samuel Johnson of Connecticut, 1696–1772* (New Haven, 1973) · P. N. Carroll, *The other Samuel Johnson: a psychohistory of New England* (Cranbury, New Jersey, 1978) · N. S. Fiering, 'Samuel Johnson and the Circle of Knowledge', *William and Mary Quarterly*, 3rd ser., 28 (1971), 199–236 · D. R. Gerlach, 'Champions of an American episcopate: Thomas Secker of Canterbury and Samuel Johnson of Connecticut', *Historical Magazine of the Protestant Episcopal Church*, 41/4 (1972), 381–414 · D. R. Gerlach and G. E. DiMille, 'Samuel Johnson: *praeis collegii regis*, 1755–1763', *Historical Magazine of the Protestant Episcopal Church*, 44/4 (1975), 417–36 · G. E. DiMille, 'One man seminary', *Historical Magazine of the Protestant Episcopal Church*, 38/4 (1969), 373–9 · D. R. Gerlach, 'Johnson, Samuel', *ANB* · F. B. Dexter, *Biographical sketches of the graduates of Yale College with annals of the college history*, 6 vols. (New York, 1885–1912), 1.123–8 · H. Schneider, *A history of American philosophy* (New

York, 1963) · I. W. Riley, *American philosophy: the early schools* (New York, 1907) · C. Bridenbaugh, *Mitre and sceptre: transatlantic faiths, personalities, and politics, 1689–1775* (1962)

Archives Christ Episcopal Church, Stanford, Connecticut, parish records · Col. U. · Connecticut Historical Society, Hartford · Episcopal Church, Austin, Texas, archives, corresp. · Yale U. | Fulham Palace, London, corresp.

Likenesses J. Smibert, portrait, 1730–39, Col. U. · portrait, *c.*1754, Col. U., King's College Room · E. P. Christie, portrait (at King's College), Col. U. · H. Pyle, portrait, Col. U.; repro. in *Harper's Magazine* (Oct 1884) · pastel, Shelburne, Museum, Shelburne, Vermont [*see illus.*]

Johnson, Samuel (1709–1784), author and lexicographer, was born in Breadmarket Street, Lichfield, on 7 September 1709 (after the change of calendar in 1752 he celebrated his birthday on 18 September), the first child of Michael Johnson (1657–1731) and his wife, Sarah Ford (1669–1759); later the couple had another son, Nathaniel (1712–1737), of whom little is known apart from the fact that he went into the family trade of bookselling and did not enjoy good relations with his elder brother. Samuel's birth took place in the Johnsons' home, a new four-storey house on the corner of Breadmarket Street and the Market Square; it survives today as the Samuel Johnson Birthplace Museum. Overlooking the property stands St Mary's Church, where Samuel may have been baptized on 17 September 1709, although he appeared so frail at first that a baptismal ceremony was carried out in his home within hours of his birth. Attending his birth was George Hector, 'a man-midwife of great reputation' (*Yale Edition*, 1.3), whose nephew Edmund Hector (1708–1794), a Birmingham surgeon, became a close lifelong friend. As godfathers the parents chose Richard Wakefield, the town clerk, and Samuel Swynfen (*c.*1679–1736), a prominent local physician. The child was named after his maternal uncle Samuel Ford.

Michael Johnson's bookshop occupied the ground floor. Originally apprenticed to a member of the London trade in 1673 and made a freeman of the Stationers' Company in 1685, he had set up business in Lichfield in 1691. He published a few books and operated in other local towns on market days. In later years he also practised as a tanner and parchment manufacturer, though with little success. Michael Johnson held a number of civic offices in the borough, including those of senior bailiff and magistrate: Samuel was born during his term as sheriff. Michael was a high-churchman and possibly, as Boswell believed, a Jacobite, although outwardly at least he conformed to the Hanoverian dispensation. Plagued by 'a vile melancholy' that he may have passed on to his son (Boswell, *Life*, 1.35), he possessed some learning and ambition. At the same time he was evidently subjected to Sarah's consciousness of her own superior social origins. Awkward in company, strictly pious, and uninterested in books, she can hardly have found an ideal companion in Michael; later in life her son respected her memory, but gave little sign that he enjoyed a warm or loving relationship with his mother.

Almost immediately the parents placed Samuel in the care of a wet-nurse named Marklew, who lived in George Lane nearby. By the time he returned home a few weeks

Samuel Johnson (1709–1784), by Sir Joshua Reynolds, 1756–7

later, he was already suffering from maladies, which affected him all his days. 'A poor, diseased infant, almost blind' (*Yale Edition*, 1.5), he had an infection in his left eye and a severe case of scrofula (tuberculosis of the lymph nodes), possibly contracted from the nurse's milk. An operation was later carried out on the glands in his neck, which left visible scars. At some stage he also underwent a bout of smallpox which caused further disfigurement. When he was two, in March 1712, he was taken by his mother to London, in order to be 'touched' for the scrofula by Queen Anne. Johnson was almost totally deaf in his left ear, and this may well have been apparent from infancy. The convulsions that marked his behaviour in adult life may have derived from congenital factors or from these infant diseases; one theory is that his condition can be diagnosed as Tourette's syndrome, where the symptoms often grow more apparent in adolescence. The only result of his contact with the queen seems to have been the gift of a gold 'touchpiece', which he wore round his neck as an amulet until his death.

Schooldays Samuel was taught to read by his mother, perhaps assisted by a maid named Catherine. He then gained the rudiments of learning at a dame-school kept by a widow, Ann Oliver, whose kindness he recalled with pleasure. Precocious from infancy, he was made to perform in public by his fond father. At the age of six or seven he studied for some time with Thomas Browne, a former shoemaker turned schoolmaster, and then in January 1717 he became a day boy at the ancient grammar school of Lichfield, to embark on Latin under the usher Humphry Hawkins. Two years later he entered the upper school, where he was placed at first under the Revd Edward Holbrooke, a less experienced and effective teacher, and then under the headmaster, John Hunter, whom the boy found 'very severe, and wrong-headedly severe' (Boswell, *Life*, 1.44). Despite Hunter's cruel discipline, Johnson came to respect his ability to drum Latin into his charges, and attributed much of his humane learning to the thorough grounding he received from the headmaster. In addition, the solitary and physically challenged boy spent much of his time leafing through the stacks of the family bookshop, and there he could explore works which would never have been on any official syllabus. Later he displayed predictable knowledge of classical literature, but also curious learning in less obvious fields, including humanistic lore.

While at school, Johnson made the acquaintance of boys who were to be among his friends, including John Taylor, subsequently a clergyman in Ashbourne, and Robert James, who became a physician celebrated on account of his fever powder. The youth's closest ally remained Edmund Hector, who lived near by in Sadler Street. Opposite the cathedral close lived the family of Captain Peter Garrick, who was on good social terms with Michael Johnson: when the captain's son David entered the school, Samuel had moved on, but the two young men (seven years apart in age) certainly knew one another from this period. In 1725 Johnson went to spend nine months near Stourbridge with his sophisticated and, some thought, dissolute cousin, the Revd Cornelius Ford (1694–1731). When the youth returned to Lichfield in June 1726, he was refused permission by Hunter to return to the school, and instead Ford arranged for him to enter King Edward VI School at Stourbridge as a boarder. It is possible that he taught the younger boys in exchange for his own advanced tuition. Meanwhile he pursued the study of literature, with a special emphasis in his exercises on translations from Horace and Virgil: he also wrote a number of English poems and consorted with Ford's circle, including a relative by marriage, Gregory Hickman, who was a leading citizen in the town.

When Johnson left Stourbridge late in 1726, apparently after suffering an illness, his regular schooling came to an end. This was the prelude to a spell of two years back in Lichfield, which he himself considered to be a period of idleness, even though he read widely in a desultory fashion. His father possibly thought that Samuel was serving an apprenticeship in the bookshop. Perhaps it was at this stage, in a fit of late adolescent moodiness, that he refused on one famous occasion to help his father on a bookstall at Uttoxeter market—a show of disobedience which shamed him so much in later life that he stood on the spot for a considerable time, bareheaded as the rain fell, to expiate his fault. This aimless existence might have continued indefinitely, but for some outside impulse. Michael's financial affairs had declined to a point at which it was impossible for him to support a university education for his son, while Samuel himself lacked the energy to take any useful initiative. A kind offer on the part of an old schoolfellow, Andrew Corbet, made the difference, although this turned out to be no more than a gesture. Corbet had proceeded to Pembroke College, Oxford, and suggested that he should pay some of Johnson's fees to allow his friend to enter the college and provide companionship for the rich young country gentleman. Though the offer was taken up, Corbet never acted upon this promise, and Johnson's days at Oxford were clouded by uncertainty over money. A small legacy which his mother received from her cousin about this time may have helped to pay his fees.

Oxford and unemployment Samuel travelled to Oxford with his father and was admitted to Pembroke College on 31 October 1728, shortly after his nineteenth birthday. His residence lasted little more than a year, and outwardly bore the marks of failure: his poverty, social immaturity, and youthful contempt for authority were compounded by renewed fears of idleness. Allegedly he was often to be found lounging around the college gate. His career was abruptly cut short, and he held no degree until the university conferred an MA on him in 1755 in recognition of the forthcoming *Dictionary*. Yet Johnson preserved for the rest of his life a deep affection for Oxford and an abiding loyalty to his college, which he termed 'a nest of singing birds' on account of the number of poets it had nurtured. Ever afterwards 'he took a pleasure in boasting of the many eminent men who had been educated at Pembroke' (Boswell, *Life*, 1.75). Equally, he 'delighted in his own partiality' for the university at large (Piozzi, *Anecdotes*, 26). In his mature years he made regular visits to Oxford: his most durable friendship from Pembroke days was with William Adams, a junior fellow who served as Johnson's nominal tutor after the rebellious young man had sparred for some time with the ineffective William Jorden. In 1775 Adams became master of the college, where he often acted as host when his former pupil visited Oxford. When Johnson was an undergraduate he resumed friendship with earlier acquaintances, relishing in particular the company of his schoolmate John Taylor, who had arrived soon after him. At this time Taylor planned to follow his father and take up a legal career—something Johnson would have loved to do. It was only a short step across the road to Taylor's college, Christ Church, and the two men shared academic interests as well as social relaxations. Johnson even borrowed notes on the lectures of an admired tutor at Christ Church. When Taylor entered the church, his intellectual concerns fell by the wayside, but at this period he provided stimulating company to his friend, who evidently left an unfavourable impression on others. Many members of the university saw no more than an impoverished Jude with a provincial accent and uncouth manners.

According to the later account by Adams, Johnson achieved some popularity with those who knew him, and even passed for a 'gay and frolicsome fellow', but when this description was reported to him he responded, 'It was bitterness which they mistook for frolic' (Boswell, *Life*, 1.73–4). Intending to fight his way to success by his literary accomplishments and his wit, he deliberately flouted authority. Moreover, his schemes for study were more grandiose than anything he actually achieved. Some of his work helped to promote his reputation in the academic community, notably a translation of Pope's already Latinate *Messiah* into Latin verse, prepared as a college exercise at Christmas 1729. This became Johnson's first published piece when it appeared in a miscellany two years later, and it allegedly impressed Pope himself. On other occasions Johnson failed to deliver required work on time, and no other substantial pieces of writing survive from this period. He probably stayed up for much of the long vacation, as was then quite usual, but pressures were mounting. His father's business was floundering more than ever, his own debts were accumulating, and he had to battle with depressive illness. A renewed burst of religious faith, derived from reading William Law, alleviated but did not dispel these problems. The exact sequence of events is not known, but when Johnson left Oxford for good just before Christmas in 1729, he was already a full term behind with his college fees and had sunk into profound dejection.

This melancholia, which probably started in the previous summer, lasted about three years. Well-placed and sympathetic observers such as Edmund Hector considered that the illness amounted to a full-scale breakdown, and wondered whether Johnson might be subject to a constitutional disease which would impair his faculties for life. The patient tried such remedies as the hapless physicians of this age prescribed, and regularly walked the 30 miles between Lichfield and Birmingham in futile attempts to dissipate his feelings of anxiety. A major symptom was what Johnson called indolence, which might be construed in modern terms as resembling clinical depression rather than laziness. For his godfather, Samuel Swynfen, now practising in Birmingham, he compiled a state of his case in Latin: this does not survive, but it went the rounds in Johnson's own day when Swynfen, impressed by the cogency with which it was written, passed it on to his acquaintances. Understandably Johnson was outraged by this circulation of private disclosures, and he was never fully reconciled to Swynfen. Meanwhile Michael Johnson had just managed to cling on to his failing business, thanks to a timely loan. But in December 1731 the bookseller died of a fever, only three months after his cousin Cornelius Ford had suddenly expired in a Covent Garden bagnio. Unemployed and suffering from nervous prostration, Samuel now had to face the loss of the two most important male mentors of his youth. It was perhaps the low point of his entire life.

Johnson had already made his first efforts to gain a regular job. A post as usher at his old school in Stourbridge had come up that summer, and Johnson went across to the town about September. Despite the support of his kinsman Gregory Hickman, which should have proved influential, he failed to obtain the appointment; this was the first of several such disappointments in the years to come. While Sarah Johnson attempted to keep the family business going, her son expanded his sorties in quest of a teaching position. Briefly he seemed to have turned the corner when he succeeded in landing a job at Market Bosworth grammar school, some 20 miles east of Lichfield.

However, he had to live with the patron of the school, Sir Wolstan Dixie, a boorish embodiment of the caricature squire, and even to act as domestic chaplain. It must have been still worse than idleness, because Johnson lasted only a few months in the post, from March to July 1732. He walked back to Lichfield, with little beyond the paltry inheritance of £19, which was all he could expect from his father's estate during the lifetime of his mother. Soon afterwards, on hearing of the death of an usher at Ashbourne School, he made efforts to gain this post and wrote to Taylor, who was now an attorney in the town. He explained to his friend that his departure from Market Bosworth had been like escaping from a prison. However, when the governors of the school met on 1 August they chose another candidate.

Late in the year Johnson was invited to stay with Edmund Hector, who had become a surgeon in Birmingham, and he remained there for more than a year. Two notable events took place during his stay: he embarked on his first sustained literary work—a translation of the account of Father Jerome Lobo, a Portuguese Jesuit, of his journey to Abyssinia—and he met his future wife. The book was based on a French translation of Lobo's account, which Johnson had read at Oxford. It was early 1735 before the work appeared, not surprisingly since Johnson's indolence had slowed its progress—so badly, indeed, that it became Hector's role to take down copy which the translator dictated as he lay in bed, and then to carry the manuscript to the printer. *A Voyage to Abyssynia*, which runs to 400 pages, earned Johnson 5 guineas from Thomas Warren, a Birmingham bookseller, although the actual publishers were members of the London trade. Again it was through Hector that a significant meeting occurred: Warren owned the house in which Johnson came to live with his friend. During 1733 Johnson stayed for a time with Warren and began to write for a newspaper which the bookseller had recently set up, entitled the *Birmingham Journal*. Here some of his first published writing, now lost, made its appearance.

Marriage An even more important contact was established when the young man changed his lodgings about June 1733. His new landlord was a certain Jervis, one of whose relatives was a woman named Elizabeth Porter, *née* Jervis (1689–1752): it was not long before Johnson made the acquaintance of Elizabeth and her husband Harry Porter. The couple's three children included a daughter, Lucy, then aged eighteen. Initially the omens looked bad since Porter, a struggling textile dealer, was the brother-in-law of Johnson's feared schoolmaster, John Hunter. However, matters took an unexpected turn in September 1734 when Harry died and Johnson began to court the widow, who was twenty years his senior. Within a few months he brought his pursuit of the lady to a successful conclusion, and the couple were married on 9 July 1735. They rode the 30 miles to Derby, perhaps stopping at Lichfield, as Johnson had once more taken up residence in his home town. The ceremony took place at St Werburgh's Church, perhaps for the simple reason that it was safely removed from Birmingham, where the widow's family had opposed her wedding: they probably thought that the young man was attracted by his bride's fortune, which amounted to something like £600 (Reade, 6.34–5). There are no grounds for believing this, as Johnson himself acknowledged that it was a love match on both sides (Boswell, *Life*, 1.96). Unkind observers drew attention to the groom's strange appearance and deportment, while portraying the bride, known as Tetty, in the guise of a blousy and ageing woman who struck absurd postures in an effort to seem youthful. The oddly assorted couple had little by way of a regular income, and family and friends on both sides showed an understandable lack of enthusiasm for the marriage.

The truth was that Johnson had still failed to advance himself in any career. He tried to interest the proprietor of the *Gentleman's Magazine*, Edward Cave, in occasional contributions to the popular new journal, which Cave had founded in 1731; however, nothing came of this for the time being. Instead he turned once again to the teaching profession, and just before his marriage he served for two months as private tutor to the family of Thomas Whitby, who lived at Great Haywood, near Stafford; there were five children in all, though Johnson's primary responsibility lay with a son of nineteen preparing to enter university. Soon afterwards he learned that the mastership of Solihull School had become vacant. Again an application failed: despite his unquestioned scholarship, the governors were put off by his reputation as 'a very haughty, ill-natured gent.', as well as by the way he had of 'distorting his face' (Reade, 6.29–30). The fresh rebuff must have wounded Johnson, especially as this time he had the backing of an old acquaintance, Gilbert Walmesley, a lawyer and official in the ecclesiastical court of Lichfield. Johnson had been familiar since boyhood with his mentor, who lived a comfortable bachelor existence in the bishop's palace adjoining the cathedral. Walmesley stands out as the most supportive member of the Lichfield community who had watched the precocious Samuel grow up in the town, and Johnson afterwards paid a warm tribute to his humanity, learning, and tolerance: 'I honoured him, and he endured me' (Boswell, *Life*, 1.81).

By the time Johnson got the news of this latest reverse, he had already formulated an alternative plan. His scheme was to set up a school, no doubt funded by his wife's small fortune. Optimistically he wrote to a friend, 'I am now going to furnish a house in the country, and keep a private boarding-school for young gentlemen whom I shall endeavour to instruct in a manner somewhat more rational than those commonly practised' (*Letters*, 1.10). The premises were duly acquired in the shape of a large brick house for rent at Edial, a village 3 miles west of Lichfield, and the would-be proprietor inserted an advertisement in the *Gentleman's Magazine*. But the enrolment of pupils was tiny, perhaps as low as three or four boys, all recruited by Gilbert Walmesley, and little more than a year after its opening in late 1735 the school had to close. The episode is remembered chiefly because one of the few students happened to be David Garrick, then aged eighteen and a favourite of Walmesley on account of his wit and vivacity. Neither the master nor the pupil was well attuned to the

process of turning Garrick into a classical scholar, and a visit to Lichfield by strolling players may have stimulated the young man more than any instruction he received from Johnson.

Life went on in this cramped fashion until the school closed in January 1737. We know nothing of the state of Johnson's marriage, apart from what may be gleaned from cruel performances Garrick later improvised to mimic the connubial dealings of Samuel and Elizabeth. Even Hester Piozzi, who reported these 'comical scenes', was not sure whether they were accurate (Piozzi, *Anecdotes*, 97). But the surviving diary entries are somewhat gloomy, suggesting that Johnson was still morbidly conscious of wasting his time on footling pursuits and still devising a harsh regimen to put himself on to a more productive track. In addition, he applied for yet another scholastic post, on this occasion at Brewood on the other side of Cannock Chase, but he met with no more success than before, as the master had heard something of the applicant's peculiar deportment and thought it might cause ridicule among the pupils. The money which Elizabeth had brought to the marriage had probably all gone. So Johnson had reached twenty-eight with very little concrete achievement. At this low point he took the decision to seek his fortune in London as a writer: his sense of the need for a fresh start may have been strengthened when his brother Nathaniel, who had been living at Frome in Somerset, died without apparent warning at the start of March 1737. But by that time the die was cast, and Johnson was already making his way to the capital.

Going to London   When Johnson left Lichfield on 2 March 1737, he had a companion—but this was not Elizabeth, who remained at home until he could find work. It was Garrick, who was due to enter a school at Rochester. The pair shared a single horse, each riding ahead in turn and tying the horse ready for his companion to arrive on foot: they were certainly impoverished, even if Johnson exaggerated in later years when he claimed that he arrived with 2½d. in his pocket, while his young friend had only three halfpence. These straitened circumstances forced him to take humble lodgings with a staymaker named Richard Norris just off the Strand, where he lived very abstemiously. He spent much of his time working on a tragedy entitled *Irene*, which he had begun at Edial. For a period he took lodgings in Church Street, Greenwich, and attempted to compose his play in the nearby park, but the task remained unfinished. Late in the summer he returned to his home town and managed to get *Irene* completed. After three months he took Elizabeth back with him to London, and he remained ever after a resident of the capital. His mother meanwhile carried on the family bookshop with the help of Samuel's stepdaughter Lucy Porter.

The overtures made to Edward Cave finally paid off in 1738, when the bookseller accepted some verse and then printed a short life of Father Paolo Sarpi in his journal. From this time forward Johnson was Cave's right-hand man in running the *Gentleman's Magazine* from its office at St John's Gate, Clerkenwell. He contributed in almost every issue to regular features of the work, including foreign and domestic news, book reviews, and illicit parliamentary reports. In this last department Johnson brought special renown to the *Magazine*: his stylized accounts of proceedings in the senate of Lilliput, which allegedly came from the pen of Lemuel Gulliver's grandson, gave the substance of the debates, even though verbatim reporting was specifically banned as a breach of privilege by a Commons resolution in April 1738. The series ran from the following June until 1745: Johnson is likely to have had a hand in the reports throughout, and he was solely responsible for their composition between 1741 and 1744. These years saw some tumultuous passages in the final phase of Robert Walpole's long political ascendancy, most notably the contentious events leading to the start of the War of Jenkins's Ear in 1739. Johnson and his collaborators evolved a complex code to record the debates, mixing allegorical byplay in the manner of Swift with studied Ciceronian oratory: speeches were put into the mouths of characters whose names transparently revealed their real identity (as 'Walelop' or 'Ptit'). For all these devices, the *Magazine's* transactions of the senate in Lilliput achieved a plausible enough effect to be cited by later historians as though they were the speakers' *ipsissima verba*. Meanwhile Cave provided his protégé with further opportunities, notably a planned translation of Sarpi's history of the Council of Trent (1619): Johnson was paid almost £50 for the work in progress, but it had to be abandoned in 1739 owing to a rival version. The same year saw him complete a translation from the French of a commentary on Pope's *Essay on Man*, written by the Swiss theologian Jean-Pierre Crousaz. Johnson is said to have worked with frenzied energy on the task, producing up to six sheets (almost fifty pages) in a single day. His version, published in 1741, provides comments on the text by way of annotation, correcting errors in Crousaz and setting out his own view of the *Essay*.

During the late 1730s Johnson's career was at last beginning to flourish, although he was unable to get *Irene* staged. His first original work of importance, *London: a Poem in Imitation of the Third Satire of Juvenal*, was issued by the leading publisher Robert Dodsley about 13 May 1738: he received 10 guineas as payment. It is a satire of 263 lines, composed in heroic couplets intended to match the vigorous Latin hexameter. The poem is closely based on its model, substituting London for Rome and France for Greece; quotations from the original are placed at the foot of the appropriate page to emphasize some of the choice effects achieved. Johnson captures some of Juvenal's bleak humour, along with his talent for terse epigrammatic phrasing and power of invective. The discontented Umbricius, fleeing the horrors of Rome, is recast as Thales, seeking repose in Wales from a London which offers little beyond urban blight, pollution, crime, and disorder: 'And now a rabble rages, now a fire'. Thales has been dubiously identified with Richard Savage, the troubled bohemian poet, whom Johnson may or may not have met at the time when the poem was written. But the work certainly contains a good deal of autobiographical reference, as in the oblique self-pity of the couplet

> This mournful truth is everywhere confessed,
> Slow rises worth, by poverty depressed.

Although *London* came out anonymously, the identity of the author was soon discovered. The greatest living English poet, Alexander Pope, whose versions of Horace had recently pushed the 'imitation' of classical models to a new level of sophistication and daring, quickly recognized the merits of the poem and sought out the name of its creator. 'He will soon be *déterré*', Pope accurately predicted to a friend (Boswell, *Life*, 1.129).

Further success came with the appearance in the spring of 1739 of two political satires. The first, *Marmor Norfolciense*, draws on Swift's methods again to attack Walpole's policies through the supposed discovery of an ancient inscription in Latin. The second, *A Complete Vindication of the Licensers of the Stage*, ironically praises the government's repressive measures against the theatre, as embodied in the Licensing Act of 1737. In addition, Johnson continued to take an active share in the monthly offerings of the *Gentleman's Magazine*. However, although he gradually became more visible in the literary world, his private life remained, and remains, shrouded in mystery. He and his wife first took lodgings near Hanover Square, and then moved to Castle Street, on the edge of the fashionable new Harley estate in the West End. By this time Johnson seems to have become friendly with Savage, and according to some reasonably dependable anecdotage the two writers took to walking the streets of the city by night 'reforming the world', as Johnson himself put it, in default of the money to pay for a drink in the taverns (Hill, 1.371). Savage was of course hardly the best role model for a young man bent on achieving worldly success, and it would be understandable if Elizabeth felt neglected. At some stage the couple appear to have separated for a period, and Elizabeth sought refuge with a friend. In July 1739 matters came to a head when Savage, racked by debts and unable to concentrate on writing, decided to leave London and rusticate in Wales; the two men never saw one another again.

As these problems beset him, Johnson came up with an answer: to resume his former quest for a post in a provincial school. In August he set off for the midlands without Elizabeth, in the hopes of becoming headmaster of Appleby grammar school in Leicestershire, 10 miles from Lichfield. He was given a letter of reference by Pope to a prominent Staffordshire peer, Lord Gower (later first earl of Gower), who in turn wrote to Dublin to see whether Trinity College might award Johnson an MA degree with the intercession of Swift. The dean was almost past such endeavours, and in any case the degree (had it been granted) would not have met the qualifications for Appleby grammar school, which required its master to be a graduate of an English university. Once more Johnson's bid failed, and in his place a certain Mr Mould was appointed. After his rebuff Johnson went on to Lichfield and then to the home at Ashbourne of John Taylor, who had now entered the church. While in the midlands he fell under the spell of some local women of exceptional charm and humanity. One of these was Mary Meynell, who 'had the best understanding he ever met with any human being' (Boswell, *Life*, 1.83); she subsequently married the politician William Fitzherbert, whom Johnson held in warm regard. Another was her pious kinswoman Hill Boothby (1708–1756); and a third was Mary Aston (1706–*c*.1765), member of a large Lichfield family. Two of Mary Aston's sisters were married respectively to Gilbert Walmesley and Henry Hervey, another close friend of Johnson by this date. All three women exercised a powerful effect on the unattached traveller, and it is generally thought that Miss Boothby was the strongest candidate when he contemplated remarriage after the death of Elizabeth, only for the chosen bride herself to fall sick and die within a short time. The visits spread over into 1740, with Johnson attempting to assure his wife in a letter that his 'rambles' had served only to confirm his 'esteem and affection' for her (*Letters*, 1.24). Elizabeth felt some jealousy over Mary Aston, although her husband assured her she had no cause (Piozzi, *Anecdotes*, 103). In April, Johnson returned to London, and he did not see Lichfield again for more than twenty years.

The couple resumed life together in the Strand, but their monetary problems caused them to move regularly over the next few years, finding lodgings generally in the area of Fleet Street. Some of Johnson's work in the *Gentleman's Magazine* now achieved a separate life in the form of pamphlets, including a life of Admiral Robert Blake (1740). Short biographies constituted his most prolific genre at this period, with subjects ranging from Francis Drake to the physicians Hermann Boerhaave and Thomas Sydenham. In the next year Johnson took over as prime author of the reports of parliamentary debates, and he wrote more of his brief lives. A larger undertaking was to compile the catalogue of the huge Harley collection of books and tracts, which the bookseller Thomas Osborne had bought when the second earl of Oxford died in 1741. The task, enlivened by a memorable passage of arms when Johnson knocked Osborne down with a hefty folio, resulted in a work of five volumes (1743–5) describing the collection in detail, as well as an eight-volume sampler of its contents known as *The Harleian Miscellany* (1744–6), on which Johnson collaborated with the noted antiquarian William Oldys. He also made a number of contributions to a large *Medicinal Dictionary* (1743–5) by his schoolfriend Robert James. Little is known of other activity until the death of Savage, which took place in Bristol gaol on 1 August 1743 and prompted Johnson to compose his famous life of the renegade poet. The author received 15 guineas from Cave for the book, which was published anonymously on 11 February 1744. Ever since, *The Account of the Life of Mr Richard Savage* has remained one of Johnson's most admired works, as a pioneering exercise in psychological biography, as a graphic sociological study of Grub Street, and as a testament of friendship. Johnson gives a vivid account of Savage's struggle to establish his parenthood, and a fair-minded narrative of the poet's trial for murder. Moreover, he manages to steer a course

between excessive praise and blame, and reveals much about his own situation through his profound identification with the financial and personal crises Savage had undergone.

Soon afterwards Johnson began to contemplate the first literary project of any scale which he had devised independently. This was an edition of Shakespeare, one of a whole series of undertakings since Nicholas Rowe's innovative venture in 1709. The most recent production was that of Sir Thomas Hanmer, and Johnson's trial publication, a pamphlet entitled *Miscellaneous Observations on the Tragedy of Macbeth*, incorporated some parting shots at Hanmer's performance when it appeared in April 1745. This appeal for subscribers to the edition might possibly have succeeded, but the project received a body blow when the publisher Jacob Tonson the younger intervened with Cave. The firm of Tonson had long claimed a perpetual copyright in the text of Shakespeare, and under threat of legal action Cave backed down. Johnson again found himself baulked: he was doing less work for the *Gentleman's Magazine*, and it appears that about this time he seriously considered entering the legal profession, even though his lack of a degree made this impossible. Underemployed as he may have been, there is no basis for the story that he joined Charles Edward Stuart (the Young Pretender) in Scotland during the failed rising of 1745–6.

The Dictionary At this juncture there arrived the most significant career opportunity of Johnson's entire life. A group of booksellers headed by Robert Dodsley perceived the need for a new English dictionary to replace the semistandard *Dictionarium Britannicum* of Nathan Bailey (1730). They found a receptive ear in Johnson, who had pondered for many years on the absence of an English equivalent to the great continental glossaries sponsored by public bodies and academies. What was envisaged was something quite different, a commercial venture financed by a consortium of leading figures in the trade, and one which would be compiled essentially by a single hand—that of a poverty-stricken journalist and pamphleteer, who had dropped out of university and who had never left England. Johnson prepared a short prospectus for the undertaking, and then signed a contract on 18 June 1746. The compiler was to be paid 1500 guineas, out of which he had to defray the cost of his copyists, and delivery was due in three years. It seems miraculous today that the job took as few as nine years to complete.

For this task, the Johnsons took a substantial house in Gough Square, which survives today off the north side of Fleet Street as a Johnson museum. The garret was fitted out as workroom for the staff, which amounted to five or six assistants, most of them Scots. Johnson used an interleaved copy of Bailey's dictionary in its 1736 edition; he also consulted a wide range of technical and specialist manuals to expand the range of vocabulary. He sought out illustrative quotations in a huge collection of books, from which his amanuenses transcribed marked extracts. Before the mammoth work was completed, a number of distractions held up its progress. Johnson quarrelled with his intended patron, the earl of Chesterfield, to whom he had dedicated a recast version of the prospectus as *The Plan of the English Dictionary* (1747); one outcome was a famous letter of dignified rebuke to the peer. 'Is not a patron, my lord' asked Johnson sardonically, 'one who looks with unconcern on a man struggling for life in the water and when he has reached ground encumbers him with help?' (Boswell, *Life*, 1.262). It is possible, too, that Johnson revised his editorial methods and made a fresh start about 1750. Ultimately the work appeared in two folio volumes on 15 April 1755, garnished with preliminary matter including a preface of extraordinary dignity and eloquence.

The *Dictionary* left an immense mark on its age. It soon became recognized as a work of classical standing, and in spite of some minor blemishes it has never lost its historical importance as the first great endeavour of its kind. Notable above all for definitions of pith and occasional wit, the dictionary was even more original in the way in which every word, as Johnson put it, had its history. Each entry is organized under the headword to exemplify graduated senses of a term, a procedure which redirected the course of English lexicography. Further, the quotations used to exemplify the usage of a given word combined to form an anthology of moral sayings and helped to define the canon of literature: they show Johnson's taste and piety, for he would not admit extracts from irreligious writers such as Hobbes, Bolingbroke, and Hume. Notoriously, a handful of entries display some of the author's prejudices, as when he glossed 'whig' as 'the name of a faction', or when he defined a 'patron' as 'commonly a wretch who supports with insolence, and is paid with flattery'. Some of the preliminary matter reaches a less distinguished level: the grammar and history of the language, for example, come over as perfunctory compared with the main entries. In addition, Johnson's etymologies betray the limit of what was possible in an age when this branch of linguistic study owed as much to inspired guesswork as to scientific enquiry. But for the most part the *Dictionary* was able to demonstrate the fecundity of the language more comprehensively than any of its predecessors. Conscious that his primary role was to record the state of English vocabulary, rather than to legislate for its usage, Johnson registered the entire sweep of words from the crude and demotic to the most rarefied scientific terms and to recent fanciful forms imported from other languages.

The work soon came to be regarded as a standard authority, almost like the statute book. There were several new printings in Johnson's lifetime, but only the 'fourth' edition of 1773 involved an extensive programme of revision, which he carried out in 1771 and 1772. After Johnson died, the cheaper quarto version continued to appear at regular intervals, while a spate of editors offered variously to augment, abstract, and otherwise improve the original work; from 1818 the main such recension was that of the Revd Henry John Todd. Meanwhile the first American edition appeared at Philadelphia in 1819. By this time the *Dictionary* stood for everything that was correct, proper, and of good report; no wonder that Becky Sharp flung a copy out of her carriage, at the start of *Vanity Fair*, in a gesture of youthful rebellion. To more staid spirits such as Noah Webster or Sir James Murray, the book proved a source of inspiration for lexicographic triumphs to come. For all the labour involved, Johnson himself would have liked to do more in this field; as a result, he was disappointed in 1774 when he did not get the chance to revise the *Cyclopedia* (1728) of Ephraim Chambers, one of the models for his own undertaking, since he admitted to having a fondness for 'that muddling work' of compiling reference books.

During the years spent on the *Dictionary*, Johnson made his name in other branches of writing. First came a curious fantasy entitled *The Vision of Theodore, the Hermit of Teneriffe*, contributed to an educational manual by Dodsley called *The Preceptor* (1748); Johnson also supplied the preface. The next year, his long-delayed tragedy *Irene* finally achieved a production. It was presented at Drury Lane by David Garrick, by then a star of the London stage as actor and producer—indeed, Johnson had written a special prologue to mark the start of Garrick's managerial reign at the playhouse on 15 September 1747. The first night of *Irene* on 6 February 1749 had its share of minor disasters, a scene rendered with appropriate dramatic energy in Boswell's account, and the play lasted for only nine performances in all, but it was not a total flop. Johnson managed to survey its fate with sang-froid, comporting himself 'like the Monument' (Boswell, *Life*, 1.199). In fact he received almost £200 from the takings, as well as £100 from Robert Dodsley when the work was published. It is perhaps the only considerable work by Johnson which has not been rehabilitated in modern times: for this we can blame the strenuous neo-classicism of its form and style, together with its remote setting in medieval Turkey. Just one month earlier, on 9 January, appeared Johnson's greatest poem, *The Vanity of Human Wishes*, a reworking of Juvenal's tenth satire. The work comprises a bitter reflection on the disappointments of mortal existence, especially those incident to writers and artists:

There mark what ills the scholar's life assail,
Toil, envy, want, the garret, and the gaol.

A particular strength of the poem lies in its compressed portraits of Wolsey and Charles XII, used within the running argument 'to point a moral [and] adorn a tale'. Dodsley paid the author 15 guineas for the copyright. Again Johnson showed a mastery of the satiric couplet which few beyond Chaucer, Dryden, and Pope in the history of English verse have equalled.

A year later, on 20 March 1750, Johnson instituted his series of 208 essays entitled *The Rambler*, which came out twice a week until 14 March 1752; he received 2 guineas for each issue. It is perhaps the most characteristic work Johnson ever wrote, addressing as it does a wide range of social, religious, political, and literary themes in a stately style. An important series of essays dealt with Milton; others addressed humanitarian issues such as prostitution and capital punishment. Johnson's moral outlook lends his papers a depth seldom attained even by his avowed model, *The Spectator* of Addison and Steele, while his criticism includes some of the first serious discussion of the emerging novel. Aptly, among the coadjutors who supplied a few of the essays for *The Rambler* was Johnson's friend Samuel Richardson, the author of *Clarissa*; others were the learned ladies Elizabeth Carter, Catherine Talbot, and Hester Chapone. By this date Johnson had become something of a champion of women writers, and he gave particular support to the novelist Charlotte Lennox, although it is unlikely that he contributed more than a few lines (if that) to *The Female Quixote* (1752). A sequel to *The Rambler* came out as *The Adventurer* (1752–4), on which Johnson assisted the editor John Hawkesworth by contributing at least thirty papers, mostly grave in tone and philosophical in scope. A thoughtful example is the essay of 16 October 1753, defending the role of visionary 'projectors' in extending human control of the world: 'Many that presume to laugh at projectors would consider a flight through the air in a winged chariot, and the movement of a mighty engine by the steam of water, as equally the dreams of mechanic lunacy' (*Yale Edition*, 2.434).

Bereavements Three days after Johnson's last issue of *The Rambler*, a moving discourse on the concept of finality, Elizabeth Johnson died at the age of sixty-three. She was buried at Bromley in Kent on 26 March 1752. Johnson, greatly distressed, did not attend the funeral, and while he wrote a sermon for the occasion Dr Taylor refused to deliver it, and it remained unpublished until 1788. The sermon takes as its text the opening words of the Anglican burial service, from St John's gospel, and admits candidly that 'to show that grief is vain, is to afford very little comfort' (*Yale Edition*, 14.267). Johnson praises his wife for her devotion, patience, and kindness—and this testimony ought to count for more than the second-hand account of scenes where Garrick mimicked a bibulous Tetty. For the remainder of his days Johnson composed special prayers in memory of his 'dear' wife, and on the last occasion, two years before his death, he wrote in his diary of the 'repentance' both partners had undergone for their faults and misdeeds (ibid., 1.319).

When the *Dictionary* came out Johnson was approaching forty-six. Now finally established as a writer, with a secure base in Gough Square, he had a growing circle of male and female friends. For a time he continued to think about remarriage, but potential brides either died or were found unworthy to succeed Elizabeth. Over the years Johnson's domestic life gradually took on an eccentric air as he admitted to his home a strange cast of derelicts and waifs. These included the blind poet Anna Williams, noted for her fractious ways; the black servant Frank Barber, who had arrived from Jamaica as a boy; the shabby Robert Levet, an unlicensed surgeon who had made a disastrous marriage; an obscure woman named Poll Carmichael, who may have been a former prostitute; and a widow called Elizabeth Desmoulins, who was the daughter of Johnson's godfather Samuel Swynfen and a conceivable candidate to be Johnson's intended second wife. It was a dysfunctional household, as Johnson told Hester Thrale: 'Williams hates everybody. Levet hates Desmoulins and does not love Williams. Desmoulins hates them both. Poll loves none of them' (*Letters*, 3.140). By the late 1770s, after the move to Bolt Court, there were at times seven awkward house-mates in residence, plus a servant. Johnson looked after this peculiar bunch of people with long-suffering kindness, and he helped Anna Williams to bring out a volume of her *Miscellanies in Prose and Verse* (1766). Those who tried to shift for themselves by leaving their protective environment soon got into trouble: Mrs Desmoulins was summoned for debt, while Frank Barber had to be rescued when he ran away to sea. Barber also made an unhappy marriage and after Johnson's death apparently frittered away the sizeable bequest made by his old master.

For all the disturbance produced by these living conditions, Johnson's career continued to blossom. He remained poor, and once in March 1756 Samuel Richardson came to his aid when he was arrested for a debt of about £5. Other signs were more hopeful: he had now been awarded the degree of master of arts by Oxford University, in time for the letters 'A.M.' to appear as an imprimatur on the title-page of the *Dictionary*. He had established a solid base in the university, and regularly visited Trinity College to call on the scholar and poet Thomas Warton, who became professor of poetry in 1757. A year before this Johnson was appointed editor of a new journal called the *Literary Magazine*. Among the most notable of his many contributions was a review published in the summer of 1757, devoted to a complacent book on metaphysics by Soame Jenyns. Johnson rips apart the Panglossian sentiments of his unfortunate adversary and substitutes his own hard-headed appraisal of life as it is actually lived by the majority of humankind. Some of Johnson's most incisive shorter pieces appeared in other journalistic outlets at this stage. The *Literary Magazine* carried forceful, if brief, essays on the opening phase of the Seven Years' War, including the martyrdom of Admiral Byng and the unsuccessful raid on Rochefort in September 1757. Johnson reviewed a wide selection of books, including a manual of beekeeping, a catalogue of Scottish bishops, a work by Stephen Hales on distilling sea water, and an onslaught on tea drinking by Joseph Hanway, which provoked a strong defence of the habit by Johnson, a confirmed addict. Hanway, he claimed, had exaggerated the harmful effects of 'this watery luxury', which he himself had not yet felt despite 'soliciting them … year after year' (*Yale Edition*, 11.252–3).

Johnson's concerns were as varied as ever at this date. One month he would be writing a short life of Frederick the Great; soon afterwards he would be attacking the management of the Foundling Hospital, London's prime charitable institution. Presciently he fixed on a work dealing with the struggles for the Ohio valley as a harbinger of imperial conflicts to come. But amid these miscellaneous writings he had a much larger undertaking now under way, although it was making slow progress: this was a renewed effort to carry out the edition of Shakespeare projected a decade earlier. Subscription proposals were issued in June 1756, with the firm of Tonson now on board as part of the promoting group of booksellers. Delivery was originally promised for 1757, but the years went by and the work remained incomplete until 1765.

This dereliction aside, Johnson had not been inactive. Between April 1758 and April 1760 he provided over 100 essays to a weekly journal called the *Universal Chronicle*. These papers, written in the guise of 'the Idler', were in a more relaxed style than those of *The Rambler*, dilating often on the follies incumbent on the literary life. The series gained great popularity and was reprinted in other organs up and down the country. Johnson made £84 from the collected edition, published in 1761. Among the best-known essays are nos. 60 and 61, satirizing the irresistible rise of a superficial man of the literary world called Dick Minim. 'Criticism', the first paper drily opens, 'is a study by which men grow important and formidable at very small expense' (*Yale Edition*, 2.184). About the same time, on 20 April 1759, a very different work came before the world: this was *Rasselas*, otherwise known as *The Prince of Abyssinia*, an adaptation of the French *conte* grafted on to the Oriental tale. The central characters embark on an educative grand tour of an imaginary Africa, proceeding into Egypt, and encounter as they go a succession of mortifying episodes which show the delusive nature of most quests for human happiness. The book cost 5 shillings for two small volumes; Johnson is said to have written the work in the evenings of a single week. He was paid £100 for the first edition, money used to defray costs of the funeral service for Samuel's mother. Sarah Johnson had died about 20 January 1759 at the age of almost ninety and had been buried in Lichfield on 23 January. Once more there was an absentee, as her son did not put in an appearance, although Samuel knew of her final illness and had written to her three times in her final week on earth. 'I am very much grieved at my mother's death', he told his step-daughter Lucy Porter soon afterwards, 'and do not love to think nor to write about it' (*Letters*, 1.183). It was not until the winter of 1761–2 that Johnson, somehow liberated by bereavement, returned to his home town after a long unbroken sojourn in London.

Pensioner and clubman The accession of George III in 1760 meant that for the first time in his adult lifetime Johnson could look on the monarchy with some approval, and hope for a loosening of the grip that the whig ascendancy had maintained for almost half a century. He began to appear in the eyes of many a figure of authority, 'Dictionary Johnson', even though financial pressures made him move to smaller lodgings, first in Gray's Inn and then in Inner Temple Lane. In July 1762 relief came when he was awarded a pension of £300 a year by the first lord of the Treasury, the earl of Bute, perhaps less for services rendered than as an encouragement to support the new administration. Opponents were quick to leap on this as an act of corrupt compliance with the unpopular Bute regime, and for many years Johnson had to endure savage attacks on his integrity as a writer.

Johnson's rise to greater prominence brought with it a widening array of social contacts. At a philanthropic meeting on 1 May 1760 he had his only recorded meeting with Benjamin Franklin. Johnson had been a member of the Society of Arts since 1756, and took a hand in promoting its major exhibition of paintings in 1760. Among his colleagues was Joshua Reynolds, whom he first met *c*.1756 and with whom he took a holiday jaunt to Devon during the late summer of 1762. The nucleus of the familiar Johnson circle was already in place: by now his acquaintances included Oliver Goldsmith, Edmund Burke, Thomas Percy, Topham Beauclerk, Bennett Langton, and Charles Burney. In May 1763 there burst into this constellation a startling newcomer named James *Boswell, who achieved a long-standing desire at the age of twenty-two when he chanced to encounter Johnson in a bookshop off Covent Garden. Something in the ambitious young man lifted the spirits of the great man, who allowed him access almost daily until Boswell left for the continent on 6 August; the two drove to Harwich, where they 'embraced and parted with tenderness' on the quayside (Boswell, *Life*, 1.472). Most of the group surrounding Johnson served as founder members of the famous Literary Club, although Boswell and Percy were forced to wait a few years for admission, as was (most pointedly) Johnson's old ally Garrick.

A different world opened up in 1765 when Johnson made the acquaintance of the rich Thrale family. The husband Henry was a businessman and MP, while his wife Hester was a well-born woman with literary interests and considerable social gifts. She soon became Johnson's most confidential friend. In addition to their home at the family brewery in Southwark, the Thrales had inherited a country estate at Streatham, 10 miles south of central London. Johnson first visited the couple in 1766, and within a few years he was allocated his own quarters at Streatham Park, where he spent prolonged periods. A chemical laboratory was even set up there in 1771 for his use, until Henry Thrale decided that the would-be scientist might have an accident owing to his short sight and go up in smoke. A library wing was added to the house, and here in 1780 Thrale hung up thirteen portraits by Reynolds, with pictures of his own wife and daughter joined by the principal members of Johnson's circle. Some of the most detailed knowledge available of Johnson's daily existence comes from the *Anecdotes* which Hester Thrale (then Piozzi) compiled after his death, drawing on their intimacy in the last fifteen years of his life. It has even been speculated that he engaged in masochistic practices with Hester. The evidence for this includes a mysterious padlock left in her care in 1768; a line in Johnson's diary for 1771, referring in Latin to some 'mad reflection on shackles and hand-cuffs' (Johnson, *Yale Edition*, 1.140); and a strange letter in French, which he addressed to her in June 1773 (*Letters*, 2.38–9) and which alludes persistently to bondage. The suggestion may go along with other 'dark hints' in the biography by Sir John Hawkins (1787) that Johnson harboured some guilty secret about his sexual past. In the present state of knowledge it is impossible to confirm or deny the stories.

Altogether, as he moved through his fifties, Johnson was travelling more. He began to pay regular visits to his old haunts in Lichfield, Birmingham, Ashbourne, and Oxford, meeting long-standing friends such as Hector, Taylor, and

William Adams. A further contact in the midlands was the local poet Anna Seward; her father, a canon of Lichfield, was married to a daughter of the schoolmaster John Hunter. In later years Anna turned violently against Johnson. Other trips took him to Lincolnshire, to Northamptonshire, and to Cambridge, where he conversed on the subject of his old acquaintance Christopher Smart. As he became less rooted in the metropolis, and found himself distracted by his social engagements, his literary productivity slowed in the 1760s, with only a few smaller items such as his exposure of the notorious Cock Lane ghost in February 1762. This brought on him the obloquy of Charles Churchill, a dissolute clergyman and friend of Wilkes, who possessed great skill as a satirist; Johnson found it hard to live down his sneering portrayal of the overbearing Pomposo. One of the more effective thrusts in Churchill's poem, *The Ghost*, concerns the long-delayed edition of Shakespeare:

He for subscribers baits his hook,
And takes their cash—but where's the book?

At last Johnson completed his work, and he was able to meet his critics in the eye when publication took place in October 1765. The eight volumes contain the full canon of accepted plays by Shakespeare, excluding *Pericles*, but none of the poems; the volumes are famous for pithy textual commentary, as well as discreet analysis of earlier editions. They contain decisive critical judgments on each play, with a masterly aside on Falstaff and a candid admission by the editor of his feelings of shock at the death of Cordelia, together with a humanely poised preface. The work further confirmed Johnson's stature, and a second edition was soon required. He obtained a total of £475 for the two editions. During the summer Johnson had received the degree of doctor of laws from Dublin University, thus permitting the designation 'Dr Johnson' which has been his regular public appellation ever since. He moved house again, taking his strange menagerie along with him to another lodging off Fleet Street which happened to be named Johnson's Court.

Although he was now comfortably into middle age, Johnson retained a sprightly and almost boyish side. With his younger friends Beauclerk and Langton he had always been ready for a 'frisk' at any hour of the day or night. According to one story he used to walk the streets at night with the Italian writer Giuseppe Baretti; there was a strange sequel in October 1769 when Baretti found himself charged with committing a murder in the Haymarket. The Johnson circle turned out in force to support their friend, and to give character references in court when he was tried at the Old Bailey. Their evidence had its effect, as Baretti was acquitted on the grounds of self-defence. More opportunities for relaxation arose when Johnson met Hester Thrale: he spent many happy hours improvising light verse and playing with her children, especially the precocious Hester Maria, known as Queeney. A great believer in pleasure, he commended innocent amusements and refused to join the fashionable clamour against the dissipations of luxury. He understood the therapeutic benefit of trifling pursuits, and as he 'delighted in exercising his mind on the science of numbers' (Boswell, *Life*, 3.207) he took great satisfaction in performing feats of mental arithmetic when feeling disturbed. Among his numerous pieces of miscellaneous writing in middle life was introductory material to the first book in English on the game of draughts, written by William Payne, 'teacher of mathematics' (1756). Characteristically Johnson remarked in his dedication, 'The same skill, and often the same degree of skill, is exerted in great and little things'.

By February 1766 Boswell had returned from an extended grand tour, and from then on he contrived to spend a good deal of time with his idol whenever he could escape his responsibilities in Scotland. The importunate Boswell arranged for Johnson's circle of acquaintance to grow. Sometimes this was agreeable, as when the Corsican patriot Pasquale Paoli was presented to Johnson in October 1769; sometimes it took more manipulation, as when Boswell lured him into dining in company with John Wilkes on 15 May 1776—a meeting Johnson enjoyed more than he expected. Another young friend was Robert Chambers, who succeeded Sir William Blackstone in 1766 as Vinerian professor of law at Oxford. Chambers found great difficulty in producing the lectures required by his post, and Johnson travelled to the university to assist in their composition. His role remained virtually an unbroken secret until the 1980s. He lent support generously to other scholars, often supplying dedications anonymously, and advising Percy in the compilation of the *Reliques of Ancient English Poetry* (1765). At the end of 1768 Johnson rejoiced to see Joshua Reynolds installed as the first president of the Royal Academy, an event that was quickly followed by a knighthood, and in the following year he himself became an honorary professor in ancient literature at the academy. Though never deeply versed in painting, he attended the presidential lectures Reynolds delivered at regular intervals, and gave his friend some help when these were published collectively as *Discourses*.

However, it was the Literary Club, formed at the instigation of Reynolds in 1764, that saw Johnson's intellect shining most radiantly in a semi-public forum. One of the founder members, John Hawkins, grated on his colleagues and soon left the group. Johnson had no regrets, as he thought Hawkins a brute and, worse, 'a most unclubable man' (*Diary and Letters*, 1.40–41). During Johnson's lifetime the group expanded from nine to thirty-five, and he had little relish for the company of some newcomers: Adam Smith was one with whom he apparently preferred not to consort. Nevertheless, he attended quite faithfully as long as health permitted, and served as the focus of conversation and collegiality. Many of the most distinguished minds of the age came together in the club, even though women were excluded and political and social factors ruled out men such as John Wilkes and Joseph Priestley. Leading practitioners in almost every field became members, ranging from Reynolds, Burke, Garrick, Goldsmith, Boswell, Burney, Edward Gibbon, Smith, Percy, and Chambers to the politicians Charles James Fox and William Windham, the orientalist William Jones, the dramatists Richard Brinsley Sheridan and

George Colman, the Shakespearian scholars Edmond Malone and George Steevens, the writers Joseph and Thomas Warton, the virtuosi Lord Charlemont and Sir William Hamilton, the lawyer William Scott, and the scientist Joseph Banks. Yet every one of these willingly ceded pre-eminence to Johnson, who was able to cow even the most self-confident speakers such as Burke, Fox, and Garrick into submission. This he did less by purely aggressive behaviour than by his stunning range of knowledge, his speed of thought, his verbal articulateness, and his command of argumentative technique. The club had no agenda, no platform, and no transactions to record, but it left an indelible mark on the high culture of the age.

Home and abroad As a new decade opened, Johnson—now into his sixties—turned again to politics. A serious proposal came from William Strahan, the publisher of major works by Adam Smith, David Hume, and William Robertson, that Johnson should join him as a member of parliament. In 1771 Strahan recommended his friend to the Treasury as one with 'perfect good affection to his Majesty'. It was a long shot, and nothing came of this bold initiative, even though Burke gave it as his opinion that, had Johnson entered the Commons early in life, he would have proved himself 'the greatest speaker that ever was there' (Boswell, *Life*, 2.137–9). At this point Johnson chose to resume the career as a political writer which he had largely abandoned a generation earlier. His first pamphlet, *The False Alarm*, published on 17 January 1770, dealt with the struggle between parliament and the renegade member John Wilkes, and put the government case with wit and energy. In the following year he wrote *Thoughts* on a territorial dispute between Spain and Britain concerning the Falkland Islands, issued on 26 March 1774. In *The Patriot*, which came out on 12 October 1774, he backed Lord North's ministry against Wilkites and other opposition groups, in the hope of assisting Henry Thrale to retain his parliamentary seat in Southwark, as did indeed occur. The last pamphlet in this sequence, *Taxation No Tyranny* (issued on 8 March 1775), was concerned with the thorny question of American independence, then just on the point of boiling over into violent insurrection. Yet amid this activity Johnson had not abandoned his old role as lexicographer: in 1773 he supervised publication of a revised 'fourth' version of his *Dictionary*, incorporating many important additions in its coverage. A fresh edition of the Shakespeare edition appeared in the same year, with help from George Steevens. At this time Johnson's physical condition and psychological health were equally fragile; his old bouts of melancholy sometimes returned to plague him. He spent much of his time with the Thrales, often visiting them in their new house at Brighton.

However, it was a much longer expedition that did most to raise his spirits. In August 1773 he set off on a three-month journey to the highlands and islands of Scotland, in company with the assiduous Boswell, who had set up the trip. Together with a servant, the two men travelled up the east coast from Edinburgh via St Andrews and Aberdeen, reaching Inverness on 28 August; from this point they encountered a much harsher world, necessitating some rugged hikes over desolate mountain regions. Passing through the western highlands to Skye, the voyagers repeatedly came across vestiges of the epic events of 1745–6, when Prince Charles Edward had mounted his unsuccessful rising and then undertaken his desperate flight through the heather. Johnson and Boswell spent a month on Skye, their stay prolonged by bad weather. Next they proceeded through the Inner Hebrides to Iona and Mull before they returned to the mainland on 22 October, not without relief after some perilous moments on their journey. They visited Glasgow and Auchinleck, Boswell's family home, before they got back to Edinburgh on 9 November. This courageous venture into an almost uncharted world resulted in two extraordinary books. Boswell's *Journal of a Tour to the Hebrides* (1785) has the chatty informality of a 'rough' guide: its focus is on Johnson, as it describes his charged encounters with the native population, whether humble cottagers or important personages like Lord Monboddo and Boswell's formidable father Lord Auchinleck. Johnson's very different work, *A Journey to the Western Islands of Scotland*, was published in January 1775; it earned him 200 guineas, as well as the admiration of George III and considerable success in terms of sales. While on the trip, Johnson had not thought it beneath himself to engage in horseplay, imitating a kangaroo (which James Cook's first voyage had recently brought to the attention of the West) and allowing Boswell to dress him up in highland costume; but the book shows nothing of these episodes.

The *Journey* aroused some adverse comment in Scotland, on account of its alleged bias against the nation, but Johnson was able to shrug off most of this criticism. In the text he had treated with disdain the supposed epics of the ancient Gaelic warrior-bard Ossian, describing the exploits of his father, Fingal, which had become an exemplar of sublime and unclassical writing. Johnson expressed his view that the poems were in fact a modern concoction by their 'editor', James Macpherson. When an incensed Macpherson complained about this treatment, Johnson repeated his challenge for the original manuscripts to be produced, if they could be. Macpherson's demand for retraction produced a famous response in which Johnson defied his opponent in the face of his 'impudent and foolish' letter. Such quarrels aside, the book is a profound meditation on the nature of primitive society, especially on one reliant on an oral culture; Johnson confronts a realm of experience foreign to the Enlightenment illuminati of London and Edinburgh, including a Gaelic legacy and vestiges of a Catholic past, as well as a degree of poverty and deprivation. The *Journey* stands as one of its author's most eloquent and challenging works, a great document of cultural studies before the topic was invented.

In the following year Johnson embarked on a more modest venture. Virtually the whole of the three months from July to September was devoted to a tour of north Wales, the home country of Hester Thrale. She joined the party along with her husband and the nine-year-old Queeney, who had long been a favourite with Johnson. This trip was less eventful than its predecessor, although there were significant stops at Lichfield and Ashbourne when the travellers met Lucy Porter, Anna Seward, and John Taylor, as well as a long-time friend, Mary Cobb, and the doctor and writer Erasmus Darwin. Johnson never turned the journal he kept into a book, although it was ultimately published in 1816; Hester Thrale wrote her own account. The final jaunt took place from September to November 1775, when the Thrales and their language tutor Giuseppe Baretti took Johnson to Paris—the sole occasion on which he left Britain. Johnson left only brief notes concerning the journey, while Hester wrote a fuller report: the accounts were published together as *The French Journals of Mrs Thrale and Dr Johnson* (1932).

Plans were subsequently laid to fulfil an ambition Johnson had long held when the Thrales and Baretti arranged to conduct him to Italy in 1776. The scheme perished when the Thrales lost their only surviving son at the age of nine, so that Johnson never made his anticipated journey to the centre of Christendom. Equally, his life had been saddened by the sudden death of Goldsmith on 4 April 1774. Against this he made some new friends among the learned ladies of the day, including Hannah More when she went to London in 1774. In March 1777 he met Frances, known as Fanny, the daughter of his old acquaintance Dr Charles Burney. Her spectacular début as a novelist with *Evelina* (1778) was encouraged by Johnson, as well as by the Thrales and their friends, and she continued to delight the circle in the following years. Another occasion of pride was the award in March 1775 of a doctorate from Johnson's alma mater. The memory of his reckless and severely curtailed spell in the university was now largely effaced.

The year 1776 witnessed great events in the world, and despite his frustration over the Italian trip Johnson too found his life full of incident. He moved a small distance to his last home at 8 Bolt Court, located in yet another alley leading off Fleet Street. A springtime ramble to Oxford, Lichfield, and Ashbourne is known from a detailed report by Boswell, who was permitted to accompany his elderly friend. Another jaunt followed to Bath, to see the Thrales: while there Johnson and Boswell took the chance of visiting Bristol, where they met Hannah More and investigated the store of manuscripts left by Thomas Chatterton, whose Rowley poems had become a *cause célèbre* of the day. Late in the year Johnson was in Brighton with the Thrales, but his health was not good. The following year saw a similar pattern: spells of sickness, interrupted by a journey to Oxford and to the midlands where he was joined for a memorable week in Ashbourne by Boswell, whose account of this episode forms a high point in the *Life*. In the summer Johnson's other main concern had been the expected execution of the Revd William Dodd, who had been convicted of forgery; even though Johnson had only a slight acquaintance with Dodd, he threw himself energetically into an unsuccessful campaign to save the clergyman's life. By comparison the following year was uneventful, although it did feature one immortal

sequence in Boswell's narrative, describing an unexpected meeting between Johnson and a forgotten college mate from his early days at Oxford, named Oliver Edwards. Though basically comic, it is an episode fraught with a range of human emotions, as Johnson struggles to recapture his youthful self amid the trite importunities of his contemporary.

The last phase As he approached seventy Johnson underwent more distressing experiences. The death of Garrick on 20 January 1779 was followed by a resplendent funeral at Westminster Abbey, which the Literary Club attended in full force. Johnson himself was in poor health and repeatedly under the doctor's care. Then in June Henry Thrale suffered the first of a number of severe strokes from which he never fully recovered. The brewery had long been mismanaged by the indolent Thrale, and for much of the time Johnson had to help Hester to keep it afloat. None the less the old man was able to initiate one more literary project, which proved to be the ultimate success in his career. This took the form of a series of prefaces to a new collection of the English poets, best-known today as *The Lives of the Poets*. In a contract signed on 29 March 1777, Johnson had agreed with a consortium of booksellers to supply 'a concise account' of some fifty poets: he undertook to do the work for £200, and though he eventually received twice this amount it is generally accepted that he could have held out for a much bigger sum. The first instalment came out in March 1779, the second in 1780, and the third in May 1781. Although Johnson's brusque treatment of well-connected nonentities gave rise to some hostile commentary, his major lives were quickly recognized as setting a new standard for English literary biography. In particular, the surveys of Cowley, Milton, Dryden, Swift, and Pope exemplify Johnson's serious concern with the deepest springs of creativity, as well as his ability to explore with considerable insight some individuals whose character and work aroused profound antipathy in him. Even in an age of greater theoretical sophistication, his reading of mainstream poetry from the seventeenth and eighteenth centuries remains canonical, by reason of its attention to verbal detail, its decisive judgments, and its robust expression.

One aspect of Johnson's career illustrated by the *Lives* is the good state of relations he maintained with the London publishing world. Born into the family of a bookseller, he enjoyed a close affinity with many of the leading figures in the trade—from Cave and Dodsley through to Andrew Millar, Thomas Longman, and William Strahan. Several of these men were personal friends: Strahan acted as his banker in later years, and the Revd George Strahan, son of the publisher, edited Johnson's prayers in 1785. A number of his later volumes were issued by Thomas Cadell, among the most respected booksellers of the age. Johnson was equally intimate with printers such as Richardson and Edmund Allen. It is natural that he should be regarded as an exemplary figure in the history of the book, one who helped to develop a strong publishing industry while advancing his own literary career by exploiting the market forces of the day.

Despite the triumphant achievement of the *Lives*, the shades were closing in on Johnson. He lost more of his friends—Beauclerk in 1780, the enfeebled Henry Thrale in 1781, and then successively his long-time house-mates Levet in 1782 and Anna Williams in 1783. One result was the noble elegy 'On the Death of Dr Levet', commending the useful life of this rough and dishevelled individual. Johnson's own health deteriorated steadily, with emphysema and dropsy added to the list of ailments. On 17 June 1783 he suffered a stroke and was rendered speechless for two days. Gradually he recovered from this blow, and he thought for a while that his general health had taken a turn for the better. But the respite was not long. A painful tumour on the scrotum made his last days excruciating, even after some courageous surgery performed by the patient on himself. It became apparent to his friends that he was unlikely to live long. In June 1784, after consulting Reynolds and other friends, Boswell approached Lord Chancellor Thurlow for the grant of a royal pension to enable the invalid to spend some time in Italy, as he dreaded the English winter, but eventually plans fell through.

One more incident clouded Johnson's final days: for a while it had been apparent that Hester Thrale was seeking to detach herself from her old friend. Any decision on her part to remarry in 1784 might well have brought a jealous reaction from Johnson, but when he learned that her new husband was to be the singing teacher Gabriel Piozzi—poor, Italian, and Catholic—his repressed feelings burst out. On 2 July he wrote her a short and bitter letter upbraiding her on the step she had 'ignominiously' taken (*Letters*, 4.338). The marriage took place on 23 July, and the Piozzis left for the continent at the start of September, with the breach between the two old friends only partially healed. For the remainder of her long life Hester Piozzi revered the memory of Johnson and did much to keep his name before the public. As for Boswell, his own final meeting with Johnson took place on 30 June, when the old man walked away into Bolt Court for ever 'with a kind of pathetick briskness' (Boswell, *Life*, 4.339). Once the news of Johnson's death reached Boswell back in Edinburgh, he was left deeply distressed. This was one reason why it took him years to make progress on the biography in which he had invested so much for so long.

The last months of Johnson's life were diversified by an occasional social outing, including dinners at the Literary Club as late as June 1784, as well as evenings with a new group which began to meet at the Essex Head tavern, off the Strand, late in 1783. He was able to make visits to Lichfield, Ashbourne, and Oxford, completing cycles of alliance and attachment which went back well over fifty years. But his illness grew worse, and on 8 December 1784 he made his final will, with a codicil on the following day. As he sank into death, numerous friends including Reynolds, Langton, Windham, and Burney called on him at 8 Bolt Court: at first he spoke about his spiritual condition, and then towards the end he lay composedly, enduring the pain with calm resignation. About seven in the evening on 13 December he died at his home, without any struggle, supposedly after uttering the words 'iam moriturus' ('now about to die'). He was seventy-five. His funeral and burial took place at Westminster Abbey on 20 December. A monument, to which his friends subscribed, was erected in St Paul's Cathedral in 1796. In his will he made many bequests to his friends, leaving the residue of the estate to his servant Francis Barber. His library of some 3000 volumes was sold by James Christie the elder on 16–19 February 1785, realizing £242.

Johnson and posterity Already a celebrity in his lifetime, Johnson was catapulted into further fame by his death. Half a dozen biographers quickly launched themselves on the market, so that the *Anecdotes* of Hester Piozzi (1786) and the life by Sir John Hawkins (1787) entered what was already a crowded and contentious field. However, it was the appearance of Boswell's magisterial biography (1791), filled with a new density of personal detail, that made the quiddities of a single individual so familiar to an immense range of readers. In the early nineteenth century Thomas Babington Macaulay gave a faintly comic reading of Johnson, deploring his bigotry while commending his mental powers, and Thomas Carlyle hailed the sage as a tragic hero embodying the destiny of the man of letters. Both these writers wove their assessments around reviews of Boswell's life, and for generations it was this 'Johnsoniad', as Carlyle termed it, that kept alive the picture of Johnson as a doughty and difficult man, battling with resilience and good humour against the onslaughts of fate. In this guise he has turned up as a character in novels, films, and television comedies, and has even made a fictional appearance as a private investigator. Overall it is not altogether a false picture, even though commentary in the second half of the twentieth century sought to roll back this stereotypical view. Academic scholarship has gone a long way to reclaim Johnson as a serious figure in intellectual history, but a stubborn popular image has grown up of a learned and aggressive conversationalist, brawling against his friends and adversaries with a bad temper but a tender heart. This version of Sam Johnson contains enough glimmerings of the complex truth to survive even today.

Almost 6 feet tall and raw-boned, Johnson towered over most of his contemporaries. His physique was as clumsy as his appearance was unprepossessing: he had a face disfigured by scrofula, and a body afflicted by involuntary convulsions. He suffered too from defective eyesight and hearing. More disconcertingly, his behaviour was marked by odd grunts and head-rolling, and despite heroic efforts at politeness, his manners and personal habits struck fastidious people as gross. A lengthening list of ailments finally made his invalid condition obvious to everyone, and often his psychological distress caused him to look still more peculiar in company. On first introduction, Johnson appeared to William Hogarth an 'idiot', until the monstrous figure began to speak with such eloquence that he seemed rather to be inspired (Boswell, *Life*, 1.147). He even contrived to master physical activities like swimming, rowing, and riding, and more than once gave evidence of prowess with his fists in self-defence. His whole life was a triumph of the mind over the recalcitrant body, a victory of an inspired savage over the timid proprieties of good breeding and complacent orthodoxy.

Wracked by acute states of anxiety and depression, doubtful of his own industry, Johnson produced works of immense scope and energy. Uncertain of his own salvation, he lived a life of almost exemplary piety. Humble before God and respectful of established authority, he was without a grain of snobbery. Never rich, he behaved with the utmost generosity to the poor, whose condition he viewed without sentimentality. He showed kindness towards the weak and the lowly, children, and animals, his attitude to the last reflected in a gesture of gruff affection towards his cat Hodge. Even his attitude to women could be called fairly enlightened by the standards of the time. Nothing is more indicative of his nature than his tenderness towards beggars and prostitutes. The *Life* contains one 'well attested' example, when Johnson found a poor woman of the town lying exhausted in the street, carried her home, and had her taken into care for a long period 'at considerable expense' (Boswell, *Life*, 4.321–2). On the other hand he had the purest scorn for foolish idlers, however well connected socially, and he showed himself willing to defy the proprieties by delivering a verbal battery on the person of Lord Chesterfield, one of the most punctilious and blue-blooded members of the aristocracy. Often irascible, he seldom bore a grudge.

Johnson was arguably the most distinguished man of letters in English history. His range as a writer is astonishing: he excelled in criticism, satire, biography, the moral essay, fiction, scholarly editing, travel writing, political pamphleteering, journalism, and lexicography. He produced distinguished poetry both in English and in Latin. Apart from this, he composed noteworthy sermons, impressive prayers, a moving diary, and superb letters. Although he did not write any sustained historical work, his library was full of books dealing with the ancient world, besides medieval and modern Europe: much of his output shows the extent of his immersion in the study of the past. Well versed in the law, theology, and medicine, plus several branches of science and practical endeavour, he had the logical rigour of an advocate, the common sense of a successful businessman (as his role in shoring up the Thrales' brewery indicates), the hands-on abilities of an engineer, and the curiosity of a research chemist. He survives both as the fount of amusing and instructive anecdotes, a tribute to his human worth, and as the author of enduring masterpieces, a tribute to his intellectual distinction. Outside Shakespeare, perhaps no one in English history has become such a representative figure of his age, and no one has done more to dignify the literary profession in Britain.   PAT ROGERS

Sources Boswell, *Life* · *The Yale edition of the works of Samuel Johnson*, ed. A. T. Hazen and others, 13 vols. (1958–) [in progress] · *The letters of Samuel Johnson*, ed. B. Redford, 5 vols. (1992–4) · A. L. Reade, *Johnsonian gleanings*, 11 vols. (1909–52) · G. B. Hill, ed., *Johnsonian miscellanies*, 2 vols. (1897) · H. L. Piozzi, *Anecdotes of Samuel Johnson*, ed. S. C. Roberts (1932) · J. L. Clifford, *Young Sam Johnson* (1955) · J. L. Clifford, *Dictionary Johnson: Samuel Johnson's middle years* (1979) · J. D. Fleeman and J. McLaverty, *A bibliography of the works of Samuel Johnson*, 2 vols. (2000) · *The works of Samuel Johnson Ll.D.*, 12 vols. (1823) · P. Rogers, *The Johnson encyclopedia* (1996) · N. Page, *A Dr Johnson chronology* (1990) · *Diary and letters of Madame D'Arblay*, ed. [C. Barrett], 7 vols. (1842–6) · *Thraliana: the diary of Mrs. Hester Lynch Thrale (later Mrs. Piozzi), 1776–1809*, ed. K. C. Balderston, 2nd edn, 2 vols. (1951) · T. Kaminski, *The early career of Samuel Johnson* (1987) · J. Hawkins, *The life of Samuel Johnson, LL.D*, ed. B. H. Davis (New York, 1961)

Archives BL, diary of a journey to France, Add. MS 35299 · BL, dictionary, Egerton MS 2329 · BL, draft of *Irene*, MS King's 306 · BL, journal of tour of North Wales, memoranda, Add. MS 12070 · BL, proofs of dictionary, vol. 1, C 45 k 3 · Bodl. Oxf., diary · Bodl. Oxf., papers · Dr Johnson's House, London, letters, printed material · Harvard U., Houghton L., scrapbooks of bills, MSS, clippings · Hunt. L., letters and literary MSS · JRL, annotated dictionary vol. 2 · JRL, notebook of a French journey [copy] · Morgan L., papers · NRA, priv. coll., diary, literary MSS, papers · NYPL, papers · Pembroke College, Oxford, corresp. and papers, prayers, and meditations · Royal Arch., his notebook with annotations by George III · U. Wales, Aberystwyth, MSS relating to Shakespeare · V&A NAL, proof sheets (with corrections) of his *Lives of the English poets*, 2 vols., corresp. · Yale U., annotations on Spence's *Anecdotes* | BL, corresp. with Thomas Birch, Add. MS 4310 · BL, letters to Charlotte Lennox and Alexander Lennox, MS RP 183 · BL, letters to John Nichols, Add. MS 5159 · BL, letters to John Perkins, RP 476 [copies] · BL, corresp. with Francis Reynolds, RP 186 [copies] · BL, letters to Susan Arabella Thrale, RP 5318 · Four Oaks Farm, Somerville, New Jersey, Hyde collection · JRL, corresp. with Hester Lynch Thrale · Samuel Johnson Birthplace Museum, Lichfield, letters to Hester Lynch Thrale · Trinity College, Oxford, letters to Thomas Warton · Yale U., Beinecke L., corresp. with James Boswell, papers, verses; documents connected with Lichfield

Likenesses miniature?, *c*.1736, repro. in J. L. Clifford, *Young Samuel Johnson*, 313 · J. Reynolds, oils, 1756–7, NPG [*see illus.*] · J. Reynolds, oils, 1769, Knole, Kent; copy, Tate collection · J. Reynolds, oils, *c*.1775, Rothschild collection · J. Nollekens, clay bust, 1777, repro. in Boswell, *Life*, ed. Hill, vol. 4, p. 555 · J. Nollekens, marble bust, *c*.1777, Westminster Abbey · J. Barry, oils, *c*.1777–1780, NPG · J. Reynolds, oils, *c*.1778, Tate collection; on loan to NPG · J. Trotter, etching, pubd 1782 (after J. Harding), BM, NPG · J. Opie, oils, *c*.1783–1784, Harvard U. · J. Flaxman, Wedgwood medallion, 1784, Wedgwood Museum, Stoke-on-Trent · J. Reynolds, oils, *c*.1784, Haverford College, Pennsylvania · J. Heath, line engraving, 1786 (after J. Opie), BM, NPG · T. Trotter, line engraving, pubd 1786, BM, NPG · J. Hall, line engraving, 1787 (after J. Reynolds), BM, NPG · J. Sayers, caricature, etching, pubd 1788, NPG · C. Townley, mezzotint, pubd 1792 (after J. Opie), NPG · J. Bacon senior, marble statue, 1796, St Paul's Cathedral, London · J. Neagle, line engraving, pubd 1806 (after J. Reynolds), NPG · J. Neagle, line engraving, pubd 1810 (after J. Reynolds), NPG · J. Barry, group portrait, oils (*The Society for the Encouragement of the Arts*), RSA · J. Hoskins, bust, NPG · O. Humphry, etching (after J. Reynolds), NPG · attrib. F. Reynolds, oils, Trinity College, Oxford; also separately attrib. to T. Palmer · S. W. Reynolds, mezzotint (after J. Reynolds), BM, NPG · T. Rowlandson, double caricature, chalk caricature (with Boswell), V&A · oils (after J. Opie), NPG · wax sculpture, NPG

Wealth at death approx. £2300; residuary legatee (F. Barber) received approx. £1500: will, Hawkins, *Life*

Johnson, Thomas (1595×1600–1644), apothecary and soldier, was born at Selby in Yorkshire, probably between 1595 and 1600, of unknown parentage. All that is known of his early life is that at some time he lived 'in the further side of Lincolnshire' (Gerard, 74). Presumably he received a good education for in 1620 he was apprenticed to William Bell, a London apothecary, and in 1628 took his freedom in the Society of Apothecaries.

Johnson was keenly interested in botany, and in 1626, while still an apprentice, he travelled not only into Kent but also north as far as Yorkshire and Durham, searching for plants and finding several not previously recorded in Britain. In the spring of 1629 he visited Hampstead Heath. Later that year he made a five-day journey into Kent and paid a second visit to Hampstead Heath, on each of these occasions in the company of nine companions, mostly fellow apothecaries. These excursions are recorded in *Iter plantarum investigationis … in agrum Cantianum 1629* and *Ericetum Hamstedianum*, published together in 1629. Also that year he contributed a Latin address to John Parkinson's *Paradisi in sole paradisus terrestris*, a measure of the standing he had already achieved among his contemporaries. In addition to pursuing his profession as an apothecary on Snow Hill, in London, Johnson continued to be active as an author and editor and in 1632, after another journey into Kent, he published an enlarged edition of the 1629 plant lists as *Descriptio itineris plantarum investigationis … in agrum Cantianum 1632*.

In 1633 he produced his most important work, *The herball … gathered by John Gerarde … very much enlarged and amended by Thomas Johnson, citizen and apothecarye of London*. In editing this book Johnson used various signs to indicate his additions and major alterations so that it is possible to distinguish the revised from the original text. It was reprinted in 1636.

In 1634 Johnson spent two months in Bath, acting privately in a medical capacity, but also preparing plans and descriptions of the city and its warm springs. He left in July to join a group of distinguished apothecaries on a plant-hunting tour of southern England and published an account of this journey under the title *Mercurius botanicus* (1634). This included a 62-page catalogue of plant names in alphabetical order, and represents an important step towards the compilation of a complete list of British plants. Following the catalogue is the separate section on Bath entitled *Thermae Bathonicae*. Also published in 1634 was a translation from the French of a book by the surgeon Ambroise Paré, which most although not all authorities attribute to Johnson. In the summer of 1639 Johnson, accompanied by a few companions, travelled into north Wales in order to record the plants growing there. The results of this journey were published in *Mercurii botanici pars altera* (1641), Johnson's last publication.

By 1642 conditions in London had worsened and Johnson, a firm supporter of the royalist cause, left for Oxford where the king had established his court. In May 1643 he was created honorary doctor of physic, doubtless in recognition of his loyalty as well as for his learning. He joined the king's forces, and in November 1643, with the rank of lieutenant-colonel, he took part in the defence of Basing House in Hampshire. The following year parliamentary forces renewed their attacks on this royalist stronghold, and on 14 September 1644, during a particularly fierce encounter, Johnson was shot in the shoulder, contracted a fever, and died a fortnight later, presumably at or near Basing House.   C. J. KING

Sources H. W. Kew and H. E. Powell, *Thomas Johnson — botanist and royalist* (1932) · J. S. L. Gilmour, ed., *Thomas Johnson: botanical journeys in Kent and Hampstead* (1972) · J. Gerard, *The herball, or, Generall historie of plantes*, rev. T. Johnson (1633) · N&Q, 11 (1855), 204–5

Johnson, Sir Thomas (*bap.* 1664, *d.* 1728), merchant and politician, the son of Thomas Johnson (*c.*1630–1700) of Bedford Leigh, Lancashire, and his wife, Elizabeth Sweeting, was baptized at St Nicholas's Church, Liverpool, on 27 October 1664. His father was elected to Liverpool's common council during the interregnum, and served as town bailiff in 1663 and as mayor in 1670, but withdrew from corporate affairs when the borough charter issued in 1676 ended the right of freemen to vote in mayoral elections. He maintained his seclusion for nearly two decades until a new charter issued in 1695 restored popular election, and his steadfast advocacy of this right was recognized in his appointment as mayor by this charter. The younger Thomas Johnson became one of the port's leading merchants; during the 1680s he established himself as a tobacco trader and in the following two decades he diversified into the sugar trade and the salt industry. His local standing was recognized in 1689 with his appointment to the council, but though willing to serve Johnson supported his father's advocacy of popular mayoral elections; the 1695 charter named him to succeed his father as mayor. During this period Johnson was married twice, first to Lidia Holt (*d.* 1696), with whom he had two sons, who both predeceased him, and two daughters. Less than a year after her death, which was in August or September 1696, Johnson married, by licence dated 7 April 1697, Elizabeth Barrow, who died childless in 1718.

The rise through the Liverpool élite evidenced by Johnson's appointment as mayor in 1695 continued in December 1701 with his election as the town's MP. Though a staunch whig, he had inherited his father's independence of mind. His support for the War of the Spanish Succession was tempered by his concern for its effects on trade, and in 1702 he criticized the proposed grant of £5000 per annum to the duke of Marlborough. During his early years in parliament he was frequently a harsh critic of professional politicians, be they whig or tory, but on crucial matters of state almost invariably supported the whigs. At no time was this more evident than on 20 March 1708, when he presented to Queen Anne an address of thanksgiving from Liverpool for the nation's deliverance from the threatened Jacobite invasion and was rewarded with a knighthood. Johnson's concern was, however, as much for the development of Liverpool as for affairs of state. Much of his time in parliament was spent defending the interests of Liverpool's traders, and in the first decade of the eighteenth century he played a crucial role in the building of two churches, St Peter's and St George's. He also obtained for the corporation grants of the site of Liverpool Castle and the right to hold a weekly market, and guided through the Commons a bill to establish the port's first dry dock.

However, Johnson's personal fortunes failed to match the rise of the port with which he was intimately associated. Rumours of his dubious business practices were rife among contemporaries, and after 1715 his position among Liverpool's colonial traders went into sharp decline.

Though in 1717 he attempted to purchase the West Indian island of St Kitts for £61,000, he was by this time experiencing financial difficulties. By that year he and his partner and son-in-law, Richard Gildart, owed the Treasury £7000 for unpaid custom bonds. Johnson's straitened circumstances were again evident in 1722, when it was claimed that he no longer satisfied the property qualification to sit in parliament. The following year he resigned his seat to accept the place of customs collector on the River Rappahannock in Virginia, but it is uncertain if he ever took up this post (Liverpool's council minutes record his presence in England from 1725 until 1728). The debt on unpaid customs bonds remained unsettled, and Johnson's need for financial assistance is suggested by a series of payments he received from the government for the last four years of his life. He died at lodgings in Charing Cross, London, on 28 December 1728, and was buried at St Martin-in-the-Fields on 5 January 1729. Johnson was one of Liverpool's founding fathers, and his contribution to the city's development is commemorated by a plaque in the council buildings and in the name of Sir Thomas Street.

RICHARD D. HARRISON

Sources DNB · 'Johnson, Sir Thomas', HoP, *Commons, 1690–1715* [draft] · E. Cruickshanks, 'Johnson, Sir Thomas', HoP, *Commons, 1715–54* · T. Heywood, ed., *The Norris papers*, Chetham Society, 9 (1846) · Lpool RO, Norris papers · A. C. Wardle, 'Sir Thomas Johnson: his impecuniosity and death', *Transactions of the Historic Society of Lancashire and Cheshire*, 90 (1938), 181–94 · A. C. Wardle, 'Sir Thomas Johnson and the Jacobite rebels', *Transactions of the Historic Society of Lancashire and Cheshire*, 91 (1939), 125–42 · *Country Journal, or, The Craftsman* (4 Jan 1729) · R. Muir and E. M. Platt, *A history of municipal government in Liverpool* (1906) · H. Peet, 'Thomas Steers, the engineer of Liverpool's first dock', *Transactions of the Historic Society of Lancashire and Cheshire*, 82 (1930), 163–242 · W. A. Shaw, *The knights of England*, 2 vols. (1905) · IGI

Archives Lpool RO, Norris MSS

Johnson, Thomas (*d.* 1746), classical scholar, was born at Stadhampton, Oxfordshire; further details of his upbringing and parentage are unknown. He was educated at Eton College from where he was elected to a scholarship at King's College, Cambridge, on 13 August 1683. He held this until 1695, having graduated BA (1688) and MA (1692). In 1689 he was usher of Ipswich School. Johnson then fell heavily into debt after divorcing his wife, details of whom are unknown. He was committed to prison and upon his discharge in 1705 was appointed an assistant master at Eton, but continued to be harassed by creditors. In September 1711 he was keeping a school at Brentford, Middlesex, and in 1715 he was chosen headmaster of Archbishop Harsnett's Grammar School at Chigwell. In 1718 the bishop of London made a new year's gift to the school so as to enable the governors to obtain, by purchase, Johnson's resignation. Johnson was a capable scholar, but egotistical and conceited (*Remarks*, 2.98, 120).

Johnson none the less gained considerable reputation for his edition of Sophocles, with a Latin version and notes. The year 1705 saw the publication of his edition of *Ajax* and *Electra*, followed in 1708, by *Antigone* and *Trachiniae*; however, his edition of *Oedipus tyrannus*, *Philoctetes*, and *Oedipus Coloneus* did not appear until after his death. A collective edition of the seven tragedies was issued in 1745, and was frequently reprinted. Johnson also edited *Gratii Falisci cynegeticon, cum poematio cognomine M. A. Olympii Nemesiani Carthaginensis*, (1699). Among his other works are *Novus Graecorum epigrammatum et poemation delectus* (2nd edn, 1699), *Phaedri fabularum Aesopiarum libri quinque* (1701), and *Decerpta ex Ovidii fastis* (1711?). A translation of Saint-Evremond's *Essay in Vindication of Epicurus and his Doctrine*, appended to John Digby's version of Epicurus's *Morals* appeared in 1712, and was followed, possibly a year later, with his *Collection of [Latin] Nouns and Verbs … together with an English Syntax*, and *Selections from Ovid's 'Metamorphoses'*. Due to his dissolute lifestyle, Johnson lived many of his later years in poverty. He died in 1746. This Thomas Johnson should not be confused with another classical scholar of the same name who printed at his own expense an edition of Cebes's *Tabula*, in 1720. Likewise Johnson has been mistaken for a third scholar of this name, Thomas *Johnson (1702/3–1737), classical scholar and moral philosopher.

GORDON GOODWIN, *rev.* PHILIP CARTER

Sources *Remarks and collections of Thomas Hearne*, ed. C. E. Doble and others, 11 vols., OHS, 2, 7, 13, 34, 42–3, 48, 50, 65, 67, 72 (1885–1921) · Nichols, *Lit. anecdotes*, 4.494; 8.410 · Nichols, *Illustrations*, 4.386

Wealth at death in extreme poverty: DNB

Johnson, Thomas (1702/3–1737), classical scholar and moral philosopher, was born at Debenham, Suffolk, the son of Thomas Johnson (*b.* 1674/5), Church of England clergyman of that parish. He was educated at Monk Soham School, Suffolk, and Magdalene College, Cambridge, which he entered aged eighteen on 3 June 1721. He graduated BA in 1724 and MA in 1728. He was ordained deacon on 19 December 1725 and priest on 11 June 1727. He was senior university taxor at Cambridge in 1732 and was afterwards chaplain at Whitehall. Johnson was one of four editors of Stephens's *Latin Thesaurus* (1734–5) and in 1735 he published an edition of Pufendorf's *De officio hominis et civis*. His other writings include *An Essay on Moral Obligation* (1731), written in answer to the deist Thomas Chubb. In the same year he published *The Insufficiency of the Law of Nature*, followed three years later by *A Letter to [Samuel] Chandler* and *Quaestiones philosophicae in justi ordinem dispositae*. Thomas Johnson died in July 1737. He should not be confused with the contemporary classical scholar Thomas *Johnson who published a well-respected edition of the works of Sophocles and who died in 1746.

PHILIP CARTER

Sources Venn, *Alum. Cant.* · *Fasti Angl., 1541–1857*, [Ely]

Johnson, Thomas (1732–1819), judge and revolutionary politician in the United States of America, was born on 4 November 1732 near St Leonard's Creek in Calvert county, Maryland, the fifth child of Thomas Johnson (1702–1777), planter, and his wife, Dorcas (1705–1770), daughter of Joshua Sedgwick. Johnson had two older and five younger brothers and two older and two younger sisters; one brother died in infancy. Both his parents were Maryland natives of English descent; his paternal grandfather emigrated from Yarmouth, Norfolk.

After receiving his primary education at home Johnson moved to Annapolis where he obtained employment with the land office, under the register, Thomas Jennings. Johnson left this position to study law with noted attorney Stephen Bordley. Johnson was first admitted to practise in the Annapolis mayor's court in 1756 and subsequently gained admittance to various county courts and to the provincial and chancery courts by 1767. Having established himself as a successful lawyer, Johnson married Anne Jennings (1745–1794), daughter of his former employer, on 16 February 1766. The couple had seven children—three sons and four daughters.

In addition to his law practice Johnson was a partner with Annapolis merchant Lancelot Jacques in a western Maryland iron furnace from the 1760s to the early 1770s. He also formed a partnership with three of his brothers in an ironworks that included several furnaces, forges, glassworks, and mills, principally the Catoctin Furnace near the town of Frederick.

Johnson's public career began in 1762, with election as the Anne Arundel county representative to the lower house of the Maryland general assembly. Serving in that body until 1774, he participated in committees to guide the Stamp Act congress (raised to resist parliament's taxation of the colonies), to resolve the constitutional rights of freemen, and to supervise building of a new state house. In 1774 Thomas Johnson was elected to represent Maryland in the first continental congress. On 15 June 1775 during the second continental congress, he had the honour of nominating George Washington as commander-in-chief of the continental army. From January 1776 to February 1777 Johnson was a senior brigadier-general in the Maryland militia, and commanded troops sent to aid Washington during his retreat through New Jersey in the winter of 1776–7.

On 13 February 1777 the legislature elected Johnson as the first governor of the independent state of Maryland. His inauguration, held in the state house which he had helped to create, followed on 21 March 1777. Johnson was re-elected unanimously in November 1777 and November 1778 (the statutory limit for consecutive terms). As governor during the American War of Independence, Johnson prepared for possible invasion by British forces and secured provisions for Washington's troops.

Upon leaving office Johnson settled at Richfield, his Frederick county estate. Although elected to represent Maryland in congress in both December 1779 and October 1780, he declined to serve. Instead, in December 1780 he accepted a seat from Frederick county in the house of delegates, where he encouraged a vote in favour of the articles of confederation, the document that bound the thirteen colonies until the ratification of the federal constitution. He resigned this post in December 1781 and resumed the practice of law, but returned to the house in 1787 and 1788 to shepherd the federal constitution through the ratification process and to support George Washington in his bid for the presidency. On 20 April 1790 Johnson accepted an appointment as chief judge of the general court, serving until October 1791 when Washington appointed him to the United States supreme court. He also headed the board of commissioners of the federal city, helping to choose a site and a name for the new national capital.

Johnson left the bench in 1793, and declined an appointment as secretary of state. He came out of retirement for a final time on 22 February 1800 to deliver a funeral oration for his friend George Washington. Johnson died on 26 October 1819 at Rose Hill, the Frederick home of his son-in-law. He was buried in the family vault in All Saints' parish cemetery, but in 1913 his body was removed to Mount Olivet cemetery where a monument was erected in his honour.

JEAN B. RUSSO

Sources E. C. Papenfuse and others, eds., *A biographical dictionary of the Maryland legislature, 1635–1789*, 1 (1979) [pt of the Maryland State Archives biography project] • E. S. Delaplaine, *The life of Thomas Johnson* (New York, 1927) • F. F. White, *Governors of Maryland, 1777–1970* (Annapolis, Maryland, 1970)

Likenesses J. Hesselius, oils, 1765–1775?, Daughters of the American Revolution Museum, Washington • C. W. Peale, group portrait, oils, 1772, Baltimore Museum of Art • C. W. Peale, oils, 1824, Maryland State Archives

Wealth at death approx. 23,000 acres in Maryland and a one-half interest in 1300 acres in Virginia: Papenfuse and others, eds., *Biographical dictionary*, vol. 2, p. 495

Johnson, Thomas Burgeland (*c*.1778–1840), writer on field sports, seems to have spent his schooldays in Leicestershire. He started his working life as a printer in Liverpool. In 1809 he published the *Shooter's Guide* (4th edn, 1814) under the pseudonym of B. Thomas. In 1817 he published *The Complete Sportsman* (under the pseudonym of T. H. Needham). His *Shooter's Companion* (1819), which celebrates the patent wire cartridge, drew on his experience in breeding pointers 'equal, if not superior, to any in the world'; but although Johnson excelled at the art of shooting over dogs, the new sport of battue shooting is barely mentioned. *The Hunting Directory* (1826) was based on hunting tours he made over the north of England and the midlands in 1824–6. Although he hunted with the fashionable Leicestershire packs, Johnson wrote little about the new fast riding and much about hounds, quoting Peter Beckford at length; his work thus shows little trace of the transformation being wrought on sporting journalism at the time by the writing of Nimrod (Charles Apperley) in the *Sporting Magazine*. In 1831 Johnson published his most successful work, *The Sportsman's Cyclopaedia*, a compendium of information on field sports, racing, and cock-fighting, with engravings by the Landseers, J. F. Herring, Philip Reinagle, and Abraham Cooper. He followed this with a bid to break into sporting journalism, launching the *Sportsman's Cabinet and Town and Country Magazine* in 1832. After struggling through twelve monthly numbers, it failed in October 1833. Sporting journalism was then at its most competitive (Surtees had brought out the *New Sporting Magazine* in May 1831 as a rival to the *Sporting Magazine*) and Johnson was a provincial outsider, hostile to metropolitan sporting fashion.

Johnson seems to have lost money by the failure of his magazine, and in 1834 he moved to London in a vain attempt to improve his blighted prospects. Here he published *Physiological Observations on Mental Susceptibility* (1837), an eccentric compilation of anecdotes, quack science, and racial chauvinism. Soon after the move to London his health gave way, and he died of consumption at 6 York Street, Strand, on 5 May 1840, leaving a wife, Martha, and their 21-year-old daughter in considerable distress. He was 'a difficult man, disappointed, cranky, vain, envious and ill-tempered' (Higginson). JANE RIDLEY

Sources GM, 2nd ser., 15 (1841), 102–3 · A. H. Higginson, *British and American sporting authors* (1949) · d. cert.
Likenesses portrait, repro. in T. B. Johnson, *The sportsman's cyclopaedia* (1831)

Johnson, Thomas Lewis (1836–1921), missionary evangelist and author, was born into slavery in Virginia, on 7 August 1836. He was moved to Washington, DC and around Virginia at the whim of his owners, who prohibited any formal education. As education might enable him to escape, he learned by subterfuge, using the Bible after his conversion to Christianity.

Resident in Richmond, Virginia, at the beginning of the civil war, Johnson cooked for his owner's son in the Confederate army. In Richmond in 1863 he married Henrietta Thompson (d. 1879), a maid of commander Robert E. Lee's sister. The Johnsons witnessed the fall of the Confederacy in April 1865. After moving, as a waiter, to New York, his search for knowledge, anxiety to assist other former slaves, and religious faith took him to Chicago, and then to Denver as pastor of its black Baptists until 1872.

Contacts with Britons who knew of his ambition to be a Christian missionary in Africa brought the Johnsons to England by 1876, where he studied at Spurgeon's Baptist college, in Stockwell, south London. Joined by Calvin Harris Richardson (whose wife was Henrietta Johnson's youngest sister) in 1877, the four went to the Cameroons in November 1878.

After his wife's death the following year Johnson was invalided back to England. He had served little over a year for the Baptist Missionary Society, whose secretary, Alfred Baynes, had largely sponsored his college studies. On returning to Chicago, he worked encouraging black American missionary efforts towards Africa, and married Sara Artemico McGowan on 28 July 1881. Together they moved to Manchester and then travelled around Britain, often at YMCA meetings, gathering funds to send black Christian missionaries to Africa. Their only daughter, Ruth, died in 1892, aged six. In 1882 his autobiographical *Africa for Christ: Twenty-Eight Years a Slave* was published in London. In 1884 he spoke at an Anti-Slavery Society meeting chaired by Edward, prince of Wales. He worked with Jamaica-born medical doctor Theophilus Scholes, and in 1885 the Johnsons toured Ireland with Sara's sister, Ora McGowan, and Dr Scholes. Scholes and a Jamaican carpenter named John Ricketts left for the Congo in 1886. Johnson returned in triumph to the USA, touring into 1887, then settled in England for the rest of his life, with occasional tours of America.

Johnson's mission work led to co-operation with William Hughes, a returned Congo Baptist whose African Institute in Colwyn Bay brought black people to Wales for a practical and religious education. Johnson, Scholes, Sir Samuel Lewis of Sierra Leone, and other black people supported Hughes.

Too ill to visit Africa from the 1890s, Johnson settled in Bournemouth at 66 Paisley Road, Pokesdown, renamed Liberia. Bournemouth residents supported his successful application to become a British citizen in 1900.

His autobiography was extended and republished in 1909; a hymn was published in 1897 (republished 1903) and *Consecration Thoughts for the New Year* in 1903. Johnson died at his home in Bournemouth, aged eighty-four, on 11 March 1921, and was buried in the town's Boscombe cemetery. A witness to slavery and a pioneer missionary in Africa, Johnson was remembered for his sincerity into the 1980s. JEFFREY GREEN

Sources T. L. Johnson, *Twenty-eight years a slave, or, The story of my life in three continents* (1909) · private information (2004)
Likenesses photographs, 1878–1908, repro. in Johnson, *Twenty-eight years a slave*
Wealth at death £1005 14s.: probate, 8 June 1921, CGPLA Eng. & Wales

Johnson, Thomas Ryder (1872–1963), trade unionist and politician, was born on 17 May 1872 at 10 South Hunter Street, off Maryland Street, Liverpool, the only child of Thomas Johnson, foreman sail maker, and his wife, Margaret Boardman. His parents were both English. Although his father was Anglican by upbringing, Johnson was enrolled in a nonconformist school in Hope Street, Liverpool in 1876, and father and son attended a Unitarian chapel. In adult life Johnson regarded himself as a freethinker. He left Hope Street School, Liverpool, in 1885 to become a messenger boy in a solicitor's office and, from 1887 to 1892, an office boy for a salt merchant. In 1892 he found employment with an Irish fish merchant, and spent part of each year buying fish in Ireland, where in 1896 he met a Cornish teacher, Marie Annie Tregay (b. 1874), the daughter of James Tregay, a basket-maker. They were wed on 24 March 1898 in St Philip's Anglican Church, Liverpool. Their only child, Fred, was born on 5 August 1899. In 1902 Johnson became north of Ireland agent for Day, Son, and Hewitt Ltd, London, distributors of veterinary medicines and animal feed.

Johnson's strict religious upbringing had given him a lifelong aversion to alcohol, smoking, and gambling, and a concern with social injustice. After reading Robert Blatchford, Robert Owen, and William Morris, he had joined the Independent Labour Party in 1893. On settling in Belfast, he was soon active on Belfast trades council, in socialist groups, and in the Belfast Co-operative Society. Though not powerful in his union, his talents as an administrator and facilitator brought him to prominence in the Irish Trade Union Congress (ITUC). Having first attended the ITUC in 1911, he became president of congress from 1914 to 1916, treasurer from 1918 to 1920, and secretary from 1920 to 1928. Johnson favoured an allied victory in

Thomas Ryder Johnson (1872–1963), by Keogh Brothers

the First World War, yet opposed the war as a socialist, and helped to lead the ITUC's campaign against the application of conscription to Ireland in 1918, which earned him national recognition and dismissal from Day, Son, and Hewitt. From May to November 1918 he worked as full-time secretary of the Mansion House committee, the co-ordinating body of the national anti-conscription campaign. Subsequently, he was employed by the ITUC, and his family resided permanently in Dublin from 1920.

Congress was also the Irish Labour Party from 1914 to 1930, and Johnson, as its only leader unencumbered with a trade union job, became its chief political guide. He had long come to identify with Ireland, supporting home rule, opposing partition, and applying for citizenship of the republic in 1919. Among the twelve pamphlets he wrote was *A Handbook for Rebels* (1918), an ironic appraisal of unionist defiance of the British government. He was particularly proud of drafting the *Democratic Programme*, adopted by Dáil Éireann as its nominal social manifesto in January 1919. However, he disliked militant nationalism and revolution. Owing largely to his often contradictory proclivities for appeasement and constitutionalism, Labour gave qualified backing to republicanism from 1918 to 1922, but declined either to challenge or ally formally with Sinn Féin, and abstained from the general elections of 1918 and 1921, a policy which historians have variously described as skilful, a subordination of Labour interests to nationalism, or a wasted opportunity to help shape the emergent Irish state. Johnson's honesty has also been

questioned for his rhetorical endorsement of contemporary trade union direct action, while trying quietly to moderate radical impulses. Johnson hoped that the Anglo-Irish treaty of 1921 would resolve the national question and clear the decks for socially based politics.

Under Johnson's leadership Labour contested its first general election in 1922, and he was returned as a TD for co. Dublin. With typically Johnsonian ambivalence, the party proclaimed its neutrality on the treaty, but helped to legitimize the Irish Free State by entering Dáil Éireann as official opposition, despite its minority status. The abstentionist republicans were furious. Ignoring Johnson's vigorous condemnation of government repression against them, they—and Larkinites—attacked him viciously, and his English origins were invariably raised. Though an able parliamentarian, he was criticized too by the Labour left for placing constitutional stability above party interests. In 1925 he pleaded with congress to abandon all lingering attachment to class politics for an inclusive 'community-ist' outlook and, suffering from overwork, offered to resign as secretary. Over the next two years he tried hard to entice republicans to abandon abstentionism. Ironically, Fianna Fáil's entry into Dáil Éireann in August 1927 precipitated a general election in September and the loss of his Dáil seat.

Johnson was elected to Seanad Éireann from 1928 to 1936, and served on various public bodies into the 1950s. As an elder statesman of the movement, he welcomed Labour's backing for the Fianna Fáil governments of 1932–8—though initially apprehensive about de Valera's constitutional policies; he encouraged ITUC initiatives to restructure trade unionism in the mid-1920s and 1930s but opposed the Trade Union Act (1941); and he was again secretary of the ITUC from May to October 1945, following the breakaway of the Congress of Irish Unions. In September 1946 he was appointed a trade union representative on the labour court. He resigned from the court on health grounds in December 1955. In retirement he continued to be involved with charities and the Irish Labour Party. He died in Dublin, after a short illness, on 17 January 1963 and was buried in Clontarf, survived by his wife and son.

EMMET O CONNOR

Sources J. A. Gaughan, *Thomas Johnson, 1872–1963: first leader of the labour party in Dáil Éireann* (1980) • private information (2004) [J. Anthony Gaughan] • b. cert. • m. cert. • *CGPLA Ire.* (1963)
Archives NL Ire., MSS • University College, Dublin, pamphlet collection | SOUND Radio Telefís Éireann, sound archives, 'Older and wiser: Mrs Thomas Johnson', Dublin 4, 30 June 1973, aa 227
Likenesses two photographs, 1920–32, repro. in *Irish Independent* • photograph, 1925, Walter Scott, Dublin • S. C. Harrison, oils, 1928, Hugh Lane Municipal Gallery, Dublin • photograph, 1946, repro. in *Irish Press* • photograph, 1952, repro. in *Irish Times* • photograph, 1956, Green Studio, Dublin • Keogh Brothers, photograph, NL Ire. [see illus.]
Wealth at death £6443: probate, 17 June 1963, *CGPLA Eng. & Wales*

Johnson, Tom [*real name* Thomas Jackling] (*c*.1750–1797), prize-fighter, was born Thomas Jackling in Derby. He was known as Tom Johnson throughout his professional life. He was working in London as a corn porter in 1781 when he took on his first professional fight, beating the once great veteran Stephen Oliver, who rejoiced in the nickname of Death. The fight linked two great eras of boxing as Oliver had appeared in the old amphitheatres of Figg, Taylor, and Broughton in its first age and Johnson was to become the first champion of the next, though before then he had several minor bouts, all for stakes of 50 guineas at most.

In 1786 the prince of Wales and his two brothers, the dukes of Kent and Clarence, began to take an active interest and pugilism became the fashion. Johnson was clearly the best boxer of the day and in January 1787 he met Will Ward for a fight for 200 guineas a side before a large crowd at Oakingham, Berkshire. The vogue proved strong enough to survive a disappointing fight which Johnson won easily, but he himself failed to appreciate the change in his sport's fortunes, and took on the ponderous slogger Fry for a mere 50 guineas in the following summer when most of the new gentry enthusiasts were out of town and little interest was aroused. This was the last of his old-style skirmishes. The stake money that he attracted grew impressively, from 300 guineas for the two fights with the Irish challenger Michael Ryan, to 500 for the fights against Isaac Perrins and Ben Bryan. By the time of the Perrins fight Johnson was beginning to show his age and won only after a hard struggle over sixty-two rounds. This contest in particular brought him riches such as he had never known before. His backer, Thomas Bullock, a well-known sportsman, won £20,000 on the fight and made his fighter (who also took two-thirds of the gate money) a present of £1000.

As a boxer Johnson was one of the earliest to make justifiable claims to be 'scientific' in that he would cautiously assess the strengths and weaknesses of an opponent and concentrate attacks on his most vulnerable areas, a discretion and care which did not, however, extend to his life outside the ring. He was said to have had property worth £5000 by the late 1780s but money slipped rapidly through his fingers. He found himself forced to defend his championship against Ben Bryan in January 1791 when he was over forty and unfit. He injured his hand on a ring railing, lost his usual composure, and was defeated. Thereafter his decline was both sad and rapid. It was said of him that while working as a porter in his younger days he once took the place of a sick colleague by carrying twice a normal load, covering for the absentee so that his wages would continue to be paid and his wife and children sustained. Unfortunately there was little sign of such generosity of heart in his post-ring life.

Johnson took over The Grapes, Duke Street, Lincoln's Inn Fields, and soon turned it into what was little short of a gambling den and resort of criminals. He gave reluctant and shifting evidence at Chelmsford assizes at the trial of John Wiltshire, accused of robbing two travellers from Newmarket. Johnson was then reduced to taking his gambling table to fights and making a nuisance of himself at the cockpit, refusing to pay up on losing bets and offering to fight instead. He moved to Ireland, first to Dublin then to Cork, found attempts to profit from his pugilism unrewarding, and again took to his gambling table. His deterioration was rapid. Both his health and his spirit were broken and he died there on 21 January 1797.

DENNIS BRAILSFORD

Sources *Pancratia, or, A history of pugilism*, 2nd edn (1815) · H. D. Miles, *Pugilistica: the history of British boxing*, 3 vols. (1906) · *Sporting Magazine*, 2nd ser. (1793–6) · F. Henning, *Fights for the championship*, 2 vols. (1902) · *The Times* (15 July 1793) · D. Brailsford, *Bareknuckles: a social history of prize fighting* (1988)
Likenesses drawing, repro. in Henning, *Fights for the championship*, vol 1, p. 74 · drawing (with Isaac Perrins), priv. coll.; *see illus. in* Perrins, Isaac (1750x57–1801)

Johnson, Sir William, first baronet (1715?–1774), colonial official, was born at Smithtown, near Dunshoughlin, co. Meath, Ireland, one of the eight children of Christopher Johnson (*b.* 1679?, *d.* in or after 1745) and his wife, Anne (1696?–1744), daughter of Michael and Catherine Warren and sister of Admiral Sir Peter *Warren. Little is known of Johnson's early years, but by 1736 he was handling some of his uncle Sir Peter's business. About 1738 he emigrated to manage Warren's estate on the Mohawk River in present-day New York, bringing with him twelve families of tenants. Through trade with the neighbouring Mohawk Iroquois, shrewd land speculations, and income generated by the increasing numbers of tenants he imported, he built a fortune. By 1743 he had moved to several thousand acres of his own land near present-day Amsterdam, New York, where he called his home Fort Johnson. Since 1739 he had been living with Catherine Weisenberg (*c.*1722–1759), a German servant who had run away from her New York city master at the age of seventeen. There is no record of a legal marriage, but Johnson called her his wife, and he was buried with what those who later exhumed his corpse assumed to be her wedding ring, engraved with the date 16 June 1739. The couple had three children: Ann (Nancy), John, and Mary (Polly). Catherine died in April 1759. Perhaps even before that date, Johnson began a relationship with his housekeeper, Mary (Molly) *Brant (*c.*1736–1796), sister of the Mohawk leader Joseph Brant. Johnson acknowledged paternity of her eight children—Peter, Elizabeth, Magdalene, Margaret, George, Mary, Susanna, and Anne—and in his will (which called their mother merely his 'prudent & faithfull Housekeeper') promised each the equivalent of a farmstead and an additional 2000 acres of unimproved land.

Johnson's kinship and economic ties with the Mohawks created enormous potential influence among their fellow Six Nations Iroquois. Since the 1720s that confederacy, strategically located between New France and New York, had become alienated from Albany merchants, who concentrated on more lucrative trades to their north and west. During the War of the Austrian Succession (1744–8), New York governor George Clinton, fearing the Iroquois would join the French, found Johnson—who had become a justice of the peace in 1745—a natural candidate to mend relations. Performing Iroquois rituals and liberally distributing supplies, Johnson recruited a small force of Mohawks to raid the French. Donning war paint, he led some of them to a conference at Albany in 1746, where Clinton issued him a colonel's commission that in effect gave him the powers previously exercised by the Albany commissioners of Indian affairs. The military fruits of Johnson's efforts were disappointing, but he cultivated a loyal Iroquois following (receiving the council title Warraghiyagey—'he who does much business') and forged a close relationship with Clinton, who had him appointed to the provincial council in 1750. A year later, when the New York assembly refused to reimburse more than a tiny portion of Johnson's wartime expenses, he resigned his Indian affairs post.

In 1755, as the conflict that would become the Seven Years' War developed, Johnson was reappointed, but as an agent of the crown rather than New York, by commander-in-chief Edward Braddock, who also placed him in charge of an expedition against Fort St Frédéric (Crown Point) on Lake Champlain. Johnson's provincial and American Indian troops failed in their ultimate objective, but in September defeated French forces under Jean-Armand Dieskau in the battle of Lake George. Although wounded early and taking little part in the fighting, Johnson thus became a war hero, rewarded with £5000 from parliament and a baronetcy from the crown. In February 1756, as part of a general imperial reorganization, Sir William Johnson became superintendent of Indian affairs for the northern department. Although never able to win all Iroquois, much less their Indian neighbours, to the British side, Johnson raised substantial Native American forces. At the battle of Niagara in 1759, assuming command when General John Prideaux was killed, he led British and American Indian troops to victory. After the surrender of the French in North America, Johnson unsuccessfully opposed commander-in-chief Jeffrey Amherst's disastrous policy of curtailing the Indian trade, banning the distribution of diplomatic presents, and shunning traditional diplomatic formalities, which sparked the decentralized attacks on British posts known as the Pontiac War (1763–6). None the less, Johnson's diplomacy kept most Iroquois from the fray, and, especially in a treaty with Pontiac at Oswego in 1766, helped to restore peace.

Subsequently, as superintendent, Johnson advocated clear boundaries between Indian and European territories, and argued that intercultural trade should be closely regulated to prevent abuse of Native American customers. When disputes over land or trade arose, he carefully observed Indian diplomatic protocol and spared no expense in distributing compensatory gifts. Less successfully, he tried to simplify diplomacy by endorsing the Six Nations' pretensions to authority over all the Native American peoples of the Great Lakes and Ohio region and centralizing negotiations under imperial instead of provincial control. His approach was hard-headed and frequently self-serving, particularly regarding land claims. 'I have laid it down as an invariable rule …', he wrote in 1765, 'that wherever a Title is set up by any Tribe of Indians of little consequence or importance to his Majesty's Interest … that such Claim unless apparently clear had better remain unsupported than that Several old Titles of his

Majesty's Subjects should thereby become disturbed' (*Papers*, 11.911–12).

In 1763 at Johnstown, New York, the baronet built Johnson Hall, a grand residence in modified Georgian style. There he presided over a remarkable neo-feudal, multiracial community, more reminiscent of the imperial Ireland of his birth than reflective of trends elsewhere in the middle colonies. Ensconced on estates totalling nearly 400 square miles, he presided over legions of Euro-American tenants and Native American retainers. Envisioning a family dynasty, he arranged for his son **Sir John Johnson**, second baronet (1742–1830), colonial official and army officer, to bear the title of knight. In addition, Guy *Johnson, husband of his daughter Mary, was to succeed him as superintendent; while the interpreter Daniel Claus, spouse of his daughter Ann, was to consolidate the clan's hold on Indian affairs. And he turned Johnson Hall not only into the site of elaborate Indian treaty conferences but also an oasis for visitors of all sorts, entertaining them with fine wines and a 'cabinet of curiosities' featuring Iroquois artefacts. Culturally, he worked for causes as diverse as a North American Anglican bishopric and the establishment of a masonic lodge. Ignoring the provincial leaders he disdained, his political connections ran straight to Whitehall.

Both the crowning achievement and the ultimate downfall of the diplomacy Johnson waged for his empire was the Fort Stanwix treaty of 1768. Building on agreements with Native American leaders during the Seven Years' War and principles articulated in the royal proclamation of 1763, the treaty established a 'line of property' bisecting present-day New York and Pennsylvania from north-east to south-west and following the Ohio River almost to its junction with the Mississippi. Along with a boundary that fellow superintendent John Stuart negotiated with southern Indians in the same year, Johnson's treaty opened much of present-day West Virginia and Kentucky to British settlers, while supposedly safeguarding Native American lands to the north-west. At least three flaws marred the scheme, however. First, the line of property was clearly a project of the imperial government, not the provinces whose borders it redefined. Colonists who decried the Stamp Act of 1765 and the Townshend duties of 1767 were no more likely to accept what they saw as an arbitrary boundary than what they considered unjust parliamentary taxes. Moreover, the treaty failed to specify which colonists, from which province, would claim rights to the ceded lands; a mad scramble among speculators and squatters from Virginia and Pennsylvania became almost inevitable. Equally vexing, most of the territory the Iroquois yielded was not theirs to give; its Shawnee and Cherokee owners scorned the Six Nations' pretended hegemony. In 1774 the problems converged in Dunmore's War, a Virginian attempt to pre-empt Ohio country lands by provoking conflict with the Shawnees. Seeking to limit the bloodshed, Johnson summoned Iroquois leaders to a council at Johnson Hall. On 11 July, after a long day of negotiations, he collapsed. Within two hours he lay dead in his room. He was buried on 13 July at St John's Episcopal Church, Johnstown.

Although much of Johnson's diplomatic legacy would survive through the work of his sons-in-law in the British Indian service, within a decade the neo-feudal, multiracial enclave he had built would be swept away by the American War of Independence. Nearly all in his sphere of influence—kin and tenants, Euro-Americans and Indians alike—became militant loyalists, ultimately forced to relocate in Canada or elsewhere. John Johnson, in particular, staunchly defended the empire his father had served, raising troops to raid his former neighbourhood and receiving a brigadier-general's commission in 1782. Succeeding Guy Johnson as head of the Indian department the same year, he held the post until his death at Montreal on 4 January 1830. In New York the revolutionaries had long since confiscated his and the rest of the family estates—including, as befitted the white man's republic they were creating, those pledged to Molly Brant's children.   DANIEL K. RICHTER

Sources M. W. Hamilton, *Sir William Johnson: colonial American, 1715–1763* (1976) · *The papers of Sir William Johnson*, ed. J. Sullivan and others, 14 vols. (1921–65) · E. B. O'Callaghan and B. Fernow, eds. and trans., *Documents relative to the colonial history of the state of New York*, 15 vols. (1853–87), vols. 6–8 · W. L. Stone, *The life and times of Sir William Johnson, Bart*, 2 vols. (1856) · M. J. Mullin, 'Sir William Johnson, Indian relations, and British policy, 1744 to 1774', PhD diss., U. Cal., Santa Barbara, 1989 · F. Jennings, 'Johnson, Sir William', *ANB* · M. Kammen, *Colonial New York: a history* (1975) · R. White, *The middle ground: Indians, empires, and republics in the Great Lakes region, 1650–1815* (1991) · B. Graymont, *The Iroquois in the American revolution* (1972) · I. T. Kelsay, *Joseph Brant, 1743–1807: man of two worlds* (1984) · J. T. Flexner, *Lord of the Mohawks: a biography of Sir William Johnson*, rev. edn (1979) · A. Pound and R. E. Day, *Johnson of the Mohawks: a biography of Sir William Johnson, Irish immigrant, Mohawk war chief, American soldier, empire builder* (1930)
Archives BL, corresp. and papers, Add. MS 29237 · L. Cong., corresp.; letter-book · NA Canada · New York Historical Society, corresp. and papers · NRA, priv. coll., biographical papers | BL, letters to John Blackburn, Add. MS 24323 · BL, corresp. with Colonel Bouquet and Frederick Haldimand, Add. MSS 21650–21670 · Hunt. L., letters to James Abercromby · PRO, corresp. with Lord Amherst, WO34 · U. Mich., Clements L., corresp. with Thomas Gage
Likenesses J. Wollaston?, portrait, c.1751, Albany Institute of History and Art, New York · C. Spooner, mezzotint, pubd 1756 (after T. Adams), BM · T. McIlworth, portrait, 1763 (original portrait now lost), New York Historical Society; copy by E. L. Mooney, 1837 · M. Pratt, portrait, 1772–3, Johnson Hall, Johnstown, New York · line engraving, BM, NPG
Wealth at death moveable items value £2383 3s. 6d. (New York currency?): inventory, repr. in *Papers of Sir William Johnson*, ed. Sullivan and others, 13.647–69 · Johnson Hall mansion; two other houses and lots; six other farmsteads; also approx. 170,000 acres (mostly unimproved): will, repr. in *Papers of Sir William Johnson*, ed. Sullivan and others, 12.1062–76

Johnson, William (1784–1864), schoolteacher, was born in Cumberland. In 1811 he was curate at Grasmere, and teacher of the school there. In September 1811 Dr Andrew Bell, the inventor of the Madras system of education by which older children undertook much of the teaching of their juniors, came over from Keswick to see William Wordsworth, who was a friend of Johnson's. He had an interview with Johnson, and was so impressed by the running of his school that in January 1812 he offered him, through Wordsworth, an appointment at the new model school that the National Society for the Education of the Poor in the Principles of the Established Church was building in London; the salary was £100 a year. Johnson accordingly moved to London, took charge of the temporary school in Holborn, and afterwards of the permanent establishment in Baldwin's Gardens. He described his work in evidence to the 1816 select committee on the education of the lower orders in the metropolis. He entered St John's College, Cambridge, as a sizar, on 30 April 1817, and graduated BD in 1827, as a ten-year man.

Johnson was an able teacher, and as Bell's system attracted much interest at the time, he was almost daily called on to explain its merits to visitors. He was presented with a diamond ring from the tsar of Russia in 1821 following a successful visit by four Russian students. To Johnson was largely due the success of both the Madras system and the National Society. For many years he was 'trainer of masters, travelling organiser, and inspector of schools', and afterwards 'cashier and comptroller of the accounts of the society'. In that capacity he gave evidence to the 1834 select committee on the state of education. He earned the sobriquet the Patriarch of National Education. He was on intimate terms with Southey, Wordsworth, and George, Lord Kenyon. On 19 October 1820 he was appointed rector of St Clement, Eastcheap, with St Martin Orgar. He married in 1822 Mary, daughter of Robert Tabrum; they had two sons and a daughter. In 1840 he retired from his scholastic work. He died at his rectory in St Martin's Lane, London, on 20 September 1864. His son Andrew Johnson (1830–1893) was headmaster of St Olave's School, Southwark.   W. A. J. ARCHBOLD, rev. M. C. CURTHOYS

Sources Venn, *Alum. Cant.* · Boase, *Mod. Eng. biog.* · *GM*, 3rd ser., 17 (1864), 526, 661 · *Guardian* (28 Sept 1864) · private information (1891) · R. Southey, *Life of the Rev. Andrew Bell*, 3 vols. (1844), vol. 2 · *GM*, 1st ser., 93/1 (1823), 82
Wealth at death under £6000: probate, 30 Nov 1864, CGPLA Eng. & Wales

Johnson, William Ernest (1858–1931), logician, was born at 1 Millington Road, Cambridge, on 23 June 1858, the fifth child and second son of William Henry Farthing Johnson, proprietor and headmaster of Llandaff House School, Cambridge, and his wife, Harriet, daughter of Augustine Gutteridge Brimley, of Cambridge, and half-sister of the essayist George Brimley. He was the brother of the writers George William Johnson and Reginald Brimley Johnson. Educated at his father's school, at the Perse School, Cambridge, and at the Liverpool Royal Institution School, he entered King's College, Cambridge, as a mathematical scholar in 1879, and was eleventh wrangler in the mathematical tripos of 1883. For some years he gained his living as a mathematical coach in Cambridge, until openings were found for him in teaching for the moral sciences tripos and as a lecturer in psychology and in the theory of education to the Cambridge Women's Training College and for the university teachers' training syndicate. He married in 1895 Barbara Keymer, daughter of Charles William Heaton, lecturer in chemistry at Charing Cross Hospital, London. After his wife's death in 1904 his sister Fanny made a home for him and his two sons. Johnson had no permanent position at Cambridge until 1902, when he was appointed to the newly created Sidgwick lectureship in moral sciences in the university and was elected to a fellowship at King's College. He held these positions for the rest of his life.

Johnson suffered all his life from ill health: bronchial troubles, together with a natural shyness, kept him to his house or college rooms. But he was none the less recalled by John Maynard Keynes as a sociable man who loved conversation. He would sit by a fire at Llandaff House, wrapped in the red shawl which became so characteristic of him, conversing with undergraduates. His pupils (who numbered a large proportion of those reading moral sciences in the university) and people who attended his lectures, which were delivered conversationally and with frequent digressions, were aware of a lovable personality and were infected with his exacting subordination of originality to clarity and truth. He was an accomplished pianist, and often entertained students and guests by playing a large grand piano. He was also interested in football and mountain climbing. He was nonconformist in religion, and remained a free-trader all his life.

From 1884 Johnson was an associate and a member of the Society for Psychical Research (SPR), which was founded in 1882 and whose first president was Henry Sidgwick. He was also mathematical assistant to the first research officer of the SPR, his sister Alice Johnson; he initiated experiments on cross-correspondence in automatic writing. Another sister of his, Fanny, was also a member of the SPR.

As well as lecturing on logic, Johnson lectured on philosophical and mathematical economics (he published a substantial article on 'The pure theory of utility curves' in the *Economic Journal of Science*, December 1913); but it was as a logician that he became known to the learned world when he published 'The logical calculus' (*Mind*, 1892), 'Analysis of thinking' (*Mind*, 1918), and above all when he developed his ideas in three volumes of a treatise on *Logic* (part 1, 1921; part 2, 1922; part 3, 1924), assisted by a pupil, Naomi Bentwick. A fourth volume, dealing with probability, was projected but never completed; its first three chapters were published posthumously in *Mind* in 1932. The *Logic* brought Johnson fame outside Cambridge: the universities of Manchester (1922) and Aberdeen (1926) conferred honorary degrees upon him, and in 1923 he was elected a fellow of the British Academy.

Johnson's 'Logical calculus' starts from the proposition as the unity of thought and introduces the logic of terms as subsidiary to the logic of propositions, making a significant reversal of the customary logical order developed subsequently by W. MacColl and B. Russell. Moreover, using primitive propositions rather than algebraic symbols, his work on logic is in the tradition of philosophical logicians such as Jevons, Venn, and J. M. Keynes rather than that of mathematical logicians, such as George Boole

and Russell. Johnson was not in full sympathy with these last developments, and devoted time and energy to providing a critique of Russell; but his definition of logic as 'the analysis and criticism of thought' did much to break down previous restrictions upon its scope.

Johnson's logic presents two crucial aspects: formal calculus and philosophical analysis. His emphasis on the concepts of meaning and significance induced him to distinguish between inference and implication, usually both expressed by 'if ... then'. It also caused him to attach great importance to the relation of the thinker to the proposition which is the object of thought, thus showing that this 'epistemic' aspect could not be ignored in logic. In his discussion of deduction he emphasized, at a time when the symbolic logicians had not realized its importance, the difference between the premisses of a deduction and the logical principles in accordance with which the conclusion is drawn.

Johnson introduced an illuminating distinction between properties of different degrees of generality now best known as the theory of determinables. A 'determinable' is one of the broad bases of distinction which may be found in objects, such as colour, shape, size. The theory introduces a new form of names (categorical) by which propositions such as 'red is a colour' can be expressed, where a determinate is linked to a determinable in a very different way from that which links a member to a class, for example, 'Plato is a man'. His treatment of probability as a field of rational but not certain belief was similar to that of J. M. Keynes, who in his *Treatise on Probability* (1921) acknowledged his debt to Johnson. Probability expresses a certain degree of rational belief, between two propositions which Johnson called 'supposal' (an evidence given as certain) and 'proposal' (a hypothesis).

From a technical point of view Johnson made some other interesting contributions to the theory of probability: for instance, that known later as R. Carnap's principle, and one subsequently referred to as 'exchangeability' or 'symmetry', named by Johnson 'Postulate of permutation' (Postulate 3). He remained an active philosopher to the end of his life, and continued to lecture until a few months before his death, which took place at St Andrew's Hospital, Northampton, on 14 January 1931. He was buried at Granchester, Cambridgeshire.

R. B. BRAITHWAITE, *rev.* RAFFAELLA SIMILI

Sources R. B. Braithwaite, 'W. E. Johnson', *Cambridge Review* (30 Jan 1931) • C. D. Broad, 'William Ernest Johnson', *PBA*, 17 (1931), 491–514 • C. D. Broad, review, *Mind*, new ser., 31 (1922), 496–510 • C. D. Broad, 'Mr Johnson on the logical foundations of science', *Mind*, new ser., 33 (1924), 242–61; new ser., 33 (1924), 369–84 • R. Simili, 'W. E. Johnson e il concetto di proposizione', *Atti convegno storia della logica* (1983) • G. H. von Wright, 'Broad on induction and probability', *The philosophy of C. D. Broad*, ed. P. A. Schlipp (*c.*1959) • A. N. Prior, 'Determinables, determinates and determinants', *Mind*, new ser., 58 (1949), 1–20, 178–94 • C. A. Mace, ed., *British philosophy in the mid-century* (1957), 11–61 • R. B. Braithwaite, 'Philosophy', *University studies, Cambridge, 1933*, ed. H. Wright, 1–32 • R. Simili, ed., *L'epistemologia di Cambridge* (1987) • *Proceedings of the Society for Psychical Research*, 2 (1884)
Archives CUL, notes on his 'Advanced logic' lectures taken by G. E. Moore

Johnson, William Percival (1854–1928), missionary and translator, was born at St Helens, Isle of Wight, on 12 March 1854, the third son of John Johnson, solicitor, of Ryde, and his second wife, Mary Percival. He was educated at Bedford grammar school, where he won an appointment to the Indian Civil Service, and at University College, Oxford, where he was an exhibitioner. In 1874 and in 1875 he was stroke for the University College boat, which won the colleges' competition for head of the river. At university he also became close friends with Chauncy Maples, afterwards second bishop of Nyasaland. In 1874 Johnson abandoned the possibility of a career in India, to join the Universities' Mission to Central Africa under Bishop Edward Steere. After taking a second-class BA degree in theology in 1876, he set sail for Zanzibar in August of the same year.

In Zanzibar, Johnson was ordained deacon, in September 1876, and priest in 1878. It was not until 1881 that he reached the shores of Lake Nyasa, where he worked for the next forty-seven years. A violent attack of ophthalmia in 1884 blinded him for a time; an operation performed in London restored partial sight to one eye, but he was only able to read in strong light through a narrow slit formed by putting two fingers together. In spite of this handicap he devoted much of his remaining life to the study of African languages. His translations of the Bible and other works formed the beginning of a written literature in several African languages.

Johnson's most considerable work as a linguist was done in Nyanja, into which he translated the whole of the Bible, the Apocrypha, the Book of Common Prayer, *Pilgrim's Progress*, commentaries on the Acts and other portions of the New Testament, a short church history, and a short life of Muhammad. After he was fifty he produced translations of considerable portions of the New Testament in three other African languages.

Johnson's great passion as a missionary was to build up a truly African church, with minimal expenditure on central stations and European agents. This put him at odds with a succession of bishops who frequently expressed exasperation at his inarticulate but obstinate pursuit of his goals. His preferred instrument for evangelization was the steamship, which he envisaged as a floating platform for itinerant preaching on the shores of Lake Nyasa. In 1884 his appeal for funds to launch the UMCA's first ship met with spectacular success; within a matter of months, the SS *Charles Janson* was manufactured, transported to Africa, pieced together, and launched. A second, much larger ship, the *Chauncy Maples*, was dedicated in 1902, largely as a result of Johnson's advocacy. It served for a time as a theological college under his care. Johnson was appointed archdeacon of Nyasa in 1896. In 1911 he received an honorary degree of DD from the University of Oxford, and in 1926 he was made an honorary fellow of

University College, Oxford. After five weeks' illness he died on 11 October 1928 at Liuli, on the shores of Lake Nyasa. He was buried in the lady chapel there. His two books, *Nyasa the Great Water* (1922) and *My African Reminiscences* (1924), left an account of the early history of Nyasaland.

Johnson's scholarship, with all its limitations, bears witness to his indefatigable powers of application, which were much remarked upon by his contemporaries. As much as any of his generation, he represented 'muscular Christianity' in the service of foreign missions. He lived with great simplicity and could endure great hardship. He took little part in the great political or theological debates of his time. While supporting Britain's claims to the shores of Lake Nyasa in preference to those of Portugal, he was happy to work in the territory of Tanganyika when the vicissitudes of the European partition of Africa delivered an important section of his mission field into German hands. According to Robert Laws, the celebrated Presbyterian missionary of southern Nyasaland, Johnson was 'the true apostle of the Lake' (Livingstone).

E. F. SPANTON, rev. NORMAN ETHERINGTON

Sources B. H. Barnes, *Johnson of Nyasaland* (1931) · W. P. Johnson, *My African reminiscences* (1924) · A. E. M. Anderson-Morshead, *History of the Universities' Mission to Central Africa, 1859–1909*, 6th edn, 1 (1956) · E. Maples and E. G. Maples Cook, *Chauncy Maples, D.D., F.R.G.S., pioneer missionary in east central Africa* (1897) · W. P. Johnson, *Nyasa, the great water* (1922) · A. J. Hanna, *The beginnings of Nyasaland and north-eastern Rhodesia, 1859–95* (1956) · *The journals and papers of Chauncy Maples, bishop of Likoma*, ed. E. Cook (1899) · W. P. Livingstone, *Laws of Livingstonia* (1922)
Archives Bodl. RH, Universities' Mission to Central Africa MSS
Likenesses photographs, repro. in Barnes, *Johnson of Nyasaland*

Johnson, William Samuel (1727–1819), lawyer and politician in America, was born on 7 October 1727 in Stratford, Connecticut, to the Revd Samuel *Johnson (1696–1772), the Church of England clergyman and president of King's College (later Columbia University), and Charity Floyd Nicholl (d. 1756). His mother, a widow with a substantial inheritance and three children from her first marriage, provided a comfortable and loving home for Johnson and his younger brother. Thanks to his mother's hospitality and social network, Johnson was equally comfortable with Anglicans and Congregationalists in Stratford. As students at Yale College, William Samuel's father, Samuel Johnson, along with his classmate Timothy Cutler, had defected from the Congregational church to become the first Church of England clergymen in Connecticut. A philosopher as well as a cleric, Samuel criticized the puritan child-rearing practice of subduing a child's stubborn will: instead he recommended indulgence of children's 'intellectual curiosity, … candor, patience, and care' (McCaughey, 12). This kind of nurture shaped Johnson's character all the more because it occurred within Connecticut's culture of 'steady habits' and augmented Anglican decorum.

Upon graduation with a BA degree from Yale College in 1744, William Samuel studied theology with his father, but found the tensions between the Church of England and the Congregational church unsettling, and decided to follow the example of his Yale classmate William Smith junior, and pursue a career in law. He read law in 1748 and opened his practice the following year, the first lawyer in Connecticut to support himself entirely at the bar. In 1748 he married Ann Beach (d. 1796), whose staunch Church of England family complicated Johnson's relationships with Congregational judges and clients.

In 1765, as a Connecticut delegate to the Stamp Act Congress, which assembled in reaction to parliament's highly controversial attempt to tax internal American trade, Johnson asked the delegates to acknowledge 'due subordination ... to the Crown and Parliament' with the proviso that 'this subordination and dependency is sufficiently secured ... by the general superintending power and authority of the whole empire ... so far as ... is consistent with ... our essential rights as freemen and British subjects' (McCaughey, 56–7). That carefully balanced acknowledgement of imperial authority and vindication of colonial rights echoed his Anglican and Connecticut heritages. When the delegates declined to endorse such a conservative position, he acquiesced in their whiggish defence of colonial liberty. Johnson's conciliatory behind-the-scenes approach and the respect in which he was held by people across the political spectrum set the pattern for the rest of his life.

In 1766 Connecticut sent Johnson to London to represent the colony before the privy council in a legal dispute between the Connecticut government and the Mason family, over the legality of a Mohegan tribal land grant to the Mason family. The Connecticut government denied that the tribe could make a legal grant to the Masons without its consent and the Masons appealed to the privy council. The litigation dragged on until 1771, when Johnson finally had the opportunity to present his case. Only after his return to America did the privy council rule in his favour.

The years in London were formative for Johnson. Pestered with requests from friends in America to handle their political and business affairs in London—and also drawn into the Susquehanna land dispute between Connecticut and Pennsylvania, which was also pending before the privy council—Johnson saw British politics and society at close range. He appreciated the salutary role of 'a supreme power in the British Parliament to regulate and direct the general affairs of the Empire', but 'general affairs' did not extend to deprivation of long-standing constitutional privileges. 'Virtual representation' and 'taxation without representation' were alike anathemas to Johnson. In Britain he came to realize that the distinction between customary superintendence of the empire and prescriptive legislation by parliament had been eroded under the Declaratory Act (1766), by which parliament declared its right to tax the American colonies as it saw fit, and that, as a political matter, the shortest route to repeal of the Townshend duties—another parliamentary attempt at taxing American internal trade—would be a colonial waiver of the alleged rights of the colonists not to be taxed but by their own representatives (Kammen, 163). Waiver did not mean disavowal, only tactical, painful

silence. Privately, Johnson applauded John Dickinson's denunciation of the Townshend duties. 'Our enemies', he reported to the Connecticut governor, William Pitkin, 'labor ... to render the cause of the colonies unpopular', and make 'friendship for America constitute an odious character' (McCaughey, 93). In this atmosphere, he feared, the Susquehanna Land Company's claim that the 1661 charter gave Connecticut sea-to-sea boundaries might provoke the crown to suspend the colony's chartered autonomy.

Back in Connecticut, Johnson watched helplessly as 'the ill-advised measures that have been taken with respect to the colonies' threatened to sever 'the connection between the two countries'. As the imperial crisis came to a head in 1774, Johnson agonized: 'Will no hand be stretched forth to prevent these two countries, perhaps the finest in the universe, from ... injuring each other?' In 1775 he withdrew from politics because 'I could not join in war against England and much less ... against my own country' (Calhoon, 184–5).

Having been gaoled briefly in 1779 when he tried to mediate between Connecticut residents and a British raiding party, Johnson decided the time had come to make peace with the American patriots, and complied with official demands that he swear allegiance to the new regime. He returned to public life in 1782, and represented Connecticut when the continental congress heard the old Susquehanna land case. Although Pennsylvania finally won the dispute, Johnson's reputation did not suffer. In 1784 he was elected to the continental congress and represented Connecticut in 1787 in the constitutional convention. There he played a key role in compromises over representation and slavery. Having been elected to the first United States senate in 1788, he supported the secretary of the treasury, Alexander Hamilton, on the national assumption of state debts and the need for a pro-British foreign policy. He left the senate in 1791 to assume the presidency of Columbia University, where, in an era of campus unrest, he was popular with students. He resigned in 1800 because of illness, but revived and later that year married his first wife's sister-in-law, Mary Beach. He died of heart failure on 14 November 1819 in Stratford, where he was buried. ROBERT M. CALHOON

Sources E. P. McCaughey, *From loyalist to founding father: the political odyssey of William Samuel Johnson* (1980) · M. G. Kammen, *A rope of sand: the colonial agents, British politics, and the American revolution* (1968) · R. M. Calhoon, *The loyalists in revolutionary America, 1760–1781* (1973) · E. S. Morgan and H. M. Morgan, *The Stamp Act crisis: prologue to revolution* (1953) · Connecticut Historical Society, Hartford, William Johnson MSS

Archives Connecticut Historical Society, Hartford

Likenesses T. McIlworth, portrait, 1761, Hirsch and Adler Gallery · four portraits, 1761–1814, repro. in McCaughey, *From loyalist to founding father* · R. E. Pire, portrait, 1788, University of Columbia · S. I. Wells, portrait, 1792, University of Columbia · J. W. Jarvis, portrait, 1814, University of Columbia

Johnston. *See also* Johnstone.

Johnston, Sir Alexander (1775–1849), colonial official and judge in Ceylon, was born on 25 April 1775, the elder son of Alexander Johnston (*b.* 1750?), landowner brother of Peter

Sir Alexander Johnston (1775–1849), by John Cochran, pubd 1831 (after Thomas Phillips)

Johnston (1749–1837), laird of Carnsalloch and MP for Kirkcudbright, and his wife, Hester (d. 1819), only surviving daughter of Francis, fifth Lord Napier (according to the *Gentleman's Magazine*, however, Johnston's father was Samuel, and there are date discrepancies in the sources concerning the father). Reportedly his father obtained civil employment at Madras under Lord Macartney, and in 1781 settled at Madura. Johnston was partly trained by Christian Friedrich Swartz, the Society for the Propagation of Christian Knowledge German missionary, and Thomas (afterwards Sir Thomas) Munro (1761–1827). He learned Tamul, Telugu, and Hindustani, and imbibed a lifelong sympathy with Indians.

When only eleven Johnston was offered a cornetcy of dragoons, but as the regiment was ordered on active service he resigned the commission, and in 1792 returned to Europe with his parents. On Lord Macartney's advice he trained for the law, and studied at Göttingen, Hanover, then at Lincoln's Inn, where he was called to the bar on 23 June 1800. He went on the home circuit until an accidental interview with Charles James Fox turned his thoughts again to India. He needed more income, having on 14 June 1799 married Louisa (d. 7 May 1852), only surviving daughter of Captain Lord William Campbell RN, son of John, fourth duke of Argyll; they had four sons and three daughters. He obtained the post of advocate-general of Ceylon. In 1805 he succeeded to the chief justiceship. In 1809 he was summoned to England to give suggestions to the government, many of which were embodied in the renewed charter issued to the East India Company in 1813. In 1810

he was knighted by the prince regent and elected FRS (22 November), and returned to Ceylon in 1811 as president of the council. In 1817 he acted as Admiralty judge, but declined to accept any salary.

Under Johnston's impulse Ceylon led the vanguard of Indian reform. A system of universal popular education was set on foot, religious liberty was established, and many owners of slaves were persuaded to agree to their gradual emancipation; public employment was largely opened to Sinhalese and Eurasians, while Europeans were permitted to acquire land; trial by jury was established, and a considerable advance was made in the preparation of a code of law, in which provision was made for the due preservation of the views and usages of Hindus, Muslims, and Buddhists. When Johnston returned to England in 1819, Lord Grey declared in the House of Lords that his 'conduct in the island of Ceylon alone had immortalised his name' (GM, 424).

In England, Johnston was instrumental in the foundation in 1823 of the Royal Asiatic Society, of which he became vice-president. In 1832 he was made a privy councillor, and it was chiefly owing to his advice that the judicial committee of the privy council established as a court of ultimate appeal in colonial litigation. Appointed to that court on 4 September 1833, he became distinguished as a supporter of native rights and an interpreter of native laws. His services were acknowledged in a petition to the House of Commons from the leaders of Indian society in the presidency of Bombay; Johnston declined to draw the salary attached to his office.

In 1832, when the East India Company's charter came up for renewal, Johnston was again examined at great length before the committee of the commons; and his evidence contained strong recommendations for extending the rights of Indians. In October 1837 his uncle Peter died and Johnston succeeded him. Latterly Johnston resided largely on his family estate of Carnsalloch, Dumfriesshire, where, according to the *Gentleman's Magazine*, 'he was ever conspicuous for his munificent acts, his kindness to the poor, and his endeavours to promote the rising talents of his countrymen' (GM, 424). It also described him as 'a handsome person, a perfect gentleman in manners, and a very intelligent and agreeable companion' (ibid.). In 1840 he unsuccessfully contested as a Liberal the Dumfries burghs. He died at Great Cumberland Place, London, on 6 March 1849, and was buried at Carnsalloch.

Alexander Robert Campbell Johnston (1812–1888), colonial official, Alexander Johnston's younger son, was born at Colombo, Ceylon, on 14 June 1812. 'The modestly talented offspring of a distinguished and influential father, who constantly exercised himself on his son's behalf' (Welsh, 66), Johnston was in the Mauritius civil service from 1828 to 1833. From 1833 to 1835 he acted as private secretary to his cousin, William John *Napier, ninth Lord Napier (1786–1834), on the latter's mission to China. Johnston received a medal for services on the armed iron paddle-steamer *Nemesis* in the 1841 Anglo-Chinese War.

Hong Kong was occupied by the British in January 1841,

but initially the British government was undecided on its future: not until June 1843 was it formally declared a British colony. Johnston—since 1837 deputy superintendent of trade of British subjects in China—in the absence of the first administrator, Captain Charles Elliot, and of his successor, Sir Henry Pottinger, unexpectedly from 1841 to 1842 was in charge of Hong Kong. Apparently assuming the colony was to be permanent, on his own initiative and with great energy he pressed ahead with the infrastructure, so presenting his superiors with something of a *fait accompli*. He built fortifications, barracks, stores, and roads, held a census, and, contrary to instructions, sold more land—much of it below its real value—to merchants and others, and encouraged non-official development. As Frank Welsh has written, 'He got few thanks for it, then or later, but it is largely due to Johnston's initiative that Hong Kong was allowed to develop' (Welsh, 142). From 1843 to September 1852 he was secretary and registrar superintending in China. On Pottinger's return Johnston continued in the administration, serving on the legislative council and, like other officials and officers, speculating in land. Following two and a half years away on sick leave, in 1846 he was not appointed consul at Shanghai. Humiliated by failure to gain a superior post, he soon sought retirement on health grounds, but not until 1852 did the Treasury agree to pension arrangements he would accept. He left Hong Kong in 1852.

In 1856 Johnston married Frances Helen, daughter of Richard Bury Palliser. They had nine sons and two daughters; the sons included Conway Seymour Godfrey Campbell-Johnston (1859–1915), drowned with his wife on the *Lusitania*, and Malcolm Campbell-Johnston (1871–1938), Conservative MP for East Ham (South) from 1931 to 1935. A. R. Campbell Johnston resided in Suffolk (where he was a JP) and in London, but died at St Raphael Ranch, Los Angeles, California, on 21 January 1888.

H. G. KEENE, rev. ROGER T. STEARN

Sources *GM*, 2nd ser., 31 (1849), 424 · Burke, *Gen. GB* (1937) · *Dumfries Times* (12 March 1849) · W. P. Baildon, ed., *The records of the Honorable Society of Lincoln's Inn: the black books*, 4 (1902) · *The Athenaeum* (18 Feb 1888), 216 [obit. of Sir William Johnston] · private information (1891) [P. F. Campbell-Johnston] · C. R. De Silva, *Ceylon under the British occupation, 1795–1833*, 1 (1941) · F. Welsh, *A history of Hong Kong*, rev. edn (1997) · G. B. Endacott, *A history of Hong Kong* (1973) · D. Wright, 'Swartz of Thanjavur: a missionary in politics', *South Asia*, new ser., 4 no. 2 (Dec 1981), 94–103 · *WWBMP*, vol. 3 · Boase, *Mod. Eng. biog.* · P. D. Coates, *The China consuls: British consular officers, 1843–1943* (1988)
Archives CUL, notebooks · Department of National Archives of Sri Lanka, PO Box 1414, 7 Reid Avenue, Colombo 7, corresp. and papers · NYPL, corresp. and papers · Royal Commonwealth Society, notebooks | Derbys. RO, letters to the governor of Ceylon, Ref D 1881 · Derbys. RO, letters to Sir R. J. Wilmot-Horton
Likenesses T. Woolnoth, stipple, pubd 1821 (after W. M. Craig), BM, NPG · J. Cochran, stipple (after T. Phillips), BM, NPG; repro. in W. Jerdan, *National portrait gallery of illustrious and eminent personages of the nineteenth century, with memoirs* (1831) [see illus.]
Wealth at death £81,853 1s. 4d.—Alexander Robert Campbell Johnston: probate, 19 May 1888, *CGPLA Eng. & Wales*

Johnston, Alexander (1815–1891), painter, was born in Edinburgh, the son of an architect. At the age of fifteen

Johnston was apprenticed to a seal engraver. He studied at the Trustees' Academy from 1831 to 1834 and exhibited at the Royal Scottish Academy portraits, landscapes, and one religious scene between 1833 and 1837. In 1836 he travelled to London where, with a letter of introduction from Sir David Wilkie, he entered the Royal Academy Schools under William Hilton in 1836. At this early stage in his career Johnston was principally a portrait painter and he brought with him to London portraits of the family of Dr Morison which he exhibited at the Royal Academy in 1836 and 1837. In the following year he exhibited his first subject picture, *The Mother's Prayer*. Subsequent exhibits, including *The Mother's Grave*, *A Thought of Love* (1843; Liverpool Museums and Art Galleries), and *Family Devotions* (Glasgow Art Gallery and Museums) appealed to a sentimental Victorian audience, and his work proved popular. Although Johnston had settled in London and soon ceased to exhibit his work in Scotland, Scotland continued to be a major inspiration for his work. In 1841 he exhibited his first historical picture, *The Interview of the Regent Murray with Mary Queen of Scots*, which was purchased by the Edinburgh Art Union. This was followed by numerous paintings based on Scottish historical events and literary works, such as *The Introduction of Flora Macdonald to Prince Charles Edward Stuart after the Battle of Culloden* (1846; Liverpool Museums and Art Galleries), *Burns and Highland Mary* (1862), and *The Cottar's Saturday Night* (1863). J. L. Caw admired Johnston's 'sound drawing and expressive composition' which, he felt, when combined with Johnston's reticent colour, gave his work a 'severe stateliness' (Caw, 120–21).

Johnston's paintings were engraved: *The Covenanter's Marriage* by Charles Lightfoot for Gems of Modern Art; *Archbishop Tillotson Administering the Sacrament to Lord William Russell in the Tower* (Tate collection) by T. L. Atkinson and C. H. Jeens. Johnston also contributed illustrations for Charles Mackay's *The Home Affections* (1858). His son, Douglas Johnston, worked as a successful musician in Glasgow but predeceased his father. Johnston died at his home, 21 Carlingford Road, Hampstead, after a short illness on 31 January 1891.   L. H. CUST, rev. JENNIFER MELVILLE

Sources P. J. M. McEwan, *Dictionary of Scottish art and architecture* (1994) · J. L. Caw, *Scottish painting past and present, 1620–1908* (1908) · J. Halsby, *Scottish watercolours, 1740–1940* (1986) · W. Hardie, *Scottish painting, 1837–1939* (1976) · d. cert. · *CGPLA Eng. & Wales* (1891)
Wealth at death £364 15s.: probate, 4 March 1891, *CGPLA Eng. & Wales*

Johnston, Sir Alexander (1905–1994), public servant, was born on 27 August 1905 at 32 Comely Bank Street, Edinburgh, the elder child of Alexander Simpson Johnston (1873–1960), stationery salesman, and his wife, Joan, née Macdiarmid (1872–1949). After the Flora Stevenson School, Comely Bank, Edinburgh, he attended George Heriot's School, Edinburgh (1914–23), where he was dux, and then Edinburgh University (1923–7), where he obtained a first-class degree in history. In 1928 he travelled to London for the first time and took top place among those taking the highly competitive examination for the administrative grade of the home civil service. For the rest of his life he was based in London and near the centre of public affairs. He became a devoted member of St Columba's Church (Church of Scotland) in Pont Street, London.

Between 1928 and 1943 Johnston served in the Home Office, latterly being involved in civil defence preparations. Then, as a rising star, he was recruited to Lord Woolton's Ministry of Reconstruction, where as principal assistant secretary he dealt until 1945 with issues arising from the Beveridge report on national insurance and with the orderly dismantling of wartime controls. It was while doing this work that he met Betty Joan Harris [**Betty Joan Johnston**, Lady Johnston (1916–1994)], an assistant parliamentary counsel. She was born on 18 May 1916 at 29 Pentre-poeth Road, Morriston, Swansea, the daughter of Edward Harris, solicitor, and his wife, Catherine Anne Williams. She was educated at Cheltenham Ladies' College and St Hugh's College, Oxford, graduating with a first-class degree in jurisprudence in 1937 and a second class in the Bachelor of Civil Law examination the following year. She was called to the bar by Gray's Inn in 1940, and served in the Treasury from 1940 to 1942, before becoming an assistant parliamentary counsel in 1942. She married Alexander Johnston in Swansea on 7 August 1947. They had a son and a daughter.

In 1946 Alexander Johnston was chosen to help Herbert Morrison, then lord president of the council, and he later served between 1948 and 1951 as deputy secretary of the cabinet. He was a key figure during the high point of twentieth-century collectivism under the Labour government of 1945–51. For the lengthy period between 1951 and 1958 he returned to the Treasury as third secretary, a position in which he showed outstanding capacity for financial control. He was appointed CB in 1946 and KBE in 1953.

In 1958 Johnston became chairman of the Board of Inland Revenue. This was an intensely specialist department, but Johnston mastered its intricacies with great distinction. He successfully advised the Macmillan government to abolish the unpopular schedule A property tax, and was chiefly responsible for implementing capital gains tax and corporation tax when Labour was in power after 1964. He was responsible for the volume entitled *Inland Revenue* in the New Whitehall series (1965); in addition to its descriptive value this book illustrated Johnston's intellect and authority as a public servant. Colleagues spoke of his devastating logic, warmed however by a temperament that left no resentment or malice in his wake. He was made GCB in 1962.

Johnston retired from the Inland Revenue in 1968, but remained intensely active for many years. From 1969 until 1976 he was deputy chairman of the Monopolies Commission (from 1973 the Monopolies and Mergers Commission), and from 1970 until 1983 he was deputy chairman of the Panel on Takeovers and Mergers. The rationale and the developing procedures of the Takeover Panel were explained in his *The City Takeover Code* (1980). Johnston's work with the panel required the highest powers of practical comprehension and rapid decision. From 1978 until 1983 he was also deputy chairman of the Council for the Securities Industry. In addition he was a member of Lord Cromer's important committee on the working of Lloyds, and later an adviser to the chairman of Lloyds. He was chairman from 1970 until 1987 of the universities' academic salaries committee, and from 1975 until 1990 of the joint negotiating committee of the universities' superannuation scheme.

Johnston's third book, *Presbyterians Awake*, appeared in 1988. It argued that the Church of Scotland was failing to maintain its historic conviction of the supremacy of scripture and of equality among all church members. Ecumenism, sacramental emphasis, and unwarranted church pretensions in public debate were among its targets. The book expressed the integrated convictions of a lifetime. To read it is to meet Johnston the expatriate rather than Johnston the powerhouse of Whitehall and the City. 'To many of us', he wrote, 'the essence of being Scottish lies in the Church of Scotland—Calvinist in cast of mind and presbyterian in government' (*Presbyterians Awake*, 26). Johnston applied this energetic and principled point of view to his own life.

Betty Johnston left the office of the parliamentary counsel in 1952 in order to bring up her family. In 1955 she became associated with the Girls' Public Day School Trust, for whose schools girls could qualify under the direct grant system without regard to their parents' ability to pay fees. She served on the trust's education committee from 1955, its council from 1959, and its finance committee from 1964; and became the first woman chairman of the trust's finance committee in 1972 and chairman of its council in 1975. This was a critical time, because the direct grant system was withdrawn in 1976. The trust first had to seek stopgap scholarship money, and then, with Lady Johnston as prime mover, prepare an assisted places scheme for both boys and girls, which was adopted by the Conservative government after 1979. In 1975 she became a parliamentary counsel, seconded to the Law Commission, where she produced several measures which were subsequently enacted. She retired in 1983, and then served until 1988 as standing counsel to the general synod of the Church of England. She retained the chair of the Girls' Public Day School Trust until 1991 and was then president from 1992 to 1994. She served on many of the main bodies concerned to promote private education, and was chairman of the governing bodies of the Girls' School Association (1979–89) and of the Independent Schools' Joint Council (1983–6). She was appointed CBE in 1989. She, like her husband, was remembered for her ability, her seriousness, and her warmth.

Sir Alexander Johnston died of heart failure at his home, 18 Mallord Street, Chelsea, London, on 7 September 1994, and was buried at Redstone cemetery, Redhill, Surrey, eight days later. Lady Johnston died at 18 Mallord Street of non-Hodgkins lymphoma on 28 November 1994; she too was buried at Redstone cemetery. The couple were survived by their two children.

ARTHUR GREEN

Sources *The Independent* (12 Sept 1994) · *The Times* (22 Sept 1994) · *The Times* (29 May 1995) · *The Times* (3 Dec 1994) [Betty Joan Johnston] · H. Kent, *In on the act* (1979) · private information (2004) [Ms Catherine Johnston; Mrs Sheila Byrde] · *WWW, 1991–5* · b. cert. · b. cert. [Betty Joan Johnston] · m. cert. · d. cert. · d. cert. [Betty Joan Johnston] · *CGPLA Eng. & Wales* (1994) [Betty Joan Johnston]
Likenesses photograph, repro. in *The Independent* · photograph, repro. in *The Times* (22 Sept 1994) · photograph (Betty Joan Johnston), repro. in *The Times* (3 Dec 1994)
Wealth at death £242,567: *The Times* (29 May 1995) · £1,757,575—Betty Joan Johnston: probate, 1995

Johnston, Alexander James (1820–1888), judge in New Zealand, the eldest son of James S. Johnston of Wood Hill, Kinnellar, Aberdeenshire, was born at Kinnellar on 15 January 1820. He entered Lincoln's Inn on 12 November 1838, migrated to the Middle Temple on 21 December 1842, and was called to the bar by the latter society on 27 January 1843. He practised for several years in Westminster Hall, and went on the northern circuit until 1857, when he was appointed deputy recorder of Leeds. In 1859 he emigrated to New Zealand, and the following year was appointed one of the judges of the supreme court in the Wellington district; in 1876 he was transferred to the Canterbury district.

As judge Johnson tried many of the Maori prisoners captured during Te Kooti's and Tito Kowaru's campaigns during the New Zealand wars. He also presided over one of New Zealand's most infamous and publicized criminal cases, Nelson's Maungatapu murders, in 1866. He occupied a dignified position during the aftermath of the New Zealand wars, opposing the outcry for summary trials by court-martial and quoting with great effect the words of Chief-Justice Cockburn (in *R. v. Nelson and Brand*) against lightly superseding the ordinary tribunals. He was a member of several commissions appointed for legal purposes, the most important being the Statute Law Consolidation Commission, which met in 1879. With the solicitor-general, he reported in 1883 on the codification of criminal law, and his recommendations were largely followed in the 1893 Criminal Code Act. He had wide cultural interests and wrote two books on legal matters and one on art. Johnston returned to England for health reasons in 1888, and died in Down Street, Piccadilly, London, at the home of his son, A. R. Fletcher Johnston, on 1 June in the same year. No more is known of his family life.

THOMAS SECCOMBE, *rev.* JANE TUCKER

Sources P. Mennell, *The dictionary of Australasian biography* (1892) · R. S. Hill, *Policing the colonial frontier: the theory and practice of coercive social and racial control in New Zealand, 1767–1867* (1986) · R. S. Hill, *The colonial frontier tamed: New Zealand policing in transition, 1867–1886* (1989) · R. Cooke, ed., *Portrait of a profession: the centennial book of the New Zealand Law Society* (1969) · *The Times* (6 June 1988) · *The Argus* [Melbourne] (5 June 1888) · *Law Journal* (9 June 1888), 322 · *CGPLA Eng. & Wales* (1888) · d. cert.
Likenesses photographs, NL NZ, Turnbull L., 22674 1/2, F97061 1/2
Wealth at death £5243 5s. 6d.: probate, 25 Aug 1888, *CGPLA Eng. & Wales*

Johnston, Alexander Robert Campbell (1812–1888). *See under* Johnston, Sir Alexander (1775–1849).

Johnston, Sir Archibald, Lord Wariston (*bap.* 1611, *d.* 1663), lawyer and politician, was baptized at Edinburgh on 28 March 1611, the son of James Johnston, a wealthy Edinburgh merchant, and his wife, Elizabeth, second daughter of the eminent lawyer Sir Thomas *Craig of Riccarton, the author of *Jus feudale*.

Early years: education, marriage, and religion, 1611–1636 As someone born into the burgh élite Wariston, as he is always known, knew the leading lawyers and merchants of Edinburgh from childhood. His family was prosperous, successful, and deeply religious. His grandmother Rachel Arnot, who lived until 1626, was a devoted patron of presbyterian ministers such as Robert Bruce. According to Burnet, 'she was counted for many years the chief support of the party' (*Burnet's History*, 1.31). Wariston's father appears to have had a classic puritan conversion experience, and his mother was a zealous supporter of the presbyterian faction in the church. On at least one occasion she fasted and prayed for eight to ten days for her son. Wariston himself recalls being 'of the seed of the faithful' at a very early age, and records intense spiritual experiences at fasts and communions when he was fifteen and sixteen. His sister Rachel Johnston was also a staunch presbyterian. She married Robert Burnet, and became the mother of the bishop and historian Gilbert Burnet, who wrote that his mother 'was bred to her brother Wariston's principles and could never be moved from them' (*Burnet's History*, 1.434).

Little is known of Wariston's childhood, but he describes having had 'many diseases in my bairne age' (Johnston, *Diary*, 1.378). He was educated at Glasgow University, where he was listed among the students in the academic year 1628–9, and again in March 1630. His tutor was his kinsman Robert Baillie. After graduating from Glasgow he went to France to continue his education, living at Castres and Paris. On 23 October 1632, in the Old Kirk of St Giles, he married his first wife, Jean (*c.*1618–1633), daughter of Lewis Stewart, a leading advocate. Wariston was twenty-one, and his bride was probably only fourteen, but he agreed to the marriage on the advice of friends and in the knowledge that the girl was from a godly family. On the Sunday morning after their wedding he examined Jean on her knowledge of religion, and was 'ravisched with hir ansuears and blissed God for hir' (Johnston, *Diary*, 1.11). However, on 12 June 1633, less than a year after their marriage, she died.

In the wake of his wife's death Wariston began his famous *Diary*. The earliest extant volume, 'Memento quamdiu vivas', is a chronicle of his religious life, written as an address to the soul in the manner of Augustine's *Confessions*. Even by seventeenth-century standards Wariston was unusually devout. Wodrow recorded that Wariston once prayed from six in the morning to eight at night having lost awareness of the passage of time, and noted that he would often pray for up to three hours at a time. In 1633 Wariston recorded three occasions on which he had experienced 'extraordinar motions' in his spiritual life: 'quhen I was an Latiner, in Castres after my coming to France, and in Edimbrugh after my hoomecoming' (Johnston, *Diary*, 1.136). However, the loss of his wife plunged

Sir Archibald Johnston, Lord Wariston (*bap.* 1611, *d.* 1663), by George Jamesone

him into a dark night of the soul, and he devoted himself to intensive rounds of praying, fasting, meditating on the scriptures, listening to sermons, and attending communions. He immersed himself in works of practical divinity by English puritans such as John Dod, Nicholas Byfield, John Preston, and John Downame. He was desperately lacking in the assurance that he was one of the elect, and he spent months searching for peace. In painstaking detail he recorded his extremes of despair and rapture, his hours of weeping and wrestling with God. In a typical entry he wrote that he had 'roared, groaned, sobbed unutterably' and 'schouted' unto God (Johnston, *Diary*, 1.65).

Surprisingly, many of the ministers from whom Wariston drew spiritual comfort at this time were staunch episcopalians who later opposed the covenanting movement. One of those to whom he turned for counsel was the Aberdeen doctor Robert Sibbald, and he was also warmly appreciative of the sermons of James Fairlie and Thomas Sydserf, both of whom were soon promoted to bishoprics. Indeed, most of the ministers whose churches Wariston attended were deposed by the Glasgow general assembly. Despite their differences, presbyterians and episcopalians still shared a common evangelical protestant piety. 'Memento quamdiu vivas' contains 250 pages on the period between 1632 and September 1634, but it is perfectly silent about the controversies raging within the kirk. In 1633 Wariston was also trying to decide whether to become a minister or a lawyer. After reading *A Treatise of Callings* by William Perkins he concluded that he did not have the qualities necessary in a good pastor. He had been trained as a lawyer, and felt that his mind was better suited to the law. He appeared before the chancellor and

the judges, and made a good impression. On 6 November 1633 he was admitted an Edinburgh advocate. Wariston's other major concern was remarriage. He seems to have struggled with sexual temptation after the death of his first wife, and referred to 'the abominations of my heart in my widouhood' (Johnston, *Diary*, 1.217). Believing that it was better to marry than to burn, he began to look around for a possible bride. On 11 January 1634 he pledged himself to marry Helen Hay, daughter of Lord Fosterseat, a member of the court of session, and she 'suore the lyk unto me' (Johnston, *Diary*, 1.193). The marriage was celebrated on 4 September 1634.

The birth of the covenanter movement, 1637–1638 Wariston's extant diary stops shortly after his marriage, and it does not resume until 7 February 1637. In the meantime he had begun to establish himself as a successful lawyer. At the outset of his legal career he found little work, and thought seriously about changing his profession. However, by 1636–7 the cases were beginning to flow in, and he was gaining a reputation as an effective pleader. His clients included the chancellor, the earl of Kinnoull, and the lord treasurer, the earl of Traquair. He also acquired the Wariston property in the parish of Currie from his brother-in-law Alexander Hay. His eldest child, Elizabeth, was probably born some time between September 1634 and August 1636, and his eldest son, James, was born on 20 April 1637 and baptized on the same day by Henry Rollock in the Old Kirk, though he died before he reached his first birthday. His next son, Archibald, was born on 11 January 1639 and named after Archibald Campbell, Lord Lorne. His youngest son, James *Johnston, was born on 9 September 1655 and became a politician and government official.

Besides becoming a busy lawyer and father, Wariston was also starting to take a serious interest in national affairs. The introspection of the first volume of his diary was still present, but it was now combined with a new political awareness. The imposition of the book of canons in 1636 and the prayer book in 1637 galvanized a man who had previously been caught up in matters of personal piety. By this stage he was in close contact with radical presbyterian ministers such as David Dickson, John Livingstone, and Robert Blair. His first reference to the controversies within the church comes on 31 May 1637, when a synod met in Edinburgh 'for to receave the service book, the image of the beast, against the quhilk som gaive ane testimonie to the treuth'. On 13 June he conferred most of the day with Dickson 'about living by faith and praeparation for subsequent tryels'. On 7 July he again met with Dickson and Livingstone to discuss the prayer book controversy and pray 'for strenth in the day of tentation' (Johnston, *Diary*, 1.258–9, 262). When the Edinburgh riots against the prayer book blew up on 23 July he was gratified that 'This uproar was greater nor [than] the 17 December [1597]', when the presbyterians had last rioted in the city. He was convinced that 'if we licked up this vomit of Romisch superstition again, the Lord in his wrayth wald vomit us out' (Johnston, *Diary*, 1.267).

Despite the growing political crisis, Wariston continued with his everyday work as a lawyer, though he was being drawn into the heart of the movement of opposition to Charles I. At the end of September he read and expounded to his family the king's confession of 1581, the document that was to form the first section of the national covenant. He discovered that the council was secretly planning to meet in Edinburgh on 17 October, and quickly wrote to the other petitioners, summoning them to the capital. Although many thought he was being 'too rash' his information proved correct (Baillie, 1.34). On 18 October Wariston was present when the disaffected nobles, gentry, burgesses, and ministers signed a supplication against the service book, canons, and bishops. He was convinced that he should use his talents for 'the rebuilding of Gods house, and casting doune of the Kingdome of Antichryst, by collecting togither a note of the most remarkable acts of Parlement for thir defective tymes' (Johnston, *Diary*, 1.275). He read George Gillespie's *Dispute Against the English Popish Ceremonies* (1637), and began to make a serious study of the king's prerogative. Although he worried about the effects on his private law practice, he agreed in early December to devote himself to defending the cause of the supplicants. As clerk to the tables he quickly established himself as a key figure in the movement, meeting regularly with noblemen such as Rothes, Loudoun, and Balmerino. Baillie referred to him as 'the only advocate who in this cause is trusted' (Baillie, 1.48). During December Wariston worked on the latest petition of the supplicants, helped to draw up a declinator arguing that the bishops on the council should not be allowed to judge the matter since it directly concerned their own conduct, and prepared a protestation which would be sent to the king if the council refused to receive the supplicants. He urged the nobles to avoid 'any mitigatorie declaration in favors of the bischops persons', and was ably assisted by Alexander Henderson, who took an equally firm line against bishops (Johnston, *Diary*, 1.287–8).

As his diary shows, Wariston continued to spend hours in prayer and biblical meditation amid this political activity. Indeed, he insisted that 'the disposition of our awin hearts towards God in al our ways, especaly in the exercises of his worschip and our privat retyrings' would be the key to the movement's success or failure (Johnston, *Diary*, 1.313). As well as rummaging through the acts of the Scottish parliament and historical manuscripts, he also set out to dig for corroborative arguments from various books: Knox's *History of the Reformation* and Buchanan's *History of Scotland*, histories of the Dutch revolt and the French wars of religion, commentaries on Roman law, the anti-episcopal writings of Thomas Cartwright, William Ames, Robert Parker, Henry Burton, William Prynne, and David Calderwood, and works of resistance theory by Philip and David Pareus, Theodore Beza, 'Junius Brutus', and Johannes Althusius. From an early date he was willing to contemplate radical measures against bishops and the king.

In January and February 1638, Wariston gathered intelligence information from sympathizers in England and Scotland regarding the latest moves of the court, and drew up further documents laying out the supplicants'

position. Since December he had been revising the historical information prepared by the earl of Rothes, and eventually to be published as Rothes' *Relation*. When it was finished the supplicants' advocates 'condemned it altogether as superfluous and danger-rubbing on the King, his Counsel, his gouvernement'. Wariston was angered, but after Andrew Ramsay had made some minor alterations the information was formally accepted (Johnston, *Diary*, 1.304). By 25 January he had already written a test piece for the national covenant, calling for fundamental checks on the royal prerogative. He also drafted a proclamation, and read it out at the Mercat Cross in Edinburgh in the presence of the nobility. This act of defiance by the supplicant leadership reportedly angered Charles I more than the riots on 23 July and 18 October 1637. On Friday 23 February Wariston spoke eloquently in defence of the proclamation in a series of meetings, 'first with the pryme foor noblemen, Rothes, Lindsay, Balmerino, Laudin; then befor the whol noblemen; and thairafter before the whol barones'. According to his diary, 'my opinion was universally applauded to and imbraced both be the nobilitie and the gentrie' (Johnston, *Diary*, 1.318–19). He may also have been the one to suggest a renewal of the covenant of 1581.

Before dinner that evening Wariston and Henderson were landed with 'the insupportable burden of drauing up the Band, quherby al should be linked together after subscryving of the Confession of Fayth' (Johnston, *Diary*, 1.319). That evening he drafted what became the final section of the national covenant, explaining why the supplicants felt compelled to renew their 'Band' with the Lord. On the morning of Saturday 24th he drafted the beginning and middle sections of the document, which contained the king's confession of 1581 and the supporting acts of the Scottish parliament. After showing his work to Rothes, Loudoun, and Balmerino, he agreed to 'compendize' the acts. On Tuesday 27th he read the three parts of the covenant (the confession, the acts of parliament, and the band) to the nobles and the ministers, who made some minor alterations. He then copied the whole document onto parchment, ready for subscription. He was overjoyed that the Lord had 'maid me, the wickedest, vyldest, sinfullest, unworthiest, unaiblest, servant, to be ane instrument in his hand of … so glorious a work' and described Wednesday 28 February as 'that glorious marriage day of the Kingdome with God' (Johnston, *Diary*, 1.321–2). In the morning he took part in last-minute meetings about the covenant, and at 2 p.m. he was at Greyfriars Kirk, where he publicly read the document and answered questions about it. Then, after Henderson's prayer, 'The Covenant was subscryved first be the noblemen and barons that night til 8 at night'. Scotland had become a new Israel: 'ye will find a verrie near paralel betuixt Izrael and this churche, the only tuo suorne nations to the Lord' (Johnston, *Diary*, 1.322, 344).

In the weeks that followed the signing of the covenant Wariston recorded the religious fervour of the covenanters. In Edinburgh, on 1 April, a meeting for subscription of the covenant turned into a revivalist rally, convincing him that the nation's covenant was being internally renewed. 'O Edr., O Edr.', he wrote, 'never forget this first day of Apryle, the gloriousest day that ever thou injoyed' (Johnston, *Diary*, 1.330–31). A week later he noted that 'after tuentie yeirs interruption the Comunion was celebrat purly in the College and Grayfrears churche'. Providentially, the prayer book had become 'Gods dishclout to scoure the vessels of his sanctuarie from the filthines of the ceremonies'. This time was 'the honymoneth betuixt the Lord and his runaway spous' (Johnston, *Diary*, 1.334–6).

At the same time Wariston continued to act as legal adviser, intelligence gatherer, and draftsman for the covenanters. In late March he revised Henderson's draft of the eight covenanter demands given to Traquair. He was at the forefront of moves to restore the power of presbyteries to ordain ministers without the assistance of bishops, and in April wrote 'tuo treatises' on the subject. He regarded himself as 'the sole principal instrument in [God's] hand for the legal recovering of his churches liberties'. By early May he had concluded that God would lead the covenanters to 'the highest step of reformation … the utter overthrou and ruyne of Episcopacie, that great grandmother of al our corruptions, novations, usurpations, diseases and troubles … the root of papacie … that chaire of Antichryst in the world' (Johnston, *Diary*, 1.34, 347–8).

Above all, Wariston acted as a propagandist for the cause. He continued to write the covenanters' official protestations in reply to royal proclamations, and from July 1638 some of these began to be printed. In May he spent a week studying Althusius in order to write *An Answere to M. J. Forbes of Corse, his Peaceable Warning* (1638). In June, when the marquess of Hamilton demanded that the covenanters abandon or modify the terms of the covenant, Wariston vigorously condemned any such compromise. Hearing that the covenanters were to be accused of treason, he quickly penned yet another protestation, and then drew up a supplication with the approval of Rothes and the help of Loudoun. When the king's delegation suggested changes to the supplication, Rothes, Montrose, Loudoun, and Henderson seemed prepared to make concessions, and Wariston 'went home almost despairing of our business; seing I was my alon'. The next day, however, he secured the agreement of the other covenanters, and the potential rift was averted (Johnston, *Diary*, 1.353–4). On 4 July the latest royal proclamation was read out at the cross in Edinburgh, and Wariston responded by reading out the covenanters' protestation. He then set to work with David Dickson on a much more detailed refutation. On 11 July he began work on a text entitled 'Ane information to all good Christians within the kingdom of England', which was eventually circulated in England in early 1639. At the end of the month he was among a group of covenanters who visited Glasgow, and persuaded the principal of the university and others to take the covenant.

In the middle of August Hamilton made his second visit to Scotland as the king's commissioner. The situation was increasingly tense, for the covenanters had begun to train men for war, and Wariston himself was helping to secure military supplies. The main point of discussion with Hamilton was the calling of a general assembly of the kirk. There was deep disagreement about the composition of the assembly, with both sides wishing to ensure that their representatives would be in control. Wariston drew up reasons in defence of the burghs ratifying the covenant, and argued in favour of the right of lay elders to elect commissioners from presbyteries to go to the general assembly. The covenanters were in danger of dividing on the matter, with many ministers disturbed at the prospect of lay control of the church. However, Wariston acted quickly along with Loudoun, Rothes, and Henderson, and drew up directions on how the commissioners from presbyteries were to be elected. Along with Dickson, Henderson, and Calderwood, he 'dreu up the publik letter to be sent to presbyteries, and reasons for ruling elders, and against constant moderators' (Johnston, *Diary*, 1.378). He then arranged for the papers to be subscribed by members of the four tables and distributed them among the ministers. The ground had been prepared for a successful election campaign which would allow covenanters to dominate the general assembly.

In September Hamilton arrived on his third diplomatic mission to the covenanters, bringing news of some dramatic concessions by the king. Hamilton was now proposing a king's covenant, ostensibly to demonstrate the king's faithfulness to the reformed faith, but also to draw the Scots away from the national covenant. Wariston was furious, and described it as 'perfect anti-christianism, and the battel betuixt the draigon and Michael' (Johnston, *Diary*, 1.392). His attitudes were hardened by the prophetess Margaret Mitchelson, who predicted the triumph of 'Covenanting Jesus'. He first heard her prophecies on 13 September, and was deeply impressed. Over the next few months, he kept in close contact with Mitchelson, even inviting her to speak in his house. With the assembly due to open on 21 November, Wariston was at the centre of the covenanter campaign against episcopacy. He sent out letters to presbyteries informing them that complaints had been made against their bishop. In accord with his instructions, the presbyteries referred the complaints to the assembly and then announced the matter in all the churches. The covenanters were also willing to use strong-arm tactics, and Wariston received letters urging him to make sure that bishops who appeared in public were met with terror and disgrace.

When the assembly finally met Wariston was appointed as clerk and Henderson as moderator. Between 12 November and 20 January Wariston proved to be too busy to keep his diary. He pulled off a major coup by producing several manuscript volumes which contained the minutes of previous general assemblies since 1560 and which had been missing for many years. Drawing on this material he drew up a large treatise arguing that episcopacy had always been condemned in the reformed Church of Scotland. He claimed that many had come to the assembly inclined to vote for episcopacy, and had been swayed by the evidence he produced. The existing bishops were deposed, and on 8

December the institution of episcopacy was declared to be abjured by the 1581 confession and removed from the church. Although more than fifty members simply declared that episcopacy should be removed, as clerk Wariston recorded everyone as agreeing to abjuration, a procedure which drew criticism from Robert Baillie. At the close of the assembly he was unanimously chosen as procurator of the kirk, responsible for the publications issued on its behalf.

Relations with England, 1639–1647 In January 1639 Wariston wrote to Lord Johnston warning him that if he travelled to court and abandoned the covenant he would provoke God's vengeance and 'be infamous in all stories' as a traitor. Even if all the nobility deserted the cause, 'the great God, the patron of this work, will trample them down, and erect over their bellies the trophies of his victory' (Dalrymple, 49–53).

Because of his work for the covenanters Wariston was no longer enjoying a steady income from his private law practice, and his wife had become ill, partly out of worry about their finances. In order to make some money he published the acts of the assembly and sold them at a substantial profit, provoking accusations of profiteering. In February 1639 his extant diary ends, though we possess a fragment for May and June 1639, when he was immersed in the first bishops' war and the subsequent negotiations with the king. Unlike earlier volumes, this fragment is exclusively focused on politics. In late May Wariston was with the Scottish army as it marched south to Dunbar. He was one of those responsible for drafting letters from the army to the government and the people, calling for further support. In early June he recorded his depression on considering 'the wants of money, munition, victual, order and discipline', and the army's confusion over its strategy (Johnston, 'Fragment', 58). However, the 'war' proved to be a damp squib, and on 13 June Wariston and Henderson were sent to the English camp to meet the king, where they debated the legitimacy of the Glasgow assembly and started to negotiate a settlement. On several occasions during the negotiations the king commanded the outspoken Wariston to be silent, and when the covenanters rose to leave, he warned Wariston to 'walk more circumspectly in tyme coming' (Johnston, 'Fragment', 85). On 18 June, however, the king and the covenanters signed the treaty of Berwick, bringing an end to the first bishops' war. Wariston returned to Edinburgh on 21 June, 'wher we found many greived with our proceidings' (Johnston, 'Fragment', 95). The covenanters had agreed to disband their army, but had gained relatively little in return.

Between 17 and 20 July 1639 Wariston and five other covenanter leaders had further discussions with the king at Berwick. The talks ended in stalemate, with each side accusing the other of breaking the treaty, and Charles returned to London at the end of the month. In the general assembly which began on 12 August in St Giles, Wariston was again appointed clerk, and he employed his knowledge of the acts and constitutions of the kirk to argue against episcopacy and the five articles of Perth. On

14 November he read out a protestation in parliament, complaining that it was being prorogued by Traquair without the consent of the estates. In December Baillie joked that because 'you ar become great, a prim member of our Church and Stat also' he had to be satisfied with a few 'blenks of your ey in the streits one a yeir' (Baillie, 1.237). However, in April 1640 Wariston still found time to read Baillie's book against the Canterburians before it went to the press.

Before it sat again in June 1640 there was some debate as to whether a parliament could meet in the absence of the king and his commissioner, but Wariston, Argyll, Rothes, and Balmerino argued against Montrose that it could. Wariston was awarded a salary of 1000 merks per annum as procurator to the kirk, and 50 merks per annum as clerk. The parliament also appointed him a member of the section of the committee of estates which accompanied the army. His task was to provide expert advice on treaties, consultations, and public declarations in the run-up to the second bishops' war. On 23 June he wrote to Loudoun in London urging him to persuade sympathetic English peers to invite the covenanters to enter England and join them in arms if they did. In early August he also helped to orchestrate the successful appeal to the people for money and tents for the army. The Scottish army entered England on 20 August and occupied Newcastle ten days later. In October Wariston was one of the eight Scottish commissioners who secured the highly favourable treaty of Ripon.

On 10 November 1640 Wariston and the Scottish commissioners arrived in London for further negotiations. He campaigned vigorously for the king's 'evil counsellors' to be sent to Scotland for trial as incendiaries, though eventually the covenanters accepted the king's statement that he would no longer employ or listen to these counsellors. In February 1641 Henderson wrote a paper designed to reassure English puritan MPs who feared that the Scots were softening in their attitudes to moderate episcopacy in England and to Strafford and Laud. Henderson explained in no uncertain terms that this was not the case. Although intended for private circulation only, the paper was published without the Scots' permission. 'The King has run stark mad at it', wrote Wariston. The paper, 'because of its bitterness', was being dubbed 'Johnston's paper', an indication of his reputation as the most hardline of the covenanter commissioners (Dalrymple, 2.107–8). He continued to insist that Traquair and other royal councillors be prosecuted and on 21 April he and the other commissioners had a stormy meeting with the king in which 'he raged' at their papers, 'called us Jesuitical', and threatened to retaliate by exempting leading covenanters from oblivion if they persisted with trying to prosecute Traquair. Wariston had, however, already claimed that he was ready to be put in chains rather than see Traquair go free, and despite these stormy exchanges, negotiations progressed and were largely completed by the end of June. Wariston returned to Edinburgh on 26 June 1641.

The Scottish parliament met on 15 July, with Wariston present during the opening days in his capacity as clerk to the general assembly. He argued that some commissioners appointed by the assembly should be allowed to sit in the parliament, but this motion was denounced by Argyll, who feared that it would open the way to greater clerical control of parliament. The general assembly met in St Andrews from 20 July to 9 August, with Wariston once again acting as clerk. Baillie had asked him to hold discussions with the two parties involved in the dispute over conventicles in the kirk, but his role seems to have been fairly limited.

The king arrived in Edinburgh on 14 August 1641. He had already ratified the treaty of London, though Wariston was not a signatory, probably because he did not represent one of the three estates. When the king appeared before parliament Wariston sprang another surprise by producing the records of the parliament in order to demonstrate that it had the power to appoint officers of state. Determined to restore his authority in Scotland, Charles handed out honours, offices, and pensions to the covenanters. In November 1641 Wariston was knighted, appointed a lord of session as Lord Wariston, and awarded a pension of £2400 sterling (£28,800 Scots) per annum. However, contrary to widespread expectation, he did not become clerk register, probably because the king opposed his appointment, and Argyll was willing to back Alexander Gibson. In late 1641 Wariston was 'very infirme, and dangerouslie sick', though he still managed to draw up a paper on the trial of incendiaries and plotters (Baillie, 1.394). On 6 November the committee of estates appointed him one of the commissioners to continue negotiations with the king and the English parliament, including about sending troops to suppress the Irish rising. On 15 January 1642 the commissioners called for the abolition of episcopacy in England, a move which the king saw as aligning them with the English opposition. On 12 April he wrote to Wariston telling him to stop 'laying an aspersion on our actions, though clouded under the name of evil counsellors', and warning of retaliation if he continued to try to unite the two kingdoms against their king (Russell, 492–3). In May Wariston was back in Edinburgh, where he responded to the royalist 'banders' by issuing a paper in defence of the covenanters' actions. When the general assembly began at St Andrews on 27 July he was appointed a member of the moderator's committee designed to control the assembly's agenda.

On 18 January 1643 Wariston was commissioned to go to the king and the English parliament to campaign for the abolition of episcopacy in England and the establishment of an assembly of divines to discuss religion. In May he helped to persuade the commissioners of the kirk to send remonstrances to the convention of estates urging it to provide assistance to the English parliamentarians. In the run-up to the opening of the general assembly in Edinburgh on 2 August, leading covenanters met in Wariston's chamber and chose Henderson as moderator. When commissioners from the English parliament arrived in August Wariston was the only person to be on the welcoming committees of both the church and the state. He persuaded other covenanters that they could not remain neutral between royalists and parliamentarians, and took an active part in the negotiations over the solemn league and covenant, which was signed on 17 August 1643. Two days later Wariston was appointed one of the Scottish commissioners to the Westminster assembly.

Wariston delayed his journey south, but in January 1644 the convention of estates nominated him to proceed to London to work for religious uniformity between the two kingdoms. Although he left most of the debating in the assembly to Henderson, Gillespie, and Rutherford, he did make a few speeches against independency and Erastianism, and in February Baillie noted that 'we gett good help in our Assemblie debates of our Lord Wariston' (Baillie, 1.140). He persuaded Rutherford to complete *Lex, rex* (1644), a work of resistance theory calculated to encourage the Scots to take a hard line with the king. He also sat on the committee of both kingdoms for managing the war, and was largely responsible for drawing up articles of peace in April 1644. He returned to Scotland for the general assembly in May and stayed on for the first session of the first triennial parliament in June and July. Of the eighteen committees in this session, Wariston sat on six. On 2 June he demanded that justice be executed on the main protagonists in the recent royalist rebellions.

On 16 July 1644 Wariston was ordered to return to London, and in August he delivered a passionate speech to the Westminster assembly emphasizing the Scots' urgent desire for covenanted uniformity. On 26 December 1644 he left England to attend the second session of the Scottish parliament and the general assembly which on 22 January 1645, where he was reappointed to the commission of the kirk. In the middle of the year he was back in London, where Baillie claimed he was indispensable to the Scottish commissioners. On 24 October he was sent to the Scottish army in Newcastle, and from there to Scotland. He once again took an active part in parliament, in the fifth session at St Andrews, from 26 November 1645 to 4 February 1646. On the first day of this session he delivered a 'longe harrang' against malignants, urging parliament to purge 'the enimies of the comonwealthe' from their midst (Balfour, 3.311–12). This sparked off a debate that culminated in January 1646 with the first Act of Classes, which ejected Montrose's sympathizers from public office. Wariston returned once more to London in March, and on 1 May delivered a significant speech to the Westminster assembly, apologizing that he could not attend more of its sessions but calling on it to make Christ king of the church by presenting 'a full, clear, plenary declaring of the truth' (Mitchell and Struthers, 458–9). After the civil war ended in England, the Scots suspected that the English parliamentarians aimed to dispose of Charles I without reference to their allies. In October 1646 Baillie wrote that 'In three solemn meetings, the Chancellour, Waristoune, and Lauderdale, did so outreason them, that all the hundreds of hearers did grope their insolent absurdities' (Baillie, 2.402–3). In late October Wariston returned to the Scottish army at Newcastle and thereafter to Scotland. On 30 October, when Charles I had joined the Scots at Newcastle, he nominated Wariston to the office of lord advocate. Wariston sat on five committees in the sixth session of parliament, held from 3 November 1646 to 27 March 1647, and was awarded £3000 sterling (£36,000 Scots) in reparation for his losses on behalf of the covenanting cause.

The rise and fall of the kirk party, 1647–1650 Between 29 March 1647 and 28 February 1648 Wariston attended eighty-four out of 107 meetings of the committee of estates. However, the radicals' grip on Scottish politics was loosening. On 8 September he was present when the committee voted in favour of Hamilton's policy of disbanding the army. In the first session of the second triennial parliament, between March and May 1648, Wariston sat as representative of the shire of Argyll, having satisfied that property qualification because Argyll had provided him with the necessary land. Baillie recorded that Wariston was one of the few to speak out against the engagers, supporters of the treaty signed by covenanter representatives and Charles I in December 1647. However, the defeat of the engagers at Preston and Cromwell's incursion into Scotland put the radicals back in charge. According to Balfour, Wariston later 'confest publickly in open parliament' what he had previously denied, that the English 'cam into Scotland with consent' (Balfour, 3.388). When parliament sat again in January 1649 Wariston and Argyll made it clear in their speeches that they expected a programme of retribution against malignants, with Argyll suggesting that Wariston's proposals would 'brecke their jaws' (Balfour, 3.377). As a result of their agitation, the draconian Act of Classes was passed against the engagers on 23 January. It was widely assumed that the act was largely Wariston's work, and he was given a key role in implementing it and purging malignant royalists from public office. On 6 January he had moved that an appointed fast be observed by the whole parliament, including its committees, and that discussion of the king's position in England be delayed for several days. In view of the extremity of the king's plight, the parliament disagreed, but it has been speculated that 'Argyll and Johnston of Wariston were attempting to delay the parliamentary process aimed at saving the king's life in order to facilitate the trial and subsequent execution' (Young, 223). Wariston may well have sympathized with James Guthrie and Patrick Gillespie who were passionately opposed to proclaiming Charles II king after the execution of his father. Despite this, he was present when Charles II was proclaimed king at Edinburgh on 5 February. On 9 March he supported the parliamentary act which abolished lay patronage in the church and the following day was appointed clerk register, a position he had coveted for some years. He acted as president of the court of session in June and July.

According to Balfour, Wariston was one of the militant critics of the plan to bring Charles II to Scotland, though Blair quotes James Sharp as saying that Wariston 'drew up the articles' of the treaty of Breda (*Life of Robert Blair*, 330).

Both may well be right, for although Wariston argued against sending commissioners to the king as late as February 1650, he may have concluded that since this was inevitable he should work for as tough a deal as possible. In May he was appointed to examine Montrose after the captured royalist was brought to Edinburgh, and on the day before Montrose's execution read out the death sentence against him. In the summer of 1650 he encouraged the purging of the Scottish army, and was present at the battle of Dunbar on 3 September 1650. Burnet claims that in his desire to see the English sectaries vanquished Wariston rashly encouraged the army to move from its strong position on Doon Hill, an error which led to crushing defeat for the Scots. However, Wariston refused to acknowledge that his actions or the purges lay behind the defeat. Although the rumours that he was the author of the radical western remonstrance were false, he did defend it 'for bothe maner and matter' (Balfour, 4.169–70), arguing that the proper response to defeat lay in further purging, not in compromise with royalists and engagers. In December parliament voted to readmit engagers to public office, and Wariston walked out. From this point on he was estranged from the mainstream of Scottish politics. Although he retained his seat on the committee of estates, he refused to participate in the coronation of Charles II in January 1651.

Protester, 1651–1656 During the first eight months of 1651 Wariston was preoccupied with the recovery of the Scottish registers captured by the English army. He worked tirelessly for their return, raising the issue repeatedly with Cromwell and other English commanders, but his close contact with the occupying forces raised suspicions that he was working with the enemy. In mid-February he had a 'privey conference with his Maiestey, an houer and a halffe' at Perth, but he remained opposed to any compromise with malignants and was accused of dissuading magistrates in Culross and Stirling from supporting the new king (Balfour, 4.250). In August, despite all his efforts, the registers were taken from Stirling Castle and transported to London. Meanwhile, Wariston had become more convinced than ever that Charles II was simply offering 'mock repentance' (Johnston, *Diary*, 2.56), and that the covenanters were allowing malignants to destroy the work of God. When the general assembly met at St Andrews on 16 July he sent a personal testimony against the compromises, and the hardline clergy issued a protest. From now on he was to be firmly aligned with the protesters against the resolutioners, who supported the resolutions of church and state to admit malignants into the army. When the Scots were defeated at Worcester on 3 September 1651 Wariston was convinced that it was God's judgment on a compromising nation. At the Edinburgh general assembly in July 1652 he drafted a protestation and remonstrance, and presented it on the opening day. The resolutioners regarded Wariston as 'the cause of al the distance and division', and described him as 'the ruyner of the Kirk of Scotland' (Johnston, *Diary*, 2.180, 198). Wariston helped to draft numerous protester papers, and in 1652 he published *The Nullity of the Pretended Assembly* *at St Andrews and Dundee*, which according to Robert Blair led to 'a great heightening of our woeful divisions' and made them 'incurable' (*Life of Robert Blair*, 304). He also wrote the first draft of the *Causes of the Lord's Wrath*, which was then completed by James Guthrie and published in 1653. In 1655 Guthrie and Wariston also promoted the concept of a new covenant that would bind together the godly in the land; Baillie claimed that they wished to omit all reference to the king, parliament, liberties of the land, or mutual defence (Baillie, 3.297). Lord Broghill described Wariston and Guthrie as 'Fifth-Monarchy-Presbyterians', implying that their opposition to the government was inspired by apocalyptic expectations of the imminent rule of Christ through the saints. In June and November 1655 Wariston participated in conferences aimed at ending the protester–resolutioner controversy, but he showed a characteristic unwillingness to compromise, and the mutual hostility of the two sides continued to grow.

On a personal level, Wariston's situation was bleak. In the wake of the English invasion he had lost £11,450 sterling and his well-paid employment as clerk register, and those who had bought offices from him were now demanding their money back. His finances were now lower than in 1637, he found it very difficult to borrow money, and his wife had literally sold the family silver to make ends meet. He was also widely hated, and records being publicly abused in church by a woman who accused him of killing Montrose, betraying the king like Judas, and trying to make himself king instead.

Compromise with the English, 1656–1660 On 31 May 1656 Wariston received a letter from Argyll informing him that if he agreed to look after the Scottish registers, the English would award him a salary. The offer presented him with an agonizing dilemma, for he was sorely tempted by the prospect of regaining public office, but did not wish to alienate his protester friends or appear hypocritical after having denounced the English usurpers since 1651. In October he received news that Cromwell had agreed to pay him an annual pension of £300 sterling per year without demanding that he take up public office. He was delighted and now described the protector as 'the man whom Thou hes providentially maid Thy depute on earth' (Johnston, *Diary*, 3.54).

At the end of 1656 Wariston was chosen to go to London as a representative of the protesters. He arrived on 5 January 1657, and as he had feared, became increasingly comfortable in his relations with the English. His changing attitudes led to angry arguments with Guthrie, who was also in London and now described Wariston as 'our Independent'. When the two men debated before Cromwell with the resolutioner James Sharp, Guthrie took a staunchly presbyterian line, but Wariston's speech impressed Cromwell, who spoke of giving him a place in the admiralty. Wariston still longed to recover his position as clerk register, and in March he resorted to casting lots, which confirmed that he should seek the post. After a number of interviews with Cromwell he finally accepted the post on 9 July. In October he returned to Scotland, and

quickly secured the return to Scotland of Scottish records relating to private matters. On 3 November he was made one of the commissioners for the administration of justice in Scotland, and in January 1658 was appointed to the new upper chamber or 'other house'. He spoke frequently in debates there before returning to Scotland. His decision to raise the price of decreets, acts, bills, and other writs was very unpopular, and he was accused of being an extortioner who enriched himself at the expense of the people. When the news of Cromwell's death reached Edinburgh he incurred the further wrath of Guthrie by attending the proclamation of Richard Cromwell as the new lord protector.

In January 1659 Wariston returned to London to take up his seat in Richard's parliament. In May the Rump Parliament was restored, and Wariston was the only Scot appointed to the new council of state. In June he was made president of the council, though it was rumoured that this was to prevent him making long speeches and presenting inappropriate motions. His power was less impressive than his title. In October the army dissolved the Rump, and Wariston was now made president of the new army-sponsored committee of safety. Soon, however, he found himself at loggerheads with Sir Henry Vane and other radicals over their proposals for toleration and the abolition of tithes. By December opposition to the republic was growing; realizing that he was on a sinking ship, Wariston started to regret his apostasy in associating with the English sectaries. His return to political office had been a failure, and was later satirized in Aphra Behn's play *The Roundheads* (1681), which lampooned him for his Scottish dialect and his unprincipled willingness to follow whichever party would offer him a small pension.

Final years and execution, 1660–1663 On 9 April 1660 Wariston arrived back in Edinburgh, where he was now 'disgusted and haitted of all men' for his compliance with the English and 'his great oppressioun in Scotland' (Nicoll, 279). To add to his woes, his eldest son, Archibald, was suffering from a serious mental illness. In April, Archibald had been found covering himself with 'wryting over al the letters of his covenant with God … with his awen blood, and covering himself with ashes and with his awen dung, and marking with his blood many passages of his Byble' (NL Scot., MS 6258, fol. 92). Despite Wariston's attempts at exorcism, his son got no relief. On 1 May, Wariston wrote ominously of 'Montrosiasme running throw the body of the nation'. The next day he described himself as 'a broken man' in 'a broken family' (NL Scot., MS 6258, fols. 130, 133). In July the government of the restored Charles II tried to arrest him, and he was forced to flee for his life to the continent. On 13 May 1661 a decree of forfeiture and death was issued against him, and he was accused of high treason in accepting office from Cromwell and sitting in the upper house after having been king's advocate. He initially fled to Hamburg, but then took cover in France, where he complained, 'I am flitting from place to place for saifty and sees litle settlement' (Johnston, *Diary*, 3.185). However, in May 1661 he did enjoy the welcome of the reformed church in Bulbek. Eventually, in January 1663, he was arrested at Rouen. According to Kirkton, the king's council debated whether to 'retain him or give him up', but Louis XIV decided to hand him over to the British authorities (Kirkton, 169–70). In February he was imprisoned in the Tower of London. Middleton, who examined him, claimed that he was so desperate that he offered to put the register to order and settle the king's prerogative 'from old records' (Kirkton, 170). In June he returned to Scotland and was imprisoned in the Tolbooth in Edinburgh. On 8 July he appeared before the Scottish parliament, 'so disordered both in body and mind, that it was a reproach to a government to proceed against him. His memory was so gone that he did not know his own children' (*Burnet's History*, 1.364). He claimed that his condition was a result of deliberate poisoning by his enemies. However, his old friend Lauderdale protested against any delay in the prosecution, and on 22 July he was brought to the Mercat Cross in Edinburgh to be hanged on 'ane gallous of extraordinar heicht' (Nicoll, 394). He read out a long speech defending the covenant but repenting of his association with the English while insisting on the sincerity of his intentions. After his hanging, his head was fixed on the Netherbow, near that of James Guthrie, and his body was buried with his family in 'the kirk yaird of Edinburgh' (Nicoll, 395). His wife survived him; the date of her death is unknown.

Historical significance Wariston and Alexander Henderson were the chief draftsmen of the Scottish revolution, the covenanter equivalents of Jefferson and Madison. Between December 1637 and the Restoration, Wariston had a hand in countless documents issued by the covenanters and the protesters. His greatest achievement was the national covenant, which he co-authored at the age of twenty-seven, with Henderson. By fusing his religious fervour and legal caution in the text, Wariston ensured that the document appealed widely beyond the ranks of zealous presbyterians, binding the Scottish opposition together, at least temporarily. Peter Donald has noted that 'Wariston's prominence relied on the collaboration of others' (Donald, 136), and certainly most of the documents he drafted were written at the behest of the covenanting leadership, and were revised by other covenanters. Yet although Wariston could not dictate the direction of the movement, he was more than a mere scribe. His work as the covenanters' spin-doctor guaranteed a rapid response to royal proclamations. More importantly, he was always one step ahead of the majority, coming to radical conclusions and then persuading others to follow. He was among the earliest to advocate a national covenant, the abolition of episcopacy, triennial parliaments, alliance with the English parliament, and the purging of malignants. He epitomized the militant zeal that was instrumental in both the rise and the fall of the covenanters, and his extraordinary *Diary* provides a unique insight into the fervent protestant world-view that lay near the heart of the movement. Ultimately, his ideological thirst for purging alienated most of his contemporaries and helped to split the covenanters. Discussing the king's counsellors in 1641, he had declared: 'I think they

deserve justice rather than mercy' (Dalrymple, 2.122). This could serve as Wariston's motto—and his epitaph, for at the Restoration he himself received justice rather than mercy. 'He was a godly, learned man', wrote Robert Blair, 'but of too fiery, and hasty temper of spirit, in our shameful and sinful divisions' (*Life of Robert Blair*, 446).

Wariston's posthumous reputation as a covenanting hero and martyr was established by Kirkton and Wodrow and reached its apogee in the Victorian period. After the publication of his *Diary* in four parts between 1896 and 1940 he was largely neglected for the next half century, though several articles appeared in the 1990s. Despite his importance, and the wealth of material about him, there has been no scholarly biography.   JOHN COFFEY

Sources *Diary of Sir Archibald Johnston of Wariston*, ed. G. M. Paul and others, 3 vols., Scottish History Society, 61, 2nd ser., 18, 3rd. ser., 34 (1911–40) • 'Fragment of the diary of Sir Archibald Johnston, Lord Wariston, 1639', ed. G. M. Paul, *Wariston's diary and other papers*, Scottish History Society, 26 (1896), 1–98 • *The letters and journals of Robert Baillie*, ed. D. Laing, 3 vols. (1841–2) • P. Donald, 'Archibald Johnston of Wariston and the politics of religion', *Records of the Scottish Church History Society*, 24 (1990–92), 123–40 • D. Stevenson, *King or covenant* (1996), chap. 11 • L. Yeoman, 'Archie's invisible worlds discovered: spirituality, madness and Johnston of Wariston's family', *Records of the Scottish Church History Society*, 27 (1997) • W. Morison, *Johnston of Warriston* (1901) • G. W. T. Omond, *The lord advocates of Scotland from the close of the fifteenth century to the passing of the Reform Bill*, 2 vols. (1883) • *The historical works of Sir James Balfour*, ed. J. Haig, 4 vols. (1824–5) • J. Nicoll, *A diary of public transactions and other occurrences, chiefly in Scotland, from January 1650 to June 1667*, ed. D. Laing, Bannatyne Club, 52 (1836) • *The works of Aphra Behn*, ed. J. Todd, 7 vols. (1992–6), vol. 6 • *The life of Mr Robert Blair ... containing his autobiography*, ed. T. M'Crie, Wodrow Society, 11 (1848) • *Bishop Burnet's History of my own time*, new edn, ed. O. Airy, 2 vols. (1897–1900); H. C. Foxcroft, *A supplement to Burnet's History of my own time* (1902) • *The writings and speeches of Oliver Cromwell*, ed. W. C. Abbott and C. D. Crane, 4 vols. (1937–47) • D. Dalrymple [Lord Hailes], ed., *Memorials and letters relating to the history of Britain in the reign of Charles the First* (1766) • J. Kirkton, *The secret and true history of the Church of Scotland*, ed. C. K. Sharpe (1817) • *The diary of Mr John Lamont of Newton, 1649–1671*, ed. G. R. Kinloch, Maitland Club, 7 (1830) • R. Wodrow, *The history of the sufferings of the Church of Scotland from the Restoration to the revolution*, ed. R. Burns, 4 vols. (1828–30) • R. Wodrow, *Analecta*, 4 vols. (1842–3) • A. Maccinnes, *Charles I and the making of the covenanting movement* (1991) • C. Russell, *The fall of the British monarchies, 1637–1642* (1991) • D. Stevenson, *The Scottish revolution, 1637–44* (1973) • D. Stevenson, *Union, revolution, and rebellion in seventeenth-century Scotland* (1997) • J. R. Young, *The Scottish parliament, 1639–1661: a political and constitutional analysis* (1996) • NL Scot., MS 6258, fols. 92, 130, 133 • A. F. Mitchell and J. Struthers, eds., *Minutes of the sessions of the Westminster assembly of divines* (1874)

Archives Mellerstain House, diaries • NL Scot., diaries [transcript] • U. Edin., corresp.

Likenesses G. Jamesone, oils, Scot. NPG [*see illus.*]

Johnston, Arthur (*c*.1579–1641), poet, was born at Caskieben, Aberdeenshire, the fifth son of George Johnston of Caskieben (*d*. 1593) and Christian (*d*. 1622), the daughter of William, seventh Lord Forbes (*d*. 1622). The eldest of his five brothers, John, was sheriff of Aberdeen in 1630, and the youngest, William, was, first, professor of humanity and philosophy at Sedan, and then professor of mathematics in Marischal College, Aberdeen. On the evidence in his *Encomia urbium*, Arthur Johnston was educated at

Arthur Johnston (c.1579–1641), by George Jamesone, c.1629

school in Kintore and thereafter at the University of Aberdeen. It is not clear whether he attended King's College or Marischal College; however, since he was later elected rector of King's College, it seems likely that this had been his college of education.

From Aberdeen, Johnston went first to Casimir College in Heidelberg, where he acted as a professor at a scholastic disputation in 1601. His status in Heidelberg at this date means that his traditional birth year of 1587 cannot be correct, and that it must be placed about 1579, a date supported by the inscription on the portrait of Johnston belonging to Marischal College. Johnston moved to Sedan, northern France, in 1603 at the invitation of Henri de la Tour, the duc de Bouillon. The duc was the uncle of the elector palatine, and it was probably through his connections in that part of Germany that he heard of Johnston and his compatriot, Walter Donaldson, who was invited to Sedan at the same time. Later they were joined by Andrew Melville, in exile in Sedan from 1611 to 1622.

Johnston was first a regent of the third class at the college at Sedan, and then regent of the second class and professor of logic and metaphysics in 1604. In 1608 he presided at the delivery of a thesis, dedicated to James VI and I. As well as being a writer of Latin verse, Johnston was also a doctor, and he received his medical qualification from Padua in 1610. After his qualification as MD, he was appointed as professor of physic at Sedan in October 1610, following the promotion of Donaldson to the post of principal. About this time he began to publish Latin verse; among his first productions was a criticism on George Eglishem MD, who had attacked George Buchanan's

translations of the Psalms. At first, Johnston published anonymously, although later he acknowledged his authorship of these and other poems. Despite his talent for composition, Sir Thomas Urquhart's assessment of Johnston's early success—'[he] had been so sweetly imbued by the springs of Helicon that before he won fully three and twenty years of age he was laureated poet at Paris and that most deservedly'—however must be exaggerated (Urquhart, 164).

Johnston's last years in Sedan were marred by a court case against a *miles* of the region, called Hampté. The nature of the case is unclear, but it seems from the poems that Johnston was hard pressed, until his eventual victory (A. Johnston, *Parerga*, 1632, 13–18). Afterwards Johnston returned to Scotland, accompanied by his first wife, Marie de Cagniol or Kynuncle (d. 1624), who bore him thirteen children, of whom six seem to have survived. His second wife was Barbara Gordon, who outlived her husband, dying in 1650. Little is known for certain of any of his children. Two by his first marriage were baptized in Sedan, Daniel (b. 1606), and Françoise (b. 1608). Another daughter, Margaret, was married to George Dalgarno in 1652, while a son of his second marriage, William (b. 1636), became regent professor in King's College in 1657 and then civilian in 1669.

Johnston became a burgess of Aberdeen in 1622, and appears in various records in a locally important capacity, including acting as a witness and as surety for relatives. In a poem he implied that he was appointed *medicus regius* by James VI and I (*Parerga*, 43, 5–6), and he was certainly using the title in 1625 in the publication of his elegy for the king. After the publication of his *Parerga* and *Epigrammata*, both by Edward Raban in Aberdeen in 1632, Johnston turned his attention to a translation of the Song of Solomon, which he dedicated to Charles I, and of the seven penitential psalms, which he dedicated to Laud. These works were published in London in 1633, and Laud seems to have encouraged Johnston to translate all the psalms, although whether he was motivated by the quality of Johnston's verse or because Johnston was sympathetic to episcopalianism is unclear. The full translation of the psalms was published in 1637. In the same year Johnston demonstrated his interest in Scottish Latin poetry other than his own, for he edited a collection of Latin poetry written by his contemporary Scots, called the *Delitiae poetarum Scotorum*, which was published at Amsterdam, again in 1637.

In the same year Johnston was also elected rector of King's College, and became involved in the campaign to introduce a new constitution to the university. The other Scottish universities had been reformed under the influence of Andrew Melville several decades earlier; Aberdeen had gained exemption from King James. Nevertheless, the desire for reform in some quarters of the university remained strong, and Johnston supported it. However, after an appeal was made to King Charles on behalf of the mediciner, the canonist, and civilist, whose posts were forfeit under the new plans, the matter was settled against Johnston's party.

Johnston died in 1641 in Oxford, while visiting a daughter married to an English clergyman. By then he had written and published a substantial amount of Latin verse, mostly in elegiac couplets, but covering a wide range of topics, from his early attack on Eglishem, to the *Encomia* on Scottish burghs. His fame as a poet continued in the next centuries, when his work was republished by Thomas Ruddiman. He was also judged by Samuel Johnson as holding 'among the Latin poets of Scotland the next place to the elegant Buchanan' (Johnson, 11). He was a good and fluent poet, but his importance is enhanced by his publication of the work of other Scottish poets as well as his own.   NICOLA ROYAN

Sources W. G. Geddes, 'Memoir of Arthur Johnston', *Musa Latina Aberdonensis*, ed. W. G. Geddes, 2, New Spalding Club, 15 (1895) · W. Benson, 'Life of Arthur Johnston', *Arturi Jonstoni Psalmi Davidici* (1742) [trans. in *Musa Latina Aberdonensis*, 1, ed. W. G. Geddes, New Spalding Club, 9, (1892)] · W. Johnston, *The bibliography and extant portraits of Arthur Johnston M.D., physician to James VI and Charles I* (1895) · A. M. Munro, ed., 'Register of burgesses of guild and trade of the burgh of Aberdeen, 1399–1631', *The miscellany of the New Spalding Club*, 1, New Spalding Club, 6 (1890), 1–162 · P. J. Anderson, ed., *Officers and graduates of University and King's College, Aberdeen, MVD–MDCCCLX*, New Spalding Club, 11 (1893) · R. S. Rait, *The universities of Aberdeen: a history* (1895) · *Reg. PCS*, 1st ser., vols. 12–13 · *Miscellaneous privy council papers* · S. Johnson, *A journey to the western islands of Scotland*, ed. J. D. Fleeman (1985) · T. Urquhart, *The jewel*, ed. R. D. S. Jack and R. J. Lyall (1983)
Likenesses G. Jamesone, oils, 1621, U. Aberdeen · G. Jamesone, oils, c.1629, U. Aberdeen [*see illus.*] · J. M. Rysbrack, terracotta bust, 1739, Scot. NPG · Vandergucht, engraving, 1740 (after bust by J. M. Rysbrack), repro. in *Arturi Jonstoni Psalmi Davidici* [folio] · Vertue, engraving, 1740 (after bust by J. M. Rysbrack), repro. in *Arturi Jonstoni Psalmi Davidici* (1741) [quarto] · R. Cooper, line engraving, 1741 (after G. Jamesone), BM, NPG; repro. in *Arturi Jonstoni Psalmi Davidici* (1741) · eleventh earl of Buchan, pencil and chalk drawing, 1794 (after G. Jamesone), Scot. NPG · J. Melvin, glass window (after G. Jamesone, c.1629), U. Aberdeen · J. Wales, oils (after G. Jamesone), Scot. NPG · J. Wales (after G. Jamesone, 1621), Scot. NPG · engraving, repro. in A. Johnston, *Poemata Omnia* (Middelburg, 1642), frontispiece · engraving, repro. in W. Lauder, ed., *Poetarum Scotorum musae sacre* (1739), frontispiece · photogravure photograph (after G. Jamesone, c.1629), repro. in W. D. Geddes, ed., *Musa Latina Aberdonensis*, 1 (1892), frontispiece · photogravure photograph (after G. Jamesone, 1621), repro. in Geddes, ed., *Musa Latina Aberdonensis* (1895), frontispiece

Johnston, Betty Joan, Lady Johnston (1916–1994). *See under* Johnston, Sir Alexander (1905–1994).

Johnston, Brian Alexander [*nicknamed* Johnners] (1912–1994), broadcaster, was born on 24 June 1912 at the Old Rectory, Little Berkhamsted, Hertfordshire, the third son and youngest of four children of Lieutenant-Colonel Charles Evelyn Johnston (*d.* 1922/3), City merchant and army officer, and his wife, Pleasance, younger daughter of Colonel William John Alt, army officer. His grandfather Reginald Eden Johnston (1847–1922) was governor of the Bank of England from 1908 to 1913. The family business, however, was in Brazilian coffee, Johnston's great-grandfather Edward Johnston having founded it in Santos in 1842. Johnston's childhood was spent in a Hertfordshire property, Little Offley, bought by his father before the

Brian Alexander Johnston (1912–1994), by Sten Rosenlund, 1991

First World War. At eight he was sent to join his brothers, Michael and Christopher, at Temple Grove preparatory school, Eastbourne. Two years later, in view of his family, his father was drowned off a Cornish beach attempting to rescue another bather in difficulties. Apart from the shock of her loss, his mother was left in straitened circumstances. Hence Johnston was put to attempting an Eton College scholarship. He failed but nevertheless went to Eton, entering the house of a revered sporting figure, R. H. de Montmorency. He was gregarious and well liked at school, where he enjoyed 'some of the happiest times of my life' (Johnston, *It's been a Lot of Fun*, 20). His lifelong friendship with the dramatist William Douglas-Home began at Eton. He was elected to Pop, and made the rugby football fifteen, but to his everlasting regret failed to get into the Eton eleven because his rival wicket-keeper stayed on beyond his nineteenth birthday. He captained the second eleven, and the New College team after going up to Oxford in 1931. He might in some years have gained his blue. As it was, he became much in demand in club cricket for the Eton Ramblers, Oxford Authentics, and I Zingari. It was a great delight in his last years to assist Sir Paul Getty in entertaining these and other clubs who played against the latter's sides on his beautiful ground at Wormsley. He graduated from Oxford with a third-class degree in history in 1934, and then joined the family firm, the Brazilian Warrant Co. Ltd, working in London and Santos, and became assistant manager of the London office by the outbreak of the Second World War.

In 1939 Johnston joined the 2nd battalion of the Grenadier Guards, with an emergency commission. He had a testing war, as the officer responsible for mechanical maintenance of the grenadier tanks when in 1941 the 2nd battalion became part of the guards armoured division. In the winter of 1944 and early spring of 1945 they were in the thick of the allied advance, crossing the Rhine and fighting their way up to Bremen and Hamburg. According to General Sir David Fraser, writing in the *Guards Magazine*:

> Brian probably did more than any other human being to maintain morale in any circumstances, to encourage, cheer and induce laughter in soldiers, however dark the day. He was widely and deservedly loved, and among his own men in the technical department he was a being entirely unique. It was impossible to mention his name to anybody, in any context, without an answering grin.

It was this contribution, maintained unfailingly under fire, rather than any special act of gallantry, which won him the Military Cross. He ended the war as a major. His last army exertion, following VE-day, was to keep the units of the division happy awaiting their return home, by producing and compèring a broad, uproarious travelling revue.

In 1945 Johnston met in the officers' mess two broadcasters, Wynford Vaughan-Thomas and Stewart MacPherson, who were covering the allied advance. Impressed by his reputation as a licensed jester among troops of all ranks, they encouraged him to apply to join the BBC. Having no inclination to return to the coffee trade, Johnston needed little persuasion, and on 13 January 1946 he was recruited by Seymour de Lotbinière into the outside broadcast department of the BBC. His love of the theatre and especially the music-hall found a ready outlet when from 1946 onwards his job came to include, in addition to taking part in *In Town Tonight* and other regular programmes, selecting plays and comedy material for broadcasts. Backstage he made friends with the comedians he so greatly admired, such as Arthur Askey, Max Bygraves, and, perhaps above all, Bud Flanagan and Chesney Allen. On 22 April 1948 he married a fellow member of the BBC staff, Pauline, daughter of Colonel William Tozer of Sheffield and his wife, Eileen, *née* Sykes. They had three sons and two daughters, the second of whom was born with Down's syndrome.

Within a few months of joining the BBC, Johnston was recruited by a pre-war cricket friend, Ian Orr-Ewing, who as head of outside broadcasts in the fledgeling BBC television service was looking for commentators to cover the tests against India. For the next twenty years Johnston and E. W. (Jim) Swanton, joined later by Peter West, developed the techniques of commentary and summaries suitable for television. That Johnston was in his element was quickly apparent. In 1963 he became the first BBC cricket correspondent. When in 1970 he was transferred to the permanent *Test Match Special* programme, broadcasting every ball of the day's play, his transparent love of the game and cheerful benevolence towards everyone connected with it, and indeed the world in general, earned a unique popularity to which there seemed scarcely a limit. After retiring from the BBC in 1972 at the statutory age of sixty, he returned as a freelance, continuing his cricket commentary for *Test Match Special*, and chairing Radio 4's *Trivia Test Match*.

Johnston's skills as a commentator were employed to good effect when he was made part of the BBC teams covering the funeral of George VI, the coronation of Elizabeth II, and the royal weddings of Princess Margaret, Princess Anne, and the prince of Wales. He also chaired the radio quizzes *What's It All About*, *Sporting Chance*, and *Treble Chance*, and appeared in numerous other radio and television programmes. In 1972 he took over the radio programme *Down Your Way* following the sudden death of Franklin Engelmann, and starred in it for fifteen years. In 1993, his last summer, he undertook a demanding series of one-man autobiographical appearances at provincial theatres (thirty-two in all, over nine months). Though they put an inevitable strain on his physique, he greatly enjoyed these appearances, entitled *An Evening with Johnners*, which invariably played to full houses. That he was a compulsive communicator is apparent from the seventeen reminiscent, light-hearted books he wrote between 1952 and 1992, the chief being the revealing autobiography *It's Been a Lot of Fun* (1974). He was appointed OBE in 1983 and CBE in 1991.

Johnston's death in London on 5 January 1994, a few weeks after a severe heart attack, was the signal for widespread expressions of affection and tribute. These culminated in a service of thanksgiving in Westminster Abbey on 16 May 1994 which was oversubscribed and at which addresses were given by the prime minister, John Major, and Sir Colin Cowdrey. The mood of the occasion was the public response to his irrepressible good nature and sense of fun, his corny jokes and appalling puns, which had an appeal transcending gender, age, and class. In his speech and dress—the invariable brown and white shoes at test matches, for instance—he had much in common with P. G. Wodehouse's Bertie Wooster. A BBC colleague composed this epitaph:

> The Cherubim and Seraphim are starting to despair of him,
> They've never known a shade so entertaining.
> He chats to total strangers, calls the Angel Gabriel 'Aingers',
> And talks for even longer if it's raining.
>
> When St. Peter's done the honours he will pass you on to Johnners,
> Who will cry 'Good morning, welcome to the wake.
> You're batting Number Seven for the Heaven fourth eleven,
> And while you're waiting, have some angel cake'.

Johnston was survived by his wife and five children.

E. W. SWANTON

Sources B. Johnston, *It's been a lot of fun* (1974) · B. Johnston, *It's been a piece of cake* (1989) · B. Johnston, *45 summers* (1991) · B. Johnston, *Someone who was* (1992) · *The Times* (6 Jan 1994) · *The Times* (17 May 1994) · *The Independent* (6 Jan 1994) · *WWW, 1991–5* · personal knowledge (2004) · private information (2004) · b. cert.
Archives SOUND BL NSA, performance recordings

Likenesses S. Rosenlund, photograph, 1991, Rex Features Ltd, London [*see illus.*] · photograph, repro. in *The Times* (6 Jan 1994) · photograph, repro. in *The Independent*
Wealth at death £258,976: probate, 23 Feb 1994, *CGPLA Eng. & Wales*

Johnston, Sir Charles Hepburn (1912–1986), diplomatist and writer, was born on 11 March 1912 in Hampstead, London, the eldest in the family of four sons and two daughters of Ernest Johnston, an underwriter at Lloyd's, and his wife, Emma Florence Hepburn. (The family later moved to a larger house in Reigate, Surrey.) Studious and competitive, he won scholarships to Winchester College and then to Balliol College, Oxford, where at first he was lonely and unhappy. He took first classes in both classical honour moderations (1932) and *literae humaniores* (1934) and taught for a term at his old school before choosing the diplomatic service, which he entered at the second attempt (1936).

For twenty years Johnston's career followed a conventional course, except that in Tokyo he and the rest of the embassy staff were interned for several months when Japan entered the war. Later, as first secretary in Cairo, he tried but was not allowed to transfer to the armed forces; he felt this keenly, especially after his brother Duncan was killed in action. He became first secretary in Madrid (1948), and counsellor at the Foreign Office (1951) and the embassy in Bonn (1955).

In 1956, aged only forty-four, Johnston was picked to be ambassador to Jordan. His first task was to wind up the outdated Anglo-Jordan treaty, which he accomplished with skill and tact (1957). A year later, when King Hussein's position was threatened, it was his advocacy, backed by the prime minister, Harold Macmillan, which overcame the doubts felt elsewhere in London and led to the brief but successful deployment of British troops to Jordan. He was appointed KCMG in 1959. These events are described in his book *The Brink of Jordan* (1972), for which Macmillan wrote a preface awarding him 'a secure place in the list of great envoys who have represented Britain overseas'.

Johnston's next appointment, unusual for a non-member of the colonial service, was as (the last) governor of Aden. He worked to merge the colony of Aden with the Federation of South Arabia, promoting constitutional advance but keeping the British military base. So long as he was there (1960–63) this line was maintained, with some difficulty but on the whole with success, as he related in *The View from Steamer Point* (1964).

After Aden, Johnston might have risen higher but for Labour's victory in the general election of 1964. As it was, the top posts to which he aspired went to others, and those offered to him did not match his own estimate of his abilities. Finally, in 1965 he agreed to go as high commissioner to Australia, where he was more effective and more popular than many had expected. He continued to reject offers of other posts and retired with a GCMG in 1971, a year earlier than normal, with the idea of entering politics.

Johnston's last years brought some disappointments. He was judged too old to stand for the House of Commons. A peerage was mentioned but not offered. A company chairmanship lapsed when the plan to build an airport in the Thames estuary was dropped. Despite his hopes he became neither chairman of the BBC nor poet laureate. A book of reminiscences built round the character of his long-serving Egyptian butler, *Mo and other Originals* (1971), had a brief success, but his other prose and poetry found little market outside magazines.

Two things consoled Johnston: his social work at Toynbee Hall, for which he showed an unexpected talent; and the world opened to him by his marriage. In Cairo he had met Princess Natasha Bagration, daughter of Prince Konstantin Bagration-Mukhransky and of Princess Tatyana Konstantinovna, descended respectively from the royal house of Georgia and from Tsar Nicholas I of Russia. They were married in London in 1944. Though childless, it was a strange but successful union until her death in 1984 after several years of intermittent illness. Arrestingly tall, possessed of magnetic charm, and connected with royal families all over Europe, she vastly enlarged his mental and especially social horizons. From their flat in Knightsbridge they continued, almost to the last, to sustain their parts in the social round which he called 'the Belgraveyard'.

In collaboration with his wife Johnston had produced in 1948 what is perhaps still the best English translation of Turgenev's *Sportsman's Notebook*. But his masterpiece is his rendering of *Eugene Onegin* into English verse preserving Pushkin's metre and rhyme scheme (1977). This received unqualified critical acclaim. His success as a translator did not help, and perhaps even hindered, the fortunes of his other work, though he continued to write, print, publish, and circulate it to his friends, convinced that posterity would be kinder. *Poems and Journeys* (1979) contains much of his best work.

Johnston developed a boisterous manner for social purposes, but remained shy and reserved at heart. The strong emotions reflected in his poetry, together with his deep vein of self-doubt, were well concealed. Physically tall, energetic but somewhat awkward, he was a good sailor and a keen shot. He managed his savings astutely and generously, and was a good judge of a painting. He died in his sleep on 23 April 1986 at his home in London, 32 Kingston House, South Ennismore Gardens.

JULIAN BULLARD, *rev.*

Sources WW · FO List · private information (1996) · personal knowledge (1996) · *CGPLA Eng. & Wales* (1986)
Archives King's Lond., Liddell Hart C., corresp. and papers; corresp. with his parents; corresp. about his poetry
Wealth at death £677,851: probate, 16 July 1986, *CGPLA Eng. & Wales*

Johnston, Sir Christopher Nicholson, Lord Sands (1857–1934), judge, was born on 18 October 1857 in the mansion house at Sands, Kincardine, Perthshire, the second son of James Johnston, of Sands, and his wife, Margaret, youngest daughter of Christopher Nicholson, minister of the parish of Whithorn, Wigtownshire. After education at Madras College, St Andrews, and the universities of St Andrews, Edinburgh (the only university from which he graduated), and Heidelberg, Johnston was admitted in

1880 to the Faculty of Advocates. His progress at the Scottish bar was steady and conventional. He held appointments as junior counsel to various government departments. He then entered crown office in 1892 as an advocate-depute, a post which he was obliged to vacate (following the practice then) on the change of government after the general election. He returned, however, in 1895, when the Conservatives regained power, and he remained there until 1899, when he was appointed sheriff of Caithness, Orkney, and Zetland. In 1900 he was transferred to the sheriffdom of Inverness, Elgin, and Nairn, and in 1905 to that of Perth. In 1902 he took silk.

Johnston was always a keen politician. In 1892 he unsuccessfully contested Paisley as a Conservative but, at a by-election held in December 1916, having resigned his sheriffdom he was returned to parliament as member for the universities of Edinburgh and St Andrews. In 1917 he was knighted and he succeeded Lord Dewar as a senator of the college of justice in Scotland, taking the judicial title of Lord Sands.

Sands had not had a large practice as a silk; this allowed time for his work as a sheriff and churchman, which brought him considerable contact with ordinary Scottish people. The value of this training was seen in his work as a judge. He had a wide knowledge of law and much common sense. He grasped quickly the essential points in a case and had a mastery over facts. It was stimulating to appear before him because he had a fondness for testing discussion by helpful hypothetical cases. His written judgments are admirable in form and sound in substance, full of quaint illustrations and touches of humour. Underlying them all were his characteristic understanding of the Scot and human sympathy.

Outside the courts Sands found his chief interest in the work of the Church of Scotland. In 1907 he was elected procurator of the church, and he remained its official legal adviser until 1918. He served on its principal committees, and he was a licensed lay preacher for many years. But his reputation as a churchman rests chiefly on his part in the long negotiations which in 1929 brought about the union of the Church of Scotland and the United Free Church of Scotland. In 1903 he had edited and largely rewritten J. M. Duncan's *Parochial Ecclesiastical Law of Scotland*, and he was a recognized authority on that subject. He was also a theologian of considerable attainments. His views were listened to with respect, and a memorandum which he drew up became the basis on which union was effected. For his services the University of Edinburgh conferred upon him in 1928 the honorary degree of DD, an unusual distinction for a layman. He received the honorary degree of LLD from the universities of St Andrews, in 1909, and Glasgow, in 1930.

Sands was also interested in social and educational work, especially in that which concerned youth. Among other activities he was from 1921 chairman of the Carnegie Trust for the Universities of Scotland. From 1919 he was president of the Edinburgh battalion of the Boys' Brigade.

Sands wrote much on all kinds of topics—legal, theological, biographical, and general. His style was easy and pleasant. Apart from contributions to periodical literature and to manuals on the various acts dealing with smallholdings, he was the author of a considerable number of books, such as *Major Owen and other Tales* and *St Paul and his Mission to the Roman Empire* (1909), and *Off the Chain* (1924).

Sands married in 1898 Agnes Warren, second daughter of James Ebenezer Dunn, of Dunmullin, Strathblane, Stirlingshire. They had two sons and two daughters. He died at his home, 4 Heriot Row, Edinburgh, on 26 February 1934, and was survived by his wife.

M. G. FISHER, rev. ROBERT SHIELS

Sources *Scots Law Times: News* (3 March 1934) · *CCI* (1934)
Likenesses H. Lintott, portrait, 1930; known to be at the Church of Scotland Assembly Hall, Edinburgh, in 1934 · H. Lintott, oils, Faculty of Advocates, Parliament Hall, Edinburgh
Wealth at death £50,659 7s. 7d.: confirmation, 18 April 1934, *CCI*

Johnston, David (1734–1824), Church of Scotland minister and benefactor, was born on 26 April 1734 at the manse, Arngask, Fife, the second son of John Johnston (*d*. 1746), minister of that parish, and his second wife, Margaret Brown (*d*. 1768), daughter of the Revd John Brown of Abercorn. Details of Johnston's education are unknown but the University of Edinburgh awarded him a doctorate of divinity on 6 March 1765. He was licensed by the Selkirk presbytery on 12 July 1757 and ordained (11 May 1758) to Langton parish, Berwickshire. Once established he married Elizabeth Todd, daughter of John Todd, a Leith shipbuilder, on 5 July 1759. They had two children: John, who died in 1786, and Elizabeth, who married Glasgow merchant William Penney on 15 September 1800. Johnston was translated on 12 June 1765 to the parish of North Leith. Nicknamed the Bonnie Doctor by Newhaven fishwives of his parish, and noted for his devotion to his parishioners' interests, he showed evangelical leanings as an associate and was a forerunner to figures such as the philanthropist and minister Thomas Chalmers (1780–1847).

Like many late-century Scottish evangelicals Johnston was keen to promote a spirit of self-help at the parish level. With the kirk session serving as trustees he invested the church property in feus for commercial development. North Leith became one of the wealthiest parishes in Scotland and the congregation moved to a new church in Madeira Street.

Johnston is principally remembered for his role in the foundation of Edinburgh's asylum for blind people, later renamed the Royal Blind Asylum and School. The idea of the blind poet Thomas Blacklock, it operated like a similar institution in Liverpool, as an asylum or community for work, education, and religious development. Focused on the very young and middle-aged it aimed to remove the able-bodied blind as a burden to society and themselves by encouraging them to save part of their wages for a retirement fund. Johnston, who acted as the asylum's secretary from its opening in 1793, was an active fund-raiser with money coming from sales of his published sermons. Although officially retired by the 1790s Johnston, from 1793 chaplain in ordinary to George III, was given the accolade 'father of the Church of Scotland' as the then oldest living minister. In 1812 he declined a knighthood as it would have required him to wait in London for two weeks. Actively engaged in running the blind asylum until near the very end of his life, Johnston died at Leith on 5 July 1824 aged ninety. He was buried at North Leith parish churchyard at a ceremony attended by all the members of the blind asylum. CAMPBELL F. LLOYD

Sources DNB · NA Scot., SC 70/1/48, fols. 847–60 · 'Royal Blind Asylum, Edinburgh', U. Glas. L., special collections department, David Murray collection, MU25-a.12 [pamphlet] · J. Marshall, *North Leith parish church, the first 500 years* (1993) · *Fasti Scot.* · M. E. Forster, *A model pastor of the old school* (1878)

Likenesses J. Kay, etching, 1814, repro. in J. Kay, *A series of original portraits and caricature etchings … with biographical sketches and illustrative anecdotes*, ed. H. Paton and others, new edn, 2nd edn, 1 (1842), facing p. 370 [2nd edn] · G. Dawe, mezzotint, pubd 1825 (after H. Raeburn), BM · G. Dawe, mezzotint, 1825 (after H. Raeburn), Royal Blind Asylum and School, Edinburgh · A. Handyside Ritchie, marble bust, Session house, North Leith, Edinburgh · H. Raeburn, oils, priv. coll.

Wealth at death £1676 9s. 9d.: inventory, 1833, NA Scot., SC 70/1/48, fols. 847–60

Johnston, Edward (1804–1876), merchant, was born in London in 1804, one of the nine children (seven sons and two daughters) of Francis Johnston (1757–1828) and his wife, Elizabeth Ellis (1771–1856). Johnston's father, who worked in the Royal Navy pay office, was of Scottish border extraction, while his mother came from a Bedfordshire family. At the age of seventeen Edward Johnston left London for Brazil, arriving just as Brazil gained independence from Portugal, and at a time when British commercial firms were beginning to take an interest in the country. He joined the Jersey-based merchant house of F. Le Breton & Co. in Rio de Janeiro, where he rose quickly to become one of the managers. In 1827, as if to indicate that he was now established in business, Edward Johnston married Henrietta (Harriet) Marie (1808–1885), the daughter of Dr Charles Alexander Moke, the owner of a showpiece coffee plantation at Tijuca, near Rio. There were fourteen children from the marriage, eight sons and six daughters, of whom two children died in infancy.

Although he was offered a one-third partnership in Le Breton's, Johnston's ambition and family responsibilities persuaded him to become his own master. He left Le Breton's in 1831 to set up his own commission house, handling anything from hides to small arms for principals in both Brazil and Europe. In 1842 with two partners, William Havers and João Tavares, he formed E. Johnston & Co. in Rio de Janeiro to trade on his own account. Two years later Johnston returned to England, and in Liverpool went into partnership with Charles Ironside & Co. At the same time he formed a second, short-lived partnership in Brazil at Bahia, which traded under the name of Johnston, Napier & Co.

Subsequent developments left the Johnston family in sole control of these related businesses. Only Edward Johnston remained of the original Rio partnership in 1848, by which time Tavares had left the firm and Havers had died. Johnston became the senior partner in Liverpool after Ironside retired from business in 1853 and Napier (Johnston's partner in Brazil) returned to England in 1857. Thereafter, Edward Johnston either employed salaried managers or went into partnership with members of his family, including his brother Henry, his brother-in-law, George Moke, and subsequently four of his sons. During the 1850s Johnston opened houses in the United States, namely, at New York and at New Orleans, where his eldest son, Charles Edward, who was born in Brazil, took over after a period in the Rio office.

The main business remained at Rio, where the house handled increasing quantities of coffee for the North American and European markets. Broadly favourable factors, especially on the demand side, undoubtedly boosted Johnston's business, but it required a combination of both luck and hard work to overcome the competitive conditions prevailing among the merchant houses of various nationalities which traded in coffee. During the 1847 financial crisis, for example, the Liverpool partnership was fortunate to survive. However, by the early 1870s E. Johnston & Co. was recognized as the leading exporter of Brazilian coffee, with a market share of 10 per cent of shipments from Rio de Janeiro. Nevertheless, Johnston, especially in the early days, was generally prepared to handle any commodity which could show a profit. Like hundreds of similar firms, the house shipped a wide range of British manufactured goods, especially textiles, to Brazil, and it also became involved in a variety of complementary service activities—insurance, shipowning, agency work, banking, and finance.

In 1862 Johnston, now an important figure in the Brazilian trades, left Liverpool for London, where he went into partnership with his third son, Francis John, under the style of Edward Johnston, Son & Co. In the same year he was invited to become a director of the London and Brazilian Bank, inaugurating his family's links within City banking circles, which subsequent generations of Johnstons carried on. His reputation was such that he was able to arrange a credit of £200,000 in Brazil for the newly formed bank to begin business. Three years later he became the bank's deputy chairman. Furthermore, Johnston was building an impressive share portfolio of railway and insurance stock on a scale which yielded more directorships. Although he established this substantial City presence, Edward Johnston seems to have left little mark on Liverpool. He rented the country estate of Allerton Hall for a time but there is no evidence of the notable philanthropic work typical of many Liverpool merchants of the period. Nevertheless, he seems to have been a fair employer, sympathetic to those less fortunate than himself and not motivated purely by profit. Edward Johnston died on 9 November 1876 at 21 Adelaide Crescent, in Brighton, where he was buried. He was survived by his wife. ROBERT G. GREENHILL

Sources *A Johnston family record* (1938) · G. C. W. Joel, *One hundred years of coffee* [1942] · P. J. Johnston, A Johnston Family History, unpublished MS, 1957 · E. Bacha and R. Greenhill, *150 años de cafe* (1992) · d. cert. · *CGPLA Eng. & Wales* (1877)

Archives priv. colls.

Likenesses Ouless?, portrait, priv. coll.

Wealth at death under £70,000 0s. 0d.: probate, 1 March 1877, *CGPLA Eng. & Wales*

Johnston, Edward (1872–1944), calligrapher and designer of lettering, was born on 11 February 1872 in San José province, Uruguay, the second of the four children of Fowell Buxton Johnston (*b. c.*1839) and his wife, Alice Douglas (*d.* 1891). There were Quakers and philanthropists among Fowell Johnston's forebears, but he was something of a ne'er-do-well. Returning to Britain in 1875, the Johnstons moved restlessly from house to house, the father often absent and rarely in work, the mother an invalid. The children were looked after by an aunt with a neurotic fear of draughts, and they grew up in an atmosphere of real and imagined sickness, with no formal education and little contact with the outside world. Edward's greatest pleasures were in gadgets, electricity, and mathematics, and in writing pages of illuminated lettering, which he called 'parchments'.

In 1891 Johnston's mother died. An uncle took charge of the children and Edward, who was still a child at nineteen, worked for him for some years. In 1896 he began to study medicine at Edinburgh University, but his family soon decided that he was not strong enough for such a career.

The direction of Johnston's life and work were settled in the next three years. In September 1897 he saw some illuminated manuscripts by the architect W. H. Cowlishaw in a magazine. In October he bought a copy of Edward F. Strange, *Alphabets: a Handbook of Lettering* (1895), which included lettering by Walter Crane, Selwyn Image, and C. F. A. Voysey, designers of the Arts and Crafts movement. Johnston worked steadily through it, imitating the alphabets. In April 1898 friends in London introduced him to Cowlishaw who told him about William Morris's illuminated manuscripts of the early 1870s, and introduced him in turn to W. R. Lethaby, principal of the Central School of Arts and Crafts, and a luminary of the Arts and Crafts movement. Lethaby admired Johnston's 'parchments', told him to study manuscripts in the British Museum, and, despite his inexperience, proposed to put him in charge of a new lettering class at the Central School. In the autumn Johnston moved to London and began studying in the British Museum, advised by Sydney Cockerell. He was drawn to late antique and early medieval scripts of the sixth to the tenth centuries, and by this time had perhaps reached the conclusion that the character of these scripts derived from the use of a broad-edged nib. This settled the nature of his work. He was not particularly interested in printing types, display lettering, or ordinary handwriting, though he would have to do with all of these during his career. He was interested in formal writing with a broad-edged nib.

In September 1900 Johnston met a lively, sociable Scottish schoolmistress called Greta Grieg (*d.* 1936). After his loveless childhood, he was ready for the security she offered, though he had perhaps already learned too well

Edward Johnston (1872–1944), by Arthur Henry Knighton-Hammond, exh. Royal Society of Portrait Painters 1937

to be alone. They were married on 20 August 1903. Priscilla Johnston's moving biography of her father is also a tribute to her parents' love for each other, shyly acknowledged on Johnston's part. They lived at first in a flat in Gray's Inn; from 1905 in Hammersmith Terrace, by the Thames; and from 1912 in Ditchling in Sussex, always surrounded by friends and colleagues of the Arts and Crafts movement, notably Eric Gill, who was for many years Johnston's closest friend. Between 1904 and 1911 they had three daughters.

With marriage Johnston became what he would always be, the man who gets up late, drained of energy, appears downstairs and potters distractedly, putting off some necessary work, and then disappears again to his workroom where he sits at a sloping desk, writing medieval letters in a medieval way, surrounded by clutter, unanswered letters, and cups of cold tea, pondering the movements of his hand and the meaning of the words in a slow, speculative, analytical way that has more to do with the Enlightenment than the middle ages. He wrote out public addresses, rolls of honour, devotional and literary texts as required, working always within a circle of domesticity. This was the centre of his life. It was also, with his teaching and a small private income, how he paid the bills.

Johnston always practised a number of different hands, but in the early years he mainly wrote rounded, upright letters based on half-uncials of the sixth and seventh centuries, believing that they came most naturally to the broad-edged nib. Then, around 1906, his preference shifted to a more flowing, sloped hand based on tenth-century models. He called this the 'foundational hand' and in teaching recommended it as better adapted to modern needs than half-uncials. This is the hand for which he is best-known, both in his own work and in the tradition he created among his pupils. But then, in 1923–4, he introduced another hand, still curved but compressed, with the density of Gothic scripts. The sweep and sharpness of this late, virtuoso hand is dazzling. Johnston did not set it before students as a model because, as he said, it broke the rules.

Johnston's teaching began in September 1899 with a small vocational class in lettering at the Central School of Arts and Crafts, as Lethaby had proposed. Over the next thirteen years Johnston made it a nursery for some of the most distinguished British designers, calligraphers, and letter-cutters of the early twentieth century. From 1901 until the late 1930s he also taught on Monday afternoons at the Royal College of Art, where his classes were larger but less focused, being part of the general curriculum. Standing at the blackboard in a well-cut but increasingly battered tweed suit, forming great sweeping letters with the chalk, he was inspirational. Stooping over a student's shoulder to inspect her work, he was dauntingly objective but still inspirational. His teaching, and the handbook *Writing & Illuminating, & Lettering* which he wrote with painful deliberation between 1902 and 1906, were grounded, like his calligraphy, on the example of early medieval scripts and the use of a broad-edged nib. And they were enriched by a commentary at once practical and speculative. Students watched the movements of his hand, absorbing perhaps the movements of his mind. In the 1920s he began work on a second book, but the richness of his thought was now too great for the quasi-scientific exactness of his writing to encompass. It remained unfinished at his death.

Johnston stood aloof from the industrial world, distrusting its purposes and holding that nothing could be satisfactorily designed by one man and made by another. But occasionally he made what Priscilla Johnston called 'anxious excursions' into the world of design and mechanical reproduction (P. Johnston, 199). He designed headings and initial letters for T. J. Cobden-Sanderson's Doves Press, and an italic and a Gothic typeface for Count Harry Kessler's Cranach Presse in Germany. These tasks did not take him far from his orthodoxy. In 1913, however, he was asked by Frank Pick, commercial manager of the Underground Electric Railways of London, to design an alphabet for use in the Underground. Pick wanted a block letter of the sort used by humble jobbing printers in the nineteenth century: bold, of uniform thickness, and without serifs. This was a long way from early medieval exemplars and the broad-edged nib. In 1916 Johnston produced a simple, rational design which has become an exemplar for twentieth-century lettering and typography, and is still in use. He continued to work for Pick until the late 1930s, contributing to the visual identity of what became London Transport. The success of this excursion reveals more clearly than his calligraphy the rational quality of Johnston's lettering. Interestingly, the calligrapher Graily Hewitt, the star among his early pupils, thought his work for the Underground a betrayal.

For someone who lived so much in a world of his own, Johnston was remarkably influential. His teaching and example created a whole school of calligraphy in Britain, whose leading lights were Hewitt and Irene Wellington. Beyond calligraphy, his profound investigation of letter forms influenced the work of Harold Curwen and Stanley Morison in printing and typography, Alfred Fairbank in italic handwriting, and Eric Gill in type design, display lettering, and monumental letter-cutting, to mention only the best-known names. Beyond that again, his influence extended to America and parts of Europe. In Germany and Austria, then changing painfully from Gothic to roman letters in their public prints, Johnston's foundational hand was of particular interest. Anna Simons from Düsseldorf trained under Johnston and carried his influence back to Germany; Johnston lectured in Dresden in 1912; and at an international exhibition of book design and graphic arts in Leipzig in 1914, one observer saw his influence 'in every stall and wall' of the German pavilions (P. Johnston, 186).

From the early 1930s Johnston did little formal writing and his Monday afternoons at the Royal College of Art began to be irregular. After Greta Johnston's death in 1936 he became something of an ailing hermit, and when he was made a CBE in 1939, could not attend the investiture. Edward Johnston died at his home, Cleves, Ditchling, on 26 November 1944 and was buried with his wife in Ditchling churchyard. The roman lettering on their headstone, carved by Eric Gill's first apprentice, Joseph Cribb, preserves his memory.

ALAN CRAWFORD

Sources P. Johnston, *Edward Johnston* (1959) · E. Johnston, *Writing & illuminating, & lettering* (1906) · E. Johnston, *Formal penmanship and other papers*, ed. H. Child (1971) · E. Johnston, *Lesson in formal writing*, ed. H. Child and J. Howes (1986) · J. Howes, *Edward Johnston: a catalogue of the Crafts Study Centre collection and archive* (1987) · R. Kinross, *Modern typography: an essay in critical history* (1992) · C. Banks, *London's handwriting: the development of Edward Johnston's Underground Railway block-letter* (1994) · A. Simons, *Edward Johnston und die englische schriftkunst* (Berlin and Leipzig, 1937) · W. Blunt, *Cockerell: Sydney Carlyle Cockerell, friend of Ruskin and William Morris, and director of the Fitzwilliam Museum, Cambridge* (1964) · A. S. Osley, ed., *Calligraphy and palaeography: essays presented to Alfred Fairbank on his 70th birthday* (1965) · CGPLA Eng. & Wales (1945) · T. Harrod, *The crafts in Britain in the 20th century* (1999)

Archives Holburne Museum of Art, Bath, papers · Newberry Library, Chicago, papers, MSS · Ransom HRC, papers · V&A NAL, corresp. and papers | Bodl. Oxf., letters to Alfred Fairbank · NL Scot., corresp. with Sir D. Y. Cameron · V&A NAL, corresp. with Miss Ironside

Likenesses W. Rothenstein, drawing, 1922, priv. coll. · A. H. Knighton-Hammond, oils, exh. Royal Society of Portrait Painters 1937, NPG [*see illus.*] · E. X. Kapp, pencil drawing, 1940, NPG · photograph, Holburne Museum of Art, Bath, Edward Johnston collection and archive · photograph, repro. in Johnston, *Edward Johnston*

Wealth at death £13,255 15s. 10d.: probate, 3 May 1945, CGPLA Eng. & Wales

Johnston, Ellen (*c*.1835–1874?), power-loom weaver and poet, was born at the Muir Wynd, Hamilton, Lanarkshire, the only daughter of James Johnston, stonemason from Lochee, a linen-weaving and quarrying village on the outskirts of Dundee, and Mary Bilsland, second daughter of James Bilsland, a Glasgow dyer. When Ellen was only seven months old, her father emigrated to America, dying there apparently by the time she was eight. Her mother then married a power-loom tenter.

Through her stepfather Ellen Johnston got a job in a power-loom factory, where she worked from the age of thirteen. She was an avid reader as a child and greatly influenced by the writings of Sir Walter Scott. Precocious (with aspirations to be an actress), and even wilful (a trait which can also be interpreted as an admirable spirit of rebellion, at odds with the Victorian prescription of the submissive woman), Johnston gave birth to an illegitimate daughter in September 1852. Partly as a result of these factors and perhaps also from a tendency to seek too overtly the approval of her employers, she was not always popular with her fellow weavers and for a time in 1863 was unable to obtain work in Dundee.

Johnston is best known as a poet. During the 1850s, under the pseudonym the Factory Girl, she submitted her verse to several weekly newspapers. Her first poem, 'Lord Raglan's address to the allied armies', appeared in the *Glasgow Examiner* in 1854. Ill health forced her to give up factory work for a time, during which she wrote poems in an attempt to support herself. But necessity seems to have driven her back to factory work in Glasgow, Belfast (1857–9), and Manchester (for three months in 1859). Following her mother's death in May 1861 Ellen Johnston returned to Dundee to live with an aunt. There she continued to write and, aided by subscriptions from England as well as Scotland, published her *Autobiography: Poems and Songs of Ellen Johnston, the 'Factory Girl'* (1867).

Although successful in attracting the (sometimes patronizing) praise and support of eminent individuals, including the duke of Buccleuch, the Revd George Gilfillan, and even a professor of Anglo-Saxon at Oxford University, Ellen Johnston's work was considered to be ephemeral. Her poems were described by one near contemporary as being 'mainly on such subjects as Mills, Factories, Foremen, Masters, Friends etc', and as of 'little account except to those upon whom they bear' (Reid, 241). Like much popular poetry of the time, her poems owed much in form and stylistic character to Robert Burns and the Romantics, and some appear to late twentieth-century taste as rather mawkishly sentimental. Yet Ellen Johnston's most effective poems were those written in dialect. One of the latter, 'The Last sark' (shirt), a powerful and biting indictment of 'the gentry' set within the context of acute household poverty, was recognized as having considerable lasting merit and was reprinted in *An Anthology of Scottish Women Poets* (1991).

Ellen Johnston was one of only a relatively small number of Victorian women of her class to have written an autobiography, albeit a short one. Significantly, much of her poetry rejected the Victorian ideal of domesticity, and was instead a celebration of the mills and factories of the industrial age, which to Johnston appear to have represented freedom from the drudgery of the home. Concerned to promote 'the moral and social elevation of humanity' (Reid, 241), Johnston's poems in praise of 'Dear Chapelshade factory' or Napier's dockyard on the Clyde, and tributes to respected foremen, combined with a sprinkling of radical and popular patriotic poems, say much about working-class attitudes in the manufacturing towns of Victorian Britain. Nothing is known about her

later life. She is probably identifiable with the Helen Johnston who died in Barnhill poorhouse, Springburn, Glasgow, on 12 April 1874. CHRISTOPHER A. WHATLEY

Sources E. Johnston, *Autobiography, poems, and songs* (1867) • A. Reid, *The bards of Angus and the Mearns* (1897) • S. Zlotnick, '"A thousand times I'd be a factory girl": dialect, domesticity and working women's poetry in Victorian Britain', *Victorian Studies*, 35 (1991–2), 7–27 • C. Kerrigan, ed., *An anthology of Scottish women poets* (1991) • D. Vincent, *Bread, knowledge and freedom: a study of nineteenth-century working class autobiography* (1981) • d. cert.

Johnston, Francis (1760/61–1829), architect, was one of four sons of William Johnston, architect and builder, and his wife, Margaret, *née* Huston, of Armagh, co. Armagh. His eldest brother, Richard Johnston (d. 1806), architect, in 1785 designed the assembly room in the gardens of the Lying-in Hospital at Dublin.

Johnston was brought up to be an architect by his father, but when he was eighteen he was sent to Dublin by Richard Robinson, the archbishop of Armagh, to work and study with Thomas Cooley of Dublin. He remained there until Cooley died in 1784. He then took his master's position as architect to Primate Robinson. He completed some of Cooley's unfinished projects and went on to erect several buildings for the primate including the Armagh observatory. He was resident in Armagh from 1786 to 1793, during which time he supervised the building of the cathedral tower, and built the church at Ballymakenny, co. Louth (1785–93).

Subsequently Johnston returned to Dublin, where he continued to practise as an architect. In 1794 he designed Townley Hall, co. Louth, which demonstrates a severity in Johnston's work, intensified by his borrowing from Greek architecture. In 1801 work began on the construction of Charleville Castle, King's county, which, with its picturesque skyline of towers and turrets, bartizans and machicolations, forms a striking example of Johnston's work in the early Gothic revival style. It was for his restrained neo-classical designs, however, that he was described as the successor to James Gandon as Dublin's most important architect (Harbison and others, 189). In Dublin he designed St George's Church (1802–13), to which he presented a peal of eight bells. He made many alterations and additions to existing buildings, including the Bank of Ireland (1804), for which he built a new cash office. In 1805 Johnston was appointed architect to the Dublin board of works and civil buildings. He went on to build the infirmary of the Foundling Hospital, James Street (1810), the castle chapel (1807–16), the Richmond General Penitentiary (1812–20), alterations in the Bermingham Tower, Dublin Castle (1813), the General Post Office (1815–17), and additions to the viceregal lodge, and Kilmainham Hospital.

The Royal Hibernian Academy of Painting, Sculpture, and Architecture was incorporated in 1813, mainly owing to the efforts of Johnston. In 1824 he laid the foundation-stone of the buildings intended for the home of the institution, which were erected at his own expense. After their completion in 1826 Johnston was elected president of the new academy, a post he held for many years. He died in

Francis Johnston (1760/61–1829), by Henry Hoppner Meyer, pubd 1823 (after Thomas Clement Thompson)

Eccles Street, Dublin, where he had lived, on 14 March 1829, and was buried in the graveyard of St George's Church, Dublin.   L. H. CUST, rev. KAYE BAGSHAW

Sources E. McParland, 'Francis Johnston, architect, 1760–1829', *Quarterly Bulletin of the Irish Georgian Society*, 12 (1969), 62–139 · F. Johnstone, 'A letter from Francis Johnston', *Quarterly Bulletin of the Irish Georgian Society*, 6/1 (1963), 1–5 · M. Craig, 'Francis Johnston and others', *Dublin, 1600–1860* (1992), 279–90 · 'Informative lecture on famous Irish architect: notes from a lecture by John Betjeman', *Irish Builder*, 84 (1942), 121–2 · M. Colley, 'A list of architects, builders, surveyors, measurers and engineers extracted from *Wilson's Dublin Directories* from 1760 to 1837', *Bulletin of the Irish Georgian Society*, 34 (1991), 7–68 · P. Harbison, H. Potterton, and J. Sheehy, *Irish art and architecture from prehistory to the present* (1978); repr. (1993) [illustrations of Townley Hall and Charleville Castle] · *IGI* · [W. Papworth], ed., *The dictionary of architecture*, 11 vols. (1853–92)
Archives PRO NIre., diary [copy] | BL, letters to Sir Robert Peel, Add. MSS 40221–40278, *passim* · Museum of Scotland, Edinburgh, letters to Sir William Jardine
Likenesses H. H. Meyer, stipple, pubd 1823 (after T. C. Thompson), probably NPG, NG Ire. [*see illus.*] · M. Cregan, oils, Royal Hibernian Academy, Dublin · T. Kirk, marble bust, Royal Hibernian Academy, Dublin · T. C. Thompson, oils, Ulster Museum, Belfast

Johnston, Gabriel (1698–1752), political writer and colonial governor, was born in Southdean, Roxburghshire, Scotland, where he was baptized on 28 February 1698, the son of the Revd Samuel Johnston and his wife, Isobel Hall. His father, a minister of the Church of Scotland parish of Southdean and, later, that of Dundee, was probably a descendant of the Elsieshields branch of the Johnstons of Annandale.

After studying Greek and philosophy at the University of Edinburgh from 1711 to 1715 Johnston entered the University of St Andrews in 1717 as a divinity student, holding the Patrick Yeaman bursary; he graduated MA in 1720. The following year he studied medicine, briefly, at the University of Leiden but within a month of his arrival in the Netherlands he applied for a patent to teach Hebrew at St Andrews. He received the royal appointment and in November 1722 was once more at St Andrews, occupying the chair in Hebrew. In 1724 he was made burgess and guild brother (gratis) of the city of Glasgow. Three years later he resigned his chair and went to London, where he lived in the household of Spencer Compton, earl of Wilmington, for seven years. During this time Johnston wrote political articles for *The Craftsman*, an anti-Walpole publication to which such famous tory critics as Daniel Pulteney, Robert Harley, third earl of Oxford, and Henry St John, Viscount Bolingbroke, contributed.

Appointed governor of North Carolina on 27 March 1733, Johnston took the oaths of office in London that August, probably in hopes of making his fortune in America, but he did not arrive in Brunswick Town, at the mouth of the Cape Fear River, until 27 October 1734, to assume his duties on 2 November. Signalling the departure of his unpopular predecessor, George Burrington, Johnston's arrival was hailed with almost unanimous delight by the Carolinians. Soon, however, the inevitable frictions arose between a chief executive sworn to promote the interests of the crown and an assertively independent citizenry, equally determined to maintain the rights granted them by the lords proprietors. Johnston's most troublesome problems during his eighteen-year tenure, the longest of any North Carolina governor, were the conflict between the northern and southern sections of the colony, the misuses of blank patents, and the quitrent controversy. Because his own salary and those of other crown officials were paid from quitrents this, of the three, most nearly touched his own well-being. At his death his salary of £1000 per year was found to be in arrears to the amount of £13,462. The last of the debt was not collected by his heirs until forty-six years later.

Colonists were antagonized by Johnston's stand on the collection of quitrents, double the amount paid by the settlers under the lords proprietors and now to be collected *in specie* in designated places instead of in produce at the farms, as formerly. His arbitrary removal of the government offices to New Town (later Wilmington) caused the eventual decay of Brunswick, making implacable enemies of the powerful Moore family and their adherents on the Cape Fear. Members of 'the family' were also among the landholders who sought blank patents. (These left the owner of the patent to fill in the amount and location of the property he claimed; purchasers regularly failed to report claims, which aided them in the avoidance of quitrents.) Johnston's spirited opposition to these misuses of the patents further disturbed this element.

Despite almost constant opposition in North Carolina and lack of support from London, Johnston accomplished many reforms. James Davis, the first printer of the colony, was brought to North Carolina and published its first newspaper. The laws of the colony were codified and printed. The old precincts came to be called counties and a sheriff was appointed for each. Forts were built along the coast for protection from Spanish depredation. A rent roll was drawn up. New counties were formed as the colony expanded westwards. The governor introduced new agricultural methods at his plantation, Brompton, in Bladen county. Above all he encouraged immigration, notably of his fellow Scots, so that the population of the province increased threefold during his tenure. His earnest attempt to establish free schools and to encourage the work of the Church of England in the colony met with apparent failure during his lifetime but laid the groundwork for future success.

Penniless and deeply in debt to his patrons when he arrived in North Carolina, Johnston soon made a most propitious marriage, about 1740, to Penelope Goland (d. 1741), stepdaughter of Charles Eden and one of the wealthiest women in the province; she had been successively the widow of William Maule, John Lovick, and George Phenney. Their only child, Penelope, married John Dawson of Williamsburg, son of the president of William and Mary College. After the death of his first wife in 1741 Johnston married Mrs Frances Button. His will mentions their son, Henry, and daughter, Carolina; 'Polly', probably a natural daughter, predeceased him.

Johnston was bitterly criticized by his political opponents for what he himself called management. They had stronger words for it: sharp practices, trickery, and fraud. In contrast to his predecessors' violent and profane behaviour Johnston's demeanour seems to have been consistently marked by self-control. He stated that he had known confusion and disorder but had not made a single personal enemy in North Carolina. Something of Johnston's personal standards may be learned from his instructions in his will concerning his 'dear little girl', Penelope. He desired that she be brought up:

> in the Fear of God and under a deep Sense of being always in His Presence, confining her desires to things Plain, Neat and Elegant … not aspiring after the Gayety, Splendor and Extravagance and Especially to take care to keep within the Bounds of her Income and by no Means to Run in Debt.

Governor Johnston died on 17 July 1752 and was buried at Eden House, his plantation in Bertie county, near Edenton. Johnston county and Fort Johnston, at the mouth of the Cape Fear River, perpetuate his name in North Carolina.
WILLIAM S. POWELL

Sources J. D. Nash, 'Johnston, Gabriel', *Dictionary of North Carolina biography*, ed. W. S. Powell (1979–96) • M. S. R. Cunningham, 'Gabriel Johnston, governor of North Carolina, 1734–1752', MA diss., University of North Carolina, 1944 • B. Hill, 'Provincial reminiscences', *North Carolina University Magazine*, 9/2 (1890) • J. Schaw, *Journal of a lady of quality: being the narrative of a journey from Scotland to the West Indies, North Carolina, and Portugal, in the years 1774 to 1776*, ed. E. W. Andrews and C. M. Andrews (1939) • J. H. Wheeler, *Historical sketches of North Carolina* (1851) • Longleat House, Wiltshire, Granville MSS • J. B. Grimes, ed., *Abstract of North Carolina wills* (1910) • University of North Carolina Library, Chapel Hill, Southern Historical Collection, Hayes MSS • will, North Carolina State Archives, Raleigh, Charles Johnston MSS • C. L. Raper, *North Carolina: a study in English colonial government* (1904) • R. J. Cain, ed., *The Church of England in North Carolina: documents, 1699–1741* (Raleigh, NC, 1999) • W. L. Saunders and W. Clark, eds., *The colonial records of North Carolina*, 30 vols. (1886–1907), vols. 4–5, 23 • J. Sprunt, *Chronicles of the Cape Fear River* (Raleigh, NC, 1914) • *Letters of James Murray, loyalist*, ed. N. M. Tiffancy (1901) • *Virginia Gazette* (17 Oct 1771)
Archives North Carolina State Archives, Raleigh, MSS • University of North Carolina, Chapel Hill, personal and family papers | BL, Newcastle and Townshend MSS • University of North Carolina, Chapel Hill, Southern Historical Collection
Wealth at death extensive lands in three North Carolina counties

Johnston, George (1764–1823), army officer and agriculturist in Australia, was born on 19 March 1764 at Annandale, Dumfriesshire, Scotland, the son of Captain George Johnston, aide-de-camp to Lord Percy, later duke of Northumberland. There is no substance to the accusation made by Governor William Bligh that he was 'Percy's bastard', but the patronage of the Percys supported Johnston throughout his career and probably saved his life in 1811. On 6 March 1776, with his patron's help, Johnston secured a second lieutenancy in the 45th company of marines. He served in New York and Halifax, purchased a first lieutenancy, and then saw service in the East Indies against the French; he was severely wounded in an action in which his ship, HMS *Sultan*, was involved.

Following a period on half pay and in the absence of any war, Johnston decided that the distant penal colony of New South Wales offered full pay and some hope of promotion. He also had an interest in botany and zoology which could be furthered by a sojourn in the Antipodes, although later claims that he knew he would make his fortune are false. To Johnston this was indeed *terra incognita*. He sailed for the new colony aboard the first fleet in 1787. His ship, the 338 ton *Lady Penrhyn*, carried female convicts, including the fifteen-year-old Jewish milliner Esther Abrahams, transported with her infant daughter, Rosanna, for stealing 24 yards of silk lace; from the time of the voyage she became Johnston's common-law wife. The couple were eventually married on 12 November 1814, probably as part of Governor Lachlan Macquarie's plan of moral example by officers. They had three sons and four daughters, and were a powerful couple—sociable, intelligent, popular, and economically successful.

Johnston adapted well to Australian life. He avoided the endemic quarrels between the officers of the detachment, dodged his irascible superior, Major Robert Ross, and stayed on good terms with Governor Arthur Phillip, acting as adjutant of orders. Similarly, he was aide-de-camp to the second governor, John Hunter, a client of Lord Howe, and judiciously steered clear of the bitter personal quarrels which wracked this administration. When the marines returned home in 1790, Johnston chose to stay in the colony, commanding a company of his marines who had volunteered for service in the New South Wales Corps. His troops also included a number of emancipated convicts, later another source of conflict with Bligh.

Johnston's career suffered a set-back in 1800, when he was sent to England for illegal trading in spirits. However, he was never court-martialled, being protected by the Northumberland interest and the difficulty of obtaining witnesses in London, and he returned to Sydney in 1801. While away he had cemented his patronage links by gifts of Australian animals, flowers, plants, and birds; he also renewed his relationship with his former commander, Colonel Francis Grose, and through him met Grose's powerful patron, Henry Phipps, earl of Mulgrave, a link which he found critical in later years.

Despite friction with Governor P. G. King over the control of the corps and the status of the governor's ex-convict bodyguard, Johnston and the governor were on good terms. The relationship was strengthened in 1804 when Johnston crushed an armed insurrection organized by the United Irishmen. After leading his troops from Sydney—they ran all night—Johnston found the rebels near Vinegar Hill (later Rouse Hill) on the road to Windsor. He organized a meeting with the leaders of the insurgents, buying time until his troops were in position, then seized the rebels and ordered his men to cut their followers to ribbons. After hanging the leaders, summary justice heartily approved of by King, he had only one complaint—'the blood lust' of his men, with whom he was immensely popular. Throughout the incident his own convicts, many of whom were Irish, remained loyal to their master and would have defended his farm against the rebels.

Johnston's actions in 1804 brought him closer to King and to Government House. However, the new governor, Bligh, caused him considerable irritation between 1806 and January 1808, largely because of the latter's attempts to interfere with the administration of the corps. Constant references by Bligh to Johnston's men as 'sons of bitches' and vice-regal threats to remove the corps and separate the men from their 'whores and bastards' further inflamed the situation, although Johnston counselled caution and calm. The storm broke late in January 1808, when, in the midst of an acrimonious court case against John Macarthur, Bligh threatened the six corps officers sitting as the court with charges of sedition. Johnston now acted, though the previous day he had told Bligh that an accident had made it impossible for him to move. With the support of the key economic and political groups in the colony, united in temporary coalition, on 26 January he drove in from his home at Annandale, 4 miles out, marched his men to Government House, seized control of the colony as acting governor, and placed Bligh under arrest.

There is no evidence that Johnston's actions were manipulated by John Macarthur; he acted to defend the corps, the crown, and his officers. He also genuinely believed he was supported by the popular will, although his coalition shattered almost as soon as Bligh was removed from his residence, and Johnston found himself at the centre of the internecine quarrels which marked one of the most litigious places on earth. He was glad to hand over the governorship to his friend and superior, Lieutenant-Colonel Joseph Foveaux, who arrived from Van Diemen's Land on 28 July 1808.

In June 1811 Johnston was court-martialled in London for his part in the overthrow of Bligh. His life was possibly in danger, but he had powerful interests—Northumberland, Mulgrave, and Foveaux's patron, General Richard Fitzpatrick—active on his behalf, as well as Fletcher Christian's family who had never forgiven Bligh for the *Bounty* affair. Although Sir Joseph Banks tried hard for Bligh, the weight of evidence swung behind Johnston and, as a result, he was sentenced only to be cashiered. He found support in the Colonial Office, and was free to return to New South Wales, where the new governor, Macquarie, was friendly. The action against Bligh cost Johnston his commission and upwards (he claimed) of £6000. It convinced him that promises of support were rarely translated into action; in future he resolved to avoid politics, and, although close to Macquarie—he gave the governor a stallion, Sultan, a gift from the Percys—he played no further part in administration.

Johnston had begun farming in New South Wales in 1793, when he received a 100 acre grant from Grose, which he named Annandale. By the end of his life his holding amounted to more than 4000 acres, with land at Annandale, Bankstown, Cabramatta, and Lake Illawarra. A good farmer, Johnston favoured Irish convicts—whom he believed were close to the land—to work his properties; he was also a large grazier, preferring meat sheep to the fine wool breeds favoured by others, and benefiting from Northumberland's gifts of Teeswater ewes and a ram. His patron's gifts of horses added immeasurably to Johnston's colonial status.

A good family man, Johnston treated his wife's illegitimate daughter as his own and had strong links with all of his children. His love affair with his wife was enduring and his grief when his popular, highly intelligent son George junior, a favourite of Macquarie, who had tamed the 'wild cattle' in the colony, was killed in a riding accident in 1820 shows a man of deep affection.

Johnston's death on 5 January 1823 was regretted by all sections of the deeply divided colonial society. Throughout his life the handsome officer had many friends and few enemies. He was popular with his colleagues, soldiers, and convicts. As a master he was generous and humane; he disliked the lash and used it rarely. Indeed, the most violent episode of his life in New South Wales was his hanging of the Irish insurrectionists in 1804. Johnston drank heavily but, by the standards of his own time, was not a drunkard; he read widely, liked dancing, music, and singing, and, judging by his children, he and his wife encouraged education. He was survived by his wife, who died on 26 August 1846 and was buried beside him at Annandale in the family vault designed by Francis Greenway.

Johnston had served the British crown with great distinction. Somewhat ingenuous and too trusting, nevertheless he made a lasting contribution to the land he came to love. He was, as his friend Macquarie said, 'a good, honourable man'. In early New South Wales few could claim as much.   GEORGE PARSONS

Sources [F. Watson], ed., *Historical records of Australia*, 1st ser., 2–8 (1914–16) · F. M. Bladen, ed., *Historical records of New South Wales*, 7 vols. (1892–1901), vols. 1–7 · J. Ritchie, ed., *A charge of mutiny: the court-martial of Colonel George Johnston* (1988) · *AusDB*, 2.20–22 · M. H.

Ellis, *John Macarthur* (1955) · R. Fitzgerald and M. Heara, *Bligh, Macarthur and the rum rebellion* (1988) · B. H. Fletcher, *Landed enterprise and penal society: a history of farming and grazing in New South Wales before 1821* (1976)

Archives State Library of New South Wales, Sydney, Dixson Wing | Mitchell L., NSW, Macarthur and King MSS · PRO, WO and CO MSS
Likenesses oils, Mitchell L., NSW
Wealth at death 4162 acres of land

Johnston, George (1797–1855), physician and naturalist, was born on 20 July 1797 at Simprim, Berwick, the tenth of the fifteen children of Peter Johnston, a farmer, and his wife, Margaret Thomson. His family moved to Ilderton in Northumberland during his infancy, and Johnston was educated first at Kelso and then at Berwick grammar school. He later moved to the high school in Edinburgh before entering university there.

While a medical student at Edinburgh University, Johnston lodged with the family of the Revd Thomas McCrie (probably Thomas McCrie the elder (1772–1835), the Scottish divine and historian). Johnston chose medicine as his profession, and became apprenticed to Dr Abercrombie, under whose tuition he gained the diploma of the Royal College of Surgeons of Edinburgh in 1817 (he became a fellow in 1824). A brief period in London followed, during which he gained further hospital experience under the anatomist Joshua Brookes (1761–1833). Johnston subsequently began a short-lived medical practice at Belford, Northumberland. In 1818 he returned to Berwick where he set up as a physician; he returned briefly to Edinburgh in 1819, graduating MD. In November of that year he married Catherine Charles (1794–1871). The couple had a son and three daughters, one of whom married Philip Whiteside Maclagan (1818–1892), brother of the archbishop of York. Johnston's second daughter, Margaret (*b.* 1823), translated as *On the Geography of Plants* the work by Meyen.

Johnston was three times mayor of Berwick. He was very fond of the town and seldom left it; those journeys that he did make included a trip to Sutherland (with the botanist Robert Graham) and to the Great Exhibition of 1851. Increasingly, he devoted his spare time to studying natural history, in particular botany and, subsequently, marine biology. His home, The Anchorage, 35 The Woolmarket, became a focal point for local naturalists. In 1831 he founded the Berwickshire Naturalists' Club, of which he was the first president. One member of the club, Ralph Carr-Ellison, was inspired to start the Tyneside Natural History Club, and soon a nationwide network of such clubs was established.

Johnston made lists and notes of the specimens he found during field trips, with the view to making the information available to interested parties. He was in correspondence with many contemporary naturalists and marine biologists including John Edward Gray (1800–1875), Alfred Merle (Mark) Norman (1831–1918), and Albany Hancock (1806–1873), and was close friends with Joshua Alder (1792–1867), William Thompson (1805–1852), and Edward Forbes (1815–1854). Nevertheless, despite these connections, he was frustrated by the lack of availability of books and references which could equip naturalists with detailed information. The problem appears to have come to a head about 1843, when Alder and Hancock sent Johnston a set of nudibranch illustrations. Johnston was impressed by the pictures, and recommended that Alder and Hancock have them published in colour. However, the cost of such an undertaking was prohibitive. Johnston's solution to the problems facing Albany and Hancock (and doubtless many other naturalists in their position) was a proposal for the foundation of the Ray Society—'to print works illustrative of the Natural History of Great Britain'. With his clear vision for a new club, Johnston worked with the naturalists Sir William Jardine (1800–1874) and Prideaux John Selby (1788–1867) to launch the Ray Society—officially founded on 2 February 1844 at 22 Old Burlington Street, London. Shortly thereafter the society agreed to undertake publication of Alder and Hancock's work, *A Monograph of the British Nudibranchiate mollusca* (1845–1855), in seven parts (the first of many taxonomic works printed by the society).

Johnston's considerable influence on nineteenth-century marine biology, at both the local and national levels, was a result not only of his extensive network of naturalists, but also of his sound scientific works. In 1838 he was the first to detect the presence of the North American water plant *Anacharis* which spread across Britain, clogging canals and rivers. His first major publication was *The Flora of Berwick-upon-Tweed* (1829–31), which was illustrated by his wife who often botanized with him. This work was followed by 'A history of the British Zoophytes', from the *Transactions of the Natural History Society of Newcastle* (1838), 'The molluscous animals', which appeared in the English edition of Georges Cuvier's *The Animal Kingdom* (1840), *A History of British Sponges and Lithophytes* (1842), *An Introduction to Conchology, or, Elements of the Natural History of Molluscous Animals* (1850), *Terra Lindisfarnensis: the Natural History of the Eastern Borders* (vol. I), the Botany (1853), of which the zoological volume was not completed, *A Catalogue of the British non-Parasitical Worms in the Collection of the British Museum* (1865), which was published ten years after his death, and 'Catalogus animalium et plantarum quae in insula Lindisfarnensi visa sunt mense Maio' (1854), issued in the *Proceedings of the Berwickshire Naturalists' Club* in 1873.

Johnston contributed some ninety papers to a number of scientific periodicals, including the *Edinburgh Philosophical Journal*, Loudon's *Magazine of Natural History*, the *Transactions of the Natural History Society of Newcastle*, the *Proceedings of the Berwickshire Naturalists' Club*, and the *Magazine of Zoology and Botany* (later the *Annals and Magazine of Natural History*). He was editor of the last journal, and also edited the *Transactions of the Berwickshire Naturalists' Club*, the *History of the Berwickshire Naturalists' Club*, and some early publications of the Ray Society.

Johnston died at Berwick on 30 July 1855; he was survived by his wife. One of his sons-in-law, Maclagan, an army surgeon, succeeded to his medical practice, and another of his daughters, Jane Barwell-Carter, compiled a selection of her father's correspondence for publication, *Selections from the Correspondence of George Johnston* (edited by James Hardy), which appeared in 1892.

YOLANDA FOOTE

Sources GM, 2nd ser., 44 (1855), 323 · *History of Berwickshire Naturalists' Club*, 3.202, 215 · P. Davis, 'George Johnston (1797–1855) of Berwick upon Tweed and the pioneers of marine biology in northeast England', *Archives of Natural History*, 22 (1995), 349–69 · R. Welford, *Men of mark 'twixt Tyne and Tweed*, 3 vols. (1895) · E. Platts, ed., *In celebration of the Ray Society, established 1844, and its founder George Johnston (1797–1855)*, Ray Society, 163 (1994) · bap. reg. Scot. · *DNB*
Archives Berwick upon Tweed Borough Museum and Art Gallery, letters and papers · NHM, papers relating to annelids · NHM, invertebrate collections · NRA, priv. coll., diary · Royal Botanic Garden, Edinburgh, plant collections | BL, letters to Daniel Solander, Add. MS 29533 · U. Newcastle, Robinson L., letters to Sir Walter Trevelyan
Likenesses engraving (after photograph, 1851), repro. in Platts, *In celebration of the Ray Society* · mezzotint, RBG Kew · photograph, repro. in Davis, 'George Johnston' · portrait, repro. in Welford, *Men of mark*

Johnston, George (1814–1889), obstetrician, was born in Dublin on 12 August 1814. His father, Andrew Johnston, a brother of Francis Johnston (1760–1829), founder of the Royal Hibernian Academy, was an army surgeon who served in the 44th regiment in Egypt under Sir Ralph Abercromby. He was also professor of midwifery and treasurer to the Royal College of Surgeons in Ireland, and in 1817 president. Johnston was educated at Trinity College, Dublin, became a member of the College of Surgeons in 1837, and subsequently studied at Paris and at Edinburgh University, where he obtained his MD in 1845. Devoting his attention mainly to obstetric practice, he was appointed assistant master of the Rotunda Lying-in Hospital at Dublin in 1848, under Robert Shekleton, holding the post for the following seven years.

During this period Johnston was a regular contributor to the Dublin *Quarterly Journal of Medical Science*, and collected detailed clinical records of all the deliveries taking place in the Rotunda, published in 1858 as *Practical midwifery, comprising an account of 13,748 deliveries which occurred in the Dublin Lying-in Hospital, during a period of seven years, commencing November, 1847*, in conjunction with Edward B. Sinclair. Johnston was appointed seventeenth master of the Rotunda Hospital in 1868, holding office until 1875, and drawing up the annual *Clinical Reports*. In the fourth report, for 1872, he ascribed the cause of puerperal peritonitis and fever to mental anxiety and 'fretting'. He encouraged cleanliness and proper ventilation in the wards, but slight improvements in maternal mortality were attributed by contemporaries to the early discharge of his midwifery cases. He also prepared a special 'Report of 752 cases of forceps delivery in hospital practice'. He advocated the early use of forceps, though only by an experienced practitioner. Elected fellow of the King and Queen's College of Physicians in Ireland, in 1863, he was president in 1880–81. He also served as president of the Obstetrical Society of Dublin, and was fellow of the Royal Geographical Society and of the Royal Dublin Society. Between 1840 and 1850 he held the post of surgeon-superintendent to the emigration commissioners for the South Australian colonies,

and also served as physician to the Whitworth Medical and Surgical Hospital, Drumcondra. With his wife, Henrietta, he had four sons and two daughters. Johnston died at his house, 15 St Stephen's Green North, Dublin, on or about 7 March 1889, aged seventy-four.

THOMAS SECCOMBE, *rev.* HILARY MARLAND

Sources *The Lancet* (16 March 1889), 559 · *BMJ* (16 March 1889), 612 · *The Times* (14 March 1889) · A. Browne, ed., *Masters, midwives, and ladies in waiting: the Rotunda Hospital, 1745–1995* (1995) · O. T. D. Browne, *The Rotunda Hospital, 1745–1945* (1947) · T. P. C. Kirkpatrick, *The book of the Rotunda Hospital*, ed. H. Jellett (1913) · *CGPLA Eng. & Wales* (1889)
Likenesses photograph, repro. in Browne, *Rotunda Hospital*
Wealth at death £4431 9s. 9d.—effects in England: probate, 9 April 1889, *CGPLA Eng. & Wales*

Johnston, George Henry (1912–1970), journalist and author, was born on 20 July 1912 at Malakoff Street, Caulfield, Melbourne, Australia, the fourth child of John George Johnston (1876–1950), a tram repairer, and his wife, Minnie Riverina (1877–1964), the daughter of William Wright, a journalist, of Bendigo, Victoria, and his wife, Sarah. He attended Brighton Technical School, Melbourne, before starting in 1926 as an apprentice lithographer with the art printers Troedel and Cooper in Melbourne, for which he took art classes at the National Gallery School. He developed an interest in the history of sailing ships, and at the age of sixteen he offered an article on local shipwrecks to the Melbourne *Argus*, which led to his joining that paper in 1933 as a cadet reporter with responsibility for the shipping round. On 19 March 1938 he married Elsie Esme Taylor (1916–1997), and a daughter, Gae, was born in 1941.

Tall and with fair good looks, Johnston was nicknamed Golden Boy among the journalist fraternity. In 1941 he became a war correspondent, and was the first to gain accreditation. He wrote on Australian participation in the war in a popular, racy style, reporting from New Guinea, Asia, the USA, and Europe, and published several quasi-documentary books, including *Grey Gladiator* (1941), *Australia at War* (1942), and *New Guinea Diary* (1943). His travels in Asia are chronicled in *Journey through Tomorrow* (1947). On returning to Melbourne in 1946 he was appointed the first editor of the magazine *Australasian Post*.

Disapproval by the management of *The Argus* of his relationship with a colleague, Charmian Clift (1923–1969), caused Johnston to resign in 1946. Clift was born in Kiama, New South Wales, and was educated at Wollongong high school. She joined the Australian Women's Army Service in 1942 and was later posted to Melbourne, where she edited the ordnance corps journal, *For your Information*. After the war she joined *The Argus*, where she met Johnston. They moved to Sydney together in 1946 and began writing fiction in collaboration. Their first novel, *High Valley* (1949), won the *Sydney Morning Herald* prize. Johnston divorced his wife in April 1947 and married Clift later the same year, on 31 August. Their son Martin was born in 1947, followed by a daughter, Shane, in 1949; a second son, Jason, was born in 1956. During this time in Sydney, Johnston wrote a feature column for the Sydney *Sun*, and in 1951 he was appointed to head the London branch of Australian Associated Newspaper Services.

In London, Johnston and Clift continued to publish fiction, but the strain of maintaining the two careers of newspaper executive and novelist began to tell on Johnston's health. In 1954 he resigned from journalism and moved with his family to the Greek islands, first to Kalymnos, and a year later to Hydra. Here he and Clift successfully established themselves as writers of international reputation, with novels such as the collaborative *The Sponge Divers* (1956), Johnston's *The Darkness Outside* (1959) and *Closer to the Sun* (1960), and numerous short stories. He also produced a series of detective novels under the pseudonym Shane Martin. Clift's own travel books *Mermaid Singing* (1958) and *Peel me a Lotus* (1959) won popular recognition, particularly in the USA. At this point Johnston's fiction was marked by its exotic settings and lack of innovation, and though at times it was favourably reviewed it won no serious literary recognition.

Despite their hard work, the life on Hydra did not prove to be the idyll that Johnston and Clift had hoped for. Financial and marital strain, alcoholism, and a reckless lifestyle affected Johnston's health, and in 1959 he was diagnosed with tuberculosis of the lung. He attempted a return to journalism in England in 1961, but failed and went back to Hydra, where his mixed fortunes continued. Yet it was all this suffering and struggle that led to his break from literary mediocrity. In near desperation to get the mistakes of his life in focus, he began in 1962 to write his first directly autobiographical novel, *My Brother Jack* (1964). It was hailed as an Australian novel of rare distinction and has been exceptionally popular with two generations of readers. In it, David Meredith conducts a quest for the meaning of his life. Beginning with his childhood, he sees himself as an oversensitive, duplicitous child of artistic temperament, developing in contrast to his more manly and honest brother, Jack. In presenting two Australian figures, the novel thoughtfully explores two Australian myths—success and mateship. It also gives a richly detailed picture of Melbourne between the wars and provides a telling contrast between its working-class and middle-class lifestyles.

In 1964 Johnston returned with his family to Australia, where his literary reputation finally blossomed. *My Brother Jack* was adapted by Clift for television, and Johnston set to work on *Clean Straw for Nothing* (1969), the second volume of what was to be a Meredith trilogy. His health continued to be a problem, and he underwent lung surgery in 1966 and 1968. Clift was herself experiencing considerable strain writing a column for the *Sydney Morning Herald*, and on 9 July 1969, suffering depression and the effects of alcohol, she died from a self-administered overdose of barbiturates. She may also have been afraid of possible personal revelations in the forthcoming *Clean Straw for Nothing*. Like its predecessor, this novel won the Miles Franklin award.

Johnston was appointed OBE in January 1970. He lived another six months, writing the final volume of the trilogy, *A Cartload of Clay* (1971). This novel continued David Meredith's life journey, setting itself the specific task 'to plot the arabesque that linked everything together'. It was incomplete at the time of Johnston's death, which took place on 22 July 1970 at his home, 112 Raglan Street, Mosman, New South Wales, from the combined effects of tuberculosis and emphysema. He was cremated at Chatswood on 24 July with Methodist forms. His son Martin Johnston (1947–1990) subsequently achieved recognition in Australia as a poet and novelist.

As a novelist, Johnston belongs in the tradition of journalistic realism. However, the autobiographical element in his best work gives it uncommon power and honesty, and in its blend of truth and the fictive his method sometimes produces modernistic results, as in the case of *Clean Straw for Nothing*. Characteristically, Johnston's narrative voice is that of an educated Australian male, better at dealing with material detail than with expressions of emotion.

Johnston bore the marks of his time and background: he had only a basic formal education, experienced the depression and the war, joined the expatriate exodus to post-war Europe, and returned to participate in, and benefit from, the increased sophistication of Australian culture in the 1960s. The psychological legacy of all this was a deep insecurity about his talent and indeed his right to fame, and the chief victims of this legacy were his own health and his marriage. He writes about this with strength, honesty, and descriptive brilliance in the Meredith trilogy, which through the personal odyssey of its central character manages to express a varied and crucial era of Australian life.

GARRY KINNANE

Sources G. Kinnane, *George Johnston: a biography* (Melbourne, 1986) · NL Aus., Johnston Estate papers · Ransom HRC, David Higham Archive · Indiana University, Bloomington, Indiana, Lilly Library, Bobbs-Merrill files · student records, Brighton Technical School, Melbourne, Australia · enrolment records, National Gallery School, Melbourne, Australia · registry of births, deaths, and marriages, Melbourne, Australia · registry of births, deaths, and marriages, Sydney, Australia · C. Clift, 'My husband George', *POL Magazine* (July 1969), 83 · C. Tolchard, 'My husband George: my wife Charmian', *Walkabout* (Jan 1969), 28 · records of the Royal North Shore Hospital, Sydney, Australia

Archives NL Aus., MSS, personal papers, corresp. | Indiana University, Bloomington, Lilly Library, Bobbs-Merrill files · U. Texas, David Higham archive

Likenesses R. Drysdale, oils, 1967, NL Aus. · R. Crooke, oils, 1969, Art Gallery of New South Wales, Sydney

Wealth at death modest; mostly furniture (approx. A$1000); personal effects; Raglan Street residence, Sydney (approx. A$15,000)

Johnston, George Lawson, first Baron Luke (1873–1943), food manufacturer and philanthropist, was born on 9 September 1873 at 2 Blacket Place, Newington, Edinburgh, the second son of the thirteen children of John Lawson *Johnston (1839–1900), nutrition promoter and food manufacturer, and his wife, Elizabeth, daughter of George Lawson, baker and confectioner of Newington, Edinburgh. Both parents were Scottish.

Lawson Johnston was initially educated privately in Canada, where his father had significant business interests. He subsequently attended Dulwich College for one academic year, and then Blair Lodge in Scotland, after his

George Lawson Johnston, first Baron Luke (1873–1943), by Lafayette, 1929

parents had returned to live in Britain. He worked for Bovril, his father's company, even before leaving full-time education, and was a cashier at the Paris International Exhibition of 1889. On joining the firm, he was trained on the job and travelled extensively in South America, the main source of raw materials. In 1896 Bovril was floated as a public company by Ernest Terah Hooley (1859–1947), and Lawson Johnston joined the board. Following the death of his father in 1900 he became vice-chairman. He succeeded to the chairmanship in 1916, and in 1932 became joint managing director, both of which positions he held until his death. On 4 December 1902 he married the Hon. Edith Laura St John (1879–1941), fifth daughter of Beauchamp Moubray St John, seventeenth Baron St John of Bletso. They had four daughters and two sons, both of whom joined Bovril.

Lawson Johnston became the main decision maker in the firm after the death of his father, showing especial care in the marketing and financial fields, and diversifying the company into related products. He considered Bovril's sources of raw materials to be so insecure that it needed to acquire them itself, and so large tracts of land in both South America and Australia were purchased and stocked with beef cattle. Subsidiary companies were established in 1908 and 1909 to run these operations, and in subsequent years he arranged for prize bulls, purchased in England, to be shipped out to improve the quality of the herd. The estates in Argentina eventually exceeded 1½ million acres, and included a fully fitted factory and river boats to carry the cattle to it. Lawson Johnston took a personal interest in these *estancias*, visiting them most years. The estates in Australia were never as productive or as important to Bovril, because rainfall was inadequate and transport facilities poor.

The other policy pursued by Lawson Johnston was to reduce Bovril's reliance on a single product by diversifying the range of commodities offered to the public. This strategy concentrated on other foodstuffs with a 'healthy' image. In 1899 a malt tonic, Virol, was introduced and became so popular that a separate company was formed and a new factory was built at the junction of Western Avenue and the North Circular in London. This was soon followed by Stelna corned beef, a by-product of making the meat extract; it was later renamed Bovril corned beef to cash in on the well-known brand name. In the 1920s Bovril acquired the Marmite Company, which had been established in Burton upon Trent in 1902 by Frederick Wissler, a Swiss citizen, to manufacture yeast extract with similar uses to Bovril, but catering for a vegetarian clientele. However, in order to keep the two companies separate in the public mind, no formal announcement of this was made and the shares were owned by a family trust. In the same decade Bovril (through Virol) bought into Ambrosia, which manufactured a range of milk-based products, thus further diversifying its product range.

Lawson Johnston also reorganized the finances of Bovril, as the flotation by Hooley had left the company over-capitalized and illiquid. Lawson Johnston set about building up a reserve fund and ensuring that the family, who had become only minority shareholders after the launch, albeit holding the single largest block, retained control of the destiny of the firm. The annual profits rose from £125,000 in 1899 to £400,000 in the late 1920s and the reserve fund grew to over £1 million by 1940. Lawson Johnston rearranged the capital base of Bovril, raising finance via eight-year notes, and then redeeming those and the debentures via an issue of pre-preference shares taken up mainly by the family, and giving them greater control by means of double voting rights. When Lawson Johnston died Bovril was financially secure, diversified into a number of strong brands, and had large holdings abroad providing the raw materials.

Lawson Johnston was on many boards of directors by virtue of large shareholdings, family or business relationships, and his knowledge of certain areas of business. The companies of which he was a director included the *Daily Express*, Sir Isaac Pitman & Sons, Lloyds Bank, the Ashanti Goldfields Corporation, the Forestal Land, Timber, and Railways Company, and the Australian Mercantile, Land, and Finance Company. He was also chairman of the national committee of the International Chamber of Commerce and attended many general congresses. Politically Lawson Johnston began as a Liberal, serving on several committees to do with raw materials in the First World War, for which in 1920 he was knighted. He switched allegiance after the war to the Conservatives, supporting Baldwin and Neville Chamberlain, and helping to establish the Conservative Research Department. In Baldwin's 1929 dissolution honours he was ennobled as Baron Luke. He was throughout his life an active and committed Christian, moving to the Church of England on his marriage, but remaining low church, and abhorring all ritual in church services. Luke endowed the Scripture Knowledge Foundation, sat on its committee, and was president at the time of his death. He also supported the *Boy's Own Paper* and *Girl's Own Paper*, and established the Luke Trust, the income from which endowed Christian charities.

A governor of the Regent Street Polytechnic from 1915 to 1943, and a tireless worker to raise funds for voluntary hospitals, Luke served on a number of hospital boards, including those for King Edward's Hospital Fund, the Royal Northern Hospital, and the Thankoffering Fund for George V's recovery. He also introduced clauses to bills in the House of Lords to allow hospitals to recoup from insurance companies the costs of treating accident victims. He was chairman of the Ministry of Health's advisory committee on nutrition from 1935 to 1941 and of the ministry of information's advisory committee on advertising agents from 1941 to 1943.

Luke was a great patriarch, placing immense store on his large extended family. He took responsibility for the family's financial stability, involving members in his own financial successes through shareholdings, directorships, and other investments. An inveterate worker, perpetually making notes and jotting down ideas, he rarely relaxed, except in the countryside, which he loved. He enjoyed riding to hounds, in spite of an aversion to dogs. He was a poor public speaker, but a firm and effective chairman. The death of his wife in 1941 was a great blow to him, and he himself died from lung cancer on 23 February 1943 at 2 Weymouth Street, London; he was buried at St Paul's Church, Bedford, on the 26th.

Luke's elder son, **Ian St John Lawson Johnston**, second Baron Luke (1905–1996), food manufacturer and company director, was born on 7 June 1905. He attended Eton College and read history at Trinity College, Cambridge, graduating in 1927. He then joined Bovril, with the understanding that eventually he would take over running the business, and studied beef production in Australia and South America. He married on 4 February 1932 Barbara (b. 1911), the younger daughter of Sir Fitzroy Hamilton Anstruther-Gough-Calthorpe, first baronet; they had four sons and one daughter. Lawson Johnston served in the Territorial Army and on the outbreak of the Second World War in 1939 became second in command of the 5th battalion, the Bedfordshire and Hertfordshire regiment. In 1940 he was transferred to the 9th battalion, which he commanded, and so escaped the appalling fate of the 5th in Malaya. Released from the army following the death of his father, Luke became chairman of Bovril and its subsidiaries. Under his leadership the business, including Ambrosia and Marmite, expanded and prospered. He continued his family's interest in advertising. He retired in 1970 (shortly after which Bovril was acquired by Sir James Goldsmith's

company Cavenham). His other appointments included directorships of Electrolux, Lloyds Bank, IBM, the Gateway Building Society, the Ashanti Goldfields Corporation, and other companies. Like his father, Luke was a devoted Anglican and did much voluntary work, in particular for hospital charities. A friend, admirer, and host of Billy Graham, he criticized Michael Ramsay, the archbishop of Canterbury, in 1967 for unenthusiastic remarks about the evangelist. He was British member of the International Olympic Committee (1951–88) and after his retirement was replaced by the princess royal. He lived at Odell Castle, near Pavenham, Bedfordshire, which had been bought by his father in 1934, and was a county councillor, JP, and deputy lieutenant for Bedfordshire. He was appointed KCVO in 1976. He died on 25 May 1996, survived by his wife and their five children, and was succeeded as third baron by his eldest son, Arthur Charles St John Lawson Johnston (b. 1933).

JOHN ARMSTRONG

Sources *The Times* (24 Feb 1943), 7 · J. Armstrong, 'Hooley and the Bovril Company', *Business History*, 28 (1986), 18–34 · PRO, MH 56/49, 79/343, 79/345 · PRO, INF 1/341 · GL, MS 14164/1–7 · Companies House, files 50, 220; 141, 748 · Beds. & Luton ARS, LJ1/1, 1/2, 1/6 · Viscount Camrose [W. E. Berry], *British newspapers and their controllers*, rev. edn (1948) · *Evening Standard* (23 Feb 1943) · *Boy's Own Paper* (April 1943) · J. Armstrong, 'Johnston, George Lawson', *DBB* · G. Lawson Johnston, 'John Lawson Johnston, 1873–1896' [typescript] · A. J. P. Taylor, *Beaverbrook* (1972) · b. cert. · *CGPLA Eng. & Wales* (1943) · private information (2004) · Burke, *Peerage* · *WWW* · *The Times* (28 May 1996) · *Daily Telegraph* (31 May 1996) · *CGPLA Eng. & Wales* (1996)

Archives Companies House, file 50, 220 · GL, MS 14164 · PRO, MH and INF files

Likenesses Lafayette, photograph, 1929, NPG [*see illus.*] · W. Brealey, oils, Shire Hall, Bedford · portrait, repro. in *Grocery*, 2/2 (2 Feb 1900), 117

Wealth at death £411,606 17s. 5d.: probate, 25 June 1943, *CGPLA Eng. & Wales* · £395,575—Ian St John Lawson Johnston, second Baron Luke: probate, 1996, *CGPLA Eng. & Wales*

Johnston [*née* de Beaulieu; *other married name* Dering], **Henrietta** (*c.*1674–1729), pastelist, was born in France, the daughter of Francis de Beaulieu (*d.* in or before 1694) and his wife, Susannah. She arrived with her family in England on 16 December 1687 and in March 1694 married Robert Dering, son of Sir Edward Dering, after receiving her mother's permission as she was only 'about 20'. Afterwards they lived in Dublin, where Dering died before 1700. He had cousins and brothers there, one of whom, Daniel, was married to Helena Percival, a daughter of Sir John Percival, later first earl of Egmont. Robert Dering's sister, Elizabeth, was married to Sir Edward Southwell, a relation of the Percivals. The earliest pastels drawn by Henrietta Dering are of these Irish connections and their friends. Details of her training are unknown. In 1704 she drew Sir Emmanuel Moore and Sir John Percival, resplendent in red coats, and the fourth earl of Barrymore, whose portrait shows her fresh colouring, notably in the face and wig. Henrietta Dering signed and dated her work on the wooden backings of her pastels, which survive as most are in their original frames. Her pastels of General Earle and Sir John Percival of 1705 are stiff in pose; a third dated

1705, of a member of the Southwell family, is signed 'Henrietta Johnson Fecit', indicating that it was painted after she married the Revd Gideon Johnston (1668–1716) on 11 April 1705, as his second wife. He had two young sons and she two daughters by their respective first marriages.

At some time in 1705 Gideon Johnston was recommended to the bishop of London as bishop's commissary in South Carolina. After a long delay the couple arrived there in spring 1708. They encountered many difficulties, including financial ones, and in 1709 Gideon Johnston wrote home saying, 'were it not for the Assistance my wife gives me by drawing of Pictures (which can last but a little time in a place so ill peopled) I shou'd not have been able to live' (papers of the Society for the Propagation of the Gospel). Other problems arose: on 5 July 1710 Johnston wrote again, 'My wife who greatly helped me, drawing pictures, has long ago made an end of her materials' (ibid.). In his reply to this letter, John Chamberlayne of the Society for the Propagation of the Gospel said, 'I have clubb'd wth Mr Shute in sending a small present of Crayons to Mrs Johnston in acknowledgement of the Rice etc which was lost wth poor Capt Cole' (American papers of the Society for the Propagation of the Gospel)—a fascinating sidelight on an artist's problems in a new colony.

There is a distinct difference between Henrietta Johnston's Irish pastels and most of those done in Charles Town which may partly be attributed to her shortage of materials. The Irish work is strong and colourful, while, with exceptions, her colonial work is much paler and sometimes lacks detail. Her Charles Town sitters are shown bust length, not waist length, the usual format for her portraits drawn in Ireland. Some forty of her works are known, of which many drawn in America were of Huguenots. In its brilliant lively colour, her pastel of Henriette Charlotte de Chastaigner (Gibbes Museum of Art, Charleston), dated 1711, may be the result of the gift of crayons sent the previous year. It remains in perfect condition.

Henrietta Johnston was in London in 1711 with documents, letters, and other items for the Society for the Propagation of the Gospel before returning to America in mid-1712. The lack of portraits from 1712 to 1714 is probably due to two hurricanes and a war between British colonists and local mainly Yamasee Indians. The subsequent portraits of Colonel and Mrs Samuel Proleau of 1715 (Museum of Early Southern Decorative Arts, North Carolina) are among her best American works.

In April 1716 Gideon Johnston was accidentally drowned. With her four children and other family members, Henrietta lived on in Charles Town. On 19 September 1719 she charged 2 pistoles for a portrait of Mr Clapp, but he paid £10 (Mrs Elizabeth Sindrey's estate account book, 1705–21, South Carolina Historical Society). This was more than she would have got in Ireland. In 1725 she was in New York drawing the Moore family, but she returned in 1726 to Charles Town, where she lived until her death on 9 March 1729. She was buried in St Philip's churchyard, Charles Town. Most of her pictures are in private collections.   ANNE CROOKSHANK

Sources W. Batson, *Henrietta Johnston, 'who greatly helped … by drawing pictures'* (1991) [exhibition catalogue, Winston-Salem, NC, and Charleston, SC, 12 Oct 1991 – 2 Feb 1992] • LPL, Society for the Propagation of the Gospel papers • correspondence, 1711, South Carolina, LPL, Society for the Propagation of the Gospel, American papers • F. J. Klingberg, ed., *Carolina chronicle: the papers of commissary Gideon Johnston, 1707–1716* (Berkeley, California, 1946) • W. A. Shaw, ed., *Letters of denization and acts of naturalization for aliens in England and Ireland, 1603–1700*, Huguenot Society of London, 18 (1911) • Mrs Elizabeth Sindrey's estate account book, 1705–21, South Carolina Historical Society, Charleston • M. Bond, 'Diaries and papers of Sir Edward Dering', in *Parliamentary diaries of Sir Edward Dering*, ed. B. D. Henning (1940), 208–9 • will, London, 1747, PRO [Mary Dering, daughter] • E. G. Miles, 'Johnston, Henrietta Branlieu Dering', *ANB*

Archives LPL, papers of Society for the Propagation of the Gospel • Society for the Propagation of the Gospel, South Carolina, American papers of the Society for the Propagation of the Gospel, corresp.

Johnston, Henry [*name in religion* Joseph] (*d.* 1723), Benedictine monk and antiquary, was born at Methley, near Leeds, Yorkshire, one of at least three sons of the Revd John Johnston (*d.* 1657) and his wife, Elizabeth Hobson, and brother of Nathaniel *Johnston MD. From 26 May 1666 to 31 May 1669 the antiquarian and herald Sir William Dugdale employed him as one of his clerks at the College of Heralds, London, at the request of his brothers Samuel and Nathaniel, copying pedigrees and visitation returns. Between May 1669 and January 1671 he travelled around Yorkshire collecting historical material on behalf of his brother Nathaniel. The date of his conversion to Roman Catholicism is not known, but he had become a Benedictine postulant at Dieulouard in Lorraine by March 1674. Here he was clothed on 14 April 1674, taking the name Joseph, and was professed for the English priory of St Edmund the King at Paris on 26 May 1675, and became MA of Paris in 1678.

Johnston was sent on the mission in the Benedictine south province, and during the reign of James II he was stationed in the monastery at St James's Palace, London. At St James's, he was responsible for making some important converts to Roman Catholicism, including Ralph Weldon and perhaps the poet Jane Barker. During the reign of James II, he became the principal editor and translator of the apologetical works of J. B. Bossuet, with whom he was acquainted. His patron seems to have been James Drummond, fourth earl of Perth, and he went on to publish a number of pamphlets defending Bossuet from the attacks of William Wake, later archbishop of Canterbury. He remained in London after the revolution, sheltering in Somerset House. He was certainly working as a Jacobite agent by 1691, and was thereby drawn into the circle of conspirators behind the assassination plot of 1696. Although he admitted he was privy to the plan to capture King William, he always insisted, perhaps disingenuously, that he was ignorant of any conspiracy to assassinate him.

A proclamation for his arrest forced Johnston back to France, where he was briefly prior of St Edmund's in Paris, but had to resign on account of his notoriety, meanwhile drawing up a vindication of his conduct. It was thought imprudent for him to return to England. After a brief sojourn at the abbey of St Faron, near Meaux, and the priory of St Gregory at Douai, he returned to Paris, becoming prior of St Edmund's again in 1705 and titular prior of Durham in 1717. At St Edmund's Priory, Paris, where the remains of James II had been deposited after his death in 1701, he acted as 'protonotary apostolic', being responsible for registering the testimonies of alleged miracles credited to the king's intercession as a preliminary to his beatification. Johnston died at St Edmund's on 22 June 1723 and was buried at the priory.   GEOFFREY SCOTT

Sources G. Scott, 'A Benedictine conspirator: Henry Joseph Johnston (c.1656–1723)', *Recusant History*, 20 (1990–91), 58–75 · J. D. Martin, 'The antiquarian collections of Nathaniel Johnston (1629–1705)', BLitt diss., U. Oxf., 1956 · J. Garret, *The triumphs of providence: the assassination plot, 1696* (1980) · J. Kirk, *Biographies of English Catholics in the eighteenth century*, ed. J. H. Pollen and E. Burton (1909) · F. Cabrol, 'Bossuet, ses relations avec Angleterre', *Revue d'Histoire Ecclesiastique*, 27 (1931), 535–71 · W. Beamont, ed., *The Jacobite trials at Manchester in 1694*, Chetham Society, 28 (1853) · *The life, diary, and correspondence of Sir William Dugdale*, ed. W. Hamper (1827) · *Sixth report*, HMC, 5 (1877–8) · *Reliquiae Hearnianae: the remains of Thomas Hearne*, ed. P. Bliss, 2 vols. (1857) · T. H. Clancy, *English Catholic books, 1641–1700: a bibliography* [1974]; rev. edn (1996) [for Johnston's bks and his trans. of Bossuet] · G. Sitwell, 'A crisis of authority in English Benedictine history', *Recusant History*, 16 (1982–3), 221–303 · W. Dugdale, *The visitation of the county of Yorke*, ed. R. Davies and G. J. Armytage, SurtS, 36 (1859) · profession book of St Edmund's, Paris, Douai Abbey, France
Archives BL, Add. MS 10118 · Bodl. Oxf., corresp. and papers relating to Yorkshire · LPL, 922/57; 933/V/84; 1029/72 | Archives Nationales, Paris, depositions relating to the miracles of James II · Douai Abbey, Reading, profession book; B. Weldon's 'Memorials'

Johnston, Henry Erskine [Hendry Erskine] (**1775?–1845**), actor, was probably born in Edinburgh on 3 August 1775, the son of Robert Johnston, barber and wigmaker, and his wife Elizabeth, daughter of William Watson Johnston, whose first forename was given as 'Hendry' in the parish record of his birth, began performing in private plays while still at school. On leaving school he was first placed by his father in the office of a writer to the signet and then apprenticed to a linen draper, with whom he remained for three years before going on the stage. He made his début in Edinburgh in 1794 reciting Collins's 'Ode on the Passions', which impressed Stephen Kemble into engaging him to appear as an amateur in the part of Hamlet in the city (9 July 1794). His success was immediate and enthusiastic: he was extravagantly fêted, and dubbed the Scottish Roscius. After playing for a few nights he went to Dublin, where he acted for twelve nights, appearing on seven of them as Norval in John Home's *Douglas*, in which he was very well received. His first appearance in London took place at Covent Garden, as 'H. Johnston from Edinburgh', also in *Douglas* (23 October 1797). He was praised in the *European Review* for his figure, countenance, and voice, but was said to lack the art to conceal art. The part of Romeo was followed by Dorilas in *Merope*, Achmet in *Barbarossa* (1798), and an original character in *Curiosity*, an unprinted play, said to have been translated from a work by Gustavus, king of Sweden. In June 1798, at the Haymarket, he

was the original Alberto in Thomas Holcroft's *The Inquisitor*. He remained at Covent Garden, with summer engagements at the Haymarket, until the season of 1802–3, playing Sir Edward Mortimer, Polydore in Thomas Otway's *The Orphan*, Lothario, Octavian, and other roles, and creating various characters in plays by Thomas Morton, W. G. Holman, Elizabeth Inchbald, Thomas Dibdin, and others.

Johnston married in 1796 a Miss Parker (*b.* 1782), with whom he had six children. Mrs Johnston belonged to a theatrical family and acted with her husband in Ireland as Lady Contest in *The Wedding Day* and Josephine in *The Children in the Wood*. She appeared as Ophelia to her husband's Hamlet at the Haymarket (September 1798) and repeated the character at Covent Garden, where she played many parts in comedy and in tragedy, including Lady Macbeth. With Holman, J. H. Johnstone, John Fawcett, Alexander Pope, Edward Knight, J. S. Munden, and Charles Incledon, Johnston signed the famous statement of grievances against the management of Covent Garden, and owed his re-engagement to the loyalty of Fawcett, who refused to renew his contract without Johnston's reinstatement. As Norval in *Douglas* he made his first appearance at Drury Lane in September 1803; he also played there Anhalt in Inchbald's *Lovers' Vows* to the Amelia of his wife. He remained at Drury Lane for two years, among other characters appearing as Petruchio and Duke Aranza, and returned to Covent Garden in October 1805 as the original Rugantino, the Bravo of Venice, in Monk Lewis's play of that name. He was seen again at Covent Garden in December 1816, and in June 1817 he was the original Baltimore at the English Opera House (the Lyceum) in an operatic version of Joanna Baillie's *The Election*. At Drury Lane he appeared as Pierre in Otway's *Venice Preserv'd* in 1817 and as the original Rob Roy Macgregor in Soane's adaptation from Scott in 1818. On 24 November 1821, at the Olympic, he was the Solitary in *Le solitaire, or, The Recluse of the Alps*. This seems to have been his last appearance in London. It has been said that his career in the capital came to an end as a result of his having horsewhipped George IV when the latter was prince of Wales for an insult to Johnston's wife.

At the beginning of 1823 Johnston became manager of the Caledonian Theatre in Edinburgh. He opened in January with *Gilderoy*, in which he played the hero, and with an address written by himself. He then played Jerry Hawthorn in W. T. Moncrieff's *Tom and Jerry* and other parts, but resigned his management in April 1823. On 20 October 1830 he was engaged for four nights at the same house, after which time he seems to have disappeared. Little is known of his later life. He separated from his wife and died in Gillingham Street, Belgrave, London, on 8 February 1845.   JOSEPH KNIGHT, rev. NILANJANA BANERJI

Sources *The thespian dictionary, or, Dramatic biography of the present age*, 2nd edn (1805) · T. Gilliland, *The dramatic mirror, containing the history of the stage from the earliest period, to the present time*, 2 (1808) · J. C. Dibdin, *The annals of the Edinburgh stage* (1888) · P. Hartnoll, ed., *The concise Oxford companion to the theatre* (1972) · P. Hartnoll, ed., *The Oxford companion to the theatre* (1951); 2nd edn (1957); 3rd edn (1967) · Hall, *Dramatic ports.* · Genest, *Eng. stage* · M. Richardson, letter to

Sir Sidney Lee, 27 March 1914, Oxford University Press, Oxford DNB archives · d. cert.

Likenesses W. Allan, oils (as Young Norval in *Douglas*), Garr. Club · H. Singleton, oils (as Douglas), Garr. Club · portrait, repro. in *Thespian dictionary* · portrait, repro. in *British Stage* (July 1820) · portrait, repro. in *Theatrical Inquisitor* (1817) · portrait, repro. in *Monthly Mirror* (1800) · portrait, repro. in *British Drama* (1817) · portrait, repro. in Oxberry, *New English Drama* (1817) · prints, BM, NPG

Johnston, Sir Henry Hamilton [Harry] (1858–1927), explorer and colonial administrator, was born in London on 12 June 1858, the eldest of twelve children of John Brookes Johnston, secretary of the Royal Exchange Assurance Company, and his second wife, Esther Laetitia, daughter of Robert Hamilton, merchant. His parents belonged to the Catholic Apostolic (Irvingite) Church, and they educated their children very largely from home, and in an unusually intelligent and liberal way. At the age of ten Johnston had a year away from school to develop his precocious talents, drawing and painting at the Lambeth School of Art and studying animals and birds at the London Zoological Gardens. From 1870 to 1875 he attended the Stockwell grammar school and in 1876 studied French, Italian, Spanish, and Portuguese at evening classes at King's College, London. In the same year he entered the Royal Academy Schools to study painting. He made long painting expeditions, to Spain in 1876 and France in 1878, and in 1879–80 spent eight months in Tunis, painting and contributing illustrated articles to *The Globe* and *The Graphic*. He reported on the preparations for a French take-over of the country and visited eastern Algeria to observe the build-up of French military forces along the frontier. He later claimed that it was in Tunis, in 1880, that he resolved to devote himself to the extension of the British empire in Africa.

In 1882–3 Johnston accompanied a geographical and sporting expedition to Angola, serving as artist, naturalist, and Portuguese interpreter. The party travelled slowly from Mossamedes to the upper Cunene, where Johnston left it, making his own way to the Congo estuary. There he was befriended by H. M. Stanley, who was then establishing the Congo Independent State for Leopold II of the Belgians. With Stanley's help, Johnston ascended the river as far as Bolobo, and spent some weeks collecting plants, birds, and insects, and vocabularies of the local Bantu languages. Back in England, he published an attractively written and illustrated account of his journey, which established his reputation as an African explorer and led to his appointment by the Royal Society to conduct an expedition to study the flora and fauna of Mount Kilimanjaro in 1884.

Preparations for the Kilimanjaro expedition brought Johnston into contact with officials of the Foreign Office, whom he alerted to the commercially exclusive treaties being negotiated by Stanley with the chiefs of the Lower Congo, and also to the purchase of slaves, ostensibly to free them, for road building, porterage, and military service. At Zanzibar, Johnston was welcomed by the powerful consul-general, John Kirk, who made what arrangements were possible for his safety in the interior. However, it was

Sir Henry Hamilton Johnston (1858–1927), by James Russell & Sons

to the Foreign Office rather than to Kirk that Johnston, a few weeks after his arrival, sent an absurdly optimistic proposal to turn his naturalist's camp near Moshi into the nucleus of a British colony of agricultural settlers to be chosen by himself, who would not need any government, nor by implication any defence, for many years to come. Arriving in London just at the moment when Germany was unveiling far-reaching colonial claims in Africa, Johnston's proposal was approved by the colonial committee of the cabinet, and was stopped only by the personal intervention of Gladstone. On his return to England, however, 'Kilimanjaro Johnston' was lionized and rewarded with the offer of a double vice-consulship in the recently gazetted British Protectorate of the Oil Rivers, in the south-east of modern Nigeria, and in the adjacent German protectorate of the Cameroons.

Johnston spent two and a half years in west Africa, during which he travelled widely in the hinterland of Old Calabar and the Cross River explaining the implications of British protection to peoples of whom most had no previous contact with the outside world. During the intervals between these journeys he studied the current partition of Africa and speculated about the interior frontiers which were still to be drawn. He embodied his thoughts in a series of dispatches, well illustrated by maps, which attracted the attention of Lord Salisbury, who, on Johnston's return to England, invited him to Hatfield, and kept him in London for almost a year as an informal adviser. Johnston's publication of *The River Congo* (1884) and *The Kilimanjaro Expedition* (1885) confirmed his reputation as an authority on Africa.

In 1888 and 1889 Salisbury was revising his policy on African partition in the light of his desire to retain control of Egypt, and therefore to encourage France in her west African ambitions, while increasing British claims in the east and the south. The new direction was epitomized in Johnston's slogan 'From the Cape to Cairo', and his own role in it was as consul in Mozambique, a post from which it was secretly intended that he should organize and direct the making of treaties with African chiefs in the region between Mozambique and Angola, where the Portuguese were known to be preparing to make treaties themselves. The main problem was that Salisbury depended for his parliamentary majority on the support of Liberal Unionists who opposed expenditure on imperial expansion. The plan became suddenly more viable when Johnston, on the eve of his departure, happened to meet Cecil Rhodes, who immediately offered to pay the expenses of Johnston's treaty making, if the areas so acquired could be assigned to the sphere of his British South Africa Company. The arrangement was sanctioned by Salisbury for the area that was to become Northern Rhodesia, but, in the area which was to become Nyasaland, where British missionaries were already established, he insisted on retaining control.

From July 1889 until March 1890 Johnston was engaged in this treaty making, travelling up the Zambezi and the Shire to Lake Nyasa and on to Lake Tanganyika, while a locally engaged assistant, Alfred Sharpe, took a more westerly route towards Katanga and Lake Mweru. In May Johnston was in Kimberley for consultations with Rhodes. He then returned to England for almost a year, while Salisbury negotiated boundary agreements with Germany and Portugal, and while arrangements were made for the administration of the newly acquired territories. In February 1891 Johnston was appointed commissioner and consul-general for the territories under British influence to the north of the Zambezi, while the British South Africa Company agreed to contribute £10,000 a year for three years towards the cost of administration. With this subsidy he recruited an armed force of seventy Sikhs from the Punjab and eighty Zanzibaris from the east coast, with whom he sailed up the Zambezi in July 1891 to begin the occupation of 400,000 square miles of central Africa, populated by some 2–3 million people.

Given such meagre resources, Johnston had to concentrate his efforts on the imperial protectorate rather than the company's sphere, and within that on a small area in the Shire highlands between Blantyre and Zomba, where a Church of Scotland mission had been operating since 1875, and where a small number of European planters were already established. Northwards, around and beyond Lake Nyasa, Yao and Ngoni, Bemba and Swahili were raiding weaker peoples for ivory and slaves, and building up their own strength in imported firearms.

Johnston's early attempts to control the Yao round the southern shore of Lake Nyasa resulted in the loss of one of his two military officers and one fifth of his armed force, and put his finances so far into deficit that he had to go to Rhodes for more money. At last, in 1894, the new Liberal government of Lord Rosebery rescued him with a grant-in-aid, and the effective occupation of the northern two-thirds of the protectorate could begin. In 1895 Johnston visited India to recruit more soldiers, and during the next eighteen months he took a personal lead in deploying his troops in one district after another of the centre and the north, marching in the middle of the column under a white umbrella that was never lowered. Operations culminated in the destruction of the Swahili settlements in the far north which had defied all attempts at peaceful incorporation.

The Treasury grant led to the separation of the protectorate from the company's sphere and the end of personal relations between Johnston and Rhodes. It enabled Johnston to develop the idea of a system of 'protectorate government', based on the education of the black man rather than his economic exploitation by the white. Traditional societies should be disturbed as little as possible. Modernization would develop around the centres of colonial government, to which progressively minded Africans could move to join the modern economy. His ideas aroused much interest in England, but unfortunately he was unable to realize them in Nyasaland. The telegram from Salisbury congratulating him on his military victories and on the appointment as KCB found Johnston prostrate with his third attack of blackwater fever. It was clear that he would have to take extensive sick leave, and seek his next post outside the tropics.

Aged thirty-seven, and the youngest member of any of the orders of knighthood, Johnston seemed set to climb yet higher, but it was not to be. After waiting for more than a year, he accepted the consulate-general at Tunis and used it as a retreat from which to pursue his literary and scientific interests. At last, in 1899, there came the tempting offer to go for two years as special commissioner to Uganda, to establish civilian administration there after seven years of disastrous and very expensive military rule. It seemed a chance to climb back on to the ladder of high preferment, and his performance, though eccentric, was highly successful. Eight months out of eighteen were spent on the march, as much in the cause of science as of good government. At Entebbe, as earlier at Zomba, government house was overrun with wildlife, from snakes to crested cranes, from monkeys to a baby elephant. Johnston had the vision of a fertile country of peasant farmers, capable of producing tax revenues necessary to support a light form of colonial overrule as soon as the completion of the Uganda Railway should give them the means of exporting their produce. He concluded an agreement with the ruling chiefs of Buganda which made them privileged allies of the British, thereby enabling him to halve the military expenditure incurred by his predecessors. At the end of his tour of duty, Johnston got a GCMG, and his book *The Uganda Protectorate* was published in 1901, following *British Central Africa* in 1897, but he got no further offers of employment under the crown.

For Johnston, during his middle years, nothing seemed to go right. In 1896 he had married the Hon. Winifred Mary Irby, daughter of Florance George Henry Irby, fifth Baron Boston, and stepdaughter of Percy Anderson, head of the Africa department of the Foreign Office. In 1902 she was delivered prematurely of twin boys, who both died within hours; there were no more children. In 1903 and in 1906 he stood unsuccessfully for parliament—his small stature and rather high-pitched, squeaky voice made him a poor platform speaker. From 1904 until 1909 he was associated with two companies interested in the development of Liberia, both of which failed.

In 1906 the Johnstons moved from London to Poling, near Arundel. Here he engaged in ceaseless literary activity, much of it ephemeral. His longest-lasting books were the early ones, describing his own explorations on the Congo and Kilimanjaro. The large works which he published during his official service, on British Central Africa and on the Uganda Protectorate, were too encyclopaedic to be of lasting value, as were his later works on Liberia and King Leopold's Congo, the latter based on the papers of George Grenfell. His *History of the Colonisation of Africa by Alien Races* (1899) deserves respect as the first attempt at a history of the entire continent and remained without a rival until the 1950s. The best monument to his scholarship, however, was without doubt his *Comparative Study of the Bantu and Semi-Bantu Languages* (2 vols., 1919–21), which set out the equivalents of some 250 words in 300 languages and dialects, for many of which he had himself collected the primary data. His classificatory analysis and historical interpretation of the evidence, though now outdated, were remarkable for the time. His natural history collections, which he sent to Kew, the British Museum, and the London Zoo, are more difficult to trace in detail, but his name is attached to many species and genera new to science at the time, notably the giraffe-like okapi of the Ituri Forest and the montane variety of the shrub senecio. In 1902 the University of Cambridge awarded him an Honorary Doctorate of Science, principally for his contributions to ornithology.

Johnston was for most of his life a social Darwinist, deeply dyed in racism, who talked about 'savages' and wrote comic verses about cannibals. However, his outlook was much changed by a journey to the United States and the Caribbean in 1908–9, when he met many distinguished people of African descent. In *The Negro in the New World* (1910) and in many of his later publications he stressed the importance of treating individuals as equal, regardless of their race. An agnostic in religion, he praised the work of Christian missionaries, whom he regarded as worthy agents in the evolutionary process. In 1923 he published his *Story of my Life*. In 1925 he suffered two strokes, which left him partly paralysed. He died on 31 July 1927 at Woodsetts House, near Worksop, and was buried at Poling.   ROLAND OLIVER

Sources R. Oliver, *Sir Harry Johnston and the scramble for Africa* (1957) • A. Johnston, *The life and letters of Sir Harry Johnston* [1929] • Burke, *Peerage* • *CGPLA Eng. & Wales* (1927) • Gladstone, *Diaries*
Archives CUL, notes on African languages • National Archives of Zimbabwe, Harare, corresp. and papers • NRA, priv. coll., corresp. and papers • RGS, travel journal • SOAS, papers relating to Bantu language | BLPES, corresp. with E. D. Morel • Bodl. RH, Cawston MS • Bodl. RH, letters to R. T. Coryndon • Bodl. RH, corresp. with Lord Lugard • Bodl. RH, Rhodes MS • CAC Cam., letters to W. T. Stead • Christ Church Oxf., Salisbury MS • National Archives of Zimbabwe, Harare, British South Africa Company MS • PRO, Foreign Office archives • RGS, letters to Sir J. S. Keltie • SOAS, letters to Sir William Mackinnon • U. Leeds, Brotherton L., letters to Sir Edmund Gosse • U. Newcastle, Robinson L., letters to Frederic Whyte
Likenesses T. B. Wirgman, pencil drawing, 1894, NPG • H. Pegram, bust, 1904 • H. Furniss, pen-and-ink caricature, NPG • J. Russell & Sons, photograph, NPG [*see illus.*]
Wealth at death £8047 7s. 11d.: probate, 5 Oct 1927, *CGPLA Eng. & Wales*

Johnston, Ian St John Lawson, second Baron Luke (1905–1996). *See under* Johnston, George Lawson, first Baron Luke (1873–1943).

Johnston, James (1655–1737), politician and government official, was born on 9 September 1655, the younger son of Sir Archibald *Johnston, Lord Wariston (*bap.* 1611, *d.* 1663), and his second wife, Helen, daughter of Alexander Hay, Lord Fosterseat. Following the execution of his father by the Restoration regime in Scotland, Johnston and his family went to the Netherlands. Later he studied civil law, having 'the character of the greatest proficient in the university of Utrecht' (*Carstares State Papers*, 92), and after the completion of his studies went to Italy. It was perhaps in Italy, where his cousin Gilbert Burnet and Henry Sidney were both travelling in 1686–7, or earlier in Utrecht or The Hague, that Burnet introduced Johnston to Sidney, the erstwhile courtier, diplomat, MP, and soldier in Dutch service, as a man 'both faithful and diligent … and very fit for the employment he was now trusted with' (*Bishop Burnet's History*, 3.278). This employment, on which Johnston was engaged at least by late 1687, was to assist Sidney with gathering intelligence of opposition in England to James II to convey to the prince of Orange.

After accompanying Sidney to England, Johnston made energetic use of extensive connections with, among others, leading Anglican clergy (whether personal or through Burnet or some other link is unclear) to report back to the Netherlands in encoded messages detailing the course of resistance to the government's religious and political policies. Acting 'with virtually plenipotentiary powers' (Jones, 234) he and Sidney engaged in long-running negotiations on William's behalf with figures such as William Penn. Johnston became the 'chief figure responsible' (Greaves, 318) for distributing literature expounding William's views on religious toleration, and following the birth of King James's son on 10 June 1688 advised the prince of Orange to sponsor a pamphlet casting doubt on the royal birth. The object was propaganda as much as conversion of those convinced of its authenticity: 'Even those that beleeve that there is a trick put on the nation will be glad to know why they themselves

James Johnston (1655–1737), by Thomas Gibson, c.1700

thinck so, and those that only suspect the thing, will be glad to find reasons to determine them' (Schwoerer, 70). Some time in the summer Johnston yielded to advice to him and to Sidney to leave England in case they were captured and their critical knowledge of William's clandestine correspondence revealed. However, according to Burnet, both men returned in October 1688, bringing 'a full scheme of devices, together with the heads of a declaration, all which were chiefly penned by Lord Danby' (*Bishop Burnet's History*, 3.284).

Following the accession of William and Mary, Johnston had his reward. In February 1689 he was sent as the king's extraordinary envoy and principal commissioner to Berlin, where he presented the elector of Brandenburg with the Order of the Garter on 6 June 1690. Johnston gave a speech at this ceremony where he commented on the military struggle with Louis XIV's France. He strongly argued for the need for continued military action as 'it is the sense of Mankind, that the Publick quiet can be no longer secured by the Faith of Treaties; and therefore, that a firm Peace is only to be obtained by a thorough War' (*An Account of … the Garter*, 16). In 1692 Johnston gave 'great service' to the strategic security of the Williamite regime in England by 'discovering the La Hogue descent' and it was reckoned that Johnston 'had better intelligence from France than any about King William' (*Carstares State Papers*, 93). This gave Johnston 'great credit at court, but created zealous enemies in both kingdoms' (ibid.).

The same year Johnston was recalled from Berlin and appointed one of the two secretaries of state in Scotland, the other being Sir John Dalrymple of Stair. Johnston was in charge of royal policy for the 1693 session of the Scottish parliament as Stair had gone to the continent.

During his tenure as secretary of state Johnston was described as 'always a zealous promoter of men of revolution-principles, and a faithful servant to that cause' (*Carstares State Papers*, 93), but he fell out of favour in 1695–6. Johnston was dismissed from office in 1696, alongside John Hay, first marquess of Tweeddale, high commissioner, for his role in allowing the royal assent to be given to the act for a company trading to Africa and the Indies which had been passed by the Scottish parliament on 26 June 1695. William stated that he had been 'ill served in Scotland, but that he would try to find a remedy for the evil which had been brought to his notice' (Macaulay, *History of England*, 1884, 2.733). Macky observed that 'what was very strange' about Johnston's dismissal was that the whigs, 'whose Interest it was to support him, joined in the Blow' (*Memoirs of the Secret Services*, 205). According to Macky, 'this soured him so, as never to be reconciled all the King's reign, tho' much esteemed' (ibid., 206); he was certainly never again employed by William.

Johnston had retained some connections with England. Following the death of his first wife, of whom nothing is known apart from that she was a relative of Adam Cockburn of Ormiston (revealed by Johnston in a letter to Carstares on 27 April 1693), in 1696 he married again in Salisbury, where Burnet was now bishop. His second wife was Catherine, third daughter of John *Poulett, second Baron Poulett (c.1615–1665) [see under Poulett, John, first Baron Poulett]. In 1702 Johnston took up residence at Orleans House, Twickenham, Middlesex. Having emerged as one of the leading advisers on Scottish affairs to Sidney, first earl of Godolphin, his political career was resurrected in 1704. The main objective of the court in the forthcoming parliamentary session was to secure the Hanoverian succession. Johnston was taken by the court ministers 'into a new management' and 'in concert with the marquis of Tweeddale and some others in Scotland' (*Bishop Burnet's History*, 5.171), Johnston proposed that the queen should empower her high commissioner to the 1704 session to agree to the type of constitutional settlement enacted by the Scottish parliament and accepted by Charles I in 1641. A revival of this settlement was to be in return for settling the Hanoverian succession. In return for this suggestion John Hay, second marquess of Tweeddale, was appointed as high commissioner to the forthcoming parliamentary session and Johnston was appointed as lord register and 'was sent down to promote the design' (ibid., 5.172). The office of lord register was described as 'the most lucrative employment' in Scotland (*Carstares State Papers*, 93). Ironically, the office of lord register had been held by Johnston's father under Cromwell and it was this political collaboration with the Cromwellian regime which had been one of the grounds for his father's execution.

Following the failure of the Tweeddale ministry to secure the Hanoverian succession in Scotland, Johnston was dismissed from office in 1705 along with Tweeddale, when 'the Duke of Queensberry and his friends were restored to favour' (*Carstares State Papers*, 93). Johnston played an important role in the *squadrone volante*, the group whose votes secured the ratification of the treaty of union in the Scottish parliament in the winter of 1706–7. From his house at Twickenham, Johnston was in correspondence with another leading figure in the *squadrone*, George Baillie of Jerviswood, throughout the union crisis. Johnston informed Jerviswood of the mood in London in the winter of 1706 and of preparations for a military invasion of Scotland to secure the union. Thus he informed Jerviswood that 'there shall be troops at hand on the Borders and in Ireland and from Flanders too, if they need them; and it's say'd ships of war too are order'd to your coasts' (*Correspondence of George Baillie*, 170). Johnston later informed Jerviswood of the glee in London following the securing of an incorporating union in 1707 and he also noted that in London 'the Whig Lords indulge themselves mightily in vilifying the Scottish nobility for their part in the Union' (ibid., 190).

Following his retirement from public affairs Johnston 'amused himself with planting and gardening, in which he was reckoned to have a very good taste' (*Carstares State Papers*, 93). Macky thought Johnston had 'the best collection of fruit of all sorts of gentlemen in England' and that one Dr Richard Bradley of the Royal Society 'ranks him among the first-rate gardeners in England' (J. Macky, *Tour through England*, 2nd edn, 1.63–4). In addition to possessing these skills he remained 'naturally active and restless in his temper' and he made 'frequent journeys into different kingdoms' (*Carstares State Papers*, 93). He went to Hanover on several occasions when George I was there and he 'often conversed with him very familiarly' (ibid.). Johnston was 'a great favourite of Queen Caroline, who was much entertained with his humour and pleasantry' although 'the freedom of his manners' had been 'rather disgusting to king William, who was often fretful and splenetic' (ibid.). One John McClaurin said of Johnston to Robert Wodrow, the famous minister of the Church of Scotland, that 'he keeps out a very great rank, and frequently has Mr. Walpool and the greatest courtiers with him at his country house near London; and the King sometimes does him the honour to dine with him' (*Diary of Sir Archibald Johnston*, 10).

Johnston died at Bath in May 1737 at the age of eighty-one and he was buried at Twickenham on 11 May. His son from his first marriage, James Johnston, was served heir-general on 13 March 1744. Writing in 1704 Macky described him as 'very honest, yet something too credulous and suspicious; endued with a great deal of Learning and Virtue; is above little Tricks, free from Ceremony; and would not tell a Lye for the World' (*Memoirs of the Secret Services*, 206). Macky also complimented Johnston as 'the first who shewed the Commons' of Scotland 'their Strength, and to establish them on a Foot independent on the Nobility (to whom they have always been Slaves) on the surest way to make their Constitution lasting, and to make them a flourishing People' (ibid., 205). From his Jacobite perspective, however, George Lockhart of Carnwath described him as a 'vile and execrable … wretch', although he was 'a shrewd, cunning fellow' (Szechi, 65).

JOHN R. YOUNG

Sources *State papers and letters addressed to William Carstares*, ed. J. M'Cormick (1774) · *Memoirs of the secret services of John Macky*, ed. A. R. (1733) · *Correspondence of George Baillie of Jerviswood, 1702–1708*, ed. G. E. M. Kynynmond (1842) · 'Fragment of the diary of Sir Archibald Johnston, Lord Wariston, 1639', ed. G. M. Paul, *Wariston's diary and other papers*, Scottish History Society, 26 (1896), 1–98 · *Bishop Burnet's History* · *The diary of Alexander Brodie of Brodie and of his son, James Brodie of Brodie, 1652–1685* (1740) · D. Szechi, ed., *'Scotland's ruine': Lockhart of Carnwath's memoirs of the union* (1995) · P. W. J. Riley, *King William and the Scottish politicians* (1979) · P. W. J. Riley, *The union of England and Scotland* (1978) · R. L. Greaves, *Secrets of the kingdom: British radicals from the Popish Plot to the revolution of 1688–89* (1992) · J. R. Jones, *The revolution of 1688 in England* (1972) · L. G. Schwoerer, ed., *The revolution of 1688–1689: changing perspectives* (1992) · *An account of the ceremony of investing his electoral highness of Brandenburgh with the order of the Garter: performed at Berlin on 6th June 1690* (1690)

Archives NA Scot., letter-book · NL Scot., corresp. with first and second marquesses of Tweeddale | BL, letters to W. Colt, Add. MSS 36662 · NA Scot., letters to Lord Melville · NL Scot., corresp. with first and second marquesses of Tweeddale · NRA, priv. coll., letters · NRA, priv. coll., letters to George Baillie · PRO, state papers, SP 3

Likenesses T. Gibson, portrait, *c*.1700, Orleans House, Richmond [*see illus.*]

Johnston, James (1819–1905), missionary and minister of the Presbyterian Church of England, was born in Sweethorpe, Berwickshire, on 18 December 1819, the son of Peter Johnston, of Sweethorpe, and Agnes Wilson. The family moved to Girrick Farm, Nenthorn, when Johnston was five. At the age of sixteen he was apprenticed to a draper in Nenthorn, and according to the practice of the time lived with his employer. After a five-year apprenticeship he went to London and found employment in the drapery firm of Swan and Edgar. During his time in London, Johnston associated with the group of young men, many of whom were employed in the drapery trade, whose prayer meetings and organizations for self-improvement led to the formation of the YMCA.

Johnston decided to enter the ministry in 1843 at the time of the Disruption of the Scottish church. His sympathies were with the Free Church faction but, as he was in England, he pursued his initial formal theological training there, attending King's College, London. He then went to Edinburgh University, and finally to the English Presbyterian College, London, where he took his theology degree. He was licensed by the presbytery of London and in 1853 was ordained into the Christian ministry as an educational missionary to China. It was Johnston's intention to establish a school in China on the model of Alexander Duff's English-medium institution in Calcutta, where the students were drawn mainly from the indigenous upper classes. After arriving in China he soon concluded that the conditions were not right there for such an endeavour. He joined the small Presbyterian mission headed by William Chalmers Burns at Paishui (Baishui), about 20 miles upstream from Amoy (Xiamen). His colleagues were forced to leave China for reasons of health, and Johnston, with the help of American Presbyterian missionaries, organized the small group of converts into a church. Johnston is credited with building the first 'gospel boat', manned by Christian sailors and designed for easy access to villages along the bays and inlets and upstream from coastal towns. Johnston himself had to leave China for reasons of health after little more than a year. After his return to Britain in 1855 he raised over £2500 towards the establishment of a college at Amoy.

Johnston next accepted an invitation in July 1858 to work at St James's Free Church in Glasgow, and for the rest of his career he combined his pastoral duties with activity on behalf of Christian missions, serving for some time as secretary to the Missionary Association of Scotland. Johnston was twice married: first on 4 August 1858 to Margaret Carson of Dumfries, and second on 6 January 1859 to Ellen Bland of Dryhorn. Ellen and James had four children; their two daughters, Jessie Marcia and Caroline, were both missionaries to China in the service of the English Presbyterian church, and both sons, George Patrick Noel and James Horace, entered the English Presbyterian ministry.

Johnston was attracted to modern statistical methods. In 1870 he conducted a survey of the population and ecclesiastical provision in Glasgow which led to the establishment of the church-extension movement in that city. In June 1877 he retired from his Glasgow ministry and moved with his wife to Norwood, Surrey. Here he continued his statistical work, largely on behalf of Christian missions. In the late 1870s he organized a political agitation to persuade the Government of India to spend more money on elementary education and to transfer management of high schools and colleges to private agencies, in accordance with principles first articulated in the education dispatch of 1854. The group called itself the council on education in India and brought together representatives of the various British missionary societies and a few former India hands, notably Lord Halifax who, in his capacity as president of the Board of Control, had been the author of the 1854 dispatch. Johnston was the public spokesman and chief publicist for the council. He presented its argument in 1880 in a large pamphlet called *Our Education Policy in India*, and he addressed the Statistical Society using the government's figures to demonstrate the high cost of direct government operation of schools when compared to aided schools under private management. The agitation led to the formation by the viceroy, Lord Ripon, of a commission on education in India (which reported in 1882 and shaped educational policy for the next decades). In 1881 Johnston was elected a fellow of the Statistical Society.

Johnston published more than twenty books and pamphlets on behalf of missions, most prominent among them his history of the English Presbyterian mission in China, entitled *China and Formosa* (1897). He was instrumental in calling and organizing the Centenary Conference on Protestant Missions of the World, held in London in 1888, and he edited the two-volume report of the conference for publication.

Johnston moved his residence to Willesden, London, and later to St Leonards, Sussex, where he died on 16 October 1905. He was buried at Willesden parish church.

DAVID W. SAVAGE

Sources records, United Reformed Church History Society, London · J. Johnston, *China and Formosa* (1897) · C. Binfield, *George Williams and the YMCA: a study in Victorian social attitudes* (1973) **Archives** U. Birm. L., Church Missionary Society archive **Likenesses** photograph, United Reformed Church History Society, London **Wealth at death** £3133 11s. 4d.: probate, 7 Nov 1905, CGPLA Eng. & Wales

Johnston, James Finlay Weir (1796–1855), chemist, was born at Paisley on 13 September 1796, the eldest son of James Johnston, merchant of Kilmarnock. At the University of Glasgow, where he supported himself by tutoring, he won prizes and medals in both science and humanities. After graduating MA in 1826 he went to Durham and opened a school. In 1829 he married Susan Ridley of Park End North, who was nineteen years older than he and from a wealthy Northumberland family. That year he visited the great Swedish chemist J. J. Berzelius, and ultimately convinced him that paracyanogen (which Johnston had analysed) had the same components in the same proportions as cyanogen. Johnston went on to attend the annual meeting of German men of science, and on his return to Britain allied with his friend and patron Sir David Brewster to proclaim the decline of science here and the need for an organization which would promote science, especially in the provinces. He was thus one of the founders of the British Association for the Advancement of Science, which met first in York in 1831, though never in the inner circle of scientific gentlemen who took charge of this important body.

In 1832 Johnston paid another visit to Berzelius's kitchen laboratory. This brought him prestige and fuelled his interest in the way atoms might be arranged in compounds; though chemical atomic theory was still very hypothetical in the 1830s, some inferences could be made. In 1837 he wrote an important report for the British Association meeting at Newcastle upon Tyne, on the relationship between chemical constitution and properties.

In 1833 Johnston was appointed reader in chemistry at the newly founded and staunchly Anglican University of Durham, despite belonging to the Church of Scotland. At Durham he strenuously promoted a course in engineering, which involved highly practical work and some advanced chemistry and mathematics. However, because industrialists refused to recognize paper qualifications from a university, the course, which was at first popular, did not ultimately succeed. In June 1837 he was elected fellow of the Royal Society, and was described in its list as professor of chemistry and mineralogy, which he was not; his (unopened) volumes of the society's *Philosophical Transactions* were bequeathed to New College, Edinburgh, indicating that at the Disruption he joined the Free Church.

Johnston became a successful popular lecturer and writer at a time when such activity did not diminish a professional reputation. In 1851 he published *Notes on North America*, following a visit there in 1849–50. This was concerned particularly with agriculture, on which he had become an expert—a good move in the 'hungry Forties'. His brief *Catechism of Agricultural Chemistry and Geology*

(1844) went through more than thirty editions in his lifetime, was widely translated, and was recommended by Tolstoy among others, and his more formal *Elements of Agricultural Chemistry and Geology* (1842) was also a great success, with a nineteenth edition in 1895. He provided introduction and notes for the Dutch professor G. T. Mulder's *Chemistry of Vegetable and Animal Physiology* (1845) and for Mulder's controversial claims against Liebig published in the following year. His *Chemistry of Common Life*, which was completed in 1855 just before his death, was a classic popularization of up-to-date science.

Johnston died at Durham on 18 September 1855 of a lung infection caught on the continent in the summer, and was buried at Croxdale, near Durham (as a sanitary reformer, he was an opponent of urban interments). He bequeathed the residue of his estate, after the death of his wife, for educational purposes in Durham; in 1899 part of this money was used to found the Johnston Technical School in Durham, which was still in being, as a comprehensive school, a century later.   DAVID KNIGHT

Sources G. R. Batho, 'A man of science: James Finlay Weir Johnston (1796–1855)', *The Johnstonian*, 27 (1976), 8 · C. Preece, 'The Durham Engineer Students of 1838', *Transactions of the Architectural and Archaeological Society of Durham and Northumberland*, new ser., 6 (1982), 71–4 · D. M. Knight, *The transcendental part of chemistry* (1978), 189–91 · J. Morrell and A. Thackray, *Gentlemen of science: early years of the British Association for the Advancement of Science* (1981) · J. Morrell and A. Thackray, eds., *Gentlemen of science: early correspondence of the British Association for the Advancement of Science*, CS, 4th ser., 30 (1984) · private information (2004)
Archives RS, articles and letters | NL Scot., corresp. with Blackwoods
Likenesses photograph, repro. in Batho, 'A man of science' · photograph, U. Durham

Johnston, James Henry (1787–1851), naval officer and developer of steam navigation, entered the navy in 1803 on the *Spartiate*, under the successive captains George Murray, John Manley, and Sir Francis Laforey. In her he was present at Trafalgar, and in 1809 at the operations on the coast of Italy. In December 1809 he was promoted lieutenant of the *Canopus*, still on the coast of Italy, and, after being invalided from her in the following year, was in September 1811 appointed to the sloop *Kite* employed in the North Sea, and afterwards in the Mediterranean. In December 1814 he was appointed to the *Leveret* (10 guns) on the home station, but in July 1815 was placed on half pay. Seeing no probability of further employment, and having friends in Calcutta, he went there in 1817, and obtained command of the ship *Prince Blucher*, in which he made two voyages to Britain. In 1821 he attempted to establish a sailors' home at Calcutta; it failed, but Johnston was favourably noted by the marquess of Hastings, who appointed him marine storekeeper, and, before he could enter on the duties, commissioner of the court of requests. However, Johnston returned to England to arrange his private affairs and never filled either office.

Johnston then turned his attention to steam navigation, and drew up a proposal for establishing steam communication with India via the Mediterranean and Red Sea. In 1823 he returned to India to lay his plans before the governor-general. They were not accepted, and Johnston, returning to England, was appointed to the *Enterprise*, a private steam-vessel, in which he sailed via the Cape of Good Hope to India, and arrived at Calcutta in December 1825. The steamer was immediately purchased for the East India Company's service, and sent to Burma, for the last nine months of the First Anglo-Burmese War. In 1829 Johnston was requested to report on the practicability of steam navigation on the Ganges, and after surveying the river was ordered to England to confer with the East India Company's court of directors. His plans, drawn up in concert with Thomas Love Peacock, were approved in 1831, and for many years the navigation of the Ganges was carried on in iron steamers built to his design. After returning to India in 1833, he was appointed controller of the company's steamers, which post he held until 1850. He was an important pioneer of the practical application of steam to oceanic and riverine service. On 8 July 1849 he was placed on the retired list of the Royal Navy with the rank of commander. On his passage home from Calcutta, after retirement, he died on 5 May 1851. He was married, and had at least one child.

J. K. LAUGHTON, *rev.* ANDREW LAMBERT

Sources J. Sutton, *Lords of the east: the East India Company and its ships* (1981) · E. C. Smith, *A short history of marine engineering* (1937) · R. Gardiner and B. Greenhill, eds., *The advent of steam: the merchant steamship before 1900* (1993) · *United Service Gazette* (19 July 1851) · O'Byrne, *Naval biog. dict.* · private information (1891) · Boase, *Mod. Eng. biog.* · GM, 2nd ser., 36 (1851)
Likenesses E. Morton, lithograph, NPG

Johnston, James William (1792–1873), politician and lawyer in Canada, was born on 29 August 1792 in Jamaica, the youngest son of William Martin Johnston (*d.* 1808), a surgeon, and his wife, Elizabeth, the daughter of John Lichtenstein and Catherine Delegal. The Johnston family migrated from Scotland to Georgia in the mid-eighteenth century and became prominent in government, but, being loyalists, they forfeited their estates at the end of the American War of Independence, and William Martin Johnston accepted a position in Jamaica. James Johnston was sent to Scotland to be privately educated. After his father's death in 1808 he went to live in Annapolis Royal, Nova Scotia, with his sister Elisabeth and her husband, Thomas Ritchie, a lawyer and member of the house of assembly. After serving as a clerk in Ritchie's office, Johnston was admitted to the bar in 1813 and practised in the Annapolis area.

In 1815 Johnston moved to Halifax, where his striking appearance (he was an angular man over 6 feet tall) and his penetrating intelligence helped him become established in society, though his position as a member of a prominent loyalist family undoubtedly played a part in his success. His status was further enhanced when he formed a partnership with Simon Bradstreet Robie, the provincial secretary and speaker of the assembly, which enabled him to establish strong political and economic links with those involved in such enterprises as the Bank of Nova Scotia. His élite connections were cemented in 1821, when he married Amelia Elizabeth Almon, the daughter of an influential Halifax doctor. She died on 20 March 1837, and on 4 August 1845 Johnston married Louisa Pryor Wentworth.

Nova Scotian society in the 1820s and 1830s was undergoing important changes as the traditional roles of church and state were challenged by the rise of sectarian politics. When, in 1824, Bishop John Inglis refused to recommend the appointment of an evangelically minded minister as rector of St Paul's Anglican Cathedral, Johnston unsuccessfully pleaded the minister's case in the court of chancery. This defeat led Johnston and a number of associates to establish in 1827 a Baptist church in Halifax, which became a dominant force within the provincial Baptist movement and helped to establish the credibility of a denomination which had hitherto been marginal. Johnston suffered no loss of social or political standing for joining the Baptists, possibly because his respect for social proprieties kept him from voicing publicly criticism of the bishop or the policies of the established church. He was appointed provincial solicitor-general in 1834, and his elevation in 1837 to the newly created legislative and executive councils clearly marked him as the leader of the anti-reform forces in the province. The two councils, which replaced the old council of twelve, were created by the British government in response to the demands from the house of assembly for greater political influence. As one of four delegates from Nova Scotia, Johnston met with Lord Durham in Quebec the following year and became a convert to the latter's concept of a legislative union of the British North American colonies, a position to which he adhered throughout his career.

As far as immediate political issues were concerned, Johnston, a firm believer in social order, feared that the programme of the reformers, or Liberals, would create social anarchy, and that, in particular, their demands for political patronage to reward supporters would undercut the class structure and lead to social instability. But, as a pragmatist, he agreed in 1840 to form a coalition with Joseph Howe, the effective leader of the Liberals in the executive council. This coalition arose after dissatisfaction at the limited extent of government reform had led the house of assembly to demand the recall of the governor, Colin Campbell. Johnston, who had strongly opposed this move, became attorney-general in 1841. He believed that the executive council must consist of representatives of a variety of interest groups, and was prepared to modify his political views in order to make the coalition a success. In 1843, however, when Howe supported a proposal to withdraw provincial grants from all denominational colleges, including Acadia University, a Baptist institution, he went into opposition. During the election campaign of autumn 1843 he resigned from the legislative council and won a seat in the assembly, where he managed to hold the Liberals at bay for two years as leader of the 'rump' administration. In 1846, after failing to resuscitate the coalition, he called an election, at which the Liberals secured a majority. The establishment of ministerial government on the British model followed shortly thereafter.

As opposition leader in the early 1850s Johnston opposed speculative railway building projects and proposed a series of measures, such as an elected legislative council as a check on the executive branch. Ideas such as this illustrated his shrewd and sophisticated intelligence, but it was Dr Charles Tupper, and not Johnston, who increasingly determined the policy of the Conservative Party. Tupper had absolutely no compunction about using political patronage, nor did he share Johnston's concern about social order. In 1857 Johnston once more became attorney-general and premier, after the Roman Catholic members of the assembly had defected from the Liberals to the Conservatives. His party was defeated in the 1859 elections but returned to office in 1863, and in May 1864 he was appointed to the newly created post of judge-in-equity. For Johnston this was at best a consolation prize, because he had long sought the position of chief justice; however, Sir William Young, his bitter rival since the early 1830s, had won this position in 1862. Although he retired from formal politics upon his judicial appointment, he remained thoroughly linked to the Conservatives and to the supporters of confederation. While in France in May 1873 he received an invitation to succeed Howe as lieutenant-governor of Nova Scotia. Although he accepted at first, ill health forced him to decline, and he died at Cheltenham, Gloucestershire, on 21 November.

Perhaps the most remarkable achievement of Johnston's career was his reshaping of the tory party to suit changing times. Although he much preferred a division of powers over the British model of cabinet government, he also appreciated when growing political unrest required a degree of flexibility and pragmatism. He knew the importance of reconciling sectarian politics with a deferential society. This achievement had a marked impact on the tone and nature of Nova Scotian politics in the 1830s and 1840s.

K. G. PRYKE

Sources D. A. Sutherland, 'Johnston, James William', *DCB*, vol. 10 · K. G. Pryke, 'Nova Scotia and Prince Edward Island consider an effective upper house', *Dalhousie Review*, 50 (1970–71), 330–43 · P. B. Waite, *The lives of Dalhousie University: Lord Dalhousie's college*, 1 (1994) · W. A. Calneck, *History of the county of Annapolis*, ed. A. W. Savary (1897) · J. Doull, 'Four attorney-generals', *Collections of the Nova Scotia Historical Society*, 27 (1947), 1–16 · B. Russell, 'Reminiscences of the Nova Scotia judiciary', *Dalhousie Review*, 5 (1925–6), 499–512 · M. C. Ritchie, 'The beginnings of a Nova Scotian family', *Collections of the Nova Scotia Historical Society*, 24 (1938), 135–54 · G. E. Levy, *The Baptists of the maritime provinces, 1753–1946* (1946) · G. W. Hill, 'History of St Paul's Church', *Collections of the Nova Scotia Historical Society*, 3 (1883), 13–70
Archives Public Archives of Nova Scotia, Halifax, family papers; letters | NA Canada, Sir Charles Tupper MSS, CO217/175; CO218/115; CO218/116; CO218/119; 218/125
Likenesses H. Sandham, portrait · H. Sandham, portrait (posthumous), Provincial House, Halifax, Canada

Johnston, John (*c.*1565–1611), scholar and poet, was born in Aberdeen, the son of Robert Johnston, merchant, and Isobell Boyes (*d.* 1616). He was educated at Aberdeen grammar school and King's College, and matriculated at the University of Rostock in August 1584, probably aged about nineteen.

After a year at Rostock, Johnston proceeded to the recently founded University of Helmstädt, and from there in 1587 to Heidelberg, where he was appointed a regent. At both universities he was the first Scottish student to matriculate. His first published work (no longer extant) belongs to this period, a rebuttal of an attack by the professor of philosophy at Helmstädt on the French humanist scholar Ramus.

In 1590 Johnston travelled to Zürich, where a municipal banquet was given in his honour, and to Bern and Geneva. However, the ongoing conflict between Geneva and Savoy caused him to decide in 1591 to return to Scotland. During his years on the continent he had gained a high reputation as a scholar and teacher, and had made the acquaintance of some of the leading philosophers and theologians of the period. On 8 November 1598 he married Catherine Melville (d. 1607).

At St Andrews, Johnston earned the regard of the presbyterian divine Andrew Melville, who secured his appointment as a master in St Mary's College; and for the next few years he was active as Melville's loyal ally in Scottish ecclesiastical and educational politics. During this period he wrote his *Inscriptiones historicae regum Scotorum*, a sequence of Latin verses on the Scottish monarchs from Fergus to James VI, and *Heroes ex omni historia Scotica lectissimi*, a similar series of verses mostly on heroes of war (Amsterdam, 1602, and Leiden, 1603). Those two books afterwards provided Alexander Garden with the models for his *Theatre of the Scotish Kings* and *Theatre of Scottish Worthies*. His power and influence, however, were undermined by the religious policy of James VI. James showed no personal animosity to Johnston, and even presented him with a ring for the dedication of his *Inscriptiones* to Prince Henry, but the king's determination to curb the power of the Presbyterian church overcame Melville's and Johnston's public protests. Johnston's diminished status was confirmed when Melville, deposed as principal of New College (St Andrews) in 1607, was succeeded at James's insistence not by Johnston but by Johnston's lifelong friend and associate, the Episcopalian scholar Robert Howie.

This disappointment, the death of his wife in the same year (two sons had already died in childhood), and his chronic and worsening ill health, clouded the last years of Johnston's life. His works of this period include *Consolatio Christiana sub cruce* (1609), a prose theological commentary prefaced by a personal memoir, and *Iambi sacri* (1611), a series of meditations in hexameters on points of faith and doctrine. Johnston died at St Andrews on 20 October 1611: his bequests included 1000 marks to Marischal College for the founding of a scholarship. Despite his active and dedicated life and the respect which he earned in his time, Johnston's lasting influence was slight, and the interest of his writings is mainly historical. He deserves to be remembered, however, as an admirable example of the cosmopolitan Scottish scholar. J. DERRICK McCLURE

Sources *Letters of John Johnston, c.1565–1611 and Robert Howie, c.1565–c.1645*, ed. J. K. Cameron (1963) • *DNB* • T. M'Crie, *The life of Andrew Melville*, 2 vols. (1819) • D. Irving, *The history of Scottish poetry*, ed. J. A. Carlyle (1861)

Archives Landesbibliothek, Gotha, corresp. • Staatsarchiv des Kantons, Zürich, corresp. • U. Glas., collection of continental theses • University Library, Hamburg, corresp. • Zentralbibliothek, Zürich, corresp.

Johnston, Sir John, third baronet (1647/8–1690), army officer and kidnapper, was born in Kirkcaldy, Fife, the son of Sir George Johnston, second baronet, of Caskieben, Scotland, and his wife, a daughter of Sir William Leslie, third baronet, of Wardes. According to an account written in 1714 Johnston was sent 'very young' into the army to 'raise his fortune' (Lucas, 29). He probably served abroad, possibly in the foot regiment of George Douglas, first earl of Dumbarton, which after 1678 was incorporated into the army of Charles II as the royal Scottish regiment. It was in this regiment that Johnston was commissioned as a first lieutenant in 1684. He was commissioned a captain of the new Scottish regiment under Colonel Wachop on 17 March 1688. Details of his military service are hazy at best: he appears to have served in the Netherlands where he was accused of rape, a charge he denied on the scaffold, and accused of the same offence while on a tour of duty in Chester in 1689, a charge he again denied. He may have been present at the battle of the Boyne.

Johnston was party to the abduction of Mary Wharton, daughter of Philip Wharton, an heiress worth £1500 p.a., from a coach outside the home of her aunt, Anne Byerley, in Great Queen Street, on 14 November 1690, following a dinner at the home of another conspirator, Archibald Montgomery. The girl, aged only thirteen, was taken to the home of a coachman named Watson in Westminster, and there married by William Clewer to the Hon. James Campbell, fourth son of Archibald, ninth earl of Argyll, and brother of Archibald, the tenth earl. The couple spent the night at Campbell's lodgings and the whole of the next day together. On the latter day, 15 November, a proclamation was issued for the arrest of Campbell, Montgomery, and Johnston, and on the 16th Johnston was taken and committed to Newgate, apparently after being betrayed by his landlord for the reward money. Mary Wharton was returned to her aunt and Campbell escaped abroad.

While Johnston languished in gaol awaiting trial, moves were afoot to annul the marriage. On 3 December 1690 the House of Commons rejected a clause to this effect in the bill preventing clandestine marriages. The bill was lost but a specific bill annulling the marriage was ordered to be brought in. This passed both houses despite a petition from the earl of Arygll on behalf of his brother claiming that the bill was 'to his brother's prejudice and dishonour of his family' (*JHC*, 10.503), and that the affair had been misrepresented to the house. In the Lords evidence was given by several witnesses and a deposition received from Dr Clewer that Mary Wharton had consented to the match.

Meanwhile, Johnston had gone on trial at the Old Bailey sessions of 10–17 December 1690. His basic defence agreed with Arygll's petition: 'I saw nothing in the whole affair but what I thought was justifiable by the laws of the kingdom' (*An Account*), as the lady had showed no sign of being forced or unhappy. However, Watson seems to have testified against him, and Clewer and several other witnesses he wished to call in his defence were on trial with him. Johnston was found guilty, although Clewer and the others were acquitted.

Great efforts were made to save Johnston's life, but the king would not do so unless appealed to by Mary's friends. Mary Wharton was in fact very well connected: her great-uncle was the aged Philip Wharton, fourth Baron Wharton, whose son, Thomas Wharton, was the king's comptroller of the household. Despite sixteen maids dressed in white appealing to the king, Johnston was executed at Tyburn on 23 December 1690, aged forty-two. His long dying speech denied the charges and brought tears to the eyes of many onlookers. His body was released to his friends and he was buried at St Giles-in-the-Fields on 24 December in a funeral attended by about thirty coaches of the Scottish nobility and gentry. Subsequently several printed papers retold the story of his life and death.

Perhaps significantly Mary Wharton married, in 1692, her cousin Robert Byerley MP, the son of Mrs Anne Byerley. Johnston was succeeded as fourth baronet by his cousin, John, who assumed the title about ten years after Johnston's death.   STUART HANDLEY

Sources GEC, *Baronetage* · *A proclamation for apprehending and seizing the persons that stole Mrs Mary Wharton* (1690) · *A brief history of the memorable passages and transactions that have attended the life and untimely death of the unfortunate Sir John Johnston* (1690) · W. Smythies, *A true account of several passages relating to the execution of Sir John Johnston* (1690) · *An account of the behaviour, confession and last dying speech of Sir John Johnston* (1690) · *The Proceedings … in the Old Bailey, 10–13 and 17 Dec. 1690*, 5–6 · *The manuscripts of the House of Lords*, 4 vols., HMC, 17 (1887–94), vol. 3, p. 217 · *JHC*, 10 (1688–93), 493–503 · N. Luttrell, *A brief historical relation of state affairs from September 1678 to April 1714*, 6 vols. (1857), vol. 2, pp. 128–48, 394 · *The life and times of Anthony Wood*, ed. A. Clark, 3, OHS, 26 (1894), 348 · T. Lucas, *Memoirs of the lives, intrigues, and comical adventures of the most famous gamesters and celebrated sharpers in the reigns of Charles II, James II, William III and Queen Anne* (1714), pp. 29–39 · C. Dalton, ed., *English army lists and commission registers, 1661–1714*, 6 vols. (1892–1904), vol. 1, p. 318; vol. 2, p. 153

Johnston, John Harold [Johnny] (1919–1998), songwriter and composer of advertising jingles, was born on 10 July 1919 in Paddington, London. His parents' names were James and Florence, and his father was a policeman. Johnston's early life was spent in and around the Praed Street area, and he received his schooling in Star Street. A self-taught pianist, in his early teens he formed a musical trio playing at neighbourhood pubs, taverns, and clubs.

The outbreak of the Second World War interrupted this developing talent. Johnston joined the Essex regiment, ultimately achieving the rank of major. He was initially posted to Kenya where, playing the piano in out-of-bounds Nairobi nightclubs, he was so frequently run in by the military police that he decided to join them. He was mentioned in dispatches in September 1945. While in Kenya he met and married in 1945 Nona Reine, *née* Sapiro (d. 1975), a White Russian by birth, who was educated in France and was a woman of considerable style and elegance. She was soon to run his office and mastermind the books. They had one daughter.

After demobilization Johnston was ever present in that hallowed London street of popular music dreams and instant stardom, Denmark Street, plugging songs to give them exposure on such outlets as jaunty Radio Luxemburg. An instinctive and intuitive musician, he formed the Keynotes group in 1948, rapidly winning national recognition with the fondly remembered signature tune to *Take it from here*, which featured Jimmy Edwards, Dick Bentley, and June Whitfield. Other signature tunes for well-received BBC light music and humorous programmes followed and in the 1950s he ran a veritable stable of musical groups. To stimulate sales of sheet music and, later, recordings, to cinema organists and singers, with Mickey Michaels he formed in 1951 his own production company, Michael Reine Partners. His first hit song, 'The Homing Waltz', was recorded by Vera Lynn, followed by the equally simple, sentimental, and popular 'Parting Brings Sorrow' and in 1953 by 'The Wedding of Lily Marlene', a sequel to the wartime international hit. Other national icons of the time, Alma Cogan and the Billy Cotton Band, also recorded his material. As a songwriter and arranger he worked for major stars Anne Shelton, Joy Nichols, and Dickie Valentine, and his backing groups the Johnston Singers and Johnston Brothers gave resonance to such runaway hit songs as 'Hernando's Hideaway', 'That Lucky Old Sun', and 'Tennessee Waltz', the last of which was, nearly half a century later, an enduring bitter-sweet memory for couples of a certain age. Hardly ever off the air, the Keynotes also made their first film appearance in a minor musical, *Melody in the Dark*. They were voted the country's top vocal group several times, but the advent of rock and roll killed off the group.

Johnston's imprint on 30 second snappy tunes was evident from the birth of television commercials on 22 September 1955, and as 'king of the jingles' for the next thirty years he could claim 4500 memorable and hummable snatches of song that added potency to advertising. No advertising agency had experience of jingle composition and so, with his friend and rival Cliff Adams, Johnston was first to capitalize upon a brand new marketing tool. In his first year he composed, arranged, and produced accompaniments to advertisements for Kleenex tissues, Stork margarine, and New Zealand butter. One of his earliest compositions was for a 'time spot'—a 7 second advertisement—that achieved a special kind of celebrity. Over a visual of a 'smiling mug' were sung the words 'Sleep sweeter, Bournvita', followed by a yawn and the word 'goodnight'. From Johnny Johnston Jingles Ltd came a cascade of classics. Singing to music from the *Nutcracker* suite, Frank Muir, for Cadbury's chocolate, made a memorable tribute to everyone's being a 'fruit and nut case'; legions of housewives sang along with 'mild green Fairy Liquid', and Bing Crosby warbled 'You can be sure of Shell'. Motorists, too, never tired of 'The Esso sign makes happy motoring', but perhaps his best ever was aimed at the kitchen millions who picked up a tin of beans and cried 'Beanz meanz Heinz'.

Lauded within the commercial radio and television industry, Johnston made his home in Boxmoor, Hertfordshire, a venue for friends and glitterati. While he remained largely anonymous to the wider public whose lives he coloured and touched, his business expanded to Europe and South Africa, leading to a period of tax exile in Geneva. On the death of his wife Johnny settled in London where, effervescent to the end, he died at 27 Circus Road, Westminster, on 10 June 1998. Due tribute was paid to him in 'Jingles all the way', a BBC Radio 4 *Archive Hour* documentary first broadcast on 18 December 1999.

GORDON PHILLIPS

John Lawson Johnston (1839–1900), by Elliott & Fry, pubd 1900

Sources 18 Dec 1999, BBC Radio 4, 'Jingles all the way', *Archive hour* · *The Independent* (12 June 1998) · *The Times* (13 June 1998) · J. Gable, *Tuppeny Punch and Judy show* (1980), pt 18 · private information (2004) [family] · d. cert.
Likenesses photographs, priv. coll.
Wealth at death £776,655—gross; £766,225—net: 21 Dec 1998, *CGPLA Eng. & Wales*

Johnston, John Lawson (1839–1900), nutrition promoter and food manufacturer, was born in Roslin, Midlothian, Scotland, on 28 September 1839, the eldest son of William Johnston and his wife, Jane, *née* McWilliam. His father was employed in the nearby gunpowder works until he was injured, after which he worked as a cobbler. Johnston was educated in Edinburgh and may have been intended for a medical career, but he served an apprenticeship in his uncle's butcher's shop in Canongate, Edinburgh. He subsequently studied with Lyon Playfair (1818–1898), then professor of chemistry at Edinburgh University, and this gave him an abiding interest in food chemistry and preservation. Johnston married Elizabeth Lawson (*d.* after 1900) in 1871; she was the daughter of George Lawson, a baker and confectioner based in Newington, Edinburgh. Johnston appears to have adopted his wife's surname on their marriage. They had thirteen children, six daughters and seven sons, two of whom went into their father's business.

A commercial opportunity occurred in 1874, in the aftermath of the Franco-Prussian War, when Lawson Johnston secured a contract from the French government to supply a large quantity of canned beef as emergency rations for its forts. He went out to Canada in 1874 to execute this order, and while he was there, he began a tomato-canning business, and also produced Johnston's Fluid Beef, a meat extract. This sold well in Canada as a hot drink, and Lawson Johnston demonstrated an appreciation of the value of marketing by offering tastings at the ice carnivals held every winter in Montreal.

A fire in his factory at Sherbrooke, Quebec, led Lawson Johnston to sell his North American business in 1880 and return to London. Within a few years he had established a factory at 10 Trinity Square, Tower Hill, from which he sold what was called 'Johnston's Fluid Beef (brand Bovril)'. The product was right for the time, when real wages were rising and a wider range of products could be included in the average shopping basket. It was also promoted as an alternative to alcoholic beverages at a time when there was growing publicity in favour of teetotalism. This, combined with Lawson Johnston's flair for publicity and marketing, led to a rapid growth in sales and it was not long before the clumsy appellation was shortened simply to Bovril.

In March 1889 the firm became a limited liability company with a paid-up capital of £120,000. Lawson Johnston's old Edinburgh friend, Andrew Walker, joined the company as managing director and a new factory was acquired in Farringdon Street, London. The product's success grew partly as a result of its innovative and striking advertising, aided by S. H. Benson (1854–1914), who joined Bovril in the early 1890s and then went on to establish his own business as an advertisers' agency; Bovril was among his first clients. Profits rose from £20,000 in 1894 to £90,000 in 1896, when the capital of the company was raised to £400,000 by means of a scrip issue. In that year the business fell into the hands of the notorious company promoter Ernest Terah Hooley (1859–1947), who bought the firm for £2 million and then relaunched it for £2.5 million. Lawson Johnston was persuaded to sell out to Hooley by various cronies, by his own desire to retire, and by the fact that George Lawson *Johnston, the son most involved in the firm, was away in South America seeking raw materials for Bovril. There was undoubtedly some financial chicanery from which Hooley and his associates made additional sums, such as 'puffing' the value of the shares by favourable comment in friendly newspapers and journals, insider dealing, creaming off the company's working capital, and careful manipulation of the allotment procedures. The relatively *laissez-faire* rules of the stock exchange allowed such devices and put little restriction on the honesty of the prospectus or of statements made by the promoter and his friends. The craze for industrial issues, sparked off by the bicycle boom of the mid-1890s, also meant that the public was favourably inclined to such shares, anticipating good returns from booming sales.

After the re-launch of Bovril, Lawson Johnston continued to serve as chairman. He was the single largest shareholder and remained the principal entrepreneur, for Hooley was not really interested in the internal working of the company and did not interfere. Lawson Johnston recruited impressive figures to the board such as Lyon Playfair, by that time Baron Playfair, and Dr Robert Farquharson, an MP and medical man interested in dietetics. Such directors encouraged the public perception of the product as one having medical value, and as an aid to healthy living. Lawson Johnston's careful canvassing of the medical profession, with the offer of trips around his factory, free samples, and similar inducements, reinforced the recommendation of Bovril as a restorative for invalids and recuperating patients. At the same time, any manufacturer who imitated Bovril's product, or any retailer who sold a substitute masquerading as Bovril, was swiftly prosecuted. The patriotic card was also played, with the firm providing rations to expeditions, to explorers, and to the British army, particularly in the Second South African War.

Throughout his life Lawson Johnston was an ardent teetotaller, and this fuelled his determination to find a nutritious substitute for alcohol. He was a lifelong Liberal, although he never stood for parliament, despite several invitations to do so. A committed nonconformist Christian, he attended Brighton Street Evangelical Union Church in his early days in Edinburgh, and Upper Norwood Presbyterian Church, London, later in life; and he remained an inconspicuous philanthropist. He retained his Edinburgh connections, rented Inveraray Castle regularly for the summer, and collected Scottish memorabilia. Lawson Johnston died on board his yacht, *White Ladye*, in Cannes harbour on 24 November 1900. He was buried in Norwood cemetery in London on 6 December, and was survived by his wife and thirteen children. He left an estate valued at £850,197. Lawson Johnston's significance lay in his commercial promotion of dietetics. He invented a product and founded a firm which became a household name, and he established a lucrative market for healthy foods.

JOHN ARMSTRONG

Sources Fortunes made in business: life struggles of successful people (1901–2), 203–8 • J. Armstrong, 'Johnston, John Lawson', DBB • P. Hadley, The history of Bovril advertising [n.d., 1970?] • J. Armstrong, 'Hooley and the Bovril Company', Business History, 28 (1986), 18–34 • H. H. Bassett, ed., Men of note in finance and commerce [1901], 128 • [Pentagon], 'Bovril and its new home in London', Grocery, 2/2 (1900), 115–28 • WW (1899), 554 • F. Harris, My life and loves, new edn, ed. J. F. Gallagher (1964) • J. Dicks, The Hooley book: the amazing financier, his career and his crowd (1904) • E. T. Hooley, Hooley's confessions (1925) • 'The great Bovril conversion', Chemist and Druggist (21 Nov 1896), vii–ix • The Times (26 Nov 1900), 11 • CGPLA Eng. & Wales (1901) • Daily Express (7 Dec 1900) • Daily Mail (26 Nov 1900)
Archives Companies House, Bovril Ltd
Likenesses Elliott & Fry, photograph, NPG; repro. in ILN, 117 (1900), 801 [see illus.] • engraving, repro. in Fortunes made in business • photograph, repro. in 'Bovril and its new home in London', frontispiece
Wealth at death £850,197 3s. 3d.: probate, 25 Jan 1901, CGPLA Eng. & Wales • over £1,000,000: Fortunes made in business: life struggles of successful people (1901–2), 203–8

Johnston, (Alexander) Keith, the elder (1804–1871), geographer and cartographer, was the fourth son of Andrew Johnston and his wife, Isabel, daughter of Archibald Keith of Newbattle. He was born on 28 December 1804 at Kirkhill, Midlothian, and was educated at the High School and the University of Edinburgh. Abandoning plans to study medicine, he was apprenticed in 1820 to the Edinburgh engraving firm of James Kirkwood & Sons, and in 1826 went into partnership as an engraver with his brother William *Johnston (1802–1888). On 3 August 1837 he married Margaret, daughter of Robert Gray of Edinburgh; they had eleven children, of whom six survived their father. In 1842 Johnston, who used the forename Keith throughout his life, made a tour of Germany and met some of the most eminent German geographers. For the rest of his life he lived mainly in Edinburgh, but visited Paris, where he met Alexander von Humboldt in 1845.

Johnston's first work of importance was the *National Atlas* (1843), which represented five years' work; most of its forty-five maps were drawn by Johnston himself. His most important work was the *Physical Atlas* (1848), intended originally as a version of Heinrich Berghaus's, but in fact an independent work. He collected much of the material for the *Atlas* in Germany and August Petermann came to Edinburgh to help with the work. Johnston knew he could expect no financial profit from the *Physical Atlas*, since physical geography was scarcely taught in Britain at this date. Among his other works a map of health and disease showed the influence of German thematic cartography and won the commendation of the medical profession. The use of lithography allowed the Johnstons to produce cheap educational and popular maps and atlases, through which Johnston hoped to establish the same respect for geography in Britain as it commanded in Germany. His multiple-sheet wall maps were of high quality and widely used in schools and other public institutions. The *Royal Atlas* (1861) became the firm's standard. Honours were heaped upon Johnston from an early date in recognition of his services to geography: he was geographer at Edinburgh in ordinary to the queen, fellow of the Royal Society of Edinburgh, honorary doctor of the University of Edinburgh, and medallist, honorand, or member of most of the world's important geographical societies. In 1851 he was awarded a medal by the London exhibition for his globe, the first to show the geology, meteorology, and hydrography of the earth. He was honorary secretary and one of the founders of the Scottish Meteorological Society.

Johnston died on 9 July 1871, at Ben Rhydding, Yorkshire, after what was probably a brain haemorrhage, and was buried on 14 July in the Grange cemetery, Edinburgh. He was a member of the congregation and a personal friend of Robert Candlish, whom, on the disruption in 1843, he followed to his new Free St George's Church, with which he remained closely connected throughout his life. He brought a religious zeal to his work in physical geography, hoping that it would give knowledge of God's

(Alexander) Keith Johnston the elder (1804–1871), by Maull & Polyblank

power in creation to a wider audience, especially to children. The Johnston partnership—which also encompassed William's and Keith's younger brother, Thomas Brumby (d. 1897); Thomas's sons Archibald, Thomas Ruddiman, James Wilson, and George Harvey; and Johnston's only son, (Alexander) Keith *Johnston, the younger—was one of the most important map-publishing firms of the nineteenth and twentieth centuries. Although best known for its geographical works, the firm did other types of engraving, notably, after 1862 when the Johnstons acquired the business of W. H. Lizars, the engraving of Scottish banknotes.   ELIZABETH BAIGENT

Sources *One hundred years of map making: the story of W. & A. K. Johnston* [1923] · F. Herbert, 'The Royal Geographical Society's membership, the map trade and geographical publishing in Britain, 1830 to ca 1930', *Imago Mundi*, 35 (1983), 67–95 · G. Engelmann, 'Der Physikalischer Atlas des Heinrich Berghaus und Alexander Keith Johnston's Physical Atlas', *Petermann's Mitteilungen*, 108 (1964), 133–49 · 'Presentation of the Royal Awards', *Proceedings* [Royal Geographical Society], 15 (1870–71), 241–51, esp. 247–51 [presentation to Johnston of the Victoria Medal, and summary of his work] · H. C. Rawlinson, *Proceedings* [Royal Geographical Society], 16 (1871–2), 304–6

Archives NL Scot., corresp. and papers | U. St Andr. L., corresp. with James David Forbes

Likenesses D. O. Hill, oils, 1866 (after calotype), Free Church of Scotland, Edinburgh · D. O. Hill, calotype, repro. in *One hundred years of map making*, frontispiece · Maull & Polyblank, photograph, RGS [*see illus.*]

Wealth at death £10,620 6s. 8d.: inventory, 19 Jan 1872, NA Scot., SC 70/1/156/265

Johnston, (Alexander) Keith, the younger (1844–1879), geographer and map publisher, was the only son of (Alexander) Keith *Johnston, the elder (1804–1871), and Margaret, daughter of Robert Gray of Edinburgh. He was born in Edinburgh on 24 November 1844, was educated at the Edinburgh Institution and the Grange House School, and was trained as a geographer and cartographer by his father and private tutors. From 1866 to July 1867 he was employed by the firm of Edward Stanford as superintendent of the drawing and engraving of maps. In 1867 he went to Germany to study the language and German geographical methods, notably those of August Petermann. On his return to Edinburgh in February 1868 he was employed in his uncle's and father's firm W. and A. K. Johnston, and was in charge of the geographical department of the London branch from June 1869. He was elected a life member of the Royal Geographical Society, of which he was map draughtsman and assistant curator from April 1872 to November 1873. Many of his maps from this period were published in the *Geographical Journal*.

In November 1873 Johnston was appointed geographer to an expedition commissioned by the government of Paraguay to survey the interior of the country. The expedition was much hampered by want of money, but Johnston none the less gathered some useful information, notably on the country's physical geography, which he published in the Royal Geographical Society's publications in 1875 and 1876. In June 1878 he was appointed leader of the Society's expedition to lakes Nyasa and Tanganyika and, leaving England in November 1878, reached Zanzibar in January and Dar es Salaam in May of 1879. The caravan of 150 men had scarcely left Dar es Salaam when Johnston contracted dysentery, and, too ill to walk, had to be carried on a stretcher. At Berobero, near what is now Kwa Mhinda along the northern banks of the Rufiji River, 120 miles from Dar es Salaam, he died from dysentery and malaria on 28 June 1879 and was buried beneath a fig tree on the trunk of which his initials and the date of his death were carved. Johnston's family later arranged with the then German administration for the erection of a large granite table with his name on it over his grave. The expedition was successfully completed by Joseph Thomson, geologist and general assistant to the party. Johnston's expedition diary (at the Royal Scottish Geographical Society) remained in private hands for over a hundred years, making Johnston's one of the least well-known African expeditions of the nineteenth century.

Johnston did not marry and his early death left his promising geographical work unfinished. Although his exploration attracted considerable notice at the time, his main legacy is his maps. Following his father's example, he published general and educational works with an emphasis on physical geography. Examples are his *Handbook of Physical Geography* (1870) and the *Book of Physical Geography* (1877). Other works, such as his 1870 'Map … showing the sources of the Nile recently discovered by Dr Livingstone', show his interest in exploration and discovery. He also revised the geographical works of others, as in his edition of T. Milner's *Universal Geography* (1876) and of

(Alexander) Keith Johnston the younger (1844–1879), by unknown engraver, pubd 1879 (after C. Henwood)

J. Bryce's *Library Cyclopaedia of Geography* (1880). Although many of his maps were published by the family firm, he continued to prepare maps, such as the African section of *Stanford's Compendium of Geography* (1878), for Stanford's until his death. ELIZABETH BAIGENT

Sources *Proceedings* [Royal Geographical Society], new ser., 1 (1879), 598–600 · J. Thomson, 'Notes on … the East Africa expedition', *Proceedings* [Royal Geographical Society], new ser., 2 (1880), 102–22 · *One hundred years of map making: the story of W. & A. K. Johnston* [1923] · private information (2004) [J. McCarthy] · J. McCarthy, *Journey into Africa: the life and death of Keith Johnston, Scottish cartographer and explorer (1844–79)* (2003)
Archives NL Scot., corresp. and papers | RGS, letters to Royal Geographical Society and papers
Likenesses portrait, repro. in Thomson, 'Notes on … the East Africa Expedition' · wood-engraving (after C. Henwood), NPG; repro. in *ILN* (23 Aug 1879) [*see illus.*]

Johnston, Lawrence Waterbury (1871–1958), garden designer and plantsman, was born in Paris on 17 October 1871, the only surviving child of Elliott Johnston (1826–1884), a banker from Baltimore, New Jersey, and his wife, Gertrude Cleveland Waterbury (*c*.1852–1926), a well-connected American heiress. He was brought up mainly in France, where his mother preferred to live; after his father's death his mother married in 1887 a New York lawyer, Charles Winthrop (*d.* 1898). Gertrude Winthrop dominated her son's life, allowing him no friends and little freedom; when he was twenty years old they moved to Great Shelford, near Cambridge, where he became a pupil of a Mr J. Dunn and prepared to enter the university. In June 1894 he entered Trinity College as a pensioner; he matriculated at Michaelmas of that year and graduated BA in 1897. He had enjoyed the friendships which Cambridge afforded, and one of his friends encouraged him to study farming and buy a farm at Crookham, Northumberland, near Coldstream. He became a British citizen in order to serve in the Second South African War, and received a commission in the Northumberland Fusiliers.

Mrs Winthrop found Northumberland remote and chilly; she persuaded her son that they should buy the small estate of Hidcote Bartrim, near Broadway in the Cotswolds, in 1907. It was Johnston's nature to study thoroughly and master his interests, and he turned first to architecture in order to restore the Hidcote Manor house and buildings, and then to garden design for the enlargement of the garden. In appearance he was small and militarily smart, combining a shy and reserved manner with birdlike energy; he loved to paint and play tennis and was welcomed into Broadway society by the artist Alfred Parsons and the American actress Mary Anderson de Navarro; he also formed links with many of the distinguished local gardening fraternity. Johnston set about the restoration of the old garden at Hidcote, enclosing adjoining fields to create wide vistas to the west and south and planting hedges of every variety to form small sheltered 'rooms'. Although he was nearly forty-three when the war started in 1914 he went to the western front as a major in the fusiliers: he later told his friend Alvilde Lees-Milne how he was wounded and left for dead until the officer of the burial party recognized him and saw him move. He was invalided home in 1915 and saw no further service.

While continuing to develop his garden at Hidcote Manor (with his head gardener, Frank H. Adams, from 1922 until 1939) Johnston also acquired a French property in a valley near Menton, La Serre de la Madone, where the winters were spent for the sake of Mrs Winthrop's health. She died in 1926, releasing Johnston to pursue his plant hunting in South America, South Africa, and the Far East. In 1930 Hidcote Manor garden was featured in an article in *Country Life*, which showed the well-grown structure of hedges and avenues of beech, holly, hornbeam, and yew and exhibited Johnston's wisdom in planning and planting them all so carefully. During the 1930s he concentrated upon filling the garden rooms with a lavish collection of rare and beautiful flowers and shrubs, his tastes and enthusiasms being shared with his closest gardening friend of those years, Norah Lindsay. Johnston maintained the garden throughout the Second World War, but it was still known to only a comparative few outside the horticultural world. However, it attracted much attention when Johnston announced that he wished to retire to his French home for the sake of his health, leaving Hidcote Manor to Mrs Lindsay. She died suddenly in 1948, and it was largely because of a campaign by Vita Sackville-West that the National Trust acquired Hidcote Manor on behalf of the nation, entirely on the merit of the garden. Johnston, who never married and remained a devout Roman Catholic throughout his life, died at La Serre de la Madone on 27 April 1958 and was buried there. His garden in Hidcote, maintained to his design and with many of his favourite planting schemes, is now regarded as one of the most influential of twentieth-century gardens, of enduring appeal and inspiration as a network of small private garden rooms. It became one of the most visited of British gardens. JANE BROWN

Sources A. Lees-Milne, 'Lawrence Johnston', *National Trust year book* (1977–8), 18–29 · E. Clarke, *Hidcote: the making of the garden* (1989) · J. Brown, *Eminent gardeners* (1990), 48–59 · V. Sackville-

West, 'Hidcote Manor garden', *RHS Journal*, 74/2 (1949), 476–81 •
H. A. Tipping, 'Country homes, gardens old and new—Hidcote
Manor, Gloucestershire', *Country Life*, 67 (1930), 286–94 • H. A. Tip-
ping, 'Early summer at Hidcote Manor', *Country Life*, 68 (1930), 231–
3 • *House and Garden*, 3/4 (1948), 47–51 • S. Lacey, *Gardens of the
National Trust* (1996), 139–44 • *CGPLA Eng. & Wales* (1958)
Likenesses photograph, repro. in *House and Garden*
Wealth at death £2922 19s. 4d.: probate, 30 Oct 1958, *CGPLA Eng.
& Wales*

Johnston, Nathaniel (*bap.* 1629?, *d.* 1705), political theorist and antiquary, was the eldest son of John Johnston (*d.*
1657) and Elizabeth Hobson, and was the brother of Henry
*Johnston. John was Scottish and lived for some time at
Reedness in Yorkshire; he was also apparently rector of
Sutton upon Derwent. Nathaniel (born in 1627 according
to the *Dictionary of National Biography*) was probably the
Nathaniel Johnston, son of John Johnston, who was baptized on 9 January 1629 at Whitgift, Yorkshire, which is
very close to Reedness. Nathaniel was probably admitted
at St Leonard's College, St Andrews, in 1647. In 1653 he
married Anne (*d.* 1681), daughter of Richard Cudworth of
Eastfield, Yorkshire, and had four sons, and one daughter,
Anne. He was incorporated MA in 1654 at Cambridge, and
graduated MD from King's College in 1656. He practised
medicine at Pontefract in Yorkshire, but moved to London
in 1686, where he at first lived 'at the iron balcony' in
Leicester Street, by Leicester Fields; Anthony Wood dined
here with him in September 1688. He was created a fellow
of the Royal College of Physicians by the 1687 charter of
James II, being admitted on 12 April that year.

In 1686 Johnston made a mark as a political theorist. His
480-page folio *The Excellency of Monarchical Government* was
the last major statement of absolutism prior to the fall of
the house of Stuart, a book dedicated to James II and
placed 'at Your Sacred Feet' (sig. A1*r*). It was printed at his
own charge, and sold for 8s. in sheets and 12s. bound; a
manuscript draft survives in the Wellcome Library. Johnston's topics are patriarchalism, the divine origin of government, the evils of democracies and republics, the virtues of princes and hereditary monarchy, the attributes of
sovereignty, the duty of non-resistance, and the
'prognosticks' of faction and sedition. The book is satur-
ated with erudition, but, unlike the clerical tories, this is
chiefly of a classical rather than scriptural kind. Above all,
he relies on Aristotle, 'the Philosopher', but also Cicero
and Tacitus. The classical ideal of citizenship is skilfully
moulded into a vision of good magistracy, counsel, and
courtiership. Bodin and Lipsius are invoked, as are also
English and Scottish absolutists such as John Nalson and
Sir George Mackenzie; but absolute though Johnston's
monarch is, he repudiates the oriental despotism he identifies with Hobbes, and absorbs the legal constitutional
tradition of Bracton, Fortescue, and Coke. The fallen whig
leader, the earl of Shaftesbury, is never named; instead
Tacitus's story of Sejanus is retold.

While most high tories abandoned the crown in defiance of James II's Catholicism, Johnston stuck loyally to
the king's cause. In 1687 he published *The Assurance of
Abbey and other Church Lands*, a promise that a Catholic
regime would never reclaim the church lands laicized at
the Reformation. (It answered a tract by Sir William Coventry which was in turn answered by John Willes.) The
next year Johnston issued *The King's Visitatorial Powers Asserted*, a vindication of the crown's assault on Magdalen College, Oxford. He recounts the affair in every detail, and
provides a large tranche of earlier precedents by which
university statutes were dispensed by royal mandate, and
often at the request of the university itself. These two
works were commissioned by the king and published by
the king's printer.

All this guaranteed Johnston's ruin at the revolution of
1688. From 1693 he was receiving charitable gifts from the
earl of Huntingdon in return for newsletters about political affairs in London. In 1695 Ralph Thoresby reported
that he had visited 'poor Dr Johnston, who, by his
unhappy circumstances, is little better than buried alive'
(*Diary of Ralph Thoresby*, 1.301). In the following year Abraham de la Pryme recorded that 'The doctor is exceeding
poor … He has been forced to skulk a great many years,
and now he lives privately with the Earl of Peterborough,
who maintains him. He dare not let it be openly known
where he is' (*Diary of Abraham de la Pryme*, 114). Among his
friends were the deposed Irish nonjuror bishop William
Sheridan and the Jacobite bishop of St David's, Thomas
Watson. The marquess of Halifax allowed him access to
his library.

Johnston's *Dear Bargain* (*c.*1690) is one of the most
important and most quoted of early Jacobite treatises, a
comprehensive indictment of the new Dutch tyranny of
William of Orange, its arbitrary acts, its fiscal exactions,
its Calvinist indifference to Anglicanism. It predicted 'a
long train of war, famine, want, blood and confusion,
entailed upon us and our posterity' as divine punishment
for rebellion (p. 24). Yet it also cleverly played upon 'country' hostility to the Williamite court, and the sense of disil-
lusion with the revolution among its supporters. It helped
forge a tradition that can legitimately be called 'whig Jacobite'.

From the 1660s Johnston was an indefatigable antiquary. For three decades he collected materials on the history of Yorkshire, most of which he kept at his house at
Pontefract, but he never managed to complete the writing
of a history, which was to have been modelled on Sir William Dugdale's *Warwickshire* and Robert Plot's *Natural History of Staffordshire*. He proposed to write up his 'antiquities' parish by parish, describing the owners of estates,
their pedigrees and seats, their arms, monuments, and
funerary inscriptions. In this project he made extensive
use of the manuscripts of Roger Dodsworth. In turn he
befriended and encouraged Ralph Thoresby, a Yorkshire
antiquary of the next generation; they met in 1682. He
wrote, but never published, substantial histories of the
earls of Shrewsbury. Johnston's notebooks ran to over 100
volumes. They were described in *Catalogi MSS Angliae*
(1697); Bishop Gibson had access to them in the eighteenth century. Many were lost; some survive, but scattered in several archives. Extensive correspondence is

extant: particularly with Thoresby, the earl of Huntingdon, Peter Le Neve, and Thomas Smith. Johnston's interests were scientific too. In the 1670s he corresponded with Martin Lister on such subjects as dissections of animals, bladder stones, mine drainage, sulphur, alum stone, and marcasite. With Thoresby, he also studied coins and medals.

Johnston died in London at some point between 17 September 1705, when his will was dated, and 25 September, when it was proved. His will notes that he was of the parish of St Margaret, Westminster, and bequeaths his worldly goods to his son Nathaniel, an oilman of Watling Street. Johnston's Pontefract estate was ordered to be sold by chancery in 1707.

Johnston's grandson, **Pelham Johnston** (1671–1765), physician, was born in York, the son of Nathaniel's eldest son, Cudworth Johnston (1654–1692), a physician, and his wife, Margaret, the daughter of John Pelham of Hull. He was educated at the Sedbergh School, and was admitted as a sizar at St John's College, Cambridge, on 2 May 1700. He proceeded MB in 1711 and MD in 1728, and was made a fellow of the Royal College of Physicians on 30 September 1732. He may also have had some foreign training, as a Pelham Johnston was noted at the University of Padua in January 1715. He married Anne, the daughter of Maximilian Western of Abington, Cambridgeshire, with whom he had two daughters, Anne and Frances. He outlived his wife, dying at Westminster on 10 August 1765. The administration of his estate was granted to his daughters on 13 August.   MARK GOLDIE

Sources *The diary of Ralph Thoresby*, ed. J. Hunter, 2 vols. (1830) · [J. Hunter], ed., *Letters of eminent men, addressed to Ralph Thoresby*, 2 vols. (1832) · J. R. Bloxam, ed., *Magdalen College and James II, 1686–1688: a series of documents*, OHS, 6 (1886) · *The diary of Abraham de la Pryme, the Yorkshire antiquary*, ed. C. Jackson, SurtS, 54 (1870) · Wood, *Ath. Oxon.*, new edn · *Report on the manuscripts of the late Reginald Rawdon Hastings*, 4 vols., HMC, 78 (1928–47), vol. 2 · *Sixth report*, HMC, 5 (1877–8) · Munk, *Roll* · LondG, 4317 (1707) · IGI · Venn, *Alum. Cant.* · J. Hunter, *Familiae minorum gentium*, ed. J. W. Clay, 3, Harleian Society, 39 (1895), 927 · J. Ingamells, ed., *A dictionary of British and Irish travellers in Italy, 1701–1800* (1997) · administration, PRO, 6/141, fol. 327v [P. Johnston]

Archives Bodl. Oxf., corresp., collections, transcripts, notes, extracts, abstracts, antiquarian and genealogical notes and papers · Magd. Oxf., papers, MS 418 · W. Yorks. AS, Leeds, corresp. and MSS · W. Yorks. AS, Leeds, medical corresp., notebook, antiquarian notes, MSS, collections relating to Pontefract and Yorkshire · Wellcome L., medical MSS, prescription book, and MSS, MSS 3083–3086 | BL, genealogical account of the Lovetot, Furnival, and Verdon families, Harley MS 6158 · BL, collections relating to the Talbot, Lovetot, Furnival, and Verdon families, Add. MS 18446 · BL, genealogical accounts of Yorkshire families, Egerton MS 3402 · Bodl. Oxf., notes and pedigree of Constable family · Bodl. Oxf., indexes and MSS relating to Dodsworth MSS · Bodl. Oxf., letters to Thomas Smith · Hunt. L., letters to the earl of Huntingdon · Norfolk RO, letters to Peter Le Neve · Notts. Arch., genealogical account of the Foljambe and Reigate families · Sheff. Arch., antiquarian notes and papers, incl. genealogical collections relating to the earls of Shrewsbury and topographical notes relating to wapentakes of Tickhill and Strafforth · U. Nott., deeds relating to the Talbot family [transcripts] · W. Yorks. AS, Leeds, letters to Ralph Thoresby

Johnston, Pelham (1671–1765). *See under* Johnston, Nathaniel (*bap.* 1629?, *d.* 1705).

Johnston, Priscilla. *See* Buxton, Priscilla (1808–1852).

Johnston, Sir Reginald Fleming (1874–1938), colonial administrator and Sinologist, was born at Goshen House, Jordan Lane, Morningside, Edinburgh, on 31 October 1874, the second of three children of Robert Fleming Johnston (1840–1902), writer to the signet, and Isabella Anne Catherine, *née* Irving (1853–1916). He was educated privately, and at Falconhall, Edinburgh, then at the University of Edinburgh (1892–4) and Magdalen College, Oxford (1894–8). To Oxford he remained somewhat romantically in thrall for the rest of his life—the poems in his first published work, *The Last Days of Theodoric the Ostrogoth* (1904), bear out this affection.

Administrator and traveller, 1898–1918 Scotland, and an unhappy home life, were left rapidly, and with some alacrity. After graduating with a second in history in 1898, Johnston, desperate to avoid returning home but failing to enter the Indian Civil Service, settled for a cadetship in the Hong Kong colonial service. This scheme combined Cantonese language training with fast track promotion: Johnston served variously as acting assistant colonial secretary (1899–1904), and private secretary (1900–02) to Governor Sir Edward Blake (1840–1918). He also made the first of the journeys which punctuated his career, travelling overland from French Indo-China, through China's Yunnan province and Laos, to Bangkok in 1902. On this trip he discovered enjoyment in the solitude of wandering, and visiting places rarely seen by Europeans; indeed, Johnston found his ideas about what constituted 'civilization' uprooted. In fact, such was his bad luck that he had no choice in the matter, being at one point abandoned by his luggage bearers and forced to continue with only what he could carry himself.

In 1898 Britain acquired the lease of Weihaiwei, on the coast of China's northern Shandong province. Here Johnston was seconded in 1904 at the behest of the governor, Sir James Stewart Lockhart. Isolation in Weihaiwei initially appealed because it shielded Johnston from the possible exposure in Hong Kong of the scandal of his late father's bankruptcy—revealed only after his death in July 1902. Johnston stayed for fourteen years, serving as secretary to the government (1904–6), then senior district officer and magistrate (1906–17), and acting administrator (1917–18). Stewart Lockhart and Johnston became firm friends; both were interested in China as administrators, but also as scholars. Johnston's fine linguistic abilities smoothed his move, and he developed a keen intellectual interest in Chinese social and religious practices in the territory. About these he later wrote *Lion and Dragon in Northern China* (1910), a sympathetic and enduringly useful portrait. Early plans for development of Weihaiwei withered and it became a relative backwater; an important summer base for the Royal Navy's China station, it became chiefly known as a summer resort. Amicable relations with the newly acquired Chinese subjects were established through the principle of governing them less by the Colonial Office book, and more like traditional Chinese magistrates. Johnston took to this smoothly, happily quoted the Confucian classics in his court judgments, and in time came to be living out an isolated and almost orientalist fantasy life in the small town of Wenquantang, where he was based.

Quiet even by the unexacting standards of British official posts in China, Weihaiwei proved an ideal location for Johnston's developing literary career, and a good base for further expeditions. Almost his first official duty was to deliver a photograph of Edward VII to Qufu, the ancestral home of Confucius. He found such work more than congenial, revelling in the ceremonial, and in the rare journey he was able to make. In 1906 he travelled—accompanied by his bull terrier, Jim—for six months across China to Burma (written up as *From Peking to Mandalay* in 1908). Johnston's attempt to penetrate to Tibet on this physically arduous hike was thwarted, but he did become the first Briton to meet the thirteenth Dalai Lama in July 1908, when on another trip to Buddhist sites in central China.

Fiercely anti-Christian, he also found time to publish, under the pseudonym Lin Shao Yang, an attack on protestant missions in China, *A Chinese Appeal to Christendom Concerning Christian Missions* (1911). Another volume, *Letters to a Missionary* (1918), expanded on correspondence with Stanley P. Smith, who had been expelled from the China Inland Mission in 1902. Johnston's atheism was humourless, and privately coarse. His anger with Christianity was a reaction against the high-church Anglicanism of his early upbringing; his was a quarrel with God, as much as with the mission enterprise—although he claimed the latter was as morally indefensible as the opium trade. Upsetting the mission establishment in China undoubtedly cost him one position at Hong Kong University in 1918; Johnston later claimed that the missionary dominance of the senate also lost him the vice-chancellorship.

When not sparring with Christianity, Johnston's was an important voice in the foreign discovery of Chinese Buddhism—not the popular Buddhist folk religion practised in China (although he argued against prevailing foreign prejudices concerning monasteries and their inhabitants), but the philosophical and religious system. He developed a keen interest in contemporary movements in the Buddhist community, developed close relations with its leaders, and published a useful volume, *Buddhist China*, in 1913. Johnston delighted in the reputation he thereby acquired among his horrified British colleagues and acquaintances as a Buddhist, and mused at length about retiring to the Buddhist complex at Putuoshan. Johnston always revelled in nonconformity, whether it was his praising of the elegance of the traditional Chinese *kowtow*, which most Europeans considered demeaning, or his enthusiastic approval for the Men's Dress Reform Party (1929). Many of Johnston's views and activities were certainly distorted in the re-telling (not least by himself), but

he evidently did not play the game, as a colonial civil servant or as a Briton.

Imperial tutor Unsurprisingly, Weihaiwei proved a career dead end, and Johnston concentrated instead on travel, and contemplation of meditative retirement. His fate was sealed in a different way, however, in November 1918, when he was appointed English tutor for three years to Asin Gioro Puyi, the Xuantong emperor, whose abdication in 1912 in the face of revolution had seen the establishment of the Chinese republic. Puyi had been allowed to live on with his retinue in the imperial palace. Johnston was seconded from the colonial service to begin what can only be labelled a passionate love affair with the person and idea of the former Manchu emperor. The experience warped his judgement, and ruined his official career—but it brought him lasting fame.

The three years turned to five. From teaching the young man English, and British constitutional history, introducing him to opticians (1921) and tennis (1923), Johnston became a confidante and adviser in internal palace affairs (notably a long struggle to outwit the imperial eunuchs) and relations with the merry-go-round of warlord presidents. His linguistic talents, and sensitivity and sympathy for traditional China, had attracted those who sought him out as tutor, and their choice was well rewarded. Johnston, too, benefited handsomely; Puyi showered him with gifts, appointments (warden of the Summer Palace in 1924), and titles. The former senior district officer—and well-known snob—took no small pleasure in addressing his letters from 'The Forbidden City'.

In Beijing, Johnston played out his affectations and passions on a larger stage than was possible in backwoods Weihaiwei. He became actively involved in the small local circle of foreign Sinologists, and met not only Chinese scholars of the old school—such as his fellow tutors—but contemporary writers and thinkers in one of the most turbulent periods of modern Chinese cultural history. He also deepened his reputation as a serious scholar of Chinese, publishing *The Chinese Drama* (1921), and articles on cultural and contemporary topics. Enjoying, for example, his status as wearer of the 'Hat Button and Robes of the First Rank', and delighting in his imperial access, he found time for more studied eccentricity. At a temple built for him west of Beijing by one president of the republic, Johnston erected memorial tablets to Shelley, Blake, and Keats (offerings to Shelley's memorial apparently proving satisfactory for infertile Chinese women supplicants). At this rural retreat he wooed, intellectually, a succession of women visitors to Beijing, including the historian Eileen Power and the novelist Stella Benson.

Puyi's position was far from secure. Already once used as a puppet in a short-lived restoration in 1917, the emperor was a suspect figure. On 5 November 1924 warlord troops expelled him from the Forbidden City. Johnston became decisively involved in the young man's flight shortly thereafter to what proved to be the ambiguous security of the Japanese legation, and then to the Japanese concession at Tianjin. For the best part of the succeeding year he appears to have busied himself with advising his protégé.

Johnston's deep involvement in and sympathy for the imperial sideshow to Chinese politics won him no friends among British officials. It led to his being passed over for the position of colonial secretary in Hong Kong in 1926, and Sir Miles Lampson, then British minister to China, vetoed his proposed appointment as governor of the colony in 1929.

Return to Britain Johnston re-entered British employ discreetly, as secretary to the Boxer Indemnity Delegation in 1926, a job he found disagreeable but which took him to Britain where he rediscovered the Scottish countryside of his youth. The following year he returned to Weihaiwei as commissioner. His last years in this 'nondescript appendage' to the British empire (R. F. Johnston, *Lion and Dragon in Northern China*, 1910, 2) were quiet, enjoyably sociable, but somewhat bitter as it became clear that the Colonial Office had no further use for him. Responsible for overseeing the territory's transfer to Chinese rule in 1930, Johnston governed his charges in a decent and patrician manner, and still found time to attempt to play on the larger political stage. Weihaiwei was handed over smoothly in October 1930, and Johnston returned to Britain, which he had visited only twice in thirty-two years, and to his fiancée. Johnston had become engaged to Eileen Power in 1928, but she finally called off the marriage in 1932, largely in reaction to Johnston's bullish timorousness. Despite a number of serious love affairs, Johnston spent much of his life in personal (and where possible professional) seclusion, and his fear of intimacy is clearly recorded in the papers of his friend Stella Benson. He remained a bachelor.

Having from very early in his career considered an academic appointment, Johnston applied successfully for the chair of Chinese at London's School of Oriental Studies in 1930. This was a high-profile appointment for the school, as Johnston was publicly well known and well connected, but his years there (1931–7) were hardly satisfactory. He baulked at administration, and at his colleagues, although he survived an attempt to unseat him in 1934 and by all accounts was an inspiring teacher. During his professorship Johnston published two encomiums for the vanishing China he so loved. *Confucianism and Modern China* (1934) mingled attacks on the Chinese New Culture movement and the republic with support for the Confucian principles underpinning the new Japanese-sponsored regime in Manchuria. Johnston had kept up his close ties with Puyi, despite the latter's accession to the throne of this puppet state. Sir Reginald (CMG, 1928; KCMG, 1930) published *Twilight in the Forbidden City* in 1934; this was partly a memoir and partly a propaganda text supporting Puyi's enthronement. His affection for traditional China, although perfectly consistent, led him to a position quite out of sympathy with his times. A visit to Japan and Manchuria in 1935 was viewed with horror by the Foreign Office, and proved once and for all the essential naïvety of his political thinking.

Johnston dreamed of retreat and reverie in China, but civil strife and disorder, and Japanese invasion, made such plans impossible. Instead he started looking for an island closer to home, buying Eilean Righ, on Loch Craignish, near Kilmartin, Argyll, in 1934, and constructing a house and a building for his extensive library. He retired from the professorship in 1937, but died shortly thereafter, on 6 March 1938, in a nursing home at 19 Drumsheugh Gardens, Edinburgh, from complications arising from an operation to remove a kidney stone. Johnston's ashes were scattered on the loch by Mrs Elisabeth Sparshott—the last of the women he almost married—to whom he left everything in his will. The library was donated to the School of Oriental Studies but his personal papers were destroyed on his instructions.

Sir Reginald Johnston was a complex and intriguing figure. Essentially a solitary man with a few intensely close friendships, he was a lover of conversation, and by all accounts an adept flirt. His dignity was easily upset, his vanity easily appealed to. Johnston was deeply sensitive to place, to mountains, islands, and to nature in the wild, but most of all to a China that faded in tandem with his career. New China's nationalism and iconoclastic modernity he found antipathetic, and this is reflected in his writings, political sympathies, and political misjudgements. Johnston's sensitivity of spirit was not, however, moved by the protestantism of his native Scotland, and his public spats with the mission enterprise were extraordinary for their time, and his position. His record as an administrator was honourable, although success and serious responsibility eluded him; his record as a scholar is longer lasting. Johnston's efforts as a sympathetic communicator to a Western audience of the realities of Chinese life, society, culture, and most importantly religion, remain his greatest achievement, but he is remembered most of all—not least because of Peter O'Toole's affectionate portrayal of him in Bertolucci's film *The Last Emperor* (1987)—as tutor to Puyi, and as a stolid Scottish foil to an 'exotic' Chinese anachronism.   ROBERT BICKERS

Sources correspondence with J. H. S. Lockhart, NL Scot., vols. 9–10, 10a · administrative files, SOAS, R. F. Johnston file · R. F. Johnston, *Twilight in the Forbidden City* (1934) · M. Berg, *A woman in history: Eileen Power, 1889–1940* (1996) · *DNB* · S. Benson, diaries, CUL · R. A. Bickers, '"Coolie work": Sir Reginald Johnston at the School of Oriental Studies, 1931–37', *Journal of the Royal Asiatic Society of Great Britain and Ireland*, 3rd ser., 5 (1995), 385–401 · S. Airlie, 'The Scottish mandarin', unpubd MS · Colonial Office and Foreign Office papers, PRO · S. Airlie, *Thistle and bamboo: the life and times of Sir James Stewart Lockhart* (1989) · b. cert. · d. cert. · private information (2004)

Archives NL Scot., corresp. | Bodl. RH, letters to Sir Matthew Nathan · Magd. Oxf., letters to Sir James Stewart Lockhart [copies] · Mitchell L., NSW, letters to G. E. Morrison

Likenesses photographs, repro. in Johnston, *Twilight* · photographs, NL Scot., Stewart Lockhart collection; repro. in Airlie, *Thistle and bamboo*

Wealth at death £1978 19s.: confirmation, 12 July 1938, *CCI*

Johnston, Robert (*c*.1567–1639), historian and philanthropist, the son of an Edinburgh burgess, was born about 1567, either in Edinburgh or some part of Annandale. He attended Edinburgh University, graduating MA in 1587. He was described in later life as doctor of civil and canon law, a degree which he may have obtained at Paris, where he was a contemporary and acquaintance of Robert Gordon of Straloch. On the accession of James VI to the English throne he seems to have left Scotland for London in the train of a relative, Sir Robert Johnston. He had been in correspondence with Cecil in 1601 and 1602. On 8 December 1604 he was appointed clerk of the deliveries of the ordinance, on surrender by Sir Thomas Johnston. He is known to have held the post as late as 1618, and may have retained it until his death. In the will of his friend George Heriot, 1623, he is described as a gentleman of London. In 1637 he was involved in a dispute with the crown over the execution of Heriot's will. As well as being a historian Johnston was, like Heriot, a philanthropist. In some quarters he found greater favour for the latter activity than for the former. Anti-puritan in outlook, his writing was humanist and royalist. As such it was admired by Robert Gordon of Straloch, but met with less approbation from Robert Baillie, the covenanting leader and principal of Glasgow University. Of the 1642 edition of Johnston's major work, published in Amsterdam under the title *Scoto-britanni, historiarum libri duo, continentes rerum Britannicarum vicinarumque regionum historias maxime memorabiles*, Baillie wrote

> Johnstoun is one of the poorest pedants and most unable for storie, of any I ever saw in print: yow would deall, and I shall also endeavour it, for the credite of the nation, and for the poor man's also, who hes left in legacie to diverse places in our countrie large soumes of monie that the rest of his books may be suppressed.   (*Letters and Journals of Robert Baillie*, 2.9)

Baillie was not successful in this endeavour, and later translations and editions of the work appeared in 1646 (as *The History of Scotland in the Minority of King James*) and 1655.

Johnston was a keen proponent of the ideal of civic virtue, leaving, as Baillie had indicated, several benefactions to good causes in Scotland. These benefactions reflected his views on the necessity of discipline and obedience for the maintenance of good order and the furtherance of the public good. By the time of his death between 12 and 18 October 1639, Johnston, as revealed by his will which is printed in Constable's *Memoir of George Heriot*, had amassed a considerable fortune. The total amount actually disposed of in charities by his will was slightly more than £13,000. Of this £1000 sterling (£12,000 Scots) was left for the maintenance of eight poor scholars in the University of Edinburgh, another £1000 sterling for setting the poor of Edinburgh to work, £1000 sterling for the foundation and endowment of a grammar school in Moffat, Annandale, £600 sterling for setting the poor of Aberdeen to work, and a bequest was also made to the burgh of Glasgow. He was unmarried and childless.

W. A. SHAW, rev. SHONA MACLEAN VANCE

Sources Chambers, *Scots.* (1835), vol. 3 · J. Man, *Introduction … to the projected work memoirs of Scottish affairs from 1624 to 1651 by Robert Gordon of Straloch, James Gordon of Rothiemay, and others* [n.d., 1741?] · *Modifications under the charge of the provost, magistrates and town council of Aberdeen* (1884) · T. Craufurd, *History of the University of Edinburgh from 1580 to 1646* (1808) · Edinburgh town council register, vol. 30, Edinburgh City Archives · *The letters and journals of Robert Baillie*, ed. D. Laing, 2 (1841) · J. D. Marwick, ed., *Extracts from the records of the burgh of Glasgow*, 2, Scottish Burgh RS, 12 (1881) · D. Allan, *Virtue, learning and the Scottish Enlightenment: ideas of scholarship in early modern history* (1993)
Wealth at death £13,000: *DNB*

Johnston, Samuel (1733–1816), planter and revolutionary politician in America, was born on 15 December 1733 in Dundee, the son of Samuel Johnston (1702–1757) and Helen, *née* Scrymsoure (d. 1750). In 1735 his parents moved to North Carolina where his uncle, Gabriel Johnston, was the royal governor. Gabriel had recently named Samuel surveyor-general of the colony. The newly arrived family promptly acquired land in Craven county and afterwards at Poplar Plains plantation in Onslow county where the elder Johnston established himself as a planter. At the time of his death in 1757 he owned over 10,000 acres in several counties on which he grew corn, cotton, and indigo, and produced naval stores. He also served as a justice of the peace in Bladen, Craven, and New Hanover counties; as overseer in the construction of a coastal fort; and as public treasurer of the colony from 1747 to 1751.

In the year of his mother's death, when he was aged seventeen, the young Samuel Johnston was sent to a school in New Haven, Connecticut. There he received letters from his father between 1750 and 1753, but there is no record of his having attended Yale College. After returning to North Carolina he studied law in Edenton with Thomas Barker and in November 1756 he was licensed as an attorney. First elected to the general assembly in 1759, he was re-elected and served in every session thereafter until 1775. This marked the beginning of a period of fifty-four years of varied service to the state and nation. In 1768 he was made clerk of the court for the Edenton district and in 1770 was appointed deputy naval officer of North Carolina. After five years in the latter post, however, he was removed by the royal governor, Josiah Martin, because of his activity in the growing revolutionary movement.

Thereafter Johnston's political activities were wholly pro-independence in nature, though he refused to pursue the cause through illegal means. In December 1773 the general assembly appointed him a member of the committee of correspondence for North Carolina to keep in touch with and co-ordinate the activity of the other colonies. Johnston also served in the first four provincial congresses, was elected president of the third and fourth, and the congress in September 1775, when he was not a member, selected him to be treasurer of the northern district of North Carolina. Late in 1776 the provincial council, the executive body of the revolutionary government, chose Johnston as both its member-at-large and paymaster of troops in the Edenton district. Just a few days before the end of the same year he was made a commissioner to codify the laws of the new state, which was no longer subject to British rule. He represented Chowan county in the state senate in 1779, 1783, and 1784, and in 1781 when he was not a member of the legislature he was elected a delegate to the continental congress.

Clearly Johnston's abilities were recognized at home, but they were also known elsewhere. The states of New

York and Massachusetts chose him as one of the commissioners to resolve a boundary dispute between them. Soon after completing this service, Johnston in 1787 was elected governor of North Carolina and re-elected for two more terms in succeeding years. He resigned during his third term, however, to take office as the first United States senator from North Carolina. Seemingly a man of boundless energy and never willing to decline a call to public service, Governor Johnston presided at the convention of 1788 to consider the ratification of the federal constitution. When it was not approved, the following year he presided at a second convention which approved the constitution in anticipation of certain amendments. A few days later, on 11 December 1789, when the University of North Carolina was chartered, Johnston was named one of its trustees. His final public service was rendered from 1800 to 1813 when he was a superior court judge.

Throughout his life in North Carolina, Johnston was active in field and forest as well as in the halls of government and law. In 1765 he bought Hayes, a plantation of 543 acres near Edenton, and over the years added to it. He also held very large tracts of land in Halifax and Martin counties on which he grew rye, oats, rice, peas, and potatoes. He was related to several important families—his sister, Hannah, was the wife of James Iredell, who was appointed by President Washington to the supreme court. Johnston married Frances Cathcart in 1770; they were the parents of nine children, only four of whom survived childhood. A member of St Paul's Church in Edenton, Johnston was a member of the vestry and served as churchwarden. He died on 17 August 1816 at Hayes and was buried in the family cemetery on the plantation.　WILLIAM S. POWELL

Sources DNB · University of North California, Chapel Hill, Southern Historical Collection, Hayes MSS · North Carolina State Archives, Raleigh, North Carolina, Samuel Johnston MSS · Duke U., Johnston MSS · W. L. Saunders and W. Clark, eds., *The colonial records of North Carolina*, 30 vols. (1886–1907), vols. 6–25 · A. W. Bair, 'Samuel Johnston and the ratification of the federal constitution in North Carolina', MA diss., De Paul University, 1969 · R. D. W. Connor, *Revolutionary leaders of North Carolina* (1906) · L. S. Butler, 'Johnston, Samuel', ANB
Archives North Carolina State Archives, Raleigh, North Carolina, MSS · University of North Carolina, Chapel Hill, corresp. and papers | Duke U., Charles E. Johnston MSS · University of North Carolina, Chapel Hill, Southern Historical Collection, Hayes MSS
Likenesses C. W. Peate, portrait on ivory, priv. coll.

Johnston, Thomas (1881–1965), politician and journalist, was born on 2 November 1881 at Cowgate Street, Kirkintilloch, Dunbartonshire, Scotland, the eldest of the four children of David Johnston, a licensed victualler, and his wife, Mary Blackwood Alexander. Little is known about his parents beyond their Conservative political disposition and their Presbyterianism. Tom Johnston was educated at Lairdslaw public school and, later, Lenzie Academy, and by his own account received a solid grounding in the classics, especially the history of ancient Greece and Rome. The town of Kirkintilloch had emerged around the site of a fort on Antonine's wall, and it seems that proximity to the remains of the Roman conquest whetted Johnston's appetite for local history from an early age. It was

Thomas Johnston (1881–1965), by Sir James Gunn, exh. RA 1956

certainly to be one of his life's passions. As a schoolboy he was successful in essay-writing competitions and published stories in comic books.

Socialism and journalism　On leaving school Johnston became a clerk first in an iron-founding business and then in an insurance office. By this time he had become attracted to the politics of the Fabian Society and the Independent Labour Party (ILP), and in 1903 stood successfully for a local election on the latter's platform. The commencement of his political career was marked by his great enthusiasm for municipal experiments, and he might happily have pursued a long career in local government. As it was, he was to bring to fruition some of his ideas, including that of a municipal bank, in a later period as councillor in Kirkintilloch between 1913 and 1922. However, he also had journalistic ambitions, and the fortuitous inheritance from a relative of a printing press enabled him to launch a weekly paper, *The Forward*, in 1906.

It was not long before *The Forward* acquired the reputation as the leading socialist paper in Scotland and Johnston that of an astute editor and crusading journalist. *The Forward* advanced essentially a Fabian socialist outlook, flavoured with the passion and humanitarianism of the ILP, but it was no mere party mouthpiece. Johnston encouraged debate and dissent, and commissioned the thoughts of intellectual mavericks of the day such as Bernard Shaw and H. G. Wells. Johnston's own style was punchy, blunt, ironic, and often satirical. He was perhaps more in the tradition of radical liberal polemic than socialist exegesis. A moralistic tone was also a notable feature: *The Forward* carried no alcohol advertisements and reflected Johnston's teetotalism and his baleful regard for many of the raffish aspects of urban working-class culture. Johnston prided himself in producing a paper for the respectable, self-improving working class. His socialism, if such it was, certainly owed more to the formative influences of small community life, Presbyterianism, and ethical values than to Marxist political thought and ideas of class warfare. Neither was he particularly close to the trade union movement.

Johnston edited *The Forward* until 1933, snubbing offers from Fleet Street, and combining journalism with a political career which was to take off at national level in the 1920s. In the early days of his paper he also combined his editorial duties with attendance as a mature student at Glasgow University. He left in 1909 without completing his degree, but the experience brought him into contact with a brilliant generation of students, including Walter Elliot, James Maxton, and the playwright James Bridie, and involved him in a memorable if unsuccessful campaign to get the ILP leader, Keir Hardie, elected rector. Hardie proved to be a profound influence on Johnston; indeed, the latter came to embody much of the former's spirit of integrity and drive for social justice. On 26 June 1914 Johnston married Margaret Freeland (1890–1977), the daughter of James Cochrane, a wholesale provision merchant; the couple had two daughters.

Besides the weekly examples of his propaganda skills on behalf of the labour movement in *The Forward*, Johnston made his literary reputation through a series of short booklets and pamphlets and the much more substantial *History of the Working Classes in Scotland*, which was published to a fanfare of praise in 1920 and which reflected a prodigious amount of research in local archives and libraries throughout Scotland. The volume remains a milestone in Scottish labour history. Of the shorter works, *Our Scots Noble Families*, published in 1909, made the greatest impact on account of its excoriating treatment of the major landed families of Scotland, who were depicted in its pages as nothing short of titled brigands and exploiters of the poor. In later life this short philippic was to prove something of an embarrassment to Johnston, as he formed close working relationships with several Scottish aristocrats. *Our Scots Noble Families* testified to Johnston's primary concern with land reform and other issues of essentially rural significance before the First World War, and was related to the leisure pursuits of fishing and hill-walking which filled the tall and well-built Johnston's happiest hours. It was also linked to a large extent to an espousal of Scottish home rule, although Johnston's support for the latter cause perhaps owed something to the need to appease one of *The Forward's* wealthiest backers, the nationalist Roland Muirhead.

Johnston viewed the outbreak of war in 1914 as an indictment of 'secret diplomacy'—which he made the subject of another incisive pamphlet—and an opportunity for unscrupulous profiteers to exploit the working class. He marshalled *The Forward* in the cause of peace and democracy while keeping its pages open to pro-war argument and complying with government directives not to publish material which might be interpreted as hampering the war effort. This included coverage of industrial disputes which proliferated on Clydeside for the duration of the conflict. Nevertheless, *The Forward* fell foul of the government in 1916 when it reported the raucously agnostic reception accorded to the minister of munitions, Lloyd George, by Glasgow workers opposed to the government's dilution plans. The paper had to cease publication for five weeks until Johnston had personally resolved the matter with Lloyd George, a man with whose practical and radical energies he ironically felt much affinity. While other leadership figures of the left in Scotland during the war, most notably John Maclean and Jimmy Maxton, relished confrontation, Johnston's priority was to keep his channel of political education open so that progressive arguments could be read and mindsets changed. He believed in no revolutionary short cut and remained a pronounced gradualist in his approach to politics, even in the intense climate of wartime. Nobody on the left, however, was more effective in attacking war profiteers; his pamphlet *The Huns at Home*, published in 1917, was a masterpiece of its kind.

Labour politician between the wars Johnston stood unsuccessfully for the ILP in West Stirlingshire in the general election of 1918, but triumphed in 1922 when Labour won twenty-nine seats in Scotland. At Westminster he was identified with the Clydeside group of Labour MPs around Maxton and John Wheatley, the latter a thinker of some repute and long-time friend of *The Forward*. When Labour formed a minority government in 1923–4 Wheatley became health minister, but Johnston, to his chagrin, was passed over by the party leader, Ramsay MacDonald, another close colleague and contributor to *The Forward*. At the election of 1924 Johnston narrowly lost his seat, only to return to parliament shortly afterwards following a by-election for Dundee.

Increasingly during the 1920s Johnston applied the under-consumptionist school of economic thinking inspired by J. A. Hobson to questions of empire. He became one of Labour's main spokesmen on colonial questions and rapidly began to develop a positive concept of empire in relation to the possibilities of international co-operation and of raising the purchasing power of workers in different countries. His interest in imperial matters culminated in his involvement in the Empire Marketing Board and co-operation with politicians from other parties, including his old friend (and Conservative) Walter Elliot and a Conservative fellow Scot, John Buchan. In this period Johnston moved significantly towards acceptance of the benefits of working in a non-partisan consensual political context, and indeed advocated that the task of resolving the problem of unemployment be taken out of the arena of party politics. As his outlook thus evolved Johnston looked with a jaundiced eye on the attempts made by Wheatley and Maxton to fashion a more doctrinally socialist Labour opposition via their influence on the ILP. Johnston defended MacDonald's leadership and was rewarded with the office of under-secretary of state for Scotland when Labour returned to power in 1929. In the election Johnston was returned for his old seat of West Stirlingshire, having decided to abandon Dundee.

Johnston performed impressively in his post, overshadowing his senior partner at the Scottish Office, William Adamson. To Johnston must go much of the credit for important legislation such as the Housing (Scotland) Act of 1930. Achievements such as this were all the more notable for the context of the economic depression and the chronic unemployment which resulted. Johnston in fact was a member of the 'Thomas committee' on unemployment in which he inclined towards many of the radical remedies advanced by Oswald Mosley, but found him too temperamental to work with. Johnston would have preferred an all-party arrangement which included the wasting asset of Lloyd George.

After moving to the post of lord privy seal (and a seat in cabinet) in March 1931 Johnston was brought squarely up against the complexities of the unemployment issue and compelled to defend the government's fidelity to orthodox economic canons. However, on the matter of cutting unemployment benefit, which eventually split the cabinet, Johnston was emphatically opposed. He declined to follow MacDonald into a national coalition government and railed against the machinations of international financiers. In the 1931 election, at which he lost his seat, Johnston called for national control over finances, and he turned *The Forward* over to debate on monetary schemes and financial reforms above all other issues. His stock in the Labour Party was high and there may have been opportunities to press claims for the leadership, but Johnston seemed disinclined. There was always a marked degree of reluctance in him about leading a politician's life.

Johnston regained the seat of West Stirlingshire in 1935 and resumed his parliamentary career focused on the dangers of another war. He championed the role of the League of Nations, opposed any increase in armaments expenditure, and called for moves to establish an international police force to settle disputes between nations. Ultimately Nazi aggression forced him to conclude that preparations had to be made for civil defence, and in May 1939 he became regional commissioner for Scotland. The outbreak of war found him at his most ingeniously resourceful in this role, and when Winston Churchill became prime minister he identified Johnston as one of the Labour figures he wanted in his coalition.

Scottish secretary Johnston, anxious to retire from party political life, was persuaded with difficulty by Churchill to become secretary of state for Scotland in February 1941. Shrewdly, he accepted only once he had wrung from Churchill the concession of forming a council of state composed of ex-secretaries of state for Scotland of all parties. Johnston insisted that, when this council was decided on something, cabinet would be obliged to acquiesce. This proved to be an administrative master stroke, allowing Johnston to expedite his agenda for Scotland and enabling him to convince Scottish public opinion that Scottish interests were being well served within the system. For his trouble Johnston would accept no ministerial salary, a selfless gesture perhaps unique in recent British political history.

Johnston seized the opportunities the extraordinary circumstances of wartime presented. His achievements in creating the North of Scotland Hydro-Electric Board and bringing war work to Scotland, among many other constructive initiatives in areas such as health, education, housing, and agriculture, have ensured his reputation as one of the greatest Scottish secretaries. He gave the state a natural role in Scottish economic life which has proved enduring and a marked contrast to developments in England. He was adept at channelling energies and expertise to a common purpose, and engendering self-belief. He believed genuinely that the kind of schemes he brought to fruition would enhance the cause of Scottish home rule, although his nationalism was politically ambiguous and he was no separatist. Criticisms have been advanced of his secretaryship from across the political spectrum, but his stature and ability have not been questioned.

Johnston retired from politics in 1945 but continued to play an active role in Scottish public life, particularly in regard to the Hydro-Electric Board and the Scottish Tourist Board. He refused a peerage offered to him in 1945 but accepted the Companion of Honour in 1953, one of many honours received in his latter years. In 1952 he published his memoirs, a surprisingly lightweight volume which conveys his mischievous sense of humour but does not do justice to his political odyssey. After a period of ill health he died at his home, Caledon, 9 Lynn Drive, Milngavie (close to Kirkintilloch), on 5 September 1965.

GRAHAM WALKER

Sources G. Walker, *Thomas Johnston* (1988) · W. Knox, ed., *Scottish labour leaders, 1918–39: a biographical dictionary* (1984) · T. Johnston, *Memories* (1952) · C. Harvie, *Scotland and nationalism*, 3rd edn (1998) · M. Fry, *Patronage and principle* (1987) · *The Scottish socialists* (1931) · b. cert. · m. cert. · d. cert.
Archives Mitchell L., Glas., corresp. · NL Scot., corresp. and papers | Dundee Central Library, letters to Garnet Wilson · NL Scot., Hughes MSS, Dep. 176 · NL Scot., Muirhead MSS, Acc. 3721 · NL Scot., letters to J. A. A. Porteous | FILM BFI NFTVA, documentary footage · IWM FVA, actuality footage | SOUND BL NSA, oral history interview
Likenesses W. Stoneman, photograph, 1941, NPG · G. Barron, bronze head, 1953, Scottish Hydro-Electric · J. Gunn, oils, exh. RA 1956, Scot. NPG [*see illus.*] · photograph, Hult. Arch.
Wealth at death £12,411 3s. 8d.: confirmation, 16 Nov 1965, NA Scot., SC 65/38/78/953

Johnston, William (*fl.* 1516–1550). *See under* College of justice, procurators of the (*act.* 1532).

Johnston, William. *See* Veitch, William (1640–1722).

Johnston, Sir William, of Hilton, seventh baronet (1760–1844). *See under* Johnston, Sir William (1773–1844).

Johnston, Sir William (1773–1844), army officer, entered the army as an ensign in the 18th foot on 3 June 1791. His promotions were: lieutenant on 7 January 1794, captain on 4 April 1795, major on 27 February 1800, lieutenant-colonel on 25 April 1808, colonel on 4 June 1814, major-general on 27 May 1825, and lieutenant-general on 28 June 1838.

Johnston served at Gibraltar until October 1793, when he was sent to take part in the defence of Toulon; he then proceeded to Corsica, where he was wounded, and became captain in Smith's Corsican regiment. In 1797 he took part in the expedition against Tuscany, and in 1798, having returned home, he was placed on half pay though he saw some service during the Irish uprising with a yeomanry corps. In 1800 Johnston joined the 68th foot as a major; and in 1801 he embarked with his regiment for the campaign against the Danish and Dutch West Indies. He commanded the 68th at the siege of Flushing (August 1809) during the Walcheren expedition. Johnston later distinguished himself in the Peninsula, and led the 68th at Salamanca, Vitoria, and Orthez; he was seriously wounded at Vitoria, and received a medal with two clasps.

On 2 June 1837 Johnston was made a KCB. The colonelcy of the 68th was given to him on 6 April 1838. He died at Orchard Place, Southampton, on 23 January 1844, and was survived by a widow, a son in the 8th foot, and six daughters.

Johnston must be distinguished from **Sir William Johnston of Hilton**, seventh baronet (1760–1844), son of Sir William Johnston of Hilton (1714–1794), the sixth baronet, and a collateral descendant of Sir John *Johnston (d. 1690), and his second wife, Elizabeth (d. 25 Aug 1772), daughter of Captain William Cleland RN of Lanark. The sixth baronet was a naval officer who purchased the Hilton estate, Aberdeen, with prize money. Born on 3 August 1760 and educated at Harrow School, William Johnston entered the army and served in India. On 19 March 1794 he succeeded his father as baronet. In 1798 he raised a regiment of fencibles, which was disbanded in 1802. From 1801 to 1806 he was MP for New Windsor. He married, first, on 24 February 1784, Mary (d. 25 July 1802), daughter of John Bacon of Shrubland Hall, Suffolk. He married, second, on 15 December 1802, Maria (d. 27 Oct 1847), daughter of another John Bacon, of Friern House, Middlesex, and they had three sons and four daughters. He was said to have become insolvent and to have lived within the precincts of Holyrood Abbey, Edinburgh. He died at The Hague on 13 January 1844. He was succeeded as baronet by his son William Bacon Johnston (1806–1865), army officer.   W. A. J. ARCHBOLD, rev. S. KINROSS

Sources GM, 2nd ser., 21–2 (1844) • The Times (24 Jan 1844) • Annual Register (1844) • W. Anderson, The Scottish nation, 3 vols. (1880) • Irving, Scots. • T. C. W. Blanning, The French revolutionary wars, 1787–1802 (1996) • R. Muir, Britain and the defeat of Napoleon, 1807–1815 (1996) • Burke, Peerage (1959) • D. R. Fisher, 'Johnston, Sir William', HoP, Commons, 1790–1820

Johnston, William (fl. 1792–1817), newspaper proprietor and radical, was a half-pay officer in the armed forces. Some time before the 1790s he married a Miss Home, niece of Francis Home, physician. By at least 1811 he owned property in North Charlotte Street in Edinburgh's expanding New Town. Between 1792 and 1794 he was resident at 20 North Frederick Street, also in the New Town, another indication of his gentle status. Henry Cockburn

later noted that Johnston had been 'a respectable man, and a gentleman in his manners' (Cockburn, 118).

Although Johnston chaired the meeting which saw the birth of the Scottish Friends of the People, held in Edinburgh on 26 July 1792, his importance in Scottish and Edinburgh radical circles was principally owing to his establishment of the Edinburgh Gazetteer in September 1792—one of only two radical papers founded in Scotland in the 1790s. (The other was the Caledonian Chronicle.) Two months later he was voted the thanks of the Friends of the People at a meeting in Edinburgh of delegates from constituent radical societies throughout Scotland. In the proposals for the paper Johnston promised early and impartial news of international events; to convey early and prompt intelligence of public abuses; full coverage of important developments in the worlds of commerce, the arts, sciences, politics, and amusements of the nation; and to devote special attention to events in France. This last promise was given added importance because of the hostile comment on, and coverage of, the French Revolution and French military fortunes in the rest of the contemporary Scottish press. In July of the following year delegates of all the radical societies of the county of Renfrew voted thanks to both the radical papers for 'the impartial manner in which they disseminated truth and political knowledge' (Meikle, 129 n. 1). Look before ye Loup, a loyalist pamphlet of 1793, also alluded to the eagerness with which French news carried by the Gazetteer was digested by weaver radicals. The proposals also made clear the reformist intent of the paper. It was, they declared, attached to the 'British constitution for which our fathers shed their blood' and 'not to those defects produced by time and by the efforts of bad men' (NA Scot., RH 2/4/64, fol. 320).

The Gazetteer quickly became the mouthpiece of the Scottish Friends of the People, being used as the vehicle for the circulation of radical addresses and motions and the advertisement of radical pamphlets and handbills, as well as the dissemination of information about radical activities throughout the British Isles, not least Ireland. As early as November 1792 one informant from Montrose told Lord Advocate Robert Dundas that they believed the paper 'has done more hurt than anything else' (NA Scot., RH 2/4/65, fols. 156–7). Copies of both the Gazetteer and the Caledonian Chronicle were also regularly forwarded to the home secretary, Henry Dundas, in London. From November Johnston's mail was being intercepted and he was being 'closely watched' by the authorities (NA Scot., RH 2/4/65, fols. 48–53; RH 2/4/68, fols. 11–12).

Although he was, by late 1793 certainly, a supporter of universal suffrage and annual parliaments, Johnston's temperament and disposition were those of a moderate. In a series of letters to the leading Scottish radical William Skirving, written some time before the third general convention of the Scottish Friends of the People, held in the Scottish capital in the autumn of 1793, he urged a posture of 'candour, firmness and constitutional integrity'. He also counselled the need for unanimity and a conciliatory attitude towards those who supported more moderate measures of reform. In the same correspondence he characterized his position as that of 'intrepid moderation' (*State trials*, 23.65–70).

Johnston displayed essentially the same attitude at both the first and the third conventions of the Scottish Friends of the People. At the former, held in Edinburgh in December 1792, he proposed two resolutions, the first of which recommended that all radical societies expunge from the roll of membership any individual who acted 'illegally, tumultuously, or in any way to the disturbance of the public peace'. The subject of the second was the defence of those who, despite having behaved 'legally and orderly', found themselves 'prosecuted by the arm of power for adhering to the cause of the people'. The previous month had seen a series of riots in Dundee, Perth, and other places in Scotland, which appeared to ministers and their supporters to be linked to, if not promoted by, the Friends of the People. As chairman of the convention—this was a rotating office—Johnston also led a number of delegates to Goldsmiths' Hall to sign a loyal address being promoted by a newly established loyal association in the capital, the Goldsmiths' Hall Association. In 1793 Johnston was no longer a delegate but a visitor to the convention. He participated in a debate on 29 October opposing a proposal to petition the king on the subject of reform as unconstitutional and likely to lead to 'ruin' (NA Scot., JC 26/276). He later claimed that he did not attend from 19 November, when the convention was reconvened following the arrival in Edinburgh of several English radicals. He was, however, present on 30 November. By this stage the convention, under the influence in part of the bolder English delegates, had taken on a more strident radical edge, symbolized by the change of title, on 23 November, to the British Convention of the Delegates of the People, Associated to Obtain Universal Suffrage and Annual Parliaments.

Johnston's caution was reflected in the contents of the *Gazetteer*. Against a background of official anxiety about radical activity and a marked disposition to use the courts to suppress it, it is striking that the paper escaped hostile attention, at least from ministers, until the end of 1793, by which time Johnston had severed his links with it. On 22 January 1793 the editor declared that he had refused to publish a letter from a 'constant Reader' in Montrose on the ground that it 'seems to espouse Republican sentiments, with which we can never coalesce'. Johnston's enthusiasm for the venture, moreover, dampened in February after he was called, along with the paper's printer, Simon Drummond—also a member of the Friends of the People—to attend the high court of justiciary to answer a charge of contempt of court for a report in the paper of the trial of three journeymen printers for sedition in the previous month. Although Johnston claimed that he had been ill at the time of publication (15 January 1793)—a story lent weight by an inflammation of the eye which prevented his initially attending court—both he and Drummond were found guilty and sentenced to three months' imprisonment. Johnston also had to find sureties

for £500 for three years for good behaviour on his release. Bonds for that purpose were entered into by fellow radical James Campbell, a writer to the signet, and Francis Home, his wife's uncle. That Johnston was chastened by this experience was evident when he refused in March 1793 to publish resolutions in the paper opposing the war against France drawn up by Thomas Fyshe Palmer, who was himself to become a victim of judicial repression later in the same year. Johnston had taken the precaution of submitting the resolutions to his lawyer, 'who rejected them in *toto*' (NA Scot., RH 2/4/70, fol. 82).

By March 1793 Johnston was exploring ways of divesting himself of the paper. On 27 March one of Lord Advocate Robert Dundas's regular informants wrote that he had 'certain information' that the *Gazetteer* and *Caledonian Chronicle* were to be given up, unless a plan was settled on for their rescue (NA Scot., RH 2/4/70, fols. 139–40). A meeting of radicals, including Skirving, was held for this purpose on the following day. Johnston was willing to give up the paper for £400 in ready cash; he claimed to have invested around £700 in its establishment. There appears to have been considerable support for some sort of rescue package, from Skirving and from radical societies outside of Edinburgh, reflecting the value of the paper to the movement. There was, however, no quick solution. On 2 April Johnston was succeeded as publisher by **Alexander Scott** (*fl.* 1793), printer and radical. By June it was being reported that Johnston was about to leave for America. His terms were by now considerably easier; he was willing to make over to Scott the types and printing apparatus upon payment of simple interest on the sum he had invested. The principal was not to be paid back for at least three years. On 20 June Johnston's terms were agreed to by the Edinburgh general committee of Friends of the People; £500 was to be raised through subscriptions to fund running expenses, and this money was to be managed by committee.

In 1794 Johnston, together with Campbell and Home, was forced to answer a petition in the High Court that his sureties for good behaviour should be forfeit because of his attendance at the British convention of radicals. In the counter-petition, Johnston claimed to have lost a considerable sum through his involvement with the *Gazetteer*. He also claimed that his health and family had suffered considerably through his imprisonment. He also declared that the paper had already been proving profitable when he gave it up, and showed every sign of becoming more so. This may have been special pleading to gain favour from the court. What is certain is that under Scott's management—and facing harassment of potential advertisers and readers—the paper lurched from one financial difficulty to the next. In July the price of the paper was raised to 4*d.* from the original 3½*d.* At some time in October or November Scott wrote to Maurice Margarot explaining that only a loan would enable him to continue publication of the paper. Scott also claimed to be publishing between 1000 and 2000 copies per edition, a relatively modest total for the period. There is also a hint in another letter from

Scott to Margarot from around the same time that Johnston had continued to provide the paper with financial support (NA Scot., JC 26/270). The only help the British convention provided was to recommend that radical societies do all in their power to raise money and send it to the editor, or at least to remit payment for the paper in advance.

The action to have Johnston's sureties for good behaviour declared forfeit was dropped. Scott and the *Gazetteer* were not so lucky. Scott was charged with seditious libel for reports on the British convention carried in the *Gazetteer* for 26 November and 3 and 10 December 1793, and for a paragraph entitled 'An extraordinary instance of public spirit in the cobler of Messina', which could be read as encouraging the assassination of the 'oppressors' of the country (NA Scot., JC 26/281). Scott was outlawed for non-appearance. He fled to London where he was arrested but subsequently released on agreeing to act as a government spy. Johnston nursed a strong sense of injury about his prosecution for contempt of court in 1793 over many years. In 1817 he presented a memorial to the first division of the court of session in which he declared again his innocence. Details of the date or place of his death are unknown.   BOB HARRIS

Sources *State trials*, 23.1793–4 · copies of state correspondence relating to Scotland, NA Scot., RH 2/4/64–71 · High court of justiciary papers, NA Scot., JC 26/270 · Treasury solicitor's papers, PRO, TS 11/956 · Home Office papers, PRO, HO 42/33 · H. W. Meikle, *Scotland and the French Revolution* (1912) · J. D. Brims, 'The Scottish democratic movement in the age of the French Revolution', PhD diss., U. Edin., 1983 · H. Cockburn, *An examination of the trials for sedition … in Scotland*, 2 vols. (1888) · *Edinburgh Directory*

Johnston, William (1800–1874), minister of the United Presbyterian church, was born in Biggar, Lanarkshire, on 18 February 1800, the youngest of nine children of Thomas Boston Johnston (*b.* 1742) and his wife, Janet Brown (*d.* 1847). He attended school locally before studying at Glasgow University, where he graduated MA in 1817. Under the influence of his mother and of his minister, John Brown (1784–1858), he decided to train for the ministry and from 1816 he attended the Divinity Hall of the Associate Synod at Selkirk. He was selected by his fellow students, as a representative of the student body, to receive the freedom of the burgh of Selkirk at the same time as Prince Leopold. Johnston was licensed in May 1821 and ordained to a congregation in the small seaport of Limekilns, near Dunfermline in Fife, on 27 August 1823. The ordination took place in a field, as the church building was inadequate for the numbers gathered. A new church was erected soon afterwards.

During his long pastorate Johnston had opportunities to move. In 1841 he was called by the congregation of Eglinton Street in Glasgow, a call repeated the following year. A call from a congregation at Montego Bay, Jamaica, was received in 1849 together with a request to become professor of theology in that island. Finally, he was called by the congregation of Shamrock Street, Glasgow, in 1850, but in spite of great efforts to persuade him otherwise, Johnston stayed put. The devotion of his congregation, which included the Bruce family, earls of Elgin, and the

contentment he felt as 'bishop of Limekilns' kept him in a humbler position than many felt that his talents merited. Although he published little of consequence, Johnston was influential in church courts where his judicial demeanour was deployed to good effect. He made a telling contribution to the defence of Robert Balmer and John Brown during the atonement controversy. From 1847 until his death he was convener of the United Presbyterian Church's committee on education and in 1854 he served as moderator of its synod. Glasgow University honoured him with the degree of DD in 1849.

Johnston was a man of medium height, spare frame, and reserved manner; one observer recalled 'his large round, head—his cold, wakeful, blue eyes—his firm mouth, that could remain shut for hours' (*United Presbyterian Magazine*, 303). He was long afflicted by an inflamed condition of the face, only latterly corrected by surgery. An abstainer and temperance promoter, he remained a staunch opponent of church establishments; in politics he was a Liberal. On 24 October 1865, at Edinburgh he married Helen B. Johnston (*d.* 1876?) of Biggar. His ministerial jubilee, which was attended by Dean Stanley, was marked by the presentation of an epergne and 1000 guineas from the congregation. At the following year's synod he became unwell. He was taken to his lodgings in Hanover Street, Edinburgh, where he died, after a short illness, on 24 May 1874; he was buried in Limekilns churchyard on 29 May.   LIONEL ALEXANDER RITCHIE

Sources *Memorials of the life and work of … W. J.* (1876) · *The Scotsman* (25 May 1874) · *United Presbyterian Magazine*, new ser., 18 (1874), 337–44 · *United Presbyterian Magazine*, new ser., 20 (1876), 303–6 · J. Smith, *Our Scottish clergy*, 2nd ser. (1849), 334–9 · R. Small, *History of the congregations of the United Presbyterian church from 1733 to 1900*, 1 (1904), 371 · *Literary World* (2 June 1876) · *DNB*
Likenesses photograph (in later life), repro. in *Memorials of the life and work of … W. J.*
Wealth at death £1540 14*s.* 4*d.*: inventory, 7 Aug 1874, NA Scot., SC 20/50/47, 672

Johnston, Sir William (1802–1888), geographical publisher and lord provost of Edinburgh, was the third son of Andrew Johnston and Isabel, daughter of Archibald Keith of Newbattle. He was born at Kirkhill, Midlothian, on 27 October 1802 and educated at Edinburgh high school. After serving apprenticeships to the Edinburgh engravers Kirkwood & Sons and William Home Lizars, he set up in business as an engraver on 1 December 1825. At Kirkwoods he gained some experience of map printing and his geographical interest was strengthened in May 1826 when his younger brother (Alexander) Keith *Johnston, the elder, became his partner. Keith was always the more distinguished geographer, but William maintained his interest in the family firm and on 2 December 1837, as its senior partner, was appointed engraver and copperplate printer to the queen. Johnston strengthened his connections with exploration and geography through his marriages. With his first wife, Margaret, daughter of James Pearson of Fala, Midlothian, whom he married on 13 March 1829, he had a daughter, Elizabeth Whyte (*b.* 1830), who married Robert Scoresby Jackson, nephew and biographer of the Arctic explorer William Scoresby. After Margaret's death on 13

June 1865, Johnston married Georgiana Augusta Wilkinson, youngest daughter of William Ker of Gateshaw, Roxburghshire, and widow of William Scoresby.

Johnston's main public career, however, was in Edinburgh civic life. Heads of Edinburgh publishing houses at the time often held civic office and Johnston became successively burgess, high constable, city councillor, and, from 1848 to 1851, lord provost of Edinburgh. At the end of his term as lord provost he was knighted. In 1842 he was president of the Edinburgh relief committee which, at his suggestion, organized public works which gave lasting improvements such as the Meadows and Queen's Drive round Arthur's Seat. In 1852 he was elected fellow of the Scottish Society of Antiquaries. In 1867 he retired from business to an estate at Kirkhill House, Gonebridge, Midlothian, which he had bought in 1848 and where he died on 7 February 1888. He was buried on 10 February in the Grange cemetery, Edinburgh.   ELIZABETH BAIGENT

Sources One hundred years of map making: the story of W. & A. K. Johnston [1923] · DNB

Archives NL Scot., corresp., diaries, and papers

Likenesses J. W. Gordon, oils, exh. 1852, Royal Scot. Acad.

Johnston, William (1829–1902), Orangeman, was born in Downpatrick, co. Down, on 22 February 1829, the son of John Brett Johnston (d. 1853) of Ballykilbeg, co. Down, and his wife, Thomasina (d. 1852), daughter of Thomas Scott, a local surgeon: he was the eldest of a family of seven. He was educated at the diocesan school, Downpatrick, and at Trinity College, Dublin, from which he graduated BA in 1852. He inherited the small and encumbered estate of Ballykilbeg on the death of his father in March 1853, and thereafter lived the life of an impecunious Irish gentleman, possessing social position but little cash. He studied law, but was not called to the Irish bar until 1872: he does not appear to have practised his profession. He married three times: his first marriage, on 22 February 1853, was to Harriet Allen, with whom he had two sons and two daughters; he married his second wife, Arminella Frances Drew, on 10 October 1861. On 4 May 1863 he married Georgiana Barbara, younger daughter of Sir John Hay, with whom he had three sons and four daughters: he remained happily united with Georgiana until her death on 6 August 1900.

William Johnston's fame rests primarily on his success as a radical Orange politician and polemicist. Although a minor landlord, Johnston was intellectually rooted in popular protestant evangelicalism and in the demotic Orange movement of the north of Ireland. Sharing the religious and party convictions of his tenants, Johnston was too poor and too paternalistic to be socially removed from the most disadvantaged sections of protestant society. He joined the Orange Society in May 1848, at a time when the movement was not conspicuously popular with the Irish gentry: in 1855 he was elected deputy grand master of the grand Orange lodge of Ireland; he was the master of his own Orange district between 1857 and his death in 1902. Throughout the 1850s he devoted his meagre income to the propagation of Orange values through an ill-fated newspaper venture (the *Downshire Protestant*, July

1855 – September 1862) and a series of 'Ballykilbeg protestant tracts'. He was an enthusiastic but unrecognized novelist, who specialized in melodramatic tales of Anglican maidens and vulpine Jesuits: the most successful of his four tendentious works of fiction was *Nightshade: a Novel*, published in 1858.

It was the Party Processions Act (1850), rather than his own prose, which won for Johnston a national celebrity. This measure was designed to ease sectarian conflict in Ireland by banning provocative marches and displays; but Orangemen believed that it was oppressive in theory, as a constraint on their right to demonstrate, and unfair in practice—because (they argued) it was more vigorously applied in the north of Ireland than in the south or west. On 12 July 1867 Johnston led an illegal procession of 9000 Orangemen from Newtownards to Bangor in north co. Down, for which he was convicted and imprisoned for two months (March–April 1868) in Downpatrick gaol. Johnston's self-sacrifice in the interests of Orangeism won him massive popularity among the newly enfranchised artisans of Belfast, and in November 1868 he was returned as one of the two members of parliament for the city. He cut a decidedly more impressive figure in the Orange lodges of Ulster than in the House of Commons: he was recognized as a political force by the Belfast Conservative Association, but not by the parliamentary leadership. However, he was instrumental in winning the repeal of the hated Party Processions Act in 1872.

Financial pressure forced Johnston out of the Commons in 1878, when he accepted a minor government appointment, the inspectorship of fisheries. He was dismissed from this post in May 1885, having contravened the terms of his employment through a series of party speeches. This action, at the hands of a Liberal government, recalled his earlier political martyrdom, and made him an object of interest to the Conservative managers in Belfast, who allocated him one of the four new Belfast constituencies, South Belfast, to contest as a Conservative candidate. In November 1885 he was returned at the head of the poll, and he retained the seat until his death.

Johnston was active in the creation of a separate Irish Unionist parliamentary party in January 1886, and was an outspoken critic of the home rule bills of 1886 and 1893. He remained prominent within his beloved Orange order, journeying to North America three times as an Irish loyalist emissary, and defending the protestant cause in parliament. But his career of independent dissent had come to an end with his election. For his expenses as a parliamentary candidate in 1885 and in 1886 were paid by the Conservative managers, and in 1887 he was further compromised through accepting a salary of £200 p.a. from Conservative central office. In return the party demanded his loyalty; the proud and independent martyr of 1868 ended his years as a minor tory retainer, bound to central office by his poverty and by his quarterly cheque.

Johnston died at Ballykilbeg on 17 July 1902. He was among the most prominent Orange politicians of the nineteenth century. A minor landlord, his financial distress and *déclassé* embarrassment serve to illustrate the fate of his once-significant social caste in post-famine Ireland. A hero for Orange artisans and labourers after his imprisonment, he helped to carry these newly enfranchised classes into a Conservative Unionist alliance in 1885–6. Johnston's obligations to Conservative central office also helped to tie the ostensibly independent Irish unionist movement to British Conservatism, for he was simultaneously a tory retainer and a loyalist activist. A mild-mannered fanatic, often outrageous in the pursuit of his convictions, Johnston won much affection in the House of Commons, but exercised little influence. By way of contrast, he was revered by the Orange movement in Ulster. His career illustrates with brutal clarity the distance between the Victorian House of Commons and its Irish hinterland.   ALVIN JACKSON

Sources A. McClelland, *William Johnston of Ballykilbeg* (1990) · Walford, *County families* · Burke, *Gen. GB* · A. Jackson, *The Ulster party: Irish unionists in the House of Commons, 1884–1911* (1989)
Archives PRO NIre., diaries | Bodl. Oxf., letters to Disraeli · Hatfield House, Hertfordshire, Salisbury MSS
Likenesses B. Stone, photograph, 1898, NPG · lithograph, pubd 1902, BM · photographs, repro. in McClelland, *William Johnston of Ballykilbeg*
Wealth at death £111 17s. 0d.: probate, 13 Oct 1902, CGPLA Ire.

Johnstone, Andrew James Cochrane- (1767–1833?), politician and fraudster, was born on 24 May 1767 at Belleville, a house in Edinburgh, the eighth surviving son of Thomas Cochrane, eighth earl of Dundonald (1691–1778), and his wife, Jean, *née* Stewart, of Torrance, Lanarkshire (1722?–1808).

The eighth earl's debts stood at £7500 at the time of his death, and Andrew's prospects rested upon family connections rather than wealth. An uncle, General James Stewart, obtained him a cornetcy in the 23rd light dragoons (10 June 1783), stationed in India, but he lacked the resources to secure smooth promotion. He became a lieutenant in the 19th dragoons in 1786, but in 1790 was back in England soliciting the prime minister, William Pitt, for promotion. Perhaps as a result he was commissioned captain in the 60th regiment of foot (10 November 1790). On 4 May 1791 he was returned as MP for the Stirling Boroughs, and, now in a position to support the government, applied again to Pitt for help in gaining further promotion. Nevertheless, he had to wait until May 1794 to achieve a lieutenant-colonelcy in the 79th regiment of foot.

Cochrane's fortunes were transformed by his marriage, on 20 November 1793, to Lady Georgiana Hope Johnstone (d. 1797), daughter of James, third earl of Hopetoun, on which occasion he adopted the surname Cochrane-Johnstone. His wife was connected to Henry Dundas, Lord Melville, a powerful magnate and ally of Pitt, and Cochrane-Johnstone now advanced rapidly. He became governor of Dominica in 1797 (upon which he resigned his parliamentary seat), colonel of the 8th West India regiment (23 January 1798), and brigadier of the Leeward Islands (12 April 1799).

Cochrane-Johnstone's governorship of Dominica was controversial. He was blamed by some for a mutiny among the black troops in 1802. The Dominican assembly petitioned for his recall, which occurred in 1803. Major John Gordon, an officer of Cochrane-Johnstone's regiment, accused his commander of using black soldiers as unpaid labour, wrongfully arresting citizens, and of corruption, but he was acquitted by a court martial in March 1805. However, the commander-in-chief of the army, the duke of York, remained dissatisfied, and Cochrane-Johnstone was passed over for promotion and resigned his commission.

His wife having died in 1797, Cochrane-Johnstone married on 21 March 1803 (during the peace of Amiens) Amelia Constance Gertrude Etienette, widow of Reymond Godet and daughter of Baron de Clugny, governor of Guadeloupe, but after the resumption of war between Britain and France the union appears to have been dissolved. Evidently there were no children of this marriage, though there was a daughter of the first marriage, Elizabeth, who became the wife of the ninth Baron Napier. Cochrane-Johnstone also had three children by an unknown woman, among them apparently John Dundas *Cochrane, the traveller.

Cochrane-Johnstone remained in Britain, campaigning for his rehabilitation and alleging the prejudices of the duke of York and others against him and abuses in military administration. His cause attracted radical politicians, then eagerly exposing government corruption. William Cobbett used it to attack the duke of York in his *Weekly Political Register* in 1806, while the parliamentary assaults it inspired on the judge-advocate-general of the navy were aborted only by the fall of Pitt's ministry. The whig Samuel Whitbread presented a petition to the Commons on Cochrane-Johnstone's behalf on 10 March 1807.

Unsuccessful in restoring his military career, Cochrane-Johnstone was elected member of parliament for Grampound in 1807. Declaring himself independent of party in the radical tradition, he attacked West Indian and army abuses, including the sale of commissions. In July he seconded his nephew, Thomas, Lord *Cochrane, in demanding a list of members holding government pensions and sinecures. In March 1808 he was disqualified from sitting in the house by reason of his failure to possess the necessary property qualifications. By then he had returned to the West Indies, where his brother, Sir Alexander Cochrane, was naval commander-in-chief in the Leeward Islands. Cochrane-Johnstone supported Francisco Miranda's plan to liberate Spanish America and open it to British commerce, writing on his behalf to Lord Castlereagh. For his own fortunes, he obtained from his brother an appointment as prize agent at Tortola, where he represented the navy in the matter of prize arising from the capture of the Danish islands of St Thomas, St Croix, and St John in 1807. He was soon accused of bribing the vice-admiralty court at Tortola to condemn property in the interests of the captors, of refusing to surrender public property to the civil authorities, and of using captors' money to buy estates and other property on St Croix. Sir Alexander confessed, 'I shall ever sincerely regret that my attachment to him as a brother induced me to repose in him the trust that I did' (Alexander to Basil Cochrane, 26 Feb 1809, NL Scot., MS 2572, fol. 173).

Legal proceedings against him drove Cochrane-Johnstone back to England. In 1809 he visited Seville and Vera Cruz, buying Spanish dollars for the British Treasury. Allegations were made that he was involved in smuggling, but the incident may have been the fault of one Captain Maling, who attempted to ship dollars from Vera Cruz under Cochrane-Johnstone's name without paying appropriate duties, and whose activities Cochrane-Johnstone sought to check. It has also been said that Cochrane-Johnstone defaulted on a deal to export British muskets to Spain in return for sheep that he would sell in the United States. Apparently his London agent had difficulty in securing an export licence for the muskets. The venture proved disastrous throughout, for most of the sheep perished on arrival in New York in 1810, while others failed to make the expected price.

On 7 July 1812 Cochrane-Johnstone replaced his brother, George, as one of the members of parliament for Grampound, retained the seat in the general election of that year, and endeavoured to resume a parliamentary career. He was, however, in deep financial trouble. In 1813 five creditors were pursuing him for a total of £16,301. His Dominican property—four houses and 671 acres of land, with 62 slaves, crops, and livestock—was seized and offered for sale in the summer of 1814.

On 21 February 1814 Charles Random de Berenger, in the guise of an aide to the British ambassador in Russia, travelled from Dover to London spreading news that the French had been defeated and Napoleon killed. Word drove up stocks of omnium on the London exchange, and among the principal beneficiaries were Cochrane-Johnstone, his nephew Lord Cochrane, and their stockbroker, arousing the suspicions of the stock exchange. According to a report published by the stock exchange Cochrane-Johnstone's profits were £4931. On 22 March he told the house that he could establish his innocence of fraud, but at a trial at the court of king's bench on 8–9 June 1814, which he did not attend, he and the other defendants were convicted. While Lord Cochrane remained to suffer imprisonment and protest his innocence, Cochrane-Johnstone fled. He never returned to Britain.

The case aroused enormous controversy, largely on account of the question of Lord Cochrane's guilt. There was ample evidence that Cochrane-Johnstone had instigated the hoax, colluding with Berenger, with whom he was on close terms and for whom he had attempted to set up a false alibi. But many believed that Lord Cochrane had innocently suffered because of his association with his uncle, among them Cochrane-Johnstone's daughter, Elizabeth, and her future husband, Lord Napier. Napier feared that Lord Cochrane would suffer for 'keeping low company' and observed that 'Cochrane-Johnstone lost his character many years ago' (William, Lord Napier, to William Guthrie, 12 March 1814, William Guthrie MSS, NMM). As late as 1859 Elizabeth wrote to Lord Cochrane, then tenth earl of Dundonald, remarking that 'ever since that miserable time I have felt that you suffered for my poor

father's fault' (Elizabeth, Lady Napier, to earl of Dundonald, Christmas 1859, Dundonald Muniments, NA Scot., GD 233/177/103). Lord Cochrane himself privately referred to his uncle as 'that greatest of all scoundrels' (Thomas, Lord Cochrane, to William Jackson, Dundonald Muniments, NA Scot., GD 233/44/XXIII).

At the time of Cochrane-Johnstone's inevitable expulsion from parliament on 5 July 1814 it was reported that he had been seen in Calais. He went to Lisbon, and in January 1815 to the West Indies, where he discovered that his Dominican estates had been sold for less than he owed. He unsuccessfully attempted to recover his property, and transferred his operations to Demerara, where he had a coffee plantation in 1819. In 1829, when a fraudulent claim he had made upon the French government was exposed, he was in Paris. He was living at 96 rue du Faubourg St Honoré, Paris, at the time of his death, which had occurred by August 1833, when his possessions were inventoried.

Cochrane-Johnstone possessed undoubted talent, and a personality that enabled him to survive constant controversy. William Beckford found him a 'confounded, mawkish, pompous braggart' (Alexander, 119) but others liked him, including William Cobbett, who wrote after the final flight from London: 'I have had the pleasure to know him for about eleven years. ... I shall always be anxious to hear from him, and learn that prosperity and happiness attend him' (Cobbett's Weekly Political Register, 2 July 1814). Nevertheless, an opportunistic self-seeker of doubtful principles, he destroyed his own reputation and blighted the brilliant naval career of his more famous nephew.

JOHN SUGDEN

Sources A. J. Cochrane-Johnstone, *Proceedings of the general court-martial in the trial of Major John Gordon* (1804) · A. J. Cochrane-Johnstone, *Correspondence between Colonel Cochrane-Johnstone and the departments of the Commander-in-Chief and the Judge-Advocate-General* (1805) · A. J. Cochrane-Johnstone, *Defence of the Hon. Andrew Cochrane-Johnstone* (1805) · A. J. Cochrane-Johnstone, *The calumnious aspersions contained in the report of the sub-committee of the stock exchange, exposed and refuted* [1814] · *The trial of Charles Random de Berenger …* (1814) · A. Mackenrot, *Secret memoirs of the Hon. Andrew Cochrane-Johnstone …* (1814) [a hostile sketch] · C. R. de Berenger, *The noble stock-jobber* (1816) [an exposé of the 1814 hoax] · HoP, *Commons, 1790–1820* · J. B. Atlay, *The trial of Lord Cochrane before Lord Ellenborough* (1897) · J. Sugden, 'Lord Cochrane, Naval Commander, Radical, Inventor', PhD diss., 1981, University of Sheffield · A. D. Harvey, *Britain in the early nineteenth century* (1978), 234–7 · A. Cochrane, *The fighting Cochranes* (1983) · W. Beckford, *Life at Fonthill, 1807–1822: with interludes in Paris and London*, ed. B. Alexander (1957) · *Cobbett's Weekly Political Register* (1806); (2 July 1814)

Archives NL Scot., corresp. and papers, MS 9049 | Beds. & Luton ARS, letters to Samuel Whitbread · BL, Add. MS 35145 [9–11] · Bodl. Oxf., corresp., mainly with William Beckford · NA Scot., Dundonald muniments · NL Scot., corresp. with Sir Alexander Cochrane

Wealth at death see inventory of belongings in Paris; NL Scot., MS 9049, fol. 57

Johnstone, Bryce (1747–1805), Church of Scotland minister, was born on 2 March 1747, the son of John Johnstone (d. c.1780) of Gutterbraes, provost of Annan, and his wife, Elizabeth (1706/7–1804), the daughter of Thomas Howie, minister of the parish of Annan. He studied at the University of Edinburgh and was licensed as a preacher by the presbytery of Annan on 4 October 1769. Two years afterwards, on 22 August 1771, he was ordained as assistant and successor to the Revd Thomas Hamilton, minister of the church of Holywood, in the presbytery of Dumfries. When Hamilton died, on 24 November 1772, Johnstone succeeded to the full charge of the parish, and shortly afterwards a new church was built to replace the existing one, which had been used as a place of worship since before the Reformation and which was almost a ruin. On 12 June 1786 the University of Edinburgh conferred the degree of Doctor of Divinity upon him, and he remained minister of Holywood for the rest of his life.

Johnstone took a leading part in the management of ecclesiastical affairs and was regarded as one of the prominent supporters of the popular party in the general assembly. He was actively involved with the Society in Scotland for Propagating Christian Knowledge. Acting on his advice the society purchased several estates, which turned out to be valuable investments, and he was thus highly valued as a counsellor. Johnstone also took a lively interest in agricultural improvement. In 1794 he wrote *A General View of the Agriculture of the County of Dumfries* for the board of agriculture in London, from which he received a vote of thanks and a piece of silver plate in appreciation of his work.

Johnstone published several sermons during his lifetime, as well as a commentary on Revelation and an essay in 1801 on how to restore peace and prosperity to Britain. He also wrote the account of Holywood parish for John Sinclair's *Statistical Account*. A collection of his sermons was published in Edinburgh two years after his death, unmarried, on 27 April 1805 at the manse, Holywood.

A. H. MILLAR, rev. ALEXANDER DU TOIT

Sources *Fasti Scot.*, new edn, 2.242, 276 · F. Miller, *A bibliography of the parish of Annan* (1925), 49–50 · *Scots Magazine and Edinburgh Literary Miscellany*, 67 (1805), 565 · G. Gilchrist, ed., *Memorials in Annan old burial ground* (1963), 23 · D. Laing, ed., *A catalogue of the graduates … of the University of Edinburgh*, Bannatyne Club, 106 (1858), 246
Archives NL Scot., single items and collections, MS 10279
Wealth at death presumably did not inherit Gutterbraes estate; not known as 'of Gutterbraes'

Johnstone, Charles (*c.*1719–*c.*1800), novelist and journalist, was born at Carrigogunnell in the county of Limerick. Apparently descended from a branch of the Johnstones of Annandale, Dumfriesshire, but lacking the financial wherewithal to make good his claims, Johnstone was educated at Trinity College, Dublin, but appears not to have taken a degree before moving to England. He was called to the bar, but his extreme deafness restricted his legal career to that of a chamber lawyer, to supplement the income from which he began a literary career. His chief work, *Chrysal, or, The Adventures of a Guinea*, appeared in four volumes between 1760 and 1765. The first and second volumes were written during a visit to the earl of Mount-Edgcumbe in Devon and had already gone through three editions before Johnstone was prevailed on to write the last two volumes, and the whole work was frequently reprinted during the eighteenth century (and translated into French). An excoriating satire that won Johnstone respect as a wit but few friends, the novel is set roughly during the period of the Seven Years' War (1757–63) and pretends to reveal political secrets, and to expose the private profligacy of many of the well-known—and highly colourful—public characters of the time.

In addition to *Chrysal*, Johnstone published a number of other novels: *The Reverie, or, A Flight to the Paradise of Fools* (2 vols., 1762); *The History of Arbases, Prince of Betlis* (2 vols., 1774); *The Pilgrim, or, A Picture of Life* (2 vols., 1775); *History of John Juniper, Esq., alias Juniper Jack* (3 vols., 1781). The British Library catalogue and *ESTC* also attribute *The Adventures of Anthony Varnish* (1786) and a tragedy, *Buthred* (1779), to Johnstone. Despite this, Johnstone faced an old age of poverty (at least in part, according to Baker, due to Johnstone's being a victim of an unscrupulous publisher and a dishonest theatrical producer).

Accordingly in May 1782 Johnstone sailed for India aboard the *Brilliant*, hoping to prevail on the generosity of those he had helped into positions of favour during more prosperous times (for example, Johnstone had helped the son of one Luke Sparks of the Covent Garden Theatre into a position as a writer in Bombay (*GM*, 1st ser., 77, 1807, 631), and in particular, Johnstone hoped to renew his acquaintance with an old friend from his Temple days, Lord Macartney, now governor of Madras. After an eventful journey—the *Brilliant* foundered off Africa and Johnstone and the other survivors suffered considerable deprivation before rescue—Johnstone found employment by writing for the Bengal newspaper press under the signature of Oneiropolos. He became joint proprietor of a journal, and it is said that the profits from this, and a number of property speculations, allowed him to amass something of a fortune for the first time in his life. He died in Calcutta about 1800 and left the balance of his fortune to the family of his wife, about whom nothing is known but that she died in England before Johnstone sailed for India.

D. R. MOORE

Sources *GM*, 1st ser., 77 (1807), 631 · *GM*, 1st ser., 80 (1810), 311 · *Ryan's worthies of Ireland* · A. J. Webb, *A compendium of Irish biography* (1878), 267 · *GM*, 1st ser., 64 (1794), 591 · C. Johnstone, *Chrysal, or, The adventures of a guinea*, ed. E. A. Baker (1904) [incl. introduction] · *British Museum general catalogue of printed books … to 1955*, BM, 30 (1965) · *DNB* · *ESTC*
Wealth at death said to have acquired considerable property: *DNB*

Johnstone [*née* Todd; *other married name* M'Leish], **Christian Isobel** (1781–1857), journalist and author, was born in the parish of St Cuthbert's, Edinburgh, on 12 June 1781, to James Todd, a medical student, and his wife, Jean, *née* Campbell. She was married, first, to a Mr M'Leish, from whom she obtained a divorce, and second, in Edinburgh on 24 June 1815, to John Johnstone (1779–1857), a teacher in Dunfermline. That year she published her first novel, *Clan-Albin*, anonymously. The Johnstones moved to Inverness and became co-editors of the weekly newspaper, the *Inverness Courier*, when it began publication in October 1817, on a joint salary of £100 a year. She gave the paper a literary distinction not usually found in provincial newspapers, wrote on domestic topics and did the usual 'cut and paste' of London newspapers to fill the *Courier*'s columns. Indeed, many of her domestic articles were published as *The cook and housewife's manual … by Mistress Margaret Dods of the Cleikum Inn, St. Ronan's*, in 1826, and provided her with both the pseudonym, Meg Dods, and a steady income for nearly thirty years, as the *Manual* was reprinted in several subsequent editions.

In 1827 the Johnstones returned to Edinburgh and John established a printing business and, together with William Blackwood, purchased the *Edinburgh Weekly Chronicle*, with Mrs Johnstone as editor. But their political liberalism ran counter to Blackwood's old-fashioned tory values, and the partnership was dissolved in 1832. Then, at his wife's suggestion, Johnstone founded the *Schoolmaster and Edinburgh Magazine*, a 1½d. weekly journal. With William Tait as publisher, Mrs Johnstone wrote most of the content between 4 August 1832 and 29 June 1833, and continued to do so after the journal became the monthly 8d. *Johnstone's Edinburgh Magazine*. Meanwhile Tait had begun publishing the monthly *Tait's Edinburgh Magazine*, on sale at 2s. 6d., with John Johnstone as the printer, in March 1832, hardly a month before the enactment of the first Reform Bill, as an organ of Liberal principles. Mrs Johnstone contributed to the periodical and may also have served as sub-editor. According to Leigh Hunt, the magazine's London readers complained of 'the excess of politics in the New Monthly' and he suggested to Tait that 'its ground be broken up into smaller and more flowery beds' (Brewer, 198).

In June 1834 *Johnstone's* was incorporated into *Tait's Edinburgh Magazine*, and the latter's price was reduced from a half-crown to 1s., making it the first of many later shilling monthlies. Tait appointed Mrs Johnstone as editor, giving her a half-share in the business, and he ran the business side and correspondence with the contributors, while she was responsible for editorial decisions and choosing and arranging the contents of each issue. But the merger did not increase circulation, which remained about 4000, with 2800 copies shipped monthly to London. The literary content of *Tait's* now took precedence over the political and, while Mrs Johnstone was editor, such women writers as Catherine Gore, Mary Howitt, and Mary Russell Mitford regularly contributed over half the journal's most interesting articles. Mrs Johnstone's fiction and criticism comprised nearly all the magazine's 'Literary register', filling twenty of each issue's 138 pages.

Thomas De Quincey, a contributor of over forty articles under her editorship, spoke of her as 'the Mrs Jameson of Scotland … cultivating the profession of authorship with no … loss of feminity' (Conolly) and her contemporaries stated that she 'was to *Tait's* what Professor [John] Wilson was to *Blackwoods*' (Anderson, *Scot. nat.*). She was 'extremely popular with Scottish readers in the early Victorian era [who] supported her conduct of *Tait's* … and many of her articles were explicitly feminist, in a moderate respectable way' (Hyde, 135–40). In fact Mrs Johnstone was the only woman journalist to edit a major Victorian periodical before the 1860s.

Perhaps her 'unassuming disposition [which] shrank from anything like publicity or conspicuousness' (Anderson, *Scot. nat.*, and substantiated in her only letter in the Blackwood MSS, MS 4012, fols. 210–12) contributed to her disappearance from Scottish cultural history. As well, she had to endure the stigma which society attached to a divorced, and remarried, childless woman. As a full-time journalist, Mrs Johnstone was well aware 'that the woman who turns her talents to any profitable use, is … in our Society, *degraded*' (C. I. Johnstone, *Edinburgh Tales*, 1846). Forty years after her death an Englishwoman was proud to announce she was the 'first woman journalist in Edinburgh since Mrs Johnstone's day' (White, 168).

Her literary output embraced three books for children, as well as her two novels and three historical surveys, some under the name of Aunt Jane. From *Tait's* she gathered together three volumes by (mainly) feminine contributors, including some of her best fiction, and published them as *Edinburgh Tales*. By the time the last of these volumes was published in 1846 both Mrs Johnstone and Tait had decided to retire and sell *Tait's*. She enjoyed ten years of retirement, saw some of her books reprinted by her major publisher, Oliver and Boyd, and died on 26 August 1857, of heart disease and bronchitis, at her home, 12 Buccleuch Place, Edinburgh. Her husband died a few months later, on 3 November. Both were buried in the Grange cemetery, where an obelisk was erected to their memory.   FRED HUNTER

Sources [M. W. Hyde and W. E. Houghton], 'Tait's Edinburgh Magazine, 1832–1855', *Wellesley index*, 4.475–85 • M. A. Weinstein, 'Tait's Edinburgh Magazine', *British literary magazines*, ed. A. Sullivan, [2]: *The Romantic age, 1789–1836* (1984), 401–5 • M. Hyde, 'The role of "Our Scottish readers" in the history of *Tait's Edinburgh Magazine*', *Victorian Periodicals Review*, 14 (1981), 135–40 • Anderson, *Scot. nat.* • *Inverness Courier* (4 Dec 1917), centenary suppl. • Mrs Johnstone's letter to W. Blackwood, 1824, Ministry of Defence, Whitehall, London, army historical branch, Blackwood MSS, MS 4012, fols. 210–12 • *The Scotsman* (27 Aug 1857) • *Inverness Courier* (3 Sept 1857) • *Tait's Edinburgh Magazine*, new ser., 24 (1857), 573–5 • J. Bertram, *Some memories of books, authors and events* (1893), 1, 10, 11, 25, 29, 30, 31 • L. A. Brewer, *My hunt library* (1938), 198 • F. White, *A fire in the kitchen: the autobiography of a cook* (1938), 168 • M. F. Conolly, *Biographical dictionary of eminent men of Fife* (1866) • bap. reg. Scot. • m. reg. Scot. • E. Barron, 'A highland newspaper and its links with Edinburgh', *University of Edinburgh Journal*, 34 (1989–90), 98–101 • A. Easley, *First-person anonymous: Victorian print media and the woman writer, 1830–70* (2003) • C. Johnstone, *Clan-Albin: a national tale*, ed. A. Monnickendam, Association of Scottish Literary Studies, 32 (2003)

Archives NL Scot., Blackwood MSS • NL Scot., Oliver and Boyd MSS

Johnstone, Edward (1757–1851), physician, born at Kidderminster, Worcestershire, on 26 September 1757, was the second of the nine children of James *Johnstone, physician (1730–1802), and his wife, Hannah, *née* Crane (1733–1802); John *Johnstone was his brother. Having spent his early years with his grandparents at the family seat near Annan, in Scotland, Edward Johnstone entered Kidderminster grammar school in 1766. When assisting his father in practice in Kidderminster he caught typhus in the 1774 epidemic and later, while at Edinburgh University, described this and a subsequent (1777) outbreak in his

MD thesis, *De febre puerperali* (1779). He also wrote an account of his experiments (1775–6) with Droitwich brine. In 1778, while he was still a student at Edinburgh, his *Case of Obstinate obstipatis Depending on a Stricture of the Rectum* was published. From his correspondence with William Withering it is clear that he had used digitalis therapeutically.

After graduating, Johnstone began practice at New Street, Birmingham, in the summer of 1779; on 13 September he was appointed as one of the first four physicians to the new General Hospital, where John Ash was the senior consultant. Johnstone quickly developed a very successful practice in the area and among his patients were Sarah Siddons and Samuel Johnson. After sharing premises with John Ash, Johnstone moved in 1783 to the fashionable medical quarter of Birmingham, Temple Row, which was attacked in the Priestley riots of 1791. He then moved to a house in the country, Moor Green, Moseley, later the home of Joseph Chamberlain, and on 2 October 1792 at Solihull he married by licence a local heiress, Catherine Weardon, a cleric's daughter. Their eldest daughter, Catherine, was born and baptized on 13 February 1794. After the birth of a third daughter, Hannah, in 1798, Mrs Johnstone became a permanent invalid.

Three weeks after his wife's death in 1801 Johnstone resigned his post at the General Hospital and his brother John was appointed in his place. Johnstone and his two surviving daughters moved to Leamington Priors, where they all caught scarlet fever, from which Hannah died in October 1801. Johnstone's father died six months later and his friend, the Revd Samuel Parr, advised him to resume medical practice. Johnstone therefore moved back to Birmingham, taking Ladywood House, then in a rural area, where St Vincent Street was later to run.

Johnstone remarried by licence on 5 October 1802, at Tettenhall, Staffordshire; his bride was an heiress, Elizabeth Pearson (1779–1823), daughter of Thomas Pearson, who was William Withering's cousin. Their son, Edward Johnstone [see below] was born at Ladywood House on 9 April 1804. Johnstone changed his professional premises from Temple Row to 12 The Square, until 1823, when he acquired consulting rooms at 104 New Street. In 1805 the family moved to Edgbaston Hall; Johnstone had invested his marriage settlement in land and leased Edgbaston Hall at £300 a year; William Withering had earlier rented it from the Gough family. His second son, James Johnstone [see below], was born at Edgbaston Hall in 1806; also born there were two daughters, who both died young, and a third son, Charles Johnstone (1815–32). Johnstone remained there for the rest of his life.

Johnstone had a considerable interest in the education of the poor and from 1816 he began Sunday evening adult literacy classes at Edgbaston Hall for some forty men, as well as a day school for girls of the parish, held in an estate lodge which he had built for the purpose. During the depression of 1816 he provided work in the area by ordering substantial improvements to the grounds, to which he permitted a degree of public access. He served on the committees of the Birmingham Mechanics' Institute and of the Deaf and Dumb School; he was a governor of King Edward VI's School in the city. His own scholarly interests led him to start learning Old English at the age of fifty. His taste in art ranged from owning a portrait, dating from 1578, of Sir Francis Walsingham, to encouraging local artists to paint in the park. In 1821 he served on the committee for establishing a society of arts.

After the death of his second wife Johnstone became actively involved in the new medical school which William Sands Cox, a local surgeon, founded in 1825. Johnstone was a council member and a generous benefactor of the institution; he laid the foundation stone when it became Queen's College in 1843 and was the first principal until 1845. In 1840 he helped to found the Queen's Hospital in Birmingham and was honorary physician there until his death.

A large public dinner was held in 1829 to mark Johnstone's fifty years of medical practice in Birmingham. He served as a magistrate until 1832. Johnstone actively promoted the dispensary, which provided medical attention for the poor in their own homes. In 1832 he was the first president of the Provincial Medical and Surgical Association (later the British Medical Association) when it was founded at Worcester. A street was named after him in the centre of Birmingham. Johnstone died, apparently of 'a slight cold', at Edgbaston Hall, on 4 September 1851 and was buried in Edgbaston Old Church on 10 September. His and Elizabeth's portrait medallions can be seen in the church. **Edward Johnstone** (1804–1881), claimant to the Annandale peerage, was born at Ladywood House, Birmingham, on 9 April 1804, the eldest son of Edward Johnstone and his second wife, Elizabeth (*née* Pearson). He gained his BA at Trinity College, Cambridge, in 1825 and his MA in 1828. He was called to the bar at Lincoln's Inn on 6 May 1828 and later entered the Inner Temple, but never practised law. With the poet Thomas Campbell, Lord Dudley Stuart, Lord Ilchester, and others he was co-founder in 1832 of the Literary Association of the Friends of Poland and in 1836 published a pamphlet, *What is Poland?*, an abridged translation of *La Pologne et ses frontières*, by the marquis de Noailles.

Johnstone never married. On the death of his half-sister in 1860 he inherited Fulford Hall, Solihull, and Dunsley Manor, near Kinver, Staffordshire. Six years later he was one of the three claimants to the dormant Annandale peerage, all of whom were rejected by the House of Lords in 1881. He died at Worcester on 20 September 1881, and was buried in the family burial place in Edgbaston, Birmingham.

James Johnstone (1806–1869), physician, was born at Edgbaston Hall, near Birmingham, on 12 April 1806, the second son of Edward Johnstone, and his second wife, Elizabeth (*née* Pearson). Following a private education, he was admitted to Trinity College, Cambridge, in 1822, gaining his MB in 1828, an ML in 1830, and an MD in 1833. He then studied in Edinburgh and briefly in Paris. On returning to England he spent a period at St Bartholomew's Hospital, London, before moving to Hastings, Sussex, for six months to study tuberculosis. He became an FRCP in 1834.

In the same year, on 7 January, he married Maria Mary Payne Webster (1813–1859), daughter of Joseph Webster, an ironmaster from Penns, Sutton Coldfield; they had thirteen children.

Johnstone wished to practise in London, but was persuaded by his father to settle in Birmingham and he moved to 9 Old Square. He served as a special constable during the town's Chartist disturbances in 1839, and as honorary physician at a temporary hospital there during a cholera epidemic. In 1841 Johnstone was appointed at Queen's College as the first professor of materia medica, a subject on which he had published in 1835; his *Discourse on the Phenomena of Sensation* appeared in 1846. He was extraordinary physician to the General Hospital and senior governor of King Edward VI's School. In September 1865, when the British Medical Association met for the first time at Birmingham, Johnstone was elected its president. His portrait, by W. T. Roden, hung in the General Hospital.

Johnstone retired from medical practice in 1867 and went to live in Leamington Spa, where he died on 11 May 1869. Of his five sons, the eldest, James (1841–1895), knighted in 1887, was a professional soldier in India, the third joined the navy, and the fourth became a cleric; none entered medicine. JOAN LANE

Sources C. L. Johnstone, *History of the Johnstones* (1909) • B. T. Davis, 'Edward Johnstone', *The Queen's Medical Magazine*, 55/1 (March 1963), 6–9 • W. H. McMenemey, *A history of the Worcester Royal Infirmary* (1947) • C. Gill, *Manor and borough to 1865* (1952), vol. 1 of *History of Birmingham* (1952–74) • J. A. Langford, ed., *Modern Birmingham and its institutions: a chronicle of local events, from 1841 to 1871*, 2 (1877) • GM, 2nd ser., 36 (1851), 436–8 • *VCH Warwickshire*, vol. 7 • T. Nash, *Collections for the history of Worcestershire*, 2 vols. (1781–2) • T. W. Peck and K. D. Wilkinson, *William Withering of Birmingham* (1950) • Venn, *Alum. Cant.* • Burke, *Gen. GB* (1898) • Pigot and Co., *Pigot and Co.'s national commercial directory for 1828–9* (1828) [Warwickshire section] • *History, gazetteer, and directory, of Warwickshire*, F. White and Co. (1850) • *London and Provincial Medical Directory* (1852) • *Aris's Birmingham Gazette* (8 Sept 1851) • *Birmingham Daily Post* (12 May 1869) • *The Lancet* (15 May 1869) [James Johnstone] • *The Times* (24 Sept 1881) [Edward Johnstone (1804–1881)] • parish registers, Edgbaston, Warks. CRO • J. Horsfall, *The iron masters of Penns* (1971)

Likenesses W. T. Roden, double portrait, oils, 19th cent. (with James Johnstone); Birmingham Hospital • W. Radclyffe, stipple, 1839, Wellcome L. • H. Room, oils, 1844, Birmingham Medical School

Johnstone, Edward (1804–1881). *See under* Johnstone, Edward (1757–1851).

Johnstone, George (1730–1787), naval officer, colonial governor, and politician, was born in Dumfriesshire, the fourth of the seven sons of Sir James Johnstone of Westerhall, third baronet (1697–1772), and his wife, Barbara Murray (d. 1773), daughter of the fourth Lord Elibank. Choosing a career in the Royal Navy, Johnstone first went to sea in 1744 and served in George II's war. By the time he had passed his lieutenant's examination in 1749 he had, while serving in the *Canterbury*, earned a reputation for bravery. On one occasion he boarded an enemy fireship so that it could be towed away from a British squadron that it threatened to destroy off Port Louis, Hispaniola. Peace in 1748 curtailed Johnstone's activities in the king's service,

though he captained at least one merchant vessel to the Caribbean in the inter-war years. In addition it seems likely that, before being summoned to serve once more in the Royal Navy in 1755, Johnstone furthered his self-education at Ballencrieff, the seat of his uncle Patrick Murray, fifth Lord Elibank, whom he called 'my adoptive father' (G. Johnstone to W. Pulteney, 18 Feb 1761, Pulteney MSS, Hunt. L.).

When he was at sea again in the *Bideford* Johnstone's insubordinate behaviour caused him to be court martialled for disobedience. Despite favourable evidence from the ship's acting mate, his younger brother Gideon Johnstone, the court found against George. He was reprimanded but ordered back to duty. On the *Dreadnought* he received further commendations for bravery in action off Santo Domingo. In addition he gained the praise of Captain Arthur Forrest, who admired his diligence, though his lack of respect for naval hierarchy also earned him the ill will of Rear-Admiral Thomas Cotes, the result of a dispute over prize money. By 1759 Johnstone was in poor health, without a ship, and looking for preferment. After some delay Lord Anson, the first lord of the Admiralty, gave him command of the sloop *Hornet* (14 guns). Initially she engaged in mostly profitless escort duties in the North Sea. Such voyages were usually dull. Exceptional was one in which Johnstone skilfully put down a mutiny of pressed men with minimal loss of life. Orders to take the *Hornet* to Lisbon changed Johnstone's luck. He took prizes on his way to the Portuguese station and captured more after his arrival. Of more importance strategically was his early notice, in January 1762, to Admiral George Rodney, that Britain had declared war on Spain. Rodney, a lifelong friend then on duty in the Caribbean, made useful captures from the Spanish before they knew that the British had become formal enemies. Such successes did not satisfy Johnstone, who coveted the security and opportunities afforded by promotion to post captain. Not until May 1762 did he achieve this ambition, too late to see active service again before peace preliminaries ended combat in the Seven Years' War.

In 1761 George III's appointment of John Stuart, third earl of Bute, as prime minister had a substantive impact on Johnstone's career. Through his friendship with Bute's secretary, the dramatist John Home, Johnstone became governor of the new British colony of West Florida. Bute's decision to appoint fellow Scots to all four of the new British colonies created after the Seven Years' War aroused much derision and criticism in the opposition press. Johnstone personally became notorious for seeking out a writer for the *North Briton* and cudgelling him for his comments on Bute's Floridian appointments. West Florida's vast area included the ports of Pensacola, reluctantly surrendered by the Spanish, and Mobile, more willingly ceded by the French in the wake of their defeat in the Seven Years' War. The province's location on both the Gulf of Mexico and the Mississippi River caused Johnstone to foresee a profitable future for West Florida, that he envisaged as 'The Emporium of the New World' (*Georgia Gazette*, 10 Jan 1765).

It was with optimism and energy that Johnstone arrived at his capital, Pensacola, on 21 October 1764. Once there, he encouraged immigration; kept order among a lawless pioneer population; negotiated, initially rather skilfully, with the local Indian peoples; and established the forms of civil government. Unlike his counterpart in British East Florida, Johnstone organized the election of representatives to a provincial legislative assembly with which he worked reasonably well, despite its becoming a forum for opposition to British policies such as the Stamp Act. Even so, Johnstone achieved a solid working relationship with the assembly and implemented an ambitious programme of legislation. During Johnstone's short governorship the assembly enacted fifteen laws, whereas no more than thirty-two were passed during the remaining fourteen years of the colony's existence. By contrast the governor's relations with the military, a dominant element in West Florida society, were awkward from the first and in the end bitter. Johnstone claimed an authority over the soldiers that his commission seemed to justify, but which was contrary to accepted practice in the colonies.

In 1766, while the British government strove for peace in North America, Johnstone was bent on a war with the Creek Indians. In August the earl of Shelburne became the secretary of state responsible for colonial affairs. Angered by Johnstone's provocative stance, Shelburne called for the governor's removal. Frustrated in his expectations of commercial prosperity in his province, and enjoying little popular support for war from outside the assembly, Johnstone applied for a leave of absence. He sailed from Pensacola on 13 January 1767, never to return. If he had any desire to do so, of which there is some doubt, the ministry's decision to remove him permanently made his resumption of the office impossible.

On his return to England, Johnstone re-entered the politics of the East India Company. Three years previously as a member of a faction of proprietors including other family members, he had supported Robert, Baron Clive. In 1767 he reversed his position, and successfully spoke and voted against Clive, who was persecuting George's brother John Johnstone, a member of the company's council in Bengal. Having established a reputation as a 'man of business' and an orator, Johnstone looked for election to the House of Commons. The patronage of Sir James Lowther enabled Johnstone to become a member for Cockermouth in 1768. Thereupon he joined 'Sir James's nine pins', a parliamentary group dedicated to Lowther, and he renewed his membership of the group in 1774 as member for Appleby. In the Commons, Johnstone maintained his interest in the affairs of the East India Company. In the early 1770s he made scorching speeches in parliament against various of the North administration's schemes for Indian reform. He blamed Clive with particularly savage obloquy for the chaos in Bengal. These attacks made Johnstone a hero of the company's court of proprietors. He was chosen to chair a proprietary committee, whose purpose was to thwart plans for company reform, whether devised by the North government or by the East India Company's directorate, which that administration largely dominated. In spite of Johnstone's philippics, however, and the backing of the earl of Richmond, Johnstone's ally on Indian affairs, North finally did obtain passage of a parliamentary act to regulate the East India Company in 1773.

On American affairs in parliament Johnstone worked with, rather than belonged to, Rockingham's faction in attacking Lord North's American policies. With characteristic extremity he branded the Tea Act of 1773 'criminally absurd', and predicted that the Boston Port Bill would serve to unite not just New Englanders, but all Americans, in hostility to Britain. He voted against North's bill to alter the charter of Massachusetts and against the Quebec Act of 1774. Johnstone was a talented obstructionist, better at denunciation than support, but his eloquence was not always for purely political ends. A streak of humanitarianism may also be discerned. For instance he spoke at length and with feeling in parliament against the penalization of Irish Catholics, of imprisonment for debt, and of using impressment to man the navy. The slave trade he described as 'a commerce of the most barbarous and cruel kind that ever disgraced the transactions of any civilised people' (Cobbett, *Parl. Hist.* 17.1186–9, 1281, 1391; 19.61, 98). On the main constitutional questions of the day he was pragmatic rather than idealistic. Taxing Americans he thought legal but inexpedient. Sending troops to America would do no good. To maintain obedience to British laws would require the military to remain there permanently at great expense. Conciliation, he believed, was a wiser option.

In 1778 Johnstone returned to America in this capacity. North chose him, probably in the belief that he would be acceptable to Americans, as a member of Lord Carlisle's peace commission designed to patch up relations before the consolidation of a threatened French alliance. Johnstone was confident of success. He wrote letters to Americans of influence. How obviously preferable, he suggested, would be reconciliation with Britain to dependence on the traditional French enemy: those who helped secure it, he hinted vaguely, but with unmistakable intent, could be sure of reward. Once in America, Johnstone was accused of more blatant bribery—of offering the American general Joseph Reed 10,000 guineas. Although the charge was never proved, congress voted to have nothing to do with Johnstone. In 1778 he sailed home before the rest of the commissioners. They stayed on, vainly proffering mutual concessionary schemes and achieving nothing.

In the following year Johnstone accepted a naval commodoreship from the ministry he had vilified for years. He alleged by way of justification that the entry of France had transformed the American conflict into a war he could support. No longer was the struggle about redressing the grievances of North Americans. Instead it had assumed a familiar form: a struggle against one, and potentially two, Bourbon monarchs who could threaten Britain with invasion. Before taking up his promised assignment on the Portuguese station, Johnstone cruised off the French coast, looking for evidence of enemy invasion preparations. Once the union of the French and Spanish fleets was known to be imminent, he took his flagship, the *Romney*, to join the Channel Fleet of Sir Charles Hardy, whose task was to thwart the enemy fleets. Johnstone wanted to do so by seeking battle, but Hardy preferred, successfully in the outcome, to wear out the Franco-Spanish fleet with Fabian tactics. For Johnstone there followed a Portuguese interlude fruitful in prize money, but diplomatically disappointing: Johnstone sought, without known backing or observable result, to interest the Spanish in abandoning their war on Britain in exchange for Gibraltar.

In 1781 Johnstone took a sizeable collection of vessels that included a strong war squadron, transports, and East-Indiamen on what was supposed to be a secret expedition. Its purpose was to seize the strategically important colony at the Cape of Good Hope from the Dutch who, in 1780, had entered the war against Britain. Discovering what was afoot, the French sent Admiral Pierre André de Suffren to thwart Johnstone. He caught up with and attacked Johnstone's fleet as it lay untidily at anchor in Porto Praya in the Cape Verde Islands. Suffren damaged it enough to hinder an effective response from Johnstone, who pursued tardily and without significant success. Suffren had ruined all chance of his surprising and capturing the colony at the Cape. After late arrival there, Johnstone found a consolation prize in nearby Saldanha Bay: six rich Dutch East-Indiamen. Johnstone showed expertise in taking his warships to the Dutch hideaway. As though re-enacting a triumph of his youth, he personally attached a boat to a burning East-Indiaman and then had it towed to a lee shore shortly before it exploded. The consequence was his capture of five intact Dutch ships.

On his return voyage Johnstone stopped in Lisbon to marry, on 31 January 1782, Charlotte Dee, daughter of the British vice-consul; the couple had one son, John Lowther Johnstone. Johnstone had already fathered four sons and a daughter out of wedlock. Hodgkin's disease may have been partly responsible for some of Johnstone's lapses of judgement on his Cape expedition. Its aftermath was vexed. Johnstone had blamed a subordinate, Captain Evelyn Sutton, for his warships' delay in chasing Suffren, and had deprived Sutton of his command and of much prize money. Sutton brought a suit against the commodore. Protracted by appeals, it preoccupied Johnstone for most of the remaining years of his life and was decided in his favour only two days before his death.

Johnstone returned to parliament as MP for Lostwithiel in 1781. In his final years he spoke for lost causes, opposing American independence and any further government intervention in the affairs of the East India Company. In particular he strongly opposed Charles James Fox's scheme, potentially the most intrusive of several, for tighter control of that organization. Finally, in defiance of all his previous opinions, Johnstone accepted the need for some government control by agreeing to the reform proposals of William Pitt the Younger. Pitt's scheme allowed the East India Company's directors, as Fox's did not, to retain power over company appointments. It was perhaps in exchange for a promise of Pitt's help in obtaining the directorship, to which Johnstone was elected in 1784, that Johnstone was persuaded to collaborate with Pitt on Indian affairs. Their co-operation was limited. Pitt neither brought Johnstone into his government, nor even found him a pocket borough for the general election of 1784, in which Johnstone failed in his bid to represent the Haddington burghs. He returned to the Commons only in 1785, serving briefly, for poor health compelled him to apply for the Chiltern Hundreds a year later.

During a multifaceted career, shaped by influence and ability, Johnstone enjoyed some spectacular small-scale successes as a naval officer, but failed when given major command. Both his forays into diplomacy were failures, one very publicly so. In parliament he was respected for the effectiveness of his destructive oratory in opposition, but he was never asked to join an administration. The East India Company prized his spoken and written defence of its interests, and he did finally obtain a directorship of that company, but only at the end of his life, when health and energy had failed. He seems to have rated his work as the founder of the colony of West Florida more highly than his comparative success in East India House, and was proud to be known as Governor Johnstone for the last two decades of his life. He died at Hotwells, Bristol, possibly from Hodgkin's disease, on 24 May 1787, survived by his wife.   ROBIN F. A. FABEL

Sources DNB · R. F. A. Fabel, *Bombast and broadsides: the lives of George Johnstone* (1987) · C. Johnson, *British West Florida, 1763–1783* (1971) · I. R. Christie, 'Johnstone, George', HoP, *Commons, 1754–90* · Cobbett, *Parl. hist.* · R. Beatson, *Naval and military memoirs of Great Britain*, 2nd edn, 6 vols. (1804); repr. (1972) · L. S. Sutherland, *The East India Company in eighteenth century politics* (1952) · *Town and Country Magazine*, 13 (1781), 513–14 · *Scots Magazine*, 25 (1763), 626 · J. B. Starr, *Dons, tories and rebels* (1976) · R. R. Rea and M. B. Howard, jun., *Journals and acts of the general assembly of British West Florida* (1979) · S. F. Bemis, *The Hussey–Cumberland mission and American independence* (1968) · N. A. M. Rodger, *The wooden world: an anatomy of the Georgian navy* (1986) · N. A. M. Rodger, *The insatiable earl: a life of John Montagu, fourth earl of Sandwich* (1993) · N. A. M. Rodger, 'The mutiny in the *James and Thomas*', *Mariner's Mirror*, 70 (1984), 293–8 · Hunt. L., Pulteney papers

Archives BL OIOC, corresp., photo Eur. 63 [copies] · Lancs. RO, corresp. · NL Scot., corresp. · Plymouth and West Devon RO, MSS | BL OIOC, Orme MSS · Glamorgan Central Library, Bute MSS · Hunt. L., Pulteney MSS · Hunt. L., letters to Sir William Johnstone · NMM, letters to Lord Sandwich · PRO, CO5/574, 582–587, 618, 622 · U. Mich., Clements L., corresp. with Thomas Gage

Likenesses attrib. Raeburn, oils, NMM · group portrait, caricature · oils (after J. Boyle, *c.*1768–1794), NMM

Wealth at death London properties sold to provide widow with £500 p.a.; £200 p.a. to only legitimate son; £2000 to natural daughter; £1500 to each natural son: will, PRO, PROB 11/1154

Johnstone, Henry Alexander Butler- (1837–1902), politician, was born in Edinburgh on 7 December 1837, the only son of the Hon. Henry Butler-Johnstone (1809–1879) and his wife, Isabella, only daughter of Sir Alexander Munro. She was the niece and heir of General Johnstone of Auchen Castle in Dumfriesshire, which Butler-Johnstone inherited. In 1874, following the death of his mother the previous year, Butler-Johnstone adopted the surname Butler-Munro-Johnstone. He was educated at Eton College and matriculated in 1856 at Christ Church, Oxford, where he gained a first in classics in 1861. In May 1862 he was elected as Conservative MP for Canterbury, the constituency that his father had represented between 1857 and 1859. He spoke against the extension of the franchise during the parliamentary debates of 1866–7. Otherwise he often supported liberal causes, such as the disestablishment of the Irish church. In his pamphlet *Ireland* (1868) he rejected demands for the creation of an Irish republic but allowed the possibility that a Dublin parliament might be created with powers to legislate on specifically domestic issues, as long as Westminster retained control of financial and foreign policy matters. After 1868 he declared himself independent of any party identification.

Butler-Johnstone's main interest as an MP was foreign affairs. He urged a maritime alliance with France and was on the council of the Maritime League for the Resumption of Naval Rights, a pressure group demanding Britain's withdrawal from the declaration of Paris (1856) with its abolition of privateering. He was an ardent imperialist and advocated the maintenance of a strong army and navy. During the Eastern crisis of 1875–8 he became a leading Russophobe and philo-Turk, influenced by David Urquhart. He warned against Russia obtaining access to the Dardanelles and supported the work of Turkish constitutional reformers. In 1876 he answered Gladstone's pamphlet on the Bulgarian atrocities by denying the responsibility of the Turkish government and by claiming that Gladstone's portrait of the Turks was a travesty. In *The Turks* (1876) he countered the popular view of the Turks as barbarians and went on to defend such institutions as the harem (which he pointed out was only the name for a Turkish home). During the Russo-Turkish War, he actually lent money to the Turkish government for attacks on the Russian army and sent over military advisers (who were not employed). He resigned his parliamentary seat in 1878 in order to visit Turkey but later came to despair of the nation.

In the early 1880s Butler-Johnstone became an acquaintance of Karl Marx. He gave his friend Henry Hyndman a copy of *Das Kapital*, which led to Hyndman's conversion to Marxism. Butler-Johnstone was present in 1881 at the early meetings of the Democratic Federation, which was to become the Social Democratic Federation in 1884, the first major organization in the revival of British socialism. However, it seems unlikely that Butler-Johnstone was ever a socialist.

On 17 November 1877 Butler-Johnstone married Maria Irma Gabrielle, countess of Soyres, who died in 1880. In 1896 he married a widow, Mrs Skipp Lloyd. He was a JP for Dumfriesshire, where he owned nearly 3000 acres, though he spent the last twenty years of his life on the continent, writing for British and European newspapers on the need for a British imperial federation. Butler-Johnstone died at a hotel in Paris on 17 October 1902; his body was returned to England. Butler-Johnstone was a maverick figure on the right who ironically played a brief role in the origins of British socialism. At one time, he was 'the hope of the Conservative party' according to Henry Hyndman, who believed that he misused his talents and 'made a sad end of his promising life' (Hyndman, 207, 209).   ROHAN MCWILLIAM

Sources Burke, *Peerage*, Dunboyne • T. F. Gallagher, 'Butler-Johnstone, Henry Alexander', *BDMBR*, vol. 3, pt 1 • *The Times* (17 Oct 1902) • H. M. Hyndman, *The record of an adventurous life* (1911) • Walford, *County families*

Johnstone, James [*known as* Chevalier de Johnstone] (1719–c.1800), Jacobite sympathizer and army officer in the French service, was the son of James Johnstone, an Edinburgh merchant; details of his upbringing are unknown. In 1738 he visited his uncles Hewitt and General Douglas Johnstone in Russia. James also desired to enter into the tsar's service, but his father objected. In 1745, also against his father's wishes, he joined the Jacobite rising in Scotland, and served as an aide-de-camp to Charles Edward Stuart, the Young Pretender, and the army's tactical commander, Lord George Murray. Johnstone admired Murray, writing in his memoirs that the general 'possessed a natural genius for military operations'. The young warrior was, however, highly critical of the Young Pretender's martial skills. Johnstone himself seems to have acquitted himself well during the campaign. Sir Walter Scott described him as a 'military man having some turn of observation' (Jervis, 36). Johnstone demonstrated his military talents at the battle of Prestonpans (20 September 1745), reconnoitring the positions of 3000 troops under Sir John Cope, and fighting at the prince's side during the rout of the British army. Johnstone also fought in the ranks of the highlanders' left wing at Culloden, and describes, in detail, the defeat as well as the massacres and executions inflicted on the retreating army.

Johnstone escaped after the Jacobite defeat at the battle of Culloden on 16 April 1746. Rather than hide out in the highlands he was prompted to return to Edinburgh, apparently guided by a dream in which he saw himself relating his adventures to Lady Jane Douglas, a distant relative of his mother. After a series of narrow escapes he met in secret his father, who arranged for him to hide in Lady Jane's house. Two months later he made his way to London and some time later left for the Netherlands disguised as Lady Jane's servant.

In 1746 Johnstone went to Paris, where he rejoined the court of the Young Pretender in the hope of participating in a second expedition to recapture the Stuart crown. The Stuart cause, however, remained moribund. In 1749 as a Jacobite refugee Johnstone received a 2200 livres grant from the French court. A year later, as an ensign in the French marines, he survived shipwreck to reach Louisbourg, the fortress at Cape Breton Island in French Canada (Nova Scotia). He returned from France to Louisbourg in 1752 and was there promoted to lieutenant two years later. When the British captured the fortress in 1758, part of military operations during the Seven Years' War, Johnstone escaped to Quebec, where he served as aide-de-camp to General François de Lévis. When Lévis departed for Montreal, Johnstone became aide-de-camp to Marshal

Louis Joseph de Montcalm. In 1760 the French forces in Quebec capitulated to a British army under the command of Brigadier-General James Murray. Despite his Jacobite service, Johnstone was allowed to return to France where, claiming that he was disgusted that juniors were promoted over him, he quit the French service. Johnstone then received a fixed pension of 1485 livres. In the early 1770s this pension was reduced when the Abbé Terray assumed the post of controller-general and introduced financial measures to improve the solvency of the French government. Throughout this period Johnstone remained estranged from his parents and family, including an older sister named Cicely, wife of the sixth Lord Rollo, who all subsequently died, apparently leaving James with little or no inheritance. His pension ceased altogether during the French Revolution. After several petitions it was restored and he was awarded the cross of St Louis. His exact date and place of death are uncertain.

Johnstone related his adventures in the 'Forty-Five and his service in Canada in manuscript. Evidently composed late in life, but prior to the French Revolution, it is uncompromisingly critical of the Young Pretender and his advisers. In 1820 the manuscript was purchased by the publishers Longman from Robert Watson, who was distantly related to Johnstone by marriage. Chapters relating to the rebellion were published as *History of the rebellion of 1745–46, translated from a French manuscript originally deposited in the Scots College Paris*. The book went through three editions. The manuscript was subsequently purchased by John Lewis of Powis, a great-grandson of Jean Johnstone, James's younger sister, and his brother Hugh Leslie. A fresh translation of the entire memoir appeared in 1870. Portions of the memoir, *The Campaign of 1760 in Canada: a Narrative Attributed to Chevalier Johnstone* and *A dialogue in Hades: a parallel of military errors, of which the French and English armies were guilty, during the campaign of 1759, in Canada. Attributed to Chevalier Johnstone*, were published by the Quebec Historical Society in 1887. Nevertheless Johnstone's work has come to represent only a minor contribution to the history of the period.

J. G. ALGER, rev. JAMES JAY CARAFANO

Sources J. Johnstone, *Memoirs of the Chevalier de Johnstone*, trans. C. Winchester, 3 vols. (1870–71) · J. Johnstone, *Memoirs of the rebellion in 1745 to 1746*, 3rd edn (1822) · R. C. Jervis, *Collected papers of the Jacobite risings*, 1 (1971)

Johnstone, James, of Galabank (1730–1802), physician, the fourth son of John Johnstone (1688–1774), laird of Galabank, and Anna, *née* Ralston (1695–1776), was born at Annan, Dumfriesshire, on 14 April 1730. The Johnstones owned considerable lands in the borders. James Johnstone was educated at Dr Robert Henry's school in Annan before going to Edinburgh University to study medicine in 1747. There he was taught by such celebrated figures as Alexander Monro, Robert Whytt, and John Rutherford. Johnstone gained his MD in June 1750 and then travelled to Paris to learn dissection. He decided to practise in Kidderminster, Worcestershire, on hearing from his brother, who had preached there, that many children in the locality had

recently died in an epidemic of diphtheria, of which James Johnstone had made a special study.

Johnstone arrived at Bewdley, Worcestershire, on 12 September 1751, and soon moved to the nearby substantial town of Kidderminster. On 10 September 1753 he married Hannah Crane (1733–1802), whose dying brother he had attended and whose father, Henry Crane, was a prosperous local carpet manufacturer. The Johnstones had seven children who survived infancy. Three of their sons, James Johnstone (1753–1783) [see below], Edward *Johnstone (1757–1851), and John *Johnstone (1768–1836), became medical practitioners. Johnstone had an extensive practice area, well beyond the town, reaching to Lichfield, Stafford, Shrewsbury, Birmingham, and Wolverhampton. Among his illustrious patients were Lord Lyttelton of Hagley, Lord Chesterfield, Sarah Siddons, Lord Hertford, and Samuel Richardson. He was a close friend of the Revd Job Orton (1717–1783) and was made a county magistrate in 1779.

In 1774, on his father's death, Johnstone inherited the substantial Annandale estate and became the laird of Galabank. Following his son's sudden death at Worcester he accepted the vacant hospital appointment there and on 3 October 1783 was elected as physician (a post he held until December 1799); he moved to Worcester to practise, and occupied a large family house at 55 Foregate Street, which was demolished in 1849 to make room for a railway station to be built.

In politics Johnstone was a whig; he was presented to George III and Queen Charlotte on a royal visit to Worcester in 1788. He was a friend of William Withering, Erasmus Darwin, and Joseph Priestley, and had corresponded between 1761 and 1775 with Baron Haller. He belonged to a local literary circle and was interested in astronomy. Johnstone's writings were considerable: in *An Historical Dissertation Concerning the Malignant Epidemical Fever of 1756* (1758), he described a new form of disinfectant for typhus; *An Essay on the Use of the ganglions of the Nerves* (1771) was translated into German in 1787; and *A Treatise on the Malignant Angina, or Putrid and Ulcerous Sore Throat* (1779) was based on his MD thesis. He also published *Some Account of the Walton Water, Near Tewkesbury … and Diseases of the Lymphatic Glands* (1787) and *Medical Essays and Observations … Relating to the Nervous System* (1795). In 1789 Johnstone wrote on the abolition of slavery, and in 1795 he reported on a recent earthquake; he contributed an account of Kidderminster to T. R. Nash's *History of Worcestershire*. Johnstone was an honorary member of the Manchester Literary and Philosophical Society, a fellow of the Royal Medical Society of Edinburgh, and a member of the Bath Philosophical Society, and as a corresponding member of the Medical Society of London he was the first to receive its medal.

Johnstone died at his home in Foregate Street, Worcester, on 29 April 1802, just four days after the death of his wife. Johnstone, who continued to practise until a few days before his death, died a wealthy man, owning property, land, and shares. He was buried on 4 May 1802 at Kidderminster in St Mary's churchyard. A memorial to him, bearing the caduceus emblem, was erected on the south wall of the nave of Worcester Cathedral.

His eldest son, **James Johnstone** (1753–1783), was born at Kidderminster, Worcestershire, in August 1753, and was baptized there on 20 December that year. He was educated at the town's grammar school and, for three years, at Dr Caleb Atwood's academy in Daventry. In October 1770 he began to study medicine at Edinburgh University, where he was taught by William Cullen and by John Gregory, to whom he was clinical clerk. He received his MD in September 1773 for a thesis, entitled 'De angina maligna', which was later translated into English and published in 1779. Thanks to his father's considerable local influence he moved to Worcester and was elected a physician at the infirmary on 29 June 1774. Johnstone served in the Worcestershire militia and was a special constable during a local riot. He became engaged to be married to the sister of his hospital colleague, William Russell, a surgeon. He wrote the account of Droitwich and its spring in T. R. Nash's *History of Worcestershire* (1799).

In 1783 Johnstone agreed to attend prisoners in Worcester Castle, the county gaol, who were suffering from typhus, from which the governor, his wife, and the gaol surgeon had already died. However, Johnstone contracted the infection and was taken by his brother Henry to their father's house in Kidderminster, where, aged thirty, he died on 16 August. John Howard commented on his death in *The State of the Prisons* (1784), and gave a copy of the volume to James Johnstone senior. James Johnstone junior was buried at St Mary's, Kidderminster, on 19 September 1783; a monument to him was erected in Worcester Cathedral, recording the cause of his death.   JOAN LANE

Sources C. L. Johnstone, *History of the Johnstones* (1909) · W. H. McMenemey, *A history of the Worcester Royal Infirmary* (1947) · J. Chambers, *Biographical illustrations of Worcestershire* (1820), 473–8, 563–6 · *Medical Register* (1779), 141–2 · *Medical Register* (1783), 117, 136 · J. R. Burton, *History of Kidderminster* (1890) · *Worcester Journal* (29 April 1802) · *GM*, 1st ser., 72 (1802), 475 · J. Lane, *Worcester infirmary in the eighteenth century*, Worcestershire Historical Society, occasional paper, 6 (1992) · Worcester Infirmary, Worcs. RO, MSS 010:6, BA 5161 · registers, Kidderminster, Worcs. RO [baptism, burial] · will, PRO, PROB 11/1374 · J. Chambers, *A general history of Worcester* (1819), 189, 192
Likenesses T. Gainsborough?, portrait, priv. coll. · portrait (after T. Gainsborough), Worcester Royal Infirmary; repro. in McMenemey, *History*, facing p. 136
Wealth at death wealthy; incl. land, houses, paintings, and silver: will, PRO, PROB 11/1374

Johnstone, James (d. 1798), Icelandic scholar, is of obscure origins and his date and place of birth have not been firmly established. His own letters and those of others indicate that he was a Scot; he titled himself master of arts in his published works, but he has not been definitively identified with any of the men of that name who are recorded as having studied at the Scottish universities or at Cambridge during the relevant decades of the eighteenth century. He was also in orders, but nothing is known of his career in the Church of England before his appointment as chaplain and secretary to Morton Eden, British envoy-extraordinary in Copenhagen from 1779 to 1782, and to his successor Hugh Elliot from 1783 to 1789.

From at least 1783 his two patrons tried to influence Whitehall to provide Johnstone with a pension or church living but were unsuccessful. In 1785 he was nominated by the bishop of Clogher, who was probably responding to the good offices of Morton Eden's brother William, to a living at Magheracross, co. Fermanagh, Ireland, and was collated on 22 June 1785, returning to Copenhagen shortly afterwards to continue his duties as chargé d'affaires during Hugh Elliot's lengthy absence. In late 1786 or early 1787 he settled in Ireland at Ballinamallard near Enniskillen, but in July 1788 and again from November 1789 until the arrival of a new British envoy in June 1790 was back in Copenhagen in charge of the British diplomatic mission. Thereafter he returned to Ireland and his '400 acres' (NL Scot., MS 13000, fols. 129r–129v, Johnstone to Hugh Elliot, 30 March 1790), and remained there for the rest of his life. By 1792 he had married and had a daughter, Allison (or Alis), with his wife, Johanna (b. c.1748, d. in or after 1810). On 3 July 1794 he was collated to the prebend of Donacavey (Fintona, co. Tyrone).

The eleven years Johnstone spent at the British diplomatic mission in Copenhagen gave him access to books and manuscripts relating to medieval Scandinavia and enabled him to establish friendships with like-minded Scandinavian scholars, among whom was Grímur Jónsson Thorkelín. Much of the Johnstone–Thorkelín correspondence survives and shows that Thorkelín assisted Johnstone with the understanding of Old Icelandic, especially poetry, and the acquisition of books, and that Johnstone, in his turn, provided Thorkelín with introductions to British scholars, patrons, and institutions when the latter visited Britain in 1786–9. In June 1783 Thorkelín was made an honorary member and Johnstone a corresponding member of the Society of Antiquaries of Scotland, and Johnstone was also made a member of the Royal Society of Copenhagen in the same year.

Between 1780 and 1786 Johnstone, with Thorkelín's help, published several pioneering works of scholarship which, although they were not very well received by the British critics of the day, advanced British knowledge and understanding of Old Icelandic literature considerably. His first two publications, *Anecdotes of Olave the Black King of Man and the Hebridean Princes* (1780) and *The Norwegian Account of King Haco's Expedition Against Scotland* (1782), both published in Copenhagen, were translations of parts of Sturla Þórðarson's *Hákonar saga Hákonarsonar*, and thus the first saga texts translated into the English language, preceding Sir Walter Scott's abstract of *Eyrbyggja saga* (1814) by some years. Both show Johnstone's great interest in the Scandinavian side to Scottish history and his conviction of the strong affinity between English and Old Icelandic. In 1782 he also published in Copenhagen a fully annotated text, and both Latin and English translations, of the Old Icelandic poem *Krákumál*, in his *Lodbrokar qvida, or, The Death-Song of Lodbrok*. This edition of a then very popular poem was significant for its extensive and detailed notes on poetic language, which Thorkelín had supplied. Johnstone also published in 1786 two compilations of medieval sources, *Antiquitates Celto-Scandicae* and

Antiquitates Celto-Normannicae, as well as *The Robbing of the Nunnery*, the very first English translation of a Danish ballad, *Hr Mortens klosterrov*.

Johnstone died on 28 July 1798, probably in Fintona, co. Tyrone. His will was proved on 14 February 1799 and his extensive library, which contained many works relating to medieval Scandinavia, was sold at auction in Dublin on 16 April 1810.

MARGARET CLUNIES ROSS and AMANDA J. COLLINS

Sources [W. Scott], 'Abstract of the *Eyrbyggja saga*; being the early annals of that district of Iceland lying around the promontory called Snæfells, by W. S.', *Illustrations of northern antiquities from the earlier Teutonic and Scandinavian romances*, ed. R. Jamieson and H. Weber (1814) • Betham's abstracts of wills, NA Ire., BET 1/38 • IGI • M. Eden, letter to G. J. Thorkelin, 16 Oct 1792, U. Edin. L., MS La III.379/437 • E. H. Harvey Wood, 'Letters to an antiquary: literary correspondence of G. J. Thorkelin (1752–1829)', PhD diss., U. Edin., 1972 • H. Elliot, letter to marquess of Carmarthen, PRO, FO 22/6, fols. 264r–266v • J. Johnstone, letter to H. Elliot, 30 March 1790, NL Scot., MS 13000, fols. 129r–129v • G. J. Thorkelin, letters, transcripts, and book catalogues to J. Johnstone, TCD, MS 1016, items 1, 2, and 4–6 • *Catalogue of an extensive and valuable collection of books … of a gentleman of distinction; also the northern part of the library of the late Rev. James Johnstone* (annotated copy), 1810, TCD, R.q.29 • private information (2004) [S. Hood] • T. K. Abbot, *Catalogue of the manuscripts in the library of Trinity College, Dublin* (1900) • *GM*, 1st ser., 57 (1787), 565–7 • *The journal and correspondence of William, Lord Auckland*, ed. [G. Hogge], 4 vols. (1861–2), vol. 1, p. 345 • S. T. Bindoff and others, eds., *British diplomatic representatives, 1789–1852*, CS, 3rd ser., 50 (1934) • M. Clunies Ross, 'The Norse muse in Britain, 1750–1820', *Hesperides, Letterature e Culture Occidentali*, 9 (1998) • D. B. Horn, ed., *British diplomatic representatives, 1689–1789*, CS, 3rd ser., 46 (1932) • W. I. Addison, *A roll of graduates of the University of Glasgow from 31st December 1727 to 31st December 1897* (1898) • K. S. Kiernan, 'Thorkelin's trip to Great Britain and Ireland, 1786–1791', *The Library*, 6th ser., 5 (1983), 1–21 • J. B. Leslie, *Clogher clergy and parishes* (1929) • B. Mitchell, *A guide to Irish parish registers* (1988) • B. Mitchell, *A guide to Irish churches and graveyards* (1990) • G. Stephens, 'The Rev. James Johnstone', *N&Q*, 3rd ser., 3 (1863), 107 • A. Vicars, ed., *Index to the prerogative wills of Ireland, 1536–1810* (1897) • G. Waterhouse, 'G. J. Thorkelin and the Rev. James Johnstone', *Modern Language Review*, 26 (1931), 436–44 • J. Worm, *Forsøg til et Lexicon over danske, norske og islandske lærde Mænd: som ved trykte skrifter have giort sig bekiendte, saa velsom andre ustuderede, som noget have skrevet, hvorudi deres fodsel, betydeligste levnets omstændigheder og dod ved aarstal kortelig erindres, og deres skrifter, saavidt mueligt, fuldstændig anføres*, 3 vols. (1771–84)
Archives PRO, FO 22/7, 22/8, 22/11, 22/12 • TCD, diplomatic corresp. | BL, letters to Lord Auckland, Add. MS 34431, fol. 451 • BL, letters to marquess of Carmarthen, Egerton MS 3505 • BL, letters to Sir Robert M. Keith, Add. MS 35535, fols. 157, 186 • NL Scot., letters to marquess of Carmarthen • NL Scot., letters to Hugh Elliot • NL Scot., corresp. with William Fraser • NL Scot., letters to Robert Liston • U. Edin. L., letters to Grímrur J. Thorkelin

Johnstone, James (1753–1783). *See under* Johnstone, James, of Galabank (1730–1802).

Johnstone, James (1806–1869). *See under* Johnstone, Edward (1757–1851).

Johnstone, James (1815–1878), newspaper proprietor, the son of James (1785/6–1865) and Elizabeth Johnstone, was born at Charles Street, Old Street, London, on 26 June 1815. His father was a messenger of the court of bankruptcy in Basinghall Street from 1820 to 1840; Johnstone succeeded him in 1842 and served until 1861.

While a senior partner in the firm of Johnstone, Wintle,

Cope, and Evans, accountants, in March 1857, following the bankruptcy of Edward Baldwin, the son of the founder of *The Standard*, Johnstone purchased that newspaper and the *Morning Herald*. James Grant later described the transactions: 'The price which he [Johnstone] paid for the *Morning Herald* and *The Standard* together, including what is called the plant—that is presses, types, everything, indeed, necessary for working the papers—was £16,500' (Grant, 2.11). The circulation of *The Standard* at that time was just 700.

A shrewd businessman, cheery, and fond of his job, Johnstone was probably on more familiar terms with his staff than most modern proprietors, who are largely isolated from their employees by the division of labour. After a few weeks, on 29 June 1857, he reduced the price of *The Standard* from 4d. to 2d., doubled the pagination to eight, and converted it into a morning paper. The paper soon became a formidable rival to *The Times*; in the official history of that paper, it was opined that: 'The ability with which the twopenny *Standard* was conducted—Lord Robert Cecil, later Lord Salisbury, was one of its leader writers—constituted an undeniable threat to the supremacy of *The Times*' (*History of The Times, 1841–1884*, 1939, 298). The following year, on 4 February 1858, Johnstone reduced the price of *The Standard* to 1d. He had also launched a Conservative evening paper, the *Evening Herald*, in connection with the long-established *Morning Herald*. Priced at 2d., it was not a success—even though much of the material was lifted from its sister paper—and it expired on 21 May 1865.

However, encouraged by the success of the new-style *Standard*, and the extra capacity from his new presses, Johnstone revived the evening edition, which had ceased publication three years earlier; at 3 p.m. on Monday 11 June 1860 the *Evening Standard* was launched. Unfortunately, in his bid to overtake *The Times*, Johnstone had overstretched himself, and in 1858 he had been pleased to accept tory funds in the form of a mortgage on his premises and machinery. For this he and Thomas Hamber (d. 1904), his editor, were pledged to follow the party line. However, the paper's coverage of the American Civil War—it supported the South—was to bring about a huge increase in circulation, and in October 1862 sales were more than 100,000 on special occasions, with an average of 50,000 a day. By 1869 the debt to the tory party had been paid. *The Standard* included among its (anonymous) contributors such figures as G. A. Henty (1832–1902), later a well-known boy's author, the prolific Thomas Escott (1844–1924), and Alfred Austin (1835–1913), a future poet laureate.

On 14 February 1874 Johnstone—a slightly portly figure, with a full head of hair, side whiskers, and pince-nez—was featured in *Vanity Fair's* caricature gallery of 'Men of the day'. The cartoon by Ape, simply entitled *The Standard*, showed the proprietor, paper in hand, pointing to the daily average sales of 185,276. The accompanying text described Johnstone's character: 'He has an even temper and is an excellent host and a vivacious talker; restless and active and suffering from gout'. Unfortunately, Johnstone did not live long enough to enjoy the fruits of his labour. He died on 21 October 1878 at Hooley House, Coulsdon, Surrey, and was buried at Coulsdon on 26 October. He had been married twice. In his will he directed that his friend William Mudford should serve as editor and manager of *The Standard* for as long as he desired. Johnstone's son, another James, also served briefly as its editor from 1872 to 1874.   D. M. GRIFFITHS

Sources *The Standard* files, British Newspaper Library • D. Griffiths, *Plant here The Standard* (1996) • J. Grant, *The newspaper press: its origin, progress, and present position*, 3 vols. (1871–2) • J. Hatton, *Journalistic London* (1882) • H. R. Fox Bourne, *English newspapers: chapters in the history of journalism*, 2 vols. (1887) • VF (14 Feb 1874) • DNB
Likenesses Ape [C. Pellegrini], caricature, NPG; repro. in VF • portrait, repro. in Hatton, *Journalistic London* • portrait, repro. in Fox Bourne, *English newspapers*
Wealth at death under £500,000: probate, 3 Dec 1878, CGPLA Eng. & Wales

Johnstone, James Hope-, third earl of Hopetoun and *de jure* fifth earl of Annandale and Hartfell (1741–1816), landowner and army officer, was born James Hope on 23 August 1741 at Hopetoun House, Linlithgowshire, the second son and fourth child of John Hope, second earl of Hopetoun (1704–1781), and his first wife, Anne Ogilvy (1717–1759), second daughter of James, fifth earl of Findlater and second earl of Seafield. He was educated at home by his tutors John Ritchie and John Tainsh. Commissioned as ensign in the 3rd regiment of foot guards in 1758, he fought at the battle of Minden in 1759. From 1762 to 1766 he travelled with his ailing brother Charles, Lord Hope, around Europe, including Italy, and then to Carolina and Jamaica. Charles died in 1766, after which Hope took the courtesy title Lord Hope. On 25 August 1766 he married Lady Elizabeth Carnegie (1750–1793), daughter of George, sixth earl of Northesk. Together they had six daughters.

During the 1760s and 1770s Hope spent his time managing his father's estates, attending to his family's education, and preparing for a political career. His family was often ill, and this placed Hope in frequent contact with the famed botanist Dr John Hope (1725–1786), who was both a relative and the family physician. Hope succeeded to the earldom on his father's death in 1781 and was soon nicknamed 'the Improving Earl' for his efforts to increase the economic potential of his land. He was duly elected vice-president of the Highland Society of Scotland in 1791. His lead mines in Leadhills, Lanarkshire, were arguably the largest in Scotland and attracted the mineralogical interest of naturalists like Thomas Pennant, R. E. Raspe, and John Walker (1731–1803). Likewise, Hopetoun made donations to Edinburgh University's natural history museum and was involved in the politics surrounding the foundation of the Royal Society of Edinburgh in 1783.

From 1784 to 1790 Hopetoun served as a Scottish representative peer. He was an independent voter, opposing the 1788 Regency Bill and arguing against the taxation of Scottish distilleries. On 18 May 1787 Hopetoun successfully introduced a motion to reaffirm the Scottish Peerage Bill of 1709—effectively limiting the power of the government by preventing Scottish peers with British titles from being representative Scottish peers. He was not re-elected

in 1790 and, along with several other Scottish peers including Dunbar Douglas, fourth earl of Selkirk, unsuccessfully contested the election. In 1792, upon the death of his maternal great-uncle George Johnstone, third marquess of Annandale, who had been declared a lunatic by chancery in 1748, he inherited a £12,000 p.a. estate. Hopetoun took the additional surname of Johnstone and in 1795 proceeded to claim the earldom of Annandale and Hartfell, a subsidiary title of his great-uncle, as senior heir female of the first earl. His claim was unsuccessful but began a series of attempts to secure the peerage by his descendants over the next 190 years; this ended in 1985 when his great-great-great-great-grandson, Patrick Hope Johnstone, was recognized as eleventh earl. Hopetoun's wife died on 19 August 1793. In that year he raised and commanded the Hopetoun fencibles, one of seven Scottish home regiments commissioned by George III in response to the French Revolutionary Wars. The fencibles served in both Scotland and England and, at one point, refused to be transported in ships for fear of being sent to the continent. In 1794 Hopetoun was made lord lieutenant of Linlithgowshire, raised both a yeomanry corps and a volunteer infantry regiment, and was re-elected to the House of Lords, where he served until 1796. The fencibles were disembodied in 1798, but Hopetoun's collective military efforts won him the British title of Baron Hopetoun in 1803.

After leaving parliament, Hopetoun concentrated on Scottish politics, where he used his influence in Linlithgowshire to ensure that Henry Erskine failed to be elected there in 1806 and 1807, Erskine finally withdrawing in 1812. He spent the last years of his life as an invalid and died at Hopetoun House on 29 May 1816; he was buried on 5 June 1816 at Abercorn kirk. During his life, Hopetoun was known as a religious man, and it was appropriate that Hugh Meiklejohn, Edinburgh's professor of church history, gave his funeral address. His half-brother John *Hope, Baron Niddry, inherited the British barony and Scottish earldom of Hopetoun. Hopetoun's only surviving child, Anne (1768–1818), who had married Admiral Sir William Johnstone *Hope in 1792, inherited Hopetoun's Annandale estates and his claim to the earldom of Annandale and Hartfell.   M. D. EDDY

Sources *Train up a child: three hundred years of educating the Hopes*, Hopetoun Research Group (1994) • *Wives and children of the 1st and 2nd earls of Hopetoun*, Hopetoun Research Group (1988) • T. C. Smout, *Report on the lead mining papers at Hopetoun House* (1962) • M. W. McCahill, 'The Scottish peerage and the House of Lords in the late eighteenth century', *Peers, politics and power*, ed. C. Jones and D. L. Jones (1986), 283–307 • G. M. Ditchfield, 'The Scottish representative peers and parliamentary politics, 1787–1793', *Peers, politics and power*, ed. C. Jones and D. L. Jones (1986), 309–326 • *Scots peerage* • Lords Selkirk and Hopetoun, *To the Right Honourable the lords spiritual and temporal in parliament assembled: the petition of Dunbar, Earl Selkirk, and James, earl of Hopetoun* (1790) • Cobbett, *Parl. hist.*, 26.1158–67 • J. Kay, *A series of original portraits and caricature etchings … with biographical sketches and illustrative anecdotes*, ed. [H. Paton and others], new edn [3rd edn], 1 (1877), 196–9 • H. Mackenzie, 'List of members of the Highland Society of Scotland, March 1893', *Prize Essays and Transactions of the Highland Society of Scotland*, 2 (1803), 21–47, esp. 27 • M. Melvin, *The Hopes at war in the 18th century* (1788) •

GM, 1st ser., 36 (1766), 390 · *GM*, 1st ser., 86/2 (1816), 569, 634 · S. Shapin, 'Property, patronage, and the politics of science', *British Journal for the History of Science*, 7 (1974), 1–41 · R. G. Thorne, 'Linlithgowshire (West Lothian)', HoP, *Commons, 1790–1820*, 2.557–8 · Burke, *Peerage* (1999) · GEC, *Peerage*
Archives Hopetoun House, Lothian region, corresp. and papers · NA Scot., earls of Annandale and Hartfell MSS, corresp. and papers · NA Scot., Hopetoun MSS, corresp. and papers · priv. coll., corresp. and papers | NL Scot., corresp. with Sir Thomas Graham · U. Edin., corresp. with John Walker
Likenesses N. Dance, group portrait, oils, 1763, Hopetoun House, Lothian region · N. Dance, oils, 1763, Hopetoun House, Lothian region · D. Martin, oils, 1785, Hopetoun House, Lothian region · J. Kay, caricature, etching, 1795, NPG; repro. in Kay, *Series of original portraits*, 196

Johnstone, John (1603–1675), naturalist, was born on 3 September 1603, at Szamotuly, near Poznań, Poland, the son of Simon Johnstone (*d.* 1617), who had emigrated with his two brothers to Poland in the sixteenth century, and his wife, Anna Becker (*d.* 1618). His grandfather was John Johnstone of Craigieburn, Dumfriesshire.

Johnstone received his education in Ostroróg (School of the Moravian Brothers), Bytom, and Toruń, and then proceeded in 1622 to the University of St Andrews. Here he matriculated as *Polonus Patre Scoto Prognatus* on 29 January 1624, and studied Hebrew, divinity, and philosophy until March 1625. Johnstone spent the next four years abroad but returned to England towards the close of 1629, taking courses in botany and medicine at Cambridge, and continuing his studies in London during 1630, when he wrote the greater part of his first important work, the *Thaumatographia*. He next proceeded to study medicine at Leiden, where he graduated MD in 1632. In a visit later that year to England he was admitted to the same degree *ad eundem* at Cambridge.

After more travel on the continent, Johnstone appears to have settled in Leiden about 1634. He practised medicine there for several years and gained a great reputation. He wrote in Latin on a number of subjects, and was considered a polymath by a number of his contemporaries. He was twice married: first, in 1637, to Rosina, daughter of Samuel Hortensius of Fraustadt, and second, in 1638, to Anna, daughter of Mathias Vechner, with whom he had four children.

Johnstone was offered the chair of medicine at the University of Leiden in 1640, and two years later a similar offer was made by the elector of Brandenburg. Johnstone, however, declined these offers, preferring instead to study independently. His works were considered by some to be laborious compilations, while Chaufepié and other critics suggested they exhibited more learning than judgement. However, in England his efforts were much esteemed during the seventeenth century. His chief works included *Thaumatographia naturalis, in decem classes distincta* (1632), which was dedicated to Prince Janusz Radziwill and his son, Boguslas, *Systema dendrologicum* (1646), *De piscibus et cetis* (1649), *De avibus* (1650), *De quadrupedibus* (1652), *De serpentibus et draconibus* (1653), *Naturæ constantia* (1652), which was translated by J. Rouland (1657), *Notitia*

regni vegetabilis … (1661), *Notitia regni mineralis* (1661), and *Dendrographias, sive, Historia naturalis de arboribus et fructibus* (1662). He also published a number of works on history, medicine, and ethics.

Johnstone was tutor to a number of young Polish nobles, with whom he travelled abroad for four years. He resided at Leszno, near Poznań, for several years, where he acted as surgeon. He retired about 1655 to his private estate, near Legnica, in Silesia, where he continued to pursue his studies until his death there on 8 June 1675. He was buried at Leszno. One daughter, Anna Regina, who married Samuel von Schoff, a noble of Breslau, alone survived him. THOMAS SECCOMBE, *rev.* YOLANDA FOOTE

Sources J. P. Niceron, *Mémoires pour servir à l'histoire des hommes illustres dans la république des lettres* (1729), 41.269–76 · *Allgemeine Encyclopädie der Wissenschaften und Künste*, 2nd section, H–N, 22 (1843), 325–6 · J. F. Michaud and L. G. Michaud, eds., *Biographie universelle, ancienne et moderne*, 85 vols. (Paris, 1811–62); new edn, ed. L. G. Michaud and E. E. Desplaces, 45 vols. (1843–65) · D. Irving, *Lives of Scotish writers*, 2 (1839), 41 · A. Chalmers, ed., *The general biographical dictionary*, new edn, 19 (1815), 85 · BL cat. · University matriculation register [University of St Andrews] · J. Wilkes, *Encyclopedia Londinensis*, 11 (1812), 234–5 · J. Aikin and others, *General biography, or, Lives, critical and historical of the most eminent persons*, 10 vols. (1799–1815), vol. 5, pp. 548–9 · W. Tomaszewski, ed., *The University of Edinburgh and Poland* (1968)
Likenesses portrait, repro. in Tomaszewski, ed., *University of Edinburgh and Poland*

Johnstone, John (1734–1795), East India Company servant, was born at Haddock's Hole, Edinburgh, on 28 April 1734, the fifth son of Sir James Johnstone, third baronet (1697–1772), of Westerhall, Dumfriesshire, and his wife, Barbara (*d.* 1773), daughter of Alexander Murray, fourth Lord Elibank. Johnstone received tuition in Edinburgh before being appointed a writer in the service of the East India Company in December 1750. He arrived in Bengal on 9 July 1751, and in 1754 was stationed as an assistant at the company's factory at Dacca, where he was taken prisoner in 1756 subsequent to the outbreak of hostilities between the nawab of Bengal, Siraj ud-Daula, and the company. Following his release Johnstone, whose brother Patrick died in the Black Hole, volunteered to assist in the recovery of Calcutta and served with the artillery at the battle of Plassey in June 1757. He was a member of the detachment sent by Robert Clive in pursuit of Jean Law, and following a brief return to civil employment participated in the expedition against the French in the Northern Circars which culminated in the capture of Masulipatam in April 1759.

On his return to Bengal, Johnstone was again stationed at Dacca but shortly afterwards was appointed to take charge, apparently on account of his linguistic abilities, of the company's affairs at Midnapore, a district newly ceded to the company. He was also now a member of the Bengal council. Johnstone was faced with collecting revenues in a hostile environment, but was successful, and in 1762 was transferred to Burdwan, another recently ceded district. These appointments gave Johnstone opportunities for participating in private trading ventures, particularly in salt, and he formed a partnership with two other company servants, William Hay and William Bolts. The partnership also became involved in revenue farming. These activities attracted accusations of malpractice and fraud, and Johnstone came into conflict with the governor of Bengal, Henry Vansittart, a trading rival who attempted to reach an agreement concerning private trade with the nawab Mir Kasim. It is likely that Johnstone received other financial gains in the form of presents from the raja of Burdwan. When news of his disagreement with Vansittart reached England in early 1764, Johnstone was dismissed from the company's service. In May he was, however, reinstated, a measure that was not supported by the followers of Clive, despite the encouragement that they had received from the Johnstone party in the company election a few weeks previously. The resulting breach between the Clive and Johnstone groups was the start of a feud that lasted for the rest of the decade and beyond.

Upon the arrival in Bengal of the orders which reinstated him Johnstone returned to Burdwan. In February 1765 Mir Jafar, who had replaced Mir Kasim as nawab in 1763, died, and was succeeded by his adolescent son Najm ud-Daula, whom the council, now headed by John Spencer, supported. Johnstone was recalled from Burdwan and led a delegation of the council to Murshidabad for the installation of the new nawab. Following this presents were distributed; Johnstone received approximately £36,000, the largest amount given to any of the individuals involved. His brother Gideon was in receipt of a smaller sum. Clive's arrival in Calcutta in May 1765 to take up the governorship of Bengal heralded the beginning of a programme of reform. Johnstone soon clashed with Clive, who began an inquiry into the presents which had been received by him and his colleagues despite their having received orders from the directors of the company to abstain from such activities. On 17 June 1765 a minute from Johnstone was considered by the council; this criticized Clive's style of government and stated his intention to resign from the service.

Johnstone left India with a fortune that has been put at £300,000. This was employed in the purchase of estates in Scotland, at Alva in Stirlingshire, and later in Selkirkshire and Dumfriesshire. Faced with prosecution by the East India Company, he published in 1766 *A Letter to the Proprietors of East India Stock*, which defended his activities in Bengal. The Johnstone group, who were allied to Clive's enemy Laurence Sulivan, were able to obtain the withdrawal of the prosecution in May 1767. In the years that followed, Johnstone's interests were taken up by his brother George *Johnstone, who was elected an MP in 1768. As the clamour for an investigation into the company's affairs in India grew, George Johnstone attempted to discredit Clive and was a member, along with his brother William Pulteney, of the parliamentary select committee of inquiry into the company which was appointed in 1772.

John Johnstone was elected MP for Dysart burghs in 1774 and supported the opposition to the North administration. In 1780 he lost his seat, and an attempt to be elected for Dumfriesshire in 1790 was unsuccessful. His wife, Elizabeth (*née* Keene), whom he had married on 1 September 1765 and with whom he had a son and a daughter, predeceased him. Johnstone died at Alva House, Alva, on 10 December 1795. D. L. PRIOR

Sources East India Company records, BL OIOC • J. Johnstone, *A letter to the proprietors of East India stock* (1766) • HoP, *Commons, 1754–90* • C. L. Johnstone, *History of the Johnstones* (1909) • R. F. A. Fabel, *Bombast and broadsides: the lives of George Johnstone* (1987) • M. M. Stuart, 'Lying under the company's displeasure', *South Asian Review*, 8 (1974), 43–53 • J. G. Parker, 'The directors of the East India Company, 1754–1790', PhD diss., U. Edin., 1977 • D. L. Prior, 'The career of Robert, first Baron Clive, with special reference to his political and administrative career', MPhil diss., U. Wales, 1993 • P. J. Marshall, *East Indian fortunes: the British in Bengal in the eighteenth century* (1976) • A. M. Khan, *The transition in Bengal, 1756–1775: a study of Saiyid Muhammad Reza Khan* (1969) • L. S. Sutherland, *The East India Company in eighteenth century politics* (1952)

Archives BL OIOC, corresp., MSS, photo. Eur. 063 • BL OIOC, letter-book, MSS, photo. Eur. 109 • priv. coll., MSS | BL OIOC, Verelst MSS, Eur. MS. F. 218

Likenesses H. Raeburn, group portrait, oils, *c*.1795, National Gallery of Art, Washington, DC

Johnstone, John (1768–1836), physician and biographer, was born in Kidderminster, Worcestershire, the sixth son and one of the eleven children of the Scottish medical practitioner James *Johnstone (1730–1802) and his Kidderminster-born wife, Hannah Crane (1733–1802). He was baptized on 23 November 1768 at the Old Meeting-House, Kidderminster. Among his seven brothers were Edward *Johnstone (1757–1851) and James *Johnstone (1753–1783) [*see under* Johnstone, James, of Galabank (1730–1802)], both of whom also became physicians. John Johnstone was educated at Kidderminster Free Grammar School and at Merton College, Oxford, which he entered aged seventeen on 6 April 1786. He graduated BA (1789) and proceeded MA (1792). He then studied medicine in London and Edinburgh before qualifying, again in Oxford, BM in 1793 and DM in 1800. He became a fellow of the Royal College of Physicians in 1805 and delivered the college's Harveian oration in 1819. In 1813 he was made a fellow of the Royal Society.

Johnstone practised medicine for more than forty years, initially in Worcester (1793–99) as a physician to the infirmary, and then in Birmingham, where he built up a large practice. He served as physician to the Birmingham General Hospital between 1801 and 1833. As a practitioner Johnstone emphasized the links between mental and physical health. He acquired a reputation for being a skilled diagnostician and for treating fever through the copious application of cold water and fresh air, allied with a sparing use of drugs. In 1832 he was a founder member and original council member of the Provincial Medical and Surgical Association (PMSA), which became the British Medical Association in 1855. In 1834 he was president of the association's second anniversary meeting in Birmingham. Johnstone was also a founder and vice-president of the Birmingham school of medicine, to which, also in 1834, he delivered the inaugural address.

Aside from his medical work Johnstone was a scholar of standing, classical literature being 'his favourite pursuit'

(*Transactions*, 90). He also served as a magistrate for the counties of Warwickshire and Worcestershire. Johnstone wrote a number of books, articles, and pamphlets, several of which, including his Harveian oration, were produced with the assistance of his friend Dr Samuel Parr. For his first publication, 'An essay on mineral poisons', the Royal Medical Society of London awarded him a medal; the paper, which appeared in James Johnstone senior's *Medical Essays and Observations* (1795), upheld his father's disputed claim to be the discoverer of the disinfecting power of muriatic acid gas, priority having been previously assigned to Dr Carmichael Smyth. Subsequently Johnstone continued to advance his father's claims; a few years later, however, the House of Commons voted to give Smyth the financial reward. Johnstone's other publications included *Medical Jurisprudence* (1800), and in 1828 a biography of Samuel Parr, whose voluminous collected works he also edited.

Johnstone married Anna Delicia Curtis, the only daughter of Captain George Curtis, on 26 December 1809. They had two daughters, Anna Delicia (*b.* 1811) and Agnes Mary (*b.* 1814), both of whom married clergymen; the elder daughter's husband was Walter Farquhar *Hook (1798–1875), who became dean of Chichester in 1859. In his politics Johnstone was 'a sound and inflexible Whig' (*GM*). Despite growing up in a dissenting household his religious affiliation was to the Church of England. Although Johnstone could be lively and agreeable company, he was renowned for his 'ardent temperament' (Butler, 9) and a tendency to point out the personal faults of others. He attended the PMSA's third anniversary meeting, in Manchester in 1835, apparently ill; thereafter his health gradually declined. He died at Monument House, Birmingham, on 28 December 1836. His wife outlived him by many years, dying in 1868. Both husband and wife were buried in the chancel of St Laurence's Church, Northfield, Birmingham, where one son-in-law, Henry Clark, was rector. There is a memorial on the church's interior north wall.

P. W. J. BARTRIP

Sources C. L. Johnstone, *History of the Johnstones* (1909) · DNB · *GM*, 2nd ser., 7 (1837), 547–9 · S. Butler, *An Harveian oration and other remains of John Johnstone* (1837), preface · *Transactions of Provincial Medical and Surgical Association*, 6/pt 1 (1837), 89–91 · Munk, *Roll* · J. T. Bunce, *Birmingham General Hospital* (1861), 33–7 · C. D. Gilbert, *A history of King Charles I Grammar School, Kidderminster* (1980) · Foster, *Alum. Oxon.* · *British and Foreign Medical Review*, 3 (1837), 586 · *Aris's Birmingham Gazette* (2 Jan 1837) · monumental inscriptions, St Laurence's Church, Northfield, Birmingham, Birmingham Genealogical Society · parish register (baptism), Kidderminster, 23 Nov 1768 · IGI

Archives BL, corresp. with Samuel Butler, Add. MSS 34585–34588, *passim* · Bodl. Oxf., letters to E. H. Barker

Johnstone, John Henry (1749–1828), actor and singer, was probably born on 1 August 1749 in the horse barracks in Kilkenny, Ireland, where his father, a quartermaster in a dragoon regiment, was then quartered. (The story that he was the son of a farmer in Cashel, Clonmel, or Tipperary appears to be mistaken.) After his father's death his mother apparently became a dealer in second-hand clothes. Johnstone was articled to a Dublin attorney, but after several years left and went to London, where he joined a cavalry regiment, with which he served for several years in Clonmel. On his discharge his colonel, who had once heard him sing, provided him with a letter to Thomas Ryder, the manager of the Smock Alley Theatre in Dublin. Here Johnstone made his first appearance, on 9 November 1775, as Lionel in Charles Dibdin's *Lionel and Clarissa*, and as a result was engaged for three years at a salary of 4 guineas a week. He remained on the Irish stage for ten years, performing at the Smock Alley, Crow Street, Fishamble Street, Cork, and Kilkenny theatres, with great success. A tenor, his roles were usually those of romantic young lovers, a part he imitated in life. On 22 February 1778 he married Maria Ann (*d.* 1784), the daughter of Colonel Poitier, governor of Kilmainham gaol, an actress and singer in the Crow Street company. But in 1783 he separated from his wife to live with another actress, Sarah Maria Wilson, *née* Adcock, previously mistress of Lord Hinchinbrooke, and after Wilson's death in 1786 he took another mistress. In 1791 he eloped with Ann Bolton, the daughter of a wine merchant, but, as her father was reconciled to the match, their wedding was arranged with his sanction, and took place at St Paul's, Covent Garden, on 23 December.

In 1783 Johnstone went to London, where, on the recommendation of Charles Macklin, he and his first wife were engaged by Thomas Harris at Covent Garden for three years, at a weekly salary of £12. Johnstone was enthusiastically received on his début as Lionel on 2 October of that year, and he remained at Covent Garden as a singer and actor until 1803. Between 1791 and 1800 he performed regularly in the summer season at the Haymarket. Following the success of one of his early parts (24 October 1783), Dermot in John O'Keeffe's comic opera *The Poor Soldier*, with music by William Shield, Shield wrote a series of Irish singing characters for him. He took other operatic first tenor parts, besides playing Irish characters in comedy, such as Sir Lucius O'Trigger in Sheridan's *The Rivals*. On 13 April 1790, in *The Beggar's Opera*, instead of his usual part of Macheath, he took the role of Lucy, opposite Mary Wells's Macheath and John Bannister's Polly. He took part in the earl of Barrymore's private theatricals at Wargrave in 1791–2. In 1799–1800 he joined J. G. Holman's protest against the new regulations at Covent Garden, but remained there after the lord chancellor's ruling against them. He moved to Drury Lane in 1803, and appeared as a member of the company for the first time on 20 September as Murtoch Delany in William Macready's *The Irishman in London*. He remained with the company for the remaining seventeen years of his career, accompanying them to the Lyceum between 1809 and 1812.

Johnstone's singing voice did not wear well (Haydn always considered him 'most unmusical' (*BDA*)), and he gradually abandoned operatic parts. He was welcomed in Dublin in 1803 in 'genuine' Irish roles such as Sir Callaghan O'Brallaghan in Macklin's *Love à la Mode*, and became known as 'Irish Johnstone' for his superiority in Irish parts. He made infrequent appearances in the provinces, and for a few years played during the summer season in Edinburgh. His benefit and last performance at Covent Garden was as Dennis Brulgruddery in George Colman's *John Bull* on 28 June 1820. He made his farewell to the stage at Liverpool in August of that year, but was tempted out of retirement for a charity performance on behalf of the Irish distressed districts at Drury Lane on 18 May 1822. He died at his house, 5 Tavistock Row, Covent Garden, on 28 December 1828, and was buried in a vault in the eastern angle of St Paul's, Covent Garden, on 3 January 1829.

Johnstone, a handsome man who always wore boots on account of swollen ankles, was described by Oxberry as 'tyrannical at home, inconstant abroad—mean at his table, and an interloper at the table of others'. His only legitimate child, Susan (*c*.1793–1851), married the actor James William Wallack, and her children inherited the bulk of her father's fortune of some £12,000. With Lois Mary Searles, an Edinburgh actress, Johnstone had an illegitimate daughter, Jemima Marian, who married the actor Frederick Vining in 1814. Mrs Vining was bequeathed £500.

L. M. MIDDLETON, *rev.* K. D. REYNOLDS

Sources Highfill, Burnim & Langhans, *BDA* · Genest, *Eng. stage* · *GM*, 1st ser., 99/1 (1829), 183–4 · W. T. Parke, *Musical memoirs*, 2 vols. (1830) · J. Adolphus, *Memoirs of John Bannister, comedian*, 2 vols. (1839) · L. Wallack, *Memories of fifty years* (1889) · *Oxberry's Dramatic Biography*, 4/53 (1826)
Likenesses C. Bestland, engraving, 1791, Harvard TC · M. A. Shee, oils, 1803, Garr. Club · W. Ward, mezzotint, 1803 (after M. A. Shee), Harvard TC; version BM, NG Ire. · Thomson, engraving, pubd 1816 (after Partridge), Harvard TC; repro. in Highfill, Burnim & Langhans, *BDA* · S. De Wilde, watercolour (as Mayor O'Flaherty), Garr. Club · S. De Wilde, watercolour (as D. Brulgruddery), Garr. Club · W. Wellings, watercolour (as O'Whack), Garr. Club · prints, BM, NPG · silhouette, Garr. Club
Wealth at death under £12,000: will; Highfill, Burnim & Langhans, *BDA*; *GM*, 184

Johnstone, William, first marquess of Annandale (1664–1721), politician, was born in Scotland on 17 February 1664, second son and seventh of eleven children of James Johnstone, earl of Annandale (1625–1672), and Lady Henrietta Douglas (*d.* 1673). His elder brother having died in infancy, he succeeded his father on 17 July 1672 as the second earl. His mother died very soon after and his uncle, the duke of Hamilton, became sole curator. He was educated at Glasgow grammar school (*c*.1672–77) and at Glasgow University (1677–81). On 2 January 1682 he married the thirteen-year-old Sophia Fairholm (1668–1716), daughter of John Fairholm of Craigiehall near Edinburgh, a union that greatly improved the Annandale family fortunes. The couple had five children, including Henrietta (1682–1750), from whom future earls were descended, and James, second marquess (*d.* 1730).

In 1684 Annandale received his first public appointment, as convener of commissioners who were to act against suspected covenanters in south-west Scotland, but he was almost totally inactive. In 1685 he is said to have agreed to intercede with James VII on behalf of his friend the duke of Monmouth. In 1688 James made him a member of the Scottish privy council. At the time of the revolution he was in London, where according to Balcarres he

pretended illness to avoid having to choose sides (Balcarres, 10). However, he was soon prominent on the revolutionary side in the convention of estates, which met in Edinburgh in 1689. It was he who proposed the establishment of a presbyterian Church of Scotland. He supported the 'club', led by his brother-in-law Sir James Montgomery of Skelmorlie, which was for a time the dominant political group. In September 1689 Annandale went with Montgomery and Lord Ross to London, where he was chosen to present to William a list of proposals that would increase the power of the Scottish parliament. William, however, gave a discouraging reply. Disappointed, Montgomery persuaded the others to negotiate with the exiled James VII instead. They hoped to persuade parliament to accept a Jacobite restoration, and James actually agreed to appoint Annandale as his high commissioner in Scotland. But even the Jacobite leaders were unwilling to support the conspirators, and it soon became clear that their best chance of saving their lives and estates was to confess to their dealings with King James. In August 1690 Annandale did so, blaming Montgomery, and on 9 December he was pardoned.

Gradually Annandale regained favour, assisted by his friend James Johnstone, William's Scottish secretary. In 1693 and 1694 he was created first an extraordinary lord of session, then a lord of Treasury and finally president of the privy council. In May 1695 he was appointed president of parliament, an office similar to that of speaker in the English House of Commons. In this capacity his conduct of the inquiry into the massacre of Glencoe (1692) was something of a political triumph. An earlier inquiry had been regarded as inadequate, but on this occasion there was a thorough investigation. Detailed evidence was published that blamed James Dalrymple, first Viscount Stair; the king was exonerated and proved duly grateful.

Annandale was one of the early supporters of the Darien scheme, to which he subscribed £1000. However, James Johnstone warned him of William's likely displeasure against active supporters of the colony. Subsequently, at a meeting of the company's council in September 1695, his cautious attitude so infuriated Lord Tullibardine that it was thought they would come to blows.

In February 1701 Annandale received the first of his three commissions to represent the monarch at the general assembly of the Church of Scotland (the others were in 1705 and 1711). This was an expensive honour that not all noblemen could afford and he seems to have given general satisfaction. At this time he was politically allied with Archibald Campbell, marquess of Argyll, acting in the Presbyterian interest. Their support was vital to James Douglas, duke of Queensberry, and Annandale was rewarded on 24 June 1701, when he became a marquess. Soon after Anne's accession he was appointed lord privy seal, on 6 May 1702. As an advocate of the Hanoverian succession he entered a protest in 1703 against the Act of Security, by which the Scottish parliament gave itself the option, on Anne's death, of choosing a different monarch from England's. He was a supporter of Tweeddale's government (1704–5), during which he distanced himself from responsibility for the execution of Captain Greene of the *Worcester*.

When his long-time ally Argyll took charge of the government in March 1705, Annandale was appointed joint secretary, a key position which gave him regular contact with Queen Anne and her chief minister, Godolphin. His prospects now looked excellent, but immediately things began to go wrong. He was keen to ask parliament to approve the Hanoverian succession, a demand which, as his ministerial colleagues knew, would not be accepted. Instead they proposed to discuss union with England. Disputes among the ministers continued until Annandale was dismissed as secretary, on 29 September 1705, and made president of the Scottish privy council instead. He immediately went to the queen but failed to persuade her to intervene on his behalf. His bitterness over his dismissal was due in part to a discovery that copies of his letters to Godolphin, which were critical of his colleagues, had been sent to Argyll. Despite approaches from Godolphin, the duke of Marlborough, and Queen Anne herself, he refused in 1706 to continue as president of the privy council, and allied himself with the opposition 'country' party.

From October 1706 Annandale emerged as a leading opponent in debates on the union, though he did vote for the clause favouring the Hanoverian succession; in effect he argued for what amounted to a federal rather than an incorporating union. After a disputed election in 1708 he was chosen as one of the sixteen Scottish peers to sit in the House of Lords, and was re-elected in 1710 and 1715. He still had hopes of high office, and also of a dukedom, but such offers as were made were not to his liking, and in 1712 he embarked on a European tour. He hoped to meet the Electress Sophia in Hanover, but her illness and death made that impossible. Having visited the Low Countries, Italy, France, Germany, and Switzerland, he returned to Britain in September 1714, to find that George I had appointed him to the privy council. On the outbreak of the rising of 1715 he became lord lieutenant of Dumfriesshire, Peeblesshire, and the stewartry of Kirkcudbright, and acted with great vigour to secure the area against Kenmuir's Jacobites.

Following the death of his first wife on 13 December 1716, Annandale married Charlotta Van Lore (*d.* 1762), only child of John Vanden Bempde of Hackness, on 20 November 1718. They had two children: George (1720–1792), later the third marquess, and John, born posthumously, who died young. Annandale himself died at Bath on 14 January 1721, and was buried at Johnstone kirkyard, Dumfriesshire. He was survived by his wife, who later married Colonel John Johnstone and died at Bath on 23 November 1762.

The best-known contemporary verdict on Annandale is George Lockhart's, that those who employed him did so as the Indians worshipped the devil, out of fear. Historians have similarly given him a hostile press, as typified by P. W. J. Riley, who describes him as 'a blatant, even high handed, turncoat, who could execute a *volte-face* in mid sentence without changing the tone of his voice' (Riley,

The Union, 45). Unquestionably he equivocated over the revolution of 1688 and the Darien scheme, yet in some respects he was consistent. He saw himself as for Hanover, the Presbyterian Church of Scotland, and the rights of parliament. He seems to have been easily offended and much concerned with matters of prestige. On the other hand, even hostile writers such as Lockhart preface their condemnation by acknowledging that he was very able and hard-working. Although regarded as a self-server, he in fact turned down offers of government posts.

Annandale's appearance was described as 'tall, lusty and well shaped, with a very black complexion' (*Memoirs of the Secret Services*, 185). Of his personal interests outside politics his papers reveal little. In the 1690s he favoured Mr Arnot's make of golf balls, and at school he played football. He spent a good deal of time at Craigiehall, a useful base for his political work in Edinburgh, rather than the family home at Lochwood, Dumfriesshire. He was the hereditary stewart of Annandale and helped to finance the building of a bridge over the River Annan.

DUNCAN ADAMSON

Sources DNB · Raehills, Dumfriesshire, Annandale MSS · W. Fraser, ed., *The Annandale family book of the Johnstones*, 2 vols. (1894) · P. W. J. Riley, *The union of England and Scotland* (1978) · *The manuscripts of J. J. Hope Johnstone*, HMC, 46 (1897) · *Letters relating to Scotland in the reign of Queen Anne by James Ogilvy, first earl of Seafield and others*, ed. P. Hume Brown, Scottish History Society, 2nd ser., 11 (1915) · G. Lockhart, *Memoirs concerning the affairs of Scotland*, 4th edn (1799) · P. W. J. Riley, *The English ministers and Scotland, 1707–1727* (1964) · *Memoirs of the secret services of John Macky*, ed. A. R. (1733) · *Bishop Burnet's History of his own time: with the suppressed passages of the first volume*, ed. M. J. Routh, 6 vols. (1823), vol. 2 · P. H. Scott, *Andrew Fletcher and the treaty of union* (1992) · D. Hume, *A diary of the proceedings in parliament and the privy council of Scotland, May 21, 1700 – March 7, 1707*, Bannatyne Club, 27 (1828) · *Scots peerage* · C. Lindsay [earl of Balcarres], *Memoirs touching the revolution in Scotland*, ed. A. W. C. Lindsay [earl of Crawford and Balcarres], Bannatyne Club (1841)
Archives Harvard U., Baker Library, legal and business papers · NRA, priv. coll., family papers · Raehills, Dumfriesshire, Annandale MSS | TCD, letters to Archibald Campbell
Likenesses G. Kneller, oils, 1705?, Raehills, Dumfriesshire · A. Procaccini, oils, *c.*1718, Hopetoun House, Lothian · J. Medena, oils (William Johnstone?), Raehills, Dumfriesshire · J. Smith, mezzotint (after G. Kneller, 1703), BM
Wealth at death rent from Dumfriesshire estates: Hopetoun archives; will, PRO, PROB 11/578–82

Johnstone, William (1897–1981), painter and art educationist, was born on 8 June 1897 at his parents' house above their butcher's shop in Main Street, Denholm, Roxburghshire, the only son and youngest of the three children of William Johnstone (1855–1938), farmer and butcher, and his wife, Jane Maria Greenwood (1853–1942), daughter of Robert Greenwood, textile designer and founder of the Art Gallery, Hawick, Roxburghshire. His father moved to Greenhead Farm, Selkirk, in 1902 and until Johnstone entered Selkirk high school in 1911, farm work took priority over his schooling. At school, authoritarian teaching methods proved beyond his endurance and he left to farm full-time. He had been painting since 1907 and some oils survive of only a slightly later date (priv. coll.). The guiding principles of Johnstone's life were established early: from his mother's family he learned respect for the vocation of the artist; at school he acquired a contempt for conventional educational methods; and through his father he developed a regard for the independence of the self-employed man, epitomized by the farmer, and also a love for farming technology and the land.

Saved from the First World War until its last months by his work on the family farm, Johnstone was conscripted in the spring of 1918 only to be posted back to the farm on 11 November. By the time of his discharge in 1919 he had decided on an artistic career and entered Edinburgh College of Art with an ex-service grant in October of that year. A successful, if somewhat difficult, student, he was refused the college travelling scholarship when he graduated in 1923, despite a recommendation from George Clausen. Awarded the Stuart prize, MacLaine Walters medal, and Keith award by the Royal Scottish Academy in 1924, its award of the Carnegie travelling scholarship in 1925 enabled him to settle that autumn in Paris. There he studied under André Lhote and came under the freer influence of the surrealist movement. During 1926 he spent a month in Madrid in the Museo del Prado, where the paintings of El Greco had a major impact on his work and were the source of inspiration for his major surrealist painting *A Point in Time* (1929, Scottish National Gallery of Modern Art, Edinburgh). Along with other works of this period, the painting is composed of complex patterns of organic forms and spatial voids, often with an implicit sexual content. In February 1927 in Paris he married a talented American sculpture student, Flora Macdonald (1903–1976). She was at the time studying with Émile-Antoine Bourdelle but later abandoned art. Johnstone and his wife returned to Scotland but left in August 1928 for California, where they briefly established an art school. A year later they returned to Scotland.

In March 1931 Johnstone settled in London, where he worked as a secondary school teacher and began to formulate educational theories regarding the importance of children's art for the adult artist, and the connections between art, design, and technology. His theories rest on belief in the creativity of all children and in automatic drawing, as developed by the surrealists André Masson and Joan Miró. He encouraged children to make random marks which were then refined by a process of tracing selected elements into what he termed 'developments', ultimately becoming finished drawings, elaborate figural compositions, or even portraits. Many others had expressed faith in the creative abilities of children but few had demonstrated how a teacher might encourage the development of a child's early efforts. The results were published in his book *Child Art to Man Art* (1941), which was later translated into Japanese. Johnstone differed from other educationists in his conviction that children's artistic efforts should be developed, with a teacher's involvement, into adult art and should not be shielded from adult influence. He used this method with older students, working with three-dimensional objects, and further encouraged them to be creative in all areas of art and design.

In the early 1930s Johnstone's painting was influenced by the vorticists, as in, for example, the portraits of his friends the poet Christopher Murray Grieve (Hugh MacDiarmid) and the musician Francis George Scott (both Scottish National Portrait Gallery, Edinburgh). He had known them since 1921–2 and shared their desire to stimulate a 'Scottish Renaissance'. Johnstone destroyed or reworked many of his paintings but a surviving landscape of the mid-1930s shows a reinvigoration of this traditional genre in a modern idiom. While *The Eildon Hills* (reproduced in *Paintings, Drawings and Sculpture*, sale catalogue, lot 1) also reveals his knowledge of European Romanticism, the thinly applied washes of oil allowed to flow down the canvas in an uninhibited, almost random manner are clearly from the hand of a twentieth-century painter.

Following his post as head of Hackney School of Art in 1936, in 1938 Johnstone was made principal of Camberwell School of Arts and Crafts and there he employed professional artists to teach part-time, insisting on them working in disciplines far beyond their normal areas of practice. In 1940 his wife and daughter Elizabeth Jane (*b.* 1931) were evacuated to the United States; the marriage ended and Johnstone's physical and mental health suffered. At this time his painting recapitulated his earlier styles, making the dating of these works difficult. He set up home with a former student, Mary Joan Bonning (1918–1988), an embroiderer whom he married in 1947 and with whom he had a daughter, Sarah. That year Johnstone was made principal of the Central School of Arts and Crafts in London, where he employed many successful artists including Patrick Heron, Eduardo Paolozzi, and Victor Pasmore. Of his students, Terence Conran made a distinctive impact on the design of British household goods in the latter part of the twentieth century. Johnstone made several teaching and study trips to the United States during 1948–50 and was made an OBE in 1954. This period of success was also a time of conflict with his staff, whom he ruled autocratically. In the 1950s he painted a number of large canvases whose colouristic complexity and bold, almost violent handling vividly express his thrusting, self-confident personality and have something in common with the abstract expressionist painters of New York.

Suffering from exhaustion Johnstone retired to farm in the Scottish borders in 1960, but gradually he returned to painting. In 1970 he retired from farming and settled at Crailing, near Jedburgh, where an extraordinary late flowering of his art took place and where he received the enlightened patronage of a wealthy widow, Hope Montagu Douglas Scott. In the last decade of his life he worked with great ease and on a large scale. His numerous large abstract drawings in black ink of this period were executed with extraordinary technical delicacy. Together with the series of plaster reliefs he made with his assistant, George Turnbull, a local plasterer, the drawings illustrate his long-standing interest in chance, the immediacy of the creative gesture, and a concern with placing a time-limit on the creative act which had first influenced him during his days in Paris. His assistant placed wet plaster on a board and in the few minutes before solidification, Johnstone, armed with a trowel in each hand, manipulated the plaster in much the same way as he plied his ink-loaded brush when making the large drawings. A series of these reliefs was exhibited at the Scottish National Gallery of Modern Art in Edinburgh in 1973. Two films were made of his life and art and Edinburgh University awarded him an honorary doctorate in 1980.

William Johnstone died at the Cottage Hospital, Hawick, Roxburghshire, on 5 December 1981, aged eighty-four, and was buried in the cemetery in nearby Denholm. He was survived by his second wife. Johnstone is considered by many to be one of the finest Scottish painters of the twentieth century. In addition to the National Galleries of Scotland his works are in the Tate collection; the National Portrait Gallery, London; the University of Edinburgh; the Glasgow Art Gallery and Museum, and the Hunterian Art Gallery, Glasgow; Nuffield College, Oxford; the Art Gallery of Ontario, Toronto; and Colorado Springs Fine Art Center, Colorado, USA.   DAVID MACKIE

Sources *William Johnstone* (1981) [exhibition catalogue, Hayward Gallery, London, 11 Feb – 29 March 1981] • D. Hall, *William Johnstone* (1980) • W. Johnstone, *Points in time: an autobiography* (1980) • priv. coll., William Johnstone MSS • A. Ehrenzweig, 'William Johnstone: artist and art educator', *The Studio*, 157 (1959), 146–8 • family graves, Denholm cemetery, Roxburghshire • *The studio of the late Dr William Johnstone, OBE* (1980) [Christies, Scotland, Ltd, Glasgow, sales catalogue, 12 April 1980] • *Contemporary and modern pictures and sculpture* (1991) [Christies, Scotland, Ltd, Glasgow, sales catalogue, 17 April 1991, lots 56–100] • *Paintings, drawings and sculpture by William Johnstone* (1996) [Christies, Scotland, Ltd, Glasgow, sales catalogue, 18 June 1996] • *CCI* (1982) • private information (2004) [family, friends]
Archives NL Scot., corresp. and papers | FILM 'A point in time', Sidhartha Films, Calton studios, Edinburgh, 1973, directed Susanne Neild • 'I see the image', Sidhartha Films, 1980, directed Steve Clark-Hall | SOUND NL Scot., BBC broadcasts
Likenesses W. Johnstone, self-portrait, oils, 1978–9, Central St Martin's College of Art and Design, Southampton Row, London • Oliver, photograph, Scot. NPG • B. Sowers, photograph, Scot. NPG
Wealth at death £526,000.43: confirmation, 5 May 1982, *CCI*

Johnstone, William Borthwick (1804–1868), painter and gallery curator, was born William Johnstone on 21 July 1804 in Edinburgh, the elder son of John Johnstone, an Edinburgh lawyer. He added his mother's maiden name, Borthwick, to his own in 1847. Following the early deaths of his parents, Johnstone and his brother were cared for and educated by the Revd Mr Cunningham, parish minister of Duns, Berwickshire. Johnstone qualified and practised as a solicitor in Edinburgh but, having many artist friends and a keen interest in the arts, he decided to abandon law for art. By 1836 he was contributing to the Scottish Academy exhibitions, showing talent as a landscape and history painter in both oil and watercolour. For two years he studied at the evening antique class of the Trustees' Academy before visiting Italy between 1842 and 1844. He went first to Venice, and then to Rome where he stayed with the painter Alexander Wilson, sending works to the Royal Scottish Academy exhibition from the eternal city. He was elected an associate of the academy in 1840 and a full academician in 1848, contributing every year to the

annual exhibitions but, lacking early formal training in art, 'he was never able to acquire complete and easy command over the technique of the craft' (*DNB*). He was influenced first by Sir David Wilkie until his experiences in Rome led him to imitate the early Italian masters. Latterly, perhaps because of his close friendship with the artist, his work was significantly influenced by John Phillip. He is well represented in the National Gallery of Scotland, Edinburgh, by the history painting *A Scene in Holyrood, 1566*, exhibited at the Royal Scottish Academy in 1855 together with *Louis XI of France, Attended by Olivier le Dain*, and in the Victoria and Albert Museum, London, by the watercolour *Landscape with Peasant Girl Carrying a Pitcher*. He took lessons in miniature painting from Robert Thorburn in London and carried out many miniature portrait commissions, exhibiting four at the Royal Scottish Academy exhibition of 1851 and five in 1853.

Johnstone's legal background and business experience benefited the Royal Scottish Academy; he became its fifth treasurer in 1850 and accepted acting responsibilities between 1853 and 1857 as 'Interim Librarian'. His negotiating skills were of great importance in the extensive discussions which led to the establishment of the 'Scotch' National Gallery (*sic*) in a fine classical building immediately behind the academy, on the Mound. In 1858 he became the gallery's first principal curator and keeper at a salary of £250 per annum and greatly enriched the collection. His *Catalogue, Descriptive and Historical* of the gallery, published in 1859, reveals his understanding of the pictures. He regretted that the taste of the previous generation had encouraged the importation of too many works of the later Bolognese painters. Whereas Rubens and Van Dyck had been prized for their religious subjects, now opinion had changed he stated: 'We are not infrequently compelled to shudder at the horrible details of suffering they have chosen to represent' (p. 37). He praised Etty's *Judith and Holofernes* because the artist had chosen to depict the scene prior to the decapitation of Holofernes, thus enabling him 'to avoid those revolting features' (p. 68). His criticism of eighteenth-century painting concentrated on its unreality and 'fantastic mannerism'. The intelligent art student might 'find technical qualities of manipulation, texture and colour' (p. 44) in Tiepolo's work. Bassano's *Adoration of the Kings* would be useful in providing accurate information on Venetian period costume to the history painter.

A man of wide and varied interests, Johnstone was a close friend of the antiquary David Laing and co-operated with him in ensuring the restoration of Hugo van der Goes's famous altarpiece *The Trinity Panels*, which remained at the palace of Holyroodhouse until 1911 (Royal Collection; on loan to National Gallery of Scotland, Edinburgh). He anonymously contributed, with David Laing, two articles on Scottish and English art to the *North British Review* in 1858 and 1859, and wrote on art subjects in other periodicals and the daily press. Unfortunately the completed manuscript of a history of art in Scotland was inadvertently destroyed after his death. On 13 June 1861 he married Ellen Brown, the daughter of the artist J. C.

Brown; the marriage was childless. Companion portraits were painted of Johnstone and his new wife by John Phillip and these were later presented by his widow to the National Gallery of Scotland. In the last year of his life he suffered from an increasingly painful illness but continued serving both the National Gallery and the academy until a few days before his death, at home, 3 Gloucester Place, Edinburgh, on 5 June 1868. The *Art Journal* of 1868 noted that 'the Scottish Academy never had a member more devoted to its interests or more universally useful to it' (Brydall, 428). He was buried at St Cuthbert's cemetery, Edinburgh, in June 1868. Johnstone was highly regarded as a connoisseur and antiquarian. He left a valuable collection of works of art, arms, and armour which was sold at auction over six days in Edinburgh in February 1869.

JOHN MORRISON

Sources DNB · R. Brydall, *Art in Scotland, its origin and progress* (1889) · Redgrave, *Artists* · E. Gordon, *The Royal Scottish Academy of painting, sculpture and architecture, 1826–1976* (1976) · C. B. de Laperriere, ed., *The Royal Scottish Academy exhibitors, 1826–1990*, 4 vols. (1991), vol. 2 · Wood, *Vic. painters* · Bryan, *Painters* (1903–5) · S. Cursiter, *Scottish art to the close of the 19th century* (1949) · D. Irwin and F. Irwin, *Scottish painters at home and abroad, 1700–1900* (1975) · C. Thompson, *Pictures for Scotland: the National Gallery of Scotland and its collection* (1972) · C. Thompson and L. Campbell, *Hugo van der Goes and the 'Trinity panels' in Edinburgh* (1974) · W. B. Johnstone, *Catalogue, descriptive and historical, of the National Gallery of Scotland* (1859)
Likenesses J. Phillip, oils, 1861, Scot. NPG · T. F. Heaphy, double portrait, ink drawing (with Horatio McCulloch), Scot. NPG · T. F. Heaphy, wash drawing, Scot. NPG · D. O. Hill and R. Adamson, calotypes, Scot. NPG · W. B. Johnstone, self-portrait, priv. coll.
Wealth at death £1636 1s. 0d.: confirmation, Scotland, 1868

Johnys, Sir Hugh (*b. c.*1410, *d.* in or after **1485**), soldier and administrator, was descended from a cadet branch of the Vaughans of Bredwardine, Herefordshire. Nothing is known of his career before 1436 (when, given the date of his death, he was still a young man). According to his memorial brass in St Mary's, Swansea, he had served in the wars for five years against the Turks and Saracens 'in the partis of Troy, Grecie and Turky' under John VIII, emperor of Constantinople, before he was knighted at the Holy Sepulchre in Jerusalem on 14 August 1441, and afterwards was knight marshal of France for five years under John Beaufort, duke of Somerset. Presumably he served in France under Somerset in 1443 and later under Richard, duke of York.

Johnys's memorial brass states that he was afterwards knight marshal of England 'under the good John duke of Norfolke'. Norfolk, earl marshal of England and lord of Gower, made generous grants to Johnys, including an annuity of £20 on 23 June 1446; the constableship of Oystermouth Castle and the surveyorship and approvorship of Gower on 26 February 1451; an annuity of 20 marks to Johnys and his wife, Mary, on 1 April 1451; and the manor of Landimore in Gower on 4 December 1451. On 18 April 1452 Henry VI appointed Johnys steward of Magor and Redwick, Gwent. In 1453 he was required to attend a trial by battle at Smithfield. Probably early in 1455 Johnys, then

Sir Hugh Johnys (*b. c.*1410, *d.* in or after 1485), memorial brass [with his second wife, Maud]

a widower, sought to marry a dowager, Dame Elizabeth Wodehill, daughter of Sir John Chetwode of Warkworth near Banbury. Richard, duke of York, and Richard Neville, earl of Warwick, each wrote to her warmly supporting his suit, but it was unsuccessful.

After Norfolk's death in 1461 William, Lord Herbert, took custody of Gower, and in the 1460s Johnys evidently played some part in the upbringing of Herbert's ward, Henry Tudor, who as Henry VII granted him a 'reward' of £10 on 15 October 1485 for the good service which he 'did unto us in our tendre age'. On 15 December 1468, by a grant which recalled Johnys's service to his father and himself, Edward IV appointed him one of the Poor Knights of Windsor, where he mainly resided (though with some long absences) from 1 January 1469 until at least Michaelmas 1480. In the early 1480s he apparently returned to Gower, as Henry VII's 'reward' was paid by the receiver of Kidwelly. The date of his death is unknown, but it was after 15 October 1485. His military service and visit to Jerusalem were well publicized, being mentioned in three contemporary documents. His visit to Jerusalem is also commemorated in a plaque at the head of his memorial brass depicting Christ arising from the Sepulchre.

Johnys's first wife, Mary, mentioned but not named in a papal grant of 1446, was referred to as his wife in 1451. Her parents and the date of her death are unknown. His marriage to Maud, daughter and heir of Rees Cradock, esquire, of Gower, probably took place *c.*1455. She probably died before Johnys's appointment as a Poor Knight in 1468. From this marriage Johnys had five sons and four daughters. One of his sons, Robert (*d.* 1532), inherited his house, Y Goetre, in Swansea parish, and other Gower lands, but resided in London, served in the royal household, and was knighted.

W. R. B. ROBINSON

Sources W. R. B. Robinson, 'Sir Hugh Johnys: a fifteenth-century Welsh knight', *Morgannwg*, 14 (1970), 5–34 • T. Bliss and G. G. Francis, *Some account of Sir Hugh Johnys* (1845) • *CEPR letters*, 9.519
Archives All Souls Oxf. • BL, Royal MSS • BL, Harley MSS • Bodl. Oxf. • Royal Institution, Swansea, George Grant Francis collection, property grants • St George's Chapel, Windsor, muniments relating to the Poor Knights
Likenesses memorial brass, St Mary's Church, Swansea [*see illus.*]

Joicey, James, first Baron Joicey (1846–1936), colliery owner, was born in the hamlet of Kip Hill, near Tanfield Lea, co. Durham, on 4 April 1846, the younger son of George Joicey, a mechanical engineer based in Newcastle upon Tyne, and Dorothy, daughter of Jacob Gowland, of Wrekenton, near Gateshead. His father was one of four brothers who in 1828 had invested in a colliery enterprise at Tanfield Moor; the resulting concern became known as James Joicey & Co. after 1829. George Joicey died when his son was nine.

James Joicey, who was educated at Gainford School, near Darlington, entered the family business in 1863 at the age of seventeen. Initially, he was employed as an office clerk, but in 1867 he was offered a partnership by the then head of the firm, his uncle James. He succeeded his uncle in 1881 and seven years later presided over the incorporation of the firm as a private limited company. Thereafter, Joicey embarked upon a sequence of colliery acquisitions which propelled him to a position of dominance in the north-eastern coalfield. In 1896 he purchased, from the earl of Durham, the Lambton Collieries, and this concern, in turn, purchased the Hetton Coal Company in 1911. The merged company was known as Lambton and Hetton Collieries until 1924, when the original family partnership of James Joicey & Co. was wound up voluntarily and its interests absorbed. Thereafter, until the nationalization of the coal industry, the company was known as Lambton, Hetton and Joicey Collieries. At the time of its formation this concern was the largest colliery enterprise in the north-east, with a coal output in excess of 5 million tons per annum drawn from twenty pits. The company also owned by-product works, coke works, and brick and gas works.

Joicey did not confine his interests to the coal trade; he was for many years a director of the London and North Eastern Railway Company and, until a few years before his death, he was president of the Newcastle upon Tyne chamber of commerce. He was also a director of George Angus & Co., the Montevidean and Brazilian Telegraph Company, and the Dunrobin Shipping Company, as well as being the proprietor of three newspapers in the north-east of England—the *Newcastle Daily Leader*, the *Evening Leader*, and *Northern Weekly*. In business Joicey was shrewd, sagacious, and far-sighted. He was an advocate of colliery mechanization and related programmes of capital investment, but he was also a firm believer in enforced wage reductions in periods of trade recession.

Joicey was twice married: first, in 1879, to Elizabeth Amy (*d.* 1881), only daughter of Joseph Robinson JP, of North Shields; Marguerite Smyles (*d.* 1911), whom he married in 1884, was the daughter of Colonel Thomas Drever, of the East India Company. Joicey and his first wife had two sons, and his second marriage brought two sons and a daughter. The three youngest children all predeceased their father, the elder of the two sons being killed in action in 1916. Joicey acquired first the Longhirst estates near Morpeth, Northumberland, and later on, early in the twentieth century, the Ford Castle estates in Northumberland, near the border. In 1885 he was elected Liberal member of parliament for Chester-le-Street, and he held the seat until 1906 when he was raised to the peerage as Baron Joicey of Chester-le-Street. He had been created a baronet in 1893. As a Liberal, Joicey belonged to the advanced wing of the party, supporting home rule for Ireland consistently. In 1931, however he joined the Conservative Party and began to express sympathy for Mussolini's regime in Italy. Joicey died at Ford Castle, aged ninety, on 21 November 1936, leaving an estate of more than £1.5 million. He was succeeded by the second baron, his elder son from his first marriage, James Arthur (1880–1940).

R. A. S. REDMAYNE, rev. M. W. KIRBY

Sources R. Church, A. Hall, and J. Kanefsky, *Victorian pre-eminence: 1830–1913* (1986), vol. 3 of *The history of the British coal industry* (1984–93) • R. W. Stenton, *Northern worthies*, 2 (1932) • Lord Aberconway, *The basic industries of Great Britain* (1927) • W. R. Garside, *The Durham miners, 1919–1960* (1971) • A. A. Hall, 'Joicey, James', *DBB* • *The Times* (23 Nov 1936) • private information (1949)
Archives Berwick upon Tweed RO, papers • Northumbd RO, Newcastle upon Tyne, bills and receipts | Northumbd RO, Newcastle upon Tyne, papers relating to administration of his estate
Likenesses B. Stone, photographs, 1905, NPG • W. Stoneman, photographs, 1919–33, NPG • T. Huddon, portrait; known to be in family possession in 1949 • J. Lavery, portrait, Commercial Exchange, Newcastle upon Tyne • Spy [L. Ward], caricature, NPG; repro. in *VF* (19 Dec 1906)
Wealth at death £1,519,717 10s. 5d.: probate, 15 Jan 1937, CGPLA Eng. & Wales

Joko, Lika. See Furniss, Henry (1854–1925).

Joli, Antonio (*c*.1700–1777). *See under* Venetian painters in Britain (*act.* 1708–*c*.1750).

Joliffe, Henry (*d.* 1573/4), dean of Bristol, is of unknown origins. He was educated at Cambridge, where he graduated BA in 1522–3 and proceeded MA in 1526. A fellow successively of Clare College and Michaelhouse, he served as a university proctor in 1536–7, and proceeded BTh in 1538. In the latter year he became rector of Bishop's Hampton, Warwickshire, while on 24 January 1542 he was named as one of the prebendaries of Worcester Cathedral under its charter of refoundation. In 1548 he was made rector of Houghton, Huntingdonshire. Strongly conservative in matters of faith, in 1552 he and his fellow prebendary Robert Johnson refused to subscribe the articles of religion propounded for the diocese by their bishop, the fervently evangelical John Hooper, on the grounds that they were neither Catholic nor agreeable to the ancient doctrine of the church. The two men held a public disputation with Hooper, who afterwards sent a letter of complaint to the privy council. In the preface to the account of the debate, which he published in 1564, Joliffe states that he had many disputes with Hooper concerning baptism and original sin, and that he was persecuted and imprisoned by the bishop. Joliffe is also said by Wood to have written an attack on Nicholas Ridley, but this does not appear to survive.

Joliffe prospered under Queen Mary. On 20 August 1554 he was presented by the king and queen to the deanery of Bristol, and was installed by proxy on 9 September following. He was present in London on 24 January 1555 when sentence of excommunication and judgment ecclesiastical was pronounced against Hooper and John Rogers, and also in Oxford at Thomas Cranmer's second trial the following September. But following the accession of Elizabeth he was deprived of all his benefices, and consequently he escaped to the continent and settled at Louvain, where he stayed for the rest of his life, though not perhaps without all hope of a return to England. In a paper drawn up in 1560 to help the pope fill vacant sees in England should the opportunity arise, Joliffe was named as worthy of Oxford, vacant by the death of Robert King in 1557. In 1564 he published at Antwerp an account of his and Johnson's disputations with Hooper, together with Stephen Gardiner's commentary on the exchanges, *Responsio venerabilium sacerdotum*; it is dedicated to Philip II. Following the death of Richard Pates, Marian bishop of Worcester, at Louvain on 5 October 1565, two former prebendaries of Pates's see, 'Dominus Joliffus et collega', claimed some of the property. When Cardinal Reginald Pole's treatise *De summi pontificis officio* was published at Louvain in 1569, it was with a prefatory epistle by Joliffe addressed to Pope Pius V. Joliffe died at Louvain late in 1573 or early in 1574: letters of administration were granted to the London publisher William Seres on 28 January 1574. THOMPSON COOPER, *rev.* ANDREW A. CHIBI

Sources J. Strype, *Memorials of the most reverend father in God Thomas Cranmer*, 2 vols. (1848) · J. Strype, *Ecclesiastical memorials*, 3 vols. (1822) · E. A. Macek, *The loyal opposition: Tudor traditionalist polemics, 1535–1558* (New York, 1996) · *Miscellaneous writings and letters of Thomas Cranmer*, ed. J. E. Cox, Parker Society, [18] (1846) · *The acts and monuments of John Foxe*, ed. J. Pratt, [new edn], 8 vols. in 16 (1853–70) · Wood, *Ath. Oxon.: Fasti* (1815), 133 · Cooper, *Ath. Cantab.*, 1.320 · *Fasti Angl., 1541–1857*, [Bristol] · *LP Henry VIII*, vol. 17 · *Dodd's Church history of England*, ed. M. A. Tierney, 5 vols. (1839–43) · administration, PRO, PROB 6/2, fol. 42v · *Fasti Angl., 1541–1857*, [Ely]

Joll, James Bysse (1918–1994), historian and university teacher, was born on 21 June 1918 in Bristol, the eldest son of Lieutenant-Colonel Harry Haweis Joll (1881–1950) and his wife, Alice Muriel Edwards (1889–1955). He was educated at Winchester College, where he was an exhibitioner, and spent a year at the University of Bordeaux after leaving school. In 1937 he went to New College, Oxford, to read Greats, but his undergraduate career was interrupted by the Second World War. In 1940 he was commissioned in the Devon regiment and in 1942, as an excellent linguist, was recruited by the Special Operations Executive and trained as an agent. He eventually joined the executive's Austrian and then German sections and was in Germany from April to October 1945. In that month he returned to New College, not to read Greats but philosophy, politics, and economics. Among his teachers there were Herbert Hart and Isaiah Berlin, and both had a

James Bysse Joll (1918–1994), by unknown photographer

marked effect on his intellectual development. In 1946 he was appointed by New College to teach politics and in 1948 elected a full fellow. In 1951 he joined William Deakin, the founding warden of St Antony's College, Oxford (the university's second graduate college), as sub-warden. He remained there until 1967 when he became Stevenson professor of international history at the London School of Economics, a post he held until his retirement.

These two institutions, whose academic remit was almost specifically international, ideally fitted Joll's intellectual interests. After he left the Special Operations Executive he was employed by Sir John Wheeler-Bennett to assist in the editing of the inter-war German foreign policy documents and was briefly editor-in-chief. In 1950 he published his first book, *Britain and Europe: from Pitt to Churchill, 1793–1940*, a collection of extracts from primary documents which emphasized the European dimension of British history. Thereafter virtually all his work was in European intellectual and cultural history or in the historiography—itself a form of intellectual history—of European international relations. His engagement with European culture in its broadest sense (he was himself a fine pianist) was reinforced by his long friendship with the distinguished art historian John Golding. In 1955 Joll wrote a short, but incisive study of modern socialism, *The Second International* (which became a standard text), a theme he further explored in *The Anarchists* (1964), a graceful and sympathetic study of European anarchism and its leading proponents. As a historian of political ideas the historical problem of the intellectual in politics came naturally to him. He had touched upon this in an essay for *The Decline of the Third Republic* (1959), which he edited, but treated it at greater length in *Intellectuals in Politics* (1960), a study of Léon Blum, Walther Rathenau, and Filippo Marinetti. This impressive book, in some ways his best, illustrates his remarkable familiarity with contemporary European culture and its particular national variants. He was to return to Italian political theory in his introductory but characteristically informative and elegant book *Gramsci* (1977). His command of European cultural–political history was demonstrated in *Europe since 1870: an International History* (1973)—a work whose range could be equalled by few other historians.

While by no means a conventional diplomatic historian, Joll was of primary importance in bringing before the English-speaking public the intense controversy over Germany's responsibility for the First World War which followed the publication in 1961 of Fritz Fischer's *Griff nach der Weltmacht*. Joll's 1966 article in the journal *Past and Present*, 'The 1914 debate continues: Fritz Fischer and his critics', was one of the first to introduce the controversy to an English-speaking scholarly audience, and the following year he wrote an introduction to the English translation of *Griff nach der Weltmacht*—published as *Germany's Aims in the First World War*. His inaugural lecture as Stevenson professor at the London School of Economics, published as *1914: the Unspoken Assumptions* (1968), which almost immediately became famous, attempted to explain the actions of the leading figures in 1914 by reference to their basic cultural and psychological presuppositions—things which the 'documents' conceal as much as explain. He brought together his formidable knowledge of 1914 in *The Origins of the First World War* (1984), a book frequently reprinted, and an exceptionally balanced and lucid account of the historiography of the causes of the First World War. His preoccupation with international history—of which the debate over the origins of the First World War was only one part—was intensified after he arrived at the London School of Economics. He was heavily involved in its graduate programmes, both doctoral and masters' (which were more extensive than those at Oxford), and he conducted with Professor Francis Carsten an extremely popular undergraduate course on German history from 1860 to 1945.

Although as a historian Joll was much concerned with the relationship of intellectuals to politics, in his writing his political sympathies, though apparent, tended to be implicit. He disliked overt partisanship both in scholarship and in life. There were two occasions, however, when he abandoned this reserve. In 1956 he was one of the leaders of university opposition to the Conservative government's Suez policy, and in 1979—a more fraught moment—he gave refuge to Anthony Blunt when Blunt was exposed as having been a spy for the Soviet Union. Joll had no sympathy for Blunt's politics, but Blunt was a friend (and a colleague of John Golding at the Courtauld Institute), and Joll's sympathy was for Blunt's human

rather than political predicament. A courageous act: it did not, however, earn him universal admiration.

Throughout his scholarly career Joll was an active teacher and administrator. As teacher and friend he was remembered with affection and gratitude by generations of scholars and students to whom he gave his time—often at the expense of his scholarship—unstintingly. In the establishment of those international networks which became so characteristic of St Antony's, which were indeed its *raison d'être*, he was an essential figure. As an administrator, his administration could be of the most domestic kind, literally kitchen sinks in some cases—all done with great patience and good humour. And although he held at the London School of Economics a chair of great standing he was anything but the tyrant professor of academic folklore. He was a widely travelled scholar, lecturing in Europe, North America, Asia, and Australia. Everywhere he expressed that liberal European culture which was the foundation of his own scholarly life. He died in London, of cancer, on 12 July 1994.   ROSS MCKIBBIN

Sources D. Blackbourn, 'James Bysse Joll', *PBA*, 90 (1996), 413–37 · personal knowledge (2004) · private information (2004) [Mr Peter Joll; Dr John Golding] · *The Times* (15 July 1994) · *The Times* (7 Dec 1994) · *The Independent* (18 July 1994) · *The Independent* (20 July 1994) · *CGPLA Eng. & Wales* (1994)
Archives University of Calgary Library, Alberta, letters to Erich Eyck
Likenesses photograph, repro. in *PBA*, 412 · photograph, NPG [see illus.]
Wealth at death £263,092: probate, 1994, *CGPLA Eng. & Wales*

Jollie, Ethel Maude Tawse (1876–1950). *See under* Colquhoun, Archibald Ross (1848–1914).

Jollie [Jolly], **John** (1640?–1682), nonconformist minister, was the third son of James Jollie (1600–1666) and his wife, Elizabeth (1596/7–1689), daughter of John Low of Denton and widow of John Hall of Droylsden (both in Lancashire). Unlike his two elder brothers, who were both baptized at Gorton Chapel in Manchester parish, Jollie's baptism is unrecorded. His father was a clothier in Gorton, subsequently provost-marshal-general in the parliamentarian army in Lancashire and a lay member of the Manchester classis. The nonconformist minister Thomas *Jollie (1629–1703) was an elder brother. John Jollie is reputed to have been educated at Trinity College, Dublin, about 1655, although there is no record of his entrance there. At some date, also unrecorded, Jollie married, but nothing is known about the family of his wife, Alice.

In 1659 Jollie signed the heads of agreement between ministers in Manchester. He apparently preached at Norbury chapel in the parish of Stockport, Cheshire, as he paid the clerical subsidy there in 1661. He was assistant to John Angier of Denton for a time and stayed with Angier during the winter of 1662–3. Jollie was ordained at the house of Robert Eaton on Deansgate, Manchester, in October 1672, said to be the first nonconformist ordination in the north since 1660. Although he appears to have continued to live at Gorton, in December 1672 he was licensed to preach at the house of Mr Hyde in Norbury in Stockport parish as a presbyterian teacher. Some controversy surrounded his licence. The Hydes were lords of the manor of Norbury, which had been a chapel of ease of Stockport parish since the late sixteenth century. It was presumed that he would not be allowed to preach without Hyde's consent, but in February 1673 a warrant was issued for Jollie's apprehension and presentation before the king for preaching in Norbury chapel. His defence was that, as the chapel was unconsecrated, he had committed no offence. The result of the case is unclear. He is said to have been fined or imprisoned, and that the intervention of Lord Delamere procured his discharge.

Jollie died suddenly on 17 June 1682 while on a visit to Oldham, and was buried there on 19 June. His sudden death shocked his fellow nonconformists. Oliver Heywood recorded:

> having been at a private fast June 16, 1682, came home, eat his supper, was seized of a palsy, died the next day, buryed on Monday June 19, 1682, a great loss to the church and family leaving a wife and six little children. (*Autobiography*, 2.173)

His brother Thomas described him as 'an active servant of Christ' (*Note Book*, 137). Henry Newcome preached a sermon at Jollie's house in Gorton on June 28, 1682 'on account of the death of that honest, labourious and useful man' (*Autobiography of Henry Newcome*, 241). Probably because of his sudden death, Jollie appears not to have made a will. Probate was granted on his estate at Chester in March 1683, when his goods were valued at £242 3s. 2d. His widow married again in 1692.

John Jollie's second son, also **John Jollie** [Jolly] (d. 1725), followed his father into the nonconformist ministry. His place and date of birth are unknown. He was admitted to Frankland's academy on 23 February 1687. There is some confusion over his ordination: the Altham and Wymondhouses church book records his ordination, at Wymondhouses, on 11 November 1696 (*Note Book*, 140), but Oliver Heywood writes that he was ordained, with eight others, at Rathmel, on 26 May 1698 (*Autobiography*, 2.12). However, Jollie became assistant at Wymondhouses in the parish of Altham, Lancashire, to his uncle Thomas Jollie, whom he succeeded as minister upon the latter's death in August 1702.

Jollie married Rebecca Livesey (1666–1720), daughter of Thomas and Isabel Grimshaw of Oakenshaw in Clayton-le-Moors, Lancashire, and widow of John Livesey of Wymondhouses. She died on 17 November 1720 and was buried at Altham four days later. John Jollie died on 29 June 1725 at his home, Oakengates (or Oakenhouses), Oakenshaw. In his will, proved at Chester in November 1725, he requested to be buried 'near the remains of my late excellent wife' (Lancs. RO, WCW. 1725).

CATHERINE NUNN

Sources *The note book of the Rev. Thomas Jolly, AD 1671–1693, extracts from the church book of Altham and Wymondhouses, AD 1649–1725, and an account of the Jolly family of Standish, Gorton, and Altham*, ed. H. Fishwick, Chetham Society, new ser., 33 (1894) · *Oliver Heywood's life of John Angier of Denton*, ed. E. Axon, Chetham Society, new ser., 97 (1937) · *The Rev. Oliver Heywood … his autobiography, diaries, anecdote and event books*, ed. J. H. Turner, 4 vols. (1881–5) · *The autobiography of Henry Newcome*, ed. R. Parkinson, 2 vols., Chetham Society, 26–7 (1852) · *Calamy rev.* · G. L. Turner, ed., *Original records of early nonconformity under persecution and indulgence*, 1 (1911) · *CSP dom.*, 1672–3 · R. Halley, *Lancashire: its puritanism and nonconformity*, 2nd edn (1872) · Burtchaell & Sadleir, *Alum. Dubl.* · will, Lancs. RO, WCW. 1682 · will, Lancs. RO, WCW. 1725 [John Jolly the younger] · parish register, Oldham (burial), 19 June 1682 · *DNB*
Archives Man. CL, transcript of Oldham parish register, Shaw MS misc. MF. 651
Wealth at death £242 3s. 2d.: inventory and will, Lancs. RO, WCW. 1682 · will of John Jolly of Oakenhouses, Lancs. RO, WCW. 1725

Jollie, John (d. 1725). *See under* Jollie, John (1640?–1682).

Jollie [Jolly], **Thomas** (1629–1703), clergyman and ejected minister, was born at Droylesden, near Manchester, on 14 September 1629 and baptized on 29 September at Gorton Chapel, Manchester parish. He was the second son of James Jollie (1600–1666), a wealthy clothier, and his wife, Elizabeth (1596/7–1689), daughter of John Low or Lowe of Denton, and previously wife of John Hall. John *Jollie (1640?–1682) was his younger brother; their elder half-sister, Elizabeth Hall, became the wife of Adam *Martindale (1623–1686).

In 1645 Thomas Jollie entered Trinity College, Cambridge, where he began a lifelong friendship with Oliver Heywood; he was also acquainted with Henry Newcome at St John's College. Jollie never graduated. On 16 September 1649 he was appointed pastor to the chapel at Altham, Whalley parish, Lancashire. He subsequently realized how unready he had been for the ministry, 'being raw in years and rude in parts, and but poorly principled and furnished for such an employment' (Slate, 194). The living was poor but the £10 from the rectorial tithes of Whalley was augmented in 1650 with £30 from the county committee and subsequently by £50 per annum from the committee of plundered ministers out of the sequestered estates of the Catholic Thomas Clifton. In October 1651 Jollie contracted the first of four marriages; his spouses' names are unknown. The first had two sons, Thomas (*bap.* 31 October 1652), and Samuel, at whose birth in 1653 she died. The second, whom he married in spring 1654, died on 11 October. His third wife died in 1656 or 1657 giving birth to his son Timothy. The date of his fourth marriage is unknown.

The Altham church was established on congregational lines with ruling elders and a deacon, and with visible signs of grace required for church membership. It consisted of thirty members including Jollie, and renewed its covenant on 13 July 1651. In fraternal meetings with the congregational church at Walmsley, Lancashire, in April 1653 the Altham church agreed that 'the pastoral office and relations were founded on the People's choice' (*Note Book*, 125). Strict discipline was practised; Jennet, daughter of member Robert Cunliffe, JP and former MP, was excommunicated in 1655 for promising marriage against the advice of the church. Its covenant was renewed again on 20 July 1655.

In May 1654 Jollie was in London, where he found favour

with the 'Commissioners for the approbation of Minis-ters, who made use of him as an instrument to prevent corruptions' (*Note Book*, 126). In his meetings with the triers he probably first made the acquaintance of John Owen. Between 1654 and 1656 he had a written contro-versy with John Webster of Clitheroe, Lancashire. The subject of the exchange is not known but in 1654 Webster was associated with William Erbury, the radical anti-nomian, and was proposing a radical reform of the univer-sities, for which he was denounced as a Leveller. Jollie was instrumental in promoting the closer association of inter-regnum churches, first with other avowedly congrega-tional churches but in the late 1650s with the presbyter-ians too. To this end, some time in 1657 he met ministers and brethren at Chesterfield and Wakefield to explore such links in Yorkshire, Lancashire, Derbyshire, and Not-tinghamshire. He attended and on 29 September 1658 preached to the general meeting of congregational chur-ches at the Savoy, London. On 13 July 1659 congregational ministers from Yorkshire and Lancashire, including Jollie, met with Lancashire presbyterians in the collegiate church, Manchester, to come to an accommodation. Ten articles were proposed and 'both sides seemed desirous of union' (Martindale, 131), but ratification, fixed for Septem-ber, was overtaken by events. Following the failure in August of Sir George Booth's rising, which many Lanca-shire presbyterian ministers had supported, congrega-tionalists, who like Jollie had tended to oppose it, dis-tanced themselves from their potential brethren, some even suggesting that the presbyterians had coerced them into association.

After the Restoration in May 1660 Jollie's exclusive churchmanship and his family connections made him a prominent target. In November he was arrested on a war-rant from three deputy lieutenants. He was discharged on taking the oath of supremacy. A second arrest on 15 Febru-ary 1661 was followed by an attempt forcibly to prevent his preaching. His appearance at the bishop's court at Chester on 11 November was prevented by the illness and death of the bishop, Brian Walton. Jollie was presented to the bishop's court at Chester by the churchwardens of Altham on 9 December on charges of acting as minister on uncertain authority and neglecting his functions by refusing to give communion and baptism to most parish-ioners, to read the Book of Common Prayer, or to bury the dead. After three appearances at the consistory he was condemned to suspension, effected after a delay by Cap-tain Bannister and Captain Alexander Nowell on 17 August 1662. A week later the Act of Uniformity came into force and Jollie resigned his living. The church book records that 'Upon the last Sabbath in the Publique Place, all were satisfied that neither censure in the Bishop's Court, nor Act of Parliament, did discharge the Pastor from his office' (*Note Book*, 131).

Jollie moved to Healey, near Burnley, Lancashire, possi-bly staying with the family of Robert Whitaker. On 9 Octo-ber 1663 he was arrested, taken to Bury, and interrogated by Nowell. He was placed under arrest in a private house and obliged to find surety for good behaviour. His hosts were pious and 'as he and they were ingag'd in family Wor-ship, Captain Nowel breaks into the House, and with blas-phemous Expressions plucks the bible out of his Hands, and drags him away to the guard, pretending they had kept a Conventicle' (Calamy, *Continuation*, 1.557). The next day, a Sunday, he was sent to Skipton gaol, where he was 'used badly' (*Note Book*, 133). In November 1663 he was re-arrested without a warrant and confined in York Castle for his alleged involvement in the Farnley Wood plot, but there was no evidence against him and he was released without charge. On 12 February 1665 he was seized at a conventicle and imprisoned in Lancaster Castle for eleven weeks. On 23 November 1665 he was again arrested on an order from the lord lieutenant and roughly treated by Nowell. In 1666 he was holding meetings in an alehouse and with Henry Newcome's encouragement was preach-ing to Anabaptists.

In 1667 Jollie bought the desolate farmstead of Wymondhouses on the north side of Pendle Hill, in Whal-ley parish, Lancashire. The church book records 'Preacht at one time to two women only' (*Note Book*, 134). A door at the foot of stairs leading from the sitting room could be folded back and used as a makeshift pulpit; if there was a warning of intruders, this could be dismantled, the door be closed, and the preacher escape upstairs. Jollie was nevertheless arrested by Nowell on 25 April 1669 while preaching in Altham and was gaoled in Preston for six months under the Five Mile Act. He refused to take the oath required by the Oxford act.

The king's indulgence of March 1672 offered Jollie and his congregation a brief respite. Wymondhouses was licensed on 2 May 1672 as a congregational meeting-place along with four other houses around Pendle. When the indulgence was revoked in March 1673 Jollie and the church continued to meet 'being loath to quitt this liberty soe pretious to us, rather thinking it should bee taken from us' (*Note Book*, 16). On 14 June 1674 he was taken while meeting at Slade, near Padiham, Lancashire, by Captain Nowell, who was again alleged to have sworn and threat-ened violence. Jollie was a prisoner for two days, before being dismissed on a bond and fined £20 along with the owner of the house. He narrowly escaped an attempt to imprison and banish him.

1675 was a miserable year for Jollie's church and his fourth wife died on 8 June, 'aged forty-two'. After a few years of relative quiet, in July 1679 he was prosecuted in the exchequer court under the laws against papists but escaped conviction. In December 1679 he was fined for non-attendance at parish worship. In July 1682 he was again arrested by Nowell and prosecuted under the Con-venticle Act and by June 1683 the church could only meet at night. In August 1684 he was arrested by order of the lord chief justice and taken to Preston, and required to provide sureties 'who were bound in [£200] each (Judge Jeffrys would have had it 2000) for having frequent Con-venticles in his house' (Calamy, *Continuation*, 1.559). This was reduced to a bond of £100 at the next assize. He con-tinued itinerant preaching, though with more circum-spection. Following Monmouth's rebellion in June 1685 his house was twice searched by troops and his horses taken. Until January 1687 Jollie held meetings mainly at night; he could only preach openly after the king's declaration of indulgence of 4 April 1687. On 15 May 1688 the foundations were laid of the New Chapel at Wymondhouses, which was completed on 5 July.

Despite persistent persecution, particularly at the hands of Alexander Nowell of Read Hall, Jollie maintained a vigorous ministry. He itinerated on large circuits in the West Riding of Yorkshire, through Manchester and Cheshire, and up to Kendal in Westmorland. He was sustained by his links with the puritan gentry, London dissenters, and New England congregationalists. He was intimate with the family of the former parliamentary Major-General John Lambert and visited them at Calton near Malham, Yorkshire, during the 1670s. He received money from Alderman Henry Ashurst of London and frequently celebrated the sabbath with the presbyterian Hoghtons of Hoghton Hall, Lancashire. He also received intellectual sustenance and support from Calvinists abroad, particularly in congregational New England. He corresponded with Samuel Mather of Dublin and Nathaniel Mather of London, and on 2 April 1677 began a correspondence with Increase Mather of Boston. He wrote to Increase Mather on 18 February 1678 of his unsuccessful efforts to call meetings promoting accommodation between congregationalists and presbyterians in England, and 'As for our poor church, wee are by death reduced to a small and weak number … little likelihood of our long continuance' (Calamy rev., 301).

Despite Jollie's tireless work, efforts at association between churches in Yorkshire, Lancashire, and Cheshire were largely in abeyance by the end of 1674. In August 1675 he met John Owen and other congregationalists in London to examine the grounds for accommodation with the presbyterians. Jollie claimed to have brought John Owen and Richard Baxter together in Henry Ashurst's house and in July 1682 he was again in London with Owen, working towards 'association of evangelicall reforming churches' on a plan which Jollie had drawn up (Note Book, 50). In Lancashire and Yorkshire there was little progress between 1682 and 1687 and there remained significant obstacles to association. Most protestant dissenting ministers in Lancashire tended towards presbyterianism, while Jollie was a congregationalist and uncompromising dissenter. As early as 1665 he had written against joining in common prayer. He was particularly strident in condemning occasional conformity among his ministerial brethren like Henry Newcome. Newcome in turn recorded his anger at Jollie's censure. Another area of conflict was ordination, becoming a particular issue in newly formed churches. By 1680 Jollie felt that he was neglected by friends in Craven to whom he had ministered in the later 1670s, following his refusal in 1678 to participate in the ordination as their minister of John Issot, whose spiritual state was unknown to him and whose inclination was towards presbyterianism. In August 1680 Jollie fell out with Oliver Heywood and Richard Frankland (to whom Issot was assistant) at the ordination of Timothy Hodgson,

Sir John and Lady Hewley's chaplain, Jollie rejecting Hodgson's evidence for the work of grace in his life. Heywood and Frankland were keen to ordain as many young men as possible as their generation passed away and were frustrated at Jollie's intransigence. Though his relationship with Heywood remained warm, continued disagreements over ordination troubled that with Frankland.

Jollie's efforts to promote ministerial association began again in the summer of 1687 but there was little movement until after the passing of the Toleration Act. Between 29 April 1689 and 24 March 1690 Jollie's attention was diverted by the claims of Richard Dugdale and his family that he was possessed. Jollie and neighbouring protestant dissenting ministers attempted to exorcise Dugdale in a barn at Surey, near Whalley. The exorcisms ended in March 1690 when the ministers involved were satisfied that they had been successful. The case attracted large crowds but did nothing to endear Jollie to his colleagues in the rest of the county.

On 4 March 1690 there was a meeting of ministers at Rathmell, Yorkshire, to decide on the basis of the communion of ministers but in May Jollie was still reporting hostility to ministerial meetings from those 'still to strongly byassed to a party' (Note Book, 98). His flagging hopes were revived in August when Isaac Noble of Bristol wrote to him concerning moves for association in the west country, but the Surey case and the increasingly rancorous tensions in the London Happy Union, combined with the long memories of the congregationalists' betrayal in 1659, meant there was little initial enthusiasm for association in Lancashire, where a general meeting of all ministers was only arranged in 1693. When the self-styled 'United Brethren' assembled at Bolton on 3 April, Jollie was very disappointed at their lack of commitment. In June he noted that while some in Manchester paid attention to his fraternal letter, an agreed 'solemn day' was unsatisfactorily observed and a leading colleague present treated him coolly. Jollie and his nephew John *Jollie [see under Jollie, John (1640?–1682)] were regular attenders at the provincial meetings of the Lancashire United Brethren, of which the minutes survive until 13 August 1700. On 4 September 1694 Jollie was assigned, along with Henry Newcome, to manage the correspondence for the county. On 14 April 1696 the United Brethren wrote to London to encourage those attempting to patch up the Happy Union. It is to his credit that despite the fierce opposition to the Happy Union of his influential correspondent, the congregationalist Nathaniel Mather, Jollie never wavered in his support for ministerial association between congregationalists and presbyterians.

Jollie's The Surey demoniack, or, An account of Satans strange and dreadful actings in and about the body of Richard Dugdale of Surey (1697) provoked a pamphlet war with the rector of Wigan and controversialist Zachary Taylor, who accused the protestant dissenters involved of being the dupes of the Catholics. By 1698 'the controversy mutated into a consideration of the religious and political divisions of English protestants, in the nation as a whole, and in Lancashire in particular' (Westaway and Harrison, 272). It was perhaps a last-ditch attempt by Jollie and like-minded ministers to defend the old providentialist world view from the new mechanical philosophy and it provided the protestant dissenters of Lancashire with much unwonted ridicule and attention.

Jollie made his will in June 1698 and in 1699 the church book records 'pastor badly; Son sent for' (*Note Book*, 140). He died on 14 March 1703 and was buried at Altham on the 18th. The funeral sermon preached by his son Timothy Jollie was published as *Pastoral Care Exemplified* (1704).

JONATHAN H. WESTAWAY

Sources *The note book of the Rev. Thomas Jolly, AD 1671–1693, extracts from the church book of Altham and Wymondhouses, AD 1649–1725, and an account of the Jolly family of Standish, Gorton, and Altham*, ed. H. Fishwick, Chetham Society, new ser., 33 (1894) • *The Rev. Oliver Heywood … his autobiography, diaries, anecdote and event books*, ed. J. H. Turner, 4 vols. (1881–5) • W. A. Shaw, ed., 'Minutes of the United Brethren, 1693–1700', *Minutes of the Manchester presbyterian classis*, 3, Chetham Society, new ser., 24 (1891), 350–65 • F. Nicholson and E. Axon, *The older nonconformity in Kendal* (1915), 142–52, 571 • will, 1698, Borth. Inst. [wills proved at York] • *Calamy rev.*, 216, 300, 301 • E. Calamy, *A continuation of the account of the ministers … who were ejected and silenced after the Restoration in 1660*, 2 vols. (1727), vol. 1, pp. 557–60 • Timothy Jollie, *Pastoral care exemplified, or, A funeral discourse after the interment of the Reverend Mr Thomas Jollie* (1704) • Thomas Jollie, *Thomas Jollie's papers: a list of the papers in Dr Williams's Library manuscript no. 12.78*, Dr Williams's Library Occasional Paper (1956) • J. Westaway and R. D. Harrison, '"The Surey Demoniack": defining protestantism in 1690s Lancashire', *Unity and diversity in the church*, ed. R. N. Swanson, SCH, 32 (1996), 263–82 • *The life of Adam Martindale*, ed. R. Parkinson, Chetham Society, 4 (1845) • *The autobiography of Henry Newcome*, ed. R. Parkinson, 2 vols., Chetham Society, 26–7 (1852), 108, 247 • B. Nightingale, *Lancashire nonconformity*, 6 vols. [1890–93] • R. Slate, *Select nonconformists' remains* (1814), 194–281 • A. Gordon, ed., *Freedom after ejection: a review (1690–1692) of presbyterian and congregational nonconformity in England and Wales* (1917), 61, 64 • C. G. Bolam and others, *The English presbyterians: from Elizabethan puritanism to modern Unitarianism* (1968), 102, 113, 115 • J. H. Turner, T. Dickenson, and O. Heywood, eds., *The nonconformist register of baptisms, marriages, and deaths* (1881), 74, 208, 293 • W. S. Weeks, 'John Webster, author of *The displaying of supposed witchcraft*', *Transactions of the Lancashire and Cheshire Antiquarian Society*, 39 (1921), 55–107 • C. Hill, *The experience of defeat: Milton and some of his contemporaries* (1984), 84–97 • *The diary of Abraham de la Pryme, the Yorkshire antiquary*, ed. C. Jackson, SurtS, 54 (1870), 189 • T. Whitehead, *History of the Dales congregational churches* (1930), 162–3 • J. B. Williams, ed., *The lives of Philip and Matthew Henry* (1974), 261 • W. Urwick, ed., *Historical sketches of nonconformity in the county palatine of Cheshire, by various ministers and laymen* (1864), xlvi, xlvii, 203, 272–4, 310, 312–16, 325, 492

Archives DWL, corresp. and papers | BL, Add. MS 54185, fols. 19–93 • BL, letters to O. Heywood, Add. MS 4276, fols. 4–5 • BL, notes on sermons by T. Jollie, Add. MSS 45672, fols. 1–17b; 45675, fols. 215b–223, 239–243b, 269–273; 45677, fols. 249–54, 265–268b • DWL, list of dissenting ministers and congregations in England and Wales, MS 38.4 • Lancs. RO, register of dissenting meeting-houses • Mitchell L., Glas., journal • University of York

Likenesses W. Ridley, stipple, BM, NPG; repro. in *Evangelical Magazine* (1805) • portrait, repro. in Nightingale, *Lancashire nonconformity*, vol. 2, p. 186

Wealth at death real estate at Wymondhouses, a cottage at Pendleton, and land in Oakenhurst and Lower Darwen left to grandson Thomas Jollie; Timothy Jollie received £200 and he and his wife received a piece of gold each; their children received a guinea each; further £20 15s. in small disbursements to friends, relations, and the poor: will, 1698, wills proved at Borth. Inst., York

Jollie, Thomas, the younger (1687–1764). *See under* Jollie, Timothy (1656x9–1714).

Jollie [Jolly], **Timothy** (1656x9–1714), Independent minister and nonconformist tutor, was born at Altham, Lancashire, between 1656 and 1659, according to differing sources. He was the youngest son of Thomas *Jollie or Jolly (1629–1703), an Independent minister; his mother was Thomas's third wife, whose name is unknown, who died in childbirth giving birth to him.

Education On 27 August 1673 Jollie entered the academy of Richard Frankland, then at Rathmell, Yorkshire, but which moved to Natland, Westmorland, the following spring. In February 1675 Thomas Jollie wrote to Oliver Heywood, whose sons were also at the academy, in response to Heywood's anxieties on Frankland's ability to carry out his duties: 'Some exercise I also had as to the discouragement upon my younger son in his place, but the lord hear solemn prayers in bowing his heart to obey mee and to return unto Natland' (Nicholson and Axon, 125). At Natland, Timothy Jollie struck up what was to prove a lifelong friendship with Heywood's son John, and saved John's younger brother Eliezer Heywood from drowning. Both Thomas Jollie and Oliver Heywood visited Natland to preach to and converse with the students, and Timothy dated his spiritual conversion to a sermon Heywood preached at Natland upon '2 Tim. 3. 7. Ever learning and never able to come to the knowledg of the truth'. Oliver Heywood noted that Timothy Jollie also 'took speciall notice of good he received by another sermon I preacht while he was at Mr Franklands at Natland concerning spirituallizing of all parts of human learning as Grammar, Rhetorick, Logick, Philosophy which I had forgot' (Heywood, 163–4).

Timothy Jollie left Frankland's academy in December 1675. About March 1677 Thomas Jollie recorded in his notebook that he was renewing a covenant with the Lord in preparation for a trip to London with his youngest son 'whom I intended for London' (*Note Book*, 31). There Timothy became a member of the Independent church at Girdler's Hall, Basinghall Street, under George Griffith. His education may have been completed at Theophilus Gale's academy on Newington Green; Thomas Jollie was shocked when he heard in February 1679 of the death of Gale, 'to whom the whole church generally and I in particular upon the account of my two sons were very much indebted' (*Note Book*, 36).

Sheffield ministry About March 1680 Thomas recorded that 'the lord had perswaded my younger son also to own the lord's covenant among a people at London, and there were some motions on foot for his coming to the church at Sheffield' (*Note Book*, 41). This was the newly erected meeting-house called the New Hall at Snig Hill, Sheffield. Timothy's call must have come in 1679 or early 1680. Thomas recorded in May 1680:

> My younger son being called to Sheffield, I went thither and found cause to acknowledg the speciall providence of god in bringing him among such a sober people in such a well

affected place, to such a numerous congregation though he was very young, yet had I encouragement in him both as to grace and gifts for soe great a work. (*Note Book*, 42)

Despite Thomas Jollie's cheerful prognostication the protestant dissenting body around Sheffield was riven by factions and personal animosities and Timothy Jollie was credited with being an eirenic influence. Significantly his ordination, at the house of Abel Yates in Sheffield on 26–8 April, had elements of both congregational and presbyterian practice. Timothy Jollie preached to the people on Isaiah 59: 1–2. They were then dismissed and the ministers examined him. The following day most of the congregation were present save two, who 'were dissatisfyed with that examination by presbiters, thought it should be done by ruling Elders in the name of the people, but no notice was taken of that opinion' (Heywood, 2.200). Heywood prayed over him in 'his actuall ordination by imposition of hands' (ibid.) and gave an exhortation. The elder 'spoke in the name of the people their desires that he would accept the pastorall office over them, wch the rest signified their consent to by lifting up their hands, and he assented' (ibid.). Significantly Thomas Jollie stressed the congregational nature of this ordination, noting the church call: 'my son Timothy was sett apart to the Ministry by severall ministers called to the work by the church at Sheffield, who had not teaching offices of their own, and afterwards hee was chosen to bee their pastor' (*Note Book*, 45). Oliver Heywood, however, noted that this Independent church submitted to have their minister ordained by presbyters, observing that as the previous minister, the congregationalist Robert Durant, 'was of another persuasion, I look on this as an olive-branch of peace amongst gods people' (Heywood, 2.24). Heywood noted that the congregationalist Thomas Ogle of Chesterfield did not come, though invited, because he was 'otherwise minded' (Heywood, 2.201). Heywood also thought it was a sign of reconciliation between the other officiating ministers at the ordination, Matthew Bloom and Rowland Hancock. They, along with Edward Prime, had been James Fisher's curates and had likewise been ejected. On 16 July 1676 they had founded a congregational church that met at Shiercliffe Hall outside Sheffield but had an acrimonious split over the building of a new meeting-house, Bloom separating and forming his own congregation in Attercliffe. Heywood acted as peacemaker in July 1679 but the two parties fell apart again later in 1681. Jollie extended the hand of friendship to the remnants of the Attercliffe congregation subsequently ministered to by Edward Prime, Heywood noting that Jollie entertained 'Mr Primes people to communion and some of his members sit down with Mr Prime' (Heywood, 4.164–5). Reflecting on Jollie in May 1700 Oliver Heywood wrote 'tho he be congregationall yet of an healing humble spirit—blessed be god for him—these are sweet signall mercys for which I have prayd, and cannot but take speciall notice of answers of prayers' (ibid.).

On 2 July 1681 Jollie married Elizabeth (*bap.* 1647, *d.* 1709), the daughter of James Fisher, the ejected vicar of Sheffield who had been the original pastor of Jollie's congregation until his death in 1669; their first child, Elizabeth, was born in August 1682. At that time Jollie frequently had to move about to avoid detection. On 19 January 1683 he was arrested under the Five Mile Act, taken before Sir John Reresby, and fined £20, and was taken to York and bound over to appear at the next assizes. Refusing to take the oath of good behaviour he was imprisoned for six months in York Castle. Elizabeth Jollie came to lodge in the city to be near him, and spent most days with him in prison. In June 1683 he was visited by Oliver Heywood, and was freed on 1 October 1683. Towards the end of 1683 Elizabeth and her daughter settled again in Sheffield but Timothy 'was forced to wander up and down … he was not suffered to come to Sheffield without he came that none knew of it but friends, for his enemies were so enraged against him that, if they should find him, they would send him to prison' (Manning, *Good Puritan Woman*, 9). From the fragments of diaries which Elizabeth Jollie kept for her daughter, it appears that the middle years of the 1680s were exceptionally hard for the family, their infant son Thomas dying on 26 April 1685. In the summer of 1685 Timothy Jollie:

> was strictly sought after … There were warrants out to take him. They came three several times; but blessed be the Lord he was out of their way. How they did threaten what they would do, and offered a great sum to any that would take him, but he came home when others were in prison, and did preach the Gospel to us. (ibid., 14)

Christ's College Richard Frankland had conducted his academy at Attercliffe, Sheffield, between 1686 and 1689, when he took it back to Rathmell. In 1691 Jollie started an academy known as Christ's College at his residence, Attercliffe Hall. The London Common Fund sent him some students but none after 1696. After 1695 most of the funding for students came from the Congregational Fund. By the time of his death Jollie had trained about a hundred students. The names of only about fifty or sixty are known, including: John Bowes, the future lord chancellor of Ireland; Nicholas Saunderson, the blind mathematician who was subsequently Lucasian professor of mathematics at Cambridge; and the ministers Thomas Bradbury, John Evans, Benjamin Grosvenor, and William Harris. Thomas Secker, subsequently archbishop of Canterbury, was a member of his congregation and a student of his in 1708–9. One of his students, Jeremiah Gill, who had entered Frankland's Academy on 10 January 1687, remained at Attercliffe and became Jollie's assistant, leaving to become minister to the Independent church in Hull in 1697. Another student, John Wadsworth, then became his assistant, leaving for Rotherham in 1701.

Jollie continued Frankland's adherence to Calvinist theology. A letter of his to Oliver Heywood in 1701 shows that he shared Heywood's alarm at the rise of 'novellists', or 'innovators upon the orthodoxy of Calvinism' (*DNB*). He avoided the teaching of mathematics on his curriculum as 'tending to scepticism and infidelity' but students pursued these studies surreptitiously (Bolam and others, 191).

The curriculum was perhaps deficient in logic, the classics, and Hebrew. Thomas Secker was scathing, saying that 'only the old philosophy of the schools was taught there, and that neither ably nor diligently' (McLachlan, 107). Benjamin Grosvenor conceded that 'there have been tutors of greater learning … but, that sweetness of temper, and benevolent turn of mind … are things not everywhere to be met with' (ibid.). Oliver Heywood noted:

> I doe perceive god hath made him of great use in training up Schollers in University learning in order to the ministry, he hath at this time 26 schollers, and 40 more are completely qualified, and are imployed in that sacred office. … I perceive he is well accomplist for his work, both for learning, parts, sweet temper, and soundness in the faith, not drawn away with these odde opinions, very orthodox of a moderate spirit. (Heywood, 4.164–5)

Matthew Henry held a similar opinion concerning Jollie's disposition; having participated in an ordination with Jollie at Dean Row, Cheshire, on 2 September 1707, he recorded 'Mr. Jolly is of a healing, loving spirit' (Williams, 145).

In 1700 a new meeting-house, since known as the Upper Chapel, was built for Jollie and his church; his hearers now formed the largest congregation in Yorkshire. He published little. In 1703 he preached a funeral sermon for his father, which was published in the following year as *Pastoral Care Exemplified*. In this sermon he urged the small church at Wymondhouses, Lancashire, to keep to the gospel doctrines of justification and sanctification and to the church order of his father. In 1712, along with Thomas Bradbury, he edited and saw published *Sermons on several occasions by the late Reverend and learned Thomas Whitaker, A.M. pastor to a church at Leeds in Yorkshire*. A compendium of funeral sermons and memorials, it contains a memorial of Whitaker by Jollie and four funeral sermons for him.

After a period of considerable infirmity Elizabeth Jollie died on 17 January 1709. Her funeral sermon was preached by a former student of Jollie, William Bagshaw of Stannington, Yorkshire, and was published in the same year. Timothy Jollie made his will on 10 October 1709. He died of dropsy on Easter day, 28 March 1714, and was buried on 31 March in the graveyard of the Upper Chapel. His funeral sermon was preached by his assistant John De la Rose and was published in 1715 as *A funeral sermon occasion'd by the death of the Rev. Mr. Timothy Jollie late pastor to the congregational church at Sheffield*. De la Rose's sermon was an attempted defence of ultra-orthodox predestinarian Calvinism and congregational church government. He claims that just before his death Jollie confided in De la Rose his belief in 'the Doctrine of Justification before God only by the Righteousness of Christ imputed, and receiv'd by Faith: This was the Way of Salvation that he chose, and acquiesced in for himself, and desired, and recommended to you' (De la Rose, 25). The doctrine of imputed righteousness was increasingly unpopular with urban chapel élites, who feared its antinomian tendencies and whose belief in human agency led them to promote more Arminian doctrines. Consequently there was an angry division after Jollie's death. The trust deed placed the management of the chapel entirely in the hands of the trustees, who appointed a minister against the wishes of some of the church members. The trustees retained the meeting-house and appointed Jollie's former assistant, John Wadsworth, as minister. About 200 seceded, chose De la Rose as minister, and formed the congregational church which built the Nether Chapel, Sheffield, in 1715. The academy was continued by John Wadsworth at Sheffield until at least 1736, with funding from the Congregational Fund.

Jollie's son and nephew Timothy Jollie [Jolly] (1691–1757), Independent minister, youngest son of Timothy Jollie, was born on 22 August 1691, probably at Wymondhouses, Lancashire, where his father was apparently assisting his grandfather for a period over the summer. He was baptized at the Upper Chapel, Sheffield, on 1 September 1691. The diary kept by his mother, Elizabeth Jollie, and subsequently by Timothy himself, is full of details about his early life, indicating that he had a delicate constitution for much of his life. At about four or five he started to attend school in Sheffield. At thirteen, in late 1704, he was sent to a Mr Matthews for his schooling. In 1707 he spent a year with his father's former pupil and assistant John Wadsworth in Rotherham, Yorkshire. He then pursued his education with his father and spent the years 1711–12 in London. About this time his diary records that he was 'full of convictions. Covenanted to be the Lord's. Join'd myself to the Church of Sheffield. A disorderly walker Humbled but little for it; not careful enough to improve time' (Manning, *History*, 63). He began to preach at Stannington outside Sheffield in February 1714. Following his father's death in March 1714 and the choice of John Wadsworth in his stead, Timothy consented to be Wadsworth's assistant. On 19 October 1714 he married the daughter (1690–1761) of the Sheffield bookseller and printer Nevill Simmons; her name is unknown.

Jollie became an elder in the congregation in December 1714 and settled into a house in Westbar in May 1715. In October and November 1715 he took part, along with neighbouring ministers, in an investigation of the causes of the split in the church. Blaming 'the precipitant acts of those who now adhere to Mr. Wadsworth' they found in favour of De la Rose, ordaining him to the pastorate of the Nether Chapel, Jollie preaching a sermon the day after the ordination. He left Sheffield, according to his own account, because of 'a prevailing Indolency of temper I found encreasing upon Me, from the way of living there' and also because 'The management of Pretended friends helpt to wean my Affections' (Manning, *History*, 63). In 1720 he became assistant minister to Matthew Clarke at Miles Lane, Cannon Street, London. His diary records that he was chosen 'to Mr. Braggs lecture' (ibid.) and in April 1721 'Was called to assist at the Lecture in Gravil Lane' (ibid.). Clarke died on 27 March 1726 and the search for a successor caused a split in the church. One candidate, David Some, who had been trained at Attercliffe by Timothy Jollie the elder, told Philip Doddridge that he had been tried as a ministerial candidate by the Miles Lane congregation but that 'he was hardly orthodox enough for so precise a people' (*Calendar*, ed. Nuttall, 35). Timothy Jollie recorded that 'after many warm Debates within Doors and very unwarrantable Practices without the Church by ballotting the Lot fell upon me by considerable Majority' (Manning, *History*, 63–4). Jollie was ordained pastor in September 1726, reportedly causing a breach because some members felt Jollie insufficiently orthodox. He remained the sole pastor for the rest of his life.

In April 1727 Jollie's sister Elizabeth Jollie came to live with him in London, remaining with him until she died on 17 November 1739; she was buried in Bunhill Fields on 23 November 1739.

Timothy Jollie published *Christ's Dominion* (1730). Subsequently he published *A sermon preach'd to the Societies for Reformation of Manners at Salters' Hall on Monday October 1st 1739*. He was involved in the work of the Congregational Fund. He subscribed to Doddridge's *The Family Expositor* between 1738 and 1756, and Doddridge consulted him as well as Isaac Watts and Daniel Neal about moving to Northampton. He suffered all his life from gout and died on 3 August 1757 at his house in Clements Lane. His funeral sermon was preached by his close friend David Jennings.

Thomas Jollie [Jolly] **the younger** (1687–1764), Independent minister, was born on 23 November 1687 at Wymondhouses, Lancashire, and was baptized there by his grandfather Thomas Jollie in his New Chapel on 4 December 1687. He was the son of Samuel Jollie (1653–1691), the oldest surviving son of Thomas Jollie the elder. By April 1691 Samuel, his wife, and his sister Sarah Jollie were all dead. In May 1691 Thomas Jollie travelled to York to take out 'tuition on behalf of the orphan my grandson' (*Note Book*, 106). Jollie records his retiring for prayer in July 1691 'on behalf of the orphan and the rest of my family, my son and daughter who draws near her time' (ibid.). The son and daughter in question here were Timothy Jollie and his wife, Elizabeth.

It is assumed that upon his grandfather's death in March 1703, if not before, Thomas Jollie the younger went to live with his uncle Timothy Jollie in Attercliffe outside Sheffield and undertook training for the ministry, as stipulated in his grandfather's will. He then seems to have spent time in London and Norfolk. In 1706 John Jollie recorded in the Wymondhouses church book 'A letter in Latin from cousin Thomas'. In 1709 he recorded 'Cousin Thomas,—good letter from London … Cousin's letter from Norfolk … Another of cousin Jolly's from London' (*Note Book*, 141–2).

On 30 May 1711 Thomas Jollie was chosen as the Independent minister of Bradfield, Norfolk, and ordained there on 13 June. The Bradfield church had recently split from the church at Tunstead. In May 1726 he succeeded John Jollie the younger at the Wymondhouses Independent Church, Lancashire. It was apparently always intended that he should eventually succeed Thomas Jollie at Wymondhouses: in his will of 1698 Thomas Jollie wrote 'Concerning my library, it is my will that my nephew, John Jolly, have the use of that part of it my Executor leaves at

Wymond-houses, so long as he stays at the said New Chappell, until my said Grandson comes of age' (*Note Book*, 152).

In 1737 Jollie became the minister of the Independent church at Cockermouth, Cumberland, where he died on 8 June 1764. His will, proved 17 June 1764, indicates that he held property at Wymondhouses and Pendleton, Lancashire. These were left to his son Thomas Jolly with a provision for an annuity to be paid from some of the lands to his wife, Jane Jollie. Jane Jollie made her will on 24 March 1770 and it was proved in June 1770. In it she left a guinea and a bond due to her for £84 to 'my Son in Law Thomas Jolly of Wymond Houses in the parish of Whally' (will of Jane Jolly).   JONATHAN H. WESTAWAY

Sources J. E. Manning, *History of Upper Chapel, Sheffield, founded 1662, built 1700: a bicentennial volume with an appendix containing Timothy Jollie's register of baptisms, 1681–1744* (1900), 16–62 · J. E. Manning, *A good puritan woman: pages from the diary of Mrs. Timothy Jollie, of Sheffield* (1900) · *The note book of the Rev. Thomas Jolly, AD 1671–1693, extracts from the church book of Altham and Wymondhouses, AD 1649–1725, and an account of the Jolly family of Standish, Gorton, and Altham*, ed. H. Fishwick, Chetham Society, new ser., 33 (1894) · *The Rev. Oliver Heywood … his autobiography, diaries, anecdote and event books*, ed. J. H. Turner, 4 vols. (1881–5), vol. 2, pp. 24, 200–01; vol. 4, pp. 163–5 · F. Nicholson and E. Axon, *The older nonconformity in Kendal* (1915), 250 · *DNB* · *Calamy rev.*, 216, 301 · H. McLachlan, *English education under the Test Acts: being the history of the nonconformist academies, 1662–1820* (1931), 62–70, 106–9 · J. G. Miall, *Congregationalism in Yorkshire: a chapter of modern church history* (1868), 121–2, 347–52 · J. De la Rose, *A funeral sermon occasion'd by the death of the Rev. Mr. Timothy Jollie late pastor to the congregational church at Sheffield* (1715) [DWL, Aaf (CLR) P.3017 Vp] · T. Jollie, *Pastoral care exemplified, or, A funeral discourse after the interment of the Reverend Mr. Thomas Jollie, late pastor to a congregation in Lancashire, with some brief hints of his character* (1704) · will, Borth. Inst. · will, Cumbria AS [Jane Jolly] · will, Cumbria AS [Thomas Jolly the younger] · A. Gordon, ed., *Freedom after ejection: a review (1690–1692) of presbyterian and congregational nonconformity in England and Wales* (1917), 130, 133, 293 · G. Hester, *Attercliffe as a seat of learning and ministerial education* (1893) · W. Bagshaw, *A funeral sermon for that pious gentlewoman, Mrs Eliz. Jollie of Attercliffe, who deceas'd Jan. 17. 1708/9* (1709) · C. G. Bolam and others, *The English presbyterians: from Elizabethan puritanism to modern Unitarianism* (1968), 191 · D. L. Wykes, 'After the happy union: presbyterians and Independents in the provinces', *Unity and diversity in the church*, ed. R. N. Swanson, SCH, 32 (1996), 283–95 · J. Browne, *A history of Congregationalism and memorials of the churches in Norfolk and Suffolk* (1877), 310ff. · J. H. Turner, T. Dickenson, and O. Heywood, eds., *The nonconformist register of baptisms, marriages, and deaths* (1881), 247, 263 · B. Dale, *Yorkshire puritanism and early nonconformity*, ed. T. G. Crippen [n.d., c.1909], 21 · *Thomas Jollie's papers: a list of the papers in Dr Williams's library* (1956) · [J. Hunter], ed., *Letters of eminent men, addressed to Ralph Thoresby*, 2 (1832), 158 · B. Nightingale, *Lancashire nonconformity*, 6 vols. [1890–93], vol. 2, p. 192 · *Calendar of the correspondence of Philip Doddridge*, ed. G. F. Nuttall, HMC, JP 26 (1979), 35, 331 · T. Whitaker, *Sermons on several occasions* (1712) · J. B. Williams, ed., *The lives of Philip and Matthew Henry* (1974), 145, 256 · J. Wilson, 'Statistical view of dissenters: Cumberland', *London Christian Instructor or Congregational Magazine*, 5 (1822), 276 · W. Wilson, *The history and antiquities of the dissenting churches and meeting houses in London, Westminster and Southwark*, 4 vols. (1808–14), vol. 1, pp. 345, 492–6 · D. Jennings, *A funeral sermon on occassion of the death of the Rev. Mr. Timothy Jollie* (1757) · T. Jollie, *A sermon preach'd to the Societies for Reformation of Manners at Salters' Hall on Monday October 1st 1739* (1739) · will, Borth. Inst. [Thomas Jollie the elder]

Archives BL, register of baptisms, Collectanea Hunteriana, Add. MS 24436, fol. 74 · BL, Hall papers, notes on sermon preached by Timothy Jollie, Add. MS 45677, fols. 254–256b

Jollie, Timothy (1691–1757). *See under* Jollie, Timothy (1656x9–1714).

Jolliffe, William (1745–1802), politician, was born on 16 April 1745, the first son of John Jolliffe (*c*.1697–1771), politician, of Petersfield, Hampshire, and Mary, daughter of Samuel Holden of Roehampton, Surrey. He was educated at Winchester College and at Brasenose College, Oxford, matriculating in 1764. In 1768 he was returned to parliament for Petersfield, a borough controlled by his father, and to which he succeeded as patron in 1771 on his father's death. On 28 August 1769 Jolliffe married Eleanor, the daughter of Sir Richard Hylton, fifth baronet, of Hayton Castle, Cumberland, and Eleanor Hedworth, with whom he had five sons and six daughters.

In his early years in parliament Jolliffe generally supported the ministry of the day, first that led by the duke of Grafton and then Lord North's long ministry of 1770 to 1782. In February 1772 he was rewarded with a position on the Board of Trade, a post which he held until he resigned in 1779, 'in order to oblige Government' (Jolliffe, 55) by making room for Edward Gibbon. When North's ministry fell in 1782, Jolliffe remained faithful to him in opposition and went on to support the Fox–North coalition ministry in 1783, during which he was a lord of the Admiralty. After the Fox–North coalition was turned out, he persisted in his support for its leaders in opposition. By 1790, having fallen out with his constituents at Petersfield, Jolliffe had demolished his father's house there and moved to Merstham, Surrey, although he maintained his electoral interest at Petersfield. In 1791 he was sentenced to six months in prison and fined for allegedly trying to influence a jury. He regarded his conviction as a consequence of his continued support for North through the 1780s. Eventually the sentence was commuted to a fine only. In 1794 he followed, albeit warily, his new political master, the duke of Portland, when the Portland whigs went over to Pitt, but a rumoured peerage never materialized. On the whole he was to be a supporter of Pitt's ministry in the 1790s, although he did complain of 'Pitt's monstrous injustice' (Thorne, 321) in blocking his peerage and was critical of the ministry's policy in relation to France. By 1801 he can be regarded as in opposition. Jolliffe died at Merstham on 20 February 1802, having broken his neck falling through the trapdoor of his wine cellar.   STEPHEN M. LEE

Sources H. G. H. Jolliffe, *The Jolliffes of Staffordshire and their descendants* (1892), 55–66 · L. B. Namier, 'Jolliffe, William', HoP, *Commons, 1754–90* · R. G. Thorne, 'Jolliffe, William', HoP, *Commons, 1790–1820* · GEC, *Baronetage*
Archives Som. ARS, accounts, corresp., memoranda, DD/HY

Jolliffe, William George Hylton, first Baron Hylton (1800–1876), politician, born on 7 December 1800, at 3 Little Argyle Street, London, was the eldest son of the Revd William John Jolliffe and his wife, Julia, daughter and coheir of Sir Abraham Pytches of Streatham. He was for some time in the army, and retired from the 15th hussars with the rank of captain. He was created a baronet on 20 August 1821. In 1832 he unsuccessfully contested Petersfield as a Conservative, but was seated, after a petition, in 1833. In 1835 he lost his seat, but returned in 1837 and represented Petersfield until 1866. In Lord Derby's first administration he was under-secretary of state for home affairs from March to December 1852, and from March 1858 to June 1859 he was parliamentary secretary to the Treasury and Conservative whip. As whip he was popular and wide-ranging in his activities, not only whipping in the Commons, but mediating between Disraeli and Rose and Spofforth (the solicitors who handled the day-to-day business), managing the election fund, and developing a more systematic party organization. He was sworn of the privy council on 18 June 1859.

Jolliffe's grandmother on his father's side, Eleanor, was the representative of the baronial family of Hylton of Hylton Castle, and when, on 19 July 1866, he was raised to the peerage, he took the title Baron Hylton of Hylton. He married, first, on 8 October 1825, Eleanor, second daughter of the Hon. Berkeley Thomas Paget and his wife, Sophia—she died on 23 July 1862 (they had four sons and five daughters); and second, on 19 January 1867, Sophia Penelope (*d*. 27 Aug 1882), widow of the fourth earl of Ilchester and daughter of Sir Robert Sheffield and his wife, Julia Brigida, *née* Newbolt. There were no children from the second marriage. Jolliffe's eldest son, Hylton, was a captain in the Coldstream Guards, and died at Sevastopol on 4 October 1854, leaving two daughters. Jolliffe died at his home, Merstham House, near Reigate, Surrey, on 1 June 1876. His second son, Hedworth Hylton (1829–1899), was the second baron.

W. A. J. ARCHBOLD, *rev.* H. C. G. MATTHEW

Sources *The Times* (3 June 1876) · *West Sussex Journal* (6 June 1876) · GEC, *Peerage* · R. Stewart, *The foundation of the conservative party, 1830–1867* (1978)
Archives Som. ARS, corresp. and papers | Bodl. Oxf., corresp. with Benjamin Disraeli · Herts. ALS, letters to Lord Lytton · Lpool RO, letters to fourteenth earl of Derby
Likenesses G. Hayter, group portrait, 1833 (*The House of Commons*), NPG · T. L. Atkinson, mezzotint, pubd 1865 (after F. Grant), BM, NPG · wood-engraving (after photograph by H. Watkins), NPG; repro. in *ILN* (27 March 1858) · wood-engraving, NPG; repro. in *ILN* (7 Dec 1867)
Wealth at death under £60,000: probate, 15 Aug 1876, CGPLA Eng. & Wales

Jolly. *See also* Jollie.

Jolly family (*per. c*.1820–1965), drapers, were the family who formed Jolly & Sons of Milsom Street, Bath, which was one of the best-known drapery and later department stores in the west of England. **James Jolly** (*b*. 1775) was born in Brockdish, Norfolk, and followed his father into the linen drapery trade. By the early 1800s he had opened his own warehouse in Winchester, moving to Deal in Kent in the 1810s. During the following decade he opened a branch shop (a novelty at the time) in fashionable Margate. James Jolly's son **Thomas Jolly** (1801–1889) was born on 24 September 1801 and was helping in the business by the time the Margate store opened. He seems to have become the manager in 1826 and enlarged the premises, now known as Jolly's Bazaar, in 1830. James Jolly retired to live as a gentleman at Shottenden outside Canterbury.

James Jolly was so pleased with the success of his venture in a tourist resort that in 1823 he started a seasonal branch at Bath, which quickly transferred to what was described as a 'Parisian Depot' in New Bond Street, Bath. In 1831 a new shop, managed by Thomas, was opened in the heart of Milsom Street, Bath, which was to combine 'a shop and bazaar' with the watchwords 'Economy, fashion, and variety'. Sales were to be entirely for 'ready money' with no discounts and no deliveries would be made before payment. The shop, trading as Jolly & Sons, was so successful that it was extended in 1834 with an imposing plate glass frontage and earned a mention in a series of poetical letters, *The Fusseltons of Bath*, in 1836: 'Twould take more time than I can spare if half these wonders I declare; but if you come to Bath 'twere folly not to buy all you can at Jolly'. Thomas travelled regularly to Paris and Lyons to buy the latest fashions. By 1851 he was employing sixteen male staff and forty-two female assistants.

Despite his commitments in Bath, Thomas Jolly continued to manage the Margate store through Jolly & Sons, which was referred to as one of the town's attractions in Thackeray's novel *The Adventures of Philip: a Shabby Genteel Story* (1863). Thomas opened another branch in College Green in Bristol in 1852. He handed the whole business over to his son William Cracknell Jolly [*see below*] in the late 1850s and devoted his retirement to local politics, philanthropy, and the Unitarian church which he had joined when he moved to Bath in 1831.

Although he catered for the establishment, Thomas Jolly was at heart a radical, a vigorous supporter of the reform of both local and national government, as befitting an importer of luxuries committed to free trade and as a Liberal shopkeeper an advocate of early closing. Following the Municipal Reform Act of 1835, he was elected in 1839 to the new Bath town council, serving as mayor in 1861 and again in 1868. He retired from the council in 1883, but was re-elected in 1885. As a member of the council he reorganized the local police force, pressed for lower rents on the council's properties to help encourage trade, and saved the neglected Pump Room and Roman Baths from collapse. By the time of his death on 18 October 1889 at his home, Park View Lodge, Oldfield Road, Bath, he was by far the longest standing member of the council, respected for 'his straightforwardness, his manliness and independence' (Bath city council, minutes, November 1889). He had also been a guardian of the poor, a trustee of the municipal charities which he had helped reform, a governor of King Edward's School, and one of the keenest supporters of the rebuilding of Bath's celebrated Theatre Royal (1840–45). During the Anti-Corn Law League protests in 1842–3 he had taken time off from his business to travel the south of England speaking in support of Cobden and Bright. He married Caroline Turner Evans on 26 November 1827; they had at least four sons and two daughters.

His eldest son, **William Cracknell Jolly** (1828–1904),

born on 16 September 1828, took over the business, stepping almost precisely into his father's shoes both as a shopkeeper and town councillor. Following the commercial treaty with France in 1860, he developed a speciality in silks from Lyons and Paris and later Switzerland, using local buyers who negotiated exclusive deals. Jollys won a medal for its silks at the International Exhibition in London in 1873, which encouraged the firm to extend its range to include Belgian and Irish linens and lace. The shop was enlarged in 1879, by which time over 4500 copies of the quarterly price lists were being distributed throughout the south of England with a growing mail order trade. In 1881 an agency was opened in Bombay 'for ladies who have commissions from friends in India'. The Bath shop was extensively refurbished in 1888 and by the 1890s fashion shows were being held in the midlands, the west country, and Wales with over 14,000 orders being received by post every year. The family assiduously promoted its royal connections and held a number of warranties for supplying the royal household.

In 1874 W. C. Jolly joined his father on the town council where he became a tireless protagonist of civic improvement. Immediately after the Local Government Act of 1888 he moved that the establishment of a public library should be put to the vote. The motion was overwhelmingly defeated by the electorate. W. C. Jolly played a prominent part in the construction of the new municipal buildings and of a new water supply and the conservation of the Roman Promenades. He was a charity trustee and an enthusiastic supporter of technical education. He served as mayor in 1894. He retired to Hampstead in 1899 and died at 9 Lansdowne Terrace, Eastbourne, on 22 January 1904. The Jolly family continued to have a major interest in the business in the first half of the twentieth century. When Queen Mary was resident at Badminton with her niece, the duchess of Beaufort, she patronized the store and gave it her royal warrant. The firm was acquired by Dingles of Plymouth in 1965. MICHAEL S. MOSS

Sources M. Moss and A. Turton, *A legend of retailing: House of Fraser* (1989) · Jolly & Sons archives, Milsom Street, Bath · clippings file on Thomas Jolly and W. C. Jolly, Bath Public Library · minutes, Bath city council, Bath Archives · d. certs. [Thomas Jolly, William Cracknell Jolly] · *CGPLA Eng. & Wales* (1904) [William Cracknell Jolly]

Archives Jolly & Sons, Milsom Street, Bath

Likenesses portrait (William Cracknell Jolly), Bath Guildhall

Wealth at death £22,535 0s. 7d.—Thomas Jolly: probate, 15 Nov 1889, *CGPLA Eng. & Wales* · £34,369 8s. 5d.—William Cracknell Jolly: resworn probate, 24 March 1904, *CGPLA Eng. & Wales*

Jolly, Alexander (1756–1838), Scottish Episcopal bishop of Moray, was born on 3 April 1756 at Stonehaven, Kincardineshire, one of two or three children of a struggling businessman. He attended Stonehaven School and was tutored by Alexander Gleig, the Episcopal minister. Entering Marischal College, Aberdeen, in 1771, he exhibited a particular proficiency in classical languages and Hebrew. After graduating MA in 1775 he became tutor to the family of a Mr Leslie of Rothie. Jolly then became Bishop Petrie's assistant at Meiklefolla in preparation for ordination. On 1 July 1776 he was ordained deacon by Bishop Kilgour of

Aberdeen, and priest on 19 March 1777. Subsequently he was appointed to the charge of the congregation at Turriff, Aberdeenshire. In April 1788 he became incumbent of the congregation at Fraserburgh, a position he retained until his death. A man who always seemed aged with an increasing asceticism accentuating his appearance, Jolly stood out among the Episcopal clergy for his devotion and scholarship, for which he was rewarded with an episcopal appointment. Bishop Macfarlane of Moray, Ross, and Argyll requested Jolly as his coadjutor, though his combined dioceses numbered only nine charges. Bishop John Skinner, primus of the Episcopal church, opposed the unnecessary request but was overruled by the other bishops, and Jolly was consecrated on 24 June 1796. It is ironic that a priest who set such store by ecclesiastical discipline and propriety should have allowed himself to be elevated in such an irregular manner. Normality was restored when, on 14 February 1798, the clergy of the diocese of Moray elected Jolly as their bishop, that diocese having been separated by the bishops from Macfarlane's huge geographical area.

As a bishop Jolly lived an introspective, almost eremitical life, having no servants and living alone with his door locked. He devoted his time to reading in the Hebrew Old Testament, Greek New Testament, patristic writers, Anglican high-church divines, and German sixteenth-century reformers. However, none of this resulted in publications until his old age owing to Jolly's excessive self-deprecation. Despite his reclusive lifestyle he proved an assiduous visitor of his congregation, although attending his diocese only every three years for confirmations. His paternalistic model of episcopacy meant that he kept in close touch with his clergy through regular correspondence, and was generous in responding to need. On occasions this approach could also shade into authoritarianism when he was faced with perceived threats to episcopal power. He successfully manoeuvred to have rescinded a canon of the 1828 general synod for regular diocesan and general synods on the grounds that it contradicted the apostolic authority of the bishops to govern the church. As a rule Jolly's natural conservatism acted as a brake on innovation in the Episcopal church, and probably prevented it from adapting more quickly to the changing social conditions of the nineteenth century.

However, in theology Jolly did make a major contribution which assisted the church's development. He was virtually alone among the high-church northern clergy and bishops of his time in opposing Hutchinsonianism, a system which purported to find an esoteric revelation in the Hebrew of the Old Testament. His theological refutation of the Calvinism in the Thirty-Nine Articles largely permitted their acceptance by the Episcopal church in 1804. This, in turn, enabled most of the schismatic 'English' chapels in Scotland to join the Episcopal church. In 1826 Jolly was made an honorary DD of Washington College, Connecticut. Two years later he published his most popular work, a small devotional book on the liturgical calendar entitled *Observations upon the Several Sunday Services and*

Principal Holydays. He also provided one of the few substantial works encapsulating the nonjuring theology of Scottish episcopacy in *The Christian Sacrifice in the Eucharist* (1831). This definitively set forth traditional episcopalian eucharistic theology, maintaining that all the virtue of Christ's sacrifice was present in the eucharist but that there was not a corporal presence in the sacramental species. Jolly's reputation for sanctity and scholarship enabled him to act as a moderator in the quarrels among his often fractious episcopal colleagues. He died at the Episcopal rectory, Fraserburgh, on 29 June 1838 and was buried at Turriff Episcopal churchyard on 5 July.

ROWAN STRONG

Sources W. Walker, *The life of the Right Reverend Alexander Jolly* (1878) • J. B. Craven, *History of the Episcopal church in the diocese of Moray* (1889) • R. Strong, *Alexander Forbes of Brechin* (1995) • *Fasti academiae Mariscallanae Aberdonensis: selections from the records of the Marischal College and University, MDXCIII–MDCCCLX*, 2, ed. P. J. Anderson, New Spalding Club, 18 (1898), 341–2
Archives NA Scot., Episcopal Church Records, corresp. and papers; letter-books • NRA Scotland, corresp. and papers • NRA, priv. coll., corresp. • NRA, priv. coll., corresp., papers, and sermons | U. Aberdeen L., corresp. with George Ogilvie and George Ogilvie Forbes • University of Dundee, letters to William Murray
Likenesses W. H. Lizars, stipple and line engraving, pubd 1839 (after J. Moir), NPG; version, pubd 1840, BM • A. G. Ingram Ltd, photograph (after portrait), repro. in M. Lochhead, *Episcopal Scotland in the nineteenth century* (1966), 72

Jolly, George (*bap.* 1613, *d.* in or before 1683), actor and theatre manager, was baptized at St Luke's Church on 23 March 1613 as the son of Ralph Gellye, whose origins and occupation are unknown. George Jolly's career had three distinct stages. In July 1640 he was living in the house of the actor Matthew Smith in Whitecross Street, where his son John was baptized. The baby, 'sonne of George Jolly Player', died a week later and was buried at St Giles Cripplegate. Like Smith, Jolly was undoubtedly a member of Prince Charles's Men, then acting at the Fortune playhouse, close to Whitecross Street, but his name does not appear among any surviving records of the company, and he must have still been a junior member of the troupe when playing ceased in 1642.

At some time before 1647 Jolly moved to continental Europe, and appears to have remained there until 1660, travelling considerable distances as the leader of a variety of acting troupes. Initially he may have joined his colleagues who had gone to perform for the English royalist community in exile, first at The Hague, then in Paris, between 1644 and 1646. This group has been called Prince Charles's Men, since it sought the patronage of the exiled prince; it certainly included two of Jolly's fellows from the Fortune company. By April 1647, however, Jolly had emerged as head of a troupe of fourteen players perhaps capable of playing in a variety of languages, but working principally, from 1648 onwards, in German. Jolly's theatrical activity in Germany for the next twelve years ranks among the most important contributions of the 'Englische Komödianten' to the early German stage, a cultural exchange which had begun in the early 1590s but had been interrupted by the Thirty Years' War.

In 1647 the company appears to have been in Brussels, then at Bruges, and in spring 1648 at Cologne, where they played for three months, moving to Frankfurt am Main in August. Early in 1649 they returned to Cologne; by October they were in Danzig, and by December in Sweden, returning to Danzig in August 1650. Throughout the 1650s Frankfurt and the surrounding area formed the base for Jolly's touring enterprises, chiefly in the southern German-speaking territories. His company included a growing number of native German actors, and by 1654 actresses; at the same date he advertised plays and operas produced with Italianate scenery. Most records of his playing are connected with annual town fairs and festivals, but he occasionally performed for the nobility. By November 1650 he had acted before the emperor Ferdinand III, and again in May 1653 his company entertained the imperial court in Vienna; in September 1655 he played before the visiting Prince Charles at Frankfurt, and it seems likely that he also played at the elector's court in Heidelberg: Elector Karl Ludwig von der Pfalz (Charles Lewis) was a cousin of Prince Charles and the brother of Prince Rupert, who resided in Mainz after 1652. It was probably Jolly's troupe which played Gryphius's German tragedy *Carolus Stuardus* near Frankfurt in 1656. The play dramatizes the trial and execution of King Charles I.

Jolly's reputation as a strolling manager was that of an irascible and violent man: two of his German actors made official complaints of assault at his hands, and he was expelled from Nuremberg in 1660 as the result of a quarrel. Of his personal life at this period there are very few indications. In appealing for permission to stay in Frankfurt in the winter of 1657–8 he claimed that his wife was very sick; it may be doubted whether this woman was the mother of the child born in London seventeen years earlier, but late in 1659 Jolly's second known child was baptized, in Nuremberg: the mother was recorded as Maria di Roy of Utrecht, perhaps one of the German-speaking actresses of the troupe.

Jolly returned to England late in 1660, and in December was granted a royal licence to form an acting company, in addition to the two led by Sir William Davenant and Thomas Killigrew. The licence put Jolly in a remarkably strong position in the new theatrical world, especially when one considers both his obscurity before 1642 and his social status relative to the two courtiers who were given charge of the other companies. He must have been able to argue, or had patrons to argue, that his theatrical enterprises in Europe had had some significance in supporting the royalist cause. Over the next two years Jolly played at both the Cockpit in Drury Lane and the Salisbury Court playhouses; among his repertory was at least one old play, Marlowe's *Doctor Faustus*. Killigrew and Davenant sought to maintain their joint monopoly on London theatre by buying the royal licence from Jolly, at the cost of £4 per week to be paid to him throughout his life. An agreement to this effect was signed at the very end of 1662, immediately following which Jolly obtained a licence to form a provincial company—a venture which he may already have begun at Cambridge in 1662. By April 1663, however,

his company was playing at the King's Arms in Norwich, where it remained until September, presenting a repertory of pre-war plays by Middleton, Ford, Fletcher, Massinger, and others. During 1664 the arrangement with Davenant and Killigrew collapsed, and Jolly resumed playing in London, at the Cockpit. In 1667 Killigrew contrived to have Jolly's 1660 patent recalled, but Jolly evaded compliance: warrants for his arrest were issued in April 1667 and again in January 1668, when he was acting in the company of John Russell, Paul Ryemes, and Peter Gryen. As a temporary settlement of the dispute with the other patentees Jolly was given supervision of the Nursery, a training school and theatre for young actors, with an income to be based on the company's performances. Jolly's control would appear to have been largely managerial, with the performers under the direction of Thomas Bedford, and after 1669 of John Perin.

Jolly remained involved in touring, however. He received permission to play in Norwich in September 1669, and his players seem to have stayed there for three months. Following Killigrew's appointment as master of the revels in April 1673 there was a further dispute about Jolly's position at the Nursery. Probably in the summer of 1674 Jolly lodged a complaint that Killigrew was denying him the money due to him from the 1662 agreement and the arrangements derived from it. The document speaks of the ruin of the complainant and his family—a wife and an unspecified number of children. No further records of Jolly's life and affairs survive; by March 1683 at the latest he was dead, when, at Norwich, John Coysh claimed to hold the succession to Jolly's patent to act.

JOHN H. ASTINGTON

Sources Highfill, Burnim & Langhans, *BDA* · L. Hotson, *The Commonwealth and Restoration stage* (1928) · J. Milhous and R. D. Hume, eds., *A register of English theatrical documents, 1660–1737*, 1 (1991) · J. Limon, *Gentlemen of a company* (1985) · G. E. Bentley, *The Jacobean and Caroline stage*, 7 vols. (1941–68) · J. Milhous and R. D. Hume, 'New light on English acting companies in 1646, 1648, and 1660', *Review of English Studies*, new ser., 42 (1991), 487–509 · LMA, microfilm X026/012 · parish register, Chelsea, St Luke, 23 March 1613 [baptism]

Jolly, James (*b.* **1775**). *See under* Jolly family (*per. c.*1820–1965).

Jolly, John. *See* Jollie, John (1640?–1682).

Jolly, Thomas. *See* Jollie, Thomas (1629–1703).

Jolly, Thomas (**1801–1889**). *See under* Jolly family (*per. c.*1820–1965).

Jolly, William Cracknell (**1828–1904**). *See under* Jolly family (*per. c.*1820–1965).

Jolowicz, Herbert Felix (**1890–1954**), jurist, was born in London on 16 July 1890, the third child and second son of Hermann Jolowicz (1849–1934), a Jewish silk merchant, and his wife, Marie Litthauer (1864–1948). His sister Marguerite married Martin Wolff, an international lawyer. He was educated at St Paul's School, from which he won a classical scholarship to Trinity College, Cambridge. He was placed in the first class of part one of the classical tripos in 1911 and in the first class of part one of the law tripos in 1913, a curious combination which committed him to Roman law and for the time being cut him off from almost all the more practical parts of English law. He then spent a year in Germany, sitting at the feet of two of the greatest Roman lawyers of modern times, Ludwig Mitteis at Leipzig and Otto Lenel at Freiburg. He escaped from Germany in 1914 with three days to spare and served throughout the war, for most of the time as an officer in the Bedfordshire regiment, and was in Gallipoli, Egypt, and France.

Called to the bar by the Inner Temple in 1919, Jolowicz was first a pupil, then a member of the chambers, of Henry Slesser. His name appears as counsel in the leading case of *Chester* v. *Bateson* (1920). His wide linguistic gifts, however, made him an obvious choice as a teacher of Roman law and in 1920 he became non-resident All Souls reader in Roman law at Oxford. From 1924 he combined that post with a lectureship, later readership, in Roman law and jurisprudence at University College, London. When in 1931 he became professor of Roman law at University College, he relinquished his readership at Oxford. During his London career he took his full share of tutorial work, in addition to lecturing, and thus came to know the students well. He was also dean of the faculty of law in the university in 1937–8. He retained a close connection with University College until his death and was from 1947 chairman of the library subcommittee of the Institute of Advanced Legal Studies, a part of the university. In 1924 Jolowicz married Ruby Victoria (1897–1963), daughter of Joseph Wagner. The couple had two sons and one daughter. His wife was until 1936 a research physicist.

During the Nazi persecutions Jolowicz gave much unobtrusive help to refugees; on the outbreak of war in 1939 he rejoined the army and served as an officer in the intelligence corps until 1945. In 1948 he became regius professor of civil law at Oxford. During the autumn of 1953 he was visiting professor at Tulane University, Louisiana (which conferred on him the honorary degree of DCL), and travelled extensively in the United States, lecturing at such universities as Yale, Columbia, and Chicago.

Jolowicz published a number of articles and reviews, but only two books. The one which made his name was his *Historical Introduction to the Study of Roman Law* (1932; 2nd edn, 1952). The term 'introduction' may mislead. The book is a large work of scholarship, intended as a companion to the markedly unhistorical *Textbook* of W. W. Buckland. It therefore contained, in addition to chapters on the constitution, sources, and character of the law at all periods, treatment of the substantive law in the preclassical period. It maintained a remarkable balance between the needs of the student and the advanced worker and in the citation and assessment of secondary authorities. The other book was a translation, with descriptive introduction and commentary, of a singularly intractable title of the *Digest* dealing with theft (*Digest XLVII.*2 (*De furtis*), 1940). It reflected the dominant concern of Romanists in the inter-war years: the attempt to distinguish classical law

from the law of Justinian by the search for interpolations in the *Digest*. This, as Jolowicz admitted, set him off on what was for him a wrong track and delayed the development of his main interest, the medieval and modern history of Roman law, especially in England. He left behind him a considerable fragment which was published in 1957 under the title *Roman Foundations of Modern Law*, covering the sources, the law of persons, and family law (with the exception of guardianship). The other main field of study which may be singled out from his almost universal interest in law was jurisprudence. He did not himself publish his University College *Lectures on Jurisprudence*, doubtless because, as they stood, they did not come up to his exacting standard, but they were later edited by his elder son, J. A. Jolowicz, fellow of Trinity College, Cambridge, and appeared in 1963. By then, however, the subject had moved in a philosophical direction, and the book did not have the success it might have enjoyed earlier.

Jolowicz was, indeed, first and foremost a lecturer. He loved lecturing and took immense pains in preparing his lectures. With all his breadth of interests he believed in and exemplified the most accurate scholarship and was profoundly sceptical of broad intellectual constructions. He had great natural sagacity, which he was always ready to put at the disposal of his friends and of any institution he was connected with. He was an enthusiastic member of the Society of Public Teachers of Law, of which he was president in 1936–7. His greatest service to the society and indeed one of the greatest services he performed to law in England was his editorship of the society's *Journal* from its first number in 1924 to the day of his death. He did more than anyone else to set the character and tone of the *Journal*, which is indeed his monument.

In spite of many trials Jolowicz preserved a gay spirit and a puckish humour. He made his house a centre of hospitality and left his friends with the recollection of a very lovable man. He died in the Acland Nursing Home, Banbury Road, Oxford, on 19 December 1954. His remains were cremated at Golders Green crematorium, Middlesex. A bibliography of his writings is to be found in the H. F. Jolowicz memorial number of *Butterworth's South African Law Review*, 1956.

F. H. LAWSON, *rev.* J. K. BARRY M. NICHOLAS

Sources F. H. Lawson and and others, *Journal of the Society of Public Teachers of Law*, 3/1 (June 1955), 3–8 [obituaries] · *Butterworth's South African Law Review*, 3 (1956), v–vii · personal knowledge (1971) · private information (1971) · private information (2004) · CGPLA Eng. & Wales (1955) · *The Times* (20 Dec 1954) · WWW · d. cert.
Archives Bodl. Oxf., corresp. relating to Society for Protection of Science and Learning
Likenesses I. Bing, photograph, repro. in Lawson et al., *Journal of the Society of Public Teachers of Law*
Wealth at death £42,331: probate, 28 Feb 1955, CGPLA Eng. & Wales

Joly, Charles Jasper (1864–1906), mathematician and astronomer, was born at St Catherine's rectory, Tullamore, Ireland, on 27 June 1864, the eldest son in the family of three sons and two daughters of John Swift Joly (successively rector of St Catherine's, Tullamore, and of Athlone), and his wife, Elizabeth, daughter of the Revd Nathaniel

Slator. His father's family, of French origin, had settled in Ireland in the eighteenth century. After a short attendance at school at Portarlington, and nearly four years at Galway grammar school, Joly entered Trinity College, Dublin, in October 1882, where he won a mathematical scholarship. He graduated in 1886 with the first mathematical honour of his year—the 'studentship', candidates for which were required to offer a second subject in addition to mathematics. Joly chose physics, the experimental side of which so much interested him that he went to Berlin in order to work in Helmholtz's laboratory. The death of his father in 1887 made it necessary for him to earn a living without delay, and, abandoning a design of devoting himself wholly to experimental science, he returned to Ireland to read for a fellowship in Trinity College. The conditions of the examination discouraged strict specialism in mathematics or science, and Joly failed to win election until 1894. He then engaged in tuition at the college, and was junior proctor in 1896.

Joly's career as a productive mathematician began almost as soon as he was admitted to a fellowship. In his first paper, on the theory of linear vector functions, which was read to the Royal Irish Academy on 10 December 1894, he proved his discipleship to Sir William Rowan Hamilton, the discoverer of quaternions, and first applied the quaternionic analysis to difficult and complex problems of geometry, using it as an engine for the discovery of new geometrical properties. The properties of linear vector functions were further studied in 'Scalar invariants of two linear vector functions' (*Transactions of the Royal Irish Academy*, 30, 1896, 709) and 'Quaternion invariants of linear vector functions' (*Proceedings of the Royal Irish Academy*, 4, 1896, 1), while the extension of the quaternion calculus to space of more than three dimensions was discussed in 'The associative algebra applicable to hyperspace' (*Proceedings of the Royal Irish Academy*, 5, 1897, 75); the algebras considered are those that are associative and distributive, and whose units satisfy equations of the same type as the units of quaternions. Other more purely geometrical investigations were published in the Royal Irish Academy's *Proceedings* for 1896 and 1897 under the titles 'Vector expressions for curves' and 'Homographic divisions of planes, spheres, and space'.

On 20 March 1897 Joly married Jessie Sophia, the youngest daughter of Robert Warren Meade of Dublin. In the same year, he was appointed royal astronomer of Ireland at Dunsink observatory, where the rest of his life was spent in study and research. From 1898 to 1900 he edited Hamilton's *Elements of Quaternions*, originally published shortly after its author's death in 1865. Joly made considerable additions to the new edition which was published in two volumes (1899–1901). While occupied with this work, he communicated several memoirs to the Royal Irish Academy: 'Astatics and quaternion functions', 'Properties of the general congruency of curves', and 'Some applications of Hamilton's operator in the calculus of variations' were all read in 1899; in the first, quaternions are applied to the geometry of forces, in the second to pure geometry, and in the third to some of the equations of mathematical

physics. Early in the following year he presented a paper entitled 'The place of the Ausdehnungslehre in the general associative algebra of the quaternion type', in which he showed that Grassmann's analysis for n dimensions, which is distributive but only partially associative, may be regarded as a limited form of the associative algebra of $n+1$ dimensions. Over the following five years Joly continued his work with a number of important memoirs (in the publications of the Royal Irish Academy or the Royal Society) on quaternions and geometry. One paper on 'Quaternions and projective geometry' occupied over a hundred pages in the *Philosophical Transactions of the Royal Society* for 1903. Finally in 1905, the centenary year of Hamilton's birth, he brought out *A Manual of Quaternions*, which at once superseded all other introductory works on the subject.

As royal astronomer Joly directed much observational work, the fruits of which appeared in the *Dunsink Observations and Researches*. In 1900 he accompanied an eclipse expedition to Spain, and obtained some excellent photographs of totality; an account of the results was published in the *Transactions of the Royal Irish Academy* (32, 1902–4, 271). He also edited Thomas Preston's *Theory of Light* (3rd edn, 1901).

Joly was elected fellow of the Royal Astronomical Society in 1898 and FRS in 1904. He was also a trustee of the National Library of Ireland and president of the International Association for Promoting the Study of Quaternions. He was fond of climbing, being a member of the Alpine Club from 1895. In literature he was well versed in Dante's work. He died at the observatory, of pleurisy following typhoid fever, on 4 January 1906 and was buried at Mount Jerome cemetery, Dublin. His wife and three daughters survived him.

E. T. WHITTAKER, *rev.* ADRIAN RICE

Sources personal knowledge (1912) · private information (1912) · J. J. and R. S. B., *PRS*, 78A (1907), lxii–lxix · *Monthly Notices of the Royal Astronomical Society*, 66 (1905–6), 177–8 · G. Scriven, 'In memoriam: C. J. Joly', *Alpine Journal*, 23 (1906), 158

Wealth at death £797 11s. 3d.: Irish administration sealed in London, 21 May 1906, *CGPLA Eng. & Wales*

Joly, John (1857–1933), geologist and physicist, was born at Holywood, King's county, Ireland, on 1 November 1857, the third and youngest son of John Plunket Joly, rector of Clonbulloge, co. Kildare, and his wife, Gräfin Julia Anna Maria Georgina, daughter of Graf Friedrich Wilhelm Ludwig August von Lusi. His father's family, of which Charles Jasper Joly, royal astronomer of Ireland, was a member, was of French origin; through his mother he was a kinsman of Richard Lovell Edgeworth, the Abbé Edgeworth de Firmont, and Maria Edgeworth.

Except for a year spent in France, Joly was educated at Rathmines School, Dublin. In 1876 he entered Trinity College, Dublin, where he studied modern literature and engineering, and in 1883, on graduating with first-class honours, he was appointed to a teaching post in the engineering school. In 1887 he was appointed to the chair of geology in the University of Dublin which he held for the rest of his life.

and true representation, which were exhibited at the Royal Society in 1895. They were the earliest pictures of the kind ever exhibited and were the starting point of much that was later accomplished. In a sense they were superior to many subsequent pictures, for Joly's method could allow for the actual sensibility of the eye for the three primary colours.

In 1897 Joly showed that the canals of Mars might be rationally attributed to the gravitational effects of satellites moving near the planet's surface. During his tenure of the chair of geology he published some 150 papers. Among his writings were many papers connected with seagoing activities, such as on synchronous signalling, a method for observing the altitude of a star when the horizon is obscure, a collision predictor, a method of measuring distances at sea in thick weather, an explosive sea sounder, floating breakwaters, the age of the earth estimated by the accumulation of sodium in the ocean, and the radioactivity of sea water. He was a keen yachtsman. During the First World War he submitted sixteen inventions to the Admiralty. Other subjects were: the apophorometer for studying the sublimation products of minerals, pleochroic haloes, their radioactive origin and what they tell of the age of rocks, and a quantum theory of vision.

Joly paid much attention to radioactivity in geology, pointing out how the distribution of radioactive isotopes in the earth must modify our views on its age, and, by devising a new and accurate method of estimating the quantity of thorium in rocks, he showed that that element plays a part in earth history almost as important as that of radium. The radioactive explanation of the occurrence and the action of thermal cycles in earth history was the outcome of Joly's prolonged researches on the radioactivity of the constituents of the outer crust. In *The Surface History of the Earth* (1925; 2nd edn, 1930) he showed that the slow accumulation of radioactive heat in the deeper layers of the earth's crust must in time lead to their melting and thus by establishing new isostatic conditions allow the subsidence of the continental masses and the consequent transgression of the oceans, which now deposit their sediments on the submerged tracts. Meanwhile the molten layers, losing their accumulated heat by convection, actuated by lunar tides, slowly return to their solid state. Heat accumulation recommences, expansion follows, raising the continents and buckling the sedimentary deposits on their lower levels. The continued accumulation of heat in the radioactive layers leads inevitably to the cycle being repeated again and again until the radioactivity of the deeper layers of the crust ultimately expires. Thus the grand geological problems of sedimentary succession interrupted by revolutions and unconformities, together with many lesser puzzles, found their solution and unification in Joly's theory of thermal cycles.

Scientific work by no means occupied all Joly's energy. In college life he was chiefly responsible for the appointment of the Trinity College science schools committee which, under his inspiration during thirteen years of

John Joly (1857–1933), by unknown photographer

Joly had early shown his originality and inventive powers and had published papers on reading meteorological instruments at a distance, on the volcanic ash from Krakatoa, and on photometry. From 1884 he maintained a constant flow of inventions and researches among which may be recorded a meldometer which determined the melting points of minerals and other substances, a hydrostatic balance to determine the specific gravity of small quantities of dense or porous bodies, and a condensation method of calorimetry, by which he succeeded in determining by direct measurement the specific heats of gases at constant volume, a problem of great theoretical importance in the study of the gaseous state and hitherto insoluble. His simple electric furnace, which reduced aluminium from topaz, anticipated Henri Moisson's method of producing that metal. He also made some of the earliest determinations of the volume change of rocks upon fusion, ingeniously replacing the containing vessels by the surface tension of the molten substances. In 1893 he joined Henry Horatio Dixon in investigating the ascent of sap in trees. Their cohesion theory, after much initial criticism and discussion, became the only generally accepted explanation of the rise of water to the tops of high trees.

On natural colour photography Joly's work was of great interest. He originated in 1894 the idea of making the positive image select from a particoloured transparent screen the correct amounts of three primary colours and by this invention produced transparent pictures of great beauty arduous work, and with benefactions from E. C. Guinness, earl of Iveagh, and others, built and equipped the schools of physics and botany and endowed the Iveagh Geological Laboratory. In 1907 he was one of the foremost champions in defence of Trinity College against the Bryce scheme for reorganizing university education in Ireland. He gave impressive evidence before the Fry commission in 1905–6 and in 1920 he was a member of the Geikie commission, the report of which, recommending a subsidy to Trinity College, had been adopted by the imperial parliament when the establishment of the Irish Free State put an end to the project. In university life his sympathy both with colleagues and students gave him great influence, and in teaching he inspired enthusiasm and affection by his originality of treatment and picturesque diction. During the Irish rising of Easter 1916 he took an active part in the defence of Trinity College. An account of his experiences then was published in *Blackwood's Magazine* (July 1916).

With D. J. Cunningham and William Spotswood Green, Joly developed a scheme of marine research in order to improve the Irish fisheries, and he became a commissioner of Irish lights in 1901. Working with Walter Clegg Stevenson he devised the deep seated application of radioactive preparations in hollow needles, and discussed the use of other radioactive methods in therapeutics.

Joly was elected FRS in 1892. He was honorary secretary of the Royal Dublin Society from 1897 to 1909, received its Boyle medal in 1911, and served as president from 1929 to 1932. In 1914 he had initiated the formation of the society's Radium Institute. He was awarded the royal medal of the Royal Society in 1910. In 1905 he was president of the Photographic Convention of the United Kingdom. From the London Geological Society he received the Murchison medal in 1918, and in 1908 he was president of section C (geology) of the British Association. He was elected a fellow of Trinity College, Dublin, in 1918, and in the same year he was selected by the Foreign Office to represent Irish universities on the Balfour mission to the United States of America. In 1924 he delivered both the Hugo Müller lecture at the London Chemical Society and the Halley lecture at Oxford. The universities of Cambridge and Michigan and the National University of Ireland conferred upon him the honorary degree of ScD.

Joly was a man of intensely vivid and varied personality. His poetic nature expressed itself in his diction and in some sonnets, his interest in art in a beautiful collection of modern pictures; and his unselfish consideration and sympathy for others more than matched these qualities and his inventive genius. He died, unmarried, at 40 Lower Leeson Street, Dublin, on 8 December 1933.

H. H. Dixon, rev. Isobel Falconer

Sources *Obits. FRS*, 1 (1932–5), 259–86 • H. H. Dixon, *John Joly: presidential address to the Dublin University Experimental Science Association*, 1940 (1941) • J. Joly, *Reminiscences and anticipations* (1920) • *Nature*, 133 (1934), 90–92 • L. B. Smyth, *Quarterly Journal of the Geological Society of London*, 90 (1934), lv–lvii • O. J. Lodge, 'Professor Joly', *London, Edinburgh, and Dublin Philosophical Magazine*, 7th ser., 17 (1934), 198–200 • *BMJ* (16 Dec 1933), 1132 • personal knowledge (1949) • C. Mollan, W. Davis, and B. Finucane, eds., *Some people and places in Irish science and technology* (1985), 64–5 • *DSB* • *CGPLA Eng. & Wales* (1934) • election certificate, RS

Archives TCD, corresp., diaries, and scientific papers; family papers | TCD, corresp. with Henry Horatio Dixon

Likenesses Mrs Dixon, watercolour, priv. coll. • R. Paget, watercolour, priv. coll. • L. Whelan, oils, priv. coll.; copy, Royal Dublin Society, Éire • photograph, repro. in *Obits. FRS* (1934), facing p. 259 • photograph, RS [*see illus.*] • portrait, repro. in Dixon, *John Joly*

Wealth at death £1244 2s. 0d.—in England: resworn probate, 5 Feb 1934, *CGPLA Eng. & Wales*

Joly de Lotbinière, Sir Henri-Gustave (1829–1908), politician in Canada, born on 5 December 1829 at Épernay, France, was the son of Pierre-Gustave Joly (1798–1865), a merchant and the owner of famous vineyards at Épernay, who in 1828 married Julie-Christine (1810–1887), the heir of the seigneury of Lotbinière, Quebec, and daughter of Michel-Eustache-Gaspard-Alain Chartier de Lotbinière, speaker of the Quebec assembly (1794–6). Joly senior, whose family originated in Switzerland, settled in Canada with his wife, whose grandfather, Michel Chartier de Lotbinière, marquis de Lotbinière, had served as one of Montcalm's engineers at Quebec. Henri-Gustave Joly received his education in Paris, returned to Canada in 1850, and was called to the bar of Lower Canada in 1855. With his prestigious name, his father's business connections, and his marriage on 6 May 1856 to Margaretta Josepha (d. 1904), the daughter of Hammond Gowen, a prominent Quebec City merchant, Joly made a place for himself in the upper circles of Quebec society. At the end of 1860 he became the seigneur of Lotbinière when his mother gave him title. With the sanction of the Quebec legislature, he assumed his mother's surname in 1888.

Joly espoused the Liberal cause in politics, and represented Lotbinière in the legislative assembly of the province of Canada as of 1861. In 1864 and 1865 he took part in the campaign against confederation but soon came round to the new political situation. After the passing of the British North America Act he sat for his old constituency both in the federal House of Commons at Ottawa and in the Quebec legislative assembly from 1867 to 1874. In the latter year a law was enacted that no one should hold a seat in both legislatures. Joly accordingly resigned his seat in the federal house and devoted his energies to the leadership of the Liberal opposition in the Quebec assembly. In this role he made a significant contribution to the work of the house. His speeches almost always dealt with economic issues: the need to modernize agriculture, to reform the administration of crown lands, and to abolish private sales of timber limits. An ardent champion of railway construction, he considered railways essential to economic growth.

In 1878 Luc Letellier de Saint-Just, who had been appointed lieutenant-governor of the province of Quebec by the Liberal federal government, precipitated the most notorious constitutional crisis in the history of the province. Claiming that he had not been properly informed by the Conservative premier, that he had serious doubts as to the constitutionality of the Municipalities Bill, and that he was worried about the state of the provincial budget, Letellier de Saint-Just dismissed the premier, Charles-

Eugène Boucher de Boucherville. On 2 March 1878 he called on Joly, the leader of the opposition, to form a government. The lieutenant-governor's action led inevitably to the dissolution of the legislature and to a general election. After the 1878 election the two parties were neck and neck: thirty-two Liberals, thirty-two Conservatives, and one Conservative Joly sympathizer, who became speaker of the assembly. The Joly government managed to survive for eighteen months under constant threat of defeat. As premier, Joly completed the construction of the Quebec, Montreal, Ottawa, and Occidental Railway, the most ambitious project undertaken by the Quebec government in the nineteenth century. During his term of office he was constantly involved in heated discussions about the legitimacy and constitutionality of Letellier de Saint-Just's dismissal of the Conservative ministry, until the lieutenant-governor was himself removed from office in 1879 at the request of the Conservatives, who had returned to power at the federal level. Hoping to achieve its goal of balancing the budget without resort to new taxes, Joly's government adopted a policy of austerity, and even proposed to abolish the legislative council, which reacted in August 1879 by refusing to vote supply. Finally, on 29 October 1879, five Liberal members of the house joined the Conservative ranks, and the Joly government found itself in a minority. Joly had no choice but to resign as premier. Back as leader of the Liberal opposition he suffered a stinging defeat in the 1881 election and, at the beginning of 1883, relinquished leadership of the Liberal Party to Honoré Mercier. In 1885, deeply upset by the nationalist agitation led by Mercier against the execution of Louis Riel for high treason, he withdrew altogether from public life.

In 1895 Joly de Lotbinière was made KCMG, and was persuaded by Wilfrid Laurier to emerge from retirement to take an active part in federal politics. He agreed to run in Portneuf in the federal election of 1896. He was invited to join Laurier's first cabinet and served from 1896 to 1900 as controller and then as minister of inland revenue. From 1900 to 1906 he was lieutenant-governor of British Columbia, a province experiencing serious political problems. In that capacity he entertained at Victoria, the capital, the duke and duchess of Cornwall and York (afterwards George V and Queen Mary) when they visited Canada in 1901. When his term was up in 1906 he returned to Quebec in rapidly deteriorating health. He died at his Quebec City residence, 10 rue des Grisons, on 16 November 1908, and was buried in Quebec City two days later.

Joly de Lotbinière was one of the most fascinating figures of the latter half of the nineteenth century in Canada. Throughout his life he actively promoted the interests of agriculture, forestry, and horticulture. In Quebec he brought about important reforms in the administration of timber lands and advocated the systematic preservation of Canadian forests. His disinterestedness was fully recognized among Canadian politicians. The last of the grand seigneurs, an aristocrat and yet a Liberal, Joly sympathized intensely with the ideals of self-government held by the *parti rouge*. Sometimes accused of being politically naive and portrayed as too honest a man to engage

in politics, he nevertheless had a surprisingly long and varied career, as a member of provincial or federal legislatures for twenty-seven years, as leader of the opposition and premier of Quebec, as a federal minister, and then as lieutenant-governor of British Columbia.

G. S. WOODS, rev. MARCEL HAMELIN

Sources M. Hamelin, 'Joly de Lotbinière, Sir Henri-Gustave', *DCB*, vol. 13 · M. Hamelin, *Les premières années du parlementarisme québécois, 1867–1878* (Quebec, 1974) · P. Trépanier, 'L'administration Joly, 1878–1879', MA thesis, University of Ottawa, 1972 · M. Caya, 'La formation du parti libéral au Québec', PhD thesis, York University, Ontario, 1981 · J. T. Saywell, *The office of lieutenant-governor: a study in Canadian government and politics* (1957) · L.-L. Paradis, *Les annales de Lotbinière, 1672–1933* (1933) · B. J. Young, *Promoters and politicians: the north-shore railways in the history of Quebec, 1854–85* (1978)
Archives Archives Nationales du Québec
Likenesses photographs, priv. coll.

Joly de Lotbinière, Seymour (1905–1984), broadcasting executive, was born on 21 October 1905 at Elibank, Taplow, Buckinghamshire, the younger of the two sons of Brigadier-General Henri Gustave Joly de Lotbinière (1868–1960) of the Royal Engineers and his wife, Mildred Louisa (d. 1953), daughter of Charles Seymour Grenfell, a stockbroker, of Elibank. His grandfather was Sir Henri-Gustave *Joly de Lotbinière (1829–1908), lieutenant-governor of British Columbia. As his parents were in India, de Lotbinière and his brother spent their school holidays with their aristocratic English relatives. He was educated at Eton College and Trinity College, Cambridge, where he was awarded a first class (division two) in part one of the economics tripos in 1926 and a second class (division two) in part two of the law tripos in 1927. He was called to the bar by Lincoln's Inn, but after practising at the Chancery bar for three years he left in 1932 to join the talks department of the BBC.

In 1935 de Lotbinière was appointed director of outside broadcasts. The outside broadcasts unit was responsible for any broadcast not transmitted from a BBC studio, and included the Christmas day royal broadcasts, the maiden voyage of the *Queen Mary* in 1936, the coronation of George VI in 1937, and major sporting events such as the Grand National, the boat race, and the cup final. In the early days of outside broadcasts the commentators tended to be experts, but de Lotbinière realized that it was better to use an eloquent speaker, an expert with the microphone, to describe the event, helped by a second commentator, an expert on the event being broadcast, who could be invited to add his comments as required. De Lotbinière was responsible for developing the art of the live running commentary, during which it was important to keep up the suspense, describing the action as it happened. He also believed in 'actuality', picking up the actual sounds of the event, to help the listener to picture the scene: the sounds of horses' feet at the trooping of the colour, or the roar of flames of the Crystal Palace fire. In 'The technique of the running commentary' he wrote that the commentator must 'allow the sounds to speak for themselves … In this way, listeners who never could hope to attend coronations and cup finals will get a feeling that broadcasting has enabled them to have a share in these events' (De Lotbinière, 'Technique', 37–40). He listened to all outside broadcasts, usually at home, and held weekly post-mortems.

After eighteen months in Bristol as director of the BBC west region from 1940 to 1941, de Lotbinière became director of empire programmes in October 1941, and he was among those responsible for setting up the front line reporting unit (later called the war reporting unit) in 1943. He was in charge of selecting and training two teams of reporters to cover operation Spartan, a big second front exercise in March 1943, which persuaded the War Office that the BBC would need a team of war correspondents to cover the invasion of Europe. As a result, the BBC reporters were given special training attachments with army units preparing for the second front. He was appointed head of the war reporting unit in May 1943.

De Lotbinière was sent to Canada in October 1943 as the BBC representative in Toronto, chosen partly because his family was well known in Canada. Responsible to the director-general for all BBC policy and practice in Canada, he organized the re-broadcasting by the Canadian Broadcasting Corporation of BBC programmes, and the exchange of programmes between the two countries. In 1944, in Quebec Cathedral, he married Mona (d. 1993), daughter of Professor T. Lewis of Brecon: she had been his secretary at the BBC. They had one son.

At the end of the war de Lotbinière returned to his former job as director of outside broadcasts, and built up a strong team of commentators, including Raymond Baxter, Wynford Vaughan Thomas, Brian Johnston, and John Snagge. From 1948 to 1952 he was head of outside broadcasts, in charge of both sound and television, covering events such as the wedding of Princess Elizabeth in 1947, the Olympic games in 1948, and the Festival of Britain in 1951, and in 1952 he himself did the television commentary on the funeral procession of George VI at Windsor, his first television assignment. In 1950 the outside broadcasts unit presented the first televised election broadcast, with a programme of results from the *Daily Mail* results board in Trafalgar Square. He was in charge of all BBC negotiations on sports broadcasting, and persuaded the BBC to spend more on sport, thus securing better contracts.

Sound and television outside broadcasts were split in 1952, with de Lotbinière choosing to take television, and he was in charge of the television coverage of the coronation of Elizabeth II on 2 June 1953, the biggest broadcasting operation in the history of the BBC. He was helped by his military and upper-class background in his discussions with the palace, which at first refused to allow cameras and commentators inside Westminster Abbey. De Lotbinière, who was appointed OBE in 1953 for the coronation broadcast, told Richard Dimbleby, who headed the team of commentators inside the abbey, 'we seem to have achieved something beyond most people's dreams' (J. Dimbleby, *Richard Dimbleby*, 1975, 247–8). He was appointed CVO by the queen in 1956 in recognition of the help he had given George VI with his Christmas broadcasts.

De Lotbinière left outside broadcasting in 1955 to become assistant controller of programmes, television, and in 1956 became controller of programme services, television, but he found administration less and less interesting. He was appointed controller of the west region in 1963, and retired in 1967 to Suffolk, where he bought his father's former house.

In the 1930s de Lotbinière had lived for several years at Toynbee Hall, taking a group from the East End hop picking and camping in Kent every summer. This concern for people characterized his whole life, and was one reason why he left his lucrative but personally unfulfilling career as a chancery barrister. Highly regarded and much loved by his colleagues, de Lotbinière was nicknamed Lobby. At 6 feet 8½ inches, he was the tallest man in the BBC, a source of amazement to George V, who claimed to have met the tallest man in Britain. Living in the flint-knapping country of the Suffolk–Norfolk border, de Lotbinière became a world expert on gun flints, and was called in during the excavations of the *Mary Rose* to date gun flints discovered in the wreck. He died on 6 November 1984 at his home, Brandon Hall, Brandon, Suffolk, and was cremated on 12 November following a funeral service in St Peter's Church, Brandon.   ANNE PIMLOTT BAKER

Sources A. Briggs, *The history of broadcasting in the United Kingdom*, rev. edn, 5 vols. (1995) · BBC WAC · *The year that made the day*, BBC [n.d., 1954?] · P. Scannell and D. Cardiff, *A social history of British broadcasting*, [1] (1991) · S. W. Smithers, *Broadcasting from within* (1938), chap. 8 · S. J. de Lotbinière, 'The radio commentator', *BBC handbook* (1939), 64–7 · S. J. de Lotbinière, 'The technique of the running commentary', *BBC Quarterly* (April 1949), 37–40 · S. J. de Lotbinière, 'Points of view', *BBC yearbook* (1952), 35–7 · *The Times* (9 Nov 1984) · *Daily Telegraph* (9 Nov 1984) · *The Times* (24 Feb 1994) [obit. of Sir Edmond Joly de Lotbinière] · *WW* · Burke, *Peerage* · private information (2004) · b. cert. · *The Times* (8 Nov 1984)
Archives SOUND BL NSA, performance recordings
Likenesses H. Magee, group portrait, photograph, 1949, Hult. Arch. · T. Hopkins, three photographs, 1953, Hult. Arch. · photograph, repro. in *The year that made the day*, 42 · photograph, repro. in *TV Mirror* (6 Feb 1954), 13
Wealth at death £163,898: probate, 17 June 1985, *CGPLA Eng. & Wales*

Jones. For this title name *see* individual entries under Jones; *see also* Bagnold, Enid Algerine [Enid Algerine Jones, Lady Jones] (1889–1981).

Jones, Adrian (1845–1938), sculptor, was born in Ludlow, Shropshire, on 9 February 1845, the fourth son of James Brookholding Jones (1816–1888), veterinary surgeon, and his wife, Jane Marshall. Adrian Jones was educated at Ludlow grammar school where his chief delight was the weekly drawing lesson. In addition to his passionate enjoyment of country and equestrian sports Jones nurtured the ambition to become an artist. Although he was taught briefly by Professor Zeigler, an art master to royalty, Jones's family discouraged professional artistic aspirations.

Fulfilling his father's desire that he should also be a vet, Jones qualified at the Royal Veterinary College, London, in 1866, aged twenty-one. Thirst for adventure drew him to the army, and he was gazetted to the Royal Horse Artillery on 11 January 1867. He was decorated during the Abyssinian expedition (1868), and joined the 3rd hussars in 1869. When illness forced Jones home to England in 1870 he married Emma, daughter of Thomas Beckingham, attorney, of Ross-on-Wye. Their only son, Adrian, was born in 1878. Jones served with the Queen's Bays in Ireland from 1871 to 1881, and was called to assist the 7th hussars in the First South African War in 1881. He was subsequently attached to the Inniskilling dragoons in South Africa.

Jones sketched and painted throughout his military career, chiefly portraits of horses and riders. In 1882 the sculptor Charles Bell Birch ARA offered to instruct Jones, encouraging him to combine his artistic sense and anatomical knowledge by making sculpture. Public success came in 1884, with his first Royal Academy exhibit (*One of the Right Sort*, a plaster statuette), and first prize in the Goldsmiths' Company's statuette competition for *Gone Away* (bronze, exh. RA, 1887; priv. coll.). In the same year Emma Jones died. On his return to London from Egypt, where he had selected camels for the Nile expedition in 1884, Jones joined the 2nd Life Guards. The success of *Camel Corps Scout* (terracotta, exh. RA, 1886) and *The Last Arrow* (wax, exh. RA, 1888; bronze, exh. Old Grosvenor Gallery, 1888) persuaded Jones to become a full-time artist. He retired from the army as captain in 1890.

In 1891 Jones married his second wife, also Emma, daughter of Robert Wedlake, master mariner, of Watchet, and moved to 147 Church Street, Chelsea, next door to the Chelsea Arts Club. The prince of Wales was impressed by Jones's quadriga *Triumph* (plaster, exh. RA, 1891), and suggested that an enlarged version should surmount Decimus Burton's arch at Constitution Hill in London. Jones was determined to execute this monumental work, and set out to prove his worth. When Sir Frederick Leighton, president of the Royal Academy, refused his support, somewhat scornful of Jones's ability, Jones defiantly exhibited a large equestrian group, *Duncan's Horses* (plaster, exh. RA, 1892; bronze cast of 1985 located at Royal Veterinary College, Hawkshead House, North Mimms), at the Royal Academy exhibition of 1892. The work was well received. However, in July 1892 the *Magazine of Art* claimed that a sculpture recently shown in the academy had been 'ghosted' by others and was not the work of the artist himself. Neither artist nor his accuser was named, but few doubted that Jones was the target, and Leighton was chief suspect. No case reached the courts, and many rushed to Jones's defence, but the slight to his honour and ability left permanent scars. Jones was understandably defensive following this apparent rejection by the academic establishment.

From 1907 Jones was occupied with making the renamed *Peace* quadriga for Decimus Burton's arch, greatly encouraged by Edward VII who frequently visited the studio until his death in 1910. However, he was bitterly disappointed that the work, the largest bronze sculpture in Britain, was unveiled without ceremony in 1912. Sir George Frampton was one of many who admired Jones's achievement.

Among Jones's royal commissions were paintings and bronzes of the prince of Wales's Derby winner Persimmon; a life-size bronze was commissioned by the Jockey Club and erected at Sandringham stud in 1895. His public monuments include the Royal Marines memorial at Admiralty Arch (1902), the Carabiniers' memorial, Royal Hospital, Chelsea (1905; maquette, Royal Army Museum, Chelsea), and the equestrian monument to the duke of Cambridge, Whitehall (1907), for which Jones was appointed MVO. His memorial to the South African wars was unveiled in Adelaide, Australia, in 1904. First World War memorials by Jones include those at Bridgnorth (1922), Uxbridge (1924), and the cavalry memorial unveiled at Stanhope Gate in 1924, later moved to Hyde Park (plaster panel, exh. RA, 1924; bronze maquette, exh. Sladmore Gallery, 1984; priv. coll.).

Adrian Jones was disciplined, ambitious, and hardworking. His objective was the accurate portrayal of animal action, for which horses were his chief models. Jones's lack of formal art education set him apart from his contemporaries. His work reveals his respect for the achievements of sculptors such as J. H. Foley, Carlo Marochetti, and Sir Joseph Edgar Boehm and he continued to make monuments untouched by the influence of the New Sculpture. Jones hoped for the respect and acceptance of the artistic establishment, but although royal patronage and public commissions proved him to be successful, membership of the Royal Academy always eluded him.

In his sweeping scarlet-lined campaign cloak Jones was a recognizable figure. At the Savage Club he enjoyed the convivial company of his friends James Abbott McNeil Whistler, C. B. Birch, Ford Madox Brown, and Phil May, whose wife considered Jones a sensible companion for her bibulous husband. He was chairman of the Chelsea Arts Club in 1905 and became one of its most venerated members, a passionate snooker player until he was over ninety. In 1918 he was admitted to the Royal Society of British Sculptors and was rewarded for his achievements with the society's gold medal in 1935. His autobiography, *Memoirs of a Soldier Artist*, was published in 1933. Adrian Jones died at his home, 147 Church Street, Chelsea, on 24 January 1938, aged ninety-two. A memorial plaque was laid, next to that of A. E. Housman, at St Laurence's Church, Ludlow.

SARAH CRELLIN

Sources A. Jones, *Memoirs of a soldier artist* (1933) · *DNB* · [J. Cunningham], *Adrian Jones: his life and work (1845–1938)* (1984) [exhibition catalogue, Sladmore Gallery, London, 8–26 May 1984] · *Graves, RA exhibitors* · S. Brindle, 'A history of the Wellington Arch', unpubd English Heritage report, 1999 · S. Brindle, 'Adrian Jones and the Wellington Arch Quadriga', *Sculpture Journal*, 6 (2001), 61–74

Archives Tate collection, press cuttings collection

Likenesses A. Priest, oils, 1909, priv. coll. · R. Bevan, bust; in family possession in 1949 · T. C. Dugdale, oils · photographs, repro. in Cunningham, *Adrian Jones*

Jones, Agnes Elizabeth (1832–1868), nurse, was born on 10 November 1832 in Cambridge, the elder daughter of Major Joseph Jones (1795–1850) of Londonderry and his wife, Elizabeth Smyth. Agnes Jones was the niece of John *Lawrence, first Baron Lawrence, viceroy of India and friend of Florence Nightingale. Major Jones, who served with the 12th regiment of foot, was promoted lieutenant-colonel in 1835. The regiment was posted to Mauritius in 1837, and the family spent six years there, until 1843 when Jones retired, as a lieutenant-colonel, and the family returned to the family home at Fahan, co. Donegal. Apart from two years at Miss Ainsworth's school at Avonbank, Stratford upon Avon (1848–50), Agnes Jones was educated at home. Following Lieutenant-Colonel Jones's death in 1850 the family moved to Dublin, and for three years Agnes Jones taught at the local ragged school, and visited the sick.

While on a six-month continental holiday with her family, in 1853, she spent a week at Kaiserswerth, near Düsseldorf, in Germany, where the Lutheran pastor Fliedner had founded an institution for ex-women prisoners in 1833, which had grown to include a hospital, an orphanage, a lunatic asylum, and two schools, run by a community of deaconesses.

Inspired by the work of Florence Nightingale in the Crimea, Agnes Jones was determined to become a nurse, and eventually, in 1860, she overcame her mother's opposition and embarked on eight months' training at Kaiserswerth. She was dissuaded by Pastor Fliedner from volunteering to go to the Syrian mission, and at his suggestion she finished training as a hospital sister and returned to England hoping to work for Florence Nightingale. On her return in April 1861 she took charge of the new Parker Street dormitory for girls, in London, run by the Bible Women's Mission, but this was cut short by the need for her to go to Rome to nurse her sister, who had been taken ill. In 1862 she became a Nightingale probationer at St Thomas's Hospital, London. After one year's training there, where she was Florence Nightingale's 'best and dearest pupil', she worked as a sister at the Great Northern Hospital for the first six months of 1864.

In April 1865, after months of hesitation, Agnes Jones, accompanied by twelve Nightingale nurses, went to Liverpool as lady superintendent of the Liverpool workhouse infirmary at Brownlow Hill. In 1864 William Rathbone, a wealthy shipowner and philanthropist, and a member of the Liverpool vestry, had offered to pay for a matron and trained nurses for three years, as an experiment, to be supplied by the Nightingale Fund, and Florence Nightingale had nominated Agnes Jones. Previously there had been no trained nurses in poor-law institutions, nursing being done by the paupers themselves, and there was widespread sickness among workhouse inmates. She began work in charge of the male wards only, but in 1867 her authority was extended to all the wards, and the vestry decided to make the new system permanent, and to pay for it. Brownlow Hill was the first workhouse to have its own training school for nurses. At first, her uncompromising attitude led to clashes with the governor, George Carr, but, after intervention by Florence Nightingale, relations improved. She was greatly overworked, with between 1300 and 1500 patients, several hundred more than the number of beds, and only fifty nurses. She had only four hours sleep a night.

Agnes Jones's intense religious fervour, which had led her into nursing in the first place, caused Florence Nightingale some anxiety. She took Bible-reading classes among her nurses, and tried to lead sinners to repentance, and Florence Nightingale was afraid this might damage the reputation of workhouse nursing. After Agnes Jones's death her two aunts, Georgina and Esther Smyth, wrote to Florence Nightingale with stories of miracles performed by her. Agnes Jones was very beautiful—Florence Nightingale described her as 'pretty and young and rich and witty, ideal in her beauty as a Louis XIV shepherdess'—and although partially deaf she was an excellent administrator, and determined to establish the principle that she, as lady superintendent, and not a doctor or the workhouse governor, should be in charge of the nursing.

Agnes Jones died of typhus fever in the Liverpool workhouse infirmary on 19 February 1868. She was buried at Fahan church, co. Donegal. Florence Nightingale wrote about her work in *Good Words* in 1868 under the title 'Una and the Lion', without mentioning her name. Una was Agnes Jones, and the lion represented the paupers she had to nurse. This eulogy was designed as a recruiting appeal for women to train as hospital nurses. Although the Liverpool scheme collapsed shortly after her death, as she had trained no successor and there was no one suitable to replace her, she had proved the importance of professional workhouse nursing. Within ten years of her death pauper assistants were no longer used in workhouse infirmaries, and in 1879 the Workhouse Infirmary Nursing Association was formed. A memorial erected to Agnes Jones in the Liverpool workhouse was later moved to the city's Walton Hospital. Liverpool Cathedral has a memorial window dedicated to her.   ANNE PIMLOTT BAKER

Sources J. C. Ross and J. Ross, *A gifted touch: a biography of Agnes Jones* (1988) · M. E. Baly, *Florence Nightingale and the nursing legacy* (1986) · Z. Cope, *Six disciples of Florence Nightingale* (1961), 1–9 · C. Woodham-Smith, *Florence Nightingale, 1820–1910* (1950) · B. Abel-Smith, *A history of the nursing profession* (1960); repr. (1961) · M. E. Tabor, *Pioneer women*, 2nd ser. (1927) · E. Pratt, *Pioneer women in Victoria's reign* (1897) · J. Jones, *Memorial of Agnes Jones by her sister* (1872)
Archives BM, corresp. with Florence Nightingale
Likenesses P. Trenerani, memorial, Walton Hospital, Liverpool; repro. in Ross and Ross, *Gifted touch*, 81 · drawing, repro. in Cope, *Six disciples*, facing p. 2 · memorial window, Liverpool Cathedral
Wealth at death under £2000: administration, 20 Nov 1868, *CGPLA Eng. & Wales*

Jones, Alan Payan Pryce- (1908–2000), writer and critic, was born on 18 November 1908 at 17 South Street, Mayfair, London, the elder of two sons of Brevet Colonel Henry Morris Pryce-Jones (1878–1952) of the Coldstream Guards, and (Marion) Vere (1884–1956), daughter of Lieutenant-Colonel the Hon. Lewis Dawnay, a son of William Henry Dawnay, seventh Viscount Downe. The Pryce-Joneses came from Montgomery in Wales; Alan's grandfather was Sir Pryce Pryce-*Jones (1834–1920), MP and chairman of Pryce-Jones Ltd, the woollen manufacturers based in Newtown.

Alan Pryce-Jones was educated at Eton College and at Magdalen College, Oxford, where he became an aesthete, establishing lifelong literary friendships with John Betjeman, Osbert Lancaster, Harold Acton, John Sutro, and Anthony Powell. His was a rebel generation where impish intelligence reigned over scholarship, and where, in his own words, it was fun to 'flash through the world like a firework, often leaving a smell of burning behind' (Pryce-Jones, 38). After two terms Pryce-Jones was gated, but he slipped out to a dance, was caught, and was sent down without a degree in 1928. He returned home in disgrace to be told he was unworthy even for service in the colonies. A military career was anathema to him, and he was advised to present himself to J. C. Squire, who was having his hair cut in the National Liberal Club. He was promptly employed as an unpaid assistant editor at the *London Mercury*, and worked there from 1928 until 1932. He introduced John Betjeman to the magazine, and commissioned short stories from his close friend James Stern. In 1931 he published *The Spring Journey*, inspired by his travels in the Middle East with Bobbie Pratt Barlow, a homosexual Coldstream Guards officer and a friend of his father. *People in the South* (1932), three novellas based on similar travels in Brazil, Chile, and Ecuador, and *Private Opinion* (1934), a work of 'informal' literary criticism, followed. *Pink Danube* (1939), written under the pseudonym Arthur Pumphrey, was a novel centred on the life of Adrian Bishop, at one time a high Anglican monk and friend of Maurice Bowra.

Having failed to marry Joan Eyres-Monsell (later Mrs Patrick Leigh-Fermor), because her father was unimpressed by Pryce-Jones's lack of prospects and removed her to India, on 28 December 1934 he married Baroness Thérèse Carmen May (Poppy) Fould-Springer (1914–1953), whose French-born Jewish family owned extensive property in Austria, as well as the Palais Abbatial at Royaumont, near Chantilly. They had one son, the writer David Pryce-Jones, born on 15 February 1936.

For some years until the *Anschluss*, Pryce-Jones enjoyed Viennese high life at Meidling, the Fould-Springer house in the Tivoligasse. But in 1937 he returned to Britain, joined the Liberal Party as their candidate for Louth, and also the officers' emergency reserve, ensuring that he would be called up. During the Second World War he served in the intelligence corps, being a German speaker, was in France at the time of Dunkirk, and worked on Ultra at Bletchley, in a section devoted to the battle order of the German army. He served briefly on the staff of the Eighth Army in Trentino, northern Italy, and at Caserta in 1943, becoming a lieutenant-colonel, with the territorial decoration, and ended up in Vienna as a liaison officer with the Soviet army.

In 1946 Pryce-Jones returned to literary life, joining Stanley Morison in the editorial offices of the *Times Literary Supplement*. He was its editor from 1948 until 1959, wielding considerable influence, and he set about widening the scope of the paper to include poetry and the hitherto neglected writings of other countries. He promoted Edwin Brock, Christopher Logue, W. S. Merwin, G. S. Fraser, Burns Singer, Alan Ross, and Philip Larkin, and introduced an almost totally unknown Austrian, Robert Musil, to an English readership. He became a trustee of the National Portrait Gallery and a council member of the Royal College of Music and of the Royal Literary Fund. He was president of the English PEN. He was closely involved with the early development of the Third Programme at the BBC, and wrote the libretto for Lennox Berkeley's opera *Nelson* (1954). He travelled widely for the British Council.

Pryce-Jones was widowed in 1953, but served as something of a *cavaliere servante* to his distant cousin Mary, duchess of Buccleuch. He was drama critic for *The Observer* for a year after leaving the *TLS*, but left England in 1960. Until 1963 he was adviser to the Ford Foundation in America, which distributed $15 million annually to the humanities and the arts; he was employed to help them dispose of yet more millions. He then collaborated on a musical, *Vanity Fair*, with Robin Pitt Miller, but the endeavour floundered. Pryce-Jones settled in Newport, Rhode Island, and sometimes in New York, working as a book critic for the *New York Herald Tribune* and other publications, and as drama critic for *Theatre Arts*. He continued to enjoy legendary stature in the literary hierarchy. He entertained generously and was himself lavishly entertained. He was one of the few travelling companions of Greta Garbo who did not betray her in print. A copy of his memoirs, *The Bonus of Laughter* (1987), was a rare work of literature in the shelves of her Manhattan apartment.

In 1968 Pryce-Jones married Mary Jean Thorne, a writer and a member of the Kempner family from Galveston, Texas, but she died in Paris a year later. As with his first wife's family, Alan was cherished by that of his second. Again they were rich, and in his old age he retired to Galveston, where they looked after him. He died at the University of Texas Medical Branch, Galveston, on 22 January 2000. He was buried on 13 February 2000 at Viarmes, near Chantilly, Oise, France. The recurring theme of Pryce-Jones's life was the delight of youth and the expectations of a glowing future versus talent dissipated and promise unfulfilled. He was a serious-looking man, dapper, elegant, with perfect, even rather affected manners, from whom the ready compliment sprang easily and effortlessly. His serious expression concealed an interest in gossip, of which he must have heard a great deal. Despite several tragedies in his own life, it could be argued that he led a charmed existence.   HUGO VICKERS

Sources *The Independent* (26 Jan 2000) • A. Pryce-Jones, *The bonus of laughter* (1987) • private information (2004) [D. Pryce-Jones, son] • personal knowledge (2004)

Archives BL, corresp. with Sir Sydney Cockerell, Add. MS 52743 • CAC Cam., corresp. with Monty Belgion

Jones, Sir Albert Evans- [*pseud.* Cynan] (1895–1970), Welsh-language poet and playwright, was born on 4 April 1895 at Liverpool House, Penlan Street, Pwllheli, Caernarvonshire, the eldest of the five children of Richard Albert Jones (1869–1933), shopkeeper, and his wife, Hannah Jane Evans (1871–1954), daughter of Evan Evans, schoolmaster and ship's purser. After receiving his secondary education at the grammar school in Pwllheli, he entered the University College of North Wales, Bangor, in 1913, and subsequently trained as a minister in the Calvinistic Methodist church at the Theological College, Bala. He served in the

First World War as both chaplain and combatant, seeing action with the Welsh student company of the Royal Army Medical Corps in the Macedonian campaign, about which he wrote some of his most famous poems. In 1920 he became minister of the Jerusalem and Glyn chapels at Penmaen-mawr in his native county, and on 29 September 1921 married his first wife, Ellen Jane Jones (1893–1962), a schoolmistress of Pwllheli, who was known as Nel and with whom he had two children.

Cynan, the bardic name by which he was always known in literary and eisteddfodic circles (and which was to replace Albert as his first name), came to prominence as a poet in 1921 when he won the crown at the national eisteddfod held in Caernarfon in that year with a *pryddest* (a poem in the free metres) entitled 'Mab y bwthyn' ('Son of the cottage'), which treated the First World War from a specifically Welsh point of view. The main character is a young man, the 'son of the cottage', who is uprooted from his rural community and, after enlisting, scarred by his experiences in a wider world. At times sentimental, but fluent and often lyrical, the poem is reminiscent of John Masefield's *The Everlasting Mercy* (1911). In 1921 he published his first volume of poems, *Telyn y nos* ('Harp of the Night'), and again won the crown at Mold in 1923 with 'Yr ynys unig' ('The Lonely Island'). Evans-Jones also won the chair (for a poem in the strict metres) at Pontypool in 1924 with 'I'r duw nid adwaenir' ('For the unknown God'). Another collection, *Caniadau* ('Songs'), was published in 1927. 'Y dyrfa' ('The multitude') won him the crown for the third time at Bangor in 1931. It tells the story of John Roberts, who played rugby for Wales thirteen times between 1927 and 1929 and later became a missionary in China; the poem, which amply demonstrates Evans-Jones's gifts as a balladeer, was probably suggested by J. C. Squire's 'The Rugger Match'.

In 1931 Evans-Jones left the ministry on his appointment as a tutor in Welsh literature in the Anglesey region of the extra-mural department of the University College of North Wales and later as staff tutor in drama and literature, a post in which he remained until his retirement. Also in 1931 he was appointed Welsh reader of plays for the lord chamberlain. In addition to his own plays, *Hywel Harris* (1932) and *Absalom fy mab* ('Absalom my son') (1957), he translated into Welsh works by Shakespeare, John Masefield, and Norman Nicholson. His novel *Ffarwel weledig* ('Farewell, visible things') was published in 1946, while his collected poems, *Cerddi Cynan* ('Poetry of Cynan'), appeared in 1959 and was reprinted (with new work) in 1967.

But it was as archdruid of the Gorsedd of Bards of the Isle of Britain, in which office he served twice (1950–54, 1963–6), and as president of the court of the national eisteddfod (1967–70), a body with which the gorsedd's affairs are closely associated, that Cynan found the stage most suited to his genial personality and gift for showmanship. As recorder (from 1935) he introduced several of the features now firmly part of such ceremonies, including the flower dance in which young girls proffer bouquets of wild flowers to the winning poets, and did much to improve the dignity of the gorsedd's public appearances in a country that has lacked indigenous pageantry with popular appeal. Privately, he was something of a bon viveur, an entertaining raconteur, and a keen angler.

Evans-Jones was the chief representative of the eisteddfodic culture of Wales in recent times and revelled in the limelight of the positions he held. He was made a CBE in 1949 and received the honorary degree of DLitt from the University of Wales in 1962. After the death of his first wife he married Menna Meirion Jones (*b.* 1920) on 17 April 1963. He was knighted in 1969. Cynan died of a heart attack on 26 January 1970 at Caernarfon and Anglesey General Hospital in Bangor and was buried with his first wife in the graveyard of St Tyssilio's Church on Church Island, near Menai Bridge in Anglesey, where he had lived from 1931 at Pen-maen, a house in a road now known as Ffordd Cynan. There is a commemorative plaque on Ffynnon Felin Bach, on the road known as Lôn Llyn, a well where (as recorded in *Mab y bwthyn*) as a boy he used to draw water for his grandmother.   MEIC STEPHENS

Sources I. Rees, *Bro a bywyd: Syr Cynan Evans-Jones, 1895–1970* (1982) · D. Owen, *Cynan* (1979) · Cynan [A. Evans-Jones], 'Hunangofiant', *Barn*, 97–108 (1970–71) · B. Lewis Jones, *Cynan: y llanc o dref Pwllheli* (1981) · I. Rees, ed., *Dŵr o ffynnon felin fach* (1995) · private information (2004) [Mrs Menna Evans-Jones] · m. cert.
Archives U. Wales, Bangor, papers | NL Wales, letters to Olwen Caradoc Evans · NL Wales, letters to Sir Thomas Parry-Williams | FILM BBC Wales | SOUND BBC Wales
Likenesses photographs, repro. in Rees, *Bro a bywyd*

Jones, Sir Alfred Lewis (1845–1909), shipping entrepreneur and colonial magnate, was born on 24 February 1845 at either Picton Place or Lammas Street, Carmarthen, the only surviving son of Daniel Jones (*d.* 1869) of Carmarthen, currier, and his wife, Mary, eldest daughter of Henry Williams, rector of Llanedi, south Wales. He moved to Liverpool with his parents at the age of three.

Educated at local schools where he showed an excellent head for figures, Jones went to sea as a cabin boy with the African Steam Ship Company in 1859. This voyage to west Africa left an impression that was to shape his future. The captain recommended him for a post as a junior clerk to the firm of Laird and Fletcher (from 1863 Fletcher and Parr), a small firm, which acted as managing agents of the African Steam Ship Company. He attended evening classes at the Liverpool College, encouraged and helped by the senior partner, Macgregor Laird, and became manager of the firm. However, in consequence of the loss of the African Steam Ship Company agency, on 1 January 1878 Jones started on his own account as a shipping and insurance broker.

In October 1879 Jones took the first step which led to his becoming the leading west Africa shipowner. Alexander Elder and John Dempster were Scots, who had worked alongside Jones in the firm of Fletcher and Parr. When a new line to west Africa, the British and African Steam Navigation Company, was established in 1868, to operate from Glasgow via Liverpool, Dempster was asked to act as Liverpool agent. Elder became his partner. They both knew Jones to be extremely ambitious and successful.

Therefore when he chartered a steamship to west Africa, they decided to avoid further competition by offering him a junior partnership in the Elder Dempster Line Ltd. He accepted, and until 1884 concentrated on learning every detail of their business. That year the senior partners agreed to be bought out by Jones. How he raised the money is not entirely clear, but he must have been able to wield strong influence with the shareholders. His forceful personality, abundant mental and physical energy, detailed knowledge, and visionary approach, persuaded his partners that, successful though the business was, if he were to establish himself in competition they might lose severely.

Jones achieved his dominant position by ensuring the close co-operation of the two existing west Africa lines, and negotiating an exclusive agreement with Woermann Line of Hamburg. As well as chartering, he built up a small fleet. In 1891 Elder Dempster also became managing agents for the African Steam Ship Company, in which Jones eventually acquired 75 per cent of the shares. He subsequently transferred Elder Dempster's fleet to it. In 1895 he created the west Africa shipping conference to prevent price wars, and restrict interlopers, by means of a deferred rebate system. Despite opposition, the conference was effective, and substantially enhanced his capital resources. On the strength of this Jones was able to diversify into African coastal boating and river services, hotels, cold storage, victualling, chandlery, cartage, oil mills, plantations, collieries and other mines, together with the Bank of British West Africa (founded in 1897): a complete network of businesses. Bunkers were supplied at main UK ports and at Las Palmas, Tenerife, and Freetown, utilized by British and foreign navies and over 200 shipping lines. By 1900 he was able to acquire the British and African Steam Navigation Company completely for £800,000 by means of a skilful capital reconstruction. By 1909 his firm controlled a fleet of 101 ships on a variety of routes. According to the *Journal of Commerce* he was, at his death, senior partner in at least twenty companies and chairman of five, president of the Liverpool chamber of commerce and the British Cotton Growing Association, past president of the Liverpool Steam Ship Owners' Association, chairman of the American chamber of commerce, and of the Liverpool School of Commercial Research (18 December 1909).

From 1895 until his death, Alfred Jones was the pre-eminent figure in the west African shipping trade. Despite rumbling opposition from potential rivals, he seemed to know just how far to go with them. Behind all his activities and manoeuvres, there lay a faith in the future of west Africa. His sister recalled how, on his youthful voyage to west Africa, he was so moved by the miserable condition of the natives that he resolved to spare no effort to remedy the situation. He held the native Africans in high esteem, and believed that the moral and spiritual ministry of the Christian missionary must be combined with practical help towards earning a living. 'His real reward was to see the transformation of British West Africa into a thriving economic development' (Davies, *Sir Alfred Jones*, 121).

On the road to this goal Jones revived the economy of the Canary Islands. Calling there in the course of business, he found a desperate situation because the old staple export trade, cochineal, had been replaced by aniline dyes. He assisted the islanders in growing bananas and other crops and, to provide a ready market, introduced the banana to the British people, initially giving them for free to the costermongers to sell. From this stemmed his contribution to the revitalizing of the Jamaican economy. Jones was asked by Joseph Chamberlain, the colonial secretary, to run a fortnightly service to Jamaica, mainly for carrying bananas, Jamaica's largest crop. He accepted a subsidy level at less than commercial rates, and established a shipping line which lasted until 1937.

Jones briefly entered the Canadian trade with the Beaver Line, bought in 1898. In 1903 he sold it to Canadian Pacific but retained the service from Cape Town to Canada. From 1895 to 1911 his firm, and the Woermann Line, monopolized the trade to the Congo, as a result of deft negotiations with King Leopold II. His involvements also included the foundation of the British Cotton Growing Association, in the hope of making Britain independent of American cotton. Although this did benefit west Africa, in production it never seriously rivalled that of the USA. In 1904 he became a member of Joseph Chamberlain's tariff commission.

The most enduring act of philanthropy undertaken by Jones was his foundation, in 1898, of the Liverpool School of Tropical Medicine. This sprang from his concern at levels of mortality in west Africa, which caused it to be called the 'white man's grave'. Sir Ronald Ross (who was to be awarded the Nobel Prize in 1902 for his identification of the anopheles mosquito as the carrier of malaria) became head of this institution, and was also appointed to the Alfred Jones chair in tropical medicine.

Jones's charitable interests were wide, including missionary societies, Liverpool University, and the Anglican cathedral. Honorary Treasurer of the Liverpool Hot-Pot Fund (to provide a Christmas meal for the poor), he was a generous patron of the Liverpool Navy League, and Lancashire Sea Training Home in Wallasey. His motives in this last cause were not only to give poor boys a good start in life, but also to reduce the reliance on 40,000 aliens to man the British merchant fleet. For his work for west Africa, Jamaica, and the School of Tropical Medicine, Jones was knighted in 1901. He received honours from Spain, Russia, and Portugal, and was also made an honorary fellow of Jesus College, Oxford, in 1905.

President of the Liverpool chamber of commerce, Sir Alfred was consul in Liverpool for the Congo Free State; and his failure to change his views in relation to the Congo led to adverse comment after his death. Reports of Belgian brutality in the Congo were too widespread to be totally discounted, and Jones was in a position, on account of his special relationship to Leopold II, to bring pressure to bear. 'Had Sir Alfred Jones come forward as the defender of the Congolese', wrote E. D. Morel, 'the Congo tragedy would have been terminated long years ago' (*Africa Mail*, 17 Dec 1909). Jones was also open to criticism on account of the minimum wages he paid to his extremely loyal and hard-working workforce.

According to Sir Ronald Ross, Jones was 'Rather short, dark, stout, with grey hair, moustache and tuft below the nether lip, a straight look, ready laugh and boundless energy'. Ross recalled that he was always surrounded by shorthand secretaries, 'to whom he would fling a letter in dictation, while he was talking to you on some other subject' (Ross, 372). While much of his philanthropy could be described as enlightened self-interest, his flaws were generally reckoned to be well balanced by his virtues. People outside commerce, like Mary Kingsley, esteemed him highly. She entrusted Jones with her funeral arrangements. He never married, always claiming he never had time. His sister, Mary Isabel Pinnock, a widow, kept house for him from 1878, when her husband died.

Just after Christmas in 1906, Jones took a large group of business associates and MPs to Jamaica, with the object of stimulating trade between Bristol and the West Indies. The possibility of cotton growing was on the agenda. An earthquake struck Kingston on 14 January 1907, while they were still there. Jones was unscathed, although his hotel collapsed around him, and his energies found full scope in organizing relief services. However, his decline in health dated from that time, and he defied all advice to take a rest. Clearly the habits of a lifetime, work from 7.00 a.m. to near midnight, were deeply engrained. In late autumn 1909, he caught two successive chills, and on 13 December he died of heart failure at his home, Oaklands, in Aigburth, a pleasant district of Liverpool. Sir Alfred's sudden death resulted in tributes to his commercial prowess, to his philanthropy, and to his international influence. His funeral took place at Mossley Hill parish church, and he was buried at Anfield cemetery on 17 December.

After his death, Sir Alfred's business interests were sold to a consortium consisting of Sir Owen Cosby Philipps and William James, first Viscount Pirrie. Although the valuation almost certainly undervalued the shipping operations, by the time the estate was finalized, over £325,000 had been distributed to charitable work, including funds for the School of Tropical Medicine, and to provide education for the people of west Africa.   J. GORDON READ

Sources P. N. Davies, *Sir Alfred Jones: shipping entrepreneur par excellence* (1978) · A. H. Milne, *Sir Alfred Lewis Jones, KCMG* (1914) · P. N. Davies, *Trading in west Africa* (1976) · Mersey docks and harbour company archives, antecedent file WUP/JA, Sir A. L. Jones · 'The new gospel of wealth', *Sunday Strand* (Nov 1903), iv · *Journal of Commerce* (18 Dec 1909) · *DNB* · P. N. Davies, 'Jones, Sir Alfred Lewis', *DBB* · R. Ross, *Memoirs* (1923), 372 · E. D. Morel, 'Sir Alfred Jones', *Africa Mail* (17 Dec 1909) · *Liverpool Courier* (14 Dec 1909) · *CGPLA Eng. & Wales* (1910)

Archives Merseyside Maritime Museum, Liverpool, archives of Elder Dempster Line Ltd · Merseyside Maritime Museum, Liverpool, archives of African Steam Ship Company | BLPES, letters to tariff commission

Likenesses F. Beaumont, oils, 1906, Walker Art Gallery, Liverpool · G. Frampton, memorial monument, Pierhead, Liverpool · photograph, repro. in Davies, 'Jones, Sir Alfred Lewis' · portrait, repro. in *Syren and Shipping Illustrated* (15 Dec 1909)

Wealth at death £674,259 7s.: probate, 8 Jan 1910, *CGPLA Eng. & Wales*

Jones, Alice Gray [*pseud.* Ceridwen Peris] (1852–1943), writer, journal editor, and temperance leader, was born in December 1852 in Llanllyfni, Caernarvonshire, the daughter of David and Ellen Jones, her father's family running a small woollen mill at Clynnog Fawr nearby. Both her parents were active Calvinistic Methodists. Her childhood was spent in Llanberis, where the composer Ieuan Gwyllt (Revd John Roberts; 1822–1877), the family's minister from 1865 to 1869, was a formative influence. She attended the village school at Dolbadarn, then spent three years as assistant mistress at the British School in Caernarfon, leaving in 1873 to spend two years at the training college in Swansea. In 1875 she was appointed headteacher of Dolbadarn School, a post which she held until her marriage in 1881 to the Revd William Jones, a Calvinistic Methodist minister at Fourcrosses near Pwllheli. Of the three sons and one daughter born to them, one son died in infancy and another, aged thirty-four, died in 1918. In 1919 the family left Fourcrosses and moved to Cricieth, where William Jones died aged seventy-eight in 1925.

Like many Welsh-speaking nonconformist women of her day, Alice Gray Jones had been active in the Sunday school movement as a young girl, and her interest in temperance probably first developed in that context. After her marriage she became leader of the local Band of Hope, but the founding of Undeb Dirwestol Merched Gogledd Cymru (UDMGC, the 'north Wales women's temperance union') at Blaenau Ffestiniog in 1892 provided far greater scope for her activity. That her husband was supportive of her work outside the home is shown by the fact that in 1894, when her children were still very young, she arranged and addressed thirty-nine temperance meetings for women. The following year she was appointed organizer for UDMGC, taking up the post on 27 September 1895. Between then and May 1896 she was away from home several nights a week, as her work took her to all six north Wales counties and to Welsh communities in English towns and cities, including Oswestry, London, Liverpool, Birmingham, and Manchester.

By this time Alice Gray Jones was also well known as a writer, under the pen-name Ceridwen Peris. She had begun publishing verse as early as 1874, and by the 1880s her work was appearing in a number of Welsh periodicals, both religious and secular. She wrote for adults and children, but also became a regular contributor to *Y Frythones*, the Welsh women's magazine edited by Cranogwen (Sarah Jane Rees, 1839–1916). *Y Frythones* ceased publication in 1891 and Alice Gray Jones was the obvious candidate as editor of a new illustrated monthly magazine to fill the gap; *Y Gymraes* was launched in October 1896. *Y Gymraes*, aimed primarily at women in north Wales, reflected her interest in temperance, and she soon persuaded the publisher, Evan William Evans of Dolgellau, to allow her to include regular reports of the meetings of branches of UDMGC. In January 1901 *Y Gymraes* was formally accepted as the union's official magazine, and a year later 2400 copies were being sent out to the branches for distribution.

Although the emphasis on temperance and the related

theme of 'moral purity' meant that *Y Gymraes* stressed women's responsibility for religious and moral standards within the family, under the editorship of Alice Gray Jones it also encouraged women to move into the public sphere. By including features about Welsh women of the past and present she made her readers aware of their own culture and history and provided important role models. Most of the contributors to *Y Gymraes* were women, for like others in the temperance movement Alice Gray Jones was keen to encourage more women to write. Her own verse, often didactic or sentimental, had no great literary quality, although a collection entitled *Caniadau Ceridwen Peris* appeared in 1934. She also published a number of temperance and Sunday school tracts and, in 1917, a Welsh translation of *Britania*, a patriotic play by Alice Williams, but her chief contribution to Welsh literature was undoubtedly as editor of *Y Gymraes*. She was succeeded as editor by Mair Ogwen in October 1919.

Alice Gray Jones was active in other aspects of public life, serving on many committees in Caernarvonshire in the fields of education, nursing and child welfare, war pensions, and agriculture; she was appointed OBE in 1920. She died, aged ninety, at the home of her daughter and son-in-law at 20 College Road, Bangor, on 17 April 1943.

CERIDWEN LLOYD-MORGAN

Sources [Mair Ogwen (?)], 'Ceridwen Peris', *Y Gymraes* (Oct 1919), 147–9 · I. M. Jones, 'Merched Llên Cymru, 1850–1914', MA diss., U. Wales, 1935, 144–8 · W. W. Price, 'Biographical index', NL Wales · C. Peris [A. G. Jones], *Er cof a gwerthfawrogiad o lafur Mrs Mathews* (1930) · S. R. Williams, 'The true "Cymraes": images of women in women's nineteenth century Welsh periodicals', *Our mother's land: chapters in Welsh women's history, 1830–1939*, ed. A. V. John (1991), 69–91 · C. Lloyd-Morgan, 'From temperance to suffrage?', *Our mother's land: chapters in Welsh women's history, 1830–1939*, ed. A. V. John (1991), 135–58 · d. cert.
Likenesses photograph, repro. in 'Ceridwen Peris', *Y Gymraes* · photograph, repro. in *Cymon*, 20 (1901), 10
Wealth at death £452 14s. 0d.: administration, 11 Oct 1943, CGPLA Eng. & Wales

Jones, Allan Gwynne- (1892–1982), painter, was born on 27 March 1892 in Richmond, Surrey, the only son and younger child of Llewellyn Gwynne-Jones, solicitor, and his wife, Evelyn Hooper, who translated French and German verse. He was educated at Bedales School, Hampshire, where he developed a precocious talent for calligraphy and illumination, and formed a deep and lasting admiration for the work and poetry of William Morris. In obedience to his father's wishes he studied law, and from 1911 to 1914 he was articled to William Joynson-Hicks. He was awarded a senior scholarship by the Law Society and qualified as a solicitor, but never practised. During these years he became acquainted with Albert Rutherston. It was with his encouragement that he painted a series of exquisite watercolours on silk. They were mainly of East Anglian subjects and included one of Southwold fair. This was the first of several paintings of fairs, including the large oil in the Tate collection (1937–8).

Gwynne-Jones became a student at the Slade School of Fine Art in May 1914, but his career there was cut short by the outbreak of war. He joined the army in August 1914, and served throughout the First World War. A second lieutenant in the 1st Cheshire regiment, he was wounded twice, mentioned in dispatches twice, and appointed DSO during the battle of the Somme (1916); the award was made on the spot in special recognition of his bravery, and the ribbon was pinned on his tunic as he lay wounded on a stretcher. He was later transferred to the Welsh Guards and demobilized in 1919.

Gwynne-Jones then rejoined the Slade, where he received much encouragement from Henry Tonks and won several prizes. In the years 1920–22, towards the end of his time at the Slade, he painted a number of haunting pictures of farmyard scenes. As compositions they are strikingly original, and their dramatic effect is largely due to their dark tonality.

In 1923 Gwynne-Jones was invited to join the staff of William Rothenstein at the Royal College of Art, where he became professor of painting. While teaching there he studied etching under Malcolm Osborne. Although he produced only eleven plates, most of which were executed in 1926 and 1927, they are of great beauty, and bear a distant affinity with the work of Samuel Palmer, for which he professed considerable admiration. From 1930 until his retirement in 1959 he was a senior lecturer at the Slade. In 1937 he married Rosemary Elizabeth, daughter of Henry Perceval Allan, shipbroker. She had been a pupil of his at the Slade. They had one daughter, Emily (Mrs Beanland), who, like her mother, became a gifted artist.

Many artists have paid tribute to what they owed Gwynne-Jones as a teacher. His views about painting and his practical advice are embodied in two of the books that he wrote, *Portrait Painters* (1950) and *Introduction to Still-Life* (1954). In his preface to the first of these books he defines the qualities that are required to paint a fine portrait; these are based on his profound study of the old masters. In the course of his long life he painted the portraits of many distinguished sitters such as the economist Lord Beveridge, the army officer Lord Ismay (NPG), the politician Lord Butler of Saffron Walden, and the scientist Sir R. George Stapledon. The best of these portraits have a sympathetic perception of character which few English painters have rivalled in the twentieth century. In his *Introduction to Still-Life*, Gwynne-Jones reserves his fullest praise for the 'grandeur, calm and simplicity' of Francisco Zurbarán's still-lifes. And, indeed, his own work has much in common with that of the Spanish painter, and of his other idol, J.-B.-S. Chardin. For, like them, he was a master of tonality, and could create on canvas as much beauty out of a loaf of brown bread as out of a basket of peaches. The same can be said of his countless flower paintings for he found the same inspiration in the most common wayside plants as in the rarest rose.

Gwynne-Jones was the most generous and modest of men. He loved people, conversation, food, and good wine. He was elected an associate of the Royal Academy in 1955 and Royal Academician in 1965. He served as a trustee of the Tate Gallery from 1939 to 1946. His distinguished achievements as an artist were recognized belatedly in

1980 with his appointment as CBE, two years before his death, at the age of ninety, on 5 August 1982 in the Northleach Hospital, Gloucestershire. BRINSLEY FORD, rev.

Sources *Allan Gwynne-Jones: an exhibition to mark his 80th birthday*, Thos. Agnew and Sons (1972) [exhibition catalogue, 7–30 March 1972; incl. introduction by H. Brooke] • *The Times* (6 Aug 1982) • personal knowledge (1990) • private information (1990) • I. Lowe, ed., *Allan Gwynne-Jones* (1982) [exhibition catalogue, NMG Wales, 1982]
Archives Tate collection, corresp. with Lord Clark
Likenesses A. Gwynne-Jones, self-portrait, oils, *c.*1922, Tate collection

Jones, Ambrose (d. 1678). *See under* Jones, Lewis (1560–1646).

Jones, (Holroyd) Anthony Ray- (1941–1972), photographer, was born at Wookey House, Wookey Hole, near Wells in Somerset on 7 June 1941. He was the youngest of three sons of Raymond Ray-Jones (d. 1942), a fine art printer and painter, and his wife, Effie Irene Pearce, a physiotherapist. Following the early death of his father, the family moved constantly during the early years of his life and eventually settled in Hampstead, London, in 1951. Ray-Jones was then sent to Christ's Hospital in Horsham, Sussex, but hated his schooling bitterly and was at the time temporarily deaf in one ear.

After leaving school in 1957 Ray-Jones went to the London College of Printing, where he studied graphic design. It was there that he became interested in photography and was especially influenced by social documentary photography of the time, and the work of Bill Brandt. Following his graduation in 1961 Ray-Jones was awarded a scholarship to Yale University School of Art for a graduate design programme. During this time he began to concentrate more fully on photography and more importantly encountered Alexey Brodovich (1898–1971), one of America's most creative forces in design and art direction at that time. During his final year at Yale, Ray-Jones joined Brodovich's avant-garde class called the 'design laboratory' in New York. The class, held in Richard Avedon's studio, had previously been attended by such eminent American photographers as Irving Penn, Robert Frank, and Garry Winogrand.

In 1963 and 1964 Ray-Jones covered street parades in New York, and the black community in New Haven, Connecticut. His work at this time was strongly influenced by the confrontational, realistic, and at times surrealistic work of contemporary photographers such as Diane Arbus, Lee Friedlander, and Garry Winogrand. After gaining his masters in fine art in 1964 he joined Brodovich as associate art director of the influential photographic magazine *Sky* and until his return to Britain in 1966 he also undertook a large amount of commercial work.

Once back in England Ray-Jones started to work on his long cherished ambition: a published project on the social customs and idiosyncrasies of the British during their leisure time. He wanted this to be an 'important statement about British society' (*Personal Views*, 31–2), and one which explored the class system and different geographic areas of the country. The majority of this work was done during 1966 and 1967 and was eventually published as *A Day Off: an English Journal* (1974). It is for this work that he is most famous.

The black and white photographs were carefully constructed, tightly controlled, and witty with an inclination towards the bizarre. His work could be both extraordinarily complex and subtle, and his skilful insight into British class systems and social codes anticipated the work of later British photographers such as Martin Parr. Though focusing on the foibles of human nature there is a tenderness and respect in this work which leaves his subjects' dignity intact. He wrote, 'I have tried to show the sadness and the humour in a gentle madness that prevails in people' (Ehrlich, 30). As Ray-Jones was not technically gifted most of his printing was done by John Benton-Harris. The project was shown at the Institute of Contemporary Arts, London, in 1969 in his first British solo show. Recognition also came with exhibitions abroad including 'Current report 2' at the Museum of Modern Art, New York, and a group show at the Rencontres Gallery in Paris.

Ray-Jones had to take on commercial work to fund his projects. He worked for the *Radio Times*, *Harper's Bazaar*, *The Observer*, and the *Sunday Times*. 'The Happy Extremists', a colour project dealing with British eccentrics, was supported by the *Sunday Times* and published by them in October 1970. He was, however, seen to be a 'difficult' photographer in the commercial market—often uncompromising and unwilling to let art directors and picture editors have control over his work. This resulted in him becoming blacklisted from many publications and in effect damaged his career.

In 1967 Ray-Jones met and married Anna Coates and became involved with the photography magazine *Creative Camera*, edited by Bill Jay. For the following years he continued to work on his project concerning the British and much of 1970 was taken up with commercial work for Manplan, on commissions for the *Architectural Review*. During this time he twice tried to become a member of the prestigious photo agency Magnum. On both attempts he was rejected.

In 1971 Ray-Jones returned to America to take up a post as visiting lecturer at the San Francisco Art Institute within their department of photography, despite having no teaching experience. During vacation time he was employed extensively on commercial work and also pursued personal projects—many of which were shown in the retrospective exhibition of his work, 'The English seen', at San Francisco Museum of Art in 1974.

In February 1972 Ray-Jones developed leukaemia. Almost immediately he returned to England with his wife and on 13 March 1972, aged only thirty, he died in the Royal Marsden Hospital in London. He was cremated at St John's crematorium, and was survived by his wife. The National Museum of Film, Photography, and Television in Bradford acquired the entire Ray-Jones archive in 1993. This archive includes not only his photographic work but also his prolific notes and journals. SUSAN BRIGHT

Sources R. Ehrlich, *Tony Ray-Jones* (1990) · A. Ellis, introduction, in T. Ray-Jones, *A day off: an English journal* (1974) · T. Ray-Jones, 'Photographs from America and Great Britain', *Creative Camera*, 52 (Oct 1968), 438–57 · P. Turner, 'T. Ray-Jones (1941–1972)', *Creative Camera*, 7 (July 1988), 10–13 · *Tony Ray-Jones portfolio* (1975) · G. Badger and J. Benton-Harris, *Through the looking glass: photographic art in Britain, 1945–1989* (1989) · personal notebooks, National Museum of Photography, Film, and Television, Bradford, Tony Ray-Jones archive · private information (2004) [J. Benton-Harris] · *Personal views* (1970) [exhibition catalogue, Arts Council] · b. cert. · d. cert.
Archives National Museum of Film, Photography, and Television, Bradford, MSS, papers
Wealth at death £4105: administration, 21 July 1972, *CGPLA Eng. & Wales*

Jones, Arnold Hugh Martin (1904–1970), classical historian, was born at Birkenhead, Cheshire, on 9 March 1904, the son of John Arthur Jones (1867–1939), then on the staff of the *Liverpool Post* and later (1908–24) editor of *The Statesman* of Calcutta, and his wife, Elsie Martin, daughter of a clergyman. A. H. M. Jones's grandfather was a Wesleyan Methodist minister. Jones himself, however, became an agnostic. He was educated at Cheltenham College from 1913 and, from 1922, at New College, Oxford, where he took a first class in both classical honour moderations (1924) and *literae humaniores* (1926), and won the Craven scholarship (1923). His fluency in the classical languages was such that in later years he would read the church fathers in hospital with the zest and rapidity with which others might have devoured novels.

In 1926 Jones was elected to a fellowship at All Souls, and in the following year married Freda Katharine Mackrell, a medievalist who read history at Somerville College, Oxford (1922–6). He was reader in ancient history at the Egyptian University of Cairo from 1929 to 1934, when he returned to All Souls; he always greatly valued his connection with the college. From 1939 to 1946 he was lecturer in ancient history at Wadham College, Oxford. During the Second World War he served first in the Ministry of Labour, then in intelligence at the War Office. His experience of wartime direction of labour helped to suggest to him that a shortage of manpower explained the regulations that tied all sorts of men to their occupations in the late Roman empire. He had already gained a high reputation as a historian, and became professor of ancient history, first at University College, London (1946), and then at Cambridge (1951), where he was a fellow of Jesus College.

Jones's interests lay not so much in political, diplomatic, and military history, which has mostly absorbed the attention of students of Greece and Rome, or in the history of ideas, as in social and economic conditions and still more in institutions and administration. To the analysis of these subjects he brought the most comprehensive knowledge of written texts, literary, juristic, epigraphic, and papyrological, over a period extending from classical Greece to the reign of Heraclius. In his younger days he took part in excavations at Constantinople and Jerash, and he had a keen interest in architecture, which led to his writing accounts of the buildings of New College and of All Souls and Worcester colleges for the Victoria county

Arnold Hugh Martin Jones (1904–1970), by Walter Stoneman, 1951

history of Oxfordshire, vol. 3 (1954). It is rather curious that he made little use of archaeological evidence for the ancient world, even for the social and economic history on which it can chiefly throw light. Before and during his tenure of the post at Cairo, he travelled widely in the Near East, and at all times he liked to see for himself the lands in which Graeco-Roman civilization had flourished, but topographical knowledge too is not conspicuous in his works.

In the earlier part of his career Jones read extensively in modern scholarly literature, but as time went on, he cared less to know what others had written. He did not indulge in polemic, and he was confident that in setting out what he saw as certain or probable, on the basis of his mastery of original evidence, he would have much to say that was true, which others had not discerned. This confidence was generally justified. He was indeed fairly criticized for relying too often on easily accessible collections of inscriptions rather than on the most reliable publications. In no other respect might his scholarly accuracy be impugned. Ignoring most modern works, he would invariably cite and often quote the full evidence on every problem, so that every reader could form his own judgement; as he expressly says, this often showed how little basis there is for any solution. He could indeed hardly have written so much and over so wide a range from personal scrutiny of the evidence, if he had not restricted himself as he did. His practice resembled that of Fustel de Coulanges, whom he rivalled in the range of his knowledge, which no contemporary historian of antiquity equalled.

The candour with which Jones presented his material was matched by the soberness and good sense of his judgement. To all this he added, again like Fustel, a marvellous clarity in exposition. Every sentence was crystal clear; every paragraph marshalled the facts and arguments with lucidity and force. This came so naturally to him that, once he had thought out a subject, he hardly ever needed to blot a word in the first draft. For that matter, he would not readily amend the manuscript in deference to objections, and with one exception, in republishing his works, he altered them very little. Rationally and carefully formed, his convictions were hard to shake.

Jones's first book was *A History of Abyssinia* (1935), written in conjunction with Elizabeth Monroe, and reprinted in 1955 as *A History of Ethiopia*. In 1938 he published *The Herods of Judaea*, his principal essay in narrative history, a readable survey for the general public. Meantime, in 1937 his *Cities of the Eastern Roman Provinces* had come out, a large work that was corrected and brought up to date with the help of collaborators just before he died. It traces the diffusion of the Greek city from Alexander to Justinian, and though useful, too much resembles an arid gazetteer. But it was the groundwork for *The Greek City from Alexander to Justinian* (1940), in which he not only analysed the process of diffusion, but also the relations between the cities and the Hellenistic monarchies and central government at Rome, the developments in their internal institutions, their economic basis, and their cultural functions. Replete with information, this is also a grand synoptic work, reprinted as a paperback without change in 1979. Jones developed M. I. Rostovtzev's insight, in stressing the gulf between the cities and the peasantry they exploited. The cities themselves came wholly under the control of local magnates, who he thought were chiefly landowners. In later works, too, Jones argued, against what had been received doctrine, that trade and industry were of relatively little importance in the Roman economy and were insignificant as a source for the wealth of the ruling class. He also gave a powerful exposition of the view, familiar enough, that the decay of civic patriotism, due to excessive central control and the burden of taxation, helps to explain the fall of the Roman empire; later he was to give more weight to barbarian invasions than to internal decay.

As this book shows, Jones's own mildly socialist leanings made it easier for him than for most classical scholars to discard the aristocratic prejudices of Greek and Roman writers. Hence his *Athenian Democracy* (1957) gives a sympathetic account of that system, but it was characteristic of him also to enquire how Athenian democracy actually worked. His *Studies in Roman Government and Law* (1960), another collection of seminal articles which relate to the Roman principate, betray the same concern with institutions and their operation. They first illustrate his mastery of Roman public and criminal law; a posthumously published book, *The Criminal Courts of the Roman Republic and Principate* (1972), unfortunately takes too little account of a

new and revolutionary theory. It shows some falling off of his powers, like his last excursions into the history of the classical periods, *Sparta* (1967) and *Augustus* (1970), which were designed for general readers or students. For their benefit he also compiled select volumes of evidence and a summary of his *magnum opus* on the late Roman empire. For scholars he planned *The Prosopography of the Later Roman Empire*, edited the first volume (1971), and made substantial contributions to it: this was in itself an immense work. His pen was indeed never inactive.

Meantime in 1964 Jones had issued *The Later Roman Empire, AD 284–602*, two volumes of text and one of notes, which he added when the text was in page proof. Parts of it were founded on memorable articles which were collected, with important pieces bearing on earlier periods too, in *The Roman Economy* (1974). It is subtitled 'A social, economic and administrative survey'; even the narrative sketch of some three hundred pages with which it begins contains numerous excursuses on these matters. A. Momigliano remarked that 'the unusual form of this book cannot be explained without the English tradition of Royal Commissions, social surveys, Fabian Society pamphlets. A. H. M. Jones is clearly in the direct line of the Webbs and Hammonds, indeed of Booth and Beveridge' (*Quarto contributo alla storia degli studi classici*, 1969, 645). This does not imply that the work is ahistorical. The process of evolution is everywhere on show. What is omitted is the record of sentiments and beliefs. Jones cared more about ecclesiastical organization than about saints or theologians, though he read lives of the saints with avidity for their incidental information on social conditions. That did not make him underrate the importance of ideas. *Constantine and the Conversion of Europe* (1948), the best of his books for the general reader, had totally rejected the notion that Constantine was no more than a rational political schemer; Jones later found new evidence to prove the authenticity of the documents that illustrate Constantine's religiosity. Still he now made little of spiritual developments. In *The Greek City* he had suggested that though Christianity had been a religion 'of escape', propounding 'no ideal of civic duty', in the end the onslaught of Islam infused it with 'a fighting spirit' and gave the empire 'a principle of unity and a motive for survival' in the east. He seems to have resiled from this view in *The Later Roman Empire*, where he ascribes the breakup of the empire primarily to 'barbarian pressure', which aggravated internal weaknesses, increasing the burdens on the subjects and their apathy to its fate; that it collapsed in the west but long survived in the east was the result of the greater economic resources of the east. Neither this nor any other explanation of Rome's decline is likely to command universal assent. Still, the book remains the greatest contribution in English to Roman imperial history since Gibbon, astounding not only for the abundance of information but for its acumen, sweep, coherence, and elegance in presentation.

Jones was elected a fellow of the British Academy in 1947, and was president of the Society for the Promotion of Roman Studies from 1952 to 1955. He was a fellow of All

Souls from 1926 to 1946. His contributions to Roman law and church history earned him respectively doctorates in law from Cambridge (1965) and in divinity from Oxford (1966). New College made him an honorary fellow.

Jones was a little man, somewhat bowed, with sparse, sandy hair and keen eyes; he spoke swiftly, softly, and jerkily (and lectured, not very attractively, in the same style); he used few words and had no small talk. Always known as Hugo, he was friendly and easily accessible, treated all as his equals, and was generous in praise where he thought it due; the development of social and economic study of the ancient world at Cambridge owed much to his example and encouragement. In private affairs one could turn to him for kind and judicious advice.

Shortly before his retirement was due, Jones died suddenly on a sea crossing from Brindisi to Patras on 9 April 1970. He had previously been subject to various illnesses, but they hardly disturbed the copious flow of his publications. He was survived by his wife, two sons, and a daughter.   P. A. BRUNT

Sources J. Crook, 'Arnold Hugh Martin Jones, 1904–1970', *PBA*, 57 (1971), 425–38 · private information (1981) · personal knowledge (2004) · *CGPLA Eng. & Wales* (1970) · *WWW*
Likenesses W. Stoneman, photograph, 1951, NPG [*see illus.*] · photograph, repro. in Crook, 'Arnold Hugh Martin Jones' (1971)
Wealth at death £42,761: probate, 10 Sept 1970, *CGPLA Eng. & Wales*

Jones, Arthur Creech (1891–1964), politician, was born at 11 Arthur Street, Redfield, St George, Bristol, on 15 May 1891, the second of the three sons of Joseph Jones, journeyman lithographic printer, and his wife, Rosina Sweet. Until 1905 he attended Whitehall Boys' School, winning a scholarship which enabled him to study French, mathematics, and commercial subjects for an extra year. For another year he worked in a solicitor's office while preparing for the civil service junior clerks' examination. As plain Arthur Jones he followed a respectable but dull career as a minor civil servant in the War Office and the crown agents' office until 1916. Later he used his second name as well and became known to all but his closest friends as Creech Jones.

Evening classes made Creech Jones question the teaching of the Methodist church, though he remained a subscribing member until 1912. Through lectures he organized from 1910 for the Liberal Christian League's study group, he met leading radical churchmen and politicians. He fulfilled the league's membership pledge to undertake social service by helping to found the Camberwell trades and labour council in 1913 and the Dulwich branch of the Independent Labour Party (ILP) and acting as their honorary secretary. Ultimately finding certain tenets of the nonconformist church unsupportable, he became a humanist and international socialist. For the ILP he organized anti-conscription meetings throughout London, joining both the South London Federal Council against Conscription and the No-Conscription Fellowship.

As an absolutist conscientious objector Creech Jones was imprisoned from September 1916 to April 1919.

Arthur Creech Jones (1891–1964), by Bassano, 1946

Imprisonment was particularly hard for him to bear, as rambling and sketching were his chief relaxations. However, he read history, politics, and economics as determinedly and widely as possible in the circumstances, and emerged with greater understanding of his own character, abilities, and vocation. By then he was acquainted with several rising men in the post-war Labour Party. On 23 July 1920 he married Violet May (d. 1975), younger daughter of Joseph Sidney Tidman, a second cousin, with whose family in Goose Green, Camberwell, he had lodged since 1907.

Debarred from returning to the civil service, on his release Creech Jones did some work on prisons for the Labour Party research department and was soon appointed secretary of the National Union of Docks, Wharves, and Shipping Staffs and editor of its journal, *Quayside and Office*. On the union's amalgamation with the Transport and General Workers' Union (TGWU) in 1922 he was promoted national secretary of the administrative, clerical, and supervisory section, an ideal position for him. The TGWU sent him to the Ruhr with Ben Tillett and Samuel Warren in 1923 to report on the effect of French occupation on the workers.

Although Creech Jones had long been interested in the theory of colonial rule, his first practical contact with African problems was in 1926 when he was asked to instruct Clements Kadalie, general secretary of the black South African Industrial and Commercial Workers' Union, on trade union organization. In 1928 the Workers' Educational Association published his handbook, *Trade Unionism To-Day*, which was much used in the colonies.

After unsuccessfully contesting the Heywood and Radcliffe parliamentary constituency in Lancashire in 1929, Creech Jones left the union to become organizing secretary of the Workers' Travel Association (WTA), on the management committee of which he had served since its inception in 1921. Always an ardent traveller, by 1939 he had visited Palestine and most countries in Europe and written about his experiences in the association's journal, the *Travel Log*. Through the WTA he directed the emergency rescue of hundreds of Czechoslovakian socialists and Jews by train, ship, and aeroplane from Prague after Chamberlain signed the Munich agreement.

Because of Ramsay MacDonald's assumption of leadership of the National Government in 1931, Creech Jones joined his friend Ernest Bevin, G. D. H. Cole, and Harold Laski in setting up a new political party, the Socialist League. Like Bevin's, his association with it was very brief; instead he transferred from the ILP to the Labour Party. Nevertheless, he became an active member of Cole's New Fabian Research Bureau for the promotion of radical political and institutional reforms, while remaining a member of the original Fabian Society. For a while he refused to contemplate a parliamentary career but events in Germany convinced him he should again stand for parliament and in 1935 he was elected member for the Shipley division of Yorkshire. The Parliamentary Labour Party recognized his interest in colonial affairs by co-opting him to its advisory committee on imperial questions, of which he became chairman in 1943, and nominating him to the Colonial Office advisory committee on education in the colonies. This enabled him to make an important, continuous contribution to the formation of the party's colonial policy. In 1937 he was a founder member of the Trades Union Congress colonial affairs committee, for which he had long campaigned. There were then no official Labour Party spokesmen on specific subjects, yet multifarious problems from every part of the empire were submitted to him to bring to the notice of parliament, the British public, the trade union movement, and the Labour Party. His diligence, energy, enthusiasm, and persistence established him as an acknowledged expert in colonial affairs; his warm friendliness, approachability, and 'colour-blindness' brought him the trust and affection of colonial peoples.

Meticulous attention to detail enabled Creech Jones, where others had failed, to pilot through parliament, as a private member's bill, the Access to Mountains Act in 1939—a cause very dear to his heart as an executive member of the Ramblers and the Youth Hostels associations. From May 1940 to June 1944 Creech Jones was parliamentary private secretary to Ernest Bevin; in the Ministry of Labour he worked for the interests of conscientious objectors, immigrant labourers, the disabled, and for the education and vocational training of the armed forces. In 1940, with Dr Rita Hinden, Creech Jones founded the Fabian Colonial Bureau; on their fact finding and research

from 1943 the Labour Party based much of its policy for post-war action. He paid his first visit to colonial territories that same year as vice-chairman under Walter Elliot of the commission on higher education for west Africa.

In August 1945 Creech Jones entered the Colonial Office, where he served as parliamentary under-secretary of state from October and later as secretary of state for the colonies until his narrow defeat in the general election of 1950. He did a great deal to reorganize the Colonial Office and to reshape the colonial service in order to meet the changed and increasing needs of the colonial peoples, founding the Colonial Development Corporation and fostering colonial research projects. He paid several visits to the colonies and represented Britain at the United Nations during the debates on the cession of the Palestine mandate in 1946 and 1947–8. In preparing British dependencies for political independence Creech Jones was deeply involved in reforming their constitutions and promoting their economic and social development. His memorandum on local government issued in 1948 confirmed the government's intention gradually to transform indirect rule to responsible government. Ceylon was the first colony with a non-European population to achieve independence. Creech Jones presided over the Montego Bay conference on West Indian federation in 1947 and over the first African conference at Lancaster House in 1948.

Creech Jones consistently maintained that adult education was a necessary preliminary to self-government and encouraged the development of mass education in the colonies through films, broadcasts, and education schemes run by trade unions and co-operatives. Adult education in Britain had always been one of his prime concerns since he himself had benefited so much from it. He was a governor of Ruskin College (1923–56) and from 1954 also of Queen Elizabeth House, the Institute of Commonwealth Studies in Oxford where groups of mature students from Britain and the dependencies could take specific courses of study relevant to their work. He was also a vice-president of the Workers' Educational Association and a vice-chairman of the British Institute of Adult Education.

While out of parliament (1950–54), Creech Jones worked for the Commonwealth by writing, lecturing, chairing conferences for the Fabian Colonial Bureau, editing *Fabian Colonial Essays* which defined its principles for colonial policy, acting as chairman and delegate for the British Council of Pacific Relations, and leading deputations to ministers from the Anti-Slavery Society and the Africa Bureau. Through the two bureaux he steadfastly opposed the federation of British central Africa, helped reconcile Tshekedi and Seretse Khama, and supported their petition to the government to rescind their exile.

Defeated in Romford, Essex, in the 1951 general election, Creech Jones won a by-election at Wakefield, Yorkshire, in 1954 and represented it until ill health forced him to resign in August 1964. His efforts to promote international responsibility for developing countries and international understanding in colonial affairs involved many visits to Commonwealth countries as a delegate of the Commonwealth Parliamentary Association.

Creech Jones was unimpressive in appearance; he was not a brilliant or witty speaker; but he was one whom the House of Commons greatly respected for his knowledge, integrity, and sincerity. He was sworn of the privy council in 1946. He died at the Lambeth Hospital, Kennington, London, on 23 October 1964 and was cremated at Golders Green crematorium on 28 October.

PATRICIA M. PUGH

Sources Bodl. RH, Creech Jones MSS, MS Brit. Emp.s.332 · Bodl. RH, Fabian Colonial Bureau MSS, MS Brit. Emp.s.365 · PRO, Colonial Office MSS · Bodl. RH, Africa Bureau MSS, MSS Afr.s.1681, 1712–14 · BLPES, Fabian Society MSS · London, Workers' Travel Association MSS · London, Workers' Education Association MSS · London, Labour party MSS · London, Trades Union Congress MSS · Nuffield Oxf., G. D. H. Cole MSS · Fabian Society [various pubns, incl. *Empire / Venture*] · Hull Central Library, Winifred Holtby papers · private information (1981)
Archives Bodl. RH, corresp., notes, and papers | Bodl. RH, Anti-Slavery Society MSS · Bodl. RH, corresp. relating to Africa Bureau · Bodl. RH, corresp. with Margery Perham and related papers · Hull Central Library, corresp. with Winifred Holtby · Mitchell L., Glas., corresp. with G. A. Aldred · PRO, Cabinet, Colonial Office, Dominions Office records · U. Sussex Library, Leonard Woolf MSS, Workers' Travel Association and Workers' Educational Association papers and publications | FILM BFI NFTVA, Daybreak Over Udi, Crown Film Unit 1949 and 1952
Likenesses W. Stoneman, photograph, 1945, NPG · Bassano, photograph, 1946, NPG [*see illus.*] · Sallon, portrait, 1948 · Sallon, portrait, 1948, west Africa · Gabriel, portrait, repro. in *Daily Worker* (18 March 1948) · I. Gall, cartoons, repro. in *News of the World* (29 June 1947) · Giles, portrait, repro. in *Daily Express* (16 Aug 1949) · Illingworth, portrait, repro. in *Punch*, 13 (1948) · O. Lancaster, portrait, repro. in *Daily Express* · Low, portrait, repro. in *Manchester Guardian* (25 July 1947) · Low, portrait, repro. in *Evening Standard* (17 Oct 1947) · Low, portrait, repro. in *Evening Standard* (12 March 1948) · Low, portrait, repro. in *Evening Standard* (6 Dec 1949) · Low, portrait, repro. in *Evening Standard* (18 Feb 1949) · Vicky, portrait, repro. in *News Chronicle* (28 March 1948) · Vicky, portrait, repro. in *News Chronicle* (16 Feb 1949) · Vicky, portrait, repro. in *News Chronicle* (10 March 1949) · Vicky, portrait, repro. in *Daily News* (16 Feb 1949) · S. Wolkowicki, portrait, repro. in *The Sketch* (14 Sept 1949) · photograph, repro. in *The Times* (23 March 1946) · photograph, repro. in *The Sketch* (23 March 1946) · photographs, Bodl. RH, Creech Jones MSS · photographs, repro. in *Illustrated* (5 April 1947)
Wealth at death £2210: administration, 12 Jan 1965, CGPLA Eng. & Wales

Jones [married name Brooke], **Avonia** (1836–1867), actress, the daughter of George Jones (who styled himself Count Joannes) and his wife, Melinda, was born according to her own account on 12 July 1836, in Richmond, Virginia. Her forename apparently commemorated an oration given by her father at Stratford upon Avon on the occasion of Shakespeare's birthday.

Avonia Jones's first appearance on the stage was at the People's Theatre, Cincinnati, in 1856, when she played Parthenia in Maria Lovell's *Ingomar* for the benefit of E. L. Davenport. She visited Australia in 1859, and performed at the Princess's, Spring Gardens, Melbourne, on 31 October; she remained in Australia until 1861, acting with Gustavus Vaughan *Brooke (1818–1866). She then went to England, making her début there at the Theatre Royal, Manchester, on 7 June. Her first London appearance was as Medea at

Drury Lane on 5 November 1861, in an adaptation of Legouvé's play. In 1862–3 she was at the Adelphi, where she took the title roles in *Janet Pride* and *Adrienne Lecouvreur*.

On 23 February 1863 Jones married G. V. Brooke at St Philip's Church, Liverpool; from this time she was deeply involved in his disastrous financial affairs and in futile attempts to refute gossip about his drunkenness. In 1864 she went to New York, where she played in *Romeo and Juliet* with Edwin Booth. On her return to England in 1865 she played Lady Isabel in *East Lynne* at the Surrey, and then went on a tour of the provinces, where her roles included Leah and the heroine of an adaptation of Charles Reade's *Griffith Gaunt* in Manchester. Her engagements prevented her accompanying her husband as he fled his creditors in January 1866. He was drowned when the ship on which he was travelling foundered, and his last message to his wife was washed up on Brighton beach in a bottle in March 1866. In October of that year she was performing in Dublin. She died from consumption a year later, on 4 October 1867, at her father's residence, 2 Bond Street, New York, and was buried in the Mount Auburn cemetery, Boston.

Avonia Jones was a 'moderate and rather statuesque' actress, with some capacity for tragedy, but her musical voice was marred by artificiality.

JOSEPH KNIGHT, rev. J. GILLILAND

Sources W. J. Lawrence, *Life of G. V. Brooke* (1892) · H. Morley, *The journal of a London playgoer from 1851 to 1866* (1866) · *The life and reminiscences of E. L. Blanchard, with notes from the diary of Wm. Blanchard*, ed. C. W. Scott and C. Howard, 2 vols. (1891) · Boase, *Mod. Eng. biog.* · Hall, *Dramatic ports.* · personal knowledge (1891) · *New York Clipper* (26 Oct 1867)
Likenesses portrait, repro. in *Illustrated Sporting News*, 145 (1866) · prints, Harvard TC · three portraits, Harvard TC

Jones, (William) Basil (1822–1897), bishop of St David's, was born on 2 January 1822 at Cheltenham, the only son of William Tilsley Jones (1782–1861) of Gwynfryn, Llangynfelyn, Cardiganshire, and his first wife, Jane (d. 1822), daughter of Henry Tickell of Leytonstone, Essex. Basil Jones's father remarried in 1826, and he and his wife had a son and two daughters. William Tilsley Jones was high sheriff of Cardiganshire in 1838. The future bishop was baptized at Llangynfelyn church on 18 August 1822, when he was named William Basil, but at times later in his life he was known as William Basil Tickell Jones.

After attending schools at Taliesin, near Llangynfelyn, and at Aberystwyth, Jones entered Shrewsbury School in 1834, and he was head boy there in his final year. In 1840 he gained a classical scholarship at Trinity College, Oxford, and in 1842 he won the Ireland university scholarship, defeating his friend, the future historian Edward A. Freeman. He took a second class in *literae humaniores* in 1844. In 1848 he was elected to a Michel fellowship at the Queen's College, exchanging it for a fellowship at University College in 1851. In 1854 he became assistant tutor and bursar of University College, and in 1858 he was appointed to a lectureship in modern history and classics. Jones was master of the schools in 1848 and senior proctor in 1861–2.

On 10 September 1856 Jones married Frances Charlotte (*d.* 1881), second daughter of the Revd Samuel Holworthy of Croxall, Derbyshire. During his years at Oxford he published *Vestiges of the Gael in Gwynedd* (1851), *Christ College, Brecon, its History and Capabilities Considered with Reference to a Measure now before Parliament* (1853), *The History and Antiquities of St. David's* (jointly with E. A. Freeman, 1856), *Notes on the Oedipus Tyrannus of Sophocles, Adapted to the Text of Dindorf* (1862), *The Clergyman's Office* (1864), and *The New Testament … Illustrated by a Plain Explanatory Comment* (jointly with E. Churton, 1865). He was a member of the Cambrian Archaeological Association almost from its inception, attending every meeting between 1849 and 1854 and serving as secretary between 1849 and 1851. Later in life he was president of the association in 1875 and 1878.

Jones was made deacon in 1848 and ordained priest in 1853. In 1859 he was appointed to a stall, which he retained until 1865, in St David's Cathedral by Bishop Connop Thirlwall, but more important clerical patronage came from William Thomson, himself, like Jones, a former pupil of Shrewsbury School, and tutor, chaplain, dean, and provost (1855–61) of the Queen's College, Oxford. Late in 1861 Thomson was nominated to the bishopric of Gloucester and Bristol, and at once he appointed Jones to be an examining chaplain. Early in 1863 Thomson was translated to the see of York, and in that same year he presented Jones to the perpetual curacy of Haxby, near York, and also to the prebend of Grindal in York Minster. Two years later Archbishop Thomson collated Jones to the parish of Bishopthorpe, in which the archbishop's palace was situated. Jones now moved from Oxford to Yorkshire. Further promotions soon followed. In 1867 he was appointed archdeacon of York, in 1869 rural dean of Bishopthorpe, in 1871 chancellor of York Minster and prebend of Laughton-en-le-Morthen, and in 1873 canon residentiary of York Minster and rural dean of the city of York. He published several sermons between 1866 and 1869.

In 1874 Disraeli nominated Jones to the see of St David's, vacant by the resignation of Thirlwall. His family links with the diocese and his own significant publication on the history of the cathedral and the diocese made this a very suitable appointment. He spoke Welsh, although not fluently. He was consecrated on 24 August 1874 and enthroned on 15 September. On 27 October he was awarded a DD at Lambeth by Archbishop Tait.

Jones took his seat in the House of Lords in 1878, and then, as junior bishop, he served as chaplain of the house until December 1882. This involved him in being in London for about six months in every year. Once he was no longer junior bishop, he seldom attended the House of Lords, but worked as 'an excellent stay-at-home bishop' (*The Times*, 15 Jan 1897) in his diocese, which covered Brecknockshire, Cardiganshire, Carmarthenshire, and Pembrokeshire, together with almost the whole of Radnorshire and a sizeable part of Glamorgan around the expanding town of Swansea. There was some discussion of dividing the diocese, but nothing was achieved in Basil Jones's time, although a suffragan bishop, taking his title

from Swansea, was nominated in 1890 to assist with episcopal duties, especially confirmation, in what was then the largest Anglican diocese in area in England and Wales.

Jones's immediate predecessors in the see had initiated reforms, and Jones continued their work, notably in spiritual, pastoral, and educational fields, and, most obviously, in the administration of the diocese. He established a diocesan conference in 1881 to encourage a sense of diocesan unity in this 'difficult and scattered diocese', and by 1897 there were twenty-one diocesan committees, boards, and societies reporting to the diocesan conference.

The diocese of St David's had an unenviable record for clerical non-residence in the early nineteenth century. Even in 1850 almost one-half of the incumbents were absentees. Bishop Thirlwall had donated a considerable proportion of his official income to the building of parsonages, and Bishop Jones also made this a priority, so that non-residence was almost entirely eliminated throughout the diocese in the early years of his episcopate. Bishop Jones also raised the standard required for ordination, and his enthusiastic support for retreats and parochial missions did much to raise the spiritual state of many parishes. Clerical stipends were increased, largely thanks to the establishment of the David's Diocesan Fund, and Basil Jones knew every incumbent in the diocese. He increased the number of confirmation services. In 1877 there were 924 candidates for confirmation. By 1896 the number had risen to 3100.

Jones's episcopate saw a remarkable growth in the number of churches built, rebuilt, and restored. Bishop Thirlwall had consecrated on average one new church a year during his time as bishop of St David's; Bishop Jones consecrated three a year, many of them being in the region of Swansea. As an authority on church buildings, he took a detailed interest in architectural proposals, making the point, for example, in the parish of Betws Bledrws that the new porch should not be made of wood because of the heavy rainfall in the area. The restoration of the cathedral was one of his greatest concerns. Bishop Jones was a moderate evangelical in churchmanship, content to regard many liturgical practices as things indifferent, but he confessed privately that he liked a few ritualists in the diocese, since they added colour. He established good working relationships with nonconformist leaders, and his willingness to accept the Burials Act of 1880, which permitted nonconformist ministers to conduct burials in parish churchyards, meant that there was little friction over this sensitive matter within his diocese.

As bishop of St David's, Basil Jones was visitor of St David's College, Lampeter, and he became chairman of the governors of Christ College, Brecon, in 1880. He took his duties seriously, especially in the former institution, which stood in need of considerable administrative and constitutional reform. In 1879 he provided Lampeter with a complete code of statutes and he was involved in gaining the college a new charter in 1896. He had a high regard for Llandovery College, and he founded a girls' high school in Carmarthen. Trinity College in that town, an institution for training teachers, received his strong support, and he was a keen proponent of Christian education in board schools.

Bishop Jones's gifts lay in administration rather than in controversy, and he took little part in the struggle against the disestablishment of the Church of England in Wales. He is remembered for his observation that Wales was neither geographically nor politically distinct from England. There was, as far as he was concerned, no more ethnic division between England and Wales than there was between the highlands and lowlands of Scotland.

Frances Jones died childless in 1881, and on 2 December 1886, Jones married Anne (d. 1902), fifth daughter of George Loxdale of Aigburth, Liverpool. They had a son and two daughters. After a long illness, and as he was preparing to resign from the see, the bishop died of heart failure at his residence, Abergwili Palace, on 14 January 1897. He was buried at Llangynfelyn parish church on 20 January.

Basil Jones was seen by contemporaries as a man of 'moderation, shrewdness, and good sense' (The Times, 15 Jan 1897). He was a 'small, delicate, nervous man, but with a dry wit and keen sense of humour' (Vaughan, 116), though he could appear rather cold and aloof in public. He maintained his interest in archaeology to the end, and it was wholly appropriate that the restoration of the roofless lady chapel of St David's Cathedral should be the memorial to Bishop Basil Jones and two deans. A selection of his ordination addresses, with a preface by Gregory Smith, was published in 1900.   D. T. W. PRICE

Sources The Times (15 Jan 1897) · Western Mail [Cardiff] (15 Jan 1897) · Annual Register (1897), 137–8 · Crockford (1895) · Archaeologia Cambrensis, 5th ser., 15 (1898), 88–9 · Debrett's Peerage (1896) · Burke, Gen. GB (1914) · T. Nicholas, Annals and antiquities of the counties and county families of Wales, 1 (1872), 198–9 · H. M. Vaughan, The south Wales squires (1926), 115–18, 203 · J. V. Morgan, Welsh political and educational leaders in the Victorian era (1908), 149–56 · CGPLA Eng. & Wales (1897)

Archives BL, letters to W. E. Gladstone, Add. MSS 44478–44479 · LPL, corresp. with Archbishop Benson · LPL, letters to A. C. Tait · NL Wales, Gwynfryn deeds

Likenesses E. U. Eddis, oils, 1882, priv. coll. · Messrs Bassano of Old Bond Street, photograph, repro. in Archaeologia Cambrensis, facing p. 88 · Messrs Spurrell & Son, Carmarthen, photograph, repro. in Morgan, Welsh political and educational leaders · photograph, NPG

Wealth at death £6652 11s. 10d.: resworn probate, June 1897, CGPLA Eng. & Wales

Jones, Basset. See Jhones, Basset (b. 1613/14).

Jones, Benjamin (1847–1942), co-operative movement activist and manager, was born on 9 September 1847 in Salford, Lancashire, the son of Reuben Jones, a dyer's labourer, and Mary, née Brazier, who worked as a power-loom weaver. Jones entered employment at the age of nine, working as an errand-boy and bookkeeper before joining the Co-operative Wholesale Society (CWS) in 1866. Jones was successively assistant bookkeeper, bookkeeper, assistant salesman, departmental manager, and assistant buyer of butter and cheese for the CWS in Manchester. In 1870 he married Annie White (d. 1894) at Altrincham.

Jones was chosen to establish the London branch of the CWS which opened in March 1874, directing the first enduring co-operative wholesaler to serve southern England. By his retirement in 1902 the London branch had an annual turnover of £3.25 million. Jones also oversaw CWS extension, establishing sales depots at Bristol, Cardiff, and Northampton, new productive capacity through, among others, the Silvertown flour mill and the Luton cocoa works, and overseas depots providing supplies including Danish bacon and Spanish dried fruit. Such was his success that at least one private company attempted to poach Jones away from the CWS.

The establishment of a wholesaler in London assisted co-operative growth in southern England. However, previous weakness was not immediately overcome and Jones was involved in supporting aspiring societies through the Co-operative Union. From 1874 until 1894 he was secretary to its southern sectional board and was a central board member from 1875. Jones was also the first secretary of the Guild of Co-operators, formed to stimulate propagandism in southern England. Jones's interest in producers' co-operation is reflected in his book Co-Operative Production (1894). He was also secretary to the Co-operative Aid Association, formed to promote producers' societies, and chaired the board of the London branch of the Co-operative Printing Society. Jones disagreed, however, with Christian socialists among the southern co-operative leadership in doubting the viability of independent producers' societies, successfully advocating instead production by federal wholesale societies on behalf of consumers.

Jones supported many other co-operative causes. He founded the Blackley and Harpurhey Co-operative Building Society in 1872 and a later housing society, the London Tenant Co-operators' Society of 1888. In 1884 Jones spoke for co-operation before the royal commission on the housing of the working class and again in 1887 to the town holdings select committee. He also encouraged the development of the Women's Co-operative Guild, in which his wife was involved until her death. In 1889 and 1896 Jones presided at the national Co-operative Congress. He also represented the co-operative movement abroad, including on a world tour in 1896.

An advocate of co-operative education, during the 1860s Jones continued his own schooling with evening classes at Owens College and the mechanics' institute in Manchester. He subsequently served on the education committee of the Blackley Co-operative Society and was a Sunday school teacher at the ragged school in Harpurhey. Following discussion at the 1882 Co-operative Congress, Jones, with the academics Arnold Toynbee and A. H. D. Acland, planned a programme of instruction in co-operative principles. This was used at a class taught by Jones in London and was presented to the 1883 congress which established the education committee of the Co-operative Union. Jones also wrote Working Men Co-Operators (1884), with Acland, as a textbook for co-operative classes. He later assisted Beatrice Webb with research for her book The Co-Operative Movement in Great Britain (1891), greatly influencing her thinking about co-operation.

Jones pursued wider educational interests as a member of the London Playing Fields Committee and the school board for London, and he was also involved with evening class provision and was chairman of a working men's club. His interests extended into the political arena. In 1876 he was a member of the Labour Representation League and while living in Norwood became involved in local radical politics, including the establishment of the Norwood Reform Club. Jones was also the first secretary to the parliamentary committee of the Co-operative Union. He supported co-operative representation in parliament and himself stood unsuccessfully for Labour at Woolwich in 1892 and 1895 and as a Lib–Lab candidate at Deptford in 1900.

Jones retired to Bournemouth where he owned the Queen Hotel, several cafés, and a bakery. He died on 25 February 1942 at Bensholme Tuckton, Bournemouth, and was buried at the north cemetery of the crematorium, Bournemouth, on 2 March 1942. His wife predeceased him in 1894, but he was survived by his four children. Jones was a vigorous advocate of co-operative federalism, and his pragmatic view of co-operation shaped its development, particularly in southern England, during an important phase of growth in the 1880s and 1890s.

MARTIN PURVIS

Sources [H. C. Jones], *Ben Jones, a great co-operator: his life, according to his son* [n.d., 1947?] · *Handbook for the 28th annual Co-operative Congress of 1896, Woolwich* (1896) · *Co-operative News* (7 March 1942) · P. N. Backstrom, *Christian socialism and co-operation in Victorian England: Edward Vansittart Neale and the co-operative movement* (1974) · A. Bonner, *British co-operation: the history, principles, and organisation of the British co-operative movement*, rev. edn (1970) · *DLB* · F. Hall and W. P. Watkins, *Co-operation: a survey of the history, principles, and organisation of the co-operative movement in Great Britain and Ireland* (1934) · B. Potter, *The co-operative movement in Great Britain* (1891) · 'Abstract return to the registrars of friendly societies', *Parl. papers* (1873), 61.349, no. 217 [industrial and provident societies] · *CGPLA Eng. & Wales* (1942)
Likenesses group photograph, 1875 (CWS London Branch Committee), repro. in P. Redfern, *The story of the CWS* [1913], facing p. 97 · photograph, 1895, repro. in *Handbook for the 28th annual Co-operative Congress of 1896*, 4 · photograph, 1931, repro. in Jones, *Ben Jones*, frontispiece
Wealth at death £10,011 5s. 1d.: probate, 17 June 1942, *CGPLA Eng. & Wales*

Jones, Bernard Mouat (1882–1953), chemist and university administrator, was born in Streatham on 27 November 1882, the fourth son of Alexander Mouat Jones, wine merchant, and his wife, Martha Eleanor Brinjes. He was educated at Queen's College, Streatham (1890–95), and at Dulwich College (1895–1901). In 1901 he went to Balliol College, Oxford, with a Brackenbury scholarship; in 1904 he gained first-class honours in chemistry, mineralogy, and crystallography. He worked for a year as research assistant to Professor W. R. Dunstan at the Imperial Institute, and was then, in 1906, appointed professor of chemistry at Government College, Lahore. In 1913 he returned to England as assistant professor at the Imperial College of Science and Technology.

In 1914 Mouat Jones enlisted in the London Scottish regiment as a private and was sent to France. Immediately after the first German gas attack in 1915 he was promoted to captain and became assistant director of the central laboratory, general headquarters, formed to organize defensive measures. Most of the problems were chemical, and Mouat Jones was usually able to solve them. He devised methods of protection from phosgene gas, and developed an almost uncanny skill in identifying quickly any new gas used by the enemy; he was the first to identify the chemical in mustard gas (dicholorodiethyl sulphide). For his services he was appointed DSO in 1917, was three times mentioned in dispatches, and in 1918 became director of the laboratory with the rank of lieutenant-colonel.

In 1919 Mouat Jones returned to civilian life as professor of chemistry and director of the Edward Davies Laboratory at the University College of Wales, Aberystwyth. Facing the post-war influx of students with scant resources, he soon had a lively department thanks to his witty and stimulating lectures and his energetic action to secure equipment. During this time he edited and revised the sixth edition (1923) of Roscoe and Schorlemmer's *A Treatise on Chemistry*, and carried out research in physical chemistry and the chemistry of minerals. He published several papers on these subjects in the *Journal of the Chemical Society*, the *Mineralogical Magazine*, and the *Proceedings of the Royal Society*.

In 1921 Mouat Jones became principal of the Manchester College of Technology, where his great administrative talent was revealed. It was a difficult post to fill since most of the day work of the college constituted the university's faculty of technology, whereas its general administration and finances came under the Manchester education committee and the city council. There was obviously the possibility of friction and misunderstanding; Mouat Jones, by securing the trust and confidence of both sides, reduced it to a negligible minimum. No doubt he was fortunate in that Sir Henry Miers, under whom he had worked as an undergraduate, was vice-chancellor of the university until 1926.

Mouat Jones brought about a much wider appreciation of the true status of the Manchester College as a centre of higher technical education when he won the interest and co-operation of industry, which took tangible shape in the form of scholarships and prizes. During years of continuous development, his influence was seen in many ways: the degree course in chemical engineering; the conferring of honorary associateship on distinguished scientists and technologists; and the new lecture hall, the Reynolds Hall, which served to bring the scientific societies of the district into closer contact with the college. Within the college he built up a wonderful spirit by bringing together staff and students through sports clubs and social activities. At the same time he took an active part in developing technical education in the district. He was president of a number of bodies, including the Manchester Literary and Philosophical Society (1931–3) and the Association of Principals of Technical Institutions (1932–3).

In 1938 Mouat Jones became the fourth vice-chancellor of Leeds University and the first scientist to hold that office. At the outbreak of war the following year he joined the local Home Guard, later becoming its gas officer, and for six months in 1941 he was chief superintendent of the chemical warfare research station at Porton. During the years of reconstruction after the war the university owed much to his leadership. His outlook was essentially empirical; he was more interested in meeting immediate needs than in probing the function and purpose of a modern civic university. He improved the relations between industry and academia, and secured a number of industrial endowments for the university between 1945 and 1948. Under his imperturbable chairmanship of the senate and council, and his good personal relations with the faculty, the university gained a sense of self-confidence and tranquillity. Mouat Jones was responsible for a far-reaching development plan, which resulted in academic expansion, new halls of residence, and the completion of the union. He retired in 1948, and gave the testimonial fund raised for him as an endowment for bursaries for foreign travel, which he considered an essential part of a student's education.

Part of Mouat Jones's success came from his brilliance as a speaker and raconteur. He had a remarkable flair for graceful compliment and witty turns of phrase. Although naturally reserved, he was able to use wit to point a lesson where a homily would have failed. For his services to education he received honorary degrees from the universities of Durham, Leeds, and Wales. His early experience in India made him a valuable member of a number of government committees, among them the advisory committee on education in the colonies, the Makerere–Khartoum education commission (1937), and the commission on higher education in west Africa (1944–5).

After his retirement Mouat Jones lived at Waverley Abbey House, Farnham, Surrey, where he died on 11 September 1953. He was unmarried and after a number of bequests he left the residue of his estate equally between Balliol College and Leeds University. His funeral was held at Farnham parish church on 17 September 1953.

HAROLD HARTLEY, rev. K. D. WATSON

Sources *Manchester Guardian* (16 Sept 1953), 3 · *The Times* (15 Sept 1953), 8e · *The Times* (18 Sept 1953), 10 · *The Times* (26 Nov 1953), 10e · O. Rhys Howell, *JCS* (1955), 1638–9 · W. E. Morton, 'Dr B. Mouat Jones', *Nature*, 172 (1953), 749 · *WWW* · I. Elliott, ed., *The Balliol College register, 1833–1933*, 2nd edn (privately printed, Oxford, 1934) · L. F. Haber, *The poisonous cloud: chemical warfare in the First World War* (1986) · T. L. Ormiston, *Dulwich College register, 1619 to 1926* (1926)
Archives PRO, Ministry of Munitions records · PRO, War Office records
Likenesses H. Carr, oils, 1945, U. Leeds
Wealth at death £26,265 3s. 8d.: probate, 12 Nov 1953, *CGPLA Eng. & Wales*

Jones, (Lewis) Brian Hopkin (1942–1969), musician, was born on 28 February 1942 at the Park Nursing Home, Cheltenham, Gloucestershire, the eldest of the three children of Lewis Blount Jones, an aircraft designer, and his wife, Louisa Beatrice, née Simmonds, a piano teacher. He was a member of the original Rolling Stones line-up, playing on most of their classic 1960s recordings and furthering their teen appeal as the 'pretty boy' of the band. Jones was educated at the Dean Close junior school and Pates Grammar

(Lewis) **Brian Hopkin Jones** (1942–1969), by Jan Olofsson

School in Cheltenham. He was academically bright, as well as proficient in playing the saxophone, harmonica, clarinet, guitar, and piano. Early in his musical career he played 'trad jazz' with the Cheltone Six, and rhythm and blues with the Ramrods. After leaving school he worked in a number of jobs without enthusiasm, including junior architect, bus conductor, and coal deliverer. A significant meeting was with the musician Alexis Korner, who encouraged Jones to move to London in 1962. Shortly after that Mick Jagger and Keith Richards spotted Jones playing blues slide guitar in a club, and were impressed by the young man's musical prowess.

Jones was shy, slightly narcissistic, softly spoken, and with a strong sense of fashion that helped to define the slightly foppish elegance of the quintessential mid-1960s English rock star. Friends have described Jones as psychologically troubled even before his success in the music business, and Jagger has at times characterized Jones as too sensitive to be in the pop world. Jones was certainly sensitive to the spirit of the times, and soon acquainted himself with Jimi Hendrix, Bob Dylan, and other rock luminaries. By 1967 he was a celebrity, introducing Hendrix on stage at the Monterey pop festival, and subject to several prosecutions for drug possession.

The Stones recorded their first record in 1963, a cover of Chuck Berry's 'Come On'. In the early years it was Jones who was very much the self-appointed musical leader of the group, contributing slide guitar parts influenced by Elmore James and blues harp-playing to give the Stones' initial recordings more authenticity. His broader musical interests did much to widen the band's basic blues–rhythm and blues axis and enable them to progress. The 1966 'Paint it Black' single featured a sitar line from Jones, who was ever conscious of the need for the Stones to keep up with the experiments of their arch-rivals, the Beatles. He added marimba to 'Under my Thumb' and dulcimer to 'Lady Jane'. Such multi-instrumental touches gave significant colour to the sequence of brilliant singles the Stones released between 1965 and 1968, and the albums *Between the Buttons* (1967), *Their Satanic Majesties Request* (1968), and *Beggar's Banquet* (1969). Guitars associated with Jones include the Vox Mk VI teardrop-shape and the Gibson Firebird.

Along with George Harrison and Jimmy Page, Jones deserves credit for introducing into Western popular music the first glimmerings of sensitivity to other musical traditions. He was fascinated by Moroccan music, just as Harrison drew on Indian music, in an era when 'world music' had not been invented. He recorded *Pipes of Pan at Joujouka* and a film score for Volker Schlondorff's *A Degree of Murder*. Unfortunately personal problems, an increasing drug intake, and unreliability led to tensions between Jones and the other members of the group, who distanced themselves from him. Matters were not improved when Anita Pallenberg, the German actress with whom Jones had been involved in a tempestuous relationship since 1965, left him for Keith Richards in May 1968. He was given the sack early in 1969. Supposedly his drug convictions were preventing the band from touring America, and he was replaced in the Stones by the guitarist Mick Taylor.

Jones died at his home, Cotchford Farm, Hartfield, Sussex, on 3 July 1969, apparently by drowning in his swimming pool 'whilst under the influence of alcohol and drugs' (d. cert.): the coroner's verdict was misadventure.

Jones's premature death was the first of a series (Jimi Hendrix, Janis Joplin, Jim Morrison) which silenced a number of 1960s rock icons between 1969 and 1971. Jagger read an extract from Shelley's 'Adonais' at a free concert at Hyde Park on 5 July, which turned into a requiem for Jones, who was buried at Cheltenham on 11 July. Although portrayed by the establishment of the day as an act of self-destruction typical of rock-star excess, Jones's drowning was always regarded by many as suspicious. New leads in the case were followed up in the 1990s after an apparent deathbed confession from a builder who was working on Jones's home. The mystery surrounding Jones's death is dealt with in detail in Terry Rawlings's *Who Killed Christopher Robin?* (1994) and Laura Jackson's *Golden Stone* (1992).

RIKKY ROOKSBY

Sources R. Chapman, 'The bittersweet symphony', *Mojo*, 68 (July 1999), 62–84 • T. Rawlings, *Who killed Christopher Robin?* (1994) • L. Jackson, *Golden stone* (1992) • b. cert. • d. cert. • *The Times* (4 July 1969) • 'Brian Jones: like a rolling stone', home.earthlink. net/~hobhead, Feb 2001 • R. Weingartner, 'A tribute to Brian Jones', www.angelfire.com/ny/JonesStones, Feb 2001
Archives FILM BFI NFTVA, performance footage | SOUND BL NSA, documentary recordings • BL NSA, oral history interview • BL NSA, performance recording

Likenesses L. Lewis, 'c' type colour print, 1973?, NPG • J. Olofsson, photograph, Redferns Music Picture Library [*see illus.*] • photographs, Hult. Arch.

Jones, Cain (*fl.* **1776–1795**). *See under* Edwards, John (*bap.* 1699?, *d.* 1776).

Jones, Calvert Richard (1802–1877), marine painter, traveller, and photographer, was born on 4 December 1802 at 'Veranda', near Swansea, the eldest of the five children of Calvert Jones (*d.* 1847), a civic leader, and his wife, Prudence Sproule. In 1823 he obtained a first-class degree in mathematics from Oriel College, Oxford. While at Oxford he met Christopher Rice Mansell (Kit) Talbot, the younger cousin of William Henry Fox Talbot, pioneer of photography. Kit Talbot shared interests with Jones in art, science, and musical performance. Perhaps more crucially for Jones, Talbot was the wealthiest commoner in Britain. With a shared love for fast sailing-boats and travel, Talbot's wealth made it possible for Jones to lead the life of an artistic dilettante. Their cruises of the Mediterranean and elsewhere provided ample material for Jones's sketches and watercolours. Between journeys the picturesque shipping and characters of the Swansea docks were Jones's favourite subjects.

In 1829 Jones entered holy orders, accepting the living of Loughor, near Penlle'r-gaer, Glamorgan, the home of the photographer John Dillwyn Llewelyn. He soon abandoned his clerical career and on 24 July 1837 married Anne Harriet Williams (1815–1856). Anne was an enthusiastic traveller and an active artistic partner; her diaries are the source of much information on their travels. Their daughter, Christina, was born in January 1839, on the day after Louis Jacques Mandé Daguerre startled the world with his announcement in Paris of a means for capturing nature in the camera. Kit's cousin, Henry Talbot, had devised his own photographic process five years before. The Llewelyns and Kit Talbot were interested in the new art, but nobody in this circle was more captivated by its powers than was Jones.

Jones immediately experimented with Henry Talbot's primitive process on paper but soon turned to daguerreotypy for making images. A fine daguerreotype (preserved in the National Library of Wales, Cardiff) of Kit Talbot's *Margam Castle* demonstrates his mastery of the art at least by 1841. Jones explained to Henry Talbot that he would prefer to use his process on paper (the daguerreotype was on a metal plate) but that the exposure times were too long. In 1841 Talbot announced his improved process, the calotype, which led to more reasonable exposures. Jones became more interested, but it was not until he saw the first copy of Talbot's *The Pencil of Nature* in 1844 that he was totally won over to photography on paper.

In his paper photography Calvert Jones at times worked with Henry Talbot, with Llewelyn, and with the Revd George Bridges. His subject matter and style in photography closely matched those of his watercolours. Marine subjects and architecture dominated, but he also did some portraits and studies. By 1845 he was confident enough to make the calotype his main means of recording his travels. His scientific and artistic talents, his energy, and his previous experience with the daguerreotype quickly made him one of the most proficient of the early art photographers.

From 1845 Jones increasingly sought to obtain an income from his photography. His travels to Malta and Italy produced many fine subjects, and he sold quantities of negatives to Talbot. (The inclusion of these in Talbot collections has often confused later attributions.) By 1847, his finances running short, he considered taking a more active role in promoting Talbot's photography. He experimented with watercolouring his photographic prints and considered the possibility of taking charge of Nicolaas Henneman's photographic printing establishment. The tinge of commerce began to strain his relationship with Henry Talbot, but the situation suddenly changed. His father's death in 1847 brought an unexpected large inheritance and made him financially independent for the first time in his life. He returned to a non-commercial friendship with Henry Talbot and seems to have briefly suspended his photography.

During the late 1840s Jones became active in managing his estate and in supporting civic affairs in the Swansea area. About 1850, however, he returned to travel photography, this time solely for his own artistic expression. In 1853 he and his family moved to Brussels, where he took many of the photographs which form the basis of the Victoria and Albert Museum's collection of his work. Anne Jones died prematurely there three years later; Jones returned to Britain to live in Bath and, on 20 May 1858, he married a much younger woman, Portia Jane Smith (*b.* 1832). They had two daughters, Isabella and Georgiana. Calvert Jones died at his home, 12 Lansdown Crescent, Bath, on 7 November 1877 and was buried at the chapel of St Mary's in his native Swansea. Many of his negatives and prints are in the Talbot collection at the National Museum of Photography, Film and Television in Bradford, and the Fox Talbot Museum at Lacock, Wiltshire; his drawings and paintings are in the collection of the Glynn Vivian Art Gallery and Museum, Swansea.
LARRY J. SCHAAF

Sources R. Buckman, *The photographic work of Calvert Richard Jones* (1990) · L. J. Schaaf, *Sun Pictures catalogue five: the Reverend Calvert R. Jones* (1990) · d. cert.
Archives Fox Talbot Museum, Lacock, Wiltshire, letters and photographs · National Museum of Photography, Film and Television, Bradford, letters and photographs · NL Wales, papers and photographs
Likenesses pencil sketch, *c.*1835, priv. coll. · C. R. Jones, self-portraits, photographs, National Museum of Photography, Film and Television, Bradford
Wealth at death under £18,000: probate with codicil, 1878, CGPLA Eng. & Wales

Jones, Charles Handfield (1819–1890), physician and histologist, son of Captain John Jones RN, was born at Liverpool on 1 October 1819. He was one of Thomas Arnold's pupils at Rugby School, from where he went to St Catharine's College, Cambridge, in 1836; he graduated BA in 1840. After studying at St George's Hospital, London, he took the degree of MB at Cambridge in 1843, but never proceeded to that of MD. He became a member of the Royal College of Physicians in 1845, and was elected a fellow in 1849. Jones published a paper of observations on the minute structure of the liver, which led to his election as FRS in 1850. He married on 20 May 1851 Louisa Holt, daughter of G. F. Holt; they had two sons, who both entered the medical profession.

Jones was elected physician to St Mary's Hospital, Paddington, in 1851, and continued on the staff of that institution until his death. He attained considerable reputation as a histologist and as a clinical observer. In the Royal College of Physicians he was junior censor in 1863–4 and senior censor in 1886, and in 1888 a vice-president. In 1865 he delivered the Lumleian lectures on the pathology of the nervous system. Besides numerous papers in other medical journals he published the following in the *Transactions of the Medico-Chirurgical Society of London*: 'On the liver and cholgagues' (vol. 35, p. 249); 'On morbid changes in the mucous membrane of the stomach' (vol. 37, p. 67); 'On degeneration of the pancreas' (vol. 38, p. 195); 'On haematemesis' (vol. 43, p. 353); and 'On a case of intussusception' (vol. 61, p. 301). Jones never joined the Pathological Society, but he communicated various observations on morbid histology from time to time through others which were published in the society's *Transactions* (vol. 34, pp. 55, 60, vol. 35, p. 134, vol. 36, p. 158, vol. 37, p. 203). He published with E. H. Sieveking *A Manual of Pathological Anatomy* (1854) and *Clinical Observations on Functional Nervous Disorders* (1864). The histology in which Jones was an original worker is now obsolete, but the clinical observations were of greater value; the relations of paralysis, spasm, anaesthesia, and neuralgia are ably discussed, and the close relation of neuralgia to debility was pointed out more clearly than in most previous books on nervous diseases.

Jones lived in London in Green Street, Park Lane, until his latter years, by which time he had moved to 24 Montagu Square. He died there of cancer of the stomach on 30 September 1890 and was buried in Finchley cemetery on 4 October. He was survived by his wife.
NORMAN MOORE, rev. MICHAEL BEVAN

Sources BMJ (11 Oct 1890), 874–5 · Venn, *Alum. Cant.* · Munk, *Roll* · m. cert.
Wealth at death £450 18s. 11d.: administration, 17 Dec 1890, CGPLA Eng. & Wales

Jones, Charlotte (1768–1847), miniature painter, was the daughter of Thomas Jones, merchant, of Cley, whose family had moved from Wales and settled near the north coast of Norfolk about 1680. Following her father's death, before 1800, Charlotte Jones moved to London, where she received lessons in painting in watercolour on ivory from the fashionable miniaturist Richard Cosway. In *The Princess Charlotte of Wales* (1885), which includes an account of a series of portraits that Charlotte Jones later painted, Catherine Rachel Jones (who published under the name Mrs Herbert Jones) noted that Cosway 'taught her to add softness and delicacy to her naturally vigorous touch' and that 'he made room for her in the brilliant circle in which his own talents were employed' (Jones, 4). Though Miss Jones frequently copied Cosway's portraits 'she never adopted his mode of finishing the figure in pencil, and colouring the head and flesh only' (ibid.). The celebrated portrait painter Sir Thomas Lawrence also 'brought her into notice, and helped to make her the fashion', and her later portraits are coloured 'with a fulness and richness' that shows the influence of his oil portraits (ibid., 4–5). Basil Long later noted that her work is 'soft in effect' and that 'her style varied a good deal … she was not a great miniaturist and some of her work was rather affected' (Long, 1.244).

After exhibiting at the Royal Academy from 1801 to 1810, from 75 and 55 Lower Grosvenor Street, Charlotte Jones set up her own studio at 127 Mount Street, London, where her 'lively conversation' and 'picturesque appearance' doubtless contributed towards her establishment as a successful miniaturist. 'Her abundant golden hair was raised high and slightly powdered, and contrasted with the bright black eyes, which were afterwards dimmed and ruined by the exercise of her art' (Jones, 3–4). She exhibited a total of forty-one miniatures at the Royal Academy from 1801 to 1823, the first of these being a portrait of Prince William of Gloucester. Her best miniatures include portraits of George, prince of Wales (afterwards George IV), after Cosway (c.1790–1795; Holburne Museum of Art, Bath); Lady Caroline Lamb (Walker, National Portrait Gallery: Regency Portraits, 303); Princess Charlotte Augusta of Wales (examples in the Royal Collection), and her 'Our Governess' Mrs Martha Udney (c.1802; Holburne Museum of Art, Bath), whom the princess disliked. The last portrait, in which the sitter is wearing a richly coloured deep blue gown, is highly accomplished and is engaging in its rendering of the evident liveliness and intelligence of Mrs Udney. (Her husband, Robert Udney FRS, was an art collector and friend of Cosway, who died in the carriage of their daughter, Miss Udney.)

In 1808 Charlotte Jones was appointed 'Miniature Painter to the Princess Charlotte of Wales', to whom she was also 'Preceptress in Miniature Painting', and she is now remembered chiefly for a set of twelve portraits that she called The Princess Charlotte, from her Cradle to her Grave (Royal Collection), which she collected together after the death of the princess in 1817, mounted in a black and gold triptych, and preserved as a memorial to her patron and friend. The three earliest were copied after a sketch and two miniatures of Princess Charlotte by Cosway; the first, after the sketch, shows the princess asleep in her cradle, the latter two as a child of three and then of four. Subsequent portraits in the set were taken from life and show the princess at various stages of her girlhood and as a young woman. Two three-quarter length miniatures show her at the time of her engagement to Frederick William, prince of Orange, in 1814 (subsequently engraved by J. S. Agar), and in 1816, the year of her marriage to Prince Leopold of Saxe-Coburg-Saalfeld. The final, commemorative portrait was painted in 1817. Walker notes that the set of miniatures was lent by Sir Lawrence Jones, bt, to the Guelph exhibition held at South Kensington Museum in 1891 and was sold for 44 guineas to the Royal Collection at Christies on 17 December 1945 (lot 16), when the earliest

miniature no longer formed part of the set (Walker, Eighteenth and Early Nineteenth Century Miniatures, xxiv). Of the copies Miss Jones made of her miniatures of the princess of 1814 and 1816 several have passed through the London salerooms. In a letter to Charlotte Jones written about 1816–17 from Claremont, Surrey, Princess Charlotte confided that:

> With regard to Cosway … there is no chance of his either doing one of me or of the Prince, as he refused me *as a sitter* two years ago, when I would have given anything to have sat to him. He wrote word that he could not paint out of his own house, a point which is never waived in favour of the Royal family. (Jones, 9–10)

Charlotte Jones later worked at Bath, where the Holburne Museum of Art also holds her self-portrait, signed and dated 1805, in which she is shown three-quarter length, seated, in a white dress. In 1838 she received a bequest from Cosway's wife, Maria. Suffering in later years from a partial loss of eyesight, Miss Jones died in Upper Gloucester Place, London, on 21 September 1847, in her eightieth year. Although Princess Charlotte had written to her about 1816, 'I must learn how the *suit* goes on, whether it *suits* you; at all events, I sincerely hope you will not be *non-suited*' (Jones, 9), Charlotte Jones never married.   ANNETTE PEACH

Sources C. R. Jones, *The Princess Charlotte of Wales* (1885) · R. Walker, *The eighteenth and early nineteenth century miniatures in the collection of her majesty the queen* (1992) · B. S. Long, *British miniaturists* (1929) · R. Walker, *National Portrait Gallery: Regency portraits*, 2 vols. (1985) · *The Holburne of Menstrie Museum Bath* (1926–33) [catalogue] · artist's file, archive material, NPG · artist files, notes, V&A · R. Bayne-Powell, ed., *Catalogue of miniatures in the Holburne Museum and Crafts Study Centre, Bath* [1995] · Graves, *RA exhibitors*
Likenesses C. Jones, self-portrait, miniature watercolour on ivory, 1805, Holburne Museum of Art, Bath

Jones [née Cumberbatch], **Claudia Vera** (1915–1964), communist and journalist, was born on 21 February 1915 in Trinidad. In 1924 she and her sisters joined their parents, who had emigrated to New York two years earlier. Unhealthy housing and overwork led to Mrs Cumberbatch's death in 1927; Claudia's father, Charles, died in 1958. In 1932 Claudia was hospitalized for a year with tuberculosis. Managing to complete high school despite the increasing ravages of the depression, Claudia worked at a series of unskilled jobs, but sustained what was to become a lifelong interest in drama by joining the drama club of the National Urban League (an African-American organization).

Inspired by the Communist Party's support of African-American struggles, Claudia joined the party in 1936, taking the *nom de guerre* of Jones. She rose rapidly in the party structure, becoming, for example, chair of its education committee for New York state, a columnist in the *Daily Worker*, and eventually editor of the Young Communist League's monthly *Spotlight* magazine. By 1945 Jones was 'negro affairs' editor on the *Worker* and an executive member of the party-affiliated National Negro Council, an organization which campaigned for civil rights.

Being on the second level of the party hierarchy, Claudia

Claudia Vera Jones (1915–1964), by unknown photographer

Jones suffered from the McCarthyite anti-communist 'witch-hunt' which began in 1948. Repeated arrests resulted in a heart attack in 1951. She was imprisoned for twelve months; on her release she was extradited to Britain in December 1955. Very ill on her arrival in London, she was hospitalized for some months. Though initially she received some support from the Communist Party of Great Britain, it never recognized her talents and her organizing and editorial experience. In order to continue her political life she became active outside the party. She began to publish a monthly paper, the *West Indian Gazette*, in March 1958 and organized a series of broad-based groups which led the protests after the 1958 race riots in Notting Hill, London, and the lynching of the Antiguan Kelso Cochrane in the same area the following year. In collaboration with other organizations, Jones was a leader of the struggles against the Immigration Act of 1962. Other campaigns she was involved with included the first moves against the apartheid regime in South Africa; the anti-Vietnam war movement, and the march in support of the 1963 march on Washington for civil rights. In 1959 she also began an annual indoor event to showcase Caribbean talent, which after her death was developed into the Notting Hill carnival.

On being granted a British passport in 1962 Claudia Jones visited the USSR at the invitation of the *Soviet Woman*; in the following year she returned for the World Congress of Women. In 1964 she was in Tokyo for the 10th Anti-Hydrogen Bomb Conference and went from there to visit China. This, at the height of the contretemps between the USSR and China, demonstrated her international perspective as well as her commitment to socialism. Throughout a hectic, committed, and financially impoverished life, she suffered repeated hospitalization. Her brief marriage to Abraham Scholnick ended in divorce; there were no children. Claudia Jones died of a heart attack in her sleep on 29 December 1964 at her home, 58 Lisburne Road, Hampstead, aged forty-eight. Her ashes were buried in Highgate cemetery. The *Gazette* outlasted her by only two issues.

MARIKA SHERWOOD

Sources M. Sherwood and others, *Claudia Jones* (1999) · d. cert. · *CGPLA Eng. & Wales* (1965) · private information (2004)
Archives People's History Museum, Manchester, communist party archives | SOUND BL NSA, 'Claudia Jones symposium', 28 Sept 1996, C 779/01–04 C1
Likenesses photograph, priv. coll. [*see illus.*]
Wealth at death £876: administration, 13 Jan 1965, *CGPLA Eng. & Wales*

Jones, (David Brinley) Clay (1923–1996), horticulturist and broadcaster, was born on 8 November 1923 at Glascoed, Napier Street, Cardigan, the elder child and only son of William Jones, marine engineer, and his wife, Annie Margaret, *née* Clay, the only daughter of a Pembrokeshire farming family. He was always known as Clay Jones, Clay not being, as many imagined, a later addition when his horticultural career flourished but a name given him because with no other male issue on either side of the family it was his grandmother's wish that her daughter should, through her son, perpetuate the Clay name.

Jones grew up in Cardigan, largely with his mother and grandmother, but in 1932, with his father by then unemployed, they were obliged to move out of Cardigan to a small farm 7 miles to the north, and it was there, with his own vegetable plot, that Jones first acquired his passion for growing things. He attended Glynarthen elementary school and then Cardigan county grammar school. In 1939 he joined the Home Guard and then, in 1942, enlisted 'by invitation' in the South Wales Borderers. He was later posted to the Welch regiment, with whom he saw service in India and Burma, rising to the rank of captain. His wartime experiences left him with a lifelong distaste for anything Japanese. In the same year as he enlisted, 1942, he married his childhood sweetheart, Glenys Frances Mary, and in time they were to have a daughter, Janice, and a son, Richard, who became an actor.

After the end of hostilities in 1945 Jones was able to take up a pre-war offer of a place at the University College of Wales, Aberystwyth, where he spent a year working in the university botanic garden to provide the income to enable him to complete his studies and graduate in botany and economics. In 1952 he joined a garden seeds company, Bees Seeds in Liverpool, moving two years later to become manager of their seed unit in Flintshire. In 1957 he switched to a rival company, Cuthbert's, as production manager in Llangollen, and became an authority on the seed industry. He was a great believer in gardeners raising their own plants and described the germination of seeds and their development into mature plants as 'a miracle'.

Jones was a fluent Welsh speaker, always spoke it at home with his family, and learned English only at primary school. He was immensely proud to be Welsh, but had no time for rampant Welsh nationalism. In 1960 he was invited to initiate a Welsh language radio gardening programme, *Garddio*, at first single-handedly but later as one of a panel of three, and finally as chairman. He also made regular television appearances, both on Welsh language programmes and on the BBC's national programme, *Gardening Club*, and its successor, *Gardeners' World*. In 1976 he was invited to join the panel of the immensely popular BBC radio programme *Gardeners' Question Time*, at first as an irregular panellist deputizing for the resident team members. In 1977 he left Cuthbert's Seeds to concentrate on writing and broadcasting and moved to a house overlooking the Severn estuary near Chepstow. It had a large and difficult hillside garden that he gradually tamed, although a fellow *Gardeners' Question Time* panellist once described it as 'ungardenable'.

Jones continued to make regular broadcasts on *Gardeners' Question Time* until, in 1985, the producer and chairman of the panel, Ken Ford, died. A new chairman was required, and Stefan Buczacki, a fellow panel member, suggested to the new BBC producer that Jones would be an ideal candidate. So it proved, and Jones remained chairman of *Gardeners' Question Time* until ill health brought about his premature retirement in 1993. His warm, rich, and deep voice, with its ringing Cardigan accent, endeared him to listeners, and his friendly but positive chairing gave the programme a special quality. He always adopted the maxim that no matter how easy or complex the question, no matter how straightforward or difficult the solution, the questioner (and the listeners) should always be left with a definite answer and with accurate and unambiguous guidance. His valediction at the end of each programme, 'And a very good day to you', became his trademark.

Jones was a handsome man of medium height and with strong build, an attribute that not only equipped him for digging his large vegetable garden (not until very late in his life did he have any gardening help), but also equipped him to play rugby at a high level. He was a man of the people: unpretentious, generous, and kind, never attracted by material wealth and never more content than with his family, in his garden, or at his local pub, pint and beloved pipe in hand. His favourite crop was the tomato, about which he wrote a book, *Growing Tomatoes* (1981). This was an affection that he traced back to a meal of fried tomatoes given to him when, as a child, he was recovering from a serious and potentially fatal attack of double pneumonia.

Jones took immense pride in his OBE (for services to gardening and broadcasting in Wales), awarded in 1990, and in the Veitch memorial medal in gold which he received from the Royal Horticultural Society in 1992. He died on 3 July 1996 at the Royal Gwent Hospital, Newport, following a heart attack. He was survived by his wife, Glenys, and their two children.   STEFAN BUCZACKI

Sources C. Jones, *Clay: memoirs of a gardening man* (1993) · *The Times* (5 July 1996) · *Daily Telegraph* (5 July 1996) · *The Independent* (5 July 1996) · personal knowledge (2004) · b. cert. · d. cert.
Archives FILM BBC Archive, recordings of 'Gardeners' world' | SOUND BBC Sound Archives, recordings of 'Gardeners' question time'
Likenesses photograph, 1981, repro. in *The Independent* · B. Farmer, photograph, repro. in Jones, *Clay: memoirs* · photograph, repro. in *The Times* · photograph, repro. in *Daily Telegraph*
Wealth at death £133,508: probate, 10 Sept 1996, *CGPLA Eng. & Wales*

Jones, (William) Clifford [Cliff] (1914–1990), rugby player and administrator, was born on 12 March 1914 in the Rhondda valley at Porth near Pontypridd, Glamorgan, the second son in a family of two sons and two daughters of Daniel Jones, wholesale fruit and vegetable merchant, and his wife, Elizabeth Mary Lewis. He was educated at Porth secondary school and, from the age of fourteen, at Llandovery College. From 1933 he attended Clare College, Cambridge, where he obtained a third class in part one of the law tripos (1935) and a second (division two) in part two (1936). There he proved himself to be among the very first order of rugby players, winning a blue three times.

It was at Llandovery College that Jones's extraordinary talent had been revealed. For five years, five afternoons a week, under the coaching of T. P. (Pope) Williams, he had been initiated into the arts of rugby, for which, at 5 feet 8 inches and only 10½ stone, he was not well tailored. To survive, he relied on his quick wits and his electrifying speed off the mark. His swift, breathtaking sidestep (off either foot) he attributed, as he claimed in one of the embroidered anecdotes of which he was fond, to the daily necessity of avoiding the crowd, traffic, and lamp-posts of the narrow Welsh valleys and the cluttered passages of his college. Having played for the Welsh secondary schools between 1931 and 1933, he left a legacy of virtuoso running. He played his first senior game for Wales (against England) at the age of nineteen. He continued to play for Wales while at university, but his national career lasted only four years. He was unable to escape the ravages of rugby's muscular confrontations: bones were cracked and joints displaced. He missed an international season because of injury in 1937. This prompted his early thoughts of quitting, so that he played only thirteen times for his country (as captain in 1938) and a mere twenty-two for his club, Cardiff. He was one of the greatest outside-halves to have graced the game.

While Jones was playing he insisted on assiduous preparation, bringing along his own masseur at a time when such assistance was unheard of. Although he was a supreme individualist he valued teamwork, as he emphasized in his book, *Rugby Football*, published in 1937. He benefited from the long pass from his partner at scrum-half, Haydn Tanner, while he in turn was able to utilize, as in the 1934 Oxford–Cambridge match, the powerful, long-striding skills of Wilfred Wooller outside him. This technique came to mature fruition in Wales's 13–12 victory against the New Zealand All Blacks in 1935, at Cardiff Arms Park.

Jones declared his temporary retirement in 1938 in order to concentrate on further legal studies, but he had played his last game for Wales. In 1939 he married Gwendoline Mary, daughter of Frederick Bartle Thomas, wholesale butcher in Tonypandy; they had three sons. He returned to play for Cardiff against Bridgend on the first Saturday in September 1939, and war was declared the following day. In the same year he was appointed assistant solicitor to Glamorgan county council and assistant prosecuting solicitor to Glamorgan police. However, he took up these posts only briefly, because when war broke out he joined the 77th regiment of the heavy anti-aircraft Royal Artillery (Territorial Army), where he rose to the rank of major. Stationed in Berlin at the end of the war he was assistant to the chief legal officer.

In 1946 Jones returned to Porth to join his father's business and later to start his own, Clun Fruits, in Pont-y-clun, where the family lived, before finally embarking on a property business. He had little contact with rugby for ten years and developed an enduring interest in watercolours, particularly marine and Victorian paintings.

In 1956 Jones's interest in rugby revived and he became a member of the Welsh Rugby Union committee. In the following year he became a selector, a position he held until 1978. In the 1960s he was chairman of the committee which developed, in Wales, following the Welsh team's disastrous visit to South Africa in 1964, the world's first comprehensive rugby coaching scheme, from which was established a permanent national coaching organizer, the first of its kind in the rugby world. He was the union's president in the centenary year of 1980–81. He was also a member of the Sports Council of Great Britain from 1967 to 1971, and in 1971 was a founder member of the Sports Council for Wales. He presided over the 'golden age' of Welsh rugby football in the late 1960s and 1970s, being behind the squad training system which enabled Wales to dominate their European rivals. In 1979 he was appointed OBE.

Jones was dapper, with fair hair and, in later years, nicely rounded features. He was animated and gregarious, as vibrant in his conversation as he was on the field. He invariably wore his Hawks' club tie and Cambridge blues' scarf. Jones died of a heart attack on 27 November 1990 at his home, Buttress House, Bonvilston, near Cardiff, to which he and his wife had moved in later years. He was buried in the churchyard of St Nicholas near Cardiff. His wife and sons survived him.   GERALD DAVIES, *rev.*

Sources interviews with Wilfred Wooller and J. B. G. Thomas · D. Smith and G. Williams, *Fields of praise, the official history of the Welsh Rugby Union* (1980) · W. Thomas, *A century of Welsh rugby players* (1979) · *The Independent* (30 Nov 1990) · *The Times* (30 Nov 1990) · personal knowledge (1996) · private information (1996) · *CGPLA Eng. & Wales* (1991)
Archives Llandovery College, Llandovery, memorabilia
Likenesses portrait, 1980, priv. coll. · photograph, Llandovery College, Llandovery · photograph, Welsh Rugby Union
Wealth at death £35,150: probate, 10 May 1991, *CGPLA Eng. & Wales*

Jones, (Emily Elizabeth) Constance (1848–1922), philosopher and college head, was born on 19 February 1848 at Langstone Court, Llangarren, Herefordshire, the eldest of ten children of John Jones (*b.* 1813) MD JP, and his wife, Emily Edith, daughter of Thomas Oakley JP, of Monmouthshire. Her parents were both Welsh, and her mother claimed kinship with Dr David Lewis, who became the first principal of Jesus College, Oxford, after its foundation by Elizabeth I. Constance was educated mostly at home. She spent the years 1861 to 1865 with the whole family in Cape Town, and when they came back she went to a small school, Miss Robinson's, in Cheltenham, for a year, before returning home to begin to prepare for

(**Emily Elizabeth**) **Constance Jones** (1848–1922), by Sir John Lavery, 1916

entrance to Girton. She had Greek tuition by post from one of Samuel Taylor Coleridge's granddaughters, and spent two months being coached for the entrance examination by a Miss Alice Grüner in Sydenham. She went up to Girton in 1875, but almost immediately had to withdraw in order to look after the aunt with whom she then lived, in Newton, Wales. Her undergraduate career was considerably interrupted, but in 1880 she was awarded a first class in the moral sciences tripos.

Constance Jones was fired with enthusiasm for philosophy as an undergraduate. Emily Davies, founder of the college and its mistress when Constance came up, had no difficulty in getting J. N. Keynes (the father of Maynard Keynes, and a logician) to teach her, describing her as 'an exceptionally clever girl'. But it was Henry Sidgwick who inspired her most. In her autobiographical sketch, *As I Remember*, published posthumously in 1922, she wrote of her supervisions with him: 'I was in a magic world of thought … of great thinkers and unrivalled teachers … a new heaven and a new earth.' She retained her great admiration for Sidgwick throughout her life, and one of her major works was to see through the press the sixth and seventh editions of his *Methods of Ethics* and to edit his lectures after his death in 1900. Almost the last thing she wrote was the article on Sidgwick in James Hastings's *Encyclopaedia of Religion and Ethics* (1920).

After leaving Cambridge and returning to her aunt in Wales (where she immediately began work on a translation of Lotze's *Microcosmos*, started by Elizabeth *Hamilton, who died before she had completed as much as half of it), Constance Jones was, most unusually, invited back to Girton as a research student. Emily Davies was on the whole against having research students at Girton until the number of undergraduates had grown and the college was thoroughly accepted in Cambridge. Although Miss Davies was no longer mistress, she still had a room in college and retained a determining influence over the affairs of Girton. She made an exception to her general rule in favour of Constance Jones because of her outstanding performance in the tripos. And so, in 1884, Miss Jones came back into residence and remained at Girton for the next thirty-two years. She became resident lecturer in moral sciences, then librarian, then vice-mistress, and finally mistress, a member of college and college council from 1903 until her retirement in 1916.

When Emily Davies founded Girton College she became, as a matter of course, a member of the college and the college council, but the mistress did not. When she herself was, briefly, mistress (1872–5), she remained a member of council, but not in virtue of her office. Indeed she continued to be opposed to the idea that the mistress should automatically have such membership, and voted against it in the case of Constance Jones. She preferred to think of the mistress as a servant of the council (most of whom had been instrumental in raising the money to found the college and many of whom were eminent Cambridge academics). Miss Jones certainly thought otherwise. It is not known whether she was aware that Emily Davies had (alone) voted against her membership of the council; there were no apparent hard feelings, and she frequently spoke with admiration of the founder of the college. All the same, that Miss Davies finally left Girton in 1904 must have been something of a relief, and thereafter Constance Jones became the first truly professional mistress.

Constance Jones achieved an enormous amount in her period of office. She was an exceptional administrator, and at once set to work to pay off the college debt, oversee the new buildings (named after Emily Davies), and increase the number of undergraduates, thus enabling the college to stay solvent for the foreseeable future. She did not give up her academic interests, and continued to teach, though, according to Dean Inge in his introduction to her autobiographical 'ramblings' (her word), her teaching was clear and expository rather than inspirational. She published four books while holding the office of mistress: *A Primer of Logic* (1905), *A Primer of Ethics* (1909), *Girton College* (in the Beautiful Britain series, 1913), and *The Three Great Questions: an Outline of Public and Private Duty* (1915), as well as numerous articles and reviews in philosophical journals. Besides this, she was active in the affairs of the university and a governor of the University College of Wales, Aberystwyth, which conferred on her an honorary DLitt in 1913.

Sidgwick and his circle long continued to influence Constance Jones in many ways. Both Henry Sidgwick and his wife Eleanor were interested in the then popular subject of psychical research, Sidgwick on the grounds that a direct proof of survival after death would have an effect on

ethics; he seems not to have found such a proof. He became president of the Society for Psychical Research, and both his wife and Constance Jones were active members, conducting experiments in thought transference as well as attempts to communicate with the dead through a medium. The Sidgwicks were also deeply committed to the cause of women's education, though Henry Sidgwick fell foul of Emily Davies on account of his unwillingness to see women admitted to the same examinations as men. Eleanor Sidgwick was also involved in the women's franchise movement, and both she and Constance Jones were vice-presidents of the Conservative and Unionist Women's Franchise Association. In May 1910 Mrs Pankhurst stayed at Girton when she came to speak in Cambridge during the 'truce' when the Conciliation Committee was doing its work.

Constance Jones was generally described as a charming, approachable person. She was an outstanding mistress of her college, permanently changing the nature of the office. As a philosopher, she was thoroughly professional. Though not an original thinker, she was an excellent interpreter of the thoughts of others, and her influence lay in her ability to persuade those she taught that philosophy was a subject they could tackle and enjoy. It was, for example, while she was mistress that Susan Stebbing changed from the history to the moral sciences tripos. Miss Jones loved children, perhaps on account of the number of her own younger siblings, and she gave frequent children's parties while she was mistress. She was, it seems, not without vanity. Her photograph by Lafayette, reproduced in *As I Remember*, shows someone pleased with her own appearance, and wearing the most glorious and extravagant hat. Her portrait by Sir John Lavery, the gift of the college to her after her retirement (painted after the First World War, when a retirement party could at last be held) and left to the college in her will, shows the same character—someone amiable, but by no means averse to the public eye. She sedulously concealed her own date of birth. She listed her recreations in *Who's Who* as architecture and languages. In fact she was equally interested in birds: she loved Girton gardens for the owls and the nightingales which frequented them, and she used to spend holidays in Northumberland with one of her nephews, Collingwood Thorpe of Alnwick, who was secretary and treasurer of the Farne Island Association. She was also much interested in music, and used to attend concerts in Cambridge organized by Hugh Allen, later professor of music in Oxford, given on 'authentic original instruments' at Christ's College, where he was organist. Constance Jones died at her home, St Sunnivia, 73 Bristol Road, Weston-super-Mare, Somerset, on 17 April 1922, and was buried in the town. MARY WARNOCK

Sources E. E. Constance Jones, *As I remember* (1922) · *WWW* · *Girton Review* (1922) · *The Times* (19 April 1922) · D. Bennett, *Emily Davies and the liberation of women, 1830–1921* (1990) · college council minutes, 1902–16, Girton Cam. · b. cert. · d. cert. · *Girton College Record* (1922)
Likenesses J. Lavery, oils, 1916, Girton Cam. [*see illus.*] · Lafayette, photograph, repro. in Jones, *As I remember*

Wealth at death £2681 10s. 10d.: probate, 8 July 1922, *CGPLA Eng. & Wales*

Jones, Dafydd, o Drefriw [David Jones] (**1703–1785**), poet and printer, was born on 4 May 1703 according to a note in his hand (although his gravestone recorded that he was seventy-seven when he died), the son of Siôn ap Dafydd and Jane, daughter of Dafydd ap Siôn. Jones traces his genealogy through his mother and his maternal grandmother, Elizabeth Rowland, to the Vaughans of Caer-gai, Merioneth, and could claim John Davies (Siôn Dafydd Las, (*d.* 1694)), the family bard of the Vaughans of Nannau, as his 'uncle' (his mother's cousin). Jones married Gwen, daughter of Richard ap Rhys, perhaps at Trefriw, Caernarvonshire, but it is not known when. Jones was probably a native of the Conwy valley, and spent all his life at Trefriw, where he was verger and at various times a charity school teacher, a miller, a parish constable, an assessor, and a rate collector. Nothing is known of his formal education but he was able to write English and he was a skilled copyist. In his own work and interests he represents many of the Welsh cultural activities of his day, as a poet, supporter of eisteddfods, publisher, and itinerant bookseller, friendly with many of the leading literary figures of the time.

Jones published a few ballads (1723–7), poems in chapbooks, 'carols' on topical and religious themes in the popular alliterative free-verse style, and other occasional verse, dedicatory poems in books, and elegies in the traditional strict-verse metres. Though he took pride in the title Dewi Fardd, by which the poet and antiquary Lewis Morris (1701–1765) sometimes referred to him, his poetry, though metrically competent, never attained a particularly high standard. In addition to selling books he was himself responsible for a number of titles as editor and publisher. *Histori Nicodemus*, the 'Gospel of Nicodemus', appeared from Wrexham in 1745, and his collection of religious and other folklore, *Eglurun rhyfedd*, was published at Shrewsbury in 1750.

Jones's most important book was *Blodeugerdd Cymru* (1759), an anthology of popular verse. He had been encouraged in this venture by Morris (who helped him to draw up his *Proposals* and gave him useful, but unheeded, advice), and by the London Cymmrodorion Society (of which he became a corresponding member in 1759). Rightly or wrongly Morris and his brothers, the leading lights of the Cymmrodorion, had believed that Jones's intention was to publish a collection of the verse of Huw Morus (1622–1709) and they saw in the experienced Dafydd Jones a means of promoting the Welsh literary 'canon'. For his part Jones welcomed such influential support. The anthology actually contained forty-six poems by Morus and some thirty by other well-known poets of the late seventeenth century, but most of the poems in the collection were contemporary popular free-verse songs, some by Jones himself, most by homespun local poets. Jones was roundly criticized for the defects of his edition, and accused by William Morris of 'mixing up rubbish with excellent poetry' (Jenkins and Ramage, 81). Jones's aim, however, had been to provide entertaining reading for ordinary folk, and though he claimed to have lost £20 on the book it appears to have sold well enough for him to bring out an enlarged second edition in 1779.

Jones had plans for further anthologies of poetry including a volume of *cywyddau* which he had collected and transcribed, but the only one to appear was *Cydymaith diddan* (1766), a miscellany of prose and verse, both contemporary and late medieval. Whatever their defects, both of his published anthologies are valuable today as examples of eighteenth-century popular literature composed for the most part by folk poets.

Jones was an assiduous collector of Welsh manuscripts, and transcribed many texts including his own Welsh–English dictionary and collections of *cywydd* and other poetry. He appreciated the importance of preserving classical Welsh verse and of safeguarding the literary tradition, and through his copying and publishing he played a significant role in the eighteenth-century revival of Welsh culture. Though frequently mocked and denigrated for his perceived lack of learning by Lewis Morris and his circle, he did not fall out of favour with the Cymmrodorion, who continued to help him. He corresponded with Lewis and Richard Morris, Evan Evans (curate at Trefriw between 1759 and 1761), Owen Jones (Myfyr), and Margaret Davies.

About 1765 Jones was given some of the type used by Lewis Morris in his short-lived printing venture in 1735, and in 1775 he borrowed money to buy Morris's old press. He set up the press at his home, Tan-yr-yw, in Trefriw, and embarked on a new career as a printer–publisher. He narrowly missed being the first commercial printer in north Wales, Richard Marsh having established a press in Wrexham in 1773. Between 1776 and his death in 1785 he printed a number of ballads, chapbooks, and books, mostly of a moral or religious nature, although they did include two items on the American War of Independence. Jones gave north Wales poets and writers, many of them craftsmen and farmers, the opportunity for the first time to have their work printed locally rather than at Shrewsbury or Chester. His major publication was *Histori yr Iesu sanctaidd* (1776), a 200-page edition of William Smith's *History of the Holy Jesus*, translated by Dafydd Ellis. Difficulties with the edition arose from Jones's limited supply of type; a shortage of the letter y (both a vowel and a consonant in Welsh) meant that v or u had to be substituted.

Jones died at Tan-yr-yw, Trefriw, on 20 October 1785, and was buried in the graveyard of Trefriw church on 26 October. Thomas Pennant bought his collection of manuscripts. Jones's youngest son, Ishmael Davies (1758–1817), continued his printing business at Trefriw. Ishmael was succeeded by his son, John Jones (1786–1865), who moved to Llanrwst in 1825, revived the fortunes of the business, and became an important nineteenth-century printer and publisher. In 1936, as O. Evans-Jones & Co., the firm passed out of the hands of the family.

BRYNLEY F. ROBERTS and EILUNED REES

Sources O. G. Williams, *Dafydd Jones o Drefriw (1708–1785)* (1907) · G. J. Williams, ed., 'Llythyrau at Dafydd Jones o Drefriw', *National Library of Wales Journal*, 3/2 (1943), 1–46 [suppl.] · R. T. Jenkins and H. Ramage, 'The history of the Cymmrodorion Society', *Y*

Cymmrodor, 50 (1951), 80–82 · I. Jones, *Printing and printers in Wales and Monmouthshire* (1925), 60–68 · G. Morgan, *Y dyn a wnaeth argraff: bywyd a gwaith yr argraffydd hynod John Jones, Llanrwst* (1982) · D. Jones, *Baledi Dafydd Jones* (1991) · *Cymru*, 25 (1903), 93–8, 141–6, 203–4 · G. H. Jenkins, '"Dyn glew iawn": Dafydd Jones o Drefriw, 1703–1785', *Cadw tŷ mewn cwmwl tystion: ysgrifau hanesyddol ar grefydd a diwylliant* (1990), 175–97 · G. M. Griffiths, 'Teulu Dafydd Jones o Drefriw', *National Library of Wales Journal*, 7 (1951–2), 73–4 · A. Lewis, 'Llythyrau Evan Evans at Dafydd Jones o Drefriw', *Llên Cymru*, 1 (1950–51), 239–58 · E. Rees, ed., *Libri Walliae: a catalogue of Welsh books and books printed in Wales, 1546–1820*, 2 vols. (1987) · J. H. Davies, ed., *A bibliography of Welsh ballads printed in the 18th century* (1911) [annotated copy, NL Wales; 1908–11] · *Additional letters of the Morrises of Anglesey, 1735–1786*, ed. H. Owen, 1 (1947), 300–12, 315–19, 325–30, 333–4, 343–5, 347, 368–9, 371–2, 380–81, 389, 420, 427, 432, 439–43, 468, 501–7, 521–3, 627–8, 678, 692–3, 704 · J. E. Lloyd, R. T. Jenkins, and W. L. Davies, eds., *Y bywgraffiadur Cymreig hyd 1940* (1953) · Dafydd Jones, notes, NL Wales, Cwrtmawr 98E · S. I. Wicken, 'Threat to home of Welsh printer', *North Wales Weekly News* (18 Feb 1971)

Archives BL, MSS, Add. MSS 9864–9867, 14973–14975, 14978–14987, 14989, 14997–14998, 15038–15040, 15045–15046 · NL Wales, corresp., 31, 476, 2039, 12029 · NL Wales, Cwrtmawr 98 · NL Wales, J. T. Evans MSS, 11990–12040 | NL Wales, MSS, 9, 57, 175, 255, 783, 841, 843, 2039, 3107, 11992, 11993, 11994, 13219, 21469, 11998; Cwrtmawr 39, 48, 237; Cardiff 1.2, 1.7, 4.10

Jones, Dafydd (1711–1777), hymn writer, was the son of Daniel John, a drover of Cwm Gogerddan, in the parish of Caeo, Carmarthenshire, where he was born early in 1711. A farmer and drover like his father, he lived in his native parish until *c.*1763, when he moved to Hafod Dafolog, near Llanwrda, a farm belonging to his second wife, and remained there until his death. When a young man, returning from one of his trips to England, Jones called in at the Troedrhiwdalar meeting-house, near Builth Wells, and experienced a religious conversion. He later became a lifelong member of the Crug-y-bar dissenting church and was known as the liveliest of proselytes who found it necessary to defend his physical reactions when praising his saviour. 'Why should I not leap if I do it with respect', he said in one of his poems, 'and dance like David before the ark' (*Difyrrwch i'r pererinion*, 1764, 7). His first wife was Ann Jones of Llanddewibrefi (*d.* 1748), his second a Miss Price of Llanwrda. There were two daughters of the first marriage, and a further five daughters of the second.

Jones's work as a drover had given him a good knowledge of English and before his conversion he was known as a folk poet, with a taste for lampoonery. At the request of some dissenting ministers he agreed to sanctify his talents by translating the psalms and hymns of Isaac Watts. These appeared in *Salmau Dafydd* (1753), *Caniadau dwyfol i blant* (1771), and *Hymnau a chaniadau ysbrydol* (1775). He also translated verses by Joseph Hart, John Cennick, Philip Doddridge, and Charles Wesley. His translations and adaptations proved popular, as did his original hymns, published in three parts under the title *Difyrrwch i'r pererinion o fawl i'r Oen* (1763, 1764, 1770). The versions of Watts's hymns served well as a more widely used replacement for the earlier *Salmau cân* of Edmwnd Prys. Several of Jones's longer religious songs are attempts to spiritualize the idiom of secular love songs, while his rhyming and selection of metres in his hymns often reveal his origins as a

country versifier. Above all, his best hymns are notable for their positive expression of joy and thankfulness for the gift of salvation.

Jones died at Hafod Dafolog on 30 August 1777.

E. G. MILLWARD

Sources G. M. Roberts, *Dafydd Jones o Gaeo* (1948) · B. F. Roberts, 'The literature of the "great awakening"', *A guide to Welsh literature*, ed. B. Jarvis, 4: *c.1700–1800* (2000), 279–304 · J. Thickens, *Emynau a'u hawduriaid*, rev. edn (1961) · A. Griffiths, M. Rhys, D. Jones o Gaes, and D. William, *Pedwar emynydd*, ed. B. Jones (1970), 76–91 · E. G. Millward, ed., *Blodeugerdd Barddas o gerddi rhydd y ddeunawfed ganrif* (1991), 101–10 · J. Peter and R. J. Pryse, eds., *Enwogion y ffydd*, 2 vols. (1878–84), vol. 2, pp. 145–50 · *Yr Adolygydd*, 2 (1852), 475–95 · *Y Traethodydd*, 5 (1849), 370–87 · *DNB*

Wealth at death rich: *Yr Adolygydd*

Jones, Daniel (1881–1967), phonetician, was born on 12 September 1881 at 12 Norfolk Crescent, near Marble Arch in central London, the son of a leading London barrister, also named Daniel Jones (1834–1915), and his second wife, Viola Carte (1848–1925). Jones was the third of four sons (his two elder brothers being from his father's previous marriage). His mother came from a notable musical family and was the sister of Richard D'Oyly Carte, the theatre impresario who sponsored Sir W. S. Gilbert and Sir Arthur Sullivan. Apart from his legal talents, Daniel Jones senior is also known as one of the enthusiasts who helped develop the modern game of tennis. In 1890 the Jones family moved to Wimbledon, where the Lawn Tennis Association had its headquarters, and it was there that young Daniel spent his formative years.

Education and early career Jones began his education at Ludgrove preparatory school and spent two years at Radley College; he left in 1897 to complete his schooling as a day boy at University College School, London. He went on to read mathematics at King's College, Cambridge; he obtained his BA degree in 1903 and proceeded MA in 1907. While still an undergraduate he became fascinated with language and developed his practical talents in this area by attending short language courses, first in England and later in Germany. There he spent a month at Marburg, where he was introduced to phonetics by a man whom Jones held ever afterwards in the highest respect—William Tilly, an Australian-born pioneer of what would later be known as immersion language-teaching techniques.

Intending to follow in his father's profession, on leaving university Jones began to read for the bar. But ill health forced him to interrupt his studies and he took the chance to spend a year (1905–6) in France, promising his father to continue his legal training on his return. He attended classes in phonetics and linguistics at the University of Paris, coming under the influence of Paul Passy, the leading French phonetician of his time. Passy, who remained the most significant influence on Jones's linguistic ideas throughout his life, encouraged him to join the International Phonetic Association (IPA), and to sit the IPA examination in the phonetics of French. Jones passed with outstanding marks and was persuaded by Passy to consider making phonetics his career. It is notable that he obtained no further linguistic qualifications of any sort,

Daniel Jones (1881–1967), by unknown photographer

even though he was later awarded honorary doctorates from Zürich (1936) and Edinburgh (1958).

Jones returned to London and fulfilled his filial duty by completing his legal studies, being called to the bar in 1907; but, realizing that he had no interest whatsoever in the law, he had meanwhile obtained a part-time appointment as a temporary lecturer in phonetics at University College, London. It was at this point that he also took private tuition from the Oxford phonetician and linguist Henry Sweet, already a legendary figure in his own lifetime. Sweet was to prove the third formative influence on Jones's linguistic outlook.

On 29 August 1911 Jones married Cyrille Motte (1890–1969), Paul Passy's niece; they had a son and daughter. Until 1934 Jones and his family lived in London, but he then bought a house at 3 Marsham Way, Gerrards Cross, Buckinghamshire, where he remained until his death.

For several years Jones, teaching single-handed, not only drew increasing numbers of students to his classes but also undertook research in many areas of articulatory phonetics. This included work on what were, to the Western world at that time, virtually unknown non-European languages. He was eventually allowed to take on some part-time staff at University College, and later (in 1913) set up a laboratory for experimental phonetic research.

Recognition and publications In 1912 University College recognized the significance of the work of Jones and his colleagues when a university department (the first such in Britain) was set up with Jones at its head. This also happened to be the year in which Bernard Shaw wrote *Pygmalion*, and it is known that Jones helped Shaw by advising him on technical matters. Despite what would appear to be deliberately misleading remarks in Shaw's preface, attempting to link the play to the recently deceased Henry Sweet, it is now thought likely that it was Daniel Jones who largely inspired Shaw's fictional phonetician Henry Higgins.

In 1913–14 Jones taught one day a week at Oxford University for two terms, acting effectively as Sweet's replacement, but refused the offer of a full-time post. Instead, in 1915, he accepted a readership from London. Despite the war his department was growing in size and significance, and it continued to expand after the war. Several more staff, including full-timers, were now recruited to cope with increasing student numbers, and many distinguished linguists began their careers under Jones's aegis, including Lilias Armstrong, Arthur Lloyd James, Harold Palmer, Ida Ward, and, later, J. R. Firth. In 1921 Jones was appointed to a chair in phonetics, the first in a modern linguistic discipline ever to be set up in a British university; he held this post until his retirement in 1949, when he was granted the title of professor emeritus.

Jones—like his mentors Tilly, Passy, and Sweet—was renowned for remarkable powers of auditory discrimination and imitation, and for insisting on the primacy of such practical aspects in phonetic teaching and research. This is reflected in the excellent standards of observation of phonetic phenomena to be found both in his own publications and in those of his followers. Jones's outstanding early works include *Intonation Curves*, an early quasi-instrumental study of pitch that appeared in 1909, and in the same year he published the elementary, but highly successful, *Pronunciation of English*. The first editions of the latter were characterized by a largely prescriptive elocutionary approach, together with occasional proscription of non-standard pronunciations. Despite its commercial success, Jones soon became positively ashamed of the book. He thoroughly revised the material in 1950, replacing the prescriptivism by his later liberal views on accent variation, and in this improved form it remains in print to the present day.

In 1913 Jones co-edited (with Hermann Michaelis) the *Phonetic Dictionary of the English Language*. Surprisingly, no serious attempt at a dedicated English pronunciation dictionary had been produced in Britain since the eighteenth century. But, though worthy of recognition as a pioneering effort, it was completely overshadowed in 1917 by the success of Jones's own masterly and comprehensive *English Pronouncing Dictionary*—or *EPD*, as it is often known. From his original prescriptive position, in which he advocated elocutionary training for dialect speakers in order for them to acquire standard pronunciation, Jones had quite rapidly moved to the view that all had the right to use whatever type of pronunciation they themselves preferred. He considered that it was no part of the phonetician's task to decide on speech standards, but rather to be totally objective in describing current usage, declaring pithily that a phonetician should ideally be 'a living phonograph'. Such an open-minded standpoint was decades ahead of its time, and Jones encountered much opposition to his liberal attitudes. None the less, the *EPD* set the global standard for all subsequent pronunciation dictionaries, rapidly becoming the recognized authority on British usages—a position it held unchallenged until the 1990s. In revised form, it still has large sales in many countries.

Together with the *EPD*, Jones's other most influential work proved to be the *Outline of English Pronunciation* (1918). Aimed originally at the foreign learner, this was the first reliable comprehensive description of the pronunciation of English, or indeed of any language. The non-regional variety of educated British English used as a descriptive model was later (in 1926, in the third edition of the *EPD*) designated 'Received Pronunciation'; Jones by reviving a little-used Victorian expression was the innovator, in a modern context, both of the technical term and its more common abbreviation, RP. The general phonetic descriptive framework of the *Outline* penetrated linguistics worldwide, having a profound influence on Leonard Bloomfield and the whole American structuralist school. Jones's *Outline*, completely revised and rewritten in 1932, reigned for more than forty years as the unique authority on British English pronunciation; it is still in print today.

Jones also produced seminal research on African and Asian languages—notably the *Cantonese Phonetic Reader* (1912), the *Sechuana Reader* (1916), and the *Colloquial Sinhalese Reader* (1919)—invariably written in co-operation with reliable native-speaker informants, who were given full credit as co-authors. The results were classic works that are milestones in the history of the phonetic descriptions of the languages concerned. In particular, Jones produced ground-breaking work on the analysis of tone languages for which he has yet to receive adequate recognition. His *Cantonese Phonetic Reader* was one of the earliest studies in the field. This was followed by the innovative *Sechuana Reader*, which contained a perceptive analysis of register tone in the southern African language Tswana, including the feature eventually to become known as 'downstep'. Jones's research on African languages was subsequently continued, not only at University College but also by several of his former students at the School of Oriental and African Studies.

Jones was the first writer in English to use the word 'phoneme' in its current sense of a minimal unit of sound capable of distinguishing meaning, borrowing the concept from the Polish linguist Jan Baudouin de Courtenay. It was in a lecture given to the London Philological Society in 1917 that Jones appears to have used the term publicly for the first time, though he later claimed that the theory had occupied a 'regular place in the teaching' of his department from 1915 onwards. Jones was ultimately responsible for the promulgation of the phoneme principle in the pre-1920 Western world. It was certainly owing to him and his London colleagues that phonemic concepts became firmly established in British linguistics by the early 1920s—well before the advent of either the European Prague school or the American linguistic structuralists.

The *Pronunciation of Russian*, which for long was the only reliable phonetic description of the language, appeared in 1923. In 1927 Jones was a co-author of *Colloquial French*, issued with accompanying disc recordings—a now largely forgotten *tour de force* which was a watershed in applied linguistics, being the most successful early example of the audio-lingual method in language teaching. He then turned from writing books to concentrate on producing numerous influential articles, including several on the phoneme concept. These can now be seen as leading up to *The Phoneme: its Nature and Use*, the book Jones regarded as his life's work. When the book eventually came out in 1950, many linguists considered it outdated; he was bitterly disappointed with the critical reception it received. In the immediately following years, after his official retirement, Jones produced important revisions of several of his major books and, in 1957, the historiographical *History and Meaning of the Term 'Phoneme'*.

Another significant aspect of Jones's work is his system of cardinal vowels, the underlying research for which was first made known in 1917 through an article in *Nature*. It provided an elegantly simple dual-parameter model of vowel description based on tongue-arch height and lip shape. Jones subsequently elaborated on the theory, and arrived eventually at a system of eight rounded and eight unrounded front and back vowels at articulatorily equidistant intervals, plus two close central vowels. Jones produced three recorded versions of the vowels, of which the last (1956) is the best known. Although its theoretical basis is now largely rejected, the cardinal vowel system has nevertheless been widely adopted ever since its inception; most non-instrumental methods of vowel description derive ultimately from Jones's model.

Other activities From 1906 on, Jones was, together with Paul Passy, the main force behind the IPA, and editor of its influential organ, *Le Maître Phonétique*, thus playing a leading role in spreading the International Phonetic Alphabet, and laying the foundation for the universal recognition it enjoys today. He was elected assistant secretary of the IPA in 1909 and made secretary in 1928; from 1950 onwards he was the association's president.

Jones was also a supporter of spelling reform: in 1911 he joined the committee of the British Simplified Spelling Society and in 1946 was appointed president, a position he retained until he died. He also co-operated enthusiastically on schemes for alphabets later adopted for various African languages, and subsequently devised romanized alphabets for Indian languages and Japanese.

In 1926 Jones became a founder member of the BBC advisory committee on spoken English. Perhaps because of his disagreement with the eccentrically prescriptive views of certain members of the committee—which included such eminent figures as Bernard Shaw and the poet laureate Robert Bridges—he left dealings with it largely to his former pupil and colleague Arthur Lloyd James. When, on the outbreak of war, the committee ceased to function, and later, as the result of tragic personal circumstances, Lloyd James's contacts with the BBC ceased, Jones took over. From 1942 to 1967 Daniel Jones was chief pronunciation adviser to the BBC, and in that role, paradoxically considering his libertarian linguistic views, was to a degree responsible for reinforcing the notion of 'BBC English' as a pronunciation standard. The early editions of his books now provide us with interesting information on the state of English pronunciation at the time. The first mentions of the spread of the glottal stop in English are to be found in Jones's works, as are predictions of future language change, including hints of the increasing influence of vernacular London speech on RP, thus presaging what is nowadays termed 'estuary English'.

Apart from linguistic matters, Jones's only other major preoccupation was the study of oriental religion and philosophy, in particular as interpreted by theosophists and similar groups. In his youth, religion of any kind had concerned him little, but by the time he reached middle age, theosophical ideas began to play an increasingly important part in his daily thought. Such concepts even infiltrate into his linguistic writings, and it is difficult to interpret some of his later statements on the phoneme without taking due account of them. Theosophical influences also seem to be why Jones from the 1930s onwards emphasized the benefits of applied practical phonetics, and increasingly regarded scientific approaches with suspicion.

Final years Jones continued working—writing and revising his academic publications, playing a full part in the IPA and the Simplified Spelling Society, and advising on pronunciation for the BBC—long after his official retirement, in fact well into his eighties. His very last jointly written book, the *Phonetics of Russian* (1969), did not in fact appear until after his death. In old age he came to be considered almost as a kind of elder statesman of phonetics, and scholars from all over the world came to consult him on linguistic matters. After a long period of illness, exacerbated by painful arthritis, he died on 4 December 1967 at his home in Gerrards Cross.

It is indicative that so many of Jones's books remained in print into the twenty-first century, and that he is still so frequently cited as a phonetic authority. His writings, now regarded as classic works, have proved outstanding, not only for reliability but also for lucid explication. They established him as by far the best-known phonetician of his generation. His ideas and methods, later to be propagated by his colleagues and former pupils, even now continue to influence most areas of phonetics and pronunciation teaching. Jones takes his place among the world's leading figures in twentieth-century linguistics; his claim to be the greatest of all British phoneticians is challenged only by Sweet.   BEVERLEY COLLINS

Sources B. Collins and I. M. Mees, *The real Professor Higgins: the life and career of Daniel Jones* (1999) · A. C. Gimson, 'Daniel Jones', *Le Maître Phonétique*, 3rd ser., 46 (1968), 2–6 · D. Jones, 'In the days of my youth', *T. P.'s and Cassell's Weekly* (2 Jan 1926) · D. Abercrombie, 'Daniel Jones's teaching', *Fifty years in phonetics* (1991), 37–47 · A. C. Gimson, 'Daniel Jones and standards of English pronunciation', *English Studies*, 58 (1977), 151–8 · private information (2004) [M. Stanbury, daughter; family] · records, King's Cam.
Archives UCL, papers | UCL, Roger Kingdon papers | SOUND BL NSA · BBC sound archives
Likenesses photograph, SOAS · photograph, UCL, department of phonetics and linguistics · photograph, University of Witwatersrand, South Africa [see illus.] · photographs, UCL; repro. in Collins and Mees, *The real Professor Higgins*
Wealth at death £19,562: probate, 7 March 1968, *CGPLA Eng. & Wales*

Jones, David. *See* Johns, David (*fl.* 1572–1598).

Jones, David (1662/3–1724), Church of England clergyman, was born in Caerfallwch, Flintshire, the son of Matthew Jones. He entered Westminster School in 1678 and while there gave evidence of what would prove to be his salient characteristic, a total inability to accept people or affairs on any terms other than his own. In 1679 a group of schoolboys, seeking to prevent a distraint in a neighbouring house, beat the bailiff to death. Jones was picked out at an identity parade as one of eleven boys involved. A royal pardon was obtained for all of them but Jones and two others refused it, stood trial, and were acquitted. One of the three had an alibi but it is not known whether this was Jones.

Jones matriculated at Christ Church, Oxford, in December 1681, aged eighteen, and obtained his BA in 1685. There was some incident in 1688 which resulted in his having to write a letter of apology to the dean and chapter, and he was no longer resident when he became eligible for the MA. He was, however, developing a reputation as a preacher, and in 1690 he delivered a sermon in London in which he set out his principles: he would criticize the vices of his auditory rather than complimenting their virtues. Having obtained a position as preacher to a church in Lombard Street he was as good as his word, making usury and riches his main target; he was dismissed amid controversy, one complaint being that his sermons attracted dissenters.

Jones proceeded MA at Oxford in 1693. In 1694 Christ Church named him to the cure of Great Budworth, Cheshire, but he remained there only until 1696. Back in Oxford his preaching began to draw crowds, attracted by the extravagance of his language and gestures. He became involved in a stupid dispute with a man whom he found mowing in the university parks on a Sunday, and this culminated in criticism of the vice-chancellor for his lack of religious zeal and a sentence of six months in Oxford Castle. Jones extricated himself by a writ of habeas corpus and moved on in 1699 to another Christ Church living, that of Marcham, in Berkshire.

Trouble with Jones's new parishioners began almost immediately. By 1701 the churchwardens had a presentment for the archdeacon's visitation that covered eight closely-written foolscap pages of complaint about his behaviour. He disdained the prayer book and refused the sacraments to those whom he considered unworthy. He shouted and brawled, using bad language both in and outside church. He was suspected of having illicit designs on the daughters of the village élite. He tried to reserve charity money for the godly, as opposed to the wicked, poor. He tried to suborn the churchwardens into buying excessive amounts of communion wine for his own use. Most seriously he performed the customary rites of passage reluctantly, capriciously, offensively, or not at all.

From this time onwards there was constant litigation both in the church and in the civil courts. Much of this related to insults exchanged in or out of church but the main landholders were also withholding tithes and depriving Jones of his income. In 1707 the lord of the manor made major encroachments on the churchyard, which led to Jones refusing to bury a body brought by a diverted path. He was suspended for six months by his bishop but, when he and the churchwardens both tried to introduce curates, there was a bout of fisticuffs in the church and a sequence of arrests and counter-arrests for assault and wrongful imprisonment.

In November 1709 Jones was confined within the rules of queen's bench, apparently for debt, and he does not seem to have returned to his cure until 1719; during this time the living was under sequestration and administered by the churchwardens, who paid a local man as curate. The interval did nothing to change Jones's behaviour, and drunkenness was added to the list of his failings. He was buried at Marcham on 7 August 1724. A wife, Susannah, who had been living in London, was granted administration of his estate. Jones is alleged also to have had a mistress, with whom he had two children—a boy (born c.1706) and a girl (born c.1708) (Remarks, 8.249–50).

Theologically Jones's position is difficult to assess. He was always critical of his fellow clergymen, who were unwilling to make enemies among the powerful members of their flock, whatever their vices, and always ready to claim that people he disapproved of were ineluctably damned. However, his surviving sermons suggest that this stance, while it may have translated into popularity with dissenters, did not equate with doctrinaire Calvinism. His imprisonment in 1709 could have had a political dimension, as Jones was often compared as a preacher to Henry Sacheverell, but there is no firm evidence to support this interpretation. A frustration to his congregations, Jones's motivation remains enigmatic.   MANFRED BROD

Sources Bodl. Oxf., MS Rawl. J, fol. 6, ff 298–303v · churchwardens' presentments, Berks. RO, D/A2, c. 125 · episcopal court papers, Wilts. & Swindon RO, D1/41/3/23 · Remarks and collections of Thomas Hearne, ed. C. E. Doble and others, 11 vols., OHS, 2, 7, 13, 34, 42–3, 48, 50, 65, 67, 72 (1885–1921), vol. 2, pp. 18–19; vol. 8, pp. 249–50 · J. B. Whitmore, 'A forgotten episode', The Elizabethan [magazine of Westminster School], 18 (1926), 83–4 · calendar of estate papers, Berkshire, Christ Church Oxf., 287, 300 · BL, Add. MS 39990, fol. 30 · sequestration accounts, 1712–16, Wilts. & Swindon RO · D. Jones, A sermon preached at Christ Church London, Nov 2 1690 · admon., PRO, PROB 6/100, fol. 173v · Nichols, Illustrations, 3.268 · W. Kennet, letter to Arthur Charlet, 11 May 1700, Bodl. Oxf., MSS Ballard 7, 43 · Foster, Alum. Oxon.

Jones, David (fl. 1675–1720), spy and historian, was the son of the Revd John Jones of Llanbadarn Odwyn, Cardiganshire, one of the earliest nonconformist ministers in that part of Wales. According to John Dunton, he was 'designed for the ministry, but began to teach school, and from that employment turned author and corrector for the press' (Life and Errors, 181).

In the preface to his principal work, The Secret History of White-hall (1697), Jones himself states that he went to France in 1675 with instruction from a certain 'Noble Person' to transmit information about the French court. About 1676 the secretary-interpreter to the marquis de Louvois, a Scot called Kilpatrick, died. He was replaced by a favourite of Louvois called Belou, who could speak no

English and hired Jones to assist him. If Jones's account is true, this was an ideal position for a spy to hold. According to this account Jones stayed in France until the 1688 revolution in Britain, when he returned briefly to England. He was then sent back to France, again by the unnamed nobleman, to continue his espionage. He was certainly back in England by 1696, as the preface to his Secret History is dated 'from my House in Clerkenwell, Nov. 9 1696'.

In addition to his history of Whitehall, which covered the period 1660 to 1688, Jones contributed in 1697 a further volume examining the first seven years of William III's reign. Despite the titles, these histories hardly mention Whitehall. Rather they consist of a series of letters purporting to have been written by Jones to his supposed employer, the unnamed English peer, between January 1676 and May 1695, while Jones was Louvois's secretary-interpreter. They profess to divulge the secret diplomatic transactions that had passed between the English and French courts during the period covered by the letters. Among other sensational information, they claim that money amounting to £600,000 was paid by the French king to Charles II. It has been suggested, however (N&Q), that little reliance can be placed on Jones's authenticity as it would have been difficult for an English spy to maintain his official position in France for so long.

From 1705 to 1720 Jones published annually A Compleat History of Europe, which reached a total of eighteen volumes. He also wrote a number of other histories, dealing with Anglo-French wars, Turkey, James II, William III, and the house of Brunswick. He translated Paul Pezron's Antiquité de la nation as The Antiquities of Nations (1706), and claimed to have revised and made additions to the second edition of Roger Coke's The Detection of Court and State of England, published in London in 1696. He may also (Williams, 122) have written biographies of Sir Stephen Fox, Dr South, the earl of Halifax, and Dr Radcliffe. Nothing is known about Jones after 1720.   ALEXANDER DU TOIT

Sources DNB · B. Williams [Gwynionydd], Enwogion Ceredigion (1869), 121–2 · N&Q, 4th ser., 11 (1873), 154–5 · The life and errors of John Dunton, [rev. edn], 1, ed. J. B. Nichols (1818), 181–2 · D. Jones, preface, The secret history of White-hall (1697)

Jones, David (1699–1775), politician and jurist in America, was born on 16 September 1699 at Fort Neck, Oyster Bay, Queens county, New York. He was the second of eight children of Thomas Jones (c.1665–1713) and Freelove (1674–1726), daughter of Thomas Townsend of Rhode Island. Thomas Jones of Strabane, co. Tyrone, Ireland, fought in James II's army at the battle of the Boyne (1690), the battle of Aughrim (1691), and the siege of Limerick (1691). In 1692 he escaped to France and became a privateer. He married Freelove Townsend in Rhode Island about 1695 and subsequently moved to Oyster Bay, where his father-in-law had given him a large tract of land. Thomas Jones eventually became a freeholder of Oyster Bay (1699), high sheriff of Queens county (1704), major in the county militia (1706), and ranger-general of Nassau Island (1710). Thomas died at Fort Neck on 13 December 1713; his wife died in July 1726.

Their son David Jones inherited the paternal estate and

thereby became one of the largest landowners in Queens county; by 1755 he had also acquired ten slaves, which made him a leading slave owner in Oyster Bay. He married Anna Willett (c.1704–1750) on 22 November 1722, and they had six children: Anna, Sarah, Thomas, Arabella, David, and Mary. Jones subsequently married his first wife's niece, Margaret, daughter of Colonel William Willett of Westchester county and widow of John Tredwell. They had no children.

Having trained in New York in the legal profession, Jones apparently practised law in New York city for several years, and was appointed a judge of the inferior court of common pleas for Queens county in 1734. He was elected in 1737 from Queens county to the New York assembly, where he served until 1758. While a member of that body Jones championed the privileges of the assembly against the prerogatives of the governor. To benefit his own constituents he also strenuously (though unsuccessfully) resisted lowering the taxes the province levied on New York city. With the backing of James De Lancey, who was one of the colony's most powerful politicians, Jones was elected speaker of the assembly in 1745. An Anglican in a province where Anglicans wielded considerable power, and a gifted politician who was especially skilled at charming small groups, Jones served as speaker until December 1758, when the twenty-seventh assembly was dissolved.

Jones was not elected to the next assembly because of his opposition to Governor George Clinton's policies during King George's War (1740–48), his support for the Anglican-dominated King's College in the 1750s, and the belief among many of his Presbyterian and Quaker constituents that he had become a mere tool of James De Lancey. In anticipation of this event De Lancey had already appointed Jones a puisne justice of the New York supreme court in 1758. Jones was re-elected to the assembly in 1761, but he was declared illegally returned on 3 April of that year. New elections were ordered. In the event the election was disputed, and the assembly seated his opponent. Jones remained on the bench until ill health forced him to retire in 1773. Governor William Tryon thereupon appointed Jones's son Thomas to his father's vacated seat. David Jones died at Fort Neck on 11 October 1775. He was buried in the old burial-ground of Major Thomas Jones at Fort Neck, but was later reinterred in Grace churchyard, South Oyster Bay.

David's son Thomas (1731–1792) married Anne, daughter of Lieutenant-Governor De Lancey, in 1762, and became a noted loyalist during the American War of Independence. In 1781 Thomas left for England, where he wrote his *History of New York during the revolutionary war and of the leading events in the other colonies at that period*. The book, which was published posthumously in 1879, blamed Presbyterian republicans (who had opposed his father and his father-in-law in the 1750s) for causing the revolution, and condemned corrupt and incompetent British officials for losing the war.

JOSEPH S. TIEDEMANN

Sources T. Floyd-Jones, *Thomas Jones, Fort Neck, Queens county, Long Island, 1695, and his descendants the Floyd-Jones family: with connections from the year 1066* (1906) • J. H. Jones, *The Jones family of Long Island: descendants of Major Thomas Jones (1665–1726) and allied families* (1907) • T. Jones, *History of New York during the revolutionary war*, ed. E. F. De Lancey, 2 vols. (1879) • W. Smith, *The history of the province of New-York* (1757); repr. M. Kammen, ed., 2 (New York, 1972) • E. B. O'Callaghan, ed., *Lists of inhabitants of colonial New York: excerpted from 'The documentary history of the state of New York'* (1979) • A. Tully, *Forming American politics: ideas, interests, and institutions in colonial New York and Pennsylvania* (1994) • P. U. Bonomi, *A factious people: politics and society in colonial New York* (1971) • P. Ross, *A history of Long Island from its earliest settlement to the present time*, 1 (1902) • 'New York, October 16', *New-York Gazette, and the Weekly Mercury* (16 Oct 1775) • *IGI*

Wealth at death land: will, Floyd-Jones, *Thomas Jones*

Jones, David (1736–1810), Church of England clergyman and Methodist preacher, was, according to later entries in his diary, born on 10 July 1736 at Aberceiliog in the parish of Llanllwni in Carmarthenshire, the son of Richard Jones and his wife, Gwenllian (d. 1778). A childhood accident, in which he fell into a vat of boiling milk, left him somewhat frail in his youth. As a result it was decided that he should enter the church rather than take up work on his father's farm. He was educated at Carmarthen grammar school before being ordained deacon in the Anglican church in 1758. He served for brief periods as curate of Tudweiliog in the Llŷn peninsula (1758–9) and at Llanafan Fawr in Brecknockshire (1759–60) before being ordained priest in August 1760. In 1761 he moved to the curacies of Trefeithin and Caldicot in Monmouthshire, where he began to develop evangelical tendencies. He subsequently moved to Bristol and then to Crudwell in Wiltshire in 1764. It was during this period in England that he made the acquaintance of Selina, countess of Huntingdon, through whose influence on his behalf he obtained the living of Llan-gan in Glamorgan from Lady Charlotte Edwin in 1767.

At Llan-gan Jones became well known for his ability as a preacher. In his elegy to Daniel Rowland, William Williams claimed that the sweetness and power of Jones's preaching was enough to melt stones and cause the strongest oaks to bend (Jones, 1.588). His parish became a centre for Methodists, who travelled miles to hear his sermons and to receive communion. His renown as a preacher spread and he was frequently invited to preach throughout Wales as well as in a number of the countess of Huntingdon's chapels in England. Prolonged absences on preaching trips led to complaints being made to bishops Barrington and Watson of Llandaff, neither of whom curtailed his activities. It was a mark of the respect afforded him as a preacher that he was invited to deliver a sermon at the funeral service of that other great Methodist orator, Daniel Rowland, in 1790. He also composed several hymns, mostly for his own edification. His published works consisted of two sermons, one of which was preached at the funeral service of the countess of Huntingdon at Spa Fields in 1791, and a brief biography in Welsh of the Revd Christopher Basset in 1784 (*Llythyr oddi wrth Dafydd ab Ioan y Pererin*).

Jones married twice. His first marriage to Sinah Bowen of Waunifor took place on 1 January 1771 and produced three children. Following his first wife's death in 1792 he subsequently married a wealthy widow, Mrs Bowen Parry of Manorowen, Pembrokeshire, in 1794. Following this marriage Manorowen became his permanent home, although he continued to make monthly trips to officiate at Llan-gan and spent three months of each year in the area. He remained as vicar of Llan-gan until his death in 1810 and his name is inextricably linked with that parish.

Jones was a conciliatory presence in the Methodist Association meetings and always strove to keep the peace and avoid controversy whenever possible. His complete lack of ambition may account for the fact that he did not inherit Daniel Rowland's mantle as leader of the movement following the latter's death in 1791. Despite his reluctance to countenance any split from the established church, he was active in collecting money for chapel-building and his name appears among the founding trustees of many early Methodist chapels. He was also closely involved with the endeavours of Thomas Charles of Bala to distribute bibles among the people of Wales. He died at Manorowen on 12 August 1810, the year before the Methodist movement finally established itself as a separate denomination. He thus remained both a loyal servant of the established church and a fervent Methodist throughout his life.

ERYN M. WHITE

Sources R. B. Higham, 'The life and work of the Rev. David Jones of Llangan, 1736–1810', MTh diss., U. Wales, 1981 · G. M. Roberts, ed., Hanes Methodistiaeth Galfinaidd Cymru, 2 (1978) · E. Evans, 'David Jones of Llan-gan: consolidating a work of God', Fire in the thatch (1996), 134–45 · J. Hughes, Methodistiaeth Cymru, 1 (1851) · J. Hughes, Methodistiaeth Cymru, 2 (1854) · J. Hughes, Methodistiaeth Cymru, 3 (1856) · E. Morgan, A brief account of D. Jones (1841) · Gweithiau Williams Pant-y-celyn, ed. N. C. Jones, 1 (1887)
Archives Glamorgan RO, Cardiff, corresp. · NL Wales, Calvinist Methodist archive, sermons, etc.
Likenesses line engraving, c.1778, BM, NPG; repro. in Gospel Magazine (1778) · portrait, repro. in Evangelical Magazine (1807)

Jones, David [pseud. the Welsh Freeholder] (1765–1816), barrister, was the only son of John and Margaret Jones of Bwlchygwynt, near Llandovery, Carmarthenshire, where his father farmed his own freehold. He received his early education at Pencader and Abergavenny, and in 1783 entered Homerton Academy, London, to train for the ministry among the Calvinistic Methodists. Before completing his studies, he changed his views on the Trinity and the person of Christ, and moved to New College, Hackney. There he became one of Dr Richard Price's students, and tutor and lecturer in experimental science. While at Hackney, Jones was drawn into the affairs of the diocese of St David's. Representing himself as a 'plain rustic', he adopted the pseudonym of the Welsh Freeholder, in a series of skilfully penned letters against the sharp anti-unitarian attacks of Bishop Samuel Horsley's visitation charge of 1790. He defended Joseph Priestley after the Church and King mob had destroyed Priestley's home and scientific apparatus in July 1791. However, his Thoughts on the Riots at Birmingham, a reprint of an anonymous letter written by him in the Morning Chronicle was republished under his own name without his authority.

In October 1792, Jones took charge of the New Meeting congregation at Birmingham, as successor to Joseph Priestley, who had recommended him for the post. David Jones's theology was strongly influenced by Joseph Priestley's preoccupations, as is clearly seen in his major work, published in 1792, Reasons for Unitarianism, or, The Primitive Christian Doctrine, another invective against the charge of Samuel Horsley. His politics were reminiscent of his former tutor, Dr Richard Price. He admired the republican constitution in France, and opposed war with revolutionary France. In The Welsh Freeholder's farewell epistles to the Right Rev. Samuel lord bishop (lately of St David's), now of Rochester, published in 1794, he was forced to admit, in light of the terror, that Bishop Horsley's view on the French Revolution had been correct. Nevertheless, he was still opposed to war with France and in February 1795 delivered a discourse, at the Union Chapel in Birmingham, entitled 'Reasons for peace'. This was his last public pronouncement, and he afterwards abandoned theological debate and political life.

Turning to the study of the law, Jones was admitted as a student of Lincoln's Inn on 1 May 1795 and was called to the bar on 26 June 1800. He practised mainly as a chancery barrister, but attached himself as well to the Oxford and south Wales circuits. He also became a member of Gonville and Caius College, Cambridge, graduating BA in 1800 and MA in 1803. Jones died in 1816.

HYWEL MEILYR DAVIES

Sources J. G. Jenkins, Hanfod duw a pherson Crist (1931) · D. O. Thomas, Response to revolution (Ymateb i chwyldro) (1989) · F. P. Jones, Radicaliaeth a'r werin Gymreig yn y bedwaredd ganrif ar bymtheg (1977) · F. C. Mather, High church prophet: Bishop Samuel Horsley (1733–1806) and the Caroline tradition in the later Georgian church (1992) · The correspondence of Richard Price, ed. W. B. Peach and D. O. Thomas, 3 (1994) · R. Williams, Enwogion Cymru: a biographical dictionary of eminent Welshmen (1852) · N&Q, 3rd ser., 11 (1867), 292, 409–10 · J. Kenrick, 'Memoir of the late Rev. Charles Wellbeloved of York', Christian Reformer, or, Unitarian Magazine and Review, new ser., 14 (1858), 617–34, 683–96

Jones, David (1796–1841), missionary in Madagascar, was born at Pen-rhiw, near Neuadd-lwyd, near Aberaeron, Cardiganshire. He was educated at the college of Neuadd-lwyd, chiefly by Dr Phillips, at whose suggestion he and a fellow pupil, Thomas Bevan, were ordained at Neuadd-lwyd in August 1817 as the first protestant missionaries, under the auspices of the London Missionary Society (LMS), to Madagascar. He was married twice: his first wife, who accompanied him to Madagascar, died there in 1818 or 1819 of a feverish illness; his second wife, whom he married in Madagascar in 1821, outlived him and returned to England in 1841. They had several children.

With their wives Jones and Bevan reached Mauritius in April 1818, and with the support of the governor of Mauritius, Sir Robert Farquhar, in August crossed to Madagascar. They were warmly welcomed by Fisatra, king of Tamatave, who sent his own son, with some twelve other boys, to be educated by them. Soon after their arrival, the epidemic which killed Jones's wife also caused the deaths of the Bevans (who were all buried at Tamatave), but Jones survived, returning to Mauritius for fourteen months to recuperate. He returned to Madagascar, accompanied by

Hastie, the governor's agent, and was welcomed by the ruler of the country, King Radama, on 4 September 1820. In 1822 he was joined by another LMS missionary, David Griffiths, with whom he worked on a phonetic orthography of the Malagasy language, giving each letter one sound and using Roman characters. They were helped in their work by another missionary, David Johns, and were soon able to teach writing to local people. The English colonists objected to the use of phonetic spelling, but the missionaries were resolute, and Radama gave it his royal authority. By 1824 the number of missionary school pupils and converts to Christianity had become very large. In 1827 a public examination of the children was held, and the king, a warm advocate of western education, awarded the prizes. Johns had brought a printing press from England and, shortly after, 1500 catechisms, 800 hymnbooks, and 2200 books for spelling and reading were published; in the next year the missionaries' own translation of the gospel of St Luke into Malagasy began to be printed.

During the political upheaval which followed King Radama's death on 27 July 1828 the work of the mission was interrupted. Radama's successor, Queen Ranavalona, withdrew royal support from the proselytizing aspects of the mission and came under pressure from her ministers to prevent the rise of the new religion in Madagascar. Jones and his fellow missionaries continued to translate books of the Bible into Malagasy and, when the queen sent orders that the Bible was not to be taught, managed to secure a revocation of the order. By 1830 most of the work of the mission had been able to resume and Jones and his family returned to Great Britain to campaign on its behalf. But the Jones family returned to Madagascar to find that the political climate had changed again, partly due to Griffiths's lack of tact in handling local sensitivities, and that Christians were being persecuted. The missionaries were formally expelled in 1835. In June 1840 Jones and Captain Campbell visited Ambatomanga to seek royal redress on behalf of the Christians. They were allowed a house each, but soon understood that they were prisoners. The following day a trial was held, and many converts were executed. Jones was injured in an accident, but managed to return to Mauritius, where some of the exiled missionaries had remained in order to help refugees to flee Madagascar. He died there of fever on 1 May 1841, and his widow and children returned to London.

R. M. J. JONES, rev. MARY HEIMANN

Sources B. Williams [Gwynionydd], *Enwogion Ceredigion* (1869) · G. Jones, *Enwogion Sir Aberteifi* (1868) · J. T. Jones, *Geiriadur bywgraffyddol o enwogion Cymru*, 2 vols. (1867–70) · R. Lovett, *The history of the London Missionary Society, 1795–1895*, 1 (1899) · E. H. Hayes, *David Jones: a dauntless pioneer*, 4th edn (1943) · 'Griffiths, David', *DNB* · 'Johns, David (1794–1843)', *DNB* · *DWB*
Likenesses portrait, repro. in Lovett, *History* · portrait, repro. in M. Gate, *Isle of treasures* (1920)

Jones, David James [*pseud.* Gwenallt] **(1899–1968)**, poet and literary scholar, was born in Wesley Terrace, Pontardawe, Glamorgan, on 18 May 1899, the eldest child of Thomas Jones (1867–1927), furnaceman, and his wife, Mary, *née* Jones (1867–1938), both of Carmarthenshire hill-

farming stock who moved to improve their lot in the industrial south. Soon after his birth the family crossed the River Tawe to Yr Allt Wen, from which village Gwenallt derived his bardic name. He attended Ystalyfera county school (1910–17), and after two years' imprisonment as a conscientious objector, including spells in Wormwood Scrubs and Dartmoor, he progressed in 1919 to the University College of Wales, Aberystwyth, emerging with an honours degree in Welsh and English. After a short stint as a teacher at Barry county school, starting in 1925, he returned as a lecturer to the department of Welsh at Aberystwyth in 1927, where he remained until his retirement. Jones married Nel Owen Edwards (*b.* 1908) on 27 March 1937, and a daughter, Mair Gwenallt, was born in 1947. The family lived from 1935 at Rhyd-y-môr, Penparcau.

Throughout his academic career Gwenallt was primarily interested in literary history and criticism. As his poem 'Myfyrdod' ('Meditation') testifies, he loved the scholar's life and was much attracted by eighteenth- and especially nineteenth-century Welsh literature, on which he wrote and lectured with pioneering zeal. His *Blodeugerdd o'r ddeunawfed ganrif* (1936), an anthology of eighteenth-century strict-metre poetry, remains an essential text and, together with his perceptive introductions to *Yr areithiau pros* (1934) and *Detholiad o ryddiaith Gymraeg R. J. Derfel* (1945), as well as his books *Y Ficer Prichard a 'Canwyll y Cymry'* (1946) and *Bywyd a Gwaith Islwyn* (1948), offers proof of his wide-ranging scholarship. He was also the first editor of *Taliesin*, the literary periodical of the Academi Gymreig (Welsh Academy), established in 1959, and as such brought out the first nine numbers between 1961 and 1965.

But it is as a powerful, regenerative national poet, whose verse, in the words of a fellow poet, has the tensile strength of wrought iron, that Gwenallt looms large in Welsh literature. He made his mark in 1926 when his *awdl* 'Y mynach' ('The monk') won him the chair at the Swansea national eisteddfod, and he was to win again at Bangor in 1931 with the *awdl* 'Breuddwyd y bardd' ('The poet's dream'), after his *awdl* 'Y sant' ('The saint') in 1928 had been dismissed as 'a heap of filth' by adjudicators scandalized by its depiction of lust. His first volume of poetry, *Ysgubau'r awen* ('The sheaves of the muse'), appeared in 1938, and was followed by *Cnoi cil* ('Chewing the cud') in 1942, *Eples* ('Ferment') in 1951, *Gwreiddiau* ('Roots') in 1959, and *Y coed* ('The trees'), published posthumously in 1969.

Central to an appreciation of Gwenallt's poetry and his two novels—*Plasau'r brenin* ('The king's mansions', 1934), a would-be psychological novel based on his prison experiences, and his unfinished *Ffwrneisiau* ('Furnaces'), published in 1982—is his testimony in *Credaf: llyfr o dystiolaeth Gristionogol* ('I believe: a book of Christian witness'), edited by J. E. Meredith and published in 1943. A translated version, entitled 'What I believe', appeared in *Planet*, 32 (1976). It is an impassioned retracing of his spiritual journey from a chapel-dominated upbringing, through the travails of pacifism, unbelief, socialism, and nationalism, back to a renewed faith in Christianity. He awoke to a realization of sin as a besetting evil that man, without Christ, was powerless to resist, and he espoused a nationalism rooted in his vision of a Wales fashioned by centuries of Christian belief to serve God.

Ysgubau'r awen, *Eples*, and *Gwreiddiau* are the three volumes which safeguard Gwenallt's status as a national poet. *Y coed* contains poems triggered by a visit to Israel, which are not finished pieces, and also includes his strained elegiac response to the Aberfan tragedy in 1967, which flops into bathos in parts. As his verse forms became progressively more free, so his poetry became less arresting. That he could write memorable free verse is proved by 'Rhydcymerau' in *Eples* and 'Yr hen emynau' ('The old hymns') in *Gwreiddiau*, but Gwenallt was a poet whose fervour caught fire within the confines of more regular metres, as is seen in the sonnets in *Ysgubau'r awen* and in his use of traditional strict metres, such as the *englyn* and *cywydd*. It is equally noteworthy that he fashioned some of his most powerful messages for his own age when tapping into myth and legend.

Jones retired from the department of Welsh at Aberystwyth in 1966, and the University of Wales awarded him an honorary DLitt in 1967. He died of cancer in Aberystwyth General Hospital on 24 December 1968, and was buried in the town cemetery on 27 December. He was survived by his wife. A commemorative plaque was unveiled at his former home, Rhyd-y-môr, on 15 March 1997.

Jones's inimitable voice is heard at its resonant best in the various poems he addressed to Cymru (Wales) over the years; in his inspired evocation in *Eples*, particularly in 'Y meirwon' ('The Dead'), of fraught industrial life in the Swansea valley; in the sonnets in *Ysgubau'r awen*, one of which, 'Pechod' ('Sin'), is one of the great reverberating poems of Welsh literature; and in a number of poems, 'Ar gyfeiliorn' ('Astray') being the definitive example, in which he presses upon a destructively wayward civilization that it is time to reinstate Christ at the heart of things.   HYWEL TEIFI EDWARDS

Sources D. Rowlands, ed., *Bro a bywyd: Gwenallt (David James Jones)*, *1899–1968* (1982) • D. Morgan, *D. Gwenallt Jones* (1972) • J. E. Meredith, *Gwenallt: bardd crefyddol* (1974) • *Y Traethodydd* [Gwenallt, 1899–1968 issue], 124 (1969) • D. G. Jones [D. J. Jones], 'What I believe', *Planet*, 32 (1976), 1–10 • b. cert.
Archives NL Wales, corresp. and papers
Likenesses F. R. Könekamp, oils, repro. in Rowlands, ed., *Bro a bywyd* • J. M. Morris, bronze bust, repro. in Rowlands, ed., *Bro a bywyd* • photographs, repro. in Rowlands, ed., *Bro a bywyd*
Wealth at death £5645: probate, 11 March 1969, *CGPLA Eng. & Wales*

Jones, David Martyn Lloyd- (1899–1981), Calvinistic Methodist minister, was born on 20 December 1899 in the family home at Donald Street, Cardiff, the second of three sons of Henry Lloyd-Jones (*d.* 1922) and his wife, Magdalene Evans (1872–1951). The family owned a shop and milk-round business first at Llangeitho, Cardiganshire, then in August 1914 at Regency Street, London.

Lloyd-Jones won a scholarship in 1911 to Tregaron county school, from there gaining a place in January 1915 at Marylebone grammar school. He became a medical student at St Bartholomew's Hospital, London, in October 1916. At Bart's he received his MRCS and LRCP in July 1921, later gaining his MB and BS (with distinctions) and MD. In October 1921 Lloyd-Jones was selected by Sir Thomas Horder, physician to the royal family, as his junior house physician.

While fulfilling his duties at Harley Street, Lloyd-Jones saw the emptiness of the world around him. At some point in 1923–4 he was converted to Christianity and decided to enter the Christian ministry. As he told Sir Thomas Horder, who tried to dissuade him, 'when you and I as doctors have done all that we can do for our patients, they still have to die. I am going to deal with that part of a man that never dies' (Harrison, 98).

Lloyd-Jones formally accepted a call to Bethlehem Calvinistic Methodist Chapel, Sandfields, Aberafan, south Wales, on 22 December 1926, and on 8 January 1927 married another physician, Bethan Phillips (*b.* 1898). They had two daughters.

Until July 1938 Lloyd-Jones ministered successfully in Aberafan. He preached from the Bible emphasizing the great Reformation themes of God's person, man's sin, God's free salvation, justification by faith alone, and the sufficiency of scripture. The church was soon full, and he preached to packed churches wherever he went. With his clear expository preaching style he was much sought after.

In 1938 Lloyd-Jones became colleague and then assistant to G. Campbell Morgan at Westminster Chapel, London. The war years were difficult, and the congregation dwindled to 200. As sole pastor in 1943 Lloyd-Jones began to build on the work. By the mid-1950s 2000 churchgoers regularly attended his ministry and were enthralled by his biblical message. The historian G. M. Trevelyan, after hearing Lloyd-Jones preach on 'the limit of man's knowledge and the power of Christ', congratulated him saying, 'Sir, it has been given to you to speak with great power' (Dudley Smith, 68). Emil Brunner, the Swiss reformed theologian, called him 'the greatest preacher in Christendom today'. His ministry at Westminster Chapel continued until he retired due to ill health in 1968.

Lloyd-Jones had three preaching styles: teaching for believers (morning services), evangelistic (evening services), and doctrinal (Friday night meetings). Like Charles Spurgeon before him, Lloyd-Jones's written sermons sold in their thousands, the most significant being his mammoth expository series on Romans and Ephesians and the sermon on the mount.

Lloyd-Jones was influential in reformed evangelical circles, playing an important role in a number of organizations: these included the Inter-Varsity Fellowship, the Leicester Ministers Conference, the Evangelical Library, the Evangelical Movement of Wales, the London Bible College, and also the International Fellowship of Evangelical Students. In later years Lloyd-Jones was no stranger to controversy, proposing in 1966, for example, that evangelical churches should leave their denominations, and his Westminster Chapel seceded from the Congregational Union.

In later years Lloyd-Jones remained active: preaching, editing his sermons, and advising ministers on practical and doctrinal matters. He died peacefully in his sleep on 1 March 1981 in Ealing, London, and was buried on Friday 6 March in the Cardiganshire town of Newcastle Emlyn.

J.-M. ALTER

Sources I. H. Murray, *David Martyn Lloyd-Jones: the first forty years, 1899–1939* (1982) • I. H. Murray, *David Martyn Lloyd-Jones: the fight of faith, 1939–1981* (1990) • O. Barclay, *Evangelicalism in Britain, 1935–1995* (1997) • D. M. Lloyd-Jones, *D. Martyn Lloyd-Jones: letters, 1919–1981*, ed. I. H. Murray (1994) • G. Harrison, *Westminster conference papers* (1999) • T. Dudley Smith, *John Stott, the making of a leader* (1999)
Archives NL Wales, corresp., diaries, sermon notes |SOUND NL Wales, sermons and interviews, LLGC RM 0000 72/11; LLGC CD 1095; LLGC CD 1096; LLGC CD 1097; LLGC CD 1098
Likenesses photographs, repro. in Murray, *David Martyn Lloyd-Jones* (1983) • photographs, repro. in Murray, *David Martyn Lloyd-Jones* (1990)
Wealth at death £55,265: probate, 8 May 1981, *CGPLA Eng. & Wales*

Jones, (Walter) David Michael [*pseud.* Dai Greatcoat] (**1895–1974**), painter and poet, was born on 1 November 1895 in Brockley, Kent, the younger son and youngest of three children of James Jones, printer, from Holywell, Flintshire, and his wife, Alice Ann, former governess, daughter of Ebenezer Bradshaw, a mast and block maker of Rotherhithe, London. His father's father was a master plasterer from Ysgeifiog, his mother's mother Italian. His father worked on the *Flintshire Observer* until 1883 and knew some Welsh songs; David learned what Welsh he knew later. He was baptized Walter, which name he discarded. His earliest animal drawings, some of which survive, date from 1902 or 1903. From 1910 to 1914 he attended Camberwell School of Arts and Crafts under A. S. Hartrick (who had known Van Gogh and Gauguin) and others.

After trying to join the Artists' Rifles and some new Welsh cavalry, Jones enlisted in the Welch fusiliers on 2 January 1915, serving as a private soldier until December 1918, in a London unit of Lloyd George's 'Welsh army'. He was wounded in the leg on the night of 11 July 1916 in the attack on Mametz Wood on the Somme. He returned to action in October but by chance avoided the Passchendaele offensive. He left France with severe trench fever in February 1918. On demobilization he wished at first to rejoin, but accepted a grant and some parental help to work (1919–21) at Westminster School of Art. He already spoke at that time of post-impressionist theory fitting in with Catholic sacramental theology, and in 1921 became a Roman Catholic and went to work under A. Eric R. Gill, then at Ditchling in Sussex, and from August 1924 at Capel-y-ffin in the Black Mountains near the Welsh border. Jones was brought up at home on Bunyan and Milton, but with strong touches of inherited Catholic feelings; he had been deeply moved by a mass just behind the front line glimpsed through a barn wall. He had liked the businesslike atmosphere. His first job was to paint the lettering of the war memorial at New College, Oxford.

In 1924 Jones got engaged to Gill's daughter, Petra. His close friend René Hague was in love with her sister, Joan,

and married her, but Jones had little money and no prospects; Petra broke off the engagement in 1927 to marry someone else, and Jones never did marry, though he was not homosexual and had *amitiés amoureuses*, mostly conducted on the telephone as he grew older. He visited the Gills at Pigotts in Buckinghamshire often until 1933, but he was too devoted to his work and usually too poor not to live alone. His closest friends loved him intensely; they included Tom Burns, Harman Grisewood, Douglas Cleverdon, Jim Ede, Father M. C. D'Arcy, and Helen Sutherland, his greatest patron. He spent time in the 1920s on Caldy Island, in Bristol, at Brockley with his parents, in Berkshire with Robert Gibbings of the Golden Cockerel Press, and in France. In 1928 Ben Nicholson had him elected to the Seven and Five Society, where he exhibited with Henry Moore, Christopher Wood, Barbara Hepworth, and John Piper. The same year he began *In Parenthesis* (1937), which has its climax at Mametz in the First World War. This book won the 1938 Hawthornden prize.

The delicacy and freshness of Jones's colours, and the purity and power of his forms as a painter, let alone the strength and grace of his engraving work and his occasional wooden sculpture, would be enough to win him a high place among the artists of his generation and in a tradition that goes back to William Blake, whose nature and genius with many differences David Jones recalls. His work as a poet, in *In Parenthesis*, *The Anathemata* (1952), and *The Sleeping Lord* (1974), was almost more impressive, and in the lettering and the texts of his 'inscriptions', words painted on paper, he devised a new and moving art. In his severest engravings he was warm, in painting of solemn beauty lyrical and humorous. His visions of nature were as fresh as Ysgeifiog, his poetry as thrilling and abundant as the Thames at Rotherhithe. He greatly admired the Cornish fisherman painter Alfred Wallis.

Jones's intellectual insights were profound and complex. They were based on a restless and never-ending meditation of the art of painting, of theology for which he had a brilliant flair, of the nature of technology, of heroic legends, prehistoric archaeology, and the history of the British Isles. He admired James Joyce, T. S. Eliot, Baron Friedrich Von Hügel, Christopher Dawson, and Père de la Taille; at least for a few years in the late 1930s he flirted heavily with Oswald Spengler's *Decline of the West* and unseriously with Adolf Hitler's *Mein Kampf*, although he was innocent of the faintest trace of fascism; he simply loved mankind, and hated what everyone hates about modern times. In London in the blitz he wrote a lot of poetry, painted some of his finest mythical paintings, and began his great 'inscriptions'. His *Aphrodite in Aulis* (1941) is the goddess and lover of dying soldiers both German and English. His work was grossly interrupted by eye trouble from 1930 onwards, by a severe breakdown in 1932 with chronic insomnia, and then by a worse attack in 1947. He bore all this with an uncomplaining goodness that he seemed to have learnt in the trenches.

In 1934 Jones was taken to Cairo and Jerusalem by Tom Burns. The British uniforms in Jerusalem, and the coincidence of the tenth legion having crucified Christ and served later in Britain, begot in his mind the equivalence of British and Roman soldiers, and his central statement, *The Anathemata*. In the later 1930s he lived mostly at Sidmouth, Devon. After the 1947 breakdown he lived in fine rooms on the hill at Harrow, later in a little hotel in the town, and in the end in Calvary Nursing Home, Sudbury Hill, Harrow, where he was looked after by the nuns. Among the new friends of his last years were Nancy Sandars, archaeologist, and Philip Lowry, silversmith.

Jones had a boyish gaiety and a charmingly wide smile. His conversation was full of humour and inventive parody; his sympathy and the range of his interest were extraordinarily wide. The fulcrum of his morality was the decency of the infantrymen of 1914. Under stress he would drop his shopping, lose his papers, or find himself smoking two cigarettes, one in each hand. His notes became long writings, and his letters, annotated in several colours, tumbled effortlessly from sheet to sheet and subject to subject like the dialogues of Plato. He concentrated on a friend, on a subject of conversation, on a detail of any kind, historical or technical or visual or intellectual, with uncommon intensity. His eyes twinkled and glittered deeply.

Jones's first retrospective exhibition at the National Museum of Wales and the Tate Gallery was in 1954–5, his second (posthumously) in 1981. He was appointed CBE in 1955 and CH in 1974. He won many prizes and awards, and received the honorary degree of DLitt from the University of Wales in 1960. He died at the Calvary Nursing Home, Sudbury Hill, Harrow, on 28 October 1974, after some years of increasing illness. Serious study of his work has been sustained since his death by Jonathan Miles and Derek Shiel, particularly in their *David Jones: the Maker Unmade* (1995). PETER LEVI, *rev.*

Sources R. Hague, ed., *Dai Greatcoat: a self-portrait of David Jones in his letters* (1986) · P. Hills, *David Jones* (1981) [exhibition catalogue, Tate Gallery, London, 21 July – 6 Sept 1981] · David Jones, *The Roman quarry* (1981) · C. Hughes, *David Jones: the man who was in the field* (1979) · private information (1986) · M. James, *David Jones, 1895–1974: a map of the artist's mind* (1995) · CGPLA Eng. & Wales (1974)
Archives NL Wales, corresp. and literary papers · Tate collection, drawings and watercolours, photographs, sketchbooks | Georgetown University, Washington, DC, corresp. with Harman Grisewood, papers, literary manuscripts, and artwork · Kettle's Yard, Cambridge, letters to H. S. Ede · NL Wales, letters to Douglas Cleverdon · NL Wales, letters to J. Saunders Lewis · NL Wales, letters to John Petts · NL Wales, letters to Kathleen Raine · Tate collection, letters to Douglas Cleverdon · Tate collection, letters to Pamela Donner [photocopies] · Tate collection, material collected by René Hague · University of Exeter Library, letters to W. F. Jackson · University of Toronto, letters to René Hague · Yale U., Beinecke L., corresp. with Harman Grisewood
Likenesses N. Elder, photographs, 1973, NPG · R. H. Jones, drawing, 1974, NMG Wales · J. Finzi, pencil drawing, U. Reading
Wealth at death £18,662: administration, 31 Dec 1974, CGPLA Eng. & Wales

Jones, Dillwyn Owen [Dill] (1923–1984), jazz pianist, was born on 19 August 1923 at Sunny Side, Newcastle Emlyn, Wales, the son of John Islwyn Paton Jones, a bank clerk, and his wife, Lavinia Bevan. His mother and an aunt were talented pianists and his father an accomplished singer.

At the age of eight Jones moved with his family to Llandovery, where his father took over the post of manager at the local branch of Lloyds Bank. Dill attended the local college as a day boy and it was there he became aware of jazz via recordings of American artists such as pianist Fats Waller and saxophonist Sidney Bechet.

On leaving college Jones commenced work at his father's bank. By the outbreak of the Second World War he was playing piano in the evenings at local dances. He served as a seaman in the Royal Navy from 1942 to 1946, part of the time in the Far East. While stationed in Ceylon he played piano duets with Lennie Felix on the British Forces Network broadcasts, and he made contact with other British jazz musicians while stationed at Portsmouth and Chatham awaiting demobilization. Following his release he enrolled at Trinity College of Music in London in 1946 and became a professional musician in January 1947 when he joined a band led by drummer Carlo Krahmer which also contained trumpeter Humphrey Lyttelton. A year later he played at the Nice jazz festival, an engagement which brought him into close contact with visiting Americans Louis Armstrong, Earl Hines, and Jack Teagarden.

At a time when the jazz world was split into modern and traditional factions Jones displayed a catholic taste and found no difficulty in moving from the orthodox jazz format of Krahmer's small group to the progressive big band of Vic Lewis, whose powerful orchestra was modelled on that of the American Stan Kenton. Dill remained with Lewis for a year, appearing with the band at the 1949 Paris jazz fair, where he heard what he later described as the 'electrifying music' played by the visiting Charlie Parker Quintet.

Jones's quest for more firsthand experience of American jazz was the motivation behind his working as a musician on board the *Queen Mary* in 1950. At that time a dispute between the British and American musicians' unions prevented any interchanges and only by working on transatlantic liners (in order to spend a few days in New York every two weeks) could many British jazz musicians enjoy the music played at 52nd Street clubs.

Back in London, Dill Jones found employment as a member of drummer Tony Kinsey's trio, the quintet of saxophonist Tommy Whittle, and on many recording sessions set up by producer Denis Preston. On the Preston recordings he played with the best local musicians, such as Kenny Baker and Bruce Turner, as well as with the visiting American blues singer Big Bill Broonzy. During this period Jones also presented a number of BBC jazz record programmes which displayed his wide-ranging stylistic tastes.

In October 1961 Jones emigrated to the USA, where he studied for a time with Luckey Roberts, an expert in 'Harlem-stride' piano. Dill was to spend the rest of his life based in New York, where he was frequently heard playing with small bands under the leadership of Eddie Condon, Jimmy McPartland, and Gene Krupa, and with the Harlem Blues and Jazz Band led by trombonist Clyde Bernhardt. In June 1969 he took the place of Earl Hines in the JPJ Quartet (the other members were saxophonist

Budd Johnson, bass player Bill Pemberton, and drummer Oliver Jackson), a unit which was sponsored by the Johns-Manville Corporation to play jazz for students at American and Canadian schools.

In 1982 Jones was diagnosed as having cancer of the larynx and returned to London for an operation. By now he had lost his voice but despite this set-back he returned to New York and succeeded in working occasionally. Unfortunately his condition worsened and he died at Calvary Hospital in the Bronx on 22 June 1984.

ALUN MORGAN

Sources J. Chilton, *Who's who of British jazz* (1997) · D. Griffiths, *Dill Jones discography* (1996) · b. cert.
Archives SOUND Rutgers, State University of New Jersey, Newark, New Jersey

Jones, Dilys Lloyd Glynne [*née* Dilys Lloyd Davies] (1857–1932), educationist, was born at 5 Gordon Square, London, the second daughter of William Davies (1826–1901), 'Mynorydd', an eminent sculptor and singer, who was also one of the original fifteen council members of the revived Honourable Society of Cymmrodorion in 1873. Her elder sister, Mary Davies (1855–1930), a noted singer, married W. Cadwaladr Davies, a member of the Cymmrodorion and later first registrar of the University College of North Wales, Bangor.

Dilys Davies was a pupil at the North London Collegiate School under Frances Mary Buss, and after spending a year (1877–8) in residence at Newnham Hall, Cambridge, returned to her former school as an assistant mistress in 1879. She became prominent in London Welsh circles and at the national eisteddfod for her vigorous campaigning on behalf of girls' secondary and women's higher education in Wales. She made a significant address to the Cymmrodorion section of the national eisteddfod at Denbigh in 1882, entitled 'A model school for girls', and another at Caernarfon in 1886 on the higher education of girls in Wales. She also spoke at the London national eisteddfod in 1887 and in the same year addressed the Liverpool Welsh National Society on the problem of girls' education in Wales. She also wrote a chapter, 'The education of girls: some practical suggestions', for *The Welsh Intermediate Education Act: How to Use It* (ed. W. Cadwaladr Davies, 1889). In 1886–7 she played the leading role in the formation of the Association for Promoting the Education of Girls in Wales, acting as one of the honorary secretaries until 1898 and later as vice-president.

During the 1880s, when the quest for a Welsh intermediate education bill was a major issue in Welsh political and education circles, Dilys Davies highlighted the 'manifest deficiencies' in secondary education for girls. She emphasized the need for the anticipated legislation to include equal provision of non-sectarian intermediate schools for girls and boys and to bridge 'the fatal gap' between elementary and higher education. She identified the Anglican domination of the two endowed Howell schools at Llandaff and Denbigh, and the inconveniently located Welsh Girls' School at Ashford, Middlesex, as major weaknesses. Justifying the provision of secondary and higher education for girls, she argued that the formative influence on

character and intelligence exerted by the educated mother on a child was crucial. Her address at Caernarfon in 1886 refuted the controversial views of Dr W. Withers Moore, president of the British Medical Association, who had cast doubt on women's suitability to pursue higher education; she advocated a sensible, balanced programme of secondary and higher education for women involving 'a symmetrical development of the whole, not exaggerated growth of a part' (*National Eisteddfod Association Report*, 1886, 64). She also advocated female representation on governing bodies and exhibitions tenable at institutions of higher education. She stated that examination by the University of Wales would 'thwart any possible attempt at control by the Education Department in London'. Her animating philosophy was a national education system with the Welsh people 'free to carry out their own educational development along their own lines of growth' (*North Wales Chronicle*, 24 March 1932).

Dilys Davies's marriage in 1889 to John Glynne Jones, a Bangor solicitor, was the first solemnized in the Welsh Presbyterian Chapel, Charing Cross, the spiritual home of so many London Welsh. They had three sons and two daughters. Thereafter, during her long residence at Bangor, Dilys Glynne Jones served on the governing body of Bangor County School for Girls from its inception in 1895 and also gave staunch support to the University College of North Wales. In 1910 her views were cited in the report on examinations in secondary schools produced by the consultative committee of the Board of Education. Dilys Glynne Jones died at her home, Glandyl, Menai Avenue, Bangor, on 12 March 1932. On 17 March, the day of her funeral at Glanadda cemetery, Bangor, the flags at University College flew at half-mast; she had ploughed a deep furrow in the fallow field of Welsh female education.

W. GARETH EVANS

Sources L. Twiston Davies and A. Edwards, *The women of Wales* (1935) · U. Wales, Bangor, Dilys Glynne Jones MSS · Association for Promoting the Education of Girls in Wales: annual reports, 1887–1901, NL Wales · National Eisteddfod Association reports, 1882–7, NL Wales, XAS37N27 · *North Wales Chronicle* (18 March 1932) · *North Wales Chronicle* (24 March 1932) · *Baner ac Amserau Cymru* (1880–1900) · H. M. Jones, *History of the Cymmrodorion Society* (1939) · *The County Schools Review*, 4/1 (July 1912), 10 · *South Wales Daily News* (Jan 1887) · *Transactions of the Liverpool Welsh National Society 1886–7*, 59–70 · W. G. Evans, *Education and female emancipation: the Welsh experience, 1847–1914* (1990) · J. G. Williams, *The University College of North Wales: foundations 1884–1927* (1985)
Archives U. Wales, Bangor
Likenesses portrait, repro. in Evans, *Education and female emancipation*
Wealth at death £3441 10s. 5d.: probate, 7 April 1932, *CGPLA Eng. & Wales*

Jones, Ebenezer (1820–1860), poet, was born in Canonbury Square, Islington, London, on 20 January 1820, the third of the six children of a Welshman, Robert Jones (*d.* 1837), and his second wife, Hannah Sumner, of Essex. They lived in comfortable circumstances and professed the strictest form of Calvinism. Yet if Jones's education at a dreary middle-class school was as unsuitable to a young poet as can be conceived, the alternative world conjured up by him, his elder brother Sumner, and sister Mary was much like that of the young Brontës. Sensitive, poetic, and finely endowed, the three children escaped into the trees around their house to read Scott's *Waverley* novels, Shelley's poetry, and Carlyle's *French Revolution*. They dreamed of Lascar pirates and Chinese emperors and rebelled against their Calvinist catechism, until the death of their father impoverished the family and Jones became, at seventeen, a clerk in a City firm in Mincing Lane connected with the tea trade (a position he held for six years), working twelve hours a day and obliged to witness grossly dishonest practices.

Yet despite the strains of Jones's warehouse job, his father's death and his mother's departure to Wales with the younger children freed him to spend every leisure moment in study and composition, guided by Mary who devoted her own time to John Locke and eighteenth-century writers. She encouraged both Ebenezer and Sumner to produce a mass of prose and poetry which they read to her at teatime, and it was she who first told Ebenezer to publish his verse. She died from consumption in 1838, and shortly after Ebenezer was to suffer from unrequited love. The circumstances led him in his despair 'to throw', as his brother Sumner said, 'the medley of his poems into the caldron of his ill-fated book' (Jones). *Studies of Sensation and Event* was published in 1843, when he was twenty-three years old. It met with the fate to be expected from anything so crude, so eccentric, and on a cursory inspection so ridiculous as a considerable portion of the book. 'When Jones writes a bad line', remarked Baron De Tabley, 'he writes a bad one with a vengeance. It is hardly possible to say how excruciatingly bad he is now and then. And yet at his best, in organic rightness, beauty, and, above all, spontaneity, we must go among the very highest poetic names to match him'.

If any man of acknowledged literary standing had thus written in 1843, Jones might have been preserved to English literature; but he felt utterly crushed as a poet, particularly by the cruel reception of his book by the eminent authors to whom his brother offered copies. Thomas Hood wrote a scathing letter, telling Jones he was 'shamefully prostituting' his poetry, which was 'sensual and immoral', and even the good opinion of Robert Browning and Algernon Charles Swinburne could not deter the severity of the literary press. Jones's distress was augmented by an unhappy marriage in 1844 with Caroline Atherstone, niece of Edwin Atherstone, author of *Fall of Nineveh*. Although she had great beauty and musical talent, her gifts (as William Bell Scott phrased it) 'did not ensure the domestic peace or well-being of her husband' (*The Academy*, November 1879). A short, stormy marriage was followed by a difficult separation, and in despair Jones cast all his unpublished poems into the fire and took a job as an accountant. In the coming years he assisted his friend W. J. Linton in his political journalism, worked for the radical publishers Cleave and Hetherington, and published a tract on land reform, which established him a staunch reputation as a Chartist which his biographers have tried to dispel. In fact, he wrote no more verse until the very end of his life, when, as a thin, pale man, nervous-

looking and sickly, he produced a set of poems ('Winter Hymn to the Snow', 'When the world is burning', and 'To Death') which were daringly original in conception and remarkable in expression. But plagued by dyspepsia, pulmonary disease, and consumption, he died at Brentwood, Essex, on 14 September 1860, aged forty, and was buried in the churchyard at nearby Shenfield. He had no children, and his few obituary notices assumed his reputation would be barren.

In 1870, however, Dante Gabriel Rossetti wrote a remarkable article in *Notes and Queries* which proclaimed Jones's 'vivid disorderly power' and prophesied that his reputation would be revived (Rossetti, 154). Rossetti's passionate, adulatory piece, coming at the height of his fame as a Pre-Raphaelite, renewed public interest in Jones, sparking several articles, brochures, and a most interesting series of biographical papers in *The Athenaeum* in 1878, and a nearly complete edition of *Studies of Sensation and Event* in 1879 with some additional pieces, a memoir by Sumner Jones, and reminiscences by Linton. These articles proclaimed his infirmities to be those of most young poets, which had been gradually cured over time, and that he needed nothing but fortitude to have taken a distinguished place among English poets.

RICHARD GARNETT, rev. KATHARINE CHUBBUCK

Sources T. Watts, 'Ebenezer Jones', *The Athenaeum* (21 Sept 1878), 368–70; (28 Sept 1878), 401–3; (12 Oct 1878), 466–8 · S. Jones, 'Ebenezer Jones: in memoriam', in *Studies of sensation and event: poems by Ebenezer Jones*, ed. R. H. Shepherd (1879) [with reminiscences by W. J. Linton] · D. G. Rossetti, 'Ebenezer Jones', *N&Q*, 4th ser., 5 (1870), 154 · T. M. Rees, *Ebenezer Jones: the neglected poet* (privately printed, 1909) · 'Literary revivals', *The Athenaeum* (14 Sept 1878), 331–2 · *CGPLA Eng. & Wales* (1860)

Wealth at death under £450: probate, 8 Oct 1860, *CGPLA Eng. & Wales*

Jones, Edmund (1702–1793), Independent minister and author, was born on 1 April 1702 in the parish of Aberystruth, Monmouthshire. His parents, John Lewis and his wife, Catherine Morgan, of Penllwyn, were of dissenting stock, and their son, who was largely self-taught, earned a reputation during his long life as being more Calvinist than Calvin himself. He began preaching as early as 1722 and was ordained at Pen-maen meeting-house in 1734. When his hopes of becoming minister at Pen-maen were dashed in 1740 he moved to Pontypool, where he contributed £30 to the building of a meeting-house at the Transh in 1741. For more than fifty years this pious, modest, and transparently honest man eked out a bare living as an Independent minister, but did more than anyone to ensure that dissent became a living force in south-east Wales.

Shortly before his death in 1793, Jones had embarked on an autobiography which promised to document 'what occurrences & strange events came to pass in my long life' (Nuttall, 26), but since this work was neither completed nor published we must rely on his unpublished diaries, sermons, and letters, as well as his printed works, for details of his career. He was clearly a local patriot. His *A Geographical, Historical, and Religious Account of the Parish of Aberystruth* (1779) reveals that he was acutely interested in topography, soil, climate, demography, and 'natural curiosities', and that his depth of local knowledge was a source of wonder in the parish. His knowledge of herbs, plants, and flowers was unrivalled, and an unpublished manuscript entitled 'A spiritual botanology showing what of God appears in the herbs of the earth' is eloquent testimony to his belief that God was at work in the natural world.

Edmund Jones was also known locally as yr Hen Broffwyd (the Old Prophet). His powers of prognostication were legendary and, as his *A Relation of Apparitions of Spirits in the Principality of Wales* (1780) indicates, he was vividly conscious of—and troubled by—the presence of spirits, ghosts, elves, goblins, and fairies in the world around him. Fired by the same motives that had inspired similar works by Joseph Glanvill and Richard Baxter, Jones despised those 'Sons of Infidelity' who spoke with 'levity and ridicule of Apparitions, as if they were the posterity and Scholars of the ancient Sadducees' (*Account*, 68) and remained convinced that the Devil sent evil spirits to ensnare the innocent and the godly. Jones's fund of ghost stories and prophetic utterances became embedded in oral tradition and prompted some nineteenth-century commentators to refer to him rather unkindly as 'Edmund Jones of Ghostly memory'.

Even though he was in many ways a naïve and credulous man, paradoxically Edmund Jones was also thoroughly versed in Calvinist theology and was the nearest thing to a bishop in Welsh Independent circles in the eighteenth century. A compulsive reader, he spent what little money he possessed on the sermons of seventeenth-century puritans, whose works he copiously annotated with pungent references to 'blind malignant royalists'. He abhorred the new spirit of critical enquiry fostered in the Welsh academies, notably at Carmarthen, and loudly denounced the 'blasphemous' tenets of Arminians, Arians, and deists. In order to strengthen the Calvinist tradition he was willing to travel long distances to preach the gospel. As late as 1789, when he was eighty-seven years old, he preached on no fewer than 405 occasions in various parts of Wales, and when he died four years later he proudly declared that he had served as 'a soldier against the spirit of error in this country' (Nuttall, 27). Even Baptists, in his view, were enemies of God, and his diaries are peppered with earnest prayers such as 'Lord, prosper not Anabaptism, but let it wither daily' (NL Wales, MS 7026A, fol. 117).

Although Jones's published sermons, notably *Two sermons, first shewing the misery of those who are without the light of Christ; second shewing the felicity of being in the state of the light of grace* (1776), are prosaic, plodding texts, his services were reputedly as warm and animated as any conducted by revivalist preachers. Like several dissenting colleagues in the late 1730s, Jones caught the revivalist fever and began to follow what he called 'the Methodist way'. Captivated by the enthusiasm and energy of the Welsh revivalist Howel Harris, he invited him to Monmouthshire and accompanied him on his preaching tours in the spring of 1738. Although his relations with Harris were subsequently riven with friction, Jones continued to take young Methodists under his wing, to introduce them to potential converts, and to preach regularly at Trevecca College, often in the company of the countess of Huntingdon, one of his greatest admirers. His principal concern, however, was to protect the dissenting inheritance and to strengthen the position and authority of the faith of his forefathers. He rightly chided William Williams (Pantycelyn) for claiming that 'neither priest nor Presbyter were awake' when the Methodist trumpet first rang out (NL Wales, MS 7027A).

Edmund Jones and his 'beloved spouse' Mary (who predeceased him on 1 August 1770) lived in poverty, largely because Jones was generous to a fault. It was not uncommon for him to hand over his overcoat and shirt to penurious people. His favourite motto was 'Jehova Jireh' ('The Lord will provide') and on his preaching tours householders who were aware of his selfless labours and charitable disposition plied him with shirts, handkerchiefs, wool, bags of wheat, and money to buy books. Jones died, aged ninety-one, on 26 November 1793 in Pontnewynydd, where he was buried in the graveyard of Ebenezer Chapel. When a memorial was raised to 'Prophet Jones' in 1907, a host of traditions still circulated in the locality regarding his prophecies, peculiarities, ministerial labours, and boundless generosity. Regrettably, however, he has been poorly served by twentieth-century historians.

GERAINT H. JENKINS

Sources NL Wales, MSS 7021-7030 · letters, NL Wales, Trevecka papers · T. Rees, *History of protestant nonconformity in Wales*, 2nd edn (1883) · E. Phillips, *Edmund Jones, 'the Old Prophet'* (1959) · T. Watts, 'The Edmund Jones Library', *Journal of Welsh Bibliographical Society*, 11 (1973-6), 233-43 · G. F. Nuttall, 'Cyflwr crefydd yn Nhrefddyn, Sir Fynwy (1793), gan Edmund Jones', *Y Cofiadur*, 46 (1981), 23-8 · *DWB* · parish register, Aberystruth, NL Wales · will, proved 4 Nov 1793, Llandaff, NL Wales

Archives NL Wales, corresp., diaries

Wealth at death under £100: will, Llandaff probate, NL Wales

Jones, Edward (1641–1703), bishop of St Asaph, was born in July 1641 at Llwyn Rhirid in the parish of Forden in Montgomeryshire, the son of Richard Jones (1603–1681) and his wife, Sarah (*d.* 1685), the daughter of John Pyttes of Marrington, Shropshire. He was baptized at Forden parish church on 24 July. He was educated under Dr Busby at Westminster School. In 1661 he was elected from Westminster to Trinity College, Cambridge, and matriculated there on 22 May. After winning a scholarship in 1662 he graduated BA in 1664 and was created DD a few years later. He was elected, along with Newton, as a minor fellow of the college in 1667.

After being ordained into the Church of England in 1667 Jones was selected by the duke of Ormond, the newly appointed lord lieutenant of Ireland, as one of his domestic chaplains. He married Maria Hurd (*d.* 1670), daughter of Colonel Humphrey Hurd of Lisdowney, co. Kilkenny; a licence for their marriage was granted on 2 February 1668 at Kilkenny (Leslie, 125).

At some stage about 1670 Jones was appointed the new master of Kilkenny College, which had been refounded about 1667 by the duke. As master of the college he was responsible for the preparation of boys for entry to Trinity

College, Dublin, the first of whom entered in 1671. During his tenure as master Jones oversaw the early education of Jonathan Swift, Samuel Foley, later bishop of Down and Connor, and John Hartsrong, later bishop of Ossory. In May 1677 Jones was collated to the prebend of Aghour and Freshford in the diocese of Ossory and in November 1678 he was further promoted to the deanery of Lismore. On 11 March 1683, after leaving his position at Kilkenny, he was consecrated as bishop of Cloyne at Cashel Cathedral by the archbishop of Cashel, who was assisted by the bishops of Waterford, Limerick, and Killaloe. At some stage during this time he married Elizabeth Kennedy, daughter of Sir Richard Kennedy, bt, of Newmountkennedy, co. Wicklow, second baron of the exchequer of Ireland. Their marriage resulted in the birth of six children; their youngest son became MP for New Ross (1713–14) and for Wexford (1715–34). Throughout his time as bishop of Cloyne there were concerted efforts to have Jones translated to the see of Ossory. A letter written in February 1686 by the earl of Clarendon to the archbishop of Canterbury noted:

> Dr. Jones, the present Bishop of Cloyne, whom I propose to be translated to Ossory, is a very worthy man, has done a great good in the diocese he is now in, even to his own detriment, to promote the interests of the Church (*State Letters of … Clarendon*, 58)

The arrival of the earl of Tyrconnell in Ireland and subsequent change in the government policy on matters of a religious nature in 1688 resulted in the departure of Jones and his family from Ireland to the more secure environs of England. In his haste to leave Ireland he left an estate with the value of £500 behind him (TCD, MS 847/1). In 1692 he was raised to the bishopric of St Asaph as successor to William Lloyd, who had been translated to Lichfield. The nineteenth-century antiquary Robert Williams suggested that Jones's preferment to St Asaph, 'was entirely owing to his being a native of the country' (Williams, 25–6). His time as bishop was marked by maladministration and corruption in total contrast to the previous incumbent. As the historian of the diocese has noted:

> perhaps no Bishop ever took possession of a see with more advantages as he did; for the diocese had undergone in all respects, the strictest regulation under the care of and government under Bishop Lloyd for the space of twelve years; the clergy were under exact discipline … the revenues of the bishopric increased, and the rights of the church everywhere recovered and settled. (Thomas, 92)

Jones's bad government led to thirty-eight clergy of the diocese petitioning Archbishop Tenison, in March 1697, for an inquiry. After an ecclesiastical commission had received the presentments of the clergy, in July 1698 Jones was summoned to answer the charges laid against him. The case lasted over two years and eventually culminated in Jones signing a written confession of his guilt in:

> promoting to canonry a notorious person accused of crimes and excesses; he had permitted laymen to perform the office of curates at several parishes; he had been guilty of a simonical contract in the disposal of some of his preferments … Besides which, he had been in the habit of appropriating to himself a year's profits of vacant livings. (*Montgomeryshire Collections*, 252)

The archbishop's sentence, pronounced in June 1701, suspended Jones for six months until he gave satisfaction. Some commentators have noted that this appeared to be a sentence inadequate to the offence (Thomas, 92). The deprivation lasted until May 1702. He died on 10 May of the following year at his house in College Court, Westminster. He was interred on 13 May under the communion table of St Margaret's Church, Westminster, without inscription or monument.

Matthew Jones (1654–1717), Church of Ireland clergyman, was Edward Jones's younger brother. He was born at Llwyn Rhirid in July 1654. He accompanied his brother to Ireland and was educated by him at Kilkenny College before he matriculated at Trinity College, Dublin, on 14 April 1673. He was elected to a scholarship there in 1675 after which he graduated BA in 1677. After he had been ordained a priest at Kilkenny on 17 December 1670, he held numerous ecclesiastical preferments which included vicar-choral of Lismore Cathedral in 1681, precentor of Cloyne Cathedral in November 1683, and prebendary of Donoughmore in 1687. He married Bridget Kennedy (d. 1733), a younger sister of his sister-in-law Elizabeth; Matthew and Bridget had six children together. His only son, Edward, was the great-great-grandfather of the Revd Samuel Hayman (1818–1886), the antiquarian writer. He died on 7 December 1717 and was buried in the churchyard of the old parish church in Inniscara, near Cork. On the western wall of the churchyard a tablet was erected to his memory.   H. T. WELCH

Sources W. M. Brady, *Clerical and parochial record of Cork, Cloyne, and Ross* (1864) • J. B. Leslie, *Ossory clergy and parishes* (1933) • *Montgomeryshire Collections*, 11 (1877–8), 7, 251–2, 208 • D. R. Thomas, *Diocesan histories: St Asaph* (1888) • N. Luttrell, *A brief historical relation of state affairs from September 1678 to April 1714*, 4 (1857) • *The state letters of Henry, earl of Clarendon*, ed. [J. Douglas], 2 vols. (1765), vol. 1 • H. Cotton, *Fasti ecclesiae Hibernicae*, 4 vols. (1878) • *Old Westminsters*, vols. 1–2 • J. Welch, *The list of the queen's scholars of St Peter's College, Westminster*, ed. [C. B. Phillimore], new edn (1852) • R. Williams, *A biographical sketch of some of the most eminent individuals which the principality of Wales has produced* (1836) • 'A list of such protestants in Ireland as are lately fled out of the kingdom', TCD, MS 847/1, fol. 3v • W. W. Rouse Ball and J. A. Venn, eds., *Admissions to Trinity College, Cambridge*, 5 vols. (1911–16) • *Narrative of the proceedings against the bishop of St Asaph* (1702) • DWB • DNB

Jones, Edward [called Bardd y Brenin] (1752–1824), harpist and music antiquary, was born at a farm called Henblas, Llandderfel, Merioneth, and baptized at Llandderfel on Easter day, 29 March 1752, the fourth of nine children of John Jones (b. 1721?) and his wife, Jane (1719–1803). He grew up amid a rich tradition of harp playing, and was taught the instrument by his father. John Jones is said to have been a good musician, and taught his children to play a number of instruments as well as the harp, including the spinet and the violin or the *crwth* (a Welsh form of the lyre). His second son, Robert, became a church organist at St Chad's, Shrewsbury.

Edward Jones moved to London in 1774 or early 1775, under the patronage of the London Welsh circle. The harp was very fashionable in London at the time, and Jones quickly established himself in some of the most eminent circles as a popular performer and teacher of the instrument. Among his earliest acquaintances in London was Charles Burney, and Jones appears in an entry in Fanny Burney's diary for May 1775 describing a concert in which both he and her father took part. She notes the fine quality of his harp, and praises the 'neatness and delicacy' of his playing, but considers that 'as *expression* must have *meaning*, he does not abound in that commodity' (O. Ellis, 20). Her opinion is perhaps borne out by the evidence of the many compositions he published, which are generally regarded as pedestrian and unoriginal, but demonstrating considerable technical ability. In 1778 Jones applied for and was granted membership of the Royal Society of Musicians, though his petition five years later for the admission of his brother, Thomas Jones (also a harpist), was rejected.

Jones was appointed harpist to the prince of Wales (later George IV), adopting the title the King's Bard or Bardd y Brenin on the accession of the prince to the throne in 1820. The date of his appointment is uncertain. In his biographical sketch for the 1825 edition of Jones's *Hên ganiadau Cymru*, John Parry (Bardd Alaw) gives it as 1783, though he describes the position as no more than an honorary one. However, Jones himself did not start to use the title in his publications until *c.*1788, when he published his *Three Sonnets now most in Vogue in Paris*, in which he styles himself 'Harper to His Royal Highness the Prince of Wales'.

Jones studied and collected a great variety of traditional music, publishing in addition to Welsh melodies the music not only of other parts of the British Isles, but also of many countries worldwide. The subtitle of his *Lyric Airs* (1804) lists the contents as 'Specimens of Greek, Albanian, Walachian, Turkish, Arabian, Persian, Chinese, and Moorish National Songs and Melodies', as well as a scholarly essay on the origins of music in ancient Greece. He also published the volume *Maltese Melodies* (1807?), and a collection entitled *Terpsichore's Banquet* (1813), in which he extended his researches to countries including Spain, Russia, Sweden, and Armenia.

However, Jones's most important work was in the preservation of traditional Welsh music. He collected and published over 200 traditional melodies, many of which he transcribed from having heard them sung and played at home in north Wales. His concern for the protection of Welsh cultural life is also evident in his strong belief in the eisteddfod as a safeguard of Welsh cultural traditions and the purity of the Welsh language. He invariably attended eisteddfods on his regular summer visits to Wales, often acting as an adjudicator; and on several occasions he provided and presented prizes for competitions such as singing with the harp and the best collection of *penillion*.

Jones was a serious scholar who made a notable contribution to the antiquarianism which typified much of the scholarship of his period. His library was extensive, and his research into both primary and secondary sources, including the old Welsh laws and Welsh grammars, enabled him not only to present music, but also to write in some depth about it. An emphasis on scholarly discourse is characteristic of his major works. For instance, two-thirds of his first important work, a collection of Welsh melodies entitled *The Musical and Poetical Relicks of the Welsh Bards* (1784), is devoted to a series of essays on Welsh music and the bardic tradition, including an extensive 'Historical account of the Welsh bards'.

Jones seems to have had close connections with other scholars and antiquaries, and it is probable that he worked on the research for *Relicks* with John Walters, sub-librarian of the Bodleian Library in Oxford and son of John Walters the lexicographer. Jones also worked with Edward Williams (Iolo Morganwg), and some of the material for the revised 1794 edition of *Relicks* seems to have come from Williams. Jones was among those who assisted Williams in founding a *gorsedd*, or cultural assembly of Welsh poets, musicians, and others, which met on Primrose Hill in London in 1792, though it was subsequently moved by Williams to Glamorgan. However, their relationship did not last. Williams disparaged Jones's scholarship, attributing the 'Historical account' from *Relicks* substantially to John Walters—a claim which should be treated cautiously, given Williams's reputation as a fantasist and forger.

Among his many other publications, Jones went on to produce a second and a third volume to accompany *Relicks*—*The Bardic Museum* (1802), and *Hên ganiadau Cymru: Cambro-British Melodies, or, The National Songs, and Airs of Wales* (1820). The significance of his work on traditional Welsh music lies not only in the preservation of the music itself, but also in the fact that it opened up Welsh history and culture as an area of interest for other antiquaries.

From at least as early as 1801 Jones ran into financial difficulties, having expended considerable sums on rare books and on the publication of costly folio editions of his works. In 1805 he was granted living quarters in the office of robes, but fell increasingly into debt, and was finally asked to leave his rooms in 1819 for non-payment of rent. Parry's biographical sketch describes Jones's subsequent decline into illness, loss of memory, and reclusiveness. He twice had to put part of his rare book collection up for auction, first in 1818, and then in February 1824, the latter sale making about £300. Parry and a number of others arranged for the Royal Society of Musicians to provide him with a pension of £50 per annum, their concern indicating the respect with which Jones was regarded by his peers. However, within a few days of receiving the news, which Parry felt he had in any case barely grasped, Jones had a 'fit', dying two days later at his home, 1 Great Chesterfield Street, Marylebone, Middlesex, on Easter day, 18 April 1824, without regaining consciousness. He was buried in St Marylebone cemetery the following Sunday. The rest of his collection, containing books, music manuscripts, and some instruments, was auctioned in February 1825, making about £500. Among the manuscripts were two, later given to the British Museum, in the hand of Matthew Locke, *Cupid and Death* (BL, Add. MS 17800), and 'For His Majesty's Sagbutts and Cornets' (BL, Add. MS 17801).

TREVOR HERBERT

Sources T. Ellis, *Edward Jones, Bardd y Brenin, 1752–1824* (1957) [in Welsh] · *DWB* · *New Grove* · J. Parry [Bardd Alaw], 'Biographical note', in E. Jones, *Hên ganiadau Cymru* (1825) · Royal Society of Musicians, London, archives · O. Ellis, *The story of the harp in Wales* (1991) · M. Stephens, ed., *The Oxford companion to the literature of Wales* (1986)
Archives NL Wales, corresp., papers, literary MSS | U. of Wales, Cardiff, Salisbury collection
Wealth at death collection of rare books and MSS valued at approx £500: Ellis, *Edward Jones*; Parry 'Biographical note'

Jones, Edward [*pseud.* Ned Môn] (*fl.* **1771–1840**), author, was a native of Anglesey, Wales, and wrote under the pseudonym of Ned Môn (Môn is Welsh for Anglesey). He lived chiefly in London, and described himself in some of his published works as 'of the Inner Temple', but the roll of the inn does not contain his name. He may have been a clerk in the Temple. He was a prominent member of the London Gwyneddigion Society, a Welsh cultural and social association, and was probably one of its founders; in 1781 he was elected councillor for life; in 1782 he was secretary; in 1785 president, and a member of the committee appointed to revise the rules of the society.

Jones seems to have had a reputation as an orator, and was involved in a political debate with the Caradogion Society. His brother **Owen Jones** (*fl.* 1789–1793), sometimes known as Cor y Cyrtie ('dwarf of the courts') and possibly also a laywer's clerk, was also a member of the Gwyneddigion Society in London; he acted as secretary in 1789, vice-president in 1792, and president in 1793. The brothers together helped Owen Jones (1741–1814) and W. O. Pughe to publish the poetical works of Dafydd ap Gwilym in 1789; their assistance was acknowledged in the preface. Edward Jones is said to have published several works himself: an English translation of two of Cicero's treatises (1776); *Cyfreithiau plwyf* (1794), which described the duties of parish officials; and *Index to Records … of the Exchequer* (2 vols., 1793 and 1795). Only the second of these, however, can be attributed to him with certainty.

By 1831 Edward Jones was living in Paris, the oldest living member of the Gwyneddigion, and his brother was dead. The date of Edward's death is unknown.

R. M. J. JONES, *rev.* BETI JONES

Sources *DWB* · W. D. Leathart, *The origin and progress of the Gwyneddigion Society of London* (1831)

Jones, Edward [*known as* Jones Bathafarn] (**1778–1837**), Wesleyan Methodist minister, was born on 9 May 1778 at Ruthin, Denbighshire but brought up on Bathafarn Farm, Llan-rhydd. The fifth of six children born to Edward and Anne Jones, he was educated at Ruthin grammar school, and when about seventeen years of age entered a cotton warehouse at Manchester. In 1796 he joined the Wesleyan congregation at Oldham Street, where the Revd George Marsden was minister. Returning to Wales in December 1799, and resolving to introduce the Wesleyan organization into his native country, he invited ministers from the Chester circuit to preach at Ruthin in a room which he hired for the purpose. The ministrations were at first carried out in English, but it was afterwards arranged to conduct them in Welsh, and Jones and John Bryan, a native of Llanfyllin, who had moved to Chester, undertook the services on alternate Sundays.

The movement spread rapidly; the Wesleyan conference of 1800 constituted Ruthin into a circuit, and decided on the establishment of a Welsh mission. After two years' probation as a local preacher Jones was ordained in 1802, and for the following fourteen years he was chiefly instrumental in promoting a religious revival in Wales, and the establishment of Wesleyan churches. In 1816 he was posted to England, where he served Wesleyan Methodism at ten different centres, including Knaresborough, Oldham, and Durham. He married Dorothy Roberts of Plas Llangwyfan on 4 July 1806 and they had at least five children. Jones died at Leek in Staffordshire on 26 August 1837, and was buried at Leek Methodist Church.

D. L. THOMAS, *rev.* MARI A. WILLIAMS

Sources A. H. Williams, *Welsh Wesleyan Methodism, 1800–58* (1935) · R. Hughes, 'The Bathafarn family', *Bathafarn*, 1 (1946), 17–24 · *DWB* · *Wesleyan Methodist Magazine*, 61 (1838), 704–5 · *Enwogion y Ffydd*, 4 (1880), 274–83 · O. Thomas, *Cofiant y Parch. John Jones, Talsarn* (1874), 276–81

Jones, Sir Edward Coley Burne-, first baronet (**1833–1898**), painter, was born on 28 August 1833 at 11 Bennett's Hill, Birmingham, the son of Edward Richard Jones, a framer and gilder. His mother, Elizabeth Coley (*d.* 1833), died as a result of his birth, and his father's housekeeper, Ann Sampson, looked after him while he was a child. He was baptized Edward Coley Burne Jones, and was known for much of his life as Edward, or Ned, Jones.

Education Burne-Jones attended King Edward's School, Birmingham, from 1844 until 1852. From 1848 he attended drawing classes at the Birmingham Government School of Design. As a boy, he was bookish and scholarly, taking great pleasure in the Romantic poets, and also absorbing antiquarian and theological texts. In June 1852 he matriculated at Exeter College, Oxford, going up for the Lent term of 1853.

There Burne-Jones met William Morris, a fellow student also intended for holy orders; a lifelong friendship between the two men began. Shortly afterwards both began to question their first intention of entering the church, and instead discovered an intense love of art and architecture. Together they explored the Oxfordshire countryside, looking at churches and drawing landscape. Early in 1854 Burne-Jones's first undertaking as an artist was to make designs for the collection of fairy stories by his Oxford friend Archibald Maclaren, which was published in 1857 as *The Fairy Family*. Burne-Jones made many drawings for this project, and in a variety of derivative styles, although only three were used.

In 1853 Burne-Jones began to read John Ruskin, absorbing *The Stones of Venice* and the early volumes of *Modern Painters*. In the following year he read the *Edinburgh Lectures*, and discussed with Morris Ruskin's references to Pre-Raphaelitism. In that same summer Burne-Jones had his first opportunity to study Pre-Raphaelite paintings, seeing Millais's *Return of the Dove to the Ark* (AM Oxf.) in the collection of Thomas Combe in Oxford, and Holman

Sir Edward Coley Burne-Jones, first baronet (1833–1898), by Barbara Leighton, 1890 [printed by Frederick Hollyer]

Hunt's *Awakening Conscience* (Tate collection) and *Light of the World* (Keble College, Oxford) at the Royal Academy in London. Also at about this time he discovered the work of Dante Gabriel Rossetti, the artist who more than any other inspired and influenced him in the early years of his career. Thomas Combe's collection included Rossetti's *The First Anniversary of the Death of Beatrice* (AM Oxf.), a watercolour drawing that profoundly impressed him. He also saw Rossetti's powerful illustrations to 'The Maids of Elfenmere' for William Allingham's *Day and Night Songs*.

In May 1855 Burne-Jones and Morris visited Benjamin Windus at Tottenham Green, to see Ford Madox Brown's *Last of England* (Birmingham City Art Gallery) and Millais's *Lorenzo and Isabella* (Walker Art Gallery, Liverpool). In that same summer Burne-Jones and Morris visited northern France to study cathedral architecture. In Paris, Burne-Jones was overwhelmed by Fra Angelico's *Coronation of the Virgin* in the Louvre, and in the course of their return journey, at Le Havre, he announced his intention to make art his career. Also in 1855 he first read Thomas Malory's *Le morte d'Arthur*, a book which he was to ponder and draw upon for subject matter for the rest of his life, and of which he was to say it could 'never go out of the heart' (*Memorials*, 2.168).

In January 1856 Burne-Jones visited the Working Men's College in London to seek Rossetti, who was teaching there. They met, and shortly afterwards Burne-Jones was invited to Rossetti's studio in Chatham Place. As a result Burne-Jones abandoned his degree studies and moved to London. He received lessons from Rossetti, and also

attended Leigh's school in Newman Street. From November 1856, for two years, Burne-Jones and Morris shared rooms at 17 Red Lion Square.

Burne-Jones received his first commission—for a subject from 'The Blessed Damozel'—from Thomas Plint in 1857. Then from the late summer until February 1858 he worked with Rossetti on the scheme of murals for the debating chamber (now the library) of the new Oxford Union building. In January 1858 William Michael Rossetti wrote of this project:

> Gabriel *was* at Oxford 3 or 4 months … The things there are very new, curious, and with a ruddy bloom of health and pluck about them—Gabriel's very beautiful both in expression and colour: Jones's next, and to some extent *more* exactly the right kind of thing. (*Selected Letters of William Michael Rossetti*, ed. R. Peattie, Pennsylvania, 1990, 92)

This shared venture bonded the group of artists involved more closely; new ideas emerged about how the principles of Pre-Raphaelitism might be adapted to romantic and historically remote subjects. This formative experience led to the second phase of Pre-Raphaelitism, in which hard-edge colours and meticulous detail were superseded by rich dark colours and decorative patterning.

By the late 1850s Burne-Jones was a recognized figure in progressive London-based art circles. He spent a period recuperating from some kind of health breakdown at Little Holland House in the summer of 1858, and in the process made friends with both G. F. Watts and Alfred Tennyson. Ruskin, also, took an interest in him. On one occasion, when Tennyson sought to upbraid the new school of painters, Ruskin defended Burne-Jones as 'the most wonderful of all the PreRaphaelites in redundance of delicate & pathetic fancy—inferior to Rossetti in depth—but beyond him in grace & sweetness.' Burne-Jones's cheerful demeanour in response, 'laughing sweetly at the faults of his own school as Tennyson declared them and glancing at me with half wet half sparkling eyes', was also recorded (*The Winnington Letters*, ed. V. A. Burd, 1969, 150). In 1858 Burne-Jones joined the Hogarth Club, which provided a forum for debate about art and an exhibition space until 1862. Early in 1859 he began to teach at the Working Men's College, and continued there until 1861. In September 1859 he made his first visit to Italy, staying in Venice and Milan, and meeting Robert Browning and Walter Savage Landor in Florence.

The 1860s On 9 June 1860 Burne-Jones married Georgiana Macdonald (1840–1920) [*see under* Macdonald sisters]. She was the daughter of a Methodist minister, W. G. Macdonald, and one of four remarkable sisters (each of whom married or became the mother of people in the public eye). Ned and Georgie (as they were familiarly known) had been friends since 1851, when he was eighteen and she eleven. They lived first at 24 Russell Place, Fitzroy Square, and then from 1861 in Great Russell Street, Bloomsbury, where their son, Philip, was born in that year. In 1864 there was an idea that the Burne-Jones family should set up home with William and Jane Morris at the Red House at Upton, a plan later abandoned. In 1865 they moved to 41

Kensington Square, and a year later their daughter, Margaret, was born. In November 1867 the family moved to The Grange, North End Lane, Fulham, a fine Georgian house, once the home of the novelist Samuel Richardson.

The Burne-Joneses were a gregarious and well-liked couple, counting among their particular friends Morris, Rossetti, and Ruskin. Algernon Charles Swinburne, who in the early 1860s had joined Rossetti's household at Tudor House in Chelsea, and who caused alarm by his outrageous and often drunken behaviour as well as his interest in deviant sexuality, was also a friend. Swinburne dedicated his volume *Poems and Ballads* to Burne-Jones in 1866.

Burne-Jones, who had abandoned his intention of taking holy orders in favour of becoming an artist, none the less devoted himself in the early years of his career to making paintings, drawings, and designs which were informed by the Christian faith. The ink drawing *The Wise and Foolish Virgins* (1859, priv. coll.), reflecting the influence of—but no longer dependence on—the example of Rossetti, was according to Burne-Jones's own work-list intended as a preparation for an unrealized painting. The drawing, regarded in its own right, represents a technical *tour de force*, consisting of myriad strokes of the pen in an ever-changing pattern to evoke the textures of the draperies, foliage, surface of water, and wooden construction. In the late 1850s and early 1860s Burne-Jones produced decorative furnishings for churches and received commissions for schemes of stained glass, notably the St Frideswide window at Christ Church Cathedral in Oxford, which was made by Powells in 1859, and the *Tree of Jesse* and *Christ in Majesty* windows at Waltham Abbey church, Essex, of 1860–61. Both transcend the conventions of contemporary stained-glass designing in favour of an immediacy of story-telling which depends on a fondness for incident and expression and a richness of effect in the treatment of colour. Burne-Jones also made illustrations of Bible subjects. Those that he produced in 1863 in connection with the Dalziel Bible project—showing *Noah and his Family Boarding the Ark* and *The Return of the Dove to the Ark*—are beautifully adapted to the requirements of simplicity and legibility for images that are to be transferred to the woodblock. In the first, a mass of mocking people press down on Noah as he goes aboard the ark, while the sequel shows the return of the dove that Noah had sent out in search of land. Pictorial story-telling of a kind which excited and intrigued the spectator was central to Burne-Jones's artistic purpose.

The culmination of Burne-Jones's early work for churches, as well as the project that marked his growing ambitions as an artist, was the triptych *The Adoration of the Kings and Shepherds, with the Annunciation* for St Paul's Church in Brighton. The commission seems to have come through Morris, Marshall, Faulkner & Co., which company had been set up in 1861 to provide architectural decorations for ecclesiastical and domestic settings and of which Burne-Jones was a founder partner. His first treatment of the subject, now in the Tate collection, was a spiritually powerful work of art later described by Georgiana Burne-Jones as 'by far the most important work he had done'

(*Memorials*, 1.224). However, when the three panels were placed on the high altar it became apparent that the subject was hard to appreciate from the main body of the church, so he embarked on a revised version. The composition of this second altarpiece, which was also painted in 1861 and is now in a private collection, was much simplified in the interests of clarity and legibility. Thus Burne-Jones faced up to practical considerations of how such a devotional object might best be seen by worshippers.

The two versions of the St Paul's triptych mark the arrival of Burne-Jones as a distinct and independent artistic identity. While on the one hand they reflect the powerful impact that Rossetti had made upon him (Burne-Jones inevitably was thinking of Rossetti's own triptych *The Seed of David*, made for Llandaff Cathedral in 1856), they derive also from the artist's study of religious paintings of the Renaissance in the course of his first visit to Italy in 1859. Botticelli, Ghirlandaio, Mantegna, and Signorelli were the masters whose works Ruskin had recommended Burne-Jones to seek out in the course of this journey.

In addition to the religious subjects that Burne-Jones was treating in the early 1860s, he had begun specializing in small and essentially private figurative subjects of literary inspiration in gouache. Meinhold's *Sidonia von Bork*, translated by Speranza Wilde as *Sidonia the Sorceress* (1849), provided the subject of the pair of watercolours *Sidonia von Bork* and *Clara von Bork* (both Tate collection), of 1860, which Penelope Fitzgerald described as 'his two real apprentice pieces, which mark the beginning of an individual style' (Fitzgerald, 73). According to Meinhold's story, Sidonia was a woman of great beauty who was particularly vicious and unforgiving to the men who fell in love with her. It was this mixture of beauty with evil, cruelty in sensuality, and invitation mixed with menace that Burne-Jones, Rossetti, and Swinburne found so thrilling, and the fascination that they felt with female sexual voraciousness lies behind the contemporary cult of the 'stunner'. Another favourite text among the members of the Rossetti circle was Walter Scott's collection of ballads *Minstrelsy of the Scottish Border*. Burne-Jones's watercolour *Clerk Saunders* (1861; Tate collection) reflects this preoccupation, and it too has a dark and threatening mood.

In the early summer of 1862 Burne-Jones made his second Italian tour, with Georgiana and on this occasion also with Ruskin. In Venice, where they stayed for three weeks, Burne-Jones studied and copied works by Titian, Tintoretto, and Veronese. These examples seem to have led him in the early 1860s towards a greater simplicity of form and command of painterly texture and richness of colour (with a particular fondness for soft greens mixed with grey and blue tones), and a new interest in themes of indolence and passivity in idyllic and Giorgionesque settings.

In 1864, at his second attempt, Burne-Jones was elected an associate of the Old Watercolour Society. As an artistic association, this seems a rather surprising choice, and one in which, as a painter of figurative subjects as opposed to landscapes, he must have felt rather isolated. None the less, among the watercolours that he exhibited there were many that are remarkable and challenging works of art.

Green Summer, for example, the title of which suggests an oblique link with Malory and *Le morte d'Arthur*, shows eight girls, seated together on a flower-strewn lawn, while one of their number reads aloud to her companions. The drawing was made in summer 1864 at the Red House, where the Morris and Burne-Jones families had spent so much time together, and conveys something of the enchanted life that he and Georgiana lived together during the early years of their marriage. However, there is hidden within it a darker and more fateful message, indicative of impending misfortune. Burne-Jones had first made compositions of girls seated together in a landscape setting similar to the arrangement in *Green Summer* in one of the panels of the St Frideswide window, the larger theme of which was one of fateful resistance to sexual advances. The motif of resignation in the face of impending threat was carried further in a design for the decoration of a piano—which instrument had been of all things a wedding present to Ned and Georgie. She described the subject: 'Death, veiled and crowned, standing outside the gate of a garden where a number of girls, unconscious of his approach, are resting and listening to music' (*Memorials*, 1.207). If in *Green Summer* the figure of Death has been omitted, the spectator is left to wonder what will interrupt the continuum of sight and sound. As we look for signs of a distinct identity in the young artist, we come to identify a sense of ominousness and foreboding, and a feeling of the transience of worldly contentment, as essential traits.

The Lament, dated 1866 but painted the previous year, is on one level a purely formal figurative arrangement in an architectural setting, and is as close as the artist came to the 'subjectless' compositional type characteristic of aesthetic classicism of the 1860s. Two draped female figures, one holding a dulcimer, the other with her head resting on her hands in a gesture of exhaustion, sit on the stone benches of a castle chamber with a view beyond into a courtyard. Whether the grief-stricken mood of the drawing is a response to the music that the left-hand figure has at that moment ceased from playing or indicative of some larger but unknown tragedy is not stated. In the absence of a given narrative, Burne-Jones allows himself the use of symbolic codes, such as for example the fallen rose and strewn petals beside the right-hand figure, a motif which may here be understood to signify loss (perhaps specifically the loss of virginity) and temporality.

Works of this type subscribe to the central principle of the aesthetic movement, which held that painted subjects served their own purpose in transmitting mood to the spectator and should be regarded as more than illustrations of literary texts. Both *Green Summer* and *The Lament* may be understood in symbolic terms, but neither lends itself to a literal interpretation. Ultimately, Burne-Jones equivocated in this contemporary debate about the narrative purpose of art, partly perhaps because he was himself a man of profound literary culture, and one who accepted that different media might be used in combination to tell stories to greater effect, whether these were drawn from ancient mythology, the Bible, or works of literature.

In 1867 John Ruskin pronounced on Burne-Jones's early career: 'He did not begin art early enough in boyhood; and therefore, in spite of all his power and genius, his pictures were at first full of very visible faults, which he is gradually conquering' (*The Works of Ruskin*, ed. E. T. Cook and A. Wedderburn, 39 vols., 1903–12, 19.206–7). Burne-Jones was conscious of his lack of professional training as an artist, and was perhaps stung by criticisms of his exhibited works, which asserted that they were less than properly crafted. Burne-Jones was determined to improve his command of figure subjects, which he did by making drawings from the antique, and thus he participated in the classical impetus of the mid-1860s, of which Albert Moore, James Whistler, and Frederic Leighton were notable figures. Expectations of the standard of finish in works by professional artists were denied by the looseness of form and shadowed perspectives of Burne-Jones's watercolours of the first half of the 1860s. Furthermore, it was noticed that a faction of younger artists (associated with the exhibitions held from 1865 onwards at the Dudley Gallery, and including such names as Robert Bateman, Simeon Solomon, and Walter Crane) was tending to follow Burne-Jones's example.

In 1865 Burne-Jones started work on a projected illustrated edition of William Morris's *The Earthly Paradise*, which was itself a collection of twenty-four stories linked together as tales told by a group of Norsemen. Georgiana Burne-Jones described how:

> the last visit we paid to Upton [Morris's Red House] was in September, 1865 … The talk of the men was much about The Earthly Paradise, which was to be illustrated by two or three hundred woodcuts, many of them already designed and some even drawn on the block. (*Memorials*, 2.294)

Burne-Jones devoted enormous efforts to the project, producing extraordinary sequences of drawings for specific tales, but despite this eventually the scheme to produce an illustrated volume was abandoned and the poem was published as text alone in 1868–70.

For decades to come Burne-Jones drew on the repertory of worked-up designs for figurative compositions that he had made in connection with *The Earthly Paradise*. For example, the watercolour *Cupid Delivering Psyche* (priv. coll.), which was exhibited at the Old Watercolour Society in 1867, shows the moment at the end of the legend, originally told by Apuleius in *The Golden Ass*, when Psyche, having opened the magic casket containing the secret of eternal youth, although Persephone had forbidden her to do so, falls into a deathlike sleep, but is rescued by her lover Cupid.

Burne-Jones's predisposition towards sequences of images which together convey a narrative—previously seen for example in the St Frideswide stained glass, and spurred by the experience of designing illustrations for *The Earthly Paradise*—found expression in the second half of the 1860s when he worked on a cycle of paintings on the theme of St George, commissioned in 1864 by the watercolour painter Myles Birket Foster. The series consisted of seven paintings (those towards the end of the sequence being painted in part by Burne-Jones's first studio assistant, Charles Fairfax-Murray, who was employed from 1866). In the canvases *The Petition to the King* and *The Princess Drawing the Lot* (both Hanover College, Indiana), Burne-Jones may be seen to have emerged in his full technical and creative capacity. The sense of volume of the figures, which are monumental in scale, and the richness of the draperies, reflect the intensive self-training to which Burne-Jones had subjected himself in the mid-1860s in drawing directly from and copying engravings of antique sculpture.

Burne-Jones was aware of the apparent dichotomy between the formal arrangement of pictorial elements for purely artistic purposes and the treatment of narrative in paintings, a debate that ranged widely in the mid-1860s. The St George series served to illustrate a familiar legend, and in doing so offered an outlet for Burne-Jones's genius for identifying key story-telling elements to lend excitement and animation to a narrative. Georgiana Burne-Jones was struck by their dramatic, even gory, character when she saw them again in 1894, after a long interval. She was, she said:

> surprised by their dramatic character, especially in the scenes where the King looks at the blood-stained clothes of the girls who had been devoured by the Dragon, and where the poor mothers crowd into the temple while the Princess draws the lot. (*Memorials*, 1.296–7)

During the second half of the 1860s Burne-Jones began to sell works to a small circle of collectors and patrons who were to be his most loyal supporters, notably Frederick Leyland and William Graham. Because these individuals understood and were in sympathy with Burne-Jones's artistic intentions, they valued works such as *The Wine of Circe*—which shows the mythological sorceress preparing food and wine for the sailors of Odysseus which, when it is consumed, will cause them to be transformed into swine. Originally undertaken for Ruskin in 1863, but purchased by Leyland in 1868, the drawing was regarded as morally depraved when shown at the Old Watercolour Society in 1869. Although the artist continued for the time being to send works to the summer exhibitions at the society, he was building a basis for professional independence which was to hold him in good stead when the inevitable break with that association came.

Burne-Jones's exhibited drawings of the second half of the 1860s were recognized as having great power, and were seen in some quarters as insidious attempts to undermine contemporary proprieties. The French critic Philippe Burty resorted to a literary comparison in his account of *The Wine of Circe* (1869): 'a painting of the greatest worth: for the mood, which is as disturbing and even more powerful than in certain parts of Baudelaire's *Fleurs du Mal*' ('Exposition de la Royal Academy', *Gazette des Beaux-Arts*, 1869, 54). The shocked response of the *Art Journal* to the work concluded that Burne-Jones's productions belonged 'to the realm of dreams, myths, nightmares, and other phantasms of diseased imagination', while his talent, though 'distinguished', was 'abnormal and perverted' (*Art Journal*, 31, 1869, 173). Burne-Jones himself was

bemused by this hostile criticism, asking: 'Why should people attack pictures as they do? Artists mean no harm—at least I don't; I only want to make a beautiful thing, that will remain beautiful after I'm a bogey, and give people pleasure when they look at it' (*Memorials*, 1.260).

As the 1860s drew to their close Burne-Jones's mood became even darker and more anguished. The mythological subject *Phyllis and Demophoön* (Birmingham City Art Gallery) revealed his emotional and spiritual plight with utter candour. The figure of Phyllis emerges from an almond tree to cast her arms around Demophoön, the lover who has announced his desire to be free of her. The watercolour caused outrage or distress, according to the sympathy of the individual for Burne-Jones's cause, when exhibited in 1870. In the first place, the nudity of the male figure was offensive to conservative opinion—representations of the male genitalia were simply not considered appropriate for display at the Old Watercolour Society. Burne-Jones's letter of resignation to the society concluded with the statement:

> The conviction that my work is antagonistic to yours has grown in my mind for some years past, and cannot have been felt only on my side—therefore I accept your desertion of me this year merely as the result of so complete a want of sympathy between us in matters of Art, that it is useless for my name to be enrolled amongst yours any longer. (*Memorials*, 2.12)

Furthermore, it was the recognition by Burne-Jones's friends of the figure of Phyllis as having been modelled on that of a woman called Maria Zambaco (1843–1911), with whom the painter had been in love since 1867, and the way in which the chosen mythological subject paralleled his relationship with her, that gave the watercolour a particular significance. As Georgiana Burne-Jones said of her husband, 'Two things had tremendous power over him—beauty and misfortune—and far would he go to serve either' (*Memorials*, 1.309). The affair ran on for several years, and the emotional upheavals that it caused may be seen to lie behind Burne-Jones's adoption of overtly sexual themes in a number of his works of the period. For Burne-Jones, a type of art that denied personal associations in its ostensible subject was virtually impossible; instead, he looked to mythology for subject matter in which he might explore his own predicament and state of mind, finding themes which lent themselves to the recasting of events from the artist's own experience or fantasy.

In 1867, as part of the ongoing *Earthly Paradise* project, Burne-Jones had made a sequence of drawings treating the story of Pygmalion. In these twenty-five preparatory drawings lay both the first ideas for the compositions and the division into four parts of the series of paintings known as 'Pygmalion and the Image': *The Heart Desires*, *The Hand Refrains*, *The Godhead Fires*, and *The Soul Attains* (all priv. coll.). The Pygmalion series was again a deliberate or unconscious commentary on the artist's love affair with Maria Zambaco. Their dual message is both a wish and a fear on his part. In the first place he imagines what it might be for an artist to make a woman, as Pygmalion created Galatea, who would be the fulfilment of all desires and who would be under the absolute control of her creator. The irony is that Maria was the opposite, making demands upon Burne-Jones that he was unwilling or incapable of fulfilling. The neurotic aspect of the series is that they describe both his longing for and his dread of submission to a woman of sexual authority during these years of turbulence and crisis.

The 1870s Following his resignation from the Old Watercolour Society in 1870, Burne-Jones was for a while determined to avoid public exhibitions, sending works to the Dudley Gallery on just one occasion in 1872–3, and relying instead on an inner circle of collectors who appreciated his intentions. This was a period to which Burne-Jones referred in later life as 'the seven blissfullest years' (*Memorials*, 2.13), and during which many of the single canvases and whole cycles of paintings upon which his fame as an exhibitor at the Grosvenor Gallery from 1877 and the New Gallery from 1888 rests were commenced.

In 1871 a breach with Ruskin resulted from disparaging comments the critic made on Michelangelo in his lecture 'The relation between Michael Angelo and Tintoret'. Ruskin had asked Burne-Jones to visit him at Denmark Hill to read him the text of the lecture, which was to be delivered in Oxford in June 1871. On hearing remarks such as 'In every vain and proud designer who has since lived, that dark carnality of Michael Angelo's has fostered insolent science, and fleshly imagination' (*The Works of Ruskin*, ed. E. T. Cook and A. Wedderburn, 39 vols., 1903–12, 22.104), Burne-Jones recognized a deliberate reproof to *Phyllis and Demophoön* and other works in which he had instilled Michelangelesque muscularity. As Burne-Jones recalled:

> He read it to me just after he had written it, and as I went home I wanted to drown myself in the Surrey Canal or get drunk in a tavern—it didn't seem worth while to strive any more if he could think it and write it. (*Memorials*, 2.18)

The new distance between the two men was referred to by Burne-Jones in a letter to Charles Eliot Norton of 1871:

> You know more of [Ruskin] than I do, for literally I never see him nor hear from him, and when we meet we clip as of old and look as of old, but he quarrels with my pictures and I with my writings, and there is no peace between us—and you know all is up when friends don't admire each other's work. (ibid.)

Burne-Jones's new sense of connection with a long tradition of figurative art originating in the Italian Renaissance, and his almost deliberate detachment from indigenous Pre-Raphaelitism and the innovations led by Rossetti in the late 1850s and 1860s, were confirmed when in September 1871 he made his third visit to Italy. He visited among other places Genoa, Florence, Arezzo, and Rome, and stated on his return: 'Now I care most for Michael Angelo, Luca Signorelli, Mantegna, Giotto, Botticelli, Andrea del Sarto, Paolo Uccello and Piero della Francesca' (*Memorials*, 2.26). He returned to Italy in 1873. These Italian journeys of the early 1870s brought about a sea change in the way he painted and in his aesthetic attitudes. Gradually he moved beyond the decorative classicism that he and others had explored in the 1860s, drawing on the dynamic and dramatic paintings of Michelangelo and Mantegna to introduce greater psychological and compositional power to his works.

A representative work of Burne-Jones's middle years is the gouache *Love among the Ruins*, begun in 1870 and exhibited at the Dudley Gallery in 1873. The watercolour struck Burne-Jones's first biographer as 'one of the most impressive of the painter's works, with its vague hint of an untold tragedy which haunts the memory and refuses to be banished' (Bell, 50). Although the painting borrows its title from Robert Browning's poem of 1855, it is not in any sense an illustration, but rather follows *The Lament* in suggesting a wistful mood to the spectator in terms of abstract allegory. Once again Maria Zambaco may be recognized as the model for the female figure.

Burne-Jones's voluntary withdrawal from the limelight of London exhibitions, and the peaceful obscurity that resulted and which allowed him to enter upon the most prolific and richly inventive phase of his entire career, was in due course to end. He well understood and to some extent shared the repugnance that painter friends such as Rossetti and Ford Madox Brown felt for public exhibitions and the processes to which artists resorted to try to gain the esteem of critics and collectors, but Burne-Jones combined a determination to advance his career and to become one of the celebrated figures of his generation with an apparently contrary disdain for commercial considerations. It was therefore inevitable that eventually he would look for opportunities to show his works before a wide public.

The Grosvenor Gallery opened in May 1877, occupying a purpose-built exhibition space in London's New Bond Street. Its proprietor, Sir Coutts Lindsay, wanted to provide an alternative public arena to the Royal Academy, to which he invited artists whom he thought of as the most interesting working at the time to exhibit. The range of painters whose works appeared in the first Grosvenor show included some who had previously struggled to gain a professional foothold or who had previously depended on the Dudley Gallery and other 'alternative' exhibition spaces, as well as established artists, a number of whose careers were closely linked with the academy. Burne-Jones was represented by nine paintings (mostly begun in the early 1870s) at the first exhibition in 1877. These were *The Beguiling of Merlin* (Lady Lever Art Gallery, Port Sunlight), *The Mirror of Venus* (Calouste Gulbenkian Foundation, Lisbon) *The Days of Creation* (Harvard U., Fogg Art Museum), and a watercolour in six panels lent by William Graham, as well as five further standing figure subjects: *Temperantia* (priv. coll.), *Fides* (Vancouver Art Gallery), *Spes* (Dunedin Art Gallery), *A Sibyl* (priv. coll.), and *St George* (Wadsworth Atheneum, Hartford, Connecticut).

Of all the Grosvenor artists, Burne-Jones made the greatest sensation, being acclaimed by most critics as the leader of a rising national school of art. Henry James's analysis of Burne-Jones's art conveys the sense of revelation that was felt by the Grosvenor's perceptive audience:

> It is the art of culture, of reflection, of intellectual luxury, of aesthetic refinement, of people who look at the world and at

life not directly, as it were, and in all its accidental reality, but in the reflection and ornamental portrait of it furnished by art itself in other manifestations; furnished by literature, by poetry, by history, by erudition.   (H. James, *The Painter's Eye: Notes and Essays on the Pictorial Arts*, ed. J. L. Sweeney, 1956, 144–7)

From this point forward the painter was a well-known figure, caricatured as the representative of the aesthetic movement and regarded as a national property, notwithstanding his reluctance to be drawn into the artistic establishment as represented by the Royal Academy.

Despite his fundamental diffidence, Burne-Jones began in the late 1870s to take a position and even on occasion to speak up in public on artistic matters. In 1878 he was drawn—although reluctantly so—into the Whistler–Ruskin libel trial, a case for professional damages brought by Whistler against Ruskin in response to criticism of his painting *The Falling Rocket*. Burne-Jones gave evidence on behalf of Ruskin, in the course of which he attempted to support the argument that quality in art depended on careful craftsmanship, or what Victorians called 'finish'. In 1879 he joined the international campaign, led by Ruskin and Morris to prevent the so-called restoration of the façade of St Mark's in Venice.

The 1880s During the 1880s Burne-Jones became a famous artist of the day, indeed perhaps the most widely admired British painter of his generation. Ruskin's Oxford lecture of May 1883, 'Mythic schools of painting: E. Burne-Jones and G. F. Watts', appeared to confirm this estimate, while the critical success of the Grosvenor summer exhibitions in which he participated (each year from 1877 to 1887, except for the years 1881 and 1885) underlined his wide appeal among metropolitan audiences.

The Golden Stairs (Tate collection)—exhibited at the Grosvenor Gallery in 1880—has a strange and compelling dynamic power. The composition, which was first devised in 1872 and worked on between 1876 and 1880, represents the consummation of Burne-Jones's interest in subjects that address the spectator in terms of mood rather than narrative. The fact that various alternative titles for the present painting—including 'The King's Wedding' and 'Music on the Stairs'—could have been contemplated demonstrates to what degree it fulfils a purely decorative purpose, and in this sense—in its abstract and formal character, which depends not at all on the spectator's ability to comprehend or interpret—it is remarkably modern. In 1885, in a survey of Burne-Jones's art, and dwelling on his debt to Renaissance traditions, Claude Phillips concluded: 'The spirit which informs his art is essentially and entirely modern, and as far asunder as the poles from that which inspired his great prototypes' (*Magazine of Art*, 1885, 228).

The Perseus series was envisaged as a scheme of decoration in ten parts to decorate the music room of the London house of Arthur James Balfour at 4 Carlton Gardens. The original scheme, with its division into painted and sculpted panels and its decorative surrounds, can be seen in three designs from 1875–6, now in the Tate collection. The room was to have had no windows and to be lit

entirely by candles, a pattern of lighting that would have allowed the reliefs to be seen to advantage. At some point in the late 1870s Burne-Jones decided that the entire scheme should be painted in oil, and the relief sculptures dispensed with. Once again, the project drew on imagery that Burne-Jones had devised in the mid-1860s in connection with the projected illustrated volume of Morris's *The Earthly Paradise*. He made up full-scale cartoons in gouache (Southampton Art Gallery) for each of the subjects before embarking on the oil versions, first painting the final episodes in the story: *The Rock of Doom*, *The Doom Fulfilled*, and *The Baleful Head*. Several panels remained unfinished at the artist's death, but, as it is now seen in the Staatsgalerie, Stuttgart, the cycle remains one of the most enduring and powerful of all nineteenth-century artistic schemes and a testament to Burne-Jones's vast inventiveness and originality.

A gradual cooling in relations with Coutts Lindsay, combined with encouragement from Leighton that Burne-Jones should support the Royal Academy, led in 1885 to his joining that institution as an associate member (without having had to submit to the process of election), and the following year he exhibited *The Depths of the Sea* (priv. coll.) in the Royal Academy summer exhibition. Later realizing his error, he resigned in 1893. In 1887 Burne-Jones withdrew from the Grosvenor, and the following year he exhibited for the first time at the New Gallery, showing oils from the Perseus series. In 1890 the display of the Briar Rose series (Faringdon Collection Trust, Buscot Park) at Agnew's in Old Bond Street drew great public excitement, and the paintings were then exhibited in Whitechapel, where they were seen by large numbers of people.

Late career Burne-Jones frequently found it hard to complete works, and during the last decade or so of his life he continued on projects commenced in some cases many years earlier, notably the great Arthurian subject *The sleep of Arthur in Avalon* (Museo de Arte de Ponce, Puerto Rico), commissioned originally by George Howard about 1880 for Naworth Castle. The composition went through many stages, and was expanded in scale so that eventually it was the largest painting that he ever worked on. Howard eventually abandoned hope of receiving it, and it remained unfinished in the artist's studio at the time of his death in 1898.

Arthur in Avalon was of great personal significance to Burne-Jones, representing his own sense of returning in old age to a mythic world based on Arthurian legend and overturning the allegiance to Michelangelo and Italian Renaissance art that he had felt in the 1870s. As a theme of mortality, yet in which there is the prospect of rebirth or reawakening if only there were a true awareness of the greatness and valour of the sleeping king, it derives from the artist's meditations on the pattern of his own life—in which he had come to feel that, although honoured in a public sense, he was no longer truly understood as an artist.

A shift of fashion occurred in the 1890s, which led Burne-Jones to think that he was out of step with current taste (he abominated the rising generation of English painters who adopted a degraded form of contemporary French impressionism, and could not comprehend the commercial success of these artists). None the less, he remained an esteemed figure, and one whose work as a painter and designer (not least of stained glass) was known and loved throughout the English-speaking world. In 1892–3 a retrospective exhibition of his works took place at the New Gallery, an event which aroused great interest among a rising generation and which to some extent prompted a return to Romantic figurative subjects on the part of British painters at the turn of the twentieth century.

Of all English Victorian painters Burne-Jones was the one who was best known and appreciated in France. Burne-Jones had first looked for opportunities to establish a European reputation in 1878, when he sent *The Beguiling of Merlin* (Lady Lever Art Gallery, Port Sunlight) and *Love among the Ruins* (priv. coll.) to the Universal Exhibition in Paris. Eleven years later *King Cophetua and the Beggar Maid* (Tate collection) was the sensation of the 1889 Universal Exhibition. Artists of different nationalities saw and praised the painting, and official acknowledgement of its popularity came in the award of the cross of the Légion d'honneur. In 1893 Burne-Jones sent the extraordinary *Perseus and the Graiae*, one of the panels of the Perseus series, to the Salon du Champ de Mars, where it was much admired. He corresponded with Puvis de Chavannes, exchanged drawings with Gustave Moreau, and gave a group of his drawings to the Luxembourg collection.

Burne-Jones was raised to the baronetcy in 1894, it was said because his son, Philip, cared about the title. Georgiana Burne-Jones remained an indomitable character who certainly would not have been impressed by such a trapping. Also on this occasion, the hyphenated form of the name Burne-Jones was officially adopted. Although in some degree he had become an eminent figure of his age, Burne-Jones remained at heart disaffected and unimpressed by society or the artistic establishment. All his life he indulged a fiendish sense of humour, which was utterly self-mocking as well as undermining of the pretensions of others. This is expressed quite brilliantly in the cartoon drawings that he made as illustrations to his letters, to his daughter, Margaret, and to various of the other younger women who gained his adoring friendship—most notably Helen Mary Gaskell.

In 1896 Ned and Georgie were cast down by the death of their great friend Morris. Burne-Jones had further cause to reflect upon old friendships when in 1897 he helped to organize an exhibition of works by Rossetti for the New Gallery. He seems to have grown old before his time, burdened by an awareness of so much unfinished work and a sense of life's shortness. His health was never robust, and by the late 1890s he was distinctly frail. He died of angina on the night of 16 June 1898, at home at The Grange. His ashes were placed in the churchyard at Rottingdean in Sussex, where the family had had a country house since 1880. A memorial service was held at Westminster Abbey.

In the following winter an exhibition of 235 of Burne-Jones's works was presented at the New Gallery, on which occasion once again his unique and towering contribution to British art in the second half of the nineteenth century was acknowledged. He had been the central figure in the wistful and escapist culture which derived from late Pre-Raphaelitism and the aesthetic movement. Burne-Jones himself defined the otherworldly character of his art in a letter to Helen Gaskell:

> I mean by a picture a beautiful romantic dream of something that never was, never will be—in a light better than any light that ever shone—in a land no one can define or remember, only desire—and the forms divinely beautiful.
> (C. Monkhouse, *Exhibition of Drawings and Studies by Sir Edward Burne-Jones, Bart*, 1899, vii)

In the middle years of the twentieth century Burne-Jones's reputation suffered, along with those of other British Victorian painters. However, two monographic exhibitions—the first organized by the Arts Council and held at the Hayward Gallery in London and at Southampton and Birmingham in 1975–6, and the second to mark the centenary of the artist's death, at the Metropolitan Museum of Art in New York, and subsequently shown in Birmingham and Paris—have clearly established Burne-Jones as one of the geniuses of British painting. The Tate Gallery's 1997 exhibition, 'The Age of Rossetti, Burne-Jones & Watts: Symbolism in Britain, 1860–1910', represented Burne-Jones as a key figure in the wider context of European symbolism.   CHRISTOPHER NEWALL

Sources M. Bell, *Sir Edward Burne-Jones: a record and review* (1892); 2nd edn (1893); 3rd rev. edn (1894); 4th rev. edn (1898) • F. De Lisle, *Burne-Jones* (1904) • G. B.-J. [G. Burne-Jones], *Memorials of Edward Burne-Jones*, 2 vols. (1904); repr. (1993) • A. L. Baldry, *Burne-Jones* [1909] • K. Löcher, *Der Perseus-Zyklus von Edward Burne-Jones* (1973) [exhibition catalogue, Staatsgalerie, Stuttgart, 1973] • M. Harrison and B. Waters, *Burne-Jones* (1973) • A. C. Sewter, *The stained glass of William Morris and his circle*, 2 vols. (1974–5) • J. Christian, *Burne-Jones: the paintings, graphic and decorative work of Sir Edward Burne-Jones, 1833–98* (1975) [exhibition catalogue, Hayward Gallery, London, 1975–6] • P. Fitzgerald, *Edward Burne-Jones: a biography* (1975) • J. Christian, *Burne-Jones* (1976) [exhibition catalogue, Hayward Gallery, London, Southampton Art Gallery, and City Museum and Art Gallery, Birmingham, 1976] • *Burne-Jones talking*, ed. M. Lago (1981) • D. Robinson, *William Morris, Edward Burne-Jones and the Kelmscott Chaucer* (1982) • M. T. Benedetti and G. Piantoni, eds., *Burne-Jones* (1986) [exhibition catalogue, Galleria Nazionale d'Arte Moderna, Rome, 1986] • A. Wilton and R. Upstone, eds., *The age of Rossetti, Burne-Jones & Watts: symbolism in Britain 1860–1910* (1997) [exhibition catalogue, Tate Gallery, London, 1997] • S. Wildman and J. Christian, *Edward Burne-Jones: Victorian artist-dreamer* (1998) [exhibition catalogue, Metropolitan Museum of Art, New York, 1998]
Archives FM Cam., corresp., papers, and notebooks • Hunt. L., letters • NL Wales, corresp. about design of University of Wales seal | BL, letters to Sir Sydney Cockerell, Add. MS 52708 • BL, letters to Helen Gaskell, Add. MSS 54217–54218 • BL, letters to Mary Gladstone, Add. MS 46246 • Bodl. Oxf., letters to members of the Lewis family, mainly annotated with drawings and sketches • Bodl. Oxf., letters to Dante Gabriel Rossetti • Bodl. Oxf., letters to F. G. Stephens • Castle Howard, Yorkshire, letters, mainly to ninth earl of Carlisle • Ches. & Chester ALSS, letters, mainly to Lady Leighton-Warren • Hammersmith and Fulham Archives and Local History Centre, corresp., mainly to D. H. Dearle • Harvard U., Houghton L., letters to Philip Burne-Jones • LPL, letters to Julia Ady • Morgan L., letters to John Ruskin • Princeton University, New Jersey, letters to Margaret Burne-Jones • Sheff. Arch., letters to earl of Wharncliffe • Tate collection, photocopied letters to Cormell Price, incl. illustrations • University of British Columbia Library,

letters to James Leathart · Watts Gallery, Compton, Surrey, letters to George Frederick Watts

Likenesses S. Solomon, pencil drawing, 1859, AM Oxf. · E. Burne-Jones, group portrait, self-portrait, oils, 1861 (*The annunciation and the adoration of the magi*; Burne-Jones as a shepherd), Tate collection · A. Legros, oils, 1868, V&A · G. F. Watts, oils, 1870, Birmingham Museum and Art Gallery · double portrait, photograph, *c.*1874 (with William Morris), NPG · G. Howard, pencil sketches, 1875, Carlisle Museum and Art Gallery · H. Furniss, caricature, pen-and-ink sketch, *c.*1880–1910, NPG · S. P. Hall, pencil drawing, *c.*1886–1903, NPG · B. Leighton, photograph, 1890, NPG [*see illus.*] · H. R. Stiles, group portraits, photographs, 1895, NPG · P. Burne-Jones, oils, 1898, NPG · E. Burne-Jones, self-portraits, caricatures, BM · Elliott & Fry, cabinet photograph, NPG · G. Grenville Manton, group portrait, watercolour (*Conversazione at the Royal Academy, 1891*), NPG · F. Hollyer, cabinet photograph, NPG · F. Hollyer, photograph, V&A · A. Legros, oils, Aberdeen Art Gallery · A. Legros, watercolour drawing, V&A · photograph, carte-de-visite (as a young man), NPG · photographs, Hammersmith Public Libraries · photograph, sepia print, NPG

Wealth at death £53,493 9*s.* 7*d.*: probate, 12 July 1898, *CGPLA Eng. & Wales*

Jones, Eirene Lloyd. *See* White, Eirene Lloyd, Baroness White (1909–1999).

Jones, (Frederick) Elwyn, Baron Elwyn-Jones (1909–1989), lord chancellor, was born on 24 October 1909 at 132 Old Castle Road, Llanelli, the youngest in the family of three sons and a daughter of Frederick Jones, a tin-plate rollerman, and his wife, Elizabeth, *née* Griffiths, daughter of a small farmer from Carmarthenshire. His father was a greatly respected member of the local community, an elder of the Tabernacle Congregational chapel and a life-long socialist, and his mother had an immensely strong and influential personality. The three other children all achieved success, in the worlds of science, business, and education respectively. He was educated at Llanelli grammar school, the University College of Wales at Aberystwyth, and Gonville and Caius College, Cambridge, where he became president of the Cambridge Union (1931). In the Cambridge history tripos he obtained a first class (division two) in part one (1930) and a second class (division one) in part two (1931). He went on to Gray's Inn and was called to the bar in 1935.

With his intense concern for human freedom and justice, Jones became involved with the Fabians and it was through this connection that he responded to a request to go out and give legal help to the beleaguered Austrian Social Democrats during the chancellorship of Engelbert Dollfuss (1932–4). It was then that he became greatly involved with the European problem and attended political trials in Germany, Greece, Hungary, and Romania, organizing help for those accused. He wrote to various newspapers about the problems and went on to write three books for the Left Book Club on the fascist threat: *Hitler's Drive to the East* (1937), *The Battle for Peace* (1938), and *The Attack from Within* (1939). On 28 August 1937 he married Pearl (Polly) Driberg (1904–1990), divorced wife of Jack Herbert Driberg and daughter of Morris Binder, a Jewish tailor in Salford. They had one son and two daughters. As Pearl Binder, Jones's wife was a lively and versatile writer,

(Frederick) Elwyn Jones, Baron Elwyn-Jones (1909–1989), by Walter Stoneman, 1949

artist, radio and television personality, and expert on costume and stained glass. The marriage was very happy.

In the late 1930s Jones rejected his earlier pacifism as no answer to the Nazi menace and became a Territorial Army volunteer. During the Second World War he served as a major in the Royal Artillery in north Africa and Italy but ended the war as deputy judge advocate (1943–5), attending many courts martial and inquiries into alleged Nazi brutalities. Following his election to parliament in 1945, as Labour MP for the Plaistow division of West Ham (from 1950, West Ham South), he soon became parliamentary private secretary (1946–51) to the attorney-general, Sir Hartley Shawcross, and joined the team of counsel for the prosecution at the Nuremberg war crimes trials.

In 1949 Jones was appointed recorder of Merthyr Tudful; he took silk in 1953. He became recorder of Swansea in 1953, of Cardiff in 1960 (the year he became a bencher of Gray's Inn), and of Kingston upon Thames in 1968 (holding the post until 1974). In the meantime he was reasonably active politically but still devoted a good deal of time to his practice on the Wales and Chester circuit. However, following the Labour victory in the general election of 1964 (the same year that he was knighted), he became attorney-general, a position he held until 1970, throughout the Labour government.

During Jones's period as attorney-general his most important achievement, in co-operation with the lord chancellor Gerald Gardiner, was the establishment in 1965 of the Law Commission, under the chairmanship of

Sir Leslie Scarman. As attorney-general Jones was also counsel for the tribunal in the Aberfan inquiry, when over 100 children had been killed in a Welsh village school by the movement of a coal slurry tip. He prosecuted in the moors murder case and in cases arising from the Official Secrets Act.

After the fall of the Labour government in 1970 Jones returned to his legal practice, by then mainly in London. When Labour returned in 1974 he became lord chancellor, with a life peerage, as Baron Elwyn-Jones, and severed his long-standing tie with his beloved East End constituency. As lord chancellor he encouraged the growth of law centres, whose number had quadrupled by the time he left office.

Although a lord chancellor (until 1979, when he became a lord of appeal) and attorney-general of distinction, Jones was not a profound lawyer. Law as such was not his prime interest; politics were. He was very much a political lawyer of swift intelligence, good judgement, and rare sensibility, more concerned that the legal system should provide the means of achieving true justice than with handing down great judgments himself.

Jones was a member of the bar council (1956–9) and chairman of the Society of Labour Lawyers. He was president of University College, Cardiff, from 1971 to 1988. He was made an honorary fellow of his Cambridge college (1976) and received six honorary degrees. A privy councillor from 1964, he was appointed a companion of honour in 1976.

Elwyn Jones was tall and dark-haired, with aquiline features and a ready smile. He was a man of natural charm and dignity, with a warm personality, a convivial disposition, and a fine sense of humour. He was a superb raconteur and had a very fine light baritone singing voice, with which he entertained his friends, and which he sometimes used on formal occasions. There was a disarming simplicity about his approach, and his shrewdness and capacity to grasp the essential points of a controversy, hidden behind an approach of urbanity and charming whimsicality, were often used to take the heat out of Commons debates which might otherwise have become acrimonious. However, below the surface were to be found the true convictions from which he never wavered. When put to the test, his concern for social justice would manifest itself in passionate outbursts. He died of cancer of the prostate at 17 Lewes Crescent, Brighton, on 4 December 1989, and his wife died seven weeks later. They were survived by their three children.   EMLYN HOOSON, rev.

Sources F. Elwyn-Jones, *In my time* (1983) · *The Independent* (7 Dec 1989) · *The Independent* (1 Feb 1990) · *The Times* (6 Dec 1989) · *The Times* (29 Jan 1990) · *CGPLA Eng. & Wales* (1990) · personal knowledge (2004) · *WWW* · b. cert. · m. cert. · d. cert.
Archives Denbighshire RO, Ruthin, diaries · NL Wales, corresp. and papers | NL Wales, corresp. with Lord Cledwyn
Likenesses W. Stoneman, photograph, 1949, NPG [*see illus.*]
Wealth at death £227,106: probate, 15 March 1990, *CGPLA Eng. & Wales*

Jones, Emily Beatrix Coursolles (1893–1966), novelist, was born on 15 April 1893 at 6 St John's Park, Blackheath, London, the youngest of the eight children of Major Charles Jones (1840–1896) of the Royal Artillery, formerly of Toronto, Canada, and his wife, Mary Jane Ross (1855–1936), who, with her siblings, including her brother, Robert Baldwin *Ross (1869–1918), had left Upper Canada in 1872. Nicknamed Topsy, Emily was brought up from 1900 onwards at Jesmond Hill, near Pangbourne, Berkshire, and educated by governesses and for one term at St Felix's School, Southwold.

During the First World War, E. B. C. Jones worked for the food control ministry and was assistant editor of the *Common Cause*, the suffragette weekly. Later she lived at home, a ménage described by her friend Romer Wilson in *If All These Young Men* (1919), where Susan has 'hair cut straight at the sides and twisted up at the back in the Spanish fashion … she looked like a thin modern intellectual doll with black hair and red blotched cheeks' (Wilson, 49), and with her sister Petica Robertson and her husband at 56 Bateman Street, Cambridge. Here she became friends with contemporaries such as Rosamond Lehmann and Dadie Rylands. E. B. C. Jones published twelve poems in *Windows* (1917) and her first novel, *Quiet Interior*, in 1920; this was praised by Kathleen Murry (Katherine Mansfield) for 'its distinction of style' (Mansfield, 308), while Rebecca West saw 'a sense of character that can be brilliant or touching', adding: 'Miss Jones has caught perfectly the tone of life as it is lived among pretty young people with enough money to give them power to amuse themselves, but not so much money that they need move out of Bayswater' (West, 82).

On 17 February 1921, at the register office in Cambridge, E. B. C. Jones married Frank Laurence (Peter) *Lucas (1894–1967), a fellow of King's College. They appeared compatible even though Virginia Woolf observed: 'she, I suppose, had a deeper experience of life, & somehow vouched for all sorts of things which, with his … scholar's unworldliness, he was ready to take on trust' (*Diary of Virginia Woolf*, 2.156). At their home, The Pavilion, 20 West Road, Cambridge, she 'would lead the conversation, fixing her guests with a bright, determined, searching gaze and firing leading questions at them in a deep voice … demanding frankness' (Lehmann, 139). Three more novels were published between 1921 and 1924; in 1927 *Helen and Felicia* was described by Cyril Connolly as a 'moving and conscientious study of fondness written with sobriety and grace' (Connolly). In that year an affair with 'Rex' (probably Warner) made it inevitable that the Lucases be 'separated for ever, owing to her flirtatious ways' (*Diary of Virginia Woolf*, 3.225), and E. B. C. Lucas moved to London. *Morning and Cloud* (1932) found a publisher only with difficulty although Dora Carrington, for example, preferred it to previous novels. The shock of the deaths of her and Strachey, the publishers' rejections, as well as the unsatisfactory nature of her emotional life, partially explained her ceasing to write after such a promising beginning; she did, however, write reviews and a few critical pieces and remained friends with writers such as Dorothy Richardson and Walter de la Mare.

In 1930 E. B. C. Lucas fell in love with (Frederick) Donald Livingstone (Ian) McIntyre (1905–1981), a barrister, later

QC, who had 'desperate reserve' but was 'the handsomest man I ever saw' (private information, R. Cohen). They lived at 2 Peel Street, Kensington, and after 1934 at Craston's Orchard, Yattendon, Berkshire. She had no children, saying 'she had fared much better with two much loved nephews who returned her devotion' (ibid.); these were the sons of Petica Robertson. During the war Ian McIntyre was a prisoner of war in the Far East, where he displayed enormous fortitude. Afterwards they lived in somewhat uneasy harmony until her death, at Newbury District Hospital, from a stroke on 30 June 1966. Her body was cremated at Reading crematorium on 8 July.

NICOLA BEAUMAN

Sources private information (2004) [family, R. Cohen] · R. Wilson, *If all these young men* (1919) · K. Mansfield, *Novels and novelists* (1930) · R. West, *New Statesman* (23 Oct 1920), 82 · *King's College report* (Nov 1967) · *The diary of Virginia Woolf*, ed. A. O. Bell and A. McNeillie, 2 (1978), 156; 3 (1978), 225 · J. Lehmann, *The whispering gallery* (1955), 139 · C. Connolly, *New Statesman* (12 Nov 1927) · E. B. C. Jones, letter to Lytton Strachey, 30 May 1930, BL · Blain, Clements & Grundy, *Feminist comp.*
Archives BL, letter to Lytton Strachey
Likenesses portrait, repro. in *Rosamond Lehmann's album* (1985), 36
Wealth at death £84,830: probate, 7 Nov 1966, CGPLA Eng. & Wales

Jones, (Elizabeth) Emma. *See* Soyer, (Elizabeth) Emma (1813–1842).

Jones, Enid Wyn [*née* Enid Williams] (1909–1967), religious and social worker, was born in Wrexham, Denbighshire, on 17 January 1909, the only daughter of Dr David Llewelyn Williams (1870–1947), medical officer of health for Wrexham, and his wife, Margaret (*née* Price) of Rhyl. Her brothers Eric and Alun became respectively a general medical practitioner and an adult educationist. The family moved to Cardiff in 1912, but she spent the war years in Rhyl; her father was with the Royal Army Medical Corps in France. At the end of the war the family was reunited at 33 Ninian Road, Cardiff, and in 1920 her father (who assumed the surname Llewelyn-Williams) became chief medical officer of health for Wales.

Enid Williams was educated between 1919 and 1926 at the Welsh Girls' School, Ashford, Kent, during the last years of the formidable headmistress Anne Hildred Jones, who was at the helm from 1889 to 1929. From there she proceeded to the Domestic Science College in Cardiff (1926–7) and then she trained as a nurse at Cardiff Royal Infirmary. She met her future husband, the physician Emyr Wyn Jones (1907–1999), on the first sea journey of the Welsh League of Youth in August 1933, and they were married on 9 September 1936. They became actively involved in the cultural and medical life of Wales and of the Liverpool area. They had a daughter, Carys, and a son, Richard Gareth.

The home of the Wyn Joneses at 15 Sandringham Drive, Liverpool, was rendered uninhabitable in 1941 as a result of the massive bombing attacks of the Second World War. As a mother, Enid had to make a secure place for the children at the homestead of Llety'r Eos, Llansannan, Denbighshire, but she continued to visit regularly her second home at 28 Rodney Street, Liverpool. When peace came Llety'r Eos became a lively cultural meeting place for the musicians and poets of the upland rural community of Hiraethog and the adjacent villages. Not only did many famous preachers of Wales, such as Tom Nefyn Williams, visit often, but also many international figures such as Pastor André Tromcé, Pastor Martin Niemöller, and Danilo Dolci stayed there.

An ecumenical at heart, Enid Wyn Jones belonged to the Presbyterian Church of Wales as well as the Society of Friends. At a time when women preachers were rare she gave substantial service for years to the Welsh-speaking congregations in south Lancashire. Her melodious singing voice and her ability as a pianist were additional assets. She was a fluent speaker who prepared her addresses with meticulous care. She had a great admiration for Rufus Matthew Jones, the American Quaker, and was a friend of the pacifist George Maitland Lloyd Davies and the Quaker writer Elfrida Vipont. She valued her involvement as a member of the religious panel of BBC Wales for six years.

Enid Wyn Jones's involvement in the medical world included membership of the medical executive council of the counties of Denbighshire and Flintshire, followed by service (1960–67) to the Clwyd and Deeside Regional Hospital Board and the North Wales Hospital for Nervous Diseases. She was appointed a member of the nursing advisory committee of the Welsh Regional Hospital Board in 1963, elected its vice-chairman in the same year, and took a leading role in establishing the branch in Wales of the Royal College of Nursing and in the building of its headquarters at Tŷ Maeth, adjacent to the University Hospital, Cardiff.

After several years of practical social welfare in the inner-city and dockland areas of Liverpool, under the aegis of the Young Women's Christian Association (YWCA) and the free churches, Enid Wyn Jones was drawn into wider fields of service. She was active in the New Wales Union and in the formation in 1967 of *Merched y Wawr*. From 1955 she was a justice of the peace for the county of Denbighshire and the petty sessional division of Is-Aled, and she was a member of the British Red Cross Society. Her favourite committee was the North Wales Child Guidance Service. During 1958–9 she was president of the National Free Church Federal Women's Council, being only the second Welsh woman to attain that honour. She became president of the Welsh council of the YWCA, vice-president of the council for England and Wales (1959–67), and a member of the world council of the YWCA, in which capacity she attended world conferences. Towards the end of the quadrennial world council at Melbourne, Australia, in 1967, she sustained, without any warning, a subarachnoid haemorrhage. After a measure of recovery, and accompanied by her husband on the return journey, she had a fatal recurrence on the flight home above Bangkok on 15 September 1967. She was buried at the Henry Rees Memorial Chapel cemetery, Llansannan, on 20 September.

Many of the articles which she contributed to the *Free*

Church Chronicle and the Welsh press describing her travels were included in the books published after her death and edited by her husband—the bilingual volume *In Memoriam Enid Wyn Jones* (1968) and the Welsh language volume *Cyfaredd cof* (1970). The article and address that sum up her life of service (delivered at Folkestone in March 1958) is entitled *A Housewife in Search of God* and was published as a pamphlet.

D. BEN REES

Sources E. W. Jones, ed., *In memoriam Enid Wyn Jones* (1968) · E. W. Jones, ed., *Cyfaredd cof* (1970) · E. W. Jones, 'Teyrnged serch', *Y Traethodydd*, 124 (1969), 202–16 · E. W. Jones, 'Enid Wyn Jones', *Y bywgraffiadur Cymreig, 1951–1970*, ed. E. D. Jones and B. F. Roberts (1997), 96 · private information (2004) [E. W. Jones] · D. B. Rees, *Cymry adnabyddus, 1951–1972* (1978), 113–14

Likenesses photograph, repro. in Jones, ed., *Cyfaredd cof* · photograph, repro. in Rees, *Cymry adnabyddus*

Jones, Sir Eric Malcolm (1907–1986), intelligence officer and administrator, was born on 27 April 1907 in Buxton, Derbyshire, the third in the family of four sons and one daughter of Samuel Jones, who ran the family business of Samuel Jones & Son, textile manufacturers, of Macclesfield, Cheshire, and his wife, Minnie Florence Grove, of Buxton. Jones went to King's School, Macclesfield, and left at the age of fifteen to join the business in Manchester. In 1925 he set up on his own, and built up a large textile agency. In 1929 he married Edith Mary (Meg) Taylor (1904–1984), daughter of Sir Thomas Taylor, silk merchant, of Macclesfield. They had a son and a daughter.

In 1940 Jones handed over his business to a manager in order to enlist in the Royal Air Force Volunteer Reserve. He was posted to the Air Ministry intelligence branch. In 1942, as squadron leader, he was sent to the Government Code and Cypher School at Bletchley Park to stand in temporarily for the senior RAF officer in Hut 3, which housed the group responsible for the analysis and dissemination of the deciphered German Enigma messages to the ministries and principal commands. So impressive was he to Edward Travis, director of the Government Code and Cypher School (later the government communications headquarters, or GCHQ), that in April 1943, when Travis decided that a formal head of Hut 3 was needed, he asked the RAF for Jones, who was then posted to Bletchley as head of Hut 3 and promoted to group captain. Jones provided the mainly academic staff in Hut 3 with wise leadership and demanded the highest standards of speed and accuracy in the production of their intelligence reports.

From 1945 to 1946 Jones was in Washington as representative of British signal intelligence and it was his discussions with American agencies which were the basis for American–British co-operation in this field in the future. This proved of great importance to both governments in the succeeding years, most notably in the cold-war period.

Jones was formally transferred from the RAF to GCHQ at assistant secretary level, was made deputy director in 1950, and succeeded Sir Edward Travis as director in April 1952. He stayed as director until 1960, when he took early retirement, believing that eight years was long enough in the post. During that time he established the organization and the ethos under which GCHQ was to operate in succeeding years. For a man who left school at fifteen, he had a remarkable interest in the English language; H. W. Fowler's *Dictionary of Modern English Usage* (1926) was a favourite work. Jones produced instructions, and a system for enforcing them, to ensure that GCHQ's reports and correspondence were of the highest possible accuracy and clarity.

Jones's directorship spanned a period of great expansion in Soviet military capability, encompassing conventional and non-conventional weapons and rocketry to deliver them. With colleagues in the services, he made sure that British signal intelligence had the staff and technical resources to provide information on these developments. He believed that his task was management of the intellectually brilliant and technically qualified staff by whom he was surrounded, to give them the best chance to exercise their skills. A man of the highest integrity, it was said of him that corruption was unthinkable in his presence.

Jones aimed, quite simply, to be the best, whether in his work, as a games player (he played golf at the highest amateur level), or in skiing, which he took up at the age of fifty. When GCHQ moved to Cheltenham he bought Bredons Hardwick Manor, near Tewkesbury, and with his wife and family became a keen gardener and grew high-quality carnations.

A handsome man, Jones was deliberate in both speech and gait, and some found him ponderous or pompous. Perhaps for this reason, or through a lack of empathy between Whitehall mandarins and a man from a quite different background, he was not given further government employment after his retirement in 1960, at the age of fifty-three. Thereafter he accepted non-executive directorships in a number of companies, including Simon Engineering Ltd (1966–77).

Jones was appointed CBE in 1946, CB in 1953, and KCMG in 1957. His standing among American government and service officers was very high. He was awarded the US Legion of Merit in 1946. When the US Air Force decided to have its own signal intelligence organization in the early 1950s, the British government was asked to lend Jones to set it up. He felt bound to refuse the offer, but arranged to provide advice. He died on 24 December 1986 in Wotton Nursing Home, 49 Barnwood Road, Gloucester, and his remains were cremated at Gloucester crematorium.

D. R. NICOLL, *rev.*

Sources *The Times* (1 Jan 1987) · R. Bennett, *Ultra in the west* (1979) · personal knowledge (1996) · private information (1996) [Peter Jones, son; colleagues] · *CGPLA Eng. & Wales* (1987)

Wealth at death £119,123: probate, 8 Sept 1987, *CGPLA Eng. & Wales*

Jones, (Alfred) Ernest (1879–1958), neurologist and psychoanalyst, was born on 1 January 1879 at Rhosfelyn in Llwchwr (renamed Gowerton), Glamorgan, the son of Thomas Jones (1853–1922), then a colliery manager and later a colliery proprietor, and his wife, Mary Ann Lewis (1855–1909). His parents were both Welsh. He had two younger sisters, Elizabeth and Sybil. He was brought up in

(Alfred) **Ernest Jones** (1879–1958), by James Russell & Sons

the Church of England and was educated at Swansea grammar school and Llandovery College.

Medical training and early career, 1896–1913 In 1896 Jones began the first part of his medical studies at University College, Cardiff, which he continued in 1898 at University College Hospital, London. Through his readings, and particularly through the influence of the works of Charles Darwin, Thomas Huxley, and Kingdom Clifford, he became committed to an evolutionary, materialistic, and atheistic world view. He obtained his BM (1901), BS (1902), MD (1903), and became MRCP (1904). He initially attempted to establish himself as a neurologist, and was heavily influenced by the work of John Hughlings Jackson. However, he had difficulty obtaining a secure position, and held house posts in medicine and surgery at University College Hospital, followed by various posts at the Brompton Chest Hospital, the National Hospital, the Hospital for Sick Children, the Royal Ophthalmic Hospital, the West End Hospital for Nervous Diseases, Moorfields Eye Hospital, the North-Eastern Hospital for Children, the Farringdon General Dispensary and the Dreadnought Seamen's Hospital at Greenwich. His career ran into difficulties, and he failed to obtain an expected appointment at University College Hospital. In 1905 he set up a practice as a consultant physician in Harley Street, together with his best friend, the surgeon Wilfred Batten Lewis *Trotter (1872–1939), who married Jones's sister Elizabeth in 1910. During this time Jones published a number of papers on neurological topics.

In 1906 Jones was accused of sexually assaulting two girls—a charge of which he was subsequently cleared. In 1908 he was asked to resign his post at the West End Hospital for Nervous Diseases after examining a ten-year-old girl and discussing sexual topics without the presence of a third person (Jones, *Free Associations*; Brome; Paskauskas, 'Ernest Jones'). During this period he became interested in psychopathology and in particular read widely in the French literature on hypnotism, double personality, and hysteria.

Jones first became acquainted with Freud's work in 1907. This was to become the central focus of his life. However, it was several years before he became a committed Freudian. That year he met C. G. Jung at the First International Congress of Psychiatry and Neurology in Amsterdam. He subsequently visited Jung at the Burghölzli Hospital in Zürich. He met Freud for the first time at the First Psychoanalytic Congress in Salzburg in 1908. There Jones presented a paper on rationalization in everyday life (contrary to the claims of many psychoanalysts, the term was not coined by him).

In 1908 Jones spent several months in Germany and France. In Munich he studied with the psychiatrist Emil Kraepelin at his clinic, and also became acquainted with the renegade psychoanalyst Otto Gross. Jones regarded Gross as the closest person to the romantic ideal of a genius that he had ever met, and he viewed him as his first instructor in psychoanalysis. In Paris Jones attempted to study with Pierre Janet, the abnormal psychologist, but Janet would not take him on as a student. Instead, Jones continued his neurological researches on hemiplegia and tongue deviations at the Bicêtre Hospital.

That same year Jones emigrated to Canada in search of employment. As British and Canadian medical qualifications were not interchangeable he had to resit his medical examinations. The professor of psychiatry at the University of Toronto, C. K. Clarke, had planned to set up a Kraepelinian clinic, where Jones hoped to secure a post. However, Clarke's plans fell through. In Toronto Jones held part-time appointments at the University of Toronto, the Toronto General Hospital, and the Toronto Asylum. He became the co-editor of the *Bulletin of the Ontario Hospital for the Insane*. During this period he became acquainted with members of the Boston school of psychotherapy, and in 1909 he was appointed by Morton Prince as assistant editor of the *Journal of Abnormal Psychology*. Jones's early psychological writings drew from French abnormal psychology as well as from the work of the Boston school of psychology, and he employed hypnosis as well as Jung's word association tests. In 1911 Jones was accused of sexual assault by one of his patients, Emma Goodman. Jones denied the charges but informed James Jackson Putnam that he 'foolishly paid the woman $500 blackmail to prevent a scandal' (Jones to Putnam, 13 Jan 1911, in Hale, 253).

In 1909, after the Clark conference in Worcester, USA, where honorary degrees were conferred on Freud and Jung, Jones told Freud that he intended to devote his life to psychoanalysis (Paskauskas, *Correspondence*, 29). For the next couple of years, however, he continued to publish papers on neurological as well as psychological topics.

In 1911 Jones played a role in the foundation of the American Psychoanalytic Association. He did not, as he would subsequently claim, found the American Psychopathological Association. That year his common-law wife, Loe Kann (d. c.1945), who was addicted to morphine, went to Freud for analysis. In their correspondence Freud gave Jones regular updates on the progress of the analysis, paying no regard to confidentiality. Her relationship to Jones was complicated by the fact that he had an affair with her servant.

The early psychoanalytic movement was full of dissensions. In the summer of 1912 Jones proposed to Freud the formation of a secret committee to secure the future of psychoanalysis. This group, Jones wrote, would be like the 'Paladins of Charlemagne, to guard the kingdom and policy of their master' (Paskauskas, *Correspondence*, 149). Freud responded favourably to the idea and the committee was set up. The other original members were Karl Abraham, Sándor Ferenczi, Otto Rank, and Hans Sachs. For many years the secret committee, which communicated through a series of circular letters, policed the psychoanalytic movement, co-ordinating strategies of how to deal with opponents and defectors. While Jones remained loyal to Freud, and conducted a lengthy correspondence with him, he never became as intimate with him as Ferenczi, Jung, or Rank had done.

In 1913 Jones himself underwent a seven-week analysis with Sándor Ferenczi. On his return to London he established himself in private practice as a psychoanalyst. He lived in a flat at 69 Portland Court, Marylebone, and had a consulting room in Harley Street. The psychologist Prynce Hopkins, who, together with his first wife, Eileen, had analysis with Jones in the 1920s, recalled him as a man of 'short stature, broad head and forehead, thin lips and pale but energetic appearance' (Hopkins, 94). Hopkins gave the following picture of Jones at work:

> Dr. Jones' consulting room was large, but unlike his mentor, Freud, it was nearly bare of furniture and very gloomy,—Out of sight, behind my head, Dr. Jones sat back in his big easy chair, usually with a rug across his legs, gazing at the wall or fire. (ibid.)

Jones would see up to eleven patients a day, and saw his first patient before breakfast.

Central role in British psychoanalysis, 1913–1939 Up until the Second World War Jones was the single most important figure in the institutional development of psychoanalysis in Britain, and its main public spokesman. In 1913, together with David Eder, he founded the London Psycho-Analytical Society. In its early years its meetings were stormy. For while Jung and the Zürich school had formally left the psychoanalytic movement in 1914, several members of the London society were at that stage favourable to Jung: Constance Long, David and Edith Eder, and Maurice Nicoll. As revealed by their correspondence Jones had an affair with Edith Eder shortly after her analysis with Jung (Jones / Edith Eder letters, Archives of the British Psycho-Analytical Society). In 1919 Jones dissolved the London

society and expelled what he called the 'Jung rump'. The purged and reformed society was renamed the British Psycho-Analytical Society. Shortly after its foundation Jones informed Freud that he had personally analysed six of its eleven members, which placed him in a position of 'good contact' (Paskauskas, *Correspondence*, 336). He remained its president until 1944 when new regulations were introduced which limited the term of office to three years.

On 6 February 1917 Jones married Morfydd *Owen (1891–1918), a Welsh musician, composer, and singer under her bardic name Morfydd Lwyn Owen, daughter of William Owen, an accountant. The following year, while travelling in Wales, she had an acute attack of appendicitis. On the advice of Trotter, Jones himself immediately conducted the surgery together with a local surgeon, using chloroform in the operation. They did not realize that this was contraindicated, given her medical condition, and she died a few days later of chloroform poisoning. Jones was to call this event the most painful episode of his life. The following year he met and married Katherine Jokl, an Austrian woman who had spent her life in Vienna. Together they had four children, Gwenith (1920–1927), Mervyn (b. 1922), Nesta (b. 1930), and Lewis (b. 1933). Their first child, Gwenith, died of pneumonia at the age of seven. In 1921 Jones purchased a house in York Terrace, London, where he lived until the Second World War.

In 1920 Jones founded the *International Journal for Psycho-Analysis*, which was the first English-language periodical devoted to psychoanalysis. He remained its editor until 1939. He also founded an International Psycho-Analytical Press, which briefly published psychoanalytic works. In 1924, together with John Rickman, he established the Institute of Psycho-Analysis in London. He was chairman of the board until 1944. In 1926, thanks to a donation of £10,000 from his patient Prynce Hopkins, the London Clinic of Psycho-Analysis was formed, which enabled low-cost psychoanalytic treatment. Jones became its honorary director. Arrangements were made with Leonard Woolf and the Hogarth Press to publish the International Psycho-Analytical Library. For many years Jones was the general editor of the series. In the 1920s a training programme became formalized at the British Psycho-Analytical Society, and in 1925 Jones was elected chairman of the training committee. Thus Jones effectively occupied most of the positions of power in British psychoanalysis, centralizing authority upon himself. In addition to his central role in Britain Jones was the president of the International Psycho-Analytical Association from 1920 to 1924, and again from 1932 to 1949.

Jones played a key role in arranging English translations of Freud, and in setting up what became the standard edition of Freud's writings. In 1920 he sent James Strachey for analysis to Freud as a prospective translator. Jones's correspondence with Strachey shows a high degree of collaboration, as they both set about establishing what became the orthodox and canonical presentation of Freud and his works (Archives of the British Psycho-Analytical Society).

In a letter to Freud of 19 June 1910, Jones defined his position *vis-à-vis* his master:

> The originality-complex is not strong with me; my ambition is rather to know, to be 'behind the scenes', and 'in the know', rather than *to find out*. I realise that I have very little talent for originality; any talent I may have lies rather in the direction of being able to see perhaps quickly what others point out: no doubt that also has its use in the world. Therefore my work will be to try to work out in detail, and to find new demonstrations for the truth of, ideas that others have suggested. To me work is like a woman bearing a child; to men like you, I suppose it is more like the male fertilisation.   (Paskauskas, *Correspondence*, 61)

Consequently, the bulk of Jones's writings were dedicated to the dissemination of psychoanalysis. Jones styled himself as the Huxley to Freud's Darwin, and engaged in polemics and propaganda on behalf of the psychoanalytic cause. Jones's rigidly materialistic perspective led him to recast psychoanalysis in this vein, and he disagreed with Freud over the latter's interest in telepathy, his advocacy of Lamarckian factors in evolution, and his postulation of the existence of a death drive. Jones published the following books on psychoanalysis: *Essays on Psycho-Analysis* (1912), *Treatment of the Neuroses* (1920), *Psycho-Analysis* (1928), *On the Nightmare* (1931), *Essays in Applied Psychoanalysis* (1923), *Hamlet and Oedipus* (1949), *What is Psychoanalysis?* (1949), and *Sigmund Freud: Four Centenary Addresses* (1956). As well as editing several collections and publishing more than 300 papers he also wrote a work on his favourite hobby, *The Elements of Figure Skating* (1931).

In the 1920s Jones brought Melanie Klein to London from Berlin. She analysed two of his children, as well as his wife. His advocacy of Klein's work against that of Anna Freud's was his most significant divergence from Freud. In the late 1930s Jones played a prominent role in enabling the evacuation of analysts from Germany, and in 1938 he succeeded in bringing Freud and Anna Freud to England, with their extensive entourage.

Semi-retirement and *Sigmund Freud*, 1939–1958 During the Second World War Jones moved to his country house, The Plat, at Elsted in Sussex, in semi-retirement. Some of his wealthy patients bought houses nearby to continue working with him. After the war he commenced work on his *Sigmund Freud: Life and Work*, which appeared in three volumes in 1953, 1955, and 1957. This was his most significant literary achievement. In preparation for it Jones had unrivalled access to Freud's papers, many of which remain inaccessible to scholars to this day. Jones was aided by the fact that his wife was a native German speaker and she transcribed over a thousand letters of Freud for him (Jones had trouble reading Freud's gothic handwriting). Furthermore, as his correspondence reveals, he drew to an insufficiently acknowledged extent upon the researches of the pioneer Freud historian and psychoanalyst, Siegfried Bernfeld (Jones / Bernfeld letters, archives of the British Psycho-Analytical Society).

Jones's Freud biography remains the single most important biographical source of information on Freud's life and on the early history of the psychoanalytic movement. No other single work has been more influential in shaping the subsequent perception of Freud. At the outset Jones stated that Freud would have disapproved of such a work, but claimed that it was necessitated by the mendacious legends that were being spread about him. However, subsequent research has shown that Jones himself was the initiator of many legends, and suppressed information which would shed an unfavourable light on Freud (Ellenberger; Roazen; Sulloway; Paskauskas).

Given the singular relation of psychoanalysis to its history, Jones's biography played a critical role in shaping the subsequent development of psychoanalysis, and indeed its impact on twentieth-century culture. Its portrait of Freud was effectively enshrined within psychoanalytic institutions. Jones's official history gave an identity to the field, and was the prime statement of the Freudian legend. Freud was presented as a revolutionary hero, on a par with Darwin and Copernicus. Freud supposedly discovered the tenets of psychoanalysis through a heroic and unprecedented self-analysis and through his clinical work. Freud's followers, and especially Jones himself, were portrayed as a revolutionary vanguard that fought against vicious and malevolent opponents, widespread prejudice, and obscurantism. Individuals such as Adler, Jung, and Rank, who parted from Freud, were represented as heretics, whose original ideas stemmed from personal psychopathology and character defects. Thus in his account of his former analyst Ferenczi's last years and his late theoretical developments, Jones elaborated a legend of the latter's mental deterioration and psychotic manifestations, a symptom of which included a turning away from Freud's doctrines. Jones's polemical intent is clearly revealed by his response to the legal report on the second volume, which requested many deletions and alterations on the grounds of libel (J. E. C. Macfarlane, 'Notes on defamatory passages', 27 Jan 1955, Jones–Peter Calvocoressi letters, Hogarth Press archives).

The Freud biography has been hailed as one of the most significant biographies of the twentieth century. However, several decades of Freud scholarship, commencing with Henri Ellenberger's *The Discovery of the Unconscious* (1970), have done much to challenge Jones's portrayal of events. Indeed, the larger share of subsequent Freud scholarship has consisted of corrections and revisions of Jones's account. More recently, Jones himself has come in for reappraisal (Paskauskas, 'Ernest Jones').

In 1942 Jones became an FRCP and in 1954 he received an honorary DSc from the University of Wales. He also became an honorary president of the International Psycho-Analytical Association as well as of the British Psycho-Analytical Society.

In his late years Jones suffered from chronic rheumatism. In 1956 he contracted cancer of the bladder. He was hospitalized at University College Hospital in 1958 with cancer of the liver. His widow recalled that, like Freud before him, Jones had requested that his physician would give him 'something to end the suffering' (Jones, 'Sketch', 273). He died in University College Hospital on 11 February 1958, and was cremated at Golders Green three days later.

At his death he left an uncompleted manuscript of his autobiography, *Free Associations: Memories of a Psycho-Analyst*, which was published in 1959.

SONU SHAMDASANI

Sources V. Brome, *Ernest Jones: Freud's alter ego* (1982) • T. G. Davies, *Ernest Jones: 1879–1958* (1979) • H. Ellenberger, *The discovery of the unconscious: the history and evolution of dynamic psychiatry* (1970) • P. Hopkins, *Both hands before the fire* (1962) • N. Hale jun., ed., *James Jackson Putnam and psychoanalysis* (1971) • E. Jones, *Free associations: memories of a psycho-analyst* (1959) • K. Jones, 'A sketch of E. J.'s personality', *International Journal of Psycho-Analysis*, 60 (1979), 271–3 • M. Jones, epilogue, in E. Jones, *Free associations: memories of a psycho-analyst* (1959) • P. King, 'The contributions of Ernest Jones to the British Psychoanalytical Society', *International Journal of Psycho-Analysis*, 60 (1979), 280–84 • P. Roazen, *Freud and his followers* (1976) • R. A. Paskauskas, 'Ernest Jones: a critical study of his scientific development', PhD diss., University of Toronto, 1985 • *The complete correspondence of Sigmund Freud and Ernest Jones, 1908–1939*, ed. R. A. Paskauskas (1993) • F. J. Sulloway, *Freud, biologist of the mind* (c.1979) • D. W. Winnicott, *International Journal of Psycho-Analysis*, 39 (1958), 298–304 • Archives of the British Psycho-Analytical Society • U. Reading, Hogarth Press archives • m. cert. [Morfydd Owen] • *CGPLA Eng. & Wales* (1958)

Archives British Psycho-Analytical Society, London, archives • NRA, priv. coll., corresp. and papers • University of Kansas Medical Center, Kansas City, Clendening History of Medicine Library and Museum, notebooks and papers | BL, letters to Havelock Ellis, Add. MS 70539 • L. Cong., Sigmund Freud archives • McMaster University Library, Hamilton, Ontario, William Ready division of archives and research collection, corresp. with Bertrand Russell • U. Reading, Hogarth Press archives |SOUND BL NSA, recorded talk, BBC, 1957

Likenesses R. Moynihan, oils, c.1946, British Psycho-Analytical Society, London • J. Russell & Sons, photograph, British Psycho-Analytical Society, London [*see illus.*]

Wealth at death £18,037 5s. 3d.: probate, 11 Sept 1958, *CGPLA Eng. & Wales*

Jones, Ernest Charles (1819–1869), radical and writer, was born in Berlin on 25 January 1819, the only child of Major Charles Jones, a veteran of the Peninsular War who had fought at Waterloo, and his wife, Charlotte, the daughter of Alexander Annesley, a large Kent landowner. Major Jones was equerry to the duke of Cumberland, but a few years after his son's birth he bought a small estate in Holstein, where he mainly occupied himself, as he explained in a letter written when Ernest was eleven years old 'in superintending the education of my only child, already master of the English, German, French and Italian languages'. At the age of thirteen Ernest entered the College of St Michael, an élite institution for the sons of the aristocracy and gentry, where he continued his prose and poetic writings and developed into an intensely romantic young man. The family left Germany when Ernest was nineteen, and he quickly became part of the social world of London (he was presented at court by the duke of Beaufort in 1841). Although his future was always assumed to be a literary one, he entered the Middle Temple (also in 1841) and on 19 April 1844 he was called to the bar. Why he chose to move into professional life is not clear—he did not engage in legal practice until the following decade—but in part it may have been prompted by his difficulties in persuading English editors to publish his writings.

It may also have been consequent upon his marriage in

Ernest Charles Jones (1819–1869), by unknown engraver

June 1841. Jones's wife, Jane Atherley (d. 1857), came of an old Cumberland family related to the Stanleys, and there were four sons of the marriage. What his financial position was at this time is not known, but in September 1844 he offered £57,000 for Kearnsey Abbey in Kent, a property deal that quickly collapsed into disaster. As early as November 1844 he attempted to resell the house and grounds, and his financial situation continued to worsen until he was declared bankrupt, and his London house was sold over his head.

To this point in his life politics do not seem to have interested Jones. His diaries to 1844 were almost wholly concerned with domestic and social affairs. He was obviously an affectionate husband and father. Within months of his financial troubles, however, political references in the diaries became more frequent, and within a year he was moving towards the most radical movement in British politics. According to his own account, it was during the winter of 1845 that he came across the *Northern Star*, the national Chartist weekly, and found that 'the political principles advocated harmonised with my own'. How it came about that this young man of twenty-seven years, previously dominated by literary ambitions, apparently happy in his family life, and having spent all his days in the conservative milieu of the landed gentry, so quickly accepted the radicalism of the Chartist movement is a wholly intriguing question. His financial problems were serious but not at this stage insoluble. Some Conservatives at this time were producing serious criticisms of a society dominated by the cash nexus, and certainly Jones to the end of his life, while hostile to both, still preferred a tory to a whig; but whatever the reasons, his acceptance of the programme of the Chartist movement was remarkable. His early political statements were those of mainstream Chartism, but it was as a poet and versifier that Jones first became known at the national level. A collection of poems, the *Chartist Songs*, was published in August 1846, and the works it contained were recited and sung all over Britain. After his previous disappointments with his literary work, it must have been wonderfully satisfying. Much of his poetry was never more than competent versification, but some in this early Chartist period was of a more lyrical quality.

Ernest Jones was an unusual recruit to Chartism and Feargus O'Connor quickly recognized his abilities. They worked together on *The Labourer*, the journal of the land plan, but Jones's closest friend soon became George Julian Harney, and it was through Harney that Jones first met Friedrich Engels and then Karl Marx, both of whom were to have a not inconsiderable influence on his general thinking. By the beginning of the year 1848 Jones was already one of the leading personalities of the movement. He had been a candidate for Halifax in the general election of July 1847. When the revolution in Paris in late February 1848 fired the imagination of both British and Irish radicals, Jones was one of the three-man delegation to present a congratulatory address to the provisional government in Paris—where he again met Marx—and he was the main speaker after O'Connor at the great demonstration of 10 April. This meeting on Kennington Common was the prelude to the presentation of the third national petition. Jones was quite a small man, but he had a powerful speaking voice with an eloquent and striking turn of phrase. From this time, especially in London, he was the outstanding personality of the movement and inevitably was to be among the first arrested by the whig government. On 6 June 1848 he was apprehended in Manchester, brought back to London to be charged with seditious behaviour and unlawful assembly, tried at the central criminal court before the lord chief justice, and sentenced to two years' imprisonment; he was also bound over for a further two years on release, which came on 9 July 1850.

Jones's prison regimen was harsh, and he came out weakened in health and strength. The Chartist movement was now much divided and no longer a national force. For the next few years Jones worked tirelessly to rebuild the movement upon the principles of 'the charter and something more': an English version of the ideas and policies of social democracy. There was an unfortunate quarrel with Harney at the beginning of 1852, and of all the 1848 leadership Jones was now alone. His journals and newspapers in the 1850s—above all, the *Notes to the People* (1851–2) and The *People's Paper* (1852–8)—offer essential insights into radical politics in this last decade of Chartism, and his political and intellectual career in the last two decades of his life provide a necessary introduction to these years, when there no longer existed an independent political movement of working people. Standing again for Halifax, Jones

was the only Chartist candidate to go to the poll in the general election of July 1852. The labour parliament of 1854 was an impractical enterprise, but on the third occasion when he stood for parliament, contesting O'Connor's former constituency of Nottingham in March 1857, his election address restated his support for the Charter but now also laid emphasis upon the contemporary radical concern with the land question. There was more continuity than is sometimes allowed.

Jones was in serious financial troubles all through this first decade after his release from prison, and his problems seem to have worsened as the years went by. He made two successful applications to the royal literary fund on the evidence of, mainly, his poetry, and among the individuals who responded to his appeals for financial help were Robert Owen, Thomas Allsop, and, at the end of the decade following the death in 1857 of his wife, William Ewart Gladstone. After the sale of his remaining Chartist papers in 1859 Jones began to work steadily in legal practice, and his material conditions were soon to be much improved. He accepted, beside the usual day-to-day cases, trade union briefs and poor people's actions, and his most famous appearance in the courts was his defence of the Manchester Fenians. Their final hearing began in late October 1867, and Jones was not only a leading member of the defence team, but also spoke in public support outside the court.

During this last decade of his life Jones moved towards a radical–Liberal position in British politics. His internationalism remained vigorous and he took an active part in the campaign to support the North in the American Civil War, but his most important contribution was in the reform movements that led up to the second Reform Bill of 1867. He was married again in 1867, to Elizabeth Darbyshire, and there was a daughter of the marriage. Jones died of pleurisy at Wellington Street, Higher Broughton, Manchester, on 26 January 1869, the day after his fiftieth birthday. Had he lived, he would almost certainly have become one of Manchester's Liberal MPs, having polled over 10,000 votes when he contested the seat in November 1868. His funeral was the occasion of an impressive radical and working-class demonstration. He was buried in Ardwick cemetery, Manchester.

In the decades that followed his death Jones's memory was kept alive by the publication of his speeches and commemorative meetings. It was as a radical Liberal that he was remembered in Lancashire and the West Riding of Yorkshire—there were still meetings in his name in the last decade of the century—but historians must have a different evaluation. For most of his political life, until the final demise of any movement of Chartism, Ernest Jones rejected middle-class ideas and policies; and he must be given his place as one of the most interesting of the early English socialists: a man of remarkable energy, a lively and vigorous polemicist with, above all, a deep compassion for the poor, the needy, and the downtrodden.

JOHN SAVILLE

Sources R. G. Gammage, *History of the Chartist movement, 1837–1854*, new edn (1894); repr. with introduction by J. Saville (1969) ·

W. E. Adams, *Memoirs of a social atom*, 2 vols. (1903); repr. with introduction by J. Saville (1968) • G. Howell, 'Life of Ernest Jones', *Newcastle Weekly Chronicle* (Jan–Aug 1898) • G. D. H. Cole, *Chartist portraits* (1941) • J. Saville, *Ernest Jones: chartist* (1952) • A. R. Schoyen, *The chartist challenge: a portrait of George Julian Harney* (1958) • J. Epstein and D. Thompson, eds., *The Chartist experience: studies in working-class radicalism and culture, 1830–60* (1982) • D. Goodway, *London Chartism, 1838–1848* (1982) • D. Thompson, *The Chartists: popular politics in the industrial revolution* (1984) • J. Saville, *1848: the British state and the chartist movement* (1987) • T. W. Porter, 'Ernest Jones and the royal literary fund', *Labour History Review*, 57/3 (winter 1992), 84–94 • M. C. Finn, *After chartism: class and nation in English radical politics* (1993) • A. D. Taylor, 'Ernest Jones: his later career and the structure of Manchester politics 1861–9', MA diss., U. Birm., 1984 • *The Times* (27 Jan 1869) • Man. CL, Manchester Archives and Local Studies, Ernest Jones MSS

Archives Bishopsgate Institute, London, diaries • BL, album of poems and drawings, Add. MS 61971A-C • Col. U., Rare Book and Manuscript Library, corresp., family and business papers • Internationaal Instituut voor Sociale Geschiedenis, Amsterdam, corresp. • Man. CL, Manchester Archives and Local Services, diaries, legal papers, and notebooks; MS poems and notes • NL Wales, draft letters; memoranda and papers • Russian Centre for the Preservation and Study of Documents of Recent History, Moscow • U. Hull, Brynmor Jones L. | Bishopsgate Institute, London, letters to George Howell • Chetham's Library, Manchester, corresp. with Jane Atherley • Co-operative Union archive, Holyoake House, Manchester, letters to George Jacob Holyoake • NRA, letters to Karl Marx

Likenesses woodcut, repro. in Gammage, *History*, facing p. 281 [*see illus.*]

Jones, Evan [*pseud.* Ieuan Gwynedd] (**1820–1852**), journalist and Independent minister, one of six children of Evan and Catherine Jones, was born at Bryn Tynoriaid, Brithdir, near Dolgellau, on 5 September 1820. He was extremely delicate all his life, so his schooling in the Dolgellau area between 1826 and 1836 was spasmodic. He was first employed as an elementary school teacher, and while engaged at Llanwddyn commenced preaching at the Independent chapel of Sardis in March 1838. In October 1839 he went to a grammar school at Marton, and subsequently to another at Minsterley, in Shropshire, to prepare for the ministry, and during the latter part of his stay at Marton had charge of the church both there and at Forden. In September 1841 he entered Brecon College, and was ordained minister of Saron Independent Chapel, Tredegar, in July 1845. On 14 November 1845 Jones married Catherine, third daughter of John Sankey of Rorrington Hall, Marton, Shropshire. She died on 25 April 1847, and the only child of the marriage died in infancy. In December 1848 he married Rachel, fifth daughter of the Revd Walter Lewis of Tredwstan.

Jones, who adopted the bardic name of Ieuan (the Welsh form of Evan) Gwynedd, contributed numerous articles, mainly on temperance and disestablishment, to Welsh and English journals. In 1846 a commission, formed almost wholly of churchmen unacquainted with the Welsh language, was appointed to inquire into the state of Welsh education. Its report, published in 1847, completely misrepresented the work of nonconformists and charged them with ignorance, drunkenness, and immorality. Similar charges had already been made in anonymous letters which appeared in *John Bull* early in 1847 from the pen

of John Griffith (1818–1885), vicar of Aberdâr. Jones wrote a spirited reply to Griffith in four letters, and addressed two able letters to Lord John Russell, in which he brought statistics to refute the charges of the commissioners. His arguments were carefully prepared and presented in *Facts, figures and statements in illustration of the dissent and morality of Wales: an appeal to the English people by Evan Jones* (1849). Jones also continued in Welsh and English journals to expose what was known in Wales as 'brad y llyfrau gleision' ('the treachery of the blue books'). He replied in separate pamphlets to two letters published in 1848–9 in support of the irresponsible report, and issued *A vindication of the educational and moral condition of Wales in reply to William Williams, esq., late M.P. for Coventry* (1848). This pamphlet responded to Williams's address to parliament on 10 March 1846, which had been responsible for the setting up of the inquiry.

Owing to ill health Jones resigned his pastorate at Tredegar in January 1848 and from March to September of that year edited *The Principality*, a new weekly Liberal paper of Cardiff. In October he moved to London to superintend the publication of the *Standard of Freedom* for John Cassell, and wrote much for *The Pathway*, a young people's magazine published by Cassell. In August 1849 his failing health compelled him to return to Cardiff, but he managed to continue his literary work and prepared a carefully compiled volume entitled *The Church Establishment in Wales* for the use of the Liberation Society. In January 1850 he published, under the patronage of Lady Llanover, the first number of *Y Gymraes*, a monthly magazine intended for women, and in March of the same year he started *Yr Adolygydd*, a national quarterly review conducted with ability but plagued by severe financial problems. He edited both of these magazines until his death. His poetical compositions were highly regarded in Victorian Wales; but most of his poems have been forgotten except for his hymns, which are in the free churches' hymnbooks.

Jones died of tuberculosis on 23 February 1852. He was buried at Groes-wen, near Caerphilly, where a monument, erected by penny subscriptions largely contributed by the women of Wales, was placed over his grave. A biography and collection of his poems and minor essays was edited by his friend, the publisher Robert Oliver Rees (1819–1881), of Dolgellau, in 1876, and a volume of his poetry was edited by the Revd Thomas Roberts of Llanrwst in 1876.   D. L. THOMAS, *rev.* D. BEN REES

Sources *DWB* • C. T. F. Thomas, *Ieuan Gwynedd* [n.d.] • B. Rees, *Ieuan Gwynedd: detholiad o'i ryddiaith* (1957) • M. Stephens, ed., *Cydymaith i lenyddiaeth Cymru* (1986), 310 • R. O. Rees, *Gweithiau Ieuan Gwynedd, ei fywyd a'i lafur* (1876) • *Congregational Year Book* (1854) • *Y Bedyddiwr* (1852) • *GM*, 2nd ser., 37 (1852), 423

Archives Gwynedd Archives, Caernarfon, letters • NL Wales, biographical collections, literary MSS, and sermons, MSS 1025–1036, 2694–2695, 2755–2769, 2877

Jones, Sir (David) Fletcher (**1895–1977**), clothing manufacturer and retailer, was born on 14 August 1895 at Bendigo, Victoria, Australia, the fifth child of Samuel Henry Jones, a blacksmith from Cornwall, and his Australian-born wife, Mahala, *née* Johns (*d.* 1897). Samuel remarried and had a second family. Fletcher recalled his childhood fondly: 'the greatest inheritance is to have been born into a struggling Christian household' (Jones, 168). The family, devoutly Methodist in religion and staunchly Labor in politics, and the mining community at Golden Square, inculcated in the boy a desire for personal improvement and the moral imperative to leave the world better off. His education was in state schools at Bendigo.

Jones left school early, in 1908, because of a bad stammer, worked in an auction room, and then grew tomatoes at Kangaroo Flat. He enlisted in the Australian Imperial Force in July 1915 and served in France, but was repatriated in 1917 and discharged in 1918 suffering from shellshock and with the stammer worse than ever. An avid reader, mainly of biographies, he began reciting aloud in an attempt to overcome his speech impediment. He became a door-to-door salesman and then a hawker, buying a wagon with a repatriation loan. This he stocked with Manchester cotton, and he did well among farmers and townsfolk in Victoria's western district. Later he bought a commercial traveller's drag (a heavy, horse-drawn vehicle), extended his business west into South Australia, and expanded into tailoring and dressmaking.

On 23 September 1922 Jones married his childhood friend Rena Ellen Jones (*d.* 1970); she was his mainstay. In 1924 he purchased a menswear and tailoring business in seaside Warrnambool, Victoria. Inexperience saw him financially embarrassed, but he entered into an arrangement with his Melbourne creditors and eventually repaid them in full. Quickly learning from his mistakes, he traded out of his difficulties. He paid cash for goods and materials in small quantities, initiated group buying by tender, recruited gifted tailors and salesmen, and attracted custom by clever advertising, exuberant showmanship, and delivering value for money. By 1939 his tailors' room was one of the largest in provincial Victoria. In 1941 he won a contract to supply army trousers, and he soon established a reputation for well-fitting and hard-wearing work pants. By 1945 he supplied 123 retailers in four states. He sold directly, for cash, supplied fractional sizes, and insisted on personal fittings. Customers besieged his first shop when it opened in Melbourne on 23 June 1946 as 'Fletcher Jones of Warrnambool—nothing but trousers. 72 scientific sizes. No man is hard to fit.'

Jones had decided to transform his business into a co-operative. Wesleyan principles, particularly of stewardship and social responsibility, were fundamental to this decision, but the American industrial efficiency movement was also important. He was acquainted with the ideas of the industrialists Henry Ford and Andrew Carnegie, the industrial efficiency advocates Frederick Taylor and Lillian Gilbreth, and the apostle of modern merchandising and good design, Edward Bok. From the 1920s he subscribed to Herbert Casson's *Efficiency Magazine*: 'I Believe in Casson's 12 points as Luther believed in his 95 theses, as George Fox believed in his inner light' (notes for speeches, 1960, Fletcher Jones papers). Jones abhorred the

way traditional tailoring wasted time and exploited workers, but he opposed pursuing industrial efficiency through schemes that extracted more labour without improving rewards and yielding job satisfaction. Spiritual growth could be achieved through productive and satisfying work and worker partnership. P. T. B. (Tubby) Clayton of Toc H influenced him to support the unemployed during the depression of the 1930s. Through reading analyses of capitalism by Victor Gollancz, Harold Laski, J. B. S. Haldane, and Sidney and Beatrice Webb, as well as studies of the co-operative movement, Jones had become convinced that social advance rather than individual profit was the proper object and an achievable outcome of business. Attracted by the teachings of the Japanese Christian socialist Toyohiko Kagawa, a pioneer of consumers' and farmers' co-operatives, he supported the latter's visit to Australia in 1935, formed the Kagawa Fellowship, and visited Japan in 1936. Since he was convinced that his co-operative would work only if the venture was financially successful, he placed customer benefits first in the statement of principles for Fletcher Jones and Staff Proprietary Ltd (1947). He determined to raise the quality of Australian-made clothing and to bring made-to-measure garments within the reach of the ordinary man.

Jones introduced the latest English and American production methods to a new factory that he designed and built on the outskirts of Warrnambool. Initially disparaged as a shanty town, the factory in a landscaped garden setting at Pleasant Hill became a tourist attraction. The firm expanded its product range beyond trousers (skirts and slacks in 1956, women's wear from the late 1950s, and men's suits in 1966) and was at the forefront of new ideas and technology, including methods-engineering practices, a textile-testing laboratory, and computerized tailoring systems. Accountants criticized his business methods, but Jones persisted with his extensive size range, quality raw materials, a non-profit after-sales service, a standard retail instead of a percentage mark-up, and consumer-oriented staff training, as well as staff ownership and consultative management (the last achieved through a junior board, adopted from the American McCormick system). The business prospered so much that labour shortages obliged him to open branch factories elsewhere, but Warrnambool remained the administrative centre, production base, and social heart of the 'FJ Family'. The staff held 53 per cent of the shares by the early 1950s and over 70 per cent by the 1970s.

Gregarious and affable, trim and impeccably groomed, a non-smoker and teetotaller, Jones enjoyed a simple lifestyle. He gave away most of his wealth, anonymously, and his and his wife's estates were willed to the FJ Foundation, established in 1959 for charitable purposes. That same year he was appointed OBE, and in 1974 he was knighted for services to decentralization and the community. He remained chairman until his health began to fail in 1975. Jones died at Warrnambool Hospital on 22 February 1977, and was buried in Warrnambool cemetery on 24 February after a United Methodist service, survived by his three children and by his second wife, Aida Margaret Wells, *née*

Pettigrove, a widowed friend whom he had married on 5 October 1971. His singular producers' co-operative employed some 3000 people in four factories and in thirty-three stores throughout every Australian capital city. Widely celebrated as a pre-eminent symbol of an affluent and self-confident post-war nation, and for its material success, the enterprise in fact embodied a form of Australian egalitarianism informed by Christian socialist teachings. Certainly no person or firm had done more to transform and for a time homogenize Australian dress, particularly among men, than Fletcher Jones and his staff.

JOHN LACK

Sources F. Jones, *Not by myself* (1976) · priv. coll., Fletcher Jones papers [Mr David F. Jones, Port Fairy, Victoria, Australia] · *The Age* [Melbourne] (24 Feb 1977) · *The Sun* [Melbourne] (24 Feb 1977) · *The Herald* [Melbourne] (23 Feb 1977) · *Warrnambool Standard* (23–5 Feb 1977) · private information (2004) [D. F. Jones] · *AusDB* · *Who's who in Australia* (1974)

Archives priv. coll., personal and business papers

Wealth at death A$326,795: probate records

Jones, Sir Francis Avery (1910–1998), physician and gastroenterologist, was born on 31 May 1910 at 26 Ritson Street, Briton Ferry, Glamorgan, the son of Francis Samuel Jones (1879–1947), a surgeon, and his wife, Marion Rosa, *née* Chaston (1875–1967). Both Francis and his brother used Avery as part of their surname. Avery Jones was educated at the Sir John Lemen School, Beccles, and at the medical school of St Bartholomew's Hospital in London. He qualified in medicine in 1934 and it was a sign of his distinction at that early period of his career that he was selected as house physician successively to professors Sir Francis Fraser, Leslie Witts, and Ronald Christie—three of the most distinguished academic physicians of their day. He married, on 1 September that year, Dorothea Bessie (1907–1983), a shorthand and typing teacher, the daughter of Henry Pfirter, a stockbroker; their son, John Francis Avery Jones, was born in 1940. In 1936 he obtained a Baly research scholarship and became assistant to Professor Witts, who was investigating the new technique, introduced by Meulengracht in Denmark, of liberally feeding patients who were bleeding from peptic ulcers instead of starving them. Using blood transfusion he and Witts were able to show that the mortality of the condition, then a common cause of hospitalization, could be dramatically reduced. This early interest in gastroenterology was further stimulated by an invitation in 1937 to attend the foundation meeting of a gastroenterological club, organized by Sir Arthur Hurst of Guy's Hospital, who was a major inspiration to him. The club later became the British Society of Gastroenterology.

In 1940 Avery Jones was appointed physician to the nutrition department of the Central Middlesex Hospital. Nutrition became one of his abiding concerns. During the war he organized a meals-on-wheels service to the population around his hospital. Together with his colleagues, Horace Joules and Richard Asher, he was determined that hospitals such as the Central Middlesex would play an increasingly important role in the medicine of the metropolis. But it was through his determination and quiet

encouragement of gastroenterology at his hospital that he was able to establish a department which became famous worldwide and which attracted students from all over the globe.

He was particularly adept at the technique of gastroscopy, using the semi-rigid Wolf–Schindler instrument for diagnosis and to observe the progress of healing of peptic ulcers. In 1946, with the return of young and ambitious physicians from the war, Avery Jones was joined by Richard Doll as his research assistant. Together, over the course of more than twenty years, they clearly showed that the bland diets and other now rejected treatments were of no benefit, and that stopping smoking was. At the same time Doll and Avery Jones conducted extensive surveys of peptic ulcer in the community that surrounded them. It was particularly entertaining for Avery Jones, whose natural reserve concealed a twinkling sense of humour, that when they conducted a survey in the nearby Heinz factory, whose well-known trade mark was '57', they found that the incidence of peptic ulcer symptoms was 57 per thousand.

With the establishment in 1948 of the National Health Service (NHS), which Avery Jones strongly supported, his unit became increasingly busy. Nevertheless he was able to produce *Modern Trends in Gastroenterology* (1952), the first modern textbook on the subject in Britain. Soon afterwards he played an important if unobtrusive role in the development of the fibre-optic techniques that were to transform the practice of gastroenterology during his lifetime. In 1954 Harold Hopkins, of Imperial College in London, together with his student Kapany, published their epoch making paper describing their construction of a flexible fibre-optic bundle which would transmit light and enable an image to be defined. Hopkins was always disappointed that his paper made so little impact on the medical profession. One of those, however, who at once recognized the importance of Hopkins's discovery for the investigation of the alimentary tract was Avery Jones, who immediately asked a young South African research fellow, Dr Basil Hirschowitz, to explore the possibility of using fibre optics in gastroscopy. No British firms, however, were interested, and Hirschowitz went to the United States, where he successfully developed an instrument that could not only be used to see the stomach but could also be introduced into the duodenum. This achievement was at once taken up by Japanese academics and commercial firms, bringing about a revolution in gastroenterology as almost the entire length of the gastrointestinal tract could be seen directly.

By now Avery Jones had established a remarkable department at the Central Middlesex to which all aspiring gastroenterologists came. He had also developed a highly successful private practice and so gave his expertise not only to individuals in Britain but increasingly to those from overseas. In this way his experience of his subject became unique there. Always quiet and patient, often working long hours which might bring him to the patient's bedside late at night, he would write his highly valued opinion in a characteristically scratchy hand. He became increasingly in demand not only as an expert diagnostician but also as a humane and caring physician.

During those years the élite London teaching hospitals paid little attention to gastroenterology, then not recognized as a speciality. It was Avery Jones at the Central Middlesex Hospital who provided the facilities for studies of gastrointestinal disease and teaching in the capital. By 1957—supported by the Nuffield Foundation, the Medical Research Council, and the hospital authorities—he had established a well-equipped unit with facilities for radiological investigation and screening. At the same time the Medical Research Council, which had sponsored and published much of the work of Avery Jones and Doll, was increasingly interested in supporting a centre where there was an abundance of clinical material and where a physiological approach to the study of human disease could be adopted. The unit was established alongside Avery Jones's department in 1960 under the direction of Tom Rowlands. The proposal had been strongly supported by Sir Harold Himsworth, the charismatic secretary of the Medical Research Council. The research unit played an important role in adding research training to the clinical experience of the Central Middlesex.

Avery Jones himself was increasingly in demand. In 1950 he had become civil consulting gastroenterologist to the Royal Navy. He also provided a consultant service to the Royal Postgraduate Medical School at Hammersmith and served as a physician to St Mark's Hospital, then orientated particularly to the surgery of the bowel. He always encouraged the closest co-operation between physicians and surgeons, and it was fitting that he became one of those rare physicians to be awarded the fellowship of the Royal College of Surgeons.

Avery Jones had a finely honed social conscience. He was the first to try and persuade the Royal College of Physicians to take action on the hazards of smoking. Having Richard Doll, co-discoverer with Professor Austin Bradford Hill of the dangers of the cigarette, working with him on his unit, he knew all too well the dangers of a habit which since he qualified in medicine had caused the death rate from cancer of the lung to rise from 3000 to nearly 17,000 a year. He had also persuaded a colleague, the chain-smoking Horace Joules, to abandon his pernicious habit overnight. In 1956, deeply concerned by the rising number of patients with cancer of the lung, he wrote to Lord Brain, then president of the college, to express his misgivings and ask that the college should put out a statement. Brain, however, replied that enough had already been said and that the college should play no part in advising the public. This response from a member of the specialist London élite of the teaching hospitals to a physician from a district hospital on the outskirts of London, was symptomatic of the time. It was not until Brain retired the next year that the new president, Robert Platt, established a committee on smoking and health, of which Avery Jones became a member. The committee published its epoch making report on the hazards of smoking in 1962, a major contribution to the public health.

Throughout his career Avery Jones was devoted to improving the structure of the National Health Service. He was chairman of the king's fund committee on catering and diet in hospitals and he chaired the King Edward VII Hospital fund development and emergency bed service committee, as well as the Department of Health's advisory committee on medical records. He always maintained his interest in nutrition. He had a deep interest in the dietary fibre controversy, when it was suggested that the lack of undigested material in the digestive tract might lead to all manner of illnesses. He was a member of the British Nutrition Foundation and the first chairman of the Royal Society of Medicine's forum on food and health.

Avery Jones was increasingly involved in medical education. He served on the medical subcommittee of the University Grants Committee, was a member of the council of the University of Surrey and a governor of his old medical school, St Bartholomew's medical school, an appointment which particularly delighted him. He was a devoted member of the British Society of Gastroenterology, which developed from the club whose inaugural meeting he had attended in 1937 at the age of twenty-six. He became president in 1966. He had founded the journal of the society in 1960 and was an early editor. He called it *Gut*, a characteristically straightforward choice which sometimes caused amusement among German colleagues. As Avery Jones had foreseen the journal, starting as a relative unknown in the world of medical publishing, met a need both in Britain and in the wider world, for it soon established an international reputation as its circulation climbed. Avery Jones was committed to *Gut*'s remaining a clinical rather than coldly scientific journal. He wanted to see it on physicians' desks. Asked in later years how he accounted for its remarkable success, Avery replied: 'If I see the word rat or dog in the title, I cross it out'.

Avery Jones received many national and international distinctions. He gave the first memorial lecture of the American Gastroenterological Association, was vice-president of the World Organization of Gastroenterology, and was the first medallist of a distinguished American honour, the Bockus medal. He received the CBE in 1967 and a knighthood in 1970.

After retirement Avery Jones maintained a keen interest in medicine, nutrition, and the NHS. An inveterate addict of the telephone, his many friends and pupils welcomed his continued interest and encouragement in later life. Shortly after the death of his wife Avery Jones married, on 4 August 1983, Kathleen Joan Edmunds, a retired nursing sister. At their home, 19 Peter Weston Place, Chichester, Sussex, he developed a remarkable herb garden, which included a collection of medicinal herbs. As the years passed he became increasingly frail. Nevertheless in 1997, the year before he died, he was able, though confined to a wheelchair, to attend the diamond jubilee of the British Society of Gastroenterology, and there he heard the lecture named in his honour. His own career had spanned the entire life of that society, which reflected the events of his own life. Much of what Avery Jones did was done unobtrusively behind the scenes, quietly and without fuss. But his major personal achievement was that from humble beginnings in a relatively unknown west London hospital, he became one of the leading and most influential physicians of his era. He died on 30 April 1998 at St Richard's Hospital, Chichester, and was cremated at Chichester a week later.   CHRISTOPHER C. BOOTH

Sources *The Times* (13 May 1998) · *The Independent* (13 May 1998) · *The Guardian* (18 May 1998) · C. C. Booth, 'Factors influencing the development of gastroenterology in Britain', *Gastroenterology in Britain*, ed. Bynum (1997) · R. Doll, F. Avery Jones, and M. M. Bucktozch, *MRC special report series*, no. 27b (1951) · H. H. Hopkins and N. S. Kapany, *Nature*, 173 (1956), 39–41 · private information (2004) [Harold Hopkins, J. F. Avery Jones] · S. Lock, L. Reynolds, and E. M. Towy, eds., *Ashes to ashes: the history of smoking and health* (Amsterdam, 1998) · personal knowledge (2004) · b. cert. · m. certs. · d. cert.
Archives Wellcome L., corresp. and papers | SOUND Royal College of Physicians, London, recorded interview
Likenesses L. Boden, portrait, 1990, RCP Lond., office of British Society of Gastroenterology · photograph, 1996, NPG; repro. in *BMJ* (1996)
Wealth at death £855,873: probate

Jones, Frederick Edward (*c.*1759–1834), theatre manager, was born at Vesington, co. Meath, Ireland, about 1759 to landed protestant parents. Little is known about his youth except that he apparently attended Trinity College, Dublin, before living for a while on the continent (there is no surviving record of him at Trinity College). He was over 6 feet tall and considered to have been one of the handsomest men of his day; he was well connected, of an aristocratic deportment, and displayed polished manners. In his youth he acquired the nickname Buck. His private behaviour was said to be impeccable, though in later life he was faulted for imperiousness and gormandizing.

In the winter of 1792 Jones and a friend, Lord Westmeath, planned a private theatre in Dublin, there being great dissatisfaction with Richard Daly's management of the Theatre Royal in Crow Street. Opened on 6 March 1793, the Fishamble Street Theatre was said to be one of the most beautiful in Europe, and Jones staged plays there (acting occasionally himself) for the next three years. In 1796 he solicited the lord lieutenant for a patent to open a second public theatre in Dublin on the grounds that, owing to Daly's mismanagement, the Crow Street Theatre was no longer a place of rational public amusement. The attorney-general agreed, and, rather than face competition, Daly ceded his patent to Jones in August 1797 and sold him the Crow Street Theatre in 1800.

Jones assumed the management of Crow Street Theatre in late January 1798 after spending over £12,000 on renovations. However, in May the theatre was closed for two months because martial law had been proclaimed in Dublin on account of the 1798 rising. Later Jones made an unsuccessful request for compensation for his losses to the Irish House of Commons, claiming to have been out of pocket by over £5000 as a result of the civil unrest. At about this time he married a woman about whom little is known except that her name was Susannah. They had three sons: Frederick, Richard Talbot, and Charles Horatio, all of whom were associated later with the theatre. Jones and his family lived for most of this period on a small but magnificent estate in co. Dublin called Fortick's Grove, which he later restored to its original name, Cloncliffe House.

Jones only occasionally involved himself in the day-to-day affairs of the theatre, relying instead on a series of competent actor deputies. The theatre was particularly noted for its introduction of Italian opera to Irish audiences, including first performances there of Mozart's *Così fan tutte* and *Don Giovanni*, and the presence on its stage of such singers as John Braham and Angelica Catalani. After 1799 the Theatre Royal prospered; however, the civil unrest accompanying the abortive rising in Dublin of the United Irishmen in July 1803 resulted in a curfew between 8 p.m. and 6 a.m., which again adversely affected theatre attendance. No sooner was the curfew relaxed than there appeared an anonymous satirical poem entitled 'Familiar epistles to Frederick Jones, esq., on the present state of the Irish stage', criticizing Jones's lack of attention to his duty, his lack of taste in repertory, and the deficiencies in the quality of his company. In December 1805 letters began to appear in the newspapers that were highly critical of his management of the theatre, and by March 1807 rumours circulated that Jones would soon leave Dublin. In April he accepted the offer of R. B. Sheridan to lease and manage the theatre in Drury Lane, but that theatre burnt down on 24 February 1809, before the deal could be finalized.

Jones was also active in Dublin politics and served as a magistrate of co. Dublin. Known as a liberal, in 1807 he actively supported the election of an anti-ministerial member of parliament for Dublin. He believed that the government never forgave him for his action, and he attributed the loss of his patent in 1819 to this political stand. In 1814 Jones served on a grand jury that prohibited the operation of Daniel O'Connell's Catholic board, which had been established in support of Catholic emancipation. According to Jones, the rioting that took place at Crow Street Theatre in the days following the announcement was directly attributable to that decision, although the immediate cause would seem to have been his unwillingness to relent to the demands of the owner of a dog who was starring in *The Forest of Bondy*, a popular melodrama, for an increase in the animal's fee. The public outcry was such that Jones was forced to retire from the management of the theatre, although he retained the patent and returned to manage it a year later when his replacements proved incompetent.

In 1818, when Jones applied to the Irish chief secretary for a renewal of his patent, his application met with opposition from a group calling itself 'The Friends of the Drama', who had the support of several Dublin newspapers. The last season of his direct association with the Crow Street Theatre was that of 1818–19. The frequent disruption at the theatre had reduced Jones and his family to a state of serious debt, and in November 1819 his share of the property was attached by the court of king's bench. The Crow Street Theatre opened only for brief periods during the 1819–20 season under an acting manager.

After numerous machinations the government officially informed Jones of its decision to grant a patent to

Henry Harris, one of the proprietors of London's Drury Lane Theatre. Jones was forced to accept a very inadequate offer for his property, and he was arrested for debt. Thus ended his twenty-two-year association with the Dublin stage. He spent the remainder of his life in relative obscurity, and died of cholera at his home, Portland Place, Dublin, on 5 November 1834. Ironically, in 1829 his sons Richard and Charles secured a second patent in Dublin and opened a theatre in Abbey Street which seriously challenged the Theatre Royal. JOHN C. GREENE

Sources Highfill, Burnim & Langhans, *BDA* · J. T. Gilbert, *A history of the city of Dublin*, 3 vols. (1854–9) · *DNB* · T. J. Walsh, *Opera in Dublin, 1798–1820: Frederick Jones and the Crow Street Theatre* (1993) · biographical dictionary research materials, Harvard TC
Wealth at death bankrupt in 1820: Gilbert, *History*, vol. 2

Jones, Gentleman. *See* **Jones**, **Richard** (1779–1851).

Jones, George (1786–1869), army officer and painter, born in London on 6 January 1786, was the only son of John *Jones (c.1755–1796), the mezzotint-engraver. His godfather was George Steevens, the controversial and argumentative writer on Shakespearian and other literary issues. George Jones enrolled as a student at the Royal Academy in October 1801, registering as aged seventeen; he was in fact only fifteen. Showing precocious talent, his first exhibits at the Royal Academy in 1803 included *Christ and the Woman of Samaria*. Thereafter, until 1811, he exhibited portraits, views, and literary subjects at the academy and, from 1807, at the British Institution. Taught the first principles of art by his father, he also had a sincere and enthusiastic knowledge of English and classical literature, influenced perhaps by his godfather, and he became one of the first artists to illustrate new work by Scott and Byron: Jones's illustrations to the first canto of Byron's *Childe Harold's Pilgrimage*, published in March 1812, for example, are dated 1812 and 1813 (priv. coll.; D. Brown, *Turner and Byron*, exhibition catalogue, Tate Gallery, London, 1992, nos. 10–14).

Jones was innately patriotic, and in 1808 he responded to the national mood and enlisted in the South Devon militia. Fighting in the Peninsular War, he rose to become a captain in the Montgomery militia, and in 1815 was an officer in the army of occupation in Paris. He did not fight at Waterloo, but nevertheless his love and experience of military life—and indeed his physical resemblance to the duke of Wellington and the fact that he chose to retain the title Captain—led him to draw together both his talent as an artist and his knowledge as a former soldier to paint a series of reliable and atmospheric pictures of battles in the Peninsula and of Waterloo. Battle painting as a genre had become underrated by artists and, sensing a career opportunity, Jones used his special combination of talents to good effect. He rapidly became recognized as an expert on the events of the battle of Waterloo, publishing an account of the battle in 1817 illustrated with his own etchings and maps.

In 1820 Jones's large oil *Battle of Waterloo* shared the prize (with James Ward RA) awarded by the British Institution for a painting to celebrate the great allied victory. This work was purchased by the British Institution directors and presented to the Royal Military Hospital, Chelsea, where it still hangs. 'Very good—not too much smoke', was the duke of Wellington's comment on the painting (H. Ottley, *Biographical and Critical Dictionary of Recent and Living Painters and Engravers*, 1866, vol. 1, p. 98).

Battle scenes having become Jones's stock-in-trade, he was commissioned in 1822 by George IV to paint the victories of Vitoria and Waterloo (Royal Collection) to hang in the throne room of St James's Palace. Other commissioners of Jones's battle pieces and other military subjects included Lord Egremont, his host at Petworth on many occasions, and Sir John Leicester, bt. The latter acquired Jones's *The King's Regiment of Cheshire Yeoman Cavalry Exercising on Liverpool Sands* in 1824 or 1825 (Tabley House, Cheshire, University of Manchester Collection). Jones's *Battle of Alma* and *Battle of St Vincent—Nelson Boarding the San Josef* are in the Ashmolean Museum, Oxford, and his *Battle of Borodino* (1829) is in the Tate collection. Other examples are in the Victoria and Albert Museum, the National Army Museum and the Yale Center for British Art, New Haven, Connecticut.

Expanding his ability to paint scenes of highly populous and dramatic military action, Jones also created what are probably the most reliable records of passing events such as *The Prince Regent Received by the City and University of Oxford, June 1814* (Magdalen College Oxford; sketch AM Oxf.), *The Conferment of Degrees on Allied Sovereigns in the Sheldonian Theatre, Oxford* (AM Oxf.), *The Passing of the Great Emancipation Act* (1829; Yale U. CBA), and *The Opening of the New London Bridge, 1831*, a commission for Sir John Soane (Sir John Soane's Museum, London). He travelled widely in Europe, and returned to paint and exhibit views of continental cities, such as *Malines* (1824; RA) and *The Town Hall, Utrecht* (1829; Tate collection). He became a talented portraitist (examples of his work are in the National Portrait Gallery), and latterly executed an extensive group of paintings and sepia and chalk drawings of biblical and poetical subjects (AM Oxf., FM Cam., BM, and Tate collection).

Jones was elected an associate of the Royal Academy in 1822, and two years later he became a Royal Academician. From 1834 to 1840 he held the post of librarian to the academy, where he reorganized the collections of books and prints, and from 1840 to 1850 he was the keeper, a post which concerned the administration of the academy's teaching role. During his tenure he visited art schools on the continent to explore new teaching methods. From 1844 to 1850, when the president, Sir Martin Archer Shee, was unable to serve through illness, Jones assumed the position of acting-president on public occasions. Passionately loyal to the academy, he was bitterly disappointed when passed over for the presidency in 1850 by Charles Eastlake. This prompted his resignation from the keepership, and the remark that it was impossible for him to 'serve under one who had been his inferior in rank' (C. R. Leslie, *Autobiographical Recollections*, ed. T. Taylor, 1978, pp. 195–7).

Jones, who had married in 1844 Gertrude Ann, daughter

of Major Wintringham Loscombe, took great pride in his resemblance to the duke of Wellington, and affected reluctance to go out on the day of the duke's funeral 'for fear they should bury him' (G. A. Storey, *Sketches from Memory*, 1899, p. 64). He was renowned for his 'elegant and conciliating manners' ('Living Artists—George Jones', *The Athenaeum*, 237, 1832, p. 505), and was described by F. M. O'Donoghue in the *Dictionary of National Biography* as 'a genial, well-bred man'. He was the chief adviser to the horse breeder Robert Vernon in the formation of his collection, presented to the nation in 1847, and four of his own works were included in it. Among Jones's closest friends were the sculptor Francis Chantrey and the painter J. M. W. Turner, for both of whom he acted as executor; and in 1849 he published his *Recollections of Sir Francis Chantrey*. On Turner's death Jones painted a group of three small elegiac oils reflecting on Turner's gallery and funeral (AM Oxf.). His MS 'Recollections of J. M. W. Turner' (published in J. Gage, *The Collected Correspondence of J. M. W. Turner*, 1980, pp. 1–10) are held in the Ashmolean Museum, Oxford. Jones died at his home, 8 Park Square, Regent's Park, London, on 19 September 1869; he was survived by his wife.

JAMES HAMILTON

Sources J. Hichberger, 'Captain Jones of the Royal Academy', *Turner Studies*, 3/1 (1983), 14–20 • I. Warrell, 'Jones, George', *The Oxford companion to J. M. W. Turner*, ed. E. Joll, M. Butlin, and L. Herrmann (2001) • private information (2004) • *CGPLA Eng. & Wales* (1869)
Archives AM Oxf., MSS • BM, MSS • FM Cam., MSS • NPG, MSS • RA, MSS • RIBA BAL, MS essay on architecture in Italy • Tate collection, MSS | Yale U., MSS | Bodl. Oxf., corresp. with Sir William Napier • Ches. & Chester ALSS, letters and receipts to Sir John Leicester • HLRO, letters to Lord Clifford
Likenesses C. H. Lear, pencil drawing, c.1845, NPG • H. Weekes, bust, 1870, RA • J. & C. Watkins, carte-de-visite, NPG
Wealth at death under £25,000: probate, 13 Oct 1869, *CGPLA Eng. & Wales*

Jones, George Matthew (c.1785–1831), naval officer and traveller, was the son of John Jones, general superintendent of Landguard Fort, Felixstowe, and his wife, Mary, *née* Roberts; General Sir John Thomas *Jones, first baronet, and Lieutenant-General Sir Harry David *Jones were his brothers. On 28 April 1802 he was promoted lieutenant in the navy. He was appointed to the *Amphion*, in which, in the following spring, Nelson went out to the Mediterranean, and which, on 5 October 1804, assisted in the capture of the Spanish treasure ships off Cape St Mary. In September 1805 Captain William *Hoste was appointed to the *Amphion*, and Jones, continuing with him, took part in the peculiarly active service in the Adriatic, distinguishing himself in several of the boat engagements, and being severely wounded on 8 November 1808. On 13 December 1810 he was promoted to command the brig *Tuscan*, in which, during the next year, he assisted in the defence of Cadiz. In 1817 he commanded the *Pandora* on the coast of Ireland, and was posted on 7 December 1818. The following years he spent travelling over Europe to examine the maritime resources of the different countries. Already well acquainted with the coasts of Spain and Italy, he

visited the ports and arsenals of France and the Netherlands, of the Black Sea, and of the Baltic. In 1827 he published his journals under the title *Travels in Norway, Sweden, Finland, Russia, and Turkey* (2 vols.). The account, dedicated to Sir William Hoste, by whose advice the travels seem to have been undertaken, is written intelligently, though at excessive length. Such intelligence-gathering work reflected a range of accomplishments not commonly acquired by sea officers. Sadly Hoste died the following year, ending any career hopes Jones may have entertained. After publication his health broke down. Jones suffered 'a paralysis of the limbs' (*GM*, 562) and at Malta fell down a flight of steep stone steps; he died three days later, in April 1831.

J. K. LAUGHTON, rev. ANDREW LAMBERT

Sources T. Pocock, *Remember Nelson: the life of Captain Sir William Hoste* (1977) • *GM*, 1st ser., 101/1 (1831), 560 • G. M. Jones, *Travels in Norway, Sweden, Finland, Russia, and Turkey*, 2 vols. (1827) • J. Marshall, *Royal naval biography*, suppl. 4 (1830)

Jones, Georgiana Burne-, Lady Burne-Jones (1840–1920). *See under* Macdonald sisters (*act.* 1837–1925).

Jones, Geraint Iwan (1917–1998), organist and conductor, was born on 16 May 1917 in Porth, Glamorgan, the elder son of Evan Jones, a professor of ancient languages at Cardiff University who became a minister in the Welsh Congregational church, and his wife Caroline Davies, formerly a hospital nurse. Evan Jones, a charismatic preacher with the *hwyl*, did not approve of his son's musical interests, but the boy received encouragement at Caterham School and at the age of sixteen won a scholarship to Cambridge; against his father's wishes he turned it down, and in 1935 became a student at the Royal Academy of Music. He studied the piano with Harry Isaacs and the organ with G. D. Cunningham (for whom he retained a lifelong admiration), was awarded the Sterndale Bennett scholarship in 1937, and graduated in 1939. On 24 June 1940 he married Margaret Audrie Kemp (1913/14–2001), daughter of Allen Frederick Kemp, engineer, and a fellow student at the Royal Academy. They had one daughter.

Ineligible on medical grounds for military service Jones made his début as an organist in 1940, playing the six trio sonatas of J. S. Bach at the wartime National Gallery concerts organized by Myra Hess. During the same year he gave more than thirty solo organ recitals for the BBC and soon built a reputation as one of the most remarkable organists of his generation: while not excluding the virtuoso repertory of the nineteenth and twentieth centuries, he concentrated on the baroque period, and during the London season of 1945–6 gave the complete organ works of J. S. Bach in sixteen recitals. In 1948 he made the first of many tours in the USA and Canada. After a recital tour in Germany in 1949 he was engaged by the BBC to record performances on the 1687 Schnitger organ at Steinkirchen near Hamburg; these, and subsequent broadcasts and recordings on other European organs of historical importance, did much to swing public taste away from the grandiose instruments of the Victorian period and encourage an interest in the more intimate sound of the baroque organ—in whose post-war revival he became a leading figure. His activities at this period also included work as a music producer for EMI. Meanwhile, his first marriage having ended in divorce, on 7 April 1949 he married the violinist Winifred Roberts, with whom he gave frequent recitals.

In 1951 the actor Bernard Miles invited Jones to conduct performances of Purcell's *Dido and Aeneas* at the Mermaid Theatre, a converted schoolroom in the garden of Miles's home in St John's Wood, London; the Wagnerian soprano Kirsten Flagstad, a friend of Miles's, sang the role of Dido, and the distinguished cast also included Maggie Teyte, Thomas Hemsley, Edith Coates, and Arda Mandikian. With characteristic regard for scholarly detail, Jones made his own edition of the score and directed from the harpsichord; though the casting of the principal female roles was distinctly unconventional, the performance bore the stamp of impeccable musicianship. It was recorded for the gramophone (Elisabeth Schwarzkopf replacing Maggie Teyte), repeated in the following year, and transferred to the Royal Exchange in 1953.

It was from the musicians who played in the *Dido* performances that Jones formed the Geraint Jones Singers and Orchestra, with whom he appeared as both conductor and soloist: their cycle of twelve Bach concerts at the Royal Festival Hall in 1955 marked the beginning of an annual series that lasted for over thirty years, and their many recordings included the Italian version of Gluck's *Alceste* (with Flagstad again in the title role) in 1956, and two awards of the grand prix du disque in 1959 and 1966. As well as conducting, Jones was still touring widely as a solo performer, travelling as often as possible in one of the succession of classic Rolls-Royces that he drove with such pleasure, but in 1960 he was thrown from his car in an accident and permanently damaged his back; as a result he found it increasingly difficult to maintain the posture needed to control the feet in organ playing, and in later life appeared comparatively rarely in public as an organist, though he continued to record for the BBC in Germany, Spain, and elsewhere and appeared frequently at the harpsichord (particularly in America, and often in joint recitals with his wife). He remained in demand as an organ consultant, designing instruments for the Royal Northern College of Music, the Royal Academy of Music (at Marylebone parish church), the University of St Andrews, the Tsin Sha Tsui concert hall, and the Academy for Performing Arts in Hong Kong. In 1985 he published translations of François-Henri Clicquot's *Théorie pratique de la facture d'orgues* and Robert Davy's *Les grandes orgues de l'abbatiale de St. Etienne de Caen*.

In 1960 Jones launched the annual Lake District Festival, of which he remained musical director until 1978; he later became artistic director of the Salisbury Festival of the Arts (1972–7) and the Manchester International Organ Festival (1977–87). He was appointed a fellow of the Royal Academy of Music in 1957 and taught the harpsichord there from 1961 to 1987, but his interest in young musicians found its most practical expression in his work with the Kirckman Concert Society, founded in 1963 to provide

a platform for outstanding young artists. Though he could be impatient with less gifted performers, he was a shrewd judge and generous encourager of genuine talent, and his role as the first musical director of the Kirckman Society was one that he valued highly and retained until his death.

In later life Jones was known mainly as a conductor and harpsichordist. Though widely recognized as a baroque specialist, he had little time for what he regarded as the 'authenticity craze', believing that imaginative musicianship was infinitely more important than historical dogma. As an organist he was, until his motor accident at least, a virtuoso of exceptional brilliance with a highly unconventional pedal technique; he stood quite outside the established tradition of the English cathedral organist and, apart from minor appointments in early life, never held a regular position as organist or choirmaster. His instinctive feeling for acoustics enabled him to develop a legato rare in organ playing, and he was one of the few performers capable of coaxing genuine musical expression from that notoriously intractable instrument. His love of the fine craftsmanship intrinsic to organ building extended in private life to Romanesque architecture and eighteenth-century furniture; he was a passionate traveller, a connoisseur of wine, and a convivial host with an impish sense of humour. He died, as the result of a stroke, at St Mary's Hospital, Praed Street, Westminster, on 3 May 1998, and was cremated at Marylebone crematorium. He was survived by his second wife, Winifred, and by the daughter of his first marriage.   MICHAEL ROSE

Sources *New Grove* · *International who's who in music*, 16th edn (1999) · *WWW* · 'A note on the origin of these recordings by Geraint Jones', *A tribute to Geraint Jones* (1998) [CD-ROM disc notes] · *The Times* (8 May 1998) · *The Guardian* (8 May 1998) · personal knowledge (2004) · private information (2004) [Winifred Jones, widow; Royal Academy of Music, London] · m. cert. · d. cert.
Archives SOUND BL NSA
Likenesses photograph, repro. in *The Times* · photograph, repro. in *The Guardian* · photographs, priv. coll.
Wealth at death £48,090—gross; £45,879—net: probate, 26 Nov 1998, *CGPLA Eng. & Wales*

Jones, Giles (*fl.* 1765). *See under* Jones, Griffith (1722–1786).

Jones, (Morgan) Glyndwr [Glyn] (1905–1995), poet and writer, was born at 16 Clare Street, Merthyr Tudful, Glamorgan, on 28 February 1905, the younger son of William Henry Jones (1873–1957), postal worker, and his wife, Margaret (1874–1966), teacher, daughter of Morgan Williams of Twynyrodyn in the same town. His paternal grandfather, David William Jones (1832–1900), a poet in the Welsh language, had been known locally by his bardic name, Llwch-haiarn. The Joneses had their family roots in Llan-y-bri and Llansteffan in Carmarthenshire, a district to which the mature writer felt a deep attachment. Both his parents were Welsh-speaking and their two sons were bilingual as children, but soon turned to English, the language of the street, the school, and eventually the home. Glyn Jones later recovered his command of Welsh but almost all his creative writing had to be done in English, the language in which he received his education and in which his adolescent imagination was first awakened. The writer's family background, which was radical in politics and nonconformist in religion, is described in his seminal book *The Dragon has Two Tongues* (1968), a largely autobiographical account of the emergence of a modern Anglo-Welsh literature in the years between the world wars.

Glyn Jones attended Caedraw infants' school, Twynyrodyn primary school, and Soar, a Welsh Independent (congregational) chapel, all three situated near his home. From 1916 to 1923 he was a pupil at Cyfarthfa high school in Merthyr, which was housed in the former home of the Crawshays, the local ironmasters, but he was 'a detached and self-absorbed pupil' (Jones) and did not distinguish himself academically. In later life he was to complain that the school had taught him nothing about the social history of the town or the literature of Wales. The boy spent his school holidays with Welsh-speaking relatives at a farm known as Y Lan (Tŷ-dan-lan-y-castell) in the parish of Llangynog in Carmarthenshire. At the age of fifteen he discovered the pleasures of reading English poetry in Palgrave's *Golden Treasury*, particularly the 'Additional Poems' by such later poets as William Morris and Robert Browning. He also found an escape from the grim industrialism of Merthyr in wandering the hills to the north of the town. On leaving school in 1923, he chose to train as a teacher, despite his mother's wish that he should go to art school, and entered St Paul's College, Cheltenham. The two years he spent there were unhappy, but he continued to equip himself with a knowledge of English literature by reading avidly and widely.

On leaving college Glyn Jones lived with his parents at 156 Donald Street in the Roath area of Cardiff, his father having been promoted by the Post Office to a job as sorting-clerk and telegraphist in the city in 1920. His first teaching post was at Wood Street School, situated in a slum area near what was then the Cardiff General railway station but long since demolished. The social deprivation which he observed among his pupils and their parents left an indelible mark on his sensitivity and confirmed him in his left-wing political views: war, famine, poverty, disease, and injustice were what made life, for him, almost unbearable. In 1927 the family moved to 27 Pentyrch Street in the Cathays district of Cardiff. At first lonely, but intent on becoming a writer, Glyn Jones attended the extramural classes of Catherine M. Maclean, a Wordsworth scholar who taught in the English department at the University College, and began reading verse by contemporary English and American poets. In 1929, on one of his frequent visits to Merthyr, which he still regarded as his home, he was taken ill with appendicitis and underwent surgery. While convalescing, he began writing verse in imitation of the poets whom he admired, discovered the work of Gerard Manley Hopkins, and began reading literature in the Welsh language. His first attempts at writing verse were published in the *Dublin Review*, under the editorship of Seumas O'Sullivan (James Sullivan Starkey), in 1931 and in Harriet Monroe's magazine, *Poetry*, in the year following. The poet used the pen-name M. G. J.

Gower, partly out of diffidence and partly in order to conceal his identity from uncomprehending colleagues at Wood Street School; Gower was the surname of some of his ancestors on the distaff side. He now came into contact with other Welsh writers, notably Dylan Thomas, whom he sought out in 1934, and later Caradoc Evans, Idris Davies, Jack Jones, Gwyn Jones, and Keidrych Rhys; the last two of these were to become editors of the *Welsh Review* and *Wales* respectively, magazines to which Glyn Jones was a regular contributor.

Glyn Jones married Phyllis Doreen, *née* Jones (1910–1999), at St Mary's Church in Whitchurch, Cardiff, on 19 August 1935. Their first home was at 65 Heol-y-deri in Rhiwbeina; they moved to Trawscoed, Heol-y-bryn, in the same suburb of the city, two years later. The author's first collection of short stories, *The Blue Bed*, appeared in 1937. He was by this time a member of Minny Street Chapel, a bastion of the Welsh Congregationalist cause in Cardiff, and of the Peace Pledge Union. In 1939 he and his wife moved to 158 Manor Way in Whitchurch, where they were to spend the rest of their life together; it was later marked by a commemorative plaque. There were no children to the marriage. His first volume of verse, *Poems*, was published in the same year.

Glyn Jones wrote an essay on Gerard Manley Hopkins's awareness of Welsh metrics in 1939, having himself discovered the complex formal patterning and arresting imagery of Welsh-language poetry, and he tried to reproduce its effects in his own work. 'I fancy words', he wrote in his poem 'Merthyr', and his pleasure in the music and sensuous texture of the English language is apparent in all his writing. The same quality is to be found in his prose: his stories are lyrical, mysterious, and occasionally grotesque but without the harsh tones of Caradoc Evans: himself a handsome man, he was fascinated by people's faces and never missed an opportunity in his stories to describe a man's red nose or a woman's golden hair. Contact with Dylan Thomas in the mid-1930s taught him how to use a young boy as narrator, and he often drew on his early years in Merthyr Tudful and his dismal experience of teaching in Cardiff.

Despite not being eligible for call-up on account of his age, Glyn Jones appeared before a tribunal on 18 May 1942 and was duly registered as a conscientious objector to military service on Christian pacifist grounds. Three days later he was dismissed, as he fully expected, from his post at Allensbank School, where he had been for five years, because it was the Cardiff education authority's policy not to employ conscientious objectors. He was unemployed for two months until given a job as a teacher of English by the Glamorgan education authority at Old Castle School in Bridgend; there many of the teachers refused to speak to him. Towards the end of the war he was moved to the Twyn School in Caerphilly, where he regained something of his old equilibrium. His second collection of short stories, *The Water Music*, appeared in 1944. In 1952 he was appointed to a post as English teacher at Glantaf county school in Whitchurch, where he was to remain until his retirement in 1965.

The rest of Glyn Jones's life was devoted to his writing, and he continued to write poems until well into his eighties. His translation of *Blodeuwedd*, the verse-play by Saunders Lewis, was broadcast on the Welsh Home Service of the BBC as *The Lion and the Owl* in September 1951, and his translation of Ellis Wynne's *Gweledigaethau'r bardd cwsg* as *The Sleeping Bard* in the following year. He published a further volume of verse, *The Dream of Jake Hopkins*, in 1954. Glyn Jones wrote three novels, *The Valley, the City, the Village* (1956), *The Learning Lark* (1960), and *The Island of Apples* (1965), arguably his finest, which weaves realism with fantasy in ways predating magic realism. In collaboration with T. J. Morgan he made two translations from early Welsh, *The Saga of Llywarch the Old* (1952) and *The Story of Heledd* (1994). He also wrote the libretto of Alun Hoddinott's opera *The Beach of Falesá* (1974), which was based on a novella by R. L. Stevenson. His *Selected Poems* appeared in 1975, while a third collection of stories, *Welsh Heirs*, was published in 1977. With John Rowlands he edited a collection of biographical essays on Welsh writers, *Profiles* (1980).

Glyn Jones received many honours in recognition of his literary achievement, including the honorary degree of DLitt from the University of Wales in 1974, the white robe of the Gorsedd of Bards in 1988, and an honorary fellowship from Trinity College, Carmarthen, in 1993. He was elected president of the Welsh Academy, the national society of writers in Wales, in 1994. A volume of his selected verse and prose, *Goodbye, What were You?*, also appeared that year. Despite the amputation of his right arm in 1992, he remained of cheerful disposition and keenly interested in the work of his younger contemporaries until his last year. Many acquaintances thought they perceived saintly qualities in him: he would say nothing unkind about others and seemed unconcerned about the promotion of his own work and reputation. It was only when Hugh MacDiarmid incorporated an extract from one of Glyn Jones's stories, *Porth-y-rhyd*, into a poem entitled 'Perfect' without acknowledgement, and was praised for it, that the Welsh writer, normally the most eirenic of men, felt compelled to defend himself, contributing to the ensuing debate in the correspondence columns of the *Times Literary Supplement* (December 1964 – May 1965). His love of humanity, even at its most unlovely, and his constant striving to make an affirmation of hope and compassion, shines through all his work, but it had deeper complexities: there is a note of self-disgust and despair in his long, unfinished, satirical poem 'Seven Keys to Shaderdom', in which he explores the fate of the failed artist (whether painter or writer) in the modern world. His Christianity was fundamental to him as a writer, and there is, in both his fiction and his verse, a profound awareness of human suffering and the injustice of the world, which he saw as a mixture of madhouse and torture chamber.

Glyn Jones died at his home on 10 April 1995. His funeral service was held on 19 April at Minny Street Chapel and afterwards at Thornhill crematorium, Cardiff. At his own request, the writer's ashes were interred in the graveyard of the parish church at Llansteffan, the village which had always meant most to him; the spot is marked by a slate plaque bearing his name, the years of his birth and death, and the word *llenor* ('man of letters'). His *Collected Poems* and his translations of Welsh folk-verses, *A People's Poetry*, were published posthumously in 1996 and 1997, followed by his *Collected Short Stories* in 1999. MEIC STEPHENS

Sources personal knowledge (2004) · G. Jones, *The dragon has two tongues: essays on Anglo-Welsh writers and writing* (1968); rev. edn, ed. T. Brown (2001) · M. Stephens, introduction, in *Collected poems*, ed. M. Stephens (1996) · T. Brown, introduction, in *Collected short stories*, ed. T. Brown (1999) · m. cert. · d. cert. **Archives** NL Wales, corresp., literary, family, and personal papers · NL Wales, draft of 'The island of apples' · NL Wales, letters · Trinity College, Carmarthen | NL Wales, letters to Elwyn Davies · NL Wales, letters to G. E. Evans · NL Wales, letters to A. G. Prys-Jones | FILM BBC Wales, Goodbye, what were you? 1996 · University of Glamorgan, video of interview | SOUND BBC Wales · Ports of Wales, Argo Records **Likenesses** J. Elwyn, oils, priv. coll. · P. P. Piech, caricature, priv. coll.

Jones, Sir Glyn Smallwood (1908–1992), colonial governor, was born on 9 January 1908 at 24 Edna Street, Hoole, Chester, the first of two children of Gwilym Ioan Jones (1877–1943), grocer's assistant, and his wife, Agnes (1886–1960), née Roberts, milliner. His parents were both Welsh, but moved to Chester a few years before he was born. Though Welsh-speaking Calvinistic Methodists, they sent their son to the English-speaking Methodist church. His primary education was at the local council school. His secondary education was at the King's School, Chester, a day school close to his home. At King's School he became head boy, house captain, and captain of soccer, boats, and swimming. He also sang and played the piano and organ. His academic accomplishments were good, though not remarkable. In 1927 he was admitted to St Catherine's Society, Oxford (as St Catherine's College was then called), as a non-collegiate student, reading English and financed by a government grant for training teachers. He was a leading member of St Catherine's debating society and was a soccer blue. In 1930, with a third-class degree, and failing to secure a teaching appointment, he joined the tropical services course at Oxford, and a year later was appointed administrative cadet in Northern Rhodesia.

From 1931 to 1951 Jones (or Jonas, as he was affectionately known) served as cadet, district officer, and district commissioner in the Zambezi valley, the north-west, the copperbelt (where he distinguished himself in a dangerous mine riot), the eastern province, and Barotseland. On 21 May 1938, on leave, he married Margaret Florence (*b. c.*1912), daughter of Peter McWilliam, Tottenham Hotspur Football Club's manager and a former Scottish international. His wife did not return to Africa with him. On his return he was appointed secretary of the MacDonnell inquiry into a dispute between the Lozi (Barotze) paramount chief and the Luvale chiefs. On 7 November 1942, now divorced, he married a nurse, Nancy Madoc (1909–1998), daughter of John Henry Featherstone of Cape Province, South Africa. He was made an MBE in 1944. Their daughter, Elisabeth, was born in 1944 and their son, Timothy, in 1946.

Jones became commissioner for native development in 1951. Appointed provincial commissioner in 1955, he served on the copperbelt—where again he dealt with mine riots—and as resident commissioner of Barotseland. He was appointed CMG in 1957. The governor, Sir Arthur Benson, made him secretary (later restyled minister) of native affairs in 1958, primarily because they shared a profound belief in the importance and continuing governmental role of the traditional chiefs. In 1958 the Colonial Office wished to appoint a new chief secretary in neighbouring Nyasaland. One of the two officers being considered was a Northern Rhodesia provincial commissioner junior to Jones on whose suitability his advice was sought late in 1959. Three months later Jones was himself offered the post and accepted it. He arrived in Nyasaland in February 1960. While the governor, Sir Robert Armitage, was on leave from August to November 1960 Jones was acting governor. Dr Hastings Banda, the Malawi Congress Party leader, who had been released in April after detention during a state of emergency, exerted pressure on Jones to release the remaining hard-core detainees, warning that he could not prevent major disturbances unless they were released. In exchange for an undertaking—soon broken—that Banda would control them, Jones released the detainees. Two weeks later he was advanced to KCMG.

When Armitage left Nyasaland on retirement on 10 April 1961, Jones became governor. Devoted to the welfare of the Nyasaland people, he was convinced that Banda was the only person able to secure that welfare—a view Banda shared. During the following three years his constant preoccupation was to support Banda, keep him in power and prevent him withdrawing co-operation with the British government. This task involved repeated capitulation to Banda's demands. To do otherwise would, in his judgement, have incurred widespread violence controllable only by external military forces, a prospect not to be contemplated. Given their joint belief in Banda's indispensable role, Jones and Banda developed a working relationship which took the country through self-government and secession from the Central African Federation in 1963 to July 1964 when, as Malawi, it became independent, with Banda as prime minister and Jones, now appointed GCMG, as governor-general. Shortly after independence a ministerial revolt resulted in the dismissal or resignation of all but one of Banda's ministers. Banda asked Jones if his staying on as prime minister was in Malawi's best interests and received an expected, promptly accepted, affirmative answer. Though agreeing with the ministers' objections to Banda's policies and autocratic methods, Jones tried to support him and desperately, but unsuccessfully, to effect a reconciliation. The former ministers fled the country, some with Jones's help—and Banda's agreement—and he long stayed in touch with them, trying to effect their return and a reconciliation.

When Malawi became a republic in July 1966 Jones retired to England but did not sever his African ties. He was successively head of the Malawi Buying and Trade Agency in London, adviser to the Lesotho government, deputy chairman of the Pearce commission on Rhodesian opinion (appointed to assess African opinion on the proposed constitutional settlement drafted by Sir Alec Douglas-Home and Ian Smith), observer at the Rhodesia-Zimbabwe elections in 1980, and chairman of numerous African charities, including the Friends of Malawi Association and the Zimbabwe Trust. He died of liver failure at his home, Little Brandfold, Goudhurst, Kent, on 10 June 1992. He was cremated and his ashes were taken to Malawi and placed next to the remains of his son, who had died in 1961, in Zomba cemetery.   COLIN BAKER

Sources C. Baker, *Glyn Smallwood Jones* (2000) · Bodl. RH · PRO, CO 1015, DO 158, DO 183 · private information (2004) [family, colleagues] · *The Times* (12 June 1992) · *The Independent* (23 June 1992) · *WWW* · Burke, *Peerage* · R. Short, *African sunset* (1973) · R. Welensky, *4000 days* (1964) · CGPLA Eng. & Wales (1992)
Archives Bodl. RH | Bodl. Oxf., Macmillan MSS · Bodl. RH, Armitage MSS · Bodl. RH, Welensky MSS · Trinity Cam., R. A. Butler MSS
Likenesses Stubley, portrait, St Catherine's College boathouse, Oxford; repro. in E. B. Smith, *Memorial address* (1993) · photograph, repro. in *The Times* · photograph, repro. in *The Independent*
Wealth at death under £125,000: probate, 20 June 1992, CGPLA Eng. & Wales

Jones, Griffith [known as Griffith Jones Llanddowror] (*bap.* 1684, *d.* 1761), Church of England clergyman and educational reformer, was baptized on 1 May 1684 at Cilrhedyn church, Pembrokeshire, the youngest of four sons born to John ap Gruffydd, a farmer, and Elinor John of Pant-yr-efel in the parish of Pen-boyr, Carmarthenshire. A frail and sickly child, he fell prey to smallpox and carried the pockmarks of that dreaded disease on his face for the rest of his life. Asthma caused him considerable suffering and made him a deeply melancholic, abstemious, and morose figure. Nevertheless, he bore his many ailments (both real and imagined) with great fortitude and, in many ways, he epitomized the earnest, puritanical 'improver' in mid-eighteenth-century Wales. During his youth he received a 'heavenly call', a profound spiritual conversion which persuaded him that it was God's will that he should be of service to his people. Educated at Carmarthen grammar school, he entered the Anglican ministry and was ordained deacon by Bishop George Bull on 19 September 1708 and priest on 25 September 1708. Having held the curacies of Penbryn (1708), Penrhydd (1709), and Laugharne (1709), he was made rector of Llandeilo Abercywyn, Carmarthenshire, on 3 July 1711. Five years later, on 27 July 1716, he was appointed rector of Llanddowror, Carmarthenshire, by his patron, Sir John Philipps of Picton Castle, whose sister, Margaret (*d.* 1755), he married on 11 February 1720. He retained the living until his death and is unfailingly referred to as Griffith Jones Llanddowror.

Long before Methodist evangelists began to roam Wales in search of sinners to save, Griffith Jones had acquired a reputation as a remarkably powerful and successful preacher. He defied bishops by crossing parish boundaries, preaching in the open air, publicly castigating parsons 'Dolittle' and 'Merryman', and condemning the unbridled appetite of the Welsh gentry for wealth. Bored by the tedious homilies of their pastors, people tramped miles to hear the fiery sermons of 'this busy enthusiast'. John Thomas of Rhaeadr walked 35 miles in order to meet Jones and was immediately entranced: 'his manner of speaking and his appearance won my heart and it was as though I looked upon an angel of God' (I. Thomas, *Rhad ras*, ed. J. D. Owen, 1949, 46). Saving souls became the ruling passion of his life and the two most influential Methodist leaders, Howel Harris and Daniel Rowland, regarded him as their mentor and father confessor. Dubbed 'the Methodist Pope' by his enemies, he exercised an enormous influence over the preaching styles of itinerant evangelists and encouraged them to strike out in new directions. No task was more important than preventing the souls of 'poor perishing wretches' from dropping into 'the dreadful Abyss of Eternity' (*The Welch Piety*, 1740, 32). Indeed, it could be argued that the ground in which Methodism grew had been tilled in readiness by the rector of Llanddowror. Jones strove to curb the wilder excesses of the young evangelists, and Harris in particular often felt the rough edge of his tongue. For several reasons, by the 1740s he was forced to distance himself from the Methodists because their irregular, and sometimes insolent, behaviour threatened to undermine his educational schemes. In order to gratify patrons of his circulating schools, Jones condemned the 'rude enthusiasm' of his protégés, even though he himself had often transgressed the rules and regulations of the church during his youth. Yet his extraordinary energy and zeal remained an inspiration to Methodists, and Howel Harris never forgot his debt to this 'old and much honoured soldier' (Roberts, 73). No eighteenth-century churchman in Wales was more highly revered than Griffith Jones.

Even though he was a powerful and often moving preacher, Griffith Jones came to realize that Welsh printed books could exert a much more lasting influence on people than sermons delivered in the pulpit in cold and draughty churches. He composed or translated over thirty Welsh books, mostly catechisms and works of piety. He publicly distanced himself from the official policy of the SPCK of imparting a knowledge of English to monoglot Welsh pupils in their charity schools, and in 1731, at the age of forty-seven, he launched a pioneering educational scheme based on itinerant schooling and intensive catechizing and Bible reading through the medium of Welsh. His own experience as an SPCK schoolmaster had taught him that poor children seldom attended, that the absentee rate was especially high in the summer, and that teaching by rote through the medium of English was absurdly impractical. Furthermore, his deep-seated fear of Catholicism strengthened his determination to instil into the young a proper awareness of their political and religious obligations. His anti-Popish animus was matched by his hostility towards the growing numbers of dissenting sects which threatened to undermine the established church.

His circulating schools, which were held in parish churches, farmhouses, cottages, and barns throughout Wales, were funded by well-disposed philanthropists such as Sir John Philipps and Madam Bridget *Bevan and staffed by an army of part-time schoolmasters (mostly clergymen). The scheme proved flexible, economical, and efficient, and it was a matter of considerable pride to Jones that bright pupils were able to become fluent Welsh readers within a six-week period of tuition, and that even illiterate septuagenarians were able to acquire rudimentary reading skills within three months. As each annual report, issued under the title *The Welch Piety*, made plain, throughout Wales parish churches and farmhouses echoed to the sounds of adult and infant voices chanting the alphabet aloud, spelling words, and repeating the catechism. For the first time in the history of Wales, large numbers of farmers, craftsmen, and labourers, together with their sons and daughters, were given the opportunity to learn to read. Some degree of rote learning was inevitable, but the key to the success of the schools was the use of the Welsh language as the principal medium of instruction. His 'little nurseries' strengthened and enriched the powerful revival which was sweeping through the church and also enhanced the prestige value of Welsh as a spoken and written language. Many farmhouses where schools were held were also Methodist seminaries, and the cause of revivalism prospered as increasing numbers learned to read. Most important of all, the scheme helped to create a literate peasantry. By the time of Jones's death in 1761 he had established around 3325 schools in nearly 1600 different locations in Wales. For a private enterprise, run on a shoestring, this was an extraordinary achievement. Hundreds of letters sent to Llanddowror by grateful clergymen and gentry testified to the beneficial effects of regular schooling.

Following the death of his wife on 5 January 1755, Griffith Jones settled in Madam Bevan's home in Laugharne, by which time he had become increasingly morose and cantankerous. Jones doted on his benefactor and shared all his confidences with her. For her part, Madam Bevan's last wish was to be buried by his side. Griffith Jones died, aged seventy-seven, on 8 April 1761 at Laugharne, and was buried in the chancel of Llanddowror church, where he had served the parishioners with selfless devotion for forty-five years. Anglicans, Methodists, and dissenters alike spoke of him with genuine affection, and there is a strong case for claiming that he was the greatest Welshman of the eighteenth century.　　　GERAINT H. JENKINS

Sources *The Welch piety* (1737–61) · F. A. Cavenagh, *The life and work of Griffith Jones* (1930) · T. Kelly, *Griffith Jones, pioneer in adult education* (1950) · G. Williams, 'Griffith Jones (1683–1761)', *Pioneers of Welsh education* (1964) · G. H. Jenkins, '"An old and much honoured soldier": Griffith Jones, Llanddowror', *Welsh History Review / Cylchgrawn Hanes Cymru*, 11 (1982–3), 449–68 · R. L. Brown, 'Spiritual nurseries: Griffith Jones and the circulating schools', *National Library of Wales Journal*, 30 (1997–8), 27–49 · *DWB* · G. M. Roberts, ed., *Selected Trevecka letters (1742–1747)* (1956) · parish register, Llanddowror, 1 May 1684, NL Wales [baptism] · parish registers, NL Wales
Archives NL Wales, letters · NL Wales, sermons, MSS | NL Wales, Trevecca College MSS

Jones, Griffith (1722–1786), journalist and children's writer, was probably born in London. Details of his parentage and childhood are unclear, although he is known to have served as an apprentice to the London printer William Bowyer the younger. He was later the editor of the *Daily Advertiser* and, from 1757 and 1760 respectively, of the *London Chronicle* and *Public Ledger*. During the late 1750s and early 1760s he was also involved with Samuel Johnson's *Literary Magazine* and with the *British Magazine* of Tobias Smollett and Oliver Goldsmith. Jones probably met Goldsmith through the publisher John Newbery, who in 1759 employed the latter to write for the *Public Ledger*. Alongside his work for this journal, Jones and his brother, **Giles Jones** (*fl.* 1765), author, and secretary to the York Buildings Water Company, were also involved—though their exact role is unclear—in Newbery's publication of celebrated children's stories including *The History of Little Goody Two-Shoes* (1765) and *The Renowned History of Giles Gingerbread* (1769). Griffith Jones is the recorded author of two further works, *The Jests of Beau Nash* (1763) and the popular *Great Events from Little Causes* (1767), and he produced a number of anonymously published French translations. He was described by John Nichols as 'an ingenious man' with a 'native goodness … which endeared him to a numerous and respectable literary acquaintance' (Nichols, 3.465–6). Towards the end of his life he was a neighbour of the greatest of this literary circle, Samuel Johnson, who, from March 1778, lived next to Jones in Bolt Court, Fleet Street. It is not clear how long Jones lived at this address, one of a number of unknown details about a life of which 'slighter notice has been taken by the Biographers of the time than his virtues and talents certainly merited' (ibid., 3.465). Jones was the father of three or four sons and one daughter, although nothing is known of his marriage. He died, probably in London, on 12 September 1786. His brother Giles was survived by a son from his marriage to Ellen Jane Maria Fewtrell, the author and compiler Stephen *Jones. PHILIP CARTER

Sources Nichols, *Lit. anecdotes* · *DNB* · F. J. Harvey Darton, *Children's books in England: five centuries of social life*, rev. B. Alderson, 3rd edn (1982) · H. Carpenter and M. Prichard, *The Oxford companion to children's literature* (1984) · *The letters of Samuel Johnson*, ed. B. Redford, 5 vols. (1992–4)

Jones, Griffith Rhys [*performing name* Caradog] (1834–1897), choral conductor, was born on 21 December 1834 in the Rose and Crown inn, Trecynon, Aberdâr, an address which provided him with the early nickname Griff o'r Crown. He was the son of John Jones (1789–1847), a carpenter and innkeeper, and his wife, Margaret, *née* Hughes (1797–1862). He had three brothers and three sisters, four of whom died as infants. His brother David died in Australia in 1866 at the age of thirty-six, and his sister Sarah, who stayed in Wales and married Morgan Thomas, died in 1861 at the age of twenty-two. Jones completed an apprenticeship as a blacksmith but demonstrated a precocious musical talent. He was an excellent violinist (sometimes characterized as 'the Paganini of Wales'), but it was as a choral conductor that he made his mark. At the age of nineteen he assembled a choir to compete at the Aberfan

eisteddfod. The choir took the name of the ancient Welsh prince Caradog. When announcing the winning choir as Côr Caradog (Caradog's choir), the adjudicator invited 'Caradog to come forth' to receive the prize. From that moment Jones was always identified as Caradog.

Jones's reputation as a choral conductor was quickly established, and he became the most celebrated Welsh choral conductor of the century. He conducted at various eisteddfods and formed a string orchestra in Aberdâr, where he also played harmonium at several Unitarian chapels. In 1872 the Welsh Choral Union was formed. This was an amalgam of several choirs which were assembled to compete at the Crystal Palace in Sydenham for a prize of £50 and a specially commissioned, extravagantly ornate cup, which became known as the Thousand Guinea Challenge Cup. The full choir is likely to have been of the order of 450 voices. Although no other choir competed in 1872, Côr Mawr was deemed to have 'won'. The ecstasy generated in Wales by this achievement became more frenzied a year later when it won again, after being challenged by the Paris Prize Choir, an equally large conglomerate of tonic sol-fa enthusiasts. These victories were significant because they did much to define and fix the idea that musicianship was an important element in the cultural identity of Wales. Because the Welsh choristers were drawn from a wide geographical area, Caradog's celebrity and tales of his charismatic conducting quickly spread. However, his reputation as a conductor was probably well founded. He had a good knowledge of the canonical repertory of large-scale choral works and he championed the oratorios of Handel and Mendelssohn in Wales. In 1893 he travelled to the Chicago World Fair, where his conducting of a thousand Welsh voices singing the 'Hallelujah' chorus became a focus of pride for the expatriate Welsh.

Jones's life outside music was almost as spectacular as that in it. By 1870 he had given up his trade as a blacksmith and moved to Treorci to keep the Treorky [*sic*] Hotel. Six years later, at the age of forty-one, he was able to retire, and moved to Treherbert. From that time on he is described in trade directories, census returns, and other sources as 'a gentleman'—on his death certificate, under 'occupation', he is described as being 'of independent means'. His money was made in the south Wales brewing industry. In 1873 he was one of five directors who established the Rhondda Valley Brewery Company. Over the following decades the company acquired other brewing and bottling companies, as well as properties—particularly public houses. The deft manipulation of funds and other interests (the companies were regularly wound up and instantly reconstituted under new names, so as to maximize profits) allowed Jones to accumulate a wealth sufficient for him to leave an estate valued at more than £38,000.

Caradog was married three times: on 27 May 1861 to Sarah Richards, who died at the age of twenty-two; to Gwenllian Williams (*d.* 1879); and on 1 October 1881 to Margaret Price (*d.* 1923). His only child to survive infancy—from his second marriage—was John Griffith Jones (1866–1928), who became a partner in a Cardiff accountancy firm and stood unsuccessfully for parliament as a Conservative in the 1922 general election. The son was accountant to Jones's brewing companies and he inherited his father's directorships. Following his third wedding Caradog left the Rhondda for Llanybydder, Carmarthenshire. After a short time there he lived at 5 Gordon Road, Cardiff, before moving to a house called Brynhyfryd in Court House Street, Pontypridd, where he died of heart disease on 4 December 1897.

Jones was buried at Aberdâr cemetery (plot 436) on 9 December 1897. A statue of him by W. Goscombe John was unveiled in the town square there in July 1920. He was said to be a man of great warmth, jovial, and a gifted raconteur. At the time of his death many spoke of him as a simple, straightforward man whose only eloquence was as a musician. Little was said of his considerable accumulated wealth (perhaps because it was derived from brewing at a time when the drinking habits of the working class were a focus for much moral concern), but it is obvious that he was both fortunate and skilled in matters of money. He is remembered as one of Wales's first modern musical heroes—a reputation based largely on the Crystal Palace victory. The symbolic importance of that event was further emphasized exactly a hundred years later, when, by agreement with local government authorities in London, the Thousand Guinea trophy was given a permanent home at the National Folk Museum of Wales. By that time it was known only as Caradog's cup.

TREVOR HERBERT

Sources W. W. Price, 'Biographical index', NL Wales, vol. 14 · NL Wales, B33 · W. Wynn, 'Griffith Rhys Jones (Caradog)', *Y Geninen*, 16 (1898) · *Cerddor Cymraeg* (1 March 1872) · *Cerddor Cymraeg* (1 Jan 1873) · Glamorgan RO, D/D RB H2–5, D/D RB K1–4 · W. R. Protheroe, *Griffith Rhys Jones (Caradog)* (1911) [in Welsh] · J. H. Davies, 'Rhondda choral music in Victorian times', *Rhondda past and future*, ed. K. S. Hopkins (1975) · NL Wales, MS 12353D, NLW, ex 1369 · *South Wales Daily News* (6 Dec 1897), 4 · F. Griffith, ed., *Notable Welsh musicians*, 4th edn (1896), 164–7 · *CGPLA Eng. & Wales* (1898)

Archives NL Wales, Caradog MSS

Likenesses W. G. John, statue, 1920, Aberdâr town square, Glamorgan · engraving, repro. in *South Wales Daily News* · engraving, NL Wales, MS 12353D [p. 346] · photograph, repro. in Griffith, ed., *Notable Welsh musicians* · portrait, Aberdâr Central Library, Glamorgan, funeral service programme, B33/11[i] · portrait, repro. in *Christian Freeman* (Aug 1902), 119

Wealth at death £38,743 1s. 0d.: resworn probate, Nov 1898, *CGPLA Eng. & Wales*

Jones, Gwyn (1907–1999), writer and viking scholar, was born on 24 May 1907 in Queens Road, New Tredegar, Monmouthshire, the second child of George Henry Jones (1874–1970), miner, and his second wife, Lily Florence, *née* Nethercott (1877–1960), a midwife, and brought up at 5 Gordon Road in Blackwood, also in Monmouthshire. He received his secondary education at Tredegar county school and the University College, Cardiff. On 4 December 1928 Jones married Alice Rees (1906/7–1979). After spending six years as an English teacher at schools in Wigan and Manchester he returned to Wales in 1935 as a lecturer at his old college.

In the same year Jones published his first novel, *Richard Savage*, an endlessly inventive evocation of life in Augustan England. Three very different novels followed in quick succession: *Times Like These* (1936), *The Nine Days' Wonder* (1937), and *Garland of Bays* (1938). The first is a moving account of family life in south Wales during the general strike of 1926, the second a tale of low life set near Manchester, and the last a historical novel about the Elizabethan writer Robert Greene.

While still at Cardiff, Gwyn Jones founded the *Welsh Review*, editing it (with an interregnum during the Second World War) until 1948. In his many editorials and articles he did much to define Anglo-Welsh literature at a crucial time in its development, and was to return to this work as editor of *The Oxford Book of Welsh Short Stories* (1956) and *The Oxford Book of Welsh Verse in English* (1977). Even so, he steadfastly refused to admit the work of Welsh writers to the syllabus in his own department, nor did he pay much attention to those who had made their reputations after what he considered to have been the heyday of Anglo-Welsh writing in the 1930s; they were, he thought, small fry in comparison with the big fish of his own generation.

In 1940 Jones moved to Aberystwyth, where he took the Rendell chair of English language and literature at the University College of Wales, remaining in that post until 1964. This was his 'golden period'. He continued to make distinguished contributions to Anglo-Welsh literature with his novels and collections of short stories; these included *The Buttercup Field* (1945), *The Flowers Beneath the Scythe* (1952), *Shepherd's Hey* (1953), and *The Walk Home* (1962); his *Selected Short Stories* was published by Oxford University Press in 1974 and his *Collected Stories* in 1997. His lectures, *The First Forty Years* (1957), *Being and Belonging* (1977), and *Babel and the Dragon's Tongue* (1981), are among the most perceptive and seminal statements about Anglo-Welsh writing ever published. He also published *A Prospect of Wales* (1948), *Welsh Legends and Folktales* (1955), and *Scandinavian Legends and Folktales* (1956).

The major achievement of Gwyn Jones's years at Aberystwyth was his collaboration with Thomas Jones, the college's professor of Welsh, in the translation of the *Mabinogion*, the collection of tales which was the prose masterpiece of medieval Wales. This work, published in a limited edition by the Golden Cockerel Press in 1948 and by Dent in Everyman's Library in the year following, not only managed to satisfy scholars in the Welsh departments of the university but also delighted a wider readership with its subtle rendering of the original and the unfailing elegance of its style. It was this translation, still regarded as definitive, which was largely responsible for re-awakening worldwide interest in these tales. After the death in 1979 of his first wife, Alice, on 31 August 1979 he married Mair Jones, *née* Sivell (1923/4–2000), the widow of his collaborator, and they made their last home in Castle Cottage, Sea View Place, Aberystwyth.

The other field in which Gwyn Jones spent his prodigious energy was that of Nordic literature in its early phases. For the American-Scandinavian Foundation he translated *Four Icelandic Sagas* (1935), the subject of his MA thesis, and *The Vatnsdalers' Saga* (1944); they were followed by *Egil's Saga* (1960), *Eirik the Red and other Icelandic Sagas* (1961), and *The Norse Atlantic Saga* (1964). Two more of his major works were *A History of the Vikings* (1968) and *Kings, Beasts and Heroes* (1972). The first of these is the standard history in English and the second a richly allusive study of *Beowulf*, the Welsh *Culhwch ac Olwen*, and the Norse *King Hrolf's Saga*. It was in recognition of his eminence as a scholar of the viking world that the president of Iceland, in 1963, presented Gwyn Jones with the knight's cross of the order of the Falcon and the commander's cross in 1987. He was made CBE in 1965 and received the medal of the Honourable Society of Cymmrodorion in 1991.

From 1964 until his retirement in 1975, Jones was professor of English language and literature at the University College, Cardiff. While in Cardiff for the third time in his career, he served as chairman of the Welsh committee of the Arts Council of Great Britain (1957–67), in which capacity he proved an implacable opponent to the idea of a national theatre for Wales. Ten years later, he was the first chairman of the editorial board of *The Oxford Companion to the Literature of Wales* (1986).

A man of handsome appearance, rich voice, strong principles, and autocratic manner, Jones gave the impression that, had he not been a Welshman, he would have been a viking. In a preface to the Folio Society edition of Jones's *History of the Vikings* (1995), Magnus Magnusson described him as 'the most gallant of war-horses, the most generous of friends' and his book as 'a formidable feat of eclectic scholarship' which did much to rehabilitate the vikings as a subject for academic research, by highlighting the achievements of the viking age in terms of Scandinavian art and commerce—the vikings as traders rather than raiders.

For Jones the manly virtues to be most admired were physical prowess, unremitting labour, honourable conduct, a command of lofty language, and courage in adversity, and he had them in abundance. Jones died at Bronglais General Hospital, Aberystwyth, on 6 December 1999; his remains were cremated.

MEIC STEPHENS

Sources personal knowledge (2004) · M. Stephens, *The Independent* (10 Dec 1999) · D. Slay, *The Guardian* (21 Dec 1999) · G. Jones, 'Jones, Gwyn', *British novelists, 1930–1959*, ed. B. Oldsey, DLitB, 15/1 (1983) · d. cert.

Archives NL Wales, corresp., literary and academic papers, incl. large collection of fine editions | NL Wales, letters to G. E. Evans · NL Wales, letters to Cledwyn Hughes · NL Wales, corresp. with Welsh National Opera | SOUND BBC Wales

Likenesses W. Coldstream, oils, Arts Council of Wales

Jones, Hannah Maria (1796?–1854), novelist, was the author of at least twenty-five novels over a writing career spanning thirty-two years. Very little is known about her parentage and youth. According to newspaper clippings preserved in the archives of the Royal Literary Fund (RLF), she claimed to have begun writing at nineteen, which—granting that her first novel appeared in 1821—would place her birth just after the turn of the century, but letters sent to the RLF in 1844 contradict this, as Jones describes herself as 'nearly sixty', placing her date of birth

in the 1780s. Garside holds that she was probably born in 1796.

Hannah Maria Jones rose to fame after her marriage to John Jones, a compositor, and her maiden name appears untraceable: her first two novels were issued anonymously, and by 1824 she was publishing under her married name. In the 1820s Jones's writings attracted some attention, with her first novel *Gretna Green* (1821) going into multiple editions; she also at this time collaborated with Anna M. Morgan on the serialized *Horatio in Search of a Wife* (1828–30). It was during the 1830s, however, that she particularly enjoyed literary success: her most famous novels, *Emily Moreland* (1829), *The Gipsy Mother* (1833), and *The Gipsey Girl* (1836), sold in the region of 20,000 copies, and these spawned numerous pirated versions and unauthorized reprints. Jones's works were issued in a variety of forms, usually first appearing in numbers, which were then reissued in collected form, and her early novels were occasionally reprinted to produce multi-volume editions. She seems to have caught the public's developing taste for melodrama, and her works vary in quality from turgid, contorted pot-boilers (*The Gamblers*, 1824) to novels displaying a well-educated mind and an articulate pen (*Emily Moreland*, 1829; *The Scottish Chieftains*, 1831). However varied in quality, her stories generally follow a number of set themes: the ingenuous heroine triumphing over fashionable society (*The Wedding Ring*, 1824); the contrast between sentimental values and worldly lures (*The Curate's Daughters*, 1853); and the disruptive nature of family secrets (*The Gipsy Mother*, 1833).

Despite her literary success in the world of cheap fiction, Jones's commercial success was negligible. Copyright of her works remained with her publishers, and she was paid by the sheet, earning 10½d. per page, 'considerably less than the penny-per-line usually associated with the meanest literature' (Cross, *Common Writer*, 176). As early as 1825 Jones approached the RLF for money, an appeal which launched a lifelong series of applications in the face of destitution, backed by her publishers, various physicians, and at one point Edward Bulwer Lytton, and from which she received a sum total of £40.

At the time of her first application, her husband was ill and unemployed, placing the bread-winning on Jones. Within three years, however, this situation was reversed, and John Jones appealed (successfully) to the RLF stating that his wife was 'lying in a most lamentable state of wretchedness and destitution from the nature of the affliction under which she suffers'. This history of physical and almost certain mental debilitation, together with absolute poverty, was to haunt Jones until her death. Her correspondence records that, at one stage, the couple slept on a straw bed without blankets or linen, and that this bed doubled as their table and chair during the day. As well as not obtaining royalties from the many reprints of her works, Jones's husband apparently received no regular salary from 1827 to 1831 from his employer, Thomas White, who himself fell into bankruptcy. In a letter of 1831 Jones noted that it had fallen solely on her over the previous ten years to support her family.

Having to contend not only with illnesses, but also the unscrupulous publishing practices of employers such as William Emans, Jones wrote in desperation of 'the attempts of the most ignorant and dishonest man that ever disgraced the respectable title of Publisher to compel me to accept less than half the sum I have received for former productions'. By the late 1830s Jones's limited success with the RLF had come to an end. Octavian Blewitt, then secretary of the society, was unsympathetic to female authors, especially those of cheap fiction. Between October 1844 and December 1846 Jones became involved with John Lowndes, a failed bookseller and librarian (later to suffer from a mental breakdown) and also himself an Emans writer. She began signing herself Hannah Maria Lowndes, and Blewitt challenged the validity of her claims of a second marriage, saying that application for money could be considered only on submission of a marriage certificate. Jones was unable to produce one, and Blewitt seems to have discovered that they were not married. He advised Lord Stanley not to give John Lowndes assistance, writing that the couple had 'become well known to the Mendicity Society as Begging Letter writers' (Cross, *Common Writer*, 178). Of the three women rejected by the RLF on moral grounds, Jones shared company with a courtesan and the purported mistress of the duke of Brunswick.

Plagued by sickness and allegations of impropriety, Hannah Maria Jones struggled to find a place in the developing literary market place of cheap fiction in the mid-nineteenth century. She received praise for her writings, albeit moderate, from such periodicals as *The Athenaeum*, but she died in destitution on 24 January 1854 at 17 Salisbury Place, Bermondsey, where she had been living. *The Times* remarked in a brief obituary, 'A Sad Fate—Anna Maria Jones, authoress of the *Gipsy* and other popular novels of the day, died on Tuesday ... in the most abject poverty. Her remains await, in all probability, a pauper's funeral' (27 Jan 1854). Her publishers, including George Virtue, William Emans, Edmund Lloyd, and Thomas Kelly died rich men: Kelly himself—referred to by Blewitt as one of the 'lowest class of Publishers'—later became lord mayor of London. A. A. MANDAL

Sources N. Cross, ed., *Archives of the Royal Literary Fund, 1790–1918* (1982–3), file 553 [microfilm] · N. Cross, *The common writer: life in nineteenth-century Grub Street* (1985) · P. Garside, 'Hannah Marie Jones', *The Cambridge bibliography of English literature*, ed. J. Shattock, 3rd edn, 4 (1999) · L. James, *Print and the people, 1819–1851* (1976) · M. Summers, *A Gothic bibliography* (1940) · *The Times* (27 Jan 1854)
Archives Royal Literary Fund, corresp. with Royal Literary Fund [microfilm: file no. 553]
Wealth at death abject poverty: *The Times*

Jones, Sir Harold Spencer (1890–1960), astronomer, was born in Kensington, London, on 29 March 1890, the third child and elder son of Henry Charles Jones, an accountant with the Great Western Railway Company, and his wife, Sarah Ryland, a former schoolmistress. Although without formal training in mathematics, his father acquired a considerable working knowledge of several branches of the

Sir **Harold Spencer Jones** (1890–1960), by Howard Coster, 1935

subject, and gave active encouragement to his son; Spencer Jones early showed exceptional ability, which was fostered at Latymer Upper School, Hammersmith, under the tutelage of G. M. Grace. He won a scholarship to Jesus College, Cambridge, where after a first in both parts of the mathematical tripos (1909–11) he took a first in physics in the second part of the natural sciences tripos (1912). He was elected Isaac Newton student in 1912 and in 1913 was second Smith's prizeman and elected to a research fellowship at his college. On 15 May 1918 he married Gladys Mary, the daughter of Albert Edward Owers, a civil engineer; they had two sons.

In 1913 Spencer Jones was appointed by the astronomer royal, Frank Dyson, to the Royal Observatory, Greenwich, in place of Arthur Eddington, who had been elected to the Plumian professorship of astronomy in Cambridge. In spite of his work during the war on optical instrument design for the Ministry of Munitions, he found time to undertake original research on many diverse branches of astronomy and to prepare the text for his comprehensive book *General Astronomy* (1922). It was during this active period of research that his appetite was whetted for what was to become his major research contribution to astronomy—the rotation of the earth and the so-called system of astronomical constants. In 1923 he was appointed astronomer at the Royal Observatory at the Cape of Good Hope, South Africa, to succeed S. S. Hough who had died in office.

Spencer Jones's years at the Cape were prodigiously productive—in original research, in the prosecution and inauguration of observational programmes, in leadership and administration, in literary output, and in social life. He left behind him a united and vigorous staff fully engaged on observational programmes of the foremost importance; these were later brought to a satisfactory conclusion, just as he himself had, in the great tradition, completed the programmes initiated by Sir David Gill.

In 1933 Spencer Jones returned to Greenwich as tenth astronomer royal, in succession to Dyson. He was rapidly immersed in administrative and public duties, with the direction of the work of the observatory, with the putting into service of two new instruments (the 36 inch reflecting telescope presented by W. J. Yapp and the new reversible transit circle to replace the eighty-year-old instrument designed by Sir George Airy), and with the serious problems arising from the rapidly increasing difficulties of conducting astronomical observations at Greenwich, now engulfed by the pollution and atmospheric disturbances created by London.

Spencer Jones continued to make significant contributions to many branches of astronomy, two of which, both involving the meticulous discussion of many thousands of observations, will always be associated with his name. His epoch-making paper 'The rotation of the earth and the secular accelerations of the sun, moon and planets' (1939) demonstrated conclusively that the observed fluctuations were due to irregularities in the rate of rotation of the earth. It was a landmark in the subject, and led directly to the adoption, in 1950, of the concept of ephemeris time. In 1928 Spencer Jones had been appointed president of Commission 34 (on the solar parallax) of the International Astronomical Union, with the task of organizing a worldwide programme for the observation of the minor planet Eros at its favourable opposition in 1930–31; the object of this work was to determine the value of the solar parallax, and, from that, the 'astronomical unit of distance' from the earth to the sun. Spencer Jones not only made the major contribution to the observations from the observatory at the Cape, but personally undertook the collection, reduction, and discussion of all the observations. This work, which took nearly ten years to complete, culminated in a discussion, published in 1941, of extraordinary thoroughness and depth, though the value was later shown to have been systematically in error. For this work, in 1943 Spencer Jones was awarded the gold medal of the Royal Astronomical Society and a royal medal of the Royal Society, of which he had been elected a fellow in 1930.

During this period Spencer Jones had to recommend the removal of the observatory from Greenwich, where it had been established in 1675. The observing conditions were rapidly worsening and expansion was impossible. Approval was granted, but it was not until after the war, in 1945, that he could publicly announce that 'the Royal Greenwich Observatory' would be established at Herstmonceux Castle in Sussex. The actual move was not completed until after his retirement on 31 December 1955. He also played an important part in the negotiations leading to the initial approval for the 98 inch Isaac Newton Telescope to be erected at Herstmonceux. He presented the case for the provision of a large telescope, originally drawn up by the councils of the Royal Astronomical Society and the Royal Society for a 74 inch telescope, forcibly and successfully.

Spencer Jones made notable scientific and administrative contributions to time measurement and horology, and was responsible for the great expansion of the watch-repair services and watch-manufacturing industries. He was president of the British Horological Institute from 1939 and received its gold medal, and played a leading part in founding the National College of Horology. He also made many contributions to geomagnetism, both to the theory and to the practical application to navigation; he was inaugural president of the Institute of Navigation in 1947.

In later years, and especially after his retirement, Spencer Jones played a large part in the organization of international science. He was president of the International Astronomical Union from 1945 to 1948 and, as such, began his long service to the International Council of Scientific Unions (ICSU) as a member of the executive board. He was secretary-general from 1956 to 1958 and a most enthusiastic organizer of the International Geophysical Year; he edited the *Annals of the IGY* and became director of the ICSU publication office. He also represented the ICSU at meetings of UNESCO and contributed much to the weight that is given to the part of the UNESCO programme devoted to pure science.

Spencer Jones was awarded his ScD from Cambridge in 1925 and made an honorary fellow of Jesus College in 1933. He received, among others, the Janssen, Bruce, Lorimer, and Rittenhouse medals. He was knighted in 1943 and appointed KBE in 1955. He was a foreign member of the principal academies of science and received honorary doctorates from some ten British and foreign universities.

Spencer Jones was a tall, upright, dignified figure, with a fine presence, a clear delivery, and a ready command of language. However, he was essentially a simple and kindly man, with high ideals and complete integrity of purpose, which he brought to all his many activities. He preferred logical and temperate argument to passionate advocacy; his beliefs were pursued, and generally achieved, with a quiet persistence and dignity. He also knew how to choose the right phrase, or the right compromise, to obtain agreement. He could assimilate long and complicated papers with apparently no more than a quick glance and express himself in writing with remarkable speed and fluency. Although such a busy man, he was never hurried, and treated all with kindness, consideration, and unfailing courtesy. He died at his home, 40 Hesper Mews, Kensington, London, on 3 November 1960.   D. H. SADLER, *rev.*

Sources R. v. d. R. Woolley, *Memoirs FRS*, 7 (1961), 137–45 • *Quarterly Journal of the Royal Astronomical Society*, 4 (1963) • m. cert. • d. cert. **Archives** CUL, papers • NMM, papers

Likenesses H. Coster, photograph, 1935, NPG [*see illus.*] • photographs, 1935–44, Hult. Arch. • W. Stoneman, photograph, 1943, NPG

Wealth at death £28,342 17s. 11d.: probate, 24 Oct 1961, CGPLA Eng. & Wales

Jones, Harriet Morant (1833–1917), headmistress, was born in Guernsey on 2 January 1833. On her mother's side she was of French Huguenot descent. Nothing is known about her education. When she was appointed first headmistress of the Notting Hill high school, which opened in September 1873, she was forty years old. Emily Shirreff described her as 'a lady of great experience and ability' (Sayers, 17): she had run her own school in Guernsey, and she was apparently invited to take the headship of the second of the Girls' Public Day School Company's schools (the first had opened in Chelsea in January). She was to become one of the foremost headmistresses of her day. At first, in the one large schoolroom in Norland Square, Holland Park, she taught the top class all subjects except arithmetic. As there were only ten pupils when the school opened, she had just the one assistant, her sister, 'Miss Anna'. By the end of the first school year there were some eighty children and Miss Jones set out to appoint her staff. She had the two essential qualities of a successful head: a genius for selecting promising teachers and keeping them happy, and a personality which won the respect of both parents and pupils. Although no real academic herself, she believed passionately in the education of women and in women working. Before the end of 1874 she had formed the ambitious idea of sending six of the pupils in for the Cambridge senior local examinations. She was against introducing non-academic subjects, such as needlework, into the curriculum. The school soon had a high academic reputation.

Living close to Miss Jones in Norland Square were her sister and her brother-in-law, the Revd Charles Du Port, chief inspector of schools. His daughter, Winifred, and another of Miss Jones's nieces, Edith Jones (alias de Grave), were to attend the high school. Winifred went up to Girton College, Cambridge, for two terms and then returned to teach the lower forms. Edith spent a year at Somerville College, Oxford, and did the Oxford examination for women.

Opinions vary as to Miss Jones's success as a teacher. Her specialist subjects were French and German. By the 1880s and 1890s, however, she was teaching scripture and history, and the schoolgirls of this era were decidedly less impressed than their predecessors, regarding the lessons as 'something of jokes' and 'old-fashioned even by the standards of the day' (Sayers, 19). She stuck rigidly to her notes, which she went over again and again. In any case, her strength was by now reflected in the strength of her staff. By this date old girls of the school who had been at the women's colleges were being pressed by the head to return and take up appointments. One such, Mary Adamson, recorded how she was invited back to teach science, a subject Miss Jones was 'indifferent to, or even disliked' (ibid., 104). Miss Adamson was the teacher of Dame Harriette Chick. The teaching was at this time of a very high

quality in all subjects. Before the end of Miss Jones's headmistress-ship, an inspector reported that 'every teacher of competence is only too glad, if she can, to obtain a post at Notting Hill' (ibid., 99). Many headmistresses were recruited from this source.

The physical features and the personality of Miss Jones have been described by many of the pupils, generations of whom knew her as Jonah. To look at she was imposing. She was tall, handsome, and impressive. She wore silk underskirts which rustled, and was often dressed in regal purple velvet, edged with fur, her black plaits forming a coronet on top of her head. She had a deep sonorous voice, and a 'stimulating and cheering personality' which 'inspired all who worked under her'. Miss Jones 'always saw before her the Golden Age in which the Victorians believed': in which not only were women to be properly educated, and to receive the Parliamentary vote, but the slums were to be cleared, unemployment to cease, and all abuses be reformed, and in all these things 'Notting Hillites would bear their worthy part' (Sayers, 18).

In 1887 she was co-signatory (with Frances Buss and Fanny Metcalfe) to a memorial to the University of Cambridge asking for the admission of women to degrees. In 1894 she gave evidence on behalf of the Association of Head Mistresses of Endowed and Proprietary Schools before the Bryce commission (on secondary education), and in 1897 and 1898 she served as third president of the association, following Miss Buss and Miss Beale. She had been a member of the council of the Maria Grey Training College from its early days in Bishopsgate and had an interest in the National Union of Women Workers. She retired in 1900. Harriet Morant Jones died at her home, 41 Norland Square, Holland Park, London, on 20 October 1917 and was buried at Kensal Green cemetery.

JANE E. SAYERS

Sources J. E. Sayers, *The fountain unsealed: a history of the Notting Hill and Ealing high school* (privately printed, Broadwater Press, 1973) • *Harriet Morant Jones, 1833–1917*, privately printed (John Bale, Sons, and Danielson Ltd, 1918) • *Daily Telegraph* (23 Oct 1917) • *Journal of Education*, new ser., 39 (1917), 648 • E. Gurney Salter, *Newsletter of the Friends of the Girls' Public Day School Trust* (1958), 28–30 • D. Stephen, *GPDST Notting Hill and Ealing High School Magazine* (1956), 29 • letters, Girton Cam., ED XIII/I/33a, 34; ED XIII/3/11, 12

Likenesses J. J. Shannon, oils, 1891, Notting Hill and Ealing High School, London • photographs, repro. in Sayers, *The fountain unsealed*, pls. 18–19

Wealth at death £10,598 15s. 11d.: probate, 3 Dec 1917, CGPLA Eng. & Wales

Jones, Sir Harry David (1791–1866), army officer, the youngest son of John Jones (1751–1806), of Welsh descent, 29th foot, superintendent of Landguard Fort, Felixstowe, Suffolk, and of Cranmer Hall, Fakenham, Norfolk, and his wife, Mary (d. 1816), daughter of John Roberts, 29th foot, was born at Landguard Fort on 14 March 1791. Sir John Thomas *Jones (1783–1843) was his eldest brother. Another elder brother was George Matthew *Jones (c.1785–1831). He joined the Royal Military Academy, Woolwich, on 10 April 1805, and on leaving became candidate for the corps of Royal Engineers, passed a probation of six months on the Ordnance Survey of England, and was commissioned second-lieutenant, Royal Engineers, on 17 September 1808.

Jones's first station was Dover, where he was employed on the extensive fortifications then in progress. Promoted first-lieutenant on 24 June 1809, in July he embarked with the expedition under Lord Chatham for the Scheldt, landed with it on the island of Walcheren, served at the capture of Flushing and throughout the campaign, and suffered from 'malarial fever'.

Jones returned to England in January 1810, and the following April was sent to the Peninsula. He took part in the defence of Cadiz under Sir Thomas Graham, and embarked with the force under Colonel Stewart sent to relieve the Spanish garrison of Tarragona. He then joined the army under Wellington in time to take part in the assault and capture of Badajoz (19 April 1812), and continued with Wellington's army through the campaign of 1812–13. He was at the battle of Vitoria (21 June 1813) with the 5th division under General Oswald, and so distinguished himself that he was recommended for special promotion. At the siege of San Sebastian, Jones was adjutant of the right attack. He led the 'forlorn hope' at the unsuccessful assault of 25 July 1813 and, hoping renewed efforts would be made, held the breach, with a few determined men inspired by his example, until they were all killed or wounded and taken prisoner. Jones himself was severely wounded, and remained a prisoner until the castle surrendered on 8 September 1813. The town had been captured by assault on 31 August, and during the week the castle continued to hold out, the prisoners were exposed with the garrison to the besiegers' overwhelming vertical fire. For his bravery then, and in compensation for his wound, Jones received a year's pay. He was sufficiently recovered from his wounds to join the 5th division at the passage of the Bidassoa under Sir Thomas Graham, and was at the battle of Nivelle (10 November 1813) under General Oswald; at the battle of the Nive (9–12 December 1813), where he was again wounded, under General Hay; and at the blockade of Bayonne under Lieutenant-General Sir Charles Colville. For his conduct he was officially thanked by the master-general of the ordnance and promoted second captain on 12 November 1813.

During the Anglo-American War of 1812–14, in February 1814 Jones joined at Dauphine Island the expedition against New Orleans under Sir John Lambert, and was sent on a special mission to New Orleans under a flag of truce. In 1815 he joined Wellington's army after Waterloo, was at the capture of Paris, and commanded the engineers at Montmartre. He remained in France with the army of occupation, and was a commissioner with the Prussian army under General Zieten.

On his return to England in 1818 Jones was stationed at Plymouth. In 1822 he obtained six months' leave and accompanied his brother John on an inspection of the Netherlands' fortresses. In 1823 he was moved to Jersey, and in 1824 was appointed adjutant and field-work instructor at the Royal Engineer Establishment at Chatham. In 1824 he married Charlotte, second daughter of

the Revd Thomas Hornsby, rector of Hoddesdon, Hertfordshire. On 29 July 1825 he was promoted first captain. In 1826 he was sent to Malta, and while there was sent to the north African coast to superintend the embarkation of some classic columns for George IV. In 1833 he was sent from Malta to Constantinople to report on the Dardanelles and Bosphorus defences, and after this returned overland to England. He went to Malta in 1834, then to Constantinople to prepare plans for the ambassador's residence, and back to Malta. In May 1835 he was ordered home, and on 1 July, following the Municipal Corporations Act (1835), was appointed a commissioner for municipal boundaries in England. On 2 December 1835 he was appointed a member of the commission for the improvement of the navigation of the River Shannon. He continued in this post several years, though his services were not confined to this project. On 11 February 1836 he was appointed first commissioner for fixing the municipal boundaries in Ireland, and on 20 October that year was made secretary to the Irish railway commission, which reported in 1838. He also reported on the distress in co. Donegal, and was employed on special service at Dover. On 10 January 1837 he received a brevet majority, and was employed that year on special service under the Admiralty. In April 1839 he was appointed commanding royal engineer at Jersey, but in November he was seconded and appointed to the Shannon commission. On 7 September 1840 he was promoted lieutenant-colonel. His services in Ireland were so appreciated that when in 1842 he was offered an appointment at headquarters, he was, at the urgent request of the lords of the Treasury, retained in Ireland, and on 15 October 1845 was appointed chairman of the board of public works in Ireland.

After the death of his brother Sir John Jones in 1843, he edited a third edition (published 1846) of the *Journal of sieges carried on by the army under the duke of Wellington in Spain during the years 1811 to 1814*, to which he added considerable information and a copious appendix. At the time he was a member of the relief committee under Sir John Burgoyne, and in 1847 he received the thanks of the Treasury and of the prime minister, Lord John Russell, for his exertions. In 1850, in accordance with regulations, having served ten years uninterruptedly in state civil employment, he had to revert to military duty, and was appointed in March 1850 to command the Royal Engineers in north Britain. On 1 May 1851 he was appointed director of the School of Military Engineering at Chatham. He there introduced a system by which line infantry were instructed in field works, and made the value of the pick and shovel more practically known to the army at large. In 1853 he accompanied Lord Lucan to Paris on a mission from the queen to Napoleon III. In April 1854 he was again sent to Paris by Lord Raglan, master-general of the ordnance, to report on a new pontoon adopted by the French. In May and June 1854 he was president of two committees on the Royal Sappers and Miners, which led to their name being altered to that already held by their officers—Royal Engineers, and various alterations were made in their dress and equipment.

On 7 July 1854 Jones became full colonel, and on the declaration of war with Russia he was appointed (10 July) brigadier-general. The British government wanted offensive action in the Baltic and Sir Charles Napier, considering Kronstadt and Sveaborg too strong to attack, decided to attack the Russian fortress at Bomarsund in the Åland Islands at the entrance to the Gulf of Bothnia. As there were insufficient British troops, French troops had to be used in the amphibious operation. Napier's fleet arrived in July and the British and French landed on 8 August. Initially liaison officer, Jones commanded British engineers, marines, and naval artillery ashore. Following land and sea bombardment the Russians surrendered on 16 August, and the British demolished the fortifications (by the 1856 treaty of Paris the Ålands were demilitarized). Later in August, with French generals, Jones sailed to Reval and Sveaborg to investigate possible allied attacks. He advocated attacking Sveaborg, but the French and Napier refused. Napier called his proposal an 'absurd proposition' (Lambert, Crimean War, 186), though back in England Sir James Graham favoured it. Jones received the thanks of the queen, by dispatch of the secretary of state, for his Baltic services. In October he returned to England and resumed his Chatham duties. On 12 December he was appointed major-general on the staff and ordered to Constantinople as commanding royal engineer there, but on arrival in January 1855 found orders to join the army before Sevastopol. On 24 February he replaced Sir John Burgoyne as commanding royal engineer. He advised Lord Raglan and distinguished himself by his energy, daily visiting the trenches although he suffered from sciatica. He urged more action against the Russian positions. He was present at the unsuccessful assault on the Redan on 18 June, was severely wounded in the forehead by a spent grapeshot, and was mentioned in dispatches by Lord Raglan. For his wound he received £100. Following Raglan's death (28 June 1855) there were various proposals for his replacement. Some naval officers favoured Jones but Lieutenant-General James Simpson, already acting commander-in-chief, was appointed. On 30 July Jones received the local rank of lieutenant-general. On 4 August he and General A. Niel argued for an early assault but were overruled by Pelissier. At the assault on 8 September Jones, partly because of his wound, was ill and unable to stand. Determined to be present and able to advise Simpson, he had himself carried in a litter—well muffled up and wearing his red night-cap—to the trenches. He was mentioned in dispatches. In 1855 he was made KCB, the military order of Savoy (first class), and the Mejidiye (second class). On 4 June 1856 he was made an Oxford DCL.

Soon after the fall of Sevastopol (September 1855) Jones's wound necessitated his removal to Scutari and, in October, to England. In January 1856 he was a member of the council of war in Paris, presided over by Napoleon III, who made him a commander of the Légion d'honneur. On 12 April 1856 he was awarded a good service pension of £100 per annum. On 29 April he was appointed governor of the Royal Military College, Sandhurst. He was unpopular with the cadets, and in October 1862 a mutiny

occurred. In May 1856 he was also made a member of the royal commission on the system of purchase in the army, presided over by the duke of Somerset. Intended by Palmerston essentially to preserve the status quo—Sir George de Lacy Evans was the only committed reformer appointed to the commission—its 1857 report recommended not abolition of purchase but a limited modification.

Before the Crimean War Sir John Burgoyne, other Royal Engineers officers, and Palmerston wanted improved coastal fortifications. By 1859, to counter the perceived threat from Napoleon III, Palmerston wanted a major coastal fortification programme as part of British rearmament and defence reconstruction. He encouraged and exploited the popular invasion 'panic' and secured the appointment in August 1859 of the royal commission on the defences of the United Kingdom with Jones, who favoured fortifications, as its chairman. Chosen for Palmerston's purpose, it was packed with fortificationists and army dominated. Its report (February 1860), assuming the possible absence of the fleet and rejecting coastal defence vessels and floating batteries, recommended a massive and expensive programme of fortification of naval bases. Although its proposals were controversial and were reduced by the government, the majority of the works recommended were eventually built, at Portsmouth, Plymouth, and elsewhere; 'Palmerston's follies' were later much criticized by navalists and radicals. On 6 July 1860 Jones was promoted lieutenant-general, and on 2 August that year he became a colonel-commandant, Royal Engineers. In 1861 he was appointed honorary colonel of the 4th administrative battalion of the Cheshire rifle volunteers, and was made a GCB.

Jones read papers (published in its Proceedings) to the Institution of Civil Engineers, of which he was an associate, on breakwaters (1842), a diving bell (1846), and a Shannon bridge. He also contributed to the United Service Journal in 1841 a narrative of his 1813 captivity in San Sebastian. He wrote several articles in the Professional Papers of the Royal Engineers, and in 1859 he compiled the second volume of the official journal of the 'siege of Sebastopol'. In 1861 he edited his brother Sir John's Reports relating to the re-establishment of the fortresses in the Netherlands from 1814 to 1830 (printed for private circulation).

Jones died, while still governor, at Sandhurst, admired and regretted, on 2 August 1866, and was buried in the Royal Military College cemetery. A memorial tablet was placed by his brother officers in the college chapel.

R. H. VETCH, rev. ROGER T. STEARN

Sources Corps records, Royal Engineers Institution, Chatham, Kent · LondG · GM, 4th ser., 2 (1866), 420 · Annual Register (1866), pt 2, pp. 215–16 · W. Porter, History of the corps of royal engineers, 2 vols. (1889) · M. S. Partridge, Military planning for the defense of the United Kingdom, 1814–1870 (1989) · J. Smyth, Sandhurst: the history of the Royal Military Academy, Woolwich, the Royal Military College, Sandhurst, and the Royal Military Academy, Sandhurst, 1741–1961 (1961) · E. M. Spiers, Radical general: Sir George de Lacy Evans, 1787–1870 (1983) · A. Bruce, The purchase system in the British army, 1660–1871, Royal Historical Society Studies in History, 20 (1980) · A. D. Lambert, The Crimean War: British grand strategy, 1853–56 (1990) · Boase, Mod. Eng. biog. ·

A. Lambert, 'Politics, technology and policy-making, 1859–1865: Palmerston, Gladstone and the management of the ironclad naval race', *Northern Mariner*, 8/3 (July 1998), 9–38

Archives Royal Engineers Museum, Prince Arthur Road, Gillingham, corresp. and papers | U. Nott. L., corresp. with duke of Newcastle

Likenesses E. U. Eddis, portrait, Royal Engineers Institution, Gordon Barracks, Chatham, Kent

Jones, Harry Longueville (1806–1870), inspector of schools and antiquary, son of Edward Jones of Oswestry and his wife, Charlotte Elizabeth Stephens, was born in Piccadilly, London, on 16 April 1806. His father was the second son of Captain Thomas Jones of Wrexham, who adopted the additional name of Longueville on succeeding to a portion of the Longueville estates in Shropshire. Jones was educated at a private school in Ealing whence he proceeded as sizar to St John's College, Cambridge, in 1823, but subsequently migrated to Magdalene College, where he graduated BA in 1828 (as thirty-first wrangler), and MA in 1832. He was elected fellow of his college and held the offices of lecturer and dean (1828–34); he was ordained deacon in 1829, priest in 1831, and between 1829 and 1834 served as curate of Conington in Cambridgeshire. He resigned his fellowship on his marriage in 1834 to Frances, second daughter of Robert Plowden Weston of Shropshire. Soon after this he settled in Paris (1834–46), where his mother's family had connections, and where he worked as a journalist on Galignani's *Messenger*, edited a reissue of Galignani's *Paris Guide*, and befriended the writer Thackeray, who held a high opinion of his accomplishments.

Journalism drew Jones to the study of contemporary social problems, and he made several crossings to England between 1835 and 1842 to read papers before the Manchester Statistical Society, one of which was a plea for the establishment of universities in new industrial towns, with a curriculum adapted to the needs of modern society. Although the experimental college he himself opened in Manchester proved premature, it provided a blueprint for Owens College (1851), which eventually became the founding college of the Victoria University (1880) and subsequently the University of Manchester.

Jones returned from Paris in 1846, and settled in Beaumaris, on Anglesey, to make a living by writing: he contributed twenty-six articles to *Blackwood's Magazine* between 1840 and 1849. In 1848 Kay-Shuttleworth appointed him her majesty's inspector (HMI) of church schools for the whole of Wales, a post which Jones used to urge the acknowledgement of the principality's distinctive needs. His passionate espousal of the Welsh language and its culture brought him into conflict with the education department, whose policy under R. R. W. Lingen (as permanent secretary from 1849 to 1870) and Robert Lowe (as vice-president of the council from 1860 to 1864) stressed cultural uniformity. The increasingly critical tone of his annual reports led Jones to be regarded as subversive: his report for 1861–2 was referred back for amendment, but that for 1863–4 was so unacceptable that it was suppressed and Jones was reported for insubordination to the lord president of the council, Lord Granville. Jones's subsequent action in circulating the suppressed report among backbench MPs precipitated a crisis which led to Robert Lowe's resignation as vice-president of the council, to the appointment of a select committee of the House of Commons, and to his own virtual dismissal from office.

While resident at Beaumaris, Jones (who had been elected fellow of the Society of Antiquaries in 1841) had published in January 1846 the first number of *Archaeologia Cambrensis* with the assistance of the Revd John Williams (Ab Ithel). This publication led to the founding of the Cambrian Archaeological Association in 1847. Through these agencies Jones brought the application of critical method to the study of Welsh archaeology and history, leading to a break with Ab Ithel and the obscurantist school of Welsh historians associated with Iolo Morgannwg. Thereafter Jones dedicated the journal to rigorous historical scholarship, both through his own contributions in the form of learned articles and fine pencilled drawings of cromlechs and inscribed stones, and by providing an outlet for such gifted scholars as Thomas Stephens. Although the journal caused Jones considerable financial embarrassment he continued to edit it until his death.

Jones's relentless struggle as HMI for the acknowledgement of a Welsh identity led to a breakdown of his health when, in the midst of the crisis of 1864, he suffered the first of a series of strokes which led him to leave Wales for Brighton, where he lived with his wife and two unmarried daughters before moving to Kensington, where he died on 16 November 1870 at his home, 1 Claremont Terrace, Newland Street. He left an estate valued at under £20—an indication of the sacrifices he had made for the causes in which he believed.

For many years Jones's contribution to Welsh scholarship and education was obscured by the long nonconformist domination of nineteenth-century Welsh historiography. A more recent and more generous acknowledgement of the part he played has enhanced his reputation.

H. G. WILLIAMS

Sources *Archaeologia Cambrensis*, 4th ser., 2 (1871), 94–6 · B. B. Thomas, 'The Cambrians and the nineteenth century crisis in Welsh studies, 1847–70', *Archaeologia Cambrensis*, 127 (1978), 1–15 · H. G. Williams, 'Longueville Jones and Welsh education', *Welsh History Review / Cylchgrawn Hanes Cymru*, 15 (1990–91), 416–42 · J. E. Dunford, 'Biographical details of her majesty's inspectors appointed before 1870', *History of Education Society Bulletin*, 28 (1981), 8–23 · Venn, *Alum. Cant.* · probate

Archives Bodl. Oxf., corresp. with Sir T. Phillipps · NL Scot., letters to Blackwoods

Wealth at death under £20: probate, 5 Dec 1870, *CGPLA Eng. & Wales*

Jones, Henry (1605–1682), Church of Ireland bishop of Meath, was born in Ireland, the eldest of five sons of Lewis *Jones (d. 1646), bishop of Killaloe, and Mabel Ussher (b. c.1580), daughter of Arland Ussher and Margaret Stanihurst and sister of the future archbishop of Armagh, James *Ussher. The couple's other sons included Michael *Jones (d. 1649), Theophilus *Jones (d. 1685), and Ambrose *Jones (d. 1678) [see under Jones, Lewis], later bishop of Kildare. Henry entered Trinity College, Dublin, in 1616, graduated BA in 1621, and proceeded MA in 1624, when he was elected to fellowship. In 1625 his father presented him to the deanery of Ardagh in Cavan, where he married Jane Culme, the daughter of a local settler, with whom he had two sons and two daughters. When the dioceses of Ardagh and Kilmore were divided in 1637 Jones exchanged his office for the deanery of Kilmore, probably in order to remain with Bishop William Bedell, whose controversial views on propagating the gospel in the Irish language he shared.

On the outbreak of the Irish rising in 1641 Jones was captured by the O'Reillys who sent him to Dublin early in November with a petition to the government, keeping his family as hostages. After his return he thought it 'high time to study my coming off, by all means, which by God's assistance was strangely effected' as he described in *The Beginning and Progress of the Rebellion in the County of Cavan* (1642). He returned in December to the capital, where he suggested to the government that the anxieties of his fellow refugees about future restitution or compensation should be allayed by the compilation of a systematic record of losses resulting from the rising. On 23 December he was appointed head of a commission of eight ministers charged with registering the claims of the dispossessed and issuing them with certificates of loss. The depositions taken by the commissioners quickly convinced him that the rising was part of a continuing, papally directed, international conspiracy, the work of Antichrist, and its object, he explained to the English House of Commons in March 1642, was 'the utter extirpation of the reformed religion and the professors of it' (Jones, *A Remonstrance*).

Jones shared the disquiet of many protestants when a cessation was concluded with the rebels in September 1643. He attempted to influence the ensuing negotiations by submitting a disquisition in which he used his growing collection of depositions as a basis on which to develop the theme of universal Catholic guilt against God, but he did not publish it (BL, Harleian MS 5999). Unlike many of his compatriots, his brother Michael among them, who transferred their allegiance to a parliament which could be relied upon to pursue victory in Ireland, he remained constant to the king and to his lord lieutenant, the marquess of Ormond, and he was rewarded by elevation to the bishopric of Clogher in 1645 and appointment as vice-chancellor of Dublin University in 1646 in place of his uncle, Archbishop Ussher, a position which he held until 1660, and the tacit obligations of which he more than fulfilled by the presentation to the college library of the books of Kells and Durrow. In 1646, his first wife having died some time after December 1641, he married Mary Piers, daughter of a Westmeath landowner, and niece of the antiquary and associate of Ormond, James Ware (1594–1666); they had two sons and five daughters.

After Ormond's departure from Ireland in 1647 Jones remained in Dublin to welcome the city's parliamentarian governor, his brother Michael. He took an active role in Michael's administration, acting as his secretary both before and after the execution of the king. After Cromwell's arrival Jones accepted appointment as scoutmaster-

general of the army and regularly attended meetings of the army council. He served on the special court which was set up, largely at his urging, to try those responsible for atrocities, and it was his collection of depositions that formed the prosecution's main body of evidence. He helped to administer the transplantation of Catholic proprietors to Connaught and the depositions made up part of the 'book of discriminations' which was used to distinguish degrees of Catholic guilt and to determine how much land each claimant was entitled to receive. He was involved in enforcing on the Scottish presbyterian ministers in Ulster an oath of engagement, which compelled them to deny the king and acknowledge the legitimacy of the Commonwealth. He was also one of those who worked on a contingency plan for moving the Scots from Ulster to some part of Ireland more safely remote from Scotland.

Inside Trinity, Jones was concerned with the revival of a scheme, introduced by William Bedell when he was provost, which was designed to equip students of the ministry to perform their duties in the Irish language. Jones acquired forfeited estates at Summerhill in co. Meath, together with the wardship of the heir of a wealthy landowner within the pale and grants of the tithes of nine abbeys and rectories—these last on the direct orders of Oliver Cromwell in March 1657, perhaps in compensation for a loss of favour in the period of Baptist influence under Charles Fleetwood, when he was required to exchange the office of scoutmaster for a lowlier position as official historian of recent events, at a reduced salary. Jones's collaboration was strictly secular: he retained his episcopally given title until he was ordered to desist late in 1651, and he did not minister in the new state church. While he published the following year *An Abstract of some Few of the Barbarous, Cruell Massacres and Murders* (1652), contributing to the memory of outrage against protestants, and rejoiced in the new regime's anti-Catholicism, he would not accept its version of protestantism or its tolerance of radical dissent, and he remained ultimately unreconciled.

After the overthrow of Richard Cromwell, Jones was one of three agents sent to London in May 1659 to represent the interests of the settler communities and in December, with his brother Theophilus, he was a prime mover in the *coup d'état* which took control of the government and army, acting as secretary to the council of officers. He was an influential member of the general convention of Ireland, in which he represented co. Meath, and was chosen to conduct the thanksgiving service in Christ Church on 24 May 1660 and to preach the sermon, later published. However, Jones's place in the new order was at first equivocal. He benefited from undertakings given by the king to Sir Charles Coote and was confirmed in his property acquisitions, but as the arch-collaborator and betrayer of his church and his sovereign he was removed from the vice-chancellorship of the university and, when the Irish hierarchy was reconstituted in a concelebrated consecration of two archbishops and ten bishops in January 1661, was relegated to the role of handing the Bible to the primate. Yet shortly afterwards, John Bramhall, the new archbishop of Armagh, wrote to assure the king that Jones 'hath been as instrumental as any man whatsoever in the restitution of all of us' (Russell and Prendergast, 106), and within a few months of his local humiliation King Charles publicly recognized his contribution to the Restoration by translating him on 25 May 1661 to the bishopric of Meath, which carried with it a seat on the Irish council.

Once enthroned, Jones remained compromised by his conduct in the 1650s and his public pronouncements were few. He took the opportunity of the installation of his brother Ambrose as bishop of Kildare in 1667 to counter suspicions of his own orthodoxy by arguing the scriptural and historical cases against presbyterianism and making a categorical affirmation of his belief in the apostolic nature of episcopacy. Not long after that he became involved in promoting the preparation for publication of the Gaelic translation of the New Testament which William Bedell had initiated. The direction and, in a sense, the continuity of his thought was made explicit in 1676, when he delivered and published *A Sermon of Antichrist* (1676). His purpose was to proclaim that Antichrist was still at work in Rome and to insist that the way to defeat him was, as St John had foretold, 'by the breath of the Lord's mouth': in short, to lead Catholics out of Babylon into the true church by placing the Bible in their hands, in their own language. Jones's book proved unexpectedly topical, even prophetic, not because of its evangelical thrust, but because of its invocation of ever-present danger. The Popish Plot prompted the publication of a London edition in 1678 but Jones, though he feared that the experience of 1641 was to be repeated, remained firm in his convictions and took the opportunity of a funeral sermon for Archbishop James Margetson of Armagh in 1678 (published the following year) to extol William Bedell as a model for the church, most particularly because he had had the wisdom to seek to convert the Irish through their own language. Jones associated himself with the earl of Shaftesbury and the English opposition, became involved in the proceedings against Archbishop Oliver Plunket, who was accused of complicity in a plot to bring a French invasion force to Ireland, and helped to have the trial removed to London, where Plunket was convicted and executed in 1681. Jones himself died on 5 January the following year, and was buried at St Andrew's Church, Dublin, the next day.

AIDAN CLARKE

Sources H. Jones, *The beginning and progress of the rebellion in the county of Cavan* (1642) • H. Jones, *A remonstrance of divers remarkable passages concerning the church and kingdom of Ireland* (1642) • Burtchaell & Sadleir, *Alum. Dubl.* • papers relating to the massacres of 1641, TCD, MSS 809–841 • papers, incl. letters and drafts by H. Jones, TCD, MS 844 • Piers genealogy, NL Ire., department of manuscripts, MS 2563 • R. Dunlop, ed., *Ireland under the Commonwealth*, 2 vols. (1913) • R. Cox, *Hibernia Anglicana, or, The history of Ireland from the conquest thereof by the English to the present time*, 2 (1690), appx • A. Clarke, 'The 1641 rebellion and anti-popery in Ireland', *Ulster 1641: aspects of the rising*, ed. B. MacCuarta (1993) • J. W. Stubbs, *The history of the University of Dublin, from its foundation to the end of the eighteenth century* (1889) • A. Clarke, 'The 1641 depositions', *Treasures of the library, Trinity College, Dublin*, ed. P. Fox (1986) • A. Clarke, *Prelude to Restoration in Ireland* (1999) • J. I. McGuire, 'The Dublin convention, the protestant community and the emergence of an ecclesiastical settlement', *Parliament and community*, ed. A. Cosgrove and J. I. McGuire (1983) • C. N. Russell and J. P. Prendergast, *An account of the Carte collection of historical papers* (1871) • [G. D. Burtchaell], 'Family of Jones', *Irish Builder*, 676 (15 Feb 1888)
Archives Representative Church Body Library, Dublin, notebook • TCD, papers relating to the massacres of 1641, MSS 809–841 • TCD, letters and drafts, MS 844 | BL, 'A treatise giving a representation of the grand rebellion in Ireland', Harley MS 5999 • NL Scot., letters to Robert Boyle, MS 821 [copies]
Likenesses miniature, TCD • miniature, TCD • portrait, repro. in *Paintings and sculptures in Trinity College Dublin* (1990); copy, TCD

Jones, Henry (*c*.1695–1727), scientific editor, was born at Langton, Dorset, the son of the Revd Charles Jones. He was educated on the foundation at Eton College (1709–12), whence he proceeded in 1712 to King's College, Cambridge, of which he was elected fellow, and graduated BA in 1716 and MA in 1720. He abridged the *Philosophical Transactions* from 1700 to 1720 in a two-volume work that first appeared in 1721. In his preface he is very severe on Benjamin Motte, a printer, who had issued a bad abridgement of the same portion just before his appeared. Motte published a *Reply* in 1722. On 27 June 1723 Jones was elected a fellow of the Royal Society. He died unmarried in January 1727 at the Red Lion, Kensington, where he had gone for the benefit of his health.

GORDON GOODWIN, *rev.* ROBERT BROWN

Sources *The record of the Royal Society of London*, 4th edn (1940) • T. Harwood, *Alumni Etonenses, or, A catalogue of the provosts and fellows of Eton College and King's College, Cambridge, from the foundation in 1443 to the year 1797* (1797) • R. A. Austen-Leigh, ed., *The Eton College register, 1698–1752* (1927) • T. Thomson, *History of the Royal Society from its institution to the end of the eighteenth century* (1812) • Venn, *Alum. Cant.*

Jones, Henry (1721–1770), poet and playwright, was born at Beaulieu, 2 miles north-east of Drogheda, co. Louth. Nothing is known of Jones's parentage, though his family seems to have been in low circumstances because Jones was trained as a bricklayer. After he left school to serve his apprenticeship, Jones continued reading the classics in translation and writing verses while learning his trade. By 1744 his poetic effusions had attracted the attention and support of the corporation of Drogheda, and of Lord Chief Justice Singleton, who also lived at Beaulieu. Early the following year, Jones left for Dublin to ply his trade and to court the muses. Opportunity arrived in the form of Lord Chesterfield, then lord lieutenant and general-governor of Ireland, who addressed the Irish parliament in Dublin on 8 October 1745. Jones seized the moment by addressing celebratory verses to Chesterfield which were hand-delivered by his friend and supporter Singleton. Jones's panegyric pleased Chesterfield, who rewarded Jones liberally for his efforts. Smitten with what he perceived to be Jones's natural poetic genius, Chesterfield brought Jones to England in 1748.

Under Chesterfield's immediate protection, and with his ample support, Jones prepared a collection of poems that was published by subscription in 1749. *Poems on Several Occasions* appeared both in London and in Dublin, and boasted a subscriber's list of more than 740 names. The *Monthly Review* noted retrospectively that Jones 'gained great reputation' by this volume 'which has deservedly raised him from the obscurity of a mechanical employment' (8.226). About this time, Jones returned to work on a tragedy, *The Earl of Essex*, based on John Banks's 1682 play *The Unhappy Favourite*. John Hill records that *Essex* 'was received at one of the houses, and had even a day fixed for the performance of it' in the spring of 1751 (*The Inspector*). For reasons unknown, the play was shelved until the winter season of 1753. With the help of Chesterfield and Colley Cibber, Jones's tragedy was finally acted on 21 February 1753 at Covent Garden Theatre, where it 'went off with great Applause' (Stone, 1.353). The play enjoyed an initial run of eleven consecutive nights, providing Jones with three author's benefits from which he realized 'no less than five hundred pounds' (Cooke, 259). The play was revived often and, of the several tragedies circulating on the Essex theme in the period, Jones's proved the most popular in England and America through the early years of the nineteenth century.

The combined success of the subscription and the play established Jones as an independent author at large, but he soon squandered his profits. According to Cooke, Jones's downward spiral was precipitated by drink, general dissipation, and idleness (Cooke, 349). He experienced a falling-out with his former patron Chesterfield over the matter of 8 guineas Chesterfield's servant had lent him. Having learned of his protégé's indiscretion, Chesterfield banished Jones from his house forever (Cooke, 350). Jones soon found himself in and out of sponging houses, but he continued to write poetry, producing fourteen monograph poems between 1753 and 1770. The highlights of this output include *The Relief, or, Day Thoughts, a Poem Occasion'd by 'The Complaint, or, Night Thoughts'* (1754), a parody of Young, Gray, and other popular mid-century poets, and several loco-descriptive pieces: *Kew Garden* (1763), *The Isle of Wight* (1766), *Clifton* (1767), and *Shrewsbury Quarry* (1769).

Although many of Jones's poems received favourable notice in the monthlies during his lifetime, his subsequent reputation as a poet has suffered under the burden of a bad character and later critical expectations for mid-century poets. It is true that Jones was more imitative than innovative—many poems echo Pope and Johnson—but his ability to turn an 'ingenious compliment' has been too readily equated with mere sycophancy (*Monthly Review*, 8.471). Jones also seems to have written another tragedy, entitled 'Harold' but this play was never produced, and the manuscript, left in the possession of the actor Samuel Reddish, was lost after Jones's death. *The Cave of Idra*, a tragedy left unfinished by Jones, was enlarged to five acts by Dr Paul Hiffernan and produced as *The Heroine of the Cave* on 19 March 1774 (Stone, 3.1794).

Whatever Jones's character flaws—and many came to light as he pursued his pleasures and fended off his creditors—he remained a remarkably productive author who enjoyed a degree of independence and a length of career

rarely seen in a labourer turned poet of this period. However, Jones's lifestyle apparently caught up with him in April of 1770, when, after being drunk for two days, he 'was found run over by a waggon ... in St. Martin's Lane, without his hat or his coat' (Cooke, 423). Jones died a few days later at the parish workhouse.

WILLIAM J. CHRISTMAS

Sources [T. Cooke], 'Table talk', *European Magazine and London Review*, 25 (1794), 257–60, 348–51, 422–4 • G. W. Stone, ed., *The London stage, 1660–1800*, pt 4: *1747–1776* (1962) • *Monthly Review*, 8 (1753), 225–9, 471 • [J. Hill], *The inspector*, 2 vols. (1753), vol. 1, p. 140–43 • D. E. Baker, *Biographia dramatica, or, A companion to the playhouse*, rev. I. Reed, new edn, rev. S. Jones, 3 vols. in 4 (1812) • *The letters of Philip Dormer Stanhope, fourth earl of Chesterfield*, ed. B. Dobrée, 6 vols. (1932), vol. 5, p. 2018 • *DNB*
Archives BL • Harvard U., Houghton L.

Jones, Henry [*pseud.* Cavendish] (1831–1899), writer on card games, was born in London on 2 November 1831, the eldest son of Henry Derviche Jones, surgeon, of 12 Norfolk Crescent, London, and his wife, Mary. He was educated at King's College School, London (1842–8), and afterwards studied medicine under Sir William Lawrence at St Bartholomew's Hospital. He qualified MRCS (1853) and LSA (1855), and subsequently practised at several addresses in Soho Square. He retired in 1869, but retained a connection with his profession by becoming a member of the court of the Apothecaries' Company.

Jones's interest in card games evidently stemmed in part from his father, a devotee of whist, who in 1863 became chairman of the Portland Club whist committee; this committee, in collaboration with James Clay, an authority on the game, and the Arlington Club committee, framed the *Laws of Short Whist*, edited by John Loraine Baldwin for publication in May 1864. Prior to this, in the mid-1850s, Henry Jones had joined the Cambridge set of his brother Daniel Jones (1824–1915) known as 'the little whist school', a group who had taken up the study of whist as a hobby. Having met James Clay at the Cavendish Club in Cavendish Square, London, from which he took his pen-name, he first published on the subject in *Bell's Life* of March 1857. After William Pole, another contemporary authority, had suggested in print that whist might be as amenable to 'scientific' analysis as chess, Jones wrote his most famous work, *Principles of Whist* (1862), which was based on the description of 'model hands'. This ran to four editions under that title, before being reissued as *The Laws and Principles of Whist* in 1863; it went through nineteen further editions up to 1901, with major revisions and additions in 1868, 1871, 1874 (which added a historical chapter), 1876, 1879, and 1886. The last mentioned edition introduced a section on American innovations, which was published separately as *American Leads Simplified* (1891). Most of the content of *Laws and Principles* was not new, and derived from the earlier texts of Edmond Hoyle and Thomas Mathews, but mathematical proofs were offered, and it was the first publication to lay down clearly the rules of discard and of trumps. Jones came to be regarded as the late nineteenth-century authority on the game, and the total sales of *Laws and Principles* were not far short of those of Hoyle's seminal *Short Treatise on the Game of Whist* of 1742. The popularity of the works of Cavendish is perhaps further indicated by the large number of editions listed as 'missing' in the British Library catalogue. Jones was whist editor of *The Field* and pastimes editor of *The Queen*, and wrote the entries on whist and other games for the ninth edition of the *Encyclopaedia Britannica*.

Besides the Cavendish, Jones belonged to other leading London whist clubs including the Westminster, the Portland, the Arlington, and the Baldwin, as well as the Union Club in Brighton. He visited America in 1893 and played the game in Philadelphia and Chicago. As a player he never scaled the same heights he did as a pundit: between 1860 and 1878 he won 15,648 rubbers and lost 15,020; his father was said not to have rated his abilities highly, and father and son apparently disliked taking each other on over the card table.

In 1879 Henry Jones wrote that 'whist is now the king of card games, and seems destined, for many a long year, to retain that distinction' (*Card Essays*, 1879, quoted in Parlett, 214), but the game's popularity waned in the final years of the nineteenth century, being supplanted in fashionable circles by bridge. A twentieth-century writer has noted that 'Cavendish and his friends had been accused of killing ordinary mortals' enjoyment of partnership whist with their obsession with playing the game "scientifically"' (Parlett, 210). Yet a Waddington survey of 1981 found that whist remained the second most popular card game after rummy.

Jones also subjected écarté to scientific analysis, and showed broader cultural concerns in his much reprinted book on piquet (1st edn, 1873), which touched on the historical, political, and allegorical significance of the game. He produced manuals for numerous other card games, including bezique, euchre, calabrasella, cribbage, *vingt-et-un*, and patience, and other games, among them chess, backgammon, billiards, and the Japanese import gobang: 'he made it his business to be beforehand with any game that seemed likely to be popular' (*The Times*, 16 Feb 1899). He also wrote on sports, including badminton, lawn tennis, and croquet: he and his brother were both involved in the foundation of the All England lawn tennis and croquet club. His personality was described as 'decided, not without brusqueness' (*DNB*).

Jones died on 10 February 1899 at his home, 22 Albion Street, Hyde Park, and was buried at Kensal Green cemetery. He left a widow, Harriet Louisa, but apparently no children; his papers passed to his brother Daniel, and his whist library was sold at Sothebys on 22 May 1900. His passing merited a leading article in *The Times*, which declared that he:

> was not a lawmaker, but codified and commented on the laws which had been made, no one knows by whom, during many generations of card playing. He was thus the humble brother of Justinian and Blackstone, taking for his material, not the vast material interests of mankind, but one of their most cherished amusements. (*The Times*, 17 Feb 1899)

H. J. Spencer

Sources D. Parlett, *A history of card games* (1991) · W. P. Courtenay, *English whist and English whist players* (1894) · *DNB* · Venn, *Alum. Cant.* · *London and Provincial Medical Directory* (1867) · *CGPLA Eng. & Wales* (1899)

Likenesses portrait, repro. in Portland [J. Hogg], ed., *The whist table* (1895), frontispiece

Wealth at death £11,916 8s. 10d.: probate, 7 April 1899, *CGPLA Eng. & Wales*

Jones, Sir Henry (1852–1922), philosopher, born at Llangernyw, Denbighshire, on 30 November 1852, was the third son of Elias Jones and his wife, Elizabeth, daughter of William Williams. His family were north Wales farmers and farm labourers, with the exception of his father, who was the village shoemaker. His mother was devoutly religious, but his father less so. Jones was baptized into the community of Calvinistic Methodists on the day of his birth.

Jones left school at twelve years of age, to be apprenticed to his father. After four years new ambitions were awakened within him by the help of Mrs Alexander Roxburgh and Tom Redfern, a pupil teacher. In 1869 he returned half-time to school. He had nearly two years of desperate and doubting preparation, working most nights and surviving on little sleep, until in November 1870 he qualified for admission to the Bangor Normal College. He showed no special distinction; but without difficulty he gained his 'teacher's certificate'. In 1873 he was appointed master of the Ironworks School at Ammanford in south Wales. In two years he increased the number of pupils from around 190 to 430. He left a vivid and long-enduring impression both upon his pupils and upon the town. At this time also he became a preacher in the Calvinistic Methodist denomination, and was encouraged to make it his vocation. In 1875, therefore, after a summer of hard study, he matriculated, with a Dr Williams scholarship, at the University of Glasgow. He was chiefly interested in philosophy, to which John Nichol and especially Edward Caird—by far the strongest intellectual influence of Jones's life—introduced him. On graduation in 1879 he was dissuaded by Caird from making a career in the ministry, and won the G. A. Clark fellowship to study for four years in Oxford, Germany, and Glasgow. On 11 April 1882 he married Annie, daughter of James Walker, manufacturer, of Kilbirnie, Ayrshire.

By this time, under Caird's guidance, Jones had decided upon a career in philosophical teaching. In 1882 he was appointed to a lecturership in philosophy at the University College, Aberystwyth. Two years later, after being narrowly beaten for the principalship, he was appointed professor of philosophy and political economy in the new University College of North Wales at Bangor. In 1891 he gained the chair of logic, rhetoric, and metaphysics at St Andrews; and finally, in 1894, he succeeded Caird in the chair of moral philosophy in Glasgow, which he held until his death.

Jones never really gave up his religious calling, and the philosophy he espoused was for him indistinguishable from religion. He 'preached' absolute idealism around the lecture theatres of the world, copiously illustrating his points, in the same manner as Caird, with quotations from poetry and the Bible. He subscribed to the doctrine of 'divine immanence' which taught that God expresses himself in and through the activity of individuals. He denied the divinity of no man, and Jesus was for him the first idealist. Like Hegel, Jones believed in the unity of experience, and argued that the different modes, religion, poetry, science, and philosophy, were converging upon the same truth, at the centre of which lay the idea of spiritual evolution. The fullest statement of his metaphysic is given in his last volume, *A Faith that Enquires* (1922), the substance of the Gifford lectures delivered at Glasgow in 1920 and 1921. But his earlier writings had developed one or other of the several aspects of his view. His studies *Browning as a Philosophical Teacher* (1891) and *The Philosophy of Lotze* (1895) were critical interpretations of two idealist teachers, the former from the point of view of religion and ethics, the latter from that of logic and epistemology.

Consistent with his view that a professor must provide intellectual leadership and cannot remain neutral on questions affecting the community, in later books such as *The Working Faith of the Social Reformer* (1910) Jones addressed pressing social and political problems, including the role of the state. His characteristic method was to take two opposing sides to a question, and demonstrate the falsity of the opposition. Liberty and community were in his view complementary. The individual and the state were mutually inclusive, each a reflection of the other. The state enhances the possibility of self-development, and to it the individual owes everything. His theory of political obligation, entailing moral constraints on state action, was developed in his book *The Principles of Citizenship* (1919), written for use in civics classes organized by the YMCA. Jones also entered the evolution debate with characteristic enthusiasm, arguing that T. H. Huxley was wrong to create a division between cosmic and ethical evolution. Jones denied the efficacy of naturalistic evolution because it attempted to explain the higher in terms of the lower. For him, it was the higher that explained the lower. Spirit permeates nature, not because nature is intelligent, but because it is intelligible.

A valued reader of manuscripts for Macmillan publishers, Jones was at all times an eager and helpful correspondent. Perhaps his greatest contribution to the philosophy of his generation was his own teaching. His rich and radiant personality gave him a remarkable influence over his students; and in the years between 1900 and 1915 he was unmistakably the dominant force in the speculative life both of the west of Scotland and of Wales.

Apart from his professorial work, Jones was profoundly interested in educational reform. He took a leading part in the movement which culminated in the Welsh Intermediate Education Act of 1889. He was a member of the royal commission on the University of Wales in 1916–17, and of the 1918 departmental committee on adult education. A committed Liberal, his interventions in politics concerned chiefly the free trade issue, and the 'people's budget' of 1909 with its ensuing controversies. On the outbreak of the First World War he devoted his energies to two long campaigns on behalf of recruiting and of national savings. He served on many committees and public bodies, and finally, in 1918 visited the United States as a member of the British university mission, which put a strain on his health. A severe operation for cancer in 1913 had impaired his strength, and only his unshakable courage carried him through the days of public and private anxiety that followed. Of his six children, one son and one daughter had died in youth; his three remaining sons went on active service in the war, and the youngest died in France.

Soon after the end of the war, the cancer returned, and after three years of much suffering, though also of much productive work, Jones died in his country home, Noddfa, Tighnabruaich, Argyll, on 4 February 1922. He was buried in the churchyard at Kilbride on the Isle of Bute. He was knighted in 1912; he received honorary doctorates from the universities of St Andrews (1895) and Wales (1905), and was elected a fellow of the British Academy in 1904. In January 1922, a few weeks before his death, he was made a Companion of Honour. His childhood home was opened to the public as a museum in 1934 by his friend David Lloyd George, president of the memorial fund.

H. J. W. HETHERINGTON, rev. DAVID BOUCHER

Sources H. Jones, *Old memories*, ed. T. Jones (1922) • H. J. W. Hetherington, *The life and letters of Sir Henry Jones* (1924) • J. H. Muirhead, 'Sir Henry Jones, 1852–1922', *PBA*, 10 (1921–3), 552–62 • T. Jones, *A theme with variations* (1933), 85–113 • H. Morris-Jones, 'The life and philosophy of Sir Henry Jones', *Henry Jones, 1852–1922: centenary addresses delivered at the University College of North Wales on the first day of December, 1952* (1953) • *The Times* (6 Feb 1922) • *John O'London's Weekly* (11 March 1922) • *Western Mail* [Cardiff] (6 Feb 1922) • D. Boucher and A. Vincent, *A radical Hegelian* (1993) • A. P. F. Sell, *Philosophical idealism and Christian belief*, 1 (1995) • *CCI* (1922)
Archives NL Wales, diary | BL, corresp. with Macmillans, Add. MSS 55161-55162 • Bodl. Oxf., letters to Gilbert Murray • CUL, letters to May Crom • NL Wales, corresp. with Thomas Jones • NL Wales, letters to D. R. Daniels • U. Glas., Jones and Muirhead, 'Materials for life of Caird', MS Gen. 1475
Likenesses oils, U. Wales, Bangor • oils, U. Glas.
Wealth at death £10,060 13s. 3d.: confirmation, 13 June 1922, *CCI*

Jones, Henry (1866–1925). *See under* Jones, (Henry) Paul Mainwaring (1896–1917).

Jones, Henry Arthur (1851–1929), playwright, was born on 20 September 1851 at Granborough, Buckinghamshire, the eldest son of Silvanus Jones (1827–1914), a farmer of Welsh descent, and his wife, Elizabeth (1824?–1887), daughter of John Stephens, also a farmer. At the age of twelve Jones was withdrawn from school and sent to work for his uncle, a draper and deacon of the Baptist church in Ramsgate, Kent, whom he hated. Three-and-a-half years later he was employed by Bryants, another draper, at Gravesend. When he had any leisure he read voraciously, thus beginning a remarkable lifelong self-education.

In 1869 Jones moved to London, and was employed by a draper in the City. Calling at a warehouse for making artificial flowers owned by a Mrs Seeley, he met Jane Eliza Seeley (1855–1924), her daughter, and became engaged to her that year. During this period he was an ardent theatregoer and vowed to become a dramatist himself. He set about learning his craft by careful analysis of what was current and popular. Realizing that if he was to marry he must earn more, later in 1869 he became a commercial traveller for Rennie Tetley, a Bradford textile manufacturer, covering the west of England. He married Jane Seeley on 2 September 1875 and they lived at Exwick, near Exeter. In 1881 they moved to the London area, where they stayed for the rest of their lives. They had seven children, one of whom, Doris A. Jones, wrote her father's biography, *The Life and Letters of Henry Arthur Jones*, published in 1930. She gave a long description of her father, including his physical appearance: of medium height, with reddish hair, bearded, a large head, twinkling blue eyes, and square capable hands, which he used constantly as he talked. He had a pronounced sense of humour, but suffered from black depressions, alternating with hectic bursts of activity.

The first of Jones's plays to be produced had only one act: *It's Only Round the Corner* (Theatre Royal, Exeter, 11 December 1878), and was rapidly followed at the same theatre by *Hearts of Oak* (29 May 1879). His first London production was a comedietta, *A Clerical Error* (Court Theatre, 16 October 1879). The actor–manager of the Court, Wilson Barrett, commissioned Jones in 1881 to write a 'strong' play, and he collaborated with Henry Herman on *The Silver King*, a melodrama. Jones had left the drapery trade, so this commission was welcome. *The Silver King* was a runaway success, making enough money for him to become a full-time playwright. Later, collaborating with Herman again, Jones wrote *Breaking a Butterfly*, the first English version of Ibsen's *A Doll's House* (Prince's Theatre, 3 March 1884). Nevertheless, lacking the confidence to be independent, he became 'house-dramatist' for Wilson Barrett. With the exception of *Saints and Sinners* (Vaudeville Theatre, September 1884), in which Jones pilloried his hated Ramsgate uncle as Sam Haggard, a hypocritical dissenter, he produced only unimportant hack work.

In 1884 Jones embarked on a secondary career, writing articles and giving speeches and lectures to promote the cause of a serious and more literary English drama. He toiled ceaselessly and to considerable effect; his conviction, dedication, and powerful rhetorical style made him an effective advocate. This activity continued long after his popularity as a dramatist had waned.

In 1889 *The Middleman* (Shaftesbury Theatre, August 1889), a play about the relationship between capital and labour, was well received. This began a long association with E. S. Willard, an actor employed by Wilson Barrett, chiefly renowned for his portrayal of villains. In 1889 he went into management for himself, although he continued to act. Further success followed for Jones with *Judah* (Shaftesbury Theatre, May 1890), one of his most interesting plays, exploring issues to which he was to return frequently: hypocrisy and fraud; aspects of truth and morality; the inevitable corruption of 'the pure in heart'. An even greater hit, presented and starred in by Herbert Beerbohm Tree, was *The Dancing Girl* (Haymarket Theatre, January 1891), about a Quaker girl who goes deliberately to the bad. Then Jones failed badly with the first of his satirical comedies, *The Crusaders* (Avenue Theatre, 2 November 1891). In spite of sets and costumes designed by William Morris, it was booed on the first night. Jones lost £4000 of his own money.

At this point Jones first visited the USA, acquiring considerable prestige and making many friends. After his return to England, he had a mild success with *The Bauble Shop* (Criterion Theatre, January 1893), his first play under the management of Sir Charles Wyndham. In the same year he experimented again with *The Tempter* (Haymarket Theatre, September 1893), a verse tragedy, with passages in prose. Tree played the main role, that of the Devil; Sir Edward German wrote the incidental music. It failed, and Tree lost a great deal of money. Jones, nevertheless, felt it to be one of his best works.

Undeterred, Jones moved to another experiment, *The Masqueraders* (St James's Theatre, April 1894). Produced by George Alexander, this presented for the first time one of Jones's favourite themes: the unhappily married young woman who, because of duty, is unable to find happiness with the man she truly loves. The play also showed clearly another characteristic of the author's writing: his dislike of 'society' and the landed gentry. Jones felt himself to be hampered by his rural origins and accent, and his resentment often showed in his characterizations. He also hated and despised his own background of small tradesmen and dissenters, and he frequently satirized them. At the end of his life, disappointed at not receiving a knighthood, he partly blamed his origins; but it is more likely that his caustic wit, irascible behaviour, and frequently intemperate outbursts in print had made him enemies, many in high places.

Jones's next play (which he also considered one of his best), *The Case of Rebellious Susan* (Criterion Theatre, October 1894) did well, although Charles Wyndham was concerned about its moral 'nastiness'. In it Jones tackled head-on the much debated question of the double standard of sexual morality prevalent at the time. This was also the first work in which Jones employed the *raisonneur*, a figure derived from French drama. This character, usually somewhat detached from the main action, is, in effect, the author's spokesman. Although not usually a central figure, he observes the other characters, commenting on their behaviour. Both Shaw and Pinero, Jones's contemporaries, tended to involve their equivalent character as a protagonist in the action.

Jones's first book, *The Renascence of the English Drama* (1895), was a selection of his articles, lectures, and speeches. In 1913 he published a companion volume, *The Foundations of a National Drama*. In these works he wrote on all aspects of the theatre: the need for a national theatre; municipal theatres; cinema and its relation to the stage; drama as a branch of literature, not just as popular entertainment. He inveighed against what he saw as the inadequacies of the actor–manager system, despite the fact that he was dependent on it to produce his plays. He felt that the dramatist must have authority and command over his own work. He was passionately committed to the belief that a dramatist should be able to explore any important subject, and therefore played a prominent part in the move to abolish the lord chamberlain's censorship of plays. The final success of the campaign did not come until 1968.

In 1896 Jones finished one of his most controversial plays (and his own favourite): *Michael and his Lost Angel* (Lyceum Theatre, 15 January 1896). It was dogged by disaster. Johnston Forbes-Robertson presented it and engaged Mrs Patrick Campbell to play Audrie, the lost angel who seduces the priest Michael. Forbes-Robertson wanted Jones to change the title, as 'lost angel' was a euphemism for prostitute, and Mrs Campbell wanted 'profane' lines changed: Jones refused. She then, three days before opening night, walked out. Marion Terry took over the part; although a good actress, she did not possess Mrs Campbell's fire and personality. The play failed disastrously and closed after ten days. Jones's eldest son, Philip, died during the run of the play, and Jones was not aware of what was happening at the theatre, so was unable to prevent the closure. There then followed one of Jones's greatest successes, *The Liars* (Criterion Theatre, October 1898). This was a comedy, with Charles Wyndham as *raisonneur*; the play created a cynical and contemptuous picture of marriage in 'society', and mercilessly exposed the moral values, cruelties, and conventions of a group of people representative of a wide section of English life. Nevertheless, Jones's plays, with this exception and possibly that of *The Case of Rebellious Susan*, appear to subscribe to the social mores then current. Censorship was a powerful force. After three further failures came the last of Jones's box-office hits, *Mrs Dane's Defence* (Wyndham's Theatre, October 1900). The play deals with the same themes as *The Liars*, double standards and social duplicity, but not in a satiric vein.

After *Mrs Dane's Defence* Jones produced little that was outstanding in the theatre. However, *The Hypocrites* (Hudson Theatre, New York, 1906) was perhaps his most successful play, being strong in action and social protest. He was highly thought of in America and in 1907 received an honorary degree at Harvard, but the play did not succeed in London. Jones wrote several social comedies: *Whitewashing Julia* (Garrick Theatre, March 1903); *Dolly Reforming herself* (Haymarket Theatre, November 1905); and *Mary Goes First* (Playhouse, September 1913), which starred Marie Tempest. He wrote this play in Grasse, in the south of France, where he was a frequent visitor; he particularly liked Nice. But the year before this he discovered he had cancer and underwent a colostomy operation which left him a semi-invalid. Jones's last significant play was *The Lie* (New Theatre, October 1923). The lead, Eleanour, was played by Sybil Thorndike. It was an immense success, but was taken off to make room for Shaw's *Saint Joan*.

In the final decade of his life Jones, an ardent patriot, became embroiled in a bitter controversy with Shaw, who had been a great friend, and H. G. Wells. Although himself deeply influenced by socialist ideas, Jones considered their writings to be traitorously aiding the Germans in the First World War. He spent the last years of his life attacking Shaw and Wells in print; his increasing frailty and ill health in no way diluted the ferocity of his polemic. Despite his preoccupation with the controversy Jones also contributed to early cinema in England, eleven of his plays being filmed.

In 1926, his kidneys beginning to fail, Jones had a series of painful operations. As his wife had died in 1924, his daughter Doris, already living at his home at 19 Kidderpore Avenue, Hampstead, became his constant companion and secretary. He was cheered in his sickness by the fact that Macmillan published a four-volume edition of his works, but he never recovered his health, and died at home on 7 January 1929, of acute pneumonia. He was buried on 10 January in the Hampstead cemetery, Fortune Green Road, West Hampstead, London.

Jones was an excellent, workmanlike dramatist with a talent for structure and characterization, possessed of a fine comic gift, but no genius. He outlived his reputation and died an embittered man. Some of his plays would revive well, but his ideas on the role and duties of women, and his apparent identification with the mores of a certain kind of 'Victorianism', with its social hypocrisy and masculine supremacy and superiority, obscures the interest and 'actability' of many of his works. Although he was a leading playwright in his own time, his work was rarely acted after his heyday.

PENNY GRIFFIN

Sources D. A. Jones, *The life and letters of Henry Arthur Jones* (1930) • P. Griffin, *Arthur Wing Pinero and Henry Arthur Jones* (1991) • J. P. Wearing, 'Henry Arthur Jones: an annotated bibliography of writings about him', *English Literature in Transition, 1880–1920*, 22 (1979) • H. A. Jones, *The renascence of the English drama* (1895) • H. A. Jones, *The foundations of a national drama* (1913) • C. Hamilton, 'Introduction', *Representative plays of Henry Arthur Jones*, ed. C. Hamilton (1926) • R. Jackson, 'Introduction', *Plays by Henry Arthur Jones*, ed. R. Jackson (1982) • J. L. Fisher, '"The law of the father": sexual politics in the plays of Henry Arthur Jones and Arthur Wing Pinero', *Essays in Literature* (1989) • B. Wallis, 'Michael and his lost angel: archetypal conflict and Victorian life', *Victorian Newsletter*, 56 (autumn 1979), 20–26 [Fall 1979]

Archives Bodl. Oxf. • Col. U. • LUL • Ransom HRC, corresp. • U. Leeds, Brotherton L. | BL, corresp. with W. Archer, Add. MS 45292 • BL, corresp. with Macmillans, Add. MS 55013 • BL, corresp. with Society of Authors, Add. MS 56733 • Hove Central Library, Sussex, letters to Lady Wolseley on social matters • LUL, letters to James Stanley Little and M. H. Spielmann • Richmond Local Studies Library, London, Sladen MSS • U. Leeds, Brotherton L., letters to Bram Stoker • University of Chicago Library, letters to William Moys Thomas | FILM BFI, records of 11 films made

Likenesses W. Tittle, lithograph, 1924, NPG • A. Wolmark, pen-and-ink drawing, 1928, NPG • Barraud, woodburytype photograph, NPG; repro. in *The Theatre* (Sept 1886) • W. & D. Downey, woodburytype photograph, NPG; repro. in W. Downey and D. Downey, *The cabinet portrait gallery* (1892), vol. 3 • H. Furniss, pen-and-ink caricature, NPG • W. E. Hooper, photogravure plate, repro. in W. E. Hooper, ed., *The stage in the year 1900* (1901) • H. G. Riviere, portrait, priv. coll. • J. Russell & Sons, photograph, NPG • Spy [L. Ward], chromolithograph caricature, NPG; repro. in *VF* (2 April 1892) • W. Tittle, drawing, NPG; repro. in 'Portraits in pencil and pen', *Century*, 108 (1924) • photograph, repro. in 'Our omnibus box', *Theatre*, 8 (1886), facing p.132 • portrait, repro. in *Annals of New York Stage*, 16, Index to portraits (American Society of Theatre Research) • portraits, repro. in Jones, *Life and letters of Henry Arthur Jones*

Wealth at death £20,144 14s. 2d.: probate, 12 March 1929, *CGPLA Eng. & Wales*

Jones, Henry Bence (1813–1873), physician and chemist, was born on 31 December 1813 at Thorington Hall, Yoxford, Suffolk, the second son of Lieutenant-Colonel William Jones (1776–1843), 5th dragoon guards, of Lisselane, co. Cork, Ireland, and Theberton Hall, Saxmundham, Suffolk, and his wife, Matilda (1791–1869), daughter of the Revd Bence Bence (1747–1824) of Thorington Hall, Suffolk, rector of Beccles. William Bence *Jones was his elder brother, and they both assumed their mother's maiden name as a second surname. Henry was educated privately and at Harrow School, and in 1832 entered Trinity College, Cambridge. He graduated BA in 1836, MA in 1840, MB in 1845, and MD in 1849. On leaving Cambridge he studied medicine at St George's Hospital, London, and chemistry as a private pupil in Thomas Graham's laboratory at University College, London. In 1841 he went to Giessen to work at chemistry under Liebig. He became licentiate of the Royal College of Physicians in 1842, and FRCP in 1849, and was afterwards senior censor.

In 1842 Bence Jones married his cousin, Lady Millicent Acheson (d. 1887), daughter of the second earl of Gosford, and settled at 30 Lower Grosvenor Street, London. There were three sons and four daughters of the marriage.

Bence Jones was an accomplished physician, who acquired a large and remunerative practice. He was also an excellent chemist, who carried out important research on the applications of chemistry to pathology and medicine. In 1843 he analysed all the urinary stones in St George's Hospital Museum, and began to study the chemical composition of the urine in health and disease. He was elected assistant physician to St George's Hospital in 1845 and full physician in 1846, the year in which he also became a fellow of the Royal Society. He was elected to the council of the College of Chemistry (founded 1845) and became a friend of its director, A. W. Hofmann. In 1848 he discovered a protein in the urine of patients with multiple myeloma; related to the immunoglobulins, it was later called 'Bence Jones protein'.

In 1849 Bence Jones delivered a course of lectures entitled 'Animal chemistry in its application to stomach and renal diseases', which were published in the following year and at once made him a recognized authority on those classes of disease. His views on animal metabolism, based on Liebig's theories, were superseded, but his experimental work remained valuable. Its weakness lay in an uncritical application of the laws of chemistry to the complex phenomena of the human body.

In 1851 Bence Jones purchased a house at Folkestone, Kent, from which he made summer excursions to many European spas. After visiting Emil Du Bois-Reymond in Berlin he translated and edited his papers on electrophysiology. He also helped to secure John Tyndall's appointment as professor of natural philosophy at the Royal Institution in 1853. He was keenly interested in the advancement of science generally, and, while secretary of the Royal Institution (1860–72), devoted himself to making the newest scientific discoveries known to the public. He wrote a biographical account of the founder and early professors of the Royal Institution, and his *Life and Letters of Faraday* (2 vols., 1870) is a standard biography.

Bence Jones's broad interests and genial temperament made him well known and popular in society, but his closest friends were found among scientific men at home and abroad. As physician to many prominent Victorians, he assisted Florence Nightingale in her efforts to improve standards of public and hospital hygiene, and Charles West in founding the Great Ormond Street Hospital for Sick Children. After his resignation from St George's Hospital in 1862 his private practice and interests outside medicine expanded. In 1865 he was a member of the royal commission on the cattle plague and in the following year he was president of the chemical section at the British Association meetings in Nottingham. In the winter and spring of 1866–7 he was seriously ill with fluid on the chest and, having a weak heart, he never fully regained his strength. In 1870 he received an honorary DCL at Oxford. He died on 20 April 1873 at his home, 84 Brook Street, Grosvenor Square, London; he was buried at Kensal Green cemetery.   J. F. PAYNE, rev. N. G. COLEY

Sources A. B. Bence-Jones, *Henry Bence-Jones, M.D., F.R.S., 1813–1873, an autobiography with elucidations at later dates* (privately printed, 1929) · *The Lancet* (26 April 1873), 614–15 · *Medical Times and Gazette* (10 May 1873), 505–8 · [W. Odling], *JCS*, 27 (1874), 1201–2 · Burke, *Gen. GB* · Munk, *Roll* · Burke, *Gen. Ire.* (1976), 638–51 [Bence-Jones] · N. G. Coley, 'Henry Bence-Jones, MD, FRS, 1813–1873', *Notes and Records of the Royal Society*, 28 (1973–4), 31–56 · F. W. Putnam, 'Henry Bence Jones: the best chemical doctor in London', *Perspectives in Biology and Medicine*, 36 (1993), 565–79 · Venn, *Alum. Cant.*
Archives CUL, corresp. · Royal Institution of Great Britain, London, corresp. and papers
Likenesses G. Richmond, crayon drawing, 1865, Royal Institution of Great Britain, London · E. Edwards, photograph, 1868, Wellcome L. · C. Holl, stipple, pubd 1873 (after G. Richmond), BM · R. and E. Taylor, wood-engraving, 1873 (after S. T.), Wellcome L. · T. Woolner, bust, c.1873, Royal Institution of Great Britain, London · Maull & Polyblank, photograph, Wellcome L. · J. Steward & Co, photograph, Wellcome L.
Wealth at death under £50,000: probate, 13 May 1873, *CGPLA Eng. & Wales*

Jones, Henry Cadman (1818–1902), law reporter, was born on 28 June 1818 at New Church in Winwick, Lancashire, the eldest son of Joseph Jones, vicar of Winwick and later of Repton, Derbyshire, and his wife, Elizabeth Joanna Cooper of Derby. Educated privately, he entered Trinity College, Cambridge, in 1836, and graduated BA in 1841 as second wrangler and second Smith's prizeman. He was elected a fellow in the same year. Admitted to Lincoln's Inn on 7 June 1841, and called to the bar on 24 November 1845, he became a pupil first of the conveyancer Christie and then of Sir John Rolt.

Although his abilities were admired, however, Jones was too reserved to prosper greatly at the bar, and made his name instead as a reporter. From 1857 until 1865, when the official law reports were founded, he was associated with Sir John Peter De Gex in three successive series of chancery reports. He continued to report chancery appeals for the law reports until 1899. In 1860 with J. W. Smith he drafted the consolidated chancery orders and later with Sir Arthur Wilson the rules under the Judicature Acts of 1873 and 1875. He is said to have refused a colonial judgeship.

Of deep religious conviction, Jones actively engaged in the work of the Religious Tract Society and took part, with his fellow university student Sir George Stokes, in the proceedings of the Victoria Institute, founded for the discussion of Christian evidences. Much leisure was spent on an unpublished concordance to the Greek Testament. Jones married twice. On 4 September 1851 he married Anna Maria, daughter of Robert Steevens Harrison of Bourne Abbey, Lincolnshire; they had eight children. She died on 10 May 1873, and on 4 September 1879 he married Eliza, third daughter of the Revd Frederick Money of Offham, Kent. His 'handsome countenance and courtly bearing' (*Law Journal*) made Jones a noted figure in Lincoln's Inn for many years. Jones died at 6 St Matthew's Gardens, St Leonards, on 18 January 1902, and was buried in Repton churchyard. He was survived by his second wife, and by a son and four daughters from his first marriage.

C. E. A. BEDWELL, rev. PATRICK POLDEN

Sources *Law Times* (25 Jan 1902), 298 • *Law Journal* (25 Jan 1902), 54 • *The Times* (21 March 1902) • Venn, *Alum. Cant.* • J. Foster, *Men-at-the-bar: a biographical hand-list of the members of the various inns of court*, 2nd edn (1885) • W. P. Baildon, ed., *The records of the Honorable Society of Lincoln's Inn: admissions*, 2 vols. (1896) • J. Rolt, *Memoirs of Sir John Rolt* (1939) • W. T. S. Daniel, *The history and origin of the law reports* (1884) • *CGPLA Eng. & Wales* (1902) • private information (1912)
Likenesses E. U. Eddis, portrait; known to be in family possession in 1912 • T. C. Wageman, drawing, Trinity Cam.
Wealth at death £21,372 2s. 8d.: probate, 26 Feb 1902, *CGPLA Eng. & Wales*

Jones, Sir Henry Frank Harding (1906–1987), gas engineer and businessman, was born on 13 July 1906 at Gloucester Terrace, Hyde Park, London, the only son and eldest of four children of Frank Harding Jones, gas engineer and company director, of Housham Tye, Harlow, Essex, and his wife, Gertrude Octavia, daughter of Edmund Kimber, of Plumstead, Kent. He was educated at Harrow School, where he won the Baker prize for mathematics, and at Pembroke College, Cambridge, where in 1927 he gained first-class honours in the mechanical sciences tripos. He was later elected to an honorary fellowship of Pembroke College (1973).

On leaving Cambridge, Jones enrolled as a student member of the Institution of Civil Engineers and within two years had won the Miller prize for a paper on long-distance gas transmission. A fourth-generation gas engineer, he was articled to George Evetts, a prominent consulting engineer, and until the war intervened was mainly occupied in merging more than a hundred individual gas companies into more economic units.

In December 1934 he married (Elizabeth) Angela, daughter of Spencer James Langton, of Little Hadham, Hertfordshire. They had three sons and one daughter.

Called up in 1939, Jones served as an infantry lieutenant with the Essex regiment in France and Belgium. Following Dunkirk, he served in staff appointments in Britain, India, and Burma. Promoted staff captain in 1941, major in 1942, lieutenant-colonel in 1943, and brigadier in 1945, he took part in the Arakan campaign and was appointed MBE (military) in 1943. He returned from war service in 1945 and resumed his career in gas as a director of important gas companies, including the South Metropolitan Gas Company. When gas was nationalized in 1949, he was appointed as the first chairman of the East Midlands Gas Board. He was promoted as deputy chairman of the Gas Council in 1952, and became chairman in 1960.

On nationalization almost 1000 separate companies were taken into public ownership. The immediate need was to rationalize them within the structure of twelve area boards and to integrate production, which was dominated by increasingly uncompetitive coal carbonization. Gas sales were stagnant and many saw the attempt of the Gas Council to establish new process routes as merely delaying the inevitable decline. But in the space of a decade the industry achieved two remarkable technological revolutions: first a move to the production of town gas by the total gasification of oil, and then a more fundamental change to the distribution and direct utilization of natural gas with the consequential need for the conversion of all gas-using appliances. Behind this transformation lay massive and radical changes in organization and technology.

Jones had a vision of the future, and his unrivalled grasp of technical detail, coupled with his propensity for detailed planning, a skill honed in war, bred confidence and provided the necessary drive. With the courage to allow his technical staff to make huge investments in innovative facilities, he faced, with evident imperturbability and remarkable success, the pressures of Westminster and Whitehall. It was a great team effort under a determined and inspiring leader and laid the foundations of the modern gas industry. He retired on 31 December 1971.

A quiet man, modest, at times even self-effacing, Jones was possessed of a notable inner strength. Punctilious and meticulous, his habit of making a cool clinical assessment of every situation did not prevent him from being sensitive to others and warm and generous in his friendships. He was tall, spare, upright in carriage, and from his early thirties had the characteristic pure white hair of his family. He had great pride in his family and was devoted to his wife, of whom he took especial care during the latter years of his life when she became blind.

Knighted in 1956, and appointed KBE in 1965, Jones was elevated to GBE in 1972. President of the Institution of Gas Engineers in 1956–7, he was also a fellow of the institutions of Civil and Chemical Engineers and a founder fellow of the Fellowship of Engineering. He was awarded an honorary LLD by Leeds University (1967) and honorary doctorates of science by Leicester (1970) and Salford (1971) universities. He was a member of the royal commission on standards of conduct in public life (1974–6). A liveryman of the Clothworkers' Company since 1928, he was master in 1972–3. Jones died in Great Missenden on 9 October 1987 of stomach cancer and was buried at Weston Turville, Buckinghamshire, his main post-war home.

DENIS ROOKE, rev.

Sources T. I. Williams, *A history of the British gas industry* (1981) • *The Times* (13 Oct 1987) • *The Independent* (15 Oct 1987) • personal knowledge (1996) • private information (1996) • *CGPLA Eng. & Wales* (1987)
Wealth at death £103,855: probate, 21 Dec 1987, *CGPLA Eng. & Wales*

Jones, Henry James (1812–1891), inventor of self-raising flour, was born in Bristol and baptized there on 23 January 1813 at Broadmead Baptist Church, the youngest son of Robert Jones, a Bristol confectioner, and Hannah Jefferies. Members of the Jones family had been in the bakery and grocery business in Bristol from about 1808, at various addresses such as Broadmead, Castle Street, and St Augustines Parade.

Jones was married on 15 November 1838 to Anne Pride (1811/12–1883) at Llanfihangel Rogiet, Monmouthshire. Anne came from a well-known and long-established family, being the eldest daughter of Thomas Pride and Sarah Baker of Llanfihangel Rogiet, who had substantial land holdings in that area. At the time of his marriage Jones was listed as a farmer.

Henry and Anne Jones apparently remained in south Wales until after the births of their first two children, Mary Anne (1841–1904) and Ellen (b. 1844). Their first son, Henry, was born in 1845 in Bristol, where further children were born to them: Elizabeth in 1847 and William in 1855.

Henry continued in the family flour and bakery business at 36 and 37 Broadmead, Bristol. It flourished, and on 11 March 1845 he patented his self-raising flour. The recipe was kept secret, but was thought to have contained a blend of various flours and chemical compounds. Before that time the only raising agent used in bread had been yeast, which meant that it would not keep. This was a particular problem for soldiers and seamen away on long assignments, who were forced to consume bread and biscuits which were almost inedible. Jones was concerned that these men should have access to products which were wholesome and pure, and the new invention was championed by other concerned individuals, including Florence Nightingale. At first, conservative attitudes made it difficult for Jones to sell his new product; being convinced that it would be of general benefit, he advertised its advantages. He fought a legal battle over his patented flour with the Admiralty, which for ten years refused to acknowledge it, despite the fact that in the meantime Jones had received a royal warrant from Queen Victoria to supply her household with his products. In 1845 the captain of the steamship *Great Britain* declared that Jones's was the best bread that had ever been served on the ship. In an article in *The Lancet* of 6 June 1846, Jones Patent Flour was praised for its contribution to public health and to the daily comfort of the masses. Following its eventual acceptance by those in authority, the soldiers in the Crimean War were able to enjoy food of a quality similar to that supplied to the queen herself. The result was to revolutionize British baking.

Jones's flour bags were very distinctive with their bright yellow paper and bold blue ink. The early bags carried Henry Jones's portrait and his authenticating signature. He also used the symbol of a giraffe, with the slogan 'It towers over all'.

Among Jones's other achievements were his arrowroot biscuits, which too were produced in Bristol. Their taste and low cost made them very popular. However, they also involved Jones in a dispute, as a local chemist and maltster, a Mr Herapath, claimed to have been first in producing the arrowroot biscuit, an assertion which Jones vigorously contested. But Herapath was quick to praise Henry's subsequent invention of self-raising flour.

By the 1880s Jones had probably delegated the running of his business to his elder son, also named Henry, who was assisted by the younger son, William. Henry and Anne Jones retired to Caldicot, Monmouthshire, to the home of their daughter Mary Anne, who was by then the widow of Arthur Hillier of Caldicot Court. Henry remained active: the 1881 census records him as a farmer with 53 acres, employing three men.

Anne died on 30 July 1883; Henry lived on for a further eight years before dying, aged seventy-eight, on 12 July 1891. They were buried in the churchyard of St Mary's Church, Caldicot, together with their daughter Mary Anne, who died on 15 February 1904.

DOLORES E. POWELL

Sources Henry Jones patent information and correspondence, Bristol RO, ref. 29932 • census returns for Bristol, 1861, 1871, 1881 • IGI • indenture, 10 July 1895, Bristol RO • parish register, St Mary's Church, Caldicot, Monmouthshire, Gwent RO, Cwbran, D/Pa 4.30 [burial] • Matthews Street Directories, Bristol, Bristol Central Reference Archives, 1820, 1830, 1842, 1849, 1890 • K. Chivers, 'Henry Jones versus the admiralty', *History Today*, 10 (1960), 247–54 • *The Lancet* (6 June 1846) • Liveings, 'Bristol's many industries', scrapbook of cuttings, 1995, Bristol Central Library • M. I. Batten, *English windmills*, 1 (1930) • J. Reynolds, *Windmills and watermills* (1970) • *Pigots Directories* (1831–) • gravestone, St Mary's Church, Caldicot, Monmouthshire, churchyard
Archives Bristol RO, corresp. concerning patent
Likenesses portrait (*The inventor 1849*), repro. in Chivers, 'Henry Jones versus the admiralty', 247

Jones, Sir Henry Stuart- (1867–1939), classical scholar and lexicographer, the only child of Henry William Jones (1834–1909), vicar of St Andrew's Church, Ramsbottom, Lancashire, and his wife, Margaret Lawrance Baker, was born on 15 May 1867 at Moor Crescent, Hunslet, Leeds, where his father was then curate. The family traced its roots back to Cornwall rather than Wales. Stuart was his second forename, but after his marriage he and his wife generally prefixed it to their surname: when he was knighted in 1933 he legally assumed the name Stuart-Jones.

Early years Jones was educated at Rossall School in Lancashire, where he was a member of the house under the charge of the headmaster, Herbert Armitage James. The classical scholar George Chatterton Richards, Jones's contemporary at Oxford, recalled that 'James made him an accurate and industrious scholar; his lively mind did the rest' (Myres, 467). Three of his younger contemporaries at Rossall were, like him, to obtain scholarships to Balliol

College. Matriculating in 1886, he had a distinguished career at Oxford. He won the Hertford scholarship (1886) in his first term, obtained first classes in classical moderations (1888) and *literae humaniores* (1890), and additionally won the Ireland and Craven scholarships (1888), and the Gaisford prize for Greek prose (1890) with a Platonic dialogue. At Oxford he was introduced to archaeology, and specifically Greek vases, by Percy Gardner, who had been appointed as Lincoln and Merton professor of classical archaeology in 1887.

In 1890 Jones was elected by competitive examination to a non-official fellowship at Trinity College, Oxford, and, as Craven fellow and Derby scholar (1891), spent three years (1890–93) on classical studies in Italy and Greece. Two of these years (1890–91, 1892–3) were spent as a student at the British School at Athens, where Ernest A. Gardner was director, working on Greek pottery in museum collections at Athens. His research, 'Two vases by Phintias', was published in the *Journal of Hellenic Studies* (1891). Among his contemporaries at Athens was Eugénie Sellers, who caused a stir in her support for the German Wilhelm Dörpfeld against Gardner. In his second spell in Athens, Jones (who was afflicted by malaria) met J. L. Myres, who recalled, 'antiquities, dialects and folklore, Greek wines and card games, seemed all alike to him' (Myres, 469). The Derby scholarship allowed him to study in Italy for a year, and he also travelled to Berlin with G. C. Richards to study under Adolf Furtwängler and R. Kekulé.

Jones returned to Oxford and began tutorial work by taking pupils in classics at Trinity, and in ancient history at Exeter College, in succession to Henry Francis Pelham. In 1894, after his marriage in that year to Ileen, only child of Edwyn Henry Vaughan, a well-known Harrow housemaster and a brother of Charles John Vaughan, he was transferred to an official fellowship at Trinity, and became one of the three tutors in 1896. His lecturing focused on Greek rather than Roman history, as well as on Plato's *Republic*.

Stuart-Jones (as he was now named) developed a reputation as a scholar, and was known to be the author of many brilliant reviews, such as those of Robinson Ellis's *Noctes Manilianae* and R. C. Jebb's *Ajax* of Sophocles, in the *Oxford Magazine*, of which he was for a time review editor under Charles Cannan. His main publications continued to be in the field of classical archaeology: these included a study entitled 'The chest of Kypselos' in the *Journal of Hellenic Studies* (1894), which was to be reproduced in Sir James G. Frazer's *Pausanias* (1898), and a student handbook, *Select Passages from Ancient Writers Illustrative of the History of Greek Sculpture* (1895). He also worked on a revised text of Thucydides, which appeared in two parts (1898, 1900), for the Scriptorum Classicorum Bibliotheca Oxoniensis, projected by the Clarendon Press, which he thus inaugurated. The value of such work and of his teaching was widely recognized; and it was felt that, if a vacancy occurred in any of the chairs of Greek, Latin, or ancient history at Oxford, he would be a very strong candidate, and, for the Lincoln and Merton professorship of classical archaeology, a certain choice. However, a serious breakdown in his health

occurred, which meant that he had to end his college teaching. An opportunity arose in February 1903 when Gordon McNeil Rushforth had to resign as director of the newly established British School at Rome (then located in the Palazzo Odescalchi) owing to ill health. Stuart-Jones was offered the position, and Trinity supported him financially by granting him a research fellowship. His assistant director was Thomas Ashby, a former student of Francis J. Haverfield at Christ Church.

Roman history   Stuart-Jones initiated a project to catalogue the sculpture collections of the commune of Rome, a counterpart to that of the Deutsches Archäologisches Institut (German Archaeological Institute), which was making a study of the Vatican collection (*Skulpturen des Vaticanischen Museums*, 1903, 1908). In the autumn he was joined by the Cambridge-educated Alan J. B. Wace, who had just completed a year at the British School at Athens studying Hellenistic sculpture. In Rome, Stuart-Jones consolidated his profound knowledge of Roman history and antiquities, displayed in his principal books and articles over the next twenty years. His contribution to classical archaeology was acknowledged by his election in 1904 as a full member of the Kaiserliches Deutsches Archäologisches Institut (German Imperial Archaeological Institute). The sculpture project was to appear in two volumes, edited by Stuart-Jones, *A Catalogue of the Ancient Sculptures Preserved in the Municipal Collections of Rome*, 1: *The Sculptures of the Museo Capitolino* (1912) and 2: *The Sculptures of the Palazzo Dei Conservatori* (1926).

Although Stuart-Jones had been appointed director for three years, ill health forced him to resign in February 1905, though he returned to Rome during winter 1909–10 to continue this work. In May 1905 he resumed his tutorship at Trinity College, but left Oxford in December for a country home at Saundersfoot, near Tenby in Pembrokeshire, south-west Wales, revisiting Oxford to examine in *literae humaniores* in 1909, 1910, and 1911, and during the war in 1916 and 1917, and again in 1919. He was probably the last man to examine in this school as well as in classical honour moderations (1900 and 1901). In 1908 he acted as one of the Oxford representatives at the International Historical Congress in Berlin, where he read a paper, 'The historical interpretation of the reliefs of Trajan's column', which was subsequently published in the *Papers of the British School at Rome* (1910).

Between 1906 and 1912 Stuart-Jones published some of his most significant work. His principal books on Roman history included *The Roman Empire, BC 29–AD 476* in the Story of the Nations series (1908) and *Companion to Roman History* (1912). F. J. Haverfield described the *Companion* as 'extraordinarily accurate and extraordinarily up to date … by a first-rate archaeologist who can speak with full authority and full knowledge' (*Journal of Roman Studies*, 1912, 118). He also dealt with allied subjects in the *Quarterly Review*, the *Times Literary Supplement*, and many learned periodicals, as well as contributing entries and revisions for the eleventh edition of the *Encyclopaedia Britannica* (1910–11). He reviewed volumes on Roman history for the

English Historical Review, pursued an interest in the catacombs and early Christian monuments at Rome, publishing a series of articles in the *Journal of Theological Studies* (1906, 1908, 1912), and collaborated with Haverfield on a study of Romano-British sculpture for the *Journal of Roman Studies* (1912).

Greek–English lexicon and chair of ancient history As his health strengthened, Stuart-Jones looked for an opportunity to return to Oxford. In 1910 he was a candidate for the Wykeham professorship of ancient history; Myres was appointed. From 1911 he served as a member of council for the newly established Society for the Promotion of Roman Studies, and in 1913 was elected a vice-president. In the autumn of 1911 Stuart-Jones returned to Oxford, invited by the Clarendon Press and assisted by his election to a research fellowship at Trinity College, to undertake the long-wanted revision of Liddell and Scott's *Greek–English Lexicon*, then in its eighth edition (1897). In this great task, not only his wide knowledge of Greek, but his practical ability and tact, were conspicuous. Putting aside the earlier suggestions for a *Thesaurus linguae Graecae* made in 1903, a project which would have extended over several lifetimes, Stuart-Jones at once organized a remarkable body of specialists as voluntary collaborators. The work benefited from the finds of new texts provided by archaeologists through inscriptions and papyri, and also incorporated comparatively unexplored writers. The new edition was kept within reasonable bounds as to size, print, and dates of issue in parts, by an ingenious scheme for abbreviation of references, and by drastic omission of ecclesiastical and Byzantine words. In 1915 Stuart-Jones was elected both as a vice-president of the Society for the Promotion of Hellenic Studies, and as a fellow of the British Academy; he served as a member of the latter's council in 1918.

During the First World War both Stuart-Jones and Roderick McKenzie, a former scholar of Trinity College and future assistant on the *Lexicon*, had offered their services to the Foreign Office and had undertaken confidential work in London and Geneva, in which their knowledge of eastern European languages was of great value. In 1919 Stuart-Jones was elected unanimously to the Camden professorship of ancient history in succession to his friend Haverfield. Wace supported the application, writing

> [Stuart-Jones] devotes himself whole-heartedly to his pupils; he can infect them with his own enthusiasm for his subject, while the inspiration of his personality coupled with his wonderful memory and his keen intellect can never fail to win the affection of his class.   (letter in Brasenose College archive)

This chair, to which was annexed a fellowship at Brasenose College, was by custom appropriated to Roman history. His inaugural lecture was published as *Fresh Light on Roman Bureaucracy* (1920). Frederic G. Kenyon had hoped that he would organize an edition of the *Inscriptions of Roman Britain*, thereby continuing Haverfield's earlier work on the epigraphy of the province. At Oxford, Stuart-Jones lectured mainly on Roman provincial bureaucracy, which was being illuminated by the finds of Egyptian

papyri. This interest is reflected in articles in the *Journal of Roman Studies* (1926, 1927). He also contributed several chapters on Roman history to the *Cambridge Ancient History* (vol. 7, 1928; vol. 10, 1934), partly in collaboration with Professor Hugh Last, and three chapters in J. A. Hammerton's *Universal History of the World* (1928).

The work on the *Greek–English Lexicon* also continued, with Roderick McKenzie as an extremely efficient assistant editor from 1920, and the first part of the *Lexicon* was published in 1925. This commitment may explain why Stuart-Jones concentrated on writing articles rather than books in this period. From 1921 he served usefully on the hebdomadal council, gaining administrative experience, but at the cost of overwork, and, as he was constitutionally unable to take anything quietly, some over-excitement.

Aberystwyth Stuart-Jones continued to have a home at Saundersfoot, where he was based during the vacations, and where his wife preferred to live. So in 1927 he became a candidate for the principalship of the University College of Wales at Aberystwyth; he had already expressed an interest in the position in summer 1919. His election was due as much to his impressive personality as to his eminence as a scholar; it was also a landmark, given Stuart-Jones's lack of a Welsh pedigree and his Anglican commitments. His seven years of administration in Aberystwyth were sound although not sensational. He dealt with the status and salaries of the non-professorial staff, with the extension of the library and other new college buildings, and with the establishment of courses on arts and crafts at the intermediate and subsidiary stages for the BA degree. The undergraduates were said to have formed the opinion that for Stuart-Jones 'valour was the better part of discretion' (Myres, 475). An able letter from him in *The Times* (11 July 1932) may be said to have produced the benefaction from Sir Julian Cahn for the development of the agricultural and plant-breeding station on 300 acres of hill land.

Stuart-Jones learned Welsh and served on the committees of a number of Welsh institutions, including the council of St David's College, Lampeter (then an Anglican theological college), Trinity College, Carmarthen, and the National Library of Wales. He also served as vice-chancellor of the federal University of Wales in 1929 and 1930. He was an active member of the Church in Wales which had been disestablished in 1920. Through the diocese of St David's, he served assiduously as a lay member of the governing body of the Church in Wales from 1929, first for the archdeaconry of Cardigan (reflecting his Aberystwyth links), and then from 1936 for the archdeaconry of St David's (from his home in Pembrokeshire).

In 1931 his wife, to whom he was devoted, died. They had one son, Edwyn, who served in the navy. Stuart-Jones continued as principal at Aberystwyth, and was knighted in 1933. In spite of ill health he agreed to remain in office, but in March 1934 he was obliged on medical advice to resign at very short notice.

For his seventieth birthday Stuart-Jones was presented with a special volume of the *Journal of Roman Studies* (1937) by the Society for the Promotion of Roman Studies, of which he had been president from 1926 to 1929. This contained a series of papers by British and foreign scholars as well as a full bibliography of his publications. He was elected to honorary fellowships at Brasenose (1928), Trinity (1935), and Balliol (1936) colleges, and received honorary degrees from the universities of Oxford, Wales, Leeds, and Liverpool. The work on the *Lexicon* continued especially after his retirement from Aberystwyth. McKenzie died suddenly in June 1937, which was a very serious blow to the project. By 1939 Stuart-Jones had seen the last (tenth) part of the *Lexicon* through the press, and had the necessary *Supplement of Addenda* well in hand, in spite of failing health. He died at his home, 3 Rock Terrace, Tenby, on 29 June 1939, and was buried with his wife at St Issell's churchyard, Saundersfoot, on 3 July.

As a classical scholar Stuart-Jones was polymathic, with a ready and retentive memory, and a special flair for ascertaining and estimating in a very short time all the important points in any new publication on his subjects. He was a competent linguist and a lucid expositor, and among general interests he was fond of music. The bibliography of his books, articles, and signed reviews occupies nearly eight pages of the Festschrift mentioned above but, as the prefatory note states, 'no single volume of any periodical could adequately represent all his activities and interests', and it is difficult to say to which branch of classical study his contributions, other than the *Greek Lexicon*, were most important and illuminating.

H. E. D. BLAKISTON, *rev.* DAVID GILL

Sources *The Times* (30 June 1939) · J. L. M[yres], 'Sir Henry Stuart Jones, 1867–1939', *PBA*, 26 (1940), 467–78 · *Trinity College Report* (1938–9), 2 · 'Sir Henry Stuart-Jones', *Brazen Nose*, 7 (1939–44), 15–17 · *Annual Report of the National Library of Wales* (1938–9), 11 · *DWB* · I. Elliott, ed., *The Balliol College register, 1833–1933*, 2nd edn (privately printed, Oxford, 1934) · T. F. Higham, *Dr Blakiston recalled: memories of an Oxford 'character' the Rev. Herbert Edward Blakiston, D.D. President of Trinity College, 1907–1938* (1967) · T. P. Wiseman, *A short history of the British School at Rome* (1990) · E. L. Ellis, *The University College of Wales, Aberystwyth, 1872–1972* (1972) · personal knowledge (1949) · *CGPLA Eng. & Wales* (1939)
Archives BL, letters to H. Idris Bell, Add. MS 59520, fols. 156–212 · BL, readers reports from Macmillan & Co., Add. MSS 55986–55988
Likenesses W. Stoneman, photograph, 1918, NPG · photograph, repro. in Myres, 'Sir Henry Stuart Jones'
Wealth at death £8332 2s. 1d.: probate, 2 Aug 1939, *CGPLA Eng. & Wales*

Jones, Herbert [H] (1940–1982), army officer, was born in Putney on 14 May 1940, the eldest of three sons of Herbert Jones, artist (1888–1957), and his wife, Olwen Pritchard (1902–1990), nurse. He was educated at St Peter's School, Seaford (1948–53), and Eton College (1953–8) before going to the Royal Military Academy, Sandhurst, as an officer cadet in September 1958. In July 1960 he was commissioned into the Devon and Dorset regiment. On 20 June 1964 he married Sara de Upaugh (*b.* 1941), a secretary and later a magistrate. They had two sons: David (*b.* 1966) and Rupert (*b.* 1969). Since boyhood Jones had never wanted any career except the army and had developed an enthusiasm for all things military, including war gaming. He was also a keen sportsman with a passion for physical fitness.

He rowed for Eton, sailed, skied, and enjoyed motor-racing while in the army.

After five years with the Devon and Dorset regiment Jones was seconded to the 3rd battalion, the Parachute regiment, where he commanded the mortar platoon. The next fourteen years saw the normal sequence of regimental or staff appointments—adjutant of his battalion, junior staff officer at the headquarters of the UK land forces, a student at the Camberley Staff College, company commander, brigade major in Northern Ireland (which earned him an MBE), and instructor at the School of Infantry, Warminster. Promoted lieutenant-colonel in June 1979 he took up a senior staff post back at UK land forces and was appointed OBE for his part in planning the introduction of a peace-keeping force into Zimbabwe. In April 1981 he achieved his ultimate ambition when he was appointed commanding officer of the 2nd battalion, the Parachute regiment—'2 Para'.

Jones, who disliked being called Herbert, preferring his nickname of H, moulded 2 Para into a formidable fighting unit with a zest for soldiering that mirrored his own. He was a fervent advocate of fitness and shooting, and was described as a person who did not recognize compromise. He was also an impatient man, quick to anger when thwarted. On exercises he was always to be found in front, often with the leading section, always pushing to keep things moving. On several such occasions, exercise umpires had ruled him 'dead'. There is no doubt that the way he subsequently died was typical of the man.

When Britain decided to send an expeditionary force to retake the Falkland Islands in the south Atlantic, which had been invaded by Argentina in 1982, Jones abandoned a skiing holiday to rush to the Ministry of Defence to persuade the authorities that 2 Para must go. He succeeded; his battalion became part of the 3rd commando brigade, an élite formation under Brigadier Julian Thompson, Royal Marines. On 28 May 1982 Jones led 2 Para in an attack on the Argentinian position at Goose Green. It was the first land battle of the campaign, but one that Thompson had been ordered from London to carry out for political reasons—against his professional advice. After a difficult 3000 metre night advance the battalion was held up in daylight by a strong enemy position on a ridge covering the settlement of Goose Green. Jones was concerned with the delay to A company, which was pinned down in a gorse gully. He went forward under fire to join them. For over an hour he tried to organize artillery and mortar fire support to get the attack moving, becoming increasingly frustrated when his efforts were unavailing. Finally, he stood up, yelled 'Follow me!', and dashed to his right up a re-entrant to try to get behind the enemy trenches. Unfortunately few heard his shout apart from his bodyguard, Sergeant Norman, who followed him round. Jones was shot from behind as he made a courageous solo charge on an enemy trench, dying soon afterwards. Within fifteen minutes the position was taken. For his gallantry and leadership Jones was awarded the Victoria Cross.

Whether he was, at that moment, doing the job of a commanding officer is arguable, but there was no doubt as to the personal courage, disregard for danger, and forceful leadership that won Jones the Victoria Cross, which is kept in the National Army Museum, London. He is buried at Blue Beach military cemetery, Falkland Islands. MARK ADKIN

Sources M. Adkin, *Goose Green* (1992) · M. Adkin, *The last eleven?* (1991) · J. Thompson, *No picnic* (1985) · J. Frost, *2 Para Falklands* (1983) · M. Arthur, *Above all courage* (1985) · private information (2004) [S. Jones] · the parachute regiment
Archives FILM BFI NFTVA, *Reputations*, Channel 4, 3 Aug 1998
Likenesses photograph, repro. in Adkin, *Last eleven*, facing p. 147
Wealth at death £187,908: probate, 15 July 1982, CGPLA Eng. & Wales

Jones, Sir Horace (1819–1887), architect, was born on 20 May 1819 at 15 Size Lane, Bucklersbury, London, the son of David Jones, solicitor, and Sarah Lydia Shephard. He was articled to John Wallen, architect and surveyor, of 16 Aldermanbury, and then studied ancient architecture in Italy and Greece in 1841–2. In 1843 he started practice as an architect at 16 Furnival's Inn, Holborn, initially in partnership with Arthur Ebden Johnson. His designs over the next eighteen years included the British and Irish Magnetic Telegraph Company office in Threadneedle Street (exhibited at the RA, 1859), the Sovereign Assurance office in Piccadilly (RA, 1857), a shop for Marshall and Snelgrove in Oxford Street, the Surrey Music Hall (RA, 1856), Cardiff old town-hall (all destr.), and Caversham Park, near Reading (now the BBC external monitoring service building). He was surveyor for the duke of Buckingham's Tufnell Park estate, for the Barnard estate, the Bethnal Green estate, and others.

Jones's election on 26 February 1864 as architect and surveyor to the City of London was a turning point in his career. He designed a series of renowned London markets, beginning with Smithfield, built in three sections: the central meat market (1866–7), the poultry and provision market (1873–5; burnt, 1958), and the fruit and vegetable market (1879–83). He converted the Deptford Dockyard into a foreign cattle market (1871), reconstructed the wholesale fish market at Billingsgate (1874–8; converted into offices, 1985–9), and rebuilt the retail Leadenhall market (1880–81). He also built several City police stations, of which only 1 College Hill (1885–6; converted) survives, and municipal housing, including St Andrew's House (1874) in Charterhouse Street. He completed the City Lunatic Asylum at Dartford in 1864. At the Guildhall he designed a new roof in 1864–8, a library and museum in 1870–72, described by Sir Nikolaus Pevsner as 'rock-faced, Gothic and gloomy' (Pevsner, *City of London*, 192), and the new council chamber in 1883–4 (destr. 1946). He prepared the Griffin memorial to mark the site of Temple Bar (1880). In conjunction with the structural engineer Sir John Wolfe-Barry he designed Tower Bridge. Erected mostly after his death, in 1886–94, it became one of London's most famous landmarks. His last important work was the Guildhall School of Music (1885–7) on the Victoria Embankment.

On 15 April 1875 Jones married Ann Elizabeth, daughter of John Patch, a barrister. They had one daughter. He was active in the Institute of British Architects, of which he became an associate in 1842, a fellow in 1858, and was later president in 1882–4. He was also an enthusiastic freemason, and from 1882 until his death was grand superintendent of works. On 30 July 1886 he was knighted. He died at home at 30 Devonshire Place, London, on 21 May 1887, and was buried in Norwood cemetery on 27 May. A portrait of Jones by W. W. Ouless was exhibited in the Royal Academy exhibition in 1887.

G. C. BOASE, rev. VALERIE SCOTT

Sources *London: the City of London*, Pevsner (1997) · *Dir. Brit. archs.* · J. Freeman, 'Sir Horace Jones, 1819–1887', *Victorian Society Annual* (1981), 45–55 · *Journal of Proceedings of the Royal Institute of British Architects*, new ser., 3 (1886–7), 330–31, 368, 370–73 [incl. list of works] · *The Builder*, 52 (1887), 799 · J. Lever, ed., *Catalogue of the drawings collection of the Royal Institute of British Architects: G–K* (1973), 164 · CGPLA Eng. & Wales (1887)
Archives RIBA, drawings collection · RIBA BAL, nomination papers and biography file
Likenesses W. W. Ouless, portrait, exh. RA 1887 · S. A. Walker, photograph, c.1887, NPG · F. Holl, oils, RIBA; repro. in J. A. Gotch, ed., *The growth and work of the Royal Institute of British Architects, 1834–1934* [1934] · R. T., wood-engraving (after photograph by S. A. Walker), NPG; repro. in *ILN* (4 June 1887)
Wealth at death £20,018 11s. 10d.: resworn probate, Jan 1889, CGPLA Eng. & Wales (1887)

Jones, Hugh (1508–1574), bishop of Llandaff, is traditionally said to have come from the same Gower family as Sir Hugh *Johnys of Llandimôr. He was rector of Tredynog in Monmouthshire by 1535, and to judge from the ages of his descendants by his eldest son he was already married at that time (as was common among Welsh clergy). He was admitted BCL at New Inn Hall, Oxford, in 1541, having possibly returned to study on the death of his first wife. His studies were rewarded with the additional parish of Almondsbury, Gloucestershire, and admitted him to the group of élite clergy who managed the diocese of Llandaff in the absence of bishop and archdeacon. He was personal chaplain to John ap Jevan, treasurer of the cathedral, and was bequeathed books by Henry Morgan, another canon of the cathedral.

Jones appears to have married again c.1550, when clerical marriage was legalized under Edward VI; his second wife was Anne Henson. Clerical marriage was so common in Wales that the clamp-down during the Marian restoration made it impossible to provide clergy for all the Welsh parishes. Clerics who were prepared to put aside their wives and make a token repentance were allowed to move (and even to exchange) parishes. Some were followed by their wives after a decent lapse of time; if they were identified the process had to begin again. This may explain why Jones was appointed to Llanfihangel Crucornau, Monmouthshire, in 1554, to Llanrothal, Herefordshire, in 1556, and eventually to Banwell, Somerset, in 1558. He was back in Tredynog by 1560, resident and preaching.

Hugh Jones was proposed as bishop of Llandaff in 1566, three years after the death of his predecessor Anthony Kitchin. His consecration in May 1566 was opposed by Richard Davies of St David's on the grounds of his intellectual and spiritual insufficiency, but Matthew Parker and Edmund Grindal both approved of him. Jones was reputedly the first Welsh-speaking bishop in his diocese for 300 years. His return to the privy council's inquiry in 1570 suggests he was a diligent pastoral bishop who regularly travelled through his diocese, preaching and dealing with local issues. The policies of tolerance followed by Jones and his predecessor, Kitchin, appear to have been justified by the state of the diocese. He was able to report that all were attending church and few refused communion—which is quite credible in the period before *Regnans in excelsis* (the papal bull deposing Elizabeth I), even in an area where recusancy was to be a problem. The main difficulty Jones identified in his report was the lack of preachers. The problem was ultimately one of resources, and here Jones laid the blame unflinchingly at the door of the local gentry and the queen and council.

Jones died at the episcopal palace in Matharn and was buried in the church there on 15 November 1574. No monumental inscription survives. His will mentions only his surviving wife and the children of his second marriage, but his descendants from his first marriage are in his pedigree in Bradney's *History of Monmouthshire*.

MADELEINE GRAY

Sources M. Gray, 'The cloister and the hearth: Anthony Kitchin and Hugh Jones, two Reformation bishops of Llandaff', *Journal of Welsh Religious History*, 3 (1995), 15–34 • Emden, *Oxf.*, vol. 4 • J. G. Jones, 'The Reformation bishops of Llandaff, 1558–1601', *Morgannwg*, 32 (1989), 38–69 • G. Williams, 'Wales and the reign of Queen Mary I', *Welsh History Review / Cylchgrawn Hanes Cymru*, 10 (1980–81), 334–58 • J. A. Bradney, *A history of Monmouthshire*, 4/1 (1933); facs. edn (1994) • DNB
Wealth at death est. just under £200 moveable property; no land: will

Jones, Hugh (d. 1782), ballad writer, was for most of his life associated with Llangwm in Denbighshire (and known as Huw Jones o Llangwm), but little or nothing is known about his origins. He married, but the name of his wife is unknown. References in his works suggest he had at least a son and a daughter.

Jones's literary output is known to have included five interludes, and four of these, commissioned by unknown groups of players and composed between 1760 and 1770, have survived. One, *Y Brenin Dafydd*, was written jointly with Siôn Cadwaladr. The lost interlude was based on the story of Myfanwy of Castell Dinas Brân. However, there is no evidence that Hugh Jones himself, unlike his contemporary Twm o'r Nant, acted in interludes. He would have received payment for his works, and he also profited by independently printing and selling his interludes throughout north Wales. He was imprisoned on two occasions, once, it seems, for non-payment of a printing debt. *Protestant a neilltuwr*, composed about 1769–70, appeared in 1783, following the author's death. Several references are made in his interludes to the custom of learning English and to the sending of children to schools across the border to acquire that language.

Although described as 'a comon ballad singer', Hugh Jones was one of the most prolific ballad writers in eighteenth-century Wales, and 100 or so of his ballads survive. These are based on traditional themes, and were composed mainly between 1749 and 1780. His ballads on drunkenness, for example, testify to the inventiveness of the ballad singers and their ability to rework the same themes. One presents a debate between a drunkard and his conscience, while another records the conversation between an impoverished drunkard and an innkeeper's wife. A conversation between a drunkard and his caring wife forms the basis of a third, and in another a cuckoo reprimands the drunkard as he leaves the tavern, early one Sunday morning, and advises him to change his ways.

Hugh Jones published in 1759 an anthology of ballads, composed by himself and his peers, entitled *Dewisol ganiadau yr oes hon*. The first part, however, was dedicated to the works of Goronwy Owen, Ieuan Fardd (Evan Evans), William Wynn, and others, the neo-classicists of the eighteenth century whose compositions were patterned on the works of the *cywyddwyr* of the later middle ages. In justifying the dual constitution of his volume, Hugh Jones expressed his hope that the light entertainment of the second part would lead young, uneducated (in the poetical sense) readers in the direction of the real substance found in the first.

Dewisol ganiadau was followed in 1763 by *Diddanwch teuluaidd*. The well-known writer and antiquary Lewis Morris claimed in his preface that the volume was published by Hugh Jones 'for his own benefit', and there is no doubt that the project was his own. Inspired by the success of *Dewisol ganiadau*, he approached Lewis Morris with a request for a collection of his poems for inclusion in his anthology, and it was Jones who saw to the printing of the proposals and the poems, and to the distribution of the material once published. And profit he did; the London printer, William Roberts, was never paid for his work.

Diddanwch teuluaidd was nevertheless very much a Cymmrodorion Society publication. The poets whose works were published were society members who actively sought subscribers, and Richard Morris, brother of Lewis, corrected the proofs. Since 1758 the society had contemplated publishing Goronwy Owen's work, but no progress had been made, and Lewis Morris's *Tlysau yr hen oesoedd* (1735) had long been abandoned. Although distrustful of Hugh Jones, the Cymmrodorion had no option but to co-operate with him, and the works of Goronwy Owen, Lewis Morris, and others were made available, thanks to the efforts of this humble farm labourer from Llangwm.

Jones died in December 1782, and was buried at Efenechdid, Denbighshire, on 29 December. According to the *Dictionary of Welsh Biography* 'his literary labours did a great deal to kindle and keep burning the interest of the country people in the Welsh language' (DWB).

A. CYNFAEL LAKE

Sources T. Parry, *Baledi'r ddeunawfed ganrif* (1935) • T. Parry, 'Yr hen ryfeddod o Langwm', in T. Parry, *Y Casglwr* (1982) • C. Ashton, *Hanes llenyddiaeth Gymreig o 1651 o. C. hyd 1850* [1893], 230–47 • *The letters of Lewis, Richard, William and John Morris of Anglesey*, ed. J. H. Davies, 2 vols. (1907–9) • R. Griffith, *Deuddeg o feirdd y Berwyn* (1910), 97–101 • J. H. Davies, ed., *A bibliography of Welsh ballads printed in the 18th century* (1911) [1908–11] • J. E. Lloyd, R. T. Jenkins, and W. L.

Davies, eds., *Y bywgraffiadur Cymreig hyd 1940* (1953) • Bishop's transcripts of parish register, diocese of St Asaph, Efenechdid • *DWB*

Jones, Inigo (1573–1652), architect and theatre designer, was born in London on 15 July 1573 and baptized on 29 July 1573 at St Bartholomew-the-Less, London, the eldest of the four surviving children of Inigo Jones (*d.* 1597), clothworker of the City of London. The origin of the unusual forename shared by father and son remains a puzzle. It is not known to be Welsh, nor can it have been of direct Spanish origin, for the father, in spite of the assertion of the *Dictionary of National Biography*, seems not to have been a Catholic but to have conformed to the established church.

Education and first visit to Italy   Virtually nothing of Jones's life is documented until he was over thirty. The tradition transmitted by Christopher Wren that he was apprenticed to a joiner in St Paul's Churchyard is given plausibility by the regular use in his notes of traditional English rather than Italian words for mouldings, and seems to be confirmed by Ben Jonson's caricature of him as the joiner In-and-In Medlay in *A Tale of a Tub*. The consistent secretary hand of his earliest manuscript notes suggests that he received a sound basic schooling, but his sometimes bizarrely phonetic spelling reveals its limitations. In intellectual matters he must have been largely self-taught.

Jones was in London in April 1597, when he proved his father's will. The next time he can be certainly traced is in June 1603, when he was paid £10 as a 'picture maker' by Edward Manners, fifth earl of Rutland. By 1605 he was referred to as a 'great traveller' (Cunningham, 6), and it must have been during this six-year period about 1600 that he spent enough time in Italy to become fluent in the language. His copy of Andrea Palladio's *Quattro libri dell'architettura* (1601) bears in manuscript the date 1601 and the price 'doi docati', indicating that he may have bought it in Italy as soon as it was reprinted. His subsequent masque inventions suggest that he was familiar with the printed descriptions of Bernardo Buontalenti's spectacular productions at the Medici court in Florence, but he could even have seen one, *Il rapimento de Cefalo*, staged in October 1600. According to John Webb—Jones's pupil but not an entirely reliable witness for these early years—he also visited Denmark. The most likely occasion for this would have been in connection with the visit of the fifth earl of Rutland from June to October 1603, to confer the Garter on King Christian IV in Copenhagen. Rutland's payment to Jones in June may even have been for services rendered at the start of the visit.

In spite of Jones's long stay in Italy at an impressionable age and his subsequent devotion to Italian culture, there is no evidence that he was tempted to Catholicism. The only explicit contemporary comment about his religious inclinations, made many years later (in 1636), admittedly by a Catholic, calls him 'L'Architetto il quale è di questi Puritani, o per dir meglio senza Religione' ('The architect, who is one of those Puritans, or rather people without religion'; Wittkower, 'Puritanissimo fiero', 51). The fact that he served as MP and JP must indicate that he conformed to

Inigo Jones (1573–1652), by Sir Anthony Van Dyck

the Anglican religion. So Wren's repeated statement that he died a Catholic must be treated with caution.

The early court entertainments, 1605–1613   Inigo Jones's first employment at court was as designer of the sets and costumes for *The Masque of Blackness* on twelfth night 1605. This production inaugurated the series of masques promoted by the queen, Anne of Denmark, in which she herself danced together with her ladies, and in which both her sons, Prince Henry and Prince Charles, appeared. Through the poetic invention of the librettist Ben Jonson and the stage machinery devised by Jones, the masque, a quasi-theatrical presentation, medieval in origin, enacted by tradition on twelfth night before and in honour of the monarchs, was transformed and given new life. Poet and stage designer were equally valued: Jonson and Jones received the same fee, normally £40 for their 'invention' for each production. Jones's innovations were also applied to other forms of court entertainment—plays and the stylized, armoured fights known as tilts and barriers.

Masques were normally performed only once, at Whitehall Palace, in the hall or the Banqueting House. Their costumes and scenic effects are recorded in descriptions supplied in many of the librettos subsequently printed, in comments of members of the audience, and in over 400 preparatory drawings in Jones's hand (now at Chatsworth House, Derbyshire). Costume designs for the masquers and their attendants for several of the early masques show that Jones combined features from contemporary court dress with pseudo-antique or exotic features, particularly head-dresses, copied or adapted from costume books, especially Cesare Vecellio's *Habiti antichi et moderni* (1598) and Robert Boissard's *Mascarades* (1597).

The set for *The Masque of Blackness* introduced three fundamental components of the Jonesian theatre: a layout within the rectangular space consisting of a raised stage at the lower end, concealed at first behind a curtain painted with scenery, and a dais for the king at the centre of the upper end; scenery painted in perspective so that it would have its full effect only when seen by the centrally positioned king; and machinery to achieve motion, in this case a large shell in which sat the masquers, carried forward on what appeared to be billows.

Jones's next opportunity came at the end of August 1605, when James I visited Oxford. In his honour the scholars of the university staged three Latin plays (a satire, a tragedy, and a comedy), and a play in English before the queen and Prince Henry. The court provided the designers and craftsmen, who fitted up the hall of Christ Church for the purpose, including Jones, who was in charge of staging the plays. Contemporary accounts make it clear that perspective was again employed, and moving clouds overhead. The stage was partly inclined, and scene changes were effected by means of 'periaktoi', painted cloths forming triangles mounted on spindles. These enabled complete scene changes from play to play and three changes of scenery during the course of the tragedy. This was Jones's first employment of the Vitruvian device which, as he later noted, 'I have often yoused in masques and comedies' (annotation in D. Barbaro, *I dieci libri Dell'architettura di M. Vitruvio*, 1567, 256, Chatsworth House). For the staging of the twelfth night masque of 1606, *Hymenaei*, Jones introduced further novelties. There was a turning machine (*machina versatilis*) and an upper- as well as lower-level stage. An effect of clouds was contrived, with the masquers sitting within them and conveyed by them gently to the ground.

The earliest drawing for a stage set to survive relates to an entertainment put on in May 1608 by Robert Cecil, the newly created earl of Salisbury, in his house in the Strand. This quick sketch shows a rock and part of an archway and does not imply any very sophisticated machinery. The next important production was *The Masque of Queens*, performed on 2 February 1609. Ben Jonson's unusually specific text, accounts for payments, and Jones's drawing for the main stage feature, the 'House of Fame', make it possible to visualize the production in some detail. There was the usual 4 foot high stage on trestles. The 'ugly hell' before which the antimasque took place must have been a painted curtain, fitfully lit by smoky torches up to the roof. At a blast of loud music the curtain was removed to reveal a proscenium arch decorated with figures of Honour and Virtue, and the stage occupied by the House of Fame, a two-storeyed structure in which sat the masquers, the twelve queens, on a *machina versatilis*: this throne turned to reveal the winged figure of Fame. After Fame had spoken, the masquers descended onto the stage through large double doors. They then mounted chariots, designed by Jones, before descending to dance in the normal way.

For the next major masque, *Tethys' Festival*, performed on 5 June 1610 to celebrate the creation of Prince Henry as

prince of Wales, no set design survives. The published libretto by Samuel Daniel, however, has extensive descriptions of the scenery. The masquers were seated in five niches 'of modern architecture' described in great detail, largely, it seems, in Jones's own words. The two other performances mounted in honour of Prince Henry also involved elaborately architectural sets. For *Prince Henry's Barriers*, the occasion of the prince's first bearing of arms, two drawings by Jones survive, depicting recognizable ancient Roman ruins, but also a semi-Gothic pavilion from which the prince and his companions emerged. The prince's masque *Oberon*, performed on 1 January 1611, employed a new device, of moveable shutters (*scena ductilis*), so that rocks opened to reveal Oberon's palace, rather than revolving. A two-level stage was also clearly used.

The queen's masque performed in the following month, *Love Freed from Ignorance and Folly*, had two scenes, as usual: one a cliff, the other a prison, as can be deduced from Jones's libretto. A drawing by Jones for the prison shows that the masquers were seated above it within a cloud on turning machines shaped like hillocks. This is the same principle as in *The Masque of Queens*, but with three machines instead of one.

The first phase of Jones's theatrical career terminated in February 1613 with two exceptionally lavish performances on successive days. His collaborators—Thomas Campion in *The Lord's Masque*, staged to celebrate the marriage of Princess Elizabeth to the elector palatine, and George Chapman for the masque presented by the Middle Temple and Lincoln's Inn—both included fulsome descriptions of the spectacle in their published texts. Yet none of Jones's designs for their scenery has been identified. In both he employed the usual two-level staging to allow the masquers to appear among clouds. For the inns of court Jones had to design, besides the masque sets, two triumphal cars to convey the masquers down Fleet Street and the Strand to Whitehall Palace.

Early intellectual contacts and the surveyorship to Henry, prince of Wales In this first decade of his artistic activity Jones seems to have established himself in intellectual circles in London. In December 1606 Edmund Bolton gave him a copy of G. F. Bordino's *De rebus praeclare gestis a Sixto V* (1588) inscribed 'Inigo Jonesio suo per quem spes est, Statuariam, Plasticen, Architecturam, Picturam, Mimisim, omnemque veterum elegantiarum laudem trans Alpes, in Angliam nostram aliquando irrepturas' ('To his friend Inigo Jones, through whom there is hope that sculpture, modelling, architecture, painting, acting, and all that is praiseworthy in the arts of the ancients will soon find their way across the Alps into our England'). Thomas Coryate, the traveller, whose *Crudities* appeared in 1611 with fifty-four commendatory verses edited by Jonson, including one by Jones, held a 'philosophical feast' at the Mitre tavern in Fleet Street on 11 September 1610 for eleven friends. Jones was among them, described by Coryate as 'Nec indoctus nec profanus Ignatius architectus' ('architect Inigo Jones, neither unlearned nor ignorant').

During this period Jones embarked on a steady architectural self-education using Palladio, Serlio, and Barbaro's edition of Vitruvius as his guides. His first architectural designs date from 1608–9. Highly finished elevations survive, one for the façade of the New Exchange in the Strand built in 1609 by the earl of Salisbury, the other for a classical crowning feature for the thirteenth-century crossing tower of St Paul's Cathedral, another project in which Salisbury was closely involved. Both designs reveal Jones's familiarity with the plates in Serlio's *Architettura* and Palladio's *Quattro libri dell'architettura*, and even with Antonio da Sangallo's model for St Peter's, as engraved by Antonio Labacco; but they also demonstrate his inexperience in their awkward disparities of scale. The former may have influenced what was built; the latter was not implemented.

In 1609 Jones visited France. Officially he acted as a bearer of letters to Paris but evidence among his annotations and drawings demonstrates that he travelled to Provence, where he saw the Pont du Gard and Roman antiquities at Arles and Nîmes. He also visited the château of Chambord. The earliest surviving structure based on a design by Jones shows evidence of this experience: the monument to Lady Cotton erected after 1608 in the church of St Chad, Norton in Hales, Shropshire, has a garlanded sarcophagus which seems to be based on a Roman sarcophagus at Arles.

In May 1610, the month before he was invested as prince of Wales, Prince Henry signed a book listing the offices in his household and their proposed holders. The officers of his works were headed by Inigo Jones, as surveyor. Jones served in this role, at the rate of 3*s.* per day, from 13 January 1611 until the prince's death on 6 November 1612.

However, it seems that over these two years the post involved little if any architectural work at the prince's palaces, St James's and Richmond. Some of what was done remained the responsibility of the office of the king's works, and from June 1611 the prince discussed ambitious architectural projects for Richmond not with Jones but with a newly arrived Florentine, Constantino de' Servi, who from March 1612 was granted an annuity of £200, almost four times Jones's salary. The prince's death, therefore, brought to a premature end what may have been for Jones an unsatisfactory episode. But his position at court was soon to be secured, for on 18 April 1613 he was granted the reversion of the surveyorship of the king's works.

Second visit to Italy The grant of the reversion came as Jones was preparing to leave England, one of thirty-six members of the entourage of Thomas Howard, fourteenth earl of Arundel, who was escorting Princess Elizabeth, the daughter of James I, to Heidelberg to meet her new husband, the elector palatine. Arundel had decided that, once his official duties were done, he and his wife would cross the Alps for an extended private visit to Italy. One of the four who accompanied them was Jones, who, as Dudley Carleton, the ambassador in Venice, noted, 'will be of best use to him (by reason of his language and experience) in these parts' (Orrell, 8). The visit, which extended for just over a year, provided Jones with the chance to re-examine Italian architecture ancient and modern in the knowledge that he was about to become the king's architect. He seems to have remained with the Arundels for much, but not all, of the time. The itinerary can be followed in some detail from the earl's correspondence, from ambassadorial reports, and from dated notes in Jones's copy of the *Quattro libri*.

The trip began with two weeks of intensive sightseeing in Venice in early September 1613. Here Jones made notes on Palladio's unfinished convent of the Carità. On 23 and 24 September he was in Vicenza, where he examined the Teatro Olimpico with its fixed perspective scenery, and noted that 'thear is no apparitions of nugolo [cloud]' (Allsopp, vol. 1, flyleaf). He also managed to gain entry to Palladio's Villa Rotonda, and took notes on its rich plasterwork decoration and its four open-well staircases. On 1 October Arundel's party was in Bologna on its way to Florence, and by 19 October it had established itself in Siena. Jones next appears in Rome, on 2 January 1614. From March to May the party was in Naples, where Jones greatly admired the temple of Castor and Pollux. By 31 May Jones was back in Rome, engaged in a close examination of the Pantheon. Other buildings he particularly observed in Rome were the temple of Fortuna Virilis and Bramante's circular Tempietto at San Pietro in Montorio. In June the party began to move north, which gave Jones an opportunity to see the temples at Tivoli and Trevi; but during the first half of August, while Arundel was in Genoa, Jones spent a further two weeks in the Veneto. Here he met the elderly Vincenzo Scamozzi, Palladio's former pupil, and discussed various technical points with him. He studied the Carità again, more analytically. In Vicenza he examined all Palladio's palaces, and his Loggia del Capitaniato, and made a critical study of Scamozzi's Palazzo Trissino. Of Palladio's villas he could visit only those closest to the city, at Quinto and Lisiera. Presumably he subsequently rejoined the Arundels, who after a fortnight's delay in Paris reached England in November.

The site notes which Jones made in his copy of the *Quattro libri* regularly indicate discrepancies between the published woodcuts and the buildings themselves, and also materials used and constructional details. There are a few value judgements, such as his analysis of the Palazzo Thiene's rustication, which show the subtlety of his observation. In January and February 1615 Jones went through the volume again and jotted down a wide range of generalizations based on what he had seen during the previous year. This was the time when, in his only surviving independent notebook, he composed his most elaborate theoretical statement on architecture, in which a well-designed building externally 'Sollid, proporsionable according to the rulles, masculine and unaffected' but with varied and composed internal ornaments, is compared to a wise man who 'carrieth a graviti in Publicke Places … y[e]t inwardly hath his Immaginacy set free' (Harris and Higgott, 56).

It is thanks to the piety of his pupil and deputy, John Webb, that the greater part of Jones's library has survived (mainly the forty-six volumes at Worcester College,

Oxford), together with the masque drawings already mentioned, about 100 architectural designs, and numerous drawings by Palladio. These last were acquired by Jones either in Italy in 1613 or shortly before that in London from Sir Henry Wotton, the former ambassador in Venice.

The books number about fifty, and include not only architectural treatises by Vitruvius (Barbaro's edition of 1567), Alberti, Serlio, Palladio, Vignola, and others, Giorgio Vasari's *Le vite de' piu eccellenti pittori, scultori, e architettori* (1568), and G. P. Lomazzo's treatise on the visual arts *Trattato dell'arte della pittura, scoltura, ed architettura*, but also works on fortification and mathematics, Greek and Roman history, and philosophy, together with guidebooks to major Italian cities. All are in Italian, with the exception of the already mentioned volume presented by Edmund Bolton, which has a Latin text, and two books in French: Philibert de L'Orme's architectural treatise and the *Histories* of Polybius. Most of the books had been published in the sixteenth century, but Jones acquired several new publications during his working life, most importantly Scamozzi's *L'idea dell'architettura universale*, obtained in 1617, two years after its publication.

Jones routinely annotated his books, making marginal translations and, in those that he studied most closely, independent comments. Occasionally he dated his notes, and the development of his handwriting over the decades of his active note taking, from the first years of the century to about 1640, makes it possible to assign broad dates to many other notes, and so relate them to the preoccupations of his professional career.

Surveyor of the king's works On 1 October 1615, at the death of Simon Basil, the incumbent surveyor of the king's works, Jones succeeded to the post by virtue of the reversion which he had been granted two-and-a-half years previously. He thereby became the head of a sizeable government department. He held the post for twenty-seven years. Beneath him were the comptroller, paymaster, purveyor and chief clerk, eight clerks (seven of whom had responsibility for particular palaces), and eleven master craftsmen. The office of works had been reorganized by Basil, and with Jones at its head it seems to have run smoothly. Indeed a writer in 1667 claimed that during Charles I's reign 'there was … scarcely any one office in his Mats Court of greater reputation both for able officers, good conduct, frugality of expence, and sure payment, then the office of his works' (Summerson, 'Surveyorship', 131). As surveyor, Jones received an annual salary of approximately £200, and he occupied a house in Scotland Yard, one of several built there by Basil.

The surveyor's duties comprised the maintenance in good structural condition of the king's palaces and other royal buildings, and the design and erection, as necessary, of new ones. By the time of Jones's surveyorship the years of James's greatest extravagance in building were over, but during the last ten years of the reign Jones had several opportunities to realize his ideas about a new, more rigorous classical architecture.

Between 1615 and 1617 Jones supervised the building at Newmarket of stables and other service buildings, perhaps still to Basil's design. His first important opportunity came in 1616, when he was commissioned by the queen to design a pleasure house at Greenwich Palace to replace the gateway which controlled access from the privy garden of the palace, across the Greenwich to Woolwich road and into the royal park to the south. He solved the problem by setting one half of the building in the garden and the other half in the park, linked by an upper level bridge-room across the road. Notwithstanding this plan, he conceived the building as an Italianate villa, and may even have taken the basic plan-form from the celebrated Medici villa of Poggio a Caiano, near Florence. Jones was paid for two designs, and several preliminary drawings survive; but little seems to have been built before work stopped in 1618; it was not completed until the 1630s.

Jones's new architectural idiom first became apparent in two structures erected in 1617–18. At the Prince's Buttery at St James's Palace he experimented with classical detailing in cut brickwork, and at Oatlands Palace he built for Anne of Denmark a lofty pedimented stone gateway into the vineyard, enriched with rough rustication. Neither of these structures survived beyond the seventeenth century. A third short-lived but important early royal work was the prince's lodging at Newmarket, of 1619. Two preliminary designs by Jones have been identified for a seven-bay, two-storeyed façade: one Palladian in character, the other reproportioned and crowned by a steep hipped roof in which are set tall pedimented dormer windows of French character. What was built seems to have been a reduced version of this second design, only five bays wide. The prince's lodging was Jones's first essay in the hipped-roof box type of house which was to become the dominant formula for house design throughout southern and midland England until almost the end of the seventeenth century. It is possible that the lodgings built at Whitehall Palace for George Villiers, marquess of Buckingham, in 1619–21 were a second, much more prominent, example of this formula. Both were destroyed, unrecorded, before the end of the century.

The other building erected by Jones at Whitehall Palace, the Banqueting House, was his most important royal work and still stands. It replaced a building little more than a decade old which burnt down in January 1619. So important was the Banqueting House to James I as the setting for the most significant public ceremonies of the court—including the production of masques—that he ordered immediate reconstruction. Jones, having worked in 1617 on the design for a similar free-standing great room for the Star Chamber, was able to evolve the concept and details of his scheme without delay and work started on the new building in April 1619. It was ready for use in 1622. Externally it derives from the town palaces by Palladio and Scamozzi which Jones had examined in Vicenza. The rusticated walls and superimposed orders have a sculptural quality quite new in English classical architecture. The present Portland stone facing is an early-nineteenth-century replacement of the original stonework, which was of Oxfordshire and Northamptonshire stone as well as Portland and must have created a subtle polychromatic effect. The interior is a single great space, a double cube in volume, the walls of the room treated with superimposed orders which relate to the exterior composition but also reflect Palladio's reconstructions of antique room types. The flat beamed ceiling, a geometricized version of Venetian ceilings, provided fields for paintings, probably envisaged from the beginning, and commissioned from Rubens in 1629 and supplied in 1635.

The other royal building to Jones's design which survives in central London is the chapel for Catholic worship at St James's Palace. It was begun in 1623, when there was the prospect that Charles, prince of Wales, would marry the infanta of Spain; it was completed from 1625, when, as king, he married the French princess, Henrietta Maria. The exterior is deliberately austere, the walls rendered and lined out to look like masonry, only the quoins and dressings of Portland stone. The simple block cornice, however, is derived from the upper cornice of the Pantheon, and Jones clearly intended that the interior of the chapel should evoke a Roman temple. It is covered by a segmental timber vault coffered on the pattern given by Palladio of the vaults in the temple of Venus and Rome. Again the space conforms to simple geometrical proportions, its length twice its breadth and twice the height of the vault. A grand tripartite 'Serliana' window in the east wall floods the chapel with light.

At the same time, in 1623–5, Jones remodelled the interior of the Tudor chapel at Greenwich, for protestant worship. This involved painting the walls with 'sondry workes of architecture' and the construction of a columned front to the royal closet, but nothing is known of the design's details. Another lost scheme of internal decoration was the covering of the House of Lords in 1623–4 with a plaster tunnel vault. Views taken before its destruction in 1823 show that it was painted with another antique coffer pattern. The closing commission of James's reign for the office of works was the construction of a timber and plaster hearse in Westminster Abbey for the king's lying in state. Jones's surviving design shows that it was a remarkable adaptation of a domed papal catafalque—engravings of those for Sixtus V (1591) and Paul V (1623) provided specific models—classicized to relate it to Bramante's Tempietto, so that it embodied harmonious proportions. It also evoked ancient imperial burial practices, as did the funeral oration by John Williams, bishop of Lincoln.

Towards the modernization of London's architecture, 1617–1629 In the first decade of his surveyorship, therefore, Jones had been presented with a series of important architectural commissions through which he was able to bring his ideas on architectural design to maturity and master the technicalities of building on a large scale. For visitors to London, however, the novelty of Jones's idiom was equally apparent in minor works carried out for private patrons. The most important of these was the brick façade crowned by a pedimented gable for Sir Fulke Greville's house in Holborn, Jones's reinterpretation in a classical idiom of the traditional urban gabled façade. The Italianate iron window balcony or 'pergola' set up on the front of

Sir Edward Cecil's house about 1617 was much imitated, as even more so was the 'Italian' timber casement window fitted at Arundel House in the Strand. This became the model for the standard window type in England until the adoption of the sash-window at the end of the seventeenth century. Another eye-catching feature of Arundel House was the handsome pedimented gateway into the garden, one of several erected for various patrons about 1619–23. Of these the only one to survive is that erected in 1621 at Chelsea for Lionel Cranfield, moved to the garden of Lord Burlington's Chiswick Villa in 1738. Close analysis of it has revealed consistent deviations from simple proportions in its details, exemplifying Jones's concept of 'varying with reason'.

The close acquaintance forged in Italy between Jones and the earl and countess of Arundel developed into long-term patronage and personal friendship after their return to Britain. In 1615 Jones was involved in negotiating the purchase of works of art for the earl and in the redecoration of the house in Greenwich which he had inherited from his uncle the earl of Northampton. By 1617 Jones had become a pivotal member of Arundel's household, entrusted, in the event of the earl's death, with the care of his wife and sons as well as with the task of designing a commemorative monument. In 1621 Jones became member of parliament for Shoreham, one of the parliamentary seats controlled by the earl.

The most important public activity in which Jones and Arundel were associated was the commission to control building in and around London. Royal attempts to prevent the erection of buildings on new foundation dated back to 1580. In a series of proclamations James I introduced the concept that new buildings should be an ornament to the city, principally by being constructed not of timber but of brick and stone. A new, more powerful commission was set up in 1615. Arundel and Jones were first involved in November 1618 in a special commission to promote the laying out of Lincoln's Inn Fields, for which Jones was instructed to prepare a plan. Nothing came of this, but by 1620 both were involved in the more general activities of the commission. The proclamation of 1619, which set out for the first time detailed guidelines for the storey heights and wall thicknesses of new-built houses, was presumably based on advice from Jones. The new commission appointed by Charles I within months of his accession in 1625 had Arundel's name at its head, and included that of Jones. From 1629 Jones acted as the expert member of sub-committees of the commission to advise the privy council in particular cases.

Masques and plays, 1617–1640 After Jones's return from Italy in 1614, the series of twelfth night masques did not resume until 1617. Thereafter he was involved in a production each January until the end of the reign of James I, except in 1624, when the masque was cancelled. He also designed the masque mounted in June 1620 at Greenwich Palace to mark the king's birthday. The normal venue, however, continued to be Whitehall: masques were staged in the Banqueting House of 1607 until its destruction by fire days after the twelfth night masque of 1619, then for three years in the Tudor great hall, and from 1623 in Jones's new Banqueting House.

Throughout the decade Jones's collaborator was Ben Jonson, with the exception of the masques of 1619 and 1621, for which neither poet's name nor text survives. For Jonson this was the period when his masque texts reached their greatest sophistication and wit; however, it was also a time when strains in the relationship between the two men became apparent. Whatever clash of personality there may have been between them, what was fundamentally at issue was their competing claims to the invention of the masques. Jonson's texts acknowledge Jones's contribution only erratically. Jones is not named until the king's birthday masque in 1620, where the names of the 'inventors' are given as Inigo Jones and Ben Jonson, in that order. Jonson's text of *The Masque of Augurs* (1622) states 'The invention was divided betwixt Master Jones and me', and further 'The Scene … was wholly his, and worthy his place of the Kings Surveyor and Architect, full of noble observation of antiquity, and high presentment' (Orgel and Strong, 333). The following year, by contrast, Jonson did not name Jones and barely mentioned the sets, and in the masque of 1624, *Neptune's Triumph for the Return of Albion*, he compounded the omission by introducing the character of the cook, whose first speech shows that he is meant as a satire on Jones.

Descriptions of staging in the printed texts are so rare that it is difficult to identify surviving drawings of this period. Nevertheless, it is clear that it was at this time that Jones devised the principal elements of his mature scenic presentations. From 1617 he began to model his staging on Serlio's tragic, comic, and satiric scenes, discussed and illustrated in book 2 of the *Architettura*, and on the engravings after Giulio Parigi's scenery for Florentine *intermedi* (musico-dramatic intervals performed between acts). These, together, supplied the information which enabled Jones to devise his characteristic shallow stage, with side shutters creating a continuous perspective setting and a rear 'standing scene', with scene changes effected by a *machina ductilis* operating in front of the standing scene. Parigi also illustrated apparitions of chariot-borne figures in the sky, which Jones now found more convincing ways to achieve. The proscenium arch became a standard feature, both emphasizing the illusionistic character of what lay behind it, and providing a decorative and emblematic border to the scene. For this too Jones undoubtedly had a print beside him, Jerôme Bols's chiaroscuro woodcut of 1589, which also shows the low stage with steps cut into its front face, a format which Jones regularly used to allow the masquers to descend to the dancing floor.

All these elements, and also cloud-borne masquers, are found together for the first time in the evocative pencil sketch identified by John Webb as *The Colledge of Augures*, intended for *The Masque of Augurs* of 1622. This masque is also significant as the first of several presenting real scenes familiar to the audience. In the following year the masque *Time Vindicated to himself and to his Honours*, the first staged in Jones's new Banqueting House, had three scenes, the first of which was 'a prospective of Whitehall,

with the Banqueting House', and for this Jones's squared-up preparatory drawing survives.

Little is known about the masques of the early years in the reign of Charles I. The only production for which Jones certainly made designs was the pastoral by Honorat de Bueil, seigneur de Racan, *Artenice*, staged in the hall of Somerset House at Shrovetide 1626, in which, notoriously, Queen Henrietta Maria and her ladies were actors. Jones's set design is strongly reminiscent of Serlio's satiric scene.

For the next play in which the queen took part, Walter Montagu's *The Shepherd's Paradise*, performed on 9 January 1633, numerous drawings survive. They include a measured plan of the theatre constructed for the purpose in the Paved Court at Somerset House, showing in detail how the scenery worked. There were eight changes of scene. Similar, even more explicit, visual evidence survives for the sets for the third court pastoral, *Florimène*, acted by a French company in the hall at Whitehall on the king's birthday, 21 December 1635. Jones provided sets for other plays in the mid-1630s. Those staged in the hall at Christ Church on the occasion of the visit of the king and queen to Oxford in September 1636 apparently caused some puzzlement: one of the spectators described the side flats and the entries between them as 'much resembling the desks or studies in a Library'. However, his further comment that 'The said partitions they could draw in and out at their pleasure upon a sudden, and thrust out new in their places' is the first definite evidence of side flats which were movable (A. Wood, *History and Antiquities of the University of Oxford*, vol. 2, book 1, 408–9).

The principal theatrical preoccupation for Jones in the 1630s was the final series of court masques. The purpose of these masques, presented by the king to the queen or vice versa, was quasi-political, a Platonic idealization of the policy which enabled Charles to rule without parliament and a celebration of the chaste love of the royal pair. The first two masques, *Love's Triumph through Callipolis* (performed on twelfth night) and *Chloridia* (at Shrovetide 1631), were the joint invention of Jonson and Jones. The text of *Chloridia* gives full descriptions of the scenes, providing incidentally the first clear evidence of Jones's use of a fly gallery. Even though both texts use the authorship formula 'The inventors; Ben Jonson, Inigo Jones', Jones felt that his contribution was inadequately acknowledged, and the collaboration finally broke down in acrimony. Thereafter Jonson wrote no more masque texts, and Jones took the entire 'invention' upon himself, in collaboration with a sequence of more or less complaisant librettists.

Jones made the two masques mounted in 1632 both a spectacular display of his stagecraft and a manifesto of his concept of the visual arts as carriers of meaning. The king's masque *Albion's Triumph*, with Charles I in the role of Albanactus, was acted out behind a proscenium arch against which stood figures of Theory and Practice, 'showing that by these two all works of architecture and ingining have their perfection' (Orgel and Strong, 2.454). There were as many as five complete changes of scene, all powerfully architectural, the first four antique, the last, in a telling association, the palace of Whitehall itself with part of the City of London in the distance. *Tempe Restored*, the queen's Shrovetide masque, by contrast, made do with only two scenes, but introduced the most ambitious manoeuvres so far of apparitions involving the descents and ascents of cloud machines, and dramatic lighting effects.

In February 1634 two more masques were presented. The first, *The Triumph of Peace*, was a sumptuous show of loyalty by the four inns of court after the scandal surrounding the publication of William Prynne's pamphlet against plays *Histriomastix* (1633). The spectacular procession was managed by Jones, as well as the usual stage sets and costumes. The king's masque *Coelum Britannicum*, performed a fortnight later, was recognized then and is still acknowledged as artistically the most satisfactory of the masques of the 1630s, in which the richness of Thomas Carew's verses matched the wonderful effects achieved by Jones in his scenic transformations.

The last masque presented in the Banqueting House at Whitehall was the queen's Shrovetide masque of 1635, *The Temple of Love*, which had an Indian theme. As soon as Rubens's great canvases 'figuring the acts of King James of happy memory' (I. Jones, *Britannia triumphans*, 1637, 9–10) had been fixed into the ceiling of the Banqueting House, Charles I forbade the continuing performance of masques and plays there. There was therefore a three-year hiatus in masque production until at the end of 1637 the king ordered the construction of a new timber Masquing House in the courtyard at Whitehall Palace. This seems to have provided an identical internal space to the Banqueting House, a double cube of 55 feet. It was in this building that Jones's last three masques were staged.

Britannia triumphans, the king's twelfth night masque performed on 17 January 1638, *Luminalia*, the ensuing queen's Shrovetide masque, and *Salmacida spolia*, the king's and queen's masque performed in January and repeated in February 1640, used all the previously perfected devices for scene changes, lighting effects, and carrying actors and masquers on clouds through the air, and used them with unprecedented versatility and daring. The surviving drawings for costumes and sets must constitute the great majority of those produced by Jones and his fair-copyists and, together with the detailed descriptions in the printed librettos, they enable these masques to be very fully visualized. The plan and section in John Webb's hand of the stage and scenery for *Salmacida spolia* demonstrate the exact working of pulleys, winches, and movable wings and shutters.

In taking responsibility for inventing the masques of the 1630s Jones probably consulted the king himself. The allusions in *Britannia triumphans* to the ship money crisis, and the representation in *Salmacida spolia* of the king's resignation in the face of the thoughtlessness and hostility of the people, could hardly have been introduced without the highest authority. On the other hand, Jones clearly worked under great time pressure in these productions. The librettos of *Tempe Restored* and *Luminalia* are lifted

respectively from a French and a Florentine court entertainment. For the sets Jones became heavily dependent on the engravings of Giulio Parigi's Florentine *intermedi*, of 1608, 1625, and even 1637. Even the most apparently poetical and imaginative scenes turn out to be copied or compiled from prints after, for example, Adam Elsheimer, Bril, or Veronese. On the costumes, however, effort was not skimped: for the antimasque costumes Jones turned regularly to pattern books, Jacques Callot's *Balli di sfessani* and *Capricci di varie figure* in particular, but for the masquers' costumes, above all for the queen's, Jones always made detailed sketches which were worked up by assistants. A note on his design for Henrietta Maria's dress for *Chloridia* shows that he took the precaution of consulting the queen over the cut and the colours, while making clear to her his own preferences.

Surveyorship of the works, 1625–1643 Under Charles I royal building was almost entirely concentrated on the queen's palaces; indeed from 1631 Jones received a salary of £20 a year as the queen's surveyor. The two most important works were completions of initiatives begun in the previous reign. Construction of the Queen's House, Greenwich, was resumed in 1630; its north front bears the date 1635, but the decoration of the interior was barely complete when work stopped in 1640.

When first built, the Queen's House must have looked even more starkly unfamiliar than the Banqueting House. From both the palace garden and the park it appeared as a plain balustraded rectangle, its lower storey rusticated, the *piano nobile* above given tall, vertically proportioned windows with barely enriched frames. The recessed portico on the park side, with an Ionic order derived from the temple of Concord in Rome, provided a viewing platform for the queen and her ladies to watch the hunting. Inside, the plan of the Queen's House was equally revolutionary, breaking with entrenched tradition. The hall in the centre of the north block is a cube, with mid-height balustraded gallery and massively beamed ceiling, in the idiom of the Banqueting House. The circular open-well staircase, with stone steps and metal balustrade, is another novelty, modelled on those Jones had seen at the Villa Rotonda and the Carità. The enrichment of the other rooms incorporated those 'composed ornaments' which Jones had recommended as appropriate for interiors. Little remains *in situ*, but several of Jones's drawings for chimney-pieces survive, as does one actual chimney-piece (now at Charlton House, Greenwich), which is almost a line-for-line copy of a design in Jean Barbet's *Livre d'architecture* (1633). So the composed ornaments were not all of Jones's own composition.

The palace for Henrietta Maria which received most attention was Somerset House. Here the major work was the construction in 1630–35 of a second chapel for Catholic worship. Though incorporating some of the fabric of a former tennis court and oriented north–south, the chapel nevertheless was internally of Jones's preferred double-cube proportion. The ceiling was of the flat, beamed type. Its most remarkable feature was the two-storeyed screen to the royal pew. This incorporated, over

Doric columns, a frieze of heads and reversed consoles inspired by a Hellenistic fragment in the earl of Arundel's collection—composed ornaments in the antique spirit. Within the palace Jones remodelled or created two richly decorated cabinets and a gallery with a pergola. In the garden a new river landing stage and stair were constructed (1628–31) and two fountains (1636–7). Jones's design for one of these shows him again gathering ideas from continental engravings. Parts of this fountain survive, incorporated in the Diana Fountain in Bushy Park, Middlesex. Jones also designed improvements in the 1630s to the queen's apartments at Oatlands Palace and to the garden there, and internal decoration for her at Wimbledon House in 1640–41.

Two more directly antique-inspired royal structures were executed in this period. A gallery was formed in the garden at St James's Palace in 1629–30 to house some of the antique sculptures newly acquired by the king as part of the Mantua collection. According to John Webb in the *Vindication of Stone-Heng* (1665), Jones designed this in imitation of the Tuscan atrium of the Romans, with the roof-slope extending so far beyond the supporting columns that there was space for the king to ride the length of the gallery under cover. Also in 1629–30, the octagonal cockpit at Whitehall was converted into a theatre, Jones's only attempt to create a fixed, columned set like the ancient Roman *frons scenae*. The king's dream of rebuilding Whitehall Palace to outdo Philip II of Spain's Escorial was, however, realized only on paper. The most elaborate of several schemes drawn by John Webb probably represents Jones's design conceived about 1638, when fund-raising to build the palace was under consideration.

Covent Garden and St Paul's Cathedral The two major architectural commissions of the 1630s which allowed Jones to develop his ideas about the proper vocabulary for modern buildings most fully did not come to him as surveyor of the king's works. The development by Francis Russell, fourth earl of Bedford, of his Covent Garden estate in 1629–35 was carried out, as is now known, with the approval of the king, in spite of the regulations against building in London on new foundations. Jones was involved throughout, from the devising of the site plan to the selection and provision of building materials, though the executant architect for some or all of the houses was Isaac de Caus. The design of both the terraces of houses and the church was revolutionary.

The enclosing of a rectangular space by terraces of handsome but identical houses built above arcaded walks was a concept which had been realized in several Italian cities in the sixteenth century, and recently in Paris in the place des Vosges. John Evelyn thought that the piazza d'Arme at Leghorn, where the porticoed cathedral stands in the centre of one of the short sides, was Jones's particular model. The fact that the south side of Covent Garden was occupied not by a terrace but by the wall of the earl's garden did not invalidate the comparison, though it was considered a blemish by some contemporaries.

The church of Covent Garden, built in 1631–3 and dedicated to St Paul, was provided by Bedford in response to concerns about overcrowding at St Martin-in-the-Fields. But the fact that the church was begun on a reverse orientation, with the entrance from the square at the east end, demonstrated its heterodox nature. Jones's decision to design the church as an embodiment of the Vitruvian Tuscan temple, in defiance of every Renaissance convention, gave him an opportunity to realize in brick and stone a type of ancient temple which existed only in the words of Vitruvius. The two stout, widely spaced Tuscan columns of the portico, that stand in line with the pilasters of the end walls of the church, may owe much to Scamozzi's illustration of the Tuscan portico, but Jones himself noted that the deep timber eaves were an experiment in the interpretation of a Vitruvian technical term. The rusticated flanking gateways which gave access to the churchyard, and the treatment of the terrace façades with pilaster strips rising the full height of the house-fronts above rusticated arcades, can all be interpreted as Tuscan too, so that the whole scheme was, as Sir John Summerson has argued, 'a comprehensive essay in the Tuscan mood' (Summerson, 'Lecture on a master mind', 179). Of the original buildings only the portico of the church and its east wall survive; the central doorway was blocked when the building was reoriented, before it could be brought into use. The gateways were accurately reconstructed in 1995–8, and Bedford Chambers (1877–9) is an enlarged pastiche of the terrace design. So something is still conveyed of the gravity and grandeur of Jones's scheme.

The long needed repair of St Paul's Cathedral was at last inaugurated in 1631 by William Laud as bishop of London. A determined fund-raising campaign, sustained even after Laud was translated to Canterbury, brought in over £100,000, and enabled the repair of the whole of the exterior of the cathedral in 1633–41. Charles I himself paid for the reconstruction of the west front. Jones was appointed surveyor in February 1633, and waived his fee. The fifteen volumes of detailed accounts kept by John Webb as clerk engrosser record exactly what was done: the building itself fell victim to the great fire of 1666.

The fourteenth-century choir was carefully repaired, but the walls of the Romanesque transepts and nave were recased to a new, classical design, and at the west end Jones constructed an entirely new ten-column portico. The recased walls were completely rusticated. Fenestration consisted of oculi above round-head windows. Pilaster buttresses were capped by pineapples, and the cornice was of a quasi-Doric design apparently derived from Hieronymus Cock's reconstruction of the baths of Diocletian (1558). The transept doorways were Ionic, and the gamut of the orders was completed by the Corinthian portico.

The portico type, a full-width colonnade carrying not a pediment but a balustraded platform, was once again familiar to Jones from Palladio's illustrations of antique temples, specifically the temple of Venus and Rome, and the 'temple of Peace' (basilica of Maxentius). His annotations relating to the latter show how he thought such a structure could embody what he called 'the Romain Greatnes' (Allsopp, vol. 1, IV.13). John Webb tells of the pains his master took to perfect this great structure, and how once again it formed a testing ground for his interpretation of Vitruvius. However, fragments of the portico columns discovered within the walls of the present cathedral in 1996 prove that the columns were no more than 4 feet in diameter, a size subsequently repeated by Wren in his cathedral.

The intervention of Charles I brought Jones one further cathedral commission. On visiting Winchester Cathedral in 1635 the king criticized the bulk of the pulpitum, which the dean and chapter thereupon decided to replace with a screen designed by Jones. The screen, erected in 1637–8, was removed in 1820, but the central portal was re-erected in 1911–12 in the new Museum of Archaeology and Ethnology in Cambridge; other fragments are stored in the cathedral. Those substantial remnants, having never been exposed to the weather, preserve more eloquently than anything else the elegance and precision of his architecture.

Influence on new building in the 1630s Two building developments of the end of the decade, licensed in a similar way to the earl of Bedford's Covent Garden, probably reflected Italianate models provided by Jones. These were the schemes promoted by William Newton in Great Queen Street in 1636 and on the west side of Lincoln's Inn Fields in 1638. In both locations brick terraces were built with continuous eaves cornices, and pilasters rising through the upper storeys. At Lincoln's Inn Fields pilasters were used on the central house only. This, Lindsey House, is the sole survivor from either scheme, and is detailed in a way that suggests a design of Jones's executed without his close oversight.

The way in which Jones was able to influence the design of a new building is documented by the case of Goldsmiths' Hall, rebuilt in 1635–8 to the design of Nicholas Stone, whom Jones recommended as architect to the Goldsmiths' Company, having encouraged the company to set its hand to total rather than partial rebuilding. Stone furthermore acknowledged Jones's assistance at all stages of the design. The hall, damaged in the great fire of 1666 and pulled down in 1829, revolutionized the design of livery company halls.

On the other hand, the authority of the privy council itself was powerless to force the designs of the king's surveyor on those who rejected them, as is demonstrated by the case of the church of St Michael-le-Querne, rebuilt on its prominent site at the west end of Cheapside in 1638–40, apparently ignoring designs which Jones had produced at the council's behest. Drawings relating to two free-standing, hipped-roofed houses in the City of London give further indication of Jones's ideas for the architecture of the capital. But if Sir Peter Killigrew's house in Blackfriars and a house or office for Lord Maltravers in Lothbury (1638) were built to Jones's designs, they were destroyed in 1666.

Jones's responsibilities towards the crown and the privy council left him with little time or inclination to undertake work outside London for private patrons. Evidence of his involvement in the design of country houses is meagre. He made designs in 1622–3 for the marquess of Buckingham at New Hall, Essex; the impressive drawing for Buckingham, for a coffered vault, apparently of a chapel, may be associated with this commission. Most important was his involvement in the design for the remodelling by Philip Herbert, the fourth earl of Pembroke, of Wilton House, Wiltshire, and the creation of the gardens there. It was, however, only as an adviser, for John Aubrey reports that Jones was too occupied with the Queen's House at Greenwich to attend to Wilton when the works were first proposed in 1636 and recommended Isaac de Caus, who made the designs, 'but not without the advice and approbation of Mr. Jones' (Colvin, 'The south front of Wilton House', *Archaeological Journal*, 111 (1954), 181). The reconstruction by John Webb of the state apartment after a fire in 1647 also drew on the now elderly Jones's advice. Wilton as built and rebuilt clearly embodies many of Jones's ideas. But, of the dozens of country houses attributed to Jones during the eighteenth century, not one has been shown to have been definitely designed by him.

Stone-Heng Restored and Jones's principles of architectural design In spite of the extent of Jones's marginal annotations, only one publication was based on his writings. In 1655 John Webb published *The most Notable Antiquity of Great Britain, Vulgarly called Stone-Heng on Salisbury Plain, Restored by Inigo Jones Esquire*. This presents a continuous text which purports to be by Jones, though Webb admits that he had compiled it from no more than 'some few indigested notes'. When in 1663 Dr Walter Charleton published, in *Chorea gigantum*, a comprehensive rebuttal of Jones's conclusions, Webb returned to the fray with a long and impassioned defence, *A Vindication of Stone-Heng Restored* (1665). This second work throws a great deal of further light on the reasoning behind Jones's theory about the origin and purpose of Stonehenge.

Jones's study of the monument originated in 1620, when James I, in progress at Wilton House, Wiltshire, set him to the task. However, his ideas did not come together until after 1637. He concluded that Stonehenge, since it was a structure of 'elegancy and proportion', had been erected, not by the native Britons but by the Romans. He interpreted it, in being a circular, roofless structure in open country in what he argued was the Tuscan order, as a temple to the Roman god of the sky, Coelus. He confirmed himself in this belief by reconstructing the plan in such a way that the positions of the stones in the outer circle and inner hexagon were defined by four superimposed equilateral triangles inscribed in a circle, in exactly the same way as Vitruvius recommended for constructing the orchestra and stage of a Roman theatre. Webb, in the *Vindication*, points out several parallels between the analysis of Stonehenge and the design principles underlying Jones's major buildings of the 1630s. His studies of Stonehenge, however implausible historically, must have confirmed for Jones the validity of his own architectural ambition, to bring, or rather to bring back, to Britain the monumental and mathematically ordered architecture of the Romans.

Connoisseurship of paintings The basis of Jones's under-standing of the theory and practice, as well as the history, of painting lay in his reading of Vasari's *Vite* and G. P. Lomazzo's *Trattato dell'arte della pittura, scoltura, ed architettura* (1585). His copy of Vasari's third book, part 1, bears annotations which show that he had studied it at the outset of his artistic career, and even took the volume with him to Italy in 1613–14; his copy of Lomazzo also bears early annotations. In these early years Jones also began to make what became a very extensive collection of prints primarily by Italian masters of the sixteenth century, or after paintings by them. His enthusiasm seems to have been greatest for Raphael and his school. A volume of etchings by Andrea Schiavone after Parmigianino, once owned by Jones and now in the Metropolitan Museum, New York, is inscribed 'Inigo Jones so fond of Parmegiano, that he bought the Prints of the Imperfect Plates, which are no[w] here in this book' (Wood, 253).

Jones was involved in the purchase of paintings for the earl of Arundel, and the collection of Charles I included several paintings, admittedly minor ones, given to or acquired for him by Jones. In 1640 delicate negotiations over paintings by Rubens and his pupil Jacob Jordaens for the Queen's House at Greenwich were dependent on Jones's ability to distinguish between their hands. Jones's enthusiasm for paintings and his pride in his own skill at identifying artists' hands are also recorded.

Towards the end of his life Jones reread Lomazzo and made a sustained effort to improve his own skill at figure drawing. Nearly 800 sheets or fragments of pen sketches survive, particularly of heads, old and young, male and female. These demonstrate that he made use of drawing manuals by Odoardo Fialetti and Guercino, and that he copied and adapted drawings in Lord Arundel's collection, and prints by or after not only Raphael and Parmigianino but also Titian, Baccio Bandinelli, Federigo Barocci, and others.

Last years At the beginning of the civil war Jones's survey-orship was terminated when, in July 1643, he was declared a delinquent. A year previously he had lent the king £500, and then concealed money and plate, and left London. He was present at the siege of Basing House, Hampshire, where he probably advised on its defences, and where on 14 October 1645 he was ignominiously captured by the parliamentary forces and taken to London. The fine for his delinquency was first set at £1000, then in May 1646 reassessed at £557 18s. 6d., payable on his estate, officially assessed at £4958 11s. 6d. However, he offered to pay the full £1000, thus both clearing his delinquency and no doubt deflecting any further investigation of concealed property. During the last six years of his life Jones seems to have lived quietly in London. In 1649–50 he was back in Scotland Yard, but his death, on 21 June 1652, took place, by tradition, at Somerset House. He was unmarried. In his will, proved on 20 August 1652, he left no less than £4140. By it John Webb was richly rewarded for his loyal service, for his wife, Anne, Jones's kinswoman, and their five children together received almost three-quarters of the total. Jones was buried on 26 June 1652 at St Benet Paul's

Wharf and the monument erected in the church under his will consisted of a tomb chest, its ends carved with reliefs of the Banqueting House and the west front of St Paul's Cathedral, and upon it a portrait bust between two obelisks. It was damaged in the fire of 1666 and subse-quently destroyed. Its appearance is known from a sketch by John Aubrey.

Character and appearance Jones's commitment to his art and his humility before it are expressed by the motto he adopted: 'Altro diletto che imparar non trovo' ('I have no other delight but to learn'). In public, however, Jones could appear arrogant. His troubled relationship with Ben Jonson over the masque productions had its roots in the conflicting claim each made for the primacy of his own art, but was also a clash of two egotistical personalities. Jonson's satires on his rival, in *A Tale of a Tub* (1633) as a joiner who 'will joyne with no man' and in *Love's Welcome at Bolsover* (1634) as 'Coronell Vitruvius', clearly reflected Jones's personality. Jones's flaunting of his technical vocabulary is also tellingly lampooned in *A Tale*. These accusations find their counterparts in the complaints at his high-handedness made by the parishioners of St Greg-ory by Paul's, when Jones was determined to clear the ground for the new west end of the cathedral.

When it came to art connoisseurship the same self-assurance was in evidence. In 1636 the papal agent Gre-gorio Panzani observed with amused distaste the spec-tacle of Jones parading before the king and queen his knowledge of Italian painting. Yet Panzani also describes Jones's almost physical excitement on seeing fine paint-ings; and in the same year the earl of Arundel's son reported bringing a collection of Neapolitan paintings 'to show Mr Survayor here, whoe is madde to see them' (Springell, 230).

Another of Jonson's accusations, however, that Jones was a social climber and envied the marquessate con-ferred on his Spanish counterpart G. B. Crescenzio by Philip IV, is undermined by the record that in 1633 he refused a knighthood. Among those whose interests he shared he undoubtedly inspired respect, affection, and loyalty. This is as true of his patron the earl of Arundel as of his pupil John Webb. The admiration shown by George Chapman was reciprocated by Jones when in 1634 he set up for the poet a tombstone, shaped like a Roman altar, in the graveyard of St Giles-in-the-Fields.

There are a number of records of Jones's appearance. The earliest portrait is the engraving by Francesco Villa-mena, which must be based on a study made in Rome in 1614. The presentation of the bust-length figure in an illu-sionistic oval recessed into a Roman altar is completely unlike Villamena's normal florid style, and suggests the sitter's involvement in its design. The presumptuous tenor of the inscription—'Inigo Jones architector / Magnae Britaniae'—is also noteworthy. Villamena emphasizes the northern-ness of Jones's physiognomy, the long face, large nose, and bulbous eyes. The other por-traits are all much later. Van Dyck's black chalk drawing at

Chatsworth—preparatory to the engraving in his *Iconographiae* (1640)—is a sympathetic image of the successful artist. Among the hundreds of sketched heads by Jones are three self-portraits (two at Chatsworth, one at the RIBA). They confirm Van Dyck's depiction, showing that Jones regularly wore his hair at shoulder length under a skull-cap, and had a lightly trimmed beard and moustache. The circular oil painting at Chiswick Villa, Middlesex, of an ageing Jones attributed to William Dobson was probably painted about 1644, when the court was at Oxford.

Artistic influence John Webb's piety led him to make exaggerated claims for his master as 'the Vitruvius of his Age' (J. Webb, 'To the favourers of antiquity', *The most Notable Antiquity of Great Britain, Vulgarly called Stone-Heng*, 1655), and in *A Vindication of Stone-Heng Restored* (1665) as 'not only the Vitruvius of England, but likewise, in his Age, of all Christendom; and it was vox Europae that named him so, being, much more than at Home, famous in remote Parts' (p. 8). For this last claim there is no evidence whatever. However, Christopher Wren's respect for his predecessor is evident in his works; the design of his St Paul's Cathedral in particular owes much to Jones. But Wren did not feel Jones's awe of antiquity, and by the end of the century a shrewd observer, Roger North, compared both Webb and Wren unfavourably with the 'grand maniere' of Jones (Colvin and Newman, 23).

The first published biography of Jones was John Bowack's brief account in the *Monthly Miscellany* for April 1708 (vol. 2, 149–51), which initiated the eighteenth-century penchant for speculative attributions. Of far greater importance was the introduction to Colen Campbell's *Vitruvius Britannicus* (vol. 1, 1715), where a patriotic polemic sets Jones and Palladio alongside one another as models for imitation. This ushered in the architectural programme commonly known as Palladianism. It was fed by imitation, even copying of Jones's designs, many of which passed, from John Webb's descendants, via John Oliver and William and John Talman, into the hands of Richard Boyle, third earl of Burlington, Campbell's pupil and subsequent arbiter of the movement. Other drawings, and the bulk of Jones's books, including his annotated copy of Palladio's *Quattro libri*, already celebrated in the early eighteenth century, were acquired by the amateur architect and fellow of All Souls College, Oxford, Dr George Clarke, but not made widely accessible. Some of the annotations were finally published in 1742, in the third edition of Giacomo Leoni's English translation of Palladio.

The publication of many drawings by Jones and Webb from Burlington's collection by William Kent (1727), Isaac Ware (1731), and John Vardy (1744) provided a wealth of models for architects to the mid-century and beyond. The emphasis by the new movement on order and proportion was in Jones's spirit, but there was little creative response to his studies of the monuments of antiquity. Anyway these were superseded in the 1750s and 1760s by much more wide-ranging archaeological investigations. From that point Jones lost his cult status, though so long as classical architecture flourished in England his buildings were held in high regard.

Jones's achievement as a theatre designer, if not his fame, was even longer-lived. Charles II did not revive the court masque, but in the 1660s John Webb and William Davenant, one of Jones's collaborators on the masques of the 1630s, were both in the forefront of theatrical production. Jonesian scenic arrangements, the proscenium arch, side flats, and back shutters thus passed into the common currency of stage design. Jones's name did not, however, retain its resonance in the world of the theatre as it did in architecture.

The myths which had grown up round Jones's reputation and *œuvre* began to be stripped away by the documentary researches of Peter Cunningham (1848) and later of H. P. Horne (writing in the *Dictionary of National Biography*). J. A. Gotch's life of the architect (1928) draws on their discoveries to present a generally credible picture of his achievements.

More thorough and rigorously scholarly research in the second half of the twentieth century has clarified matters further. Howard Colvin in his *Biographical Dictionary of British Architects, 1600–1840* (1978) has reduced Jones's architectural *œuvre* to a credible body of works. The researches undertaken by John Summerson for *The History of the King's Works* volumes 3 (1975) and 4 (1982) have demonstrated Jones's administrative success in his long tenure of the surveyorship of the king's works and documented in detail the architectural commissions, both major and minor, which he carried out for the crown. Summerson's analysis of Jones's major works, in particular Covent Garden and the remodelling of St Paul's Cathedral, has emphasized Jones's devotion to the achievements of Roman antiquity and the inspiration he drew from that source.

The interpretation of Jones's achievement as a masque designer remains more debatable, though D. J. Gordon's article of 1949 demonstrated that the quarrel with Ben Jonson was about serious artistic principles, not mere personalities. The publication by S. Orgel and R. Strong in 1973 of all Jones's masque drawings, together with texts of the masques and contemporary evidence for their production and audience reaction, is a model of its kind. John Peacock has shown that the masque drawings were copied or adapted from a wide range of continental engravings—in particular, in his book of 1995. Jeremy Wood's comparable analysis (1992) of the hundreds of surviving fragmentary figure drawings confirms that Jones was very widely knowledgeable in continental art, both of the Italian Renaissance and of contemporary masters.

The other material which has been examined in detail since about 1970, particularly by Gordon Higgott and John Newman, is the annotations in Jones's books, above all in his copy of Palladio's *Quattro libri*. The dating of the notes to the various phases of Jones's career has enabled a picture to emerge of his developing mastery of architectural design and practice. More remains to be done in this area; but during the last quarter of the twentieth century it was possible to disentangle to a considerable degree the lines of Jones's thinking about his art.   JOHN NEWMAN

Sources P. Cunningham, *Inigo Jones: a life of the architect* (1848) · Vertue, *Note books* · J. A. Gotch, *Inigo Jones* (1928) · J. Summerson, *Inigo Jones* (1966) · Colvin, *Archs.* · J. Summerson, 'The surveyorship of Inigo Jones, 1615–43', *The history of the king's works*, ed. H. M. Colvin and others, 3 (1975), 129–59 · S. Orgel and R. Strong, *Inigo Jones: the theatre of the Stuart court*, 2 vols. (1973) · J. Harris and G. Higgott, *Inigo Jones: complete architectural drawings* (1989) · J. Summerson, 'Inigo Jones: lecture on a master mind', *PBA*, 50 (1964), 169–92 · J. Harris, S. Orgel, and R. Strong, *The king's arcadia: Inigo Jones and the Stuart court* (1973) · J. Webb, *The most notable antiquity of Great Britain, vulgarly called Stone-Heng on Salisbury Plain, restored by Inigo Jones esquire, surveyor-general to his late majesty* (1655) · J. Webb, *A vindication of Stone-Heng restored* (1665) · *DNB* · J. Peacock, *The stage designs of Inigo Jones: the European context* (1995) · J. Orrell, *The theatres of Inigo Jones and John Webb* (1985) · B. Allsopp, ed., *Inigo Jones on Palladio, being the notes by Inigo Jones in the copy of I Quattro libri dell'architettura di Andrea Palladio, 1601, in the library of Worcester College, Oxford*, 2 vols. (1970) · H. M. Colvin and J. Summerson, 'The king's houses, 1485–1660', *The history of the king's works*, ed. H. M. Colvin and others, 4 (1982), 48–9, 114–22, 159–60, 176–9, 213–17, 246–52, 260–71, 277, 299–300, 326–41 · *The parish of St Paul, Covent Garden*, Survey of London, 36 (1970) · D. Duggan, '"London the ring, Covent Garden the jewel of that ring": new light on Covent Garden', *Architectural History*, 43 (2000), 140–61 · G. Higgott, 'Inigo Jones in Provence', *Architectural History*, 26 (1983), 24–34 · R. Wittkower, 'Inigo Jones, architect and man of letters', *RIBA Journal*, 60 (1952–3), 83–90 · G. Higgott, 'Varying with reason: Inigo Jones's theory of design', *Architectural History*, 35 (1992), 51–77 · J. Newman, 'Inigo Jones's architectural education before 1614', *Architectural History*, 35 (1992), 18–50 · J. Newman, 'Italian treatises in use: the significance of Inigo Jones's annotations', *Les traités de la Renaissance*, ed. J. Guillaume (1988), 435–41 · J. Wood, 'Inigo Jones, Italian art, and the practice of drawing', *Art Bulletin*, 74 (1992), 247– · J. Peacock, 'Inigo Jones's catafalque for James I', *Architectural History*, 25 (1982), 1–5 · M. Whinney, 'John Webb's drawings for Whitehall Palace', *Walpole Society*, 31 (1942–3), 45–107 · J. Harris and A. A. Tait, eds., *Catalogue of the drawings by Inigo Jones, John Webb and Isaac de Caus at Worcester College, Oxford* (1979) · J. Peacock, 'Inigo Jones and Florentine court theater', *John Donne Journal*, 5 (1986), 201–34 · A. A. Tait, 'Inigo Jones's "Stone-Heng"', *Burlington Magazine*, 120 (1978), 154–9 · D. J. Gordon, 'Poet and architect: the intellectual setting of the quarrel between Ben Jonson and Inigo Jones', *Journal of the Warburg and Courtauld Institutes*, 12 (1949), 152–78 · D. Howarth, *Lord Arundel and his circle* (1985) · J. Newman, 'Strayed from the Queen's House?', *Architectural History*, 27 (1984), 33–5 · H. Colvin, 'Inigo Jones and the church of St Michael le Querne', *London Journal*, 12 (1986), 36–9 · J. Newman, 'A draft will of Lord Arundel', *Burlington Magazine*, 122 (1980), 692–6 · H. Colvin, 'The south front of Wilton House', *Essays in English architectural history* (1999), 136–57 · J. Newman, 'Nicholas Stone's Goldsmiths' Hall', *Architectural History*, 14 (1971), 30–39 · R. Wittkower, 'Inigo Jones, puritanissimo fiero', *Burlington Magazine*, 90 (1948), 50–51 · *Of building: Roger North's writings on architecture*, ed. H. Colvin and J. Newman (1981) · R. C. Strong, *Henry, prince of Wales, and England's lost Renaissance* (1986) · *Ben Jonson*, ed. C. H. Herford, P. Simpson, and E. M. Simpson, 11 vols. (1925–52), vol. 10 · E. S. de Beer, 'Notes on Inigo Jones', *N&Q*, 178 (1940), 292 · D. Howarth, *Images of rule* (1997) · 'Abraham van der Doort's catalogue of the collections of Charles I', ed. O. Millar, *Walpole Society*, 37 (1958–60) · W. Sainsbury, *Original unpublished papers illustrative of the life of Sir Peter Paul Rubens* (1859) · F. Springell, *Connoisseur and diplomat: the earl of Arundel's embassy to Germany in 1636 as recounted in William Crowne's diary, the earl's letters and other contemporary sources with a catalogue of the topographical drawings made on the journey by Wenceslaus Hollar* (1963) · E. Chaney, 'Inigo Jones in Naples', *The evolution of the grand tour* (1998)

Archives Worcester College, Oxford, volumes from his library, many bearing his marginal annotations | Canadian Centre for Architecture, Montreal, annotated volume of S. Serlio, *Architettura*, quarto edn · Chatsworth House, Derbyshire, collection of the duke of Devonshire, copy of D. Barbaro, ed., *I dieci libri dell'architettura di M. Vitruvio* (1567) with numerous marginal annotations by Jones · Chatsworth House, Derbyshire, collection of the duke of Devonshire, notebook and sketchbook, entitled 'Roma 1614' · Queen's College, Oxford, annotated volume of S. Serlio, *Architettura*, folio edn · V&A, annotated volume of G. P. Lomazzo, *Trattato dell'arte della pittura, scoltura, ed architettura* (1585)

Likenesses F. Villamena, line engraving, *c*.1614, Chatsworth House, Derbyshire, BM; repro. in Harris, Orgel, and Strong, *The king's arcadia* · I. Jones, self-portrait, drawing, 1630–39, RIBA; repro. in Harris, Orgel, and Strong, *The king's arcadia* · I. Jones, two self-portraits, drawings, 1630–39, Chatsworth House, Derbyshire; repro. in Harris, Orgel, and Strong, *The king's arcadia* · A. Van Dyck, oils, *c*.1632–1635, The Hermitage, Leningrad; copy, NPG · R. van Voerst, engraving, 1635 (after A. Van Dyck), BM, NPG; repro. in A. Van Dyck, *Iconographiae* (1640) · W. Dobson, oils, *c*.1644, Chiswick House, London; version, NMM · V. Green, mezzotint, pubd 1775 (after A. Van Dyck), BM, NPG · R. Earlom, mezzotint, pubd 1811 (after A. Van Dyck), BM, NPG · C. F. Carter, sculpture medal, 1849, NPG · W. Hollar, print (after A. Van Dyck), NPG · A. Van Dyck, black chalk drawing, Chatsworth House, Derbyshire [*see illus.*]

Wealth at death £4140—money legacies: will, PRO

Jones, Isaac (1804–1850), translator, was born on 2 May 1804 in the parish of Llanychaearn, near Aberystwyth, Cardiganshire. His father, a weaver, was able to teach him Latin, and he also attended a small school in his native village. He afterwards went to the grammar school at Aberystwyth, where he became first an assistant and in 1828 headmaster. He resigned the post in 1834, when he entered St David's College, Lampeter, and was elected Eldon Hebrew scholar there in 1835. He was ordained deacon in September 1836 and priest in September 1837. He held curacies first at Llanfihangel Genau'r-glyn, and then at Capel Bangor, both near Aberystwyth. In February 1840 he became curate of Llanedwen and Llanddaniel-fab, in Anglesey, where he remained until his death.

Jones was chiefly known as a translator of English works into Welsh, including Gurney's *Dictionary of the Bible* (1835) and Adam Clarke's *Commentary on the New Testament* (1847). This was valuable work at a time when the majority in Wales were monoglot Welsh speakers. He was joint editor with Owen Williams of Waunfawr of the early Welsh encyclopaedia *Y geirlyfr Cymraeg* (2 vols., 1835), the second volume being entirely written by Jones. In 1850 he edited the second edition of William Salesbury's *Welsh Testament* (originally published in 1567), and assisted the Revd E. Griffiths of Swansea with his translation of Matthew Henry's *Exposition*. He was also the author of a Welsh grammar (1832, 1841) and several tracts and pamphlets.

Isaac Jones died, unmarried, at Llanidan, on 2 December 1850, and was buried in Llanidan churchyard.

D. L. THOMAS, rev. E. G. MILLWARD

Sources R. Williams, *Enwogion Cymru: a biographical dictionary of eminent Welshmen* (1852), 559 · *Cymru*, 10 (1896), 286–7

Jones, James Felix (1813/14–1878), officer in the Indian navy and surveyor, joined the Bombay marine on 14 June

1828 when he was fourteen years old. As midshipman and lieutenant of the East India Company's ship *Palinurus*, under Commander Robert Moresby, engaged in the survey of the northern part of the Red Sea, 1829–34. Jones was a skilled draughtsman and the charts were principally drawn by him. They were critical to the development of steam communication between Britain and India through the Red Sea. He was next employed in the survey of Ceylon and the Gulf of Mannar, under Lieutenant Powell, and in May 1840 joined Lieutenant C. D. Campbell, commanding the *Nitocris*, in the survey of Mesopotamia, in the course of which he connected the Euphrates and Mediterranean by chronometric measurements for longitude. This survey examined the alternative overland route from the Gulf of Alexandretta (Iskenderun) into the Persian Gulf, as explored by Francis Rawdon Chesney in 1836–7. In October 1841 Captain Lynch commenced the survey of the Euphrates, and on his retirement in 1843 was succeeded by Jones, who continued for several years the examination of the Tigris and Euphrates. Following the disputes between Persia and Turkey in 1843, Jones, in company with Major Henry Rawlinson, was sent in August 1844 to collect information respecting the boundary, the results obtained being officially printed in 1849 as *Narrative of a Journey through Parts of Persia and Kurdistan*. Promoted commander on 13 September 1847, in 1848 Jones examined the course of the ancient Nahrwan Canal, and surveyed the once fertile region which it irrigated. In 1850 he surveyed the old bed of the Tigris, discovered the site of the ancient Opis, and made researches in the vicinity of the Median wall and Physcus of Xenophon. In 1852 he made a trigonometrical survey of the country between the Tigris and the upper Zab, including the ruins of Nineveh, the results of which are recorded in a series of maps of *Assyrian Vestiges*, and the accompanying memoir. In 1853 he completed a map of Baghdad on a large scale, with a memoir on the province. In 1854 he was named political agent at Baghdad and consul-general in Turkish Arabia. In 1855 he was appointed political agent in the Persian Gulf, and as such rendered important services during the war in 1856, and still more during the mutiny of 1857–8. He was promoted captain on 1 February 1858. In 1864 Sir Bartle Frere, governor of Bombay, criticized him and removed him from his post, despite his protests. Frere's criticism was excessive. Though Jones was not an ideal resident—his perception and discretion were limited, and he was sometimes tactless, overbearing, and short-tempered with local rulers—he was resident at a difficult time and usually worked competently. Broken health compelled him to return to England, and, though he revisited Bombay in 1873, he had no further active employment. His later years were spent in geographical work for the India Office, and in 1875 he completed a beautifully drawn map, in four sheets, of western Asia, including the valleys of the Tigris and Euphrates; it remains in manuscript in the India Office collections. FRGS (1864), he served on the Royal Geographical Society council, and was a valued contributor to the *Geographical Magazine* and a member of the Geographical Club. He was married to Sophie Takoor and they had

children. He died at his home, Fernside, Church Road, Upper Norwood, Surrey, on 3 September 1878, his wife surviving him. The *Geographical Magazine* obituary called him 'one of the greatest ornaments of the old Indian navy' (*Geographical Magazine*, 1878). The most important of his numerous memoirs are included in *Selections from the Records of the Bombay Government* (1857, new ser., 43). Jones made an important contribution to the development of safe communications between Britain and India—the basis on which the empire developed.

J. K. LAUGHTON, rev. ANDREW LAMBERT

Sources J. S. Guest, *The Euphrates expedition* (1992) • J. Sutton, *Lords of the east: the East India Company and its ships* (1981) • H. L. Hoskins, *British routes to India* (1928) • C. R. Low, *History of the Indian navy, 1613–1863*, 2 vols. (1877) • J. B. Kelly, *Britain and the Persian Gulf, 1795–1880* (1968) • Boase, *Mod. Eng. biog.* • *Geographical Magazine*, 5 (1878), 264 • *CGPLA Eng. & Wales* (1878)
Archives BL OIOC
Wealth at death under £16,000: probate, 23 Sept 1878, *CGPLA Eng. & Wales*

Jones, James Rhys Kilsby (1813–1889), Congregational minister and writer, was born James Rhys Jones on 4 February 1813 at Pen-lan, near Llandovery, Carmarthenshire, the son of Rhys Jones (1780–1862), a small farmer and local preacher, who later became Independent minister at Ffaldybrenin in the same county. Jones was educated at Neuadd-lwyd grammar school, Cardiganshire, in a college at Blackburn, and at the Presbyterian college at Carmarthen (1835–8).

After serving briefly elsewhere, Jones became minister of the Independent church at Kilsby, Northamptonshire, in January 1840, and was fully ordained there on 18 June of the same year. During his ministry here, he assumed the additional name of Kilsby, and on 22 April 1842 married Ann Southwall Chilcott of Leominster, with whom he had one son.

About 1850 Jones moved to Birmingham, and subsequently to Bolton (1851–5), before returning to Wales. He bought Gellifelen Farm, near Llanwrtyd, Brecknockshire, his mother's birthplace, where he built a house, called Glenview. Except for a short period spent in London as pastor of the Tonbridge Congregational Chapel (1861–6), he spent the rest of his life at Glenview. He served as minister at Rhayader (1857–60) and at Llandrindod Wells (1868–89), where he built Christ Church Chapel, though he did no ordinary pastoral work.

Jones's views and personality were unusually original and independent, and he was widely known by his ready wit and biting sarcasm. His sermons and lectures were practical rather than dogmatic, and whether in Welsh or English were delivered in an easy, conversational tone. He gained a great reputation as a lecturer, his best-known lectures being 'Vicar Prichard', 'John Penry, the Welsh martyr', and 'Self-made men'. He was a resolute enemy of the church establishment in Wales, and both by pen and speech he rendered an invaluable service to Welsh Liberalism. His political activities involved him in the struggle over education in Wales. The publication of the 1847 report on education in Wales led to an outcry there, given its disparaging remarks on the Welsh language and Welsh morals, and its denigration of Welsh nonconformity. Jones translated the summary of the report into Welsh and thus assisted its wide dissemination, fuelling a public outcry against its contents. An early proponent of the utilization of the Welsh language in schools, Jones insisted that bilingualism was preferable to the eradication of Welsh. In expressing these views, he contradicted the wisdom of the day which insisted that the only means by which the Welsh could gain a thorough knowledge of English was by eliminating the Welsh language from the schools of the principality.

Jones contributed extensively to Welsh periodicals, submitting articles on political, social, and educational questions to *Y Traethodydd* and *Y Byd Cymreig*. For many years he was Welsh editor for the publishing firm of William Mackenzie of Glasgow. He translated a biography of William Williams of Wern into English and produced the much used translation of John Brown's *Biblical Dictionary* as *Geiriadur beiblaidd*, published in 1869–70. He edited the works of William Williams of Pantycelyn (1868) and a Welsh version of John Bunyan's *Pilgrim's Progress* with other works (1869), as well as a Welsh *Family Bible* (1869). In addition to these publications, Jones produced several important works on educational, religious, and health matters in Wales.

Jones died on 10 April 1889 at Glenview, and was buried in the parish churchyard at Llanwrtyd, where a monument was placed over his grave by public subscription. His wife survived him.

D. L. THOMAS, *rev.* ROBERT V. SMITH

Sources DWB · D. S. Davies, 'Y diweddar Barchedig J. R. Kilsby Jones', *Y Geninen*, 7 (1889), 148–55 · *Y Geninen*, 8 (1890), 43–8 · *Congregational Year Book* (1890) · CGPLA Eng. & Wales (1889) · m. cert. · d. cert.
Archives NL Wales, letters to Lewis Edwards
Likenesses ap Caledfryn, portrait, Congregational College, Brecon · portrait, repro. in *Y Diwygiwr* (July 1889), 64
Wealth at death £154 4s. 6d.: probate, 16 May 1889, CGPLA Eng. & Wales

Jones, Jenkin (1700?–1742), nonconformist minister, was born in Trafle, Llanwenog, Cardiganshire, in or around 1700, the son of John Jenkins (d. 1759), a blacksmith, of Bryngranod, Llanwenog. His father died on 18 March 1759 and, among other legacies, he left one of £100 to endow Llwynrhydowen, the chapel founded by his son. Jenkin Jones married a daughter of David Thomas of Pantydefaid, and they had at least one child.

Nothing is known of his early life, but in 1720 Jones entered the Presbyterian college, Carmarthen, then under Thomas Perrot, a president whose own orthodoxy was unquestioned, but many of whose pupils subsequently drifted into heterodoxy. He remained there until April 1722, after which there is no record of his attendance.

On leaving college, Jones seems to have become co-pastor with James Lewis of the congregation at Pantycreuddyn, Llandysul, Cardiganshire. His views soon inclined to Arminianism, and, although his following was

large, the majority of the congregation opposed his teaching, as did Lewis, who prevented him from continuing to preach at Pantycreuddyn. He therefore resigned his co-pastorate, and about 1726 he began to preach the doctrines of Arminianism at the old farmhouse of Pen-y-banc and at his home of Wern-hir; in 1733 he built the Arminian chapel of Llwynrhydowen on his own land. For some years he was the only public advocate of Arminianism among paedobaptists in Wales, though many of the younger ministers and Carmarthen students were probably in secret sympathy with him.

In Whit week 1729 the spread of Arminian views was the subject of serious discussion at a meeting of the associated Baptist ministers at Llangloffan in Pembrokeshire, when it was resolved that certain works should be published to counteract the Arminian doctrines which, it was felt, were then beginning to disturb the churches. Towards the close of the year Jones published a pamphlet professing to give from the Arminian point of view a 'Correct account of original sin' (*Cyfrif cywir o'r pechod gwreiddiol*), arguing against the doctrine of original sin and stressing the individual's ability to secure salvation. No copy is now known to be extant, but it evoked numerous replies, among them one by Jones's old pastor, James Lewis, in conjunction with the Revd Christmas Samuel, with the title 'The most correct account of original sin' (*Y cyfrif cywiraf o'r pechod gwreiddiol*; 1730). Jones's congregation increased, and six or seven influential ministers, together with their congregations, adopted his opinions. Jenkin Jones died in 1742, in the 'mid-day' of life, according to his elegy, and was buried on 20 June in the parish churchyard at Llandysul.

After Jones's death, a further volume of his works was published under the title *Hymnau cymmwys i addoliad Duw* (1768), edited by his son-in-law and successor in the ministry, David Lloyd. Also included was an elegy in Welsh by Evan Thomas Rees. Although he once referred to himself as an unscholarly, unskilful, and unproficient Welshman, his works include a catechism for children and two translations, *Llun Agrippa* (1723) and *Dydd y farn fawr* (1727). By the time of his death, he had succeeded in laying the foundations of what would be a stronghold of Unitarianism in south-west Wales.

R. M. J. JONES, *rev.* DYLAN FOSTER EVANS

Sources O., 'Jenkin Jones, Llwynrhydowen', *Yr Ymofynnydd*, 32 (1932), 21–9 · G. H. Jenkins, *Cadw tŷ mewn cwmwl tystion: ysgrifau hanesyddol ar grefydd a diwylliant* (1990), 127–9 · E. Rees, ed., *Libri Walliae: a catalogue of Welsh books and books printed in Wales, 1546–1820*, 1 (1987), 363 · D. E. Davies, *Hoff ddysgedig nyth* (1976), 24, 28, 36–9, 101 · J. G. Jenkins, *Hanfod duw a pherson Crist* (1931), 36–42, 174–5 · R. T. Jones, *Hanes Annibynwyr Cymru* (1966), 131–9 · A. J. Martin, *Hanes Llwynrhydowen* (1977), 13–23

Jones, Jenkin (1779–1837), insurance company manager, was the son of Jenkin Jones and Sophia Jones (d. 1823) of Molesey, Surrey. In 1792, at the age of twelve, he joined the staff of the Phoenix Fire Office, Britain's second largest fire insurer, and the world's leading insurance exporter, and rose rapidly through the clerical ranks to become assistant secretary in 1802. In 1805, aged only twenty-five, he was appointed secretary to the company. He became assistant director in 1833.

Within two months of his appointment as secretary, Jones travelled to Germany and Scandinavia on the first of several trouble-shooting missions abroad, which became landmarks in his career. In 1807, following a huge fire on the Caribbean island of St Thomas, which nearly bankrupted Phoenix, with its extensive insurances of the sugar trade, Jones set sail for Barbados on his lengthiest and most difficult tour. Recognizing the danger of this wartime mission, Phoenix granted Jones £1000 in advance for his services, and effected an assurance on his life to provide a £150 annuity for his mother. Between November 1807 and July 1809 he visited some twenty cities and towns in the West Indies, Canada, and the eastern seaboard of the United States. In Grenada he fell ill with malaria, in Washington he was introduced to President Jefferson, and while in New York, Philadelphia, and Baltimore he negotiated tariff agreements with local offices, the first such agreements concluded anywhere abroad by a British insurer. On behalf of Phoenix's sister office, Pelican Life, he also appointed Phoenix's agent in Philadelphia as the first life-assurance agent in the United States.

Jones's reports to the Phoenix board, often accompanied by detailed drawings, were notable for their clarity and vigorous comment on the quality of the company's agents, the spread of risks insured, the standards of urban construction, and the level of competition from other insurance offices. The overall result of his work was to rationalize the system of foreign underwriting and to reinforce the company's belief in the market opportunities offered by the New World. Partly as a result of this, Phoenix, and by extension Britain, retained its dominance of the world's insurance exports well into the nineteenth century. Acknowledged as the foremost expert on overseas insurance, at home Jones worked for greater co-operation between provincial and London insurers. In 1830 and 1833, over months of arduous negotiations, he brought together nearly two dozen fire offices in local tariff agreements for Scotland and Liverpool, a success which foreshadowed the more comprehensive tariff co-operation of the 1840s and beyond. Jones also pioneered the development of the modern merger strategy. Beginning with Phoenix's purchase of the Glasgow Fire Office in 1811, he negotiated eight further take-overs, culminating in the purchase of the Protector Fire Office in 1837, probably Britain's biggest corporate merger of the first half of the nineteenth century. Although his underwriting instincts were not always sound, Jones had the charm and tactical judgement of a successful diplomat. His greatest strength lay in his awareness that good information is the lifeblood of good insurance practice, and that such information must be managed effectively.

From about 1820 Jones lived with his wife, Hannah Elizabeth (d. 1834), and widowed mother in the 'neat Gothic Cottage' on Holders Hill, Hendon, Middlesex. On 11 April 1837, during the final stages of the Protector negotiations, he collapsed suddenly in the street, while walking home from the London coach, and died 'almost immediately'.

An exhumation and inquest were only narrowly averted by Jones's relatives after two anonymous letters were received by the Middlesex coroner from 'an old inhabitant of Hendon' demanding, on behalf of Hendon residents, and in the name of 'legality', an inquest into the sudden death. Jones was interred in Hendon churchyard next to his wife and near his mother, both of whom had predeceased him.

ROBIN PEARSON

Sources C. Trebilcock, *Phoenix Assurance and the development of British insurance*, 1 (1985) • G. Hurren, *Phoenix renascent* (1973) • R. Pearson, 'Taking risks and containing competition: diversification and oligopoly in the fire insurance markets of the north of England in the early 19th century', *Economic History Review*, 2nd ser., 46 (1993), 39–64 • *Morning Chronicle* (27 April 1837) • *GM*, 2nd ser., 7 (1837) • burial register, Hendon, 1813–38, LMA, MS DR029 • file on Jenkin Jones, Barnet Archives, Hendon, London NW4 4BI **Archives** CUL, Phoenix Assurance Archives, corresp. **Likenesses** portrait, repro. in Trebilcock, *Phoenix assurance* **Wealth at death** £5200: will, 1835, PRO, PROB 11/1878/378

Jones, Jeremiah (1693/4–1724), Independent minister and biblical scholar, was the son of David Jones (d. 1718), Independent minister at Shrewsbury, and his wife, Maria, eldest daughter of Samuel *Jones (1628–1697). He and his younger brother Joshua [see below] were educated for the nonconformist ministry at Samuel Benion's academy (conducted in Shrewsbury from 1706 until Benion's death in 1708), before completing their education with their uncle Samuel *Jones (1681/2–1719) at his academy in Gloucester, which moved to Tewkesbury in 1713. Thomas Secker, the future archbishop of Canterbury, was a fellow student, and remarked in a letter to Isaac Watts that Jeremiah would 'in all probability make a greater scholar' than any of the other students (Gibbons, 348). Between 1715 and 1719 Jeremiah Jones was assistant to David Some, minister of the Independent congregation at Market Harborough, Leicestershire, who also supplied Ashley, Northamptonshire. In 1719 he succeeded George Fownes as minister of the Independent meeting at Forest Green, Nailsworth, in the parish of Avening, Gloucestershire. At the same time, following the death of his uncle, he took some of his students and was therefore considered his uncle's successor in the conduct of the academy. The numbers he taught, however, were small. He was a popular preacher, and the congregation increased greatly during his time, making it necessary to enlarge the meeting-house. His preaching also appealed 'to the more judicious', for his salary of £100 a year 'came from persons of superior rank in life' (J. T., 240).

Jones's considerable reputation as a scholar extended beyond dissent. In his *Vindication of the Former Part of St Matthew's Gospel* (1719; reprinted 1721, 1803), dedicated to his uncle, he successfully demonstrated that the available Greek editions of St Matthew's gospel were in the order in which they were written, and thereby refuted William Whiston's theory of 'dislocations'. He is best remembered for his remarkable *New and Full Method of Settling the Canonical Authority of the New Testament*, in which he studied for himself all the early Christian writings on the authenticity of the canonical books and demonstrated that none of the apocryphal books of the New Testament had ever been admitted into the canon. His treatment of the subject was long unique, and notable for the comprehensiveness of its scholarship. First published after his death in 1726, with a third volume in 1727 that applied his system to the gospels and Acts, it was republished by the Clarendon Press in 1748, 1798, and 1827. Parts were included in William Hone's edition of *The Apocryphal New Testament* (1820), and in many later editions. It was 'a work of original plan, and, for its day, exhaustive research', and was 'certainly the most valuable outcome of the tutorial work of the old Academies or indeed of English contemporary scholarship' (Gordon, *Addresses*, 205). Jones died at Nailsworth on 30 April 1724, aged thirty, probably of a fever brought on by overexerting himself, and was buried at Nailsworth Chapel.

Jones's younger brother **Joshua Jones** (*d.* 1740), Presbyterian minister, was probably the editor of his posthumous work. Joshua's first settlement was at Oswestry, where he received a grant of £6 a year from the Presbyterian Fund (1716–18). He left in 1718, and when he first attended the Cheshire classis in August 1719 it was as an ordained minister 'from Manchester'. He was apparently minister at Tucker Street Chapel, Bristol, in succession to John Catcott (*d.* 1719), but had left by September 1720, when William Fisher became minister. He briefly succeeded his brother Jeremiah as minister of Forest Green, Nailsworth, in 1724. From 1725 until his death he was a colleague with Joseph Mottershead at Cross Street, Manchester. The following year on 6 July he married a Mrs Walker. He published a single sermon, preached at Cross Street Chapel on 14 November 1719, the anniversary of the defeat of the Jacobites at Preston. He died at Chester on 25 August 1740. DAVID L. WYKES

Sources J. T. [J. Toulmin], 'Pieces of neglected biography', *Monthly Magazine*, 15 (1803), 240–41, 510 · J. Hunter, *Familiae minorum gentium*, ed. J. W. Clay, 1, Harleian Society, 37 (1894), 300 · H. McLachlan, *English education under the Test Acts: being the history of the nonconformist academies, 1662–1820* (1931), 127, 130 · Allibone, *Dict.* · W. Orme, *Bibliotheca biblica* (1824), 264 · T. Rees, *History of protestant nonconformity in Wales* (1861), 260 · W. W. [W. Wilson], 'Biography: some account of Mr Samuel Jones', *Monthly Repository*, 4 (1809), 651–7 · documents and memoranda relating to early nonconformist academies collected by the late Joshua Wilson, esq., of Tunbridge Wells, DWL, New College collection, L54/1/15 · 'An account of the dissenting academies from the Restoration of Charles the Second', DWL, MS 24.59, fols. 30, 60r–62r · T. Gibbons, *Memoirs of Isaac Watts* (1780), 347–52 · J. Evans, 'List of dissenting congregations and ministers in England and Wales, 1715–1729', DWL, MS 38.4, pp. 42, 58, 64, 97 · W. Davies, *The Tewkesbury Academy with sketches of its tutor and students* [1905], 29–32 · A. Gordon, *Addresses biographical and historical* (1922), 205 · C. Russell, *A brief history of the Independent church at Forest Green, Nailsworth* (1847), 15 [1912] · A. Gordon, ed., *Cheshire classis: minutes, 1691–1745* (1919), 185 · G. E. Evans, *Record of the provincial assembly of Lancashire and Cheshire* (1896), 113 · T. Baker, *Memorials of a dissenting chapel* (1884), 23, 156 · J. H. Turner, T. Dickenson, and O. Heywood, eds., *The nonconformist register of baptisms, marriages, and deaths* (1881), 221, 329 · M. Caston, *Independency in Bristol: with brief memorials of its churches and pastors* (1860), 93 · *DNB*

Jones, Jezreel (*d.* 1731), traveller and diplomatist, is of unknown parentage, though he is known to have had a brother, John, for whom he provided in his will. In 1698 he

was elected clerk to the Royal Society. This was one of the few salaried positions at the Royal Society, and Jones's election coincided with the departure of Edmond Halley, also a clerk, on his voyage to the Atlantic. In the same year Jones set out under the patronage of the Royal Society on an expedition of discovery into the interior of Africa. The society's council appeared to have had a very high opinion of him, as they gave him the large sum of £100 towards his costs and regretted that they could not do more. In 1699 Jones's 'Account of the Moorish way of dressing their meat (with other remarks) in west Barbary, from Cape Spartel to Cape de Geer' appeared in the *Philosophical Transactions* of the society (vol. 21, 248–58). He apologizes for presenting so 'tiresome and frivolous a Discourse' (p. 258). His account certainly lacks the *gravitas* of most others appearing in the *Transactions*, but it is by no means tiresome. He obviously relished his food, and the narrative is a succession of recipes, detailed enough to be followed by a cook, and giving both Arabic and Shilha names for some dishes. The recipes are interrupted by a brief digression, rather admiring in tone, about the duration and conviviality of parties in Barbary. Perhaps the society thought this account slight recompense for their £100, as on 11 November 1699 he was proposed for election to the fellowship of the society but was refused. Jones returned home at the end of the year, but in February 1701 he sailed on a second voyage to north Africa and in September reached Tetouan. He sent Hans Sloane and James Petiver many valuable specimens.

In July 1704 Jones was chosen as British envoy to Morocco, and on 28 December 1704 arrived at Tangier. He is also recorded as having acted as secretary to Paul Methuen, envoy to Lisbon, on his first mission (1697–1706). This mission involved Methuen in 1705 in a commission to treat with the king of Fez, which may explain Jones's involvement.

An excellent Arabic scholar, Jones often acted on his return to London as interpreter to ambassadors from Arabic-speaking countries. To John Chamberlayne's *Oratio Dominica in diversas linguas versa* ('The Lord's Prayer in various languages'; 1715) Jones contributed a learned dissertation, 'De lingua Shilhensi'. Written in 1713, the account is of the Shilha language spoken by the Berber people of southern Morocco and includes a glossary of some common words.

Jones died at his house, the Two Golden Arrows, in Plough Yard, Fetter Lane, Holborn, on 21 May 1731. With his wife, Edith, he had three sons, Jezreel, Henry, and Edward, the last only a baby when he made his will in 1729, and a daughter, Edith. In his will Jones gave strict instructions that he was to be buried simply, without pomp, and at a cost no greater than £10—any money saved to be given to the poor. ELIZABETH BAIGENT

Sources will, PRO, PROB 11/645, fols. 333r–334r · C. R. Weld, *A history of the Royal Society*, 2 vols. (1848) · *GM*, 1st ser., 1 (1731), 221 · M. Hunter, *The Royal Society and its fellows, 1660–1700: the morphology of an early scientific institution*, 2nd edn (1994) · D. B. Horn, ed., *British diplomatic representatives, 1689–1789*, CS, 3rd ser., 46 (1932), 96 · *DNB*
Archives BL, corresp. with John Ellis, Add. MSS 28892, fols. 182, 190, and 28916, fols. 121, 137 · BL, Sloane MSS, letters to Sir Hans

Sloane and J. Petiver • BL, letters to Edward Southwell, Add. MS 38847

Jones, John (*fl.* 1562–1579), physician, was a native of Wales. He is said to have studied at both Oxford and Cambridge universities, and Wood conjectured that he took a degree in physic at Cambridge, though no record exists. It is not known when or where Jones commenced the practice of physic, but he mentions curing a person at Louth in 1562. He was living at Asple Hall, near Nottingham, in May 1572, and at Kingsmead, near Derby, in January 1573. He also appears to have travelled, for the purposes of practice, to Bath and Buxton and to have been patronized by Henry Herbert, second earl of Pembroke, and George Talbot, earl of Shrewsbury.

Jones wrote a number of works on medical subjects, among them *The bathes of Bathes ayde: wonderfull and most excellent agaynst very many sicknesses, approved by authoritie, confirmed by reason, and dayly tryed by experience, with the antiquitie, commoditie, property, knowledge, use, aphorismes, diet, medicine, and other thinges to be considered and observed*. It was published in 1572 and was dedicated to the earl of Shrewsbury. This and *The Benefit of the Auncient Bathes of Buckstones* [Buxton], published the same year, are notable as some of the earliest works on waters and spas in English. He also translated Galen's *Bookes of Elementes* in 1574. During the same year he published *A briefe, excellent, and profitable discourse, of the naturall beginning of all growing and liuing things, heate, generation, effects of the spirits, gouernment, vse, and abuse of phisicke, preseruation, &c. ... In the ende whereof is shewed the order and composition of a most heauenly water, for the preseruation of mans lyfe* (1574). In 1579 he published a work on the care of infants and small children, *The arte & science of preserving bodie & soule in healthe, wisedome, and Catholike religion*. He dedicated the book to Elizabeth I. It contained advice on nurses, and the disciplining and education of children, and warned against 'pampering or pyning, dandling or dulling, cockering or crowning' them (*The Art of Preserving Bodie & Soule*, 50). Little else is known of Jones's life, except that he had a son, Morgan.   THOMPSON COOPER, rev. PATRICK WALLIS

Sources Foster, *Alum. Oxon.* • Venn, *Alum. Cant.* • Wood, *Ath. Oxon.* • J. Aikin, *Biographical memoirs of medicine in Great Britain: from the revival of literature to the time of Harvey* (1780) • J. Cule, 'John Jones phisition on the preservation of body and soule, 1579', *Childcare through the centuries*, ed. J. Cule and T. Turner (1984), 195–209 • B. M. Berry, 'The first English paediatricians', *Journal of the History of Ideas*, 35 (1974), 561–77 • J. Ames, *Typographical antiquities, or, An historical account of the origin and progress of printing in Great Britain and Ireland*, ed. W. Herbert, 3 vols. (1785–90) • Tanner, *Bibl. Brit.-Hib.*

Jones, John [*name in religion* Godfrey Maurice] (**1559–1598**), Franciscan friar, was born in the parish of Clynnog Fawr in Caernarvonshire. At an unknown date he entered the order of Friars Minor at Pontoise, France. In 1591 he was professed at the Observantine convent of Santa Maria in Ara Coeli, Rome, as a Riformati father, taking Godfrey Maurice as his name in religion. Challoner is wrong in stating that he was a prisoner in the Marshalsea in 1582–4 (the list of prisoners in Morris's *Life of Gerard*, p. 29, does not include Jones's name), and again in Wisbech Castle in 1587.

After remaining at Rome for about a year Jones, with the permission of his superiors and the blessing of Clement VIII, returned to England and stayed for a few months in London in a house, established by the Jesuit John Gerard and run by Ann Line, for the reception of priests. On quitting London he developed his own mission circle and continued his missionary work until he was arrested at the instance of the notorious pursuivant and torturer Richard Topcliffe, in 1596. Before his arrest Jones had visited Robert Barnes and Jane Wiseman, who were then accused of aiding a priest. After two years' imprisonment in the Clink all three were arraigned for high treason in the king's bench court at Westminster on 3 July 1598. The charge against Jones was that, being a Roman Catholic priest, he had returned to England contrary to the statute 27 Eliz. c. 2. According to an account of his martyrdom by Henry Garnet, Jones replied, 'If this be a crime I must hold myself guilty, for I am a priest and came over into England to gain as many souls as I could to Christ' (de Yepes, 712). He was sentenced to death, and on 12 July 1598 was drawn on a hurdle to St Thomas's Waterings, Southwark, and hanged. His quarters were fixed on poles at different places, and Dr Champney stated that one of the quarters found its way to the convent at Pontoise.

Jones used a number of aliases, including Griffith, Herbert, Freer, and Buckley. He is to be distinguished from the Benedictine Robert Buckley (1517–1610), who was the only surviving member of the English Benedictine community between the Marian and Jacobean reigns.

D. L. THOMAS, rev. CERI SULLIVAN

Sources D. A. Bellenger, ed., *English and Welsh priests, 1558–1800* (1984), 77, 208 • J. H. Pollen, ed., *Unpublished documents relating to the English martyrs*, 1, Catholic RS, 5 (1908), 362–75 • D. de Yepes, *Historia particular de la persecucion de Inglaterre* (1599), 710–13 • Gillow, *Lit. biog. hist.*, 3.657–60 • *John Gerard: the autobiography of an Elizabethan*, trans. P. Caraman (1951), 86

Jones, John [*name in religion* Leander a Sancto Martino] (**1575–1635**), Benedictine monk, was born at Llanfrynach, near Brecon. In the register of the English College, Valladolid, he is recorded as *natus ... honestis parentibus et de fide catholica bene sentientibus* (Henson, 43), who had some family connection with the Scudamores of Kentchurch, not to speak of an alleged descent from the Welsh princes of Brycheiniog, but in fact the family seems to have lived in modest circumstances and may have conformed to the established church. When he was scarcely one year old John moved with his family first to Herefordshire, then to London. In 1584 he entered Merchant Taylors' School, which stamped him for life, given that Hebrew was a speciality fostered by its first headmaster, Richard Mulcaster, six of whose former pupils were invited to share in the translation of the King James Bible. Sharing the same founder, the school had links with St John's College, Oxford, where Jones was elected a scholar on 28 June 1591 and admitted on 15 October, to share rooms with the young William Laud. After two years of arts Jones was admitted to a fellowship in law on 18 June 1593, but in 1595 for reasons unknown he resigned his fellowship and returned to London, only to find both his parents and his brothers dead of the plague. At some time he must have become a Roman Catholic for, on 20 December 1596, he was admitted to the English College at Valladolid and in 1597 took the customary college oath to become a missionary in England. But in 1599 he became one of a stream of students who, in the face of stiff resistance from the college's Jesuit officials, transferred their loyalties to the Spanish Benedictines, and on 20 October 1599 Jones was admitted as a novice to the abbey of San Martino at Compostela; he professed in 1600, taking the name in religion Leander. In 1601 he, along with the other English monks in the various Spanish monasteries where enclosure was taken very strictly, persuaded their superiors to obtain from Pope Clement VIII a faculty allowing them to go on missionary work in England as monks. Meanwhile he shone in his studies at the University of Salamanca, where he was awarded a doctorate in divinity.

In 1606 the Spanish Benedictines founded St Gregory's Priory at Douai, in the Spanish Netherlands, in order to realize the missionary aspirations of their English subjects who would there be collected into a single community. Leander was called to be its novice master, a position he had already been exercising when he was loaned in 1606 to the abbey of St Remy at Rheims. The new foundation, understandably in the light of what had happened at Valladolid, encountered resourceful opposition from the Jesuits and their ally, Thomas Worthington, president of the English College at Douai, where secular priests were trained, and in September 1607 Jones had to publish a refutation of the charges adduced by them against those students of Valladolid who had become Benedictines. His legal and diplomatic skills, along with the favourable impression given by the English monks' observance, their heroism as missionaries and martyrs, and their usefulness as lecturers in the colleges of Douai, won powerful support both locally and in high places, which enabled the infant monastery to survive and prosper. Leander acted as professor of Hebrew and catechetics in the University of Douai for twenty-four years, teaching in the colleges there belonging to the abbeys of Marchienne and St Vaast, and in 1617 published his *magnum opus*, the six folio volumes of *Biblia sacra cum glossa ordinaria*, which was followed in rapid succession by editions of Trithemius (1621), Vincent of Beauvais (1624), Blosius, Tacitus (1629), Arnobius (1634), and most notably the *Apostolatus Benedictinorum in Anglia* (1626), which appeared under the name of Clement Reyner but was really the work of Augustine Baker, so far as the historical researches involved are concerned, and of Leander Jones in respect of the Latinity.

But Jones's industriousness as an editor by no means isolated him from the world of action—indeed he seems to have been the inevitable choice for any position of responsibility. In 1612 he was made vicar-general, that is, superior over about a hundred Anglo-Spanish Benedictines working in England. In 1617 he was the first of the nine definitors elected to negotiate the union into a single congregation of the three independent groups of English monks who now existed—the Spanish, those who were attached to Italian monasteries, and the little group which had obtained the rights of succession to the pre-Reformation English Benedictines from their last representative, Sigebert Buckley. This led to his becoming the first president-general of the new congregation, ruling it from 1619 to 1621, and again from 1633 to 1635. Twice he was prior of St Gregory's, from 1621 to 1625 and again from 1629 to 1633. In 1629 he was appointed abbot of Cismar, a north German abbey temporarily recovered for Catholicism during the fluctuations of the Thirty Years' War only to be lost again, and in 1633 he was given by his grateful congregation the honorific title of cathedral prior of Canterbury. One of his most decisive interventions as president was to give official support to Augustine Baker, chaplain to the Benedictine nuns at Cambrai, who was encountering opposition to his revival of the medieval English mystical spirituality, then almost forgotten in an age which favoured systematized meditation and close spiritual direction.

Although Jones was usually preoccupied with the internal affairs of his congregation, in the final year of his life he stepped on to a wider stage. In 1634 he went to England with a safe conduct from the government primarily to settle some problems which had arisen among the Benedictine missionaries, but he was also asked by Cardinal Barberini, Urban VIII's secretary of state, to take the occasion to send an unofficial report on the state of Catholicism in England. In this he advised against the creation of any Catholic bishop for England and urged the pope to lift his prohibition on Catholics taking the oath of allegiance, which, he claimed, relying overmuch on private assurances he had received from Francis Windebank, the secretary of state, Charles I interpreted as requiring no more than a general profession of civil loyalty, notwithstanding the strongly anti-papal phrases which it contained. He also took it upon himself to send a very benign report on the Church of England in which he minimized its differences from the Roman communion which, he said, were no greater than those which the Council of Florence had found tolerable in the case of the Greeks, and he pressed that the Church of England be 'united but not absorbed'. There had, however, been no close conferences with Laud as was later alleged by Prynne at the archbishop's trial. Rome did not take any of his suggestions very seriously, tinged as they were with his unconscious Gallicanism. His valuation of Anglicanism was based on impressions he had received from a very restricted court circle and did not take into account the strength of puritanism. His role was taken over by the more realist Gregorio Panzani to whom Rome gave a more official standing.

Jones died at Somerset House, London, on 17 December 1635 and was the first person to be buried in the cemetery of the Capuchin friars attached to the queen's chapel there. Of all the many plaudits rendered to him the most apposite was that of Rudesind Barlow, a fellow monk: 'In all my life I have never found anyone so candid, sincere, agreeable and discreet' (Ogle and others, 1.243).

DAVID DANIEL REES

Sources J. McCann and H. Connolly, eds., *Memorials of Father Augustine Baker and other documents relating to the English Benedictines*, Catholic RS, 33 (1933) · D. Lunn, *The English Benedictines, 1540–1688* (1980) · G. Albion, *Charles I and the court of Rome* (1935) · B. Weldon, *Chronological notes … of the English congregation of the order of St Benedict* (1881) · G. Sitwell, 'Leander Jones's mission to England, 1634–5', *Recusant History*, 5 (1960–61), 132–83 · H. R. Trevor-Roper, *Archbishop Laud, 1573–1645* (1940) · T. P. Ellis, *The Welsh Benedictines of the terror* (privately printed, Newtown, 1936) · E. L. Taunton, *The English black monks of St Benedict*, 2 vols. (1897) · R. H. Connolly, 'The first six', *Downside Review*, 46 (1928), 31–49 · R. H. Connolly, 'Responsio pro monachis Anglicis by Father Leander of S Martin, 1607', *Downside Review*, 46 (1928), 144–57 · J. B. Whitmore, 'John Jones (Leander a Sancto Martino)', *N&Q*, 146 (1924), 93–4 · *Calendar of the Clarendon state papers preserved in the Bodleian Library*, 1: *To Jan 1649*, ed. O. Ogle and W. H. Bliss (1872) · P. Allanson, 'Biographies of the English Benedictines', Downside Abbey · B. Weldon, 'Collections', Downside Abbey · E. Henson, ed., *The registers of the English College at Valladolid, 1589–1862*, Catholic RS, 30 (1930)

Archives Downside Abbey, near Bath, English Benedictine Congregation archives

Likenesses oils, *c*.1630, Downside Abbey, near Bath

Jones, John (*b.* before **1585**, *d.* in or before **1658**), copyist and manuscript collector, was born in Gellilyfdy in the parish of Ysgeifiog, Flintshire, the eldest of six sons and three daughters born to William Jones (1527/8–1622) and his wife, Margaret, daughter of Thomas ap Hywel. His father and his grandfather, Siôn ap William, were also copyists and patrons of poets. Nothing is known about his education except his year in Shrewsbury School (1595–6). The copying of an arithmetical treatise onto legal documents dated 1598 suggests that he may have been apprenticed to an attorney in Shrewsbury; he may also be the 'John Jones, clerck' mentioned in April 1600 in Llanfair Dyffryn Clwyd. Between 1603 and 1610 he was in Gellilyfdy and the gentry houses of the nearby Vale of Clwyd copying the bulk of twenty-five manuscripts belonging either to members of his family or to neighbouring gentry, clergymen, and scholars.

In 1611–12 Jones compiled a list of the names of owners of manuscripts and books. In September 1612 he was in Glamorgan copying *Liber landavensis*, compiling another catalogue of the owners of manuscripts in that area, and locating Welsh manuscripts and books on both sides of the border. After that he was in Ludlow, reputedly practising as an attorney; there he would have been ideally placed for hearing about the location of manuscripts from Anglesey to Warwickshire, since it was the seat of the council in the marches and the focus of political and legal life in the principality. In 1617 he was imprisoned by the council and copying again. The pattern of copying between *c*.1613 and 1621 is revealing and establishes a pattern that remained to the end of his life—he did little while at liberty, but copied extensively during his frequent periods of incarceration. Consequently there was much copying in 1618 but little in 1620 and 1621, when he was in London dealing with a case in the court of common

pleas; back in Ludlow prison by August 1622, the copying began again. But during these years, 1622–4, Jones was only rearranging and recopying manuscripts such as his massive dictionaries, unlike the period before 1610 when he borrowed new manuscripts from other scholars. The apparently obsessive rearranging may simply indicate that he had no new materials at hand.

His father died in August 1622, and after various bequests the residue of the estate went to Jones, which resulted in almost continuous litigation with his siblings and others between 1624 and 1632, in chancery, the Star Chamber, and other courts. He incurred a fine of £200 in the Star Chamber and was committed to the Fleet prison between 1632 and 1639. Very few manuscripts were copied during 1624–32, but during the Fleet years, 1632–9, Jones worked on fifteen literary manuscripts and put the finishing touches to two others which he had compiled years previously. Some of these are his most accomplished work, but unfortunately many of the most ornamental manuscripts are disfigured by an excess of gall in the ink, which has destroyed the paper, especially where it has been laid on thickly in the ornate capitals. The facility to copy in this period raises the question of his precise status as a prisoner. He always referred to himself as a 'close prisoner' in the Fleet, but those men were usually political prisoners, denied access to pen and paper except to write petitions concerning their cases; such a prohibition did not apply to Jones. However, there are extant drafts of petitions by him to members of the privy council and House of Commons outlining his own grievances and suggesting remedies for general defects of the body politic.

After 1641 the copying virtually stopped, although Jones may have remained in the Fleet until 1643 when he was released from an unnamed prison and returned to Gellilyfdy. During the civil war Jones was in Flint gaol for refusing to pay a levy of the commissioners of array, and he petitioned the king in June 1643 on behalf of the people of Flintshire about the oppression of the commissioners. He had manuscripts in boxes and bags with him in gaol which were stolen by the parliamentary army. He remained at liberty in Gellilyfdy from the end of 1647 until 1653. In 1648 he started an action in the court of chancery for the recovery of stolen books and manuscripts, and in October 1649 another action in the same court against a Thomas Edwards which dragged on until his death. Meanwhile he was petitioning parliament obsessively.

In 1651 Jones married Elizabeth, daughter of Peter Griffiths, of Caerwys, Flintshire. Typically, the details of the marriage are known from a chancery case of 1657. In January 1654 he was again in the Fleet, but was home by September. He has left a vivid account of the night of 9 November 1654 when Thomas Edwards, on the pretext of a chancery warrant, broke into Gellilyfdy with five armed soldiers and 'theeves' and attacked Jones and his pregnant wife. He was first taken to Cheshire and afterwards to the Fleet, where he remained until he died intestate, before 6 April 1658. Elizabeth Jones was granted letters of administration in 1659, which revealed that she and her husband had had three girls, referred to as 'infants of 6 yeares or thereabouts'. His grave is unknown and there is no memorial to him save the manuscripts he copied.

Over eighty manuscripts wholly or partly in Jones's hand survive in various repositories; it is impossible to be more precise since some manuscripts have been broken up and the parts separated. The topics cover all aspects of Welsh history and literature up to the seventeenth century, for example: poetry, from copies of the earliest poems to contemporary collections, often with anecdotes about the poets and/or the circumstances of composition; bardic grammars; vaticinatory poetry and prose works; historical texts, law texts, and religious works of all kinds, including several collections of saints' lives; prose romances and ancillary materials such as triads and folk tales; genealogies and materials for family history; astrological, mathematical, and pseudo-scientific and musical texts, word-lists and dictionaries of Welsh and several other European languages, plus anything and everything else that came his way and that he could copy. Jones was the most prolific and most skilled of all the Welsh copyists.

NESTA LLOYD

Sources N. Lloyd, 'A history of Welsh scholarship in the first half of the seventeenth century, with special reference to the writings of John Jones, Gellilyfdy', DPhil diss., U. Oxf., 1970 • N. Lloyd, 'John Jones, Gellilyfdy', *Flintshire Historical Society Publications*, 24 (1969–70), 5–17 • N. Watcyn-Powel, 'Robert ap Huw: a wanton minstrel of Anglesey', *Welsh Music History / Hanes Cerddoriaeth Cymru* [Robert ap Huw issue, ed. S. Harper], 3 (1999), 5–29
Archives BL, papers • Bodl. Oxf., papers • NL Wales, papers • South Glamorgan County Library, Cardiff, papers

Jones, John (*c*.1597–1660), parliamentarian army officer and regicide, was the son of Thomas ap John ab Ieuan ap Huw of Maesygarnedd, Llanbedr, Merioneth. His mother, Ellen, was the daughter of Robert Wynn of Taltreuddyn, Llanenddwyn, in the same county. Jones's immediate forebears were modest freeholders, but his mother's family claimed kinship with the important Myddelton family of Chirk, and Jones was sent to London in his youth to serve in the Myddelton household. Through that connection he served an apprenticeship in the Grocers' Company, of which he became a freeman in 1633, and acquired a good enough grounding in the law to be described later as a solicitor. By 1639 he had married Margaret Edwards, with whom he had one son; she died on 19 November 1651. Jones was still in the service of Sir Thomas Myddelton when he enlisted as an infantry captain in the service of parliament in 1642. He was apparently among the troops driven ashore at Milford Haven in November 1644; they provided support for Rowland Laugharne in south-west Wales before moving north to join Myddelton. By 1646 Jones had become a colonel of horse in Myddelton's army, under Major-General Thomas Mytton, and was prominent in the taking of Beaumaris and Caernarfon. He was one of the parliamentary commissioners who successfully negotiated the surrender of Anglesey on 14 June 1646, and was also present at the surrender of Harlech Castle on 15 March 1647. During that year he began to appear as an

assessment commissioner in his native county and on 3 November he was elected its MP.

Jones may have been absent from the Commons on military business for the first half of 1648, and on 10 June he was required to draft letters thanking the parliamentarian commanders in north Wales for their efforts in putting down the revolt of Sir John Owen, and to join them there. Jones was on hand at Denbigh Castle to witness the foiling of an attempt to rescue Owen, and reported back to the speaker. Given authority to raise a troop to help with the final destruction of Owen's forces, he was on 22 August 1648 again given a commission to settle Anglesey. On 4 October Jones was voted £2000 arrears by the house for his services, the sum to come from estates of Anglesey delinquents. Later that month he was one of a number of north Wales commanders who wrote to assessment commissioners in English counties requesting that assigned revenue be sent them so that they could disband their forces. On 25 November he and Myddelton were ordered to bring in assessments for the army from north Wales. Jones was a regularly attending commissioner at the trial of Charles I, and signed his death warrant [*see also* Regicides]. On 27 January 1649 he was named to a committee on a bill to prohibit a royal succession. To judge from the forty-five committees to which he was named in 1649, he was an enthusiast for the Commonwealth government. On 13 February he was appointed a councillor of state, and he was among the ten most frequent attenders of council meetings. It was through his involvement in the work of the council that he began an association with Irish affairs; he was also a kinsman of Colonel Michael *Jones, governor of Dublin until his death in 1649.

John Jones shared the radical millenarian outlook of Colonel Thomas Harrison, with whom Jones conducted a mutually supportive spiritual correspondence during the years of the Rump Parliament, and he was naturally included as a commissioner for the propagation of the gospel in Wales in February 1650. As a Welsh MP, Jones had served on the committee which scrutinized the bill to authorize the scheme. Beyond attending a meeting of the south Wales commissioners at Roath near Cardiff on 6 March 1653, however, he was unable to contribute much to the propagation experiment, as he had on 2 July 1650 been appointed by parliament a commissioner for Irish affairs. His salary was fixed at £1000 in October, and by 25 January 1651 he had arrived at Waterford with his two colleagues. Jones's commission in Ireland was renewed in August 1652, and as a result he spent most of his time between 1651 and 1654 in Ireland. His approach to the native Irish was as unsympathetic as that of most of his contemporaries. He believed that Ireland should be ruled with firm military force and that transplantations of the Irish from choice estates to poorer ones should proceed apace; moreover he viewed his posting as an opportunity to improve the quality of his livestock and estates. Contemplating Wales from across the Irish Sea, he deplored the spiritual deadness of Merioneth, believing only Ireland to be in a worse condition. He hoped in vain that Welsh evangelists like Morgan Llwyd and Vavasor Powell might launch a mission to Ireland, sharing their view that only by gathered churches could godliness be fostered in such wildernesses. To judge from his commentary on the conditions of spiritual life in Wales and Ireland, and the remedies he advocated, Jones must be accounted an Independent. An assumption that he must be the Colonel Jones described as the son-in-law of the Baptist soldier and MP John Hewson cannot be substantiated. His correspondence from Dublin is tinged with regret that he could not influence events at Westminster. In November 1651 he considered a new parliament to be unnecessary and an unwarranted gamble on the security of the state, but he must have shared the frustrations of his correspondents, especially Harrison, through 1652 and 1653 that conservative forces were inhibiting the radical religious cause he held most dear. Jones was sympathetic to the nominated assembly, but was not a member of it, and was rather reluctant to embrace the protectorate. He feared its promoters were influenced more by material than spiritual considerations, and for its part the new government did not renew his Irish commission.

After his return to north Wales, probably to Wrexham, Jones began a journey of reconciliation with the protectorate that began with his appointment as a commissioner for scandalous ministers, progressed with his post as a militia commissioner under Major-General James Berry, and culminated in his marriage in 1656 to Catherine Whitstone (b. 1597), the widowed sister of Lord Protector Oliver Cromwell. There were those in the government who retained suspicions of him, however—notably Henry Cromwell, lord deputy in Ireland, who thought Jones had promoted faction by encouraging the sects, and had 'acted very corruptly' (Thurloe, State papers, 4.606) in Ireland. Neither of these allegations could be substantiated, and Cromwell's hostility subsided somewhat when Jones joined his family. His support for the avowed republican Edmund Ludlow when the latter was arrested at Beaumaris in 1655 was more a token of their former comradeship in Ireland than an act of political manoeuvring. At the parliamentary general election of 1656 Jones was returned for both Denbighshire and Merioneth, opting to sit for the latter. Although his career in that parliament is difficult to distinguish from another Colonel Jones—Philip Jones—it is unlikely that John Jones was anything like as active as Philip. Both men were elevated to the new upper house on 10 December 1657, but republican commentators thought John Jones still retained some independence from Cromwell's court. Their assessment was correct: he was unsympathetic to Richard Cromwell's government, and was among the army officers who met on 29 April 1659 to debate the prospects for a military council which could exercise a veto on the planned restored Rump. Jones was one of the military section of the committee of public safety on 7 May. On the same day, as a member himself of the restored Rump Parliament, he was among the MPs who scrutinized the list of attending members. He reported to the house from the committee of safety and on its demise was appointed a councillor of state on 14 May. On 7 June he was restored to his place as

Irish commissioner, and he was dispatched to Ireland on 16 July, sailing with Edmund Ludlow. He combined this civilian role with that of military governor of Anglesey.

When Ludlow returned to England in October 1659 he personally nominated Jones commander-in-chief in Ireland. Jones was less than enthusiastic about his own appointment, and his lack of self-confidence was shared by the military establishment in Ireland, even though Ludlow had obtained the consent of his army officer colleagues for the posting. Jones failed to manoeuvre to get alongside George Monck, whose political star was rising, and declared instead for John Lambert and the 'Wallingford House' officers who had once again turned out the Rump. On 4 November Jones and Sir Hardress Waller rejected an alliance with Monck, fearing a split in the army, but on 13 December Waller seized Dublin Castle in the name of parliament. Jones was arrested, as was Ludlow, who bitterly regretted Jones's decision to side with the army officers in London against parliament. Both were impeached for high treason against parliament. After his appearance before the recalled house on 19 January 1660 Jones was released on parole, to the irritation of Monck, who wanted the impeachment to proceed.

Jones seems not to have realized the danger he faced as a regicide, and was arrested while out walking in Finsbury on 2 June. On 6 June he was added to the list of persons excepted from the bill of indemnity, then in draft. At his trial on 12 October he submitted to his fate, confessing the fact of which he was charged, and he was executed on 17 October, displaying remarkable courage and an unshakeable Christian faith. On the day of his execution, and immediately after, there were stories of men seen in the sky in Hertfordshire, and a crab tree blossomed on his estate: such stories enhanced an impression of martyrdom fostered by the bearing of the elderly soldier during his final sufferings.

His son and heir was allowed to retain the lands Jones had held before 1646. Crown lands he had bought, including the lordship of Bromfield and Yale, Denbighshire, for over £7500, automatically reverted to the king; other extensive estates he had acquired in north Wales, valued at £265 a year and heavily mortgaged, were forfeited to James, duke of York, and those in Ireland to Arthur Annesley, Lord Valentia.

STEPHEN K. ROBERTS

Sources J. Meyer, ed., 'Inedited letters of Cromwell, Colonel Jones, Bradshaw and regicides', Transactions of the Historic Society of Lancashire and Cheshire, new ser., 1 (1860–61), 177–300 • NL Wales, Plas Yolyn papers • The memoirs of Edmund Ludlow, ed. C. H. Firth, 2 vols. (1894) • CSP dom., 1642–60 • DWB • J. R. Phillips, Memoirs of the civil war in Wales and the marches, 1642–1649, 2 vols. (1874) • State trials, vol. 5 • E. Ludlow, A voyce from the watch tower, ed. A. B. Worden, CS, 4th ser., 21 (1978) • HoP, Commons, 1690–1715 [draft] • Eniantos terastios. Mirabilis annus, or, The year of prodigies (1661) • W. S., Rebels no saints, or, A collection of the speeches, private passages, letters, and prayers of those lately executed (1661) • GL, MS 11592A • CSP Ire., 1647–60 • R. Dunlop, ed., Ireland under the Commonwealth, 2 vols. (1913) • A. N. Palmer, A history of the town and parish of Wrexham, 3: A history of the older nonconformity of Wrexham [1888] • M. Noble, Memoirs of the protectoral-house of Cromwell, 2 vols. (1787)
Archives NL Wales, corresp., letter-book, and papers

Likenesses group portrait, line engraving (*The regicides executed in 1660*), BM; repro. in W. S., *Rebels no saints* (1661) · line engraving, NPG

Jones, John (1644/5–1709), lawyer and physician, was the son or grandson of Matthew Jones of Pen-tyrch, Glamorgan. On 28 June 1662 Jones entered Jesus College, Oxford, graduating BA on 5 April 1666, proceeding MA on 11 May 1670, BCL on 9 July 1673, and DCL on 21 July 1677, and being elected a fellow. In 1677 Robert Plot described a clock invented by Jones which 'moves by the air, equally expressed out of bellows of a cylindrical form, falling into folds in its descent, much after the manner of paper lanterns' (Plot, 230). On 13 June 1678 Jones was licensed by the university to practise physic and, following his marriage (licence 29 August 1678) to Mary Starkey (*b.* 1651/2, *d.* in or before 1704) of New Windsor, Berkshire, he took up the profession in that town. His wife was well connected, being the daughter of George Starkey (*d.* 1676) MP and sister of Samuel Starkey (1649–1717), MP for New Windsor 1679–81. Indeed, a John Jones was one of the first signatories of an address from New Windsor abhorring the Rye House plot.

On the death of Sir Richard Lloyd in June 1686 Jones became chancellor of Llandaff. Lloyd had married Elizabeth, daughter of John Jones, apothecary, of London. This makes it possible that John Jones was the son of the apothecary John Jones and therefore Lloyd's brother-in-law, especially as Lloyd's will refers to his 'brother Jones'. Jones became a licentiate of the Royal College of Physicians on 22 December 1687. His chancellorship was disputed by Bishop Beaw of Llandaff, who wished to bestow the place on his own son, William. In May 1691 Jones secured possession of his office, but in January 1693 the bishop responded by exhibiting articles against him before the court of arches for 'uncanonical practices and misdemeanours'. William Beaw had to wait for the death of Jones to make good his patent for the place.

Jones died on 22 August 1709 and was buried near the west door of Llandaff Cathedral. His will, made in 1704 when he was residing at Shinfield in Berkshire, makes no reference to his wife, but does refer to a daughter. Browne Willis considered Jones

> eminent also for his skill in physic, which he sufficiently showed in a learned discourse in Latin of intermitting fevers, and also in another discourse concerning opium, written in English, which are books very much esteemed by the gentlemen of that profession. (Willis, 4–5)

The first book to which Willis referred was *De febribus intermittentibus*, published in 1683, and the second *The Mysteries of Opium Reveal'd* (1700). He may also have written a work in Welsh, *Holl dd'ledswydd Cristion … a gyfieithiwyd gan Rees Lewys* (1714), which Lewis was said to have translated from an unpublished work by Jones.

STUART HANDLEY

Sources Foster, *Alum. Oxon.* · *DWB* · G. T. Clark, *Limbus patrum Morganiae et Glamorganiae* (1886), 535 · J. L. Chester and J. Foster, eds., *London marriage licences, 1521–1869* (1887), 774 · Wood, *Ath. Oxon.*, new edn, 4.722 · *The life and times of Anthony Wood*, ed. A. Clark, 3, OHS, 26 (1894), 361–2, 413 · N. Luttrell, *A brief historical relation of state affairs from September 1678 to April 1714*, 3 (1857), 17 ·

will, PRO, PROB 11/512, sig. 290 · will, PRO, PROB 11/384, sig. 98 [Sir Richard Lloyd] · Munk, *Roll* · R. Plot, *The natural history of Oxfordshire* (1677), 230 · B. Willis, *A survey of the cathedral church of Llandaff* (1719), 4–5, 100 · S. Bond, ed., *The first hall book of the borough of New Windsor, 1653–1725* (1968), 42

Jones, John (1694–1752), schoolmaster and classical scholar, son of William Jones, an apothecary, was born in the Old Jewry, London, on 10 October 1694. He entered Merchant Taylors' School on 12 September 1703, was elected to a scholarship at St John's College, Oxford, in 1712, to a fellowship in 1716, and graduated BCL in 1720. While at Oxford he printed an (unidentified) introduction to English grammar. He was probably the same John Jones who completed William Diaper's unfinished translation of Oppian as *Halieuticks*, published at Oxford in 1722.

Jones was headmaster of Oundle School between 1718 and 1722, where he acquired the reputation of 'a very Orbilius'—a keen flogger. His 1736 edition of Orbilius' pupil Horace with Latin notes barely recovered its printing expenses, which were largely defrayed by the duke of Rutland's gift of £20 for the dedication. In 1743 he was collated to the rectory of Uppingham in Rutland through the influence of his kinsman Edmund Gibson. Possibly in return for this favour, Jones put some 'shrewd questions' to Richard Newton, which appeared in the third edition of the latter's *Pluralities Indefensible* (1745). In 1744 his wife Elizabeth (1690–1744), whom he had married in 1718, died. Jones died in Uppingham and was buried there on 20 July 1752.

D. L. THOMAS, *rev.* PATRICK BULLARD

Sources Foster, *Alum. Oxon.* · W. G. Walker, *A history of the Oundle schools* (1956) · *The correspondence of Jonathan Swift*, ed. H. Williams, 1 (1963) · N. Sykes, *Edmund Gibson, bishop of London, 1669–1748: a study in politics & religion in the eighteenth century* (1926) · R. Newton, *Pluralities indefensible: a treatise humbly offered to the consideration of parliament* (1745) · MS continuation of Wood's *Athenae Oxonienses* by Dr. Rawlinson, St John's College, Oxford · Nichols, *Lit. anecdotes*, 5.709 · C. J. Robinson, ed., *A register of the scholars admitted into Merchant Taylors' School, from AD 1562 to 1874*, 2 (1883), 11

Jones, John (1700–1770), religious controversialist, was born in Llanilar, Cardiganshire, the son of John Jones of Llanilar. He briefly attended Worcester College, Oxford, but matriculated from St Edmund Hall on 25 May 1721, graduating BA on 15 March 1725. He was ordained priest in 1726 and was curate of King's Walden, Hertfordshire, and then of Abbot's Ripton, Huntingdonshire. At this time he assisted the bookseller John Wilford in compiling *Memoirs of Eminent Persons*. About 1741 he became vicar of Alconbury, near Huntingdon. This was a poor living and difficulties in collecting the small tithes led him to resign in 1750 when he became rector of Bolnhurst, Bedfordshire. Deciding that the locality did not suit his health, at Michaelmas 1757 he became curate to Edward Young, the poet, at Welwyn, Hertfordshire, where he remained until Young's death in 1765. Jones was bequeathed £200 in Young's will, of which he was an executor. Otherwise he was unprovided for but, after the intervention of friends, he was inducted into the vicarage of Shephall, Hertfordshire, in April 1767.

In 1749 Jones published anonymously *Free and Candid Disquisitions Relating to the Church of England*. This takes the form of an address to convocation and argues for a new translation of the Bible and for modifications in the Anglican liturgy. He suggests that the three Sunday morning services (the litany, matins, holy communion) should be merged into one, and that repetitions (as in the case of the Lord's prayer) be eliminated. He questions the use of the sign of the cross and of sponsors in baptism and argues that the use of the Athanasian creed be discontinued because it is incomprehensible to most people. Conversely he argues for more occasional offices and prayers of thanksgiving, for both of which he perceived a real need. In discussing the Thirty-Nine Articles he questions the need to enforce subscription on those who cannot understand the propositions that they affirm, argues the case for subscription in more general terms, and questions the status given to the Book of Homilies. He takes the view that the Reformation's work is not yet complete and that the time has come to complete it, and argues that the canons of 1604 need modification. An appendix includes quotations from Anglican divines of the 17th and 18th centuries in support of Jones's views. A warm controversy ensued, prompting responses from John Boswell and John White. Furthermore, consideration of Jones's book played a part in the conversations on comprehension between Samuel Chandler, Philip Doddridge, and Archbishop Thomas Herring in 1750 and it influenced many of the reformed liturgies published later in the century. Jones nevertheless remained anonymous and many believed Francis Blackburne, a friend of Jones, who had seen the manuscript and had written *An Apology for the Author of the Free and Candid Disquisitions* (1751), to be the author. In *Catholic Faith in Practice* (1765) Jones developed his views on the Reformation; a biography of Cranmer was unfinished at his death.

Jones never married. Nichols says of him that he was:

> a man of very singular character, pious and regular in his deportment, diligent in his clerical functions, indefatigable in his studies, which were chiefly employed in promoting the scheme of reformation ... but not without affecting a mysterious secrecy even in trifles, and excessively cautious of giving offence to the higher powers. (Nichols, *Lit. anecdotes*, 3.15n)

He corresponded with Philip Doddridge, and was a friend of Edmund Law and Samuel Richardson. On 8 August 1770 'he fell from his horse going to his parish ... and never spoke more' (*GM*, 81, 1811, 511).   JOHN STEPHENS

Sources Nichols, *Lit. anecdotes*, 1.585–639; 3.15n.; 8.289–92 · G. F. Nuttall, 'Chandler, Doddridge and the archbishop: a study in eighteenth century ecumenicism', *Journal of the United Reform Church History Society*, 1/2 (1973), 42–56 · J. E. Lloyd, R. T. Jenkins, and W. L. Davies, eds., *Y bywgraffiadur Cymreig hyd 1940* (1953) · A. E. Peaston, *The prayer book reform movement in the 17th century* (1940), 39ff. · H. Davies, *Worship and theology in England: from Watts and Wesley to Maurice, 1690–1850* (Princeton, 1961) · E. Young, *The correspondence, 1683–1756*, edited by Henry Pettit (1971) · *Calendar of the correspondence of Philip Doddridge*, ed. G. F. Nuttall, HMC, JP 26 (1979) · E. Wilbur, *A history of Unitarianism in Transylvania, England, and America* (1952) · C. M. Spicer, *Tyme out of mind: the story of Shephall near Stevenage in Hertfordshire* (1984) · *GM*, 1st ser., 53 (1783), 924 · *GM*, 1st ser., 81/1 (1811), 510–11 · will, Sept 1770, PRO, PROB 11/960, sig. 329 · *Cylchgrawn Cymdeithas Hanes Methodistiaid Calfiiaidd* (1916), 52–5 · DNB

Archives DWL, corresp. and papers | BL, letters to T. Birch, Add. MSS 4049, 4311

Jones, John (1728?–1796), organist and composer, became organist of the Middle Temple on 24 November 1749, of the Charterhouse on 2 July 1753, and of St Paul's Cathedral from 25 December 1755. He held all three positions until his death, despite apparent weaknesses such as an inability to play from score. Before 1785 he married Sarah Chawner at Sudbury, Derbyshire; their children were baptized at the Charterhouse chapel. His chief compositions were the *Sixty Chants, Single and Double* which were published in 1785. One of them was sung during the service of thanksgiving for the recovery of George III at St Paul's on 23 April 1789, and at many of the annual meetings of the Charity Children. Haydn heard them sing this chant (no. 24 of the double chants) in 1791, and noted it in his diary, commenting that 'In my whole life nothing has moved me so deeply as this pious and innocent music' (*New Grove*). Jones published several volumes of harpsichord music (1754, 1761); the subscription lists for the 1761 volumes were extensive. Jones died in London on 17 February 1796 and was buried at the Charterhouse. It has been asserted that another **John Jones** (*fl.* 1797), the probable composer of *Six Pianoforte Trios* and a glee 'Ah! pleasing scenes' (both *c.*1797), was the sub-director of the Handel commemoration in 1784, but it seems likely that the Jones of St Paul's was in fact the Jones of the Handel commemoration as well.   L. M. MIDDLETON, rev. K. D. REYNOLDS

Sources G. Gifford, 'Jones, John', *New Grove*, 2nd edn · C. F. Pohl, *Mozart und Haydn in London*, 2 vols. (Vienna, 1867) · G. Grove, 'Jones, John', Grove, *Dict. mus.* (1927)

Jones, John (1736/7–1808). *See under* Jones, William (*bap.* 1762, *d.* 1831).

Jones, John (*c.*1755–1796), engraver, was judged by Dodd to be of 'distinctive merit' (Dodd's history, fol. 162). Nothing is known of his parentage or his training and although the *Dictionary of National Biography* and other authorities speculated that he might have been born about 1745, the date of his earliest work suggests a birth date a decade later. He exhibited with the Society of Artists in 1780, at which time he was living in Little Compton Street, London, but by 1783 he had settled in Great Portland Street, Westminster, with his wife, Elizabeth; their daughter Elizabeth Croswell Jones was baptized in September 1783. From Great Portland Street, Jones published the vast majority of the prints that he engraved in mezzotint and in stipple. He produced over two dozen plates after George Romney and was evidently his favourite interpreter. He also engraved a group of Henry Bunbury's drawings, several notable portraits and fancy pictures of children after Reynolds, and a few portraits after Gainsborough, including a lively mezzotint of the dancer Signora Baccelli (1784). A series of progress proofs of *Frances Kemble* after Reynolds in the British Museum gives an idea of the stages involved in scraping a mezzotint. He published a number of portraits of actors and actresses, sometimes in character, suggesting an interest in the theatre. He produced a few large historical pieces and genre scenes, including *Dulce domum* and *Black Monday, or the Departure to School* (1790) after William Redmore Bigg, and *Beatrice Listening to Hero and Ursula* (1791) after Henry Fuseli. These were among the plates that he exhibited with the resurrected Society of Artists in 1790 and 1791, in which years he was also appointed principal engraver to the duke of York and engraver extraordinary to the prince of Wales. His son George *Jones (1786–1869) also became an artist, known for his views of military life. John Jones died in November 1796 and was buried at St Marylebone, Middlesex, on 5 November.

TIMOTHY CLAYTON and ANITA McCONNELL

Sources 'John Jones', Dodd's history of English engravers, BL, Add. MS 33402, fols. 162–73 · Redgrave, *Artists* · will, PROB 11/1285, sig. 94 · J. C. Smith, *British mezzotinto portraits*, 4 vols. in 5 (1878–84) · E. Hamilton, *Catalogue raisonné of the engraved works of Sir Joshua Reynolds* (1874) · N. Penny, ed., *Reynolds* (1986) [exhibition catalogue, RA, 16 Jan – 31 March 1986] · H. P. Horne, *An illustrated catalogue of engraved portraits and fancy subjects, painted by Thomas Gainsborough, R.A., published between 1760 and 1820, and by George Romney, published between 1770 and 1830, with the variations of the state of the plates* (1891) · parish register, St Mary Marylebone, 5 Nov 1796, LMA [burial]
Likenesses group portrait, line engraving, pubd 1798 (*Sketches taken at print sales*), BM

Jones, John [*pseud.* Jac Glan y Gors] (1766–1821), poet and political pamphleteer, was born on 10 November 1766 at Glan-y-gors in the parish of Cerrigydrudion, Denbighshire, the eldest of the three children of Lawrence Jones (1716–1790), yeoman, and his wife, Margaret Roberts (1740–1815). According to a local tradition Jones was sent away to be educated at Llanrwst grammar school, and this seems likely in view of his early acquaintance with the poet Elis Roberts (Elis y Cowper), an inhabitant of that area. By the age of thirteen or fourteen he was at home, helping his father on the farm and spending his leisure hours composing love lyrics.

In 1789 Jones went to London, reputedly as a drover. A tradition that he left home in order to evade military service is probably without foundation. He found employment with Davison, Newman & Co., grocers and tea dealers in Fenchurch Street, and the following year he became a member of the Gwyneddigion Society of London Welshmen. Like Jones himself, most of the society's members came from Denbighshire, and many of them sympathized with the ideals of the French Revolution. By August 1790 Jones was once again in Cerrigydrudion. In his letters of this period to his friend Edward Charles (Siamas Wynedd) he mentions his poor state of health and his indecision as to whether to return to London. Early in the next year, however, soon after the death of his father, he entered the service of North and Pritchard, hat-makers, in Tooley Street, Southwark.

By April 1793 Jones had become tenant of the Canterbury Arms, in Canterbury Square, Southwark. The following year he and his fellow pamphleteer Thomas Roberts were among the twelve founders of the Cymreigyddion debating society, the most radical of the London Welsh societies. In 1795 Jones published a republican treatise entitled *Seren tan gwmwl* ('Star under a Cloud'), which attracted hostility from Welsh Methodists and other conservative elements. It provoked a heated exchange of views in the periodical *Y Geirgrawn*. According to tradition, Jones was forced to spend nine months in hiding at Cerrigydrudion in order to avoid persecution by the authorities. In 1797 he published a conclusion to this work in a second pamphlet, entitled *Toriad y dydd* ('Break of Day'). Jones was not an original political thinker and his views on war, monarchy, and the church were derived, for the most part, from Thomas Paine's *Rights of Man* (1791–2). Nevertheless, his pamphlets are distinct works of literature, appreciated today for their caustic wit and vigorous prose style.

By 1799 Jones had left the Canterbury Arms and obtained a position of some responsibility with Rock and Shute, Silkmen, 27 Ivy Lane, Newgate Street. He continued to be an active member of the Gwyneddigion, being elected vice-president in 1801 and in 1813. He was also appointed bard to the society, and would entertain his fellow members by singing his compositions to them. His most enduring works are lampoons, attacking hypocrisy and snobbery. The eponymous Dic Sion Dafydd of his most famous poem has entered the Welsh language as a derogatory term for one who believes that by affecting ignorance of his native tongue he is able to elevate his status within society. Another popular work, 'Hanes y sessiwn yng Nghymru', a farcical account of proceedings in a Welsh law court, highlights the absurdity of conducting a case in English when the plaintiff and defendant are both monoglot Welsh speakers.

On 23 July 1816 Jones married Jane Mondel of Whitehaven at Bermondsey parish church, and within two years he had become landlord of the King's Head in Ludgate Street. The tavern became a focus of London Welsh life and was for a brief period the favoured meeting place of the Cymreigyddion society. Jones died at home, highly respected and a comparatively wealthy man, on 21 May 1821. He was buried on 4 June in the London parish of St Gregory by Paul.   GERAINT PHILLIPS

Sources BL, Add. MS 14957 · M. P. Jones, 'John Jones of Glan-y-Gors', *Transactions of the Honourable Society of Cymmrodorion* (1909–10), 60–94 · E. G. Matthews, *Jac Glan-y-Gors a'r baganiaeth newydd* (1995) · introduction, J. Jones, *Seren tan gwmwl* [1932] · parish register (baptism), 10 Nov 1766, Cerrigydrudion, Denbighshire
Archives BL, Edward Charles MSS, Add. MS 14957
Likenesses T. C. Jones, oils, 1859 (after unknown artist), NL Wales
Wealth at death comparatively wealthy; had apparently acquired some of the best farms in Cerrigydrudion; left all his goods, chattels, and effects to wife: Jones, *Seren*, introduction

Jones, John (*c*.1766–1827), Unitarian minister and classical scholar, was born at Wernfelan, near Llandovery, in the parish of Llandingad, Carmarthenshire, the son of a farmer. He was educated at Christ's College, Brecon, a grammar school, from 1780 until the death of his father in 1783. From 1786 to 1792 he studied at the recently founded Hackney College, where he was a student of the classicist Gilbert Wakefield during 1790 and 1791.

In 1792 Jones became assistant tutor at the Presbyterian college in Swansea. Theological disagreements between the Arian principal tutor, William Howell, and Jones, 'who was not of an amiable disposition' (Jeremy, 71), and who,

John Jones (c.1766–1827), by Ridley, pubd 1799

moreover, was veering towards the Unitarian position of Joseph Priestley, led to the dismissal of both men, and in 1795 to the closure of the college, which later moved to Carmarthen. In 1795 Jones became minister of the nominally Presbyterian congregation at Plymouth, in succession to John Kentish, and in 1798 he moved to Halifax, where he established a school. From 1802 until 1804 he was minister of the Unitarian Northgate End Chapel, Halifax, running his school at the same time.

In 1804 Jones settled in London, where he spent the rest of his life as a classics tutor, his pupils including the sons of Sir Samuel Romilly. Soon after his move to London he married the daughter of Dr Abraham Rees, editor of *The New Cyclopaedia*, who had been his tutor at Hackney College. Mrs Jones died in 1815, and in 1817 Jones remarried. His second wife was Anna, daughter of George Dyer of Sawbridgeworth, Hertfordshire; they had two children.

Between 1800 and 1827 Jones published some twenty works of theology, classical lexicography, and grammar. Among the former were *Ecclesiastical Researches, or, Philo and Josephus Proved to be … Apologists of Christ* (1812) and the posthumously published *The Book of the Prophet Isaiah Translated* (1830). *A Grammar of the Greek Tongue* appeared in 1808; its fourth edition had the title *Etymologia Graeca* (1826). *A Latin and English Vocabulary* (1812) was enlarged as *Ananlogiae Latinae* in 1825. In 1824 he published *The Principles of Lexicography*. Before 1814 Jones had become a member of the Philological Society of Manchester. In 1818 he was made an LLD by the University of Aberdeen and in 1821 he was elected a trustee of Dr Daniel Williams's foundations.

About 1825 he became a member of the Royal Society of Literature.

John Jones died at Great Coram Street, London, on 10 January 1827, survived by his second wife. He was interred in the burial-ground of St George's, Bloomsbury.

ANNE PIMLOTT BAKER

Sources W. D. Jeremy, *The Presbyterian Fund and Dr Daniel Williams's Trust* (1885), 71, 194–5 · J. Murch, *A history of the Presbyterian and General Baptist churches in the west of England* (1835), 505 · J. G. Miall, *Congregationalism in Yorkshire* (1868), 266 · *Monthly Repository*, new ser., 1 (1827), 293–7 · *Northgate End Chapel magazine* (March 1886), 47 · private information (1891) · *GM*, 1st ser., 97/1 (1827), 371–3 · *DWB*

Likenesses Ridley, stipple, pubd 1799, NPG [*see illus.*]

Jones, John (*fl.* 1797). *See under* Jones, John (1728?–1796).

Jones, John (1772–1837), writer and translator, was born on 17 August 1772 at Derwydd, in the parish of Llandybïe, in Carmarthenshire. Little is known of his early years but it is thought that he received some classical education. As a young man he was employed as a schoolmaster at Wimbledon where Sir Robert Peel was said to have been among his pupils. He later pursued his studies in Germany and obtained, among other distinctions, the degree of LLD at Jena University. On his return to Britain he studied law at Lincoln's Inn, London, and, on being called to the bar in February 1803, he went on the Oxford and South Wales circuits. He was initially successful, but, after offending members of the legal profession while pleading the case of a poor client, he obtained little or no practice.

Jones was a good Greek scholar, and was well read in British manuscript records and in those of other countries. He published many translations, including *A Translation from the Danish of Dr Bugge's Travels in the French Republic* (1801) and an original translation of the four gospels, sometimes erroneously attributed to the Revd John Jones (*c.*1766–1827). However, his historical works were not so highly regarded and his interpretation of the religious revival in his *History of Wales* (1824) was severely criticized by the Welsh. A revised copy of this work was found among his papers after his death. He also left in manuscript a work entitled 'The worthies of Wales, or, Memoirs of eminent ancient Britons and Welshmen, from Cassivelaunus to the present time'. A letter by him on Madog, the alleged Welsh discoverer of America, appeared in the *Monthly Magazine* in 1819.

Jones died in straitened circumstances at St James's Street, Islington, London, on 28 September 1837, and was buried at St Mary's Church, Islington, on 3 October.

D. L. THOMAS, rev. MARI A. WILLIAMS

Sources *DWB* · J. T. Jones, *Geiriadur bywgraffyddol o enwogion Cymru*, 2 vols. (1867–70) · R. Williams, *Enwogion Cymru: a biographical dictionary of eminent Welshmen* (1852) · T. M. Rees, *Notable Welshmen: 1700–1900* (1908) · G. M. Roberts, *Hanes Plwyf Llandybïe* (1939) · 'John Jones, 1772–1837', *Carmarthenshire Historian*, 8 (1971), 77–8

Archives NL Wales

Likenesses R. Woodman, engraving (after drawing), repro. in J. Jones, *History of Wales* (1824)

Jones, John (*b.* 1774), poet, was born at Clearwell, near Newland, Gloucestershire, the son of Philip and Mary

Jones, and was baptized in Newland in February 1774. His father was gardener in the service of Charles Wyndham (who assumed the name of Elwin) in Gloucestershire, and his mother kept a small shop in the village. After receiving only so much education as enabled him to read and write, he became an errand-boy and afterwards, at the age of seventeen, a domestic servant at Bath. He employed his leisure time in self-education, read poetry, and began writing verses. In January 1804 he entered the service of W. S. Bruere of Kirkby Hall, near Catterick, Yorkshire, and in the summer of 1827 sent a few examples of his verse to Robert Southey, who was then at Harrogate. The result was the publication, in 1831, of *Attempts in verse by John Jones, an old servant; with some account of the writer written by himself, and an introductory essay on the lives and works of our uneducated poets by Robert Southey*. Jones's verses also form the appendix to Southey's *Lives of Uneducated Poets* (1836). Although Southey saw in the verses abundant proof of talent, his opinion of them was not high. Jones's volume was reviewed in the *Edinburgh Review* and is credited there with 'the stamp of mediocrity'.

D. L. THOMAS, *rev.* REBECCA MILLS

Sources R. Southey, 'Introduction', in *Attempts in verse by John Jones, an old servant; with some account of the writer written by himself, and an introductory essay on the lives and works of our uneducated poets* (1831) · Allibone, *Dict.* · *EdinR*, 54 (1831), 69–84 · *IGI*

Jones, John (1777–1842), politician, was born at Carmarthen on 15 September 1777, the son of Thomas Jones, an attorney and estate agent, and his wife, Anna Maria, daughter of John Jones, also an attorney. After the death of his father in 1790 he was placed under the guardianship of his kinsman John *Williams (1757–1810), a serjeant-at-law. Educated at Eton College (1791–3), and briefly at Christ Church, Oxford (1796–7), he was admitted at Lincoln's Inn in 1798 and called to the bar in 1803 after being a pupil of his guardian. He subsequently developed an extensive practice on the south Wales circuit, being considered the region's leading advocate. Although not a great rhetorician, he was a cogent speaker and had 'an unerring judgement of the temper and tastes of a Welsh jury'. One jury, indeed, is said to have announced its verdict thus: 'My lord, we are all for John Jones, *with costs*'. He practised until the abolition of the court of great sessions in 1830, and later became chairman of the Carmarthenshire quarter sessions.

Able advocate though he was, Jones was most famous as a politician. In his youth, he was apparently the 'rankest Radical' in Carmarthen (George Thomas, letter to *The Welshman*, 6 May 1842), and a fierce supporter of Charles James Fox. His early political career in Carmarthen took place in association with the whigs, and he was mayor of the town in 1809. On their refusal to support his parliamentary ambitions, however, he defected to the tories, and with their support became member for Pembroke Boroughs (1815–18), Carmarthen Boroughs (1821–32), and Carmarthenshire (1837–42). He was always a relatively poor man and his election expenses were met by subscriptions from his supporters.

In parliament, Jones followed Sir Robert Peel, even supporting Catholic emancipation in 1829. Jones's parliamentary career, however, was most interesting for his attention to local interests. Particularly important was his attempted defence of the court of great sessions, which the whigs in Wales (led by Lord Cawdor, Jones's chief opponent in Carmarthen) were seeking to abolish. Jones, in addition to urging the practical utility of the system, defended it on nationalistic grounds, arguing that the great sessions had been a gift to the nation from Henry VIII and that parliament must respect this. The court was abolished, however, in 1830.

For all his appeal to 'nationalism', Jones was no friend of the Welsh language: although he spoke Welsh himself and was instrumental in founding the Welsh Anglican Church in Carmarthen, he earnestly sought the decline of the Welsh tongue which he believed hindered the material progress of Wales. This was, however, only one instance among many of the paradoxes which were the hallmark of Jones's character. Despite the 'populist' style of his political campaigns, for example, he opposed the extension of the franchise in 1832. Hospitable and genial, he nevertheless had a most violent temper, as his antics during the 1831 election revealed. Not only did he assault a fellow lawyer in the street, believing him to be the author of a hostile article in the *Cambrian*, but he also brawled with the leader of a rioting election mob, and fought a duel with the Hon. G. F. Greville. This side of his character earned him the nickname 'Jack Slack' after the celebrated pugilist. John Jones died unmarried at his seat, Ystrad Lodge, Carmarthenshire, on 10 November 1842. His death robbed the principality of one of its most colourful public figures.

MATTHEW CRAGOE

Sources *GM*, 2nd ser., 18 (1842), 653 · *The Times* (14 Nov 1842) · R. G. Thorne, 'Jones, John', HoP, *Commons, 1790–1820*, 4.322–3 · M. Cragoe, *An Anglican aristocracy* (1996) · V. Jones, 'Through riot and duel to parliament', *Carmarthenshire Historian*, 14 (1977), 59–65 · R. D. Rees, 'Electioneering ideal current in south Wales, 1790–1830', *Welsh History Review / Cylchgrawn Hanes Cymru*, 2 (1964–5), 233–50 · R. D. Rees, 'The parliamentary representation of south Wales, 1790–1832', PhD diss., U. Reading, 1963

Archives NL Wales, letters and papers | BL, corresp. with Sir Robert Peel

Jones, John (1788–1858), poet, was born at Llanasa, Flintshire, where his parents held a small farm. From 1796 to 1803 he was apprenticed to a cotton-spinner at Holywell, Flintshire, where he learned to read and write. In 1804 he went to sea in a trading vessel sailing from Liverpool to the coast of Guinea, and in 1805 joined the man-of-war *Barbadoes*, which cruised in the West Indies. He was subsequently transferred to the *Saturn*, under Lord Amelius Beauclerk, and in 1812 to the *Royal George*, which cruised in the Mediterranean and elsewhere. At the end of the Napoleonic war he left the service, and was soon engaged once more as an operative spinner at Holywell. In 1820 he moved to a factory belonging to Robert Platt at Stalybridge in Cheshire.

While a sailor Jones read much, and also began to write poetry. He supplemented his post-naval wages by writing panegyrics addressed to his patrons, which he often published and sold as broadsheets. He also wrote a poetical version of Aesop's and other fables, and was author of two poems, *The Cotton Mill* (1821) and *The Sovereign* (1827). A collection of his works, entitled *Poems by John Jones*, was published in 1856 under the auspices of William Fairbairn of Manchester.

John Jones died on 19 June 1858, and his funeral was attended by about 8000 people; he was buried in the ground attached to the Wesleyan chapel, in Grosvenor Square, Stalybridge, where a plain gravestone was erected, and a memorial tablet placed on the wall of the chapel by public subscription.

D. L. THOMAS, *rev.* M. CLARE LOUGHLIN-CHOW

Sources *DWB* · Boase, *Mod. Eng. biog.* · *GM*, 3rd ser., 5 (1858), 202 · C. W. Sutton, *A list of Lancashire authors* (1876), 65

Jones, John (1791–1889), Church of England clergyman, son of Rice Jones (who was of Welsh descent), an army captain, and Mary his wife, was born on 5 October 1791 in the parish of St George's, Hanover Square, London. He was privately educated, entered St John's College, Cambridge, in 1811 as a sizar, was awarded a scholarship, and graduated BA in 1815 and MA in 1819. At Cambridge he came under the influence of Charles Simeon, and in February 1815 he was ordained to the curacy of St Mary's, Leicester, under the evangelical incumbent, Thomas Robinson. In 1816 he was recommended to Sir John and Anne Gladstone by Simeon as a sound and zealous clergyman, and he became the first vicar of St Andrew's Church, Liverpool, which the Gladstones had built. There was, it is said, but one evangelical minister in Liverpool before Jones's arrival (W. E. Gladstone, *Gleanings of Past Years*, 7, 1879, 213–14). His ministry, in spite of opposition, was so successful that the church had to be enlarged. He married in 1816 Hannah, daughter of John Pares, banker, of Leicester and of Hopwell Hall, Derbyshire. They had one daughter and seven sons, five of whom became clergymen.

In December 1850 Jones succeeded, on the death of his second son, C. J. Graham Jones, to the incumbency of Christ Church, Waterloo (in Liverpool), and in 1855 he was appointed to the archdeaconry of Liverpool, in succession to Jonathan Brooks, the first archdeacon. This post he held until 1887. A serious accident had incapacitated him from preaching since 1883. A collection of his sermons was published in 1829, followed by his lectures on the Acts of the Apostles (1841) and the Old Testament (1845), and by *Hints on Preaching* (1861). Many of his sermons on national occasions were separately published; the first was preached just after the battle of Waterloo, on behalf of the widows and orphans. Jones was believed to be the oldest clergyman in the Church of England at the time of his death, on 5 December 1889, at 14 Esplanade in Waterloo.

D. L. THOMAS, *rev.* M. C. CURTHOYS

Sources *Liverpool Daily Post* (6 Dec 1889) · *Pall Mall Gazette* (6 Dec 1889) · *Guardian* (11 Dec 1889) · Boase, *Mod. Eng. biog.* · D. M. Lewis, ed., *The Blackwell dictionary of evangelical biography, 1730–1860*, 2 vols. (1995) · S. G. Checkland, *The Gladstones: a family biography, 1764–1851* (1971)

Archives BL, corresp. with W. E. Gladstone, Add. MSS 44352–44474, *passim*
Wealth at death £13,471 6s. 9d.: probate, 21 Jan 1890, *CGPLA Eng. & Wales*

Jones, John [*pseuds.* Ioan Tegid, Tegid] (1792–1852), poet and antiquary, first son and third child of Henry and Catherine Jones of Bala, adopted the bardic names Ioan Tegid and Tegid, from the Welsh name of the lake near Bala in Merioneth, where he was born on 10 February 1792. He was educated at private schools at Bala and entered the Presbyterian Academy Grammar School at Carmarthen aged twelve. He returned to Bala and was admitted into Jesus College, Oxford, on 13 December 1814, and held a clerkship there from 1814 to 1817; he graduated BA in 1818, after taking a second class in mathematics, and proceeded MA in 1821. He contemplated taking up a teaching post in Calcutta in 1819 but took orders and was appointed chaplain at Christ Church that year, precentor in October 1823, and on 21 October of the same year perpetual curate of St Thomas's at Oxford. During his incumbency the church was repaired and partly rebuilt, and schools for boys and girls were established in connection with it. On 27 August 1841, perhaps at the instigation of Lady Hall of Llanover, Lord Chancellor Cottenham presented him to the living of Nevern in Pembrokeshire, and in 1848 he was made prebendary of St David's Cathedral. He held both preferments until his death in 1852. It appears that he did not marry.

Jones was a good Hebrew scholar, and in 1830 published *The Book of the Prophet Isaiah* (2nd edn, 1842), an independent translation from the Hebrew text of Van der Hooght, which was commended by Gesenius, Ewald, and other Hebrew scholars. He also had in preparation a Welsh translation of the same book, but it was never published. While in residence at Oxford he transcribed the 'Mabinogion' and other Welsh romances in the Red Book of Hergest at Jesus College for Lady Charlotte Guest (afterwards Schreiber), who adopted his transcript as the text of her edition of the 'Mabinogion' (3 vols., 1838–49), and he assisted her with her translations of these tales. Jones was co-editor with the Revd Walter Davies (Gwallter Mechain) of *The Poetical Works of Lewis Glyn Cothi* (2 parts, 1837–9), published for the Cymmrodorion Society. Davies was responsible for the pedigrees and most of the notes, while Jones transcribed the poems, unfortunately transforming them into his own orthography instead of preserving that of his originals, and also making some textual alterations. He wrote an introduction to each poem and was responsible for the glossary; he also contributed to part 2 a 'Historical sketch of the wars between the rival roses'.

Jones adopted, with some modifications, the orthographic system devised for Welsh by William Owen Pughe in 1803 and set out by him in 1808 which rejected the established conventions and which professed to explicate his own fanciful etymology of words. In 1828 Jones superintended, for the Society for Promoting Christian Knowledge, an edition of the New Testament in Welsh, into which he introduced his own system of spelling to supersede that of previous editions. This aroused much adverse criticism, to which he replied in *A Defence of the Reformed*

System of Welsh Orthography and in a *Reply to the Rev. W. B. Knight's Remarks on Welsh Orthography* (1831). Knight issued a rejoinder (1831). The best exposition of Jones's system is to be found in his *Traethawd ar Iawn-Lythyreniad, neu Lythyraeth yr Iaith Gymraeg* (a prize essay; 1830). Petitions signed by 150 Welsh clergymen against the adoption of his system were presented to the Society for Promoting Christian Knowledge, and were so far successful that the old orthography was adopted in the society's Welsh editions of the Old Testament. After his return to Wales in 1841 Jones took an active part in the eisteddfod and other literary meetings, particularly the important series held at Abergavenny, which resulted in the formation of the Welsh Manuscripts Society of which he was one of the promoters.

Jones had been tutored in Welsh poetry in his youth by Robert Williams (Y Pandy) and was a prolific poet in the traditional strict metres, in free verse, and as a hymn writer. His poems were published under the title *Gwaith Barddonawl … Tegid*, with a biography of the author by the Revd Henry Roberts (1859). Some of his lyric poems are attractive but Jones never achieved eminence as a poet. Jones was also the author of *Traethawd ar Gadwedigaeth yr Iaith Gymraeg* (1820), and translated into Welsh a portion of the government blue book of 1847 on Welsh education, including the counties of Brecon, Cardigan, and Radnor (1848). He was in correspondence with many Welsh scholars and antiquaries of the day. He frequently contributed to both Welsh and English journals, generally on questions of Welsh literature, and at the time of his death it was said that he was engaged on a commentary on the epistle to the Galatians for publication in *Yr Haul*, but only a portion was completed.

Jones died on 2 May 1852 at the parsonage at Nevern, Pembrokeshire, where he was buried.

D. L. THOMAS, rev. BRYNLEY F. ROBERTS

Sources H. Roberts, *Gwaith Barddonawl y diweddar Barch. John Jones, M.A., Tegid … ynghyd a Bywgraffiad o'r Awdur* (1859) · Hywel, 'Fy ymweliad olaf a Ioan Tegid', *Yr Haul*, new ser., 6 (1855), 339–41, 376–7; new ser., 7 (1856), 12–14, 42–4 · E. D. Jones, *Gwaith Lewis Glyn Cothi, 1837–1839* (1973) · R. Bromwich, 'The *Mabinogion* and Lady Charlotte Guest', *Transactions of the Honourable Society of Cymmrodorion* (1986), 127–41 · D. R. Hughes, '"Tegid" a syr S. R. Meyrick', *Journal of the Welsh Bibliographical Society*, 4 (1932–6), 361–3 · *GM*, 2nd ser., 38 (1852), 96–7
Archives NL Wales, corresp.

Jones, John [*known as* John Jones Tal-y-sarn] (1796–1857), Calvinistic Methodist minister and hymn writer, was born at Tan-y-castell, Dolwyddelan, Caernarvonshire, on 1 March 1796, the son of John and Elinor Jones. His father died when John was twelve years of age, and the direction of the family farm fell upon him, but he afterwards worked as a labourer and as a quarryman at Trefriw. There, he attracted the notice of the Revd Evan Evans (1795–1856), who advised him and lent him books. He began to preach about 1820 and in 1822 he was admitted to the Merioneth monthly meeting. In 1823 he moved to Tal-y-sarn and worked in the quarry. He married Frances (Fanny) Edwards (1805–1877) of Tal-y-sarn on 14 May 1823, and in 1824 he left the quarry to work in his wife's shop. He

made rapid progress as a preacher, and in 1824 he was admitted a member of the North Wales Calvinistic Methodist Association. In June 1829 he was ordained and soon became regarded as one of the greatest Welsh preachers of his time. Known as the People's Preacher, he attracted great audiences throughout Wales. He emphasized practical rather than doctrinal issues, and a musical voice and handsome appearance gave further appeal to his pulpit oratory. He was also a composer of repute and forty of his hymn tunes were published in a collection. He died at Tal-y-sarn on 16 August 1857, and was buried in the churchyard at Llanllyfni, Caernarvonshire, on 21 August.

MARI A. WILLIAMS

Sources O. Thomas, *Cofiant y Parch. John Jones, Talsarn* (1874), 17 · I. Foulkes, *Geirlyfr bywgraffiadol o enwogion Cymru* (1870) · H. Hughes, *Cofiant John Jones Talsarn* (1857) · M. O. Jones, *Bywgraffiaeth cerddorion Cymreig* (1890) · *DWB* · T. R. Roberts, *Eminent Welshmen: a short biographical dictionary* (1908) · T. Jones [Glan Alun], *Pregethwr y Bobl …* (1858) · *Y Drysorfa*, 48 (Dec 1878), 470 · d. cert.
Archives NL Wales, sermons
Likenesses W. Dickes, engraving, 1841, repro. in Thomas, *Cofiant y Parch: John Jones* · T. W. Hunt, stipple, pubd 1848 (after E. Williams), BM · engraving, *c.*1850, repro. in G. Parry, ed., *Pregethau y Parch: John Jones* (1869) · Hanhart, lithograph (after E. Williams) · Robinson and Thompson, carte-de-visite, NL Wales · J. Thomas, photograph, NL Wales · E. Williams, oils, NL Wales · photograph, repro. in Roberts, *Dictionary of eminent Welshmen*
Wealth at death under £450: NL Wales, Bangor wills (copies), 1858/1, proved 13 Jan 1858

Jones, John (1798/9–1882), art patron and collector, was born in Middlesex; nothing is known of his parentage. After serving his apprenticeship he set up in business about 1825 as a tailor and army clothier at 6 Waterloo Place, London, moving to 6–8 Regent Street about 1827. In 1850 he retired from active business but retained his interest in the firm, which benefited from a contract to supply uniforms for the army during the Crimean War. He continued to live over his business premises. He travelled frequently to Dublin, where the firm had a branch, and to the continent, particularly France. Jones began collecting soon after 1850, but the greater part of his collection was formed after his move to 95 Piccadilly in 1865. Most of the recorded information concerning his life appears to have been derived by William Maskell, author of the *Handbook of the Jones Collection in the South Kensington Museum* (1883), from Arthur Habgood, Jones's servant for over thirty years. Jones lived a retiring life, keeping no carriage or horses. He died unmarried on 7 January 1882 at 95 Piccadilly, London, and was buried at Brompton cemetery on 14 January. His tombstone gave his age as eighty-three.

Jones's estate was estimated at more than £350,000, including £250,000 said to have been spent on the collection. He appears to have had no close relatives, and apart from some legacies to friends left the bulk of his estate—except the collection—to hospitals and orphanages, including £70,000 to the Royal National Hospital for Consumption at Ventnor, Isle of Wight. His bequest to the South Kensington (later the Victoria and Albert) Museum—consisting of a total of 1034 objects (excluding the books), including 105 paintings, 137 portrait miniatures, 147 pieces of porcelain, 52 bronzes and ormolu objects, 135 pieces of furniture, 109 sculptures in marble and alabaster, and 313 prints—was subject to the condition that it should be kept as a separate collection and not distributed over the museum. Jones was an important patron of British painters of the early and mid-nineteenth century, including William Mulready, Edwin Landseer, and W. P. Frith. Yet the bulk of the collection, and the area for which it is famous, is of French art and in particular decorative arts of the eighteenth century. Paintings by Jean-François de Troy, Nicolas Lancret, Jean-Baptiste Pater, and François Boucher were bought to hang with a crowded display of French furniture, porcelain—most notably Sèvres of the period 1756–85—and objects of gilt bronze, silver, and enamel.

Not all the furniture in Jones's collection has stood the test of time: about one third of the pieces are now thought to be wholly or partly nineteenth century. Yet Jones bought at a time when there were no reference books and his judgement has been vindicated by the number of pieces which are considered to be among the most important examples of eighteenth-century French furniture anywhere in the world; these include works by David Roentgen, M. Carlin, and J. H. Riesener. In collecting *ancien regime* French art Jones followed a Victorian tradition and his collection stands comparison with those of Richard Wallace and Ferdinand de Rothschild, even though it is more modest in scale. C. M. KAUFFMANN

Sources [W. Maskell], *Handbook of the Jones collection in the South Kensington Museum* (1883) · O. Brackett, *Catalogue of the Jones collection*, 2nd edn, 1 (1930) · W. King and others, *Catalogue of the Jones collection*, 2 (1924) · B. S. Long, *Catalogue of the Jones collection*, 3 (1923) · D. Sutton and others, 'The Jones collection in the V&A Museum', *Apollo*, 95 (1972), 2–58 · *DNB* · C. Sargentson, *Catalogue of French furniture, 1640–1790* [forthcoming] [V&A] · C. M. Kauffmann, ed., *Catalogue of foreign paintings: Victoria and Albert Museum*, 2 vols. (1973), vol. 1 · R. Parkinson, ed., *Catalogue of British oil paintings, 1820–1860* (1990) [catalogue of V&A] · D. S. Macleod, *Art and the Victorian middle class: money and the making of cultural identity* (1996) · A. de Champeaux, 'Le legs Jones au South Kensington Museum', *Gazette des Beaux-Arts*, 2nd ser., 27 (1883), 425–44 · *List of the bequests and donations to the South Kensington Museum to 31 Dec. 1900* (1901)
Likenesses J. Lawler, marble bust, 1882, V&A · J. Brown, engraving (after drawing by R. Deighton), repro. in Maskell, *Handbook of the Jones collection in the South Kensington Museum*
Wealth at death £359,106 18s. 11d.: probate, 1 March 1882, CGPLA Eng. & Wales

Jones [formerly **Humffrey**], **John** [pseud. Idrisyn] (1804–1887), biblical commentator, was born near Dolgellau on 20 January 1804, the son of William Humffrey, a carpenter, and Elizabeth. Early in life he attended the local grammar school at Dolgellau before becoming an apprentice at that town with Richard Jones, printer and publisher of the Welsh Wesleyan journal *Yr Eurgrawn*, and adopting his name. He moved to Llanfair Caereinion, Montgomeryshire, in 1824, becoming by January 1827 the managing printer of the Wesleyan Methodist Connexion. In 1827 he settled at Llanidloes, Montgomeryshire, where he established his own business as a printer and publisher and continued printing *Yr Eurgrawn*; he edited the journal in 1851–2. For several years he was a member of the town's council and became its mayor. During this time he was a local preacher among the Wesleyan Methodists, but in 1853 he joined the Church of England, and was ordained a deacon by the Bishop of St David's in September of that year; he was licensed to the curacy of Llandysul in Cardiganshire. He remained there until 1858, when he was made vicar of Llandysiliogogo in the same county. He lived at 3 Church Street, New Quay, the neighbouring village to his living. In 1881 he was granted a civil-list pension of £50.

Jones's best-known work was a critical commentary on the Bible, written in a popular style, and entitled *Y deonglydd beirniadol* (1852). This ran into eight editions, and it was stated that 80,000 copies of it were sold in Britain and America. He also wrote another commentary in six volumes in 1845 and was the author of a volume of sermons and numerous pamphlets, poems, and contributions to the Welsh press. He died at home in New Quay on 17 August 1887 and was buried in the churchyard at Llandysiliogogo on the 22nd; he was survived by a daughter and five sons. D. L. THOMAS, rev. MARI A. WILLIAMS

Sources Glan Menai, 'Y Parchedig John Jones Idrisyn', *Ceninen Gŵyl Dewi*, 7 (March 1889), 64–71 · J. I. Jones, *History of printing and printers in Wales* (1925), 159 · *Yr Eurgrawn Wesleyaidd*, 101 (Feb 1909), 64–5 · *Yr Haul*, 4th ser., 3 (1887), 287–8 · *The Times* (20 Aug 1887) · *Bye-Gones Relating to Wales and the Border Counties*, 8 (1886–7) [24 Aug 1887] · *DWB* · CGPLA Eng. & Wales (1887)
Archives NL Wales | NL Wales, Dol. Corr VI MSS
Wealth at death £2262 3s. 9d.: probate, 24 Sept 1887, CGPLA Eng. & Wales

Jones, John [pseud. Talhaiarn] (1810–1869), poet and architect, was born on 19 January 1810 at The Harp, an inn kept by his parents, John Jones (d. 1832), a carpenter and smallholder, and his wife, Gwen, née Williams (d. c.1857), in Llanfair Talhaearn, Denbighshire. He attended the church school in Llanfair Talhaearn, and schools in Abergele and Rhuddlan. In 1844 he was employed by Sir Gilbert Scott and W. B. Moffat in London as an architectural draughtsman and practical superintendent of works, leaving them to join Sir Joseph Paxton in 1850. He was present at the opening of the Crystal Palace in 1851, and supervised the building of mansions for the Rothschilds at Mentmore, Buckinghamshire (1851–5), and Ferrières, près Lagny, near Paris (1856–9). Before returning to his birthplace in 1865 on the death of Paxton, he supervised the building of a mansion for Lord John Russell at Battlesden Park, Bedfordshire (1860–65).

Jones enjoyed a reputation among his countrymen as a stormy petrel at their eisteddfodau, where his abrasive toryism and Anglicanism, his iconoclasm and open contempt for temperance, set him apart. As an eisteddfod poet in the strict metres Jones, whose bardic name was Talhaiarn, was never to be a national winner, but as a writer of Welsh words to old Welsh airs he attained a popularity matched only by John Ceiriog Hughes. His skill in this respect is evident in John Owen (Owain Alaw), *Gems of Welsh Melody* (3 vols., 1860–64) and John Thomas (Pencerdd Gwalia), *Welsh Melodies*, (3 vols., 1862–70); and his two ditties 'Mae Robin yn swil' and 'Gweno fwyn gu' became both instant and lasting favourites in Victorian Wales. Three collections of his poems, interspersed with occasional pieces of racy descriptive or satirical prose, were published: *Gwaith Talhaiarn* (1855), *Talhaiarn* (vol. 2; 1862), and *Gwaith Talhaiarn* (vol. 3; 1869).

Jones had suffered from gout and an internal ailment for many years, and these complaints were doubtless aggravated by the excesses of committed bachelor carousing. His health seriously undermined, on 9 October 1869 he attempted to shoot himself with a pistol, and subsequently died in Llanfair Talhaearn at his birthplace, which had been renamed Hafod-y-gân, on 17 October. An inquest held the following day returned a verdict of natural causes, and he was buried in the village churchyard, where a monument was erected to his memory.

Jones's favoured subjects were war, wine, and love, but his insistence on the poet's duty to aim at the popular heart meant that he rarely rose above easy sentiment and commonplace expression. His rollicking adaptation of Burns's 'Tam O'Shanter', published as *Sôn am ysbrydion* (1845), and the twenty cantos of 'Tal ar Ben Bodran' in his second collection, which tell of a Welsh poet's disillusionment and deep sense of futility in the 'age of progress', show that Talhaiarn had a mastery of language and an awareness of human despair which are the attributes of a more accomplished poet than he is generally thought to be.   HYWEL TEIFI EDWARDS

Sources D. M. Lloyd, 'Bywyd a gwaith Talhaiarn', MA diss., U. Wales, 1963 · D. M. Lloyd, *Talhaiarn* (1993) · T. G. Jones, *Talhaiarn: detholiad o gerddi* (1930) · J. S. Lewis, 'Talhaiarn', *Baner ac Amserau Cymru* (23 Dec 1930), 4 · J. G. Davies, ed., *Burns ac Ingoldsby* (1931) · D. G. Jones, 'Talhaiarn', *Y Gangell*, 15 (1949), 3–8 · d. cert.
Archives NL Wales, corresp. and literary papers | NL Wales, letters to Ebenezer Thomas
Likenesses photographs, 1850–69, NL Wales, NLW MS 12353D · W. Roos, oils, 1851, NL Wales · Mynorydd [W. Davies], effigy on gravestone, Llanfair Talhaiarn, Denbighshire
Wealth at death under £450: administration, 1 Dec 1869, CGPLA Eng. & Wales

Jones, Sir John (1811–1878), army officer, was an illegitimate son of Horace St Paul (probably Sir Horace David Cholwell St Paul, baronet (1775–1840), one of the prince of Wales's set) and, presumably, a Miss or Mrs Jones. In June 1828 he was appointed ensign in the 5th regiment, and became lieutenant in December 1831. Two years later he exchanged to the 60th (King's Royal Rifle Corps), in which he became captain in July 1841 and major in July 1849. He served in the 2nd battalion of the four-company depot, of which he was left in command when the battalion went out to the Cape in 1851. In June 1854 he became lieutenant-colonel in the 1st battalion, and was at Meerut at the outbreak of the Sepoy mutiny in May 1857. He commanded the battalion in the fighting at the Hindan, 30–31 May, at the battle of Badli-ki-sarai, and at the siege of Delhi. He was at this time described as 'a fine old gentleman who might have sat for a portrait of Falstaff, he was so fat and jolly' (Hibbert, 284). Jones commanded the column of attack on the Subzee Mundi on 18 July 1857 and covered the assaulting columns at the storming of the city on 14 September; he was in command of the left attacking column from 15 to 20 September, which blew open the gates

and took the palace on 20 September 1857. He was the brigadier commanding the Roorkee field force, one of the columns of the army under Sir Colin Campbell during the hot-weather campaign in Rohilkhand and the capture of Bareilly. The successes of his column, and the heavy punishment inflicted on the mutineers, acquired for Jones the sobriquet of the Avenger. He was afterwards employed as brigadier in Oudh, at the relief of Shahjahanpur, the capture of Bunnai, the pursuit of the enemy across the Gumti, and the destruction of Mahomdi. He commanded the battalion in the action at Pusgaon. He received the thanks of General Wilson, Lord Clyde, and the governor-general in council, was made KCB (November 1858), and promoted brevet colonel. He was inspecting field officer at Liverpool from March 1864 until his promotion to major-general in March 1868. He became lieutenant-general in October 1877, and received a pension for distinguished service. Jones died at Torquay on 21 February 1878.
                              H. M. CHICHESTER, *rev.* JAMES FALKNER

Sources Army List · L. Butler, *The annals of the king's royal rifle corps*, 3 (1926) · *Hart's Army List* · N. W. Wallace, *A regimental chronicle* (1879) · Boase, *Mod. Eng. biog.* · *HoP, Commons* · C. Hibbert, *The great mutiny, India, 1857* (1978); repr. (1980)
Likenesses group portrait, photograph, 1857 (with officers, Delhi king's royal rifle corps) · oils, *c.*1860, Royal Green Jackets; black and white version, repro. in Butler, *Annals of the King's Royal Rifle Corps*

Jones, John [*pseud.* Mathetes] (1821–1878), Baptist minister and biblical scholar, the eldest son of Roger and Mary Jones, was born on 16 July 1821 at Bancyfelin, Cilrhedyn, Carmarthenshire. He was brought up at the village of Tan-yr-helyg, near Newcastle Emlyn, Carmarthenshire, where his father was a small tenant farmer. His early education at the school of Mr Davies, Newcastle Emlyn, was meagre, and in 1838–9 he went to Dowlais in Glamorgan to find work as a miner. At Dowlais he regularly attended Caersalem Baptist Church and in 1839, having returned to Carmarthenshire, he joined the Baptists. On his return to Dowlais, Jones became an active member at Caersalem and delivered his first sermon at Hirwaun in 1841. He spent a short time at Cardigan grammar school preparing himself for the Baptist college at Haverfordwest, where he spent nearly three years. He was ordained to the pastorate of Bethlehem church at Porth-y-rhyd, Carmarthenshire, on 27 May 1846. In 1848 he removed to Caersalem church, near Swansea. Subsequently he held ministerial charges at Newport (1854–7); Llangollen (1857–9), as co-pastor with John Prichard; Llanfachraeth (1859–61); Pyle (1861–2); Penuel Rhymni (1862–77), with Siloam, Tafarnau Bach; and Salem, Briton Ferry, where he remained from 1877 until his death. He married three times, burying his first two wives (Miss Williams of Wick Farm, Porth-y-rhyd, and Miss Williams of Nant-y-gwreiddyn) and marrying his third, Elizabeth Tye Williams, while he was at Rhymni. He was the father of six children.

Jones was active in radical politics, but he was best known as a littérateur, who contributed widely to the Welsh periodical press, particularly the Baptist journal

Seren Gomer. While at Llangollen he edited the denominational magazine *Y Greal* and later, while at Rhymni, was co-editor of *Yr Arweinydd*. He won many prizes at eisteddfods for his essays, several of which dealt with the geology of Wales and other related subjects. He also published a collection of sermons and sketches bearing the title of *Areithfa Mathetes* (1873). About 1860 he started a biblical and theological dictionary in Welsh, *Geiriadur beiblaidd a duwinyddol*, the third and last volume appearing (posthumously) in 1883. Jones died on 18 November 1878 at Briton Ferry, and was buried in Pant cemetery, Dowlais.

D. L. THOMAS, rev. MARI A. WILLIAMS

Sources D. Bowen, *Cofiant y Parch John Jones* (1921) · D. Powell, 'Revd John Jones (Mathetes)', *Welsh religious leaders in the Victorian era*, ed. J. Vyrnwy Morgan (1905) · *DWB* · D. Powell, ed., *Y geiriadur beiblaidd*, 3 vols. (1883) · D. Powell, *Seren Gomer*, 3 (1882), 286–97; 4 (1883), 38–46, 113–22, 219–26; 5 (1884), 57–63, 126–33, 207–13, 300–07 · *CGPLA Eng. & Wales* (1879)
Archives NL Wales | NL Wales, W. R. Jones MSS
Likenesses engraving, repro. in J. Vyrnwy Morgan, ed., *Welsh religious leaders in the Victorian era* (1905) · engraving, repro. in Bowen, *Cofiant y Parch John Jones* · photograph, repro. in Bowen, *Cofiant y Parch John Jones* · photograph on poster (*Seren yr Ysgol sul*), NL Wales · portrait, repro. in Powell, ed., *Y geiriadur beiblaidd*
Wealth at death under £600: probate, 21 Jan 1879, *CGPLA Eng. & Wales*

Jones, John (1835–1877), geologist and engineer, was born in the neighbourhood of Wolverhampton. While young he began to study the rocks of his native district, and published a short treatise entitled *Geology of South Staffordshire*. Jones was secretary of the South Staffordshire Ironmasters' Association from an early age until 1866, when he was appointed secretary to the Cleveland Ironmasters' Association, and moved to Middlesbrough. In his new position he took an active part in the formation of the board of arbitration and conciliation for the iron trade of the north of England, and served on the board as an employer representative until his death. He was also secretary of the Middlesbrough chamber of commerce and of the British Iron Trade Association; while shortly before his death he was appointed secretary to the Association of Agricultural Engineers. In 1868 he founded the Iron and Steel Institute, and acted as its secretary and the editor of its journal until his death. In addition he established a weekly iron exchange at Middlesbrough, and founded and edited two or three newspapers connected with the iron trade, including the *Iron and Coal Trades Review*. He was elected an associate of the Institution of Mechanical Engineers in 1869, and became a full member of the same body in 1873.

Jones died, after a long illness, at his residence in Saltburn by the Sea on 6 June 1877, at the age of forty-two. Having invested unsuccessfully in the iron industries of the north of England, he died penniless. A fund, however, was raised by the members of the Iron and Steel Institute for the benefit of his wife and children.

Jones wrote about twenty papers on scientific (mainly geological) subjects, the first of which, 'On Rhynchonella acuta and its varieties', appeared in *The Geologist* for 1858.

At the Middlesbrough meeting of the Institution of Mechanical Engineers in 1871 Jones read a paper on the 'Geology of the Cleveland iron district' (*Proceedings of the Institution of Mechanical Engineers*, 1871, 184). His other papers are principally contained in the *Proceedings of the Cotteswold Club* and in the *Intellectual Observer*.

W. J. HARRISON, rev. IAN ST JOHN

Sources *Journal of the Iron and Steel Institute* (1877), 414, and appx C, viii–x · *The Athenaeum* (23 June 1877), 804 · d. cert.
Wealth at death under £6000: probate, 29 Aug 1877, *CGPLA Eng. & Wales*

Jones, John Andrews (1779–1868), Particular Baptist minister, was born on 10 October 1779 at Bristol, the eldest son of a manufacturing tobacconist. His father abandoned the family when John was aged about ten. John was educated from 1789 to 1794 at Colston's School, Bristol, a charitable foundation, and was apprenticed to a Bristol merchant from 1795 to 1798. His father subsequently returned to the family, and in 1800 they moved to London. Soon after the move, however, John was obliged to leave home, and from 1801 to 1813 was employed as a bookbinder at Guildford. Here, on 10 October 1805, he married Ann (1774–1849), daughter of Elisha Turner of Bentley, Hampshire; they had seven children.

In early life Jones was, according to his own account, 'strongly Deistical', but was converted to Baptist principles in 1807 by John Gill, minister of the Baptist church at St Albans. He was baptized in July 1808 in the Old Meeting-House at Guildford, and six months later began to preach in the surrounding district; from 1811 he wrote for the *Gospel Magazine*. After preaching informally at the church at Hartley Row, Hampshire, for nearly three years, he was ordained minister there on 13 March 1816. In 1818 he was, for a short time, minister of Ebenezer Chapel in Stonehouse, Devon, and for six months subsequently at Beccles, Suffolk. The maintenance of a large family was a heavy burden, and he settled at Ringstead, Northamptonshire, in 1821, but left the congregation in 1825 because he refused to preach the moderate Calvinism known as Fullerism. He then became pastor of the Particular Baptist Church, North Road, Brentford, where his higher Calvinism accorded with the views of his flock. He remained there until June 1831, when he became pastor of the chapel in Mitchell Street, Old Street, London. In 1838 his congregation moved to Jireh Chapel in Brick Lane, and in 1861 to East Street, City Road; Jones remained there until his death in August 1868. He was buried at Abney Park cemetery on 28 August.

Jones's chief work was *Bunhill Memorials* (1849), a collection of gravestone inscriptions and short biographies of some 300 dissenting ministers buried in Bunhill Fields. A series of reprints of religious works by John Gill of London, John Owen, John Brine, and others, published by Jones between 1849 and 1854 with the title *Sacred Remains*, was intended to serve as an appendix to the *Memorials*. Jones also published pamphlets, devotional tracts, and single sermons. He edited many religious treatises, notably Gill's *Body of Divinity* (1839), and in 1833–4 engaged in a controversy in print with Joseph Irons, Independent minister of Grove Chapel, Camberwell, over the ordinance of baptism. W. A. SHAW, rev. L. E. LAUER

Sources E. C. Starr, ed., *A Baptist bibliography*, 12 (1967), 137–9 · J. A. Jones, *Grateful recollections of the life and ministry of Mr J. A. Jones* (1856) · *Baptist Messenger* (1868), 252 · private information (1891)

Jones, John Daniel (1865–1942), Congregational minister, born on 13 April 1865 at Ruthin, Denbighshire, was the third of the four surviving sons of Joseph David *Jones (1827–1870), schoolmaster and musical composer, and his wife, Catherine, daughter of Owen Daniel, a farmer of Penllyn, Tywyn, Merioneth. His father died in 1870, and in 1877 his mother married David Morgan Bynner, Congregational minister at Chorley. After schooldays spent at Towyn Academy and Chorley grammar school, Jones proceeded to Owens College, Manchester, with a Hulme exhibition supplemented by other scholarships and prizes. He graduated BA (of the Victoria University of Manchester) with honours in classics in 1886, then trained for the Congregational ministry at Lancashire College, of which in later life he was invited to become principal—an invitation which after much thought he declined. He proceeded MA in 1889 and in the same year took his BD at St Andrews, and was ordained to the ministry at Newland Church, Lincoln, where he remained until 1898.

In that year Jones accepted the invitation to become minister of Richmond Hill Church, Bournemouth. Under his leadership this church became known to a far wider circle than his own town, denomination, or even his own country. It was crowded Sunday by Sunday, not only by his own people but by the many visitors to Bournemouth from all parts of the world. They were attracted by the personality of the preacher, his appearance, the beauty of his voice, and his simple and eloquent expositions of scripture. He was pre-eminently an expository preacher with a gift of telling application to the problems and needs of practical life. During the long period of his ministry, which ended in 1937, the town extended its borders, and the church became the centre of a group of Congregational churches founded by his statesmanlike vision and by the generosity of his people. It was fitting that in 1938 Bournemouth should recognize the great part he had played in its life by making him an honorary freeman.

Jones's work for the denomination may not easily be summarized. He gave himself unsparingly to the Congregational churches throughout the country and loved nothing better than to serve the village churches at their anniversaries. It was his sympathy for the village minister which led him to the campaign for the Central Fund of £250,000 for bringing ministerial stipends up to a minimum figure, while later he was the prime mover in raising the Forward Movement Fund of £500,000, one of the objects of which was to make better provision for pensions for retired ministers and ministers' widows.

The denomination in its turn gave Jones all the honours within its power to bestow. He was elected chairman of the Congregational Union of England and Wales in 1909–10, and again in 1925–6, while in 1919 he was elected an honorary secretary of the union, a position which he held for the rest of his life. During his ministry he paid several visits to the churches in the United States and in the British Commonwealth as well as in the mission field. It was therefore natural that in 1930 he should be chosen as moderator of the International Congregational Council, an office which he still held at the time of his death. The free churches of the country also called him to high offices, and in 1921–3 he was moderator of the Free Church Federal Council, and in 1938–9 president of the National Free Church Council. He played a leading part in discussions on church unity following the Lambeth appeal of 1920, although he thought it unlikely that any specific act of union would result. He welcomed the increased understanding which these conversations afforded, and himself preached from time to time from Anglican pulpits. Through his preaching and through the many books of sermons and addresses which he published he made a vital impression on the whole religious life of his age, which was recognized by his appointment as CH in 1927. In the course of his ministry he received the honorary degree of DD from the universities of St Andrews, Manchester, and Wales. But his renown as one of the outstanding free church leaders rested not so much upon the high offices which he filled or the honours which came to him as upon the simplicity and strength of his faith and the devotedness of his service of his church.

Jones married in 1889 Emily (d. 1917), daughter of Joseph Cunliffe, a calico printer of Chorley, and they had one son and one daughter. In 1933 he married a member of his congregation, Edith Margery, daughter of the late William Wilberforce Thompson. Jones died at Bala, where he was living, on 19 April 1942, survived by his wife, and was buried in Bournemouth. An elder brother, Sir Henry Haydn Jones, Liberal member of parliament for Merioneth from 1910 to 1945, died in 1950. His younger brother, Daniel Lincoln Jones, was one of the first moderators of the Congregational church, an innovation for which J. D. Jones was largely responsible. S. M. BERRY, rev.

Sources J. D. Jones, *Three score years and ten* (1940) · A. Porritt, *J. D. Jones of Bournemouth* (1942) · *The Times* (20 April 1942) · personal knowledge (1959) · R. Tudur Jones, *Congregationalism in England, 1662–1962* (1962) · CGPLA Eng. & Wales (1942)
Likenesses W. Stoneman, photograph, 1930, NPG · E. Moore, oils, Memorial Hall, London
Wealth at death £16,272 19s. 3d.: probate, 6 Aug 1942, CGPLA Eng. & Wales

Jones, John Edward (1806–1862), sculptor, was born in Dublin on 2 May 1806, the son of the miniature painter Edward Jones (c.1775–1862). He trained there as a civil engineer under Alexander Nimmo. He worked with Nimmo on several important projects and was in charge of the construction of Waterford Bridge (1829–32). Preferring sculpture to engineering, he went to London to study and settled there. With his wife, Isabella Sophia, Jones had a son, Tennant Telford, who was baptized at St Matthew's, Brixton, Surrey, on 15 July 1839. Though entirely self-taught, he was successful, and was employed by many distinguished persons. He exhibited over 100 works, mostly portrait busts, at the Royal Academy from 1842 until his death, and the 'severe eloquence' of his style was noted in 1846 in the *Art Journal* (Gunnis, 221). Among his sitters were Queen Victoria (1854), the prince consort, Louis-Philippe (1844), Napoleon III, the duke of Cambridge (1853), the duke of Wellington, Lord Brougham, the earl of Clarendon (1852), Lord Palmerston, Daniel O'Connell, and Lord Gough. His bust of Daniel O'Connell (1843) is in the National Gallery of Ireland, Dublin. Among his few full-length statues is one of Sir R. Ferguson erected at Londonderry in 1862. He exhibited at the Royal Hibernian Academy between 1847 and 1853. His bust of the singer Signora Favanti was shown at the Louvre in 1845, and one of the earl of Carlisle at the International Exhibition of 1862. An undated bronze bust of Sir Robert Peel by Jones is in Birmingham City Art Gallery. Jones died at Finglas while on a visit to Dublin on 25 July 1862. He was described 'in wit, humour and vivacity' as 'a thorough Irishman' (Strickland, 1.558).   F. M. O'DONOGHUE, *rev.* ANNETTE PEACH

Sources W. G. Strickland, *A dictionary of Irish artists*, 2 vols. (1913); repr. with introduction by T. J. Snoddy (1989) • R. Gunnis, *Dictionary of British sculptors, 1660–1851* (1953) • *CGPLA Eng. & Wales* (1862) • IGI

Wealth at death under £300: administration, 18 Aug 1862, *CGPLA Eng & Wales*

Jones, Sir John Edward Lennard- (1894–1954), theoretical chemist and physicist, was born John Edward Jones on 27 October 1894 at Leigh, Lancashire, the eldest son of Hugh Jones, insurance agent, and his wife, Mary Ellen. He was educated at Leigh grammar school, where he specialized in classics, and at Manchester University from 1912, where he changed to mathematics, taking first-class honours in 1915. He then joined the Royal Flying Corps, became a pilot, and saw service in France. Afterwards he served as experimental officer at the armament experimental station at Orford Ness. In 1919 he returned to academic life, at first at Manchester, and then at Cambridge, where he held an 1851 Exhibition scholarship as a senior student at Trinity College. In 1925 he became reader in theoretical physics at the University of Bristol, and on 26 August of that year he married Kathleen Mary, daughter of Samuel Lennard, boot manufacturer, of Leicester. After his marriage he adopted the name Lennard-Jones. He and his wife had a son, John Edward, a medical doctor, and a daughter. In 1927 he was elected professor of theoretical physics at Bristol.

Jones's early research at Cambridge, under the influence of R. H. Fowler, was on intermolecular forces and their relationship to the properties of gases. His mathematical expression for intermolecular forces is known as the 'Lennard-Jones potential' and is much used in statistical mechanics. During a year in Göttingen in 1929, Lennard-Jones studied quantum mechanics and then introduced these new theories to the group of physicists at Bristol which A. M. Tyndall was gathering together in the newly built H. H. Wills Physics Laboratory. At this time he also began working on the development of the molecular orbital theory, which had been introduced by R. A. Mulliken in the USA, and of which Lennard-Jones became a leading exponent. In 1929 he used the theory in a paper on the electronic structure of diatomic molecules to give the first explanation of the paramagnetism of the oxygen molecule.

In 1932 Lennard-Jones was elected to the Plummer chair of theoretical chemistry in the University of Cambridge, the first chair in this subject in the UK. He built up a very successful school that specialized in applying quantum mechanics to the properties of molecules and of liquids and many of his pupils became leaders in this field. At Cambridge much experimental work was going on in adsorption and heterogeneous catalysis. Lennard-Jones collaborated in this work by developing appropriate fundamental theory.

Soon after the outbreak of war in 1939 the university mathematical laboratory became closely allied to the external ballistics department of the Ordnance board and Lennard-Jones worked with his staff on problems of ballistics. In 1942 he was appointed chief superintendent of armament research, and undertook charge of the old research department at Woolwich in its new role as the armament research department at Fort Halstead in Kent. His major contribution to the war effort was made at this department, particularly in the changes he made in its administrative machinery, and his encouragement of personal responsibility for scientific work.

Unlike many of his academic colleagues, Lennard-Jones stayed in government service for some time after the war; he was occupied with the reorganization of the department for peacetime conditions and became director-general of scientific research (defence) in the Ministry of Supply in August 1945. In spite of the offer of several positions in government service, however, he decided to return to academic life in the autumn of 1946, although he kept his connection with government science. In the post-war years he threw himself into the task of once more building up his school of theoretical chemistry at Cambridge and seldom had fewer than fifteen research students working under his direction. His main work during this period was on molecular orbital theory, and on the theory of liquids. He was also active in university policy making in the post-war situation of expansion in undergraduate and research student numbers. He strongly supported the idea of founding a graduate college to accommodate the increasing number of research students in the sciences, and he also advocated the formation of a university body concerned with the strategic development of Cambridge science, independent of the particular interests of the individual colleges.

Lennard-Jones had not intended to leave Cambridge but when he was invited to succeed Lord Lindsay of Birker as principal of the University College of North Staffordshire (later Keele University), the educational experiment involved in this project aroused his enthusiasm. After some months of hesitation he took up office in October 1953. Of his work at Keele, cut short after only a year, it is probably true that he had three things mainly in mind: the non-specialist foundation year which had been introduced as an essential feature of the course; the financial position of the college; and its relations with the outside world. With characteristic vigour he set about promoting and developing these aspects of the new institution, and was not embarrassed to give due emphasis to the public relations needed to put it on the map.

Lennard-Jones was elected FRS in 1933. In 1946 he was appointed KBE and in the same year he was awarded the degree of ScD by the University of Cambridge. In 1948–50 he was president of the Faraday Society and in 1953 he was awarded the Davy medal of the Royal Society and the Hopkins prize of the Cambridge Philosophical Society. From 1947 to 1954 he was a member of the research panel of the National Gallery. In 1954 he was president of section B for the meeting of the British Association at Oxford and he received an honorary DSc from the University of Oxford. Shortly before his death he received the Longstaff medal of the Chemical Society. He died of cancer at North Staffordshire Royal Infirmary, Stoke-on-Trent, on 1 November 1954.   NEVILL MOTT, rev. JOHN SHORTER

Sources N. F. Mott, *Memoirs FRS*, 1 (1955), 175–84 · *JCS* (1955), 1047–8 · *The Times* (2 Nov 1954) · personal knowledge (1971) · b. cert. · m. cert. · d. cert.

Archives CAC Cam., corresp., journals, and papers | Nuffield Oxf., corresp. with Lord Cherwell

Likenesses W. Stoneman, photograph, 1934, NPG · W. Stoneman, photograph, 1945, NPG · W. Stoneman, photograph, RS; repro. in Mott, *Memoirs FRS*

Wealth at death £17,580 12s. 3d.: probate, 14 April 1955, *CGPLA Eng. & Wales*

Jones, John Gale (1769–1838), politician, was born in Middlesex on 16 October 1769. After attending Merchant Taylors' School, London, where he was admitted in 1783, he became a surgeon and apothecary, having been trained by William North, a member of the Company of Surgeons, practising at Chelsea. Although he published *Observations on the Tussis Convulsiva, or Hoopping-Cough* (1798), it is doubtful whether he was fully qualified. He married c.1796, but the name of his wife is not known.

Charles Roach Smith said that Jones's public advocacy of democratic doctrines ruined his professional prospects. Certainly he is best-known for his radical political activism. He was a member of the London Corresponding Society, spoke with great effect at radical gatherings, and publicly professed his sympathy with the French Revolution. Jones is depicted in Gillray's caricature of the great meeting held at Copenhagen Fields on 13 November 1795 against the Bill for the Protection of the King's Person, and he was one of the major speakers at other such meetings. In 1796 he published the first and only part of his *Sketch of a Political Tour through Rochester, Chatham, Maidstone, and Gravesend*, and on 11 March in that year he and John Binns delivered lectures, as delegates from the *London Corresponding Society, in Birmingham, but the meeting was broken up. On 9 April 1797 Jones was tried at Warwick before Justice Grose, and, although defended by Romilly and Vaughan, was convicted on one count of seditious libel. Upon appeal, and after numerous delays, the judge at the king's bench abandoned the prosecution so that Jones escaped punishment. A description of this can be found in his *Farewell Oration* (1798).

This led to a period of prominence in Foxite radical circles, but over time this subsided. Jones, however, did

John Gale Jones (1769–1838), by unknown engraver, pubd 1798

not abandon his radical sympathies. In 1804 he published a political poem entitled 'Galerio and Nerissa'; in 1806 he published 'Five letters to George Tierney' and helped to found the British Forum, a radical debating club. Jones also remained active in the politics of the borough of Westminster, which at the time was responding to the radical message propagated by Sir Francis Burdett's Westminster committee, led by Francis Place.

Early in 1810 Charles Yorke insisted on the exclusion of strangers from the House of Commons during the debates on the expedition to Walcheren. After a debate on this proceeding in the British Forum, the result condemning Yorke was announced outside the building in a placard drawn up by Jones. Yorke brought the matter before the House of Commons as a breach of privilege (19 February 1810), and Jones was ordered to attend the house. He acknowledged the authorship, was voted guilty, and committed to Newgate, where he remained until 21 June, when the House of Commons rose. During his imprisonment, Burdett, Romilly, and Sir James Hall made motions for his release, but they were all unsuccessful. Indeed, a letter that Burdett wrote on Jones's treatment led to his own committal to Newgate.

In this same year, on 26 November 1810, Jones was sentenced to twelve months' imprisonment, and ordered to provide sureties to keep the peace for three years for a libel on Lord Castlereagh. The rumour that he was ill-treated in this prison was found, on the investigation of Coleridge and Daniel Stuart, to be groundless (*Abuse of Prisons*, 1811, and *GM*, 1838, 2nd ser., 10, 127). Jones, in the meantime, had become disillusioned with Burdett, and turned instead to Henry Hunt. In 1818 he was heavily involved in Hunt's failed campaign for a Westminster seat, and in 1820 both men assisted John Cartwright's equally unsuccessful Westminster campaign. During these years Jones published three pamphlets: *Westminster Election* (1818), *Speech at the British Forum* (1819), and *Substance of Speeches* (1819).

Meanwhile Jones's political philosophy, influenced by the heady experience of the French Revolution, had lost influence. As his speeches came under increasing attack from other radicals, he withdrew from active politics and attempted to re-establish his practice as a surgeon and apothecary in Somers Town, London. Correspondingly, his views became more conservative: he turned against William Cobbett and supported the developing Anglo-American rapprochement (he had written a panegyric to George Washington in 1797). Jones died at Somers Town on 4 April 1838.   W. P. COURTNEY, rev. PETER SPENCE

Sources GM, 2nd ser., 10 (1838), 127, 218–19 • W. D. Jones, 'Jones, John Gale', *BDMBR*, vol. 1 • C. J. Robinson, ed., *A register of the scholars admitted into Merchant Taylors' School, from AD 1562 to 1874*, 2 (1883), 151 • *The diary and correspondence of Charles Abbot, Lord Colchester*, ed. Charles, Lord Colchester, 2 (1861), 235–63 • D. Le Marchant, *Memoir of John Charles, Viscount Althorp, third Earl Spencer*, ed. H. D. Le Marchant (1876) • S. Romilly, *Memoirs of the life of Sir Samuel Romilly*, 2 (1840), 305–33 • A. Griffiths, *The chronicles of Newgate*, 2 (1884), 61–2 • *The works of James Gillray, the caricaturist, with the history of his life and times*, ed. T. Wright (1873) • J. C. Smith, *British mezzotinto portraits*, 4/1 (1882), 1735–6 • E. P. Thompson, *The making of the English working class* (1963)

Likenesses J. C. Smith, mezzotint, 1735–6 • Gillray, caricature, 1795 (on hustings) • mezzotint, pubd 1798, BM, NPG [*see illus.*] • stipple, pubd after 1810, NG Ire.

Jones, John Gwilym (1904–1988), literary scholar and author, was born on 27 September 1904 at 6 Rathbone Terrace, Y Groeslon, near Caernarfon in north Wales. He lived for the greater part of his life in a house called Angorfa, in that village. He was the only child of Griffith Thomas Jones (1875–1957), stonemason, and Jane, *née* Williams (1878–1937). He was baptized John William Jones, and renamed by the renowned Celtic scholar Ifor Williams during registration at university. He was educated in local schools, Penfforddelen primary to 1916 and Pen-y-groes grammar (1916–21). After a year as a pupil-teacher he entered the University College of North Wales, Bangor (1922–6).

Jones's interest in serious drama was aroused when he was a student. His first post as a schoolteacher was at Millfield Road primary school, Clapton, London, from 1926 to 1930, and during his time in London he became an ardent theatregoer; he remained so for the rest of his life. This gave him a sense of the highest theatrical standards. The first of the fifteen plays he published appeared in 1934, and the last in 1980. Some of these are short, and were first presented on radio or television. He is the only Welsh-language dramatist to have had his work performed off-Broadway, in early 1980. He also translated many plays.

Jones held various teaching posts after working in London—in Llandudno (1930–44), Pwllheli (1944–8), and Pen-y-groes (1948–9). He then joined the BBC as a drama producer from 1949 to 1953. It was in 1953 that he was appointed

lecturer in the Welsh department at his alma mater, University College, and subsequently he was promoted reader. He retired in 1971. He was an extremely influential literary critic and teacher of literature over the course of this career. Many of the most notable critics writing in Welsh after 1960 were his former students from the Welsh department at Bangor.

Jones was always interested in technical developments in the contemporary theatre and his work reflects this interest. This is especially true of his two most notable plays, *Hanes rhyw Gymro* ('The Story of a Certain Welshman'—Morgan Llwyd, 1619–1659; 1964) and *Ac eto nid myfi* ('And yet not I'; 1976). The characters in his plays are usually intelligent, literate, and cultured, and are able to analyse their own predicaments to a large degree. There is a preoccupation with principle and reason on the one hand and feeling on the other, with the latter being presented as a more sure guide to what is good. In religious matters John Gwilym Jones was a chapel-going Methodist agnostic. His uncertainty about matters which had been fundamental beliefs in his upbringing is apparent in his work.

An avid reader of critics' work, in university classes and in a multitude of societies Jones enthralled listeners with expositions of the major critics, but it was in the close reading of original texts that he excelled. His methods are well exhibited in *Daniel Owen* (1970)—a study of the nineteenth-century Welsh novelist—and his *Swyddogaeth beirniadaeth* ('The function of criticism'; 1977).

Jones's work at the university was varied, and also drew on his theatrical experience. The university's Welsh Drama Society (as well as many amateur dramatic societies) benefited from his association with them as drama director. His main interest was in his actors' delivery of their lines, and under his direction inexperienced actors often gave extraordinary performances.

Jones's writing was not restricted to plays and criticism, however; his own book of short stories, *Y goeden eirin* ('The plum tree'; 1946), shows his acquaintance with contemporary European and American writing, especially with the narrative method of 'stream of consciousness'. The more impressive of Jones's two novels is *Tri diwrnod ac angladd* ('Three days and a funeral'; 1979), which deals, as does some of his other work, with the intricacies of family life.

John Gwilym Jones is generally acknowledged to have been a pre-eminent Welsh dramatist, drama director, prose writer, and critic and teacher of literature. In 1973 he was awarded an honorary DLitt by the University of Wales. In personality he was genial and sociable and became practically a patriarch in his own village, but was at times—especially times of illness—prone to become despondent. Jones collapsed while reopening a chapel vestry in Groeslon on 16 October 1988 and died shortly afterwards in the county hospital. He had never married. His cremation took place in Bangor on 21 October, and his ashes were buried in his parents' grave in Llandwrog.

GWYN THOMAS

Sources M. W. Siôn, ed., *John Gwilym Jones* (1993) • W. R. Lewis, *John Gwilym Jones* (1994) • G. Thomas, ed., *John Gwilym Jones: cyfrol* *deyrnged* (1974) • J. G. Jones, *Capel ac ysgol* (1970) • J. G. Jones, *Ar draws ac ar hyd* (1986) • personal knowledge (2004) • d. cert.

Archives priv. coll. | NL Wales, corresp. with Emyr Humphreys |FILM Arts Council of Wales (Northern Region) • BBC (Wales) • HTV, Croes Cwrlwys, Caerdydd |SOUND BBC (Wales), Llandaf, Caerdydd

Likenesses K. Williams, oils, priv. coll.; repro. in Siôn, ed., *John Gwilym Jones*

Wealth at death £149,750: probate, 15 Nov 1989, *CGPLA Eng. & Wales*

Jones, Sir John Lewis (1923–1998), intelligence officer, was born on 17 February 1923 at 8 Quality Row, Shotton Colliery, Easington, co. Durham, the son of Isaac Jones, a coalminer, and his wife, Isabel Raine. He was educated at Nelson grammar school in Cumberland and in 1940 went to Christ's College, Cambridge on a scholarship. During the Second World War he served in the Royal Artillery (1942–6). He returned to Cambridge to complete his studies, taking a first in part two of the historical tripos and a certificate in education. In 1947 he joined the Sudan government service as a teacher, transferring in 1951 to the ministry of education where he became the establishment officer. In 1948 he married Daphne Redman (*d.* 1988), whose father also served in Sudan; they had no children.

In 1955 Jones returned to Britain and accepted an offer to join the military intelligence department (MI5), serving first in Hong Kong and then Singapore (1959–61). After returning to London, he carried out the first feasibility study to computerize MI5's records. He then moved to the overseas branch, which was responsible for supervising the work of MI5 agents abroad: although it was the internal Security Service, MI5 also had responsibility for security in the British empire. In 1968 Jones was seconded to the Ministry of Defence as director of the moribund British services security organization in Germany. He revitalized it, and was appointed CMG in 1972.

When he returned to Britain, Jones was for a short time director of the overseas branch before becoming head of F branch, which dealt with counter-subversion, and later the operations branch. A rising star, he was appointed deputy director-general of MI5 in 1976, and in 1981 the prime minister, Margaret Thatcher, made him director-general. He had not come up in the traditional way through the more prestigious K branch (responsible for countering Soviet espionage), and Peter Wright described him 'as an F branch man through and through, and his appointment perfectly illustrated the decisive shift in MI5's centre of gravity' (*The Guardian*, 12 March 1998), away from concern with the external security threat, and towards the 'enemy within'.

Jones was director-general of MI5 during perhaps the most controversial and politically motivated period of its history. Encouraged by Thatcher, the agency targeted groups it considered a subversive threat to national security. These included coalminers, left-wing trade unionists, the Campaign for Nuclear Disarmament, and the National Council for Civil Liberties. Resources were diverted to countering subversion from what Jones called 'the far and wide left'. Peter Wright resented this move because it

deflected attention from his own obsession, the Soviet penetration of MI5.

Shortly after Jones became director-general the prime minister learned that Anthony Blunt, keeper of the queen's pictures, had confessed fifteen years earlier to being a Soviet spy. On that occasion the matter had been covered up to save the queen and the security establishment from embarrassment. Jones advised the prime minister that she should not name Blunt, on the grounds it might dissuade other spies from confessing in return for immunity. Thatcher rejected this advice and publicly unmasked Blunt on the floor of the House of Commons. Jones had also to deal with the highly embarrassing case of Michael Bettaney, the middle-ranking MI5 officer who tried to offer his services to the KGB. Moscow Centre, which feared a set-up, did not respond to Bettaney's overtures, and treated his original approaches to the KGB in London with great suspicion. Bettaney tried again, but the KGB double agent Oleg Gordievsky eventually exposed his treachery. The subsequent security commission report was critical of MI5 for failing to spot the potential troublemaker in its ranks, particularly when it became known that Bettaney was a heavy drinker. Jones was not personally criticized, but the case led to a demand for reforms in both vetting procedures and management. Jones, who had been created KCB in 1983, resigned in 1985. He subsequently served as chairman of civil service selection boards. He lived in Boston, Lincolnshire, where he took a considerable interest in local issues and was a member of the Boston golf club. He was an intensely private man, and only his closest friends knew of his real job. In his later years he developed emphysema, which contributed to his death in Pilgrim Hospital, Fishtoft, Boston, on 9 March 1998.   PETER MARTLAND

Sources P. Wright, *Spycatcher* (1987) • *The Times* (11 March 1998) • *The Guardian* (12 March 1998) • b. cert. • d. cert.

Likenesses photograph, repro. in *The Times* • photograph, repro. in *The Guardian*

Wealth at death £463,934: administration with will, 1998, *CGPLA Eng. & Wales*

Jones, Sir John Morris- (1864–1929), Welsh scholar and poet, was born at Trefor, Llandrygarn, Anglesey, on 17 October 1864, the eldest son of Morris Jones (*d.* 1879) and his wife, Elizabeth Roberts, shopkeepers, both originally of Llanrug, Caernarvonshire. When he was three years old his parents moved to Llanfair Pwllgwyngyll, Anglesey, and he went to the local school, the Duchess of Kent's, and the board school. From 1876 to January 1879 he attended the Friars' School, Bangor, under the headmastership of Daniel Lewis Lloyd (afterwards bishop of Bangor), and when Lloyd left for Christ College, Brecon, Jones was one of the many Friars' boys to go with him.

Jones's father died at Christmas 1879, and his help was now required at home. He assisted his mother for a year in the shop, but managed to find time to read a considerable amount of Welsh literature, especially poetry, and the beauty of the old *cywyddau* and *englynion* captured his imagination so completely that he could barely tolerate any other kind of verse again. Lloyd had a high opinion of

Sir John Morris-Jones (1864–1929), by unknown photographer

his former pupil's gifts as a mathematician, and made it possible for Jones to return to Brecon early in 1881 in order to read for a mathematical scholarship at Oxford. But the old zest had gone. The year at home had roused in him such an interest in Welsh poetry that mathematics took second place. He did win a scholarship, and went to Jesus College, Oxford, in October 1883, but obtained only a third-class degree in mathematics in 1887. A Meyricke scholarship from his college, tenable for a year, then enabled him to follow his real bent. He had already attended the lectures of John Rhŷs on Celtic; he now devoted himself wholly to Welsh, and began to prepare an edition of *The Elucidarium* and other tracts in Welsh from *Llyvyr agkyr llandewivrevi*, which appeared under his name and that of Rhŷs in 1894.

Jones and six others had already (6 May 1886) founded the Dafydd ap Gwilym Society in Oxford for the discussion of Welsh language, literature, and culture. Two of the first members, Jones himself and Owen Morgan Edwards, were to play the leading parts in the revival of Welsh literature. Edwards focused upon history and Welsh prose; Jones on philology and Welsh verse. Both felt the need of a more regular and scientific orthography; both loved purity of idiom and diction, although Edwards found his models in the living dialect and Jones in the medieval poetry. Vigorous discussions at the Dafydd paved the way for the work of the orthographical committee of the Society for Utilizing the Welsh Language (Cymdeithas yr Iaith

Gymraeg), whose report on *Welsh Orthography* was published in 1893, Jones acting as secretary. He did most of the work on this report, and for years afterwards in controversy after controversy he defended this 'Oxford Welsh', as it was called, against all comers.

Jones was appointed lecturer in Welsh at the University College of North Wales, Bangor, in January 1889. The charter of the University of Wales was granted royal approval at the end of 1893, and he was elected professor of Welsh in 1895, holding the post until his death. The new University of Wales gave him students in plenty, and through them his lectures on Welsh grammar became known throughout Wales. In 1897 he married Mary, second daughter of William Hughes of Siglan, Llanfair Pwllgwyngyll, with whom he had four daughters.

Jones studied the versification of the medieval poets and dealt faithfully, if not tenderly, with Joseph Loth's *Métrique Galloise* in the *Zeitschrift für Celtische Philologie* (vol. 4, 1903). His own skill in the ancient technique of the bards was demonstrated by the ode 'Cymru fu, Cymru fydd', printed in *Cymru* (1892) and later with other poems in his only published volume of poetry, *Caniadau* (1907). Jones's exposure of the falsity of the claims made by Iolo Morganwg on behalf of the gorsedd appeared in *Cymru* for 1896, and in the same year, curiously enough, he gave his adjudication on the odes, the chief poetic competition, at the national eisteddfod held at Llandudno. This was the first of a series of pronouncements, continuing until 1927, on correct Welsh and correct prosody given by him at this popular assembly, which made his name famous throughout Wales and helped to spread his doctrines. He castigated sloppy work with ruthless severity; no man did more to raise the standard of poetic diction in the eisteddfod poetry.

Although Jones's chief interest lay in the strict alliterative metres, he also helped to perfect the form of the free lyric by his translations from Heine, J. L. Uhland, and others; in particular his translation of ʿUmar Khayyam, *Penillion Omar Khayyâm wedi eu cyfieithu o'r berseg i'r Gymraeg* (1928), merits mention. His chief contribution to the study of Welsh prosody and, in the opinion of many, his best work, is his *Cerdd dafod* (1925), a full account of Welsh metric art in which he displayed his belief that a Welsh literary and linguistic revival was impossible without a careful study of the Welsh literature of the past. It was also of immense importance for its practical demonstration that Welsh was an appropriate language for the discussion and publication of detailed scholarly material.

Another of Jones's important contributions to Welsh prose is the masterly introduction to Ellis Wynne's *Gweledigaetheu y bardd cwsc* (1898), which is significant not only for its discussion of Ellis Wynne's sources but also for its stylistic analysis, which displayed Jones's characteristic dedication to the purity of the Welsh language. He edited the quarterly magazine *Y Beirniad* ('The Critic') from start to finish (1911–19), but wrote little himself for that periodical, although he spent a great deal of time in editorial work. Occasional articles from his pen appeared in various magazines: notably his 'Tudur Aled' in the

Transactions of the Cymmrodorion (1908–9) and the review in English in *Cymmrodor* (vol. 28, 1918) of the edition of the Book of Taliesin by John Gwenogvryn Evans.

Jones's *Welsh Grammar, Historical and Comparative* (1913), although limited in that it deals only with phonology and accidence, is a key work in the scholarship of the Welsh language. It was followed by an unfinished draft, printed posthumously in 1931 as *Welsh Syntax*. Both texts display a remarkable gift of lucid exposition, and skill in the clear arrangement and presentation of grammatical facts.

Jones was knighted in 1918, when he began to style himself Morris-Jones. In 1919 Glasgow University conferred on him the honorary degree of LLD, and in 1927 the National University of Ireland that of DLittCelt. He died after a brief illness at his home, Tŷ Coch, at Llanfair Pwllgwyngyll, on 16 April 1929, and was buried in the cemetery of that village.   I. WILLIAMS, *rev.* D. BEN REES

Sources *DWB* · M. Stephens, ed., *Cydymaith i lenyddiaeth Cymru* (1986), 417–18 · H. T. Edwards, 'Cerddi Syr John Morris-Jones', *Barn*, 61–72 (1967–8), 305–6, 331–2; 73–84 (1968–9), 24–6 · W. J. Gruffydd, 'Representative Welshmen: John Morris Jones', *Wales*, 11 (1911), 647–50 · T. Parry, *John Morris-Jones (1864–1929)* (1958) · A. James, *John Morris-Jones* (1987) · *Transactions of the Honourable Society of Cymmrodorion* (1919–20) · J. Lloyd-Jones, 'The late Sir John Morris Jones, MA., LLD., D.Litt. An appreciation', *Y Cymmrodor*, 40 (1929), 265–75 · *Wales* (1896) · *Wales* (1912) · *Welsh Leader* (28 Jan 1904) · personal knowledge (1937)
Archives U. Wales, Bangor
Likenesses R. L. Gapper, sculpture, U. Wales, Bangor · photograph, NL Wales [*see illus.*]
Wealth at death £7798 15*s.* 7*d.*: probate, 30 May 1929, *CGPLA Eng. & Wales*

Jones, John Ogwen (1829–1884), Calvinistic Methodist minister, the son of David and Elizabeth Jones, was born on 2 June 1829 at Tyddyn, Llanllechid, on the banks of the Ogwen, near Bangor. He was educated at Bangor and at Botwnnog grammar schools, and was employed between 1844 and 1849 as a merchant's clerk in Liverpool, and subsequently held a similar post in London. On deciding to enter the ministry, he spent four years at the Calvinistic Methodist college at Bala (1852–6); he matriculated at London University in 1856 and graduated BA in 1858. He married Margaret, daughter of Jacob Jones of Bala, on 28 December 1858; in the following year, he was ordained at Bangor. He had ministerial charges at Birkenhead and Liverpool from June 1857 to 1867, at Oswestry (Zion Chapel) from 1867 to the autumn of 1876, and at the Clwyd Street Church at Rhyl from 1876 until his death. He gained a reputation for powerful preaching despite suffering from indifferent health. He died at his home, 1 Churton Road, Rhyl, on 22 September 1884. His wife survived him.

Jones devoted himself to the improvement of the Sunday school system, and to the establishment of similar weekday classes. He was practically the founder of the county examinations of Sunday schools in north Wales, and he prepared several small handbooks for the use of Sunday scholars. He started and successfully conducted classes in botany and chemistry at Oswestry and Rhyl under the aegis of the South Kensington Department of Science and Art; he was also largely instrumental in obtaining adequate provision for elementary education at Rhyl.

In September 1864, while at Liverpool, he edited and wrote much in a monthly magazine, *Y Symbylydd*, which was discontinued after the first volume. In 1873, at the request of the Methodist Association of north Wales, he delivered a series of lectures at Bala College entitled 'Science and biblical history', in which he showed knowledge not only of geology and biology, but also oriental archaeology. These lectures were published in a volume entitled *Hanes iaeth a gwyddoniaeth y Beibl yn wir a chywir* (1875).

Jones's greatest contribution was as the author of numerous publications on religious topics, and on the relationship between natural science and religion. Foremost among these works are *Hanes bywyd cyhoeddus Iesu Grist, o'r, Temtiad hyd at y Pasg diweddaf* (1870), and popular commentaries on the book of Genesis, and on biblical history. His *Testament y Miloedd* (1883) was considered to be one of the best works of its period on the New Testament in the Welsh language, while his contributions to *Y gwyddionadur Cymreig* were again of a high quality.

     D. L. THOMAS, *rev.* ROBERT V. SMITH

Sources *DWB* · E. Edwards, memoir, *Y Geninen*, 3 (1885) · *Rhyl Advertiser* (27 Sept 1884) · *Y Genedl Gymreig* (10 Oct 1884) · private information (1891) · private information (2004) · *CGPLA Eng. & Wales* (1884)
Wealth at death £1372 16*s.* 3*d.*: administration with will, 27 Nov 1884, *CGPLA Eng. & Wales*

Jones, John Paul (1747–1792), naval officer in the American and Russian services, was born John Paul on 6 July 1747 in a cottage at Arbigland, William Craik's estate, near Kirkcudbright, the fourth of six children of John Paul (*d.* 1767), a gardener, and his wife, Jean, *née* MacDuff, daughter of a farmer.

Early years John Paul received a rudimentary education at the Kirkbean parish church school, near Kirkcudbright, before being apprenticed aged thirteen to a merchant from Whitehaven, across the Solway Firth in Cumberland. Over the next three years he sailed to the Caribbean and Chesapeake Bay where he visited his brother, William, in Fredericksburg, Virginia. Released from apprenticeship by the bankruptcy of his master and in need of employment, John Paul made at least two voyages in slave-trading vessels. In 1768 he was sailing as a passenger from Jamaica to Scotland when the brig's master and mate died. John Paul assumed command, brought the 60-ton *John* safely to port, and was rewarded with permanent command of the vessel. On a voyage from Scotland to Tobago in 1770 Captain Paul ordered a sailor, Mungo Maxwell, flogged for neglect of duty. Maxwell later died of a fever on another ship, and his father, a prominent Kirkcudbright resident, had John Paul arrested on a charge of inflicting fatal wounds on his son. While released on bail gathering evidence that cleared his name, John Paul joined the freemasons in Kirkcudbright, establishing a relationship that later opened doors to him in Boston, Portsmouth, Philadelphia, and Paris.

By the time he was twenty-five John Paul had formed a partnership with a West Indian merchant-planter and

John Paul Jones (1747–1792), by Jean-Antoine Houdon, 1781

commanded ships in the north Atlantic trade. In 1773, acting in self-defence, he killed the ringleader of a mutiny. (During his naval career Paul, a brilliant but tough man, suffered as many mutinies as the notorious William Bligh.) Taking the advice of friends in Tobago, he moved to North America and took the additional surname Jones to cover his identity pending an Admiralty investigation into the incident. He began to sign his name Jno. P. Jones, later changed to J. Paul Jones, and came to be called Paul Jones.

Early naval service At the outbreak of the American War of Independence, Jones joined the continental navy on 7 December 1775 and was offered command of the sloop *Providence* (21 guns), but chose instead to serve as first lieutenant in the frigate *Alfred* (30 guns). Following the continental navy raid against New Providence in the Bahamas, Jones accepted command of the *Providence* and spent May and June 1776 convoying men and supplies from New England to New York and Philadelphia. During the following September and October Jones captured sixteen British prizes on the Grand Banks and burned the fishing fleets at Canso and Isle Madame in Nova Scotia. Promoted captain on 8 August 1776 and transferred to command of the *Alfred* on 10 October 1776, Jones embarked on a second cruise to the Grand Banks during which he took seven more prizes, including the transport *Mellish* with a cargo of uniforms.

Although Jones was the most successful American naval commander to date, when he returned to Boston he learned that he had been placed eighteenth on the naval seniority list revised by a continental congress whose members valued family relationships and place of residence more than proven ability. Lacking those assets, Jones did well to gain so high a position, but he felt slighted and complained bitterly. While in Philadelphia trying to regain seniority, he convinced congress to authorize raids on outposts of the British empire. These orders were subsequently cancelled and Jones was instead instructed to fit out the sloop of war *Ranger* (18 guns) and to proceed to Europe where he was to assume command of a frigate under construction in the Netherlands. Jones took two prizes while *en route* to France but soon learned that Britain had blocked transfer of the frigate to the United States, and so Jones retained command of the *Ranger*.

Cruise of the *Ranger* During February and March 1778 Jones preyed upon British shipping in the Bay of Biscay. In April he sailed to the Irish Sea with plans for a raid on the English coast in retaliation for British attacks on towns in Connecticut, and to seize one or more prisoners who could be exchanged for American seamen held in British prisons. On the night of 22 April Jones and a landing party spiked the guns of the fort at Whitehaven and set fire to colliers in the harbour. While the physical damage was small, the psychological repercussions of the landing were great. The following day Jones crossed the Solway to St Mary's Isle and led another party ashore. He intended to kidnap the earl of Selkirk, but abandoned hopes for a prisoner exchange when he learned Selkirk was away. Unhappy with the risks they had run for naught, Jones's men refused to return to the *Ranger*. Faced with mutiny, Jones proposed that a group go to the house and 'politely demand the family plate'. His plan was accepted, the silver taken, and violence averted. In a letter to Lady Selkirk dated 8 May, written upon his return to France, Jones informed her of his original intentions, promised to purchase and return the plate, and explained his motives, saying, 'I have drawn my Sword in the … Struggle for the rights of Men … I am not in Arms as an American, nor am I in pursuit of Riches … I profess myself a Citizen of the World' (Morison, 149–50).

Undeterred by his failure at St Mary's Isle or by his men's conduct, Jones crossed the Irish Sea and sought battle with the sloop of war *Drake* (20 guns) that he knew was stationed at Carrickfergus. Calculating that the two vessels were roughly equal in armament, but fearing that the *Drake* had more men, Jones hammered the *Drake* into submission from a distance. After an hour-long duel, the *Drake* surrendered, her captain dead and her rigging cut to pieces. A cautious captain might have burned his prize and fled to avoid pursuit, but Jones understood the impact of carrying a British prize into a French port and remained in the area a day repairing the *Drake*. Two weeks later he led it with 200 prisoners into Brest.

Cruise of the *Bonhomme Richard* Recognizing Jones's abilities, Benjamin Franklin, then American diplomatic agent in Paris, obtained command of an aged East Indiaman, the *Duc de Duras*, for Jones who renamed it the *Bonhomme Richard* (40 guns) and converted it into a warship. Additional vessels were added to form a squadron and plans were laid for a raid on Liverpool with Jones in command of the ships and the marquis de Lafayette in command of land forces. Subsequent cancellation of the expedition left Jones free to pursue his own strategy, and he sailed from Lorient on 14 August 1779 with three intentions: to intercept ships expected from India, to lay Leith, the port city of Edinburgh, under contribution, and to intercept a convoy from the Baltic loaded with naval stores. Proceeding clockwise around the British Isles, Jones and the five vessels under his command missed the ships from India, but took seventeen prizes before heaving to off Leith. On 13 September Jones led the *Bonhomme Richard*, the *Alliance* (36 guns), and the *Pallas* (32 guns) into the Firth of Forth and issued an ultimatum threatening destruction of Leith unless a ransom of £200,000 was paid immediately. When a strong wind blew his ships away from the city Jones abandoned the enterprise and set course southwards in search of the Baltic convoy.

At mid-afternoon on 23 September the convoy arrived as Jones lay in wait off Flamborough Head. Light winds prevented closing with the forty-one ships of the convoy until near dark. As the merchant ships scattered Jones sought their protectors, the new frigate *Serapis*, rated at 44 guns but carrying 50, and the *Countess of Scarborough* (20 guns). If supported by the *Alliance*, the *Pallas*, and the *Vengeance* (12 guns), Jones and the *Bonhomme Richard* should have had an advantage. However, during the ensuing battle, the *Vengeance* avoided battle, and the *Alliance*, captained by the erratic Pierre Landais, inflicted greater damage on the *Bonhomme Richard* than on the British. After two of his ship's 18-pound cannon exploded during an early exchange of broadsides, Jones abandoned his main battery. When Captain Richard Pearson of the *Serapis* tried to cross the *Richard*'s bow to rake her, Jones ran the *Richard*'s bow into the *Serapis*'s stern hoping to board the more powerful ship.

The two vessels locked together as their crews continued pouring fire into each other. At one point, the American flag was shot away, and Pearson shouted, 'Has your ship struck?' Jones responded with his immortal, 'I have not yet begun to fight' (Morison, 230). For what seemed an eternity devastating cannon fire from the *Serapis* ripped huge holes in the *Bonhomme Richard*, while the seamen and French marines of the *Bonhomme Richard* swept the enemy's deck with small arms and swivels. At ten o'clock the battle swung in Jones's favour when one of his men threw a grenade from the *Richard*'s yardarm into an open hatch on the *Serapis*. It exploded among a pile of loose cartridges, killing twenty British sailors and causing panic on the gundeck. British attempts to board the *Richard* were repulsed and, when the mainmast of the *Serapis* began to tremble, Pearson surrendered. Each vessel had lost almost half its 320-man crew. Survivors worked feverishly to save the ships, but the *Richard* was beyond saving. Jones transferred his flag to the *Serapis* and on 3 October limped into the Texel accompanied by the *Pallas*, her prize, the *Countess of Scarborough*, the *Alliance*, and the *Vengeance*.

The Dutch public greeted Jones as a hero, but protests by Sir Joseph Yorke, Britain's ambassador to the Netherlands, led the Dutch government to order the *Serapis* and the *Countess of Scarborough* turned over to the French and their captor to leave the Netherlands. On 27 December 1779 Jones set sail in the *Alliance*, evaded Royal Navy ships lying in wait for him, and after a cruise in the Bay of Biscay entered Lorient on 19 February 1780. Jones spent six weeks refitting the *Alliance* then set out for Paris to seek funds to pay his crew. Upon his arrival in the French capital, he was lionized by the public and honoured by the government in a ploy to divert public attention away from the failure of French arms. Louis XVI bestowed the ordre du mérite militaire on Jones and presented him with a gold-hilted sword. The ordre gave Jones the title Chevalier, though he rarely used it. France's leading masons, the brethren of the lodge of the nine sisters, engaged the renowned Jean-Antoine Houdon to sculpt a bust of Jones. His hazel eyes, reddish-tinged brown hair, soft voice, polite manners, sensitivity, and quick wit made the slim, 5½ foot tall Jones attractive to women and a welcome guest at receptions, dinner parties, and the theatre. After six weeks of such activities Jones returned to Lorient with the intention of returning to America with a cargo of military supplies.

However, a series of disputes pitting Jones against Pierre Landais, who had taken command of the *Alliance* in Jones's absence, and Arthur Lee, an American diplomat seeking passage to the United States, damaged the reputations of all three men. Outmanoeuvred by Landais and Lee, Jones took command of the *Ariel*, a smaller ship lent by France to carry war supplies to America. In February 1781 he reached America and was received courteously by the continental congress. By then nearly bankrupt, congress could do little to reward him for his achievements other than vote Jones 'the thanks of the United States … for the zeal, prudence and intrepidity with which he has supported the honor of the American flag; [and] for his bold and successful enterprises to redeem from captivity the citizens of these states'. In addition, congress voted unanimously to give him command of the *America*, the continental navy's only ship of the line.

In August 1781 Jones travelled to Portsmouth, New Hampshire, where he struggled for a year to find the supplies and skilled workmen necessary to complete construction of the *America*. By the time the vessel was ready for sea, peace negotiations were under way with the British. Doubting the need for the vessel and lacking funds to operate it, the continental congress presented it to the French navy and Jones was again without a command. In November 1782 he went to Philadelphia and obtained permission from congress to accompany a French fleet on a cruise in the Caribbean to expand his knowledge of fleet manoeuvring and naval tactics. When the fleet reached Venezuela, Jones learned of the war's end, and returned to Philadelphia.

Diplomatic and Russian service On 1 November 1783 congress commissioned Jones to go to Europe and collect prize money due the men of his squadron. During two years of negotiations with French officials he renewed friendships, wrote a *Memoir of the American Revolution*, and sent letters to Robert Morris proposing systems of administration, training, and officer education for the American navy. Jones's success in finally extracting money from the distressed French treasury in 1785 reflected both his tenacity and the prestige he continued to enjoy in Paris. In 1787 Jones returned briefly to America before travelling to Denmark to seek payment for prizes sent into Bergen during the war.

In Copenhagen agents of the Russian Tsarina Catherine II renewed offers made to Jones in Paris of a commission as a rear-admiral in the Imperial Russian navy. He accepted, and in April 1788 he proceeded to St Petersburg, stopping briefly to be received by Catherine, and then continued to the Black Sea to assume command of Russian naval forces in the Liman. On 6 and 7 June Jones assisted Prince Charles Othon of Nassau-Siegen, commander of a flotilla of gunboats and galleys, in repelling Turkish attacks during the first battle of the Liman. Ten days later Jones directed Russian forces in the second battle of the Liman, which resulted in the destruction of fifteen Turkish vessels and the death or capture of 4700 Turks at a cost of only one frigate and fewer than a hundred Russian casualties. Sailing vessels under Jones's command next cut off the Turkish fortress at Ochakov from supply by sea, thus laying the basis for its capture by Russian armies commanded by Prince Potemkin. After becoming embroiled in partisan intrigues Jones travelled to St Petersburg in December 1788 where Catherine awarded him the order of St Anne. Jones remained in the city preparing his 'Journal of the campaign of the Liman' and seeking a new command. In April 1789 conspirators, probably including Nassau-Siegen, framed Jones with the rape of a twelve-year-old butter maid, but the charges were dropped when the French ambassador, Louis Philippe, comte de Ségar, exposed their falsity.

Retirement Granted a two-year furlough from the Russian navy, Jones took leave of Catherine at a public audience on 26 June 1789. He made his way to Paris via Warsaw, Vienna, Amsterdam, and London, reaching the French capital in May 1790. In July 1790 he headed a delegation of Americans who appeared before the national assembly. After suffering from jaundice for two months he died on 18 July 1792. A committee of the national assembly organized his funeral and burial in the cemetery for foreign protestants two days later. There his body remained until 1905 when it was exhumed and returned to America to lie in a splendid marble sarcophagus in a crypt beneath the chapel at the US Naval Academy in Annapolis, Maryland.

Jones rose from humble origins, proved to be an excellent tactical commander and visionary naval strategist, but never enjoyed command of sufficient forces to fully demonstrate his abilities. His victories against British forces did not directly influence the course of the American War of Independence, but they boosted American morale at critical times and won for Jones and America the respect of France. Jones's concepts of professionalism were far advanced for his era; and his plans for a navy were too ambitious for the young United States, but he gave its navy a sense of pride. Although vilified in England he became an American hero, justly recognized as the 'Father of the United States Navy'.

JAMES C. BRADFORD

Sources *The papers of John Paul Jones*, ed. J. C. Bradford (1986) [10 reels of microfilm and printed guide] · S. E. Morison, *John Paul Jones: a sailor's biography* (Boston, MA, 1959) · J. P. Jones, *John Paul Jones' Memoir of the American revolution*, ed. and trans. G. W. Gawalt (1979) · J. C. Bradford, 'John Paul Jones: honor and professionalism', *Command under sail: makers of the American naval tradition, 1775–1850*, ed. J. C. Bradford (Annapolis, MD, 1985), 18–45 · J. C. Bradford, 'The battle of Flamborough Head', *Great American naval battles*, ed. J. Sweetman (Annapolis, MD, 1998), 27–47 · J. E. Walsh, *Night on fire: the first complete account of John Paul Jones's greatest battle* (New York, 1978) · J. Boudriot, *John Paul Jones and the Bonhomme Richard*, trans. D. H. Roberts (1987) · L. Lorenz, *John Paul Jones: fighter for freedom and glory* (Annapolis, MD, 1943) · A. De Koven, *The life and letters of John Paul Jones*, 2 vols. (1913) · R. Sands, *Life and correspondence of John Paul Jones, including his Narrative of the campaign of the Liman* (New York, 1830) · J. Malcolm, *Memoirs of Rear-Admiral Paul Jones … compiled from his original journals and correspondence*, 2 vols. (1830) · F. A. Golder, *John Paul Jones in Russia* (1927) · A. S. Mackenzie, *The life of Paul Jones*, 2 vols. (Boston, MA, 1841)

Archives L. Cong., papers · National Archives and Records Administration, Washington, DC, papers of the continental congress, 168, 132 | Mass. Hist. Soc., Adams family papers

Likenesses J. Millette, silhouette, 1776, Franklin D. Roosevelt Library, Hyde Park, New York · A. Dupré, bronze medal, 1779, Bibliothèque Nationale, Paris · A. Dupré, copper medal, 1779, Scot. NPG · etching, pubd 1779, BM · sketch, 1779, Foundation Atlas Van Stolk, Rotterdam · J.-A. Houdon, plaster bust, 1780, Boston Museum of Fine Arts; copy, Scot. NPG · Comtesse de Lowendahl, miniature, oils, 1780, US Naval Academy Museum, Annapolis, Maryland · J. M. Moreau the younger, portrait, 1780; copy, L. Cong. · C. W. Peale, oils, 1780, Independence National Historic Park, Philadelphia · wax portrait, in high relief, c.1780, US Naval Academy Museum, Annapolis, Maryland · J.-A. Houdon, marble bust, 1781, US Naval Academy Museum, Annapolis, Maryland [*see illus.*] · gouache drawing, c.1781, Morgan L. · J. Chapman, stipple, pubd 1796, NPG · C. Guttenberg, line engraving (after C. J. Notté), BM · M. Le Jeune, pastel drawing, Louisiana State Museum, New Orleans · attrib. J. M. Renaud, wax medallion, Scot. NPG · oils (*The Gombault miniature*), Masonic Library, Boston, Massachusetts

Wealth at death est. over $20,000: *Papers of John Paul Jones*, ed. Bradford

Jones, John Pike (1791–1857), political activist and antiquary, eldest son of John Jones, a mercer at Chudleigh, Devon, and his wife, Mary Pike, was born at Chudleigh on 25 February 1791. On 4 July 1809 he was admitted as sizar at Pembroke College, Cambridge, and in 1813 he graduated BA. In the following year he took holy orders, and was curate of North Bovey in Devon from 1816 until 1831.

Jones was keenly interested in politics: in 1819 he published *A true and impartial account of the parliamentary conduct of Sir T. D. Acland, by a freeholder of Devon*. His political enthusiasms, however, affected his clerical career. In 1819 he was nominated to two benefices, one in the diocese of Peterborough and the other in that of Lincoln, and he produced to the respective bishops the three testimonials which were required before institution. His diocesan at Exeter declined to countersign them on the grounds that Jones, at a county meeting at Exeter Castle on 23 April

1819, had made in his speech some inappropriate comments, apparently on the Athanasian creed, and his institution to these livings, together worth £500 a year, was refused. The matter was brought before the House of Lords by Lord Holland on 12 May 1820, on a petition from Jones; but a motion for a committee on the subject was rejected by eighteen votes to thirty-five. Jones's political zeal continued unabated: in 1821 he published *Substance of Speech at County Meeting at Exeter Castle, 16 March 1821*, advocating Catholic emancipation, and in 1828 *Substance of Speech at Meeting of Devon County Club 1 Aug. 1828*. On 12 May 1829 he was instituted, probably as a result of his advocacy of Roman Catholic claims, to the vicarage of Alton, Staffordshire, in the gift of Lord Shrewsbury, and on 12 May 1832 he was instituted to the lord chancellor's benefice of Butterleigh, Devon.

While still in Devon, Jones published several works of natural history: *A Botanical Tour through Various Parts of Devon and Cornwall* (1820; 2nd edn, 1821) and, with J. F. Kingston, *Flora Devoniensis, or, A Descriptive Catalogue of Plants Growing Wild in Devon* (1829). Antiquarian works by Jones include: *Historical and Monumental Antiquities of Devonshire* (1823), *Guide to Scenery in the Neighbourhood of Ashburton* (1823; another edn, 1830), *Observations on Scenery and Antiquities at Moreton-Hampstead and on the Forest of Dartmoor* (1823), and *Ecclesiastical Antiquities of Devon* (1828). The introduction for this last work, 'On the preservation and restoration of our churches', and the articles signed Devoniensis were by Jones, while other parts were by George Oliver. In 1840 Oliver republished a much revised edition of *Ecclesiastical Antiquities of Devon*, omitting all contributions by Jones, except the introduction.

Jones died suddenly at Cheadle, Staffordshire, on 4 February 1857. Some of his unpublished manuscripts on Devon and Cornwall passed to his sister Mary Jones (d. 1883), who was herself the author of a *History of Chudleigh* (1852). Subsequently they were purchased by the Bodleian Library, Oxford, on the sale of her library by Messrs Drayton of Exeter.   W. P. COURTNEY, *rev.* IAN MAXTED

Sources J. Davidson, *Bibliotheca Devoniensis* (1852), 9–10, 13, 36, 118, 135, 172 · *Hansard 2* (1820), 1.305–29 · *GM*, 3rd ser., 2 (1857), 368 · *Western Antiquary*, 4 (1884), 148 [note on MSS relating to Devon] · 'Third report of the committee on Devonshire records', *Report and Transactions of the Devonshire Association*, 23 (1891), 150–70, esp. 151, 162–3 [incl. lists of MSS] · Venn, *Alum. Cant.* · Boase, *Mod. Eng. biog.* · parish register (baptism), Chudleigh, 25 Feb 1791
Archives Bodl. Oxf., commonplace book, notes, and collections relating to the history and botany of Devon and Cornwall | BL, corresp. with Lord Holland and Lady Holland, Add. MS 51592 · Devon and Exeter Institution Library, Exeter, history of the antiquities of the hundred of Teignbridge · UCL, letters to Society for the Diffusion of Useful Knowledge

Jones, John Richard (1881–1955), builder and historian, was born on 29 June 1881 at 29 Barrington Road, Wavertree, Liverpool, the son of John Jones (1853–1936), a builder, and his wife, Catherine Parry (1855–1887). His mother died on 30 March 1887 when J. R. Jones was only five years of age; but his father was a remarkable individual who brought up his sons to take responsibility at an early age, in particular within the Welsh Presbyterian

chapel of Webster Road. From 1899 onwards John R. Jones shouldered every year some responsibility, beginning as secretary to the Sunday school, becoming involved in young people's activities, and acting as a temperance witness, until he himself was made an elder (like his father) in 1932. Both were heavily involved in the planning of a large new Welsh Presbyterian chapel on the border of Allerton and Wavertree overlooking Penny Lane, completed in 1927. For a short period of time both he and his father served together as elders, a rather unique situation, although his command of Welsh was not so fluent as that of his father (known in the trade as John Jones Drinkwater because he refused to allow the customary 'price of a pint', an honorarium given to bricklayers on completing the first house of a block. He would tell them to go and drink water).

Educated at Webster Road board school and Liverpool Institute, Jones became a bank clerk; but on 10 September 1912 he married Mary (d. 1974), the daughter of John Hughes of Wavertree, the successful Liverpool Welsh builder and partner of his father in the building firm of Jones and Hughes. His brother married Mary's sister. Shortly after his marriage Jones became an estate agent and a property owner, becoming in time vice-president of the Liverpool Property Owners Federation. On 11 December 1913 their only daughter, Mair, was born. In June 1917 he joined the French Transport Company and saw service to 1919 in France, and was awarded for bravery the Croix de Guerre. It was this war experience that explains why a leading free churchman had life membership of the Territorial Army rifle association.

After the war Jones became very involved in the life of Liverpool and Wales. As a Liberal politician he represented Wavertree on the city council (1936–7 and 1942–5). He became president of the Wavertree constituency Liberal Party, and served as honorary treasurer. His interests were wide. In June 1935 he was appointed a justice of the peace, serving the Liverpool bench. In addition, he served as chairman of the Liverpool Welsh Choral Union, executive member of the Liverpool National Society, and was heavily involved in the committees of the Liverpool presbytery. Jones served as chairman of the Undeb Cymry Fydd Glannau Mersi (Merseyside new Wales union) and the Young Wales Club with its premises in Upper Parliament Street. In 1932 he was a founder member of the Cylch XXV (Liverpool club), composed of up to twenty-five leaders of Welsh life, which came together monthly to discuss in Welsh subjects to do with Wales and the Liverpool area. He was behind the formation of a Welsh luncheon club that ceased in the early sixties, but the Cylch XXV continues to flourish long after his death.

Jones maintained his links with Wales, for he had a second residence in Anglesey, and in 1940–41 he was high sheriff of the county. He gave generously to Anglesey-based institutions such as the annual eisteddfod, and supported the Anglesey Antiquarian Society and the National Society for the Preservation of Rural Wales. He also gave generously and was influential in the Undeb Cymry Fydd (New Wales Union) and the Urdd Gobaith Cymru (Welsh

League of Youth), and was elected its vice-president in 1945. His lasting contribution must be his only book, *The Welsh Builder on Merseyside: Annals and Lives*, published by himself in 1946. The proceeds from the book were given to the Royal Southern Hospital, of which he was a life governor. Many of the builders mentioned were obscure individuals, but through his family contacts he was able to gather together an amazing mass of detail. It is a good example of the work of an amateur historian, and he treasured his membership of the Cambrian Archaeological Association. Jones died suddenly at his home, Cintra, 109 Menlove Avenue, Liverpool, on 28 January 1955 and was buried in Allerton cemetery, Liverpool.

D. BEN REES

Sources *WWW* · O. Evans, *Eglwys Bresbyteraidd Cymru, Heathfield Road, Liverpool: hanes, 1937–1962*, 44–5 · D. B. Rees, *Cymry adnabyddus, 1951–1972* (1978), 121–2 · Welsh Presbyterian Chapel, Webster Road, Liverpool, annual report, 1889–1909 · J. R. Jones, *The Welsh builder on Merseyside: annals and lives* (1946) · 'Death of Mr John R. Jones', *Liverpool Daily Post* (29 Jan 1955) · private information (2004) [R. Parry; J. Jones]
Archives NL Wales, accounts and corresp. relating to *The Welsh builder on Merseyside*
Likenesses photograph, repro. in Rees, *Cymry adnabyddus*, 121
Wealth at death over £60,000: private information

Jones, Sir John Thomas, first baronet (1783–1843), army officer, eldest of five sons of John Jones (1751–1806), of Welsh descent, 29th foot, general superintendent at Landguard Fort, Felixstowe, Suffolk, and of Cranmer Hall, Fakenham, Norfolk, and his wife, Mary (d. 1816), daughter of John Roberts of the 29th foot, was born at Landguard Fort on 25 March 1783. Sir Harry David *Jones (1791–1866) was his brother. He was educated at Ipswich grammar school, joined the Royal Military Academy, Woolwich, in spring 1797, and, aged fifteen years five months, was commissioned second-lieutenant, Royal Engineers, on 30 August 1798. He embarked in October for Gibraltar. He was appointed adjutant of the corps there, and remained at Gibraltar four years (lieutenant 14 September 1800). He was employed on the defences of the north front and in constructing the famous galleries; he also studied and learned French and Spanish. In May 1803 he returned to England, and was employed on the eastern coast constructing defence works against the threatened French invasion and, in 1804, constructing fieldworks from Widford to Galleywood Common, Essex (the Chelmsford lines), to defend London.

Service in Malta and Sicily On 1 March 1805 Jones was promoted second captain, and soon after embarked at Portsmouth with the expedition under Sir James Craig. After some months' cruising the troops were disembarked in July at Malta, where Jones did garrison duty until the autumn. He then accompanied the expedition to Naples, and was detached with the commanding engineer to Calabria to retrench a position at Sapri for covering a re-embarkation. From Naples the troops sailed for Sicily, and, on the dethronement of the king, garrisoned Messina and Melazzo. Jones was employed under Major Lefebure in constructing defence works. In spring 1806 Jones reported, for the king of Naples, on the forts, harbours, and military condition of Sicily. His work was commended by the Neapolitan government and by Sir John Moore. In June 1806 Jones embarked at Messina with a force under Sir John Stuart, which landed in the Bay of St Euphemia. He was present at the British victory of Maida (4 July), and marched with an advanced corps under General Oswald to sweep off the French detachments between Monteleone and Reggio, and to reduce Scylla Castle. The castle was so ably defended that its capture required the formalities of a siege. Jones successfully directed the attack, and after its capture persuaded Stuart to retain and strengthen it instead of blowing it up. Jones did this so well that it was held until February 1808, proving during that time a bar to the invasion of Sicily. When it was reduced to ruins by the French, the garrison was withdrawn in boats, without the loss of a single man, by means of a covered gallery constructed by Jones. He always considered the retention of Scylla the most meritorious achievement of his career. In December 1806, having visited Algiers *en route*, Jones returned to England, and on 1 January 1807 he was appointed adjutant at Woolwich, the headquarters of the Royal Military Artificers. The war necessitated the augmentation of the local and independent companies of engineer workmen, and Jones was occupied until 1808 in reorganizing them into one regular corps.

The Peninsular War Following the Spanish insurrection against the French, and Spanish requests to Britain for assistance, in July 1808 Jones was selected to serve as one of the two assistant commissioners under General Leith, appointed military and semi-diplomatic agent to the juntas of northern Spain. Jones was attached to the army of the marqués de La Romana, and gained a great affection for its commander. Towards the end of the year Leith was ordered to take command of a brigade and to select an officer to succeed him as commissioner. Leith offered to appoint Jones, but he declined, though the high pay was tempting, on the ground that his youth and want of rank would deprive his advice of its proper weight, and he asked instead to join the army. Leith appointed him his acting aide-de-camp. Jones continued in this capacity until after the skirmish before Lugo, when he was ordered to assist in blowing up the bridge over the Tamboya, and was employed with his own corps during the retreat to Corunna. On his arrival in England he resumed his staff appointment at Woolwich, and on 24 June 1809 was promoted first captain. On 9 July he was appointed brigade major to the engineers under Brigadier-General Fyers to accompany the disastrous expedition under the earl of Chatham to the Dutch island of Walcheren, at the mouth of the Scheldt.

Jones acted throughout the operations in Zealand as chief of the engineers' staff, and carried out the arrangements for the attack of Rammekins and Flushing. After the capitulation of Flushing, Jones remained until the defences had been repaired and strengthened, and then returned to England, 'bursting with feelings of rage and indignation' (*Military Autobiography*, 51). In his autobiography he insisted that the Walcheren expedition could have succeeded if properly commanded, but failed through Chatham's 'ignorance, incapacity, and indolence' (ibid., 43). Jones was appointed to command the engineers in the northern district.

In March 1810 Jones was ordered to embark for Lisbon, where he was employed under Colonel Richard Fletcher on the lines of Torres Vedras, the crucial defence works, ordered by Wellington, which secured Lisbon and the British bridgehead in Iberia and enabled the later British victories there. In June Fletcher joined the army headquarters at Celerico and Jones was appointed commanding engineer in the south of Portugal, entrusted with completion of the works against the threatened French invasion under Massena. The arrangements for manning the works had been so well made by Jones that they were quickly occupied.

On 17 November 1810 Jones was appointed brigade major of engineers in the Peninsula and was attached to the headquarters' staff, the details of the engineers' service in all parts of the Peninsula passing through his hands. He held the appointment until May 1812, and served at all the sieges of that period. For his conduct during the operations against Ciudad Rodrigo he was particularly mentioned by Wellington in his dispatches, and was promoted brevet major on 6 February 1812. At the siege of Badajoz, Sir Richard Fletcher, the commanding engineer, was wounded, but at Wellington's wish retained his command, and the active duties devolved on Jones, his staff officer. In the assault on Fort Picuriaz, Jones saved the life of Captain Holloway of the engineers, who had been shot down on the parapet and fell onto the fraise. For his services at the siege Jones was promoted on 27 April 1812 brevet lieutenant-colonel, and resigned his appointment as brigade major.

When it was decided to carry on operations on the eastern coast of Spain, Jones was appointed commanding engineer under General Frederick Maitland, and sailed from Lisbon at the beginning of June. On the disembarkation of the troops at Alicante, Jones received a staff appointment as assistant quartermaster-general, there being already an engineer officer senior to himself in command of the engineers. Owing to differences between the commanders of the allied forces, Jones was sent on a special mission to Madrid to explain the situation to Wellington. Travelling by night and avoiding roads, Jones reached Madrid safely and was warmly received by Wellington, who kept Jones to accompany him to the siege of Burgos. During the siege, Jones was ordered to signal to Wellington by holding up his hat when the arrangements for exploding a mine and making a lodgement were complete. As the signal was not acknowledged, Jones repeated it until the French noticed him and shot him through his ankle. He with difficulty rolled himself into the parallel, but he ordered the mine to be fired, and the operations entrusted to him were successfully carried out before he left the field. Jones was delirious for ten days, and as soon as he could be moved Wellington sent him to Lisbon in the only spring wagon at headquarters. The sufferings of this two months' journey severely tried his strength, and he remained in Lisbon until April 1813, when he was sent to England. Eighteen months of severe suffering followed. Indignant at the unnecessary loss of life 'merely for want of the most simple means for attacking fortresses being with the army' (*Military Autobiography*, 107), he published *Journal of Sieges Carried on by the Allies in Spain in 1810, 1811, and 1812* (2 vols., 1814). In this work he fearlessly exposed the deficiencies of the engineer service, blaming the ignorance and military incapacity of the Board of Ordnance and its advisers. His strictures offended the dispensers of patronage. Wellington, however, although the book was published without his sanction and criticized his siege proceedings, praised it, and remained Jones's friend.

From the Napoleonic War onward, British policy was to exclude France from the Low Countries and the naval resources of Antwerp and the Scheldt, and to prevent future French expansion and increased naval strength. Crucial to this were the British-promoted, Orange-ruled kingdom of the United Netherlands and its Belgian fortifications, partly British financed, as a barrier against France. In 1814 Jones visited the Netherlands and examined the principal fortresses. Wellington appointed him, with Brigadier-General Alexander Bryce and another engineer officer, to report on the system of defence for the new United Netherlands. The commissioners arrived in Brussels on 21 March 1815. On 4 June 1815 Jones was made a CB. On Wellington's appointment to the command in the Netherlands, Jones accompanied him round some of the principal points of defence. At the end of August the reports of the commission were taken to Paris by Bryce and Jones and submitted to Wellington, with whom all details were settled by March 1816, when the commission was broken up. Jones was then selected to be Wellington's medium of communication with the Netherlands' government for the furtherance of the objects of the report. In the previous December Jones, with Colonel Williamson, Royal Artillery, acting as commissioners of the allied sovereigns, prevented the fortress of Charlemont from falling into Prussian hands. The commissioners took possession of Landrecy for the allies and returned to Paris in January 1816.

Inspector of fortifications On 20 April 1816 Jones married, in London, Catherine Maria (*d.* 1 Dec 1859), daughter of Effingham Lawrence of New York. They had three sons and a daughter. In November 1816 a convention founded on the treaty of Paris was signed between England and the Netherlands, empowering Wellington to spend a fund of £6.5 million in constructing fortifications and to delegate his powers to inspectors. The duke named Jones sole inspector, and insisted on his choice despite strong pressure on behalf of a superior officer. Jones's duty was to make periodical inspections of each fortress, superintend the execution of approved plans, sanction modifications, and check expenditure. Wellington usually made two inspections of some weeks annually, when he was always attended by Jones alone, and became intimate with him.

On the return to England of the army of occupation Jones, promoted regimental lieutenant-colonel on 11 November 1816, was appointed to the command of the Royal Engineers and Royal Sappers and Miners at Woolwich, with a range of responsibilities including the gunpowder factories at Waltham Abbey and elsewhere, while still acting as inspector in the Netherlands. He also served on varied military committees. In 1823 he was sent by Wellington to the Ionian Islands to confer with the high commissioner, Sir Thomas Maitland, on the defences of Corfu. His plans were approved and gradually carried out. On 27 May 1825 he was appointed aide-de-camp to the king, with the rank of colonel in the army. On 19 August 1830 Wellington sent him on a special mission to the Netherlands with a view to any military arrangements advisable on account of the July revolution in France. At Ghent, Jones heard of the Brussels rising, went to William I of the Netherlands at The Hague, and at William's request joined the Dutch army and the prince of Orange at Antwerp. On his advice the prince went to Brussels, where he had a good military position and sufficient force to maintain himself. Two hours after Jones had left Brussels for London to report on his mission, the prince retired to The Hague, thus abandoning his advantages and determining the subsequent course of the revolution. Jones was shocked at the Dutch loss of the fortifications and the sudden collapse of the barrier strategy, but his own role was questionable and Wellington was displeased. From 1820, when he inherited a considerable landed property, Jones repeatedly asked Wellington for a baronetcy. Finally, on Wellington's recommendation but through the whig prime minister, Grey, on 30 September 1831 Jones was made a baronet for his services in the Netherlands. Wellington suggested a castle with the word 'Netherlands' as an addition to his armorial bearings. According to John Wade's *Extraordinary Black Book* (1832) Jones was paid £1107 per annum and a £300 wound pension. He was consulted by Palmerston on the Netherlands and the fortifications there. From 1835 to 1838 Jones's health compelled him to live in a southern climate. He was promoted major-general on 10 January 1837, and on 19 July 1838 he was made a KCB.

In the summer of 1839 Jones was requested by the master-general of the ordnance to revise and systematize the plans for the defence of British coasts and harbours against possible French attack using steam vessels, and in the spring of 1840 was a member of a commission on colonial defences. He next undertook at government request a general scheme of defence for Great Britain, in consultation with Wellington. Following anxiety at a possible French attack, in early October 1840 he visited Gibraltar to report on the defences, remaining there as major-general on the staff until June 1841, when he returned to England. His proposals for the improvement of the Gibraltar defences were approved and gradually carried out.

Writings Jones was the author of a short account of Sir John Stuart's campaign in Sicily, published in 1808. His *Account of the war in Spain and Portugal and in the south of France, from 1808, to 1814, inclusive* (2 vols., 1818), written partly in response to French accounts which he believed distorted, claimed the importance of the guerrilla war had been much overrated. He printed in 1829 for private circulation *Memoranda Relative to the Lines Thrown up to Cover Lisbon in 1810*, later published in the *Professional Papers of the Corps of Royal Engineers*. A third edition of the *Journal of Sieges*, in 3 volumes, edited and augmented by his brother Sir Harry David Jones, who incorporated the Torres Vedras memoranda, was published in 1843. Jones's 'Reports relating to the re-establishment of the fortresses in the Netherlands from 1814 to 1830' were, by permission of the secretary for war, edited by Sir Harry Jones and printed for circulation among Royal Engineers officers. Jones's publications continue to be valuable sources, still used by historians.

Jones was considered among the first military engineers of his day. He possessed talents of the highest order: great mathematical knowledge, coupled with sound judgement. He was present at six sieges, at five as brigade major, and his intimate knowledge gave great value to his publications on them. His reputation as a military engineer was not confined to Britain.

From the autumn of 1842 to February 1843 Jones wrote for his family his military autobiography. He died, after a day's illness, on 26 February 1843 at his residence at Pittville, Cheltenham, Gloucestershire. Royal Engineers officers subscribed for a memorial statue by William Behnes, in St Paul's Cathedral south transept. His son Sir Willoughby edited Jones's *Military Autobiography* (1853), 'twelve copies only printed for family perusal'. Jones's eldest son, Sir Lawrence, second baronet (b. 10 Jan 1817), was murdered by brigands on 7 November 1845 when travelling between Macri and Smyrna, and was succeeded in the baronetcy by his brother Willoughby (1820–1884), whose eldest son, Lawrence (1857–1954), was the fourth baronet.

R. H. VETCH, rev. ROGER T. STEARN

Sources *The military autobiography of Major-Gen. J. T. J.*, ed. [W. Jones] (1853) • *Colburn's United Service Magazine*, 2 (1843), 109–15 • *GM*, 2nd ser., 19 (1843), 428 • Burke, *Peerage* (1967) • *The dispatches of … the duke of Wellington … from 1799 to 1818*, ed. J. Gurwood, 13 vols. in 12 (1834–9) • *Supplementary despatches (correspondence) and memoranda of Field Marshal Arthur, duke of Wellington*, ed. A. R. Wellesley, second duke of Wellington, 15 vols. (1858–72), vols. 1–11 • J. T. Jones, *Account of the war in Spain and Portugal and in the south of France, from 1808, to 1814, inclusive* (1818) • J. T. Jones, *Journal of sieges carried on by the army under the duke of Wellington in Spain*, 2nd edn, 2 vols. (1827) • E. Longford [E. H. Pakenham, countess of Longford], *Wellington*, 1: *The years of the sword* (1969) • P. W. Schroeder, *The transformation of European politics, 1763–1848* (1994) • R. Muir, *Britain and the defeat of Napoleon, 1807–1815* (1996) • D. Gates, *The Napoleonic wars, 1803–1815* (1997)

Likenesses W. Behnes, statue, St Paul's Cathedral, London • Freebairn, engraving (after portrait medallion), repro. in Jones, ed., *Military autobiography*, frontispiece • oils, Royal Engineers, Gordon Barracks, Chatham, Kent

Jones, John Viriamu (1856–1901), university administrator and physicist, was born on 2 January 1856 at Pentrepoeth, near Swansea, the second son of Thomas *Jones (1819–1882), nonconformist minister, and his first wife, Jane Roberts. His elder brother was Sir David Brynmor Jones KC, a Liberal MP for Swansea district. John was named after John Williams, missionary of Erromango,

'Viriamu' being the pronunciation of 'Williams' in that area of the south seas. Jones was educated successively at a private school at Reading, at University College School, London, at the Normal College, Swansea, at University College, London, and finally, as holder of a Brackenbury scholarship in natural sciences, at Balliol College, Oxford.

Jones had a distinguished university career. At London he was first in honours at matriculation, graduated BSc with honours, became university scholar in geology, and was elected fellow of University College. At Balliol, where he matriculated on 24 January 1876 and was the centre of a circle of singularly able undergraduates, he won a first class in mathematical moderations in 1877, and a first class in the final schools of mathematics in 1879 and of natural science in 1880. He graduated BA in 1879, and was appointed as a demonstrator at the Clarendon Laboratory, Oxford, under Professor Robert Clifton. He proceeded MA in 1883. In May 1881 he was appointed principal of Firth College (now University College), Sheffield, acting as professor of physics and mathematics. On 18 August 1882 he married Sarah Katharine Wills (b. 1859/60), eldest daughter of W. Wills of Wylde Green, near Birmingham. They had no children. In June 1883 he was selected as the first principal of the University College of South Wales at Cardiff, and in a few years collected the sum of £70,000 for building, obtaining a grant of the site from the corporation. From that time much of his energy was devoted to the movement for creating a national university of Wales, and when the charter was granted in 1893 he became the first vice-chancellor of the new institution. In this capacity he had a preponderant influence in determining the course of studies in the arts and sciences, and in giving the new university's degrees a standard value.

Jones's position in the scientific world was strong, though he was never in the front rank of original researchers. His work was mainly directed towards the precise determination of electrical and physical standards, and to the construction of measuring instruments which should satisfy the utmost demands of engineering theory. His first paper appeared in the *Proceedings of the Physical Society* in 1888 and treated of the mutual induction of a circle and of a coaxial helix; in 1890 he published in *The Electrician* a determination of the ohm by the use of a Lorenz apparatus. From this time forward a series of more and more accurate determinations of this constant occupied the time that he had available for research. As such, his researches paralleled the earlier work by Maxwell and his successor Lord Rayleigh at the Cavendish Laboratory in Cambridge to determine the ohm. In Jones's undergraduate years precision experiments of this kind were considered the central task of laboratory physics in the universities in Britain. Jones was elected FRS in 1894; his election certificate, unusually, emphasized his engagement 'in the teaching of physics (and) the organisation of scientific studies' (Royal Society election certificate, RS). In 1897 he laid before the Royal Society a simplification and more general solution of the problem attacked in his first paper. In 1898 he described a design for a new ampere balance, which he did not live to see constructed.

Jones's sympathies were wide and his personality attractive. He was an expert mountaineer and was a member of the Alpine Club from 1887 until his death. He died at Geneva on 2 June 1901 following several years of ill health, and was buried at Swansea. The Physical Research Laboratory at the new college buildings in Cathays Park, Cardiff, was erected in his memory. His wife survived him and was granted in 1902 a civil-list pension of £75 a year.

ROBERT STEELE, rev. IWAN RHYS MORUS

Sources E. B. Poulton, *John Viriamu Jones and other Oxford memories* (1911) · *Nature*, 64 (1901), 161–2 · *The Electrician* (7 June 1901), 259–60 · W. A. W., 'In memoriam: Principal Viriamu Jones', *Alpine Journal*, 21 (1902), 36–8 · *The Times* (4 June 1901) · election certificate, RS · CGPLA Eng. & Wales (1901) · m. cert.
Archives Bishopsgate Institute, London, Howell MSS
Likenesses W. Goscombe, marble statue, 1906, U. of Wales, Cardiff · portrait, repro. in Poulton, *John Viriamu Jones*
Wealth at death £2246 7s. 3d.: administration, 19 Oct 1901, CGPLA Eng. & Wales

Jones, John Winter (1805–1881), librarian, was born in 1805, probably on 16 June, at Lambeth, London. His family came originally from Carmarthenshire; his father, John Jones, was the editor of the *Naval Chronicle* and the *European Magazine*. His mother, Mary Walker, was a cousin of the painter Robert Smirke. He was educated at St Paul's School (1813–21), and after leaving it became the pupil of Bythewood, a conveyancer, with a view to being called to the chancery bar. In 1823, at the age of eighteen, he published a translation of all the quotations in foreign languages in William Blackstone's *Commentaries on the Laws of England*. A serious illness, during which he temporarily lost his voice, ended his prospects of a career in law. He applied himself to the study of languages and literature, and about 1835 he accepted an engagement as one of the travelling clerks to the charity commissioners, hoping to restore his health through open-air exercise. In 1837 he married Susanna, daughter of M. W. Hewson of Lesson Hall, Cumberland; they had two daughters, Mary and Ellen.

Jones continued to be employed by the Charity Commission until April 1837, when, chiefly through the recommendations of two members of the commission, Patrick Johnston and Nicholas Carlisle (who was also secretary to the Society of Antiquaries and second keeper of printed books in the British Museum), Jones was appointed an assistant in the library of the British Museum. The library was about to undergo a major transformation. In the following July Antonio Panizzi became keeper of printed books; he initiated a series of reforms which made the library one of the foremost institutions of its kind. Two measures were imperative: the removal of the books from Montagu House to the new buildings which were in course of erection, and the preparation of a code of rules for the catalogue which the trustees had determined to produce. In the former undertaking Jones rendered important service, and the latter was in great measure his

John Winter Jones (1805–1881), by unknown engraver, pubd 1866 (after William Salter Herrick)

own. The famous ninety-one rules, the foundation of all subsequent achievement in the field of scientific cataloguing, were prepared by a committee presided over by Panizzi himself, but none doubted that Jones was the primary agent in their formulation. When the catalogue was begun in 1839 he acted as its general reviser, performing at the same time a vast number of other duties, and serving as Panizzi's right hand in all emergencies. He (and Thomas Watts) helped Panizzi to produce the report on the collections which caused the Treasury to agree in 1846 to a considerably increased purchase grant. In his evidence to the royal commission on the British Museum in 1849, Panizzi spoke highly of Jones's services, and, upon the death of Richard Garnett in 1850, Jones became assistant keeper of printed books, succeeding Panizzi as keeper upon the latter's appointment as principal librarian in March 1856. During his time as assistant keeper, the new reading room and its surrounding bookstacks were erected; although the idea for this was undoubtedly Panizzi's, Jones was consulted upon every detail. As a result of these improvements the grant for purchases, curtailed for several years because of lack of space for new acquisitions, was restored to its original amount. This entailed much additional work for Jones, who proved himself to be diligent and efficient.

Jones acted as deputy principal librarian from December 1862 to May 1863 while Panizzi was absent because of ill health. The enthusiastic support of Panizzi, and his own reputation for efficiency, gained for Jones the appointment of principal librarian upon Panizzi's retirement in 1866. His performance in this post recommended

him strongly to the trustees, and he was especially respected by those, such as George Grote, Sir David Dundas, and Spencer Walpole, who took a personal interest in the day-to-day running of the library. In 1873 he was a member of a group appointed by the committee of the privy council for education to consider bringing the South Kensington (now the Victoria and Albert) Museum under the management of the trustees of the British Museum, a scheme subsequently shelved. The building of the museum at South Kensington for the natural history departments of the British Museum was carried out under him; during his administration, also, the Castellani collection of antiquities was acquired for Britain, and new excavations were undertaken in Assyria. The condition of the staff, moreover, was considerably improved after protracted negotiations with the Treasury. On the conclusion of this harassing business, however, Jones's health became seriously affected, and, after failing to restore it by a sabbatical in Cornwall, he resigned in August 1878.

Jones had many interests and involvements which were peripheral to his library duties. He was elected president of the Library Association of the United Kingdom, and took the chair at its first congress in October 1877. He edited and translated three works for the Hakluyt Society and contributed largely to the unfinished *Biographical Dictionary* of the Society for the Diffusion of Useful Knowledge. His article on the British Museum Library in the *North British Review* for May 1851 was described by Richard Garnett as the best account of its administration to be found anywhere. He also contributed to the *Quarterly Review* and to the *Proceedings of the Society of Antiquaries*, of which he was a vice-president. After his retirement from the museum he delivered a lecture in Penzance on the Assyrian excavations, in which he was deeply interested; subsequently he published this lecture privately.

After his wife's death in 1876, aged sixty-eight, Jones spent his last years partly at Penzance and partly at Henley-on-Thames, where he had built a house, Underwood, and where he died suddenly of heart disease on 7 September 1881. He was buried in Kensal Green cemetery.   RICHARD GARNETT, *rev.* P. R. HARRIS

Sources R. Garnett, *The late John Winter Jones* (1884) · G. W. Porter, *John Winter Jones* (1882) · *The Times* (8 Sept 1881)
Archives BL, notes on the liturgy, Add. MSS 5363–5381, 5384–5388 · BM, papers | Bodl. Oxf., corresp. with Sir Thomas Phillipps · LPL, letters to A. C. Tait · NHM, letters to J. E. Gray concerning Gray's resignation · NHM, corresp. with Sir Richard Owen and William Clift · U. Edin. L., corresp. with James Halliwell-Phillipps · UCL, letters to Society for the Diffusion of Useful Knowledge
Likenesses R. C. Lucas, wax portrait, 1856, BM · W. S. Herrick, oils, BM · wood-engraving (after W. S. Herrick), NPG; repro. in *ILN* (3 Nov 1866) [*see illus.*]
Wealth at death £5259 12s. 6d.: probate, 27 Oct 1881, *CGPLA Eng. & Wales*

Jones, Joseph David (1827–1870), composer and singing teacher, was born in Bryncrugog, in the parish of Llanfair Caereinion, Montgomeryshire, the son of a small farmer who was a Wesleyan local preacher. Jones, in spite of his father's opposition, devoted himself as a youth to the study of music, and in 1847 published at Llanidloes the

Perganiedydd, a volume of congregational tunes, which proved to be a success. In the same year, after the death of his mother, he left home, and in the following years held singing classes in Tywyn, Merioneth, and the neighbouring villages. In 1851 he spent three months at a training college in London, and from 1857 to 1866 he took charge of the British and Foreign School Society's school in Ruthin, Denbighshire, also teaching singing. In 1866 he opened a private school in the town.

Jones's published music was popular in Wales for many years. His collection of Welsh carols for Christmas (*Caniadau Bethlehem*) appeared in 1857, and his cantata *Llys Arthur*, or *Arthur's Court*, with words by R. J. Derfel, was performed in Ruthin in 1864. This includes 'The Queen's Song', apparently one of his most effective compositions. The collection of hymns and tunes *Tonau ac emynau* (1868) took six years to complete, after the Revd E. Stephens of Tanymarian withdrew his assistance. It remained in use for a long period, and Jones made some progress with an appendix, which was helpful to Stephens when he prepared a second collection. Jones also arranged a volume of music for the use of the Methodist church, which was published posthumously. He died at Clywd Bank in Ruthin on 17 September 1870, leaving a widow, Catherine. Daughter of Owen Daniel, a farmer of Penllyn, Towyn, Merioneth, she bore him a number of children. The third of their four surviving sons was the Congregational minister John Daniel *Jones. R. M. J. JONES, rev. DAVID J. GOLBY

Sources Brown & Stratton, *Brit. mus.* · private information (1891) · *CGPLA Eng. & Wales* (1870)
Archives Flintshire RO, Hawarden · NL Wales, corresp. and papers
Wealth at death under £300: probate, 2 Dec 1870, *CGPLA Eng. & Wales*

Jones, Joshua (d. 1740). See under Jones, Jeremiah (1693/4–1724).

Jones [née Boyle], **Katherine, Viscountess Ranelagh** (1615–1691), noblewoman associated with the Hartlib circle, was born in Ireland on 22 March 1615, the fifth daughter and seventh child of Richard *Boyle, first earl of Cork (1566–1643), and his second wife, Catherine Fenton (c.1588–c.1630), daughter of Sir Geoffrey *Fenton, principal secretary of state for Ireland. Among the ten of her fourteen siblings to survive into adulthood, she was particularly close to her brothers, Roger *Boyle, Lord Broghill (later earl of Orrery) and Robert *Boyle, the natural philosopher and future luminary of the Royal Society. Among her sisters she was especially close to Mary, supporting her in her decision to marry Charles Rich, future earl of Warwick, against the wishes of her father. She was described as Mary's 'friend sister' by her sister's chaplain and, with her brother Robert, she acted as Mary's executor when she died in 1678.

As was his custom in respect of arrangements for his daughters, the earl of Cork negotiated a marriage for Katherine when she was still very young—in her case, six and a half. Like her sisters, she was sent to live in the family of her intended in-laws when she was only a few years

older. She left for England in September 1624 to live with the family of her fiancé, Sapcott Beaumont, son of Thomas Beaumont, a kinsman of the duke of Buckingham. Since her father did not make any special provision for the education of his daughters, it is possible that she owed such education as she had to the Beaumont family. However, the proposed marriage alliance did not last and she returned to Ireland in 1628. In April 1630 Katherine married Arthur Jones, later second Viscount Ranelagh, with a dowry of £3000 to be increased by £1000 if she bore a male heir. In 1631 she accompanied him to London. Her eldest daughter, Catherine, was born in 1633, and her youngest, Frances, in 1639. Her only son, Richard *Jones, was born on 8 February 1641. Her second daughter, Elizabeth, created a family scandal by marrying a footman in 1677. The Jones match does not appear to have been a happy one. Her husband had a reputation for boorishness, even at the time of their marriage. Katherine's residence in London during the 1640s and 1650s was probably, therefore, a separation of convenience, as well as a refuge from troubles in Ireland. None the less she petitioned tirelessly on her husband's behalf to obtain compensation for his losses during the Irish rising of 1641 and to secure the return of his estates in co. Roscommon. From 1658 she experienced financial difficulties because of his attempts to deprive her and her children of support. In her attempts to resolve the situation she sought the help first of Cromwell, and, after the Restoration, of the king.

As a young woman in Ireland, Katherine Boyle had impressed those who knew her. Lucius Cary, son of the lord deputy, Sir Henry Cary, was a friend in childhood and remained so after their first meeting in 1624. In 1635 Sir John Leeke records the high esteem in which she was held in Dublin. Murrough O'Brien, Baron Inchiquin, commented in 1647 that God had gifted her 'in much more than ordinary measure' (Lynch, *Roger Boyle*, 60). She was in Ireland at the time of the 1641 rising. After being besieged at Athlone Castle she negotiated a safe conduct for herself and her family in 1642 and moved to London, where she resided in Queen Street and subsequently in Pall Mall. In London her home became a refuge for her displaced relatives, in particular her sister Alice, Lady Barrimore, who arrived there with her children in 1642, and her sister-in-law, Margaret, Lady Clotworthy. Lady Ranelagh made the most of her location and connections in London to exert influence on the political scene. In 1642 she urged Sir Edward Hyde to try to reconcile the king and parliament. In 1646/7 she was paid an allowance of 6s. by the House of Lords, and was later granted a pension of £4 by the House of Commons. She used her influence to promote the protestant (and therefore English) interest in Ireland, and kept her brothers in Ireland informed of events in Westminster. In her dealings with parliament she was fortunate in the fact that her brother-in-law was the prominent presbyterian parliamentarian Sir John Clotworthy (future Viscount Massarene). Milton's nephew, Edward Phillips, regarded her as 'an Oliverian in politics'. She was acquainted with leading figures in Cromwell's government, including the president of his council, Henry Lawrence, and the Protector himself. Her assessment of Cromwell, in a letter to Lord Broghill, shows she was a woman of independent judgement and political insight. She was also on friendly terms with supporters of Cromwell, notably John Milton, Andrew Marvell, Cyriack Skinner, and Marchamont Needham. She was also a friend of Sir Henry Vane and of Henry Cromwell's wife. None the less, her political engagement cut across party lines: at the Restoration, Edward Hyde admitted that the duke of Ormond owed his protection at that time to Lady Ranelagh. The same may also be true of her brother, Lord Broghill, who had co-operated with Cromwell during his Protectorate.

Apart from her letters Lady Ranelagh left no writings from which may accurately be gauged the depth of her learning or the scope of her interests. It is, however, clear from her contacts, and from other people's appraisal of her, that she was the leading woman intellectual of her generation, actively involved in contemporary politics, and deeply interested in educational, ethical, religious, and scientific matters. Sir John Leeke attested to her prodigious powers of memory. Gilbert Burnet noted her 'vast Reach both of Kowledg and Apprehensions' and 'her great Understanding and the vast Esteem she was in' (Burnet, 33). 'The incomparable' is a recurring sobriquet among those who knew her. 'That exemplary woman' is Milton's description (Masson, 5.267). She was a lady of great piety, deeply convinced of the role of providence in human affairs, and a proponent of religious toleration. In 1647 Sir Cheney Culpeper called her an Independent. Later on she seems to have inclined towards presbyterianism: a memorandum of 1661 by Secretary Nicholas notes that she was held in great esteem by presbyterian leaders such as her brother-in-law Sir John Clotworthy, who met at her house. She apparently had a flair for languages: she seems to have known German and to have learned Hebrew, as William Robertson attests when dedicating his *A Gate or Door to the Holy Tongue* to her in 1653. Her study of Hebrew was undoubtedly linked to her pious wish, which she shared with her brother Robert Boyle, to proselytize by promoting translations of the Bible. It was also connected to the same millenarian and tolerationist interest in Judaism that led her and Robert Boyle to invite the Dutch Jewish leader, Manasseh ben Israel, to meet them during his visit to London in 1656, on his mission to persuade Cromwell to permit Jews to settle in England.

From 1643 Lady Ranelagh was closely acquainted with the Hartlib circle, especially with Samuel Hartlib, Sir Cheney Culpeper, John Dury, John Beale, Benjamin Worsley, and Robert Wood, as well as with William Petty, Gerard and Arnold Boate, and Theodore Haak. It was her aunt Dorothy Moore (*née* King) who was instrumental in persuading her to support Hartlib, and Lady Ranelagh in her turn interceded on behalf of another of Hartlib's friends, John Dury, to persuade Dorothy to marry him in 1645. The Durys' daughter, Dora Katherina, married Henry Oldenburg, the secretary of the Royal Society, in 1668. Lady Ranelagh shared Hartlib's interest in education and new

scientific investigations and was regarded by his circle as a patroness. In 1648 she made representations on Hartlib's behalf for support from parliament, suggesting that he be paid a stipend financed by income from church lands. In 1660 she tried to intercede on behalf of another of Hartlib's correspondents, John Worthington, when he was faced with ejection from the mastership of Jesus College, Cambridge.

Lady Ranelagh supported a variety of projects for educational reform in Ireland. Hartlib mentions an educational project she was engaged in with Robert Wood and William Potter. She is the probable addressee of a paper 'Of the education of girles' (MS Sloane 249, fols. 203–5) that was attributed to her friend and kinswoman Dorothy Dury. She played an important role in the education of her own family and her nephews. She employed John Milton as tutor to her nephew David Barry in 1647 and subsequently to her own son, Richard Jones. She also knew Peter du Moulin, who had tutored her nephews Viscount Dungarven and Richard Boyle, and she advised on the education of Lionel, son of her brother Richard. Through Milton she became acquainted with Henry Oldenburg, whom she engaged as tutor to accompany her son first to Oxford in 1656, and then, in 1657, on a tour of Europe.

Hartlib sent Lady Ranelagh details of many projects, including, in 1655/6, Robert Wood's proposal for decimalization of the currency. She was associated with Wood's work for a natural history of Ireland, and discussed with him proposals for increasing plantings in Ireland in 1656. One of the discussions on which she engaged with Hartlib was on the validity oaths in changed political circumstances. In 1672 she was, through the agency of William Petty, advising the English adventurers in Ireland on the issue of land settlement and offering to assist them in advancing their claims. She was also interested in law reform and universal language. In 1656 Lady Ranelagh was associated with a proposal by William Rand for liberalizing medical practice through the establishment of a college of graduate physicians. She herself appears to have considerable practical knowledge of medicine. She treated members of her own family, and some of her medical recipes are included in Thomas Willis's *Pharmocopoiea rationalis* (1684) and Robert Boyle's *Medicinal Experiments* (1692).

Lady Ranelagh's most important intellectual and family relationship was with her youngest brother, Robert Boyle. 'Such a *Sister*', Burnet commented, 'became such a *Brother*' (Burnet, 33). It was to her that Robert went first after his return from his travels, when she dissuaded him from enlisting in the royalist army, persuading him to retire to the country instead. She encouraged his literary pursuits and shared with him her religious and ethical ideals, and, for the last thirty years of their lives, her home in Pall Mall. As a result her house became a centre for the new science being promoted by Robert Boyle and the Royal Society. It was through her that Henry Oldenburg first met Boyle. In 1676, she commissioned Robert Hooke to make additions to her house, including a laboratory for her brother's use. It is difficult to judge the extent to which she may have contributed to his scientific investigations, but the few hints we have from her letters suggest that her involvement was not inconsiderable. She certainly gave him encouragement in all his projects. In return he praised her intellect and knowledge. Her son Richard is the Pyrophilus to whom Boyle's early publications are addressed. Lady Ranelagh's importance for Robert Boyle, both intellectually and emotionally, cannot be over-estimated. He appointed her one of the executors of his will, but she predeceased him by one week on 23 December 1691. They are buried next to one another in the south chancel of St Martin-in-the-Fields, London.

SARAH HUTTON

Sources G. Burnet, *A sermon preached at the funeral of the Honourable Robert Boyle* (1692) · D. Masson, *The life of John Milton*, 7 vols. (1859–94) · *The works of the Honourable Robert Boyle*, ed. T. Birch, 5 vols. (1744) · N. Canny, *The upstart earl: a study of the social and mental world of Richard Boyle, first earl of Cork, 1566–1643* (1982) · *The correspondence of Henry Oldenburg*, ed. and trans. A. R. Hall and M. B. Hall, 13 vols. (1965–86) · *The diary and correspondence of Dr John Worthington*, ed. J. Crossley, 1, Chetham Society, 13 (1847) · *The diary and correspondence of Dr John Worthington*, ed. J. Crossley, 2/1, Chetham Society, 36 (1855) · *The diary and correspondence of Dr John Worthington*, ed. R. C. Christie, 2/2, Chetham Society, 114 (1886) · Thurloe, *State papers* · C. Webster, *The great instauration: science, medicine and reform, 1626–1660* (1975) · L. Hunter, 'Sisters of the Royal Society', *Women, science, and medicine, 1500–1700*, ed. L. Hunter and S. Hutton (1997) · K. M. Lynch, *Roger Boyle, first earl of Orrery* (1965) · K. M. Lynch, 'The incomparable Lady Ranelagh', *Of books and humankind*, ed. J. Burtt (1964) · H. Brogan, 'Marvell's Epitaph on —', *Renaissance Quarterly*, 32 (1979), 197–9 · C. Fell Smith, *Mary Rich, countess of Warwick (1625–1678): her family and friends* (1901) · *Autobiography of Mary, countess of Warwick*, ed. T. C. Croker (1848) · D. Townshend, *The life and letters of the great earl of Cork* (1904) · F. P. Verney and M. M. Verney, *Memoirs of the Verney family during the seventeenth century*, 2nd edn, 4 vols. in 2 (1907) · J. G. Taafe, 'Mrs John Dury: a sister of Lycidas', *N&Q*, 207 (1962), 60–61 · *The Lismore papers, first series: autobiographical notes, remembrances and diaries of Sir Richard Boyle, first and 'great' earl of Cork*, ed. A. B. Grosart, 5 vols. (privately printed, London, 1886) · R. Scrope and T. Monkhouse, eds., *State papers collected by Edward, earl of Clarendon*, 3 vols. (1767–86) · G. H. Turnbull, *Hartlib, Dury and Comenius: gleanings from Hartlib's papers* (1947) · W. Robertson, *A gate or door to the holy tongue opened in English* (1653) · W. Robertson, *The second gate, or, The inner door to the holy tongue* (1655) · A. Walker, *The virtuous woman found* (1686) · *The diary of John Evelyn*, ed. E. S. De Beer (1959) · [J. Dury], *Madam, although my former freedom in writing might rather give me occasion to beg pardon for a fault committed …* (1645) [four letters to Lady Ranelagh by Dury and his wife concerning their marriage]

Archives BL, letter to Robert Boyle, Add. MS 4292 · BL, letter to Lord Broghill, Add. MS 46932 · BL, letters to earl of Burlington and Cork · BL, letter to Lord Hyde, Add. MS 17017 · BL, corresp. with Petty, Add. MSS 72858, 72884 · BL, Sloane MSS, 4229, 249, 1367 · Chatsworth House, Derbyshire, letters to earl of Cork · NRA, priv. coll., letters to Lord Orrery and Lady Orrery · PRO, state papers, domestic · PRO, state papers, Ireland · RSA, Boyle MSS · University Sheffield Library, Hartlib MSS · W. Sussex RO, letters to Lord Orrery and Lady Orrery · Wellcome L., Boyle family Western MSS

Likenesses oils, 1957, priv. coll. · attrib. Kneller, oils, priv. coll. · W. Sonmans?, oils, Hampton Court Palace · oils, Bolton Abbey, Yorkshire

Jones, Kathleen Letitia Lloyd (1898–1978), garden designer and nurserywoman, was born on 4 June 1898 at

Kathleen Letitia Lloyd Jones (1898–1978), by unknown photographer, 1920s

Rotherslade House at Oystermouth on the Gower peninsula in Glamorgan. Known as Kitty, she was the ninth of the ten children of Arthur Lloyd Jones (1853–1932), a physician and surgeon, and his wife, Margaret Spears (1857–1931). Margaret's father, Robert Spears, a Unitarian minister, was one of the founders of Channing School for Girls, Highgate, Middlesex. Having been brought up in south Wales, Lloyd Jones left in 1910 to be educated at Channing School. She studied for a diploma at the Royal Botanic Society's practical gardening school at Regent's Park from 1917 to 1919 and continued her studies at Reading University until 1925; she attained firstly a degree in agriculture and horticulture and then a national diploma of horticulture.

Since she was unable to obtain an academic post, Kitty Lloyd Jones's first employment was as a private gardening tutor; she soon went to work for her employer Mrs Balfour's sister, Lady Gladstone, a keen gardener who ran a nursery. Her first design commission was for a large curved border at the Gladstones' home, Dane End House, at Ware in Hertfordshire, and she lived in a cottage in the grounds there from 1925 until 1931.

This first commission led through personal recommendation to others, and by 1931 Lloyd Jones had moved to the White Cottage, Binfield, Berkshire, where she established what would now be called a garden design consultancy.

Most of her work was based in the counties near her home, Berkshire, Hertfordshire, and Oxfordshire. In addition, she won several commissions in northern France. Her most active period was from 1927 until the outbreak of the Second World War. Anecdotal evidence suggests that up to one hundred gardens around the country may owe something to Kitty Lloyd Jones, but little documentation about her work survives.

Those gardens for which detailed information is available include Upton House, near Banbury, Oxfordshire, which is the most famous of the gardens which Lloyd Jones designed. Here, between 1930 and 1936 she laid out, for the Bearsted family, a magnificent terraced garden of herbaceous borders, several linked small formal gardens, and a bog garden on the site of earlier stewponds; she returned to create a cherry orchard about 1950. At the Court House, Chipping Warden, Oxfordshire, the fine planting of many unusual trees is her work; a bog garden which she created in the 1930s has been recently restored. She designed an Anglo-Japanese garden about 1930 at Courances, near Fontainebleau, and in 1933, at Pontrancart, near Dieppe in Normandy, she planned several borders in the English style. At Greys Court, Berkshire, in the 1950s, she produced a design for a rose garden for Sir Felix and Lady Brunner.

After the war Lloyd Jones's efforts were concentrated on the garden at Achamore House, Gigha, Argyll, for Sir James Horlick. Horlick had acquired the island of Gigha in the 1940s with the intention of creating a garden full of exotic plants, and in particular rhododendrons. Lloyd Jones worked there from 1944 to about 1952, meeting the challenge of marrying the demands of a collector's garden with the aesthetics of garden design. Her glades of azaleas and rhododendrons and a bog garden still survive.

While only one plan remains in Lloyd Jones's hand (for the rose garden at Greys Court) and no complete plant lists, something about her design philosophy is known from a chapter which she contributed to *Modern Garden Craft*, published in 1936 and edited by Arthur Cobb, one of her former lecturers. In this chapter she showed a strong preference for plants with subtle colour combinations in wide borders. In addition to her obvious knowledge of and enthusiasm for herbaceous planting, Lloyd Jones became an expert on rhododendrons, shrubs, and roses: her selection of unusual trees and their planting showed a mastery in anticipating the mature form.

Kitty Lloyd Jones's importance as a garden designer lies not in any originality of style—her work resembles that of her contemporaries—but in the pioneering way in which she operated. One of the earliest graduates in horticulture, at a time when career openings for women were few, she developed a very personal approach to the newly developing profession of garden design. She would base herself at the home of her client as a house guest, and work with the gardening staff on changes to the gardens. She set very high standards and was always prepared to

show the (male) workforce how a job should be done. Despite her demanding principles, her warmth and enthusiasm earned her affection from those who worked for her. She was popular, too, among her clients because of her willingness to give advice on modifying, rather than radically changing, an established garden. When at home she worked long days outside in her nursery, where she propagated plants for her clients as well as developing new strains; her evenings were spent on correspondence. In her later years she was bronchitic and crippled by arthritis and relied on the support of family and friends, many of whom were former clients. She died of heart failure on 9 July 1978 after an illness of several months at a nursing home near Ascot, Berkshire, and was cremated on 13 July at Easthampstead Park, Berkshire. Small in stature, dark-haired and strong-featured, Kitty Lloyd Jones had a lively and likeable personality. She never married. She was for many years a close friend of Sir James Horlick of Sunninghill, Berkshire, on whose gardens in Argyll she had worked.   RACHEL BERGER

Sources private information (1998) · letters between Kitty Lloyd Jones and Lady Bearsted, Upton House, Oxfordshire · priv. coll. · A. Oswald, 'Country homes, gardens old and new, Upton House II', *Country Life*, 80 (1936), 274–9 · J. Sales, 'Valley transformation', *Country Life* (25 April 1991), 66–9 · G. Leveque and M.-F. Valery, *French garden style* (1990) · C. Quest-Ritson, *The English garden abroad* (1992) · T. Lord, *Best borders* (1994) · A. Pereire and G. van Zuylen, *Private gardens of France* (1983) · J. Horlick, 'Gigha', *RHS Journal*, 90 (1965), 236–45
Archives NRA, priv. coll., MSS | Upton House, Warwickshire, Bearsted MSS
Likenesses photograph, 1920–29, priv. coll. [*see illus.*] · photograph, *c*.1950 · photographs, 1960–78

Jones, (William) Kennedy (1865–1921), newspaper manager and editor, was born on 4 May 1865 at Glasgow, the son of Henry Jones of Newry, co. Down, and his wife, Jeanie Kennedy of Ayr. He married Hetty, daughter of James Staniland of Birmingham, in 1892, and was the father of one son and three daughters.

K. J., as Jones was known, was educated at Glasgow high school, leaving at sixteen to start a career in newspapers. He worked first as a reporter and sub-editor in Glasgow, notably with *The News* and the *Evening News*. He later moved south, and took with him the advantages of a practical apprenticeship in journalism and a sure instinct for the human-interest story that would sell newspapers.

After brief engagements in Leicester and Birmingham, Jones sought work in London. *Morning*, which he helped to start in 1892, failed to prosper, but the experience convinced him that there was a market for a halfpenny morning daily if the right formula could be found. Jones moved to T. P. O'Connor's *Sun* as news editor after a few months but, in 1894, undeterred by lack of capital, he gambled boldly, acquiring with Louis Tracy, assistant editor of *The Sun*, an option to purchase the London *Evening News*, then running at a loss despite a respectable circulation of about 100,000. The idea was to sell it on quickly to Alfred Harmsworth, whom Jones had identified as a potential buyer.

The sale secured Jones a 7½ per cent stake in the profits

(William) **Kennedy Jones** (1865–1921), by unknown photographer

of the *Evening News* and, after a short interval, the editorship, which he retained until 1900. The paper was completely refashioned, with political coverage reduced to make way for sport, prize competitions, serialized fiction, and the kind of eye-catching feature articles with which Harmsworth had successfully entertained the readers of *Answers*. Its fortunes were transformed, and Harold Harmsworth was soon referring to the *Evening News* as 'our gold brick' (Pound and Harmsworth, 172).

Alfred Harmsworth, with no previous experience of newspapers, allowed Jones to steer his early ventures as a proprietor. At Jones's suggestion the Glasgow *Daily Record* was acquired in 1895 as the first of a projected chain of provincial dailies. This project, however, was soon eclipsed by the *Daily Mail*, launched in May 1896, flagship of a new style of popular journalism which originated in Jones's vision of a halfpenny paper produced in London and wired to provincial cities for printing, distribution, and early-morning sale. Though not burdened with the routine duties of editorship Jones was given overall responsibility for content and style. The runaway success of the *Mail* owed much to Harmsworth's abrasive, ambitious deputy. It was typical of Jones that he should boast of his part in transforming journalism, once a profession, into 'a branch of commerce'. He had an instinct for news that would make newspapers sell. War, which 'not only creates a supply of news but a demand for it', featured prominently, as well as funerals, football results, and the 'First-class Murder' (Jones, 173, 198–201).

As his newspaper empire expanded Harmsworth came to rely on Jones's shrewd commercial judgement and his aggressive business mentality. Jones appeared to relish his reputation as Harmsworth's hard man and minder. 'He had', it has been observed, 'almost none of the elements of personal popularity' and 'many enemies whose existence seemed to give him pleasure' (Pound and Harmsworth, 173–4). When more subtle skills were required, however, Jones was adept, acting in 1908 as an intermediary in the negotiations which led to Harmsworth's purchase of *The*

Times. His intervention was critical in enabling Harmsworth to snatch the prize from Arthur Pearson's grasp at the eleventh hour. Jones then modernized the *Times* printing works, but was denied the editorial influence which he had anticipated. In 1912, following a period of ill health, he sold his newspaper interests. After two further years as chairman of Waring and Gillow, the London furniture store, Jones retired from business.

Jones entered politics in April 1916 as an independent candidate at the Wimbledon by-election. His robust radical right-wing campaign led to a substantial protest vote against the wartime party truce, sending a clear message to the ailing Asquith government 'on behalf of the Do-it-now party' (*The Times*, 26 April 1916). Elected unopposed as Unionist member for Hornsey a few months later, Jones spent his remaining years in parliament. He took an unpaid appointment with the Ministry of Food in 1917 and, after the war, showed a particular interest in London's traffic and transport problems. His *Fleet Street and Downing Street*, published in 1919, is a useful source, not only for the origins of popular journalism in Britain, but also for relations between politicians and the press.

Jones died of pneumonia at his home, 123 Victoria Street, London, on 20 October 1921 and was cremated at Golders Green crematorium on 24 October, after a memorial service at St Margaret's, Westminster. His wife survived him.

DILWYN PORTER

Sources Kennedy Jones, *Fleet Street and Downing Street* (1919) · R. Pound and G. Harmsworth, *Northcliffe* (1959) · P. Ferris, *The house of Northcliffe: the Harmsworths of Fleet Street* (1971) · [S. Morison and others], *The history of The Times*, 3 (1947) · D. Griffiths, ed., *The encyclopedia of the British press, 1422–1992* (1992) · M. Pemberton, *Lord Northcliffe. A memoir* (1922) · F. A. McKenzie, *The rise and progress of the Harmsworth publications* (1897) · WWW · WWBMP · *The Times* (21 Oct 1921) · *Newspaper World* (22 Oct 1921) · *The Times* (26 April 1916) · *The Times* (24 Oct 1921)
Archives BL, corresp. with Lord Northcliffe, Add. MS 62196 · News Int. RO, *The Times* archive
Likenesses photograph, repro. in Pound and Harmsworth, *Northcliffe*, facing p. 321 · photograph, NPG [*see illus.*]
Wealth at death £206,537 3s. 1d.: administration with will, 24 Jan 1922, CGPLA Eng. & Wales

Jones, Leslie Grove (1779–1839), army officer and radical writer, was born at Bearfield, near Bradford-on-Avon, Wiltshire on 4 June 1779. His father, John Jones of Frankley, near Bradford, was inspector of the board of works and died in 1807. Jones entered the navy as a youngster, but while a midshipman on the *Révolutionnaire* he incurred censure for intervening on behalf of the ship's cook whom Jones believed to have been unjustly flogged. As a result, he left the navy. The marquess of Lansdowne offered Jones a commission in the guards, and he became an ensign on 25 November 1796, lieutenant and captain on 25 November 1799, brevet major on 4 June 1811, and captain and lieutenant-colonel on 21 January 1813. He served throughout the Peninsular War, and was commandant of Brussels before Waterloo. While with the army of occupation at Cambrai, he spent his leisure time during the winter of 1817 writing a pamphlet, *Principles of Legitimacy*, published in 1827.

more likely that he is the Lewis Jones who graduated BA from Brasenose College in 1580. This tallies with Archbishop Ussher's comment that Jones was sixty-nine years old in 1629. Taken together these evidences suggest that he was eighty-six when he died rather than the staggering 104 often attributed to him. He married Mabel (b. c.1580), sister of James *Ussher, archbishop of Armagh, before 1609. His will dated 10 June 1646 shows that he then had four sons, including Henry *Jones (1605–1682), Sir Theophilus *Jones (d. 1685), and Michael *Jones (1606x10–1649), and three daughters.

By 1606 Jones had moved to Ireland and become vicar of Ardee, co. Louth. Recommended by Sir Arthur Chichester for the bishopric of Dromore, he was instead appointed dean of Ardagh in June 1606, a position which he continued to hold along with the deanery of Cashel when granted it in June 1608. He was also prebendary of Kilbragh in Emly from 1608, holding this benefice and four others until he resigned them all in 1634, most probably in the wake of a royal visitation. In 1615 the Cashel visitors criticized Jones for improvident leasing and threatened to deprive him for non-residence. Later on it was claimed that he had been responsible for restoration of the cathedral church and the establishment of a choir there. He passed his deanship of Ardagh on to his son Henry on 24 May 1625.

Despite enjoying the support of James Ussher for the archbishopric of Cashel in 1629, Jones had to wait until December 1632 for nomination as bishop of Killaloe; he was consecrated on 12 April 1633. Within a year he had been accused by Lord Deputy Wentworth of wrecking his see by ruinous leases. After John Bramhall, archdeacon of Meath, had been sent to Killaloe to investigate in March 1634, the leases were overturned on the condition that recovered revenues would be used for the construction of a new episcopal residence. Jones repeatedly denied that he had reached a secret deal with Sir Daniel O'Brien for the lands in question. Judging by his ability to lend relatively large sums of money in the 1630s, he was certainly not poor. Dublin convocation records for 1640–41 indicate that Jones was absent throughout the sessions, as he was from the House of Lords where he was represented by proxy. He may have moved to Dublin in the wake of the violence of the winter of 1641. He died there on 2 November 1646 and was buried in St Werburgh's, Dublin.

Lewis Jones's son **Ambrose Jones** (d. 1678), bishop of Kildare, was educated at Dublin. He became prebendary of Killenlick in the diocese of Emly in 1638. He became treasurer of Limerick in 1639 and precentor in 1661. In 1661 he was made archdeacon of Meath, then rector of Castletown, Meath, in 1665, and finally bishop of Kildare (consecrated 29 June 1667). He died on 15 December 1678 and was buried at St Andrew's, Dublin.　　JOHN McCAFFERTY

Sources P. Dwyer, *The diocese of Killaloe: from the Reformation to the close of the eighteenth century* (1878) · Strafford papers, Sheff. Arch., Wentworth Woodhouse muniments, vols. 6–7, 20 · *The works of the most reverend father in God, William Laud*, ed. J. Bliss and W. Scott, 7 vols. (1847–60) · J. B. Leslie, *Armagh clergy and parishes* (1911) · H. Cotton, *Fasti ecclesiae Hibernicae*, 6 vols. (1845–78) · St J. D. Seymour, *The succession of parochial clergy in the united diocese of Cashel and Emly*

Leslie Grove Jones (1779–1839), by Charles Phillips, pubd 1832 (after Abraham Wivell)

After retiring from the army, Jones became actively involved in politics, and when the agitation for political reform was in progress he became well known for his virulent letters to *The Times*, which he signed 'Radical'; he especially attacked pension-holders. His intention to stand for the new borough of St Marylebone in 1832 was thwarted by a lack of finances according to *The Age*.

Jones married, first, Jean, the youngest daughter of Patrick Miller of Dalswinton; she died on 29 October 1833, leaving two sons. His second wife, whom he married on 28 March 1838, was Anna Maria, second daughter of William Davies Shipley. Jones died in Buckingham Street, Strand, London, on 12 March 1839, and was buried on 18 March in the catacombs at Kensal Green cemetery, Middlesex. His second wife survived him.

W. A. J. ARCHBOLD, rev. S. KINROSS

Sources GM, 2nd ser., 11 (1839), 541 · *The Times* (1831–3) · *The Greville memoirs*, ed. H. Reeve, new edn, 2 (1896) · Ward, *Men of the reign*
Archives City Westm. AC, corresp., letter-book, and papers | BL, letters to J. C. Hobhouse, Add. MSS 36458–36468, *passim* · BL, letters to Francis Place, Add. MSS 36148–36150, 37949–37950, *passim* · Lambton Park, Chester-le-Street, Durham, letters to Lord Durham
Likenesses M. Gauci, lithograph, pubd 1833 (after S. M. Smith), BM, NPG · C. Phillips, stipple (after A. Wivell), BM, NPG; repro. in *Union Magazine* (Feb 1832) [*see illus.*]

Jones, Lewis (1560–1646), Church of Ireland bishop of Killaloe, was a native of Dol-y-moch, Merioneth. He attended Oxford University but confusion surrounds his early career, and while Anthony Wood gives his BA as 1569 it is

(Dublin, 1908) • Bodl. Oxf., MS Sancroft 8 • Wood, *Ath. Oxon.*, new edn • Foster, *Alum. Oxon.* • W. B. Wright, *The Ussher memoirs* (1889) • *DNB* • J. Ohlmeyer and E. Ó Ciardha, eds., *The Irish statute books, 1596–1687* (1998) • T. W. Moody and others, eds., *A new history of Ireland*, 9: *Maps, genealogies, lists* (1984)

Jones, Lewis Richard (1897–1939), political activist and novelist, was born on 28 December 1897 at 4 Sunny Bank, Blaenclydach, a mining village in a side valley of the Rhondda, Glamorgan, the illegitimate child of Jane Jones (*d.* 1940/41), a domestic servant, and was brought up by his grandmother. He lived all his life in Blaenclydach, which is the setting of both his novels, *Cwmardy* (1937) and *We Live* (1939). His attendance at the local primary school was punctuated by frequent absences during which he lived a street life in an attempt to supplement his family's meagre income. At the age of twelve he went to work underground at the Cambrian colliery and, seven years later, on 9 April 1917, married Elizabeth Mary Jones (*b.* 1898/9), the daughter of Daniel Jones, a timberman; they had two daughters, Megan and Avril. Within a year of his starting work the Cambrian Combine owned by Lord Rhondda, whom Jones pilloried in his novels as Lord Cwmardy, embroiled all the pits of mid-Rhondda in a strike which ended in defeat for the miners, and in 1910 he witnessed the Tonypandy riots, a civil disturbance by locked-out miners which is among the most famous events in the history of the south Wales coalfield.

Elected chairman of the Cambrian lodge, a hotbed of the 'advanced', mainly syndicalist thinking of the South Wales Miners' Federation, in 1918, Jones began a career as a public speaker of legendary power. During his first year at the Marxist-orientated Central Labour College (1923–5) he joined the Communist Party and, on his return to the Rhondda, became one of its most eloquent and able representatives as well as an organizer of immense talent. By the general strike, which began in May 1926, his ambition to be a mining engineer had dwindled as he became more interested in political philosophy. On the miners' ignominious return to work in the following November, after they had held out for nearly seven months against Stanley Baldwin's government, Jones—like many militants—was removed from his job as check-weighman for refusing to work with blackleg labour. He then became an organizer for the National Unemployed Workers' Movement in an area where unemployment was endemic, widespread, and long-term. In this capacity he led contingents of hunger marchers from the Rhondda to Cardiff and from south Wales to London in 1932, 1934, and 1936. He also arranged demonstrations against the hated means test which culminated in the mass movement of 1935. In that year he attended, as a British delegate, the Seventh World Congress of the Communist International in Moscow but, always a maverick, sometimes in bad odour with his party, and appalled by the cult of leader, refused to stand or clap for the person or name of Stalin.

In 1931 Lewis Jones had been elected a member of the Welsh committee of the Communist Party and, for the last three years of his life, was one of two communist members of Glamorgan county council. A fiery orator,

who served a three-month prison sentence in 1926 for his allegedly seditious speeches and was fined for 'inciting disorder' during the 1930s, he commanded a strong personal following among miners and other workers in the heavy industries of south Wales. Ardent in his support for a popular front between communists and the Labour Party against the threat of fascism at home and abroad, he also played a prominent part in the campaign in Wales on behalf of the beleaguered Spanish republic. He died of a heart attack at 12 Clare Road, Cardiff, on 27 January 1939 after addressing some thirty street meetings in the week that Barcelona fell to the fascist forces of General Franco. His secular funeral procession, the coffin draped with a scarlet banner, seemed to some observers as it wound its way through the packed streets of Tonypandy to the Judges' Hall in Trealaw to symbolize the thwarted hopes of 'Red Rhondda' and the passing of one of its most militant sons. He was buried in Trealaw cemetery, Rhondda, Glamorgan.

Like other left-wingers in south Wales during the interwar years, Lewis Jones was influenced by the syndicalism of the pamphlet *The Miners' Next Step* (1912), but the essential fact of his volatile but attractive personality, whether expressed in his stormy political career or in his writing, was the Marxism which he had embraced so wholeheartedly in his youth and to which his life was dedicated. He was remarkable not least because, during a brief, difficult, and busy life, he wrote—besides articles and stories contributed to the *Daily Worker*—two novels about the mining communities of south Wales which, though unsatisfactory in strictly literary terms, gave an authentic account of the social deprivation and political militancy which were typical of his time and place.

In a preface to *Cwmardy* (1937) the author attributed the inspiration for the book to the miners' leader Arthur Horner, who 'suggested that the full meaning of life in the Welsh mining areas could be expressed for the general reader more truthfully and vividly if treated imaginatively, than by any amount of statistical and historical research'; there he also admitted that the novel had been written hastily 'during odd moments stolen from mass meetings, committees, demonstrations, marches and other activities'. The novel's focus is divided between scenes of vivid documentary in its description of strikes, pit explosions, and the workers' clashes with troops and policemen, on the one hand, and a sensitive exploration of the psychology of the principal character, Len Roberts, and his sweetheart, Mary, and their denial of sex, on the other. Len, the archetypal wounded hero, grows increasingly sceptical about the efficacy of political action and is drawn to introspection and a quest for aesthetic beauty. His political involvement is part of the price he has to pay for not pursuing the life of the imagination, a compromise reflecting one of the main tensions in the author's own life. This theme is further developed in the sequel *We Live* (1939), which was finished after the author's death by Mavis Llewellyn, a communist with whom he shared his last years, and published posthumously. It brings an added subtlety to both books, which otherwise might be read as merely propagandist novels bristling with outrage against working-class conditions and advocating radical, even revolutionary, means of exposing and improving them.   MEIC STEPHENS

Sources D. Smith, *Lewis Jones*, Writers of Wales (1982) · J. Pikoulis, 'Lewis Jones', *Anglo-Welsh Review*, 74 (1983) · J. Pikoulis, 'The wounded bard', *New Welsh Review*, 26 (1994) · b. cert. · m. cert. · d. cert. · private information (2004)
Archives University of Swansea, South Wales Miners' Library
Likenesses photograph, repro. in Smith, *Lewis Jones* (1982)

Jones, Sir Lewis Tobias (1797–1895), naval officer, second son of Lewis Tobias Jones, captain, Royal Artillery, and his wife, Mary Gerrish Gray of Gerrish Hall, Windsor, Nova Scotia, was born on 24 December 1797. The family, originally from Denbigh, Wales, had been settled at Ardanaglass, co. Sligo, Ireland, since the Commonwealth. The elder Lewis Jones was author of a history of the campaign in the Netherlands in 1793–5, and barrack master at Sunderland until his death in September 1822. The son entered the navy in January 1808 on the brig *Thrasher* attached to the Walcheren expedition in 1809, but whether Jones was actually serving in her at the time is doubtful. Later he served with his relative, Sir Jahleel Brenton. In 1812 he was in the *Stirling Castle* off Brest, in 1816 was in the *Granicus* at the bombardment of Algiers, where he was wounded, and served continuously in the channel and on the Cape of Good Hope or West Indian stations until he was made lieutenant on 29 August 1822. He was afterwards on the North America and West Indian, home, and Mediterranean stations.

On 28 June 1838 Jones was promoted commander (second captain) of the *Princess Charlotte*, flagship of Sir Robert Stopford, and was in her during the operations on the coast of Syria in the summer and autumn of 1840, for which he was promoted captain by commission dated 4 November, the day following the capture of Acre. In 1847 he was flag captain to Commodore Sir Charles Hotham in the *Penelope*, on the west coast of Africa, where in February 1849 he commanded the boats of the squadron at the destruction of the slave barracoons in the Gallinas River. The *Penelope* was paid off in the summer of 1849, and early in 1850 Jones was appointed to the *Sampson*, again for the west coast, under the orders of Commodore Bruce. On 26–7 December 1851 he commanded the expedition detached against the slaving stronghold at Lagos which was captured and brought under British control. Bruce highly commended Jones's 'gallantry, firmness, judgment, and energy', in this desperate and bloody action and sent him home with dispatches. Still in the *Sampson*, he then went to the Mediterranean, and on 22 April 1854 was senior officer at the bombardment of Odessa. On 26 May he was made a CB. He continued actively employed in the Black Sea, and in November was moved into the ship *London* (90 guns), in which he continued until the end of the war. He received the cross of an officer of the Légion d'honneur, and the Madjidieh (third class).

On 17 June 1859 Jones was promoted rear-admiral, and in the following year was second in command on the China station, under Sir James Hope. On 28 June 1861 he

Sir Lewis Tobias Jones (1797–1895), by Elliott & Fry, pubd 1895

was made a KCB. From 1862 to 1865 he was commander-in-chief at Queenstown, and he became vice-admiral on 2 December 1865. On 1 April 1870, under Hugh Childers's retirement scheme, he was put on the retired list, and he became admiral on 14 July 1871. On 24 May 1873 he was made a GCB, and on 25 March 1884 visitor and governor of Greenwich Hospital, a nominal and honorary appointment. He died at his home, Rugby House, 10 Lennox Road, Southsea, Hampshire, after two days' indisposition without pain, on 11 October 1895, the oldest British admiral. Jones had an unusual career, with a slow start in the promotion race owing to lack of influence; but his zeal, bravery, and professionalism, notably on the highly unpopular west Africa station, brought him success.

J. K. LAUGHTON, *rev.* ANDREW LAMBERT

Sources W. E. F. Ward, *The Royal Navy and the slavers* (1969) · J. W. D. Dundas and C. Napier, *Russian war, 1854, Baltic and Black Sea: official correspondence*, ed. D. Bonner-Smith and A. C. Dewar, Navy RS, 83 (1943) · G. S. Graham, *The China station: war and diplomacy, 1830–1860* (1978) · O'Byrne, *Naval biog. dict.* · Boase, *Mod. Eng. biog.* · *The Times* (14 Oct 1895) · *The Times* (17 Oct 1895) · *Navy List* · Burke, *Peerage* (1894) · *CGPLA Eng. & Wales* (1895)
Likenesses Elliott & Fry, photograph, BM, NPG; repro. in *ILN*, 107 (1895), 486 [*see illus.*]
Wealth at death £1757 17s. 0d.: probate, 14 Dec 1895, *CGPLA Eng. & Wales*

Jones, (Patrick) Lloyd (1811–1886), socialist, was born at Bandon, co. Cork, on 17 March 1811. He moved in 1827 to Manchester, where he followed his father's trade and became secretary to the journeyman's union of fustian cutters. Influenced by E. T. Craig, he joined the Salford Co-operative Society in 1829, ran its free school until 1831, and was an Owenite missionary, lecturer, and propagandist between 1838 and 1844; he took the oath to become a dissenting minister in 1841. He dropped the name Patrick in 1837 to dissociate himself from his Roman Catholic father. In the same year he married Mary Dring.

A forceful and persuasive public speaker, Lloyd Jones persuaded Manchester Chartists to oppose the threatened 'sacred month's' strike of 1839. A moral-force Chartist himself, he visited Paris in 1848 with William Lovett and in 1849 launched the short-lived Chartist-radical National Reform League with Bronterre O'Brien and George Reynolds.

Jones joined the communitarian Leeds Redemption Society in 1846 and became director of its flour mill. He then established a business as a master tailor on Oxford Street, London, in 1847, and the following year joined the Owenite League of Social Progress. In 1850 he gave evidence before R. A. Slaney's committee on working-class savings and joined the Christian socialists, managing their London co-operative stores. He subsequently undertook several lecture tours, taught at the working men's college, and founded the Co-operative Industrial and Commercial Union. Having attended the Christian socialists' conferences in 1853 and 1854, he helped organize the inaugural annual Co-operative Congress, in 1869, and presided at the seventeenth, at Oldham in 1885. He was also a member of the inaugural central board of the Co-operative Union.

A prolific journalist, Jones wrote on co-operation, unionism, social politics, and industrial subjects in the *Spirit of the Age* (1848), *Spirit of the Times* (1849), *Glasgow Sentinel* (1850–63), *North British Daily Mail* (1859–65), *London Reader* (1863), *Industrial Partnerships Record* (1867–9), *Bee-Hive* and *Industrial Review* (1871–8), *Co-operative News* (1870s–80s), *Newcastle Daily* and *Weekly Chronicles* (1876–86), and *Miner's Watchman and Labour Sentinel* (1878). Following his management of the Leeds Mechanics' Institute (1855–6), he established the *Leeds Times* in 1857, assisted by Lord Goderich and W. E. Forster.

A member of the trades union committee deputed to help the Preston strikers in 1855, Jones subsequently worked to reform the labour laws and in 1867 co-wrote *The Progress of the Working Classes* with John Ludlow. In 1869 he became the first secretary of the Labour Representation League and in 1871 joined the first parliamentary committee of the Trades Union Congress. From 1874 he was frequently appointed arbitrator in trades union disputes, particularly in mining districts. Standing as an independent miners' representative for the constituency of Chester-le-Street in Durham in the 1885 general election, he was defeated by the Liberal candidate.

Jones died of cancer at his home, 14 St Michael's Road, Stockwell, London, on 22 May 1886, nine days before his wife. He was predeceased by his eldest son, Lloyd, but was survived by another son, William Cairns, and two daughters. His *Life, Times and Labours of Robert Owen* (1889) was published posthumously. MATTHEW LEE

Sources *Co-operative News* (29 May 1886) · *The Spectator* (29 May 1886) · *Newcastle Weekly Chronicle* (29 May 1886) · *Newcastle Weekly Chronicle* (5 June 1886) · Boase, *Mod. Eng. biog.* · J. Bellamy, J. Osburn, and J. Saville, 'Jones, (Patrick) Lloyd', *DLB*, vol. 1 · J. D. Osburn, 'Jones, Patrick Lloyd', *BDMBR*, vol. 2 · G. J. Holyoake, *Sixty years of an agitator's life*, 3rd edn, 2 vols. (1893) · *New Moral World* (1834–45) · *Christian Socialist* (1850–52) · *The Co-operator* (1860–71) · *Co-operative News* (1871–86) · *CGPLA Eng. & Wales* (1886) · *Life and letters of George Jacob Holyoake*, ed. J. McCabe, 2 (1908), 58

Archives Co-operative Union, Holyoake House, Manchester, G. J. Holyoake collection · Co-operative Union, Holyoake House, Manchester, Robert Owen collection · CUL, J. M. Ludlow MSS · Newcastle Central Library, Joseph Cowen MSS
Wealth at death £238: administration, 1886, *CGPLA Eng. & Wales*

Jones, Mark (1933–1958). *See under* Busby Babes (*act.* 1953–1958).

Jones, Sir (Edward) Martin Furnival (1912–1997), intelligence officer and civil servant, was born on 7 May 1912 at 26 Bedford Avenue, Barnet, Hertfordshire, the third and youngest son of Edward Furnival Jones, chartered accountant, later to be president of the Association of Chartered Accountants, and his wife, Kathleen Lizzie, *née* Sedgfield. He was educated at Highgate School and at Gonville and Caius College, Cambridge, where he was an exhibitioner, reading modern and medieval languages and then law. On graduating he was admitted as a solicitor in 1937, working for the firm Slaughter and May until the outbreak of the Second World War. In 1940 he was commissioned in the intelligence corps, and in 1941 he was attached to MI5, serving in the War Office and then in the counter-intelligence division of Supreme Headquarters Allied Expeditionary Force (SHAEF), where he worked on the deception operation for the D-day landings. For his work with SHAEF he was mentioned in dispatches and awarded the United States bronze star medal. By the end of the war he had been promoted to the rank of lieutenant-colonel.

In 1946 Furnival Jones became a permanent member of the Security Service (MI5), initially working in C branch (protective security), becoming director in 1953. At that time C branch was seen as a backwater within the service. Following Sir Dick White's move from head of MI5 to become chief of the Secret Intelligence Service (SIS/MI6) in 1958, Furnival Jones had an opportunity to move. Sir Roger Hollis became director-general of the Security Service, and Graham Mitchell, formerly director of D branch (counter-espionage), became his deputy. Furnival Jones replaced Mitchell as head of D branch. As head of counter-espionage, Furnival Jones was at the heart of the crisis within the British intelligence community and central government following the defections of Guy Burgess and Donald Maclean. The treachery of the Soviet 'moles' led to deep suspicion, paranoia, and poor morale. Members of MI5's counter-espionage branch, including Peter Wright, were convinced that there remained an undiscovered mole within the Security Service. The main target for the mole-hunters was initially the deputy director-general, Mitchell, and their allegations played a part in his unprecedented early retirement in 1963. Furnival Jones, who had supervised the first stages of the internal investigation, again succeeded Mitchell.

When Sir Roger Hollis retired in 1965, Furnival Jones became director-general of the Security Service. A climate of deep suspicion still pervaded the service, to the extent that Furnival Jones was in the unenviable position of having to initiate an official investigation of his predecessor, an investigation he described as 'grotesque' (Wright, 297). Despite being convinced of Hollis's innocence, Furnival

Jones felt that he had to order a detailed investigation to avoid accusations of a cover-up. Hollis was thoroughly investigated, Furnival Jones himself questioning Hollis personally, but no conclusive proof was found. Furnival Jones remained convinced of Hollis's innocence. He and former deputy director-general Anthony Simkins wrote a letter to *The Times* in October 1981, stating that 'We are wholly convinced of his innocence' (*The Times*, 21 Oct 1981). The inconclusive witch-hunt had a long-term effect on the service's morale and reputation—damage which Furnival Jones could only begin to remedy. In 1971 Furnival Jones played a key role in the expulsion of 105 Soviet 'diplomats' identified as KGB officers by the defector Oleg Lyalin. This was a triumph for Jones, who, according to Peter Wright, was convinced that his greatest challenge as director-general was 'the sheer scale of Soviet Bloc intelligence activity in Britain' (Wright, 123). The expulsions limited Soviet intelligence operations in Britain, and went some way to redressing the perceived intelligence imbalance.

Furnival Jones made a celebrated incognito appearance before the Franks committee reviewing section 2 of the 1911 Official Secrets Act in November 1971. His evidence gave a rare view of the quiet, shy man behind the veil of secrecy. He informed the committee that 'very many members of parliament are in contact with very many intelligence officers'. He also, most famously, stated that Russian spies had been readily recognizable 'because they wore long coats and curiously shaped hats', and that his definition of an official secret was that 'It is an official secret if it is in an official file' (Franks committee, evidence, 5 Nov 1971).

FJ, as he was known, was a respected intelligence officer and a solid, unassuming civil servant, who beneath his quiet and reserved exterior possessed a determined streak. During the Second World War he gained a reputation for a penetrating mind and sound judgement. As director-general of the Security Service he was the safe pair of hands the service needed in the wake of the disruptive mole-hunts. He also limited further damage to MI5's reputation following claims that the service was politically biased against the Labour government of the day, keeping disruptive elements within MI5 in check and reassuring the government. He was made a CBE in 1957 and knighted in 1967.

Furnival Jones married, on 1 October 1955, (Elizabeth) Margaret Snowball (b. 1918/19), secretary, daughter of Bartholomew Snowball, electrical engineer. They had one daughter. Furnival Jones retired from the Security Service in 1972. He then worked briefly as a security consultant to ICI and Playboy. He was a member of the panel of chairmen of the civil selection board, and chairman of the board, Frensham Heights, from 1973 to 1976 (president in 1977). He was an avid ornithologist. He died of cancer on 1 March 1997 at his home, 'Lindum', First Drift, Wothorpe, Stamford, Lincolnshire. He was survived by his wife and daughter.
MARC B. DAVIES

Sources *Daily Telegraph* (8 March 1997) · *The Guardian* (6 March 1997) · *The Times* (5 March 1997) · P. Wright, *Spycatcher* (1987) · *Departmental committee on section 2 of the Official Secrets Act 1911*, 3: *Oral evidence, mainly from government witnesses* (1972) [evidence taken 5 Nov 1971] · T. Bower, *The perfect English spy* (1995) · N. West, *Molehunt* (1987) · C. Pincher, *Their trade is treachery* (1981) · WWW · b. cert. · m. cert. · d. cert.
Likenesses photograph, repro. in *The Times* · photograph, repro. in *Daily Telegraph*
Wealth at death under £180,000: probate, 6 May 1997, *CGPLA Eng. & Wales*

Jones, Mary (1707–1778), poet, was born on 8 March 1707 in Oxford, the second of four children of Oliver Jones, cooper, of St Aldates, and his second wife, one of the daughters (probably Mary) of Thomas Penn, a yeoman of South Newington near Banbury. Two younger brothers died in infancy; her elder brother, Oliver, became chanter and senior chaplain of Christ Church.

Jones learned French and Italian and was able to translate from Italian by the age of sixteen. She may have spent some years as a governess, since by 1730 she had formed friendships with an aristocratic circle including two women of Queen Caroline's household: Martha Lovelace, who in 1739 married Lord Henry Beauclerk and later became housekeeper at Windsor Castle, and Mrs Charlotte Clayton ('Stella' in Jones's verse), who became Lady Sundon in 1735. Jones regularly visited Martha at New Lodge, Windsor, and Charlotte at nearby Fern Hill. In contrast to these wealthy friends, she lived for most of her adult life modestly with her brother.

Information on Jones's life is mostly drawn from her *Miscellanies in Prose and Verse*. She began writing verses 'at a very early age' with no view to publication. In April 1742 she found to her surprise that her ballad 'The Lass of the Hill' was published in London, and about the same time her verses on the death of Lord Aubrey Beauclerk were printed, regardless of permission, by his widow. Jones comments: 'this … one gets by letting one's friends enjoy the pleasing secrets of one's writing.'

About 1745 Jones published *A Letter to Dr Pitt*, a prose mock complaint to her neighbour at the condition of the boundary fence, with much play on the need of his medical skills to repair its 'paroxysms' and 'epilepsies'. She was now becoming reconciled to publication, and in 1748 was preparing a collection of her letters and poems. *Miscellanies in Prose and Verse* was published in 1750, with 1400 subscribers, 'for the sake of a relation, grown old and helpless … whom she had no other methods of effectually assisting'. The volume was well received; extracts were published in the *London Magazine* throughout 1752. Sixteen poems appeared in *Poems by Eminent Ladies* in 1755.

Jones's literary acquaintance included Samuel Johnson, who called her 'the Chantress' (Boswell, *Life*, 1.322). Thomas Warton remembered her as 'a most sensible, agreeable and amiable woman' (ibid.). Her poetry is well crafted and witty, her subjects typically epitaphs, mild moral counsel, and light satire. She was much influenced by Pope: 'If Mr Pope could contrive to write without a Genius, I don't know anyone so likely to hit off my manner.' Lonsdale (p. 156) regards her as 'one of the most intelligent and amusing women writers of her period'.

Jones lived in Oxford all her life, her final address being

16 Fish Street. At her death she was postmistress of Oxford. She died in Oxford on 10 February 1778, and was buried there four days later. WILLIAM R. JONES

Sources M. Jones, *Miscellanies in prose and verse* (1750) · R. Lonsdale, ed., *Eighteenth-century women poets: an Oxford anthology* (1989) · J. Todd, ed., *A dictionary of British and American women writers, 1660–1800* (1984) · H. E. Salter, ed., *Survey of Oxford in 1772* (1912) · Boswell, *Life*, 1.322 · *DNB* · parish register (baptism), Oxford, St Aldate's, Oxfordshire CRO · *Jackson's Oxford Journal* (14 Feb 1778)

Jones [*married name* Lewis], **Mary** (**1784–1866**), exemplar of godly life, was born at Tyn-y-ddôl, near the hamlet of Llanfihangel-y-Pennant, Merioneth, the daughter of Jacob (or James) Jones and his wife, Mary (Molly), who were both weavers, and members of the Calvinistic Methodist church in the village of Abergynolwyn, 2 miles away. As a dutiful child Mary undertook household tasks, fed the hens, and looked after the beehive. Her keen interest in Bible stories, and her ability to learn and recite the scriptures in Welsh, were evident from an early age, and at eight she accompanied her mother to adult meetings at church.

About 1794 the Revd Thomas *Charles (1755–1814) established one of his 'circulating schools' (day schools) at Abergynolwyn, under a schoolmaster, John Ellis, and shortly afterwards established an associated Sunday school. From the age of ten to sixteen Mary Jones attended them both, made good progress in her studies, and learned whole chapters of the Bible by heart. At that time copies of the Bible in Welsh were in short supply, and her parents did not own one, so Mary regularly walked 2 miles to read a Bible at the house of a neighbouring farmer. She longed to obtain a Bible of her own, and began to save for one by undertaking various chores for neighbours.

In 1799 the Society for the Promotion of Christian Knowledge printed 10,000 copies of a new translation of the Bible in Welsh, but since it incorporated the Apocrypha, the Book of Common Prayer, and ecclesiastical tables it was expensive. Nevertheless, Mary had by this time saved enough for the new translation and asked a local preacher, William Hugh, where she could buy one. He told her that the nearest copies were with the Revd Thomas Charles at Bala, 25 miles away, but that they were probably all sold or spoken for. Undaunted, the sixteen-year-old Mary won her parents' permission to make the long journey to Bala on foot. She set off across the shoulder of Cadair Idris carrying her shoes in a wallet and late in the day arrived at Bala. There she learned that Charles, according to his custom, had retired early, so she followed the directions given her by William Hugh and stayed overnight at the home of a local preacher, David Edwards.

The following morning Mary accompanied Edwards to Charles's house, eager to obtain her Bible. When Charles revealed that all were sold, or spoken for, she wept bitterly. Eventually, her tears, her remarkable knowledge of the scriptures, and the story of her years of saving so affected Charles that he released one of his ordered copies.

This incident, and his further enquiries regarding Mary, made a lasting impression on Charles. In December 1802,

at a meeting of the committee of the Religious Tract Society, he urged the case for setting up a Welsh Bible Society, adducing Mary Jones's story as evidence of a thirst for the scriptures. The committee was greatly moved, especially the Revd Joseph Hughes, who enlarged the concept to that of a Bible Society for the whole world. This led in 1804 to the establishment of the British and Foreign Bible Society with its aim of making the scriptures available to all races at affordable prices.

In the years that followed, Mary's story, especially her epic walk to Bala, was often recounted, and at the request of agents abroad was translated into several languages. It was seen as a seed of the great missionary movement of the nineteenth century and evidence for the potential power of the apparently weak (1 Corinthians 1: 27). Welsh patriotism, evangelical fervour, and pride in the spread of the gospel abroad led to the popular Victorian biographies.

Mary later married a weaver, Thomas Lewis, and brought up her family at the village of Bryn-crug near Tywyn. She worked as a weaver and dressmaker, and kept bees, with which she was reputed to have a remarkable rapport. Her devotion to the scriptures continued and she learned whole books by heart. She continued as a member of the adult Sunday school movement and supported foreign missions. She died on 28 December 1866 at Bryn-crug and was buried in the graveyard behind the chapel at Bryn-crug, with a monument in Welsh and in English.

In the context of Bible societies and the Sunday school movement 'Mary Jones and her Bible' was a favourite story, for both adults and children, well into the last century, and in such circles and beyond she figured as a kind of protestant saint. JOHN D. HAIGH

Sources R. O. Rees and T. Levi, *Mary Jones of Ty'nyddol*, trans. S. C. Malan (1887) [trans. from the Welsh] · M. E. R., *From the beginning, or, The story of Mary Jones and her Bible*, British and Foreign Bible Society (1882) · M. E. R., *Mary Jones and her Bible* (Gospel Standard Trust Publications, 1983) [with additional illustrations and notes]
Likenesses print (*Old Mary Jones*), repro. in M. E. R., *From the beginning*

Jones, Mary (**1812–1887**), nursing reformer, was born in Tamworth, Staffordshire, the daughter of a cabinet-maker. Her father was still alive in March 1853, when she appeared at the sisterhood of St John's House, 3–4 Queen Square, London, but nothing is known of her upbringing before this point. St John's House was one of the new Anglican sisterhoods founded in 1848 as a training school for nurses. The sisters were to be ladies who would train as nurses themselves and who would provide moral and religious discipline for the working-class nurses. Together with the doctors they would also give instruction in clinical practice in the teaching hospitals. The sisterhood had succeeded in attracting nurses but had not been able to recruit enough sisters or probationers for its training school. In March 1853 the sisterhood consisted of only the lady superintendent, Mrs Morrice, who was ill, and one resident sister. St John's House was in financial difficulties and its council was considering closing it down.

Jones so impressed the council members with her

administrative skills and overall competence that three months later they asked for Mrs Morrice's resignation. In August Jones became a sister and the acting lady superintendent, and on 7 November 1853 she became lady superintendent. A year later the Crimean War provided the sisterhood with excellent publicity, more charitable donations, and more sisters. Six St John's House nurses went to the East with Florence Nightingale's original party, and Jones agreed to provide hospital training for volunteer ladies who later went to the hospitals in Turkey and the Crimea.

By March 1856 Jones had enough well-trained staff to take over the nursing service at King's College Hospital, London. Hospital nurses were then noted for their delinquencies, most notably for leaving their wards unattended and ignoring the doctors' orders. Jones surmounted these failings, first by strict discipline; second, she removed the cleaning work from the nurses' duties so that they could concentrate on patient care; third, living and working conditions were improved; and fourth, she provided a thorough clinical training so the nurses would understand what was expected of them. She had no patience with ladies who wanted to come for short periods or who wanted only to attend the lectures and not to carry out the clinical practice. Although deeply religious herself, Jones was wary of ladies who were religious enthusiasts, finding them often unrealistic dilettantes. Many people wanted to make work for ladies in hospitals rather than making the ladies work to improve the hospitals. As for the working-class nurses, Jones said, 'We have left the poor Hospital nurse as the victim of a vicious system—and then condemn and shrink from her as degraded' (Jones to Nightingale, 16 June 1863, BL, Add. MS 47743, fols. 202–6). She wanted to advance the cause of women by training willing and capable women to achieve usefulness in life.

King's College Hospital was the first hospital with a trained nursing service and the first to introduce ladies as nurses. Almost immediately some of the other London teaching hospitals began adopting the less expensive parts of the St John's House system. In 1862 the All Saints sisters undertook the nursing at University College Hospital using the St John's House system wholesale. Jones took over the nursing at the Galignani Hospital in Paris in 1862 and the Charing Cross Hospital in London in 1866. Many other hospitals asked the sisters to undertake their nursing, but unfortunately Jones did not have the resources to do so.

The successes of St John's House were duly noted by Florence Nightingale, who consulted Jones about every possible detail when establishing her school in London at St Thomas's Hospital in 1860. Jones became one of Nightingale's dearest friends and her chief mentor in this project. Nightingale sent outstanding lady pupils at St Thomas's to work with Jones, and in 1862 she had the Nightingale Fund subsidize midwifery training at King's College Hospital under Jones's direction.

By 1868 St John's House was the recognized leader of nursing reform, but the high-church leanings of Jones and her sisters had brought them into conflict with their low-church council. In 1856 Jones became the effective head of the sisterhood, replacing the chaplain, who was known as the master. In 1865 she took the title of lady superior and divested the master of his office as treasurer, making him simply the chaplain. Matters came to a head when the sisters wished to replace their low-church chaplain with a priest who would administer vows and hear confession. The bishop of London, who was also the president of the council, refused to sanction such high-church practices. Jones and her sisters felt the council had no right to interfere in their religious life and decided to sever their connection with St John's House. Nightingale urged Jones not to do so because she saw that, once the sisters left the two teaching hospitals where they had effected such impressive nursing reforms, they would be out of mainstream nursing and no longer able to exercise the same influence.

Nightingale's urgings notwithstanding, Jones and seven of the nine members of the sisterhood left St John's House and their work at King's College and Charing Cross hospitals in January 1868. They constituted themselves as an independent sisterhood, the Community of St Mary and St John the Evangelist. By 1873 they had established themselves in a home at 39 Kensington Square, London, where they carried out social work among the poor, tended the sick in their own homes, and performed some refuge work. In 1874 they opened St Joseph's Hospital for Incurables in an adjoining house.

On 2 June 1887 Jones died of typhoid fever at 39 Kensington Square. She was buried in the sisters' plot in Brookwood cemetery, Woking.

CAROL HELMSTADTER

Sources LMA, archives of St John's House, HI/ST/SJ · BL, Add. MSS 47743–47744 · King's Lond., King's College Hospital Archives · Charing Cross Hospital Archives, London · LMA, Nightingale collection, HI/ST/NC 1 and NC 18 · Bishop Blomfield MSS, microfiches nos. 122–9, fol. 364; Archbishop Tait MSS, vols. 142, 145–6, 148–9, LPL · P. Myers, Building for the future: a nursing history, 1896–1996, of St Mary's Convent and Nursing Home, Chiswick (1996) · F. F. Cartwright, 'The story of St John's House', King's College Hospital Nurses' League Journal (1959), 29–34 · F. F. Cartwright, 'Miss Nightingale's dearest friend', Proceedings of the Royal Society of Medicine, 69 (1976), 169–75 · Archives of St Mary's Convent, Chiswick, London

Archives King's Lond., hospital archives · NRA, priv. coll., letters with records of order's hospice · St John's House | BL, papers, incl. letter to F. Nightingale, Add. MSS 47743–47744 · LPL, Bishop Blomfield MSS, microfiches nos. 122–9, fol. 364 · LPL, Archbishop Tait MSS, vols. 142, 145–6, 148–9

Jones, Matthew (1654–1717). *See under* Jones, Edward (1641–1703).

Jones, (Ronald) Maxwell [Max] (1917–1993), jazz critic and author, was born on 28 February 1917 at 9 Nightingale Road, Bushey, Hertfordshire, the youngest son and second of the three children of Theophilus Hill (Theo) Jones, an iron and scrap metal merchant, and his wife, Elsie, *née* Brierley. Both parents were English. He lived and was educated in the Primrose Hill area before attending Regent

Street Polytechnic, London, where, with his brother Clifford Hill (Cliff) Jones (b. 1914) and friends, he formed an eight-piece amateur dance band. He played tenor and soprano saxophones and learned about jazz from American records, and, although the band never progressed further than amateur standard, it continued beyond his student days. He joined the band of trumpeter Johnny Claes but abandoned the tenor saxophone after hearing the instrument's master Coleman Hawkins at first hand, and, although persevering with lessons on alto saxophone, he eventually decided to abandon playing music. He heard Louis Armstrong, Duke Ellington, Joe Venuti, and Cab Calloway on their British visits and, with Claes, got to know the small contingent of local black musicians, whose society he enjoyed. By the end of the 1930s he was involved with the rhythm club movement, giving record recitals and writing about jazz.

A lifelong social conscience, formed early on through Jones's interest in African American music, was cemented by witnessing police corruption at his father's business premises. In 1935 he joined the Communist Party. As a conscientious objector he spent most of the war years as an air raid warden in London, but he also travelled to High Wycombe, where his parents had moved, and, with Peter Duffell, started a rhythm club in the town. In 1943 he wrote about jazz for the Young Communist League weekly, *Challenge*, and formed the Challenge Rhythm Club, organizing record recitals and lectures under its auspices and concert appearances by Claes and the Trinidadian trumpeter Cyril Blake.

On 8 January 1942 Jones married Amy Alice (Sandra) Salberg (1920–2002), the daughter of George Henry Salberg, glass worker and photographer's processor; they had one daughter, Vivienne Anne Lindsey Jones (b. 1944), who was later known as Vivienne Anne Lindsey Luck. He subsequently began a long relationship with his sister-in-law Betty Elizabeth Salberg (1925–1992), who changed her name to Jones before their son, Nicholas Carl Maxwell Jones, was born in 1948; they married on 14 May 1965 after his previous marriage was dissolved.

In the summer of 1942 the publication *Jazz Music* was launched, with Jones and Albert J. McCarthy as editors. Established jazz writers were featured and Jones, in addition to his musical articles, reported on racial matters in the USA. 'A survey of slavery', written with Charles Wilford and published in *Jazz Music* in 1944, provided an educational jolt to enthusiasts for whom the blues existed only as music on a 78 r.p.m. shellac record. Although limited in size by wartime restrictions, the magazine published poetry and reprinted writings by the American jazz historian William Russell and Harlem renaissance figures Langston Hughes and Zora Neale Hurston. In April 1944 the editors formed the Jazz Sociological Society and, when *Jazz Music* temporarily ceased publication, they produced a series of erudite booklets on aspects of jazz, one of which included a report by Jones on the fight to desegregate the American armed forces. In 1945 Jones was one of several writers who formed the British Hot Record Society; he also co-edited *Piano Jazz* with McCarthy. A tribute to

the folk-singer Leadbelly (1946) presaged the reappearance of *Jazz Music*, which included new articles by musicians as well as collectors; notable features included Jeff Aldam's 'African survivals in Afro-America' (1947). He also edited Ernest Borneman's important book *A critic looks at jazz* (1946).

In 1944 Jones collaborated with Rex Harris in writing the column 'Collectors' corner' for *Melody Maker*, then, in 1945, joined the staff of that newspaper. In the ensuing years he produced a substantial body of writing about jazz, blues, and gospel music, and the lives of these musical idioms' practitioners. At the heart of this corpus was a prolific collection of interviews, many of which, through their subsequent—and uncredited—extraction in Nat Hentoff and Nat Shapiro's *Hear me Talkin' to ya* (1955), provided important building blocks in the creation of the oral jazz history. With Jones as amanuensis, the stories of pianist Mary Lou Williams, clarinettist Edmond Hall, and others were serialized at a time when no other newspaper would have considered them worthy of such coverage; these recollections were later reprinted in *Talking Jazz* (1987).

Jones was always concerned by racial injustice, whether in the United States, Britain, or South Africa. Following the 1958 Notting Hill racial disturbances he became involved in the Stars' Campaign for Inter-racial Friendship (SCIF) and, while proposing reforms, wrote a spirited defence of the new black settler community, published in *Melody Maker* in 1959. Though always associated with jazz, his musical and other interests were wide: he wrote about the folk-singer Woody Guthrie when he was unknown outside the USA, and expressed enthusiasm for the young Bob Dylan. He also wrote sympathetically about many women musicians.

Although he was himself a spirited raconteur and bon viveur, Jones had the ability to empathize with his subjects and thus get the best from them. He wrote about both major and minor jazz figures with uncommon respect, while presenting them as equally human and fallible characters. This emphasis influenced several younger acolytes. The seamless conversational style he evolved, his horn-rimmed spectacles, and the trademark black beret he always wore were known throughout the jazz world.

A long-standing admirer of Louis Armstrong, Jones paid tribute to his hero by co-writing the trumpeter's biography with John Chilton; *Louis* was published in 1971. His genuine love for the music led to lasting friendships with many of the musicians he interviewed, most notably with Armstrong and the singer Billie Holiday, and the Jones household accommodated many top names from the world of jazz; trumpeter Buck Clayton tipped his hat to his host with his composition 'Mr Melody Maker'. Motor-racing remained another passion: his long association with Claes and former drummer Les Leston encompassed shared racing-circuit activities. His other enduring interests were cricket and wine: he was vice-captain of both the Melody Maker and the Ravers cricket teams and an enthusiastic member of the Wig and Pen Club.

On retirement from *Melody Maker* in 1982 Jones became a

freelance television consultant and continued to write, and turned his collection of photographs and memorabilia into a library which his son continued to maintain. He died of heart failure at St Richard's Hospital, Chichester, Sussex, on 2 August 1993. He was survived by his two children, his wife, Betty, having predeceased him.

VAL WILMER

Sources M. Jones, *Talking jazz* (1987) · J. Godbolt, *A history of jazz in Britain, 1919–50* (1984) · *The Guardian* (4 Aug 1993) · personal knowledge (2004) · private information (2004) · b. cert. · m. certs. · d. cert.
Likenesses photographs, priv. coll.
Wealth at death £289,668: probate, 15 Aug 1994, *CGPLA Eng. & Wales*

Jones, Maxwell Shaw (1907–1990), psychiatrist, was born in Queenstown, Cape of Good Hope, on 7 January 1907, the son of William Wilson Jones, a schoolmaster. When he was five his father died and his mother took him and two older children to be educated in Scotland. He attended Stewart's College and then Edinburgh University, qualifying in medicine in 1931. He then trained in psychiatry under Sir David Henderson at the Royal Edinburgh Hospital, where he developed an interest in the biological correlates of neurosis. In 1936, with a Commonwealth Fund fellowship, he went to the USA where he spent a year successively at the University of Pennsylvania and at Columbia Medical Center, New York. On the basis of his laboratory research there, he was recruited by Aubrey Lewis in 1938 at the Maudsley Hospital, London. A year later the hospital was evacuated and he was with that part which went to Mill Hill. There, he was in charge of a unit dealing with effort syndrome in servicemen; continuing research on the biochemical aspects of the disorder, he was awarded the MD (Edinburgh) with gold medal. It was in this setting that his most important future work began.

Because there was a shortage of staff for psychotherapy, Jones experimented with group treatment; men with chronic anxiety or depressive states were also admitted in addition to those with cardiac neuroses. For the first time anywhere Jones made use of meetings of the entire community as a therapeutic measure; results, in terms of return to duty, were much better than before. The term 'therapeutic community' was coined by T. F. Main to describe a similar regime at Northfield Military Hospital in the latter years of the Second World War. At Mill Hill, large groups of patients and staff met three times weekly for a combination of educational talks about psychosomatic mechanisms with open discussion. Psychodrama, work projects, staff discussions, and a general meeting of the entire community were added. Within the unit, treatment was seen as a continuous process, effective over every aspect of the patient's life; more open communication led to a diminution of the power relationships between different kinds of staff and patients.

In 1945 Jones took charge of a 300-bed unit at a military hospital in Dartford for the rehabilitation of returned prisoners of war who were psychiatrically disabled. While the Mill Hill regime was largely reproduced, meaningful work was emphasized and links were fostered with the local community. Results were again impressive and Jones was appointed CBE in 1954 for this work and for his help to the disabled generally.

Jones became director of the industrial rehabilitation unit at Belmont Hospital, Sutton, in 1946; it later had several changes of name, eventually becoming the Henderson Hospital. At the same time, he was undergoing analysis with Melanie Klein. Belmont originally dealt with those identified as chronically unemployed, but over the course of time the clientele became more identified as psychopathic personalities. It was assumed that in this social environment patients would find opportunities to replay the problems they had experienced outside; community interaction and group psychotherapy would then help towards healing. Four cultural principles were defined: democratization, permissiveness, communalism, and reality confrontation. This therapeutic community gained worldwide notice and attracted numerous visitors.

In 1959 Jones became Commonwealth visiting professor at Stanford University and while there pioneered a programme of therapeutic communities in the prison system. This was followed by an appointment at Oregon State Hospital, with a teaching appointment at Oregon medical school. Jones attempted to transform this large, traditional hospital into one based on therapeutic principles, but was eventually dismissed. In his view, 'the new freedoms signalled dangerous signs of change to conservative, hierarchical forces in psychiatry, in politics, public opinion, big business and bureaucracy generally'. He returned to England in 1962 and became physician superintendent of Dingleton Hospital, Melrose. At Dingleton Hospital, Jones transformed the traditional hierarchical culture into one where there was open communication at all levels and where authority could be questioned in a constructive way. Overall, the therapeutic community concept made a significant contribution to professional training, to policy development in psychiatry and criminology, and to the management of institutions.

In 1969 Jones returned to the USA and spent some time at the University of Colorado before moving to Phoenix, where he worked in the psychiatric unit of a minimum security gaol, introducing the familiar elements of a therapeutic community. Moving to Wolfville, Nova Scotia, in 1982, he undertook teaching in educational psychology at a local university. He saw himself as a 'change agent', rather than as having a conventional professional role.

Jones developed an increasing interest in spiritual matters and became a regular consultant to a Roman Catholic therapeutic community for clergy in the British west midlands. He described a number of personal mystical experiences in his final years. His democratic principles did not exclude the need for leadership, though he argued that this function should involve different people over time. Jones was

always exciting and stimulating, with bubbling enthusiasm even in his eighties. He was always excited about some new discovery or person or book [though] he would rage against those who did not see his version of the truth [with] a savage delight in humiliating the pompous, the rigid, the traditional ... [A]ttempts to destroy his work were thwarted time and again by powerful protectors ... He deployed charm, intelligence and erudition in every situation, challenging, questioning, teasing those he met.   (Clark)

Jones, who married three times, died at Wolfville, Nova Scotia, on 19 August 1990.

Jones was one of the greatest pioneers of social psychiatry. He was one of the few non-Americans to receive the Isaac Ray award of the American Psychiatric Association. His therapeutic community concept transformed the culture of psychiatric institutions in many parts of the world.   HUGH FREEMAN

Sources D. Millard, 'Maxwell Jones and the therapeutic community', *150 years of British psychiatry*, ed. H. Freeman and G. E. Berrios, 2: *The aftermath* (1996) · *BMJ* (29 Sept 1990), 663 · *The Times* (30 Aug 1990) · D. H. Clark, 'Maxwell Jones and the mental hospitals', *International Journal of Therapeutic Communities*, 12 (1991), 117–24

Jones, Sir (Bennett) Melvill (1887–1975), university teacher and aeronautical engineer, was born in Rock Ferry, Birkenhead, Cheshire, on 28 January 1887, the elder son and eldest of three children of Benedict Jones of Birkenhead, a Liverpool barrister, and his wife, Henrietta Cornelia Melvill of South Africa, widow of George William Bennett, who had three other children from her earlier marriage. From Birkenhead School he entered Emmanuel College, Cambridge, in 1906 as an exhibitioner, becoming a scholar one year later and graduating with first-class honours in the mechanical sciences tripos in 1909.

After gaining some workshop experience Jones worked for two years in the newly formed aeronautical department at the National Physical Laboratory and for one year in industry on airship design. On the outbreak of the First World War in 1914 he went to the Royal Aircraft Factory at Farnborough, Hampshire, where he worked on problems of aerial gunnery and the development of instruments to assist flying in clouds. In 1916 he moved to the Air Armament Experimental Station at Orford Ness, Suffolk, where he continued his work on gunnery and qualified as a pilot. In the same year Jones married Dorothy Laxton (d. 1955), daughter of Frederick Charles Jotham, a Kidderminster wine merchant. They had one daughter and two sons, one of whom was killed in action in August 1941. In 1918 Jones served in France for about six weeks in 48 squadron of the Royal Flying Corps and the RAF as a rear gunner of a Bristol Fighter. He was awarded the AFC (1918) and attained the rank of lieutenant-colonel.

Early in 1919 Jones returned to Cambridge as a fellow of Emmanuel College, but only a few months later the Francis Mond professorship of aeronautical engineering was established at Cambridge and he was appointed to it, retaining the post until his retirement in 1952. The Air Ministry had agreed to provide aeroplanes and flying facilities, which gave Jones the opportunity to develop a very successful school of aeronautical research, using aeroplanes in flight as the major research tool. The research team was always small, usually about four people, and with characteristic modesty Jones made it clear that the members of the team were expected to work with him and not for him. After a few years working on aerial surveying he turned his attention to a detailed study of the processes occurring when an aeroplane stalls. This led to a major advance in understanding and helped to reduce accidents. His later work, from 1926 onward, was all concerned with the drag of an aircraft and ways of reducing it. In a particularly important paper in 1929 he introduced the concept of the ideal streamline aeroplane whose drag would be very much less than that of the aeroplanes then flying. This gave designers for the first time an ideal at which to aim and led to a rapid evolution of the clean monoplane with retractable undercarriage. During the 1930s the research by Jones and his small team was aimed at understanding and eventually reducing the drag experienced even by an aeroplane of good streamline form and this work was of great value in laying a foundation for later research elsewhere on reduction of drag.

Shortly before the start of the Second World War the Air Ministry asked Jones to return to his work on aerial gunnery. He worked energetically in this field for four years, laying the foundations for the development of the gyro gunsight, and in 1943 moved to the Ministry of Aircraft Production and became chairman of the Aeronautical Research Committee (later Council) until 1946. On his return to Cambridge after the war he took up again his flight research on reduction of drag. After his retirement in 1952 he worked for a number of years as a part-time consultant at the Royal Aircraft Establishment, Farnborough.

Jones was of stocky build, a strong swimmer, and an enthusiastic rock climber. Known as Bones to his friends, he was an excellent teacher and one of the kindest and friendliest of men. He was described by a former colleague, Sir William Farren, as 'a man of unsurpassed charm and simplicity'. He was appointed CBE in 1938, elected FRS in 1939, and knighted in 1942. In 1947 he was awarded the medal of freedom by the president of the USA for his work in the Second World War on aerial gunnery and in the same year he received the gold medal of the Royal Aeronautical Society, of which he became an honorary fellow in 1951. Jones died in north Devon on 31 October 1975. He was survived by his younger son, Geoffrey Jones FRS, director of the aviation medical research unit at McGill University, Montreal, Canada.

W. A. MAIR, rev.

Sources A. Hall and M. Morgan, *Memoirs FRS*, 23 (1977), 253–82 · *The Times* (6 Nov 1975) · A. V. Stephens, *Emmanuel College Magazine*, 59 (1976–7) · personal knowledge (1986) · *CGPLA Eng. & Wales* (1976)
Archives Royal Air Force Museum, Hendon, corresp. and papers
Likenesses W. Stoneman, photograph, 1944, NPG
Wealth at death £34,151: probate, 1 March 1976, *CGPLA Eng. & Wales*

Jones, Michael (1606x10–1649), parliamentarian army officer, was the second son of Lewis *Jones (1560–1646), later bishop of Killaloe, and his wife, Mabel (b. c.1580), daughter of Arland Ussher and Margaret Stanihurst. He was born between 1606 and 1610, a range of dates inferred from his elder brother's date of birth and his own likely age at university matriculation. The couple's other sons included two bishops, Henry *Jones and Ambrose *Jones [see under Jones, Lewis], and another soldier, Theophilus *Jones. Michael entered Trinity College, Dublin, in 1621, and Lincoln's Inn in 1631, commenced a legal career, and was admitted to the King's Inns in Dublin in November 1640.

In December 1641, after the start of the Irish rising, Jones was commissioned to raise a company and served in the earl of Kildare's regiment in both Munster and Leinster until the conclusion of a cessation in September 1643, rising to the rank of major. In October, with three fellow officers, he was chosen as an agent to attend the king in Oxford by an informal group of protestants who wished to ensure that their views were heard during the negotiations with the confederate representatives in the spring of 1644. In an address to Ormond on behalf of the group in January 1644 he spoke uncompromisingly of their hopes for the 'present and future settlement and security' of Irish protestants (Carte, 6.23). Shortly afterwards, on learning that he would be expected to bring his company with him to England to join the royal army, he withdrew from the delegation.

In the summer Jones joined the parliamentarian army in Cheshire where he took part in the campaign to recover control of the county after the battle of Marston Moor, making his first recorded appearance in the area when he contributed to the defeat of scattered units of Prince Rupert's command at Tarvin and Malpas on 21 and 26 August 1644. From November 1644 to February 1646, under the command of Sir William Brereton, he was continuously involved in the actions surrounding the siege of Chester. When the suburbs were stormed on 18 September 1645 and the royalists defeated at Rowton Heath six days later, Jones was in command of the cavalry in Brereton's absence in London. More moderate leaders in Cheshire vainly hoped that he would be appointed to replace Brereton. As the siege drew to an end, Jones policed the Welsh border and defeated relieving forces commanded by Sir William Vaughan at Denbigh on 1 November and by Sir William Byron at Holt Bridge a month later. When Chester capitulated on 3 February 1646 he was appointed governor.

After the confirmation of Lord Lisle's appointment as lord lieutenant of Ireland in April 1646, Jones's name was canvassed for Irish service: on 3 July he was contracted to take a regiment to Dublin where he was to serve as deputy governor under Lisle's brother Algernon Sydney. In the event Jones played no part in the plans of Lisle and his Independent associates and it was not until the presbyterian grouping recovered political control that his services were called upon. On 9 April 1647, the day on which Lisle's commission expired, Jones was appointed governor of Dublin and commander of the Leinster forces with the initial responsibility of accepting the surrender of the city from the king's viceroy, the marquess of Ormond. Accompanied by civil commissioners and 2000 men, he arrived in Dublin on 7 June and the terms of the transfer of authority were agreed on 18 June.

Jones's immediate requirements were 'bread and elbow room' (Gilbert, 7.33), but the initiative lay with Preston's confederate army which was already picking off garrisons as a prelude to the investment of Dublin. When Jones marched to the relief of Trim, Preston raised the siege and outflanked the parliamentarian army in a bid to reach Dublin in its absence. On 8 August Jones caught up with Preston's force at Dungan's Hill where cavalry superiority gave him a decisive victory. Preston's casualties were in excess of 3000, 200 of his officers were captured, and his artillery and baggage train were taken. Returning to Dublin in triumph, Jones famously refused to parade the captured enemy colours for fear that he would seem to be 'attributing unto man the glory of this great work due unto the Lord only' (Bodl. Oxf., MS Carte 21, fol. 371). The return of Owen Roe O'Neill to Leinster prevented Jones from taking immediate advantage of his success, but in October he linked up with George Monck, parliamentarian commander of the Ulster forces, and their combined armies secured control over the strongholds of north Leinster.

In 1648 the terms of politics in Ireland were changed by divisions among the confederates, Inchiquin's return to the royalist cause, the outbreak of the second civil war in England, and the realignment of the Scots. Jones's pragmatic response was to protect the position of parliament's forces by entering into an agreement with O'Neill in August 1648. His example was followed by Monck and Coote, and Ormond was successfully deprived of the services of the confederates' most capable commander. The negotiations with O'Neill, conducted by Jones's elder brother Henry, bishop of Clogher, who acted as his secretary, secured the release from captivity of his younger brother Theophilus. It is likely that Michael's wife, referred to as 'the Lady Dame Mary Culme' (d. 1660) in the parliamentary record, was connected by a previous marriage to the Cavan family of Henry's first wife, Jane Culme, whose brother Arthur had been sent to parliament by Michael with news of parliamentarian success at Dungan's Hill in 1647 and raised to a colonelcy when he purged his officer corps of the doubtfully loyal late in 1648.

Ormond's objective, after he had brought together the alliance of royalists and confederates that was formed in January 1649, was to secure control of Dublin, and he began by exploring the possibility of doing so peacefully in a letter to Jones urging him to abandon the regicides. In the exchange which followed Jones made no comment on the execution of the king and at first distanced himself and his 'work' from 'proceedings of state foreign to my charge and trust'. However, he quickly removed the professional mask to denounce Ormond who, by sending soldiers to England after the cessation of 1643, had betrayed the principle that only the English could preserve the English interest in Ireland, had seemed to accept it by surrendering Dublin to parliament, and was now 'receding from it here' (Bodl. Oxf., MS Carte 24, fol. 129). On 19 June

Ormond laid siege to the city with an army of 11,000, reinforced when Inchiquin joined him in July after reducing the remaining parliamentarian garrisons in north Leinster. Jones's forces were ill-provided and untrustworthy, but the arrival from England of one horse and two foot regiments by 26 July transformed the situation. Control of the meadows south of the city became critical. In a bid to deprive the horses of pasturage and to secure a position from which to block entry to Dublin by water, Ormond seized Baggotrath Castle on the morning of 2 August. Jones moved to recover it at once, with 1200 horse and some 4000 foot. The encounter quickly developed into a running engagement which culminated in the routing of Ormond's main army at Rathmines. Jones tried to take advantage of the victory by regaining Drogheda, but Ormond's regathered forces prevented him from investing the town.

On 15 August 1649 Cromwell arrived in Dublin and Jones became his second-in-command with the rank of lieutenant-general. He accompanied Cromwell to Drogheda and subsequently to Wexford, where he took Rosslare on 2 October and participated in the unsuccessful sieges of Duncannon and Waterford that followed. He became feverish on the march from Waterford and died at Dungarvan on 10 December, 'having run his course', Cromwell reported, 'with so much honour, courage, and fidelity, as his actions speak better than my pen. What England lost hereby is above me to speak. I am sure I lost a noble friend and companion in labours' (*Writings and Speeches*, 2.177). Protestants in Ireland were less convinced of Jones's attachment to the cause of parliament and attributed to him their own local preoccupations, believing that 'nothing so much steer'd him in the service of Ireland, as a just reflection on the murthers and insolencies committed by the Irish on the protestants, not otherwise to be pacified than by a due revenge' (Borlase, 230). After both Dungan's Hill and Rathmines, parliament ordered lands to the value of £500 to be bestowed upon Jones and shortly before his death he received a grant of the Bath estate at Balgriffin in co. Dublin. It remained in his widow's possession until her death in 1660, but was subsequently lost to the duke of York despite the efforts of Henry Jones, whose eldest son was the residuary legatee.

AIDAN CLARKE

Sources papers of H. Jones, incl. his drafts of M. Jones's letters, 1647–9, TCD, MS 844 · *CSP Ire.*, 1633–60; 1663–5 · Bodl. Oxf., MSS Carte 21–4 · *The manuscripts of the marquis of Ormonde*, [old ser.], 3 vols., HMC, 36 (1895–1909) · *Calendar of the manuscripts of the marquess of Ormonde*, new ser., 8 vols., HMC, 36 (1902–20) · *The manuscripts of his grace the duke of Portland*, 10 vols., HMC, 29 (1891–1931), vol. 1 · *Sixth report*, HMC, 5 (1877–8) [House of Lords] · *Seventh report*, HMC, 6 (1879) [House of Lords] · J. T. Gilbert, ed., *History of the confederation and the war in Ireland, 1641–53*, 7 vols. (1882–91) · [T. Carte], *The life of James, duke of Ormond*, new edn, 6 vols. (1851) · [E. Borlase], *The history of the execrable Irish rebellion* (1680) · *The writings and speeches of Oliver Cromwell*, ed. W. C. Abbott and C. D. Crane, 4 vols. (1937–47) · R. N. Dore, *The civil war in Cheshire* (1966) · J. S. Morrill, *Cheshire, 1630–1660: county government and society during the English revolution* (1974) · A. W. M. Kerr, *An Ironside of Ireland* (1923) · Burtchaell & Sadlier, *Alum. Dubl.*, 2nd edn · W. P. Baildon, ed., *The records of the Honorable Society of Lincoln's Inn: admissions*, 1 (1896) · *JHC*, 6 (1648–51) · [G. D. Burtchaell], *Irish Builder*, 676 (15 Feb 1888)
Archives TCD, corresp. with Cromwell, etc.

Jones, Michael Daniel (1822–1898), Congregational minister and college head, was born on 2 March 1822 at the Chapel House, Llanuwchllyn, Merioneth, the third of the five children of Michael Jones (1785–1853), Congregational minister, and his wife, Mary (1786–1861).

Jones was educated at the Dr Williams's School conducted by his father at Llanuwchllyn. He attended the Presbyterian college, Carmarthen, from 1839 until 1843, and studied at Highbury College, Middlesex, from 1844 to 1847. Since many of his relations had emigrated to Ohio, he joined them and was ordained minister of the Lawrence Street (Welsh) Congregational Church in Cincinnati, Ohio, on 7 December 1848. He returned to Wales in the summer of 1849 and was inducted into the pastorate of Bwlchnewydd Congregational Church, Carmarthenshire, on 27 June 1850. After the death of his father in 1853 he was appointed to succeed him as principal of the college at Bala on 26 September 1854. At the same time he was inducted into the ministry of the Congregational churches at Bala, Tyn-y-bont, Bethel, Soar, and Llandderfel. He resigned the pastorates of Bala and Tyn-y-bont in 1859, but continued principal of the college until his death.

On 20 December 1859 at Pen-dref chapel, Ruthin, Denbighshire, Jones married Anne Lloyd (1831–1925), the daughter of John and Mary Lloyd of Pistyll, Bodfari, Flintshire; Mary had been married to Hugh Davies, Plas-yn-rhal, before 1851. They had two sons and two daughters. The eldest son, Llwyd ap Iwan, a land surveyor, was murdered in Patagonia on 29 December 1909 by the notorious Sundance Kid. His brother, Mihangel ap Iwan, was a successful surgeon in Buenos Aires. One daughter, Mair, died in 1898 and the other, Myfanwy, married Professor Thomas Rhys (1852–1930) of Bala-Bangor College, Bangor.

Jones's passionate interest in radical politics soon became evident at Bala. Rural Wales had long been under the thumb of tory landlords, and typical of the class was the MP for Merioneth, W. W. E. Wynne (1801–1880), the distinguished antiquary. Jones organized the Bala Reform Society to oppose Wynne. This was the beginning of the campaign that was to secure victory for the Liberals in the election of 1868.

Jones is often called, not unjustly, the father of twentieth-century Welsh nationalism. During his stay in the United States he had noticed how soon Welsh identity was lost there and conceived a scheme to create a Welsh settlement in Argentina. The first settlers landed at Port Madryn, as they were to call it, on 28 July 1865. His hope was that a Welsh-speaking republic could be created in Patagonia, but the Argentine government would have none of it. Nevertheless the settlement, which had caused Jones much anxiety, effort, and expense, eventually began to flourish, and was still Welsh-speaking at the end of the twentieth century.

Jones realized that the struggle for the maintenance of the Welsh identity had to be fought in Wales itself. His contribution there was to politicize the older cultural nationalism, and he nurtured the hope that a Welsh nationalist party would eventually take its place in parliament. His was a moderate nationalism, inspired by the work of Kossuth in Hungary and Mazzini in Italy. He argued for a federal union within the United Kingdom and pioneered the idea that this should be part of a federal European union on the pattern of the United States. He was a sharp critic of Victorian imperialism, and like other radicals condemned what he saw as the wasteful ostentation of the royal family. Unlike other Victorian radicals, he did not approve of unalloyed *laissez-faire* capitalism and argued for an economy based on co-operative principles.

All this involved Jones in constant controversy. The most bitter of his controversies, however, had to do with his own college. A plan was launched to mark the bicentenary of the Great Ejection of 1662 by merging the Bala College with the other Congregational college at Brecon. The prime mover was the formidable John Thomas of Liverpool (1821–1892). Jones opposed the plan. In the trial of strength that followed, Jones was ejected from the principalship in 1879, but he and his supporters continued to maintain their college. This meant that there were two colleges at Bala. The controversy split the Congregational denomination, and only in 1892 was it possible to reunite the colleges at Bangor under the name Bala-Bangor College.

In theology Jones was an evangelical Arminian, and always claimed that his political principles grew out of his evangelical theology and his Congregationalism. He was a striking character. He always wore homespun clothes and ate plain food. He was a teetotaller and vigorous opponent of smoking, yet he enjoyed nothing more than a day's shooting. He was also the first Welsh nonconformist minister to wear a beard. Virtually all his writing was in articles to a variety of Welsh periodicals. He died at his home, Bodiwan, in Bala, on 2 December 1898 and was buried in the cemetery of the Old Chapel, Llanuwchllyn, on 8 December.   R. TUDUR JONES

Sources E. P. Jones, *Oes a gwaith … Michael Daniel Jones* (1903) • R. T. Jenkins, *Hanes cynulleidfa hen gapel Llanuwchllyn* (1937) • R. B. Williams, *Y Wladfa* (1962) • G. D. Owen, *Ysgolion a cholegau'r annibynwyr* (1944) • R. G. Owen, 'Brwydr y ddau gyfansoddiad, 1877–1885', MA diss., U. Wales, 1941 • I. C. Peate, 'Helynt y cyfansoddiadau', *Y Llenor*, 12 (1933), 1–10, 231–41; 13 (1934), 163–70; 15 (1936), 209–14 • R. T. Jones, *Hanes Annibynwyr Cymru* (1966), 254–7, 271–2 • R. T. Jones, 'Michael D. Jones a thynged y genedl', *Cof Cenedl*, ed. G. H. Jenkins (1985), 95–124 • G. Evans, *Welsh nation builders* (1988), 260–7 • parish records—birth, 2 March 1822, Old Chapel, Llanuwchllyn, Merioneth • parish records—baptism, 1 April 1822, Old Chapel, Llanuwchllyn, Merioneth

Archives NL Wales, general collection • U. Wales, Bangor, department of manuscripts and archives, diaries, corresp., and family papers • U. Wales, Bangor, Coetmor collection | NL Wales, D. S. Davies MSS

Likenesses oils, Congregational College, Aberystwyth

Wealth at death £111: probate, 11 March 1899, *CGPLA Eng. & Wales*

Jones, Morgan (1885–1939), educationist and politician, was born on 3 May 1885 at Rhos Cottages, Gelli-gaer, the fifth of seven children of Elias Jones (1853–1917), a collier,

and his wife, Sarah Ann Evans (1857–1946), a domestic servant. Welsh-speaking, he was educated at elementary schools at Gelli-gaer and Hengoed before winning a scholarship to Lewis' School, Pengam. Having matriculated in 1901 he began training as a pupil teacher at Gilfach School, Bargoed, before studying at University College, Reading (1905–7). A Baptist, he became a lay preacher, speaking at chapels in Berkshire and in Wales. He returned to teach at Gilfach school (1907–14) and later at Bargoed Boys' School. Initially Liberal in his politics, in 1908 he joined the Independent Labour Party (ILP) and started its first branch in the Rhymni valley. He was elected to the Gelli-gaer urban district council in 1911 (becoming chairman, 1921–2), and from 1913 to 1915 was president of the Glamorgan Federation of Teachers.

At the outbreak of war Jones became a pacifist, joining the No-Conscription Fellowship, being appointed to its national committee, and later becoming chairman of the South Wales Anti-Conscription Council. When called up in April 1916 he refused to serve, so spent most of the period until August 1919 in prison. He was also a defendant at the 1916 Mansion House trial, charged with prejudicing recruitment by urging the repeal of the Military Service Act. Lengthy spells of hard labour and solitary confinement, combined with inadequate diet, left him with poor health for the remainder of his life. His imprisonment led to his being dismissed from his teaching post, and upon release in August 1919 he found himself refused work because of his wartime record.

For a while Jones worked as a colliery labourer, but was heavily involved in organizational work for the ILP in Wales from this point on (and served on the ILP national administrative council, 1920–22). In December 1919 he was elected to Glamorgan county council, and when the Caerphilly parliamentary seat became vacant Jones defeated the preferred choice of the South Wales Miners' Federation to gain the Labour Party's nomination as candidate. In the by-election of August 1921 Jones achieved a majority of 4741 in defeating both Coalition Liberal and Communist. The first conscientious objector to be returned to the Commons after the war, he remained MP for Caerphilly until his death.

Jones married Gladys Thomas of Merthyr Tudful, a fellow schoolteacher and member of the ILP, in 1923, and they had two daughters. Though living in London, Jones maintained strong links with Wales, becoming secretary of the Welsh Labour group of MPs and, in June 1938, leading a deputation of Welsh MPs to Neville Chamberlain to argue, unsuccessfully, the case for a secretary of state for Wales.

Jones's parliamentary contribution fell into three main areas. He swiftly established a reputation as a spokesman on educational matters, joining Labour's advisory committee on education. In 1924 he served in Ramsay MacDonald's government as parliamentary secretary to the president of the Board of Education (C. P. Trevelyan), a post he filled again between 1929 and 1931. He served as parliamentary secretary to the Teachers' Labour League before its disaffiliation from the Labour Party in 1927. By the 1930s he was an advocate of multilateral (a precursor of comprehensive) schooling and technical education. He also possessed a keen eye for financial and administrative detail, serving on the public accounts select committee (as chairman from 1931 until 1938), winning cross-party respect for his conscientious approach and painstaking efforts. Finally, he took a considerable interest in international and colonial affairs. He was sympathetic to Jewish causes, and was a 'friend of India' and a supporter of the League of Nations. He served on the joint select committee on Indian constitutional reform (1933–4) and on the royal commission to the West Indies (1938–9). While in the West Indies he suffered a heart attack and returned to the United Kingdom, only to die from a further attack at his home in Finchley on 23 April 1939. He was cremated at Golders Green on 27 April.

Morgan Jones was a politician of moderate but sincere views, praised for his honesty and integrity. Upon his death it was felt that the Labour Party had lost a potential minister of education or a speaker of the House of Commons (*Western Mail*, 24 April 1939).   CHRIS WILLIAMS

Sources D. Rees, 'Jones, Morgan', *DLB*, vol. 9 · D. Rees, 'Morgan Jones, educationalist and labour politician', *Morgannwg*, 31 (1987), 66–83 · D. J. Rees, 'Morgan Jones (1885–1939) and his contribution to education', MEd diss., U. Wales, Swansea, 1985 · J. Sheaff, 'Morgan Jones: a memorial', unpublished memoir, 1986, priv. coll. · R. Barker, *Education and politics, 1900–1951: a study of the labour party* (1972) · J. Griffiths, *Pages from memory* (1969) · K. Robbins, 'Morgan Jones in 1916', *Llafur: the Journal of Welsh Labour History*, 1/4 (1975), 38–43 · *The Times* (24 April 1939) · *Western Mail* [Cardiff] (24 April 1939) · *Daily Herald* (24 April 1939) · *Guardian* (24 April 1939) · *Merthyr Express* (29 April 1939) · *Caerphilly Journal* (29 April 1939) · *Cardiff Times* (29 April 1939) · *Schoolmaster and Woman Teacher's Chronicle* (27 April 1939)
Archives Cumbria AS, Carlisle, corresp. | NL Wales, corresp. with E. T. John · PRO, Board of Education papers, ED 24/1387, 24/1525, 24/1651, 24/1757, 24/1761, 35/7129 · RS Friends, Lond. | FILM BFI NFTVA, documentary footage
Likenesses A. Wright, portrait, repro. in A. Wright, *The history of Lewis' School, Pengam* (1929), 221 · photographs, repro. in *Western Mail* (23 Aug 1921) · photographs, repro. in Rees, 'Morgan Jones, educationalist and labour politician' · photographs, priv. coll.
Wealth at death £6518: Rees, 'Jones, Morgan'

Jones, Noble (1702–1775), colonial politician and planter, was born in Lambeth, Surrey; details of his parents and education are unknown. By 1722 he had married Sarah Hack (c.1703–c.1752), with whom he had two sons and a daughter. A close friend of James Edward Oglethorpe, one of the original trustees who founded the colony of Georgia, Noble Jones accompanied him as a carpenter on the initial voyage to Savannah in 1733. Because so many of the 'chief carpenters' died in the severe Georgia heat, Jones soon found himself directing much of the building in the colony. Appointed one of two conservators of the peace (constables) by Oglethorpe, he discharged his duties with a new-found confidence. Named the colony's surveyor, he laid out the sites for Ebenezer and Augusta, two of Georgia's principal settlements. However, his limited skills could not keep up with the demands of the new colony. Amid grumbling over his late reports, inattention to detail, and inaccurate charts, and even his own interest in

landholdings, Oglethorpe relieved him of all his duties. The setback proved temporary.

Following the death of William Cox, the colony's official doctor, in 1736, Noble Jones once more found himself in demand, despite his limited training. That same year he developed an intensive interest in the cultivation of mulberry trees and the production of silk, all in keeping with the original plan of the trustees. He called his plantation Wormslow and the inlet just south of Savannah the Isle of Hope. Between 1739 and 1742 he turned his attention to military affairs, serving, at various times, as Georgia's official emissary to Tomochichi and the Yamacraw Indians, as a ranger in command of a militia company, and as the engineer in charge of a fort built on the Isle of Hope to protect Georgia from the threat of invasion by the Spanish in Florida. During the War of Jenkins's Ear (1739–42) he helped Oglethorpe with the invasion and siege of St Augustine and the repulsion of the Spanish at the battle of Bloody Marsh. From his stronghold on the Isle of Hope, Jones commanded two scout boats, the *Savannah* and the *Skidaway*, and also a company of rangers. At every opportunity, he continued to acquire substantial grants of land from the trustees. When Georgia became a royal colony in 1752, Noble Jones owned more than 4500 acres and prosperous trading interests from Charles Town to the West Indies. Eventually he became one of the colony's wealthiest and most successful planters, no insignificant feat for someone who came to colonial America as a carpenter.

The royal period saw Jones's bounties only increase. From 1752 until 1775 he served as a member of the governor's council, becoming in time its president, as well as justice of the peace for the colony, colonel and commander of the 1st Georgia regiment of militia, a vestryman of Christ Church parish, and chief justice of the general court. From the enactment of the Stamp Act until the outbreak of the American War of Independence, Jones remained an ardent loyalist and unswerving ally and friend of Sir James Wright, Georgia's last royal governor. His younger son, Inigo, steadfastly supported his father, but his elder son, Noble Wimberly *Jones, became a fiery rebel and opposed him. Noble Jones died at his beloved Wormslow on 2 November 1775, with all his children by his side. He was buried at Wormslow two days later.

Jones's life demonstrates the paradox of British rule in colonial America. Through hard work, perseverance, and limited skills Jones rose to prominence in colonial Georgia. As a holder of numerous positions through that same persistence and ambition, he came to personify the placemen reviled by Americans as a corruption of government. His two sons, Noble Wimberly and Inigo, loved their father as many colonial Americans did their beloved Britain, only to go their separate ways in 1775.

MILTON READY

Sources E. M. Coulter, *Wormsloe: two centuries of a Georgia family* (1955) · S. G. B. Temple and K. Coleman, *Georgia journeys* (1961) · H. E. Davis, *The fledgling province* (1976) · E. M. Coulter and A. B. Saye, eds., *A list of the early settlers of Georgia* (1949) · W. M. Kelso, *Captain Jones's Wormsloe* (1979) · K. Coleman and C. S. Gurr, eds., *Dictionary of Georgia biography*, 2 vols. (Athens, GA, 1983) · M. Ready, *The olonial* *records of the state of Georgia*, ed. A. D. Candler and K. Coleman, 28 (1983) · C. S. Ebel, 'Jones, Noble', *ANB*

Archives Georgia State Archives, Atlanta, papers | University of Georgia, Athens, De Renne papers

Jones, Noble Wimberly (*c.*1723–1805), physician and revolutionary politician in America, was born in Lambeth, Surrey, the eldest child of Noble *Jones (1702–1775) and his wife, Sarah Hack (*c.*1703–*c.*1752). In 1733 he accompanied his parents and younger sister Mary to Georgia aboard the ship *Anne*, with the original settlers of the colony. The senior Jones acquired a grant of 500 acres on the Isle of Hope that he named Wormslow (later changed by a descendant to Wormsloe). A second son, Inigo, was born in 1734, and a daughter, Sarah, died in infancy.

Noble Wimberly Jones learned the rudiments of medical practice from his father and applied himself to a lifelong improvement in that practice. Georgians measured success in land-holding, and Jones secured his first grant of 450 acres adjoining his father's property in 1751. Later grants amounted to 5900 acres as well as several town lots in Savannah. In 1755 he married Sarah Davis and moved from Wormslow to his own plantation on the Little Ogeechee River that he named Lambeth, after his birthplace. The marriage produced fourteen children, only one of whom, George, outlived the father.

Georgia became a royal province in 1752 and in 1755 Jones was elected to the colony's first Commons house of assembly. He served in that body continuously until its final dissolution in 1775. His services were in demand for composing addresses, framing laws, and acting on various committees. He earned the respect of his peers for his intelligence, moderation, and good judgement. From 1762 he served on the Georgia committee of correspondence and exchanged information with other provinces, which gave him more of a continental perspective than many of his colleagues. When William Knox, Georgia's agent in London, wrote a pamphlet defending the Stamp Act of 1765, by which parliament directly taxed internal American trade, Jones composed a letter of dismissal in accordance with a resolution of the house. Georgia governor James Wright and his council, on which sat Jones's father, took the position that the council as the upper house must concur on appointment of agents. The issue divided the two chambers until 1768, when both houses compromised on the appointment of Benjamin Franklin as agent. In that year the Commons house elected Jones speaker, and his first official action was to notify Benjamin Franklin of the house's objection to the Townshend duties. The unilateral action caused Governor Wright to dissolve the assembly and call for new elections.

Most of the same delegates returned to the assembly in October 1769 and again elected Jones as its speaker. He continued to maintain the right of the house to appoint and correspond with Franklin, its agent. Despite the governor's difference with the house, he allowed that body to continue in session until 22 February 1771, when he dissolved the assembly. The assembly reconvened in April 1771 and Jones resumed his role as speaker. By this time

Noble Wimberly Jones (*c.*1723–1805), by Charles Willson Peale, *c.*1781

Jones had come to personify the house's assertion of its independence, at least in the matter of selecting an agent. Governor Wright notified the house that it must select someone else as speaker. The members acquiesced to the extent of electing Archibald Bulloch, but defiantly entered in its journal a resolution praising Jones for supporting the honour of the house and the rights of the people. The resolution stated that the rejection of the speaker constituted another subversion of the liberties of the people. Governor Wright retaliated by dissolving the assembly after it had sat for only three days; later in the same year he went to London and received a baronetcy from the crown for his defence of the royal prerogatives.

In Wright's absence it fell to James Habersham, as president of the council, to convene the assembly, which, with trepidation, he did on 21 April 1772. He was under orders from the British ministry to veto anyone elected speaker in order to maintain the right. As might have been expected, the house proceeded to the election of Jones. At the same time the council elected Jones's father as its president. In an awkward position, Habersham informed the house that he had no objection personally to the election of Jones as speaker, but in accordance with his instructions he had to ask that body to choose someone else. The house defiantly re-elected Jones. Again Habersham disapproved and again the house elected Jones. By now Jones was as much a symbol of self-determination as a liberty pole. On the occasion of his third election Jones thanked his colleagues for the honour, but expressed a wish to devote his full attention to the practice of medicine. The house then elected its second choice, Archibald

Bulloch. When Habersham read the house journal and discovered that that body had elected Jones a third time, he asked the new speaker to delete the reference from the journal. The house refused to do so, whereupon Habersham dissolved the assembly.

With the business of government sadly in arrears, Habersham called for new elections and set 9 December 1772 for the next meeting of the assembly. Predictably, the house elected Jones its speaker. Jones once more declined, and the house elected William Young. Habersham might have taken offence, but he chose not to. The assembly remained in session until 29 September 1773.

On 14 July 1774 Jones, Bulloch, George Walton, and John Houstoun published a notice calling for a public meeting to denounce the British 'Intolerable Acts'—parliament's measures taken in response to the Boston Tea Party. Most Georgians were too concerned with the threat of a war with neighbouring American Indians to worry about Boston, and the meeting attracted only a few people outside the colony's lower counties. After Governor Wright's peace treaty with the powerful Creek Indians in October, the revolutionary movement gained momentum. A provincial congress met in Savannah on 18 January 1775 and elected Jones, Bulloch, and Houstoun to the second continental congress scheduled to meet in May. Because many Georgians opposed joining the continental association against trade with Britain, the delegates declined to go to Philadelphia. However, a second Georgian provincial congress, meeting in Savannah on 4 July 1775, again elected Jones, Bulloch, and Houstoun, as well as Lyman Hall and John J. Zubly, to the continental congress then in session. Because of his father's declining health, Jones did not go to Philadelphia. The senior Jones died on 2 November 1775. Father and son maintained their respect and affection for each other, despite their opposing political views.

With the onset of the war Jones played a less conspicuous political role than he had for the preceding decade. When the British army landed in Georgia on 28 December 1778, Jones sought refuge in Charles Town, only to be taken prisoner when the British took that city on 12 May 1780. He was sent to St Augustine and later exchanged to Philadelphia. An American patriot government was restored in Augusta in 1781 and the Georgia assembly named Jones to represent the state in the continental congress. He returned to Savannah after the British evacuation of that place and resumed his old role as speaker of the house.

After the war Jones eschewed politics to devote his full attention to the practice of medicine. He helped organize the Georgia Medical Society and became its first president in 1804. He died on 9 January 1805 at his Savannah home and was buried in Bonaventure cemetery in Savannah. He was survived by his wife. His early insistence on the right of the people to elect their London representative earned for him the description the Morning Star of Liberty.

EDWARD J. CASHIN

Sources E. M. Coulter, *Wormsloe: two centuries of a Georgia family* (1955) · Jones family papers, Georgia Historical Society, Savannah, coll. 440 · Noble Wimberly Jones papers, Georgia Historical Society, Savannah, coll. 442 · J. Grimes, 'Eulogy on the life and character of Dr. Noble Wymberly Jones', *Georgia Historical Quarterly*, 4 (1920), 17–32, 141–58 · K. Coleman and C. S. Gurr, eds., *Dictionary of Georgia biography*, 2 vols. (Athens, GA, 1983), 1.553–4 · J. E. Simpson, ed., 'The Jones family papers, 1760–1810', *Collections of the Georgia Historical Society*, 17 (1976) · A. D. Candler, *The revolutionary records of the state of Georgia*, 3 vols. (1908)
Archives Georgia Historical Society, Savannah, family papers · Georgia Historical Society, Savannah, papers | Wormsloe Foundation, Savannah, Elfrida De Renne Barrow collection
Likenesses C. W. Peale, oils, *c*.1781, Telfair Museum of Art, Savannah, Georgia [*see illus.*]
Wealth at death $11,875 divided between son and heirs of his daughter; payments to various others amounted to $7496; wife received rents from his properties; grandson and granddaughter received other real estate; total property (including fifty-eight slaves) amounted to $14,486: probate court records, Chatham county courthouse, Savannah

Jones, Owen [*pseud.* Owain Myfyr] (1741–1814), literary patron and furrier, was born on 3 September 1741 at Tyddyn Tudur, in the parish of Llanfihangel Glyn Myfyr, Denbighshire, the son of Hugh Jones (*d.* 1778), yeoman, and his wife, Catherine Humphreys (1700?–1795). Unlike his brother William, a student at Jesus College, Oxford, Owen Jones received little formal education. Nevertheless, he may have been made aware of the rich literary tradition of the Vale of Clwyd, sustained in earlier centuries by the patronage of the nobility. This perhaps explains his zeal in later life for the preservation of Welsh literature. By the late 1760s Jones was working in London for a prosperous firm of skinners owned by Benjamin Kidney and William Nutt, in Cannon Street and Ducksfoot Lane. Under the guidance of Richard Morris, founder of the Cymmrodorion Society and surviving member of the influential 'Morrisian circle' of antiquaries, he sought to make known the contents of the earliest Welsh manuscripts, which were locked away in the libraries of an increasingly Anglicized and indifferent Welsh gentry. In 1768 he copied the poems of Dafydd ap Gwilym from manuscripts in Richard Morris's possession; and two years later, with the aid of his friend Robert Hughes, he established the Gwyneddigion Society, whose convivial meetings became a focus of London Welsh life. As assistant secretary of the Cymmrodorion during the late 1770s he corresponded with scholars and poets in Wales and worked assiduously to promote the publication of their books. He also worked hard at his trade, becoming first a partner in the firm, and by 1782 manager of his own furrier's business at 148 Upper Thames Street, where he remained for the rest of his life.

Within a few years Jones was sufficiently wealthy to spend large sums of money on the transcription and printing of texts. He was a generous patron to gifted Welshmen such as Edward Williams (Iolo Morganwg), William Owen Pughe, and Walter Davies. Although not a scholar, he had the ability to encourage and direct the efforts of his often wayward protégés. Assuming the pseudonym Owain Myfyr, he became the central figure in the Welsh antiquarian movement that flourished in London at the close of the eighteenth century. In 1789 he paid £180 to print an edition of the works of Dafydd ap Gwilym (*Barddoniaeth*

Dafydd ab Gwilym, ed. Owen Jones and William Owen Pughe), which remained the only readily available source of the poet's work for over a century. In the same year the Gwyneddigion, with Jones's financial assistance, began organizing local eisteddfods in north Wales, thus laying the foundations of what became a national festival during the nineteenth century. In 1798 he proposed an ambitious plan to publish, at his own expense, virtually the entire corpus of early and medieval Welsh texts in a series of volumes. In acknowledgement of this he was persuaded to give the venture the title *Myvyrian Archaiology of Wales*. William Owen Pughe was engaged as editor and Edward Williams was to search Wales for further manuscripts. The first two volumes appeared in 1801 and contained the earliest poems in Welsh, together with works by the poets of the princes and some of the chronicles. Thereafter Jones suffered business losses and was forced to halt the project for a while. In or about 1806 he married his maidservant Hannah Jane Jones (1772/3–1838), who bore two daughters and a son, the architect Owen *Jones (1809–1874).

A third volume of the *Archaiology* appeared in 1807; but by then Jones had quarrelled with Williams, and, following Pughe's departure to Denbighshire, he lost interest in the undertaking and no further volumes were published. Altogether it had cost him almost £5000; but it brought the Welsh literary tradition to the attention of a much wider readership in both Wales and England at a time when many had even doubted its existence. Matthew Arnold praised Jones's industry and patriotism in *Celtic Literature* (1867), and of his contribution Robert Southey remarked: 'When a foreigner asks the names of the nobility and gentry of the principality who published the Myvyrian Archaeology [sic] at their own expense, we must answer that it was none of them, but Owen Jones, the Thames-street furrier' ('The antiquities of nursery literature', *Quarterly Review*, 21, 1819, 94). Jones died at his London home on 26 September 1814 and was buried on 1 October at All Hallows-the-Less, Upper Thames Street. He was survived by his three children and his wife, who later married Robert Roberts. GERAINT PHILLIPS

Sources letters and papers of Owen Jones, BL, Add. MSS 15024–15063 · O. Jones, letters to Walter Davies, NL Wales, MS 1806E · O. Jones, letters to Edward Williams, NL Wales, MS 21281E · G. J. Williams, 'Owain Myfyr', *Llên Cymru*, 8 (1964–5), 42–7 · G. J. Williams, 'Owain Myfyr', *Y Llenor*, 1 (1922), 252–61 · G. J. Williams, 'Hanes Cyhoeddi'r Myvyrian Archaiology', *Journal of the Welsh Bibliographical Society*, 10 (1966–71), 2–12 · W. D. Leathart, *The origin and progress of the Gwyneddigion Society of London* (1831) · M. Arnold, *On the study of Celtic literature* (1867) · will, PRO, PROB 11/1561 · parish register (birth), Denbighshire, Llanfihangel Glyn Myfyr, 3 Sept 1741 · parish register (death), London, All Hallows-the-Less, 26 Sept 1814
Archives BL, corresp. and notes, Add. MSS 15024–15063 · BL, transcripts of Welsh poems, Add. MSS 31062–31110 | NL Wales, MS 1806E · NL Wales, MS 21281E
Likenesses J. Vaughan, oils, 1802, repro. in Leathart, *Origin and progress of the Gwyneddigion Society* · lithograph, 1828, NPG
Wealth at death see will, PRO, PROB 11/1561

Jones, Owen (*fl.* **1789–1793**). *See under* Jones, Edward (*fl.* 1771–1840).

Jones, Owen [*pseud.* Meudwy Môn] (**1806–1889**), Calvinistic Methodist minister and writer, was born on 15 July 1806, the son of John and Ellen Thomas of Gaerwen, in the parish of Llanfihangel Ysgeifiog, Anglesey. His parents died when he was young, and he was brought up by his aunt and attended the village school from the age of six. He showed early promise, and was sent to Thomas Jones's school at Llangefni, and then the local national school. He spent several years as a farmworker, before becoming a tutor, and eventually a schoolmaster. He later worked as a proofreader for the firm of John and Evan in Mold, and as a colliery clerk for the Plas Argoed colliery. He also kept a bookshop in Mold where, it was said, he had plenty of books but too few customers. Jones married Ellen, only daughter of Richard Rowlands of Bryn Mawr, Llangoed. He became an assistant superintendent in the Bible Society, a post which he held for forty years.

About 1827, Jones was appointed lay preacher to the Calvinistic Methodists, and he was ordained on 8 June 1842. Serving at Mold, he became a pioneer in the temperance movement in north Wales. He was minister to the Calvinistic Methodist churches of Manchester from 1844 to 1866, when differences of opinion led him to resign and pursue his temperance interests as north Wales superintendent of the United Kingdom Alliance. In 1866 he moved from Manchester to Llandudno as pastor. He resigned from the ministry in 1869, owing to the poor pay which he received. From then until his death, he earned his living by literary activities, though continuing to work for the temperance movement and the Bible Society.

Jones had always been an industrious, if unoriginal, *littérateur*. Besides a large number of articles contributed to Welsh periodicals, he was the author, translator, or editor of over forty works in Welsh, being from 1867 Welsh editor for Blackie of Glasgow. In 1833 he superintended the publication, at Mold, of James Hughes's Welsh commentary, and in January 1834 he also became editor of a monthly review known at first as *Y Cynniweirydd*, which was converted into a weekly newspaper entitled *Y Newyddiadur Hanesyddol* in January 1835, and was subsequently known as *Cronicl yr Oes*. He started two short-lived temperance magazines, *Y Cymedrolydd* (1835) and *Y Cerbyd Dirwestol* (1837–8). His most important work was *Cymru yn hanesyddol, parthedigol a bywgraffyddol* (1875), a historical, topographical, and biographical dictionary, undertaken in conjunction with the Revd G. Parry (Gwalchmai). He also published a series of popular lectures on Welsh history (1850–53), and a concordance of the Welsh Bible (1860), which was much used in Welsh Sunday schools.

Jones died at Bryn Eisteddfod, Llandudno, on 10 October 1889 and was buried in St Tudno churchyard. Jones led an exceptionally active life: it is said that he preached 12,000 times, leaving behind him 6000 sermons in manuscript, and he delivered about a thousand addresses on behalf of the Bible Society, and 8000 temperance lectures. D. L. THOMAS, *rev.* ROBERT V. SMITH

Sources DWB · C. Ashton, *Hanes llenyddiaeth Gymreig o 1651 o. C. hyd 1850* [1893], 643–6 · *Y Geninen*, 8 (1890), 33–43, 243–8 · d. cert.
Archives U. Wales, Bangor, diaries and papers

Jones, Owen (1809–1874), architect, printer, and designer, was born on 15 February 1809 at 148 Thames Street, London, the second of the three children of Owen *Jones (1741–1814) and his wife, Hannah Jane (1772/3–1838). His father was a furrier and a distinguished Welsh antiquary. Jones was to become one of the most influential, prolific, and well-known designers of mid-nineteenth-century Britain. A man of his time, he made a major contribution to the development of design theory and education at a point when design was considered to reach beyond the aesthetic sphere and into the realms of economics and morals. And his spectacular architectural schemes and designs for consumer goods catered to the needs and desires of a growing and increasingly affluent and leisured middle class.

After a brief sojourn at Charterhouse (March 1818 to August 1819) Jones went to a private school in London. In 1825 he started an architectural career by taking articles with Lewis Vulliamy. He remained in his office for five years and in 1829 he also began to attend the architectural class at the Royal Academy.

Architecture Although he was to have more success and significance in other areas, Owen Jones always characterized himself as an architect. His most important built work was St James's Hall, between Regent Street and Piccadilly, for almost fifty years London's premier concert hall. It was completed in 1858. Jones was also responsible for the Crystal Palace Bazaar in London's West End. This great emporium, situated between Lower Regent Street, Oxford Street, and John Street, opened in 1858. In the following year he designed Osler's glassware showroom, again in the West End. The exteriors of these buildings were somewhat undistinguished, but their great glittering interiors, dedicated to leisure and consumption, were extraordinary. The barrel-vaulted ceiling of the main hall at St James's was painted red, blue, and gold and was lit from below by star-shaped gas burners, causing the whole surface to glow like stained glass. The ceilings of the other two buildings used real stained glass. In Osler's showroom the effect of space and brilliance was enhanced by large mirrors positioned opposite each other around the walls. The whole effect was fairy-like—'one of the sights of the metropolis', according to the *Furniture Gazette* (6 June 1874, 569).

Structurally, too, the concert hall and the bazaar were modern, especially in their overt use of cast iron. Although builders and architects had already taken up this material for construction purposes, it was generally concealed or disguised except in functional or industrial buildings. Jones, however, from as early as his 1835 lecture to the Architectural Society, *On the Influence of Religion upon Art* (printed for private circulation in 1863), had argued that cast iron should be widely and frankly used and that new architectural forms appropriate to it should be developed. It was not new to say that architecture was, and always had been, directly related to, and expressive of, the religion of its period, but it was radical to suggest, as Jones did, that Christianity had been superseded by science, commerce, and industry. He argued that architecture

Owen Jones (1809–1874), by Henry Wyndham Phillips, 1856

should accept this state of affairs and should use materials and forms relevant to the new 'religion'.

This approach was clearly expressed in three of Jones's largest architectural schemes: a design for the Manchester Art Treasures Exhibition of 1857; drawings and a model for a People's Palace at Muswell Hill, Middlesex, designed in 1858–9; and a series of drawings of about 1860–62 for the Palais de Cristal at St Cloud near Paris. These huge and spectacular iron and glass structures were to be places of education and entertainment for the paying public. However, probably for financial reasons, none of the projects was realized.

The Crystal Palace These schemes were clearly related to his experience as one of the superintendents of works for the Great Exhibition of 1851, which was housed in Joseph Paxton's gigantic glasshouse in Hyde Park, London. Here Jones's duties included the arrangement of the exhibits and the decoration of the building. His colour scheme for the interior—the solid parts of the structure in horizontal bands of yellow, blue, and red, separated by narrow white stripes—was highly controversial but was finally accepted and even admired. He justified his intentions in a lecture to the Institute of British Architects on 16 December 1850, stating that his aim was to enhance the grandeur of the interior, 'by a system of colouring which, by making distinct every line in the building, shall increase the height, the length and the bulk'. Colour theories were relatively new and much discussed at the time and Jones's scheme relied particularly on the work of Michel-Eugène Chevreul and the experiments of George Field. At the Crystal Palace, Jones had a magnificent chance to put theory into practice. This and his subsequent writings made a significant contribution to the accepted views on colour balance.

When the Great Exhibition closed in 1852, a Crystal Palace Company was formed to move the building to Sydenham, Kent, where it opened as a permanent pleasure and educational site in 1854. For its first thirty years it attracted about 2 million visitors a year. Jones was appointed director of decorations and was involved, together with Paxton and Matthew Digby Wyatt, in enlarging the original building. He participated in selecting works of art and sculptures to be replicated and displayed, and in designing the new Greek, Roman, Egyptian, and Alhambra courts. The Egyptian court, for example, included copies of the statues from the temple of Abu Simbel, rescaled to suit the space at Sydenham.

Influence of the Near East Jones's passionate interest in the art and architecture of Islam and the Near East had started during the grand tour he had undertaken upon completing his architectural training in the early 1830s. He and Jules Goury, a French architect, travelled to Egypt, Turkey, and Spain, following their interest in polychromy and taking it into the new areas of Egyptian and Islamic architecture and decoration. They spent six months at the Alhambra, investigating and recording its buildings and its decoration. On his return to England in 1834 Jones began the preparation of his first great work, *Plans, Elevations, Sections and Details of the Alhambra*. He issued the first three parts in 1836, but did not complete the first volume (in ten parts) until 1842. The two parts of the second and final volume were published in 1845. This was an important and impressive work, establishing his reputation as an expert on Moorish art and architecture. The magnificent colour illustrations contributed to the growing use of polychromatic detailing and decoration in nineteenth-century British architecture.

Printing In order to illustrate the *Alhambra* to his desired standards, Jones wanted to use chromolithography as well as the more expensive, and sometimes less subtle, techniques of hand-coloured engraving and block printing. But it was a new process and was beyond the abilities of English printers at this date, leading Jones to undertake the work himself. With the help of the firm of Day and Haghe, he set up his own presses in his residence at 11 John Street, Adelphi, in London.

The cost of producing the *Alhambra* was enormous and put a serious financial strain on Jones. But he established the press as a going concern and subsequently became much involved in printing and designing for the illustrated and illuminated gift books that were increasingly a feature of the affluent middle-class drawing room. One of his first, highly regarded, volumes was *Ancient Spanish Ballads*, by J. G. Lockhart (1841). *Illuminated Books of the Middle Ages*, by H. N. Humphreys (1850), with its sophisticated and detailed use of colour, was a factor in the enthusiasm for medieval illumination which itself influenced later Victorian artistic styles. The earliest of these beautifully illustrated books were rather let down by their covers, and so Jones and Humphreys developed several totally new binding styles, using materials such as papier mâché, terracotta, and embossed leather, which were more fitted to the sumptuous contents. Jones ceased to run his own press in the early 1850s, but continued his association with Day & Son (successors to Day and Haghe), becoming a director of the company by 1865.

Jones also worked with several other publishers and printers, but his most long-standing connection was with the firm of De La Rue, for whom, from the mid-1840s onwards, he designed a range of products which included playing cards, stamps, chessboards, almanacs, menus, calendars, biscuit-tin wrappers, endpapers, and diaries. Some of his designs remained in use until the twentieth century.

Decorative design But many other manifestations of Jones's work also found their way into the middle-class home. From the 1840s he was designing tiles and pavements for companies such as Blashfield, Minton, and Maw, all of whom were keenly developing new processes and products. Their coloured and patterned tiles and mosaics were so successful that such elements became a feature of many nineteenth-century houses. From the 1840s until the 1870s he designed wallpapers for several companies, including Townsend and Parker and Jeffrey & Co. His printed and woven textile designs were put into production by various manufacturers, including Warner, Sillet & Co. in the 1870s.

Examples of textiles to his design are in the Victoria and Albert Museum, London, where the department of prints and drawings has a large collection of Jones's wallpapers, which demonstrate very clearly his characteristic style and use of startling colour combinations. Some of the designs show a strong Egyptian or Islamic influence (indeed, his work was sometimes criticized for being *too* Moresque or Alhambraesque) but, whatever the source, they are always very highly stylized. Jones never used techniques like shading and perspective, and he never produced any of the naturalistic florals that were so fashionable at the time. He was adamant about respecting the flatness of the medium and, in tune with other design reformers, he thought it abhorrent to cover walls or floors with realistic representations of flowers in all their three-dimensional glory. He always translated floral or natural motifs into two-dimensional abstract forms.

Design theories Jones's wallpapers are a perfect realization of the theories of design which he had been formulating all his working life and which he expressed in a series of lectures, 'Principles of decorative art', delivered in 1852, in his articles 'Gleanings from the Great Exhibition of 1851', published in the *Journal of Design and Manufacture* (June 1851) and most notably and completely in his *Grammar of Ornament* (1856). The last-named set out, in a list of thirty-seven propositions, his principles of good design and colouring. These were illustrated and expanded in twenty chapters, each of which presented examples of fine ornament from a particular geographical area or historical period. The last chapter, 'Leaves and flowers from nature', emphasizes the importance of nature and natural growth in design.

The *Grammar* proved to be Jones's most enduring and influential work, partly because it was adopted as a set text for the schools of design which had been established in the 1830s as part of a governmental move to raise the standard of design of manufactured goods. In the late 1840s and early 1850s they were subject to a large-scale reorganization which included the setting up of a Museum of Ornamental Manufactures, for both student and public use. Owen Jones was one of those appointed to select objects for the museum from the displays at the Great Exhibition. However, as a teaching aid the museum was seen to have two disadvantages: it would encourage students to copy the examples rather than to comprehend the principles of good design, and it was not accessible to students at the provincial schools. The *Grammar of Ornament* overcame both of these obstacles, and its precepts became the doctrine of the schools. It was reissued twice and continued in use in art schools well into the twentieth century.

Interior decoration Throughout his career Jones acted as a decorator. In the 1840s he produced interior schemes for two houses that he designed in Kensington Palace Gardens, London. In his last fifteen years, when architectural commissions were not forthcoming, he took on much more of this type of work. His bigger projects included the new Langham and Charing Cross hotels. In the West End he was responsible for the interiors of several large stores: Houbigant, the perfumier; Jay's, the mourning retailers; and Hancock, the silversmith and jewellers. He worked on some enormously luxurious private homes, for example Fonthill House and 16 Carlton House Terrace, both for Alfred Morrison (of Morrison and Dillon, a department store in Fore Street, London). Here, and for many other such commissions, he collaborated with the London decorating firm of Jackson and Graham. The viceroy of Egypt's palace at Gesch, near Cairo, was perhaps his largest such undertaking. On a much smaller scale he did some work for his friends George Lewes and George Eliot at their house at The Priory, 21 North Bank, Regent's Park, in 1863 and 1871. At the time of his death he was designing interiors and furnishings for Eynsham Hall, near Oxford, the house of James Mason, a copper mining magnate. A small collection of Jones's metalwork and furniture is in the Victoria and Albert Museum, London.

Recognition and reputation Jones died at his home, 9 Argyll Place, Regent Street, London, on 19 April 1874 and was buried at Kensal Green cemetery. Obituaries such as those in *The Builder* and *The Architect* (25 April 1874, 235–6) gave recognition to his publications, to his designs, and to his importance as a colour theorist. He had been a member of the Architectural Society from 1833 until 1838. In 1836, on his presentation of the first part of the *Alhambra*, he joined the Institute of British Architects, remaining a member for the rest of his life, and becoming vice-president in 1867. In 1857 he was awarded the institute's royal gold medal in recognition of his publications and his work at the Crystal Palace at both Hyde Park and Sydenham. In the same year he was granted the order of St Maurice and St Lazare by the king of the Italians, as well as the order of King Leopold of the Belgians. His work in the decorative arts displayed at the Universal Exhibitions in Paris and

Vienna in 1867 and 1873 won gold medals. There was a sizeable section entitled 'The work of the late Owen Jones' at the London International Exhibition of 1874. But his reputation soon dimmed. He had been a very modest and unassuming man. His wife, Isabella Lucy, the daughter of the water colour painter Charles *Wild (1781–1835), whom he had married on 8 September 1842, sold the contents of his office, his drawings, and his library at Sothebys in 1876. He had no children. Little remains of Jones's architectural or decorative schemes; the Crystal Palace burnt down in 1936. His patterns, with their insistence on two-dimensional representation and their obvious repeating elements, went out of fashion when faced with the new arts and crafts and art nouveau styles that won national and international acclaim in the last quarter of the nineteenth century. Jones's reputation was, and still is, overshadowed by the designers (most notably William Morris) who worked in those idioms, but it must not be forgotten that it was his design theories and his high profile as what we would now call an industrial designer that had helped prepare the ground for their success. The *Grammar of Ornament* was his real monument. Reissued in 1867 and 1910, its importance was recognized by a further reprint in 1986. Although in the last quarter of the twentieth century several articles and catalogues on specific aspects of his work appeared, there is still no readily available overall survey. The most useful general source remains the unpublished PhD thesis of 1974, 'Owen Jones and the Eastern ideal', by Michael Darby.

LESLEY HOSKINS

Sources M. Darby, 'Owen Jones and the Eastern ideal', PhD diss., U. Reading, 1974 • *The Builder*, 32 (1874), 383–6 • M. Darby and D. Van Zanten, 'Owen Jones's iron building of the 1850s', *Architectura* (1974), 53–75 • M. Schoeser, *Owen Jones silks* (1987) • *Catalogue of the works of the late Owen Jones* (1874) [exhibition catalogue, International Exhibition, London] • *The Architect*, 11 (1874), 235–6 • *CGPLA Eng. & Wales* (1874) • *DNB* • m. cert.
Archives CUL, corresp. with Joseph Bonomi • V&A, architectural drawings and designs for wallpaper | U. Reading L., Michael Darby collection, MS 3975 • U. Reading L., Huntley and Palmer collection, MS 1490 • U. Reading L., Longman archive, MS 1393 • U. Reading L., Mason estate collection, OXF 22 • U. Reading L., De La Rue collection, MS 937
Likenesses H. W. Phillips, oils, 1856, RIBA [*see illus.*] • C. Baugniet, lithograph, BM • drawing, repro. in *The Graphic* (2 May 1874), 433 • drawing, repro. in *The Builder* (9 May 1874), 383 • wood-engraving (after photograph by Watkins and Haigh), NPG; repro. in *ILN* (9 May 1874), 445 • wood-engraving (after T. D. Scott), NPG; repro. in *The Builder* (11 Dec 1869)
Wealth at death under £8000: probate, 27 May 1874, *CGPLA Eng. & Wales*

Jones, Owen Glynne (1867–1899), mountaineer, was born on 2 November 1867 at 110 Clarendon Street, Paddington, London, the son of David Jones, a carpenter and builder, and his wife, Eliza, *née* Griffiths. He went first to a boarding-school in Ealing, then in 1881 to the Central Foundation School, Cowper Street, London, where he won several prizes and distinguished himself in science. In 1884 he was awarded the Holl scholarship and went to Finsbury Technical College, where he studied the theoretical and practical aspects of mechanical engineering, mathematics, and chemistry. A Clothworkers' scholarship then took him in 1886 to the Central Institute (City and Guilds) at South Kensington, where after three years in the engineering department he came top of his class, received the diploma of association of the institute, and was appointed assistant in the institute's mathematics department. In 1890 he passed the London University BSc exam with first-class honours, and at the time of his death was preparing for his DSc.

Of Welsh descent, Jones spent his holidays in Wales, where he developed a passion for climbing. His early serious rock climbs were in the Lake District and on Cadair Idris. He kept meticulous notebooks, with shorthand accounts of his routes and occasional sketches. His first visit to the Alps was in the summer of 1891, immediately before he obtained the newly created post of physics master at the City of London School. He also lectured at Goldsmith's Institute. He was popular with the other masters and the boys; they delighted in hearing of his exploits, which included the notable feat of climbing round the school's common room without touching the floor, except for one impossible pitch by the fireplace. Schoolmastering gave Jones the opportunity for climbing in all seasons, and henceforth this activity consumed all his spare time and money. At Easter 1893 he climbed the Dent Blanche, Switzerland (14,295 feet), with two guides and a porter, in an expedition lasting thirty-six hours with only brief rest periods, a remarkable feat. He conquered most of the great peaks at Chamonix, Grindelwald, Zermatt, and Saas Fee, and was contemplating an expedition to the Caucasus.

Although greatly attracted to the ice and snow of the high Alps, Jones exercised his rock-climbing skills in the Dolomites in 1894 and remained active in Britain, where he was a founder and committee member of the Climbers' Club. In 1896, in the English Lake District, he climbed Scafell Pinnacle from Deep Ghyll and in 1899 he conquered Walker's Gully on the Pillar Rock, both routes being hitherto considered impossible. His interest in devising such new assaults led him to compile his guide, *Rock Climbing in the English Lake District* (1897), many of whose photographs were taken by the brothers George Dixon Abraham and Ashley Perry Abraham, with whom he sometimes climbed. In this book Jones graded the climbs into four degrees of difficulty, his intention being to prevent less able climbers from undertaking routes where they might risk life and limb. The book itself remained a classic, kept in print by the Abrahams. Jones's only other publications were a few articles in *Alpine Journal*, *Climbers' Club Journal*, and *Cassell's Magazine*. Those who knew Jones and climbed with him always appreciated his good humour and steadfastness, and felt confident in his company.

In 1899 Jones and his great friend and climbing partner Frederick William Hill (1863–1935), the second master at the City of London School, were staying near Zermatt, and climbing the local peaks. Before dawn on Monday 28 August 1899 they set out with three local guides to climb the Dent Blanche by the west arête, which had been achieved only twice before. By 10 a.m. the party, roped together, had reached 14,100 feet and was only 160 feet from the top when the leading guide lost his footing, but managed to get a hold with his axe and tried to recover his position; this put a strain on the rope, which jerked Jones and the two men behind him off their feet. But the rope had been belayed between Hill and the rest of the party, and it broke at the belay, leaving Hill to watch in horror as his colleagues disappeared from view. It was impossible for Hill to get down alone by the route they had taken; he therefore continued to the top and began to descend by an easier route. But mist came down, and with no food or shelter Hill was forced to stay on the mountain overnight; after another night he reached Zermatt early on the Wednesday. A thirty-strong search party went out that evening and early next day found the mangled bodies lying some 1600 feet below the spot from which they had fallen. Jones was buried on 2 September 1899 in the graveyard of the Roman Catholic church at Evolena. Jones was unmarried, and lived at Denmark Hill with Margaret Ellen, his younger sister, whom he supported.

ANITA McCONNELL

Sources 'Alpine disaster', *City Press* (2 Sept 1899), 4f • H. C. B., 'In memoriam Owen Glynne Jones', *Alpine Journal*, 19 (1898–9), 583–4 • F. W. Hill, 'The accident on the Dent Blanche', *Alpine Journal*, 19 (1898–9), 590–4 • *Climbers' Club Journal*, 2 (Sept 1899), 48 • W. M. Crook, 'The accident on the Dent Blanche', *Climbers' Club Journal*, 2 (Sept 1899), 81–6 • W. M. Crook, 'Memoir', in O. G. Jones, *Rock climbing in the English Lake District*, 2nd edn (1900), vii–xliv • *The Times* (31 Aug 1899), 3 • *The Times* (1 Sept 1899), 4c, 4f [reports and obit.] • *ILN* (9 Sept 1899), 346–7, 361 • Boase, *Mod. Eng. biog.* • b. cert.
Likenesses photograph, repro. in H. C. B., 'In memoriam'
Wealth at death £2022 19s. 11d.: probate, 4 Oct 1899, *CGPLA Eng. & Wales*

Jones, Sir Owen Haddon Wansbrough- (1905–1982), chemist and scientific administrator, was born on 25 March 1905 at Attleborough, Norfolk, the youngest in the family of three sons and a daughter of Arthur Wansbrough-Jones, solicitor, of Long Stratton, and his wife, Beatrice Anna, daughter of Thomas Slipper, farmer, of Braydeston Hall. He was educated at Gresham's School, Holt, from where he won an open scholarship in 1923 to Trinity Hall, Cambridge. He gained first-class honours in parts one and two of the natural sciences tripos (1925 and 1926). He then became a research student financed by the Goldsmiths' Company, working in colloid science under Professor Eric Rideal. In 1930 he took his MA and PhD, and was elected a fellow of Trinity Hall; he then spent a year working under Fritz Haber in Berlin. On his return in 1932 he was appointed assistant tutor and, in 1934, tutor at Trinity Hall. These were inspired appointments; while demanding the highest academic standards, Wansbrough-Jones was greatly liked and admired by undergraduates.

On the outbreak of the Second World War, Wansbrough-Jones decided that his place was in the army, and he was commissioned in January 1940. He held a number of technical and general staff appointments and, by the time of his demobilization in 1946, had become a brigadier (1945) as director of special weapons and vehicles. He was appointed MBE (1942) and OBE (1946).

After the war Wansbrough-Jones accepted an invitation to be scientific adviser to the army council (1946). With his knowledge of the War Office, he proved the right man for the job. He established operational research sections in the British army of the Rhine and Malaya and fought successfully to enhance the standing of the Military College of Science, Shrivenham, in the academic world. He was appointed CB in 1950. In 1951 he transferred to the Ministry of Supply, becoming chief scientist in 1953. He saw his main task as the deployment of the ministry's immense scientific potential to maximum advantage. He managed the research programme with skill and tact, and fostered *esprit de corps* among the senior staff, notably by arranging regular informal dinners. He was appointed KBE in 1955.

In 1959 Wansbrough-Jones accepted an invitation from Albright and Wilson to become executive technical director and joined the company at a challenging time of rapid growth. He became vice-chairman in 1965 and was chairman from 1967 until he decided to retire in 1969.

Wansbrough-Jones had a lifelong interest in education. He served as a governor of Gresham's from 1938 until 1979 and, in recognition of his distinguished services, the Fishmongers' Company (with which the school is closely associated) made him an honorary freeman in 1973. He became a freeman of the Goldsmiths' Company in 1950 (so enabling him to call himself proudly a 'goldfish'), and was prime warden in 1967–8 and a formidable chairman of the company's education committee from 1967 to 1981. He was treasurer of the Faraday Society (1947–59), a director of British Oxygen Company (BOC) International in 1960–76, and a governor of Wellington College (1957–75) and of Westminster School (1965–80). He continued to have close links with Trinity Hall, which elected him an honorary fellow in 1957.

Wansbrough-Jones was a man of uncompromising honesty and loyalty, qualities which owed much to the influence of his mother, a woman of profound faith, who lived to 102. Although shy, he had a flair for making and keeping friends, many of whom turned instinctively to him for advice. He was a man of great kindness. He remained a countryman at heart, proud of his Norfolk roots, and loved a day's shooting. While living in London, he continued to return at weekends to the family home and his beloved garden. He was a recognized authority on silverware, and a lover of music.

Wansbrough-Jones did not enjoy the best of health in his last few years and retired to Long Stratton, where he died, unmarried, on 10 March 1982.

GEORGE LEITCH, *rev.*

Sources *The Times* (3 March 1982) · *The Times* (19 March 1982) · *WWW* · private information (1990) · personal knowledge (1990) · *CGPLA Eng. & Wales* (1982)
Archives Royal Institution of Great Britain, London, corresp. with Sir E. Rideal
Wealth at death £120,054: probate, 7 June 1982, *CGPLA Eng. & Wales*

Jones, Owen Thomas (1878–1967), geologist, was born in Beulah, near Newcastle Emlyn, Carmarthenshire, on 16 April 1878, the only son of David Jones, a farmer, and his wife, Margaret Thomas. Another child, a daughter, died at the age of six. He attended the British School at Tre-wern, Powys, until 1893 and then Pencader grammar school, Carmarthenshire. In 1896 he won the Keeling natural science entrance exhibition to University College of Wales, Aberystwyth, and, four years later, graduated with first-class honours in physics. In the same year he became an exhibitioner at Trinity College, Cambridge, and was successively Wiltshire prizeman and Harkness scholar. He took a first class in both parts of the natural sciences tripos (physics, chemistry, mineralogy, and geology in part one, and geology in part two).

In 1903, Jones joined the team from the Geological Survey of Great Britain, under Aubrey Strahan, that systematically mapped the south Wales coalfield and adjacent areas, and he spent his free time investigating the geology of the area around Ponterwyd, in north Cardiganshire. In 1910 he was awarded a DSc (Wales) and the Sedgwick essay prize (Cambridge), and took up his duties as the first professor of geology at Aberystwyth. That same year he married Ethel May, daughter of Henry Reynolds of Haverfordwest. They later had two sons and a daughter. After turning down an offer from Liverpool University (1917) he accepted the chair at Manchester in 1919 and succeeded John Edward Marr as Woodwardian professor at Cambridge in 1930. He retired in 1943.

Jones's interests were wide. At Aberystwyth, he collaborated with his colleagues in botany and agricultural botany, assessed the potential of the lead-zinc mining field of north Cardiganshire for the Geological Survey, and wrote on rural industries and the geological origins of the legends of the Welsh coast for the non-specialist. At Manchester and Cambridge he demonstrated an interest in the zonal sequence of the Carboniferous and in the borderland between geology, physics, and engineering, producing studies in rock mechanics and comprehensive surveys of geophysics and its applications. He was a geological adviser to the department of geodesy and geophysics at Cambridge. His main research interests, however, were those of his own teacher, Marr, in Lower Palaeozoic geology and geomorphology. His contributions to the former were fivefold. First, his mapping was meticulous, made possible by his well-developed three-dimensional awareness, which was equally effective in large-scale study of selected areas and in the tracing of certain geological boundaries over large areas. Second, he contributed to palaeontology and biostratigraphy, illustrated in the successful adaptation of Charles Lapworth's sequence of graptolite zones to the 'geological wilderness' of south central Wales and in the pioneer study of Silurian brachiopods, in which he demonstrated their value in correlating strata. Third, he understood sediment behaviour in the laboratory and in modern seas and oceans, which was expressed in the reinterpretation of contorted strata of Silurian age in Denbighshire. Fourth, he marshalled and synthesized large amounts of geological data, materially helped by his phenomenal memory (including a striking visual memory) and his understanding of stratigraphical classification and nomenclature. Fifth, he imaginatively applied the geosynclinal concept to the Lower Palaeozoic strata of Wales and reconstructed a remarkable Ordovician shoreline and a complex igneous intrusion in the Builth–Llandrindod area. Jones's contributions to geomorphology, particularly to the history of drainage systems and the interpretation of peneplains, started in the area made famous by Andrew Ramsay and continued in the levelling of the profiles of the headwaters of the River Tywi (expressed in mathematical equations), the comprehensive review of the physiographic history of the Bristol Channel, and the overview of the river systems of Wales and adjacent parts of England in his third address to the Geological Society (1951).

Jones was an excellent teacher, whether in the field, the laboratory, or the classroom. He appreciated and solved problems quickly and explained them simply and clearly; and he had an unusual intuition in assessing the significance of work in areas with which he was not personally familiar. He was a fierce critic of those whose ideas he did not accept, and his criticism was characteristically delivered on the parliament-like arrangement of the floor of the Geological Society and recorded in its journal. Jones was twice president of the Geological Society of London (1936–8, 1950–51), he was foreign secretary in 1948–64, and he received its Lyell (1926) and Wollaston (1945) medals. In 1930 he was president of section C of the British Association. He was elected fellow of the Royal Society (1926), served as vice-president (1940–41) and received the Royal medal in 1956. He was an honorary LLD (Wales, 1958), a fellow of Clare College, Cambridge, for nearly thirty-seven years, and an honorary fellow of geological societies in other countries.

A Welsh speaker from birth, Jones wrote and spoke the language fluently throughout his life and lost little of his Welsh accent. His last two papers were in Welsh. He died at the Evelyn Nursing Home in Cambridge on 5 May 1967.

DOUGLAS A. BASSETT

Sources W. J. Pugh, 'Owen Thomas Jones, 1878–1967', *Memoirs FRS*, 13 (1967), 223–41 · W. J. Pugh, 'Recent work on the Lower Palaeozoic rocks', *Advancement of Science*, 6 (1950) [Presidential address] · *The Times* (6 May 1967) · 'Master and fellows of Clare College', *The Times* (11 May 1967) · A. Wood, ed., *The Pre-Cambrian and Lower Palaeozoic rocks of Wales. Report of a symposium held at University College of Wales, Aberystwyth in honour of Professor O.T. Jones and Sir William Pugh* (1969) · E. H. Brown, *The relief and drainage of Wales: a study in geomorphological development* (1960) · J. Challinor, 'A review of geological research in Cardiganshire 1842–1967', *Welsh Geological Quarterly*, 4 [covers geological and physiographical work] · D. A. Bassett, 'The Welsh palaeozoic geosyncline: a review of recent work in stratigraphy and sedimentation', *The British Caledonides*, ed. M. R. W. Johnson and F. H. Stewart (1963), 35–69 · J. W. Jackson, 'Owen Thomas Jones 1878–1967', *Amateur Geologist*, 3 (1969) · m. cert. · *Bibliography and index of geology and allied sciences for Wales and the Welsh borders 1897–1958* (1961) [references to Owen Thomas's pubns in a chronological / regional context, with index] · *A sourcebook of geological, geomorphological and soil maps for Wales and the Welsh borders (1800–1966)* [details of geological (primary and secondary) and physiographic maps] · I. C. Peate, *Y Faner* (1 June 1967) · W. M.

Williams, *Y Gwyddonydd* [The Scientist], 5 (1967) · J. Idris Jones, *Y Gwyddonydd*, 7 (1969) · B. F. Roberts, ed., 'O. T.', *Y Bywgraffiadur Cymreig*

Archives BGS, corresp. · NL Wales · U. Wales, Aberystwyth, archives | BGS, letters to Finlay Kitchin · BGS, letters to William Pugh

Likenesses photograph, repro. in Pugh, *Memoirs FRS*, facing p. 223

Wealth at death £23,332: probate, 7 July 1967, *CGPLA Eng. & Wales*

Jones, (Henry) Paul Mainwaring (1896–1917), public schoolboy and army officer, was born on 18 May 1896 at 6 Cloudesdale Road, Balham, south London, the elder of two sons of Welsh parents.

His father, **Henry [Harry] Jones** (1866–1925), journalist, was born at Llanelli, Carmarthenshire, south Wales, on 27 March 1866, the eldest son of William Jones (*d.* December 1905 aged nearly eighty), variously described as a puritan artisan and a mechanical engineer. Harry Jones became assistant editor of the *South Wales Daily News*. T. P. O'Connor discovered him and appointed him acting editor of the *Weekly Sun*, then of the halfpenny evening *Sun*, which he left when it passed to Conservative ownership. In 1895 he married Emily Margaret, daughter of Thomas Mainwaring, 'a leading figure in literary and political circles in Carmarthenshire' (P. Jones, 9). In January 1897 he went to Plymouth as managing editor of the *Western Daily Mercury* (owned by Thomas Owen, Liberal MP for Launceston division, Cornwall). In summer 1904 he returned to London and became deputy editor of the *Daily Chronicle*. He was admitted to the Middle Temple in June 1900 and called to the bar in May 1906. A fellow of the Institute of Journalists, in 1912 he published a 351-page book, *Liberalism and the House of Lords: the Story of the Veto Battle, 1832–1911*, a partisan account 'in picturesque style', eulogizing Gladstone, Asquith, and Lloyd George. Later, when the prime minister, Lloyd George, resented the *Chronicle's* criticism, Jones's 'small mind' gibe (13 September 1918) was reportedly 'the last straw' (Koss, 774). After the *Chronicle* was bought at the end of September 1918 by a syndicate of Lloyd George's supporters, Jones moved to the *Daily News*, becoming parliamentary correspondent. He died on 11 January 1925.

H. P. M. Jones, known as Paul, was educated at the Hoe preparatory school, Plymouth, Brightlands preparatory school, Dulwich Common (1904–8), and as a day boy at Dulwich College from September 1908 to April 1915. He was strong and athletic, but very short-sighted and had to wear spectacles from his sixth year. Dulwich College was a large and flourishing Victorian public school, 'the most famous school in South London' (P. Jones, 14). Jones worked and played hard, and was outstandingly successful there: junior scholar (1909), senior scholar (1912), London University matriculation with honours (1911), prefect (1912), member of the first fifteen (1912–15), editor of *The Alleynian* (1913–15), head of the modern side (1913–15), and captain of football (1914–15), when he reformed the school game and Dulwich had one of its best seasons ever. In 1910, against his father's wishes, he changed from the classical to the modern side as he wanted to study English literature and modern languages. He was proudly Welsh and an advanced Liberal—in a largely Conservative school—who read Shaw and Wells and admired Lloyd George. He enjoyed varied interests and hobbies. A rugby enthusiast, he supported Wales and aspired to win a blue and play for Wales. He gloried in amateur sport, but for professional sport 'his scorn was unmitigated, and he could not endure association football with its paid players' (ibid., 51). He read widely and voraciously, played the piano and sang, and revered Beethoven and Wagner. He ran a small gas engine and an electric model railway, and studied astronomy. As a young man he was strongly built, 6 feet tall, with grey eyes. 'Essentially a man's man' (ibid., 112), he was shy and embarrassed with young women. He was a non-smoker and almost teetotal.

At the outbreak of war in 1914 Jones wanted to enlist in the public schools' battalion (16th battalion, Middlesex regiment, a 'Kitchener's army' unit) but was persuaded by his father to stay at Dulwich to take the Balliol scholarship examination and to finish the football season. He joined the Officers' Training Corps and assiduously trained with it. In December 1914 he was elected a Brackenbury history scholar at Balliol College, Oxford, the first Dulwich boy to win a Balliol scholarship. His examination showed 'strong mental grasp and excellent arrangement and method' (P. Jones, 267). At the school sports in March 1915 he won the mile, half mile, and steeplechase, and tied for the victor ludorum shield with his friend Stanley John Hannaford (killed at the third battle of Ypres in October 1917). He left Dulwich in April 1915.

Jones applied for an infantry commission but, to his great disappointment, was rejected because of his eyesight—he admitted he was 'helpless' without spectacles—and received a temporary commission as second lieutenant, Army Service Corps, in April 1915. He served in England then in July 1915 went to France, with five pairs of spectacles. In France and Belgium he served in various supply roles, working hard. Although he knew 'the War for the dull, sordid, murderous thing it is' (P. Jones, 221), spurred by the deaths of old Alleynians and other contemporaries, he made repeated unsuccessful attempts to transfer to a front line combat unit. Promoted lieutenant in May 1916, he wrote in July 1916 that he was 'longing to be in the thick of the fighting, … yet condemned to look after groceries … it is my passionate desire to share the hardships and dangers of this war' (ibid., 197–8). Like so many of his public-school contemporaries, he remained devoted to his school. Dulwich was a recurring theme in his letters home. He wrote, 'the old school has done splendidly … the more I see of life the more convinced I am of the greatness of the old school … the welfare of the school is a very precious thing to me' (ibid., 176, 240, 247). On leave he played for the old Alleynians. He also wrote that 'our Public Schools have done marvellously in this war. The system has proved its value' (ibid., 151). He wrote in January 1917 that Oxford 'would be the crowning joy of my life' (ibid., 227) but doubted if he would survive to go there.

In February 1917 his application to transfer to the front was finally successful, and to his joy Jones joined the heavy branch, machine-gun corps (from June 1917 the Royal Tank Corps). He was much happier than previously. He fought in the battle of Arras (April 1917). On the morning of 31 July 1917, advancing in his tank, north-east of Ypres, Belgium, he was killed, shot in the head by a sniper firing through a porthole. He was buried west of Zonnebeke, north-east of Ypres. Among the letters of condolence was one from a Dulwich master who wrote that Jones had been the embodiment 'of all that is best in the public-school spirit' (P. Jones, 263). His father published an edition of his letters with a biographical memoir, *War Letters of a Public-School Boy* (1918), and his parents endowed memorial prizes at Dulwich College: Paul Jones was among 506 old Alleynians killed. His name is on the war memorials of both Dulwich and Balliol.

ROGER T. STEARN

Sources P. Jones, *War letters of a public-school boy* (1918) · M. Christison, *Dulwich College war record, 1914–1919* (1923) · T. L. Ormiston, *Dulwich College register, 1619 to 1926* (1926) · *Balliol College war memorial book, 1914–1919*, 1 (1924) · E. S. Craig and W. M. Gibson, eds., *Oxford University roll of service*, 3rd edn (1920) · *WWW, 1916–28* · H. A. C. Sturgess, ed., *Register of admissions to the Honourable Society of the Middle Temple, from the fifteenth century to the year 1944*, 2 (1949) · *Hist. U. Oxf. 8: 20th cent.* · H. Jones, *Liberalism and the House of Lords: the story of the veto battle, 1832–1911* (1912) · J. M. Winter, *The Great War and the British people* (1985) · S. E. Koss, *The rise and fall of the political press in Britain*, 2 vols. (1981–4); repr. (1990) · H. Simonis, *The street of ink: an intimate history of journalism* (1917) · P. Simkins, *Kitchener's army: the raising of the new armies, 1914–16* (1988) · B. H. Liddell Hart, *The tanks: the history of the royal tank regiment and its predecessors*, 1 (1959) · I. F. W. Beckett and K. Simpson, eds., *A nation in arms: a social study of the British army in the First World War* (1985) · B. Gardner, *The public schools: an historical survey* (1973) · P. Parker, *The old lie: the Great War and the public-school ethos* (1987) · T. Wilson, *The myriad faces of war: Britain and the Great War, 1914–1918* (1986) · B. Bond, *A victory worse than defeat? British interpretations of the First World War* (1997)

Likenesses J. J. Bayfield, photograph, c.1914, repro. in Jones, *War letters* · H. V. M. Jones, photograph, c.1915, repro. in Jones, *War letters*

Jones, Sir Pendrill Charles Varrier- (1883–1941), physician and founder of Papworth Village settlement, was born at Glyn Taff House, Troedyrhiw, Glamorgan, on 24 February 1883, the only son of Charles Morgan Jones, surgeon, and Margaret Varrier, daughter of William Jenkins. He had one sister. He was educated at Epsom College, and at St John's College, Cambridge, where he was a foundation scholar and prizewinner in 1905 and 1906. He attended medical school at St Bartholomew's Hospital, and qualified MRCS, LRCP in 1910, becoming house surgeon at St Bartholomew's in 1911. In 1912 he returned to Cambridge to undertake research on the significance of temperature variation in tuberculosis, under the guidance of Sir German Sims Woodhead and Sir Clifford Allbutt. On the outbreak of war in 1914 he was appointed temporary tuberculosis officer for Cambridgeshire and there became aware of the psychological, social, and economic consequences of loss of employment resulting from tuberculosis. Supported by Allbutt and Sims Woodhead, he formulated the idea of setting up an industrial colony where people with arrested tuberculosis could work under medical supervision. In 1915 Allbutt set up the Cambridge Tuberculosis After-Care Association to raise funds for the project. In a manner which was to typify his later business dealings, Varrier-Jones bypassed the committee and 'begged, bullied and cajoled £603 out of local worthies' (Parker, 138). In February 1916 the Cambridgeshire Tuberculosis Colony was set up, with one patient, in an open-air shelter at Bourne.

In 1918 the colony, with 25 patients, moved to the newly purchased Papworth Hall at Papworth Everard, Cambridgeshire. Varrier-Jones was to remain medical director of Papworth Village settlement until his death in 1941, by which time the settlement had 500 patients in the hospital and a further 700 in hostels or cottages. The complex included 500 acres of land, with administration and hospital blocks, a sanatorium, laboratories and research institute, a home for tuberculosis nursing staff, a village settlement of more than a hundred cottages and hostels, and workshops. Papworth Industries (which included carpentry, cabinetmaking, leather goods, printing, upholstery, and building concerns) employed ex-patients at trade union rates and under medical supervision, and showed annual sales amounting to over £88,000 per annum by 1941. Papworth Village settlement and Varrier-Jones became world famous. One history of the institution claimed that the list of visitors read like *Who's Who* (Ives and Ives). Papworth's annual magazine in 1942 boasted that well over 5000 visitors had come from overseas (*Papworth Annual*, 7). Varrier-Jones himself was a great publicist for Papworth, lecturing and publishing widely throughout his career. His contributions included *Industrial Colonies and Village Settlements for the Consumptive*, published jointly with Sims Woodhead in 1920 (with a preface by Allbutt), on tuberculosis village settlements. In 1927 he delivered the Mitchell lecture to the Royal College of Physicians, in London, and in 1937 he addressed the first Empire Conference in London, on the care and aftercare of the tuberculous. Varrier-Jones was knighted in 1931 for his contributions to tuberculosis. In 1934 he was appointed fellow of the Royal College of Physicians, and in 1939 he was awarded the Weber-Parkes prize for tuberculosis. Sir Humphry Rolleston noted that his 'great assets were his organizing ability and his exceptional capacity as a good man of business' (Rolleston, 9). Not only was Varrier-Jones responsible for turning Papworth into a large and successful institution, he also helped to build up two other village settlements for tuberculosis patients: Preston Hall, in 1919, at the request of the British Legion; and Peamount, near Dublin, in 1930, at the request of Lady Aberdeen. In 1919 he also helped Sir Frederick Milner to re-establish an industrial village in Hampshire—Enham Village Centre—for ex-servicemen with nervous diseases.

Varrier-Jones never married. However, he reigned over Papworth Village settlement as a paternal figure. The patients affectionately called him the Old Man or Father, and one described him as a benevolent autocrat: 'when you saw him you had to tug your forelock' (Papworth Village Settlement Archives, G2.16). According to another patient, he had an uncanny knack of sizing up a man's personality and character simply by his answers to searching questions. One patient considered that 'his word was

law; no red tape and no other channels to go through' (ibid., G1.6). As leader of the settlement, Varrier-Jones enjoyed the loyal support of his staff, including that of Miss K. L. Borne, matron from 1915 to 1943, who was appointed OBE for her work at Papworth in 1942. She retired two years after Varrier-Jones's death.

Varrier-Jones died at Papworth of heart disease on 30 January 1941. His obituary in *The Lancet* described him as a Celt with all the Celt's fire and imagination, and with the long black hair and gestures of an impresario. He was also commonly known as the Pendragon, which later became the trademark of Papworth goods. Not only did his 'family' mourn his death, but tributes were paid to his vision in the care of tuberculosis patients and in particular to his belief in holistic medicine. The idea of placing the victims of the disease in isolated colonies such as Papworth was neither financially nor socially viable on a large scale, but the experiment was regarded as important, for Varrier-Jones's conception of illness as not only a medical but also a social problem.
LINDA BRYDER

Sources *BMJ* (8 Feb 1941), 220–21 • *The Lancet* (8 Feb 1941), 198 • *The Lancet* (22 Feb 1941), 264 • L. Bryder, 'Papworth Village settlement—a unique experiment in the treatment and care of the tuberculous?', *Medical History*, 28 (1984), 372–90 • H. Rolleston, 'Introduction', *Papers of a pioneer: Sir Pendrill Varrier-Jones*, ed. P. Fraser (1943) • R. Parker, *On the road: the Papworth story* (1977) • H. Rolleston, *The Eagle*, 52 (1941–7), 74–7 • Mr & Mrs F. W. A. Ives, The history of Papworth, unpublished manuscript, 31 March 1958, Cambs. AS, Cambridge • *Papworth Annual* (1942), 7 • Papworth Village Settlement Archives • *WWW* • b. cert. • d. cert. • *CGPLA Eng. & Wales* (1941)
Archives Cambs. AS, Cambridge, professional corresp. and papers • Papworth Village Settlement Archives, Papworth Everard, Cambridgeshire |FILM Papworth Village Settlement Archives, film on Papworth Village settlement
Likenesses photographs, Papworth Village Settlement Archives, Papworth Everard, Cambridgeshire
Wealth at death £60,165 1s. 5d.: resworn probate, 9 May 1941, *CGPLA Eng. & Wales*

Jones, Peter Rees (1843–1905), department store owner, was born in Newcastle Emlyn, Carmarthenshire, the son of Thomas Jones, a modestly successful hat manufacturer. He was educated privately, and after serving an apprenticeship in a Carmarthen drapery establishment, left Wales in 1864 to seek his fortune in London. Years later a contemporary recounted meeting the young draper on the train to the capital, and being entrusted with the latter's savings—£14. Jones seems to have been 'doubtful about the honesty of all the inhabitants of London' (Holding). On arrival in London, Peter Jones found employment with the Newington-based firm of Tarn & Co., but by 1868 had established himself in his own small shop on the Hackney Road. In the winter of that year both his young wife, Anna Maria (Annie), *née* Campion (b. 1842/3), the daughter of a London publisher, whom he had married on 9 September 1866 at St Leonard, Shoreditch, and the couple's two-year-old child died of scarlet fever. A three-month-old daughter survived, and was sent to Wales to be looked after by her paternal grandparents.

In the course of the following decade, Peter Jones moved the premises of his drapery establishment three more times: by 1870 to Southampton Row, Bloomsbury, in

1871 to Marlborough Road, Chelsea, and finally in 1877 to the King's Road, adjoining Sloane Square. The King's Road venture seems to have been a remarkably quick success: by 1884 annual turnover stood at almost £40,000, while staff numbers had grown from the original thirty to nearly fifty. The number was to double again before the end of the decade.

After six years on the King's Road site, Peter Jones began an ambitious programme of expansion and reconstruction. Having acquired premises from no. 2 to no. 14, he set about consolidating them into a distinctive whole. The result was a huge five-storey building, 'of harmonious design and handsome appearance' ('Mr Peter Jones, general draper', 86), topped by a turret and flagstaff whose object was thought to have been that of rivalling the nearby Harrod's. Extensive use was made of plate-glass windows to display stock, and the interior was luxuriously decorated. The central shop, for example, devoted to the sale of parasols and umbrellas, was ornamented with marble pillars and panelled throughout with mirrors. By 1893 Peter Jones's store was selling not only drapery goods and household linens, but also boots and shoes, ladies' underclothing, mantles, clothing and millinery, bedding and carpets, china, glass, and electroplated silverware, and more besides: a gentlemen's tailoring establishment, for example, was a recent addition.

In 1900, with profits standing at £10,802, the store was successfully floated as a public company. Peter Jones retained the position of chairman, while his two surviving sons were appointed as board directors. They were the offspring of his second marriage, to Amanda Blanche Cockayne, whom he had married on 12 April 1870. The couple had six children, of whom only four seem to have still been alive at Peter Jones's death.

Peter Jones emerges from contemporary accounts as a man of drive and ambition, and of considerable business ability, whose King's Road establishment benefited from the rise of London's West End as a fashionable shopping area. Contemporaries remarked upon the energy and degree of personal attention he devoted to his business. A colleague who had worked with him in the 1880s commented that 'he never seemed happier than when at work' ('Mr Peter Jones, 1843–1905', 229). He was thought to be a humane employer: he supported the early closing movement, and was known as the first London store owner to provide seating for female shop assistants. A Liberal in politics, although not an active one, a keen art collector, and a freemason, Peter Jones can with some justification be described as one of the 'great self-made retailing giants of his time' (ibid., 228).

Peter Jones died of a stroke at Eversley, 151 Rydal Road, Streatham, on 30 August 1905. After being cremated at Woking, his ashes were interred at Brockwood cemetery, Surrey, on 2 September 1905. In 1906 the store was sold to John Lewis, eventually becoming part of the John Lewis Partnership.   LAURA UGOLINI

Sources 'Mr Peter Jones, 1843–1905: considerate employer and draper of genius', *Gazette of the John Lewis Partnership*, 59 (1977), 228–9 • 'Mr Peter Jones, general draper, silk mercer, outfitter and furnisher', *Illustrated London and its representatives of commerce* (1893), 86–7 • T. H. Holding, 'The late Mr Peter Jones: a reminiscence', *Draper's Record* (9 Sept 1905) • *Draper's Record* (9 Sept 1905) • *West London News* (1 Sept 1905) • *West London Press* (8 Sept 1905) • *West Middlesex Advertiser and Chelsea Mail* (8 Sept 1905) • corresp., John Lewis Partnership archives, Stevenage, item 642 • Peter Rees Jones family Bible, John Lewis Partnership archives, Stevenage • *Contemporary portraits: men and women of south Wales and Monmouthshire* (1897), 303 • d. cert. • IGI

Archives John Lewis Partnership archives, Stevenage, personal records

Likenesses photograph, 1897, repro. in *Contemporary Portraits*

Wealth at death store bought 1906 by John Lewis for £20,000 (in cash, apparently): 'Lewis, John', *DBB* (1985), 764–6 • turnover peaked 1902–3 at £157,000 with profits of £12,000, but these figures not maintained seemingly: 'Mr Peter Jones, 1843–1905', 229

Jones, Philip, appointed Lord Jones under the protectorate (1617/18–1674), politician and army officer, was born at Penywaun, a farmstead in Llangyfelach parish in west Glamorgan, the son of David Philip and his wife, Elizabeth David. His father lived in the poorest part of the county but accounted himself a gentleman, and was a freeholder of prominence in his parish in the strongly Welsh uplands 5 miles north of Swansea. Philip Jones was the first generation of his family to abandon the patronymic and adopt an English style surname.

Civil war Nothing is known of Jones's career before the civil war, but it must be assumed that, like his father, he lived the life of a freehold farmer. In 1642 he married Jane Price (d. 1678) of Gelli-hir, in Ilston, which brought him into a close network of Gower families who were later to form a core of lay puritan activity. Jones's grandfather was tenant of the earl of Worcester, and Jones himself was harassed by soldiers of the marquess of Worcester during the first civil war, suggesting a continuing unhappy link between the Jones family and the Raglan interest. Beyond that the only commentary on Jones's behaviour during the earlier part of the conflict is provided by his enemies, who later alleged that at the start of the war he fled to Pembrokeshire and was interviewed there by Rowland Laugharne, who offered him a military commission in the service of parliament. Jones was said to have refused the offer on the grounds that it was 'against his conscience to fight or spill bloud' (Glamorgan Archive Service, D/DF L/8). Members of the Price family escaped across the Bristol Channel to Devon at the start of the civil war, so it is possible that Jones was part of a pro-parliamentarian diaspora from Gower.

By October 1645, as the military tide in south Wales turned in favour of parliament, Jones was back in south Wales, in Cardiff. He signed a report to the committee for both kingdoms, and travelled up to London to deliver it in person. His reward, on 17 November 1645, was the offices of governor of Swansea and commissioner in the Gloucester association, the regional army covering the south Wales counties except Carmarthenshire and Pembrokeshire. He had no military rank at the time of his appointment, and his parallel title of deputy steward of Swansea indicates that his skills were civilian, not military. In 1646 he was sworn a burgess of Swansea and was given the rank

Philip Jones, appointed Lord Jones under the protectorate
(1617/18–1674), by unknown artist, c.1655

of colonel, which provided him with the authority required to displace royalist aldermen and others from the town's government. In April 1647 he was awarded arrears of pay and repayments on his 'public faith' advances from the marquess of Worcester's estates in Glamorgan. He was active in the Glamorgan county committee, formed from Gloucester association commissioners; the vigorous levying of penal taxation by the committee provoked unrest and two revolts by the royalists of the Vale of Glamorgan, in February and June 1647.

Jones's links with the dominant Independents in parliament were evidently better than those of Rowland Laugharne, nominally the most senior commander in south Wales. He was on 17 November 1646 named as a commissioner for the three itinerant ministers dispatched by the House of Commons to Wales. Jones and John Price were among those charged with disbanding the supernumerary troops under Laugharne, and soldiers of the Swansea garrison, under Jones's command, were active in suppressing the rebellion of Laugharne and others at St Fagans, near Cardiff, on 8 May 1648. Jones thus played a leading role in aligning the military politics of south Wales with developments in the New Model Army and in parliament. In the immediate aftermath of St Fagans, when Oliver Cromwell passed through south Wales on his way to reduce Pembroke Castle he stayed with Jones at Swansea. This may have been their first meeting, but the two men already had a business relationship: Jones was a steward of the lieutenant-general's south Wales estates, including the seignory of Gower, sequestrated from the marquess of Worcester. It must have been his standing

with Cromwell which in December 1648 secured him the place as a commissioner for compounding, to be followed closely by the position of sequestration commissioner in south Wales. By early May 1649 he had become governor of Cardiff and colonel of foot in the south Wales counties, and when sections of the New Model regiment of Colonel Thomas Horton were dispatched to Ireland, Jones's garrison force was left as the Commonwealth's front line military presence in south Wales. In August 1649 the vocal royalist vicar of Llantrisant, Thomas Bassett, appealed to his kinsman John Price, as well as to Jones himself, for relief from imprisonment in Cardiff Castle, in tones that suggest that the governor was considered honourable.

Propagator and land purchases On 5 February 1650 Jones was admitted to the Commons as MP for Brecknockshire, on his interest as the regional military supremo, and ten days later he was named second on the list of lay commissioners for the propagation of the gospel in Wales. First on the list was Colonel Thomas Harrison, whose presence in south Wales was short-lived and who had none of the local credentials enjoyed by Jones. Jones's activity as a propagator was confined to south Wales, and had been presaged by his service as a commissioner for Welsh ministers from 1646 at least to November 1648. Despite the dominance of religious radicals of a millenarian persuasion within this new body, on both lay and clerical sides, Jones's own cast of mind was firmly pragmatic, and he cannot be linked convincingly to any sect or church beyond the somewhat rudderless state church of the 1650s. The allegations of Jones's arbitrary dealings in this commission depend heavily on retrospective accounts, with the drift of the influential petition of 1652 being against the whole experiment, rather than *ad hominem* against Jones. He was certainly active in this commission, however, signing orders to appoint schoolmasters and reward clergy. His appointment to the committee for plundered ministers in July 1650 was further recognition of his interest in the future of the state church.

From 1649 Jones began to buy lands in south Wales, using his involvement in the procedures for penal taxation to good effect. In January 1649 he bought lands in his native area of Glamorgan from the trustees for sale of bishops' lands, and the following month he took a lease of four manors in the richer Vale of Glamorgan. When the trustees for the brigade of Colonel Thomas Horton, of which Jones was one, were looking for estates to buy in order to satisfy parliament's award of £1000 to its members, Jones steered them towards these manors. The brigade purchased, and soon afterwards Jones's brother-in-law bought its interest and conveyed it to Jones. Many purchases were made by Jones from trustees for various classes of confiscated properties. Perhaps the most successful acquisitions were those made between 1656 and 1658 of the choice manors, again in the Vale of Glamorgan, of Fonmon, Pen-marc, and Llancadle: Fonmon Castle provided Jones with a family seat to match his rising status. What characterized his many transactions was his readiness to sell on to others his lands outside Glamorgan and Carmarthenshire, and the use of his extended family, particularly brothers-in-law, as agents and middlemen: evidence that he retained the notions of patrimony of the Welsh squirearchy, despite his moving in increasingly exalted and English circles.

Councillor of state The Rump Parliament declined to renew the propagation experiment, and thus provided Oliver Cromwell with one of several reasons with which to justify its dissolution in April 1653. Jones's seniority in the propagation commission and his general dominance of south Wales politics secured him a place in the council of state which first assumed power from the Rump and then brought into being the nominated assembly. Jones sat in this body, acting in support of the government, and was acting president between 24 June and 4 July. Re-elected to the council in November, on 3 December he became an admiralty commissioner, which confirmed a conservative trend, away from religious radicals, within naval administrative appointments. On 10 December he was a teller for the yeas in a vote in the assembly to establish a new disciplinary structure for the state church. The voting down of these proposals led directly to the resignation by members to Cromwell of their authority, an episode in which Jones was prominent. He was almost certainly in close touch with John Lambert during the drafting of the 'Instrument of government', and was thus a natural candidate for the place on the new council of state, which place he retained throughout the protectorates of Oliver and Richard Cromwell, and which he attended more frequently than all but two or three other councillors. It was because of this closeness to power that Colonel John Jones wrote to him from Ireland to warn him of worldly temptations, and to remind him to promote the interests of the 'Saints'.

Although Jones was willing to help his former Welsh propagator colleagues when he could—he helped provide the Wrexham minister Morgan Llwyd with a maintenance, for example—his attention was now concentrated on high central office. He was one of the most active of councillors, on a salary of £1000 a year, and in the first protectorate parliament, sitting for Glamorgan, acted as a government spokesman in divisions on settling the new constitution. In March 1655 he was in the west midlands and Yorkshire on state security matters, and in April he was appointed an arbitrator in a trade dispute between English merchants and the Portuguese government. In the second protectorate parliament he sat again for Glamorgan, and between September 1656 and 10 December 1657, when he was removed to Cromwell's 'other house' as Lord Jones, sat on more than fifty committees. His elevation recognized his importance in the Cromwellian establishment. His views echoed those of Cromwell on such matters as the debates on the Quaker James Nayler, where Jones argued for leniency, and in the debates on the offer of the crown to the protector he acted as a mediator between parliament and the court. His own view on this matter was that Cromwell should accept the crown, and, after the protector first declined the offer, he was one of a group of six councillors who pressed him to reconsider. When the refusal was evidently beyond recall Jones threw his weight behind the campaign to have 'The humble petition and advice' accepted as the next best thing to kingship. When he went to the 'other house' it was with the title of comptroller of Oliver Cromwell's household, and in September 1658 Jones took responsibility for organizing his master's funeral.

Censure and last years Perhaps as a result of becoming politically exposed by his prominence as a backer of Richard Cromwell, Jones had to fight off attacks on his integrity in the closing days of Cromwell's parliament, and again when the revived Rump met again, in May 1659. It was hardly a new experience for Jones to be under attack. First subject to a hostile lawsuit in 1648, he had since been the butt of various petitions: in 1651 from victims of his sequestration activities, between 1652 and 1654 from those implacably opposed to the experiment to reorganize the church in Wales, and in 1654 from Bassett Jones, whose grievance was related to Philip Jones's acquisition of estates on which the former was a tenant. Several themes in these attacks recurred and cross-referred to each other. The 1659 campaign against him fed off this previous history, and drew upon separate, though inevitably related, petitions against Jones's cronies, such as Edmund Jones of Brecon, MP and attorney-general of south Wales, first attacked in 1654 for a royalist past, and expelled from the house on 12 February 1659. Edmund Jones's fall gave heart to Philip Jones's enemies, and Jones had to stand up in the house on 23 May to clear himself of the charges against him. Inevitably not content with his reply the petitioners, led by Bledry Morgan, a former ally from Carmarthenshire, resorted to the press, publishing a broadside containing twenty articles against Jones. On 5 August Jones surrendered the keys of the state lodgings he had continued to enjoy as comptroller of the household, and on 30 September he was fined by the Commons as an absentee. Shortly afterwards he moved to East Barnet, Hertfordshire, where John Price had property. He had lost office, central and local, by January 1660, but recovered some local commissions in March, only to lose all public positions at the Restoration. His land investments were naturally affected by the return of the king. He forfeited his interests in former crown and church lands, but by the terms of the Restoration land settlement held on to four manors in the Vale of Glamorgan and the Fonmon estate, where he lived quietly. His fate after 1660 was at least partly determined by the goodwill he had shown royalists in the 1640s and 1650s, and he had no difficulty in conforming to the restored political and religious order. Enquiries into the management of Welsh church assets scarcely touched him, and in 1671 he was appointed sheriff of Glamorgan and was returned to the commission of the peace a year later. Thought to have an income of £1000 a year in his last years, Jones died at Fonmon Castle, aged fifty-six, on 5 September 1674, and was buried in the chancel of Pen-marc church, near Fonmon.

STEPHEN K. ROBERTS

Sources A. G. Veysey, *Transactions of the Honourable Society of Cymmrodorion* (1966), 316–40 · Glamorgan Archive Service, Cardiff, Fonmon MSS, NLW 1/25 · 'Jones, Philip', HoP, *Commons, 1690–1715* [draft] • C. Grant-Francis, *Charters granted to Swansea* (1867), 167–207 • *CSP dom.*, 1649–60 • M. A. E. Green, ed., *Calendar of the proceedings of the committee for compounding ... 1643–1660*, 5 vols., PRO (1889–92) • Worcester College, Oxford, Clarke MS 67 • *The copy of a petition* (1654) • T. Richards, *A history of the puritan movement in Wales* (1920) • A. G. [A. Griffith], *A true and perfect relation of the whole transaction concerning the petition of the six counties of South-Wales* (1654) • J. Jones, letter to Mrs Llwyd, 28 May 1656, NL Wales, 11441 D, fol. 9 • J. Meyer, ed., 'Inedited letters of Cromwell, Colonel Jones, Bradshaw and regicides', *Transactions of the Historic Society of Lancashire and Cheshire*, new ser., 1 (1860–61), 177–300 • BL, Lansdowne MS 821; BL, Lansdowne MS 822, fols. 160–61; BL, Lansdowne MS 823, fols. 3–4, 92–3 • NL Wales, Castell Gorfod MS 8, fol. 143 • *JHC* • *Diary of Thomas Burton*, ed. J. T. Rutt, 4 vols. (1828) • B. G. Owens, ed., *The Ilston book: earliest register of Welsh Baptists* (1996) • W. R. Williams, *The parliamentary history of the principality of Wales* (privately printed, Brecknock, 1895) • will, PRO, E112/559/29; PROB 11/347, fol. 26

Archives BL, Lansdowne MSS, letters, 821, fols. 128–9; 822, fols. 160–61; 823, fols. 3–4, 92–3 • Glamorgan RO, Cardiff, papers relating to Commonwealth military affairs, NLW 1/25

Likenesses portrait, *c*.1655, Fonmon Castle, Vale of Glamorgan [see illus.]

Wealth at death £1034 9s. 10d.; dowries of £3500 to daughters: PRO, E 112/559/29, no. 15 (1674); will, PRO, PROB 11/347, fol. 26

Jones, Philip Mark (1928–2000), trumpeter, was born on 12 March 1928 at 44 Rivers Street, Bath, the only son and eldest child of John Jones (1897–1957) and his wife, Mabel Copestake (1905–1980). He came from a family of musicians. His grandfather, his father, and an uncle all played in the Pump Room orchestra at Bath: his grandfather, formerly a trumpeter, as a percussionist; his father as a trombonist; and his uncle Roy Copestake as a trumpeter. Some time after John Jones had taken his family to London in 1933 he joined the BBC Symphony Orchestra, and he later became manager of the London Philharmonic.

Philip went to Battersea grammar school and played the trumpet and cornet in the brass band. His father introduced him to the principal trumpeter of the BBC Symphony Orchestra, Ernest Hall, who gave him lessons and continued as his teacher when Jones won a scholarship to the Royal College of Music in 1944. Three years later, while still a student, Jones heard a BBC broadcast given by the Amsterdam Koper Quartet (two trumpets, horn, and trombone) which gave him the idea that brass instruments ought to be able to play chamber music; previously they were restricted to the brass band repertory and to a subservient role in the orchestra. So in 1951 he founded the Philip Jones Brass Ensemble, which changed the course of brass history.

One of the problems with creating brass chamber music at that time was the shortage of repertory. From the earliest stages Jones realized that he would have to commission works from living composers. John Gardner wrote the first, and his successors eventually included international figures such as Henze, Takemitsu, Lutosławski, and Birtwistle. Altogether seventy-one works were specially written for the Philip Jones Brass Ensemble, and it gave eighty-seven world premières. Activity in the recording studio, with some fifty separate releases, continued to bring the work of the ensemble to an increasingly wide audience.

But Jones had an active orchestral career as well. Soon

Philip Mark Jones (1928–2000), by Hans Erni, 2000

after gaining his ARCM, he joined the Royal Opera House orchestra, in which he first played bass trumpet, then principal trumpet. From 1953 he spent two years with the London Philharmonic Orchestra, and it was at this time that he met Ursula Strebi (*b.* 1932), the Swiss-born secretary of the Philharmonia Orchestra. She liked to explain that since it was her job to engage musicians, she engaged Philip Jones, who then engaged her. From then onwards she supported his career with remarkable dedication and efficiency. They were married on 1 August 1956 at the parish church of St Bartholomew-the-Great in the City of London. The organist was the horn player Dennis Brain, and Philip's uncle played the trumpet.

From 1956 until 1972 Jones served as principal trumpeter in most of the leading London orchestras. These included the Royal Philharmonic Orchestra under Sir Thomas Beecham; then the Philharmonia under Otto Klemperer; and finally the BBC Symphony Orchestra under Pierre Boulez. During these years the Philip Jones Brass Ensemble, with some of the leading London performers, developed in parallel, gradually building an international reputation. At first it provided incidental music and joined forces with choirs in programmes of early music. The ensemble had been heard on the BBC from 1952, but its first solo programme was at the Aldeburgh Festival in 1962, its first recording in 1965, and the first British tour two years later. European tours followed, and then the ensemble toured South America and the Far East. Jones celebrated his fiftieth birthday in Australia after they had given a concert at Sydney Opera House.

After he left his orchestral positions, but with the Philip Jones Brass Ensemble still very much on the road, Jones influenced the rising generation of brass players with his work in conservatories. He was head of wind and percussion first at the Royal Northern College in Manchester (1975–7) and then at the Guildhall School of Music and Drama (1983–8). He officially retired from playing in 1986 but then expanded his commitment to education as principal of Trinity College of Music (1988–94). These were difficult years for the college, when it was trying to define its image alongside the better-funded royal institutions. Jones's inspired leadership helped pave the way for the college's eventual move to the Royal Naval College, Greenwich, in 2001. When he retired from Trinity College Jones became chairman of the Musicians' Benevolent Fund, thus supporting those who had been less fortunate in their professional careers than he. Along with his friend and colleague Elgar Howarth, Jones edited the influential series of brass publications Just Brass. His many honours included fellowships of the leading conservatories and the Royal Society of Arts and the freedom of the City of London (1988); he was awarded the OBE in 1977 and appointed CBE in 1986.

The recordings of the Philip Jones Brass Ensemble and the new works commissioned for it represent an enduring legacy from a man who set new standards in brass music. Jones had no children and died from cancer at his home, 14 Hamilton Terrace, Westminster, London, on 17 January 2000. His wife survived him.   PETER DICKINSON

Sources *Daily Telegraph* (19 Jan 2000) • *The Times* (19 Jan 2000) • *The Independent* (29 Jan 2000) • *The Guardian* (19 Jan 2000) • memorial service booklet, 26 Jan 2000 [privately printed] • private information (2004) [Ursula Jones, widow] • b. cert. • m. cert. • d. cert.
Archives Trinity College of Music, London | SOUND BBC • BL
Likenesses H. Erni, drawing, 2000, NPG [*see illus.*] • S. Maeder, photograph, repro. in *Daily Telegraph* • photograph, repro. in *The Times* • photograph, repro. in *The Guardian*
Wealth at death £54,268—gross, £54,268 net: probate, 2000, *CGPLA Eng. & Wales*

Jones, Sir Pryce Pryce- (1834–1920), draper and politician, was born on 16 October 1834 at Newtown, Montgomeryshire, Wales, the second son of William Jones, solicitor, of Newtown and his wife, Margaret Goodwin, who was related to Robert Owen. Though his *Who's Who* entry suggests that he had been privately educated other sources indicate that he attended the church elementary school in Newtown before becoming apprenticed to John Davies, a local draper, at the age of twelve. He continued in Davies's employment until 1859 when he took over the business, transforming it within two years into the Royal Warehouse, selling Welsh flannel and other woollen textiles. On 6 April 1859 he married Eleanor (*d.* 1914), daughter of Edward Rowley Morris of Newtown, with whom he had four sons and four daughters.

Pryce-Jones (as he became known from 1887, when he assumed the additional surname Pryce) was a pioneer of mail-order retailing in Britain. The Royal Warehouse, renamed the Royal Welsh Warehouse in 1869, established a 'direct mail' operation which was serving 100,000 customers by the mid-1880s. The business, which remained under Pryce-Jones's personal direction until 1895, expanded rapidly in the late nineteenth century. An impressive new warehouse was opened next to the railway station at Newtown in 1879. This was extended in 1887 when a printing works was attached, thus facilitating the production of an illustrated catalogue, first published in 1890. By this time there were over 200,000 customers.

For Pryce-Jones the 'guiding principle' of retailing was that, as far as possible, 'the public should be brought into direct contact with the producer' (*Montgomeryshire County Times*, 17 Jan 1920). He showed great enterprise in establishing an overseas market for Royal Welsh goods, exhibiting at trade fairs in Europe and the United States. His Patent Euklisia Rug, a type of sleeping bag, was a particularly successful line; 60,000 were ordered by the Russian government during the Russo-Turkish War of 1877–8. The patronage of royalty was assiduously cultivated, not least for its advertising potential. He was knighted on 6 July 1887 for his services to retailing. Acutely aware that his business depended on the development of efficient communications, he served as a director of the Welshpool and Llanfair Railway Company and was a persistent and influential advocate of the parcel post, first introduced in 1883; this proved of such importance that, in 1892, a branch of the Post Office was opened inside the warehouse to facilitate rapid dispatch.

Pryce-Jones was a staunch Anglican and an opponent of Welsh disestablishment, endowing a new parish church, All Saints, Llanllwchaiarn. He was elected to parliament as a moderate Conservative for the Montgomeryshire boroughs at the 1885 general election. His majority of eighty-three evaporated a year later when he was defeated. Though he firmly opposed Gladstone's scheme for Irish home rule he was an advocate of developed assemblies for England, Wales, Scotland, and Ireland, subject to the sovereignty of Westminster. He won the seat back with a majority of 118 in 1892. His progressive inclinations were evident in his election address, which pledged support for measures to reform the poor law and to improve housing conditions as well as measures 'to protect the working classes from working excessive hours' (*Montgomeryshire Express*, 24 June 1892). Despite his victory the election was an unhappy experience. Both he and his wife were roughly handled by a crowd at Llanidloes. After the poll his defeated opponent brought a petition to unseat him, alleging breaches of the Corrupt Practices Act. The subsequent judgment, though it allowed him to retain his seat, was decidedly lukewarm, awarding some costs against him. He did not contest the 1895 general election. Pryce-Jones, who was in poor health from about 1906, died at his home, Dolerw, Newtown, Montgomeryshire, on 11 January 1920, and was buried on 18 January at All Saints, Llanllwchaiarn. His eldest son, Edward Pryce-Jones (1861–1926), succeeded him as chairman of Pryce-Jones Ltd, held the Montgomery seat as a Unionist MP (1895–1906 and 1910–18), and was created a baronet in 1918.

DILWYN PORTER

Sources R. Freegard, 'The Royal Welsh Warehouse', 3 Oct 1984, Kay & Co., Worcester [internal memorandum] • *Montgomeryshire*

County Times (17 Jan 1920) · *Montgomeryshire County Times* (24 Jan 1920) · *Montgomeryshire Express* (10 Nov 1885) · *Montgomeryshire Express* (23 June 1886) · *Montgomeryshire Express* (28 June 1892) · *Montgomeryshire Express* (26 July 1892) · *Montgomeryshire Express* (2 Aug 1892) · *Montgomeryshire Express* (20 Dec 1892) · M. J. Daunton, *Royal Mail: the Post Office since 1840* (1985) · Burke, *Peerage* · *Dod's Parliamentary Companion*

Archives Robert Owen Memorial Museum, Newtown, Montgomeryshire, Colonel E. Pryce-Jones MP scrapbooks
Wealth at death £7902 13s. 6d.: probate, 15 March 1920, CGPLA Eng. & Wales

Jones, Reginald Teague- [*alias* Ronald Sinclair] (1889–1988), intelligence officer, was born on 30 July 1889 in Walton, Liverpool, the eldest of four children and only son of Frederick Jones, schoolmaster, and his wife, Elizabeth Deeley Smith. His father, who taught languages, died when he was about thirteen, leaving his mother in straitened circumstances. Friends living in St Petersburg, Russia, offered to take him there and oversee his education. He attended St Anne's College in the tsarist capital and was soon fluent in German, French, and Russian. On return to England he studied at King's College, London, but left without a degree. He failed to pass the Foreign Office entry examination, instead joining the Indian police in 1910. He quickly learned some Indian languages, plus Persian, and was used for frontier intelligence work—sometimes in disguise—before being transferred to the foreign and political department of the British Indian government, who had spotted his unusual talents, and for whom he was working at the outbreak of the First World War. He was then commissioned into the Indian army reserve of officers.

The nature of his duties makes Teague-Jones's career a shadowy one, but he appears to have spent most of the war as officer in charge of British intelligence in the Persian Gulf, and then as political officer in Basrah. However, following the withdrawal of Russian forces from Persia and the Caucasus as a result of the Bolshevik coup in October 1917 and the peace treaty of Brest Litovsk, he was engaged in the urgent task of assessing which groups, if any, of non-Bolshevik Russians or of the indigenous peoples would support the allies in keeping the Germans and Turks from overrunning Persia, the Caucasus, and Transcaspia—and ultimately India.

Teague-Jones himself crossed into Transcaspia disguised as a Persian merchant and travelled along the Transcaspian railway—assessing the possibility of blowing it up if necessary—to Krasnovodsk on the eastern side of the Caspian. After successfully foiling German plans to acquire a large consignment of cotton from the Bolsheviks (for use in the manufacture of explosives), he crossed by ferry to Baku to liaise with the British representative there and to organize a network of intelligence agents in the area, before reporting back to Major-General Wilfrid Malleson in Mashhad. The Bolsheviks' brutality in Transcaspia led to their being overthrown there in July 1918 by social revolutionaries and the local Turcomans, and the new government, the 'Ashkhabad committee', sought British help from Malleson, via Teague-Jones, who sent an urgent report to Mashhad before returning to

Baku, which was being hard pressed by the Turks. After a few weeks, however, Teague-Jones was summoned back to Transcaspia, where a Bolshevik force from Tashkent in Turkestan was fighting its way westwards along the railway and seemed likely to recapture the province.

A few days later Teague-Jones was hit in the thigh by a machine-gun bullet at a battle 80 miles east of Ashkhabad. He was removed to hospital in Ashkhabad and, as soon as he was able to hobble around, was appointed British political representative there. In the meantime Baku had fallen to the Turks, and in the frenzied exodus a large party of Bolshevik commissars who were making for Astrakhan, which was still in Bolshevik hands, had the misfortune to be delivered instead to Krasnovodsk, where they were seized by their enemies the social revolutionaries. The gaols of Transcaspia were already overflowing with the hated local Bolsheviks and there was little room for these new arrivals, so the Ashkhabad committee asked Malleson whether the British could take them over. Malleson suggested to his authorities that the commissars might be useful in an exchange of prisoners with the Bolsheviks, but was unsure how he could transport them to India when he was very short of men. While the debate was proceeding the social revolutionaries pre-empted any decision by taking twenty-six of the prisoners out into the desert at dead of night, summarily executing them, and shovelling their bodies into a shallow grave (20 September 1918).

At the time this seemed just one more atrocity in the Russian civil war, but it was to have the gravest repercussions for Teague-Jones. Once the First World War was over and the British had withdrawn from the region in 1919, the Bolsheviks soon recaptured Transcaspia and discovered the fate of their colleagues from Baku, some of whom had been personally known to Lenin. The social revolutionaries of the old Ashkhabad committee, eager to exonerate themselves, blamed Teague-Jones for the decision to execute the commissars, and the affair escalated to the point where the twenty-six Baku commissars became revered martyrs in the Soviet Union, and Teague-Jones was regarded as a war criminal, denounced by Stalin and Trotsky personally. Such were the fears for his safety that he was forced to 'disappear' in 1922 and re-emerge as Ronald Sinclair. Thereafter he led a shadowy life, still apparently working for British intelligence until his retirement, and keeping his true identity secret right up to his death at the age of ninety-nine. He received two honours: he became MBE (military) in 1919 as Reginald Teague-Jones, and OBE in 1923 as Ronald Sinclair.

A big ebullient man with a distinctive throaty voice, Teague-Jones was twice married: first—and very romantically—to a Russian girl, Valentina (Valya) Alekseyeva, whom he met in Transcaspia during the war. In July 1933 they were divorced in London, but remained friends. Her parents lived in Krasnovodsk. In October 1933 he married in Cairo his second wife, Else (Taddie), daughter of Hermann Ferdinand Danecker, a German engineer. They subsequently lived in New York (where he seems to have worked for British intelligence during the Second World

War), Florida, and Spain. After her death in 1986 he moved to a retirement home in Plymouth, where he was joined by Valya not long before her own death in 1988. He had no children.

Shortly before his death at his residence, Charlton House, 55 Mannamead Road, Plymouth, on 16 November 1988, his first book, *Adventures in Persia*, appeared, under the name Sinclair, and it was as Ronald Sinclair that his obituary was published in *The Times* on 22 November. A corrected one, revealing his real identity and the reasons for his change of name, appeared three days later. His Transcaspian journals were published in 1990 under his true name, with the title *The Spy who Disappeared*.

PETER HOPKIRK, rev.

Sources R. Teague-Jones, *The spy who disappeared* (1990) [with foreword and epilogue by P. Hopkirk] · P. Hopkirk, *On secret service east of Constantinople* (1994) · B. Pearce, *Sbornik*, 6–7 (1981) · B. Pearce, *Sbornik*, 9 (1983) · B. Pearce, *Sbornik*, 11 (1985) · *The Times* (22 Nov 1990) · *The Times* (25 Nov 1990) · private information (1996) · CGPLA Eng. & Wales (1989)
Wealth at death £255,551: probate, 14 Feb 1989, CGPLA Eng. & Wales

Jones, Reginald Victor (1911–1997), physicist and intelligence scientist, was born in Herne Hill, London, on 29 September 1911, the son of Harold Victor Jones (1880–1953), a sergeant of the Grenadier Guards, and his wife, Alice Margaret, née May (1890–1979).

Education and early career Jones was educated at St Jude's School, Herne Hill; Sussex Road elementary school, Brixton; Dulwich College; and Wadham College, Oxford, where he was an exhibitioner in physics. He graduated with first-class honours in 1932, and having earlier attracted the attention of Frederick Alexander Lindemann he went to the Clarendon Laboratory to study infra-red radiation. On completing his doctorate in 1934 he left Lindemann's team and was elected to a Skynner senior studentship in astronomy at Balliol College to work on the infra-red spectrum of the sun.

Jones's earlier efforts to improve the spectrometers used in the Clarendon led Commander Paul MacNeil (United States navy, retd) to seek his help in 1935. MacNeil had designed an apparatus to detect aircraft in flight by registering their infra-red emissions. The project was beyond the technology of the day, but Jones's interest came to the attention of the Air Ministry's committee, chaired by Henry Tizard, for the scientific survey of air defence. Although the committee was urgently intent on the development of radar, Tizard was, characteristically, also looking ahead to a time when night fighters might need close-range detectors. Jones was given funds to continue his experiments, and in October 1936 was recruited to the Air Ministry staff.

A brush with Robert Watson-Watt almost immediately removed Jones from the mainstream of research on aircraft detection, but he was compensated by a wide experience of the ministry's work under the aegis of Hugh Leedham, then assistant director of instrument research and development. His occasional liaison with the intelligence service enabled him to investigate, among other interests, the uses of high-frequency radio transmissions in Germany. In summer 1939 Tizard's committee urged the appointment of a scientist to survey and improve upon the gathering of intelligence of enemy weapons. The committee had in mind a figure of some eminence, but public thrift suggested that Jones, as a relatively junior and therefore inexpensive civil servant, should be seconded to the post. He was accordingly attached to the Secret Intelligence Service from 1 September 1939.

It was a timely and fortunate accident. Young as he was, Jones brought exceptional qualities of temperament and intellect to his new office, and he had two other complementary advantages. The first was unrestricted access to the highly secret intercepts, known since as Ultra, made available through the work of the Government Code and Cypher School at Bletchley Park. The second was the continuing confidence of Lindemann, which became of great consequence in June 1940 when it brought him into direct contact with Winston Churchill.

The secret war In the first days of the war Jones began to review the available intelligence reports on German weapons and their technology, which were not extensive, and to consider how they might best be augmented. He was therefore readily receptive to the extraordinary budget of material delivered anonymously, in the autumn of 1939, to the British naval attaché in Oslo, which was subsequently known as the Oslo report. The package came from Hans Ferdinand Mayer, a distinguished scientist and industrialist, then of Siemens and Halske AG, and a resolute opponent of national socialism. It contained, besides a capacitor of advanced design, a wide-ranging and well-informed review of German weaponry research and development, including the first reference to the experimental station at Peenemünde, in Mecklenburg. Received opinion was that the report was only an essay in calculated deception of the kind known as a plant, but Jones kept it as a marker, and measured it against later discoveries.

In the meantime Jones began to collect information on the German development of radar, a quest which led him in spring 1940 to conclude that the Luftwaffe had a system of radio beams which could direct its aircraft to attack specific targets even by night. It was a carefully considered hypothesis drawn from varied and fragmentary evidence, and it was entirely correct. It also exemplified a peculiarly intractable crux in intelligence work, which occurs when an enemy accomplishes something which expert opinion at home believes to be technically impossible. In this instance the problem was dramatically resolved.

Churchill, only recently persuaded that the preparations made by Fighter Command could suffice to repel a daylight assault by the Luftwaffe, was disturbed to hear from Lindemann that bombers might nevertheless be able to operate efficiently and with impunity at night. He convened a meeting on 21 June 1940 at which Jones (then aged twenty-eight) had an opportunity to set out his findings and, equally important, to suggest the possibility of some counter-measures. Churchill ordered the immediate investigation of the threat in terms that enabled Jones to overcome some administrative resistance, and on 22 June an exploratory flight high above Spalding, Lincolnshire, detected a beam laid on to the Rolls-Royce works at Derby. It was a notable vindication of Jones's reasoning, and though it did not endear him to everybody it did much to establish his reputation. He remained in Churchill's mind as 'the man who broke the bloody beam' (Jones, *Most Secret War*, 516). By others he was regarded with a wary but useful respect as a man with ready access to the prime minister.

As the war took its course Jones's work changed direction with it. From improving Britain's air defences in 1940–41 he turned to assist the aerial assault upon Germany, which for four years was the only direct action that Britain could take against the enemy's homeland. Before 1942 Bomber Command believed that it had as much scientific expertise at its disposal as it needed, but it became more clamant as the bomber offensive developed. Jones and his colleagues worked both to enhance the effects and to protect the secrecy of the sophisticated navigational aids and operational techniques which the squadrons deployed, while seeking also to investigate and counteract the German defences. The daring and productive airborne raid on the radar station at Bruneval, Seine-Maritime, in February 1942, was devised by Jones, who was appointed CBE for its planning. It was an early and uncharacteristically public feature of an intelligence campaign which continued to the last days of the war. The bitter struggle against the U-boats, in which the need to preserve the secret of the code breaking operation made constant demands on ingenuity, was equally unremitting.

In the last two years of the war the threat of the German long-range weapons, the pulse jet propelled flying bomb, or V1, and the A4 rocket, the V2, produced an extraordinary commotion in the intelligence community. By spring 1943 there was enough evidence of German activity, from a handful of reports, for Jones to propose a more closely directed search for such missiles. An alarm at the War Office, however, then set off a discussion among the chiefs of staff and at ministerial level, with the result that a formal inquiry into the threat was ordered, to be chaired by Duncan Sandys.

What followed had, the reality and gravity of the danger notwithstanding, many elements of farce about it. Sandys's committee had access to all the intelligence material that Jones and his colleagues marshalled, but also consulted a wide variety of expert opinion on the manufacture and use of rockets and on their associated technology. As the committee deliberated, fresh reports, some well founded and others wildly fanciful, came in from agents all over Europe. The ensuing farrago of speculation and apprehension was enriched by two factors, both intuitively perceived by Jones. One was that, as with the beams in 1940, but to a much greater degree, German expertise in rocketry and the automated guidance of missiles had outrun current British experience. The other, more bizarre, was that what the Germans were seeking to

do with the long-range rocket was by any rational calculation not worth doing, in the sense that the destructive power of the V2's 1 ton warhead bore no relation to the intricacy and cost of its propelling and guiding systems. A final irony was that while the German army was painfully refining the rocket, the Luftwaffe was simultaneously developing an inexpensive device of much greater efficacy, which the rocket overshadowed and obstructed. If the V1 had not been delayed by inter-service rivalries, endemic managerial incompetence, and allied interference, it could have posed a much more severe threat to southern Britain in 1943 than either weapon did when they were finally brought into use in 1944.

In the meantime the committee pursued one weapon, largely of its own devising, while Jones and his colleagues painstakingly detected and distinguished two. British experts and others, beguiled by reports of a 10 ton warhead, concluded that they were seeking a rocket which would burn great quantities of solid fuel, would therefore need a weighty steel casing, and would require an enormous launching apparatus to keep it stable in the early stages of its trajectory. In discounting the possibility that the weapon was relatively small, used liquid propellants, and could be stabilized and guided by an innovatory internal system, they made it almost impossible to interpret the evidence that was accumulating before them. There was nevertheless sufficient information available to justify a preventive strike on Peenemünde, where Jones had discovered, and was monitoring, the tracking system used to record the missiles' flight. The station was attacked by Bomber Command on the night of 17–18 August 1943. Not all the designated targets were destroyed, but enough damage was done to cause a general dispersal of work from the site, and a delay of some critical months in the development of both weapons.

At the same time further evidence brought the V1 into focus, and allowed Jones to begin to judge the relative state of the two programmes. However, the emergent threat of the flying bomb naturally intensified the sense of crisis, even though the difference between the two weapons was not generally perceived or understood. Lindemann, having decided *a priori* that a rocket of what he judged an effective striking power was a practical impossibility, which it was, dismissed the whole enterprise as a mare's nest, which it was not. At the same time he had faith in Jones's abilities and was not prepared to see him disparaged by anyone supported by Sandys, whom Lindemann deeply disliked. A kind of balance was therefore maintained in the debate. The imminent attack feared in the autumn of 1943 failed to materialize, but the Luftwaffe's preparations for the V1 produced a crop of launching sites in France and the Low Countries which gave an opportunity for positive action. The sites were attacked by bombers of the RAF and the United States air force from December 1943 onwards. The assault persuaded the Germans to disperse the launching sites and modify their design, but the offensive was delayed as much by mechanical and administrative difficulties as by the bombing. That said, the concurrent air campaign against all communications in northern France in preparation for D-day was a further serious hindrance.

The successful accomplishment of the invasion of France dispelled one fear, but when the bombardment began, in the second week of June, it proved formidable enough. The V1 was mastered first by moving the heavy anti-aircraft batteries to the coast and then by the tide of conquest in northern France, but its effect was also impaired by an intelligence campaign of misinformation which led to many of the missiles being aimed short of London. The threat of the rocket remained, however, and Churchill was at first more annoyed than impressed by Jones's acute prediction of the size, capacity, and likely numbers of the weapon. When the rockets began to fall, early in September, they caused some grievous damage, but their effect was psychological rather than material, and over a dismal winter they proved inadequate for their purpose. On the other hand, the outcome once again vindicated Jones's reasoning, and together with the robust defence which he had offered to Churchill's original strictures served to increase the regard which the prime minister and his own colleagues had for him.

In the last months of the war Jones and his colleagues were assessing captured material and the testimony of prisoners from Germany while preparing for new operations in the Far East. However, with the sudden end of the Japanese war, and the victory of the Labour Party in the election of July 1945, a general reordering of intelligence work began. It was only one of the many tasks which the new administration undertook, and the lessons of the war sat very lightly upon it. Jones's personal record was unsurpassed, but with more powerful figures at large he could not hope to maintain his privileged position in the face of a drastic reorganization. From an effective autonomy in the Air Ministry he found himself one of a committee of thirteen which was devised and chaired by P. M. S. Blackett. Blackett had proved a brilliant operational scientist but had a much blunter perception of creative intelligence and its nuances. Jones, pained but not surprised by the new dispensation, was delivered from frustration by a call to the academic life.

Professor of natural philosophy At the end of the war one of Jones's colleagues from the Air Ministry, Edward Wright, had returned to the University of Aberdeen, where he was professor of mathematics, and later principal. In the autumn of 1945 he suggested that Jones should apply for the vacant chair of natural philosophy there, which in the nineteenth century had been held by James Clerk Maxwell and from 1922 to 1930 by George Paget Thomson. Jones did so, with Thomson's ready encouragement and the enthusiastic endorsement of Churchill, who received an honorary doctorate from the university in April 1946, and left his hosts in no doubt about where their duty lay.

It proved a felicitous appointment. Jones, at thirty-five, had no experience of university teaching and his original research was more than a decade behind him. He was also a classical physicist in an age when many thought that classical physics had run its course. He had, however, a natural gift for exposition, a lively and wide-ranging

mind, and a remarkable flair for experimental investigation. He zestfully took on the professor's traditional duty to lecture to the first-year students. He also promoted a series of projects in the department, beginning with the growth of large crystals for optical instruments and other industrial uses. They continued, through a radical improvement of infra-red spectrometry by the galvanometer amplifier, to an imposing range of seismic and other micrometers. Jones's exploitation of the principle of registering minute physical displacements as changes in electrical capacitance produced some astonishing refinements of instrumentation.

In 1952–4 Jones returned to Whitehall, at Churchill's request, as director of scientific intelligence at the Ministry of Defence. He found the wartime community dispersed and divided, with nuclear and electronic intelligence in separate fiefs, and the Ministry of Defence still struggling to achieve a practical unity of purpose. He worked to improve what he could not change, but his return was chiefly important for the new contacts and friendships which it brought from abroad, and especially from the United States, where he had long been recognized as a master of his craft. His advisory work for the Allied Control Commission in Germany, on the re-establishment of German science, put him in touch both with the leading German physicists and with some of his former adversaries, but his greatest pleasure always was to meet and talk with those who had risked their lives, often at his request, in the resistance movements of occupied Europe.

Jones's public and international work continued well beyond the tenure of his chair, from which he retired in 1981. His commitment to his department and the university was matched by equally intensive concerns at large for scientific research and its applications, scientific education, and a wide variety of advisory works, marked by a comparable range of public and academic honours, fellowships, and prizes. He was made CB in 1946, and a Companion of Honour in 1994, and received the United States medal of freedom in 1946, the United States medal for merit in 1947, and the R. V. Jones intelligence award of the CIA in 1993. He was elected a fellow of the Royal Society in 1965, and was joint editor of the *Notes and Records of the Royal Society* from 1969 to 1989. He received eight honorary doctorates.

On 21 March 1940 Jones married Vera Margaret (d. 1992), a civil servant and daughter of Charles Cain. They had enduring confidence in each other, though, as Jones observed, his wife held him absolutely responsible 'for any calamity that befell the country' (*Most Secret War*, 435). They had three children: a son, Robert, and two daughters, Susan, who died, to her father's great grief, only a fortnight after her mother in 1992, and Margaret.

Jones had an imposing physical presence, with his father's stature and something of a soldier's bearing. His varied social accomplishments included a useful skill with the mouth organ. He was an impassioned fly-fisher and a formidably expert shot with a pistol, though he later came to prefer nature photography to shooting. Living sociably in Aberdeen, at 8 Queen's Terrace, he and his family also enjoyed country life at the White House, Corgarff, in Strathdon, Aberdeenshire, where they regularly attended the Lonach gathering.

Jones died of heart failure at Aberdeen Royal Infirmary on 17 December 1997, and was buried on 22 December at Corgarff, where the Lonach highlanders paid their respects to a long-standing and honoured friend. He was survived by his daughter Margaret and son, Robert. His obituary notices dwelt not only on his war service, but also on his gifts as a teacher, the keenness of his glance, and the liveliness and warmth of his conversation. A memorial service in the chapel of King's College, Aberdeen, on 27 April 1998 included, besides tributes from his academic colleagues, an address by a former director of the CIA, James Woolsey, which was a revelation of Jones's international stature to many who thought that they knew him well.

G. H. MARTIN

Sources R. V. Jones, *Most secret war* (1978) · R. V. Jones, *Reflections on intelligence* (1989) · C. McCombie, 'Reginald Victor Jones', *Aberdeen University Review*, 57 (1997–8), 287–97 · R. J. Woolsey, 'A general tribute', U. Aberdeen memorial service, 1998 · M. A. Player, 'An academic tribute', U. Aberdeen memorial service, 1998 · *The Independent* (19 Dec 1997) · *The Independent* (24 Dec 1997) · *The Scotsman* (19 Dec 1997) · *The Scotsman* (14 May 1998) · *The Guardian* (19 Dec 1997) · *The Times* (19 Dec 1997) · R. Hanbury Brown, 'R. V. Jones, 1911–1997', *Astronomy and Geophysics*, 39 (Aug 1998), 4 · *WW* · *People of Today* (1995) · R. K. Aspin, *The Broomhill squirrels* (privately printed, Grantown-on-Spey, 1997) · private information (2004) [family]
Archives CAC Cam., corresp. and papers · PRO, papers as director of scientific intelligence, DEFE 40 | Nuffield Oxf., corresp. with Lord Cherwell · University of Bristol Library, corresp. with Sir Charles Frank
Likenesses photograph, 1977, repro. in *The Times* · L. Meitner-Graf, photograph, repro. in *The Independent* (19 Dec 1997) · photograph, repro. in *The Scotsman* (19 Dec 1997) · photographs, repro. in Jones, *Most secret war* · photographs, repro. in Jones, *Reflections on intelligence* · portrait, priv. coll.
Wealth at death £444,346.22: confirmation, 31 March 1998, CCI

Jones, Sir Reginald Watson- (1902–1972), orthopaedic surgeon, was born on 4 March 1902 at 29 Devonshire Place, Brighton, Sussex, the son of Edward Henry Jones, who had a senior position with Dr Barnardo's Homes, and his wife, Alice Maud, formerly Watson. Shortly afterwards the family moved to Liverpool, where his father continued to work for Dr Barnardo's. As he grew up Watson-Jones became aware of the extensive crippling deformities caused by tuberculosis and poliomyelitis in children admitted to the homes. He studied at Liverpool University, graduating BSc in 1922 and qualifying in medicine in 1924. He became demonstrator and lecturer in Liverpool University, then house surgeon at the Royal National Orthopaedic Hospital and the Great Ormond Street Hospital for Sick Children in London, before returning in 1927 to Liverpool, where he obtained the degree of MChOrth. In the following year he was elected fellow of the Royal College of Surgeons, London. He married on 11 June 1930 a fellow student at Liverpool, Muriel Emily (1903/4–1970), daughter of Charles William Cook, freight manager. They adopted a boy and a girl.

From his position as senior surgical tutor and registrar at Liverpool Royal Infirmary, Watson-Jones was appointed honorary consultant orthopaedic surgeon to the infirmary in 1935. The infirmary was considering the establishment of a fracture clinic, drawing on the experience of Robert Jones, who had set up accident clinics for workers on the Manchester Ship Canal in 1888–93 and orthopaedic centres during the First World War, and of Harry Platt, whose first fracture clinic was at Ancoat's Hospital. Watson-Jones wished to be among the first to adopt the British Medical Association recommendations for such clinics. With typical enthusiasm he wanted to begin forthwith, and resented the obstacles which the cold hand of bureaucracy placed in his way. Eventually he was able to establish in-patient and outpatient clinics, and he persuaded several insurance companies to contribute to the cost of rebuilding his department. Temporary huts were built which remained in place until the hospital closed in 1978. Continuous patient records were kept, consisting of typewritten case notes and prints of the X-rays taken at each visit. Watson-Jones was a gifted writer: his textbook *Fractures and other Bone and Joint Injuries* (1940) was a remarkable combination of brilliant didactic instruction with an impeccable English prose style and was read by many for pleasure as well as instruction. It was reprinted fifteen times and translated into eight languages, and was for many years the Bible for management of trauma.

Unable to persuade the authorities to invest in more in-patient beds for his clinic, Watson-Jones left Liverpool for London. From 1939 to 1945 he served as consultant in orthopaedic surgery to the Royal Air Force, working tirelessly for the best treatment and rehabilitation for all those injured in the services. In 1942 he was appointed to the medical advisory committee which looked at ways to reduce the injury time away from work of miners and other war-workers. In 1943 he became director of the orthopaedic and accident service at the London Hospital, and in the same year he joined a Trades Union Congress delegation to Russia. In 1945 he was knighted for his services to the Royal Air Force.

In the late 1940s Watson-Jones founded the British volume of the *Journal of Bone and Joint Surgery*, which he edited until his death. He was regarded as a radical when it came to implementing the National Health Service, writing in 1948, by which time he enjoyed a large and world-famous London practice: 'We want freedom from medical control, and that freedom demands private practice. I saw the abolition of such freedom in Russia and it has meant the end of medical progress in that country' (*BMJ*, 1948, 1.266). He nevertheless gave generously of his time to surgical education and research, serving on the council of the Royal College of Surgeons from 1943 to 1959, being vice-president in 1952–4. In 1953 he was elected president of the British Orthopaedic Association. In addition to many visiting titled lectureships, Watson-Jones was an honorary fellow of the colleges of surgeons of Edinburgh, Australia, Canada, and America, and a member of numerous international societies connected with his specialisms, and he drew large audiences wherever he spoke.

Possessed of a warm personal character, and dedicated

to his patients and colleagues, Watson-Jones was supportive of young people and tolerant of novel ideas, though harshly critical of loose thinking. Those who met him were influenced by his intellect, drive, and imagination, his surgical and literary talents, and above all his enthusiasm for life. His wife died in 1970 and he married on 23 July 1971 Muriel Wallace Robertson (b. 1920/21), a nursing sister. He died at his home, 82 Portland Place, Marylebone, London, on 9 August 1972.   GEORGE BENTLEY

Sources H. Osmond-Clarke, *The Lancet* (26 Aug 1972), 439 • J. P. Ross and W. R. Le Fanu, *Lives of the fellows of the Royal College of Surgeons of England, 1965–1973* (1981) • *WWW*, 1971–80, 837 • J. N. Wilson, 'Watson-Jones, the book and the third world', *Proceedings of the Royal Society of Medicine*, 83 (1990), 352–5 • C. Brewer, *A brief history of the Liverpool Royal Infirmary, 1887–1978* (1980), 76 • R. Cooter, *Surgery and society in peace and war* (1993) • F. F. Cartwright, *The development of modern surgery* (1967), 157 • b. cert. • m. certs. • d. cert.
Wealth at death £62,384: probate, 27 Nov 1972, *CGPLA Eng. & Wales*

Jones, Rhys [Rice] (1713–1801), poet and literary editor, was the eldest son of John Jones of Y Blaenau (also known as Tŷ Uchaf y Blaenau and Tyddyn Mawr y Blaenau) in the parish of Llanfachraeth in Merioneth, and Sioned, the daughter of Hugh Pugh, of Garthmelan. He was educated at Dolgellau and Shrewsbury. His proposed legal career was abandoned upon the death of his father in 1731, and he returned to the family estate, where he remained until his death. He married Ann (d. 1795), daughter of Richard Griffiths, of Tan-yr-allt, Caernarvonshire, on 9 January 1742. His son, Rice Jones (1754–1790), graduated from Wadham College, Oxford, in 1778 and served as curate of Llanystumdwy, Caernarvonshire. The estate passed to Rhys's eldest daughter, Catherine, and subsequently to his grandson and only remaining heir, Rice Jones Owen, the son of his fifth daughter, Ann.

Shortly after his return to Merioneth, Rhys composed an elegy to the poet and almanac publisher Siôn Rhydderch (d. 1735). It shows that he had already mastered the techniques of the learned strict metre poets and that he was well versed in their style and subject matter. During the next thirty years he wrote several elegies and eulogies to his county's gentry, whom he would have known on personal terms. Rhys copied seventy or so of his poems about 1764, and he presented the collection to his friend and neighbour William Vaughan, of Corsygedol, whom he addressed in several poems, mostly in a light vein (bawdy poems to Vaughan's gardener, Siôn Grystal), occasionally in a more sombre mood (an elegy to Vaughan's wife, Ann). He also composed some love songs, where he reproduces themes prominent in Dafydd ap Gwilym's work, and some religious verses, again in the strict metres, together with some occasional free metre pieces. Some of his compositions were published in ballad form, nine poems appeared in Huw Jones of Llangwm's *Dewisol ganiadau yr oes hon* (1759), including his notorious diatribe on the Methodists, and Rice Jones Owen paid his respects to his grandfather by publishing in 1818 a selection of his works—omitting the ones most likely to cause offence to a sensitive nineteenth-century audience—entitled *Gwaith prydyddawl y diweddar Rice Jones o'r Blaenau, Meirion*.

Rhys Jones is remembered as compiler of the anthology *Gorchestion beirdd Cymru* (1773), elegantly printed by Stafford Prys of Shrewsbury. The opening pages contain a handful of pieces attributed to three early Welsh poets, Aneirin, Taliesin, and Llywarch Hen, but the volume is primarily dedicated to the works of the *cywyddwyr*, whose compositions between c.1350 and 1550 represent a golden era in the history of Welsh literature. Renaissance scholars of the sixteenth and seventeenth centuries, and their successors in the eighteenth, had long sought to publish this material which, having been assiduously collected by generations of copyists, remained out of sight in private libraries. The *Gorchestion*, a rare success, made public for the first time the works of sixteen *cywyddwyr*, among whom Dafydd ap Gwilym is given pre-eminence, 27 of the 103 pieces being in his name.

Evan Evans (Ieuan Fardd) has been credited with this pioneering project and indeed with the compilation. A 1761 version of the proposals in his hand names him and Rhys Jones as co-editors, the English introduction in the *Gorchestion* bears his hallmark, and several of his acquaintances (including Dr Johnson) are listed among the subscribers. Ieuan, however, is not acknowledged in any way in the *Gorchestion*. Two substantial manuscript collections of poetry containing verse by the *cywyddwyr*, in Rhys Jones's hand, are the clearest evidence of the latter's involvement—thirty-one of the *Gorchestion* poems feature here. The Merioneth gentry, Rhys's poetic patrons, are prominent among the subscribers, who interestingly include one Siôn Grystal, gardener at Corsygedol.

Rhys died at Y Blaenau on 14 February 1801. He was buried four days later in Llanfachraeth church, and a tablet was erected in the church in his memory.

A. CYNFAEL LAKE

Sources R. J. Owen, *Gwaith prydyddawl y diweddar Rice Jones o'r Blaenau, Meirion* (1818) • D. M. Ellis, 'Y Tyddyn Mawr yn y Brinaich', *Llên Cymru*, 8 (1964–5), 88–95 • B. H. Griffiths, 'Rhys Jones (1713–1801) o'r Blaenau', *Journal of the Merioneth Historical and Record Society*, 11 (1990–93), 433–45 • D. Jenkins, 'Rhys Jones o'r Blaenau (1713–1801)', *Journal of the Merioneth Historical and Record Society*, 1 (1949–51), 36–8 • A. C. Lake, 'Rhys Jones: y golygydd a'r bardd', *Ysgrifau Beirniadol*, 22 (1997), 204–26 • NL Wales, Peniarth MS 288 • R. Jones, *Gorchestion beirdd Cymru* (1773) • I. Foulkes, *Geirlyfr bywgraffiadol o enwogion Cymru* (1870) • C. Ashton, *Hanes llenyddiaeth Gymreig o 1651 o. C. hyd 1850* [1893] • M. Stephens, ed., *Cydymaith i lenyddiaeth Cymru*, rev. edn (1997) • *DWB* • NL Wales, Mostyn MS 163: NLW MS 7856D
Wealth at death under £300: Jenkins, 'Rhys Jones o'r Blaenau'

Jones, Rice (fl. 1650–1663), Quaker schismatic, was a Baptist soldier from Nottingham prior to joining the Society of Friends. According to George Fox, Jones and John Trentam of Mansfield in Nottinghamshire left the Quakers in 1650 and 'drew a great company after them & opposed the truth' (*Journal of George Fox, Journal*, 2.314). They held their meetings in the castle yard at Nottingham. When Jones was on his way to participate in the battle of Worcester the following year he visited Fox, who was then a prisoner at Derby. Having taken Fox's views about the primacy of the indwelling of Christ literally, he reputedly castigated Fox for having placed his faith in 'a man that dyed att Jerusalem & there was never any such thinge'. When Fox retorted that Christ had been persecuted by Pilate, the chief priests, and 'professinge Jewes', Jones labelled Fox a chief priest and insisted that prophets, apostles, and holy men suffered inwardly, never externally (*Journal of George Fox, Journal*, 1.10–11). Fox blamed Jones and his followers for the erroneous accusation that Quakers denied the historical Christ.

In 1654 James Nayler visited Jones, finding that in 'the things of god he is exceeding darke … many Confused words came forth, as swearing marry'. Although he apologized for offending Nayler, Jones saw no sin in swearing, nor did he repudiate oaths, without which, he argued, the 'heathen' would not believe Quakers (Swarthmore MS 3, fol. 75). About the same time he and his colleagues prophesied that Fox was at his zenith and would soon fall as rapidly as he had risen, and they distributed papers accusing the Quakers of improperly proclaiming their message in churches and markets. In an epistle to London Friends in 1654, Fox denounced Jones for having castigated the monthly meetings to assist the poor as 'moon-light Meetings'. Because Jones repudiated the Quakers' judgements and admonitions, which Fox claimed had been rendered in the spirit of God, he was denounced by the Quaker leader as a son of the devil and an opponent of gospel order (Penington MS 4, fol. 80). At Fox's invitation, approximately eighty of Jones's followers met with him at Nottingham in 1658. Similar efforts to convince the Proud Quakers, as Jones's people were known, were made by George Whitehead and Richard Hubberthorne, and in time some of them embraced mainstream Quaker tenets.

There is no evidence to determine the number of Proud Quakers, who were probably so-called because they refused to humble themselves and follow Fox. All of the information about Jones and his adherents comes from hostile sources and should be assessed with caution. They reputedly embraced worldly customs and fashion, claiming they had the freedom to do so as long as they were inwardly committed to God. Some of them were known for their skill as wrestlers and football players, and Fox accused them of playing shovel-board on Sundays. Jones had no objection to taking oaths tendered by civil authorities, and Fox accused him of profanity. The opposition of the Proud Quakers to Fox's efforts to persuade Friends of means to assist their less fortunate fellow believers suggests that they were relatively prosperous. Fox sent a letter warning the Proud Quakers of their erroneous ways in 1660. Three years later Lodowick Muggleton referred to a society at Nottingham that comprised Quakers and followers of the mystic Jakob Boehme, by which he apparently meant Jones's group. When Jones's economic fortunes declined, he opened an alehouse, and his colleague Trentam, having turned from the Spirit to spirits, became an alcoholic. The Proud Quakers probably disintegrated in the 1660s, for Fox later observed that 'most of all there people came to nought but what turned againe to ffrendes & truth' (*Journal of George Fox, Journal*, 2.314).

RICHARD L. GREAVES

Sources *The journal of George Fox*, ed. N. Penney, 2 vols. (1911) • *Narrative papers of George Fox*, ed. H. J. Cadbury (1972) • RS Friends, Lond., Penington MS 4, fol. 80 • RS Friends, Lond., Swarthmore MS 3, fol. 75 • *The acts of the witnesses: the autobiography of Lodowick Muggleton and other early Muggletonian writings*, ed. T. L. Underwood (1999), 79 • W. C. Braithwaite, *The beginnings of Quakerism*, ed. H. J. Cadbury, 2nd edn (1955) • H. L. Ingle, *First among Friends: George Fox and the creation of Quakerism* (1994) • *The Christian progress of that ancient servant and minister of Jesus Christ, George Whitehead*, ed. [J. Besse?] (1725), 120–21 • G. F. Nuttall, *The Holy Spirit in puritan faith and experience* (1946) • 'Dictionary of Quaker biography', RS Friends, Lond. [card index]
Archives RS Friends, Lond., Penington MSS; Swarthmore MSS

Jones, Richard (*fl.* 1564–1613), bookseller and printer, was admitted as a 'brother' of the Stationers' Company on 7 August 1564. Nothing is known of his parents, date of birth, or birthplace. His being admitted as a 'brother' rather than a 'freeman' suggests that he was an alien or a foreigner, and there is some evidence to suggest that Jones may have originally come from Wales. Jones's only known child, Thomas, became a freeman in the Stationers' Company by patrimony on 16 August 1596.

Jones operated out of a variety of locations in his five decades as a stationer. His initial London career seems to have been divided between a bookshop in St Paul's Churchyard and a printing house on Fleet Lane. From 1576 to 1580 Jones's imprints exclusively advertise a printing house outside Newgate near St Sepulchre's Church as the location of his business. By 1580 Jones had moved his printing shop for the last time to a location near St Andrew's Church in Holborn. There is some evidence to suggest that after 1586 Jones entered into a partnership with the bookseller William Hill. While a relatively obedient member of the Stationers' Company, Jones did get into serious trouble on three occasions: on 3 August 1579 he received a large fine for printing without a licence and was ordered to bring all copies to Stationers' Hall; on 21 January 1583 Jones was heavily fined and committed to prison for allowing an unlicensed ballad to be printed in his shop; and on 5 September 1597 Jones was fined and committed to the ward for 'printinge a booke disorderly', all copies of which were ordered destroyed (Arber, *Regs. Stationers*, 2.827).

Ballads were a staple of Jones's business and, appropriately enough, both his first and last entries in the Stationers' register were for ballads. He was a prolific producer of poetry collections as well, involved with at least ten collections of poetry as either printer, publisher, or both. He had more than a passing interest in aristocratic culture: for a span of approximately ten years he published seven books on the history and practice of chivalry. He seems to have been a publisher with literary aspirations. Not only did he produce a relatively large amount of prefatory material, penning a range of matter (poems, dedications, and addresses) for sixteen of his extant publications, but there is also evidence to suggest that he was the compiler of *A Handefull of Pleasant Delites* (1565–6), *A Gorgious Gallery of Gallant Inventions* (1577), *Brittons Bowre of Delights* (1591), *The Booke of Honor and Armes* (1590), and *The Arbor of Amorous*

Devices (1594). Along with publishing many works by Isabella Whitney, Nicholas Breton, Sir John Smythe, George Whetstone, and Francis Sabie, Jones was also the first publisher of Richard Edward's *Damon and Pithias* (1571), Philip Stubbes's *The Anatomie of Abuses* (1583), and Thomas Nashe's *Pierce Penilesse* (1592). Jones is perhaps best-known, however, for his publication of the first edition of Christopher Marlowe's *Tamburlaine* (1590), in which he wrote in a preface that he '(purposely) omitted and left out some fond and frivolous Jestures, digressing (and in my poore opinion) far unmeet for the matter' (sig. A2r). Towards the end of his career Jones often decorated title-pages with a printer's device containing his initials and depicting a gillyflower flanked by a rose and another flower. Encircling these flowers is the Welsh motto 'Heb Ddieu heb ddim' ('Without God without anything'). His involvement with the printing and publication of new works slowed in 1595, and in 1598 he seems to have sold his printing shop to William White.

Jones seems to have continued sporadically publishing new works for over a decade until 1611. He received poor relief from the company from 1608 until early 1613. Nothing is known of either the place or the date of his death.

KIRK MELNIKOFF

Sources Arber, *Regs. Stationers* · C. Marlowe, *Tamburlaine the great* (1590) · C. Blagden, *The Stationers' Company: a history, 1403–1959* (1960) · P. H. Jones, 'Wales and the Stationers' Company', *The Stationers' Company and the book trade, 1550–1990*, ed. R. Myers and M. Harris, St Paul's Bibliographies (1997), 185–202 · W. C. Ferguson, 'The Stationers' Company poor books, 1608–1700', *The Library*, 5th ser., 31 (1976), 37–51 · *STC, 1475–1640*

Jones, Richard (1603–1673), schoolmaster and translator of religious texts, was the son of John Lewis of Llansannan, Denbighshire. He matriculated at Balliol College, Oxford, on 18 March 1625, and graduated BA in February 1629 and MA in June 1633. During the Commonwealth he became an itinerant minister. At some time before February 1657 he was appointed schoolmaster at Denbigh Free School, but he was ejected from this position in 1660 on the grounds of his nonconformity.

Jones translated into Welsh a number of popular puritan English texts. The first of these was *Galwad i'r annychweledig* (1659), from Richard Baxter's *The Call to the Unconverted*, a theologically intricate work that nevertheless had sold more than 20,000 copies in the year of its publication. This work went through many editions in a number of languages, and was also translated by the missionary John Eliot into the tongue of the native Indians of Massachusetts. In 1672 a composite volume appeared, published by Stephen Hughes, containing two translations by Jones: *Amdo i Babyddiaeth*, from Baxter's *A Winding Sheet for Popery*, and *Rhodfa Feunyddiol y Christion*, from Henry Oasland's *Christian's Daily Walk*. Two further translations by Jones appeared posthumously: *Hyfforddiadau Christionogol* (1675), from *Christian Directions* by Thomas Gouge, a tireless propagator of scripture and religious works in Wales in the 1670s and published at his expense; and *Bellach neu Byth* (1677), another translation of Baxter, on this occasion his text *Now or Never*. Jones died on 15

August 1673 at Denbigh, and Mr Roberts, the conforming minister of the town, preached his funeral sermon. He was probably unmarried.

Richard Jones has often been confused with a namesake, also born in 1603, who was a cleric and author of religious works and happened to study at Oxford at the same time. This Jones, son of John Pew of Henllan, published two summaries in Welsh of the contents of the Bible in free metric form in the 1650s. *Testun Testament Newyyd ein Harglwydd … yn Benhillion Cymraeg* was published in 1653, and *Perl y Cymro neu Cofiadur y Beibl ar fesurau Psalmau Dafydd* appeared in 1655. The confusion between the two men reached its height in the *Dictionary of National Biography*, in which the entry for the subject of this article dismissed suggestions that older sources had mixed up two persons called Richard Jones, and presented a conflation of the two lives. The muddle was sorted in the *Dictionary of Welsh Biography* (1959).   NICHOLAS KEENE

Sources DWB · A. H. Williams, 'The origins of the old endowed grammar schools of Denbighshire', *Transactions of the Denbighshire Historical Society*, 2 (1953), 17–69 · H. E. Hughes, *Eminent men of Denbighshire* [1946] · Foster, *Alum. Oxon.*, 1500–1714, 2.827 · T. Richards, *A history of the puritan movement in Wales* (1920) · J. C. Morrice, *Wales in the seventeenth century: its literature and men of letters and action* (1918)

Jones, Richard, earl of Ranelagh (1641–1712), politician, was born on 8 February 1641 at the house of an uncle, Viscount Dungarvan, in Long Acre, London, the only son of Arthur Jones, second Viscount Ranelagh (d. 1670), nobleman, and Lady Katherine [see Jones, Katherine (1615–1691)], daughter of Richard *Boyle, earl of Cork. Educated in his youth by John Milton, he attended Oxford in 1656 but did not matriculate, spent 1657–60 travelling abroad with a tutor, and in 1663 was an original fellow of the Royal Society. On 28 October 1662 he married the Hon. Elizabeth (d. 1695), daughter and coheir of Francis *Willoughby, Baron Willoughby of Parham, and Elizabeth, daughter of Edward Cecil, Viscount Wimbledon. They had two sons who died in infancy, and four daughters, three of whom survived him and were his coheirs: Elizabeth, later countess of Kildare (d. 1758), and twins Frances, later countess of Coningsby (d. 1715), and Catherine (d. 1740).

Following the restoration of Charles II, Jones was returned as MP for Roscommon to the Irish parliament of 1661–6, in which he was conspicuous for his opposition to the Irish land settlement. Appointed governor of Roscommon Castle in 1661, in late 1668 he became chancellor of the exchequer (which post he held until 1674) and a privy councillor, as part of the attempts by the lord lieutenant, James, duke of Ormond, to strengthen his position in the face of the English Treasury board's investigations into Irish finances.

Having succeeded to the viscountcy on 7 January 1670, Ranelagh was appointed in May 1670 to head a new Irish council of trade and at the end of the year moved to England, where he attached himself to the interest of leading politicians such as Lord Danby and Edward Seymour, and won favour with the duchess of Portsmouth and Charles

II. The king's constant need for money prompted Ranelagh to promise that Ireland could be a rich source of royal income. His scheme, which originated out of an official inquiry into the Irish establishment pay arrears, was for payment of the crown's debts by December 1675, plus £80,000 to the king by December 1677, by means of a farm of the collection of arrears. The proposal was accepted in June 1671, at which time Ranelagh and his eight partners, or undertakers, were appointed Treasury commissioners for the management of all Irish expenditure from June 1670 to December 1675, with all Irish revenue to be paid to them during this period. The undertaking gave greater freedom of expenditure to the king, opened up the way for great corruption, and made Ranelagh a leading power-broker at court in the 1670s. During the undertaking substantial false funds were created on the establishment, large sums were paid to the king's privy purse, and any officers who complained about the low estimates for pay arrears were cashiered at Ranelagh's request. Ranelagh also had a secret indemnity against personal liability should any part of the £80,000 due in 1677 remain unpaid thereafter, which indemnity he secured by paying the king £10,000 annually throughout the undertaking.

Having been appointed constable of Athlone Castle in 1673, in 1674 Ranelagh became vice-treasurer, and by 1675 was wholly in the ascendant in Irish government. Despite the undertakers' embezzlements, the establishment was fully paid to September 1675, though the extent to which this was achieved by compounding was unclear. During Ormond's second viceroyalty Ranelagh continued to dominate financial affairs, though his attempt with Danby to conduct Irish revenue business even more privately by bypassing the signet office in relation to revenue documents was unsuccessful. In 1677 he was created earl of Ranelagh, though in that year the continued withholding of the undertakers' accounts precipitated the appointment of a commission of inquiry. The undertaking was then transferred into other hands, though the accounts were still withheld. In the meantime Ranelagh continued to compound for pay arrears, and also became involved in a dispute with the leading revenue farmer, Sir James Shaen, husband of Ranelagh's cousin Lady Frances Fitzgerald. Although appointed gentleman of the bedchamber in 1679, Ranelagh found his position undermined by Danby's fall from power and the continuing question of the accounts. It was at this time that there were rumours that he was attempting to secure his position by promoting his eldest daughter as a mistress for the king. A writ of *scire facias* was filed against him in 1679, and in 1681 an order was passed at the English council prohibiting any further payments to him. Although he had stopped the flow of English money into Ireland, supplied £128,000 for Charles II's own use in 1670–82, and provided troops for Tangier, it was clear that Ranelagh's influence with the king was on the wane. During 1681 he was excluded from discussions on the Irish revenue and was suspended as vice-treasurer, while in 1682 the debt from Ranelagh and his partners to the crown was acknowledged as £76,752.

Restored briefly as vice-treasurer during the investigation into Shaen's accounts, Ranelagh was finally dismissed in 1682, though with a pardon for his debts and compensation of £16,000.

During the 1670s Ranelagh had become active in English affairs, taking up residence in 1678 in St James's Square, were he lived until 1694. Having failed at his first attempt to enter the English House of Commons in 1679, he was returned as MP for Plymouth in 1685, in which year, on the recommendation of Lord Rochester, James II appointed him paymaster-general of the English forces. He retained the post following the revolution, despite William III's initial doubts, and indeed remained in favour throughout the reign. Returned as MP for Newtown, Isle of Wight, in 1689 and 1690, he was sworn of the privy council in 1692. In the same year the arrears of his lapsed Irish pension of £300 per annum were paid and he was freed from payment of a yearly crown rent of £100 for the manor and castle of Athlone for twenty-one years. In 1693 he was given a lease of 15 acres on grounds adjoining Chelsea Hospital (of which he was treasurer 1686–1702) to go with 7 acres already leased in 1690, upon which he built a house and gardens which later became the famous Ranelagh Gardens. Both Mary and William III dined with him at Chelsea. His first wife having died on 1 August 1695, on 9 January 1696 he married Margaret (*bap.* 1672, *d.* 1728), widow of John Stawell, Baron Stawell, and daughter of James *Cecil, earl of Salisbury, and Margaret, daughter of John Manners, earl of Rutland. It was rumoured that soon after the marriage, which remained childless, he discovered his young wife in bed with Thomas, Lord Coningsby, which may account for his decision to disinherit his daughter Frances on her subsequent marriage to Coningsby. In later life he relented, and in his will of 1710 he left Frances a quarter of his estate. He continued as an MP, for Chichester in 1695–8, for Marlborough in 1698–1701, and for West Looe in 1701–3. In 1699 he was granted a new pension of £300 a year for twenty-one years, and in 1700 he purchased Cranborne Chase, near Windsor.

Although he was retained as paymaster-general following Queen Anne's accession, the mounting pressure in parliament against Ranelagh for his failure to deliver accounts from his office, and renewed allegations of corruption, forced his resignation in December 1702. In February 1703 he was expelled from the Commons for misappropriation of funds, while in March 1704 the queen was presented with a parliamentary address requesting that he be prosecuted. He spent his remaining years endeavouring to order his accounts, though he still received favour from the crown: a substantial part of his debt was cancelled, he received Treasury grants to help with his accounts, and in late 1704 he was made a governor of Queen Anne's Bounty. Yet he also sank into personal financial hardship. He died on 5 January 1712, being buried at Westminster Abbey on 10 January. He left his estate in confusion, with a large debt to the exchequer. He was said to have died without discovering religion; it certainly appears that religion never played a leading role in his life.

Described as a great wit, capable of pleasing people of very different dispositions, he was both profligate and greedy, and although he demonstrated a great ability to avoid conclusive detection of his embezzlements, he spent a great deal more than he earned from his public offices and small Irish estate, and the truth of the accusations of corruption cannot be doubted. The earldom became extinct on his death, while the viscountcy was claimed by a cousin in 1759. His widow died on 21 February 1728 at Turnham Green and was buried on 5 March at Chiswick.

C. I. McGRATH

Sources GEC, *Peerage*, vol. 10 · S. M. W., 'Jones, Richard', HoP, *Commons, 1690–1715* [draft] · HoP, *Commons, 1660–90* [draft] · S. Egan, 'Finance and the government of Ireland, 1660–85', PhD diss., TCD, 1983 [2 vols.] · J. Lodge, *The peerage of Ireland*, rev. M. Archdall, rev. edn, 4 (1789) · *Calendar of the manuscripts of the marquess of Ormonde*, new ser., 8 vols., HMC, 36 (1902–20), vols. 4, 6 · *Seventh report*, HMC, 6 (1879) · *CSP dom.* · W. A. Shaw, ed., *Calendar of treasury books*, [33 vols. in 64], PRO (1904–69), vols. 3 [1670] – 26 [1712] · J. Redington, ed., *Calendar of Treasury papers*, 6 vols., PRO (1868–89) · N. Luttrell, *A brief historical relation of state affairs from September 1678 to April 1714*, 6 vols. (1857) · K. M. Lynch, *Roger Boyle, first earl of Orrery* (1965) · T. Carte, *An history of the life of James, duke of Ormonde*, 3 vols. (1735–6); new edn, pubd as *The life of James, duke of Ormond*, 6 vols. (1851) · *Bishop Burnet's History* · R. Lascelles, ed., *Liber munerum publicorum Hiberniae … or, The establishments of Ireland*, later edn, 2 vols. in 7 pts (1852), vol. 1, pt 2 · T. J. Kiernan, *A history of the financial administration of Ireland to 1817* (1930) · T. Barnard and J. Fenlon, eds., *The dukes of Ormonde, 1610–1745* (2000) · T. W. Moody and others, eds., *A new history of Ireland*, 3: *Early modern Ireland, 1534–1691* (1976) · S. Réamonn, *History of the revenue commissioners* (1981)

Archives Dorset RO, official accounts, 3327 · NL Ire., reports on finances · PRO NIre., corresp. and papers | BL, Carte MSS · BL, accounts, notes, etc. of Thomas Coke relating to Lord Ranelagh as paymaster of the forces, Add. MS 69959 · BL, corresp. with Lord Danby, Egerton MS 3327 · BL, Lansdowne MSS · Glos. RO, corresp. with William Blathwayt relating to payment of troops · Harvard U., Baker Library, letters to William Blathwayt

Likenesses P. Lely, oils, Royal Hospital, Chelsea · oils, Ranelagh School, Bracknell, Berkshire

Jones, Richard (1767–1840), sporting painter, was born in Reading. He exhibited animal paintings and portraits at the Royal Academy, London, in 1818, 1819, and 1820 from addresses in Reading and Leicester Square, London. In 1824 he moved to Louth, Lincolnshire, and in 1830 he relocated to the Birmingham area. He showed eleven pictures at the Royal Birmingham Society of Artists between 1832 and 1835. H. C. Pyall produced twelve prints after Jones's paintings. Four of his sporting subjects were engraved in mezzotint by Charles Turner for Ackermann's *Repository*. Jones died in 1840.

L. H. CUST, rev. MATTHEW HARGRAVES

Sources W. S. Sparrow, *A book of sporting painters* (1931) · S. Mitchell, *The dictionary of British equestrian artists* (1985) · Graves, *Artists*

Jones, Richard [*called* Gentleman Jones] (1779–1851), actor and playwright, generally known as 'Gentleman Jones', was born in Birmingham, the son of a builder and surveyor. He was educated for a career as an architect. After gaining experience as an amateur actor, he became a professional because of his father's financial difficulties, and

played such parts as Romeo, Norval, and Hamlet at Lichfield, Newcastle, and Bolton. After a season at Birmingham he went to Manchester, and through the indisposition of Ward took at short notice the part of Gossamer in Frederic Reynolds's *Laugh when you can*. This was a success, and as a result he was engaged by Frederick Edward Jones, the patentee of the Crow Street Theatre in Dublin, and appeared there on 20 November 1799. He remained in Ireland playing in all the principal towns, until he moved to London, where he appeared at Covent Garden on 9 October 1807 as Goldfinch in Thomas Holcroft's *The Road to Ruin* and Frederick in *Of Age Tomorrow*, an entertainment by Thomas Dibdin with music by Michael Kelly. His reception was unfavourable, and he was, not without justice, denounced as an imitator of 'Gentleman Lewis' (William Thomas Lewis). He played, however, steadily and conscientiously. Gingham in Reynolds's *The Rage*, first taken by Lewis, was his next part, and on 17 November 1807 he was the original Count Ignacio in Dibdin's *Two Faces under one Hood*. Jones played a variety of roles in his first season and in the season of 1808–9, when, after the fire at Covent Garden, the company migrated first to the Haymarket Opera House and then to the Haymarket Theatre. When Lewis, his predecessor and model, left the London stage in 1809, the light-comedy parts were at Jones's disposal. On 5 June 1809 he made at the Haymarket what seems to have been his first appearance as a member of that company, playing the Copper Captain in Beaumont and Fletcher's *Rule a Wife and have a Wife*, one of the most famous of Lewis's roles, but this performance was very badly received. Jeremy Diddler in J. Kenney's *Raising the Wind*, Rover in John O'Keefe's *Wild Oats*, Wilford in George Colman the younger's *Iron Chest*, and Sir Charles Racket in Arthur Murphy's *Three Weeks after Marriage* show how wide a range was now assigned him.

Jones resolutely faced opposition, and developed into one of the most popular comic actors. His attempts as a playwright, however, were not very successful. He claimed authorship of *The Green Man*, an adaptation from the French of D'Aubigny and Poujol in three acts, produced at the Haymarket in August 1818, but the claim was disputed. *Too Late for Dinner*, an adaptation of a French play which was produced at Covent Garden on 22 February 1820, is said on its title-page to be 'by Richard Jones, Esquire', but it has also been said to be by Theodore Hook. Jones played in it Frank Poppleton, a dashing young man. He wrote *The School for Gallantry*, a one-act piece, apparently unprinted, in which he played Colonel Morrsfelt, and was co-author, with Hook, of a piece entitled *Hoaxing*. An entertainment called *A Carnival*, in which he appeared for his benefit, was a failure. At the close the audience called for an apology, which, as Jones had gone to bed, was given by a colleague. On 3 June 1833, after a benefit which was not announced as a farewell, Jones took an unostentatious leave of the stage. Thereafter he gave lessons in elocution. He died on 30 August 1851, and was buried in St Peter's Church, Pimlico. A memorial tablet in the wall of the church records his virtues, and states that he was for over forty years an inhabitant of the parish. In the same grave are his sister Eliza (*d.* 29 Nov 1828, aged forty) and his wife, Sarah, who died on 18 June 1850 aged seventy-one.

Jones was a respected man. He was something of a valetudinarian, lived a comparatively secluded life, but was friendly with his associates, and was sought after in literary society. On the stage he was admirable as an eccentric gentleman, a dashing beau, and the hero of madcap farce. Recklessness on the stage marred his representation of fine gentlemen. His laugh was loud, but somewhat forced, and his acting generally wanted repose. He was one of the best-dressed actors on the stage, and was a gentleman in his manner. His manager in Dublin, Frederick Edward Jones, in some well-known verses, noted, at the outset of his career, faults in his style, which were never quite overcome.   JOSEPH KNIGHT, *rev.* KLAUS STIERSTORFER

Sources R. Jones, Memoir, *Monthly Mirror* (Aug 1809) • *Era Almanack and Annual* (1876) • *Oxberry's Dramatic Biography*, 3/43 (1825) • *The biography of the British stage, being correct narratives of the lives of all the principal actors and actresses* (1824), 99–104 • A. Nicoll, *Early nineteenth century drama, 1800–1850*, 2nd edn (1955), vol. 4 of *A history of English drama, 1660–1900* (1952–9) • *The Era* (7 Sept 1851), 16 • G. B. Bryan, ed., *Stage deaths: a biographical guide to international theatrical obituaries, 1850–1990*, 2 vols. (1991) • Genest, *Eng. stage* • *Drama, or, Theatrical Pocket Magazine* • Hall, *Dramatic ports.*, vol. 2 • J. Pollock, *Macready as I knew him* (1884) • T. Dibdin, *The reminiscences of Thomas Dibdin*, 2 vols. (1834)
Likenesses S. De Wilde, watercolour drawing, 1813, Garr. Club • S. De Wilde, group portrait, oils, exh. RA 1814, Garr. Club • G. Clint, group portrait, oils, exh. RA 1819, Garr. Club • F. Waldeck, coloured lithograph, 1822 (as Count Almaviva; after vignette), British Gallery • B. Burnell, oils, Garr. Club • G. Cruikshank, plate (as Matthew Sharpset; after etching), repro. in *The British stage* (1818) • S. De Wilde, drawing (as Jeremy Diddler in *Raising the wind*), Garr. Club • S. Freeman, stipple (after C. Robertson), BM, NPG; repro. in *Monthly Mirror* (1809) • J. D. Herbert, pencil and watercolour drawing (as Goldfinch), NG Ire. • oils, Garr. Club • two theatrical prints, NPG

Jones, Richard (1790–1855), political economist, was born on 12 August 1790 at Frant, Sussex, and baptized in September 1790 at the church of St Charles the Martyr, Tunbridge Wells. His father was Richard Jones, an eminent solicitor, whose family lived near Newtown, Montgomeryshire. After attending a private school at Chelsea, run by a Mr Ouyseau, Jones was admitted pensioner at Gonville and Caius College, Cambridge, in 1812 and held a scholarship from 1812 to 1819. He graduated BA in 1816 and proceeded MA in 1819. At Cambridge his companions included Charles Babbage, John Herschel, and William Whewell, who remained close lifelong friends, and with whom he shared an enthusiasm for the inductive and experimental method of Francis Bacon. He was ordained deacon in the diocese of Chichester on 18 December 1816 and priest on 1 November 1817. He officiated in the parishes of Lodsworth and Ferring in Sussex, and from 1822 to 1833 was curate of Brasted, near Sevenoaks, Kent, with a stipend of £100 and fees. On 22 January 1823 he married Charlotte (1789–1871), daughter of William and Frances Attree, of Brighton. Her father was also an eminent solicitor. At one stage Jones intended to pursue a career in law, and he was admitted at the Inner Temple on 18 February 1812.

In 1831 Jones published his chief work, *An Essay on the Distribution of Wealth and on the Sources of Taxation*, with the half-title 'Part 1: Rent'. The preface states that he intended to publish three further parts—on wages, profits, and taxation—but despite persistent urgings from Whewell, none of these appeared. The *Essay* was republished in 1844 with new pagination but only minor alterations. In January 1833 Jones was appointed professor of political economy in the newly established King's College, London, after the resignation of N. W. Senior, and published his introductory lecture together with a syllabus of his lecture course on the wages of labour. In 1835 he succeeded Malthus in the chair of political economy and history at the East India College at Haileybury, Hertfordshire, though he did not formally resign from King's College until 1854. He was admired by the students at Haileybury for his lucid, attractive, and instructive lectures, especially those on political economy.

Jones was an important influence in the development of an anti-Ricardian tradition in economics. He was critical of the deductive method employed by Ricardo and others, and advocated greater (but not exclusive) use of induction. Like Malthus, he warned of the dangers of hasty and premature generalizations. He was also critical of Ricardian absolutism, although he did not adopt an extreme relativist position. Against Ricardo he asserted the harmony of interests between landlords and tenants, and the role of social institutions in the determination of rents. He was much admired by Karl Marx, and is regarded as a forerunner, if not a founder, of the English historical school, the German historical school, and the American institutionalist school of economists. He was instrumental (along with Malthus and others) in establishing in 1834 the Statistical Society of London (later the Royal Statistical Society).

Between 1833 and 1840 Jones published four pamphlets on the commutation of tithes and was associated with J. E. D. Bethune in drafting the Tithe Commutation Act (1836). He was nominated by the archbishop of Canterbury as one of the three tithe commissioners, an office he held at a salary of £1500 a year from 1836 until the commission was remodelled in 1851. He was apparently disappointed not to have received a substantial ecclesiastical preferment for his service to the church and the government as tithe commissioner. He also served as a member of the episcopal and capitular revenues commission and of the Charity Commission; and he was secretary to the cathedral commission.

In physical appearance Jones was distinctive. Because of his considerable weight, he sometimes had difficulty mounting the pulpit of the East India College; and Maria Edgeworth provides a colourful description of his excessively florid complexion. But she also expressed her warm regard for his personal charm, intelligence, general knowledge, and conversation. Jones resigned his professorship at the East India College in December 1854, with a pension of £400 a year, but died at the college on 26 January 1855 and was buried on 1 February in the churchyard at Great Amwell, 2 miles from the college. He bequeathed all his property to his wife, who died in October 1871 and was buried with him on 6 November. He was succeeded at the college by Leslie *Stephen.

After his death Jones's widow gave his papers to Whewell, who in 1859 edited a selection, including some previously published items, under the title *Literary remains, consisting of lectures and tracts on political economy, of the late Rev. Richard Jones* (with portrait). Whewell stated that the main labour of editing was performed by John *Cazenove, one of Jones's most faithful friends and admirers.

J. M. PULLEN

Sources Venn, *Alum. Cant.* · J. Venn and others, eds., *Biographical history of Gonville and Caius College*, 1–2 (1897–8) · *DNB* · F. C. Danvers and others, *Memorials of old Haileybury College* (1894) · W. Whewell, preface, in R. Jones, *Literary remains, consisting of lectures and tracts on political economy*, ed. W. Whewell (1859) · N.-T. Chao, *Richard Jones: an early English institutionalist* (1930) · B. F. Reinhart, 'The life of Richard Jones and his contributions to economic methodology and theory', PhD diss., Catholic University of America, 1962 · L. G. Johnson, *Richard Jones reconsidered: a centenary tribute* (1955) · S. Rashid, 'Richard Jones and Baconian historicism at Cambridge', *Journal of Economic Issues*, 13 (1979), 159–73 · W. L. Miller, 'Richard Jones: a case study in methodology', *History of Political Economy*, 3 (1971), 198–207 · W. L. Miller, 'Richard Jones's contribution to the theory of rent', *History of Political Economy*, 9 (1977), 346–65 · will of Richard Jones, 28 Aug 1851, PRO, PROB 11/2206/135

Archives BL, Charles Babbage MSS · NRA, priv. coll., John Murray MSS · RS, corresp. with Sir John Herschel · Trinity Cam., corresp. with William Whewell

Likenesses M. Gauci, lithograph (after E. U. Eddis), NPG, BM · portrait, repro. in Whewell, *Literary remains*

Jones, Richard Roberts

Jones, Richard Roberts [called Dick of Aberdaron] (1780–1843), linguist, was born at Aberdaron, Caernarvonshire, the second son of Robert Jones and Margaret, *née* Richards. In his early adult years he called himself Richard Roberts, and later used the nickname Dick of Aberdaron which others then adopted. His father, a carpenter and fisherman, often made voyages in a small boat to Liverpool, accompanied by his son, whom he treated badly. Dick never attended school, and he was about nine years of age when he first learned from his mother to read Welsh. He afterwards acquired a practical knowledge of English, in which he was never very proficient. At fifteen he began to study Latin through the help of a friend, John Evans, at nineteen Greek, and a year later Hebrew. About 1804 he accompanied his father on a voyage to Liverpool, where he was given some books, which he lost by shipwreck off the Caernarfon coast on the return journey.

Soon afterwards Jones ran away from home. At Bangor he was befriended by Dr William Cleaver, then bishop of the see, who gave him Greek books and employed him in his gardens. He subsequently spent a year with the Revd John Williams at Treffos in Anglesey, devoting his time principally to the study of Greek, but also acquiring French, with the aid of some refugees in the neighbourhood. Later he learned Italian and Spanish, and was fluent in them. In the summer of 1807 he journeyed to London, with many books concealed in his ragged dress. He went on to Dover, where he was engaged in menial work, and paid Rabbi Nathan for instruction in Hebrew; he also gained some acquaintance with Chaldaic and Syriac. In

Richard Roberts Jones (1780–1843), by William Roos, *c*.1840

1810 he returned to Wales, and was for six months supported by the Revd Richard Davies of Bangor, for whom he copied and corrected the Hebrew words in Littleton's *Latin Dictionary*. A futile attempt to teach him a printer's trade in Liverpool followed, but he attracted attention there, and in 1822 his patron, William Roscoe, published an account of his career, and appealed for subscriptions. It is said that Jones compiled a Greek and English lexicon, a Hebrew grammar, and a volume of Hebrew extracts with vocabulary, to which were added brief Latin treatises on Hebrew music and the accents of Hebrew. But his chief work was a Welsh, Greek, and Hebrew dictionary, which he began in 1821. When it was finished in 1832 he went to an eisteddfod at Beaumaris, and tried, unsuccessfully, to have it published. The remaining years of his life were spent partly in Liverpool and partly in journeys made in search of subscribers.

Roscoe gives a vivid description of Jones's strange appearance:

> His person and dress at this time were extremely singular: to an immense shock of black hair he united a bushy beard of the same colour. His clothing consisted of several coarse and ragged vestments, the spaces between which were filled with books, surrounding him in successive layers, so that he was literally a walking library. (Roscoe, 13)

Jones's total absorption in the acquisition of languages made him quite unfitted for practical affairs, and he could never settle to a job. His interest was solely in the structure and vocabulary of the languages he learned: he had no ability to retain or discuss the content or cultural values of the texts he studied.

On 10 October 1843 Jones left Liverpool for St Asaph, where he died on 18 December of that year. He was buried on 21 December in St Asaph churchyard, and a stone with an inscription (quoted in *Bye-gones* for 16 January 1889) was placed over his grave.

D. L. THOMAS, *rev.* JOHN D. HAIGH

Sources [W. S. Roscoe], *Memoir of Richard Robert Jones* (1822) • *GM*, 1st ser., 94/1 (1824), 65–6 • *Y Gwladgarwr*, 4.223; 5.29–32 • *Chester Chronicle* (23 Dec 1843) • *Y Beirniadur Cymreig* (1845) • E. H. Rowland, *A biographical dictionary of eminent Welshmen who flourished from 1700 to 1900* (privately printed, Wrexham, 1907), 156 • *Bye-Gones Relating to Wales and the Border Counties*, 2nd ser., 1 (1889–90), 16, 20, 112, 125, 130, 164
Archives NL Wales, corresp., lectures, MSS, and notes • NL Wales, Hebrew grammar in Welsh
Likenesses A. R. Burt, etching, pubd 1823, BM, NPG; repro. in *GM*, 94/1 (1824), 65–6 • W. Roos, oils, *c.*1840, priv. coll. [*see illus.*] • W. Clements, woodcut, BM, NPG • Mrs D. Turner, etching, BM, NPG; repro. in Roscoe, *Memoir* • portrait, repro. in *Y Gwladgarwr*, 5

Jones, Robert (*c.*1564–1615), Jesuit, who employed a variety of aliases, was born in the diocese of St Asaph, either near Chirk or in Oswestry. On 20 August 1581 he arrived at the English College then situated in Rheims. On 3 September 1582 he was sent to the English College in Rome where he was accepted on 6 November. On 26 May 1583 he entered the Jesuit noviciate in Rome. He completed his philosophical and theological training at the Roman College and was ordained at an unknown date in the early 1590s. About the same time he was appointed to the philosophical faculty of the Roman College: copies of student notes from his lectures can be found in various European archives. On 11 October 1594 Claudio Acquaviva, father general of the Society of Jesus, sent Jones to the English mission and by 25 February 1595, Jones was in London. Little is known about his activities in the 1590s save that he laboured in Wales and along the marches with periodic visits to London. Somewhere outside London he was professed of the four vows on 18 October 1603.

By the accession of King James, Jones had established an organization of recusant Welsh gentry, Welsh secular priests, and Jesuits. From a centre in Monmouthshire the network extended along the marches. Official government reports claimed that Jones himself frequented the Lacons and the Draycotts of Painsley (Shropshire), the Morgans of Llantarnam, and the Griffiths of Cwm near Monmouth, and celebrated mass weekly at the Darren on the Herefordshire border. In 1604 he sent students to Valladolid and Douai from Shropshire, Worcestershire, Herefordshire, and Monmouthshire. In 1605 Sir Herbert Croft, high sheriff of Herefordshire, warned London that recusants under Jesuit influence would take up arms against the king, accusing Jones of being the instigator. Despite the increased surveillance and vigilance as a result of the fury unleashed by the Gunpowder Plot, Jones eluded capture. He was considered the most likely candidate to succeed Henry Garnet as superior of the Jesuit mission after the latter's execution on 3 May 1606, but he asked to be excused.

More severe legislation followed the plot. To avoid financial disaster the ex-Jesuit Thomas Wright urged Catholics to attend churches, according to Jones, 'not to hear service, but to hear sermons'—which, unfortunately,

happened to be commonly held during services (Foley, 4.372). To stop the spread of such error Jones asked the Jesuit Robert Persons to lobby the Catholic church for a clear, forceful condemnation of these views.

Some time in the early 1600s Jones received into the Roman church Lady Frances Somerset, daughter of Edward Somerset, the fourth earl of Worcester, who, in 1596, had married Jones's patron William Morgan of Llantarnam. Through her Jones gained admission into the Worcester household at Raglan Castle. Eventually Jones reconciled Frances's sisters and her brother Henry Somerset, the earl's son and heir. By January 1609 the Somersets and the Morgans were the principal Catholics under Jones's direction.

Despite Jones's earlier reluctance Acquaviva named him superior of the English Jesuit mission on 28 March 1609. In letters to Jesuits on the mission Jones consistently stressed the importance of prayer, mutual support, and especially poverty, as Jesuits strove to follow a religious life in a hostile environment. He urged Acquaviva to send only 'truly discreet, prudent, mortified, humble and patient' Jesuits to the mission (Foley, 4.385–6).

In 1609 Jones submitted an English translation of an unnamed treatise *de potestate papae* but Acquaviva denied permission for its publication. It is not clear from the correspondence whether Jones was the translator or simply submitting to censors the translation of another. His Italian account of the execution of Roger Cadualadr at Leominster in 1610 attempted to claim the secular priest as a Jesuit ally in the current tension between Jesuits and secular clergy in England.

Described as tall, broad faced, with a high forehead and large eyes, Jones relinquished not the office itself but its exercise to Michael Walpole on 24 November 1613 presumably for reasons of health. Two successive accidents within a short period as he hastened through the night to baptize a baby resulted in his death on 20 August 1615.

THOMAS M. McCOOG

Sources H. Foley, ed., *Records of the English province of the Society of Jesus*, 7 vols. in 8 (1875–83) • W. Kelly, ed., *Liber ruber venerabilis collegii Anglorum de urbe*, 1, Catholic RS, 37 (1940) • T. F. Knox and others, eds., *The first and second diaries of the English College, Douay* (1878) • T. M. McCoog, ed., *Monumenta Angliae*, 1–2 (1992) • T. M. McCoog, 'The Society of Jesus in Wales; the Welsh in the Society of Jesus: 1561–1625', *Journal of Welsh Religious History*, 5 (1997), 1–27 • M. C. Questier, *Newsletters from the archpresbyterate of George Birkhead*, CS, 5th ser., 12 (1998) • F. Stegmüller, 'Jesuitentheologie in schwedischen Bibliotheken', *Archivum Historicum Societatis Iesu*, 18 (1949), 173–6
Archives Archives of the British Province of the Society of Jesus, London, MSS • Archivum Romanum Societatis Iesu, Rome, MSS • Westm. DA, MSS

Jones, Robert (*fl.* 1597–1615), composer and theatrical entrepreneur, graduated BMus at Oxford in 1597; nothing is known of his family. In January 1610 he was, together with three others, granted a patent to found a children's theatre company, 'Children of the revels to the Queen within Whitefriars', and in May 1615 permission to build a playhouse for their performances on the site of Jones's house near Puddle Wharf in Blackfriars was added. But objections from the civic authorities to the privy council caused the nearly completed building to be demolished, and the patent was withdrawn.

Beyond this, nothing is known of Jones except what may be gathered from his publications. In 1600 he issued *The First Booke of Songes & Ayres*—the first of his five books of lute songs. Each volume comprised twenty-one items. Since three supporting vocal parts were also printed in this first volume, and its title-page allowed that an orpharion (a lute-like instrument) and viola da gamba might participate, each piece could be performed as a solo with lute, as a four-part vocal arrangement (with or without selective instrumental participation), or as a full ensemble. It seems to have been highly successful, for Jones's second volume followed the very next year. This time there were no supporting vocal parts, but these were reinstated in the eight central songs of Jones's third volume, *Ultimum vale* (1605), though the opening six pieces (solos) and the concluding seven (duets) were provided with accompaniment only for the lute and/or viola da gamba.

Jones now changed direction. In 1601 he had contributed a madrigal, 'Fair Oriana seeming to wink at folly', to *The Triumphes of Oriana*, the collection of madrigals honouring the aged Queen Elizabeth, and in 1607 he returned to the form, publishing twenty-six in *The first set of madrigals of 3, 4, 5, 6, 7, 8 parts, for viols and voices, or for voices alone, or as you please*. It was Jones's sole madrigalian print (unfortunately its contents survive incomplete), and the only English madrigal volume to present works for such a wide-ranging number of voices; as in some of his earlier collections Jones was clearly intent on encouraging sales by providing a broad spread of performance options.

Whether Jones's madrigals enjoyed success is unknown. Whatever the case, he decided to rescind the 'final farewell' announced in his 1605 print, and in 1609 his fourth volume of lute songs, *A Musicall Dreame*, appeared. Except that its final section comprised solos instead of duets, the pattern of contents was the same as in *Ultimum vale*. But in his fifth volume, *The Muses Gardin for Delights* (1610), there are signs that Jones's interest in the lute song was fading; it was his plainest collection, scored only for solo voice with lute and/or bass viol, and it proved to be his last. That he composed no more songs probably resulted from his new involvement in theatrical enterprises. Nevertheless, he contributed three anthems to Sir William Leighton's *The Teares or Lamentacions of a Sorrowful Soule* (1614); a single anthem survives incomplete in a manuscript source.

Jones was not one of the more distinguished composers of his time. His harmonic technique was limited (though some of the blatant inaccuracies in his lute parts may arise from printers' errors) and he showed little interest in the more radical trends already displayed in some of John Dowland's songs. But he had a flair for the simple, tuneful lute air, and, judging from his unmatched flow of volumes, he was the most popular composer of such songs in the first decade of the seventeenth century.

DAVID BROWN

Sources *New Grove*, 2nd edn · E. H. Fellowes, *The English madrigal composers*, 2nd edn (1950)

Jones, Robert (1745–1829), schoolmaster and author, was born on 13 January 1745 at Suntur, a farm in Rhos-lan, in the parish of Llanystumdwy, Caernarvonshire, the only child of John Williams (*d.* 1783), a smallholder, and his wife, Margaret Owen (*d.* 1776). His mother taught him to read the Bible and the Book of Common Prayer. Apart from that the only education which he had was at a school conducted by Thomas Gough, who based the lessons on the catechism published by Griffith Jones of Llanddowror (*bap.* 1684, *d.* 1761). He also taught him the rules of the strict metres of Welsh poetry.

In his adolescence Jones suffered from acute agonies of conscience, but was converted after studying once again a copy of Griffith Jones's catechism that he had bought and through hearing an unknown preacher in 1762. He then joined the Calvinistic Methodist society meeting at Brynengan in the parish of Dolbenmaen, Caernarvonshire. He became deeply concerned about the ignorance and immorality of young people and persuaded Bridget Bevan (1698–1779) to set up one of her circulating schools in north Wales. In 1768 he opened a school at Capel Curig and then moved to Rhuddlan, Flintshire, where he suffered much public opposition. Later at Brynsiencyn, Anglesey, the incumbent of the parish wrote to Madam Bevan asking her to dismiss him. She took no notice of the request and Jones continued to conduct schools at Llangybi, Caernarvonshire, and Brynengan.

Jones was a very successful schoolmaster despite the harassment and had an instinctive talent for teaching children. His first published work was a satirical attack on the Revd Zaccheus Hughes, a graduate from Jesus College, Oxford, who resided at Trefan, Llanystumdwy, and died on 1 January 1796. Hughes had instigated a disturbance during a service conducted by Jones. The first edition bore the title *Ymddiffyn Cristionogol* ('Christian defence') and appeared in 1770, but the second edition in 1776 had a more colourful title, *Lleferydd yr asyn* ('The voice of the ass'), and ran to six editions during the author's lifetime. On 2 December 1772 Jones married Magdalen Prichard (*c.*1750–1813), the daughter of Richard Griffith (*d.* 1779) of Cae'rtyddyn in the parish of Llangybi, Caernarvonshire, and his wife, Mary Francis. Robert Jones and his wife had two daughters and two sons, including Samuel (1789–1875), one of the most prominent figures among the Calvinistic Methodists of Liverpool.

In 1774 Jones took a seven-year lease upon Tir-bach, a farm in the parish of Llanystumdwy, and added to it a room that could be used as a chapel. In 1776 Robert Roberts, the incumbent of the parish, reported to the bishop of Bangor, John Moore, that it was where the Methodists assembled every Sunday and twice in the week, but the house was not licensed. The landlord ejected Jones and he moved to Tŷ Bwlcyn in the parish of Llaniestyn, Caernarvonshire, and remained there until 1815.

Jones had begun to associate with the Calvinistic Methodists in 1768 and in time became one of the leaders of second-generation Methodists. He was a constant attendant at their assemblies and his services as a preacher were in demand all over the country. In 1784 he came into contact with Thomas Charles (1755–1814) of Bala and became one of his closest confidants. He produced an elementary manual for use in Charles's schools in 1788, entitled *Drych i'r anllythyrennog* ('Mirror for the illiterate'), as well as the first miscellaneous collection of hymns for use in the private societies, the *Grawn-syppiau Canaan* ('Cluster of Canaan's grapes') of 1795. After some initial hesitation, he supported the decision of the Methodists to sever their links with the Church of England by ordaining their own ministers. He declined to be ordained himself but took a prominent part in the first ordination at Bala in 1811. He also assisted Charles in editing the Welsh Bible, the first to be published by the British and Foreign Bible Society. Jones's literary reputation today rests on his book *Drych yr amseroedd* ('Mirror of the times') (1820). It has come to be recognized as a minor literary classic on account of Jones's mastery of strong, idiomatic Welsh. A historic document of continuing value, it preserved snippets of information, mainly about Methodism in north Wales, that would otherwise have been lost, and as a piece of Methodist historiography the work exemplifies both the belief that at the beginning of the evangelical revival religious life was all but extinct and the large part played by the rhetoric of martyrdom in later Methodist thinking.

After 1815 Jones left Tŷ Bwlcyn and spent some time in lodgings until a house was built for him next to the chapel at Dinas, Llaniestyn, where he spent the remainder of his life. He died there on Saturday 18 April 1829, at eighty-four years of age, and was buried alongside his wife on 21 April in Llaniestyn churchyard.   R. TUDUR JONES

Sources J. Elias and T. Charles, *Cofiant o fywyd a marwolaeth y diweddar Mr Robert Jones* (1834) ['Biography … Robert Jones'] • G. M. Ashton, ed., introduction, in R. Jones, *Drych yr amseroedd*, ed. G. M. Ashton (1958) ['Mirror of the times'] • *DWB* • D. E. Jenkins, *The Reverend Thomas Charles of Bala*, 3 vols. (1908) • J. Jones, *Cofiant y Parch. Thomas Jones* (1897) ['Biography of Rev. Thomas Jones'] • E. Jones, *Y gymdeithasfa* (1891) • *Transactions of the Calvinistic Methodist Historical Society* • parish registers, Llanystumdwy and Llaniestyn and Llangybi, Caernarvonshire
Archives NMG Wales, Church in Wales archives, Bishops' transcripts, Bangor, B/QA/5 • NMG Wales, NLW 12793C; NLW 12794C • NMG Wales, Wheldon MSS
Likenesses portrait, NL Wales

Jones, Robert (1810–1879), writer on Welsh literature and Church of England clergyman, was born on 6 January 1810 at Llanfyllin in Montgomeryshire, the eldest son of Robert Jones, a bailiff. He was educated at Oswestry grammar school and at Jesus College, Oxford, where he matriculated on 12 December 1833 and graduated BA in 1837. Ordained deacon by the bishop of St Asaph on 1 July 1837, he was licensed to the curacy of Northop, Flintshire, received priest's orders on 5 May 1838, and held a curacy at Barmouth from 1840 to 1842. He was appointed vicar of All Saints', Rotherhithe, in London, in 1842. After the death of his first wife (about whom nothing is known), he married Eliza Lucretia Mousley on 16 May 1849. They had at least

one son, Charles Edward Jones (b. 1850). Robert Jones remained at Rotherhithe until his death.

While at Barmouth Jones published a small collection of Welsh psalms and hymns, including several of his own composition. He was a regular contributor to Welsh periodicals, and in 1876 he was appointed the first editor of *Y Cymmrodor*, the transactions of the Honourable Society of Cymmrodorion. His scholarly work on Welsh literature includes reprints of John Davies's *Flores poetarum Brittanicorum* (1864) and William Salesbury's Welsh–English dictionary (1876), and a two-volume edition of the poetry and letters of Goronwy Owen (1876). His editorial work on the poetry of Iolo Goch was left unfinished, although a portion was published as supplements to the first two volumes of *Y Cymmrodor*. He had a fine collection of Welsh printed books, now preserved in the Swansea Central Library. He is said to have taught Welsh to Prince Louis Lucien Bonaparte, and to have accompanied him on a tour of Wales in search of the purest dialect.

Jones was a prominent member of the London Welsh community, and also contributed much to the cultural life of Wales, supporting the national eisteddfod and the University College of Wales at Aberystwyth in its early years. He died at All Saints' vicarage, Rotherhithe, on 28 March 1879, and was buried in All Saints' churchyard. In his devotion to Welsh learning he was typical of several generations of scholarly parsons in nineteenth-century Wales.

DAFYDD JOHNSTON

Sources *Y Cymmrodor*, 3 (1880), 126–9 • R. Williams, *Montgomeryshire worthies*, 2nd edn (1894) • *DWB* • W. Baker and K. Womack, eds., *Nineteenth-century British book-collectors and bibliographers*, DLitB, 184 (1997) • m. cert. • d. cert. • b. cert. [Jones, Charles Edward]
Wealth at death under £800: probate, 7 April 1879, *CGPLA Eng. & Wales*

Jones, Robert. See Derfel, Robert Jones (1824–1905).

Jones, Sir Robert, first baronet (1857–1933), orthopaedic surgeon, was born at Rhyl, in north Wales, on 28 June 1857, the eldest child and eldest son of Robert Jones (1836–1875), freelance journalist, and his wife, Mary, daughter of Edward Hughes, of Rhuddlan, Flintshire. In 1873, after three years at Sydenham College, London, where he excelled at cricket, he was sent to Liverpool to be apprenticed to his uncle, the general practitioner Hugh Owen *Thomas, and to begin studies at the Liverpool school of medicine, from which he graduated in 1878. His uncle's extensive practice among Liverpool's dockers and his expertise in the treatment of locomotor injuries and deformities provided Jones with a unique apprenticeship. From Thomas he learned the first principles of modern orthopaedics. Besides inheriting his uncle's private clinic at 11 Nelson Street, Liverpool, on the latter's death in 1891, he acquired his uncle's appetite for hard work, perseverance, and innovation in therapeutic techniques, tools, and work procedures. Blessed with a generous, open personality and immense vitality, Jones failed to acquire any of his uncle's combative, dogmatic nature.

In 1881 Jones was appointed honorary assistant surgeon

to the Stanley Hospital, Liverpool; he rose to full surgeon in 1886. In 1887 he married Susannah (d. 1918), daughter of William Evans, a Liverpool merchant; they had a son and a daughter. In 1888, three years after establishing his own private practice, Jones was invited by the Manchester Ship Canal Company to act as its consulting surgeon during the construction of the 35-mile canal to Liverpool. Responsible for the well-being of the 10,000–20,000 navvies annually employed on this five-year project, Jones designed a comprehensive accident service which provided near-continuity of care for patients, from the moment of injury to recovery. In many ways this model of organization was replicated in the orthopaedic service for disabled soldiers that Jones implemented during the First World War.

In the course of this work, in 1889, Jones was elected honorary surgeon and dean of the clinical school at Liverpool's Royal Southern Hospital. There in 1906 he established one of the first hospital orthopaedic outpatient clinics in Britain, the only one at the time to deal both with injured workers and with disabled children. As at the Nelson Street clinic, he devised a meticulous division of labour among his surgical assistants, which enabled him to undertake staggeringly heavy caseloads. He also made use of social workers, physiotherapists, and limb-fitters, integrating them into his therapeutic system. The efficiency achieved through this organization made his work in Liverpool the focal point of worldwide interest.

Jones's involvement with the physically handicapped made him acutely aware of the lack of adequate long-term curative provision for children with chronic conditions such as polio and tuberculosis of the bone and joints. Thus in 1898, with the help of his colleague at the Royal Southern Hospital, Charles Macalister (1860–1943), he established a rural hospital for such children at Heswall, Liverpool, the first of its kind in Britain. Shortly afterwards he was recruited by Agnes Hunt to act as the consulting surgeon to her children's convalescent home in Oswestry. Impressed as much by Hunt's strength of character as by the results she obtained through her open-air therapy, Jones helped to transform her 'home' into an internationally renowned orthopaedic hospital. Jones sent many of his Liverpool assistants and most of his distinguished medical visitors to observe the work carried out at Oswestry. Among those who became involved with the hospital before the First World War was the young Shropshire general practitioner Gathorne Girdlestone, subsequently Britain's first professor of orthopaedics. Beginning about 1910, Jones, Girdlestone, and Hunt pioneered the development of outlying orthopaedic clinics which would feed into the central hospital at Oswestry. In 1919 Jones and Girdlestone developed this organization on a national basis, fulfilling their plans partly under the auspices of the Central Council for the Care of Cripples, established that same year with Jones as chairman.

The First World War consolidated Jones's international reputation. With 65 per cent of war casualties suffering impairments to the locomotor system, the war presented him with myriad professional opportunities. In January 1915, as government concerns over recruitment and pensions mounted, he obtained permission from the War Office to secure up to 400 beds at the requisitioned poor-law infirmary at Alder Hey, Liverpool, for the rehabilitation of injured soldiers. The success of this venture contributed to his appointment as director of military orthopaedics in March 1916. The appointment, made by the director-general of the Army Medical Service, Sir Alfred Keogh, is alleged to have been insisted upon by the eminent Leeds surgeon Sir Berkeley Moynihan, who threatened to resign from Keogh's advisory body if Jones was not appointed. Once installed, Jones rationalized and standardized military orthopaedic procedures and techniques, and organized more than twenty special military orthopaedic centres in Britain, staffing them mainly with young orthopaedists from the United States and the Commonwealth. The flagship of the orthopaedic centres was that established in May 1916 at Shepherd's Bush, London, where no fewer than a 1000 of the first 1300 disabled recruits were rehabilitated to active military duty.

Jones's wartime work gained him the titles of CB (1917) and KBE (1919) and a host of other honours. It also effectively transformed the practice and public understanding of orthopaedics. Hitherto, outside Liverpool, the specialism mostly comprised the treatment of disabled children and, institutionally, the treatment of club-foot. Jones expanded the specialism, redefining it to encompass the treatment of acute locomotor injuries. He also played a major part in founding the British Orthopaedic Association in February 1918, over which he presided from 1920 to 1925. However, he had no interest in developing an autonomous specialism; rather, he wanted to see orthopaedics fully within the structure of medical education and the voluntary hospitals. Although from about 1910 almost all of his work was confined to the treatment of locomotor disorders, he remained a general surgeon committed to surgical expertise within a conceptually unified medical system.

Predictably, however, Jones's efforts to capture for orthopaedics such generalist practices as fracture treatment were repulsed by powerful sectors of the London medical establishment. His appointment as director of military orthopaedics was opposed by senior members of the Royal College of Surgeons, and in July 1918 a committee of the college insisted that the military orthopaedic centres be relabelled 'special military surgical hospitals' to avoid the implication that only orthopaedic specialists were capable of carrying out the surgery conducted there. The metropolitan defenders of traditionalism in general surgery, fearful of losing lucrative areas of private practice to orthopaedists, also exerted pressures on some of the London teaching hospitals to reduce their beds for civilian orthopaedics. Partly because of these pressures Jones was compelled after the war to develop orthopaedics around the uncontested territory of disabled children. The campaign for the orthopaedic control of fracture treatment in general hospitals, though bolstered by an important publication by him in the *British Medical Journal* in 1925, gained momentum only in the 1930s. Jones was created a baronet in 1926.

After the death of his wife in 1918, Jones suffered personal sorrow at the very moment of his greatest professional triumphs. Thereafter he drew heavily on the friendship of Agnes Hunt, who later nursed and comforted him during the final months of his life. Increasingly he resided with his daughter and son-in-law and biographer, Frederick Watson, at Bodynfoel Hall, Llanfechain, Montgomeryshire, near Oswestry, where he died on 14 January 1933. He was buried in Liverpool Cathedral two days later. Jones was succeeded as second baronet by his son, Arthur Probyn (1882–1951), who changed his name by deed poll to Probyn-Jones in 1933.

ROGER COOTER

Sources F. Watson, *The life of Sir Robert Jones* (1934) · R. Cooter, *Surgery and society in peace and war: orthopaedics and the organization of modern medicine* (1993) · 'A chronological list of Sir Robert Jones's contributions to surgical literature', *Journal of Joint and Bone Surgery*, 39B (1957), 212–17 · G. R. Girdlestone, 'The Robert Jones tradition', *Journal of Bone and Joint Surgery*, 30B (1948), 187–95 · C. Macalister, *The origin and history of the Liverpool Royal Southern Hospital with personal reminiscences* (1936) · *The heritage of Oswestry: the origin and development of the Robert Jones and Agnes Hunt Orthopaedic Hospital* (1900 to 1975), 3rd edn (1975) · WWW
Archives British Orthopaedic Association
Likenesses F. Cornall, oils, RCS Eng. · R. E. Morrison, oils, RCS Eng. · W. C. L., pencil drawing, Wellcome L. · photographs, repro. in Watson, *The life of Sir Robert Jones* · photogravure (after Lafayette), Wellcome L. · photogravure, Wellcome L. · silhouette, Wellcome L.
Wealth at death £75,976 5s. 0d.: probate, 16 March 1933, CGPLA Eng. & Wales

Jones, Robert Ambrose [*pseud.* Emrys ap Iwan] (1848–1906), writer and Calvinistic Methodist minister, was born at the cottage of Ffordd-las, Bryn Aber, Abergele, on 24 March 1848 (not 1851 as in references prior to 1987), the eldest of the five children of John Jones (1807/8?–1883) and his wife, Maria (1816/17?–1876). His father was employed at Bryn Aber as a gardener. Following his school years at two elementary schools in Abergele and periods of shop work in Liverpool and gardening back in Wales, Jones studied at the Bala Calvinistic Methodist college (1868–72), showing a particular interest in foreign languages, though there is no truth in the assertion that he had a French great-grandmother. He went to Lausanne in 1874 to teach English and improve his French and German, returning to Wales after eighteen months and thereafter visiting the continent frequently. On his return he began writing for the weekly Liberal newspaper *Baner ac Amserau Cymru* and the Welsh encyclopaedia *Y gwyddoniadur Cymreig*. During the late 1870s and 1880s the *Baner* published a series of his letters on controversial subjects, including 'A capital for Wales', 'Wales for the Welsh', and 'The English fever in Wales'. His attacks on his own denomination's policy of creating English-language congregations in Welsh-speaking communities were particularly sardonic; as a result, when he sought ordination in 1881 he was rejected, but a second application in 1883 was accepted. He was minister successively at Ruthin, at Trefnant (near Denbigh), and then, until his death, at Rhewl in the Vale of Clwyd. Though sometimes perceived by his contemporaries as either shy or distant by nature, and certainly as of a challenging and independent intellect, he was popular with his congregations and particularly with children. It was only after his death that his influence on Welsh literature and politics began seriously to manifest itself, particularly after the publication of a memoir (*Cofiant*) by T. Gwynn Jones in 1912.

Emrys ap Iwan's published letters and articles show a developing range of satirical and polemical skills, influenced by Pascal and especially by the French pamphleteer Jean-Paul Courier. Among his targets were English imperialism and arrogance, Welsh Anglomania and political servility, and sentimental emotionalism in nonconformist preaching and hymn singing. He was one of the first modern thinkers to identify the status and future of the Welsh language as a political issue; although he is known to have favoured home rule, the future of the language was for him more important. From 1886 he began contributing to the literary periodical *Y Genhinen*, which in 1890 serialized his only extended satirical work, *Breuddwyd pabydd wrth ei ewyllys* ('A papist's reverie'). This purports to be the text of a lecture delivered in 2012 by a Roman Catholic, explaining the collapse of Welsh protestantism, the triumph of Catholicism, and the achievement of Welsh dignity and self-respect; the work is a remarkable challenge to the conformities of Victorian Wales in religion, politics, and language.

At a time when the dominant style of Welsh prose was frequently turgid, bombastic, and Anglicized, Emrys ap Iwan fashioned a limpid but trenchant and sophisticated style, combining the better features of spoken Welsh with his extensive study of Welsh prose classics. He published a Welsh grammar (1881) and a popular edition of the earlier classic *Gweledigaethau'r bardd cwsc* (1898), and had prepared a volume of his sermons, which was published posthumously as *Homilïau* in 1906, with second and third volumes following in 1909 and 1928. He took great pains over his sermons, delivering them word for word as originally composed; he was determined that his addresses should be as polished and well reasoned as possible, avoiding the rhetorical and emotional excesses of many contemporary Welsh preachers. Three volumes of selections from his articles, letters, and sermons appeared from 1937 to 1940. Modern Welsh writers, especially Saunders Lewis, co-founder of the Welsh Nationalist Party, have acknowledged his profound influence on them. Emrys ab Iwan died, unmarried, at his home in Rhewl of liver cancer on 6 January 1906, and was buried in his chapel graveyard.

ENID R. MORGAN

Sources H. O. Hughes, 'Emrys ap Iwan', *Y Genhinen* (1906), 133–40 · T. G. Jones, *Emrys ap Iwan, dysgawdr, llenor, cenedlgarwr: cofiant* (1912) [incl. bibliography of periodical writings supplemented in *National Library of Wales Journal*, 1 (1939–40)] · B. Wynne-Woodhouse, *Hel Achau* [Clwyd Family History Society journal], 21 (spring 1987), 15 · D. M. Lloyd, *Emrys ap Iwan* (1979) · E. Morgan, 'Rhai agweddau ar waith Emrys ap Iwan', MA diss., U. Wales, 1973
Archives NL Wales, notebooks · U. Wales, Bangor

Jones, Sir Robert Armstrong- (1857–1943), psychiatrist, was born at Llwyn-y-mafon-isaf, Ynyscynhaearn, Caernarvonshire, Wales, on 2 December 1857, the second child and eldest son of the ten children of the Reverend Thomas Jones, Independent minister and farmer, of Eisteddfa, Cricieth, and his wife, Jane Elizabeth, daughter of Robert Jones, also of Eisteddfa. His mother claimed to be twenty-first in lineal descent from Collyn ap Tangno, lord of Eifionydd. He assumed the additional surname of Armstrong in 1913. Jones was educated at Porthmadog grammar school, at Grove Park School, Wrexham, and at the University College of Wales, Aberystwyth. After six months' apprenticeship to a Dr Roberts at Porthmadog, he entered St Bartholomew's Hospital, London, in 1876, where he gained the Wix essay and Hitchens prize. He qualified as LSA (1880), MB (London, 1880), and MD (1883). He was admitted MRCP in 1900 and FRCP in 1907. Leaving St Bartholomew's in 1880 he was junior medical officer at the Royal Earlswood Institution for Idiots for two years, and then at the Colney Hatch Asylum for six years. He had an early inclination towards surgery and in 1885 took the FRCS, but soon decided that psychiatry was to be his life's work. In 1888 he returned to Earlswood as medical superintendent, and then in 1893 became the first medical superintendent of the London County Council's new asylum at Claybury, in Essex. In that year he also married Margaret Elizabeth (*d.* May 1943), daughter of Sir Owen Roberts who was a justice of the peace and deputy lieutenant for the counties of London and Caernarfon. They had one son and two daughters.

Armstrong-Jones remained at Claybury for twenty-three years, resigning in 1916. His medical and administrative ability, and the research work of his colleague Frederick Mott spread the renown of Claybury far and wide. It was the first asylum under municipal control to receive paying patients and the first to institute a systematic course of training for psychiatric nurses. His work to promote psychiatric nursing was recognized by the order of St John of Jerusalem, who awarded him a knighthood of grace. As Claybury's directing genius, Armstrong-Jones played a crucial role in ushering in more scientific methods of treating mental illness. He was also noted for his support of occupational therapy and for his teaching of students. He was for many years consulting physician in psychological medicine to St Bartholomew's Hospital, and during the First World War he acted in a similar role to the London and Aldershot commands, with the rank of lieutenant-colonel.

From 1921 until 1931 Armstrong-Jones was one of the three lord chancellor's visitors in lunacy. He was a justice of the peace for Essex and justice of the peace and deputy lieutenant for the counties of London and Caernarfon and in 1929 high sheriff of Caernarvonshire. Armstrong-Jones had firmly held religious beliefs and in 1910 he gave evidence on behalf of the British Medical Association to the royal commission on divorce and matrimonial causes,

and in 1920 he served on the archbishop of Canterbury's special committee on spiritual healing. Armstrong-Jones was Gresham professor of physic (1917–27), general secretary of the Royal Medico-Psychological Association (1897–1906), and its president (1906–7), president of the section of psychological medicine of the British Medical Association (1903), and of the section of psychiatry of the Royal Society of Medicine (1929). He was knighted in 1917 and made CBE in 1919 in recognition of his war services. He received the honorary degree of DSc from the University of Wales in 1920. He travelled as far afield as Russia, Poland, and Tunisia to visit psychiatric hospitals, and was keenly interested in social questions, on which he wrote vigorous letters to *The Times*. He published a *Text-Book of Mental and Sick Nursing* (1907) and contributed many articles to encyclopaedias, treatises, and journals. Armstrong-Jones was well known and admired for his tact, enthusiasm, and energy. His grandson, Anthony Charles Robert Armstrong-Jones, earl of Snowdon, married Princess Margaret (Rose), younger sister of Elizabeth II. Armstrong-Jones died on 30 January 1943 at his home at Plas Dinas, Caernarfon.

W. J. BISHOP, *rev.* NICK HERVEY

Sources *BMJ* (6 Feb 1943), 175 · *The Lancet* (6 Feb 1943), 189 · *The Times* (1 Feb 1943) · b. cert. · m. cert. · d. cert. · CGPLA Eng. & Wales (1943)
Likenesses F. Whiting, portrait; known to be at Plas Dinas, Caernarfon, in 1959
Wealth at death £68,717 10s. 6d.: probate, 8 May 1943, CGPLA Eng. & Wales

Jones, Robert Thomas (1874–1940), trade unionist, was born on 14 October 1874 in Blaenau Ffestiniog, Merioneth, the son of David Jones, a quarryman, and his wife, Ellen Parry. His formal education was largely confined to the elementary school at Ffestiniog, but the chapel Sunday school also contributed to his early education and he remained a staunch advocate of the Sunday school and of temperance. He started work in the local slate mines at the age of thirteen. He was a regular attender of evening classes and was influenced by the socialism of a local minister, Silyn Roberts. Together they established a branch of the Independent Labour Party (ILP) in the district.

Jones was an active leader of the Blaenau Ffestiniog lodge of the North Wales Quarrymen's Union (NWQU) and served as its president before he became its financial secretary in 1908 and general secretary in 1909. His professional approach to the organization of the union transformed the NWQU from a loose collection of lodges into a more centralized and generally effective union. The union's leadership since its foundation in 1874 had been characterized by the involvement of a number of middle-class Liberals. Jones was the first general secretary who was not only a quarryman himself but also a full-time professional trade union official. His policies led to the union adopting a common programme, the 'Quarryman's Charter', in 1911, which was finally accepted by the owners in 1918. Jones conducted long amalgamation negotiations with Ernest Bevin which finally resulted in the amalgamation of the NWQU with the Transport and General Workers' Union in 1923. The union continued to use its own name, however, and continued to conduct much of its business in an autonomous fashion. Virtually all the union's business was conducted in the Welsh language. Jones continued to be the general secretary until his retirement in 1933. Nationally he served as a member of the general council of the Trades Union Congress from 1921 to 1932, where he was considered to be a moderate, anti-left-wing trade unionist. Under his leadership the NWQU avoided the prolonged and ruinous strikes which had characterized the period from 1874 to 1903; in 1896–7 and again in 1900–03 the quarrymen had been locked out of the world's largest slate producer, the Penrhyn quarries at Bethesda in Caernarvonshire.

Jones's political views were certainly moderate and he took an actively pro-war stance during the First World War. Despite his earlier membership of the ILP he was the leading opponent of moves to affiliate the NWQU to the Labour Party and he succeeded in delaying affiliation until 1920 despite pressure from within the union; this might have been connected to his parliamentary ambitions. In 1915 the Liberal Party refused to nominate him as a Liberal parliamentary candidate and in 1918 he stood in the Caernarvonshire constituency as a Labour and nationalist candidate. In 1922 he stood again, this time as an official Labour candidate, and, taking advantage of Liberal divisions, he was elected as member of parliament. He lost the seat in the election of December 1923 and Labour was not to triumph again in the constituency until 1945. Jones had succeeded, however, in establishing a substantial, if minority, Labour vote in this Liberal stronghold. R. T. Jones, who was also a prominent freemason, was therefore a crucial figure in establishing the labour movement in Welsh-speaking north Wales. He served on a number of public bodies including the royal commission on metalliferous mines and quarries (1910–14). He died on 15 December 1940 at Caernarfon. He was unmarried.

R. MERFYN JONES

Sources DWB · R. M. Jones, *The north Wales quarrymen, 1874–1922* (1981) · C. Parry, *The radical tradition in Welsh politics: a study of liberal and labour politics in Gwynedd, 1900–1920* (1970) · *Who's who in Wales*, 3rd edn (1937) · O. Parry, *Undeb y Chwarelwyr, 1908–1929* (1930) · *North Wales Chronicle* (20 Dec 1940) · *The Labour who's who* (1927)
Archives Gwynedd Archives, Caernarfon, North Wales Quarrymen's Union MSS
Wealth at death £1188 0s. 7d.: probate, 3 Feb 1941, CGPLA Eng. & Wales

Jones, Sir (George) Roderick (1877–1962), news agency director, was born at Whitehead Street, Dukinfield, Cheshire, on 21 October 1877, only son of Roderick Patrick Jones, hat salesman, of Manchester, and his wife, Christina Drennan (d. 1897), second daughter of William Gibb of Kilmarnock, cotton agent; Gibb was a cousin of Archbishop A. C. Tait. He had two younger sisters. His parents married just five weeks before his birth. Throughout his life Jones overcompensated for his socially uneasy beginnings, and he rarely spoke about his father, who died in 1887. Despite his Welsh surname he regarded himself as a Scot because of his mother's superior background, descended from the earls of Cassillis. However, she had lost her money in the 1878 crash of the Bank of Glasgow, and this meant that he could not attend a major school or a university. He was educated at home by his maternal grandfather.

In 1894 Jones was sent to live with his mother's married sister in Pretoria, Transvaal republic, where he became a reporter on the only English-language daily newspaper. Intelligent and well informed, precise but engaging in manner and voice, Jones became a good journalist. He taught himself Afrikaans, and he got to know such politicians as Louis Botha and Jan Christian Smuts. Throughout his career Jones cultivated contacts in high places, not only for journalistic purposes but also for self-advancement. On 2 January 1896 he obtained the first press interview with Dr L. S. Jameson after the failure of the Jameson raid. In 1902 he began his long career at Reuters, taking charge of its new South African section in London. At the end of 1905 he returned to Cape Town as regional general manager. Jones made the business highly profitable, and he overcame a determined attempt by leading Cape Town and Johannesburg newspapers to break the agency's virtual monopoly of overseas news.

After the suicide in 1915 of the managing director, Baron Herbert de Reuter, Jones was called to London to take charge. The First World War was raging, and although Baron Herbert had left Reuters in a weak financial position, Jones knew that, as the news agency of the British empire, the British government could not do without the agency's news-gathering and distribution network. In return for covert government backing, financial and otherwise, Jones wound up the old public company, and installed himself as chief executive (and soon also chairman and principal shareholder) of a private company. He also undertook unpaid propaganda work at the Department (later Ministry) of Information. Throughout the war—and then between the wars and into the Second World War—he always contended that he had never permitted the traditional independence of Reuters to be compromised: that the agency under his direction was patriotically ready to work *with* successive British governments, but never *for* any British government. He believed that it was not contradictory for Reuters to claim that its news was objective even though deliberately presented 'through British eyes' (Read, *The Power of News*, 133).

As a reward for his wartime services Jones was made a KBE in 1918. He readily admitted that he ran the company as an autocrat. At first his dominance was beneficial, but later it became stifling. Recognizing that the agency could not make money out of selling general news, Jones encouraged a great worldwide expansion of the Reuters commercial services of stock and commodity prices; the profits from these services largely paid for the general news side. To speed the transmission of news Jones also encouraged the global use of wireless. And for the long-term protection of Reuters, he brought the Press Association, representing British provincial newspapers, into the ownership of the agency in two stages in 1926 and 1930. Although Jones could fairly claim that this was in the public interest, he never revealed that he had made a personal fortune from the transaction.

Jones lived in high style at 29 Hyde Park Gate, London, in a house elaborately redesigned by his friend the architect Edwin Lutyens. Jones also owned North End House at Rottingdean, Sussex, once the home of Edward Burne-Jones. The Press Association's provincial newspapermen knew little about the handling of world news, and after 1926 Jones kept control. But during the mid-1930s it became clear that Reuters was falling behind the two thrusting American news agencies Associated Press and United Press. Associated Press wanted to quit the international news cartel which Reuters had led since 1870, and Jones mishandled the crisis. He began to lose the confidence of his board, and also of the Foreign Office. Yet he refused to retire, despite hints of a peerage. Internal pressure upon him increased when several able new members joined the board. These included William Haley from the *Manchester Guardian* group. At the start of the Second World War Jones urgently negotiated news management arrangements with the British government which he believed left Reuters sufficiently independent. But there were ambiguities; and when the position was fully revealed to the Reuters board early in 1941, Haley and the other directors claimed that Jones had deceived them about the extent of his concessions. Yet paradoxically the Ministry of Information remained dissatisfied with Jones, and the decisive disclosure came from its director-general, Sir Walter Monckton. Haley summed up later: 'the Ministry deliberately betrayed him' (*DNB*).

On 4 February 1941, under threat of imminent dismissal, Jones resigned. In retirement he remained an active member of the Council of the Royal Institute of International Affairs, and from 1950 he was chairman of the governors of Roedean School, near his Rottingdean home. At Reuters he had worn built-up shoes to add to his 5 feet 5 inches, and he always preferred tight-waisted suits and looked too carefully dressed, as shown in his posthumous portrait (at Reuters) by Reginald Lewis. After 1941 he became increasingly overshadowed by his wife, Enid Algerine *Bagnold (1889–1981), the popular novelist and playwright, only daughter of Colonel Arthur Henry Bagnold, whom he had married on 8 July 1920. They had three sons and a daughter. Jones died from uraemia at his London home, 29 Hyde Park Gate, on 23 January 1962, and was buried at St Margaret's, Rottingdean, on 27 January.

DONALD READ

Sources Reuters Archive, London, Jones MSS · D. Read, *The power of news: the history of Reuters*, 2nd edn (1999) · R. Jones, *A life in Reuters* (1951) · D. Read, 'Reuters and South Africa: "South Africa is a country of monopolies"', *South African Journal of Economic History*, 11 (1996), 121–35 · A. Sebba, *Enid Bagnold* (1986) · *DNB* · *The Times* (24 Jan 1962) · J. Lees-Milne, *Another self* (1970), 122–31 · CGPLA Eng. & Wales (1962)
Archives Reuters Archives, London, papers
Likenesses W. Stoneman, 1920, NPG · R. Lewis, portrait, oils, 1962, Reuters archive · photograph, Reuters archive; repro. in Read, *Power of news*, pl. 25 · photographs, Reuters archive

Wealth at death £38,042; 36,439: probate, 14 May 1962, *CGPLA Eng. & Wales*

Jones, Ronald Christopher Hope- (1920–2000), diplomatist, was born on 5 July 1920 at 39 High Street, Eton, Buckinghamshire, the fourth child of William Hope-Jones, assistant master at Eton College, and his wife, Winifred Murton Harvey Coggin. He showed early academic promise and won a scholarship to Eton, where he won the leading classics prize (the Newcastle) and went on to become captain of the school, as well as being a prominent athlete—winning the school half-mile in what was to be a long-standing record time of 1 minute 59.8 seconds. From Eton he won another scholarship to King's College, Cambridge.

With the onset of the Second World War Hope-Jones was commissioned in the army, and served in the north African campaign in 1942. The following year he took part in the invasion of Sicily, and had a narrow escape when the glider in which he was being transported into action was released prematurely and ditched in rough seas at night. Having been a strong swimmer at Eton, he survived. In 1944 he again participated in a glider assault, this time at Arnhem in Holland where his unit (the 1st battalion of the Border regiment) was involved in operation Market Garden; this time the outcome was less fortunate for Hope-Jones and he was captured, spending the rest of the war in captivity. On 12 February 1944, shortly before his capture, he married Pamela Muriel Hawker, who was at the time serving in the WAAF, the daughter of Harry George Hawker, airman; there were two sons and one daughter of the marriage.

After the war Hope-Jones returned to Cambridge to finish his degree, graduating with first-class honours. In June 1946 he joined the foreign service. After an initial spell in the Foreign Office he was posted in 1947 to Paris, where he was promoted second secretary in 1948. Transferred to Beirut in 1949, he returned to the Foreign Office in 1952, being promoted first secretary in November. He was appointed consul at Quito in September 1955. By the time he arrived in Ecuador he was already speaking fluent Spanish after studying the language on the voyage out. He was greatly attracted to the outdoor aspects of Ecuador, exploring its jungles and climbing Andean peaks. Further postings followed to Budapest (1959) and the Foreign Office again (1961). He was promoted counsellor in 1963.

With his appointment to Vienna in 1964, as British representative to the International Atomic Energy Agency, Hope-Jones began a preoccupation with the moral and practical aspects of nuclear deterrence and disarmament which was to characterize much of his subsequent career. On return to London he was appointed head of the atomic energy and disarmament department in the Foreign Office (later the Foreign and Commonwealth Office) in 1967 (the disarmament department after 1968) and in that capacity was an architect of the international treaty banning the use of biological and chemical weapons, encouraging and implementing British leadership in that field. His achievement was acknowledged by his appointment as CMG in 1969. Hope-Jones would have liked the British government to give a similar lead in banning the use of CS anti-riot gas; but this non-lethal substance had been used both by the British in Northern Ireland and by the Americans in Vietnam, and his arguments failed to carry the day. In the circumstances Hope-Jones felt unable to carry on as head of the disarmament department and was relieved to be posted to the north African department in London in 1970. A further posting as counsellor in Brasilia followed in 1972—his fifth appointment in the same rank, which reflected some deceleration in a formerly promising career. His last post—as ambassador to Bolivia from October 1973 to September 1977—was a return for four years to a part of South America for which he already had a great affection, but which did not stretch his intellectual powers as much as some previous jobs.

In retirement Hope-Jones continued to pursue the altruistic principles that had guided his professional life: he edited and contributed to a book of essays, *Ethics and Nuclear Deterrence* (1982), and he actively supported the Liberal Democrats, the British Legion, and Oxfam. He lived in the country in Headley, Hampshire, and died at the North Hampshire Hospital, Basingstoke, on 18 February 2000. He was survived by his wife and three children.

Hope-Jones was widely respected as a physically and morally courageous man who showed that within the diplomatic service there remained officers who were prepared to jeopardize their own careers for principles in which they believed.   JOHN URE

Sources *The Times* (3 March 2000) · *WWW* [forthcoming] · *FO List* · personal knowledge (2004) · b. cert. · m. cert. · d. cert.
Likenesses caricature, 1942, repro. in *The Times*
Wealth at death £420,781—gross; £419,468—net: probate, 1 March 2000, *CGPLA Eng. & Wales*

Jones, Rowland (*bap.* 1722, *d.* 1774), philologist, was second of the twelve children of John Williams (1692–1755), of Bachellyn, Llanbedrog, Caernarvonshire, a prosperous farmer and lawyer, and his wife, Mary Trygarn (*d.* 1754), daughter of Rowland Parry. Jones was baptized at Llannor in 1722 and educated at Llannor School and Botwnnog grammar school. Having trained in law at his father's office at Bachellyn he moved to London and, despite his father's surname, was admitted as attorney under the name Rowland Jones from Symonds Inn on 27 November 1741. He was enrolled as a member of the Inner Temple on 20 October 1751. He married Elizabeth Brown, a Welsh heiress, and they had two daughters, Elizabeth and Ann, and a son, Rowland. By marriage and inheritance Jones became a rich man and acquired an estate known as Y Weirglodd Faur (Broom Hall) in the parish of Aber-erch, Caernarvonshire. The extraordinarily young age of his admission as a solicitor has led to conjecture that Jones was in fact born about December 1716 (*DWB*, 511).

A highly accomplished linguist with a sound knowledge of several modern and ancient languages, Jones laboured indefatigably at his chosen task of uncovering the original tongue spoken before the events at the tower of Babel. With meticulous reference to his historical source, the Bible, he reached the conclusion, not rare among philologists of the period, that this had been Celtic. By extension,

he thought that Welsh held the key to primeval speech, propounding in the preface to his first book, *The Origin of Language and Nations* (1764), his theory that the people of Wales 'continue to speak a language which will define all European languages'. The volume forms the basis for all his later work and contains, established upon his notions of comparative philology, two lexica in which he demonstrates that all words are derived from monosyllabic roots, as well as some speculation on the meaning embodied in the shape of letters. While not always ill-founded, Jones's theories often go unexplained and much of his conjecture, particularly on the aetiology of writing, appears arbitrary and fanciful. Consequently the work was poorly received. An article in the *Critical Review* (18, 1764, 303–6) quotes his musings on the letter 'O': 'the indefinite circle of time and space … representing the globe, the sun, a wheel, &c. in a primary sense … and in a secondary sense, motion, heat, light &c.' 'The author', concludes the reviewer, 'talks like a druid rising out of the grave after eighteen hundred years sleep. No man dares disbelieve him, and no critic can contradict him'.

Still convinced of the importance of his work, Jones published *Hieroglyfic* in 1768 and *The Philosophy of Words* the following year. An intriguing treatise, the latter takes the form of two dialogues conducted with Crito (a character borrowed from Plato) through whom Jones, clearly stung by his previous critical reception, takes the opportunity to attack his detractors. Contained within the first dialogue is his *Plan for an Universal Philosophical Language*, an expression of Jones's belief that linguistic regression would lead to the foundation of a universal language and the repair of the 'great disorders, disputes and disunion among mankind' that had resulted from the loss of a common tongue.

Jones's idea that English could become the universal language is put forward in his 1771 treatise, *The Circles of Gomer*. The book's main body, however, is a disastrous attempt to discover the original meanings of place names. With even more than his characteristic abstruseness, Jones resolved virtually every toponym into a reference to sea- or spring-water and, not surprisingly, took another critical hammering. Thoroughly discouraged, the author took his leave of the presses in the preface to *The Io-Triads* (1773) with a condemnation of the 'disingenuous party politicians and still more illiberal biblio-pagans', who had thwarted his 'endeavours of introducing to the world secrets of the utmost utility and concern'.

If Jones's place in English linguistic history is assured only on grounds of his eccentricity, it is to the neglect of his ingenious theorizing and rational, if subjective, methodology. His work on a universal language revived that of George Dalgarno and the 'universalists' of the Royal Society such as John Wilkins and Francis Lodowyck, while his ideas on original speech were similar to those of L. D. Nelme, the champion of Anglo-Saxon (whom he attacks, along with Locke, in *The Io-Triads*, 5, 44). However, by combining both the notion of instituting a philosophically perfect language and the search for the lost tongue of Adam, Jones represents a unique synthesis of two of the key propositions in eighteenth-century linguistics. Similarly, while the idea of linguistic filiation had been used by the French *philosophes* to refute the orthodox, theological explanation of language, Jones manages to reconcile the two viewpoints. His proposal that English is a medium for enshrining all knowledge places him in opposition to such continental contemporaries as Antoine Rivarol, who advocated French. In addition he exerted a great influence on W. O. Pughe, especially on his Welsh dictionary. Were it not for the stubbornly difficult presentation of his theories, Jones might have enjoyed greater recognition and avoided the criticism to which he was so sensitive.

Jones died at his home in Hamilton Street, Hanover Square, London, in February 1774. His wife survived him. In 1859 a lawsuit in chancery, brought to contest a claim to the estate of Broom Hall, attempted unsuccessfully to prove that he was the son of William Jones of Crugan, near Llanbedrog, and not the son of John Williams.

ROSS KENNEDY

Sources J. E. Griffith, *Pedigrees of Anglesey and Carnarvonshire families* (privately printed, Horncastle, 1914), 331 · *DWB* · PRO, PROB 11/995, fols. 66v–68r
Wealth at death wealthy

Jones, Samuel (1628–1697), nonconformist minister and founder of a nonconformist academy, was born near Chirk Castle, Denbighshire, the son of John Roberts of Corwen, Merioneth. According to Welsh custom he adopted his father's forename for his surname. Nothing further is known with certainty of his immediate family, and there is no record of his early education. He matriculated at All Souls College, Oxford, in 1647, but migrated to Merton College soon afterwards. As a scholar of Merton he appeared before the parliamentary visitors in May 1648; refusing to submit to their authority, he was ordered to be expelled from the university. Due possibly to the intervention of his patron, Sir Thomas Myddelton, and Jones's subsequent submission, the decision was reversed, and it was ordered in November 1648 that he be admitted as a scholar of Jesus College. Unhappily the college was in a state of domestic strife throughout Jones's residence, but his academic progress was not impeded. He graduated BA in 1652, was elected a fellow in 1652–3, and proceeded MA in 1654. He also served as senior moderator. By means which remain unknown his nominal puritanism deepened into conviction, leading him to relinquish his fellowship in 1656. He was ordained by the presbyterians at Taunton and, on the protector's authority, admitted to the vicarage of Llangynwyd, Glamorgan, on 4 May 1657. His local sponsor was Rice Powell of Coytrahen, a magistrate and parliamentary commissioner, whose later friendship and support meant much to Jones. There followed a five-year ministry at Llangynwyd, of which little is known. About 1660 Jones married Rice Powell's daughter Mary (c.1638–1676), and they took up residence at Brynllywarch in Llangynwyd parish, renting the property from the Powells. They had fourteen children, of whom only three survived their father. He married, secondly, on 14 August 1677, Mary David of St Lythans; they had no children.

Jones found the conditions of the Act of Uniformity unacceptable, and was obliged to give up his living in 1662; he remained, however, at Brynllywarch for the rest of his life. His moderation, courtesy, and scholarship attracted the notice of the bishop of Llandaff, who offered him a living if he would conform. Jones declined, and made his position clear in a (surviving) list of objections. He resolved to continue his preaching, probably beginning at the house of Rice Powell, who remained a staunch puritan. Under the declaration of indulgence of 1672 he held licences to preach also at his own house, and at Cildeudy (near Coytrahen), Margam, and Cowbridge—more than anyone else in Wales. Having some means of his own, Jones always enjoyed gentleman status, enhanced by his association with the Powells, and possibly with Sir Edward Mansel of Margam, a puritan sympathizer. There is no evidence as to how Jones's conventicles fared under the penal code; it is said that he himself suffered imprisonment during the episcopate of Francis Davies at Llandaff (1667–75). On the whole, however, it seems that his lot under the persecution was not especially severe: his status and connections with people of quality were much in his favour.

Jones's great service to the nonconformist cause was to establish at Brynllywarch an academy for the education of dissenting ministers. His excellent academic credentials drew numerous able men to the academy, for example, James Owen, who was in fact the first known ministerial student, in 1672–3. The academy continued its work until near the end of Jones's life. Concurrently, he also taught, at a more elementary level, sons of the gentry. In the final seven years or so the presbyterian and congregational funds supported ministerial students at Brynllywarch, preserving their names in their records. With hindsight Brynllywarch was recognized as the first dissenting academy in Wales—indeed, its first 'university'—bringing Jones an enduring fame. It was succeeded by a series of other academies, in different places, finally settling at Carmarthen.

Though clear in outline, Jones's life is not well documented, and areas of uncertainty remain. Strangely, and unlike many of his puritan contemporaries, he produced no published work. He is said to have been a rather corpulent person; in his last years he suffered considerably from stone in the bladder. He died at Brynllywarch in early September 1697, and was buried at Llangynwyd churchyard on 10 September. His second wife survived him.

D. R. L. JONES

Sources D. R. L. Jones, 'Fame and obscurity: Samuel Jones of Brynllywarch', *Journal of Welsh Religious History*, 1 (1993), 41–65 · E. Calamy, ed., *An abridgement of Mr. Baxter's history of his life and times, with an account of the ministers, &c., who were ejected after the Restauration of King Charles II*, 2nd edn, 2 vols. (1713), vol. 2, p. 721 · T. Rees, *History of protestant nonconformity in Wales*, 2nd edn (1883) · W. D. Jeremy, *The Presbyterian Fund and Dr Daniel Williams's Trust* (1885) · T. C. Evans, *History of Llangynwyd parish* (1887) · *DWB*
Wealth at death estate in Abergavenny and Llanellen; money and goods in parish of Mynyddislwyn left to wife: will, NL Wales, Llandaff probate records, proved 28 Oct 1697

Jones, Samuel (*d.* 1732), poet, has been assumed to be a son-in-law or natural child of Hugh Machell of Crackenthorpe Hall, Appleby, Westmorland. This assumption was based on his description of himself, in the dedication to Machell in his *Poetical Miscellanies on Several Occasions*, as 'His most obedient Son'. Jones was a clerk and afterwards, from 1709 to 1731, queen's searcher in the custom house of Whitby. Besides the *Poetical Miscellanies*, which was published by Curll in 1714, Jones wrote *Whitby: a poem occasioned by Mr. Andrew Long's recovery from the jaundice by drinking of Whitby spaw waters* (1718). The poem is said to have 'shown the Virtues and Nature of the Waters, the wholesomeness of the Air, and the Beauty of the Piers' (Gent, addenda). The volume was of such rarity in the nineteenth century that the *Whitby Repository* speculated that 'some rival Spa, envious of the glory of Whitby as a curer of jaundice, bought up, burnt, or otherwise destroyed every copy' (p. 96). According to Nichols's *Illustrations* Jones's writings were much commended in his day. Jones died at his house in Grape Lane, Whitby, and was buried in the parish church of St Mary on 24 December 1732.

THOMAS SECCOMBE, *rev.* FREYA JOHNSTON

Sources GM, 1st ser., 98/2 (1828) • T. Gent, *Annales regioduni Hullini* (1735) • *Whitby Repository*, 2 (1867) • L. Charlton, *The history of Whitby, and of Whitby Abbey* (1779) • N&Q, 4th ser., 3–4 (1869) • Nichols, *Illustrations*, 3.787

Jones, Samuel (1681/2–1719), nonconformist tutor, was the son of Malachi Jones (*d.* 1729), nonconformist minister in Herefordshire until he emigrated to America about 1711. In February 1704 the Congregational Fund board examined him as a candidate for the ministry and resolved to grant him the full allowance. He was educated for the nonconformist ministry first at Roger Griffiths's academy at Abergavenny, Monmouthshire, and then, following Griffiths's sudden conformity, under James Owen (*d.* 1706) at Shrewsbury. On 7 August 1706 he entered Leiden University, where he studied under Jacobus Gronovius, Jacobus Perizonius, and Hermanus Witsius, whose lectures he was later to use himself when teaching. He never entered the ministry, but settled first at Gloucester, where he opened a nonconformist academy in Barton Street in the house of Henry Wintle, a trustee of the nearby Presbyterian meeting.

Jones, in common with most other nonconformist tutors in this period, was harassed, and in September 1712 presented at the ecclesiastical correction court for keeping a private unlicensed school or seminary. He was accused of corrupting his students with 'seditious and antimonarchical principles … very prejudicial to the present Establishment in Church and State' (articles against Samuel Jones, Glos. RO). He moved the academy to Tewkesbury in spring or early summer 1713, ostensibly to find larger premises, and was lent £200 by one of his students to finance the move, which was repaid 'by Degrees, in a Course of several Years' (*Autobiography of Thomas Secker*, 4). Jones did not escape the attentions of the high church even at Tewkesbury. In 1714 his house was attacked by the mob on the day of George I's coronation.

In 1711, not long after Jones's academy had opened,

Thomas Secker, the future archbishop of Canterbury, entered as a divinity student. Writing to Isaac Watts in November 1711 he provided an account of the academy, which he believed was the largest in England at the time. Jones maintained a strict discipline: the students rose at five and were required to speak Latin except when with the family. Secker's autobiography attests to the wide range and excellence of Jones's teaching. He had an excellent library with many foreign books. 'There I recovered my almost lost Knowledge of Greek & Latin; and added to it that of Hebrew, Chaldee & Syriack.' Secker also studied logic, mathematics, geography, and 'a Course of Lectures, Preparatory to the Critical Study of the Bible' (*Autobiography of Thomas Secker*, 3). In his lectures on logic Jones covered all of Heereboord and the greater part of Locke's *Essay Concerning Human Understanding*. Although he was 'no great admirer of the old *Logic*, yet he has taken a great deal of pains both in explaining and correcting Heereboord, and has for the most part made him intelligible, or shewn that he is not so' (Gibbons, 349). He also used his notes from Perizonius's lectures on Terence, Gronovius's on ancient geography, and Witsius's on Jewish antiquities, which he had made as a student at Leiden. About a dozen volumes of notes made by various of Jones's students survive for his lectures on logic, mathematics, and geography, his observations on the New Testament, and his course on Jewish antiquities, which was derived from Thomas Godwin's *Moses and Aaron*. Their survival points to their continuing value to later scholars, and his notes on Godwin were subsequently used by John Jennings and Philip Doddridge. Jones himself published nothing.

The academy, despite its short life, established a reputation for learning as great as any among dissenters in this period because of the scholarship of its tutor and the distinction of many of its students in later life. Besides Secker, they included Joseph Butler, later bishop of Durham, and John Bowes, lord chancellor of Ireland, and among the dissenters Samuel Chandler (1693–1766), the Baptist Andrew Gifford, Edward Godwin, the grandfather of William Godwin, author of *Political Justice*, Vavasor Griffiths (1698?–1740), nonconformist tutor in Wales, and Jeremiah Jones, the noted New Testament scholar. In all the names of about sixty students are known, though there were more. Secker suggests that Jones in his later years took to drink. Jones married Judith Weaver (*d.* 1746), but the marriage appears to have been brief because of his premature death. He died at Tewkesbury on 11 October 1719 aged thirty-seven, and was buried in Tewkesbury Abbey. His widow subsequently married Edward Godwin, who declined to become Jones's successor as tutor. Instead, Jones was succeeded by his nephew Jeremiah *Jones of Nailsworth.

DAVID L. WYKES

Sources DWB • W. W. [W. Wilson], 'Biography: some account of Mr Samuel Jones', *Monthly Repository*, 4 (1809), 651–7 • *The autobiography of Thomas Secker, archbishop of Canterbury*, ed. J. S. Macauley and R. W. Greaves (1988), 3–4 • T. Gibbons, *Memoirs of Isaac Watts* (1780), 347–52 • H. McLachlan, *English education under the Test Acts: being the history of the nonconformist academies, 1662–1820* (1931), 126–31, 191–2, 299 • Articles exhibited against Samuel Jones of the parish of St

John the Baptist, Gloucester, 1712, Glos. RO, GDR B4/1/1056 · consistory court detection causes, 1712, Glos. RO, Gloucester diocese, GDR 272 · 'Attorney and solicitor generals' report on a riot at Tewkesbury', 1714, PRO, SP 35/74/5 · A. Gordon, ed., *Freedom after ejection: a review (1690–1692) of presbyterian and congregational nonconformity in England and Wales* (1917), 294 · documents and memoranda relating to early nonconformist academies collected by the late Joshua Wilson, esq., of Tunbridge Wells, DWL, New College collection, L54/4/52–57, vol. 4 · 'An account of the dissenting academies from the Restoration of Charles the Second', DWL, MS 24.59, pp. 25–6, 60–62 · historical notes and abstracts from printed sources and from Walter Lloyd's papers in the Gloucestershire Library, Records of the Unitarian Chapel, Barton Street, Gloucester, Gloucester Central Library, Gloucestershire Collections, 3793, D4270/7/1, p. 140 · 'Memoirs to serve for a history of protestant dissent', BL, Collectanea Hunteriana, Add. MS 24442, fols. 77v–78r, 102r · J. Hunter, *Familiae minorum gentium*, ed. J. W. Clay, 1, Harleian Society, 37 (1894), 299 · *VCH Gloucestershire*, 4.319, 8.165–6 · W. Davies, *The Tewkesbury Academy with sketches of its tutor and students* [1905] · *DNB* · monumental inscription, Tewkesbury Abbey
Archives BL, lecture notes and annotations, Add. MSS 23915–23919 · U. Birm., special collections department, MS textbooks and lecture notes · U. Leeds, Brotherton L., 'Logic sive ars ratiocinandi'

Jones, Samuel (1770–1859). *See under* Jones, William (*bap.* 1762, *d.* 1831).

Jones, (James) Sidney (1861–1946), composer, was born in Islington, London, on 17 June 1861, the eldest son and second of the six children of (James) Sidney Jones, a military bandmaster, and his wife, Ann, *née* Eycott. He spent his childhood in various military towns (Colchester, Aldershot, York, Dublin) before the family settled in Leeds, where the elder Jones became an important figure in local musical life, conducting the orchestra at the Grand Theatre and presiding over the municipal band. The young Sidney Jones began his musical life playing clarinet in his father's orchestra and band, but in his early twenties he turned to conducting and went on the road with a series of increasingly substantial theatre companies—with a *Fun on the Bristol* company, with Alfred Hemming's comedy and burlesque company, as music director to the Vokes family, and as conductor of Kate Santley's *Vetah* (1886). He then spent four years as principal touring conductor for the highly successful Henry Leslie, playing *Dorothy*, *Doris*, and *The Red Hussar*. In 1891 he conducted a tour of the Gaiety musical *Little Jack Sheppard*, and as a result was hired by George Edwardes as music director for the Gaiety company's trip that year to America and Australia. He subsequently conducted *In Town* for Edwardes at London's Prince of Wales Theatre, then another of the earliest and most popular musical comedies of the era, *Morocco Bound*, at the Shaftesbury, and the London production of the major provincial hit *The Gay Parisienne*, at the Duke of York's.

From his earliest days as a music director Jones also worked as a composer and songwriter, providing incidental music and songs as required for the shows he conducted. In 1889 he composed the score for the Leeds pantomime *Aladdin II*, in 1892 he had a little operetta, *Our Family Legend*, played at Brighton, and the following year his song 'Linger Longer, Loo' was a considerable success when interpolated in Edwardes's production of the burlesque

Don Juan. It was Edwardes who gave the young composer his big chance when he asked him to compose the music to Owen Hall's snappy libretto for *A Gaiety Girl*. The show was a major hit, going on from its original long London run to be produced in America, Australia, Germany, and elsewhere and proving to be a cornerstone in what was to become the famous tradition of Gaiety musicals.

Jones was commissioned to provide the score for the successor on Edwardes's schedule to *A Gaiety Girl*, *An Artist's Model* (Daly's Theatre, 1895), and in the following years he became the recognized house composer for the producer's series of shows at Daly's. *The Geisha* (1896), *A Greek Slave* (1898), and *San Toy* (1899) were musical plays written in a more musically substantial style than the featherweight entertainment given at the Gaiety. Their librettos sported a solid and serious romantic backbone (confided to the baritone hero Hayden Coffin and the soprano Marie Tempest) alongside their comic and *soubrette* elements, and the scores which Jones provided included, alongside the lighter material, numbers sentimental and dramatic, as well as some impressive and vocally demanding concerted ensembles and finales of a kind not heard in the musical comedies of the period. Although *San Toy* achieved the longest run of the series at Daly's, it was *The Geisha* that proved the biggest winner. Following its triumphant London run, it was produced all round the world, scoring a major success in America, and above all on the continent, where it proved to be by far the most successful English-language musical (the works of Gilbert and Sullivan not excepted) of the nineteenth century. Only *Die Fledermaus* was more often played in Germany and Austria than was *Die Geisha* in the first thirty years of its existence. It remained in the repertory for many, many years, and not until nearly a century later, and the days of such international successes as *The Phantom of the Opera*, did any other imported musical even challenge its record.

After *San Toy* Jones left Daly's to try his hand at producing his own work, with a period piece called *My Lady Molly*. It did extremely well, but he did not pursue this line, and his next work was a commission for the newly very rich producer of *Florodora*, Tom Davis. *The Medal and the Maid* (1903) gave Jones the first flop of his career. A pretty Chinese-style piece for Edwardes called *See See* (1906) did fairly well, but Jones had another big hit in 1908 when he wrote the score to Freddie Lonsdale's book for *King of Cadonia*. A thoroughly romantic Ruritanian piece, in which, as in Jones's work for Daly's, the comic and lighter side of affairs decorated rather than predominated, *King of Cadonia* allowed the composer to spread himself into the kind of colourful lyrical music at which he excelled. The successor to *King of Cadonia*, *A Persian Princess* (1909), was a severe failure, and Jones, who was still working in parallel as a theatre conductor, somewhat surprisingly switched next to turning out something like a Gaiety score for Edwardes. *The Girl from Utah* (1913) provided simple songs for the pretty voice of Ina Claire, the light comedian Joe Coyne, and the Gaiety comic Teddy Payne rather than music for the stronger tones of Isobel Jay and Bertram

Wallis of *King of Cadonia*. In 1916, after Edwardes's death, the former lead tenor at Daly's, Bobbie Evett, took over the now struggling theatre. For his first essay he produced a romantic musical which strove to follow the style established more than a decade earlier by Jones's famous shows: Jones provided the score for *The Happy Day* (1916), Wallis starred, alongside the soprano José Collins, but the show was only a partial success. By now the fashion in music and musical theatre had thoroughly changed, and the theatre music of the nineteenth century was giving way to the syncopated dance rhythms invading Europe from across the Atlantic. With such music Sidney Jones was not in sympathy and so, his time having apparently passed, he simply withdrew from the world of the theatre, and for the last thirty years of his life—while productions of *The Geisha* and *San Toy* continued to flourish all round the world—he wrote no more.

Jones died at his home, 17 Lichfield Road, Kew, Surrey, on 29 January 1946. None of his five children from his marriage (on 14 March 1885) to the actress Kate Linley became involved in the theatre. His younger brother Guy (1875–1959), however, conducted many major musical productions and composed the scores for a number of musicals, the most successful of which was *The Gay Gordons* (1907).

KURT GÄNZL

Sources K. Gänzl, *The encyclopedia of the musical theatre*, 2 vols. (1994) · K. Gänzl, *The British musical theatre*, 2 vols. (1986) · *The Era* (1886–1916) · *The Times* (27 April 1946) · DNB · A. Lamb, 'Jones, (James) Sidney', *New Grove* · b. cert. · m. cert.
Likenesses portrait, repro. in Gänzl, *Encyclopedia of the musical theatre*
Wealth at death £14,766 2s. 6d.: probate, 25 June 1946, CGPLA Eng. & Wales

Jones, Stephen (1763–1827), journal editor and compiler of reference works, was born in London and baptized at St Martin-in-the-Fields on 25 October 1763, the son of Giles *Jones [see under Jones, Griffith], author, and Ellen Jane Maria Fewtrell. His uncle was Griffith *Jones, whose daughter Christian Jones later became Jones's first wife. He entered St Paul's School, London, in April 1775, and was afterwards apprenticed to a sculptor, but having left 'on account of some difference' (GM, 90–91) he moved closer to family tradition by becoming apprenticed to a printer in Fetter Lane. He was subsequently employed as a press corrector by Strahan, and afterwards as a reader by Thomas Wright of Peterborough Court. On the death of the latter in March 1797 Jones became editor of the *Whitehall Evening Post*. This was not a commercial success and he moved to the *General Evening Post*, of which he was joint proprietor, but this enterprise was similarly ill-fated and eventually merged with Charles Baldwin's *St James's Chronicle*. From 1807 Jones edited the *European Magazine*, and from 1797 to 1814 he produced *The Spirit of the Public Journals*, an annual compilation.

Jones's most enduring literary achievement was his updated edition of the *Biographica dramatica, or, A Companion to the Playhouse*; originally compiled to 1764 by David Erskine Baker, and continued to 1782 by Isaac Reed. It was heavily criticized by Octavius Gilchrist in the *Quarterly Review*, mainly on the score of the entries that had been republished unchanged from the earlier editions. Jones defended himself in *Hypercriticism Exposed* (1812), and posterity has largely vindicated him, for nearly two centuries later his work is still cited in bibliographies of the theatre as the standard authority for the period concerned.

Others among Jones's more significant works were *A New Biographical Dictionary* (1794), which ran to eight editions; *Sheridan Improved: a General and Pronouncing Dictionary of the English Language* (3rd edn, 1798), which was likewise much reprinted; an edition of the poems of Thomas Gray, published in 1800; a memoir of David Garrick (1808); and a self-penned history of Poland (1795). A contemporary directory commended him as 'an industrious compiler' (A. Chalmers, *Appendix to the General Biographical Dictionary*, 1820).

Jones was an enthusiastic freemason. For a time he was editor of the *Freemason's Magazine* (c.1807), and he wrote *Masonic Miscellanies in Poetry and Prose* (1797) and *A Vindication of Masonry from a Charge of Having Given Rise to the French Revolution*, which was posthumously published in 1847. He was a fully instructed member of the Harodim lodge and the Harodim chapter; he also belonged to the lodge of antiquity and was married, it appears for the second time, to the niece of William Preston (1742–1818), its deputy grand master. This was almost certainly the Jemima mentioned in his will of 28 June 1821, in which he described himself as being of Red Lion Passage, off Fleet Street. Jones was nominated the first lecturer in a series of masonic lectures endowed by Preston and produced an updated edition of the latter's *Illustrations of Masonry* (1821). Such patronage notwithstanding, his devotion to the craft appears to have contributed largely to his professional ruin; an obituarist wrote that 'he devoted too larger portions of his evenings to the lodge and other convivial parties, being himself a very good-tempered and agreeable companion and singing and excellent song', and that this, compounded by his spat with Gilchrist, meant that in later life 'nearly all literary employment was denied to him' (GM, 90–91).

Jones died of dropsy in Upper King Street (later Southampton Row), Holborn, on 20 December 1827. He left his wife stock in the Stationers' Company and some property in Serjeant's Inn, but the absence of a valuation for his estate in the death duty register suggests that he died impecunious.

H. J. SPENCER

Sources GM, 1st ser., 98/1 (1828), 90–91 · DNB · D. Griffiths, ed., *The encyclopedia of the British press, 1422–1992* (1992) · R. A. Wells, *The rise and development of organised freemasonry* (1986) · will, PRO, PROB 11/1739/209 · death duty register, PRO, IR 26/1165/174 · C. J. Lowe, *A guide to reference and bibliography for theatre research* (1971) · IGI
Wealth at death see will, PRO, PROB 11/1739/209; PRO, death duty registers, IR 26/1165/174

Jones, Sir Theophilus (d. 1685), army officer, was born in Ireland, the son of Lewis *Jones (1560–1646), Church of Ireland clergyman and later bishop of Killaloe, and Mabel (b. c.1580), daughter of Arland Ussher and Margaret Stanihurst. He was a younger brother of Henry *Jones (1605–1682) and Michael *Jones (d. 1649); another brother,

Ambrose *Jones [see under Jones, Lewis], died in 1678. Nothing is known of Theophilus's early life.

Jones, who was in the service of the absent lord lieutenant of Ireland, the earl of Leicester, when rebellion broke out in October 1641, was successively captain, major, and lieutenant-colonel of Lord Conway's 'British regiment', which was established for service in Ulster by the English parliament in December 1641. He commanded the garrison in Dungannon after its capture by General Leslie in September 1642, and yielded it after a five-week siege some twelve months later. Jones was one of two men knighted by the marquess of Ormond after his appointment to the lord lieutenancy in January 1644. When the Scots entered the English civil war and Robert Monroe received a parliamentary commission to command all the Ulster forces, Jones refused to admit him to Lisburn (Lisnegarvey) in May 1644. Thereafter, he co-operated with Monroe militarily, while supporting Ormond's attempts to assert authority over the royalist forces in Ulster. He refused to subscribe to the covenant, defied the authority of the parliamentary commissioners who arrived in Ulster in October 1645, and resisted the parliamentary appointment of Lord Blaney as colonel of the 'British regiment', acting as its commander in place of Ormond's absent appointee, Edward Conway. With other officers, Jones published a declaration protesting against the proceedings of the commissioners in January 1646.

Jones came to Dublin after the proclamation of the first Ormond peace in July 1646, and was sent in December to garrison Kells, where he was surprised and captured some months later by Henry Roe O'Neill. Despite efforts to secure his release he remained in captivity until a cessation was agreed between Owen Roe O'Neill and Michael Jones in August 1648. By October he was in London, where he received permission to recruit soldiers for his brother Michael's regiment and a troop for himself. Also in 1648 Jones married Alicia (1625–1690), daughter of Arthur Ussher and his wife, Judith, daughter of Sir Robert Newcomen.

In the early summer of 1649 Jones was sent to Ireland with provisions and money in advance of Cromwell's expeditionary force. When Cromwell left Dublin for Drogheda, he remained behind as governor. Having been replaced by Colonel Hewson, he returned to the north and contributed to the defeat of Munroe and the royalists near Lisburn in November 1649. He was given a regiment shortly afterwards, apparently taking over his brother Michael's command after his death, and remained in continuous action thereafter. It was Jones who accepted the surrender of the last garrison to fall, Cloghoughter, in co. Cavan, on 27 April 1653. Although his regiment was disbanded in the same year, he became major of Lieutenant-General Ludlow's regiment and retained command of a troop throughout the protectorate, latterly of Henry Cromwell's life-guard.

In 1654 Jones received a grant of the forfeited Sarsfield estate at Lucan in co. Dublin. He was a member of all three protectorate parliaments, representing the King's county–Longford–Westmeath constituency in 1654 and 1656–7, when he voted in favour of the kingship petition, and co. Dublin in 1659. He was also appointed a commissioner in the act for the security of the lord protector's person passed on 27 November 1656.

When the Irish army was 'remodelled' by the restored Rump in the summer of 1659, Jones was cashiered. He was one of the prime movers in the surprise of Dublin Castle on 13 December following, served as a member of the ad hoc commission that assumed control of the army, and played a leading part in the meeting of the council of officers which anticipated General Monck by declaring for the readmission of the excluded members of the Long Parliament on 16 February 1660. He represented co. Dublin in the general convention of Ireland, was among the signatories of an invitation to Charles II to come to Ireland, and was one of the commissioners sent to negotiate with the restored king in May 1660. His extensive campaigning links, in particular with the royalist 'old Scots' in the north, and his connections with the Dublin office-holding élite, reinforced by his marriage to Sir William Ussher's granddaughter, gave him considerable influence, and he and his brother Henry, together with Colonel Arthur Hill, were reported to have effective control over the army during the critical months of transition.

Although his services were acknowledged and rewarded after the Restoration, Jones's part in public life was short-lived. On 30 July 1660 he was appointed clerk of the pells; in December he was created a privy counsellor; on 21 January 1661, with the Coote brothers and his brother Henry, he was confirmed in all the lands 'settled or intended to have been settled' upon him 'by any gift, grant or order of any power or usurped power' (CSP Ire., 1660–62, 189); on 28 February he was nominated as scoutmaster general; and in April he was appointed to the commission for executing the king's declaration for settling Irish lands. In the Restoration parliament he represented County Meath, and moved the private bill to raise £30,000 for the use of the duke of Ormond on his appointment to the lord lieutenancy in 1662. In the following year he disclosed an attempt on the part of discontented former army officers to secure his support for a plot to seize Dublin Castle and kidnap Ormond.

Jones had acquired substantial interests in co. Sligo, and these were confirmed to him in February 1670, but his chief prize eluded him. In 1663 the court of claims confirmed him in possession of the Sarsfield estate only for the life of the Catholic claimant. This decision was incorporated in the Act of Explanation (1665), where it was qualified by a proviso that not only stipulated that he should be reprised with lands of equal value elsewhere but exempted him from the general obligation to relinquish one-third of his acquisitions to provide for the restitution of lands to innocent Catholics. In the event, the reversionary heir married the duke of Monmouth's sister, and the crown purchased Jones's interest in the estate in 1674 and granted him £800 a year in concealed land to be discovered elsewhere. Jones's grudging response was to relinquish the estate by degrees, surrendering only as much at a time as he had succeeded in discovering in concealed lands. The process seems to have been complete by the time of his death, on 2 January 1685. Jones was buried on 8 January at Naas, co. Kildare. He was succeeded by his son, Arthur, and was also survived by his wife and two daughters, Judith and Mabella.   AIDAN CLARKE

Sources papers, incl. Jones's account of the 1663 conspiracy, TCD, MS 844 · *The manuscripts of the marquis of Ormonde*, [old ser.], 3 vols., HMC, 36 (1895–1909), vols. 1–2 · *Calendar of the manuscripts of the marquess of Ormonde*, new ser., 8 vols., HMC, 36 (1902–20), vols. 1–2 · *CSP Ire.*, 1660–70 · *CSP dom.*, 1648–50; 1653–4; 1670–85 · *The memoirs of Edmund Ludlow*, ed. C. H. Firth, 2 vols. (1894) · T. Carte, *An history of the life of James, duke of Ormonde*, 3 vols. (1735–6); new edn, pubd as *The life of James, duke of Ormond*, 6 vols. (1851) · *The journals of the House of Commons of the kingdom of Ireland*, 1 (1796) · [E. Borlase], *The history of the execrable Irish rebellion* (1680) · A. Clarke, *Prelude to Restoration in Ireland* (1999) · L. J. Arnold, *The Restoration land settlement in county Dublin, 1660–1688* (1993) · D. Stevenson, *Scottish covenanters and Irish confederates: Scottish-Irish relations in the mid-seventeenth century* (1981) · *Mercurius Politicus* (1–8 July 1652) · [E. Hogan], *The history of the warr of Ireland from 1641 to 1653* (1873) · W. A. Shaw, *The knights of England*, 2 (1906), 217 · [G. D. Burtchaell], *Irish Builder*, 676 (15 Feb 1888)
Archives NA Ire., account books, deeds · TCD, account of the conspiracy to seize Dublin Castle, MS 844

Jones, Theophilus (1759–1812), county historian, the son of Hugh Jones (d. 1799), Church of England clergyman, and his wife, Elinor (d. 1786), elder daughter of the historian Theophilus *Evans (1693–1767), was born in Lion Street, Brecon, on 18 October 1759. His father, curate of St David's Church, Brecon, was subsequently vicar of Llangamarch (in succession to his father-in-law, who resigned the living in his favour in 1763), vicar of Llywel, and prebendary of Boughrood. Theophilus Evans had a small estate, Llwyneinon, at Llangamarch and there is no doubt that the young Theophilus was deeply influenced and inspired by his grandfather, who bequeathed the estate and many of his books and papers to him. He was educated at Christ College, Brecon, and following articles with a local solicitor, he became a partner in a solicitor's office in the town and deputy registrar of the archdeanery of Brecon. On 13 November 1783 he married Mary Price (d. 1828) at St Brides, Pembroke.

Hugh Jones died in 1799 and the degree of security which his inheritance afforded Theophilus Jones, together with the support of his wife, allowed Theophilus to devote his time to researching and writing the history of his native county, although his partnership with Samuel Church was not formally dissolved until 1808. He was elected FSA in 1810. His post as deputy registrar, which he retained, enabled him to become thoroughly conversant with a range of documents relating to Brecknockshire parishes and to learn a great deal about their history, while his legal training had taught him to scrutinize this and other evidence closely and critically. Although he used other documents, including Hugh Thomas's manuscript 'Essay towards a history of Brecknockshire' (1698) and pedigrees (BL, MS Harley 2289), he did not restrict himself to written sources but collected legends and folklore and visited every parish, with the result that he was

able to draw also on topographic and place-name evidence. *The History of Brecknockshire* was published in two quarto volumes in 1805 and 1809 and was subsequently reprinted in one volume (1898), and 'enlarged by the notes collected by Sir Joseph Russell Bailey, bart., first Baron Glanusk' in four volumes (1909–1930), the 'Glanusk edition'.

Jones's work, which was conceived on an ambitious and wide-ranging scale, describes the general history, 'religion, laws, customs, manners, language and system of agriculture' of the county in the first volume and in the second describes the natural history, antiquities, and history of the individual parishes, their incumbents, and gentry families. Standing in the tradition of the new county histories of Wales of the late eighteenth and early nineteenth centuries, his *History* has been praised by Sir Glanmor Williams as the most systematic and best organized, 'decidedly the best of them' (Williams, 'Romantic and realist', 23). Jones was criticized for his neglect of puritanism and he was taken to task by Edward Williams (Iolo Morganwg), whose fabricated history of the bards Jones rejected uncompromisingly. He became one of the earliest and most severe critics of Edward Williams, condemning the 'meretricious ornaments' and 'senseless pantomime' which he perceived in his imagined history. Jones was in correspondence with a number of Welsh antiquaries, including Iolo Morganwg and his son Taliesin, Walter Davies (Gwallter Mechain), Edward Davies of Olveston, J. M. Treharne, and William Owen Pughe. He also wrote some essays, reviews, and published letters on Welsh history, tours, and antiquities in the *Cambrian Register* (1795, 1796) and in *Archaeologia* (1814), but a projected history of Radnorshire was not written and a translation of Ellis Wynne's *Gweledigaetheu y bardd cwsc* (1703) which Jones is said to have attempted and left unfinished was never published. He died on 15 January 1812 in Lion Street, Brecon, where he had lived since 1800, and was buried in the church of Llangamarch. His widow died on 22 July 1828.
                                                                          BRYNLEY F. ROBERTS

Sources *Theophilus Jones, FSA, historian: his life, letters, and literary remains*, ed. E. Davies (1905) · G. E. F. Morgan, *Biography of Mr Theophilus Jones* (1902) · G. Williams, 'Romantic and realist: Theophilus Evans and Theophilus Jones', *Archaeologia Cambrensis*, 140 (1991), 17–27 · G. J. Williams, *Iolo Morganwg a chywyddau'r ychwanegiad* (1926), 269–70 · *IGI* · *DNB* · *GM*, 1st ser., 82/1 (1812), 190
Archives NL Wales, corresp., MSS 1806, 1891, 4954, 6556, 13222–13224, 15257, 16098 · NL Wales, notes, MS 6543 · NL Wales, papers relating to Brecknockshire and Glamorganshire history and genealogy; proof sheets and MS notes of *History of Brecknockshire*, MSS 6611, 9599, 14553 | Cardiff Central Library, Tonn collection, corresp. with Edward Davies · NL Wales, Iolo Morganwg MSS
Likenesses Carnhuanawc [T. Price], sketch, repro. in Morgan, *Biography* · Carnhuanawc [T. Price], sketch, repro. in Davies, *Theophilus Jones*

Jones, Thomas [*known as* Twm Siôn Cati] (1532–1608/9), Welsh-language poet and genealogist, was born either on Lammas day or St Lawrence's day (1 or 10 August) 1532, the illegitimate son of Siôn ap Dafydd ap Madog ap Hywel Moethe of Porth-y-ffynnon, Tregaron, and Catrin, an illegitimate daughter of Maredudd ab Ieuan ap Robert (great-grandfather of Sir John Wynn of Gwydir). He is sometimes referred to by the ancestral name Moethe, and by 1559 was already known as Twm Siôn Cati (taking his mother's name in addition to his father's).

In 1559, described as 'gentleman', Jones was granted a pardon for *omnia escapia et cautiones* but two years later he appeared before Glamorgan great sessions on suspicion of felony. The uncalendared records of great sessions in Wales will probably reveal more of his felonious early years. Tradition (by about 1615) recounts his prospering in Brecon in early life (he later married a sister of Richard Price of Brecon); one Thomas Jones was bailiff of Brecon in 1569. By 1572 he was a buyer of land near Porth-y-ffynnon, his ancestral home.

The earliest reference to a pedigree drawn by Jones is by Gruffudd Hiraethog (d. 1564) in Peniarth MS 133 in the National Library of Wales (page 25), the earliest to a dated roll is in 1572. He may have been the first to perceive that there was a good market among the Welsh gentry for attractive heraldic pedigree rolls. At least fifteen original rolls compiled by him survive, and there is evidence in copies for well over twenty more. These rolls date from 1572 to 1608. The rolls up to about 1600 are written in italic by several good scribes, one of whom is known by name, Richard Adams, 'paynter of Ludlow, servant to Mr Thomas Jones', active in 1590–91. To judge by Thomas Jones's coarse signature in Egerton MS 2585, folio 80, in the British Library, none of these rolls is in the hand of the compiler himself, nor any of the genealogical manuscripts that have sometimes been attributed to him. The later rolls are by other scribes in secretary script. In a roll of 1608 he describes himself as 'principal heraulde for all Wales'. Whatever may have been his relationship to the College of Arms, it must have been an informal one.

That Jones in his later years was more than a mere genealogist, and was probably an engaging companion, is attested by the quality of his associates. He was on friendly terms with John Dee (a distant cousin) by 1579, and visited him as late as 1596 during Dee's sad last years in Manchester, 'and rode back toward Wales again—13 day—to meet the cattle coming' (Dee's diary). He is extravagantly praised by Siôn Dafydd Rhys in his *Cambrobrytannicae Cymraecaeve linguae institutiones* (1592), for his pre-eminence in knowledge of bardic art; a copy of a bardic grammar of his survives in University of Wales, Bangor, MS 2. Poems show his intimacy with the bards Dafydd Benwyn, Sils ap Siôn, Siôn Tudur, Siôn Mawddwy, and others. The few of his own poems that survive suggest that satire and bawdry may have been his forte. Among his antiquarian associates were George Owen, Sir John Wynn, and Lewys Dwnn. He claimed to have been acknowledged as a kinsman by Lord Burghley (also descended from Hywel Moethe). His local standing is indicated by his stewardship of the lordship of Caron in 1601 in which year, so he alleged in a long complaint to the Star Chamber, the vicar of Tregaron led several attacks by armed mobs against him and his household, and tried to hang John Moethe, his son.

Jones's will mentions his son-in-law, Griffith David, and his base son, John Moethe (also a genealogist). Nothing is known of Jones's daughter, or the mother of John. In 1607 he married, within weeks of her husband's death, Joan (b. 1542), the aged widow of Thomas Williams of Ystrad-ffin, a daughter of Sir John Price or Prise. This led to accusations in the court of Star Chamber that he had tried to alter the will of Thomas Williams to Joan's advantage. He made his own will on 17 May 1608. It was proved on 25 May 1609. Within a year Joan married Sir George Devereux.

The posthumous fame of Twm Siôn Cati as robber and wit and friend of the poor was for two centuries sustained, and doubtless coloured, by oral tradition, though a few references occur in manuscripts, in connection with Welsh poetry, the earliest about 1615. His fame reached a wide public in 1823 through a sketch, *Twm John Catty, the Welsh Robin Hood* (1822), and a play, *The Welsh Rob Roy* (1823), both by W. F. Deacon, and was firmly established by the often reprinted novel of T. J. Llewelyn Prichard, *The Adventures and Vagaries of Twm Shon Catti* (1828). It found a new audience in a trilogy by T. Llew Jones, *Y ffordd beryglus* (1963), *Ymysg lladron* (1965), and *Dial o'r diwedd* (1968), which has become a Welsh children's classic.

DANIEL HUWS

Sources J. F. Jones, 'Thomas Jones of Tregaron alias Twm Shon Catti (1530–1609)', *Transactions of the Carmarthenshire Antiquarian Society*, 29 (1939), 77–87 · D. H. Evans, 'Twm Siôn Cati', *Coleg Dewi a'r fro*, ed. D. P. Davies (1984) · M. P. Siddons, *The development of Welsh heraldry*, vols. 1–3 (1991–3) · M. P. Siddons, *Welsh pedigree rolls* (1996) · F. Jones, 'An approach to Welsh genealogy', *Transactions of the Honourable Society of Cymmrodorion* (1948), 303–466 · great sessions, NL Wales, 22/31 · probate records, NL Wales, SD 1609/20 · Gogerddan deeds, NL Wales, 614, 670 · *Welsh Gazette* (24 May 1928) · *Welsh Gazette* (31 May 1928) · *N&Q*, 2 (1850), 12 · S. R. Meyrick, *The history and antiquities of the county of Cardigan* (1808) · D. C. Rees, *The history of Tregaron* (1936) · John Dee's diary, Bodl. Oxf., MS Ashmole 487 · R. J. Roberts, 'John Dee and the matter of Britain', *Transactions of the Honourable Society of Cymmrodorion* (1991), 129–43
Wealth at death goods and chattels £139 5s.; also land: will and inventory

Jones, Thomas (c.1550–1619), Church of Ireland archbishop of Dublin and lord chancellor of Ireland, was born in Middleton, Lancashire, the younger son of Henry Jones of Middleton. Lodge's *Peerage* and Mason's history of St Patrick's Cathedral both state that his father was Sir Roger Jones, alderman of London, but other sources suggest that Sir Roger was Thomas's brother. Thomas matriculated sizar from Christ's College, Cambridge, in November 1565. He commenced his BA studies in 1569 and took his degree in 1570. He proceeded MA in 1573.

Jones went to live in Ireland in 1574, shortly after his ordination. He was immediately taken under the wing of Adam Loftus, archbishop of Dublin. It is clear that Jones spent many years as part of the household of the archbishop and may have received some of his early education there. In 1577 he became chancellor of St Patrick's Cathedral, Dublin, an office he held until 1611; in 1581 he also became dean of St Patrick's. Jones married Margaret, the widow of John Douglas. She was the sister of Loftus's wife and the daughter of Adam Purdon of Lurgan Race, co. Louth. Jones and his wife had five children, but two died young. Their son Roger Jones was made a peer in 1628, becoming Viscount Ranelagh. Their daughter Margaret was married to Gilbert Domville, clerk of the hanaper, and their daughter Jane was the wife of Henry Piers or Pierce of Tristernagh, with whom she had eight children.

Jones was an active preacher during his early years in Ireland. From 1580 until 1582 he was employed by the Dublin administration to visit Roman Catholics imprisoned for association with the Baltinglass and Nugent conspiracies. His task was to encourage confessions and exhort them to conform to the established church. Jones also escorted a number of prisoners to the scaffold, and his report on the deaths of three of these captives is one of the most vivid accounts of judicial execution to be found among the Irish state papers. On 18 April 1584 Queen Elizabeth wrote to the lords justices of Ireland that Jones should receive the bishopric of Meath, left vacant by the death of Hugh Brady. He was promoted by letters patent dated 10 May 1584 and consecrated on 12 May. On 6 June the Irish privy council expressed its wish that Jones should become a member; he was sworn in on 22 June.

As bishop of Meath, Jones was frequently accused of venality. During the late 1580s, when the Dublin administration made an attempt to collect arrears of first fruits from the Irish bishops, he was one of the most vociferous opponents of the effort, using the collectors 'most hardly' and being 'content to take anything but unwilling to part with any duty to Her Majesty' (PRO, SP 63/150/52, ii). In 1591 Roman Catholic recusants believed that Jones had brought about the execution of a Catholic schoolmaster, Michael Fitzsimons, in order to obtain Fitzsimons's lands in co. Meath. It was the view of some of the queen's councillors that the bishop paid insufficient attention to the religious well-being of his diocese. In 1589 he was forced to defend himself against charges of dilatoriness, assuring Secretary Walsingham that he was not 'unmindful' of his duty to his diocese and promising to be 'more diligent hereafter' (PRO, SP 63/149/28). In 1600 the queen was informed that between Dublin and Athlone there were 'so few churches standing as will scarcely make a plural number and so few pastors to teach or preach the word, as in the most of them there is not so much as a reading minister' (CSP Ire., 1600, 273). The bishop of Meath was urged to 'give over his former profane way of life and to give himself more to preaching and travailling in the ways of his calling' (ibid.). Jones pleaded that many church buildings had, in fact, been pulled down by soldiers.

Bishop Jones was probably more effective in secular affairs. He had brought odium on his head by officiating at the marriage of the earl of Tyrone to Mabel Bagenal, which alliance had been violently opposed by the bride's brother, the military commander Sir Henry Bagenal. However, during the Nine Years' War (1594–1603), though he was more than once accused of having passed information to Tyrone, Jones seems to have played an energetic role in the prosecution of hostilities. He participated in negotiations with Tyrone and was frequently present at the diocesan house at Ardbraccan in co. Meath, though

military skirmishes took place not far away. He gathered intelligence at the episcopal house, with several individuals passing information to the administration through him. Towards the end of 1599 Tyrone drew up a proclamation and twenty-two articles listing his demands. It was framed in a manner which he hoped would gain him the support of the gentry of the English pale. It is uncertain how widely the material was published and, though copies were acquired by messengers and spies, it appears that it may not, in fact, have reached the palesmen. Bishop Jones, however, was present at a meeting of the Dublin council when it received a copy of the documents and he put aside all business in order to compose a reply, entitled 'The answer of a faithful servant to his sovereign prince to a seditious libel signed by Tyrone'. In the event it was felt by the Irish secretary Geoffrey Fenton and others that, as the populace had for the most part not seen Tyrone's proclamation, Jones's answer would merely cause confusion and it was therefore not published. Nevertheless, it reveals interesting information about Jones's own political and religious thinking. Central to his philosophy was the idea that a prince drew his authority from God and must always be obeyed. The sword, he declared, was 'by God's divine ordinance' committed to the prince and subjects had 'no warrant in the book of God' to take up the sword against their prince. Such action was never 'just and laudable war but an unjust commotion and rebellious uproar' (Marsh's Library, MS 23/1/19, no. 767, 'Answer', fol. 5).

This comment reflects the contemporary acceptance of divinely imposed hierarchy and the necessity for a prescribed structure of duties so that order could be preserved. As Jones made clear, this encompassed the duty of servant to master, child to parent, wife to husband, subject to prince. No absolution from such duties was possible. This was the case even if a prince were judged to be a heretic. Jones recounted the fate of Ladislav of Hungary who broke his oath to the Islamic Turkish emperor, showing that it was the Turk who successfully called on God to strike down his enemy, thereby restoring order. Deposing princes, he wrote, 'is a particular thing belonging unto God … he taketh away kings and setteth up kings' (Marsh's Library, MS 23/1/19, no. 767, 'Answer', fol. 8). Both scripture and the church fathers upheld this view, while the apostles never claimed the power to depose a prince. Thus Jones denied the right of the pope to excommunicate Queen Elizabeth, noting that 'God doth expressly command us even to obey wicked princes'. He stressed that the temporal power of the clergy was limited, adding that:

> such as are called to the service of God in his church have a regiment indeed but it is distinct from the temporal power and state and the regiment of theirs is by counsel and persuasion not by terror or compulsion. It reaches not into the goods or lands of private men.   (ibid., fol. 9)

Shortly after the accession of James I in 1603, Jones joined with Archbishop Loftus in composing a plea to the new monarch urging the banishment of Roman Catholic priests and that the people be compelled to hear reforming preachers. On the death of Loftus, Jones, with the support of Lord Deputy Chichester, was appointed archbishop of Dublin on 8 November 1605—the king also having issued, on 14 October, letters decreeing his appointment as lord chancellor of Ireland. On 22 November 1605 a group of recusants appeared before the Dublin Star Chamber and were committed to Dublin Castle until they should conform and take the oath of supremacy. Most were eventually fined and released upon recognizances. This was the beginning of a series of stern anti-recusant measures supported by Jones which, though likened by the Jesuit Christopher Holywood to 'the fury of the wolves' (Lennon, 181), are generally judged to have encouraged the Catholic counter-Reformation rather than increased conformity.

A claim by Archbishop Jones that Lord Howth had visited Kate Fitton, a married lady in co. Meath, for the purposes of an intrigue, opened an extraordinary and lengthy quarrel between the two men which occupied much of Jones's attention between 1608 and 1610. In 1614 Jones received the degree of doctor of divinity *honoris causa* from Trinity College, Dublin. A diocesan visitation in 1615 revealed that Jones had by then acquired thirty-eight preachers for Dublin's archdiocese, along with forty reading ministers, though it is clear that the archbishop by no means considered these sufficient. He also maintained a school in Dublin city and another at St Patrick's. Between 1613 and 1615 Jones twice held office as lord justice. He died at the episcopal palace of St Sepulchre's, Dublin, 'at five of the clock' on the morning of 10 April 1619 and was buried at St Patrick's Cathedral.

HELEN COBURN WALSHE

Sources PRO, state papers Ireland (Elizabeth I), SP 63 · CSP Ire., 1509–1625 · H. Morgan, 'Faith and fatherland or queen and country? An unpublished exchange between O'Neill and the state at the height of the Nine Years' War', *Dúiche Néill*, 9 (1994), 9–65 · Marsh's Library, Dublin, MS 23/1/19, no. 767 [copy of Bishop Jones's 'Answer'] · J. S. Brewer and W. Bullen, eds., *Calendar of the Carew manuscripts*, 6 vols., PRO (1867–73) · J. Morrin, ed., *Calendar of the patent and close rolls of chancery in Ireland for the reigns of Henry VIII, Edward VI, Mary, and Elizabeth*, 2 vols. (1861–2) · J. Lodge, *The peerage of Ireland*, rev. M. Archdall, rev. edn, 7 vols. (1789) · W. M. Mason, *History … of the cathedral of St Patrick's* (1819) · Venn, *Alum. Cant.* · M. V. Ronan, ed., 'The royal visitation of Dublin, 1615', *Archivium Hibernicum*, 8 (1941), 1–55 · C. Lennon, *The lords of Dublin in the age of the Reformation* (1989) · W. A. Phillips, ed., *History of the Church of Ireland*, 2 (1934) · DNB

Wealth at death considerable property and chattels: CSP Ire., 63 ser.; Mason, *History*

Jones, Sir Thomas (1614–1692), judge and law reporter, born on 13 October 1614, was the second son of Edward Jones (*d.* 1648), of Sandford, Shropshire, and Mary, daughter of Robert Powell, of Whittington Park, Shropshire. He was educated at Shrewsbury School and admitted as a pensioner at Emmanuel College, Cambridge, on 9 November 1629 (BA 1632). He became a student of Lincoln's Inn on 6 May 1629 and was called to the bar on 17 March 1634. About 1640 he married Jane, daughter of Daniel Barnard of Chester, and they had five sons and six daughters. Jones started his political and legal career in Shrewsbury, was

elected alderman in 1638, and was appointed town clerk (1660–62). During the civil war he was a moderate royalist, but he conformed to the Commonwealth. With the Restoration he trimmed again and became a devoted loyalist to the crown. Jones, 'a great countenancer of the Presbyterian party' (HoP, *Commons, 1660–90*, 665), was an elected member of the Convention for Shrewsbury in 1660 and was re-elected to the Cavalier Parliament in 1661. During this decade he was comparatively inactive at Westminster and he pursued his legal career in Wales and the marches. At Lincoln's Inn he was called to the bench in May 1660 and was advanced to the degree of serjeant-at-law in 1669. He served on circuits for north Wales (1662–70). In the next decade Jones's career took an upward turn. In 1671 he was promoted to be chief justice of the north Wales circuit, became a king's serjeant, and was knighted. An opponent described Jones as 'almost famished for preferment, and a great wheeler to the projectors' (ibid.). On 13 April 1676 his political services in parliament were rewarded by appointment as a judge of the king's bench and on 29 September 1683 he was advanced to be chief justice of the court of common pleas.

Roger North in his *Examen* described Jones as:

> a very reverend and learned judge, a gentleman, and impartial, but being of Welsh extraction was apt to be warm, and when much offended often showed his heats in a rubor of countenance set off by his grey hairs, but appeared in no other disorder, for he restrained himself in due bounds and temper, and seldom or never broke the laws of his gravity. (North, 563)

Lord Nottingham, addressing Jones on his king's bench appointment, also spoke of 'your great learning and ability … and of a very rare and unusual qualification, which accompanies it, a singular modesty and quietness of temper' (*Lord Nottingham's Chancery Cases*, 323). As a judge Jones took part in many cases that factional politics brought before the courts, being, as Foss puts it, 'engaged in most of the political trials that disgraced the latter part of Charles's reign, and the commencement of that of James II' (Foss, *Judges*, 378). In 1677 Jones refused to interfere with the imprisonment of the earl of Shaftesbury by order of the House of Lords. In Trinity term 1680 the House of Commons ordered his impeachment and that of Chief Justice Scroggs for dismissing the Middlesex grand jury who were about to present the duke of York as a papist recusant, but he was saved by the prorogation of the second Exclusion Parliament. He took part in the trials of Fitzharris, Dr Plunket, and Stephen Colledge in 1681 and that of William, Lord Russell, in 1683. During the Popish Plot trials Jones appears to have been a believer in the testimony of Titus Oates and other informers, but as with Scroggs and others he later found reason to change his mind. He pronounced judgment in the *quo warranto* proceedings against the City of London in 1683 and was rewarded by succeeding Francis North as chief justice of the common pleas. He continued to display considerable severity in the subsequent trials of Fernley, Ring, Elizabeth Gaunt, and Alderman Cornish (the attainder of the latter being reversed at the revolution of 1688). But eventually he found himself unable to comply with the king's wish to enforce the royal prerogative of dispensation: on 21 April 1686 he and three other judges were dismissed. According to his son he told the king that

> he was not sorry for himself to be laid aside, being old and worn-out in his service, but that his Majesty should expect such a construction of the law from him, as he could not honestly give, and that none but indigent, ignorant, or ambitious people would give their judgments as he expected. (HoP, *Commons, 1660–90*, 666)

Another less well-authenticated account credits Jones with even more forthright language, for when the king said that he would have the twelve judges of his opinion, he is said to have replied that his majesty might find twelve judges of his opinion but scarcely twelve lawyers.

Jones then retired to his home, Carreghofa, Montgomeryshire, but faced at the revolution of 1688 an accusation by the House of Commons that in 1680 he had rejected a plea by their serjeant-at-arms who, on trial for extortion, had pleaded that he had acted under orders of the house. This was voted a breach of privilege and Jones (together with the former chief justice Pemberton) was taken into custody on 19 July 1689, but was released on prorogation a fortnight later. Thereafter he was undisturbed and he died at Carreghofa on 31 May 1692. He was buried on 3 June at Shrewsbury in St Alkmund's Church, in which there is a monument to his memory. Jones's political career earned for him something of the character of a time-server and his judicial career has been often adversely criticized for harshness and severity in the conduct of criminal trials, but it is clear that on the critical question of dispensations he was not afraid to assert his judicial conscience. His principal contribution to the law was not so much in his work as a judge as in his authorship of a useful volume of law reports that covered the years 1667–85, published posthumously in 1695 in the professional law French, but afterwards, in 1729, with translations into English.   D. E. C. YALE

Sources HoP, *Commons, 1660–90*, 2.665–6 · DWB · E. Foss, *Biographia juridica: a biographical dictionary of the judges of England … 1066–1870* (1870), 378–9 · D. E. C. Y. [D. E. C. Yale], 'Jones, Sir Thomas', *Biographical dictionary of the common law*, ed. A. W. B. Simpson (1984) · Holdsworth, *Eng. law*, vol. 6 · *Lord Nottingham's chancery cases*, ed. D. E. C. Yale, 1, SeldS, 73 (1957), 317, 322–4 · R. North, *Examen, or, An enquiry into the credit and veracity of a pretended complete history* (1740) · VCH *Shropshire*, 3.264 · IGI · Venn, *Alum. Cant.*
Likenesses W. Claret, oils, Lincoln's Inn, London · R. Thompson, mezzotint (after W. Claret?), BM

Jones, Thomas (1618/19–1665), classical and Hebrew scholar, was born at Nanteos, Cardiganshire, the son of Edward Jones of Nanteos and Margaret, daughter of James Lewis of Aber-nant bychan. He matriculated from Oriel College, Oxford, on 29 May 1635, aged sixteen, graduated BA on 12 February 1639, and was elected in that year to a fellowship at Merton College, proceeding MA on 4 June 1644. During 1647 he travelled in France and Italy as tutor to George, son of Sir Nathaniel Brent, warden of Merton.

He returned to Oxford in 1649, submitted to the parliamentary visitors, and was given a fellowship at Jesus College while apparently retaining that at Merton. On 18 May 1659 he proceeded BCL and DCL.

Jones was recognized as a Greek and Hebrew scholar, and published in 1660 *De origine dominii* and *Prolusiones academicae: hisce praemittitur oratio inauguralis*. Having been deputy to Richard Zouch, professor of civil law, in 1661, following Zouch's death he unsuccessfully petitioned Charles II for the post; his appeal was supported by Brian Duppa, bishop of Winchester, and Thomas Clayton, regius professor of medicine. In his turn, Jones nominated Clayton for the wardenship of Merton College. Clayton, as a 'stranger', was not the first choice of the other senior Merton fellows, and the sub-warden, Alexander Fisher, himself a candidate of the majority of fellows, was asked to exclude Jones from the voting. He refused, but the resulting disputed election left the decision in the hands of the visitor, Archbishop William Juxon. Juxon, dying and under pressure from Clayton's brother-in-law, the master of ceremonies, Sir Charles Cotterell, chose Clayton. The fellows barred the gate of Merton College against Clayton; Jones attempted twice to install Clayton in the warden's lodgings but was unsuccessful. Only after three weeks' 'siege' did the fellows give way, under threat of force, and allow Clayton to take up his wardenship. Anthony Wood suggests that Jones was 'ambitious, discontented, covetous, and destitute of preferment' (*Life and Times*, 1.394) and that, knowing this, Clayton used him to achieve his aims. Any rewards that Clayton might have promised Jones for his support in the election were not forthcoming, and Jones seems to have had a mental breakdown.

Jones moved to London in 1661 or 1662 to follow a career in law at Doctors' Commons but rumours of his mental condition preceded him. Work was not forthcoming and Jones's mind deteriorated further. He died of the plague in Bread Street or Wood Street in the autumn of 1665 which, according to Anthony Wood, was 'a just reward for a knave and a rogue' (*Life and Times*, 1.395).

D. L. THOMAS, rev. J. H. CURTHOYS

Sources B. W. Henderson, *Merton College* (1899) · G. H. Martin and J. R. L. Highfield, *A history of Merton College, Oxford* (1997) · G. C. Brodrick, *Memorials of Merton College*, OHS, 4 (1885) · *The life and times of Anthony Wood*, ed. A. Clark, 1, OHS, 19 (1891) · Foster, *Alum. Oxon.* · Wood, *Ath. Oxon.*, new edn, 3.707–9

Jones, Thomas (d. 1682), Church of England clergyman, was born in Oswestry, Shropshire, the son of John Williams of Oswestry. Following the Welsh custom he took his surname from the first name of his father, whose family were originally from Pwllheli, Caernarvonshire. Thomas received his early education in Oswestry and entered Jesus College, Oxford, in 1641. However, he left the city on the outbreak of civil war in the following year and did not return until its surrender to parliamentarian forces in 1646. He subsequently subscribed to the covenant and by the authority of the university visitors obtained a fellowship at University College in 1649, graduating BA in 1650 and proceeding MA in 1651.

On 4 September 1654 Jones was approved by the triers and was certified to hold the rectory of Castle Caereinion in Montgomeryshire, and seems to have mastered enough Welsh to preach in that language. He was ejected after the Restoration in 1661 and was replaced by Rice Wynne, who had been dispossessed of the living in 1645 by the propagators for scandalous living. Some time after he was appointed chaplain to Richard Vaughan, second earl of Carbery, lord president of the council in the marches, at Ludlow, and his conformity to the established church became evident with his appointment in 1663 as domestic and naval chaplain to James, duke of York. When Anne Hyde, the duke's wife, announced her intention of converting to Roman Catholicism, Jones accused George Morley, bishop of Winchester and her chaplain, of misguiding her and of being disloyal to the Church of England. He was dismissed from his post but, on 11 November 1665, obtained the rectory of Llandyrnog (then within the diocese of Bangor) under the great seal by the duke of York, where he remained in retirement.

The dispute with Morley continued, however. In 1670 Jones was fined £300 in the king's bench for slandering Morley in the presence of Robert Morgan, bishop of Bangor, calling him a 'promoter of popery and a subverter of the church of England' (Wood, *Ath. Oxon.*, 4.51). Matters did not end there because conflict arose between Jones and Morgan, who had supported Morley, following complaints by the churchwardens of Llandyrnog that Jones had refused to read the service from the accustomed reading desk. More importantly, Morgan wished also to see the rectory return to the bishops of Bangor since it had been held *in commendam* by them in the past. To pay Jones's slander fine his living was sequestered in 1670 which left him totally impoverished: 'I have had my fortunes wholly ruined', the embittered priest maintained in June 1681 in a letter to Dr Turner, his successor as York's chaplain, 'my good name wounded, my calling disturbed, my converse straitend, my senses questioned, and my truth and testimony at last attempted to be wrested from me' (*CSP dom.*, *1680–81*, 319).

Jones's ardent protestantism was demonstrated during the Popish Plot, engineered by Titus Oates in 1678, when he published a number of tracts defending the Church of England, including *Of the Heart and its Right Sovereign; and Rome No Mother-Church to England* (1678) and *A remembrance of the rights of Jerusalem above, in the great question, where is the true mother-church of Christians?* (1678). In 1681 he wrote *Some letters and papers from a late chaplain to the duke of York … touching the beginning of this plot and danger to the nation from masquerade protestants*. Although Jones was said to have refused the bishopric of Bangor in 1665 and then avidly to have sought it through the patronage of the duke of York in 1681 (on the false rumour of the then bishop's death), in both cases the allegations rest on insufficient evidence. Indeed, his consistent anti-popery, as displayed in his works, makes the latter story seem all the less likely. His final publication, which amounted to a recital of the charges against Morley, was entitled *Elymas the sorcerer, or, A memorial towards the discovery of the bottom of this Popish-Plot,*

publish'd upon the occasion of a passage in the late dutchess of York's declaration for changing her religion (1682). This work was answered by Richard Watson in July 1682 and later in *A Fuller Answer to Elymas the Sorcerer* (1683); Morley published his own vindication in prefaces to treatises published in 1683.

Jones's latter years were dismal, for his sight had deteriorated and his mental state had become a cause of concern. In his letter of 18 June 1681 to Turner he bemoaned his depressed state as a result of losing his chaplaincy for his anti-popish stance, and reiterated his bitter feelings towards his enemies. In a period of heightened religious tension and insecurity he took the opportunity to censure Morley and Morgan, both of whom he mistrusted as 'masquerade Protestants' in places of power in the church. He died on 8 October 1682 at Totteridge in Hertfordshire while a guest of Francis Charlton, brother-in-law of the puritan Richard Baxter. J. GWYNFOR JONES

Sources LPL, MS 997, bk 2, fol. 168 · Wood, *Ath. Oxon.*, new edn, 4.51–3 · Wood, *Ath. Oxon.: Fasti* (1820), 120, 162 · *CSP dom.*, *1680–81*, 319–20 · M. A. E. Green, ed., *Calendar of the proceedings of the committee for compounding … 1643–1660*, 5, PRO (1892), 3235 · *Bye-Gones Relating to Wales and the Border Counties*, [2] (1874–5) [4 Mar 1874] · *Bye-Gones Relating to Wales and the Border Counties*, [2] (1874–5) [20 Jan 1875] · D. R. Thomas, *Esgobaeth Llanelwy: the history of the diocese of St Asaph*, rev. edn, 2 (1911), 414; 3 (1913), 730 · T. Richards, *Religious developments in Wales, 1654–1662* (1923), 23, 111, 319 n. 2, 374, 440–42 · J. C. Morrice, *Wales in the seventeenth century: its literature and men of letters and action* (1918), 207–8 · DNB

Jones, Thomas [*known as* Thomas Jones yr Almanaciwr] (1648–1713), publisher and almanac maker, was born on 1 May 1648 at Tre'r-ddôl, near Corwen, Merioneth. His parents' names are unknown, but his father was a tailor, a trade which his son inherited. At some time in 1666 he joined the stream of masterless men who journeyed to London in search of fame and fortune. Having gained little success as a tailor, he turned to bookselling and began to describe himself as 'a lover of Learning, and Student in Astrology, and Autodidactus' (Jenkins, 'Sweating Astrologer', 163). In January 1679 he was granted sole rights for the compilation, printing, and publishing of an annual Welsh almanac, and from then until his death in 1713 he was known throughout Wales as Thomas Jones yr Almanaciwr (Thomas Jones the Almanac Maker).

Jones lived in Lower Moorfields and sold his wares in a variety of shops in Paul's Alley, Cobbs Court in Blackfriars, and Tower Hill. He rubbed shoulders with celebrities of Grub Street fame, including Tom Brown, Francis Moore (compiler of *Old Moore's Almanack*), and Tom D'Urfey, but came to despise the cut-throat world of printers and publishers and the crime and debauchery prevalent in the capital. Although he was a sharp and resourceful businessman, he was seldom able to steal a march over his rivals, and in faraway Wales shameless pedlars and booksellers made off with his profits. He yearned for the opportunity to return to his native land, and when the Printing Act was allowed to lapse in 1695, thereby enabling printers and publishers to set up presses in the provinces, he and his wife, Mary, packed their bags and established a printing office in the fashionable residential area of Hill's Lane in

Shrewsbury, a thriving provincial town which served as the natural capital of mid-Wales. From that time onwards until his death in 1713 Jones established a reputation as the most inventive and successful publisher of Welsh books. Indeed, he was chiefly responsible for Shrewsbury's pre-eminence as the printing capital of Wales in the first half of the eighteenth century.

Between 1680 and 1713 Jones published an annual Welsh almanac, and became widely known in Shrewsbury as the Stargazer and in his native land as the Sweating Astrologer. An irremediable hypochondriac, he contracted a variety of ailments and maladies, including a bizarre version of the sweating sickness which, he claimed, drew from his body twenty-eight barrels of sweat over a period of six years in the 1690s. His eagerly awaited almanacs sold much better than other ephemera not only because of their intriguing astrological guides (which were invariably couched in obscure and delphic language) but also because they included fascinating details of his medical condition. The Welsh almanac was also sprinkled with passages of wry humour and biting satire. Jones's forthright views about Welsh quislings and popish traitors, together with his running battles with rival almanac makers, kept sales buoyant and enlivened the printing scene in Wales and the borders.

Jones's thriving press, however, was not exclusively concerned with the production of entertaining, hastily prepared, and shoddily bound almanacs and ballads. An ardent patriot and champion of his ailing native tongue, Jones was determined to infuse new life into 'the old and most excellent British language'. His most valuable contribution in this direction was the publication of *Y Gymraeg yn ei disgleirdeb / The British Language in its Lustre* (1688), a substantial Welsh–English dictionary, and an enlarged version of Foulke Owen's *Cerdd-lyfr* (1696), an anthology of Welsh poems. He feared that the Welsh had been 'blotted out of the Books of Records' and that they were in serious danger of losing their language, literature, and history. As the patronage of the gentry dwindled alarmingly, he believed that it was necessary for the Welsh press to print the works of leading poets such as Huw Morys, Dafydd Manuel, and Owen Gruffydd, and also to publicize the newly revived eisteddfods, which were held annually in convivial taverns in Welsh market towns from around 1700 onwards. His prefaces to his books and almanacs invariably extolled the merits of the Welsh language and disparaged the Anglicizing gentry who were swiftly abandoning their native tongue.

A devout churchman and a fierce enemy of Catholicism and dissent, Jones ensured that his publications not only stiffened the cause of Anglicanism but also nourished anti-popish sentiments and Francophobia among readers. He published a Welsh version of the Popish Plot in 1684, a Welsh edition of the book of matins in 1683, a Welsh prayer book in 1687–8, and large numbers of devotional books, the most successful of which was a Welsh translation of Bunyan's *Pilgrim's Progress* in 1699. Even his bestselling ballads, which included tales of monstrous births,

grisly murders, and ill-fated courtships, had a moral sting in the tail.

Apart from the pecuniary motive, Jones's principal aim as a publisher was to provide humble readers with cheap, popular, and accessible reading material. With the aid of agents, booksellers, clergymen, and shopkeepers he established a remarkably successful system of book distribution which enabled his publications to reach the growing numbers of farmers, craftsmen, and artisans who were acquiring the reading habit in late Stuart Wales. During the 1680s the only literate parishioner in Llanfihangel Tre'r-beirdd, Anglesey, was a cooper, who taught the father of the celebrated Morris brothers to read by using Thomas Jones's publications. 'Who knows', wrote William Morris, 'but that you and I would be illiterate were it not for that old fellow … who taught our father … and so started the blessed gift' (Jenkins, 'Sweating Astrologer', 175). Welsh poets, understandably pleased to see their work in print, sang his praises loudly, though highbrow Welsh scholars were fiercely critical of him. Moses Williams was so infuriated by Jones's plagiarism and arrogance that he annotated his personal copy of *Y Gymraeg yn ei disgleirdeb* with the epithets 'Tom the Tailor' and 'Tom-ass'.

Thomas Jones died in Shrewsbury, aged sixty-five, on 6 August 1713, and was buried two days later in St Mary's parish church, Shrewsbury. A man of considerable, if sometimes misplaced, energy, Jones was rather more than a plausible rogue. His books, almanacs, and ballads reached a wider cross-section of Welsh society than ever before, and his contribution to the cultural and religious life of Wales was not inconsiderable. There is much truth in William Morris's grudging posthumous tribute: '[he was] an old fellow who, in spite of his ignorance, did a lot of good' (Jenkins, 'Sweating astrologer', 175).

GERAINT H. JENKINS

Sources T. Jones, *Almanac* (1680–1712) · G. H. Jenkins, *Thomas Jones yr Almanaciwr, 1648–1713* (1980) · G. H. Jenkins, '"The Sweating Astrologer": Thomas Jones the Almanacer', *Welsh society and nationhood*, ed. R. R. Davies and others (1984), 161–77 · M. Stephens, ed., *The Oxford companion to the literature of Wales* (1986), 324 · DWB · inventory, 1713, Lichfield RO, Staffordshire · NL Wales, MS 1244D, fol. 49 · W. Rowlands, *Cambrian bibliography / Llyfryddiaeth y Cymry*, ed. D. S. Evans (1869), 244
Likenesses engraving, 1683, NL Wales
Wealth at death £48 6s. 6d.: inventory of Thomas Jones, 1713, Lichfield Joint RO, Staffordshire.

Jones, Thomas (1742–1803), landscape painter, was born on 26 September 1742 at Trefonnen, near Llandrindod, Radnorshire, the second of sixteen children (nine surviving infancy) of Thomas Jones of Trefonnen (1711–1782), landowner, and his wife (and first cousin), Hannah Jones (1721–1789). Both his parents were dissenters. Thomas Jones grew up on his father's estate of Pencerrig, Radnorshire, for him a much-loved place. He was well educated by tutors and ministers in local grammar schools. In 1759 he entered Jesus College, Oxford, financed by a maternal uncle who intended him to enter the church (contrary to Jones's own inclinations). On the uncle's death in 1761,

Thomas Jones (1742–1803), by Giuseppe Marchi, 1768

Jones left Oxford, free to pursue his chosen career as a painter.

The chief source for Thomas Jones's life and work is his own highly entertaining journal (MS, priv. coll.; published as *Memoirs of Thomas Jones*, ed. A. P. Oppé; cited here as Jones). Jones explains that his journal was concluded in 1798, 'from short hints and *Memoranda* of a Diary which for many years I had been in the habit of keeping' (Jones, 140).

Training, and first fifteen years of exhibited work, 1761–1776
From November 1761 Jones spent a year in William Shipley's drawing school, where he became a firm friend of John Hamilton Mortimer, his frequent collaborator as well as companion on high-spirited excursions. Later he attended the life class in St Martin's Lane Academy, but gained no confidence in his ability to depict figures. Convinced that his 'natural bias' was towards landscape painting (Jones, 9), in March 1763 he persuaded Richard Wilson to take him as a pupil for two years. His journal includes a glimpse of Wilson rebuking Jones and his fellow pupils William Hodges and Joseph Farington for rowdiness: 'Gentlemen, this is not the way to rival Claude' (Jones, 10).

Jones exhibited over fifty works at the Society of Artists between 1765 and 1780. Some were specific views in England and Wales; others are less identifiable, such as the *View, after Nature* singled out by Horace Walpole in 1770 as a 'very fine picture' (Graves, *Soc. Artists*, 132). For a few years from 1769 Jones specialized in large landscapes designed as settings for episodes from history and literature. In

many of these Mortimer added the figures (his collaboration always being acknowledged). Jones himself considered *A Land-Storm, with the Story of Dido and Aeneas* (figures by Mortimer) to be 'one of the best Pictures I ever painted' (Jones, 19); exhibited in 1769, engraved by William Woollett in 1787, by *c*.1790 it had been acquired by Catherine the Great of Russia (Hermitage Museum, St Petersburg). Collaboration with Mortimer also produced *A Landscape, with the Death of Orpheus* (exh. 1770; two versions, one Yale U. CBA, the other priv. coll.). *The Bard, from Mr Gray's 'Ode'* (exh. 1774; engraved in mezzotint by John Raphael Smith, 1775; NMG Wales) treated a subject which Paul Sandby among others had already painted but which Jones, with his lifelong pride in being Welsh, invested with the full force of a national tragedy. Numerous commissions included view-painting (combined with amateur theatricals) for Oldfield Bowles of North Aston, Oxfordshire, and painting for Dr Benjamin Bates (patron of Mortimer, Wright of Derby, and others) *A View of the House … where Milton Resided during the Plague, and where he Wrote his 'L'allegro'* (exh. 1775; priv. coll.). Dr Bates also requested 'companion' oval landscapes in the two contrasting Miltonic moods of 'L'allegro' and 'Il penseroso' (exh.? 1775 or 1776), a commission congenial to Jones, who had already exhibited companion landscapes whose titles (for example *A Sunset*; *An Evening*, 1772) suggest response to atmosphere.

By 1770 Jones enjoyed some success as a landscape painter; in 1771 he was elected fellow of the Society of Artists, and served as a director of the society in 1773–4. He continued to work on commissioned and/or exhibitable pictures; but by 1770, when painting for his own pleasure, he had begun the unconventional habit of making small oil studies out of doors, painting 'little picturesque bits' of nature on primed paper small enough to fit into the lid of a painting-box (Jones, 22). In Radnorshire in 1772 he mentions making 'a good many Studies in Oil on paper' (ibid., 27). The most strikingly original of these are two views of the hillside from the terrace of Pencerrig (Tate collection; Birmingham Museum and Art Gallery). In these Jones surveys the landscape he loves and paints it directly, with 'the serene objectivity that he had extracted from the habit of painting outdoors' (Gowing, 20). On a long tour of England and Wales during 1775–6, executing commissions and painting (for himself) a very beautiful *View of Carneddau Mountain, from Pencerrig* (canvas; NMG Wales), Jones mentions that he made 'a number of Studies in Oil on thick primed paper—after Nature' (Jones, 38); but the fact that he neither lists nor describes them indicates that his small oils on paper were personal to himself, and would hardly have been deemed 'pictures' by contemporaries.

Italy, 1776–1783 By September 1776 Jones had resolved on a 'project that had been in agitation for some Years, and on which my heart was fixed' (Jones, 37): his visit to Italy. Having embarked on 16 October 1776, he arrived in Rome on 27 November ('a wet cold gloomy day', ibid., 53). Within weeks he recorded his delight in the new and uncommon Sensations I was filled [with] on my first traversing this beautiful and picturesque Country—Every scene seemed anticipated in some dream—It appeared Magick Land—In fact I had copied so many Studies of that great Man, & my Old Master, Richard Wilson … that I insensibly became familiarized with Italian Scenes, and enamoured of Italian forms.   (12 Dec 1776, ibid., 55)

Many of the canvases Jones painted in Italy pay homage to Wilson, but as a landscapist Jones is less meditative than his master. For Jones, the Roman Campagna seemed 'formed in a peculiar manner by Nature for the Study of the Landscape-Painter' (ibid., 66); but his countryman's interest in vegetation and the lie of the land overcrowds many of his large landscapes with detail. Few other painters in Italy took such pains over distinguishing between ilex and olive trees. Some of his landscapes in oil on canvas are on a large scale, such as *View of Lake Nemi* (priv. coll.) and *The Bay of Naples* (NMG Wales). Jones frequently painted in watercolour in Italy (and later, when working up his Italian sketches); it was the medium for some of his finest and most expressive works, such as *View of Ariccia* and *The Lake of Nemi with Genzano* (both Whitworth Art Gallery, Manchester). He developed a distinctive watercolour palette, notably using blues which range from the inkiest darks of deep water to the clear blues of soaring skies. In colour, as in much else, he was a nonconformist. Observing some Italian views which Jones showed at the Royal Academy in 1798, Joseph Farington RA remarked that they were 'very cold—like china' (Farington, *Diary*, 3.996): but Farington tended to agree with the art patron Sir George Beaumont, that landscapes should be predominantly brown.

Jones enjoyed the company of many artists in Rome, including William Pars, Jacob More, John Robert Cozens (always referred to as 'little Cousins'), Henry Tresham, and the sculptor Thomas Banks, to whom, in return for a picture, Jones sat in May 1778 for a bust (now unknown; possibly uncompleted). Ebullient, gregarious, occasionally truculent, and never forgetful of St David's day, Jones enjoyed excursions and diversions (vividly recounted in his journals); but he worked hard, filling his sketchbooks (notably a large Italian sketchbook of 1777–8; NMG Wales) with views often worked up years later. He writes sardonically of the 'English cavaliers' in Rome: 'Milordi Inglesi … who moved in a Circle of Superior Splendour' but, spoiled for choice, failed to buy his work (Jones, 56, 71); but he found a rewarding patron in Frederick Augustus Hervey, bishop of Derry (and later also fourth earl of Bristol), who in 1778 bought the large *View of Lake Albano, a Sun Set* (Yale U. CBA), the first picture Jones painted in Italy ('it took me 41 days'; ibid., 62) and the one which established his status among fellow artists then in Italy.

In the summer Jones found Rome intolerably hot; with the thermometer reading 95–7 degrees in the shade, he devised a near equivalent to painting in the open air: 'sitting in my Shirt and thin linnen Drawers without Stockens—with the Windows open—and in this dress I sat down to paint' (Jones, 63). He does not specify that he painted in oil on paper, but it is likely that he produced

some small, confrontational views in that medium which (like much of his work) are now untraced.

Jones twice visited Naples. On his first visit, travelling with the sculptor Giuseppe Plura, he arrived in Naples on 15 September 1778; the next day he climbed (and later memorably described) the slopes of the recently erupted Vesuvius. He stayed in Naples for five months, making numerous sketches of its surroundings, including Pozzuoli, Posilippo, Pompeii, Portici, and Sorrento; he also enjoyed the friendship of the Storace family of musicians. On 29 December 1778 his patron the bishop of Derry arrived (accompanied by 'Soane the Architect'). Waiting on the bishop the next morning, Jones found him 'combing and adjusting a small single Curl which was fixed by a String to his own Short Hair' (Jones, 83), before commissioning two large pictures: *A View on the Coast of Baja Including Mt Vesuvius and ye Islands* and *A View of the Rock at Terracina—a Storm* (both delivered in December 1781; now untraced).

Jones returned to Rome on 26 January 1779. Six months later he records taking on a 'Maid Servant'. This was in fact the start of twenty years' happy cohabitation with Maria Moncke (*née* Turnstaat), a young Danish widow, who bore him two daughters, in 1780 and 1781; but 'for family reasons' (Maria was a Roman Catholic, and Jones evidently feared disinheritance), he was for many years nervous about 'owning the connexion' (Jones, 89).

On a second visit to Naples, begun in May 1780 and lasting three years, Jones was accompanied by his young family. He could not range far in search of new subjects, and diminishing funds enforced 'a frugal Stile of living' (Jones, 97). In improvised studios he completed paintings in oil and watercolour; and during 1781 he found, within walking distance of his lodgings, a lane overhung with trees and plants, offering to his eye a peculiarly interesting combination of natural growth and picturesque arrangement; he made at least thirteen drawings of this lane (*On the Road to Santa Maria de Monti*), chiefly in watercolour (examples are in the Tate collection; Whitworth Art Gallery, Manchester; Yale U. CBA; and priv. colls.). Occasionally his friends William Pars and Francis Towne accompanied him on such excursions; but mostly Jones felt that he moved 'in a Cloud of Obscurity' (ibid., 113), until he formed a friendship with G.-B. Lusieri, who specialized in panoramic views.

Jones's last fifteen months in Naples produced, almost fortuitously, the group of small oils on paper for which he is now best-known. By April 1782 he knew that he could not long delay his return home. Needing cheap lodgings on short leases, he had to move frequently, often to higher (and cheaper) floors in insalubrious streets. He found that many of the tenements he occupied had flat roofs offering wide views of the city and its surroundings; from such vantage points he 'spent many a happy hour in painting from Nature', in oil on primed paper (Jones, 112). The wholly original works he produced during 1782 include four small 'rooftop views' which are now the most prized of his entire life's work: *Buildings in Naples* (NMG Wales);

Rooftops in Naples (AM Oxf.); *Houses in Naples* (BM); and perhaps most extraordinary of all, *Wall in Naples* (National Gallery, London), which is about the size of a postcard. In each of these, Jones paints what directly confronts him, from a close viewpoint. Other small works on paper painted in and around Naples during 1782 include *Hillside with the Monastery of St Martino* (FM Cam.), *Naples* (a chalk cliff-face with houses on top) and *The Capella nuova fuori della porta di Chiaja* (both Tate collection) and *The Grotto at Posilippo* (priv. coll.).

It is unlikely that any of Jones's contemporaries saw his small oils on paper. Jones happened to be out when William Beckford 'called with all his Retinue at my house to see the Pictures' in July 1782 (Jones, 112); but he would hardly have shown his small oils on paper to such a great collector. Nor did he show them to the British envoy at Naples, Sir William Hamilton, who came to see his 'Pictures' on 3 August 1782, and later allowed Jones to use the billiards room in his palazzo as a painting room during his last four months in Naples. It did not occur to Jones to exhibit any of his oils on paper on his return to London. They remained unknown for over a century and a half. Jones's daughters married, but neither left surviving issue; his works passed to their husbands (who remarried), and eventually to the auction room. When offered for sale at Christies in 1954, Jones's oils on paper caused something of a sensation among collectors and museums in England and Wales.

Return to London; inheritance of Pencerrig On 3 August 1783, after seven years in Italy, Jones left Naples, with his family, and with his paintings 'rolled round a large hollow Cylinder'. On reaching London (3 November) he found that the books, prints, and drawings which he had put in store in 1776, including all his studies 'from Nature', had been destroyed by damp into 'one undistinguished heap of Rubbish' (Jones, 124). Prospects of professional employment were gloomy, and he admits to painting imitations of Wilson and G. F. Zuccarelli, 'innocent impostures' which, however, found buyers (ibid., 141). He had inherited a small estate worth about £300 per annum from his father, on which he lived for a few years, renting houses in London (in Charlotte Street, and from 1785 in Tottenham Court Road) but was increasingly drawn to Wales. Between 1784 and 1798 he exhibited ten paintings at the Royal Academy; these were mostly views in Italy, but included two views in Thomas Johnes's landscape garden at Hafod, Cardiganshire (paintings destroyed by fire 1807; but Jones's *Hafod* sketchbook of 1786–92 survives; priv. coll.). A small *View Looking towards Queen Square* (1784; Tate collection) shows that he retained the habit of painting in oil on paper: it is 'in pink and green, like a foretaste of Camden Town colouring' (Gowing, 56). But by 1785 Jones felt that his professional career was at an end.

Jones's last six years were spent contentedly at Pencerrig. His elder brother Major John Jones had inherited most of the family estates (worth about £4000 a year); on his death on 2 May 1787, they passed to Thomas Jones. For him Pencerrig (which he always spells Penkerrig) was the supreme prize. Secure in his inheritance, Jones finally

married Maria Moncke in September 1789, at St Pancras Church. Francesco Renaldi's group portrait *Thomas Jones and his Family* (1797; NMG Wales) portrays Jones as a middle-aged country squire with his wife and daughters at Pencerrig; Jones is posed with his palette and a painting on an easel, but looks away from them. In his last years he painted only occasionally, mostly in watercolour, his chief subjects being trees on his estate and views of the Carneddau Mountains from Pencerrig. His last, unmistakably characteristic work may be the small watercolour *Study of Rocks*, inscribed *Penkerrig 1796* (priv. coll.). Maria Jones died in spring 1799. Thomas Jones died on 29 April 1803, and was buried on 6 May 1803 in the family chapel at Caebach.　　　　　　　　　　　　　　　　　JUDY EGERTON

Sources T. Jones, journal, MS, priv. coll. · A. P. Oppé, ed., 'Memoirs of Thomas Jones, Penkerrig, Radnorshire', *Walpole Society*, 32 (1946–8) [whole issue] · L. Gowing, *The originality of Thomas Jones* (1985) · P. Morgan, 'Thomas Jones of Pencerrig', *Transactions of the Honourable Society of Cymmrodorion* (1984), 51–76 · P. Galassi, *Corot in Italy* (1991), 9, 18, 37, 21, 31–5, 38–9, 128 · P. Conisbee and others, *In the light of Italy: Corot and early open-air painting* (1996) [exhibition catalogue, National Gallery of Art, Washington, Brooklyn Museum, and St Louis Art Museum, 1996–7] · J. Egerton, 'Thomas Jones: a wall in Naples', *The British paintings*, rev. edn (2000), 186–93 · R. C. B. Oliver, *The family history of Thomas Jones the artist of Pencerrig, Radnorshire* (1970) · R. Hallet, 'The Hafod sketchbook of Thomas Jones', *Friends of Hafod Newsletter*, 5 (1991) [cyclostyled] · F. Jones, diary, MS, priv. coll.

Archives NL Wales, daybook [copy] · NL Wales, memoirs and account book · priv. coll., MSS, journal, daybooks, etc.

Likenesses G. Marchi, oils, 1768, NMG Wales [*see illus.*] · F. Renaldi, group portrait, 1797 (with his family), NMG Wales

Jones, Thomas (1752–1845), Church of England clergyman, was born on 2 April 1752 at Cefn-yr-esgair, near Hafod, Cardiganshire, where his father farmed a small freehold. Like many another Cardiganshire smallholder's son, Jones sought a career in the church. In 1765 he entered Ystradmeurig grammar school, and in September 1774 became curate of Eglwys Fach and Llangynfelyn, near Aberystwyth, at an annual salary of £20. Here he distinguished himself, according to the later memoir by the Revd John Owen, by his strong opposition to the 'barbarous and heathenish customs' (Owen, 13) of the inhabitants, particularly cock fighting and dancing on Sundays. However, he acknowledged that few of his parishioners were evangelized and turned to God by their suppression.

Quitting the parish in frustration in 1779 Jones embarked upon a peripatetic existence, briefly holding a succession of curacies: Leintwardine in Herefordshire (August 1779–December 1780); Longmore, Shropshire (December 1780–July 1781); Oswestry (July 1781–January 1782); Loppington, near Wem (January–November 1785). His earthy, evangelical preaching style, however, seems to have made him unpopular: at Oswestry, the annual church collection for the curate fell from an average of £30 to just 2s. 6d. when Jones was to be its beneficiary.

In November 1785, however, Jones became curate of Great Creaton in Northamptonshire, a notable evangelical church which attracted a congregation from miles around. Here he stayed for the rest of his professional life:

as a curate until 1828 (serving also Spratton from 1810), on a salary which never rose above £60, and then as rector of Great Creaton alone. At Creaton, Jones instituted many beneficial reforms: in 1788 he established both a sick club and a clothing club for the labourers of the parish, and a year later, in 1789, started the first Sunday school in Northamptonshire. Despite his discouraging experience at Oswestry, Jones himself became a very popular and powerful preacher: a collection of notes made from his sermons, edited under the title *Basket of Fragments* (2 vols., 1832–3), passed through several editions.

Despite his long residence in England, Jones remained interested in the affairs of the Welsh church and, indeed, longed to move back to north Wales. He recognized the need of the Welsh church to reform itself: in 1789, writing to his friend Thomas Charles of Bala, he commented:

> The Lord have mercy upon the Clergy in North Wales; they are surely at the worst; blinder they cannot be. The people perish for lack of knowledge. The blind Indians cannot need instruction more than the people of this country. (Owen, 108)

It was in this context that Jones and Charles first conceived the idea of forming Bible societies in the principality. In 1799, Jones persuaded the Society for Promoting Christian Knowledge (SPCK) to publish 10,000 copies of the Welsh Bible. Though these quickly sold out, his repeated applications for another edition were refused. His proposal to form a new society for Wales, similarly, proved a failure. However, Thomas Charles mentioned Jones's project to the committee of the SPCK in December 1802, and the British and Foreign Bible Society was forthwith established.

Jones became rector of Creaton in 1828, but increasingly suffered from ill health, and in 1833 he was obliged to retire. By 1839 he was almost completely blind. He died on 7 January 1845 and was buried at Spratton churchyard, leaving £12 a year to St David's College, Lampeter, to be given for the best essay in Welsh.

A prolific author, Jones produced works in both English and Welsh. The *Scriptural Directory* appeared in 1811, and went through ten editions. In the following year, *The Welsh Looking Glass … by a Person who has Travelled through that Country* (1812) included a remonstrance against the secession of the Welsh Calvinistic Methodists from the established church. *Jonah's Portrait* (1819) was followed by three other devotional works, *The Prodigal's Pilgrimage* (1825), *The True Christian* (1833), and *The Christian Warrior* (1837). His books in Welsh were chiefly translations of works by Richard Baxter, William Romaine, John Berridge, and Sir Richard Hill.   D. L. THOMAS, rev. MATTHEW CRAGOE

Sources J. Owen, *Memoir of the Rev. Thomas Jones, late of Creaton, Northants* (1853) • *DWB*
Archives NL Wales, letters to Thomas Charles • NL Wales, letters mainly to Thomas Richards
Likenesses G. Clint, oils, *c*.1814, NPG • G. Clint and W. H. Mote, engraving (aged sixty-two), repro. in Owen, *Memoir*

Jones, Thomas (1756–1807), college teacher, was born at Aberriw, in Montgomeryshire, on 23 June 1756. His parentage is uncertain: he may have been the illegitimate son of Owen Owen, of Tyncoed, and of his housekeeper, who married a Mr Jones of Traffin and brought up Thomas as Jones's son. He was educated at local schools in Aberriw and Ceri before going to Shrewsbury School, where he remained for nearly seven years. In 1774 he was admitted a pensioner to St John's College, Cambridge, but he migrated on 27 June 1776 to Trinity College because of the limited number of fellowships at St John's. He was senior wrangler in 1778, having acted as tutor to the second wrangler, Herbert Marsh, the future bishop of Peterborough, who became his lifelong friend. In 1779 he graduated BA and was appointed assistant tutor at Trinity; he was elected fellow on 1 October 1781 and proceeded MA in 1782. From 1787 until his death he was head tutor. He enjoyed a very high reputation as a mathematical tutor, and his lectures were clear, methodical, and interesting. As moderator in the philosophical schools in 1786 and 1787 he introduced William Paley's *Principles of Moral and Political Philosophy* into the examinations.

Jones was ordained deacon at Peterborough on 18 June 1780 and priest at Ely on 6 June 1784; he became curate to the parishes of Fen Ditton and Swaffham Prior in 1784. He published *A Sermon on Duelling* (1792), which he had preached before the university on 11 December 1791, soon after a fatal duel had taken place on Newmarket Heath between two undergraduates of Pembroke College, Henry Applewhaite and Richard Ryecroft. Jones was an enthusiastic advocate of political and religious reform, and together with the bursar of Trinity, James Lambert, gave his support to William Frend, a pupil of his, in his trial before the university in 1794 for promoting Jacobinism.

Jones died on 18 July 1807 in lodgings on the Edgware Road, London, where he had gone to seek medical treatment. He was buried in Dulwich College burial-ground, and a bust and tablet to his memory were placed in the ante-chapel of Trinity College.

D. L. THOMAS, rev. S. J. SKEDD

Sources H. Marsh, *Memoir of the late Revd. Thomas Jones* (1808) • Venn, *Alum. Cant.* • J. Gascoigne, *Cambridge in the age of the Enlightenment* (1989), 226–7, 232, 234, 243 • P. Searby, *A history of the University of Cambridge*, 3: 1750–1870, ed. C. N. L. Brooke and others (1997), 309–10
Likenesses bust, Trinity Cam.

Jones, Thomas (*bap.* 1756, *d.* 1820), Calvinistic Methodist minister, was born at Penucha, Caerwys, Flintshire, and baptized in Caerwys on 20 February 1756, the eldest son of Edward Jones (1713–1802), a comparatively wealthy farmer, and his wife, Jane (1732–1764). He was educated at the grammar school of John Lloyd, curate and later rector of Caerwys, where he acquired some proficiency in the classics, before he entered the grammar school at Holywell in 1769, where he remained until 1771. His father intended him to become a clergyman of the established church but he came under the influence of the Calvinistic Methodists, whom he joined in 1772.

Jones began to preach with the Methodists in September 1783 and he was appointed supervisor in charge of the Methodist societies at Mold and Denbigh. In 1784 he became acquainted with Thomas Charles (1755–1814) of

Bala, one of the prime leaders of Welsh Calvinistic Methodism and the main architect of the Sunday school movement in Wales. Both men realized that continuous and progressive instruction was essential to consolidate and make permanent the results of the evangelical revival, and they were to work in the closest collaboration for a period of over twenty-five years. In April 1799 they founded and co-edited the quarterly *Trysorfa ysprydol* ('Spiritual treasury'), the first religious and denominational periodical in Welsh that provided reading material for itinerant preachers, Sunday school teachers, and their pupils. Charles and Jones also drew up *Rheolau a dybenion … y Methodistiaid yn Nghymru* ('Rules and designs … of the Methodists in Wales') in 1801. The Methodist societies were nominally within the Church of England, whose clergy ministered the sacraments to society members, but during the first decade of the nineteenth century there grew a demand to ordain Methodist lay preachers. Thomas Jones was one of the first group of men to be ordained a minister of the new Methodist Connexion in 1811, an act which marked the severance of the Methodists from the Anglican church as a separate denomination.

Jones's literary output was large, as a theologian, church historian, lexicographer, translator, poet, and hymnist, commencing in 1788, when he published an elegy to Anne Parry of Llanrhaeadr. In 1793 he published his *Sylwiadau [sic] ar draethawd a elwir undeb crefyddol* ('Observations on an essay entitled religious unity'), which was an attempt to answer a pamphlet published anonymously by Richard Jones, curate of Ruthin. This work shows that Jones was familiar with the writings of the early church fathers as well as later theologians. *Gair yn ei amser* ('A word in season'), published in 1798, is a rebuttal of the charges of sedition brought against the Methodists during the French Revolution. His *Geiriadur Saesoneg a Chymraeg: an English and Welsh Dictionary* first appeared in 1800 and ran to its fourth edition in 1843. Among his translations are *Y Cristion mewn cyflawn arfogaeth* ('The Christian in complete armour') by William Gurnall, which he completed in four volumes, in 1796–1819, and *Catecism eglwys loegr* ('Catechismus, sive, Prima institutio') by Alexander Nowell, in 1809. Most of Thomas Jones's publications between 1796 and 1802 were printed at Chester, but in May 1803 he entered into a short-lived partnership with Thomas Charles and his wife, Sarah, and established a printing press at Bala; the partnership was dissolved in September 1804. Jones set up his own printing press at Ruthin in October 1808 but removed it to Denbigh in April 1809. There he commenced work on his influential *Diwygwyr, merthyron, a chyffeswyr Eglwys Loegr* ('Reformers, martyrs and confessors of the Church of England'), which was completed in August 1813; it was to be reprinted twice before the end of the century. In 1813 Jones sold his printing office to Thomas Gee (1780–1845), who had been employed as its overseer since its inception.

Jones also took a prominent part in the leading theological controversies of his day. When Wesleyan Methodism was introduced to north Wales in the first decade of

the nineteenth century he became involved in a fierce theological dispute with Owen Davies (1752–1830), superintendent of the Welsh Mission. He also became embroiled in similar debates with High Calvinists, such as the Baptist Christmas Evans (1766–1838), and these controversies resulted in a spate of books and pamphlets, among which are *Y drych athrawiaethol* ('Doctrinal mirror'), 1806; *Ymddiddanion crefyddol* ('Religious discourses'), 1807; and *Ymddyddanion rhwng ymofynydd a henwr ar brynedigaeth* ('Discourses between an inquirer and an old man on redemption'), 1819.

Jones was married three times; first, in October 1795, to Elizabeth Jones of Mold, a woman of considerable wealth who left him most of her property on her death in November 1797; second, in March 1804, to A. Maysmor of Llanelidan, who died on 14 August 1805; and finally, on 6 October 1806, to Mary Lloyd of Llanrwst (1772–1848), who survived her husband. There were no children from any of the marriages. Jones suffered from ill health for many years and underwent surgical lithotomy—an operation to remove stones from the urinary tract—in 1797 and in 1802. He died at his home, Bryn Disgwylfa, Denbigh, on 16 June 1820, and was buried at Eglwys Wen, Denbigh, three days later.

As a denominational leader Jones was wise and moderate and, next to Thomas Charles, the most influential in the Calvinistic Methodist Connexion. He was a diligent and scholarly writer and as a church historian he occupies the front rank in his generation. He was also a most accomplished poet in traditional metres. His *Cofiant* ('Autobiography'), published after his death in 1820 (reprinted 1937), which chronicles the experiences of a gentle and sensitive man, has long taken its place among the classics of Welsh literature. It also contains a wealth of material for the social historian in its descriptions of surgical lithotomy and the use of leeches in medicine.

HUW WALTERS

Sources J. Jones, *Cofiant y Parch. Thomas Jones, o Ddinbych* (1897) • F. P. Jones, *Thomas Jones o Ddinbych, 1756–1820* (1956) • I. Jones, ed., *Hunangofiant y Parch. Thomas Jones* (1937) • I. Jones, 'Thomas Jones o Ddinbych awdur a chyhoeddwr', *Journal of the Welsh Bibliographical Society*, 5 (1937–42), 137–209 • G. P. Jones, 'Thomas Jones a'r Maen Tostedd', *Newyn a haint yng Nghymru a phynciau meddygol eraill* (1963), 158–65 • I. Jones, *A history of printing and printers in Wales to 1810* (1925), 177–9, 196–7 • D. Ll. Morgan, 'Llenyddiaeth y Methodistiaid, 1763–1814', *Hanes Methodistiaeth Galfinaidd Cymru*, ed. G. M. Roberts, 2 (1978), 456–528 • F. P. Jones, '"Gair yn ei amser" Thomas Jones o Ddinbych', *Radicaliaeth a'r werin Gymreig yn y bedwaredd ganrif ar bymtheg* (1977), 17–40 • E. Rees, ed., *Libri Walliae: a catalogue of Welsh books and books printed in Wales, 1546–1820*, 2 vols. (1987)
Archives Flintshire RO, Hawarden, accounts, corresp., and papers | NL Wales, letters to Thomas Charles, Daniel Jones, and Joseph Tarn, MSS 4797, 4836, 12775C, 12790C
Likenesses J. Blood, stipple, pubd 1817, NL Wales; version, BM • R. Burt, engraving (after H. Hughes), repro. in *Cofiant neu hanes bywyd a marwolaeth y Parch. Thomas Jones* (1820), frontispiece • miniature, priv. coll.; photographic copy, NL Wales

Jones, Thomas [*pseud.* Bardd Cloff] (1768–1828), Welsh-language poet, was probably born at Llandysilio in Denbighshire in 1768. In later life he became known as Bardd

Cloff, or the lame bard, because of an accident he had suffered in his early childhood. At the age of fifteen he entered the counting-house of Mathew Davies, in his coach-builder's establishment at 90 Long Acre, London, and resided there, becoming a partner in the business in 1813.

For a long period Jones was closely connected with the Gwyneddigion Society of London. He was elected member in 1789; acted as secretary for 1790 and 1791, in which capacity he was 'most zealous and businesslike'; and was president for three terms, on the last occasion in 1821. Several of his poetical compositions were dedicated to the society, such as his ode on the celebration of its anniversary, on 15 July 1799, published in Welsh and English (1799), and his ode for St David's day (1802). Jones also gained several prizes at eisteddfods. A benevolent man, who subscribed to many charities, Jones died at 90 Long Acre, London, on 18 February 1828, and was buried in the churchyard of St Martin-in-the-Fields. His elegy was written for the Cymmrodorion Society by Robert Davies (Bardd Nantglyn), who received a silver medal marking its excellence.

D. L. THOMAS, rev. M. CLARE LOUGHLIN-CHOW

Sources W. D. Leathart, *The origin and progress of the Gwyneddigion Society of London* (1831), 73–4 · *DWB* · R. Williams, *Enwogion Cymru: a biographical dictionary of eminent Welshmen* (1852), 264–5 · H. E. Hughes, *Eminent men of Denbighshire* [1946], 185

Jones, Thomas (1775–1852), maker of scientific instruments, was born on 24 June 1775, eldest son of William Jones and his wife Catherine, *née* Nicoll, probably in the parish of St George, Hanover Square, Westminster. He was apprenticed from 1789 to 1796 to Jesse Ramsden of Piccadilly, the most eminent scientific instrument maker of the day, who declared that Jones was 'the most ingenious and the most assiduous' of his many apprentices (L. Dutens to J. Banks, 4 Dec 1800, Royal Society Misc. MSS 8.24). Jones continued to assist Ramsden until the latter's death in 1800, and he subsequently developed and wrote on several instruments which had originated in Ramsden's workshops. With his brother, Jones worked for private customers and for the trade, in particular for Edward Troughton of Fleet Street, who succeeded Ramsden as London's master craftsman. Troughton also thought highly of Jones, and his recommendation secured for the younger man several of the prestigious commissions which Troughton declined in his old age. Jones always traded in Westminster, and had no need to be free of any guild. His first shop was in Mount Street, off Berkeley Square, where he was in 1806. In 1811 he moved to 21 Oxenden Street, and in 1816 to 62 Charing Cross, where he remained until 1850 when he went to 4 Rupert Street.

From Ramsden and Troughton, Jones had learned the difficult art of accurately graduating scales, and major national observatories at home and overseas ordered from him their principal astronomical instruments, consisting at that time of transit telescopes and mural circles, as well as any of the lesser instruments for astronomy, and for magnetic or meteorological observations that they required. He received two important orders for 6 foot diameter mural circles in 1820, one for the new Cape of Good Hope observatory, which he was to construct under Troughton's supervision, the other, along with a transit telescope and a clock, for the Spanish naval observatory at San Fernando, near Cadiz. He completed the Cape circle in the agreed time of two years but when it was set up for testing at Greenwich observatory, John Pond, astronomer royal, asked to keep it. Jones was instructed to make a duplicate circle for the Cape, which was ready for shipment in 1826, part of a consignment of thirteen cases of assorted instruments and apparatus from his workshop. He was then asked to make a 5 foot circle for Armagh observatory; when this circle was found to have a defective pivot, Jones went to Armagh in 1832 to correct it and to recut the graduations, an exercise he had to repeat in 1834. Other circles were made for the observatories of Oxford and Cambridge universities.

Meanwhile the sum of £1576, which had been sent to London to pay for the Spanish instruments, disappeared when the commercial agent holding it was declared bankrupt, and it was 1825 before the contract was revived. The telescope reached Spain in 1832, the circle in 1834, but another year passed before Jones, as his contract required, arrived in San Fernando to supervise its erection and lastly to graduate it, thereby avoiding the risk of the graduated scale's being distorted in transit.

The Cape circle was never satisfactory, despite Troughton's assurance to Fearon Fallows, the Cape astronomer, that, judging from the one Jones had made for the Royal Observatory, he might reckon on having a first-rate instrument. Fallows, who considered that 'Jones was a very good sort of man, only that he was such a knave' (CUL, RGO 15/31/9), had endless problems with it, and in 1839, some years after Fallows's death, it was shipped back to Greenwich for examination. George Biddell Airy, then astronomer royal, wrote to Francis Beaufort, hydrographer of the navy: 'Jones turned the pivot scandalously ill and has done so in several other instances, his graduation also in this case is very bad and in another case is infamous. I have no confidence in him' (CUL RGO 15/28, fol. 167r). The steel collar of the pivot, inadequately fastened only with soft solder, had probably come loose when the case containing the circle was roughly handled as it was unloaded at Table Bay. Airy, notwithstanding these harsh criticisms, continued to employ Jones for numerous small tasks at Greenwich. His reputation remained high and in general his precision apparatus was excellent in design and construction. He made geodetic pendulums, theodolites, and geomagnetic apparatus for various Admiralty expeditions. Among the minor instruments which he devised were an all-metal travelling barometer and a transit instrument for Sir Henry Englefield, a lactometer for Sir Joseph Banks, and for Henry Kater, a small azimuth compass.

Jones was one of the founder members of the Astronomical (later Royal Astronomical) Society, and a member (briefly) of the Society of Arts, the Royal Geographical Society, and the Statistical Society of France. In 1835 he was elected FRS. It is not known when he married his wife, Emma, but their son Thomas worked with his father, attended the London Mechanics' Institute in 1834, and continued the business until 1861. W. H. Jones, whose signature receipted some of Thomas Jones's invoices, may have been another son or a relative. The family resided in later years at Beaufort Street, Chelsea, but the elder Thomas Jones, being in poor health, had been sleeping at his shop in Rupert Street, where he died, intestate, on 29 July 1852. He was buried at St James's Church, Piccadilly.

ANITA MCCONNELL

Sources *Monthly Notices of the Royal Astronomical Society*, 13 (1852–3), 112 • W. Pearson, *An introduction to practical astronomy*, 2 (1829), 317–21, 434–5 • F. J. G. González, *El observatorio de San Fernando, 1831–1924* (1992), 96–106 • B. Warner, *Royal Observatory, Cape of Good Hope, 1820–1831: the founding of a colonial observatory* (1995) • CUL, Airy MSS, RGO 6/715, 717, 719, 724, 725 • CUL, Board of Longitude MSS, RGO 15 • L. Dutens, letter to Joseph Banks, 4 Dec 1800, RS, Misc. MS 8.24 • minutes of committees, 1816–17, RSA, 232, 269, 275 • Evening minute book (Nov 1830 – June 1834), RGS, minutes for 24 Jan 1831 and 11 April 1831 • parish register (birth), Westminster, Hanover Square, St George, 24 June 1775 • parish register (baptism), Westminster, Hanover Square, St George, 9 July 1775 • parish register (burial), Piccadilly, St James's, 2 Aug 1852
Archives Armagh Observatory • Cape Observatory • CUL, board of longitude MSS, RGO 15 • CUL, Airy, corresp. with tradesmen series, RGO 6

Jones, Thomas (1810–1875), librarian, was born at Margam, Glamorgan, in 1810, the third son of Philip Jones. He was educated at Cowbridge grammar school and (from 1827) at Jesus College, Oxford, where he graduated BA in 1832. Although he had originally intended to take holy orders, he abandoned the idea in favour of the world of books. In 1842 he compiled a catalogue of the Neath Library, and in 1845 was appointed librarian of Chetham's Library, Manchester. Under his care Chetham's Library increased its holdings from 19,000 to 40,000 volumes and Jones used his personal influence to obtain works for the library. He compiled two volumes of the catalogue of the institution (1862–3) in continuation of those published by J. Radcliffe in 1791 and W. P. Greswell in 1821. James Crossley said that he was 'one who seemed designed by nature for the place and whose whole soul was in his work'. He wrote *Catalogue of the collection of tracts for and against popery (published in and about the reign of James II) in the Manchester library founded by Humphrey Chetham*, which was published by the Chetham Society in 1859, and he began extensive collections for a life of Dr John Dee, a former warden of the collegiate church at Manchester.

Jones was a witness before a committee of the House of Commons on public libraries in 1849, and was elected FSA in 1866. He died unmarried at Southport, Lancashire, on 29 November 1875, and was buried at St Mark's Church, Cheetham Hill, Manchester.

C. W. SUTTON, *rev.* ALAN G. CROSBY

Sources W. E. A. Axon, 'In memoriam: "Bibliothecarius Chetamensis" (Thomas Jones, BA, FSA)', *Papers of the Manchester Literary Club*, 2 (1876), 59–65 • A. Nicholson, *The Chetham Hospital and library* (1910), 84 • Foster, *Alum. Oxon.* • CGPLA Eng. & Wales (1876)
Archives U. Edin. L., letters to James Halliwell-Phillipps • U. Edin. L., letters to David Laing

Likenesses J. H. Walker, oils, c.1875, Chetham's Library, Manchester
Wealth at death under £3000: probate, 12 Feb 1876, CGPLA Eng. & Wales

Jones, Thomas [*known as* Jones Treforris] (1819–1882), Congregational minister, was born at Rhayader, Radnorshire, on 17 July 1819, the son of John Jones (*d.* 1829), a commercial traveller. After attending the village school at Rhayader, he was apprenticed about 1831 to a flannel manufacturer named Winstone at Llanwrtyd. In 1837 he obtained work as a collier and later a check weigher at Bryn-mawr, Brecknockshire, and in 1839 he moved to Llanelli, Carmarthenshire. There he started preaching among the Calvinistic Methodists, but in 1841 he joined the Independents. During the following three or four years he attended a private school at Rhyd-y-bont, kept by Jones Llangollen and later a school kept by the Revd Thomas Roberts at Llanelli. In July 1844 he was ordained pastor of Capel-y-Bryn, near Llanelli, but in 1845 moved to take charge of the churches of Hermon and Tabor, near Llandeilo. In 1850 he became pastor of Libanus church, Morriston, near Swansea.

As Jones Treforris he became known throughout Wales for his eloquence and originality as a preacher and lecturer. In September 1858, after much hesitation, he accepted the pastorate of Albany Chapel, Frederick Street, London. In 1861 he moved to a larger church, called Bedford Chapel, near Oakley Square, where he ministered successfully until December 1869; the poet Robert Browning was a seat-holder in Bedford Chapel. Owing to failing health Jones returned to Wales, and in January 1870 he undertook the charge of the new Congregational church at Walter Road, Swansea. He was chairman of the Congregational Union of England and Wales in 1871–2. For the sake of his health he moved to Australia in 1877 and held the pastorate of the Congregational church at Collins Street, Melbourne, from May 1877 to May 1880. After his return to Swansea he resumed the pulpit at Walter Road and from 1881 until his death he remained as pastor, assisted by the Revd E. Jenkins.

Jones attained a unique position as a popular preacher in Welsh, being often classed with William Williams of Wern (1781–1840). His reputation rests mainly on the eloquent and undogmatic sermons he preached in English at Bedford Chapel, where he avoided a strictly 'popular' style. Jones was also a poet of some repute and published several pieces of Welsh poetry. A volume of his sermons, *The Divine Order*, was published in 1884. The volume contains a preface by Robert Browning and a short memoir by his son, the editor.

Jones was twice married; firstly to Jane Roberts of Morriston, and secondly, to Annie Howell of Pembroke Dock, who survived him. He had five sons and one daughter. The two sons from his first marriage were Sir David Brynmor Jones KC, MP (1852–1921), and John Viriamu *Jones (1856–1901), first principal of the University College, Cardiff. Jones died on 24 June 1882 at his home in Eaton Terrace, Swansea, and was buried on 30 June in Swansea cemetery.

D. L. THOMAS, *rev.* MARI A. WILLIAMS

Sources T. Rees and J. Thomas, *Hanes eglwysi annibynol Cymru*, 5 (1891) • *DWB* • D. B. Jones, 'Memoir', in T. Jones, *The divine order* (1884) • A. H. Jones, ed., *Lyric thoughts of the late Thomas Jones, the poet-preacher* (1886) • *The Cambrian* (30 June 1882), 8 • *The Times* (27 June 1882), 10 • W. Dorling, *Great modern preachers* (1875) • *CGPLA Eng. & Wales* (1882)

Likenesses photograph, *c.*1880, repro. in Jones, *The divine order*, frontispiece

Wealth at death £6068 19s. 2d.: probate, 11 Nov 1882, *CGPLA Eng. & Wales*

Jones, Thomas (1870–1955), civil servant and benefactor, was born on 27 September 1870 in the valley town of Rhymni, a pocket of Welsh-language culture in north-west Monmouthshire. He was the first of the nine children of David Benjamin Jones (d. 1919) and his wife, Mary Ann (d. 1903), the daughter of Enoch Jones, who managed the truck shop owned by the Rhymney Iron Company. On his father's promotion within this shop, he was moved from the Upper Rhymni board school to the fee-paying Lewis School, Pengam, where he showed considerable academic promise; but on his grandfather's insistence he was withdrawn from school at fourteen to work as a clerk in the ironworks so that his bookishness could be tempered by a knowledge of the world. By 1890, however, he had started to establish a reputation as a preacher and, having won the Calvinist Methodist scripture gold medal, he left to study for the ministry at the recently established University College of Wales at Aberystwyth.

Academic life in Scotland, marriage, and return to Wales It was to be some eleven years before Jones graduated, and then it was from the University of Glasgow with a first-class honours degree in economics. The length of his studies, financed to an extent by his own preaching, was partly involuntary. He consistently failed examinations in mathematics. It was due more significantly, however, to a life of 'perpetual motion' in student activities and in particular political and philanthropic work: at Glasgow, for instance, he joined the Independent Labour Party and founded the local Fabian Society as well as living in the university settlement between 1896 and 1899. One of his fellow students at Aberystwyth was Eirene Theodora (1875–1935), the daughter of Dr Richard John Lloyd, reader in phonetics at Liverpool University, whom he married on 31 December 1902 and with whom he enjoyed a rewarding partnership until her death in 1935. Of their three children, Eirene *White became a Labour minister and Tristan became manager of *The Observer*. A second son, Elphin, died tragically in 1928.

At Glasgow, Jones gradually lost his Christian faith, although its ethical values (reinforced by the teaching and continuing friendship of Henry Jones, the professor of moral philosophy there) were to govern his public life. Consequently it was not to the chapel but to an academic career that he turned. In 1899 he was appointed a part-time assistant in political economy in Glasgow and, after gaining his honours degree in 1901, he became a full-time lecturer. He specialized in practical issues, such as unemployment and juvenile labour, which informed his continuing immersion in philanthropic and political work. He acted as a special commissioner in Scotland for the

Thomas Jones (1870–1955), by Ivor Williams, 1939

royal commission on the poor law, of which his professor (William Smart) was a member. Earlier in 1904 and 1905, to supplement his income, he had become the Barrington visiting lecturer in Ireland, which required him during his vacations to deliver some fifty lectures in small towns; and, after flirting with several other possibilities such as the principalship of Ruskin College, Oxford, and standing as the parliamentary Labour candidate for Merioneth, he returned to Ireland in 1909 as the first professor of political economy at Queen's University, Belfast. There he threw himself into his usual social commitments, including the foundation of a local branch of the Workers' Educational Association.

While in Scotland and Ireland, Jones remained drawn to the vitality of civic and cultural life in south Wales which, at a time of exceptional economic prosperity, was the key to the forging of a new Welsh national identity. This was the reason for his superficially surprising decision to leave Belfast after only a year and return to south Wales as secretary to a new philanthropic initiative: the King Edward VII Welsh National Memorial Association, financed by David Davies MP, the millionaire coal owner, and designed to reduce the incidence of tuberculosis. The association was an embodiment of the new Welsh consciousness. So too was the organization to which he next became secretary in 1912, the Welsh National Insurance Commission, which was responsible for the implementation of the Liberal government's new health insurance scheme. This was a job that he did not wholly enjoy. He had applied to be a commissioner and, impatient of office routines, he was not a born bureaucrat; but the principal reason for his exasperation was the intrigue centring on John Rowland, the Welsh commissioner and protégé of Lloyd George. At this time, however, he was able to make a favourable impression on Lloyd George, when persuading him to include state financing of tuberculosis sanatoriums in the 1911 legislation. He was also able to consolidate his friendship with David Davies, who—together with his sisters Gwen and Margaret—was to become one of his greatest benefactors. It was Davies, for instance, who provided the financial backing for *Welsh Outlook*, a monthly magazine committed to promoting a wider appreciation of political and cultural developments in Wales, which continued in publication until 1933 and of which Jones was the initial honorary editor between 1914 and 1916. It was Davies also who took him to London in 1916 to work for Lloyd George in his bid to become prime minister. This placed him, together with many other Welshmen, on a wholly new stage.

Whitehall: the cabinet secretariat Jones, or T.J., as he quickly became known, was to remain in Whitehall from December 1916 to 1930. There he served four very different prime ministers in the unique capacity—as he had originally hoped—of 'a fluid person moving among people who mattered and keeping the P.M. on the right path so far as is possible' (Jones, *Whitehall Diary*, 1.15). He acted as the liberal conscience of successive governments, best expressed by Baldwin (with whom he developed a remarkable empathy despite a fundamental disagreement over the virtues of Lloyd George) when he admitted:

> I am a Tory P.M., surrounded by a Tory Cabinet, moving in Tory circles. You don't let me forget or ignore the whole range of ideas that normally I should never be brought up against if you were not in and out of this room. You supply the radium. … You have such an extraordinary width of friends in all classes, and so many interests that through you I gather impressions of what is being thought by a number of significant people. … I think every Tory P.M. ought to have someone like you around the place. (Jones, *Whitehall Diary*, 2.167–8)

The one prime minister with whom he did not initially have such an intimate relationship was ironically the leader of the party for which T.J. almost always voted, Ramsay MacDonald.

Officially, T.J. was first assistant and then deputy secretary to the cabinet, responsible for domestic issues while Maurice Hankey, as secretary, concentrated on military and foreign affairs. He took and circulated cabinet minutes, acted as secretary to many cabinet committees, and deputized for Hankey on his frequent absences abroad. As a member of many informal groupings of officials and public figures, such as 'The Family' and the Romney Street group, he kept abreast of progressive opinion, which he discussed candidly with Lloyd George. He used his extensive contacts within the labour movement to act as a go-between in the continuing industrial unrest, particularly in the coal industry. Even more importantly, he used his knowledge of Ireland to participate actively in the formal discussions and informal negotiations which ultimately led to the Anglo-Irish peace treaty of 1921 and the creation of the Irish Free State. As secretary to the British delegation in the negotiations between October and December 1921, he could converse with Lloyd George in

Welsh both to maintain secrecy and to impress Sinn Féin. He also acted as a vital go-between between Lloyd George and the Irish leaders, most notably securing Arthur Griffith's pledge to accept a boundary commission which was to prove critical to the eventual success of the negotiations (Jones, *Whitehall Diary*, 3.156–7).

On Lloyd George's downfall, the future of the cabinet secretariat was uncertain and in both Bonar Law's and Baldwin's first ministries T.J. acted, on Hankey's admission, virtually as a 'political secretary', writing speeches and providing general political assistance (Ellis, 258). The speeches included virtually all Baldwin's election speeches in 1923 advocating protection which, given T.J.'s commitment to free trade, was—in the words of his biographer—as 'bizarre as a confirmed teetotaller writing advertising copy for the brewers' (ibid., 259). His closeness to Baldwin, publicized in a press photograph of the two walking together, aroused MacDonald's suspicions and consequently he was consigned to more conventional civil service duties during the first Labour government. Indeed, it was the accuracy of his cabinet minutes that MacDonald dishonestly tried to challenge in an attempt to disguise his misleading of the House of Commons over the decision not to prosecute in the Campbell 'incitement to mutiny' case, which brought the government down in October 1924.

On Baldwin's return, T.J. reverted to a more political role advising on the membership of the cabinet, acting as go-between (especially through J. H. Thomas) during the build up to and duration of the general strike and then trying to reinforce Baldwin's aversion to any punitive legislation. More conventionally he became secretary to the committee of social research which was intended, but failed, to stimulate the scientific examination of pressing domestic issues, as a counter to official negativity. It evolved under the second Labour government into the economic advisory committee, of which T.J. was also initially secretary. By this time, however, his faith in the ability of political action to instil greater moral responsibility into both public and private life had been undermined as thoroughly as had been his religious faith in the 1890s. He was ready for other challenges.

Welsh appointments, appeasement, and unemployment T.J. did not totally abandon a political role after his resignation from the civil service. He continued to move widely in political circles and was so regularly consulted on Welsh appointments and honours that he earned the sobriquet of the unofficial secretary of state for Wales—a position he used to press for greater devolution and for a separate BBC Welsh service. He also met Baldwin regularly and—despite voting Labour in 1935—wrote most of his election speeches including the one controversially committing the future government to 'no great armaments'. Baldwin remained, however, as deaf to his advice on the readmission of Lloyd George to office as he was inactive in the face of pleas arising from two other of T.J.'s independent actions. Both exposed T.J.'s political naïvety. The first was his use by Von Ribbentrop in an abortive attempt in 1936 to arrange a meeting between Baldwin and Hitler. T.J. met Hitler—as notoriously he was to do again in the same year in the company of Lloyd George—and was temporarily convinced of his good faith in seeking to revise the treaty of Versailles. This was despite his awareness of Nazi brutality, not least through the assistance he arranged for Jewish refugees. His continuing association both with All Souls and the Cliveden set eventually led to an attack upon him as a 'mystery man' advocating appeasement in high places as late as April 1938 (*Daily Herald*, 6 April 1938). Second, as a member of the Unemployment Assistance Board, which was established in 1935 to take unemployment relief 'out of politics', he was irate when the government—as a result of public unrest, not least in south Wales—suspended the initial benefit scales of the supposedly 'independent' board and permitted the uninsured for two years to receive whichever was the more generous: the new board benefits or the old payments made by local authorities. Aware of the corruption that had resulted in illegally high payments by local councils in south Wales and of the danger to the self-reliance of claimants which over-generous government handouts could pose, he refused to accept the advice of his closest friends that the concession was politic at a time of exceptional distress. Thereafter, his interventions were mainly limited to advocating Lloyd George's return to government in 1940 and advising Cripps in his battle against Churchill in 1942. As a result of his friendship with the Astors, he also became a founding trustee of the Observer Trust in 1946.

Philanthropy and education Most of Jones's time after 1930, however, was spent as the linchpin for a wide range of philanthropic, cultural, and educational activities, particularly in Wales, to which he had remained devoted despite his heavy workload in Whitehall. From 1930 to 1945 he was secretary to the Pilgrim Trust and served later as a trustee (1945–52) and chairman (1952–54). Financed by the American oil tycoon Edward Harkness, the trust distributed some £2 million in the 1930s on the relief of the unemployed and longer-term protection of the heritage. Among its achievements was the 1938 report *Men without Work*, which exceptionally concentrated on the psychological and moral problems faced by the unemployed. As a member of various subcommittees of the National Council of Social Service, the main authority for co-ordinating official and voluntary relief, Jones also helped to direct further resources to schemes designed to promote self-reliance and self-belief in areas of high unemployment. His principal cultural achievements centred on Gregynog Hall in Montgomeryshire, the home of the Davies sisters. Here a press was established in 1926 which produced some forty-two books of high quality and a series of annual musical events was held, under the inspiration of Sir Walford Davies, which exposed the vibrancy of Welsh culture to the wider world. The success of these initiatives led him in 1939 to promote another joint venture between the national government and the voluntary sector, the Council for the Encouragement of Music and the Arts, of which he became deputy chairman. The council was later transformed into the Arts Council.

Education, however, was T.J.'s overriding interest. Here the initiative with which he was 'divinely obsessed' (Ellis, 299) was Coleg Harlech, a residential adult education college in north Wales. He masterminded its establishment in 1927 and 220 full-time students (largely manual workers) had passed through it by 1937. It epitomized his abiding faith in the power of education, through its demonstration of 'the many-sided nature of truth', to foster self-knowledge, individual responsibility, and mutual understanding. Targeted above all at 'the future leaders of tomorrow', this, he was convinced, was the principal way in which democratic society could be enriched and safeguarded from the twin evils of moral rootlessness and class warfare. More prosaically, it was also designed as an alternative to the Marxist-inspired Central Labour College in London, to which the South Wales Miners' Federation made a sizeable financial contribution. A similar initiative was launched with T.J.'s assistance in 1937 at Newbattle Abbey in Scotland. In addition, as secretary of the York Trust (1934–40), funded by the Astors, and of the Elphin Lloyd Jones Trust (1933–45) he was also to disburse grants to needy students. T.J. was also closely involved in formal education in Wales. He was deeply disappointed not to be selected as principal of the University College of Wales, Aberystwyth, in 1919 and rejected a similar post at Cardiff in 1928; but in 1944 he became president at Aberystwyth (where one of his less commendable actions was the appointment of Goronwy Rees as principal). It was a year after his retirement from there that he died on 15 October 1955 at 6 Heather Gardens, Golders Green, Middlesex. He was cremated at Golders Green.

Assessment T.J. was a small man (a self-styled 'microbe') with a quick and alert manner and yet with a certain lack of physical co-ordination and a notorious carelessness about his appearance. Grey–blue eyes gave a hint of the steel which lay beneath his infectious enthusiasm, his easy naturalness, and his genius for friendship. This made him particularly attractive to women, especially after his wife's death. Energy and integrity were his key qualities. 'His industry was immense', as his close friend Ben Bowen Thomas wrote in the *Dictionary of National Biography*, 'his use of time remorseless'. His integrity derived from his Calvinist Welsh upbringing, 'which never left him': significantly, despite the many official honours that were offered him, he accepted only the CH (in 1929) and, despite the immense amount of money that passed through his hands, he left an estate of barely £5000. It was this integrity that made him a trusted adviser to successive governments. 'I believed a little in each of the three parties', he once wrote, 'more in the Left than the Right' (Jones, *Diary with Letters*, xxiii); but what really created the trust was the certainty that his advice was based on clear principles and was wholly disinterested.

This integrity also provides the best defence against those criticisms which the apparent contradictions provoked. A believer in high moral principles in public life, Jones parleyed with Hitler. Committed to relieving poverty, he moved regularly and easily among the opulent and sought to reduce benefit payments in the 1930s, while opposing many of the more radical initiatives to reduce unemployment. Committed also to the political and cultural renaissance of Wales, he became embattled with Labour leaders in south Wales and scorned popular passions such as rugby. In addition he exercised considerable political influence at a time when Welsh fortunes, as reflected by exceptional depopulation, were at their nadir. As a pronounced democrat, moreover, his influence was wielded with all the secrecy that brought his friend Sir Horace Wilson such obloquy. Finally, it could be argued, all his philanthropic and educational initiatives—advanced with a certain degree of self-congratulation—benefited relatively few people. However, in everything he did he personified the principles of 'public service' and 'active citizenship' which inspired leading civil servants and philanthropists at this time as they sought to adapt to a period of rapid social and political change; and, if the motivation of others may have been to protect their class interests, this patently was not the case with T.J. His actions never involved personal gain and, even if they did arguably contain an element of self-delusion, they were always driven by deeply held beliefs.

One final service T.J. rendered was as an author and diarist. Among his books are the first full biography of Lloyd George (1951) and a series of memoirs based on his extensive diaries: *Rhymney Memories* (1938), *Cerrig Milltir* (1942), *Leeks and Daffodils* (1942), *Welsh Broth* (1951), and *A Diary with Letters, 1931–1950* (1954). The pamphlet *The Native Never Returns* (1942) includes a powerful indictment of Plaid Cymru. Equally important are his detailed diaries for 1916–30, published in three volumes as *Whitehall Diary* between 1969 and 1971. Together with his private papers held in the National Library of Wales in Aberystwyth, these books provide an unrivalled insight into high politics and policy making, political and cultural life in Wales, and the world of philanthropy during a critical period in Britain's recent history.   RODNEY LOWE

Sources NL Wales, Thomas Jones papers · T. Jones, *Whitehall diary*, ed. K. Middlemas, 3 vols. (1969–71) · E. L. Ellis, *T. J.: a life of Dr Thomas Jones* (1992) · T. Jones, *A diary with letters, 1931–1950* (1954) · *DNB* · V. Markham, *Friendship's harvest* (1956) · K. O. Morgan, *Rebirth of a nation: Wales, 1880–1980* (1981) · R. Griffiths, *Fellow travellers of the right: British enthusiasts for Nazi Germany, 1933–9*, pbk edn (1983) · d. cert.
Archives NL Wales, corresp. and papers · U. Wales, Aberystwyth, papers relating to Workers' Educational Association | Bodl. Oxf., corresp. with L. G. Curtis · Bodl. Oxf., letters to E. J. Thompson · JRL, letters to the *Manchester Guardian* · NA Scot., corresp. with Sir James Morton · NL Wales, letters to Thomas Iorwerth Ellis and Annie Hughes Griffiths · NL Wales, letters to T. G. Jones · NL Wales, letters to Sir Ben Bowen Thomas · NL Wales, corresp. with Sir Daniel Lleufer Thomas · TCD, corresp. with Erskine Childers
Likenesses P. Artot, drawing, 1914, NMG Wales · W. Rothenstein, chalk drawing, 1924, NPG · L. S. Merrifield, bust, c.1928, NPG · W. Stoneman, photograph, 1930, NPG · S. Morse-Brown, drawing, 1938, NMG Wales · S. Charoux, bronze bust, 1939, Newport Museum and Art Gallery, Monmouthshire · I. Williams, oils, 1939, NMG Wales [*see illus.*] · E. Perry, oils, 1951, U. Wales, Aberystwyth · S. Mrozewski, wood-engraving, NPG
Wealth at death £9319 3s. 5d.: probate, 12 Jan 1956, *CGPLA Eng. & Wales* · barely £5000 (net)

Jones, Thomas [Tom] (1908–1990), trade unionist and Spanish republican volunteer, was born on 13 October 1908 in Ashton in Makerfield, Lancashire, the second of three children of William Jones, coalminer, and his wife, Mary Jones, a kitchen maid. His father had earlier left Wrexham to work in the mines in Lancashire, but returned to north Wales in 1915 due to the health of his wife. After attending elementary schools in Ashton and in Rhosllannerchrugog, he followed his father into the mines at the age of fourteen, working at Hafod colliery in the Wrexham coalfield. His father had been active in the minimum wage strike in 1912, and from an early age Tom became interested in politics.

The 1921 lock-out was a formative influence on Jones, who believed that the government was continually undermining the rights of the miner. He had started work at Hafod colliery in 1922, moving to Bersham two years later. In the 1926 general strike and subsequent miners' lock-out, the Rhos became an area of acute distress. He became a socialist after hearing a rousing speech by A. J. Cook at the Wrexham racecourse. Owing to the decline in the coal industry after 1926 many Wrexham miners went to the United States, but Jones opted to join the army. On release after a year, he again entered the coal industry, this time at Bersham colliery, where he was elected to the lodge committee. He became chair of the Rhos Labour Party, complementing the small socialist movement in the village, which contained A. R. Jones of the co-operative movement and James Idwal Jones, the future MP for Wrexham.

Jones moved between the various collieries in Wrexham and by 1930 had become a delegate to the Wrexham Trades Council after completing a number of courses run by the National Council of Labour Colleges and the Workers' Educational Association. The failure of the Labour government in 1931 pushed Jones towards the Communist Party, but although he met Harry Pollitt he refused to join the organization, as the perceived atheism of the Soviet Union stood in opposition to his Welsh Methodist Christianity. The north Wales coalfield, which had a history of moderation, was becoming increasingly radicalized in the 1930s. A five-week strike at Bersham in 1935 led to violent clashes between pickets and police. The district union was also moving towards a coalfield-wide stoppage to gain representation at the Point of Ayr colliery, where an industrial union had displaced the North Wales Miners Association in 1927. Jones played an active role in these campaigns, moving closer to the politics of Arthur Horner and Aneurin Bevan in south Wales.

Jones had been the secretary of the Rhos Peace Council, but at the outbreak of the Spanish Civil War he was convinced of the republican cause because of the threat of fascism. Along with other Welsh volunteers picked for their military background Jones served in the élite anti-tank battery. He arrived in Spain in April 1937 and was captured in 1938, detained in Burgos prison, and sentenced to death. Soon after his capture he was called to court again, and the death sentence was commuted to thirty years' imprisonment. In prison Jones, who shared a cell with the

Irish republican Frank Ryan, suffered a number of harrowing experiences. For a long period he was presumed dead. His parents received a death certificate, and a memorial meeting was held in Bangor and a poem was composed by T. E. Nicholas to honour his memory. When it was discovered that Jones was still alive, pressure by the South Wales Miners' Federation and Will John, the Labour MP for Rhondda West, finally secured his return to Britain in April 1940, the last International Brigades member to come home. In 1942 he married Rosa Thomas, with whom he had two sons and two daughters.

Jones did not return to the mining industry but became an official of the Transport and General Workers' Union (TGWU) in north Wales in 1944. In 1953 he took over from Huw T. Edwards, who had himself replaced Arthur Deakin as regional secretary for north Wales and the border counties at the union's Shotton office on Deeside. Jones fitted neatly into the shoes of Edwards, who had been a critic of Deakin's right-wing leadership of the Transport and General Workers. Although Jones was politically to the left and a follower of Aneurin Bevan, Deakin probably favoured his appointment on the basis that both shared a background of trade union activity in north-east Wales. He was the TGWU's regional secretary for Wales from 1969 until his retirement in 1973. He worked closely with Dai Francis of the South Wales National Union of Mineworkers in bringing about the formation of the Welsh TUC in 1974. In 1962 he was appointed OBE and in 1974 CBE. The Spanish government in exile made him a knight of the order of Loyalty in 1974. The University of Wales awarded him an honorary MA in 1989. Jones died at his home, 2 Blackbrook Avenue, Hawarden, Flintshire, on 21 June 1990.   KEITH GILDART

Sources J. Pugh, *A most expensive prisoner: Tom Jones, Rhosllannerchrugog's biography* (1988) · H. Francis, *Miners against fascism: Wales and the Spanish Civil War* (1984) · F. Beckett, *Enemy within: the rise and fall of the British communist party* (1995) · WWW · d. cert.
Archives Flintshire RO, Hawarden, MSS, incl. recollections of service in Spanish Civil War | Flintshire RO, Hawarden, MFGB/ NUM North Wales archive

Jones, Thomas Gwynn (1871–1949), poet and scholar, was born on 10 October 1871 at Gwyndy-uchaf, Betws-yn-Rhos, Denbighshire, the eldest of the four children of Isaac Jones (1842–1929), farmer, poet, and lay preacher, and his wife, Jane, *née* Roberts (1845–1896). At birth he was given the name Thomas, but adopted Gwynn as a second name in his early twenties and thereafter went by the name T. Gwynn Jones.

After elementary education in country schools and a little private tuition Gwynn Jones's early attempts to prepare for Oxford entrance came to nought when he fell ill on the eve of the matriculation examination. The autodidact in him overcame this set-back, and when ultimately he obtained a university chair he did so unencumbered by a day spent in a seat of higher learning. Between 1891 and 1909 he was a journalist in north Wales and Liverpool, working mainly for Welsh-language weekly newspapers, including *Baner ac Amserau Cymru* in Denbigh and *Yr Herald Cymraeg* and *Papur Pawb* in Caernarfon. On 8 June

Thomas Gwynn Jones (1871–1949), by unknown photographer, 1936

1899 he married Margaret Jane (Megan; 1872–1963), the daughter of Thomas and Anne Davies of Denbigh: they had a daughter and two sons. After wintering in Egypt on medical advice in 1905–6 he returned briefly to journalism until, in 1909, he became a cataloguer at the new National Library of Wales in Aberystwyth. In 1913 he was appointed reader in Welsh literature at the University College of Wales, Aberystwyth, and in 1919 was promoted to the Gregynog chair of Welsh literature, remaining in that post until he retired in 1937. Gwynn Jones's late entry to academic life was fostered by supporters such as Sir John Williams, the national library's principal benefactor, and the influential scholar and critic Sir John Morris-Jones, his academic guru.

Gwynn Jones was a prolific writer of exceptional energy and versatility. His scholarly works include an introduction to *Dwyfol gân Dante*, a translation of Dante's *Divina commedia* by Daniel Rees, his sympathetic editor in Caernarfon (1903); 'Bardism and romance' (1914); *Llenyddiaeth y Cymry* (1915); *Llenyddiaeth Gymraeg y bedwaredd ganrif ar bymtheg* (1920); *Gwaith Tudur Aled* (2 vols., 1926); and *Welsh Folklore and Folk Custom* (1930). He wrote acclaimed biographies of two men who had a profound influence upon him. The first, published in 1912, was of Emrys ap Iwan (the Revd Robert Ambrose Jones), a forthright critic and writer on religious and political matters, who had encouraged him to study early Welsh literature and kindled his interest in European languages. The second biography appeared in 1913, and took as its subject Thomas Gee, owner and campaigning editor of *Baner ac Amserau Cymru* in Denbigh and mentor of the young Lloyd George, who had given him his start in journalism.

Gwynn Jones also turned his linguistic and literary gifts to translating works from English, Irish, and languages of mainland Europe. They include *Macbeth* (1902 and 1942), translations from Irish in *Peth nas Lleddir* (1921) and *Awen y Gwyddyl* (1922), works by Ibsen and von Hofmannsthal, and, notably, *Faust* (1922). With H. J. Rose he translated a selection of Greek and Latin epigrams (1927). In 1940 the Gregynog Press published *Visions of the Sleeping Bard*, his translation into English of Ellis Wynne's prose masterpiece. During his years in journalism he produced fifteen novels in serial form, of which four subsequently appeared as books, *John Homer* (1923) and *Lona* (1923) being the best-known. His winter in Egypt provided material for a travel book, *Y Môr canoldir a'r Aifft* (1912). Collections of his essays appeared in *Traethodau* (1910), *Cymeriadau* (1933), *Beirniadaeth a Myfyrdod* (1935), *Astudiaethau* (1936), and *Dyddgwaith* (1937).

Despite these substantial achievements it is as a poet that Gwynn Jones is remembered by the Welsh people. He was generally recognized as the leading poet of his generation, and is one of the major figures of Welsh poetry from its beginnings to the present day. Part of Gwynn Jones's genius lay in his remarkable complexity—a Romantic who said profound things about the tragedy of his own times; a poet of 'pure bitterness' and of lyrical nostalgia; in prosody a conservative and an innovator; a pacifist 'with the emphasis on the fist'; a semi-detached believer; a melancholiac with a sense of humour.

The classical diction and economy of medieval Welsh poetry captivated Gwynn Jones, and their imprint is clear in his later work. He was a consummate master of the strict metres and of *cynghanedd* (alliteration and sometimes internal rhyme in a line of verse). Most of his major poems are dramatic narratives which draw upon Celtic legend, although he adapted the stories freely, grafting on inventions of his own and exploiting their timelessness to relate them to his own day. He came to prominence in 1902 when, still a struggling journalist, he won the first of his two national eisteddfod chairs for his ode 'Ymadawiad Arthur' ('The passing of Arthur'), which captured the spirit of an age of national reawakening. There followed a majestic sequence of mythological poems—'Gwlad y bryniau' (1909), 'Tir na n'óg' (1916), 'Madog' (1918), 'Broséliáwnd' (1922), 'Anatiomaros' (1925), 'Argoed' (1927), and 'Cynddilig' (1935)—which chart the transition from his early optimism to bitter disillusionment, a process hastened by his reaction to the First World War and to contemporary cultural and moral disintegration. He devised new metres, dispensing with rhyme but retaining *cynghanedd* until, finally, metre gave way to *vers libre*. Although Gwynn Jones saw contradictions in his poems, and said that it was 'idle to seek in them either teaching or philosophy', their recurring themes are the tragedy of simple societies and the personal dilemmas of their heroes under the threat of oppression, and the quest for

Arcadia (famously Ynys Afallon in 'Ymadawiad Arthur'). They appear in one or more of his six volumes of verse—*Gwlad y gân a chaniadau eraill* (1902), *Ymadawiad Arthur a chaniadau ereill* (1910), *Detholiad o ganiadau* (1926), *Manion* (1932), *Caniadau* (1934), and *Y dwymyn* (1944). Most of the poems in *Y dwymyn*, stark and full of foreboding, first appeared pseudonymously in the 1930s, when their style and content caused a stir. They mark his final weaning from Afallon.

Some have suggested that Gwynn Jones's search for his Afallon led him to an ivory tower far from the social realism found in later poets. But he was no cloistered scholar: his early socialism and years in journalism taught him something of the world, and he had seen what the industrial age had done to traditional society. His poems, he said, were 'an attempt to recount experiences': his Afallon allegorically suggests his condemnation of the unbearable present. The stories, the majestic diction with its archaisms, the effortless mastery of *cynghanedd*, and the vivid evocation of nature and scenes of human action combine to make some of the most artistically satisfying passages in Welsh literature. But at the same time his symbolism precisely suggests the old world's loss of innocence and the corrosive materialism of the new.

When he retired in 1937 Gwynn Jones was appointed CBE. Both the University of Wales and the National University of Ireland conferred upon him the honorary degree of DLitt. He was granted the medal of the Honourable Society of Cymmrodorion in 1939, and in 1944 received the traditional tribute of the Welsh people in the form of an illuminated address and generous testimonial. He died at his home, Willow Lawn, at Caradog Road in Aberystwyth, on 7 March 1949, and was buried on 10 March in the town's public cemetery.

EMRYS WYNN JONES

Sources DNB · D. Jenkins, *Thomas Gwynn Jones: cofiant* (1973) · G. ap Gwilym, ed., *Thomas Gwynn Jones*, Cyfres y Meistri, 3 (1982) · D. H. E. Roberts, ed., *Llyfryddiaeth Thomas Gwynn Jones* (1981) [Bibliography] · D. Ll. Morgan, *Barddoniaeth T. Gwynn Jones* (1972) · *Y Llenor*, 28/2 (1949), 54–164 [Thomas Gwynn Jones memorial number] · *Y Traethodydd* [T. Gwynn Jones issue], 126 (1971), 3–91 · W. B. Davies, *Thomas Gwynn Jones* (1970) · A. Llewelyn-Williams, *Y nos, y niwl a'r ynys* (1960) · R. M. Jones, *Llenyddiaeth Gymraeg, 1902–1936* (1987), 115–48 · G. Williams, *Y Rhwyg: arolwg o farddoniaeth Gymraeg ynghylch y Rhyfel Byd Cyntaf* (1993) · J. Rowlands, 'Dau lwybr T. Gwynn Jones', *Y Traethodydd*, 148 (1993), 69–86 · [R. T. Jenkins, E. D. Jones, and W. L. Davies], eds., *Y bywgraffiadur Cymreig, 1941–1950* (1970), 33–4 · A. Llywelyn-Williams, 'T. Gwynn Jones: gorchest y bardd', *Transactions of the Honourable Society of Cymmrodorion* (1971), 119–27 · D. Jenkins, ed., *Bro a bywyd: Thomas Gwynn Jones, 1871–1949* (1984) · D. Johnston, ed., *A guide to Welsh literature, 6: c.1900–1996* (1998) · D. Ll. Morgan, 'T. Gwynn Jones: "Broseliawnd"', *Trafod cerddi*, ed. B. Jarvis (1985) · J. G. Jones, 'T. Gwynn Jones, R. W. Parry a W. B. Yeats', *Ysgrifau Beirniadol*, 8 (1974), 226–39 · W. B. Davies, *T. Gwynn Jones* (1962) · G. Bowen, 'T. Gwynn Jones', *Gwŷr llên*, ed. A. T. Davies (1948) · J. Hunter, 'Y nos, y niwl a'r ynysig: estheteg fodernaidd T. Gwynn Jones', *Taliesin*, 98 (summer 1997), 37–54 · T. Parry, *Llenyddiaeth Gymraeg, 1900–1945* (1945) · G. Williams, *An introduction to Welsh literature* (1978) · G. Jones, *The Oxford book of Welsh verse in English* (1977) · T. Conran, *Welsh verse* (1992) · R. G. Jones, *Poetry of Wales, 1930–1970* (1974) · J. P. Clancy, ed., *Twentieth century Welsh* *poems* (1982) • H. I. Bell, *The development of Welsh poetry* (1936) • E. M. Humphreys, 'Dr T. Gwynn Jones', *Gwŷr enwog gynt* (1950), 132–43 • T. H. Parry-Williams, 'T Gwynn Jones', *Y bardd yn ei weithdy* (1948), 11–16 • E. W. Jones, 'Rhai o feddyliau'r hil: edrych yn ôl ar T. Gwynn Jones', *Taliesin*, 94 (summer 1996), 77–100 • m. cert. • personal knowledge (2004)

Archives NL Wales, corresp. and papers • NL Wales, corresp. and papers, incl. poems, articles, and adjudications [II–VI, 1992–3] • U. Wales, Aberystwyth, papers • U. Wales, Bangor, papers and corresp. | NL Wales, letters to John Glyn Davies; letters to Thomas Iorwerth Ellis and Annie Hughes Griffiths; letters to W. J. Gruffydd • NL Wales, letters to J. W. Jones • NL Wales, corresp. with Thomas Jones • NL Wales, letters to Richard Morris Lewis and Sir Daniel Lleufer Thomas • NL Wales, letters to Evan Rees (Dyfed) | SOUND BBC Wales, Llandaff, Cardiff, Rhan o 'Madog', 8 Dec 1947, Disk 5636 • BBC Wales, Llandaff, Cardiff, 'Melwl', 8 Dec 1947, Disk 5636

Likenesses D. Bell, pencil drawing, *c.*1935, NL Wales • photograph, 1936, priv. coll. [*see illus.*] • E. Walters, oils, 1945, NMG Wales • P. Evans, charcoal drawing, NL Wales

Wealth at death £7159 13*s.* 3*d.*: probate, 14 June 1949, *CGPLA Eng. & Wales*

Jones, Thomas Rupert (1819–1911), geologist and palaeontologist, was born on 1 October 1819 in Wood Street, Cheapside, London, the son of John Jones, a silk merchant, and his wife, Rhoda Burberry (originally from Coventry). He was educated at Foster's School in Taunton and by the Revd John Allen at Ilminster. He became interested in geology through collecting fossils in the Lias quarries around that district.

In 1835 Jones was apprenticed to Hugh Norris, a Taunton surgeon; following Norris's death he moved to Newbury, Berkshire, to continue his training with Dr Joseph Bunny. He carried on geological research in the Thames valley and this formed the basis for papers published in 1854 and 1871. Between 1842 and 1850 he was engaged as a medical assistant, working around Taunton and later in London. Continuing his natural history studies, Jones was introduced to various specialists: Bowerbank (London Clay), Harris (Chalk), Morris (Tertiary), and Parker (Foraminiferida). Sorting material for the conchologist John Pickering, he began to pay particular attention to the associated foraminifera and entomostraca (lower orders of Crustacea), and obtained other examples from the chalk fossils of William Harris (whose daughter, Mary, Jones married). He published a *Monograph on the Cretaceous Entomostraca of England* in 1849 and was recognized as the authority in Britain for several entomostracan orders as well as foraminifera.

On becoming established in London's scientific world, Jones was appointed assistant secretary of the Geological Society in 1850, editing its *Quarterly Journal* from 1850 to 1865. He became a fellow in 1852 and, as librarian–curator, in 1855 was responsible for starting the regular reference lists of works acquired by the library. During this period he also produced revised editions of several of Gideon Mantell's works. In 1858 he was appointed lecturer on geology at the Royal Military College, Sandhurst, and moved to nearby Farnborough, resigning from his position at the Geological Society. Professor of Geology from

1862, he was retired 'on reduction' in 1870 when the college's junior department was closed but continued to lecture at the Staff College until he finally retired in 1880, on the abandonment of the teaching of geology by the military authorities.

Throughout this period Jones continued his research on microzoa, contributing numerous papers to geological and natural history journals, often in collaboration with other specialists. He also prepared two other Palaeontographical Society monographs, *The Tertiary Entomostraca of England* (1856) and *The Fossil Estheriae* (1862). Later he co-operated with others in contributing to three more: *Crag foraminifera* (1866–97), *Carboniferous Entomostraca* (1874–84) and *British Palaeozoic Phyllopoda* (1886–99). In 1864, with H. B. Woodward, he founded the *Geological Magazine* (which superseded and incorporated *The Geologist*) acting as an editor until July 1865. During the 1870s he edited and revised other works producing a second edition of Dixon's *Geology of Sussex* (1878) and the *Reliquiae Aquitanicae* of Lartet and Christy (1875). Following retirement he continued his research and augmented a pension by lecturing and writing. An extensive knowledge of many subjects enabled him to produce numerous articles for periodicals, popular dictionaries, and encyclopaedias. He became very interested in South African geology, and so conversant with the literature that he was able to assist those working in the country, despite never visiting it himself.

Jones served on the council of the Geological Society for four periods: 1865–70, 1876–7, 1878–81, and 1883–9. He was awarded the balance of the Wollaston Fund in 1860 (with Professor Parker); the Murchison Fund in 1882; and the Lyell medal in 1890 (in recognition that existing knowledge of various fossil organisms was solely based on his research). In 1872 he was elected FRS, and he served as president of the Geologists' Association in 1879–81, and as president of section C (Geology) of the British Association for the Advancement of Science at Cardiff in 1891, later attending the meeting in Montreal (1894) as vice-president.

Physically of sturdy build, though below average height, Jones had a cheery disposition, and although prone to jocularity was a clear and fluent lecturer. He regarded proof-correcting and editing as a recreation. In common with many other eminent geologists, he was a supporter of the organic origin of the Laurentian *Eozoon canadense* that was finally disproved in 1894.

Jones had two sons and three daughters from his marriage to Mary Harris; the eldest son, William Rupert, was assistant librarian at the Geological Society from 1872 until 1912. His second wife was Charlotte Ashburnham, daughter of Archibald Archer (an instructor in portrait painting at the Royal Academy); they had two sons and three daughters. During the later years of his life he lived at Penbryn, Chesham Bois Lane, Chesham, Buckinghamshire, where he died on 13 April 1911. After his death the Geological Society considered a memorial to aid his family in 1911, but his widow was granted a civil-list pension in 1912.

Jones was part of what has been termed the 'English school' of foraminiferal research, a group of British workers distinguished by its philosophical ideas on variation that led to an important contribution to classification. However, Robinson has indicated that his influence on ostracod studies was probably of more consequence, since 'his name crops up in all quarters, … with faunas of all ages' (Robinson, 1) and with 'an unswerving adherence' to taxonomy rather than palaeoecological speculation. Yet, some of his work, even that of classic districts, still remains the only account available. Through his professional positions, Jones was often the 'prop' (ibid., 5) for a great number of other workers and co-ordinated research through a 'harmonious' joint authorship. It resulted in a swing away from freshwater ostracod studies to the treatment of marine faunas. It also introduced the technique of washing residues of bulk samples (in which the microfossils were not readily apparent) in significant quantities. H. B. WOODWARD, *rev.* R. J. CLEEVELY

Sources E. Robinson, 'An outline history of ostracod studies in Britain', in R. Bate and E. Robinson, *A stratigraphical index of British Ostracoda, Geological Journal special issue*, no. 8 (1978), 1–20 • 'Familiar faces no. 53: Professor T. Rupert Jones', *Mining Journal* (20 Feb 1892), 195 • A. S. W. [A. S. Woodward], *Quarterly Journal of the Geological Society*, 68 (1912), lviii–lxi • 'Eminent living geologists, no. 7: Professor Thomas Rupert Jones', *Geological Magazine*, new ser., 3rd decade, 10 (1893), 1–3 • R. Hodgkinson, 'Professor Thomas Rupert Jones, 1819–1911', 1993, NHM, fossil protozoa section • H. B. Woodward, *Nature*, 86 (1911), 287 • R. Cifelli, 'A history of the classification of foraminifera, 1826–1933', *Special Publication Cushman Foundation for Foraminiferal Research*, 27 (1990) [pt 1] • *Men and women of the time* (1899) • 'The annual report of the Geologists' Association for the year 1911', *Proceedings of the Geologists' Association*, 23 (1912), 92–3 • J. R. Norman, *Squire: memories of Charles Davies Sherborn* (1944) • H. B. Woodward, *The history of the Geological Society of London* (1907)
Archives Geologists' Association • Institute of Geological Sciences, Keyworth, Nottinghamshire • NHM, catalogue and drawings; papers and drawings relating to ostracods | NHM, corresp. with Sir Richard Owen and William Clift • NHM, corresp. among a collection of letters of naturalists belonging to Charles Davies Sherborn • U. Edin. L., letters to Sir Archibald Geikie • U. Edin. L., letters to Sir Charles Lyell • Wellcome L., letters to Henry Lee
Likenesses Adams and Stilliard, photograph, repro. in G. A. Prestwich, *Life and letters of Sir Joseph Prestwich* (1899), facing p. 376 • Maull & Co., photograph, GS Lond.; repro. in E. V. Brunton, *The Challenger expedition, 1872–1876* (1994), 11 • Maull & Fox, photograph, GS Lond.; repro. in *The Graphic* (5 Oct 1907) • Maull & Fox, photograph, repro. in '90th birthday congratulations – Professor Thomas Rupert Jones, F.R.S., F.G.S., etc.', *Geological Magazine*, 6 (Nov 1909), 481 • A. J. Melhuish, photograph, repro. in *Mining Journal*, 195 • A. J. Melhuish, photograph, repro. in 'Eminent living geologists', frontispiece • photograph, repro. in Cifelli, 'History of the classification of foraminifera', fig. 13 • photograph, Newcastle upon Tyne Libraries, Bray family photograph album
Wealth at death £4417 9s. 11d.: resworn probate, 14 July 1911, *CGPLA Eng. & Wales*

Jones, Thomas Rymer (1810–1880), morphologist and physiologist, was born at Whitby on 20 March 1810, the son of Thomas Jones, a captain in the navy, and his wife, Margaret. Nothing is known of his early education but in 1831 he became one of the first students to attend the newly formed medical department of King's College, London. He also studied at Guy's Hospital and in Paris and was admitted to the College of Surgeons in 1833. Chronic deafness made it impossible to practise medicine so he concentrated on the study of comparative anatomy and physiology. In 1835 he was appointed demonstrator of anatomy at King's College, becoming professor of comparative anatomy the following year, a position he occupied with distinction until his retirement in 1874.

Jones earned a solid reputation as a skilful dissector and lecturer during his tenure at King's. From 1840 to 1842 he was also Fullerian professor of physiology at the Royal Institution. He was elected FRS in 1844. He was assistant secretary to the zoology and botany section of the eighth meeting of the British Association, held at Newcastle upon Tyne in 1838, where he publicly took issue with the views of most colleagues concerning the structure of polygastric infusoria. His paper on the digestive apparatus of infusoria, published in the *Annals of Natural History* in 1839, incorporated many of the ideas discussed at this conference relating to the digestive system of these protozoans.

Jones's earliest publications, however, were his 'Notes on the dissection of a tiger (*Felis tigris*, Linn)' and his 'Notes on the dissection of an agouti (*Dasyprocta aguti*, Ill.)', both published in the Zoological Society's *Proceedings* in 1834. Other important publications were his *General Outline of the Animal Kingdom and Manual of Comparative Anatomy* (1839–41), a work accompanied by many fine woodcut illustrations; *The Natural History of Animals* (2 vols., 1845–52), the substance of his lectures at the Royal Institution; *The Animal Creation: a Popular Introduction to Zoology* (1865); *The Natural History of Birds: a Popular Introduction to Ornithology* (1867); and *Mammalia: a Popular Introduction to Natural History* (1873). Jones died from heart disease on 10 December 1880 at his home, 22 Castletown Road, Barons Court, West Kensington. He was survived by his wife, Elizabeth Neville Jones. JOEL S. SCHWARTZ

Sources election certificate, RS • Boase, *Mod. Eng. biog.*, vol. 2 • H. Willoughby Lyle, *King's and some King's men* (1935) • F. J. C. Hearnshaw, *The centenary history of King's College, London, 1828–1928* (1929) • *Nature*, 23 (1880–81), 174–5 • Allibone, *Dict.* • S. Wilks and G. T. Bettany, *A biographical history of Guy's Hospital* (1892), 150–52 • E. S. Barr, *An index to biographical fragments in unspecialized scientific journals* (1973) • d. cert.
Archives NHM, Owen Collection, letters | American Philosophical Society, Philadelphia, William Hutton letter
Wealth at death under £300: administration with will, 14 April 1881, Boase, *Mod. Eng. biog.*

Jones, Thomas Wharton (1808–1891), physiologist and ophthalmic surgeon, was born in St Andrews, Fife, on 9 January 1808, the second of three sons (there were also three daughters) of Richard Jones (*d.* 1821), sometime secretary of customs for Scotland, and his wife, Margaret Cockburn of Ayton Mains, Berwickshire. Through his maternal grandmother Jones fancied he could trace a distinguished ancestry back to the Norman conquest, but he grew up in straitened circumstances, and money remained a problem throughout his life. After early education in Stirling, Dalmeny, and Musselburgh, he enrolled in arts classes at Edinburgh University in 1822. After switching to medicine, he distinguished himself, and qualified LRCS in 1827. Jones's appointment as demonstrator in the extramural anatomy school of Robert Knox coincided with the scandal of William Burke and William Hare, and Jones left Edinburgh for Glasgow in 1829. There his interests in ophthalmology and embryology were cultivated. About 1835 he moved to a practice in Cork; after an extended tour of continental universities, he settled in London in 1838.

Never a particularly successful medical practitioner, Jones brought a sound scientific reputation with him. In May 1841 he was appointed lecturer in physiology at Charing Cross Hospital medical school. He had been elected FRS in 1840 and became FRCS in 1844. From 1851 to 1881 he was professor of ophthalmic medicine and surgery at University College, London, and although he influenced the earliest microscopical investigations of Joseph Lister, he never took much part in college life. Eventually he became an object of derision among medical students, who called him 'Mummy Jones'. For many years he lived with his mother.

Jones's scientific work was mostly microscopical, and included important observations on the blood circulation through capillaries, the mammalian ovum, the pathophysiology of inflammation, and the nature of the white blood corpuscles. Much of this was summarized in his 'State of the blood and blood-vessels in inflammation, as ascertained by experiments, injections, and observations under the microscope', his Astley Cooper prize essay (*Guy's Hospital Reports*, 1850). His *Failure of Sight from Railway and other Injuries of the Spine and Head* (1869) was a speculative attempt to apply his theories of inflammation to clinical problems.

Jones was a competent eye surgeon, and his *Manual of the Principles and Practice of Ophthalmic Medicine and Surgery* (1847) reached its third edition in 1865. He published in addition shorter primers aimed at medical students and general practitioners. His views on the nature of astigmatism were important and he improved the treatment of acute glaucoma. After Hermann von Helmholtz introduced his ophthalmoscope, Jones became adept at using it, though he had earlier failed to recognize the significance of an ophthalmoscope devised by Charles Babbage.

Jones was a religious man who published a treatise on natural theology and was hostile to the evolutionary work of Charles Darwin. He was saved in old age from extreme poverty by a private subscription and, on the recommendation of T. H. Huxley, a civil-list pension. This permitted him to retire in 1881 and to settle at Swiss Cottage, Ventnor, Isle of Wight, where he died, unmarried, on 7 November 1891.   W. F. BYNUM, *rev.*

Sources R. J. Goodlea, 'Thomas Wharton Jones', *British Journal of Ophthalmology*, 5 (1921), 97–117, 145–56 · C. Snyder, 'Charles Babbage and his rejected ophthalmoscope', *Archives of Ophthalmology*, 71 (1964), 591–3 · J. Hirschberg, *The history of ophthalmology*, trans. F. C. Blodi, 8a (1987) · *BMJ* (14 Nov 1891), 1058–9; (28 Nov 1891), 1175–7 · V. G. Plarr, *Plarr's Lives of the fellows of the Royal College of Surgeons of England*, rev. D'A. Power, 2 vols. (1930) · *The Lancet* (28 Nov 1891), 1256–8

Wealth at death £876 12s. 9d.: probate, 12 Dec 1891, CGPLA Eng. & Wales

Jones, Vicky Veronica Clement- [*née* Vicky Veronica Yip] (1948–1987), physician and founder of the British Association for Cancer United Patients, was born on 23 December 1948 in Hong Kong, the third child of Teddy Yip, a successful Chinese businessman, and his wife, Susie Ho. Her early life was spent in Hong Kong, and after a period in Rangoon she returned to Hong Kong in 1954. Of her four brothers and sisters—Tina, George, Betty, and Ronnie—George, who was slightly older, was the most important for her as he inspired her love of learning. The family became wealthy and lived in elegant style in Hong Kong. The transition that occurred when their mother brought the children to East Grinstead, Sussex, in 1957, could have been daunting, but Vicky performed well at Nôtre Dame Convent School. Academically brilliant, she was also a talented violinist and played hockey for the county. From school she obtained an exhibition to Girton College, Cambridge, where she read for the medical science tripos, obtaining a first-class honours degree in 1970 and a first in part two archaeology and anthropology in 1971. She was awarded the Cambridge University Elizabeth Walter prize for 1970, the Pfeiffer graduate scholarship for 1971, and the Raemakers prize for 1971.

A quiet determination to succeed did not prevent Vicky from making many friends. One of these friendships was with Timothy Francis Clement-Jones (*b*. 26 Oct 1949), son of Maurice Llewelyn Clement-Jones, personnel manager, whom she married on 16 June 1973, two years after she left Cambridge; there were no children. By this time Vicky was well into her clinical training at St Thomas's Hospital, London, where she qualified MB, BChir, in 1974. Junior appointments at St Thomas's and the Brompton Hospital followed. In 1976 while working in the department of medicine at St Bartholomew's Hospital, she passed the MRCP examination. She had become increasingly interested in research and was awarded an Aylwen bursary at Bart's to study the naturally occurring opioid peptides which are concerned with the body's response to pain. She was successful in devising a radioimmunoassay for one of these and reported it in *Nature* (17 January 1980, 295). Publications leading to a better understanding of pain mechanisms followed. It was a strange irony that in 1982 she was struck by one of the most painful of diseases, carcinoma of the ovary. The shock of the diagnosis was overwhelming. Later, in a BBC radio interview with Professor Anthony Clare, she said she thought she would be dead in a few months. A few days after the diagnosis had been confirmed, a medical oncologist at Bart's was able to restore her hope, but almost certainly this fearful episode and her ignorance about cancer resulted in her major achievement, the formation of a help and advisory service for patients with cancer, the British Association for Cancer United Patients (BACUP). This became the largest and most successful organization of its kind in the United Kingdom, helping over 100,000 patients a year through the provision of a telephone information service, personal counselling, and the publication of a range of booklets and leaflets.

Before this took place Vicky passed through the fire of

her own treatment for cancer, with intractable vomiting, loss of hair, depression, and curtailment of every aspect of her life. Through this experience she was able to help others. Amazingly, she told Professor Clare that as a result of her illness she felt her life had been enriched. Those who knew this vibrant, dark-eyed, intense young doctor testified to her relentless pursuit of establishing BACUP. The inaugural meeting took place in October 1984 and the official launch was exactly a year later. In the months ahead, as the success of BACUP became assured, it became evident that Vicky would not survive a recurrence of the disease. She died in Bart's on 30 July 1987, exactly five years from the day of her diagnosis. Her body was cremated at Croydon crematorium, London.

J. S. MALPAS

Sources C. Faulder, *A special gift* (1991) · *BMJ* (12 Sept 1987), 677 · T. J. McE., *The Lancet* (15 Aug 1987), 407 · transcript of interview with Professor Anthony Clare for the BBC programme 'In the Psychiatrist's Chair', July 1985 · private information (2004) · V. Clement-Jones, 'Cancer and beyond: the formation of BACUP', *BMJ* (12 Oct 1985), 1021–3 · personal knowledge (2004) · b. cert. [Timothy Clement-Jones] · m. cert.
Archives SOUND BBC Sound Archive, London, interview with Anthony Clare
Wealth at death £16,281: probate, 3 Nov 1987, *CGPLA Eng. & Wales*

Jones, William (1561–1636), Church of England clergyman, attended Cambridge University, having matriculated as a sizar from Trinity College at Easter 1576. He graduated BA from Clare College in 1579–80, proceeded MA in 1583, and was awarded his BTh (1590) and DTh at Emmanuel College. He was one of the founding fellows of Emmanuel and in December 1589 was a petitioner in favour of the imprisoned Francis Johnson.

Ordained as priest in the diocese of Lincoln on 23 September 1585, Jones was instituted as rector of East Bergholt, Suffolk, on 28 December 1591, and was licensed there on the 6 March following. However, in law the church was a mere chapel of ease, and it seems that in instituting Jones the bishop was doing little other than formally confirming the choice of the parish. Soon afterwards 141 inhabitants wrote to their new minister. Recalling that it had 'pleased God to move us heretofore to send for you', they promised to submit themselves 'to all that counsel of God which you shall truly deliver to us out of his written word'. This was essentially a contract or covenant between Jones and his 'flock'; it was 'not a document which would readily have recommended itself to the hierarchy of the church, and many gentlemen would have found it fairly threatening as well' (MacCulloch, 319). At the time of Bishop Redman's visitation in 1597, Jones was also rector of Frostenden, Suffolk, where it was reported that the chancel and parsonage houses were in a state of disrepair, and that Jones 'readeth not the injunctions', which may suggest that his outlook was no better liked by the authorities than his covenant. It may be assumed that he married, though nothing is known of his wife. A son William was admitted in 1615 to Gonville and Caius College, Cambridge, aged sixteen.

As an old man Jones published *A Commentary upon the*

Epistles of St Paul to Philemon and the Hebrewes (1636), which he dedicated to Sir Thomas Jermyn, and to Henry, earl of Holland. In 1641 Sir Edward Dering protested that remarks relating to sabbath observance had been excised from this book by Dr Samuel Baker, chaplain to the bishop of London. In 1646 William Prynne alleged that Baker, 'a great instrument of the Archbishop's', had 'purged out all the principal clauses in it against altars, images, mass, transubstantiation, popery, papists, and for the sanctification of the Lord's day', giving references both to the manuscript copy and the printed book (Prynne, 255). It is clear that excisions were made, and that these also included references to arbitrary government. Laud responded to Prynne's charge that he could not be made 'answerable for every fault that is committed by every man that I employ in my visitation, though it be a fault committed at another time' (*Works*, 4.283). Prynne further claimed that Jones 'was so much discontented at the alterations and purgations made therein without his privity, that he disclaimed it to be his work, saying that it was the licencer's only, not his' and that he 'fell sick through discontent and soon after died' (Prynne, 255). Whatever the cause, William Jones died on 12 December 1636, and was buried in the church of East Bergholt, where a monument was erected to his memory in the north wall of the chapel.

Jones is to be distinguished from another Church of England clergyman, **William Jones** (b. 1581/2, d. in or before 1636), from Chacombe in Northamptonshire. Educated at Eton College, he entered King's College, Cambridge, as a scholar on 25 August 1599 at the age of seventeen. He graduated BA in 1604, proceeded MA three years later, and on 31 May 1607 was ordained as a priest in the diocese of Lincoln. He was a fellow at King's from 1602 and 1616, and received his BD degree in 1613. He may have been the 'William Iones Master of Arts', who in Dorchester on Christmas day in 1613 preached a sermon which was published the following year as *The Mysterie of Christes Nativitie*. An earlier work on how to make a will, entitled *A Pithie and Short Treatise* (1612), has also been attributed to him.

Jones became chaplain to the countess of Southampton, to whom he preached following the deaths in 1624 of her husband and son. The sermon was expanded and published in 1625 together with a collection of memorial poems, *The Teares of the Isle of Wight*, edited by Jones, who was described as the 'P[reacher?] of Arraton in the Isle of Wight'. This, along with three further religious works by Jones, published in the 1630s, were all printed in London by his namesake and fellow Northamptonshire man, William Jones. It is not known when Jones died, but his *True Inquisition, or, The Sad Soules Search* described him as 'late preacher to Arreton' (W. Jones, *Time Inquisition*, 1636, title-page).

STEPHEN WRIGHT

Sources D. MacCulloch, *Suffolk and the Tudors: politics and religion in an English county, 1500–1600* (1986) · *The works of the most reverend father in God, William Laud*, 4, ed. J. Bliss (1854) · *The Registrum vagum of Anthony Harison*, ed. T. F. Barton, 2 vols., Norfolk RS, 32–3 (1963–4) · J. F. Williams, ed., *Diocese of Norwich, Bishop Redman's visitation, 1597*, Norfolk RS, 18 (1946) · W. Prynne, *Canterburies doome, or, The*

first part of a compleat history of the commitment, charge, tryall, condem-
nation, execution of William Laud, late arch-bishop of Canterbury (1646) •
C. Hill, Society and puritanism in pre-revolutionary England (1964) •
H. C. Porter, Reformation and reaction in Tudor Cambridge (1958) •
W. Jones, A commentary upon the epistles of St Paul to Philemon and the
Hebrewes (1636) • Venn, Alum. Cant. • STC, 1475–1640 • DNB

Jones, Sir William (1566–1640), judge, was the eldest son
of William Jones of Castellmarch, Caernarvonshire, and
his first wife, Margaret, a daughter of Humphry Wynn ap
Meredith of Hyssoilfarch. Jones matriculated at St
Edmund Hall, Oxford, in the early 1580s, but he did not
take a degree. He was admitted to Lincoln's Inn on 5 July
1587, having spent some years previously at Furnival's
Inn, and was called to the bar on 28 January 1595. He married Margaret, the daughter of Griffith ap John Griffith of
Cefnamwlch, Tudweiliog, Caernarfon, about 1587, and by
the end of the 1590s had built up a substantial clientele
among friends and relations in north Wales, including the
Wynns of Gwydir. About 1600 he was made crown bailiff
of Cafflogion commote, a position once held by his great-
grandfather. From 1601 until his death he was a member
of the commission of the peace for Caernarvonshire, and
in 1604 he was made recorder of Beaumaris. Having been
returned as a member of parliament for Beaumaris in
1597 and Caernarvonshire in 1601, he sat again for Beaumaris in 1604 and 1614.

Though not a particularly active parliament man, Jones
made an impact on the impositions debates in 1610 and
1614, reportedly saying that:

> I thinke the kinge cannot by the Comon law of the land
> impose. The reason is: the common law of the land hath
> geven a propriety to every man of his owne goodes and the
> kinge cannot charge or have any interest therein but by the
> grant of the partie either in person, or by representation in
> parliament wherin all men are parties.   (Ellesmere MS 2511)

The attribution is not completely secure, but he is also
likely to be the William Jones who participated in the discussions of the Society of Antiquaries in London, and who
on one occasion outlined the role of the druids as civil and
ecclesiastical magistrates before they were driven into
Wales and then suppressed by the Romans.

Jones gave the Lent reading (on 43 Eliz. c. 1) at Lincoln's
Inn in 1616. In the following year he became a serjeant-at-
law, was knighted, and was appointed chief justice of the
king's bench in Ireland, having impressed the new lord
keeper, Sir Francis Bacon, despite his opposition in the
earlier parliaments. He resigned the Irish post early in
1620, probably because it was not sufficiently lucrative,
but his return to private practice was short-lived since he
was made a justice of the common pleas in England in
1621, perhaps through the good offices of Bacon's successor, Bishop John Williams. At the instigation of Lord Treasurer Lionel Cranfield, Jones was appointed in 1622 and
1623 to high-profile commissions that were charged with
investigating the state of the kingdom of Ireland. With
the help of his son Charles and his law clerk Roger Haswell, Jones was largely responsible for presenting the
privy council with a comprehensive and conscientious
report that covered the conditions of the plantations as
well as the administration of civil and ecclesiastical law.

The programme of reform with which the commissions
were associated came to an end as a result of factional conflict between the duke of Buckingham and Cranfield that
led to the latter's fall in 1624, but Jones continued to be
consulted from time to time about Irish affairs until Wentworth became lord deputy in 1632.

Repeatedly appointed between 1622 and his death to
commissions for gaol delivery at Newgate and as a justice
of assize on the Oxford circuit Jones is often mentioned in
manuscript and printed law reports of the period. Always
maintaining his connections in Wales as well as London
he became a member of the council of the marches, and
in October 1624 was transferred from the common pleas
to the king's bench. Though he displayed considerable
independence of thought, Jones was also an active servant
of the crown in the later 1620s and 1630s. At the trial of the
five knights imprisoned at the king's command for failing
to contribute the forced loan of 1626 he questioned
Attorney-General Heath about the king's position, but did
not dissent from the court's ruling that they could be held
without charges being specified. Following the dissolution of parliament in 1629 he gave the decision against
the members accused of holding the speaker down in the
chair, and he was appointed to nearly all the commissions
set up during the 1630s for raising revenue by enforcing
the forest laws. On the other hand in 1631 Jones was reprimanded for speaking against the earl marshal's court.
Though unsympathetic to religious nonconformity he disliked the political pretensions of some of the clergy, and
irritated Archbishop Laud in 1633 by maintaining the
right of the common law judges to grant prohibitions.
Acutely aware of the divide in public opinion that surrounded the test case brought by John Hampden in connection with the royal attempt to levy ship money, Jones
'fluttered in his argument' (Cope, 119), but eventually concluded that if the country was in danger then there was an
obligation on all subjects, as well as the king, to defend it.
Trusting the king to determine the extent of the threat he
declared the writs legal so long as the rate was used to
build ships and not merely to contribute to the general
revenues of the crown.

Following the death of his first wife in 1609 Jones married Catherine, daughter of Thomas Powis of Abingdon
and widow of Robert Hovendon, historian and sometime
warden of All Souls College, Oxford. He died at his house
in Holborn on 6 December 1640 and was buried at Lincoln's Inn chapel. He made bequests to his wife and two
daughters, Dorothy and Luce Jones, in a will made four
days before his death. Though he built a new house at Castellmarch in 1625 he was said not to have added more than
£200 p.a. to the inheritance he had from his father. A collection of his reports, covering the years from 1621 to
1640, was published from autograph manuscripts in
1675.   CHRISTOPHER W. BROOKS

Sources 'Jones, Sir William', HoP, Commons, 1604–29 [draft] • HoP,
Commons, 1558–1603 • DNB • State trials, vol. 3 • T. Hearne, A collection
of curious discourses, written by eminent antiquaries upon several heads in
our English antiquities, 2 vols. (1720–71) • V. Treadwell, Buckingham
and Ireland, 1616–1628: a study in Anglo-Irish politics (Dublin, 1998) •

Hunt. L., Ellesmere MS 2511 · *Les reports de Sir William Jones chevalier … un des justices del banck le roy* (1675) · E. S. Cope, *Politics without parliament, 1629–1640* (1987) · will, PRO, PROB 11/185, sig. 28
Archives Exeter College, Oxford, MSS | BL, 'Divers reports concerning the state of the kingdome of Ireland upon the views of certain commissions sent thether by King James in the year 1622', Add. MS 4756 · BL, Lent reading on 43 Eliz. c. 1, confirmation of grants made by the king and of letters patents made by the crown, Harley MS 1692, fols. 82ff.
Likenesses W. Sherwin, line engraving, BM, NPG; repro. in *Reports* (1675) · oils, Lincoln's Inn, London
Wealth at death will, PRO, PROB 11/185, sig. 28 · maintained at least two houses: *Reports*

Jones, William (*b*. 1581/2, *d*. in or before 1636). *See under* Jones, William (1561–1636).

Jones, Sir William (*bap*. 1630, *d*. 1682), lawyer and politician, was baptized on 3 July 1630, second son of Richard Jones (1605–1692) of Stowey Court, Chew Magna, Somerset, and of Joyce (*d*. 1644), *née* Woodward. His father, also a lawyer, supported parliament in the 1640s and held county office and sat in parliament in the 1650s. On 6 May 1647 the younger Jones entered Gray's Inn, being called to the bar in 1655.

At St Margaret Patterns in London, on 11 September 1661, Jones married Elizabeth (*d*. 1699), daughter of Edward Alleyn of Hatfield Peverel, Essex, and widow of John Robinson of Senston Hall, Suffolk. The young barrister was already one of the leading members of his profession, particularly in the court of king's bench, where his rise was matched only by Francis North, the protégé of Attorney-General Sir Geoffrey Palmer. Jones's and North's simultaneous advance brought them into competition, and Jones was reportedly jealous in 1671 when North was made solicitor-general rather than himself. As a sop to Jones and his patron, the duke of Buckingham, Jones was made a king's attorney instead. A knighthood followed on 15 July 1671. Financial success paralleled professional success, and in 1673 Jones bought the manor of Avington in Berkshire, buying further properties in Berkshire and in Wiltshire in the years following, culminating in his purchase of Ramsbury, where he began construction of a new house in 1681.

On 14 November 1673 Jones at last became solicitor-general as North advanced to the attorney-general's place. Jones succeeded as attorney-general on 23 June 1675 when North became chief justice of common pleas. As attorney-general Jones argued against the release of the earl of Shaftesbury on his habeas corpus in 1677. He also directed the early Popish Plot prosecutions, frequently joined as counsel by Sir John Maynard and Sir Francis Winnington, who, like Jones, would soon become prominent foes of the duke of York's succession to the throne. Jones reportedly played a leading role in the extensive remodelling of the bench in Westminster Hall in the spring of 1679.

Jones's elder son, also William, died in October 1679 in an accident while playing with a servant. His death, and suggestions of ill health, were the pretexts for Jones's request to the king to be relieved of office, which was granted on 21 October 1679. Others suspected that Jones's opposition to the court, his desire for a judgeship, or both motivated his departure from office. Jones retained close contacts with the king and even the duke of York while he apparently tried to use his alliance with court opponents as a wedge to force himself back into office. Talk arose in 1680 that Jones might become lord chancellor as part of a bid to bring the earl of Halifax and others into a broader royal ministry. Further gossip suggested that Jones might become chief justice of common pleas. Nothing came of either of these rumours. Even as late as October 1680 some considered Jones to be 'a firm friend to the court' (*Le Fleming MSS*, 163).

In November 1680 Jones was elected MP at a by-election for Plymouth, perhaps having stood on the interest of Sir John Maynard. Though he had no previous parliamentary experience, Jones immediately assumed a leading role in bringing the House of Commons to support a bill intended to exclude the Catholic duke of York from the succession. Jones attacked the king's servants, including Sir George Jeffreys and his old rival Sir Francis North, for allegedly writing the king's proclamation against petitioning. He was active in a Commons committee investigating what some considered the arbitrary proceedings of Sir William Scroggs, chief justice of king's bench. Jones joined with Maynard, Winnington, and George Treby in prosecuting the Commons' impeachment of Viscount Stafford for plotting against the king's life. Those who witnessed the trial spoke of their expert management, and especially of Jones's summation, as a result of which Stafford was executed.

Jones was chosen again as MP for Plymouth in March 1681 and played a prominent part in the Oxford parliament, where one observer considered Jones and Winnington 'the privy councilors' to the disaffected (*Letters of Humphrey Prideaux*, 99). Those who sought some expedient to settle the controversy over the duke of York short of barring his succession were stymied by Jones's argument that whoever succeeded would by law have the full power of the prerogative vested in him: it was because of the enormous theoretical authority he accorded to the king that Jones insisted that exclusion was the only solution. With the failure of the exclusion effort, and with the king's well-received declaration explaining why he had dissolved the Oxford parliament, Jones assisted Algernon Sidney in writing *A Just and Modest Vindication of the Proceedings of the Last Two Parliaments*, a vigorous assertion of parliamentary power.

Jones died on 2 May 1682, competing reports placing his death at his chambers in Gray's Inn, his house in Southampton Square, or in Buckinghamshire. The lease of his London house went to his widow. The residue of his extensive landed estate went to his only surviving son, Richard, who died in 1685 aged seventeen, after which the properties descended through the line of his brother, Samuel Jones. Bishop Burnet declared that Jones 'had a roughness in his deportment that was very disagreeable' (*Burnet's History*, 2.106). Many, including Roger North, brother of Sir Francis North, condemned Jones for 'using all the arts of his profession against the lives of so many poor men as he convicted to death for the plot' (North, 1.100). Yet even

North, like most of his generation, recognized Jones's professional ability as being equal with, 'if not superior to, the rest of his contemporaries' (ibid., 101).

PAUL D. HALLIDAY

Sources HoP, *Commons, 1660–90* · N. Luttrell, *A brief historical relation of state affairs from September 1678 to April 1714*, 6 vols. (1857) · *Burnet's History of my own time*, ed. O. Airy, new edn, 2 vols. (1897–1900) · M. Knights, *Politics and opinion in crisis, 1678–1681* (1994) · J. Scott, *Algernon Sidney and the Restoration crisis, 1677–1683* (1991) · M. Landon, *The triumph of the lawyers* (1970) · R. North, *The lives of … Francis North … Dudley North … and … John North*, new edn, 3 vols. (1826) · *State trials*, vols. 6–8 · F. A. Wood, *Collections for a parochial history of Chew Magna* (1903), 175–8 · Sainty, *Judges* · *Calendar of the manuscripts of the marquess of Ormonde*, new ser., 8 vols., HMC, 36 (1902–20), vols. 4–5 · *Seventh report*, HMC, 6 (1879) · *The manuscripts of the duke of Beaufort … the earl of Donoughmore*, HMC, 27 (1891) · *The manuscripts of S. H. Le Fleming*, HMC, 25 (1890) · *Report on the manuscripts of Allan George Finch*, 5 vols., HMC, 71 (1913–2003), vol. 2 · *CSP dom.*, 1675–6; 1679–80; 1682 · *The diaries and papers of Sir Edward Dering, second baronet, 1644 to 1684*, ed. M. F. Bond (1976) · *Letters of Humphrey Prideaux … to John Ellis*, ed. E. M. Thompson, CS, new ser., 15 (1875) · E. M. Thompson, ed., *Correspondence of the family of Hatton*, 2 vols., CS, new ser., 22–3 (1878) · *VCH Berkshire*, vols. 3–4; *VCH Somerset*, vol. 3; *VCH Wiltshire*, vol. 12 · will, 18 Oct 1861, PRO, PROB 11/370, fols. 29v–30 · J. Foster, *Register of admissions to Gray's Inn, 1521–1881* (privately printed, London, 1887), 244
Likenesses S. Dubois, oils, 1682, Dulwich Picture Gallery, London · tomb effigy, 1682, Holy Cross Church, Ramsbury, Wiltshire
Wealth at death lands in Berkshire, Wiltshire, and Somerset; lease of house in London; Ramsbury, a house in Wiltshire, then under construction: will, PRO, PROB 11/370, fols. 29v–30

Jones, William (c.1675–1749), mathematician, was born about 1675 on the small farm of Y Merddyn, Llanfihangel Tre'r-beirdd, Anglesey. He was the elder son of Siôn Siôr and Elizabeth Rowland; his mother came from Bodwigan, Llanddeusant. The family moved into the parish of Llanbabo, to Tyddyn Bach, and, after his father's death, to Clymwr. Jones (an Anglicized form from Siôn) showed his calculating skill while at the charity school at Llanfechell, leading the local landowner, Lord Bulkeley, to send him to London, to work in a merchant's counting-house. In this employment he went to the West Indies, probably thereby acquiring a taste for the sea and an interest in navigation, for he next became mathematics master on a man-of-war. Leaving the navy after participating in the capture of Vigo in 1702, he published his *New Compendium of the Whole Art of Navigation* in the same year; a second edition in 1706 was entitled *A New Epitomy*.

As a peripatetic teacher in London, within a year or two Jones was engaged as tutor to Philip Yorke, the future lord chancellor Hardwicke. Lodging with John Harris FRS, author of the *Lexicon technicum* (1704), Jones probably contributed the navigational articles in the volume. In 1706 his teaching notes were printed under the title *Synopsis palmariorum matheseos, or, A New Introduction to the Mathematics*. It used the work of John Wallis, Isaac Newton, and others to establish the current state of mathematical analysis and mechanics, demonstrating his grasp of the significance of Newton's discoveries. In it he introduced the symbol π, earlier used slightly differently by Oughtred. Maybe the book, with possibly a recommendation

from Harris, brought Jones to the attention of Newton. At this point, aged about thirty, Jones had delineated the two themes of his life—tutor to prominent figures and disseminator of Newton's writings.

Responsibility for Yorke's mathematical education probably lasted no more than two or three years. Early in 1709 Jones unsuccessfully applied for the mastership of Christ's Hospital Mathematical School, with a testimonial from Halley, and one from Newton, who wrote as if he knew Jones only by repute. In 1706 Yorke had embarked on a legal career and presently developed a close relationship with Thomas Parker, later first earl of Macclesfield. Through this connection Jones entered the Parker household as tutor to the son, George.

In 1708 Jones acquired the mathematical papers of John Collins. At that time, the priority dispute between Newton and Leibniz, publicly ignited by Fatio in 1699, was still smouldering. While unequal to evaluating Newton's work critically, Jones had a good command and appreciation of it; he was already contemplating an extensive edition when he found a Collins transcript of a Newton manuscript, 'De analysi' (1669). Using this and other transcripts, together with guidance from Newton and borrowed autographs, he published *Analysis per quantitatum series, fluxiones ac differentias* (1711). This bore neither Jones's name nor Newton's, but the preface to a second edition from Amsterdam in 1723 has Jones's signature. Jones had been sufficiently confident to fill gaps and to make minor amendments to Newton's texts. Included was a 1676 Newton letter to Collins, used by Keill as the kernel of his attack on Leibniz. In his preface Jones presented 'powerful evidence of Newton's mathematical originality as far back as 1665' (*Correspondence of Isaac Newton*, 5.95). It was a key element in the escalating dispute.

Jones was admitted FRS on 30 November 1711, and was included on a committee appointed on 6 March 1712 by the Royal Society to inspect the letters and papers relating to the dispute. The documents came largely from the Collins papers. Selection, annotation, and editing were performed by Newton himself, with Jones helping to take care of the impression. The resulting publication, ostensibly from an impartial standpoint, was the anonymous *Commercium epistolicum* (1712). Jones deposited the bulk of the Collins papers with the Royal Society, retrieved them in the 1730s, and in 1741 returned them bound, but with some missing.

Jones had married the widow of the merchant, his former employer; in 1711 he was using the accommodation address of Child's Coffee House, St Paul's Churchyard. He became acquainted with other prominent fellows, and acted as intermediary with Newton for some, specifically Brook Taylor and Roger Cotes, whose relationship with Newton had cooled. His letters to Cotes are in Trinity College, Cambridge. Jones transcribed many tracts or extracts that he had from Newton and circulated them among his contacts, although James Wilson MD, presumably one of his pupils, later wrote of the 'transpositions and interpolations, as Mr Jones was wont to make' so that 'none might make a perfect book out of them' (*Mathematical Papers of Isaac Newton*, 1.400). In the early 1720s 'Will Jones, the mathematician, & others of the heathen stamp' participated weekly in 'an infidel Club' hosted by Martin Folkes (*Family Memoirs*, 100). About 1725 Jones became a member of the freemasons' lodge at the Queen's Head, Hollis Street; George Parker, too, was a freemason.

Jones may have been editor of Newton's *Lectiones opticae* (1729). Briefed by James Logan, between 1732 and 1734 he was championing before the Royal Society the claim of Thomas Godfrey to be independent inventor of the double-reflecting quadrant. The introduction to Gardiner's *Logarithms* (1742) was compiled from Jones's papers, and it is reported that the 'Account of logarithms' prefixed to Dodson's *Anti-Logarithmic Canon* (1742) was also by him (Wilkinson, 189). Jones also had three articles in the *Philosophical Transactions*, two of them transmitted, long after his death, by John Robertson, (1712–1776), former pupil, later Royal Society librarian, who inherited some of Jones's papers. Charles Hutton, author of an influential mathematical dictionary, praised the neatness, brevity, and accuracy of Jones's mathematical writings; while not a great mathematician, Jones left a considerable mark on the mathematical world.

Although early in life Jones's manners were said to be 'agreeable and inviting' (Jones, 4), John Robertson, describing him as a little short-faced Welshman, spoke of his harsh manner in the late 1730s (Wilkinson, 518).

During Jones's long association with the Parkers he spent much time at their castle at Shirburn. The epigram 'Macclesfield was the making of Jones, and Jones the making of Macclesfield' testifies to Jones's services in resolving the family's 'disturbance' over an 'Italian marriage' (Hutton) of George Parker, although there is another interpretation. Jones lost heavily when his banker failed, but was supported by sinecures of secretary of the peace, procured by Hardwicke, and deputy teller to the Exchequer, by George Parker. Jones's first wife apparently having died some years previously, he married, on 17 April 1731, Mary (*c*.1705–1780), daughter of George Nix, a prominent London cabinet-maker and friend of Thomas Parker; he was fifty-six, she, twenty-five. Of their three children two survived, Mary (1736–1802) and William *Jones (1746–1794). Their London address was 11 Beaufort Buildings, Strand.

Jones served as council member of the Royal Society, and in 1743 on the committee to compare its new standard yard and weights with exchequer standards and others, witnessing the proceedings. He died at his London home on 1 July 1749, attended by Richard Mead for a 'polypus in the heart' (Jones, 6). He was buried on 7 July at St Paul's, Covent Garden. His collection of some 15,000 books was considered to be the most valuable mathematical library in England and was bequeathed to George Parker, the second earl of Macclesfield. His papers were not in the bequest; nevertheless many are at Shirburn, where they have remained (1995) with access extremely restricted. Almost the only permitted publication has been those papers contained in the two-volume Rigaud *Correspondence*. Among Jones's manuscripts was another projected mathematical book, which his son, Sir William, had intended, but failed, to publish.   RUTH WALLIS

Sources A. Llwyd, *A history of the island of Mona* (1833) · *Memoirs of the life, writings and correspondence of Sir William Jones*, ed. J. Shore, 1 (1806) · C. Hutton, *A mathematical and philosophical dictionary*, 2 vols. (1795–6) · *The mathematical papers of Isaac Newton*, ed. D. T. Whiteside, 8 vols. (1967–80), vols. 1, 3, 8 · *The correspondence of Isaac Newton*, ed. H. W. Turnbull and others, 1 (1959); 5 (1975); 7 (1977) · Ll. G. Chambers, *Mathemategwyr Cymru* (1994) · private information (2004) · T. T. Wilkinson, 'Mathematics and mathematicians, the journals of the late Reuben Burrow [pt 1]', *London, Edinburgh, and Dublin Philosophical Magazine*, 4th ser., 5 (1853), 185–93, esp. 189 · T. T. Wilkinson, 'Mathematics and mathematicians, the journals of the late Reuben Burrow [pt 2]', *London, Edinburgh, and Dublin Philosophical Magazine*, 4th ser., 5 (1853), 514–22, esp. 518 · *The family memoirs of the Rev. William Stukeley*, ed. W. C. Lukis, 1, SurtS, 73 (1882), 100 · S. P. Rigaud and S. J. Rigaud, eds., *Correspondence of scientific men of the seventeenth century*, 1 (1841) · R. V. Wallis and P. J. Wallis, eds., *Biobibliography of British mathematics and its applications*, 2 (1986) · J. R. Clarke, 'The Royal Society and early grand lodge freemasonry', *Ars Quatuor Coronatorum*, 80 (1967), 110–19 · R. T. Jenkins and H. M. Ramage, *A history of the Honourable Society of Cymmrodorion* (1951), 45 · G. Cannon, *The life and mind of Oriental Jones* (1990) · G. Harris, *The life of Lord Chancellor Hardwicke*, 1 (1847) · *General Advertiser* (3 July 1749) · GEC, *Peerage*, new edn

Archives RS, commonplace book · Shirburn Castle, Oxfordshire · Trinity Cam.

Wealth at death approx. £3000; books left to the earl of Macclesfield; £1000 to each of the two children on reaching age of twenty: will, PRO, PROB 11/772, sig. 252; Wilkinson, 'Mathematics and mathematicians'

Jones, William [*pseud.* Gwilym Cadfan] (*bap.* 1726, *d.* 1795), poet and radical, was baptized on 18 June 1726 at Llangadfan parish church, Montgomeryshire, the youngest of three sons born to William Siôn Dafydd (1666–1758), a farmer and stagecoach guard, and his second wife, Catherine (*d.* 1760). He took up his father's tenancy of Dolhywel in 1750, a decision which consigned him to a life of unremitting toil and poverty. Yet, in an age which prized versatility, he was an unusually gifted all-rounder and a remarkably intelligent, sophisticated, and well-read man. His fellow parishioners could only marvel at his gifts as a country healer, musician, poet (his bardic name was Gwilym Cadfan), raconteur, linguist, eisteddfod adjudicator, historian, and amateur astronomer. He offered his services as a collector and transcriber of Welsh manuscripts to leading Welsh and Celtic scholars in London, and Walter Davies, his bardic disciple, believed that in Welsh prosody and syntax Jones 'ranked among the profoundest critics that Wales has ever produced' (*Cambrian Register*, 11, 1796, 239).

Well versed in free-metre and strict-metre Welsh poetry, Jones also translated from Latin into Welsh some of the odes of Horace and parts of Ovid's *Metamorphoses*. Much of the content of the enlarged edition of Edward Jones's *Musical and Poetick Relicks of the Welsh Bards* (1794) was the fruit of William Jones's tireless research. Not the least of his achievements, too, was to record and revive the traditional country dances associated with the parish of Llangadfan and his efforts to rid the Welsh of their musical amnesia.

Although Jones was deeply interested in Welsh literature, his researches on behalf of London Welsh scholars were also prompted by the need to make ends meet. Trapped by his penury in the barren upland wastes of mid-Wales and by the illness of his wife, Ann, he was obliged to seek ways of supplementing his income. As a part-time country healer (he despised the term 'quack') he earned considerable respect in the county, not least because of the deft use he made of herbal lore. The Llangadfan vestry books bear witness to his care for sick people by purging, bloodletting, excising tumours, extracting teeth, and healing malignant fevers and agues. All his patients were informed in considerable detail of his success in conquering scrofula and those who cast doubt on his competence were shown his scars.

Jones was much in demand as an adjudicator in national and local eisteddfods, and also participated in some of Iolo Morganwg's gorsedds in London. He was remarkably well informed about current affairs, partly because members of the Gwyneddigion Society visited him regularly but mainly because he pestered members of parliament and foreign ambassadors for information. Letters, books, magazines, squibs, and ballads were sent by the score to Cann Office, a staging post at Llangadfan, and Jones developed a particular interest in astronomy, physics, geography, topography, and navigation. He traced the voyages of Captain Cook, familiarized himself with the terrain of Africa, Arabia, Brazil, and Egypt, and few in Britain were better acquainted with the civilization of the Incas and the culture of the elusive Padoucas (white-skinned Welsh Indians, the alleged descendants of Madoc, son of Owain Gwynedd), who were believed to dwell in the upper reaches of the Missouri.

Like many cultural nationalists and myth-makers in eighteenth-century Europe, Jones was determined to enhance the self-image of his people by campaigning on behalf of Welsh national institutions. He was among the first to call for a national library and a truly national eisteddfod. He composed a robust Welsh national anthem—the first of its kind in modern Wales—based on the refrain 'And join in joyful song on the fair break of dawn'. Stirringly patriotic, the anthem was his riposte to the jingoism of 'Rule Britannia' and 'The Roast Beef of Old England'.

Jones's political radicalism owed much to the inspiration of the French Revolution. In many ways, he discovered his political voice in 1789, and his correspondence is riddled with barbed references to fleecers, tyrants, and oppressors. A self-styled sans culotte, he prized the works of Voltaire above all others, so much so that he became known as the Rural Voltaire. Jones bore more than a passing resemblance to Voltaire and he also shared his Ranter-like fondness for satire, blasphemy, and vulgar jokes. Jones's penchant for bawdiness is best exemplified in his unpublished poem 'The Enraptur'd Lover to the Tune of Jack ye Latin', and the rector of Llangadfan, who dubbed him 'a rank republican [and] a Leveller' (NL Wales, MS 1806E, fol. 786), believed that he deserved to be peppered with gunshot and powder. During William Pitt's 'reign of terror' government spies intercepted, opened, and destroyed letters to and from Jones, and doubtless many of them were horrified by his scabrous comments about despotic Saxons and Normans. One of Jones's most loyal friends reckoned that he was 'the hottest arsed Welshman he had ever known' (NL Wales, MS 13221E, fol. 256).

Weary of poverty, persecution, and neglect, William Jones resolved to emigrate to the Land of Liberty. His aim was to purchase cheap and fruitful land in Kentucky and also to embark on an expedition in search of the Lost Welsh Brothers. But illness and old age conspired against him, and the Welsh Voltaire died in November 1795. The final wish of this incorrigible infidel was that he should be laid to rest in unconsecrated ground in the graveyard of Llangadfan parish church.   GERAINT H. JENKINS

Sources G. H. Jenkins, 'A rank republican [and] a leveller: William Jones, Llangadfan', *Welsh History Review / Cylchgrawn Hanes Cymru*, 17 (1994–5), 365–86 · G. H. Jenkins, *Y Chwyldro Ffrengig a Voltaire Cymru* (1989) · E. P. Roberts, 'William Jones, Dolhywel', *Montgomeryshire Collections*, 70 (1982), 40–46 · *DWB* · NL Wales, MS 1806E, fol. 786; MS 13221E, fols. 256, 416 · parish registers, Llangadfan, Montgomeryshire, Wales
Archives NL Wales, corresp., MSS 1641B, 1806E, 13221E, 13222C
Likenesses engraving, repro. in *Cambrian Register*, 2 (1796)

Jones, William [*known as* William Jones of Nayland] (1726–1800), Church of England clergyman and religious controversialist, was born at Lowick, Northamptonshire, on 30 July 1726, the son of Morgan Jones and his wife, Sarah Lettin. That he was descended on his father's side from the regicide Colonel John Jones was a source of regret in later life, when Jones was a leading spokesman for the very values against which his ancestor had taken arms.

Jones was educated at Charterhouse School, matriculated from University College, Oxford, on 9 July 1745, and graduated BA in 1749. At Oxford he formed some of his most significant personal and intellectual friendships, notably with George Horne, subsequently dean of Canterbury and bishop of Norwich, and Charles Jenkinson, later first earl of Liverpool. At Oxford, too, Jones, Horne, and some of their other friends were drawn to the semi-mystical writings of the anti-Newtonian and anti-Lockian John Hutchinson, and developed a high-church theology which was entirely consistent with the predominantly tory mentality of their university. Although by no means an uncritical Hutchinsonian, Jones shared Hutchinson's admiration for the nonjurors and his notions of the English constitution as divinely sanctioned. Jones was ordained deacon in the diocese of Peterborough on 24 September 1749 and priest in the diocese of Lincoln two years later. At this time he accepted his first curacy, of Finedon, Northamptonshire. In 1754 he married Elizabeth (d. 1799), daughter of the Revd Nathaniel Bridges and cousin of Sir Brook Bridges of Goodnestone Park, Kent. They had a son. Jones then became curate to his brother-in-law, the Revd Brook Bridges, at Wadenhoe, Northamptonshire, although the Kentish connections of his wife's family were to be of significance for the rest of his life.

In 1756 Jones published his *Catholic doctrine of a Trinity*

William Jones (1726–1800), by Robert Mitchell Meadows, pubd 1801

proved by … arguments expressed in the terms of the holy scripture, which went through seven editions in the next forty years and drew him to the attention of the church authorities as a champion of orthodoxy at a time when antitrinitarian speculation was fashionable in some latitudinarian and rational dissenting quarters. In 1764 Archbishop Secker presented him to the living of Bethersden in Kent, with an estimated value of £100 per annum. Jones himself believed that the income was insufficient and that the location was detrimental to his health. The following year Secker presented him to the rectory of nearby Pluckley, worth some £200 per annum. Here, according to his fellow clergyman Joseph Price, Jones attracted pupils from wealthy families (Ditchfield and Keith-Lucas, 337, 339). By publishing in 1770 a reply to Francis Blackburne's markedly latitudinarian *Confessional*, Jones consolidated his reputation as a defender of the traditional authority and dogma of the church. Several of his fellow Hutchinsonians, moreover, had Kent connections; George Horne and William Stevens (subsequently Jones's biographer) both attended school at Maidstone. Joseph Price described him as 'As high a churchman as if he had lived in the last 4 years of Queen Anne' (ibid., 338).

In 1777 Jones became perpetual curate of Nayland, in Suffolk, where he resided until his death and with which his name became closely associated. At the same time he exchanged Pluckley for Paston in Northamptonshire. In 1782 he proceeded to the degree of MA at Sidney Sussex College, Cambridge. Natural science was one of his intellectual interests: his *Essay on the First Principles of Natural Philosophy* (1762) was followed by a larger work, *Physiological Disquisitions*, in 1781. In 1771 he published *Zoologica ethica: a discourse concerning the Mosaic description of animals into clean and unclean*. In this work he pursued his interest in the Jewish religion, arguing that, rather than abstaining from the consumption of swine's flesh, it was more pleasing to God to avoid 'the earthly, unclean and grovelling *affections*' of the swine. Joseph Price described his methods of enquiry: 'Every peddling Jew that comes to his house with a box at his back Jones has him into the parlour and disputes with him about his Religion' (Ditchfield and Keith-Lucas, 340). Jones's scientific work was rewarded by his election as a fellow of the Royal Society in 1775. His *Six Letters on Electricity* was published after his death.

Jones's principal publications, however, concerned the Anglican tradition and its justification through scripture and established practice. He was a strong admirer of the Caroline divines and in his *Essay on the Church* (1780) he defended the idea of the apostolic succession. The values espoused by a high-churchman of Jones's type have been neatly summarized by a recent scholar: 'he tended to cultivate a practical spirituality based on good works nourished by sacramental grace and exemplified in acts of self-denial and charity rather than on any subjective conversion experience or unruly pretended manifestations of the Holy Spirit' (Nockles, 26). Accordingly, Jones disapproved both of popular evangelicalism and of Socinianism; in *A Preservative Against the Publications Dispersed by Modern Socinians* (1786), he claimed that:

> The change from Christianity to Socinianism is as little to be envied as the transmigration of those who should leave the scenery of Paradise and the plenty of Canaan, to associate with the savages of the South on a weather-beaten Rock in the Magellanic Ocean.

As a subsequent commentator averred, 'The very name of "Nayland Jones" makes all the Unitarians and Methodists tremble' (*Kenyon MSS*, 563). One of his particular targets was the Unitarian bookseller Joseph Johnson, whom Jones described in 1789 as having 'kept the grand shop for heresy, schismatology, and rebellion' (ibid., 550).

By this time the French Revolution had inspired Jones and his associates to heightened energy in defence of the church against what they saw as anarchy, irreligion, and Antichrist. In 1792 Jones founded the Society for the Reformation of Principles to promote high-church values, which resulted in the publication of the *British Critic*. He edited in 1795 an expanded version of a collection of tracts previously published fifteen years earlier and now entitled *The Scholar Armed Against the Errors of the Time*. He sought to popularize his views, in a manner later adopted with immense success by Hannah More, in his *Letter from Thomas Bull to his Brother John* (1792) and similar works. That his type of orthodoxy was becoming increasingly integrated into the ecclesiastical establishment was seen in the elevation of his close friend George Horne to the bishopric of Norwich; Horne promptly made Jones one of his chaplains. On Horne's death in 1792 Jones wrote a eulogistic biography, published in 1795. At Nayland he took immense trouble over his parochial duties. Two volumes of his sermons were published in 1790 and he maintained a keen interest in the technicalities of musical notation and its applicability to church services. He published a sermon entitled *The Nature and Excellence of Music* (1787) and prepared 'Ten Church Pieces for the Organ … for the Use of the Church of Nayland'. Music to Jones enhanced the value of ecclesiastical rites and ceremonies, which deepened the understanding of scripture. Hence priests and choristers in church should wear white as symbols of purity; candles symbolized the illumination offered by the gospel (Nockles, 208).

During the 1790s Jones experienced poverty and ill health. Through the intercession of William Stevens he received financial succour from Archbishop John Moore, who allowed Jones to renew his Kentish connections by presenting him to the sinecure rectory of Hollingbourne in 1798. Its income undoubtedly eased his closing years, although he continued to reside at Nayland. The death of his wife in February 1799 was a devastating blow to him, and in a most pathetic and moving letter, conveyed to the *Gentleman's Magazine* by his friend and fellow Hutchinsonian Samuel Glasse, he lamented 'I have lost the manager, whose vigilant attention to my worldly affairs, and exact method in ordering my family, preserved my mind at liberty to pursue my studies without loss of time, or distraction of thought' (*GM*, 1st ser., 69/1, 1799, 294). Jones himself died at Nayland of a paralytic stroke on 6 January 1800, and was buried there. The following year his collected works were published, in twelve volumes, with a 'life' by William Stevens. His career illustrates the ways in which the high-church mentality, with its connotations of sacerdotalism and respect for divinely constituted authority, was more influential in the eighteenth century than has sometimes been appreciated. The threats to order posed by the American War of Independence, and even more by the French Revolution, gave Jones and his contemporaries a wide readership. They drew upon a corpus of Anglican doctrine which enabled them to mount an effective ideological counter-attack against the challenge of Jacobinism and heterodoxy at home and abroad. Jones's ideas were readily received by the Hackney Phalanx, a group of high-churchmen who commanded very considerable influence within the church during the first thirty years of the nineteenth century (Nockles, 271–2). Clergymen of Jones's ilk deserve to be considered as much more than precursors of the Oxford Movement; Jones himself was greatly admired by J. H. Newman, but his churchmanship remains of considerable historical importance in its own right.

G. M. DITCHFIELD

Sources W. Stevens, 'Life', *Works of William Jones*, 12 vols. (1801), vol. 1 · G. M. Ditchfield and B. Keith-Lucas, 'Reverend William Jones "of Nayland" (1726–1800): some new light on his years in Kent', *N&Q*, 238 (1993), 337–42 · *GM*, 1st ser., 70 (1800), 183–4, 459–60, 231 · P. B. Nockles, *The Oxford Movement in context: Anglican high churchmanship, 1760–1857* (1994) · *The manuscripts of Lord Kenyon*, HMC, 35 (1894) · J. C. D. Clark, *English society, 1688–1832: ideology, social structure and political practice during the ancien régime* (1985) · *The autobiography of Thomas Secker, archbishop of Canterbury*, ed. J. S. Macauley and R. W. Greaves (1988) · W. H. Teale, *Lives of English divines* (1866), 345–419 · Foster, *Alum. Oxon.* · N. Sykes, *Church and state in England in the XVIII century* (1934) · R. Hole, *Pulpits, politics and public order in England, 1760–1832* (1989) · V. H. H. Green, 'Religion in the colleges, 1715–1800', *Hist. U. Oxf. 5: 18th-cent. Oxf.*

Archives Pusey Oxf., sermons | BL, letters to George Berkeley, MSS 39311, 39312 · BL, corresp. with first earl of Liverpool, Add. MSS 38216–38225; 38307–38309; 38472, *passim* · BL, letters to Charles Poyntz · Magd. Oxf., corresp. with George Horne

Likenesses R. M. Meadows, stipple engraving, pubd 1801 (after portrait), AM Oxf., BM, NPG [*see illus.*] · S. Davenport, engraving (after J. Thurston), repro. in *Rev. William Jones's letters to his pupils*, new edn (1863) · T. A. Dean, engraving (after J. Basire), priv. coll. · R. Graves, line engraving, NPG · G. Murray, engraving (after J. Basire), repro. in *Rev. William Jones's letters to his pupils*

Wealth at death small personal estate; bequeathed manuscripts to son-in-law; residue to William Stevens: will, PRO, PROB 11/1337, fols. 195r–196r

Jones, Sir William (1746–1794), orientalist and judge, was born at Beaufort Buildings, Westminster, on 28 September 1746, the youngest child of William *Jones (c.1675–1749) and Mary Nix (c.1705–1780), the gifted daughter of a cabinet-maker. His father, a distinguished Welsh mathematician and a friend of Sir Isaac Newton and Edmond Halley, died before he was three, leaving him well connected but lacking financial resources. His intellectual patrimony linked the young Jones with the cultural and intellectual tradition of his Anglesey relation Lewis Morris, whose polymathic and entrepreneurial approach influenced the future orientalist. His mother's enlightened educational ideas helped to stimulate his young mind; a wide range of books was always available to facilitate her guiding maxim: 'read, and you will know'. Jones, already something of a prodigy at seven, won a scholarship to Harrow School, which he entered in Michaelmas term 1753; he rapidly displayed his prowess in languages, translating and imitating the Greek and Roman classics, teaching himself Hebrew, learning Arabic script, taking the lead in a tragedy he wrote entitled 'Meleager', and, having acquired more Greek than the headmaster, Robert Carey Sumner, gaining the nickname 'the Great Scholar'.

On entering University College, Oxford, where he matriculated on 15 March 1764, Jones was not over-impressed by the standard of public lectures, but his election as one of the college's four Bennet scholars on 31 October 1764 enabled him to improve his Arabic by employing a Syrian named Mirza to help him translate the *Arabian Nights* back into its original tongue. His exertions were fuelled by intellectual excitement as he uncovered the manuscript treasures of the Pococke collection in the Bodleian. Fascinated by the linguistic connections between Arabic and Persian, he found his study of the latter accelerated by his enthusiasm for the thirteenth-century Persian poet Sa'di. He made the acquaintance of Robert Lowth, bishop of Oxford from October 1766 and former professor of poetry, whose *De sacra poesi Hebraeorum* (1753) encouraged Jones to read the Old Testament as a masterpiece of oriental literature. Researching

Sir William Jones (1746–1794), by Arthur William Devis, c.1793

at Oxford, and passing the vacations in London—where he read European classics in Italian, Spanish, and Portuguese, learned fencing from Domenico Angelo and the Welsh harp from a musician called Evans—he was, in his own words, 'with the fortune of a peasant, giving himself the education of a prince' (Teignmouth, 'Memoir', in *Works*, 1.59). His subsequent studies were supported by his acceptance in 1765 of the post of tutor to George John Spencer, Viscount Althorp, eldest son of John, first Earl Spencer, whereby he gained a lifelong friend and correspondent, access to one of the foremost private libraries in Europe, and an entrée into the society of influential whig magnates. In summer 1766 he met Anna Maria Shipley (1748–1829), daughter of Jonathan *Shipley (1713–1788), afterwards bishop of Llandaff and of St Asaph, who had recommended him to the Spencers, and sister of William Davies *Shipley (1745–1826). Jones fell in love with Anna Maria, but felt he could not marry her until he had become sufficiently independent to avoid reliance on the Shipleys and their relatives for advancement.

'Selim' Jones Jones's reputation as an orientalist was rapidly established, and earned him the nickname Selim Jones. On 7 August 1766 he was elected a fellow of University College. In that summer he was offered the post of interpreter for Eastern languages at the Treasury by its new first lord, Augustus Fitzroy, third duke of Grafton, which he refused, suggesting instead with characteristic generosity and youthful unworldliness that the post instead be given to his friend Mirza; his first biographer, John Shore, first Baron Teignmouth, later observed that Jones must not have realized that he could have accepted the post and appointed Mirza his deputy on full salary. He graduated BA in Michaelmas term 1768, at about which time he received a prestigious commission from King

Christian VII of Denmark to translate from Persian into French what became the *Histoire de Nader Chah*, an account of the life of the Persian monarch Nadir Shah (d. 1747). The book was published in 1770; Christian rewarded Jones with nomination to the Royal Society of Copenhagen and a recommendation to George III. The irony implicit in the fact that the translation of a biography sympathetic to a Persian despot should constitute the first published work of a scholar who later argued for universal manhood suffrage was compounded by many aspects of the career of a man who was both radical whig and colonial administrator. Jones was already highly regarded, but his ambition was not limited to oriental literature and tutoring the aristocracy, and on 19 November 1770 he entered the Middle Temple, London, to begin studying for the bar.

The work which Jones shrewdly appended to *Histoire de Nader Chah*, 'Un traité sur la poësie orientale', was designed to destroy the absolute sway which Graeco-Roman classicism held over European literature. He argued that access to alternative classical traditions might prove reinvigorating. Organized on comparative principles illustrated by prose and verse translations of odes by the fourteenth-century Persian poet Hafiz, the 'Traité' proved a timely curtain-raiser to Jones's *Grammar of the Persian Language* (1771), a text which simultaneously established his international reputation as Oriental or Persian Jones, inaugurated the literary trend later identified as romantic orientalism, and represented a work of utility in the training of East India Company writers. Persian was the official language at the courts of nawabs and Mughal princes, and the fact that a grammar might prove valuable intellectual property was evidenced by the attempted piracy of Jones's proofs. In his preface Jones attempts to combat prejudice, asserting that the Eurocentric philistines are the real savages:

> We all love to excuse, or to conceal, our ignorance, and are seldom willing to allow any excellence beyond the limits of our own attainments: like the savages, who thought the sun rose and set for them alone, and could not imagine that the waves, which surrounded their island, left coral and pearls upon any other shore. (*Works*, 5.166)

While he appreciated that commercial and colonial interest 'was the charm which gave the languages of the East a real and solid importance' (ibid., 173), Jones provided a poets' grammar which transcended utility and served as a primer of Persian verse for generations of writers from Lord Byron and Thomas Moore to Edward FitzGerald and Alfred Tennyson.

1771 also saw Jones publish the important *Dissertation sur la littérature orientale*, in which he further illustrated the elegant beauty of Arabic and Persian verse, comparing oriental authors such as Hafiz and Abu'l-Fida to the classical writers Horace and Xenophon. His third publication of 1771, the *Lettre à Monsieur A*** du P****, is a work which, though well received at the time, blotted Jones's scholarly integrity as surely as it blighted the academic career of his opponent, Abraham-Hyacinthe Anquetil-Duperron. Despite his stated conviction that international scholarly co-operation should rise above disputes between the ruling dynasties of Europe, Jones was stung to patriotic anger by the Frenchman's criticisms of Oxford scholarship. In applying the weight of his reputation to his misguided assertion that Anquetil-Duperron had been duped by the Parsis with modern forgeries, Jones seriously retarded studies of the Zend-Avesta for many years.

The success in 1772 of *Poems, Consisting Chiefly of Translations from the Asiatick Languages* owed much to the fashionable craze for things oriental; according to Elizabeth Montagu, 'The descriptions are so fine, & all the objects so brilliant, that the sense aches at them!' (quoted in *Letters*, 1.111) As a poet Jones blended philosophical allegory and dramatic narrative into the genre of the oriental verse tale, but as a scholar he created, through his concern for accuracy of translation and comparative linguistic method, a demand for genuine Eastern products while significantly adjusting racial and political stereotypes. His representation of the East includes a translation from Saʿdi's *Bostan* of the advice of King Nushirvan to his son Hormuz; such poems 'a century or two ago … would have been suppressed in *Europe*, for spreading with too strong a glare the light of liberty and reason' (*Works*, 10.354). For each stanza of an ode by the fifteenth-century Turkish poet Mesihi, Jones supplied a verse translation, a transliteration in Roman letters, and a more precise prose translation, so that his readers might have access to a product of Turkish civilization at a range of levels.

Two essays which Jones included in this volume are highly significant in terms of the history of criticism, as they install the lyric at the centre of poetry. 'On the poetry of the Eastern nations' establishes Jones as a major precursor of the Romantics. His desire to revive the pastoral involved not faint shepherds but full-blooded Bedouin, and in his attempt to inject a certain primitive energy and a basic reality into the genre he anticipated William Wordsworth's preface to *Lyrical Ballads*. Ten years later Jones's acclaimed translation of the pre-Islamic *The Moallakát, or, Seven Arabian poems* (1782) demonstrated a radical strain of pastoral, a mature and confident portrayal of the Bedouin mentality, its heroism, and its hedonism. Such, in the second poem of the series, are the pleasures of the poet Tarafa:

First, to rise before the censurers awake, and to drink tawny wine, which sparkles and froths when the clear stream is poured into it.
Next, when a warrior, encircled by foes, implores my aid, to bend towards him my prancing charger, fierce as a wolf among the Gadha-trees, whom the sound of human steps has awakened, and who runs to quench his thirst at the brook.
Thirdly, to shorten a cloudy day, a day astonishingly dark, by toying with a lovely delicate girl under a tent supported by pillars.
('The poem of Tarafa', verses 58–60; *Works*, 10.32–3)

The second essay appended to *Poems* (1772), 'On the arts, commonly called imitative', is remarkable for its proto-Wordsworthian definition of poetry as 'originally no more than a strong and animated expression of the human passions' (*Works*, 10.363), an emotionalist concept of art which can be seen as paving the way for the subjectivity of the Romantic writers.

On 30 April 1772 Jones was elected a fellow of the Royal Society, and, although he was unsuccessful in his somewhat ambitious attempt to gain the post of ambassador to Turkey, he was admitted to Dr Johnson's prestigious Turk's Head Club when it opened in the following spring. He thus became an intimate of the great and the good, among them Edmund Burke, Edward Gibbon, Oliver Goldsmith, David Garrick, and Thomas Percy. He graduated MA at Oxford in 1773. He had intended to use the occasion to make an oration that would 'vindicate learning from the malevolent aspersion of being destructive of manly spirit, unfavourable to freedom, and introductive to slavish obsequiousness' (Teignmouth, 'Memoir', in *Works*, 1.197), but the sentiments proved too controversial for the university.

Barrister in Wales Jones felt acutely the tensions and frustrations implicit in being a radical intellectual dependent on aristocratic connections. As he wrote to Henry Schultens, a Dutch orientalist friend: 'My temperament cannot stomach the arrogance of princes and nobles, which has to be swallowed by poets and lovers of literature' (*Letters*, 1.167). On 28 January 1774 he was called to the bar at the Middle Temple, and so was able to embark on a career in which intellectual merit and effort might rival aristocratic privilege and allow him to escape dependence. Jones gained his early experience on the Oxford circuit, but from 1775 to his eventual appointment to the Bengal supreme court in 1783, he chose to practise on the Welsh circuits. Lessons learned in the principality prepared him for his role as an imperial administrator. His legal thinking was firmly grounded in the common-law tradition, and he shared the objections of bourgeois radicals to the growth of statute law and summary jurisdiction. In the great and petty sessions of Welsh towns he championed the rights of a peasantry oppressed by the arbitrary and discretionary power exercised by the largely Anglicized landowners, a rack-renting squirearchy, and English-speaking monoglot magistrates and judges. Jones's egalitarian principles aligned him with the underprivileged, frequently representing impoverished Welsh clients gratis. At Haverfordwest in 1780 he defended a man charged with alarming a Pembrokeshire village with a report of a French invasion. The indictment had been brought by two local magistrates, one of whom, John Zephaniah Holwell, was a former governor of Bengal. Jones believed that the magistrates were abusing their power in an attempt to cover up for their own foolishness in believing reports of an invasion, and the incident confirmed to him that despotism was by no means an oriental preserve. His letters to the Spencers describing the oppression of the 'yeomanry and peasantry of Wales' (ibid., 1.354) applied a powerful corrective to contemporary patrician conceptions of Wales as a little-visited haven of pastoral quietude and quietism where a contented pauper peasantry managed to combine independence with obedience.

Jones's perspective on Wales was shaped both by his social mobility as a barrister and tutor to the aristocracy, and by the cultural diversity of his family background. It was as the grandson of an Anglesey sheep farmer that he deprecated rural tyranny, but it was with the ease of a London Welsh celebrity–scholar that he socialized with the more enlightened gentry. Inspired by the researches into the *cynfeirdd* (early poets) and *gogynfeirdd* (poets of the princes) undertaken by his Anglesey relations, fellow Cymmrodorion (he had joined the society of Cymmrodorion by 1778), and London Welshmen, Jones indulged in recreational Celticism. He initiated among his fellow lawyers the society of the 'Druids of Cardigan', and the druidical meetings, by the picturesque banks of the River Teifi, became indistinguishable from fashionable outdoor society assemblies, the entertainment provided by Jones's bardic skills of extempore composition. The hedonism of lyrics such as 'The damsels of Cardigan' (1779) anticipated the themes of Wordsworth:

> Leave Year-books and parchments to grey-bearded sages,
> Be Nature our law, and fair woman our book
> (*GM*, 52, 1782, 446)

but was balanced by the topicality of 'Kneel to the goddess whom all men adore' (1780), a mock-heroic address to Muslims, Christians, Hindus, Parsis, pagan Greeks, and Romans who all worshipped the same goddess, be she called Diana, Mary, or Astarte. In early June 1780 Jones had been appalled by first-hand experience of the anti-Catholic Gordon riots, and this poem supplies a humorous corrective, characterized by a tolerant deism and a syncretic approach to world religions.

To add to his skill as an advocate, Jones was also placing at the disposal of his Welsh clients a distinguished reputation as a legal scholar. Jones's *Speeches of Isaeus Concerning the Law of Succession to Property in Athens* (1779) and *The Mahomedan Law of Succession to the Property of Intestates* (1782) established him as one of the first comparative lawyers and underlined his priorities in the protection of the individual, his person, and property. His major contribution to British jurisprudence was his accurate and elegant *Essay on the Law of Bailments* (1781), which has been described as 'one of the most remarkable books' of the eighteenth century (Holdsworth, *Eng. law*, 12.393). It exerted a profound influence on the principles of commercial law, and was still cited in judicial decisions at the end of the twentieth century, including some dealing with sexual harassment in the workplace. In the *Essay on the Law of Bailments* Jones suggested that he might follow it with works on similar principles that would eventually subject the entirety of English law to comparative analysis, but other studies took priority.

Radical whig Jones sought to be free of patronage, yet to be independent required the support of highly placed friends and acquaintances who respected his talents. In 1775 Jones was appointed a commissioner of bankrupts by the lord chancellor, Henry Bathurst, second Earl Bathurst, who admired him; the post provided him with extra income, but further advancement in the legal profession could not be expected so soon after his call to the bar. He achieved more success in the intellectual and social environment of Johnson's club. In 1778 he was able to turn the

tables of patronage by nominating his former pupil Viscount Althorp for admittance, and two years later, while president, he secured the election to the club of Jonathan Shipley. Jones maintained his close connections to the Spencer household; as well as continuing his close friendship with Lord Althorp he assisted Georgiana, Countess Spencer, with her philanthropic work.

Jones was sufficiently conventional to associate himself with traditional country ideology in regarding landed property as the ultimate guarantee of personal independence and civic autonomy. His reaction early in 1778 to learning of a vacancy on the bench of the supreme court in Calcutta with its salary of £6000 per annum was in many respects indistinguishable from that of the would-be nabob, a figure then much maligned for his mushroom wealth and pretensions. Thoughts of independence, a handsome fortune, a country estate, and a parliamentary seat ran in his mind. In Bengal he might combine his linguistic and legal expertise; his work on Muslim law was highly regarded, and his advice upon the Bengal Judiciary Bill of 1781 would prove invaluable to his friend Edmund Burke. He was eminently qualified for the post, yet for the next five years Jones seemed to do his utmost to disqualify himself. His supporter Bathurst was replaced as lord chancellor in 1778 by Edward Thurlow, first Baron Thurlow, who disliked Jones's liberal opinions. Jones failed to proceed with the political caution which advancement under Thurlow demanded. Although his principled inflexibility and independence of mind unsuited Jones for any courtly role, his success in advocacy encouraged him to adopt the role of self-appointed intermediary in the American War of Independence. In 1779 he travelled to France, where he met Benjamin Franklin at Passy. He presented 'A fragment of Polybius', which enlisted invented classical precedent to formulate a treaty establishing grounds of compromise between America and Britain. It revealed Jones as more of a scholar than a politician, but his movements between London and Paris created intense press speculation that he was involved in international diplomacy with the support of Lord North's ministry. In fact, it marked him out further as one of the government's radical opponents.

Frustrated by delays concerning the Calcutta post, in 1780 Jones applied for the lord almoner's professorship of Arabic at Oxford. The university appreciated the reflected glory of Jones's international scholarly reputation, but ministerial supporters at Oxford recalled how the withdrawn oration of 1773 had failed to contain the requisite praise for North as chancellor, and were chary of Jones's growing reputation as a radical whig. In the event nepotism combined with politics; Jones was passed over for the Arabic chair in favour of a comparative nonentity, Henry Ford, who was married to the niece of Bishop Robert Lowth.

Undeterred, Jones in May 1780 astonished Oxford by his decision to stand as a whig candidate for the university in the next parliamentary election, then expected in 1781. An ill-judged circular letter, written by his friend the linguist John Paradise, the inclusion of copies of his pro-

American ode 'Ad libertatem', and the fact that the canvassing efforts of Georgiana Cavendish, duchess of Devonshire (sister of Lord Althorp), Elizabeth Montagu, Charles James Fox, and John Dunning were supplemented by the active London support of John Wilkes and Richard Price, did not impress the staid Oxford voters. They resented the way in which Jones's campaign relied upon non-resident MAs, perhaps echoing academic irritation at how his linguistic expertise had relied upon native speakers from outside Oxford. Jones's political convictions were reinforced by his experiences during the Gordon riots in London in June 1780, when he led a volunteer company of barristers and students in defence of the Middle Temple and by implication of reason against superstition. This experience, confirming his opposition to a standing army, produced in July his first political tract, *An inquiry into the legal mode of suppressing riots, with a constitutional plan of future defence* (1780), which advocated the idea of a civilian militia. It encountered praise and support in London, but did little to advance his cause in Oxford. As Jones wrote to Countess Spencer on 16 June, he realized 'the late disturbances have contributed very unreasonably to make the resident Oxonians more adverse than ever to the advocates for Liberty, which they absurdly confound with Licentiousness' (*Letters*, 1.417). By the end of August it was clear that there was going to be an early election, and on 2 September, the day after the dissolution of parliament, Jones withdrew from the contest. Within a few days, Jones was energetically supporting Wilkes on the hustings, and his *Speech on the Nomination of Candidates to Represent the County of Middlesex*, advocating the reformist agenda of the association movement, attacking government policy in India, and inveighing against the horrors of the slave trade, was judged by a correspondent to the *Gentleman's Magazine*, twenty-four years later, 'to the full as bold as the boldest of Mr. Wilkes's' (*GM*, 74/2, 1804, 1214).

Jones's political poems were originally distributed to fellow members of the Club of Honest Whigs such as Richard Price and Joseph Priestley, Charles Dilly, Ralph Griffiths, Thomas Day, and Benjamin Franklin. His 'Ode in imitation of Alcaeus' (1781), 'composed in my chaise between Abergavenny and Brecon', however, was initially sent to his former pupil, addressed in the first line: '*Althorp*, what forms a state?' The poem, with its answering declaration:

Men, who their duties know,
But know their rights, and knowing dare maintain
(*Selected … Works*, ed. Franklin, 78)

was given a huge popular audience through being distributed gratis by Major John Cartwright's Society for Constitutional Information (to which Jones was elected in March 1782), and subsequently republished by Thomas Spence in the radical journal of the 1790s *One Penny Worth of Pig's Meat* (the voice of Burke's 'swinish multitude'). Even an epithalamium on the occasion of his former pupil's marriage written at the insistence of Georgiana, duchess of Devonshire (the groom's sister), and printed by Horace Walpole at the Strawberry Hill Press under the direction of Charles Bingham, first Baron Lucan (the bride's father),

was elegantly laced with oppositional ideology. The climax of *The Muse Recalled; an Ode on the Nuptials of Lord Viscount Althorp and Miss Lavinia Bingham* (1781) scourges contemporary decadence; Freedom and Concord are depicted departing to the 'purer soil' and 'more congenial sky' (*Works*, 10.388) of Delaware in a radical paean saluting America as the asylum of liberty. At this time Jones was also contemplating emigration westwards, and his association with Americans such as Henry Laurens and Arthur Lee in London and John Adams and Benjamin Franklin in Paris made it seem more likely that the future would see him a legislator on the banks of the James river than (as remained his expressed ambition) a judge on the banks of the Hooghly.

For many establishment figures, Jones was lingering under the liberty tree. His powerful *Speech on the Reformation of Parliament* (1782) revealed both his suspicion of uncontrolled aristocratic power and his confidence in commodity exchange and the market. He attacked the dependence of a client upon a patron in the economic as well as the social and political spheres, and moved closer than many of the Wilkesite radicals to the idea that market relations were a viable alternative to aristocratic patronage. Jones argued that political rights were not co-inherent with the ownership of land, and so aligned himself with the thinking of the radical dissenting middle class. Another pamphlet, *The Principles of Government, in a Dialogue between a Scholar and a Peasant* (1782), began as an essay written at the Paris house of Benjamin Franklin to convince Franklin that the mysteries of the state might be made intelligible to the working man. Developing Lockean concepts of voluntary association, Jones observed that 'a free state is only a more numerous and more powerful club, and that he only is a free man, who is a member of such a state' (*Works*, 8.537), maintaining that the qualification for membership was the property which every man possessed in his own life and liberty. Its emphases upon popular education, parliamentary reform, and co-operative association anticipated the works of Thomas Paine and William Godwin. The work was seized upon by Major Cartwright and published as a free pamphlet by the Society for Constitutional Information. William Shipley, dean of St Asaph and shortly to become Jones's brother-in-law, reprinted this tract at Wrexham in January 1783, replacing the words 'scholar' and 'peasant' with 'gentleman' and 'farmer'. The high sheriff of Flintshire, Thomas Fitzmaurice, promptly prosecuted Shipley for publishing a paper 'seditious, treasonable, and diabolical'.

Ironically, however, while Fitzmaurice was attempting to blacken Jones's name in Flintshire, Fitzmaurice's brother, William Petty, second earl of Shelburne, then prime minister, was at Windsor, recommending Jones for the Indian judgeship. Jones's radicalism had delayed his departure for Calcutta by five years, but he had seen in Shelburne a possible ally, and had lobbied Shelburne for the judgeship for several months. He wrote to Lord Althorp that:

The friends of lord North were too monarchical, and those of the late Marquis [of Rockingham], in general, far too aristocratical for me; and, if it were possible to see an administration too democratical, I should equally dislike it. There must be a mixture of all the powers, in due proportions weighed and measured by the laws, or the nation cannot exist without misery and shame   (*Letters*, 2.577)

Shelburne, to Jones, represented the best hope of achieving this balance. On 4 March 1783 his appointment as a judge of 'his Majesty's supreme court of judicature at Fort William in Bengal' (*GM*, 53/1, 1783, 274–5) was announced, and on 20 March he was knighted. On 8 April he finally married Anna Maria Shipley, and on 12 April they departed from Portsmouth for Bengal.

Jones left the Shipley case behind him, but *The Principles of Government* left its mark both on English law, inspiring the confirmation of the right of a jury to decide on the libellous tendency of any publication in Fox's Libel Act of 1792, as well as on Welsh politics. The north Welsh radicals boosted the audience of Jones's pamphlet beyond the 10,000 copies distributed by the Society for Constitutional Information, by incorporating the text, together with a history of the trial, into an *anterliwt* (interlude) to be performed at fairs and markets to the literate and illiterate alike. The robust language of *Barn ar egwyddorion y llywodraeth, mewn ymddiddan rhwng pendefig a hwsmon*, 'Gan fardd anadnabyddus o wynedd' (*A Judgement on the Principles of Government, in a Dialogue between a Gentleman and a Farmer*, 'By an obscure poet of Gwynedd'; 1784), argues the authorship of Thomas Edwards (1739–1810), known as Twm o'r Nant. Jones's text subsequently received a new English edition in the wake of the Peterloo massacre of 1819, and another Welsh translation at the height of the Chartist movement of the 1840s.

The Asiatick Society of Bengal and the emergence of Indology

After his arrival in Calcutta on 25 September 1783, Jones's response to the intellectual prospect presented by 'the vast regions of Asia' (*Works*, 3.2) was profoundly visionary, but this was balanced by an eminently practical awareness of the difficulties inherent in transforming such a vision into a functioning reality. 'Clubbable' Jones loved to associate, and by January 1784 he galvanized the scholarship encouraged by Warren Hastings into the pioneering Asiatick Society of Bengal. He offered a small but dedicated group of East India Company employees a vast sphere of intellectual and imaginative space exceeding that available in London. Money had brought them to Bengal as it offered the ambitious bourgeois an alternative route of social mobility, but Jones, stressing the unique advantages of their position for introducing Indian ideas into Europe, demonstrated that the society could represent an alternative, intellectual, route of aspiration. Their investigations, bounded 'only by the geographical limits of *Asia*' (ibid., 3.4), should encompass 'MAN and NATURE; whatever is performed by the one, or produced by the other' (ibid., 3.5). In seeking the election of Hastings as president, Jones acknowledged his awareness of the governor-general's pre-eminence in the promotion of

oriental learning, but his refusal, on the grounds of insufficient leisure, led to the election of Jones as founder-president. In his project to codify Muslim and Hindu law, Hastings had successfully encouraged close collaboration with native informants, and Jones, like many other society members, benefited from this initiative. Hastings's departure in February 1785 precluded any long-term co-operation, but Jones, who shared Hastings's interest in the *Mahabharata*, admired the vision of the governor-general who, in his prefacing letter to Charles Wilkins's *Bhāgvāt-Gēētā* (1785), declared that Indian writings 'will survive when the British dominion in India shall have long ceased to exist, and when the sources which it once yielded both of wealth and power are lost to remembrance' (Hastings, 13). Convinced of both its political utility and cultural value, Hastings had fostered the production of orientalist knowledge to increase his comprehension of the complexities of the subcontinent; understanding of Hindu tradition and Mughal precedent seemed essential if Hastings was successfully to inherit the syncretic mantle of the emperor Akbar. The first two observations of Jones's 'The best practicable system of judicature', which he sent to Edmund Burke in the spring of 1784, underscored the thinking of the Hastings administration:

> 1. A system of *liberty*, forced upon a people invincibly attached to opposite *habits*, would in truth be a system of cruel *tyranny*.
> 2. Any system of *judicature* affecting the natives in *Bengal*, and not having for its basis the old *Mogul* constitution, would be dangerous and impracticable.
> (*Letters*, 2.643)

That the middle-class British, with their respect for the extension of liberty in their own country, should have to realize power in India by operating a despotism was a situation fraught with ideological tensions, especially for a radical whig such as Jones. A humane despotism, whether Akbar's or Hastings's, required a self-justifying dialectic. And, if the information which Jones gleaned from orientalist researches was immediately relevant in the formation of government policies, the prestige of such scholarship when published in Calcutta and London and translated throughout Europe might reinforce the authority of Hastings's regime in both the East and the West. Although sympathetic to the governor-general's ideological objectives, Jones attempted to maintain a judicial impartiality. On learning from England that Burke had threatened to remove him from his judicial post should he side with Hastings, Jones was furious with his friend, and this breach was never effectively healed.

As the first European to have mastered 'the language of the gods' for several generations, it was Charles 'Sanskrit' Wilkins rather than 'Persian' Jones who first opened up the path of modern Indology. Reliance upon Persian or other intermediary languages was effectively redundant, and it was inevitable that Jones should follow Wilkins's lead, acknowledging his debt to his friend and fellow founder member 'without whose aid I should never have learned [Sanskrit]' (*Selected … Works*, ed. Franklin, 219).

Jones's *A Discourse on the Institution of a Society*, together with his 'First charge to the grand jury at Calcutta' and his 'Hymn to Camdeo', was published in London in 1784, whetting metropolitan appetites for what was to come from Calcutta. Knowledge produced by the Asiatick Society would be, in Hastings's terms, both 'useful to the state' (Hastings, 13) and 'the gain of humanity' (ibid.). Jones's inclusion of the hymn to the Hindu god of love signalled not so much his affirmation of the power of knowledge as his commitment to the knowledge of power, and to the sources of power in Indian culture, so that the British administration could provide better government through its mastery of Indian law and customs. One reviewer commented: 'How grand and stupendous is the following plan! … We may reasonably expect to enlarge our stock of poetical imagery, as well as of history, from the labours of the Asiatic Society … to combine the useful and the pleasing' (*Critical Review*, 59, 1785, 19–21).

Jones's discovery of the beauties of Sanskrit literature proved an even greater revelation than his earlier discovery of Arabic and Persian poetry; it too was one which displaced the primacy of the Graeco-Roman heritage, and one he was anxious to communicate to the European reading public:

> I am in love with the *Gopia*, charmed with *Crishen*, an enthusiastick admirer of *Rām*, and a devout adorer of *Brimha-bishen-mehais*: not to mention that *Jūdishteir*, *Arjen*, *Corno*, and the other warriours of the *M'hab'harat* appear greater in my eyes than Agamemnon, Ajax, and Achilles appeared, when I first read the Iliad. (*Letters*, 2.652)

To the society's journal, *Asiatick Researches*, which was distributed and pirated throughout Europe, Jones himself contributed papers upon a vast range of subjects: Indian anthropology, archaeology, astronomy, botany, ethnology, geography, music, literature, physiology, languages and inscriptions, mythology and religion. This represents a phenomenally polymathic output achieved despite long hours in court, and his major task of codifying Indian laws. The leading essay in the first volume of *Asiatick Researches*, 'A dissertation on the orthography of Asiatick words in Roman letters', pioneered a system of transliteration for Sanskrit, Persian, and Arabic characters, which proved to be of lasting utility, coming to be known as the Jonesian system. He was responsible for over a third of the papers read to the society during the years of his presidency. It was Jones's European reputation that sold *Asiatick Researches* in the West, and the society members in Calcutta deferred not to his intellectual egotism, but to his enormous erudition and enthusiasm.

The birth of Indo-European linguistics On 2 February 1786, only about six months after he had begun to study Sanskrit, Jones's 'Third anniversary discourse' (1786) introduced startling ideas of linguistic and familial relationship between the rulers and their 'black' subjects, and the equally disconcerting conception of classical India as the *fons et origo* of world understanding. His emphasis upon roots and grammatical structure, rather than speculative etymology, rejected the philosophical *a priori* method of

the eighteenth century for a new historical and comparative *a posteriori* method:

> The *Sanscrit* language, whatever be its antiquity, is of a wonderful structure; more perfect than the *Greek*, more copious than the *Latin*, and more exquisitely refined than either, yet bearing to both of them a stronger affinity, both in the roots of verbs and in the forms of grammar, than could possibly have been produced by accident; so strong indeed that no philologer could examine them all three, without believing them to have sprung from some common source, which perhaps no longer exists: there is a similar reason, though not quite so forcible, for supposing that both the *Gothick* and the *Celtick*, though blended with a very different idiom, had the same origin with the *Sanscrit*; and the old *Persian* might be added to the same family. (*Works*, 3.34)

In maintaining that the classical languages of India, the Near East, and Europe descend from a common source, Jones was making an imaginative leap which effectively marked the beginning of Indo-European comparative grammar and modern comparative-historical linguistics. This developed the syncretic ramifications of the earlier path-breaking essay, 'On the gods of Greece, Italy, and India' (1784), which exploited cultural relativism to familiarize Europe with the 'alien' beliefs of the subcontinent. Jones presented Europe 'with the mighty challenge of the Hindus as teachers of the Egyptians … herald[ing] the Aryan thesis to which nineteenth-century German scholars devoted themselves' (Manuel, 114). Eurocentric thinking was also challenged when Jones concluded in the same 'Third anniversary discourse' of 1786 that it is not possible 'to read the Vedanta, or the many fine compositions in illustration of it, without believing that Pythagoras and Plato derived their sublime theories from the same fountain with the sages of India' (*Works*, 3.37).

Jones's mind spanned the pragmatic as well as the speculative, and he was fascinated by historical chronology. It was no part of the Asiatick Society's project to essentialize Asia's timelessness and fixity, and therefore its inferiority to western Europe. Instead, in his discourse 'On Asiatic history, civil and natural' of 1793, by identifying the Greek name Sandrocottus cited in classical histories of Alexander the Great's invasion of north-western India in 326 BC with Chandragupta, the founder of the Mauryan empire, and connecting the key site named by the Greeks as Palibothra with Pataliputra, Jones facilitated the accurate correlation of eastern and western history.

Sacontalá and the Hindu pantheon Inspired by his researches into Hinduism and wishing to attract a wider readership, Jones wrote a series of odes addressed to Hindu deities (1784–8). Dignified by their development of Pindaric forms and their use of Miltonic resonances, they explored analogies between poetic and divine acts of creation and perception, foreshadowing and facilitating romantic fascination with beauty, power, and knowledge:

> Wrapt in eternal solitary shade,
> Th'impenetrable gloom of light intense,
> Impervious, inaccessible, immense,

Ere spirits were infus'd or forms display'd,
BREHM his own Mind survey'd,
('A hymn to Náráyena', 1786, lines 19–23)

Jones's prefatory argument to this hymn claimed that the essence of Vedic doctrine was compatible with Platonic thought, and also with most of the central philosophical features of Romanticism. Jones's translations, his academic discourses, and his own poetry including the 'Hymns to Hindu deities', together with his earlier experimentation with the genre of the oriental verse tale, provided both fascinating materials and formative models for the orientalizing of Walter Savage Landor, Samuel Taylor Coleridge, Robert Southey, Byron, Percy Bysshe Shelley, and Thomas Moore, their Romantic subjectivity underpinned and weighted by Jones's scholarly objectivity.

Jones's poetic treatment of the goddess in his 'Hymn to Durgá' (1788) exemplifies the subtle cultural tact with which he made Indian civilization available to the West. He avoids representing Durga in her Kali aspect—black, four-armed, standing on a corpse, holding a severed head, and wearing only a necklace of skulls—as such unpalatable iconography might have created reader resistance. He portrays her instead as the gentle and devout Parvati, the lady of the mountain, and daughter of Himalaya, and in this was inspired by the *Kumarasambhava* of Kalidasa, the flower of Gupta high culture. Jones reveals an enlightened understanding of traditional constructions of womanhood in India, especially the concepts of *prakriti* (nature seen at the female principle) and *sakti* (the female embodying active power). While he can be accused of evading the misogynism apparent in *sati* and female infanticide, he did so in the knowledge that the West had exclusively focused upon such abhorrent and aberrant practices in order to blacken Hindu culture and religion.

A much easier task of creating cultural empathy faced Jones in his translation of Kalidasa's *Sacontalá* (1789), a revolutionary contribution to orientalism, which went into six editions between 1790 and 1807, and received, in the century following its publication, no fewer than forty-six translations in twelve different languages. The play concerns the aesthetic and erotic entrancement of King Dushmanta by the beauty of Sacontalá, the daughter of a Brahman sage and a heavenly courtesan, and the level of identification by a European audience was quite remarkable. The literature of sensibility was much in vogue, and the blend of the divine and the erotic in this story which Kalidasa had adapted from the *Mahabharata* was at once delightfully pagan and profoundly religious. Reviewers in Britain such as Mary Wollstonecraft fell under its spell, but in Germany its translation by Georg Förster caused a sensation, inspiring Johann Gottfried Herder, Friedrich Schiller, Novalis, Friedrich Schlegel, and Johann Wolfgang Goethe. Kalidasa's play, as interpreted by Jones, became a vibrant source of archetypal values linking ancient and modern, East and West, making Goethe rethink his strictures and preconceptions concerning Indian art, Vedic thought, and Aristotelian dramatic theory. Although Goethe's planned adaptation of *Sacontalá*

never materialized, he used its introductory scene as a model for the 'Vorspiel auf dem Theater' of *Faust* (1797).

The rapturous European response which greeted *Sacontalá* established it as the representational icon of Indian civilization, a European judgement which exactly reflected that of the Hindu poetic tradition. Western longing for the East was simultaneously sacred and profane; there was a specifically sexual charge to much of the enraptured enthusiasm for this Hindu play. The demands upon Jones's sensitivity as a cultural translator were even greater when he decided to translate the *Gitagovinda*, the devoutly erotic poem of the twelfth-century Bengali poet Jayadeva.

Jones appended his *Gitagovinda* to his paper 'On the mystical poetry of the Persians and Hindus' which was published in the third volume of *Asiatick Researches* (1793), prefacing the poem with the explanation that he had censored 'only those passages, which are too luxuriant and too bold for an *European* taste' (*Works*, 4.235). He had earlier observed in 'On the gods of Greece, Italy and India' (1784) that 'it never seems to have entered the heads of the legislators or people that anything natural could be offensively obscene; a singularity, which pervades all their writing and conversation, but is no proof of the depravity of their morals' (ibid., 3.367), but caution was still required in interpreting this evocation of the love of Krishna and Radha. Consequently he removed references to love bites and nail wounds, regarded in Hindu tradition as marks of refinement and social distinction. In many respects Jones's translation is faithful to the spirit of the original, in which the duality of Krishna and Radha continually recalls the cosmic coitus on the causal waters, as the blue (ether) and gold (sun) of Vishnu mingle with the water lily and lotos of Lakshmi:

> [H]is heart was agitated by her sight, as the waves of the deep are affected by the lunar orb. His azure breast glittered with pearls of unblemished lustre, like the full bed of cerulean Yamunà, interspersed with curls of white foam. From his graceful waist, flowed a pale yellow robe, which resembled the golden dust of the water-lily scattered over its blue petals. His passion was inflamed by the glances of her eyes which played like a pair of water-birds with azure plumage, that sport near a full-blown lotos on a pool in the season of dew. (*Works*, 4.264)

Unlike many of his colleagues in the Asiatick Society, and despite his own deistic sympathies, Jones refused to dismiss contemporary Hinduism as a degraded falling-away from an original and pristine monotheism. Neither subscribing to the common prejudice against popular Hinduism, nor supporting a caste-based dichotomy between a rational ethical Brahman élite and the superstitions of the masses, Jones viewed Bengal as a crucial site in the evolution of Hinduism reflecting a vigorous continuity between a classical devotional text such as the *Gitagovinda* and contemporary Hindu devotees. He appreciated how the doctrine of *bhakti* (loving devotion) could in some respects link popular fetishism and learned Vedantism. His interest in the cult of Vaishnavism (devotion to Vishnu, especially in his important eighth *avatar*, or incarnation, as Krishna) was apparent in his own 'A hymn to Lacshmí' (1788), and in his keen awareness of a living tradition of religious performance of the *Gitagovinda* enlivened by village pride and rivalry.

In Europe the power of Jones's *Gítagóvinda*'s blend of mystic and sensual love was received as a key to universal religion. In many respects the Romantic image of India was to reflect India's own self-image. If Jones's translation ensured that the *Sacontalá* represented the capstone in the construction of the Romantic conception of India, it also helped establish the work as a defining text of Indian civilization accessible to all Indians. In collecting, translating, and printing Sanskrit materials, Jones and his fellow orientalists were making accessible in the secular public domain texts formerly subject to exclusive Brahmanical control. Orientalism, through its retrieval of Sanskrit texts and its reconstruction of India's past, shaped the way Indians perceived themselves, ushering in the Bengal renaissance. These texts were subsequently seized upon by the Hindu national movement as symbols of *Hindutva* (Hindu-ness), ultimately constituting defining symbols of Hindu resistance to British rule.

The Ordinances of Menu Jones's key project was his preparation of an exhaustive digest of Hindu and Muslim law, a foundation stone of the policy of legitimizing British rule through the recovery of native traditions. In attempting to arrive at what was universal and authoritative, Hastings had turned to texts embodying ancient or high-culture law, and this focus was, of course, at the expense of diverse customary law of the villages. The laws of Manu (called Menu by Jones) undoubtedly possessed great prestige among all Hindus and were respected by Muslim rulers; as it represented the only indigenous system of jurisprudence, it was, in some respects, understandable for Hastings and Jones to concentrate upon this law of the higher castes. Work on the digest began formally three years after the departure of Hastings, in 1788, when Jones stressed its necessity to Governor-General Cornwallis, and volunteered to edit it. The emphasis Jones placed upon inheritance, contracts, disputed accounts, and debts was at the centre of his vision of reinforcing private property rights, both real and personal. This reflected not only the commercial concerns of the East India Company, but his everyday courtroom experience of contract and litigation which were functions of the dynamic commercialism of the natives of Calcutta. The fruit of his long co-operation with Indian legal scholars appeared in the early 1790s. *Al Sirájiyyah, or, The Mohammedan law of inheritance*, which firmly settled the question of the existence of property rights under the Mughal constitution, and which formed an important part of the Muslim digest, was published in 1792. Two years later, the *Institutes of Hindu Law, or, The Ordinances of Menu* in 1794 helped to produce a renaissance in *dharmasastra* literature in India.

In Europe the great antiquity of the *Ordinances*, added to the fact that they possessed the sanction of religion, fascinated the philosophers, poets, and scholars of emergent Romanticism, among whom regard for ancient religions had never been so intense.

Death and legacy With the completion of *The Ordinances of Menu*, Jones was anxious to follow his wife, Anna Maria, who, for reasons of health, had left Calcutta on 7 December 1793. He could not, however, contemplate the abandonment of his project, for which his close collaboration with a skilled team of Indian legal scholars was essential. He wrote to the home secretary, Henry Dundas, on 1 March 1794:

> If I had obtained His Majesty's leave to resign my office, nothing would now keep me here, but the Digest of Indian Laws, consisting of nine large volumes, two of which remain to be collated and studied with the learned Brāhmen, who assists me: he is old and infirm; but, should he be able to attend me another year, or two years at the very utmost, the whole work will be finished. (*Letters*, 2.928)

Within two months Jones had succumbed to a swift and fatal liver infection; he died at his home, Gardens, later 8 Garden Reach, in Alipore, a suburb of Calcutta, on 27 April 1794, before Anna Maria had reached Portsmouth. He was buried on 28 April at the South Park Street burial-ground, Calcutta. The result of Jones's supervisory, editorial, and collaborative labours, Jagannatha Tarkapancanana's *Vivadabhangarnava*, or 'Oceans of resolutions of disputes', was completed shortly after his death. This digest of Hindu law, to which Jones had dedicated over six years of tireless effort, was translated by the Sanskrit scholar Henry Thomas Colebrooke, and published in 1798. The digest was eagerly cited by court pandits, and it represented a profound contribution to the integration and organization of a vast body of belief, myth, ritual, custom, practice, and law into the Hinduism of modern India.

Jones's initial reasons for learning Sanskrit were based in his desire to remedy his dependence upon supreme court pandits, but his increasing confidence in the language, and his meeting with Radhakanta, the pandit of John Shore, transformed his low opinion of Bengali Brahman pandits. Intense collaboration with his team of legal informants, many of whom were Brahmans, led to a real and reciprocated respect. He consulted pandits and informants in a wide range of disciplines, and a certain ambivalence of attitude was the product of a scholarly reluctance to accept uncorroborated scientific 'evidence' which only occasionally deserted him. Concerned that contemporary Indian scholarship should not be neglected by the Asiatick Society, Jones had raised the question of membership for Indians at the inaugural meeting. His suggestions regarding their admittance were ignored (it was not until 1829 that Indians were admitted as members), but *Asiatick Researches* became the first 'European' journal to publish papers written by Indian scholars, such as Govardhan Kaul's 'On the Vedas' and Ali Ibrahim Khan's 'On the cure of the elephantiasis'. Pioneering ecological anthropology and avoiding the universalizing taxonomic vision of Eurocentric natural historians, Jones consulted indigenous knowledge about landscape, flora, and fauna. His 'Botanical observations on select Indian plants' was deeply sensitive to both the Sanskrit names of species and the place they occupied in Hindu culture, and this sensitivity extended to his investigations of Hindu medicine. A similar empathy illuminates 'On the musical modes of the Hindus', the first Western study of Indian music; the practicality and syncretism of its approach is everywhere apparent. His enthusiasm for contemporary Hindustani poets such as Mir Taqi Mir, Sauda, and Mir Muhammad Hussein, or the female Hindi poet Gunna Begam, balanced his antiquarian fascination with Gupta culture. Jones's close co-operation with Hindu pandits and Muslim maulavis provides a model of cultural contact between the European and Asian intelligentsia ignored by some modern scholars of orientalism who stress the inequality of such meetings.

The sharp contrast between the Sir Joshua Reynolds portrait of a youthful, confident, and full-faced Jones at twenty-two and the drawn and angular forty-seven-year old of Arthur Devis's painting testifies to the accuracy of Anna Maria's anguished comment to the duchess of Devonshire: 'his business is all day & every day: in a temperate climate it would be reckon'd hard duty[;] think what it is in this!' (*Letters*, 2.689). His complete works, edited by Anna Maria and with a lengthy biographical preface by Lord Teignmouth, were published in 1799; a second edition followed in 1807. Anna Maria survived until 1829. The colossal John Bacon statue erected by the East India Company in St Paul's Cathedral may be seen to represent an invasion of the metropole by alien wisdom and exotic poetry in the sculpted shapes of the *dharmasastra* of Manu and Vishnu's kurma avatara (tortoise incarnation). John Flaxman in his monument to Jones at University College, Oxford, depicts three native scholars sitting at the orientalist's feet, but Jones's anti-Eurocentric reversal of these roles illustrated that the production of colonial knowledge could involve Western enquirer and Eastern informant in a dialogue characterized by reciprocity, pluralism, and equality. This remains his lasting memorial.

MICHAEL J. FRANKLIN

Sources *The works of Sir William Jones*, ed. A. M. Jones, 13 vols. (1807); facs. repr. (1993) · *The letters of Sir William Jones*, ed. G. Cannon, 2 vols. (1970) · *Sir William Jones: selected poetical and prose works*, ed. M. J. Franklin (1995) · M. J. Franklin, *Sir William Jones*, Writers of Wales (1995) · G. Cannon, *The life and mind of Oriental Jones* (1990) · G. Cannon, *Sir William Jones: a bibliography of primary and secondary sources* (Amsterdam, 1979) · S. N. Mukherjee, *Sir W. J.: a study in C18th British attitudes to India* (1968) · R. Rocher, 'Weaving knowledge: Sir William Jones and the pandits', *Objects of enquiry: the life, contributions, and influences of Sir William Jones*, ed. G. Cannon and K. R. Brine (1995), 51–79 · J. Drew, *India and the romantic imagination* (Delhi, 1987) · D. Kopf, *British orientalism and the Bengal renaissance* (Berkeley and Los Angeles, 1969) · L. A. Willson, *A mythical image: the ideal of India in German Romanticism* (Durham, N.C., 1964) · P. J. Marshall, *The British discovery of Hinduism* (1970) · P. J. Marshall, 'Warren Hastings as scholar and patron', *Statesmen, scholars and merchants: essays presented to Dame Lucy Sutherland*, ed. A. Whiteman, J. S. Bromley, and P. G. M. Dickson (1973), 242–62 · C. A. Bayly, *Empire and information: intelligence gathering and social communication in India, 1780–1870* (1996) · T. R. Trautmann, *Aryans and British India* (1998) · M. J. Franklin, 'Accessing India: orientalism, anti-"Indianism" and the rhetoric of Jones and Burke', *Romanticism and colonialism: writing and empire, 1780–1830*, ed. T. Fulford and P. Kitson (1998), 48–66 · M. J. Franklin, 'Cultural possession, imperial control, and comparative religion: the Calcutta perspectives of Sir William Jones and Nathaniel Brassey Halhed', *Yearbook of English Studies*, 32 (2002), 1–18 · F. E. Manuel, *The eighteenth century confronts the gods* (Cambridge,

Mass., 1959) · R. Schwab, *The oriental renaissance: Europe's rediscovery of India and the East, 1680–1880*, trans. G. Patterson-Black and V. Reinking (New York, 1984) · G. Shaw, *Printing in Calcutta to 1800* (1981) · E. Said, *Orientalism* (1978) · O. P. Kejariwal, *The Asiatic Society of Bengal and the discovery of India's past, 1784–1838* (Delhi, 1988) · D. Figueira, *Translating the Orient: the reception of Śakuntalā in nineteenth-century Europe* (Albany, 1991) · T. Raychaudhuri, *Europe reconsidered: perceptions of the west in nineteenth-century Bengal* (1988) · J. D. M. Derrett, *Religion, law and the state in India* (1968) · L. Siegel, *Sacred and profane dimensions of love in Indian traditions as exemplified in the Gītagovinda of Jayadeva* (Delhi, 1978) · M. J. Franklin, ed., *Representing India: Hindu culture and imperial control: the writings of British orientalists in the eighteenth century*, 9 vols. (2000) · R. Rocher, 'British orientalism in the eighteenth century: the dialectics of knowledge and government', *Orientalism and the postcolonial predicament*, ed. C. Breckenridge and P. van der Veer (Philadelphia, 1993), 215–49 · I. Kramnick, *Republicanism and bourgeois radicalism: political ideology in late eighteenth-century England and America* (1990) · B. S. Miller, 'The divine duality of Rādhā and Krishna', *The divine consort: Rādhā and the goddesses of India*, ed. J. Stratton Hawley and D. M. Wulff (Boston, 1986), 13–26 · R. Inden, *Imagining India* (1990) · W. Hastings, preface, *The Bhăgvăt-Gēētā*, trans. C. Wilkins (1785) · H. A. C. Sturgess, ed., *Register of admissions to the Honourable Society of the Middle Temple, from the fifteenth century to the year 1944*, 1 (1949) · Foster, *Alum. Oxon.* · Holdsworth, *Eng. law*, 11.220–21; 12.393; 13.670, 673 · J. A. Cannon, 'Oxford University', HoP, *Commons*, 1754–90, 1.359–60
Archives BL, letters and papers, Add. MSS 7033–7034, 8885, 8889, 8896 · BL OIOC, Chinese–Latin dictionary, probably compiled by Jones, MS Eur. C 119 · BL OIOC, official records, reels 759–80 [microfilm] · BL OIOC, papers, parcel 699 · Bodl. Oxf., Sanskrit MSS · NL Wales, letters · NL Wales, notes on legal cases · Royal Asiatic Society, London, drawings and papers · Texas A&M University, papers, parcel 698 · University College, Oxford, oriental MSS · Yale U., Beinecke L., notebook | BL, letters to second Earl Spencer and Countess Spencer, incl. MS journal for 1787 · BL OIOC, letters to Sir Charles Wilkins, MS Eur. C 227 · NA Scot., letters to H. Dundas and C. W. Boughton Rouse · NL Wales, letters, mainly to Richard Johnson · NL Wales, letters to Samuel Parr and J. Miller · Sheff. Arch., letters to Edmund Burke
Likenesses attrib. J. Northcote, oils, *c.*1767, Welsh Folk Museum, St Fagans, near Cardiff · J. Reynolds, oils, *c.*1769, Althorp House, Northamptonshire · J. Heath, stipple, pubd 1779 (after J. Reynolds), BM · A. W. Devis, oils, *c.*1793, BL OIOC [*see illus.*] · J. Bacon, effigy on marble monument, *c.*1795, St Paul's Cathedral, London · J. Flaxman, effigy on marble monument, exh. RA 1797, University College, Oxford · J. Hatchard, engraving, 1806 (after A. W. Devis), BL
Wealth at death £30,000–£40,000

Jones, William (*bap.* 1762, *d.* 1831), maker of scientific instruments, who was baptized at St Andrew's, Holborn, London, on 27 June 1762, was the elder of two sons of **John Jones** (1736/7–1808) and his wife, Elizabeth, *née* Dillon. John Jones, the son of a stay maker of St Martin-in-the-Fields, had been apprenticed as a mathematical instrument maker and was made free of the Spectaclemakers' Company in 1758, the year of his marriage. He was in the Holborn area by 1776 and trading as an optician at 135 Holborn by 1782. William was apprenticed to his father in 1776, and was in partnership with him by 1784, not taking his freedom in the Spectaclemakers' Company until 1794.

In 1786 Thomas Jefferson (1734–1824), later third president of the United States, patronized the Jones business on his only visit to London. Jefferson acquired a number of scientific instruments from some of the most eminent London makers, among them Peter Dollond and Jesse

Ramsden, and this first link with a prestigious foreign customer must have assisted the Jones firm with subsequent overseas sales. Jefferson corresponded with the Joneses in 1787 and again in 1793. John Jones retired in 1791 to end his days at Islington, where he died on 15 August 1808. Apart from minor bequests, including £10 to his nephew John Dillon, a printer, then working for his sons, he left everything to his wife during her lifetime and then to his sons William and Samuel. William was forced by ill health to retire early from business and also removed to Islington. He died, unmarried, in Brighton, on 17 February 1831, and was buried at St Andrew's, Holborn.

Samuel Jones (1770–1859) was baptized at St Andrew's, Holborn, on 18 February 1770. He does not appear to have served an apprenticeship and, indeed, is a far more insubstantial figure than his elder brother; like him, he was a bachelor. He joined his brother in partnership in 1791 on the retirement of their father, obtaining his freedom of the Spectaclemakers' Company by patrimony in 1806. He continued to trade as W. and S. Jones long after his brother's departure. In his latter years he lived at Dalton House, St Albans, Hertfordshire, where he died on 10 October 1859, at the age of eighty-nine. The firm ceased to trade after this date.

W. and S. Jones traded under the sign of Archimedes, at 135 Holborn, next to Furnival's Inn, moving across the road to 30 Holborn around 1800. The firm was extremely prolific, selling a wide range of optical, mathematical, and philosophical instruments and apparatus in the middle ranges of price and quality, as detailed in their comprehensive catalogues, issued at frequent intervals. William Jones was a friend and pupil of the prominent lecturer and instrument maker Benjamin Martin, who effectively introduced Jones into a wide society of like-minded people. A major opportunity for the Jones business occurred in 1782, as a result of Martin's bankruptcy and death, and the subsequent sale of his business; in 1795–6, a second, perhaps larger, boost resulted from the death of the younger George Adams and subsequent sales by his wife, Hannah. W. and S. Jones's trade must have benefited from the reduced competition after the cessation of two of the largest and apparently most successful contemporary London businesses. More important was its purchase of the copyright of the influential textbooks written by the two George Adamses, father and son: from 1797 onwards catalogues of the wares of W. and S. Jones, as illustrated in these texts, were priced and bound in the back of every volume. As a form of advertising, this appears to have had considerable success. It is possible that the copyright of Benjamin Martin's popular textbooks had also been purchased, as a number of these were revised by William Jones, and catalogues bound with them.

Among W. and S. Jones's more prestigious customers were the college at Harvard, supplied with apparatus to order between 1797 and 1817, and the prolific American collector Charles Nicholl Bancker, a customer during the 1820s. The company also drew up the auction catalogue for disposal of the third earl of Bute's magnificent collection, in 1793. Items bearing the firm's signature can be found in collections all over the Western world.

A. D. MORRISON-LOW

Sources G. Clifton, *Directory of British scientific instrument makers, 1550–1851*, ed. G. L'E. Turner (1995) • *GM*, 1st ser., 101/1 (1831), 275 • *GM*, 1st ser., 78 (1808), 758 [obit. of John Jones] • *GM*, 3rd ser., 7 (1859), 545 [obit. of Samuel Jones] • will, PRO, PROB 11/1485, sig. 740 [John Jones] • will, PRO, PROB 11/1784, sig. 222 • will, principle probate registry (died 1859) [Samuel Jones] • A. Simpson, 'A subcontractor of W. and S. Jones identified', *Bulletin of the Scientific Instrument Society*, 39 (1993), 23–7 • parish register, Holborn, St Andrew's, 1762 [baptism] • parish register, Holborn, St Andrew's, 1770 [baptism; Samuel Jones] • S. A. Bedini, *Thomas Jefferson, statesman of science* (1990) • D. P. Wheatland, *The apparatus of science at Harvard, 1765–1800* (1968) • A. D. C. Simpson, ''La plus brillante collection qui existe au monde': a lost American collection of the nineteenth century', *Journal of the History of Collections*, 7 (1995), 187–96 • G. L'E. Turner, 'The auction sales of the earl of Bute's instruments, 1793', *Annals of Science*, 23 (1967), 213–42 • d. cert. [Samuel Jones]
Archives American Philosophical Society, Philadelphia • Harvard U. • Harvard U., instruments | L. Cong., Jefferson MSS • MHS Oxf., instruments • Museum of Scotland, Edinburgh, instruments • Sci. Mus., instruments • Whipple Museum of the History of Science, Cambridge, instruments
Wealth at death under £25,000—Samuel Jones: probate, 1859

Jones, William (1762–1846), author and Scotch Baptist minister, was born at Gresford, near Wrexham, on 17 June 1762, and married Maria Crane about 1785. Under the influence of Archibald McLean, he became a Scotch Baptist in Chester, and was baptized in 1786. From 1793 he was a bookseller in Liverpool and from 1812 carried on the same trade in London. In both cities he was an elder in the Scotch Baptist church, and from 1812 took McLean's place as the chief writer of that movement. He edited a series of religious periodicals, and published a *History of the Albigensians and Waldensians* (1811), *Biblical Cyclopaedia* (1826), *Lectures on the Apocalypse* (1829), *Sermons on Primitive Christianity* (1837), and various memoirs of religious leaders. Jones helped in 1834–6 to introduce the ideas of Alexander Campbell to Britain, thus involuntarily opening the way for the establishment of the Churches of Christ, which drew members from the Scotch Baptist communities. Later he parted company with Campbell on theological grounds. Jones was important for publishing the essays and letters of those who taught primitive Christianity (that is, New Testament belief and customs stripped of later accretions), and was deeply opposed to religious establishments. His periodicals had a wide circulation, especially in Scotland; they included the *New Evangelical Magazine* (1815–24) and the *Millennial Harbinger and Voluntary Church Advocate* (1835–6). He died in London on 21 January 1846, as the result of a fall in the street in which he lived.

DEREK B. MURRAY

Sources *Autobiography of William Jones*, ed. J. Jones (1846) • R. Taylor, 'English Baptist periodicals, 1790–1865', *Baptist Quarterly*, 27 (1977–8), 50–82 • D. M. Thompson, *Let sects and parties fall* (1980) • E. C. Starr, ed., *A Baptist bibliography*, 12 (1967)

Jones, William (1784–1842), Congregational minister, was born in Brighton on 6 February 1784, his father being the inventor of the carriage spring and his uncle a pioneer in the design and manufacture of weighing machines. He was educated in Oxfordshire and in 1800 was converted in Carr's Lane Chapel, Birmingham. He was trained for the ministry at Hoxton Academy, and in September 1807 received a call to a second Independent church in Bolton which had just broken away from the Dukes Alley Chapel and was meeting in the Cloth Hall. He began his formal ministry on 28 July and was ordained on 3 September 1808. His congregation grew very rapidly, and in 1809 a new chapel in Mawdsley Street was built. Of Welsh ancestry and a mixed Anglican and Independent background, Jones was a tall man, a powerful preacher, a tireless itinerant—preaching in the leading London churches, and a determined foe of instrumental music in worship. He received more than 400 persons into membership at Mawdsley Street, oversaw the erection of a Sunday school in 1819, and founded the Rose Hill cause in 1841 as an offshoot of his own church. Jones published a number of sermons, tracts, books for children and Sunday-school workers, and improving works, some of them, such as *Improper and Unhappy Marriages* (1842), of a strongly moralistic kind. He died on 19 October 1842.

T. B. JOHNSTONE, *rev.* IAN SELLERS

Sources 'Memoir of the late Rev. William Jones', *Evangelical Magazine and Missionary Chronicle*, new ser., 21 (1843), 157–63 • B. Nightingale, *Lancashire nonconformity*, 6 vols. [1890–93], vol. 3 • F. Baker, *Rise and progress of nonconformity in Bolton* (1854) • J. Johnson, *Mawdsley Chapel, Bolton le Moors* (1908) • J. C. Scholes, *Bolton bibliography* (1886)
Likenesses R. Woodman, stipple, pubd 1826, NPG • Blood, stipple, 1830 (after J. R. Wildman), NPG • portrait, repro. in Johnson, *Mawdsley Chapel, Bolton le Moors*

Jones, Sir William (1808–1890), army officer, was the only son of William Jones of Caernarvonshire. He was educated at the Royal Military College, Sandhurst, and joined the 61st regiment as ensign on 10 April 1825. His subsequent steps were: lieutenant (December 1826), captain (24 November 1835), major (26 July 1844), lieutenant-colonel (29 December 1848), colonel (28 November 1854), major-general (1 April 1863), lieutenant-general (31 December 1871), and general (1 October 1877). Jones was with the 61st throughout the Punjab campaign of 1848–9. He took part in the passage of the Chenab and the battles of Sadulapur, Chilianwala, and Gujrat. After Gujrat (March 1849) he pursued the enemy as far as the Khyber Pass, in command of his regiment and a troop of Bengal horse artillery. He was made a CB. During the Indian mutiny Jones commanded the 3rd infantry brigade at the siege of Delhi, and was one of the officers selected to lead the storming parties on 14 September 1857. During the assault, owing to the death of General Nicholson, he commanded the 1st as well as the 2nd column, and remained in charge during the ensuing six days' fighting. He was mentioned in dispatches and awarded a good-service pension. He married in 1857 Elizabeth, second daughter of John Tuthill of Kilmore House, co. Limerick. On 2 June 1869 he was made a KCB and on 29 May 1886 a GCB. From 2 January 1871 until his death he was colonel of the Duke of Cornwall's light infantry. Jones

died at his home, Lansdown Lodge, Lansdown Road, Dublin, on 8 April 1890, and was buried in Mount Jerome cemetery.

W. A. J. ARCHBOLD, *rev.* JAMES FALKNER

Sources *Army List* • *The Times* (11 April 1890) • Burke, *Peerage* • *Broad Arrow* (12 April 1890)
Wealth at death £15,742 5s. 6d. in England: Irish probate sealed in England, 13 May 1890, *CGPLA Eng. & Wales*

Jones, William Arthur (1818–1873), antiquary and Unitarian minister, born on 1 May 1818 at Carmarthen, was the youngest son of William Jones, corn merchant, of Carmarthen. He was educated at Carmarthen College and at Glasgow University, where he graduated MA with honours in 1841. He entered the Unitarian ministry, and settled first at Northampton, where he remained from 1842 to 1849. He became a close friend of George Baker (1781–1851), the Northamptonshire antiquary. In 1849 he moved to Bridgwater, Somerset, and in 1852 he moved to Taunton, where he became minister of Mary Street Unitarian Chapel. He soon afterwards became honorary secretary of the recently founded Somerset Archaeological and Natural History Society, an office he held until his death; he was largely responsible for guiding the society in its early years. He served as editor of the society's *Proceedings* and contributed to it many papers on the geology, archaeology, and history of the county. He succeeded in establishing at Taunton a successful school of science and art, to which he was honorary secretary, and was also active as chairman of the management committee of the Taunton and Somerset Hospital. It was through his persuasion that the town's grammar school was opened to those of all religious denominations. To Taunton people he was best-known as president of the working men's Liberal association, and as a tireless promoter of the Liberal cause.

In 1866 Jones resigned his position at Mary Street Chapel, and after travelling for two years on the continent finally gave up the ministry, though he remained a member of the Unitarian community. Thereafter he devoted himself exclusively to the affairs of Taunton, and to literary and scientific studies. He married, first, Mary, sister of William Fitchett Cuff of Merriott, Somerset, who died within a year of the marriage without children; and, second, Margaret, sister of William Blake JP, of South Petherton, Somerset, who also died before him. They had three sons. He became a justice of the peace in 1871, was elected a fellow of the Geological Society, and compiled, with the Revd Wadham P. Williams, vicar of Bishop's Hull, a 'Glossary of the Somersetshire dialect'. After a short illness, he died at his home, Tauntfield, on 23 April 1873. He was buried five days later in the cemetery at Wellington Road, Taunton. A monument was erected to his memory in the grounds of Taunton Castle.

Jones was widely remembered in Taunton for his great energy and ability, as well as for 'a kindness of heart and amenity of manner which endeared him to all who had the pleasure of knowing him'.

G. F. JONES, *rev.* T. W. MAYBERRY

Sources personal knowledge (1891) • *Somerset County Gazette* (26 April 1873) • *Somerset County Gazette* (3 May 1873) • *Taunton Courier*

(30 April 1873) · *Proceedings of the Somersetshire Archaeological and Natural History Society*, 19/1 (1873), 4
Archives Som. ARS, collections and private papers
Likenesses photograph (in later life), Somerset Archaeological and Natural History Society Library, Taunton
Wealth at death under £5000: probate, 23 June 1873, *CGPLA Eng. & Wales*

Jones, William Bence (1812–1882), agriculturist, was born on 5 October 1812, at Beccles, Suffolk, the eldest son of William Jones (1776–1843) of Beccles, a lieutenant-colonel of the 5th dragoon guards, and his wife, Matilda (1791–1869), daughter of the Revd Bence Bence (1747–1824) of Thorington Hall, Suffolk. He was the brother of Henry Bence *Jones, MD. He was educated at Harrow School and matriculated on 31 March 1829 at Balliol College, Oxford. He proceeded BA in 1834 and MA in 1836, and was called to the bar at the Inner Temple in 1837.

In 1838 Bence Jones took over the management of the estate at Lisselan, near Clonakilty, co. Cork, in Ireland, bought by his grandfather, an absentee landlord. In 1843 he married Caroline, daughter of William Dickinson MP, of Kingweston, Somerset. They had at least two sons and one daughter, and lived at Lisselan from 1843 to 1880.

Using the knowledge of farming which he had acquired in Suffolk, Bence Jones made great improvements on the 4000 acre estate and farmed 1000 acres himself. He hired a man to teach his tenants how to grow turnips and clover, he improved the roads, reclaimed nearly 400 acres, and consolidated the farms, in order to make the estate profitable. He was never popular in the district, and had a reputation as a harsh JP. In the severe winter of 1879 he gave employment to the local labourers, but opposed the establishment of public relief works, and when the Land League agitation began he was attacked as an unjust and rack-renting landlord. In December 1880 he refused to accept as rent from his tenants the valuation placed on his land by Sir Richard Griffith's government valuation, in place of the stipulated rent; he was consequently boycotted, the first landowner to suffer a boycott. Most of his employees left him, but he managed to run his farm with the help of labourers brought in from England and elsewhere.

Although successful in his resistance to the Land League, Bence Jones left Ireland in January 1881 and settled in London. He gave evidence to the Bessborough commission (1881), and opposed Gladstone's Irish Land Act of 1881, proposing emigration and state drainage of wetlands as alternative solutions to the Irish problem. In 1880 Bence Jones published *The Life's Work in Ireland of a Landlord who Tried to do his Duty*, a collection of articles contributed to journals between 1865 and 1880. In these he defended the Irish landlords, arguing that they were responsible for the only progress in farming in Ireland, and that it was a delusion to think that the peasants were keen to carry out improvements and were kept back by the landlords. He also wrote about the Irish church, in *The Irish Church from the Point of View of its Laymen* (1868), *The Future of the Irish Church* (1869), and *What has been Done in the Irish Church since its Disestablishment* (1875).

Bence Jones died at his home, 34 Elvaston Place, Queen's Gate, London, on 22 June 1882, and was survived by his wife.　　　　　　　D. L. THOMAS, *rev.* ANNE PIMLOTT BAKER

Sources C. Annesley, 'The land war in west Cork: the boycott of William Bence Jones', *Journal of the Cork Historical and Archaeological Society*, 2nd ser., 99 (1994), 1–22 · B. L. Solow, *The land question and the Irish economy, 1870–1903* (1971) · Boase, *Mod. Eng. biog.* · *The Times* (24 June 1882) · IGI · Foster, *Alum. Oxon.* · P. Bew, *Land and the national question in Ireland, 1858–82* (1978), 25 · *CGPLA Eng. & Wales* (1884)
Archives LPL, letters to A. C. Tait
Likenesses portrait, repro. in Annesley, 'The land war in west Cork', 1 · portrait, repro. in *Agricultural Gazette* (3 March 1882)
Wealth at death £30,924 13s. 6d.: resworn probate, Jan 1883, *CGPLA Eng. & Wales* (1882) · £16,312 2s. 3d.: probate, 9 Oct 1882, *CGPLA Ire.*

Jones, William Ellis [*pseud.* Gwilym Cawrdaf] (1795–1848), Welsh-language poet, born on 9 October 1795 at Tyddyn Siôn in the parish of Aber-erch, Caernarvonshire, was the second son of Ellis Jones and Catherine Hughs. His father was then a fuller, but subsequently became a schoolmaster. William worked as a journeyman printer at Caernarfon and Dolgellau, where he printed the work of Dafydd Ionawr (David Richards) and Dafydd Ddu Eryri (David Thomas). The latter taught Jones the rules of Welsh poetry. William moved to London in 1817. About this time he studied landscape painting, and soon after accompanied a gentleman to France and Italy in the capacity of a draughtsman. On his return to England he carried on the business of a photographer at Bath and Bristol, but after an illness returned to Wales and resumed the occupation of printer. In January 1824 he entered the office of *Seren Gomer* at Carmarthen. In the same year his ode (*awdl*) on the regency of George IV won him the chair at the eisteddfods.

Jones was the author of at least eleven odes (*awdlau*), besides several other shorter poems written according to the rules of Welsh assonance. A short lyrical poem entitled 'Nos Sadwrn' ('Saturday Night') and his ode 'Hiraeth Cymro am ei wlad' ('The Welshman's Longing for his Home') are full of a nervous tender feeling. He was also the author of a romance of high merit, *Y bardd, neu, Y meudwy Cymreig* ('The poet, or, The Welsh hermit') (1830). This story of a dream in which a hermit is led by Providence around the world has been described as the first Welsh novel; but with its lack of characterization and plot, and its high moral purpose, it belongs more to the genre of religious allegory. From 1836 to 1838 Jones worked for the Revd Josiah T. Jones, first at Merthyr, then at Cowbridge, and finally at Carmarthen. He was for many years a lay preacher among the Wesleyans, and while at Cowbridge was editor of and chief contributor to *Y Gwron Odyddol*, the monthly organ of the Welsh Oddfellows. He also contributed prolifically to *Hanes y Nef a'r Ddaear* (1847–8), and translated into Welsh John Williams's *A Narrative of Missionary Enterprises*. The last few years of his life were spent in Cardiff, where he resumed printing work. He died at Carmarthen on 27 March 1848, and was buried there in St Peter's churchyard. A collected edition of his poetical works was published in 1851 under the title *Gweithoedd Cawrdaf*, to which is appended a reprint of *Y meudwy Cymreig* and a memoir by his brother, Ellis Jones.

D. L. THOMAS, rev. CLARE L. TAYLOR

Sources T. R. Roberts, *Eminent Welshmen: a short biographical dictionary* (1908) • W. E. Jones, *Gweithoedd Cawrdaf, sef y diweddar W. E. Jones, yn cynnwys Gwyddfa y bardd a'r Meudwy Cymreig* (1851) • T. Parry, *A history of Welsh literature*, trans. H. I. Bell (1955); repr. (1970) • M. Stephens, ed., *The Oxford companion to the literature of Wales* (1986) • IGI
Likenesses portrait, repro. in Jones, *Gweithoedd Cawrdaf*

Jones, William Henry Rich (1817–1885), Church of England clergyman and antiquary, eldest son of William Jones, solicitor and chief secretary of the Religious Tract Society, was born in the parish of Christchurch, Blackfriars, London, on 31 August 1817. He was educated at a private school at Totteridge, Hertfordshire, at King's College, London, and (from 1836) at Magdalen Hall, Oxford. At Oxford he won the Boden scholarship for proficiency in Sanskrit in 1837; he graduated BA in 1840 and proceeded MA in 1844.

In 1841 Jones became curate of St Andrew's, Holborn, in the following year rector of St Martin-in-the-Fields, in 1845 incumbent of St James's, Curtain Road, Shoreditch, and in 1851 vicar of Bradford-on-Avon in Wiltshire. From 1861 to 1873 he acted as rural dean of Potterne. In 1872 he was appointed surrogate of the diocese of Salisbury and prebendary of Netheravon. On 28 September 1842 he married Elizabeth Woodhouse Perks, daughter of Edward Perks, a chemist. After her early death he married on 9 October 1849 Mary Caroline Lydia (b. c.1825), daughter of William Osborne Rich, and in 1883 he prefixed his wife's maiden name to his surname. She survived him with their son and three daughters.

An active parish priest and an erudite antiquary, Jones was elected a fellow of the Society of Antiquaries in 1849. He carefully restored the Anglo-Saxon church at Bradford-on-Avon, and made a significant contribution to the study of the early history of Wiltshire. He wrote a number of articles for the magazine of the Wiltshire Archaeological Society, of which he was elected vice-president in 1882. His books included an edition of Domesday for Wiltshire (1865) and an account of the Saxon church at Bradford-on-Avon (1878); his *Fasti ecclesiae Sarusberiensis: a History of the Cathedral Body at Sarum* was published in 1879. With Canon Dayman, Jones edited the *Statutes of Salisbury Cathedral* (1882). He also edited the *Registers of St. Osmund* (2 vols., 1883–4) for the Rolls Series. At the time of his death he had collected for the Rolls Series the ancient documents relating to the diocese and city of Salisbury. He died suddenly at home at the vicarage, Bradford-on-Avon, on 28 October 1885, and was buried in the town cemetery on 3 November.

W. C. SYDNEY, rev. PENELOPE RUNDLE

Sources *Salisbury and Winchester Journal* (31 Oct 1885) • Foster, *Alum. Oxon.* • *The Guardian* (4 Nov 1885) • census returns, 1851 • Crockford (1885) • m. certs. • *CGPLA Eng. & Wales* (1886) • Bradford-on-Avon urban district council cemetery register, W.R.O./ G13/204/3
Archives Bodl. Oxf., notes on Salisbury Cathedral
Wealth at death £1724 9s. 9d.: probate, 5 Feb 1886, *CGPLA Eng. & Wales*

Jones, William Ronald Rees [*pseud.* Keidrych Rhys] (1915–1987), journalist and poetry editor, was born at Blaensawdde, near Llanddeusant, Carmarthenshire, on 26 December 1915, the only son of Morgan Jones, a tenant farmer, and his wife, Margaretta, *née* Evans. The name by which he was known in literary and journalistic circles was taken from a small river, the Ceidrych, which ran near his home; for a while in the 1960s he used this spelling. Educated at Llandovery grammar school, he found his first job in a local bank, but after an incident involving a shot-gun was dismissed, and shortly afterwards, at the age of twenty, left Wales for London to seek a career in journalism; he worked as a public relations consultant to various animal welfare charities.

Rhys launched the magazine *Wales* in 1937 as 'an independent pamphlet of creative work by the younger progressive Welsh writers', taking as his motto, 'Though we write in English, we are rooted in Wales.' The first series (1937–40) ceased publication during the war but the second, started three years later, ran for eighteen numbers and was edited from Rhys's home at Llan-y-bri and then from the famously cluttered office of the Druid Press in Lammas Street in Carmarthen.

In October 1939 Rhys married, in a secret ceremony and against his parents' wishes, Evelyn Beatrice Roberts (1909–1995), known as Lynette, a poet whose Welsh parents had emigrated to Argentina from Australia; the best man was Dylan Thomas, who once referred to him as 'the best sort of crank'. They lived first at Penybont, a farm near Llangadog where his parents lived, and then rented a whitewashed cottage known as Tŷ Gwyn at Llan-y-bri on the Tywi estuary. The marriage was put under strain by Rhys's prolonged absences from home while serving with the 53rd London Welsh regiment and then the Royal Artillery, during which time his wife suffered a miscarriage; for refusing to serve overseas while she was unwell, he was held in Woolwich arsenal for a few weeks. After his own health broke down, he worked with the Ministry of Information but saw the war out as a correspondent in France, the Netherlands, and Germany.

Rhys published only a small booklet of his own poems, *The Van Pool* (1942), in which he wrote mainly about the farming community of his youth and separation from his wife during war service. He also edited three anthologies of verse: *Poems from the Forces* (1941), *More Poems from the Forces* (1943), and *Modern Welsh Poetry* (1944), of which the last-named was the most influential. Among its thirty-seven contributors were Dylan Thomas, Alun Lewis, Glyn Jones, Idris Davies, Vernon Watkins, Emyr Humphreys, and R. S. Thomas. Quixotically, Rhys stood as the Independent Progressive candidate in the Carmarthen county elections of March 1946. His marriage ended in divorce in 1948; the couple had a son and a daughter. He resumed his career as a journalist, notably as a Welsh columnist with *The People* from 1954 to 1960. In 1954 he was married again, this time to Eva Smith, with whom he had a son. From 1956 until 1960 he served as London editor of Tambimuttu's intermittent magazine *Poetry London–New York*. The third and final series of *Wales* (1958–60), published as a monthly

679 JONES, WILLIAM WEST

from London, was less literary than the early numbers, though it continued to carry poems and stories by some of the best Welsh writers of the day such as Rhys Davies.

Keidrych Rhys, an indefatigable impresario on behalf of Welsh writers, was a generous and gifted editor who was often short of money and could not always pay his printer's bills or his contributors. His was an ebullient personality which delighted in anecdote and controversy, and he was an inveterate purveyor of scandal, especially about members of the Welsh establishment, among whom his paranoia detected many a plot against him. A fluent Welsh speaker, he was a lifelong supporter of Plaid Cymru, for which he arranged publicity in London. In his later years, he dealt in antiquarian books. Rhys died at his home, 40 Heath Street, Hampstead, London, on 22 May 1987.

MEIC STEPHENS

Sources personal knowledge (2004) · *The Times* (27 Sept 1987) · M. Stephens, ed., *The new companion to the literature of Wales*, rev. edn (1998) · G. Jones, 'Letter to Keidrych', *The dragon has two tongues: essays on Anglo-Welsh writers and writing* (1968) · CGPLA Eng. & Wales (1987)
Archives NL Wales
Likenesses photograph, repro. in *Wales*, 25 (1947)
Wealth at death under £70,000: administration, 10 Nov 1987, CGPLA Eng. & Wales

Jones, William West (1838–1908), archbishop of Cape Town, was born in South Hackney, Middlesex, on 11 May 1838. He was the sixth and youngest son of Edward Henry Jones, wine merchant, of Mark Lane, London, and his wife, Mary Emma, *née* Collier. He was educated at Merchant Taylors' School, London, from April 1845, and from 1856 at St John's College, Oxford, where he was a foundation scholar. He was awarded a second-class mark in his first set of exams, classical moderations, in 1858, but barely scraped a degree, being awarded an honorary fourth in the final exams in classics and mathematics in 1860, by which time he had already been elected a fellow of St John's. His poor result was said to be due to illness from overwork. After graduating BA, Jones proceeded to an MA in 1863 and BD in 1869, and was made an honorary DD on being consecrated a bishop in 1874. He was made an honorary fellow of his college in 1893. After being ordained deacon in 1861 and priest in 1862, he was licensed to the curacy of St Matthew's in the City Road, and from 1864 to 1874 held the living (in the gift of St John's College) of Summertown, in the suburbs of Oxford. Jones was diocesan inspector of schools, preacher at the old Whitehall Chapel in London (1870–72), and rural dean of Oxford (1871–4). In 1879 he married Emily, the daughter of John Allen of Altrincham, Cheshire, at which point he was obliged to give up the fellowship at St John's College which he had held from 1859; they had two sons.

On 17 May 1874, in Westminster Abbey, Jones was consecrated as the second bishop of Cape Town, the first bishop of Cape Town and metropolitan of South Africa having been Robert Gray. Jones, who had already refused appointments as bishop of the Orange Free State and Hong Kong, accepted the difficult post only because of the urging of

William West Jones (1838–1908), by S. B. Barnard, c.1880s

Samuel Wilberforce, bishop of Oxford, who was concerned that the continuing dispute over the status of the South African church's relationship to the Church of England (which had been sparked by the Colenso affair) should be resolved. When at his consecration Jones took his oath of allegiance to the archbishop of Canterbury, A. C. Tait, he and the archbishop signed a document which safeguarded the independent rights and privileges of the South African church. The thirty-four years of Jones's episcopate were years of constant racial violence in South Africa. But he worked persistently to encourage peace in both church and state without sacrificing his high-church principles or concealing his own views. His courtesy, friendliness, dignity, and business sense gained him the respect of nonconformists and members of the Dutch Reformed church, as well as of his own high-church party and the English Church Union to which he belonged. In 1897 Cape Town was raised from a bishopric to an archbishopric as an acknowledgement of its rising importance. Jones also encouraged missionary work among the Cape Malays, and during his episcopate the church became more attuned to the African people.

At the end of the Second South African War in 1902 Jones took part in the great peace thanksgiving service held in Pretoria. Before his death he was busy raising funds for the completion of the Anglican cathedral at Cape Town, dedicated to the memory of those who had died in the war. The future George V laid the foundation-stone in 1901. Early in 1908 Jones returned to England for the Lambeth conference, and died at the Lizard peninsula, Cornwall, on 21 May 1908. His body was then moved to Oxford, where it was buried in Holywell cemetery. A recumbent statue of Jones was placed in the memorial chapel of St George's Cathedral, Cape Town.

C. P. Lucas, *rev.* Lynn Milne

Sources *The Times* (22 May 1908) · *The Guardian* (27 May 1908) · *Cape Church Monthly* (June 1908) · *Cape Church Monthly* (July 1908) · A. T. Wirgman, *History of the English church and people in South Africa* (1895) · P. B. Hinchliff, *DSAB*

Archives LPL, corresp. | Bodl. Oxf., corresp. with Lord Kimberley · LPL, corresp. with E. W. Benson; corresp. with A. C. Tait

Likenesses S. B. Barnard, photograph, *c.*1880–1889, NPG [*see illus.*] · W. Orpen, oils, 1909, St John's College, Oxford · C. L. Hartwell, bronze effigy, exh. RA 1911, St George's Cathedral, Cape Town · P. T. Cole, watercolour, Diocesan Library, Cape Town · C. W. Furse, oils; known to be in family possession in 1912 · C. H. Thompson, oils, Diocesan College, Cape Town

Jones, (Frederic) Wood (1879–1954), anatomist, was born on 23 January 1879 at West Hackney, London, the youngest of the three children of Charles Henry Jones, architect, of Welsh descent, and his wife, Lucy Allin. He entered the London Hospital in 1897 as a medical student and qualified MB, BS in 1904. While a student he contributed to the *Journal of Anatomy and Physiology*, and won a succession of prizes in anatomy, physiology, and clinical medicine. He was throughout life active and restless, and did not retain any of his academic posts (including six chairs of anatomy) for more than a few years. This adventurous spirit was first shown when in 1905 he became medical officer to the Eastern Extension Telegraph Company in the Cocos Islands. He stayed for fifteen months and made an important study of reef-building corals, the results of which appeared in *Coral and Atolls* (1910). In 1907 he returned to England to take up the post of demonstrator in anatomy at the London Hospital under Arthur Keith, but soon afterwards he left for Egypt to undertake field anthropological studies on behalf of the Egyptian government's archaeological survey of Nubia.

Jones returned to England in 1909 to become lecturer in anatomy at Manchester University, and a year later he went to St Thomas's Hospital medical school as senior demonstrator in anatomy. In this year also, he was awarded the DSc degree of London University. In 1910 Jones married Gertrude (d. 1957), daughter of George Clunies *Ross. They had no children. There were, however, five children of her previous marriage to Axel Wilhelm Blom, whom Gertrude had divorced.

In 1912 Jones transferred to the London School of Medicine for Women, first as director and then as professor of anatomy. In 1915 he delivered the Arris and Gale lectures at the Royal College of Surgeons, entitled 'The influence of the arboreal habit in the evolution of the reproductive system', proving a lecturer of unusual ability, with an original approach to the evidence of comparative anatomy in human evolution. He amplified his lectures in *Arboreal Man* (1916). Later, he expounded the view that there is no close relationship between humans on the one hand and apes and monkeys on the other, but that the segregation

of the evolutionary line leading to humans occurred as far back as the Eocene period. This thesis met with considerable criticism from other comparative anatomists.

During the First World War, Jones was a captain in the Royal Army Medical Corps, and was stationed at the Military Orthopaedic Hospital at Shepherd's Bush. He made some useful observations on the effects of partial paralysis of limbs following gunshot wounds, and in 1920 he published one of his best and most widely read books, *The Principles of Anatomy as Seen in the Hand*.

In 1919 Jones went to Australia as professor of anatomy at Adelaide University, where he remained for eight years and engaged largely in field studies, taking part in several expeditions in South Australia. On these expeditions extensive zoological, botanical, and anthropological collections were made, some of which led to the discovery of new marsupial species as well as many new species of invertebrates. The results were published in the *Records of the South Australia Museum* and the *Transactions of the Royal Society of South Australia*. Between 1923 and 1925 he published a systematic catalogue of the mammals of South Australia—probably his most important work on comparative anatomy with 311 illustrations, drawn by himself.

In 1927 Jones accepted the Rockefeller chair of physical anthropology in the University of Hawaii, where he remained for two years. During this time he published a general systematic account of the comparative anatomy of the primates in *Man's Place among the Mammals* (1929), in which he expounded in detail his unorthodox view of the relationship of humans to the higher primates. In 1930 he returned to Australia to take the chair of anatomy at Melbourne University, and during the next few years he took part in further zoological and anthropological expeditions, and completed papers on strictly anatomical subjects. At the end of 1937 he left Australia to take up the professorship of anatomy at Manchester University, where he continued to publish papers on anatomical subjects, as well as editing the seventh edition of Buchanan's *Manual of Anatomy* (1946). His stimulating book, *Structure and Function as Seen in the Foot* (1944), was a work of considerable value for orthopaedic surgeons. His biological essays, *Design and Purpose* (1942), *Habit and Heritage* (1943), and *Trends of Life* (1953), affirmed his modified Lamarckian interpretation of evolution and expressed strongly anti-Darwinian views.

In 1945 Jones assumed his last academic office, that of the Sir William H. Collins professor of human and comparative anatomy at the Royal College of Surgeons, which he held until 1949. Thereafter he served as curator of the Hunterian collection of the college and was a Hunterian trustee. He had been elected to the fellowship of the college in 1930. Jones died of lung cancer at his London home, 20 Marsham Court, Westminster, on 29 September 1954, his wife surviving him. He was remembered for his vigorous personality, his strictly scientific contributions, and for the healthy stimulus he gave to controversy by the occasional unorthodoxy of his opinions. His reputation as a lecturer brought him many requests to deliver memorial lectures and orations. He was elected FRS in 1925 and received the honorary degree of DSc from Adelaide (1920) and Melbourne (1934).

W. E. Le Gros Clark, *rev.* Harold Ellis

Sources A. Keith, 'Frederic Wood Jones, 1879–1954', *Annals of the Royal College of Surgeons of England*, 15 (1954), 335–9 • B. Christophers, 'Frederic Wood Jones as a teacher and on teaching', *Australian and New Zealand Journal of Surgery*, 64 (1994), 710–20 • B. Christophers, 'Frederic Wood Jones: corals and atolls', *Australian and New Zealand Journal of Surgery*, 65 (1995), 749–60 • W. Le Gros Clark, 'Frederic Wood Jones', *Journal of Anatomy*, 89 (1955), 255–60 • W. E. Le G. Clark, *Memoirs FRS*, 1 (1955), 119–134 • private information (1971) • personal knowledge (1971)

Archives RCS Eng., corresp. and papers | RCS Eng., letters to Ulrica Hubbe • RCS Eng., corresp. with Sir Arthur Keith

Likenesses A. E. Cooper, portrait, RCS Eng. • W. McInnes, portrait, Royal Australian College of Surgeons, Melbourne

Wealth at death £2949 14s. 0d.: probate, 23 Feb 1955, *CGPLA Eng. & Wales*

Jonghe, Adriaen de. *See* Junius, Hadrianus (1511–1575).

Jonson, Benjamin [Ben] (1572–1637), poet and playwright, was born on 11 June 1572, probably in or near London. He was of Scottish descent, and retained a keen interest in the country of his forebears. 'His Grandfather came from Carlisle and he thought from Anandale to it' noted the Scottish poet William Drummond of Hawthornden, after meeting Jonson on his travels north of the border in 1618–19; 'he served King Henry 8 and was a Gentleman' (*Conversations with William Drummond*, ll. 234–5). The Johnstones or Johnstouns—the name is spelt in thirteen different ways in Scotland in this period, but always with a t—were a powerful family of brigands and aristocratic warlords who had played a major part in skirmishes in Annandale and along the Scottish borders over several centuries. Jonson was sufficiently impressed by their reputation to have adopted their armorial bearings of 'three spindles or Rhombi' as his own (ibid., l. 588; Symonds, 2–3). Jonson's grandfather may have been one of the Scottish prisoners seized by the English from Annandale during the battle of Solway Moss in November 1542, brought south to the English garrison at Carlisle, and wooed into loyal service of Henry VIII: a 'Maister Johnston' is recorded among this company (*LP Henry VIII*, vol. 17, 1900, 625–6). About Jonson's father, who died a month before the birth of his son, little is known. According to Drummond's memoir, he had lost 'all his estate under Queen Marie' (a phrase that appears to imply initial prosperity) and suffered imprisonment and forfeiture; on his release, he 'at last turn'd Minister' (*Conversations*, ll. 236–9). The date and circumstances of his marriage are unknown. In its southward progress, his family name had shifted to the commoner English spelling, 'Johnson'; yet 'Jonson' was to be the poet's own favoured spelling in all surviving examples of his autograph, and in his published work from 1604 onwards. 'Ben' was the version of his forename by which he would be universally known.

Early life Jonson was 'brought up poorly', according to his own report (*Conversations*, l. 239). His earliest years would have been difficult for his recently widowed mother: a

Benjamin Jonson (1572–1637), by Abraham van Blyenberch, *c*.1617

clergyman's wages in this period were modest, and her husband can have had little accumulated wealth to leave her. While Jonson was still a '*little child*' in '*his long coats*', however, his mother married again, this time to a bricklayer, and the family moved to Hartshorn (or Christopher) Lane, a narrow alleyway which ran from the Strand to Thames-side wharves, not far from Charing Cross (Fuller, *Worthies*, 243). The bricklayer has been plausibly identified as Robert Brett, a contractor of comfortable means who had risen to become master of the Tylers' and Bricklayers' Company by the time of his death on 29 August 1609 (Bamborough). No record of Brett's marriage or will has been found, and little is known about Jonson's mother, apart from a single anecdote, recorded by Drummond, of her bravery at the time of her son's imprisonment in 1605 for his part in the writing of *Eastward Ho!* Fearing a fatal sentence, she prepared a poisoned draught for him, and 'that she was no churle she told she minded first to have Drunk of it herself' (*Conversations*, ll. 282–3). It has been conjectured that she may have been the Rebecca Brett who was buried at St Martin-in-the-Fields on 9 September 1609, just a few days after Robert Brett's own death (Kay, *Life*, 2). Brett may have had other children, to judge from the recurrence of the family name in the parish records: they certainly included John (1582–1618) and Robert (1584–1618), who were eventually to inherit their father's business. Ben would thus have been the oldest child in a busy and growing household.

At an early age Jonson attended a small elementary school maintained by the church of St Martin-in-the-Fields, not far from Hartshorn Lane; here he learned to read and write in English, along with elementary rules of grammar. At the prompting of an unidentified 'friend' (sometimes thought to be the lawyer John Hoskyns) he was sent off as a day boy to Westminster School, perhaps at the age of seven, where he was fortunate enough to study under William Camden, who was at that time the school's second master (*Conversations*, ll. 239–40). In later life Jonson spoke warmly of his pupillage and friendship with the great antiquary—'Alumnus olim, aeternum Amicus', 'a pupil once, a friend for ever'—acknowledging Camden as the source of:

> All that I am in arts, all that I know
> (How nothing's that?)
> (*Ben Jonson*, ed. Herford, Simpson, and Simpson, 4.4–5; Jonson, *Epigrams*, no. 14, ll. 1–3)

Other friendships formed at Westminster were to prove equally enduring: with the young Robert Cotton, for example, another protégé of Camden's, from whose superlative collection of books and manuscripts Jonson was later to profit; and with the future poet and fellow convert to Catholicism Hugh Holland, whose verses to the memory of Shakespeare would eventually stand beside Jonson's at the head of the 1623 first folio. Like other Westminster poets after him—Richard Corbett, George Herbert, Henry King, Abraham Cowley, John Dryden—Jonson benefited deeply from the school's traditions of rhetorical and classical training, and, in particular, from the exercise of rendering Greek and Latin verse and prose into their equivalent English forms. Camden, who had a good knowledge of earlier English poetry, seems also to have encouraged his boys to write verses of their own in English. Noting Jonson's 'opinion of Verses' in 1618–19, William Drummond observed 'that he wrott all his first in prose, for so his master Cambden had Learned him' (*Conversations*, ll. 376–8). Through the Latin play, a regular event in the life of Westminster School, Jonson had early experience in a medium he was eventually to make his own. He was to retain a special fondness for the comedies of Plautus and Terence which were commonly performed on these occasions, and for the school's traditions of dramatic performance, to which he refers familiarly in two later plays, *The Staple of News* (1626) and *The Magnetic Lady* (1632).

Fuller believed that Jonson 'was statutably admitted into Saint *Johns colledge* in *Cambridge*' but, for want of funds, was obliged to return after a few weeks to London to help his stepfather with new building works at Lincoln's Inn (Fuller, *Worthies*, 243). Though Jonson's name does not appear in the records of the college or the university, Fuller's prodigious memory and local knowledge of Cambridge make the story credible; and the possibility of a connection with St John's is strengthened by a request to Jonson from its president, Robert Lane, that he 'penne a dyttye' to celebrate the visit of King James to the college in 1615 (Mullinger, 1–4). The building work at Lincoln's Inn with which Jonson was involved has been dated to the summer of 1588 (Eccles, 'Marriage', 264). It has been suggested that Jonson might have lingered at Westminster a year or two longer—his *English Grammar* shows a familiarity with Hebrew, which was taught only at seventh form—and that he began to work as a labourer as late as 1590. But

tuition in languages such as Hebrew was easily available in London at this time, and Drummond's observation that Jonson was 'taken from' Westminster suggests an earlier departure (*Conversations*, l. 240).

His stepfather's trade proved one that Jonson 'could not endure' (*Conversations*, l. 242). Fuller pictures him with trowel in hand and book in pocket, labouring reluctantly at his uncongenial task. John Aubrey tells of a lawyer overhearing Jonson reciting verses from Homer while working on the new buildings at Lincoln's Inn; 'discoursing with him and finding him to have a Witt extraordinary', he provided 'some Exhibition to maintaine him at Trinity College in Cambridge' (*Ben Jonson*, ed. Herford, Simpson, and Simpson, 1.178). No evidence of Jonson's connection with Trinity has been found, however, and Aubrey (or his informant, Richard Hill) may have been muddled in their memories of the timing of Jonson's stay at Cambridge. Taunts about his early work as a bricklayer followed Jonson throughout later life. As late as 1633, after the failure of *The Magnetic Lady*, Alexander Gill abusively suggested it was time the ageing Jonson abandon the theatre, and return to his former trade. Yet Jonson had in fact been attached to this trade throughout a surprisingly long period of his life. The quarterage book of the Tylers' and Bricklayers' Company shows him making payments to the company from 1595, and still paying his dues as late as 1611, when he was at the height of his career as a dramatist and writer of court masques. It is possible, as David Kay has suggested, that Jonson's continued membership of the guild was a hedge against unemployment, and that he returned to bricklaying during periods of financial need, when work for the court and the theatres was slack (Kay, 'Bricklayer'). But guild membership was also an avenue to citizenship, and a warrant therefore of social standing. In 1618 Jonson was welcomed to the city of Edinburgh not as a celebrated writer, but as 'inglisman burges and gildbrother in communi forma' (*Ben Jonson*, ed. Herford, Simpson, and Simpson, 1.233). 'Burges' (a Scottish term) implies that Jonson had served his apprenticeship to full term, and 'gildbrother' that he was still associated with the Tylers' and Bricklayers' Company at this advanced stage of his career. Such qualifications may have eased his ready acceptance by the civic community in Edinburgh; later still, in 1628, they made possible his appointment as chronologer to the City of London.

At some time in the early 1590s, however, Jonson abandoned his work as a bricklayer, and joined the English expeditionary forces to the Low Countries. The dates of this period of service, as of other events in his early life, have been disputed, but it is likely that he was recruited during the early months of 1591, when special efforts were made to reinforce the English presence in the Netherlands. In the spring of that year Maurice of Nassau, commander of the army of the states general, began his first campaign to drive the Spanish out of the inland provinces of the north. The English general Sir Francis Vere, accompanied by his younger brother, Sir Horace, whom Jonson was later to celebrate in *Epigrams*, no. 91, gave brilliant support and tactical advice. Zutphen fell in May,

Deventer in June, and Nijmegen in October. English troops were also involved the following year in the successful siege of Steenwijk in June, and the capture of Coevorden in September. Jonson may have seen service at all or several of these sites. One notable feat he described to William Drummond with evident pride almost thirty years later: 'In his servuce in the Low Countries, he had in the face of both the Campes Killed ane Enimie and taken opima spolia from him' (*Conversations*, ll. 244–6). *Opima spolia* are the arms traditionally taken by victors from the vanquished on the field of battle: the Latin phrase hints at the antiquity of the custom. Single-combat fighting of the kind suggested here, originally undertaken by opposing kings or leaders as a way of avoiding wider bloodshed among their men, was rarely practised in this period; Jonson's victory would have brought him to the notice of his superior officers. But it was also the forerunner of other, less happy, fights in which he was later to be involved.

Entering the theatre After 'returning soone' to England—probably with the first contingent of homecoming troops in autumn 1592—Jonson 'betook himself to his wonted studies' (*Conversations*, l. 243). Where and at what date he chose to enter the theatre is unclear. Aubrey believed that on his return from the Low Countries Jonson 'acted and wrote at *The Green curtaine* but both ill, a kind of nursery or obscure Play house, somewhere in the Suburbes (I think towards Shoreditch, or Clarkenwell' (*Ben Jonson*, ed. Herford, Simpson, and Simpson, 1.179). It is possible that Aubrey (or his informant, J. Greenhill) was again confused about the exact sequence of events in Jonson's early life. (Later in the decade Jonson was certainly to be associated with the Curtain Theatre, Shoreditch, where *Every Man in his Humour* was performed in 1598.) Aubrey's assertion that Jonson 'was never a good Actor, but an excellent Instructor' (ibid., 1.182) nevertheless has the ring of truth. Once he had firmly established himself as a writer, Jonson (unlike Shakespeare) chose to abandon his career as an actor altogether. In several of his plays, however, he gives an amusing glimpse of his own anxious presence behind the scenes. Gossip Mirth in the 'Induction' to *The Staple of News* (1626) speaks of the author in the tiring house '*rowling himselfe up and downe like a tun*' (ll. 61–74) in sweaty agitation as he issues last-minute directions to the actors.

The gibes of Captain Tucca in Thomas Dekker's *Satiromastix* (1601) suggest that early in his career Jonson may have worked as 'a poore Jorneyman Player' with a travelling company, playing the part of the royal marshal Hieronymo, crazed by the murder of his son and his thwarted search for justice, in Thomas Kyd's *The Spanish Tragedy*: 'thou hast forgot how thou amblest (in leather pilch) by a play-wagon, in the high way, and took'st made Jeronimo's part, to get service among the mimickes' (*Satiromastix*, IV.i, ll. 161–5). It has been plausibly suggested that the troupe with which Jonson was travelling was Pembroke's Company, who were on the road in 1595–6 (Bowers, 396–7). *The Spanish Tragedy* was to leave a strong, though not entirely positive, impression on Jonson's creative imagination: humorous and parodic echoes of the play are to be found throughout his later work. In 1601 and

1602 the theatre manager Philip Henslowe was to pay Jonson for writing 'adicians' to Kyd's play. Whether Jonson is in fact the author of the surviving additions to *The Spanish Tragedy* is still however an open question.

On 14 November 1594 Jonson was married to Anne Lewis in the church of St Magnus the Martyr, by London Bridge. Mark Eccles has argued that the location of this church, adjoining the theatrical parish of St Saviour, Southwark, suggests that by this date Jonson was working as an actor on or near the Bankside: at the Rose Theatre, or Newington Butts, or the Paris Garden—where, according to Dekker (*Satiromastix*, IV.i, ll. 150–53), he played the part of Zuliman in a tragedy (Eccles, 'Marriage', 261). Jonson's earliest surviving play, *The Case is Altered* (published in quarto in 1609, but not included in the 1616 folio) was performed by Pembroke's Company probably during the first half of 1597. Modelled on two of Plautus's comedies, *Captivi* and *Aulularia*, the play has elements that Jonson would later ridicule, but to which he would return in his final years: cross-wooings, lost children, happy reunitings. 'The Isle of Dogs', written in collaboration with Thomas Nashe, was performed by the company at the new Swan Theatre on the Bankside in July of the same year. For unknown reasons, this play caused grave offence. It may have glanced at members of the court circle and possibly at the queen herself, whose palace at Greenwich lay opposite the Isle of Dogs, down river from the city. On 28 July the privy council, in apparent response to its performance, ordered the closure of all the London theatres because of the 'greate disorders' caused 'by lewd matters that are handled on the stages, and by resorte and confluence of bad people'. Jonson and two of his fellow actors, Gabriel Spencer and Robert Shaa, were arrested and imprisoned at the instigation of Elizabeth's interrogator, the notorious Richard Topcliffe, and charged at Greenwich on 15 August with 'Leude and mutynous behavior' (*APC*, 22.346; *Ben Jonson*, ed. Herford, Simpson, and Simpson, 1.217–18). Nashe had fled to the safety of Great Yarmouth, but his rooms were raided and papers seized. Throughout this episode, as Jonson later told Drummond, 'his judges could gett nothing of him to all their demands bot I and No'; though 'they plac'd two damn'd Villans to catch advantage of him, with him', he was warned of their intentions by the prison keeper, and evaded their enquiries (*Conversations*, ll. 256–60). The affair subsided as mysteriously as it had begun. Jonson and his companions were released on 2 October, and a few days later Henslowe's company, the Lord Admiral's Men, began to perform again at the Rose Theatre with impunity, in defiance of the closure order which was still officially in place. Pembroke's Men were effectively destroyed, however, by the closure, and several members of this company were recruited by Henslowe for the Admiral's Men.

An exchange of payments recorded on 28 July, the very day of the privy council order, suggests that Henslowe had been attempting to attract Jonson himself to become a sharer in the Admiral's Men. The absence of further recorded payments suggests that this move came to nothing. Over the next two years, however, Henslowe employed Jonson regularly as one of his writers, noting payment for a number of plays that today are known only through their titles. These include 'Hot Anger Soon Cold', written with Henry Porter and Henry Chettle, and perhaps performed in August 1598; 'Page of Plymouth', with Thomas Dekker, a year later; and 'Robert II, The King of Scots Tragedy', with Chettle, Dekker, and others, for which payments were made in August and September 1599. During the early part of his career Jonson undoubtedly wrote, in part or in whole, other plays that have now disappeared. In September 1598 Francis Meres in *Palladis tamia* nominated Jonson among those he reckoned 'our best for Tragedie' (G. Gregory Smith, ed., *Elizabethan Critical Essays*, 2 vols., 1904, 2.319), but no tragedies of Jonson's from this period have survived. A play called 'Richard Crookback', for which Jonson received payment from Henslowe in 1602, has similarly vanished. By 1619 Jonson was able to report to Drummond 'that the half of his comedies were not in Print' (*Conversations*, l. 393). Many of these unpublished comedies probably dated from the 1590s; like most of his other lost plays, they may have been collaborative or commissioned pieces, which he felt little need to preserve.

Early successes *Every Man in his Humour*, performed in the autumn of 1598 at the Curtain Theatre in Shoreditch by Shakespeare's own company, the Lord Chamberlain's Men, with Shakespeare himself and Richard Burbage in leading roles, marked a different level of achievement. This skilfully constructed city comedy, wittily exploiting the fashionable notion of 'humours', clearly established Jonson as the coming dramatist of the 1590s. In its radically revised form—the locale shifted from Florence to London, its action more thoroughly domesticated—the play was to occupy pride of place at the head of the folio edition of Jonson's collected works in 1616, symbolically marking the beginning of his career as a dramatist, and the arrival of a new kind of vernacular comedy. Bobadilla, the comedy's impoverished, smooth-tongued veteran, is an engaging braggart worthy of comparison with Shakespeare's Falstaff—who had made his first stage appearance just a few months earlier in *1 Henry IV*, presented by the same company. Burbage, who was from now on to be Jonson's leading man as well as Shakespeare's, may perhaps have played Musco, the ingenious servant, while Shakespeare himself may possibly have taken the part of Lorenzo, a father anxious about his son's ventures into poetry and high-spirited company.

On 22 September 1598, while *Every Man in his Humour* was probably still in performance, Jonson was indicted at Shoreditch on a charge of manslaughter, having killed in a duel the actor Gabriel Spencer, with whom he had been imprisoned during the previous summer. Years later Jonson was to tell William Drummond that Spencer had challenged him to this fight, and, with a sword 10 inches longer than his own, had wounded him in the arm before being overcome; and that for this offence he himself 'was Emprisoned and almost at the Gallowes' (*Conversations*, ll. 246–51). Jonson escaped by reading the so-called neck-

verse (Psalm 51: 1), possibly after the intervention of Henslowe or a member of his company (Dekker, *Satiromastix*, IV.iii, ll. 252ff.; *Henslowe's Diary*, 286). His goods were confiscated, and he was branded on the thumb as a convicted felon. While in prison, Jonson was converted to Catholicism, perhaps by Father Thomas Wright, a learned Jesuit who had studied in Rome and Milan and was now himself living in semi-detention in London's gaols. Jonson's earliest surviving poems can be dated from this period; some are addressed to fellow Catholics or show other traces of his new-found faith.

Every Man out of his Humour was performed at Burbage's recently built Globe Theatre on the Bankside in November or December 1599, and again at court about Christmas of the same year. Though the play's title appeared to promise a sequel of sorts to Jonson's earlier success, the new piece proved very different from its predecessor in tone and structure. In the revised ending written for court performance, the envious figure Macilente declares himself to be wholly redeemed by the sudden appearance of the queen herself: a hopeful, if implausible, conclusion that awkwardly anticipates the subtler structural transformations of Jonson's Jacobean court masques. *The Fountain of Self-Love, or, Cynthia's Revels* was performed by the then Children of Queene Elizabeths Chappell' at Blackfriars Theatre some time between 2 September 1600 and May 1601, and again on 6 January 1601 at court. The court performance was evidently not liked. Despite the play's famous lyric in praise of the Virgin Queen ('Queene and Huntresse, chaste, and fayre'), its references to her hounding of Actaeon may have aroused political suspicion, on the very eve of Essex's rebellion, while the ambitions of Criticus 'A creature of a most perfect and divine temper' (II.iii) to ingratiate himself at the court of Cynthia may have seemed too close to the ambitions of the author himself. Jonson was to revise the play extensively for publication in his 1616 folio, reversing the play's title and subtitle, and including much satire on court behaviour that is not to be found in the quarto of 1601.

Poetaster, performed at Blackfriars by the Children of Her Majesty's Chapel probably in the spring of 1601, seems to have been prompted in part by personal antagonisms. Jonson later informed Drummond that 'he had many quarrells with Marston beat him and took his Pistol from him, wrote his Poetaster on him the beginning of them were that Marston represented him in the stage' (*Conversations*, ll. 284–6). Reacting, perhaps over sensitively, to Marston's portraits of him in *What you will* and *Jack Drum's Entertainment*, Jonson retaliated with a portrait of Marston in the character of Crispinus, who at the end of *Poetaster* is forced to vomit up a number of hard words, known to have been favoured by Marston himself. Dekker, also glanced at in *Poetaster* in the character of Demetrius, took revenge in *Satiromastix*, a comedy performed privately that autumn by Paul's Company and publicly at the Globe by the Lord Chamberlain's Men. Dekker's play, of which Jonson appears to have had advance information while writing *Poetaster*, presents 'Horace', alias Jonson, as a self-promoting, self-creating figure, shooting his quills like a porcupine and flicking 'inke in everie mans face' (*Satiromastix*, iv.ii, ll. 128, 102).

Despite the vividness of such exchanges, the so-called 'war of the theatres' may have been a less substantial combat than an earlier generation of literary historians imagined. Recent scholars have stressed the collaborative ties that actually united the rival companies and dramatists, and the presence of other, political, currents within a play such as *Poetaster*—whose original title, *The Arraignment*, may well have reminded early audiences of the celebrated trial earlier that year of Essex and Southampton. Like many of his friends, future patrons, and fellow Catholics—John Selden, Sir Henry Goodyere, Sir Henry Neville, Lord Monteagle, the earls of Bedford, Rutland, and Pembroke—Jonson seems to have looked expectantly to Essex, and to have been dismayed by his sudden downfall. The world invoked by the figure of Envy at the opening of the play, of:

> wrestings, comments, applications,
> Spie-like suggestions, privie whisperings,
> And thousand such promooting sleights as these
> (*Poetaster*, 'Induction', ll. 24–6)

is not merely that of Augustan Rome, but hints also at the condition of contemporary England following the death of Essex. It was a world with which Jonson himself would become increasingly and uncomfortably familiar in the years that followed.

Domestic life In the 'Apologetical Dialogue' to *Poetaster* Jonson depicts himself in monkish seclusion, working

> halfe my nights, and all my dayes,
> Here in a cell, to get a darke, pale face,
> To come forth worth the ivy, or the bayes.
> (ll. 233–5)

Here as elsewhere in his writing Jonson gives little sense of the possible companionship of his marriage and family life. Little is known about Anne, the wife whom Jonson many years later was tersely to describe as 'a shrew yet honest' (*Conversations*, l. 254). For increasing periods of time, the couple appear to have lived apart. During the early years of the new century Jonson lodged with various friends and patrons. 'Ben. Johnson the poet nowe lives upon one Townesend' observed John Manningham the diarist in February 1603—referring to Sir Robert Townshend, at some stage the patron also of John Fletcher—'and scornes the world' (*Diary of John Manningham*, 187). '5 yeers he had not bedded with her', noted Drummond, 'but remained with my Lord Aulbanie' (*Conversations*, ll. 254–5). Though the precise dates of Jonson's five-year residence in Blackfriars with the king's cousin Esmé Stuart, seigneur d'Aubigny, have been variously assigned, the stay may well have begun in 1603, not long after Aubigny's arrival in London from Scotland with the royal party in May of that year. It is possible that Jonson was working on his Roman tragedy, *Sejanus*, while lodging in turn with these two patrons: a copy of the 1605 quarto of the play is inscribed to Townshend, and the play itself is gratefully dedicated to Aubigny, who may have offered significant protection during the troubles that followed the staging of that play and of *Eastward Ho!*, and in the aftermath of

the Gunpowder Plot in late 1605 and early 1606. Jonson's residence with Aubigny may thus have been prompted as much by practical necessity as by any domestic unhappiness. The separation of the Jonsons during this period seems in any case not to have been absolute: the 'Epistle Dedicatory' printed with the quarto edition of *Volpone* in 1607 is signed 'from my house in the Blackfriars', while the baptism of an infant, Benjamin Jonson, 'son to Benjamin', in February 1608 suggests that about this time the couple were at least in intermittent contact.

They had several other children before this date. An earlier Benjamin, probably born in 1596, had died of the plague in 1603. Jonson was once more away from home, staying this time in William Camden's company with Sir Robert Cotton in Huntingdonshire. Jonson told Drummond he had had a vision of the boy appearing before him in adult shape, with the mark of a bloody cross on his forehead, as if cut by a sword. He described the vision to Camden, who persuaded him it 'was but ane appreehension of his fantasie', but letters arrived later from his wife, informing him of the boy's death (*Conversations*, ll. 261–72). The episode was to inspire one of Jonson's most touching epitaphs ('On my First Son', *Epigrams*, no. 45). The death at six months of a daughter, Mary, had prompted another moving epitaph, perhaps in 1600 ('On my First Daughter', *Epigrams*, no. 22). Another boy, Joseph, 'the sone of Beniamyne Johnson', had been baptized at Cripplegate on 9 December 1599. Jonson is likely to have fathered other children, both legitimate and illegitimate. If the Elizabeth, 'daughter of Ben Johnson', whose baptism is recorded in the register of St Mary Matfelon on 25 March 1610 and the 'Benjamin Johnson fil. Ben', baptized at St Martin-in-the-Fields on 6 April of the same year were both his children, then they were almost certainly born of different mothers. 'In his youth given to Venerie', noted Drummond laconically in his account of Jonson's early life (*Conversations*, l. 287).

Celebrating James Jonson made no attempt to mourn the death of Queen Elizabeth on 24 March 1603; 'His Muse an other path desires to tread', as one contemporary pointedly remarked (H. Chettle, *England's Mourning Garment*, 1603, sigs. D2v–D3r). King James's accession, on the other hand, prompted in Jonson a burst of energetic writing. He composed speeches for three of the eight pageants for the royal entry to the City of London on 15 March 1604, working in uneasy collaboration with Dekker, and a *Panegyre* to James on his progress to Westminster Hall four days later to open his first parliament, along with a series of epigrams saluting the new monarch, his policies, and even his early poetry—about which, in private conversation with Drummond, he was later to express misgivings. The previous summer Jonson had devised an entertainment at Althorp for Queen Anne and Prince Henry in their progress south from Edinburgh, and more royal entertainments were now to follow: at Highgate in May 1604, to divert the king and queen at the home of Sir William Cornwallis; at Theobalds, Sir Robert Cecil's estate, in July 1606, in celebration of the visit to England of King Christian of Denmark and his meeting with King James; and at

Theobalds once more in May of the following year, in honour of another royal visit. Other entertainments which Jonson wrote during this same period in connection with civic occasions have largely vanished, though a manuscript of 'Britain's Burse', performed in the king's presence to mark the opening of Cecil's New Exchange in April 1609, has recently come to light, as have three surviving songs from the 'Merchant Taylors' Entertainment', also staged in the king's presence in July 1607.

Jonson's firm acceptance into royal favour was achieved on 6 January 1605 with the presentation of *The Masque of Blackness* in the old Banqueting House at Whitehall. Queen Anne herself had proposed the masque's central and surprising device: that she and eleven of her ladies should emerge from a scallop shell, 'all paynted like Blackamores face and neck bare', dazzlingly bejewelled and 'strangely attired', to dance with members of the court. The shell was borne in to the hall on a mobile wave, 'stuck with a *chev'ron* of lights', and escorted by six huge sea monsters (*Ben Jonson*, ed. Herford, Simpson, and Simpson, 10.449, 8.171). Though it shocked more demure observers, this audacious and costly affair, the first of Jonson's collaborations with Inigo Jones, secured their commissions for the masquing season for many years to come. Through Jones's and Jonson's combined genius the Stuart court masque achieved its most sophisticated form—though temperamental differences, compounding tensions intrinsic in the form itself, drove the two men increasingly apart. *Hymenaei* was presented at court on 5 January 1606 in celebration of the marriage of the young earl of Essex and Frances Howard—and, through Jonson's deft contrivance, James's parallel 'marriage' of the two kingdoms. The printed version of the masque, published later that year, contained Jonson's provocative comparison of the outward 'show' of the court masque—Jones's scenes and machines—to the transitory human body, and the poetic text of the masque—his own contribution—to the enduring soul. *The Masque of Beauty*, a companion piece to *Blackness*, was performed at the new Banqueting House on 10 January 1608, and *The Haddington Masque*, marking the marriage of Elizabeth Radcliffe, daughter of Robert, fifth earl of Sussex, with James Ramsay, Viscount Haddington, a mere month later.

The Haddington Masque had presented a comical or 'antique' dance of Cupid and his companions, in light-hearted parody of the more graceful dancing of the main masquers that was to follow. In *The Masque of Queens*, performed at court on 2 February 1609, Jonson developed this device more fully into 'a *magicall Daunce*, full of praeposterous change, and gesticulation' executed by a coven of witches, as an 'antimasque' (or 'foyle, or false-*Masque*') to set off the masque's main entry of heroic women, personated by Queen Anne and her ladies. This sharply antithetical form became a regular feature of Jonson's subsequent masques, in which a rabble of threatening or grotesque antimasquers would miraculously vanish at the entry of the principal masquers; as vice, in an ideal world, might be conquered by the very sight of virtue. This glitteringly optimistic view of the power and majesty of the court was further elaborated in *The Speeches at Prince Henry's Barriers* (6 January 1610), *Oberon* (1 January 1611), and *Love Restored* (6 January 1612). It was a court superbly endowed—so the latter masque asserts—with the ten ornaments of Honour, Courtesy, Valour, Urbanity, Confidence, Alacrity, Promptness, Industry, Ability, and Reality.

Fame and trouble, 1603–1612 In his dealings with the court over these years Jonson had not invariably encountered these virtues, though Promptness and Alacrity may well have been in evidence on 6 January 1604 when he and his friend Sir John Roe were thrown out of the performance of an unnamed masque at Hampton Court (possibly Daniel's *Vision of the Twelve Goddesses*), perhaps for revealing too openly their opinion of its qualities. During the first decade of James's reign, the most productive period of his long career, Jonson was involved in recurrent troubles with authority. Despite his favoured position at court, his writing, like his personal life, was regularly subjected to the closest scrutiny.

Sejanus, 'Acted, in the yeere 1603' (or probably early in 1604, by modern dating) with Shakespeare himself in a leading role, brought Jonson into immediate collision with a powerful enemy, Henry Howard, first earl of Northampton, at whose instigation he was summoned before the privy council to answer charges 'both of popperie and treason' (*Conversations*, ll. 325–7). The basis for these charges cannot easily be deduced from the 1605 quarto and 1616 folio texts, which differ, on Jonson's admission, from the play as originally performed. These revised texts excised offensive references as well as the work of 'a second pen'. (The unnamed collaborator is sometimes thought to have been George Chapman, though Shakespeare, who acted in the tragedy, has also plausibly been proposed.) It is likely that some of the play's lines about the behaviour of princes and court favourites were more sharply pointed in the acting text. In the character of Cremutius Cordus, the chronicler whose work is seized and burnt by suspicious authorities, Jonson possibly hinted at his own recent experiences, while the atmosphere of constant surveillance that Silius notes in the house of Agrippina, where:

> every second ghest your tables take,
> Is a fee'd spie, t'observe who goes, who comes,
> What conference you have, with whom, where, when
> (*Sejanus*, II, 444–6)

is one with which Jonson, through his Catholic connections, might well have had personal acquaintance.

Eastward Ho!, a collaboration between Jonson, John Marston, and George Chapman performed by the Children of Her Majesty's Revels at Blackfriars probably in July or August of 1605, occasioned further and even more threatening trouble. In Jonson's own account, he was impeached 'by Sir James Murray to the King for writing something against the Scots' in this play, and 'voluntarily Imprissonned himself with Chapman and Marston, who had written it amongst them. The report was that they should then had their ears cutt and noses' (*Conversations*, ll. 273–7). It is not clear whether this response was provoked by an unlicensed performance during the absence of the king and lord chamberlain at Oxford during the summer months or by the preparation of the play for printing in September, when the printers were obliged to cancel a number of offensive passages. The play's references to James's lavish distribution of knighthoods among his Scottish followers must have been especially galling to such Scottish knights as Murray, whose disgruntlement may have been deepened by the actors' mimicry of Scottish accents, and other byplay. A group of ten letters written from prison by Chapman and Jonson to Aubigny, Salisbury, Suffolk, Pembroke, Montgomery, as well as to other unnamed figures and to the king himself (Washington, DC, Folger Shakespeare Library, MS V. a. 321), is almost certainly related to this episode, though the letters do not name the play which had given offence, or confirm Jonson's statement to Drummond that his imprisonment was voluntary, or suggest the involvement of Marston.

Released from prison, Jonson attended a supper party on or about 9 October 1605 at William Patrick's house in the Strand, along with many of the leading conspirators in the Gunpowder Plot, now in its final stages of preparation: Robert Catesby, Jocelyn Percy, Francis Tresham, Lord Mordaunt, Thomas Winter, John Ashfield, and another unidentified guest. Jonson's precise role in relation to this conspiracy is obscure and ambiguous. The plot was finally revealed by a warning from Tresham to his Catholic brother-in-law, Lord Monteagle, that he should stay away from Westminster Hall on 5 November; Monteagle raised the alarm, and twenty barrels of gunpowder awaiting detonation were discovered in the basement of Westminster Hall. Jonson prudently directed a congratulatory epigram to Monteagle (*Epigrams*, no. 60), whom he praised as the saviour of his nation, and agreed to assist Robert Cecil, newly created earl of Salisbury, in his investigation of the conspiracy. On 7 November Jonson received a warrant from the privy council allowing him to escort an unnamed priest to visit the Lords, and give testimony about the conspiracy to members of the council. Jonson failed in the end to locate this priest, who, it has plausibly been suggested, may have been Father Thomas Wright, the Jesuit who is thought to have converted Jonson some years earlier (F. Teague, 'Jonson and the Gunpowder Plot', *Ben Jonson Journal*, 5, 1998, 249–52). On 8 November Jonson wrote to Salisbury describing the wide ramifications of the conspiracy, and suggesting that its exposure would convince many Catholics quickly to change their religion: 'So that to tell your Lo: playnly my heart, I thinke they are All so enweav'd in it, as it will make 500 Gent: lesse of the Religion within this weeke, if they carry theyr understanding about them' (*Ben Jonson*, ed. Herford, Simpson, and Simpson, 1.202).

Jonson himself was not, however, among those who carried their understanding about them, and chose to change their faith. On 10 January 1606, just a few days after the performance at court of *Hymenaei*, Ben and Anne Jonson were presented before the consistory court on charges of recusancy, and on 26 April they returned to answer those charges. Jonson vigorously denied an accusation of

'seduceing of youthe … to the popishe religion', and declared that he had abstained from receiving communion on account of a religious 'scruple' that the minister of the parish or some suitably qualified person might perhaps now help him to resolve (*Ben Jonson*, ed. Herford, Simpson, and Simpson, 1.220–23). Of his wife's recent habits, he professed imperfect knowledge, though he vouched for her general piety. The couple were required in future to produce a certification of attendance at communion, and Ben was ordered to discuss his theological difficulties with the dean of St Paul's, the archbishop of Canterbury's chaplain, and other learned men. These advisers were evidently unable to persuade him to a conversion, for in May and June of the same year he and Anne were back in the consistory court to answer the same charges.

Jonson's comic masterpiece, *Volpone, or, The Fox*, was written at unusual speed ("Tis knowne, five weekes fully pen'd it': prologue, l. 16) in the aftermath and interstices of these events. The play's plots and counter-plots may seem at times as labyrinthine as those in which Jonson himself had lately been embroiled, its dazzling depiction of Venetian fraud and judicial corruption being tinged with some knowledge of the processes of crime and punishment in contemporary London. *Volpone* was performed at the Globe by the King's Men, probably about mid-March 1606, with Richard Burbage possibly in the title role. The 'Epistle Dedicatory' printed with the quarto edition of 1607 speaks delightedly of the play's reception at Oxford and Cambridge, though there are no surviving records of its performance in either university. The tributory verses prefixed to the quarto text give some sense of Jonson's social and intellectual friendships at this moment; admirers of the play included the historian and poet Edmund Bolton, who had been summoned on recusancy charges with Jonson in January of that year; George Chapman, Jonson's recent collaborator and cell mate; Lord Aubigny, his Catholic patron and protector; and John Donne, himself a recent convert from the Roman church, with whom Jonson seems to have been on close and friendly terms since the 1590s. A few years later (*c*.1611), Donne and Jonson were to be fellow members of a club, composed largely of lawyers and politicians, that met regularly at the Mermaid tavern in Bread Street. (Contrary to popular legend, Shakespeare was not a member of the Mermaid Club, and the lively 'wit-combates' between Jonson and Shakespeare to which Thomas Fuller famously referred must have occurred elsewhere—if they occurred at all (Fuller, *Worthies*, 126).)

Epicene, or, The Silent Woman was performed by the Children of Her Majesty's Revels at Whitefriars in December 1609 or January 1610. The play's wittily discursive style anticipates in some respects that of Etherege and Congreve, as does its highly contemporary setting in the newly developing West End of London. (Jonson was living at this time in Blackfriars, not far from the Strand, where the play itself is set—and where John Donne's and Jonson's patron, Lucy, countess of Bedford, and Donne himself, also resided.) John Dryden in *An Essay of Dramatic Poesy* was admiringly to analyse the play's structural complexity, though elsewhere he expressed distaste for its more boisterous elements. *Epicene* brought Jonson once again into conflict with the authorities: by February 1610 the play had been banned after complaints from the king's cousin Arabella Stuart concerning a reference to 'the Prince of *Moldavia*, and … his mistris, mistris EPICOENE' (v.i, ll. 24–5). The 'prince' in question was Stephen Janiculo, a claimant to the throne of the Romanian province of Moldavia, who, though already married, had announced his intention of marrying Arabella Stuart. Arabella herself had some claim of succession to the English throne, and was later to play an 'epicene' role of sorts through making her escape in male dress from the custody of the bishop of Durham. Jonson strenuously denied that he had revised the piece to include any reference to contemporary events, and complained characteristically of those who:

> with particular slight
> Of application … make a libell, which he made a play.
> (*Epicene*, second prologue, ll. 11–12, 14)

The Alchemist was performed in 1610 by the King's Men probably at the Blackfriars Theatre, in the very district in which the play itself is set. Through internal references the action can be assumed to occur in the very year of the play's presentation—a year in which London was affected by the plague, a fact crucial to its brilliantly contrived plot—and precisely dated to 1 November 1610. From mid-July to late November the London playhouses were actually closed in order to curb the spread of the infection; the play was presented in Oxford in September, but its London performance must have occurred at some point before this period of closure.

The assassination in Paris on 14 May 1610 of the French king, Henri IV, further increased fears in England of similar extremist action, and led to a further tightening of anti-Catholic laws. Jonson returned to the Church of England about this time. Later he reported to Drummond that at 'his first communion in token of true Reconciliation, he drank out all the full cup of wyne' (*Conversations*, ll. 314–16). Despite this decisive gesture, Jonson seems to have retained certain Catholic sympathies and associations for the remainder of his life, his close friendship in particular with Sir Kenelm and Lady Venetia Digby in the 1630s drawing him into renewed contact with Catholic circles. Drummond in 1619 had noted with evident displeasure that Jonson was 'for any religion as being versed in both' (ibid., l. 690).

Catiline his Conspiracy was presented by the King's Men in the summer of 1611. Despite Jonson's high expectations, the play was badly received, Cicero's long orations in the fourth act evidently straining the patience of its audiences. Jonson quickly published a quarto text of the play which he commended to 'the Reader extraordinary' and dedicated to Lord Pembroke, deploring the ignorance of '*these Jig-given times*'. The play, which gained wider admiration later in the century, has been thought by one scholar to offer a veiled 'parallelograph' of the complex events of the Gunpowder Plot in which Jonson during his Catholic years had been enmeshed (B. N. De Luna, *Jonson's Romish*

Plot, 1967). While it is unlikely that the play's references are quite as specific or detailed as here claimed, the tragedy, like much of Jonson's work from this period of his life, bears evident marks of his own recent experiences of conspiracy and interrogation.

The middle years, 1612–1625 During the summer of 1612 Jonson set off for France and the Netherlands in the company of Walter Ralegh (*b.* 1593), mischievous son of a distinguished father. Jonson was employed as 'governor' or tutor to the young Ralegh, as he may also recently have been to another high-spirited scion of a well-known family, the young Sir William Sidney (*b.* 1590), whom Jonson in *The Forest*, no. 14, sternly addresses in November 1611 on the occasion of his twenty-first birthday. At the age of fifteen Sidney had stabbed a schoolmaster, with near fatal consequences. Jonson too had a reputation for physical violence:

> didst thou not put out
> A boies Right eye that Croste thy mankind poute?

asked Chapman years later in 'An invective wrighten … against Mr Ben: Johnson' (lines 29–30; *Poems*, ed. P. B. Bartlett, 1941, 374)—and may therefore have been considered an aptly intimidating tutor for these wild youths. In the case of young Ralegh, however, any confidence of this kind was misplaced. Drummond notes that the 'knavishly inclyned' Ralegh caused Jonson:

> to be Drunken and dead drunk, so that he knew not wher he was, therafter laid him on a Carr which he made to be Drawen by Pioners through the streets, at every corner showing his Governour stretched out and telling them that was a more Lively image of the Crucifix then any they had. (*Conversations*, ll. 296–302)

A trace of these experiences is perhaps to be found in Jonson's next play, *Bartholomew Fair*, performed at the recently opened Hope Theatre on 31 October 1614 and at court the following day, in which the irascible Humphrey Wasp, 'governor' to Bartholomew Cokes, proves equally incapable of maintaining authority over his feckless charge.

On 4 September 1612 (25 August, by English dating) Jonson attended a debate in Paris between the protestant minister Daniel Featly (Ralegh's old Oxford tutor) and a Catholic adversary, D. Smith, future bishop of Chalcedon, concerning the nature of the real presence, and was appointed—along with his acquaintance from London, John Pory—to testify formally concerning the arguments advanced. At some point during his stay in Paris, perhaps through the mediation of Pory, Jonson also encountered the learned Cardinal Duperron, and informed him bluntly that his free translations of books 1 and 4 of the *Aeneid* 'were naught' (*Conversations*, ll. 69–71). Letters dispatched from Jean Beaulieu in Paris to his fellow agent in Brussels, William Trumbull, on 3 and 11 March 1613 (21 February and 1 March by English dating) advised Trumbull that Jonson and Ralegh had 'taken a resolution to passe, by Sedan [in the Ardennes], into your partes'. In an open testimonial Beaulieu commended Jonson's 'extraordinarie and rare partes of knowledge and understanding', but in a supplementary note he referred privately to 'some crosse busynes' in which Jonson had recently been employed (BL, Add. MS 72250). By early April Jonson and Ralegh had moved on from Brussels to Antwerp, and shortly thereafter appear to have visited Leiden, where Jonson met the great Dutch scholar and poet Daniel Heinsius (D. McPherson, *English Language Notes*, 44, 1976, 105–9). By 29 June they were back in London, as a reference in 'An Execration upon Vulcan' (*The Underwood*, no. 43, ll. 129–38) implies that Jonson witnessed the burning of the Globe that day after cannon misfired into the thatched roof of the theatre during a performance of Shakespeare's *Henry VIII*.

Absent from England during the crucial period of 1612–13, Jonson had been unable to observe the initial moves in the swiftly developing affair between James's favourite, Robert Carr, and Frances Howard, divorced countess of Essex. On 21 April 1613 Carr's secretary and intimate friend, Sir Thomas Overbury, who opposed the couple's plans to marry, had been placed in close confinement in the Tower, where he was to die in suspicious circumstances five months later. Jonson may have known Overbury at least since 1602, and in an epigram written about 1610 had praised his ability to set a moral example in a court beset by temptation: 'Where, what makes others great, doth keepe thee good!' (*Diary of John Manningham*, 187; Jonson, *Epigrams*, no. 113, l. 4). The two men had later quarrelled after Overbury—author of *The Wife*, a poem advocating marital loyalty—attempted to use Jonson as a go-between in a suit to the (already married) countess of Rutland (*Conversations*, ll. 213–19). Jonson and Overbury nevertheless shared many political aims and friendships with former followers of the second earl of Essex, including the earls of Pembroke and Southampton, Sir Benjamin Rudyerd, Sir Henry Neville, and others opposed to the Howard faction. On 26 December 1613 Frances Howard was married to Robert Carr, newly created earl of Somerset, and was led to the altar by Jonson's old enemy, her great-uncle Henry Howard, the earl of Northampton. Jonson, who had written *Hymenaei* in celebration of Frances Howard's first marriage in 1606, was now required to help celebrate her dubious second match. *A Challenge at Tilt* (performed on 27 December 1613 and 1 January 1614) and *The Irish Masque* (performed on 29 December 1613 and 3 January 1614) were the result. Whether Jonson was aware of the already circulating rumours that the couple had conspired to poison Overbury, it is impossible to say. The precise facts of the situation would at this stage have been far from clear, but the extreme awkwardness of Jonson's position must have been very evident.

Even before his departure for the continent Jonson had been gathering together many of his writings from the past two decades with a view to publication. 'A booke called Ben Johnson his Epigrams' was entered in the Stationers' register on 15 May 1612 by the publisher and bookseller John Stepneth. Stepneth died later in 1612, and no copies of such a book survive, though Drummond includes 'Ben Jhonsons Epigrams' among the 'bookes red by me anno 1612' (*Ben Jonson*, ed. Herford, Simpson, and Simpson, 8.16). Conceivably this was a manuscript collection. Jonson was also planning a folio edition of his collected works. It has been guessed (without much evidence) that he intended to publish this collection in 1612 or 1613, dedicating the work to the young Prince Henry, and was thwarted by Henry's unexpected death in November 1612. The handsome folio edition of Jonson's *Workes* was finally published by William Stansby between 6 and 25 November 1616 (M. Bland, 'William Stansby and the production of the *Workes* of *Beniamin Jonson*, 1615–16', *The Library*, 20, 1998, 10). Jonson himself appears to have taken an unusually close interest in its production, though recent scholarship has shown that he did not exercise control over typographical detail to the degree imagined by his twentieth-century Oxford editors, C. H. Herford and Percy and Evelyn Simpson (who placed great trust in the folio's authority as copy-text).

Jonson's decision to include nine plays, generally regarded as an ephemeral form of literature, within a volume whose title promised more serious matter was a seeming paradox that attracted the amused attention of several observers. The volume was not however designed to present Ben Jonson uniquely or even primarily as a man of the theatre. It included also more than a dozen masques, a smallish group of court entertainments, the *Panegyre* written for the king's entry to parliament in 1604, and two substantial collections of poems, *Epigrams* and *The Forest*. The catalogue, with its carefully organized column of distinguished patrons, friends, and institutions to whom the various works within the folio are dedicated— William Camden; the inns of court; Richard Martin; Esmé Stuart, Lord Aubigny; the two universities; Sir Francis Stuart; Mary, Lady Wroth; William Herbert, earl of Pembroke—stresses the range and versatility of Jonson's accomplishments, and his ability to command the respect of those in crucial positions of power. Pembroke, to whom both *Catiline* and the *Epigrams* are dedicated and a poem of praise (*Epigrams*, no. 102) addressed, had recently been appointed lord chamberlain, and would continue to provide crucial protection and support for Jonson, providing him with £20 each new year for books, and probably contriving his award of an honorary degree from Oxford in 1619.

Jonson placed a high valuation on his *Epigrams*, which he described in his dedication to Pembroke as 'the ripest of my studies' (l. 4). The title-page of this collection announces it as a first book; evidently more such books were contemplated. Though Jonson continued to experiment with the form, and to speak sharply of the shortcomings of other epigrammatists, such as Owen, Harington, and Sir John Davies (*Conversations*, ll. 223–5, 37–40, 381–3), no second book of epigrams was to appear in his lifetime. *The Forest*, a group of fifteen (formally more various) poems written between 1600 and 1612, included the imaginative addresses to Sir Robert Sidney's estate at Penshurst and to Sir Robert Wroth at Durrants. Both these estates are adduced, in idealized form, as models of an alternative social community, removed from the competitive anxieties of court and urban life.

The publication of the 1616 folio in the very year of Shakespeare's death consolidated Jonson's position as England's foremost living author. Shakespeare had died on 23 April from a fever contracted, according to dubious Stratford legend, after a 'merry meeting' with two visitors from London, Ben Jonson and Michael Drayton (J. Ward, *Diary*, recorded 1662, in Schoenbaum, 120). On 1 February Jonson was granted a royal pension of 100 marks (£66 13s. 4d.) per annum, payable in quarterly instalments, establishing him in fact if not in name as Britain's poet laureate. Late payment of this pension would cause him much anguish in the years to come. In *The Devil is an Ass*, performed at Blackfriars by the King's Men in the autumn of 1616, Jonson glances at royal practices with a characteristic mix of admiration and critical amusement. James's recent triumph in exposing a case of sham diabolical possession during a witchcraft trial in Lincolnshire is flatteringly recalled in the comedy's final dénouement, but the comedy also looks more sharply at the king's manner of granting knighthoods and monopolies, and included satire on 'the Duke of Drown land' which James asked Jonson to suppress (*Conversations*, ll. 414–15).

Now in his late forties and at the height of his fame, Jonson chose to abandon the metropolis for almost a year. 'Ben Jonson is going on foot to Edinburgh and back, for his profit' wrote George Gerrard to Sir Dudley Carleton on 4 June 1617 (*CSP dom.*, 1611–18, 472). James and his entourage were visiting Edinburgh at this moment, and reports of their warm reception in that city were already reaching London. Jonson may have been spurred by these accounts, and was also no doubt curious to see the country of his father's family. He planned to write a versified account of his travels entitled *A Discovery*, along with 'a fisher or Pastorall play' set on Loch Lomond (*Conversations*, ll. 406, 402–3). A slender man in his youth, Jonson was now almost 20 stone in weight, with 'Mountaine belly' and 'rockye face' (ibid., l. 677). He set off the following summer (1618), and walked by stages along the Great North Road, arriving by early August in Edinburgh, where he was feasted by the town council, and visited a number of prominent families. John Taylor the Water Poet followed Jonson's journey by a more westerly route, having been (so Jonson supposed) 'sent along here to scorn him', but the two men had a friendly meeting at Leith, and parted on amicable terms (ibid., l. 607; J. Taylor, *The Pennyless Pilgrimage*, 1618, 58–9).

At the year's end Jonson stayed with William Drummond at Hawthornden Castle on the River Esk, 7 miles south of Edinburgh. Drummond, a learned bachelor thirteen years younger than Jonson, had studied in France, mastered a number of European languages, and amassed a fine library; he took a keen interest in contemporary English, Scottish, and continental writing. Drummond's notes of Jonson's 'informations' during this stay—the so-called *Conversations with William Drummond of Hawthornden*—were apparently made for private use, but were finally published in an abridged and reordered form in the 1711 folio edition of Jonson's works, and in a fuller

state, from a newly discovered eighteenth-century transcript, by David Laing in 1833. They vividly record Jonson's literary opinions and ambitions, his jokes, dreams, and personal reminiscences, along with much social gossip. His sharper verdicts—'that Done for not keeping of accent deserved hanging. That Shakesperr wanted Arte', etc. (*Conversations*, ll. 48–50)—shocked many eighteenth-century readers, reinforcing the myth of Jonson's supposed malignity towards (in particular) his greatest rival. They should be seen, however, as argumentative moments within more extended, now irrecoverable, private conversations, and weighed against Jonson's more generous public tributes, in particular the poem to his 'beloved' Shakespeare which stands at the head of the 1623 first folio.

Drummond and Jonson had many interests in common, and their subsequent correspondence is unfailingly affectionate. Their temperamental differences are nevertheless clearly apparent in the final sketch of Jonson's character which Drummond added after his guest's departure from Hawthornden in January 1619. 'He is a great lover and praiser of himself', wrote Drummond:

a contemner and Scorner of others, given rather to losse a friend, than a Jest, jealous of every word and action of those about him (especially after drink, which is one of the Elements in which he liveth) a dissembler of ill parts which reign in him, a bragger of some good that he wanteth, thinketh nothing well bot what either he himself, or some of his friends and Countrymen hath said or done. He is passionately kynde and angry, carelesse either to gaine or keep, Vindicative, but if he be well answered, at himself. (*Conversations*, ll. 680–89)

By early May 1619 Jonson was back in London, where he was warmly welcomed by James, who had taken a close interest in his northern travels. For a period following his return Jonson devoted himself to quiet scholarship, removed from the pressures of public life. While in Scotland he had informed Drummond that 'He was Master of Arts in both the Universities by their favour not his studie' (*Conversations*, ll. 252–3). No records concerning Jonson's honorary degree from Cambridge or of the Oxford conferral survive, but in July 1619 Jonson was formally inducted into the Oxford degree, and, according to Anthony Wood, spent some time in residence at Christ Church at the invitation of his old friend Richard Corbett (Wood, *Ath. Oxon.*, 1st edn, 1.518). Jonson later extended the circle of his Oxford friendships to include the learned group (of which Hobbes, Chillingworth, and Clarendon, were prominent members) which gathered at the house of Lucius Cary, Lord Falkland, at Great Tew.

Whether Anne Jonson was still alive in the 1620s is doubtful. It is just possible that the marriage of 'Benjamyne Johnson and Hester Hopkins' recorded in the register of St Giles Cripplegate on 27 July 1623 is that of the poet, but there is no other evidence of his having entered into a second marriage about this time. Giving testimony in a chancery case on 20 October 1623, he is described as '*Beniamin Johnson* of Gresham Colledge in London gent. aged 50. yeares and vpwards' (*Ben Jonson*, ed. Herford,

Simpson, and Simpson, 11.582). C. J. Sisson has conjectured that Jonson may have remained for a period of time at Gresham College, deputizing for Henry Croke, who held the office of professor of rhetoric from 1619 to 1627; and that sections of Jonson's commonplace book, *Discoveries*, may represent notes for lectures he delivered at that time (*TLS*, 21 Sept 1951). But it is possible that Jonson was merely taking temporary refuge at the college after the fire that damaged his library late that year. In 'An Execration upon Vulcan' (*The Underwood*, no. 43) Jonson ruefully lists a number of his unpublished writings that perished in the fire, including a history of the reign of Henry V, a commentary on Horace's *Ars poetica*, a translation of Barclay's Latin romance *Argenis*, and the works he had begun on his Scottish journey.

Jonson's scholarly standing was now clearly recognized. His name was reportedly listed among the eighty-four 'Essentials' or founding members of an 'Academ Royal', first proposed to the crown in 1617 by his friend Edmund Bolton: a scheme encouraged by James, but slow to progress, and finally collapsing at his death. Other, more surprising, honours and offices hovered and receded in similar fashion. Writing to Sir Martin Stutevile on 15 September 1621, the Revd Joseph Mead declared that Jonson was to be knighted, but escaped it narrowly, 'for that his Majestie would have done it, had not been means made (himself not unwilling) to avoid it' (*Ben Jonson*, ed. Herford, Simpson, and Simpson, 1.87). Soon afterwards Jonson was granted a patent for the reversion of the mastership of the Revels, in the event that Sir George Buc, the present master, and Sir John Astley, who was next in line, died before he did, but in the event Jonson died first.

Jonson continued throughout this period to produce court masques in every year except 1619, when he was absent in the north. The most popular of these was *The Gypsies Metamorphosed*, a daringly satirical piece that was performed on three occasions in the late summer of 1621 at Burley on the Hill, Belvoir, and Windsor. During the final years of James's reign, however, Jonson came to feel increasingly marginalized from the life of the court. His sense of alienation is clearly evident in 'An Epistle to one that Asked to be Sealed of the Tribe of Ben' (*The Underwood*, no. 47), written in the late summer of 1623 while elaborate preparations were under way in London and Southampton for the reception of Prince Charles and his intended bride, the infanta of Castile. Jonson's collaborator, Inigo Jones, was playing a central role in these events, while Jonson himself was not. Jonson consoles himself by describing another, more exclusive, group, 'the tribe of Ben', that met convivially under his presidency in the Apollo Room of the Devil and St Dunstan tavern near Temple Bar, with rules of conduct and standards of friendship more rigorous and exacting (so the poem implies) than those of the court itself. The failure of Charles's and Buckingham's unpopular mission to Madrid was soon however to be public knowledge. Eighteen months later, James would be dead, and Charles himself would soon be married to a French bride.

The final years, 1626–1637 *The Staple of News*, Jonson's first new play for a decade, was performed at the Blackfriars Theatre by the King's Men early in 1626, not long after Charles's coronation on 2 February, to which the play makes oblique reference. Ostensibly a satire on newsmongering, *The Staple of News* also boldly touches on questions of filial inheritance and succession that might well have seemed relevant to the political moment. The personal tastes and character of the new king were in some ways less congenial to Jonson than those of his robustly learned father, and his own position at court might have appeared less secure. Ideologically, however, Jonson was not greatly at variance with Charles, whose unpopular counsellors (such as Lord Weston, lord high treasurer from 1628) and policies he continued loyally to support. In an epigram addressed to Charles on his anniversary day (27 March) 1629, as troubles and debt were mounting throughout the land, Jonson deplored the public's failure to appreciate the value of their monarch:

'Tis not alone the Merchant, but the Clowne
Is Banke-rupt turned! the Cassock, Cloake, and Gown
Are lost upon accompt! And none will know
How much to heaven for thee, great CHARLES, they owe!
(*The Underwood*, no. 64)

It has been suggested that, in disenchantment with the state of England during the final decade of his life, Jonson turned nostalgically back to the England of Elizabeth; this taste for retrospection being evident in the themes and structure of such late plays as *The New Inn*, presented by the King's Men early in 1629, and *A Tale of a Tub*, performed by Queen Henrietta's Men at the Cockpit 'as new' in May 1633 (see A. Barton). Yet in the scornful 'Ode to Himself' written after the failure of *The New Inn* Jonson vowed to 'leave the lothed stage' and direct his remaining energies to praising the present king, 'tuning forth the acts of his sweete raigne' (ll. 1, 59). It was seemingly with the theatre, not with his monarch, that Jonson's quarrel chiefly lay.

An engraving of Jonson made in the mid-1620s by Robert Vaughan (possibly based on a portrait by the Dutch artist Abraham van Blyenberch, a version of which hangs in the National Portrait Gallery, London) shows a scraggily bearded, heavily built figure, with 'one eie lower, than tother, and bigger' (as Aubrey was later to describe him; *Ben Jonson*, ed. Herford, Simpson, and Simpson, 1.180). He is plainly dressed and crowned with laurel, and stares gloomily through an oval border whose inscription proclaims him 'doctissimi poetarum anglorum', the most learned of English poets. The melancholic look may perhaps reflect the sharp decline in Jonson's health that began in these years. Late in 1627 or early in 1628 he appears to have suffered a paralytic stroke. He was by now grossly overweight, and further affected by a 'palsy' (possibly Parkinson's disease) which, in Clarendon's words, 'made a deep Impression upon his Body and his Mind' (*The Life of Edward, Earl of Clarendon*, 1759, 16). In a late poem he wryly views himself as:

a tardie, cold
Unprofitable Chattell, fat and old,
Laden with Bellie

who:

> doth hardly approach
> His friends, but to breake Chaires or cracke a Coach.
> (*The Underwood*, no. 56, ll. 7–10)

Poverty compounded these afflictions. On 19 January 1628 a grant of £5 was made by the dean and chapter of Westminster 'to Mr Beniamin Jhonson in his sicknes and want', and in March of the same year Jonson thanked King Charles in verse for 'A Hundred Pounds He Sent Me in My Sickness' (*Ben Jonson*, ed. Herford, Simpson, and Simpson, 1.244; *The Underwood*, no. 62). Jonson's poems and letters written during the last period of his life—especially those to his new and watchful patron, William Cavendish, earl of Newcastle—return touchingly to these practical problems now besetting his life.

> *Disease*, the Enemie, and his Ingineeres,
> *Want*, with the rest of his conceal'd compeeres,
> Have cast a trench about mee, now, five yeares,

he writes in 1631 in an 'Epistle Mendicant' addressed to the lord treasurer (*The Underwood*, no. 71, ll. 4–6). Jonson's poverty at this and other stages of his life must have been attributable in part to his style of living. The generous habits that Drummond had noted in 1619 evidently continued into old age. James Howell in the 1630s speaks of a 'solemne supper' given by Jonson in which 'there was good company, excellent chear, choice wines, and joviall wellcome' (*Ben Jonson*, ed. Herford, Simpson, and Simpson, 11.419). From September 1628 Jonson enjoyed a further income of 100 nobles a year as city chronologer, being appointed in succession to Thomas Middleton 'To collect and set down all memorable acts of this City and occurences thereof' (ibid., 1.241), a task he evidently performed with such inefficiency that from November 1631 to September 1634 payment of the stipend was suspended. In 1630 Jonson's court pension was increased from 100 marks to £100 per year, augmented by a tierce (42 gallons) of Canary Spanish wine from Charles's store at Whitehall. Izaak Walton gives a vivid glimpse of Jonson in his final years in his lodgings near the Abbey, tended by 'a woman that govern'd him … and that nether he nor she tooke much Care for next weike: and wood be sure not to want Wine: of which he usually tooke too much before he went to bed, if not oftner and soner' (ibid., 1.182).

Despite all difficulties, the last phase of Jonson's life was still remarkably productive, and his work still marked by fresh energy and invention. *Love's Triumph through Callipolis* (9 January 1631) and *Chloridia* (22 February 1631) were to be his final masques at court, and the unhappy end of his long collaboration with Jones. When Jones took objection to his name appearing after Jonson's on the title-page of *Love's Triumph* ('The Inventors, Ben Jonson, Inigo Jones'), Jonson retaliated by omitting his name entirely from the title-page of *Chloridia*, and by ridiculing his more spectacular scenic inventions (and social ambitions) in 'An expostulation with Inigo Jones' (*Ungathered Verse*, no. 34). But in two subsequent entertainments to regale King Charles on his progress to and from his coronation in Scotland—the first at Welbeck on 31 May 1633, the other at Bolsover on 30 July of the same year—as in the unfinished pastoral,

The Sad Shepherd, Jonson drew imaginatively on northern traditions (including the stories of Robin Hood) and memories of his own Scottish journey many years earlier. In their rural settings and occasional employment of romance conventions, the comedies of Jonson's last period are strikingly different from the bustling city intrigues of his early maturity. None of his late plays, however, was to enjoy theatrical success. In the 'Induction' to *The Magnetic Lady* (staged at Blackfriars in October 1632 with noisy disruptions from three of Jonson's old adversaries, Alexander Gill, Nathaniel Butter, and Inigo Jones) the Boy who serves as the author's apologist speaks of the steady progress of Jonson's comic writing since the late 1590s to this present moment, as he approaches 'the close, or shutting up of his Circle' (ll. 104–5). Jonson's insistence, here as elsewhere, on the constancy of his own artistic and moral life has tended however to obscure the many shifts, experiments, and renewals to be found within his long career, and the many contradictions within his complex character.

Jonson died in mid-August 1637. His funeral procession was attended by 'all or the greatest part of the nobilitie and gentry then in the town' (Sir Edward Walker, Garter, 17 Aug 1637, in *Ben Jonson*, ed. Herford, Simpson, and Simpson, 1.115). He was buried in the north aisle of Westminster Abbey, beneath a square of blue marble with the inscription 'O Rare Ben Jonson', 'donne at the chardge of Jack Young afterwards knighted, who walking there when the grave was covering gave the fellow eighteen pence to cutt it' (Aubrey, ibid., 1.179–80). *Jonsonus virbius*, a volume of memorial verses edited by Dr Brian Duppa and dominated by tributes from Jonson's Oxford friends, was published early in 1638, and other commemorative poems continued to appear in the following months, mourning the passing of the supreme literary figure of his age. A second folio edition of Jonson's works was published in 1640–41 in three volumes: the first being a reprint of the 1616 folio, the second containing *Bartholomew Fair*, *The Devil is an Ass*, and *The Staple of News* (a volume prepared for publication, but left unpublished, in 1631), and the third presenting a number of hitherto unpublished masques and plays, along with the *English Grammar*, *Discoveries*, a verse translation of Horace's *Ars poetica*, and a third major collection of poems, *The Underwood*. A quarto containing 'An Execration upon Vulcan' and other poems and a duodecimo edition of another version of the *Ars poetica* were published by John Benson in 1640; while a third folio, containing a number of texts not published in 1640–41 (including *The New Inn* and *Leges convivales* and a recast version of the *English Grammar*) was to appear in 1692.

'Remembrance with posteritie' Unlike Shakespeare, with whom it has been his fate continually to be compared, Jonson did not choose to work continuously for a single theatrical company, or indeed primarily within the theatre. His ambitions, befitting a pupil of William Camden, were to excel in the many branches of Renaissance humanistic endeavour: as a poet, historian, philologist, rhetorician, as well as writer for the stage. His intellectual energies were expressed not only in his poetry and dramatic work, but in writings as various as the *English Grammar*, the account of the reign of Henry III contributed to Ralegh's *History of the World*, the translations of Horace, and the miscellaneous meditations on statecraft, social conduct, literary criticism, and theology to be found in his commonplace book, *Discoveries*. He moved warily but ambitiously between three main professional sites: the court, the playhouse, and the printing house. Under James, he and Jones were soon clearly established as the leading providers of royal masques and entertainments. In the theatre, where his two surviving tragedies met with initial failure, Jonson perfected a kind of comedy more technically perfect in design, more sharply contemporary in subject matter, than that of his greatest rival. The power of the printed book, which might carry his writings and those he celebrated to '*remembrance with posteritie*' (*Epigrams*, dedication), also deeply attracted him. Skilfully wresting his play texts out of the hands of the theatre companies, to whom they technically belonged, and publishing them, often in revised form, under his own name, Jonson created a notion of authorial ownership and identity that is recognizably modern. His 1616 folio was to serve as an important model for similar collected editions later in the century.

Throughout much of the seventeenth century Jonson was commonly regarded as a writer whose literary distinction equalled, and perhaps outshone, that of Shakespeare himself. His dramatic practice was closely studied by immediate disciples such as Nathan Field, Richard Brome, William Cartwright, and other so-called 'sons of Ben', and by most of the major Restoration dramatists. His poetry was widely admired throughout the century, being read with particular affection and attention by Robert Herrick and John Suckling, Abraham Cowley and John Milton, John Oldham and the earl of Rochester. John Dryden's deep respect for Jonson's writing was tempered only by his greater regard for Shakespeare; 'I admire him, but I love Shakespeare', says one of the speakers apologetically in 'An essay of dramatic poesy' (*'An Essay of Dramatic Poesy' and other Essays*, ed. G. Watson, 2 vols., 1962, 1.70). Throughout the eighteenth century this comparative assessment was further weighted by a growing conviction, stirred by Rowe's biographical speculations in his edition of Shakespeare in 1709, that Jonson was chronically envious of his rival's more fluent genius, and that Jonson's writings were coldly laborious, lacking Shakespeare's spontaneity and generous warmth. Despite the efforts of William Gifford in his edition of Jonson's works in 1816 to scotch these perceptions, Jonson was commonly regarded in the nineteenth century as an uncongenial classic, best sampled in small doses. His shorter lyrics were often praised, but his dramatic works, which David Garrick had enterprisingly adapted for the eighteenth-century stage, were by and large neglected. Coleridge praised *The Alchemist* as having one of the world's three most skilful plots, but never saw the play in performance.

The gradual modern recovery of Jonson has built upon the monumental labours of his Oxford editors, C. H. Herford and Percy and Evelyn Simpson (*Ben Jonson*, 11 vols.,

1925–52), and has been aided by an ever-growing body of criticism and scholarship. It has been stimulated by the appreciation of writers such as T. S. Eliot, who in an influential review for the *Times Literary Supplement* of 13 November 1919 commended 'intelligent saturation in his work as a whole'; by James Joyce, who named Jonson as one of the four writers whose work he had read comprehensively; by the poet Thom Gunn, who has edited a selection of his poems, and the dramatist Peter Barnes, who has adapted several of his plays for stage and radio. The Royal Shakespeare Company has successfully performed a number of his plays, including works such as *The New Inn* and *The Devil is an Ass*, which had never or scarcely ever been staged since the seventeenth century. At the beginning of the twenty-first century a major new edition of his complete works was in preparation for publication by Cambridge University Press in 2005.   IAN DONALDSON

Sources *Ben Jonson*, ed. C. H. Herford, P. Simpson, and E. M. Simpson, 11 vols. (1925–52) · *The Cambridge edition of the works of Ben Jonson*, ed. D. Bevington, M. Butler, and I. Donaldson, 25 vols. [forthcoming] · *Conversations with William Drummond of Hawthornden*, in *Ben Jonson*, ed. C. H. Herford, P. Simpson, and E. Simpson, 11 vols. (1925–52), 1.128–78 · Fuller, *Worthies* (1662) · *Henslowe's diary*, ed. R. A. Foakes and R. T. Rickert (1961) · Wood, *Ath. Oxon.*, 1st edn, vol. 1 [Benjamin Johnson] · D. Riggs, *Ben Jonson: a life* (1989) · W. D. Kay, *Ben Jonson: a literary life* (1995) · J. B. Bamborough, 'The early life of Ben Jonson', *TLS* (8 April 1960), 225 · W. D. Kay, '"Rare Ben": the bricklayer of Westminster and his family', unpubd typescript · W. D. Kay, 'The shaping of Jonson's career: a re-examination of facts and problems', *Modern Philology*, 67 (1970), 224–37 · M. Eccles, 'Jonson's marriage', *Review of English Studies*, 12 (1936), 257–72 · M. Eccles, 'Jonson and the spies', *Review of English Studies*, 13 (1937), 385–91 · I. Donaldson, *Jonson's walk to Scotland* (1993) · M. Butler, 'Late Jonson', *The politics of tragicomedy: Shakespeare and after*, ed. G. McMullan and J. Hope (1992), 166–88 · *DNB* · R. Miles, *Ben Jonson: his life and work* (1986) · I. Donaldson, *Jonson's magic houses: essays in interpretation* (1997) · M. Butler, '"Servant, but not slave": Ben Jonson at the Jacobean court', *PBA*, 90 (1996), 65–93 · W. H. Phelps, 'The date of Ben Jonson's death', *N&Q*, 225 (1980), 146–9 · J. Bass Mullinger, 'Was Ben Jonson ever a member of our college?', *The Eagle*, 25 (1904), 1–4 [St John's College, Cambridge] · I. A. Shapiro, 'The Mermaid Club', *Modern Language Review*, 45 (1950), 6–17 · T. A. Stroud, 'Ben Jonson and Father Thomas Wright', *ELH: A Journal of English Literary History*, 14 (1947), 274–82 · *The diary of John Manningham of the Middle Temple, 1602–1603*, ed. R. Parker Sorlien (1976) · S. Orgel and R. Strong, *Inigo Jones: the theatre of the Stuart court*, 2 vols. (1973) · M. Butler, ed., *Re-presenting Ben Jonson: text, history, performance* (1999) · R. Dutton, *Mastering the revels: the regulation and censorship of English Renaissance drama* (1991) · A. Barton, *Ben Jonson: dramatist* (1984) · F. T. Bowers, 'Ben Jonson the actor', *Studies in Philology*, 34 (1937), 396–7 · C. J. Sisson, 'Ben Jonson of Gresham College', *TLS* (21 Sept 1951), 604 · A. R. Braunmuller, ed., *A seventeenth-century letter-book: a facsimile edition of Folger MS V.a321* (1983) · D. Lindley, *The trials of Frances Howard: fact and fiction at the court of King James* (1993) · J. A. Symonds, *Ben Jonson* (1886) · E. M. Portal, 'The "Academ Roial" of King James I', *PBA*, [7] (1915–16), 189–208 · R. Lander Knutson, *Playing companies and commerce in Shakespeare's time* (2001) · J. Loewenstein, 'The script in the marketplace', *Representing the English Renaissance*, ed. S. Greenblatt (1988), 265–78 · S. Schoenbaum, *Shakespeare's lives* (1970) · J. H. Penniman, ed., *Ben Jonson, 'Poetaster', and Thomas Dekker, 'Satiromastix'* (1913) · *CSP dom.*, 1611–18, 472 · W. Bang and L. Krebs, *Ben Jonson's 'The fountaine of self-love, or, Cynthias revels'* (1908) [1601 quarto] · T. Mason, ed., *A register of baptisms, marriages and burials in the parish of St Martin's-in-the-Fields … from 1550 to 1619* (1898)

Archives NRA, commonplace book attributed to Jonson · NRA, corresp. and literary MSS
Likenesses A. van Blyenberch, oils, c.1617, NPG [*see illus.*] · R. Vaughan, line engraving, c.1625, BM; repro. in *The workes of Beniamin Jonson* (1640), vol. 1, frontispiece · W. Marshall, line engraving, 1640, BM · G. Vertue, line engraving, 1711 (after A. van Blyenberch), BM, NPG · A. van Blyenberch, oils, second version, Knole, Kent · W. Elder, engraving (after R. Vaughan), repro. in *B. Jonson's execration against Vulcan* (1640), frontispiece · mezzotint (after A. van Blyenberch), NPG
Wealth at death £8 8s. 10d.: *Ben Jonson*, ed. Herford, Simpson, and Simpson, 1.249 (act books of the dean and chapter of Westminster, no. 4, 1632–44; second entry under date 'Vicesimo secundo die mensis Augusti Ano dni 1637', fol. 53)

Jooss, Kurt (1901–1979), choreographer and teacher of dance, was born on 12 January 1901, in Wasseralfingen, a suburb of Stuttgart, Germany. His father owned a farm, but as a child Jooss felt vague inclinations toward several arts. While studying at the Stuttgart Academy of Music in 1918, he encountered the great modern dance teacher and theorist Rudolf Laban, and from then on he devoted himself to the art of dance. He worked with Laban in Mannheim, Stuttgart, and Hamburg from 1919 until 1924, when in Hamburg he met Sigurd Leeder, another disciple of Laban. Jooss and Leeder began to collaborate on a series of dance concerts featuring only themselves, 'Zwei Tänzer'. But a knee injury to Jooss prevented him from emerging as a star dancer.

In 1924 Hanns Niedecken-Gebhardt, artistic director of the Münster Opera, invited Jooss to form a new company, the Neue Tanzbühne, with members of the recently disbanded Tanzbühne Laban. In Münster, Jooss received acclaim for his choreographic skill in providing bold, innovative dances to support modernist stage works by the composers Egon Wellesz, Paul Hindemith, and Ernst Toch; his dance concerts moved away from Laban's expressionism toward a satiric-grotesque commentary on the encoding of social identity in movement. In 1926 Jooss and Leeder travelled to Vienna and Paris to study ballet, which Jooss soon considered an outmoded and inert art. Nevertheless, for the rest of his career he presented his aesthetic under the concept of a 'new ballet', rather than as a category of German *Ausdruckstanz* ('expressive dance', in which movement was meant to signify the 'inner' emotional condition of the dancer or choreographer). In the following year the city of Essen invited Jooss to establish a dance school closely affiliated with the Essen Municipal Opera, and there, at the Folkwangschule, he choreographed perhaps his greatest dances, including *Pavane auf den Tod einer Infantin* (1929), *Der verlorene Sohn* (1931), *Grossstadt von Heute* (1932), and *Ein Ball in Alt-Wien* (1932).

The success of Jooss's dances owed much to his close collaboration with the designer Hein Heckroth, the composer–arranger Fritz Cohen, and the Estonian dancer Aino Simola (1901–1971), whom Jooss had met through their work with Laban. Jooss and Simola married in 1929, and she became his chief partner in all his enterprises until her death. She gave birth to their daughter Anna in March 1931, but a subsequent illness compelled her to give up her performing career. Jooss, meanwhile, sought to intensify the right of modern dance to incorporate theatrical effects (*Tanztheater*) by collaborating with Arturo Toscanini in the 1930 Bayreuth production of Wagner's *Tannhäuser* in 1931 and by acting in productions of George Kaiser's *Europa* and Shakespeare's *Midsummer Night's Dream*. In 1932 Jooss created his most famous ballet, *The Green Table*, in which expressionist use of masks, brilliantly exaggerated movement, and violent scenic effects produced a powerful satire on bureaucracy, diplomatic gesturing, and political hypocrisy. But the tremendous international success of this piece failed to resolve differences between Jooss and the city of Essen in the funding of the Folkwangschule. Jooss therefore established the Ballets Jooss as a private institution that did not rely on public funds. The Nazis, however, began attacking Jooss for protecting and supporting Jews within his company. Throughout 1933 the Ballets Jooss toured Holland, Belgium, France, and Switzerland; in June the company gave its first performances in London, at the Savoy Theatre.

Unable to return to Germany without facing persecution, the Ballets Jooss toured constantly (1934–8) in northern and eastern Europe, the United States, and eventually South America. But Jooss found his strongest support in England; there in April 1934, Leonard and Dorothy Elmhirst financed the founding of the Jooss Leeder School of Dance at Dartington Hall, Devon, which in 1935 additionally became the headquarters of the Ballets Jooss. Jooss's works of the mid- to late 1930s, such as *The Prodigal Son* (1933), *Persephone* (1934), *Ballade* (1935), *The Mirror* (1935), *Seven Heroes* (1937), and *Chronica* (1939), show his expressionism evolving from grotesque social critique to more abstract, symbolic-allegorical images that blended historical detail with dreamlike moods. The war stranded the Ballets Jooss in New York, while Jooss himself in 1940 was interned in London for six months as an 'enemy alien'. In the following year he and Leeder moved headquarters to Cambridge, England. In 1942 the Sadler's Wells Opera company commissioned him to direct highly successful productions of Mozart's *The Magic Flute* and *The Marriage of Figaro*, and in July of that year his daughter Christina was born. By January 1946 he was in British uniform to guide the Ballets Jooss on a tour of European cities occupied by the British army, and in 1947 he received British citizenship. But financial difficulties continued to plague the Ballets Jooss, which dissolved in 1948, when Jooss went to Chile for eight months to teach at a school established there by former members of the company. Upon his return to England early in 1949, he received an invitation from the city of Essen to revive the dance section of the Folkwangschule. From then until his death his career unfolded entirely in Germany, where he enjoyed increasing glory for his achievements as a master choreographer and teacher of German modern dance. His most distinguished student at the Folkwangschule was the great choreographer Pina Bausch. He died in a car accident in Heilbronn on 22 May 1979.

Jooss introduced Europe to a unique perception of modern dance. He rejected the expressionist focus on movement as the projection of individual personality; instead, he saw dance as an image of modern social reality or communal interaction, in which movement exposed the essence of social identities and relations. He taught that choreographic inspiration should derive from exaggerating the observation of movement within a particular social milieu, rather than from perfecting a set of movement tropes peculiar only to dance or to the 'inner' life of a dancer. His idea of *Tanztheater* required modern dance to abandon the quest for purity and autonomy and to absorb the benefits of theatricality (masks, props, captivating costumes, powerful lighting effects), as well as the fascination of gestures 'taken from life itself'. But his influence in England was much less than that of his teacher, Rudolf Laban, who migrated there in 1937 and succeeded in showing how movement theory could be applied outside dance, for example to worker efficiency and improved social interaction and group performance. This limited impact was due partly to the need of the Ballets Jooss to tour extensively outside England and partly to Jooss's rural background, which inspired him to pursue dance education and aesthetic perfection in a pastoral or manor environment rather than in the big-city culture where modern dance otherwise flourished. KARL TOEPFER

Sources A. V. Coton, *The new ballet: Kurt Jooss and his work* (1946) · A. Markard and H. Markard, *Jooss* (1985) · K. Toepfer, *Empire of ecstasy: nudity and movement in German body culture, 1910–1935* (1997) · S. Walther, *The dance of death: Kurt Jooss and the Weimar years* (1994) · S. Walther, ed., *The dance theatre of Kurt Jooss* (1994)

Joplin, Thomas (*c*.1790–1847), banker and author, was born about 1790 at Newcastle upon Tyne, the second son of Thomas Joplin (*d*. 1808), timber merchant of that city. Joplin had two brothers, although the younger died at an early age; he also had one sister. On his father's death the timber business, based at 'Egypt' in the New Road, Newcastle, passed to Thomas and his elder brother, William, the firm being known as W. and T. Joplin & Co. In the early 1800s Joplin met and married Jane, whose parentage is unknown. They had no children.

By the early 1820s Joplin had left the timber concern, and he devoted the rest of his life to the study of monetary questions and the promotion of joint-stock banking companies. He published more than twenty pamphlets on banking and political economy, the most influential of which, *An essay on the general principles and present practices of banking in England and Scotland; with observations upon the justice and policy of an immediate alteration in the charter of the Bank of England, and the measures to be pursued in order to effect it*, was first published at Newcastle in 1822. This work explained the system of Scottish banking, and suggested the establishment of a joint-stock bank; it went through several editions, and attracted the notice of many statesmen, although the design was not then carried out. In 1824 the Provincial Bank of Ireland was formed in London, and Joplin became actively concerned in its management. In 1826, when joint-stock banks were permitted 65 miles from London, Joplin left the Provincial Bank of Ireland and submitted a scheme to his cousin, George Fife *Angas,

for the association of a number of provincial banks together under a central management, but with considerable local freedom of action. He proposed to call the new concern the National Provincial Bank of England. The estimated expense of initiating the scheme was only £300, which Angas sought to raise in 1829. However, owing to the disturbances surrounding the reform agitation, the plan was not carried out until 1833, when the National Provincial Bank was established. On 23 September in that year Joplin's name was placed in the deed of settlement as one of the directors and as the originator of the bank. However, following a series of disagreements with his fellow directors, Joplin resigned from the National Provincial Bank in March 1835. He also helped to establish banks at Lancaster, Huddersfield, Bradford, Manchester, and several other places, some of which were very successful, but he derived little pecuniary benefit from his efforts.

Joplin is recognized as having played a formative role in the introduction of joint-stock banking to England and Wales. None the less, his relations with the many joint-stock banks which he helped to establish were frequently acrimonious. Standing at 6 feet 2 inches, Joplin was remembered by contemporaries as a man of commanding presence, with a forceful and frequently dogmatic temperament. His single-minded belief in the superiority of his own ideas often caused friction among those with whom he worked. By 1843 his health began to trouble him and he visited Gräfenberg, in Austrian Silesia, to take a water treatment. Any improvement was short-lived, however, and he died on 12 April 1847 at Böhmischdorf, Silesia, while on a return visit to the spa. He was survived by his wife. FRANCIS WATT, rev. IAIN S. BLACK

Sources M. Phillips, *A history of banks, bankers and banking in Northumberland, Durham, and North Yorkshire* (1894), 102–9 · T. E. Gregory and A. Henderson, *The Westminster Bank through a century*, 1 (privately printed, London, 1936), 335–53 · H. Withers, *National Provincial Bank, 1833 to 1933* (1933) · E. Hodder, *George Fife Angas* (1891), 85–8 · W. F. Crick and J. E. Wadsworth, *A hundred years of joint stock banking*, 3rd edn (1958) · B. L. Anderson and P. L. Cottrell, *Money and banking in England: the development of the banking system, 1694–1914*, 1st edn (1974) · *GM*, 2nd ser., 29 (1848), 320 · J. E. Wadsworth, 'Thomas Joplin and his amanuensis', *Institute of Bankers Journal*, 73 (1952), 249–54 · PRO, PROB 11/2065/854 · death duty register, PRO, IR 26/1776/888

Likenesses portrait, repro. in Phillips, *History of banks*, 104

Wealth at death £1500; nephew chief beneficiary: PRO, death duty registers, IR 26/1776/888; will, PRO, PROB 11/2065/854

Jopling, Joseph Middleton (1831–1884), watercolour painter, was born in 1831, the son of Charles Jopling, a clerk in the Horse Guards, Whitehall, and Ann Middleton. Though apparently self-taught, he enjoyed early success as an artist and made his début at the Royal Academy exhibition in 1848. He was to show regularly at the academy for the rest of his life, mostly watercolour portraits and genre subjects. From the age of seventeen he worked as a civil servant like his father. After a few years, however, he left his post in the adjutant-general's office, with a pension, in order to pursue art as a full-time career. By 1858 he was living in chambers at 130 Piccadilly, where he remained until his marriage in 1874. He was an associate of the New Watercolour Society (later Institute of Painters in Water Colours) from 1859 until he resigned in 1876. He also drew cartoons for the magazine *Vanity Fair*. In his leisure time Jopling was an active member of the 3rd Middlesex volunteers; he was a celebrated shot, and distinguished himself frequently in the national rifle competitions at Wimbledon, winning the queen's prize in 1861.

On 24 January 1874 Jopling married Louise Romer (1843–1933) [*see* Jopling, Louise], also an artist, whom he had met through his old friend John Everett Millais. She had been married before, separated, and widowed with a son. With Jopling she had another son, Lindsay Millais Jopling, born in 1875; the boy's godfathers were Millais and another close friend, Coutts Lindsay, who was to found the Grosvenor Gallery. From about 1879 the Joplings lived at 28 Beaufort Street in Chelsea, working in studios designed for them by William Burges.

Jopling served as superintendent of the British art section at the Philadelphia International Exhibition of 1876. He also held a position with the Fine Art Society on Bond Street, where he organized a Millais retrospective in 1881, and advised the Art Gallery of New South Wales in Sydney on purchases of works of art. Millais's son and biographer John Guille Millais described Jopling as 'a man of considerable talent whose progress in his profession was hindered only by his habitual *laissez-faire* and an inordinate love of amusement' (Jopling, 427). In his last years he suffered from epileptic fits, and died at his home, 28 Beaufort Street, Chelsea, after a prolonged attack, on 10 December 1884. MALCOLM WARNER

Sources L. Jopling, *Twenty years of my life, 1867 to 1887* (1925) · J. G. Millais, *The life and letters of Sir John Everett Millais*, 2 vols. (1899) · m. cert. · d. cert. · *IGI*
Likenesses J. E. Millais, pen-and-ink drawing, 1861, priv. coll.; repro. in H. Zimmern, 'John-Everett Millais', *Grands peintres français et étrangers: ouvrage d'art*, 2 (1886) · photograph, repro. in Jopling, *Twenty years of my life*
Wealth at death £1132 3s. 7d.: administration, 26 March 1885, *CGPLA Eng. & Wales*

Jopling [*née* Goode; *other married names* Romer, Rowe], **Louise Jane** (1843–1933), portrait painter, was born on 16 November 1843 at 10 Heath Field, Moss Side, Manchester, one of the nine children of Thomas Smith Goode, a railway contractor who held strict views on education, and his wife, Frances Wickstead Pinker. In 1861 at the age of seventeen she married Francis (Frank) Romer, secretary to Baron Nathaniel de Rothschild in Paris, and they had three children. Encouraged by the baroness, Louise Romer began to study art in Paris. Her classes at a state technical school and in Charles Chaplin's studio included anatomy and nude life study. In 1869, when her husband lost his appointment, she returned to London, where she attended Leigh's School of Art and led a fashionable life in London's artist community. Her friends included Frederick Leighton, Val Prinsep, and Kate Perugini. *Punch* published her first drawing, *A Sketch from Nursery History*, in 1869 as well as her journalism, poems, and stories. She

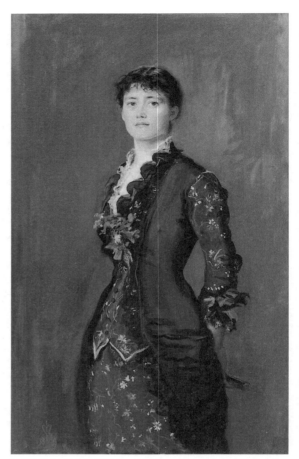

Louise Jane Jopling (1843–1933), by Sir John Everett Millais, 1879

separated from her husband, a compulsive gambler, in 1871, and returned to Paris for a brief period where she met the artists Alfred Stevens and James Tissot. Despite the deaths of Frank Romer (in 1873) and two of her children, her subject painting, for which friends modelled in Japanese robes, *Five O'Clock Tea*, was exhibited at the 1874 Royal Academy exhibition where it was well received and purchased by Agnews. That same year she married Joseph Middleton *Jopling (1831–1884), a watercolour painter, and they had one son. Although he was a less successful painter than his wife, Joseph Jopling was superintendent of the fine arts for the Philadelphia International Exhibition in 1876 to which she sent *Five Sisters of York* based on Charles Dickens's novel *Nicholas Nickleby*. Sir Coutts and Lady Blanche Lindsay invited her to exhibit at the Grosvenor Gallery, London, from 1877 and, drawing in the fashionable society that attended exhibitions at the Grosvenor, she began to give preview exhibitions of her work in her studio. Her self-portrait from this year is now in Manchester City Galleries. Joseph Jopling introduced his wife to James MacNeill Whistler who painted her portrait, *Harmony in Flesh Colour & Black: Portrait of Mrs Jopling* (1877; Hunterian Art Gallery, University of Glasgow). She was also a friend of John Everett and Effie Millais; Millais painted her portrait in 1879 (priv. coll.). Jopling produced many portraits of intelligent and fashionable women including *Phyllis* (1883, oil on canvas; formerly collection of Sir Merton and Lady Russell-Cotes, Bournemouth) and worked extensively in pastel; one of her few drawings of men is a portrait of the biographer Samuel Smiles (NPG). Her theatrical portraits included *Ellen Terry as Portia*, exhibited at the Grosvenor Gallery in 1883, and purchased by Sir Henry Irving for the Alhambra theatre. *Blue and White* (exh. RA, 1896; Lady Lever Art Gallery, Port Sunlight, Cheshire, repr. Lambourne, pl. 373) was purchased by W. H. Lever with the humorous intention that the graceful middle-class women washing blue china would advertise the benefits of Sunlight soap. (An advertising poster, entitled *Home Bright—Hearts Light*, reproduced the painting and included on the table a packet of Sunlight soap.) Lionel Lambourne notes that Leverhulme saw 'its interest as a document in aesthetic taste' (Lambourne, 311). Joseph Jopling died in 1884 and in 1887 Louise married George William Rowe, a lawyer, and that year she set up a professional art school for women in Clareville Grove, London. The students were trained in perspective and anatomy, drawing, and painting from nature—nude and clothed models, and casts—and modelled in clay. In *Hints for Amateurs* (1891) she outlined basic techniques and materials for drawing, painting, photography, modelling, anatomy, colour, and perspective. Jopling was a member of the Society of Women Artists, the Pastel Society, and the Women's International Art Club. The Royal Society of Portrait Painters, founded in 1891, included a few women whose membership did not grant voting rights, so Jopling led a successful lobby that pressurized the society to reform. She was the first woman member of the Royal Society of British Artists in 1902 and a founder and president of the Society of Immortals. In 1889 Jopling signed the 'Declaration in favour of women's suffrage'; she also supported the National Union of Women's Suffrage and signed a 'Letter from ladies to members of parliament' (published in the *Woman's Suffrage Journal*, June 1885, 125), which highlighted the fact that male suffrage had initially been granted on the basis of property rights. She published *Poems* in 1913 and *Tête à tête Bridge* in 1916; in 1925 her autobiography entitled *Twenty Years of my Life, 1867–87* was published. Louise Jopling died on 19 November 1933 at her home, Manor Farm, Bois Common, Chesham Bois, Buckinghamshire.   MEAGHAN E. CLARKE

Sources L. Jopling, *Twenty years of my life, 1867–87* (1925) • C. E. Clement, *Women in the fine arts* (1904) • D. Cherry, *Painting women: Victorian women artists* (1993) • Graves, *Artists* • Graves, *RA exhibitors* • P. G. Nunn, ed., *Canvassing women: recollections by six Victorian women artists* (1986) • D. Gaze, ed., *Dictionary of women artists*, 2 vols. (1997) • E. Morris, *Victorian and Edwardian paintings in the Lady Lever Art Gallery* (1994) • L. Lambourne, *Victorian painting* (1999) • CGPLA Eng. & Wales (1934) • b. cert. • m. cert. [Francis Romer] • m. cert. [Joseph Middleton Jopling] • d. cert.

Archives NYPL, Anna Lea Merritt papers, MSS

Likenesses L. Jopling, self-portrait, 1877, Man. City Gall. • J. M. Whistler, oils, 1877, U. Glas., Glasgow, Hunterian Museum and Art Gallery • J. E. Millais, oils, 1879, NPG [*see illus.*]

Wealth at death £4716 6s. 9d.: probate, 12 Feb 1934, CGPLA Eng. & Wales

Jordan, Abraham (*c.*1666–1715/16), distiller and organ builder, was the son of Abraham Jordan (*d.* in or before 1669), vintner, and grandson of William Jordan, yeoman, of Ratbey, Leicestershire, and was probably born either there or in London. The tradition that the family came from Maidstone was invented in the nineteenth century and has no basis in contemporary documentation. Jordan was apprenticed distiller in the City of London on 21 February 1679, apparently to his twice-widowed mother, if she was the 'Elizabeth Jorden widow' who had married William Leywood, distiller, at Chelsea in 1669. His father had been apprenticed vintner there on 4 June 1656, to an Abraham Jordan, son of John Jordan, yeoman, also from Ratbey. On 29 April 1686, at St Mary Aldermary, London, Jordan married Ann Greenhill. She had died before 11 April 1689 when Jordan married Elizabeth Butler (*b.* 1667, *d.* in or after 1715) at St Luke, Chelsea. By 1694 they had settled in St George's, Southwark.

Sir John Hawkins recorded that 'Jordan, a distiller ... betook himself to the making of organs, and succeeded beyond expectation', although he 'had never been instructed in the business, but had a mechanical turn' (Hawkins, 4.356n.). However, Jordan's fine instruments, all now altered or lost, showed influences from each of the leading contemporary London-based rival builders, Bernard Smith and Renatus Harris, and he was the first organ builder to add a Swell division to English organs.

On 12 December 1702 'Abraham Jordan Distiller' of St George's, Southwark, signed articles of agreement for his new organ there, already 'erected and Sett up ... being in full perfection and approved of by Dr. John Blow and Jeremiah Clerke' (Southwark archives, Surrey, deed 1232) and valued by them at £600. As part payment, Jordan was to accept the old organ.

In 1683 'Mr. Smith' had been paid £3 12s. 'in Arreares' for organ work carried out in 1682, and in 1690, 'Mr Smith Organ Maker for 2 Stopps' £5 (Southwark archives, Surrey, accounts 787). Therefore by 1702 Jordan had gained an organ which had possibly been through Bernard Smith's hands. If reused, such pipes could explain some possible Jordan pipe-markings using an alphabet consistent with Smith's north European experience.

By 1707 Jordan was insuring houses with the Hand-in-Hand Company, on the west side of the Borough at Jordan's Court 'by the Rules alley' (insurance registers of Hand-in-Hand Company, Guildhall MS 8674/4.333; 5.352) opposite St George's Church—one his own dwelling and one (behind his 32-foot-long workshop) occupied by William Stephens. A 'rough' parish register of 1704 (London Metropolitan Archives, X092.031) names Stephens as an organ builder by the Rules alley. If this man was 'Mr. Smith's man Mr. Stevens' (Canterbury Cathedral archives, DCc TB 34) who worked at Canterbury Cathedral in 1699, Jordan had another link with Bernard Smith.

Early in 1705 a Jordan organ was approved at St Saviour's, Southwark, subsequently Southwark Cathedral. Its similarity to Renatus Harris's 1696 organ at St Bride's, Fleet Street, suggests familiarity with Harris's practice. On 16 February 1727 Jordan's son Abraham [*see below*] entered into articles of agreement to 'Clean Repaire Tune and Fin-ish' (LMA, P92/SAV/147) this St Saviour's organ. The stop list must include his father's organ of 1705: 'In the great Organ' numbers 1–13: 'double Diapazon; open Diapazon; Stopt Diapazon; Principall; Cornet Mounted of Five Ranks; great Twelfth; Fifteenth; Tirce; Flagalute; Sexquialtra; Furniture; Trumpet; Clarion'. 'In the Choire Organ' numbers 14–19: 'Open Diapazon; Stopt Diapazon; Flute; Tirce; Mixture; Vox humaine'. To this, the younger Jordan proposed to add 'An Intire New Swelling Organ containing from C in the Middle of the Keys to C in Alt' numbers 20–26: 'Open Diapazon; Stopt Diapazon; Principall; Twelfth; Fifteenth; Tirce; Trumpet and Violin by Mixture'. However, this 'new' work probably adapted his father's Echo manual, being identical to the Echo at St Bride's except that the last stop there is simply 'Trumpet'. This (rare) Jordan stop list reflects Harris's 'French' habit, notably in provision of a separate Tirce on each manual, and (as at St Bride's) in listing the mounted Cornet amid the chorus stops.

Jordan's expanding activities were revealed in a letter to the steward of Hugh, second Viscount Cholmondeley, signed in Chester on 3 June 1705. He 'desiers to know if my Lord has any Sarvis [Service] to Com'and of him for he has finish ye Organ he sent ye Dean & Mended ye Choire Organ so wayts my Lords Answer or Else on Tueseday next designes for London' (Chester Diocese RO, DCH/L/50/30). The Jordans' finest achievement was the four-manual organ built in 1712 'joynery excepted' for St Magnus the Martyr, north of London Bridge. One manual was 'adapted to the art of emitting sounds by swelling the notes, *which never was in any organ before*' (*The Spectator*, 8 Feb 1712, quoted in Hopkins and Rimbault, 140). Presumably they realized that the sliding sash-shutters provided by Bernard Smith at St Paul's Cathedral as dust protection would affect the volume of sound, and had fitted a pedal to control a similar mechanism. The addition in 1702 of glazed sashes to enclose Harris's organ at St Sepulchre in London and a proposal in 1706 by the vestry of St Saviour's for Jordan 'to skreene the Organ from the Sun by Glass' (LMA, P92/SAV/452) may also have been factors. By 1714 Johan Knoppell was proposing 'Swelling to each Stop' (Canterbury Cathedral archives, DCc Fabric 8/18) for a new seven-stop echo at Canterbury.

Jordan's other recorded activities included building an organ for Bath Abbey in 1708, and one for £400 for St Benet Fink, London, in 1714. He has been confused with Abraham Jordan, carpenter, of St Michael Royal, London, who worked at St Magnus from 1686 to 1707, and whose will was proved in September 1712. Abraham Jordan 'Organ Builder ... Freeman of the City of London' wrote his will on 10 April 1715, 'being weak in Body'. He named as his children Abraham, James, Elizabeth, and Butler. Probate was granted on 9 February 1716 to his eldest son, **Abraham Jordan** (1690–1755/6), born in the parish of St Mary Aldermary in the City of London on 21 March 1690, who successfully developed the business further and was organist at St George's, Southwark, probably from the age

of twelve. On 7 January 1731, at St Stephen Walbrook, London, he married Lucy Goodjerd (d. 1763/4), spinster, of St George the Martyr, Holborn. Insurance and land tax records show that the Southwark workshop continued in use after 1731, when he changed his business address to Budge Row, St John Baptist, City of London. By 1745 he resided in Camberwell 'on the east side of the road a little south from the College at Dulwich' (Guildhall MS, 6874/68, 48).

The younger Jordan was also inventive, inviting visitors to his Southwark workshop to inspect a one-manual organ built so that the player could face the listener; it also introduced some stop-control by pedals (*London Journal*, 7 Feb 1730, quoted in Hopkins and Rimbault, 141). New organs built by him included instruments at Fulham (1733) and Maidstone (1746), one at the duke of Chandos's house at Cannons, Edgware, that was known to Handel, and an organ sent to Boston, Massachusetts, in 1744 with informative instructions for erection. He adapted Swell divisions for earlier instruments, including one in 1736 for Shrider's 1730 organ at Westminster Abbey (Knight, 40).

In 1754 a 'Parlytick Disorder' curtailed Jordan's work on his new organ at the Royal Naval Chapel, Greenwich, which the *Universal Magazine* of August 1751 'esteemed one of the best in England' (S. Jeans, 'An organ by Abraham Jordan, junior, at the Old Chapel at Greenwich Hospital', *The Organ*, 46, 1966, 70). He died, probably at Dulwich, Surrey, and was buried at Dulwich College on 10 January 1756. His wife, Lucy, continued business from Lime Street, and was carried from St Dionis Backchurch 'to be buried at Dulwich' (Guildhall MS 17603) on 12 January 1764. Their 'servant' John Sedgwick was paid £160 in 1761 for repairing the St Magnus organ after disastrous fire damage.

Hawkins noted a 'coalition' (Hawkins, 4.357n.) between Jordan, Byfield, and Bridge, intended to maintain standards but their exact relationship is not clear. An organ combining eighteenth-century English tonal characteristics was built in 1990 at the Grosvenor Chapel, London, for which Jordan's casework was reused.

JOAN JEFFERY

Sources J. Hawkins, *A general history of the science and practice of music*, 4 (1776), 356–7n. · Southwark Archives, Surrey, deed 1232 · parish of St George, accounts, Southwark Archives, Surrey, 787 · parish register, Southwark, St George, LMA · parish register, Southwark, St Saviour, LMA · vestry minutes, Southwark, St Saviour, LMA, P92/SAV/451 (1670–1703); P92/SAV/452 (1704–1738) · insurance registers of Hand-in-Hand Company, 1706–65, GL, Guildhall MSS, 8674 · land tax, GL, 11316 · parish accounts, St Magnus the Martyr and St Margaret, New Fish Street, City of London, GL, Guildhall MSS · S. Bicknell, *The history of the English organ* (1996), 122–71 · E. J. Hopkins and E. F. Rimbault, *The organ*, 3rd edn (1877) · B. Owen, 'Colonial organs', *British Institute of Organ Studies Journal*, 3 (1979), 92–107 · N. Plumley, 'The Harris/Byfield connection', *British Institute of Organ Studies Journal*, 3 (1979), 108–34 · M. Lindley and W. Drake, 'Grosvenor Chapel and the 18th century English organ', *British Institute of Organ Studies Journal*, 15 (1991), 90–117 · N. Thistlethwaite, 'Grosvenor Chapel, London', *British Institute of Organ Studies Journal*, 16 (1992), 112–15 · D. Knight, 'The Shrider organ from Westminster Abbey', *British Institute of Organ Studies Journal*, 22 (1998), 40–51 · N. Plumley, *The organs of the City of London* (1996) ·

D. Dawe, *Organists of the City of London* (1983) · parish register, London, St Mary Aldermary, GL [birth, baptism] · Vintners' Company, City of London, apprentice bindings · City of London, Distillers' Company, apprentice bindings · will, PRO, PROB 11/550/29/238 [Abraham Jordan, senior] · will, PRO, PROB 11/820/13 [Abraham Jordan, junior] · will, PRO, PROB 11/825/18 [Lucy Jordan] · will, PRO, PROB 11/925/28 [Penelope Sparham]

Wealth at death several leases of houses and other property in and near London: insurance registers of Hand-in-Hand Company, 1706–65, GL, Guildhall MSS, 8674

Jordan, Abraham (1690–1755/6). *See under* Jordan, Abraham (*c.*1666–1715/16).

Jordan, Dorothy [*real name* Dorothy Phillips] (1761–1816), actress, one of reputedly nine children of Francis Bland and Grace Phillips, was born on 22 November 1761 in London, in the neighbourhood of Leicester Square and Covent Garden. Her parents' permanent home was in Ireland. Captain (later Colonel) Francis Bland was heir to Derriquin Castle, co. Kerry, but was disinherited by his father, a judge of the prerogative court, Dublin, when he began his liaison. Grace Phillips, the daughter of the vicar of Trelethyn, St David's, South Wales, was an actress, as were her two sisters. The couple possibly went through a form of marriage, invalid as both were under age. In 1774 Bland left his family in Ireland and made a legal marriage in London to Catharine Mahoney of Killarney. The Bland family made Grace an allowance on condition that the children did not use their father's name.

Early acting and relationships Richard *Daly (d. 1813), the manager of the Smock Alley Theatre, Dublin, invited Dorothy (or Dora, as she was often known) to join his company, and she made her début, billed as Miss Francis, on 3 November 1779. Shortly afterwards the company toured Cork and Waterford, where she was courted by Lieutenant Charles Doyne. However, she became Daly's mistress in an unhappy and subservient relationship in which she conceived his child (Francis Daly) in February 1782. She owed him a considerable sum of money and, lacking the ability to pay, was threatened with the debtors' prison.

In the July of that year, with her mother, her sister Maria, and her brother Francis, Dorothy fled Dublin and at Leeds applied to Tate Wilkinson, the manager of the York company, for work. He engaged the beleaguered actress, giving her the stage name Jordan and, 'for pregnant reasons', the title Mrs (*Thespian Dictionary*). Cornelius Swan, a critic and Shakespeare scholar in York, not only coached the neophyte in her roles but also raised the money to pay Daly a waiver on her articles of apprenticeship. For three years she played in Wilkinson's company until she was seen at York by the actor William ('Gentleman') Smith, who recommended her to Richard Sheridan of the Theatre Royal, Drury Lane.

In London, Jordan stayed at 8 Henrietta Street, Covent Garden, until she found a protector in Richard *Ford (1758–1806), the son of the court physician and a major shareholder at Drury Lane, with whom she lived as wife at 5 Gower Street. Ford fathered three of Jordan's children, two daughters, and a son who died at birth. He appears to

Dorothy Jordan (1761–1816), by John Hoppner, exh. RA 1791 [as Hypolita in *She Would and She Would Not, or, The Kind Imposter* by Colley Cibber]

have intended to marry Jordan at some point in their relationship but never did.

The duke of Clarence In the spring or summer of 1790 Prince William Henry, duke of Clarence (later *William IV), who for a year had noticed Jordan at Drury Lane, learning that she was unmarried, took her to live with him at Clarence Lodge, Roehampton. No stranger to mistresses, the duke found Jordan an admirably domesticated companion and a woman whom he could love, protestations of which he regularly made in his letters. Jordan was allowed an annuity of £1200 and an equipage, and provision was made for her children, whatever their paternity. Even with this income, the actress continued to work not solely at Drury Lane but also at Covent Garden and a vast number of provincial theatres on tours of lengthy duration, sharing her salary with the duke:

> As Jordan's high and mighty squire
> Her playhouse profits deigns to skim
> Some folks audaciously enquire:
> If *he* keeps her or *she* keeps him.
> (Ziegler, 80)

Clarence was appointed in January 1797 ranger of Bushy Park, a position which included the use of Bushy House, to which he and Dorothy Jordan repaired. Eventually the mother of ten of the duke's children, all surnamed Fitz-Clarence, among them George Augustus Frederick *Fitz-Clarence and Adolphus *FitzClarence, Mrs Jordan possessed the attributes and the status of a wife; visiting Bushy, Horace Walpole was surprised to find her acting as hostess there. Scurrilous cartoons appeared in newspapers as a comment on the couple's concubinage; many of these featured a huge chamber pot, or 'jordan', on which the duke of Clarence figured.

On 2 October 1811 Jordan was appearing at the Cheltenham theatre when she received a letter from Clarence asking her to meet him at Maidenhead; there he stipulated that they must part. Debts were mounting, and his immediate need was to find an eligibly rich woman whom he might marry. He began to negotiate for the hand of Catherine Tylney-Long, the target of every fortune-hunter in London. Although the plan fell through and the duke did not marry until 1818, the separation with Jordan was final. Popular opinion, however, was against the break:

Return to Mistress J....n's arms
Soothe her, and quiet her alarms;
Your present differences o'er,
Be wise, and play the fool no more.
(Tomalin, 247)

In a deed of settlement drawn up in November, Jordan was to receive £4400; she would look after the duke's daughters, to whom he was to have free access, until they reached the age of thirteen. Should the morals of the children be endangered by Jordan's return to the stage, that part of her allowance relating to them (£2200) would be stopped.

An acting career For the next four years Jordan lived at Cadogan Street, Chelsea; in spite of poor health and fatigue she performed in London and the provinces, and finally made her farewell to the stage at the Margate theatre in July 1815.

Throughout her professional life Dorothy Jordan worked feverishly to earn an ample salary, with which she was generous and extravagant. On her entry into Wilkinson's company she was paid 15s. per week. The Drury Lane account book (Folger Shakespeare Library, Washington, DC) reveals that in her first season (1785) Sheridan paid her £4 per week of six performances, and by the end of that season the salary was doubled. From 1792 she was paid £31 10s. per week, and by 1795 she commanded 10 guineas per night, performing four or five nights per week. To this weekly salary must be added the benefits. That of her first season at Drury Lane grossed £205 2s. 1d. By 1796 this increased, as she had gained the right to a 'clear' benefit (one unencumbered with the deduction of the charges of the house for the night), to £658 19s. 6d. In 1799 the benefit grossed £706 5s. 6d. For acting in the benefits of her fellow performers Jordan made a charge of £10 or £15.

Jordan's provincial tours were made primarily for financial reasons. In 1788 John Boles Watson I invited her to the Cheltenham theatre on the occasion of the visit of George III and Queen Charlotte. So great was her popularity in the spa town that a commemorative medal depicting the comic muse was struck. Henry Thornton was another manager in whose playhouses Jordan performed; she appeared at the first season of the newly built Reading theatre in 1788 and from that time made regular visits around the circuit along the Bath and Portsmouth roads. After her break with Clarence she relied on Thornton, among other provincials, for work, and she performed during 1812 and 1813 at his and Thomas Collins's theatres at Gosport, Southampton, Ryde, and Portsmouth, in spite of her dismay at the rowdiness of the seafaring audiences.

The demands of touring are hinted at in a listing of Jordan's principal provincial engagements. In 1786 and 1787 she returned to Wilkinson's circuit. In Edinburgh in 1789 she played to houses with seats to spare. She returned again to the York circuit in 1791, promised by Wilkinson the same financial terms that Mrs Siddons and Miss Farren had enjoyed, travelled to Margate in the summer of 1797 for her first season there at £50 per week, and in 1801 was in Canterbury, where there were protests at the higher priced seats for her nights. Liverpool and Preston were her hosts in 1802 and Birmingham was visited the following year. She began the first of her annual seasons at Bath in 1808, the following year adding Bristol for alternate performances; also in 1809 she played at Liverpool, Chester, and Leicester, netting £971. In 1810 she was in Manchester at £50 per week. 'This is a dismal, gloomy theatre and the performers shocking' (Aspinall, 186), wrote Jordan in 1811 of Hoy and Crisp's company at Worcester; 200 guineas gained in Coventry over five nights on the same tour helped to compensate for a mere 140 guineas at Worcester. All of this was accomplished in the face of debilitating illnesses and travel difficulties.

Dorothy Jordan took a while to discover the kind of role which suited her distinctive abilities; her years in Ireland and on the York circuit were a time of experiment. Both Thomas Ryder and Richard Daly presented plays at their theatres with 'reversed' casts, men playing women's roles and vice versa. This convention was applied to the Crow Street production of Sheridan's *The Duenna*, in which Jordan played Lopez. Her first biographer, James Boaden, wrote of her capability in transvestite roles: 'The neatness of her figure in the male attire was for years remarkable; but the attraction, after all, is purely feminine, and the display of female, not male perfections' (Boaden, 1.46). Here was one trait on which Jordan would capitalize in the future in her Rosalind (*As You Like It*), Viola (*Twelfth Night*), and Sir Harry Wildair (*The Constant Couple*). In Ireland, too, Jordan essayed a comedy role, Priscilla Tomboy in Isaac Bickerstaff's *The Romp*, which she was to sustain for many years. The opportunity arose in Dublin to play in tragedy against John Philip Kemble: Jordan was Anne to his Richard III and Adelaide to Kemble's title role in *The Count of Narbonne*, Robert Jephson's dramatization of *The Castle of Otranto* by Horace Walpole. Such a rounded apprenticeship was given in Dublin that when Wilkinson asked her whether she specialized in comedy, tragedy, or farce, she instantly replied 'All!'. On the York circuit there were further opportunities to master a wide repertory, and it was not until she was confronted with the challenge of appearing at Drury Lane, where Sarah Siddons had reached an eminence in the portrayal of tragic figures, that Jordan decided she must apply her skill to comedy if she was also to scale the peaks. She had been impressed by David Garrick's *The Country Girl*, an adaptation of *The Country Wife* by William Wycherley, and she chose this for her

London début on 18 October 1785. Mary Tickell, present at the revival (the play had not been seen for eleven years), described her appeal in the role of Peggy:

> little she is and yet not insignificant in her figure, which, though short, has a certain roundness and embonpoint which is very graceful. Her voice is harmony itself … and it has certain little breaks and indescribable tones which in simple archness have a wonderful effect. (W. Fraser Rae, *Sheridan: a Biography*, 1896, 2.12–13)

Leigh Hunt recorded that in later life a stout Jordan still gave an agreeable portrayal, wearing a pinafore on her buxom figure and dividing 'sobs of sorrow with the comforts of a great slice of bread and butter' (L. Hunt, *The Dramatic Works of Wycherley, Congreve, Vanbrugh, and Farquhar*, 1840, xxi). It was as the Country Girl that Romney painted her in 1787.

The boldness and rusticity of her humour made Jordan a natural for the part of Hoyden in *The Relapse* by John Vanbrugh; Byron judged she was 'superlative' in this. A further hoydenish character which she undertook, but this time a mature woman, was the Widow Cheerly in Andrew Cherry's comedy *The Soldier's Daughter*. Again she was highly successful, and Lord William Pitt Lennox wrote:

> the lively, good-humoured and delightful widow is a very pleasing madcap, with an air of novelty … Mrs Jordan's widow was all that vivacity and sensibility could make it … The enthusiasm with which they [the audience] seized the following words can scarcely be adequately described: 'It is said of me that I have a facility in raising the spirits and creating good humour where ever I am'. (W. Pitt Lennox, *Plays, Players and Playhouses*, 1881, 1.52)

Last years and death When nearing forty Jordan could still bring credibility to the role of the young melodramatic heroine: she created Imogen in Matthew Gregory Lewis's *Adelmorn the Outlaw* and Angela in the same playwright's popular drama *The Castle Spectre*. The actress was highly conscious of the theatrical moment, whether it consisted, in the latter play, of standing by a gothic window casement in a reverie lit by the moonlight or abasing herself in the candle-lit oratory of Conway Castle before the apparition of her murdered mother.

Jordan was less successful in playing women of some social standing. To her Lady Teazle in *The School for Scandal* she brought a dimension of spontaneity and innocent charm, but she lacked the artifice and incisiveness of her two predecessors in the role at Drury Lane, Frances Abington and Elizabeth Farren, although Charles Lamb made the qualification: 'When we say she never did or could play the Fine Lady, we mean it to her honour. Her mind is essentially above the thing' (W. McKenna, *Charles Lamb and the Theatre*, 1978, 87). The contrast between the studied acting of Siddons and the immediacy of Jordan was noted in the preparations for Sheridan's historical drama *Pizarro*. Siddons's speaking delighted the playwright, whereas during Jordan's scenes he beat on the ledge of the stage box the rhythm inherent in his prose which, he judged, Jordan ignored. This illustrates the innovatory nature of Jordan's acting: she abandoned the stiff attitudes and mannered speaking of the Kemble school and brought to the stage immediacy and a natural vivacity. A full list of her roles may be found in Tomalin, *Mrs Jordan's Profession*, 323–30.

When she retired from the stage, Jordan sold her London house and sailed to Boulogne, where, as Mrs James or Mrs Johnson, she lived in premises just outside the town at Marquetra. Biographers offer two reasons for her self-imposed exile: her worsening health may have necessitated it; and she had very little money left after lending large sums to her eldest daughter, Frances, and her son-in-law, Thomas Alsop, who had defrauded her. Jonah Barrington claimed that a flight from creditors was inconceivable as in Jordan's last year of working she had earned £7000; however, his is a minority view. When her bank account was closed, it contained £10 14s. 1d.

Mrs Jordan made two further moves, to Versailles and then to St Cloud, near Paris. There, on 5 July 1816, she died alone and was buried beneath an acacia in the town cemetery. Mr and Mrs Henry Woodgate, two English visitors, paid for a memorial stone for which the Revd John Genest composed a Latin epitaph.   PAUL RANGER

Sources J. Boaden, *The life of Mrs Jordan*, 2 vols. (1831) • C. Tomalin, *Mrs Jordan's profession* (1994) • A. Aspinall, *Mrs Jordan and her family* (1951) • B. Fothergill, *Mrs Jordan, portrait of an actress* (1965) • *The great illegitimates!! by a confidential friend of the departed* (1830) • Highfill, Burnim & Langhans, *BDA* • Genest, *Eng. stage* • T. Wilkinson, *The wandering patentee, or, A history of the Yorkshire theatres from 1770 to the present time*, 4 vols. (1795) • *The thespian dictionary, or, Dramatic biography of the present age*, 2nd edn (1805) • P. Ziegler, *William IV* (1971) • *Jordan's elixir of life and cure for the spleen* (1789) • *Oxberry's Dramatic Biography*, 1/12 (1825) • *Mrs Jordan—the duchess of Drury Lane*, English Heritage (1995) [exhibition catalogue, Kenwood House, 1995]
Archives BL • CKS, letters • Hunt. L. • NRA, priv. coll., letters relating to her | Folger, the Drury Lane account books • Hunt. L., letters to the duke of Clarence • NRA, priv. coll., corresp. with William Adam • Royal Arch., letters to the duke of Clarence • Royal Arch., Munster MSS
Likenesses J. Hoppner, sketch, exh. RA 1785, Gov. Art Coll. • J. Hoppner, oils, exh. RA 1786, Royal Collection • G. Romney, oils, 1786–7, Waddesdon Manor, Buckinghamshire • T. Park, mezzotint, pubd 1787 (after J. Hoppner), NG Ire. • P. Thomas, mezzotint, pubd 1787 (after J. Hoppner), NG Ire. • J. Ogborne, stipple, pubd 1788 (after G. Romney), BM, NPG, NG Ire. • J. Hoppner, oils, exh. RA 1791, Tate collection [*see illus.*] • J. Jones, mezzotint, pubd 1791 (after J. Hoppner), NPG, BM, NG Ire. • J. Hoppner, oils, *c.*1796 (as Viola in *Twelfth Night*), Kenwood House, London • S. De Wilde, oils, *c.*1799, Trinity College of Music, London, Mander and Mitchenson Theatre Collection • J. Heath, stipple, pubd 1802 (after J. Russell), NPG, BM • J. Godby, stipple, pubd 1806 (after R. K. Porter), NPG • J. Rogers, stipple, pubd 1824 (after O. Steeden), NPG, BM • F. Chantrey, statue, 1834, Royal Collection • F. Chantrey, statue, AM Oxf. • S. De Wilde, oils (as Peggy in *The country girl*), Garr. Club • S. De Wilde, oils (as Phaedra in *Amphitryon*), Garr. Club • attrib. G. Dupont, oils, Garr. Club • line engraving, NPG
Wealth at death £10 14s. 1d. bank balance on death

Jordan, John (1746–1809), local historian and poet, eldest son of John Jordan (1718–1775), wheelwright, and Elizabeth Lock (1716–1777), was born at Tiddington, in Alveston, near Stratford upon Avon, on 9 October 1746. He was educated at the village school until 1756, but then was put to learn his father's trade. In 1759 his father moved the family to Stratford, where John continued to work for him, before taking over the business on his father's death in 1775. But his evident academic abilities led him to seek advancement by way of antiquarian and Shakespeare studies. He played various Shakespearian characters in local theatrical productions, and by 1776 had composed *Welcombe Hills, Near Stratford upon Avon; a Poem, Historical and Descriptive*. This work, on which Joseph Greene, headmaster of the town's grammar school, gave him considerable assistance, was published by subscription the following year. John Jordan married, at St Philip's, Birmingham, on 2 June 1783, Sarah (*bap.* 1750, *d.* 1799), daughter of Samuel Smith; with her he had two children.

By 1786 Jordan had compiled a history of Stratford and entered into correspondence with Mark Noble, with a view to its publication. Noble found much to criticize, but in return for Jordan's carrying out researches into his ancestry, he reworked the manuscript, returning it to Jordan, it seems, in 1788. It was not, however, published in the author's lifetime, eventually appearing in 1864 as *Original Collections on Stratford-upon-Avon, by John Jordan*, edited, but with many omissions, by James Orchard Halliwell. During 1790 Jordan was in correspondence with Edmond Malone when the latter was collecting material for his biography of Shakespeare, sending him a manuscript account of Shakespeare and his relatives. This was also later edited by Halliwell under the title *Original Memoirs and Historical Accounts of the Families of Shakespeare and Hart* (1865). These two works are the earliest written source for much of the Shakespearian folklore then circulating in the town (some of which Malone treated with scepticism), but the former also represents the first attempt to write a history of Stratford, and contains useful information on the late-eighteenth-century town, particularly in an expanded version (largely ignored by Halliwell) which Jordan wrote after Noble had returned his manuscript. In 1792 Samuel Ireland visited Stratford, and Jordan showed him the principal sights in and near the town. Ireland also proved a more gullible recipient of Jordan's collection of Shakespearian folklore, some of which appeared in print for the first time in his *Picturesque Views of Shakespeare's Avon* (1795).

Though none of Jordan's other verse was published, manuscript copies survive of various commemorative orations which he composed and delivered, mostly on behalf of the Old Friendly Society, of which he was secretary and bookkeeper. His drawings, several of which were published in the *Gentleman's Magazine*, though crude, are still of value. By his own account, poor health led, in the late 1780s, to the failure of his wheelwright's business and both Noble and Malone made some effort to find him a position, the latter also raising £40 for him by subscription. Nothing came of this, however, and Jordan became dependent for work on his brother Samuel, also a wheelwright. He died on 25 June 1809 in Stratford, and was buried three days later alongside his wife in the churchyard of Holy Trinity, Stratford upon Avon. Most of his manuscripts were acquired by the Stratford antiquary Robert Bell Wheler, passing later to the Shakespeare Birthplace Trust. ROBERT BEARMAN

Sources manuscript of autobiographical material, Shakespeare Birthplace Trust RO, Stratford upon Avon, ER 1/2, 118, 122 · *Original letters from Edmond Malone to John Jordan*, ed. J. O. Halliwell (1864) · manuscript copy letters to John Jordan from Mark Noble and Samuel Ireland, Shakespeare Birthplace Trust RO, Stratford upon Avon, ER 1/9 · R. B. W. [R. B. Wheler], biographical preface, in J. Jordan, *Welcombe Hills, near Stratford upon Avon: a poem, historical and descriptive* (1827) · W.-H. Ireland, *The confessions and additional lies of William-Henry Ireland* (1805) · S. Schoenbaum, *Shakespeare's lives*, new edn (1991) · *Letters of the Reverend Joseph Green*, ed. L. Fox, Dugdale Society, 23 (1967) · E. K. Chambers, *William Shakespeare: a study of facts and problems*, 2 vols. (1930)

Archives Shakespeare Birthplace Trust RO, Stratford upon Avon, corresp. and papers · U. Birm., Shakespeare Institute | Folger, Halliwell MSS · Shakespeare Birthplace Trust RO, Stratford upon Avon, collection started by John Hughes, continued by John Jordan · Shakespeare Birthplace Trust RO, Stratford upon Avon, Saunders collection · Shakespeare Birthplace Trust RO, Stratford upon Avon, Wheler MSS

Likenesses J. Saunders, watercolour (after lost portrait by G. Grubb, *c.*1790) · engraving, repro. in Jordan, *Welcombe Hills* · pen-and-ink silhouette, Shakespeare Birthplace Trust RO, Stratford upon Avon

Jordan, Sir John Newell (1852–1925), diplomatist, was born at Balloo, co. Down, Ireland, on 5 September 1852, the second son of John Jordan and his wife, Mary Newell, both of substantial Presbyterian farmer stock. To his upbringing Jordan owed the diligence and conscientiousness that marked his career. Following education at the Royal Belfast Academical Institution and Queen's College, Belfast, where he gained first-class honours, and Queen's College, Cork, he joined the Chinese consular service in 1876 as a student interpreter. He married in 1885 Annie Howe Cromie, also of co. Down. They had three sons and one daughter. After consular posts in south China he moved to the British legation in Peking (Beijing), where by 1891 he had become Chinese secretary, a post he owed to general ability as well as to proficiency in the Chinese language.

In 1896 Jordan was appointed consul-general at Seoul. He became chargé d'affaires in 1898 and minister-resident in 1901. British interests in Korea were, in the main, limited to commerce, but Jordan also held a watching brief over the contest for influence between Russia and Japan. He remained at Seoul until November 1905, when Japan was moving towards full control of Korea. He was created KCMG in 1904.

In 1906 Jordan was appointed minister to China, a post for which he was recommended by G. E. Morrison, the influential correspondent of *The Times* in Peking. He returned to a scene much changed from 1896. Then, a weak China was becoming the field of fierce competition among imperialist powers for economic and territorial prizes. By 1906 China had gained confidence, for Russia and Japan, the most dangerous threats to her integrity, were both exhausted following their conflict in 1904–5. The central government had embarked on a programme of reform and modernization. National consciousness had awakened and was reflected in determination to recover rights and privileges extorted in China's weakness. Recognition of this new confidence was one reason for co-operation among foreign powers, particularly for railway business, replacing rivalry. By 1910 German and American syndicates had joined British and French groups (linked since 1905), forming the China consortium to secure and finance contracts. These developments were supported by the Foreign Office for reasons of general policy as well as to meet a situation in which competition could be turned to advantage by China. Jordan did not welcome this trend, which he saw as permitting infiltration into British preserves. He did not allow for the broader issues of policy involved, as he recognized when in 1908 the importance of the French entente was pointed out to him; he wrote to F. A. Campbell, 'It is not always easy for the man on the spot to "think imperially"' (Jordan to Campbell, 20 Aug 1908, FO 305/5). By 1911, however, when the consortium reached agreement with China on a major railway project, the Hukuang (Huguang) loan, he admitted that the principle of international co-operation had proved a 'triumphant success' and thought prospects good for the railway programme.

Jordan's optimism was ill-founded. Within a few months China was in revolution which both toppled the imperial regime and disrupted the railway schemes. It also set back the most successful of the Chinese government's reforms which Jordan had applauded—the campaign against the cultivation and use of opium. Jordan, anxious to secure a strong central government in China, saw the only hope in a regime with Yuan Shih-k'ai in control. The Foreign Office, where Jordan was held in high esteem, took the view that the nature of the new structure, monarchy or republic, was immaterial so long as Yuan was its effective head. By 1912 China was a republic, with Yuan as provisional president. Jordan supported him in his successful struggle with the opposition led by Sun Yatsen, which cleared the way for a strong government.

There were other matters to concern Jordan in the aftermath of the revolution. The China consortium fell into disarray and competition between lenders returned to the industrial field. He was alarmed at the threat to British interests mounted by French and particularly by Japanese projects in the Yangtze (Yangzi) valley. He was said to be diffident in presenting his views, but his trenchant criticism of British financiers for failure to support purely British schemes reflects something of the forthright speech he was capable of using on occasion. He gained support in the Foreign Office for a British economic policy in China detached from international connections, but he and his allies had misjudged the attitude of British industry, which was not attracted to group combinations on the continental model and, in general, not much interested in the China market. Yet, though ground had been lost, British investment had continued to expand, and in 1914 still surpassed all competitors in China.

The defence of the British position became more difficult as war in Europe absorbed the Western powers and left China open for Japanese advance. The twenty-one demands (particularly Group V) presented by Japan to President Yuan in January 1915 threatened to make China virtually a Japanese protectorate. Jordan in his official capacity kept detached, recognizing that there was little Britain could do to restrain Japan, but in private letters to the Foreign Office he denounced Japanese policy. When in

May 1915 Japan presented modified terms in an ultimatum, Jordan on his own initiative realistically advised Yuan to accept. The crisis, followed by Yuan's attempt to create a monarchy, placed Jordan under heavy strain. The death in 1916 of Yuan, the one man he believed who could hold China together and whom he valued as a friend, was a personal loss. Towards the end of 1917, though he had just returned from a long leave, G. E. Morrison found him 'tremulous, petulant and overburdened' (Pearl, 345).

Jordan, by now KCB (1909), GCIE (1911), privy councillor (1915), and GCMG (1920), retired in 1920. He had been a stalwart defender of British interests and privileges, and was regarded by most Chinese opinion as a foreign imperialist still more tarnished by his support of Yuan Shih-k'ai. By 1918, however, his views had changed under the influence of the new currents of international co-operation. He looked to revision of the policy of competition and suspicion pursued by foreign powers in China and to their future co-operation as the basis for reconstruction.

Jordan had maintained his links with Ireland and, it is said, his brogue. He became a freeman of Belfast in 1910 and was pro-chancellor of Queen's College 1912–22. He died at 99 Cannon Street, London, on 14 September 1925 during a committee meeting of the China Association after an active retirement which included membership of the British delegation at the Washington conference in 1921–2. He was survived by his wife.   E. W. EDWARDS

Sources C. L. Kit-Ching, *Anglo-Chinese diplomacy in the careers of Sir John Jordan and Yuan Shih-k'ai, 1906–1920* (1978) • E. W. Edwards, *British diplomacy and finance in China, 1895–1914* (1987) • P. Lowe, *Great Britain and Japan, 1911–1915* (1969) • I. H. Nish, *Alliance in decline* (1972) • *The Times* (15 Sept 1925) • C. Pearl, *Morrison of Peking*, new edn (1971) • *DNB* • *CGPLA Eng. & Wales* (1925) • Burke, *Peerage* • PRO, FO 305/5

Archives PRO, diplomatic corresp., FO 350 | CUL, corresp. with Lord Hardinge and others • Mitchell L., NSW, letters to G. E. Morrison

Likenesses W. Stoneman, photograph, 1920, NPG • London Electrotype Agency, photograph, repro. in Lowe, *Great Britain and Japan* • pencil sketch (after photograph), Queen's University, Belfast

Wealth at death £39,409 11s. 10d.: probate, 31 Oct 1925, *CGPLA Eng. & Wales*

Jordan, Sir Joseph (1603/4–1685), naval officer, was probably a member of a Thames shipowning family. He was bred to the sea and first appears in 1637 as master of the *Amity*, importing tobacco from Nevis and Barbados. He served in the parliamentary navy from the beginning of the civil war, commanding the merchantman *Caesar* in the summer guard of 1642. In August of that year he was engaged in securing castles on and about the Isle of Wight. In 1643 he served as rear-admiral in the Irish guard and, in the *Expedition*, took a Hamburger laden with salt. In the following year he was active off the Channel Islands and at the relief of Lyme. He was at the siege of Weymouth in 1645 and in 1647 was still commanding the *Expedition*. In 1648 he was keeping the Irish sea and the channel; he remained loyal to parliament during the naval revolt that summer, and accepted the new republican regime in 1649. In February that year he was among the naval officers who signed a remonstrance congratulating the army and the

Commons for restoring liberty. During and after the civil war he supplied timber for the navy.

In September 1650 Jordan was made captain of the *Pelican*, intended for support to the army in Scotland but diverted to Penn's Mediterranean squadron, which returned in March 1652. After Blake's rear-admiral was wounded on 11 August, Jordan replaced him. After the battle of Portland (18 February 1653) he was given the *Vanguard*, receiving instructions from Blake, Deane, and Monck on 29 March. In this ship he served as flag captain and then vice-admiral of the blue at the first battle of North Foreland on 23 June and the engagements off Katwijk and Scheveningen on 29–31 July. In the latter his ship was disabled and he transferred to the *George*. He received the flag officers' gold chain and medal for his services and Monck praised him as 'godly and valiant' (PRO, SP 46/115, fol. 15). In 1654 he was rear-admiral aboard the *Unicorn*, sailing with Blake and Badiley to the Mediterranean. On 1 September 1655 Blake gave him leave to return to England 'about some extraordinary business' (*Letters of Robert Blake*, 311). Perhaps it was now that Jordan married; his eldest son, finding employment in 1672, could have been born about 1656. But since Jordan was past fifty, he may already have established himself as a family man and country squire. Nothing more is heard of him in public life for almost a decade.

Jordan must have retained contacts in naval circles, for in July 1662 he supported a seaman's petition for his master's ticket. In 1664, as another conflict with the Dutch approached, Jordan was introduced to the king's service by his old colleague Penn, now a navy commissioner. By 7 April, Jordan was back in the *St George* (its full name now restored), in which he was at the battle of Lowestoft on 3 June 1665. When Lawson, who was hit, asked to be relieved of command of the *Royal Oak*, the duke of York sent Jordan to take his place, where he did 'brave things' (Pepys, *Diary*, 6.122). The master had been killed and the ship had sprung her luff, but Jordan quickly restored order and took her back into action. His conduct was rewarded with a knighthood when the king welcomed his fleet home to the Nore on 29 June. Jordan's portrait by Lely in the Flagmen of Lowestoft series was seen by Pepys in the artist's studio on 18 April the following year. Meanwhile on 2 July 1665 Jordan was promoted rear-admiral of the white. In September he took command of the *Royal Oak* in his own right and, with Harman and Berkeley, chased the Dutch to Texel, but was ordered by Sandwich to withdraw when night closed on them.

At the start of the 1666 campaign Jordan was advanced to rear-admiral of the red, still flying his flag in the *Royal Oak*. Following the division of the fleet he was further promoted to the vice-admiral's place in his squadron, and as such served in the Four Days' Battle on 1–4 June. His account of this great action, written to Penn on 5 June, makes modest reference to his own battle (in which 100 of his ship's company were killed or wounded). Only the loss of the *Royal Prince*, run on to the Galloper and an easy target for enemy fireships, was particularly recalled. He shared the widespread view that victory might have been

achieved had Rupert been with them from the start. But he was thankful to have survived 'the greatest passes, I think, that ever was fought at sea', and asked Penn to tell his wife he was safe. He would not write to her or any others, but only to Penn 'who knows how to make use of it; as truth is not always to be writ' (Powell and Timings, *Rupert and Monck*, 251–2). On 2 July he was sent with the judge advocate to deal with disorders in the *Crown*. He saw action again on St James's day (25 July). A ballad dubbed him 'Heart of Oak' on this occasion (Firth, 73). He would name one of his sons Hartoake, presumably in commemoration of his ship.

As the war neared its end in June 1667 Jordan commanded a detachment of small vessels in Harwich, where he lay waiting for a chance to annoy the Dutch; he made several forays. On 23 June he and four other ships exchanged fire with thirty Dutchmen. On the following day he tried again, but the enemy were out of his range. On the 29th the wind was wrong and on the 30th the tide was against him. In July, when he could hear the guns from the Thames (where the Dutch were in the process of inflicting on the Royal Navy perhaps its greatest humiliation), he was itching to be out again. On the 24th he sailed with all the forces at his disposal (sixteen fireships and six small warships according to one of the more precise accounts) to intercept the homebound Dutch fleet. The action off the Kent coast on 26 July, called the second battle of North Foreland, was a fiasco. One of the fireships would not catch fire, while several others destroyed themselves without attaching to the enemy. Contrary winds and tides were blamed, as was the shipwright, Deane, for packing the fireships without high explosive. The commanders of these were said to be 'some idle fellows' (Pepys, *Diary*, 8.357); one of them was subsequently shot for cowardice and three others were dismissed the service. Jordan, who was much criticized for his indiscretion and for failing to maintain liaison with the squadron at sea under Spragge, limped home by 1 August, the day after the war ended.

In the following year Jordan was offered new commands, but it was to be a year of peace. When war with the Dutch resumed in 1672, Jordan was made rear-admiral of the red, being promoted vice-admiral of the blue before the fleet went into action. At the battle of Solebay on 28 May he led the van from the *Sovereign*. Between 8 a.m. and 9 a.m. Sandwich (admiral of the blue) sent his barge to order Jordan to weather the Dutch who were firing heavily on Sandwich's *Royal James*. Jordan received the message, but was then observed to pass by his embattled admiral and to stand in support of the duke of York, commander-in-chief, in the *Prince*. Sandwich and his ship were lost. An eyewitness on the shore commented on Jordan's manoeuvre: 'I like not his fighting nor conduct' (*CSP dom.*, 1672, 92). Haddock, Sandwich's flag captain, thought Jordan 'took no notice at all of us' (Anderson, 167); Haddock later commissioned a painting from Willem van de Velde the younger which shows the *Royal James* signalling for the help which never came. But most commentators have accepted that Jordan acted honourably, and it may be that he saved not only the future James II: also aboard the *Royal James* that day was John Churchill, later duke of Marlborough, ancestor of Winston but then still childless.

Jordan remained at sea in 1672 as commander at Sheerness. Thereafter he retired to his house at Hatfield Woodside, Hertfordshire, rewarded with a crown pension of £500 a year. He died at Hatfield Woodside on 2 June 1685, in his eighty-second year, leaving the house to his wife, Mary, and most of his other properties, in London and adjacent counties, to his elder son Joseph (who was married to another Mary, with sons Joseph and Burghill). His other surviving son—two others predeceased him—was Hartoake, who received £1200 in cash and £50 a year during his minority. Jordan was buried in Hatfield church.

C. S. KNIGHTON

Sources J. R. Powell and E. K. Timings, eds., *Documents relating to the civil war, 1642–1648*, Navy RS, 105 (1963), 9, 39, 40, 71, 88, 126–7, 142, 190, 276, 294, 359, 384 • B. Capp, *Cromwell's navy: the fleet and the English revolution, 1648–1660* (1989), 117 (n. 12), 158 • *The letters of Robert Blake*, ed. J. R. Powell, Navy RS, 76 (1937), 311 • W. L. Clowes, *The Royal Navy: a history from the earliest times to the present*, 7 vols. (1897–1903); repr. (1996–7), vol. 2, pp.157 and n. 2, 188, 194–5, 210 • *CSP dom.*, 1663–4, 589; 1667, 227, 230, 244, 249, 324–5, 327–9, 331–2, 334, 340, 342, 351, 356; 1672, 92, 103, 109, 115, 164, 658 • *The journal of Edward Mountagu, first earl of Sandwich, admiral and general at sea, 1659–1665*, ed. R. C. Anderson, Navy RS, 64 (1929), 174, 226, 236, 272 • Pepys, *Diary*, 6.122, 147; 7.102; 8.354, 357–60 • A. W. Tedder, *The navy of the Restoration* (1916); repr. (1970), 141, 189–90 • J. R. Powell and E. K. Timings, eds., *The Rupert and Monck letter book, 1666*, Navy RS, 112 (1969), 16, 84, 196, 237, 250–52 • C. H. Firth, ed., *Naval songs and ballads*, Navy RS, 33 (1908), 73 • R. C. Anderson, ed., *Journals and narratives of the Third Dutch War*, Navy RS, 86 (1946), 10 (n. 1), 17, 21–2, 166–7, 170–72, 173–4 • M. S. Robinson, ed., *Van de Velde: a catalogue of the paintings of the elder and the younger Willem van de Velde*, 2 (1990), 578 • R. Clutterbuck, ed., *The history and antiquities of the county of Hertford*, 2 (1821), 368 • D. Lysons, *The environs of London*, 4 (1796), 125 • J. Charnock, ed., *Biographia navalis*, 1 (1794), 108–11 • Magd. Cam., Pepys Library, MS 2611, 215–16 • Magd. Cam., Pepys Library, MS 2873, 165–7 • BL, Add. MS 28937, fol. 201 • S. Pepys, *Naval minutes*, ed. J. R. Tanner, Navy RS, 60 (1926), 69–70 • PRO, PROB 11/380, fols. 173v–175 • PRO, SP 46/115, fol. 15

Archives NMM, journal of *Vanguard*; account of battle with Dutch, 1666 | NMM, letter to Penn with account of four days' fight, 5 June 1666, W.7.N/14/1

Likenesses P. Lely, oils, c.1666, NMM; repro. in F. Fox, *Great ships: the battlefleet of King Charles II* (1980), 35 • R. Tompson, mezzotint (after P. Lely), BM • engraving, Magd. Cam., Pepys Library, MS 2979, 233

Wealth at death lands in Hertfordshire, Middlesex, Essex, and London: will, proved 12 June 1685, PRO, PROB 11/380, fols. 173v–175 • cash bequests of £1554, incl. quantity of funeral rings at 10s. each; £800, from mortgage on Thames dock and much anticipated from crown pension of £500 p.a.: BL, Add. MS 28937, fol. 201

Jordan, Joseph (1787–1873), surgeon and lecturer, was born on 3 March 1787, at 116 Water Street, Manchester, the sixth and youngest child of William Jordan and his wife, Mary Moors. He was educated at the Revd J. Birchall's school, Manchester, and in 1802 was apprenticed to Mr John Bill, surgeon to the Manchester Infirmary. Jordan became dissatisfied and joined instead Mr William Simmons, an ambitious and progressive surgeon who was also on the honorary staff of the infirmary. He completed his professional education by attending the lecture courses in Edinburgh.

In 1806 Jordan joined the Royal Lancashire regiment, achieving the rank of assistant surgeon in the following year. Jordan did not see any active service and in 1811 he resigned his commission. After spending a year in London continuing his medical studies, he returned to Manchester and joined the practice of Stewart and Bancks. He also began offering lecture courses on anatomy at a small house near Deansgate. In 1814 he resigned from the practice and in September of that year announced in the local press that he was opening 'rooms for the study of anatomy' in Bridge Street. In 1816 the school moved to larger premises in the same street where Jordan also had private apartments. Initially, teaching was devoted entirely to anatomy and involved lectures, demonstrations, and dissection. Later, Jordan was joined by other teachers and a broader range of subjects was offered.

Before the Anatomy Act of 1832, few bodies were available for dissection. Jordan, by his own admission, was involved, with students from his school, in stealing bodies from graves. He also bought corpses from professional 'resurrectionists' who charged about £10 per body. On one occasion Jordan was fined £20 by a magistrate for his involvement in 'bodysnatching'; on another, angry crowds smashed windows in Jordan's school after a consignment of bodies was discovered. However, Jordan managed to secure a reasonable supply of corpses, which ensured the early success of his school.

In 1815 the Apothecaries' Act established the licence of the Society of Apothecaries, the LSA, as a legal requirement for general practitioners in England and Wales. To obtain the licence students had to attend a prescribed number of lecture courses. In 1817 Jordan's school was recognized by the Society of Apothecaries; four years later the Royal College of Surgeons also recognized its teaching as acceptable towards their membership diploma, the MRCS. The regulations concerning the MRCS had been revised following the Apothecaries' Act, along similar lines to the LSA. In 1819 Jordan was involved in establishing the Lock Hospital for Unfortunate Women with Drs Hull, Simmons, Brigham, and Stewart.

In 1824 Thomas Turner opened a school of medicine in Pine Street, Manchester, offering courses on all the subjects required by students aiming for the LSA and MRCS qualifications. His school is regarded as the first complete school of medicine in the provinces. There was intense rivalry between Turner and Jordan, both for students and for staff. In 1826 Jordan moved his school into purpose-built premises in Mount Street. However, his colleagues often found him difficult to work with and in 1828 most resigned and set up a rival school. Although Jordan continued to operate the Mount Street School with the assistance of his nephew Edward Stephens, he was never able to challenge Turner's school in Pine Street.

In 1828 and again in 1833 Jordan put himself forward for election to the honorary staff of the Manchester Infirmary. On both occasions he failed to win sufficient votes. Infirmary elections were invariably hard fought and the support of influential individuals among both staff and subscribers was crucial. In 1834 Jordan negotiated with Turner, who had been elected honorary surgeon in 1830, to transfer his pupils to the Pine Street School if the school's staff would support him in a future election. He also later transferred his anatomical museum to the school. In 1835 William Whatton, who had been the successful candidate in the 1833 election, died, and Jordan put himself forward again. He spent an enormous amount of money and invested tremendous energy in his election campaign. He won and remained on the staff of the Infirmary until 1866. He became FRCS in 1843.

Jordan was active in a number of Manchester organizations. In 1843 he became a founding member of the Chetham's Society. In 1857 he served as vice-president of the Manchester Royal Institution. In 1869 he became consulting surgeon-extraordinary to the Salford Royal Hospital. Jordan continued to live in Bridge Street until 1871, when he began to suffer serious ill health. He moved first to West High Street, Salford, then to Stroud, Gloucestershire, and finally to South Hill Park, Hampstead, London, where he died, a bachelor, on 31 March 1873.

STELLA BUTLER

Sources F. W. Jordan, *Life of Joseph Jordan, surgeon* (1904) • W. Brockbank, *The honorary medical staff of the Manchester Royal Infirmary, 1830–1948* (1965), 4–7 • *The Lancet* (31 May 1873), 790–91 • M. C. H. Hibbert Ware, *The life and correspondence of the late Samuel Hibbert Ware* (1882), 453–4 • *CGPLA Eng. & Wales* (1873) • *London and Provincial Medical Directory* (1867)
Likenesses photograph, repro. in Jordan, *Life of Joseph Jordan* • photograph, JRL, Manchester Collection
Wealth at death under £9000: probate, 29 April 1873, *CGPLA Eng. & Wales*

Jordan, (Heinrich Ernst) Karl (1861–1959), entomologist, was born at Almstedt, near Hildesheim, Hanover, on 7 December 1861, the youngest of the seven children of a farmer, Wilhelm Jordan, and his wife, Johanne Vosshage. He was educated at Hildesheim high school and the University of Göttingen, where he obtained his degree in botany and zoology, *summa cum laude*, and a diploma in teaching. In 1888 he was appointed a master at Münden grammar school, and in 1891 married Minna Brünig (*d.* 1925), a childhood friend; they had two daughters.

In 1893 Jordan went to England, to take up the post of entomologist at the zoological museum at Tring which was being created by Lionel Rothschild. On arrival, Jordan found a vast collection of beetles, butterflies, and moths, all in the utmost confusion. By working far into the night, a habit he never lost, he reduced these to order in an incredibly short space of time, and as a result he found himself with just the array of material he needed for the study of the causes of variation and evolution. He was director of the Tring Museum from 1930 to 1939, and president of the Royal Entomological Society of London from 1920 to 1930; he was elected FRS in 1932.

Jordan was a prolific writer. By the end of 1903 he had published, either alone or jointly with Rothschild, profusely illustrated papers, to a total of more than 2500

pages. The best known were the *Revision of the Papilios of the Eastern Hemisphere* (1895), the *Monograph of Charaxes*, and the *Revision of the Sphingidae* (1903), all of which long remained standard works of reference. Jordan also found time to publish several papers of a more philosophical nature on such subjects as mechanical selection and mimicry, and a critique of the theory of orthogenesis as applied to Papilionidae by Eimer. As early as 1898 and before much was known of the laws of heredity, Jordan showed reproductive divergence not to be a factor in the evolution of species. All this was the result of his first ten years' work at Tring. Between 1903 and 1958 he published a further 420 papers, which were frequently interspersed with pointed reflections on their bearing on the problem of evolution. He deplored the amount of time taken up with descriptions of new genera and species, but knew it was a prerequisite for a sound classificatory basis for the study of evolution.

About 1900 Jordan took up the study of fleas, and with Charles Rothschild began to publish on the systematics of this much neglected order. Their work on the plague fleas of the genus *Xenopsylla* provides a perfect example of the importance of precise taxonomic work. Gradually they built up the immensely valuable collection of fleas which now belongs to the British Museum, and provided through their writings the knowledge of these insects, subsequently proved of such value to medical entomologists.

Beetles also claimed a large share of Jordan's interest. In particular, especially in later life, he was fascinated by the Anthribidae. He described 150 new genera and nearly two-thirds of the known species, but never achieved a system of classification which satisfied him.

In science Jordan was an internationalist. To help to break down the isolation of entomologists of different nationalities and interests, he founded in 1910 the International Congress of Entomology, remaining permanent secretary until 1948, when he was elected honorary life president. Jordan also unobtrusively rendered great service in the field of zoological nomenclature. Confusion and bitter argument prevailed, until at the congress at Monaco in 1913 he succeeded in reaching a compromise which subsequently proved most beneficial. Until 1950 he was on the Commission on Zoological Nomenclature, and was president for nineteen years.

Many of Jordan's major contributions to zoological thought appeared in scientific publications little consulted by zoologists not primarily concerned with entomology. His introductory note to the revision of the oriental swallowtails (1895) sets out clearly the taxonomic concepts and general principles which guided all his work. The soundness of his concepts was celebrated in a Festschrift to mark his ninety-fourth birthday (*Transactions of the Royal Entomological Society*, 107, 1955).

A rather shy man, Jordan was somewhat overshadowed by his surroundings at Tring, but colleagues quickly recognized his friendliness, helpfulness, humour, and his unqualified devotion to the pursuit of truth and the advancement of knowledge. His most incisive criticism never hurt.

Jordan was naturalized in 1911 and died in St Paul's Hospital, Hemel Hempstead, Hertfordshire, on 12 January 1959. N. D. RILEY, *rev.*

Sources N. D. Riley, *Memoirs FRS*, 6 (1960), 107–33 · W. T. Stearn, *The Natural History Museum at South Kensington: a history of the British Museum (Natural History), 1753–1980* (1981) · *CGPLA Eng. & Wales* (1959)
Likenesses photograph, repro. in Riley, *Memoirs FRS*, 107
Wealth at death £5634 1s. 4d.: probate, 6 March 1959, *CGPLA Eng. & Wales*

Jordan, Thomas (*c*.1614–1685), actor, poet, and playwright, was born possibly in London or Eynsham, in Oxfordshire, where a branch of the Jordan family held lands. His parentage is unknown, though he may have been the son of Samuel Jordan baptized on 9 November 1614 at St James's, Clerkenwell (*Harleian Society Registers*).

During the 1630s Jordan was a member of the King's Revels Company, which played at the Salisbury Court and Fortune theatres. Founded about 1629 by Richard Gunnell, the troupe was notable for its large number of boy actors. Some time between 1634 and 1636 Jordan played the role of Lepida, mother of the Roman empress, in Thomas Rawlins's *The Tragedy of Messallina* (1640). On 10 March 1635 he was one of twenty-eight players forbidden by the mayor's court to act within the city of Norwich. Jordan's first comedy, *Money is an Asse* (1668; reissued as *Wealth Out-Witted*, n.d.), which he claims to have written at the age of fifteen, was performed by a boy company, possibly the King's Revels, with Jordan in the part of Captain Penniless. He was one of six adult actors named in the entrance warnings in the anonymous Caroline play *The Waspe* (Lever). Jordan's theatrical background is much in evidence in his earliest publication, *Poeticall Varieties* (1637), a collection of love poems and elegies. The volume was dedicated to John Ford of Gray's Inn, cousin of the dramatist, and contains commendatory verses by the playwrights Thomas Heywood, Richard Brome, and Thomas Nabbes, and the actor Edward May.

The seventeen-month closure of the London theatres from May 1636 brought to an end Jordan's association with the King's Revels Company. On 23 August he performed in Thomas Bushell's royal entertainment staged to celebrate the completion of the renowned Enstone Marvels, a grotto incorporating elaborate water effects. Jordan's poem, 'composed, and spoken by the Author to the … King … in the person of Calliope', was written to complement *The Severall Speeches and Songs at the Presentment of Mr Bushells Rock* (1636), and survives in his Restoration print *Wit in a Wildernesse of Promiscuous Poesie* (n.d.).

Nothing is known about Jordan's activities in the late 1630s. He may have been attached to the Werbergh Street Theatre in Dublin, built by Sir Thomas Wentworth, lord deputy of Ireland. *The Royall Master* (1638), written for the Irish playhouse by its resident dramatist, James Shirley, contains a commendatory verse signed 'T. I.' (sig. A4r–v). The poet's conceit, 'I Like some petty Brooke scarse worth

a name', is similar to a number of other verses in which Jordan alludes to his surname. The lines:

> Thy Muse I honor'd, e're I knew by sight
> Thy person; oft I've seene with much delight
> Thy sweet composures

suggest a degree of familiarity with Shirley, but whether that friendship was fostered in London or Dublin remains uncertain. Jordan's 1640 miscellany, 'Sacred Poems' (Trinity College, Dublin, MS 433), dedicated to James Ussher, archbishop of Armagh and primate of all Ireland, lends weight to an Irish connection. However, there is no hint in Jordan's hyperbole of a personal relationship with the prelate. Ussher spent very little time in Dublin during this period, having retired to his palace at Drogheda early in 1636 ostensibly on financial grounds, though Wentworth suspected that the primate's disapproval of official religious policy was the real cause. Coupled with his hostility towards theatrical performance, he is unlikely to have encountered Jordan at the Werbergh Street Theatre. However, the poet may have admired Ussher from afar. Despite his lack of effective influence in the political arena prior to his involvement in the Long Parliament, Ussher was widely recognized as a scholar of considerable import. Moreover, his moderate Calvinist stance may have struck a chord with the poet. For example, less than a month before the outbreak of civil war Jordan attacked Archbishop Laud and the Arminian bishop Matthew Wren in his pamphlet *Rules to Know a Royall King* (1642). Jordan's connection with the Werbergh Street Theatre is an attractive possibility, but in the absence of further evidence a career on the Irish stage remains inconclusive.

Jordan contributed commendatory verses to *The Tragedy of Messallina* and Nathaniel Richards's *The Rebellion* (1640), both of which were entered in the Stationers' register in autumn 1639. By 1641 he was acting with the Red Bull–King's Company at their playhouse in Clerkenwell. His second comedy, *Youths Figaries*, was written for the troupe that year, when it was 'publikely Acted 19. days together, with extraordinary Applause' (published as *The Walks of Islington and Hogsdon*, 1657, a reference to the many taverns frequented in the course of the play). In 1642 Jordan, his wife, Susan, and their daughter Martha were living in Moullins Rents in Shoe Lane in the parish of St Andrew, Holborn (GL, MS 6667/2, baptismal entry dated 29 April). Phelps suggested that six other children mentioned in the records of St Bride's, Fleet Street, the parish of the Salisbury Court Theatre, might also be the poet's offspring (Phelps, 431–3; GL, MS 6536).

Despite his commitment to 'lay my life down' in defence of the king, there is no evidence that Jordan played an active military role during the civil war, but he fervently supported the royalist cause through the pen. For example, between July and November 1642 he published several political tracts, including the satirical pamphlet *A Diurnall of Dangers*, which pokes fun at the emerging news books. Between 1641 and 1668 he reissued four collections of verse, a ballad entitled *The Anarchie* (published twice in 1648), and two plays. His verse miscellany *Pictures of Passions* was issued twice in 1641. *Poeticall Varieties* reappeared in 1646 under the title *Loves Dialect*, presented on this occasion to Henry Coggaine, 'Master Comptroller of his Majesties Mint in the *Tower of London*'. Jordan's Restoration miscellany, *A Royal Arbor of Loyal Poesie* (1663), was reissued no fewer than five times. The whole volume reappeared twice under the same title (n.d. and 1664) and once as *A Rosary of Rarities* (n.d.). The first part ('Poems') was issued separately as *A Nursery of Novelties* (n.d.) and the second ('Songs') as *Musick and Poetry, Mixed in Variety of Songs, and Poems* (n.d.). Jordan presented copies of his printed works to several dedicatees, the majority of whom were strangers to him. By leaving the dedication blank he was able to insert an alternative name. For example, copies of *Wit in a Wildernesse* were dedicated to at least five different individuals, George Griffith, bishop of St Asaph, Thomas Turner, dean of Canterbury, Solomon Seabright, Robert Boyle, and Sir Thomas Hussey.

In the late 1640s Jordan plagiarized the works of two of his contemporaries. In 1646 he reissued under his own name *Divine Raptures*, a collection of religious verse by the minor poet James Day, first published in 1637 as *A New Spring of Divine Poetrie*. Three years later he published *Death Dis-Sected*, this time the work of the puritan clergyman Edward Buckler (1610–1706). The collection was published originally in 1640 under the title *A Buckler Against the Fear of Death*.

In 1654 his only surviving masque, 'Cupid his Coronation' (Bodl. Oxf., MS Rawl. B165, fols. 107–13), was presented 'with good Approbation at the Spittle diverse tymes by Masters and yong Ladies that were theyre scholers'. The educational institution in question was probably Christ's Hospital, the foundling school near St Paul's. Heavily revised and expanded, the masque was printed in 1657 as *Fancy's Festivals*. During the 1650s Jordan compiled a manuscript of royalist verse with music, containing a mixture of thirty-four political medleys and ballads, love songs, drinking songs, and civic eclogues (Nottingham University Library, MS PwV 18), which substantially predates the analogous 1685 anthology of political verse, *A Choice Collection of 180 Loyal Songs*. Several of the lyrics in the John Gamble manuscript (New York Public Library, Drexel MS 4257, dated 1659), a collection of over 300 songs composed during the Caroline and Commonwealth periods, are also in Jordan's hand.

The surviving epilogue to Jordan's lost romance, *Love hath Found his Eyes*, suggests that the work might have been performed at the Red Bull in the 1640s, despite the parliamentary ban on unlawful acting (1642–60). In September 1655 several actors, including one Thomas Jay, alias Thomas Jordan, were arrested in a raid on the playhouse. This notorious event was commemorated in a ballad published in *Sportive Wit* (1656, sigs. Ff4*v*–5*r*). There is no record of *Youths Figaries* being performed at the Red Bull during the interregnum, but the play must have been revised after 1641 for there is a reference in act III, scene iii, to the Quaker movement (*The Walks of Islington and Hogsdon*, sig. E3*v*). The play was reissued in 1663 as *Tricks of Youth*. The verse of dedication in the latter implies that the comedy was performed in 1661, though a second, dated

copy of the 'Prologue to the King', printed in *A Royal Arbor*, suggests that the play might even have been staged the previous year. Jordan is not included among the Restoration list of 'gentlemen Actors of the Red Bull', but it is clear from his printed works that his association with the playhouse continued for some time. *A Royal Arbor of Loyal Poesie* (1663, 20–24) contains a number of verses written for the Red Bull, including a prologue 'to introduce the first Woman that came to act on the Stage' in a production of Shakespeare's *Othello*.

Jordan is remembered chiefly for his activities as City poet and pageant writer. His earliest civic verse, dating from the late 1650s, includes an eclogue in four parts for the lord mayor, Sir Thomas Allen, and a jig, *The Cheaters Cheated*, composed for the sheriffs of London (*A Royal Arbor*, 29–55). In spring 1660 Jordan wrote speeches and songs for at least five of the great livery company feasts given in honour of General Monck: Drapers (28 March), Skinners (4 April), Goldsmiths (10 April), Vintners (12 April), and Fishmongers (13 April). Between 1671 and 1684 he was responsible for devising the lord mayor's show, adapting each to the changing political situation. *Londons Glory* (1680), for example, stresses the dangers of popery. But in the main his civic entertainments are imbued with 'moderation and peace, coupled with Protestantism, patriotism, the promotion of trade, and a socially inclusive vision in which the city and its government have an important role in the nation' (Owen, 299).

Jordan died intestate, but a letter of administration issued in April 1685 in the prerogative court at Canterbury almost certainly pertains to the poet (PRO, PROB 6/61, fol. 45*v*). He was buried on 17 April 1685 in the parish of St Michael, Wood Street, where he had been residing since July 1682 with his daughter and son-in-law, Mary and Thomas Yeardley (GL, MS 6532; PRO, PROB 5/3909/1–6). According to the probate inventory submitted by his daughter to the prerogative court, his possessions were valued at £219 1*s*. 6*d*., and included various items of furniture and bedding, clothing, books, three mourning rings, a watch, a picture of a coat of arms, and £201 10*s*. 6*d*. in cash.

LYNN HULSE

Sources L. Hulse, 'Cavalier songs: Thomas Jordan's collection' • L. Hulse, '"Musick and poetry, mixed": Thomas Jordan's manuscript collection', *Early Music*, 24/1 (1996), 7–26 • W. H. Phelps, 'Thomas Jordan and his family', *N&Q*, 224 (1979), 431–3 • Harleian Society Registers, 9 (1884), 70 • J. W. Lever, ed., *The wasp* (1976) • A. Stevenson, 'James Shirley and the actors at the first Irish theatre', *Modern Philology*, 40 (1942), 155–7 • GL, MSS 6667/2, 6536, 6532 • P. Dobell, 'A catalogue of a collection of poetical, dramatic and other manuscripts', *The Oldenburgh House Bulletin*, no. 3 (1934) • S. J. Owen, *Restoration theatre and crisis* (1996) • PRO, PROB 6/61, fol. 45*v*; PROB 5/3909/1–6

Archives Bodl. Oxf., MSS Rawl. • Harvard U., Houghton L., Divine Poesie, MS Eng. 159 • NYPL, Drexel collection, Drexel MS 4257 • TCD, Ussher MSS • U. Nott., Portland collection, MS PwV 18

Wealth at death £219 1*s*. 6*d*.: inventory, PRO, PROB 5/3909/1–6

Jordan, Thomas Brown (1807–1890), engineer, was born at Bristol on 24 October 1807, the son of a Quaker engineer, Thomas Jordan. He began life as an artist, moving in his early twenties to Falmouth where he became drawing master to Barclay, son of Robert Were *Fox. He participated in Fox's magnetic and physical researches, and in his house met many of the leading scientists of the day. Fox encouraged his mechanical bent and by 1836 an exhibition of inventions held at the Royal Cornwall Polytechnic Society in Falmouth (of which Jordan became secretary in 1835) included a 'galvano-motive' engine constructed by him. He set up as an instrument maker, improving the miners' dial, and constructing for Admiral Beaufort the portable magnetometers which Fox had designed in 1834 and which were by that time in demand for naval scientific expeditions. Jordan became interested in the new art of photography, and in 1839 he showed the Polytechnic Society his photographically recording barometer, and a photographic sunshine recorder. His pioneering work on the application of photography to meteorology was acknowledged by Charles Wheatstone and Sir John Herschel, whose own ideas on this subject were still taking shape.

Jordan married Sarah Dunn in 1837, a marriage that may have taken him out of the Quaker community, and they raised eleven children. In 1840 Sir Henry De la Beche, who had met Jordan when he was engaged on the geological survey of Cornwall, secured his appointment in London as the first keeper of mining records. Jordan's interest in electrometallurgy developed during this period; he produced some electrotype prints and in 1841 made an egg-cup of electro-deposited copper, plated with silver outside and gold inside, which was considered a model of workmanship. He resigned from the post of keeper of mining records in 1845, having devised a method of carving by machinery, which he patented in February that year, which replicated plaster originals in wood or stone. He set up a factory at Lambeth, where he manufactured much of the carving destined for the new House of Lords. He was elected to the Royal Society of Arts in 1847 and in June of that year received for his invention the society's Isis medal, which was presented by Prince Albert. The machinery was also displayed at the Great Exhibition of 1851. Later, first in Manchester and then in Glasgow, he collaborated with various other engineers, designing and constructing rock drills and other mining machinery. At Glasgow he also devised and patented machinery for the production of school slates.

By 1868 Jordan was back in London, trading with his sons as mechanical and mining engineers and manufacturers of machinery, with a City office and works in south-east London and at Wigan. His last invention, patented in 1877, was a portable machine for boring blast-holes in rock. To the end of his life he retained an interest in meteorology; in 1889 he described to the Meteorological Society his new recorder which provided an index of cloudiness by registering light from each quarter of the sky, on every hour throughout a week. One of his sons, Thomas Rowland Jordan, continued the machinery business. Another, James B. Jordan, was clerk of mineral statistics at the Home Office; he also had an interest in meteorology, proposing in 1885 an improved version of his father's sunshine recorder. Jordan died at Carlyle Villa, St John's Wood Road, Bournemouth, on 31 May 1890. His wife survived him.

ANITA MCCONNELL

Sources *The Times* (19 June 1890), 6f · *Iron*, 35 (20 June 1890), 541 · Boase & Courtney, *Bibl. Corn.*, 1.280, 3.1250 · *Barclay Fox's journal*, ed. R. L. Brett (1979) · T. B. Jordan, 'On carving by machinery', *Transactions of the Society of Arts*, suppl. (1852), 124–36 · C. G. Scott, 'T. B. Jordan's photographic recording instruments', *History of Photography*, 15 (1991), 241–2 · A. McConnell, 'Nineteenth century geomagnetic instruments and their makers', *Nineteenth-century scientific instruments and their makers* [Amsterdam, 1984], ed. P. R. de Clercq (1985) · trade directories, 1840–90 · patents, 1844–77 · RSA · DNB · d. cert.

Jordan, William (*fl.* 1611), scribe, is supposed to have been the author of the Cornish language mystery play *Gwreans an bys, or, The Creacion of the World with Noye's Fludde*. Scholars are uncertain, however, whether he was actually the author of this work or merely the transcriber of an existing text. At the end of the earliest manuscript of the play (Bodl. Oxf., MS 219) it is stated that it was written by William Jordan on 12 August 1611. The most detailed consideration of this question has been by Neuss, who dates the play later than 1500 (Neuss, lxxiv) on the basis of language and a possible link to the re-establishment of Catholicism under Mary after 1553. Others have suggested a pre-Reformation date of about 1530 because of the presence of Roman Catholic doctrinal elements such as limbo. Neuss sees the 1611 version as a third-generation copy, perhaps the start of a commonplace book by someone seeking to preserve a record of the declining Cornish language. This would explain why it was apparently deposited in the Bodleian Library within four years of this date. The earliest discernible version of the play included directions to the actors. A later version was produced for use as prompt-book, with notes on what props had to be ready several lines ahead of the scene in which they were required. Neuss suggests that the 1611 version was transcribed from the prompt-book by someone unable to distinguish between these different kinds of stage directions, strongly suggesting that Jordan was not himself involved in mystery play production.

Virtually nothing is known of William Jordan himself apart from the fact that he was said to come from Helston in Cornwall. The family seat was said by Polsue to have been at Higher Trelill, in Wendron parish. He may be the William Geordaine baptized at Redruth on 26 February 1576, son of John. John may be the John Jordyn mentioned in the 1569 muster-roll in Penryn borough. There could be an intriguing link to Glasney College, which was in Penryn. The college, suppressed in 1549, is considered on internal evidence to be where the late medieval Cornish dramas were composed, and could have provided the intellectual milieu in which an earlier version of *Gwreans an bys* was written.

There are several later manuscript transcriptions of the Bodleian text, including John Keigwin's 1693 translation (Bodl. Oxf., MS Corn. e.2). A botched version of this was printed by Davies Gilbert in 1827, with many typographical errors. A new edition and translation by Stokes was published to remedy this in 1864. Neuss's critical edition and translation is the most recent. Jenner suggested that the play was in fact published between 1642 and 1662, an opinion based on a list of books published 'in Welsh' in Bagford's collections for a history of printing (BL, Lansdowne 808). However, no printed copy from this period is known to exist. Whether Jordan was or was not the author of the work it is to him that its survival is certainly owed as one of the rare examples of Cornish language drama. Scholars of the language and literature of Cornwall are thus forever in his debt.   MATTHEW SPRIGGS

Sources P. Neuss, *The creacion of the world: a critical edition and translation* (1983), lxiv–lxxxix · *Gwreans an bys. The creation of the world*, ed. and trans. W. Stokes (1864) · *The creation of the world, with Noah's flood: written in Cornish in the year 1611*, ed. D. Gilbert, trans. J. Keigwin (1827) · H. Jenner, 'The Cornish language', *Transactions of the Philological Society* (1873–4), 176–7 · J. Polsue, *A complete parochial history of the county of Cornwall*, 4 (1872), 312 · parish registers, Redruth, Cornwall RO · H. L. Douch, ed., *The Cornwall muster roll of 1569* (1984), 77 · M. Harris, ed., *The Cornish ordinalia* (1969), ix

Jorden, Edward (*d.* 1632), physician and chemist, was born at High Halden, Kent, the younger son of Edward Jorden, of Cranbrook, Kent. He studied at Oxford, probably at Hart Hall, but left the university without apparently taking a degree. Jorden continued his studies at Peterhouse College, Cambridge, where he obtained his BA in 1583 and MA in 1586. He then travelled to Padua, where he was awarded an MD in 1591. On his return he practised in London, and became a licentiate of the College of Physicians on 7 November 1595, and a fellow on 22 December 1597.

In 1602 Jorden testified at the trial of Elizabeth Jackson, who was accused of bewitching Mary Glover. Jorden argued unsuccessfully that Glover's symptoms had natural, rather than supernatural, causes. Following the trial Jorden published *A Briefe Discourse of a Disease called the Suffocation of the Mother* (1603), in which he claimed that persons thought to be possessed by evil spirits were more likely to be suffering from hysteria. Three years after the Jackson trial, in 1605, Jorden testified in the case of Anne Gunter, who was also believed to be possessed.

Jorden was known and respected by James I, and when Jorden moved from London to Bath it was he who treated Queen Anne on her visits to the city. He also tried, unsuccessfully, to persuade James to give him a monopoly on the profits of alum. Jorden's keen interest in chemistry led him to write *A Discourse of Natural Bathes and Mineral Waters* (1631), which explored the causes of the growth of minerals and the heating of mineral waters. The book, which ran to five editions, shows Jorden to have been intelligent and widely read. In his preface to the third edition of the *Discourse* (1669), Thomas Guidott claimed that Jorden was 'a learned, candid, and sober physician'. This appears to be a just assessment.

Edward Jorden married the daughter of a Mr Jordan. The couple had five children, one of whom failed to survive infancy. Their eldest daughter, Elizabeth, married Thomas Burford, a Bath apothecary, who later became mayor of the city. Jorden, who suffered from the stone and gout, died in Bath on 7 January 1632, and was buried in the abbey church. His rejection of the supernatural as a cause in nature, and his work as a chemist, entitle him to be considered a physician and natural philosopher of note.

J. F. PAYNE, *rev.* MICHAEL BEVAN

Sources T. Guidott, 'Preface', in E. Jorden, *A discourse of natural bathes and mineral waters*, 3rd edn (1669) · M. Macdonald, ed., *Witchcraft and hysteria in Elizabethan London: Edward Jorden and the Mary Glover case* (1990) · A. Debus, 'Edward Jorden and the fermentation of metals: an iatrochemical study of terrestrial phenomena', *Towards a history of geology*, ed. C. J. Schneer (1969) · Venn, *Alum. Cant.* · Wood, *Ath. Oxon.* · K. Thomas, *Religion and the decline of magic* (1971)

Jorden, William (1685–1739), college teacher, was born and baptized on 19 November 1685 at Newland, Gloucestershire; his mother, Catherine Jorden (*d.* 1685), died in childbirth. His father, the Revd Humphrey Jorden (*b.* 1651/2, *d.* in or after 1715), lecturer of Newland, was of a Staffordshire family. Jorden matriculated from Corpus Christi College, Oxford, on 28 March 1702, but migrated to his father's old college, Pembroke, where he was founder's kin, and graduated BA in 1705, before proceeding MA in 1708, and BD in 1728. A fellow of the college, he served as bursar, chaplain, and vicegerent, but he is now remembered only as Samuel Johnson's tutor. Johnson disparaged Jorden's scholarship and absented himself from lectures; it was to Jorden that Johnson admitted he had been sliding in Christ Church meadow instead of attending his lectures. Johnson none the less loved and respected the man. 'Whenever (said he) a young man becomes Jorden's pupil, he becomes his son' (Boswell, *Life*, 1.61). Johnson's first published poem, a Latin version of Pope's *Messiah*, was written as an exercise for Jorden in the Christmas vacation of 1728.

On 14 November 1729 Jorden was presented to the rectory of Standon, Staffordshire, by William Vyse (1709–1770), his pupil and Johnson's friend. He resigned Standon on 18 October 1733, having been instituted to the vicarage of nearby Seighford on 1 December 1731. He died, unmarried, at Seighford in January 1739 and was buried there on 17 January that year.   JAMES SAMBROOK

Sources Boswell, *Life*, 1.59, 61, 79, 272; 2.537 · D. Macleane, *A history of Pembroke College, Oxford*, OHS, 33 (1897), 178, 331–4, 339, 393 · A. L. Reade, *Johnsonian gleanings*, 5 (privately printed, London, 1928), 123–9 · Foster, *Alum. Oxon., 1500–1714* · parish register, Newland, 19 Nov 1685 [baptism] · parish register, Newland, 20 Nov 1685 [burial] · *Johnsonian miscellanies*, ed. G. B. Hill, 1 (1897), 164, 170, 362 · *The works of Samuel Johnson, together with his life*, ed. J. Hawkins, 11 vols. (1787), vol. 1, p. 9 · E. Salt, *The history of Standon* (1888), 156 · W. M. Warlow, *A history of the charities of William Jones at Monmouth and Newland* (1899), 281–2 · *GM*, 1st ser., 1 (1731), 502 · *Remarks and collections of Thomas Hearne*, ed. C. E. Doble and others, 10, OHS, 67 (1915), 108 · parish register, Seighford, 17 Jan 1739 [burial]

Jortin, John (1698–1770), ecclesiastical historian and literary critic, was born on 23 October 1698 in the parish of St Giles-in-the-Fields, London, the son of a French Huguenot, **Renatus Jortin** (*d.* 1707), government official, who had been educated at Saumur, and Martha, daughter of the Revd Daniel Rogers of Haversham, Buckinghamshire. His father, a refugee from the persecutions of Louis XIV who had settled in England in 1687, was talented and ambitious, and became a gentleman of the privy chamber to William III in 1691. He was in turn secretary to three admirals—Lord Orford, Sir George Rooke, and Sir Cloudesley Shovell—with the last of whom he perished when the *Association* ran aground off the Isles of Scilly on 22 October 1707. Renatus Jortin had changed the spelling of his surname to Jordain; his wife reverted to the original spelling shortly after his death. The family spoke French at home.

John Jortin was educated at Charterhouse School, and was admitted a pensioner at Jesus College, Cambridge, on 16 May 1715. An able mathematician, he studied under Saunderson, the celebrated professor of geometry. It was as an undergraduate at Jesus that he was given his first literary commission: his tutor, Styan Thirlby, had him produce a translation of Eustathius for the notes to Pope's translation of Homer. Jortin never met Pope, who nevertheless made good use of Jortin's anonymous work. Jortin graduated BA in January 1719, was elected fellow of Jesus College on 9 October 1721, and graduated MA in 1722; in that year he was moderator, and in 1723 taxator, to the university. He was ordained deacon by Bishop Kennett on 22 September 1723 and priest by Bishop Green on 24 June 1724. In January 1726 he was presented to the college living of Swavesey, Cambridgeshire, which he held with his fellowship and which he vacated on his marriage, on 15 February 1728, to Ann Chibnall (d. 1778) of Newport Pagnell. They had two children: a son, Rogers (1731/2–1795), of Lincoln's Inn, who practised at the court of the exchequer; and a daughter, Martha (1730/31–1817), who married the Revd Samuel Darby—like his father-in-law a former fellow of Jesus College, Cambridge.

Having resigned his living on 1 February 1731 Jortin was reader and preacher at a chapel of ease in New Street, in his native parish of St Giles-in-the-Fields. The earl of Winchilsea presented him to the living of Eastwell, in Kent, in 1737, which he was quickly obliged to resign on grounds of ill health. Zachary Pearce, rector of St Martin-in-the-Fields, secured him (20 March 1747) the preachership at a chapel of ease in Oxenden Street, on which he resigned the chapel in New Street. Thomas Herring, archbishop of Canterbury, had been deeply impressed by the consecration sermon preached by Jortin at Kensington church on 21 February 1748 on the occasion of Pearce's appointment to the see of Bangor; it was subsequently published on Herring's orders. Herring, acting alongside Bishop Sherlock of London, procured the Boyle lectureship for Jortin from the earl of Burlington in 1749. Earlier, while archbishop of York, Herring had sought a living for him in the north, which Jortin had not wished to accept; Herring was also unsuccessful when he later sought the mastership of Charterhouse for Jortin, just as when earlier seeking the librarianship to Queen Caroline for him. Herring presented him to the rectory of St Dunstan-in-the-East in 1751 and conferred a Lambeth degree of DD on him in 1755. The living of St Dunstan's had been offered to Jortin at a feast for the sons of the clergy at which he had failed to retrieve his hat, allowing him to tell his fellow diners 'I have lost my hat; but I have got a living' (Nichols, *Lit. anecdotes*, 6.561). He resigned his chapel in Oxenden Street in 1760 and was appointed chaplain to his friend Thomas Osbaldeston, bishop of London, on 10 March 1762. Osbaldeston gave him the prebendal stall of Harleston, in St Paul's Cathedral, and the vicarage of Kensington, which he held with St Dunstan's. Jortin declined the living of St James's, Piccadilly, in November 1763 and was made archdeacon of London in April 1764.

As his career attests Jortin was always more interested in writing than in seeking out preferment; he noted that 'Habits, titles, and dignities, are visible signs of invisible merits' (J. Jortin, *Tracts*, 2 vols., 1790, 2.533). His first publication took the form of some Latin hexameters that he contributed to the Cambridge collection of verses on the death of George I, and he published a small volume of elegant verse in Latin: *Lusus poetici* (1723). He continued to enjoy the discipline of writing Latin verse, and a delightful *Epitaphium felis* was posthumously published in his son's edition of Jortin's *Tracts, Theological, Critical and Miscellaneous* in 1790. Jortin was a committed man of letters and started a magazine, *Miscellaneous Observations upon Authors, Ancient and Modern*, in 1731. It came to an end in 1732 but was republished in 1732–4, and subsequently continued in a Latin translation in Amsterdam. His most significant work for *Miscellaneous Observations* took the form of critical observations on the poetry of Milton and Spenser, both of whom he greatly admired; he published *Remarks on Spenser*, to which he appended some observations on Milton, largely concerned with the poet's sources, in 1734. *Four Sermons* appeared in print in 1730, and in 1746 they were considerably expanded as *Discourses Concerning the Truth of the Christian Religion*. These laid out the grounds for Christian belief by presenting a providential reading of the time of Christ's appearance, the miraculous propagation of the faith by unlettered followers, and the assuredly divine testimony of the scriptures—all of which were typical resources for eighteenth-century apologetic, and were presented by Jortin with eloquent and economic conviction.

By far Jortin's most important contribution to learning began to appear in 1751: his *Remarks on Ecclesiastical History* amounted to five volumes, concluding with two posthumous volumes in 1773. They constitute the most significant Anglican ecclesiastical history of the eighteenth century and were written from a markedly latitudinarian perspective (Jortin had given up reading the Athanasian creed in the 1730s). Edward Gibbon treated them and their author with considerable respect; he noted that Jortin had treated the apologetically sensitive Arian controversy 'with learning, candour, and ingenuity' and he described him as 'a correct and liberal scholar' (E. Gibbon, *The History of the Decline and Fall of the Roman Empire*, ed. D. Womersley, 3 vols., 1994, 1.779 n. 45; 2.28 n. 25). Jortin saw the purpose of the work as establishing evidence for the Christian religion, especially in support of convincing arguments for the interposition of providence in both its establishment and its preservation. Many of his readings of the early Christian centuries (as in his treatment of the demoniacs and the date of the cessation of miracles) were those of advanced Anglicans, and he was a firm critic of 'tradition' in the scholarly study of ecclesiastical history. Indeed his criticism of Roman Catholicism was such that he argued that it was only the direct supervision entailed by divine providence that had preserved Christianity up to the era of the Reformation—at which point, in 1517, his history ended. Something of his attitude to Roman Catholic humanism and to the work of the reformers can be discerned in his two-volume *Life of Erasmus*, which appeared between 1758 and 1760—a work much indebted to Jean Le Clerc's studies on the same subject; Jortin, a fellow product of the Huguenot diaspora, was a great admirer of Le Clerc and his writings. Jortin's belief in the apologetic significance of ecclesiastical history formed the basis of three of the four charges that he delivered to his clergy as archdeacon of London between 1765 and 1770; the first, significantly, had been delivered on the revealing subject of 'Christianity, the preserver and supporter of literature'. Jortin was in many ways a late representative of Christian humanism, as well as an active citizen in the protestant republic of letters.

Jortin was a gifted musician (he played the harpsichord) and this informed his letter *Concerning the Music of the Ancients*, which was included in Charles Avison's *Essay on Musical Expression* (1753). Musical analogies are to be found in several of his writings, as in his observation in the *Discourses* that 'The understandings of men are as the chords of musical instruments: when a string sounds, the strings which are unisons to it, if within proper distance, will vibrate' (J. Jortin, *Discourses*, 1746, vi–vii). He contributed miscellaneous observations on Archbishop Tillotson's sermons to Thomas Birch's *Life of Tillotson* (1752); they comprise a late latitudinarian defence of the theology of a latitudinarian hero. His classical preoccupations remained a constant part of his literary endeavours, and he helped to see through the press in 1763 the edition of Euripides' *Supplices mulieres* made by Jeremiah Markland, a fellow Cambridge scholar; his own critical remarks on Virgil, a confirmed favourite, appeared in Donaldson's *Miscellanea Virgiliana* in 1825.

The generally happy reception of Jortin's writings was contradicted by only one instance, the controversy that raged over the last of the *Six Dissertations upon Different Subjects* (1755). The dissertations were concerned with theological, moral, and historical topics, and the sixth described the treatment of the state of the dead by Homer and Virgil. This subject fascinated Jortin, and he sermonized on the theme of death and eternal life several times, rebutting the heresy of mortalism in a sermon that he preached in the 1750s, a decade which saw a semi-revival of the doctrine spearheaded by his Cambridge friend Edmund Law. Jortin's examination of Virgil contradicted the readings of the *Aeneid* made by Warburton, for whom he had acted as an assistant at Lincoln's Inn between 1747 and 1750. Richard Hurd, Warburton's closest disciple, therefore chose to attack Jortin as an ingrate in a seventh dissertation, richly entitled *On the Delicacy of Friendship*.

This met with Warburton's approval, and he characteristically wrote to Hurd that 'next to the pleasure of seeing myself so finely praised, is the satisfaction I take in seeing Jortin mortified' (Hurd, 21 Dec 1755). The distance between the former benefactor and his now disgraced assistant is all too apparent in a comment that Warburton made in a subsequent letter to Hurd: 'Jortin is himself as vain as he is dirty, to imagine I am obliged to him for holding his hand' (ibid., 30 Dec 1755). This was, however, a controversy that benefited Jortin more than it undermined him. As he noted in some observations that he jotted down for himself, 'I have examined "The State of the Dead, as described by Homer and Virgil," and upon that Dissertation I am willing to stake all the little credit that I have as a critic and philosopher' (J. Jortin, *Tracts*, 1790, 2.444).

Jortin, who had never enjoyed good health, died of bronchitis in Kensington rectory on 5 September 1770. He was buried, following his instructions, in the new churchyard in Kensington. His sermons were widely praised during his lifetime but he chose not to publish them, saying to an interested clerical friend 'They shall sleep till I sleep' (Nichols, *Lit. anecdotes*, 6.570). He had a taste for the laconic statement, and it is appropriate that his last words, spoken to a nurse who had offered him refreshment, were 'No; I have had enough of every thing!' (ibid.). An edition of his sermons, in seven volumes, the last of which also printed his archidiaconal charges for the first time, appeared in 1771 and 1772. Jortin's lively style and frame of mind can be summed up in a terse statement from a commonplace book that his son published in the *Tracts*: 'The man who is not *intelligible* is not *intelligent*. You may depend upon this, as upon a rule which will never deceive you' (J. Jortin, *Tracts*, 1790, 2.529). Jortin was a considerable, if quietly celebrated, hero of the later Cambridge latitudinarians, and memoirs of him appeared from the pens of Ralph Heathcote in 1784 (originally an entry in the *Biographical Dictionary*, which was then prefixed to an edition of Jortin's sermons in 1787), and of John Disney, who praised his forthrightness, in 1792. Disney assumed that as a non-subscriber and one who had never written explicitly on the precise nature of Christ's divinity Jortin was a Socinian, a claim that had been made as early as 1773 in the *Gentleman's Magazine* (GM, 43.388). Heathcote ably conveyed Jortin's personality and the way in which it inflected his writings when he wrote of him that 'Besides great integrity, great humanity, and other qualities which make men amiable as well as useful, this learned and excellent person was of a very pleasant and facetious turn, as his writings abundantly shew' (Heathcote, 1.xi–xii). The popularity of the sermons was further attested in their distillation by J. Burden as *Subjects of religion, illustrated in extracts from the sermons of the late Doctor Jortin: to which are added occasional prayers* (Salisbury, 1792). Jortin's critique of Roman Catholicism was praised by William Trollope in an edition of *Remarks* in 1846, to which he prefixed a short life of the author. Jortin's writings enjoyed a considerable afterlife in the closing decades of the eighteenth century before falling into undeserved obscurity in the mid-nineteenth century; they offer an attractive insight into the workings of the literary and religious culture of the eighteenth century.

B. W. YOUNG

Sources Nichols, *Lit. anecdotes*, 6.550–77 · R. Heathcote, 'An account of the life and writings of Dr Jortin', in J. Jortin, *Sermons on different subjects*, ed. R. Jortin, 1 (1787), i–xvi · R. Jortin, advertisement, in J. Jortin, *Tracts, theological, critical and miscellaneous*, 1 (1790), v–xxii · J. Disney, *Memoirs of the life and writings of John Jortin* (1792) · [W. Warburton], *Letters from a late eminent prelate to one of his friends*, ed. R. Hurd, 3rd edn (1809) · W. Trollope, 'A brief account of the life and writings of the author', in J. Jortin, *Remarks on ecclesiastical history*, 2nd edn, ed. W. Trollope, 2 vols. (1846), vol. 1, pp. xxv–xxviii · *GM*, 1st ser., 43 (1773), 387–8; 54 (1784), 826 · W. Whiston, *Memoirs of the life and writings of Mr William Whiston: containing memoirs of several of his friends also*, 2nd edn, 2 vols. (1753) · J. Gascoigne, *Cambridge in the age of the Enlightenment* (1989) · *DNB*
Archives BL, letters to Thomas Birch, Add. MS 4311
Likenesses A. Smith, line engraving, pubd 1805 (after R. Crosse), BM · J. Hall, line engraving (after E. Penny), BM, NPG; repro. in Jortin, *Tracts* · oils, Jesus College, Cambridge

Jortin, Renatus (d. 1707). See under Jortin, John (1698–1770).

Jorz [Joyce], **Thomas** (c.1260–1310), cardinal, possibly identifiable with the figure known as Thomas Anglicanus, is of obscure origins. One suggestion is that he came of good family in London, although perhaps of Welsh descent. But it could be that he originated in Nottinghamshire, where early in Edward III's reign a William Jorz was joint holder of half a knight's fee at Carlton and a Robert Jorz acted as coroner. He was one of six brothers who became Dominicans, two of whom, Walter *Jorz and Roland, succeeded one another as bishop of Armagh (r. 1307–11 and 1312–22 respectively).

Quite when Thomas Jorz joined the Oxford Dominicans is not known, but he preached in Oxford on 4 February and 16 December 1291, and on the first Sunday in Advent in the following year he delivered the *sermo communis*. It was probably also in 1291 that he was incorporated DTh. Prior of the convent in 1294, he was still in office in 1297 at the time of his election as prior provincial of the order in England. As diffinitor of the English order Jorz was granted safe conduct to attend the general chapters at Strasbourg in 1295, and at Marseilles in 1300. Before leaving for Strasbourg he was sworn of the king's council, together with another Dominican, William of Hotham, but the chapter was abandoned owing to the death of the master-general. On 1 January 1304 Jorz had safe conduct to go to Rome for two years on the order's affairs and on the 'secret business' of Edward I. In the first year of his absence he attended the chapter that met at Toulouse. Clement V created him cardinal-priest of Santa Sabina on 15 December 1305, and four years later Jorz was granted an extension to his licence, dating from the previous pontificate, which enabled him to hold benefices *in commendam* to the value of 1000 marks. Among those so held were the abbacy of Acquapendente (26 March 1309) and a canonry of Salisbury with the prebend of Grantham Australis. The latter he received on the nomination of Cardinal Ruffati, who surrendered it on becoming dean of Salisbury in 1308. In the same month that Jorz became nominal abbot

he received a pension of 100 marks for expediting the king's business at Avignon.

As prior provincial Jorz was zealous in taking advantage of the canon *Super cathedram*, enabling friars to secure licences to preach and to hear confessions in the dioceses. Archbishop Robert Winchelsey alleged that the friars were guilty of serious abuses by granting absolution in cases reserved to diocesan bishops. In his courteous reply to the archbishop, dated 8 November 1297, Jorz detailed the steps he had taken to correct the matters brought to his attention. Even before the archbishop's letter, he claims, he had begun of his own accord to caution the brethren concerning the various points at issue, sending letters throughout England and Wales, and commissioning the visitors to see that they achieved a salutary effect in the individual priories. He did, however, suggest that not all complaints from the lower clergy were to be believed! The unease on this score was widespread and John Dalderby, bishop of Lincoln, alarmed by the number of friars being presented, became irritated with Jorz, who apparently claimed to make such presentations throughout the diocese, rather than, as in the case of the Oxford convent, just for the Oxford archdeaconry. The bishop restricted the numbers to fifty from each of the Franciscan and Dominican orders.

A notable conflict of another kind erupted in 1301 between the dean and chapter of Exeter and the Dominican convent there over the burial of a knight, Henry Ralegh. The chapter, claiming that before burial in the convent a corpse should be presented at first mass in the cathedral, sent two canons, one of them Walter Stapledon (a future bishop of Exeter), to secure the body. In the event it was forcefully removed by the executors and friends, whereupon the Dominicans refused to readmit it. In February of the following year Jorz appeared as one of the arbiters for the friars. An agreement was reached, but the conflict continued. Jorz disputed the alleged custom, and argued that unless it had the consent of the master of the order and general chapter it was contrary to canonical legislation. The Dominicans, on the grounds that Stapledon had acted to their detriment and was thereby excommunicate, protested against his inception as doctor of civil and canon law at Oxford. The Oxford chancellor urged that peace be made with Cardinal Jorz and with Dalderby, the bishop of Lincoln, within whose diocese the university lay. Ill feeling was short-lived, for in 1308 Stapledon occurs as the cardinal's chaplain.

Like many other Dominicans, Jorz was pressed into royal service. He became confessor to Edward I who, in October 1305, sent him to Lyons with Henry de Lacy, Hugh Despenser, and others to treat with the newly elected Clement V. Subsequently he acted for Edward I and Edward II at the curia where, urged on by Bishop Richard Swinfield, he was active in urging the canonization of Thomas of Hereford, a former bishop of Hereford (r. 1275–82), and, at Edward I's request, that of Robert Grosseteste, as well as the promotion of John Ros DCL, subsequently bishop of Carlisle. For his services Edward II on 4 March

1309 granted him a pension of 100 marks. Jorz died at Grenoble on 13 December 1310 while on a mission as papal envoy to the emperor, Heinrich VII, and was buried in the choir of the Dominican church in Oxford.

Various works have been attributed to Jorz by Bale and others, mostly inaccurately. He did compose a *Traité de la pauvreté de Jésus Christ*, but this, like his other works, has been lost, with the exception of elements of a commentary on the first book of the *Sentences*—identified by Grabmann—in which he argues against Duns Scotus, among others, in support of Thomist opinions then current among the Oxford Dominicans. The *Commentary on 27 Psalms* published in Venice (1611) under his name properly belongs to Thomas Waleys. ROY MARTIN HAINES

Sources J. Bale, *Illustrium Maioris Britannie scriptorum … summarium* (1548) · J. Pits, *Relationum historicarum de rebus Anglicis*, ed. [W. Bishop] (Paris, 1619) · M. Grabmann, 'Neu aufgefundene lateinische Werke deutscher Mystiker', *Sitzungsberichte der Bayerischen Akademie der Wissenschaften* [Philosophisch-philologische und historische Klasse], 3 Abh. (1922) · A. G. Little, *Franciscan papers, lists, and documents* (1943) · W. A. Hinnebusch, *The early English Friars Preachers* (1951) · M. H. MacInerny, *History of the Irish Dominicans*, 1 (1916) · D. E. Sharp, *Franciscan philosophy at Oxford in the thirteenth century*, British Society of Franciscan Studies, 16 (1930) · F. C. Copleston, *A history of philosophy* (1966), 2: *Mediaeval philosophy: Augustine to Scotus* (1966) · G. Leff, *Paris and Oxford universities in the thirteenth and fourteenth centuries* (1968) · A. G. Little and F. Pelster, *Oxford theology and theologians*, OHS, 96 (1934) · A. G. Little, 'The friars v. the University of Cambridge', *EngHR*, 50 (1935), 686–96 · J. C. Russell, 'Dictionary of writers of thirteenth century England', *BIHR*, special suppl., 3 (1936) [whole issue] · J. Quétif and J. Echard, *Scriptores ordinis praedicatorum recensiti*, 1 (Paris, 1719) · Emden, *Oxf.*, 2.1023–4

Jorz [Jorse], **Walter** (d. 1321), archbishop of Armagh, had early connections with Nottinghamshire. He was a brother of Thomas *Jorz (d. 1310), cardinal-priest of Santa Sabina, and was a member of the Dominican convent in Oxford c.1300. At the same period he appears in the records of the diocese of Lincoln, where he was granted licence to hear confessions by Bishop Dalderby in 1300 and 1301.

In August 1307 Jorz was provided to the archbishopric of Armagh by Pope Clement V, and his episcopacy marked the beginning of a period of English rule in that diocese. His appointment provoked the displeasure of Edward II who fined the new archbishop £1000, claiming that the papal bull of appointment contained words prejudicial to his crown and dignity. The fine was afterwards remitted and the temporalities of the see were restored to the new archbishop by September 1307. Little is known of his activities in Armagh. In 1310 he was apparently instrumental in the Irish parliament's decision to repeal its recent enactment debarring Irishmen from admission to any religious house in a territory at peace or in English land. In the same year he complained of harassment by royal officials, and sought protection for one year to go to the Roman curia at Avignon. By November 1311 he had obtained permission to resign his see with a yearly pension of £50. He was succeeded in Armagh by another brother, Roland. The appointment to archbishoprics of the two Jorz brothers probably reflects the influence wielded at the curia by their other brother Thomas.

Walter Jorz ended his career back in Lincoln, where he is found in 1320 acting as coadjutor to the bishop. He died at the Dominican convent in Lincoln in February 1321, and requested burial in the convent church. His will was proved on 7 February 1321. Three works—*Promptuarium theologiae*, *De peccatis in genere*, and *Questiones variae*—were ascribed to him by John Bale but none is known to be extant. MARGARET MURPHY

Sources *CEPR letters*, vol. 2 · *CPR*, 1307–13 · J. A. Watt, *The church and the two nations in medieval Ireland* (1970) · J. F. Ferguson, 'The "mere English" and the "mere Irish"', *Transactions of the Kilkenny Archaeological Society*, 1 (1850–51), 508–12 · A. Gibbons, ed., *Early Lincoln wills* (1888), 6 · A. G. Little, *Franciscan papers, lists, and documents* (1943) · Bale, *Cat.*, 1.368

Joscelin [Joscelyn], **John** (1529–1603), Old English scholar and Church of England clergyman, was the third surviving son of Sir Thomas Joscelin (d. 1562), of Hyde Hall, Sawbridgeworth, Hertfordshire, and High Roding, Essex, and his wife, Dorothy, daughter of Sir Geoffrey Gate (d. 1526) of Rivenhall, Essex. The Joscelins were Hertfordshire gentry of some antiquity, said to be of Breton origin. John Joscelin was probably born at High Roding, and matriculated as a pensioner at Queens' College, Cambridge, in 1545. He graduated BA in 1549, and was admitted a fellow of Queens' by the Edwardian commissioners to the university. He became Latin lecturer there in 1550–51 and Greek lecturer in 1551–2, proceeding MA at the end of that year. He subscribed to the Marian articles in 1555, and was bursar of the college in 1556–7, when he was again Greek lecturer. He resigned his fellowship in 1557, however, and subsequently evinced a robust protestantism.

When Matthew Parker was made archbishop of Canterbury in 1559 he appointed Joscelin to a chaplaincy as his Latin secretary. At the head of the writing office Joscelin at once became an influential figure in the archbishop's household. His early work was rewarded in 1560 with a prebend at Hereford, which he held until 1577, when Parker's successor Edmund Grindal presented him to the sinecure rectory of Hollingbourne, Kent. He died, unmarried, on 28 December 1603, probably at High Roding; he was buried there, at All Saints' Church. He had property there and in the neighbourhood, and may have been the tenant of the manor for some years between 1584 and his death.

Joscelin's scholarly interests extended to Hebrew, a serious accomplishment in his day, and he bequeathed £100 to provide a Hebrew lectureship at Queens'. It was presumably his general reputation and his classical learning that recommended him to Parker, who was well informed about talent in Cambridge. Thereafter, however, his distinction lies in his contributions to medieval studies, and particularly in the revival of Old English. Parker, like other protestant divines, was interested in the early history of the church, and in the growth of the papal government in the middle ages. He paid particular attention to the pre-conquest church in England, however, because of its use of the vernacular, its practice of clerical marriage, and its views on the eucharist. To study those matters he assembled all the Old English material he could find, including three texts of the gospels, and began a programme of publication. He found an able collaborator in Joscelin, who served him well, both in seeking and acquiring manuscripts and in preparing copy for the press. Together with George Acworth, Joscelin wrote a substantial part of *De antiquitate Britannicæ ecclesiæ*, which Parker published privately in 1572, including all seventy lives of the archbishops.

Joscelin also undertook much critical work of his own. Parker's library included some forty Old English texts, and a wide range of medieval chronicles. Joscelin, who had helped to collect many of them, made extensive notes on the authors and the previous owners of the manuscripts as well as preparing extracts. He was interested in manuscript books and acquired some skill in palaeography, but he also made the Old English language an object of study. He attained a remarkable knowledge of the laws of the Anglo-Saxon kings, and used them extensively in compiling an Old English–Latin dictionary in collaboration with Parker's son John, which, however, was never completed. He is also credited with having constructed a grammar.

In Parker's household there was a general interest in Old English hands and the runic accretions of their alphabet. The interest was not reverential. Joscelin interpolated some paper leaves into the D manuscript of the Anglo-Saxon Chronicle in a simulated script, and he annotated texts freely, but he was also anxious to see manuscripts properly bound and safely housed. What was distinctive was his scientific approach to the language. He contributed additional texts and translations to Parker's edition of Ælfric of Eynsham's Easter homily (1566 or 1567), and, although William Lisle included and refined them in *A Saxon Treatise* (1623), Joscelin's vocabulary was not superseded until William Somner published his *Dictionarium Saxonico-Latino-Anglicum* in 1659.

Joscelin also published a critical edition of Gildas's *De excidio* (1568), and at Parker's suggestion wrote a short history of Corpus Christi College, edited for the Cambridge Antiquarian Society by J. W. Clark in 1880. His papers are distributed between Corpus Christi and the Cottonian collection in the British Library. Joscelin's epitaph at High Roding says that the credit for his work was appropriated by others, which has been read as a criticism of Parker. However, his own references to Parker are friendly, and there are errors in the inscription, such as attributing his fellowship to King's, which make it unlikely that it reflects his own opinions. The collaboration of the archbishop with his secretary is more justly reflected in Joscelin's substantial contribution to *A Testimonie of Antiquitie*, Parker's edition of Ælfric's Easter homily—it is the earliest known printed book to contain passages of Old English.

G. H. MARTIN

Sources *DNB* · Cooper, *Ath. Cantab.*, 2.366 · M. McKisack, *Medieval history in the Tudor age* (1971) · P. Morant, *The history and antiquities of the county of Essex*, 2 vols. (1768) · M. R. James, *A descriptive catalogue of the manuscripts in the library of Corpus Christi College, Cambridge*, 2 vols. (1912) · F. G. Emmison, ed., *Feet of fines for Essex*, 6: *1581–1603* (1993) · J. Bately, 'John Joscelyn and the laws of the Anglo-Saxon kings', *Words, texts, and manuscripts: studies in Anglo-Saxon culture presented to Helmut Gneuss on the occasion of his sixty-fifth birthday*, ed. M. Korhammer and others (1992), 435–66
Archives BL, Cotton MSS

Joseph of Exeter. *See* Exeter, Joseph of (*fl. c.*1180–1194).

Joseph Scottus (*d.* 791x804), abbot and scholar, was of Irish origins. Educated under the renowned Colcu, probably at Clonmacnoise in central Ireland, he later studied at York with Alcuin, probably in the 770s. The Frisian Liudger (later bishop of Münster) was also a student at York at this time, and Joseph's friendship with Liudger is recorded in a poem in which he requests from Liudger the gift of a polished staff. In the 780s Alcuin left York to take up residence at the court of the Frankish king (later emperor) Charlemagne, and Joseph seems to have accompanied his teacher.

Joseph's career on the continent shows evidence of intellectual achievement—modest compared to the more renowned luminaries of the court, but none the less distinguished for his time—and also of the trust and esteem he enjoyed from both Alcuin and Charlemagne. Whether he was himself the target of any of the sometimes vitriolic anti-Irish humour documented in the Carolingian court poetry of the 790s is unknown.

In 787 or 788 Charlemagne sent Joseph and several companions as *missi* (emissaries) to Rome, Spoleto, and Benevento. The legation almost ended in disaster when the members of the party were separated from each other and threatened with ambush and death by southern Italians disloyal to Charlemagne. In 790 Joseph was entrusted with Alcuin's continental affairs when the latter's journey back to Northumbria was unexpectedly extended for political reasons. Joseph's career is otherwise so poorly documented that, although it is known that he became an abbot, where and when are unknown, as is the precise year of his death, though this is likely to have been between 791 and 804. The possibility that he was briefly abbot of Monte Cassino has been canvassed; such an appointment would make sense after his service as *missus* in Italy, but the evidence is too equivocal to allow any certainty.

Four acrostic poems by Joseph are found alongside those of Alcuin and Theodulf in a collection of acrostic religious poems (Bern, Burgerbibliothek, MS 212) dedicated to Charlemagne and modelled on the panegyrics which the fourth-century poet Optatianus Porfyrius addressed to the Roman emperor Constantine. The whole collection is a remarkable demonstration of technical virtuosity, and the inclusion of Joseph in this endeavour is a reminder not to underestimate the intellectual contribution to the Carolingian revival of learning even by those who seem to have written little. Joseph's other extant writings include a clear and competent abridgement of Jerome's commentary on Isaiah drafted at Alcuin's behest (unprinted; manuscripts listed by Bischoff, 'Wendepunkte', no. 8). With less certainty, two other texts have been attributed to him which typify the intellectual diversions of an educated man of his time: a collection of riddles, now lost, but attested before 903 in a Passau manuscript and perhaps more convincingly to be attributed to Joseph, bishop of Freising between 749 and 764; and a list of the characteristic noises produced by various animals, in partially alphabetical order and glossary format (Madrid, Biblioteca Nacional, MS 19 (formerly A 16), fol. 189v). Such *voces animantium* lists were a staple of Latin grammatical lore, but alphabetization is unusual. The list associated with Joseph would seem to have been taken from his personal notebook or commonplace book. Joseph Scottus exemplifies the internationalism of the Carolingian Renaissance and has been called an early example of 'the scholar in public life' (Bullough, 'Aula renovata', 141).   MARY GARRISON

Sources E. Dümmler, ed., *Epistolae Karolini aevi*, MGH Epistolae [quarto], 4 (Berlin, 1895) · E. Dümmler, ed., *Poetae Latini aevi Carolini*, MGH Poetae Latini Medii Aevi, 1 (Berlin, 1881), 149–59 · 'Codex Carolinus', *Epistolae Merowingici et Karolini aevi*, ed. W. Gundlach, 1 (Berlin, 1892), 469–657, nos. 82–3, appx 1–2 · M. Manitius, *Geschichte der lateinischen Literatur des Mittelalters*, 1 (1911), 547–9 · J. F. Kenney, *The sources for the early history of Ireland* (1929); repr. (1966), 536, no. 341 · D. A. Bullough, 'Aula renovata: the Carolingian court before the Aachen palace', *Carolingian renewal: sources and heritage* (1991), 123–60, esp. 140–41 · D. A. Bullough, *Alcuin: achievement and reputation* [forthcoming] · D. Schaller, 'Die karolingischen Figurengedichte des Cod. Bern. 212', *Medium aevum vivum: Festschrift für Walter Bulst*, ed. H. R. Jauss and D. Schaller (1960), 22–47 · B. Bischoff, 'Wendepunkte in der Geschichte der lateinischen Exegese im Frühmittelalter', *Mittelalterliche Studien*, 1 (1966), 205–73, no. 8 · J. F. Kelly, 'The originality of Josephus Scottus' commentary on Isaiah', *Manuscripta*, 24 (1980), 176–80 · B. Bischoff, 'Die Bibliothek im Dienste der Schule', *Mittelalterliche Studien*, 3 (1981), 213–33, esp. 220–21 · J. Semmler, 'Karl der Grosse und das fränkische Mönchtum', *Karl der Grosse: Lebenswerk und Nachleben, Das Geistige Leben*, ed. B. Bischoff (1965), vol. 2 of *Karl der Grosse: Lebenswerk und Nachleben*, 255–89, at 276 n. 50 · O. Bertolini, 'Carlo Magno e Benevento', *Karl der Grosse: Lebenswerk und Nachleben, Persönlichkeit und Geschichte*, ed. H. Beumann (1965), vol. 1 of *Karl der Grosse: Lebenswerk und Nachleben*, 637–661, at 637–47 · K. Hallinger and M. Wegener, eds., *Initia consuetudinis Benedictinae, consuetudines saeculi octavi et noni*, Corpus Consuetudinum Monasticarum, 1 (1963), 157–75, esp. 173 · A. Reifferscheid, *C. Suetonius Tranquillus: Praeter Caesarum libros reliquiae* (1860), 251–2 [incl. Joseph's *voces animantium*] · J. Iriarte, *Regiae Bibliothecae Matritensis Codices Graeci MSS* (1769), 310–13 · W. von Hartel, G. Loewe, and Z. García, *Bibliotheca patrum latinorum Hispaniensis* (1886), 316 · C. E. Ineichen-Eder, *Mittelalterliche Bibliothekskataloge Deutschlands und der Schweiz 4.1: Bistümer Passau und Regensburg* (1977), 24–6

Archives Biblioteca Nacional, Madrid, MS 19, fol. 189v · Burgerbibliothek, Bern, MS 212

Joseph [*née* Hodson; *other married name* Hastings], **Anthea Esther** (1924–1981), publisher, was born on 6 March 1924 in London, the only daughter of Francis Lord Charlton (Charles) *Hodson, Baron Hodson (1895–1984), barrister and later a lord of appeal in ordinary, and his wife, Susan Mary (d. 1965), daughter of Major William Greaves Blake. Educated at Queen's Gate School, London, she worked at the American embassy in London during the Second World War. In 1946 she became secretary to Michael *Joseph (1897–1958), the publisher, who had founded the company bearing his name ten years earlier. They married on 15 November 1950, following the death of Michael Joseph's second wife.

Eight years of marriage saw Anthea Joseph do a great deal to establish the family home at Brown's Farm, Old Basing, Hampshire. She had two children, Charlotte and Hugh, and was a sympathetic stepmother to Michael Joseph's children (three sons and a daughter) from his earlier marriages. During this period she lacked time to work closely with her husband in his business but accompanied him on visits to the United States and South Africa, events which broadened her circle of friends and professional acquaintances to her benefit in later years.

Michael Joseph's death was the start of Anthea Joseph's real career in publishing. The years 1958–61 were difficult for the company. They culminated in the resignation of the majority of the board, leaving her and one other director in charge. It was largely due to Anthea Joseph's energy and determination that the company survived intact to settle down as a part of the Thomson Organization and to enjoy two decades of very successful publishing.

Anthea Joseph was not a publisher in the broadest sense of the word. The mechanics of the business, the printing and binding, the marketing, and other commercial aspects of publishing interested her only to the extent that they were the means of presenting the work of an author she believed in to the public. That her judgement often proved to be correct and commercial criteria were met was secondary: the act of publication meant everything to her. This somewhat romantic attitude towards her profession could be a trial to her colleagues at times, but her lively sense of humour, her subtle powers of persuasion, and, above all, her enthusiasm invariably disarmed her keenest critics. She was, however, far more than an editor: rather, she believed that the true task of the publisher is to inspire and support creators of literature, a position that was becoming difficult to sustain towards the end of her life.

Anthea Joseph was a particularly sensitive judge of fiction: Stan Barstow, Dick Francis, James Baldwin, James Herriot, H. E. Bates, Barry Hines, Alun Richards, and Julian Rathbone were among the writers she worked with and published. Many others, lesser known, enjoyed equal dedication, understanding, and sympathy for their work. She was a critic of the 'hyped' book that in the 1970s became a prominent feature of publishing in both the UK and the USA. While accepting that some were necessary for the income they produced, she argued consistently that a part of their profits should be set aside to support creative literature.

Anthea Joseph had an outstanding flair for friendship, which stemmed from her deep interest in people. She was an excellent listener. Her loyalty to friends, authors, colleagues, and her family was widely acknowledged. A committed Christian who was modest about her faith, she was determined that her religious belief should shape every aspect of daily life.

In 1962 Anthea Joseph became deputy chairman of Michael Joseph Ltd, and chairman in 1978. On 30 March

1963 she married a close friend of her first husband, (Douglas) Macdonald Hastings (1909/10–1982), the son of Basil Macdonald Hastings, playwright. They had one daughter, Harriet. Anthea Hastings died after a long struggle with cancer on 23 January 1981 at her home in Hampshire, Brown's Farm, Old Basing, Basingstoke.

VICTOR MORRISON, rev.

Sources *The Times* (26 Jan 1981) • *The Bookseller* (31 Jan 1981) • *At the sign of the mermaid: fifty years of Michael Joseph* (1986) • personal knowledge (1990) • private information (1990) • m. certs • d. cert. **Wealth at death** £164,627: probate, 2 March 1981, *CGPLA Eng. & Wales*

Joseph, George Francis (1764–1846), portrait and subject painter, was born on 25 November 1764. He may have been the George Francis Joseph who was baptized on 16 December 1764 at St Botolph Aldgate, London, the son of Thomas Joseph and his wife, Ann. He entered the Royal Academy Schools as an engraver on 3 December 1784, when his age was given as twenty on '25th last Novr' (Hutchison, 148), and in 1792 gained the Royal Academy's gold medal for a *Scene from Coriolanus*. He sent his first contribution to the Royal Academy in 1788, and became a constant exhibitor both there and at the British Institution. In 1797 he painted *Mrs. Siddons as the Tragic Muse*. In 1811 the directors of the British Institution awarded him one-third of their combined premiums of 350 guineas for his *Return of Priam with the Dead Body of Hector*, and, in 1812, 100 guineas for his *Procession to Calvary*. In 1813 he was elected an associate of the Royal Academy. His portrait *Eliza O'Neill as Melpomene* at the Royal Academy in 1815 is now in the Garrick Club, London. Joseph also painted fancy pictures and made designs for book illustrations. His portraits in both oil and miniature are very numerous, and some of them have been engraved. He practised in London until 1836, when he retired to Cambridge; there he died in 1846, having continued to exhibit at the Royal Academy until that year, and was buried in St Michael's churchyard, Cambridge. His portraits *Spencer Perceval* (1812) and *Sir Stamford Raffles* (1817) are in the National Portrait Gallery, London; his *Henry Grattan* portrait is in the Hugh Lane Municipal Gallery of Modern Art, Dublin, and the print room of the British Museum possesses his watercolour portrait *Charles Lamb*, executed when Lamb was forty-four.

F. M. O'DONOGHUE, rev. J. DESMARAIS

Sources Redgrave, *Artists* • *N&Q*, 6th ser., 4 (1881), 541 • W. Sandby, *The history of the Royal Academy of Arts*, 2 vols. (1862) • [G. Scharf], *Catalogue of the pictures in the National Portrait Gallery* (1859) • Graves, *RA exhibitors* • Bryan, *Painters* (1866); (1886–9) • R. N. James, *Painters and their works*, 3 vols. (1896–7) • Ward, *Men of the reign* • S. Houfe, *The dictionary of British book illustrators and caricaturists, 1800–1914* (1978) • Waterhouse, *18c painters* • *Checklist of British artists in the Witt Library*, Courtauld Institute, Witt Library (1991) • R. Walker, *National Portrait Gallery: Regency portraits*, 2 vols. (1985) • *IGI* • S. C. Hutchison, 'The Royal Academy Schools, 1768–1830', *Walpole Society*, 38 (1960–62), 123–91, esp. 148

Joseph, Horace William Brindley (1867–1943), philosopher, was born at Chatham, Kent, on 28 September 1867, the second and eldest surviving of the three sons of Alexander Joseph (*d.* 1890), rector of St John's Church, Chatham, and honorary canon of Rochester Cathedral, who, although brought up a Christian, was on both sides of Jewish descent, and his wife, Janet Eleanor (*d.* 1917), daughter of George Acworth, solicitor, a member of his congregation. A woman of great intelligence and strong character, she was a first cousin of Sir William Acworth, railway economist, and was lineally descended from a half-brother of Mr Ackworth, the Woolwich storekeeper often mentioned by Pepys.

Horace Joseph's home, after ill health had compelled his father to give up parish work, was successively at Croydon, Wimborne (where he attended the grammar school as a day boy), Malvern, and Clevedon. In 1877 he was sent as a boarder to Allhallows School, Honiton, and in 1880 he was elected, first on the roll, to a scholarship at Winchester College. He developed an enduring loyalty towards his school and was elected a fellow of Winchester in 1942. After a distinguished career at school, winning three gold medals (an unprecedented honour) and becoming prefect of hall, Joseph passed in 1886 to New College, Oxford, with the first Winchester scholarship of the year. He obtained first classes in classical moderations (1888) and *literae humaniores* (1890), the junior Greek Testament prize (1889), and the Arnold historical essay prize (1891). In 1891 he was elected a fellow of New College.

In view of new family responsibilities which the death of his father had brought upon him, Joseph accepted with his fellowship a lectureship in philosophy, but not without characteristic diffidence and with some hankering after a career in the Indian Civil Service. On the death of Alfred Robinson in 1895 he became the senior philosophy tutor of the college and also junior bursar. The former position he occupied for thirty-seven years; the latter office he held until 1919. To his obituarist in the *Oxford Magazine* he:

> incarnated, more than any man of his time, the essential characteristics of 'Greats' Philosophy: a philosophy firmly rooted in the teachings of Plato and Aristotle, and continuing that tradition as a living thing, applicable to the problems of our own day. (*Oxford Magazine*, 98)

The academic successes of his students soon reconciled him to teaching. He always preferred private work with his pupils to lecturing, but spared no pains with the latter, and for a long time was the principal lecturer in the university on Plato's *Republic*. In 1932 he exchanged his official fellowship as tutor for a supernumerary fellowship which he retained until his death. His retirement did not bring leisure: while still pursuing his philosophical studies, continuing to teach, and taking a full share in the affairs of his college, he became a member of the city council and the active chairman of its education committee. He was elected FBA in 1930.

Until her death in 1917 Joseph's home in vacations (to which he would often welcome his students as guests) was with his mother, first at Holford in Somerset and from 1912 at Dinder near Wells. In the summer he frequently went abroad with a sister or a friend; in 1901, on medical advice, he took a year's holiday, and visited India (where his younger brother was a civil servant) and the Far East. In 1919 he married Margaret, younger daughter of the poet laureate Robert Bridges, and he enjoyed seven years of great happiness with her. There were no children of the marriage. She died in 1926, and he founded in her memory—she was an accomplished musician—a scholarship in music at New College. He made the college his residuary legatee. He died in the Acland Home, Banbury Road, Oxford, on 13 November 1943. A tablet to himself and his wife was placed in the cloisters of New College by the warden and fellows.

Joseph made a profound impression of intellectual integrity upon many generations of his pupils. He was, they felt, a man 'to whom truth and right meant all the world'. In his teaching, to use words quoted by himself of John Cook Wilson, he 'was always pricking some bubble of language or thought'. To some he recalled Socrates:

> in the determination to clear up confusion, in his ruthless exposure of half-knowledge and pretentious verbiage, in his humility and courtesy and wit, most of all in his absolute consecration to his duty, and his utter disregard of comfort and convenience.

'All his qualities seemed to be expressed in his powerful head, and his short, square, strongly built and rapidly moving body'. Many pupils found him intimidating:

> it was the pupil's part to deliver the goods; it was Joseph's to turn them inside out, and he did so with remorseless skill, energy, and accuracy, till hardly a shred was left. The pupil left Joseph's rooms hardly knowing whether he stood on his head or his heels … This drastic method was somewhat of the 'kill or cure' variety. (*Oxford Magazine*, 98)

He was singularly free from self-consciousness and conventional inhibitions.

Joseph left no systematic account of his philosophy. In his earlier writings at least, he was a realist in the school of Cook Wilson. But his doubts concerning the independent reality of space and the nature of solidity and magnitude caused a gradual return to a position similar to the idealism which had prevailed in Oxford during his undergraduate days. He was hostile towards formalism in logic, particularly towards Russell, and argued against the attempt to establish mathematics as the model of all thought. In *An Introduction to Logic* (1906; 2nd edn, 1916), which had a large circulation on both sides of the Atlantic, he sought to re-establish a version of Aristotelian logic. In 1923 appeared his only published work on economics, a subject always of much interest to him. This was a discussion entitled *The Labour Theory of Value in Karl Marx*. In *Some Problems in Ethics* (1931) he intervened in a discussion begun by his friend H. A. Prichard and attempted to mediate between a rigid discrimination of the 'right' from the 'good' and a utilitarianism which would reduce 'right' conduct to a choice of means-to-an-end 'good' only in the sense of satisfying desire, by the Platonic doctrine of an absolute good, whose form would determine how our lives ought to be led. Most of the writings in *Essays in Ancient and Modern Philosophy* (1935) had appeared before, among them the Herbert Spencer lecture of 1924 entitled 'The concept of evolution', perhaps the most important of his philosophical writings. *Knowledge and the Good in Plato's Republic* was published posthumously in 1948. To *Mind* he contributed several remarkable papers on our perception of things in space. In philosophical debate he displayed an extraordinary grasp of the points at issue, an unfailing memory for the course taken by the argument, and a readiness in meeting opponents which impressed those who heard him for the first time.

Joseph was of a deeply religious disposition, and *pietas* towards the religious traditions of his home and his school inspired his character and conduct, leading him to take all opportunities permitted him by his sensitive intellectual conscience to join in worship with his family and his college. Familiarity with the Bible was obvious in his writings and conversation, while his constant reference in both to the thought of God, although used only by way of illustration or as, in Kantian phrase, a 'regulative idea', imparted to his representation of the world a theistic colouring. Joseph's possession of a true poetic gift is evidenced in the verses addressed to his wife which were included in a small collection privately printed after his death. CLEMENT C. J. WEBB, *rev.* C. A. CREFFIELD

Sources *The Times* (15 Nov 1943) • A. H. Smith, 'Joseph, Horace William Brindley, 1867–1943', *PBA*, 31 (1945), 375–98 • H. A. Prichard, *Mind*, new ser., 53 (1944), 189–91 • J. Passmore, *A hundred years of philosophy* (1957), 253–4 • funeral address [privately printed, 1943] • *Oxford Magazine* (2 Dec 1943) • *The Wykehamist* (16 Dec 1943) • personal knowledge (1959) • private information (1959) • CGPLA Eng. & Wales (1944)

Archives New College, Oxford, diaries and travel journals | Bodl. Oxf., corresp. with Gilbert Murray • Bodl. Oxf., letters to Sir Alfred Zimmern

Likenesses W. Stoneman, photograph, 1932, NPG • K. Knowles, drawing, New College, Oxford • J. Russell & Sons, photograph, repro. in Smith, 'Joseph, Horace William Brindley'

Wealth at death £34,001 16s. 6d.: probate, 24 June 1944, CGPLA Eng. & Wales

Joseph, Keith Sinjohn, Baron Joseph (1918–1994), politician, was born on 17 January 1918 at 63 Portland Place, London, the only child of Samuel Gluckstein Joseph (later Sir Samuel George Joseph, first baronet, of Portsoken in the City of London) (1888–1944), businessman, and his wife, Edna Cicely (1896–1981), younger daughter of Philip Alexander Solomon Phillips (1867–1934), partner in a Bond Street firm of antique silversmiths. Both sides of the family belonged to the affluent Ashkenazi Jewish commercial aristocracy. Samuel Joseph's mother, Sarah Gluckstein, was a member of the family which owned the catering company J. Lyons, some of whose building contracts went to Bovis, of which Samuel Joseph became co-chairman and managing director. Samuel Joseph (who changed his middle name from Gluckstein to George in the 1930s) was twice mentioned in dispatches in the First World War. He was twice mayor of St Marylebone (in 1928 and 1930), sheriff of the City of London in 1933–4, and lord mayor in 1942–3. Knighted in 1934, he was created baronet in 1943, taking his territorial designation from the City of London ward for which he became an alderman in 1933.

Family and early years In the absence of an autobiography, the early formative influences integral to understanding anyone, let alone a public figure as reticent and as unusual as Keith Joseph, may never be known. His childhood—

quite enough for me', he later recalled (Denham and Garnett, 79).

Joseph's earlier thoughts of becoming an architect gave way to the idea of a career at the bar, but the war intervened. At Harrow he had been in the Officer Cadet Corps and at Oxford he joined the Territorial Army, so in September 1939 he reported for duty. He served from 1939 to 1946, rising from second lieutenant (1940) to captain (1943) in the Royal Artillery. In Italy during 1943–4 he taught himself shorthand, and learned Italian through reading Shakespeare in the language. He volunteered for the most dangerous missions; like his father he was mentioned in dispatches, and he was wounded slightly in the leg. After a brief spell in the Middle East and a second spell in Italy during 1944, he was recalled to Britain. On his father's death (on 4 October 1944) he became second baronet. Joseph was much cleverer than his father, but in his public life he followed at first in his father's footsteps. Having been elected a prize fellow of All Souls College, Oxford, in 1946 (his fellowship was renewed until 1960, and then again from 1972) he industriously set about acquiring qualifications, as barrister-at-law at the Middle Temple in 1946, and as licentiate of the Institute of Builders in 1947. His research at All Souls on tolerance was never completed, but he pushed himself hard. He became common councilman for the ward of Portsoken in the City of London in 1946, and was alderman for the ward from 1946 to 1949, but resigned because of pain from a stomach ulcer; something close to a starvation diet after 1944 may have been the cause, and major stomach surgery was eventually needed, in 1968.

On 6 July 1951 at the West London Synagogue, Marylebone, Joseph married the serious-minded, self-improving American university student Hellen Louise (b. 1930/31), daughter of Sigmar Guggenheimer, businessman. They had a son, James Samuel (b. 1955), and three daughters—Emma Catherine Sarah (b. 1956), Julia Rachel (b. 1959), and Anna Jane Rebecca (b. 1964). By the 1960s, however, his wife's interests had begun to diverge: whereas Joseph was becoming increasingly interested in politics, she was devoted to her family and was winning a reputation for her sculpture. They separated by mutual consent in 1978 and were divorced in 1985.

Beginnings in politics In 1948 Joseph joined the Young Conservatives, and as a Conservative candidate at the general election of May 1955 he contested Barons Court; in a straight fight he was only 125 votes behind his rival. In February the following year at the Leeds North-East by-election he came comfortably ahead of his Labour rival. He remained MP for Leeds North-East until he retired in 1987, triumphing in straight fights up to and including 1970, and thereafter finding his majority boosted by divisions among his opponents. He was at first one of only two Jewish Conservative MPs. His initial stance was to favour the political consensus founded on the mixed economy and the welfare state, and his maiden speech on 9 May 1956 rocked no boats. It was, however, courageous during the Suez crisis in November for a new

Keith Sinjohn Joseph, Baron Joseph (1918–1994), by Nicholas Posner, 1987

affluent, with parents devoted to one another and indulgent towards their only child—seems to have been happy. It was a cultivated background, helping to mould Joseph's lifelong taste for literature and the arts. The Josephs and Glucksteins belonged to the Anglicized and up-market Liberal Jewish Synagogue, and so were half-way towards an assimilation which Samuel Joseph carried further by denying his son the customary barmitzvah at age thirteen. The boy was edged towards further assimilation through his education, which began at Gibbs Wagner's School in Sloane Street. Joseph's social conscience was already alert: he regularly sneaked food out of the house to feed a beggar he saw on the way to school. From there in 1926 he went as a boarder to Lockers Park School in Hemel Hempstead, where his lifelong digestive problems (which seem to have had a psychosomatic component) and his youthful obsession with cricket became manifest. At Harrow School (1931–6) he was shy and serious, but his habit of self-deprecation, already well developed, did not preclude his becoming a monitor in his final year. In 1936 he went to Magdalen College, Oxford, where he received tuition from its formidable law tutor, John Morris. Hitherto academically rather a late developer, he gained a first-class degree in jurisprudence in 1939, one of only six in his year. Unlike his undergraduate contemporaries Roy Jenkins and Edward Heath, he showed no interest in the Oxford Union or in university party politics. In one vacation, though, his serious-mindedness took him for a week's work in a mine near Rotherham; 'one week was member to sign (with only ten other backbenchers) a letter to the prime minister urging that British forces in Egypt be placed under the orders of the United Nations. Joseph made himself a specialist in social security issues, and combined compassion with conscientiously getting up his brief—displaying a considerable faith in the expert, in statistics, and in organizational change. It was no surprise that he soon joined the One Nation group of progressive Conservatives, or that his contribution to its important pamphlet, *The Responsible Society* (1959), was on the social services.

Joseph's rise up the parliamentary ladder began early, his first post being in 1957 as parliamentary private secretary to Cuthbert (Cubby) Alport, parliamentary under-secretary of state at the Commonwealth Relations Office. Joseph saw civil servants as allies in his enthusiastic quest for an expertise and information that he reinforced with the notebook and pencil which accompanied him on ministerial visits. Energetic, and with a good grasp of the issues, he then did well as parliamentary secretary to the minister of housing and local government (1959–61) and as minister of state at the Board of Trade (October 1961–July 1962). His ministerial grasp was enhanced by the business interests that he had not been neglecting. Director of Bovis Ltd from 1951 to 1959, he was chairman from 1958 to 1959, and deputy chairman of Bovis Holdings Ltd from 1964 to 1970. He also co-founded and was first chairman of the Foundation for Management Education (1960), a pioneering cause which by the end of his life had become mainstream.

In and out of office, 1962–1974 Following Macmillan's 'night of the long knives' in July 1962 Joseph entered the cabinet as minister of housing and local government and minister for Welsh affairs. He enjoyed office. Immensely hard-working like his father, and invariably well-briefed and courteous, he believed that problems could be solved through rational discussion between intelligent men, and he consulted widely among his civil servants, who liked and respected him. His earlier instincts favoured freeing up the rented sector from state control, but the public outcry against exploitative landlords, including the notorious Peter (Perec) Rachman, helped to render this impracticable, and Joseph's policies as minister involved active collaboration between industry and an interventionist government. New towns, low-rise slum clearance, high-rise alternatives, new building techniques, erosion of the green belt, local government reform, public acquisition of development land—all were grist to his mill. In later years he felt that the Conservative Party's housing policy before 1964—rent control, slum clearance, and council house building—had made things worse by reducing the supply of low-cost housing and by increasing dependence on the state. 'The right hon. Gentleman is not fully a Socialist yet', said James Callaghan on 4 December 1963, 'but he is coming along' (*Hansard 5C*, 685.1268, 4 Dec 1963). Congratulating a newly appointed housing minister, Joseph in the 1980s said: 'Well done. You'll find lots of problems in your new job. I caused many of them' (*The Times*, 12 Dec 1994). In his disarming honesty, his belief in the power of

reason to solve problems, and his anxious and public self-criticism, Joseph was in many ways not a politician at all.

In the contest for Conservative leader in 1965 Joseph backed Edward Heath; 'Ted has a passion to get Britain right', he told Margaret Thatcher, persuading her to do the same (Thatcher, *Path to Power*, 136). Heath had already asked Joseph to review the Conservative Party's policy on social services, and now added labour questions. At this time Joseph wanted to complement state pensions by extending occupational old-age pensions to all, and to co-ordinate occupational pensions, health, and national insurance through setting up a mega-department: the Department of Health and Social Security. After the party's general election defeat in 1966 Heath relieved Joseph of social services, and soon afterwards moved him on from labour questions to trade and power.

In 1964 Joseph paid his first visit to the Institute of Economic Affairs (IEA), and his regular subsequent visits there reflected the relief felt by a non-economist that his free-market instincts could win respectable intellectual backing. There was a foretaste of his later economic stance when, to the surprise of his colleagues, he announced—in a speech at Reading on 26 April 1967—that private enterprise, far from failing, 'has not been properly tried' (Denham and Garnett, 159). In the same year he invited colleagues to seminars addressed by economists from the Chicago school. Unlike Enoch Powell, however, he was too cautious, too responsive to the ideas of others, to carry these insights as yet into public debate. Early in 1970, however, he made libertarian speeches on economic matters which acquired an edge from his new-found collaboration with Alfred Sherman, a Jewish former Marxist who (unlike Joseph) had begun life in the East End, but had prevailed against antisemitic prejudice and worked his way out. Here Joseph again came close to diverging from what was then the mainstream Conservative approach to economic policy, but neither party nor country were as yet in sufficient trouble for such desperate remedies to seem necessary. And although in 1968 Powell's 'rivers of blood' speech caused the party serious difficulty on race, Joseph on this topic seems to have blown hot and cold; an unexplained illness may well have been in the long term convenient by keeping him out of trouble at a crucial moment.

As secretary of state for social services (in charge of the Department of Health and Social Security) in Heath's government from 1970 to 1974 Joseph was accessible, open-minded, inquisitive, industrious, and less abrasive than his predecessor, R. H. S. Crossman. He was as usual an obsessive worker, keen to encourage initiatives, though sometimes indecisive. He was at one with Heath on the major issue of the day—British entry to the EEC—and was too preoccupied with departmental duties to diverge markedly from the government's economic strategy. He was aware of IEA arguments for scaling down state welfare, but—fully exposed as he was to 'the political difficulty of the short term' which he had drawn to the institute's attention in 1965 (Cockett, 168)—he did not act upon them. Sherman saw him as 'a lion in opposition and a lamb in government' (*The Times*, 12 Dec 1994). Indeed, Conservatives at this time cited his period of office, during which social expenditure rose as a proportion of gross national product, as exemplifying Conservative compassion. Joseph was undeniably compassionate, being unusually preoccupied with the welfare of vulnerable groups such as the disabled, the old, and the mentally ill. 'I recall him telling me at the time that he wished to provide free chiropody to poor pensioners', Nigel Lawson recalled; 'I cannot recall any other minister even having chiropody on his radar screen' (private information). His solution at this time for the National Health Service's growing problems was not to retreat from state provision but to pursue efficiency by counter-productively adding all the complexity and cost of an additional managerial layer.

Pioneering 'Thatcherism', 1974–1979 After his government's defeat at the general election of February 1974 Heath rather unexpectedly failed to make Joseph shadow chancellor. Joseph, seeking no other ministerial area of responsibility, opted to remain in the shadow cabinet without portfolio to conduct a radical policy review across the board, establishing the Centre for Policy Studies with Sherman as its first director. 'It was only in April 1974', he wrote, 'that I was converted to Conservatism' (Joseph, 4). Hitherto his career had succeeded only in conventional terms, but now his moment in British history had come: he could at last transcend the short term and launch a shift in the political agenda whose importance is comparable in twentieth-century Conservative politics only to Joseph Chamberlain's bid for tariff reform in 1903. The shift was remarkable because (unlike R. A. Butler's centrist shift of 1945–51) it ultimately reshaped all three major parties, went against the grain of fashionable opinion, was fiercely resisted from within his own party, and was at first conducted single-handedly among former ministers. Of the party's leading figures a few (notably Sir Geoffrey Howe) were in cautious and mostly silent sympathy, and it was Joseph not Thatcher who blazed the trail; furthermore, her position as leader after 1975 set limits to how publicly and rapidly she could support him. Moral courage—the quality Joseph prized above all others, and which he had earlier reproached himself for lacking—was in no way lacking now.

Words, the politician's stock-in-trade, were central to Joseph's achievement, but the words gained impact in the mid-1970s because of the conjuncture between the serious plight of the party and (as many saw it) the desperate situation faced by the country. The interventionist economic policies of the 1960s had come more naturally to socialists than to Conservatives, who found themselves in policy terms placed at a permanent disadvantage by Labour's superior claims on trade-union loyalty. Furthermore, under governments of both parties in the 1970s, interventionism failed to arrest relative economic decline, seemed to entail mounting centralization and control, and ultimately delivered both rising unemployment and escalating inflation, both of which they were designed to prevent. Joseph characteristically blamed himself: 'I was a very bad member of Heath's Cabinet', he

recalled in 1987, 'in the sense that I was obsessed with my departmental job and never raised my head either to recognize, let alone protest about, the monetary incontinence which we adopted' (*The Independent*, 13 Nov 1987).

Like Tony Benn at the opposite end of the political spectrum, Joseph's aim was nothing less than to save the nation with remedies unorthodox and drastic. When the two men met by chance on a train journey in February 1981, their long conversation revealed that their diagnosis had much in common, including the belief (in Benn's words) 'that the last thirty-five years have been a disaster' (Benn, 93). Apart from their shared doubts about incomes policies, their remedies were, however, at opposite poles; besides, the traditions and structure of British party institutions left no room for any formal alliance between them. So Joseph had few allies: after October 1974 the Labour Party had electorally prevailed twice over the Conservatives, the Heath government had failed in all but its central objective—getting Britain into the European Economic Community—and there were as yet few anticipations of the subsequent slow anti-corporatist shift in British intellectual opinion. Joseph claimed that a 'socialist ethic of institutionalized envy' was being 'fostered by many politicians, communicators and academics'; they were creating 'an anti-enterprise climate' which must now be confronted (*The Times*, 7 Oct 1976). Churches, schools, universities, the civil service, and the political parties had diffused within the establishment the notion that 'business is fine, but really it's for the tradesman's entrance' (M. Charlton and K. Joseph, interview, BBC Radio 4, 30 July 1979). Talent was being drawn disproportionately into the professions, teaching, the civil service or the armed forces, but insufficiently into industry and commerce. In crusading for socialism earlier in the century the Webbs had at least been able to rely upon the London School of Economics and the *New Statesman*: not so Joseph in 1974. 'We must fight the battle of ideas in every school, university, publication, committee, TV studio even if we have to struggle for our toehold there', he argued in October: 'we have the truth—if we fail to make it shine clear, we shall be to blame no less than the exploiters, the casuists, the commercialisers' (*The Times*, 21 Oct 1974).

A less likely crusader than Joseph could hardly be imagined: unclubbable and self-tormented, he preferred reading to lobbying. He banned television from his home, and hated being televised. In interviews he did not always appear to advantage because of the almost physical pain he experienced when trying to answer questions: before any answer emerged there were anguished expressions, with a vein noticeably throbbing in his forehead, or long silences, head in hand. Yet Joseph had important assets. His political innocence, even naïvety, was not in this exceptional party-political and national situation necessarily a drawback. Besides, Joseph was something of a phrase-maker, and liked to cut a dash. Nor was significant opinion as hostile as appeared on the surface. Bagehot had long ago pointed out that many people's opinions come from what they think that others think, but that 'in secret, each has his doubts, which he suppresses, because he fancies that others who have thought more about the matter have no such misgivings'; 'if a shrewd examiner were to scrutinise each man's mind', Bagehot continued, 'they would find much tacit, latent, accumulated doubt in each' (*The Collected Works of Walter Bagehot*, ed. N. St John Stevas, vol. 8, 1974, 50). The all-party corporatist orthodoxy had by the 1970s gone so long unchallenged that it was going stale; Joseph's role was to give latent contrary opinion the necessary prod. Conservatives should not feel on the defensive, he said in a speech at St Ermin's Hotel in London on 15 January 1975; arguing their case courteously and intelligently, they should 'not … be deterred by … sneers of those who consider that any idea which is more than a couple of decades old is bad by definition, unless it was written by Marx or Lenin' (Joseph, 63).

Joseph was no original thinker, nor is original thinking the politician's role, but he was interested in ideas, and possessed the creative politician's essential quality: knowing when new ideas are needed, what they are, where to look for them, and how to project them. 'Thatcherism', of which Joseph was more than anyone else the creator in its domestic rather than overseas dimension, needed recruits from other political parties and from none if it was to have any hope of success, and Joseph's contacts were wide. A key influence at this time was his resumed contact with Sherman, whose disillusioned familiarity with the left's panaceas sharpened Joseph's rejection of prevailing orthodoxies. As a former housing minister, Joseph had been impressed by Sherman's two uncompromisingly disparaging articles published in the *Daily Telegraph* on 10 and 29 August 1973 about the impact of social engineering on the new towns and of public subsidies on urban transport. Enoch Powell had challenged interventionist orthodoxy earlier and more publicly, but by 1974 he had left the party, thus freeing up space for Joseph and Thatcher to occupy; besides, Joseph needed a warmer, more evangelical and didactic backroom adviser who could shame him out of his self-confessed political timidity. Sherman behind the scenes, and Thatcher in public, bolstered Joseph with their complete lack of self-doubt and of middle-class guilt.

With Sherman's help Joseph read voraciously: Hayek, Friedman, and the publications of the Institute of Economic Affairs. Several keynote speeches soon followed, the first three between the two general elections of 1974, the rest later. By October 1974 Joseph felt ready to announce that he had 'only recently started to become a Conservative', in that he had 'only recently become a believer, a passionate believer in the virtues of decentralization and individual responsibility and in the indispensability of incentives and rewards' (*The Times*, 25 Oct 1974). This was, in truth, not Conservatism at all, but the radical variant of free-market Liberalism which individualist Liberal refugees from the left since the late-Victorian period had gradually been infusing into the Conservative Party. To former cabinet colleagues, the beguiling innocence of such a public 'conversion' seemed an implied rebuke to

their own lack of vision, and their scepticism was reinforced by knowing how different his private ministerial stance had been in 1970–74. Others felt that Joseph too nonchalantly ignored the impact of his public self-questionings on the party's electoral chances. Still, all Joseph's speeches at this time contained ideas sufficiently dense and arresting to be worth publishing in full in *The Times* at the time, and in booklets later. Cumulatively, courageously, he used them to educate the nation, to create a new policy agenda, even to generate a new political vocabulary. In the process he discredited the claims often made then and since that only the populist and undemanding speech will gain a hearing.

Joseph's instrument was the Centre for Policy Studies (CPS). Originating in his conversations with Sherman before the general election of February 1974, it struck a theoretical note unfamiliar in British politics and still less familiar within the Conservative Party. The CPS soon drew in Thatcher, and promoted collective brainstorming among supporters from other parties and from none. Several of its key figures were unknown in government circles let alone elsewhere, and some were, to say the least, strong meat. Jews were prominent, for the CPS marked a significant episode in Jewish businessmen's move away from Labour; they included not only Joseph and Sherman, but also David Young, Norman Strauss, and David Wolfson. The party's official policy mechanism, the Conservative Research Department, was wary of the upstart CPS, if only because the department's strategy was to devise short-term policies to conciliate prevailing opinion in the hope of winning the next election, whereas the CPS aimed to broaden the terms of public debate so as to free the party from longer-term constraints.

Joseph did not run the Centre for Policy Studies from day to day because between 1974 and 1977 he was preoccupied with what he later called 'my mission': speaking at over 150 university and polytechnic campuses. Some forcibly denied him a hearing, for British universities were not at this time secure homes for free speech; indeed, Joseph found that some university authorities paid only lip-service to it. Far from combative by nature, he none the less enjoyed these encounters; the adrenalin flowed, the microphone usually enabled him to get a hearing, and he was exhilarated to find his private doubts dispelled when he discovered the weakness of the anti-capitalist case. He retained throughout life a youthful inquisitiveness, enjoyed argument, responded vigorously to hecklers, and aimed to unsettle his critics by always claiming his right to ask them a question. Socratically he honed his ideas by conducting what was in effect a nationwide public tutorial, for like Joseph Chamberlain after 1903 his aim was to draw lay people into a complex economic debate.

Joseph's overall strategy soon became clear. His three major speeches before the general election of October 1974 did not deter the party from pursuing the 'middle ground' (a point midway between the existing policies of the Conservative and Labour parties), but thereafter he branded this continuously shifting 'middle ground' as a will-o'-the-wisp which drew pragmatic Conservatives ineluctably into Labour territory: this 'socialist ratchet' must be halted by moving the terms of debate on to safer free-market territory. But with what policies? Joseph aimed instead for what he called the 'common ground': a consensus that reflected, not a lowest common denominator between existing party views, but a more stable set of new policies that might attract people from all parties and from none. Central to his new direction was a bold move towards the free market which had hitherto been almost universally thought impracticable. Given Joseph's earlier corporatist entanglements, such a new direction entailed recantation, for in February 1964 Harold Wilson had labelled him 'Little Sir Echo', frequently espousing policies pioneered by Labour (Denham and Garnett, 125). However, by the mid-1970s there were rich pickings to be made in this area, and Joseph, in a multi-dimensional approach, seized the moment.

Seeking to rescue Keynes from the Keynesians, Joseph emphasized that inter-war unemployment had unduly influenced politicians' attitudes to the very different economic situation which prevailed after 1945. Inappropriate policies had been the result: 'we talked ourselves into believing that those gaunt, tight-lipped men in caps and mufflers were round the corner, and tailored our policy to match these imaginary conditions', as he put it in a speech at Preston on 5 September 1974 (Joseph, 21). Like all the pioneers of Thatcherism he was influenced by overseas comparisons which, they claimed, exposed socialist Britain's relatively poor growth rate and high levels of poverty. Rather than spending the economy out of unemployment, thereby accelerating inflation, Joseph argued that it would be better to rein in the money supply and risk generating the short-term unemployment which would establish a more stable equilibrium. To monetarism he brought all the enthusiasm of the recent convert, with too little thought for the complications, but neither in his Preston speech nor in his Stockton lecture (*Monetarism is not Enough*, 1976) did he claim that a monetarist squeeze was alone sufficient. Working practices, returns on investment, levels of pay, rates of taxation, and the incidence of welfare should all, he thought, be adjusted in the face of an increasingly global market for goods and services.

Joseph identified 'six poisons' wrecking British prosperity: excessive government spending, high direct taxation, egalitarianism, excessive nationalization, politicized trade unions associated with Luddism, and an anti-enterprise culture. The United Kingdom was, he said, the only country in the world with all six. 'We are over-governed, over-spent, over-taxed, over-borrowed and over-manned', he declared (K. Joseph, *Monetarism is not Enough*, 19). The British economy, unduly politicized, was too readily distorted by politicians' short-term vote-catching priorities. Nationalized concerns did not benefit the general public but only the trade-union leaders and the interventionist governments which they locked into a partnership of mutual short-term self-interest. In the longer term nationalized industries demanded subsidies, which in turn pushed up taxes, thereby weakening further the more competitive parts of the economy. Each

well-intentioned intervention distorted the economy further, mobilizing further needs, precedents, and vested interests behind an unending socialistic spiral; foredoomed incomes policies, with all their centralized and impracticable intrusiveness, were the dénouement.

The alternative for Joseph was the Victorian free-market ideal, Liberal in origin, Conservative by adoption. He felt that the entrepreneurial case should be robustly re-stated so that a new 'common ground' consensus could assemble behind it, for he believed that competitive business values were more popular even among trade unionists than the Labour Party allowed: free collective bargaining and free enterprise went together and could each draw recruits into the new 'common ground'. Democratic priorities required the politician to defend consumer against producer, and to readjust the balance between the voter's selection in the polling booth and the consumer's selection in the marketplace. Beneath this lay a view of human nature, readily misrepresented, that elevated self-interest among the incentives to action. Joseph believed that trade unions, for all their socialist pretensions, were as driven by self-interest as anyone else, but that socialist policies were converting them from being genuinely representative structures into agencies of an increasingly centralized state. For Joseph as for Powell before him, trade unionists who opposed incomes policies were not being irresponsible: they were performing their traditional and necessary role of defending their members' interests.

Joseph accompanied his economic prescription with at least three supplementary policy options, not all of them subsequently pursued. Briefly in March 1975 he advocated strengthening government authority against revolutionary movements while simultaneously enacting a Bill of Rights, but he and Thatcher later viewed experiments with all-party coalition, devolution, electoral reform, and other attempts to fend off the state as half-admissions of defeat, and preferred to face the enemy head on. A second policy option had been pioneered by Powell: exploiting hostility to immigration, and in 1978 Joseph backed Thatcher in her scaled-down variant of it which aimed to conciliate anti-immigrant sentiment by enacting legislation which would remove unnecessary apprehension. Yet for him any approach towards resisting immigration had a double drawback: it was particularly difficult for a Jew to espouse, and it was still more difficult to reconcile with commitment to the free market.

A third policy option, ultimately rejected, seemed at times more promising: to exploit the reaction against the 'permissive society' of the 1960s and tar socialism with its brush. This Joseph attempted in his somewhat shrill speech at Edgbaston on 19 October 1974, arguing that legislation could succeed only if founded upon a remoralized community. He urged his audience to 'take inspiration from that admirable woman Mary Whitehouse … a shining example of what one person can do singlehandedly when inspired by faith and compassion' (*The Times*, 21 Oct 1974). Her response was to tell reporters that 'until this speech, the people of Britain have been like sheep without a shepherd. But now they have found one'

(Denham and Garnett, 267). This third strategy was soon scotched, however, by critics' distorted interpretation of one section in his speech. Crime could be reduced, he said, through reducing the number of problem families; this could be achieved through encouraging birth control among unmarried mothers at some social levels. Some chose to view this as eugenic prescription: he was accused by the miners' leader Jo Gormley of saying that 'we should put down the kids produced by what he calls the lower classes', and the TGWU's leader Jack Jones reminded him of the need to improve social justice rather than preach morality (The Times, 21 Oct 1974). Such responses were hasty, politically self-interested, and crude, but Joseph's attempt to correlate permissiveness with socialism was undoubtedly simplistic; nor was religious and traditionalist fundamentalism strong enough in Britain to support the American conservative strategy of mobilizing the 'moral majority'.

Joseph's attack—soon abandoned—on sixties values was none the less significant because it permanently damaged him as a candidate in the contest of 1975 to challenge Heath for the Conservative leadership. It did not, however, do damage to the Conservative Party or to Joseph's long-term role—because for both of these Joseph's apparent setback constituted a blessing in disguise. Although he remained a contender for the leadership until 21 November 1974, Joseph on his own admission would not have made a good party leader, whereas with Thatcher as leader he enjoyed ready access to and respect from the party's longest-serving twentieth-century prime minister. In the contest to succeed Heath, Joseph had at first been the candidate of the right, William Whitelaw that of the left. But Joseph then backed Thatcher for the leadership— the only member of the shadow cabinet openly to do so— bringing some of his supporters with him. The historic Thatcher–Joseph partnership was improbable: both had, it is true, attended Oxford University, but there the similarities ceased. Joseph was a brilliant and wealthy but diffident metropolitan Jew drawn from the élite, whereas Thatcher was an opinionated and self-made but decisive provincial drawn from a Methodist shopkeeping family.

Following her victory in the leadership election of February 1975, Thatcher did not make Joseph shadow chancellor, as some had predicted, perhaps because she doubted his political judgement: instead he was asked to remain responsible for policy and research. He was now free to focus on his economic policy option, where in the longer term the Labour Party was most vulnerable. Joseph's pronouncements gained the more weight after February 1977 when he succeeded John Biffen as Conservative spokesman on industry. In the party's reorientation after 1975, wrote Hugo Young, 'Joseph articulated ideas, Howe formulated policies, and Mrs Thatcher was the essential conduit from one to the other' (Young, 107). The implications of such a major shift in the political agenda ramified far beyond the economic sphere. A multi-layered historiographical revolution was one consequence: Conservative Party history now needed revaluation, and there was an unexpected rejuvenation of interest in Victorian values

and institutions such as self-improvement, entrepreneurship, rigorous control of public spending, the respectable artisan, and the libertarian trade union. In January 1975 Joseph welcomed the possibility of universal embourgeoisement, oriented round an almost forgotten ideal: the 'artisan of Victorian days, who read serious literature, supported radical causes, was sober and self-improving' (The Guardian, 16 Jan 1975). In 1986 his introduction to the Penguin reissue of Samuel Smiles's Self-Help (originally published in 1859) as a 'management classic' saw the book as 'deeply expressive of the spirit of its own times' but also as 'a book for our times' (introduction, S. Smiles, Self-Help, 1986, 16). It was, he said, a salutary corrective to the 'perceptible depressing limpness in individual attitudes' (p. 11) flowing from public welfare and high taxation. 'Only when we match the ... moral qualities ... of our more productive competitors abroad can we hope to employ all those here who seek work' (p. 13).

Joseph's new agenda also carried implications for political institutions and for the politician's role within them: if politicians attempted less, he thought, they would fail less often, and political institutions would then be less vulnerable to the indignation that flows from disappointed expectations. Politicians would then be more likely to succeed in the somewhat diminished role for which they were better qualified. Joseph's stance also had implications for a political vocabulary which Conservatives needed to recapture from the left. 'Unemployment', for example, should no longer be an emotive, inflated, and global figure: it should be resolved into sub-categories— frictional, voluntary, fraudulent, regional, short-term, long-term, and so on—a procedure which Keynes would have found entirely acceptable. Thence flowed relatively diverse and at first sight irrelevant remedies such as reviving the rented housing sector, new incentives to move between jobs, and reformed procedures for welfare payment. The 'customer' and the 'taxpayer' now received a new prominence in public discussion. Using words and phrases that were often unfamiliar, even eccentric, Joseph sometimes ended up by inverting accepted values. Jobs could not be created, they 'occurred'; trade unions did not create employment, they destroyed it; welfare payments pauperized; and planning produced chaos and stagnation. None of these ideas made much immediate impact on public opinion at large, but they gained credibility from the Labour governments' mounting difficulties between 1974 and 1979, and influenced an ever-widening band of significant opinion.

Secretary of state for industry, 1979–1981 No subsequent achievement of Joseph's could compare with his role in promulgating what came to be called Thatcherism; indeed, there was something anticlimactic about his career thereafter, though not about the impact of the policy revolution that he had pioneered. He continued to preach in office the same free-market message, and no small part of his achievement after 1979 lay in his staunch backing for Thatcher at a time when she was fighting on that basis for supremacy within her party. In his two ministerial posts, however, he experienced all the difficulty that flows from trying to implement innovative policies hitherto somewhat abstractly conceived. Former allies accused him of caving in before his civil servants, but this underestimated both the scale of his task and the courage of his refusal to sound any public retreat. None the less, his open-mindedness was a hindrance when it came to taking decisions, and his civil servants often prevailed.

As secretary of state for industry from May 1979 Joseph began bravely enough, questioning early on whether his department really needed to exist. He presented his senior civil servants at their request with a reading list, subsequently famous, which listed twenty authors, including Tocqueville, Adam Smith, and Schumpeter, as well as several publications from the Institute of Economic Affairs and the Centre for Policy Studies. 'Cuts in state spending of sufficient magnitude to reduce inflation substantially will require strong nerves', he had argued in his Stockton lecture; 'but the alternative would be accelerating decline in standard of living and in employment within the next few years' (K. Joseph, *Monetarism is not Enough*, 1976, 17). He immediately set about cautiously dismembering subsidies and redrawing the map of regional aid: 'nothing will do more for the prosperity of a region', he told parliament on 17 July 1979, playing down the impact of subsidies, 'than a reputation for effective work, high productivity and co-operation between work force and management' (*Hansard 5C*, vol. 970, col. 1307, 17 July 1979). Government job-creation schemes he described as 'Dead Sea fruit', and he was fond of saying that 'there should be a monument to the unknown unemployed, the men who have lost their jobs because of state aid elsewhere' (*The Observer*, 22 July 1979). None the less, when in the key position of power after 1979 he did not split up or sell off British Leyland, he failed to close down the National Enterprise Board, and he did not break up the Post Office monopoly of the telephone system; nor can he be credited with edging the Conservatives towards the privatization that lent such drive to Thatcher's second government.

In some ways Joseph got the worst of both worlds. He did not push fully home the policies in which he believed, and he continued to prop up with public funds such concerns as British Steel and British Leyland. Yet at the same time he reaped no credit with those who favoured such handouts because he was too honest to conceal his distaste for what he was doing. Often photographed at this time in his impeccably tailored suits—Joseph was once voted one of the top ten best-dressed men in the country—this was not a happy time for him, and the photographs often revealed tortured features. He was in the front line in the government's ultimately successful battle to defeat the strike in the steel industry which began in January 1980; for him this was 'a clear example of the British disease—a demand for higher pay without readiness to co-operate in financing that higher pay by higher productivity' (*Hansard 5C*, 976.1893, 17 Jan 1980). For his forthright dismissal of predicted governmental 'U-turns' in policy he became intensely unpopular, and was often beset by angry pickets and hecklers: 'for generations to come the name Joseph will stink in the nostrils of the

people of South Wales', the Labour MP for Newport declared (ibid., 976.1933, 17 Jan 1980). It was with some relief that in Thatcher's reshuffle of September 1981 he swapped the Department of Industry for the Department of Education and Science. In the latter department, as in the former, much of his achievement was concealed at the time, but it bore rich fruit later.

Secretary of state for education and science, 1981–1986 Joseph's period at the Department of Industry had been, in policy terms, a mere postscript to what he had achieved before 1979. At the Department of Education and Science, however, he resumed the role of pioneer. He had asked Thatcher for his new post because he had come to see education as central to Britain's economic plight. He had, after all, for years been condemning what he called Britain's 'anti-enterprise culture', and relished the idea of challenging it at its heart. Once again Joseph's new move rested upon overseas comparisons unfavourable to Britain, and once more he offered guidance to his civil servants: this time only one booklet, *Lessons from Europe: a Comparison of British and West European Schooling* (1977), which he had commissioned for the Centre for Policy Studies from the educational journalist Max Wilkinson. Its recommendations coincided markedly with Joseph's ministerial initiatives, which challenged the many vested interests and traditionalist attitudes that clustered round and within his department. British educational traditions were non-interventionist, and some pride had long been taken in the weakness of central control over curricular matters. Soon after his appointment, a journalist asked Joseph how he was settling into his new job; 'I haven't found the levers yet', he replied (Denham and Garnett, 397). Like Wilkinson, Joseph knew that as education minister he lacked powers comparable to those of his European counterparts; much of the control lay with local authorities, teachers' unions, educational experts, and the civil servants with whom they were allied. Indeed, for Joseph's successor, Kenneth Baker, the department epitomized 'producer capture' at the expense of the consumer (Baker, 168).

Hard-working as usual, Joseph was also cautious, conducting departmental business 'by endlessly (and courteously) arbitrating between the views of ministers and officials as though he were conducting a seminar' (*The Times*, 12 Dec 1994). As always, he loved the debate and hated making the decision. Furthermore his desire to improve educational standards coincided with his reluctance to seek more money for his department, and this provoked on 4 December 1984 what *The Times* described as 'one of the angriest grillings given to a minister for many years' by a parliamentary committee. Over 250 Conservative backbenchers attended a one-hour meeting on Joseph's proposal to cut by £39 million the taxpayer subsidy to students whose parents were in high income brackets; only 3 of the 33 backbench speakers supported him, and one commented that 'Keith is just sitting there silent and slightly aghast' (*The Times*, 5 Dec 1984). His stance also provoked one of the longest disruptions to schools in British history—the strikes organized from February 1985 by the teachers in England and Wales. And despite his belief in student loans, backed by Nigel Lawson as chancellor of the exchequer, he was slow to propose them (he did so in 1985) and was forced to retreat.

Yet a minister's success cannot be judged solely by success in avoiding controversy; indeed, the creative politician must sometimes court it. In contrast with his conduct at the Department of Industry, though not at all inconsistently with it, Joseph at the Department of Education and Science was an interventionist. His first requirement was information and means of influence before he could hope for effective reform; his response would have won whole-hearted approval from J. S. Mill, whose governmental vision entailed 'the greatest dissemination of power consistent with efficiency; but the greatest possible centralization of information, and diffusion of it from the centre' (*Liberty* in *The Collected Works of John Stuart Mill*, ed. J. M. Robson, vol. 18, 1977, 309); power might not be centralized, but information could be. Like Wilkinson, Joseph felt that surveys of schools' performance could be conducted, reports on them encouraged and publicized, standards set, and financial and other rewards channelled to schools that moved in the desired direction. He equipped himself with a far more powerful machine to inspect schools and provide the department with information about them. Many more inspectors were appointed, their influence was increased, regular appraisal of teachers was required, and (against opposition from within the department) the inspectors' reports received wide publicity. Also under Joseph the department lost important functions to other departments: technical and vocational education to the Department of Employment and the Manpower Services Commission, and provision of computers in schools to the Department of Trade and Industry (as his old department had become, following its merger with the Department of Trade in June 1983). Within the schools Joseph made some progress in diverting power from the local authority to the parent. All this empowered the minister against the sceptics who initially beset him.

Joseph accompanied structural change with moves towards important detailed reforms, many of them implemented by his successor. He felt a special concern for the non-academic child labelled as a failure when trapped within a system that had been unduly moulded by university needs, and sympathized with parents who wanted schools to encourage basic vocational skills and more practical subjects. There were moves to issue records of achievement to all pupils, as well as to provide formal vocational qualifications and enhance their status. The merger in 1986 of CSEs and O-levels into the GCSE examination aimed to convert a threshold hitherto used to divide the academic sheep from the non-academic goats into a gateway which opened onto opportunities for all, so that all children would have a chance to get a worthwhile national school-leaving certificate. Also under Joseph moves towards a national core curriculum were launched. 'Where other education ministers tinkered,

fudged or shelved difficult education issues', wrote Wendy Berliner, 'Keith Joseph plunged in' (*The Guardian*, 22 May 1986). Holding office for four years and eight months, Joseph was the longest-serving education secretary since H. A. L. Fisher (1916–22). In the short term he was both less popular and legislatively less successful than many of his predecessors. But in seeking to widen the agenda of practical politics in education he was more ambitious than most, and his long-term impact was greater. As an obituarist pointed out, 'it is … for his courageous and quietly persistent efforts to make people think about educational standards, and then raise them, that he should be properly remembered' (*The Times*, 12 Dec 1994).

Last years Joseph asked to be relieved of his post in spring 1986, nor did he wish to continue in the cabinet as minister without portfolio—this despite Thatcher's need to ensure that there were 'more of us' in a cabinet which now included too few among her inner circle of supporters. He was made a Companion of Honour, and the dissolution honours of 1987 brought him a life peerage, as Baron Joseph, of Portsoken in the City of London. He became a regular speaker in the House of Lords, defending the Thatcherite position, turning increasingly against the European connection, and on the welfare front getting more and more interested in voluntarism—especially in Home-Start, which aimed to mobilize volunteers to defend children in broken homes who were at risk of being taken into care. Yet on the welfare front he was no longer pushing forward the Thatcherite frontier. She had been turning her mind to social welfare issues from summer 1982 onwards, and towards the end of the decade these were rising among her priorities. What Thatcherism needed by then was an adventurous doctrinal advance into this Labour territory. Joseph lacked the energy or the inspiration to make what for him would have been a third policy breakthrough. For this he can scarcely be blamed, for Thatcher and her admirers from the late 1980s became too preoccupied with Europe to contribute much in this area either. Instead, Joseph contented himself with assuming an almost protective role towards Thatcher, whose achievements prompted him to display a tutor's pride in a pupil far more successful than himself. 'She is the best prime minister we could have had, and overwhelmingly the best for this parliament and the next', he declared in *The Times* on 7 May 1990. By then there was much to be said against that view, yet so greatly did he resent Sir Geoffrey Howe's role in Thatcher's downfall that at the meeting of Conservatives held on 4 December 1990 formally to endorse Major as leader, he turned courteously but firmly away from Howe, saying 'I'm sorry, Geoffrey: we're not friends any more' (Howe, 676).

Joseph's intensely nervous disposition was related to a chronic, persistent, and often painful set of physical ailments, but an unfamiliar serenity attended his final years. On 16 August 1990 he married Yolanda Victoria Sheriff (*b.* 1924), whom he had known since the 1940s. The daughter of the late Charles Vita Castro, engineering merchant, and herself a divorcee, she had been living in Connecticut, USA. Joseph had a stroke in 1993 and was partly paralysed; in a debate on the family on 23 February 1994 he gave from a wheelchair his last speech in the House of Lords. Early in December, in a two-hour visit from Thatcher, they discussed similar subjects, but it was their last meeting. 'As he approached the end in hospital, Keith, though mortally weak, was still alert', she wrote; 'characteristically, after what would be our final discussion, he asked whether I would find it useful if he recorded his views in a memorandum. Sadly, it never came' (Thatcher, *Path to Power*, xiv). On 10 December 1994, in the presence of his second wife and his children, Joseph died at the Royal Brompton and National Heart Hospital, Chelsea, of bronchopneumonia and chronic obstructive airways disease. He was buried near his wife's farm in Connecticut. His only son, James Samuel Joseph, succeeded to the baronetcy in 1994 but chose not to use the title.

Assessment Listing the 'full members' of 'the group of Tory radicals' who 'were the Government's driving force during the first two Thatcher parliaments', Nigel Lawson included Sir Geoffrey Howe, Norman Tebbit, and himself as among the most important, but also Joseph (Lawson, 599). Although the overall shift in the political agenda that Thatcherism entailed owed most to Thatcher herself, she was the first to acknowledge that in its domestic aspect it had been pioneered by Joseph, not simply as the first major politician to embrace it and promote it with courage and energy, but as her staunch backer in the difficult early years of her premiership. 'You, more than anyone else, were the architect who, starting from first principles and involving many people, shaped the policies which led to victory in two elections', she wrote on Joseph's retirement, in an exchange of letters less insincere than is customary on such occasions: 'our debt to you is great indeed' (*The Guardian*, 22 May 1986). While Joseph's ministerial career in 1979–86 saw many disappointments and failures, these partly reflected his courage in tackling the difficult tasks which most ministers push to one side, and in ministerial posts where new thinking was essential. In both posts he set in train policies and attitudes fruitful enough to become an all-party orthodoxy after 1997.

The personality lying behind this unusual achievement remains something of a mystery. Joseph was tense and intense, enormously conscientious, and ever willing to listen—eagerly recording people's remarks in his notebooks, and energetically seeking and following up people's recommendations on what to read. Howe found it extraordinary to go on a long journey with him: it 'was like travelling with a foraging squirrel: he was constantly tearing articles out of newspapers, writing notes to himself and stowing them about his person' (Howe, 39). There was no doubt a domestic price to pay for all this, but Joseph hated publicity, and his wives and children maintained a reticence about him that he would have welcomed. The two biographies which had appeared by 2001 (by Halcrow and by Denham and Garnett) were therefore necessarily confined to his public personality. Joseph puzzled his fellow politicians, and the sobriquet 'mad monk'

gained some currency—a label more discreditable to its inventor than to Joseph. However convinced politicians may be on entering politics that they can make a difference, their sense of purpose and their belief that problems can be solved often gets worn down by the pluralism, the uncertainties, and the manipulation that inevitably accompany achievement in a democratic society. Only in a very exceptional situation can an impact be made by a politician who lacks artifice, who dislikes personal publicity, who lacks a personal following, who refuses to blur political issues, and who dislikes the media. In the 1970s Joseph had the intelligence to see that such a situation existed and the courage to seize the opportunity.

To important sections of the general public—traditionalists on the shop floor and in the board-room—Joseph became from 1974 a hate figure. Yet to those politicians who knew him he was kind and diffident in the extreme, courteous, and painfully scrupulous. He 'never seems to be more at home', wrote T. E. Utley, 'than when apologising for something which is not his fault' (*Sunday Telegraph*, 22 May 1986). On day-to-day matters Joseph was approachable, considerate, generous, loyal, upright, and a good colleague: according to Norman Fowler, 'one of the best men that I knew in fifteen years on the front bench' (Fowler, 9), for Michael Heseltine 'one of the kindest men I ever met in British politics' (Heseltine, 157), for Nigel Lawson 'a secular saint' (Lawson, 599), and for Norman Tebbit 'one of the kindest, most highly principled, thoughtful and decent men in politics—or anywhere else' (Tebbit, 173). Kenneth Baker recalled how Joseph's innate courtesy led him to accompany his visitors from the top floor of the Department of Education and Science down in the lift to the main door, something Baker had never seen done by any other minister (private information). He was personally generous, too. The housing minister who in the early 1960s worried about the scarcity of low-cost accommodation, for example, created the non-profit-making Mulberry Housing Trust, of which he was founder and first chairman (1965–9); it refurbished in Rachman's area of Paddington dilapidated residential property which was then let and ultimately sold to the poor and elderly, and was eventually responsible for about 800 properties. But Joseph was too trusting: the trust collapsed in the 1970s after serious fraud by senior staff. Joseph was an essentially decent man, ambitious not for himself but for his country, and distressed at the scale of its relative economic decline during his lifetime. He was not content merely to have ideas about remedies, but was courageous enough to act upon them.

Despite the fact that Joseph exerted profound long-term influence, his name was in eclipse by the end of the century in Conservative circles. Partly this was because he was too intelligent and too open-minded ever to be a safe party man. Although the policy shift to which he contributed more than anyone was effectively anti-socialist, antisocialism does not constitute the mainstream within British Conservatism, whose overall outlook transcends such short-term purposes. Like the most famous among his Jewish Conservative predecessors, he possessed considerable creative political imagination, but he lacked Disraeli's romantic attachment to party for its own sake. Joseph was not the sort of dependable, stolid, unmovable Wellington, Salisbury, or Baldwin likely to enthuse the right; furthermore, his major and unconcealed mid-career shift was to a line of domestic policy whose pedigree was more Liberal than Conservative. Joseph's was a nervous, restless, rationalistic, questing temperament that is more often found on the left. His self-doubt made him seem wayward—though to the charge of careerism and of pursuing power for its own sake he was much less vulnerable than Peel, Joseph Chamberlain, or Winston Churchill. He 'had no beliefs or gut instincts', John Redwood (who knew him well and admired him) recalled. 'This made life an agony for him—he was travelling without a map or compass, constantly asking the way of sages living and dead ... I remember him saying to me once "I admire your certainty"—he certainly had no inner certainty about life' (private information). Though Joseph voiced no public doubts, Conservatives may have sensed that, had he been a younger man, he might have moved on again, forsaking in his open-mindedness the Thatcherism to which he had contributed so much.

Besides, Joseph's career did not seem relevant to what the Conservative Party viewed as its particular need after 1997, for by then it was in hot (and, Joseph would have said, mistaken) pursuit of the comfortable centrist 'middle' ground rather than of the 'common' ground that in the 1970s he had thought it important to occupy—and whose Thatcherite potential for the party was far from exhausted. Viewed from the post-Thatcher Conservative perspective, therefore, Joseph was an uncomfortable figure, for after 1974 he had never aimed merely to pursue an ephemeral and shifting consensus: his aim was to re-locate the political agenda on territory more congenial to his party and to the long-term prosperity of his country. Again, at the Department of Industry in 1979–81, he was resisting—with ultimate success—a corporatist trend that his predecessors since the 1930s had all endorsed. At the Department of Education and Science in 1981–6 he was resisting, again with ultimate success, a deeply engrained distancing of school and university education from the needs of the economy, and was defending children and their parents against the resistance to change and the short-term articulated self-interest of their teachers. Conservatives, seeking by the late 1990s a lost consensual image, thought that their electoral chances required them to forget as much as possible about their party's recent history: Joseph was dispensable because he could hardly be seen as standing for comfortable consensus. Thatcherism within the Conservative Party, like Blairism within the Labour Party, was a minority strain, continuously battling against traditionalists and the easy option, and vulnerable after her departure. With one prominent Conservative, however, Joseph's memory remained green. 'Keith and I have no toes', Thatcher once said; so close was their partnership that in argument each had no fear of offending the other (*The Independent*, 12 Dec 1994).

The first volume of Thatcher's autobiography was dedicated to Joseph, and in its acknowledgements she took care to record 'a debt ... which can never be repaid' (Thatcher, *Path to Power*, xiv). BRIAN HARRISON

Sources M. Halcrow, *Keith Joseph: a singular mind* (1989) • A. Denham and M. Garnett, *Keith Joseph* (2001) • *The Times* (12 Dec 1994) • *The Independent* (13 Nov 1987) • *Daily Telegraph* (12 Dec 1994) • *The Guardian* (12 Dec 1994) • *The Independent* (12 Dec 1994) • *Keith Joseph, CH, PC, MA, 17 January 1918–10 December 1994: addresses delivered at the commemorative gathering on Saturday, 3 June 1995* (All Souls College, Oxford) • K. Joseph, *Reversing the trend* (1975) • M. Charlton and K. Joseph, interview, BBC Radio 4, 30 July 1979 • B. Harrison and K. Joseph, tape-recorded interview, 7 Aug 1992 • R. Cockett, *Thinking the unthinkable: think-tanks and the economic counter-revolution, 1931–1983* (1994) • J. Hoskyns, *Just in time: inside the Thatcher revolution* (2000) • B. Harrison, 'Mrs Thatcher and the intellectuals', *Twentieth Century British History*, 5/2 (1994), 206–45 • K. Baker, *The turbulent years: my life in politics* (1993) • T. Benn, *The end of an era: diaries, 1980–90*, ed. R. Winstone (1992) • N. Fowler, *Ministers decide: a personal memoir of the Thatcher years* (1991) • M. Heseltine, *Life in the jungle: my autobiography* (2000) • G. Howe, *Conflict of loyalty* (1994) • N. Lawson, *The view from no. 11: memoirs of a tory radical* (1992) • N. Tebbit, *Upwardly mobile* (1988) • M. Thatcher, *The Downing Street years* (1993) • M. Thatcher, *The path to power* (1995) • H. Young, *One of us: a biography of Margaret Thatcher* (1989) • WWW • Burke, *Peerage* • personal knowledge (2004) • private information (2004) • b. cert. • m. cert. [Hellen Louise Guggenheimer] • m. cert. [Yolanda Victoria Sheriff] • d. cert.
Archives BLPES, corresp. with J. E. Meade • Bodl. Oxf., corresp. with Lionel Curtis • NL Wales, corresp. with Leo Abse
Likenesses N. Posner, photograph, 1987, NPG [*see illus.*] • photograph, repro. in *The Times* • photograph, repro. in *The Independent* • photograph, repro. in *The Guardian* • photograph, repro. in *Daily Telegraph* • photographs, repro. in Halcrow, *Keith Joseph* • photographs, repro. in Denham and Garnett, *Keith Joseph*

Joseph, Sir Maxwell [*formerly* Max] (1910–1982), hotelier and property dealer, was born Max Joseph on 31 May 1910, at 21 Whitechapel Road, London, the second of the three sons of Jack Joseph, a journeyman tailor and property dealer, and his wife, Sarah Orler, a schoolteacher. His education was a failure until his father sent him to Pitman's Business School, where he learned shorthand, typing, and bookkeeping. At the age of nineteen, with £500 from his father, he set up his own Bayswater estate agency, Connaught Hooper, and a small private property company. In 1932 he married Sybil, the daughter of Harry Nedas, a clothier. They had one son and one daughter. Sybil's sister Edna in 1936 married another property developer, Harold Samuel, afterwards Baron Samuel of Wych Cross. One spur to Joseph's early efforts was the success of his wife's sister and brother-in-law. Always a heavy gambler, he took risks in his trading: in the period between the Munich crisis and the declaration of war he came near to bankruptcy.

Joseph was released from the army in 1946 after serving as a lance-corporal in the Royal Engineers. Having managed service chambers in St James's, he bought small hotels in Kensington, such as the Milestone, then acquired the Mandeville in St Marylebone, and other hotels around Mayfair. He had keen intuitions about the potential value of properties and was prescient about the growth of mass tourism. His purchase of the Mount Royal Hotel at Marble

Sir Maxwell Joseph (1910–1982), by Elliott & Fry

Arch for £1 million (1957) was a breakthrough in his status. It was during the 1950s that he adopted the forename Maxwell in preference to the more spivvy Max. He merged the Mount Royal company in 1962 with Grand Hotels (Mayfair) Ltd, which he had formed with associates in 1957, to create Grand Metropolitan Hotels Ltd. Although he revelled in the role of luxury hotelier, he learned that his hotels were most successful when he delegated their operational management. Essentially a great entrepreneur, he stood out from contemporaries such as Jack Cotton by organizing a consummately efficient business bureaucracy under himself. As a result of his skill in delegation, Joseph was able to relax in his office and give expansive thought to new possibilities as well as attend to the minutiae of his deals.

Grand Metropolitan catered to the upper bracket of travellers, and centralized the renting of hotel rooms rather than delegating it to individual hotel managers, as had hitherto been customary. It reduced the number of empty rooms attributable to seasonal fluctuations by promoting 'mini-holidays' priced to cover only marginal costs. By 1974 more than 140,000 customers a year took mini-holidays at Grand Metropolitan hotels, accounting for 70 per cent of the British market in such holidays. In the mid-1960s Joseph complained that the Treasury underestimated the importance of hoteliers as earners of foreign exchange, and he resented the selective employment tax introduced by the Wilson government in May 1966. In that year he cancelled British projects worth £3.5 million and pursued a policy of foreign acquisitions,

including three hotels in Paris (1967) and the Royal Manhattan in New York (1969). His favourite hotel in the group became the Carlton at Cannes.

During the 1950s Joseph dealt in rented property. Following the relaxation of rent controls, in 1958 he bought the Dolphin Square buildings, Pimlico, containing 1200 flats, for £2.5 million. His sale of this property to a dubious company called Lintang Investments, whose leader Friedrich Grunwald was afterwards convicted of fraud, caused a scandal which injured Joseph's reputation. He continued to speculate in property independently of Grand Metropolitan's business, and made a second fortune in this way. Among other interests, he became chairman of the merchant bank of Robert Fraser & Partners (1966), joint chairman of Lombard Banking (1966), chairman of Union Property Holdings, owners of the Classic cinema chain (1969–70), and a director of the Cunard shipping line (1966–71).

Grand Metropolitan bought Express Dairies for £32 million in 1969, the Berni Inn chain of 130 steakhouses and fifteen hotels for £15 million in 1970, and the Mecca betting shops, dance-halls, and bingo houses for £33 million. After a furiously contested battle, it gained control of the brewery Truman Hanbury Buxton in 1971, and soon afterwards acquired the Watney Mann brewery for £400 million. This coup, which had previously eluded Charles Clore, was then the largest recorded British take-over. By 1975 Grand Metropolitan had a debt of over £500 million; interest charges of £54.3 million exceeded pre-tax profits of £41.9 million. These problems were surmounted, and in 1980 Grand Metropolitan resumed its campaign of take-overs by buying the Liggett Group Inc., an American tobacco and drinks company. Joseph was expeditious: in 1981, when Pan American Airways' difficulties became evident, he settled terms to buy their eighty-three Intercontinental hotels in forty-six countries before other hoteliers had finished their plans or mustered their forces. In the City of London, Joseph's acquisitions were considered rash, and he reciprocated the mistrust.

Edward Erdman described Joseph as 'a slim, soft-voiced courteous man with a friendly smile … in order to appease his impulsive disposition, he would start reading half a dozen or more books at once and keep them all going by delving into each in turn' (Erdman, 128). Joseph was a keen philatelist. Diminutive in stature and sensitive by disposition, he preferred understatement to histrionics, and regarded the world with ironic vigilance. He was capable of small, attentive kindnesses, and was the most prepossessing of his generation of property tycoons and the most humane in his pursuit of take-over bids. In his office life he was protected by a succession of formidably able and intelligent secretaries: the calibre and responsibilities of his last assistant, Judith Bowen, surpassed those of many managing directors.

Joseph separated from his wife in 1953, but was unable to settle terms for a divorce before accepting a knighthood in the new year honours of 1981. For many years he had lived with a woman of great charm and character, who was known as Eileen Joseph (1922–1994). She was

Eileen Olive Simpson, a divorcee, the daughter of Arthur Scott Warrell, a clerical officer. They were finally married in 1981. She designed the interiors of many of Grand Metropolitan's hotels and restaurants, and Joseph gave her La Mas Candille, a superior restaurant at Mougins in the south of France. Joseph, who took great pleasure in his cigars, retired as chairman of Grand Metropolitan in July 1982 after a diagnosis of cancer, and died on 22 September at his home, Park House, Pelham Street, Kensington.

RICHARD DAVENPORT-HINES

Sources personal knowledge (1990) [DNB] · private information (1990) · The Times (24 Sept 1982) · E. L. Erdman, People and property (1982) · N. Broackes, A growing concern (1979) · CGPLA Eng. & Wales (1982) · C. Shaw, 'Joseph, Sir Maxwell', DBB · DNB

Archives Grand Metropolitan plc, St James's Square, London, Grand Metropolitan MSS

Likenesses Elliott & Fry, photograph, NPG [see illus.] · photograph, Grand Metropolitan plc, Brighton; repro. in Shaw, 'Joseph, Sir Maxwell'

Wealth at death £17,315,831: probate, 17 Dec 1982, CGPLA Eng. & Wales

Joseph, Michael [called an Gof] (d. 1497), rebel, was probably born in the parish of St Keverne on the Lizard in Cornwall. A blacksmith by trade, Joseph was chosen to be the 'hede capitayne' of the angry demonstrations in west Cornwall against the government of King Henry VII in mid-May 1497. These swiftly escalated into a full-scale uprising across the south-west, the first of two major insurrections in the region that year, and the decision was taken to march on Exeter and London. His epithet (an Gof, the smith) implies that Joseph spoke Cornish rather than English as his first language, an attribute which would have made him an ideal leader of the commons from the still largely monoglot western peninsulas of Penwith and the Lizard. As the rebels moved east, Joseph was joined in command by Thomas Flamank, a Bodmin gentleman who had served in parliament as a burgess of the town in 1492.

The story of Michael Joseph and the 1497 western rebellion was first told in Polydore Vergil's *Anglica historia* and two of the manuscript London chronicles, the Vitellius and 'great' chronicles. These accounts were reviewed and embellished in Edward Hall's printed *Chronicle* of 1548. All blame the insurrection on the excessive taxation imposed in 1496 to fund Henry VII's military and naval campaign against Scotland. Of these four sources, Hall comes the closest to alleging that Joseph entertained any designs against the king's person. Writing fifty years after the event and building on Vergil's picture of the 'wretched Cornish' and their infertile land, Hall claimed that 'the Cornish men inhabityng the least parte of the realme, and thesame sterile and without all fecunditee, forgettynge their due obeysaunce, beganne temerariously to speake of the kyng him selfe'. In this they were encouraged by Joseph and Flamank, 'men of high courages & stoute stomackes', who 'cast oyle & pitche into a fyre & ceased not to provoke & prick theim forward like frantique persons to more mischiefe' (*Hall's Chronicle*, 477). By contrast, the London chronicles contain no hint that the western rebels contemplated deposing Henry VII.

Joseph led his retinue successfully through Devon and into Somerset, where more men adhered to the rebel cause and James Tuchet, Lord Audley, was recruited as a third leader. Audley took charge of a contingent marching to Wallingford, while Joseph travelled the road from Wells to Winchester and on to Guildford. By mid-June the rebels had reached Blackheath, overlooking the Thames at Greenwich. Support for Michael Joseph, both within and beyond his army, had so far remained high, a tribute to his remarkable powers of leadership. The rebels' decision to pay for their provisions and supplies, rather than forcibly requisition them from the country through which they passed, had helped them to achieve the outskirts of London virtually unopposed. Southern England was plainly sympathetic to their stand against excessive taxation. It remains unclear, however, what Joseph hoped to do when he reached the capital. Had his plan been to replace Henry VII with the pretender Perkin Warbeck, this would surely have been highlighted by contemporary observers. The rebels themselves maintained that their grievance was not with the king but his ministers—Cardinal Morton, Sir Thomas Lovell, and Sir Reynold Bray. King Henry, however, observed no such distinctions, and took to the field in person against the insurgents. This alarmed them greatly, and Joseph's leadership began to waver. A number secretly contacted the commander of the royal army, Giles, Lord Daubeney, offering to surrender Joseph and the other leaders in exchange for a pardon, although nothing came of it. In the words of the Vitellius chronicler, the eve of the battle the rebels:

> lay all that nyght in great agony and variaunce; for some of theym were myended to have comyn to the kyng, and to hav yolden theym and put theym fully in his mercy and grace, but the Smyth was of the contrary myende. (Kingsford, 214)

Many deserted under cover of darkness.

Joseph and the other captains headed a force of some nine or ten thousand on the day of battle, 17 June 1497. Drawn up at Deptford Strand, the rebels fought with more courage than Polydore Vergil alleged, at one stage capturing Daubeney and releasing him unharmed; but they faced a much larger royal army. Flamank and Audley were captured on the field. Joseph escaped and tried to reach the friary at nearby Greenwich, but was apprehended before he could make sanctuary. In the face of certain execution for treason, he acted his role with memorable spirit. The 'great' chronicle of London described the captured rebel captain riding behind a yeoman of the guard, 'the Smyth beyng clad in a jakett of white & grene of the kyngis colours and held as good countenaunce and spak as boldly to the people as he had been at his lyberte' (Thomas and Thornley, 277). All three rebel commanders were examined before king and council in the Tower on 19 June. The two Cornish were arraigned at Whitehall a week later, and on 27 June 1497 were drawn through the streets from the Tower to Tyburn and hanged—until they were dead, according to the Vitellius chronicler, perhaps a small gesture of leniency on the king's part. Hall alone expands on the last hours of Michael Joseph, who 'was of such stowte stomack & haute courage, that at the same time that he was drawn on the herdle toward his death, he sayd … he should have a name perpetual and a fame permanent and immortal' (*Hall's Chronicle*, 479). His head was displayed on London Bridge with those of his fellow leaders. King Henry's next intention was to send Joseph's quartered corpse to be exhibited in Cornwall as a lesson in obedience, but the still rebellious temper of the region dissuaded him.

Over the next fifty years, Michael Joseph's native parish of St Keverne would witness several further popular disturbances, implying that his stand against the encroachment of central government was not locally forgotten. Reporting news of a planned demonstration against religious change in the parish in April 1537, William Godolphin reminded Cromwell that the rising of 1497 had begun there at the hands of 'the blacke smyth' (PRO, SP 1/118, fol. 248). In April 1548 a mob from St Keverne murdered the avaricious archdeacon of Cornwall, William Body, at Helston; a local priest who had been among the rioters, Martin Geoffrey, was executed in London the following July. Joseph also achieved a degree of national fame early in Elizabeth's reign with the inclusion of a verse tragedy, 'The Wilfull Fall of Blacke Smyth', in the second edition of the *Mirror for Magistrates* (1563). This poem reworked Vergil's account of the 1497 rising in order to stress the underlying theme of Tudor royal propaganda, that there 'Was never rebell before the world, nor since, that could or shall prevayle agaynst his prynce' (Campbell, 409). Joseph's name then passed into obscurity. He found no place in the *Dictionary of National Biography*, perhaps because of his plebeian origins. Both Flamank, a gentleman, and Audley, a peer, enjoyed their own articles in the *Dictionary of National Biography*; and yet several of the sources, including the *Mirror for Magistrates*, imply that Joseph was the true leader of the 1497 uprising.

The regional politics of later twentieth-century England breathed a curious new life into Michael Joseph. In search of a local hero, the Cornish nationalist party Mebyon Kernow found him in an Gof, and placed a commemorative plaque in Cornish and English on the wall of St Keverne churchyard. The five-hundredth anniversary of the 1497 rising saw a march by many local people from Cornwall to London to protest at Cornwall's economic and constitutional status, the part of Michael Joseph played by an actor. A statue of Joseph and Flamank, unveiled in 1997, stands on the road to Coverack just outside St Keverne village. The smith's arm is raised in defiance, or perhaps encouragement; his foot rests upon an anvil. His Cornish name, an Gof, has also been connected with a shadowy direct action group, and is occasionally still to be seen spray-painted on bridges and underpasses in Cornwall.

J. P. D. COOPER

Sources C. L. Kingsford, *Chronicles of London* (1905) · A. H. Thomas and I. D. Thornley, eds., *The great chronicle of London* (1938) · *Hall's chronicle*, ed. H. Ellis (1809) · PRO, SP 1/118, fols. 247–8 · *The Anglica historia of Polydore Vergil, AD 1485–1537*, ed. and trans. D. Hay, CS, 3rd ser., 74 (1950) · A. L. Rowse, *Tudor Cornwall* (1941) · I. Arthurson, 'The rising of 1497: a revolt of the peasantry?', *People, politics and community in the later middle ages*, ed. J. Rosenthal and C. Richmond (1987), 1–18 · I. Arthurson, *The Perkin Warbeck conspiracy, 1491–1499* (1994) · A. Fletcher and D. MacCulloch, *Tudor rebellions*, 4th edn (1997) · L. B. Campbell, ed., *Mirror for magistrates* (1938)
Likenesses statue, St Keverne, Cornwall

Joseph, Michael (1897–1958), publisher, was born on 26 September 1897 at 123 Osbaldeston Road, Upper Clapton, Hackney, London, the elder of two sons of Moss Joseph, a diamond merchant, and Rebecca Davis. At eleven Joseph won a London county council scholarship to the City of London School, where he excelled in classics. He left in 1914 and had intended to go on to the University of London but the outbreak of the First World War disrupted this plan. Instead, he joined the University of London Officers' Training Corps and from there volunteered for service in the army. In 1915 he was gazetted to the Wiltshire regiment, and from 1916 to 1919 served as a lieutenant and a captain in the machine-gun corps. He then returned to the University of London to take a part-time course at University College for a diploma in journalism. He did not take the examination, however, as he found the course 'sadly academic and hopelessly unpractical' (M. Joseph, *Journalism for Profit*, 1924). By now Joseph had already started writing, and his first book, *Short Story Writing for Profit*, to which Stacy Aumonier contributed a foreword, was published in 1923. The directness of the title reflected the book's purposeful nature.

In 1918 Joseph married the actress Hermione Ferdinanda *Gingold (1897–1987); they had two sons: Leslie, born in 1919, and Stephen (1921–1967), founder of the Stephen Joseph Theatre in the Round in Scarborough. Michael Joseph started working for the literary agents Curtis Brown in 1924 and became a director in 1926. In the same year his first marriage was dissolved and on 11 March he married Edna Victoria Nellie Frost (1899/1900–1949), daughter of Thomas Richard Frost, solicitor. They had a daughter, Shirley, born in 1927, and another son, Richard, born in 1940. Meanwhile, further books followed, among them *The Commercial Side of Literature* (1925) and *The Magazine Story* (1928). Joseph's lasting love of cats resulted in a quite different work, *Cat's Company* (1930).

On 5 September 1935 Joseph founded his own publishing house, Michael Joseph Ltd, as a subsidiary of Victor Gollancz, with Gollancz himself and Norman Collins as directors and Joseph as managing director. The enterprise was highly risky, as it fell in a difficult decade when many established publishers were closing or experiencing financial restraints. In his semi-autobiographical work *The Adventure of Publishing* (1949), Joseph recorded that he was one of the few young publishers who held on 'by the skin of their teeth'. His firm not only survived but prospered, bringing out books by H. E. Bates and by a number of other well-known authors, among them C. S. Forester's *The General* (1936), Monica Dickens's *One Pair of Hands* (1939), and Richard Llewellyn's *How Green was my Valley* (1939). (Joseph persuaded Llewellyn to change his proposed title, 'The land of my fathers', to something more biblical and nostalgic.) Other authors 'discovered' by Joseph include Paul Gallico, Richard Gordon, Vicki Baum, Joyce Cary, and Vita Sackville-West. Relations between

Joseph and Gollancz were not always smooth, and the two were quite different in character. Gollancz was 'fiery … arrogant and excitable', while Joseph was 'cool, persuasive, charming and rather cautious' (Dudley Edwards, 197). Joseph was constrained by Gollancz's economic objectives, and the pair did not agree on many aspects of publishing. Joseph offended Gollancz by accepting 'lowbrow' manuscripts such as *Pink and Blue: an Anthology of Babyhood* (ibid.) while he resented Gollancz's interference and criticism. In 1938 Joseph bought Gollancz out when he attempted to censor Sir Philip Gibbs's *Across the Frontiers* on political grounds.

Although now a full-time publisher, Joseph continued as a writer. *This Writing Business* had already appeared in 1931, while cats resurfaced in two collaborations—*Puss in Books* (1932), written with Elizabeth Drew, and *Heads or Tails* (1933), with Selwyn Jepson—and in one of his most personal accounts, *Charles: the Story of a Friendship* (1943), about his beloved Burmese cat. A play, *Discovery*, followed in 1934, the plot centring on a woman who is capable of dreaming the future. In the Second World War, Joseph served as a lieutenant and captain in the Queen's Own Royal Kent regiment from 1940 to 1941. A further book, *The Sword in the Scabbard*, came out in 1942, based on Joseph's army experiences in both world wars.

On 15 November 1950, a year after Edna's death, Joseph married Anthea Esther Hodson (1924–1981), his secretary and later a publisher, the daughter of Lord Justice Hodson, a High Court judge [see Joseph, Anthea Esther]. They had two children, Charlotte in 1952 and Hugh in 1954, and settled at Brown's Farm, Old Basing, Hampshire.

Joseph was a member of the Savage Club and president of the Siamese Cat Society of the British Empire. He gave his recreation in *Who's Who* as cats, but they were really much more than that. A heavy smoker from boyhood, Michael Joseph died of heart failure and a perforated duodenal ulcer on 15 March 1958 at 20 Devonshire Place, Marylebone, London. His business was plunged into a crisis that culminated in the resignation of most of the board. Only Anthea Joseph remained, together with one other director, and it was largely thanks to her determination that its reputation was restored.

ADRIAN ROOM

Sources *At the sign of the mermaid: fifty years of Michael Joseph* (1986) • *The Times* (17 March 1958) • 'Hastings, Anthea Esther', *DNB* • R. Dudley Edwards, *Victor Gollancz: a biography* (1987) • *WWW, 1951–60* • R. Joseph, *Michael Joseph: master of words* (1986) • b. cert. • m. cert. [Edna Frost] • m. cert. [Anthea Esther] • d. cert.
Likenesses photographs, 1927–54, repro. in Joseph, *Michael Joseph* • photograph, *c.*1935, repro. in *The Bookseller* (29 May 1935) • H. Coster, photographs, 1938, NPG • photograph, *c.*1950, repro. in *At the sign of the mermaid* • H. M. Bateman, portrait, repro. in Joseph, *Michael Joseph*, dust jacket
Wealth at death £73,734 17s. 3d.: probate, 27 June 1958, CGPLA Eng. & Wales

Joseph, Morris David (1848–1930), Jewish minister and theologian, was born on 28 May 1848 at 17 Green Street, Long Acre, London, one of the seven children (four girls and three boys) of David Joseph and his wife, Amelia Levi. The son of a schoolmaster who was also the minister of Maiden Lane Synagogue in central London, Morris Joseph spent his professional life as a member of the Jewish clergy, following a path which travelled from Orthodox to Progressive Judaism.

Joseph was educated at the Westminster Jews' Free School, a co-educational school located in the heart of London's Soho district. From there he graduated to Jews' College, a seminary which was established in 1855 following a proposal by the chief rabbi, Nathan Adler, for the setting up of a college where aspiring rabbis in Britain could receive the 'requisite theological and scholastic education and the necessary preparation for their future offices' (Lipman, 24). It was during his time at Jews' College, under the tutelage of the principal, Dr Michael Friedlander, that the young Joseph developed his love of learning. Following his period at the college Joseph—who did not receive *semichah* (the ordination of rabbi)—was appointed minister–secretary to the newly established Orthodox North London Synagogue, situated in the comfortable working- and middle-class area of Barnsbury.

On 30 October 1872, while still at North London, Joseph married Frances Amelia Henry (1851–1914), daughter of Michael Henry, a merchant, the marriage ceremony being performed by Chief Rabbi Adler. Two years later Joseph took up the post of minister to the Orthodox, though progressive, Old Hebrew Congregation of Liverpool, which had just moved to its newly opened synagogue in the city's Princes Road. A previous incumbent of the post had been David Woolf Marks, who in 1841 left Liverpool to become first minister of the newly created West London Synagogue of British Jews. Joseph was to follow in Professor Marks's footsteps yet again when, in 1893, he was appointed senior minister of west London when Marks stepped down. It was while at Liverpool that Joseph developed the oratorical and intellectual skills for which he became renowned. Sadly his term in office in Liverpool was cut short. In 1881 he was forced to return to London and enter into semi-retirement due to ill health. But these were no years in the wilderness: he wrote regularly for the *Jewish Chronicle* and taught homiletics at Jews' College, while freedom from the demands of clerical office enabled him to sit back and examine his beliefs and determine his future direction.

By 1890, fully restored to good health, Joseph was eager to re-enter his chosen profession. He began by arranging religious services for those Jews who had moved to the rarefied and intellectual middle-class pastures of Hampstead in north-west London, an area at that time void of synagogues. He organized a series of sabbath afternoon services which began at 3 p.m. at the Town Hall, Broadhurst Gardens, West Hampstead; these attracted Jews of all shades of opinion. Joseph tried to combat the growth of religious apathy within the Jewish community, many members of which perceived Orthodox Judaism as medieval and the cause of gradual intellectual alienation. He recognized that there was a need to inject spiritual uplift into the services while at the same time bowing to progress, although he stopped short of accepting the suggestion of a shared Christian–Jewish service.

It was Joseph's modernism, his concern about the 'melting away' (Joseph, ix), and his support for the use of instrumental music at sabbath services that determined his future and the appointment which was to be his for the remainder of his active life. In 1892 an Orthodox synagogue was opened in Hampstead. It was a foregone conclusion that Joseph would apply for, and be appointed to, the position of minister. However, his published views, which were at variance with traditional Judaism, resulted in the new chief rabbi, Hermann Adler, refusing to sanction the appointment. The rejection coincided with the semi-retirement of David Woolf Marks, now senior minister of the West London Synagogue of British Jews. Joseph was encouraged to apply for the post at the same time as a collection of his Saturday afternoon service sermons was published under the title *The Ideal in Judaism* (1893). In the volume Joseph's beliefs in a return to Israel without the restoration of the sacrifices and that the 'Messiah is always moving amongst us' received a public airing, as did his conviction that 'True religion is reason'. While the collection of sermons was favourably reviewed by the national press and an article in the *Jewish Chronicle* pronounced the sermons to be powerful aids to devotional faith and practical Judaism, the members of the West London Synagogue reacted to the publication with mixed feelings. Some were approving but others were sceptical, stating that the sermons were 'interesting but not Jewish' (Kershen and Romain, 112–13). However, when the other contender for the position, the Revd Simeon Singer, dropped out of the running these concerns were overruled and Joseph was appointed senior minister to the West London Synagogue of British Jews.

In his inaugural sermon Joseph called upon his congregants to 'be devoted to the principles of enlightened religion'. He also stated his intention to narrow the rift between Reform and Orthodox Jewry which had been a distressing facet of the Jewish community's life for the past fifty years (*Jewish Chronicle*, 15 September 1893). That he achieved this latter aim was manifest when, in 1911, he was given the honour of delivering the *hesped* (memorial sermon) at Chief Rabbi Hermann Adler's funeral.

Joseph served west London as senior minister until 1925, during which time he earned a reputation as a 'forceful and lucid preacher' who was 'no orator in the ordinary sense' but a man whose sermons were 'literary gems' (*Jewish Chronicle*, 25 April 1930). These sermons were published in a series of volumes: *The Ideal in Judaism* (1893), *Judaism as a Creed* (1903), *The Message of Judaism* (1907), and *The Spirit of Judaism* (1930). In addition to the published volumes of sermons Joseph wrote articles for the *Jewish Quarterly Review*, *Jewish Chronicle*, and the *Hastings Encyclopaedia of Religion*, and translated the introduction to the *Rokeach* (a collection of medieval religious writings). Joseph also took a concerned interest in current affairs and to this end, in 1895, established the West London Synagogue Association as a

'religious and philanthropic Centre and as a forum for debate of topical issues' (Kershen and Romain, 124).

Joseph personified the Englishman who followed the Mosaic religion. He was determined that immigrant eastern European Jews should become part of the mainstream as rapidly as possible; indeed he saw it as their duty to do so. In the same way he was totally opposed to the concept of political Zionism, and 'abhorred the notion of a nationalist Jewish state' (Kershen and Romain, 116). Anti-Zionism created strange bedfellows: Chief Rabbi Adler and the Revd Morris Joseph joined forces to attack pro-Zionists at the universities of Oxford, Cambridge, and London. In addition to his anti-Zionist beliefs Joseph was a pacifist and chairman of the Jewish Peace Society. He was also a member of the executive committee of the League of Religions and sat on the council of the Metropolitan Hospital Sunday Fund.

Joseph retired from the West London Synagogue in 1925, aged seventy-seven. He lived for a further five years and though denied the pleasure of grandchildren, as he and his wife were childless, he was cared for by devoted nieces and nephews, his wife having died in 1914. He died at his home, 11 Gloucester Terrace, Hyde Park, London, on 17 April 1930 from carcinoma of the bladder, and was buried on 21 April at the Golders Green Jewish cemetery, Middlesex. He was remembered as 'a scholar in the finest sense of the word', as a 'lover of peace', and 'a man of optimism whose oratory was most outstanding'. In his eulogy at the burial the Revd Vivian Simmons recalled how Joseph 'spoke often with the insight of a prophet ... fired with the spirit of the greatest rabbis of old' (*Jewish Chronicle*, 23 April 1930).   ANNE J. KERSHEN

Sources A. J. Kershen and J. A. Romain, *Tradition and change: a history of Reform Judaism in Britain, 1840–1995* (1995) · *Jewish Chronicle* (15 Sept 1893) · *Jewish Chronicle* (13 April 1906) · *Jewish Chronicle* (25 April 1930) · M. Joseph, *The ideal in Judaism* (1893) · *Encyclopaedia Judaica*, 12 (1997) · V. Lipman, *History of Jews in Britain since 1858* (1990) · b. cert. · m. cert. · d. cert. · CGPLA Eng. & Wales (1930)

Likenesses photograph, repro. in Kershen and Romain, *Tradition and change*

Wealth at death £5396 13s. 11d.: resworn probate, 1930, CGPLA Eng. & Wales

Joseph, Nathan Solomon (1834–1909), architect and social worker, was born on 17 December 1834 at The Crescent, The Minories, London, one of nine children of City merchant Solomon Joseph (1805–1868) and his wife, Jane Selig (d. 1893). Nathan was educated at home under private tutors and from 1852 to 1854 at University College, London, where he was an excellent student, taking first prize for civil engineering. On graduation, on the advice of a friend of his father, he turned to architecture, which in the mid-nineteenth century was a very unusual choice of profession for Jews.

Joseph became the most prominent of the first generation of Anglo-Jewish synagogue architects that included Davis and Emanuel, Hyman Henry Collins, and Edward Salomons. The latter, Manchester based, acted as one of his proposers for ARIBA on 9 March 1863; another was Daniel Addington Cobbett, to whom he had been articled between 1855 and 1858 and with whom he remained as principal assistant. Having travelled abroad in France, Belgium, Germany, and later Italy, Joseph went into independent practice in London in 1860, in partnership with George Pearson (1846–1934) between 1871 and 1886, and afterwards with Charles James Smithem. He was elected FRIBA on 16 June 1890.

Joseph was brother-in-law of the chief rabbi, Hermann Adler, a connection that greatly advanced his architectural career. The establishment of the United Synagogue by act of parliament in 1870 triggered a boom in synagogue building. This was the golden age of the 'cathedral synagogue' in Britain, and as architect-surveyor to the United Synagogue Joseph became the leading exponent of the type. His first commission was for Bayswater Synagogue (1862–3) in conjunction with Edward Salomons. This was followed by the Central Synagogue (1868–70) and Dalston Synagogue (1884–5). He also worked on the New West End Synagogue (1877–9), the only one of his synagogues which has survived, now a grade II* listed building, but its gorgeous orientalist interior was largely the work of the non-Jewish George Audsley of Liverpool, with whom Joseph shared the commission.

It is perhaps surprising that in 1870 the future architect of the United Synagogue championed the independence of the immigrant *hevrot* (small congregations) in the East End against the big City synagogues that sought to absorb them. Joseph attacked the patronizing snobbery of the City synagogues, which were prepared to bestow free seats on poor Jews. 'This will not do', he wrote. 'In such a synagogue, all men would be equal in the sight of God, but not in the sight of the beadle' (*Jewish Chronicle*, 9 Sept 1870). He was responsible for remodelling the eighteenth-century chapel in Sandys Row, Bishopsgate, for use by the fledging Dutch Jews' congregation.

Joseph married twice. His first wife, Alice, daughter of Sampson Samuel, died on 3 March 1879, aged only thirty-one. She was mother of their three sons and three daughters. His second wife, Elizabeth (Lizzie), daughter of Sylvester Samuel of Liverpool, died in March 1899, aged forty-three. Joseph hailed from a family that for several generations had been involved in the affairs of the élite Ashkenazi Great Synagogue. He had a social conscience inherited from his mother, an active charity worker in the East End. Joseph's own welfare concerns were to be expressed, throughout his career, both in his architectural practice and in his work for the Jewish and general community.

A large part of Joseph's practice was occupied with early progressive housing projects for the working classes. He designed Rothschild Buildings (1885) and other developments in the East End for the Jewish-owned Four Per Cent Industrial Dwellings Company. He was responsible for the original Jews' Free School Buildings, Bell Lane, London (1883), whose Great Hall, bombed during the Second World War, he considered his best work. He was vice-president and honorary architect of the Jews' Hospital and Orphans' Asylum, Norwood, and designed that institution's Centenary Hall in 1897.

Joseph was active in the Jewish Board of Guardians from 1861 as a founder member and chairman of its visiting committee (1895–1900). In 1865–6 he initiated the establishment of its medical (later styled sanitation) committee. His housing experience was applied more widely on behalf of the Guinness Trust, several London boroughs, the London county council, and the Iveagh Trust of Dublin. He became an authority on public-health issues in an age when cholera and typhoid were rampant.

Joseph was a founder and lifelong member of the Russo-Jewish Committee, set up in 1882 in response to the pogroms in Russia following the assassination of Tsar Alexander II, which stimulated mass emigration of Jews to the West. While sympathetic to the plight of the East End poor, Joseph was in favour of restricting Jewish immigration to 'the able-bodied' at the expense of 'helpless paupers'. He was prepared to countenance re-emigration and even repatriation of immigrants who could not easily be absorbed. He was keen to encourage the rapid dispersal of Jews away from the slums of the East End. His views, expressed in a policy document entitled *The New Departure in Jewish Charity* (1892), brought him into conflict with other members of the Jewish Board of Guardians with which the Russo-Jewish Committee, with Joseph as chairman, had formed a 'conjoint' partnership.

The manager of several East End board schools, Joseph took a close interest in the welfare of both pupils and teachers. He was honorary secretary of Jews' College from 1860 to 1869 and of the Jewish Association for the Diffusion of Religious Knowledge. He wrote a number of religious tracts and a widely circulated textbook entitled *Religion, Natural and Revealed* (1879) in which he advocated a non-dogmatic approach to Judaism. A member of the council of the United Synagogue, chairman of its visitation committee (concerned with the welfare of Jewish prisoners), and originally a worshipper at the Central Synagogue, in later life he experimented with religious reform. He regularly attended services at the West London Synagogue (Reform) on the new year and *yom kippur*. He was a founder member of the Jewish Religious Union (1902) which soon after his death evolved into the Liberal Synagogue.

Joseph was the founder of something of an architectural dynasty: his nephew Delissa Joseph (1859–1927) designed synagogues in greater number, but most were architecturally less successful than his uncle's. Delissa's talents lay elsewhere, and he became more widely known for offices and hotels built over tube stations in Edwardian London. In 1887 he married Lily Solomon, a sister of Solomon J. Solomon RA. Exhibiting under the name Lily Delissa Joseph (1863–1940), she was an accomplished painter as well as a suffragette. Nathan Joseph's sons by his first marriage, Charles Sampson Joseph (1872–1948) and Ernest Martin Joseph (1877–1960), went into their father's practice. Ernest is chiefly remembered for the design of the art deco Shell Mex house on London's Embankment (1931).

Nathan Joseph retired on 1 January 1904. He died on 11 June 1909 at home at 18 Porchester Terrace, Hyde Park, and was buried on 14 June between his two wives at Will-esden Jewish cemetery, whose Gothic style *ohel* (chapel) complex he had designed in 1873.   SHARMAN KADISH

Sources *Jewish Chronicle* (9 Sept 1870) · *Jewish Chronicle* (23 Sept 1870) · *Jewish Chronicle* (11 Nov 1870) · *Jewish Chronicle* (16 Dec 1904) · *The Times* (14–15 June 1909) · *Jewish Chronicle* (18 June 1909) · *The Builder*, 96 (19 June 1909), 737 · *RIBA Journal*, 16 (1908–9), 607–8 · *RIBA Journal*, 41 (1933–4), 419–20 [obit. of George Pearson] · *The Times* (20 July 1909) · *Jewish Chronicle* (4 Dec 1868) · *Jewish Chronicle* (7 March 1879) · *Jewish Year Book* · *Dir. Brit. archs.* · biographies file and nomination papers, RIBA BAL · L. Fraser, '"Four Per Cent Philanthropy": social architecture for East London Jewry, 1850–1914', *Building Jerusalem: Jewish architecture in Britain*, ed. S. Kadish (1996), 166–92 · V. D. Lipman, *A century of social service, 1859–1959: the Jewish Board of Guardians* (1959) · C. Magnus, ed., *EMJ: the man and his work* (1962) · J. Glasman, 'London synagogues in the late 19th century: design in context', *London Journal*, 13 (1988), 143–55 · J. Glasman, 'Assimilation by design: London synagogues in the 19th century', *The Jewish heritage in British history*, ed. T. Kushner (1992), 171–209 · E. Jamilly, 'Anglo-Jewish architects, and architecture in the 18th and 19th centuries', *Transactions of the Jewish Historical Society of England*, 18 (1953–5), 127–41 · E. Jamilly, 'Synagogue art and architecture', *A century of Anglo-Jewish life, 1870–1970*, ed. S. S. Levin (1970), 75–91 · J. White, *Rothschild Buildings* (1980) · CGPLA Eng. & Wales (1909) · d. cert. [Jane Joseph, mother] · d. cert. [Lizzie Joseph, wife] · tombstones, Willesden Jewish cemetery
Archives RIBA BAL, nomination papers and biography file
Likenesses I. Cohen, crayon, repro. in Lipman, *Century of social service* · photograph, repro. in *Jewish Chronicle* (18 June 1909)
Wealth at death £52,848 13s. 11d.: probate, 16 July 1909, *CGPLA Eng. & Wales*

Joseph [*formerly* Becham; *later* Wyllys], **Robert** (1500–1569), Benedictine monk and letter writer, was probably born at Evesham, where he attended the grammar school before entering the Benedictine abbey in 1517 or 1518, when he changed his name from Becham to Joseph. In 1523 he was sent to Gloucester College, Oxford, and was recalled to Evesham in early 1529 after graduating BA. He became the abbot's chaplain, but was demoted in 1530 by the new prior to teacher of the novices. He spent his spare time manoeuvring for a return to Oxford and writing letters to monastic friends in the regions of the Severn and Avon and at his old university. In December 1532 he was permitted to return to Oxford where, in January 1533, he wrote his last two epistles. On 23 April 1535 he was granted his BTh. He was mentioned as prior of Gloucester College in December 1537 and replaced in early 1538 when he returned to Evesham, where he remained until the dissolution, when he changed his name to Wyllys, possibly the name of his mother's family. For nineteen years he was a secular priest at All Saints' Church in the former monastic precincts. In 1559 he was presented to the vicarage of Cropthorne, 3 miles west of Evesham, where he remained until his death, and where he was probably buried, in July 1569. He bequeathed his Latin books, and probably his collection of 170 letters and some Latin verses, to two priests with whom he had corresponded forty years earlier.

Joseph's letter-book (NL Wales, Peniarth MS 119; published in 1967, edited by Dom Hugh Aveling and W. A. Pantin), which has survived by chance, illuminates university and monastic life just before the Reformation—the entire collection dates from between 1530 and 1533.

Joseph's attempts to point out when he was being ironic and playful, and his request to recipients that they return letters for copying, suggest that he was compiling a guide to letter writing for the novices under his charge, displaying his skills in rhetoric and in the composition of elegant and idiomatic Latin in the style of Erasmus. He required his correspondents to reply in Latin, and his references were from Cicero, Augustine, Virgil, Terence, Plautus, and contemporary humanists such as Erasmus and Baptista Manteanus. Little interest was shown in the scholastic theology of the middle ages—Scotus was the butt of frequent jokes—and little attention was paid to the more strident reforming aspects of even Erasmus's thought, such as church reform and the application of learning to a life of inner commitment to Christ. The writings of antiquity were read and imitated as models of persuasion; Joseph lectured to novice monks, displaying rhetoric and teaching appreciation of the comedies of Terence and Plautus. However, his letters also chart the erosion of the regency system within the university, as temporary public lecturers were being superseded by a more formal system of tutorials and lectures within the colleges. Joseph wrote letters on behalf of his younger relatives to the tutors whom he felt could supply them with a suitable humanist education.

The core of this humanist, literary life was friendships sustained by letter writing. To his closest friend, John Feckenham of Evesham, who was also at Gloucester College, Joseph wrote: 'If I could not exchange letters with you my heart would break' (letter 111). Friendship and communication through letters attained for Joseph a religious significance. He remembered his friends in his daily prayers; mass was an opportunity to meditate on absent friends; and letters from a friend could be read many times, like the scriptures. Little interest was shown in this collection in rationalizing the monastic life and none in asceticism. Joseph enthusiastically endorsed Erasmus's secular ethic and frequently expressed irritation with the rituals and duties of the Evesham community when they distracted him from the joys of letter writing. By instinct conservative in religious matters, he reacted with horror to heresy while showing scant interest in doctrinal debate and merely expressed a desire to follow the custom and footsteps of 'our fathers' (letter 104). He was able to adapt to the dissolution of his house in 1540 by becoming a secular priest near his monastery (a vocation for which he always expressed the highest regard) because it allowed him to maintain his friendships. There was nothing of the martyr in his temperament.

Joseph's letters are also of literary interest. He expressed the joys of creative writing. To John Dorell at Oxford he wrote: 'See how many words your little letter has given rise to. Keep writing: send whatever comes into your head' (letter 15). For Joseph this could include memories of his Oxford youth, and humorous references also abound: for instance to the quality of Westminster sausages, likened to candles. The letters attest the spread of Erasmian humanism into possibly unexpected places, and also bear witness, in the frequency with which he asks his friends to reply to his messages, and the anxiety with which he seeks reassurance that he has not offended anyone, to the sensitive temperament of their author.

JONATHAN HUGHES

Sources The letter book of Robert Joseph, ed. H. Aveling and W. A. Pantin, OHS, new ser., 19 (1967) • NL Wales, Peniarth MS 119 • W. A. Bruneau, 'Humanism and the university and the monastic life: the case of Robert Joseph, monk of Evesham', British Journal of Educational Studies, 20 (1972–3), 282–301 • J. K. McConica, English humanists and Reformation politics under Henry VIII and Edward VI (1965) • D. Knowles [M. C. Knowles], The religious orders in England, 3 (1959) • G. Marchadour, 'Dom Robert Joseph: le moine inconnu d'Evesham à la veille du schisme anglican', Rivista di Letteratura Moderna et Comparate, 17 (1964) • R. B. Dobson, 'The religious orders, 1370–1540', Hist. U. Oxf. 2: Late med. Oxf., 539–79 • Worcs. RO, Reg. 31, fol. 32
Archives NL Wales, Peniarth MS 119
Wealth at death moveable property, blankets, books; 4d. to every householder in his parish of Cropthorne; 10d. to poor of All Saints, Evesham: will, Letter book, ed. Aveling and Pantin, appx IV

Joseph, Samuel (1790/91–1850), sculptor, about whose parents, and early life nothing is known, was a cousin of George Francis *Joseph (1764–1846), the portrait painter. It is known that Samuel Joseph had a wife and seven children, but not details survive of them either. In London he was a pupil of Peter Rouw the younger, a leading modeller of miniature portraits in wax, a medium which encourages realistic rendering. In 1811 Joseph trained at the Royal Academy Schools, London; he won silver medals in 1811 and 1812 and a gold medal in 1815 for a Miltonian subject entitled Eve Entreating Forgiveness of Adam (untraced). Failure to gain a Royal Academy travelling scholarship to Rome in 1817 exacerbated his isolation from the ideal classicism of portrait sculpture then in vogue, and propelled him instead towards a rarer, idiosyncratic naturalism expressed in the portrayal of a sudden alertness of facial features and a flamboyant treatment of hair, at times bordering on caricature, as in the bust of the divine Sir Henry Wellwood Moncrieff (1825, National Gallery of Scotland, Edinburgh). The catalyst in this approach to portraiture was Joseph's involvement with the pseudo-science of phrenology, in which the mental powers of the individual are read by feeling and interpreting cranial bumps. He was admitted a member of the Edinburgh Phrenological Society on 26 December 1820 (minute book, 1.10) and was diagnosed on 7 July 1822 by the society's founder, George Combe, who reported that the sculptor was 'a great lover of truth' and susceptible 'to talk of himself, and his own feelings' (Friedman, 'Samuel Joseph phrenologized', 24). Subsequently, he produced a series of life masks in plaster of notorious criminals, including the murderers Burke and Hare (minute book, 1.146). Joseph began exhibiting at the Royal Academy in 1811; between 1815 and 1823 he resided at 68 Newman Street, London, but from 1821 he was also working in Edinburgh, and was the first sculptor of significance to set up a studio there, first at 139 George Street in 1823, then at 9 Windsor Street, and subsequently at no. 22.

Joseph exhibited at the Institute for the Encouragement of the Fine Arts in Scotland (1821–6), the Northern Society for the Encouragement of the Fine Arts in Leeds (1822),

and the Royal Scottish Academy in Edinburgh (1827–44). Early successes included busts of the Edinburgh crown attorney Henry Mackenzie (1822, National Gallery of Scotland, Edinburgh) and of Sir Walter Scott (1824, priv. coll.). Equally memorable are his female portraits, such as Lady Belhaven (1827, Victoria and Albert Museum, London). Other celebrated sitters included the Revd Archibald Alison (1825, Fitzwilliam Museum, Cambridge), author of Essays on the Nature and Principles of Taste; Dugald Stewart, professor of moral philosophy (1827, University of Edinburgh); and the civil engineer Robert Stevenson (1828, Royal Museum of Scotland, Edinburgh). A later writer rightly regarded these as 'superior to any examples ... produced in Scotland previous to his practice' (Graham, 448). Joseph was a founder member in 1826 of the Scottish (subsequently the Royal Scottish) Academy, and some of its formative meetings were held in his Windsor Street studio. A portrait of him (1827–8) shows handsome but reticent features, and letters of the period reveal an unsettled life plagued by financial debt (National Library of Scotland, MS 7208, fols. 137, 133).

Joseph returned to London in 1828, set up studios at a succession of addresses, and attracted a distinguished clientele of professionals, divines, statesmen, and artists. His bust of George IV (1831, Victoria and Albert Museum, London), commissioned by the monarch, is a swaggering, Berninesque portrayal; that of the painter Sir David Wilkie (1842, National Gallery of Scotland, Edinburgh), a friend since 1822, is wind-tossed and Byronic. On Wilkie's death in 1841, he was commissioned to execute a life-size statue (1843) for the National Gallery, London (now in the Tate collection). His masterpiece is the life-size figure of the reformer William Wilberforce (1838–40) in Westminster Abbey, its unconventional pose based on Jean-Antoine Houdon's seated Voltaire (1781, Comédie Française, Paris). Although one of the best British sculptors practising during the first half of the nineteenth century and a regular exhibitor at the Royal Academy from 1811 to 1846, where he showed a total of 100 works, Joseph nevertheless failed to secure popular success or lasting fame. William Bell Scott, in The British School of Sculpture (1871, 81), was 'unable to give an account' of his life for lack of information . Perhaps his portraits were too eccentric and psychologically highly charged. Declared a bankrupt in 1848, Samuel Joseph died on 1 July 1850 leaving his family penniless and dependent on a Royal Academy pension. His widow died in 1863.

TERRY FRIEDMAN

Sources R. Gunnis, Dictionary of British sculptors, 1660–1851, new edn (1968) • T. Friedman, 'Samuel Joseph phrenologized', Leeds Arts Calendar, 86 (1980), 20–28 • T. Friedman, 'Samuel Joseph and the sculpture of feeling', Virtue and vision: sculpture and Scotland, 1540–1990, ed. F. Pearson (1991), 58–63 • F. Pearson, 'Phrenology and sculpture, 1820–1855', Leeds Arts Calendar, 88 (1981), 14–23 • Graves, RA exhibitors, 4 (1906), 286–8 • C. B. de Laperriere, ed., The Royal Scottish Academy exhibitors, 1826–1990, 4 vols. (1991); vol. 2, pp. 385–6 • T. Friedman, 'Aspects of nineteenth century sculpture in Leeds', Leeds Arts Calendar, 70 (1972), 21–2 • M. Whinney, Victoria and Albert Museum English sculpture, 1720–1830 (1971), 160–61 • J. M. Graham, An historical view of literature and art in Great Britain (1871), 448 • Redgrave, Artists • W. B. Scott, The British school of sculpture (1871), 81 •

Literary Gazette (27 July 1850), 508 • minute books of the Edinburgh Phrenological Society, U. Edin. • NL Scot. • RA

Archives NL Scot. • U. Edin. L., minute books of the Edinburgh Phrenological Society | NL Scot., letters to W. H. Lizars

Likenesses G. F. Joseph, portrait, exh. RA 1824 • pencil and wash, 1827–8, repro. in Friedman, 'Samuel Joseph phrenologized', 21; priv. coll. • T. Smith, wax portrait, exh. RA 1828

Wealth at death declared bankrupt in 1848: Gunnis, *British sculptors*, 222

Josi, Christian (1768–1828), printmaker and art dealer, was born in Utrecht, Netherlands, on 27 March 1768 and baptized the same day, the son of Christiaan Josi and Bertje van Doren, of whom nothing else is known. In 1784 he entered the Renswoude Institute in Utrecht as an orphan, and in 1786 he became a pupil of a local printmaker, Pieter Hendrik Jonxis. In August 1791 Josi went to London to study engraving under John Raphael Smith (and, it is said, Francesco Bartolozzi and Conrad Martin Metz). After marrying in 1795 Carolina Susanna, the daughter of the printmaker Jan Chalon, he returned to the Netherlands in October of that year and established himself as an engraver in Amsterdam. He worked briefly for his wife's step-uncle, Cornelis Ploos van Amstel, who had engraved a series of prints after old master drawings by Dutch and Flemish artists. About 1800 poor health and the overriding popularity of British prints forced him to retire from printmaking, and he became instead a dealer in prints and paintings and earned himself a great reputation among connoisseurs. By 1802 he had acquired Ploos's stock and began collecting drawings in order to continue Ploos's print series. In July 1810 Josi sold Ploos's collection of Rembrandt etchings and produced an important accompanying catalogue.

The French occupation of the Netherlands affected Josi's business adversely. This, combined with the trauma of fathering ten children who died in infancy, led him to consider relocating to London. In 1815 he was appointed to a committee sent to Paris to reclaim artworks appropriated by Napoleon from the Netherlands. Josi sold his stock in April 1818 and emigrated to Britain in 1819, settling in the house in London formerly occupied by Dryden at 42 Gerrard Street, Soho, where he continued as a renowned art dealer. In 1821 he published his most important work, *Collection d'imitations de dessins*, containing more than a hundred prints (forty-five of them from Ploos's plates) reproducing Dutch and Flemish drawings with extraordinary fidelity. Josi engraved three of the plates and wrote the lengthy texts. The whole forms one of the earliest histories of Netherlandish drawing. Josi died at Ramsgate, Kent, in November 1828. His large art collection was sold at auction over fifteen days in 1829–30.

Henry Josi (1802–1845), museum curator, son of Christian Josi, was born in Amsterdam. From about 1819 he attended Dr Burney's academy in Greenwich, and he became his father's assistant before establishing his own print shop on Newman Street, Soho. On 25 February 1823 he married Lucy Levett at St Saviour's Church, Southwark; presumably following her death, on 31 July 1832 he married Jane Levett at St Anne's, Soho. Also in 1832 he exhibited at the Society (later Royal Society) of British Artists

from the family's Gerrard Street address (his relation to the painter Charles Josi (*fl.* 1827–1852), of the same address, is unknown). In that year he was also an unsuccessful candidate for the post of keeper of prints and drawings in the British Museum, but he was appointed in 1836, after the death of the new keeper, William Young Ottley. Josi increased the department's significance, producing a thorough inventory of the collection and overseeing its first major acquisitions, including key collections of Dutch and Flemish art and of early German and Italian engravings. A sympathetic individual who recognized its importance to artists and connoisseurs, he broadened public access to the department's print room, and he is considered the founder of the department in its modern guise. After a long illness he died at his house in Upper Wharton Street, Pentonville, on 7 February 1845.

SARAH MONKS

Sources C. Josi, *Collection d'imitations de dessins d'après les principaux maîtres hollandais et flamands, commencée par Ploos van Amstel continuée et portée au nombre de cent morceaux. Avec des renseignements historiques et détaillés sur ces maîtres et sur leurs ouvrages. Précédés d'un discours sur l'état ancien et moderne des arts dans Les Pays Bas* (1821) • T. Laurentius, J. W. Niemeijer, and G. Ploos van Amstel, *Cornelis Ploos van Amstel, 1726–1798: kunstverzamelaar en prentuitgever* (1980) • GM, 1st ser., 98/2 (1828), 572 • A. Griffiths, ed., *Landmarks in print collecting: connoisseurs and donors at the British Museum since 1753* (British Museum Press, 1996) [exhibition catalogue, Museum of Fine Arts, Houston, TX, 1996, and elsewhere] • GM, 2nd ser., 23 (1845), 320 • *Art Union*, 7 (1845), 69 • A. Griffiths, 'The department of prints and drawings during the first century of the British Museum', *Burlington Magazine*, 136 (1994), 531–44 • DNB • A. de Luise, 'Ploos van Amstel and Christian Josi: two generations of printmakers working in the artful imitation of drawings', *Quérendo*, 25 (1995), 214–26 • E. Miller, *That noble cabinet: a history of the British Museum* (1973) • G. Ploos van Amstel, *Portret van een koopman en uitvinder Cornelis Ploos van Amstel: maatschappelijk, cultureel en familieleven van een achttiende-eeuwer* (1980) • A. Griffiths and R. Williams, *The department of prints and drawings in the British Museum: user's guide* (1987), 8–9 • G. Meissner, ed., *Allgemeines Künstlerlexikon: die bildenden Künstler aller Zeiten und Völker*, [new edn, 34 vols.] (Leipzig and Munich, 1983–) • Bénézit, *Dict.*, 4th edn • P. A. Scheen, *Lexicon nederlandse beeldende kunstenaars, 1750–1950*, 2 vols. (1969–70) • F. G. Waller, *Biographisch woordenboek van Noord Nederlandsche graveurs* (1938) • J. Immerzel jun., *De levens en werken der hollandsche en vlaamsche kunstchilders, beeldhouwers, graveurs en bouwmeesters, van het begin der vijftiende eeuw tot heden*, 3 vols. (1842–3), 2.93 • Thieme & Becker, *Allgemeines Lexikon* • R. Lister, *Prints and print making: a dictionary and handbook of the art in nineteenth-century Britain* (1984) • F. Lugt, *Répertoire des catalogues de ventes publiques*, 1–2 (The Hague, 1938–53) • J. Johnson, ed., *Works exhibited at the Royal Society of British Artists, 1824–1893, and the New English Art Club, 1888–1917*, 2 vols. (1975) • M. H. Grant, *A dictionary of British landscape painters, from the 16th century to the early 20th century* (1952) • bishop's transcripts, 1759–1835, Southwark, St Saviour • parish registers, 1686–1931, Soho, St Anne

Archives BM, corresp. and minutes

Likenesses W. H. Carpenter, etching, 1845, BM; repro. in Griffiths, ed., *Landmarks in print collecting*

Josi, Henry (1802–1845). *See under* Josi, Christian (1768–1828).

Josse, Augustin Louis (1763–1841), Roman Catholic priest and Hispanic scholar, was born in France and ordained priest in the diocese of Vannes. During the reign of terror he narrowly escaped falling victim to the French Revolution. He first sought asylum in Spain, where he remained for four years, during which time he thoroughly mastered the Spanish language. Towards the close of the century he settled in London, where he established himself as a teacher of languages and published a series of successful textbooks as well as editions of works by Spanish writers.

Josse's innovative *Nouvelle grammaire espagnole raisonée*, first published in London in 1799 as *Éléments de la grammaire espagnole*, was reprinted many times in London, Paris, and the United States, where a revised edition by F. Sales, Spanish instructor at Harvard, was still current in the late nineteenth century. The fourth London edition (1817) was supplemented by the text of Jovellanos's *El delincuente honrado* and selected letters of P. Isla. He also published an anthology of Spanish prose, *El tesoro español* (1802), and a guide to Spanish prose composition, *Cours de thèmes adaptés aux principes fondamentaux de langue espagnole* (1804), as well as a revision of the French grammar of Nicolas Wanostrocht (1827). In 1809 he produced editions of the *Fabulas literarias* of Tomás de Iriarte and the *Historia de la conquista de Mexico* by Antonio de Solis. His *Juvenile Biography, or, Lives of Celebrated Children*, 'with moral reflections addressed to the youth of both sexes', translated from the original French by Mrs Cummyng, appeared in 1801.

In 1813 Josse was appointed professor of French literature to Princess Charlotte of Wales. Among his other pupils were the duke of Wellington and the actor John Kemble. In February 1828 Bishop William Poynter persuaded Josse to take charge of the Catholic mission at Gloucester, where he spent the last twelve years of his life in the presbytery attached to the church of St Peter's in London Road. He died there on 28 January 1841, and was buried in the churchyard of St John the Baptist.

G. MARTIN MURPHY

Sources DNB · G. Oliver, *Collections illustrating the history of the Catholic religion in the counties of Cornwall, Devon, Dorset, Somerset, Wilts, and Gloucester* (1857), 118–19, 337 · A. Bellenger, *The French emigré clergy* (1986) · *Gloucester Journal* (6 Feb 1841)

Likenesses Gauci, oil on panel; formerly priv. coll., in 1891

Josselin, Ralph (1617–1683), Church of England clergyman and diarist, was born on 26 January 1617 at Roxwell in Essex, the first son and third child of John Josselin (*d.* 1636), farmer, and his wife, who was probably called Anne.

Education and early career Josselin's early education was at Bishop's Stortford. By his own account he was an eager pupil, with a special love of books and histories, both secular and biblical. From his early days, he claimed, he showed a desire to become a clergyman. He loved to hear ministers preach and afterwards to imitate them—'acting in corners' (*Diary*, 1)—and to walk home solitarily to meditate on the sermon. His mother died in 1624 when he was not yet eight and when Josselin was in his early teens his father—an unsuccessful farmer—married again. Josselin seems not to have got on with his stepmother and in 1633 he was sent to Jesus College, Cambridge. Despite interruptions to his studies caused by lack of money, he received his BA in 1636–7 (and his MA in 1640). His father died in 1636. Having toyed with thoughts of becoming either a farmer or a lawyer, Josselin decided on a career in the

church, and spent the next three years trying to support himself in a succession of posts as schoolteacher and curate. In March 1641 he became vicar of the parish of Earls Colne, Essex, where he was to spend the rest of his life.

Josselin as clergyman Josselin described himself as, at birth, 'the seed of the righteous' (*Diary*, 1). His own record of his passage into the ministry makes clear his religious identity as a puritan. He disapproved of the religious changes introduced by Charles I's archbishop, 'that great stickler for all outward pomp' (ibid., 31) William Laud, changes that were making their mark on the Cambridge he attended. At his ordination in February 1640 Josselin refused to bow towards the altar. Having been encouraged to enter the church by John Borodale, vicar at his father's parish and himself a man questioned for his nonconformity, he was well suited to be minister at Earls Colne. This was a parish which had acquired a reputation for nonconformity under Thomas Shepard, who had been forced to flee to New England, and under its godly patrons and lords of the manor, the Harlakenden family, with whom Josselin was to form a very close relationship.

Josselin's arrival at Earls Colne coincided with the beginnings of parliament's attack on the Caroline church, and his long tenure with the prolonged period of instability precipitated by the failure to agree on the structure of a reformed church and later the growth of nonconformity following the reimposition of Anglican uniformity at the Restoration. His diary provides an intimate picture of the hopes and fears that these changes brought to a deeply religious man.

Josselin welcomed the religious freedom parliament's reforms brought, signing the 1642 petition to parliament from Essex in support of further reform. He rejected the 'heavy burden' of the prayer-book service and he ensured that at the earliest opportunity the parish swept away idolatrous imagery from the church. But thereafter he was caught between his desire, in accordance with his strict Calvinist beliefs, to exclude from the sacrament of the communion those who were not in the company of God's saints, and his pressing concern to promote throughout his parish a moral reformation that required regular and universal church attendance. In the absence of an effective national church he found himself also worried by those separatists who regarded liberty as an invitation to form their own churches and to worship after their own fashion.

In the early 1640s Josselin found comfort in his ability to meet together regularly with a select group of his honest and godly neighbours in voluntary prayer and discussion. By 1647 this had come to be formalized in what Josselin termed 'the society'. There are repeated references in the diary to its meetings, especially for the period from 1647 to 1657. With his patrons the Harlakendens and other leading families active in the meetings, it provided Josselin with significant spiritual assistance throughout the turbulent days of civil war, revolution, and Restoration. Josselin needed support since he faced challenges in his ministry from both spiritual enthusiasm and what he termed spiritual apathy. By 1647 he was noting in his diary that his 'congregacion growes very thinne' (*Diary*, 93), but this had less to do with spiritual apathy than with the spiritual antipathy that Josselin faced from some of the parish. For, although it is clear from his diary that Josselin was an effective and active preacher, receiving invitations to preach elsewhere in the county and at Paul's Cross in London, his policies within Earls Colne made him unpopular with a section of the parish. (It may be significant that the only time Josselin recorded preaching to a full church, with parishioners outside the church forced to listen through the windows, was in a dream.) Like other godly ministers Josselin was anxious to suppress popular festivities. These were occasions of sin in the eyes of the godly, what Josselin himself attacked as 'the jollity and vanity of the time that custome hath wedded us unto' (ibid., 30). That Josselin used the pulpit to attack such practices, intervening personally on one occasion to scatter the youth at play on the green, probably did little for his popularity. But an important consequence of his readiness to find spiritual support in the more select gathering of 'the society' probably had a larger role to play. Josselin's worries that universal communion might mean that those who lacked evidence of grace and salvation would endanger the purity of the sacrament had led him to abandon communion in the early 1640s. It is clear that this decision caused him considerable soul-searching. When communion was restored early in 1651 his moving entry in his diary provides powerful testimony of the importance of the sacrament to the godly. But when communion was restored, it was done only after considerable discussion with other members of Josselin's immediate religious circle, and the restrictions placed on those who could receive effectively made it a closed communion available to only a minority of parishioners. Reintroduction led to a period of prolonged worry for Josselin as to what would happen if parishioners presented themselves for communion who were thought unworthy.

Josselin's consciousness of what he termed confusions and disorders in parish and country help to explain his recognition of the need for a national church and his support for a presbyterian church settlement. Josselin was an eager signatory of the solemn league and covenant and confided in his diary his disappointment that parliament did not ensure its full implementation. He was one of the signatories to the 1648 petition in support of the church settlement proposed by the Westminster assembly, *A testimony of the ministers in the province of Essex to the truth of Jesus Christ and to the solemn league and covenant, as also against the errors, heresies and blasphemies of these times and of the toleration of them.* He discussed the establishment of parochial classes with Matthew Newcomen and he was named as minister for Earls Colne in the proposed presbyterian church settlement for Essex. But in his practice, as in the petition he signed, Josselin was prepared to allow for the tender consciences of dissenting brethren. He was hostile, however, to those who wished to separate altogether from the church. Almost from the start of his ministry he was troubled by separatists within the parish; while this led to another source of anxiety in the diary, it later became something of a preoccupation with the emergence of the Quakers in the 1650s.

With the failure of a national settlement, entries in Josselin's diary reveal the intensity with which he, in association with other ministers and with his immediate religious circle, debated both matters of faith and church government. Confronted by enormous changes both in the kingdom and abroad, from 1647 Josselin began to exhibit in the diary an active belief in millenarianism, recording and seeking to interpret both his and his children's dreams, as well as major episodes in the Europe-wide battle between Catholics and protestants and rumours of the return of the Jews to England, as evidence for the imminence of Christ's second coming.

After the Restoration, Josselin—to his continuing surprise and puzzlement—was allowed to continue as vicar of Earls Colne, while all around him his fellow godly ministers were expelled. Although references to 'the society' cease after 1662, it is clear that Josselin still had a circle of godly friends with whom he could pray and seek advice. It is also clear that he continued quietly to resist the reintroduction of an Anglican liturgy. He only reintroduced the prayer book communion service into the parish in 1665 after being summoned before the church courts the previous year, in what was to be the first of several appearances for his unwillingness to conform. But when communion was restored, Josselin recorded only a small number of communicants—usually less than twenty in a parish where several hundred were eligible. These well-known figures have led some historians to use Josselin as a witness to growing plebeian indifference, but they suggest perhaps that Josselin and his godly circle may have continued to exercise—albeit informally—restrictions on eligibility.

Josselin as diarist Ralph Josselin's main claim to fame lies in the detailed diary he kept. This diary, one of the richest and most important to survive for the seventeenth century, has suffered various vicissitudes. It was lost or stolen in the nineteenth century and recovered by a chance purchase for 6*d.* by the Victorian novelist Mrs Oliphant. A scholarly edition prepared for the Camden Society in the first decade of the twentieth century omitted almost three-quarters of the original with the justification that only the repetitive 'many entries of no interest whatever' had been excised. The Josselin that emerged from this edition of the diary was very much the public man, whose comments on the great religious and political issues of his day were what most merited attention. He was a moderate parliamentarian, active in electioneering and petitioning and worried by the emergence of more radical groups like the Levellers, and served for a brief spell as a chaplain in the parliamentarian army and assisted locally with the implementation of measures for the reform of the church and augmentation of livings; he suffered plundering by royalist troops for his active organization of the defence of the village in 1648 at the siege of Colchester. Although unhappy at the king's execution, he retained his support for what he called the 'honest party' even after the Restoration. Josselin's well-informed comments on political events both in England and on the continent (on which he made an annual end-of-year report in his diary) reflect the social depth to political knowledge in mid-seventeenth-century England.

Renewed examination of the manuscript diary in the 1960s disclosed how much had been excluded. It revealed the possibilities for a rich and intimate portrait of the man and the social, cultural, and mental worlds he inhabited. Such was the quality of the evidence that Josselin became perhaps the first man in British history whose biography formed the subject for 'an essay in historical anthropology' (Macfarlane), and this in turn led to a pioneering large-scale study of his parish of Earls Colne. Finally, a complete edition of the diary appeared in 1976.

After a retrospective of his early life in its early pages, the diary offers a detailed (and for the core years often daily) account of Josselin's life. The picture that emerges allows the reader to see Josselin properly in context, to sympathize with much that seems familiar in his life, and to puzzle over much that is foreign and strange. Married and family life feature strongly. He writes of falling in love and marrying a wife—Jane (c.1621–1693), daughter of Thomas Constable of Olney, Buckinghamshire, whom he married on 28 October 1640 and with whom he was to spend all but a few months of the forty-three years of their marriage living and working together. He writes with pride and affection of his relations with his children and of his evident concern to see them settled, but with irritation when relationships with them (or his wife) did not go the way he planned or expected. He writes movingly of their illnesses and deaths; two of his ten children died soon after birth, and one—his beloved Mary—in early childhood. A sense of loss and sensitivity to the psychological needs of the survivors clearly informed the counselling he offered in a funeral sermon of 1652, his only published sermon. But in seeking explanations for why God took away his ten-day-old son Ralph, Josselin opens a window on to another world when he finds the explanation in a punishment for his playing too much chess. As his references to a monstrous birth and parishioners who had seen the devil reveal, for all the intimate familiarity of his family life, Josselin inhabited a very different mental world.

The Josselin of the restored diary is a man himself vulnerable to the threats posed by illness, anxiously and endlessly noting the condition of his urine or the recurring problems he had with an infected navel. He was a man who needed to combine his pastoral duties, his scholarship, and his love of books (of which he was a frequent purchaser) with the need to secure a living. A worry over money is a constant theme. Earls Colne as a living never quite lived up to his expectations and this led to hard negotiations with his parishioners on whose tithes and voluntary (but, for many in the parish, often reluctant) donations he much depended, and it prompted threats and thoughts of moving to other livings, which were scotched by the renewed generosity of his patrons, the Harlakendens. A generous bequest from a wealthy parishioner helped to establish him as a farmer from the mid-1640s.

Frequent references to the weather and state of the harvest are but the most common of the many other topics noted in Josselin's detailed diary. But his references to the weather reveal a deeper significance, one that clearly informed the purpose of his diary-keeping. He saw in the weather, especially that causing a run of poor harvests in the later 1640s and coinciding with the greatest period of religious and political uncertainty, worrying evidence of divine displeasure. Running through the diary is a concern to understand the ways of God in relation to events in his world and in his own life, and to the question of his own salvation. As frequent entries make clear, Josselin subscribed to a providentialist reading of the world as one in which God intervened directly in the lives of individuals and the societies in which they lived, punishing sin and rewarding right living. Keeping a diary allowed Josselin to reflect on evidence of divine interventions— general through sword, famine, and plague and particular in the manifold mercies that he and his family enjoyed in escaping illness or accident. For all its rich detail of a past life, the primary purpose of Josselin's diary-keeping reflected the rigorous self-inspection by which the godly were expected to live their lives. Thus, when he survived a bee sting on the nose, Josselin was moved to record the incident in his diary, noting unselfconsciously that 'divine providence reaches to the lowest things' (*Diary*, 19).

Josselin died in August 1683, and was buried at Earls Colne on 30 August. By the time of his death he had secured a comfortable material existence. But even to the end, his diary, maintained until the month before his death, reveals a man trying to fulfil his parochial duties, continually concerned with his children's lives, receptive to political news (particularly of the fate of godly dissenters), and still, amid entries increasingly caught up with documenting his failing health, continuing to note, 'God good to me' (*Diary*, 645). JOHN WALTER

Sources *The diary of Ralph Josselin, 1616–1683*, ed. A. Macfarlane (1976) · A. Macfarlane, *The family life of Ralph Josselin, a seventeenth-century clergyman: an essay in historical anthropology* (1970) · 'Earls Colne: records of an English village, 1375–1854', linux02.lib.cam.ac.uk/earlscolne//, June–July 2002 · will, Essex RO, Chelmsford, D/ACR/10/144 · parish register, Earls Colne, Essex, Essex RO, Chelmsford, D/P 209/1/3 · H. Smith, *The ecclesiastical history of Essex under the Long Parliament and Commonwealth* [n.d.] · R. J. [R. Josselin], *The state of the saints departed* (1652)
Archives Essex RO, diary [typescript]
Likenesses portrait (of Josselin?), repro. in Macfarlane, *Family life*, frontispiece · portrait (of Josselin?), priv. coll.
Wealth at death over £540: 1 June 1683, will, Essex RO, D/ACR/10/144 · lands: Macfarlane, *Family life*

Josselyn, Henry (1606–1683). *See under* Josselyn, John (c.1608–1704?).

Josselyn, John (c.1608–1704?), travel writer, was a younger son of Sir Thomas Josselyn (b. 1559/60, d. in or after 1639), landowner, of Willingale Doe, Essex (later of Littleport, Isle of Ely), and his second wife, Theodora (d. 1635), daughter of Edmund Cooke of Erith and Bexley, and widow of Clement Bere of Dartford, Kent. In 1638 John accompanied his father to New England. On arrival in Boston in early

July, John called on Governor John Winthrop and the clergyman John Cotton, delivering to the latter for approbation (which it did not receive) a metrical version of six of the Psalms by the poet Francis Quarles. Father and son then went to Black Point, Scarborough, Maine, where John's elder brother Henry [*see below*] was settled. Sir Thomas had been appointed the colony's deputy governor, but he and John soon returned to Britain, reaching England in October 1639. John paid his second visit to New England in 1663, arriving in Boston in late July. He joined his brother in Maine and stayed with him for almost eight and a half years.

Josselyn returned to England in December 1671, and in 1672 published *New-England's rarities discovered in birds, beasts, fishes, serpents, and plants of that country, together with the physical and chyrurgical remedies wherewith the natives constantly use to cure their distempers, wounds, and sores ... illustrated with cuts.* His second work, licensed by Roger L'estrange on 28 November 1673, was published in 1674, with a second edition appearing in 1675: *An account of two voyages to New-England: wherein you have the setting out of a ship, with the charges ... A description of the countrey, natives and creatures, with their merchantil and physical use; The government of the countrey ... A large chronological table of the most remarkable passages, from the first discovering of the continent of America to the year 1673.* Josselyn's first work, a small volume noticed by the Royal Society, was dedicated to Josselyn's kinsman Samuel Fortrey, who had sponsored the author's recent visit. The second, larger work was dedicated to the president and fellows of the Royal Society, though election to the society failed to follow. This outcome is not wholly surprising, for Josselyn's two works blend dispassionate and useful observations with a retailing of marvels that he would neither read as providences nor explain, nor omit. Despite his failure to impress the Royal Society he apparently enjoyed the patronage of the queen. At Willingale Doe the tombstone of a John Josselyn dated 1704 may be his.

Josselyn's elder brother **Henry Josselyn** (1606–1683), colonial governor, entered Corpus Christi College, Cambridge, in 1623 but was not awarded a degree. Styled lieutenant, he was an agent for the Council for New England in 1631, admitting patentees to their lands. In 1634 he was at Piscataqua (now Portsmouth), New Hampshire. When Captain John Mason, that colony's patentee, died in 1635, Henry took service with Sir Ferdinando Gorges, and from 1636 was a member of the Maine government: at first a commissioner, by 1639 he was a councillor and steward-general and by 1645 a magistrate. Like his brother John, Henry was an Anglican and no friend to the puritan Massachusetts Bay colony. By 1638 he was at Black Point with Captain Thomas Cannock, and when Cannock died in 1643 Henry married his widow, Margaret, and inherited Cannock's patent there. He became deputy governor of Maine in 1645, an office he still held in 1648; in the late 1650s Massachusetts confirmed him as a councillor, an appointment confirmed by the king in 1665. In 1660 he was a deputy to the Massachusetts Bay general court.

Defeated by the Indians in October 1676, Henry Josselyn retired westwards. By 1682 he was at Pemaquid, where he died in 1683, some time before 10 May.

GORDON GOODWIN, *rev.* DAVID R. RANSOME

Sources J. Josselyn, *New-England's rarities discovered in birds, beasts, fishes, serpents, and plants of that country* (1672) · J. Josselyn, *An account of two voyages to New-England: wherein you have the setting out of a ship, with the charges* (1674); 2nd edn (1675) · R. C. Anderson, *The great migration begins*, 2 vols. (1995), vol. 2 · P. J. Lindholdt, ed., *John Josselyn: colonial traveler* (1988) · *VCH Cambridgeshire and the Isle of Ely*, vols. 2, 4, 9 · Venn, *Alum. Cant.* · P. Morant, *The history and antiquities of the county of Essex*, 2 (1768), 478–9 · Essex RO, T/P 195/15 [for Willingale Doe tombstone of 1704] · D. Wharton, 'Josselyn, John', *ANB* · P. Baxter, ed., *The Trelawny papers*, Collections of the Maine Historical Society, Documentary History, 2nd ser. 3 (1884) · IGI

Joubert de la Ferté, Sir Philip Bennet (1887–1965), air force officer, was born in Darjeeling, India, on 21 May 1887, the fourth child of the family of four daughters (two of whom died young) and two sons of Colonel Charles Henry Joubert de la Ferté, of the Indian Medical Service, and his wife, Eliza Jane, eldest daughter of Philip Sandys Melville, of the Indian Civil Service. He was of partly French descent, his grandfather having come to England in 1840 and, after being naturalized in 1885, distinguished himself by designing and engraving a fourpenny Inland Revenue stamp which was used for over forty years.

The Joubert children had a sound upbringing, but had a reputation for recklessness. At the age of nine, Philip was sent to school in England at Elstree, a severe test for a youngster brought up in the East. However, he found solace by reading novels about flying and submarine adventures, books which undoubtedly coloured his future outlook. Since it was impossible to return to India for school holidays, he went to family friends in the country and to an aunt in the south of France. These visits developed in him those qualities of self-reliance which became evident later, since by the age of eleven he was travelling alone between England and France and was thrown entirely on his own resources.

It was intended that Joubert should join the army, though he himself was keen to join the navy. Parental influence prevailed and he was dispatched to Harrow School. He qualified for the Royal Military Academy, Woolwich, at his second attempt and passed out at the lower end of his term, gaining a commission in the field gunners in 1907. After five years as a second lieutenant, Joubert regained his desire to fly or to operate a submarine. By chance, his parents had taken a house at Weybridge, adjacent to Brooklands racetrack. Brooklands soon afterwards became an aerodrome. In 1912 Joubert set out to learn to fly and was given official permission to do so at his own expense. He was soon granted Royal Aero Club certificate no. 280. After a course at the Central Flying School at Upavon, he was attached to the Royal Flying Corps (RFC) (military wing) in March 1913 as a flying officer. He was at last financially independent, and had joined the RFC at a time which favoured his future prospects. He was a fully qualified young army officer, fit and keen to believe in the importance of powered flight, and with the added advantage of being able to speak French.

Joubert was promoted to the rank of temporary captain when war began in 1914, and proceeded to France with 3 squadron. Within a week, flying a Blériot and armed with a pistol, he made aviation history by being one of the two pilots to make the first reconnaissance of enemy lines. He was mentioned in dispatches for the first time two months later—in all he was to be mentioned seven times. He was then recalled to England in 1915 to raise a new squadron. That task completed, he was promoted to the rank of temporary major and given command of 15 squadron in France.

Events moved swiftly as the war developed and Joubert was fortunate to be given command of 1 squadron, in succession to (William) Geoffrey Salmond, at a significant time because it covered the battle of Loos. His younger brother, John Claude—also of 1 squadron and also a pilot—had had the misfortune to be shot down in March 1915 over Holland and remained a prisoner of war for the rest of the war.

Early in 1916 Joubert was invalided out of France with trench foot. When he recovered he was ordered to form a new squadron, 33. Very shortly afterwards he was promoted temporary lieutenant-colonel and given command of 5 wing in Egypt. There his experience and flair for improvisation were put to good use since 5 wing's resources were not large and its aircraft were out of date. Joubert left Egypt early in 1917 with many important lessons learned from the fighting in Sinai, particularly in handling both air and ground operations. He was appointed DSO for his efforts.

After only a few months in England in command of 21 wing, Joubert was transferred to 14 wing, which he took to Italy after a short stay in France. The move to Italy was an important step in his career as he had now established himself as a leader, a practical airman, a sound administrator, and a good commander in the field—all essential qualities for higher command. These qualities were recognized in 1918 by his appointment to command the RFC in Italy. At this time he was awarded the order of Sts Maurice and Lazarus, the *cavaliere*, and the *croce di guerra*. Later he was appointed CMG in 1919, CB in 1936, and KCB in 1938. During the war he married, on 19 May 1915, Marjorie Denison, youngest daughter of Frederick Joseph Hall, of Sheffield. They had two daughters.

When the war ended Joubert was given command of 2 group at Oxford and received a permanent commission as a wing commander in the Royal Air Force (created in April 1918 by the amalgamation of the RFC and the Royal Naval Air Service). 2 group was moved to the recruits depot at Uxbridge where Joubert's administrative and leadership qualities were tested to the full because he had both to deal with 1500 restless and undisciplined dominion cadets anxious to return home, and to participate in the country's milk distribution during the nationwide railway strike. He emerged from both tests with an enhanced reputation. In the following year, 1920, he attended the Staff College, Camberley; his happy days there were a welcome respite.

In 1922 Joubert was promoted group captain and appointed an instructor to the recently formed RAF College at Andover. This period was vital for his subsequent career, as it provided a forum for the formulation of future air policy. On leaving Andover he served as deputy director of personnel and in the directorate of manning at the Air Ministry. In 1926 he became the first RAF instructor at the Imperial Defence College, another milestone. He remained there for three years, being promoted air commodore when he left. After about nine months in flying training, during which he took every opportunity to modernize his airmanship, he was posted as commandant of the RAF Staff College, where he remained for three years. This was an admirable post because it enabled him to witness the implementation of the plans made by the Air Council in 1922, and the development of an air policy, broadly conceived and flexible in its application. Above all, Joubert sought to bring the other two services into closer co-operation with the RAF. His quick brain infused both a spirit of enthusiasm and a sense of urgency into staff and pupils alike.

In 1933 Joubert was promoted air vice-marshal and a year later he was appointed air officer commanding the fighting area of Great Britain—the forerunner of Fighter Command. In this post he devoted much time to studying the air tactics which were gradually evolving from the techniques employed by fighters during the war of 1914–18 into those of the more modern fighters then in service. It was during this period that he took charge of British air defence during the annual air exercises. Promoted air marshal in 1936, he was appointed for the first time as air officer commanding-in-chief Coastal Command, a post in which he hoped to stay for some time in view of his earlier affection for the sea. But this was not to be: in 1937 he was sent to India as air officer commanding. This was the least satisfying of his appointments because the authorities in London were inevitably preoccupied with the dangerous course of events in Europe. Although Joubert made his needs known, he was frustrated by his superiors' inability to face the military facts of life in the Far East, where even the nucleus of a modern air force was lacking. Fortunately for Joubert himself, his stay in India was cut short when he was recalled to England at the outbreak of the Second World War and appointed air adviser on combined operations. There were, however, more pressing needs for his services elsewhere, and he became assistant chief of air staff with special responsibility for the practical application of radar in the RAF. Much of the ultimate success of the radar war was due to Joubert's realization at this early stage of its great possibilities, in both defence and offence. It was also during this period that he gave his regular broadcasts on the air war; the large audience for these was evidence of his talent in this medium.

In June 1941 Joubert was promoted air chief marshal and became, for the second time, air officer commanding-in-chief Coastal Command, his own favourite (if not his most successful) command. During the seventeen months he was there, much needed to be done to reduce the very heavy U-boat attacks on allied shipping in the Atlantic.

The command became better equipped, with more aircraft and superior weapons, the most important of which were aircraft of very long range (B-17s and B-24s) and improved air-to-surface vessel radar. These innovations had a profound effect upon the command in the days ahead. This period in his life was not free from criticism. His relationship with civilian scientists, especially those in operational research, was not as close as it had been in his predecessor's time, and he came close to sinking his command's anti-submarine effort by advocating the bomb rather than the depth charge as the prime weapon. His outspokenness on the use of air power also led to a clash with the head of Bomber Command, Sir Arthur Harris, who resented any diversion of long-range aircraft to Coastal Command. Joubert was moved on and became inspector-general of the RAF, a post he held until his retirement in 1943.

Fortunately for Joubert, he was recalled after only a month of retirement to join the staff of Admiral Mountbatten in the south-east Asia command as deputy chief of staff (information and civil affairs), reverting to the rank of air marshal. Perhaps his most successful venture in this posting was to create a south-east Asia command newspaper, delivered almost daily to the troops throughout the command. After the fall of Rangoon, Joubert returned to England for hospital treatment. He finally retired from service in October 1945.

After some nine months of rest and recuperation Joubert returned as a civilian to the Air Ministry for another year as director of public relations. He permitted himself the luxury of only a short rest before embarking on a most successful but exhausting coast-to-coast lecture tour of the United States on his favourite subject, air power. Joubert also gave frequent expression to his thoughts in print; one book, *The Third Service* (1955), provoked considerable controversy among the various services and ministries. Nor was he universally popular within his own service. During the early 1960s he alienated many former Bomber Command personnel by his comments on the effectiveness of the bomber offensive during the war, and, in particular, by his judgement that the 'official historians' of the bomber offensive had mishandled the subject and failed to draw the right conclusions.

In appearance Joubert was just under 6 feet tall, broad in proportion, with a fine complexion, sparkling eyes, and a very healthy look. He had a strong character combined with great charm and an engaging personality. His first marriage was dissolved in 1947, and on 30 April 1948 he married Joan Catherine (b. 1915/16), the divorced wife of Terence Cripps and the daughter of Fred Bucknell, a retired merchant seaman. He died at the RAF Hospital, Uxbridge, on 21 January 1965.

EDWARD CHILTON, rev. CHRISTINA J. M. GOULTER

Sources *The Times* (22 Jan 1965) · *Daily Telegraph* (22 Jan 1965) · P. Joubert de la Ferté, *The fated sky: an autobiography* (1952) · private information (1981) · Air Historical Branch (RAF) records, London · Burke, *Peerage* (1959) · m. certs. · N. Frankland, *History at war: the campaigns of an historian* (1998) · M. Dean, *The Royal Air Force and two world wars* (1979)

Archives Royal Air Force Museum, Hendon, logbooks, corresp., diaries | Bodl. Oxf., letters to Lord Monckton · IWM, corresp. with Tizard and memorandum | FILM BFI NFTVA, documentary footage · IWM FVA, news footage | SOUND IWM SA, oral history interview · IWM SA, recorded lecture
Likenesses H. Coster, photographs, 1930–39, NPG · W. Stoneman, photographs, 1934–56, NPG · J. Gunn, oils, 1941, IWM · O. Birley, portrait; formerly at Headquarters Coastal Command but destroyed by fire · J. Hughes-Hallett, oils, RAF Museum, Hendon; on loan
Wealth at death £2156: probate, 28 Oct 1965, CGPLA Eng. & Wales

Joule, James Prescott (1818–1889), physicist, was born on 24 December 1818 in New Bailey Street, Salford, the fourth of seven children of Benjamin Joule (1784–1858), a Salford brewer, and his wife, Alice (1788–1836), elder daughter of Thomas and Grace Prescott of Wigan. The first two children died in infancy, leaving Benjamin as eldest and James as second son. Delicate in health, James was educated by private tutors at the new family residence, Broom Hill, near Manchester. About 1834 his father decided that he and Benjamin should study under the celebrated chemist John Dalton who taught pupils on the premises of the Manchester Literary and Philosophical Society, of which he was then president. Following two years of arithmetic and geometry, they had just begun chemistry when Dalton suffered a serious stroke. Dalton's personal influence on James Joule was nevertheless considerable, being most conspicuous in the distinctive experimental style of quantitative measurement that characterized the laboratory practices of both men. Within a short time, Joule's father provided him with a room at Broom Hill for use as a laboratory. After Dalton, Joule was tutored by John Davis, medical lecturer and co-founder in 1839, with the electrical showman and inventor William Sturgeon, of Manchester's Royal Victoria Gallery for the Encouragement and Illustration of Practical Science.

The motive power of electricity Joule's first publication, 'Description of an electro-magnetic engine' (1838), appeared in a new British periodical with the grandiose title *Annals of Electricity, Magnetism and Chemistry; and Guardian of Experimental Science*, edited by Sturgeon. The *Annals* placed great emphasis on 'the rise and progress of electromagnetic engines for propelling machinery', controversially claiming in 1839 that developments in the design of electromagnets offered 'new and inexhaustible sources of force which appear easily and extensively available as a mechanical agent' (Sturgeon, 430). Joule addressed his initial contributions as letters to the editor, reporting on his own experimental arrangements to improve the economic working of electromagnetic engines.

These early contributions typically promoted the advantages, especially compactness, of Joule's arrangements for locomotives and steamships: 'A great saving of room is effected and, consequently, the power relative to the weight of the engine is increased'. Visual and practical throughout, the accounts concerned geometrical systems rather than philosophical explanations and, when he promised to communicate upon completion of the engine

James Prescott Joule (1818–1889), by Lady Roscoe, c.1876

'a particular account of its duty', he spoke both the language of Sturgeon the inventor, and of engineer–inventors in general (Joule, *Annals*, 122–3). Sturgeon quickly endorsed Joule's invention as an 'exceedingly ingenious arrangement of electro-magnets of soft iron … Mr. Joule proposes to apply his engine both to locomotive carriages and to boats' (Sturgeon, 436).

In a second letter, however, Joule signalled that he aspired to something higher than ingenious invention. Presenting a report on the disappointing performance of his electromagnetic engine, he announced an intention to conduct experiments comparing the performance of different arrangements of iron in the electromagnet. He now began to represent himself as an experimental philosopher. 'On electro-magnetic forces' (1840), published in Sturgeon's *Annals*, expressed fully Joule's shift from descriptions of ingenious apparatus to experimental natural philosophy with a strong emphasis on the measurement of physical quantities. The paper included, for example, Joule's definition of a unit current as one which, if allowed to pass for an hour through a water voltameter, would decompose nine grains of water. Furthermore, his whole mode of presentation changed from that of personal letters to that of a series of consecutively numbered paragraphs. It was hardly coincidence that Joule's second communication under the same title followed immediately after a reprint of some of Michael Faraday's 'Researches in electricity' with its distinctive numbering of paragraphs. Joule's new and less personal style, appealing to the forces of nature rather than to human artefacts,

suggests that Faraday, not Sturgeon, had become his role model.

Consistent with this shift, Joule attempted in the same year to present himself as a gentlemanly natural philosopher to the nation's premier scientific society. 'On the production of heat by voltaic electricity' appeared in summary form in the *Proceedings of the Royal Society* (1840) and announced what subsequently became known as Joule's 'i^2R' law of the heating effects of an electric current: 'when a current of voltaic electricity is propagated along a metallic conductor the heat evolved in a given time is proportional to the resistance of the conductor, multiplied by the square of the electric intensity [current]' (Joule, *Papers*, 1.65). But the aloof reporting of the *Proceedings*, combined with the non-appearance of the paper in the *Philosophical Transactions*, suggests that Joule was very far from possessing the authority required to persuade the Royal Society of the importance of his investigation. Furthermore, an accompanying theoretical speculation on the electrical nature of chemical combustion transgressed the strict experimental ethos of the society's *Transactions*.

Taking advantage of his continuing links with Sturgeon, Joule delivered early in 1841 his first public lecture at the Victoria Gallery (of which Sturgeon had become superintendent two years previously). His special concern was to investigate 'a novel form of electro-magnetic engine', based on the increase in length of an iron bar on being magnetized, suggested to him by 'an ingenious gentleman of this town' (Joule, *Papers*, 1.48). Here was the voice of the aspiring philosopher seeking to investigate and pronounce upon the principles and practicality of that which the merely ingenious individual, a local wheelwright, G. Arstall, had suggested.

In his lecture Joule deployed a measure of 'economical duty' (understood as the number of pounds raised to the height of 1 foot by the agency of 1 pound of coal in the steam engine or of 1 pound of zinc consumed in the battery used to power the electromagnetic engine) to assess the viability of electromagnetic engines as potential contenders to replace steam engines. He also pointed out the importance of battery resistance (alongside other forms of resistance in the electromagnet or conductors) as a principal obstacle to efficiency. His conclusions made sombre reading for ingenious inventors. In the case of his own experimental engine, the economical duty was some 331,400 pounds raised to the height of 1 foot for every pound of zinc consumed in a Grove's battery. In contrast 'the duty of the best Cornish steam engines is about 1,500,000 lbs. raised to the height of 1 foot by the combustion of each pound of coal, or nearly five times the extreme duty that I was able to obtain from the magnetic engine by the consumption of a pound of zinc' (Joule, *Papers*, 1.48).

This public lecture also gave Joule an opportunity to enhance his local philosophical credibility by considering the possible mechanical causes of the increased length of the magnetized iron bar in the case of Arstall's proposed engine. He adopted a version of the theory put forward by an eighteenth-century German natural philosopher, F. U. T. Aepinus (1724–1802), which proposed atoms of iron surrounded first by atmospheres of magnetism and, beyond these, still rarer atmospheres of electricity. The space between each of these 'compound atoms' was filled with 'calorific ether in a state of vibration' or in some manner allowing vibration of the atoms themselves (Joule, *Papers*, 1.52). Under a magnetic inductive influence, the atmospheres accumulated on one side of the atom in line with the axis of the bar. This theory explained the various phenomena of magnetism (saturation, increased length, destruction of magnetic power by heating) in simple mechanical terms of matter, space, and motion.

In this respect Joule committed himself to a fundamentally mechanical conception of nature whose basic building blocks of matter, together with its mechanical properties, had been created by God and thus admitted of no further human explanation or analysis. Although he shared with Faraday the belief that only God could create or destroy the basic entities of nature, he differed radically from Faraday in his assumptions concerning the mechanical character of those building blocks. His mechanical commitments also differed strikingly from the assumptions of the German physician Julius Robert Mayer, subsequently his rival claimant to 'discovery' of the mechanical equivalent of heat. On the other hand, his perspective would appeal strongly to Scottish-centred natural philosophers within an engineering context, notably William Thomson and Macquorn Rankine.

In the same year, Joule published his investigations into the heating effects of electric currents in a well-established scientific periodical with national and international readerships. Unlike the *Philosophical Transactions*, the *Philosophical Magazine* tended to welcome contributions of a more speculative character in which, for example, hypotheses were developed to account for physical and chemical effects. For its readers Joule extended his investigations from solid conductors to electrolytes and arrived at an identical law for the heating effects. He quickly followed up this publication with three further studies, all of which shared a common investigation of electrical resistances, whether in metallic conductors, batteries, electrolytic cells, or chemical combustion. The theme strongly suggests that in this period Joule's researches were motivated by a desire to improve the economical duty of electromagnetic engines through a philosophical understanding of the sources and nature of electrical resistances.

The mechanical value of heat In November 1841 Joule read a paper on the electric origin of the heat of combustion before the Manchester Literary and Philosophical Society. The ailing Dalton moved the vote of thanks. On 25 January 1842 Joule was elected to that élite, if provincial, body, which represented the city's most eminent and wealthy citizens. In subsequent years he served as the society's librarian, honorary secretary, and vice-president, being twice elected president (1860 and 1868).

Joule's electrochemical researches found a receptive audience through the strong chemical interests of Lit. and Phil. members. 'On the heat evolved during the electrolysis of water', read to the society in January 1843, pursued the theme of electrical resistances and concluded with a number of general observations on the subject. In the third such observation Joule inferred that whatever the arrangement of the apparatus 'the whole caloric of the circuit is exactly accounted for by the whole of the chemical changes' (Joule, *Papers*, 1.119), that is, he wanted to persuade himself and his readers that he had traced the heat produced or absorbed in every part of the circuit and had found that the gains and losses of heat were all balanced.

Use of the term 'caloric' here suggested that Joule's interpretation was still compatible with a material view of heat: that heat was simply transferred from one part of the circuit to another without net production or annihilation. But, in adopting Aepinus's theory of magnetism, he had previously accounted for the loss of magnetic power with increased temperature in terms of a vibrational view of the nature of heat. Furthermore, his recent series of papers had favoured an electrical theory of chemical heat (attributed to Humphry Davy and the Swedish electrochemist J. J. Berzelius) by which 'Electricity may be regarded as a grand agent for carrying, arranging, and converting chemical heat' (Joule, *Papers*, 1.120). Heat could thus be interpreted as vibrations within an electrical atmosphere.

Having focused exclusively on the production and absorption of heat with respect to chemical changes, Joule shifted attention in his fourth general observation to the relation of heat and mechanical power. The fifth general observation then introduced into the hitherto 'closed' electrical circuit 'external' factors in the form of an electromagnetic engine and generator. On the one hand a generator driven by mechanical power would produce an electric current which in turn yielded heating effects in the circuit, while on the other an electromagnetic engine producing mechanical power would, in Joule's view, 'convert' a proportionate amount of heat into that mechanical power.

In a footnote of February 1843 Joule indicated that he was 'preparing for experiments to test the accuracy of this proposition' (Joule, *Papers*, 1.120 n.). The outcome was his paper 'On the calorific effects of magneto-electricity, and on the mechanical value of heat' presented to the chemistry section (Section B) of the Cork meeting of the British Association for the Advancement of Science six months later. The full paper, dated July with a postscript of August 1843, appeared in three instalments in the *Philosophical Magazine* during the same year.

Having implemented in practice his own suggestions made in the fifth observation of his 'Electrolysis of water' paper, Joule could now communicate news of experiments relating to the revolution of a small electromagnet immersed in water between the poles of a powerful magnet. Using the electromagnet as a magneto-electric machine (generator), he carried out measurements both of the electricity generated (using an accurate galvanometer) and the calorific effect of the coil (measured by the change of temperature in the water surrounding it). He also introduced a battery into the magneto-electrical circuit. His main conclusion was that 'heat is *generated* by the magneto-electrical machine, and that by means of the inductive power of magnetism we can *diminish* or *increase* at pleasure the *heat* due to chemical changes' (Joule, *Papers*, 1.149). The heat was not merely transferred from one part of the arrangement to another as might be expected from a caloric theory of heat. This conclusion then prompted the further enquiry as to whether or not a constant ratio existed between the heat and the mechanical power gained or lost, that is 'a mechanical value of heat'.

Adopting the mean result of thirteen experiments, Joule presented his answer thus:

> The quantity of heat capable of increasing the temperature of a pound of water by one degree of Fahrenheit's scale is equal to, and may be converted into, a mechanical force capable of raising 838 lb. to the perpendicular height of one foot.

He admitted that there was a considerable difference between some of the results (which ranged from 587 to 1040) but the differences were not, he asserted, 'greater than may be referred with propriety to mere errors of experiment' (Joule, *Papers*, 1.156). Joule's experimental results hardly spoke for themselves, requiring instead a trustworthy experimenter to assure his uneasy readers that the errors were indeed due to mere errors of experiment and not to some more fundamental cause.

If the meaning of 'mechanical value' is understood not simply in the numerical but also in the economic sense, then Joule's investigations can be seen as being shaped by a continuing search for the causes of the failure of his electromagnetic engine to match the economy of heat engines. His primary concern was not with the conversion of work into heat as in frictional cases—the 'waste of useful work' which was of most interest to the brothers James and William Thomson who would soon find common cause with Joule—but with maximizing the conversion of heat from fuel into useful work in various kinds of engines, that is, with 'economical duty'.

In a postscript of August 1843 Joule also connected his conclusions with the earlier work of Count Rumford which focused on the frictional production of heat during the boring of cannon, which had previously met with largely critical reaction from scientific experts. Perhaps recognizing the limited gains to be made here, Joule quickly cited his own attempt at measuring the generation of heat by frictional means. This method measured the 'heat evolved by the passage of water through narrow tubes'. With a mechanical value of about 770 lb, Joule claimed his result to be 'very strongly confirmatory' of his other results, and pledged to 'lose no time in repeating and extending these experiments, being satisfied that the grand agents of nature are, by the Creator's fiat, *indestructible*; and that wherever mechanical force is expended, an exact equivalent of heat is *always* obtained' (Joule, *Papers*, 1.157–8).

Guided by this powerful conviction that the exercise of divine will had established the unchangeable character of

nature's fundamental agents, Joule now fashioned himself as a regular player on local and national stages. As yet, however, he had not received significant critical acclaim. In 1844 he embarked on a third method of construing the relationship between heat and mechanical force, a method which he would deploy for a second assault on the metropolitan stage. An abstract, prepared by the Royal Society's secretary, P. M. Roget of *Thesaurus* fame, appeared in the *Proceedings* but once again the *Philosophical Transactions* rejected the full paper.

The method offered a very different (non-electrical and non-frictional) approach to the mechanical value of heat. The apparatus consisted of a condensing pump and receiver immersed in a large quantity of water, the changes in the temperature of which were ascertained by a thermometer of extreme sensitivity. Joule's method relied upon the accurate measurement of the heat produced by work done in compressing a gas. Conversely, the expansion of a gas against a piston would result in a loss of heat equivalent to the work done. On the other hand, his assertion that no work was done by a gas expanding into a vacuum rested on the contentious claim that no change in temperature had been or could be detected. Everything thus seemed to depend upon one's faith in the accuracy of the thermometers employed. As Otto Sibum has argued, Joule's own exacting thermometric skills can be located in the context of the family brewing business (Sibum, 73–106). Such personal skills, however, as yet carried little weight with Joule's peers.

Joule's rejected paper appeared in the *Philosophical Magazine*. There Joule framed the presentation of his new method within concerns about a theory of the motive power of heat. 'It is the opinion of many philosophers', he wrote, 'that the mechanical power of the steam-engine arises simply from the passage of heat from a hot to a cold body, no heat being necessarily lost during the transfer'. In the course of its passage, the caloric developed *vis viva* (measured now as half the mass times velocity squared). Joule, however, asserted that 'this theory, however ingenious, is opposed to the recognized principles of philosophy, because it leads to the conclusion that *vis viva* may be destroyed by an improper disposition of the apparatus' (Joule, 'Changes of temperature', 382). Aiming his criticism at the French mining engineer Emile Clapeyron for a cleverly contrived theory (the Carnot–Clapeyron theory of the motive power of heat), Joule explained that the Frenchman had inferred that the fall of heat from the temperature of the fire to that of the boiler leads to an enormous loss of *vis viva*. Invoking a shared belief with his Royal Society mentors, Joule countered: 'Believing that the power to destroy belongs to the Creator alone, I entirely coincide with Roget and Faraday in the opinion that any theory which, when carried out, demands the annihilation of force, is necessarily erroneous' (Joule, *Papers*, 1.189). Roget in particular had already written of the impossibility of perpetual motion for the benefit of the Society for the Diffusion of Useful Knowledge. Joule's own theory, then, substituted the straightforward conversion into mechanical power of an equivalent portion of the heat contained in the steam expanding in the cylinder of a steam engine.

Relentlessly pursuing his conviction that the grand agents of nature were indestructible, Joule began work about 1845 on a fourth method for determining the mechanical value of heat. His latest efforts received a polite but unremarkable reception at the Cambridge meeting of the British Association. This time the experiments involved a paddle wheel placed in a can filled with water. Weights attached over pulleys working in opposite directions communicated motion to the paddle wheel. Joule argued that 'the force spent in revolving the paddle wheel produced a certain increment in the temperature of the water' and concluded that:

> when the temperature of a pound of water is increased by one degree of Fahrenheit's scale, an amount of *vis viva* is communicated to it equal to that acquired by a weight of 890 pounds after falling from the altitude of one foot. (Joule, *Papers*, 1.202)

Joule had now firmly introduced the language of *vis viva* to describe the conversion of the motion of the falling weights into the heat of the water. He was identifying his analysis with a by now well established point of view in engineering mechanics, though with the new claim that the motion 'lost' was in fact converted into heat, understood as another form of *vis viva*. It is likely that Joule's adoption of *vis viva* here was contingent upon the fact that his engineering friend, Eaton Hodgkinson, had read to the Lit. and Phil. as recently as April 1844 'Some account of the late Mr. Ewart's paper on the measure of moving force' which discussed the principle of *vis viva* in relation to the effects of machines.

Undaunted by the apparent indifference to his claims, Joule seized an opportunity in the spring of 1847 to deliver a popular lecture entitled 'On matter, living force [*vis viva*] and heat' to a Manchester audience. A lifelong tory in politics, so always concerned with the need for order and stability in a society frequently threatened by radical forces for social change, he offered a conservative vision of the divinely ordained system of nature. His vision of the universe was of machinery working in the most ordered way imaginable, with no tendency to failure or decay. The principles of continual conversions or exchanges, established and maintained by God as the basis of nature's currency system, guaranteed this dynamic stability in nature's economy. In this respect, Joule's perspective harmonized with John Playfair's system of nature earlier in the century (Joule had been collaborating with Playfair's nephew Lyon). Indeed, Joule took care to explain that his was a cyclical cosmos, a dynamic equilibrium, where 'the phenomena may be repeated in endless succession and variety' (Joule, *Papers*, 1.273). The lecture was published in the Conservative *Manchester Courier*.

In 1847 Joule at last attracted the attention of élite philosophers of a new generation during the British Association meeting held in Oxford. The positive atmosphere contrasted with the sense of decline that had pervaded the Cambridge meeting two years earlier. Although forced by pressure of business within Section A (mathematics and physics) to make an abbreviated presentation, Joule nevertheless received welcome public attention from the media, most notably *The Athenaeum* and the *Literary Gazette*, which both summarized his results. The annual *British Association Report*, however, placed the summary of Joule's presentation in Section B (chemistry) and published slightly different mechanical equivalents from those reported at the time.

It was not, however, the public reporting, nor indeed the presence of a distinguished list of mathematicians and astronomers, but the notice of a young professor of natural philosophy which conferred upon Joule the credibility that he had long sought. Joule himself recollected in 1885 that:

> the chairman suggested that as the business of the section pressed I should not read my paper, but confine myself to a short verbal description of my experiments. This I endeavoured to do, and discussion not being invited, the communication would have passed without comment if a young man had not risen in the section, and by his intelligent observations created a lively interest in the new theory. The young man was William Thomson. (Joule, *Papers*, 2.215)

Thomson's retrospective account suggested that the significant encounter took place after the session, when he recalled that 'Joule's paper at the Oxford meeting made a great sensation'; G. G. Stokes soon told Thomson that he was 'inclined to be a Joulite'; Faraday was 'much struck with it' but not wholly persuaded (Bottomley, 619). A couple of weeks later Joule and Thomson met again by chance near Chamonix. Joule had married Amelia (d. 1854), daughter of John Grimes (comptroller of customs in Liverpool) on 18 August 1847, and the couple were on their wedding tour. Thomson recalled in 1882 that Joule was carrying a long thermometer with which to try for a rise of temperature in waterfalls and that the two men had arranged to conduct a joint experiment a few days later at the Cascade de Sallanches which was found to be too much broken with spray. In a letter to his father a few days after the meeting, however, Thomson made no mention of these specific events. But, whatever the detailed circumstances, the friendship between the two natural philosophers was now firm and enduring.

The conservation of energy Subsequent to these meetings, Thomson's attention focused on Joule's claim to have shown the conversion of mechanical effect into heat in fluid friction. Before long, Thomson had devised a variant of Joule's paddle-wheel apparatus and was even considering the use of a steam engine to demonstrate in dramatic fashion the heating effects of fluid friction. For his part, Joule began work in the cellar of the brewery on a fresh set of results (yielding a mechanical equivalent of 772) which Faraday communicated to the Royal Society on 21 June 1849. In 1850 'On the mechanical equivalent of heat' appeared in the *Philosophical Transactions*; Joule was elected FRS in June of the same year.

The appearance of a rival claimant to the mechanical equivalent doctrine, however, threatened to rob Joule of some at least of his hard-won credit. In 1848 Julius R. Mayer (1814–1878) became acquainted with Joule's papers. Seizing his opportunity to impress upon the scientific establishments the importance of his own contributions during the 1840s, Mayer wrote to the French Académie des Sciences pointing out his claims to priority. Published in the *Comptes Rendus* (the académie's official reports), his letter drew a rapid defence from Joule. Joule's tactics, agreed in consultation with his new advocate William Thomson, were to acknowledge Mayer's priority with respect to the idea of a mechanical equivalent, but to claim that he (Joule) had established it by experiment. The controversy in fact also aided Joule's cause by drawing international scientific attention to his claims.

Eager for the reform of British physical science, William Thomson and a growing network of associates (including Macquorn Rankine, James Thomson, James Clerk Maxwell, and Peter Guthrie Tait) made Joule's results the foundation for the new doctrine of conservation of energy from the early 1850s. In the 1860s, however, the Royal Institution's John Tyndall elevated Mayer to at least equal status with Joule in the history of energy, while in response Tait caricatured the German physician as the embodiment of speculative and amateurish metaphysics compared with the trustworthy and gentlemanly producer of reliable experimental knowledge from Manchester.

Later years Despite his growing iconic role after 1850, Joule continued to be experimentally active for another three decades. In 1863 he joined the British Association committee on standards of electrical resistance and was entrusted with the task of determining the mechanical equivalent from the thermal effects of electric currents using the new standard of resistance provided by the committee. The result (783) was announced in 1867. Joule's last determination of the mechanical equivalent by frictional means in 1878 yielded a figure (772.55) close to that of the 1850 Royal Society paper. The Johns Hopkins physicist Henry Rowland (in 1878) and the Cavendish physics professor John William Strutt, Baron Rayleigh (in 1881–2), accounted for the discrepancy in terms of the standard of resistance which, when adjusted, showed the two methods to yield almost identical values.

Mayer's method of calculating the mechanical equivalent had become associated with what Thomson labelled as 'Mayer's hypothesis', which assumed that the effect of intermolecular forces could be ignored in the expansion and compression of gases. The label simultaneously detracted from Mayer's competence as an experimentalist. In a series of famous experiments on the physical properties of gases (particularly when expanding through small orifices), Joule and Thomson sought to test the validity of 'Mayer's hypothesis' in the 1850s. Slight cooling effects, for example, were measured in the case of the expansion of air and carbonic acid, while slight heating effects were observed with hydrogen. These results were communicated to the Royal Society and published as 'On the thermal effects of fluids in motion' in the *Philosophical Transactions* (1853). Altogether Joule and Thomson published at least ten papers on their joint experimental researches up to the early 1860s.

Contrary to the claim of Osborne Reynolds (Joule's earliest biographer) that Joule had little connection with the family brewery business, it now seems certain that he played a very active role in its management in the decade or so before its final sale in 1854. As Sibum has argued, there are good grounds too for seeing his laboratory practice and brewery management as mutually reinforcing activities: on the one hand, a purpose-built laboratory provided for James by his father at a new residence at Oak Field in 1843 could draw upon the repertoire of craft skills, including temperature measurement, characteristic of a modern brewing industry, while on the other, the brewery itself was probably being subjected to a regime of scientific reform with imperatives of exact control and quantitative measurement, especially with respect to processes of heat conversion in germination, fermentation, and mashing. Equally important for Joule's experimental practice was John Benjamin Dancer, a Manchester instrument maker and a master of the construction of highly accurate thermometers, who supplied most of the equipment for the fluid friction experiments in the 1840s.

Joule was awarded a royal medal (1852) and the Copley medal (1870) by the Royal Society. He received the honorary degrees of LLD from Dublin (1857), DCL from Oxford (1860), and LLD from Edinburgh (1871). He also received a civil-list pension of £200 from 1878 in recognition of his services to science, while in 1880 he was awarded the Albert medal of the Society of Arts by the prince of Wales. In 1885–7 the Physical Society of London sponsored a two-volume edition of his scientific papers, edited by Joule himself.

By 1854 James and Amelia had a son and daughter but in the summer of that year another son died some days after his birth. Amelia herself failed to recover and died early in September. Joule's own state of health was never robust. Twice he was to have presided over the British Association (at Bradford in 1872 and Manchester in 1887), but on both occasions ill health prevented him from taking the chair. Indeed, from 1872 he lived quietly at his home, 12 Wardle Road, Sale, until his death there on 11 October 1889. He was buried in Brooklands cemetery, Sale, on 16 October and the headstone bears the number '772' as well as the inscription from John's Gospel (ch. 9, v. 4): 'I must work the works of him that sent me, while it is day: the night cometh, when no man can work'. A statue by Alfred Gilbert, funded by public subscription, and unveiled by William Thomson (by then Lord Kelvin) was placed in Manchester town hall in 1893 as a companion to that of Dalton. A memorial tablet was placed in Westminster Abbey.

CROSBIE SMITH

Sources J. P. Joule, 'Description of an electro-magnetic engine', *Annals of Electricity*, 2 (1838), 122–3 · J. P. Joule, *The scientific papers of James Prescott Joule*, 2 vols. (1884–7); repr. (1963) · W. Sturgeon, 'Historical sketch of the rise and progress of electro-magnetic engines for propelling machinery', *Annals of Electricity*, 3 (1838–9), 429–37 · W. Thomson, 'On the mechanical antecedents of motion, heat, and light', *Report of the British Association for the Advancement of Science* (1854), 59–63 · C. Smith and M. N. Wise, *Energy and empire: a biographical study of Lord Kelvin* (1989) · O. Reynolds, *Memoir of James Prescott Joule* (1892) · D. S. L. Cardwell, *James Joule: a biography* (1989) ·

R. Fox, 'James Prescott Joule, 1818–1889', *Mid-nineteenth-century scientists*, ed. J. North (1969), 72–103 • H. O. Sibum, 'Reworking the mechanical value of heat: instruments of precision and gestures of accuracy in early Victorian England', *Studies in History and Philosophy of Science*, 26 (1994), 73–106 • H. J. Steffens, *James Prescott Joule and the concept of energy* (1979) • J. Forrester, 'Chemistry and the conservation of energy: the work of James Prescott Joule', *Studies in the History and Philosophy of Science*, 6 (1975), 273–313 • *DNB* • J. T. Bottomley, 'James Prescott Joule', *Nature*, 26 (1882), 617–20 • J. P. Joule, 'On the changes of temperature produced by the rarefaction and condensation of air', *London, Edinburgh, and Dublin Philosophical Magazine*, 3rd ser., 26 (1845), 369–83

Archives Inst. EE, MS description of a current meter • Museum of Science and Industry, Manchester, letters and papers • RS, letters and papers • Salford City Archives, papers • University of Manchester Institute of Science and Technology, letters and papers | CUL, corresp. with Lord Kelvin • CUL, letters to Sir George Stokes • Manchester Literary and Philosophical Society, letters to Lord Playfair • RS, corresp. with Sir John Herschel • U. Glas. L., corresp. with Lord Kelvin • Whitby Museum, Whitby Literary and Philosophical Society Library, letters to William Scoresby

Likenesses G. Patten, oils, 1863, Manchester Literary and Philosophical Society, Churchgate House, Manchester • Lady Roscoe, photograph, *c.*1876, NPG [*see illus.*] • J. Collier, oils, 1882, RS • A. Gilbert, marble statue, 1890–94, Manchester town hall • Daiziel, woodcut, BM • C. H. Jeens, stipple, BM, NPG; repro. in *Nature*, 617

Wealth at death £12,765 6s. 4d.: probate, 30 Oct 1889, *CGPLA Eng. & Wales*

Joules, Horace (1902–1977), physician, son of Richard Edgar Joules (1872–1949), master grocer, and his wife, Emily Ann Hyatt (*b.* 1875), was born at Woodseaves, High Offley Road, Newport, Shropshire, on 21 March 1902. He was educated at Newport grammar school before studying medicine at Cardiff and at Middlesex Hospital medical school; he qualified MB, BS, in 1925. In 1928 he was awarded the MD from London University, with gold medal. In 1930 he married Mary Sparrow (*b.* 1906); they had two sons and a daughter.

After a period as registrar to the Middlesex and Brompton hospitals, and as resident physician to the Selly Oak Hospital, Birmingham, Joules became the first senior physician at the Central Middlesex Hospital in north-west London in 1935 and was appointed its medical director shortly after the outbreak of the Second World War. He was elected FRCP in 1943. By the start of the National Health Service in 1948, Joules had helped to raise the Central Middlesex to a dominant place among the non-teaching hospitals of the country. His passion for preventive medicine came from his experience with his own patients: young women with pulmonary tuberculosis, older men with chronic bronchitis or lung cancer, miners crippled with silicosis. He was indignant when he saw his patients suffering needlessly from their environment or their own habits. After the black smog of December 1952, which caused 4000 extra deaths in London, Joules, as a member of the Central Health Services Council, pressed for a Clean Air Act. It became law in 1956 and resulted in the disappearance of this type of smog from London and other cities.

At the end of the war tuberculosis was a serious problem and 11,000 patients were awaiting treatment in British hospitals. The high incidence of tuberculosis and the consequent risk to nurses caused many general hospitals to refuse admission to these patients. In 1945 Joules opened two wards for tuberculosis at the Central Middlesex but he took great care to safeguard nurses' health by insisting on masks and protective clothing. As a result very few nursing staff became infected, far fewer than in the London teaching hospitals or in those of the London county council. Following the work of Richard Doll and Austin Bradford Hill in 1952, Joules also campaigned strongly against cigarette smoking. A heavy smoker for thirty years, he managed to break himself of the habit.

Joules was inspired by Somerville Hastings and was a founder member of the Socialist Medical Association. During the Spanish Civil War he worked with the Spanish medical aid committee. He visited the Soviet Union and China where some aspects of their health services greatly impressed him. Many students remembered Joules best, however, for his popular Friday afternoon teaching rounds. He towered above all others, wagging his finger for emphasis. There was a dynamic cut and thrust at the bedside, and woe betide the student who did not know the occupation and social background of his patient.

In private life Joules was a keen gardener. He also enjoyed birdwatching in the Essex marshes, accompanied by a volume of the writings of his favourite poet and natural philosopher, John Clare. In 1962 the illness that had first shown itself during the war returned and forced him into early retirement. When his manic depression was at last controlled he lived quietly at home. He died in Colchester on 25 January 1977 and was cremated at Colchester crematorium on 30 January. KEITH BALL

Sources Munk, *Roll* • J. S., *The Lancet* (5 Feb 1977) • *The Times* (28 Jan 1977) • M. W. McNicol, ed., 'Progress in the prevention of chest diseases: conference in memory of Horace Joules, 27 Jan 1978, at Central Middlesex Hosp.', *British Journal of Diseases of the Chest*, 73 (1979), 45–54 • M. Orbach, 'Dr Horace Joules—a profile', *Socialism and Health* (July–Aug 1971) • H. Joules, 'Health from the health service', *The Lancet* (8 Dec 1956), 1171–4 • *BMJ* (12 Feb 1977), 449 • J. A. Gray, *The Central Middlesex Hospital* (1963) • private information (2004) • b. cert. • m. cert.

Likenesses photograph, *c.*1957 • bronze bust, Central Middlesex Hospital, London NW10 • photograph, repro. in J. S., *The Lancet*, 317

Wealth at death £6326: probate, 14 March 1977, *CGPLA Eng. & Wales*

Jourdain, Eleanor Frances (1863–1924), author and college head, was born on 16 November 1863 at Derwent Woodlands, Derbyshire, the eldest of ten children of the Revd Francis Jourdain (1834–1898), subsequently vicar of Ashbourne, and his wife, Emily, daughter of Charles *Clay, a Manchester surgeon. It was a poor, proud, talented family of Huguenot descent. Eleanor grew up in a country vicarage; her orthodox high-church parents were cultivated but lacking in warmth towards the children, who were driven to achieve by a sense of duty, financial necessity, and family rivalries. Of her five brothers, Francis *Jourdain became eminent as an ornithologist and Philip *Jourdain as a mathematician; a sister, (Emily) Margaret *Jourdain became an authority on domestic arts and artefacts. Unlike some of her siblings Nelly was no rebel against this austere Anglican childhood. Educated at first

Eleanor Frances Jourdain (1863–1924), by unknown photographer, c.1915

at home, she played her part in educating, and later supporting, the younger children (the two youngest were partially paralysed by multiple sclerosis). Between the ages of fourteen and eighteen she attended a private day school in Manchester, financed by her mother's parents, who also enabled her to go to Lady Margaret Hall, Oxford, as a scholar in 1883. Her father, though by some accounts no enthusiast for women's education, nevertheless supported the opening of Oxford undergraduate examinations to women, and three Jourdain daughters studied at Oxford. Eleanor was in 1886 one of the first women examined in the modern history school and the first woman to undergo a viva. She was placed in the second class.

Eleanor was an accomplished woman, with musical, literary, and philosophical interests, and artistic gifts that developed strikingly in later life. Teaching was, however, the only secure profession then open to women. She embarked on it in a more ambitious spirit than her sisters Charlotte and May, who became governesses. After a brief period as secretary to Minnie Benson, wife of the archbishop of Canterbury and mother of a contemporary at Lady Margaret Hall, she became an assistant mistress, first at Tottenham high school and then at Clifton high school. In 1892 the Clifton headmistress, Miss M. A. Woods, joined her in founding Corran Collegiate School, Watford, a private boarding- and day school offering 'a thorough education of the best type for girls of all ages', where Miss Jourdain was soon sole headmistress. She proved to be, in the words of one former pupil, 'a born teacher' (Evans, *Prelude and Fugue*, 35). The success of this school, which had by 1900 more than 100 pupils, launched her on the next phase of her career. In Paris she rented a Rive Gauche flat—270 boulevard Raspail—in partnership with the daughter of a Sorbonne professor who had been on the Corran staff, where older girls could spend a year studying. There Miss Jourdain spent vacations between 1900 and 1914. She acquired the French elegance and style for which she was remembered and found opportunities to develop her work on the symbolism in Dante's *Divina commedia*, on which she had published articles, into a study published in English (1902) and in French (1903), for which she was in 1904 awarded a doctorate by the University of Paris. An early guest at this Paris flat was an acquaintance from her Oxford days, Charlotte Anne Elizabeth *Moberly, principal of St Hugh's Hall (later College), where Charlotte Jourdain had studied, who suggested that Eleanor should move to St Hugh's as vice-principal.

An experience shared by Miss Jourdain and Miss Moberly during a visit to Versailles on 10 August 1901 drew them together in friendship and gave rise to one of the best-known of all ghost stories. They came upon figures in eighteenth-century dress near the Petit Trianon: later researches convinced them that these were ghosts of Marie Antoinette and members of her court and that the landscape and buildings they had seen were just as they had been in 1789. Both women believed they had psychic powers, though repudiating any associations with spiritualism, and the prevailing interest in the paranormal (which extended to Edwardian academic and church circles) encouraged them to publish their story. *An Adventure* (1911) appeared under the pseudonyms Elizabeth Morison and Frances Lamont but the authors' identity was known to acquaintances and some reviewers. It became a best-seller, attracting lasting interest as an instance of 'haunting' involving two reputable eyewitnesses. Subsequent editions appeared in 1913, 1924, 1931, 1955, and 1988. Contemporary sceptics included the Jourdain family and exponents of the scientific methods of the Society for Psychical Research (SPR). A courteous but devastating review by Eleanor Sidgwick noted that the authors' methods of recording and investigating the incident—described privately by an SPR researcher as 'rather fishy'—gave much scope for tricks of memory and imagination (Iremonger, 203). Later critics have speculated that behind their collaboration lay a repressed lesbian relationship (ibid., 86; Castle). Joan Evans, who knew both women well, dismissed that as inconceivable and hers is perhaps the most plausible explanation of the 'adventure': they may have interrupted rehearsals for a *tableau vivant* in preparation for one of the fancy-dress parties given at Versailles by the *belle époque* rake Robert de Montesquiou (Evans, 'An end to *An Adventure*', 45–7).

Miss Jourdain left Corran in 1903 to become vice-principal and, from 1905, tutor in French at St Hugh's, at a sacrifice of income and status that was rewarded when she succeeded Miss Moberly as principal in April 1915. In these years she emerged as a complex, controversial, and powerful personality. Short and, as a young woman, rather plain, she developed a strong likeness to Queen Victoria—stout, dignified, *soignée*, bejewelled, always dressed in black, her grey eyes bright and prominent, the sandy hair now silver and worn in a chignon. Her charm and vivacity, her watercolours and piano playing, and the range of her ideas lent her an air of distinction even while she held a subordinate position. From 1908 she led the St Hugh's contingent at London suffrage demonstrations arrayed in her doctoral robes. Papers she gave to student societies were published as *On the Theory of the Infinite in Modern Thought* (1911). Of her stimulating qualities as a tutor, administrative ability, and commitment to the collegiate development of St Hugh's there was no doubt. But she divided opinions. She fascinated admirers and showed them much kindness. Those who did not find favour thought her manipulative, devious, and domineering. Unresolved tensions permeated her own values—an orthodox churchwoman who cultivated a reputation for second sight, an exponent of 'bracing common sense' who dabbled in mysticism and the modish intuitionism of Henri Bergson (*Oxford Magazine*, 1 May 1924, 400; Evans, *Prelude and Fugue*, 99). Conscious of a self-sacrificing dedication to duty, she was incapable of self-criticism. Even admirers questioned her rigour as a scholar.

In her lifetime, however, Eleanor Jourdain built up a considerable professional and public reputation. Oxford was late in taking up French studies and she took advantage of openings to publish work drawing on her knowledge of the country and her lectures: 'Methods of moral instruction and training of girls in France', in *Moral Instruction and Training in Schools*, edited by M. E. Sadler (1908, 2.85–112); *An Introduction to the French Classical Drama* (1912); *Dramatic Theory and Practice in France, 1690–1808* (1921); *The Drama in Europe in Theory and Practice* (1924). In the First World War she was commissioned to undertake translating and deciphering work for the government. In 1919 she served on the election committee for the university's (notoriously anti-feminist) Conservative MP, Sir Charles Oman. She was among the first women to hold university lecturerships at Oxford, as Taylorian lecturer in French, 1920–22, and in 1922 was the first woman to examine undergraduates in the schools. At the peak of her career she was president (1921–2) of the Modern Language Association. At the time of her death she was working on a history of Burgundy.

As principal of St Hugh's, Miss Jourdain presided over the college's move to new purpose-built premises and a rapid growth in student numbers, from about 50 to over 150. Autocratic by nature, she was a forceful leader. But staff and students acquired new aspirations when women were admitted to membership of Oxford University in 1920. Although sympathetic in principle to the claims of women tutors to participate in governing the college, Miss Jourdain resisted their initiatives in practice. Her decisions on student discipline were sometimes harsh. Always subject to migraine and now worn down by a severe attack of influenza, her judgement became increasingly erratic. In November 1923 she persuaded the college's council to dismiss a tutor, Cecilia Ady, formerly an intimate friend but now believed by Miss Jourdain to be disloyal. The 'St Hugh's row', widely reported in the press,

raised issues that concerned not only the professional standing of female dons but also the future of women's colleges—would they develop on collegiate lines or as autocracies modelled on girls' schools? All St Hugh's tutors resigned in support of Cecilia Ady, as did six council members; women tutors at other Oxford colleges boycotted teaching of its students; undergraduates demonstrated; parents and senior members pressed for an independent enquiry. Miss Jourdain, confident as always (and badly advised, as a successor pointed out, by the head of house, J. A. R. Munro of Lincoln College, who chaired her council), was happy when the university's chancellor, Lord Curzon, was brought in to investigate, and sanguine even when his report exonerated Miss Ady and suggested the need for changes of both constitution and personnel at St Hugh's (Griffin, 55). On 6 April 1924, shortly after hearing that her resignation was expected, she died of a coronary thrombosis at the home she shared with Miss Moberly in vacations, 4 Norham Road, Oxford. She was buried on 9 April at Wolvercote cemetery, Oxford. There is no evidence to support later rumours of suicide.

Devoted as she was to St Hugh's, Eleanor Jourdain left a legacy of division and embarrassment—protracted by sensational interest in both the 'row' and the ghosts of Versailles. Her reputation suffered, too, at the hands of hostile colleagues and relatives. A tragic figure, she was destroyed by a scandal that overshadowed real gifts and achievements. There is much to be said for the contemporary verdict that, had she ceased to be principal two years earlier, she would 'have left a splendid record in Oxford' (*Proceedings of the Huguenot Society*).

JANET HOWARTH

Sources J. Evans, *Prelude and fugue: an autobiography* (1964) · J. Evans, 'An end to *An adventure*: solving the mystery of the Trianon', *Encounter*, 47/4 (1976), 33–47 · J. Evans, ed., *An adventure* (1955) · L. Iremonger, *The ghosts of Versailles: Miss Moberley and Miss Jourdain and their adventure, a critical study* (1957) · R. Tricket, 'The row', *St Hugh's: one hundred years of women's education in Oxford*, ed. P. Griffin (1986), 55 · H. Spurling, *Secrets of a woman's heart: the later life of Ivy Compton-Burnett* (1984) · T. Castle, 'Contagious folly: an adventure and its skeptics', *Questions of evidence: proof, practice and persuasion across the disciplines*, ed. J. Chandler, A. I. Davidson, and H. Harootunian (1994), 11–42 · *The Guardian* (26 March 1884) · *Oxford Magazine* (1 May 1924), 399–401 · *Oxford Magazine* (8 May 1924), 420–21 · *The Imp*, 16 (1924) · *St Hugh's Club Paper* (1899) · H. G., 'Eleanor Frances Jourdain', *Brown Book* (1924), 51–2 · *Proceedings of the Huguenot Society*, 13 (1923–9), 10–11 · *Hampton's scholastic directory and hotel guide*, 2nd edn (1894), 217 · St Hugh's College archives, Oxford

Archives Bodl. Oxf., diary, corresp., and papers relating to psychic experiences at Versailles | St Hugh's College, Oxford, council minutes, college scrapbook, Rogers file, Ady file

Likenesses photograph, *c.*1915, priv. coll. [*see illus.*] · Elliott & Fry, photographs, *c.*1917, repro. in Evans, *Prelude and fugue* · R. Levi-Strauss, oils, 1922, St Hugh's College, Oxford · F. Sanderson, drawing, *c.*1924, St Hugh's College, Oxford · photographs (in youth and middle age), repro. in Castle, 'Contagious folly: an adventure and its skeptics'

Wealth at death £3837 5s. 1d.: probate, 12 May 1924, *CGPLA Eng. & Wales*

Jourdain, Francis Charles Robert (1865–1940), ornithologist and Church of England clergyman, was born on

4 March 1865, at Adenshaw Lodge, near Manchester, the eldest of the five sons of Francis Jourdain (1834–1898), later vicar of Ashbourne, Derbyshire, and his wife, Emily, daughter of Charles *Clay. He was educated at Ashbourne grammar school and at Magdalen College, Oxford, graduated in 1887, and was ordained in 1890. He was vicar of Clifton by Ashbourne, Derbyshire, from 1894 to 1914. In 1896 he married Frances Emmeline (d. 1933), daughter of William Richard Smith, of Clifton, Derbyshire. They had two sons, the younger of whom predeceased his father, and a daughter. Between 1914 and 1925 he was rector of Appleton, Berkshire. After his retirement in 1925 he devoted most of his time to ornithology.

Jourdain's primary preoccupation in ornithology was the collecting and study of eggs, but he was interested in almost every aspect of the breeding habits of birds and was an excellent general field ornithologist. He travelled widely in Europe and north Africa, collecting eggs and studying breeding habits and distribution. The extensive first-hand experience he thus acquired, combined with an encyclopaedic knowledge of the literature of his subject, resulted in his recognition as a leading authority on the breeding biology of the birds of the western palaearctic region. He was one of the first to recognize fully the importance of obtaining accurate data on all phases of the breeding of birds, including incubation and fledgeling periods and the share of the sexes in parental duties; and he devoted much of his time for many years to this task. As a result, when *A Practical Handbook of British Birds* appeared (2 vols., 1919, 1924), in the authorship of which he collaborated with Harry Forbes Witherby, Ernst Johann O. Hartert, and others, his concise and systematic treatment of these matters set a new standard in the literature. It also stimulated further investigation, which led to the remarkable increase in precise information on breeding biology recorded in *The Handbook of British Birds* (5 vols., 1938–41), the enlarged successor of *A Practical Handbook*.

Jourdain's work in *The Handbook*, the product of a lifetime of study, was his greatest contribution to ornithology, but he was also the author of important faunistic papers on Corsica, Spitsbergen (he led the Oxford University expedition to Spitsbergen in 1921), Cyprus, Spain, and north Africa, as well as many other ornithological publications. The list of those under his own name, although extensive, represents only a fraction of his scientific output. Apart from *The Handbook*, he supplied material to or collaborated in some of the principal standard works on British ornithology of the twentieth century and constantly assisted other ornithologists from his unique fund of knowledge. His 'A study on parasitism in the cuckoos' (*Proceedings of the Zoological Society*, 1925, 639–67) was a valuable contribution to general evolutionary biology, and he encouraged much local faunistic work on birds of the British Isles. For many years Jourdain was assistant editor to his friend Witherby of the journal *British Birds*.

Jourdain's caustic style in controversy was famous in ornithological circles, but there was another side to him. His ready sympathy and helpfulness towards younger ornithologists reflected his real character much more

accurately. This attractive trait found full play through his close association with Oxford while he was rector of Appleton and afterwards, and contributed greatly to the development of ornithological studies there. Jourdain died at his home, Whitekirk, 4 Bellevue Road, Southbourne, Bournemouth, on 27 February 1940.

B. W. TUCKER, rev. V. M. QUIRKE

Sources B. W. Tucker, 'Francis Charles Robert Jourdain: an appreciation', *The Ibis*, 14th ser., 4 (1940), 504–18 • B. W. Tucker, 'The Rev. F. C. R. Jourdain', *Nature*, 145 (1940), 885 • H. F. W., 'Obituary: the Rev. F. C. R. Jourdain', *British Birds*, 23 (April 1940), 286–93 • *CGPLA Eng. & Wales* (1940)
Archives U. Oxf., Edward Grey Institute of Field Ornithology, papers • University Museum, Oxford, entomological notebook
Likenesses portrait, repro. in Tucker, 'Francis Charles Robert Jourdain', plate ix
Wealth at death £23,937 14s. 3d.: probate, 17 Oct 1940, *CGPLA Eng. & Wales* • English probate resealed in Vancouver, 7 Aug 1941, *CGPLA Eng. & Wales*

Jourdain, John (c.1572–1619), merchant navy officer, was born at Lyme Regis, the fourth of six children of John Jourdain (d. 1588), merchant, and Thomazin, whose maiden name was probably Jones. By the mid-1590s he had begun to conduct trade between Lyme Regis and Portugal and the Azores, but in 1607 he chose to abandon this activity in favour of service with the newly established East India Company. He was appointed by the court of directors as one of their factors on 7 December 1607 and sailed on the ill-fated fourth company voyage in the *Ascension* on 14 March 1608. The *Ascension* was the first English ship to visit Aden, and it then called at Mocha and the island of Socotra before being lost en route for Surat on 3 September 1609 when it struck a shoal in the Gulf of Cambay near Diu. The crew reached Gandava in the boats, and marched to Surat. A few weeks later most of them set out for Agra, but Jourdain remained at Surat in order to develop the company's trade.

In January 1611 Jourdain joined Captain William Hawkins (d. 1613) at Agra, and after six months' stay there he returned to Surat. Portuguese pressure on the local authorities forced the company's representatives to abandon Surat, and on 6 February 1612 Jourdain sailed for the Red Sea in the *Trade's Increase*. From Mocha he moved on to Bantam, where he was appointed to remain as chief factor, or 'president of the English', although shortly afterwards, in February 1613, he volunteered to take command of the *Darling* on a voyage to Amboyna and Ceram. This brought him into repeated conflict with the Dutch and, having had little success in establishing trade, Jourdain was forced to return to Bantam where he reluctantly accepted the post of agent.

Jourdain had intended to go home at the end of 1615, but the death of Captain Nicholas Downton delayed his return for a year. He eventually sailed for England in the *Clove* in December 1616 and arrived home in the early summer of 1617. In November he entered into another term of service with the company for five years, and at his prompting it was agreed that the company should secure its position at Bantam against the Dutch through the adoption of an aggressive forward policy. To this end a small fleet was assembled under the command of Sir Thomas Dale, with Jourdain appointed to act as principal agent or first president at Bantam. Such a demarcation of authority gave control over the ships to Jourdain, not Dale, and this subsequently led to disputes between the two men. By the end of 1618 Jourdain was at Jakarta, to where the factory had been moved from Bantam, and was busy directing operations against the Dutch, with whom active hostilities had broken out.

On 24 April 1619 Jourdain went in the *Sampson*, with the *Hound* accompanying, to arrange the company's affairs at Patani (on the Malay peninsula), and on 16 July was surprised there by a Dutch squadron of three or four ships. Both the *Sampson* and the *Hound* were captured after a brief skirmish, in which Jourdain was killed, on 17 July 1619. It is likely that Jourdain was buried on the shore at Patani with two of his nephews, John Jourdain and Jonas Viney, present as mourners. He was survived by his estranged wife, Susan, and his son, John, but his sister, Susan Viney, was left as sole executor of his estate.

J. K. LAUGHTON, rev. H. V. BOWEN

Sources *The journal of John Jourdain, 1608–1617*, ed. W. Foster, Hakluyt Society, 2nd ser., 16 (1905) • F. C. Danvers and W. Foster, eds., *Letters received by the East India Company from its servants in the east*, 6 vols. (1896–1902), vols. 1–5 • *CSP col.*, vols. 2–3 • S. Purchas, *Purchas his pilgrimes*, 4 vols. (1625), vol. 1, p. 228 • will, PRO, PROB 11/136, sig. 87
Archives BL, 'Journal of a voyage to the East Indies 1607–8 with addition of travels in Arabia 1617', Sloane MS 858

(Emily) Margaret Jourdain (1876–1951), by unknown photographer, 1910

Jourdain, (Emily) Margaret (1876–1951), historian of English furniture and decoration, was born on 15 August 1876 in Derwent, Derbyshire, the eighth of ten children of the Revd Francis Jourdain (1834–1898) and his wife, Emily, daughter of Charles *Clay, a Manchester surgeon. As the hard-up daughter of a hard-up country parson, surrounded by caustic and highly competitive siblings, Margaret grew up sardonic, independent, and unorthodox. She rejected Christianity at an early age, declaring firmly to her governess, 'I don't want to hear any more about that poor man' (Spurling, *Ivy when Young*, 1.260).

Margaret shared her scholarly approach with her eldest brother, Francis Charles Robert *Jourdain—himself a comparable pioneer in the field of ornithology—and her refusal to acknowledge sexual restrictions with her eldest sister, Eleanor Frances *Jourdain, principal of St Hugh's College, Oxford (and author, with C. A. E. Moberly, of *An Adventure*, 1911). Another brother was Philip Edward Bertrand *Jourdain, historian of mathematics and logic. Margaret herself read classics at Lady Margaret Hall, Oxford, left with a third-class degree in 1897, and afterwards earned a precarious living as editor, translator, and book reviewer. Her chief patron was Lord Alfred Douglas, who, as editor of *The Academy*, published her collection of prose poems, *An Outdoor Breviary*, in 1909.

But literary ambition was overtaken by a growing interest in the still virtually unexplored history of interior decoration and furnishing. In the early years of the century Margaret began writing up her researches in a steady stream of articles covering the field from chintzes to Chinese wallpapers, stumpwork to samplers, tea caddies, knife cases, card tables, and cradles. It was her knowledgeable and authoritative contributions that helped transform *Country Life* from a relatively lightweight, romantic magazine into what Walter Runciman called 'the keeper of the architectural conscience of the nation' (Spurling, *Secrets of a Woman's Heart*, 90). She spearheaded a shift in taste away from Victorian ostentation, fussiness, and clutter to an earlier simplicity and severity. In *Furniture in England from 1660 to 1760* (1914), together with its companion volume on decoration, she was the first to rediscover English Palladian design, to insist on the importance of historical context, and to rehabilitate the virtually forgotten William Kent (her monograph, *The Work of William Kent*, appeared in 1948).

Margaret Jourdain published her first two furniture books under the name of the fashionable interior decorator Francis Lenygon, and her *Decorative Arts in England* (1760–1880) under the name of a Birmingham coachbuilder called H. H. Mulliner. Both men profited from her literary abilities, providing her in return with a practical expertise that she could have got nowhere else. In the furniture world she had, in the words of Ralph Edwards, keeper of the Victoria and Albert Museum's woodwork department, 'few rivals and no superiors' (private information). Edwards was one of a whole generation of young men, trained by Margaret in the 1920s and 1930s, who went on to fill major posts in the national museums, the

National Trust, and the great London auction houses. Younger women whose careers blossomed under her guidance included Joan Evans, Freya Stark, and Ivy Compton-Burnett.

Margaret Jourdain set up house in 1919 with Ivy Compton-Burnett, who published the first of her singular novels six years later. Contemporaries maintained that Ivy owed much as a novelist to Margaret's dry, deflationary wit and profoundly sceptical intelligence. Margaret's own books remained erudite, austerely factual, and frequently first in the field. She was one of ten contributors to the three-volume *Dictionary of English Furniture* (1924-7), edited by Edwards and Percy Macquoid, and her *Georgian Cabinet-Makers* (1944), written with Edwards, gave long overdue recognition to designers other than Thomas Chippendale, George Hepplewhite, and Thomas Sheraton.

Margaret Jourdain in her prime inspired terror, awe, and in some bold spirits affection. Squat, broad, and plain, she wore dashing plumed hats, lace jabots, feather boas, and a Georgian spyglass on a gold chain. Teatime anecdotes from the hospitable table she and Ivy kept at their flat in South Kensington have passed into London literary legend. Margaret never married for the same reasons as the character in one of Ivy Compton-Burnett's novels, who said, when asked if she would not have liked a full, normal life, 'No. I don't want the things it would be full of' (I. Compton-Burnett, *Parents and Children*, 1972, 86). Margaret Jourdain died from heart failure on 6 April 1951 in Charing Cross Hospital, London.

JAMES LEES-MILNE, rev. HILARY SPURLING

Sources H. Spurling, *Ivy when young* (1974) · H. Spurling, *Secrets of a woman's heart* (1984) · private information (2004) [R. Edwards, P. Thornton, V. King, S. Jenyns, J. Kiddell, J. Evans, P. Wilson, G. Reynolds, S. Coffin (for F. Lenygon)] · *CGPLA Eng. & Wales* (1951)

Archives priv. coll., account books · priv. coll., photo album and papers · V&A, papers

Likenesses photograph, 1910, repro. in Spurling, *Secrets* [see illus.]

Wealth at death £4813 13s. 8d.: probate, 20 Sept 1951, *CGPLA Eng. & Wales*

Jourdain, Philip Edward Bertrand (1879-1919), historian of mathematics and logic, was born on 16 October 1879 at Ashbourne vicarage, Derbyshire, one of the large family of Francis Jourdain, vicar of Ashbourne, and his wife, Emily, formerly Clay. Among his siblings, an elder sister, Eleanor Frances *Jourdain, was a principal witness of the alleged vision in 1901 of Marie Antoinette and members of her court at Versailles; she was later principal of St Hugh's Hall (as it was then called) in Oxford. Another sister, (Emily) Margaret *Jourdain (1876-1951), was a well-known authority on furniture, and a brother, Francis Charles Robert *Jourdain (1865-1940), on birds.

After education at Cheltenham College, Jourdain studied mathematics at Trinity College, Cambridge, and took a course in mathematical logic—the first of its kind in a British university—given by Bertrand Russell. Thereafter he specialized in set theory and logic, and their histories. His research work was indifferent, in that he persisted in trying to prove the 'axiom of choice', a controversial

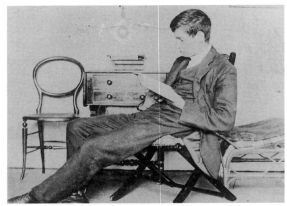

Philip Edward Bertrand Jourdain (1879-1919), by unknown photographer

assumption made in set theory introduced in 1904 but fairly soon accepted by everybody else as unavoidable. However, his historical work was not only very scholarly but also important both in its erudition and in publishing the views of major figures which he obtained by correspondence. One of these was the German mathematician Georg Cantor (1845-1918), the main creator of set theory; Jourdain published English translations of two main papers in 1915. He also translated and studied the logician Gottlob Frege (1848-1925), then not widely known. He published in 1916 a new edition of George Boole's *The Laws of Thought* (1854), but did not live to prepare an edition of Boole's other logical writings.

These editions were put out by the Open Court Publishing Company, an American house devoted to the furthering of science and philosophy, especially of German origin. Jourdain became its English editor in 1912, and was active in executing or arranging translations of works by major figures (above all of the physicist Ernst Mach), commissioning articles for its principal journal *The Monist* (from T. S. Eliot and Ezra Pound, among others), and writing and reviewing himself there frequently. He also published there and elsewhere on various aspects of the history of mathematical analysis, mechanics, and mathematical physics, and (with less significance) on aspects of the philosophy of mathematics and science, but a plan for a 'national edition' of the works of Newton did not advance.

Two of Jourdain's best known products were short books, not placed with Open Court. *The Nature of Mathematics* (editions of 1912 and 1919) gave a heuristic treatment of some aspects of the subject strongly informed by history. *The Philosophy of Mr. B*rtr*nd R*ss*ll* (1918) may seem to be light relief, but in fact many sharp observations are made about issues addressed by Russell, Frege, and other philosophers and logicians of that time; a few of the contributions are by Russell himself. In an appendix Jourdain revealed many fine anticipations of these issues by Lewis Carroll, especially in the *Alice* books. He also published some satire and verse.

On 26 June 1915 Jourdain married Laura Cross, daughter

of the deceased Revd Walter Horace Insull of Girton. She helped him as a secretary; they had no children. After the death of Paul Carus, editor of *The Monist*, in 1919, Jourdain succeeded him, but he died at Basingbourne Road, Crookham, Hampshire, on 1 October, from a creeping paralysis called Friedreich's ataxia. This illness had prevented him from taking the part two tripos at Cambridge and thus hoping for an orthodox academic career, so he had always worked freelance.

While not a major figure, Jourdain made lone but durable contributions to the history of mathematics and logic. He also brought several noteworthy titles to the Open Court list, some of which (his translation of Cantor, for example) were kept in print for many years. His own main historical writings on logic and set theory were reprinted in 1991.   I. GRATTAN-GUINNESS

Sources J. Arden [Millicent Jourdain], *A childhood* (1913) · E. R. Eames, 'Philip E. B. Jourdain and the Open Court papers', *ICarbS*, 2 (1975), 101–12 · I. Grattan-Guinness, *Dear Russell—Dear Jourdain: a commentary on Russell's logic* (1977) · P. E. B. Jourdain, *Selected essays on the history of set theory and logics, 1906–1918*, ed. I. Grattan-Guinness (1991) · A. E. Heath, *The Monist*, 30 (1920), 161–82 · G. Loria, 'Philip E. B. Jourdain: matematico e storico della scienza, 1879–1919', *Archivio di Storia della Scienza*, 2 (1921–2), 167–84 · G. H. Moore, *Zermelo's axiom of choice* (1982) · G. Sarton and L. Jourdain, 'Philip E. B. Jourdain, 1879–1919', *Isis*, 5 (1922–3), 126–36 · b. cert. · d. cert. · m. cert. · Southern Illinois University at Carbondale, Open Court archives, 32A/9
Archives Institut Mittag-Leffler, Djursholm, Sweden, notebooks of letters and draft replies | Southern Illinois University, Carbondale, Open Court archives, folder 32A/9; *passim* in general corresp. files 27 and 32
Likenesses M. Jourdain, pastel sketch, 1909, repro. in Sarton and Jourdain, 'Philip E. B. Jourdain' · photograph, Trinity Cam. [*see illus.*] · portrait, repro. in Grattan-Guinness, *Dear Russell*, pl. 1 · portraits, repro. in Jourdain, *Selected essays on the history of set theory and logics*, figs. 1–3
Wealth at death £1149 16s. 6d.: probate, 13 Feb 1920, *CGPLA Eng. & Wales*

Jourdain [Jourdan], **Silvester** (*bap.* **1565**, *d.* **1650**?), merchant, was baptized on 14 February 1565 at Lyme Regis in Dorset, the son of John Jourdain (*d.* 1588), merchant, and his wife, Thomazin, whose maiden name was probably Jones. Little is known of his background or early career. His father was a wealthy merchant who served as mayor of Lyme Regis in 1584; at his death in 1588 he left £400 to his wife, and various lands and tenements to his four sons, including Silvester and his brother John *Jourdain. Ignatius Jourdain, who has previously been identified as one of their brothers, was a cousin.

During the later sixteenth and early seventeenth century Jourdain became a leading overseas merchant in Lyme Regis. In 1598, however, he was instructed to stay in the guild hall for five hours, apparently for 'some contumacy' (Wanklyn, 193). Much of his overseas trade appears to have been with France and the Canary Islands; from 1599 to 1602 he was exporting small cargoes of cloth from Lyme Regis and Exeter, despite the disruption caused by the war with Spain. In June 1609 he sailed with a relief expedition to Virginia, set out by the Virginia Company of London. Sir George Somers, the commander of the expedition, came from Lyme Regis and was probably well

known to Jourdain. After seven weeks at sea the expedition was scattered during a violent storm, and the *Sea Adventure*, in which Jourdain sailed with Somers and Sir Thomas Gates, the new lieutenant-governor for Virginia, was wrecked on the Bermudas. Under the leadership of Somers and Gates, the company of 150 men survived by living off the resources of the islands; they also constructed two pinnaces, which were used to complete the journey to Virginia in May 1610. According to Jourdain's account of the voyage, they found only sixty settlers alive when they reached the settlement. In difficult circumstances Gates decided to abandon the enterprise and return to England; in June, however, as the survivors were sailing downriver, they met an expedition of fresh supplies, led by Lord De La Warr, governor of Virginia, which encouraged the leaders to re-establish the settlement. Gates returned to London, apparently accompanied by Jourdain, in an attempt to persuade the company to maintain its interest in Virginia, despite a discouraging start.

It was against this background that Jourdain wrote a brief account of the expedition, published as *A Discovery of the Barmudas, otherwise called the Ile of Divels* in London in 1610. It provides a summary report of the voyage and shipwreck on the Bermudas, including an account of the survivors' experience on the island and their subsequent arrival at Virginia. It was reprinted anonymously in 1613, under the title *A Plaine Description of the Barmudas, now called Sommer Ilands*, and with a dedication by W. C. to Sir Thomas Smith. It included an additional account of the first colonizing expedition sent out to the Bermudas in April 1612 by the Virginia Company. Jourdain's work aroused English interest in the colonization of the Bermudas by helping to destroy the islands' reputation as a dangerous and enchanted place. Rather than a 'habitation of Divells' it was one of the 'sweetest Paradises' on earth which could serve as a nursery for the colonization of Virginia (Jourdan, *A Plaine Description*, A3). John Smith drew on Jourdain's work for *The Generall Historie of Virginia, New-England, and the Summer Isles* of 1624, and material from the *Plaine Description* was used in Samuel Purchas's *Purchas his Pilgrimes* (1624). Jourdain's work may also have had some influence among the playwrights of Jacobean England, but in this context it was of less significance than the work of William Strachey, another member of the 1609 expedition, who included a description of the shipwreck at the Bermudas in his account of Virginia.

Little evidence survives of Jourdain's later career. He is not known to have married, and possibly lived in London in St Sepulchre's parish until 1650, when the estate of a Silvester Jourdain was administered by a John Jourdain. However, this identification is not certain, and one modern scholar has suggested that he may have been dead by 1615.   JOHN C. APPLEBY

Sources S. Jourdan, *A discovery of the Barmudas, otherwise called the Ile of Divels* (1610) · [S. Jourdan], *A plaine description of the Barmudas, now called Sommer Ilands* (1613) · *The journal of John Jourdain, 1608–1617*, ed. W. Foster, Hakluyt Society, 2nd ser., 16 (1905) · exchequer, port books, PRO, E.190/868/7, E.190/937/6 · P. L. Barbour, ed., *The complete works of Captain John Smith (1580–1631)*, 3 vols. (1986) · L. E.

Pennington, ed., *The Purchas handbook: studies of the life, time and writings of Samuel Purchas*, 2 vols., Hakluyt Society, 2nd ser., 185–6 (1997) · C. Wanklyn, *Lyme Regis: a retrospect* (1927) · T. L. Stoate, ed., *Dorset Tudor subsidies granted in 1523, 1543, 1593* (1982) · K. R. Andrews, *Trade, plunder and settlement: maritime enterprise and the genesis of the British empire, 1480–1630* (1984) · H. Wilkinson, *The adventurers of Bermuda* (1933) · J. Parker, *Books to build an empire* (1965) · R. R. Cawley, 'Shakspere's use of the voyagers in *The Tempest*', *Publications of the Modern Language Association of America*, 41 (1926), 688–726 · PRO, PROB 6/25

Jowett, Benjamin (1817–1893), master of Balliol College, was the eldest son and second child of Benjamin Jowett (1788–1859) of Camberwell in London and Isabella Langhorne (1790–1869). The elder Benjamin Jowett seems to have tried his hand at several kinds of small business but was described by Francis Turner Palgrave as having 'the manner, more easily recognized than defined, of one who had not been successful in his profession' (Abbott and Campbell, 1.20). The son was born in Camberwell on 15 April 1817 and is said to have taken after his mother: a pale, delicate child with little physical strength but remarkable intelligence. He was educated privately with his Langhorne cousins, showing a precocious aptitude for Greek. In these early years his chief companion seems to have been his elder sister, Emily, who shared his pleasure in reading and study. His father was to live until 1859 and his mother for a decade beyond that. He was always a devoted and affectionate son and brother, but once he had set out upon an academic career his family played less and less part in his life. His parents were to settle in Paris, Bonn, and Aix-la-Chapelle in the late 1840s, but Benjamin was not impressed by French religion nor, in spite of his later admiration for much German scholarship, did he become fluent in the German language.

School and university Jowett was admitted to St Paul's School, London, in June 1829. He was later to attribute his own ability in the Greek and Latin languages to two disciplines he acquired at the school: he learned by heart large quantities of poetry in those languages; and when he had translated a passage into English he regularly practised translating it back into the original. By the time he gained a scholarship to Balliol College in November 1835 he had come to be regarded by Dr John Sleath as the best Latin scholar the school had produced in his time as highmaster. Jowett went up to Balliol in October 1836. The scholars then at Balliol formed a brilliant group, which successive generations of entrants tried to emulate. They included A. P. Stanley (who was to be Jowett's closest friend for at least a decade), Stafford Northcote (the future Lord Iddesleigh), and W. C. Lake and J. G. Lonsdale, who were to become fellows of the college when Jowett did. He was tutored by A. C. Tait, Robert Scott, and W. G. Ward. Through the last of these he became, at first, very much inclined towards the ideas of the Oxford Movement, but it was Tait who exercised the most influence over him in the long run. Long afterwards Jowett was to write to Tait, 'Supposing that the Tutors of Balliol had been all like Ward, where should I have been … at the time of my election to the fellowship you helped to keep up some light of common sense in me' (Hinchliff, 20). Surprisingly he managed

Benjamin Jowett (1817–1893), by Julia Margaret Cameron, 1865

to remain on relatively friendly terms with both Ward and Tait. After Tait had become archbishop, and when Jowett himself was master of Balliol, he conceived a plan for a private dinner party to reunite the three of them.

Reforms instituted at the beginning of the century, in which John Parsons, the master of Balliol, had been a protagonist, shaped the Oxford of Jowett's undergraduate years. The honour school of *literae humaniores* (Greats) had been set up, together with a network of prizes and scholarships, to raise the university's standards. Jowett won the Hertford scholarship for Latin after six months at Balliol, was elected a fellow of the college in November 1838 before he had even taken his degree, and gained a first class in Greats in the summer of the following year. The master of Balliol, Richard Jenkyns, was—like his predecessor—determined to raise the academic standards of the college. Jowett was plainly as much a beneficiary of their achievements as he was, in turn, to be the architect of further advances in the intellectual quality of the college.

College tutor Jowett began to coach private pupils even before he took up his fellowship. He graduated BA in 1839 and continued his classical studies, being awarded the chancellor's prize for the Latin essay in 1841. In the following year he took his MA, was ordained deacon, and was appointed by Jenkyns to one of the tutorships in the college. This last was a considerable recognition of his ability. Most fellows of colleges had no obligation to concern themselves with the undergraduates at all. A small number of tutors was usually appointed by the head of the house and it was their responsibility to provide both teaching and pastoral care of the undergraduates allotted to them. Jowett used, at regular intervals, to deliver a devotional address to his pupils in his rooms.

The undergraduates seem to have held very varied opinions as to Jowett's abilities as a classical scholar. The young Algernon Charles Swinburne complained of howlers in his translations, and many years later A. E. Housman refused to attend his lectures because of his gross ignorance of Greek. But Edward Caird, who was eventually to succeed him as master of Balliol, and was tutored by him in Greek and Latin composition in the 1860s, thought him 'the very best in the University' (H. Jones and J. H. Muirhead, *The Life and Philosophy of Edward Caird*, 1921, 27). There is little doubt, however, about his effectiveness as a tutor, his personal concern for his pupils, or about his kindness towards them—a kindness which was plainly returned in their devotion to their tutor. Jowett may, indeed, have come to regard his former pupils as owing him a personal loyalty and felt betrayed if he did not receive it.

University reform Though Jowett had escaped from Ward's influence he had not escaped, nor wished to escape, from theological controversy altogether. He came from an evangelical background and, perhaps, always defined religion in evangelical terms. But by the 1840s he had become something of a liberal. Alongside, yet related to, the debate about the 'catholic' nature of the Church of England was another debate about the nature of truth and the means of arriving at it. For exponents of the older view, authority guaranteed truth: for the new school, influenced by the developing natural sciences, truth was what one arrived at by enquiry. The debate, therefore, indirectly concerned the nature of education and of the university, and was related to the growing pressure for university reform. In particular, it affected the nature of theology and underlay much of the developing liberal theology of the 1840s. Jowett and Stanley worked together on a history of the university, which was intended to bolster arguments for its reform, of which all that has survived is a pamphlet, published in 1848, *Suggestions for an Improvement of the Examination Statute*. In its preface, arguing for a new kind of theology after the manner of Thomas Arnold, Jowett used a phrase that he was later to make notorious, saying that the New Testament should be studied 'like any other book'. Two years later some measure of reform was introduced into the Greats syllabus, so that Greek and Latin texts were examined in moderations, and history and philosophy in the final examination. Jowett's chief concern, in this aspect of the university's curriculum, was that Plato's thought should occupy a more important place in this revised syllabus.

Jowett and his friends, loosely a group of people associated with Rugby School and Balliol, including Arthur Stanley, Robert Lingen, and Frederick Temple, became known as educational reformers. After the commission for the reform of the university had reported in 1852, Jowett submitted detailed proposals to Gladstone, who had been entrusted by the cabinet with the task of drafting legislation based on the commission's recommendations. Some of his suggestions found their way into the bill but he failed in his chief purpose, which was to ensure that the university was reformed as a whole in order to prevent individual colleges doing separate deals with the administration. In the event, an executive commission was appointed to work out how each college should be reformed. When it came to appointing a secretary to this commission both Jowett and Temple were considered, but it was Stanley who was appointed. In this period Jowett was also consulted about the reform of the Indian Civil Service and the manner in which its recruits were trained, a matter which remained one of his concerns throughout his life. He had begun to influence public affairs.

When the mastership of the college became vacant in 1854 Jowett, though he was not yet thirty-five, was one of the candidates. Robert Scott, who had become the incumbent of a college living, was the other. It is not entirely clear why Jowett was unsuccessful, but his growing reputation as a radical may have had something to do with it. He took his defeat very badly, withdrew from much of the life of the senior common room, and made himself virtually permanent leader of opposition to the master within the college. For ten years the fellows were divided into two parties, Scott's and Jowett's, until a hotly contested fellowship election in 1864 gave Jowett a permanent majority in the governing body. From then on he was able to promote his own plans for the college over Scott's head.

Liberal theology Meanwhile Jowett and Stanley were working on a projected series of commentaries on the Pauline epistles. The first (and, in the event, the only) volumes were published in 1855, the year in which Jowett was appointed to the regius chair of Greek: Stanley on 1 and 2 Corinthians and Jowett on Romans, Galatians, and 1 and 2 Thessalonians. Stanley's volumes were uncontroversial, though both men used the Greek text of the New Testament edited by Lachmann rather than the text used by the translators of the Authorized Version. But Jowett, particularly in a number of essays within the volumes, expressed radical theological views which were widely attacked. His theology of the atonement, in which he rejected not only the evangelical penal substitutionary view but also the Anselmian satisfaction theory beloved by high-churchmen, was particularly controversial. His work also showed some knowledge of Kant and Locke and he was to proceed, in a way that was unusual at this date, to read Schleiermacher and Hegel. His university lectures also dealt with Hegel, one of the very few ways in which Hegelian ideas were accessible to English undergraduates. It is not easy to be sure how profound an understanding of these thinkers he possessed. He was always eclectic and a hater of systems. He maintained that Kant confused 'sensation with the objects of sense' (Hinchliff, 89) and that Hegel's philosophy was splendid if one could 'only get it out of its dialectical form' (Abbott and Campbell, 1.130).

In the furore which followed the publication of the commentaries, Jowett was subjected to both petty persecutions and more serious attacks. At the instigation of J. D.

Macbride and C. P. Golightly he was required by the vice-chancellor (R. L. Cotton) to subscribe the Thirty-Nine Articles afresh in December 1855, and a prize was offered in the university for an essay controverting his theology. Scott, to his credit, refused to take any action against him in the college. Jowett's own views, and particularly his subjectivist theology of the atonement, only became firmer and clearer.

In 1860 Jowett contributed an article, 'On the interpretation of scripture', to *Essays and Reviews*, a typically broad-church volume, with no overall editorial policy, in which each contributor chose his own theme without regard to, or even knowledge of, the work of the others. Jowett regarded the volume as an opportunity to challenge the way in which traditionalists were trying to terrorize liberals into hiding their opinions. His essay, which he had originally intended to include in the second edition of his commentaries, was an attempt to expound a rational explanation of the authority and inspiration of the Bible. He did not employ, and hardly even referred obliquely to, critical biblical scholarship. But he insisted that biblical writings should be treated as other books; that is to say, as one would treat classical texts. They should be read as far as possible in the sense in which they had been intended, without the overlay of traditional and sometimes forced meanings which they had often acquired. At the heart of his argument was the concept of progressive revelation, so that the books of the Bible should, he thought, be placed in a continuum which came to its climax with Christ, and to which climax the epistles and other New Testament writings looked back. What disturbed his critics, however, was his suggestion that revelation was still going on, and that each generation should interpret holy scripture afresh after its own fashion.

In 1860 *Essays and Reviews* was attacked as being neither religious nor rational by a reviewer (Frederic Harrison) in the radical *Westminster Review*, a great blow to the contributors, who thought of themselves as proponents of a rational religion. But this was also a time when conservatives, and particularly the clergy, were in any case angry about what they saw as attacks upon religion. The Huxley/Wilberforce debate about evolution and the attempt to have Max Müller elected to the new chair of Sanskrit at Oxford aroused their fury, which was further fuelled by a review of *Essays and Reviews* by Bishop Samuel Wilberforce of Oxford (though published anonymously) in the *Quarterly Review* in January 1861. Jowett and Temple (who had also contributed to the volume) went to see Tait, now bishop of London, on 20 January, and believed they would have his support. But when the bishops met early in February Tait was persuaded to sign an episcopal letter expressing disapproval of views such as those contained in the book. For this Jowett never completely forgave him, and when Temple, in due course, withdrew his contribution on becoming bishop of Exeter he also incurred Jowett's displeasure. Jowett was himself delated to the vice-chancellor's court in 1863 for teaching contrary to the doctrines of the Church of England, but the vice-chancellor's assessor refused to proceed with hearing the case.

Jowett had suffered no actual penalty for his part in the book but felt he had been vilified for being honest about his beliefs. It was a period when liberals were in decline within the university, and Jowett was also caught up in an unseemly wrangle about the salary attached to his professorship, which had not been increased since the original endowment in the sixteenth century. After six years of controversy, through the intervention of Dean Liddell and in spite of the opposition from those who thought that a heretic should not be paid from what was originally a pious foundation, his salary was raised from £40 p.a. to £500 in 1865.

Editor of Plato The 1860s marked the end of a phase in Jowett's life. Most of his friendships with other young and liberal clergymen were coming to an end. He had become convinced that public theological debate was unproductive. He turned his academic attention to editing Plato and his theological energies to preaching rather than publishing. The occasional nature of the sermon was, in any case, more suited to his eclectic approach and he could propagate his liberal ideas more subtly without their unconventional character being so evident. Sermons in college chapel were a comparatively recent innovation, and in 1869 Jowett got himself appointed official college preacher.

Jowett had been devoting much of his time to work on Plato throughout the decade. His first intention was to produce a commentary on the *Republic*. But, concluding that this text was to be understood only through an analysis of Plato's other works, he commenced what eventually became his translations of the dialogues, with introductions in which many of his own theological and philosophical ideas were embedded. The translation appeared in 1871 in four volumes and in a revised edition in five volumes in 1875. There followed a translation of Thucydides, with notes on the Greek text, in 1881, and of Aristotle's *Politics* in 1885. A third edition of his translations of Plato appeared in 1892, but the edition of the *Republic*, which had been in a sense the foundation and starting point of all his work as an editor and translator of the Greek classics, was still unfinished at his death and was completed and published by his friend and biographer Lewis Campbell. For thirty years the work had occupied the chief place among his interests. He often noted that he hoped and intended to get back to theology, and perhaps especially to writing a life of Jesus, but the business of constructing translations and commentaries on the classics seemed to expand to fill every available moment.

In the nineteenth century Jowett's work in this respect, as in so many others, broke new ground and established new norms. The several editions of his commentaries and translations, like his commentaries on the Pauline epistles, were both less systematic and less precise than had been usual. His admirers thought that his translations of Plato and Thucydides superseded all previous translations in elegance and polish, and even some modern translators have been content to use Jowett's version as a basis for their own work. But one of his twentieth-century successors in the chair has asserted that any page of Jowett's translation of Plato 'will supply some evidence of Housman's stern judgment' (Lloyd-Jones, 16).

Master of Balliol Jowett had been elected master of the college in 1870 on Scott's appointment by Gladstone (who intervened in order to release Scott with dignity from what had become an intolerable position in the college) to the deanery of Rochester. Jowett was now where he had always wanted to be, not merely because it was his personal ambition but also because it enabled him to achieve what he had long believed to be desirable, an educational institution which was genuinely religious but in a sense very different from what he regarded as Oxford's formal and empty ecclesiasticism. He was not a secular person and did not regard the mastership as a secular office, but his concept of religion was one in which the enquiring spirit must be free to reach whatever conclusions seemed to correspond with reality and experience. He seems to have learned from the example of Dr Arnold at Rugby, perhaps through his friendship with Stanley, that it was possible to establish an undogmatic and liberal Christian institution to which the middle classes would nevertheless be more than willing to send their children. He was very proud of the fact that the chapel services which he devised as master (and they were not very radical adaptations of parts of the Book of Common Prayer) regularly drew an entirely voluntary congregation of undergraduates.

As master Jowett's closest friends were not, as had been the case earlier, other liberal clergymen, but people of character and strength of personality likely to be much involved with the world's affairs. He acquired the reputation of being a great picker, trainer, and placer of able young men, whom he sent from the college into positions of influence in government and civil service. Jowett has often been accused of being a snob, but he would have said that it was important that able and potentially influential young people, just because they were going to be of significance in public affairs, should be trained to understand the importance of morality. Otherwise their influence might be entirely disastrous. The secret of his ability to befriend the young, even when he was over seventy, seems to have rested on two things. He could be kind and generous, often when it was least expected or deserved; and he remained interested always in current concerns rather than reverting at every opportunity to the things that had been of significance in his own youth.

Jowett was not, of course, universally liked by undergraduates. Those of them who were conservative or traditionalist found him as uncongenial as did many of his contemporaries. W. H. Mallock, who was an undergraduate at Balliol when Jowett was master, constructed a cruel but clever parody of Jowett as Dr Jenkinson in *The New Republic* (1877), a satire on liberal intellectual circles. But many former Balliol undergraduates did become important in the world of government and remained his friends; and there was a very real sense in which Jowett used friendship as a mode of exercising the mastership and of influencing society as a whole. Throughout his life he created a network of friends as genuinely close as they were influential. They included Tennyson and Browning, the duke of Bedford, Lord Lingen and Lord Selborne, Milner the pro-consul, and above all the diplomatist Sir Robert Morier. Stanley, almost the only one of his close friends to have survived since the early days, became dean of Westminster. Many of his academic colleagues were his former pupils who had matured into being his friends.

Jowett's close confidante even before he became master, and the person with whom, perhaps, he was able to be most open and honest, was Florence Nightingale, whom he seems to have found congenial because she possessed an independent, enquiring mind and stood outside his usual circle. But she was not his only female friend. The formidable Lady Stanley of Alderley was another and so were George Eliot and Queen Victoria's first and Prince Albert's favourite child, Victoria, the crown princess of Prussia, 'my princess'. Many of his surviving letters were addressed to women such as these, strong-minded, unconventional, and interested in ideas. He was a firm believer in education for women, though he was not, curiously, a supporter of their admission to Oxford University, for he thought it desirable that they should live at home while studying. But his concern for university extension was genuine and he played a considerable part, for instance, in the establishment of the university in Bristol.

It is chiefly as an outstanding master of Balliol that Jowett is remembered. Because of the considerable degree of autonomy enjoyed by colleges and the real power of their heads, he was able to impose a shape on Balliol. The college, he said, existed for the benefit of the young men. He encouraged candidates from middle-class homes; he was always anxious to make it possible for poorer undergraduates to live more cheaply in Oxford. He created a science laboratory in the college and he cajoled the fellows into buying a piece of land which would eventually become playing fields. His fear of systems made him very suspicious of tutors who embraced schools of thought, and he feared that they would be too anxious to make disciples among the young. For that reason, though he was largely responsible for the interest which T. H. Green and Edward Caird took in Idealism, he was also always very critical of them. This fear may also account for the fact that he created no school of liberal theology. For all that he valued the loyalty and friendship of his pupils, he was too much the inculcator of individualism.

Jowett seems to have lost some of his enthusiasm for university reform. Perhaps he believed that the essential things had been done. He was not inclined to support research (indeed he thought that so few were capable of it that it was not worth endowing), though he had begun to say that it might be a good thing to establish readerships so as to be able to reward faithful college tutors. As vice-chancellor, between 1882 and 1886, he was responsible for putting into effect reforms designed by government to redistribute college income, open fellowships to married and lay persons, and create faculty boards to control university lecturing. These reforms he largely welcomed, since they reduced the power of the clergy within the university, and devoted himself to their smooth introduction. He also encouraged the provision of facilities for non-collegiate students, drew up a plan (which was never achieved) for draining the low-lying area around the river, and devised a pension scheme for the employees of the university press.

Jowett seems to have been exhausted by his years as vice-chancellor and, after a severe illness in 1887, his health never really recovered. He was again seriously ill in 1891: the illness recurred in 1893 and he became very weak. He died on 1 October of that year while staying at the home of a former pupil, a judge, Sir Robert Wright, and Lady Wright at Headley Park in Hampshire. It was symbolic. For thirty years, since the talk of prosecuting him for his part in *Essays and Reviews*, he had felt more comfortable in the company of lawyers than of clergymen. He had published no more controversial essays about religion. He was left out of the panel of translators working on the *New English Bible*. Apart from the occasional invitation from the dean, A. P. Stanley, to preach at Westminster Abbey, he restricted himself to sermons about the great religions of the world in Balliol College chapel, or 'Platonism flavoured with a little Christian charity' as Henry Scott Holland unkindly put it (Hinchliff, 116).

Jowett never married (though he told Miss Sorabji that he had proposed to Florence Nightingale and been refused), and his brothers and sisters were all dead. The funeral service was conducted in the college chapel, and the interment followed in St Sepulchre's graveyard, Oxford, where he was laid close to T. H. Green.

Reputation and assessment Jowett's name had become synonymous with Balliol, which he turned into the leading college in the first university in the United Kingdom at the height of its world power. How had he done this? He was fortunate that Balliol was already a comparatively well-run institution, where the scholarships were open and where men were encouraged to take honours degrees and to distinguish themselves and gain high classes in the schools. To this Jowett himself added educational zeal and a sense of duty. 'When we think of what is and what might be', he wrote to Earl Russell, 'of the endless possibility of improvement in all human creatures during the first years of life we feel that if there is such a thing as national guilt it is incurred in the neglect of education' (27 Oct 1867). Young men were very impressionable when they left home. Christ's ministry had not begun until he was thirty years old and had lasted, at most, three years, and in that time he had changed the world. Jowett was struck by how many men, when they reached the university, brought with them 'no high aim in life'. But none 'while young' was 'incurable', and none of these 'good blossoms' must be allowed to fall (*Dear Miss Nightingale*, 139, 12). The work of the dedicated college tutor was holy, almost, and the college tutor, rather than the coach or the professor, was the figure round whom the university should revolve. Jowett, as Florence Nightingale said, 'was always intent on improving his own character for the sake of his undergraduates'. When he became master he went further, and

aimed to make Balliol 'an ideal college' where the link with active life would be formed (ibid., xxxiv, 188–9).

To the high-born like Lord Lansdowne, Jowett stressed that hell, as Robert Browning said, was the consciousness of opportunities lost. Among the middle classes even the most intelligent young men, he observed, needed to overcome three obstacles if they were to be successful in their careers: shyness, religious fanaticism, and ignorance of the world. In identifying shyness Jowett was speaking from personal experience. Memoirs concur that meetings with the master, and still more walks, were punctuated by long silences. In addressing fanaticism he was perhaps too outspoken. But he can be excused. He knew, because the young men told him so, that the liturgy and the creeds of the church were becoming incomprehensible with the passage of time. His object was to identify what was still credible (not miracles) and could be passed on to the next generation: that 'the death, and not the resurrection of Christ, is the really strengthening and consoling fact— that human nature could have risen to that does show that it is divine' (*Dear Miss Nightingale*, 52). Most important of all was knowledge of the world. Of course 'all the mischief in the world' was 'done by conservatism' while 'the world always cunningly pretends that it is really done by radicalism' (ibid., 94). But Jowett believed we could not 'strengthen our lives by eccentricity' (ibid., 229), and that was why he was never going to leave the Church of England, as many people thought he should, and become a dissenter. Dissenters had adopted oppositional attitudes and placed themselves outside the mainstream. We must never allow the mind 'to decompose itself into sympathy and antipathy' (ibid., 279) lest 'we become hopeless and isolated, antipathetic to all things, sympathetic with nothing', and 'we must accept faits accomplis' (ibid., 97).

Jowett enlarged the college from about twenty-five admissions a year in the 1850s to about sixty in the 1870s. He strengthened existing connections with the great schools such as Eton, Harrow, and Rugby. But he was convinced that it was 'important to provide a means of giving the best education to the best intelligences in every class of Society' (to Earl Russell, 27 Oct 1867), and he threw the college open to talent wherever it could be found. Simultaneously he began to attract men from beyond the United Kingdom, the sons of British nationals engaged in business overseas, of British emigrants domiciled in the colonies, and even the indigenous inhabitants themselves (Balliol's famous black men). Students arrived, too, from France, Germany, and the United States, and the college began to enjoy a reputation for the international character of its admissions. In the early 1870s, when a Siamese prince and the son of the Japanese prime minister came to study at Balliol, Jowett's aspiration 'to govern the world' through his pupils (*Dear Miss Nightingale*, 249) appeared on the verge of being realized. However that may have been, he did govern India through three successive viceroys, Lansdowne, Milner, and Curzon, and the scores of probationers or future members of the Indian Civil Service whom he attracted to the college. The presence of men from so many different countries combined with the stance taken by the master in chapel (Christianity is not absolutely true and other religions are not absolutely false) to ensure that students at Balliol were exposed to a variety of ideas, alternative ways of thinking, and an extended range of beliefs. The college thus became the first institution in England (would Jowett have supposed the first institution in the world since the fourth century BC?) formed around the idea that education consists not in growing up among others like ourselves and in the fortification of received opinions, but in living among others unlike ourselves and learning to make up our own minds in a plural society.

Recruit by ability. Train character. And then launch your students upon the world. The great achievement of Jowett's life lay, Florence Nightingale thought, in 'connecting University education with a man's future career'. He had no equal in cultivating his acquaintance and 'making University the entrance to life' (*Dear Miss Nightingale*, xxxv). Jowett met and knew the great figures of the age. Of Lord John Russell, who consulted him about education, he said, 'I always like him; he is so simple and natural. I wish that he had not done so many foolish things' (ibid., 134). Russell's opponent, Lord Derby, he described as 'a schoolboy of magnificent proportions all his life' (ibid., 111). Derby's son Lord Stanley, though 'cut off from the religious world, and equally from the jolly world', was still 'a man with higher aims than any other politician' (ibid., 27). Disraeli was 'a rascal whom I rather like for his pluck and his cleverness' (ibid., 143). Gladstone puzzled him: he had 'a sort of madness akin to genius'. Jowett added that he did not like 'being ruled by a man who has such unsound views about Homer' (ibid., 108, 174). These were wonderfully acute but uncensorious judgements. Little wonder then that Jowett made friends in high places and that he was able to start so many of his pupils off upon the fast track within their professions.

Outside the college members of the university found Jowett overbearing. He engaged in one long and unsuccessful struggle to persuade Bodley's librarian to allow readers easier access to the books and in another more rewarding one with the university press, which he thought should publish cheap standard texts for schools and make a profit. His worst fault, as Mark Pattison pointed out, was that he championed the tutorial system, not in conjunction with research but almost independently of it, and discounted new lines of scholarly enquiry. Members of other colleges did not enjoy having Balliol held out to them as an example, did not look forward to 'little Benjamin' becoming vice-chancellor, and did not welcome the vice-chancellor's support for the newly founded Oxford University Dramatic Society. Other colleges Balliolized themselves notwithstanding, and in the way Jowett himself would most have hoped, by the election of Balliol men to their fellowships. Seven of Jowett's pallbearers were Balliol heads of other colleges. They did not agree in politics or form a school in philosophy, and Jowett would not have wished them to. But each in his own way was a modernizer, helping to lay the ghost of ancient clerical Oxford and preparing men for the present and the future. Jowett had arrived in Oxford when the mould was already breaking, and he had created a new model, no less high-minded, and much more open to a worldwide aristocracy of liberal intellects.

At the end of the twentieth century Jowett's translations of Plato's *Dialogues*, Aristotle's *Politics*, and Thucydides—though heavily revised—were still in print. In 1895 P. L. Gell edited and printed a book entitled 'Essays on men and manners by the late Benjamin Jowett'. This was not published, but is available, together with many manuscripts of his sermons, his letters to Florence Nightingale, and other papers, in Balliol College Library. A two-volume *Life and Letters* begun by Evelyn Abbott and finished by Lewis Campbell was published in 1897, and this was followed two years later by a further volume of *Letters*. Leslie Stephen published a chapter entitled 'Jowett's life' in his *Studies of a Biographer* (2, 1898, 123–59). Jowett's achievement is now taken for granted, and only one more life, G. Faber's *Jowett, a Portrait with Background* has been published, in 1957. This was a long time in the writing, larded with speculation about Jowett's libido (which was low), and completed in a race against illness. Peter Hinchliff, *Benjamin Jowett and the Christian Religion* (1987), was the first work to examine Jowett's theology carefully and to discover traces of his influence in the thought of Charles Gore and William Temple. The attractive side of Jowett's character comes across in his letters to Florence Nightingale published in E. V. Quinn and J. M. Prest (eds.), *Dear Miss Nightingale: a Selection of Benjamin Jowett's Letters, 1860–93* (1987). *Jowett's Correspondence on Education with Earl Russell in 1867*, edited by J. M. Prest, was published as a supplement to the *Balliol College Record* in 1965.

PETER HINCHLIFF and JOHN PREST

Sources E. Abbott and L. Campbell, *Life and letters of Benjamin Jowett*, 2 vols. (1897) · *DNB* · G. Faber, *Jowett, a portrait with background* (1957) · P. Hinchliff, *Benjamin Jowett and the Christian religion* (1987) · J. Jones, *Balliol College: a history, 1263–1939* (1988), 202–24 · E. Caird, 'Professor Jowett', *International Journal of Ethics* (Oct 1897), 43–8 · J. Prest, *Robert Scott v Benjamin Jowett*, supplement to *Balliol College Record* (1966) · H. F. G. Swanston, *Ideas of order: Anglicans and the renewal of theological method in the middle years of the 19th century* (1974) · *Dear Miss Nightingale: a selection of Benjamin Jowett's letters, 1860–93*, ed. E. V. Quinn and J. M. Prest (1987) · F. M. Turner, *The Greek heritage in Victorian Britain* (1981) · H. Lloyd-Jones, *Blood for the ghosts* (1982), 13–32 · W. R. Ward, *Victorian Oxford* (1965) · Gladstone, *Diaries* · *Hist. U. Oxf. 6: 19th-cent. Oxf.* · *Hist. U. Oxf. 7: 19th-cent. Oxf. pt 2*

Archives Balliol Oxf. · Bodl. Oxf., lecture notes · Bodl. Oxf., letters | Balliol Oxf., letters to Claude Montefiore · Balliol Oxf., corresp. with Robert Morier · Balliol Oxf., corresp. with A. L. Smith · Baylor University, Waco, Texas, letters to Robert Browning · BL, corresp. with W. E. Gladstone, Add. MSS 44333–44430 · BL, corresp. with Florence Nightingale, Add. MSS 45783–45785 · BL OIOC, letters to Lord Curzon, MSS Eur. F 111–112 · BL OIOC, letters to Cornelia Sorabji, MS Eur. F 165 · Bodl. Oxf., letters to Henry Acland · Bodl. Oxf., corresp. with Lord Kimberley · Bodl. Oxf., letters to Edwin Palmer · Bodl. Oxf., letters to Henry Taylor and Theodisia Taylor · Derbys. RO, letters to Philip Gell; papers relating to literary executorship · Hove Central Library, Sussex, letters, mainly to Viscount Wolseley and Lady Wolseley · ICL, corresp. with Thomas Huxley and his wife · LPL, letters to Edwin Hatch · LPL, letters to A. C. Tait · NL Scot., letters to John Stuart Blackie · NL Wales, letters to T. C. Edwards · NPG, letters to George Frederic

Watts • NRA Scotland, corresp. with Lord Wemyss • Pusey Oxf., letters to Robert Scott • U. St Andr. L., letters to Wilfrid Ward • W. Sussex RO, letters to Frederick Maxse

Likenesses G. Richmond, pencil and chalk on paper, c.1855, Balliol Oxf. • J. M. Cameron, photograph, 1865, priv. coll. [see illus.] • G. Howard, drawing, 1868, Balliol Oxf. • D. Laugée, drawing, 1871, Balliol Oxf. • Taunt & Co., photograph, c.1890, NPG • Lady Abercromby, watercolour drawing, 1892, NPG • H. H. Cameron, photograph, 1893, Balliol Oxf. • H. R. Hope-Parker, marble bust, 1896, Balliol Oxf. • E. O. Ford, miniature memorial effigy, exh. RA 1897, Balliol Oxf. • G. F. Watts, oils, 1899, Balliol Oxf. • Lady Abercromby, oils (after G. F. Watts), Balliol Oxf. • Elliott & Fry, photograph, NPG • H. Furniss, pen-and-ink caricature, NPG • S. P. Hall, pencil drawing, NPG • Hills & Saunders, carte-de-visite, NPG • H. R. Hope-Parker, marble bust, U. Oxf., Examination Schools • C. M. C. Ross, pastel drawing, Balliol Oxf. • T. & G. Shrimpton, carte-de-visite, NPG • Spy [L. Ward], chromolithograph caricature, NPG; repro. in VF (26 Feb 1876)

Wealth at death £20,217 5s. 8d.: probate, 1893, CGPLA Eng. & Wales

Jowett, Frederick William (1864–1944), socialist and politician, was born on 31 January 1864 at 108 Clayton Street, Bradford, one of eight children (three of whom died in infancy) of Nathan Jowett, cotton warp dresser, and his wife, Emma Gerry. Born into a working-class household, his education was limited, and at the age of eight he started work in the Bradford textile trade as a half-timer, before transferring to full-time employment at the age of thirteen. His education was continued through a mixture of self-directed reading and attendance at classes at the mechanics' institute and the technical college. He made rapid progress in the textile trade and became a power-loom overlooker at the age of nineteen. On 19 July 1884 he married Emily Foster, the daughter of a Bradford wool waste dealer, and through his marriage he became a partner in a small textile firm. However, by this point his interests were already more clearly related to trade unionism and the infant labour movement, which were to dominate the remainder of his life.

In 1886 Jowett joined William Morris's Socialist League, and on the closure of the Bradford branch in 1889 he was a founder member and secretary of the Labour Electoral Association, an organization committed to the selection and election of working men as parliamentary candidates. His acceptance of socialism grew out of reading Carlyle, Ruskin, and Morris (influences which he later acknowledged in the Review of Reviews, June 1906, 575), combined with observing working-class life: his direct experience of the social, economic, and political situation in late Victorian Bradford dominated his political career. In that period the textile industry was undergoing increasing difficulties, which led to worsening labour relations and culminated in the Manningham mills strike (December 1890–April 1891). Out of that strike emerged a growing demand for independent working-class political activity, which, faced by locally a conservative Liberalism and a weak trade unionism, led to the formation in the spring of 1891 of the Bradford Labour Union, subsequently the Bradford Independent Labour Party. Jowett, who was a founder and first president of the Bradford labour church, was a key figure in this burgeoning movement; in November

1892 he was the party's first candidate for Bradford town council to win a contested election. For the next fifteen years his major sphere of activity was Bradford town council, and from 1897 the city council. As chairman of the sanitary committee and later the health committee, he was a driving force behind municipal socialism, particularly municipal housing. His thinking in this field was outlined in his book The Socialist and the City (1907).

But even before this publication Jowett's main area of activity had moved to Westminster. He had been a delegate to the founding conference of the Independent Labour Party (ILP) in 1893, and had stood as an ILP candidate for Bradford West in 1900, when he was narrowly defeated. He was elected in 1906 and represented Bradford West until the 1918 general election. Although he remained deeply involved in Bradford issues, for much of the remainder of his political life his primary role was in the House of Commons and within the central administration of the ILP. He wrote a parliamentary column in The Clarion until 1909 and then in the Labour Leader.

Small in stature, Jowett was a fiery speaker who, unlike many of his contemporaries, retained his radicalism until the end of his life. In the period before the First World War he was an active spokesman in parliament on most issues affecting working-class life, notably the provision of school meals. During this period two of the key issues which were to dominate much of his political thinking emerged. The first was his concern to democratize parliament, for which he advocated a central role for committees of MPs to scrutinize all legislative and administrative matters relating to each department of state, as described in What's the use of Parliament? (1909) and in his evidence to the select committee on House of Commons procedure (1913–14). The second was his active opposition to secret diplomacy in international relations. On the left of the party, he was strongly suspicious of Ramsay MacDonald, and of attempts to stifle the rights of Labour members to vote according to conscience. He campaigned against the National Insurance Bill in 1911, objecting to its contributory principle, and this stand placed him at odds with the majority of the Parliamentary Labour Party. As a member of the select committee appointed to investigate the Putumayo scandal, he was deeply impressed by the evidence of the exploitation of the local labour force in the Amazon rubber collecting industry. Having previously been chairman of the ILP in 1909–10 he was re-elected for a further three-year term in 1914.

Throughout his life Jowett passionately opposed war. He spoke out against the Second South African War, and during the First World War he was a bitter opponent of its conduct. He was never a pacifist, though, and believed in the right of national defence. As well as being a member of the executive of the Union of Democratic Control, he spoke out against secret diplomacy, which he believed responsible for the outbreak of war, and was a constant advocate for British war aims to be defined and peace negotiations to be entered into.

Defeated at the 1918 general election, Jowett concentrated on his work within the central party apparatus: he was the ILP representative on the Labour Party executive and was chairman of the Labour Party in 1921–2. During this period he was often a member of overseas delegations: he made visits to Hungary to investigate reports of a 'White terror', to Geneva for the International Socialist Conference held to consider the post-war situation, and to Ireland to inquire into the policies of the British state during the war of independence. Jowett and his fellow Labour Party delegates recommended the withdrawal of British forces and the recognition of the right of the Irish to self-determination.

In 1922 Jowett was elected for Bradford East, and in parliament he was chairman of the public accounts committee. After being re-elected at the general election of 1923, he became in January 1924 the first commissioner of works, with a seat in the first Labour cabinet. With John Wheatley he refused to wear morning dress and a top hat when receiving the seals of office from the king. As commissioner of works he was best remembered for authorizing Epstein's statue of *Rima* as the central feature of the W. H. Hudson memorial in Hyde Park. He advocated socialist policies and opposed collaboration with the Liberal Party to keep the government in office.

Jowett lost his Bradford seat at the general election of 1924, and during the next five years out of parliament he was closely associated with the leftward movement of the ILP, in conjunction with James Maxton and John Wheatley. He was again chairman of the ILP (1925–6) and was party treasurer from 1927 until his death. His thinking as expressed in the pamphlet *Parliament or Palaver?* (1926) returned to the need for the democratization of both the party and parliament, and was coupled with a deep hostility to cabinet government as a result of his experience of the first Labour government. He restated his arguments for the reorganization of parliament on the basis of a committee system, and carried these proposals at the ILP conference in 1926. But they were opposed by Ramsay MacDonald and other Labour leaders who feared that they would make parliament a permanent coalition, and would emasculate a future Labour government (Morrison, 169). He worked for the ILP's 'socialism in our time' programme, and was a powerful supporter of the miners both during 1926 and after. He firmly opposed another west Yorkshire labour pioneer, Ben Turner, in his involvement in the Mond–Turner talks, which were concerned to develop a more co-operative relationship between employers and trade unions in the context of pressures for industrial rationalization.

Jowett regained his seat at Bradford East in the general election of 1929. During the second Labour government he was associated with the left ILP rebels: he proposed a socialist amendment to the king's speech at the opening of the session in 1930 and opposed restrictions on entitlement to unemployment benefit. He also refused to sign a declaration that, if elected, all candidates should accept the standing orders of the Parliamentary Labour Party. For Jowett, as for a small number of MPs sponsored by the ILP, such a declaration would prohibit support in parliament for ILP policy when this was in conflict with the position of the majority of Labour MPs. He was defeated in the general election of 1931 and never sat in parliament again. At a special conference at Jowett Hall in Bradford (opened in 1927 by James Maxton in his honour) in July 1932, the ILP disaffiliated from the Labour Party. Jowett recognized that this was likely to lead to an increased marginalization of the ILP, but believed that commitment to principle was more important. The issue of standing orders was the basis of Jowett's support for disaffiliation. He did not share some ILP members' beliefs that disaffiliation in a context of capitalist crisis would permit the party to become an effective revolutionary alternative to both the Communist and Labour parties. For Jowett, this period, following the death of his wife of over forty-five years in September 1931, was not a happy one. Politically, he remained committed to the parliamentary road to socialism, and was appalled by the ILP's subsequent flirtation with ultra-left tendencies and willingness to co-operate with communists. He stood as an ILP candidate for Bradford East in 1935 but was defeated.

During the 1930s Bradford was Jowett's major focus of activity, and he wrote a weekly article of 1000–1500 words for the Bradford *ILP News*. In these articles he reflected on his political career and pushed forward a number of key issues: the reform of parliament, the 'living wage' and 'socialism in our time', anti-militarism, and—arising out of the experience of the second Labour government—an increasing concern with the role of finance and the need for a clear socialist policy in this area. He never embraced the populism of the ILP Clydesiders and was unusual on the left in taking a powerful interest in the reform of existing political institutions.

In 1939 Jowett opposed the declaration of war, once again arguing for the clear articulation of war aims and proposing immediate peace negotiations. He died at his home, 10 Grantham Terrace, Bradford, on 1 February 1944, survived by two daughters, a son, and five grandchildren. He was cremated at Scholemoor cemetery. His memorial service was conducted in Bradford's nineteenth-century cathedral of nonconformity, Horton Lane Congregational Chapel, where James Maxton paid a glowing tribute to a friend and colleague, referring to him as one of the giants of the labour movement.

J. A. JOWITT

Sources F. Brockway, *Socialism over sixty years: the life of Jowett of Bradford (1864–1944)* (1946) · *Manchester Guardian* (2 Feb 1944) · *DLB* · J. A. Filkins, 'Jowett, Frederick William', *BDMBR*, vol. 3, pt 1 · F. W. Jowett, *What made me a socialist* (1925) · M. Hardman, *Ruskin and Bradford: an experiment in Victorian cultural history* (1986) · J. Reynolds and K. Laybourn, 'The emergence of the independent labour party in Bradford', *International Review of Social History*, 20 (1975), 313–46 · K. Laybourn, 'The issue of school feeding in Bradford, 1904–1907', *Journal of Educational Administration and History*, 14 (1982), 36–8 · H. Morrison, *Government and parliament: a survey from inside*, 3rd edn (1964) · E. P. Thompson, 'Homage to Tom Maguire', *Essays in labour history*, ed. A. Briggs and J. Saville (1960), 276–316 · D. Howell, *British workers and the independent labour party, 1888–1906* (1983) · G. Cohen, 'The independent labour party: disaffiliation, revolution and standing orders', *History* (2001) · b. cert. · d. cert.
Archives BLPES, corresp. and papers · Labour History Archive and Study Centre, Manchester, corresp. and papers · W. Yorks. AS, Bradford, corresp.

Likenesses W. Scott, photograph, 1943, repro. in Brockway, *Socialism* · J. Southall, portrait, Bradford City Art Gallery
Wealth at death £1009 8s. 11d.: probate, 19 April 1944, *CGPLA Eng. & Wales*

Jowett, John Henry (1863–1923), Congregational minister, was born in Beaumont Town, Northowram, Halifax, on 25 August 1863, the fourth child of Josiah Jowett (d. c.1905), tailor and draper, and his wife, Hannah Marshall (d. 1911). Both his parents were members of Halifax's Square Congregational Church, whose minister, Enoch Mellor, provided J. H. Jowett with the model for his own career.

After four years at Hipperholme grammar school, Halifax, Jowett became, at the age of fourteen, a pupil teacher at Victoria Street board school, and in 1882 entered the Airedale Congregational College in Bradford to prepare for the ministry. During his first year at Airedale he won a scholarship to the University of Edinburgh, from which he graduated in 1887. Twenty-three years later Edinburgh conferred on him the honorary degree of doctor of divinity. After returning to Airedale in 1887 he spent two terms at Mansfield College, Oxford, and in October 1889 began his first ministry at St James's Congregational Church, Newcastle upon Tyne. After six years in Newcastle he was called to the pastorate of Carr's Lane Congregational Church, Birmingham, following the death of R. W. Dale. While in Birmingham, Jowett took the initiative in raising £25,000 for the establishment of the Digbeth Institute, in one of the city's poorest districts, which opened in January 1908 as a community centre for worship and recreation.

A holiday in the United States in the summer of 1909 led to an invitation to the pastorate of the Fifth Avenue Presbyterian Church, New York, reputedly the wealthiest church in the city. Despite a petition signed by 1400 members and worshippers at Carr's Lane and a memorial from Birmingham magistrates, Jowett accepted the invitation from New York in January 1911. It was this invitation that brought Jowett to the notice of the secular press, and he was reputed to have been enticed across the Atlantic by the offer of a large salary. In fact Jowett accepted the call to Fifth Avenue only on condition that his salary should be no more than the equivalent salary he had received at Carr's Lane. In New York, Jowett preached regularly to congregations of 1200–1500 people, and although at times he regretted not being in England during the First World War he argued the justice of the allied case in the New York press.

In February 1917 Jowett received an invitation to return to England to succeed Campbell Morgan at the Congregational Westminster Chapel. While the British prime minister, David Lloyd George, wrote to Jowett urging him to return to England, the American president, Woodrow Wilson, urged him to remain in the United States. He accepted the call from Westminster Chapel, but only on condition that, with the United States entering the war in April 1917, he delay his return until the spring of 1918. Jowett began his ministry at Westminster Chapel on Whit Sunday 1918, preaching to a congregation which included David Lloyd George and his wife, but the ministry was to

last only four years. In the summer of 1917 there appeared the first signs of the pernicious anaemia that would ultimately kill him. Ill health obliged him to retire from the pastorate of Westminster Chapel in December 1921, though he continued to preach at Sunday morning services until May 1922. In November 1922 he was made a Companion of Honour.

Jowett was a shy, humble man who was always slightly puzzled by the amount of public interest he aroused. He was tall, lean, balding with a full moustache, and always dressed fastidiously. He married, on 20 May 1890, Lizzie Ann, daughter of Francis Winpenny of Barnard Castle, and although they had no children of their own they adopted a daughter, Monica, in 1910.

Jowett's power as a preacher derived from a powerful, rich, musical voice and a masterly use of language. The burden of his message was 'the grace and love of our Lord and Saviour Jesus Christ', and having experienced no intellectual difficulties with Christianity himself he had little to say to those who had. From 1907 until 1922 he wrote a monthly devotional article for the *Christian World*, and published some twenty-five books, consisting largely of revised versions of his sermons. He served as chairman of the Congregational Union in 1906 and as president of the National Council of Evangelical Free Churches in 1910–11. He was an enthusiastic advocate of church unity and caused a storm of protest when, in February 1920, he accepted an invitation from the dean of Durham to preach in the cathedral—the first dissenter to preach in an English cathedral since the Commonwealth.

The last six months of Jowett's active life were devoted to a campaign designed to prevent another world war. In August 1922, despite growing weakness, he attended the conference, at Copenhagen, of the World Alliance for Promoting International Friendship through the Churches. And in the autumn he persuaded the archbishop of York, Cosmo Gordon Lang, to join him in a series of meetings designed to persuade British Christians to enlist as 'an act of personal dedication … in the cause of international brotherhood' (*Christian World*). The campaign reached its climax with a meeting in London's Queen's Hall in December, but Jowett's speech there was to be his last. A few days later his health collapsed and he died on 19 December 1923 at Belmont, Surrey, survived by his wife. His funeral was held at Westminster Chapel on 22 December, followed by cremation at Golders Green.

MICHAEL WATTS

Sources A. Porritt, *John Henry Jowett* (1924) · A. H. Driver, *Carr's Lane, 1748–1948* (1948) · J. D. Jones, *Three score years and ten* (1940) · *WWW* · *Christian World* (30 Nov 1922) · b. cert. · m. cert. · *CGPLA Eng. & Wales* (1924)
Likenesses photograph, repro. in Porritt, *John Henry Jowett*, frontispiece
Wealth at death £20,566 4s. 3d.: probate, 1924

Jowett, Joseph (1751–1813), jurist, was born in London on 27 October 1751, the second surviving son of Henry Jowett (1719–1801), furrier, then of Smithfield, and his first wife, Sarah Woodman (d. 1771). After moving with his family to Leeds in 1757 Jowett was educated at Leeds grammar school, and admitted a sizar at Trinity College, Cambridge, on 24 June 1769. In January 1773 he migrated to Trinity Hall, having been recommended to Dr Samuel Hallifax, then regius professor of civil law, who offered him the post of assistant tutor, with the prospect of a fellowship and tutorship, and of the regius professorship itself upon the anticipated appointment of Dr Hallifax to a bishopric. Jowett proceeded LLB in 1775, and became fellow and tutor in the same year on Dr Hallifax's vacating his fellowship by marriage. After taking his LLD in 1780 Jowett succeeded Dr Hallifax as regius professor in May 1782, upon the latter's appointment as bishop of Gloucester. An elegant Latinist, Jowett lectured regularly with solid sense, basing himself upon Hallifax's syllabus, and attracting particular commendation for his comparison of Roman and English law. Ordained deacon at Peterborough on 19 December 1773, and priest on 16 June 1776, Jowett held the Trinity Hall living of St Edward's, Cambridge, from 1785, and in 1795 accepted the college living of Wethersfield, Essex. His fellowship lapsed in the same year, but he continued as professor until his death, spending term in Cambridge and vacations in Wethersfield.

Jowett's sincerity and high moral character gained him general respect and much influence, though he became the victim of a well known epigram upon a little garden which he had laid out at Trinity Hall:

A little garden little Jowett made …
If you would know the mind of little Jowett
This little garden don't a little show it.
(Willis and Clark, 1.228, n.2)

The epigram exists in several versions, its authorship variously ascribed. One attribution is to Francis Wrangham, a moderate but decided whig who had migrated to Trinity Hall from Magdalene College at Jowett's suggestion in 1787, to be defeated in 1793 by John Vickers of Queens' College in competition for a divinity fellowship of Trinity Hall; Vickers was re-elected in short order after resigning ecclesiastical preferment which had rendered him ineligible at the time of his first election. Vickers was patronized by Jowett's closest friend, Dr Isaac Milner, president of Queens' College, an influential figure in academic politics in the tory interest, who also had been educated at Leeds grammar school and with whom Jowett invariably spent two evenings each week while in Cambridge. The junior fellows of Trinity Hall at the time were wont to describe their college as 'a fief of Queens'' (Gunning, 32).

Possessed of a fine alto voice, Jowett was passionately fond of music and was responsible, perhaps with the assistance of William Crotch, for the composition and installation of the quarter-hour chimes in the clock of Great St Mary's Church, Cambridge, copied in 1859 for the great clock of the Palace of Westminster. Jowett's strict evangelical opinions, which he shared with Dr Milner, led to his close involvement with the newly formed Cambridge Auxiliary Bible Society. Having written the society's second annual report the previous day, Jowett was suddenly taken ill in the street and died in his rooms at Trinity Hall on 13 November 1813. He was buried in the chapel of Trinity Hall on 18 November, immediately before the second anniversary meeting of the Bible society; its secretary and Charles Simeon were among his pallbearers. He never married.   N. G. JONES

Sources *Christian Observer*, 12 (1813), 820–23 · Venn, *Alum. Cant.*, 2/3 · G. Faber, *Jowett*, rev. 2nd edn (1958) · H. Gunning, *Reminiscences of the university, town, and county of Cambridge, from the year 1780*, 2 (1854) · C. Crawley, *Trinity Hall: the history of a Cambridge college, 1350–1975* (1976) · W. D. Bushell, *The church of St Mary the Great* (1948) · *Cambridge University Calendar* · *Cambridge Chronicle and Journal* (19 Nov 1813) · M. Milner, *The life of Isaac Milner*, 2nd edn (1844) · *GM*, 1st ser., 83/2 (1813), 624 · *Trinity College Admissions Book, 1740–87* · R. V. Taylor, ed., *The biographia Leodiensis, or, Biographical sketches of the worthies of Leeds* (1865) · register of baptisms, St Sepulchre, Holborn · *DNB* · R. Willis, *The architectural history of the University of Cambridge, and of the colleges of Cambridge and Eton*, ed. J. W. Clark, 1 (1886), 228

Jowett, William (1787–1855), missionary, was the son of John Jowett of Newington, Surrey, and nephew of Joseph *Jowett. He was educated by his uncle, the Revd Henry Jowett, and at St John's College, Cambridge, matriculating in 1806, graduating BA as twelfth wrangler in 1810, and proceeding MA in 1813. He was a fellow there 1811–16. In 1810 he won the Hulsean prize for an essay on the Jews and idolatry, published in 1811.

Jowett was the first Anglican clergyman who volunteered in 1813 for the foreign service of the Church Missionary Society. In 1815 he married Martha (d. 1829), daughter of John Whiting of Little Palgrave, Norfolk; they had seven children. From 1815 to 1820 he worked in the countries of the Mediterranean, and in 1823–4 in Syria and Palestine. He published *Christian Researches* on the Mediterranean in 1822 and on Syria and Palestine in 1825, and a considerable variety of religious treatises and memoirs. He was clerical secretary of the Church Missionary Society from 1832 to 1840, and was successively lecturer at St Mary Aldermanbury, St Peter, Cornhill, and Holy Trinity, Clapham. In 1851 he became incumbent of St John's, Clapham Rise. He died at Clapham on 20 February 1855, and was buried in Lewisham churchyard.

GORDON GOODWIN, rev. H. C. G. MATTHEW

Sources *GM*, 2nd ser., 43 (1855), 436 · Venn, *Alum. Cant.* · E. Stock, *The history of the Church Missionary Society: its environment, its men and its work*, 1–3 (1899) · T. E. Yates, *Venn and Victorian bishops abroad: the missionary policies of Henry Venn and their repercussions upon the Anglican episcopate of the colonial period, 1841–1872* (1978)
Archives U. Birm. L., special collections department, Church Missionary Society archive, corresp. and journals as missionary in Mediterranean

Jowitt [*née* Crawford; *other married name* Glover], **Jane** (1770–1846), poet, was born on 14 May 1770 at Harcourt Street, Dublin, daughter of Counsellor Crawford and of his wife (d. 1778), the daughter of a surgeon who was a native of Derbyshire. She was educated initially at home and, aged eight, could 'write a decent copy, and behave myself better than could be expected at my age' (*Memoirs*, 2). At this time her mother, who had been confined to bed after childbirth, died two days after being shown by her husband the picture of a well-known actress, Ann Barry, whom he intended to marry on her death. With help from a grandmother Jane next attended Mrs Frances Knowles's school in York Street. Following her father's return to

Dublin from London in 1782 she worked for a brief period as waiting-maid to her stepmother. She then boarded at a school at Clontary; the fees were met from interest on an inheritance from her grandmother, the capital of which she was to receive on marriage or maturity.

On attaining her majority Jane obtained a small property on the coast and spent £400 on furnishing it with a view to letting 'to respectable people in summer' (Memoirs, 13). For several years this proved a successful venture; but the rising of 1798 and the imposition of martial law led to a fall in the number of clients, and after settling her debts she determined to try her fortune in England. Having travelled via Liverpool and then on foot to London, she established herself in Knightsbridge and traded as a hawker, buying silk handkerchiefs and muslins in quantity and selling in many of the surrounding villages. Later, however, she travelled on to Dover, and almost on her arrival met at the Flying Horse inn a builder, Michael Glover (c.1758–1820/21), a Roman Catholic whom she had known four years earlier in Dublin and who, having enlisted in the Corps of Royal Sappers and Miners, had been assigned work on the fortifications at Dover. After a period of courtship they married, at St James's Church, Dover, on 17 December 1810. They spent several happy years in Dover, where Jane occupied herself with needlework for officers' ladies, and two years in Bermuda, where her husband again worked on fortifications and she was employed as a cook of plain English food for the wife of the governor. On the declaration of peace in 1817 they returned to England on the frigate *Pactolus*, and on her husband's discharge at Woolwich determined to pursue a future in Sheffield, since several of their acquaintance came from Yorkshire.

Three years later Jane's husband died, 'a martyr to his Industry' (Memoirs, 25), and she was again thrown upon her own resources. Having obtained a small house in Chapel Walk, Sheffield, she placed a notice in the window—'Letters wrote here'—and within about three months 'knew almost half the secrets and love affairs of the town [for] poor countrylads and lasses came from the villages, and I had many tender epistles to read and answer' (ibid., 29), her fee for each being 3d. In due course her modest demeanour and studious attention to writing attracted the attention of a regular passer-by, a man called Jowitt, a hand for twenty years at the silver-plate manufactory of Smith, Holt & Co. Jane appreciated his attention, and when he paid his respects she enquired locally of his character; being satisfied of his honesty and industry she agreed to marriage. After a wedding in Sheffield they set up home in the parish of St Paul's. But Jane had been deceived; within six months her second husband had taken to drink and lost his job. Arraigned by his wife to live on his pension or take to the workhouse, he brought in a broker, sold his wife's furniture, drank the proceeds, and, after living briefly on the parish, died.

Once more Jane was forced to look to her own resilience and learning. Forswearing experience as landlady, hawker, seamstress, cook, and letter-writer, she recalled her enjoyment at school of Milton, Thomson, and Young,

and hit upon a future as a poet. Her first subject was at hand; sadly afflicted by the death of the incumbent at St Paul's, she wrote 'Lines on the Death of the Rev. T[homas] Cotterill' (1823). Despite their being mawkish in tone Cotterill's widow was pleased with the verses and paid Jane 'a guinea and a gown' (Memoirs, 31). This satisfaction confirmed Jane's aptitude for poetry, and for the final twenty years of her life, much of which she spent in Doncaster, she regularly wrote memorial verses on the death of local citizens and gentry. Her most successful poem was lines on the death of the wife of 'the present Earl Fitzwilliam', for she sold over 800 copies to tenantry and others in the neighbourhood.

In 1840, aged almost seventy, Jane turned her mind to a different subject: 'On the Approaching Marriage of Queen Victoria'. Contrasting her own experience with that of the young queen she begins:

> An aged widow now presents her lay,
> All Albion hails the bright, auspicious day

addresses her queen as 'fair Victoria, sweetest flower of May', expresses the hope that the land may be blessed with true religion and that trade and culture may flourish 'hand in hand', and concludes:

> Oh may thy *roses* bloom, thy *shamrocks* spread,
> Thy *stately* thistles raise their loyal heads;
> May Heav'n vouchsafe to give thee length of years
> To dry the widow's and the orphan's tears.
> (Memoirs, 39–40)

Shortly afterwards, on 15 April 1840, she suffered a paralytic stroke. She recovered sufficiently to write a few further poems and her *Memoirs*, which include her only topographical poem, on 'Harrogate sulphur well'. She died in the Union Workhouse at Sheffield on 3 August 1846, of a 'decay of nature' (d. cert.). Her remains were her memoirs, written, she there avers, solely 'to gratify the desire of many most respectable families who have befriended me on many trying occasions'. PAUL FOSTER

Sources *Memoirs of Jane Jowitt, the poor poetess, aged 74 years, written by herself* (1844) · *Freeman's Journal* (July 1778) · parish register, Dover, St James's, 17 Dec 1810 [marriage, Michael Glover] · captain's log, *Pactolus* · d. cert.
Wealth at death inconsequential, but perhaps a few personal possessions and a few copies of her *Memoirs*

Jowitt, John (1811–1888), wool-stapler, was born on 15 September 1811 at Carlton House, Leeds, the eldest of the seven children of Robert Jowitt, cloth manufacturer and wool-stapler, and his wife, Rachel, daughter of Thomas and Cicely Crewdson of Kendal. Jowitt was educated at Mr Mercer's day school in East Parade, Leeds, then from 1823 at Josiah Forster's school at Tottenham, Middlesex, a Friends' school. Both his father's and his mother's family were Quakers. His grandfather, also John Jowitt, had been a prominent member of the Society of Friends in Leeds. In 1837, however, John Jowitt made the decision to break his allegiance to the Society of Friends, and joined the Congregational Leeds Salem Chapel. In later years he became a deacon at East Parade church, Leeds, and superintendent of the Sunday schools. For forty-three years he was secretary of the Leeds town mission, which he helped form in

1837. In the years before his death he was its president. He was closely connected with the Bible Society and the Religious Tract Society.

The family wool-stapling business was founded at Churwell, near Leeds, in 1776, although the family had much longer connections with the wool textile trade. Jowitt entered the business in 1826 and appears quickly to have gained a reputation as an astute businessman. He closely monitored the state of the wool textile industry, assiduously collecting statistics and developing a reputation for his speed and accuracy with figures. Some of his detailed calculations for the state of trade in the 1820s and 1830s survive. He was taken into partnership with his father, and revived what was later described by his son as a somewhat somnolent concern. Jowitt travelled extensively on behalf of the business—he expanded its activities in the home wool trade and was at the forefront of the early trade in wool to Europe from Australia, New Zealand, and South Africa. The family firm gained an important, and much-respected, role in the British wool textile industry, through its activities in wool merchanting, top-making, wool combing, wool scouring, carbonizing, and fell-mongering. It opened branches in Australia and South Africa.

On 5 May 1836 Jowitt married Deborah, eldest daughter of Robert and Dorothy Benson of Parkside, Kendal, another Quaker family. They had eleven children, six boys and five girls. Five of the boys, born between 1843 and 1852, died soon after birth. Their first son, Robert Benson, joined his father in the business and in 1874 was taken into partnership; he gradually took over the management of the business during his father's failing health.

Although a Liberal by persuasion, Jowitt took no very active role in local or national politics, except that he devoted time and money to the campaign for the abolition of slavery. His philanthropic interests in the Leeds area were, however, very varied. He was an early member of Leeds chamber of commerce, serving for many years as vice-president. For a short period he was a member of Leeds city council. He was one of the founders of Ilkley Hospital, and a founder committee member of Cookridge convalescent hospital and the reformatory at Adel, both near Leeds. He believed in voluntary education and gave support to W. E. Forster's Education Bill. In 1870 he joined the first Leeds school board, served as its vice-chairman for eight years, and was its chairman in 1879. He was appointed a JP for the West Riding of Yorkshire in 1870. His chief recreation was riding.

Jowitt was recognized by his contemporaries as a man of sound judgement. He was a good public speaker. An obituarist wrote of him: 'No citizen of Leeds has left a simpler or a purer record in his life' (*Leeds Mercury*, 31 Dec 1888). From the mid-1870s his health began to fail, and he gradually retired from the business. He died on 30 December 1888 at his home, Harehills, Potternewton, Leeds, and was buried in Roundhay churchyard, Leeds, on 3 January 1889. The business was continued by Robert Benson Jowitt, who was joined by his sons F. McCulloch Jowitt, Edward Maurice Jowitt, and Robert Jowitt.   D. T. JENKINS

Sources *Leeds Mercury* (31 Dec 1888) · *Leeds Mercury* (4 Jan 1889) · D. T. Jenkins, 'Jowitt, John', *DBB* · R. B. Jowitt, *Reminiscences of John Jowitt by his children* (1889) · *Wool Record and Textile World*, 30 (1926), 851–3 · *Wool Record and Textile World*, 79 (1951), 2197–8 · R. J. Morris, 'The middle class and the property cycle during the industrial revolution', *The search for wealth and stability*, ed. T. C. Smout (1979) · d. cert.
Archives U. Leeds, business records of Robert Jowitt & Sons Ltd
Wealth at death £111,735: Jenkins, 'Jowitt, John'

Jowitt, William Allen, Earl Jowitt (1885–1957), lord chancellor, was born on 15 April 1885 at Stevenage rectory, Hertfordshire, the only son and tenth child of the Revd William Jowitt (1834–1912) and his wife, Louisa Margaret, daughter of John Allen of Oldfield Hall, Altrincham, Cheshire. In 1892 he was sent to Northaw Place School, Potters Bar, Hertfordshire, where Clement Attlee was his contemporary. In January 1899 he went to Marlborough College, where he stayed until 1903. Here he taught himself Russian. He entered New College, Oxford, where in 1906 he gained first-class honours in jurisprudence. He was made an honorary fellow of his college in 1947. He was admitted to the Middle Temple on 15 November 1906, was called to the bar in June 1909, and practised on the western circuit.

Jowitt entered political life immediately, and in the general elections of 1910 he was active as a Liberal. On 19 December 1913 he married Lesley (d. 1970), the second daughter of James Patrick M'Intyre. (The M'Intyre family were neighbours of the Attlees in Putney.) They had one daughter. In 1914 Jowitt enlisted in the Royal Naval Air Service and served as an able seaman until, having repeatedly been declared medically unfit, he was discharged. In later life it was said against him that, because he had not done military or civilian service, he was able to build up a successful commercial practice.

In 1918 Jowitt was adopted as Liberal candidate for Hartlepool. He was elected to parliament in 1922, in the same year in which he took silk. However, he lost his seat in the 1924 general election. While he was out of parliament he served as a member of the royal commission on lunacy and mental disorder. In 1927, when informally approached by the Labour Party, Jowitt declared his willingness to serve a future Labour government. In 1929 he was elected Liberal MP for Preston, a seat to which he had been allocated at his own request. However, immediately after the election he received a personal appeal from Ramsay MacDonald, a close friend, to be attorney-general in the new Labour government, because of the shortage of suitable Labour lawyer MPs. After a painful interview with Lloyd George, Jowitt accepted, and received the usual knighthood on taking office. He resigned his seat and stood again as a Labour candidate, and on 31 July he was returned as Labour MP for Preston, with a greatly increased majority. This episode did Jowitt lasting damage, as he received severe criticism from the bar and from all political parties, and he and his wife were ostracized. Reflecting on his career in November 1931, he expressed a wish 'to have some convictions', which goes some way to explain the lack of trust in him (*Political Diary of Hugh Dalton*, 163).

William Allen Jowitt, Earl Jowitt (1885–1957), by Sir Gerald
Kelly, exh. RA 1957

As attorney-general, Jowitt prosecuted Clarence Hatry
for fraud, and in 1931 he appeared for the crown in the
prosecution of Lord Kylsant, the chairman of the Royal
Mail Steam Packet Company. This inevitably high-profile
prosecution of a member of the House of Lords had to be
handled with great delicacy, as Jowitt was anxious not to
put forward a case that might fail, as had the Campbell
case in 1924, with disastrous consequences for the government. Kylsant was convicted of having published a false
prospectus.

Jowitt was sworn of the privy council in 1931. In August
of that year, with Sankey, he supported MacDonald on the
break-up of the Labour government and supported the
new National Government to which he was reappointed
attorney-general. He was expelled from the Labour Party,
and in October stood as National Labour candidate for the
Combined English Universities, although he had previously advocated the abolition of the university franchise.
He was defeated and returned to the bar. A year later Mac-
Donald put some pressure on the Conservative Party to
find a seat for Jowitt, but without success, and at this
moment, he seriously considered retiring from politics.

In 1934 Jowitt appeared for the defence in the successful
case for libel brought by Princess Yousoupoff against
Metro-Goldwyn-Mayer. In 1936 he was readmitted to the
Labour Party and in 1939 he was re-elected to parliament
for Ashton under Lyne in an unopposed by-election.

In May 1940 Churchill appointed Jowitt solicitor-general
in the wartime coalition government. He remained there
until March 1942, when he was appointed paymaster-
general. In that capacity he was made chairman of the
reconstruction problems committee, and commissioned

a survey on public opinion about issues to be faced after
the war. The results went far to support the recommendations of the Beveridge report, which was published later
that year. As minister without portfolio from November
1942, Jowitt served on the 1944 reconstruction committee,
chaired by Woolton. He had been offered another more
important position, thought to be chief justice of India,
but this he had declined. For the last months of the war,
from October 1944 until May 1945, he was minister of
national insurance. He introduced a white paper on
national insurance, and in March 1945 brought forward
the Family Allowances Bill which was delayed by the
general election. He took a leading role in the preparation
of the Industrial Injuries Bill which was later introduced
by the Labour government.

Lord chancellor and after After the general election in July
1945, Jowitt was pessimistic about his future, but Attlee
made him lord chancellor. He received the great seal on 28
July 1945 and took the title Baron Jowitt, of Stevenage,
Hertfordshire. In January 1947 he was made Viscount
Jowitt. The new government's legislative programme was
unprecedentedly heavy, and the burden on Jowitt, as one
of the leading ministers in a largely hostile House of
Lords, was great. He saw through the Town and Country
Planning Act 1947 and the Companies Act 1948, both
major acts outside his own departmental responsibilities.

Within his own field, Jowitt oversaw a burst of legislative activity. The government had accepted the recommendations of the Rushcliffe report on legal aid. Jowitt
introduced the Legal Aid and Advice Bill, which gave the
poor the full protection of the law for the first time, and
was an important plank in the government's welfare programme. Following the report of a royal commission,
Jowitt reformed the system of appointment of justices of
the peace. His aim was to ensure that only the best candidates were appointed, whatever their politics, and to
underline the lord chancellor's superiority over the local
advisory committees. In 1948 he brought forward the
Criminal Justice Bill. He had been opposed to the suspension of the death penalty, but a free vote in its favour had
been taken in the House of Commons and Jowitt advised
that a suspension should be tried. However, the proposal
was defeated by a large majority in the House of Lords.

The size of the civil service and the armed forces and
crown estate increasingly emphasized the difficulties
caused by the fact that it was impossible to sue the crown
in tort and in contract except by a petition of right. Jowitt
met these problems with the Crown Proceedings Act 1947,
a major reform of administrative law. Heuston has
praised Jowitt for taking an unusual interest, not just in
reform by statute, but in the reform of statute (Heuston,
128). He tackled the long-running problem of the condition of the statute book, which he described as 'a scandal'
(ibid., 116). Jowitt's Consolidation of Enactments (Procedure) Act, 1949, provided an improved procedure for consolidation bills in every session of parliament to remove
anomalies, doubts, and unnecessary provisions from
existing legislation.

The Labour government was fortunate to have Jowitt in the House of Lords for his political skills, especially his diplomacy and his effective advocacy, which stood the government in good stead. He was a loyal, if detached, member of cabinet, though he was not appreciated by some. Dalton considered him to be weak, 'useless as a politician' and with 'an unfailing capacity to accept impossible jobs under undignified circumstances' (*War Diary of Hugh Dalton*, 668). However, Jowitt had strong views on some matters. He shared with Chuter Ede, the home secretary, misgivings about the Roman Catholic faith. In 1949 Pope Pius XII appeared to say that judges who were Roman Catholics were unable to grant civil divorces. Jowitt threatened to bar the appointment of Catholic judges until he exacted confirmation that the pope's remarks did not have this effect in practice (Stevens, 86–88). However, his judicial appointments are regarded as fair and without political bias. He took pride in the fact that it was now firmly established that the man best able to fill the position was appointed, and that in so doing, both 'politics' and 'influence' were disregarded (Heuston, 119).

After the defeat of the Labour government in October 1951, Jowitt, who surrendered the great seal on 30 October, was created Earl Jowitt (24 December 1951). In retirement he became leader of the opposition in the House of Lords, where the work load was heavy. He took part in the debates on Suez in 1956, criticizing the government for bringing the country's reputation into disrepute. He continued his interest in law reform, and he also sat judicially. He was treasurer of the Middle Temple in 1952.

Jowitt was a considerable patron of the arts. He had a fine private collection of paintings by Matisse, Boudin, Bonnard, and Duncan Grant, and he was a trustee of both the National Gallery and the Tate Gallery. (He is depicted in his lord chancellor's robes in the mosaic by Boris Anrep at the entrance of the National Gallery.) Jowitt and his wife had friends in the Bloomsbury group, and their circle included such continental politicians as Jan Masaryk.

In retirement Jowitt published three books. The first, *Some were Spies* (1954), was on cases in which he had been involved at the bar. He also edited a *Dictionary of English Law* which was published after his death. His most controversial book, published in 1953, was a study of Alger Hiss. In this he doubted the conviction of Hiss, but he was criticized both in England and America for being ingenuous about the nature of communist conspiracy. Jowitt died at West Lodge, Bradfield St George, Suffolk, on 16 August 1957, and was buried in his parents' grave at St Nicholas Church, Stevenage. He was survived by his wife.

THOMAS S. LEGG and MARIE-LOUISE LEGG

Sources R. F. V. Heuston, *Lives of the lord chancellors, 1940–1970* (1987) · *The Second World War diary of Hugh Dalton, 1940–1945*, ed. B. Pimlott (1986) · *The political diary of Hugh Dalton, 1918–1940, 1945–1960*, ed. B. Pimlott (1986) · D. Marquand, *Ramsay MacDonald* (1977) · Lord Shawcross, *Life sentence: memoirs* (1995) · H. A. C. Sturgess, ed., *Register of admissions to the Honourable Society of the Middle Temple, from the fifteenth century to the year 1944*, 2 (1949) · *WWBMP* · R. Stevens, *The independence of the judiciary: the view from the lord chancellor's office* (1993)

Archives NRA, priv. coll., corresp. and papers · PRO, corresp. and MSS, CAB 127/159–193 | CUL, corresp. with Samuel Hoare · HLRO, corresp. with Lord Beaverbrook · JRL, corresp. with Ramsay Macdonald · Welwyn Garden City Central Library, corresp. with Frederick Osborn | FILM BFI NFTVA, news footage · BFI NFTVA, records footage | SOUND BL NSA, performance recording
Likenesses A. McEvoy, oils, 1912, Tate collection · G. C. Beresford, photograph, 1914, NPG · W. Stoneman, two photographs, 1923–42, NPG · H. Coster, photographs, 1930–31, NPG · B. Anrep, gouache drawing, c.1952, V&A · B. Anrep, mosaic, 1952, National Gallery, London · G. Kelly, oils, exh. RA 1957, Middle Temple, London [*see illus.*] · W. Coldstream, oils
Wealth at death £104,727 18s. 2d.: probate, 8 Oct 1957, CGPLA Eng. & Wales

Joy, David (1825–1903), engineer and inventor, was born on 3 March 1825 in Leeds, one of the five sons of Edward Joy, oil-mill owner of Leeds, and his wife, Ruth. He showed keen interest in machinery from his early days and made ship and engine models, including a charcoal-fired model locomotive which ran at the Leeds exhibition in 1838. In 1840 he went to Wesley College, Sheffield, where he studied engineering drawing and read in particular Thomas Tredgold's *The Steam Engine* (1st edn, 1827).

Joy entered his father's seed-crushing and oil-refining works in 1841. He then started an apprenticeship with Fenton, Murray, and Jackson, locomotive builders. When this firm closed down in 1843 he transferred to the locomotive drawing office of the railway foundry works, Leeds, of Shepherd and Todd, where he became acting chief draughtsman. Here in 1847 he designed the famous Jenny Lind 2-2-2 type express locomotive for the London, Brighton, and South Coast Railway. Tested on the Midland Railway in the following year, one of these machines averaged 56 m.p.h. for 65 miles. This type had considerable influence on locomotive design for many years. In 1850 Joy and Edward Wilson patented twin boilers working in parallel within the same casing.

In 1850 Joy became superintendent of the Ambergate, Nottingham, Boston, and Eastern Junction Railway and in 1853 of the Oxford, Worcester, and Wolverhampton, both of which were operated under contract by E. B. Wilson & Co. Here all his skill and experience were fully stretched in keeping the service running despite frequent breakdowns of second-hand and unsatisfactory locomotives. Returning to the railway foundry in 1855, he was involved in the building of the 'farm engine' of Robert Willis, the forerunner of the tractor and road locomotive, and in 1857 built a double expansion marine engine with innovative features. In 1859 he became manager of De Bergue's, bridge builders of Manchester, and took out patents for an improved steam hammer, whose manufacture was started in his own Cleveland engine works in Middlesbrough.

In 1874 Joy went to the Barrow Shipbuilding Company as manager of the water-tube boiler department, becoming secretary in 1876. In 1879, following several years' work, he patented his radial valve gear, of simple and compact design, to give improved steam distribution in locomotive and marine engines. This was applied in 1880 to a new London and North Western Railway (LNWR) design of 0-6-0 freight locomotive. Well over 3000 loco-motives of the LNWR, Lancashire and Yorkshire, and other railways were fitted with Joy's valve gear, which was also applied by Maudslay & Co. to marine engines, where a saving of 25 per cent in space and weight was achieved.

In 1867 Joy married Kate, daughter of C. F. Humbert of Watford. They had three sons and two daughters. In 1882 Joy, with his sons, set up an engineering consultancy prac-tice in Westminster to continue and develop applications of his inventions, which included a revolving gun and an organ blower. Among his many inventions one of the most important, for which he was awarded a gold medal at the 1885 inventions exhibition, was the conjugating mechanism enabling the three valves of a triple-expansion marine engine to be driven by only two sets of valve gear. Thirty years later this principle was applied by others to locomotives, and over 3000 were so equipped in Britain, Germany, and elsewhere. He was a member of the Institution of Civil Engineers, of the Institution of Mech-anical Engineers, and of the Institution of Naval Archi-tects in England and in the USA.

Joy died at his home, 118 Broadhurst Gardens, Hamp-stead, London, on 14 March 1903. He was survived by his wife. GEORGE W. CARPENTER, rev.

Sources Institution of Mechanical Engineers: Proceedings (1903), 357–60 • C. Hamilton Ellis, 'Famous locomotive engineers, 14, David Joy', Locomotive, Railway Carriage and Wagon Review (15 June 1940) • H. A. V. Bulleid, The Aspinall era (1967) • CGPLA Eng. & Wales (1903) • The Oxford companion to British railway history (1997)
Archives Institution of Mechanical Engineers, London, collected locomotive engineering drawings | Sci. Mus., diaries with dia-grams and drawings
Likenesses photograph, repro. in Hamilton Ellis, 'Famous loco-motive engineers'
Wealth at death £1595 19s. 7d.: probate, 24 April 1903, CGPLA Eng. & Wales

Joy, Francis (1697–1790), printer and paper manufacturer, was born on 3 August 1697, probably in Belfast. Family legend claimed that he was descended from Captain Thomas Joy, a follower of Arthur Chichester, Baron Chich-ester of Belfast, but this has not been firmly established. Joy's early career is unclear. He may possibly be the Fran-cis Joy of Carrickfergus, gentleman, who signed a deed of lease dated 9 October 1727. A fanciful account in A Series of Genuine Letters between Henry and Frances (1757) states that Joy had been a tailor and that on becoming a printer he 'made the types, the ink, the paper and the press' (Griffith and Griffith, 98). This tale may have its origin in his later petition to the House of Commons of Ireland in which he claimed to have had printing presses constructed in Bel-fast. Madden described him as a notary public and convey-ancer, and claimed that he received a printing establish-ment in payment of a debt. At some point before 1719 or 1720, Joy married Margaret (1690–1745), daughter of Rob-ert Martin of Belfast; together they had at least two sons: Henry *Joy (1719/20–1789) and Robert *Joy (1722–1785) [see under Joy, Henry].

Joy's name appears on book imprints between 1737 and 1749, but he is most famous for the founding in 1737 of Bel-fast's first newspaper (and Ireland's second provincial newspaper), the Belfast News-Letter, of which the earliest extant issue is no. 152 for 16 February 1738, printed by Joy at the sign of the Peacock in Bridge Street. Joy had moved to the Peacock premises in 1737 and remained there until 1746. Paper was in short supply and in 1740, in partnership with two other Belfast printers, Samuel Wilson and James Magee, Joy took leases of a paper mill at Ballymena and two paper mills at Ballygrooby near Randalstown, co. Antrim. A deed of the partnership dated 19 January 1741 stipulates that Joy was to be the operator of the mills. It is unclear how soon Joy was using his own paper for print-ing, but the first acknowledgement by the Belfast News-Letter that it was being printed on paper made at these mills came on 10 June 1746. Joy twice petitioned the House of Commons of Ireland for assistance in his paper mak-ing, with his first petition of 10 November 1747 boasting that he had erected three paper engines in the previous four years. His bid in this instance proved unsuccessful but in his second petition, dated 6 November 1749, Joy pro-duced a more elaborate recital of his benefit to the public in printing, press manufacture, paper making, and involvement in linen bleaching, and on 9 November 1749 he was granted £200. By now, however, his sons were run-ning the printing business, having taken charge of the Bel-fast News-Letter from 1745, although it was not until 12 March 1746 that it displayed 'F. Joy and Sons' on the mast-head, the imprint specifying that it had been 'printed by Henry and Robert Joy'.

Griffith suggested Joy 'retired upon an easy fortune' before 1752 (in which year he was living in Antrim town) but this is misleading, as he continued to work in paper manufacturing (Griffith and Griffith, 98). He leased one of his mills to William Courtney, a linen draper, in January 1760 (when he was recorded as a resident of Feehoge in co. Antrim) and the other two in May 1780 to Henry and Her-cules Ellis (by which time he had moved to Randalstown). Joy died in Randalstown on 10 June 1790, the notice in the Belfast News-Letter of 11 June giving his age (erroneously) as ninety-three. He had evidently remarried, to a woman named Ann, and he had at least four children. Both Henry and Robert predeceased their father, with the Belfast News-Letter being passed to Henry, Robert's son; the family retained control of the newspaper until 15 May 1795, when it was sold to a Scotsman named George Gordon. C. J. BENSON

Sources Belfast News-Letter (1738–95) • registry of deeds, Dublin, Memorials 54/490/36526, 107/32/73078, 154/324/107072, 207/25/135061, 254/483/169162, 332/148/223771 • R. Griffith and E. Griffith, A series of genuine letters between Henry and Frances, 3 (1770), 98 • G. Benn, A history of the town of Belfast, 2 vols. (1877–80) • The journals of the House of Commons of the kingdom of Ireland, 21 vols. (1796–1802) • R. Maddan, The United Irishmen: their lives and times (1843) • 'The note-book of an Irish barrister, no.IX', Metropolitan Magazine, 22 (1838), 337–55 • Burtchaell & Sadleir, Alum. Dubl., 2nd edn • F. E. Ball, The judges in Ireland, 1221–1921, 2 vols. (1926) • ESTC [web page, consulted Jan 2002]

Joy, Henry (1719/20–1789), newspaper proprietor and benefactor, was born in Belfast, the first of three children of Francis *Joy (1697–1790), printer and paper maker, and his wife, Margaret (1690–1745), daughter of Robert Martin of Belfast. The family was descended from Calvinist stock who moved to Ireland in the early seventeenth century. Nothing of Henry's early life is known except that he trained as a lawyer. The family's fortunes changed when in 1737 Francis Joy founded the *Belfast News-Letter* (Ireland's second oldest provincial newspaper) after apparently receiving the printing press in lieu of a bad debt. Faced with a shortage of paper, Francis Joy developed the family business to include papermaking, first in Ballymena and then in 1745 at Randalstown, where he installed a larger mill.

Henry Joy and his brother, **Robert Joy** (1722–1785), took charge of the *Belfast News-Letter* from their father in the same year, and gained full control several years later. In 1767 the brothers acquired a site at Cromac for a new paper mill (Joy's paper mill, now commemorated by Joy Street, Belfast). In the following decade the newspaper became a mouthpiece for Henry Joy's support of the pro-Fox whig cause, and carried articles defending the American revolutionaries. In addition to the *Newsletter* the firm of Henry and Robert Joy also printed and published books, with Henry acting as the company's notary. Paper printed by the firm bore a watermark with their name, the initials in the form of a ligature.

Over the following decade the Joys emerged as one of Belfast's most notable entrepreneurial families. In 1777 Robert Joy conceived a scheme to introduce cotton manufacture into Ireland, and, together with Thomas McCabe, he installed the machinery necessary to teach poorhouse children to spin and weave cotton. Two years later the first cotton spinning mill was built in Whitehouse by Nicholas Grimshaw, followed by that of Messrs Joy, McCabe, and McCracken (the Joys' brother-in-law and father of the radical politician Henry Joy *McCracken). This mill, opened in Belfast, was the first in Ireland powered by water.

Alongside entrepreneurship the Joys combined public duty and charity. In 1745 Henry Joy was one of the volunteers who garrisoned Carrickfergus Castle when it was rumoured that the Young Pretender (Charles Edward Stuart) was attempting an invasion of the Antrim coast from Scotland. Henry was also a leading member of the Belfast Charitable Society (founded in 1752), acting as one of three 'key carriers' of the society's chest, kept at his house in High Street, Belfast; his press also printed the lottery tickets by which the society raised funds. In addition the Joys were involved in building the north Belfast poorhouse, for which Henry signed the lease and Robert drew the architectural plans in 1771; both brothers provided money and materials for the building. Between 1759 and 1772 Henry Joy served as Belfast's deputy town clerk. In 1778 he and Robert were among the first members of the 1st Belfast volunteer company, a local defence force established after the declaration of war with France; both brothers remained members after the volunteers became a political force campaigning for the legislative independence of Ireland. In 1781 Henry was elected a burgess of the town and two years later a founding member of the Belfast chamber of commerce. Heavily involved in providing facilities for marketing white linens in Belfast, he contributed in the same year (1783) to the building of the town's White Linen Hall.

Henry Joy was married to Barbara Dunbar (*d.* 1777?), daughter of George Dunbar of Belfast; they had ten children, six daughters and four sons, including Henry Joy (1766–1838), who became chief baron of the Irish exchequer in 1831. Joy died, aged sixty-nine, on 20 January 1789, in Belfast, where he was buried. Just before his death the citizens of Belfast honoured him with a cup, expressing to him their 'gratitude for the innumerable services rendered by him in a long series of years to his fellow citizens'. His obituary in the January edition of *Walker's Hibernian Magazine* likewise emphasized his philanthropy, describing him as a man of 'correct, amiable, and engaging' manners, 'an invaluable friend of all … [who] died without the enmity of any'. On his death the proprietorship of the *Belfast News-Letter* passed to Henry, the son of Robert Joy, who had died in 1785.

BRIGITTE ANTON

Sources Linen Hall Library, Belfast, Blackwood pedigrees, no. 24 · M. McNeill, *The life and times of Mary Ann McCracken, 1770–1866: a Belfast panorama* (1960); repr. (1988) · G. Benn, *A history of the town of Belfast from the earliest times to the close of the eighteenth century*, 2 vols. (1877–80) · R. W. H. Strain, *Belfast and its charitable society* (1961) · R. M. Young, *Historical notes of Old Belfast and its vicinity* (1896) · Linen Hall Library, Belfast, Joy MSS · *Walker's Hibernian Magazine* (Jan 1789), 56

Archives Linen Hall Library, Belfast, papers · NL Ire., department of manuscripts, pedigree of Joy of Belfast, MS. 173, pp. 96–7 · Ulster Museum, Belfast, indenture for lease of ground in High Street, Belfast | PRO NIre., lease given by earl of Donegal for a building in High Street, D. 652/26 · PRO NIre., Donegal estate documents, leases to Henry and Robert Joy, D. 509/255–7 · PRO NIre., genealogical notes on the Joy, Beatty, Cowan, Bingham, Close, Cunningham and Norwood families, T. 1289 · TCD, Madden papers: McCracken letters

Wealth at death property on east side of Linenhall Street, and on south side of High Street; 'a considerable sum' of money advanced to son George, and sums to sons Henry and James, and daughter: will, PRO NIre.

Joy, John Cantiloe (1806–1859). *See under* Joy, William (*b.* 1803, *d.* in or after 1859).

Joy, Robert (1722–1785). *See under* Joy, Henry (1719/20–1789).

Joy, Thomas Musgrave [Thomas Musgrove] (1812–1866), genre and portrait painter, born on 9 July 1812 at Boughton Hall, Boughton Monchelsea, near Maidstone, Kent, was the only son of the local squire, Thomas Joy, and his wife, Susanah Tomkin. Although at first discouraged in his early predilection for art, he was sent to London to study under Samuel Drummond. In 1831 he exhibited at the Royal Academy for the first time; from the following year, until his death, he exhibited frequently at the Society of British Artists and at the British Institution. His charming conversation and appearance attracted the patronage of Lord Panmure, who placed John Phillip with him as a pupil and encouraged him to study in Paris. A commission from Lord Panmure to paint the portraits of Grace and William Darling, and a dramatic re-creation of

Thomas Musgrave
Joy (1812–1866),
self-portrait, c.1839

the *Wreck of the 'Forfarshire'* (1839, McManus Galleries, Dundee), was particularly welcome: it enabled him to marry Eliza Rohde Spratt in the autumn of 1839, after a seven-year engagement.

In 1841, following a visit by Prince Albert to his studio, Joy was commissioned by Queen Victoria to paint portraits of the young prince of Wales and the princess royal (Royal Collection, Windsor Castle, Berkshire). He also painted several portraits of the queen's favourite dogs. Although he was best-known for his subject pictures—such as *Le bourgeois gentilhomme* (exh. RA, 1842), *A Medical Consultation* (exh. RA, 1853), and *Prayer* (1865)—throughout the 1840s and early 1850s he was also in some demand as a portrait painter. His sitters included Sir Charles Napier and the duke of Cambridge. In 1864 he painted *Meeting of the Subscribers to Tattersall's before the Races*, which contained portraits of the most noted characters in horse-racing at the bloodstock auctioneers. His successful career as a portrait painter was brought to a close when he began to withdraw from society following the death of his young son (possibly in 1857). However, he continued to produce genre and literary pictures, and his *Art Journal* obituary suggested that his habits of overwork contributed to a fatal attack of bronchitis. He died suddenly at his home, 32 St George's Square, Pimlico, London, on 7 April 1866; his wife survived him. A sale of his remaining works was held at Christies on 18 June 1866; examples of his work are in the Victoria and Albert Museum, London. One of his two daughters, Mary Eliza *Haweis (1848–1898), was herself a portrait painter as well as a writer and illustrator.

SUZANNE FAGENCE COOPER

Sources *Art Journal*, 28 (1866), 240 • *Catalogue of the remaining pictures and sketches of that talented artist, the late T. M. Joy* (1866) [sale catalogue, Christie, Manson, and Woods Ltd, London, Monday 18 June 1866] • B. Howe, 'A forgotten Victorian painter', *Country Life*, 132 (1962), 792–5 • Graves, *Brit. Inst.*, 312–5 • Graves, *RA exhibitors* • P. McEvansoneya, 'Joy, Thomas Musgrave', *The dictionary of art*, ed. J. Turner (1996) • Bryan, *Painters* (1903–5) • M. A. Wingfield, *A dictionary of sporting artists, 1650–1990* (1992), 162 • R. Parkinson, ed., *Catalogue of British oil paintings, 1820–1860* (1990) [catalogue of V&A] • *CGPLA Eng. & Wales* (1866) • D. Millar, *The Victorian watercolours and drawings in the collection of her majesty the queen*, 2 vols. (1995), 127–8
Likenesses T. M. Joy, self-portrait, oils, c.1839, priv. coll. [*see illus.*]

Wealth at death under £3000: administration, 5 Sept 1866, *CGPLA Eng. & Wales*

Joy [Joyce], **William** (1675?–1734), strongman, was apparently born on 2 May 1675 at St Lawrence, near Ramsgate, Kent. He first attracted public attention about 1699 when he held a series of performances at the Dorset Garden Theatre in London. The theatre had previously seen the original productions of many of Thomas Otway's plays, and its debasement by the 'English Samson' excited adverse comment: the satirist Tom Brown remarked in a letter to George Moult of 12 September 1699 that:

> the strong Kentish man (of whom you have heard so many stories) has, as I told you above, taken up his quarters in Dorset Gardens, and how they'll get him out again the Lord knows, for he threatens to thrash all the poets if they pretend to disturb him. (*Works*, 4.217–18)

Likewise, George Farquhar complained of the wrong done to the theatre by 'that strong dog Samson', who 'snaps rope like thread', in the prologue to *The Constant Couple*, written late in 1699.

Joy, who was by all accounts no particularly large man, performed feats of strength, such as breaking a rope which had borne 3500 pounds in weight, lifting a stone weighing 2240 pounds from the ground, pulling up a tree whose trunk was a yard and a half in circumference, and competing with carthorses in tests of strength. On 7 December 1699 he was billed to perform with Richard Joy, who was possibly his brother, and in January 1700 his sister was also advertised for feats of strength. On 15 November 1699 he performed for William III at Kensington Palace, and in December the king went to see him at the playhouse. In 1701 he took a booth at the Bartholomew fair, but his vogue was relatively short-lived. Joy was reported to have later 'followed the Infamous Practice of Smugling [sic]' (Lewis, 189), and to have drowned in 1734.

THOMAS SECCOMBE, rev. K. D. REYNOLDS

Sources Highfill, Burnim & Langhans, *BDA* • J. Caulfield, *Portraits, memoirs, and characters of remarkable persons, from the reign of Edward the Third, to the revolution*, 2 vols. (1794–5) • *Kirby's wonderful … museum*, 6 vols. (1803–20), vol. 1, p. 359 • *The works of Mr Thomas Brown*, ed. J. Drake, 3rd edn, 4 vols. (1715) • J. Lewis, *The history and antiquities, ecclesiastical and civil, of the Isle of Tenet, in Kent* (1723)
Likenesses J. F., etching, 1699, BM; repro. in Caulfield, *Portraits, memoirs, and characters* • P. van den Berge, etching, BM

Joy, William (*b.* 1803, *d.* in or after 1859), marine painter, was born in Great Yarmouth, Norfolk. His younger brother, **John Cantiloe Joy** (1806–1859), also a marine painter, was also born in Great Yarmouth; they were known as the brothers Joy in the nineteenth-century art world. Their mother's maiden name was Cantiloe, and their father was for many years guard on the Great Yarmouth to Ipswich mail coach. They both showed an early talent for drawing, and while attending Mr Wright's Southtown Academy in Great Yarmouth made sketches of the school which were engraved. Recognizing their potential, the barrack-master, Captain G. W. Manby, gave them the use of a room overlooking the sea in the Royal Hospital at Great Yarmouth; here they practised drawing and painting the sea and shipping from life.

About 1830 the brothers Joy moved to the south of England, under the patronage of the earl of Abergavenny, and, while living in London, studied the work of established painters. They gained a considerable reputation and received commissions from naval patrons such as Admiral Sir Charles Cunningham and Sir Jaheel Brenton. Although they often worked together on the same composition, they also produced individual works. Both exhibited, but not regularly, William at the Royal Academy in 1824 and 1832 and the British Institution in 1823 and 1845, and both at the Suffolk Street Gallery. Unusual among their works is an early collaborative watercolour, *King George IV Passing Great Ormesby, Yarmouth, on his Return from Edinburgh, 1822* (V&A). A contemporary commented that 'they greatly excelled in depicting water in motion, they put their vessels well upon it and were accurate in the display of sails and rigging' (Palmer). Examples of their work can be found in a number of national and regional collections, including the Victoria and Albert Museum, the National Maritime Museum, Greenwich, and the Maritime Museum for East Anglia, Great Yarmouth.

The brothers Joy spent their later years working in Chichester, Sussex. They are generally believed to have died within a short space of one another: a death certificate for John Cantiloe Joy establishes that he died on 9 August 1859 at 15 King Street, Soho, London; his brother William was present at his death.

LINDSEY MACFARLANE

Sources C. J. Palmer, *The perlustration of Great Yarmouth*, 3 (1875), 278 · Redgrave, *Artists*, 2nd edn · C. Miller, 'Captain Manby and the Joy brothers', diss., U. Cam., 1975 · L. Lambourne and J. Hamilton, eds., *British watercolours in the Victoria and Albert Museum* (1980) · d. cert. [J. C. Joy]

Joyce, Archibald (1873–1963), composer, was born on 25 May 1873 in Belgravia, London, the son of a band sergeant in the Grenadier Guards. He went to school in Paddington, sang as a boy chorister, and learned the piano and violin. From his teens, Joyce worked as a pianist at various dance schools in the West End, occasionally also playing for music-halls, hotels, restaurants, transatlantic liners, and private balls. About 1900 he began taking bookings for his own ensemble, the Archibald Joyce Dance Orchestra, whose reputation grew until he needed no other employment. Its numbers varied: a large orchestra supplied music for aristocratic balls during the London season; the core musicians then went on tour, performing at seaside pavilions and great houses.

From arranging dance medleys, Joyce progressed to composing. His first publication, a two-step, 'The Moke's Parade' (1905), made no great mark. The waltz 'Sweet Memories' did better in 1908, when he hit on his winning formula with 'Songe d'automne'. A succession of similar waltzes followed: 'Vision d'amour' (1909), 'A jamais' (1909), 'A Thousand Kisses' (1910), 'Charming' (1912), 'Maiden's Blush' (1913), 'Entrancing' (1914), 'Love's Mystery' (1915), and others. The appeal of 'Vision of Salome' (1909), with transient modulations to minor keys to evoke the mysterious East, warranted three sequels with her name in the title. By far his greatest triumph, however,

was 'Dreaming' (1911), which swept the ballrooms of the world, selling a million copies in a decade. Over forty different recordings of it were made in the twentieth century.

Joyce's publishers, Ascherberg, Hopwood, and Crew, marketed him as 'The English Waltz King', implying a comparison to Johann Strauss the younger that cannot be taken seriously. He was more directly inspired by Franz Lehár—in particular, by the waltz duet from act II of *The Merry Widow* (running in London 1907–9), which established the vogue for dreamy smoothness as opposed to exuberant brilliance. The typical Joyce waltz comprised a very brief introduction followed by three slow, sentimental melodies, with the main one much repeated before a soft coda. Even if he never quite equalled the sensuous quality achieved by Lehár or Leo Fall, he did well to compete at all, for British composers had failed to produce much original dance music in the nineteenth century. Joyce announced himself the first Englishman to have waltzes published on the continent. Then, in 1912, Sydney Baynes's 'Destiny' and Charles Ancliffe's 'Nights of Gladness' joined Joyce's 'Dreaming' as defining examples of 'the English waltz'.

The Archibald Joyce Dance Orchestra ceased to be a permanent body after 1914, as many of its members enlisted. By then, its founder owned a large house beside Clapham Common and a car (for motoring was his hobby). He married Florence Mary (b. 1888/9), daughter of William Alfred Latter, a farmer's manager, on 28 July 1919.

Though Joyce had sometimes conducted in the theatre, notably for Ellen Terry, and his style echoed musical comedy, he wrote only twice for the stage. *Toto*, a flimsy tale of 'Gay Paree', jointly composed with Merlin Morgan, ran a mediocre seventy-seven nights in London in 1916 but toured until 1920. He collaborated with G. H. Clutsam on *Gabrielle*, which, without ever reaching the West End, did good enough business in the provinces 1921–4.

The visit of the Original Dixieland Jazz Band to London in 1919 transformed popular dance music. Like many Edwardian musicians, Joyce fled saxophones, banjos, and syncopated foxtrots, leaving the dance-halls to younger men. He found refuge in the emergent genre of British light music, and, although he was no Albert Ketèlbey or Eric Coates, resort orchestras and amateur pianists happily filled out their repertories with his polka 'Frou Frou', suites like 'Caravan', and sundry marches and novelty pieces.

Joyce abandoned inner London in 1927, moving to Bexhill-on-Sea and then in 1932 to his last home in Sutton, Surrey. After a fallow decade, the advent of 'old tyme' dancing in the 1940s elicited a flurry of late works, such as 'Brighton Hike', a sprightly military two-step, but even the nostalgia market had faded away by the time of his death from heart failure at 75 Langley Park Road, Sutton, on 22 March 1963. Thereafter his name appeared only in connection with the claim that 'Songe d'automne' was the final piece played on the *Titanic*. However, a compact disc in 1996 salvaged a selection of his music from oblivion.

JASON TOMES

Sources P. Scowcroft, *British light music* (1997) · *WW* · K. Gänzl, *The British musical theatre*, 2 (1986) · *The Times* (23 March 1963) · *The Gramophone* (March 1996) · m. cert. · d. cert.

Joyce, Eileen Alannah (1912–1991), pianist, was born Eileen Joyce (she acquired her middle name, Alannah, later) on 21 November 1912 near Zeehan, Tasmania, the only child of Joseph Joyce, a failed mining prospector and itinerant labourer of Irish descent, and his wife, Alice, of Spanish descent. She was reportedly born in a tent, her only home during her earliest years, and went barefoot with only a pet kangaroo named Twink for company. Later she was taken by her parents to the Australian mainland, where the family lived in an iron shack in the outback of Western Australia, between Perth and the town of Boulder. A priest found her a place at the Loreto Convent School, Osborne, where one teacher was Esther Pickering (mother of Sir John Drummond, controller of BBC Radio 3 and director of the Henry Wood Promenade Concerts). She was obliged to sit with other non-paying pupils at the back of the class and was usually known as Ragged Eilie. An instinctive musicality began to appear unbidden whenever she was near a piano, and she soon learned the rudiments of music (and of civilized living) from the instruction she received there. The school authorities brought her to the attention of the Australian composer–pianist Percy Grainger when he was visiting the area in 1926 (she was then aged fourteen). The 'rebellious red-head' (as Esther Drummond remembered her) was to Grainger 'the most transcendentally gifted child' he had ever heard, an opinion endorsed by the famous German pianist Wilhelm Backhaus while on an Australian tour.

Backhaus urged that Joyce should be sent to his own alma mater, the Leipzig conservatory, an idea that could not be entertained in her existing circumstances until Grainger added deeds to words and took it on himself to lead a fund-raising campaign for her. In due course the inexperienced girl was shipped out alone to what must have been the terrifying environment of a leading European music centre, where not merely the language was alien; she regrettably left no account of how she adjusted to this change. She spent three years in Leipzig as a pupil first of Max Pauer, the conservatory director, and then of the redoubtable Robert Teichmuller, a martinet-style teacher whose methods almost broke her spirit but effectively laid the foundations of her astonishing technical facility. This was polished later in London by Tobias Matthay (Uncle Tobs to her) and Adelina de Lara, the last surviving pupil of Clara Schumann, who featured Eileen Joyce in some duet performances, then by the distinguished Artur Schnabel in Berlin.

Joyce's brief but brilliant professional career began in earnest when Teichmuller introduced her to the conductor Albert Coates, for whom she performed Prokofiev's third concerto, then a rarity on account of its technical difficulty. Much impressed, Coates recommended her to Sir Henry Wood, with whom she made her major début at his 1930 Promenade Concerts playing the same concerto, followed some months later by the even rarer Busoni *Konzert-Fantasie* for piano and orchestra, and

Eileen Alannah Joyce (1912–1991), by Elliott & Fry, 1946

then by Franck's *Symphonic Variations* under Sir Thomas Beecham. During the 1930s her repertory multiplied at a prodigious rate and came to number some seventy-five concertos and over 500 solo works.

Joyce had begun to make gramophone records even in advance of her formal concert début as a result of the odd circumstances of her fortuitous introduction to the medium. To prepare herself for an audition she went to the Parlophone studios to make a private recording of the Liszt F minor étude, *La leggierezza*, to check on her performance. Returning to collect the disc and pay the fee, she was politely refused and instead invited by the label's director to record something else for the other side. This she did, playing a dazzling flamboyant study in A♭ by Paul de Schlozer. Parlophone, amazed, paid her a fee and turned the recordings into her first public issue. Her performances of both pieces were included on a CD issued much later by EMI Records, *The Eileen Joyce Album*.

On 16 September 1937 Joyce married Douglas Legh Barratt (1899/1900–1942), stockbroker, son of Legh Barratt, stockbroker. They had one son before Barratt's death in 1942. After her marriage, Joyce continued performing under her maiden name. Shortly before the destruction of London's Queen's Hall in an air raid in 1941, she appeared there in the 'manifesto concert' devised by J. B. Priestley to stimulate support for cultural activity in wartime and to boost the ailing London Philharmonic Orchestra. She later toured with the orchestra to a succession of blitzed cities, often to perform in the most improvised conditions at best. During this time she developed a liking for playing three (sometimes four) concertos in one programme, accompanied by corresponding changes in the glamorous concert gowns she favoured to set off her striking physical image, a tactic which somehow drew sceptical critical views of her musical achievement. (According to Sir John Drummond, she 'had destroyed her serious standing through her obsession with changing her dresses. It was a bonus for the popular press, but did nothing for the music' (Drummond, 495).) She countered such views by claiming to suit the colour of her dress to her own esoteric views of the music concerned, as well as to relieve habitual nervousness before the next item. Most in demand were the more popular classics, notably the concertos of Grieg, Chopin, and Rakhmaninov, but she kept an interest in some newer trends, and gave the UK premières of both the concertos by Dmitry Shostakovich.

After the war ended in 1945, Joyce moved on to the international circuit, returning as a celebrity to her native Australia in 1948. She later visited South Africa, the USA (where she was dubbed by a leading New York critic 'the world's greatest unknown pianist'), the Soviet Union, India, and many areas in the Far East, where in 1960 she suddenly announced her impending retirement. Her heavy performing schedule (she sometimes gave fifty concerts a season in London alone) took its toll: her fingers at times required taping for their protection, and associated muscular stress obliged her to seek increasing medical attention. Apart from giving an isolated charity concert in 1966, she moved into retirement with her second husband, Christopher Mann (whom she had married in or before 1951), on a farm near Sir Winston Churchill's old home at Chartwell, Kent. In 1981 she was appointed CMG, an unusual distinction for a performing artist. Her academic honours included honorary degrees from Cambridge and from the universities of Western Australia and Melbourne. She died on 25 March 1991, and was survived by her husband and the son of her first marriage.

NOËL GOODWIN

Sources WWW, 1991–5 · *The Times* (29 March 1991) · *The Independent* (1 April 1991) · J. Siepmann, 'Pianists of the past: Eileen Joyce', *Classical Piano* (March–April 1996), 34 · B. Morrison, 'Rare Joyce', *Gramophone* (Nov 1987), 695 · J. Drummond, *Tainted by experience: a life in the arts* (2000) · m. cert. [Douglas Legh Barratt] · *CGPLA Eng. & Wales* (1991)
Archives SOUND BL NSA, performance recordings · BL NSA, recorded talk
Likenesses photographs, c.1931–1952, Hult. Arch. · Elliott & Fry, photograph, 1946, NPG [see illus.] · J. Bratby, charcoal, 1959, NPG · photograph, repro. in *The Times* · photograph, repro. in *The Independent*
Wealth at death £885,155: probate, 1991, *CGPLA Eng. & Wales*

Joyce [née Rice], **Ellen** (1832–1924), organizer of women's emigration, was born on 12 January 1832, the first of two children of Francis William Rice (1804–1878) and his wife, Harriet Ives (d. 1854), daughter of Daniel Raymond Barker. Ellen's father was vicar of Fairford, Gloucestershire, from 1827 to 1878. His second marriage, to Eliza Amelia Knox in 1856, produced a clerical son and three more daughters. Rather fortuitously he inherited the title of fifth Baron Dynevor in 1869, from a cousin who had five daughters and six sisters, and passed it on to Ellen's full brother, Arthur de Cardonnel Rice (1836–1911). The Dynevor connection linked Ellen to moderate estates in Carmarthenshire and Glamorgan, and to an ancient family name. In later years she took pride both in her courtesy title, 'the Honourable', and in her Welsh ancestry.

Ellen became involved from an early age in parish philanthropy. She claimed to have begun her emigration work at the age of fourteen by preparing the outfit of a child about to emigrate. On 20 September 1855 she married James Gerald Joyce (1819–1878), rector of Stratfieldsaye, Hampshire, from 1855 until his death. He tended his parish and his antiquarian interests while Ellen raised their only son, Arthur Gerald, born in 1856. Arthur Joyce became rector of Winnall in 1887 and shared a comfortable home with his mother at St John's Croft, Winchester, for the rest of her life.

During the early 1880s Ellen Joyce deepened her involvement in emigration work. She had been among the seventy-five founding associates of the Girls' Friendly Society (GFS), launched in 1875. After working with the Winchester Emigration Society in 1882 she urged the formation of a GFS emigration department to protect and assist members who chose to emigrate, and in 1883 she became the official GFS emigration correspondent. Her earliest concern was with the moral dangers of unprotected travel. Colonial contacts were urged to meet incoming parties of women, supervised during their journey by GFS-appointed matrons, and to place them in suitable employment through a system of introductions and written testimonials. Soon GFS parties were travelling with the added protection of an 'anchor cross' on their luggage, chosen to symbolize 'baptized fortitude' and 'stability amid the waves of this troublesome world' (Heath-Stubbs, 71).

In 1884 Ellen Joyce travelled with her son to Canada, crossing the Atlantic with eighty GFS emigrants and eventually following the incomplete Canadian Pacific railroad to its western extreme. On her return she reported not only to the GFS but also to the United Englishwomen's Emigration Association, which she had helped to found in February 1884. The new association soon moved decisively beyond the small-scale and individualist approach of previous emigrators. In 1885 a finance committee was appointed to raise funds and allocate loans to deserving emigrants. In 1888 Scottish emigrators agreed to join the retitled United British Women's Emigration Association (BWEA). Ellen Joyce became the undisputed leader of this national organization, which arranged the emigration of about 20,000 women between 1884 and 1914.

As organizing referee Ellen Joyce exercised the right of final decision over all arrangements for individual emigrants. This role was used both to enforce her own views on 'the right sort' of emigrant and to exert her authority over fellow emigrators. In a succession of published speeches to church congresses in the late 1880s and the 1890s she expounded the benefits of female emigration, both for the women themselves and, increasingly, for the building of a strong, morally pure, and Christianizing British empire. The philanthropic slant of her early emigration work was gradually overtaken by her determination to place quality above quantity: to emigrate only the best of British womanhood so that overseas colonies should inherit their civilizing powers and their potential as mothers of an imperial race. The Second South African War (1899–1902) gave renewed impetus to emigration. However, it also coincided with unaccustomed challenges to Ellen Joyce's expertise as a new generation of emigrators took up the cause. Both South African employers and government officials tried to impose their own priorities, in particular by maximizing the emigration of domestic servants. She was forced to countenance the formation of a separate South African Colonisation Society in 1903.

During the 1900s Ellen Joyce laboured on as head of the GFS emigration department, as president of the BWEA, and as senior voice of organized female emigration. Some of her more personal initiatives failed (for example, attempts to emigrate East End factory workers to Canada in 1903 and to revive child emigration as a BWEA project in 1904). However, she made good use of the propaganda opportunities afforded by the expanding press of the GFS and the female emigration associations. In the first edition of the BWEA journal, *The Imperial Colonist* (January 1902), she interviewed Colonel Baden-Powell on South Africa's need for women workers, while outlining the association's aims and methods, and announcing her own future column, 'Emigration notes'. This contained practical advice on jobs, fares, and general conditions for emigrants in South Africa, Australia, New Zealand, and Canada. She frequently contributed to other contemporary newspapers and magazines, and wrote a continuous flow of emigration pamphlets. She was also a prolific, and sometimes passionate, public speaker and was listened to with respect by politicians at home and abroad. In 1905 she gave evidence to Lord Tennyson's emigration committee, and in 1907 she led a BWEA deputation to the colonial premiers' conference. In 1908 she retired as BWEA president but four years later gave evidence to the royal commission on the dominions. Her address to the GFS Imperial Conference in York (17 July 1912) was perhaps the most eloquent statement of her imperialist faith. 'Empire building ought not to be left to accident', she told her audience; 'It is the finest, the most interesting, the most satisfactory bit of work an English woman can lay her hands to do' (E. Joyce, *Thirty Years of Girls' Friendly Society Imperial Work*, 1912, 5).

The First World War caused an abrupt suspension of organized emigration but strengthened its longer-term prospects. From her retirement the octogenarian Ellen Joyce helped to promote a new Joint Council of Women's Emigration Societies (1917). The government eventually promised regular funding and an acknowledged official status to a fully amalgamated Society for the Oversea Settlement of British Women (1919). Ellen Joyce's contribution was recognized by her appointment as an honorary vice-president and the appointment as CBE in 1920. A final honour was her nomination as president, shortly before her death on 21 May 1924 at St John's Croft, Winchester. After a funeral in Winchester Cathedral she was buried at Stratfieldsaye, on 31 May.

Ellen Joyce was in many ways a highly conservative woman. She was convinced of the religiously ordained centrality of marriage in women's lives and promoted an essentially maternalist ideal of female imperial citizenship. There is nevertheless some evidence in her writings and speeches that she acknowledged women's developing ambitions and needs as well as their duties. Emigration to the colonies appeared to offer an ideal combination of opportunities, for the individual and for the empire itself. Ellen Joyce's achievement lay both in publicizing and in bringing about opportunities for emigration. She was inspired by a grand vision, and achieved organizational success through determined leadership and close attention to practical detail.   JULIA BUSH

Sources Girls' Friendly Society archive, GFS central office, London • Female Emigration Societies archive, Women's Library, London • *Imperial Colonist* (1902–24) • Burke, *Peerage* (1999) • Crockford (1926) • *The Times* (26 May 1924) • M. Heath-Stubbs, *Friendship's highway* (1926) • U. Monk, *New horizons* (1963) • J. Bush, *Edwardian ladies and imperial power* (2000) • Boase, *Mod. Eng. biog.*, vol. 5 • E. Lodge, *The peerage and baronetage of the British empire*, 57th edn (1888) • GEC, *Peerage*, new edn, vol. 4 • d. cert. • *CGPLA Eng. & Wales* (1924)

Archives Girls' Friendly Society, London, Girls' Friendly Society archive • Women's Library, London, Female Emigration Societies archive

Likenesses photograph, repro. in Heath-Stubbs, *Friendship's highway*

Wealth at death £11,903 17s. 3d.: probate, 10 Sept 1924, *CGPLA Eng. & Wales*

Joyce, George (*b.* 1618), parliamentarian army officer, was born on 13 July 1618, probably the son of George Joyce, a Londoner. Nothing is known of his mother. His date of birth is known because he had his horoscope cast by an astrologer. According to one source he was a tailor in London and joined the parliamentarian army under the influence of a local puritan preacher; another source describes his father as an alehouse keeper at Cranborne, Dorset (and possibly a tenant of the earl of Salisbury). Dorset parish records show many Joyces but no George of the right date.

Details of his family life are similarly obscure. The name of his wife, Elizabeth, is known from an entry in the parish register of St Dunstan and All Saints, Stepney, recording the baptism of their child George in 1656. Most London tradesmen and artisans served in the foot regiments of the city's trained bands, but Joyce was in Cromwell's horse regiment by 1644–5, and held the lowest commissioned rank of cornet in Captain General Fairfax's regiment by 1647. He is not listed among the junior officers elected as 'agitators', or delegates, during the army's growing confrontation with the Long Parliament (April–May 1647), who then formed part of the general council of the army (June–November), but he was closely associated with the elected soldier agitators (among whom Edward Sexby was the leading figure) and spoke once in the general council debates at Reading on 16 July.

Joyce and other radical sympathizers later alleged that he had had Cromwell's personal authority for leading a force of some hundreds, drawn from different regiments, first to secure the artillery train and munitions at Oxford and then to replace the king's existing guards at Holmby, in order to forestall a projected counter-coup by the presbyterian majority in the House of Commons and their Scottish allies. Colonel Graves (or Greaves), then in command at Holmby, was a strong supporter of Denzil Holles, the presbyterian leader, who the army feared was planning to bring the king to London, in order to conclude a treaty between him and the parliament from which they would be excluded, thereby losing much of what they had fought for. So there were clear grounds for some kind of pre-emptive strike. Otherwise, even in the unsettled, near mutinous state of many units, someone of such junior rank could scarcely have led so considerable a force across the country to undertake these vital tasks. Although certainty will never be established, the likeliest sequence of events is that the original initiative came from the agitators, but that Cromwell and his son-in-law Commissary-General Henry Ireton had given their tacit approval to the securing first of the guns, then of the monarch. The cornet and his force reached Holmby and took control on 3 June 1647, but the subsequent decision to move Charles was forced on Joyce by those he was leading, after they had seized Holmby and Graves had escaped to London. Although Fairfax was said to have wanted him to be court martialled, no action was ever taken against Joyce. In view of later accusations against him, the evidence suggests that he had addressed the king respectfully and had treated him with consideration. Ironically it was Charles's own preference which led to his arrival near the army's headquarters at Newmarket, thus greatly strengthening the army's bargaining position in relation to king and parliament.

When a committee of senior officers recommended Joyce for a vacant captaincy in another regiment, this was vetoed by Fairfax; none the less early in 1648 Joyce was promoted and given command of Southsea Castle under the governor of Portsmouth. By this time the king was a prisoner on the Isle of Wight, to which he had gone after making his escape from Hampton Court in November 1647. Riding up from Hampshire to London, Joyce met one of the king's closest confidants, and told him that Charles should be brought to trial, in order to uphold the army's honour in having fought against him, but that he was not to be harmed. The following winter (November 1648 to January 1649) again saw Joyce playing a very active part in events. He took a confidential message and letters from Ireton and others at army headquarters near London to Cromwell, who was then conducting a siege operation in Yorkshire, besides taking part in the renewed debates of the army council at Whitehall. After the famous purge of the House of Commons, known after one of its leading organizers, Colonel Thomas Pride, Joyce apparently led a body of men into the City and arrested the sheriff of London, Major-General Richard Browne, a top military figure in the presbyterian party, who had somehow escaped arrest after the Purge. When asked by Browne how he dared to treat him like this, Joyce is quoted as saying that someone who had arrested the king was not afraid to do the same for the king's sheriff. In the debate on 13 January 1649 he called on Lord General Fairfax and the army council, acting as the instruments of God's people, who could 'by belief remove Mountains', to do 'such things as were never yett done by men on earth' (Firth, *Clarke Papers*, 2.182). But in spite of these apocalyptic tones, the subsequent testimony of the astrologer William Lilly, given to a parliamentary committee after the Restoration in 1660, that Joyce was one of the two masked axemen on the scaffold at Charles's execution on 30 January 1649, is unlikely to be true. In his autobiography Lilly named his source as Cromwell's personal secretary, Robert Spavin, who had asserted that Joyce's role was known only to himself, Cromwell, and Ireton; by 1660 all three of them were dead, while Spavin had been disgraced before that for forging his master's signature and trafficking in pardons to royalists. So, whether or not Lilly was a liar, Spavin certainly was.

In view of Joyce's later opposition to Cromwell it is noteworthy that he took no part in the Leveller-inspired army mutinies of May 1649 (nor had he in the earlier troubles of November 1647). Like the former Levellers John Wildman and Sexby, he speculated in confiscated lands, including the joint purchase with Sexby of the manor of Portland in Dorset; by 1651 he had become a lieutenant-colonel, succeeded his partner as governor there, and bought out Sexby's share of the property. In July of that year Joyce published a short pamphlet calling for justice on the presbyterian conspirator the Revd Christopher Love, more generally admonishing crypto-royalist backsliders, and in particular attacking the leading Dorset republican politician Denis Bond MP over local appointments and implying that Bond was secretly working in the presbyterian interest. Parts of the pamphlet referring to the late king suggest a mood of extreme religious exaltation. 'My love', he wrote, 'is to mankinde, and that all should turn from their evil ways and be saved, this doctrine I held forth to the late king, who justified himself, and stood upon his innocency, and dyed a Martyr or sufferer for truth (and his people) as he would have made the world believe' (G. Joyce, *A Letter or Epistle to All Well-Minded People …*, 1–2).

Joyce's downfall came with his political opposition to Cromwell during the Barebones Parliament in September 1653, when he was stripped of his commission and temporarily imprisoned; Colonel Pride is said to have offered to stand bail, and thereby to have incurred disapproval. In a rambling, self-exculpatory pamphlet published nearly six years later, after Cromwell's death and the fall of the protectorate, Joyce ascribed his own overthrow less to political differences than to a collision with Cromwell's son Richard for possession of a former royal park in Hampshire. He had in fact received a grant of other confiscated lands, in settlement of his arrears and expenses, at the beginning of the protectorate in December 1653; but according to Joyce his imprisonment and loss of army rank had led to financial ruin with his creditors foreclosing on him. The summer of 1659, under the restored Commonwealth, saw Joyce's re-emergence as a freelance military-cum-political activist. In 1660 the blacksmith of Marlborough in Wiltshire wrote a lengthy but vivid and convincing account of how he had been 'trepanned' by Joyce and his associates, being tricked into the expression of proroyalist sentiments and then pressed to incriminate others suspected of planning an uprising on behalf of Charles II. This had led to the blacksmith's incarceration in Newgate and his repeated cross-examination by John Bradshaw and other republican councillors. The whole story reads like a picaresque novel.

Nemesis followed the king's return. Whether on account of Lilly's story or his role in 1647, Joyce's arrest was ordered in June 1660, but he escaped and by the year after was living with his wife and children as an exile in Rotterdam. Nine years later, partly as a counter-intelligence drive against former republicans, partly as deliberate provocation of the Netherlands authorities, the English ambassador at The Hague was ordered to secure Joyce's extradition, no doubt with a view to his trial for treason. Both the Rotterdam magistrates and the provincial estates of Holland dragged their feet, claiming lack of legal grounds for Joyce's arrest, and describing him as—in effect—a harmless lunatic. Eventually they pretended to have organized his capture, but made sure that he had time to get away. He is last heard of in August 1670. How much longer he lived, indeed how he subsisted as a refugee, remain impenetrable mysteries. His whole career is unthinkable except during a revolution; perhaps historians should join Dame Veronica Wedgwood and salute Joyce 'the gallant little tailor' (Wedgwood, 23) as he flickers like an erratic meteor across the pages of English seventeenth-century history.   G. E. AYLMER

Sources *The Clarke papers*, ed. C. H. Firth, [new edn], 2 vols. in 1 (1992) • [G. Joyce], *A true impartiall narration, concerning the armies preservation of the king*, in J. Rushworth, *Historical collections*, 2nd edn, 4/1 (1701), 513–17 [presumed to be Joyce's own account of events] • *A letter or epistle to all well-minded people ... written by Lieut.-Col. Joyce*, 7 July 1651, BL, E. 637/3 • *A true narrative of the occasions and causes of the late Lord Gen. Cromwell's anger and indignation against Lieut. Col. George Joyce* (1659); repr. in W. Oldys, *The Harleian miscellany*, 8 (1746), 293–6 • 'Memoirs of Sir John Berkeley', *Select tracts relating to the civil wars in England*, ed. F. Maseres, 1 (1815), 353–94 • R. Huntington, ed., *Sundry reasons inducing Major Robert Huntingdon to lay down his commission* (1648); repr. F. Maseres, ed., *Select tracts relating to the civil wars in England*, 2 (1815) • *Calendar of the Clarendon state papers preserved in the Bodleian Library*, 2: *1649–1654*, ed. W. D. Macray (1869), 254, 260 • W. Lilly, *Mr William Lilly's history of his life and times*, 2nd edn (1715); repr. (1822), 202–3 [1st edn 1715] • *The works of Sir William Temple*, new edn, 2 (1757), 138–48 • A. Woolrych, *Soldiers and statesmen: the general council of the army and its debates, 1647–1648* (1987) • I. Gentles, *The New Model Army in England, Ireland, and Scotland, 1645–1653* (1992) • C. H. Firth and G. Davies, *The regimental history of Cromwell's army*, 2 vols. (1940) • C. V. Wedgwood, *The trial of Charles I* (1964) • IGI • *Calendar of the manuscripts of the most hon. the marquess of Salisbury*, 22, HMC, 9 (1971) • T. C. Dale, ed., *The inhabitants of London in 1638*, 1 (1931), 55 [MS, p. 105, St Ethelburga's parish, shows a George J. rated at 12s. (*recte* £12, since tithe paid was 14s)] • Dr. F. Bernard, 'Scheme of Nativities', BL, Sloane MS 1707, fol. 11v

Likenesses T. Athow, wash drawing, AM Oxf., Sutherland collection

Joyce, James Augustine Aloysius (1882–1941), writer, was born at 41 Brighton Square, West Rathgar, Dublin, on 2 February 1882, the eldest surviving son of John Stanislaus Joyce (1849–1931) and his wife, Mary Jane (May) (1859–1903), daughter of John Murray and Margaret Theresa Murray. The Joyces were a Catholic middle-class family who had enjoyed moderate commercial prosperity in Cork and Dublin throughout the nineteenth century. The family was aligned on both sides with constitutional nationalism, although the Joyces were the more substantial property-owners and the more socially secure representatives of the emerging Catholic bourgeoisie. They boasted a connection with Daniel O'Connell through Joyce's paternal grandmother. Purportedly descended from Thomas de Jorce, John Stanislaus laid somewhat specious claim to a heraldic coat of arms bearing the legend *Pernobilis et pervetusta familia* ('Most famous and ancient family').

Joyce called his father 'the silliest man I ever knew', but he also attributed to him his own 'good tenor voice, and an extravagant licentious disposition' (Ellmann, *Joyce*, 643). John Joyce is the model for Simon Dedalus in *A Portrait of the Artist as a Young Man* (1916) and *Ulysses* (1922), and—somewhat more diffusely—the model for Earwicker in *Finnegans Wake* (1939). He plays a larger role than any other relative in an œuvre which T. S. Eliot considered pervasively autobiographical. Interest in Joyce's family background seems 'not only suggested by our own inquisitiveness, but almost expected by [Joyce] himself' (preface to S. Joyce, *My Brother's Keeper*, 11–12). Throughout his life James Joyce tirelessly revisited his own family history as well as the wider life of the city in which he was born, transforming the 'sluggish matter' of experience into the 'imperishable' substance of art—as his autobiographical *alter ego* Stephen Dedalus pronounces in the *Portrait*.

John Stanislaus Joyce was born on 4 July 1849. After a short time at school, and to improve his health, he was sent out on pilot ships of the transatlantic steamers from Queenstown (Cobh), which coloured his vocabulary in ways he transmitted to the next generation. His taste for operatic music also greatly influenced the novelist's sensibility. He became active in Fenian politics before moving in the mid-1870s to Dublin, where he sang in public and private to such effect that he earned the name 'a successor to Campanini'. He also sang in the company of Barton M'Guckin at the Antient Concert Rooms—a distinction echoed by his son when he sang at the same venue in company with John McCormack some thirty years later.

At the end of the 1870s John Stanislaus entered into partnership with one Henry Alleyn in the Dublin and Chapelizod Distillery but lost his £500 investment when Alleyn embezzled the company's funds (an injury that James Joyce avenged in naming the disagreeable solicitor in 'Counterparts' after him). In 1880 he became collector of

James Augustine Aloysius Joyce (1882–1941), by Jacques-Émile Blanche, 1935

rates for Inns Quay and Rotunda wards, a reward for services to the United Liberal Club. On 5 May 1880 he married Mary Jane (May) Murray, ten years his junior. She was the daughter of an agent for wines and spirits from co. Longford—a family background that John Stanislaus Joyce considered inferior to his own and often disparaged: 'O weeping God, the things I married into' (*Ulysses*, 47). They married against the wishes of both their parents, and John Stanislaus's mother never forgave him for it. But May was brought up well enough to have been a fellow pupil of Katharine Tynan at Misses Flynn School, where dancing, *politesse*, and the piano were taught (providing the setting for 'The Dead'), and May's sister-in-law Josephine (*née* Giltrap) was the older relative for whom Joyce had the most respectful, good-humoured, and affectionate regard throughout his life.

John Stanislaus and May Joyce settled at 47 Northumberland Avenue, Kingstown (now Dun Laoghaire). A first child, John Augustine Joyce, was born in 1881 but did not survive. In December of that year John Stanislaus took out the first of a succession of mortgages which marked his economic decline in future years. James, the first surviving child, was born in Rathgar on 2 February 1882 and baptized at St Joseph's Chapel of Ease, Roundtown, Dublin (now St Joseph's Church, Terenure), on 5 February, when he was erroneously registered as James Augusta Joyce. In the ensuing twelve years, May Joyce endured thirteen more pregnancies, bearing four boys and six girls, with three miscarriages. The writer's siblings were Margaret Alice (Poppie) (1884–1964); (John) Stanislaus (1884–1955), the writer's 'whetstone'; Charles (1886–1941); George Alfred (1887–1902); Eileen (1889–1963); Mary Kathleen (May) (1890–1966); Eva (1891–1957); Florence (1892–1973); Mabel (1893–1911); and Freddie (born and died in 1894). Her son was probably thinking of May Joyce when he called the long-suffering maternal principle of *Finnegans Wake* 'Crippled-with-Children'.

Childhood and schooling In May 1887 the family moved to 1 Martello Terrace in Bray, co. Wicklow, a rapidly developing seaside resort. The household now included William O'Connell, a widowed uncle of Mr Joyce who had failed in business, and Elizabeth Conway, who was reduced to family dependence when her husband absconded with her inheritance. Called 'Dante' in the family (from 'Auntie'), she served as governess to the children and taught Joyce his letters. There were lively visits from friends including Alf Bergan, Tom Devin, and—a somewhat sensational acquaintance—John Kelly, a Fenian who had been incarcerated by the government and came to recuperate with the Joyces. Kelly was a man of forceful character whose sense of conviction inspired the writer. There were also convivial singing parties with the neighbouring protestant family of James Vance. The young Joyce attended Miss Raynor's infant school with Vance's daughter Eileen.

In 1888 Joyce went to Clongowes Wood College, a boarding-school for Catholic gentry at Clane, co. Kildare. He soon acquired the nickname 'Half-Past Six', arising from his answer to a query about his age. As the youngest boy Joyce suffered from homesickness and feelings of insecurity, and the class bully pushed him into a square ditch (a cesspool). He was also beaten on the hands for offences including the use of vulgar language. Father James Daly, the director of studies who administered one such punishment, is the model for Dolan in the *Portrait*, where he is depicted as an ignorant and brutal man. In daring to take his grievance to the rector of the college, Father John Conmee, the young Joyce demonstrated a self-possession and an independence which characterized him throughout his life. The fact that Conmee apologized to him reflected the esteem in which he was already held as a gifted student, although the sincerity of the apology is undermined in the *Portrait*.

The school practised a version of the Jesuits' *ratio studiorum* (programme of study). The ethos was both Catholic and 'west-Briton' in so far as the boys were prepared for the higher ranks of the British imperial administration in Ireland and beyond. Joyce also learned the piano, and though liking cricket, took little part in school games. On 21 April 1889 he made his first holy communion, and he took the name Aloysius at confirmation in spring 1891. Early in October 1891 he appears to have been in the infirmary again, possibly with amoebic dysentery resulting from his immersion in the ditch. This illness may have coincided with the death of Parnell on 6 October 1891, an event which he conveys through the young boy's fevered vision of his own demise in the *Portrait*. He was taken home, and because of his father's deepening financial problems did not return to Clongowes.

The death of Parnell marked a watershed in Irish cultural and political life, when a new impetus was given to the national movement by W. B. Yeats, Douglas Hyde, and others. The fall of Parnell was the occasion for a dramatic quarrel in the Joyce household over Christmas dinner when John Stanislaus and Dante clashed over their respective loyalties to the home-rule leader and the Catholic bishops. In the *Portrait* this became one of the most celebrated episodes in modern Irish literature. John Kelly (on whom Mr Casey was modelled) was the catalyst for those violent verbal exchanges, ending with Mr Joyce's grief-stricken cry: 'Poor Parnell! … My dead king!' Mrs Conway left the household four days later. It is uncertain whether the dinner row took place in Bray or at Leoville, the new family home at 23 Carysfort Avenue, Blackrock, to which the Joyces were forced to move between late November 1891 and the beginning of 1892. Almost certainly before the removal (if not as early as July 1891), Joyce wrote a sentimental elegy for Parnell which his father printed and circulated under the title 'Et tu, Healy'.

By this time John Joyce was in growing trouble at the rates office. Although he courageously defended his collector's pouch from attackers in Phoenix Park in 1887, his mismanagement of funds prompted his transfer to the less congenial North Dock ward area in 1888. In May 1892 the Dublin corporation resolved to take the rates collection office under its own aegis. A series of court actions for settlement of debts culminated in John Joyce's name appearing in *Stubbs' Gazette* on 2 November 1892. This resulted in his immediate suspension from duties by the collector-general, which put his pension settlement in jeopardy, and (tradition has it) it was only after a personal appeal from his wife that a sum of £132 per annum was assigned. In November the Joyces were forced to move to 14 Fitzgibbon Street, Mountjoy Square, a less salubrious address which bordered on the area that Joyce made world-famous as 'Nighttown' in the 'Circe' chapter of *Ulysses*.

Throughout 1892 James Joyce conducted his own education at home in Blackrock, with some assistance from his mother. Once settled in the city, he briefly attended the school on North Richmond Street run by the Christian Brothers—a lowly order that was social anathema to both father and son. Release came through the good offices of Father Conmee, now director of studies at the Jesuit day school Belvedere College, and on 6 April 1893 James and his brother Stanislaus entered the school. He faced few intellectual challenges, and his attitude to his studies was at once competitive and debonair. When he won a £20 award in intermediate examinations for 1894 he characteristically doled it out in 'loans' to his siblings and spent even more on a dinner for his parents at a fashionable Dublin restaurant. His potential as a breadwinner was seized on by the family, though it was increasingly resisted by the gifted boy himself, who realized that the

'slight thread of union' between father and son was breaking because of the 'gradual rustiness [of] the upper station' (*Stephen Hero*, 101). The family moved regularly from 1884 to 1899, in a downward spiral, and by autumn 1902 were at 7 St Peter's Terrace in Cabra, the last address Joyce shared with his father.

Adolescence: 'shaking the wings of their exultant and terrible youth' John Joyce's drunkenness and his increasing violence added to the family's woes: shortly after the birth and death of Freddie in July 1894, James stopped a physical attack on his mother by jumping on his father's back. Meanwhile at school, James began to enjoy special favour with the new rector, Father William Henry, who was also director of the Sodality of the Blessed Virgin Mary. On 7 December 1895 Joyce was admitted to the sodality as a member, and on 25 September 1896 he was elected prefect. His devotion to the Virgin Mary was evidently sincere, but a shadow fell across his reputation for devoutness when Father Henry winkled it out of Stanislaus that his brother had engaged in spanking games with a housemaid in his parents' home. Father Henry warned Mr Joyce that he would have trouble from the boy, yet that did not prevent his probing Joyce for signs of a vocation to the priesthood—an episode which became the linchpin of the *Portrait*. There the priest's skull, silhouetted against the window, together with a noose he makes from the cord of the 'crossblind', amply prepares the reader for the young man's realization that 'His destiny was to be elusive of social or religious orders … to learn his own wisdom apart from others … wandering among the snares of the world [which] were its ways of sin'.

The annual school retreats at Belvedere, with their sermons on the agonies inflicted on sinful souls by the fiends of hell, instigated in Joyce a period of strict chastity which lasted into spring 1897, when an obsessive round of 'pious ejaculations' (short prayers designed to stave off carnal temptation) and decades of the rosary were observed by his siblings. It was not until 1898, when Joyce encountered a 'gay' girl in the street, that he engaged in sexual intercourse in the manner suggested at the close of chapter 2 of the *Portrait*. This amorous offence is juxtaposed with the 'hellfire sermon' that scarifies young Stephen Dedalus.

Joyce's adolescent religious conviction soon gave way to an increasing enthusiasm for modern literature. The works of Thomas Hardy and George Meredith along with the anti-conventional writings of George Bernard Shaw were part of his self-administered diet, but the transforming influence was Henrik Ibsen, whose 'spirit he encounters in a moment of radiant simultaneity', as Joyce later recalled in the autobiographical draft novel *Stephen Hero* (1944). Joyce found in Ibsen 'a spirit of wayward boyish beauty' (*Portrait of the Artist as a Young Man*, 179)—a phrase that suggests that his powers of intellectual apprehension were still bounded by the reflexes of *fin de siècle* aestheticism. But much sterner forms of egoism were flexing their muscles—or as Stephen Dedalus would have it, 'shaking the wings of their exultant and terrible youth'. When Joyce saw Hermann Sudermann's *Magda* with his parents in March 1899, he told them that they need not have bothered going to see a play about genius flourishing in the home, since they would soon witness 'genius breaking out' in their own household (Ellmann, *Joyce*, 54).

Such a mind was unlikely to mix easily with schoolboys, yet aside from defending Byron against asinine criticism in the tussle recounted in chapter 2 of the *Portrait*, Joyce was on good terms with his most able peers, including Richard and Eugene Sheehy, sons of the MP David Sheehy. He shared with them musical entertainments, played charades, and mounted burlesque versions of plays and operas. Joyce was generally more reserved than the others, and evinced no partiality towards girls, though biographers since Ellmann have asserted that he was shyly infatuated with Mary, the youngest and reputedly the prettiest of the Sheehy girls. She is, indeed, the generally favoured model for Emma Clery in *Stephen Hero* (Miss M. E. Cleary is another), and her counterpart, 'E. C.', in the *Portrait*.

Joyce was the educational and social equal of his contemporaries, but was essentially *déclassé* and prone to wander deeper into the disreputable side of Dublin life than any of his friends. Those odysseys precluded his returning to the ordinary fold of middle-class youth, and gave him a frankness of appetite, and a desire to find frankness reciprocated in a way impossible with his educational peers. The obsolescent Parnellite opinions and improbable gentry pretensions of his father, both of which Joyce perpetuated in a sublimated form, provided a further barrier.

Neither Joyce's agnosticism nor his sexual libertinism was known to his mentors at Belvedere, and he remained to the end a prefect of the Sodality of the Blessed Virgin Mary. His intellectual interest in mysticism was still sufficient in October 1897 for him to buy Thomas à Kempis's *Imitation of Christ*. Towards the end he fell out with Father Henry when he refused to sit the bishops' examination, considering the senior intermediate a more important occasion. In the event he won £30 for a second year along with £4 for English composition, but failed to win a university exhibition.

University years and intellectual development, 1899–1902 Having spent a year on the matriculation course of the Royal University of Ireland during 1898–9, Joyce entered University College, Dublin, as an undergraduate in October 1899, reading modern languages with Latin and logic as additional subjects. The reserved but self-possessed young man was acknowledged to be exceptional in both temperament and intellect by his peers. He was certainly the best-read student in his year, yet his examination results were invariably undistinguished and he emerged in 1902 with only a pass degree. He had decided that the college syllabus was far too narrow, and set about educating himself with the help of the National Library of Ireland and Dublin book-barrows.

While at university Joyce took part in the sodality's literary conference, attended the Thomas Aquinas Society, and apparently did not leave off Easter duties until his brother George died on 3 May 1902. Up to this point his agnosticism was more a tendency of mind than an intellectual conviction or an artistic premise. He was wary and increasingly disdainful of the Jesuit authorities in the college but responded warmly to individual teachers. The celebrated account of an exchange on the theme of beauty conducted by Stephen with the dean of studies in the *Portrait* reveals a strategy that was by then second nature to him: the use of 'one or two ideas of Aristotle and Aquinas' to frame his own philosophical intuitions. Stephen's colloquy also depicts the young Joyce's growing unease with the condition of received language, his awareness of 'heaps of dead language'.

The chief of Joyce's friends and associates at University College who modelled for characters in his autobiographical fiction were Vincent Cosgrave, perceptive but coarse of mind (Lynch in the *Portrait*); John Francis (Jeff) Byrne, thoughtful but capable of conventional disapproval (Cranly in the *Portrait* and *Ulysses*); George Clancy, a naïve exponent of Irish-Ireland *purismo*, later assassinated by the Black and Tans (Davin in the *Portrait*); Francis Sheehy-Skeffington, pacifist–feminist–vegetarian and sporter of knickerbockers, who was murdered in custody by British soldiers after he quixotically attempted to prevent looting in the rising of 1916 (McCann in the *Portrait*); and Constantine Curran, later author on Georgian Dublin architecture, who produced the most complete memoir of the period (after Stanislaus Joyce's). The chief forum for intellectual debate was the Literary and Historical Society, where Joyce, who was co-opted to the executive committee, first spoke in January 1899.

Joyce was not, however, training for public and professional life as the others were: his immediate purpose was to become a recognized writer, and to that end he composed a review article on the painting *Ecce homo* by Mihály Munkácsy. On 20 January 1900 Joyce delivered the first of two papers to the Literary and Historical Society entitled 'Drama and life'. In it he castigated as mistaken the insistence on the religious, moral, and idealizing tendencies of art as well as the 'boyish instinct to dive under the blankets at the mention of the bogey of realism'. He ended by echoing Lona in Ibsen's play *Samfundets stotter* ('The Pillars of Society'): 'I will let in fresh air'. This clarion call was 'very seriously intended to define his own position for himself', as Joyce wrote in *Stephen Hero*. Its delivery coincided closely with publication of his article 'Ibsen's new drama' in the *Fortnightly Review* (1 April 1900). A fee of 12 guineas enabled him to travel to London with his father and visit William Archer, Ibsen's English translator. He heard from Archer a month later that the playwright had written a note of earnest appreciation when he read the article. Joyce learned Dano-Norwegian so that he could read the plays in the original and write to Ibsen in time for his birthday in March 1901.

Joyce's reading of the works of Gabriele D'Annunzio at this time resulted in a play entitled *A Brilliant Career* dealing with the experience of a young doctor caught up in an epidemic in a midland town. Joyce called it 'the first true work of my life' and dedicated it 'To [His] Own Soul'. Archer thought it immature. Joyce then turned to the sterner stuff of Gerhart Hauptmann and produced stiff translations of *Vor Sonnenaufgang* and *Michael Kramer* during the following twelve months. (A taste for Hauptmann's drama was later used as an indication of Mr Duffy's emotional sterility in 'A Painful Case'.) Archer was equally discouraging about *Shine and Dark*, Joyce's first poetry collection, which he sent him in September 1901.

About this date Joyce wrote the first of a series of short prose records that he called his epiphanies. He defined the term as 'a sudden spiritual manifestation, whether in the vulgarity of speech or of gesture or in a memorable phase of the mind itself', adding that 'it was for the man of letters to record these epiphanies with extreme care, seeing that they themselves are the most delicate and evanescent of moments' (*Stephen Hero*, 188). The earliest example, preserved with others on the verso of Stanislaus's commonplace book, concerns a butcher-boy observed making a commonplace gesture in Glengariff Parade; others dealt with psychological moments in their author's life and tokens by which his middle-class associates and siblings revealed the ignobility of their minds. What was most important about the technique was, perhaps, the absence of authorial voice: description was cut to a minimum, and hiatus also used for unheard words. The effect was to carry Joyce away from poetry and drama in the generic sense towards a kind of prose which entailed the suggestive power of the one and the actuality of the other. It also posed an epistemological riddle about how the writer gains insight into the 'soul of the object'. The epiphanies that Joyce wrote between 1900 and 1904 were later incorporated into his novels, beginning with the autobiographical draft *Stephen Hero* and ending with *Ulysses*. (The method was revived, though with some alteration in tone, for the manuscript record of a love affair in 1911–14 later published as *Giacomo Joyce*.)

Joyce attended all the productions of the fledgeling Irish Literary Theatre as a student. Yeats's *The Countess Cathleen*, one of the first plays produced in May 1899, was particularly influential. At the deathbed of his brother George in 1902 Joyce sang some lyrics from the play, which he invoked at the end of the 'Nighttown' episode of *Ulysses*. On 14 October 1901 he wrote to protest that Douglas Hyde's *Casadh an tSugáin* and the George Moore–W. B. Yeats collaboration *Diarmuid and Grania* were to be staged in contravention of its professed policy of bringing the best of modern continental drama to the Irish capital. Joyce published the broadside in November 1901, hinting in it that the literary heir to Ibsen who 'Even now … may be standing by the door' might be himself. In his paper delivered at the Literary and Historical Society on 15 February 1902 on the Irish Romantic poet James Clarence Mangan, Joyce rejected the idea that the rebirth of an Irish nation was a necessary condition of the 'affirmation of the spirit' in literature, and lamented Mangan's plight in writing 'for a public which cared for matters of the day, and for poetry only so far as it might illustrate these'. Whatever else Joyce had to say about nationalist Ireland he reserved for *Stephen Hero*, while he wrote a verse play, 'Dream Stuff' (now lost), and made contact with the leaders of the literary revival.

On 18 August 1902 he walked to Rathgar to introduce himself to George Russell ('Æ'), who told him famously that he had not enough chaos in him to be a poet. He met W. B. Yeats in October 1902 and read to him a 'beautiful though immature and eccentric harmony of little prose descriptions and meditations' (Ellmann, *Identity of Yeats*, 86), which Yeats praised. But Joyce professed not to care for Yeats's opinion, and regretted that the poet was too old—a sentiment that he uttered to his face. Joyce also made it abundantly clear that he did not intend to be suborned by the theosophically minded literati gathered around Russell any more than by the nationalist enthusiasts of his own class.

Paris and back On completion of his studies Joyce followed several college friends into medicine at the Cecilia Street Medical School, Dublin, and on 18 November 1902 applied to the Faculté de Médecine of the University of Paris. Joyce borrowed money from friends and acquaintances including Lady Gregory, to whom he wrote that he 'found no man yet with a faith like mine' (*Selected Letters*, 8). On her recommendation he was given book reviewing by E. V. Longworth, editor of the Dublin *Daily Express*. His notices on Irish literature over the next six months were uncompromising assertions of his own literary standards. Joyce appraised Lady Gregory's *Poets and Dreamers* as a work in which the author 'has truly set forth the old age of her country … a land almost fabulous in its sorrow and senility'. Buck Mulligan in *Ulysses* voices the obvious objection: 'She gets you a job on the paper and then you go and slate her drivel to Jaysus. Why can't you do the Yeats touch?'

Joyce reached Paris on 3 December, only to discover that he lacked the necessary qualifications for the Faculté de Médecine. While in Paris he did however write some epiphanies and amassed the continental experiences which Stephen Dedalus recalls in the 'Nestor' episode of *Ulysses*, notably a cameo of the Jewish traders at the Bourse and a visit to Joseph Casey, formerly a prominent Fenian. Joyce's father found the price of his ticket home in time for Christmas 1902 by raising a further mortgage. In Dublin he met Oliver St John Gogarty, who provided him with an archetypal example of the 'gay betrayer' immortalized as Buck Mulligan in *Ulysses*. Once back in Paris he applied himself to Aristotle's *De anima* in J. Barthélemy Saint-Hilaire's translation (*Psychologie d'Aristote, traité de l'âme*), which he 'Englished' to produce a spare but focused record of philosophical sentences. These anchored his own aesthetic and epistemological syllogisms in the so-called 'Paris notebook' before he resigned them to his autobiographical persona Stephen Dedalus: 'Thought is the thought of thought. Tranquil brightness. The soul is in a manner all that is: the soul is the form of forms.' None the less, bouts of hunger and begging letters home were part of Joyce's life in Paris until the telegram arrived in April 1903 with news that his mother was dying.

Joyce returned to Dublin, but his mother did not die until 13 August; in the interim there were more than the usual distresses, including the outbursts of his father, who once shouted, 'If you can't get well, die … and be damned to you!' (S. Joyce, *My Brother's Keeper*, 230). Joyce refused to yield to his mother's pleadings that she take the sacraments and later refused even to kneel at her death-bed. May Joyce appears in *Ulysses* as a ghoul terrorizing her son from beyond the grave. In the *Portrait*, where she expresses the hope that he will learn 'what the heart is and what it feels', she is more like her living self and the personality expressed in her letters to him in Paris. Her wry scepticism about masculine opinions, and her unfailing pride in and concern for her brilliant but wilful son, produced the only confession of faith he ever made, when he professed to believe in nothing but 'the love of a mother for her child and the love of a man for lies' (Ellmann, *Joyce*, 293). Joyce was greatly affected by his mother's death but remained unsentimental. Following the funeral, at which his father surpassed himself in self-commiseration, Joyce embarked on a series of half-baked plans intended to support a career in literature. He then became a preparatory school teacher for a few weeks in summer 1904 at Clifton School, established in Dalkey by Francis Irwin (Mr Deasy in *Ulysses*).

The experiences of December 1903 to September 1904 make up the immediate background of *Ulysses*. Oliver St John Gogarty helped Joyce to deepen his familiarity with the 'kips' (brothels), and together they refined the arts of bawdy poetry. But Joyce's relationship with Gogarty had become intensely barbed, as each assumed himself superior. Hoping to launch into a singing career, Joyce equipped himself with a respected voice teacher, a first-floor room at Shelbourne Road, and a grand piano. He missed the first prize at the annual Feis Ceoil held in the Antient Concert Rooms on 16 May 1904 because of his inability to sight-sing. On his return to Dublin, Joyce's slight contact with the city's literati had been unamiable: he crashed Lady Gregory's literary gathering and was written off by George Moore, whose poetry he likened to that of Arthur Symons, as a 'beggar'.

The beginnings of *A Portrait of the Artist as a Young Man* and *Dubliners* But Joyce was far from abandoning writing. On 7 January 1904 he composed in one day an early version of *A Portrait of the Artist as a Young Man*, intended as a contribution to John Eglinton's new journal *Dana*; it was refused as unintelligible. Indeed, the 1904 'Portrait' is meaningless other than as an indicator of Joyce's artistic and imaginative development, and even then it is febrile and obscure. At the outset he speaks of the human personality as 'a fluid succession' of moments, and suggests that this debars literary portraiture of the kind that retails 'beard and inches'. He promises a better way of conveying identity 'through some art, by some process of mind as yet untabulated, to liberate from the personalised lumps of matter that which is their individuating rhythm, the first or formal relation of their parts'. The importance of this declaration is that it links his Aristotelian interests with his search for a literary form that would trace the reality of psychological life, which he here describes as 'the curve of an emotion'.

It was many years before Joyce began to approach that point when, in a bold revision of his interminable auto-biographical novel (the remnant of which appeared post-humously as *Stephen Hero*), he adopted the method of character-specific style, moulding the narration to the state of mind, age, and emotional state of his central protagonist. In 1904, however, the nascent autobiographical *alter ego* was hardly more than an explosion of literary and psychic self-importance which ends by proclaiming:

> Man and woman, out of you comes the nation that is to come, the lightning [*sic*] of your masses in travail; the competitive order is employed against itself, the aristocracies are supplanted; and amid the general paralysis of an insane society, the confederate will issues in action.

There is a sense that James Joyce himself is expected to be the one 'who would give the word' to the 'multitudes, not as yet in the wombs of humanity but surely engenderable there'.

Immediately and over the next few years, Joyce expanded on his essay, and the conviction that 'life is such as I conceive'. As *Stephen Hero* it swelled to 200,000 words before grinding to a halt in 1913. A panoply of Christological images points to the messianic stature of the artist. The 'Hero' owed something to Thomas Carlyle's 'Hero as Man of Letters' (a point often contested by Joyce commentators), for he was 'the intense centre of the life of his age to which he stands in a relation than which none can be more vital', as Stephen holds of the true poet and himself. The extant portions (chapters 15–25) roughly correspond to the last chapter of *A Portrait of the Artist as a Young Man*. They deal with Stephen's days at University College, Dublin, and are full of opinions about his teachers and his peers. Anti-clericalism reaches an extraordinary pitch in passages where he compares Ireland's priests to 'black tyrannous lice' who imposed 'Contempt of human nature, weakness, nervous tremblings, fear of day and joy, distrust of man and life, hemiplegia of the will' on those in their power. While his supine contemporaries are reduced to 'terrorized boys, banded together in a complicity of diffidence', he would 'live his own life according to what he recognised as the voice of a new humanity, active, unafraid and unashamed'. Already burdened by this deadening declamation, the novel also suffers from a radical instability of tone. It is impossible to know what the author understands—or expects his reader to understand—by the account that he gives of his literary manner at the date of the events recounted: 'Stephen's style of writing, though it was over affectionate towards the antique and even the obsolete and too easily rhetorical, was remarkable for a certain crude originality of expression.' The trouble is that the style of *Stephen Hero* is entirely of a piece with it.

By way of relief from such an arduous task, Joyce assembled a collection of 'Elizabethan' poems, which he called *Chamber Music* (on a scatological hint from Gogarty when they were in earshot of a micturating prostitute). Arthur Symons placed one such poem ('Silently, she's combing') in the *Saturday Review* on 8 April 1904—thus bearing out George Moore's estimate of Joyce's poetical character. During summer 1904 he began a set of 'epiclets' for the

Irish Homestead, a newspaper of the Irish co-operative movement fostered by Horace Plunkett and 'Æ', which eventually constituted the stories of *Dubliners* (1914). If 'Æ' wanted something 'simple, rural, live-making [with] pathos', what he got was a subtle, damning exposé of the network of hypocrisy and deception, tyranny and abuse, moral cowardice and self-contempt which Joyce regarded as the symptoms of 'spiritual paralysis' in Ireland. 'The Sisters' (13 Aug 1904), 'Eveline' (10 Sept 1904), and 'After the Race' (17 Dec 1904) appeared successively over the pseudonym Stephen Daedalus, before the editor, H. F. Norman, rumbled the writer's subversive bent and terminated the understanding. 'The Holy Office', written in verse, plotted his relation to the literary revival and the Catholic-nationalist purists of the period; he styled himself 'Katharsis-Purgative' in jejunely Aristotelian terms:

Thus I relieve their timid arses,
Perform my office of Katharsis.

Nora and 'exile' Joyce's dissolute mode of life had reached an advanced stage when on 10 June 1904, walking in Nassau Street, he was struck by the auburn hair of Nora Barnacle (1884–1951) [*see* Joyce, Nora Joseph], a chambermaid in Finn's Hotel. Joyce persuaded her to walk out with him in the neighbourhood of the botanical gardens in Ringsend, when on 16 June she offered him the 'kind of satisfaction' that filled him with 'amazed joy' to recollect, as he told her in a letter. Nora, though still a churchgoing Catholic, was free from the sexual restraints of Joyce's educational class. Joyce supplemented his physical and emotional passion for her with a good deal of intellectual fancy: he came to regard her as his 'soul' and his 'Ireland'—a portable Ireland, as the event would prove. He promptly told her about his religious apostasy and his general disdain for Irish society and his contemporaries, as well as his limitless faith in his own genius. For a while he doubted her response but their unlikely relationship grew closer.

In summer 1904 Joyce's living arrangements were unsettled. In September he spent one week in the Martello tower at Sandycove with Gogarty and Samuel Chenevix Trench. This Anglo-Irishman is accurately portrayed as Haines in *Ulysses*, whose dream of panthers provided Gogarty with a pretext to rattle off some shots from his revolver in the main chamber of the tower. Joyce took this as his notice to quit, eventually returning to the family home in Cabra. The Martello tower sojourn forms the basis for the opening of *Ulysses*. As the novel goes on to relate, late in September Joyce met medical friends at the National Maternity Hospital in Holles Street and proceeded to the 'kips' of the Montgomery Street area in company with Vincent Cosgrave (who earned the name Lynch for standing by when Joyce was beaten in a drunken fight). There Joyce appears to have encountered Alfred Hunter, the model for Leopold Bloom, who rescued him in 'orthodox Samaritan fashion' after he had been beaten by two soldiers. Hunter was an Ulster Presbyterian and commercial traveller who had converted to Catholicism at marriage, but was nevertheless an outsider—though not a Jew

as represented in the novel. Joyce later sought detailed information of him from his brother when planning a story to be called 'Ulysses' for the *Dubliners* collection.

By the end of September Joyce was convinced of the hopelessness of staying on in Dublin. Besides lack of money, the strain of his passionate relationship with Nora in an unsympathetic milieu and his increasingly rocky friendships with Curran and Byrne precipitated a paranoid sense of isolation which became a recurring note in his dealings with Dublin acquaintances and with publishers. Once he had planned to leave, he accepted Byrne's advice to ask Nora to come with him, rather as Eveline is asked by her untrustworthy lover Frank in the *Dubliners* story named after her. Pausing only to send *Chamber Music* to the publisher Grant Richards the day before he left, they reached Paris on 9 October 1904, and then set off for Zürich, where Joyce wrongly understood he had a teaching appointment.

On reporting to the Berlitz School, Joyce found no job awaiting him and was sent onwards to Trieste, in Habsburg Austria. After finding no post there either, he was redirected to the new establishment at Pola, under the deputy director Alessandro Francini. Acclimatization was not easy. Joyce began by being locked up when he tried to help three drunken British sailors, and difficulties with money were such that they often moved before settling at via Giulia 2, near the school. There Joyce and Nora established the domestic pattern that characterized their family life for years to come: intense periods of literary work alternating with conviviality among colleagues and pupils, and intermittent bouts of drunkenness. There was much strain and solitude for Nora, and a wide gulf of intellectual interests that cut her off from his writing. Joyce had a fascination with her 'untrained' mind, and a delight in her body, which provided him, if not her, with some compensation.

When, early in 1905, Joyce and Nora moved to via Medolino 7, at the invitation of the Francinis, there were eighteen chapters of *Stephen Hero* (Stanislaus received the manuscript for strictly limited circulation among relatives in mid-January 1905). In November he wrote the carefully meditated aesthetic entries of the 'Pola notebook' which turn St Thomas's sentences 'bonum est in quod tendit appetitus' ('the good is that towards the possession of which an appetite tends') and 'pulchra sunt quae visa placent' ('those things are beautiful the apprehension of which pleases') into an ingenious account of the 'act of apprehension', while dismantling the conventional distinction between the 'beautiful' and the 'ugly'. Friendship with Francini flourished to the extent that they embarked on a translation of George Moore's *Celibates* in autumn 1905 while Francini taught Joyce his superior Tuscan in place of the classical Italian that Joyce had learned (so he said) from Dante. But early in March 1905 Joyce's sojourn in that 'queer old place' was abruptly terminated when the Austrian authorities expelled all aliens on the discovery of an Italian spy ring in the city. Having been offered work at the Berlitz School in Trieste, where he proved a popular teacher, Joyce settled with Nora at 31 via San

Nicolò, Trieste, where their son Giorgio (1905–1976) was born.

Dubliners in Trieste, Rome, and Dublin As in Pola, Joyce had much time to write, and he produced nine more stories for the *Dubliners* collection as well as a spate of letters to Stanislaus describing his growing affinity with irredentism and socialism. He was flush enough in June to have 'The Holy Office' printed for distribution by his brother in Dublin. The birth of Giorgio on 27 July 1905 brought domestic strains which are obliquely reflected in 'A Little Cloud'. But the 'legal fiction' of paternity released in Joyce a new consciousness of self which led inevitably to the abandonment of the Dedalian persona and the adoption of a mentality more like that of Leopold Bloom. Nora was forced to take in washing, while Joyce began to drink again, supposedly as a form of contraception. He embarked on a series of fruitless money-making schemes, including a new attempt to make a living as a singer which entailed lessons with a Triestino teacher and composer, Francesco Sinico (who remained unpaid and unwittingly bestowed his name on the tragic central figure of 'A Painful Case' in *Dubliners*). In October Stanislaus joined the household, and acted as his 'brother's keeper' at endless sacrifice to himself until the First World War. The arrangement brought its own tensions, and Stanislaus turned into a resentful memorialist. In February 1906 the Joyce ménage moved to via Giovanni Boccaccio, sharing with the Francinis, by then also established in Trieste.

On 3 December 1905 Joyce sent twelve stories to Grant Richards, who agreed to publish them as a collection, thus setting in motion an eight-year saga which Joyce later described as the 'fiasco' of *Dubliners*. Encouraged at this time, he quickly added two more stories, 'Two Gallants' and 'A Little Cloud', while carefully revising 'A Painful Case' and 'After the Race'. On 23 April 1906 Richards wrote to say that his printer had red-pencilled the epithet 'bloody' in 'Two Gallants', and in ensuing exchanges further objectionable passages were noted, including aspersions on the prince of Wales and—more likely to offend the censor—sado-masochistic hints in 'An Encounter'. Richards revoked the agreement in September 1906. In letters to the publisher that summer, Joyce defended his stories as a 'first step towards the spiritual liberation of [his] country' (*Letters*, 1.63), in the portrayal of the 'centre of paralysis' that was Dublin. In the same spirit he disclaimed responsibility for the 'odour of ashpits and old weeds and offal' (ibid., 1.64) which hung about his stories on the grounds that no artist dares 'alter in the presentment what he has seen or heard' while condemning the censorship laws of England.

In August 1906 Joyce took up a post in the international banking house of Nast-Kolb and Schumacher in Rome. Nora's and Joyce's seven-month stay in Rome taxed Joyce's resources, nerves, and relationship with Nora (which he considered to be a marriage) more than any other period of his self-styled 'exile' so far. Hours at the bank were long and the work entirely unsympathetic. He found a private pupil before taking on part-time hours at the École des Langues late in November 1906. He frequently dined out and drank without coming to like the city any better, comparing its denizens to a man who makes his living by exhibiting his grandmother's corpse. No progress was made with *Stephen Hero*, and his interest in *Dubliners* began to wane. 'A Painful Case' and 'After the Race', in particular, now seemed poor stuff to him. In Trieste he had contemplated a collection called *Provincials* to follow *Dubliners*; yet in Rome he conceived several new stories in the urban vein, 'The Last Supper', 'The Street', 'Vengeance', 'At Bay', and 'Catharsis', and planned one other called 'Ulysses'. This 'never got forrarder than its title' as a short story, but came to serve as the germ for the novel *Ulysses*. By Christmas, however, Joyce was working on 'The Dead', a final story for the stalled collection *Dubliners*. This classic example of the genre was inspired by a growing sense that he had underrated the tradition of hospitality in his native city, and supplied a redemptive air at the end without diminishing the emphasis on 'paralysis' that governs all the stories.

On 7 January 1907 the publisher Elkin Mathews wrote to propose terms for the publication of *Chamber Music*. Joyce took this as an omen and abruptly resigned from the bank with effect from 5 March. But Rome had not finished with Joyce yet: *Dubliners* was rejected by John Long on 21 February, and shortly before his departure Joyce was mugged in the street, losing 200 crowns. He returned to Trieste and the Berlitz School in early March, his mouth 'full of decayed teeth' and his soul full of 'decayed ambitions'. In addition, Nora was pregnant again notwithstanding their habit of sharing the bed head-to-toe—the method of contraception also practised by Leopold and Molly in *Ulysses*.

The Joyces settled at via S. Caterina, sharing cramped quarters there until a row over debts resulted in Stanislaus's moving out in autumn 1908. Joyce taught reluctantly for a lowly rate. He was commissioned by his pupil Roberto Prezioso to write three articles on Ireland in Italian for *Il Piccolo della Sera*: 'Il Fenianismo: l'ultimo feniano' (22 March), 'Home rule maggiorenne' (19 May), and 'L'Irlanda all sbarra' (16 Sept 1907). At the invitation of Dr Attilio Tamaro, another pupil, Joyce presented three lectures at the Università Popolare in April–May 1907: 'Irlanda, isola dei santi et dei savi', 'Giacomo Clarenzio Mangan' (May 1907), and a third on the Irish literary revival (now lost). In addressing a Triestino public with strongly irredentist leanings, Joyce showed himself surprisingly unwilling to advance the claims of Irish nationhood against those of British unionism. Ireland was not a new country asserting its independence, but 'a very old country' trying 'to renew under new forms the glories of a past civilisation'. In this archaic guise he doubted whether the Irish nationalists could establish a modern state of the sort he might wish to inhabit. In addition, he bore the old Parnellite grudge against parliamentary nationalists and equally, while clearly admiring its determination, he discounted the military capacity of Fenianism, the 'physical force' movement which he expressly identified with Sinn Féin. Ascribing blame to the colonial regime interested him less than understanding the paralysed condition of his country—hence his assertion that, while Ireland's 'soul has been weakened by centuries of useless struggles and broken treaties', the real deficit lay in the fact that the 'economic and intellectual conditions do not permit the development of individuality'. Separatist politics were marred by a 'hysterical nationalism', and cultural revivalism by an equally fantastical delusion, since in his view 'Ancient Ireland is dead just as ancient Egypt is dead'.

Joyce considered Anglo-Saxon and Roman Catholic authority to be equally 'foreign powers' in Ireland. In his lecture on Mangan—a version of the one he gave in Dublin five years earlier—he warned that 'The poet who would hurl his lightning against tyrants would establish upon the future a crueller and more intimate tyranny', thus revealing his suspicions of the form of stateship that an independent Ireland might embody. There is an obvious reference to himself in the melodramatic assertion that 'No one who has any self-respect stays in Ireland, but flees afar as though from a country that has undergone the visitation of an angered Jove'. Yet the difference between 'flight' and the notion of the artist in exile that he cultivated in Trieste is less significant than that between Joyce's insistence that Ireland remain the hamstrung nation which he left and the attempts, constitutional or otherwise, of those at home to remedy the situation. The well-known pacificism of certain episodes in *Ulysses* has its origins in such differences—as has the vagary that Bloom keeps a furled union flag near the ingleside of his front room. In his journalism of 1907, Joyce showed himself out of step with his Irish contemporaries, and preferred to remain so even at the cost of being out of step with his Triestino neighbours.

A published writer, 1907–1914 With *Chamber Music* Joyce became a published writer in May 1907, but not before he had considered withdrawing the thirty-six poems in view of their archaic air and literary slightness. The book was generously reviewed by Arthur Symons but was largely ignored by readers, fewer than 200 copies selling in the ensuing five years, though Geoffrey Molyneux Palmer requested permission to set the lyrics to music. As Nora's term approached, Joyce drank more than previously and was rescued from the gutter on one occasion by Francini. Financial hardship was such that he even applied for a post with the South Africa Colonisation Society early in July, but he was soon ill with rheumatic fever. On 26 July 1907, while he lay in one bed in the Ospedale Civico, Nora gave birth to their daughter (Anna) Lucia in the paupers' maternity ward. The child had a perceptible squint, about which she became very self-conscious as she grew older.

Joyce's illness actually spurred creative activity, and he emerged from hospital with the text of 'The Dead', which he completed on 6 September 1907. During convalescence he planned future writing including—at least in embryo—*Ulysses* (he told Stanislaus that the novel would be a Dublin *Peer Gynt*). He also planned to rewrite *Stephen Hero* in five long chapters, leaving out the sections leading up to schooldays. By 29 November he had finished the first chapter of what became *A Portrait of the Artist as a Young Man*. When Artifoni leased the Berlitz School, Joyce took on his own private pupils, among them Ettore Schmitz,

who wrote as Italo Svevo and received crucial encouragement from his friend Joyce.

In April 1909 Joyce sent the manuscript of *Dubliners* to George Roberts at Maunsel, in Dublin, and in July he returned there. He looked in vain to his friend Tom Kettle to secure him a post at University College, and a meeting with Cosgrave proved painfully shocking. His claim to have enjoyed Nora's favours while Joyce was courting her in Dublin triggered an acute attack of jealousy in Joyce, who bombarded Nora with letters questioning her virginity, his paternity, and the trust upon which their relationship was founded, asking her on 6 August, 'is it all over between us?' Byrne assured him that the whole episode was the result of a plot between Cosgrave and Gogarty to break his spirit. Joyce's next letters to Nora were full of self-abasement and erotic longing. The event had however sparked off a train of thought on the question of jealousy, the subject of his play *Exiles*. After an initial meeting with George Roberts he signed a contract for *Dubliners* with Joseph Maunsel Hone, and managed to extract an advance of £300 from Roberts. On 13 September he returned to Trieste with his sister Eva (who returned to Dublin in July 1911).

Joyce's mind turned again to money-making schemes, and he went into partnership with Triestino businessmen to establish a cinema in Dublin. After returning there in October, Joyce found suitable premises at 45 Mary Street and fitted them with electricity, gained a licence, and recruited staff. When two of the partners came over to complete the business they lodged initially in Finn's Hotel. A visit to Nora's former room stimulated Joyce to write her a letter in a lyrical tone that characterizes the final chapter of the *Portrait*. As the separation from her lengthened, his letters expressing sado-masochistic impulses compounded by coprophiliac tendencies and an obsession with women's underwear summoned a willing response in Nora. The Volta Cinema opened on 20 December 1909, first showing films such as *The Tragic Story of Beatrice Cenci*, which were received with general enthusiasm but had limited appeal for an Anglophone audience. The Volta later succumbed to the influx of more exciting fare from America by July of the following year, when it was peremptorily sold off at 40 per cent loss to the investors. Before departing Joyce secured an agency from the Dublin Woollen Company to import tweed to Trieste.

Back in Trieste by January 1910 with his sister Eileen, Joyce resumed teaching, though he passed the mornings 'at his thoughts' in bed. His relations with George Roberts deteriorated after the publisher insisted on changes to *Dubliners*. Joyce eventually agreed, but when Roberts pronounced them inadequate Joyce wrote on 10 July threatening to take legal action against the publisher. A letter from Roberts in December bore a promise of publication on 20 January 1911 and gave notice that proofs for *Dubliners* were on the way, but they were never sent. Roberts wrote again in February 1911 renewing his objections to 'Ivy Day in the Committee Room' and calling for more radical revision. Joyce's frustration reached such a pitch that he allegedly threw the manuscript of the *Portrait* in the fire, from where it was rescued by Eileen. At the beginning of August, Joyce wrote to George V to find out whether he objected to the contested phrases about Edward VII in 'Ivy Day' and received a predictably anodyne letter from his secretary. He then sent Roberts an open letter documenting the history of *Dubliners* which was printed in the *Northern Whig* (Belfast) in late August and in *Sinn Féin* (Dublin) in early September 1911.

In March 1912 Joyce gave a second series of lectures at the Università Popolare entitled 'Verismo ed idealismo nella letteratura inglese: Daniele De Foe e William Blake'. His account of each author maps out the territories in which he was coming to stake his own claim as a writer as well as prefiguring the mind and temperament of Leopold Bloom and Stephen Dedalus in complex and interchangeable ways. In April he took examinations to become a teacher in the state school system, but his admission to the profession was blocked by the unwillingness of the authorities to acknowledge his university degree.

In July Joyce joined Nora in Dublin to try to settle the matter of *Dubliners*. Together at Oughterard in co. Galway they visited the grave of Michael Bodkin, the young boy who had 'died for her' as related in 'The Dead'. Joyce, who was moved to see a grave inscribed for one 'J. Joyce' nearby, wrote the moving poem 'She Weeps for Rahoon'. Their two days on the Aran Islands resulted in an article for *Il Piccolo della Sera* in which Joyce evinced a new interest in native Irish life and folklore. Face to face with George Roberts again, Joyce found that his arguments in favour of the collection as it stood resulted in a demand for a bond of £1000 to indemnify the publisher against libel. Joyce's friend Tom Kettle declared the stories harmful to Ireland and promised to 'slate' them if they appeared. He particularly disparaged 'An Encounter', and Joyce agreed to delete it. On 18 August he suffered a further set-back when Padraic Colum called 'An Encounter' a 'terrible story'. Fortified by this, the Maunsel publisher demanded the wholesale omission of several other stories.

Joyce engaged a solicitor who wrote a damning legal opinion warning that the vigilance committee would set upon the collection. Roberts's own solicitor warned of libel charges and advised two sureties of £500. At this point Joyce pawned his watch and chain to stay in Dublin. On 30 August Roberts—by now toying with him—responded to Joyce's point-by-point defence by demanding that he rewrite whole paragraphs in 'Grace', 'Ivy Day', and 'The Boarding House' as well as changing every proper name in the book. When, on 5 September, Roberts finally offered to sell the galleys of *Dubliners* for £30, Joyce accepted on a ten-day bill to be paid from Trieste, planning to publish the collection under his own imprint, which he would call the Liffey Press. At this point Joyce apparently secured one set 'by a ruse', as he later wrote. In the event, the printer, Falconer, refused to part with the galleys when asked on 10 September, and the following day he destroyed 1000 sets of the so-called 1910 Maunsel edition of *Dubliners*. Joyce left Dublin with his family on the same evening, and

stopped briefly in London to offer the book to the *English Review* and Mills and Boon. He never returned to Ireland.

At Flushing station in the Netherlands, Joyce wrote 'Gas from a Burner', a verse invective replete with allusions to fatuous and supine practices of Dublin publishers and literati, printed in Trieste shortly after his return. In the meantime Stanislaus had rented a new apartment at 4 via Donato Bramante, after the Joyces had been evicted from their previous residence; it became their home for the remainder of their time in Trieste. Joyce took up a post at the Scuola Revoltella Superiori de Commercio in 1913, but continued afternoon lessons at the homes of private pupils. One of these was Amalia Popper, possibly the object of those yearnings which formed the basis of a new collection of epiphanies written between 1911 and 1914 and ultimately published in 1968 as *Giacomo Joyce*—after the ironic name he used for the slightly aged lover faced with the bitter-sweet discovery that 'youth has an end'. Lessons with Paolo Cuzzi's younger sister and her teenage friends ended abruptly when Signora Cuzzi caught Joyce and the girls sliding down the bannisters at the end of the lesson.

Joyce lectured on *Hamlet* at the Università Popolare between 11 November 1912 and 11 February 1913. Throughout 1913 his preparatory work on *Exiles* and *Ulysses* continued alongside *Giacomo Joyce* (several epiphanies from which were used in the novel when he had resolved against issuing it as a discrete literary text). Martin Secker and Elkin Mathews having refused *Dubliners*, Joyce wrote to Grant Richards, who wrote back. In December 1913 his fortunes changed. Both Yeats and Ezra Pound were struck by Joyce's poem 'I Hear an Army', which Pound wanted to reprint in his anthology *Des Imagistes*. Joyce sent a revised first chapter of the *Portrait* to him, along with the manuscript of *Dubliners*. Pound was so impressed that he immediately placed the novel with *The Egoist*, an originally feminist journal edited by Dora Marsden and Harriet Shaw Weaver. Joyce's explanation of the publishing history of *Dubliners*, which included his letter to the Irish press, appeared as 'A Curious History' in the January issue of *The Egoist*. The first chapter of the *Portrait* began to appear in the next, coming out on Joyce's birthday and thus establishing a tradition to which he adhered for the rest of his career. It also established the pattern that characterized the publication of *Ulysses* and *Finnegans Wake*. Publishing serially in journals gave Joyce the opportunity to revise his work endlessly, and to evolve the idea of the modern novel as a 'work in progress' which in its most extreme form was never fully 'finalized'.

Emboldened by his success with the *Portrait*, Joyce asked Richards for an immediate decision, and received his undertaking on 29 January 1914 to publish *Dubliners*. The agreement signed in March committed Joyce to taking the first 120 copies and gave Richards first option on his next work. Richards used page proofs from the Maunsel edition as copy for the first edition, which was published in 1250 copies on 15 June. Meanwhile serialization of the *Portrait* in *The Egoist* continued between February and August 1914; in the August issue one passage which offended the printer ('Fresh Nelly is waiting on you') was removed. Serialization was completed under a different printer between November 1914 and 1 September 1915.

The war years, 1914–1918 On 1 March 1914 Joyce began the long-prepared writing of *Ulysses*, without abandoning the composition of *Exiles*, which had developed its own momentum by this time. (He also worked part-time as English correspondent to the Gioacchino Veneziani paint factory.) Joyce's *annus mirabilis*, however, coincided with the outbreak of European war. In January 1915 Stanislaus was arrested as an outspoken irredentist, and in August he was interned for the duration of the war. Notwithstanding their British citizenship, Joyce and Nora remained unaffected until Italy declared war on Germany in May 1915. The Austrian authorities began a partial evacuation of Trieste. Eileen, now married, moved to Prague. Joyce managed to gain American visas from the US consulate then catering for British citizens in the region, and the Joyces were permitted to leave Austria for Switzerland, where they reached Zürich on 30 June 1915. With him Joyce had the manuscript of 'Calypso', possibly the first episode of *Ulysses* to be written.

On entering Switzerland Joyce, with no Stanislaus to depend on, was virtually without funds. But through the solicitude of Pound and Yeats he received £75 from the Royal Literary Fund, and through Siegmund Feilbogen, editor–proprietor of the *International Review*, he took on editorial work for some months at the end of 1915. Although he spent recklessly, his income increased during the war years as a result of the indulgence of his pupils (who often paid for lessons that they did not receive) and the munificence of patrons. The sum of £100 reached Joyce from the civil pension list in August 1916, while Pound secured a further £2 weekly from the Society of Authors. Late in February 1917 he received notification from an English solicitor that he was to receive a quarterly income of £50 from an anonymous admirer, who turned out to be Harriet Shaw Weaver of *The Egoist*. Miss Weaver also settled on him £5000 in war loan bonds in May 1919. From March 1918 to October 1919 he received a monthly stipend of 1000 francs from Mrs Edith Rockefeller McCormick, but the payments ended after he refused her request that he be psychoanalysed by Carl Jung. (Joyce was always sceptical about psychoanalysis, and caricatured its chief exponents as the 'Swiss Tweedledum' and the 'Viennese Tweedledee'; *Selected Letters*, 282.) All of this Joyce accepted as his due, spending his time at operas and concerts, and with Frank Budgen—a painter working for the Ministry of Information whom he met in 1918, and who subsequently wrote *James Joyce and the Making of 'Ulysses'* (1934) guided by Joyce himself. At the height of these regalements the Joyce children complained that they were left at home unattended.

There were madcap schemes in Zürich also. In spring 1917 Joyce was caught up in a plan of Jules Martin (real name Juda de Vries) to form a film company in order to extract funds from wealthy women intent on appearing in their films. (Before the year was out Martin had been arrested for embezzlement.) Irregular living—Joyce was

drinking absinthe at the time—led to increasingly frequent attacks of the iritis which he had experienced first in Trieste and later in Dublin during summer 1912. In mid-August he was diagnosed with glaucoma and synechia. During convalescence from an iridectomy on his right eye Joyce suffered a nervous collapse and recovered in Locarno from October 1917 to January 1918. Yet throughout this period writing of *Ulysses* went on relentlessly. Friends were constantly drawn in as conversational sounding boards, couriers, and typists. One such was Claud Sykes, an actor whom Joyce had met through the abortive film company scheme. During November and December 1917 Joyce sent back to Zürich the first three chapters of *Ulysses*, and Sykes produced the typescript, which was forwarded to Pound for serial publication.

Joyce's reputation as a writer of stature was advancing steadily all the while among the 'little magazines' through the dogged literary networking of his supporters. In May 1914 Grant Richards, however, decided not to exercise his option on the *Portrait* for lack of an audience in time of war, and it was rejected by Secker in July 1915. Through J. B. Pinker, his literary agent from February 1915, Joyce secured Richards's sales of *Dubliners*: disappointingly, by mid-1915 only 525 copies had been sold. In January 1916 Edward Garnett radically misjudged the originality of the *Portrait*, regarding it as a formless piece of work, and rejected it for Duckworth. Reeling from this, Joyce instructed Pinker to place the *Portrait* with Miss Weaver following an offer made the previous November, although no printer could be found after D. H. Lawrence's *The Rainbow* (1915) was banned for obscenity. At this juncture B. W. Huebsch agreed to publish it in New York if Miss Weaver would take 750 copies from him for publication in England. With this agreement in place by October, *A Portrait of the Artist as a Young Man* appeared on 29 December 1916 in New York and on 22 January 1917 in London.

From the *Portrait* to *Ulysses* In the *Portrait* Joyce had brought to its furthest development the 'embryological' method of tracing the development of his hero's 'soul' that he had glimpsed in the 1904 'Portrait' essay. The 'young man' embraces by turns religious ardour and literary aestheticism and finally discovers in himself the capacity and the will to 'forge in the smithy of [his] soul the uncreated conscience of [his] race'. This sentence, which is the climax of the last chapter of the novel, is very like another that Joyce actually wrote to Nora during his struggles with George Roberts in 1912 when he spoke of 'creating a conscience' of this 'wretched race' despite the perfidy that surrounded him. To draw out the line of his own artistic development further, however, Joyce had to wrench himself free from the unlimited egoism of Stephen Dedalus, who, as he told Frank Budgen, during the writing of *Ulysses* had 'a shape that can't be changed' (Budgen, 105). It is difficult to know exactly when Joyce arrived at this new estimate of the character whose creation and development had engaged him for ten years before he wrote '1904–1914' at the bottom of the last page of the *Portrait*. Certainly there are signs that he regarded the messianic self-exaltation of his *alter ego* as a dangerous show of hubris, comically foreshadowing the 'lapwing poet' that Stephen became in the opening chapters of *Ulysses*, where he is more like Icarus than like the masterful 'old artificer' Daedalus.

Yet, along with the shift in values that brought Leopold Bloom into existence as a counterbalance to the youthful hero in *Ulysses*, the abandonment of a privileged standpoint from which the social world could be surveyed and judged plunged Joyce into an epistemological maelstrom. He was, of course, never seriously tempted to adopt the narratorial voice of an urbane, knowing author. The nature of the colonial world from which he sprang dictated that the only authentic representation of reality in language must follow the contours of a divided world. In *Ulysses* he played out the logic of this inheritance remorselessly. None of his original supporters—Pound, Eliot, and Miss Weaver—could accept that stylistic experimentalism should be taken so far, and there was a parting of the ways after the 'Sirens' chapter in which his *fuga per canonem* struck Pound as wilful and absurd. But Joyce believed in his perception that what we know as reality, like religious doctrine, is founded 'on the incertitude of the void'—the void being the phenomenal diversity of human perceptions, points of view, *Weltanschauungen*, habits of expression, intentionalities, and idiolects. This intense relativism is unsustainable without a corresponding belief that the relativized order of experience overlies a spiritual unity accessible only through the multiplex channels of living language.

Just as the radically socialized world of *Ulysses* developed from the *Portrait*, so *Ulysses* led on to the cosmic universe of *Finnegans Wake*, in which all diversity is bound into a vast system of correspondences: mythic, stereotypical, accidental, homophonic, but always testimony to the 'continual affirmation of the human spirit' (a phrase which Joyce used in his essay on Mangan and in *Ulysses* and *Stephen Hero*). The plot and execution of *Ulysses* make it clear that the human spirit can be affirmed by two means, thought and action; and by two types, the artist and the 'citizen'. When, in the penultimate chapter, Joyce represents Stephen and Bloom at the moment before parting, pouring out their 'sequent, then simultaneous urinations' by the faint glow of a bedroom window, he is able to square the circle by demonstrating that what seems divided is actually united and what seems united is perpetually falling into division. Significantly, the two are standing in the garden, dimly lit by 'The heaventree of stars hung with humid nightblue fruit'—an arrangement that recalls the end of Dante's *Purgatorio*. At the same time the faintly illumined presence of Molly in the position of a moon is a symbol of the eternal female whose sensual affirmation in the last word of the novel ('yes') stands for the continual *exitus et reditus*, the coming and going, of human love, 'that word known to all men'.

Serialization in the *Little Review* undoubtedly contributed to the growing complexity of style that made *Ulysses* the ultimate work of literary experimentalism until *Finnegans Wake*. In each episode Joyce carried formal invention further than before, and he was increasingly obliged to

explain to his patrons and supporters the reasons for those methods which were so much at variance with Pound's promotion of him as the 'nearest thing we have to Flaubertian prose in English' (*The Egoist*, 4/2, Feb 1917, 21–2). In September 1920 he defended his novel to Miss Weaver: '[*Ulysses*] is my epic of two races and at the same time the cycle of the human body as well as a little story of a day', adding:

> It is also a sort of encyclopaedia. My intention is to transpose the myth *sub specie temporis nostri*. Each adventure (that is, every hour, every organ, every art being interconnected and interrelated in the structural scheme of the whole) should not only condition but even create its own technique.
> (*Letters*, 1.146–7)

In June 1921 he still struggled to justify the daunting texture of the novel:

> The task I set myself technically in writing a book from eighteen different points of view and in as many styles, all apparently unknown or undiscovered by my fellow tradesmen, that and the nature of the legend chosen[,] would be enough to upset anyone's mental balance.
> (*Selected Letters*, 284)

Joyce nevertheless insisted to Frank Budgen that though the methods were complicated, the thought was always simple.

Apart from Joyce's governing theme—the necessary place of love in human society—an important factor was his steady adherence to the Homeric parallel, taking the simplified narrative in Charles Lamb's *The Adventures of Ulysses*, which he read as a child, as a template for a very modern novel. Behind this lay a conviction that Odysseus, not Christ (or any other hero), was the proper model for modern man: sceptical yet able, longing for home when away and aching to wander when at home; uxorious but open to erotic stimulus and female blandishment. Such a conception involved an imaginative and occasionally jejune review of the *Odyssey* and all related texts, in antiquity and later times, notably those of Victor Bérard and other pioneers of modern archaeology and classical exegesis. At times his hermeneutic method was unashamedly whimsical—he turns the brand with which Odysseus blinds the Cyclops into a 'knockmedown cigar'. But that simply demonstrates that he kept his gaze fixed on the image of a modern man who, though unaided by any dogma other than his belief in his moral superiority, can face life's challenges with adequate understanding and practical assurance. Exploring this idea in the 'Ithaca' chapter, Joyce proffered his most ingenious, perspicacious, and light-hearted contrivance when Leopold Bloom finds he has left his latchkey in his other trousers and must let himself in by dropping into the front area of his house. Just when Stephen is affirming his own nature as 'an animal proceeding syllogistically from the known to the unknown and a conscious rational reagent between a micro- and a macrocosm ineluctably constructed upon the incertitude of the void', Bloom finds himself 'comforted' by the apprehension 'that as a competent keyless citizen he had proceeded energetically from the unknown to the known through the incertitude of the void'.

Ulysses first appeared in the *Little Review* (USA), edited by

Margaret Anderson and Jane Heap, between March 1918 and December 1920. In the opening chapters ('Telemachus', 'Nestor', and 'Proteus'), Stephen Dedalus begins his hegira from the Martello tower to the school in Dalkey where he teaches for the last time, and goes onwards to the city, 'walking into eternity along Sandymount Strand'. 'Calypso' and 'Lotus-Eaters', appearing in June and July 1918, introduced the reader to Leopold and Marion (Molly) Bloom, starting the day at their house in Eccles Street. Bloom crosses the city to the Westland Row post office to collect a letter from his clandestine correspondent Martha, before entering the turkish baths. The 'Hades' episode, set at Glasnevin cemetery, was published in September 1918, with 'Aeolus' appearing the month later. 'Lestrygonians' (January–March 1919), which takes the characters as far as lunchtime in the single day that spans the whole of the novel, was the first to raise real misgivings about the 'arsthitic' tendency of *Ulysses*, as Pound called it, suggesting in his pun that Joyce's artistic integrity was being compromised by his attention to lower matters. Katherine Mansfield and Virginia Woolf thought the author 'low-bred' for all his self-evident genius.

'Scylla and Charybdis' (April–May 1919), which takes Stephen Dedalus to the National Library of Ireland, was followed by 'Wandering Rocks' (June–July 1919), a *tour de force* in literary logistics. The movements of the characters are carefully timed by Joyce, who asked friends in Dublin how long the different itineraries would take. In 'Sirens' (August–September 1919), stylistic experimentalism begins in earnest. The device of *fuga per canonem* rests on a questionable analogy between the musical and literary arts. It was, however, the phallocentric eroticism of the chapter that alienated its contemporary readers. 'Cyclops' (November 1919–March 1920) is a brilliant parody of Irish nationalism in the personage of Michael Cusack, founder of the Gaelic Athletic Association (here called 'the citizen'), and the Irish-Ireland mania of which he is a prime representative.

'Nausicaa' (April–August 1920) was started in Zürich and continued in Trieste in October 1919. Following a period of three weeks during which he claimed not to have read, written, or spoken, Joyce resumed working on the chapter in November and finished it in time for his thirty-eighth birthday in February 1920. The episode centres on Gerty MacDowell, a lame girl who leads Leopold Bloom on through the 'wondrous revealment' of her 'nansook knickers'. (Early in 1919 Joyce was sexually drawn to a Marthe Fleischmann, an attractive young woman with a slight limp, who reminded him of a girl he had seen in Clontarf in 1898.) In 'Nausicaa' Joyce evolved the technique that he characterized in a letter to Frank Budgen as 'namby-pamby jammy marmalady drawersy (*alto là!*)', examples of which could be found in novelettes and hymnbooks he asked his Aunt Josephine to send from Dublin. (Hearing that his aunt thought *Ulysses* unfit to read, he said: 'If *Ulysses* isn't fit to read, life isn't fit to live'; Ellmann, *Joyce*, 537.) 'Oxen of the Sun' (September–December 1920), which proved to be the last serialized portion of the novel, has Stephen and Bloom in the National Maternity Hospital on very different pretexts. In it Joyce parodied canonical prose styles to highlight the embryological development of English. The result is a literary fabric which he frankly admitted to be the 'most difficult … to interpret and to execute' in his odyssey of style so far (*Letters*, 1.137). It is also the most resolutely Aristotelian. T. S. Eliot considered it a revelation of the 'futility of all styles'—a judgement related to his own conviction that the 'mythic method' of *Ulysses* was 'a way of controlling, of ordering, of giving shape and a significance to the immense panorama of futility and anarchy which is contemporary history' (Eliot, 201). It is far from certain that Joyce shared Eliot's anxiety.

The composition of 'Circe'—a *Walpurgisnacht* in which Stephen and Bloom confront their inner demons in the brothel quarter of Dublin—engaged Joyce from June to December 1920, spanning the period of his move to Paris in October 1920. Like the remaining three chapters of the novel, it did not appear in print until the publication of the completed novel in February 1922. 'Eumaeus' follows Stephen and Bloom from Nighttown to the cabman's shelter, where questions of history and politics visit their tired minds. It is a skilful sampler of clichés and misleading information from the social and political consciousness of contemporary Ireland together with a peculiarly Joycean vision of Parnell and the Invincibles. 'Ithaca' is conducted in catechetical form—an encyclopaedia crossed with family charades and tinged with cosmological awe. It brings Stephen and Bloom to Bloom's kitchen, before the younger man goes out into the night to become (presumably) the author of *Ulysses* ten years later. In 'Penelope', Joyce created a virtually unpunctuated stream of consciousness: the unexpurgated contents of Molly Bloom's mind flow around the day's events and the events of other days, finally returning to Leopold, whom she recalls choosing because he 'understood or felt what a woman is and I knew I could always get round him'. Her life-affirming 'yes' added in October 1921 is conditional, but an affirmation none the less. (Inspiration came from Lillian Wallace, the wife of his friend Richard Wallace, who repeatedly employed the 'yes' in conversation.) After long meditation, Joyce had written *Ulysses*, mostly in Zürich. This gave Tom Stoppard grounds for the retort he puts in the novelist's mouth in *Travesties* (1974), where he rebuts the usual question about what he did during the war with the answer, 'I wrote *Ulysses*. What did you do?'

Publication of *Ulysses* During the Zürich years Joyce had formed a theatrical company with Claud Sykes. The first production was Wilde's *The Importance of Being Earnest* at the Theater zu den Kaufleuten on 29 April 1918. The evening was a profitable success largely owing to the acting of Henry Carr, who had a minor post in the consulate, but Carr was upset to receive so small a share of the profits, and pursued Joyce in the courts. Joyce won the first case on 15 October 1918 but lost the second on 11 February 1919, with costs and damages totalling 120 francs. Fortunately there soon arrived gifts of $1000 from millionaire friends of Padraic and Mary Colum in New York, from which Joyce paid $200 towards the upkeep of the English Players. In spring 1919 his attempts to stage Purcell's *Dido and Aeneas* were hindered by the British consulate, which confirmed his contempt for such officials. In *Ulysses* Carr's name was used for the coarse and belligerent soldier in the 'Circe' episode and Horace Rumbold, British minister to Switzerland, for the semi-literate hangman. Notwithstanding Carr's defection, Joyce took the English Players on tour to Lausanne, Geneva, Montreux, and Interlaken. In mid-June the company staged Synge's *Riders to the Sea*, with Nora as Catheleen. His own play *Exiles* reached the stage in a German translation by Hannah von Mettal, made at the instigation of Stefan Zweig. Produced as *Verbannte* in Munich on 7 August 1919, it ran for only one night, adjudged 'a flop' by Joyce to forestall criticism.

On 19 October Joyce returned to Trieste with his family and moved in with his sister Eileen at 2 via Sanità, where Stanislaus was already ensconced, having been released from internment. Joyce gave a few lessons at the Istituto di Commercio 'Revoltella' (the last time he taught), and socialized with Ettore Schmitz and the Francinis—though Clotilde Francini found his manner altered. Relations with Stanislaus were cooler too; indeed, the brothers were never close again. Stanislaus's resentment of Joyce's exploitation over many years and his disappointment with Joyce's recent works were beginning to harden in Stanislaus's mind. Joyce's view is portrayed in the Shem-Shaun relationship of *Finnegans Wake*, in which the over-regulated and authoritarian character of the one is pitted against the chaotic yet creative temperament of the other.

Early in June 1920 Joyce for the first time met Pound, who found him 'stubborn as a mule or an Irishman' but not 'at all *unreasonable*' (Ellmann, *Joyce*, 480). On Pound's suggestion the Joyce family moved to Paris on 8 July, into a tiny flat close to the Bois de Boulogne. Without income, they lived on Pound's personal generosity. The world of Parisian letters began to make a place for Joyce: within three days of reaching the city, he had met Paul Valéry at the home of Natalie Clifford Barney. In John Rodker he found a genial admirer who became the nominal publisher of the Egoist edition of *Ulysses*. On 11 June, at the home of André Spire, Joyce was introduced to Sylvia Beach, proprietor of Shakespeare & Co., who became his most important supporter after Miss Weaver. In August he met T. S. Eliot and Wyndham Lewis at the Hôtel Élysée, Eliot bearing a parcel of shoes from Pound to replace the tennis shoes that Joyce was reduced to wearing. This drove him to pick up the bill for an expensive meal while otherwise displaying what Eliot called 'punctilious reserve'.

Joyce soon, however, moved to a luxurious apartment at 5 boulevard Raspail using £200 supplied by Miss Weaver. (Her support did not fail in his lifetime and even extended to his family afterwards.) On Christmas eve Sylvia Beach arranged a meeting between Joyce and the influential critic and translator Valery Larbaud, who 'raved' about *Ulysses* and acted as its chief publicist in France, giving the book an immense impetus by means of a pre-launch lecture at La Maison des Amis des Livres on 7 December 1921. In the interim, however, the 'Nausicaa' episode became the object of a formal complaint by the Society for the Prevention of Vice in New York, and issues of the *Little Review* were confiscated and burnt by the US post office in September 1920, others having been previously sequestered in January and May 1919. In the hearing at the court of special sessions in February 1921, the editors of the magazine were fined $50 on the understanding that the lapse would not be repeated. Although the lawyer John Quinn believed that the entire book might be more easily defended than a single episode, Huebsch was sufficiently rattled to withdraw his undertaking to publish *Ulysses* in America.

Joyce's despondency at these events led Sylvia Beach to request 'the honour of bringing out your *Ulysses*' in Paris. It was agreed that an edition of 1000 copies would be produced using the Dijon printer Maurice Darantière. It was simultaneously agreed that the Egoist Press in London would buy the Darantière plates to publish a London edition as soon as the Paris imprint was sold out. Yet the book had still to be completed; and, though Joyce confidently predicted that he would finish writing it by the summer, iritis and other difficulties intervened in the months ahead.

Calamity struck when a Mr Harrison, employed in the British embassy, indignantly grabbed a portion of the 'Circe' episode of *Ulysses* from his wife, who was typing it from manuscript, and thrust it in the fire. John Quinn reluctantly repaired the loss with a photostat of the fair copy, which he purchased as Joyce produced it. Joyce's health now deteriorated dramatically. In July and again in August he lost consciousness, with fear of rats being the proximate cause, though drinking bouts stood behind each occasion. A serious attack of iritis prevented work for five weeks in July and August. Robert McAlmon, who with Djuna Barnes and Wyndham Lewis was a drinking companion, provided Joyce with a monthly stipend of $150 throughout 1921 and assisted with some typing. Another boon companion was Arthur Power, the Irish painter whom Joyce met in Montparnasse and who carefully recorded their conversations for posterity. A visit from Con Leventhal, who later introduced Samuel Beckett to him, soon resulted in the sole enthusiastic notice that *Ulysses* received in Dublin in his lifetime.

From June to October 1921 Joyce worked on the galley sheets from Darantière, embarking on the habit of marginal revision that characterizes so much of the textual history of *Ulysses*. In places he added one-third as much again to the margins, poring over his notebooks for additional material. With 'Penelope' and 'Ithaca' finished in October, and the passages omitted by *The Egoist*'s printer all reinstated, *Ulysses* was published on 2 February 1922. It was Joyce's fortieth birthday, and Sylvia Beach gave one copy, in its distinctive cobalt blue covers with white lettering (chosen after the Greek flag), to Joyce. Though it was promised to Miss Weaver, Joyce inscribed his copy to Nora, who never read it. As a result of Larbaud's advocacy, the subscription list for the first edition is a veritable almanac of leading French and English authors, though André Gide and George Bernard Shaw pointedly abstained. On 16 June 1922 Joyce celebrated the first 'Bloomsday', as the day on which the action of *Ulysses* occurs was known from that time, and on 12 October the Egoist edition was published in London. Within four days the agreed print run of 2000 was fully subscribed, although problems with delivery resulted in some copies being smuggled across borders. Confiscations accounted for some 400–500 copies in America, while the British customs seized 499 at Folkestone shortly after a further run of 500 had been printed in 23 January to make up for the American losses.

'Work in Progress' begins In 1922 and 1923 Joyce's health was again precarious. While Nora was in Ireland, following a period of domestic tension, he suffered an acute attack of iritis late in May 1922 and a physician observed him living in considerable squalor at rue de l'Université. On an endocrinologist's recommendation all his teeth were extracted, and shortly afterwards he underwent a sphincterectomy on his left eye. But meanwhile Joyce showed signs of bestirring himself in new writing. To Miss Weaver he had said that he was thinking of composing 'a history of the world' (Ellmann, *Joyce*, 537)—the first intimation of the ground plan of *Finnegans Wake*. In February 1923 he sorted out 12 kilograms of notes for *Ulysses*, and he began about this time a notebook later published as *Scribbledehobble*, which consisted largely of unused material from earlier works under headings based on the *Dubliners* stories. It was the first of nearly seventy such notebooks which went towards the making of *Finnegans Wake*. Though Joyce may have shown Larbaud a very early draft of the 'Tristan and Isolde' passage of the *Wake* in March 1922, it was not until 10 March 1923 that Joyce made a formal departure in sketching the 'King Roderick O'Conor' episode—the so-called first fragment of *Finnegans Wake*—writing to Miss Weaver, 'the leopard cannot change his spots' (*Letters*, 1.202). His benefactor soon demonstrated her commitment to his genius—to be tested hard in the ensuing seventeen years—by settling a further £12,000 on Joyce. After 'St Kevin' and 'The Colloquy of St Patrick and the Druid' swiftly followed, he produced 'Mamalujo' (*Finnegans Wake*, II.iv) as a framing chapter for the revised version of 'Tristan and Isolde'. Six of the eight sections of book 1 were written consecutively during 1923, with sections 1 and 4 being added in 1926–7.

Ford Madox Ford offered to publish part of 'Work in Progress'—as Ford dubbed it—in *transatlantic review*, where a draft of 'Tristan and Isolde' appeared as a 'literary supplement' in April 1924. In November T. S. Eliot's essay 'Ulysses, order, and myth' appeared in *The Dial* (1923), announcing that the 'mythic order' of Joyce's *Ulysses* had the importance of a scientific discovery'—a distinct compensation for the fact that Eliot had been unwilling to review *Ulysses* when it appeared. Joyce, meanwhile, was determined to sustain his reputation as an author adept at more conventional forms of literature and permitted five poems from *Chamber Music* to appear in the Frankfurt magazine *Der Querschnitt* (1923). Shakespeare & Co. reprinted *Ulysses* in the first unlimited edition in the new year, incorporating a list of corrections which had been supplied by Joyce himself but which were not applied to the text until the reset Bodley Head edition in 1960. On 7 March 1924 he sent 'Anna Livia Plurabelle' to Miss Weaver, with a letter explaining its narrative framework: 'a chattering dialogue across the river [Liffey] by two washerwomen who as night falls become a tree and a stone' (*Letters*, 1.213). Joyce had completed 'Shaun the Post' by late May and composed the moving poem 'A Prayer!', expressing the masochistic but not abject relation to Nora from which much of his energy as a writer may have proceeded: 'Blind me with your dark nearness … beloved enemy of my will!'

Recurrent health problems did not prevent Joyce's carrying 'Work in Progress' forward dramatically during 1925. A four-page section on 'the Earwickers of Sidlesham in the Hundred of Manhood' (I.ii) appeared in McAlmon's *Contact Collection of Contemporary Writers* in May, while a sample of the 'Mamafesta' chapter (I.v) was published in Eliot's *Criterion* in July 1925. Anna Livia Plurabelle (I.viii) made her first appearance in *Navire d'Argent* (1 Oct 1925), and Ernest Walsh published a draft of the 'Shem' chapter (I.vii) in *This Quarter* (1925–6). Early in June the Joyces moved to 2 square Robiac, off rue de Grenelle, where they remained until 1931; this was their most lasting residence in Paris. By November Joyce was near the end of 'Fourth Watch of Shaun' (bk III). In February 1926 the first English-language production of his play *Exiles* was staged at the Neighbourhood Playhouse in New York, followed in the same month by a London première by the Stage Society, after an inordinately long delay, which elicited praise from Bernard Shaw.

The writing of book 2 and emendations to other sections occupied Joyce from 1926 to 1938, but he was preoccupied with eye trouble (he worked with a magnifying glass), the mental illness of his daughter Lucia, and the growing alienation of supporters. No new sections of 'Work in Progress' were published during 1926. For much of the year Joyce was busy revising the 'Mime of Mick, Nick and the Maggies' and the other three chapters of book 2. Besides that he produced the new episodes 'Triangle'—later part of 'Night Lessons' (II.ii)—and the opening pages of *Finnegans Wake*. About this time Ezra Pound stated that 'nothing short of divine vision or a new cure for the clapp' could be worth 'all that circumambient peripherisation' (Read, 228).

In summer 1927 Joyce wrote the 'Questions' section of 'Work in Progress' (I.vi). Between April and November, Eugene and Maria Jolas, Joyce's greatest literary allies in advancement of 'Work in Progress', published the first eight sections in *transition*, their 'international quarterly for creative experiment', resuming again in 1928 and 1929 with 'Night Lessons' and 'Four Watches of Shaun'. The Jolases adopted the work as the icon of their 'revolution of the word', a 'mantic' conception of language which, since free from any positive metaphysics, proved easier to combine with Freudianism, surrealism, and ultimately post-structuralism than with religion or theosophy, which proved convenient to contemporaries, and even more so to later Joycean commentators. With a definite literary forum, Joyce secured the support of Stuart and Moune Gilbert (Stuart Gilbert helped with the French translation of

Ulysses in 1929, and in 1930 wrote a study of *Ulysses* based on Joyce's information), Paul and Lucie Léon, Louis Gillet, Nino Frank, and Samuel Beckett, while older friends dropped away. One such was Wyndham Lewis, who in autumn 1927 published in *Time and Western Man* an unflattering 'analysis of the mind of James Joyce', whom he accused of introducing a 'suffocating, neotic expanse of objects, all of them lifeless' into his work. Joyce retaliated in a scathing portrait of Lewis as an antisemitic, pro-fascist woman-hater in 'The Mookse and the Gripes' and the fable 'The Ondt and the Gracehoper' (III.i).

Crisis and consolidation, 1928–1939 By September 1928, having returned to Paris from a trip to Salzburg, Frankfurt, Munich, and Le Havre, Joyce found his eyes deteriorating to an extent that virtually prevented him from working in 1931. A hostile review from Sean O'Faolain in *Criterion* in the autumn upset him greatly, especially as he feared that T. S. Eliot was also turning against him. In October 1928 *Anna Livia Plurabelle* came out as a pamphlet in New York. Meanwhile, Joyce had organized the compilation of a book that appeared in May 1929 under the title *Our Exagmination round his Factification for Incamination of Work in Progress* with essays from Beckett, Budgen, Gilbert, McAlmon, Thomas MacGreevy, Marcel Brion, Victor Llona, Elliot Paul, John Rodker, Robert Sage, and William Carlos Williams, as well as letters of protest from G. V. L. Slingsby and Vladimir Dixon—the latter an illiterate correspondent long thought to be Joyce, but in fact real. In August the Black Sun Press in Paris issued *Tales Told of Shem and Shaun*, comprising 'The Mookse and the Gripes', 'The Muddest Thick that was Ever Heard Dump', and 'The Ondt and the Gracehoper', with a foreword by C. K. Ogden and a 'symbol' of Joyce's 'sens du pousser' by Brancusi, which caused John Stanislaus Joyce to remark that 'the boy seems to have changed a good deal' (Ellmann, *Joyce*, 614).

In England during summer 1929 Joyce met Eliot to discuss the forthcoming publication of *Anna Livia Plurabelle* (1930), and made a recording from it at the BBC in what Harold Nicolson later called his 'Anna Livia voice' (Hutchins, 176). Joyce, who had for some time thought he might hand over *Finnegans Wake* to another writer, visited James Stephens, who offered to complete it if his eyesight should fail. The appearance of 'Fourth Watch of Shaun' in *transition* in November 1929 marked a change of tempo for Joyce, since financial problems obliged the Jolases to discontinue publication until 1933. Henry Babou and Jack Kahane brought out *Haveth Childers Everywhere* in Paris and New York; this was the only fragment to be published in 1930 (Faber issued it in 1931). Further eye operations in Zürich markedly improved Joyce's sight. His suspicions about psychoanalysis were confirmed when Jung wrote a foreword for the third German edition of *Ulysses* that was both irrelevant and offensive. Jung subsequently mollified Joyce, calling the 'Penelope' chapter a 'non-stop run of psychological peaches' (ibid., 182). In December he found a willing hagiographer, Herbert Gorman (*James Joyce* was not published until 1939), and himself worked on the French translation of *Anna Livia Plurabelle* started by

Samuel Beckett and Alfred Péron (it was completed by Paul Léon, Eugene Jolas, and Ivan Goll).

In 1931 Sylvia Beach accepted the *Ulysses* manuscripts in lieu of world rights, and the novel was brought out in America by Random House in 1934 having been judged 'honest' and 'sincere' by a United States district court judge. Albatross Press took over publication of the novel in Europe, issuing the Odyssey Edition of 1932, which was seen through the press by Stuart Gilbert. (An English edition published by John Lane appeared in 1936.) In 1931 Joyce also signed a contract for the English edition of *Finnegans Wake* with Faber and with B. W. Huebsch at New York's Viking Press.

On 4 July 1931 Joyce and Nora were married, 'for testamentary reasons', at Kensington register office, Joyce singing 'Phil the Fluther's Ball' and 'Shule Aroon' in celebration. The date, intentionally, was Joyce's father's birthday, but nearly six months later on 29 December John Stanislaus Joyce died. Surprisingly, the old man left an estate of £665 0s. 9d. gross, of which £36 12s. 1d. remained to Joyce, the sole beneficiary, after debts were paid. Joyce experienced 'self-accusation' and 'prostration of mind', but this was alleviated when Giorgio (now George) and his wife Helen Fleischman, whom he had married in December 1930, provided him with a grandson, Stephen, on 15 February 1932. Joyce marked the occasion with the poem 'Ecce puer', which contained the lines:

> Young life is breathed
> On the glass
> The world that was not
> Comes to pass …
> O, father forsaken,
> Forgive your son!

Lucia's troubling behaviour at this period reached a crisis on Joyce's fiftieth birthday, when she threw a chair at her mother and was removed by George to a *maison de santé*: this was her first entry into medical care. Her unrequited love for Samuel Beckett, and a disastrous engagement to Alex Ponisovsky, who had taught Joyce Russian, had added to her distress, and she was diagnosed—possibly mistakenly—with hebephrenia, a type of schizophrenia. Joyce was racked with anxiety and guilt about his daughter ('Whatever spark of gift I possess has been transmitted to Lucia, and has kindled a fire in her brain'; Ellmann, *Joyce*, 650), and he arranged for her to design 'lettrines' for *A Chaucer ABC* (1936). With his right eye virtually beyond repair, he worked on through the autumn with the children's chapter of 'Work in Progress' (II.i). The mordant humour of its celebrated conclusion—'Loud, heap miseries upon us yet entwine our arts with laughters low'—triumphantly reflects its author's humour at that period. (It was issued by the Servire Press in June 1934 with designs by Lucia.) *Two Tales of Shem and Shaun* was also published as a pamphlet in 1932. In 1933 Joyce suffered from colitis, an indication of the illness that eventually killed him, but the news of the American edition of *Ulysses* inspired some jubilation. With his daughter in a sanatorium early in 1934, Joyce worked 'every day alone at my big long wide high deep dense prosework' (Ellmann, *Joyce*,

673). But on 15 September Lucia, now also suffering from leucocytosis, set fire to her room and was transferred to Zürich Mental Asylum before being moved to a private sanatorium at Küsnacht where Jung was a consultant. Despite Joyce's misgivings about Jung as a critic he thought he might be able to help his daughter. Indeed for a time Lucia responded well to Jung and Joyce was reassured. When Jung suggested that Lucia was her father's *anima inspiratrix*, Joyce removed her in January 1935. He later told Jung that he and his daughter were both innovating a new literature. Jung believed however that they 'were like two people going to the bottom of a river', but Lucia was drowning while her father was diving (Ellmann, *Joyce*, 679). Meanwhile Lucia was temporarily put in the care of her aunt Eileen in Bray and Miss Weaver in London, who were tested to the limit. Joyce himself was melancholic, doubting if 'anything lies ahead of us except ruin' (*Letters*, 3.332), as he wrote to Budgen.

Throughout this period Joyce strenuously resisted the idea that Lucia was mad or that her fixation on him was anything more than the hypersensitivity of an affectionate daughter for whose disordered state of mind he felt immense responsibility and a profound compassion. His letters to Miss Weaver mingled anger and scepticism at the disturbing information given him, while she, attempting to obey his injunction that Lucia be spoken of as normal, understated the extremity of her behaviour. Late in 1935 Lucia was removed in a straitjacket from an establishment at Neuilly after further violent behaviour, and was threatened with incarceration in a state asylum. Joyce, now recognizing that she was in 'the abyss of insanity', was able to have her transferred to a *hôtel de santé* at Ivry-sur-Seine, where she remained until 1951. (She was then moved to St Andrew's Hospital, Northampton, where she remained until her death in 1982.)

With Lucia safe at Ivry—where he visited her each week—Joyce, notwithstanding attacks of colitis and the usual financial troubles, was more relaxed than for some years previously, expressing himself on life and literature with uncharacteristic freedom to friends and visitors. He spent much time in 1937 conferring with Nino Frank about the Italian translation of *Anna Livia Plurabelle*, and Samuel Beckett was also in his company. *Storiella as She is Syung* was published by the Corvinus Press in London in October 1937, containing passages from 'Night Lessons'. 'Work in Progress' was drawing to conclusion with galley proofs, page proofs, and the last manuscript pages of book 4 keeping Joyce occupied for sixteen hours a day, by his own estimation. In Zürich in late summer 1938 Joyce ignored advice to undergo examination after severe stomach cramps, and returned to Paris as war loomed. Joyce barked at Stanislaus: 'Don't talk to me of politics, all I am interested in is style.' His indifference did not prevent his helping Herman Broch to reach England in March 1938, nor, as Bernard McGinley points out, his involvement with Giuseppe Bertelli in trying to help Jewish refugees to get to America. But his unwillingness to protest against Nazism in print disappointed several friends.

In the fraught atmosphere after the Munich pact, the last passage of 'Work in Progress', or *Finnegans Wake*, as it was now to be known, was composed, ending on 13 November 1938 with the inscription 'un rien, l'article the'. Joyce's sense of pride and relief was such that, for some days afterwards, he carried the manuscript with him. Joyce had hoped to publish *Finnegans Wake* on his father's birthday in 1938, but instead one unbound copy reached him on 30 January 1939. Faber in London and the Viking Press in New York simultaneously published his final work on 4 May 1939.

Finnegans Wake The most conspicuous innovation of *Finnegans Wake* is its use of 'dream-language'. After *Ulysses* Joyce believed that he had 'come to the end of English', and his last novel is a pervasive layering of multilingual puns in successive drafts which produces a fabric rich in semantic possibilities but almost impenetrable to the general reader. Joyce's method is demonstrably modern, having more to do with philology and psychoanalysis than with symbolism and magic, but it is none the less informed by a sacral relation to language as a kind of 'broken heaventalk' in which truth subsists in a dismembered way. He was unorthodox in his beliefs but he used the terms 'soul' and 'spirit' passionately, and he did not accept the premises of a vacuous form of relativism. *Finnegans Wake* is patently the most relativistic of all literary texts, yet it is also the most absolute in that it attempts to reconstruct 'the reality of experience' through a vast system of correspondences. If developed to the uttermost, these produce a representation of humanity whose claim to truth is its completeness as a 'selfbounded and self-contained' entity whose 'soul' 'leaps from the vestment of its being'. In order to effect this Joyce made H. C. Earwicker, a publican in Chapelizod, co. Dublin, and reincarnation of Finn MacCool, the 'dreaming subject'. Like the Joyces, who spoke Triestino Italian at home, the Earwicker family is multilingual. No one language dominates in *Finnegans Wake*, except Hiberno-English, which has a comic vibrancy and lyricism. The characters occupy different times and places in the same (or opposite) person. The question 'Who is dreaming *Finnegans Wake*?' is not ultimately rewarding, yet it does point to the fundamental innovation, which is to let language itself constitute the reality of experience.

The relationship between the various textual stages of *Finnegans Wake* is even more anomalous than is the case with *Ulysses*. There was no fair copy, and multiple versions exist in notebooks, drafts, typescripts, and corrected proofs (now held at the British Library and the State University of New York at Buffalo). Moreover, many of the episodes were published in magazines and pamphlets, often not in their final state. *Finnegans Wake* therefore seems less like a book '*about* something; *it is that something itself*', as Samuel Beckett wrote of it (Beckett and others, 14). In one respect the final text of *Finnegans Wake* is, however, stable.

The title of the book—which was kept secret until 1938—was taken from an Irish-American ballad, a party piece in the Joyce household in Dublin, about Tim Finnegan, a drunken bricklayer who falls to his death from a ladder but returns to life when accidentally splashed with whiskey at his wake. Around this song, with its suggestion of reincarnation and eternal return, Joyce constructed a vast edifice of corresponding myths and narratives. Some of these were hallmark Irish and Judaeo-Christian, but other sources, including the Egyptian Book of the Dead and the comic-strip banter of Mutt and Jeff, provide an astonishing symphony of human voices to construct a universal history. Joyce's chief inspiration is Giambattista Vico, who divided human history into divine, heroic, and human ages followed by a *ricorso* (or return), setting the whole cycle in motion once again. In *Finnegans Wake* these ages correspond to the four books which constitute the whole work, as well as internal cycles within them. At the same time the *Wake* is structured by the idea of interdependent and mutually generating opposites which Joyce derived from Giordano Bruno and Samuel Taylor Coleridge, who wrote: 'Every power in nature or in spirit must evolve an opposite as the sole condition and means of its manifestation; and every opposition is, therefore, a tendency to reunion' (*Critical Writings*, 134).

Joyce's central 'characters' represent human life in a more comprehensive way than literary realism—and naturalism in particular—admits. They are archetypal while being located in a dense matrix of disparate and even contradictory literary and historical allusions. At the centre stands Humphrey Chimpden Earwicker with his consort Anna Livia Plurabelle, respectively embodied by the Hill of Howth and the River Liffey. In the central 'Night Lessons' chapter, Joyce presents a chart of 'the whome of your eternal geomater' which doubles as a map of Ireland and a diagram of the dynamic and often hostile relations between genders and siblings and (more problematically) between fathers and their daughters. The events that befall the Earwicker family in the *Wake* primarily concern a sexual misdemeanour committed by Humphrey in Dublin's Phoenix Park. This involves two girls and three soldiers, who are counterparts of Issy on the one hand, and Shem and Shaun on the other. Just as Issy becomes her mother, so the boys become their father. Earwicker is a male principle who readily bifurcates into his warring sons, while Issy represents the sexually attractive principle through whom the sons are reattached to the source of life. It is through loss of innocence that these necessary processes in the chain of reproduction are effected—a *felix culpa*, or happy fall.

By 21 May 1926 Joyce had been able to write, 'I have the book fairly well planned out in my head' (*Letters*, 1.241). He insisted that the labour of composition was like tunnelling through a mountain from two sides, implying a general symmetry between the four latter sections of book 1 and those of book 3. For instance, Anna's soliloquy at the end of book 1 ('Anna Livia Plurabelle') is balanced by Earwicker's soliloquy at the end of book 3 ('Haveth Childers Everywhere'). 'The Mookse and the Gripes' in book 1 is a companion piece to 'The Ondt and the Gracehoper' in book 3. The structure of the text is a 'simple equilibrium of two symmetrical half-arches supporting a keystone of greater complexity', as Roland McHugh has remarked

(McHugh, 6)—the keystone being the barely penetrable chapters of book 2.

Book 1 concerns Earwicker's crime, betrayal, demise, and burial. The fifth section offers a palaeographer's account of Anna's letter and a pastiche of Sir Edward Sullivan's preface to the Book of Kells, which serves also as a caricature of *Finnegans Wake* itself. The sixth poses twelve conundrums of great ingenuity, including 'The Mookse and the Gripes'. In the next section Shaun offers a portrait of the artist in which Stephen Dedalus is disparaged as a 'supreme prig', and the *Wake* itself as an 'epical forged cheque', comprising 'once current puns, quashed quotatoes, messes of mottage'. The last section is a *tour de force* with its 'chattering dialogue' between two washerwomen across the Liffey, discoursing on the scandalous failings of Earwicker. The episode ultimately included the names of more than 500 rivers.

The first half of book 2 concerns the children, initially engaged in a charade-cum-matinée performance and afterwards at their homework. The third section, set in the public house, features two more Joycean fables—'The Norwegian Captain' and 'How Buckley Shot the Russian General'. It also frames Joyce's response to the invention of television and the splitting of the atom (respectively 'the bairdboard bombardment screen' and 'the abnihilisation of the etym' by 'the first lord of Hurtreford'). In the last section of book 2, the story of Tristan and Isolde is retold by the four evangelists ('Mamalujo'), who hover above the lovers' boat in the form of seagulls, each connected with a different province, as their accents reveal. These voyeurs also represent the four masters (compilers of the seventeenth-century Irish *Annals*) and, as such, all important redactors of hotblood conquests. The section ends with the tragic history of 'King Roderick O'Conor', last high king of Ireland, whose 'babel tower and beamer' are reduced to 'diversed tonguesed', signifying the cultural disorder of a colonized realm. This was the first episode to be written and reveals the centrality of cultural hybridity to *Finnegans Wake*.

Book 3 traces the passage of Shaun the Post 'backwards through the events already narrated' while 'rolling up the Liffey in a barrel', as Joyce told Miss Weaver (*Letters*, 1.214). The first section, containing 'The Ondt and the Gracehoper', is followed by 'Jaun', who preaches moral hypocrisy to Issy and falls ignominiously to earth from his 'soapbox', while Issy turns to the more romantically interesting Shem ('Coach me how to tumble, Jaime'). As 'Yawn' in the third section, the eponymous postman is stretched out at the hill of Uisneach, a druidic centre of ancient Ireland, and becomes a conduit for contesting Irish voices from St Patrick to Parnell until, at last, being revealed as Earwicker. (The final passage was published as *Haveth Childers Everywhere* in 1930.) In the fourth watch, Earwicker's children witness a 'culious epiphany' as their father, wakened in the night, unsuccessfully attempts sexual intercourse with his wife ('You never wet the tea!').

After this, the lowest ebb, Joyce takes his universal history back to dawn with the 'Ricorso' (book 4), conceived as a stained-glass window through which the sun rises at the pagan equinox. St Patrick, in legend associated with that season, contends with the archdruid Balkelly, in whom Bishop Berkeley and Johannes Erigena are equally mixed. Pantheism gives way to monotheism when the missionary ignites the paschal fire, bringing in a new cycle, just as life begins again when 'dawnfire' touches the 'tablestoane ath the centre of the great circle of the macroliths' at Tara (or, more exactly, Newgrange). In spite of these masculine enactments of the idea of rebirth, it requires Anna's soliloquy at the end to usher in the new cycle of birth, marriage, and death, as she does with her imperative call: 'Finn, again!'

Last years, 1939–1941 When war was declared on 3 September 1939 Joyce and Nora were in Brittany awaiting Lucia. From late 1939 to early 1940 they were on the move, from La Chapelle with Maria Jolas to Vichy. Joyce passed his time preparing corrections for *Finnegans Wake* with Paul Léon (or 'adding commas', as he told George Pelorson), and telling Homeric stories to his grandson Stephen. In Paris Léon rescued Joyce's papers and saved other possessions which an unpaid landlord auctioned. He deposited them with Count O'Kelly, the Irish ambassador, on the understanding that they should be given to the National Library of Ireland if he did not return to collect them. Léon soon afterwards fell into the hands of the Gestapo, and was murdered by a concentration camp guard in April 1942.

The Joyces left France for Switzerland, and arrived in Zürich on 17 December 1940. From the Pension Delphin Joyce issued messages of thanks to those who had assisted him—Jacques Mercanton, who signed the deposition denying that he was Jewish (which had led to his initially being refused a Swiss visa); Edmund Brauchbar (a businessman who had been a student of Joyce's in 1915), who had deposited 20,000 francs in a Zürich bank for which Joyce's friend Paul Ruggiero still worked; Ruggiero himself, who galvanized a support group; and Armand Petitjean and Louis Gillet, who gained permission for the Joyces to leave France. In the afternoons he walked in the snow with Stephen, stopping on one occasion to buy him books on Greek mythology.

On 7 January 1941 Joyce sent his last written communication, a card with a list of useful names for Stanislaus, who had been forced to move to Florence. After Ruggiero's birthday dinner on 10 January he suffered acute abdominal pains—the 'cramps' that had been troubling him periodically for many years. When a dose of morphine proved inadequate he was carried on a stretcher to the Schwesterhaus vom Roten Kreuz, 'writhing like a fish' according to his grandson's memory of the event (Ellmann, *Joyce*, 741). An X-ray revealed a perforated duodenal ulcer, and an operation was performed on 12 January. Joyce woke from anaesthetic and appeared to be recovering but started losing strength on Sunday and was given blood transfusions. Before Nora and George were sent away by the medical staff, he asked for Nora to lie down beside him. At 1 a.m. he woke and asked for them before slipping into a coma. James Joyce died at the Schwesterhaus vom Roten Kreuz at 2.15 a.m. on 13 January

1941, before his family could arrive. The sculptor Paul Speck was commissioned to make a death mask. Joyce was buried at Fluntern cemetery in Zürich on 15 January, Nora refusing Catholic rites. The expenses of the funeral were paid by Miss Weaver, who readdressed to Nora the sum of £250 she was preparing to send to him. At the graveside were the British minister Lord Derwent, who made an address, the poet Max Geilinger, Professor Heinrich Straumann, and Max Meilor, a tenor, who sang 'Addio terra, addio cielo' from Monteverdi's *Orfeo*. Lucia received the news of her father's death with all the marks of her condition and a curious echo of Joyce's theme in his last book, saying, 'What is he doing under the ground, that idiot? When will he decide to come out? He's watching us all the time' (Ellmann, *Joyce*, 743).

The young Joyce who had arrived at University College, Dublin, in 1899 was 'tall, slim, and elegant' with 'an erect yet loose carriage; an uptilted, long, narrow head, and a strong chin that jutted out arrogantly; firm, tight shut mouth; light-blue eyes [that] could stare with indignant wonder' (Curran, 4), as Con Curran remembered him from that time. In later years he grew conspicuously slighter but always retained a dandified air which he enhanced by a cane and rings. His hair was severely swept back, and he wore broad felt hats in the fedora style. He had the 'stork's legs' that he attributed to Leopold Bloom, and on these he occasionally danced an Irish jig of his own invention—the celebrated 'spiderdance'. The thin lips, determined chin, and prominent forehead of the young artist produced in time a somewhat concave physiognomy in the ageing writer which, when surmounted by the thick lenses of his round spectacles that magnified the conspicuous effect of repeated surgery to his left eye, oddly anticipated the aspect of the death mask. For Louis Gillet it captured 'a double expression of Noli me tangere and Non serviam', yet displayed also 'a smile mischievous and somewhat waggish' on his 'ironic mouth' as if to say, 'where I am, you'll never catch me … I slip away, unseen, unknown' (Potts, 178). But Joyce is neither unseen nor unknown today. Indeed, no figure in twentieth-century literature represents the idea of the literary artist more completely than the great Shem, in whom so many extraordinary elements of passion, observation, rebellion, invention, tenacity, and incomparable literary ability were combined.

The Joyce archive In view of the uniquely complex development of James Joyce's literary texts in notebooks, manuscripts, and typescripts, along with the author's practice of composing extensively on the printers' galleys, the study and appreciation of his art calls for an exacting examination of the written and printed materials involved at every stage. Voluminous materials of this kind have been dispersed throughout libraries and collections in Ireland, Britain, and the USA. Many of Joyce's papers are now held at the Lockwood Memorial Library of the State University of New York at Buffalo, together with the Joyce family portraits. The manuscript of *Stephen Hero*, which was edited and introduced by Theodore Spencer in 1944 and revised by John J. Slocum and Herbert Cahoon to incorporate some additional pages, is at Harvard. The fair-copy manuscript of *A Portrait of the Artist as a Young Man* was presented to the National Library of Ireland by Harriet Shaw Weaver, while a definitive edition of the novel based on it was published in America in 1964 (and in the United Kingdom in 1968). The *Ulysses* manuscript which Joyce sold to John Quinn after a triplicate typescript had been produced from it remains intact at the Rosenbach Museum and Library in Philadelphia. After her offer to permit the repatriation of her husband's body was turned down by the Irish government, Nora Joyce ensured that Miss Weaver would donate the manuscript of *Finnegans Wake* to the British Museum rather than to the National Library of Ireland. In order to make the sum of such materials available to scholars, notebooks, manuscripts, typescripts, and corrected galleys for all Joyce's work were published in black-and-white facsimile by the Garland Press of New York as *The James Joyce Archive* (1977–9). A colour facsimile edition of the *Finnegans Wake* notebooks at Buffalo is now in progress (ed. V. Deane, D. Ferrer, and G. Lernout, 2001–).

Joyce's essays, lectures, reviews, and some of the extant notebooks were edited by Ellsworth Mason and Richard Ellmann as *The Critical Writings of James Joyce* in 1959. The poetry collections with sundry shorter writings including the 1904 'Portrait' essay were collected by Ellmann and others as *Poems and Shorter Writings* in 1990, a further critical compilation being issued by Kevin Barry as *Occasional, Critical, and Political Writings* in 2000. J. C. C. Mays's edition of *Poems and 'Exiles'* (1992) is also notable. A volume of Joyce's letters was edited by Stuart Gilbert in 1957, with two further volumes and a *Selected Letters* appearing under the hand of Richard Ellmann respectively in 1966 and 1975. (Joyce's so-called 'black letters' to Nora of 1909 are printed in the latter only.) In 1984 the Garland Publishing Company issued a controversial 'Critical and Synoptic Edition' of *Ulysses*, edited by Hans Walter Gabler on the basis of a hypothetical 'genetic text' comprising variants in working manuscripts, typescripts, complete editions, and serial publications whether within the direct line of textual transmission or not. The validity of this method and the authenticity (or even accuracy) of the result has been widely disputed, and conservative readers still adhere to the corrected Odyssey Edition and its successors as bearing the imprimatur of the author. *Finnegans Wake* has never been reset, though Joyce's corrections (which Maria Jolas carried out of France during the Second World War) were applied to the Viking Press and Faber editions in the 1950s. (In all editions the pagination and font are identical to those in the 1939 editions and each other.) In December 2000 a 'lost' typescript of the 'Circe' episode of *Ulysses* was purchased by the National Library of Ireland for $1.5 million at auction in New York. The papers rescued from the Joyces' flat in Paris in autumn 1941 were lodged in the National Library of Ireland, as agreed, and became available for inspection by scholars fifty years later. A further body of papers in the possession of Paul Léon (including the lost 'Paris notebook' of 1904) was acquired by the Irish government in 2001. In 1967 the first Annual James Joyce International Symposium was held in Dublin. A James Joyce Centre was established at 35 North Great George's Street, Dublin, adjacent to Belvedere College, in the 1990s. Plaques reset in the pavement mark the major points in Joyce's Ulyssean hero's itinerary on Bloomsday in the modern city, and Joyce himself has featured on an Irish banknote.

Critical and cultural heritage James Joyce's standing as a major writer in world literature was established during his lifetime. After the Second World War his promise to 'keep the professors busy' was widely realized in American and British universities. The 'guide' to *Ulysses* which Joyce had himself provided through the books of Frank Budgen and Stuart Gilbert made that novel less off-putting than it might otherwise have been for many readers. Thus heralded, *Ulysses* could be treated either as a modernist and experimental text offering a new vision of society and a new method of literary representation, or as a classical affirmation of the humanist principles deemed to underlie all great literature. Hence, those among the first generation of 'Joyceans' who devoted themselves to the arcana of the texts—symbol and motif, structure and significance, mythic parallels, and psychoanalytical hypotheses—sat comfortably with those who exalted Leopold Bloom as the modern Ulysses, 'an all-round man' and 'a keyless competent citizen'.

Finnegans Wake was a more daunting challenge, but the work of early exegetes made it clear that, for all its complexity, it shared the same world of literary and popular consciousness as its readers. Archetypal readings dominated the early reception of the book yet, like *Ulysses*, it seems to require an immense amount of local knowledge also. The gleaning of sufficient Irish background became a badge of honour for the rapidly growing tribe of Joyceans, enabled by the comparative rarity of a philosemitic modernist. There was a distinct element of cultural tourism in all of this, given that the establishment which embraced Joyce was predominantly protestant and Anglo-American. Joyce's agnosticism was, of course, a help. That his mind was 'Irish', 'Catholic', and even 'medieval' thus seemed less important than the fact that he conceived of the world of culture as a huge jigsaw of interlocking pieces in which no one narrative, still less one national tradition or one religious dispensation, easily prevailed. In this way he came to represent a syncretic view of human culture that began to dominate the increasingly liberal and sceptical orthodoxy of Western democracies in the second half of the twentieth century.

By the 1960s Joyce's reputation stood at the apex of a pyramid of international renown, with modernism, humanism, and psychoanalysis at its intellectual foundations. With only the Soviet realists standing out against him, he was hailed as an intrinsically democratic writer in the climate of cold war cultural politics even though the actual contents of his works (and to a great extent their manner) were at odds with the prevailing ethos of Western society at many material points. Thus Joyce posthumously managed to become both the epitome and the antithesis of cultural conformism though all the while a writer centrally respected for the magnitude of his talent and the scale of his achievement.

In 1926 Mary Colum told Joyce that *Anna Livia Plurabelle* was 'outside of literature', to which he replied, 'it may be outside literature now, but its future is inside literature' (Colum and Colum, 130). That he was proved right illustrates the coincidence between his idiosyncratic form of innovation and an anti-conventional impulse at the heart of much critical thought in late twentieth-century culture. From the 1960s onwards the 'deconstruction' of bourgeois certainties in ethics and belief increasingly characterized intellectual life first in Europe and then in America. Joyce's affinity with the 'Revolution of the Word' made him an ideal literary talisman. It was as the battering-ram of post-structuralism that he first figured in the writings of Jacques Lacan and others, who discovered in 'la jouissance de Joyce' an image of their own rebellion against the fixity of language and meaning.

For an anti-authoritarian movement such as feminist studies, the connection between the political agenda and the texts themselves was intrinsically unstable. If *écriture féminine* was the very definition of Joyce's way of writing from 'Penelope' onwards, Molly Bloom was nevertheless the creation of a writer who did not seem to accord intellectual dignity to women (although Mary Colum refuted this), whatever grandeur Joyce attached to her sensual vitality and however highly he prized her amenity to mythopoeic elevation in the quasi-divine capacity of domestic Gea-Tellus. Certainly Joyce believed that women's liberation was the central revolution of the twentieth century (as he told Arthur Power), but if he valued their subjectivity and regarded union with them as a necessary measure for the creative imagination, it did not mean that he endowed them with a plenitude of artistic power in their own right.

The rise of post-colonial studies in the 1990s provided a more rewarding means of analysing Joyce's subversive attitude towards the dominant form of Anglophonic culture—an attitude readily ascribed to him by Anglo-Saxon contemporaries whether inside or beyond the avant-garde movement. The point was epitomized by H. G. Wells when he wrote to Joyce: 'while you were brought up under the delusion of political suppression I was brought up under the delusion of political responsibility.' The difference indicated here is national. On the question of style, Wells admitted his desire to keep 'language and statement as simple and clear as possible', hence implying that Joyce, to the contrary, was inspired by Fenian malice towards the well of English undefiled. Joyce offers some support for this by means of a counter-reformational thrust in *Finnegans Wake*, where he appears to describe the linguistic outcome of the book as 'One sovereign punned to petery pence'. In fact the differences instanced by Wells are very real. Where his ideal is 'a big unifying and concentrating process' resulting in a kind of '*progress* not inevitable but interesting and possible', Joyce dismisses progress as the self-aggrandizing fantasy of Shaun-types who exercise power through the abuse of language. It is clear

today that Wells's talk of 'increase of power and range by economy and concentration of effort' (*Selected Letters*, 364–5) is the stuff of textbook imperialism, as his *History of the World*, for all its liberality, reveals on every page. From this standpoint, the difference in their outlooks is actually that between the colonizer and the colonized no less than that between Enlightenment and modernist epistemologies, or that between protestant and Catholic, as Wells openly concedes.

Joycean criticism began—like Joycean biography—with American scholars whose arrival in Ireland to investigate his formative conditions resembled an anthropological expedition. Richard Ellmann's biography saw Irish literary life in the wider context of Western literary values—as can be seen in how he glosses Joyce's great discovery in *Ulysses* in terms of the word 'love' in all its human ramifications. It is a view which sets Leopold Bloom—sceptical, kindly, ordinary, imaginative, human—against the nationalist 'citizen' of the 'Cyclops' chapter—an embodiment of prejudice, bitterness, and hatred of the Anglo-Saxon. Ellmann goes so far as to cite the Irish nationalists who fought for independence as exemplifying those traits in the Irish national character least like the liberal secularism that Bloom (and, by implication, Ellmann himself) embodies.

In this way teams were formed with Joyce and Anglo-America on one side and Irish separatists on the other. Not surprisingly, recent Irish criticism has been much concerned with repudiating Joyce's Bloomian pacifism (if it is such) while emphasizing the 'Fenian' sympathies of the novelist in his incidental writings. This allies them with the post-colonial critics everywhere who argue that colonial peoples can attain authentic self-representation only when they shed the chains of imperial hegemony and, if possible, the language which sustains it; it does not, unfortunately, consolidate their bond with James Joyce, the chief writer to emerge from Catholic–nationalist Ireland at any time in its history. While Joyce as an eccentric Irishman, or at least a writer of genius at a tangent to the main line of national development (if not indeed the colonial remainder), has obvious attractions, it is also possible to accord him a great measure of ethical sense and political precedence in the context of the European Union. In any case, some further thinking about the underlying issues of colonial, anti-colonial, and post-colonial thinking is in order before the convincing critical repatriation of James Joyce can be completed.

It is clear that, in spite of the desires of Irish separatists at any period, post-colonial cultures are generally forced to acknowledge their own hybridity, thereby ending up more like Bloom than like Michael Cusack. Equally, in modern Irish society, Bloom stands nearer to the consensual view than the Fenians of *Ulysses*. Joyce undoubtedly offered a difficult nettle for Irish nationalists to grasp if they wished to see the half-Jewish and half-Irish advertising agent with a foothold in at least three religious camps as the best kind of modern Irishman. More than that: he clearly meant to antagonize those whom he had accused of circulating 'the pap of racial hatred'. In this sense, *Ulysses* bears the stamp of his own subtly rebarbative personality and inveterate resistance to the encroachments of religion, nationality, language, and family (in a germane sense).

Post-colonialism, properly conceived, suggests an open approach to Joyce that allows for the best response to the facts of text and context. Yet '-isms' are only limited guides to works as complex as this author's and the worlds that he inhabited in structure and significance. There is much in Joyce that eludes liberal humanist and post-structuralist ways of thinking while also giving sustenance for one or the other kind of reading. Joyce's 'medievalism', which critics have often put aside as an unfortunate relic of his Irish Catholic (and, more specifically, Jesuit) education, is a case in point. This consisted in the incessant effort to make the intensely relative facts of reality and consciousness correspond in some large symbolic way to a unified image of reality. In view of an evident lack of engagement with this impulse, truly 'Joycean' criticism has arguably never yet been attempted. If it is to be written, it must be grounded primarily in the context of Irish literary history and the Irish cultural experience.

It has often been said that Joyce's experimentalism placed him in the vanguard of anti-bourgeois thinking. Yet, if so, it also placed him in an anomalous yet fertile relation to contemporary Irish nationalism. Ironically, in the light of the divergent courses of James Joyce and the modern Irish nation, his art carries forward the cultural project of the revivalists *vis-à-vis* the English canon, and the values that it supposedly embodies, in a far more radical way than any of his Irish contemporaries in literature or in arms. Joyce effectually overcame that canon by appearing to ignore it. With the exception of Rudyard Kipling, he professed that he had 'nothing to learn' from the English novelists, and made Flaubert and Ibsen his primary models. This did not signify an allegiance to one or other continental tradition so much as a commitment to what he called in 1904 a 'process of mind as yet untabulated' ('A Portrait of the Artist', *James Joyce: Poems and Shorter Writings*, 211): that is, an imaginative activity which disintegrates norms and standards in its attention to the sheer 'whatness' of experience and language.

The post-colonial concept of hybridity is the most accurate response to this in reflecting the essentially provisional methods of the writer, in this respect perfectly adapted to a reality which is radically unstable, and which affords no easy foothold to the consensual style of the liberal conscience—hence Stephen Dedalus's insistence on 'the incertitude of the void'. Positioned on the periphery of a powerful cultural formation such as English national literature, Joyce was well placed to discover the endless fissuring of experience in its received versions and conventional forms. At the same time he disdained the concrete alternative of an essentially reactive 'national' ideal which preoccupied his Irish coevals as well as those who came after him in Ireland, Samuel Beckett being the great exception.

It was thus that Joyce differed from those Irish contemporaries who wrote the orthodoxy of the revival and especially its Irish-Ireland wing comprising the Gaelic League and Sinn Féin. Hence the double aspect of his literary character: on the one hand he stands as a conservative exponent of the idea of literary value in the face of national chauvinism; on the other he is more radical than any nationalist in dismembering the cultural hegemony upon which the colonial state is founded. That Joyce saw so deeply into the social, psychological, and linguistic nexus that constituted the greater and the lesser worlds into which he had been born was the measure of his intellect. That he constructed a literary universe which admits of benefaction, trespass, and transcendence, and abasement, individuality and community, and the dream of a world/word as an ultimately integral thing, is the measure of his humane art. That he conceived and executed an entirely new form of writing in which waking and dreaming minds throw up an integral vision of the world as word is the measure of his genius.   BRUCE STEWART

Sources R. Ellmann, *James Joyce* (1959); new and rev. edn (1983) • *Letters of James Joyce*, vol. 1, ed. S. Gilbert (1957); new edn (1966) • *Letters of James Joyce*, vols. 2 and 3, ed. R. Ellmann (1966) • *Selected letters of James Joyce*, ed. R. Ellmann (1975) • F. Budgen, *James Joyce and the making of 'Ulysses'* (1934); repr. (1960) • C. P. Curran, *James Joyce remembered* (1968) • J. Joyce, *Ulysses* (1967) • J. Joyce, 'A portrait of the artist as a young man': the definitive edition, ed. C. Anderson and R. Ellmann (1968) • J. Joyce, *Stephen Hero: part of the first draft of 'A portrait of the artist as a young man'*, ed. T. Spencer, J. J. Slocum, and H. Cahoon (1956); rev. (1977) • *The critical writings of James Joyce*, ed. E. Mason and R. Ellmann (1959) • *James Joyce: poems and shorter writings*, ed. R. Ellmann, A. Walton Litz, and J. Whittier-Ferguson (1990) • T. S. Eliot, *'Ulysses', order, and myth*', *James Joyce: two decades of criticism*, ed. S. Givens (1948) • S. Beckett and others, *Our exagmination round his factification for incamination of work in progress* (1929) • S. Gilbert, *James Joyce's 'Ulysses'* (1930) • H. Gorman, *James Joyce* (1939) • H. Levin, *James Joyce* (1941) • *Pound / Joyce: the letters of Ezra Pound to James Joyce*, ed. F. Read (1967) • P. Colum and M. Colum, *Our friend James Joyce* (1958) • J. Campbell and H. Robinson, *A skeleton key to 'Finnegans wake'* (1944) • R. McHugh, *The sigla of 'Finnegans wake'* (1976) • R. M. Kain, *Fabulous voyager: James Joyce's 'Ulysses'* (1947) • H. Kenner, *Dublin's Joyce* (1955) • P. Hutchins, *James Joyce's world* (1957) • S. Joyce, *My brother's keeper* (1958) • S. Joyce, *The complete Dublin diary of Stanislaus Joyce* (1971) • R. Ellmann, *'Ulysses' on the Liffey* (1972) • R. Ellmann, *The consciousness of Joyce* (1977) • R. Ellmann, *The identity of Yeats* (1954); pbk edn (1964) • J. Atherton, *The books at the wake: a study of literary allusions in James Joyce's 'Finnegans wake'* (1959) • S. L. Goldberg, *The classical temper* (1961) • R. M. Adams, *Surface and symbol: the consistency of James Joyce's 'Ulysses'* (1962) • C. Hart, *Structure and motif in 'Finnegans wake'* (1962) • A. Walton Litz, *The art of James Joyce* (1961) • M. C. Solomon, *Eternal geomater: the sexual universe of 'Finnegans wake'* (1969) • R. H. Deming, ed., *James Joyce: the critical heritage*, 2 vols. (1970) • A. Power, *Conversations with James Joyce* (1974) • H. Cixous, *The exile of James Joyce* (1976) • M. Norris, *The decentred universe of 'Finnegans wake'* (1976) • M. French, *The book as world* (1976) • J. Garvin, *James Joyce's disunited kingdom and the Irish dimension* (1976) • C. H. Peake, *James Joyce: the citizen and the artist* (1977) • M. Groden, *'Ulysses' in progress* (1977) • A. Glasheen, *A third census of 'Finnegans wake'* (1977) • W. Potts, ed., *Portraits of the artist in exile: recollections of James Joyce by Europeans* (1979) • C. MacCabe, *James Joyce and the revolution of the word* (1978) • S. Brivic, *Joyce between Freud and Jung* (1980) • D. Hayman, *'Ulysses': the mechanics of meaning* (1982) • D. Attridge and D. Ferrier, eds., *Post-structuralist Joyce* (1984) • F. Senn, *Joyce's dislocations: essays on reading as translation* (1984) • B. K. Scott, *Joyce and feminism* (1984) • B. Benstock, *James Joyce* (1985) • R. Brown, *James Joyce and sexuality* (1985) • K. Lawrence, *The odyssey of* style in 'Ulysses' (1981) • J. Bishop, Joyce's book of the dark (1986) • V. Mahaffey, Reauthorising Joyce (1988) • S. Henke, James Joyce and the politics of desire (1990) • B. Arnold, The scandal of 'Ulysses' (1991) • D. Attridge, ed., The Cambridge companion to James Joyce (1990) • P. Myers, The sounds of 'Finnegans wake' (1992) • M. Beja, James Joyce: a literary life (1992) • P. Costello, James Joyce: the years of growth, 1882–1915 (1992) • J. Fairhall, James Joyce and the question of history (1993) • J. Valente, James Joyce and the problem of justice: negotiating sexual and colonial difference (1994) • T. C. Hofheinz, Joyce and the invention of Irish history: 'Finnegans wake' in context (1995) • E. Nolan, James Joyce and nationalism (1995) • V. J. Cheng, Joyce, race, and empire (1995) • C. van Boheemen-Saaf, Joyce, Derrida, Lacan and the trauma of history: reading, narrative and postcolonialism (1999) • M. Keith Booker, 'Ulysses': capitalism and colonialism (2000) • P. McGee, Joyce beyond Marx: history and desire in 'Ulysses' and 'Finnegans wake' (2001) • M. Hodgart, James Joyce: a student's guide (1978) • J. McCourt, The years of Bloom: James Joyce in Trieste, 1904–1920 (2000) • B. Maddox, Nora: a biography of Nora Joyce (1988); repr. (2000) • J. McCourt, James Joyce: a passionate exile (2000) • J. Lidderdale and M. Nicholson, Dear Miss Weaver: Harriet Shaw Weaver, 1876–1961 (1970) • B. McGinley, Joyce's lives: uses and abuses of the biografiend (1996) • B. Bradley, James Joyce's schooldays (1982) • J. B. Lyons, James Joyce and medicine (1973) • C. Fahy, ed., The James Joyce–Paul Léon papers in the National Library of Ireland: a catalogue (1992)

Archives BL, papers relating to Finnegans wake, Add. MSS 47471–47489 • BL, papers incl. draft of autobiography, Add. MS 49975 • Cornell University, Ithaca, New York, Olin Library, corresp., literary MSS, and papers • Harvard U., Houghton L., corresp., literary MSS, and papers • Hunt. L., letters • New York State University, Buffalo, Lockwood Memorial Library, MSS • NL Ire., letters • Ransom HRC, papers • Southern Illinois University, Carbondale, Morris Library, corresp., literary MSS, and papers • Yale U., Beinecke L., corresp., literary MSS, and papers | BL, letters to Harriet Shaw Weaver, Add. MSS 57345–57352 • Harvard U., Houghton L., letters to Grant Richards • TCD, corresp. with Thomas MacGreevy • University College, Dublin, letters to D. J. O'Donoghue | FILM Museum of Modern Art, New York, film taken by Robert Kastor showing James, Nora, and Stephen Joyce in a Paris garden, 1937? | SOUND University of Tulsa, Oklahoma, McFarlin Library, James Joyce collection, 'Ulysses' (Shakespeare & Co., Paris, 1924), 'Anna Livia Plurabelle' (Orthological Institute, Cambridge), 'Bid adieu' (Radiodiffusion et Television Françaises, Paris), 'Bid adieu, Anna Livia Plurabelle, Ulysses' (Microsillon, Paris)

Likenesses photographs, 1904–c.1938, Hult. Arch. • W. Lewis, pen-and-ink drawing, 1921, NG Ire. • B. Abbott, two photographs, 1926, NPG • B. Abbott, photograph, 1928, Museum of Modern Art, New York • P. Tchelitchew, oils, c.1928–1930, NG Ire. • J. Davidson, bronze head, 1929, U. Texas • A. John, pencil drawing, c.1930, U. Texas • D. Harmsworth, pen-and-ink drawing, 1932, U. Texas • J.-É. Blanche, oils, 1934, NG Ire. • J.-É. Blanche, oils, 1935, NPG [see illus.] • H. Kernoff, pastel drawing, 1935, U. Texas • S. O'Sullivan, chalk drawing, 1935, NG Ire. • G. Freund, photograph, 1939, NPG • P. Speck, plaster death mask, 1941, International James Joyce Centre, Zürich; also at Library of Congress, Washington, DC • F. Budgen, oils, U. Texas • F. Budgen, oils, State University of New York, Buffalo, Lockwood Memorial Library • G. Freund, photographs, repro. in G. Freund, Three days with James Joyce (1985) • D. Harmsworth, pen-and-ink drawing, U. Texas • M. Hebald, sculpture, Fluntern cemetery, Zürich • T. Silvestri, oils, State University of New York, Buffalo, Lockwood Memorial Library

Wealth at death £1212 gross; £980 net: Maddox, Nora, 464

Joyce, Jeremiah (1763–1816), Unitarian minister and writer, was born on 24 February 1763 at Cheshunt, Hertfordshire, son of Jeremiah Joyce (d. 1778), a wool comber, and his wife, Hannah (d. 1816), the daughter of John Somersett of Mildred's Court, London. He claimed that from his father he 'learned to consider the cause of America as the cause of Man' (Joyce, 45). He was educated at a local school before being apprenticed to a painter and glazier in the Strand, Westminster. Private study in mathematics and theology and the assistance of the dissenting minister Hugh Worthington drew him into a metropolitan dissenting élite. His own theological sympathies were firmly Unitarian, and from 1786 to 1790 he studied at the new and short-lived New College, Hackney, under Worthington, Richard Price, and Andrew Kippis. Here he imbibed both religious and political radicalism in an atmosphere fashionably sympathetic towards the French Revolution. As a student he was supported by a patrimony of £200 per annum and further assisted by his brother Joshua Joyce (d. 1816), a tallow chandler.

Joyce was a member of the Society for Constitutional Information and his political views brought him to the attention of Charles, third Earl Stanhope, cousin of the prime minister, William Pitt, but also a prominent aristocratic radical. In 1790 Joyce was appointed tutor to Stanhope's two sons and resided with the earl at his seat at Chevening, Kent. At the very time when Stanhope's strong opposition to the war against revolutionary France led to his political isolation, Joyce himself became involved with such radical figures as Thomas Hardy and John Horne Tooke of the London Corresponding Society. He preached regularly to small dissenting congregations in Kent and used his sermons to attack the European reaction against the French Revolution. These activities brought him under official suspicion, and on 4 May 1794, at the time of the treason trials of Thomas Hardy and Horne Tooke, he was arrested at Chevening, his property was searched, and he was interrogated by the privy council. He refused to answer questions, on the ground that to do so would injure the constitution of the country. He was imprisoned in the Tower and, on 6 October, was indicted on a charge of high treason. He was then detained in Newgate prison, but after the acquittals of Hardy and Horne Tooke, Joyce was released on 23 November. He was immediately welcomed back to Chevening by Stanhope with a vast celebration party, and remained in the earl's employment until 1800. He wrote a narrative of his arrest and imprisonment, in which he identified himself fully with the reforming movements of the 1790s.

In later life Joyce resided at Holly Terrace, Highgate, and preached regularly to the Unitarian congregation at Essex Street Chapel and to a small Unitarian congregation in Hampstead. However, perhaps because of his political notoriety, he failed to secure a regular position as a dissenting minister. According to Robert Aspland, moreover, Joyce was a man of 'remarkable plainness of appearance' whose 'bluntness of manner' and warmth of expression 'sometimes led superficial and distant observers to form an erroneous notion of his temper' (Aspland, 703). Much of his income was derived from literary work; he published scientific, mathematical, and religious works (often under the pseudonym J. J.), notably the Scientific Dialogues (1807). He co-operated with Lant Carpenter and William Shepherd in the compilation of Systematic Education (1816). He was secretary to the Unitarian Society and a Dr

Williams's trustee. In his will he instructed his wife, Elizabeth, to destroy his papers, except those upon which he had left specific instructions for publication or preservation. His daughter Hannah (who was subsequently adopted by Shepherd) appears to have been his only child. He died at 4 Holly Terrace, Highgate, on 21 June 1816 and was buried in Cheshunt churchyard on 24 June.

G. M. DITCHFIELD

Sources R. Aspland, *Monthly Repository*, 12 (1817), 697–704 · J. Seed, 'Jeremiah Joyce, Unitarianism, and the radical intelligentsia in the 1790s', *Transactions of the Unitarian Historical Society*, 17 (1979–82), 97–108 · J. Joyce, *A sermon preached on Sunday, February the 23rd, 1794 … to which is added an appendix containing an account of the author's arrest for … treasonable practices* (1794) · GM, 1st ser., 86/1 (1816), 634 · *State trials*, 25.565ff. · J. A. Hone, *For the cause of truth: radicalism in London, 1796–1821* (1982), 68, 139, 184, 231–2 · H. Ridyard, *A selection from the early letters of the late Revd. William Shepherd* (1855) · C. Bewley, *Muir of Huntershill* (1981) · A. Newman, *The Stanhopes of Chevening: a family history* (1969) · will, PRO, PROB 11/1582, fols. 227–9
Archives DWL, Millar, Belsham, Wilson MSS · JRL, Theophilus Lindsey MSS
Likenesses stipple, pubd 1794, NPG
Wealth at death several hundred pounds; leasehold of house, 4 Holly Terrace, Highgate; securities in Equitable Insurance office; household goods: will, PRO PROB 11/1582, fols. 227–9

Joyce, Sir Matthew Ingle (1839–1930), judge, was born on 17 July 1839 at Breedon on the Hill, Leicestershire, the fourth son of John Hall Joyce, yeoman farmer, of Blackfordby, Leicestershire, and his wife, Mary, daughter of Matthew Ingle, of Ashby-de-la-Zouch. He was educated at Ashby-de-la-Zouch grammar school and at Gonville and Caius College, Cambridge, where he graduated eighth wrangler in the mathematical tripos of 1862. He was elected a fellow of Caius in 1862, a position which he held until 1875. He was made honorary fellow in 1900.

Joyce was called to the bar by Lincoln's Inn in 1865, and was junior equity counsel to the Treasury from 1886 until 1900 when he was appointed a judge of the High Court and knighted. In 1891 he married Miriam Bertha (*d.* 1922), the eighth daughter of Sir William Jackson, first baronet, a contractor. They had one daughter. A somewhat brusque manner concealed a kind heart.

As a judge, Joyce was unshowy and straightforward. His cases were not particularly noteworthy; perhaps the most important was *Colls* v. *Home and Colonial Stores* (1904), concerned with the nature and extent of the easement of light, a case in which his decision was reversed by the Court of Appeal, but restored by the House of Lords. In *Grierson* v. *National Provincial Bank* (1913) he made a contribution to the law on priorities among different mortgagees of the same land. He was considered a sound lawyer with a wide knowledge of real property and equity jurisprudence and to have prized simplicity and common sense over subtlety or technicality of argument. Particularly among conservatives, he was considered a just and upright judge. Among his most notable pupils were Lord Parker of Waddington and the younger Lord Russell of Killowen.

Joyce retired as a judge in 1915, when he was sworn a member of the privy council. He died at Liverpool on 10 March 1930 and was buried on 15 March at Breedon on the Hill.

H. G. HANBURY, *rev.* HUGH MOONEY

Sources *The Times* (12 March 1930) · *Solicitors' Journal*, 74 (1930), 159 · *Law Journal* (15 March 1930), 177 · *Law Times* (15 March 1930), 249
Likenesses Spy [L. Ward], caricature, chromolithograph, NPG; repro. in *VF* (23 Jan 1902)
Wealth at death £63,573 2s. 0d.: probate, 5 May 1930, CGPLA Eng. & Wales

Joyce [*née* Barnacle], **Nora Joseph** (1884–1951), wife and muse of James Joyce (1882–1941), was born on 21 or 22 March 1884 at the Galway union workhouse hospital, co. Galway, Ireland, the second of eight children born to Thomas Barnacle (1846–1921) and Honoraria (Annie) Healy (*c.*1859–1939), of Sullivan's Lane, Galway. Nora was educated at the Convent of Mercy national school in Galway. Fostered as a child with her grandmother, she worked from the age of twelve at the Presentation Convent, Galway; then, having run away from home in 1904, as a chambermaid at Finn's Hotel, Leinster Street, Dublin. On 10 June 1904 on Nassau Street in Dublin her auburn hair, confident figure, and bold walk caught the eye of the young writer James *Joyce. Their first evening together so changed Joyce's life that he later set the entire action of his great novel *Ulysses* (1922) on that day, 16 June 1904.

The young couple ran away unmarried to the continent on 8 October 1904, settling in Habsburg Austria—first in Pola, next in Trieste, where Joyce taught English in a Berlitz school. Their first child, Giorgio (1905–1976), was born, and they were soon joined by Joyce's brother Stanislaus (1884–1955), who became a permanent resident there. In the following year the family moved to Rome, where Joyce worked in a bank and also wrote 'The Dead', the last and greatest of his short story collection *Dubliners* (1914). Nora is widely thought to be the model for the red-haired Gretta Conroy in that story. When they returned to Trieste, the couple's second child, (Anna) Lucia Joyce (1907–1982), was born, and two of Joyce's unmarried sisters, Eileen (1889–1963) and Eva (1891–1957), came from Dublin to join the household (Eva stayed only briefly). By now the Joyce family spoke Italian at home and Nora ceased active practice of her religion out of respect for Joyce's apostasy.

During the Trieste years Nora's portrait was painted by the artist Tullio Silvestri, who said she was the most beautiful woman he had ever seen. She also attracted the attentions of Roberto Prezioso, editor of the *Piccolo della Sera*, and Joyce broke with this good friend out of jealousy. Joyce's terror of being cuckolded underlay the novel *Ulysses*, which he had begun to write, and also his play *Exiles* (1918).

With the outbreak of the First World War, the Joyces (without Stanislaus and Eileen) took refuge in Zürich. Joyce continued to work on *Ulysses*, and in 1918 Nora played Cathleen in the English Players' production of J. M. Synge's *Riders to the Sea*, directed by Joyce. In Zürich, Ottocaro Weiss (a Triestine banker) made his admiration of Nora known. There is no evidence that she was ever unfaithful to Joyce, rather that he was manipulating his jealousy for his own literary purposes. She wept to Frank Budgen, a close friend of Joyce's, 'Jim wants me to go with other men so that he can write about it' (Budgen, 188).

With the war's end, the Joyces returned to Trieste but the city, now part of Italy and no longer a major port, was dull. Ezra Pound persuaded Joyce to move his family to Paris, which he did in 1920. Nora began mastering her third foreign language, and with the money lavished on them by Joyce's selfless English patron, Harriet Shaw Weaver, she learned the delights of the Paris couture houses. Joyce, increasingly troubled by failing sight and more than ever dependent on Nora's strength, indulged her. She was never over-respectful. She refused to read *Ulysses*. When he became a literary celebrity after the publication of *Ulysses*, she told friends, 'I've always told him he should give up writing and take up singing' (Ellmann, 561). Of 'Work in Progress', the developing *Finnegans Wake*, she said to him 'Why don't you write sensible books that people can understand?' (Ellmann, 590).

Nora made a full recovery from two operations for uterine cancer in November 1928 and February 1929. With Joyce she moved briefly to London in 1931. They married on 4 July at the Kensington register office, 'for testamentary reasons', Joyce told the press. (Both Nora and James Joyce remained British subjects all their lives.) Nora was happy to be married at last. However, the unexpected press publicity upset her family in Galway and also Lucia Joyce, who had thought her parents were married already. Shortly afterwards the Joyces returned to Paris, where they lived during the 1930s. Those years were marred for Nora by her daughter's severe mental collapse, but brightened by the marriage of her son to Helen Kastor Fleischman of New York, and by the birth of her grandson Stephen James Joyce on 15 February 1932.

The Joyces left Paris in late 1939 in advance of the Nazis' entry, leaving Lucia behind in a psychiatric clinic in Brittany, but accompanied by their son (whose wife too had suffered a psychiatric illness) and their grandson. They lived in the village of St Gérand-le-Puy near Vichy. In December 1940, with the help of Swiss friends, they moved back to Zürich. A month later Joyce died unexpectedly from a perforated ulcer and was buried in Zürich's Fluntern cemetery.

As a widow Nora remained in Zürich, with her loyal son nearby. She resumed the practice of her Catholic religion. In the post-war years she hoped to have her husband's body returned to Ireland in honour, as W. B. Yeats's had been in 1948, but in the puritanical Ireland of Eamon de Valera, Joyce remained a scandalous writer. From Zürich, living in pensions, Nora was sought out by the increasing numbers of Joyce scholars, who experienced the tart tongue and Irish common sense so prized by Joyce, for whom, as they wandered Europe, she had been his portable Ireland. Asked her opinion of André Gide, the widow replied, 'When you've been married to the greatest writer in the world, you don't remember all the little fellows' (Ellmann, 743). As for Joyce's favourite authors, she replied, 'He spent a good deal of time reading himself' (Maddox, 475). Upon her death on 10 April 1951, from

uraemic poisoning, she too was buried in Fluntern cemetery, though in a separate grave; in 1966 the bodies were reinterred in a new joint grave.

Nora's influence on Joyce, both personal and literary, was long underplayed by Joyce scholars, who tended to see her as an unworthy and uneducated consort of the great writer. Yet she was the model for his principal women characters, including Bertha in his play *Exiles* and Anna Livia Plurabelle in *Finnegans Wake*. In time, however, scholars came to note the connection between Nora, with her unpunctuated writing and uninhibited speaking styles, and Joyce's most famous female creation, Molly Bloom, whose earthy rambling soliloquy brings *Ulysses* to a close. Nora was the subject of portraits by at least two painters, Tullio Silvestri and Myron Nutting, and the photographer Berenice Abbott, while two biographies and a film (*Nora*, directed by Pat Murphy) have chronicled her life. Her mother's home at Bowling Green in Galway is now a museum.   BRENDA MADDOX

Sources B. Maddox, *Nora: a biography of Nora Joyce* (1988); repr. (2000) • F. Budgen, *Myselves when young* (1970) • R. Ellmann, *James Joyce*, rev. edn (1982) • P. Ó Laoi, *Nora Barnacle Joyce: a portrait* (1982) **Archives** Cornell University, James Joyce collection • Ransom HRC, James Joyce collection • State University of New York, Buffalo, University Libraries, poetry/ rare books Collection | BL, Manuscript Room, Harriet Shaw Weaver papers • Harvard U., Houghton L. • NL Ire. • NYPL, Manuscript Room • NYPL, Berg collection • Southern Illinois University, Morris Library, Croessman collection • UCL, Manuscript Room, James Joyce collection • UCL, Manuscripts Room, Lucia Joyce bequest • Yale U., Beinecke L., Slocum collection | FILM Museum of Modern Art, New York, film taken by Robert Kastor showing James, Nora and Stephen Joyce in a Paris garden, 1937? **Likenesses** B. Abbott, photograph • F. Budgen, portrait, State University of New York, Buffalo • M. Nutting, portrait, Northwestern University, Evanston, Illinois • T. Silvestri, portrait, State University of New York, Buffalo **Wealth at death** £4024 2s. 11d.: probate, 23 July 1951, CGPLA Eng. & Wales

Joyce, Valentine (1768/9–1800), seamen's spokesman during the Spithead mutiny, was born in Jersey. His parents were probably Valentine and Elizabeth Joyce, to whom a further ten children were born; those children were baptized in Portsmouth. He joined the *Perseverance* in Portsmouth as able seaman in 1788 and became quartermaster's mate in the *Royal George* in 1793. During the Spithead mutiny in April and May 1797 he was the effective leader of thirty-two elected delegates who referred all decisions for the seamen's approval. All were senior ratings whose skills were crucial to the mutiny's success. This hazardous campaign to improve pay and conditions, involving 30,000 men and eighty-two ships, was influenced by merchant seamen (the largest element of the Royal Navy), rather than quota men.

Edmund Burke, and authors writing for the *Sun* and *The Times* libelled Joyce, describing him as a subversive Irish quota man. Many modern historians unquestioningly accepted this description but Joyce denied it.

I beg leave to say, that in the *Sun* of the 11th instant, the Editor is pleased to mention my name jointly with a supposititious one of *Evans*, and to describe me as a

Tobacconist of Belfast in Ireland, who for seditious harangues, had been shipped on board a tender by Lord Carhampton. The above statement is totally erroneous—I am now twenty-eight years old, and have been seventeen years in his Majesty's Navy—am a *Seaman*, who from his soul, wishes well to his King and Country, and whose conduct, I flatter myself, has and will free his character from the effects of malice or misrepresentation. (*Portsmouth Gazette*, 10 July 1797)

Manwaring and Dobrée describe him as 'a sound, experienced, authoritative sailor, or he would not have been Quarter Master's Mate', whose 'family lived in Portsmouth' (Manwaring and Dobrée, 35, 68, 98, 101).

Aaron Graham, a magistrate sent by the home secretary to discover Jacobin inspiration for the mutiny, planned to persuade Joyce to reveal 'incendiaries' through 'possession' of his mother. He would 'prevail upon the sister to join her influence to the mothers; and as the father likewise is said to belong to the Invalid Corps in this Garrison there can be little doubt of his assistance being had if it should be wanted'. On 22 May Graham claimed to have found no such evidence, and testified to Joyce's arranging 'good order' (ADM 1/4172).

Joyce and his fellow delegates ensured the seamen's commitment 'to the plan laid down at Spithead' (ADM 1/811). They won public support and increased pay and provisions from the Admiralty and government. Their determination to act humanely after three seamen were shot on the *London* (7 May), prevented further bloodshed. Earl Howe, sent by George III to conclude negotiations, assessed one delegate as

of a temper, character, & degree of intelligence, that I think I could have employed to good purpose, if I had continued in Service. Joyce in the *same station* in the Royal George, much as he has been spoken to his disadvantage, prejudiced me by his conduct, equally in his favour. (Lord Howe to Lord Keith, 24 June 1797, Royal Naval Museum, MS 1998/2)

After the mutiny it was asserted: 'There would allways be a private Corryspondance Carried on between them by Letters all though it Was all settled with them ... for it was agreed Upon at there Community ... Joyce of the Royal george ... will have all ...' (28 May 1797, ADM 1/3974, fol. 261).

Joyce's subsequent promotion to quartermaster and midshipman confirmed his leadership qualities. Tragically, on 26 January 1800, his ship was wrecked on Ave Rocks near Newhaven in a storm, with the loss of all but one of the crew. The *Portsmouth Gazette* (3 February 1800), recalled his historic role: 'Valentine Joyce, who bore so conspicuous a part in the mutiny at Spithead in the year 1797, was drowned when the Brazen sloop was lost a few days since on the coast of Sussex'. Of the recovered bodies, twenty-nine were buried at Newhaven, 'in a spot of ground adjoining the church-yard' (*Portsmouth Gazette*, 10 Feb 1800).   ANN VERONICA COATS

Sources G. E. Manwaring and B. Dobrée, *The floating republic: an account of the mutinies at Spithead and the Nore in 1797* (1935) · C. Gill, *The naval mutinies of 1797* (1913) · A. T. Patterson, *The naval mutiny at Spithead* (1978) · *Naval Chronicle*, 3 (1800), 147–8 · *Portsmouth Gazette and Weekly Advertiser* (10 July 1797) · *Portsmouth Gazette and Weekly Advertiser* (3 Feb 1800) · *Portsmouth Gazette and Weekly Advertiser* (10 Feb 1800) · PRO, ADM 36/11146; 36/11148; 36/11697; 36/11702; 36/11704; 36/12218; 36/12700; 36/14141 · PRO, ADM 1/4172; 1/3974, fols. 251, 261; 1/1039; 1/811 · Lord Howe to Lord Keith, 24 June 1797, Royal Naval Museum, Portsmouth, MS 1998/2 · *IGI* · *The Times* (12 May 1797) · St Thomas' baptism register, Portsmouth City RO, Portsmouth, CHU2/1A/7 · D. Hepper, *British warship losses in the age of sail, 1650–1859* (1994) · M. Elliott, *Partners in revolution: the United Irishmen and France* (1982) · R. Wells, *Insurrection: the British experience, 1795–1803* (1983) · J. Dugan, *The great mutiny* (New York, 1965); repr. (1966) · M. Lewis, *A social history of the navy* (1960) · W. J. Neale, *History of the mutiny at Spithead and the Nore* (1842) · W. G. Glascock, *Tales of a tar* (1830)

Archives Portsmouth City Museum and RO, Portsmouth, St Thomas's baptism register, CHU2/1A/7 · PRO, ADM 36/11146; 36/11148; 36/11697; 36/11702; 36/11704; 36/12218; 36/12700; 36/14141; ADM 1/4172; 1/3974, fols. 251, 261; 1/1039; 1/811; WO 97/1239 · Royal Naval Museum, Portsmouth, Lord Howe to Lord Keith, 24 June 1797, MS 1998/2

Joyce, William Brooke [*known as* Lord Haw-Haw] (1906–1946), fascist and propaganda broadcaster, was born on 24 April 1906 at 1377 Herkimer Street, Brooklyn, New York, USA, the first of three sons of Michael Francis Joyce (1869/70–1941), builder and contractor, originally of co. Mayo, Ireland, but naturalized as an American citizen in 1894, and his wife, Gertrude Emily Brooke (*d.* 1944), of Shaw, Lancashire. The family returned to Ireland in 1909, where Joyce was educated in Roman Catholic schools, including the Jesuit St Ignatius Loyola College. The Joyces were, however, ardent loyalists, and Joyce later claimed to have fought as a boy alongside the Black and Tans.

In December 1921 the family moved to England, where Joyce enlisted, first, in the British army (from which he was discharged when found to be under age), and then the London University Officers' Training Corps (when, to facilitate his application, his father falsely claimed that the family were British citizens). He studied at Battersea Polytechnic (1922–3), then at Birkbeck College, University of London, where he graduated with a first-class honours degree in English in June 1927. On 30 April 1927 he married Hazel Katherine Barr at Chelsea register office. They had two daughters, but the marriage was dissolved in 1937.

While at Birkbeck, and still in his teens, Joyce became heavily involved in extreme right-wing politics. From 1923 to 1925 he was a member of the British Fascisti (and first came to the notice of special branch), and during an affray between fascists and communists at Lambeth during the general election of 1924 received the razor slash that permanently marked his face: the scar extended from his right ear to the corner of his mouth. Although he joined the Conservative Party in 1928, Joyce joined Sir Oswald Mosley's British Union of Fascists (BUF) in 1933, and became area administrator for the home counties, then director of propaganda and Mosley's deputy leader, with a reputation as a ferocious orator. In 1934 he obtained a British passport, after falsely declaring his birthplace to be Galway, Ireland. He married Margaret Cairns White (1911–1972), another active BUF member, at Kensington

William Brooke Joyce [Lord Haw-Haw] (1906–1946), by unknown photographer, c.1942

register office on 13 February 1937. However, Joyce and Mosley fell out (Joyce considered Mosley insufficiently antisemitic), and shortly after standing as a BUF candidate in Shoreditch in the London county council elections of March 1937 (when he received fourteen per cent of the vote) Joyce set up his own party, the National Socialist League (NSL), which called for Britain to unite with Hitler's Germany against the 'twin Jewish manifestations' of Bolshevism and international finance. Margaret Joyce became the NSL's assistant treasurer. Fearing certain detention should war come, the Joyces travelled on 26 August 1939 to Berlin, and on 18 September Joyce began broadcasting in the Reichsrundfunk's English-language service, initially as a newsreader. Within a few years he had become Germany's principal English-language broadcaster.

The original Lord Haw-Haw (a name coined by Jonah Barrington of the *Daily Express* in September 1939) was almost certainly one Wolff Mittler, the Reichsrundfunk's chief English-language broadcaster in the early part of the war, though the name was also applied to several other broadcasters, including Norman Baillie Stewart. Although Joyce's accent ('some sort of hybrid between a Yankee twang and an Irish brogue', according to J. W. Hall (Hall, 1)) differed markedly from Mittler's stilted aristocratic manner, his distinctive sardonic tones and call-sign ('Jairmany calling') made him the most instantly recognizable of German propagandists to Britain and the nickname stuck to him. By May 1940 he was using it himself on air and his true identity had been revealed in the British press. His broadcasts from Zeesen, Bremen, and especially Hamburg rapidly made him a celebrity of sorts in Britain, inspiring, for instance, a popular song ('Lord Haw-Haw, the Humbug of Hamburg') and a musical revue starring Max Miller, and they concerned the British government sufficiently to commission a BBC listener research report in December 1939. It found that two-thirds of the British public listened to Joyce at least occasionally—although apparently more out of curiosity than defeatism. Although listening appeared to decline from mid-1940, public fascination with the broadcasts continued, and apocryphal 'Haw-Haw rumours' (for instance, that Joyce had correctly predicted local air raids, or demonstrated a sinisterly precise knowledge of town clocks) persisted throughout the war. Despite little evidence that these broadcasts did undermine

British morale as intended, Goebbels himself rated Joyce's wartime propaganda contribution highly. In June 1942 Joyce was promoted to chief commentator in the English-language service, with his own programme, *Views on the News*. In September 1944 he was awarded Nazi Germany's war merit cross first class.

While in Germany Joyce also published a propaganda tract, *Twilight over England* (1940), wrote extensively for the 'black' propaganda stations the New British Broadcasting Station and the Workers' Challenge Station, and was active in recruiting other broadcasters from among British prisoners of war. Margaret Joyce also worked for German English-language radio, writing women's features and from November 1940 to May 1942 broadcasting (as 'Lady Haw-Haw') weekly talks aimed at British women. After being granted German nationality in September 1940, the two were divorced in August 1941 (he citing adultery, she cruelty), but they remarried at the Berlin-Charlottenburg register office on 11 February 1942.

Joyce's final broadcast was from Hamburg on 30 April 1945. He and his wife went into hiding near the Danish border, but he was shot and arrested on 28 May 1945 after a British soldier recognized his voice. Although Joyce had never legitimately held British nationality, he was tried on three counts of treason at the central criminal court, London, on 17–19 September 1945, with the prosecution (led by Sir William Hartley Shawcross) arguing that his youthful claims of British citizenship and, above all, his fraudulent holding of a British passport from 1933 to 1940 were sufficient proof in law that he had placed himself 'under the protection of the British crown' and thus owed the crown allegiance in return. After direction to this effect from the trial judge, Mr Justice Tucker, and with Joyce refusing to give evidence, the jury took just twenty-three minutes to convict him of the third count, that he had 'adhered to the King's enemies' by broadcasting for them between 18 September 1939 and 2 July 1940 (the date his British passport expired). Despite some disquiet in legal and other circles, appeals to the High Court and the House of Lords were dismissed (the latter with one dissentient), and Joyce was executed by hanging on 3 January 1946 at Wandsworth prison, London, one of only three people to be convicted by a British court of treason after the war and of only two to be executed (the other being John Amery). Margaret Joyce was detained in military custody for some months but was not prosecuted, and later moved to Ireland. She died in 1972.   SIÂN NICHOLAS

Sources T. Chapman, 'William Joyce "Lord Haw Haw" 1906–1946: a biographical introduction', in W. Joyce, *Twilight over England* (1992), v–xiv · J. W. Hall, ed., *Trial of William Joyce* (1946) · M. A. Doherty, *Nazi wireless propaganda: Lord Haw-Haw and British public opinion in the Second World War* (2000) · J. A. Cole, *Lord Haw-Haw — and William Joyce: the full story* (1964) · R. West, *The meaning of treason*, new edn (1982) · J. Gottlieb, *Feminine fascism* (2000) · F. Selwyn, *Hitler's Englishman: the crime of 'Lord Haw-Haw'* (1987)
Archives BBC WAC, listener research reports on propaganda broadcasts · University of Sheffield, notes and letters to C. C. Lewis |SOUND BL NSA · BL NSA, documentary recordings · BL NSA, news recordings

Likenesses photograph, *c*.1942, Hult. Arch. [*see illus.*] • photograph, repro. in Hall, ed., *Trial of William Joyce*, facing p. 32

Joyce, Yootha [*real name* Yootha Joyce Needham] (1927–1980), actress, was born at 19 Bolingbroke Grove, Battersea, London, on 20 August 1927, the only child of Percival Henry John (Hurst) Needham, a singer who was appearing as part of the long summer season at the Grand Theatre, Clapham Junction, and his wife, Jessie Maud (*née* Revitt). Her father had been robbed of much of his bass-baritone voice after contracting emphysema in the First World War and was forced to move into musical comedy, revue, and finally variety. Her mother's own singing career had been halted by her marriage; she gave up her voice to concentrate on her piano playing as an accompanist to her husband. This sacrifice of a wife's talent to the arguably less important career of her husband, who was often out of work, seems to have left its mark on the adult Joyce's attitude to her own work. She acknowledged that she subordinated her private life to the pursuit of her professional ambitions.

Determined to become an actress, Joyce overcame a degree of parental opposition, as well as the difficulty of achieving her ambition while being shunted around schools in Battersea, Petersfield, and Croydon, and was accepted by the Royal Academy of Dramatic Art (RADA). RADA seems to have been something of a disappointment to her because it favoured a particular breed of Shakespearian actress. Rather more to her taste was a summer job, about 1944, as assistant stage manager at the Grand Theatre, Croydon, and a tour with the Entertainments National Service Association in the following year's long vacation. Knowing from these experiences that she could earn money by acting, she left RADA before her final year was complete, and embarked on more than a decade of repertory, radio work, and touring. During this period she took on her familiar stage surname Joyce.

On 8 December 1956 Joyce married the actor (John) Glynn Edwards, the son of John Walters Edwards, a licensed victualler, and he recommended her to Joan Littlewood, then at the height of her success with the Theatre Workshop, for a small role in her version of Jaroslav Hašek's *The Good Soldier Schweik*. The production went briefly to Paris, and on its return Littlewood offered Joyce a permanent place in the company. Three years later she took part alongside Edwards in the original production of Frank Norman's and Lionel Bart's East End gangster play *fings ain't wot they used t'be* [*sic*], at the Theatre Workshop's home, the Theatre Royal, Stratford East. He had been cast in the leading role, Frederick Cochran, while in support was what amounted to an academy of future television actors, including Miriam Karlin, Brian Murphy, George Sewell, and a very young Barbara Windsor. Joyce was given two characteristic roles, the 'strapping policewoman' who appears briefly in the first act, and Myrtle, a caricatured upper-class girl who appears, to general ridicule, towards the end of the play. After a long series of performances in Stratford, the play moved to the Garrick Theatre in London's West End, where it opened in February 1960.

These performances were crucial for Joyce's career: among the audience late in the run were Frank Muir and Denis Norden, the writers of a forthcoming BBC situation comedy, *Brothers in Law*, broadcast between April and July 1962. An appearance in one episode launched her TV career: within a year she was regularly being given character roles in the series of single comedy dramas that comprised *Comedy Playhouse*, performing scripts by writers of the calibre of Alan Plater, and Ray Galton and Alan Simpson. In 'Impasse', a Galton and Simpson script broadcast in March 1963, two drivers meet in a narrow country lane, one in a small cheap car, the other in a much grander Bentley, and refuse, for half an hour, to let each other pass. Joyce played the poorer man's wife, looking on sardonically and forging an uneasy bond with her richer counterpart. This confrontation encapsulated the great themes of British sitcom: male stupidity, female frustration, and above all, the English class divide, developed in some of the great television sitcom series that followed it.

Man about the House, the Thames Television show in which Yootha Joyce became a major star, and which began the first of its six series in August 1973, takes on all these major themes. Its gender skirmishes are, openly, about sex as much as misunderstanding: the comedy is fuelled by what now seems a rather quaint sense of dismay at a young man (Richard O'Sullivan) sharing a house with two pretty young girls (Paula Wilcox and Sally Thomsett). But any potential hanky-panky is only implied and the centre of sexual gravity is shifted, rather oddly, to the older, and initially more peripheral, figures of their landlords, Mildred and George Roper, played, in a Theatre Workshop reunion, by Joyce and Brian Murphy.

As *Man about the House* developed, the fractures in the Ropers' marriage of more than twenty years—his absent libido, her resultant sexual frustration, her desire to be middle-class, and his to be lazy—became its central preoccupations, and increasingly diverted attention from its ostensible stars. In 1976 the writers, Johnnie Mortimer and Brian Cooke, created two complementary spin-offs, separating the two groups of characters. O'Sullivan went off to set up a bistro in *Robin's Nest*, while Joyce and Murphy became owner–occupiers of a house in Teddington for their eponymous series *George and Mildred*. Here the Ropers could fight their battles of sex and class undistracted. Joyce had greatly intensified her performance, turning her character into 'a mass of twitchily frustrated sexuality', Mildred verbally demolishing George 'as an alternative to the sex act' (Crowther and Penfold, 157). Their private class struggle was centred on the house, a semi-detached on a new development—in reality, just around the corner from Thames Television's Middlesex studios. *George and Mildred* ran for five series, between September 1976 and Christmas day 1979, and was complemented by a stage play, performed during the 1977 summer season at the Pier Theatre, Bournemouth, and succeeded in 1980 by a feature film version, to a script by Dick Sharples.

Joyce's marriage ended in divorce in 1968; there were no children. She was a keen supporter of animal charities.

After her death, from cirrhosis of the liver, in a London clinic on 24 August 1980, it emerged that she had been for the last ten years of her life an extremely heavy drinker. The depression that led her to drink derived from a fear of being eternally typecast. She may well have been justified: the strength she had identified in herself when younger, which had disqualified her from playing Desdemona during her time at RADA, had settled by her fifties into a square-jawed hardness of feature, which immediately and irrevocably suggested the kind of terrifying battleaxe epitomized by Mildred. It was perhaps the tragedy of Yootha Joyce's career that her greatest success only confirmed what seems to have been her greatest fear.

STEPHEN FOLLOWS

Sources *Daily Telegraph* (25 Aug 1980) · *Daily Telegraph* (16 Sept 1980) · *The Guardian* (25 Aug 1980) · *Daily Mirror* (25 Aug 1980) · *Daily Mail* (25 Aug 1980) · *Daily Express* (25 Aug 1980) · *The Sun* (25 Aug 1980) · *The Times* (16 Sept 1980) · *Evening News* (11 Oct 1976) [preview of *George and Mildred*] · B. Crowther and M. Penfold, *Bring me laughter: four decades of TV comedy* (1987) · P. Curran, ed., *Ropermania*, 2 (1995) [Liverpool: George and Mildred/Yootha Joyce Memorial Society] · Y. Joyce and A. Coleman, 'Yootha—I've never cried in bed and I never will', *TV Times* (22 Oct 1976) · M. Lewisohn, *Radio Times guide to TV comedy* (1998) · F. Norman and L. Bart, *fings ain't wot they used t'be* (1960) · b. cert. · *CGPLA Eng. & Wales* (1981) · m. cert.
Likenesses group photograph, 1976, Hult. Arch. · photograph, 1976 (with Brian Murphy), Hult. Arch. · photograph, repro. in *Daily Mirror*
Wealth at death £101,536: probate, 19 March 1981, *CGPLA Eng. & Wales*

Joye, George (1490×95–1553), evangelical author, was born in Bedfordshire, and educated in Cambridge, where he graduated BA in 1513, and on 27 April 1517 was elected a fellow of Peterhouse. He took the degree of BTh in 1524–5, but soon afterwards his religious beliefs brought him into conflict with the Henrician government. In 1526 his rooms were searched for heretical and prohibited literature, and it seems that it was through the intervention of Stephen Gardiner that Joye escaped persecution. In his *Refutation* of 1546 Joye would have hard words for Gardiner on his backsliding in the intervening years. Further investigations followed in 1527 after John Ashwell, the prior of Newnham Abbey near Bedford, informed John Longland, bishop of Lincoln, that Joye held heretical and suspect opinions. Joye was summoned to London to appear before Wolsey in December 1527—at the same time as Thomas Bilney and Thomas Arthur were also under investigation. Directed to Longland at Lincoln, Joye sensed danger and fled abroad, probably to Antwerp. In 1531 he printed there a copy of the letter sent by Ashwell to Longland, along with a defence of his views, under a title drawing attention to the fact that he was responding publicly to charges made covertly against him—*The letters which Johan Ashwel priour of Newnham Abbey sente secretely to the bishope of Lyncolne*. Joye rejected the papal power to bind and loose, and argued that faith alone without works justified. He rejected Ashwell's claim that he supported clerical concubinage, but argued in favour of the marriage of priests.

Joye's literary output was prolific, and included a number of translations of the works of continental reformers, or texts based upon their writings. In 1529 he completed his first psalter, a translation from Bucer's Latin edition. In 1534 he produced a revised psalter, this time following Zwingli's Latin one. Joye had also composed a primer, probably in 1529, and although no copies are extant it is clear from the writings of Thomas More that Joye was thought to be the author. In July 1530 he issued a second primer, the *Hortulus animae*, prefaced by a new calendar which excluded many of the traditional saints' days. Instead Joye inserted contemporary references, adding Thomas Hitton, who had been executed for heresy as recently as 23 February, to the calendar and giving him the title of 'sei[n]te'. The work was probably a revision of the lost primer of 1529, and drew heavily upon Luther, Brunfels, and Bucer. It also followed Zwinglian practice in stressing the prohibition of graven images in the decalogue. It was condemned in England in 1530, and it has been suggested that subsequent changes in the calendar reflected this initial condemnation. The primer, the psalter, and the *Hortulus* were all condemned by Stokesley in a list of prohibited works circulated in December 1531.

Alongside the primers and psalters, Joye also produced a number of translations of books of the Bible. The first to be printed was his edition of Isaiah, issued from the press of Martin de Keyser in Antwerp in May 1531. Joye appended an introductory prologue to the volume, which included an exhortation to improve the availability of scripture: just as Isaiah had battled against the idolatry of the world in which he lived, so Joye's world suffered while the words of scripture were stifled. In May 1534 Joye's translation of Jeremiah was completed, and his introduction to the work picked up on the themes explored in the prologue to Isaiah. There were parallels to be drawn between what Joye viewed as contemporary backsliding in religion and the religious attitudes which Jeremiah had criticized. But there was also room for hope: Joye rejoiced in the rejection of papal authority in England, and celebrated the arrest and imprisonment of Thomas More. Further translations followed: English editions of Proverbs and Ecclesiastes were printed in London (ESTC 2752).

Of all Joye's translations, however, it was the revision of Tyndale's English New Testament of 1526 which was to be the most controversial, not least because Joye's interventions created a serious rift with Tyndale. Joye had been approached to produce a revision of Tyndale's New Testament, probably in the spring of 1534. The book appeared later that year, and there are clear similarities between the two editions, suggesting that Joye's work was indeed one of revision and not one of rewriting. In his *Apology* of 1535 Joye gives his own account of events, and claims that he had simply revised parts of Tyndale's translation to ensure that readers were not deceived by any mistranslations which might be in circulation. It was expected that Tyndale would then revise the whole work, but until then it was vital that uncorrected editions should not reach England. However Joye had also used his revisions to set out his own views on a number of subjects, especially the fate of the soul after death. Where Tyndale had used the word 'resurrection', Joye substituted the phrase 'the life after this', a rewording which Tyndale rejected. When

Tyndale's own revised New Testament was printed only three months later, in August 1534, it was prefaced by two introductions to the reader. The first was an implicit condemnation of Joye's intervention, and the second a more personal attack, focused on the whole question of the resurrection. Joye took up the challenge, and in the 'address to the reader' appended to the second edition of his own work he launched a spirited defence of his choice of the phrase 'the life after this'. Joye's final defence in the *Apology* did little to advance the debate, and his hostile tone made it less likely still that the rift would be healed.

Joye's enemies and fellow exiles suggested that he had colluded with Henry Phillips in securing the arrest of Tyndale in 1535, and his subsequent execution. It seems that the allegations were unjustified: in a letter addressed to Archbishop Cranmer in July 1535, Thomas Tebolde denied that Joye had any involvement in the arrest of Tyndale, 'I write this because Joye is greatly blamed and a[bu]sed among merchants and others who were his friends falsely and wrongfully' (*LP Henry VIII*, 8, no. 1151). After Tyndale's arrest Joye lodged with Edward Foxe in Calais, and Foxe interceded on his behalf with Cromwell, assuring him of Joye's orthodoxy on the question of the eucharist. In part this may have reflected the controversy which surrounded the publication of the *Souper of the Lord*, a tract on the eucharist which modern scholarship attributes to Joye. Five editions were printed, making it perhaps Joye's most influential work. Thomas More condemned the opinions advanced in the *Souper*, and Joye retaliated with the publication of *The Subversion of Moris False Foundacion* in 1534 (ESTC 14829). However in June 1535 Foxe told Cromwell that Joye 'will never again say anything contrary to the present belief concerning that sacrament and is conformable in all points as a Christian man should be' (*LP Henry VIII*, 8, no. 823). Joye returned to England later that year, but had clearly fled again by the summer of 1540, in the aftermath of the Act of Six Articles and the threat of persecution in 1539.

Throughout the 1540s Joye composed a number of popular works which criticized the state of the church in England, and in particular the bishop of Winchester, Stephen Gardiner. The controversy with Gardiner opened in June 1543 with the publication of *George Joye Confuteth Winchester's False Articles*. It was Gardiner's involvement in the events of 1539–40, and particularly in the execution of Barnes, which had turned Joye against him. Late in 1545 Gardiner voiced suspicions that Joye was the author of the scurrilous *Lamentacyon of a Christian Agaynst the Cytye of London*, published under the name of Roderyk Mors, noting darkly that it 'everywhere prints the word Joye with a great letter' (*LP Henry VIII*, 20/2, no. 732). In fact the tract was the work of Henry Brinklow, and in any case Gardiner did not respond to Joye's polemic until 1546 (*A Declaration of such True Articles*). Joye soon retaliated with the publication later that year of *The Refutation of the Bishop of Winchester's Derke Declaration*, in which he compared Gardiner to Pontius Pilate and argued that the bishop was responsible for the more conservative direction of the 'Kings Book' of 1543.

Between 1541 and 1546 some ten books were attributed to Joye, including two works on clerical marriage. The *Defence of Matrimony* was a translation of Melanchthon, but in 1541 Joye also published his own work on the subject, *The Defence of the Mariage of Priestes*. It appeared at Zürich under the pseudonym James Sawtry, one which concealed Joye's identity so successfully that his authorship was only established in the twentieth century. For Joye the question of clerical marriage was an issue of personal concern as well as doctrinal importance, for by 1532 he had married in breach of the discipline of both Catholicism and the Henrician church, and would have been vulnerable to persecution in the aftermath of the six articles of 1539. Thomas More was well aware of Joye's circumstances: in his *Confutation of Tyndale's Answer* he had noted of Joye that 'beynge preste he hath bygyled a woman and wedded her' (More, 1.8). Joye argued for the scriptural foundations of the married priesthood, and suggested that the rejection of married priests in England reflected Gardiner's preference for clerical concubinage, which fitted well with the vested interests of secular powers, such as the duke of Norfolk, who feared that the clergy would acquire too much land through marriage dowries.

Alongside his work on the Bible and polemic against Gardiner, Joye also produced a number of devotional tracts. *Our Saviour hath not Overcharged his Churche* criticized the proliferation of ceremonies and extra-scriptural traditions in the church. A translation of Zwingli's *Christianae fidei expositio* repeated Joye's criticisms of the church in England and included a prayer of complaint from 'the pore pe[r]secuted maryed Preistis' (sigs. D6–8). *The Unite and Scisme of the Olde Churche* (1543) contrasted, through the words of the prophets, the early purity of Israel with her fall into idolatry, and warned of the threat which was posed to Christianity by superstition and false doctrine. In 1544 *A Present Consolacion for the Sufferers of Persecution* described the triumph of truth in adversity, the endurance of the persecuted and the fall of their persecutors, illustrated with contemporary examples, with More and Wolsey as the contemporary figures of evil. This blend of biblical history and contemporary events was explored at greater length in *The Exposicion of Daniel the Prophete*, a work of some five hundred pages which drew upon Melanchthon, Oecolampadius, and Pelikan. The prophecies of Daniel were applied to events past and present, and Joye showed that he believed that he lived in the age of the tyranny of the Antichrist, epitomized in the persecution of the faithful and the promotion of false religion.

Joye's works were condemned again at Smithfield in 1546, but after the death of Henry VIII he returned to England, and secured ecclesiastical promotion, to the rectory of Blunham, Bedfordshire, in 1549, and to that of Ashwell, Hertfordshire, in 1552. He died in 1553, apparently in his native Bedfordshire. He left a son, George, who was educated in Cambridge, and held a number of ecclesiastical preferments.   H. L. PARISH

Sources C. Butterworth and A. Chester, *George Joye, 1495?–1553: a chapter in the history of the English Bible and the English Reformation* (1962) · W. A. Clebsch, *England's earliest protestants, 1520–1535*

(1964) • W. D. J. Cargill Thompson, 'Who wrote "The supper of the Lord"?', *Harvard Theological Review*, 53 (1960), 79–91 • G. Joye, *An apolgye made by George Joye to satisfye, if it maye be, W. Tindale* (Antwerp, 1535) • *The letters which Johan Ashwel … sente secretely to the bishope of Lyncolne in … MDXXVII. Where in the sayde priour accuseth George Joye … of fower opinios* (1531?) • J. Sawtry, *The defence of the mariage of preistes* (1541) • St Thomas More, *The confutation of Tyndale's answer*, ed. L. A. Schuster and others, 3 vols. (1973), vol. 8 of *The Yale edition of the complete works of St Thomas More* • *LP Henry VIII* • Cooper, *Ath. Cantab.*, 1.114–15 • C. Butterworth, *The English primers, 1529–1545* (Philadelphia, 1953) • D. MacCulloch, *Thomas Cranmer: a life* (1996) • D. Daniell, *William Tyndale* (1994)

Joye, Peter (1636–1721), merchant, was born in August 1636, the son of Peter Joye, senior, a Dutch-born tailor of Blackfriars, London. Apprenticed by the Merchant Taylors' Company in 1653, Joye was brought into trade by the merchant Charles Marescoe in 1669, soon after his marriage in 1668 to Marescoe's sister, Elizabeth. Joye provided a quarter share in the firm's capital of £28,000 and their business prospered until Marescoe's death in 1670. Joye then took a one-fifth share in a partnership set up by Marescoe's widow, Leonora, but its £10,000 capital proved inadequate to sustain the scale of its predecessor's activities and he withdrew or was ousted from the partnership in 1675.

By then Joye had acquired useful experience of the Swedish iron, pitch, and tar imports in which Marescoe had specialized and he was able to set up his own flourishing trade with the major suppliers. He dealt particularly in the long iron bars known as 'voyage' iron or 'Guinea' iron, which was in demand for sale in the west African slave trade. Joye invested £400 when the Royal African Company was floated in November 1671 and he was to serve in its court of assistants as a director in 1678–80, 1683, 1683–5, 1688–9, and 1691–5. He soon became one of the company's major contractors, agreeing in 1685 to supply it with 450 tons of bar iron and 40,000 bars of copper. In 1683 he was admitted to the Eastland Company which dealt mainly in Scandinavian and Baltic commodities. He acquired an interest in shipping and in 1676 secured the British government's diplomatic support to recover one of his vessels after its seizure by a Dutch privateer. His specialization in iron, copper, pitch, tar, and hemp made him a valued and increasingly prosperous supplier of naval goods to the Admiralty, and he made substantial loans to the government of William III.

Although he was baptized into the Dutch church at Austin Friars, Joye was a long-standing parishioner of St Dunstan-in-the-East, where he became churchwarden. Living close to the wharves through which passed London's overseas trade, Joye paid rates as one of the most substantial citizens of the Dice Quay precinct, and he later inhabited a large house in Mincing Lane. In 1682–3 and 1689–93 he was a member of the common council as a representative for Tower ward and he was commissioned in the militia lieutenancy for the City of London in 1690 and 1694. He became treasurer of St Bartholomew's Hospital, to which he bequeathed £1000. Politically his sympathies were evidently tory–Anglican, for although he was listed as 'good' in a government survey of councilmen in 1681 he

was among those liverymen purged by James II in 1687 as hostile to his plans for the toleration of Roman Catholics and protestant dissenters.

With his first wife, who died in April 1680, Joye had a son, named Charles, born in March 1670. He evidently remarried, as he and his wife, Ellen, had one son, James; but some coolness may be deduced from Joye's will of June 1718, in which he pointedly left Ellen and James the smaller share in his estate. However, although Charles had followed in his father's footsteps and established himself as a successful Eastland merchant, he had also become heavily involved in the South Sea Company, of which he became deputy governor. He thus shared in the catastrophe of the South Sea Bubble of 1720 and was among those held chiefly responsible. Shrewdly anticipating the confiscation of Charles's estate, valued at £40,105 by a punitive parliament, Peter Joye's last act, on 2 January 1721, was to add a codicil to his will, transferring to James its execution and principal benefits. He died at his house in Mincing Lane on 11 January, and his estate, which included lands in Northamptonshire bought for about £36,000 and financial investments exceeding £56,000, thus passed unscathed to its very numerous beneficiaries, who included the poor of Stockholm, Hamburg, and Malaga, as well as the French and Dutch churches of London, Sion College, and the charity school of St Ann Blackfriars. A memorial to Peter Joye and his first wife was placed in St Dunstan-in-the-East, where he was buried.

H. G. ROSEVEARE

Sources *Markets and merchants of the late seventeenth century: the Marescoe–David letters, 1668–1680*, ed. H. Roseveare, British Academy, Records of Social and Economic History, new ser., 12 (1987); repr. (1991) • J. R. Woodhead, *The rulers of London, 1660–1689* (1965), 100 • K. G. Davies, *The Royal African Company* (1957), 67, 171–2 • probate records: will, inventories, sentence, witnesses, PRO, PROB, 11/578, sig. 51 (will); PROB 11/582, sig. 240 (sentence); PROB 5/4169 (inventories); PROB 24/58 (witnesses) • register (baptism), Dutch church, Austin Friars, London • register (marriage), Dutch church • parish register (burial), St Dunstan-in-the-East, Billingsgate

Archives PRO, chancery masters exhibits, C.114/63–78 • Riksarkivet, Stockholm, Momma-Reenstierna Sammlung

Wealth at death over £56,000; incl. lands in Northamptonshire at approximately £36,000; variety of bonds, loans, and investments, incl. £2875 in Bank of England stock, £12,000 in East India Company stock, and £19,336 2s. 7d. in South Sea Company stock: will, PRO, PROB 11/578, 402; inventories, PRO, PROB 5/4169

Joyliffe, George (1621–1658), anatomist and physician, was born at East Stower in Dorset, the son of John Joyliffe. He matriculated from Wadham College, Oxford, in 1637, aged sixteen, graduating BA in 1640 and MA in 1643, the latter through Pembroke College, where he remained until 1648. In 1643 he served as lieutenant in the royalist army under Lord Hopton. Joyliffe's interest and skill in anatomy, which had increased while he was at Oxford, was encouraged by his mentor, Thomas Clayton, regius professor of medicine, who, while trained in the Galenic tradition, was nevertheless moderately receptive to change. It was first reported in 1642, by a colleague, that Joyliffe had discovered the lymphatics and had demonstrated them in dissections in Oxford. In 1648 he moved to

Sussex, where he carried on anatomical and botanical work, as indicated in letters to the diarist and virtuoso John Evelyn between 1648 and 1649. In 1652, as a member of Clare College, Cambridge, Joyliffe obtained his MD under the tutelage of Francis Glisson, regius professor of medicine, and subsequently he established a practice in London.

It was through Glisson's monograph on the liver, *Anatomia hepatis* (1654), that Joyliffe's discovery of the lymphatics generated new controversy. The work was dedicated to Cambridge University and to the College of Physicians as the culmination of extensive dissection and discussion at the college. Glisson suggested considerable prominence for the lymphatic system, which increasingly had replaced circulation of the blood as a topic of European medical controversy. While many other writers focused on the priority dispute between Bartholin and Rudbeck in Scandinavia on this issue, Glisson further complicated the debate. He repeated the view, widely held in England, that his former student Joyliffe—who was now a candidate for the College of Physicians and lectured on the lymphatic system in 1653, when the priority controversy was at its height—had independently discovered the lymph ducts.

The same claim was to be revived by Joyliffe's friend and former Oxford colleague Timothy Clarke in the Royal Society's *Philosophical Transactions* of 1668. Clarke had been given an Oxford DM in 1652 and had become a physician in London where, in the same year as the *Transactions* article was published, he was nominated as physician-in-ordinary to the king. In an undated letter to Henry Oldenburg, secretary to the Royal Society, which circumstantial evidence suggests was written in the spring of 1668, Clarke recounts:

> even before 1652, while studying the spermatic vessels, [Joyliffe] squeezed the testicle and its covering with his hand after he had tied a ligature higher up so as to cause the vessels to swell up, and thus for the first time witnessed the swelling of the lymphatic vessel, quite inadvertedly and without contemplating such a result. (*Correspondence of Henry Oldenburg*, 361)

This account of accidental discovery was also conveyed by Joyliffe to Robert Boyle, the chemist and leading corpuscularian, in the early 1650s. Robert Plot, in his *Natural History of Oxford-Shire* (1677), was likewise to defend Joyliffe's priority in discovering the lymphatics.

Joyliffe's association with Boyle, who became successor to John Wilkins as leader of the Oxford physiological community from late 1655, finds expression in a dissection the two performed together in London between April and May of 1656. Boyle described Joyliffe on this occasion as 'that dexterous Dissector', who helped him to 'take the spleen of a dog without killing him', while Joyliffe 'cut asunder the vessels reaching to it, that I might be sure there was not the least part of the spleen unextirpated' (*Works of … Boyle*, 2.67–8). The puppy in question was reported to be in excellent health a fortnight later. Joyliffe became a fellow of the College of Physicians in 1658.

Joyliffe was one of many figures whose anatomical activities were built upon an Oxford physiological community that flourished, from the early 1640s to the late 1660s, under the leadership of William Harvey, John Wilkins, and Robert Boyle. Like many of his contemporaries, Joyliffe set up a medical practice in London, where he died, unmarried, at his home at Garlick Hill, on 11 November 1658. He was buried at St James Garlickhythe.

MALCOLM OSTER

Sources R. G. Frank, *Harvey and the Oxford physiologists* (1980) · C. Webster, *The great instauration: science, medicine and reform, 1626–1660* (1975) · *The correspondence of Henry Oldenburg*, ed. and trans. A. R. Hall and M. B. Hall, 4 (1967), 361 · F. Glisson, *Anatomia hepatis* (1654) · R. Plot, *The natural history of Oxford-shire* (1677) · *DNB* · Munk, *Roll* · Venn, *Alum. Cant.* · *The works of the Honourable Robert Boyle*, ed. T. Birch, new edn, 2 (1772), 67–8

Joyner [*alias* Lyde], **William** (*bap.* 1622, *d.* 1706), writer and playwright, was baptized on 24 April 1622 in the parish of St Giles', Oxford, the second son of William Joyner, alias Lyde (*d.* 1626) and Anne, daughter of the physician Edward *Lapworth. William's grandfather Richard Lyde lived at Cuddesdon, Oxfordshire, and his uncle John Lyde owned land at Horsepath near Oxford. William was educated at the free schools of Thame and Coventry before entering Magdalen College in 1636, matriculating on 6 May aged fourteen. He was a demy from 1636 to 1642, was awarded his BA on 3 November 1640, and was a fellow of the college from 1642 to 1645. At this time he was writing Latin and English poems, typical being his verses in *Musarum Oxon. charisteria* (1638) and *Horti Carolini rosa altera* (1640).

However, troubled by the religious practices of the time, in 1645 Joyner resigned his fellowship, changed his name from Joyner to Lyde, and became a Catholic. He then joined Edward, earl of Glamorgan, as his secretary and went with him to Ireland. When the royal cause was lost there, he accompanied the earl through France and Germany. For a time he was also in the service of Queen Henrietta Maria, widow of Charles I. For several years Lyde was domestic steward in the household of the Hon. Walter Montagu, abbot of St Martin at Pontoise, and youngest son of Edward, first earl of Manchester. He was esteemed by the abbot for his learning, sincere piety, and great fidelity.

Subsequently Lyde returned to England and spent several years in strict retirement in London, devoting his time to study. One product of this was that in 1671 *The Roman Empress, a Tragedy: Acted at the Royal Theatre by his Majesties Servants* was published. Dedicated to Sir Charles Sedley, it was well received.

However, the persecution brought about by the Popish Plot in 1678 caused Lyde to move to the family estate at Horsepath. Shortly afterwards, John Nicholas, vice-chancellor of Oxford, had him arrested as a priest to appear at the quarter sessions in Oxford in January 1679. Cleared of the accusation, Lyde retired to the house of his sister Mrs Mary Phillips in the quiet village of Ickford, Buckinghamshire, and continued his devout life. By 1686, when he was living in Wales, he published the biography *Some observations upon the life of Reginaldus Polus, cardinal of the royal bloud of England, sent in a pacquet out of Wales.*

In 1687, when James II conceived the project of making Magdalen College a Catholic institution, Lyde was restored to his fellowship on 16 November by royal mandate, replacing Dr Fairfax. On 7 January 1688 he was admitted as bursar again by royal mandate. But on 20 October 1688 he was removed from his fellowship by the college visitor, and he retired again to Ickford where he lived in poverty in a dilapidated thatched cottage. In a letter to Wood, dated 12 April 1692, he wrote humorously that he 'was never guilty of paying chimney tax' (Wood, *Ath. Oxon.*, new edn, 4.588). Lyde also sustained a friendship with Thomas Hearne who saw him as a large man, very cheerful and pleasant as well as devout and religious. Lyde later lived in obscurity near Brill, Oxfordshire, and also used part of a house adjoining the north part of St Cross Church, Holywell, Oxford, where he died, unmarried, while singing a hymn on 14 September 1706. He was buried at Holywell two days later.   F. D. A. BURNS

Sources DNB · Foster, *Alum. Oxon.*, 1500–1714, 2.835 · Wood, *Ath. Oxon.*, new edn, 4.587–9 · Gillow, *Lit. biog. hist.*, 4.355–6 · parish register, St Giles', Oxford · parish register, Holywell, Oxford · J. R. Bloxam, ed., *Magdalen College and James II, 1686–1688: a series of documents*, OHS, 6 (1886), 169, 175, 184–5, 191–2, 207, 210, 212–14, 231–2, 252, 265

Archives University College, Oxford, letters to A. Wood

Wealth at death £300–£400: DNB

Juan y Santacilla, Jorge (1713–1773). *See under* Industrial spies (*act. c.*1700–*c.*1800).

Jubb, George (1717–1787), Church of England clergyman, was the youngest of at least three sons of Thomas Jubb of York and was baptized at St Michael-le-Belfry in the city on 19 November 1717. He was educated at Westminster School from 1729, where he became a king's scholar in 1731. In 1735 he was elected to a studentship at Christ Church, Oxford, whence he matriculated on 9 June 1735, aged seventeen. He graduated BA (1739) and proceeded MA (1742), BD (1748), and DD (12 April 1780). A poem by him in hexameters is included in the Oxford verses on the death of Queen Caroline in 1738. After his ordination he was appointed chaplain to Thomas Herring, archbishop of York, who was related to Jubb's sister-in-law, the wife of Robert Jubb of York; he remained as chaplain on Herring's translation to Canterbury. He was presented by Herring to the rectory of Cliffe, near Rochester, Kent, which he held until 1751, when he exchanged it for that of Chenies in Buckinghamshire. In the same year he received from Lord Stafford the neighbouring living of Toddington in Bedfordshire. A Latin ode, dated 1752, addressed by him to Thomas Herring on his marriage to the daughter of Sir John Torriano, appeared in the *Gentleman's Magazine* (44, 1774, 232).

In 1754 Jubb was appointed joint registrar of the prerogative court of Canterbury, and from 1774 was the sole occupant of this sinecure, which brought him about £600 per annum. In 1755 he received the Lambeth degree of DD. He was made archdeacon of Middlesex in 1779, but resigned on being appointed to the prebend of Sneating in St Paul's Cathedral in September in 1781, in which year he was also appointed chancellor of York Minster. He was

chosen regius professor of Hebrew and canon of Christ Church on 25 March 1780. His inaugural dissertation had the title *Linguae Hebraicae studium juventuti academiae commendatum* (Oxford, 1781).

Jubb was twice married: on 20 November 1775 he married Mrs Mason (*d.* 4 Feb 1782) of Porters in Hertfordshire, who was the widow of George Mason, a malt distiller of Deptford; on 6 March 1784 he married Mrs Anne Middleton of Windsor. Jubb died suddenly at Oxford of gout in the stomach on 12 November 1787, and was buried in Christ Church Cathedral. His wife, who appears to have survived him, was bequeathed an annuity of £350 in Jubb's will. He left some 'written remarks on the 9th Chapter of Daniel' to Cyril Jackson, dean of Christ Church, with a request that he should prepare them for the press, or burn them; these seem not to have been published.

E. J. RAPSON, *rev.* JOHN D. HAIGH

Sources GM, 1st ser., 57 (1787), 1031–2 · Foster, *Alum. Oxon.* · GM, 1st ser., 44 (1774), 232 · will, PRO, PROB 11/1159, fols. 76r–77v · IGI · *Old Westminsters*

Archives BL, corresp. with first earl of Liverpool, Add. MSS 38206–38207, 38307–38309, 38470–38473, *passim*

Wealth at death bequests of several hundred pounds: will, PRO, PROB 11/1159, fols. 76r–77v

Jubbes, John (*fl.* 1643–1649), parliamentarian army officer, apparently came from Norfolk. Nothing is as yet known of his parentage or education, though he may have been a kinsman, and possibly even brother, to the William Jubbs of Wymondham who appears in the herald's visitation of Norfolk in 1664. He had no professional military experience before the English civil war though he may have obtained some military training through association with the Military Company in Norwich, a noted voluntary group formed in emulation of the Society of the Artillery Garden in London. He described his reasons for enlisting in the parliamentary cause:

> in apr. 1643. in conscience and judgement I drew forth my sword for the recovery of my Countries Rights & Freedom; and continued engaged both before and in all the war of the Earl of Manchester's Army, and since with you, in my Lord Generals Army that now is, until April 1648 in which time (although through many weaknesses) I neither coveted Honour or Riches, but a happy Peace. (Jubbes, *Apology*, 2)

On 14 April 1643 Jubbes was commissioned captain in Sir Miles Hobart's infantry regiment in the army of the eastern association. Colonel Hobart raised his regiment in Norfolk, where his family had strong connections, and Jubbes was active in recruiting soldiers for the company he commanded. Jubbes commented later, when seeking to assist his men to obtain their arrears of pay, that his veterans were 'old Soldiers (which at my first engageing, I brought from their trades' (Jubbes, *Apology*, 1), which suggests that he had some influence in his local community. During 1643 he was one of several officers appointed by the earl of Manchester to raise funds for the army and he recorded that he together with 'his servants and horses' were employed 'in the Countys of Norfolk, Suffux and Essex by order of the Earl of Manchester the care of which three countys was referred wholly unto me in cheife'.

Jubbes appears to have performed his duty enthusiastically, expanding it to include iconoclastic attacks on 'ungodly' images in churches, as Thomas Windham, a Norfolk resident, complained in December 1643 that 'the oppression practised by Jubs and his Associatts is very odious, Their fury in churchjes detestable' (Ketton-Cremer, 51). On 16 March 1644 Jubbes was promoted sergeant-major (major) in the puritan Colonel John Pickering's regiment, also in the army of the eastern association. At the creation of the New Model Army Pickering was appointed colonel of one of twelve infantry regiments and brought most of his senior officers with him, including Jubbes as sergeant-major; his lieutenant-colonel, John Hewson; and five out of his seven captains. Pickering's regiment served with the army of the eastern association at the battle of Marston Moor (2 July 1644), the second battle of Newbury (28 October 1644), and with the New Model Army at the battles of Naseby (14 June 1645) and Langport (10 July 1645) and a series of successful sieges during the remainder of 1645. Colonel Pickering, and a number of his men, died of plague in November 1645 during the siege of Exeter. John Hewson then became colonel and Jubbes was promoted lieutenant-colonel.

As the first civil war ended with the defeat of the king's armies Jubbes became closely associated with the unrest in the New Model Army as officers and men resisted efforts by the presbyterian party in parliament to re-organize the army. New Model Army veterans were unwilling to enlist for service in Ireland or to disband without satisfaction of their arrears of pay and indemnities for acts committed during the war. Jubbes was one of the signatories to a statement of the grievances of Colonel Hewson's regiment dated 13 May 1647 and attended the general council of the army at Putney in October 1647 (now known as the Putney debates). On 4 November 1647 he was one of the signatories to a document, 'The humble remonstrance and desires', which promised the regiment's support to the army's commander, the lord general, Sir Thomas Fairfax. Jubbes had fought in some of the bloodiest battles of the English civil war and the experience had instilled in him a growing desire for a peaceful settlement involving the various factions within the three kingdoms of England, Scotland, and Ireland and within the army itself. He distrusted the ambitions of Oliver Cromwell and was concerned over the changing perspectives of some officers and soldiers as the New Model Army began to evolve from a revolutionary to a professional army. His convictions led him to resign his commission in April 1648, and he became active in promoting a more moderate version of the Leveller *Agreement of the People* within the City of London and among a broad group of leading army officers.

Jubbes was not closely linked to any of the numerous factions within the army and his proposals, printed in December 1648, were based on the concept that a compromise consisting of a range of reforms offering something to every party was the best way to achieve a lasting peace and move on. His proposals included satisfaction of soldiers' arrears of pay, land reform, extension of the right to vote, freedom of conscience in religion, and a settlement with King Charles I. He published a second pamphlet in December 1648 and his original proposals were reprinted in May 1649 but by then the opportunity for compromise solutions had passed as soldiers' attitudes had hardened during the second civil war (March to August 1648) and army unrest had become the driving force behind the execution of the king (on 30 January 1649). Thereafter John Jubbes returns to obscurity and details of the rest of his life have not survived.

KEITH ROBERTS

Sources [J. Jubbes], *Severall proposals for peace and freedom by an agreement of the people* (1648) [Thomason Tract E477(18)] • Veritie Victor, gent [J. Jubbes], 'A plea for moderation in the transactions of the army, or, Weighty observations upon the late proposalls for peace presented to commissary generall Ireton', 28 Dec 1648, BL [Thomason Tract E536(12)] • J. Jubbes, 'An apology unto the honorable and other the honored and worthy officers of his excellencies the lord generals army, by Lieut. Col. John Jubbes', 4 May 1649, BL [Thomason Tract E552(28)] • three documents relating to John Jubbes's petition to the committee for accounts for his arrears of army pay, PRO, SP28/257 unfoliated • D. M. Wolfe, ed., *Leveller manifestoes of the puritan revolution* (1944) • H. N. Brailsford, *The Levellers and the English revolution*, ed. C. Hill (1961) • W. Schenk, *The concern for social justice in the puritan revolution* (1948) • G. Foard, *Colonel John Pickering's regiment of foote, 1644–1645* (1994) • *The Clarke papers*, ed. C. H. Firth, 1, CS, new ser., 49 (1891) [of 4 vols, CS, new ser. vols. 49, 54, 61 and 62 (1891–1901)] • *The humble remonstrance and desires of divers officers and souldiers in the armie under Colonel Hewson* (4 Nov 1647) [BL, Thomason Tract E413] • I. Gentles, *The New Model Army in England, Ireland, and Scotland, 1645–1653* (1992) • C. H. Firth and G. Davies, *The regimental history of Cromwell's army*, 2 vols. (1940) • A. W. Hughes Clarke and A. Campling, eds., *The visitation of Norfolk … 1664, made by Sir Edward Bysshe*, 1, Harleian Society, 85 (1933) • R. W. Ketton-Cremer, 'A note on Thomas Windham', *Norfolk Archaeology*, 32 (1961), 51–3 • I. Gentles, 'The agreements of the people and their political contexts, 1647–1649', *The Putney debates of 1647: the army, the Levellers and the English state*, ed. M. Mendle (2001), 148–74

Judd, John Wesley (1840–1916), geologist, was born on 18 February 1840 in Bath Square, Portsmouth, the son of George Judd, civil servant, and his wife, Jannette (*née* Meldrum). After the family moved to London, where his father worked in Somerset House, Judd attended school at Camberwell before training as a teacher at Westminster College. In 1863 he enrolled at the Royal School of Mines, and later won a royal exhibition for advanced study. However, he decided instead to take a job as an analytical chemist in Sheffield, where in 1866 he met the eminent geologist Henry Sorby, who introduced him to the use of thin rock sections and the polarizing microscope in the study of rocks and minerals.

Judd was involved in a serious railway accident in 1864, but after recovering from his injuries, in 1867 joined the geological survey as a temporary field officer and mapped much of the English midlands. Wishing for more freedom he became a school inspector in 1871, mapping the Wealden deposits of southern England in his spare time. He extended his study of Jurassic rocks to Scotland and studied the igneous complex of the Hebrides, producing many papers from 1873 onwards.

Judd's published works attracted the attention of Charles Lyell, Charles Darwin, and George Scrope, who commissioned him to investigate the volcanic districts of Europe, which he did from 1874 to 1876. On his return to England he was appointed professor of geology at the Royal School of Mines, where he established an innovative and integrated course. In 1896 he was elected dean, a position which he held until his retirement in 1905. Two years after his return to England, Judd married on 10 August 1878 Jeannie Frances Jeyes, daughter of John Jeyes of Great Harrowden. The couple later had one son and one daughter.

Judd was elected a fellow of the Geological Society in 1865, subsequently serving as both secretary (1878–86) and president (1886–8). He received the Wollaston medal in 1891. In 1877 he was elected FRS and later served twice on council. In 1885 he was president of section C when the British Association met in Aberdeen. In 1895 he was created CB, and, in 1913, was appointed emeritus professor of the Royal College of Science.

During his career Judd published ninety-seven papers and books. Almost all appeared in either the *Quarterly Journal of the Geological Society* or the *Geological Magazine*. His earlier papers concerned the Neocomian (the earliest epoch of the Cretaceous), the most noteworthy correlating the Speeton Clays with the Neocomian of the Lincolnshire wolds and north central Europe. A number of other papers, resulting from his European travels, dealt with the volcanic regions of central Italy and Hungary, in addition to the older volcanic districts within the alpine system. A third group of papers investigated igneous rocks on both the Scottish mainland and the Hebrides and was part of the controversy over the Skye intrusions involving Archibald Geikie. Although Judd's papers were detailed and comprehensive, his findings were not accepted by the geological survey. Judd's 1885 presidential address to section C of the British Association dealt with this controversy over the north-west highlands of Scotland, and in it he was highly critical of the survey.

Judd had a reputation as a specialist petrographer, and he wrote extensively in this area. As one of the new generation of vulcanologists, in 1888 he was asked by the Royal Society to write a report on the 1883 eruption of Krakatoa. Judd also produced important concepts in igneous petrology, modifying Bunsen's classification of acid and basic by the addition of 'intermediate' and 'ultrabasic' categories, and also the concept of 'petrographic provinces' to explain the presence of consanguineous rock types. He died of cancer on 3 March 1916, at 30 Cumberland Road, Kew. He was survived by his wife.

BERYL AMBROSE-HAMILTON

Sources 'Eminent living geologists: John Wesley Judd', *Geological Magazine*, new ser., 5th decade, 2 (1905), 385–97 · A. Harker, *Quarterly Journal of the Geological Society*, 73 (1917), lvii–lx · A. J. C. Grenville, *Mineralogical Magazine*, 18 (1916–19), 140–43 · T. G. Bonney, *Geological Magazine*, new ser., 6th decade, 3 (1916), 190–92 · *Nature*, 97 (1916), 37–8 · D. R. Oldroyd, *The highlands controversy: constructing geological knowledge through fieldwork in nineteenth-century Britain* (1990) · b. cert. · d. cert.
Archives BGS, maps of Northamptonshire · ICL, corresp. and papers | Elgin Museum, letters to George Gordon · U. Edin. L., special collections division, letters to Sir Charles Lyell

Likenesses photograph, repro. in 'Eminent living geologists', p. 384, pl. xxi
Wealth at death £4910 7s. 5d.: probate, 11 April 1916, *CGPLA Eng. & Wales*

Judde, Sir Andrew (*c.*1492–1558), merchant, was the third son of John Judde (*d.* 1493), gentleman, of Tonbridge, Kent, and his wife, Margaret, daughter of Valentine Chiche and great-niece of Archbishop Henry Chichele. He was apprenticed in 1509 to John Buknell, a skinner of London and merchant of the staple of Calais, and took up his freedom as a member of the Skinners' Company in 1520 (he was master in 1533 and five times thereafter). Judde married three times: first, in 1523, Mary, daughter of Sir Thomas Mirfyn, himself a skinner and lord mayor of London in 1518; second, by 1542, Agnes, about whom nothing is known; and third, in 1552, Mary, daughter of Thomas Mathews of Colchester and wealthy widow of another skinner, Thomas Langton. Three children survived from the first marriage, John, Richard, and Alice, who married Thomas *Smythe (1522–1591) the customs official, and one daughter from the third, Martha, who married Robert Golding in Essex.

Judde profited initially from exports of English wool through Calais, and he remained heavily involved there: he was mayor of the staple in 1552, 1555 (when he entertained King Philip of Spain in the city), and 1558. But he also had interests in the cloth trade; he dealt in lead, alum, and bullion; he lent money, arranged loans for the crown, and bought and sold former monastic land; he was a promoter of early voyages to Russia and west Africa, and a founder member of the Russia Company. It is highly unlikely that he himself travelled to Muscovy and Guinea, as a later epitaph alleged (though he had an elephant's head displayed as a curiosity in his house), but he was certainly one of the richest and most prominent of overseas merchants in early Tudor London.

Judde was also a public figure of some note, being alderman from 1541 and lord mayor in 1550–51, when he had to deal with the problems caused by dearth and by the 1551 'calling down' of the coinage. 'Judde's Law', regulating the estates and marriages of orphan children of freemen of London, was passed during his mayoralty. He was knighted on 15 February 1551. He was a member of commercial deputations to the council, one of the City élite who gave nominal assent to the accession of Lady Jane Grey by signing the letters patent of 1553 in her favour, and then one of those organizing the defence of London in 1554 on behalf of Queen Mary against rebels led by Sir Thomas Wyatt. Nothing is known of his religious inclinations, but, like his friend Sir Thomas White, he had many charitable interests. He was treasurer of St Bartholomew's Hospital when it was remodelled in 1547, and surveyor-general of all the London hospitals in 1557–8. At the end of his mayoralty he founded six almshouses at St Helen's, Bishopsgate, with the Skinners as trustees, and in May 1553 he obtained letters patent for the erection of a free school, Tonbridge School, again with the Skinners' Company as trustees. The founder stressed the importance of instruction in Latin, Greek, and Hebrew; the school was built by the time of Judde's death and endowed with property worth £60 3*s.* 8*d.* a year. Its first master was John Proctor, fellow of All Souls, Chichele's foundation, and author of the account of Wyatt's rebellion which notes Judde's part in the defence of London Bridge. Sir Thomas *Smythe (*c.*1558–1625), Judde's grandson, was a later benefactor of Tonbridge School. Judde died on 4 September 1558, leaving lands in Kent, Surrey, and Hertfordshire worth £141 p.a. to his widow, with reversion to John and Richard. He was buried in St Helen's, Bishopsgate, London.

PAUL SLACK, *rev.*

Sources H. S. Vere-Hodge, *Sir Andrew Judde* (1953) · T. S. Willan, *The Muscovy merchants of 1555* (1953) · W. K. Jordan, 'Social institutions in Kent, 1480–1660: a study of the changing patterns of social aspirations', *Archaeologia Cantiana*, 75 (1961) [whole issue] · F. Lambard, 'Sir Andrew Judde', *Archaeologia Cantiana*, 43 (1931), 99–101 · will, PRO, PROB 11/42A, sig. 54

Jude, Martin (1803–1860), trade unionist, came to prominence during disputes in the Northumberland and Durham coalfields in the late 1830s, but nothing is known about his parentage or upbringing. He belonged to a small coterie of young men who assisted Thomas Hepburn, the miners' leader, during the unsuccessful disputes of 1831–2 in the great northern coalfields. Though there is no evidence he received any formal education, Jude demonstrated impressive skill and ability in formulating a cogent case and expressing ideas coherently. Consequently when another, more successful, attempt was made in 1842 to succeed where Hepburn failed, Jude emerged as a prominent figure.

The Miners' Association was formed at the end of 1842 and quickly grew into a trade union of unprecedented power, with 100,000 members. In March 1843, six months after its formation, when Jude became its treasurer, the association had attained national dimensions, and was represented in every coalfield. Remarkably, Jude ran its financial affairs in his spare time, working as a publican to secure his livelihood. This was an age when trade unions did not possess either strong leaderships or coherent policies, and Jude's difficulties were compounded by the fact that pitmen in each coalfield were preoccupied by their own particular grievances—such as the 'bond', the 'butty system', child labour, and the 'tommy shops'—to the exclusion of the overall national situation. Getting a policy that would be followed throughout the coalfields proved virtually impossible.

This was one reason why Jude counselled caution. He sought to dampen the ardour of pitmen in Northumberland and Durham, where the union was strongest, when they wanted to strike against the 'bond'. This was the year-long contract entered into by miners, who increasingly felt that the system unduly favoured the coal owners, and should be scrapped. At the Manchester and Glasgow union conferences in 1844, Jude cast doubt on the legality of the contemplated strike, questioning whether all avenues of negotiation had been exhausted, and if the ultimate outcome was likely to be what they desired. When the pitmen disregarded his strictures and stopped work, however, Jude threw himself wholeheartedly into the fight. Besides addressing mass meetings and writing to other workers' organizations for financial support, he even let the union borrow his life savings of £100 which it never repaid.

After five months Jude's prediction proved correct. The union treasury exhausted, and donations from elsewhere drying up, the 34,000 north-east pitmen, some of whom had been evicted from their cottages and forced to subsist in roadside encampments, admitted defeat and sought their old jobs back. But the influx of strikebreakers during the dispute, combined with the dislocation of coal sales, meant fewer miners were needed. The labour surplus led to the imposition of wage cuts which, Jude calculated, varied between 15 and 33 per cent.

Wanting where possible to eschew industrial conflict, Jude sought to direct pitmen towards campaigning for mining legislation. He addressed many public meetings, wrote widely, and appeared before numerous parliamentary inquiries. He always advanced his arguments in a clear, rational manner. Assisted by W. P. Roberts, the miners' attorney-general, and Thomas Duncombe MP, in 1847 he arranged for the Mines and Collieries Bill to be introduced to parliament. Containing a comprehensive list of pitmen's demands, which every miner could endorse, although it was not passed by parliament, the bill represented an attempt to secure change through legislation, and had the effect of broadening miners' mental horizons, making them think of themselves on a national rather than local level. It also made them behave in a more respectable, moderate way, hopeful that it would influence parliament. Jude repeatedly stressed that better wages and shorter hours would also have beneficial knock-on effects, improving family life and providing an opportunity for educational pursuits.

Jude was aware of the coercive control of colliery owners, and argued that pitmen, fearful of losing their jobs, were often reluctant to raise safety matters. He therefore advocated the appointment of mines inspectors on a permanent basis, assisted by scientists where needed. Such an informed and independent body would, he argued, be able to express an impartial opinion on vital health and safety issues. The soundness of his argument was in time recognized.

Bringing pressure to bear on parliament was only part of Jude's strategy. He also sought to secure democratic rights for working people, which would give them the vote and allow them to elect their own representatives. In 1842 he was one of those nominated by Byker, a suburb of Newcastle upon Tyne, to the Chartist grand council, and in 1847 he was elected by Newcastle as delegate to the Chartist convention. In the 1850s he joined the short-lived Northern Political Union and then the much more influential Northern Reform Union, both of which strove to obtain political rights for working people.

The effects of the failure of the strike were long-lasting. Despite many attempts, Jude failed to restore union organization in the great northern coalfields to its pre-1844 strength. He was due to speak, along with W. P. Roberts, at a rally in 1858 which could be regarded as the beginning of the ultimately successful campaign, but was taken ill. Two years later, on 30 August 1860, Jude died in very abject circumstances at the Old Highlander public house in Liddell Street, North Shields, Northumberland. The ceremony marking his burial three days later at Elswick cemetery, Newcastle upon Tyne, was attended by only a few personal friends.

Revival of interest in Martin Jude came with the publication in 1873 of *The Miners of Northumberland and Durham*. Its author, Richard Fynes, knew Jude personally and refers to him as a moving spirit among the pitmen for nearly a quarter of a century. He ends his tribute: 'Of great and varied intelligence, his conduct was characterised by an entire lack of egotism. Firm yet conciliatory to opponents, his modest and respectful manner gained him many friends amongst those who differed with him in opinion.' (Fynes, 186).   RAYMOND CHALLINOR

Sources R. C. Challinor and B. Ripley, *The Miners' Association: a trade union in the age of the chartists* (1968) · R. Fynes, *The miners of Northumberland and Durham* (1873) · R. P. Arnot, *The miners: a history of the Miners' Federation of Great Britain*, 1: … 1889–1910 (1949) · E. Welbourne, *The miners union of Northumberland and Durham* (1923) · S. Webb, *The story of the Durham miners* (1921) · S. J. Webb, B. P. Webb, and R. A. Peddie, *The history of trade unionism* (1894) · *Daily Chronicle and Northern Counties Advertiser* (1 Sept 1860) · d. cert.
Archives Newcastle upon Tyne Central Library, local biography | Newcastle upon Tyne Central Library, pitmen's strike MSS · Northumbd RO, Newcastle upon Tyne, Bell and Biddle MSS
Likenesses statue, 1877; known to be outside the headquarters of the Durham Miners office, in 1877
Wealth at death died in very abject circumstances: Fynes, *Miners of Northumberland*, 186

Judge, Roy Edmund (1929–2000), historian and folklorist, was born on 24 July 1929 at 79 London Road, St Leonards, Hastings, Sussex, the elder son of the two children of Albert Edmund Judge (1899–1970), a watchmaker, and his wife, Lilian Winter, née Woolnough (1900–1971). Most of his years at Hastings grammar school were spent in war evacuation at St Albans; in 1947 he won a place at St Catherine's Society, Oxford, to read history. Here he met his future wife, Betty Rose Jones (b. 1929), when folk dancing. His national service posting to nearby Cowley after graduation in 1950 enabled the relationship to continue; they were married in Tilbury on 30 July 1954 and over the following nine years had a daughter and two sons.

After national service Judge completed a postgraduate certificate of education and in 1953 began teaching at Dovedale secondary modern school, Peckham. While there he took a diploma in biblical and religious studies, and in 1958 he was appointed to Erith grammar school to teach history and religious studies. Pious even in his youth, he moved fully to religious education upon accepting appointment as lecturer in religious studies at Furzedown College of Education in 1963.

Judge's career to this date had been undistinguished, but in 1974 he took the opportunity of a sabbatical to pursue at the Institute of Dialect and Folk Life Studies at the University of Leeds the study of the Jack-in-the-green, the perambulatory bush which was the traditional May-day custom of sweeps in the nineteenth century, and which

was maintained by Oxford University Morris Men at Oxford's May morning celebrations. Judge had joined the morris team (and also the London Pride team) in 1959, and become their archivist. Here he found his métier. His MA in 1975 became a book, *The Jack-in-the-Green* (1979). This brought a historian's skills to bear on earlier interpretations of the Jack which had gone beyond the evidence (if they had assessed it at all); in Judge's typically uncensorious words, 'problems can arise when too much reliance is placed on … intuitive insight' (*The Jack-in-the-Green*, 2nd edn, 84).

The work did not just bring sound historical method to folklore studies, it made use of the wealth of local sources that historians themselves were only just beginning to appreciate, including local newspapers and manuscript collections, printed ephemera, and school logbooks. He also looked beyond the historical sources to literature, art, and drama in works investigating the reception of folk custom in society and how that in turn influenced the ways in which early collectors approached the material when passive interest turned to active engagement.

In 1980 Furzedown closed, and Judge took early retirement to become a latter-day gentleman scholar. Two themes dominated his work over the next twenty years: the history of May-day customs and of the morris dance. The first formed the subject of his doctoral dissertation, 'Changing attitudes to May day, 1844–1914', submitted at Leeds in 1987, and developed in a series of lectures and articles. One demolished the myth that the plaited maypole dance was introduced to England by John Ruskin at Whitelands Teacher Training College in 1888; another showed that the impression of a timeless quality given by the Oxford May morning celebrations masks a history of continuous development and change over several centuries. His 'May day and merrie England' (*Folklore*, 102, 1991, 131–48) took the 'visionary, mythical landscape where it is difficult to take normal historical bearings' and provided those bearings, starting with the nature and sources of the ordinary person's knowledge of May day in early Victorian times and tracing its development over a hundred years.

The second strand of research concerned the history of the morris dance, and specifically of its revival. Here Judge showed that Cecil Sharp's encounter with morris dancers in Headington in 1899 was not an isolated event from which a revival sprang *ab initio*, but was merely the turning point in a convergence of currents in theatre, pageant, and antiquarianism which had been under way for most of the previous century. He revealed how representations of morris in nineteenth-century theatre—hitherto virtually unknown to scholarship—contributed to their development in 'Merrie England' pageantry, and how the quest for authenticity in re-creation led to the pageant master D'Arcy Ferris's revival of the Bidford morris and Percy Manning's similar reactivation of the Headington team shortly before Sharp met them. He also investigated how the knowledge and attitudes of Sharp and others developed in the early days of the revival.

Judge served as president of the Folklore Society from

1990 to 1993, but was not naturally an organization man. His strengths were his eirenic geniality, a characteristic 'Why, bless you!' whenever friends performed an unasked service, a hesitancy in putting forward his views, which did not undermine an animated and dramatic lecture style, and an unfailingly positive response to life which extended even to his prostate cancer, the diagnosis and subsequent spread of which did not prevent his continuing to work until the last few weeks of his life. He died at Guy's Hospital in London on 17 November 2000, surrounded by his family. His funeral service was held at St Swithun's Church, Hither Green, Lewisham, on 30 November, and was followed by committal at Lewisham crematorium.   MICHAEL HEANEY

Sources personal knowledge (2004) · private information (2004) · *The Guardian* (5 Dec 2000) · *The Independent* (11 Dec 2000) · *Folklore*, 112 (2001), 89–91 · *Folk Music Journal*, 8 (2001–5), 251–5 · d. cert.

Archives Cecil Sharp House, London, Vaughan Williams Memorial Library, collection · priv. coll.

Likenesses C. Sheffield, photograph, *c*.1985, repro. in *Folk Music Journal*, cover · A. Bennett, photograph, *c*.1990, repro. in *Folklore*, 90 · J. Gilpin, photograph, *c*.2000, repro. in *The Independent* · J. Gilpin, photograph, *c*.2000, repro. in *Folk Music Journal*, 251 · photograph, *c*.2000, repro. in *The Guardian*

Wealth at death under £210,000: probate, 8 Feb 2001, CGPLA Eng. & Wales

Judith (*b.* after 843, *d.* *c*.870). *See under* Æthelwulf (*d.* 858).

Judith of Flanders, duchess of Bavaria (1030×35–1095), noblewoman, was the daughter of Baudouin (IV), count of Flanders (988–1035), and his second wife, Eleanor, daughter of Richard (II), duke of Normandy (*d.* 1026). She was born between 1030, the year that Baudouin's first wife, Ogiva, died, and 1035, the year of Baudouin's own death. In the autumn of 1051 she married *Tostig, later earl of Northumbria (*b.* *c*.1029), while he and his parents, Earl *Godwine and Gytha, were in exile in Flanders. Judith and Tostig were benefactors of Durham from where they acquired relics of St Oswine and St Oswald, while in 1061 they went on an embassy to Rome. By November 1065 Tostig, his sons (who may have been Judith's as well), and Judith were back as exiles in Flanders. Tostig returned to England for the final battle with his brother King Harold at Stamford Bridge where in September 1066 he was killed. Several years later, *c*.1070, Judith was married off by her half-brother Baudouin (V), count of Flanders (1035–1067), to Welf (IV) (*d.* 1101), the newly created duke of Bavaria; they had two sons, Welf (V) (*d.* 1119) and Henry (*d.* 1126). On 12 March 1094, together with her husband and with the approval of her sons, Judith drew up a list of bequests to the family monastery of Weingarten. She died there on 5 March in 1095 or—unlikely because of the date of her bequest—in 1094. Among her gifts were four Anglo-Saxon gospel books and the relic of Christ's blood that she had received from her father. Weingarten (where she was buried) remembered Judith as a widowed queen of England, an important testimony to Tostig's one-time closeness to the English throne.   ELISABETH VAN HOUTS

Sources P. Grierson, 'The relations between England and Flanders before the Norman conquest', *TRHS*, 4th ser., 23 (1941), 71–

112 · P. McGurk and J. Rosenthal, 'The Anglo-Saxon gospelbooks of Judith, countess of Flanders: their text, make-up and function', *Anglo-Saxon England*, 24 (1995), 251–308 · F. Barlow, ed. and trans., *The life of King Edward who rests at Westminster*, 2nd edn, OMT (1992) · 'Historia Dunelmensis ecclesiae', Symeon of Durham, *Opera*, 1.94–5 · *ASC*, s.a. 1061, 1065 [text D] · 'De inventione et translatione sanguinis Domini', [*Supplementa tomorum I–XII, pars III*], ed. G. Waitz and W. Wattenbach, MGH Scriptores [folio], 15/2 (Stuttgart, 1888) · *Württembergisches Urkundenbuch* (1849), 1.302–3 (no. 245) · F. L. Baumann, ed., *Dioeceses Augustensis, Constantiensis, Curiensis*, MGH Necrologia Germaniae, 1 (1886–8), 221–2 [Weingarten necrology]

Likenesses illumination, 11th cent., Morgan L., no. 709, fol. 105; repro. in C. R. Dodwell, *Anglo-Saxon art: a new perspective* (1982), pl. 10

Jugge, Joan (*d.* 1588). *See under* Jugge, Richard (*c*.1514–1577).

Jugge, John (*d.* 1588). *See under* Jugge, Richard (*c*.1514–1577).

Jugge, Richard (*c*.1514–1577), bookseller and printer, born in Waterbeach, Cambridgeshire, was the son of Richard Jugge. He was educated at Eton College (*c*.1527–1531) and King's College, Cambridge (1531–*c*.1534), to whose library he bequeathed many books. He left the university without taking a degree. On 4 October 1541 he was admitted to the Stationers' Company as a freeman, and began printing about 1547 at the sign of the Bible at the north door of St Paul's Church, probably working as a bookseller in the interim. His wife, Joan [**Joan Jugge** (*d.* 1588)], may have been the Joan Merrye who married a Richard Jugg at St Lawrence Jewry and St Mary Magdalen, Milk Street, London, on 14 June 1543. The couple lived in London near Newgate Market, in the parish of Christ Church. They had seven children: two sons, Richard and John [*see below*]; and five daughters, Anne, Joanne, Elizabeth, Susan, and Katherine, who married the printer Richard Watkins in 1569. Jugge had another daughter, Elizabeth Symons, who was probably illegitimate.

In January 1551 Jugge had licence to print the New Testament in English, and produced a beautiful edition of Tyndale's version, 'with the kynge his mooste gratious lycences', in the following year. It is believed that a patent to print all books of common law for seven years was granted to him on 5 May 1556. He was an original member of the Stationers' Company at its incorporation in 1557, and he served as warden of the company in 1560, 1563, and 1566; and as master in 1568, 1569, 1573, and 1574.

On the accession of Queen Elizabeth, Jugge printed a proclamation for the crown on 17 November 1558. John Cawood, who had been printer to Queen Mary, joined him on 7 February and from that time the two printed state documents together. They were appointed queen's printers on 24 March 1560, with a salary of £6 13*s.* 4*d.*, and they jointly rented a room in Stationers' Hall at 20*s.* per annum from 1560 to 1572. On 10 April 1561 the petty canons of St Paul leased to Jugge 'their shop with a chymney in it', then in his possession, and other premises, for a term of thirty-one years (*CSP dom.*, *1547–80*, 173). The highlight of his career came in 1568, when he received an exclusive patent to print Matthew Parker's Bishops' Bible. Given the high price of the bible, 27s. 8d., the requirement of all cathedrals to possess a copy, and the strong encouragement of all churches and ecclesiastical dignitaries to do likewise, this was a lucrative patent. Archbishop Parker wrote to Cecil on 5 October 1568 regarding the publication of the Bishops' Bible:

> I pray your honour be a mean that Jugge only may have the preferment of this edition; for if any other should lurch him to steal from him these copies, he were a great loser in this first doing, and, Sir, without doubt he hath well deserved to be preferred. (*Correspondence*, 337)

The *Short-Title Catalogue* lists 153 entries for Jugge and an additional 254 items for which he and Cawood were jointly responsible. Jugge's output is largely confined to proclamations, injunctions, bibles, new testaments, prayer books, and official documents arising from his position as queen's printer. Notable departures from church and state publications were Thomas Raynalde's translation of Eucharius Roesslin's pioneering medical text on obstetrics, Henry Cheke's translation of a tragedy by Francesco Negri de Bassano, and Richard Eden's translation of a Spanish navigational work. All Jugge's books, and in particular his folio bibles and quarto new testaments, are of an exceptionally high quality. The abundant use of elaborate woodcuts and decorated initials is characteristic of Jugge's work: for instance his prayer book of 1564 contains 398 richly decorated initials. One of his devices was a pelican feeding her young; another consisted of an angel holding the letter 'R', with a nightingale bearing a scroll inscribed with 'Jugge, Jugge'.

After Cawood's death in 1572 Jugge became the sole queen's printer. Given the abundance of official publications for which he was responsible, without Cawood's assistance Jugge was unable to produce religious texts at a satisfactory rate, and so, in 1575, his printing patent was limited to quarto bibles and testaments in 16mo. He died at some point between 23 August 1577, when a codicil was added to the will he had drawn up six days earlier, and 3 October, when it was proved, and was buried at the north side of the parish church of St Faith's under St Paul's.

His widow, Joan, took over her husband's business, premises, and apprentices. She printed four volumes, all of which were reissues of Richard's publications: the fifth edition of *A ... History ... of the Jewes Commune Weale* in 1575; the fourth and fifth editions of *The Arte of Navigation* in 1579 and 1584; and the eighth edition of Raynalde's medical text issued from her press in 1585. Her own will is dated 13 June 1588 and was proved on 2 September 1588. She asked to be buried near Richard at St Faith's.

Their son **John Jugge** (d. 1588), contrary to previous belief, did not inherit his father's business and had a career only tangentially linked to the printing industry. Only one book was printed by him, and even that was a co-operative endeavour with J. Allde. Furthermore, *Gerilean* was entered to him but was printed by John Kingston in 1577; and *A Briefe Treatise, Concerning the Use and Abuse of Dauncing* was printed for him by John Charlewood, probably in 1580. John Jugge was admitted into the livery of the Stationers' Company at some point between July 1573 and

July 1574 and received his first apprentice in 1576. His premises were apparently at the same address as his father's had been. John died in September or early October 1588: he was alive when Joan's will was proved on 2 September 1588 but is referred to as deceased in the Stationers' register on 7 October.
       H. R. TEDDER, *rev.* JOYCE BORO

Sources will, PRO, PROB 11/59, sig. 40 · will, PRO, PROB 11/72 [Joan Jugge], sig. 56 · Arber, *Regs. Stationers* · W. Sterry, ed., *The Eton College register, 1441–1698* (1943) · T. Harwood, *Alumni Etonenses, or, A catalogue of the provosts and fellows of Eton College and King's College, Cambridge, from the foundation in 1443 to the year 1797* (1797) · Venn, *Alum. Cant.*, 1/2 · *CPR, 1549–51* · *CSP dom., 1547–80* · *Correspondence of Matthew Parker*, ed. J. Bruce and T. T. Perowne, Parker Society, 42 (1853) · J. Ames, T. F. Dibdin, and W. Herbert, eds., *Typographical antiquities, or, The history of printing in England, Scotland and Ireland*, 4 vols. (1810–19) · C. Blagden, *The Stationers' Company: a history, 1403–1959* (1960) · C. Clair, *A history of printing in Britain* (1965) · H. R. Plomer, *Abstracts from the wills of English printers and stationers from 1492 to 1630* (1903) · *Printing in England from William Caxton to Christopher Barker*, Glasgow University Library (1976) [exhibition catalogue, Glasgow University Library, Nov 1976 – April 1977] · H. G. Aldis and others, *A dictionary of printers and booksellers in England, Scotland and Ireland, and of foreign printers of English books, 1557–1640*, ed. R. B. McKerrow (1910) · C. H. Timperley, *Encyclopaedia of literary and typographical anecdote*, 2nd edn (1842) · *STC, 1475–1640* · *IGI*
Wealth at death quite well off: will, PRO, PROB 11/59, sig. 40

Juggins [Jugins], **Richard** (1843–1895), trade unionist, was born on 16 July 1843 at New Street, Darlaston, Staffordshire, the son of a miner, Samuel Jugins, and his wife, Elizabeth, *née* Emery. His father was killed in an accident at work when Richard was only eleven. His only education was at Sunday school and night school. He started work as a nut and bolt maker at the age of seven and followed this occupation for the next twenty years. In November 1870 he played a leading part in forming the Nut and Bolt Makers' Association and was elected its part-time secretary. Fourteen months later, in January 1872, he was dismissed from his job for organizing a strike and became full-time secretary of the union. Under his leadership the union grew steadily and expanded far beyond its Black Country heartland. By 1877 it had 2000 members in 31 branches as far apart as Glasgow, Cwmbrân, and Wolverton.

The other Black Country metal-using trades remained largely unorganized: constant downward pressure on employment volumes and wage levels generated by intense competition in product markets meant that most attempts at association were foredoomed to failure. In a bid to bolster such unions as existed and to foster new ones Juggins formed the Midland Counties Trades Federation in May 1886. He was appointed its secretary and combined this position with that of union secretary. Initially, only his own association and two others joined the federation, but by the time of its fourth annual meeting 66 unions with 10,000 members were affiliated. This success was due very largely to Juggins's dedicated work and in 1889 the executive council of the federation voted him a salary of £52 per annum. In the following year the members presented him with a purse of 100 gold sovereigns, a clock, and an illuminated address in appreciation of his efforts.

The spread of organization, and hence discipline,

among workers encouraged Juggins to initiate discussions with employers about establishing conciliation machinery in some industries: hitherto even minor disputes had often led to strikes or lock-outs, sometimes accompanied by violence. His first success came, appropriately, in the nut and bolt industry. In February 1889 the employers agreed to participate with the union in the south Staffordshire nut and bolt wages board. This set the pattern for other industries and within a few years there was a sprinkling of such boards across the Black Country.

In March 1889 Juggins gave evidence to the select committee of the House of Lords on the sweating system and three years later he was called before the royal commission on labour. He also represented the Nut and Bolt Makers' Association and the Midland Counties Trades Federation at the annual conference of the Trades Union Congress many times and attended some meetings of the International Labour Congress.

Juggins was among those trade union leaders who believed that industrial organization should be supported by direct labour representation in parliament and from 1886 he was a member of the TUC's labour electoral committee for the Birmingham area. In 1891 the executive council of the Midland Federation resolved that Juggins himself 'be recommended to the electors of Dudley as the labour candidate' at the next general election (*Dudley Herald*, 30 May 1891), but this came to nothing. There was opposition from within the federation and from Dudley Liberal Association so the proposal was dropped.

Juggins did, however, make an important contribution to public life in his local community. He served on the Walsall board of guardians, the Darlaston urban district council and the Darlaston school board, as well as being a member of the local court of the Ancient Order of Foresters and a Methodist lay preacher.

Juggins died at his home, 60 New Street, Darlaston, on 5 March 1895 and was buried at James Bridge cemetery, Darlaston, on 11 March 1895. He was married twice. His second wife survived him, together with five sons and two daughters, apparently from both marriages. In November 1896 a marble headstone was erected over his grave, paid for by contributions from members of the Nut and Bolt Makers' Association and the Midland Counties Trades Federation.   ERIC TAYLOR

Sources reports of the Nut and Bolt Makers' Association and Midland Counties Trades Federation activities, *Wolverhampton Chronicle* (1870–95), *Dudley Herald* (1870–95), *Midland Advertiser* (1872–95), *Free Press* [West Bromwich] (1875–95), *Wednesbury Herald* (1876–95), *Labour Tribune* (1886–94) · annual reports, 1887–95, Midland Counties Trades Federation · 'Select committee … on the sweating system: third report', *Parl. papers* (1889), 13.27–59, 89, 161–3, 218–19, no. 165 · 'Digest of evidence … mining, iron, engineering, and hardware', *Parl. papers* (1892), 36/3.188–9, C. 6795-I [royal commission on labour] · *Midland Advertiser* (9 March 1895) · *Wednesbury Herald* (9 March 1895) · *Wolverhampton Chronicle* (13 March 1895) · *Ironworkers' Journal* (April 1895) · *Wolverhampton Chronicle* (11 Nov 1896) [memorial to Juggins] · E. Taylor, 'Juggins, Richard', *DLB*, vol. 1 · E. Taylor, 'The Midland Counties Trades Federation, 1886–1914', *Midland History*, 1 (1971–2), 26–40 · E. Taylor, 'The working class movement in the Black Country, 1863–1914', PhD diss., University of Keele, 1974 · J. A. C. Baker, 'History of the nut and bolt industry

in the west Midlands', MComm diss., U. Birm., 1965 · H. A. Clegg, A. Fox, and A. F. Thompson, *A history of British trade unions since 1889*, 1 (1964) · G. C. Allen, *The industrial development of Birmingham and the Black Country, 1860–1927* (1929); repr. (1966) · *CGPLA Eng. & Wales* (1895) · b. cert. · d. cert.
Wealth at death £47 10s. 7d.: probate, 29 July 1895, *CGPLA Eng. & Wales*

Jukes, (Joseph) Beete (1811–1869), geologist, was born at Summer Hill, near Birmingham, on 10 October 1811, the eldest child and only son of John Jukes and his wife, Sophia. Members of a dissenting family, his father and paternal grandfather were involved in button manufacturing, and his maternal grandfather—Joseph Beete—had been in trade in Demerara. His father died when Jukes was seven and his mother was left to support him and his three sisters on somewhat slender means. He was educated at Wolverhampton grammar school, a school at Pattingham, Staffordshire, and King Edward's School, Birmingham, where he lived in the house of Rann Kennedy (1772–1851).

At his mother's insistence Jukes resolved to prepare for ordination within the established church. To that end he entered St John's College, Cambridge, in 1830. He preferred perambulations and punts to paragraphs and praelections, but was saved from intellectual idleness by the fact that he possessed an interest in geology acquired from his aunt Jane Jukes (1791–1873) and his uncle Frederick Jukes (c.1796–1857), who had published several articles on fossils. At St John's his tutor considered geology to be an unsuitable study for a prospective ordinand, but Jukes none the less enrolled in the geological class of Adam Sedgwick. This proved to be Jukes's moment of rebirth. Visions of the cloth vanished, and throughout the remainder of his life he commonly addressed Sedgwick as 'my dear father'. Jukes proceeded to the BA degree in 1836 and the MA in 1841.

On leaving Cambridge Jukes in 1837 and 1838, devoted himself to pedestrian geological tours of England, paying his expenses by delivering courses of geological lectures in places such as Birmingham, Derby, and Liverpool. Early in 1839, on the recommendation of the president of the Geological Society of London (William Whewell) and Sedgwick, he was appointed geological surveyor to the colony of Newfoundland. He sailed for St John's on 11 April 1839, and on arrival began a one-man reconnaissance geological survey of the colony. The results of his labours were presented in reports to the colony's house of assembly and in Jukes's *Excursions in and about Newfoundland* (2 vols., 1842). However, his appointment was discontinued in 1840 as he had failed to satisfy a local expectation for the speedy discovery of mineral wealth; he returned to England during November that year.

Further English geologizing and lecturing followed, but Jukes failed to secure the chair of geology in University College, London, during the summer of 1841. In December of that year he was appointed as naturalist to HMS *Fly*, commanded by Captain Francis Price Blackwood (1809–1854), which was under orders to chart the Australian and New Guinea coasts around the Torres Strait. The *Fly* cleared Falmouth on 11 April 1842, and over the next four years Jukes pursued his science in locations such as Madeira, Cape Colony, New Guinea, Australia, and the Great Barrier Reef. By the time the *Fly* dropped anchor at Spithead on 19 June 1846 he was a geologist of global experience. His narrative of the voyage was published in two volumes in 1847.

During Jukes's absence in the antipodes, the Geological Survey of Great Britain had been formally instigated with Sir Henry De la Beche (1796–1855) as its director. Jukes applied for a post with the new survey and was appointed as geologist as from 1 October 1846. He presented himself at Bala, Merioneth, for training under Andrew Crombie Ramsay (1814–1891) and William Talbot Aveline (1822–1903). For four years he mapped in north Wales and the English midlands. He was in his element; as a field surveyor he was an outstanding success. Meticulous in attention to detail, and possessed of a superb eye for country, he became perhaps the finest British field geologist of his day.

At Harborne, near Birmingham, on 22 September 1849, Jukes married Georgina Augusta Meredith, and during the following summer his new financial responsibility rendered attractive De la Beche's offer of the local directorship of the Geological Survey of Ireland in succession to Thomas Oldham (1816–1878). The Irish salary was no higher than that already achieved by Jukes in Britain, but the wily De la Beche, fully aware of the deceit, assured Jukes that the cost of living in Ireland was lower than that in Britain. For Jukes a scientific issue also had to be placed upon the scales of decision. The survey's British field mapping was mostly being conducted at a scale of 1 inch to 1 mile (1:63,360), but in Ireland all the survey's field operations were based on the Ordnance Survey's lavish 6 inch (1:10,560) sheets. Ireland thus offered Jukes a unique scientific opportunity.

Jukes became the local director of the Geological Survey of Ireland on 30 November 1850, and director after 1 April 1867. Personally he had made a mistake. Within days he discovered the hollowness of De la Beche's financial assurances, and neither Jukes nor his wife was ever entirely happy in Ireland. Oldham had held the chair of geology in Trinity College, Dublin, concurrently with his local directorship and Jukes had hoped to do likewise, but the chair instead went to Samuel Haughton. In 1854 Jukes did, nevertheless, combine his survey duties with a second office, of professor of geology in the Government School of Science Applied to Mining and the Arts attached to the Museum of Irish Industry, an institution which in 1867 became the Royal College of Science for Ireland. He also conducted courses in many Irish towns as an instructor under the Department of Science and Art committee of lectures.

As the head of the Irish survey Jukes was outstandingly successful, first under De la Beche and then under Sir Roderick Impey Murchison (1792–1871). He refined the field techniques put in place by Oldham, and he possessed a deep understanding of the scientific importance of the survey's 6 inch field sheets. Between 1856 and his death he supervised the publication of 120 1 inch geological sheets, representing more than half of Ireland, most of them being accompanied by a descriptive memoir which he edited. To problems of Irish geology he brought an incisive mind, and his paper of 1862 on the southern Irish rivers possesses seminal significance for the history of geomorphology. Among his contemporaries, his *Student's Manual of Geology*, first published in 1857, was regarded as worthy of comparison with the famed *Manual of Elementary Geology* by Sir Charles Lyell.

On 27 July 1864 Jukes was inspecting his officers' work in south-western Ireland when he fell, in a Kenmare inn, and was concussed. He was never the same man again. He had to take sick leave during 1864 and again during 1869, he suffered periodic blackouts, his temper became uncertain, and his scientific judgement was impaired. On 8 May 1869 Augusta and two physicians committed him to Hampstead House, Glasnevin, a private lunatic asylum in Dublin, where he died on 29 July. He was buried at St Mary's churchyard, Selly Oak, Birmingham, on 3 August 1869. Among his contemporaries there seems to have been some reluctance to accept the 1864 accident as the cause of his demise and it has to be conceded that his correspondence reveals signs of mental deterioration antedating the Kenmare incident by four years.

Jukes and his wife had no children but had instead devoted themselves to domestic pets and to the animals in Dublin Zoo, where Jukes served on the council. He was of patrician appearance, with a full beard, and in his earlier years his sturdy frame endowed him with remarkable powers of endurance. Of an open and guileless character, he lived for his science. He was elected to fellowship of the Royal Society in June 1853, and was president of the Geological Society of Dublin (1853–5) and of the Geology Section of the British Association for the Advancement of Science in 1862.   GORDON L. HERRIES DAVIES

Sources C. A. Browne, ed., *Letters and extracts from the addresses and occasional writings of J. Beete Jukes* (1871) · G. L. Herries Davies, *North from the Hook: 150 years of the Geological Survey of Ireland* (1995) · parish records, Birmingham, St Mary, Selly Oak · CGPLA Eng. & Wales (1869) · private information [Jukes family scrapbook, in possession of contributor]
Archives BGS, notebooks; corresp. · Geological Survey of Ireland, Dublin · NHM, autobiographical notes · University of Oklahoma | CUL, Sedgwick MSS · ICL, letters to Sir Andrew Ramsay · NMG Wales, De la Beche MSS · U. Edin. L., special collections division, letters to Sir Archibald Geikie
Likenesses engraving · photographs, BGS · plaster bust, Geological Survey of Ireland, Dublin
Wealth at death under £3000: probate, 1 Nov 1869, CGPLA Eng. & Wales

Jukes, Francis (1745–1812), aquatint engraver, was born at Martley, Worcestershire, of unknown parentage. Specializing at first as a topographical painter, probably in watercolours, he was one of the first English artists to exploit the newly discovered method of aquatint engraving. In 1775 he exhibited with the Society of Artists two aquatints of stormy landscapes that he had engraved the previous year and that had been published by William Wynne Ryland that January. Jukes is said to have learned the method from Paul Sandby who got it from Charles Greville who got it from France. Some of Jukes's early aquatints reproduced drawings by Sandby and one pair of elevations of Somerset House (1777) was executed under Sandby's supervision. Subsequently both Sandby and Jukes developed the potential of aquatint as a means of reproducing drawings with colour washes, and Jukes became a most renowned and prolific exponent of this art over the next thirty years. Sometimes he added an aquatint ground to a plate etched by another artist, most famously to *Vauxhall* (1785) after Thomas Rowlandson, where he collaborated with Robert Pollard. He aquatinted a number of other caricatures, as well as sporting prints and literary or genre subjects, but for the most part he produced landscapes or seascapes. His sporting and livestock prints included Charles Ansell's *Life and Death of a Race Horse* (1784), *The Pytchley Hunt* (1790–91) after Charles Loraine Smith, and several animals after John Boultbee, including portraits of a ram and a ewe of the new Leicestershire breed (1802). He was a prolific aquatinter of ships in storms and naval engagements and he engraved and published many maritime and coastal views as well as picturesque landscapes of the kind popularized by the Revd William Gilpin, whose *Observations on the River Wye* (1782) was illustrated by Jukes. His topographical views include some important early records of colonial settlements. His large oval aquatints of Cape Town (1794) after Alexander Callender are among the finest early views of South Africa, and he also produced prints of New York (1800) and Sydney Cove, New South Wales (1804).

Jukes published his early prints in partnership with Valentine Green, who also came from Worcestershire, and together they issued a series of large aquatints of ruins in the Welsh borders, cathedrals, and other scenes. His obituarist's remark that Jukes's hopes of establishing a trade with Basel were dashed by the French Revolutionary Wars suggests that, like Green, Jukes was exporting prints to Chrétien de Mêchel, the leading printseller in Switzerland, who was ruined by the French invasion. He also collaborated in a number of projects with Robert Pollard, notably in some fine views of elegant developments in London such as *Hanover Square* (1787). Jukes appears never to have achieved the prosperity that his application merited. He lived for over twenty years in Howland Street, Westminster, before moving to nearby Upper John Street, where he published in partnership as Jukes and Sarjent. A lifetime of inhaling the fumes given off by the strong acid with which he pursued his craft made him ill. He died in 1812, probably in March.

TIMOTHY CLAYTON and ANITA MCCONNELL

Sources Dodd's history of English engravers, BL, Add. MS 33402, fol. 176, 'Francis Jukes' • C. Le Blanc, *Manuel de l'amateur d'estampes*, 2 (Paris, 1855–6), 438–9 • *GM*, 1st ser., 82/1 (1812), 300 • J. R. Abbey, *Scenery of Great Britain and Ireland, 1770–1860* (1952) • J. R. Abbey, *Life in England in aquatint and lithography, 1770–1860* (privately printed, London, 1953) • J. R. Abbey, *Travel, 1770–1860*, 2 vols. (1956) • F. G. Stephens and M. D. George, eds., *Catalogue of political and personal satires preserved … in the British Museum*, 5–11 (1935–54) • D. Snelgrove, *British sporting and animal prints, 1658–1874* (1981) • 'Catalogue of prints and drawings', www.nmm.ac.uk, 7 May 2001

Archives Birm. CA, letters to Boulton family

Julian of Norwich (1342–*c*.1416), anchoress and mystic, may have taken her name from the parish church of St Julian at Conisford in Norwich, where she had her cell; however, the name Julian (also spelt Ielyan or Latinized to Juliana) was not uncommon at the time and might have been hers from birth. No other information concerning her identity or origins has come to light, although the partly northern dialect of one manuscript of her work, combined with an affectionate reference to St John of Beverley, has suggested a connection with Yorkshire; but the mixed dialect may owe more to the northern associations of the scribe.

Julian is known through her one work, usually referred to by its modern title of *Revelations of Divine Love*, which she composed in both a short and a long version. This work contains her profound reflections on a series of sixteen visions of the crucified Christ, which she received in 1373 as she lay apparently dying, on either 8 or 13 May (according to different manuscripts), when, she relates, she was thirty and a half years old. This would place her date of birth late in 1342.

Julian reveals nothing of her life up to that point, and there is much debate as to whether she was then already an anchoress, or perhaps a nun of the nearby Benedictine priory of Carrow (who held the advowson of St Julian's), or still a laywoman. The circumstances of her near death experience, as given in the short text, suggest that she was in her own home. In that case, Julian was either unmarried or possibly a widow, who might have lost a husband and even children, perhaps in the plague epidemics of 1362 or 1369.

Such speculations seek to clarify the origin of Julian's distinctive blend of orthodoxy and startling originality. For example, her important discussion of Christ as Mother might flow naturally from her own experience of motherhood, rather than from reading Latin authors, such as Anselm of Canterbury, who also touch on this idea. In her parable of 'The Lord and the Servant' she also appears to offer a new interpretation of the fall, in which Adam sins more through zeal than through disobedience, while her assertion that finally 'alle maner of thyng shalle be wele' depends on a 'grett deed' which the Trinity will accomplish at the end of time (Julian of Norwich, *Book of Shewings*, 422, 424). Even her visions of the crucified Christ, where she is on more traditional ground, have an unusual emphasis on the dehydration of Christ's body, and a unique emotional stress on the pure joy and self-abandonment with which Christ poured himself out for mankind on the cross.

The quality of her thought has prompted some critics to dismiss as rhetorical her claim that she was 'a symple creature vnlettyred' (*Book of Shewings*, 285), and argue that she must have been exceptionally learned, this being perhaps more likely if she were a nun. However, there is little evidence of learning among nuns in England at this time, and among the nuns of Carrow there is no Julian who fits her dates. Furthermore, the near disappearance of her work after her death argues against connection with any religious order: there seems to have been no community behind her with the wherewithal to preserve and publicize her works.

At some point before 1394, when a bequest was made to 'Julian anakorite', she became a solitary, and also recorded her visions in the two texts of her work. The short text is generally assumed to have been written soon after the event, but could have been produced at any time before the completion of the long text. It might even represent an edited version of the latter, in which some of her more unusual ideas, such as the parable of the lord and the servant, are omitted. However, its general tenor is that of an initial record, whereas, at the end of the long text Julian states that not until 'twenty yere saue thre monthys' (*Book of Shewings*, 520) had passed did she understand the full meaning of what she had received. This gives 1393 as the earliest date for the long text.

Two references to Julian reveal something of her reputation in her lifetime. In 1413 the scribe of the short text asserts that Julian is a 'devoute womann', 'that is recluse atte Norwyche and ʒitt is onn lyfe, anno domino millesimo CCCC xiij' (*Book of Shewings*, 201). And in this same year she was visited by the visionary Margery Kempe of Bishop's Lynn, because 'þe ankres was expert in swech thyngys and good cownsel cowd ʒeuyn' (Meech, introduction, 42). An annotator of Margery's *Book* writing c.1500, has noted 'Dame Ielyan' in the margin, suggesting that her reputation outlived her for some time.

Further small bequests to Julian in 1404, 1415, and 1416, some including her maids Sarah and Alice, imply that she was still alive at seventy-three. References then cease, unless a bequest to an anchoress at St Julian's in 1428 was to her rather than to a successor in her cell—several such are known. The unlikely dating of Julian's death to 1443 which is occasionally made derives from an apparent misreading of the short text; nor, probably, should she be confused with the later Juliana Lampett, anchoress at Carrow from 1428 to 1478. In fact, the exceptional number of solitaries in Norwich, after a gap of fifty years before Julian, might itself reflect her influence.

Since then, in contrast, the long text (her major work) has been handed down principally through three seventeenth-century manuscripts, copied by the English nuns of Paris and Cambrai, without whom knowledge of her would have been lost. Through them the text was also printed by Serenus Cressy in 1670, almost certainly in England. It is only now, however, that the range of her thought is widely appreciated. Her cell at Norwich has been rebuilt on its putative medieval foundations, and the Anglican calendar commemorates her on 8 May.

SANTHA BHATTACHARJI

Sources Julian of Norwich, *A book of shewings*, ed. E. Colledge and J. Walsh, 2 vols. (1978) [Short text; long text: Paris MS; Introduction 1–198] · N. P. Tanner, 'Popular religion in Norwich with special reference to the evidence of wills, 1370–1532', DPhil diss., U. Oxf., 1973 · S. B. Meech, introduction, in *The book of Margery Kempe*, ed. S. B. Meech and H. E. Allen, EETS, 212 (1940), 42–3 · Julian of Norwich, *A revelation of love*, ed. M. Glasscoe (1976) [Long text: MS Sloane 2499] · B. Ward, 'Julian the solitary', *Signs and wonders* (1992) · B. Ward, 'Mine even-Christian', *The English religious tradition and the genius of Anglicanism*, ed. G. Rowell (1992), 47–63 · S. Upjohn, *In search of Julian of Norwich* (1989) · Julian of Norwich, *Shewings*, trans. E. Colledge and J. Walsh (1978), 17–119 · F. Blomefield and C. Parkin, *An essay towards a topographical history of the county of Norfolk*, [2nd edn], 11 vols. (1805–10), vol. 4, pp. 81, 524–30 · *VCH Norfolk*, 2.352 · W. Rye, *Carrow Abbey* (1889)
Archives Bibliothèque Nationale, Paris, MS fonds anglais 40 · BL, Sloane MS 2499 · BL, Sloane MS 3705 · Westminster Cathedral, selections from long text | BL, Amherst MS, Add. 37790 · St Joseph's College, Upholland, near Skelmersdale, Upholland MS, selections from long text
Wealth at death several small bequests: *Book of shewings*, ed., Colledge and Walsh; Tanner, 'Popular religion'

Juliana. *See* Julian of Norwich (1342–c.1416).

Julien, Louis Antoine. *See* Jullien, Louis (1812–1860).

Julius, Churchill (1847–1938), bishop of Christchurch and archbishop of New Zealand, was born in Richmond, Surrey, on 15 October 1847, the second son of Dr Frederic Gilder Julius MD, a surgeon at the Richmond Infirmary, and his wife, Ellen Hannah Smith. He attended a local preparatory school and the junior department of King's College, London, and then went up to Worcester College, Oxford, graduating BA in 1869. His vocation was to the Church of England, and he was ordained deacon in 1871 and priest in 1872; his first curacy was in St Giles, Norwich. On 18 June 1872 he married Alice Frances, the daughter of Lieutenant-Colonel Michael John Rowlandson. Their son Sir George Alfred *Julius was born in 1873. Julius's second curacy, from 1875, was in South Brent, Somerset, not far from his wife's home in Bournemouth. He was then appointed vicar of Shapwick, also in Somerset. He had attended St Aldates Church in Oxford under Canon Christopher when a student, and he was appointed to the well-known evangelical parish of Holy Trinity, Islington, from 1878 to 1884; however, he caused some offence there when he wore a surplice and mixed in broad company.

In 1883, after the bishop of Ballarat preached in his pulpit, Julius accepted a surprise invitation as vicar and archdeacon of the pro-cathedral parish of Ballarat, one of the country dioceses of Victoria, Australia. He was in effect the dean. Having adjusted well to this position, he was then nominated bishop of the diocese of Christchurch, which had been created by an Anglican association in 1851. A strong and vigorous young man, he was consecrated on 1 May 1890 and served with great distinction; as senior bishop of the province of New Zealand, he also acted as primate (1920–25), to which was added the title archbishop in 1922.

Julius is a striking example of the liberal evangelicals of the late Victorian age and early twentieth century. He sought to enhance the structure and order of the church and to maintain the distinctiveness of Anglicanism and its traditions. So he was interested in the revival of deaconesses and sponsored the formation of the Community of the Sacred Name, and in other respects adopted a Tractarian outlook. He defended the right of clergy to wear vestments and elevate the host, but insisted that 'neither Evangelical nor High Churchman, faithfully doing God's work, shall ever suffer at my hands' (Peters, 111). Insisting on the bishop's authority to take patterns of worship beyond the strict letter of the prayer book, he increased the diversity in the New Zealand Church of England.

Julius also had a growing concern for the conditions of labour and welfare of the poor. He had begun to describe himself as a Christian socialist while in London, having been deeply moved by conditions in the City's dockland slums. He became notorious for supporting the great dock strike of London while in Ballarat, and early in his Christchurch episcopate, preaching in the cathedral to the trades and labour council, he declared, 'I look therefore for a change from the system of individualism to the higher one of socialism'—although he saw socialism as a model of harmony and therefore criticized union exclusiveness. He worked to attract working people back to the church, and established a special evening service in Christchurch Cathedral to suit them. As well as social justice, religious education for the young remained a consistent concern of his episcopate.

A large man with a firm and sturdy appearance, a ready wit and brilliant conversation, sensitivity to others but a rather plain bluff philosophy, Julius was every inch the colonial bishop. He retired in 1925, and died on 1 September 1938.   PETER J. LINEHAM

Sources 'Unionism', *Lyttleton Times* (4 May 1891), 6 · *President's report to general synod* (1922) [22nd synod] · *President's report to general synod* (1925) [23rd synod] · M. Peters, *Christchurch-St Michael's: a study in Anglicanism in New Zealand* (1986) · G. M. McKenzie, *The history of Christchurch Cathedral … New Zealand* (1931) · S. Parr, *Canterbury pilgrimage: the first hundred years of the Church of England in Canterbury, New Zealand* (1951) · b. cert.

Julius, Sir George Alfred (1873–1946), engineer and public servant, was born on 29 April 1873 in Norwich, the eldest son of Churchill *Julius (1847–1938), who later became the Anglican archbishop and primate of New Zealand, and his wife, Alice Frances, daughter of Colonel Michael John Rowlandson. After moving to Ballarat, Victoria, Australia, in 1884 Julius was educated at the Church of England grammar school, Melbourne; he later attended Canterbury University College, Christchurch, New Zealand, where, deriving an interest in engineering from his father, he graduated BSc in engineering in the University of New Zealand in 1896. On 7 December 1898 Julius married Eva Dronghsia Odierna, third daughter of Charles Yelverton O'Connor, engineer-in-chief for Western Australia. They had three sons, the eldest of whom became a partner in his father's firm. Julius joined the engineering staff of the Western Australian Government Railways and investigated the properties of West Australian hardwoods. His reports on the subject, and on Australian hardwoods generally, remained important for many years.

In 1907 Julius moved to Sydney and established the firm of Julius, Poole, and Gibson, consultant engineers, to which came a variety of work from many public and private bodies. His extraordinarily versatile intellect was brought to bear on many engineering problems and he found the frequent laudatory references to himself as the inventor of the automatic totalizator for racecourse betting an amusing commentary on the public lack of appreciation of his other services to the community.

In addition to his consulting practice, Julius sacrificed much in time, money, and energy in supporting the development of the Australian commonwealth. In 1926 he became the first chairman of the Commonwealth Council for Scientific and Industrial Research, an appointment which he held until 1945. Although his training and experience had been in engineering subjects, he at once appreciated that the most urgent problems facing the council at that time related to Australian primary products, particularly food supplies, wool, and timber, and the investigation of diseases affecting them. He and his colleagues, in particular the chief executive officer, David Rivett, and Professor Arnold Richardson, combined into a powerful team which blended strong leadership with scientific distinction. Rapid practical results were achieved, especially in the control of animal disease so that, before a decade had passed, the council readily obtained from the Commonwealth government greatly increased capital sums and annual monetary grants which enabled the growing activities of the council to be put on a substantial and permanent footing. These grants were voluntarily increased by financial support from farmers and graziers.

Some years before the outbreak of war in 1939 Julius turned his attention towards the requirements of secondary and manufacturing industries, and with his colleagues was again successful in persuading the Commonwealth authorities to assist in providing for physical testing, engineering, and chemical investigations, and the standardization of fundamental measurements, in conformity with those established in Great Britain. He was president of the Australian National Research Council from 1932 to 1937, and chairman of the Standards Association of Australia from 1926 to 1940. An industrial chemical laboratory was built in Melbourne, a national standards laboratory in Sydney, and Julius gave his personal attention to the details of an aeronautical research laboratory which came into service by the outbreak of war. During most of the war years he was the chairman of the Australian Council of Aeronautics.

Julius held very strong opinions which he did not hesitate to express, and he seldom failed to gain his point when facing an audience, large or small. He had a very engaging personality, and although hardly an orator of the conventional kind, his clear and precise diction, together with the persuasive logic of his views and his obvious earnestness had their effect, enhanced no doubt by his rather gaunt face, his crop of curly brown hair, and his very luminous blue eyes. Many honours came to Julius, who was knighted in 1929. He was president of the Institution of Engineers, Australia, in 1925, and received its Peter Nicol Russell memorial medal in 1927. He was also awarded the William Charles Kernot memorial medal by the University of Melbourne in 1938. He declined the university's invitation to present a public lecture at the medal presentation in 1939, stating that he had had a very difficult year. One of his sons had been killed in a light aircraft crash in New South Wales earlier in the year. In 1940 he received the honorary degree of DSc from his old university of New Zealand. Julius died on 28 June 1946 at his home, 39 Stanhope Road, Killara, Sydney. After a service at St Mark's Church, Darling Point, the following day, he was cremated at the Northern Suburbs crematorium. He was survived by his wife.

W. H. MYERS, rev. C. BORIS SCHEDVIN

Sources C. B. Schedvin, *Shaping science and industry: a history of Australia's Council for Scientific and Industrial Research, 1926–49* (1987) · *Sydney Morning Herald* (31 Jan 1939) · *Sydney Morning Herald* (29 June 1946) · *Sydney Morning Herald* (1 July 1946) · J. A. Alexander, ed., *Who's Who in Australia*, 10th edn (1938) · *Journal of the Institution of Engineers, Australia*, 18 (1946), 171 · G. Currie and J. Graham, 'G. A. Julius and research for secondary industry', *Records of the Australian Academy of Science* (Nov 1970), 10–28 · Kernot memorial medal file, University of Melbourne, central records · personal knowledge (1959) · private information (1959)
Likenesses N. Carter, oils, 1947, Commonwealth Scientific and Industrial Research Organisation, Australian Capital Territory

Julius Agricola, Gnaeus [*known as* Agricola] (AD 40–93), Roman governor of Britain, was born of provincial stock on 13 June AD 40 at Forum Julii (Fréjus) in the Roman province of Gallia Narbonensis (Provence). His native city had been founded as a settlement of Roman citizens by Julius Caesar and refounded as a *colonia* by Augustus, with the title Colonia Octavanorum Pacata, to accommodate veterans of the eighth legion. Agricola's family name, Julius, probably indicates that Roman citizenship had been acquired through a forebear who had either served as an officer of Julius Caesar or Augustus, or achieved prominence as a rich and influential native inhabitant of Forum Julii. Agricola thus belonged to that sector of western provincial society which played an increasingly important role in urban administration and the manning of the ranks of army officers. This was a social milieu of relative affluence and was not devoid of cultural pursuits. Agricola's father, Lucius Julius Graecinus, achieved senatorial rank under Tiberius and was appointed praetor at the end of that reign. He had a taste for practical literature, writing on viticulture with learning and humour. His agricultural interests are probably reflected in the cognomen he gave to his son. Seneca had a high opinion of Graecinus as a man of principle, telling how he would not take favours from political figures of dubious reputation. Highmindedness was not a safe virtue in the reign of Gaius (Caligula). Having refused that unstable emperor's request to prosecute Marcus Silanus, Graecinus was put to death shortly after Agricola's birth, in circumstances which remain obscure. His tomb monument was apparently set up on the Esquiline Hill in Rome.

Education and early military career in Britain Agricola's mother, Julia Procilla, bore a name which is suggestive of Gaulish descent, probably from landed stock derived from the tribal nobility. When Agricola reached the appropriate age for schooling his mother dispatched him to Massalia (Marseilles), the ancient Graeco-Roman city where cultural pursuits created a favourable climate for the education of the young provincial élite in rhetoric and philosophy, the usual training for upper-class youth. As a senator's son, Agricola could aspire, if he wished, to imperial service. The first stage of that career, duty as a tribune of a legion, Agricola passed in Britain when he was eighteen to twenty years of age, under the governor Suetonius Paullinus. During the terrifying upheaval of the Boudiccan revolt in AD 60 to 61, he served on the governor's own staff, where he must have learnt much about provincial administration and what could result from its abuse, as well as the conduct of military affairs in a far from quiescent part of the empire. The sequence of offices which followed in Rome was conventional enough: quaestor in AD 64, tribune in 66, praetor in 68. But unusual duties fell to him during the civil wars of AD 68 to 70: under Galba the recovery of treasures stolen from temples, and under Vespasian the raising of legionary conscripts in Italy. That Agricola was viewed as a wholly reliable adherent of the Flavian cause of Vespasian is clear from his appointment in AD 70 as legate of the twentieth legion in Britain under the governor Petillius Cerialis. This regiment had recently been in turmoil, its commander being instrumental in driving out the previous governor of the province. Under Agricola's command the twentieth presumably took part in the major extension of Roman control in northern Britain which involved the conquest of the Brigantes of the Pennines and the Vale of York. Agricola's subsequent elevation to the ranks of the patricians and his appointment as governor of Aquitania, probably in AD 75, reveals that his command of the legion had been effectively discharged and he was seen as an imperial servant who, still in his mid-thirties, could go much higher. Election as suffect consul for a few months in AD 77 carried him into the pool of candidates from whom the holders of the highest military commands were drawn. Nevertheless, his appointment as governor of Britain, either late in AD 77 or in 78, represented something of a leap, for he had governed no province which contained a legionary army and the military task which Britain presented was still great. No doubt Agricola's excellent knowledge of Britain, as well as his all-round competence, earned him this senior command. It is difficult to identify anyone who was better qualified.

Tacitus's *Agricola* Agricola had married Domitia Decidiana in AD 62 and in 77 their daughter was married to **Tacitus** [Cornelius Tacitus] (*b.* AD 56/7, *d.* in or after 113), a young man then taking his first steps in official life. Since almost all that is known of Agricola is relayed by this writer, the position and outlook of the man are worth more than passing comment. Cornelius Tacitus was born of provincial stock in northern Italy or southern Gaul; the latter is more likely to have been his origin as his writing reveals a close knowledge of that province. He may thus have belonged to the same provincial circle as Agricola himself. His father was of equestrian rank (a step lower than the senatorial class), quite probably the procurator of Gallia Belgica. In the reign of Vespasian (AD 69–79) Tacitus embarked on the usual minor magistracies held by the young Roman bound for the senate. He served as quaestor in AD 81 or 82, either tribune of the people or aedile three years later, and praetor in 88. He should then have served as legate of a legion for about three years, but this phase in his career is not recorded. He next appears as consul in AD 97, when he was forty or forty-one. This succession of offices had been rapid for the son of an *eques* and there is no evidence that his progress had been slowed by changes in the Flavian regime. The later stages of his official career are largely unknown, but he attained the proconsulship of Asia (a small portion of western Anatolia), the pinnacle of the senatorial *cursus*, in 112–13. His talents were not confined to the field of provincial administration. He was an outstanding orator and advocate; and by his early forties, if not before, he had begun his literary career. The *Agricola* was fairly certainly his first published work, compiled in AD 97–8, immediately before the *Germania* and immediately after his consulship. The circumstances of its writing—the recent death of Domitian, the accession of Nerva, and the adoption of Trajan—have left their mark on the tenor of the work.

As a source for Roman Britain, especially in the Flavian period, the *Agricola* stands alone. No other text provides a consecutive narrative from the invasion of Britain in AD 43 to the high-water mark of conquest in the north. But the very nature of the work and the purposes of the writer impose their own conditions on the use that can be made of it. The literary models for this form of biography are ultimately Greek, but a distinctively Roman tradition had evolved by Tacitus's day in which the qualities and character of the subject were given priority over historical context. While the *Agricola* is much more than a laudation of a distinguished life not wholly fulfilled, it is something less than a biography. Herein lies a central problem of interpretation. Much of the treatment is historical, especially in relation to early Roman Britain. In style as well as in content the work is reminiscent of the narratives of Sallust and Livy of the previous century. Nevertheless, Agricola and his achievements are the dominant theme; he is rarely absent for more than a sentence or two. Interwoven into the fabric of the text there are also themes and references relating to the final years of the first century. It is matter for debate as to how much should be read into these, how 'political' were Tacitus's motives in writing as he did. Was the *Agricola* to some extent an apologia and a justification for the provincial élite who had served Rome, rather than the regime of Domitian, in the previous two decades? Certainly there is a clear and deliberate contrast between the dedicated servant of the state and the paranoid despot whom he served. But there is more individuality in the delineation of Agricola than this. Tacitus had portrayed a man in his time, not with warts and all, but equally certainly not a stereotype of the good governor and soldier.

Given the primacy of the text, the debate on the reliability of the *Agricola* for its subject's governorship and for the wider history of Roman Britain in its first half-century will continue. Modern attitudes have ranged from acceptance tempered by caution to scepticism tempered by a measure of approval. On Agricola's work and achievements in Britain the account contains no obvious exaggeration or invention, even though the figure of Agricola naturally enjoys an enhanced status. There is general archaeological endorsement of the veracity of Tacitus in his account of the conquest of northern Britain, though it must be admitted that the geographical setting is very weakly presented. There is support, too, for the Flavian programme of urban and social development in Britain to which Agricola is said to have contributed and which is evident at London, St Albans, Cirencester, Silchester, Winchester, and elsewhere. There is no obvious discord between the archaeological record and the text of the *Agricola* as it relates to Agricola's own administration. The account of Britain before the Flavian period is more suspect. There is foreshortening in the chronology here and the work of governors in Nero's reign is not given its due. Some achievements and developments are omitted altogether. From the early Flavian period onward, however, when Tacitus himself began to hold offices of state, the work can be used with much greater confidence and not merely *faute de mieux*.

Military successes: 'Mons Graupius' Agricola's arrival in Britain followed upon, and was evidently intended to continue, forward movement in the west and north, prosecuted by his predecessors Petillius Cerialis and Julius Frontinus. Agricola's first task was to complete the subjugation of the Welsh tribes. He was swiftly into action soon after his arrival in the province. The Ordovices of north Wales had all but annihilated a Roman cavalry regiment shortly before. The new governor struck deep into their territory, destroyed their military strength, and seized the rich island of Mona (Anglesey). This bold stroke was followed by the routine garrisoning of north Wales, thus completing the work begun by Julius Frontinus between AD 74 and 77. No further resistance by the tribes of Wales is recorded. The northern regions of Britain posed greater problems, of logistics as well as of conquest, and the campaigns conducted there by Agricola from AD 78 to 84 were arduous and demanding. They were also highly successful and must be ranked among the finest feats of the Roman army in the western provinces at any date. While it is self-evidently true that Agricola's reputation has been enhanced by Tacitus's account of his career, there is no serious doubt that his military operations in Britain were highly successful. In six years of campaigning, the tribes of northern Britain, from the Pennines to the southern fringe of the Scottish highlands, were subdued and their territory firmly held by strategic roads and garrisons. The culmination of this forward movement came in a pitched battle against the Caledonians at 'Mons Graupius' in AD 84, a site which cannot be identified with certainty, but which must have lain in the coastal plain of north-east Scotland, probably in what is now Aberdeenshire or Banffshire. Agricola's battle position was far from favourable, the Caledonian host having the advantage of higher ground. By allowing the Roman centre to engage the enemy on the slopes, however, he tempted the northerners to descend to lower ground where four regiments of cavalry held in reserve were able to rout and disperse them. Roman legionary forces were not called upon to join in the battle. Auxiliary troops alone carried the day. Against Roman losses of only 360, the Caledonians were said to have lost 10,000 men. After brief forays further north and a voyage to the Orkneys to receive the surrender of those islands, Agricola withdrew to winter quarters.

The Roman conquest of northern Britain had reached its highest point and so had Agricola's career. Shortly after the victory at 'Mons Graupius', he was recalled by Domitian and awarded the ornaments of a triumph—the highest military honour he could have expected. He had been governor of Britain for seven years, an unusually long term for any province, especially one which contained so large a legionary army. His northern conquests were not to last for long. Pressures on other frontiers in mainland Europe, notably on the Danube, enforced a withdrawal of forces from Scotland. At the nodal point of his general disposition of forces in Scotland, Agricola had planned and begun the construction of a new legionary base at Inchtuthil on the Tay, possibly for his old legion, the twentieth. This base was largely complete when, in AD 86 or at the latest in 87, the decision was taken to abandon most of the territory north of the Cheviot hills. The legionary base was given up and carefully dismantled, along with the auxiliary forts between the 'highland line' and the Tweed basin. It is entirely credible, as Tacitus reported, that Agricola felt bitter about the turn of events. But no blame can be attached to him or to the emperor and his advisers for an enforced withdrawal from the northernmost conquests. The demands of frontiers under threat elsewhere could only be met by drafting in troops from secure provinces. That Britain could be so regarded was itself a measure of Agricola's achievement.

Probably a much greater disappointment was Agricola's failure to receive one of the commands which crowned the senatorial career: Syria, Africa, or Asia. Domitian, or a confidant, made it plain that he should not put his name forward for the proconsulship of Africa or Asia. This is not wholly incomprehensible. Most of Agricola's years of service had been spent in the specialized conditions of Britain, far removed from the civilities of old proconsular provinces. He may also have lacked powerful connections at court and there may be some truth in Tacitus's assertion that Domitian harboured jealous sentiments about Agricola's achievements. The emperor may well have felt that he had received honours enough in the ornaments of a triumph, a public statue, and a long, honorific citation.

Death and reputation Virtually nothing is known of Agricola's last years. He died nine years after his recall from Britain, on 23 August AD 93 after an illness. Tacitus reports a rumour that he was poisoned and hints, no more, at Domitian's involvement. In the fervid atmosphere of Domitian's later reign such rumours were frequent and there is no good reason for believing that this one held substance. Domitian (named as coheir in Agricola's will) had nothing to gain by removing from the scene a long-retired provincial governor.

Agricola the effective and successful general is a figure whose fame is secure. Agricola's merits and achievements as a provincial administrator are less easily assessed, as the account of Tacitus is almost all there is. His all-round competence is entirely credible. Whether or not he was possessed of greater talents is more difficult to ascertain. His origins in a western *colonia* may have made him more sensitive to provincial feeling than many of his Italian peers in the imperial service. His checking of abuses in the supply of grain to Roman forces may thus have been motivated by a sense of fairness, but it also made good administrative sense not to push newly subjected provincials too far. Similarly, his encouragement of Roman culture and education among the rising generation of British leaders may have been motivated as much by pragmatism as by a desire to Romanize the province. This was the social group upon which the further development of Britain would depend. There is evidence to support the statement of Tacitus that Agricola gave active assistance to the development of cities, though in this too he was building on the work of earlier governors. The famous dedicatory inscription for the forum at Verulamium (St Albans), dating to either AD 79 or 81 and naming Agricola, is striking confirmation of his general care for urban development, but this text records the completion of work which must have begun years earlier.

The personality of Agricola remains elusive; it could hardly be expected to emerge from Tacitus's encomium. The figure there depicted is somewhat bland and bloodless; an efficient subordinate rather than a born leader; a man of duty not vision. That judgement may seem harsh. To have served emperors as diverse as Nero, Vespasian, Titus, and Domitian, and to have passed through a civil war, were achievements which proved to be beyond many. Agricola's career may not have reached the topmost pinnacles of the imperial service, but he does worthily represent that large and significant body of provincials who served the Roman empire with competence and distinction. Few provincial governors are better known to us. None could better exemplify their all-round achievements.   MALCOLM TODD

Sources Tacitus, *De vita Agricolae*, ed. R. M. Ogilvie and I. Richmond (1967) · Dio's *Roman history*, ed. and trans. E. Cary, 3 (1914), xxxix.50, 4; 8 (1925), lxvi.20, 1 · C. Tacitus, *The histories [and] the annals*, ed. and trans. C. H. Moore and J. Jackson, 1 (1925), i.2, 1 · W. Roy, *Military antiquities of the Romans in north Britain* (1793) · O. G. S. Crawford, *Topography of Roman Scotland north of the Antonine Wall* (1949) · L. F. Pitts and J. K. St Joseph, *Inchtuthil: the Roman legionary fortress* (1985) · G. S. Maxwell, *The Romans in Scotland* (1989) · W. S. Hanson, *Agricola and the conquest of the north* (1987) · S. S. Frere, 'The Flavian frontier in Scotland', *Scottish Archaeological Forum*, 12 (1981), 89–97 · B. Dobson, 'Agricola's life and career', *Scottish Archaeological Forum*, 12 (1981), 1–13

Julius Caesar, Gaius. *See* Caesar (100–44 BC).

Julius Classicianus [Julius Alpinus Classicianus], **Gaius** (*fl. c.*AD 60), procurator of Britain, was married to Julia Pacata, daughter of Julius Indus; he died in office at an unknown date and was buried in London by his widow. To judge from his names and from what may be inferred about his wife, Classicianus was a Gaul, probably from the province of Gallia Belgica. His father-in-law, Indus, was the Treveran noble (that is, from the Trier region) who remained loyal to Rome during the Gallic revolt of AD 21 and helped to suppress the rebel leader Julius Florus. Her cognomen suggests that Julia Pacata was born soon after this event. Classicianus himself may be assumed to have been in his forties at the time of his appointment to the post in Britain. Family recollections of the revolt of AD 21, provoked by heavy indebtedness among the Romanized élite in Gaul (similar problems are said to have contributed to the revolt of Boudicca) may conceivably have influenced Classicianus's conduct in Britain. But this is naturally speculative. Apart from his tombstone (Collingwood and Wright, RIB 12)—two parts of which were found in 1852 and 1935, reused in a bastion of the Roman wall of London, north of Tower Hill, and now in the British Museum—the only record of this man is supplied by a brief passage in Tacitus's *Annals*.

Classicianus was appointed procurator (chief financial officer) of Britain in AD 60 or 61 as the successor of Decianus Catus, who had fled the province in panic after Boudicca's rebels had sacked Camulodunum (Colchester). Catus himself had been partly responsible for the outbreak of the revolt by his harsh treatment of the queen; and the governor, Suetonius Paullinus, after his hard-fought victory, had moved against any of the British peoples whose loyalty was uncertain or who were still hostile 'with fire and steel'. The situation was aggravated by a food shortage, for no crops had been sown during the rebellion, and the Britons tried to divert to their own use supplies reserved for the Roman army. According to Tacitus, Classicianus caused 'the fierce natives to postpone making their peace by holding out hopes that Paullinus would soon be replaced by a milder governor' (Tacitus, *Annals*, xiv.38). Meanwhile he reported to Rome that there was no hope of an end to hostilities unless Paullinus was given a successor. He attributed Paullinus's setbacks to his own perverse character, his successes simply to luck. Nero reacted by dispatching a senior imperial freedman, Polyclitus, to inspect. Following Polyclitus's report, although Paullinus was retained in office for a short time, he was replaced early in AD 61 by Petronius Turpilianus (Tacitus, *Annals*, xiv.39), a nephew of the first governor of Britain, Aulus Plautius. The policy adopted both by Turpilianus and by the next governor, Trebellius Maximus (AD 63–9), was indeed one of clemency, combined with which the 'barbarians' were encouraged to 'acquiesce in the blandishments of vice' (Tacitus, *Agricola*, 16.2–4), presumably a sarcastic reference to baths, banquets, and other aspects of the Roman way of life; and active campaigning ceased for a decade.

It may be that the procurator Classicianus, himself of Celtic origin and hence with some sympathy for the Britons, played an important role in reconciling them to Roman rule. He could well have stayed in office as procurator for several years; but it is quite unknown how long he lived. No descendants are known, but a Treveran named

Alpinius Montanus, who served as an equestrian officer in the army of Vitellius, in AD 69, could have been a son of Classicianus.   A. R. BIRLEY

Sources C. Tacitus, *The histories [and] the annals*, ed. and trans. C. H. Moore and J. Jackson, 2 (1931) · R. G. Collingwood and R. P. Wright, eds., *The Roman inscriptions of Britain*, 2 vols. (1965), RIB 12 · A. R. Birley, *The fasti of Roman Britain* (1981)

Julius Frontinus, Sextus (d. 103/4), Roman governor of Britain, held that appointment from AD 73 or 74 to 77. His service in Britain is attested only by a single sentence in Tacitus's *Agricola*, and his date of birth, origin, and early career are unknown. But as the author of a work on land-surveying (*Libri duo argumenti gromatici*, preserved only in excerpts), of the *Stratagemata*, and of the *De aquis*, as a patron and friend of the younger Pliny, and as a leading figure in the reigns of Nerva and Trajan, he was to become one of the most prominent persons of the age. Aelian, author of the *Tactica*, visited him to discuss military matters at Formiae, near Rome, and the poet Martial refers to his country retreat at Anxur (Tarracina); but there is no reason to suppose that Frontinus's original home was in Latium. Rather, his names and connections suggest strongly that he was of Gallic origin, probably from Nemausus (Nîmes). His wife's name is unknown. A daughter married the leading general Sosius Senecio (consul for the second time in 107), a granddaughter was the wife of Pompeius Falco, governor of Britain at the beginning of Hadrian's reign. Frontinus also had links with the Calvisii, the family of Marcus Aurelius's grandmother.

Frontinus first appears in the historical record as praetor in AD 70. In this capacity he had to convene the important meeting of the senate on 1 January, in the absence of the consuls, who were the new emperor Vespasian and his elder son Titus, both still in the east. It has been conjectured that Frontinus had recently been promoted to the senate, perhaps by the emperor Galba (r. AD 68–9), after service as an equestrian officer and procurator. Later in AD 70 he served in the campaign against the Batavians and other rebel tribes of northern Gaul and the Rhineland, probably as a legionary legate. He mentions in the *Stratagemata* that he received the surrender of 70,000 rebel Lingones, whose chief town was Andematunnum (Langres). An altar dedicated at Vetera (Xanten) to Jupiter, Juno, and Minerva for Frontinus's welfare may belong to this time, if not to his later participation in a campaign in Germany (*Corpus inscriptionum Latinarum*, 13, no. 8624). He presumably held the consulship (the necessary qualification for the governorship of Britain) at latest in AD 73, in which year he probably succeeded Petillius Cerialis in the province.

To equal Cerialis was a difficult task, so Tacitus wrote, but Frontinus:

> took up and sustained the burden; he was a great man— insofar as greatness was then permitted; and he subdued by arms the powerful and pugnacious people of the Silures, overcoming not only the courage of the enemy but the difficulties of the terrain.   (Tacitus, 17)

Archaeological evidence suggests, if it cannot prove, that

Frontinus founded the legionary fortresses at Isca (Caerleon), in Silurian territory, and Deva (Chester), and that he added substantially to the network of auxiliary forts in mid-Wales. Apart from dealing with the refractory inhabitants of south Wales, Frontinus clearly, as Tacitus indicates, carried on where Cerialis had left off, in northern Britain. He may also deserve credit for giving the Silures a new urban centre, at Venta Silurum (Caer-went), and for fostering urban development in southern Britain, for example at Verulamium (St Albans). In midsummer of AD 77 he was succeeded by Julius Agricola. His next known activity was in 83, when he accompanied the emperor Domitian on his campaign against the Chatti (of Hesse) in Upper Germany, either as governor of Lower Germany or as a member of the emperor's general staff (*comes Augusti*). Several important passages in the *Stratagemata* recall aspects of this service, including a much discussed description of the driving of *limites*, the word later used to describe Roman frontier works, through the German forest. A few years later Frontinus became proconsul of Asia: a massive arch set up at Hierapolis (Pamukkale) during his term of office is dated to AD 86 (Eck, 77ff.).

The Asian proconsulship generally marked the final stage in a senatorial career and Frontinus probably devoted himself mainly to writing in the following decade. But the assassination of Domitian in September AD 96 and the accession of Nerva led to his re-emergence, as a senior statesman. In AD 97 he was made *curator aquarum*, and undertook the overhaul of Rome's aqueducts with great conscientiousness, to judge from his manual on the subject. His praise of Rome's practical engineering, as the best testimony to the greatness of the empire, in contrast to the 'idle pyramids' and the 'useless' works of Greek architecture (Frontinus, *De aquis*, 16), has often been quoted. In the same year he was one of the first two men chosen to serve on a special economy commission and early in AD 98 held a second consulship. His colleague was Trajan, who had been adopted by Nerva as his heir in October AD 97 and succeeded him in January AD 98. Frontinus's son-in-law Senecio was consul in AD 99 and Frontinus himself held a third consulship, a very rare distinction, as colleague of Trajan, in 100. It may be inferred that Frontinus played an important part in securing the choice of Trajan as Nerva's heir. Frontinus died in 103 or 104, when Pliny recalled with satisfaction that he had been elected to the vacant place in the college of augurs which Frontinus's death had created. Frontinus had doubtless held this prestigious priesthood for many years, a further sign of his great distinction.   A. R. BIRLEY

Sources Tacitus, *Agricola*, ed. and trans. M. Mutton (1914), 17 • Martial, *Epigrams*, ed. and trans. W. C. A. Ker (1919), 10.58 • 'Aelianus' theorie der taktik', *Griechische Kriegsschriftsteller*, ed. and trans. H. Köchley and W. Rüstow, 2 (1855), 218–471, *praef*.3 [Ger. trans.] • Pliny, *Letters*, ed. and trans. B. Radice (1969), 4.8, 9.19 • Frontinus, *The 'Stratagems' and 'Aqueducts of Rome'*, ed. and trans. C. E. Bennett, M. B. McElwain, and C. Herschel (1950) • R. Syme, *Tacitus* (1958) • A. R. Birley, *The fasti of Roman Britain* (1981) • W. Eck, *Senatoren von Vespasian bis Hadrian* (1970) • O. Hirschfield and C. Zangemeister, eds., *Inscriptiones trium Galliarum et Germaniarum*, 6 vols. in 9 (Berlin, 1899–1943)

Julius Severus, Sextus (*fl. c.*130–133). *See under* Roman officials (*act.* AD 43–410).

Julius Verus, Gnaeus (*fl. c.*155–158). *See under* Roman officials (*act.* AD 43–410).

Jullien [Julien], **Louis** (1812–1860), conductor and composer, was born at Sisteron, France, on 23 April 1812, the son of a military bandsman. Although he later publicized a fanciful account of his childhood (*Musical World*, 1853), he seems to have been brought up in barracks and trained by his father to play piccolo in the band; he also studied the violin. In 1833 he entered the Paris Conservatoire, but he left early in 1836, having shown more aptitude for dance music than counterpoint. The vogue for dance-halls, where orchestras played adaptations of new operas and other topical numbers, gave him his chance. After conducting at least one small dance-hall orchestra and taking many other minor engagements, Jullien was by 1838 in charge of a large orchestra at the Jardin Turc, where he made his name by concocting a quadrille based on tunes from the popular opera *Les Huguenots* and accompanied by gas flares, alarm bells, and musketry. He then moved to the fashionable Casino Paganini. But by 1839 he had fled to England to escape imprisonment for debt, and the rest of his career was spent in English-speaking countries.

Low-priced Promenade Concerts mixing 'classical' and popular music and lasting four or five hours were not new to London, but Jullien gave them new appeal and found a new audience. From June 1840 to early 1859 he conducted winter and summer seasons of such concerts, mainly in leading theatres (most often Drury Lane), interspersed with tours of the main British and Irish cities. From 1845 to 1857 most of the summer seasons were held at the Surrey Zoological Gardens; at the first 'monster concert' there, 12,000 people heard Bellini's 'Suoni la tromba' played by twenty each of cornets, trumpets, trombones, ophicleides, and serpents, as well as 'God Save the Queen' with each bar punctuated by cannon. Profusion and noise marked much of Jullien's conducting, as they did his topical compositions, such as his *British Army Quadrille* and *Siege of Sebastopol Quadrille*. Yet his concerts from the start included entire Beethoven symphonies—at times titivated with effects like peas rattling to simulate hailstones in the 'Pastoral', but played with brio and precision, as, later, were works by Mozart and Mendelssohn.

Jullien combined belief in his own genius and some mental imbalance (he seems to have been manic-depressive) with a nose for advertising in a raw, newly urbanized society. His dandyish dress and a manner shifting from the solemn to the enthusiastic—he would conduct in white gloves with a jewelled baton presented to him on a silver salver, but at the climax might climb onto a plush and gilt armchair—endeared him at once to the audience. His concerts were lavishly presented, the house bedecked with coloured drapes and with flowers provided by his English wife, a former florist. (After Jullien's death his wife, whose name is unknown, was destitute and given a job in the Drury Lane box office.) As 'the Mons', Jullien became a cartoon figure in *Punch*; by 1854 his friend the critic J. W. Davison could write that he 'had created a new taste for music among the middle class' (*Mendelssohn to Wagner*, 85).

Jullien's manic side, however, as well as bad luck, brought successive disasters. In 1847–8 an ill-planned season of opera at Drury Lane, with excellent singers and Berlioz conducting, provoked his first bankruptcy. Berlioz's comments as the venture unfolded were typical of people who dealt with Jullien: he first praised the man's boldness, intelligence, and understanding of the English audience, but just over two months later he was calling him incompetent and mad. Jullien, however, quickly recovered, as he did from the failure of his ambitious opera *Pietro il Grande*, the production of which at Covent Garden he financed in 1852. By touring his orchestra (with 11 tons of luggage) to New York and the main cities of the north-eastern and southern United States for nearly a year from August 1853 he did much to repair his fortunes; already about 1851 he had been able to buy a country house in Belgium near Waterloo, the Abbaye d'Aywiers. The fire of 1856 at Covent Garden, however, destroyed most of his scores and parts; a year later, mismanagement at the Surrey Zoological Gardens, for which he was not responsible, brought the failure of that venture, the seizure of his music, a personal loss of £6000, and a second bankruptcy.

Although Jullien again bounced back and took up his routine, he began to show signs of megalomania, planning a world tour that would instil 'universal harmony'. In Paris in May 1859—perhaps on the run from his British creditors—he was arrested for debt, but was released in July. On 6 February 1860 he could write lucidly about his plans, but by the 22nd he had suffered a breakdown and apparently stabbed himself. He was placed in a private asylum at Neuilly, where he died on 14 March of causes still unclear. Thought by some a charlatan, by others an educator, Jullien is notable as the first conductor to have imposed himself on the audience even more than on the music.   JOHN ROSSELLI

Sources A. Carse, *The life of Jullien* (1951) · F.-J. Fétis, *Biographie universelle des musiciens, et bibliographie générale de la musique*, 2nd edn, 8 vols. (Paris, 1860–65) · *From Mendelssohn to Wagner: being the memoirs of J. W. Davison, forty years the music critic of The Times*, ed. H. Davison (1912) · *Correspondance générale: Hector Berlioz*, ed. P. Citron, 1 (Paris, 1972), 679; 3 (1978) · H. F. Chorley, *Thirty years' musical recollections*, 2 (1862), 187–8 · J. E. Cox, *Musical recollections of the last half-century*, 2 (1872), 157–8 · B. Lumley, *Reminiscences of the opera* (1864), 425 · G. L. Duprez, *Souvenirs d'un chanteur* (Paris, 1880), 260–65 · J. Rivière, *My musical life and recollections* (1893) · 'A sketch of the life of Jullien', *Musical World* (14 May 1853), 307; (21 May 1853), 314; (28 May 1853), 331–2; (4 June 1853), 347–8; (11 June 1853), 363–4; (18 June 1853), 380–81; (25 June 1853), 396–8; (2 July 1853), 412; (9 July 1853), 428–9; (16 July 1853), 444–6; (23 July 1853), 466–9 · Boase, *Mod. Eng. biog.*

Likenesses J. P. Dantan, caricature, plaster statuette, 1836, Musée Carnavalet, Paris · N. Hanhart, coloured lithograph, NPG · Mayall, photograph, NPG · D. J. Pound, stipple and line engraving (after photograph by Mayall), NPG · lithographs and woodcuts,

Harvard TC · portraits, repro. in Carse, *The life of Jullien* · woodcuts, NPG

Wealth at death probably little or nothing; bankrupt in England (for second time) in 1858; had been arrested for debt in Paris; subscription was raised for him in London which after death produced £500–£600 for widow

Julyan, Sir **Penrose Goodchild** (1816–1907), civil servant, was born on 30 December 1816, the first of two children of Captain Robert Julyan RN (*d.* 1857), and his wife, Anne Veale (*d.* 1878), daughter of Richard Thomas. His father became harbour master at Quebec, and Julyan seems to have spent his early life in Canada. After serving in the corps of gentleman volunteers during the Canadian uprising of 1838, he became the special commissioner of roads and bridges in Lower Canada, and in 1845 was appointed to the British army commissariat. His organization of an immigrant quarantine station on Grosse Island in the St Lawrence River and his invention of a mechanical appliance for the disinfection of hospital bedding saved many lives. Impressed by his initiative and organizational skill the lords commissioners of the Treasury appointed him in 1848 assistant financial secretary to the board of works in Ireland. Ill health, however, caused him to relinquish the post after only a few months. On his recovery he was dispatched to Malta, where he helped to place the island's currency on a sound and uniform basis, and then to Australia as the director of the Royal Mint's Australian branch. He married in 1848 Marianne, the daughter of Charles Brocklesby of Lincolnshire, who died childless in 1878.

At the outbreak of the Crimean War Julyan was recalled to London by the army commissariat. He served first as an engineer, and was then given the task of designing a floating flour mill and bakery. Constructed within the shells of steamers, the flour mill contained grinding machinery driven by the screw shaft of the vessel, and the bakery four ovens, hot and cold cisterns, and steam machinery for the kneading of dough. The ships, the first of their kind, greatly improved the diet and morale of the army, and earned Julyan promotion to assistant commissary-general. In his spare time he also invented a compressor to reduce the bulkiness of cavalry hay before shipment, and a preparation of chopped hay, bruised oats, and bran, which he called 'amalgamated field forage'. The latter halved forage shipping costs, and was subsequently used by the army in China, Abyssinia, and New Zealand.

In 1858 Julyan was appointed senior agent at the office of the crown agents for the colonies, a quasi-government department that purchased crown colony public goods, issued crown colony and responsible government colony loans, and performed a myriad of other duties. Charged with the reorganization of the office, Julyan set about his work with, Frederic Rogers noted, 'remarkable energy' (5 March 1870, PRO, CO 323/299). In the years 1858–60 to 1875–7 the annual disbursements of the agency rose more than ninefold to £9.481 million, and from 1863–6 to 1876–82 the average annual income almost doubled. In 1874 he was appointed KCMG. Besides his work as an agent Julyan also, in 1873, travelled to Mauritius and the Seychelles, and in 1878 to Malta, to report on the state of the civil service in those colonies. He also accepted the role of loan agent to the New Zealand government, for which, unknown to the Colonial Office, he received remuneration. On discovering the gratuities paid, the secretary of state fined him £1000 and required him to take no further paid employment. Undeterred, Julyan immediately before his retirement in 1879 again acted as paid New Zealand loan agent, causing much Colonial Office anguish and the under-secretary Sir Robert Herbert to describe him as 'honest, but fond of money' (28 July 1881, PRO, CO 537/219).

Free of government restraints Julyan spent the final years of his career as a leading City figure. From 1879 to 1896 he was financial adviser and loan and stock agent to the New Zealand government, for a time director of the New Zealand Bank and the Wellington and Manawatu Railway Company Ltd, and from 1879 to 1890 a director of the London and Westminster Bank. He spent his long retirement in Torquay where, apart from the occasional trip to his London club, the Junior United Services, he devoted his time to painting. Julyan died at his home, Stadacona, Torquay, Devon, on 26 April 1907.

DAVID SUNDERLAND

Sources D. Sunderland, 'Agents and principals: the crown agents for the colonies, 1880–1914', DPhil diss., U. Oxf., 1996 · WWW · A. T. C. Pratt, ed., *People of the period: being a collection of the biographies of upwards of six thousand living celebrities*, 2 vols. (1897) · *The Times* (24 April 1907), 6 · Walford, *County families* (1898)
Archives PRO, CO, CAOG
Likenesses photograph, repro. in 'Devonshire historical descriptions' (1907)
Wealth at death £36,619 14s. 2d.: probate, 28 May 1907, CGPLA Eng. & Wales

Jumièges, Godfrey of (d. c.1106). See under Malmesbury, William of (b. c.1090, d. in or after 1142).

Jumièges, Robert of. See Robert of Jumièges (d. 1052/1055).

Jumièges, William of (fl. 1026–1070), Benedictine monk and author, wrote the *Gesta Normannorum ducum* ('The deeds of the dukes of the Normans'), written between the 1050s and 1070. Little is known about his person. In the dedicatory letter of his work, addressed to William the Conqueror, he refers to himself as a monk of Jumièges, a Benedictine monastery on the Seine in Normandy. In book 6, chapter 1, he mentions that he writes as an eyewitness from 1026–7 onwards, which suggests that he was born about the year 1000. The only other details about him derive from Orderic Vitalis (d. c.1142) who in his *Ecclesiastical History* three times refers to him as author of the *Gesta*, calling him by his cognomen Calculus. The name may mean that William was in charge of computus (time calculations) in his monastery, or that he suffered from the calculus or stone. The year of his death is unknown but must have occurred after 1070 when he finished the *Gesta*.

William of Jumièges's chronicle of the Norman dukes is important for English history for two reasons. In the first place book 7, chapters 13 to 21, contains the earliest Norman prose account of the conquest of England in 1066. This justifies the use of violence and conquest by battle on the grounds that Harold was a perjurer. William probably wrote it at the request of the Conqueror himself when he visited Jumièges in the summer of 1067 and then added it to the *Gesta*, which was already in an advanced stage of completion. He was not an eyewitness but based his account on other people's information. It is very brief in its details on the logistics of the conquest, very uninformative about the crossing and actual battle, and unreliable in its unique information that King Harold died early on during the battle. It becomes more informative when William relates the campaign leading to the English surrender, the Conqueror's coronation on Christmas day 1066, and the conquest of the north up to 1070. Since he makes no reference to King William's second coronation at Winchester at Easter 1070, nor to Lanfranc's election as archbishop of Canterbury that summer, William of Jumièges must have laid down his pen early in 1070.

The second reason for the relevance of the *Gesta Normannorum ducum* for English history is William of Jumièges's treatment of pre-conquest Anglo-Norman relations of the early eleventh century as described in books 5, 6, and 7. For a long time it was thought that these sections had been written at the same time as the account of the conquest, with all the hindsight that allowed. They form, however, part of the bulk of the chronicle which dates from the pre-conquest period. Consequently, for example, the reference to Edward the Confessor (r. 1042–66) as king in the 1030s supports the evidence of several pre-1041 continental charters which bear Edward's attestation as king.

Despite his addition of the account of the conquest to what is an overwhelmingly Norman history, William of Jumièges had no intention of embarking on further English historiography. On the contrary, in his epilogue he promised to write a sequel on the Conqueror's son Robert Curthose 'in whom at present we rejoice as duke and advocate', an unambiguous statement confirming the delegation of (temporary) ducal power to Robert after 1066. The *Gesta* was a popular chronicle: it was revised and updated several times between 1070 and c.1139, by, among others, Orderic Vitalis and Robert de Torigni (d. 1186), prior of Bec and abbot of Mont-St Michel, and has survived in more than fifty manuscripts.

ELISABETH VAN HOUTS

Sources *The Gesta Normannorum ducum of William of Jumièges, Orderic Vitalis, and Robert of Torigni*, ed. and trans. E. M. C. van Houts, 2 vols., OMT (1992–5) · S. Keynes, 'The æthelings in Normandy', *Anglo-Norman Studies*, 13 (1990), 173–205
Likenesses O. Vitalis, portrait, illuminated initial, Bibliothèque Municipale, Rouen, MS 1174 (Y14), fol. 116r; repro. in *Gesta Normannorum ducum*, frontispiece

Jumper, Sir William (bap. 1660, d. 1715), naval officer, was baptized on 8 January 1660, the second son of William Jumper of Weybridge, Surrey, and his wife, Elizabeth. He was apprenticed to John Love, captain in the Royal African Company, and sent to the African coast in 1678, where he probably stayed for nearly ten years. He was back in England by 1688 when George Legge, Baron Dartmouth, appointed him master's mate of the *Resolution*; he rose to first lieutenant in 1689 and probably sailed with Henry Killigrew to the Mediterranean. In October 1690 he married Elizabeth Willis of Hoo, near Rochester. In December Killigrew appointed him first lieutenant of the *Duke* and the following year he was commissioned a lieutenant in Killigrew's marine regiment.

Appointed captain of the fireship *Hopewell*, Jumper took part in the battle of Barfleur on 19 May 1692, his ship being burnt in the attempt to set fire to the French ships at anchor. He was a volunteer in one of the boats that succeeded in this task a few days later. Jumper was moved to command the fireship *Cygnet* in June, the *Saudadoes* in October, the *Adventure* in July 1693, and the *Weymouth* in March 1694. Jumper gained a reputation as a successful cruiser captain of the *Weymouth*, attacking the French privateers and capturing eleven of their ships, and he was celebrated in verse:

> Be it spoke of the praise of the bold Captain Jumper,
> when he met a French ship he bravely would thump her.
> (C. H. Firth, *Naval Songs and Ballads*, 1908, lxiv)

He served as Sir Cloudesley Shovell's flag-captain on the *Swiftsure* from 30 October 1698 to 13 July 1699 and from 13 September to January 1700. Five months later he wrote to Josiah Burchett, the Admiralty secretary,

> I am always ready on the suddenest occasion to serve His Maj^{tie} and Present Government … and humbly beseech their Lordships (if there be occasion for manning a number of ships) will please permit me to comman one of them.   (PRO, ADM 1/1979, 10 May 1700)

Appointed to the *Lennox* (70 guns) in 1701, he was in Sir George Rooke's fleet sent to Cadiz in 1702, and in 1703 he was in the Mediterranean under Shovell.

Jumper was prominent in the reduction of Gibraltar, leading boats ashore. The Spanish blew up the Round Tower just as Jumper entered it, leaving him, as he related, 'severe battered and bruised' when a wall fell on him, 'broke his head' and gave him 'a very large scar' which 'afflicts him with Pains in Open Weather' (PRO, ADM 1/1980, Jumper's petition). At the battle of Malaga on 13 August 1704 Jumper in the *Lennox* was at the head of Shovell's division. His ship was severely damaged, twenty-three men were killed, and seventy-eight wounded, including Jumper, who suffered injuries to his back and shoulder which continued to trouble him long after his return to England. He was rewarded with a knighthood in 1705. He returned with Shovell in October 1707, but having stood away from the fleet escaped its shipwreck on the Isles of Scilly on 22 October and only learnt later of Shovell's death. Ordered to refit at Plymouth, Jumper seems finally to have desired a less strenuous posting; he petitioned Prince George on 8 January 1708 to bear his many services in mind, and later wrote to Burchett asking to be appointed commissioner or superintendent at Chatham, which was granted. In 1714 he was appointed resident commissioner at Plymouth. He died there on 12 March 1715 and was buried three days later at St Andrew, Plymouth. He was survived by his wife.

J. K. LAUGHTON, *rev.* PETER LE FEVRE

Sources captains' letters, 1698–1708, PRO, ADM 1/1979–1981 · letters to navy board, 1692, 1696, PRO, ADM 106/420, 490 · captains' logs, *Weymouth* and *Lennox*, PRO, ADM 51/4391, 4238 · Plymouth dockyard letters, 1705–40, PRO, ADM 174/101 · PRO, Royal African Company papers, T 70/78, fol. 127v · paybook of *Resolution*, 1688, PRO, ADM 33/136 · parish register, St Werburgh, Hoo, Kent, Medway Archives and Local Studies Centre, Rochester, Kent, Oct. 1660 [marriage] · parish register, Weybridge, Surrey HC, 8 Jan 1660 [baptism] · A. Boyer, *The history of the reign of Queen Anne, digested into annals*, 3 (1705), 55 · BL, Add. MS 70087, fol. 296v
Archives PRO, ADM 1, ADM 106, ADM 174

June, John (*fl. c.*1744–1775), printmaker, flourished in London between about 1744 and 1775. Throughout his career he worked at the cheaper end of the print trade and was dependent upon publishers for his livelihood. He turned his hand to numerous graphic genres, including portraits, topography, and book illustration, and regularly engraved watch papers and royal sheets for the London publisher Robert Sayer.

June's first known prints are small portraits, and that of *F. Richter* (1744) was both drawn and engraved by him; indeed, he designed most of his own engravings, except for a few reproductions which he made after the work of John Collett. Generally, in the 1740s, he specialized in fashion plates and popular genre scenes. His skill in the first is typified by a fashion calendar, published in 1749, by D. Voisin, where each of twelve plates depicts a woman dressed according to the season and situated in a different London location. During a period when Hogarth's prints had popularized the satire of fashionable life, June exploited his skill to produce cheap and often bawdy satiric compositions which ridiculed fops and harlots on the streets of London. One such is his sixpenny print *The Lady's Disaster* (1749), where a woman, wearing an over-large hoop skirt, is embarrassed on 'tossing her Hoop too high' and thus revealing her petticoats in front of a crowd of onlookers. On account of the comic potential and commercial mileage in the English taste for all things French, many of June's plates display his sensitivity to the rococo style and subject matter. This is also seen in his illustrations for K. Brooke's *The Art of Angling* (1766), which are small light-hearted etched vignettes of rustic scenes with organic-motif borders. His two plates of the rice and silk manufactory in China also capitalized on this taste, and, although they first appeared in Sayers and Bennett's catalogue of 1775, their republication in *A New Book of Landscapes* (1794) by the firm of Laure and Whittle suggests the continuing viability of June's work.   LUCY PELTZ

Sources Bénézit, *Dict.* · Anderton catalogues [exhibition catalogues, Society of Artists, BM, print room] · T. Dodd, 'Memoirs of English engravers, 1550–1800', BL, Add. MS 33403, fols. 79, 177 · H. Hammelmann, *Book illustrators in eighteenth-century England*, ed. T. S. R. Boase (1975) · *Engraved Brit. ports.* · L. Peltz, 'The merchant, the Frenchified fop, and the anti-Gallican, "The fate of the country is in these hands": graphic satire and the production of merchant identity during the Seven Years' War', MA diss., Courtauld Inst., 1994 · J. Strutt, *A biographical dictionary, containing an historical account of all the engravers, from the earliest period of the art of engraving to the present time*, 2 vols. (1785–6) · Thieme & Becker, *Allgemeines Lexikon* · Bryan, *Painters* (1903–5) · I. Maxted, *The London book trades, 1775–1800: a preliminary checklist of members* (1977)

Jung, Meir Zvi (1858?–1921), rabbi, was born in Tisza Eszlar, near Tokay, Hungary, then part of the Austrian empire, the son of Rabbi Abraham Jung, a businessman and landowner. He studied in a *yeshivah* (Talmudic college) in Pressburg under Rabbi Samuel Ehrenfeld and Rabbi S. B. Schreiber. He also studied in Huszt under Rabbi Moses Schick. He gained *semichot* (rabbinical ordinations) in Pressburg, as well as from Rabbi Isaac Glick of Tolscva, Rabbi Judah Leib Julius of Shebesh, and from Rabbi Solomon Spitzer of Vienna. He received his secular education in the *Gymnasium* of Budapest. He then studied philosophy, history, and Semitics at a string of German universities including Marburg (under Professor Hermann Cohen), Heidelberg, and Leipzig, gaining his doctorate from the latter under the protestant theologian Professor Franz Delitzsch. He published a study of the *Pirke avot* ('ethics of the fathers') based on his dissertation.

Some time in the 1880s Jung was appointed rabbi in Mannheim, where he staunchly opposed the growing influence of Reform Judaism. In 1891 he took up a position in Ungarisch-Brod, Moravia. He was probably the earliest pioneer in Europe of Jewish day schools that offered secular as well as religious instruction, in the German-Jewish spirit of *Torah im Derekh Eretz*. He began a network of *Gymnasia* in Austria-Hungary, the first opening in Ungarisch-Brod (1901), followed by Lemberg (Lwów) (1908), Storozynetz, Bukovina (1906 or 1909), and Vienna (1911). He saw these institutions as a means of counteracting assimilation brought about by attendance at state schools. Jung's schools flourished until 1915 and the dislocation caused by the First World War.

However, another school established in Cracow in September 1906 was short-lived. Jung's schools offered a classical education in Greek and Latin alongside traditional *yeshivah* training. This combination aroused bitter opposition from the local Hasidim, with the support of Rabbi Issachar Dov Rokeakh of Belz and other Hasidic groups throughout Hungary, and they plastered the streets with posters proclaiming in Hebrew 'HaMashchit bo el HaIr' ('The destroyer has come to town'). Jung responded by issuing a Hebrew *kol koré* or open letter addressed to the *rebbes* (heads of Hasidic sects), appealing to them to support his work. It fell on deaf ears. An unholy alliance was formed between the Hasidim and assimilationist Jews in the city and they made a successful joint appeal to the Galician authorities to have the school closed down.

In 1912, on the recommendation of Rabbi Moritz Gudemann, chief rabbi of Vienna, Jung was selected out of some twenty or thirty applicants to succeed Rabbi Moses Avigdor Chaikin as chief minister of the Federation of Synagogues in London. Within a year Rabbi Jung, a native German speaker, had mastered both Yiddish and English. He founded and was first president of the Va'ad ha Rabbonim (council of rabbis) set up to bolster both standards of religious observance and the influence of the rabbinate in Anglo-Jewish life. He was particularly critical of the inadequate standards of *kashrut* (kosher food provision) of the chief rabbi's *bet din* (Jewish ecclesiastical

court). Between 1912 and 1915 he acted as unofficial spiritual guide to the Machzike Hadas ('upholders of the faith') or Spitalfields Great Synagogue, when this was the most influential east European style Orthodox congregation in Britain. However, the authority of the Va'ad and of Jung in particular was never accepted by the rival United Synagogue, which represented the interests of establishment Anglo-Jewry.

Jung continued his educational work in London. In December 1912 he opened a Jewish trade school for the sons of poor East End Jewish immigrants. The curriculum combined paid apprenticeship training with traditional religious studies. However, the school, which settled in premises in Cambridge Heath, Bethnal Green, foundered not for want of potential pupils but for lack of funding from the lay leaders of Anglo-Jewry. Unlike the Jews' Free School, the ethos of Jung's establishment was an unfashionable loyalty to traditional Judaism, not rapid Anglicization designed to smooth passage into British society. In addition, Jung encouraged the introduction of secular studies into the curriculum of the Etz Chaim Yeshiva, the first Talmudic college founded in Britain, in order to widen its appeal.

The Sinai League was another educational initiative of Rabbi Jung's. This was an informal association of youth clubs that combined social activities with Jewish learning, aimed at school leavers, the sons and daughters of the first generation of immigrants who were defecting from their Jewish roots. The clubs, which segregated the sexes, usually met on the premises of synagogues affiliated with the federation and developed a strongly Zionist complexion.

In 1886 Rabbi Jung married Ernestine Silbermann (*b.* 1860/61), a daughter of Jacob Silbermann of Eperjes (Presov), Slovakia, and sister of Abraham Silbermann, translator and publisher of London. They had six children: four sons and two daughters. The eldest child, Lolla, was born in Mannheim and the rest in Ungarisch-Brod. Two of the sons, Professor Moses Jung (1891–1960) and Rabbi Leo Jung (1892–1987), emigrated to the United States where they both became leading figures in Jewish education, the elder as an academic, eventually professor of comparative religion at Columbia University, New York, and the younger as a congregational rabbi. A third brother, Julius Jung (1894–1975), remained in London; following in his father's footsteps, albeit in a lay capacity, in 1925 he became secretary, and in due course executive director, of the Federation of Synagogues (1952–9). In 1914 Rabbi Jung set up a branch of the non-Zionist Orthodox political party Agudat Yisrael in the East End and invited a number of Hasidic leaders to join, his Cracow experience notwithstanding. When the Aguda was revived after the First World War, he served as secretary of the London branch in 1920–21.

Jung's wife died on 30 January 1915. He married Regina Silbermann (*b.* 1870/71), his late wife's sister, on 13 April 1921, only weeks before his death. This took place on 10 June 1921 in 'tragic circumstances' in his bathroom at home at 14 Bancroft Road, Mile End. An inquest recorded a verdict of 'accidental death' caused by 'bronchial pneumonia accelerated by coal-gas poisoning': there had been a gas leak. He was buried on 14 June at the Federation Jewish cemetery, Edmonton, Middlesex.

SHARMAN KADISH

Sources *Jewish Chronicle* (31 May 1912) · *Jewish Chronicle* (17 June 1921) · *Jewish Chronicle* (21 Oct 1960) [Moses Jung] · *Jewish Year Book* · S. Wininger, ed., *Grosse jüdische National-Biographie*, 3 (1928), 359 · G. Bader and M. Jung, 'Meir Tsevi Jung', *Jewish leaders*, ed. L. Jung (1953), 295–316 · J. Jung, *Champions of orthodoxy* (1974), 180–253 · G. Alderman, *The Federation of Synagogues* (1987), 46–50 · B. Homa, *Orthodoxy in Anglo-Jewry, 1880–1940* (1969), 43 · H. Rabinowicz, *A world apart: the story of the Chasidim in Britain* (1997), 35 · C. Roth, *The Federation of Synagogues: a record of twenty-five years, 1912 to 1937* (1937), 11–12 · private information (2004) [M. Z. Jung, grandson] · d. cert. [Ernestine Jung] · m. cert. [Regina Jung and Meir Jung]
Archives U. Southampton, Julius Jung papers, MS 167
Likenesses photograph, repro. in Alderman, *Federation* · photographs, repro. in Jung, *Champions*

Junge, Alfred August (1886–1964), film production designer, was born on 29 January 1886, in Görlitz, Silesia, the only child of August Junge (d. 1897), a house painter, and his wife, Emma Hulda (1858–1943), a seamstress. When he was eleven his father died, and at fourteen he left school to be apprenticed to a local house painter. While attending evening classes he found he had a talent for design and two years later he joined an art club, where he studied life drawing. Stagestruck, at the age of eighteen he started working at the local Görlitz Stadttheater, trying his hand at everything from acting to special lighting effects. After further art studies in Germany and Italy he began to work as a scenic artist and designer at various provincial theatres in Germany and Switzerland, finally ending up with the Berlin Staatsoper and the Berlin Staatstheater, until the First World War intervened. Junge served in the German army until he was invalided out in 1917. On 13 November 1918 he married Elsbeth (Else) Gebhardt (1886–1964), the daughter of a cabinet-maker from Frankfurt an der Oder, whom he had met when she was a flower girl in Berlin in 1912. The couple settled in an apartment on Bismarckstrasse in Berlin-Hermsdorf, their home until 1932. By 1922 they had two sons, Helmut (1921–1989), who became an architect in America, and Ewald (1922–2000), who had a varied career, encompassing arts journalism (including work in the 1950s for the BBC German Service and as an arts correspondent for *The Times*), classical music recording, and numismatics.

About 1920 Junge entered the film industry, working as an art director at the famous UFA studios in Berlin alongside some of the leading creative talents of the era, notably director E. A. Dupont. After the great success of *Variété* in 1926, Dupont was courted by British International Pictures (BIP), and in 1928 Junge accompanied him to Elstree, where he designed two elaborate Dupont productions, *Moulin Rouge* and *Piccadilly*. The team remained at BIP until 1930. Junge then returned briefly to Germany, with a stopover in France to work on Alexander Korda's *Marius* (1931), the first film of the classic Marcel Pagnol trilogy. But it was England that was to be Junge's home base for the rest of

Alfred August Junge (1886–1964), by unknown photographer, 1951

his career. In 1932, on the strength of his experience at UFA and his much-admired work at BIP, he was brought to England once again, by producer Michael Balcon, on a five-year contract to head the new Gaumont-British art department at the Lime Grove studio in Shepherd's Bush in west London, where he was immediately put in charge of designing an ambitious Hollywood-style production programme. At Gaumont-British, Junge really came into his own with his invaluable organizational skills, Prussian sense of discipline and efficiency, and technical expertise, overseeing an extensive production schedule and deploying a whole army of draughtsmen and technicians. Junge was almost single-handedly responsible for bringing professional management and modern organization to British cinema design and he also supervised the studio's pioneering design apprenticeship programme, training and influencing many of Britain's future top film designers, including Michael Relph, Peter Proud, and Elliot Scott.

As Britain's first real supervising art director or 'production designer', as the role came to be described, Junge worked on an amazing range and number of films during his six years at Shepherd's Bush: Jessie Matthews musicals such as *Evergreen* (1934) and *It's Love Again* (1936), George Arliss character vehicles such as *The Iron Duke* (1935), Aldwych farces, Jack Hulbert comedies, and classic Hitchcock thrillers such as *The Man Who Knew Too Much* (1935) and *Young and Innocent* (1937). After his stint at Gaumont-British, Junge was summoned to be supervising art director for MGM's new British operations at Denham, where he created the quaint English public school atmosphere of the nostalgic *Goodbye, Mr Chips* (1939).

During the 1940 invasion scare Junge was sent as an enemy alien to Huyton near Liverpool, where he was interned from May to July 1940. (Junge had applied for British citizenship in 1938, but had to wait to become a British citizen until just after the end of the Second World War.) He was soon released and back at work, this time with visionary director Michael Powell, who naturally turned to Junge to head the art department for the new production unit, the Archers, that he was assembling with Emeric Pressburger at Denham. Junge rose magnificently to the challenge of their first Technicolor production, the beautifully crafted *The Life and Death of Colonel Blimp* (1943). The Powell–Pressburger films, among the most memorable of the 1940s, marked an outpouring of Junge's creative spirit. The poetic and quirky *A Canterbury Tale* (1944) was followed by the Scottish romance *I Know Where I'm Going!* (1945; Junge's own personal favourite, shot partly on the Isle of Mull), and the striking fantasy, set during the war, *A Matter of Life and Death* (1946), with its monumental 'stairway to heaven' and its inspired artistic conceit of a black and white heaven contrasting with the earthly pleasures of Technicolor. Junge's rich use of colour reached its height in the extravagant exoticism of *Black Narcissus* (1947), which won him an Academy award for design and the personal accolade of an autographed photo from its star, Deborah Kerr, inscribed 'To Alfred Junge, of all art directors the most brilliant'.

Junge was in great demand after his Oscar, and MGM, which was resuming its British operations at Borehamwood, Elstree, made him the enticing offer of a lucrative seven-year contract as supervising art director. He accepted, heading the MGM British art department from 1947 to 1955, realizing a series of historical spectacles (*Ivanhoe*, 1952; *Knights of the Round Table*, 1953) in the colour and widescreen processes of the 1950s, as well as working with a variety of Hollywood stalwarts such as John Ford (*Mogambo*, 1953) and George Cukor (*Edward, my Son*, 1949). By now himself a legend in the British film industry, Junge belonged to several professional organizations, notably the Society of British Film Art Directors and Designers (of which he was a founder member), the British Film Academy, and the British Kinematograph Society, and he published articles about film design in the British journals *The Artist*, *Film & TV Technician*, and *British Kinematography*. After his MGM contract expired Junge went freelance. His last film work was helping to select Italian locations for David O. Selznick's *A Farewell to Arms*; he left early into this fraught production, exasperated by Selznick's incessant memo-writing.

Junge retired in 1957, at the age of seventy-one. Very much a family man, he spent his final years pursuing his main hobbies, photography and gardening. In 1948, with the money from his MGM contract, he had bought a magnificent rambling house designed by Giles Gilbert Scott, Greystanes, on a hilltop in Hendon, in north London. After his retirement Junge built a smaller house, Sunset Lodge, on a small parcel of his former domain, where he tended a lovely rose garden. But the golden years at Sunset Lodge proved to be short. A longtime sufferer from diabetes, the portly Junge also began to have heart problems. A first stroke in 1962 was followed by another in early 1964, and Junge went to a clinic at Bad Kissingen, West Germany, to recover. He died there suddenly of a stroke on 16 July 1964, less than six weeks after the death of his beloved wife, Else, in Hendon; both were cremated and were buried at Paddington new cemetery, Mill Hill, Middlesex. At his death Junge left more than 1000 set designs, mainly from his British period. These form the basis of four major Junge collections now in public archives at the British Film Institute, London; the Cinémathèque Française, Paris; the Stiftung Deutsche Kinemathek, Berlin; and the Harry Ransom Humanities Research Center, at the University of Texas at Austin, USA.

CATHERINE A. SUROWIEC

Sources private information (2004) [Ewald Junge, son] · C. A. Surowiec, *Accent on design: four European art directors* (1992) · E. Carrick, *Art and design in the British film* (1948) · *CGPLA Eng. & Wales* (1965)
Archives BFI, corresp. and papers relating to Academy award for *Black Narcissus* · BFI, collection · Cinémathèque Française, Paris, collection · Ransom HRC, designs and photos · Stiftung Deutsche Kinemathek, Berlin, set designs | FILM BFI NFTVA, performance footage
Likenesses photograph, 1951, BFI [*see illus.*] · photographs, BFI
Wealth at death £60,554: administration with will, 12 Feb 1965, *CGPLA Eng. & Wales*

Junius (*fl.* 1768–1773), political writer, was the pseudonym adopted by the author (or possibly authors) of a series of letters which appeared once or twice monthly (sometimes more often) in the *Public Advertiser*, a leading London newspaper owned by Henry Sampson *Woodfall, between 21 January 1769 and 21 January 1772. In this series Junius—named after the popular republican hero Lucius Junius Brutus—opposed the policies of George III and the administrations of the serving prime ministers, the duke of Grafton and Lord North. Now a classic of English political commentary, the correspondence owes its influence to three interrelated factors: the high whig philosophy espoused to attack tory policies and celebrated political personalities; the literary power of the letters, one of the most effective uses of slanderous polemic ever employed in English political controversy; and, finally, the uncertainty surrounding their authorship.

In the complex political context of the period Junius was, in principle, a supporter of the former prime minister, George Grenville. On all public questions Junius positioned himself on the popular side, supporting the radical politician John Wilkes and the right of constituencies to elect to parliament anyone who had not previously been disqualified. (Junius's name had earlier appeared on a letter printed in the *Public Advertiser* in defence of Wilkes on 21 November 1768, though this was not one he included in the collected edition of March 1772; Junius and Wilkes also conducted a private correspondence in the late summer and autumn of 1771.) Junius was equally critical of the overgrown privileges of parliament under which arbitrary imprisonment of a citizen might occur without appeal or redress. He vigorously supported the right of the press to report parliamentary business, in addition to the unrestricted right to petition the crown and the inviolability of private papers against arbitrary search in cases of libel. He argued for citizens to have their property undisturbed by interested and obsolete claims of the crown, to tell their rulers of their duties and liberties, and to threaten them if these freedoms were challenged. While accepting that parliament had the abstract or theoretical right to tax the colonies, Junius believed that this so-called right would never be exercised. The letters themselves provide no clear reason for Junius's conclusion of the series in January 1772, though private correspondence with Woodfall in the following year suggests his diminishing faith in the power of his attacks and declining public interest. Though the quality of the later letters is often considered less effective than the early campaign, the dominant tone of the series identifies Junius as a highly opinionated, shrewd, ironic, vituperative, even arrogant individual schooled in classics and the law.

The letters proved an enormous success and were reprinted in other London newspapers, in weeklies, magazines, and pamphlets, and in the provincial and colonial press. The circulation of Woodfall's *Public Advertiser*, typically about 3000 copies daily, grew considerably as a result, with particularly substantial sales for specific letters (1750 extra copies, for example, were printed of the issue containing Junius's letter to George III of 19 December 1769 in which he warns the king that as the crown 'was acquired by one revolution, it may be lost by another'). Such comments prompted reviews from leading political observers both shocked at the tone and impressed by the power of the letters. 'How comes this Junius', Edmund Burke asked the Commons on 27 November 1770,

> to have broke through the cobwebs of the law, and to range uncontrolled, unpunished, through the land? … No sooner has he wounded one than he lays down another dead at his feet. For my part, when I saw his attack on the King, I own my blood ran cold … King, Lords and Commons are but the sport of his fury.   (*Parl. hist.*, 16.1154)

Lord North in reply spoke of 'this mighty Junius' as 'the great boar of the wood', while the tory Samuel Johnson maintained, with an abusiveness second only to that of Junius himself, that 'he cries *havock* without reserve, and endeavours to let slip the dogs of foreign and civil war, ignorant whither they are going, and careless what may be their prey' (Johnson, *Thoughts on the Late Transactions Respecting Falkland Islands*, 1771, in the *Yale Edition of the Works of Samuel Johnson*, ed. D. Green, 1958–90, 10.376).

Junius's concern over the effects of unauthorized collections prompted the publication of his own edition of his letters as the *Letters of Junius* (3 March 1772) which, printed by Henry Sampson Woodfall, superseded twenty-eight partial and unauthorized volumes. In addition to a preface and a 'Dedication to the English nation', this edition included forty-two letters signed by Junius, sixteen by Junius but signed 'Philo Junius', three unsigned letters, and eight replies, five of them from Sir William Draper,

whom Junius had mercilessly attacked in the correspondence, and three from the Revd John Horne Tooke, who had been accused of covert work for the government.

Following Woodfall's death in 1805, his son George Woodfall resolved to publish a new and more complete edition comprising the letters of the original 1772 edition together with further 'miscellaneous letters' by Junius from the *Public Advertiser* (many of which are believed not to be genuine), and Junius's private correspondence with Henry Sampson Woodfall and John Wilkes. This edition, which appeared in 1812, was edited by John Mason Good, who added numerous notes and a 'preliminary essay'; usually referred to as 'Woodfall's edition', it is often confused with that of the elder Woodfall. In 1850 the publisher Henry George Bohn undertook publication of a new edition, *Junius: Including Letters by the same Author under other Signatures*, based largely on the 1812 volume and edited by John Wade. The two-volume Bohn edition, part of Bohn's Standard Library, was reprinted without change well into the twentieth century and, on account of its easy availability, became the standard edition despite its many deficiencies. The most recent and authoritative collection is John Cannon's 1978 edition published by Oxford University Press.

Common to successive editors and reviewers has been a fascination with Junius's true identity. The mystery of authorship was established in the dedication to the 1772 edition. Adopting the motto *Stat nominis umbra* (taken from Lucan, *Pharsalia*, 1.135: 'stat magni nominis umbra', 'he stands the shadow of a great name'), Junius maintained that 'I am the sole depository of my own secret, and it shall perish with me.' Few questions in literary or political history have given rise to so much debate as Junius's identity. In over two centuries some sixty candidates have been proposed, including persons eminent and obscure, those with views similar and antithetical to Junius's and those whom he favoured or attacked in his correspondence. Speculation began soon after the appearance of the first letter and included, among others, William Petty, second earl of Shelburne (later marquess of Lansdowne), and his political allies Isaac Barré, John Dunning, first Baron Ashburton, and William Greatrakes; Richard Grenville (later Grenville-Temple), second Earl Temple, and his brothers George Grenville and James; Lord George Sackville; Hugh Macaulay Boyd (who was connected with the letters only after his death in 1794); Philip Dormer Stanhope, fourth earl of Chesterfield; Edward Gibbon; Edmund Burke; the poet Richard Glover; Horace Walpole; Lauchlin Macleane (*c*.1728–1778); and Sir Philip *Francis (see Cannon's edition of the letters, 540, for a more complete list).

The 'Franciscan theory', proposing Francis as Junius, originated with John Taylor in his *A Discovery of the Author of the Letters of Junius* (1813), which identified Sir Philip and his father the Revd Philip Francis as the authors. In 1816 Taylor attributed the letters to the younger Francis alone in his *The identity of Junius with a distinguished living character [Sir Philip Francis] established* (2nd edn, corrected and enlarged, 1818), followed a year later by his *A Supplement to*

Junius Identified. Taylor's scholarship gave the Franciscan theory a special significance but it would not have achieved any special status (as against that of other claimants) had it not been for the attention of Thomas Babington Macaulay, whose widely read and much reprinted essay on Warren Hastings (originally in *Edinburgh Review*, 74, 1841, 227–41) elucidated 'five marks' in favour of Francis's claim to the Junian authorship.

None the less several contemporaries, including Abraham Hayward and Charles Wentworth Dilke, rejected any connection between Francis and Junius. Dilke, the doyen of Junian scholars, achieved a knowledge of the subject subsequently unsurpassed in his efforts to disprove the authorship not only of Francis but also of Isaac Barré. A series of essays by William Fraser Rae in *The Athenaeum* of 1888 further distanced Francis and others from Junius while failing to provide a credible candidate in their place. Even so, the second half of twentieth century saw a renewed confidence, based on Alvar Ellegård's *A Statistical Method for Determining Authorship: the Junius Letters* (1962) and John Cannon's 1978 edition for Oxford University Press, that Francis was indeed the most likely author. Cannon's argument draws attention to the parallels between Francis's and Junius's political views, frequent references in the letters to the War Office (Francis's workplace), and close commentaries on Lords debates at which Francis was present. Corroborative evidence includes the connection between the dates of Junius's private letters to Henry Sampson Woodfall and the times when Francis was in and out of the country, Francis's proximity to London, and similarities (albeit inconclusive) between Francis's and Junius's handwriting. Needless to say, while the Franciscan theory has recently enjoyed new life, it remains contested and impossible to demonstrate categorically.

In the light of this ongoing if now perhaps less heated debate, the comments of two leading nineteenth-century Junians are of continued relevance. Thus Charles Wentworth Dilke cautioned scholars 'never to believe a Junius "rumour"', never to believe any story of or concerning Junius, no matter how confidently or circumstantially told, which is not proved (Dilke, 2.176), while for Abraham Hayward, 'The Junius secret [like buried treasure] … lies in the search, in the industry it stimulates, in the discriminating spirit of inquiry it promotes, in the biographical and historical harvest for which it prepares the ground' (A. Hayward, *More about Junius: the Franciscan Theory Unsound*, 1868, 1). FRANCESCO CORDASCO

Sources F. Cordasco and G. Simonson, *Junius and his works: a history of the letters of Junius and the authorship controversy* (1986) • F. Cordasco, *Junius: a bibliography of the 'Letters of Junius' with a checklist of Junian scholarship and related studies* (Fairview, N.J., 1986) • *The letters of Junius*, ed. J. Cannon (1978) • C. W. Dilke, ed., *The papers of a critic: selected writings by Charles Wentworth Dilke*, 2 vols. (1875) • A. Ellegård, *Who was Junius?* (1962) • J. Maclean, *Reward is secondary: the life of a political adventurer and an inquiry into the mystery of 'Junius'* (1963) • A. Hayward, *Biographical and critical essays*, new ser., 2nd edn, 2 vols. (1873) • J. Parkes and H. Merivale, *Memoirs of Sir Philip Francis*, 2 vols. (1867) • T. H. Bowyer, *A bibliographical examination of the earliest editions of the 'Letters of Junius'* (1957) • C. Chabot, *The handwriting of Junius professionally investigated* (1871) • *The Grenville papers: being the correspondence of Richard Grenville … and … George Grenville*, ed. W. J. Smith, 4 vols. (1852–3) • W. F. Rae, 'Sir Philip Francis', *Temple Bar*, 87 (1889), 171–91 • J. T. Boulton, *The language of politics in the age of Wilkes and Burke* (1963)

Archives BL, private letters to H. S. Woodfall, Add. MS 22774 • PRO, letters to Lord Chatham, PRO 30/8/3 pt 2, fols. 357–8; PRO 30/8/4 pt 1, fols. 136–7

Junius [Du Jon], **Franciscus** [Francis] (**1591–1677**), philologist and writer on art, was born at Heidelberg, Germany, on 29 January 1591, the youngest of the five children of Franciscus Junius (or Du Jon; 1545–1602), a French nobleman and protestant theologian, and his third wife, Joanna (d. 1591), daughter of the Antwerp nobleman Simon l'Hermite. After the family had moved to Leiden in the Netherlands in 1592, Junius was educated with his future brother-in-law Gerard Vossius at the Dordrecht Latin school, and having matriculated at Leiden University on 23 April 1608, studied *artes* and presumably theology. This thorough philological grounding was to inspire all his future studies. In 1614 and 1615 he trained for the ministry in Middelburg, and early in 1615 visited England. Two years later, at Hugo Grotius's instigation, he was appointed minister to Hillegersberg, near Rotterdam. However, his refusal to take sides in the crisis that divided the Dutch church caused him to resign the ministry in the spring of 1619.

After a ten-month stay in Paris, in May 1621 Junius crossed the channel. For the next twenty years he made England his home and forged friendships with such scholars as John Selden, Patrick Young, William Oughtred, and Matthew Wren. With Bishop Lancelot Andrewes's help he entered the service of the notable art collector Thomas Howard, earl of Arundel, as tutor to his son William, to his grandchildren, and to his protégé Aubrey de Vere, earl of Oxford, for whom in 1644 Junius composed an admonition to virtuous conduct (1654). References to Junius's librarianship to Arundel only date from 1639. At his patron's behest, Junius compiled an encyclopaedia of artists and artefacts from classical quotations, which was eventually published by Johannes Graevius (1694). His extensive research also resulted in the unprecedented art theory *De pictura veterum* (1637), which he dedicated to Charles I. Moulded from quotations, it was concurrently a philological treatise about classical conceptions of art, an art history, defence of art, and instruction for artists. His friends Peter Paul Rubens and Anthony Van Dyck acclaimed it highly. He himself translated it into English (1638) and Dutch (1641). A bookish person, who nevertheless enjoyed a lifestyle which relieved scholarship with pastimes, Junius preferred to pursue his studies than to accede to Arundel's wish that he search the Mediterranean for antiquities.

Accompanying Oxford and the Arundel family to the Netherlands in the spring of 1642, Junius stayed there for most of the next thirty-three years. From the mid-1640s, when aged about fifty-five, Junius began to study the northern languages with a mind to revealing the origin of Dutch. His working knowledge of the older stages of the Germanic languages became unrivalled. By 1654 his acquaintance with Gothic led him to view the Germanic languages as a separate family and to study them from a comparative perspective. Principally an etymologist and lexicographer, however, Junius never attempted to formulate paradigms. A substantial component of his studies consisted in his collecting data from sources found in Friesland in 1646–7, in England between 1647/8 and 1651 and on repeated visits there between 1652 and 1659, in Heidelberg in 1653, and at home in the rich library of his nephew Isaac *Vossius. In England he made transcriptions from Old English manuscripts of the Cottonian library and from the Rushworth gospels, and co-operated with Sir Simonds D'Ewes and William Somner. Junius's diverse philological projects include annotations on Williram's Old High German paraphrase of the Song of Solomon (1655), a transcript of the Old English 'Boethius' (published by Christopher Rawlinson in 1698), a comprehensive Latin–Old English glossary (on which Edward Lye based *Dictionarium Saxonico* (1772), without acknowledgement), a new glossary on Chaucer, and various glossaries of Old Germanic languages, which, however, suffer from repetitions. Junius initiated the study of Gothic with the *editio princeps* of the Gothic gospels and an accompanying detailed dictionary (1664/5), for which Thomas Marshall produced the commentary. He excused his work on an English etymological dictionary to Sir William Dugdale as 'a wilde and flying fancy proceeding out of my good wishes towards a countrie and language I have bene conversant with the greater part of my life' (*Life … of Sir William Dugdale*, 356). His monumental work was finally published as *Etymologicum Anglicanum* (1743) by Lye.

In the 1650s Junius was based with his sister Elizabeth, Vossius's widow, first in Amsterdam and then at The Hague. From 1663 to 1666 he lived in Dordrecht, but then returned to The Hague, to live with his nephew Isaac Vossius. In 1675 his studies took him again to London, and towards the end of 1676 he settled, close to Thomas Marshall, in Oxford, where his presence stimulated comparative Old Germanic studies. He died of a fever on 19 November 1677 in Windsor at the house of his nephew Isaac, who had become canon there, and was buried in St George's Chapel, Windsor. A tablet was provided by Oxford University. While he divided much of his property between his nieces and nephews including Isaac Vossius, Junius bequeathed to Oxford his books and manuscripts pertaining to Germanic studies, and the types, punches, and matrices he had had made for the printing of early Germanic languages. His collection has proven a treasure trove to students of Germanic languages ever since. It includes important texts such as the *Ormulum* and the 'Caedmon' poems, which Junius had received from James Ussher and was the first to edit (1655), initiating the traditional attribution of these texts to Caedmon. Another part of his library became fused with Isaac's and remained in Leiden.

A modest, amiable bachelor, 'dressed in granito with silver trimmings, at his side a precious poniard that formerly belonged to the old earl of Essex' (Bodl. Oxf., MS Rawlinson letters 84b, fol. 117), Junius dedicated his life to the Muses, reportedly rising each day at four to work at several lecterns simultaneously until eight at night, only interrupted by a break for lunch and walking exercises from noon until three (Graevius). In his convictions he followed his father's eirenicism, which allowed him to feel at home in puritan and Roman Catholic environments alike. William Nicolson remembered him as 'very kind and communicative, very good, and very old' (*Letters on Various Subjects*, 1.105).

SOPHIE VAN ROMBURGH

Sources S. van Romburgh, ed., *'For my worthy freind Mr Franciscus Junius': an edition of the complete correspondence of Francis Junius F. F. (1591–1677)* [forthcoming] · F. Junius, *The painting of the ancients: 'De pictura veterum' according to the English translation (1638)* (1991), vol. 1 of *Franciscus Junius: the literature of classical art*, ed. K. Aldrich, P. Fehl, and R. Fehl · F. Junius, *De pictura veterum libri tres: livre 1*, ed. and trans. C. Nativel (Geneva, 1996) · P. H. Breuker, 'On the course of Franciscus Junius's Germanic studies, with special reference to Frisian', *Franciscus Junius F. F. and his circle*, ed. R. H. Bremmer (1998), 129–57 · R. H. Bremmer, ed., *Franciscus Junius F. F. and his circle* (1998) · K. Dekker, *The origins of Old Germanic studies in the Low Countries* (1999) · J. G. Graevius, 'Vita Francisci Iunii F. F.', *F. Junius: De pictura veterum … accedit catalogus artificum* (1694), xv–xix · *The life, diary, and correspondence of Sir William Dugdale*, ed. W. Hamper (1827) · *Letters on various subjects … to and from W. Nicolson*, ed. J. Nichols, 2 vols. (1809) · J. Vossius to G. Vossius, 1628, Bodl. Oxf., MS Rawl. letters 84b, fol. 117 · *DNB* · *A lexicon of artists and their works: 'Catalogus architectorum' … translated from the original Latin of 1694* (1991), vol. 2 of *Franciscus Junius: the literature of classical art*, ed. K. Aldrich, P. Fehl, and R. Fehl · letters to Gerard Vossius, Bodl. Oxf., MS Rawl. letters 79, 84

Archives BL, corresp., Hl 4935 · BL, corresp., Hl 7011, 7012 · BL, corresp., Bcern 36g. · Bodl. Oxf., corresp., collections, and papers · Harvard U., Houghton L., copies of antiquarian notes · Nationaal Archief, The Hague, corresp. · University of Amsterdam Library, corresp. · University of Leiden, book collection, corresp. | BL, letters to Gerard Vossius, Add. MS 34727 · Bodl. Oxf., letters to Thomas Marshall, MS Marshall 134 · Bodl. Oxf., letters to Gerard Vossius, MS Rawl. letters 79, 84 · LPL, MS 783

Likenesses group portrait, oils, c.1639 (after A. Van Dyck), Knole, Kent · A. Van Dyck, oil on wood, 1640, Bodl. Oxf.; repro. in www.rsl.ox.ac.uk/imacat/img 0022.jpg · P. van Gunst, line engraving, 1694 (after Van der Werff), BM; repro. in F. Junius, *De pictura veterum libri tres* (Rotterdam, 1694) · A. van der Werff, etching, 1694 (after Hollar), repro. in F. Junius, *De pictura veterum libri tres* (Rotterdam, 1694) · M. Burghers, etching, 1698 (after Van Dyck), repro. in Boethius, *An. Manl. Sever. Boethi Consolationis philosophiae libri V*, ed. and trans. C. Rawlinson (1698) · G. Vertue, etching, 1743 (after Van Dyck), repro. in F. Junius, *Etymologicum Anglicanum*, ed. E. Lye (1743) · W. Hollar, etching (after Van Dyck), BM, NPG; repro. in F. Junius, *De Schilder-konst der oude* (1641) · W. Hollar, etching (after Van Dyck), repro. in F. Junius, *De Schilder-konst der oude* (1659)

Junius, Hadrianus [Adriaen de Jonghe] (1511–1575), physician and historian, was born on 1 July 1511 at Hoorn, Netherlands, the son of Petrus Junius (Pieter de Jonghe; d. 1537), scholar and burgomaster of Hoorn, and Marij Dircx. Junius, whom Justus Lipsius thought the most erudite Dutchman since Erasmus, studied at the Latin school at Haarlem and Louvain University before graduating in philosophy and medicine at the University of Bologna in 1540. There he became acquainted with the count of Pepoli and Andrea Alciato. After spending two years in Paris, he settled in England in early 1544, thanks to Edmund Bonner, the later bishop of London. He earned his living as a private physician to the Howard family in Norfolk and also served as a tutor to the children of Henry Howard, earl of Surrey, who became an intimate friend.

When Henry Howard was executed in 1547, Junius lost his job and library. He found a post as personal physician of a lady in Bridewell, London. When, hoping for patronage, he dedicated his *Lexicon Graecolatinum* (1548) to the young King Edward as *fidei defensor*, all his works were put on the papal index. The commission removed his name from the index only in 1569, after Junius had written a letter of defence to the pope himself on the advice of his friend Benito Arias Montano.

In 1550 Junius was back in the Low Countries. At the end of that year he bought a house in Haarlem, where he worked successfully as a town physician, but less successfully as rector of the Latin school (1550–52). He married Maria Wilhelmina Keizers after 1554. After Maria's death he married Hadriana Simonsdochter Hasselaer, a sister of the famous Kenau Simonsdochter Hasselaer. Junius became acquainted with the poet and engraver Dirck Volkertszoon, Coornhert, the painter Maarten van Heemskerck, and the engraver and print publisher Philips Galle, who engraved his portrait for publication. Junius provided numerous Latin verses which were engraved on biblical, allegorical, and mythological prints after the design of Maarten van Heemskerck. This was also a prolific period for his scientific work. In 1565 Plantin published his *Emblemata*; the woodcuts were made after the designs of Geofroy Ballain and Pieter Huys. Emblems, which consisted of a motto, a picture, and a subscript that together conveyed the meaning of the whole, became the rage in the sixteenth century. The author of the first English emblem book, Geoffrey Whitney, would borrow twenty of Junius's emblems for his own *A Choice of Emblems* (1586). Among Junius's other important works from that period—in addition to his many editions of and commentaries on a variety of classical writers (including Horace, Plutarch, Seneca, Juvenal, and Martial)—are the *Adagiorum ab Erasmo omissorum centuria octo* (1565) and the *Nomenclator* (1567). In the meantime Junius had not forgotten England. He wrote a long poem celebrating the wedding of Mary Tudor and Philip II, *Philippeis* (1554), and crossed to London to present it to the court, but was disappointed with its reception. Nevertheless he dedicated his *De anno & mensibus commentarius* (1556) to Queen Mary.

In April 1564 Junius accepted in Copenhagen the appointment as physician to the Danish king Frederick II and to a chair of medicine at the university. He unexpectedly left Denmark only a few weeks later, because he did not receive his promised pay and did not like the country at all, according to his letters. Shortly afterwards he got a better offer: in September 1565 the states of Holland appointed him as their official historiographer. From that year he worked on his *magnum opus*, the *Batavia*, the first history of Holland, in which he tried to give the northern Netherlands a national image and a history of its own. He therefore attributed the invention of typography to his fellow-townsman Lourens Janszoon Koster. Being familiar with the visual arts, he also mentioned several contemporary Dutch painters and engravers. The *Batavia* was completed at the end of 1569, and dedicated to the states of Holland. The book was not published until 1588, posthumously.

Junius visited London again in 1568. Having dedicated his *Eunapius Sardianus* (1568) to Queen Elizabeth I (an English translation was published in 1579), he tried once more—in vain—to offer his services as a teacher to the Howard family in Norfolk. Junius's friends and acquaintances in England also included Walter Haddon, Nicholas Wotton, William Cecil, and Daniel Rogers. In February 1573 he was summoned to treat Prince William at Delft and stayed in his service until 1574. During the capture of Haarlem by the Spaniards his library was sacked. He died in Arnemuiden on 16 June 1575, and was officially buried in Middelburg four years later.   ILJA M. VELDMAN

Sources T. Velius, *Chroniik van Hoorn*, 4 (1617), 294–97 • H. Junius, *Epistolae* (1652) • P. Scheltema, *Diatribe in Hadriani Junii, vitam, ingenium, familiam, merita literaria* (1836) • P. Scheltema, 'Het leven van Hadrianus Junius', *Oud en Nieuw uit de Vaderlandse Geschiedenis en Letterkunde*, 1 (1844), 133–75 • I. M. Veldman, 'Enkele aanvullende gegevens omtrent de biografie van Hadrianus Junius', *Bijdragen en Mededelingen Betreffende de Geschiedenis der Nederlanden*, 89 (1974), 375–84 • M. Aston, *The king's bedpost: reformation and iconography in a Tudor group portrait* (1993), 176–99 • I. M. Veldman, *Maarten van Heemskerck and Dutch humanism of the sixteenth century* (1977), 97–112 • D. Gordon, 'Veritas filia temporis: Hadrianus Junius and Geoffrey Whitney', *Journal of the Warburg and Courtauld Institutes*, 3 (1939–40), 228–40 • J. A. van Dorsten, *The radical arts: first decade of an Elizabethan renaissance* (1973), 131–4
Likenesses P. Galle, engraving, 1562, Municipal Archives, Haarlem

Junor, Sir John Donald Brown (1919–1997), journalist, was born on 15 January 1919 at 12 Shannon Street, Glasgow, the youngest of the three sons of Alexander Junor, iron roofer (later a foreman, and later still manager of a steel constructors), and his wife, Margaret, *née* Dickie. His father came originally from Ross and Cromarty and was largely deaf, the result not of any single accident but of his working conditions. His mother was the force in the family and was addicted to whist: hence the title of Junor's memoirs *Listening for a Midnight Tram* (1990), which referred to the little boy waiting for his mother to return late from a whist drive across the city. She was determined that all her sons should go to university, as they did.

Beginnings in politics and journalism After North Kelvinside secondary school, Junor was admitted to Glasgow University at seventeen to read English literature. There in 1938 he became president of the university Liberal club. In this capacity he was invited, with the president of the Edinburgh University Liberal Club, to help the newly selected candidate for Orkney and Shetland during the summer vacation. The candidate was Lady Glen-Coats, of the Coats cotton family (also the providers of the wealth of Lord Clark and his son Alan). In June 1939 she invited Junor to become her private secretary until October at £4 a week with a car. He accepted and they toured Europe (including Germany), only just managing to return safely to the United Kingdom before the outbreak of war.

Junor joined the Royal Naval Reserve in 1939 as a midshipman on HMS *Canton*, a newly converted P. & O. liner which patrolled the Denmark Strait. From there he joined the Fleet Air Arm, where he became a lieutenant. Later in life he admitted he had not been a natural pilot and had often been frightened. In 1944 he suggested to his station commander that it might be a good idea to have a station magazine. The captain concurred; a magazine was produced under Junor's auspices; and a copy was dispatched to the Admiralty in London. By coincidence the commander of the Fleet Air Arm was then planning a magazine for that entire branch of the service. He had already invited A. P. Herbert (independent MP for Oxford University) to become editor. Herbert then decided he did not want the job after all. So Junor (who was to have been his assistant) became editor of the magazine, which he named *Flight Deck*. It was, by all accounts, a success. While he was still editing *Flight Deck* he became a London sub-editor for the news agency Australia Associated Press, where his task was to condense stories from the British press and transmit them to Sydney. He also worked as a freelance for the *Sydney Sun*, where he remained on a full-time basis after the war had ended. Meanwhile, on 21 April 1942, he had married Pamela Mary, daughter of Squadron Leader George Hedley Welsh, RAF officer and flying instructor. They had a son, Roderick, and a daughter, Penelope (Penny), both of whom became journalists.

Junor's ambition was still to become a Liberal MP rather than a journalist. In 1945 he was invited to contest Kincardine and West Aberdeenshire. He lost to the Conservative by only 642 votes. In 1947 he fought a by-election in Edinburgh East, coming a creditable third with 3379 votes. In the general election of 1950 he wanted to fight the Labour minister John Strachey in Dundee East. But the Conservatives and the Liberals in the constituency made a pact whereby only one party was to fight Labour, and the Conservative was chosen. Junor extracted a promise that next time it would be his turn to fight. The time came sooner than expected. At the 1951 election Junor lost to Strachey by 3306. Lord Beaverbrook, proprietor of the *Daily Express*, the *Sunday Express*, and the *Evening Standard*, had already advised Junor that he would have to make a choice: 'If it is politics, you will reach the highest echelon. But if it is journalism, I will put on your head a golden crown' (Junor, *Listening for a Midnight Tram*, 54).

Beaverbrook's protégé It had taken Junor only slightly over three years to find himself confronted with this choice. In 1947 he had been sacked by the *Sydney Sun*. He was fortunate in having written beforehand to Arthur Christiansen, editor of the *Daily Express*; more fortunate still that Christiansen saw him, liked him, and offered him a job as a reporter at 18 guineas a week, less than he had been earning with the *Sydney Sun*, but relatively good money none the less. Junor did not take to general reporting. Christiansen sensibly used him to cover by-elections on account of his interest in and experience of politics. Christiansen also introduced him to the proprietor, Lord Beaverbrook, who similarly warmed to him. Shortly afterwards, Christiansen suggested that he should write the 'Crossbencher' column in the *Sunday Express* while the joint authors (Conservative MPs Anthony Marlowe and Beverley Baxter) were away on a three-week holiday.

Christiansen always claimed that this idea was his rather than Beaverbrook's, but Junor doubted it. Both were sufficiently impressed with the result that Junor displaced the previous authors. He certainly made the column a livelier production than it had been for the previous few years. 'To write "Crossbencher",' he remarked later, 'you've got to be a bit of a shit' (personal knowledge).

It was in his 'Crossbencher' period that Junor came to know Beaverbrook well: partly because Beaverbrook's interest in contemporary politics and in the *Sunday Express*'s political column was greater in the 1940s and 1950s than it was subsequently, but mainly because Junor and his young family were given the occupancy of a cottage on Beaverbrook's estate at Cherkley, Surrey. (He moved later to a more commodious farmhouse, Wellpools Farm, Charlwood, near Dorking. Despite a sentimental regard for his native land, Junor remained resolutely a man of Surrey for the whole of his long working life.) While at Cherkley he went for walks with Beaverbrook and attended Sunday luncheons when there were present such figures as Brendon Bracken, Pamela Churchill (later Harriman), Michael Foot, and Patrick Hennessy. He also paid his first visit to Beaverbrook's villa at Cap d'Ail in the south of France.

In 1951 Beaverbrook asked Junor to return to the *Daily Express* as an assistant editor, mainly to stiffen the leader column. Junor agreed. In 1953–4 he was deputy editor of the *Evening Standard*. In both posts he was successful, but in neither was he wholly comfortable. The trouble was, he subsequently explained, that his time was never his own. He was always liable to be interrupted. Though he was for the whole of his life an immensely hard worker, he liked to know he had set periods when he could enjoy his favourite activities: sailing, golf, tennis (which he played less as he grew older), and, above all, lunch, usually with one of the day's leading politicians. He was on particularly good terms with Quintin Hogg (later Lord Hailsham) and R. A. Butler. He had various principles of lunching which he would adumbrate to his younger colleagues: always to choose first from the table d'hôte menu; never to order additional vegetables; above all, to have no truck with vintages and wine waiters but to order the house wine. This could be red or white, but never on any account rosé: 'Only poofs drink rosé.' 'Poofs' played a disproportionate part in Junor's demonology, though when he was editor of the *Sunday Express* he employed several homosexuals on the staff. He later claimed that he had never taken anybody on unless he liked him or (rarely) her personally.

The *Sunday Express* Beaverbrook made Junor editor of the Sunday paper in 1954. He succeeded Harold Keeble, who had done the job briefly. But his true predecessor, whom he regarded almost as a rival, was his fellow Scotsman John Gordon, who had edited the paper from 1928. Gordon wrote a curmudgeonly column called 'Current events', which was one of the most widely read features in the paper. He was provided with an office, a secretary, a Rolls-Royce, meals at the Savoy Hotel, and the service of a young reporter to investigate any stories in which he might be interested. Junor treated him distantly. Though

Gordon bore the formal title of editor-in-chief, he was allowed no say, even if he had wished to exercise it, in what went into or was kept out of the paper. But Junor made no change in Gordon's fundamental formula. The *Sunday Express* was for middle-aged or elderly readers who were conservative in their inclinations, even though they might vote Liberal or Labour. They were patriotic—Junor ran seemingly endless series of articles on British deeds of derring-do in 1939–45—but this did not mean they were uncritical admirers of the royal family, the House of Lords, and the bench of bishops: all matters on which Junor and Beaverbrook were at one. There was both a uniformity and a predictability about Junor's *Sunday Express*. As one member of his staff, Robert Pitman, remarked in the 1960s: 'Not only does John want the same feature articles week after week, but he wants the same news stories too' (personal knowledge). For a period, from the mid-1950s to the late 1960s, the formula worked. But in the end time caught up with him. Under his editorship the circulation declined from 4.5 million to 2.2 million.

Two years after becoming editor Junor found himself in conflict with the House of Commons. The occasion was the Conservative government's imposition of petrol rationing as a consequence of the Suez crisis. Under the scheme, constituency parties were to receive a generous allocation. The *Sunday Express* wrote a leader on the subject: 'Tomorrow a time of hardship starts for everyone. For everyone? Include the politicians out of that … the tanks of the politicians will be brimming over' (*Sunday Express*, 16 Dec 1956). The article was raised in the house as a contempt of parliament. The matter was referred to the committee of privileges, where Junor was examined by the attorney-general, Sir Reginald Manningham-Buller. The committee found that a contempt had indeed been committed. Junor was ordered to appear before the bar of the house on 24 January 1957. He agreed to apologize, though in his statement to the house he reiterated his opinion that 'these allowances were a proper and indeed an inescapable subject of comment in a free press'. The house agreed to take no further action. It was universally held that Junor had comported himself with distinction. Throughout the entire episode Beaverbrook did not communicate with Junor, whether in encouragement or in reproof. It is likely that Junor would not have apologized at all if he had been given the support by his proprietor to which he felt entitled.

In an era when journalists on national newspapers came and went more or less according to their inclinations, provided they completed their work satisfactorily, Junor was an exigent editor. He insisted they kept office hours: from ten to six, with a generous two hours for lunch between one and three, which was what he took himself. He could be an appalling bully with his 'executives' such as foreign, home news, features, and sports editors—sometimes, indeed, reducing them to tears—but was indulgent towards young members of the staff: the more so if he had been responsible for bringing them on to the paper in the first place. To them he would impart one or more of his numerous journalistic maxims: an ounce of emotion is worth a ton of fact; no one ever destroyed a man by sneering; always look forward, never back; everybody is interested in sex and money; when in search of a subject, turn to the royal family; it is not libellous to ask a question (a perilous maxim legally). Another Junorism was popularly supposed to be: 'Never trust a man with a beard.' What he said was: 'No first-class journalist ever has a beard.' He also said: 'No one ever has sex in the morning' (personal knowledge).

Despite or perhaps because of Junor's early familiarity with Beaverbrook, there was on both sides a certain wariness in the relationship. Junor would employ his assistant editor, Robert Pitman, to decode the strange, garbled messages that issued from Arlington House, Cherkley, the Waldorf Towers, Montego Bay, Cap d'Ail, or wherever Beaverbrook happened to be staying. But Junor was by no means an obedient follower of his proprietor's instructions. After they had been deciphered he would sometimes procrastinate or deliberately misunderstand them. In 1963 they fell out—not over any specific instruction but over support for Harold Macmillan, the Conservative prime minister. A subsidiary cause was that Junor suspected Beaverbrook of wanting Pitman to succeed Gordon when he relinquished his column. (As matters turned out, both Junor and Gordon outlived Pitman, who died in 1969.) Junor opposed Macmillan because of his handling not only of the Profumo affair (in which, owing to Beaverbrook's influence, the *Sunday Express* had been restrained, even laggardly) but also of the Vassall case in the previous year, when two journalists had gone to prison for refusing to answer questions about their sources before a tribunal of inquiry. Possessing, as he did, a highly developed sense of the dignity and importance of his own trade, Junor was thereafter determined to campaign against Macmillan. But Beaverbrook would not allow it. Moreover, it was made clear to him that, unless he supported Macmillan, he would cease to be editor. Junor chose to leave. Then followed a period of limbo when, at Beaverbrook's request, Junor remained on the premises to induct his designated successor, Arthur Brittenden—shortly replaced by Derek Marks—into the mysteries of editorship, until the resignation of Macmillan, in October 1963. Junor was then restored to the editorship. In the six months that were left to Beaverbrook, he and Junor resumed their former closeness, and dined together twice a week.

In December 1974 John Gordon died. Though Junor, knowing Gordon was ill, had made efforts to find a replacement, he had always in his heart wanted to write the column himself. So he did, under the title J. J. It was a great success, transforming Junor from a Fleet Street celebrity into a national figure. His column was determinedly illiberal, except in matters of free speech, apart from 'filth', to which he remained resolutely opposed. Two of its stock phrases became popular. One was: 'Pass the sickbag, Alice'. The other was: 'I do not know the answer to this question, but I think we should be told'. In particular, 'I think we should be told' caught on, and subsequently turned up in a variety of unlikely contexts. J. J.'s equivalent of the nineteenth century's man on the Clapham omnibus was the citizen of Auchtermuchty, a real village in Fife with which Junor had no connection and whose inhabitants had little idea of the honour that had been bestowed upon them, if honour it was. They were depicted as hostile to homosexuals, sociologists, and other inhabitants of Junor's private menagerie of modern liberal error. 'I wanted,' Junor wrote in his memoirs, 'a sort of Brigadoon place which had been bypassed by the modern world and in which old-fashioned virtues still persisted' (*Listening for a Midnight Tram*, 280). Auchtermuchty also illustrated Junor's capacity for simultaneous belief in contradictory propositions; demonstrated as much in political matters as in sexual.

After Macmillan's departure Junor certainly showed his ability to get on with, or at any rate to have lunch with, a succession of prime ministers: Alec Douglas-Home, Harold Wilson, Edward Heath, and, most productively of all, Margaret Thatcher, who was responsible for his knighthood in 1980 and to whom he was closest politically. In 1964 Beaverbrook died. After some twists and turns, in 1977 Express Newspapers fell into the hands of the Trafalgar House group. Junor got on well with the overseer of the newspaper side of the group's activities, Victor Matthews. Trafalgar, renamed Fleet, then fell victim in 1985 to United Newspapers, whose chief, David Stevens, did not attract Junor as Matthews had done, even though Stevens asked him to stay on.

Final years In 1986 Junor resigned as editor, to be replaced by Robin Esser, a former *Sunday Express* journalist of whom Junor approved, inasmuch as he could bring himself to approve of any successor. Stevens gave Junor a contract to continue as a columnist at the same salary. It was also agreed that he would move out of the *Express* building in Fleet Street to the headquarters of United Newspapers in Tudor Street. Junor liked this new arrangement. But it did not last long. After three years he resigned, following the replacement of Esser. His complaint was that he was not consulted about the succession. He took his column to the recently established *Mail on Sunday*. In 1997, still writing it, he was given the Gerald Barry award of the television programme *What the Papers say*. At the luncheon at the Savoy Hotel when it was presented to him, he complained loudly to his neighbour because he was not being honoured specifically for his column but, rather, for long service.

Junor was a tall, heavily built man, with a prominent nose, slightly protuberant light-blue eyes, and a ruddy, weather-beaten complexion. Working to the end, he died unexpectedly at Epsom General Hospital, Epsom, Surrey, on 3 May 1997, after a routine operation. He was survived by his wife, Pamela, from whom he lived separately for the last years of his life, and by their two children.

ALAN WATKINS

Sources J. Junor, *Listening for a midnight tram* (1990) · J. Junor, *The best of J. J.* (1981) · A. Watkins, 'John Junor', *Brief lives* (1982) · A. Watkins, *A short walk down Fleet Street* (2000), chap. 3 · P. Junor, *Home truths: life around my father* (2002) · *The Times* (5 May 1997) · *The Independent* (5 May 1997) · *Daily Telegraph* (5 May 1997) · *The Guardian* (5 May 1997) · *WWW* · personal knowledge (2004) · private information (2004) · b. cert. · m. cert. · d. cert.
Archives JRL, Labour History Archive and Study Centre, corresp. with William Gallacher | FILM BFI NFTVA, documentary recordings
Likenesses photograph, 1951, Hult. Arch. · photograph, 1968, repro. in *The Independent* · photograph, 1981, repro. in *Daily Telegraph* · photograph, repro. in *The Times* · photograph, repro. in *The Guardian* · photograph, repro. in *The Scotsman* (5 May 1997) · photographs, repro. in Junor, *Best of J.J.* · photographs, repro. in Junor, *Listening for a midnight tram*
Wealth at death £2,226,796: probate, 1997, CGPLA Eng. & Wales (1997)

Jupp, Edward Basil (1812–1877). *See under* Jupp, Richard (1728–1799).

Jupp, Richard (1728–1799), architect and surveyor, born in London, was the elder son of Richard Jupp (*fl. c.*1700–*c.*1770) of St John's parish, Clerkenwell, master of the Carpenters' Company in 1768, to whom he was apprenticed, and possibly Sarah Bibings (*fl. c.*1700–*c.*1734). Jupp spent some time studying abroad; the Architects' Club, of which he was one of the fifteen founders in 1791, required its members to have studied architecture in Italy or France. Appointed architect to Guy's Hospital in 1759, he supervised construction of the west wing (1774–7) and remodelled the main front (1774–8). He also designed Dyers' Hall, Dowgate Hill (1768–70, rebuilt 1839), and designed or remodelled at least four country houses, including Painshill House, Cobham, Surrey, for Benjamin Bond Hopkins (the design for which was exhibited at the Royal Academy in 1778); Wilton Park, Beaconsfield, Buckinghamshire (*c.*1790) for Josias Dupré, governor of Madras; and Park Farm Place, Eltham, for Sir William James, bt, a director of the East India Company, for whose widow he constructed a commemorative triangular Gothic tower, Severndroog Castle, Shooter's Hill, Kent (1784).

Jupp's principal employment, however, was as surveyor to the East India Company from 1768: he designed several London warehouses, starting with the Old Bengal Warehouse, New Street (1769–71), with extensions towards Cutler Street and Middlesex Street in the 1790s (largely rebuilt 1978–82). When in 1796 a greatly extended front building to East India House, Leadenhall Street, was proposed, Jupp was instructed to take the advice of leading architects, including John Soane. Fearing that the aggressive Soane would obtain the commission for himself, Jupp secured his exclusion; but in trying to dissociate himself from anonymous attacks on Soane, he succeeded only in kindling Soane's enduring hostility. However, reminding the East India directors of his long service, Jupp obtained the commission for the new building (at an estimated cost of £47,000). It was 190 feet long, with Ionic portico. Surviving drawings indicate that Jupp owed the design of the façade to Henry Holland, who carried out Jupp's designs for the interior after his death. In his last years he canvassed for election to the Royal Academy.

Jupp married Rebekah Allen (*d.* in or after 1802), to whom he left the life interest in his substantial estate, said to amount to £35,000. He died suddenly on 17 April 1799 at his house, 6 King's Road, Holborn, leaving instructions to be buried very privately at midnight in Bunhill Fields. He was buried there six days later.

His brother, **William Jupp the elder** (1734–1788), architect, born in London, was likewise apprenticed to their father. He was made free of the Carpenters' Company in 1753, and became a warden in 1781. He exhibited country house designs at the Society of Artists in 1763 and 1764, but his principal works were in the City of London. He rebuilt the London tavern, Bishopsgate Street Within (dem. 1876), after a fire in 1765, and was employed in making plans for the Carpenters' Company's Stratford estate (1769), and improvements to their London Wall property (1777 and c.1784). About 1780 he designed the entrance hall and staircase of Carpenters' Hall, London Wall (dem. 1876). He married Mary Webb (c.1745–1809) in 1765; they had five sons and five daughters. He died at his house in St Clement, Eastcheap, London, on 16 November 1788.

William Jupp's son **William Jupp the younger** (1770–1839), architect, born in the parish of St Nicholas Olave, exploited his family connections, becoming architect and surveyor to four City companies—the Skinners' (altering their hall in Dowgate Hill in 1801–3), the Merchant Taylors' (building almshouses at Lee, Kent, in 1826), the Ironmongers', and the Apothecaries'. He was also district surveyor for several East End districts. In 1821 he designed a house at Great Gains, Upminster, Essex, for the Revd John Clayton. He was master of the Carpenters' Company in 1831. About 1798 he married Matilda (*fl. c.*1780–1802), who predeceased him, leaving three daughters. He died at Upper Clapton, Middlesex, on 30 April 1839.

The elder brother of William Jupp the younger, **Richard Webb Jupp** (1767–1852), lawyer, was born on 29 July 1767 in the parish of St Nicholas Olave. He was elected clerk to the Carpenters' Company in 1798, several years after his marriage to Sarah (*d.* 1844), daughter of the Revd Morgan Jones DD, with whom he had six sons and five daughters. When he died, at home at Carpenters' Hall, London Wall, London, on 26 August 1852, he was the senior member of the corporation of London.

Richard Webb Jupp's youngest son, **Edward Basil Jupp** (1812–1877), lawyer and antiquary, was born on 1 January 1812 at Carpenters' Hall. A partner in his father's law firm, in 1843 he was associated with him as joint clerk to the Carpenters' Company, succeeding him on his death. A fellow of the Society of Antiquaries, he compiled a history of the Carpenters' Company (1848). He also collected and grangerized catalogues of English art exhibitions, publishing descriptive lists of his collections in 1866 and 1871. His notable collection of the work of Thomas Bewick was sold at Christies in February 1878. He married on 10 May 1845 Eliza Margaret, daughter of Joseph Kay, architect, with whom he had five sons and three daughters; she survived him. He died at 4 The Paragon, Blackheath, London, on 30 May 1877 after a few days' illness.   M. H. PORT

Sources C. H. L. Woodd, *Pedigrees and memorials of the family of Woodd … and of the family of Jupp, of London and Wandsworth*, London (1875) [privately printed] • will, PRO, PROB 11/1324, fol. 365 • Colvin, *Archs.* • IGI • parish register, London, St Nicholas Olave [baptism] • J. T. Squire, *Mount Nod: a burial ground of the Huguenots*
(1887) • will, PRO, PROB 11/1496, fol. 285 [Mary Jupp] • will, PRO, PROB 11/1911, fol. 303 [William Jupp the younger] • A. T. Bolton, ed., *The portrait of Sir John Soane* (1927), 59–79 • Farington, *Diary* • N. Brawer, 'The anonymous architect of the India House', *Georgian Group Journal*, 7 (1997), 26–36 • Graves, *RA exhibitors*, 4 (1906), 297 • W. Foster, *The East India House* (1924), 139–43 • will, PRO, PROB 11/2159 [Richard Webb Jupp], fol. 711 • Index of probates of wills, Family History Centre [Edward Basil Jupp] • *GM*, 1st ser., 69 (1799), 357
Archives V&A, drawings for rebuilding of East India House
Wealth at death £35,000; incl. £5000 to wife, plus income from estate; £10,000 to nieces and nephews; £10,000 in trusts: Farington, *Diary*, vol 4, p. 1269; will, PRO, PROB 11/1324, fol. 365

Jupp, Richard Webb (1767–1852). *See under* Jupp, Richard (1728–1799).

Jupp, William, the elder (1734–1788). *See under* Jupp, Richard (1728–1799).

Jupp, William, the younger (1770–1839). *See under* Jupp, Richard (1728–1799).

Jurdain, Ignatius (*bap.* 1561, *d.* 1640), politician and civic reformer, was baptized on 17 August 1561 at St Michael's Church, Lyme Regis, one of the eight children of William Jurdain of Lyme; his mother's name is unknown. In his youth Jurdain was sent to Exeter 'to be brought up in the profession of a Merchant' (Nicolls, 2). He was apprenticed to Richard Bevis, a wealthy merchant of St Mary Arches parish, to whom he was in all probability related, and about 1576 dispatched on a trading trip to Guernsey. Here Jurdain underwent a spiritual conversion, or 'new birth', and the rest of his life was to be directed by a burning protestant zeal. On 24 June 1589 he married Katherine Bodley (*bap.* 1570, *d.* 1593), the daughter of an Exeter goldsmith, and later that same year he was admitted as a freeman of the city. Three children were born to the couple, but in May 1593 Katherine died. Within four months, on 5 August, Jurdain married again. His second wife was Elizabeth Baskerville (*bap.* 1576, *d.* 1649), daughter of Thomas Baskerville of St Mary Arches, apothecary. No fewer than fourteen children were born to Elizabeth and Ignatius, the last of them in 1620, when she was forty-four and he fifty-nine.

As Jurdain's family grew and his business prospered he began to ascend the *cursus honorum* of civic office at Exeter. In 1599 he was appointed as one of the city bailiffs and in 1608 he was chosen to be a member of the chamber, the body of twenty-four rich and powerful townsmen which governed Exeter's affairs. Further distinction swiftly followed. In 1610 he served as receiver (or treasurer) and in 1611 as sheriff, while in September 1617 he attained the peak of civic eminence when elected as mayor for the forthcoming year by the assembled Exeter freemen. Jurdain's mayoralty was to prove a turbulent one. He and his allies were determined to 'reform' the civic community of Exeter, to turn it into a godly 'city upon a hill', and during 1617–18 they encouraged the city officials to launch a sustained assault against drinking, swearing, sabbath-breaking, fornication, and every other form of 'prophaneness'. Jurdain's drive for moral reformation provoked great opposition in Exeter, both among ordinary citizens and among more conservative members of the civic élite, but it is clear that he had many supporters too.

In 1620 Jurdain won enough votes among the freemen to be elected as MP for Exeter. He attended assiduously the 1621–2 parliament, where he spoke out against scandalous and non-resident ministers. Following parliament's dissolution Jurdain returned to Exeter, where the power struggle between the godly and their conservative-conformist adversaries continued to rage. In 1623 he opened himself up to attack when he caused a more-or-less respectable townsman to be savagely whipped at the house of correction for adultery, and remarked soon afterwards that 'it would never be well' until adultery was punished with death (PRO, STAC 8/161/10). A prosecution in Star Chamber followed, during the course of which it was claimed that Jurdain was 'the principall patron of factious and seditious persons in all the Westerne parts' (ibid.). Rather surprisingly Jurdain was eventually cleared on all charges—a crushing blow for his domestic enemies—and in May 1625 he was again elected to represent Exeter in parliament.

The events of the following year were to make Jurdain's position in Exeter almost unassailable. In autumn 1625 the city was hit by a devastating outbreak of the plague which killed perhaps a fifth of the population and prompted the mayor-elect and most of the town élite to flee for their lives. Jurdain refused to follow their example and remained behind in the stricken city, assuming the role of lieutenant-mayor and doing all he could to ease the sufferings of the distressed inhabitants. Jurdain's behaviour during 'the plague year' made him a popular hero in Exeter, and in 1626 and 1628 he was twice re-elected as MP for the city, in direct opposition to the chamber's wishes. During the late 1620s he became increasingly bold in his attacks on the drift of royal policy, speaking out against leniency towards Catholics and calling for the removal of the duke of Buckingham. In 1629 he was bracketed alongside John Pym and William Prynne as one of the most intransigent of the crown's puritan critics, while in 1633 he dared to write a letter to Charles I demanding that the king withdraw the Book of Sports—a letter which caused that usually undemonstrative monarch to exclaim that Jurdain should be hanged. Six years later Jurdain—by now seventy-eight—publicly demonstrated his opposition to the king's war against the Scots. It was to be his last act of defiance. He had been ill for some time and in 1640 he died in Exeter, having done more than any other individual of his generation to influence the course of public affairs in that city. He was buried at St Mary Arches church on 18 June 1640. 'The Arch-Puritan' was commemorated by the minister of St Mary Arches, Ferdinando Nicolls, in a biography published in 1654 and later printed in Samuel Clarke's *Lives*.   MARK STOYLE

Sources F. Nicolls, *The life and death of Mr. Ignatius Jurdain* (1654) • F. Rose-Troup, 'An Exeter worthy and his biographer', *Report and Transactions of the Devonshire Association*, 29 (1897), 350–77 • M. Stoyle, *From deliverance to destruction: rebellion and civil war in an English city* (1996) • Exeter quarter sessions order books, 61–3, 1618–42, Devon RO • Exeter chamber act books, 1600–40, Devon RO • PRO, STAC 8/161/10 • M. M. Rowe and A. M. Jackson, eds., *Exeter freemen, 1266–1967*, Devon and Cornwall RS, extra ser., 1 (1973) • J. J. Alexander, 'Exeter members of parliament, pt 3', *Report and Transactions of the Devonshire Association*, 61 (1929), 193–215 • W. Notestein, F. H. Relf, and H. Simpson, eds., *Commons debates, 1621*, 7 vols. (1935) • R. C. Johnson and others, eds., *Proceedings in parliament, 1628*, 1–4 (1977–8) • *Diary of John Rous*, ed. M. A. E. Green, CS, 66 (1856) • C. A. T. Fursdon, ed., 'Parish register of St Mary Arches, Exeter, 1538–1837' [transcript of 1926, kept at West Country Studies Library, Exeter]
Archives Devon RO, Exeter city archives

Jurin, James (*bap.* 1684, *d.* 1750), physician and natural philosopher, son of John Jurin, citizen and dyer of London, and his wife, Dorcas Cotesworth, was baptized on 15 December 1684. In April 1692 he was admitted from St Leonard, Shoreditch, to the Royal Mathematical School at Christ's Hospital, London, where he distinguished himself and earned a full scholarship to Trinity College, Cambridge. Jurin graduated BA in 1705, and was elected fellow of Trinity in 1706. Richard Bentley, master of Trinity, became his patron and arranged for him to travel as tutor to Mordecai Cary (later bishop of Killala) in 1708–9. During his travels Jurin enrolled at Leiden University, but did not receive a degree. In 1709 he received an MA from Trinity and was appointed headmaster of the grammar school at Newcastle upon Tyne. While in Newcastle he delivered a series of public lectures on mathematics and Newtonian natural philosophy, and updated Newton's edition of Bernhard Varenius's *Geography* (1672) by adding supplements on meteorology, tides, and properties of air.

In 1715 Jurin resigned his position as headmaster and returned to Cambridge to study medicine, receiving his MD in 1716. He established a successful medical practice in London and in Tunbridge Wells during the summer months. He was elected fellow of the Royal Society in 1717 and became secretary in November 1721. He served as secretary until 1727 and edited volumes 31–4 of the *Philosophical Transactions*. He was admitted a candidate of the Royal College of Physicians in 1718, and was made a fellow in 1719. In 1722 Jurin delivered a series of lectures on anatomy to the Company of Surgeons, and in 1725 was appointed physician to the newly established Guy's Hospital, a position he held until 1732, when he resigned and became governor to the hospital. Jurin served as censor to the Royal College of Physicians five times during the period 1724–50, was made an elect of the college on 17 July 1744, served with Richard Mead as consiliarius in 1749, and became president of the college on 19 January 1750.

In the autumn of 1724 Jurin married Mary Douglas, *née* Harris (*d.* 1784), the wealthy widow of a Northumbrian landowner. They had five daughters—Frances, Mary, Ann, Catherine, and Jane—and one son, James (*d.* 1782).

Jurin occupied a central place in British medical and scientific circles during the first half of the eighteenth century. He was witty, satirical, ambitious, and professionally and financially successful. His dispassionate, yet forceful advocacy of smallpox inoculation using an innovative statistical approach brought him widespread recognition both in Britain and abroad. Initially a folk practice, inoculation consisted of placing matter taken

James Jurin (*bap.* 1684, *d.* 1750), by James Worsdale

from the pocks of an individual with smallpox in a small incision made on a limb of a healthy individual. A mild case of smallpox typically ensued, which generally gave the inoculated individual immunity from natural smallpox. Occasionally, however, inoculated individuals died from the severity of the infection. During the first decades of the eighteenth century in England smallpox inoculation was debated fiercely on medical, ethical, and religious grounds. Jurin approached the issue differently by calculating the risks of inoculated and natural smallpox. Using his position as secretary to the Royal Society, he placed an advertisement in the *Philosophical Transactions* inviting readers to send accounts of their experiences with inoculation. Over sixty individuals responded, the majority either physicians or surgeons who performed the inoculations themselves. From these accounts Jurin calculated the relative odds of dying from smallpox inoculation (roughly 1 in 50) and natural smallpox (roughly 1 in 7 or 8). He published the results of his calculations in a series of annual pamphlets entitled *An Account of the Success of Inoculating the Small-Pox*, which appeared from 1723 until 1727. Contemporaries were generally persuaded by Jurin's figures and his pamphlets were acknowledged as central to the establishment of smallpox inoculation in England.

Jurin was an ardent Newtonian. (His portrait in the Royal Society portrays him holding a copy of Newton's *Principia*.) Although not taught by Newton, he studied with two early Newtonians at Trinity, Roger Cotes and William Whiston, and proved an able mathematician. Jurin developed his relationship with Newton at the Royal Society, especially as secretary to the society during the last seven

years of Newton's presidency. During the 1730s and 1740s he corresponded with leading French Newtonians, including Voltaire, Buffon, and Mme du Châtelet, and throughout his life he championed Newton and Newtonian ideas in the most important scientific debates of the time, including the *Analyst* controversy with Bishop Berkeley over the calculus, the *vis viva* controversy over how to measure force, and the iatromechanical disputes over the force of the heart.

As secretary to the Royal Society, Jurin initiated a project to collect meteorological reports in order to learn more about the weather, or in his words, to create 'a natural history of the air'. He recruited observers from Britain, the European continent, and the North American colonies; he also persuaded the Royal Society to send meteorological instruments (thermometers and barometers) as gifts to more distant observers, to facilitate standardization among observations. This project was significant in its thoroughness and in the degree to which it encouraged co-operation among an international group of natural philosophers.

Jurin's most important scientific papers, initially published in *Philosophical Transactions*, concerned capillarity, and were well received by natural philosophers throughout Europe. Much of his early work discussed iatromechanical topics, such as the force of the heart and the specific gravity of blood, and he debated the former with John Keill and Jean-Baptiste Sénac. He wrote several treatises on hydrodynamics, published both in the *Philosophical Transactions* and separately, which criticized Jean Bernoulli's and Daniel Bernoulli's work on the topic. In 1738 Jurin appended an essay *On Distinct and Indistinct Vision* to Robert Smith's *Opticks*, which provoked an extended exchange in print with the mathematician Benjamin Robins.

Jurin participated in a lively controversy among British mathematicians about the calculus triggered by Berkeley's *The Analyst* (1734), which argued that the calculus was as much a doctrine of faith as was religion, because the new mathematics was not based on rigorous demonstration. Jurin took this as an attack on Newton and proceeded to defend Newton's approach to the calculus. Between 1734 and 1742, the most heated period of debate, Jurin penned over 300 pages, many satirical, on the topic. Two pamphlets, published under the pseudonym Philalethes Cantabrigiensis and entitled *Geometry no Friend to Infidelity, or, A Defence of Sir Isaac Newton & the British Mathematicians* (1734) and *The Minute Mathematician, or, The Freethinker no Just Thinker* (1735), responded directly to Berkeley. After this exchange Berkeley withdrew from the debate, and Jurin's later writings on the subject (published in the *Republick of Letters*, 1728–26, and the *History of the Works of the Learned*, 1737–43, under the same pseudonym) were directed against the mathematicians Benjamin Robins and Henry Pemberton.

Near the end of his life Jurin became embroiled in yet another controversy, this one involving the death of Robert Walpole, first earl of Orford. Orford suffered from the stone, and Jurin was one of the physicians he consulted.

Jurin prescribed lixivium lithontripticum, a medicine he developed while treating his own case of bladder stones. Walpole died, and Jurin was accused of causing his death. He was forced to defend himself in a heated exchange of pamphlets.

Jurin died in London on 29 March 1750, at sixty-six years of age, and was buried at St James Garlickhythe in London; he was survived by his wife. He left £35,000 in stock for his family and rings of remembrance for his friends Edward Hulse, Richard Mead, Robert Smith, and Shallett Turner.   ANDREA RUSNOCK

Sources [J. Jurin], *The correspondence of James Jurin, 1684–1750: physician and secretary to the Royal Society*, ed. A. Rusnock (1996) · Munk, *Roll · DNB ·* A. Rusnock, 'The weight of evidence and the burden of authority: case histories, medical statistics and smallpox inoculation', *Medicine in the Enlightenment*, ed. R. Porter (1995), 289–315
Archives RS, corresp. and meteorological journal · Wellcome L., corresp.
Likenesses P. Scheemakers, bust, Trinity Cam. · J. Worsdale, portrait, RS [*see illus.*] · portrait, Trinity Cam.
Wealth at death £35,000—stock: will, PRO, PROB 11/778

Just, John (1797–1852), archaeologist and botanist, eldest son of Jonathan Just and his wife, Mary, was born at the family farm in the village of Natland, near Kendal, Westmorland, on 3 December 1797. After attending the village school he was employed on a farm, but, showing an aptitude for study, he went at the age of fourteen to Kendal grammar school. The philanthropist William Carus Wilson of Casterton Hall noticed his ability, in 1812 took him into his house, and sent him to Kirkby Lonsdale grammar school for five years. While at Casterton Hall, Just engraved ciphers upon the family plate and scales for barometers, and commenced his investigations on Roman roads. About 1817 he became for a short time classical assistant to the Revd John Dobson at Kirkby Lonsdale School, and pursued his favourite study of botany in the neighbourhood. From 1832 until his death he was second master of Bury grammar school, devoting much of his leisure to private teaching, and acting as actuary of the Bury Savings Bank.

Just was elected lecturer on botany at the Pine Street (afterwards the Royal Manchester) school of medicine and surgery in September 1833, and lectured annually from 1834 to 1852. On 22 January 1839 he was chosen a corresponding member of the Literary and Philosophical Society of Manchester. In October 1848 he was appointed honorary professor of botany at the Royal Manchester Institution; he delivered three courses of lectures there in 1849–51. He closely studied chemistry and its application to the analysis of soils and manures. Three of his agricultural essays were printed in the *Transactions of the Literary and Philosophical Society of Manchester*, and his lecture of 27 September 1850 to the Bury Agricultural Society, on the value and properties of lime for agricultural purposes, was printed as a pamphlet.

Just acquired a good knowledge of ancient and modern languages, and specially studied Old English, on which he also contributed to the Manchester society. His last essay, contributed to a local society in the month before his death, was on the derivation of local names. He left

unpublished four quarto manuscript volumes, an unfinished dictionary or lexicon of English words and their derivations, with similar words of similar meanings in cognate and kindred languages, and compiled *A Glossary of the Westmoreland Dialect as Spoken in the Neighbourhood of Kendal*. He also succeeded in deciphering some runic inscriptions in the Isle of Man.

Just's knowledge of the Roman roads which traverse Lancashire—the subject of many of his papers for learned societies—led to his collaboration with the officers of the Ordnance Survey for the county. For the British Archaeological Association congress, held at Manchester and Lancaster in August 1850, Just superintended excavations at Ribchester which led to the discovery of interesting Roman remains. He died at Bury on 14 October 1852, aged fifty-five, and was buried there in St Paul's churchyard on 20 October. He left a widow and a daughter aged fifteen, but no further details of his family are known.

G. C. BOASE, *rev.* ANITA McCONNELL

Sources J. Harland, 'Memoir of the late Mr John Just of Bury', *Memoirs of the Literary and Philosophical Society of Manchester*, 2nd ser., 11 (1854), 91–121 · *GM*, 2nd ser., 38 (1852), 652–3 · *Journal of the British Archaeological Association*, 9 (1854) · IGI

Justel, Henri (1620–1693), librarian, was born in Paris, the son of Christophe Justel (1580–1649), a learned Calvinist and canonist, and his wife, Olympe, *née* de Lorme. His father's reputation and office of *sécretaire du roi* ensured for Henri an entrée to high Huguenot society. He inherited the office, which carried nominal duties and also opportunities for influence, but made a mark in his own right as a man who was learned, insatiably curious about facts and ideas, and at ease with sceptics and Roman Catholics though staunch in his own protestantism. This 'cultivated man of the world' (Engel, 19) brought interesting and clever people together at his regular suppers, and was specially generous to visiting foreigners. From theology to clocks, sermons to sonnets, talk round his hospitable table led to significant friendships, often followed up in his large correspondence. Leibnitz and Locke were among his admirers.

For many years Justel worked on a projected book on useful commodities and recent inventions. Leibnitz encouraged him to persist, but it never appeared. He edited and published his father's weighty *Bibliotheca juris canonici veteris* (1661). *Un recueil de divers voyages faits en Afrique et Amérique* (1674) may have been his: it is compiled from English works. Also anonymous, *Answer to the bishop of Condom's book, entitled 'An exposition of the doctrine of the Catholic church'* (translated, 1676) is almost certainly not his, though Agnew claimed that Justel was 'chieftain of protestant controversialists' (Agnew, 149). Justel was undogmatic, and unwilling to compromise his position: indeed, between 1668 and 1670 he was in receipt of a royal pension for services to scholarship. His self-appointed role as cultural intermediary is hard to evaluate. It certainly made for friendly relationships between French and foreign scholars. The good offices of English ambassador Henry Savile in Paris and of Henry Compton, bishop of

London, eased his passage to England and enabled him to continue there his useful work.

In 1675 Justel presented through George Hickes to the Bodleian Library at Oxford three valuable manuscripts of the seventh century in uncial characters containing the acts of the council of Ephesus. The DCL was conferred on him by a grateful Oxford on 23 June 1675. To Dr Hickes, Justel confided about December 1680 his presentiment about the fate of the Huguenots: 'We must all be banished from our country or turn papist' (Ancillon, *Lettres*, 1.37). He had married in 1676 a much younger cousin, Charlotte de Lorme. With two children, one daughter sick and about to die, it seems she urged him to leave. He had already received a letter (2 December 1680) from Charles II inviting him, 'in consideration of his vast knowledge', to sort out the royal manuscripts. Principle and prudence pointed to England. In April 1681 he sold his library of 7000 volumes. Somehow he secured permission from Louis XIV to depart. By the end of the year he was installed in a house in Piccadilly, with the post of assistant keeper of royal manuscripts. On 7 December, proposed by Christopher Wren, he was unanimously elected fellow of the Royal Society, to which he had been so valuable a correspondent.

His twelve years in London were busy and useful. A particular friend was John Evelyn, who called him 'that great and knowing virtuoso'. In March 1691 the diarist recorded: 'went to visit Mr Justell and the library at St James in which that learned man had put the MSS which were in good number into excellent order, they having lain neglected for many years' (*Diary of John Evelyn*, 2.203). Justel was formally naturalized on 15 August 1687. He assumed the keepership in July 1689, with a salary of £200 a year. He died, in office, at Eton in September 1693, and was buried at Eton parish church. His wife survived him.

Justel was clearly an assiduous librarian. There is uncertainty, however, about the value of his work. Hearne declared that his library was useless for want of a catalogue and that Justel was 'a very ingenious man, but far from being learned' (*Remarks*, 3.54). In any case Justel's greatest contribution to the intellectual life of his time was as promoter, through hospitality and correspondence, in circles in Paris and London, of the optimistic spirit of enquiry which would be a feature of the European Enlightenment.　　　　　　　　　　　GEOFFREY TREASURE

Sources D. C. A. Agnew, *Protestant exiles from France in the reign of Louis XIV, or, The Huguenot refugees and their descendants in Great Britain and Ireland*, 2nd edn, 2 (1871), 149–50 · M. Ancillon, *Mémoires concernant la vie et les ouvrages de plusieurs modernes* (1730), 220–32 · M. Ancillon, *Lettres choisies de M. Simon* (1730) · J. Lough, ed., *Locke's travels in France, 1675–9* (1953) · H. Brown, 'Un cosmopolite du grand siècle: Henri Justel', *Bulletin* [Société de l'Histoire du Protestantisme Français], 82 (1933) · C. E. Engel, 'Henri Justel', *XVIIe Siècle*, 61 (1963), 19–30 · E. R. Briggs, 'Some Huguenot friends of Saint-Evremond', *Proceedings of the Huguenot Society*, 23 (1977–82), 13–17 · *Remarks and collections of Thomas Hearne*, ed. C. E. Doble and others, 3, OHS, 13 (1889), 54 · *The diary of John Evelyn*, ed. W. Bray, new edn, 2, ed. H. B. Wheatley (1906), 202–3

Archives Bodl. Oxf., corresp., mainly letters to John Locke · RS, letters to Henry Oldenburg, etc.

Likenesses line engraving, BM, NPG; repro. in *GM* (1788)

Justice [*née* Surby], **Elizabeth** (1703–1752), author, was the eldest child of Dorset Surby of Hatton Garden, London, and his second wife, Ann Ellis. The major source for her biography is her novel *Amelia, or, The Distress'd Wife* (1751), which was a thinly disguised autobiography. If its account is reliable, Elizabeth was educated in a boarding-school in Hackney and at home with a private tutor. At sixteen she married a barrister and Cambridge graduate some seven years her senior, Henry Justice (*d.* 1763), with whom she had three children. After they married, she discovered that her husband, an avid book collector, was unwilling to divert much of his earnings from his hobby to maintaining his family. *Amelia* describes the breakdown of the marriage under her growing indebtedness. Although she eventually secured a settlement from her husband of £25 annually, this was not enough to pay her creditors. In order to devote the sum to servicing her debts, she began looking for employment as a governess. As she did not speak French, she was advised to go abroad. She readily accepted a position in Russia as governess to the children of Hill Evans (*d.* 1740), a member of the English merchant community in St Petersburg, for whom she worked for three years.

Justice returned reluctantly to England in 1737 as a result of the scandal which enveloped her estranged husband after he was sentenced to transportation to America for stealing sixty rare books from the Cambridge University Library. Her writing appeared in print for the first time in that year when, without her permission, the unscrupulous publisher Edmund Curll published in the fifth volume of *Mr. Pope's Literary Correspondence* four letters she had written from St Petersburg to a friend in London. Two years later she published by subscription her *Voyage to Russia*, the first British eyewitness account of the country that had appeared since John Perry's *The State of Russia under the Present Czar* (1716), and the first that reflected the condition of the country after the death of Peter the Great in 1725. The 600 copies she had printed eventually sold out, and she was encouraged by a 'Lady of Quality' to issue a second edition in 1746, which was slightly enlarged through the inclusion of the letters Curll had published in 1737.

On this occasion Justice assembled an impressive list of subscribers representing a cross-section of the provincial gentry. Altogether she managed to interest 281 subscribers, including the Wisbech Book Club (and dozens of other subscribers from this area—King's Lynn, Peterborough, and Stamford), in her endeavour. The *Voyage* went unnoticed by the metropolitan intellectual community. It was neither reviewed by the periodical press nor acknowledged by subsequent travellers. It is probably of more interest to readers today as the first travel account in English written by a woman. According to Anthony Cross the *Voyage* offered an 'account of Russian customs and habits ... seen from somewhat lower down the social scale than usual' (Cross, 339). In 1751 Justice's continuing financial desperation led her to publish, again by subscription, *Amelia*, the tale of the hardship brought on her by her unfortunate marriage. She died in the following year.

JAMES PATERSON

Sources E. Justice, *Amelia, or, The distress'd wife* (1751) · P. Gaskell, 'Henry Justice: a Cambridge book thief', *Transactions of the Cambridge Bibliographical Society*, 1 (1949–53), 348–57 · E. Kraft, 'The two Amelias: Henry Fielding and Elizabeth Justice', *ELH: a Journal of English Literary History*, 62 (1995), 313–28 · A. Cross, *By the banks of the Neva* (1997) · Blain, Clements & Grundy, *Feminist comp.*

Justice, James Norval Harald Robertson (1907–1975), actor, was born at 39 Baring Road, Lee, Lewisham, on 15 June 1907, the son of James Norval Justice, mining engineer, and his wife, Edith Burgess. He was educated at Marlborough College and went on to the University of Bonn, where he was awarded a PhD. Intended (by his parents at least) for a career in the diplomatic service, Robertson Justice joined Reuters as a young journalist and was sent out to Canada in 1927. Over the next ten years he found work around the globe variously as a reporter, a schoolmaster, an insurance salesman, a lorry driver, a sailor, and the manager of an ice rink. He had a great facility with languages: said to speak ten, he himself admitted to French, German, Italian, Dutch, and Gaelic.

Robertson Justice was called up into the Royal Navy at the outbreak of the Second World War. After the war he drifted into acting, and was appearing as the chairman in music-hall at the Players Theatre Club when Harry Watt, the film director, spotted his talent and gave him a role in his film *Fiddlers Three* (1944), followed by other films produced at Ealing Studios. He made notable screen appearances in Peter Ustinov's *Vice Versa* (1947), as Commander Evans in *Scott of the Antarctic* (1948), and in *Whisky Galore* (1948).

In 1951 James Robertson Justice went to Hollywood, where he appeared in *David and Bathsheba* (1951), and also in *Land of the Pharaohs* (1955) and *Moby Dick* (1956). A Second World War drama for British Lion was *Orders to Kill* (1958). However, his career changed decisively when he played the irascible surgeon Sir Lancelot Spratt in the sequence of film comedies which started in 1954 with *Doctor in the House*.

An actor of more than 20 stone in weight, with a grizzled, once red beard, and the voice of an educated foghorn, Robertson Justice was typecast as 'the heavy' in countless films, as 'a peppery doctor, professional lawyer, sailor, senior spy' (*The Times*).

Seldom tempted towards the stage or radio or television, James Robertson Justice spent thirty years or so in regular film work, which he seemed to find of diminishing interest. His real concerns were ornithology, ecology, and conservation, and his passion was falconry; he published learned papers on all these subjects, and noted proudly that he had invented a rocket-propelled net method of catching wildfowl for marking purposes.

Robertson Justice lived for many years in his beloved highlands, contesting North Angus and Mearns unsuccessfully as a Labour candidate in 1950. He had rather better luck at Edinburgh University, where students elected

James Norval Harald Robertson Justice (1907–1975), by Georges Maiteny

him their rector in both 1957 and 1963; he served a total of six years and was rewarded with an honorary doctorate.

In later life Robertson Justice took to compèring opera and ballet programmes for BBC television, but unnerved colleagues by occasionally appearing on the set with a remarkably tame eagle tethered to his wrist. A difficult man, loyal to the Scottish nationalist cause long before Sean Connery made that position fashionable, he was a rich and rare addition to the gallery of great British character-acting eccentrics.

Robertson Justice lived in his later years with the former actress Baroness Irina Margarethe Pauline Isabelle Caecilie von Meyendorff. Their long-standing relationship was responsible in 1968 for his divorce from his first wife, Dillys. Robertson Justice and Irina married on 29 June 1975, only a few days before his death. He died on 2 July 1975 at his home, Top House, Ashley, Stockbridge, Hampshire, from heart failure. He was cremated.

SHERIDAN MORLEY

Sources *The Times* (3 July 1975) · *WWW* · b. cert. · m. cert. [Irina von Meyerdorff] · d. cert.
Archives FILM BFI NFTVA, advertising film footage · BFI NFTVA, performance footage | SOUND BL NSA, performance recordings
Likenesses G. Maiteny, photograph, NPG [*see illus.*]

Justus [St Justus] (*d.* 627×31), archbishop of Canterbury, was the first bishop of Rochester and the fourth archbishop of Canterbury. Almost everything that is known about him derives from Bede's *Historia ecclesiastica*. He had been sent in 601 from Rome by Pope Gregory along with Mellitus and others to reinforce Augustine's mission. In 604 he was consecrated as bishop of Rochester by Augustine, and, according to a charter of uncertain authority, on 28 April he received from Æthelberht, king of Kent, a grant to his church of the south-eastern quarter of the walled town. He was later said by St Boniface to have helped Augustine in his ecclesiastical government. After Augustine's death he was associated with bishops Laurence and Mellitus in sending a letter to the Irish bishops and abbots urging them to conform to the customs of the universal church. In 614 he attended a council of the Frankish church at Paris. On the relapse into paganism which followed the accession of Eadbald in Kent in 616 or 618, he fled with Mellitus into Francia, and remained there a year until he was recalled to his bishopric by the king. He and Mellitus both received letters of exhortation from Pope Boniface V (r. 619–25). On the death of Mellitus on 24 April 624 Justus succeeded to the see of Canterbury, and received a pallium from Boniface with a letter acknowledging his work in strengthening the faith of King Eadbald (erroneously called 'Adulwald') and conveying the right to consecrate bishops. He then consecrated Romanus to succeed him at Rochester. Another letter, purportedly from Boniface V to Justus and giving the primacy of the whole English church to Canterbury, is a forgery based upon the genuine letter preserved by Bede. On 21 July 625 he consecrated Paulinus as bishop, purportedly in order to accompany Æthelburh to Northumbria on her betrothal to King Eadwine. One or two further details given by Thomas of Elmham can scarcely be considered historical. There are short lives of Justus by Goscelin, William of Malmesbury, and Gervase, and in a manuscript martyrology in Lambeth Palace Library. None of them adds anything to Bede's account. Justus died on 10 November, between 627 and 631; he was buried in the porch of St Peter's and St Paul's Monastery (later St Augustine's), Canterbury.

WILLIAM HUNT, rev. N. P. BROOKS

Sources Bede, *Hist. eccl.* 1.29; 2.3–9, 16, 18, 20 · A. Campbell, ed., *Charters of Rochester*, Anglo-Saxon Charters, 1 (1973), no. 1 · *Concilia Galliae*, 2: *A. 511–A. 695*, ed. C. De Clercq (Turnhout, 1963), 274–89 · N. Brooks, *The early history of the church of Canterbury: Christ Church from 597 to 1066* (1984), 9, 11–13, 64, 66, 265 · Thomas of Elmham, *Historia monasterii S. Augustini Cantuariensis*, ed. C. Hardwick, Rolls Series, 8 (1858), 116, 121 · *Willelmi Malmesbiriensis monachi de gestis pontificum Anglorum libri quinque*, ed. N. E. S. A. Hamilton, Rolls Series, 52 (1870), 6, 47–9, 134 · *The historical works of Gervase of Canterbury*, ed. W. Stubbs, 1: *The chronicle of the reigns of Stephen, Henry II, and Richard I*, Rolls Series, 73 (1879), 332–3 · T. D. Hardy, *Descriptive catalogue of materials relating to the history of Great Britain and Ireland*, 1, Rolls Series, 26 (1862), nos. 600–02 · T. Tatton-Brown, 'Buildings and topography of St Augustine's Abbey, Canterbury', *Journal of the British Archaeological Association*, 144 (1991), 61–91

Justyne, Percy William (1812–1883), painter and book illustrator, the son of Percy and Anne Justyne, was born at Town Malling in Kent. He was educated for the Royal Navy, and went on a surveying expedition in HMS *Nimble*, but left the service for health reasons. Having completed his education at a school at Mitcham, Surrey, he began painting landscapes. In 1837 he sent a landscape to the Suffolk Street exhibition, and the following year he exhibited *A Scene in the Alps by Moonlight* at the Royal Academy. From 1841 to 1845 he was private secretary to Major-General Charles Joseph Doyle, governor of the island of Grenada in the West Indies; he afterwards served as acting stipendiary magistrate on the island, and on Doyle's death in 1848 he returned to England.

Justyne then turned to book illustration and was employed on the *Illustrated London News* (1849–50), *The Graphic*, the *London Journal*, the *National Magazine*, the *Floral World*, and *Building News*. He illustrated the *Art Journal* catalogues of the International Exhibitions in 1851 and 1862, Dr Smith's *History of Greece* and *Biblical Dictionary*, James Fergusson's *The Illustrated Handbook of Architecture*, George Rawlinson's *The Five Great Monarchies of the Ancient Eastern World*, Dean Stanley's *Memorials of Westminster Abbey*, Cassell's Bible and *Bible Dictionary*, Charles Kingsley's *Christmas in the Tropics*, and Miss Meteyard's *Life of Josiah Wedgwood*. In 1881 Justyne was living at Avondale Road, Camberwell, London, with his wife, Matilda (b. 1812/13); they had at least one daughter, who married a W. H. Arnold. He died on 6 June 1883 at 70 Crofton Road, Camberwell, Surrey, and was buried at Norwood cemetery.

L. H. CUST, rev. DENNIS HARRINGTON

Sources private information (1891) · Bénézit, *Dict.*, 4th edn · Thieme & Becker, *Allgemeines Lexikon* · Graves, *RA exhibitors* · S. Houfe, *The dictionary of British book illustrators and caricaturists, 1800–1914* (1978) · d. cert.

Juta, Jan Carel (1824–1886), bookseller, was born at Zaltbommel, Netherlands, on 23 March 1824. He studied law before entering the book trade in Holland. He emigrated to the Cape on the suggestion of his brother, a Dutch sea-captain whose ship had been wrecked in Table Bay and who had, after swimming ashore, fallen in love with a Cape Town woman. Before leaving for the Cape, Juta married Louisa Marx (d. 1893), the sister of Karl Marx, one result of which is that some of the more obscure writings of Marx are to be found in Cape Town newspapers, where they were placed by his sister. In Cape Town, Juta joined the congregation of the Groote Kerk, the main Dutch Reformed church, where his children were baptized.

Within a few months of his arrival, Juta had established a bookselling and publishing house in the centre of Cape Town. The first work he published concerned the constitution ordinance which granted the Cape representative government (1853). He later published widely in both English and Dutch, including textbooks and more popular works. He initiated and published the influential *Cape Monthly Magazine* (1857–81), and the *Descriptive Handbook of the Cape Colony* (1875) compiled by John Nobel, clerk of the house of assembly. It was in the 1860s that his firm began to specialize in the production of legal works, for which it was to remain famous. He both encouraged local writers, and, through importing books from Britain and Holland, the growth of a reading culture in Cape Town.

In poor health, Juta returned to England in 1884 and settled in Chiswick, Middlesex, where he died on 8 April 1886. His wife then returned to Cape Town; she died in Rondebosch in 1893. One of their sons, Henricus Hubertus (Henry Hubert), became speaker of the Cape legislative assembly and judge president of the Cape division of the supreme court.

CHRISTOPHER SAUNDERS

Sources S. A. Rochlin, 'J. C. Juta: bookseller and publisher', *Africana Notes and News*, 12 (June 1957), 222–8 · M. Arkin, 'Juta, Jan Carel', *DSAB* · M. C. Juta, *Boundless privilege: an autobiography* (1974) · S. A. Rochlin, 'A link between Karl Marx and Cape Town', *Africana Notes and News*, 2 (Dec 1944), 23 · A. B. Caine and L. Leipoldt, *Bibliography of the publications of J. C. Juta and J. C. Juta and Co., 1853–1903* (1954) · F. Rossouw, *South African printers and publishers, 1795–1925, from a South African bibliography to the year 1925* (1987) · *CGPLA Eng. & Wales* (1886)

Wealth at death £1004 13s. 6d.: probate, 2 June 1886, *CGPLA Eng. & Wales*

Jutsum, Henry (1816–1869), landscape painter, was born in London, the son of John Jutsum and his wife, Elizabeth, and was baptized on 4 October. He was educated in Devon, where he also became interested in landscape painting. On returning to London he drew from nature, most frequently in Kensington Gardens. He first exhibited at the Royal Academy in 1836. Three years later he became a pupil of James Stark. He devoted himself for some time to watercolour painting, and in 1843 was elected a member of the New Watercolour Society. He continued, however, to exhibit works, mainly landscape subjects, at the Royal Academy from 1836 to 1868 (except 1867). In 1847 he resigned from the New Watercolour Society to concentrate on painting in oil. He was a frequent contributor to the chief exhibitions up to his death, including those of the Society of British Artists, and his works were always much admired. Examples of his work are held in Blackburn Art Gallery, Cartwright Hall, Bradford, Coventry Art Gallery, Leeds City Art Gallery, Maidstone Museum, and Newport Art Gallery; *The Foot Bridge* is in the Victoria and Albert Museum, London. He died at the home he shared with his brother Rowland, 88 Hamilton Terrace, St John's Wood, London, on 3 March 1869. Many of his own drawings in his possession and others collected by him were sold by auction at Christies on 17 April 1882.

L. H. Cust, rev. Jocelyn Hackforth-Jones

Sources Graves, *Artists*, 3rd edn · Mallalieu, *Watercolour artists*, vol. 1 · J. Johnson, ed., *Works exhibited at the Royal Society of British Artists, 1824–1893, and the New English Art Club, 1888–1917*, 2 vols. (1975); repr. (1993) · Redgrave, *Artists*, 2nd edn · Graves, *RA exhibitors* · d. cert. · *CGPLA Eng. & Wales* (1869)

Likenesses J. Watkins, carte-de-visite, NPG · watercolour drawing, BM

Wealth at death under £4000: administration, 1869

Juxon, Thomas (1614–1672), parliamentarian activist and diarist, was born in London on 24 June 1614, the second son of John Juxon (1579–1626) of St Stephen Walbrook and later East Sheen, Surrey, a prosperous sugar baker of genteel lineage, and his first wife, Elizabeth Kirrell (*c*.1593–1619), daughter of John Kirrell of St Michael Queenhithe, London, and East Sheen. He was to be married twice: first, on 2 March 1647 at St Giles-in-the-Fields, to Elizabeth Carent (*d*. September 1669), daughter of Maurice Carent of Toomer Park, Somerset, with whom he had a son, William (*b*. December 1647), and a daughter, Elizabeth (1649–1722); and second, to Elizabeth Meredith (*d*. June 1698), daughter of Sir Robert Meredith of Greenhills in co. Kildare, Ireland, with whom he had no children.

Both of Juxon's parents, who were godly protestants, died during his childhood, and his uncle, Arthur Juxon,

became his guardian. With a father free of the Merchant Taylors, he received his initial education at the company's school in 1619–21, after which he was apprenticed to one of its liverymen in 1630 and gained his freedom in 1637. His father had bequeathed a house and approximately 100 acres in East Sheen to Juxon, who by 1640 had begun his rise in wealth and influence by becoming a partner of his half-uncle, Matthew Sheppard, who like Juxon's father was a prosperous London sugar baker. By 1642 he was serving as colonel's ensign in the Green regiment of the City trained bands; promotion to captain followed in 1643 and to major and lieutenant-colonel in 1647. He was also admitted to his company's livery in 1646 and, during the last four years of his life, served on its governing body. Yet there is no evidence that he ever became a member of common council despite his familiarity with its internal politics in the mid-1640s.

Irish interests were to loom large during the second half of Juxon's life. He invested substantially in Irish land, mainly in Leinster, under the Irish adventurers' scheme to finance the reconquest of Ireland, and during the 1650s he purchased land from other investors to consolidate his holdings. This accumulation of property periodically took him to Ireland, where he could enjoy his status as one of the kingdom's new generation of English landowners, a fact that was to be underlined by his second marriage into a leading English settler family. At the Restoration he was to be found in Dublin working as a key figure among Irish adventurers seeking secure titles to their lands in what became the Act of Settlement of 1662.

However, Juxon's chief claim to historical recognition is the journal he kept in London during the eventful years 1644–7 (DWL, MS 24.50), which enables the reader to view those years from the perspective of a godly London tradesman who was also a radical parliamentarian activist. The journal reveals a strong belief in a providential God combined with a marked Erastianism and a rejection of a coercive presbyterianism. Yet he was not a religious Independent and was totally opposed to a legal recognition of religious toleration. His political analysis displayed a deep-seated antipathy to kings and lords in general, and to Charles I and the current peerage in particular, while stopping short of a principled advocacy of republicanism. Nevertheless, he was no Leveller and did not advocate a wider social distribution of political rights. Although traditionally described as a political Independent, he was never a rigid supporter of any party, for this would have run counter to both his convictions and his temperament. This did not prevent a royalist attack on him as 'a most violent ass' (Harley MS 986, fol. 19) and a presbyterian description of him as 'that swearing phantastic fool' (*A Pair of Spectacles for the City*, 9). He made one brief and final appearance on the English political stage in 1659 when he was elected MP for Helston, Cornwall, yet his parliamentary career was fairly nondescript.

Juxon died on 2 October 1672 in Dublin, and was buried on 14 October in St James's Church, Dublin, having apparently returned to Ireland to set up a new household with his second wife and to be near his only son, who was being treated in Dublin for mental illness. His daughter, Elizabeth, was the executor of his will of 6 June 1672, which bequeathed lands and properties at East Sheen and in Ireland, Essex, and London. The will was subsequently disputed by two of his nephews, but in 1674 judgment went in Elizabeth's favour. His widow was to marry in 1675 the nonconformist divine Daniel Williams, and the library established by the latter was eventually to acquire Juxon's manuscript journal in 1850.   KEITH LINDLEY

Sources T. Juxon, journal, DWL, MS 24.50 · *The journal of Thomas Juxon*, ed. K. Lindley and D. Scott, CS, 5th ser., 13 (1999) · will, PRO, PROB 11/340, sig. 147 · BL, Harley MS 986, fols. 19, 21 · *The visitation of London, anno Domini 1633, 1634, and 1635, made by Sir Henry St George*, 2, ed. J. J. Howard, Harleian Society, 17 (1883), 23 · K. S. Bottigheimer, *English money and Irish land* (1971), 185, 205 · apprentice binding book, 1629–35, GL, Merchant Taylors' Company MSS, fol. 120 · presentment book, GL, Merchant Taylors' Company MSS, vol. 2 · court minute books, GL, Merchant Taylors' Company MSS, vol. 9, fol. 233r–v; vol. 10, pp. 245, 248, 321, 445–7 · C. J. Robinson, ed., *A register of the scholars admitted into Merchant Taylors' School, from AD 1562 to 1874*, 1 (1882), 100 · CSP Ire., 1625–60, 22, 188, 215, 284, 343, 344, 347, 353; 1660–62, 337 · DNB · *Diary of Thomas Burton*, ed. J. T. Rutt, 4 vols. (1828), vol. 3, p. 560; vol. 4, p. 211 · will of John Juxon, PRO, PROB 11/150, quire 112 · *A pair of spectacles for the city*, 1647, BL, E419/9, p. 9 · funeral entries vol. 4, NL Ire., department of manuscripts, MS 67, fol. 178 · funeral entries vol. 11, NL Ire., department of manuscripts, MS 74, fol. 8 · W. B. Bannerman and W. B. Bannerman, jun., eds., *The registers of St Stephen's, Walbrook, and of St Benet Sherehog, London*, 1, Harleian Society, register section, 49 (1919), 14 · W. A. Littledale, ed., *The registers of Christ Church, Newgate, 1538 to 1754*, Harleian Society, 21 (1895), 28 · GL, MS 7670, fols. 106, 111 · S. Denison, *The monument or tombstone* (1620), 79 · J. L. Chester, ed., *The parish registers of St Thomas the Apostle, London … from 1558 to 1754*, Harleian Society, register section, 6 (1881), 57 · St Giles-in-the-Fields, parish register (marriages), 1615–1713, 2 March 1647, fol. 30v · 'Boyd's index of Inhabitants of London', Society of Genealogists, London, 35385

Wealth at death lands and property in Ireland, Essex, London, and East Sheen, Surrey; £1000 owing to him; plate: will, PRO, PROB 11/340, sig. 147

Juxon, William (*bap.* 1582, *d.* 1663), archbishop of Canterbury, was baptized in the church of St Peter the Great, Chichester, on 18 October 1582, the second son of Richard Juxon, registrar and receiver-general of the bishops of Chichester. His grandfather, John Juxon, was a Londoner, and the family had long been settled in the city of London, with close associations with the Merchant Taylors' Company. After attending the prebendal school in Chichester, Juxon joined his cousins Arthur and Rowland Juxon at the Merchant Taylors' School in London, entering on 30 June 1595; his uncle Thomas Juxon was then warden of the company.

The Oxford years On 11 June 1598 Juxon was elected to St John's College, Oxford, having been awarded one of Sir Thomas White's scholarships, and he matriculated on 7 May 1602. Unlike John Buckeridge, William Laud, and Matthew Wren—other future bishops, who all graduated BA from St John's—Juxon proceeded to the degree of BCL on 5 July 1603 and very probably entered Gray's Inn soon afterwards, as a comment he made in the House of Lords in 1641 suggests. He stayed there only briefly, however, preferring an academic career within Oxford University even though he already held the reversion of his father's

William Juxon (*bap.* 1582, *d.* 1663), after unknown artist, *c.*1640

offices of bishop's registrar and dean's registrar at Chichester and must have been aware of parental expectations. He was elected a fellow of his college and lost little time in fulfilling the requirement of its statutes that within ten years of starting the study of law he should be ordained deacon (as he was in September 1606), and within fourteen become priest (as he did in September 1607). On 20 January 1610 he was appointed vicar of St Giles's, Oxford, a living in his college's gift; he resigned it in January 1616 on his presentation by Benedict Hatton to Somerton, Oxfordshire, where he served as rector for nearly six years. He eventually took his DCL in 1622.

During 1611 Juxon played a useful, but not decisive, part in securing the election of William Laud, as president of St John's in succession to Buckeridge, after a hotly disputed contest with John Rawlinson. Juxon was one of a group of five senior fellows of the college who decided to vote as a block in accordance with the will of the majority among them; although their role was investigated on James I's orders by the college visitor, Thomas Bilson, bishop of Winchester, and was further considered by the king, the election was allowed to stand. John Towse's floating vote had been crucial. Immediately after Laud's appointment, Juxon served a year as vice-president of St John's, but he may well have had an obligation to do so, in keeping with the college's requirement that a civil lawyer had to fill the office once in every three years. Ten years later, Laud was reticent about his part in Juxon's own election to the presidency of St John's on 10 December 1621. In his diary Laud simply recorded his resignation from the presidency on 17 November 1621, and in a letter to Sir Robert Cotton in

November 1623, which acknowledged that the college had still not recovered from the contest, he suggested that his role was less than Juxon's opponents supposed: 'the heat that was then struck is not yet quenched in the losing party', yet arose merely 'out of an opinion that I had some hand in the business' (*Works*, 6.242). He did not elaborate on his part in proceedings, but Juxon, meanwhile, may have reflected on the hazards of close identification, real or imagined, with Laud. Lancelot Andrewes, visiting the college as Bilson's successor in June 1624, referred to the detrimental effects of its continuing 'unhappy disagreement at home' (Mason, 33). Perhaps to bolster the new president Andrewes may, as dean of the chapels royal, already have had some part in the invitation from the clerk of the closet, Richard Neile, to Juxon to contribute to the series of Lenten sermons at court in both 1623 and 1624, as one of the few preachers who was not yet a royal chaplain. Laud, increasingly active at court as Andrewes's health declined, may also have helped.

Juxon, however, came more frequently to royal notice during the two academic years he served as vice-chancellor of the University of Oxford, in 1626/7 and 1627/8. In this role he received Charles I at Woodstock in August 1627, greeting him with a Latin oration (PRO, SP 16/73/2, Laud's copy), and by the end of the year had become a royal chaplain and received nomination as dean of Worcester (instituted 7 January 1628); as dean he repaired his cathedral and, at court, gave Lenten sermons each year between 1628 and 1631. His enthusiasm for hunting, although he was by now less often in the saddle, and knowledge of local woodlands, also commended him to the king. A letter of October 1627 from Charles to the chancellor of Oxford, Pembroke, asking him to instruct his vice-chancellor to order the heads of colleges to control their students' activities in the forest around Woodstock, may have been suggested by Juxon. A year later, Juxon was named among commissioners appointed to survey Shotover Forest, east of Oxford, on the king's behalf. As vice-chancellor, however, he proved quite unable to counter the Calvinist emphasis of the acts, and his difficulties may have prompted the final paragraph of the king's declaration on the articles of religion of November 1628, just after his term of office had ended, which specifically banned doctrinal disputations within the two universities.

At Charles I's court When Richard Neile was translated to York in March 1632 and resigned from the clerkship of the closet which he had held since 1603, Juxon succeeded him, on 10 July, and Laud for the first time mentioned Juxon by name in his diary (the only previous entry, in July 1625, had simply referred impersonally to the president of St John's). Laud, who seemed to see the clerkship as about Juxon's mark, did however claim that it was 'at my suit' that he was chosen, 'That I might have one that I might trust near his Majesty, if I grow weak or infirm; as I must have a time' (*Works*, 3.216). There is at least a hint here of a more immediate concern about losing Charles's ear, for Laud was aware he must soon succeed Archbishop George Abbot across the river at Lambeth. Juxon, at almost fifty,

was only nine years Laud's junior, and the decision was surely the king's. Charles may have thought it appropriate for a past president of St John's to make a formal request on behalf of his successor, but it is inherently unlikely, given the king's concern over church appointments, that he had not made up his own mind first, especially as the clerk's privy closet was placed between the presence chamber and the privy chamber, bringing him as physically close to the king as a servant not of the privy chamber or bedchamber could be. Juxon's resignation from the presidency of St John's on 5 January 1633, when still dean of Worcester and with no preferment within the church immediately in view, indicated his confidence in the continued flow of royal favour.

In the event Juxon did not have long to wait. The deaths of Francis Godwin, bishop of Hereford, in April 1633 and archbishop Abbot on 4 August 1633 prompted his swift elevation. The king initially intended him for Hereford, where his election was confirmed late in July 1633, but before his consecration could take place Laud's translation to Canterbury brought Juxon the succession both to the deanship of the chapels royal (an office previously held under the Stuarts only by James Montagu, Lancelot Andrewes, and Laud) on 12 August 1633 and to the see of London, to which he was nominated on 22 September and confirmed eight days later. In the space of a few months Juxon had acquired two of the most coveted offices in the English church, and done so with a discreet certainty which, as the privy seal office warrants and signet office docquet books confirm, indicated the exercise of the king's will. A normally well-informed London newsletter writer, John Flower, in reporting on 21 September that Laud would hold on to the see of London until Michaelmas (29 September), was still unaware who the new bishop might be. More notably, neither Laud's diary nor his surviving correspondence records Juxon's rapid rise or reflects on the potential which the deanship of the chapels royal gave for further advancement. Within five years of becoming a royal chaplain Juxon had, as much by his accommodating personality as by any demonstration of competence, confirmed his place close to the king at court just as Laud was moving across the water to Lambeth. As clerk of the closet in succession to Juxon, Charles had chosen Matthew Wren, his chaplain since 1622 and an old friend of Francis, Lord Cottington.

In March 1636 Juxon became lord treasurer of England, the first bishop in an office of state since John Williams held the lord keepership between 1621 and 1626, and the first churchman in the treasury since 1470. After the death of Portland in March 1635, the treasury had been placed in commission while Charles considered his options; friction between its two principal members, Laud and the chancellor of the exchequer, Cottington, soon undermined its effectiveness. The differences between them ran much deeper than a clash of personalities. Laud became obsessed with the need to root out impurities within the system of financial management, which the sometimes self-serving and aggrandizing Portland had come to epitomize and which his associate Cottington threatened to perpetuate. It was here, if anywhere in England, that 'Thorough' joined issue with what it took to be corruption, and Laud had high hopes that his ally, Thomas Wentworth, lord deputy of Ireland, would show an active interest in the succession to Portland. Wentworth, however, recognized from the outset that this would be politically unwise, and by the autumn of 1635 Laud, regarding himself as isolated at court by his abhorrence of what he saw as graft and corruption on all sides, was left to press his own case upon the king. His failure was a severe blow. Charles's preference for Juxon as lord treasurer compromised his own position, as primate, within the state. Yet Laud seems to have had no inkling that Juxon was in the running, and ignored him in correspondence with Wentworth at this time. It was as though the treasury was regarded as business beyond his compass. Juxon himself may have thought so. Charles afterwards remarked that he had spent most of the year in which the treasury was in commission trying to persuade Juxon to take it on and there is some evidence that the bishop was being encouraged to think of redefining his responsibilities. Laud himself implied in September 1635 that Matthew Wren was by then standing in for Juxon as dean of the chapels royal and that same month George Garrard, whose friendship with Cottington sharpened his perceptions of court activity, reported a rumour that Juxon was about to be made a privy councillor. A few days earlier the queen had informally consulted Cottington at Hanworth, no doubt confirming the identity of the prospective treasurer, and found him ready to remain in the less onerous post of chancellor of the exchequer. She knew that what Charles wanted was an amenable treasurer with some appreciation of financial priorities, who would work smoothly with Cottington, whose services he was anxious to retain. That November, in the Star Chamber case of *Pell* v. *Bagg*, which the queen attended in support of the wily and hard-dealing Bagg, Juxon duly aligned himself with Cottington among a narrow majority of judges who found in Bagg's favour, in contrast to Laud who trustingly supposed that the king would, like him, see the force of Pell's arguments. Juxon proved adept at grasping the ways of the court and his amiable disposition, and evident royal favour, were already bringing him a range of contacts more varied than Laud's own. As bishop of London he was well placed to strengthen his contacts with his kinsmen, some of them working in the church courts, and others associated with City companies.

As lord treasurer Juxon soon demonstrated his readiness to fall in with established practices. He saw no reason why customs farms, which allowed the crown to draw extra concessions from the bidders, should be abandoned and the customs returned to direct management by the crown as Laud and a disgruntled London merchant, John Harrison, maintained. Harrison never regarded Juxon as a financial innocent, later recalling Juxon's practice of referring to his brother John of St Gregory by Paul, a proctor in the London church courts:

> all business of profitt, as offices in his disposall and what else; unto all which he gave despatch when his brother and

> the party were agreed; by which course (although he seemed never to meddle in those things) he made a greater benefit then any of the former treasurer upon like occasions had made.   (BL, Stowe MS 326, fol. 62r)

Among Juxon's cousins was Nicholas Crisp, the rising Guinea merchant, who was brought into Sir Paul Pindar's syndicate for the great farm of customs in July 1637. Another who joined the farm was the queen's master of horse, George, Lord Goring, who had hopes of extending his interests in the tobacco trade, and who had lost no time in securing the appointment of his kinsman Philip Warwick as the new lord treasurer's secretary. As early as December 1637 Henry Percy assured Wentworth that Warwick 'governs his master as he pleases' (Strafford MS 17/259), seeming to fulfil the prediction of the earl of Clare that it would be left to Cottington to do the business of the treasury. But Juxon had also shown that he was not entirely unfamiliar with the practices of high finance—Percy indeed thought him 'the best for them [projectors] we ever had' (Strafford MS 17/263).

In most respects Juxon proved a tidy and effective peacetime administrator, under whom the king's finances continued to increase in yield: he and Cottington ultimately secured a substantial improvement in the value of the customs farms (the great farm up to £172,000 per annum, the petty to £72,500 per annum), and by using the 1635 book of rates they increased revenue from trade to an average of £425,000 per annum, during the later 1630s, almost half the crown's ordinary revenue. They encouraged the effective management of both the court of wards and the soap monopoly and curbed the tendency for treasury officials to employ the king's revenues for their own purposes by promptly examining the declared accounts; in 1639–40 they reduced pensions and annuities. Yet the king's decision to take military action against the Scottish covenanters quickly demonstrated the limits to these financial improvements. In neither bishops' war was the king's campaign securely or promptly funded, in part because support from the peers and gentry was not as readily forthcoming as Juxon supposed it would be. Unlike Cottington and Wentworth, he did not relish the urgency and uncertainty of war financing. As early as December 1638 Laud had ruffled the king by remarking that Juxon 'would use providence enough were he left alone … were I in his place, they should command the [white] staff when they would, but not a penny of money till these difficulties were over' (*Works*, 7.511). Juxon's resignation from the treasury on 17 May 1641, shortly after Wentworth's attainder (which he had advised against) and execution, must have come as a relief. Cottington resigned from the exchequer the same day.

On his appointment as lord treasurer on 6 March 1636 Juxon had been made a privy councillor and found himself involved in the king's government across a broad front. As treasurer he was *ex officio* a member of all the council's standing committees as well as the commission for the admiralty, and was also likely to serve on the council's *ad hoc* committees. On 9 May 1637 he was among those nominated to the new council of war. The extant evidence does not allow for an accurate estimate of his overall commitment, but attendance lists for the administrative meetings of the council (in PRO, PC 2, and in the council clerks' papers in SP 16) indicate that he was very seldom absent from its board, and between March 1636, when he gave his last Lenten sermon at court (PRO, LC 5/134, fol. 1v), and his final pre-war appearance at the board on 27 April 1641, his presence was noted at well over 500 of these routine meetings, more than any other councillor. There was much other business besides, and it was not long before diocesan responsibilities began to lose ground to ship money and then the Scottish troubles.

This may not have entirely displeased Juxon. His preoccupation with council and treasury matters meant that he could, more legitimately than his fellow bishops, place responsibility for carrying out church policy on his officials. To be at a remove from the enforcement of policy suited his cautious nature. He took a liberal view of reading the reissued Book of Sports in the parishes, and merely wanted assurance that it had been published, and did not enquire when and by whom it had been read. His attitude to altar rails was circumspect—perhaps like Laud he was aware that the practice did not entirely have canonical sanction. He did not stand in the way of firm action by local officials but, as his commissary, Dr Robert Aylett, once complained, left them without adequate backing. Juxon visited his diocese in 1634, 1637, and 1640 but his annual diocesan returns, as summarized by Laud as part of his provincial reports to the king, read feebly, and point to a lack of firm direction, in much the same way as visitors' reports on St John's, Oxford, under his presidency had done. In 1634 he acknowledged some inconformity in the diocese of London, 'but proofs came home only against four: three curates and a vicar'. In the next year 'three of his [four] archdeacons have made no return at all to him, so that he can certify nothing but what hath come to his knowledge without their help'. In 1637 Laud again reported that 'my lord treasurer complains that he hath little assistance of his archdeacons', and may have taken satisfaction in adding 'I believe it to be true, and shall therefore, if your Majesty think fit [as Charles did], cause letters to be written to them to awake them to their duties' (*Works*, 5.327, 332, 348).

In his own dealings, Juxon took a pragmatic line. He sparingly granted licences to preach, but was on occasion accommodating to existing lecturers. He viewed Richard Mountague's enthusiasm for closer relations with Rome with caution, but from 1635 expected clergy new to his diocese, at least, to subscribe on institution to a set of eleven Arminian articles, the last of which stated bluntly that the 'Church of Rome is a true Church and truly so called' (Fincham, *Visitation Articles*, 2.126). He also knew how to make himself inconspicuous. He sought in February 1636 to allay Scottish fears over the changing character of the new Scottish prayer book but, pleading treasury commitments, left Laud and Wren to scrutinize James Wedderburn's notes which, for the first time, dealt with the interpretation of the eucharist. Juxon was among the five bishops absent from the Lords on the day the canons of 1640 were due to be signed, and thus was not named in the impeachment proceedings of 4 August 1641.

Retirement and restoration Given the sensitivity of the two posts he held, as lord treasurer and bishop of London, Juxon attracted remarkably little attention from either MPs or constituencies during the parliamentary reckoning against Charles I's personal rule. As Lord Falkland conceded early in the Long Parliament, Juxon 'in an unexpected and mighty place and power … [had] expressed an equal moderation and humility, being neither ambitious before, nor proud after, either of the crozier's staff or white staff' (Rushworth, 3/1.185). Because during the civil war Juxon did not take up arms against parliament or voluntarily assist the king's army he was allowed to remain at Fulham with his secretary, Philip Warwick, until the sale of the bishop's palace, after which he lived for much of his time as a discreet country cleric at either Aldbourne in Sussex or Little Compton in Gloucestershire with his brother John who, an informer told the committee for the advance of money in 1647, had 'all or the most part of the bishop's plate and goods, for all things are in common between them' (Mason, 143). Juxon nevertheless defended Laud at his trial in 1644 against the charge that he had been treasonably close to the Church of Rome, and attended the king, at his request, at successive peace negotiations, the last at Newport in September 1648. He was present at the king's trial and was with him on the scaffold. Later he supervised his interment at St George's Chapel, Windsor, having been refused permission to bury the body in Henry VII's chapel or to read the burial service.

During the 1650s Juxon hunted frequently despite his advancing years, and on one occasion was allegedly defended by Cromwell after his normally well-ordered hounds had disturbed worshippers at Chipping Norton by excitedly chasing a hare into the churchyard. Nearby, at Little Compton, he continued with impunity to conduct services according to the Anglican rite.

When Juxon returned to London in August 1660 he was in his late seventies and out of touch with current politics and Anglican thinking. Appointed primate by Charles II that September, he was overshadowed in church affairs by Gilbert Sheldon, bishop of London, and had little influence on the religious settlement. His attitude to nonconformity never became clear. He was restored to the privy council only in April 1663, an indication perhaps of the new king's coolness towards him. He did what he could to revive the material condition of the church, spending freely on clergy incomes, furniture, and, especially, fabric: over £10,000 was spent on the great hall at Lambeth Palace alone. He also, characteristically, appointed his kinsmen to administrative posts within the diocese of Canterbury. His metropolitan visitation of the southern province in 1663, carefully carried out by his vicar-general, Sir Richard Chaworth, was to be the last of its kind.

Juxon died, unmarried, at Lambeth on 4 June 1663, and was buried at Oxford on 9 July with more pomp than he had asked for in St John's College chapel, next to the college's founder, Sir Thomas White. Laud's body was brought from Barking to lie with them. Juxon's will showed how far he had outlived his generation. Personal bequests, such as that to Philip Warwick, were few, and apart from £6000 to members of his family the bulk of his estate went to institutions with which he had been associated: St John's College received £7000 to purchase lands 'for the increase of the yearly stipends of the fellows and scholars', St Paul's £2000 for repairs, and Canterbury Cathedral, by way of a codicil, £500. His nephew Sir William Juxon, as executor, was charged with overseeing the completion of the hall at Lambeth, if need be (PRO, PROB 11/311/89).

Juxon, according to Philip Warwick, was 'of a meek spirit and of a solid and steady judgement' (Warwick, 100), very different from his supposed mentor, Laud, whose shortcomings as a courtly cleric his own advance does much to point up. Where Laud consoled himself with being a principled but lonely and thwarted reformer, Juxon, true to his training as a civilian, preferred to work quietly within the system. Even though Wentworth in Ireland almost always dealt directly with Cottington, Juxon was an inspired choice for lord treasurer in the context of reducing friction at court. He was on good terms with both the fractious senior treasury commissioners, Laud and Cottington, and he was someone the king and queen felt comfortable with. But despite the distinction visited on the church, Laud was less than happy with the outcome, and in the later 1630s continued to snipe at the management of the king's finances, suggesting that Juxon lacked the firmness to assert himself when it mattered. Charles acknowledged that he found it difficult to elicit Juxon's own views from him, despite making it plain that he valued them; political confidences between them must have been few. Juxon's reserve brought him durability in high office but left his beliefs less clearly visible than they might have been. His theology is defined largely by the Arminian circles within which he moved. He does not seem to have been asked to make declarations on the king's behalf from the pulpit. None of his sermons was ever ordered to be printed by either James or Charles, unlike those of Andrewes and Laud, and none appears to have been otherwise published. Juxon had become the king's man but, for all his apparent authority, his role remained circumscribed. With that he prudently rested content.

BRIAN QUINTRELL

Sources PRO, PROB 11/311/89; SP 16; SO 3/10; PSO 2/94; PC 2; LC 5/132, 134; C 115 · J. Flower, letter to Viscount Scudamore, 21 Sept 1633, PRO, C 115/M31/8159 · BL, Stowe MS 326 · GL, GL 9531/15, GL 9537/14 and 15 · LMA, DL/C/88–90 · Strafford papers, Sheff. Arch., Wentworth Woodhouse muniments · Essex RO, D/ALV 2 and D/AXA 2 · muniment book 15, Westminster Abbey Muniment Room and Library · The works of the most reverend father in God, William Laud, ed. J. Bliss and W. Scott, 7 vols. (1847–60) · P. Warwick, Memoirs of the reign of Charles I, ed. W. Scott (1813) · K. Fincham, ed., Visitation articles and injunctions of the early Stuart church, 2 vols. (1994–8) · W. D. Peckham, ed., The acts of the dean and chapter of the cathedral church of Chichester, 1545–1642, Sussex RS, 58 (1959) · The life and letters of Sir Henry Wotton, ed. L. P. Smith, 2 vols. (1907) · The diary of Thomas Crosfield, ed. F. S. Boas (1935) · The autobiography of Phineas Pett, ed. W. G. Perrin, Navy RS, 51 (1918) · The letters and journals of Robert Baillie, ed. D. Laing, 3 vols. (1841–2) · Letters of John Holles, 1587–1637, ed. P. R. Seddon, 3 vols., Thoroton Society Record Series, 31, 35–6 (1975–86) · J. Rushworth, Historical collections, 5 pts in 8 vols. (1659–1701) · E. Cardwell, ed., Documentary annals, 2 vols. (1839) · The manuscripts of the Earl Cowper, 3 vols., HMC, 23 (1888–9) · G. Radcliffe, The earl of Strafforde's letters and dispatches, with an essay towards his life, ed. W. Knowler, 2 vols. (1739) · Pepys, Diary · The diary of Bulstrode Whitelocke, 1605–1675, ed. R. Spalding, British Academy, Records of Social and Economic History, new ser., 13 (1990) · T. A. Mason, Serving God and mammon: William Juxon, 1582–1663 (1985) · N. Tyacke, Anti-Calvinists: the rise of English Arminianism, c.1590–1640 (1987); repr. (1990) · B. Quintrell, 'The Church triumphant? The making of a spiritual lord treasurer, 1635–6', The political world of Thomas Wentworth, ed. J. Merritt (1996) · P. E. McCullough, Sermons at court: politics and religion in Elizabethan and Jacobean preaching (1998) [incl. CD-ROM] · A. Milton, Catholic and Reformed: the Roman and protestant churches in English protestant thought, 1600–1640 (1995) · J. Davies, The Caroline captivity of the church: Charles I and the remoulding of Anglicanism, 1625–1641 (1992) · K. Sharpe, The personal rule of Charles I (1992) · H. R. Trevor-Roper, Archbishop Laud, 1573–1645, 2nd edn (1962) · M. C. Fissel, The bishops' wars: Charles I's campaigns against Scotland, 1638–1640 (1994) · R. Ashton, The crown and the money market, 1603–1640 (1960) · I. M. Green, The re-establishment of the Church of England, 1660–1663 (1978) · G. Donaldson, The making of the Scottish prayer book of 1637 (1954) · P. S. Seaver, The puritan lectureships: the politics of religious dissent, 1560–1662 (1970) · K. Fincham, Prelate as pastor: the episcopate of James I (1990) · W. C. Costin, The history of St John's College, Oxford, 1598–1860, OHS, new ser., 12 (1958) · W. H. Marah, Memoirs of Archbishop Juxon (1869)

Archives CKS, De L'Isle and Dudley MSS, papers, HMC 77 | BL, Coke papers · PRO, state papers domestic, Charles I, SP 16

Likenesses oils, c.1640, NPG [see illus.] · portrait, St John's College, Oxford · portrait, LPL · portrait, Longleat, Wiltshire · portrait, Fulham Palace

Wealth at death over £18,000—bequests: will, PRO, PROB 11/311/89

Kaberry, Phyllis Mary (1910–1977), anthropologist, was born on 17 September 1910 in San Francisco, not long after her family migrated to the USA from Yorkshire. Her father, Lewis Kaberry (1878–1962), was an architect who specialized in designing theatres and cinemas. Her mother, Hettie Emily, née Coggins (1884–1975), was a Christian Scientist (as was Kaberry's father) and lived to the age of ninety-one. Within the family Kaberry was nicknamed Tip. She and her two brothers migrated with their parents from the USA to Australia when they were young children. Educated at Fort Street Girls' High School in New South Wales, Kaberry entered Sydney University in 1930, graduating BA in 1933 and MA (first-class honours) in 1935. Following a short period as honorary lecturer in anthropology at Sydney University, and fieldwork among the Aboriginal peoples in northern Australia (1934–6), she travelled to England and completed a doctoral thesis entitled 'The position of women in an Australian aboriginal society' (1939) at the London School of Economics under the supervision of Bronislaw Malinowski, the noted anthropologist. When not in the field, she lived in London, from about 1950 mostly in a flat in Nevern Square, Earls Court. She never married, and she had no children. By all accounts, the rest of her family remained in Australia.

Kaberry was a pioneer in the systematic study of women. Between 1935 and 1975 she published widely in international journals such as *Africa*, *Man*, and *Oceania*. She is best known for two classic texts, both of which focus on women. The first, *Aboriginal Woman Sacred and Profane* (1939), emerged as a result of her 1930s Australian field-work in the remote Kimberley region. Kaberry—who was incorporated into Aboriginal social life by allocation to the Nadjeri (Nyapajarri) sub-section—showed that Aboriginal women experienced an important and rich religious life which complemented that of the men. Her findings provided new substantive insights on indigenous gender relations and religion in Australia and elsewhere. The second, *Women of the Grassfields* (1952), focused primarily on the Nsaw in the Bamenda region of the Cameroons in west Africa. Kaberry first worked there in 1945, initially for the Colonial Social Science Research Council in London, and later for the Wenner-Gren Foundation. She documented the socio-economic position of Nsaw women, in part by recording detailed accounts of subsistence activity. The results of her work were highly valued by the Nsaw, among whom she was celebrated as Yaa Woo Kov (Lady of the Forest) and Queen Mother. From 1958 she often collaborated with friend and historian E. M. (Sally) Chilver, and together they published a number of articles on the Cameroons. In between working in Australia and Africa, Kaberry conducted field research in 1939 and 1940 among the Abelam, in the Sepik district of Papua New Guinea, where she concentrated on conflict resolution and dispute settlement.

From 1949 to 1976 Kaberry held the position of lecturer and reader in anthropology at University College, London. A rigorous and practical scholar, especially when in the field, she received a number of academic awards, such as the Stirling international fellowship which took her to Yale University, the Rivers memorial medal of the Royal Anthropological Institute for outstanding fieldwork, and the Wellcome medal in applied anthropology, which she shared with Sally Chilver. She also received a Carnegie fellowship to enable her to edit with Malinowski a collection devoted to cultural change. She completed this task on her own, following Malinowski's untimely death, and it appeared in 1945 as *The Dynamics of Cultural Change*.

Kaberry's less well-known personal qualities included her love of literature (especially poetry) and the arts, her sense of humour, her unpretentiousness and tenacity, and her dedicated role as tutor of apprentice anthropologists. She was physically slight (though clearly not frail), smoked cigarettes and occasionally a pipe, and in later life was increasingly prone to bouts of depression and melancholia. She was a keen and loyal correspondent, as evidenced by the letters she exchanged with friends and colleagues, including Australian writer Dame Mary Durack Miller, with whom she corresponded for four decades. Kaberry was also renowned for caring deeply about the people among whom she worked, and for maintaining close and active contact. Her advocacy on behalf of the Nsaw, in particular, is legendary.

In 1976 Kaberry retired from University College, London. She died suddenly at her Bloomsbury flat at 142 Bedford Court Mansions, Adeline Place, on 31 October 1977. A memorial service was held in February 1978 at the university church of Christ the King in London. Sir Raymond Firth, who had first met Kaberry when she was a student at Sydney University in the 1930s, delivered the address. Some months later in west Africa, a Nsaw mourning ceremony (*diiy kpu*) was undertaken where Kaberry's death was 'cried'. She was honoured again in 1987 when a resource centre in Cameroon was named after her. The Centre for Cross-Cultural Research on Women at Oxford University also set up a Phyllis Kaberry commemorative lecture, to be delivered every three years. Anthropological thought and practice, and future students of anthropology, owe much to the rich intellectual legacy of Phyllis Mary Kaberry.   SANDY TOUSSAINT

Sources C. H. Berndt and E. M. Chilver, 'Phyllis Kaberry: field worker among friends', *Persons and powers of women in diverse cultures*, ed. S. Ardener (1992), 29–39 · private information (2004) · C. H. Berndt, 'Phyllis Mary Kaberry (1910–1977)', *Women anthropologists: a biographical dictionary*, ed. U. Gacs, A. Khan, J. McIntyre, and R. Weinberg (1988), 167–74 · C. Cheater, 'From Sydney schoolgirl to African queen mother: tracing the career of Phyllis Mary Kaberry', *First in their field: women and Australian anthropology*, ed. J. Marcus (1993), 137–52 · *CGPLA Eng. & Wales* (1977) · BLPES, Kaberry MSS · Australian Institute of Aboriginal and Torres Strait Islander Studies (AIATSIS), Canberra, Australia, Kaberry MSS · Battye State Library, Perth, Western Australia, Kaberry MSS · University of Western Australia, Berndt Museum of Anthropology, Kaberry MSS · d. cert.

Archives Australian Institute of Aboriginal and Torres Strait Islander Studies, Canberra, Australia, Australian field notes · Battye Library of West Australian History, Perth, field notes and commentary on Aboriginal circumstances · BLPES, Cameroons, west Africa, field notes, reports, corresp. · Royal Anthropological Institute, London, report on farmer–grazier relations in Nsaw · University of Western Australia, Perth, Berndt Museum of Anthropology, corresp. | BLPES, letters from Bronislaw Malinowski · UCL, ethnographic collection, artefacts from west Africa and Papua New Guinea |SOUND IWM SA, oral history interview

Likenesses photographs, BLPES · photographs, UCL · photographs, Institute of Social and Cultural Anthropology · photographs, Centre for Cross-Cultural Research on Women · photographs, Australian Institute of Aboriginal and Torres Strait Islander Studies, Canberra, Australia · photographs, University of Western Australia, Perth, Australia, Berndt Museum of Anthropology · photographs, priv. coll.

Wealth at death £62,343: probate, 15 March 1978, *CGPLA Eng. & Wales*

Kable, Henry (1766/7–1846), transported convict and merchant, was born and lived in Suffolk, like his father, Henry Cabell (*d.* 1783). Both were illiterate and unskilled labourers, and little is known of Henry Kable's early life. He joined a rural gang notorious for thefts from farms, and in 1783 he, his father, and an accomplice were found guilty of house burglary and sentenced to death. The elder two were hanged on 5 April 1783, but sixteen-year-old Kable was reprieved on condition of transportation.

Confined to Norwich Castle gaol, Kable fathered a son, Henry, in 1786. The mother, another convict, Susannah Holmes (*c.*1765–1825), was an illiterate Norfolk spinster of no trade, also reprieved from execution and awaiting transportation. With her baby a few months old, Susannah was ordered to Plymouth to join the first fleet bound for New South Wales. When her baby was refused permission to join her and Kable refused permission to marry her, the English press reported the distress of this young convict family so sympathetically that a public subscription was opened and £20 subscribed to assist the family in their exile. Lord Sydney himself was approached and intervened, personally ordering that both father and son should embark with Susannah.

After arriving at Sydney Cove in January 1788, Kable married Susannah at the first religious service performed by the colony's chaplain, on 10 February 1788. They subsequently had ten children, all baptized by the Church of England chaplains. Such close family life was both unexpected and unrecognized in a penal colony reputed infamous for the criminality, depravity, and immorality of its convict inhabitants.

In July 1788 Kable and Susannah issued a writ against the master of the *Alexander* for withholding the goods that they had bought in England. Their case was the first to be heard in the colony's court of civil jurisdiction. Although convicts were arguably ineligible to sue or be sued, they won their case and the master was ordered to make restitution. It is argued by legal historians that this favourable verdict was Kable's 'greatest impact' (Neal, 177) on England's convict colony, the verdict 'establishing a foothold … for the rule of law tradition' (ibid., 190), thus ensuring that the exercise of power by an arbitrary governor was not automatically dependent on either prison discipline or martial law but rather on legal principles.

Kable's working life did not conform with the traditionally accepted pattern for convicts. In 1789 Kable and some of his associates established the night watch to maintain law and order. He was overseer of the watch (1791) and chief constable (1794–1802) and was deeply involved in procedures and practices in both civil and criminal cases. Business prospered. By 1800 Kable's colonial-built vessels promoted sealing, whaling, and inter-colonial trade, and by 1807 Cable & Co. owned both colonial and foreign-built ships carrying goods and passengers to England. In 1820 he was one of twenty 'most important emancipist land-holders' in New South Wales (PRO, CO 201/123/D5).

In 1805 Kable clashed with Governor William Bligh, who refused permission to trans-ship goods between two of Cable & Co.'s vessels. Bligh imprisoned Kable and his wealthy ex-convict partners in Sydney gaol for one month and fined them £100 each for addressing him 'improperly' and in a derogatory manner. After Bligh's deposition (1808) Kable energetically supported the rebels, and, with his two partners, publicly subscribed £500 to assist John Macarthur's English defence against charges of rebellion. (Macarthur later wrote to his wife that this promissory note could not be honoured in England.) During the interregnum (1808–10) Kable continued to increase his land grants and town allotments, and all his grants were confirmed by Governor Macquarie in 1810. By 1819 Kable was one of the colonial emancipists who, describing themselves as the 'wealthy middle class', petitioned the prince regent for civil rights denied them in the colony to whose economic development they had contributed so greatly.

The accumulated wealth and landholdings of these ex-convicts far exceeded those of the free settlers.

After the death of his wife (8 November 1825) Kable lived with his son John at Windsor until his own death, at Hawkesbury, on 16 March 1846. He was buried with Susannah at St Matthew's, Windsor. They had been married for thirty-seven years, during which time Kable, the notorious transported felon, had become the wealthy colonial settler. The text at that first marriage ceremony at Sydney Cove had been: 'What shall I render to the Lord for all his benefits towards me?' (Psalm 116: 12) which would have been more appropriate at his funeral. Despite lack of education or skill, and despite the infamy of being a convict, his positive response to and exploitation of the unique colonial environment was influential on the economic and social development of early Australia. As an entrepreneur, a businessman, and a family man, Kable, the ex-convict first fleeter, helped to lay the foundations for the new and respectable society which was to become Australia. PORTIA ROBINSON

Sources [F. Watson], ed., *Historical records of Australia*, 1st ser., 6, 10 (1916–17) • F. M. Bladen, ed., *Historical records of New South Wales*, 3–6 (1895–8) • *Sydney Gazette* (1804–29) [esp. 16/8/1807] • *Norfolk Chronicle* (11 Nov 1786) • *English Chronicle* (2 Dec 1786) • T. D. Mutch, 'Register of births, deaths and marriages, 1788–1814', 1815, Mitchell L., NSW • parish registers, St Phillip's, Sydney, Mitchell L., NSW • parish registers, St Matthew's, Windsor, Mitchell L., NSW • *Musters of the population, land and stock, of New South Wales, 1800, 1806, 1811, 1814, 1819*, 3 vols. (1820–24) • *Population of Richmond, Windsor, Castlereagh and Evan*, 3 vols. (1820) • census of New South Wales, 1828, PRO, Home Office MSS, 10/21-8 • New South Wales court of civil jurisdiction, rough minutes of proceedings and related case papers, 1788–1809, Archives Authority of New South Wales, 1092 • 'Lists of all grants and leases of land registered in the colonial secretary's office between 26th day of January 1788 and the 31st day of December 1809', Archives Authority of New South Wales, 7/2731 • PRO, CO 201/123/D5 • R. Clark, journal, 1787–92, Mitchell L., NSW • R. Clark, letter-book, Mitchell L., NSW • J. Cobley, ed., *The crimes of the first fleet convicts* (1970) • J. Cobley, ed., *Sydney Cove*, 5 vols. (1962–86) • P. Robinson, 'The victualling list, New South Wales, 1788', *Sydney Morning Herald* (14–18 Dec 1980) • D. Neal, *The rule of law in a penal colony* (1991) • A. Atkinson, *The Europeans in Australia: a history*, 1: *The beginning* (1997) • C. M. H. Clark, *A history of Australia*, 1 (1962) • P. Robinson, *The hatch and brood of time: a study of the first generation of native-born white Australians*, 1 (1985) • P. Robinson, *The women of Botany Bay*, 2nd edn (1993) • T. J. Robinson, 'A quantitative analysis of conflict in New South Wales … 1806–10', diss., Macquarie University, 1979 [2 vols.] • colonial secretary's in-letters (memorial land grants)

Kadoorie, Sir Horace (1902–1995). *See under* Kadoorie, Lawrence, Baron Kadoorie (1899–1993).

Kadoorie [*formerly* Kelly], **Lawrence**, **Baron Kadoorie** (1899–1993), businessman, was born Lawrence Kelly on 2 June 1899 in Upper Richmond Road, Hong Kong, the eldest of the three sons of Sir Elly Kadoorie (known until 1901 as Eleazar Silas Kelly) (1867–1944), and his wife, Laura Samuel (*d.* 1919), daughter of A. Mocatta of Mocatta and Goldsmid, whose family had emigrated to Britain from Spain in the seventeenth century. The Kadoories, a Sephardi Jewish family, emigrated from Baghdad, Elly arriving in

Hong Kong in 1880, where he was first employed as a clerk in E. D. Sassoon & Co., became a broker, later founded Sir Elly Kadoorie & Sons, and earned a reputation both for his consequent directorships in several key Hong Kong and Shanghai companies, including China Light and Power, and for his widespread philanthropy.

The family moved to England in 1910, but Sir Elly returned to Shanghai in 1911 where, in co-operation with the Hongkong and Shanghai Bank, he was key to the reconstitution of rubber companies. Meanwhile, the youngest son having died in infancy, Lawrence and his brother Horace [see below], whose joint bank account symbolized their intertwined lives, attended school at Ascham St Vincents, Eastbourne, and at Clifton College in Bristol. In 1914 they ventured to Banff, Canada, for a family reunion, but, unable to return to England, the boys continued on to Shanghai and its cathedral school.

After their mother died in 1919 (attempting to locate the family governess in their burning home) the two brothers took on the responsibility of building up the Kadoorie name in Asia, reaching an 'understanding of what it was to become a citizen of the world' (Kadoorie, 87). While Horace in Shanghai ran Marble Hall, a family home of great magnificence which since 1949 has been utilized as the Children's Palace, Lawrence, after studying law at Lincoln's Inn and strengthening the family's connections in France—he would later foster the development of the Alliance Française in Hong Kong—became a virtual aide-de-camp to his father, an intensive business experience which would stand him well in the future.

After returning to settle in Hong Kong in the 1930s Kadoorie became chairman of the family-managed China Light and Power Company and the prestigious Peninsula Hotel. On 9 November 1938 he married Muriel (b. 1915), daughter of David Gubbay of Hong Kong. With the fall of Hong Kong in 1941 they, with their infant son and daughter, were interned by the Japanese in Stanley Camp, but in 1942 the family were transferred to Shanghai, living with relatives until they were interned in Chapei (Zhabei) Camp.

Kadoorie made use of the RAF plane which brought Alwyne Ogden, Britain's first post-war Shanghai consul-general, to the newly liberated city, and, after an adventurous trip, finally reached Hong Kong in November 1945. There he took charge of China Light and Power, and, with a contagious optimism coupled with sound judgement (which subsequently included the foresight to move from coal to oil), made possible through the supply of electric power the recovery and development of Kowloon and the New Territories. Believing family control important he fought off take-over bids. Following objections to the tariff rates the 1959 report of a British-led commission of inquiry included a recommendation for nationalization. Nationalization, however, had not been the Hong Kong government's intention; instead tariffs and dividends were frozen, Lawrence came to timely financial arrangements with Esso (then Standard Oil, NJ), and together they worked out a government-agreed scheme of control.

Indeed, China Light and Power's capacity grew from 19.5 mW in 1946 to 2656 mW in 1981; consumers increased from 24,000 to 949,000; and issued capital from HK\$13.2 million to HK\$2400 million, confirming the ability of a private sector, family-led utility both to provide the essential leadership and to keep vital supplies just ahead of the growing demands of Hong Kong's economic revolution.

Operating from his base as chairman of Sir Elly Kadoorie & Sons, Kadoorie was a member of the colony's legislative and executive councils; he held in all some fourteen chairmanships, twenty directorships, and twenty memberships in important Hong Kong committees and/or companies, including the general committee of the Hong Kong general chamber of commerce and government planning and advisory committees. Of particular importance was his leadership in Nanyang Cotton Mill Ltd, Hong Kong Carpet Manufacturing Co., and Schroders Asia Ltd. In 1957 he was invited to become a director of the Hongkong Bank, a position he was virtually forced to resign in 1967, despite his recognized contribution and patronage, when the British Bank of the Middle East (owned by the Hongkong Bank) became the target of riots allegedly fuelled by the presence of a Jew on the parent company board. But he retained a high profile with his life chairmanship of China Light and with such Hong Kong landmarks as the Peak Tram and the Hong Kong and Shanghai hotels (including the Peninsula) firmly within his jurisdiction.

As well known for his deep humanitarianism and philanthropic contributions as for his role as business *taipan* and adviser, Lawrence with his brother Horace founded the Kadoorie Agricultural Aid Association to improve conditions for villagers and encourage development in the New Territories. Their contribution to agriculture, based on their experimental farm, included the training of Gurkha soldiers stationed in the territory and due for return to Nepal and discharge. Kadoorie was, in keeping with his interest in and contributions to education, a member of the University of Hong Kong's council and court, and his work with Hong Kong's Ohel Leah Synagogue, of which he was a trustee after 1937 and chairman during the last four years of his life, confirmed his strong religious roots. A justice of the peace from 1936, Kadoorie accumulated honours, including the Ramón Magsaysay award (of the Philippines, 1962), appointment as CBE (1969), a knighthood (1974), and appointment as commander of the Légion d'honneur (of France, 1982). He still found time for sports cars, patronage of St John Ambulance, photography (he was chairman of the Hong Kong Photographic Society), and a serious interest in Chinese works of art, the collection of jade in particular.

In 1981, at the commencement of the largest single project in the history of Hong Kong, China Light and Power placed orders totalling £600 million with British industry. Meanwhile the governor, Sir Murray MacLehose, had become convinced that an increasingly politically aware Hong Kong needed a presence in the House of Lords. Later the same year Kadoorie was elevated to the peerage. In his maiden speech he spoke appropriately, regretting recent government moves which distanced Britain from Hong Kong. 'We are losing our Britishness', he complained (*The Times*, 21 Oct 1981, 9b). With negotiations proceeding relating to the retrocession of Hong Kong in 1997, Kadoorie later argued for measures to ensure the retention of British citizenship for the non-Chinese minority, the beginning of a difficult struggle only partially won. In 1985, through a 25 per cent investment by China Light and following six years of negotiations, he supported a controversial but successful joint project with China for a nuclear plant at nearby Daya Bay, reflecting a long-term constructive relationship with the Chinese leadership.

Kadoorie's health declined in 1993, though he was active virtually to the end; he died following chemotherapy treatment for non-Hodgkin's lymphoma and cancer of the prostate at St Teresa's Hospital, Hong Kong, on 25 August 1993, and was buried on the 27th in the Jewish cemetery, Happy Valley. Senior Chinese leaders were reported to be 'deeply saddened'; he had forged links across the border, and, as former governor Sir Murray MacLehose wrote, 'With his wisdom and courtly charm he was respected and liked all over the world' (*South China Morning Post*, 1993). *Fortune* magazine had listed him as the third richest of Hong Kong's US$ billionaires, but for Hong Kong another link with the 'economic miracle', the dramatic post-war recovery and industrialization, personalized in *taipans* of Kadoorie's calibre—Sir William (Tony) and Sir John Keswick of Jardines, Sir Arthur Morse of the Hongkong Bank, Sir Alexander Grantham, the governor—had been lost.

Kadoorie's younger brother, **Sir Horace Kadoorie** (1902–1995), businessman and philanthropist, was born on 28 September 1902 in London. During the 1920s and 1930s he looked after the family's interests in Shanghai, where he engaged in many charitable activities including, in the late 1930s, establishing a school for the children of Jewish refugees who had reached the city. Following Japan's entry into the Second World War he was interned. After the war he joined his brother in successfully rebuilding the Hong Kong businesses. He was a director of China Light and Power, but took a more active interest in the group's hotels. His great passion was philanthropy. It was said of the brothers that Lawrence made the money and Horace gave it away. He supported a range of charities in Hong Kong—including the Hong Kong Anti-Cancer Association and the RSPCA—and in South Africa and Israel. He was particularly closely involved in the Kadoorie Agricultural Aid Association, through which the brothers helped settle many Chinese refugees as smallholders in the New Territories, providing training at the Kadoorie Farm and giving each family a pair of chickens and a pair of piglets. Horace Kadoorie became known as 'Mr New Territories'. He also provided similar training for Gurkha soldiers and financed livestock and horticultural projects in Nepal. He was appointed CBE in 1976 and knighted in 1989, and received French, Belgian, and Nepalese honours. A connoisseur of antique Chinese ivory and bronze, he formed one of the finest private collections in the world, and published *The Art of Ivory Sculpture in Cathay* (1988). He retired from China Light and Power in 1992. Suffering from Parkinson's disease, he died unmarried on 22 April 1995 in Hong Kong.   FRANK H. H. KING

Sources L. Kadoorie, 'The Kadoorie memoir, being a letter from Lord Lawrence Kadoorie of Hong Kong to Mrs Luba Arkin of Israel, dated 6 February 1979', in D. A. Leventhal, *Sino-Judaic studies: whence and whither, an essay and bibliography* (1985) • *South China Morning Post*, personality microfiche file, University of Hong Kong Library, special collections • *South China Morning Post* (1993) [CD Rom] • F. H. H. King, *The history of the Hongkong and Shanghai Banking Corporation*, 4 (1991) • 'Certainty of power', *Far Eastern Economic Review* (9 Sept 1993), 64–5 • N. Cameron, *Power: the story of China Light* (1982) • *The Times* (13 June 1981), 4 • *The Times* (21 Sept 1981), 15g • *The Times* (25 Sept 1981), 16f • *The Times* (21 Oct 1981), 9b • *The Times* (23 May 1984), 5a • *The Times* (29 March 1985), 4b • *The Times* (17 May 1986), 4 • *The Times* (26 Aug 1993) • V. England, *The quest of Noel Croucher, Hong Kong's quiet philanthropist* (1998) • B. Baker, 'Lady Kadoorie remembers', in B. Baker, *Shanghai: electric and lurid city, an anthology* (1998), 290–91 • private information (2004) [family, Sir Jack Cater, Lady Cater, Carl Smith, Caroline Plüss] • *WWW* • b. cert. • d. cert. • *Daily Telegraph* (28 April 1995) • *The Times* (5 May 1995)

Likenesses Constantine, photographs, University of Hong Kong, Hong Kong collection • photographs, repro. in Cameron, *Power*, pp. 90, 199, 227, 240 • photographs, University of Hong Kong, Hong Kong collection • portrait, repro. in *The Times* (26 Aug 1993), 19

Wealth at death $3.3 billion: *South China Morning Post* quoting *Fortune* magazine survey

Kagan, Joseph [*formerly* Juozapas Kaganas], **Baron Kagan** (1915–1995), textile manufacturer, was born in Kaunas, Lithuania, on 6 June 1915, the second of the three children of Benjaminas (Benjamin) Kaganas (1879–1988), textile manufacturer, and his wife, Mira (Miriam; 1893–1965), daughter of Shlomo and Chaia Nannes. His parents were Orthodox Jews, who had made a fortune in textiles by selling grey cloth to the Kaiser's army during the early years of the First World War. Joseph received a technical education at Kaunas high school and at a German boarding-school in East Prussia. He hoped to train as a barrister, but was persuaded by his father to study textiles in England. He travelled to west Yorkshire, chaperoned by his mother, and gained a bachelor of commerce honours degree in textiles at Leeds University.

After returning home to Lithuania to take charge of the family textile business, Kagan was stranded in Lithuania with his mother when the Russians invaded the independent Baltic republic in 1940, but was allowed to remain manager of the family firm by the Soviet authorities. This extraordinary concession later led to suspicion that he was being groomed as a KGB agent. In June 1941 when the Nazi forces invaded Lithuania he was stripped of his belongings and placed in a ghetto with his mother in the suburb of Vilijampole, Kaunas, where on 23 October 1943 he married Margarita (Margaret) Stromas (*b.* 1924), the daughter of a middle-class Lithuanian family, at a makeshift register office in the ghetto. It was only after the war that the couple formally exchanged rings at a Jewish ceremony in Bradford in 1946. Kagan escaped a pogrom and became a foundry worker, and when the ghetto became a concentration camp he planned an ingenious escape by constructing a secret hideout in the underdrawing of the foundry, where he hid with his wife and mother for nine months until Russian troops liberated Kaunas. They then travelled across Europe with other refugees to Romania, where Kagan worked in the British mission at Bucharest as a pest-control officer for a year. They then proceeded, via Italy, to west Yorkshire, where Benjamin Kagan had transferred part of the family textile business in 1940.

After working as a salesman for his father's business, Kagan tried his hand in the motor trade before setting up on his own account in textiles, with his wife, Margaret, manufacturing rough blankets in a hastily erected shed with a corrugated iron roof at South End, Elland, near Halifax. In 1951 he acquired the century-old firm of J. T. and T. Taylor of Batley, a pioneering profit-sharing company, and produced his first Gannex raincoat. Kagan's distinctive Gannex designs, patented in 1956, ingeniously sealed air between a waterproof nylon exterior and a woollen lining to create warm, fully insulated, stylish, lightweight coats and jackets. They became world famous after the opposition trade spokesman, Harold Wilson, wore a Gannex coat on a world tour in 1956, and they were subsequently sported by world leaders such as Lyndon Johnson, Mao Zedong, and Nikita Khrushchov, whom Wilson presented with a coat in 1963, Khrushchov's measurements having been gauged from his waxwork at Madame Tussaud's. The garments were also worn, on more relaxed occasions, by Queen Elizabeth and the duke of Edinburgh, and even by the royal corgis. In addition they were worn by Arctic and Antarctic explorers, Himalayan climbers, the armed services, and police forces in Britain and Canada. The success of the new fabric made Kagan a multi-millionaire and a series of mergers, takeovers, and outright purchases put Kagan Textiles in control of one of the most efficient combines in the textile and clothing industries.

For Harold Wilson the Gannex coat became a kind of personal trademark. Indeed, the satirical magazine *Private Eye* suggested mischievously in September 1971 that Wilson had been in effect in the employment of 'his good friend' Joseph Kagan 'as a commercial traveller and male model' for Gannex coats 'the last seven years' (Ziegler, 359). Kagan certainly developed a close friendship with Harold Wilson, who became prime minister in 1964, and he had become part of Wilson's political entourage by the time of the 1966 election, which gave Wilson a second term of office. Roy Jenkins, chancellor of the exchequer from 1967 to 1970, recalled the duty policeman at 10 Downing Street remarking that Joseph Kagan was 'very well known here' (ibid., 184). Kagan received a knighthood on 7 August 1970 in Harold Wilson's resignation honours' list.

Wilson and Kagan were of a similar age, and shared a love of the West Riding and a common industrial philosophy. Wilson admired the innovative Yorkshire entrepreneur for his business success and his interest in profit-

sharing at a time when his government was desperately seeking to promote industrial enterprise as part of his anticipated technological revolution in the 1960s. Before Wilson took office as prime minister, Kagan Textiles was paying him £100 a month in 1963 'for consultations and technical advice … in respect of Gannex sales to the USSR' (Ziegler, 91), and Wilson's official biographer maintained that Kagan subsequently made erratic contributions towards the running of Wilson's political office, though his name did not appear on the list of trustees established to fund the office. Kagan also helped Wilson's private secretary, Marcia Williams, to buy a flat close to Downing Street in 1967 by providing a deposit and underwriting her mortgage. His ennoblement as a life peer in Wilson's resignation honours' list in 1976, drafted by Marcia Williams on lavender notepaper, created a political furore, though Williams insisted that the nominations were Harold Wilson's 'and his alone' (Ziegler, 496).

Within two years Kagan was at the centre of further controversy, when he was charged with stealing twenty-three drums of indigo dye from Kagan Textiles Ltd (which had by then been taken over by another firm) and defrauding the public revenue, after absconding abroad with his 23-year-old secretary, Angela Radford. After lying low in Israel, he was finally arrested in Paris, extradited, and returned to face trial. He was fined £375,000 and served a ten-month sentence in Rudgate open prison, Yorkshire. He survived his prison ordeal by teaching fellow inmates to play chess and demonstrating his dexterity as a prodigious sewer of mailbags. Stripped of his knighthood by the queen, he was allowed to retain his life peerage, which could have been rescinded only by a special act of parliament, and he returned to the House of Lords in 1982, where he spoke effectively from his personal experience on penal issues. He also supported the War Crimes Bill and was deeply disappointed when it suffered defeat in the upper chamber.

Dark-haired, short, and stocky in stature, with a slight limp, Kagan was usually photographed wearing large, black-framed spectacles, and sporting a flamboyant bow tie and pipe. Naturally ebullient and charmingly persuasive, he gained a reputation as a womanizer, allegedly claiming to have had forty mistresses by the age of sixty. He acknowledged fathering an illegitimate son, Joshua Astor, by Judy Moynihan (wife of the sports journalist John Moynihan), in the 1960s. However, he retained a deep and abiding affection for his devoted and understanding wife, with whom he had two sons and a daughter between 1950 and 1965, insisting that 'no-one has ever taken her place in my life' and that 'marriage is for keeps' (*Daily Telegraph*, 19 Jan 1995). He died of heart failure and chronic lymphatic leukaemia at his home, 14 Queen's Court, Queensway, London, on 18 January 1995, following a heart attack in the House of Lords the previous month. He was cremated at Golders Green the next day after a ceremony conducted by Rabbi Hugo Gryn, and his ashes were preserved for later interment. He was survived by his wife and children. A memorial meeting was held in the

House of Lords on 10 May at which tributes were paid by Lord Glenamara, Viscount Tonypandy, the earl of Longford, and Baroness Masham. It was attended by members of his family and friends from inside and outside parliament, though not by the ailing Harold Wilson, whose elevation of Kagan to the House of Lords was now regarded by many as an embarrassing error of judgement.

Kagan was remembered in west Yorkshire as an enterprising industrialist who had given a timely boost to the ailing regional textile industry after the Second World War. However, his industrial legacy was short-lived. Although he introduced new lines in denims and jeans when the appeal of Gannex began to fade, his reputation never fully recovered after his gaol sentence and his core business interests suffered a lingering death. The *Halifax Courier* commented in an obituary tribute that his reputation had been sullied by 'dishonest and manipulative' flaws in his character. But Tam Dalyell, his obituarist in *The Independent*, while acknowledging that Kagan had made serious errors of judgement, concluded that he was 'a man whose contribution to Britain far and away outweighed any of the naughty things he may have done' (*The Independent*, 19 Jan 1995). Moreover, Dalyell maintained that Kagan's controversial relationship with Richardas Vaygauskas, a fellow Lithuanian based at the Soviet embassy between 1969 and 1971, who was an officer of the KGB expelled from Britain for espionage in 1971, sprang from their mutual love of chess and Kagan's concern for his remaining relatives in Soviet-controlled Vilna. For his part, Wilson denied that Kagan ever had access to official secrets. MI5, alarmed at the possibility of Soviet contact within the premier's entourage, had kept Kagan under close surveillance. In reality, as his moving maiden speech in the House of Lords made abundantly clear, Kagan was a democrat at heart, suspicious of dictatorships of both the left and the right, and believed passionately in the rights of the individual.   JOHN A. HARGREAVES

Sources J. Burns, 'Knight of the ghetto: the story of Lord Kagan', unpublished typescript, [n.d.], United States Holocaust Memorial Museum, Washington, DC, USA • *The Times* (19 Jan 1995) • *The Independent* (19 Jan 1995) • *Daily Telegraph* (19 Jan 1995) • *The Guardian* (19 Jan 1995) • *Evening Courier* [Halifax] (18 Jan 1995) • *Yorkshire Post* (19 Jan 1995) • M. Williams, *Inside number 10* (1972) • A. Roth, *Sir Harold Wilson, Yorkshire Walter Mitty* (1977) • T. Benn, *Against the tide: diaries, 1973–1976* (1989) • K. O. Morgan, *Callaghan: a life* (1997) • 'Gannex: the best all-weather cloth in the world', *Manufacturing Clothier* (Aug 1969) • newspaper cuttings file, Halifax Courier Library, Halifax • C. Pincher, *Too secret too long* (1984) • P. Ziegler, *Wilson* (1995) • *WWW, 1991–5* • d. cert. • private information (2004) [Lady Kagan]
Archives priv. coll., news cuttings, corresp., etc. | Halifax Courier Library, Halifax, news cuttings • Industrial Museum, Halifax, West Yorkshire • priv. coll. • United States Holocaust Memorial Museum, 100 Raoul Wallenberg Place, Washington, DC, J. Burns, 'Knight of the ghetto: the story of Lord Kagan' (unpublished typescript, n.d.) • W. Yorks. AS, Calderdale, Kagan textiles (Gannex mills), plans, ELL: 443-444 • W. Yorks. AS, Calderdale, Gannex cartoon collection |FILM priv. coll., various amateur films (1966–73)
Likenesses D. Flynn, oils, 1964, priv. coll. • photograph, 1970, repro. in *The Independent* • photograph, 1970, repro. in *Yorkshire Post* • photograph, 1976, priv. coll. • photograph, repro. in *The Times* • photograph, repro. in *Manufacturing Clothier* • photograph

(with Harold Wilson), priv. coll. • photographs, priv. coll. • photographs, Halifax Courier Library, news cutting file
Wealth at death £261,041: probate, 1995, *CGPLA Eng. & Wales*

Kahan [*née* Langridge], **Barbara Joan** (1920–2000), social worker, was born on 18 March 1920 at Station House, Horsted Keynes, Sussex, the youngest child of Alfred George Langridge, railway clerk and later station master, and his wife, Emily Kathleen, *née* Bromley. She grew up in a bookish home. The family's Methodism, which she later forswore for agnosticism, inculcated a strong sense of social justice and a taste for public service. She participated in her mother's local good works, and remembered the workhouse where she took part in a Christmas pantomime and the plight of the strikers and their families in 1926. In the 1930s, at her prompting, a refugee Jewish girl came to stay, who became her 'foster sister'.

Barbara Langridge was educated locally, and in 1939 she won a state scholarship to Cambridge University to read English. She was active in student politics: the University Labour Club, Richard Acland's leftist Common Wealth Party, and the Peace Pledge Union. On graduation she moved to the London School of Economics (billeted in Cambridge) to gain her diploma in social science. In 1943 she became a factory inspector, but in 1948 she was appointed, by Dudley borough council, one of the first children's officers, a post created under the Children Act of the same year. Children's officers were a remarkable group of (mainly) women who, often against institutional odds, pioneered a new service; this was one of the less prominent but enormously far-reaching reforms of the immediate post-war years. In Dudley she opened the authority's first children's home.

In 1950 Langridge became the children's officer in Oxfordshire. She had one room and piles of public assistance files to wade through; after six weeks she had permission to appoint a seventeen-year-old secretary. The departments were small and centralized, and she was not alone among children's officers in shouldering a caseload as well as managerial responsibilities. She abolished corporal punishment in children's homes in 1951, and imaginative fostering was introduced. Preventative work was the cornerstone of child care policy; staffing ratios were high and there was close liaison with families. She always sought to unite children with their families when possible. This was unusual when the prevailing professional ethos was that children needed to be permanently removed from 'bad' family circumstances. Her ideas bore the mark of the child-rearing theories of George Lyward, David Wills, John Bowlby, Donald Winnicott, and her own husband, the child psychiatrist Vladimir Leon Kahan (1907/8–1981), whom she married on 9 July 1955. He was the son of Leon Kahan, medical practitioner. There were no children of the marriage.

In Barbara Kahan's view young people in trouble needed help, not punishment, and she believed that there was an artificial distinction between deprived young people and young offenders. Both in Oxfordshire and in her extramural activities, with bodies including the Association of Children's Officers, she, with others, paved the way for the Children and Young Persons Act of 1969, with its belief in the welfare model of working with young people in trouble, seeing them as deprived, not depraved. It was partly her 'obsessional antagonism' (as one colleague called it) to the approved schools that helped to bring about their abolition. She was a member of the Finer commission on single-parent families from 1969 to 1973. She stayed in Oxfordshire until 1970, when the children's department was absorbed into the new social services department. She then joined the Home Office as deputy chief inspector of the children's department but in the next year transferred to the Department of Health and Social Security, as assistant director of the Social Work Service. She remained there until her retirement in 1980.

Kahan then became director (and the only staff member) of the charitably funded Gatsby Project, to pioneer distance learning for residential child care workers. In 1991, when the work was absorbed into the Open University and was renamed the Child Care Open Learning Project, she gave up the directorship. The project was innovative and promoted her long-cherished ideas—recognizing the specialist skills of residential care staff, raising their status, and expanding their training. But she was also much concerned about those in care. Her book *Growing up in Care* (1979) was a pioneering work in allowing young people to give their views. Her other books were *Childcare Research, Policy and Practice* (1989) and *Growing up in Groups* (1994). She also co-edited two volumes on residential care and staff selection. She served as professional adviser to the House of Commons select committee on social services from 1983 to 1990 and as chair of the National Children's Bureau from 1985 to 1994 (vice-president thereafter). She was appointed OBE in 1990 and received honorary degrees from the Open University and the University of Victoria, British Columbia.

In 1991 Kahan produced, with Alan Levy QC, *The pindown experience and the protection of children: the report of the Staffordshire Childcare Inquiry, 1990*. It not only drew attention to the neglect of residential care by management that allowed abuse to flourish but also prompted the first of a series of government reports into residential care. In her last years she worked as an expert witness for firms of solicitors representing those who had been abused in the residential care system. She was nevertheless a steadfast proponent of residential care for children long after it had gone out of fashion, and she believed that it foundered for lack of advocates among directors of social services. Hers was perhaps a necessary corrective to the wholesale disfavour in which residential care found itself with both statutory and voluntary agencies.

Kahan never suffered fools gladly and often showed little patience with those whom she perceived as her intellectual inferiors. She could easily be dismissive, but for her friends she was delightful, amusing, and stimulating company, especially at her beloved home in Cassington, Oxfordshire. She was not always the easiest of employers but she nurtured talent. Many men and women who later distinguished themselves as academics or directors of

social services departments could thank her for the start and encouragement that she gave them.

Kahan had an unwavering faith in children and their potential combined with an appreciation of the need for first-class services to care for them. To these ends she brought courage, considerable gifts, great spirit, passion, extraordinary energy, and relentlessness. She died at the John Radcliffe Hospital, Oxford, on 6 August 2000. Her funeral was held at St Peter's Church, Cassington, on 16 August, followed by cremation. A memorial meeting took place in London on 25 January 2001.   TERRY PHILPOT

Sources *The Guardian* (9 Aug 2000) · *The Times* (10 Aug 2000) · T. Philpot, 'Championing the children's cause', *Community Care* (7 Sept 1977) · *WWW* · private information (2004) · personal knowledge (2004) · b. cert. · m. cert. · d. cert.
Archives Bessell's Leigh School, Oxfordshire, staff library
Likenesses photograph, repro. in *The Guardian* · photograph, repro. in *The Times* · photograph, repro. in *Community Care* (10–16 Aug 2000)
Wealth at death £1,924,215: probate, 7 March 2001, *CGPLA Eng. & Wales*

Kahane, Jack (1887–1939), publisher, was born on 20 July 1887 at 59 Bury New Road, Broughton, in Salford, near Manchester, the seventh of the eight children of Selig Kahane (d. 1893), a shipper, and his wife, Suzy, née Sufrin (d. 1896). Although registered as Jonas, he was always known as Jack. His parents were of Jewish origin and his forebears had prospered in the cotton trade. Both Kahane's father and mother died when he was young and he was brought up by an elder sister. He was educated at Manchester grammar school from 1900 to 1903, and then went to work in a cotton trader's office before setting up his own successful business. A tall, good-looking man, Kahane indulged a natural taste for the good life with fashionable clothes and frequent visits to London. The archetypal Edwardian dandy, he carried a cane and wore a monocle.

Kahane joined the army on the outbreak of the First World War and was gassed and wounded at the battle of Ypres. During his convalescence he met his future wife, Marcelle Eugénie Girodias, whose father was a French civil engineer and whose mother was Spanish, and they were married in 1917. In 1919 their first son, Maurice, was born and over the next seven years three more children followed: Nicole, Sylvie, and Eric.

During a bout of tuberculosis Kahane wrote a light and slightly *risqué* novel called *Laugh and Grow Rich* which was published in England, where it was banned by lending libraries. He sent a spirited letter defending the novel to a British newspaper, good and bad reviews followed, and the book sold well. Noting that spicy stories invoked censorship, which triggered protest, which produced sales, Kahane turned his attention to publishing.

In 1928 Kahane joined a French publisher as a junior partner and persuaded Sylvia Beach, owner of the bookshop Shakespeare and Company, who had recently published James Joyce's *Ulysses*, to allow his firm to publish a 5000 word fragment of Joyce's work in progress, *Haveth Childers everywhere*. In 1931 Kahane decided to set up his own publishing house, rented offices in the elegant place

Vendôme, and named his publishing house the Obelisk Press after the Egyptian obelisk in the centre of the nearby place de la Concorde.

Aware of both the pitfalls and the opportunities created by censorship in Britain, Ireland, and the United States, Kahane devised a double-sided publishing strategy. He would publish popular and sexually titillating novels to pay the bills but also actively search for serious authors who could not have their works published in their own countries. It was this simple formula that underpinned the Obelisk Press during its short life in the 1930s, as well as that of its successor, the Olympia Press, founded and run by Kahane's son, Maurice *Girodias, after the Second World War. Between them they published some of the landmark avant-garde novels of the twentieth century.

In 1933 Kahane launched the new venture with *The Young and the Evil* by Parker Tyler and Charles Henri Ford, an interracial homosexual novel set in New York; Radclyffe Hall's crusading lesbian novel, *The Well of Loneliness*; and Frank Harris's four-volume *My Life and Loves*, an exaggerated and bombastic account of his literary, political, and sexual adventures. Kahane's great coup, however, was to publish Henry Miller's *Tropic of Cancer* in 1934, followed by *Black Spring* (1936), *Max and the White Phagocytes* (1938), and *Tropic of Capricorn* (1939). Through Miller, Kahane met Lawrence Durrell and Anaïs Nin. He published Durrell's first serious novel, *The Black Book*, in 1938 and Nin's *Winter of Artifice* in 1939. He also put out Cyril Connolly's novel *The Rock Pool*, and wrote engagingly about his own life in *The Memoirs of a Booklegger*. Jack Kahane died in Paris of a heart attack on 2 September 1939. A fitting epitaph came from Henry Miller, recalling the birth pangs of *Tropic of Cancer*. 'It was something of a miracle', he said, 'that I found in Paris the one publisher … courageous enough to sponsor such a book: Jack Kahane and the Obelisk Press' (E. de Grazia, *Girls Lean Back Everywhere: the Law of Obscenity and the Assault on Genius*, 1992, 367). JOHN DE ST JORRE

Sources J. Kahane, *The memoirs of a booklegger* (1939) · H. Ford, *Published in Paris: American and British writers, printers, and publishers in Paris, 1920–1939* (1975) · M. Girodias, *The frog prince: an autobiography* (1980) · J. de St Jorre, *Venus bound: the erotic voyage of the Olympia Press and its writers* (New York, 1996)
Likenesses photograph, priv. coll.; repro. in de St Jorre, *Venus bound*

Kahn, Franz Daniel (1926–1998), astrophysicist and mathematician, was born on 13 May 1926 in Nuremberg, Germany, the only son and the younger child of Siegfried Kahn (1894–1967), a company director, and his wife, Grete, *née* Mann (1896–1980). His parents were German Jews; his father was a successful manufacturer of children's toys. In 1938 the family moved to England, where his father, with Jewish colleagues, had already set up a branch of their firm (Trix Ltd, manufacturers of toy trains). Kahn was educated at St Paul's School from 1940 to 1944, during his evacuation to Crowthorne. He won a form prize for English after he had been in England for less than two years, and in 1944 secured an open scholarship to Queen's College, Oxford. After graduating with first-class honours in

mathematics in 1947 he continued at Oxford with research under Sydney Chapman, then moved in 1948 to Balliol College as a Skynner senior student. His DPhil thesis was a study of the expulsion of corpuscular streams in solar flares. He was awarded the degrees of MA and DPhil in 1950.

Kahn was appointed assistant lecturer in mathematics at the University of Manchester in 1949 and remained in Manchester for the rest of his life. On 22 March 1951 he married Carla Vivienne Copeland (1928/9–1981), a schoolteacher and the daughter of Benjamin Copeland, a textile merchant. It was a happy marriage, and they had two sons and two daughters. In the same year as Kahn's marriage, a new astronomy department was formed at Manchester, under Zdeněk Kopal, complementing the development of radio astronomy at Jodrell Bank under Bernard Lovell. Kahn joined the new department in 1952 as a Turner and Newall fellow, and was appointed in succession lecturer (1955), senior lecturer (1958), reader (1962), and professor (1966). He was elected a fellow of the Royal Society in 1993 and retired in the same year as professor emeritus. He continued active in research until his death.

Kahn's DPhil dissertation on solar streams marked the beginning of his seminal theoretical work on astrophysical gas dynamics. His classic paper 'The acceleration of interstellar clouds', published in the *Bulletin of the Astronomical Institute of the Netherlands* in 1954, analysing the effect of radiation from hot stars on interstellar gas, was written during a year in Leiden, where he collaborated with Jan Oort, Henk van der Hulst, Lyman Spitzer, and Bengt Strömgren. Photoionization by ultraviolet light from hot stars occurs in narrow zones; Kahn introduced the widely used classification of these ionization fronts into four types, according to their velocities of propagation. Many papers on related subjects followed; a frequently quoted paper (published in *Astronomy and Astrophysics* in 1976) was on the temperature and cooling rate of supernova remnants. On the larger scale of the dynamics of whole galaxies, Kahn suggested that the collective effects of many supernova explosions may be to drive hot gas away from the disc of a spiral galaxy, creating a 'galactic fountain': this was the subject of an introductory lecture to a symposium of the International Astronomical Union (IAU), subsequently published with its proceedings in 1991. Other especially notable research topics were the formation of massive stars by accretion within dusty molecular clouds, the electrodynamics of pulsar magnetospheres, and the effect of intergalactic gas on the dynamics of the local group of galaxies.

In 1975 Franz and Carla Kahn wrote an important historical paper, published in *Nature* that year, on the correspondence between Einstein and de Sitter, which they found in the archives of the Leiden observatory during a sabbatical year. In a series of letters, dated 1916–18, Einstein asked de Sitter to make his relativity theory more widely known; in England de Sitter later published papers in the *Monthly Notices of the Royal Astronomical Society*, which attracted the attention of A. S. Eddington. The letters included discussion of cosmical repulsion during a period when Einstein was introducing the so-called cosmical constant.

Kahn was an inspiration to all astrophysicists, contributing at least as much by his quiet and thoughtful remarks at discussion meetings as in his formal papers. He was a council member of the Royal Astronomical Society (1967–70) and an editor of the *Monthly Notices of the Royal Astronomical Society* (1993–8). He was president of the IAU's commission on interstellar matter (1970–73), and the IAU named an asteroid, Kahnia, after him. He also served on committees of the Science and Engineering Research Council, chairing the theory panel (1976–9), the panel for allocation of telescope time (1979–81), and the astronomy II committee (1981–4). Following the death of his wife, Carla, in 1981 he developed a warm friendship with Junis Davis, but did not remarry. He died suddenly of a heart attack in Bourne End, Buckinghamshire, on 8 February 1998 and was buried in the south Manchester Jewish cemetery. He was survived by his four children.

F. Graham-Smith

Sources J. E. Dyson and D. Lynden-Bell, *Memoirs FRS*, 45 (1999), 255–67 · J. Dyson, 'Franz Daniel Kahn', *Astronomy and Geophysics*, 39 (1998), 32–3 · *The Independent* (7 March 1998) · *The Guardian* (16 March 1998) · *WWW* · personal knowledge (2004) · private information (2004) · m. cert. · d. cert.
Likenesses photograph, repro. in *Memoirs FRS*, 254 · photograph, repro. in *The Independent*
Wealth at death £261,068: probate, 13 May 1998, *CGPLA Eng. & Wales*

Kahn, Richard Ferdinand, Baron Kahn (1905–1989), economist, was born in London on 10 August 1905, the second child and only son of four surviving children (two younger sons died) of Augustus Kahn, inspector of schools, and his wife, Regina Rosa Schoyer, of Germany. Kahn was educated at St Paul's School, London, and at King's College, Cambridge. He read mathematics for one year, obtaining a first in part one in 1925, physics for two years, obtaining a second in part two of the natural sciences tripos in 1927, and economics, obtaining a first in part two in 1928, a remarkable performance after only one year. John Maynard *Keynes and Gerald Shove, his King's supervisors, and Piero Sraffa encouraged Kahn to write a fellowship dissertation for King's, of which he became a fellow in 1930.

In only a year and a half, Kahn produced 'The economics of the short period', a remarkable contribution to the then emerging theory of imperfect competition. It was associated with the beginning of Kahn's close intellectual friendship with Joan Robinson. Kahn's dissertation contained many of the results in her *The Economics of Imperfect Competition* (1933) and the subsequent literature spawned by it and Edward Chamberlin's *The Theory of Monopolistic Competition* (1933): the use of a reverse L-shaped cost curve, the kinked demand curve, and the procedure of explaining empirical observations in terms of business people's perception of their situations rather than starting from a simple axiom. Showing that the unfit were not purged in a slump was the most grievous blow dealt to *laissez-faire* until Keynes established the possibility of under-

Richard Ferdinand Kahn, Baron Kahn (1905–1989), by Ramsey & Muspratt

employment equilibrium in 1936. Kahn's dissertation was not published in English until shortly after his death in 1989. (An Italian translation was published in 1983.) In retrospect Kahn regretted that he had not published it at the time. In his introduction to the 1989 book he described it as an impressive performance for its time and (economic) age of its author.

Kahn became a university lecturer in the faculty of economics and politics in 1933, second bursar to Keynes in 1935, and a teaching fellow at King's in 1936. He was the key figure in the famous 'circus' which 'argued out' the propositions of *A Treatise on Money* (2 vols., 1930) and discussed and criticized Keynes's drafts as Keynes moved from the *Treatise on Money* to *The General Theory of Employment, Interest and Money* (1936). Kahn also went regularly with Keynes to Tilton (the Sussex home of Keynes and his wife, Lydia Lopokova) to give him 'stiff supervisions' on the emerging drafts.

Cambridge was the scene for two theoretical revolutions in economic theory in the 1920s and 1930s. Kahn played crucial roles in both. His lifelong scepticism about the quantity theory of money as a causal explanation of the general price level increasingly sapped Keynes's acceptance of it (and Say's law) from his teacher Alfred Marshall. In a famous article in 1931 on the multiplier, 'The relation of home investment to unemployment' (*Economic Journal*, vol. 41), Kahn used the apparatus of Keynes's *Treatise on Money* to put a precise order of magnitude on the total increase in employment that would ultimately occur if a primary increase were created by public works. He showed, under carefully specified conditions, that the investment expenditure itself would create a matching volume of new savings. This concept allowed Keynes to create a key innovation, the propensity-to-consume schedule, which became an integral part of the theory of employment as a whole in *The General Theory*. That it was the investment dog which wagged the savings tail, rather than the other way around, owes much to Kahn's article. A mystery remains, though, as to why Kahn, who had provided a realistic and better alternative in his dissertation, allowed Keynes to return to Marshall to provide the theory of prices in *The General Theory*.

During the 1930s Kahn wrote a number of seminal papers on imperfect competition, welfare economics, and international trade. The Second World War saw Kahn, on Keynes's recommendation, in Whitehall. He started as a temporary principal in the Board of Trade. Oliver Lyttelton liked his work and had Kahn seconded to him in a number of different sections: the Middle East supply centre (as economic adviser, 1941–3), then the Ministry of Production, the Ministry of Supply, and finally the Board of Trade again in 1945. Kahn ended the war with the administrative grade of principal assistant secretary. He took to Whitehall like a duck to water, drafting memos, scheming to get his views through, while still having enough time and energy for the minutiae of administration. This intense interest in detail and a reluctance to delegate stayed with Kahn for the rest of his life. He had excellent ideas, was an acute and incisive critic, but was often difficult to work with, especially when his notorious anger was aroused.

After the war Kahn returned to Cambridge for the rest of his life (there were extended periods away working for the United Nations in the 1950s and 1960s). He became first bursar of King's in 1946 when Keynes died, a position which he held until he was elected to a chair in 1951. (He retired from this post in 1972.) He was appointed CBE in 1946, elected a fellow of the British Academy in 1960, and created a life peer in 1965. He remained, as he himself wished to be known, a disciple of Keynes, devoting himself, particularly through his selfless input into the work of others, to extending Keynes's ideas into the theory of the long period—especially with Joan Robinson and also with Nicholas Kaldor, Sraffa, and Luigi Pasinetti—and to extending and defending Keynes's ideas on money and the stock market generally. Kahn had a substantial impact on the views of the committee of inquiry into the monetary and credit system (1957–9), chaired by Sir Cyril Radcliffe. He also discussed the need for an incomes policy as he spelt out the implications for inflationary pressures and the balance of payments of successfully sustaining full employment, as opposed to reaching it (for obvious reasons, Keynes's main objective in the 1930s). In the 1970s and 1980s Kahn turned increasingly to the history of theory, providing authoritative evaluations of Keynes's achievements for the British Academy (1974), in the *Journal of Economic Literature* (1978), and in his Raffaele Mattioli

Foundation lectures in Italy, *The Making of Keynes' General Theory* (1984).

Kahn lived in a splendid set of rooms in Webb's Court at King's until his final illness. To those who did not know him well, he seemed an intensely private person. Deafness and ill health in his last years made him a rather solitary public figure. In reality, he was kind, generous, and hospitable, a meticulously considerate host and, in his younger days, a vigorous walker and rock climber. He never lost his interest in what was happening in King's and the faculty, or ceased to disapprove if things did not turn out as he would have wished.

Kahn came from a deeply religious Jewish family who were devoted to education. Up until the Second World War Kahn's orthodoxy was a byword among Jewish students and others. After the war his strict observance fell away. In his last years, though, he returned to his earlier faith and asked that he be buried in the Jewish section of the Cambridge cemetery. Kahn never married but he never lacked agreeable female company either. He died at the Evelyn Hospital, Cambridge, on 6 June 1989, and was buried in accordance with his wishes.

G. C. HARCOURT, *rev.*

Sources *Annual Report of the Council* [King's College, Cambridge] (1990) · L. L. Pasinetti, 'Kahn, Richard Ferdinand', *The new Palgrave: a dictionary of economics*, ed. J. Eatwell, M. Milgate, and P. Newman (1987) · L. L. Pasinetti, 'Richard Ferdinand Kahn, 1905–1989', *PBA*, 76 (1990), 423–44 · C. Marcuzzo, interview with Kahn, 1988, King's Cam. [mimeo] · *The Independent* (10 June 1989) · *The Times* (8 June 1989) · personal knowledge (1996) · private information (1996) · G. C. Harcourt, 'R. F. Kahn: a tribute', *Quarterly Review* [Banca Nazionale del Lavoro], 44 (1991), 15–30 · G. C. Harcourt, 'Kahn and Keynes and the making of *The General Theory*', *Cambridge Journal of Economics*, 17 (1994), 11–23

Archives BLPES, corresp. relating to Royal Economic Society and the *Economic Journal* · King's AC Cam., corresp. and papers | BLPES, corresp. with J. E. Meade · Bodl. Oxf., corresp. with Sidney Dell · King's AC Cam., corresp. with John Maynard Keynes · King's AC Cam., letters to G. H. W. Rylands · Trinity Cam., corresp. with Piero Sraffa

Likenesses Ramsey & Muspratt, photograph, British Academy [*see illus.*]

Wealth at death under £100,000: administration, 2 Feb 1990, CGPLA Eng. & Wales

Kakungulu, Semei Lwakirenzi (1868–1928), war leader and administrator in Uganda, was probably the son of Semuwemba, a chief in Koki, then a small principality to the south of Buganda. Seeking greater opportunities, Kakungulu moved to the court of Kabaka (king) Mutesa I of Buganda, who rewarded his skill as an elephant hunter with a minor chieftaincy. He went on to make his name as a recklessly brave war leader, helping to place Mutesa's successor, Mwanga (c.1866–1903), back on the throne in 1889 after the kingdom had been shaken by religious conflict. His reward was marriage about 1889 to Princess Nawati, a sister of Mwanga: she died of smallpox not long afterwards. Apolo Kagwa (1864–1927), however, not he, became *katikiro* (chief minister) of Buganda, and rivalry between these two men marked Kakungulu's career. He was baptized an Anglican in 1889 or 1890, with the Christian name Semei, and on 15 October 1894 he entered into a

Christian marriage with Princess Elizabeth Semiramis Nakalema, another relative of Kabaka Mwanga. Kakungulu went on to distinguish himself in the campaign fought by the British and the newly emerging Christian chiefly hierarchy in Buganda against reactionary forces led by Mwanga and by Kabarega, the *mukama* (king) of Bunyoro, which resulted in their capture and exile in 1899.

In the 1890s Kakungulu was rewarded with chiefly appointments, first a minor chieftaincy and then a senior chieftaincy, but the latter brought him into renewed conflict with Apolo Kagwa. Dissatisfied, he resigned and began to build up his own power base around the shores of Lake Kyoga. Recognizing his talents, the protectorate administration appointed him to bring under British control a vaguely defined area lying between Lake Kyoga and Mount Elgon, known at the time as Bukedi, which fell within the boundaries of Uganda, but was not yet effectively administered: the British had neither money nor personnel to do so themselves and were willing to use what historians later called the sub-imperialism of the Baganda. Accompanied by a considerable number of Baganda, Kakungulu established his first headquarters near Mbale, settling his followers on the surrounding land, but was then moved to Budaka, further west, when the government post was established there. Kakungulu organized the area into Ganda-type chieftaincies after raiding parties had subdued the people, sometimes with unnecessary brutality. Literacy as well as guns helped him to assert his authority. In 1900 Sir Harry Johnston (1858–1927), special commissioner in Uganda, was impressed by this fine figure of a man, by Kakungulu's well-organized headquarters, the roads he had built, and his energy and administrative skills. He encouraged Kakungulu to believe that he had been appointed *kabaka* of Bukedi, a position entirely foreign to the peoples of eastern Uganda. He had the strong support of the (Anglican) Church Missionary Society for the way in which he encouraged his followers to act as evangelists.

As the British gradually increased their presence in the area, they became wary of Kakungulu's power and ambitions. In their eyes he was a junior salaried employee, appointed only to meet a temporary need. He was moved around by a succession of inexperienced protectorate officials, chiefs he had appointed were demoted and replaced, and, forced to seize cattle in lieu of hut tax when people had no money to pay, he became a scapegoat for trouble that arose from this. In 1904 his powers were curbed. He was moved back to Mbale, given 20 square miles of land for himself and his followers, and limited to administering that small area, a demotion he fretted under. The administration feared him as a potential rebel, yet found him a useful counterweight to Apolo Kagwa. He could not simply be sacked, so in 1906 it was decided to move him to Busoga to become president of the Busoga council of chiefs, a post which, it was hoped, would give him prestige without too much power.

Reluctantly Kakungulu agreed. There was conflict with the protectorate authorities over the amount of land he

was to be allowed, and they disapproved of his ambitious house-building plans. He had less scope to organize the administration of Busoga than he had possessed in the early days of his time in Bukedi. His power was steadily eroded as literate Basoga emerged who could take over many roles. There was conflict with Apolo Kagwa over land Kakungulu owned in Buganda. In 1905 he had divorced his Christian wife for adultery and married on Ganda customary terms a Muslim princess, Dimbwe, daughter of Kalema, who had briefly been *kabaka* of Buganda in 1888; following her adultery with his brother he separated from her in 1918. This marriage earned him the disapproval of the missionaries who had previously supported him. There were problems with the protectorate government when Kakungulu was reluctant to clear land he owned by the lake, as ordered by the medical authorities, who were concerned about the spread of the fly (*Glossina palpalis*) which was the vector of sleeping sickness. A quarrel with Frederick Spire, the provincial commissioner, led to his final downfall and forced resignation in 1913. No successor was appointed.

Having no alternative, Kakungulu now returned to Mbale, but his power base there had disappeared, so he moved to Gangama in the Elgon foothills. Unsurprisingly he was in no mood to co-operate with the British authorities. The first major clash came in August 1914 when he was refused permission to enter Buganda unless inoculated against plague. Roughly handled, he refused and turned back. He now turned to the teaching of the Bamalaki, a group who had broken with other Christians over the need for lengthy instruction before baptism and the use of medicine. The Luganda Bible unfortunately used the same words for witchcraft and wizards as for medicine and doctors. As the former were forbidden, so should the latter be, according to the Bamalaki. They saw that European medicine was powerless against sleeping sickness; many who entered hospitals died there; one should trust in God alone. A further clash occurred over cattle vaccination: the authorities gave up trying to apply the regulations around Mbale. In 1920 Kakungulu and a small band of followers separated from the Bamalaki over circumcision, which they came to believe was necessary, calling themselves Bayudaya (Jews). Kakungulu married several more wives, living polygamously. The final major clash with the authorities came over the compulsory purchase of land for Makerere College, Kampala, which Kakungulu resisted, and for which he therefore received little compensation. He died probably of pneumonia on 24 November 1928 and at his funeral a few days later Ham Mukasa (c.1871–1956) gave the eulogy. The evaluation of Kakungulu's controversial career is still a matter for debate among Ugandans.

M. LOUISE PIROUET

Sources M. Twaddle, *Kakungulu and the creation of Uganda, 1868–1928* (1993) · H. B. Thomas, 'Capax Imperii: the story of Simei Kakunguru', *Uganda Journal*, 6/2 (1939), 125–36 · J. M. Gray, 'Kakunguru in Bukedi', *Uganda Journal*, 27/1 (1963), 31–60 · H. B. Welbourn, *East African rebels: a study of some independent churches* (1961) · J. V. Taylor, *The growth of the church in Buganda* (1958) · H. B.

Thomas and R. Scott, *Uganda* (1935) · M. L. Pirouet, *Black evangelists: the spread of Christianity in Uganda, 1891–1914* (1978)
Likenesses J. B. Purvis, photograph, repro. in Twaddle, *Kakungulu*, 189

Kaldor, Nicholas [Miklós], **Baron Kaldor** (1908–1986), economist, was born in Budapest on 12 May 1908, the youngest in the family of three sons (two of whom died in infancy) and one daughter of Gyula Kaldor, Jewish lawyer and legal adviser to the German legation in Budapest, and his wife, Jamba Adler. Miklós (he later Anglicized his name) was educated at the Minta Gymnasium in Budapest (1918–25), the University of Berlin (1925–7), and the London School of Economics (LSE) (1927–30), where he obtained a first-class honours degree in economics and a research studentship to study the problems of the Danubian succession states. In 1932 he joined the staff of the LSE as an assistant in economics (later assistant lecturer), then lecturer (1938), and reader (1945). He became an honorary fellow of the LSE in 1970. In 1947 he resigned his post to become director of the research and planning division of the Economic Commission for Europe in Geneva. In 1949 he was appointed a fellow of King's College, Cambridge, and a lecturer in economics at Cambridge, where he taught and researched for the rest of his life. He became a reader in economics in 1952 and a professor in 1966, until his retirement in 1975.

During his academic life Kaldor held several advisory posts and visiting positions. In the war he worked on the two reports by Lord Beveridge, *Social Insurance* (1942) and *Full Employment in a Free Society* (1944). After the war he took on several advisory roles as chief of the economic planning staff of the American strategic bombing survey (1945), adviser to the Hungarian government (1946), adviser to the French commissariat général du plan (1947), member of the Berlin currency and trade committee (1948), and member of the United Nations group of experts on national and international measures for full employment (1949). In 1951 he was appointed to the royal commission on the taxation of profits and income and was the author of a famous memorandum of dissent attacking the majority report (1955) for its conservatism on matters relating to the taxation of capital gains, company taxation, and the treatment of expenses under schedule D. There followed several invitations from developing countries to give tax advice: India (1956), Ceylon (1958), Mexico (1960), Ghana (1961), British Guiana (1961), Turkey (1962), Iran (1966), and Venezuela (1976). He was also special adviser in 1964–8 and 1974–6 to the chancellor of the exchequer in two British Labour governments. He accepted a life barony in 1974 and he contributed frequently to economic debates in the House of Lords, being a trenchant critic of Conservative economic policy during the early years of Margaret Thatcher's government. Like J. M. Keynes, Kaldor was a public figure, but, unlike Keynes, he was a socialist. He had a passionate concern for the underdog, and was the most prolific newspaper-letter-writing economist of his generation. His membership of

Nicholas Kaldor, Baron Kaldor (1908–1986), by Godfrey Argent, 1970

the House of Lords gave him enormous pleasure. In many ways he was more English than the English. He admired their history and culture and revelled in their institutions.

Kaldor's advisory work never seemed to interfere with his academic research and may even have enhanced it. In his early years at the LSE he made significant breakthroughs in several key areas including the theory of the firm, capital theory, trade cycle theory, and welfare economics. In 1936 Keynes produced his *General Theory* and Kaldor was an immediate convert. He later had close links with Keynes during the Second World War when the LSE was evacuated to Cambridge, and in the 1950s he was joint architect of the 'Cambridge school' which extended Keynesian modes of thinking to the analysis of growth and distribution in capitalist economies. At this time he also became a prominent tax expert, publishing a minor classic, *An Expenditure Tax* (1955). In the 1960s and 1970s he turned his attention to the applied economics of growth. He emphasized particularly the role of manufacturing industry in the growth process and argued that the ultimate constraint on growth in the world economy is the rate of land-saving innovations in agriculture. He was a strong critic of general equilibrium theory, regarding it as barren for an understanding of the dynamic and cumulative processes that propel economies in the real world. Kaldor also led the attack on the doctrine of monetarism, which he regarded as simply a euphemism for deflation, that afflicted both governments and the economics profession in the 1970s and 1980s. Between 1960 and 1980 he published eight volumes of collected essays which are testimony to his endeavour and creativity.

Kaldor was a unique figure in twentieth-century economics. It was not only his intellect and his non-orthodox approach to economics that made him dominant and controversial; it was also his style, charm, and sense of fun, which made it impossible not to listen to what he had to say. In lectures and seminars he would captivate his audience by the heavily accented flow of English prose which was so much a feature of his personality and an endearing quality in itself. The image of a rotund and jovial medieval monk holding forth in intellectual discourse fits him perfectly. While Kaldor worked in his ground-floor study, the ever open door of his spacious Edwardian house would see a succession of family and friends coming and going. Kaldor might appear or not depending on the urgency of the task at hand. He was egocentric, but could also afford to be generous with his time. He liked to compartmentalize his intellectual effort, working for long periods and then relaxing. He had money enough to enjoy the summers at a residence in the south of France.

Many honours came Kaldor's way, including honorary doctorates from the universities of Dijon (1962) and Frankfurt (1982), fellowship of the British Academy (1963), the presidency of section F of the British Association for the Advancement of Science (1970) and of the Royal Economic Society (1974), and honorary membership of the American Economic Association (1975) and of the Hungarian Academy of Sciences (1979). He gave the Mattioli lectures (1984) and the Okun lectures (1985). Inexplicably, the Nobel prize eluded him.

Kaldor's love for economics and politics was superseded only by the love for his family, from which he derived so much of his self-confidence and inner happiness. In 1934, the year he was naturalized, he married Clarissa Elisabeth, daughter of Henry Frederick Goldschmidt, stockbroker. They had four daughters. Kaldor died from cardiac asthma at Papworth Hospital, Cambridge, on 30 September 1986.   A. P. Thirlwall, *rev.*

Sources A. P. Thirlwall, 'Nicholas Kaldor, 1908–1986', *PBA*, 73 (1987), 517–66 · *The Times* (2 Oct 1986) · *CGPLA Eng. & Wales* (1987) · F. Targetti, *Nicholas Kaldor* (1992)
Archives BLPES, corresp. relating to Royal Economic Society and the *Economic Journal* · King's AC Cam., corresp. and papers | Bodl. Oxf., corresp. with Sidney Dell · CAC Cam., corresp. with Ralph Hawtrey · JRL, letters to the *Manchester Guardian* · King's AC Cam., corresp. with Richard Kahn
Likenesses G. Argent, photograph, 1970, NPG [*see illus.*] · photograph, repro. in Thirlwall, 'Nicholas Kaldor', 516
Wealth at death £603,080: probate, 26 Jan 1987, *CGPLA Eng. & Wales*

Kalecki, Michał (1899–1970), economist and policy adviser, was born on 22 June 1899 into a Polish-Jewish family in Łódź, now in Poland, then occupied by Russia. He was the only child of Abram Kalecki (*d.* 1933), the owner of a small cotton mill, and his wife, Klara Segalla, who died in unknown circumstances during the Second World War. His father, described by Kalecki as a 'victim of technical progress', lost the mill in 1913 and became a bookkeeper

in his brother's company. Kalecki enrolled in the I Philological Lycée in Łódź, where he completed four grades before the outbreak of war. The German occupation authorities closed the school in 1914–15, but Kalecki then enrolled at the Father Ignacy Skorupka II Philological Lycée in Łódź. After receiving his secondary school certificate in 1917 he began studying at the Warsaw University Engineering College. His studies were interrupted after two terms when he was drafted into the army, and he served for seven months in the VI telegraph battalion in Lwów: he was later discharged from the army in 1921 on health grounds.

Kalecki was able to begin mathematical studies at the department of philosophy of Warsaw University in February 1920, and transferred to the engineering college of Danzig University a year later. He received the first degree certificate in 1923, but discontinued his studies in 1925 shortly before graduation to support his family because his father had lost his job. He returned to Łódź where he undertook some tutoring and worked for a number of firms including one in the field of credit intelligence. He began his own study of economics about this time, studying first such writers as Rosa Luxemburg, Turan-Baranovski, and Marx. Only at a relatively late stage was he exposed to the ideas of neo-classical economics then dominant in Polish academic circles. His attitudes were also strongly influenced by the prevailing levels of unemployment in Poland. In 1927 he moved to Warsaw and earned his living in a range of jobs, including making engineering calculations of reinforced concrete constructions. He also started writing for the journals *Preeglad Gospodarczy* and *Przemysł I Handel*, mainly on the operations of large businesses and on business conditions in particular markets. In December 1929 he became a research fellow at the Institute for the Study of Business Cycles and Prices (ISBCP), headed by Edward Lipiński. Initially he studied the structure and operation of cartels, and later business fluctuations and national income in Poland. He was also involved in political journalism and maintained close connections with left-wing socialist movements. He married Adela (Ada) Szternfeld (1903–1994) on 18 June 1930.

In 1933 Kalecki published a paper in Polish under the title 'Outline of a theory of the business cycle' (reprinted as chapter 1 of M. Kalecki, *Selected Essays on the Dynamics of the Capitalist Economy, 1933–1970*, 1971) in which he presented the basic idea of the importance of fluctuations in investment expenditure as a generator of business cycles. This and some related papers form the basis of the claim that Kalecki published some of the key ideas of Keynes before Keynes himself (1933 versus 1936).

In 1935 Kalecki received a twelve-month Rockefeller scholarship to enable him to study abroad. He visited Sweden for the first three months of 1936, and then travelled to England in April 1936. There he made contact with leading British economists such as Keynes, Joan Robinson, and others who were developing ideas similar to his own. He resigned from the ISBCP in November 1936, protesting against limits on the freedom of research. He received an extension of his Rockefeller scholarship, and then a scholarship from Cambridge University to enable him to complete his first book, *Essays in the Theory of Economic Fluctuations* (1939), based on papers written in the late 1930s. In this book, as well as providing a theory of the business cycle, Kalecki also advanced a theory of the distribution of income (between wages and profits) based on the market power of firms. The idea of the 'principle of increasing risk' was developed, whereby the investment undertaken by a single firm is limited by the increasing risk which would be entailed by more investment reflected in a rising cost of finance.

Kalecki was appointed a statistical assistant for the economics department of Cambridge University and the National Institute of Economic and Social Research from October 1938 to February 1940. This was followed by a move to Oxford where he was employed at the Oxford University Institute of Statistics. There he worked on the British war economy, particularly rationing, war finance, and then post-war reconstruction, and made frequent contributions to the three weekly reports on economic matters published by the institute. He contributed to the major and influential study *The Economics of Full Employment: Six Studies in Applied Economics* (1944). He argued that full employment could be achieved through deficit spending by government, through redistribution of income from higher- to lower-income groups, but that the stimulation of private investment was not a satisfactory way to achieve full employment. During this period he developed the arguments that the political and social problems involved in the achievement of full employment were much greater than the economic problems involved.

In 1945, after some time working for the French ministry of national economy, Kalecki moved to the International Labour Office in Montreal, Canada, where he worked mainly on post-war reconstruction and full employment. In July 1946 he returned to Poland for three months as an adviser to the ministry of reconstruction, the ministry of finance, and the central planning office. At the end of 1946 he was appointed deputy director of a section of the economics department of the United Nations secretariat. During his time at the UN he supervised a range of studies on food shortage and inflationary pressures, and made major contributions to the annual *World Economic Report*. He spent two months in 1950 as economic adviser to the Israeli government. He resigned from the UN at the end of 1954 in response to the restrictions placed on himself and others by the intervention of the USA under the influence of McCarthyism.

From the beginning of 1955 Kalecki's home was in Poland. The first two years of his return to Poland coincided with the growth of overt political opposition to the Polish government; the Poznan workers' uprising in June 1956 and the spread of strikes across Poland; and the spontaneous creation of workers' councils in October 1956 (the 'Polish October'). In April 1955 Kalecki was appointed chief adviser to Hilary Minc, the deputy prime minister. From December of that year he was also employed by the Institute of Economics of the Polish Academy of Sciences where he headed research on the capitalist economies. In October 1956 he was appointed deputy chairman of a joint Polish United Workers' Party (PUWP) and the government 'commission to assist the proper development of workers' initiative in workplace management' established in response to the spontaneous formation of workers' councils. In June 1956 he received his first academic title as professor of economics, conferred by the central qualifications commission, and in July he was appointed professor of economics in the Institute of Economics of the Polish Academy of Sciences. In January 1957 he was appointed one of the deputy chairmen of the economic council at the Council of Ministers. In September 1957 Kalecki was appointed chairman of the commission of perspective planning, but his official role effectively ended in 1960. During a visit to India as an economic adviser on financing the third five-year plan there, the perspective plan for which he had supervised the preparation was heavily criticized and rejected. In May 1960 he was dismissed from the board of the planning commission, but appointed scientific adviser to the chairman of the planning commission with a much narrower range of powers. In 1959 he was awarded the officer's cross of the order of the Rebirth of Poland.

In the last decade of his life Kalecki was heavily involved with problems of economic development, including seminars organized at the academy of sciences, Warsaw University, and the central school for planning and statistics. By 1968 the political climate in Poland had changed considerably for the worse, and Kalecki's outspokenness and disagreement with the country's heavy industry investment programme (and an element of antisemitism) brought him into disfavour.

Kalecki made substantial contributions to the analysis of developed capitalist, socialist, and developing economies. His writings on the economics of socialism were undertaken only after his return to Poland in December 1954. He was directly involved in many of the debates of the mid-1950s on the development and organization of the Polish economy. His general approach could be summarized as seeking a departure from the system of bureaucratic centralism, the main lines of development in the economy being centrally planned, with the market mechanism used in a subordinate role. He further advocated a substantial increase in self-management by workers (under a system of workers' councils), while acknowledging that there would be tension between central planning and workers' councils. He was heavily involved with teaching and research in the area of development planning from the late 1950s to the late 1960s, organizing courses and seminars on underdeveloped economies.

Many of Kalecki's major writings on capitalism, socialism, and developing economies were republished after his death in *Selected Essays on the Dynamics of the Capitalist Economy, 1933–1970* (1971), *Selected Essays on the Economic Growth of the Socialist and the Mixed Economy* (1972), and *Essays on Developing Economies* (1976). He died on 17 April

1970 of a cerebral haemorrhage and was buried in the Alley of the Meritorious in the Powązkowski cemetery in Warsaw.   MALCOLM SAWYER

Sources *Collected works of Michał Kalecki*, ed. J. Osiatyński, trans. C. A. Kisiel, 7 vols. (1990–97) [incl. 'Main dates and facts of Kalecki's life', vol. 7, pp. 586–605; 'Bibliography of Kalecki's pubns 1927–87', vol. 7, pp. 606–67] · M. Sawyer, *The economics of Michał Kalecki* (1985)

Kalicho (*d.* **1577**). *See under* American Indians in England (*act. c.*1500–1609).

Kalisch, Marcus Moritz (**1825–1885**), Hebraist and biblical commentator, was born of Jewish parents at Treptow, Pomerania, on 16 May 1825. He was educated in Berlin, first at the *Gymnasium* of the Grauer Kloster, then at the University of Berlin, where he studied classical philology and Semitic languages, and finally at the rabbinical seminary. In 1848 he gained doctorates at the universities of Berlin and Halle. In the same year he became engaged in the struggles in Germany for democracy, and when those hopes were disappointed he emigrated to England. From 1848 to 1853 he was secretary to the chief rabbi, Dr N. M. Adler. He was then engaged as a tutor and literary adviser to the Rothschild family, a position which made it possible for him to take up research and writing.

In 1855 Kalisch published the first volume of a projected *Historical and Critical Commentary on the Old Testament*. This volume, on Exodus, and that on Genesis in 1858, drew largely on traditional Jewish interpretation; however, the Genesis volume was sensitive to recent scientific discoveries and argued that the genius of the biblical writers lay with religious and not scientific matters. Eight years elapsed before the appearance of part one of the commentary on Leviticus, during which time Kalisch published a *Hebrew Grammar* (2 vols., 1862–3). If the previous volumes of the *Commentary* had been more traditional, the Leviticus volumes (published in 1867 and 1872) were revolutionary. Drawing on the critical work of German scholars such as W. M. L. de Wette and Wilhelm Vatke (one of his teachers in Berlin), Kalisch argued that Leviticus had been composed in several stages, mainly after the exile. However, he went beyond the earlier critics in proposing, apparently independently, the view of Israelite priesthood and sacrifice that was given classical expression by Julius Wellhausen in 1878 and whose first published account was that of Abraham Kuenen in 1870. Kalisch dated the Levitical system of priesthood and sacrifice to the post-exilic period as against the view of the Old Testament that these ordinances were given by Moses. Thus Kalisch was not only a pioneer of modern Old Testament criticism; he also worked from within a Jewish tradition— a fact that must be set against the claim that modern criticism has its roots in antisemitism.

Kalisch's plans to complete his commentary were interrupted by illness in 1873, and his remaining works concerned the prophecies of Balaam (in 1877) and Jonah (in 1878). In 1880 his *Path and Goal: a Discussion on the Elements of Civilisation and the Conditions of Happiness* dealt with religious systems.

Kalisch married Clara, daughter of S. Stern of Frankfurt am Main, director of the *Realschule* in Frankfurt am Main; they had a son and a daughter. Kalisch died on 23 August 1885 at a clinic in Rowsley, Derbyshire, which practised hydropathy, and he was buried in the Jewish cemetery in Willesden, London. His wife survived him.

J. W. ROGERSON

Sources J. Klatzkin, ed., *Encyclopaedia Judaica: das Judentum in Geschichte und Gegenwart*, 10 vols. (Berlin, 1928–34) · *Grosse Jüdische Nationalbiographie*, 3 (1929), 377 · I. Singer and others, eds., *The Jewish encyclopedia*, 12 vols. (1901–6), vol. 7, p. 420 · J. Rogerson, *Old Testament criticism in the nineteenth century: England and Germany* (1984), 242–4 · H. S. Morais, *Eminent Israelites of the nineteenth century* (1880), 170–73 · *Jewish Chronicle* (28 Aug 1885) · *Jewish World* (28 Aug 1885) · *The Times* (31 Aug 1885) · *CGPLA Eng. & Wales* (1885) · *DNB*
Archives ICL, letters to Thomas Huxley
Wealth at death £601 19s. 7d.: administration, 9 Dec 1885, *CGPLA Eng. & Wales*

Kalm, Pehr (**1716–1779**), botanist, was born in Ångermanland, Sweden, in March 1716, the son of Gabriel Kalm, minister of Korsnäs chapel, Närpes, Vasa county, in Österbotten, and Catharina Ross. His father died before Kalm was born, but with the help of relatives Kalm was able to attend elementary school in Vasa, and to matriculate in 1735 at Åbo Academy, both in the Swedish-speaking part of Finland and the latter then a flourishing centre for the study of natural history. In 1740 he gained the patronage of Friherre Sten Carl Bielke who took him to live on his estate near Uppsala, at which university Kalm matriculated on 5 December 1740. Here his teachers were Linnaeus and Anders Celsius. Their example and the support of Bielke, who was keenly interested in natural history, particularly as applied to agricultural improvement, led to Kalm's undertaking several journeys for research purposes between 1740 and 1745 through Finland, Sweden, Russia, and Ukraine. He graduated doctor of natural history and economics of Åbo Academy in 1746 and became on 31 August 1747 its first professor of *oeconomie*, a subject which included mineralogy, botany, zoology, and chemistry, and their economic application. At the instigation of Linnaeus, who had himself hoped to make the journey, and with the support of the Åbo Academy, Kalm travelled in North America between 1747 and 1751 with explicit instructions to gather information and specimens such as seed which would be of practical economic use to Sweden. To this end he was to go particularly to areas in the north with climates similar to that of Sweden. Setting off in November 1747 he travelled first to England. The English leg was always seen as an important part of his journey since British botanists had had considerable experience and success in introducing North American plants and they had important contacts with American botanists. He stayed and met with British scientists, particularly Peter Collinson, a botanist with American contacts who introduced Kalm to the Royal Society, Mark Catesby, a botanist with extensive American contacts, Philip Miller, keeper of the Chelsea Physic Garden, and John Mitchell, the Virginian natural historian, then in London, who was Kalm's chief guide in England. He made a visit into the Chilterns to see William Ellis whose works on agricultural improvements he had read in Åbo and Uppsala, but came away

Pehr Kalm (1716–1779), by Johann Georg Geitel, 1764?

sharing the poor opinion of Ellis held by some of his neighbours. He sent quantities of seed and specimens back to Sweden and made detailed notes of all he saw.

The War of the Austrian Succession disrupted shipping but Kalm finally sailed for America on 6 August 1748, arriving there in November. He visited Philadelphia, where on 1 January 1750 he married Anna Margareta (d. 1787), daughter of Johan Sjöman, commissioner at the Stockholm arsenal, and widow of John Sandin, dean of the Swedish congregation in Philadelphia. He was warmly received into the leading scientific circles in Philadelphia. He then went on to Canada, where he arrived in the summer of 1749, and travelled extensively in areas of British and French settlement. He was particularly well received in New France, then the focus of much French scientific attention. He reached home in 1751, having been away four instead of the projected two years. He brought back plants and seeds of medicinal use and of benefit to agriculture and industry. All were planted enthusiastically, notably in his new botanical garden at Åbo. Although few flourished the practice of systematic cultivation and experiment with plants gained wide currency among the well educated and the well born and his efforts were in this way very influential.

Kalm reached a wider audience through his publications. Reports of his travels were published in Swedish, German, Dutch, and English in the eighteenth century, some in his lifetime, and a French and other editions followed in the nineteenth and twentieth centuries. These reports, although containing detailed and pertinent observations, were less detailed than his journals (fair copy in Helsinki University Library), which were published in the twentieth century in Swedish and English

and further consolidated his reputation. All his writings show his thirst for information, and his thoughtfulness in interpreting what he saw, particularly in the light of his scientific and medical knowledge. He was the first European traveller with scientific knowledge to visit and report on many areas; his report of Niagara Falls, for example, published by Benjamin Franklin and John Bartram in 1751, was the first English description of the falls. Though his primary aim was scientific Kalm was no less acute an observer of the economic, ethnographic, and social characteristics of the lands through which he travelled, and his comments on Native Americans, European colonists, and the relations between the two are of particular interest on both sides of the Atlantic. Kalm intended a Flora Canadiensis, but this eagerly awaited work was never completed. Most of the material for it was recorded in his travel diaries and Kalm's students and Linnaeus and his students made considerable use of the information in their writings.

In 1763 Kalm declined the offer of the chair of botany from the academy of sciences in St Petersburg and remained at Åbo, where he took his duties very seriously. Under his direction 146 dissertations were completed. His emphasis on the applied and the empirical and on communicating in Swedish set his school apart from the old academic tradition and foreshadowed the later establishment of agricultural, economic, and technical colleges. Most of his students became clergymen and, by adopting new practices on their church farms, helped to raise the standards of Finnish agriculture and husbandry. He was made doctor of theology at Lund University in 1768. He died on 16 November 1779 in Åbo.

Kalm was important as a link between the natural history communities of England, North America, and Sweden, the last being in the mid-eighteenth century of crucial importance because of Linnaeus. Scientific links between Sweden and England were well established, not least by Linnaeus himself and his pupil Daniel Solander, Joseph Banks's secretary. Connections between North America and England were similarly well developed, for example by John Ellis, Peter Collinson, and John Mitchell; but Kalm linked all three. These links make him important in the development of eighteenth-century natural history, and the quality and early date of his descriptions, economic and social as well as botanical, give them continuing importance as a historical source.

ELIZABETH BAIGENT

Sources P. Kalm, *Resejournal över resan till norra Amerika*, ed. M. Kerkkonen, J. E. Roos, and H. Krogerns, 4 vols. (1966–88) · P. Kalm, *Travels into North America*, trans. J. R. Forster, 3 vols. (1770–71) · M. Kerkkonen, 'Kalm, Pehr', *Svenskt biografiskt lexikon*, ed. E. Grill, 20 (1973–5), 598–601 · M. Kerkkonen, *Peter Kalm's North American journey* (1959) · B. Hildebrand, *Pehr Kalms amerikanska reseräkning* (1956) · G. W. R. Mead, 'Geographical reflections beside the memorial to Pehr Kalm', *Terra* [Journal of the Geographical Society of Finland], 101 (1989), 62–6 · W. R. Mead, 'Pehr Kalm in the Chilterns', *Acta Geographica* [Helsinki], 17 (1962–3), pt 1 · P. Kalm, *Kalm's account of his visit to England on his way to America in 1748*, trans. J. Lucas (1892) · R. A. Jarrell, 'Kalm, Pehr', *DCB*, vol. 4 · *Pehr Kalms brev till Friherre Sten Carl Bielke*, ed. C. Skottsberg (Abo, Finland, 1960) · private information (2004) [W. R. Mead]

Archives Kgl. Vetenskapsakademiens Bibliothek, Stockholm, MSS · Linn. Soc., papers · LUL, papers relating to rural economy · University of Helsinki, diary | Karolinska Institutet, Stockholm, letters to A. Bäck · Kungliga Biblioteket, Stockholm, letters to C. C. Sjöwall · Nationalarkiv, Stockholm, letters to N. Tessin · Uppsala University, letters to S. C. Bielke
Likenesses J. G. Geitel, portrait, 1764?, Satakunta Museum, Pori, Finland [*see illus.*]

Kalmeter, Henrik (1693–1750). *See under* Industrial spies (*act. c.*1700–*c.*1800).

Kames. For this title name *see* Home, Henry, Lord Kames (1696–1782).

Kandel, Isaac Leon (1881–1965), educationist, was born in Romania, the son of Abraham Kandel, a velvet merchant, and his wife, Fanny. The family moved to Manchester when he was a child, and he attended Manchester grammar school from 1892 to 1899. He won a university scholarship and studied classics at Manchester University from 1899 to 1902, graduating with first-class honours. Four years later he was awarded the MA and in the same year completed the teacher's diploma course where he came under the stimulating influence of Professor J. J. Findlay and the academic study of pedagogy, and of Michael Sadler, the professor of the history and administration of education. Both shared an admiration for the Jena educationist Wilhelm Rein, whom Kandel visited in 1907. At Manchester University he had met Jessie Sara Davis (*b.* 1891/2), a classicist and trained teacher; they married at the Great Synagogue, Prestwich, on 27 July 1915, and had a daughter and a son.

Kandel taught his subject briefly at the Royal Belfast Academical Institution before moving to America in 1908 (where he became a citizen in 1920), studying at the Teachers' College, Columbia University, for a PhD, which was awarded in 1910 for a dissertation on the training of elementary school teachers in Germany. He worked with Paul Monroe, head of the Teachers' College, on the important *Cyclopaedia of Education* from 1909 until 1913, when he was appointed a lecturer at the Teachers' College. Concurrently acting as a researcher for the Carnegie Foundation for the Advancement of Teaching from 1914 to 1923, he explored many aspects of education and, in contributions to the United States bureau of education's *Bulletin*, deepened his interest in foreign systems, particularly those of Germany, France, and Britain. His studies were assisted by his exceptional linguistic ability. The international institute of the college had links with the New Era Fellowship with which Kandel had sympathies, particularly with its emphasis on human fulfilment, peace, and co-operation, although he disliked the dogmatism of some progressive educators. The views of Findlay and Sadler on the vital role of the teacher and the cultural aspects of education were reinforced by a colleague, W. C. Bagley, a leader of the essentialist movement in education. In 1923 Kandel was promoted from associate professor to the chair of the history of education, and he remained in that post until his retirement in 1946.

Kandel wrote numerous papers and books. Early studies were a *History of Secondary Education* (1930) and *The Making of*

Nazis (1935). A complex historical perspective underlay all his work and contributed to his understanding of comparative studies:

> The history of education has in the main been devoted to a study of theories and practices in isolation instead of being what it should be, a study of the relationships between education and cultural backgrounds in the fullest sense of the term, concerned with the history of culture and politics and their impact on education.   (*Universities Quarterly*, 3/3, May 1949)

Such an approach ensured that comparative education as taught by Kandel was an academically robust form of analysis far removed from the mere collection of data on foreign systems. His pioneering reputation was established in 1933 with the publication of the classic and widely translated *Studies in Comparative Education*, which laid a basis for the increasingly sophisticated analysis of educational systems during the rest of the century. *The New Era in Education* (1955) was complementary, as it picked up and developed 'trends already in the making' (preface, ix) when the earlier volume was published. Other influential methodological statements, both called *Comparative Education*, appeared in 1936 and 1939.

Always seeking to understand underlying causes in education despite superficial similarities and wary of transferring practices from one country to another, Kandel in his books *Conflicting Theories of Education* (1938) and *Education in an Era of Transition* (1948) reflected the social and political complexities of the 1930s and 1940s; on the other hand his *The Impact of the War upon American Education* (1948) and *American Education in the Twentieth Century* (1955) focused on his own society. He was in demand as a visiting professor and taught at Johns Hopkins, Yale, and the universities of California, Maine, and Pennsylvania; his lectures at Harvard and the University of London in the 1930s resulted in the books *The Dilemma of Democracy* (1934) and *The Outlook in Education* (1933). His scholarship and international outlook were recognized by honorary degrees from the universities of Melbourne and North Carolina, while France conferred on him the Légion d'honneur. As well as many contributions to works of reference he was editor from 1924 until 1944 of Colombia University's influential *Educational Year Book*, and from 1946 to 1953 edited the weekly journal *School and Society*. Kandel's reputation was recognized by his election to the distinguished National Academy of Education. His stature as an internationalist and a prudent educationist drew him into the orbit of government and from 1937 to 1946 he was a member of the United States national committee on intellectual co-operation, and he was invited to join a Jamaican committee to reform secondary education. In 1946 he was part of the United States education mission to Japan.

After so long at Columbia University, Kandel had a brief but notable second career when he returned in 1947 to Manchester University as a Simon research fellow. His intellectual energy was at once apparent both in the university and outside, and in 1947 he presided over the North of England Education Conference. America's importance in the war had encouraged the British government in 1941 to encourage greater understanding of American life through education. Manchester responded and set about what proved to be a frustrating attempt to secure a suitable person to head a proposed department of American studies. During his fellowship year Kandel's ability was quickly recognized, and he was the first professor of American studies from 1948 to 1950. He created an innovative department which drew on and co-ordinated the academic resources of the university. His experience and wide knowledge were of value to Lord Simon of Wythenshawe, the founder and editor of the *Universities Quarterly*, and on Simon's appointment as chairman of the BBC Kandel became editor. His work and personality were so highly regarded at Manchester that his resignation in 1950 was greatly regretted.

This was not the end of Kandel's career. He continued to write and travel extensively and consolidated the internationalist approach advocated in his *International Co-operation: National and International* (1944). From 1946 he was an effective consultant with UNESCO, writing particularly on education as a human right and compulsory education, themes continued in work for the United Nations human rights division in 1955. In a period of decolonization he turned his attention to the educational issues of independence and development. In 1960 he attended a conference at Natal University in South Africa, where he witnessed the effects of apartheid. Kandel died in Geneva, Switzerland, on 14 June 1965.

A. B. ROBERTSON

Sources E. Pollack, 'Isaac Leon Kandel (1881–1965)', *Prospects*, 23 (1993), 775–87 · *The Times* (1 July 1965) · R. Aldrich and P. Gordon, *Dictionary of British educationists* (1989) · P. Gordon and R. Aldrich, *Biographical dictionary of North American and European educationists* (1997) · W. Boyd and W. Rawson, *The story of the new education* (1965) · Manchester University archives · m. cert. · census returns, 1901

Archives Stanford University, California, Hoover Institution, personal papers

Kane, John (*d*. 1834), army officer, adjutant in the Royal Invalid Artillery, was promoted to that rank from sergeant on 1 July 1799. He was the compiler of lists of officers known as *Kane's List*. These contained the names of Royal Artillery officers serving between 1763 and the date of publication (1815). Revised editions were published at Woolwich in 1869 and 1891. Kane died at Woolwich on 29 August 1834. Another John Kane, presumably the son of the above, a first lieutenant Royal Artillery, died at Calcutta in December 1818.

H. M. CHICHESTER, *rev.* S. KINROSS

Sources *Army List* · *N&Q*, 2nd ser., 6 (1858), 257 · *Kane's list*, rev. edn (1891)

Kane, John (1819–1876), trade unionist, was born on 18 July 1819 at Alnwick, Northumberland. His father was the son of a Methodist minister and had served as an attorney but Kane's prospects of a comfortable upbringing were destroyed when he was orphaned while still very young. He started work in a tobacco factory at the age of seven and between the ages of nine and twelve he attended school in Alnwick. He was then apprenticed to a gardener but ran away after being beaten for refusing to take part in a contrived demonstration of welcome for the estate owner. Kane subsequently found work in the mills of Hawks, Crawshay & Sons, iron manufacturers, of Gateshead and soon became well known as a forceful speaker and astute negotiator in disputes with the management. In 1842 he formed a union in Gateshead and though it soon collapsed he remained convinced that it was possible to establish effective organization among the ironworkers and the rest of his life was dedicated to this end.

The strongly cyclical nature of the industry and the ruthless opposition of the ironmasters kept Kane's ambition in abeyance for the next twenty years and during this time his restless energy was diverted into a variety of working-class causes. He was involved in the later stages of the Chartist movement on Tyneside and subsequently became a leading figure in the Northern Reform Union. He was also a founder member of the Cramlington Co-operative Society, helped set up a working men's reading room in Newcastle, and lectured on temperance (he was a lifelong teetotaller).

Kane finally achieved his ambition to establish a lasting union in 1862, when he formed the National Association of Ironworkers with headquarters in Gateshead. He was elected the paid president at a salary of £140 per year and set out to extend the National Association into other ironmaking districts but in doing so he encountered fierce opposition from two unions based in south Staffordshire. There were some bitter battles until, in 1868, depression brought about the collapse of both Staffordshire unions, leaving the National Association as the sole focus of organization but with its membership and finances at a desperately low ebb.

Kane set about rebuilding the union by taking the position of general secretary so that he could exercise tighter control over day-to-day administration, moving the headquarters to Darlington and launching a fortnightly newspaper, the *Ironworkers' Journal*, which he edited. These moves were followed by a massive increase in membership, which rose from under 500 in 1868 to 35,000 by the later months of 1873. This dramatic growth certainly owed something to Kane's drive and organizing ability but the main factor was the great industrial boom of the early 1870s which *inter alia* carried trade union membership generally to unprecedented heights. Kane's wife, Jane, shared his union interests and 'laboured heart and hand with her husband in every sphere in which he was engaged' (*Northern Echo*, 22 March 1876). From 1862 she was responsible for much of the administration of the ironworkers' unions.

While overseeing his union's recovery Kane was also engaged in establishing a completely new relationship between the ironworkers and their employers. He said in evidence to the royal commission on trades unions in 1867 that strikes and lock-outs were very prejudicial to all classes and, like war, left a trail of misery behind them, and went on to advocate that conciliation boards should be set up in the iron industry. He found a powerful ally in

David Dale, the Quaker managing director of the Consett Iron Company, and in 1869 the two came together to establish the board of arbitration and conciliation for the manufactured iron trade of the north of England. The rules did not allow union representation but Kane was appointed the paid secretary to the workmen's panel. The formation of the board was widely welcomed on both sides of the industry and in 1870 the ironworkers acknowledged Kane's contribution to leading them out of chaos by presenting him with a gold watch, gold guard and seal, an illuminated address in a gold frame, and a purse of gold sovereigns. His wife was also presented with a gold watch and gold guard, and a locket.

During these years Kane was also active in the wider trade union movement. He was present at the Manchester conference in 1868 which inaugurated the TUC and subsequently became a leading member of its parliamentary committee, serving as joint chairman in 1875. The main concern of the TUC in its early years was the ambiguous legal status of the unions and Kane was among those who felt that direct labour representation in parliament was needed to remedy the situation. He accordingly contested Middlesbrough at the 1874 general election with the support of his union and the Labour Representation League, finishing a creditable second ahead of the Conservative in a three-cornered fight.

By this time the great industrial boom was over and as it collapsed so did trade union membership. The ironworkers' union was no exception and Kane's ceaseless efforts to shore up its crumbling organization undermined his health and brought about his premature death. Kane died in Birmingham, where he was on union business, on 21 March 1876, following a stroke two days earlier. He was buried in the west cemetery, Darlington, on 24 March 1876. His wife and at least one son survived him. His obituary in the *Darlington and Richmond Herald* on 25 March 1876 described him fittingly as 'an indomitable man'.

ERIC TAYLOR

Sources *Ironworkers' Journal* (1869–76), esp. 15 April 1876 · N. P. Howard, 'The strikes and lockouts in the iron industry and the formation of the ironworkers' unions, 1862–1869', *International Review of Social History*, 18 (1973), 396–427 · J. H. Porter, 'David Dale and conciliation in the northern manufactured iron trade, 1869–1914', *Northern History*, 5 (1970), 157–71 · A. J. Odber, 'The origins of industrial peace: the manufactured iron trade of the north of England', *Oxford Economic Papers*, 3 (1951), 202–20 · 'Commissioners appointed to inquire into … trades unions: fifth report', *Parl. papers* (1867–8), 39.1–15, 37–9, 138–41, no. 3980-I [minutes of evidence] · E. Taylor, 'Kane, John', *DLB*, vol. 3 · F. Harrison, 'The iron-masters' trade union', *Fortnightly Review*, 1 (1865), 96–116 · *Annual Report* [Trades Union Congress] (1869–76) · G. D. H. Cole, 'Some notes on British trade unionism in the third quarter of the nineteenth century', *International Review for Social History*, 2 (1937), 1–27; repr. in *Essays in economic history*, ed. E. M. Carus-Wilson, 3 (1962), 202–19 · B. C. Roberts, *The Trades Union Congress, 1868–1921* (1958) · J. C. Carr and W. Taplin, *History of the British steel industry* (1962) · A. W. Humphrey, *The history of the Labour Representation League* (1912) · *Northern Echo* (22 March 1876) · *Northern Echo* (25 March 1876) · *Darlington and Richmond Herald* (25 March 1876) · CGPLA Eng. & Wales (1876)
Likenesses line drawing, repro. in Carr and Taplin, *History of the British steel industry*

Wealth at death under £450 0s. 0d.: administration, 15 April 1876, CGPLA Eng. & Wales

Kane [*formerly* O'Cahan], **Richard** (1662–1736), army officer, was born Richard O'Cahan at Duneane, co. Antrim, Ireland, on 20 December 1662, the only son of Thomas O'Cahan the younger (1600–1665), landowner, and his wife, Margaret (1630–1693), daughter of James Dobbin and his wife, Mary. On reaching his majority he was advised to adopt the surname of Kane.

Kane entered the Royal regiment of Ireland about 1689; he was with the regiment at the battles of the Boyne, Athlone, and Aughrim, and the siege of Limerick, and afterwards on board the fleet and in Flanders. He was wounded as a captain in Lord Cutts's desperate assault on the castle of Namur on 1 September 1695, on which occasion the regiment won the Nassau lion badge and motto, the oldest in the British armed forces. He served under Marlborough in the campaigns of the War of the Spanish Succession; as a major he was wounded at Blenheim, and commanded the regiment as lieutenant-colonel at Malplaquet. In 1710 he was appointed colonel of a regiment of Irish foot which had been raised by Lieutenant-General George Macartney. He formed part of the Canadian expedition in 1711, under Brigadier-General John Hill.

The regiment was disbanded in 1712, when Kane was appointed lieutenant-governor of Minorca (ceded to Britain under the treaty of Utrecht). He was very active in dealing with the complaints made against him by the Minorcan clergy, incited by the bishop of Majorca. Kane's proposal—a bishopric of Minorca, independent of Majorca—did not materialize. Memorials from the clergy are included in his own correspondence at the time of the dispute. Full particulars of the dispute are to be found in a pamphlet published in London in 1720 entitled *A vindication of Colonel Kane, lieutenant-governor of Minorca, against the late complaints made by the inhabitants of that island*. He was appointed acting commander-in-chief, Gibraltar, during disputes with Spain in 1720–21 and again in 1725–7. He became colonel of the 9th (Norfolk) foot on the death of Colonel Otway in 1725. He was relieved in Gibraltar by General Jasper Clayton, before the siege of 1727, when he returned to Minorca.

Among Kane's achievements as lieutenant-governor of Minorca were proposals for a constitution (Tyrawley MSS) and reforms in the administration of justice, although these were not implemented until 1754. He also transferred the capital from Ciudadela to Mahón, constructed a highway between the forts of those towns, and imported new breeds of cattle and clover as their fodder. In 1714–17 and again in 1732 he was concerned with the problem of the reception of a Spanish consul in the island. In 1733 he was appointed governor of Minorca and in 1735 was promoted to the rank of brigadier-general.

Kane died a bachelor at Mahón on 31 December 1736 and was buried in the chapel of the castle of San Felipe, Minorca, on 3 January 1737. A monument with bust was erected to his memory in Westminster Abbey. Kane was an accomplished soldier. He wrote *Narrative of All the Campaigns of King William and the Duke of Marlborough*, which was autobiographical up until his arrival in Minorca, and *A New System of Military Discipline for Foot on Action*, both of which were first published in 1741. General James Wolfe, writing in 1751, expressed a high opinion of these works, and their value was fully recognized by the *United Services Journal* for October 1836 (p. 172). However, it is on his governance of Minorca during a period of almost 25 years that his place in history depends. He was a colonial governor truly devoted to the people he administered.

BRUCE LAURIE

Sources will of Richard Kane, governor of Minorca, 29 May 1735, PRO, PROB 10/1848 [registered copy, PROB 11/683, sig. 111; sentence, PROB 11/698, sig. 224] · G. Hill, *An historical account of the MacDonnells of Antrim* (1873) · B. Laurie, *The life of Richard Kane* (1994) · B. Laurie, *Richard Kane y Menorca en la Historia de Europa* (1996) · R. Kane, *Narrative of all the campaigns of King William and the duke of Marlborough* (1741) · R. Kane, *A new system of military discipline* (1741) · R. Cannon, ed., *Historical record of the eighteenth, or the royal Irish regiment of foot* (1848) · R. Cannon, ed., *Historical record of the ninth, or the east Norfolk regiment of foot* (1848) · W. Kingsford, *The history of Canada*, 10 vols. (1888–98) · BL, Egerton MSS 2171–2174 · BL, Add. MSS 32766, 32779 · R. Wright, *The life of Major-General James Wolfe* (1864) · J. A. Houlding, *Fit for service: the training of the British army, 1715–1795* (1981) · D. Chandler, *Marlborough as military commander* (1973) · M. Mata, *Menorca Britanica* (1997) · J. Armstrong, *History of Menorca* (1756) · Colonel Pinfold, letter to the duke of Newcastle, PRO, WO 1/294, fol. 345 · BL, Tyrawley MSS, Add. MSS Harlem no. 35; Tyrawley 23638, item 3, p. 154
Archives BL, account of campaigns and method of discipline for a regiment of foot, Add. MS 41141 | Archivos de Mahón de Ciudadela, MSS · Archivos Diocesanos de Ciudadela, Minorca, MSS · Archivos Municipales de Ciudadela, Minorca, MSS
Likenesses J. M. Rysbrack, bust, 1736, Westminster Abbey

Kane, Sir Robert John (1809–1890), chemist and educationist, was born at 48 Henry Street, Dublin, on 24 September 1809, the son of John Kane, a manufacturing chemist. He was educated at Trinity College, Dublin (1828–35), and studied medical and practical science in both Dublin and Paris. He became a clinical clerk at the Meath Hospital, and obtained the prize offered by Dr Graves at Dublin in 1830 for the best essay on the pathological condition of body fluids in typhoid fever. The previous year he had identified an unknown mineral as an arsenide of manganese, which was named kaneite in his honour. In 1831 he was appointed professor of chemistry to the Apothecaries' Hall, Dublin (leading to the sobriquet 'the boy professor'), and in the same year he published *Elements of Practical Pharmacy*. He retained the chair of chemistry until 1845.

Kane became a licentiate of the King and Queen's College of Physicians in 1832, and a fellow in 1841. In the former year he founded the *Dublin Journal of Medical Science*, but closed his connections with it in 1834. From that year until 1847 he was professor of natural philosophy to the Royal Dublin Society. In 1838 he married Katherine (1811–1880), daughter of Henry Baily of Newbury, Berkshire, and a niece of the astronomer Francis Baily. She was the author of *The Irish Flora* (1833). Their five children included the lawyer Robert Romney *Kane (1842–1902) and Admiral Sir Henry Cory Kane (1843–1917).

Like other chemists in the 1830s, Kane struggled with the problem of classifying organic compounds. In 1833, one year before Liebig, Kane suggested that alcohol, ether, and many esters contained an ethyl radical. In 1836 he visited the chief laboratories and scientific institutions in France and Germany, including Liebig's laboratory at Giessen, where he isolated acetone from wood spirit. Soon afterwards he devised a process for the production of methyl alcohol (methanol) from wood spirit and synthesized mesitylene by reacting acetone with sulphuric acid. In 1841 a royal medal was awarded to Kane by the Royal Society of London for his elucidation of the chemical nature of archil and litmus, the natural dyes extracted from lichens. He had become the Irish editor of the *Philosophical Magazine* in 1840, and was elected a fellow of the Royal Society in 1849. In 1842 he was appointed secretary of the council of the Royal Irish Academy, which awarded him its gold prize medal in 1843 for an investigation of the nature and constitution of compounds of ammonia that had appeared in the academy's *Transactions*. His chemical work was summarized in *Elements of Chemistry* (1841), which was used by Faraday as a text at the Woolwich Academy, and was also used in the United States, where an edition was brought out in 1843 under the editorship of John William Draper.

Kane paid much attention to the development of industries in Ireland, and delivered a course of lectures on the subject in Dublin in 1843. These were published in 1844 as *Industrial Resources of Ireland*. The work met with much success, and a second edition was published in 1845. In it he directed attention to the various sources of wealth in the fuel, water-power, mines, agriculture, and manufactures of Ireland, and indicated the most economical modes of exploiting them; for example, he urged the formation of small farms. On Kane's suggestion the government established in 1846 the Museum of Irish Industry at St Stephen's Green, Dublin, of which he was appointed director. In 1845, despite his Roman Catholicism, Kane was appointed president of the Queen's College at Cork (opened in 1849), and was much criticized for the fact that he continued to reside in Dublin. After passing some months on the continent in investigating methods of higher education, he was knighted by the viceroy of Ireland, Lord Heytesbury, in February 1846. By then effectively the government's chief scientist in the country, he became a member of the commissions appointed in 1845 to inquire into the potato blight and the relief of Irish distress. He was granted the honorary degree of LLD by the University of Dublin in 1868, was appointed a commissioner of national education in Ireland in 1873 (when he resigned his post at Cork), and was elected president of the Royal Irish Academy in 1877. In 1880 he was made vice-chancellor of the newly created Royal University of Ireland. A man of strong views, Kane's influence on the development of science and education in Ireland was considerable. He died at 2 Wellington Road, Dublin, on 16 February 1890.

J. T. GILBERT, *rev.* W. H. BROCK

Sources J. E. R., *PRS*, 47 (1889–90), xii–xvii · D. O'Reilly, *Sir Robert Kane* (1942) · C. Mollan, W. Davis, and B. Finucane, eds., *More people and places in Irish science and technology* (1990), 24–5 · T. S. Wheeler, 'Sir Robert Kane', *Endeavour*, 4 (1945), 91–3 · D. O'Reilly, 'Robert John Kane', *Journal of Chemical Education*, 32 (1955), 404–6 · B. B.

Kelham, 'Royal College of Science for Ireland', *Studies*, 56 (1967), 297–309 · B. B. Kelham, 'Science education in Ireland', PhD diss., University of Manchester, 1968
Archives Royal Dublin Society · Royal Irish Acad.
Likenesses H. Meyer, stipple, pubd 1849 (after C. Grey), NPG · S. Freeman, stipple (after G. F. Mulvany), NPG, RS; version, NG Ire. · C. Grey, pencil on paper, NG Ire. · G. F. Mulvany, portrait, NPG · engraving, repro. in J. S. Muspratt, *Chemistry … as applied and relating to the arts and manufacturers*, 1 [n.d., c.1854]

Kane, Robert Romney (1842–1902), lawyer, was born at Gracefield, Blackrock, co. Dublin, on 28 October 1842. He was the eldest son of Sir Robert *Kane (1809–1890), first president of the Queen's College, Cork, and his wife, Katherine, *née* Baily, author and the daughter of Henry Baily, of Berkshire; her uncle was Francis Baily, president of the Royal Astronomical Society. Kane attended Dr Quinn's private school in Harcourt Street, Dublin, and then went to Queen's College, Cork, where he graduated MA in 1862. In 1882 he was also awarded the honorary degree of LLD. He became a member of Lincoln's Inn, London, on 12 January 1864, and studied law in London in the chambers of an eminent conveyancing lawyer, W. H. G. Bagshawe. In 1865 Kane graduated LLB with honours at London University, was called to the Irish bar, and commenced practice on the Munster circuit. In 1873 he was appointed professor of equity, jurisprudence, and international law at the King's Inns, Dublin. On 29 December 1875 he married Ellinor Louisa Coffey; they had two sons and three daughters.

Professionally, Kane gained a reputation as an expert on Irish land legislation, and he was appointed a legal assistant commissioner under the Land Law Act of 1881, a post which he retained until 1892, when he was made county court judge for the united counties of Kildare, Carlow, Wexford, and Wicklow. Together with Francis Nolan QC, Kane wrote the treatise *Statute Law of Landlord and Tenant in Ireland* (1892). He also had a keen interest in Irish history, literature, and antiquities. In 1887 he published his own edition of his friend A. G. Richey's work, *Lectures on Irish History*, under the title *A Short History of the Irish People*.

Kane was a member of the Royal Irish Academy, a trustee of the National Library, a fellow of the Royal Society of Antiquaries of Ireland, and an honorary secretary of the Royal Dublin Society. After some years of poor health he died at his home, 4 Fitzwilliam Place, Dublin, on 26 March 1902, survived by his wife.

ROBERT DUNLOP, rev. SINÉAD AGNEW

Sources J. S. Crone, *A concise dictionary of Irish biography*, rev. edn (1937), 108 · *Annual Register* (1902) · W. P. Baildon, ed., *The records of the Honorable Society of Lincoln's Inn: admissions*, 2 (1896), 310 · *Irish Times* (4 Oct 1901) · *The Times* (28 March 1902) · CGPLA Ire. (1902) · CGPLA Eng. & Wales (1902)
Wealth at death £9389 13s. 10d.: probate, 30 April 1902, CGPLA Ire. · £851 13s. 1d. in England: Irish probate sealed in England, 9 Sept 1902, CGPLA Eng. & Wales

Kane, Sarah Marie (1971–1999), playwright, was born on 3 February 1971 in Brentwood Maternity Home, Essex, the only daughter and second child of Peter Terence Kane, journalist, and his wife, Jeannine, *née* Potter. She grew up in Kelvedon Hatch, near Brentwood, and was educated at Shenfield comprehensive school. Her parents were Christians, and she became evangelical for a while as a teenager. After acting with the Basildon youth theatre group, she took drama at the University of Bristol (1989–92). At first she wanted to be an actor, but then changed her mind and turned to directing, working on several student productions. She also wrote three 20-minute monologues, which she performed at the Edinburgh fringe festival in 1991–2. After leaving Bristol with a first-class honours degree, she took the MA in playwriting at the University of Birmingham (1993). Stories from her student days tend to emphasize the provocative side of her character. On one occasion, after a tutor had called one of her monologues 'pornographic', she took a couple of magazines to his class to show him what real pornography was like—and suggested he make use of them.

Kane moved to Brixton, south London, and became literary associate at the Bush fringe theatre in early 1994. Her first full-length play, *Blasted*, was put on by the Royal Court Theatre in January 1995, directed by James Macdonald. Although staged in a small studio space, the play caused the biggest theatrical controversy of the decade. Raw in style, horrific in content, and experimental in form, *Blasted* received exceptionally hostile reviews. The *Daily Mail* headline read 'This Disgusting Feast of Filth' (19 Jan 1995) and *The Guardian* listed the play's content as 'scenes of masturbation, fellatio, frottage, micturition, defecation—ah, those old familiar faeces—homosexual rape, eye gouging and cannibalism' (20 Jan 1995). Amid calls for the theatre's funding to be cut, Kane was hounded by the media but defended by senior playwrights such as Harold Pinter, Caryl Churchill, and Edward Bond. Most critics failed to see that what was really disturbing about her play was its radical structure, in which a naturalistic first half suddenly explodes into a more symbolic second part.

Six months after the furore over her début, Kane completed the final drafts of *Skin*, a screenplay for a 10-minute film directed by Vincent O'Connell. It was made in September 1995, previewed at the London film festival the following month, and was eventually broadcast by Channel Four television on 17 June 1997, causing controversy because of its violent content. In May 1996, Kane's *Phaedra's Love*—a modern updating of Seneca's play directed by Kane herself—was staged by the Gate Theatre in west London, but its critical reception was skewed by the notoriety of *Blasted*. In August she was appointed writer-in-residence at Paines Plough theatre company, where she ran a series of writers' workshops. In October 1997 Kane returned to the Gate Theatre to direct George Büchner's *Woyzeck*.

By 1998 Kane's unique voice—which combines a rawness of tone with austere economy and visceral power—had begun to achieve wider recognition. Her work continued to tackle extreme subjects, but critics gradually became more attuned to the theme of passionate love in her plays. In April her innovative *Cleansed*, put on at the Royal Court, once again pushed against the limits of naturalism. In August *Crave* marked a further experiment in terms of structure, being more of a tone poem divided into four voices than a conventional drama. Kane thought it was her most pessimistic work. In the last two years of her life she ran workshops and attended conferences all over Europe. In 1998 she was awarded the annual Arts Foundation fellowship in playwriting.

Although appreciated and loved by her peers, Kane suffered from clinical depression, becoming a voluntary patient at London's Royal Maudsley Hospital on more than one occasion. On 20 February 1999, while recovering in King's College Hospital, London, from a suicide attempt, she hanged herself during the night. The following year, her last play, *4.48 Psychosis*—which painfully explored the subject of suicidal depression—was performed at the Royal Court.

Kane was a slight, spiky-haired blonde with watchful eyes and gentle manners. Typically dressed in androgynous black, she was always great fun to be with, mixing scabrous humour with immense empathy. Often contradictory, she was a vegetarian who fantasized about eating bacon sandwiches. She hated being labelled a 'woman writer' or a 'moralist', and distrusted the clichés of politically correct discourse. She avoided writing introductions to her work because she believed that her plays spoke for themselves. And while she was a student of theatre traditions—influenced by writers such as Shakespeare, Samuel Beckett, Edward Bond, and Howard Barker—she also loved the drama of the football pitch. Friends remember her exuberance, and the highly articulate way in which she defended herself and her work. She never married, and had both male and female lovers. Since her death, Kane has been widely seen as an icon, symbolizing the uncompromising writer who is true to her inspiration, meticulous about her craft, and provocative in her attitude.   ALEKS SIERZ

Sources A. Sierz, *In-yer-face theatre* (2001) · D. Rebellato, 'Sarah Kane: an appreciation', *New Theatre Quarterly*, 60 (Nov 1999), 280–81 · J. McGloan, 'The mark of Kane', *The Scotsman* (13 March 1999) · S. Hattenstone, 'A sad hurrah', *The Guardian* (1 July 2000) · personal knowledge (2004) · private information (2004) · D. Dromgoole, *The full room: an A–Z of contemporary playwriting* (2000)
Archives priv. coll., papers | SOUND interviews held by various journalist and academics
Likenesses J. Bown, photograph, repro. in *Marie-Claire* (Feb 2001) · S. Politis, photograph, repro. in *Daily Telegraph* (27 May 2000)
Wealth at death under £200,000: administration, 18 May 1999, *CGPLA Eng. & Wales* · under £25,000: probate, 18 May 1999, *CGPLA Eng. & Wales*

Kantababu. *See* Krishna Kanta Nandy (*c.*1720–1794).

Kapitza, Peter Leonidovich [Pyotr Leonidovich Kapitsa] (1894–1984), physicist, was born in Kronstadt (near St Petersburg) on 9 July 1894, the younger son of General Leonid Petrovich Kapitsa, a military engineer, and his wife, Olga Ieronimovna, daughter of General Ieronim Ivanovich Stebnitsky. His mother was a specialist in children's literature and folklore. In 1912 he graduated with honours from the local *Realschule* and entered the electro-technical faculty of the St Petersburg Polytechnical Institute. After two years of military service during the First World War Kapitza returned to the institute in 1916 and

Peter Leonidovich Kapitza (1894–1984), by Boris Mikhailovitch Koustodieff, 1926

participated in a seminar series organized by physics professor A. F. Joffé. In 1916 he married Nadezhda Kirillovna Chernosvitova, daughter of General Kirill Kirillovich Chernosvitov. Upon graduation in 1919 Kapitza was appointed to a research position at Joffé's newly founded Physico-Technical Institute.

Kapitza lost his father, wife (in 1920), and two children to epidemics during the difficult conditions of the civil war. Partly in order to take Kapitza's mind off this devastating blow Joffé arranged for him to take part in a Soviet mission to renew scientific contacts with western Europe. He and Joffé visited Cambridge in 1921. Sir Ernest Rutherford agreed to have Kapitza in the Cavendish Laboratory for a winter to gain research experience and was much impressed by Kapitza's success in tackling his first problem. Kapitza would remain in Cambridge for thirteen years. He married, in 1927, Anna Alekseyevna Krylova, daughter of Admiral Aleksey Nikolayevich Krylov, mathematician and naval architect. They had two sons.

To study the loss of energy by alpha particles Kapitza required high magnetic fields. In 1924, with engineer M. P. Kostenko, he conceived of a large dynamo for producing such pulse fields on short circuit. These would be sufficiently high to curve tracks of fast particles, but would not last long enough to overheat the magnet coil. The development of this equipment brought the Cavendish Laboratory into contact with industry and the Department of Scientific and Industrial Research, and signalled its transition to the physics of big machines. Once Kapitza managed to produce record high magnetic fields his interest shifted from Rutherford's favourite nuclear radiations to the study of magnetic phenomena. Magnetic properties of substances become more distinct at very low temperatures and Kapitza developed ingenious methods of liquefying hydrogen and helium to cool specimens to temperatures close to absolute zero. To house all this new activity more space was needed and Rutherford persuaded the Royal Society to provide £15,000 from the Ludwig Mond bequest for the building of the Royal Society Mond Laboratory, which opened in 1933 in the courtyard of the Cavendish Laboratory.

Kapitza rose rapidly in the scientific establishment. He gained his PhD in 1923; in 1925 he was appointed assistant director of magnetic research and was elected to a fellowship at Trinity College. In 1929 he was elected FRS and became a corresponding member of the Soviet Academy of Sciences (he became a full member in 1939); in 1931 he was appointed Royal Society Messel professor. During his years in Cambridge, Kapitza became somewhat of a legend, not only for the originality of his scientific achievements, but also for his ebullient and sometimes eccentric personality, and for establishing at the Cavendish a model of informal discussions about physics at his weekly personal seminar, which was known as the Kapitza Club and which introduced the Russian style of close scientific discussion into the more formal and individualistic culture of British academia. He brought his early engineering training to bear on problems of fundamental physics and initiated—in competition with the Oxford team led by Lindemann—the tradition of low temperature and solid-state physics in Cambridge. His machines were still in use there until the early 1950s, and the Kapitza Club continued meeting regularly until 1958, long after Kapitza had left Cambridge.

Unfortunately, Kapitza himself had little opportunity to exploit the facilities of the Mond Laboratory. In the summer of 1934, following a routine holiday visit to the USSR he was refused permission to return to Cambridge. In spite of many appeals, the Soviet authorities would not revoke their decision. Eventually Kapitza agreed to become director of a new Institute for Physical Problems in Moscow, built specially to his requirements.

After the institute was built and fitted with replicas of his Cambridge equipment, in early 1937 Kapitza began to investigate the strange behaviour of liquid helium at very low temperatures. In the course of a series of ingenious experiments he discovered the phenomenon of superfluidity and provided further basis for a fundamental theory of quantum liquids to be developed from 1941 on by Lev Landau, the institute's house theoretician. Treated by Soviet officials with suspicion, as half-foreigner, Kapitza strove for the patronage of high politicians, including prime minister V. M. Molotov and Stalin. He sent them long personal letters about his work and problems, often including some cleverly calculated criticism on political and administrative issues related to science and technology. Though this strategy was unusually brave by the standards of the time and certainly carried risks, it helped him to achieve a high visibility among politicians, to secure some privileges for his institute, and, last but not least, to plead for arrested colleagues in the time of the

great purges of 1936–8. Through his active intervention Kapitza succeeded in saving the lives of V. A. Fok and Lev Landau, two of the nation's foremost theoretical physicists.

Kapitza also made important contributions to the techniques of gas liquefaction, and his turbine method of liquefying air had many applications during the Second World War and especially afterwards for the bulk production of oxygen for the steel industry. Towards the end of the war he was in charge of the Soviet oxygen industry and received the highest government decoration, the hero of socialist labour. Soon, however, his fortunes again suddenly changed, apparently because of a conflict with L. P. Beria, the deputy prime minister and former chief of secret police who also headed the Soviet atom bomb project. In the autumn of 1945 Kapitza wrote two long letters to Stalin in which he demanded more authority for Soviet scientists and criticized Beria's style of administration and the way the atomic project was organized. This time he lost his battle and was released from his duties on the government's special committee on the atomic problem. In mid-1946 he was dismissed from his position in industry and from the directorship of the institute, allegedly for shortcomings in his oxygen work. Though fired from all his positions he was not arrested, and for the next seven years he lived at his dacha outside Moscow, where he set up a home laboratory.

After Stalin's death in 1953 and Khrushchov's victory over Beria in the subsequent struggle for the Kremlin, Kapitza was reappointed to his institute. He resumed large-scale scientific work, but in a direction which shifted his interests from very low to very high temperature physics. His main effort went into developing powerful new microwave sources for the intense heating of plasma, with the hope of reaching temperatures high enough to produce thermonuclear fusion. Kapitza continued this plasma work to the end of his life, but although he made interesting contributions to plasma physics he did not achieve his aim of producing thermonuclear fusion. Nevertheless, powerful machines such as the Tokamak seemed to offer great promise.

Though in the post-Stalin era Kapitza never again established a close link with the highest politicians, he became an important figure in the Soviet scientific and cultural establishment and often quite outspokenly promoted liberal causes. His work was recognized by many awards and academic honours both in the USSR and in the West, culminating in the Nobel prize in 1978. Kapitza died in Moscow on 8 April 1984. He was survived by his wife and sons.

ALEXEI B. KOJEVNIKOV

Sources D. Schoenberg, *Memoirs FRS*, 31 (1985), 325–74 • A. Kozhevnikov, 'Piotr Kapitza and Stalin's government: a study in moral choice', *Historical Studies in the Physical and Biological Sciences*, 22 (1991–2), 131–64 • *Kapitza in Cambridge and Moscow: life and letters of a Russian physicist*, ed. J. W. Boag, P. E. Rubinin, and D. Schoenberg (1990) • *Collected papers of P. L. Kapitza*, ed. D. ter Haar, 4 vols. (1964–85) • P. L. Kapitza, *Pis'ma o nauke, 1930–1980* (1989) • P. E. Rubinin, ed., *Piotr Leonidovich Kapitza: vospominaniia, pis'ma, dokumenty* (1994) • L. Badash, *Kapitza, Rutherford and the Kremlin* (1985) • P. L. Kapitza,

Experiment, theory, practice: articles and addresses (1980) · F. Kedrov, *Kapitza: life and discoveries* (1985) · *DNB*
Archives Institute for Physical Problems, Moscow · Russian Academy of Sciences, Moscow | Cambridge, Rutherford MSS
Likenesses B. M. Koustodieff, portrait, 1926, FM Cam. [*see illus.*] · photograph, 1966, RS · G. Bollobás, bust, 1970–79, RS · photograph, 1973, RS · colour negative (after B. M. Koustodieff, 1926), RS

Kapp, Gisbert Johann Eduard [Gilbert John Edward] (1852–1922), electrical engineer and university teacher, was born on 2 September 1852 in Mauer, Austria, the first of the two children of Johann Gisbert Sebastian Kapp, a senior civil servant, and his wife, Aloisia Theresia Young, a professional singer, born in Linz of Scottish descent. He was educated at parish and secondary schools in Vienna, and from 1864 to 1869 in Prague at the Deutsche Oberrealschule. From 1869 he studied mechanical engineering at the Eidgenössisches Polytechnikum, Zürich, and received his diploma in December 1871. After a year's service in the Austrian navy, Kapp went to England and accepted the post of chief draughtsman at Gwynne & Co., Hammersmith, London, a firm which manufactured centrifugal pumps, where he was concerned chiefly with the design and installation of pumps and turbines. In 1879 he joined the firm of Hornsby, manufacturers of agricultural machinery at Grantham, Lincolnshire, as a sales representative in Italy, Russia, and north Africa.

After visiting the Paris electrical exhibition in 1881 Kapp decided to become an electrical engineer. Electrical engineering was in its infancy: the incandescent electric light had been demonstrated in 1879, and the demand for electric power, leading to the rapid development of centralized power-generating stations in the next two decades, was just beginning. Despite his lack of electrical engineering knowledge, Kapp was engaged in 1882 by R. E. B. Crompton (1845–1940) as manager of his Chelmsford works. He became involved in all aspects of the design of electricity supply systems and patented a number of inventions jointly with Crompton. While with Crompton, Kapp began writing technical papers and articles on a variety of electrical subjects, which he continued throughout his life. He joined the Society of Telegraph Engineers and Electricians (later the Institution of Electrical Engineers) in 1883, and took an active part in its affairs. On 5 December 1881 he became a naturalized British subject. Three years later, on 20 August 1884, he married, in Lambeth parish church, Theresa ('Treasy') Mary, the daughter of John Baptist Krall (1828–1900), a London coffee merchant. They had two sons, Reginald Otto (*b.* 1885) and Norman Gisbert (*b.* 1887).

In 1884 Kapp left Crompton to establish his own practice as a consulting electrical engineer, and the next twelve years marked his most productive period. He designed electrical equipment for W. H. Allen & Co., Lambeth, and supervised their electrical department. From 1886 to 1889 he was the London editor of *Industries*, a weekly technical journal. Towards the end of the decade he undertook some consultancy work for the Brush Company. His dynamos were widely used, and some of his designs were installed in the St Pancras power station, London, in 1891.

From April 1891 to 1893, working with W. H. Preece (1834–1913), he designed a new electric power station and distribution scheme for Bristol corporation.

In 1894 Kapp moved to Berlin on appointment as general secretary of the new Verband Deutscher Elektrotechniker (VDE) and editor of its journal *Elektrotechnische Zeitschrift*. The object of the society was to establish electrical standardization, in which Kapp's technical knowledge and experience were invaluable. He also taught part-time at the Technische Hochschule at Charlottenburg.

Kapp returned to England in 1905 on his appointment as the first professor of electrical engineering at Birmingham University, where he remained until his retirement in 1919. As a professor he encouraged independent thought from his students and ensured that the electrical engineering laboratories were exceptionally well equipped. Throughout his career, Kapp's advice was much sought after, and in 1909 he was elected president of the Institution of Electrical Engineers. He published nine monographs and more than fifty-five technical papers on electricity and dynamo design. He realized that there was a need to apply quantitative scientific principles, rather than trial and error, to the design of electrical machinery, and he contributed much to the quantitative design of machinery and generating systems. His most important contribution, however, was his work in 1885 on the theory of the magnetic circuit—a concept which was also developed independently at about the same time by John Hopkinson (1849–1898).

Kapp and his wife were sociable people who enjoyed entertaining colleagues at home. Both were musical, and Kapp enjoyed sailing and golf. He had been ill for several years before his death, from nephritis and uraemia, on 10 August 1922 at his home, Treganor, 43 Lepland Road, Selly Oak, Birmingham. ELEANOR PUTNAM SYMONS

Sources G. Kapp, 'Autobiography', U. Birm., archives · D. G. Tucker, *Gisbert Kapp, 1852–1922* (1972) · D. G. Tucker, 'A new archive of Gisbert Kapp papers', *Seventeenth IEE weekend meeting on the history of electrical engineering* [Swansea 1989] (1990) · U. Birm., Gisbert Kapp MSS and correspondence · d. cert. · *CGPLA Eng. & Wales* (1922) · baptism cert.
Archives Inst. EE, notebooks of machine design · U. Birm. L., corresp. and papers | Inst. EE, archives, A. J. Lawson MSS
Likenesses B. Munns, oils, 1923, U. Birm. · photograph, Inst. EE · photographs, U. Birm.
Wealth at death £11,210 7*s.* 1*d.*: probate, 2 Dec 1922, *CGPLA Eng. & Wales*

Kapp [*née* Mayer], **Yvonne Hélène** (1903–1999), writer and political activist, was born on 17 April 1903 at 170 Tulse Hill, Norwood, London, the daughter of Max Alfred Mayer (1871–1948) and his wife, Clarisse Fanny, *née* Bielefeld (1878–1960). Her parents were of Jewish immigrant stock: her father was a prosperous vanilla merchant and her mother enjoyed a life of leisure. Yvonne proved to be precocious and defiant, and referred to her childhood as 'a campaign of civil disobedience' against her parents and older brother, whose values she despised (*Time Will Tell*, 14). At thirteen, horrified by the casualties of war, she announced to her mother and father that she was an atheist.

Yvonne Mayer's early education was disrupted by tuberculosis. She was sent to a number of schools in London and on the continent, including Queen's College, in Harley Street, and a finishing school in Lausanne. In 1921 she left home, despite parental protestation, and enrolled on a diploma course in journalism at King's College, London, editing the college magazine though never graduating. A letter to Alec Waugh led to a job on the *Evening Standard*, followed by a post on the *Sunday Herald* as assistant to the editor. Her next act of rebellion was to announce her intention to marry the artist and caricaturist Edmond Xavier Kapp (1890–1978), in defiance of a law which prevented young women under the age of twenty-one from marrying without parental consent. Her parents dropped their case when newspaper publicity threatened to escalate. Six months after the marriage at Marylebone register office on 2 August 1922 the newspapers reported the Kapps' departure on a walking tour of the French and Italian riviera after an all-night party in Fitzrovia.

Life for the Kapp ménage (a daughter, Janna, was born on 5 June 1924) was bohemian. Often in the company of friends, patrons, and volunteer nannies, they spent eight years travelling across Europe and shifting from studio to country house to hotel, relying on patronage, luck, resourcefulness, and Yvonne's journalism. Their friends and acquaintances from these times included Clifford Allen, Max Beerbohm, Quentin Bell, Desmond Bernal, Sybil Colefax, John Collier, W. H. Davies, Mark Gertler, Gordon Craig, Kathleen Hale, Edward Heron-Allen, Elsa Lanchester, C. K. Ogden, Francis and Vera Meynell, and Edward Wolfe. Following a recommendation from Rebecca West, Kapp spent a number of months as literary editor of Paris *Vogue*, but left after a dispute with her employers about the low pay of technical staff.

The Kapps' marriage broke up in 1930, after which Yvonne spent six months as part of Nancy Cunard's entourage. She turned to writing prose, as she had done when she was a child. Her first novel, *Nobody Asked You* (1932), was a *succès de scandale*. Cecil Harmsworth had written on the galleys, 'I cannot sanction the publication of this book' (private information); Kapp acquired the type and paper stock, set up her own press, and published the book herself. It was praised by Gerald Gould in *The Observer* and promptly sold out. By 1939 Kapp had published eight books—four of them novels—under the *nom de plume* Yvonne Cloud.

The 1930s also saw a raising of Kapp's political awareness: 'I became fully awake to the social scene around me: the misery of widespread unemployment, the hideous state of malnutrition from which children were suffering; the poverty and degradation in which millions of my compatriots were forced to live' (*Time Will Tell*, 140). In summer 1935 she visited the Soviet Union, accompanying friends who were attending a physiology conference. On the boat home she spent time with Harry Pollitt, secretary of the Communist Party of Great Britain, who was returning from the Seventh World Congress. Upon her return she signed up with the party.

Kapp's political life was typically active. From 1933 she

housed refugees while they sought a more permanent home. In the mid-1930s she and a band of local party women formed a care committee for the children of impoverished families. In 1937 she worked with the largest influx of refugees in British history: 4000 Basque children encamped at Stoneham near Southampton. Upon her return to London she wrote *The Basque Children in England* (1938) and organized the speakers for the celebrated 'Spain and culture' fund-raising event at the Albert Hall. Before the outbreak of the Second World War she worked full time with the main Jewish refugee organization. This was followed by her appointment as assistant to the director of the Czech Refugee Trust. However, as a communist she was dismissed from her job in 1940. Meanwhile, in autumn 1938 she had met Margaret Mynatt who became Kapp's partner until her death in 1977. Mynatt was a fellow communist (later the editor of the *Collected Works of Marx and Engels*) who had also fallen foul of Home Office policy. Together they wrote an account of their findings, *British Policy and the Refugees* (completed 1941, published 1968).

Blacklisted, Kapp found it difficult to get work, and in spring 1941 offered her services to the Labour Research Department as a volunteer. This led to the post of research officer at the Amalgamated Engineering Union (AEU), where for seven years she wrote speeches for the president of the union, Jack Tanner. She also launched three significant production inquiries, lobbied the royal commission on equal pay for women, and assembled the John Burns Library of working-class movement literature (now housed by the TUC). After leaving the AEU in 1947 she worked for the Medical Research Council. Her work took her to factories in Luton, Birmingham, and Cowley. Bored, however, by what she felt was inconsequential research, she undertook independent investigation into working conditions and health care in West Ham, a report which cost her her job.

Between 1953 and 1960 Kapp worked as a translator. She was dismissive of this late métier, with the exception of two projects: her work on the translations of Brecht's plays published in the UK; and a commission that resulted in her discovery of correspondence between Friedrich Engels and Marx's daughter Laura. The latter fired her interest in Marx's youngest daughter, Eleanor, leading to her acclaimed two-volume biography, *Eleanor Marx* (1972 and 1976). Kapp said that the book 'drew in one way or another upon my whole accumulated experience' (*Time Will Tell*, 237). She kept meticulous notes on her subject in case a revised edition was required.

Kapp died of kidney failure on 22 June 1999 at her home, 39 North Road, Highgate, London, in the presence of her companion of later years, Betty Lewis, and was cremated on 10 July at Golders Green crematorium. She remained quick-thinking until the end, and continued to write and publish. In her memoirs, which she began writing at eighty-seven, she reflected:

> Above all, I have learnt in old age that, despite what appear
> to be sudden dramatic spurts, the march of history is
> unconscionably slow; but that a love of justice and a belief in

the potential for human progress is inextinguishable. (*Time Will Tell*, 238)

She was survived by her daughter, Janna.

MATTHEW McFALL

Sources Y. Kapp, *Time will tell* (2003) · S. Alexander, 'Yvonne Kapp', *Writing lives: conversations between women writers*, ed. M. Chamberlain (1988), 99–119 · C. Brinson, foreword, in Y. Kapp and M. Mynatt, *British policy and the refugees, 1933–1941* (1997), ix–xxvi · *The Guardian* (29 June 1999) · *The Independent* (1 July 1999) · *The Times* (2 Aug 1999) · personal knowledge (2004) · private information (2004) · b. cert. · m. cert. · d. cert.
Archives Women's Library, London, corresp. and papers | Amalgamated Engineering and Electrical Union, Bromley, archives · Labour History Archive and Study Centre, Manchester, papers relating to meetings of the communist party psychology group · Medical Research Council, London, archives · People's History Museum archive, Manchester, Labour Research Department
Likenesses photograph, 1932, repro. in *The Independent* (1 July 1999) · photograph, repro. in *The Guardian* (29 June 1999)

Kar [*formerly* Karamian], **Ida** (1908–1974), photographer, was born in Tambov, Russia, the daughter of Melkon Karamian, a professor of science and mathematics. It is not known from what date she became known as Kar rather than Karamian. Her early childhood was spent in Russia and Persia and the family eventually settled in Alexandria, Egypt, when Kar was thirteen. There she was educated at the Lycée Français and then in 1928, aged twenty, she was sent to Paris to study medicine and chemistry. In Paris, Kar abandoned her studies and took courses in singing and the violin. Much of her time was spent working and socializing with avant-garde writers and artists in the Left Bank of the city. She was exposed to the work of international artists and photographers and it was during this time that she became aware of the potential of photography and established an interest in left-wing politics. She returned to Alexandria in 1933.

Kar began to lose her singing voice and so abandoned her musical career and began to work as a receptionist and assistant in a local photographer's studio. In the late 1930s she married Edmond Belali, an Egyptian government official and a very keen amateur photographer. They moved to Cairo and set up their own studio, Idabel. In 1943 and 1944 their work was exhibited in two surrealist exhibitions staged in Cairo. Her photographs attracted the attention of Victor Musgrave (*d.* 1984), the British artist, art dealer, curator, and critic, and in 1944, when Kar was thirty-six, she divorced Belali and married Musgrave.

In 1945 Kar and Musgrave moved to London and Kar pursued her career as a photographer. The portraits she took of the many artists and writers living and socializing in Soho during the early 1950s were to become the foundation of her subsequent work. Her most famous portraits include those of Jacob Epstein (1953), Bertrand Russell (1952), and Gino Severini (mid-1950s). Throughout her life she craved recognition as an artist and continuously struggled financially. At times she isolated herself by her autocratic and somewhat overbearing personality: 'everyone started off loving her and her personality but they ended up saying, "My God, I can't stand any more of this"' (Williams, *Ida Kar—Photographer*, 18).

In 1954 Kar held an exhibition entitled 'Forty artists from Paris and London' at Gallery One but it received little critical acclaim. Her portraits were confrontational, simple, but dramatic, showing none of the glamour of earlier portrait photography. Surrealist elements were apparent in some of the work and she often placed her subjects in their studios and homes using only natural lighting. She used a large old plate camera for these portraits but later changed to a rolleiflex for her documentary work. In 1956 Kar embraced a more documentary style and a number of her pictures of London life were published in *Tatler* and *The Observer*. In 1957 she returned to Armenia on a commission from *The Observer*. There she exhibited her photographs of local rural communities and found that she and her work were respected and revered. Optimistic, she returned to London and for the next three years embarked on a period of intense work and travel.

In 1960 Kar exhibited her work at the Whitechapel Art Gallery—it was the first solo photography show held in a major public art gallery in London. The show concentrated on her portraits of artists and writers with a small number of images from Russia and Armenia. It was a great success for Kar and for the future status of photography, generating a huge amount of press. The exhibition was the pinnacle of her achievement and the catalyst for some of her best work. The exhibition design was also innovative, with some of the photographs blown up to a huge scale—in some cases as large as 4 by 5 feet. In 1962 Kar held another successful exhibition at Moscow's House of Friendship but her biographer, Val Williams, recorded that 'her major projects were invariably accompanied by storms and upsets … to many potential clients and gallery curators, she was a difficult woman, and better avoided' (Williams, *Ida Kar—Photographer*, 53). In 1963 Kar became a regular photographer for *Animals* magazine—but it was a post that lasted only a year. During this time she exhibited some work in Birmingham and London and opportunities for teaching and lecturing were frequent. However, her rather formal approach to portraiture was becoming increasingly unfashionable and financial worries continued to dominate her life.

After a trip to Cuba in 1964 Kar began to show signs of acute manic depression, paranoia, and obsessive behaviour. She separated from her husband in 1969. After this, and up until her death, Kar suffered several breakdowns and was frequently hospitalized. She died on 24 December 1974 of thrombosis, virtually forgotten, at Inverness Terrace, a Bayswater bedsit. She was cremated at Golders Green. Her work did much to advance the status of photography in Britain and provided an important social record of London in the 1950s. Her archive is now held at the National Portrait Gallery and her work is widely collected by museums around the world.

SUSAN BRIGHT

Sources V. Williams, *Ida Kar—photographer, 1908–1974* (1989) · A. Inselmann, ed., *A second look: women photographers of the Gernsheim collection* (Frankfurt am Main, 1993) [exhibition catalogue, Deutscher Werkbund e.V., Frankfurt am Main, 26 Aug – 2 Sept 1993] · N. Rosenblum, *A history of women photographers* (1994) · H. Gernsheim, 'The photographs of Ida Kar', *Motif*, 9 (1962), 90–95 ·

V. Musgrave, Knoedler Gallery invite (with text), 1982 • V. Williams, 'Ida Kar: the decade before pop', *Sunday Correspondent* (15 Oct 1989) • M. Gerson, 'Ida Kar at the Knoedler Gallery', *British Journal of Photography* (14 Jan 1983), 50–55 • C. MacInnes, *Ida Kar* (1960) [exhibition catalogue, Whitechapel Art Gallery, London, March–April 1960] • J. Findlay, 'The photographs of artists and writers', PhD diss., Duncan of Jordanstone College of Art, Dundee
Archives NPG, archive
Likenesses photographs, repro. in Williams, *Ida Kar*
Wealth at death £1583: administration, 30 April 1975, *CGPLA Eng. & Wales*

Karim, Abdul (1862/3–1909), Queen Victoria's Indian secretary, was the son of an Indian Muslim, Sheikh Mohammed Waziruddin of Agra, India, a hospital assistant at Rs60 a month. Records suggest he had an older brother and four sisters, a wife and one child. Having been employed as a vernacular clerk in Agra gaol (salary Rs10 monthly), in 1887, aged twenty-four, he came as a servant to Queen Victoria's household.

Slim and strikingly good-looking, Abdul Karim, promoted the queen's munshi in 1889, gave Victoria lessons in Hindustani, with 'instructive' discussions in Indian religion and culture. Graduating to the position of the queen's Indian secretary, with the title hafiz, in 1894, he assisted with her 'boxes', handling Indian petitions which required 'merely a civil refusal' (Longford, 638). His official residences were at Frogmore Cottage, Windsor, and Arthur Cottage, at Osborne. At the latter, he gave a party every Christmas for the children of the estate. Rewards followed: a grant of land in the suburbs of Agra and permission to attend the durbar. He was painted twice by Rudolf Swoboda (1888 and 1889) and by von Angeli in 1890. Accorded high social position at court, he was made a companion in the Order of the Indian Empire.

Such social elevation caused much controversy and resentment in the royal household, especially among the private secretaries. Abdul Karim was snubbed socially, while the queen was shown an Indian report depicting his low origins. A sensitive man, the munshi was deeply hurt. According to a biographer of Queen Victoria there was a 'running battle' between the queen and her advisers (Longford, 674), with the queen determined to promote 'her excellent and much esteemed Munshi and Indian Clerk', and the court putting him down (Victoria to Lansdowne, 29 Oct 1890, MS Eur. D/558/1). The court alleged that giving the munshi access to state papers was dangerous, leading to his movements being watched and reports being compiled on him in India. The climax came in 1897: the viceroy was wired for details of his family status and Henry Frederick Ponsonby, the queen's private secretary, requested gossip from 'native' and European papers. Finally, the government called a halt. Instead the queen was 'plainly' spoken to by some trusted Indian officers in her court, and the munshi put into his 'proper place' (George Hamilton to Lord Elgin, 7 May 1897, Longford, 678).

Like the court at the time, some historians have suggested that Abdul Karim saw 'more confidential papers

Abdul Karim (1862/3–1909), by Hills & Saunders

than he should have' and 'probably influenced' the queen on Indian 'problems' (Plumb, 281). But, given the fact that, according to the queen, he saw 'no political papers' and did not 'read English fluently enough to be able to read anything of importance', it is unlikely he could have influenced policy or posed any danger to the state (Victoria to Salisbury, 17 July 1897, Longford, 678). The row over the munshi (similar in ways to the earlier rows about the role of John Brown) is more an illustration of race and class prejudice in Victorian England: of the munshi not being kept in what was perceived as his proper place. More significantly, however, his presence may have made Queen Victoria 'more sensitive' to race prejudice, as seen from a long letter urging the future viceroy to be 'more free' of the 'red-tapist narrow-minded Council' (Plumb, 282).

Following Queen Victoria's death, a bonfire of the munshi's papers was ordered by King Edward at Frogmore. Abdul Karim retired to Agra, where he died in 1909. All his papers were burnt, except for a few letters allowed to his widow as a memento of the queen. ROZINA VISRAM

Sources E. Longford, *Victoria RI* (1964) • R. Visram, *Asians in Britain: four hundred years of history* (2002) • R. Visram, *Ayahs, lascars and princes: Indians in Britain, 1700–1947* (1986) • J. H. Plumb, *Royal heritage: the story of Britain's royal builders and collectors* (1977), 281–2 • F. Ponsonby, *Recollections of three reigns* (1951) • BL OIOC, MS Eur. D/558/1 • BL OIOC, MS Eur. F 84/126a • BL OIOC, L/P and S/8/61
Archives BL OIOC, IOR, MS Eur. F 84/126a • BL OIOC, IOR, MS Eur. D/558/1 • BL OIOC, IOR, L/P and S/8/61
Likenesses R. Swoboda, portrait, 1888, Osborne House, Isle of Wight; repro. in R. Visram, *The history of the Asian community in Britain* (1995), 9 • R. Swoboda, portrait, 1889 • von Angeli, portrait, 1890 • Hills & Saunders, photograph, NPG [*see illus.*]

Kark [*née* Gordine], **Evelyn Florence** [*known as* Lucie Clayton] **(1928–1997)**, college head, was born on 5 December 1928 at 50 Hague Street, east London, the elder of the two daughters of William Gordine (*d.* 1937), a factory labourer and later an insurance agent, and his wife, Emily Mildred Winifred, *née* Mallott. She was educated at Chandos School, in the north London suburb of Queensbury, before being evacuated to Ilkley, Yorkshire, during the Second World War. After the war she won a scholarship to Pitman's, and trained as a secretary, becoming assistant to the associate editor of *Courier Magazine*, (Arthur) Leslie Kark (*b.* 1910). When Leslie Kark left in 1950 to launch *Model*, a directory of British models, she went with him as his personal assistant; they were joined in the office by Muriel Spark, not yet known as a writer. After the success of *Model*, Kark bought the Lucie Clayton Model and Charm School and Agency, at 449 Oxford Street, founded in 1928 by Sylvia Golledge. He appointed Evelyn principal of the school in 1952, and she took the name Lucie Clayton for publicity purposes. She married Kark, son of Victor Kark, company director, of Johannesburg, on 8 November 1956; they had one son and one daughter.

Within a decade the Karks had revived the Lucie Clayton Model and Charm School, and by the time it moved to 66 New Bond Street in 1960 it had become extremely fashionable, thanks partly to the growing respectability of a career in modelling following the success in the 1950s of models such as Fiona Campbell Walter (later Baroness Thyssen). In the 1960s many of the most beautiful and glamorous models, including Jean Shrimpton, the top model of the 1960s, and Sandra Paul, Celia Hammond, and Joanna Lumley, were trained at the Lucie Clayton School. Only a few of the applicants were accepted as trainee models and taken on to the agency's books at the end of the month-long course: most came not to become models, but in order to look like models. As Evelyn Kark explained, 'most students come to me because they want to acquire a model-girl finish before launching into other careers' (Clayton, 19). Lucie Clayton's agency became the top model agency in London, and in 1966 it was one of the six leading agencies to form the Association of London Model Agencies (ALMA), with Leslie Kark as chairman.

In 1961 the Karks opened the Lucie Clayton College of Dressmaking and Fashion Design in the Bond Street premises, and in 1965, in South Kensington, launched the Lucie Clayton Secretarial College at 4 Cornwall Gardens, henceforth known as Lucie Clayton House. When they surrendered the lease on Bond Street in 1974 they moved the college of dressmaking to Lucie Clayton House, along with the grooming school, which all the students attended, while the model agency moved to 168 Brompton Road, which they had bought in 1965, and which also housed some of the students from the secretarial college. The model agency closed in 1988. Lucie Clayton's became the most successful and socially exclusive of the English finishing schools, teaching deportment and social skills, and gradually enlarging its syllabus to include cookery (Evelyn Kark, herself a cordon bleu cook, presided in the kitchen), flower arranging, table laying and party giving, art appreciation, and current affairs. In the mid-1980s a new course was launched for those who wanted to change their accent, while students were taken to the theatre and the ballet, and on trips to such London institutions as Sothebys, Harrods, and de Beer's diamond house. Etiquette was an important part of all the courses, and Lucie Clayton's came to be regarded as the authority on this. Girls who were about to come out as débutantes trained at Lucie Clayton's for the NSPCC fashion show, produced every year by the staff of the school.

Beautiful and glamorous, Evelyn Kark was never a model herself—she was too short—but her charismatic and warm personality helped to make the school a success. She published *The World of Modelling and how to Get the Model Girl Look* (1968) and *Modelling and Beauty Care Made Simple* (1985). When her husband sold the business in 1995 Evelyn Kark retired, and they moved to Burford, Oxfordshire, where she enjoyed old-fashioned pursuits such as tapestry making and *petit point*. She also loved jazz and the music of the 1960s. She died of heart disease on 8 March 1997 at her home, Roche House, 29 Sheep Street, Burford, Oxfordshire, survived by her husband, and was buried a week later.   ANNE PIMLOTT BAKER

Sources *The Times* (15 March 1997) · J. Shrimpton, *The truth about modelling* (1964), 33–41 · L. Clayton [E. F. Kark], *The world of modelling* (1968) · private information (2004) [Leslie Kark, husband] · *WW* · b. cert. · m. cert. · d. cert.
Likenesses D. Anthony, photograph, repro. in Clayton, *World of modelling*, frontispiece · photograph, repro. in *The Times*
Wealth at death £523,600: probate, 12 Nov 1997, *CGPLA Eng. & Wales*

Karkeek, William Floyd (1802–1858), veterinary surgeon, the son of George and Elizabeth Karkeek, was born at Truro on 9 September 1802. On 10 November 1823, at the age of twenty-one, he entered the London Veterinary College (later known as the Royal Veterinary College); he obtained his diploma as a veterinary surgeon on 31 January 1825, and then returned to Cornwall to practise. On 12 March 1836, at Clifton, Bristol, he married Jane Quick (1815–1870), daughter of Paul and Grace Quick; they had at least one son.

Karkeek became a leading authority in the west of England on the practice of scientific farming, and did much to promote his ideas in Cornwall through his writings and by reading papers at lectures and meetings of agricultural societies. He also acted as a judge of horses for meetings of the Royal Agricultural Society of England. For twenty years Karkeek was secretary to the Cornwall Agricultural Association. During the years 1829 to 1855, Karkeek was one of the major contributors of learned and scholarly articles to *The Veterinarian*, eventually as co-editor, from 1838 to 1841. In 1844 Karkeek published *An Essay on Artificial and other Manures* and *An Essay on Fat and Muscle*. The latter won a prize from the Royal Agricultural Society of England and was published separately, later appearing in the fifth volume (1845) of the *Journal of the Royal Agricultural Society of England*. In the same year he published an elaborate report, *The Report of the Farming of Cornwall*, which appeared in volume 6 of the same journal, before being published separately; this essay was reviewed at a later date in *The Veterinarian* (vol. 20, 1847). In 1851 another of Karkeek's prize essays, entitled *Diseases of Cattle and Sheep Caused by Mismanagement*, was published as a separate item after appearing first in the *Journal of the Royal Agricultural Society of England*. He also published essays on similar subjects for the *Journal of the Bath and West and South Counties Association Society*, which, again, were subsequently reprinted. In the spring of 1848, according to the Royal Veterinary College minute books, he consented to become an examiner of the students educated at the college.

Karkeek was also interested in the welfare of horses, and according to Sir Frederick Smith 'the system of ventilation [of military stables], [was] generally attributed to Coleman, whereas we now know it was that of Karkeek' (Smith, *History of the Royal Army Veterinary Corps*, 1927). It was Karkeek's concern for the care of horses that led to his untimely death at the age of fifty-five. He had been called out to attend an urgent case near Camelford, where some horses had been struck by lightning, and on his return home he was thrown out of the gig in which he had been travelling. He suffered severe bruising and an abscess appeared on the bruised area. Karkeek died twelve days later, on 25 June 1858, at Pantreve, Truro, Cornwall, and was buried in St Mary's burial-ground. He was survived by his wife. On the day of his funeral 'shops in Truro were spontaneously closed, and a long procession of sorrowing friends and neighbours acknowledged his worth, and lamented his early death' (*The Veterinarian*, 478–80).

LINDA WARDEN

Sources F. Smith, *The early history of veterinary literature and its British development*, 4 vols. (1919–33); repr. (1976), vol. 4 · F. Smith, *A history of the royal army veterinary corps, 1796–1919* (1927) · E. Cotchin, *The Royal Veterinary College, London: a bicentenary history* (1990) · I. Pattison, *The British veterinary profession, 1741–1948*, [another edn] (1984) · minute books, 1804–52, Royal Veterinary College, London · register of pupils, 1794–1907, Royal Veterinary College, London · d. cert. · *The Veterinarian*, 31 (1858), 478–80 · *CGPLA Eng. & Wales* (1858) · *CGPLA Eng. & Wales* (1871) · *West Briton and Cornwall Advertiser* (2 July 1858) · *DNB* · *IGI*

Wealth at death under £7000: administration, 23 Aug 1858, *CGPLA Eng. & Wales* · under £5: further action, 19 July 1871, *CGPLA Eng. & Wales*

Karloff, Boris [*real name* William Henry Pratt] (1887–1969), actor, was born in Camberwell, London, on 23 November 1887, the son of Edward John Pratt of the Indian salt revenue service, and his wife, Eliza Sara Millard. He was the youngest of nine children, eight of them boys; one brother became a judge in the high court of Bombay and another was Sir John Thomas Pratt, an expert on China for the Foreign Office. Young William gained his first interest in the stage from a third brother, who acted under the name George Marlowe. In 1894 the family moved to Enfield, Middlesex, and William was educated at Merchant Taylors' School, London, and at Uppingham School; in 1906 he moved to King's College, London, and studied for the consular service. In fact he elected instead for a stage career, but in deference to family feeling he sailed to

Boris Karloff (1887–1969), by Ben Pinchot, 1940s?

Montreal, Canada, before beginning it. Despite his striking looks and inimitable voice, his young manhood was not a period of great success. He acted with repertory companies all over Canada, and when jobs were hard to find he worked on farms and fairgrounds. In 1911 he adopted Karloff, an old family name, adding Boris to it because it seemed to fit. The new name got him a steady job at Kamloops, where he worked until 1912, subsequently joining a company in Prince Albert, Saskatchewan. In 1917 he joined a touring company of the play *The Virginian* in the United States, starting in Chicago and ending in Hollywood, where he stayed. He was to be married three times, in 1923 to Helene Vivian Soule, in 1929 to Dorothy Stine, and in 1946 to Evelyn Helmore (*née* Hope), who survived him. There was one daughter of the second marriage.

Gradually extra work came Karloff's way, and by 1919 he was playing villains in Douglas Fairbanks films. During the twenties he worked fairly steadily without being at all well known. His best role in silent films was as the mesmerist in *The Bells* (1926), but the first years of sound found him again reduced to playing bandits and minor gangsters. In 1930 he was fortunate to find a good stage role in Los Angeles in *The Criminal Code*. When this was filmed he was offered the same part of a convict who—with gait and gestures that were to become very familiar—kills a stool-pigeon. This led to several roles in 1931, including the unexpected one of the hypocritical effeminate reporter in *Five Star Final*.

When James Whale was casting *Frankenstein* (1931) he saw something unusual about the shape of Karloff's head that he thought might make him effective as the monster.

Weighed down under much uncomfortable make-up, Karloff was sensationally effective in the role, extracting pity as well as revulsion for the monster. His name did not appear on the credits, the intention being to surround the role with mystery, but immediately the film was released he was a star, and in his next films, *The Old Dark House* (1932, in which he played the deaf-mute butler) and *The Mummy* (1932), his name appeared on the bills in larger letters than the titles. In 1932 he was also very effective as the Chinese villain in *The Mask of Fu Manchu*, and in 1933 he returned to England for *The Ghoul*. This period, though exciting, had typecast him, and in his occasional non-horror roles (*The Lost Patrol*, 1934; *The House of Rothschild*, 1934) he showed that he had become an over-emphatic actor.

Returning to horror films Karloff was excellent in *The Black Room* (1935) and *The Bride of Frankenstein* (1935), although he himself felt that the monster should not have been allowed to talk. Lean years followed, horror films being out of fashion, and he was reduced to playing Mr Wong in a low-budget series of detective films. In 1939 *Son of Frankenstein* revived his stature somewhat, though he played the monster, for the last time, rather disappointingly as a soulless killer. The popularity of horror films revived during the Second World War and Karloff starred in a series of 'mad doctor' films, in which his intentions at least were always honourable. It was clear that he was never to find another role like the monster, and that Hollywood regarded him as no more than a useful addition to low-budget offerings; yet ironically his name was known throughout the world.

Karloff determinedly made a name for himself in other fields, notably the Broadway stage. He successfully caricatured his own image in *Arsenic and Old Lace* (1941), was a kindly professor in J. B. Priestley's *The Linden Tree* (1948), and was Captain Hook in *Peter Pan* (1950). He issued several recordings in which he recited fairy tales and ghost stories, and edited volumes of similar material; he was also a noted Hollywood cricketer. At the end of the Second World War Hollywood began to offer him more distinguished roles, such as the leading part in his first colour film, *The Climax* (1944), smooth comedy villainy in *The Secret Life of Walter Mitty* (1947), and, curiously, an Indian chief in *Unconquered* (1947). He had also some success with Val Lewton, a producer of 'intellectual horror' films: *The Body Snatcher* (after Robert Louis Stevenson, 1945), *The Isle of the Dead* (1945), and *Bedlam* (1946). Thereafter he was unsuccessful in Hollywood, except in television.

In Britain between 1953 and 1955 Karloff played patch-eyed Colonel March of Scotland Yard in the eponymous television series, and in 1958 he secured two thrillers better than Hollywood was likely to offer: *Corridors of Blood* and *Grip of the Strangler*. In 1959 he retired to a Sussex village to enjoy cricket. Despite failing health, he continued to accept small roles, appearing in several television commercials and even playing a transvestite villain in the television series *The Girl from UNCLE* (1966). He died at Midhurst, Sussex, on 2 February 1969, shortly after completing a moving performance in a television series, *The Name of the Game*, as a Czech writer caught in the cold war. His remains were placed in the garden of remembrance, Mount cemetery, Guildford, Surrey. Karloff's deep and cultured voice was widely imitated. He deserved better roles, although his acting range was limited.

LESLIE HALLIWELL, *rev.* K. D. REYNOLDS

Sources R. Bojarski and K. Beals, *The films of Boris Karloff* (1974) · P. Underwood, *Horror man* (1972) · D. Gifford, *Karloff, the man, the monster, the movies* (1973) · *The Times* (4 Feb 1969) · www.findagrave.com
Archives SOAS, corresp. with his brother John
Likenesses B. Pinchot, bromide print, 1940–1949?, NPG [*see illus.*] · photographs, Hult. Arch.
Wealth at death £2480: administration with will, 7 April 1971, CGPLA Eng. & Wales

Karno, Fred [*real name* Frederick John Westcott] (1866–1941), comedian, was born on 26 March 1866 at Paul Street, Exeter, the eldest of the six sons and the seven children of John Westcott, cabinet-maker and french polisher of Exeter, and his wife, Emily Bowden, also of Exeter. He had a perfunctory elementary education in Exeter and Nottingham. He began as a circus acrobat and gymnast as one of the Three Carnoes with Bob Sewell and Ted Tysall. This became the Karno Trio, from which he took his stage name in the 1880s. By the 1890s he had developed his flair for low comedy, and established himself as an entrepreneur of often 'speechless' sketches. From Karno's Fun Factory in Camberwell he sent forth teams of comedians to perform his endless series of slapstick mini-shows as set pieces on music-hall bills. He had an early success with 'Jail Birds', while other favourites were 'The Football Match', starring Harry Weldon as Stiffy the goalkeeper, and 'Karno's Komics'. However, the cameo which won everlasting fame was 'Mumming Birds', first performed in 1904 at the Star Music Hall, Bermondsey. This is reputed to be the funniest burlesque of music-hall there has been, and, with its stage within a stage, it ran in one form or another for thirty years.

In 1913 Karno expended a huge part of the fortune he had gathered on buying Tagg's Island on the Thames in Hampton and there built his 'Karsino' at a cost of £70,000. The outbreak of the First World War ruined all chance of its success—he had hoped to sell it after two years to the Lyons company—and he never quite recovered financially or professionally. He ran an off-licence in the latter part of his life.

Karno's 'army' gave either a solid start or valuable experience to dozens of comedians. Charles Chaplin was spotted as a film prospect when with a Karno company, while other famous names associated with him include Stan Jefferson (Laurel, of Laurel and Hardy), Fred Kitchen (of the famous catchphrase, 'Meredith, we're in') Will Hay, Sandy Powell, Wee Georgie Wood, and Max Miller. Immortalized by the soldiery in the First World War, Fred Karno's army lives on as a descriptor of chaotic organization. To a famous hymn tune the troops irreverently sang: 'We are Fred Karno's army, Fred Karno's infantry; we cannot fight, we cannot shoot, so what damn good are we?'

Karno married Edith (1867/8–1926/7), theatre assistant

and daughter of John Cuthbert, journeyman rope manufacturer of Stockport, in Lambeth, on 15 January 1889. They had eight children, of whom six died in extreme infancy and only two sons, Frederick Arthur and Leslie, survived. On 16 June 1927, after the death of his first wife, whom he had treated with some cruelty, he married his long-time mistress, Marie Theresa Laura, daughter of Thomas William Moore of London, theatrical manager and co-founder of the Moore and Burgess Minstrels. Fred Karno died on 17 September 1941 at his home, 24 Wharfedale Road, Parkstone, Dorset.   ERIC MIDWINTER

Sources J. P. Gallagher, *Fred Karno: master of mirth and tears* (1971) · S. T. Felstead, *Stars who made the halls* (1946) · b. cert. · m. cert. · *CGPLA Eng. & Wales* (1941)
Archives Theatre Museum, London, cuttings | FILM BFI NFTVA, performance footage
Wealth at death £42 7s. 4d.: probate, 29 Oct 1941, *CGPLA Eng. & Wales*

Karpeles, Maud Pauline (1885–1976), folk music collector and scholar, was born on 12 November 1885 at Lancaster Gate, London, the third of five children of John N. Karpeles (*d.* 1926?), merchant and stockbroker, a naturalized German from Hamburg, and his wife, Emily Annette (1861–1914), daughter of the banker Henry Lewis *Raphael. The family was Jewish by descent but not practising, and Karpeles had little religious education. At fourteen she converted to Christianity, although she was not baptized into the Anglican church until 1938. From 1900 to 1905 she attended Hamilton House School, Tunbridge Wells, then spent six months in Berlin, studying the piano. When she returned to London at the end of 1906, she began charitable work for the Mansfield House Settlement, Canning Town, and joined the Fabian Society.

Maud Karpeles and her sister Helen encountered folk-dances and -songs at the Stratford upon Avon festival in 1909, whereupon they enrolled in Cecil *Sharp's folk-dance classes in London in order to acquire the skills to teach their Canning Town children. The Folk Dance Club they formed, based at their home in Westbourne Terrace, became the nucleus of the English Folk Dance Society (EFDS) founded two years later in December 1911; Helen became secretary and Maud a committee member. In the following two years Karpeles and Sharp became increasingly close as they worked together: Karpeles assisted Sharp in demonstrations, accompanied him on folk-dance collecting expeditions, and in 1913 became his amanuensis, effectively taking up residence in his household; she lived there for twenty years.

When Sharp travelled to America in 1914 Karpeles was 'bereft', and Sharp's letters to her, especially at the beginning of his extended period in America from February 1916, emphasized how dependent on her assistance he felt. In April 1916 he summoned her to join him for what she described as 'the great event of my life: collecting folk songs in the Southern Appalachian Mountains'. They endured many discomforts during their Appalachian trips; Karpeles recorded sleeping on the floor next to Sharp's bed to nurse him through attacks of illness. The

Maud Pauline Karpeles (1885–1976), by unknown photographer

pair returned to England in December 1918; it fell to Karpeles to publish the Appalachian material in 1932.

On Sharp's death in 1924 Karpeles was appointed his literary executor. She strove to ensure that the EFDS continued Sharp's policies, but resigned as EFDS secretary in 1928, after disagreements with its director (her brother-in-law Douglas Kennedy). She oversaw, and virtually ghost-wrote, Sharp's biography in 1933 (and published her own version in 1967). At the meeting approving the amalgamation of the EFDS and the Folk Song Society (to form the English Folk Dance and Song Society, EFDSS) in 1931, Karpeles spoke of the benefits for international co-operation in having a single national body. She now had international connections as secretary to the British National Committee on Folk Arts, formed after an international League of Nations conference. This accomplished little itself but paved the way for future developments. The culmination of Karpeles' pre-war international activity came when, as its secretary, she played a key role in organizing the International Folk Dance Festival held in London in July 1935, at which the spectacular procession of dancers from eighteen nations excited much interest nationally.

During the 1930s Karpeles, as Sharp's literary executor, found herself in dispute with the EFDSS over the copyright in dances collected by him, and she resigned from its committee. In the period since Sharp's death Karpeles herself had collected much. She collected folk-songs in Canada and the United States, most notably in Newfoundland. Visiting areas neglected by Sharp, she had found morris dances in the west midlands and Lancashire, and country dances in Northumberland and Devon.

During the Second World War, Karpeles held several posts in charitable organizations and afterwards reactivated the dormant pre-war international body, transforming it into the International Folk Music Council. From then on she devoted most of her energy to its activities. In the 1950s she returned to the Appalachians to record singers, and although she found many singers had died and much had been forgotten since her visits with Sharp, she was able to record over 200 items there.

Karpeles served as secretary to the International Folk Music Council from 1947 to 1963, and was honorary president thereafter; she also edited its journal. But her interest lay in having folk-songs and -dances performed, and it was not until the 1970s that she finally brought to publication the songs she had collected in Newfoundland, and two volumes of the songs collected by Sharp over fifty years before. Throughout she remained steadfast to the concept of folk music as elaborated by Sharp, regretting that its study—particularly when redefined as ethnomusicology—had moved on. Bemoaning the confusion which she thought existed between 'popular' and 'genuine classical' folk music, she maintained that folk-songs belonged to a pre-literate stage of mankind, and could not be created in an industrialized society. The review of her *An Introduction to English Folk Song* in the council's journal (1973) characterized this as 'a certain nostalgic preciousness' (p. 195), while recognizing her personal power to imbue others with her own enthusiasm, and her 'abiding gentility' (p. 196). She was awarded honorary doctorates by Laval University in 1961 and the Memorial University of Newfoundland in 1972, and was appointed OBE in 1960 for her services to folk music. Active until her death and unmarried, she died from heart failure on 1 October 1976 at her home, 43 Cadogan Place, London.

MICHAEL HEANEY

Sources M. Karpeles, autobiography, c.1970, DWL · *Yearbook of the International Folk Music Council*, 8 (1976), 9–11 · *Journal of American Folklore*, 90 (1977), 455–64 · *English Dance and Song*, 39/1 (1977), 30 · *Folk Music Journal*, 3 (1975–9), 292–4 · D. Atkinson, 'Resources in the Vaughan Williams Memorial Library: the Maud Karpeles manuscript collection', *Folk Music Journal*, 8 (2001–5), 90–101 · M. Karpeles, 'The distinction between folk and popular music', *Journal of the International Folk Music Council*, 20 (1968), 9–12 · private information (2004) · *CGPLA Eng. & Wales* (1976)
Archives Memorial University, Newfoundland · Vaughan Williams Memorial Library, London | FILM English Folk Dance and Song Society, London, performance footage, film 2, Kinora no. 934, film 3, Kinora no. 935, film 5, Kinora no. 937, film 6, Kinora no. 939 · Morris Ring Archive, film 11 | SOUND L. Cong., Archive of Folk Culture, recordings from the Appalachian Mountains
Likenesses Times Newspapers, photograph, repro. in B. Nettl, ed., *1975 Yearbook of the International Folk Music Council*, 7 (1976), frontispiece · photograph, Vaughan Williams Memorial Library, London, leaflet advertising the Maud Karpeles Memorial Lecture, 11 Nov 1977 · photograph, Vaughan Williams Memorial Library, London [*see illus.*]
Wealth at death £18,028: probate, 16 Dec 1976, *CGPLA Eng. & Wales*

Karr, Heywood Walter Seton- (1859–1938), soldier and game hunter, was born on 2 June 1859 at Belgaum, Bombay, India, the third son of three sons and a daughter of George Berkeley Seton-Karr and his wife, Eleanor, daughter of H. Osborne of Suffolk. His brothers were Sir Henry Seton-Karr MP and Walter Seton-Karr, lawyer. George Seton-Karr, member of an old Scottish family formerly of Kippislaw, a civil servant in the Bombay presidency, had been resident commissioner of Baroda during the Sepoy

mutiny of 1857–8. Seton-Karr was educated at Eton College from 1873 to 1877, matriculated at Oriel College, Oxford, in 1878, then underwent military training at Sandhurst before being gazetted lieutenant in 1882 in the Berkshire regiment, which was then stationed at Gibraltar. By July that year the regiment was in Alexandria. It took no part in the battle of Tell al-Kebir and by 1883 Seton-Karr was back in Gibraltar 'having earned a rather easy medal' (Myatt, 69). He transferred to the Gordon Highlanders but left the army by the end of 1884.

While still in Egypt, Seton-Karr discovered in the eastern desert the ancient flint mines whose location had been lost. The flint strata had been excavated into the cliff face, and he collected implements of several periods, which he later gave to Liverpool Museum. In December 1897 he examined ancient emerald mines south-east of Edfu on behalf of Streeter & Co. Ltd, to whom the government had leased the mines. He found the Roman shafts largely filled with washed-in rubble and discovered a few fragments of emerald around the ore heaps.

In 1896 Seton-Karr, in search of game in Somaliland, came across numerous small worked flints, which he recognized as resembling palaeolithic tools previously found in France. He showed examples to John Evans and studied Evans's collections of flints from various parts of the world, and on revisiting Somaliland he found many large hand-axes resembling those from the Somme gravels. These tools, and others from the 'lost flint mines', were exhibited to the Royal Archaeological Society at their meeting in London on 2 June 1897. Seton-Karr's discoveries in Somaliland were the first evidence of Stone Age man in tropical Africa, and, in Evans's view, tended to prove the unity of races in Asia, Europe, and Africa in palaeolithic times. For his contributions to archaeology, Seton-Karr was awarded the Galileo gold medal by the University of Florence.

Rifle shooting had been Seton-Karr's passion since his Eton schooldays, and he went to Norway on his first hunting expedition before his first army posting. Thereafter he went in pursuit of big game almost every year: he made nineteen expeditions to tropical Africa, more than twenty to India, and the same to Arctic Europe, sometimes with a few European or American companions, at other times only with local guides and servants. These exploits were written up in magazines and as a series of books. *Shores and Alps of Alaska* (1886) described his journey as one of the first passengers to cross Canada by the new Canadian Pacific Railway, then a steamship journey north, and an abortive attempt to scale the 18,000 ft Mount St Elias in Alaska, where the party was forced to turn back at 7200 ft. *Ten Years' Wild Sports in Foreign Lands, or, Travels in the 1880s* (1889) described adventures ranging from Canada and Scandinavia, including its northern areas, to Sardinia (which he visited with the earl of Mayo in 1884 and 1885), Corsica, and Mount Athos, and to Persia and India. He had three companions for the expedition by canoe and sled that was described in *Bear Hunting in the White Mountains, or, Alaska and British Columbia Revisited* (1890). Seton-Karr had considerable artistic ability: his own sketches illustrate these books, and a number of his watercolours were presented to the Imperial War Museum.

When in London, Seton-Karr was a familiar figure at meetings of the Royal Geographical Society. From an early age he saw himself as possessing the power of passing messages from the dead to those remaining, and from his considerable estate he bequeathed modest sums to the International Institute of Psychical Research, the Eugenics Society, and the Birth Control Clinic, leaving the remainder to be shared by his sister, Eleanor, and his nephews and nieces. Latterly he lived at 8 St Paul's Mansions, Hammersmith, London; he died, unmarried, at St Mary's Hospital, Paddington, on 12 January 1938, and was buried on 17 January at Fulham cemetery, Mortlake, Surrey.

ANITA McCONNELL

Sources *Nature*, 141 (1938), 319 · *Report of the British Association for the Advancement of Science* (1895), 824 · H. W. Seton-Karr, 'Discovery of evidences of the Paleo-stone age in Somaliland', *Journal of the Anthropological Institute*, 25 (1895), 271–5 · H. W. Seton-Karr, 'Discovery of the lost flint-mines of Egypt', *Journal of the Anthropological Institute*, 27 (1897), 90–92 · H. W. Seton-Karr, 'Further discoveries of ancient stone implements in Somaliland', *Journal of the Anthropological Institute*, 27 (1897), 93–5 · *The Times* (14 Jan 1938), 16b · *The Times* (18 Jan 1938), 15c · J. Evans, 'On some palaeolithic implements found in Somaliland by Mr W. H. Seton-Karr', *PRS*, 60 (1896–7), 19–21 · F. Myatt, *The royal Berkshire regiment* (1968) · d. cert.

Archives Salisbury and South Wiltshire Museum, letters to A. H. L. F. Pitt-Rivers

Wealth at death £14,773 17s. 4d.: probate, 13 May 1938, resealed British Columbia and Penang

Karsavina, Tamara Platonovna (1885–1978), ballet dancer, was born in St Petersburg on 9 March (25 February os) 1885, the daughter of Platon Karsavin. She grew up with her brother, Lev, in an artistic family (her father was a danseur, mime, and ballet teacher with the Imperial Ballet) in a flat overlooking the Fontanka Canal. Her interest in dancing was encouraged by her mother, who saw Karsavina's excitement at watching *La sylphide* when she climbed onto a chair to get a better view. She therefore arranged for her daughter to take lessons from Mme Zhukova. Seeing her natural aptitude for ballet, her father, reluctant to subject his daughter to the gruelling training of a dancer, was won over. He began to teach her himself, and on 26 August 1894 she auditioned for and was accepted by the Imperial Russian Ballet School. Karsavina's thrill at performing on the Maryinsky stage in the crowd for *Coppélia* and as a page in *The Sleeping Beauty* was immense.

Karsavina's training is singularly well documented, for in a series of articles for the *Dancing Times* (1964–5) she described her studies with a succession of great teachers. Pavel Gerdt (her godfather) was influential in developing her style; Karsavina was noted for her artistry rather than virtuoso technique. Yevgeniya Sokolova developed Karsavina's pointe work, speed, and precision of movement; while the Italian Caterina Beretta, with whom she studied for three months in summer 1907, strengthened her technique and stamina.

Karsavina was proud of dancing ballerina roles at the Maryinsky Theatre in St Petersburg. Having graduated, she made her official début in the 'Pearl and Fisherman'

Tamara Platonovna Karsavina (1885–1978), by Emil Otto Hoppé, *c*.1911 [in the title role of *The Firebird* by Michel Fokine]

pas de deux added to *Javotte* on 1 May 1902. But it was five years before she received a leading role in a full-evening ballet: dancing Medora in Petipa's *Le corsaire*, she felt that she had fulfilled her ambitions.

Other major roles at the Maryinsky included Odette/Odile in *Swan Lake* (1908), the title role in *Raymonda* (1909), Nikiya in *La bayadère* (1910), Aurora in *The Sleeping Beauty* (1911), the title role in *Paquita* (1912), and Lise in *La fille mal gardée* (1915). An early marriage to Vasily Mukhin ended in divorce. Then in 1917 Karsavina married the British diplomatist Henry James Bruce (1880–1951), with whom she had a son. She danced at the Maryinsky until she left Russia for good, giving her last performance there in *La bayadère* on 15 May 1918. Her escape from Russia during the revolution reads like a film script. With her husband and son Nikita, she travelled by boat then through dense forest in a horse-drawn cart, and finally on a coal ship to reach Middlesbrough.

Michel Fokine was a major influence on Karsavina's career. She supported him at the time of the revolution in October 1905, when the dancers campaigned to improve their conditions, and she became a muse to him when he choreographed new ballets. Her artistry enhanced his productions, which aimed at dramatic truth and coherence. It was to dance in Fokine's ballets that Karsavina was invited to join Serge Diaghilev's Ballets Russes and overnight won stardom in Paris. After performing the *pas de trois* in *Le pavillon d'Armide* at the company's première on 18 May 1909, she became eulogized as La Karsavina. In his unexpected star (the season had been planned around the talents of Anna Pavlova rather than Karsavina) Diaghilev found an intelligent woman. Their mutual respect and affection enabled her to undertake her own engagements alongside returning to his company.

Although Karsavina created roles for Vaslav Nijinsky (*Jeux* in 1913), for Léonide Massine (the Miller's Wife in *The Three-Cornered Hat* and Pimpinella in *Pulcinella*), and for Bronislava Nijinska as Juliette in the surreal *Roméo et Juliette*, she was much happier dancing the roles Fokine had created for her and in which she was never simply typecast. Fokine was always willing to discuss his plans with Karsavina, taking her completely into his confidence and making her feel a real artist. For him she became an ethereal sylph dancing the mazurka in *Les sylphides* (1909); a powerful and exotic bird in the title role of *The Firebird* (1910); a maturing, innocent girl in *Le spectre de la rose* and a thoughtless doll in *Petrouchka* (both 1911); a cruel, imperious ruler in *Thamar* (1912); and the oriental queen of Shemakhan in *Le coq d'or* (1914). She was also acclaimed in the title role of *Giselle* (1910).

In the first years of the Ballets Russes Karsavina also danced in divertissements at the Coliseum in London, where Diaghilev bullied her with his unending telegrams to rejoin his company as promoters demanded her presence with it. In the 1920s she undertook recital tours through central Europe, and in 1924 in America. In planning these later programmes, which involved either a partner or a small group of dancers, she sought Edwin Evans's advice on music and retained Eric Wollheim (Diaghilev's agent) as her agent. Friends including Claude Lovat Fraser, Mstislav Doboujinsky, and Alexandre Benois were asked to design her costumes. J. M. Barrie wrote his play *The Truth about the Russian Dancers* (1920), a work of delicious nonsense, so that Karsavina could mime the role of Karissima. Karsavina's dancing was filmed but the extracts that survive of her dancing recorded towards the end of her career do not do her justice. Unfortunately prints of the feature films she made in Germany appear to be lost.

During the early 1930s Karsavina encouraged the development of British ballet. She served on the committee of, and danced with, the Camargo Society as well as with the Marie Rambert Dancers; not only in the Fokine ballets *Les sylphides* and *Carnaval*, but in new choreography by Susan Salaman and Frederick Ashton. Karsavina also, bravely, danced on television in its very earliest days. Later recordings of interviews and introductions for television and radio preserve her fruitily captivating voice.

Karsavina's demonstrations of classical ballet mime were legendary, and in 1954 she helped to devise a unique syllabus for the teacher-training course of the Royal Academy of Dancing which preserved the best elements of ballet from the turn of the century. She coached dancers in roles she had created, including Margot Fonteyn in *The Firebird* and *Le spectre de la rose*. She also helped the Royal Ballet with its production of *Giselle* and gave Ashton full details of the action for *La fille mal gardée* in 1960. She showed him the mime scenes, leaving him free to choreograph it as he wished.

Karsavina wrote extensively. Her autobiography, *Theatre Street* (1930), concentrates primarily on her career at the Imperial Theatre, St Petersburg, but her later performing career is covered in a series of articles she wrote for *Dancing Times* (1966–7). She was loved and admired by all who met her. She was charming and cultured with a lifelong passion for Russian literature, especially for the works of Pushkin and Lermontov. After her beloved husband died in 1951 she continued to live in her Queen Anne Hampstead house until 1974, when increasing infirmity forced her to a nursing home, 38 Longfield Drive, Amersham, near Beaconsfield, where she died on 26 May 1978; she was buried in Hampstead cemetery.

Karsavina's career encompassed the Imperial Russian Ballet in St Petersburg and the foundation of British ballet; but she is best remembered for her work with the Ballets Russes. As the French critic Robert Brussel recognized, Karsavina's importance came in uniting the traditions of Russian academic ballet with the artistic revolution wrought by Diaghilev and his company in the early twentieth century. Arnold Haskell in an obituary in *Dance Gazette* described her as 'the first modern ballerina' (Haskell).

In his tribute at Karsavina's service of thanksgiving in London at St Martin-in-the-Fields, Frederick Ashton spoke of her stunning beauty, with enormous, luminous Russian eyes and the wondrous carriage of her head. She was, without doubt, one of the great beauties of her age. It was hardly surprising that her likeness was captured by a wealth of artists. JANE PRITCHARD

Sources H. J. Bruce, *Silken dalliance* (1946) · H. J. Bruce, *Thirty dozen moons* (1949) · R. Buckle, *Diaghilev* (1979) · J. Drummond, *Speaking of Diaghilev* (1997) · A. Haskell, 'Tamara Karsavina: a personal note', *Dance Gazette* (Oct 1978), 8 · T. Karsavina, *Theatre Street* (1930) · N. MacDonald and F. Francis, *Tamara Karsavina* · C. Wildman, 'Conversation with Karsavina: an inspiration and a legend', *Dancing Times* (June 1965), 458–63 · WWW · CGPLA Eng. & Wales (1979)

Archives FILM BFI NFTVA, Dance collection · NYPL · performs *Sylvia pas de deux* with Piere Vladimirov in *Wege zu draft und Schönheit (Back to Nature)*, 1926 | SOUND BBC Archives (radio and TV archives)

Likenesses E. O. Hoppé, photograph, c.1911, Hult. Arch. [see illus.] · L. Bakst, portrait · J. Blanche, portrait · J. Cocteau, portrait · M. Doboujinsky, portrait · W. de Glehn, portrait · G. Philpot, portrait · J. S. Sargeant, portrait · R. Schwabe, portrait · V. Serov, portrait

Wealth at death £5353: probate, 1979, CGPLA Eng. & Wales

Karslake, Sir John Burgess (1821–1881), lawyer, was born at Bencham, near Croydon, the second son of Henry Karslake, solicitor to the duke of Kent, and his wife, Elizabeth Marsh, eldest daughter of Richard Preston QC, an eminent conveyancer and MP for Ashburton. Having been educated at Harrow School, Karslake was articled to his father without proceeding to a university. He went on to join the Middle Temple, and was called to the bar in January 1846. He joined the western circuit, where he became the rival of John Duke Coleridge at every step in his career. He was appointed a queen's counsel in 1861, and was then elected a bencher of his inn. He became solicitor-general in November 1866 (though without a seat in the Commons) and was knighted in January 1867. He was promoted by Lord Derby to the attorney-generalship the following July, and was elected unopposed for Andover. He unsuccessfully contested Exeter at the general election in 1868 and went out of office with the tory government. In 1873 he was elected at a by-election for Huntingdon, which he held until February 1876, when he resigned. He was again briefly attorney-general, from February to April 1874, when failing eyesight forced him from office. He was sworn of the privy council in March 1876. He continued to act on the judicature commission of which he was a member.

Karslake enjoyed a large and lucrative practice at the bar, and was also an effective parliamentary debater. After a long illness he died, unmarried, at his house, 7 Chester Square, London, on 4 October 1881. Karslake revised for publication Charles P. Collyn's *Chase of the Wild Red Deer* (1862), of which he was erroneously reported to have been the author.   J. A. HAMILTON, *rev.* JOANNE POTIER

Sources *The Times* (6 Oct 1881), 9f · *Annual Register* (1881), 144 · *Solicitors' Journal*, 25 (1880–81), 887 · *The Times* (10 Oct 1881), 86 · *Men of the time* (1875) · J. B. Atlay, *The Victorian chancellors*, 2 (1908), 323–4 · WWBMP · Ward, *Men of the reign* · Boase, *Mod. Eng. biog.* · d. cert.
Likenesses Faustin, caricature, chromolithograph, NPG · W. V. [W. Vine], watercolour caricature, NPG; repro. in *VF* (22 Feb 1873) · wood-engraving, NPG; repro. in *ILN* (29 Dec 1866)
Wealth at death £234,990 16s. 3d.: probate, 11 Nov 1881, CGPLA Eng. & Wales

Kater, Henry (1777–1835), geodesist and metrologist, was born on 16 April 1777 in Bristol, the son of Henry Kater (*d.* 1795), a sugar baker of German descent, and his wife, Anne Collins. Intended for a legal career by his father, Kater was articled as a clerk in the office of the Bristol attorney Matthew Mills Coates on 24 September 1794. His father's death in February 1795 enabled him to leave the office before the end of his five-year term to resume his mathematical studies in preparation for a military career. At the beginning of 1799 he was made a freemason before becoming an ensign by purchase in the 12th foot (25 April 1799) and sailing to join his regiment in Madras. For several years he assisted William Lambton, a subaltern in the 33rd foot, who was surveying the country between the Malabar and Coromandel coasts for the Madras government. This laid the foundation for what became the great trigonometrical survey of India under George Everest. Kater was promoted to lieutenant on 3 November 1803.

During his years in India Kater demonstrated his care and precision in the use of instruments in the field and his inclination to devise improvements to instruments, the prominent characteristics of his subsequent scientific career. He returned to England due to ill health and was promoted to a company without purchase in the 62nd foot on 13 October 1808. Kater undertook further training in the senior department of the Royal Military College, High Wycombe (1806–10), and then joined the 2nd battalion of his regiment in Jersey. Following recruiting service in Uxbridge he was for several years brigade major at Ipswich, headquarters of the eastern military district.

In 1814 Kater was placed on half pay, bringing his military career to an end. Having already published several scientific papers, he was elected a fellow of the Royal Society of London on 15 December 1814. The society was the

Henry Kater (1777–1835), by George Richmond, 1831

focus for much of his scientific work for the remainder of his life and brought him into contact with many of the leading scientific figures of his day. He was for some years on the council of the society, serving as treasurer (1827–30) and on occasion as vice-president.

The government in 1816 sought the assistance of the Royal Society in determining the length of a pendulum beating seconds in the latitude of London to provide a physical basis for a standard of length. Kater was a member of the committee set up to investigate the problem. He undertook much of the practical work involved. Using Huygens's theorem he devised a reversible pendulum with knife edge supports near each end and conducted a series of experiments and measurements himself. Kater received the society's Copley medal in 1817 for his contribution to the pendulum work which led to experiments with Kater invariable pendulums being carried out by British scientists in many parts of the world, to improve the understanding of the figure of the earth.

In 1819 a royal commission was set up to report more fully on weights and measures. Kater was appointed a commissioner along with several prominent fellows of the Royal Society. He once again undertook much practical work including a careful comparison of several standards of length. The commission's final report was presented in 1821 leading to the introduction of imperial standards as defined in the Weights and Measures Act of 1824. Kater subsequently undertook the supervision of the construction and adjustment of the multiple sets of the new standards required under the act. For this delicate and protracted work he received £1000 in 1828. Later the Russian government commissioned Kater to supervise the production in London of a series of linear measures. In 1833 he was awarded the order of St Anne for this work of which he had published an account the previous year.

Kater returned to trigonometrical work in 1821 when the Académie des Sciences in Paris invited the Royal Society jointly to remeasure the difference in longitude between the Paris and Greenwich observatories. Kater was appointed with Colby to work with their French counterparts Arago and Mathieu. For a period Kater was a member of a committee advising the board of longitude.

Kater's interest in the design, graduation, testing and use of precision instruments was evident throughout his career. While in India he had observed that a native grass could provide the basis for a very sensitive hygrometer. The hygrometer was described in *Asiatic Researches* (1807) and produced commercially. The comparative light capture of Cassegranian and Gregorian telescopes formed the subject of his first two contributions to the *Philosophical Transactions* of the Royal Society. By then he had already invented the azimuth compass (1811) bearing his name, consisting of a mirror for reading the scale while simultaneously sighting through a sighting vane on the opposite side of the compass box. Compasses incorporating Kater's designs were manufactured by Thomas Jones. The mirror was soon superseded by the prism, as patented by Schmalcalder in 1812. Kater's later investigations into the best kind of steel and form for a compass needle were presented as the Royal Society's Bakerian lecture for 1821.

Kater's method of dividing astronomical circles (1814) was later applied at Armagh observatory but was not generally adopted. A more widely appreciated contribution to astronomical technique was the floating collimator on which Kater published two papers (1825, 1828). He also devised a portable altitude and azimuth instrument that was produced in some numbers by T. C. Robinson from 1826. His investigations into a clock escapement mechanism were published posthumously (1840) by his son Edward, who was elected FRS in the same year.

Kater's practical contributions to the science of his day were recognized by the awarding of honorary membership of numerous scientific societies in Britain and abroad. For his work on the floating collimator he was in 1831 awarded the gold medal of the Royal Astronomical Society of which he became a fellow two years later. The majority of Kater's scientific papers were published in the *Philosophical Transactions* of the Royal Society. He also published some astronomical observations, and contributed a chapter on balances and pendulums to Dionysius Lardner's *Treatise on Mechanics* (1830).

On 31 May 1810, in St Mary's Church, Marylebone Lane, Marylebone, London, Kater married Mary Frances Reeve, daughter of Edward Reeve and Frances Elizabeth Reynardson. They had three children, (Mary) Agnes (b. 1811/12), Henry Herman (bap. 1813), and Edward (1816–1866). Mary Frances Kater was an intelligent, observant, and articulate woman who charmed her husband's scientific colleagues; she published a *History of England* for young people in 1824. Henry and Frances Kater shared an interest in music, sometimes singing together. 'I never heard any voice so touching as Mrs. Katers' remarked the novelist Maria Edgeworth, who became intimately acquainted with the Katers during a visit to London in 1822 (*Letters from England*, 387). The Katers formed an intimate friendship with William and Mary Somerville and the chemist William Hyde Wollaston. Kater's scientific acumen and genial manner enabled him to form ready friendships with the many local and foreign scientists with whom he came into contact.

For many years Kater was dogged by ill health, regarded by some as verging on hypochondria. The Katers sought relief in spa towns and seaside resorts. Their later years were overshadowed by the death on 5 August 1827 of their sixteen-year-old daughter Agnes, who had shown a strong aptitude for science.

Frances Kater died at Hastings in February 1833. Kater died at his home, 12 York Gate, Regent's Park, London, on 26 April 1835. They were both buried, together with their daughter, in the then new church of St Mary-in-the-Castle, Hastings.   JULIAN HOLLAND

Sources G. Jones, 'The scientific publications of Henry Kater', *Centaurus*, 11/3 (1965), 152–89 • C. R. Weld, *A history of the Royal Society*, 2 vols. (1848), vol. 2 • H. Lyons, *The Royal Society, 1660–1940: a history of its administration under its charters* (1944) • M. B. Hall, *All scientists now: the Royal Society in the nineteenth century* (1984) • D. S. Macmillan, *The Kater family, 1750–1965* (1966) • V. F. Lenzen and R. P. Multhauf, 'Development of gravity pendulums in the 19th century', *US National Museum Bulletin*, 240 (1965), 301–48 • R. D. Connor, *The weights and measures of England* (1987) • A. McConnell, *Geophysics and geomagnetism* (1986) • *Maria Edgeworth: letters from England, 1813–1844*, ed. C. Colvin (1971) • E. C. Patterson, *Mary Somerville and the cultivation of science, 1815–1840* (1983) • election certificate, RS • private information (2004)

Archives NRA, priv. coll., paper relating to him and Edward Kater • RCS Eng., papers relating to cholera • RS, notebook • University of Sydney, Fisher Library, letters | RS, corresp. with Sir J. Herschel

Likenesses G. Richmond, wash drawing, 1831, NPG [*see illus.*] • J. F. Skill, J. Gilbert, W. and E. Walker, group portrait, pencil and wash drawing (*Men of science living in 1807–08*), NPG

Katherine. *See also* Catherine.

Katherine (*fl. c.*1272–*c.*1273). *See under* Women medical practitioners in England (*act. c.*1200–*c.*1475).

Katherine [*née* Katherine Roelt; *married name* Katherine Swynford], **duchess of Lancaster** (1350?–1403), mistress and third wife of John of Gaunt, duke of Lancaster, was the daughter of Sir Payn Roelt, a knight of Hainault who travelled to England in the service of Philippa, queen of Edward III, and subsequently rose to be Guyenne king of arms. By 1365 Katherine was in the service of Blanche, duchess of Lancaster, and soon afterwards she married Sir Hugh Swynford of Coleby and Kettlethorpe, Lincolnshire, a tenant of *John of Gaunt who served abroad with him on the campaigns of 1366 and 1370. Katherine became governess to the duke's children after the death of Blanche of Lancaster in 1369 and, following the death overseas of her own husband in November 1371, she was soon openly acknowledged as the duke's mistress. A precise date for the start of the liaison is, in the nature of things, hard to establish, though there was a significant increase in Katherine's status and rewards within the Lancastrian household in the spring of 1372; the later allegation that the relationship began while Katherine's husband was still alive, so that her eldest son with the duke was 'in double advoutrow goten' (Ellis, 1.164) consequently seems unlikely. Between 1373 and 1377 Katherine and Gaunt had four children, who were given the dynastic name of Beaufort, and she remained at the Lancastrian court, acting as governess to the duke's legitimate daughters, Philippa and Elizabeth of Lancaster. In February 1377 she had a grant of the manors of Gringley and Wheatley, Lincolnshire, worth more than £150 p.a., from the duke. Such public acknowledgement of Katherine's position, and the slight to Gaunt's second wife, the Duchess Constance, that it implied, caused great scandal to contemporary chroniclers, who denounced Katherine as 'une deblesce et enchauntresce' (*Anonimalle Chronicle*, 153), and seems to have been widely and unfavourably remarked upon. As a result, in June 1381 Gaunt responded to the public mood that saw in the recent rising of the commons God's chastising of the sins of England's rulers by renouncing his relationship with Katherine and staging a reconciliation with his wife. Katherine gave up her post as governess in September and retired from the Lancastrian household, with a further pension of 200 marks p.a., to live in some style at Kettlethorpe and Lincoln, where she rented a town house in the Minster Yard.

It seems likely that this renunciation was largely formal and that the liaison between Katherine and Gaunt continued on a more discreet and occasional footing. Katherine's relations with the duke and the rest of his family remained cordial: she lent him money for his Castilian expedition in 1386, received a new year's gift from the countess of Derby, his eldest son's wife, in 1387, and in the early 1390s was still a frequent presence at the duke's court, where a stable of a dozen horses was kept for her convenience. It was nevertheless a surprise to contemporaries when, following the death of his second wife, Gaunt married Katherine in Lincoln Cathedral in January 1396. The marriage caused dismay in court circles, where it was viewed as a spectacular *mésalliance*, but it had an unsentimentally practical end in view: the further advancement of John and Katherine's children. The Beauforts were legitimated by papal bull in September 1396 and by royal patent the following February. Following the death of her husband in February 1399 the dowager duchess once again retired to Lincoln, where she died on 10 May 1403 and was buried in the 'angel choir' of the cathedral.

With Sir Hugh Swynford, Katherine had a son, Sir Thomas Swynford [*see below*], and a daughter, Blanche, to whom John of Gaunt stood as godfather. From her liaison with the duke of Lancaster, Katherine had four children: John *Beaufort, earl of Somerset; Henry *Beaufort, cardinal-bishop of Winchester; Thomas *Beaufort, duke of Exeter; and Joan *Beaufort, wife of Sir Robert Ferrers and of Ralph Neville, earl of Westmorland. Katherine was unusual, perhaps unique, in English aristocratic society in making a successful transition from mistress to wife. Comparison of her career and reputation with that of

Edward III's mistress, the unpopular Alice Perrers, suggests that she managed a difficult task with some skill. This is not altogether surprising: as her countryman, Jean Froissart, remarked, she was well suited to her role as duchess of Lancaster, for she had lived in princely courts since her youth. Indeed Katherine seems to have been readily accepted as the matriarch of the whole Lancastrian family, in both its Plantagenet and its Beaufort branches, and the notable cohesion of the Lancastrian dynasty, vital to its survival in the early years of Henry IV's reign, can in part be ascribed to the general respect in which she was held.

Sir Thomas Swynford (1368–1432), soldier and administrator, Katherine's eldest child with her first husband, was brought up in the household of Henry, earl of Derby, whom he accompanied on his first Prussian expedition in 1390–91, before moving to the household of John of Gaunt, where he served as a chamber knight. He received an annuity of 100 marks p.a. from the duke and, as a sign of royal favour, was granted an exchequer pension of a further 100 marks in May 1393. The usurpation of *Henry IV, his stepbrother, brought Swynford to greater prominence. Granted the custody of Somerton Castle, Lincolnshire, in October 1399, he was entrusted with the sensitive task of keeping the deposed Richard II in captivity at Pontefract. Steward of the duchy honour of Tickhill by 1401, he appears as a royal chamber knight by the following year. In 1404–5 he acted as keeper of Calais, in the stead of John Beaufort, earl of Somerset, and was closely involved during the next two years in the difficult negotiations leading to the reaffirmation of the maritime truces between England, France, and Burgundy. After 1406, however, Swynford disappears abruptly from royal employment, serving instead in the household of his halfbrother, Thomas Beaufort, duke of Exeter. Part of his time was taken up with attempts to vindicate his mother's inheritance in Hainault, for in 1411 he obtained a declaration of legitimacy in order to facilitate this, but it may also be that the responsibility for the death of Richard II later attributed to him by some chroniclers had earned the disfavour of Prince Henry. Swynford married first Joan Crophull in March 1383; and second Margaret Grey (d. 1454), widow of John, Lord Darcy, before July 1421. He had one son, Thomas, with his first wife, who served as an esquire in the household of Thomas Beaufort, and another son, William, with his second wife. He died on 2 April 1432.

SIMON WALKER

Sources PRO, DL 28; DL 29/738/12096 m.10; DL 42/15 fol. 150v · *Chancery records* · *John of Gaunt's register*, ed. S. Armitage-Smith, 2 vols., CS, 3rd ser., 20–21 (1911) · *John of Gaunt's register, 1379–1383*, ed. E. C. Lodge and R. Somerville, 2 vols., CS, 3rd ser., 56–7 (1937) · E. Sussex RO, MS GLY 3469 · S. Bentley, ed., *Excerpta historica, or, Illustrations of English history* (1833) · F. C. Hingeston, ed., *Royal and historical letters during the reign of Henry the Fourth*, 1, Rolls Series, 18 (1860) · A. Goodman, *John of Gaunt: the exercise of princely power in fourteenth-century Europe* (1992) · G. L. Harriss, *Cardinal Beaufort: a study of Lancastrian ascendancy and decline* (1988) · V. H. Galbraith, ed., *The Anonimalle chronicle, 1333 to 1381* (1927) · [T. Walsingham], *Chronicon Angliae, ab anno Domini 1328 usque ad annum 1388*, ed. E. M. Thompson, Rolls Series, 64 (1874) · J. Hunter, 'Remarks upon two deeds relating to Sir Thomas Swynford, the son of Catherine Swinford', *Archaeologia*, 36 (1855), 267–9 • H. Ellis, ed., *Original letters illustrative of English history*, 2nd ser., 4 vols. (1827) • *Itineraries [of] William Worcestre*, ed. J. H. Harvey, OMT (1969) • S. Jones, K. Major, J. Varley, and C. Johnson, *The survey of ancient houses in Lincoln*, 1 (1984) • GEC, *Peerage* • CIPM, 13, no. 206 • CPR, 1401–5, 218; 1436–41, 137 **Wealth at death** £1300 p.a., value of assignment from duchy of Lancaster: PRO, DL 29/738/12096, m. 10

Katherine [Catalina, Katherine of Lancaster] (1372–1418), queen of Castile, consort of Enrique III, was the youngest of the three daughters of *John of Gaunt, duke of Lancaster (1340–1399), and his second wife, Constanza (1354–1394), daughter and heir of Pedro I of Castile, whose death at the hands of his half-brother Enrique of Trastámara (Enrique II) in 1369 gave John a claim to the Castilian throne in his wife's right. Probably born at Hertford, as an infant, in January 1375, Katherine had her own household at Melbourne, Derbyshire, but from mid-April 1380 until at least 1382 she lived with Joan Burghersh, Lady Mohun, a widowed kinswoman of her father. In 1381 she was recorded as Katerine d'Espaigne, suggesting that a role in Iberian affairs was foreseen for her, and in 1386 she and her sisters accompanied their parents on an expedition to Castile to press John's claims to its throne. He occupied Santiago with ease, but in 1387 withdrew to Portugal after an unsuccessful invasion of León, and subsequently accepted the proposal of King Juan, Enrique's son, that Katherine should marry his son, another Enrique, and that he and his wife should renounce their claims. A final treaty was ratified at Bayonne in Gascony on 8 July 1388.

On 5 August 1388 Katherine declared that she entered freely into the marriage and accepted the treaty arrangements. These included a dower of the towns of Soria, Almazán, Atienza, Deza, and Molina, and licence to adhere in her private worship to the Urbanist papal obedience (in September 1390 she succumbed to pressure to accept the authority of the Avignon papacy, of which she became a staunch supporter). On 17 September 1388 she was married to the nine-year-old Enrique in Palencia Cathedral. Her husband succeeded to the throne in 1390, and began to rule in 1393. Katherine—in Spanish Catalina—was of minor political importance during Enrique's reign, except in bearing three children, Maria (1401), Catalina (1402), and the future Juan II (1405). Her remaining energies seem to have been devoted to religious patronage, especially of the Dominicans. All this changed when Enrique died in 1406. According to the terms of his will, his brother Fernando and his widow were to be joint regents during Juan's minority, but the custody of his son was to be entrusted to two nobles, Diego López de Stúñiga and Juan Fernández de Velasco. Rather than hand over her son, in 1407 Catalina prepared to defend herself and her household in the Alcázar at Segovia, but Fernando eventually brokered a deal that enabled her to keep her son. Nevertheless, distrust between the regents was exacerbated by Fernando's plans to lead his brother's planned campaign against the kingdom of Granada, separating the two regents and consequently, under Enrique's will, necessitating a division of rule. The royal council awarded Catalina control of the northern kingdoms of Castile and

León. Tensions between the regents persisted, not least over Catalina's favours to Velasco and Stúñiga, and in 1409 Fernando insisted on their expulsion from her court. Thereafter she became co-operative in providing financial support for his costly Granadan campaigns.

In consequence of her increasing involvement in wars in the south, Castile's alliance with France languished, and Catalina was able to cultivate better relations with Portugal (where her half-sister *Philippa was queen) and with England, along lines her father would have approved. She was on good terms with Richard II, while her dealings with her half-brother *Henry IV, infused with personal warmth, had beneficial effects. Although there was no peace treaty, the two rulers fostered Anglo-Castilian trade by granting numerous safe conducts, while Catalina, who herself bought costly fabrics in London, sponsored a series of unilateral truces between 1410 and 1416. Her international policies boosted the prosperity of Castilian communities, whereas her co-regent's were a drain on it. However, although as a result of Fernando's pursuit of the throne of Aragon, Seville, Córdoba, and Jaén were brought within her sphere of control, his attainment of his ambition in 1412, and his death in 1416, had the effect of reducing Catalina's authority, by depriving his rivals of incentives to support her. Government became increasingly conciliar, and Catalina—who may have been partially incapacitated by a stroke—relinquished the custody of her son.

A vivid account of Catalina towards the end of her life was later recorded by Fernán Pérez de Guzmán. It suggests that she may have inherited physical characteristics from her father, and also that she was a sick woman:

> The queen was tall of body and very fat. She was pink and white in her complexion and fair. In her figure and her movements she seemed as much like a man as a woman. She was very virtuous and reserved in her person and in her reputation; generous and magnificent in her ways but very much devoted to favourites and greatly ruled by them—a thing which, in general, is a vice common to royal personages. She was not very well ordered in her body and had a serious affliction of the palsy which did not leave her tongue properly loose or her bodily movements free. (Guzmán, 19–20)

Whatever the effects of her favouritism—she was twice obliged to banish ladies from her household—they should not be allowed to obscure either the constructive effects of her initiatives in foreign policy, or the concern to protect the interests of Juan II which infused her domestic statecraft. Catalina died at Valladolid on 2 June 1418, and was buried with her husband in the capilla de los reyes nuevos in Toledo Cathedral. Her monumental effigy portrays her with a long face and highly arched forehead.

ANTHONY GOODMAN

Sources A. Echevarria, 'Catalina of Lancaster, the Castilian monarchy and coexistence', *Medieval Spain: culture, conflict and coexistence. Essays in honour of Angus MacKay*, ed. R. Collins and A. Goodman [forthcoming] • J. Torres Fontes, 'La regencia de Don Fernando de Antequera', *Anuario de Estudios Medievales*, 1 (1964), 375–429 • R. Menéndez Pidal, ed., *Historia de España*, 15: *Los trastámaras de Castilla y Aragón en el siglo XV*, ed. L. Suárez Fernández, A. Canellas López, and J. Vicens Vives (Madrid, 1964) • L. de Ayala, 'Crónica del rey don Juan', *Crónicas de los reyes de Castilla*, ed. C. Rosell, 2 (Madrid, 1953) • J. J. N. Palmer and B. Powell, eds., *The treaty of Bayonne (1388) with preliminary treaty of Trancoso (1387)* (1988) • L. Corell Ruiz, *Una copia del testamento de Catalina of Lancaster* (Valencia, 1952) • F. Pérez de Guzmán and others, *Generaciones y semblanzas*, 3rd edn (Madrid, 1954) • P. E. Russell, *The English intervention in Spain and Portugal in the time of Edward III and Richard II* (1955) • 'Crónica del serenísimo príncipe don Juan, segundo rey deste nombre en Castilla y León', *Crónicas de los reyes de Castilla*, ed. C. Rosell, 2 (Madrid, 1953) • *John of Gaunt's register*, ed. S. Armitage-Smith, 2 vols., CS, 3rd ser., 20–21 (1911) • *John of Gaunt's register, 1379–1383*, ed. E. C. Lodge and R. Somerville, 2 vols., CS, 3rd ser., 56–7 (1937) • W. R. Childs, *Anglo-Castilian trade in the late middle ages* (1978)

Likenesses stone effigy on tomb, Toledo Cathedral, Spain

Katherine, countess of Devon (1479–1527), princess, was probably born at Eltham Palace, the sixth of the seven surviving children of *Edward IV (1442–1483) and his queen *Elizabeth, *née* Woodville (c.1437–1492). Following her father's death in 1483 Katherine shared with the rest of her family in the traumatic events that followed the seizure of the throne by her uncle Richard, duke of Gloucester. Her two brothers disappeared in the Tower, and the proclamation that her parents' marriage was invalid made her and her siblings illegitimate. Later she and her sisters returned to live in the royal household, ostensibly under Richard III's protection, while after the battle of Bosworth her eldest sister, *Elizabeth, became queen to the new king, Henry VII, and the family's honour was restored.

Like all princesses Katherine was a potential pawn in the marriage market. Soon after her birth there were proposals for a match with a Spanish prince, and in 1487 for her marriage to James, marquess of Ormond, second son of the Scottish king James III. Eventually, however, Katherine took a less exalted husband, when in 1495 she married Sir William *Courtenay (c.1475–1511) [*see under* Courtenay, Edward], the son and heir of Edward *Courtenay, first earl of Devon (d. 1509), a great landowner in Devon and Cornwall and a staunch supporter of Henry VII. They had two sons: Edward, who died in 1502, and Henry *Courtenay, who eventually succeeded his father as earl. They also had a daughter, Margaret. Apparently in favour with the king, the young couple settled at court. In 1502, however, William came under suspicion of involvement in the conspiracy of the Yorkist claimant Edmund de la Pole, a suspicion doubtless magnified by his own marriage to a Yorkist princess. The charge was probably unjust, but Courtenay was attainted and imprisoned for the rest of the reign. Katherine received some assistance from her sister the queen, and was chief mourner at Elizabeth's funeral in February 1503.

Following the accession of Henry VIII in 1509 William Courtenay was released. His father died shortly after the old king, and proceedings began to restore him to his lands and titles. One condition of his restoration was that Katherine should renounce her claim to the lands of the earldom of March, inherited from the Mortimers through her father. But before negotiations could be completed Courtenay, who had been created earl of Devon on 10 May 1511, died of pleurisy shortly afterwards, on 9 June. Left a widow at the age of thirty-seven, Katherine almost at once (on 6 July) completed the transfer of her rights in the earldom of March to the crown, and to ensure her future freedom took a vow of chastity. On 3 February 1512 she received from the king, in her own right, all the estates of the earldom of Devon for her lifetime. On 4 November following her ten-year-old son Henry received the title of earl of Devon, and in due course became established in the king's circle at court.

Countess Katherine made occasional appearances at court, notably as a godmother to Princess Mary in 1516, but normally she resided at Tiverton Castle in Devon. There her position as head of the county's principal family and owner of its largest estate provided full scope for the emergence of her robust personality. Her estates, which were administered by a network of officials, brought her an annual income of around £2750, from which she maintained a large household. Accounts from the early 1520s show that Katherine lived in a style befitting her rank, with regular purchases of luxury goods—spices, French and Rhenish wines, and fine cloths like velvet and satin. Her chapel was similarly well equipped, with a handsome array of vestments, sacred vessels, service books, and images of saints. She was clearly on good terms with the prelates of Devon, receiving gifts from the bishop of Exeter and from the abbots of Ford, Buckland, and Newenham. But religious devotion did not preclude sports and relaxation. Katherine is recorded as hunting in the early 1520s, she made several payments to minstrels, and she employed three fools, named Dick, Mug, and Kit; the new year festivities for 1524 included visits from troupes of players and from the Exeter waits.

The fact that an inventory of Countess Katherine's goods made after her death included a horse litter may indicate declining mobility in her later years. Her will, drawn up on 2 May 1527, was largely devoted to ensuring the safety of her soul. She made elaborate provision for £21 per annum to be paid in perpetuity to three priests who were to say three masses daily in St Peter's Church, Tiverton, in the presence of three poor men receiving 8*d.* each per week, and also a weekly requiem. She died at Tiverton Castle on 15 November 1527, aged forty-nine, and was buried with much ceremonial in St Peter's on 2 and 3 December. She had directed that all her servants and officers were to have a black gown, as well as a year's wages. The abbots of Ford, Montacute, and Torre attended; a canon of Exeter Cathedral preached. Eight thousand poor people each received 2*d.* to offer prayers for Katherine's soul. In their scale and solemnity her exequies constituted an appropriate valediction to a woman whose armorial bearings had combined Courtenay with the royal arms of England, and who on her seal and in her documents had styled herself 'the excellent Princess Katherine, Countess of Devon, daughter, sister and aunt of kings' (Westcott, 23).   MARGARET R. WESTCOTT

Sources M. A. E. Green, *Lives of the princesses of England*, 6 vols. (1849–55), vol. 4, ch. 1 • F. Sandford, *A genealogical history of the kings and queens of England*, ed. S. Stebbing (1707) • G. Oliver, 'The will of

Katharine, countess of Devon, daughter of Edward IV', *Archaeological Journal*, 10 (1853), 53–8 • M. Westcott, 'Katherine Courtenay, countess of Devon, 1479–1527', *Tudor and Stuart Devon … essays presented to Joyce Youings*, ed. T. Gray, M. Rowe, and A. Erskine (1992), 13–38 • Katherine, countess of Devon, household accounts, Michaelmas 1522–3, PRO, state papers general series, Henry VIII, SP 1/28 • Katherine, countess of Devon, household accounts, Michaelmas 1523–4, PRO, exchequer, lord treasurer's remembrancer's books, E 36/223 • Tiverton Castle, inventory, Jan 1528, PRO, SP 1/46, 51–6 • BL, Lansdowne MS 978 • D. MacGibbon, *Elizabeth Woodville (1437–1492): her life and times* (1938) • C. Ross, *Edward IV* (1974) • F. J. Snell, *Chronicles of Twyford* (1892) • M. Dunsford, *Historical memoirs of the town and parish of Tiverton* (1790) • R. Holinshed, *The chronicles of England, Scotland and Ireland*, 6 vols. (1807–8); facs. edn (New York, 1965) • *Hall's chronicle*, ed. H. Ellis (1809) • *The Anglica historia of Polydore Vergil, AD 1485–1537*, ed. and trans. D. Hay, CS, 3rd ser., 74 (1950) • *RotP*, vol. 6 • *LP Henry VIII*, vols. 1–4 • GEC, *Peerage*, 4.330

Archives Devon RO, Katherine, countess of Devon, will, L 1508 M/family/test/1 • PRO, Katherine, countess of Devon, household accounts, Michaelmas 1522–3, SP 1/28 • PRO, Katherine, countess of Devon, household accounts, Michaelmas 1523–4, exchequer, lord treasurer's remembrancer's books, E 36/223 • PRO, Tiverton Castle, inventory, January 1528, SP 1/46, 51–6

Wealth at death £2760 1s. 2d. income from estates 1527–8: existing manorial account rolls for 1527–8

Katherine (1485–1536), by Lucas Horenbout, c.1525–6

Katherine [Catalina, Catherine, Katherine of Aragon] (1485–1536), queen of England, first consort of Henry VIII, was born in the archbishop of Toledo's palace at Alcalá de Henares, north-east of Madrid, on 16 December 1485.

Upbringing The youngest daughter of the 'Catholic monarchs', Ferdinand of Aragon (1452–1516) and Isabella of Castile (1451–1504), she was named after Isabella's grandmother Catalina, or Katherine, of Lancaster, daughter of John of Gaunt and his second wife, Constanza, and wife of Enrique III of Castile. Both her parents were descended from Enrique II of Castile, the founder of the Trastamaran dynasty. A contemporary chronicler, Alfonso de Palencia, commented that they would have preferred a son, as they feared the consequences of depending for the future of their dynasty on the life and health of their male heir, the Infante Juan, and on the fecundity of their daughters, Isabella, Juana, Maria, and now Catalina.

During her early years Catalina followed her parents, and in particular her mother, in their travels through large parts of Spain, as the war against the Muslim emirate of Granada continued. As a small child she was present at the ceremonial conquest of the capital of the former Nasrid kingdom, on 2 January 1492. The pomegranate ('Granada apple', in Castilian *granada*) later became her personal emblem, ironically symbolizing fertility. Along with her older sisters, Catalina received an education fitting for one who was intended for marriage with foreign rulers, bearing children for them and thus linking Castile and Aragon to neighbouring powers by ties of blood as well as friendship. Isabella was especially conscious of her own educational limitations (she learned Latin only as an adult) and was especially insistent on a proper education for her daughters. The team of scholars chosen by Isabella and Ferdinand to educate their children included the notable Dominican reformer Pascual de Ampudia, his fellow Dominican Andrés de Morales, and, in the case of Catalina, the Italian humanist brothers Alessandro and Antonio Geraldini. In accordance with the principles of Spanish scholarship in the period, emphasis was placed on Latin, as well as modern languages, but always within a Catholic Christian context, based on the Bible and liturgical texts. In addition to her acquisition of the domestic arts thought suitable for a princess, Catalina's skill in Latin, and knowledge of classical and vernacular literature, brought her the admiration of the Spanish humanist Juan Luis Vives and of Erasmus of Rotterdam, who regarded her as a model of Christian womanhood.

Negotiations with England, 1487–1489 The notion of a marriage between Catalina and the heir to the English throne, *Arthur, prince of Wales (born on 19 September 1486), seems to have originated in the mind of Arthur's father, Henry VII, when the princess was only two. Like his predecessors, the new and insecure Tudor monarch needed Spanish friendship, although relations between the two countries had never been entirely untroubled. Ferdinand and Isabella, meanwhile, had already begun, in 1481, to arrange marriages for their son and daughters in order to raise the prestige of their Castilian and Aragonese monarchies in Europe. In the latter part of 1487 they agreed to send ambassadors to England, not only to discuss political and economic relations but also to negotiate the marriage of Catalina and Arthur. First to arrive was Rodrigo (Ruy) Gonsales Puebla, a doctor of civil and canon law who possessed a solid record of achievement in local government in Castile, as did a number of Jewish Christians (*conversos*) in the Spain of Ferdinand and Isabella.

The Trastamaran dynasty largely owed its royal status to the French, and the Castilian rulers had subsequently looked to their northern neighbour for support. As late as 1487 Ferdinand and Isabella still secretly hankered after a marriage between their eldest daughter, Isabella, and Charles VIII of France. It was only when the French regency government spurned the suggestion that negotiations were begun to marry Isabella to Alfonso of Portugal and Catalina to Prince Arthur. In these circumstances, France was the main enemy and, despite the help he had received from that quarter during his exile under Richard III, Henry VII responded with alacrity. On 10 March 1488 he appointed representatives to negotiate with Castile and Aragon on three issues: trade, a political alliance, and the royal marriage.

Isabella and Ferdinand gave priority to the marriage because they regarded it as the best cement for a political relationship, and on 30 April 1488 they gave Puebla power to negotiate on the subject. The relevant document was brought to England by a second ambassador, Juan de Sepúlveda, who arrived in London on 1 June, to promote a political alliance against France. Puebla agreed with his colleague's objective, but his greater experience of English politics led him to urge that if the marriage were arranged first, political and economic benefits would quickly follow. On 6–7 July a draft agreement was duly reached concerning Catalina's dowry, fixed at 200,000 Spanish escudos. Ferdinand and Isabella undertook to send Catalina to England at their own expense, with an adequate wardrobe, and to pay the dowry in two instalments, the first on her arrival in England and the second when the marriage was solemnized.

Almost at once Anglo-Spanish mistrust and misunderstanding emerged. The Spanish rulers wanted to pay less, and found the English offers for Catalina's maintenance (a third of the rents from the principality of Wales, the duchy of Cornwall, and the earldom of Chester) inadequate. Nevertheless, the desire of both parties for an alliance against France overcame these objections and negotiations continued for the rest of the year. In spring 1489 Henry VII's ambassadors spent a month at the court of Ferdinand and Isabella in Medina del Campo. The result was the treaty agreed at Medina on 27 March 1489, which replaced the century-old Franco-Castilian alliance by a link with England which was to be almost as long-lived. Many of the twenty-five articles concerned international politics and trade, while the marriage of Catalina and Arthur was deferred until the two children came of age.

Marriage settlement, 1489–1501 During the early 1490s the projected marriage of Catalina and Arthur was overshadowed by the eruption on the European scene of a pretender to the English throne who claimed to be Edward IV's younger son Richard, duke of York, generally held to have perished in the Tower of London in 1483. Edward IV's sister Margaret of York, the dowager duchess of Burgundy, was determined to do all in her power to remove the Tudor 'usurper', Henry VII, and may genuinely have regarded the pretender as her lost nephew. Continuing support from Margaret and her Habsburg relatives for Perkin Warbeck, as various witnesses stated that he was in fact called, played a significant part in delaying implementation of the treaty of Medina del Campo. At various times between November 1491, when he landed at Cork, and October 1497, when he was finally captured and imprisoned by Henry, the supposed 'duke of York' was exploited by the enemies of the house of Tudor. Warbeck received support from Ireland, Scotland, and France, and above all from Maximilian, king of the Romans, and Archduke Philip of Austria. But Isabella and Ferdinand showed no such credulity; indeed they played a vital part in exposing the false 'duke of York'. Anxious to secure the alliance with England, and Catalina's marriage to Arthur, her parents reacted sharply when accused by Henry of harbouring Warbeck. They obtained a Portuguese investigation into the pretender's true identity, dated 25 April 1496, which supposedly revealed his Flemish origins, and used the document to reassure Henry; they also gave their daughter Juana the task of weaning her new husband, Archduke Philip, away from Warbeck, and thus neutralizing the anti-Tudor fervour of Margaret of York.

Anglo-Spanish discussions became more intense at this time, until a new agreement was reached in London on 1 October 1497. The marriage would not take place until Arthur reached fourteen, though either side might request it up to two years earlier. The papal dispensation, which would in that case be required because of the prince's youth, would be requested jointly by the English and Spanish. The dowry remained at 200,000 escudos, the trousseau consisting of 15,000 escudos in gold, gold and silver plate to a similar value, and precious stones worth 20,000 escudos. Catalina would receive the revenues from Arthur's lands as soon as the marriage took place. The revised treaty was confirmed on 1 January 1497. Ratification by Ferdinand and Isabella was kept secret and, as a second option, Catalina was offered to James IV of Scotland, to whom Pedro de Ayala was sent as ambassador. Nevertheless, on the same day, Catalina empowered Puebla to act as a proxy in her marriage to Arthur, which was evidently still her parents' real aim. The threat of the Scottish marriage was not removed for several years, however.

Ferdinand and Isabella were sufficiently concerned, both with Henry VII's attitude to the marriage and with Puebla's conduct as ambassador, to send further ambassadors to England, Sancho de Londoño and Tomás de Matienzo. While the new envoys took a hostile line towards Puebla, they failed to speed the negotiations with Henry, though in 1499 Catalina's departure for England appeared to be imminent, after a proxy marriage ceremony between herself and Prince Arthur had taken place on 19 May at Tickhill Manor, near Bewdley. Isabella and Ferdinand were still insistent that Catalina would be sent to England only when Arthur reached fourteen. Final agreement on the dowry, which would amount to 200,000 escudos in cash and plate, was made at this time. During 1500 disputes continued over the valuation and payment of the dowry and the timing of Catalina's arrival in England, which was being delayed on the Spanish side. In October a list of the princess's proposed Spanish household of about fifty was sent to England, where King Henry tried to reduce it. But in March 1501 serious preparations at last began for Catalina's journey from Granada to England, and after delays caused first by the uprising of the Muslim Alpujarras in Spain and then by bad conditions at sea, the princess landed at Plymouth on 2 October. Catalina's arrival evidently took Henry VII by surprise, for it was not until 7 October that the lord steward, Baron Willoughby de Broke, was ready to receive her at Exeter. Then began a ceremonious progress to London, during which Henry and Arthur intercepted her at Dogmersfield, near Farnborough in Hampshire, on 4 November. Overriding the (probably feigned) insistence of ambassador Ayala that Catalina should observe Spanish etiquette and remain secluded until her wedding, Henry insisted on seeing her 'even if she were in her bed', before introducing his son to her (Mattingly, 32–7). King and prince then departed and Catalina continued her journey. She was greeted in London on 12 November with a lavish series of pageants provided by the city authorities. Two days later her marriage was solemnized at St Paul's, after which there followed another week of unprecedentedly elaborate banquets and tournaments.

Marriage and widowhood, 1501–1506 There was some discussion of whether Catalina, or Katherine, as her name was invariably spelt in England in accordance with contemporary usage, should accompany her husband on his return to his duties as prince of Wales at Ludlow. Puebla and some of Katherine's entourage would have preferred her to stay in London and not begin full marital relations immediately. Her former tutor, now confessor, Alessandro Geraldini, thought otherwise. Katherine refused to give an opinion; Henry VII eventually took the decision, and the couple set off for the marches on 21 December. Almost thirty years later Katherine deposed, under the seal of the confessional, that they had shared a bed for no more than seven nights, and that she had remained 'as intact and incorrupt as when she emerged from her mother's womb' (Brewer, 2.303). Arthur died, still aged only fifteen, on 2 April 1502.

As soon as the news of Arthur's death reached Katherine's parents they mooted the possibility of her marrying the new heir to the throne, Arthur's younger brother Henry [see Henry VIII (1491–1547)]. The English were equally eager. Inevitably both sides resumed the hard bargaining which had characterized the original negotiations; neither, however, seems to have had doubts about either the legality or the feasibility of a marriage 'in the first degree of affinity' between brother- and sister-in-law. In spite of complaints about Henry VII's niggardly treatment of his daughter-in-law and threats by the Spanish monarchs to take her home, a draft treaty was ready by September 1502, and a formal treaty was concluded in June 1503. The treaty specified a betrothal ('matrimonium per verba de praesenti') to take place within two months, while the marriage would be solemnized following receipt of the necessary papal dispensation, the payment of the second portion of the dowry agreed for the first marriage, and Henry's reaching fifteen, in June 1506. (Interestingly, this was one year older than in Arthur's

case and perhaps resulted from the discussions of December 1501.) The betrothal followed immediately on the conclusion of the treaty, on 25 June 1503.

The treaty assumed that Katherine's first marriage had been consummated. This was apparently reported by Puebla, on the authority of Geraldini, but it was vehemently denied by Katherine's duenna, Doña Elvira Manuel, in a letter to Ferdinand and Isabella, and Geraldini was hurriedly recalled to Spain. Ferdinand, however, accepted the English position, that the papal dispensation should cover all eventualities. The dispensation was held up by the deaths of popes Alexander VI and Pius III (on 18 August and 18 October 1503). In spite of pressure from both Spain and England, no document was made available by the new pope, Julius II, until one was sent to Isabella shortly before her death on 26 November 1504. This 'brief' was dated 26 December 1503, but this may well represent a subsequent back-dating. A copy may have been sent by Ferdinand to England, to Julius's displeasure; if so it was subsequently lost. The eventual papal bull, also dated 26 December 1503, did not arrive in England until March 1505. (Historians have generally accepted the date 26 December 1503 for both bull and brief, but that they were back-dated is borne out by Castellesi's report of 4 January 1504 that the matter was still under consideration.) The reason for papal procrastination is unknown. It may indicate caution about the canonical issues involved. Immediately after his election Julius had indicated that 'prima facie, he did not know if he had power to dispense in this case' (Pocock, 1.1–4). Perhaps more plausibly, the dispensation was a useful card in Julius's diplomatic game against Ferdinand's control of Naples. The 'brief' stated bluntly that Arthur had consummated his marriage. The bull was more circumspect, granting dispensation for the new marriage 'even if' ('forsan') the previous one had been consummated.

By this time the international situation had changed once more. Isabella died on 26 November 1504. The heir to Castile was Katherine's elder sister Juana, married to Archduke Philip, the ruler of the Low Countries. Juana and Philip had aroused some antagonism on a visit to Spain in 1502. Isabella left a will naming her husband, Ferdinand, as governor of Castile, so excluding Juana and Philip from rule in that kingdom. Opinion in Castile rapidly polarized into anti-Habsburg and anti-Aragonese factions. In these circumstances there was no point in Henry VII's tying himself too closely to Ferdinand. Indeed in February 1505 he lent Philip £108,000 'for his next voyage to Spain' (Chrimes, 289). On 27 June 1505, just before his fourteenth birthday, Prince Henry formally repudiated his betrothal to Katherine, alleging lack of necessary consent on his part. Neither she nor the Spanish representatives were informed of this development. The English were not intending a final repudiation of the marriage. Rather the manoeuvre was designed to keep options open, at least until the situation in Castile was clearer, and to preserve the valuable diplomatic card of the prince's marriage.

The Castilian question divided Katherine's own advisers; Doña Elvira worked for an alliance between

Henry VII and Philip, involving Katherine in the plot, until Puebla persuaded Katherine to write to Henry repudiating her expressed wish for a meeting with Juana, in August 1505. In November Doña Elvira was banished from Katherine's household. In January 1506, however, Philip and Juana were forced by a storm to land in England while on their way to claim their rights in Castile. Katherine met Juana, while Henry VII and Philip concluded a close alliance. Ferdinand bowed to circumstances and welcomed Philip and Juana to Castile. Philip's sudden death at Burgos on 25 September 1506, however, restored Ferdinand's rule, Juana being sidestepped on the grounds of her apparent mental instability. But Henry VII continued to cherish his diplomatic freedom. Invoking Ferdinand's failure to pay the second instalment of the dowry, he continued to offer Prince Henry's hand on the international market, as well as his own (which included a proposition of marrying Juana himself), and to court a Habsburg alliance with Maximilian rather than an Aragonese one.

Remarriage, 1506–1509 Katherine had been allocated Durham House, the bishop of Durham's house in London, to live in as dowager princess of Wales, with an almost entirely Spanish entourage under the direction of Doña Elvira as duenna. Her parents and Henry insisted she should keep 'rule and observance and seclusion', though Katherine herself hoped for some lightening of the regime (*CSP Spain, 1485–1509*, 420). She was frequently ill, probably with tertian ague, at least until the spring of 1507. Curiously, there is evidence that she was thought by the English court to be indulging in religious austerities in a way likely to damage her health and capacity for child bearing. A papal letter of October 1505 empowered her 'husband' to curb these proclivities; he was described as Arthur, prince of Wales, so presumably the complaint had originated in 1501–2. Her knowledge of English was still imperfect in 1505, to Ferdinand's displeasure; she could speak 'some' and understand 'more' (Scarisbrick, 437). Since only part of her dowry had been paid before her marriage, Katherine could not claim the dower, a third of Arthur's lands, to which she would otherwise have been entitled. In any case her rights were explicitly repudiated in the treaty of 1503 for the second marriage. Instead she was allocated an allowance of £1200 p.a. by Henry VII. When Doña Elvira was banished in November 1505, Henry withdrew the allowance; Puebla, presumably backed by Henry, persuaded Katherine to give up Durham House and to lodge at court, adducing the impropriety of her keeping a separate household without proper chaperonage. Her regular allowance gave way to spasmodic payments by Henry VII.

Katherine complained volubly to her father about her poverty and shabby treatment, her inability to pay her servants, and her demeaning dependence on Henry's charity. She went so far as to pawn some of the plate and jewels which, on some interpretations, were to form part of the second instalment of her dowry. She was kept apart from Prince Henry, complaining in 1507 that she had not seen him for four months, although they were both living in the palace at Richmond. At the same time Henry VII told

her that he no longer regarded his son as bound by the earlier betrothal; Puebla and Katherine's confessor conceded that Henry's position was justified. Katherine complained bitterly of Puebla. Ferdinand decided to involve her directly in negotiations, in parallel with the ambassador, and she received formal credentials. She was provided with a cipher, painfully deciphered Ferdinand's letters, and eventually managed to encipher her own replies, although with so little confidence that she also sent the same letter *en clair*. She evidently lacked any sort of confidential secretary, at least one she could trust, and her letters to Ferdinand are in her own hand.

This curious arrangement came to an end in February 1508 with the arrival of a new ambassador, Gutierre Gómez de Fuensalida, sent to join Puebla with specific instructions to conclude the marriage, bringing the means to pay the remainder of the dowry. Henry VII's eyes were still on a Habsburg alliance (especially through a marriage of his daughter Mary to the future Emperor Charles V). The English council quibbled over details of the payment, and especially the question of Katherine's plate and jewels. By late 1508 both Fuensalida and Katherine's household were convinced that her marriage would never take place, and plans were made for her return to Spain. Only Katherine, supported by her confessor, Diego Fernández, was adamant that it was her duty to remain in England and marry Prince Henry. By March 1509 even she despaired, asking to return to Spain to lead the religious life. Henry VII, however, died on 21 April 1509. Before 8 May Fuensalida was summoned and told that the new king wished the marriage settled quickly, without quibbles. Possibly Henry VIII was acting, as he alleged, in obedience to his father's dying wish. But more likely the new policy was his own. On 11 June Henry VIII and Katherine were married at the Franciscan church at Greenwich. Katherine's persistence in discouraging, even at times humiliating, circumstances had triumphed. Her experience in these vital years, between the ages of sixteen and twenty-four, may well explain her reluctance in later years to yield her position as queen of England.

Queen and mother, 1509–1525 The first years of her marriage saw Katherine's hold on her husband, and her political influence, at their height. Henry was ostentatious in his attentions. Katherine was frequently pregnant, though her gynaecological history is uncertain, reports of miscarriages and stillbirths being largely derived from ambassadorial reports. She miscarried a girl on 31 January 1510. A boy, named Henry and created prince of Wales, was born on new year's day 1511, but died on 22 February. There is an unsubstantiated report of a live birth shortly after the battle of Flodden in September 1513; if this happened the child must have died almost immediately. A male child was stillborn in November or December 1514. Only on 18 February 1516 was a healthy child born, Princess *Mary. Katherine's last delivery, on 9–10 November 1518, was a stillborn daughter.

Katherine played some part in foreign affairs. She engineered the recall of the Spanish ambassador Fuensalida in August 1509, and received a commission from Ferdinand to be his official channel of communication with Henry. She evidently reported in cipher. A new ambassador, Don Luis Caroz, arrived in March 1510. He, too, incurred Katherine's wrath. He blamed Katherine's confessor, Diego Fernández, for this, accusing him of exercising undue influence over her. How far, in fact, Katherine influenced English policy is hard to judge. The alliance with Ferdinand was a natural consequence of Henry's enmity towards France. It culminated in Henry's joining the Holy League in November 1511 and in plans for joint military action. An English army was shipped to the Basque country in May 1512 to join with a Spanish force to reconquer Guyenne for England. Ferdinand, however, used his army to conquer Navarre for himself, and failed to support the English, until Henry's troops mutinied and sailed home in October. Katherine played a part in smoothing over the resulting recriminations. But the English belief that they were tricked by Ferdinand in 1513 and again in 1514 made Katherine's position difficult. In December 1514 Caroz reported that she had been persuaded by Diego Fernández 'to forget Spain and everything Spanish to gain the love of the King of England and of the English' (*CSP Spain, 1509–25*, 201).

Katherine was governor of the realm and captain-general during Henry's absence on campaign in France between 30 June and 21 October 1513. She had authority to raise troops and to make appointments, and was provided with a council headed by Archbishop Warham, the lord chancellor. None the less, a good deal even of routine business was handled by Henry's council in the field. Katherine wrote letters to Wolsey (but not to the king), giving some news, but mostly expressing her anxiety about Henry's welfare and safety, and apologizing for intruding on Wolsey's valuable time. She did refer to being 'horribly busy with making standards, banners and badges'; the level of irony in this perhaps self-deprecating reference to traditional feminine pursuits is hard to gauge (*LP Henry VIII*, 1/2, no. 2162). (Isabella supervised the making of banners on campaign.) She faced a crisis when James IV of Scotland invaded England on 22 August. On 9 September Thomas Howard, earl of Surrey, appointed to the command of the north by Henry before his departure, defeated the Scots at Flodden, leaving James and a large number of Scottish nobles dead on the field. Katherine was heading a reserve army on its way north; news of the victory led to its disbandment at Buckingham. A Spanish source credits Katherine with a rousing speech to the troops, but there is no English evidence in support. She did, however, write triumphantly to Henry, in her own hand and in English: 'In this your grace shall see how I can keep my promys, sending you for your banners a King's coat. I thought to send himself unto you, but our Englishmen's hearts would not suffer it' (ibid., no. 2268).

A new Anglo-Spanish alliance was concluded in 1515. In January 1516, however, King Ferdinand died, effectively succeeded by his grandson Charles, Juana's son. Charles was too busy establishing his position in Spain to pursue an English alliance, while Katherine's relations with her nephew were inevitably less close than they had been

with her father. She ceased to be either an informal or a formal channel of communication. From 1514, if not earlier, there was talk of Henry having a mistress, while by 1519 Elizabeth Blount had borne him an acknowledged son, Henry Fitzroy. His marital relations continued with Katherine (witness her 1518 pregnancy), but the five-year age gap between husband and wife was becoming more significant; a Venetian ambassador thought her 'rather ugly than otherwise' in 1515 (*CSP Venice, 1509–19*, 248). Certainly the undated National Portrait Gallery portrait shows her as a rather substantial lady, by contrast with the youthful prettiness depicted by Michel Sittow in 1505 in a portrait now in Vienna (though the identity of the sitter is not entirely certain). Perhaps Katherine, at thirty, was settling into dignified early middle age, presiding over court ceremonial, supervising her household, attending to her considerable powers of patronage as queen. In 1517 she took the role scripted for her when she publicly pleaded for pardon for prisoners accused of taking part in the 'evil May day' riots in London.

Katherine had already been fluent in French and Latin when she arrived in England, and she now became proficient in English. She built on and developed the interest in Latin education she had acquired at Isabella's court, more than fulfilling what was expected of her in the field of scholarly patronage. She defended the interests of Queens' College, Cambridge, and interceded with Henry to protect Lady Margaret Beaufort's benefaction to St John's College. She visited both Oxford and Cambridge, and received the plaudits habitually bestowed on royal visitors by the universities. She provided exhibitions for poor scholars and contributed to the support of lectureships. She may have been involved in trying to persuade Erasmus to prolong his stay in England beyond 1514, and was habitually praised by him; he dedicated his *Christiani matrimonii institutio* (1526) to her. Her patronage included Richard Pace, Thomas Linacre, and John Leland. She asked Sir Thomas Wyatt to translate Petrarch on 'Ill fortune'; he produced instead a version of Plutarch as *Of the Quyete of Mynde*.

In 1523 Katherine brought the Spaniard Juan Luis Vives to England to finish his commentary on Augustine (dedicated to Henry VIII), and commissioned him to write his *De institutione foeminae Christianae* (presented to Katherine in 1523, printed in 1524). She was praised in Vives's preface as a model of maid, married woman, and widow. The book advocates a classical education for noblewomen (the education of Isabella's daughters and their ability in Latin was mentioned), although, since women would not have to devote themselves to business, and having due regard to feminine modesty, only a selection of classical writings is recommended. The scriptures, the church fathers, Plato, Cicero, and Seneca are thought especially suitable. Women should be prepared to converse, although not to thrust themselves forward, and should submit to the precepts of fathers and husbands. Nor are they to neglect needlework, household management, or the nurture of children. Given Vives's subsequent involvement with Princess Mary's education, it seems reasonable to assume that Katherine shared these views. Vives reported a conversation with Katherine in January 1524 as they returned on a boat from Syon to Richmond. The talk was of the vicissitudes of life. Katherine claimed to have experienced many turns of fortune. If forced to choose between bad fortune and good, she would prefer the former: 'faced with disaster men need consolation, but excessive prosperity undermines their character' (McConica, 53–4).

Katherine was concerned with the education, in the widest sense, of her daughter, although since Mary was heir apparent and a valuable piece in the international dynastic game, its direction was largely out of her hands. She commissioned from Vives in 1524 a supplementary treatise, addressed to the particular problems faced by Mary as a princess and possible ruler (*De ratione studii puerilis*, 1524). Vives's solution was the mixture as before, modified only by the inclusion of more political texts and histories. When in 1525 Mary was dispatched, at the age of nine, to keep a princely household at Ludlow, Katherine wrote that she was glad that in future 'Master Federston [Richard Fetherston]' rather than herself would be teaching her Latin, although she hoped that Mary would continue to show her mother her Latin letters, 'for it shall be a great comfort to me to see you keep your Latin and fair writing and all' (Ellis, 1st ser., 2.19).

Diplomacy and divorce, 1525–1527 Charles V's election as holy Roman emperor in 1519 had simplified the international scene by creating a polarization between the French and (imperial) Habsburg interests. English policy in the next ten years played off the parties against each other. Katherine naturally sympathized with the imperialists, but her influence was muted and hardly significant among the contending factors which determined policy. She played her due part in the Field of the Cloth of Gold of 1520, the ceremonial meeting between Henry and François I. But she had also pleaded family reasons for the brief English visit by Charles V which preceded that event, and which led to a further meeting between Henry and Charles at Gravelines, at which an Anglo-imperial alliance was forged. In 1521 Charles was betrothed to the five-year-old Princess Mary. In 1522 and 1523 English armies invaded northern France, to little effect. In spite of a second English visit by Charles in 1522, English policies were moving in favour of France when, on 24 February 1525, Charles's forces took François prisoner at Pavia. Henry's attempt to take advantage of this situation by mounting an immediate invasion of France foundered on the difficulty of funding it, and on an unwillingness by Charles to play things Henry's way. Instead England and France made peace at the treaty of The More in August 1525. Katherine was powerless to influence events. Indeed she complained about never hearing either from Charles or from Spain. Charles's ambassador Iñigo de Mendoza reported that he was not allowed to see Katherine on her own, nor to communicate with her on anything except family matters. Even if they did set up a secret channel of communication it would, she thought, do more harm than good. 'She will do her best to restore the old alliance between Spain and England but though her will is good her means

are small' (*CSP Spain, 1527–9*, 37). An Anglo-French treaty was concluded on 30 April 1527, and in January 1528 England was formally at war with Charles.

The first moves in the procedure to annul Katherine's marriage took place in 1527 (the convenient, if inaccurate, term 'divorce' will be used hereafter). The specific problem was not merely that Henry and Katherine were related in the first degree of affinity, but that sexual relations with a brother's wife were among those specifically forbidden in Leviticus 18: 1–19; while Leviticus 20: 21 threatened that no children would be born to such a union. However, according to Deuteronomy (21: 5) it was the duty of a man to generate a son by his brother's widow if the marriage had not produced a son. This duty of the 'levirate' did not apply to Christians, but did at least call in question the absolute nature of the prohibition in Leviticus. The question of whether a pope could dispense from the Levitical prohibition may have explained the apparent reluctance of Julius II to grant the bull in 1504. In 1509, in the immediate aftermath of Henry VII's death, the Spanish ambassador was told by an English courtier that Katherine's marriage to the new king was unlikely since Henry VIII himself had a difficulty in conscience about marrying his brother's wife. Ferdinand wrote back in alarm, invoking the papal bull to counter the objection, and instancing the marriage, in 1500, of Katherine's sister Maria to Manuel, king of Portugal, who was the widower of her elder sister Isabella. Ferdinand added encouragingly that the couple had numerous progeny, a possible reference to the Levitical curse. Of course Ferdinand's letter was overtaken by events. Katherine had married Henry, with, apparently, no mention of the affinity problem. A rumour circulated in Rome in 1514 that Henry meant to repudiate Katherine; this was probably unfounded, but significantly gave as a reason Henry's inability to have children with his brother's widow. An awareness of the Levitical prohibition and of doubts about the papal right to dispense from it was known in diplomatic circles from 1503 and, probably, equally known to Henry.

Henry later claimed that his conscience was first pricked by a French embassy raising the question of Mary's legitimacy during negotiations for her possible marriage; but since the embassy concerned seems to have been that of April 1527, this is too late to explain the sequence of events, although again testifying to the knowledge in diplomatic circles that the validity of Henry's marriage was open to question. It seems more likely that Henry had been brooding on the subject since it became apparent that he would have no son from his marriage to Katherine, especially as the possible strategy of marrying Mary to an acceptable husband could not take effect until she was fourteen, in 1530. Henry said in 1531 that he had not slept with Katherine for seven years. He may have been keeping his options for the succession open in 1525, when his illegitimate son Henry Fitzroy was created duke of Richmond and sent to keep his household in the north, at the same time as Mary was being sent to the Welsh marches. The first move towards a divorce was the examination, on 5–6 April 1527, of the elderly Bishop Richard Fox about Katherine's marriage to Arthur, the papal bull, and Henry's repudiation of his betrothal in 1505. On 17 May 1527 Wolsey, as papal legate, summoned Henry before himself and Archbishop Warham to defend the validity of his marriage. The trial was adjourned on 31 May while expert opinion was consulted; it was never resumed. The popular assumption is that the intention was to rush through a verdict against the marriage and so face Katherine with a *fait accompli*. This is unlikely. Since Katherine had not been summoned as a party to the proceedings (though by 18 May she was aware of what was happening), she would have had unimpeachable grounds for an appeal. More probably, the intention was to establish the foundations of the case for further proceedings. On 22 June Henry told Katherine personally of his 'scruples', and demanded formal separation; faced with her fury, he retreated, assuring her that his hope was that his scruples would be set at rest. Katherine immediately sent to Charles V in Spain, asking him to intervene personally with Henry, to rouse the pope to summon the case to Rome, and to revoke Wolsey's legatine authority in England. She continued to preside at court and to occupy her apartments as queen. Anne Boleyn was also for much of the time prominent at court. On at least one occasion Katherine and Anne are said to have played cards together, Katherine allegedly remarking 'You have good hap to stop at a king, but you are not like others, you will have all or none' (Ives, 119).

Appeals to Rome and the legates' court, 1527–1529 Charles V's troops had sacked Rome and, effectively, made the pope a prisoner, on 6 May 1527. This was known in England by about 1 June and offered Henry both an obvious obstacle, and an opportunity. Wolsey was sent to France in July 1527 with, among other aims, the hope of convening a meeting of cardinals to run the church during the pope's incapacity. At the same time the king sent William Knight to Rome with various suggestions, to be kept secret from Wolsey. The document does not survive, but it seems to have included a request that Henry be permitted to marry immediately, presumably in confident expectation of a subsequent annulment of the first marriage; in effect it amounted to a dispensation for bigamy. That document was countermanded while Knight was travelling through France. Under new instructions he was to procure a bull allowing Henry to marry within the first degree of affinity, whether that resulted from licit or illicit intercourse (provided it was not to a brother's widow). The dispensation was also to cover the possibility that the bride had already contracted marriage to another man, provided that the marriage had not been consummated. The intended bride was plainly Anne Boleyn, to whom Henry was related within the first degree because her sister had been his mistress.

Meanwhile Henry's case was also being set out in papers by various scholars. In part, these took a 'high' line, that the marriage to Katherine being against divine law, Julius II had had no power to dispense. To the objection that he had not been punished by childlessness, as threatened in

Leviticus, Henry's party argued that, correctly interpreted, the Hebrew referred to male children. In part, more modest, technical objections were canvassed, such as the argument that since there had been no prospect of war between England and Spain in 1503, the 'preservation of peace' was not an adequate ground for a dispensation; or that while the bull did indeed cover a consummated marriage between Katherine and Arthur, it had omitted to deal with the issue of 'public honesty', which even a non-consummated marriage required.

Katherine's position seems to have been much simpler than Henry's. She contended that her marriage to Arthur had never been consummated, that she had come to Henry a maid, that her marriage to Henry was therefore valid in the sight of God and man, and, moreover, that Henry knew this. She argued this at her confrontation with Henry on 22 June 1527, and stuck to it unalterably thereafter. In fact this argument undercut the arguments of her advisers and defenders of the papal cause, who had to support the view that Julius II had not exceeded his powers in dispensing for a possibly consummated marriage. For them Katherine's position was unprovable and irrelevant to the real issue. It was clearly, however, the emotional core of her position.

Early in 1528 the papal brief, issued to Isabella in 1504, surfaced in Spain, and it was cited by Katherine's counsel from October onwards. The brief, in fact, pointed in a different direction from Katherine's own tactic, in that it assumed unequivocally that the marriage to Arthur had been consummated. Katherine gave notice that, in propounding the brief, she did not admit this assumption. Rather she intended to use it to throw dust in the eyes of her opponents, by making it impossible for them to be sure that any technical objections they might produce against the bull were not guarded against in the brief. It was impossible for the English to argue that the latter was a forgery, since the Spaniards refused to let them have the original.

Pope Clement VII had been released from captivity in December 1527, though with Charles dominant in Italy, he was still liable to imperial pressure. Through 1528 Henry's agents agitated for a 'decretal' commission, to examine the case in England without the danger of its verdict being appealed to Rome. The commission was eventually brought to England by the specially appointed papal legate, Cardinal Campeggi, in October 1528, empowering him and Wolsey to try the case. Campeggi, however, had orders to prevaricate, and to find another solution. To that end he and Wolsey saw Katherine on 24 October. Three days later she sought Campeggi under the seal of the confession. She told him that she had shared Arthur's bed on up to seven occasions, but that she had none the less remained a maid. She rejected utterly the suggestion that she might enter the religious life, and affirmed 'that she intended to live and die in the estate of matrimony, to which God had called her'. Henry, worried at reports of popular support for Katherine, called a meeting of courtiers and prominent Londoners to Bridewell on 8 November. He expounded his case of conscience. According to

Edward Hall he also professed his admiration for Katherine's noble qualities, so that 'if I were to marry again, if the marriage might be good, I would surely choose her above all other women' (Brewer, 2.306–7).

Eventually the legatine court met at Blackfriars on 31 May 1529. On 16 June, in the presence of Archbishop Warham and six other bishops, Katherine appealed formally to the pope for the case to be heard in Rome. On 18 June she appeared in person at the legatine court at Blackfriars to read a protest to be entered on the record, indicating her denial of the impartiality of the legates and her appeal to Rome. On 21 June she and Henry both appeared. The sources differ considerably in their accounts of what happened, but it is clear that Henry, Wolsey, and Katherine all spoke, Henry setting out his case, Wolsey defending his own impartiality, and Katherine appealing to her honour and that of her daughter and of the king to justify her appeal to Rome. It is clear that she knelt before Henry, and that she protested that she had lived twenty years as his lawful and faithful wife. Whether or not she went on to assert that she had been 'a true maid' at the time of their marriage, and to challenge Henry to deny it, as so vividly presented by Shakespeare, must remain in question. The earliest source is George Cavendish's life of Wolsey; although Cavendish was an eyewitness, he did not write until 1556–8. Katherine then left the court in spite of a summons to remain. On 25 June she was declared contumacious. This was known in Rome by 9 July. By 16 July Clement VII had issued the advocation to Rome. There may have been (again Cavendish is the source) a further attempt by Wolsey and Campeggi to persuade Katherine to co-operate. Wolsey meanwhile feared that the advocation would be granted before the court could come to a verdict. On 23 July Campeggi, with Wolsey's agreement, adjourned the court, following the Roman custom, for the summer vacation. Clearly there was no intention of reconvening it.

Last years as queen, 1529–1533 Formally, Katherine's position was unchanged by these proceedings. She remained at court, though she and Henry rarely dined together except on great occasions, and Henry was frequently elsewhere, in the company of Anne Boleyn. On one occasion when they did dine informally, on 30 November 1529, there was a blazing row; Anne pointed out subsequently that 'whenever you disputed with the Queen, she was sure to have the upper hand' (Ives, 154–5). In June 1530 Henry was still having Katherine make his shirts, to Anne's fury. Henry's case ground interminably on as he collected opinions from foreign universities, organized a petition to the pope from peers and a selection of leading clergy, and began to press the clergy to agree that the English church was self-sufficient and could proceed in the case regardless of the pope. Katherine meanwhile pressed Clement through Charles V's agents (and especially through Charles's new ambassador, Eustache Chapuys) to settle the case quickly in her favour, trusting, so she claimed, that Henry would thereby see the error of his ways. Clement, however, prevaricated; the furthest he would go, in January 1531, was to forbid Henry to remarry before the case was settled at Rome, and to forbid English authorities, ecclesiastical or secular, to meddle.

Following the acknowledgement by the clerical convocations in February 1531 that Henry was 'Supreme Head' of the English church 'as far as the law of Christ allowed', Clement offered Henry a compromise to allow the trial to take place on supposedly neutral ground. A deputation of some thirty councillors saw Katherine on 31 May 1531, but she refused any compromise and spiritedly defended both the papal supremacy and her marriage, citing, as always, her maidenhood in 1509. In a story related by Chapuys, perhaps too good to be true, the duke of Suffolk reported to Henry that Katherine was ready to obey 'but she owed obedience to two persons first'; to Henry's supposition that these were pope and emperor, Suffolk retorted 'God was the first; the second her soul and conscience' (*CSP Spain, 1531–3*, no. 739; Katherine certainly used this formula in a later exhortation to Mary). On 11 July 1531 Henry and Katherine saw each other for the last time. The queen and her daughter were also separated; Katherine was ordered to The More in Hertfordshire, where, however, she continued to keep considerable state, Mary to remain at Windsor. Mother and daughter never met again (suggestions that they did so in September 1534 derive from a mistranscription).

In October 1531 Katherine faced another conciliar deputation to persuade her to agree to a trial in England. She was forbidden to write to the king, and her new year gift was brusquely refused. Further pressure was put on the English church early in 1532, with the passing in parliament of the supplication against the ordinaries and the threat to cut off the payment of annates to Rome. Yet another weak papal admonition to Henry, in January 1532, led Katherine to appeal for help from God's vicar to God himself. Then the death of Archbishop Warham on 22 August opened the way to a settlement in England. Henry took Anne Boleyn to meet François I in October 1532. Katherine, meanwhile, had left The More and seems to have been leading a peripatetic life from August to November 1532, moving between Hertford, Hatfield, and Enfield. By the end of the year Anne was pregnant, and Henry married her in January. On 9 April 1533 the dukes of Norfolk and Suffolk waited once more on Katherine, now installed at Ampthill, in Bedfordshire, to tell her that Henry and Anne were already married and to require her to give up her title as queen. On 8 May Thomas Cranmer, the new archbishop of Canterbury, summoned Katherine to his court at Dunstable, close to Ampthill. She refused to appear and was declared contumacious. On 23 May Cranmer pronounced her marriage null, finding that her marriage to Arthur had been consummated, and that no dispensation could remove an impediment resulting from divine law.

In July 1533 Katherine again refused to accept the title 'princess dowager'; the same month she moved, with a much reduced household, to Buckden in Huntingdonshire. She urged Chapuys to press for a definitive papal sentence; however, while Chapuys hoped to stimulate rebellion in England, Katherine refused to countenance resort to force. She also avoided entangling herself with Elizabeth Barton, the Nun of Kent, whose treasonable prophecies about Henry's marriage were revealed in November. There was clearly a good deal of sympathy for Katherine in England as wronged wife and rightful queen, as numerous indictments and reports to Cromwell make clear. Support for her seems to have been particularly marked among women, whether they were great ladies like Henry's sister Mary, duchess of Suffolk, or 'gossips' in London and elsewhere. But it is difficult to assess the extent or the potential political significance of such apparent goodwill. There were reports that Londoners showed themselves sullen or even disrespectful to Anne Boleyn during her coronation procession, refusing to cheer or even pull off their caps. But these stories derived from imperial sources. Chapuys's belief that were Katherine to give the signal England would rise in revolt to defend her rights was never put to the test.

A mission by Suffolk in December to remove Katherine to Somersham in Cambridgeshire foundered on her obduracy and Suffolk's reluctance to carry out a forcible removal, although he did imprison some of her English household. On 23 March 1534 Rome at last pronounced on Katherine's marriage, decisively in her favour, but too late to influence events in England. In May Katherine declared that she would refuse to swear the oath recognizing Anne Boleyn's children as Henry's legitimate succession, professing her readiness to accept the capital penalty for refusal, and advising Mary to do likewise, to Chapuys's disquiet. In the event the oath was not pressed on either Katherine or Mary, although their servants were sworn. In May 1534 she was removed to the more secure house at Kimbolton, also in Huntingdonshire, described as smaller but more convenient than Buckden.

Katherine's household had now been reduced to a core largely made up of Spaniards: her confessor, her *maestresala* (hall-steward), physician and apothecary, two grooms of the chamber, three maids of honour, and six to eight other women. Even so, her yearly expenses came to rather over £3000. Katherine kept to her apartments, including a private garden, perhaps to spare her servants embarrassment, since she insisted on being addressed as queen. Sir Edmund Bedingfield and Sir Edward Chamberlayn acted as steward and chamberlain, with instructions to allow no visits without Henry's licence. In July 1534 Chapuys, despite having been refused permission to visit, nevertheless took a large retinue, including many Spaniards, to make a demonstration outside the walls. In his dispatches Chapuys mentioned possible threats to Katherine's life, especially by poison. Written communication, however, seems to have been maintained relatively freely. Mary was ill in September 1534 and again in February–March 1535; Katherine pleaded that she should be allowed to nurse her daughter, or at least that Mary should be moved closer to her. Henry refused; in part, at least, because he feared that Mary might be spirited away to Charles V's dominions, a suspicion justified where Chapuys, though not Katherine, was concerned.

In March 1535 Henry called Katherine 'a proud and intractable woman' who might, in her daughter's interests, 'carry on a war against him as openly and fiercely as Queen Isabella, her mother, had done in Spain' (*CSP Spain*, 1534–5, no. 142), and throughout that year she continued to urge the new pope, Paul III, to publish the excommunication Henry had incurred by his non-compliance with papal directions; whether because she still believed that Henry would eventually recognize his sin, or to justify rebellion or intervention, is a moot point. The move was sabotaged by Charles V's ambassador in Rome. At the end of December Katherine was dangerously ill. Chapuys was allowed to visit her at Kimbolton. She seemed better when he took his leave on 4 January 1536, but sickened during the night of Thursday the 6th. She heard mass in the morning, dictated letters to Charles V and to Henry, the latter as always protesting her continued love, her anxiety for her daughter, and concern for her servants. She died at Kimbolton about 2 p.m. on Friday 7 January 1536.

The chandler whose duty it was to embalm the body reported to Katherine's physician that the organs were sound, except for the heart, which was black all through. It has been suggested that this was a secondary from a melanotic carcinoma, but the physician deduced 'slow poisoning', and her friends needed little persuading. The precise cause of death is probably now beyond investigation. Henry greeted the news of Katherine's death with relief, regarding it as ending the risk of war with the emperor. Next day he and Anne, dressed in yellow (for mourning, according to Hall), paraded the infant Elizabeth around the court. Katherine was buried, as princess dowager, at Peterborough Abbey on 29 January 1536. No monument was ever erected.

Personality Katherine has enjoyed a good historical reputation. The tragic heroine of Shakespeare's *Henry VIII* is ultimately derived, through Holinshed, from the publication in Mary's reign of the final part of Polydore Vergil's *Anglica historia* and also of George Cavendish's *Life and Death of Cardinal Wolsey*: both feature her speech at the Blackfriars court and her interview with the two cardinals in 1529. The picture was enhanced by the publication in the nineteenth century of Chapuys's extremely sympathetic and admiring dispatches covering the period from autumn 1529; Chapuys, indeed, appointed himself her champion not only with Henry but also with the emperor. Undoubtedly from her late teens Katherine displayed a tenacious will, to the annoyance of successive Spanish ambassadors. Before 1509 she was heavily influenced by close friendships with members of her household, most notably Doña Elvira, her duenna, and her confessor Diego Fernández. As queen she performed her role with dignity, presiding at court functions, dispensing patronage to churchmen and writers; while Vives was perhaps of these recipients the closest to Katherine herself, the flavour, even in his case, was more international-humanist than specifically Spanish, although Katherine evidently took pleasure in speaking Spanish with him. Although she was perceived in diplomatic circles as a symbol of Anglo-Spanish alliance against France, her direct political influence was limited, even in the early years of Henry's reign, and from about 1514 minimal. Indeed her views on the public role of a great lady would have precluded any different stance as long as she was under the authority of a husband. She was convinced from 1503 that it was her duty to marry Henry. The sudden turn in her fortunes in 1509 must have confirmed her sense of providential mission. She believed to the utmost of her being that she was Henry's wife, and that belief helped her cut through the legal complexities of the divorce proceedings.

Although Katherine became fluent in English, circumstances after 1529 drove her increasingly into the Spanish core of her household; she always confessed in Spanish. She was meticulous in her observance of public worship, as befitted her position. When she gave birth to a son in 1511 she promised to visit the shrine of Our Lady of Walsingham (Henry made the pilgrimage immediately), but did not fulfil her vow until after the victory at Flodden, almost three years later. She repeated the visit in 1517, and in her 'will' asked that a representative be sent there on her behalf after her death. In the same document she requested 500 masses for her soul. But while honouring conventional religious practices, Katherine seems not to have displayed the credulity so often associated with the cults of saints, nor to have been concerned with such manifestations of devotion as the collection of holy relics. She had a keen eye for the failings of churchmen, including those of popes and cardinals. The Spanish atmosphere of her private devotions may have accentuated the essential inwardness of her piety, which revolved around mass, prayer, confession, penance, in a manner characteristic of the Spanish court and especially of her mother, though also found in some great English ladies like Lady Margaret Beaufort. Her conversation with Vives in 1524 suggests Christian resignation, even Christian stoicism.

Among the religious orders Katherine especially supported the Observant Franciscans; she was a member of their third order. Popular in Spain, the Observants were established in England from 1482 under the auspices of the court, as an élite group of mature and well-motivated religious. Her marriage to Henry had taken place in their church at Greenwich. She asked to be buried in one of their churches but by the time of her death the order in England had been dissolved.

C. S. L. DAVIES and JOHN EDWARDS

Sources CSP Spain, 1485–1538 • LP Henry VIII, vols. 1–11 • CSP Venice, 1202–1554 • L. Suárez Fernández, ed., Política internacional de Isabel la Católica, 5 vols. (Valladolid, 1965–72) • J. Gairdner, ed., Letters and papers illustrative of the reigns of Richard III and Henry VII, 2 vols., Rolls Series, 24 (1861–3) • G. Cavendish, 'The life and death of Cardinal Wolsey', Two early Tudor lives, ed. R. S. Sylvester and D. P. Harding (New Haven, 1962) • H. Ellis, ed., Original letters illustrative of English history, 1st ser., 3 vols. (1824) • Correspondencia de Gutierre Gómez de Fuensalida, ed. duque de Berwick y de Alba (Madrid, 1907) • N. Pocock, ed., Records of the Reformation: the divorce, 1527–33, 2 vols. (1870) • S. Ehses, ed., Römische Dokumente zur Geschichte der Ehescheidung Heinrichs VIII (Paderborn, 1893) • A. H. Thomas and I. D. Thornley, eds., The great chronicle of London (1938) • G. Mattingly, Catherine of Aragon (1942) • M. A. Ladero Quesada, La España de los reyes católicos (Madrid, 1999) • J. J. Scarisbrick, Henry VIII, rev. edn (1997) • H. A. Kelly, The matrimonial trials of Henry VIII (Stanford, 1976) • D. Loades, Mary Tudor: a life (1989) • J. E. Paul, Catherine of Aragon and her friends (1966) • E. W. Ives, Anne Boleyn (1986) • J. K. McConica, English humanists and Reformation politics (1965) • L. Suárez Fernández, Isabel I, reina (1451–1504) (Barcelona, 2000) • C. G. Noreña, Juan Luis Vives (The Hague, 1970) • P. Gwyn, The king's cardinal (1990) • M. Dowling, Humanism in the age of Henry VIII (1986) • J. S. Brewer, The reign of Henry VIII from his accession to the death of Wolsey, ed. J. Gairdner, 2 vols. (1884) • W. Busch, England under the Tudors: King Henry VII (1895) [Eng. trans.] • S. B. Chrimes, Henry VII, rev. edn (1999) • S. Anglo, Spectacle, pageantry and early Tudor policy (1969) • J. C. Dickinson, The shrine of Our Lady at Walsingham (1956) • G. R. Elton, Policy and police: the enforcement of the reformation in the age of Thomas Cromwell (1972)

Archives PRO, state papers • Simancas, archive • Brussels, archive • Vienna, archive

Likenesses stained-glass window, c.1518–1528, The Vyne, Hampshire • L. Horenbout, miniature, c.1525–1526, Buccleuch collection [see illus.] • oil on panel, c.1530, NPG; version, Museum of Fine Arts, Boston; many later versions • miniature, c.1530–1536, priv. coll. • miniature, c.1530–1536, priv. coll. • attrib. L. Horenbout, miniature, NPG • M. Sittow, oils (identification uncertain), Kunsthistorisches Museum, Vienna • two miniatures, Buccleuch estates, Selkirk, Scotland

Wealth at death chattels only

Katherine [Kateryn, Catherine; née Katherine Parr] (1512–1548), queen of England and Ireland, sixth consort of Henry VIII, was born in 1512, probably in August, the second child and elder daughter of Sir Thomas *Parr (1478–1517) [see under Parr family (per. c.1370–1517)] of Kendal, Westmorland, and Maud Green (1492–1531), daughter of Sir Thomas Green of Greens Norton, Northamptonshire, and his wife, Jane Fogge. Although Parr inherited an estate centred in the north-west, he was raised at Great Harrowden, Northamptonshire, the home of his stepfather, Sir Nicholas Vaux. A charming, athletic, well-educated man, Parr became a favoured courtier of *Henry VIII on his accession in 1509, and his young wife Maud became lady-in-waiting to the queen, Katherine of Aragon. Maud's elder daughter, Katherine, born some three years later, either at Great Kimble, Buckinghamshire, or Blackfriars, London, was named after Henry's first queen.

Early years and education, 1517–1529 During Katherine's early childhood the Parrs led an itinerant life, moving between such temporary homes as Great Kimble near Aylesbury, Moor's End at Potterspury, Northamptonshire, Rye House, Hertfordshire, and a London house in Blackfriars. Between 1516 and 1517 Sir Thomas Parr served with Sir Thomas Lovell as associate master of the court of wards and the family seems to have divided its time between Blackfriars and Rye House. Parr died in London on 11 November 1517 and was buried at St Ann Blackfriars, under an elaborate monument erected for him by his widow. In his will he left £800 to be divided between his two daughters as marriage portions.

At their father's death the guardianship of Katherine and her two siblings, William *Parr (1513–1571), later earl of Essex and marquess of Northampton, and Anne (c.1515–1552), later countess of Pembroke, was left in the hands of their mother, who set up a school in her household to educate them. Maud Parr was an independent, capable, and unusually articulate woman, who in the years after her husband's death managed the family estates, oversaw her

Katherine [Katherine Parr] (**1512–1548**), attrib. Master John, c.1545

children's education, arranged marriages for her two eldest, and set an example of female independence that was to have a lifelong effect on her elder daughter, and through her, on Katherine's stepdaughter, Elizabeth Tudor.

On the advice of her husband's cousin, Cuthbert Tunstall, later bishop of London and Durham, Maud selected tutors for her children who stimulated their interest in scholarship. Katherine's interest in medicine is well documented, and Tunstall may have introduced her to his particular hobby, numismatics, as she had a considerable collection of antique and foreign coins in her possession at her death. The Parrs' educational programme was organized along the lines devised by Sir Thomas More for his own children. As an adult Katherine was fluent in French, Latin, and Italian, and while she was queen she undertook

the study of Spanish. Her fluency in Latin, often a matter of contentious debate among historians, is amply supported by the number of scholars—people like Sir Thomas Smith, Roger Ascham, Francis Goldsmith, and the young Prince Edward—who corresponded with her in that language. Unfortunately no holographic letter of hers in Latin has survived. Her capabilities with her own language, exemplified by her books and letters, were extraordinary for a non-royal woman of the sixteenth century.

First two marriages, 1529–1543 Between April 1523 and March 1524 Maud Parr attempted to arrange a marriage for Katherine with Henry Scrope, son and heir of Lord Scrope of Bolton, but this failed to materialize owing to Lord Scrope's lack of enthusiasm. About May 1529, however, she took as her husband Edward Borough (c.1508–1533), the son of Thomas Borough, third Baron Borough of Gainsborough, Lincolnshire. Although few facts about the marriage are known, it is unlikely to have proved a happy experience for Katherine. Her father-in-law was an overbearing bully whose children lived in fear of his temper; moreover insanity ran in the family. But in October 1530, probably under pressure from Maud Parr, Lord Borough was persuaded to allow Katherine and her husband to take up residence at the manor of Kirton in Lindsey, Lincolnshire, where they resided until Edward Borough's death, shortly before April 1533.

Maud Parr had died on 1 December 1531, and, as neither of her siblings was in a position to offer her a home, according to tradition Katherine took refuge with her cousins, the Stricklands of Sizergh Castle, Westmorland. In the summer of 1534 she married as her second husband John *Neville, third Baron Latimer (1493–1543), of Snape Castle, Yorkshire. Latimer had been married twice before and had two young children. Unlike the Boroughs, who had evangelical sympathies, Lord Latimer was conservative in matters of religion. On 1 October 1536 the Pilgrimage of Grace began at Louth in Lincolnshire. Shortly afterwards a rebel mob appeared at Snape and carried Latimer off, forcing him to join their ranks. Latimer equivocated, trying to appease both his rebel captors and the king, who now considered him a traitor. In January 1537, believing that Latimer would betray them to the king, a mob stormed Snape and took Katherine and the children hostage. Although Latimer managed to secure their freedom, the experience intensified Katherine's antipathy towards the north. When the revolt was finally crushed in March 1537, Latimer barely escaped prosecution for treason. His kinship with his wife's family who had opposed the rebels helped to protect him from arrest. By mid-1537 the Latimers had left Yorkshire and moved to their manor of Wick, near Pershore. Although Latimer returned frequently to the north on both government and personal business, it appears that, after the Pilgrimage of Grace, Katherine spent most of her time in the south.

Queen and regent Lord Latimer died on 2 March 1543. In the previous winter Katherine had secured a position in the household of Princess Mary as one of her ladies. Mary had been in favour with her father since her submission to him in 1536, and she and her household were frequently at court. This had the result of bringing Katherine to the notice of the king. Although she had cherished the hope that after her failing husband's death she would be able to marry Sir Thomas *Seymour (b. in or before 1509, d. 1549), brother of Queen Jane, the king's interest changed the course of Katherine's life. It was made clear to her, no doubt by her reform-minded family, that her reluctance to accept the king as her husband was to defy God's will: 'my mind was fully bent the other time I was at liberty to marry you before any man I know,' she later wrote to Seymour. 'Howbeit, God withstood my will therein most vehemently … [and] made me to renounce utterly mine own will, and to follow his most willingly' (Dent-Brocklehurst MS).

Print and film alike have represented Katherine as an ageing, plain-faced, pious widow with few attractions, selected by the king for her talents as a nurse. This is a misleading image that does not hold up beneath the weight of contemporary evidence. She was of medium height, with red hair and grey eyes. She had a lively personality, was a witty conversationalist with a deep interest in the arts, and an erudite scholar who read Petrarch and Erasmus for enjoyment. She was a graceful dancer, who loved fine clothes and jewels, particularly diamonds, and favoured the colour crimson in her gowns and household livery. Katherine also conveyed a sense of her own value, independent of the marital relationship, which was rare for a woman of this period. As queen, her signature invariably included the initials of her maiden name, 'KP'. Henry had a finely developed eye for beauty and it is highly unlikely that he would have married a woman he did not find physically attractive. Her clandestine romance in the winter of 1542–3 with Sir Thomas Seymour, one of the most dashing bachelors at the Tudor court, together with its renewal in 1547, constitutes a further tribute to her attractions.

Katherine Parr was married to Henry VIII (1491–1547) on 12 July 1543 in the queen's closet at Hampton Court with eighteen people in attendance. From the beginning the new queen's position at court was difficult. The only one of Henry's queens without either royal background or court service to train her for her new position, she was forced to learn quickly the duties and obligations of queenship, as well as its prerogatives. Among her first acts were her efforts to secure the friendship of Henry's children. Already on good terms with her former mistress, Princess Mary, Katherine soon befriended Princess Elizabeth and the young prince of Wales. Both were of a scholarly bent and they found a kindred spirit in their stepmother, who took an active and personal interest in their education. Edward wrote frequently to her regarding his progress at his studies, and of the five surviving letters that Elizabeth wrote before the age of sixteen all are either to or about Katherine. The new queen also used the increasingly popular iconographic medium of secular portraiture to reinforce the royal position of her stepchildren, and at her behest not only was Edward painted but the first

portraits en large of Mary and Elizabeth were commissioned. Her kindness to and championship of the royal children had long-lasting consequences for English politics, since Katherine used her growing influence with the king to persuade him to include both Mary and Elizabeth in the line of succession, thereby validating their future rule.

During summer 1544 Henry VIII led a military expedition to France to join with the emperor Charles V against François I. During his absence Henry appointed his queen regent-general, together with a regency council dominated by the queen's fellow religionists. Katherine took this opportunity to bring Princess Elizabeth back to court from de facto exile at Ashridge, Hertfordshire, and reinstate her in her father's favour. From the middle of July until the middle of September the queen kept the royal children with her at Hampton Court and made every effort not just to preside over the regency council but to rule in the king's name. This assumption of power, not merely by a woman but by a woman who only a year before had been a Yorkshire housewife, made the queen enemies, particularly among the religious conservatives who resented her evangelical beliefs. For Katherine, who understood only too well how rapidly the king's health was deteriorating, the protectorship was a trial run for a minority regency. Should the king die before Prince Edward was of age, under the terms laid down for transfer of power, a regency council would be appointed headed by the young king's mother. Rightly or wrongly, Katherine certainly saw herself in this role.

Katherine signed five royal proclamations while regent, most of them dealing with war-related matters such as the pricing of armour and the arrest and trial of military deserters. While her husband besieged Boulogne, the queen had to contend with a wide variety of issues, including the provisioning of English troops in France, pardons for imprisoned Gypsies, petitions from French nationals, as well as potentially devastating attacks on the English herring fleet, and unstable conditions along the Scottish border. Katherine's capable management of the protectorship earned her the king's approval, and when Boulogne surrendered on 13 September she celebrated by taking her stepchildren on progress into Surrey. An interesting commentary on these months can be found in Nicholas Udall's satire, Ralph Roister Doister, which he wrote for the queen at this time and in which he portrays her as Christian or Kitte Custance, a woman effectively running her own affairs and those of her household while dealing with the plots of an amorous courtier, the 'Ralph' of the title.

The plot against Katherine Henry's foray into France had made him enemies across Europe. In February 1545, apparently at the queen's instigation, secret overtures for a new alliance were made on behalf of the crown to the protestant princes of the Schmalkaldic league, using Katherine's trusted personal secretary, Walter Bucler, and Christopher Mont as envoys. Although the plan failed to materialize, the queen's zealous evangelical position combined with her influence on the king, the recent precedent of her regency, and Henry's deteriorating health to ring alarm bells among religious conservatives at court.

In February 1546 these conservatives, led by Stephen Gardiner, bishop of Winchester, began plotting to destroy her. Rumours of her imminent demise were circulated, together with gossip about possible candidates for her replacement. As Henry's health worsened, his temper became ever shorter and his wife's assertiveness began to irritate him. He particularly resented the queen's spirited debates with him in matters of religion and voiced this resentment openly to Gardiner. The bishop, who, like the queen, knew that the king could not survive much longer and that a minority regency under her control would give ample scope for a vigorous enforcement of the new religion, joined with the lord chancellor Sir Thomas Wriothesley, Sir Richard Rich, and his own protégé, William Paget, to compromise the queen with such proofs of heresy as would lead to her arrest and execution. Katherine and some of her ladies kept proscribed books in their chambers—the queen hid hers in her garderobe—and if this fact could be proven, charges could be laid against her. Wary of attacking her openly, Gardiner sought to implicate the queen through the interrogation of a self-confessed sacramentarian heretic, Anne Askew. Under extreme torture, however, Askew refused to implicate anyone and went to the stake on 16 July 1546 without giving Gardiner the evidence he needed for an open attack on the queen.

Gardiner nevertheless managed to procure evidence regarding Katherine's heretical library and a warrant of arrest was issued, probably at about the same time as Askew's execution. According to John Foxe one of the court doctors (possibly Robert Huicke, medical adviser to both king and queen) chanced to see the warrant when it was accidentally dropped and immediately informed the queen of its existence. Terrified, Katherine took to her bed, giving it out that she was mortally ill, and when the king rushed to her side she explained that her illness stemmed from fear that she had displeased him. Henry taxed her with her outspokenness in matters of religion and Katherine mollified him by explaining that if she argued it was only to take his mind off his own ailments and to learn by his responses. In a speech that bears a strong resemblance to Katherine's speech of submission to Petruccio in Shakespeare's *The Taming of the Shrew*, which, indeed, it may have influenced, Katherine submitted all her spiritual and worldly wisdom to her husband's guidance. Henry was convinced by this show of submission and cancelled the warrant. The queen's obvious terror at having come so close to arrest caused her to play a far more subdued role during the final months of Henry's life. She appeared at the celebrations given in honour of the French emissary Admiral Claude d'Annebaut at Hampton Court in August 1546 and later that month went on a brief progress with the king. In the first week of December 1546 Katherine went to Greenwich to keep Christmas while Henry travelled to London. It was the last time she saw him alive. The king died on 28 January 1547 at Hampton Court and three days later, Edward Seymour, earl of Hertford, made himself duke of Somerset and protector of England, and contrary to her expectations excluded the queen completely from the regency.

Patronage and public works Katherine's income as queen derived from dower manors inherited from her first two husbands and an extensive package of lands and manors located principally in the southern shires and London, once the dowry of Katherine Howard. This gave her a considerable income and she took a keen interest in her estates, ordering a complete survey of them after marrying Henry VIII. She also had a passion for gardens, and her household accounts show payments for various plantings at Greenwich and at her dower manor of Chelsea. The arrangement of the queen's household in the early days of her marriage included finding positions for Parr cousins, for former retainers, for her uncle and stepdaughter, and for others close to her such as Henry Seymour, the brother of Sir Thomas. In addition to patronage arranged for family and friends through employment in her household, the queen found numerous other avenues to engage her interest and income. Katherine probably involved herself in more aspects of the English Renaissance and Reformation than any other of Henry's queens. Her love of music and the arts led her to take the Bassano family of court musicians into her household, as well as scholar and author Nicholas Udall, and the Flemish artists Susanna Horenbout and Levina Teerlinc. She patronized all the chief portraitists of the day including John Bettes, Lucas Horenbout, William Scrots, and one Master John, as well as the engraver Giles Gering, and the jeweller Peter Richardson. Two of the queen's favourite gifts to family or close friends were miniatures of herself and the king and presentation copies of her own books. In the evolving world of printing Katherine patronized Thomas Berthelet, the king's printer, and helped to advance the careers of new publishers of reformed religious literature such as Richard Grafton and Edward Whitchurch. Her orders for a wide array of bindings for her books in stamped leather, coloured velvets, and enamelled gilt helped promote the art of bookbinding. In the performing arts the queen maintained her own acting troupe and patronized Nicholas Udall, who wrote a number of plays, such as *Ralph Roister Doister*, for her amusement. Her interest in architecture is evidenced by the splendid new apartments that she commissioned for herself at Hampton Court.

Katherine's involvement in intellectual and scholastic patronage was equally extensive. In 1544–5 she appears to have been involved in the publication of an 'ABC' or reading primer for children, and she took an active interest in the education of her tenants in her honour of Clare in Suffolk and in the curriculum of the college of canons at Stoke. In February 1546, at the special request of the University of Cambridge, which was fearful of losing considerable income owing to an act passed on 23 December 1545 giving the king power over colleges, chantries, and hospitals, she became its advocate to the king. Her influence was a factor in the foundation of Trinity College in the same year. Where religious publications were concerned she was particularly committed to providing cheaply priced works in the vernacular as support for religious reformation. To this end she worked with Archbishop Thomas Cranmer on the publication (29 May 1545) of the *King's Primer* which contained both Cranmer's *Litany* and *Psalms or Prayers Taken out of Holy Scripture*, Katherine's translation of the late Bishop Fisher of Rochester's work. The queen also delegated Nicholas Udall to oversee her most cherished religious project, *Paraphrases upon the New Testament*, translated from Erasmus, the first volume of which was published on 31 January 1548 and dedicated to the queen. Three of the translators are known: Udall himself, Thomas Key, the queen's oratorian, and Princess Mary. The translator of the book of St Matthew was in all likelihood the queen herself, who may additionally have worked on all or part of the book of Acts. The *Paraphrases* had a circulation of some 20,000 volumes between 1548 and 1551.

Published works One of the first literary projects financed by Katherine was the publication in Latin of Fisher's *Psalmi seu precationes*, issued on 18 April 1544 by Berthelet. Apparently encouraged by her almoner and spiritual mentor, George Day, bishop of Chichester, who had once been Fisher's chaplain, Katherine's first effort as a writer was the English translation of this work which appeared in print a week later, on 25 April, and had run through eighteen editions by 1608. Although the translation was published anonymously, her second effort, *Prayers or Meditations*, issued on 29 May 1545, appeared under her own name, the first work ever published by an English queen. *Prayers or Meditations* consists of two parts, a paraphrase of portions of chapter 3 of Thomas à Kempis's *The Imitation of Christ*, with interpolated original material, and a compilation of five original prayers written by the queen, particularly an extraordinary one for men to say when going into battle. Princess Elizabeth translated Katherine's work into French, Italian, and Latin as a new year's gift for her father in 1546. The second book to appear under the queen's name was *The Lamentation of a Sinner*, a markedly Lutheran work with Calvinist flourishes, which was published on 5 November 1547, and describes the queen's search for religious truth and the soul's salvation initiated by divine grace. This work was translated into French by Jean Bellemain, Edward VI's French tutor. Also credited to the queen is an English translation of Savonarola, *A goodly exposition, after the manner of a contemplation upon the li psalm called 'Miserere mei Deus'*.

Queen dowager, 1547–1548 Within weeks of the death of Henry VIII Katherine had taken the handsome, dashing, but fatally reckless Sir Thomas Seymour as her lover and secretly married him some time in May 1547. This impetuous action, when it became known, alienated her from her stepson, Edward VI, and caused much salacious gossip, exacerbating a series of bitter public and private quarrels between Seymour and his new wife and his brother, the protector, and his wife. Despite this, Katherine managed to secure the guardianship of Princess Elizabeth while her new husband purchased the wardship of Lady Jane Grey from her father, the marquess of Dorset, for £500. Although Elizabeth resided with Katherine at her dower manors of Hanworth and Chelsea, Lady Jane was installed at Seymour Place in London. Seymour was careful to maintain the size and estate of his wife's household, both to enhance his own consequence with the privy council and to remind the court that Katherine was still the only queen in England. The teenaged Elizabeth soon developed a crush on Seymour, actively encouraged by her governess, the garrulous Katherine Ashley. This, combined with Seymour's indiscreet behaviour and Katherine's loving indulgence, caused yet another scandal. Rumours of an illicit affair between Elizabeth and Seymour, now lord admiral, circulated at court. Then in December 1547 Katherine became pregnant, and the following spring she sent Elizabeth to Cheshunt, Hertfordshire, to live with Katherine Ashley's sister, Lady Denny. A few weeks later, on 13 June, with Lady Jane Grey in her train, Katherine travelled down to her husband's castle of Sudeley, Gloucestershire, to await confinement. On 30 August she was delivered of a daughter, who was baptized Mary, but Katherine soon developed puerperal fever. She died 'between two and three of the clock in the morning' (Coll. Arms, MS RR21/C, fol. 98a) on Wednesday 5 September, leaving to her husband all of her possessions, 'wishing them to be a thousand times more in value than they were' (PRO, PROB 11/32/19). She was buried the same day in Sudeley chapel with Lady Jane Grey as chief mourner. For nearly 250 years her body lay forgotten until it was accidentally unearthed by some workmen in May 1782. Opening the lead casket, they found the body in perfect condition but it rapidly disintegrated with rough handling and exposure. Queen Katherine's remains now lie beneath a modern effigy in the chapel at Sudeley.

Queen Katherine's influence on the politics and culture of her time was diverse and wide-reaching, far greater than has usually been appreciated. Her patronage extended to many of the architects of religious and educational reform; her active interest in the latter is especially clearly shown by her role in the foundation of Trinity College, Cambridge. Politically she contributed to the re-establishment of her stepdaughters, Mary and Elizabeth, in the line of succession, and her exercise of power as queen regent may have furnished a model for the latter. An enthusiastic patron of the arts in the fields of drama, miniature painting, and music, she was herself the first known Englishwoman to publish a work of prose in the sixteenth century, as well as being an energetic advocate of the publication of affordable vernacular religious writings. Her commitment to religious reform in particular, reinforced as it was by her position of queen, made her a singularly important player in the power politics of the last three years of Henry VIII's reign.   SUSAN E. JAMES

Sources S. E. James, *Kateryn Parr: the making of a queen* (1999) · *LP Henry VIII*, vols. 18–21, addenda · *CPR, 1547–53* · *CSP dom., 1547–53* · *CSP Spain, 1541–9*, p. 6, nos. 2–9 · J. Foxe, *The acts and monuments of*

John Foxe, ed. S. R. Cattley, 5 (1838); repr. (1866), 553–61 • J. Strype, *Ecclesiastical memorials*, 2/1 (1822) • PRO, exchequer accounts, E101/423/12–15; E101/424/1–3 and 12; E101/426/2–3; E314/22; E315/160–61 and 340 • lord chamberlain's department, records of special events, PRO, LC2/2 • Parr–Seymour letters, PRO, state papers domestic, Edward VI, SP 10/1 • Katherine Parr's jewels and personal possessions at death, BL, Add. MS 46348, fols. 167b–171b; 205a–209a • S. James, 'Was Kateryn Parr born at Kendal Castle?', *Abbot Hall Quarto*, 27/1 (April 1989), 11–13 • *A collection of state papers … left by William Cecill, Lord Burghley*, ed. S. Haynes, 1 (1740) • P. L. Hughes and J. F. Larkin, eds., *Tudor royal proclamations*, 1 (1964) • M. Hatch, 'The Ascham letters: an annotated translation of the Latin correspondence', PhD diss., Cornell University, 1948 • G. Scheurweghs, *Materials for the study of the Old English drama*, 16 (1939) • F. Rose-Troup, 'Two book bills of Katherine Parr', *The Library*, 3rd ser., 2 (1911) • Coll. Arms, MS RR21/C, fols. 98–9 [burial of Katherine Parr] • T. Nash, 'Observations on the time of death and place of burial of Queen Katherine Parr', *Archaeologia*, 9 (1789) [exhumation of Katherine Parr's body] • S. E. James, 'Lady Jane Grey or Queen Kateryn Parr?', *Burlington Magazine*, 138 (1996), 20–24 • A. Strickland and [E. Strickland], *Lives of the queens of England*, new edn, 3 (1851) • S. James, 'Parr occupancy at Kendal Castle', *Abbot Hall Quarto*, 30/3 (Oct 1992), 17–18 • D. Scott, *The Stricklands of Sizergh Castle* (1908) • will, PRO, PROB 11/32, sig. 19 • Dent-Brocklehurst MS, Sudeley Castle • S. E. James, 'A new source for Shakespeare's *The taming of the shrew*?', *Bulletin of the John Rylands University Library*, 81 (1999), 49–62 • S. E. James, 'Susanna Horenbout, Levina Teerlinc, and the mask of royalty', *Jaarboek Koninklÿk Museum voor Schone Kunsten, Antwerpen* (2000)

Archives BL, letters • CUL, prayer book as child, INC.4.J.1.2 (3570) • PRO, chamber records, E101/423, 424, 426; E314; E315; LC2/2 | BL, Lansdowne MSS; Add. MS 46348, fols. 167b–171b and fols. 205a–209a • Bodl. Oxf., MSS Ashmolean and Rawlinson • Hatfield House, Hertfordshire, Cecil MSS • PRO, corresp. with Sir Thomas Seymour, SP 10/1 • Sudeley Castle, Dent-Brocklehurst collection

Likenesses pen-and-ink drawing, *c.*1517–1518, BL, Add. MS 45131 fol. 190b • oils, *c.*1534, LPL • L. Horenbout, miniature, 1544, Sudeley Castle, Gloucestershire • attrib. Master John, oils, *c.*1545, NPG [*see illus.*] • oils, *c.*1545–1546 • W. Scrots?, oils, *c.*1546, NPG

Katherine [Catherine; *née* Katherine Howard] (1518x24–1542), queen of England and Ireland, fifth consort of Henry VIII, was the daughter of Lord Edmund Howard (1478x80?–1539), an impecunious younger son of Thomas *Howard, second duke of Norfolk, and his first wife, Elizabeth Tilney, and of Joyce or Jocasta Legh (*b. c.*1484, *d.* after 1527), widow of Ralph Legh of Stockwell and daughter of Sir Richard Culpeper of Aylesford, Kent.

A tainted upbringing The date of Katherine's birth is uncertain, but sources which include the few extant family records suggest that she was born between 1518 and 1524, probably nearer the latter year. Her mother, who may have had five children in her second marriage, as well as about five from her first, died when Katherine was young. Her father, who remarried twice, was in 1531 made comptroller of Calais. Consequently the youthful Katherine was brought up by her father's stepmother, Agnes Tilney [*see* Howard, Agnes, duchess of Norfolk], at Chesworth House near Horsham and at Norfolk House, Lambeth. Agnes supervised her education: instruction in reading and writing and in playing the virginals and lute. About 1536 Katherine's music teacher, Henry Manox, a member of a Sussex gentry family, was found to have taken sexual advantage of his position, although he

stopped short of intercourse. However, although Lady Norfolk struck Katherine when she found the couple embracing—presumably blaming the victim—she was herself at fault for failing to guard her granddaughter's honour as custom dictated. Manox continued to pursue Katherine after the duchess and her household moved to Lambeth.

Late in 1538 Katherine became sexually involved with Francis Dereham, a kinsman and formerly a gentleman pensioner of her uncle Thomas *Howard, third duke of Norfolk, who had recently entered the dowager's service. Katherine and her bedmate, Katherine Tilney, received Dereham and Manox's cousin Edward Waldgrave in their bedchamber several times during a period of perhaps three months. Dereham addressed Katherine as his wife; they exchanged gifts and became sexual partners, prompting the jealous Manox to co-operate in writing an anonymous letter to Lady Norfolk warning her about secret goings-on in the maids' bedchamber. When Katherine showed this message to him Dereham guessed its author, suggesting that he knew about Manox's relationship with her. Tilney and Dereham later testified that the duchess had struck her granddaughter and Dereham when she found them embracing. After Katherine was made a maid of honour to Anne of Cleves late in 1539, Dereham left for Ireland.

The death of Katherine's father in March 1539 may have prompted her uncle, who was anxious to promote the interests of his extended family, to seek this prized position for her—it was politically advantageous to have a relative employed in the queen's privy chamber. That Katherine herself became queen has traditionally been attributed to a competition for power between court factions divided by religious allegiance, a conservative group led by Norfolk and Stephen Gardiner, bishop of Winchester, against reformers led by Thomas Cromwell, the lord privy seal, and Archbishop Thomas Cranmer; the conservatives allegedly took advantage of Henry's disappointment with Anne of Cleves early in 1540 to direct his attention towards Katherine. Not all historians have accepted this scenario, however, and it has even been denied that Norfolk and Gardiner were allies. In any case, Henry does not seem to have required assistance in choosing his wife, for the dowager duchess later recalled that he had taken a fancy to Katherine the first time he saw her, perhaps on 19 December 1539, when he travelled to Greenwich to await Anne's arrival. As Katherine was already then receiving a maid of honour's stipend, she was probably in residence when he reached the palace, where he would have had ample opportunity to admire her. Besides attending the new queen's reception at Blackheath on 3 January 1540, Katherine is highly likely to have been present at Anne's other festivities, including the Londoners' welcome in February and the May day celebrations.

Queenship Exactly when Henry [*see* Henry VIII (1491–1547)] began to consider marrying Katherine is uncertain. The grant to her on 24 April 1540 of the possessions of two murderers and the purchase for her on 18 May of twenty-three sarcenet quilts are the earliest known signs of his favour. On 20 June, however, Anne complained to Carl Harst, the duke of Cleves's ambassador in England, that the king was attracted to Katherine, and in a letter to his employer Harst claimed that the affair had been going on for months. His early knowledge of Henry's affection for Katherine is noteworthy because it was not until July that Charles de Marillac, the French ambassador, made his first recorded comment on the new royal favourite, whose identity was then unknown to him. Meanwhile, on 22 June, Anne referred to Henry in kinder terms, probably because she had learned of Katherine's departure from court. Two days later, however, the privy council instructed the queen to remove to Richmond, leaving Henry free to cross the Thames in his barge to court Katherine at her grandmother's Lambeth residence. Richard Hilles, a London merchant, later claimed that the bishop of Winchester entertained Henry and Katherine at his house in Southwark.

As she awaited marriage, Katherine reportedly sent a message to Cranmer, advising 'that you should not care for your businesses, for you should be in better case than ever you were' (MacCulloch, 272)—a reassuring gesture, in the light of the archbishop's alleged opposition to the king's marriage with Anne of Cleves. It is also possible, however, that as Anne's maid of honour Katherine had learned that Cranmer sometimes communicated with the Cleves ambassador about court politics, and that she wished him to know that his association with Harst would not hinder her from favouring him. Maintaining secrecy about the Dereham liaison, she married Henry at Oatlands Palace in Surrey on 28 July, three weeks after the annulment of his union to Anne and the day on which Cromwell was executed, along with his client Walter, Lord Hungerford of Heytesbury. On 8 August Katherine was acknowledged as queen at Hampton Court, and a week later prayers were said at matins for her, the king, and Prince Edward. Many observers noted that Henry doted on Katherine, even though Marillac describes her as short and graceful in appearance rather than beautiful. In letters patent of 9 January 1541 Henry confirmed to her a jointure which included the property that had belonged to Queen Jane, as well as some of the estates of Cromwell and Hungerford. He also allotted to her more than £4600 per annum for her household, in which she found posts for friends from her past like Katherine Tilney. Whether Katherine similarly appointed people like Joan Bulmer, to whom Dereham had also been romantically attracted, because she wished either to reward them or to bribe them to silence about her sexual history, cannot now be determined.

In November 1540 Richard Jones dedicated to Katherine his *The Byrth of Mankynde*, a study of childbirth which was subsequently reprinted several times, though without the dedication. In the same month she sought from Edward Lee, archbishop of York, the advowson of the archdeaconry of York for one of her chaplains. Lee responded on 7 December that he never disposed of advowsons except on the king's orders, but undertook to keep an earlier promise to provide for another of her chaplains when an appropriate position became available. The queen also had a disagreement with her stepdaughter, Princess Mary. On 5 December, Eustace Chapuys, the imperial ambassador, told the emperor's sister that he had informed Mary that Katherine had tried to remove two of her attendants because she believed that the princess was showing less respect to her than to her two predecessors. How far Mary succeeded in mollifying Katherine is unclear—on 6 February 1541 Chapuys reported that one of the princess's maids had died of grief after being dismissed by the king.

During the Christmastide holidays of 1540–41 Henry presented Katherine with jewellery and arranged entertainments for her. On 3 January 1541 she greeted Anne of Cleves, who knelt before her in recognition of her royal status. After banqueting with them Henry departed, leaving the queen and Anne to dance together. The next day he dined with them again, and Katherine transferred to Anne a ring and two small dogs that he had given her. On 19 March he escorted Katherine down the Thames from Westminster to Greenwich on her first passage through London, sailing on decorated barges; the citizens welcomed the king and queen with peals of gunshot. At Greenwich, following the convention for royal consorts, Katherine successfully pleaded with Henry to pardon Sir Thomas Wyatt, Sir John Wallop, and John Mason, who had been arrested on charges of treasonable correspondence with Cardinal Reginald Pole. She also at various times interceded for Helen Page, accused of felony, obtained the release from prison of her kinsman John Legh, and helped to secure the position of ambassador to France for her uncle Lord William Howard.

The advent of Thomas Culpeper By March 1541, however, when Henry departed for a brief visit to Dover, leaving her at Greenwich, Katherine's life had become complicated. Francis Dereham, who had returned to England and was pestering her for office, began boasting to her councillors that she favoured him. In addition a gentleman of the king's privy chamber, the younger **Thomas Culpeper** (*c*.1514–1541), was seeking favours from her. He was distantly related to Katherine on her mother's side, for they shared a Culpeper ancestor who had lived in the reign of Edward II. Thomas was the second of the three sons of Alexander Culpeper of Bedgebury, Kent (*d*. 1541), and his second wife, Constance Harper (*née* Chamberlain); his elder brother, also named Thomas, was a client of Thomas Cromwell. Perhaps the younger Thomas served as a page to the king, as George Cavendish was later to recall in his *Metrical Visions* of the 1550s, but the first definite evidence for Culpeper as a courtier comes in 1535, when he began acting on behalf of Arthur, Viscount Lisle, the lord deputy of Calais, and his wife, Honor. In October 1537 Honor obtained a hawk for Culpeper, and about that time he successfully requested from her two bracelets of her 'colours', while in May 1538 he promised to obtain for her some of the king's cramp rings. He was a gentleman of the privy chamber no later than November 1537, and the following January a boy of his who had been condemned to death for theft at Westminster Palace was reprieved from the gallows when a royal pardon arrived just as the hangman was removing the ladder. In June 1538 he co-operated with Richard Cromwell in obtaining a hawk for the king. In the same month he was made keeper of the armoury for the king's body, and in September 1539 he was appointed to several positions at Penshurst Place, Kent, including that of keeper of the manor. Between 1537 and 1541 the king granted him, mostly ex-monastic, property in Kent, Essex, Gloucestershire, and Wiltshire.

Culpeper apparently had a reputation for lechery. Five months after Culpeper's execution Hilles alleged to Bullinger that a chamberlain of the king (unnamed) who had been hanged (except that Culpeper was beheaded) for adultery with Queen Katherine had two years earlier raped the wife of a park-keeper, and that one of the villagers who tried to arrest him was killed. The king was said to have pardoned him for these offences. In March 1541, moreover, some of his servants, together with men of Sir Thomas Paston, his colleague in the privy chamber, were imprisoned for their role in an affray at Southwark. Culpeper had attended the same court functions as Katherine in 1540, including the May day tournaments, in which he was defeated by Richard Cromwell, and on Maundy Thursday 1541 was given a velvet cap by her. For their meetings, which probably began about this time, they required the assistance of Katherine's lady of the privy chamber, Jane *Boleyn, Viscountess Rochford, the financially straitened widow of Queen Anne's brother George. On these occasions only Lady Rochford, who was probably bribed, and Katherine Tilney, who later denied knowing the visitor's identity, were allowed to enter the queen's chamber.

Problematic relationship Culpeper continued to meet the queen after 30 June when she accompanied Henry on his progress to the northern counties, where rebellion had recently been suppressed and where he hoped to meet James V of Scotland at York. Bad weather delayed their entry into Lincoln until 9 August. Katherine permitted Culpeper access to her chamber there and again at Pontefract Castle, where the court arrived on 23 August. Crucial to all interpretations of their relationship is the letter addressed to 'Master Culpeper', undated but probably dispatched during this progress, perhaps at Liddington or Lincoln, endeavouring to arrange their meetings—Katherine asks that he send a horse for her postman. In this letter (calendared as *LP Henry VIII*, 16, no. 1134) Katherine sympathizes about Culpeper's illness, hopes that he will 'be as' he had 'promised' her, expresses dismay that they are not together so that they can talk, and wishes that he could see the 'pain' she takes in writing to him—'It makes my heart die to think I cannot be always in your company'. Signing off 'Yours as long as lyffe endures', this message has for many historians served as prima facie evidence for the queen's passion for Culpeper, and by extension for an adulterous affair between them.

It is possible, however, to put a different interpretation upon Katherine's letter, that its emotional tone was fuelled less by sexual ardour than by the desperation of a young woman who was seeking to placate an aggressive, dangerous suitor, one who, moreover, as a member of the privy chamber had close contact with the king. The promise she mentioned could have concerned the Dereham affair. Culpeper, it may be suggested, had established some form of threatening control over the queen's life, and although he—as he admitted—was seeking sexual satisfaction with her, Katherine was trying to ensure his silence through a misguided attempt at appeasement. The letter makes it clear that she wished for his presence, but she never refers to him as her 'lover' or 'darling', and expresses a desire for no more than verbal conversation with him. Far from initiating relationships, Katherine's attitude to Culpeper, as to the other men in her life, the king included, can be seen as essentially passive, reactive to their demands.

Four days after her arrival at Pontefract not only did Katherine meet with Culpeper, she also appointed Dereham her secretary. She later insisted that this appointment was at her grandmother's urging, and was probably intended to silence him, too, about their former relationship. She could reasonably hope for success in this, for Dereham later confessed that on two occasions she bribed him to hold his tongue. All this while the king and queen were publicly moving triumphantly through the north, extravagantly celebrating the majesty of the monarchy. By 16 September they had reached York, where Katherine met Culpeper in Lady Rochford's chambers. At some point, she could not recall when, Katherine's growing fear of discovery caused her to send word to him through Rochford that she would not meet with him again. She did remember calling him 'little sweet fool' when he refused to accept her decision as final (*Bath MSS*, 2, 9–10). James V failed to appear at York, and by the end of September the royal party had turned south toward Hampton Court. Unbeknownst to them, as they left Hull on 6 October, trouble was brewing in London.

Disclosures and discoveries Early in October 1541 John Lassells told Archbishop Cranmer about Katherine's premarital behaviour. His informant was his sister Mary Hall, who had been employed at Horsham and Lambeth by Lord William Howard and the latter's mother, Lady Norfolk. Cranmer consulted the earl of Hertford and the chancellor, Lord Audley, who persuaded him to convey these disclosures to Henry when he arrived at Hampton Court. On 2 November, therefore, Cranmer presented a written statement of the allegations to a disbelieving king, who sent the earl of Southampton to interview Lassells and Hall, and dispatched Sir Thomas Wriothesley, the principal secretary, to question Dereham and Manox. The two men confirmed Hall's testimony, and on 6 November, Henry deserted Katherine, never to see her again.

In the days that followed Norfolk, Audley, Cranmer, and the marquess of Winchester interrogated the queen, who had been confined to her chambers, about her relations with Manox and Dereham. At first she denied the allegations, but on 8 November she confirmed them to Cranmer, who recorded her testimony and who later reported to Henry that he had found her in 'lamentation and heaviness, as I never saw no creature' (Jenkyns, 308). She claimed that the encounters with Manox had occurred when she was a 'young girl', and that Dereham had aggressively pursued her. Although Dereham had addressed her as his wife, she denied that they were married, an opinion that Cranmer doubted, since under canon law a union was valid if a couple took vows to wed in the future and then had sexual relations. Her denial might indicate an ignorance of canon law, a proud reluctance to relinquish the queenship, or even a conviction that a marriage was unlawful if one of the vowtakers had not felt free to withhold consent. Possibly Dereham had used his knowledge of Manox's previous intimacy to seduce her.

Katherine and Dereham, who was tortured, both denied that their relationship had continued after she became queen. In her statement Katherine begged the king's pardon and asked that he remember her youth, ignorance, and frailty. Following this interview Cranmer visited her again and found her almost out of her mind with fright. He had learned from her attendants that the 'vehement rage' he had witnessed earlier had continued from his departure until his return. In his letter to the king he pointed out that her emotional state had been such that instead of first emphasizing how 'grievous' were her transgressions and then holding out hopes of royal clemency, as Henry had instructed, Cranmer decided to offer the hopes of forgiveness first. This promise failed to ease her mind for very long because, as she finally admitted, 'this sudden mercy' made her offences seem even more 'heinous'. About 6 o'clock, Cranmer recalled, after he had brought her into 'quietness', she fell into another 'pang' because it was the time when Sir Thomas Heneage ordinarily brought her a message from the king (Jenkyns, 308–9).

The inquisition was far from over, however, and if Henry had been serious about the offer of clemency he was soon to change his mind. In his confession Dereham alleged that Culpeper had replaced him in the queen's affections, a surprising revelation given Katherine's extreme secrecy concerning her meetings with the latter. Interrogated about this by councillors on 11 November, Katherine denied the allegation, but subsequently admitted to the rendezvous, blaming Culpeper as the aggressor in their relationship. Next day Cranmer and the council signed her statement, and Audley informed the judges of her unchaste life. On the 13th her household was informed of her misconduct. The privy council also questioned some of her attendants, especially Lady Rochford, who speculated that Culpeper and the queen, whom she blamed equally for the meetings, had committed adultery. By contemporary standards the argument was a reasonable one. Wives who met secretly with men other than their husbands earned dishonourable reputations, for women were assumed to be more driven by lust than men.

Although Culpeper accused Katherine of initiating their meetings, he did admit to intending to do ill with her, albeit without success. As the French ambassador reported to his king, the admission was sufficient to condemn him, since the Treason Act of 1534 recognized intent to harm the king as high treason. The queen's motives remain opaque, not least because her questioners never pressed Katherine to explain why she met with Culpeper or needed to converse with him, beyond her excuse that he insisted on seeing her. Perhaps they were indeed physically attracted to one another, but it is just as probable that she was attempting to purchase his silence about her past; it seems unlikely to be mere coincidence that her association with him began in the spring of 1541 after Dereham had been boasting of her favours to himself. An admission that she had been attempting to deceive the king by concealing her relationship with Dereham would not have bolstered her defence, a consideration that could account for her silence as to why she agreed to meetings with Culpeper. Seen against a background of court life in which mutual espionage was routine, such an interpretation may offer a more plausible explanation for her conduct than the ill-advised passion and even 'imbecility' which most historians have accepted as the causes of her downfall.

The king's reaction when the charges against his queen were confirmed was one of enormous sorrow. On 12 November the privy council described his deep distress in a letter to Sir William Paget, the resident ambassador in France, telling how at first Henry was so choked up with emotion that he could not express his feelings, but had finally released 'plenty of tears' (*LP Henry VIII*, 16, no. 1334). As late as April 1542 Chapuys reported to the emperor that 'Since he heard of his late wife's conduct he has not been the same man, and Chapuys has always found him sad, pensive and sighing' (*LP Henry VIII*, 17, App. B no. 13).

Deaths and judgments On 14 November 1541 Katherine was moved to the former monastery of Syon, and eight days later was deprived of her queenship. On 1 December a special commission sitting at the Guildhall convicted Culpeper and Dereham of treason. Nine days later Culpeper was beheaded at Tyburn after requesting the bystanders to pray for him. The place was unusual for such a sentence—beheadings were normally carried out in relative privacy at Tower Hill—but the council had required that he be drawn on a hurdle to Tyburn in order to make his execution 'notable'. His body was buried in St Sepulchre Holborn. Then Dereham endured the usual penalties of treason, being hanged, disembowelled, beheaded, and quartered. The privy council next rounded up some of Katherine's other relatives and associates. The arrests were so numerous that space ran out in the Tower's prison quarters, making it necessary to house some of the accused in the royal apartments. Lady Norfolk, who had opened two of Dereham's coffers, allegedly looking for evidence for the crown, was suspected of attempting to destroy incriminating manuscripts. Under intensive questioning she admitted to having known of Katherine's unchaste past, and subsequently she, her widowed daughter Katherine, countess of Bridgewater, her son Lord William, the latter's wife, Margaret, Katherine's sister-in-law Anne, and a number of attendants were indicted for misprision of treason, on the grounds of their having concealed Katherine's sexual history from Henry. All pleaded guilty and threw themselves on the king's mercy, and all were eventually pardoned and released.

A different fate awaited Katherine, one she suffered primarily because she had possessed neither the courage nor the wisdom to confess her illicit past to Henry when he proposed marriage. Since Lady Norfolk and Katherine's other relatives who knew about her relationship with Dereham conspired to remain silent, she followed their example, probably acting upon their advice. That her step-grandmother had warned her of dire consequences if Henry ever learned of the Dereham affair could account for Katherine's great distress after admitting it to Cranmer. Fear of disclosure would also have made her vulnerable to the machinations of seasoned courtiers like Culpeper, for as she said in her confession about Dereham, 'the sorrow of my offenses was ever before my eyes' (*Bath MSS*, 2, 9).

Although they were indicted, neither Katherine nor Lady Rochford was brought to trial. Instead they were condemned under a bill of attainder introduced into the House of Lords on 21 January 1541. There seems to have been uncertainty among the judges, however, about whether the former queen's offence constituted treason, and when the bill returned for its second reading on the 28th its further passage was postponed, with Audley warning against moving too hastily, as Katherine was not merely a private lady. Subject to royal approval, the lords agreed to send a deputation from both houses to her. But on the 30th Audley announced that the council had advised against this procedure, and the bill resumed its parliamentary journey. It received the king's assent, given *in absentia* by letters patent, on 11 February. The bill proclaimed the high treason of Katherine and Lady Rochford and upheld the convictions of Culpeper, Dereham, and various Howard relatives. It stipulated that any future queen who failed to disclose her unchaste past would be guilty of treason, and that others who remained silent about such illicit behaviour would be guilty of misprision of treason. Before Henry assented to it, the earl of Southampton and duke of Suffolk met Katherine, who confirmed her testimony, asked that her relatives should not be blamed for errors, and petitioned Henry to distribute some of her clothes to her maidservants. On 10 February she travelled by barge to the Tower of London, passing under London Bridge on which were displayed the rotting heads of Culpeper and Dereham. Three days later, at 9 a.m., although so weak that she had to be assisted up to the scaffold, she mustered the strength to admit before the axe fell that her execution was just. After a cloth had been placed over Katherine's corpse, Lady Rochford was also beheaded. They were buried under the altar of St Peter ad Vincula, the chapel of the Tower, the same day.

Because Katherine had confessed to illicit communications with Manox and Dereham and to the rendezvous with Culpeper, contemporary and later reporters basically accepted her guilt. Writing in the 1550s, George Cavendish blamed her fall on her 'beawtie' and 'wanton youth', and Culpeper's misdeeds on his 'prid and viciousness' and 'Courtly lyfe' (Cavendish, ll.897, 942, 945). In 1585 the Catholic priest Nicholas Sander, writing about England's break with Rome, delivered himself of the opinion that 'As the king himself was faithful neither to God nor to his first wife, so also his wives were not faithful to him.' So it was, explained Sander, that the adulterous Katherine and 'her companions in sin', Culpeper and Francis Dereham, 'were put to death' (Sander, 153–4).

RETHA M. WARNICKE

Sources W. B. Bannerman, ed., *The visitations of Kent, taken in the years 1574 and 1592 by Robert Cooke, Clarenceux*, Harleian Society, 75 (1924) · M. St C. Byrne, ed., *The Lisle letters*, 6 vols. (1981) · *CSP Spain, 1538–43* · GEC, *Peerage*, new edn · *DNB* · *Calendar of the manuscripts of the marquis of Bath preserved at Longleat, Wiltshire*, 5 vols., HMC, 58 (1904–80), vol. 2 · R. Jones, *The birth of mankind* (1540) · J. Kaulek, ed., *Correspondance politique de MM. de Castillon et de Marillac, ambassadeurs de France en Angleterre (1537–1542)* (Paris, 1885) · A. Müller, 'Die Beziehungen Heinrichs VIII zu Anna von Cleve', DPhil diss., Tübingen University, 1907 · G. Redworth, *In defence of the church catholic: the life of Stephen Gardiner* (1990) · L. B. Smith, *A Tudor tragedy: the life and times of Catherine Howard* (1961) · *State papers published under … Henry VIII*, 11 vols. (1830–52) · R. M. Warnicke, *The marrying of Anne of Cleves: royal protocol in early modern England* (2000) · *LP Henry VIII*, vols. 14–17 · J. G. Bellamy, *The Tudor laws of treason* (1979) · S. E. Lehmberg, *The later parliaments of Henry VIII, 1536–1547* (1977) · D. MacCulloch, *Thomas Cranmer: a life* (1996) · exchequer, king's remembrancer, accounts various, PRO, E101/422/15 · G. Cavendish, *Metrical visions*, ed. A. S. G. Edwards (1980) · H. Jenkyns, *The remains of Thomas Cranmer, D.D., archbishop of Canterbury*, 4 vols. (1833) · N. Sander, *The rise and growth of the Anglican schism*, ed. D. Lewis (1877) · C. Wriothesley, *A chronicle of England during the reigns of the Tudors from AD 1485 to 1559*, ed. W. D. Hamilton, 1, CS, new ser., 11 (1875) · R. Strong, *The English Renaissance miniature*, rev. edn (1984)

Archives Longleat House, Wiltshire · PRO, state papers

Likenesses window (of the Queen of Sheba), King's Cam.

Katheryn of Berain [called Mam Cymru] (*c*.1540–1591), gentlewoman, was born at Berain, Llanefydd, Denbighshire, the only child of the soldier and courtier Tudur ap Robert Fychan (*d.* 1564) and his wife, Jane, daughter of Sir Roland de Veleville (*d.* 1535) and his wife, Agnes, daughter of William Gruffudd of Penrhyn, Llandygái, chamberlain of Gwynedd. It was firmly, if incorrectly, believed that Sir Roland was the son of Henry Tudor (later Henry VII) and a Breton lady; he was knighted at the coronation of Henry VIII in 1509, appointed constable of Beaumaris Castle, and given the king's moiety of the Tudor property in Penmynydd together with other lands in Anglesey. These he bequeathed to his wife, all of which later devolved to Katheryn.

Folk-story motifs and unfounded malicious rumours became attached to Katheryn's history; equally unfounded is the supposition that she was the ward of Elizabeth I. She is remarkable for having married four times, and her descendants became connected with so many families of north Wales that later generations called her Mam Cymru ('Mother of Wales'). The final arrangement of her child-marriage to John Salisbury (*c*.1542–1566), eldest son and heir to Sir John Salisbury, Lleweni, Denbighshire, and his wife, Dame Jane, made on 5 February 1558, proves that Katheryn had been living at Lleweni for some time; they were to go together as man and wife between then and Christmas. Their elder son, Thomas

Katheryn of Berain [Mam Cymru] (*c*.1540–1591), by Adriaen van Cronenburg, 1568

*Salisbury, was born at Lleweni in 1561 and the second son, John, in 1566. Katheryn's first husband died of a sudden illness, at Berain, in the early summer of 1566. By the arrangements made on 12 July and 14 September 1566 all her lands were secured to descend to her son Thomas and his heirs, with remainder to his brother John. Sir John Salisbury was to have the custody of her two sons.

Katheryn's second marriage, to Sir Richard Clough (*d.* 1570), a native of Denbigh and a knight of the Holy Sepulchre, factor to Sir Thomas Gresham at Antwerp, had taken place before 6 May 1567. They lived at Antwerp, then the centre of world trade; they visited Spain and Denmark; and they moved to Hamburg because of the disturbed conditions in Flanders. Two daughters were born of this marriage: Ann (1568) who married Roger Salisbury, her mother's brother-in-law, and Mary (1570) who married William of Melai, Denbighshire. Clough died of a lingering sickness, in 1570, and his widow and young daughters returned to Berain. It was then that Katheryn commissioned the poet Wiliam Cynwal to compile all the poems composed to members of her family and others connected by marriage (Oxford, Christ Church, MS 184).

The attempt made by John Vaughan of Golden Grove, Carmarthenshire, the following year to secure Katheryn as wife for his son Walter came to nothing. Before the end of January 1573 she had married Maurice Wynn (*d.* 1580) of Gwydir, Caernarvonshire. Like so many marriages, this was a dual arrangement. On 20 September 1574 a settlement was drawn up between Sir John Salisbury and his wife, Dame Jane, and Maurice Wynn of Gwydir before the marriage of Thomas Salisbury, Katheryn's son from her first marriage and heir apparent to Sir John, to Margaret, daughter of Maurice Wynn from his first marriage. A son, Edward Wynn, and a daughter, Jane Wynn, were born of Katheryn's third marriage. Maurice Wynn died on 10 August 1580, and Katheryn returned once more to Berain.

Katheryn married fourthly Edward Thelwall (*d.* 1610) of Plas-y-Ward, Denbighshire. A draft of the arrangement of a double marriage, whereby Katheryn was to marry Edward Thelwall, while Simon, Edward's son from a previous marriage, was to marry Jane Wynn, was drawn up at Berain on 5 January 1583. The family resided at Berain until Edward's father died in April 1586, when they moved to Plas-y-Ward. The following September Katheryn's eldest child, Thomas Salisbury, was executed for high treason for his involvement in the Babington plot. There were no children from the fourth marriage. Edward died on 29 July 1610, having survived his wife by nineteen years.

Undoubtedly amassing a great landed estate was a consideration in all four marriages. The Salisburys, Wynns, and Thelwalls were well-established landed gentry. Their eagerness to obtain more land becomes obvious in all the marriage settlements, particularly so in the dual arrangements where detailed alternative provisions were made to ensure the union of the two families in the case of death on either side before the marriage was solemnized. Clough came of a mercer family, and was immensely rich, but his great ambition was to own a landed estate; Sir John Salisbury had 'conveyed or morgaged' some of his lands to him. The Berain estate consisted of some 3000 acres with about a further 1000 acres in Anglesey; rentals from the Berain estate totalled £300 per annum. Katheryn was a much desired heiress.

Katheryn of Berain died at Plas-y-Ward on 27 August 1591 and was buried on 1 September at Llanefydd.

ENID ROBERTS

Sources J. Ballinger, 'Katheryn of Berain', *Y Cymmrodor*, 40 (1929), 1–42 · E. Roberts, 'Priodasau Catrin O Ferain', *Transactions of the Denbighshire Historical Society*, 20 (1971), 31–56 · E. Roberts, 'Siôn Salsbri, Lleweni', *Transactions of the Denbighshire Historical Society*, 19 (1970), 66–102 · [J. Ballinger], ed., *Calendar of Wynn (of Gwydir) papers, 1515–1690, in the National Library of Wales* (1926) · B. G. Charles, ed., *A schedule of the Lleweni collection* (1971) · J. W. Burgon, *The life and times of Sir Thomas Gresham*, 1 (1839), 235; 2 (1839), 382 · R. G. Jones, 'Sir Richard Clough of Denbigh', *Transactions of the Denbighshire Historical Society*, 19 (1970), 24–65; 20 (1971), 57–101 · Christ Church Oxf., MS 184 [copy in NL Wales, Aberystwyth, MSS 6495–6496] · *Report on manuscripts in the Welsh language*, 2 vols. in 7, HMC, 48 (1898–1910), vol. 2, pp. 419–782 · Chester City Archives, Combermere Abbey MSS, CR 72/82/23/2 A

Likenesses A. van Cronenburg, oils on panel, 1568, NMG Wales [*see illus.*]

Wealth at death Berain estate almost 3000 acres; *c.*1000 acres in Anglesey; Lleweni 658 acres (1566); £300 p.a. rentals from Berain: NL Wales, 1600E, 373–9 (*c.*1560)

Katial, Chuni Lal (1898–1978), physician and politician, was born in the Punjab, India. He graduated MBBS in 1922 from Lahore University, with honours in medicine and surgery, then joined the Indian Medical Service (IMS) and for five years, as a captain in the service attached to the Royal Air Force, served in Baghdad. In 1927 he moved to Britain. In 1928 he obtained both his diploma in tropical medicine from Liverpool University and his licentiate in medicine from the University of Dublin, before settling in London. He was elected a fellow of the Royal Society of Tropical Medicine.

Thin and 'rather distinguished-looking, with a head that was narrow in elevation' (Allan, 331), Katial was deeply influenced by the Gandhian ideal of service for the benefit of humanity without personal reward. He established his first medical practice in 1929 in the East End of London, before moving to Finsbury in the 1930s. He was so respected by his working-class patients that it was said that 'the difference between East and West did not exist' at his Spencer Street surgery (News Chronicle, 19 June 1948). He also had a Harley Street practice for some years. A Hindu, he was a trustee and director of the Hindu Association of Europe, founded in 1935. He was also a member of Krishna Menon's India League.

In 1934 Katial entered on a public career when elected as a Labour member of Finsbury borough council, for St John's ward: he was alderman from 1938 to 1946, and deputy mayor in 1936 and 1938. He was elected mayor of Finsbury for 1938–9, the first Indian to reach that position. In 1946 he was elected to the London county council, as one of the two borough representatives. His most significant work as councillor, however, was as chairman of the public health committee, when he became instrumental in creating a health centre that was ahead of its time.

Medical facilities in Finsbury were haphazard and scattered around the borough in a variety of dispensaries, voluntary hospitals, private clinics, and clubs. In 1931 the Labour council under Harold Riley drew up the Finsbury plan, a programme for health and housing, with a new health centre at its heart. By 1933 the plan had been abandoned, but in 1935 Katial revived the plan for a health centre and became its driving force, securing the overwhelming support of the council. He commissioned Berthold Lubetkin of the Tecton group as architect, so impressed had he been with Tecton's design of the TB clinic unveiled at the British Medical Association in 1932, and it was Katial's vision which influenced the provision of services in the new health centre. Opened in 1938, the Finsbury health centre in Pine Street introduced a new concept in medicine: a centralized health service. Apart from doctors' surgeries, there was a TB clinic, a foot clinic, a dental surgery, a women's clinic, and a solarium, as well as disinfectant rooms and a mortuary. Administrative offices, case records, and statistics were all housed in the same building. In the words of Katial, the Finsbury health centre marked 'the dawn of a new era' ('Opening of the Finsbury health centre'). It anticipated the 1948 National Health Service reforms by ten years, and became 'almost universally famous' at the time (Islington Gazette, 11 June 1948).

During the Second World War Katial's public service work on Finsbury council increased. He was chairman of the air raid precautions medical service and food control committee, a civil defence first aid medical officer, a lecturer on first aid for the St John Ambulance Brigade, and a member of the City division medical emergency committee. He was said to be 'completely fearless' in the blitz and 'never had his clothes off for a week' (Daily Telegraph, 31 Oct 1975). He was also on the executive committee of the British Medical Association. In 1948, in recognition of his services to public health, housing, and social welfare, Katial was made a freeman of the borough of Finsbury—only the third person to receive the honour (Islington Gazette, 11 June 1948).

In 1948 Katial went back to India to become director-general of the Employees' State Insurance Corporation of India, a position he held until 1953. In the 1970s he returned to live in London. In his last years he lived in a flat in Kenilworth Court, Lower Richmond Road, Putney. He died of cancer of the prostate at Putney Hospital on 14 November 1978. It is thought that he was unmarried.

ROZINA VISRAM

Sources J. Allan, Berthold Lubetkin: architecture and the tradition of progress (1992) • R. Visram, Asians in Britain: four hundred years of history (2002) • medical directories, 1929–48 • Holborn Guardian (4 Nov 1938) • Islington Gazette (25 Oct 1938) • Islington Gazette (11 Nov 1938) • Islington Gazette (11 June 1948) • News Chronicle (19 June 1948) • Daily Telegraph (31 Oct 1975) • 'Opening of the Finsbury health centre by Rt Hon Lord Horder, 21/10/1938', Finsbury archives • council minutes, Finsbury archives • d. cert.
Likenesses group portrait, photograph (1934 Finsbury council members), Finsbury archives; repro. in R. Visram, The history of the Asian community in Britain (1995), 32 • photograph, repro. in Finsbury Citizen (1 Nov 1937) • portrait (as mayor), Finsbury archives
Wealth at death £96,991: probate, 27 Sept 1979, CGPLA Eng. & Wales

Katterfelto, Gustavus (d. 1799), itinerant popular lecturer, claimed to have been born in Prussia of a military family (Norfolk Chronicle) and to have travelled widely in Europe. He probably lived continuously in England from at least 1777, when he lectured in Gloucester, and may have toured the country before arriving in London in December 1780. He performed first at Cox's former museum in Spring Gardens, and then successively at rooms in 22 and 24 Piccadilly. Most often styling himself Doctor Katterfelto, he initially leapt to fame by treating patients during the influenza epidemic of 1782. For the next couple of years he gave numerous didactic performances to metropolitan audiences, and became a household name. Charging from 1s. to 3s. a seat, he gave different three-hour shows each night of the week.

In June 1784 Katterfelto allegedly delighted George III and other members of the royal family, but cartoons and advertisements suggest that his appeal had already plummeted. By the end of 1783 he was advertising his equipment for sale, and he left London less than a year later. In November 1784 he was in Norwich, where he gave lectures until January, before leaving for Cambridge. Although a caricature shows him clutching bags of gold, he spent most of the rest of his life striving to support his wife and children as an itinerant provincial entertainer, charging between 6d. and 2s. for a ticket. Announcing his arrival

Gustavus Katterfelto (d. 1799), by unknown engraver, pubd 1783

advertisements headed 'Wonders! Wonders! Wonders!'. Thus William Cowper described him in *The Task* as:

> Katterfelto, with his hair on end
> At his own wonders, wondering for his bread,

and John Wolcot mentioned him several times in his Peter Pindar poems. Katterfelto was probably the model for William Blake's Inflammable Gass the Windfinder in his satire 'An Island on the Moon' (the hydrogen in balloons was called inflammable air). Although in contemporary cartoons Katterfelto was derided as a quack, because of his great notoriety he was also utilized for mocking prominent political figures. In 1875 George Whyte-Melville published a romanticized novel of Jacobite intrigue featuring Katterfelto as a villainous doctor.   PATRICIA FARA

Sources BL, Sophia Banks' collection of broadsides, L.R.301.h.3, fols. 192–206 · DNB · A. S. Brown, 'Gustavus Katterfelto: mason and magician', *Ars Quatuor Coronatorum*, 69 (1956), 136–8 · J. Money, *Experience and identity: Birmingham and the west midlands, 1760–1800* (1977), 140–41 · advertisements, *Norfolk Chronicle* (4 Dec 1784–15 Jan 1785) · G. J. Whyte-Melville, *Katterfelto: a story of Exmoor* (1875)
Archives BL, Sophia Banks's collection of broadsides, L.R.301.h.3, fols. 192–206
Likenesses woodcut, BM, NPG; repro. in *European Magazine and London Review*, 3 (1783), 406 [*see illus.*]

Katz, Arthur (1908–1999), toy manufacturer, was born on 21 March 1908 in Johannesburg, Transvaal, the son of Hermann Katz (1876–1917) and his wife, Regine, *née* Ullmann (1885–1977). Both parents were of Jewish descent and had been born in Nuremberg, Germany. Two years after his father's death Katz was taken to Germany by his mother to complete his schooling. Following a commercial apprenticeship with a Nuremberg exporter, he worked in a major chain store, becoming one of its youngest ever managers, before joining Tipp & Co., a leading firm of lithographed pressed-metal toy manufacturers owned by his cousin Philip Ullmann. Although the German toy industry had by then largely recovered from the post-war difficulties associated with currency instability, raw-material shortages, and increased foreign competition, it was plunged back into crisis by the Wall Street crash of 1929. Hitler's rise to power presented a different but no less dangerous threat to an industry in which Jewish entrepreneurs were prominent. In 1933 Ullmann joined the growing number of German businessmen relocating in Britain; Katz—who on 3 June 1933 married Erna Baer (1907–1989), the daughter of Solomon Baer of Münster—followed shortly afterwards.

Although the world slump also caused casualties among British toy makers, rising real incomes and the protection provided by the Import Duties Act of 1932 helped to attract some 1200 new businesses into the industry in the course of the 1930s. Among them was Mettoy, established by Ullmann in Northampton, initially to design and market lithographed tin-plate toys, although the firm soon began to manufacture in its own right. Katz was employed as company secretary. With the coming of war in 1939 the metal pressing skills of Mettoy's 600 strong workforce were applied to munitions production, work which became so demanding that new premises had to be found, near Swansea.

with long series of advertisements in local papers, Katterfelto travelled all over England. He lectured successfully at Birmingham in 1792, but was jailed in at least two other towns as a vagrant and an impostor. His performances were acclaimed many times at Whitby, and he probably eventually settled in Bedale, also in Yorkshire, where he died on 25 November 1799. His widow subsequently married John Carter, a Whitby publican.

Katterfelto compiled a great variety of flamboyant newspaper advertisements and wall posters, many of them incorporating long poems. Their two major themes were his fame as an international freemason with secret knowledge of occult mysteries and his expertise as a natural philosopher. Correspondingly, his two renowned props were his necromantic black cat and his solar microscope, a device which projected magnified displays onto a white surface for public viewing. By revealing thousands of 'insects' writhing in a drop of water, he persuaded Londoners terrified of catching influenza to purchase his patent medicine at 5s. a bottle. In addition, his diverse equipment included a lecturer's standard natural philosophical apparatus—some of it quite expensive—such as compasses and globes, an orrery, a telescope, an air pump, and an electrical machine. To attract his declining audiences he proclaimed ever more exotic devices, including a perpetual-motion machine, a magnetic copying apparatus, and sympathetical clocks. One celebrated trick entailed lifting his daughter to the ceiling by using a large magnet for attracting a steel helmet on her head. Katterfelto also owned a large hydrogen balloon, and charged people to watch him ascending with his two black servants for making astronomical observations.

Like James Graham, with whom he was often bracketed, Katterfelto was marginalized as a quack, and mocked for his colourful puffery. By ingeniously combining the fascination of mystery with the vogue for rational self-improvement, he competed against other travelling performers and conjurors, and also against rival lecturers on natural philosophy who similarly relied on spectacle to attract their audiences. Satirists rendered Katterfelto the epitome of charlatanry, referring particularly to his

Arthur Katz (1908–1999), by unknown photographer

At the end of the war Katz, by now managing director, was appointed a colonel and was commissioned to assess the state of the German toy industry. Concluding that early resumption of German production was unlikely, and well aware of the British government's drive to raise aggregate export levels, he set about directing Mettoy's activities towards overseas markets. Yet he was shrewd enough to understand that toy making was hardly a national priority, even though government controls did ensure that scarce tin plate went only to those firms producing primarily for export. In 1949, therefore, he opened another plant to develop new techniques of plastic injection moulding, brought from the United States by Philip Ullmann's son. Other successful diversifications included the establishment of a plant to manufacture Wembley Playballs using rotational plastic moulding, and the founding of Playcraft Ltd to give Mettoy an outlet into the market for pre-school toys.

However, it was Katz's encouragement of another product which propelled Mettoy into the forefront of the British toy industry. Ever since the 1930s Meccano had been producing its famous line of Dinky die-cast model vehicles. Katz oversaw Mettoy's move into this market, with model vehicles incorporating plastic windows, treaded tyres, and other details lacking in the Dinky product. This greatly enhanced the play value of the toys, an important consideration for a man who openly admitted his love of working in an industry catering for children. Under the brand name Corgi, these products were phenomenally successful both at home and abroad following their launch in 1956. The company's model of the gadget-packed Aston Martin featured in the *James Bond* films sold almost 4 million units between 1965 and 1968. When Mettoy offered a quarter of its ordinary shares on the stock market in 1963, they were oversubscribed ninety-one times, and *Management Today* ranked the company as the second most profitable in Britain.

Mettoy's success made Katz a major figure in the industry. As chairman (1955–7) and then president (1971–6) of the British Toy Manufacturers' Association he represented toy makers to government, played a leading role in wage negotiation, and sought to persuade a generally conservative industry of the advantages of European co-operation. He served on the Welsh Design Council, the Welsh committee of the Confederation of British Industry, and the Institute of Directors. He was appointed OBE in 1961 and CBE three years before he finally retired in 1976. By this time, Mettoy had won three queen's export awards, employed some 3500 people, and had an annual turnover of almost £20 million.

Katz was succeeded as managing director in 1972 by Bernard Hanson and later by his son Peter, one of the two children from his first marriage. But the firm did not long survive his own formal retirement from the board. In 1983 it was declared bankrupt, the last of five major British toy manufacturers swept away in the space of a few years, victims in the main of the much tougher export conditions in which British firms were operating from the late 1970s.

Katz's first marriage ended in divorce, and on 13 May 1946 he married Margaret Bowers (1908–1973). Following her death he married, thirdly, on 22 December 1976, (Ursula) Agnes Lipmann (b. 1920), the daughter of Carl Lipmann. Honoured in 1996 as one of the first two recipients of a lifetime achievement award from the British Toy and Hobby Association, his final years were clouded by the onset of Alzheimer's disease. He died on 25 June 1999 at the Royal Free Hospital, Camden, of bronchopneumonia, survived by his third wife, Agnes, and the son and daughter of his first marriage.   KENNETH D. BROWN

Sources Toy Trader · Toys International · K. D. Brown, *The British toy business: a history since 1700* (1996) · *The Times* (27 July 1999) · *The Independent* (27 July 1999) · private information (2004) [Peter H. Katz, son] · d. cert.
Likenesses photograph, News International Syndication, London [*see illus.*] · photograph, repro. in *The Independent*
Wealth at death £258,296—gross; £255,763—net: probate, 12 Jan 2000, *CGPLA Eng. & Wales*

Kauffman, (Anna Maria) Angelica Catharina (1741–1807), history and portrait painter, was born on 30 October 1741 in Chur, Graubünden, Switzerland, the only child of Johann Joseph Kauffmann (1707–1782), an Austrian painter from the region of Bregenz, and his second wife, Cleofea Luz, or Lucin (1717–1757), a native of Chur. She was baptized in the Roman Catholic faith on 6 November 1741 as Anna Maria Angelica Catharina Kauffmann. In her early years she signed her name Maria Angelica Kauffmann, though later she shortened it to Angelica Kauffman.

Training in Italy In 1742 Johann Joseph moved his family to Italy, first to Morbegno in Lombardy and ten years later to Como. As a girl Angelica demonstrated precocious talent for drawing and painting, so her father instructed her in these arts. She made rapid progress, and at the age of eleven produced a pastel portrait of the bishop of Como. In 1754 they travelled to Milan where she portrayed the archbishop, the duke and duchess of Modena, and Count

(Anna Maria) Angelica Catharina Kauffman (1741–1807), self-portrait, *c.*1770–75

Firmian, among others. After her mother's death in 1757, Kauffman returned with her father to Schwarzenberg, his native village, where the bishop of Constance commissioned Johann Joseph to paint frescoes in the parish church. Angelica assisted him and produced her first frescoes, half-length figures of thirteen apostles copied from a set of engravings after Giambattista Piazzetta. Early descriptions of Kauffman's youth note her musical talent and fine singing voice. In her thirteenth year she portrayed herself (1753; Tiroler Landesmuseum Ferdinandeum, Innsbruck) holding a sheet of music. Kauffman's first biographer, her brother-in-law Giuseppe Carlo Zucchi, recorded a memorable anecdote regarding her artistic abilities, a story repeated by De Rossi and all subsequent biographers. According to Zucchi's account, Kauffman was equally talented in music and art, yet she chose to forgo a chance of a promising musical career to pursue the profession of painting. She made this difficult choice, against the wishes of her friends, with the help of a priest who advised her that a career in painting would be more rewarding and less fleeting than music. This tale of Kauffman's wise judgement—a rather fanciful version based on truth—has become part of her almost legendary place in history as an unusually successful woman artist. Kauffman herself helped to create this image when she commemorated her youthful choice many years later in 1791—about the time Zucchi was preparing his biography—in a large allegorical self-portrait known in two versions (1791; Pushkin Museum, Moscow; 1794; Nostell Priory, Yorkshire). She portrayed herself hesitating between female personifications of Music, who implores her to stay, and Painting, who points prophetically up the

rocky path to the Temple of Glory. Having made this choice, in 1759 Kauffman and her father returned to Italy so she could further develop her artistic skills, especially in perspective and proportion. They visited royal collections and other important galleries where Kauffman was granted permission to study and copy paintings in Milan, Modena, Venice, Piacenza, Parma, Bologna, Florence, Rome, and Naples. In 1762 she met the American painter Benjamin West in Florence, and the following year in Rome she became acquainted with the German antiquarian Johann Joachim Winckelmann, whose portrait she painted (1764; Kunsthaus, Zürich). She also befriended the British neo-classical painters Gavin Hamilton and Nathaniel Dance. These contacts influenced her aspiration to create history paintings of classical, mythological, and historical subjects, a rare ambition for a female artist, since very few women could receive training in this most demanding and highly regarded branch of the art. Among her early history paintings in Rome were *Bacchus Finding the Abandoned Ariadne* (1763; Rathaus, Bregenz) and *Penelope at her Loom* (1764; Hove Museum and Art Gallery, Sussex). Kauffman produced her earliest etchings, and she painted portraits in Naples of several English travellers. These included the actor *David Garrick* (1764; exh. Society of Artists, 1765; Burghley House, Northamptonshire) and *Brownlow Cecil, Ninth Earl of Exeter* (1764), who became an important patron. Her sketchbook (MS *c.*1762–5; V&A) contains portrait drawings, figure studies, and sketches of antique statuary. She learned anatomy by studying classical statues and nude drawings by other artists, for women were prohibited from the common practice of working directly from living models. As a female prodigy who was fluent in English and French as well as Italian and German, Kauffman attracted much attention. She was honoured with memberships in the Accademia del Disegno in Florence (1762), the Accademia Clementina in Bologna (1762), the Accademia di San Luca in Rome (1765), and later the Accademia delle Belle Arti in Venice (1781).

England and the Royal Academy of Arts, 1766–1781 Kauffman was especially popular with the English residents and grand tourists in Italy, so she readily accepted the invitation of Lady Wentworth to pursue her career in England. With plans for her father to follow later, the two women travelled via Paris to London, arriving on 22 June 1766. Within a week Kauffman visited Joshua Reynolds in his studio, and the two artists became friends. They made portraits of one another, and Reynolds, an advocate for history painting in England, became instrumental in promoting her career. He encouraged his boyhood friend John Parker, first Lord Boringdon, whom Kauffman had already painted in Naples, to purchase more of her pictures, most notably her portrait of Reynolds (1767) and several classical history paintings which include *The Interview of Hector and Andromache* (exh. RA, 1769) and *Venus Showing Aeneas and Achates the Way to Carthage* (exh. RA, 1769). These pictures and others are still at Saltram House, Devon, now in the collection of the National Trust.

Kauffman developed a reputation as a fashionable painter and was in great demand for portraits and subject pictures. She made a life-size portrait of the king's sister, *The Duchess of Brunswick* (1767, Royal Collection), whose mother, the dowager princess of Wales, visited Kauffman's studio. After lodging in London with a surgeon in Suffolk Street, Charing Cross, Kauffman took a house in Golden Square. Her father joined her in the summer of 1767 accompanied by his sister's daughter, Rosa Florini, who came to live with them until she married the architect Joseph Bonomi ARA, in 1775. In 1768 Kauffman was one of thirty-six founding members of the Royal Academy of Arts, one of only two women (the other was Mary Moser). From 1769 to 1782 she sent a variety of pictures each year to the annual Royal Academy exhibitions and after she left England more sporadically until 1797. Her pictures ranged from portraits and allegories to mythology, history, and literary subjects from a variety of authors including Homer, Tasso, Spenser, Shakespeare, Metastasio, Alexander Pope, and Laurence Sterne. She tended to favour sentimental themes, but she was among the first in London to exhibit classical subjects, such as *Cleopatra Adorning the Tomb of Mark Anthony* (exh. RA, 1770; Burghley House), and the first artist to send British history subjects to the Royal Academy exhibitions. Examples of these are *Vortigern, King of Britain Enamoured of Rowena at the Banquet of Hengist* (exh. RA, 1770; Saltram House, Devon), *Tender Eleanora Sucking the Venom out of the Wound of Edward I* (exh. RA, 1776; priv. coll.), and *Lady Elizabeth Grey Imploring of Edward IV, the Restitution of her Deceased Husband's Lands* (exh. RA, 1776).

In 1773 Kauffman was one of five artists selected to paint the interior of St Paul's Cathedral in London, a project that was never carried out, and in 1774 she was in the group invited to decorate the Great Room of the Society of Arts, another abandoned scheme. In 1775 the Irish painter Nathaniel Hone tried to exhibit a satirical painting called *The Conjuror* (1775; National Gallery of Ireland, Dublin), intended to mock Reynolds. It offended Kauffman because of a nude female figure in the background thought to represent her. She complained to the academy, and as a result the picture was removed and Hone painted over the offending figure. Kauffman made four oval ceiling paintings for the council chamber of the academy's new premises at Somerset House in 1780. As part of an extensive didactic programme, they represent the four parts of painting as allegorical figures: *Invention, Composition, Drawing (Design)*, and *Colouring* (1779–80; Royal Academy, London).

Portraiture, prints, and decorative arts Portraits continued to provide a large part of Kauffman's income. In 1771 George, first Marquess Townshend, the lord lieutenant of Ireland, invited Kauffman to visit Dublin to paint his family (1771–2; priv. coll.). She remained in Ireland for six months and received many more commissions, including the portrait of *Henry Loftus, the Earl of Ely, with his Wife and Two Nieces* (1771; National Gallery of Ireland, Dublin). In the mid-1770s Kauffman painted several informal portraits of ladies dressed in pseudo-Turkish attire, such as *Mary, Third*

Duchess of Richmond (exh. RA, 1775; Goodwood House, Sussex). Kauffman also collaborated with printmakers, especially Francesco Bartolozzi, William Wynne Ryland, Thomas Burke, and John Boydell, in the production of stipple engravings and mezzotints after her paintings. She was directly involved in the production and marketing of her prints, and was one of the few contemporary artists whose works were used to make 'mechanical paintings'—a relatively inexpensive process of colour reproduction invented in the 1770s that was especially suited for incorporation into decorative schemes. Matthew Boulton, an inventor and manufacturer, reproduced several of Kauffman's classical pictures through this process, in which an aquatint printed on coated paper was transferred onto canvas and then touched up by hand to create the appearance of an original painting. Kauffman's style has been much associated with the decorative arts, in particular the neo-classical interior designs of Robert Adam. However, though many eighteenth-century walls, ceilings, porcelains, and furniture are ornamented with Kauffman's compositions, the vast majority were actually copied or reproduced by others after her pictures or simply based on her style. Kauffman may have provided some sketches for Adam, but she was not directly responsible for the many decorative works attributed to her. Nevertheless, the suitability of her neo-classical figures for such decoration ensured her continuing popularity, and her graceful style has made a permanent mark on the decorative arts, especially in England and Austria.

Marriage Kauffman worked steadily and profitably, but she also enjoyed an active social life. Her alleged flirtations and relationships have been the subject of much speculation. She was an attractive though not beautiful woman, described as modest, intelligent, and charming. Contemporary references note her engagement to marry Nathaniel Dance in Rome in 1765. Gossip suggested she jilted Dance after she arrived in England in hope of marrying the more prominent artist Joshua Reynolds, but there is scant evidence to support this rumour. Her only documented relationship was a brief, disastrous marriage in 1767 to an impostor and bigamist, the so-called Count Frederick de Horn (or von Horn). This unfortunate and rather mysterious episode in her life was related at length in De Rossi's biography and has been corroborated by more recently discovered documents. Kauffman was deceived by this handsome man who claimed to be a wealthy Swedish nobleman. He persuaded her to marry him in secret without her father's consent, but then the scoundrel confronted her father with demands for money and threats of violence. Finally he was exposed as a fraud, arrested, signed a separation agreement (10 February 1768), and was released after promising to leave England forever. The parish register of St James's Church, Piccadilly, London, confirms a marriage on 20 November 1767 between Angelica Kauffman and Frederick de Horn, and according to Helbok there is evidence of a prior clandestine Roman Catholic ceremony in the San Jacopo Chapel of the Austrian embassy in London on 13 February 1767. It is noteworthy that despite the scandal and her personal distress, Kauffman never stopped working, her patrons and friends remained loyal, and her career prospered. She stayed single until 14 July 1781 when, after receiving a papal annulment (1778) and news of de Horn's death (1780), she married the Venetian painter Antonio Pietro *Zucchi (1726–1795), who had long resided in England. A contract ensured Kauffman's continued control of her considerable wealth—over £14,000 by the time she left England—and she retained her own name.

Rome, 1782–1807 Five days after the marriage the couple and her father, whose health was failing, departed from England for the continent. They visited Schwarzenberg, Austria, and spent the winter in Venice, where her father died in January 1782. Kauffman and Zucchi settled in Rome in a large house on the via Sistina near the church of Santa Trinità dei Monti. Except for several sojourns in Naples, where she produced paintings for King Ferdinand I and Queen Carolina and taught the princesses to draw, Kauffman lived in Rome for the remainder of her life as a celebrated and well respected member of the international arts community. Zucchi took care of business matters and kept a list of her commissions ('Memorie delle pitture', 1782–95, MS, London, RA) and a record of their accounts (BL, MS Egerton 2169). After his death on 26 December 1795 her cousin Johann Kauffmann came to live with her and run the household. She continued to send pictures to England, especially for George Bowles, an enthusiastic patron who eventually owned over fifty of her works, which included *Pliny the Younger, with his Mother at the Eruption of Vesuvius* (exh. RA, 1786; Princeton Art Museum, New Jersey), *Cornelia, Mother of the Gracchi, Pointing to her Children as her Treasures* (exh. RA, 1786; Virginia Museum, Richmond), and *Self-Portrait in the Character of Design Embraced by Poetry* (1782; Iveagh Bequest, Kenwood House, London). She presented another self-portrait to the prestigious Medici collection of artists' portraits (1787; Uffizi Gallery, Florence). Kauffman's studio was a popular stop for fashionable visitors on the grand tour. Her clients and guests who came to enjoy conversation and music included artists, writers, aristocrats, and dealers from England, Germany, Austria, Russia, Sweden, and Poland. She developed friendships with international luminaries such as Johann Wolfgang von Goethe, with whom she corresponded after his departure from Italy in 1788, Antonio Canova, and Sir William Hamilton. Kauffman's long list of noble patrons included Catherine of Russia, Joseph II of Austria, Ludwig I of Bavaria, Prince Poniatowski, and King Stanislaus of Poland. Until the end of her life she painted both portraits and history paintings, including some religious subjects such as *Christ and the Woman of Samaria* (1796; Bayerische Staatsgemäldesammlungen, Munich) and *The Madonna Crowned by the Holy Trinity* for the high altar of the church in Schwarzenberg (1802). During the French invasion of Rome in 1798 she never stopped working, although her health and fortune suffered. In 1802 Kauffman visited Florence, Milan, Como, and Venice for the last time. She died in Rome after an illness on 5 November 1807. Her elaborate funeral, arranged by Canova, was attended by members of the Accademia di San Luca and other foreign academies. She was buried on 7 November in the church of Sant' Andrea delle Fratte, Rome, beside her husband. Joseph Bonomi received a letter from Rome (7 November 1807) that described Kauffman's final illness, death, and the funeral. On 23 December 1807 Benjamin West read Bonomi's translation of the letter to the general assembly of the Royal Academy, and a copy of this letter was entered into the academy records. A manuscript inventory of her possessions (25 January 1808; Getty Research Institute, Santa Monica) documents her wealth and fine taste, and her will (17 June 1803) is a testament to both her industriousness and her generosity. Kauffman's surviving paintings and prints confirm her reputation as one of the most accomplished, productive, resourceful, and influential women in the eighteenth century.   WENDY WASSYNG ROWORTH

Sources G. G. De Rossi, *Vita di Angelica Kauffmann, pittrice* (Florence, 1810) · G. C. Zucchi, 'Memorie istoriche di Maria Angelica Kauffman Zucchi riguardanti l'arte della pittura da lei professata', 1788, Vorarlberger Landesmuseum, Bregenz, inv. n. A. G. 10 [transcription, German translation, and commentary by H. Swozilek, ed., *Memorie istoriche di Maria Angelica Kauffmann Zucchi riguardanti l'arte della pittura da lei professata scritte da G. C. Z. [Giuseppe Carlo Zucchi], Venezia MDCCLXXXVIII, Schriften des Vorarlberger Landesmuseums, Reihe B, Kunstgeschichte und Denkmalpflege, 2, im Eigenverlage des Vorarlberger Landesmuseums, Bregenz* (1999)] · W. W. Roworth, ed., *Angelica Kauffman: a continental artist in Georgian England* (1992) · C. Helbok, *Miss Angel: Angelika Kauffmann, eine Biographie* (1968) · V. Manners and G. C. Williamson, *Angelica Kauffman, RA: her life and her works* (1924) · B. Baumgärtel, ed., *Angelika Kauffmann* (Ostfildern-Ruit, 1998) [exhibition catalogue, Kunstmuseum, Düsseldorf, 15 Nov 1998 – 24 Jan 1999, Haus der Kunst, Munich, 5 Feb – 18 Apr 1999, and Bundner Kunstmuseum, Chur, 8 May – 11 July 1999] · O. Sandner, ed., *Angelica Kauffman e Roma* (Rome, 1998) [exhibition catalogue, Accademia Nazionale di San Luca, Istituto Nazionale per la Grafica, Rome, 11 Sept – 7 Nov 1998] · D. Alexander, 'Kauffman and the print market in eighteenth-century England', *Angelica Kauffman: a continental artist in Georgian England*, ed. W. W. Roworth (1992), 141–89 [incl. list of prints] · C. Knight, ed., *La 'Memoria delle piture' di Angelica Kauffman* ([Rome], 1998) [orig. text of memorandum of paintings in the RA] · W. W. Roworth, 'Anatomy is destiny: regarding the body in the art of Angelica Kauffman', *Femininity and masculinity in eighteenth-century art and culture*, ed. G. Perry and M. Rossington (1994), 41–62 · P. Walch, 'An early neoclassical sketchbook by Angelica Kauffman', *Burlington Magazine*, 119 (1977), 98–111 · P. Leisching, 'Von böser und von guter Ehe. Die beiden Heiraten der Angelika Kauffmann', *Jahrbuch Vorarlberger Landesmuseumsverein* (1991), 373–8 · W. S. Sparrow, 'Angelica Kauffman's amazing marriage', *The Connoisseur*, 92 (1933), 242–5 · M. Butlin, 'An eighteenth-century art scandal: Nathaniel Hone's "The conjuror"', *The Connoisseur*, 174 (1970), 1–9 · [C. Helbok], ed., *Angelika Kauffmann und ihre Zeit: Graphik und Zeichnungen von 1760–1810* (Düsseldorf, 1979) [exhibition catalogue, Düsseldorf, 1–22 Sept 1979] · F. Romagnoli, MSS relating to the estate of Angelica Kauffmann, 25 Jan 1808, Rome, Getty Research Institute, Santa Monica, special collections 90-A136M · W. T. Whitley, *Artists and their friends in England, 1700–1799*, 2 vols. (1928) · M. F. Adams and M. Mauchline, 'Ut pictura poesis: Angelica Kauffman's literary sources', *Apollo*, 132 (1992), 345–9 · A. Rosenthal, *Angelika Kauffmann, Bildnismalerei im 18 Jahrhundert* (1996)

Archives BL, account of expenses, Eg. MS 2169 · RA, 'Memorie delle pitture', description of works and patrons · V&A, sketchbook | Getty Research Institute, Santa Monica, Romagnoli MSS, special collections 90-A136M · RA, Zucchi MS · Vorarlberger Landesmuseum, Bregenz, Zucchi MS, inv. n. A. G. 10

Likenesses A. Kauffman, three self-portraits, oils, 1753–81, Tiroler Landesmuseum Ferdinandeum, Innsbruck · A. Kauffman, three self-portraits, oils, c.1758–1787, Uffizi Gallery, Florence · N. Dance, oils, 1764, Burghley House collection, Stamford, Northamptonshire · J. Reynolds, oils, 1766–77, Althorp, Northamptonshire · A. Kauffman, self-portrait, oils, c.1770–1775, NPG [*see illus.*] · A. Kauffman, group portrait, oils, 1771, NG Ire. · R. Samuel, group portrait, oils, 1779 (*The nine living muses of Great Britain*), NPG · F. Bartolozzi, stipple, 1780 (after J. Reynolds), repro. in Roworth, ed., *Angelica Kauffman* · A. Kauffman, self-portrait, c.1780, Bünder Kunsthaus, Chur, Switzerland · A. Kauffman, self-portrait, oils, c.1780–1785, The Hermitage, Leningrad · A. Kauffman, self-portrait, oils, 1782, Iveagh Bequest, Kenwood House, London · A. Kauffman, self-portrait, 1784, Bayerische Staatsgemäldesammlungen, Munich · A. Kauffman, self-portrait, oils, 1794, Nostell Priory, Yorkshire · C. Hewetson, bust, 1795–6, parish church, Schwarzenberg, Austria · J. P. Kauffmann, bust, 1809, Protomoteca Capitolina, Rome · W. Ridley, stipple, pubd 1809 (after A. Kauffman), NG Ire. · N. Dance, double portrait, drawing (with J. Reynolds), Harewood House, West Yorkshire · H. Singleton, group portrait, oils (*Royal Academicians, 1793*), RA · J. Zoffany, group portrait, oils (*Royal Academicians, 1772*), Royal Collection

Wealth at death £3350 from stock invested at 3.5 per cent; 17,790 florins (in currency of Austrian Empire); unspecified funds in Rome; furniture, household items, jewellery, books, paintings, drawings, prints, and painting materials: will, Manners and Williamson, *Angelica Kauffmann*

Kauffman, Niklaus. *See* Mercator, Nicolaus (1620?–1687).

Kauffmann, Angelica. *See* Kauffman, (Anna Maria) Angelica Catharina (1741–1807).

Kaushal, Baldev Sahai (1906–1992), general practitioner, was born at Partoki, Punjab, India, on 2 August 1906, the son of the physician to the household of the governor of the Punjab. He undertook his medical training at King Edward Medical College, Lahore, and completed his postgraduate qualifications at Middlesex Hospital, London, during the 1930s. Following this he decided to settle in Britain, and found work as a general practitioner in Bethnal Green in the East End of London. His kind and compassionate nature was soon recognized by local people, as was his considerable skill as a physician.

Kaushal acquired the reputation of a folk hero during the blitz. Bombs began to fall on Bethnal Green on the night of 24 August 1940 and this onslaught continued for many months. Kaushal was active in civil defence throughout this time. On one occasion he crawled beneath some debris in an attempt to reach a woman who clearly could not be saved but who asked for a cup of tea. He decided that the only practical way of fulfilling her last wish was to pour this through an enema tube. London civil defence subsequently recommended this as standard equipment for such situations.

The most serious incident in which Kaushal was involved was the Bethnal Green underground disaster of 1943. The disused underground station made ideal shelter from enemy bombing. On 3 March 1943, after an air-raid warning at 8.17 p.m., people made for the shelter from all directions; 1500 people were said to have been admitted within the first ten minutes. At 8.27 p.m. a salvo of rockets was discharged from a nearby battery in Victoria Park, creating a noise which many mistook for the sound of exploding bombs, and several hundred more people

rushed to the shelter. Then, according to the official report, a woman, said to have been holding a child, fell on the third step from the bottom and a man fell on her left. Those impeded by the bodies were forced down on top. Within seconds there was an 'immovable and interlaced mass of bodies five or six deep' against which the people above and on the stairway continued to be pressed. Although Kaushal attempted to descend into the shelter to tend to casualties, he found it impossible to make headway. His task rather became to certify the corpses as they were brought up. One hundred and sixty-one people died from suffocation and twelve more subsequently died in hospital. It was 11.40 p.m. before the last casualty was cleared from the stairway.

On 20 September 1944 *The Times* reported that a young Indian doctor had just gone to bed after touring the shelters when the blast from a flying bomb injured him and wrecked his home. In spite of his injuries he refused to go to hospital until he had administered morphine to mortally wounded fire watchers as well as tending to other wounded civilians for eight hours. This and other incidents were mentioned in Kaushal's citation for the MBE, which was gazetted in March 1945. The citation also mentioned the fact that he had served in civil defence since the beginning of hostilities, and 'on more than one occasion, has entered confined spaces in dangerous debris in order to give aid to a casualty … Dr Kaushal has shown courage and devotion to duty and has been the means of saving many lives' (regional commissioners, London civil defence region, to Dr Baldev Kaushal, 5 March 1945).

Kaushal ended the war as divisional surgeon for the local St John Ambulance Brigade and medical officer of the St James-the-Lesser Church Approved Society and of several other local organizations. He continued to work hard and devotedly until his retirement in 1965, when he became involved in charitable work. Frugal in his habits, shrewd with his investments, and a lifelong bachelor, he made substantial donations to hospitals and schools in his native Punjab, in particular to the Ludhiana Medical College. An active member of the Arya Samaj denomination of Hinduism, he was a founder member and president of the Hindu Association of Europe and his donation enabled the founding of an Arya Samaj medical centre in Greater Kailash, New Delhi, which he opened in 1984. His visits to India were of great importance to him, but he remained devoted to Bethnal Green and its people. He died of bronchopneumonia and chronic obstructive airways disease at his home, 36 Merceron House, Victoria Park Square, Bethnal Green, London, on 14 July 1992 and was cremated at Manor Park crematorium.

SHAKUN BANFIELD

Sources L. R. Dunne, 'Report on an inquiry into the accident at Bethnal Green tube station shelter on 3/3/43' [Ministry of Home Security, 1945] · *The Times* (5 March 1943) · *The Times* (20 Sept 1944) · *Bethnal Green News* (20 July 1935) · *Hackney Gazette* (12 March 1945) · *Daily Telegraph* (18 July 1992) · personal knowledge (2004) · private information (2004) [letter sent to Kaushal on 5 March 1945 from regional commissioners, London civil defence region] · d. cert.
Archives priv. coll., papers

Wealth at death £125,087: probate, 13 Nov 1992, *CGPLA Eng. & Wales*

Kavan, Anna [*née* Helen Emily Woods; *married name* Helen Emily Ferguson] (**1901–1968**), writer, was born at Les Delices, Cannes, France, on 10 April 1901, the only child of Claude Charles Edward Woods (*d.* 1915/16), a gentleman whose family owned property in Northumberland, and Helen Eliza Bright (*d.* 1955), a socialite, who was the illegitimate granddaughter of Dr Richard Bright, discoverer of Bright's disease. Helen was put out to a wet-nurse, and spent most of her childhood at various boarding-schools in the United States (where her father had bought an orange grove), then in Lausanne, and, finally, at Malvern Girls' College. She hated all her schools, but was often left on her own at them during the holidays. She longed to go to Oxford, but due to the family's straitened circumstances (her father reputedly jumped to his death from a boat bound for South America when Helen was fourteen) her mother encouraged her to marry, on 10 September 1920, Donald Harry Ferguson (*b.* 1889/90), a thirty-year-old engineer on the Burma railway employed by the colonial administration. Donald Ferguson is fictionalized in Helen's second novel, *Let me Alone* (1930), as Matthew Kavan, a man who persistently rapes his wife and whose favourite pastime is bludgeoning rats to death with a tennis racquet. The marriage, which they spent in a small village near Mandalay, ended after two years, but it resulted in one son, Bryan, born in 1922, and started Helen Ferguson off on her writing career. Under her married name she wrote six novels, beginning with *A Charmed Circle* (1929), ostensibly about romantic and family life in the home counties but always overshadowed by far darker themes.

At some time after Helen's marriage had ended, she was introduced to heroin. She claimed that a tennis coach had advised her it would improve her serve, but it was much in use in the racing-driver circles which she frequented in the south of France. She enjoyed their company hugely. 'Out of their great generosity they gave me the truth, paid me the compliment of not lying to me. Not one of them ever told me life was worth living' (Callard), she wrote. It was in the south of France, between 1925 and 1926, that Helen met Stuart Edmonds, a bohemian and a painter. She described their relationship as 'the only time I have ever been in love' (ibid.). After both she and Stuart had become divorced from their respective spouses, they lived together in the Chilterns. Stuart painted, while Helen—who was such a talented painter that she managed to have an exhibition in 1935 at the Wertheim Gallery, London—also painted, and bred bulldogs. It is unclear whether they married, but she called herself Helen Edmonds. The relationship failed in the late thirties, as Helen took more and more drugs, and Stuart Edmonds relapsed into alcoholism and philandering.

It was after a suicide attempt—she made six in her life—and the first of many detoxification treatments, that Helen Edmonds decided to re-invent herself. She renamed herself Anna Kavan from her novel *Let me Alone* (though never officially, it seems), and changed her appearance. The boyish-looking woman with brown hair became a glamorous platinum blonde. In 1940 Jonathan Cape published *Asylum Piece*, the first of the books she wrote under her new name, a collection of sinister and surreal short stories dealing with topics like paranoia, drug addiction, mental illness, and the inmates of private clinics. This was followed by an equally dark collection of stories, *I am Lazarus* (1945).

From 1939 Anna Kavan travelled the world, spending time in New York, Los Angeles, Cape Town (to stay with her mother), Norway, and New Zealand, on her own and with various different men. But when her son was reported missing in 1942 on an RAF bombing raid, she returned to England and attempted suicide once again. It was while she was in hospital that she met her mentor, the psychiatrist Dr Karl Theodore Bluth. He persuaded her to register with the Home Office as a heroin addict—there were only around 200 registered addicts in 1949—so that he could legally supply her with the drug.

Although Dr Bluth was married, he and Anna Kavan maintained an intense but probably platonic friendship, and through Dr Bluth she met Peter Watson, who financed Cyril Connolly's *Horizon* magazine, for which she wrote short stories and reviews. One piece for *Horizon*, 'The case of Bill Williams' (May 1944), was based on her work with a military psychiatric unit specializing in the psychological casualties of war. In 1950, to supplement her income, she set up Kavan Properties to buy and renovate properties, mainly in streets off Kensington Church Street, between London's Notting Hill Gate and Kensington, where she lived.

Dr Bluth's death in 1964 prompted another suicide attempt. Much to her fury she was rescued in time, and continued to live privately, surrounded by a group of mainly homosexual friends, her closest being the writer Rhys Davies and the critic Raymond Marriott, who rented the lower flat in her house. Her mother, who died in 1955 and whom Anna Kavan blamed for much of her unhappiness, left her virtually nothing except her harp and a portrait of herself by Vladimir Tretchikoff, both of which Kavan kept in her sitting-room. Kavan's last publisher was Peter Owen, whom she met in 1956, and it was for him that she wrote novels with an increasingly science fiction flavour, like *Ice* (1967), nominated by Brian Aldiss as best science fiction novel of 1967.

Anna Kavan wrote: 'Life is just a nightmare and the universe has no meaning', and 'Real life is a hateful and tiresome business' (Callard). Her inner landscape, of which she wrote, was bleak. And yet of *Asylum Piece* Sir Desmond MacCarthy wrote: 'There is a beauty about these stories which has nothing to do with their pathological interest and is the result of art. … There is beauty in the stillness of the author's ultimate despair' (quoted in Owen). On 5 December 1968 Anna Kavan was found dead from a heart attack, lying on her bed at 19A Hillsleigh Road, Kensington, her head resting on a box of heroin. In the house the police later found enough stockpiled heroin to kill the whole street. The day before, she had failed to turn up to a party given by Peter Owen to introduce her to one of her greatest admirers, Anaïs Nin, who had described her as 'an equal to Kafka'. Later that month she was cremated at Golders Green crematorium, and her ashes were interred at her home at Hillsleigh Road.   VIRGINIA IRONSIDE

Sources D. Callard, *The case of Anna Kavan: a biography* (1992) · R. Davies, introduction, *Julia and the bazooka* (1970) · P. Owen, introduction, *Asylum piece* (2001) · B. Aldiss, introduction, *Ice*; repr. (1970) · m. cert. · d. cert. · *CGPLA Eng. & Wales* (1969)
Archives Ransom HRC, papers · University of Tulsa, Oklahoma, McFarlin Library, papers | NL Wales, Rhys Davies papers, letters
Wealth at death £16,327: probate, 1969, *CGPLA Eng. & Wales*

Kavanagh, Arthur Macmorrough (1831–1889), politician, born at Borris House, co. Carlow, on 25 March 1831, was the second son and third child of Thomas Kavanagh (1767–1837) and his second wife, Lady Harriet Margaret Le Poer Trench (d. 1885), daughter of Richard *Trench, second earl of Clancarty. His father was MP for Kilkenny in the last Irish parliament, and for co. Carlow in the House of Commons. His family traced its descent to the kings of Leinster. Born with severely under-developed arms and legs, Kavanagh nevertheless, by indomitable resolution and perseverance, and with the sympathetic help of Francis Boxwell, the local physician, triumphed over his physical difficulties, and learned to do almost everything as well as, or better than, an able-bodied person. He had a mechanical chair made so that he was able to move about the room. His chest was broad, but he could make the stumps of his arms meet across it, and by long practice he made his arms so supple, strong, and sensitive that, with the reins round them, he could manage a horse as well as if he had the reins between his fingers, and even make good use of a whip. When riding he was strapped on a chair saddle, and rode to hounds and took fences and walls as boldly as any in the field. He was also an expert angler and a good shot. He became a fair amateur draughtsman and painter, and wrote more legibly than many who suffer from no physical handicap. He was, moreover, a keen sailor, publishing *The Cruise of the RYS Eva* (1865).

As a child Kavanagh was educated under private tutors at Celbridge, co. Kildare, and by his mother at St Germain-en-Laye and at Rome. He also travelled with his mother and his tutor, the Revd David Wood, in Egypt, ascending the Nile as far as the third cataract, and in Asia Minor, visiting Sinai, Jerusalem, and Beirut in 1846–8. On his return to Ireland in 1848 Kavanagh acted as a volunteer scout during Smith O'Brien's rebellion, riding sometimes many miles unattended in the dead of night. During 1849–51 he travelled with his eldest brother, Thomas, and his tutor to India by way of Russia and Persia, arriving at Bombay on 5 January 1851. Here Kavanagh gained some experience of tiger hunting. In December his brother, attacked by consumption, left India for Australia. He died on the voyage, and Kavanagh, who had remained behind, was for a time short of money, and maintained himself by carrying dispatches in the Aurangabad district. He afterwards obtained a post in the survey department of the Poona district, but returned to Ireland in 1853, and succeeded to the family estates on the death of his brother Charles in that year. On 15 March 1855 he married in Dublin his cousin,

Arthur Macmorrough Kavanagh (1831–1889), by unknown engraver, pubd 1891

Frances Mary, with whom he may have fallen in love before leaving on his travels. She was the only surviving daughter of the Revd Joseph Forde Leathley, rector of Termonfeckin, co. Louth. They had six children.

Kavanagh was a constructive landlord; a 'landlord of landlords', said Sir Charles Russell. He rebuilt in great part the villages of Borris and Ballyragget, on the basis of plans drawn by himself, which won the Royal Dublin Society's medal, and in other ways sought to promote the well-being of his tenantry. In this he was ably helped by his wife, who taught the villagers floriculture and lace making, the latter having been started by his mother. Kavanagh subsidized and managed the railway line from Borris to Bagnalstown until it was taken over by the Great Southern and Western Railway. He was a justice of the peace for the counties of Wexford, Kilkenny, and Carlow, high sheriff of co. Kilkenny in 1856 and of co. Carlow in 1857, and a member (and from 1862 chairman) of the board of guardians of the New Ross poorhouse, in which, though himself a strong protestant, he had a chapel provided for the benefit of Roman Catholic inmates, the first of its kind in Ireland. Daily he was to be seen seated under an old oak in the courtyard of Borris House, administering justice, adjusting differences, making up quarrels, and even arranging marriages. Here, also, in the winter he distributed beef and blankets among the poor. Kavanagh represented co. Wexford in parliament from 1866 to 1868, and co. Carlow from 1868 to 1880. During the Fenian rising he fortified and provisioned Borris House for a siege, and patrolled the country nightly, as he had done in 1848.

Kavanagh was a Conservative, voted against the disestablishment of the Irish church, and took an active part in its reorganization upon a voluntary basis. On the other hand, he supported the Land Bill of 1870. He spoke seldom in the house, but with great weight; his maiden speech decided the fate of the Poor Law (Ireland) Amendment Bill of 1869. He supported the peace preservation bills of 1870 and 1875. Uniquely, he was excused from standing in the lobby to vote, the tellers coming to him for his verdict. He lost his seat at the general election of 1880, even his own tenantry (largely Catholic) voting against him; he was appointed lord lieutenant of co. Carlow in 1880, and sat on the Bessborough commission of 1880–81. Dissenting from the report of his colleagues, he drew up one of his own, in which the principal feature was a proposal to extend the land purchase clauses of the act of 1870. Foreseeing the storm, he initiated the Irish Land Committee, of which he became one of the honorary secretaries. He was also an energetic member of the Property Defence Association, and founded in 1883 the Land Corporation. In 1886 he was sworn of the Irish privy council and set out a plan of Irish government deriving from a representative Irish privy council (MacCormick, 196). In that year he developed diabetes and with it acute depression. Worn out by anxiety and overwork, he succumbed to an attack of pneumonia at his London house, 19 Tedworth Square, Chelsea, on Christmas day, 1889. He was buried in the ruined church on Ballycopigan, a wooded hill in the demesne of Borris.

J. M. RIGG, rev. H. C. G. MATTHEW

Sources S. L. Steele, *Arthur Macmorrough Kavanagh* (1891) · G. D. K. MacCormick, *The incredible Mr Kavanagh* (1960) · *The Lancet* (14 March 1891) · K. T. Hoppen, *Elections, politics, and society in Ireland, 1832–1885* (1984) · *Dublin Gazette* (1886) · M. J. MacCarthy, *Handicaps: six studies* (1936) · *CGPLA Eng. & Wales* (1890)
Archives NL Ire. · NRA, priv. coll., corresp., travel diaries, and family papers | Birr Castle, Offaly, letters to Laurence Parsons, fourth earl of Rosse · HLRO, letters to Ashbourne
Likenesses Morris & Co., lithograph, pubd after 1889, NG Ire. · engraving, repro. in Steele, *Arthur Macmorrough Kavanagh* [*see illus.*] · portraits, repro. in MacCormick, *The incredible Mr. Kavanagh*
Wealth at death £700—in Killarney: probate, 6 June 1890 · £700—in England: probate, 24 Oct 1890

Kavanagh, Cahir Mac Art, baron of Ballyann (*d.* 1554?), chieftain, was the eldest son of Art Kavanagh of St Mullins, co. Carlow. The available secondary works on Cahir's life are frequently contradictory. The position of MacMurrough, a title to which Cahir aspired, was not strictly hereditary; the holder was the person thus recognized by the 'eldest and wealthiest' from among the *derbfine* (descendants of a common male ancestor in four generations) of the clan. None of Cahir's line had recently been MacMurrough, and his rise to prominence among his kinsmen was probably connected to his marriage to Lady Alice, the daughter of Gerald Fitzgerald, ninth earl of Kildare. Cahir first appears in the historical record when he was taken as a hostage following the Kavanaghs' involvement in the Geraldine rebellion of 1534. He escaped—with the connivance of the lord deputy, it was later said. With the subsequent execution of Silken Thomas, the tenth earl of Kildare, and the eclipse of that house, Leinster entered a period of political turmoil which had both advantages and disadvantages for Cahir. He was forced to give hostages to Lord Leonard Grey in 1537, and was accused of rebellion, but he quickly made a submission.

Now regarded as a 'principal captain' of the Kavanaghs, Cahir came to find that Dublin could provide a bolster for his claims against local rivals, both other Kavanaghs and those English 'captains' who had been appointed to secure the pale and its border after the fall of Kildare. He

proposed to Lord Deputy St Leger that the northern portion of what was by English law co. Wexford should be shired as the county of Ferns with himself as sheriff. This suggestion was never taken up, but Cahir was soon keenly occupied with the process known as surrender and regrant, whereby Gaelic property titles were, under government pressure, substituted for new titles under English law. The first stage of this took place at New Ross on 3 September 1543 when the principal men of the nation of the Kavanaghs agreed to make a new partition of all their lands. Notably absent from the normal terms was any provision for a representative of the Kavanaghs to attend parliament. This process was not without its opponents among the Kavanaghs, and probably lay behind the inter-Kavanagh battle near Hacketstown in 1545, from which Cahir emerged victorious. At this time Cahir's prominence among the Kavanaghs is witnessed by the regional nature of his alliances, such as that cemented by a bond of £100 to serve the earl of Ormond with his kinsmen.

Cahir 'became MacMurrough, apparently in succession to Murtough, son of Art Boy, who died in 1547, and certainly held that position by 6 November 1548' (Nicholls, 442). In the late 1540s he once again fell foul of Dublin over his continuing feud with the Wexford gentry and his insistence on applying Brehon law within his lands. He was pardoned in 1549, and when pardoned again the following year Dublin's terms included the renunciation of the title of MacMurrough: this was done before St Leger on 4 November 1550. Cahir's creation as baron of Ballyann for life in 1554 was by way of compensation. He was also made 'captain of his country', this title being a much desired legitimation of his position in the face of the inroads being made into Kavanagh authority and property by those deputed to secure the pale and its borders after the fall of Kildare. The final division of the Kavanagh lands was effected in 1552, Cahir securing a very substantial estate.

According to the seventeenth-century annals of the four masters, Cahir, 'a successful and warlike man, and worthy to have become Lord of Leinster had it not been for the invasion of the English', died shortly after his creation as a baron (*AFM*, *sub anno* 1554). He was succeeded as MacMurrough by Murrough McMaurice. By letters patent Cahir's son Dermot McCahir McArt was created *tanist* (successor apparent to the chief), although it was Brian, a younger son, who eventually became MacMurrough. Other children were Turlough, Art, Donogh, Criffin, Murtough, and Una. The substantial estate established by Cahir passed by primogeniture to Brian (*d.* 1572) who passed it to his eldest son, Morgan. Successfully kept intact through the penal period, the estate was only finally dispersed under the Tenant Land Acts at the end of the nineteenth century. The nominal title of MacMurrough was used by descendants of Cahir in the nineteenth and twentieth centuries.

MIHAIL DAFYDD EVANS

Sources H. Goff, 'English conquest of an Irish barony: the changing patterns of land ownership in the barony of Scarawalsh, 1540–1640', *Wexford: history and society*, ed. K. Whelan (Dublin,

1987), 122–49 • J. Hughes, 'The fall of the clan Kavanagh', *Journal of Ireland*, 4th ser., 2 (1874), 282–305 • C. Brady, *The chief governors: the rise and fall of reform government in Tudor Ireland, 1536–1588* (1994) • 'Reason why Cahir Mac Art Kavanogh was created baron for his life only in 1552', 1612, Bodl. Oxf., MS Laud Misc. 612 • K. Nicholls, 'The Kavanaghs, 1400–1700', *Irish Genealogist*, 5–6 (1974–9), 435–47, 573–80, 730–34 • GEC, *Peerage*, new edn, 1.387–88

Kavanagh, Henry Edward [Ted] (1892–1958), scriptwriter, was born on 1 March 1892 in Auckland, New Zealand, the younger son of Henry Paul Kavanagh (d. 1926), and his wife, Jane Lorigan. Both parents were Roman Catholics, and his paternal roots were in co. Carlow, Ireland. His father worked as a crown lands ranger, and by the end of his career was chief surveyor of forests. Kavanagh was educated at Sacred Heart College, Auckland, and at Auckland University. He went to Britain in 1914 to study medicine, at St Bartholomew's Hospital, London, and in Edinburgh, but his studies were interrupted by the First World War. In 1919 he married Agnes (Sally) O'Keefe, and they had two surviving sons.

Kavanagh (who was always known as Ted in Britain) never returned to medicine. To support his family he worked as a medical journalist for Burroughs Wellcome, as an advertising copy-writer, and as a cartoon contributor. He wrote an occasional comic column for a religious magazine, *New Witness*, and also for its successor, *GK's Weekly*. A keen wireless listener from the earliest days of the BBC, Kavanagh liked the work of Tommy *Handley. He was inspired to write a script which the comedian bought, and this was the beginning of a long and fruitful partnership, culminating in the outstanding BBC radio comedy success of the Second World War, *ITMA* (*It's that Man Again*, a phrase alluding to Adolf Hitler). In those early days of radio scriptwriting was not well paid and in 1940, according to his son P. J. Kavanagh, he was 'a hard ridden hack' earning a meagre £10 for writing such now long-forgotten shows as *Send for Doctor Dick*, *Lucky Dip*, as well as *ITMA*.

All comedy successes are created by a triumvirate of writer, performer, and producer; and when all three are first class the result is invariably success. It is certainly true that the combination of Ted Kavanagh, Tommy Handley, and Francis Worsley, their BBC producer, was a world-beater: *ITMA* became, in the words of *The Times*, 'the most highly successful and popular entertainment any nation has ever enjoyed' (*The Times*, 28 Sept 1958). Yet the programme was not an instant success. Its first series in July–August 1939 was set on a cruise ship and had none of the characters that subsequently made it famous. The coming of war stopped it dead in its tracks, as a series set on a cruise ship could not possibly work in wartime.

In 1939 the BBC's variety department was evacuated to Bristol, and in the blitz of 1940 the city was heavily bombed. The variety department then moved to Bangor in north Wales and it was there in comparative tranquillity that Ted Kavanagh's genius for popular comedy came into its own and he invented a number of new characters for the third series. In July 1941 the title was changed to *It's that Sand Again* and it was set in the Middle East but it soon

reverted to *ITMA* and stayed that way until Tommy Handley's death in 1949 ended *ITMA* for ever. By 1942 *ITMA* was a firm favourite and Ted Kavanagh was able to concentrate on that one show (at the considerably enhanced fee of £50 per programme). A very fast writer (and in his £10 a week days he needed to be), it was said that he could write an *ITMA* script (thirty minutes of material) in three hours—an amazing achievement.

Kavanagh loved puns, alliteration, and all forms of word play, but he also had the knack of creating three-dimensional characters. Although they were creatures of radio, his characters stood out in stark relief—quirky, opinionated, and complete in their brief catch-phrase-ridden existence. They included Colonel Chinstrap, Mrs Mopp, Mona Lott, Funf, Sam Scram, Signor So-So, and the Squire of Much Fiddling. The catch-phrases, repeated ad nauseam, entered the national vocabulary. They included 'Can I do you now, sir?', 'I don't mind if I do', and 'Boss, boss, something terrible's happened'.

ITMA was far and away Kavanagh's most successful show, and after it he never had another hit; but by then he had started a literary agency. He had long cherished a dream of combining radio writers under one roof for their better comfort and protection, and in 1945 he founded Kavanagh Associates. Many writers lined up under the Kavanagh banner, including Denis Norden who joined the agency in 1947, followed only a few weeks later by Frank Muir. They became directors in the 1950s along with Sid Colin, himself one of the agency's earliest clients. The business side of the agency was handled by John Hayes and Kavanagh's son Kevin, with Ted Kavanagh as a sort of talent spotter.

Frank Muir became involved with Kavanagh Associates while he was still in the RAF. Having seen an article in the London *Evening Standard* saying that Ted had formed an agency for writers, he sent him some material that he had written: 'He asked me to write a piece for a clarinettist who wanted to become a comedian. I did, and Ted paid me £10 out of his own pocket, I found out later. He was the kindest of all kind men' (Took, 30). Kavanagh was also very gregarious, at home, in pub and club, and an affable, witty companion; friendly and accessible to would-be scriptwriters. 'He was red-faced and red-haired, balding, with a huge dome', recalled his son (Kavanagh, *People and Places*, 100). With keen insight P. J. Kavanagh has also written that his father 'spent his life, earned his living, presenting a sort of inspired, zany disorder as a source of true heart's ease … and every kind of authority as ludicrous' (ibid., 101).

A devout Catholic, Kavanagh devoted a great deal of time in his later years to promoting charitable causes, including the Catholic Stage Guild and the Catholic Writers' Guild. He was awarded a papal knighthood by Pius XII. Asked what there was in his father's life, his son replied that 'There was God, there was fellowship, and there were jokes' (Kavanagh, *People and Places*, 102). Kavanagh died on 17 September 1958 at the Hospital of St John and St Elizabeth, Marylebone, London.

Kavanagh will be remembered as part of the trio that

produced *ITMA*. Listening to recordings of *ITMA* years after the event, one might be forgiven for wondering why audiences found it so funny—but it was about *then*, when it happened. Although saddened by Handley's sudden death in 1949, which brought the series to an end, Kavanagh 'said he felt he'd been released from a life sentence' (Kavanagh, *People and Places*, 108). A sentence of over 300 scripts, of what was in its day a national institution.

BARRY TOOK

Sources P. J. Kavanagh, *Finding connections* (1990) · P. J. Kavanagh, *People and places: a selection, 1975–1987* (1988) · B. Took, *Laughter in the air: an informal history of British radio comedy*, rev. edn (1981) · *The Times* (18 Sept 1958) · *Manchester Guardian* (18 Sept 1958) · T. Kavanagh, *Tommy Handley* (1949) · C. Andrews, ed., *Radio who's who* (1947) · F. Muir, *A Kentish lad* (1997) · d. cert.
Archives BBC WAC | SOUND BBC WAC · BL NSA, performance recording
Likenesses photograph, repro. in *The Times*
Wealth at death £1702 1s. 11d.: probate, 1 Dec 1958, CGPLA Eng. & Wales

Kavanagh, Julia (1824–1877), novelist and biographer, was born on 7 January 1824 at Thurles, co. Tipperary, Ireland, the only child of **Morgan Peter Kavanagh** (1800–1874), poet, novelist, and philologist, and his wife, Bridget Fitzpatrick (*d.* 1887). Morgan Kavanagh also was born in Thurles, and married Bridget in 1819. He was an applicant to the Royal Literary Fund between 1820 and 1830, and published a variety of badly received works, including *The Wanderings of Lucan and Dinah: a Romance* (1824); *The Reign of Lockrin* (1838), a poem written in Spenserian form; and *Discovery of the Science of Language* (1844), a ridiculous work on philology that provided highly dubious evidence for the origin of all languages. It was translated into French in the same year as publication and was developed in *Myths Traced to their Primary Source through Language* (1856) and *Origin of Language and Myths* (1871).

In childhood Julia Kavanagh accompanied her parents to London and then to France; eventually they settled in Paris, where they remained until 1844. Her father having abandoned them, she and her mother returned to London, where, to support them, Julia embarked on a literary career that overshadowed her father's faltering efforts in the same sphere. She wrote tales and essays for periodicals, and works for children, such as *The Three Paths* (1848). Her first novel for adults, *Madeleine* (1848), which depicts the life of a peasant girl in Auvergne, is influenced by her early French experiences. Of her many published novels the best-known is arguably *Nathalie* (1850). In this work she again draws on the familiarity with French life for which she was noted and admired by such contemporary critics as Katharine S. Macquoid, who remarked on the 'truth of [her] observation, as well as the quality of her style' (Macquoid, 255). *Nathalie* relates the experiences of a rebellious, passionate, independent young schoolmistress at a girls' school in northern France who subsequently falls in love with and marries an older man. Critics have noted both Kavanagh's debt to Charlotte Brontë's *Jane Eyre* (1847) and Brontë's subsequent debt to Kavanagh, as *Nathalie* appears to have strongly influenced *Villette* (1853). Kavanagh's admiration of *Jane Eyre* prompted her to write to

Brontë, and the two novelists corresponded for several years; the editor W. S. Williams arranged for them to meet in London in June 1850. When *Nathalie* was published in November of that year Brontë wrote directly to Kavanagh, telling her how 'thoroughly interested and highly pleased' she was by the novel, especially its characterization (Foster, 179).

Although connected with France in the popular imagination Kavanagh also wrote several novels with an English setting, including *Rachel Grey* (1856), a condition-of-England novel with an orphaned working-girl heroine. In her review of the novel for *The Leader* (5 January 1856) George Eliot criticized Kavanagh's depiction of the speech and manners of ordinary people; Eliot's *Adam Bede* (1859), however, may well have been influenced by a passage in which Kavanagh uses Dutch painting as an analogy.

Kavanagh's collective biographies of famous women also were very popular, and were remarkable for their time. *Woman in France during the Eighteenth Century* (1850), *Women of Christianity* (1852), *French Women of Letters* (1862), and *English Women of Letters* (1862) all argue against idealized, sentimental portrayals of female experience. She intended these biographies to provide a corrective to the silence of male historians on the topic of female influence in a variety of spheres beyond the domestic.

In the late 1850s Julia Kavanagh was involved in a high-profile literary dispute involving her father. On the title-page of his novel *The Hobbies* (1857) he claimed that his daughter, who had by this time achieved literary fame and widespread popularity, had edited the work. A heated correspondence in *The Athenaeum* ensued between Julia Kavanagh and her father's publisher, Newby, in which Julia denied any connection to the work and threatened legal action (*The Athenaeum*). This attempt by her father to trade on her name did in fact temporarily damage her reputation. Having lived mainly in London he died in an accident on 10 February 1874.

Kavanagh never married. She travelled frequently between England and the continent throughout her life, finally settling at Nice with her mother, with whom she wrote *The Pearl Fountain*, a collection of fairy stories, in 1876. She died suddenly, on 28 October 1877 in Nice, and was buried there, in the Catholic cemetery.

THOMPSON COOPER, *rev.* MEGAN A. STEPHAN

Sources Blain, Clements & Grundy, *Feminist comp.* · E. A. Langstaff, 'Julia Kavanagh', *An encyclopedia of British women writers*, ed. P. Schlueter and J. Schlueter (1998), 360–61 · S. Foster, 'A suggestive book: a source for *Villette*', *Études Anglaises*, 35 (1982), 177–84 · E. Langstaff and G. Smith, 'Kavanagh, Julia', *Dictionary of British women writers*, ed. J. Todd (1989), 376–7 · R. Colby, *Fiction with a purpose* (1967) · *The Athenaeum* (13 June 1857) · *The Athenaeum* (20 June 1857) · *The Athenaeum* (27 June 1857) · *The Athenaeum* (4 July 1857) · *The Athenaeum* (17 Nov 1877) · K. S. Macquoid, 'Julia Kavanagh', *Women novelists of Queen Victoria's reign: a book of appreciations*, ed. M. Oliphant and others (1897) · J. Sutherland, 'Kavanagh, [Miss] Julia', *The Longman companion to Victorian fiction* (1988), 343–4 · J. Sutherland, 'Kavanagh, Morgan Peter', *The Longman companion to Victorian fiction* (1988), 344 · J. Shattock, 'Kavanagh, Julia', *The Oxford guide to British women writers* (1993), 240–41 · d. cert. [Morgan Peter Kavanagh]
Archives NL Scot., letters to Leitch Ritchie and others

Likenesses H. Chanet, portrait, 1884, NG Ire.

Kavanagh, Morgan Peter (1800–1874). *See under* Kavanagh, Julia (1824–1877).

Kavanagh, Patrick Joseph (1904–1967), poet and writer, was born on 21 October 1904 at the family home in Mucker, a townland in the parish of Inniskeen, co. Monaghan, Ireland, the elder son and fourth of the ten children of James Kavanagh (1855–1929), a cobbler, and his wife, Bridget (1872–1945), daughter of Patrick and Mary Quinn, farmers. James Kavanagh bought a 9 acre farm in 1910 and Patrick was removed from school at the age of thirteen to embark on the career of cobbler-cum-subsistence farmer. Though the rest of his siblings left home in their teens and early twenties, most entering the nursing or teaching professions, he lived and worked on the family smallholding until he was thirty-five.

As a schoolboy Kavanagh was rather lackadaisical and displayed no particular aptitude for literature, but he developed a passion for poetry in his teenage years and secretly pursued a literary education, reading and versifying in his spare time. Books, other than school texts, were scarce in this hard-pressed society and he knew nothing about contemporary literature until 1925, when by chance he picked up a copy of the *Irish Statesman* in a newsagent's. From then until it folded in 1930, this weekly journal of arts and ideas, edited by George Russell (A. E.), was his main educational resource. By 1929 he had learnt to write the kind of vague religio-rural rhymed verse that A. E. favoured and three of his poems were accepted for publication, among them 'Ploughman'.

In December 1931 Kavanagh visited Dublin for the first time to meet A. E.—walking there rather than taking the train, to exaggerate his peasant status. A. E., who had a reputation for fostering young talent, lent him books, dispensed literary advice, and introduced him to other writers such as Frank O'Connor. He became a frequent visitor to Dublin and was soon *au fait* with what was happening on the Irish literary scene. The *Dublin Magazine* began publishing his verse in 1931, and from that year it also began to appear in English journals such as *The Spectator* and *John O'London's*. His first collection, *'Ploughman' and other Poems* (1936), consists for the most part of slight apprentice offerings, the chief exception being the sonnet, 'Inniskeen Road: July Evening', a rueful, yet playful, meditation on the anomaly of being a poet in his native village.

In 1937 Kavanagh went to London for a time to seek literary employment and was commissioned to write *The Green Fool* (1938), an autobiography with an anthropological dimension, combining a portrait of the artist with a portrait of his society. The mandate to provide a narrative about small-farm life in Ireland compelled Kavanagh to attend to the subject which was closest to him but which he had so far virtually ignored. *The Green Fool*, which took a fresh and light-hearted approach to life in an Irish village and modulated easily from the comic to the lyrical, received rave reviews in the Irish and English press, but was withdrawn in 1939 following a successful libel suit by

Oliver St John Gogarty. Gogarty, a practising doctor as well as an author, took offence because on page 300 Kavanagh had commented that on his first visit to the city he had called at his house and was unsure whether the white-robed maid who answered the door was his wife or mistress.

Kavanagh moved to Dublin in 1939 to become a full-time writer and, apart from some lengthy stays in London and Inniskeen, he lived there for the rest of his life. During his first Dublin years he benefited from the cult of peasantry which had been a feature of the Irish literary revival and was welcomed and patronized by the city's literati as a harmless naïf. In dress and appearance he still looked like a farmer. Not particularly tall at 5 feet 10½ inches, he none the less conveyed an impression of ungainly size because of his broad frame, large hands and feet, and ploughman's gait. Under the influence of Sean O'Faolain, editor of a new monthly journal, *The Bell* (October 1940–1946), and Frank O'Connor, its first poetry editor, he soon began to perceive himself as a post-literary revival and post-independence writer, one of a new generation of disillusioned realists intent on portraying contemporary Irish life, warts and all. He projected himself as the 'voice of the people', the authentic and articulate expresser of a rural Catholic Ireland that he saw as grossly misrepresented by literary revival writers such as W. B. Yeats, Lady Gregory, and, especially, J. M. Synge. Possessed by a missionary zeal to counter inherited literary images of the peasant, he quickly progressed from brief, affectionately realist lyrics such as 'Spraying the Potatoes', 'A Christmas Childhood', and 'Art McCooey' to *The Great Hunger* (1942), a rhetorically powerful poem of 758 lines offering an authoritative and shocking indictment of small-farm Ireland.

Its central protagonist, Patrick Maguire, a typical Irish subsistence farmer, is an elderly bachelor who has sacrificed sexuality to agricultural productivity, living 'that his little fields may stay fertile'. The poem criticizes the contemporary Irish small-farm ethos in which a puritanical Catholicism and a preoccupation with economic security combine to render men's and women's lives joyless and unfulfilled. Technically as well as thematically daring, it is written in a mix of free-verse paragraphs and rhymed stanzas, and exploits cinematic strategies of montage. Though some Dublin critics were uncomfortable with *The Great Hunger*'s innovative techniques and disruption of literary pieties about the peasantry, Kavanagh was now widely recognized as a force to be reckoned with in Irish letters.

In another long and only posthumously published poem, *Lough Derg* (1978), he experimented with broadening his cultural analysis to present an anatomy of Catholic Ireland, urban and rural, north and south. He then abandoned socio-realist verse. His post-war collection of poems, *A Soul for Sale* (1947), was respectfully received and *The Great Hunger*, which many English and American critics were reading for the first time in that volume because it had previously appeared in a limited edition, was singled out as a major twentieth-century poem.

Since he could not survive on the pittance he earned from his poetry, Kavanagh had been assiduously seeking a well-paid job or sinecure since his first days in Dublin. Lack of academic qualifications and political connections rendered him ineligible for most positions, and the only regular employment he was offered in the 1940s was as a twice-weekly columnist with a daily newspaper, the *Irish Press* (September 1942–February 1944), and as a staff journalist (August 1945–April 1947) and film critic (February 1946–July 1949) with a Catholic weekly paper, *The Standard*. Embittered by middle-class Dublin's refusal to proffer him patronage or at times even the means of earning a livelihood while writers whose work he despised were salaried and secure, he produced a series of satires excoriating Dublin as a cultural mediocrity and casting himself in the role of outcast genius. The best of these was 'The Paddiad' (1949), based on the *Dunciad*. Satire, as he gradually came to recognize, was 'unfruitful prayer' ('Auditors In'), corroding him spiritually as well as frittering his talent. The supreme literary virtue which he endeavoured, often vainly, to cultivate from the late 1940s was what he termed comedy, a humorous, affectionate, yet disengaged art.

Tarry Flynn, the autobiographical novel about the life of a farmer–poet he had been attempting to write since 1940, eventually appeared in full in 1948; it was a realistic but mellow and often very funny portrayal of his Inniskeen milieu. This novel had its advocates from the beginning but its shelf life was short because the London publisher, the Pilot Press, went into liquidation. Its present status as a classic of Irish fiction dates from its reissue as a paperback in 1962 and its many subsequent reprintings.

One of the cultural legacies of the Irish struggle for independence was an emphasis on ethnicity and nationalism in literature, a trend so antipathetic to Kavanagh that he once declared, 'Irishness is a form of anti-art' (*X*, August 1961). His opposition to an ethnic aesthetic, evident from 1947, took two contrary forms. First, he countered the 'myth of Ireland as a spiritual entity' (*Studies*, spring 1959)—which he attributed to the literary revival writers, especially Yeats—with a 'parish myth' presenting the country as a mosaic of distinctive parishes rather than as a monolith. *Tarry Flynn* is the finest instance of what Kavanagh called 'parochialism' (*Kavanagh's Weekly*, 24 May 1952), an art that has the courage to focus on the local and familiar. In his sonnet 'Epic', Homer makes the Iliad out of a 'local row'. Second, and more persistently from 1950 onwards, he demanded that writing should reveal the personality rather than the nationality of the writer. A new Irish monthly journal of arts and letters, *Envoy* (December 1949–July 1951), to which he contributed a monthly diary, gave him a platform to communicate his subversive views on contemporary Irish life and letters. He indulged this vein even further in *Kavanagh's Weekly*, a short-lived journal which he edited and co-wrote with his brother Peter (12 April 1952–5 July 1952). *Kavanagh's Weekly*, which was critical of the government, of almost every state institution, and of many prominent figures in Irish public and

artistic life, won him numerous enemies and its collapse left him destitute and unemployable.

Kavanagh's own life as a Dublin writer and character was becoming his poetic theme from 1950 onwards. A distinctive figure about town because of his unkempt, countrified appearance, abrasive turn of phrase, and booming voice, he took to boozing and gambling on horses in middle age. Among his intimates he was an entertaining and humorous companion. His cultivation of a crusty and abusive public manner was largely a way of fending off intrusiveness, but he had also been soured by financial insecurity. Though widely recognized as Ireland's leading poet he was pathetically poor and dependent for survival on loans and handouts from well-off supporters and on the nurture and sympathy of numerous women friends, 'Rescue work with kiss or kitchens' ('Prelude'). In a frank, laid-back, casual vernacular verse that drew on metaphors from racecourse, betting shop, street, and pub and blended journalistic cliché and literary allusion, he analysed his daily experiences and his psyche: his insolvency, alcoholism, temperamental cussedness, failures as a lover, and abiding belief in the importance of poetry. Among the best of these lyrics centring on the persona of an endearing, fallible figure, usually intent on self-reform, are 'Auditors In', 'Prelude', and 'If ever you go to Dublin town'.

In the hope of making some easy money Kavanagh took a libel action against *The Leader*, an Irish journal which had printed an unsigned 'profile' of him in October 1952. The profile depicted him hunkered on a bar stool surrounded by young disciples whom he verbally abused, but it went on to praise his poetry, especially *The Great Hunger*. The case, heard in February 1954, was a *cause célèbre* and earned Kavanagh considerable notoriety but no money. He lost, later won the right to appeal, and eventually settled out of court, only to discover that the defendants had virtually no assets.

The stress of this court case also took a severe toll on his health. A heavy cigarette smoker all his life, he was found to be suffering from lung cancer in March 1955. He was operated on, had a lung removed, and made a good recovery, though he never regained his former robustness. That period of his convalescence spent lying day after day on the bank of Dublin's Grand Canal in the warm July of 1955 entered his self-mythologizing as a time when he was born or reborn as a celebratory, lyrical poet whose role was to:

> be reposed and praise, praise, praise
> The way it happened and the way it is.
> ('Question to Life')

In the late 1950s he published a series of sonnets expressing this rapturous mood and written in an improvisatory, colloquial style, among them 'The Hospital', 'Canal Bank Walk', 'Lines Written on a Seat on the Grand Canal, Dublin', 'October', 'Come Dance with Kitty Stobling', and 'The One'. These were collected in *Come Dance with Kitty Stobling* (1960), which was widely and enthusiastically reviewed and was a British Poetry Society choice for summer 1960.

Equally at home among the literary and artistic sets in

Soho and Dublin, Kavanagh was held in high esteem and affection by the upcoming generation of Irish poets in the 1960s. His years of penury and near-destitution were at an end: a regular income came from an extra-mural lectureship at University College, Dublin, from May 1955, a weekly column of reminiscences about his farming days in the *Irish Farmers Journal* (June 1958–March 1963), and a chat column in the *RTE Guide* (April 1963–June 1967). His *Collected Poems* was published to much critical acclaim in 1964, his *Collected Prose* followed in 1967, and *Tarry Flynn*, adapted for Dublin's Abbey Theatre by P. J. O'Connor in 1966, was a box-office hit.

On 19 April 1967 Kavanagh married a long-time friend, Katherine Barry Maloney (1928–1989), and they settled in Dublin. A niece of the martyr patriot Kevin Barry, Katherine came from a prominent republican family in Dublin but had been working in London as a book-keeper since the late 1950s. Kavanagh lived with her during his frequent stays in London from about 1960 onwards. They had many friends in common in literary and artistic circles, shared an interest in all forms of sport, were drinking companions, and, in addition, Katherine was devoted to his welfare.

In the final years of his life Kavanagh was plagued by poor health, largely consequent on the alcoholism to which he had been succumbing since the early 1950s, and he was frequently hospitalized. He died of pneumonia in the Merrion Nursing Home, Dublin, on 30 November 1967 and on 2 December was buried, as he had requested, in his native Inniskeen.

Too little known outside Ireland because of disputes over copyright and consequent limitations on the distribution of his poetry, Patrick Kavanagh is acknowledged by most Irish poets who began writing in the 1960s and thereafter as a pivotal figure in twentieth-century Irish literature and as a seminal influence on Irish verse. By precept and example he steered Irish poetry away from its post-colonial obsession with ethnicity in theme and language and its preference for the historical and national rather than the contemporary and personal. He advocated that poetry should be confessional yet carefree; draw its images from the trivia of everyday life and its language from the argot of street and pub; cultivate a casual, relaxed vernacular style, avoiding the bardic or technically intricate; above all, that it should convey personality, capture a mood or an attitude—wonder, love, delight, pain. His message to Irish poets was to de-nationalize and 'try to be more human'. ANTOINETTE QUINN

Sources A. Quinn, *Patrick Kavanagh: a biography* (2001) · A. Quinn, *Patrick Kavanagh: born-again Romantic* (1991) · P. Kavanagh, *Selected poems*, ed. A. Quinn (1996) · *CGPLA Éire* (1968)
Archives NL Ire., MSS, incl. family papers · State University of New York, papers and letters · University College, Dublin, commonplace book, corresp., and literary papers | FILM Radio Telefis Eireann Archive, Dublin | SOUND BBC Sound Archive, London · Radio Telefis Eireann Archive, Dublin · TCD
Likenesses S. O'Sullivan, pencil drawing, 1939, NG Ire. · P. Swift, lithograph, 1956, priv. coll. · P. Swift, oil on board, 1961, priv. coll. · J. Coll, sculpture, 1991, Grand Canal bank, near Baggot Street Bridge, Dublin · photographs, University College, Dublin, Kavanagh archive · photographs, NL Ire., Wiltshire collection
Wealth at death £712: administration, 23 Sept 1968, *CGPLA Éire*

Kavuma, Paulo Neil (1901–1989), administrator and first minister of Buganda, was born in Ssingo county, Buganda (Uganda), the son of Saulo Balirete Munako, a protestant minor chief, and his wife, Samali Saba Webwa. In 1909 he was sent to live with the Revd W. B. Gill of the Church Missionary Society, working as a servant to earn his school fees, following a traditional practice whereby children were educated by serving in the household of a chief. From 1910 to 1917 he attended Mityana School, and came top in the scholarship entrance examination to the prestigious King's School (later College), Budo. He achieved a first-grade certificate in 1920, having reached what was then the pinnacle of education in Uganda. He became a clerk in government service and was posted to the office of the district commissioner in Kampala, where he worked for the next four years. In 1920 he was promoted to the office of the provincial commissioner of Buganda. In the same year he married Abigaeri, 'who helped me in all the difficulties I had to face' (Kavuma, 6): she predeceased him.

In 1930 Kavuma was promoted African assistant to the provincial commissioner, a responsible position he held for thirteen years during which he became exceptionally well versed both in the ways of the protectorate government and of the Buganda government under indirect rule, acting as interpreter of one system to the other. In 1943 his competence was rewarded when he was appointed country chief of Buruli, and in 1945 he moved to the important post of county chief of Kyagwe, the area around the capital, Kampala. During the following difficult years, in which there was much unrest in Buganda, Kavuma showed himself level-headed and even-handed, and in 1950 he was made first minister (*katikiro*) of Buganda at a time when changes were being introduced in the conduct of the Buganda government and popularist pressures were mounting.

In 1952 relations between the newly appointed governor, Sir Andrew Cohen, and Mutesa II, the kabaka (king) of Buganda, and his government reached crisis point. When the kabaka finally refused to accept an ultimatum from the governor, the agreement of 1900, under which Buganda's special status was defined, was suspended, and in 1953 the kabaka was exiled to Britain. Kavuma refused to consider the appointment of a new kabaka or the appointment of regents until these matters could be put to the council of chiefs. For the same reason he refused to resign as first minister and agreed to become regent only on the exiled kabaka's urging lest the British placed Buganda under direct rule. He then had the delicate task of trying to keep the peace while at the same time sharing the grief and anger of the populace, sometimes in fear of his life as he negotiated between Buganda and the protectorate authorities. A slow face-saving climb-down was organized by the British government when it became obvious that Buganda would remain virtually ungovernable unless the kabaka returned. On the kabaka's return

Paulo Neil Kavuma (1901–1989), by Fergus Wilson, c.1963–4

on 17 October 1955 Kavuma lost his position as first minister. He was unfairly traduced and a faction remained suspicious of his intentions.

Nevertheless, Kavuma was still widely respected and trusted. From 1963 to 1965 he was deputy mayor and then mayor of Kampala, held numerous directorships and was a member of the board of governors of several schools, including King's College, Budo. He remained president of the Uganda Red Cross until his death.

In the run-up to independence (1962) Kavuma supported Kabaka Yekka, the Ganda royalist party which allied itself with Milton Obote's Uganda People's Congress. In 1966, after Buganda tried to secede, Obote dissolved the kingdoms. In 1980, threatened with the possibility of Obote's return to power after the overthrow of the dictator Idi Amin, Kavuma, though nearly eighty, became a regional vice-president of the Democratic Party in order to campaign against Obote because of his treatment of Buganda. His *Crisis in Buganda, 1953* had been published in 1979 and is a valuable historical document, shot through with his integrity and his loyalty to Buganda. He died in 1989.

M. LOUISE PIROUET

Sources P. Kavuma, *Crisis in Buganda, 1953: the story of the exile and return of the kabaka, Mutesa II* (1979) • R. C. Pratt, 'The politics of indirect rule: Uganda, 1900–1955', in D. A. Low and R. C. Pratt, *Buganda and British overrule: two studies* (1960) • D. E. Apter, *The political kingdom in Uganda: a study of bureaucratic nationalism* (1961) • D. A. Low, *Buganda in modern history* (1971) • J. J. Jorgensen, *Uganda: a modern history* (1981) • K. Ingham, *The making of modern Uganda* (1958) • E. G. Wilson, *Who's who in East Africa, 1963–64* (1964) • E. G. Wilson, *Who's who in East Africa, 1965–66* (1966) • E. G. Wilson, *Who's who in East Africa, 1967–68* (1968) • F. A. W. Bwengye, *The agony of Uganda: from Idi Amin to Obote* (1985) • P. Mutibwa, *Uganda since independence: a story of unfulfilled hopes* (1992) • D. Brown and M. V. Brown, eds., *Looking back at the Uganda protectorate: recollections of district officers* (1996)

Likenesses group photograph, c.1953, repro. in Kavuma, *Crisis in Buganda* • F. Wilson, colour photographs, c.1963–1964 [*see illus.*]

Kay. *See also* Kaye.

Kay, Arthur (1861–1939). *See under* Cameron, Katharine (1874–1965).

Kay, Sir Edward Ebenezer (1822–1897), judge, was born at Meadowcroft, near Rochdale, Lancashire, on 2 July 1822, the fourth son of Robert Kay of Brookshaw, Bury, Lancashire, and Hannah, daughter of James Phillips of Birmingham. He was educated at Patricroft, near Salford, and later at Trinity College, Cambridge, where he matriculated on 16 October 1839 and graduated BA in 1844 and MA in 1847. On 22 April 1844 he was admitted as a student at Lincoln's Inn, where he was called to the bar on 8 June 1847. He took silk in 1866, and after leading in Vice-Chancellor Bacon's court, confined his practice to the House of Lords and the privy council. He was elected bencher at Lincoln's Inn on 11 January 1867, having learned about the law in the capacity of a reporter. He was elected treasurer of his inn in 1888.

On the retirement of Vice-Chancellor Malins in 1881, Kay was appointed justice of the High Court, Chancery Division (30 March) and knighted (2 May). He proved a tough-minded judge who was strongly in favour of the simplification of court procedure and appeared to be as competent on circuit as he was in chambers. On 13 November 1890 he succeeded Sir Henry Cotton as lord justice of appeal. A painful illness forced his retirement from the Court of Appeal after seven years in office. During his legal career he showed independence of thought and was the author of Kay's and Johnson's reports (of cases adjudged in the high court of chancery before Vice-Chancellor Wood) from 1854 to 1858.

On 2 April 1850 he married Mary Valence French, daughter of Dr William French, master of Jesus College, Cambridge; they had two daughters. After Mary's death in 1889 or 1890 Kay founded several divinity scholarships at Jesus College, worth over £4500, to perpetuate her memory. He died at his London house, 37 Hyde Park Gardens, on 16 March 1897 and was buried on 23 March in the churchyard at Brockdish, near Scole, Norfolk, close to his county seat of Thorpe Abbotts.   J. M. RIGG, rev. SINÉAD AGNEW

Sources WWW, 1897–1915 • J. Foster, *Men-at-the-bar: a biographical hand-list of the members of the various inns of court*, 2nd edn (1885), 251 • *Annual Register* (1987), pt 2, p. 145 • W. P. Baildon, ed., *The records of the Honorable Society of Lincoln's Inn: admissions*, 2 (1896), 215 • Venn, *Alum. Cant.* • *Men and women of the time* (1899), 394–5 • Boase, *Mod. Eng. biog.* • Allibone, *Dict.* • A. T. C. Pratt, ed., *People of the period: being a collection of the biographies of upwards of six thousand living celebrities,*

2 (1897), 30 • *Law Journal* (20 March 1897), 155, 170 • *Law Journal* (27 March 1897), 186 • *Law List* (1848) • *Law List* (1867) • *VF* (28 Aug 1886) • *VF* (7 Jan 1888) • *Whitehall Review* (27 March 1897) • Burke, *Peerage* (1896) • *Times Law Reports* (1891) [appeal cases]

Likenesses S. Evans, ink drawing, 1877, NPG • Lock & Whitfield, woodburytype photograph, NPG; repro. in T. Cooper and others, *Men of mark: a gallery of contemporary portraits* (1883), 7 • Spy [L. Ward], caricature, watercolour study, NPG; repro. in *VF* (7 Jan 1888) • photograph, repro. in *ILN*, 60 (1897), 379

Wealth at death £206,990 7s. 1d.: probate, 12 May 1897, *CGPLA Eng. & Wales*

Kay [Caius], **John** (*fl. c.*1482), translator, who describes himself as 'poete lawreate' of Edward IV, dedicated to him a prose translation of the *Obsidionis Rhodie urbis descriptio*, an eyewitness account of the siege of Rhodes by the Turks in 1480 by Guillaume Caoursin, the vice-chancellor of the order of the knights of St John of Jerusalem, the town's defenders. He is otherwise unknown, and it is not clear that the title of 'poet laureate' implied any official position at court. In the case of Skelton it seems to have been a kind of graduate 'degree' in rhetoric, conferred on him by Oxford (probably in 1488), but John Kay is not recorded as a member of Oxford or Cambridge—unless he is the same person as Caius Auberinus, recorded from autumn 1483 until 1504 in Cambridge, and from 1488 as professor of humanities there. This identification is possible—John Kay's remark that he has 'seen and red in Italye' of the 'oppressyng and captyvyte' of Constantinople might suggest that he had studied in Italy—but is not supported by more certain evidence.

John Kay's book was probably written *c.*1482: it refers to the death of Muhammad II in May 1481, and, although the printer is unknown, according to Duff 'the type appears for the most part identical with that used by Lettou and Machlinia *c.*1482–4' (Duff, 2). Kay's introduction gives a brief account of the Turkish conquests of the preceding forty years, leading up to the siege of the island ('the key and yate of all crystendome'; *The Dylectable Newesse*). God rescued his people: the attackers were repelled, and the 'grete Turke' was smitten down 'in his moste pryde and his moste hope' by sudden death. Kay's translation will bring to the king's people 'the dylectable newesse and tithynges of the gloryous victorye of the Rhodyans agaynest the Turkes' so that they will rejoice and see the great power of the Christian faith. The work is a direct and vigorous translation which emphasizes both the emotional and the exemplary aspects of Caoursin's narrative. Three copies of the printed text survive, together with a manuscript fragment (almost identical with the print) in BL, Cotton MS Vitellius D.xii (but originally from BL, Cotton MS Titus A.xxvi).   DOUGLAS GRAY

Sources G. Caoursin, *The dylectable newesse and tithynges of the gloryous victorye of the Rhodyans agaynest the Turkes*, trans. J. Kay [n.d., *c.*1482]; facs. edn as *The siege of Rhodes* (1975); ed. H. W. Fricham as *Caoursin's account of the siege of Rhodes in 1480* (1926) • R. H. Robbins, 'Good gossips reunited', *British Museum Quarterly*, 27 (1963–4), 12–15 • G. G. Duff, *Fifteenth-century English books*, Bibliographical Studies (1917) • D. Gray, ed., *The Oxford book of late medieval verse and prose* (1985) • D. R. Leader, 'Caius Auberinus: Cambridge's first professor', *A distant voice: medieval studies in honor of Leonard E. Boyle, O.P.*, ed. J. Brown and W. Stoneman (1997), 322–7 • Emden, *Cam.*, 23

Archives BL, Cotton MS Vitellius D.xii • BL, Cotton MS Titus A.xxvi

Kay, John (1704–1780/81), inventor of textile manufacturing machinery, was born at Park Farm in the township of Walmersley in the parish of Bury, Lancashire, on 16 July 1704, the fifth son of Robert Kay (1651–1704) and his wife, Ellen, *née* Entwistle, of Quarlton. His father was a prosperous farmer who died three months before his birth and left an estate of £82 13s. 6d. John left school at the age of fourteen to be apprenticed to a maker of reeds—devices which separate the threads of a warp and beat up the weft after each shot. Reputedly he abandoned his master after one month, believing that he had learned all that he could about the art. A natural inventor, whose mechanical genius always surpassed his commercial ability, he was able and confident to excess, but fractious and quarrelsome in disposition. Anticipating a legacy of £30 when he reached the age of twenty-one, he married on 29 June 1725 Ann Holt (d. 1747); they had six sons and six daughters.

Kay's first invention was an improved reed for the loom, made perhaps in 1726, which substituted thin wire for the usual strips of cane or reed. Those wire reeds proved more durable, reduced breakages in the warp, and facilitated the weaving of finer, stronger, and more regular fabrics. They were never patented but were widely known as Kay's reeds. His first patent was taken out in 1730, for an engine for twisting reed twine. In 1733 he patented a shuttle, which was much lighter than the existing one, ran upon four wheels, and could be used for weaving woollen or linen broad-goods. Termed at first a wheel-shuttle, a spring-shuttle, or a bobbin-shuttle, it was called a fly-shuttle only in 1780 (in [D. Rasbotham], *Thoughts on the Use of Machines in the Cotton Manufacture*, 1780, 9). Its significance has been misunderstood and exaggerated, especially by exponents of the heroic theory of invention, who exalted Kay as 'the father and founder of the British textile industry' (Wood, 77). A balanced assessment of its significance was eventually made by Paulinyi in 1986. The original patent described an extended sley (or batten) with at each end a shuttle box containing a spring-powered picker (or mechanical hand), together with a shuttle race-board, a picking card, and a picking peg. This design proved, however, to be imperfect, and it was improved in 1735 by the introduction of a fixed and larger spool, so making the shuttle heavier as well as longer. The patent shuttle was then introduced into the local woollen industry for which it had been devised and so became a true innovation, enabling Kay to set up in business as a shuttle maker. He sought to profit from his invention by charging an annual rent for its use but set the rental so high as to encounter inevitable resistance from his clients. Instead of negotiating an acceptable price, Kay embarked upon the worst possible course of action and launched three successive suits in the court of chancery against some fifty-two woollen weavers of Rossendale in the years 1737, 1740, and 1743. He incurred heavy legal costs and failed to recoup any rents from those who had pirated his invention. It has been claimed that the new

John Kay (1704–1780/81), by unknown engraver

shuttle doubled a weaver's production, created 'a yarn famine' (B. Woodcroft, *Brief Biographies of Inventors*, 1863, 3), and so necessitated the development of spinning machinery by Wyatt, Hargreaves, and Arkwright. No evidence has so far been produced to support such a hypothesis, which assumes that a weaver would prefer to increase his production rather than his leisure time. It remains certain that a weaver spent only one-third of his time at the loom in passing the shuttle through the shed and that he required considerable practice in order to master the effective use of the new picking peg. The shuttle was devised to serve the needs of the woollen industry, wherein the weaving of broadcloth had already entered upon a process of long-term decline. It came into use in the manufacture of baize in Rossendale and Rochdale from 1735 and was also adopted from the 1750s in the cotton industry, especially in the fustian trade of Bolton, where warps proved more resistant to breakage than in the woollen industry. It had come into general use in the trade of Lancashire by 1780 and was introduced into the woollen industry in Yorkshire from about 1763 but into that of the west country only from 1792.

In 1738 Kay patented a windmill for raising water from mine shafts, and in 1745 he took out a joint patent with Joseph Stell of Keighley for an improved Dutch or swivel loom, driven by water power, for weaving tapes and other narrow goods; it made the first use of tappets in order to control the pedals. In those patents he described himself in 1738 as an engineer and in 1745 as a gentleman. Then in 1747 he emigrated to France. Several factors may have influenced this decision: the failure of the 1745 rising, given the Jacobite tradition of his family, the impending

expiry of his fourteen-year patent of 1733, the heavy burden of accumulated debts, and the failure of his application to parliament for financial relief.

In France Kay learned of the death of his wife in childbirth, but he also secured the encouragement which he had been denied in England. He obtained in 1747 a patent for the sole manufacture and sale in France of his wheelshuttle for fourteen years, and in 1749 he was granted a government subsidy and life pension, upon condition that he severed all ties with England. To help him in the task of manufacture in a Paris workshop he brought over three of his sons from England—**Robert Kay** (1728–1802), James Kay, and John Kay (1740–1791)—but he soon found that French weavers were diligently counterfeiting 'the English shuttle' (*la navette anglaise*, as it was styled in a French publication of 1763). He also resumed the efforts to improve the process of carding which he had first made in the early 1730s. Between 1750 and 1754 he perfected and manufactured a superior card-making machine. His machines came into use in both the woollen and cotton industries of France; while the card-making machine proved of great benefit to the spinning industry, the shuttle secured general acceptance only in the 1800s. Kay may well have been adversely affected by the outbreak of the Seven Years' War in 1756. He revisited England not once but at least five times, in 1753–4, 1757–8, 1759–60, 1764–8, and 1773–4, suffering the revocation of his pension in 1759.

Robert Kay extended the use of his father's wheelshuttle from a single shuttle to two or more shuttles, housed in a drop box to the side of the loom, so permitting the easier weaving of cross-striped fabrics. The drop box was invented in 1760 but was never patented. Robert also improved the capacity of the wheel-shuttle for weaving checks and bed ticks and, in 1773, the card-making machine. In 1764 he appealed to the Society of Arts for a reward for his father's invention, but the application proved untimely, since the society criticized Kay for his activities in France. Ten years later, in 1774, the Society of Arts awarded a bounty of 50 guineas to Kay for his cards but not for his shuttle. In 1770 John Kay's French pension was restored and thereafter he thought up six new inventions relating to canal excavation, dock cleansing, temperature regulation, and silk manufacture. He outlined an impressive programme to the French authorities in 1779, when the minister Mignot de Montigny recognized him as a 'genius'. Kay also aroused the interest of Richard Arkwright about 1780 because of his efforts to maintain his patent rights against opponents. He wrote his last recorded letter from Sens in Burgundy on 8 June 1779, but was reported in 1780 to be living 'in credit and affluence' ([D. Rasbotham], *Thoughts on the Use of Machines in the Cotton Manufacture*, 1780, 10). He died in the south of France during the winter of 1780–81. The exact date and place remain unknown, as does the site of his grave; the reason for the absence of information may well be found in the Anglo-French war of 1778–83.

In some respects the life of John Kay resembles that of William Lee, another inventor of genius who emigrated to

France and died there, and who for long remained an obscure figure. Kay, however, became the subject of more legends than any other inventor, legends which seem to have been largely created during the nineteenth century. The first centenary of the patent passed in 1833 without any attendant publicity. The efforts made from 1843 by the inventor's great-grandson Thomas Sutcliffe (1791–1849) to raise a subscription for the benefit of Kay's descendants proved fruitless but set in motion the elaboration of the Kay legend. That legend was embodied in the biographies published in 1863 by Bennet Woodcroft and in 1874 by Francis Espinasse, *Lancashire Worthies*, in the fresco of *John Kay ... AD 1753* painted in 1890 by Ford Madox Brown for Manchester's town hall, and in the Kay memorial inaugurated in Bury in 1908, inscribed with the phrase 'died in exile and poverty'. In that legend Kay became the personification of 'merit neglected and genius unrewarded' (Sutcliffe) and the archetype of the heroic inventor who failed to profit from his own invention. That legend was dispelled by the meticulous research of John Lord (1839–1903) and Julia Mann (1891–1985), published in 1903 and 1931, but nevertheless continues to be reiterated with a dogmatic fervour. It may be well, therefore, to mention some dozen associated myths which have long been refuted. It is untrue that Kay was of gentle birth and was the grandson of a Yorkshire baronet, that he was educated abroad, that his father became a Levant merchant and died in 1727 or 1728, that his family owned a woollen 'factory' at Colchester in Essex, that he invented the fly-shuttle in the year 1738, that he also invented spinning machines (the product of confusion with the clockmaker John Kay of Warrington), that he resided for seven years in Leeds, that his shuttle provoked riots and plunged the whole country into uproar, that he was driven by hostile weavers out of Leeds in 1745 and out of Bury in 1753, that he was forced to sell the family estate to the first Robert Peel in 1745, that his brother William became a founder in 1754 of the Society of Arts, that Kay fled to France in order to escape from the wrath of hostile weavers, and that he died in Paris in poverty in 1762.

In reality Kay was an inventor of supreme talent, resource, and vision but sadly lacking in business capacity. His inventions were both simple and practical as well as the first to be made in the region, justifying his description as 'the Christopher Colombus among the mechanical inventors of Lancashire' (Lord, 156). Their adoption in France proved them to be commoners of nature, belonging to no single place or country. The wire reeds secured universal acceptance. The fly-shuttle was never modified after the 1760s and remained a device of fundamental importance. It came into use in the 1870s in Japan, in the 1890s in India, and in the 1900s in China, where it enhanced the productivity of the world's largest stock of hand-looms and enabled them to withstand the competition of mill-made goods, whether emanating from Manchester, Bombay, or Shanghai. The shuttle remained even more significant for its indirect influence upon the mechanization of weaving. The picking peg replaced for the first time the human hand by a mechanical device and so took the first historic step towards the creation of a wholly automatic loom. The negative drive incorporated in the shuttle's action became universal in the later power-loom. The Kay–Stell Dutch loom was first driven by a water wheel at Keighley in 1750 and then at Garratt Hall on the Medlock in Manchester about 1760, so creating the town's first true factory. Kay's card-making machine was improved by his sons and stimulated other inventors from the 1760s. In Bury itself the firm of loom makers Robert Hall & Sons was established in 1844 and erected in 1877 a statue of Kay upon the gable of the offices of Hope foundry. The Kay memorial, inaugurated in 1908 in the Kay Gardens, bore a medallion portrait together with a list of inventions: it was surmounted by a statue symbolizing fame, surrounded by four lesser figures representing agriculture, engineering, mining, and weaving. That memorial was listed as a historic monument in 1985. In 1974 the statue from Hope foundry was transferred to the premises of Wilson and Longbottom in Barnsley, Yorkshire. In 1989 a memorial plaque was fixed to the wall of Park farmstead.

D. A. FARNIE

Sources J. Lord, *Memoir of John Kay of Bury* (1903) · J. de Lacy Mann, 'The introduction of the fly shuttle', in A. P. Wadsworth and J. de Lacy Mann, *The cotton trade and industrial Lancashire, 1600–1780* (1931), 449–71 · [A. Barlow], 'Weaving, no. VI: hand loom weaving', *Engineering* (12 June 1874), 422–4 [repr. in *The history and principles of weaving by hand and by power* (1878), 81–97] · A. Paulinyi, 'John Kay's flying shuttle', *Textile History*, 17 (1986), 149–66 · H. T. Wood, 'The inventions of John Kay (1704–1770)', *Journal of the Royal Society of Arts*, 60 (1911–12), 73–86 · J. R. Harris, *Industrial espionage and technology transfer. Britain and France in the eighteenth century* (1998), 79–94 · X. Linant de Bellefonds, 'John Kay et l'essor des textiles français', *Les techniciens anglais dans l'industrie française au XVIIIe siècle*, LLD diss., Université de Droit de Paris, 1971 · J. de L. Mann, 'The card making machine', *Textile History*, 7 (1976), 186–9 · J. de L. Mann, *The cloth industry in the west of England from 1660 to 1880* (1971), 139–41 · 'The textile inventor John Kay', *Bulletin of the John Rylands University Library*, 48 (1965–6), 9–12 · R. Hirst, 'The life of John Kay', 1983, Bury Historical Society · G. M. Ramsden, 'A record of the Kay family of Bury, Lancashire, in the 17th and 18th centuries', 1978, Lancs. RO · T. Sutcliffe, 'Address to the merchants, manufacturers, etc., respecting the invention of J. Kay' (1846)

Likenesses T. O. Barlow, engraving, 1863, repro. in W. S. Murphy, *The textile industries*, 8 vols. (1910–11) · F. M. Brown, fresco, 1890 · engraving, Sci. Mus. [*see illus.*] · portrait; loaned to V&A, 1877 · portrait, repro. in Lord, *Memoir*, 54

Kay, John (1742–1826), portrait etcher and miniature painter, was born in April 1742 in a small house known as Gibraltar, near Dalkeith, Scotland, the son of John Kay (*d.* 1748), a mason, and his wife, Helen Alexander. Kay was only six when his father died, and he was placed in the care of some relatives of his mother in Leith. When he was thirteen he began a six-year apprenticeship with George Heriot, a barber in Dalkeith. He married in 1762 Lilly Steven (*d.* 1783), with whom he had ten children, all of whom predeceased him, including a son, William Kay, who showed an aptitude for art and etched several plates. For seven years Kay worked as a barber in Edinburgh; on 19 December 1771 he purchased the freedom of the city of Edinburgh and was enrolled as a member of the Society of

Surgeon–Barbers, which enabled him to start his own business.

During his years as a barber, Kay had devoted his spare time to art. He was self-taught and produced many portrait sketches which are marked by their quaint originality and convey the true likeness of the sitter. He found a generous and encouraging patron in William Nisbet of Dirleton. Nisbet died in 1784 having neglected his promise to remember Kay in his will, but his heir arranged for Kay to receive an annuity of £20. Two years after the death of his first wife, Kay married, in March 1785, Margaret Scott (d. 1835); there were no children of this marriage.

The annuity enabled Kay in 1785 to relinquish his barber's trade for caricature portraiture. He drew and etched many portraits, which he sold from his little shop at 10 Parliament Close, Edinburgh, and these singly issued impressions show his prints at their best; however, he was never an accomplished draughtsman or a master of the technicalities of etching. His work, which is solely of antiquarian value, affords a quaint picture of Edinburgh society in his time. Although nothing is explicitly known of Kay's political views, his depiction of persons known for their liberalism and association with the French Revolution, coupled with his satirical renderings of those in opposition, suggest that he himself favoured the liberals. Kay etched in all nearly 900 plates and drew almost every notable Scotsman of his time, with the exception of Burns. His etchings of Adam Smith are, with the posthumous medallions by Tassie, the only authentic likenesses that exist of the great economist. Kay's caricatures provide light relief in the field of portraiture at the end of the eighteenth century. He quickly and deftly summed up the characters of those living in a very prosperous Georgian Edinburgh.

The artist made some arrangements with a view to the publication of his works. He was aided, it is said, by James Thomson Callender, who compiled some descriptive letterpress, including a slight autobiographical sketch, but the work was unfinished at the time of Kay's death. In 1837–8 a quarto edition of his plates, under the title *A series of original portraits and caricature etchings by the late John Kay, miniature painter, Edinburgh*, was published in monthly numbers by Hugh Paton of Edinburgh. A second edition, in four volumes, was issued in 1842 by the same publishers. The plates then passed into the hands of A. and C. Black of Edinburgh, who had them retouched, and in 1877 published a third edition in two volumes, after which the coppers were destroyed. A 'popular letterpress edition', in two volumes, which very inadequately reproduced the more interesting plates, and reprinted only a portion of the letterpress, was published in London and Glasgow in 1855.

Kay contributed portraits to each of the exhibitions of the Edinburgh Associated Artists from 1811 to 1816, and to the fourth exhibition of the Institution for the Encouragement of the Fine Arts in Scotland in 1822. An interesting collection of his drawings, which are somewhat more artistic than his etchings, is preserved in the library of the Royal Scottish Academy. Kay is also represented in the Scottish National Portrait Gallery and the Metropolitan Museum in New York. The department of prints and drawings in the British Museum has *A Complete Collection of the Portraits and Caricatures*, 'Drawn and Engraved by John Kay Edinburgh From the Year 1784 to 1813', and a miscellaneous volume of portraits and caricatures. Both volumes show that, while his etching technique did not necessarily improve, the size and scope of the caricatures broadened throughout his career, and his portrayal of Edinburgh society increased in wit and humour.

A self-portrait, inscribed 1786 (now in the City of Edinburgh Art Collection), is one of Kay's earliest dated etchings; other likenesses of the artist are in the Scottish National Portrait Gallery, which has an oil self-portrait, and the British Museum, which has two engravings. In his later years Kay was described as 'a slender, straight old man, of middle size, usually dressed in garb of antique cut, of simple habits and quiet unassuming manners' (Evans and Evans, 23). He died at his house, 227 High Street, Edinburgh, on 21 February 1826 and was buried in the Greyfriars churchyard. His widow, Margaret, ran their picture-dealing business until her death in November 1835, having disposed of the plates to Hugh Paton of 27 Horse Wynd, who, finding many of the plates hardly used, proceeded to issue collections of Kay's figures.

LUCY DIXON

Sources J. Halsby and P. Harris, *The dictionary of Scottish painters, 1600–1960* (1990) • P. J. M. McEwan, *Dictionary of Scottish art and architecture* (1994) • H. Smailes, *The concise catalogue of the Scottish National Portrait Gallery* (1990) • [E. Cumming], *Catalogue of the city of Edinburgh art collection*, 2 vols. (1979) • K. Andrews and J. R. Brotchie, *Catalogue of Scottish drawings* (1960) • D. Foskett, *A dictionary of British miniature painters*, 1 (1972) • *Engraved Brit. ports.* • B. Stewart and M. Cutten, *The dictionary of portrait painters in Britain up to 1920* (1997) • S. Houfe, *The dictionary of 19th century British book illustrators and caricaturists*, rev. edn (1996) • M. Bryant and S. Heneage, eds., *Dictionary of British cartoonists and caricaturists, 1730–1980* (1994) • D. Daiches, P. Jones, and J. Jones, *A hotbed of genius: the Scottish enlightenment, 1730–1790* (1986) • M. Campbell, *The line of tradition: watercolour drawings and prints by Scottish artists, 1700–1900* (1998) • J. L. Caw, *Scottish painting past and present, 1620–1908* (1908) • H. Evans and M. Evans, *John Kay of Edinburgh* (1980) • *DNB*
Likenesses J. Kay, self-portrait, engraving, 1786 (after his portrait), City of Edinburgh Art Collection • J. Kay, self-portrait, etching and aquatint, 1786 (after his earlier work), BM, NPG • J. Kay, self-portrait, etching, 1792 (after his earlier work), NPG • C. Butterworth, engraving (after J. Kay), BM • J. Kay, self-portrait, oils, Scot. NPG

Kay, Joseph (1821–1878), economist and lawyer, the third son of Robert Kay of Brookshaw House, near Bury, Lancashire, cotton merchant, and his wife, Hannah Phillips, was born at Ordsall Cottage, Salford, on 27 February 1821. Sir James Phillips Kay-*Shuttleworth (1804–1877) and Sir Edward Ebenezer *Kay (1822–1897) were his brothers. He was educated together with the sons of Sir Thomas Fowell Buxton and attended school at Patricroft, Lancashire, and matriculated from Trinity College, Cambridge, in 1840; he graduated BA in 1845 and proceeded MA in 1849. He was admitted at the Inner Temple in January 1844 and was called to the bar on 5 May 1848. From 1845, as a travelling bachelor of his college (a post endowed by the will of William Worts), his duties included travelling abroad and writing reports in Latin and English. He consequently travelled, encouraged by his brother James and accompanied by W. F. Campbell, in France, Switzerland, the Netherlands, Germany, and Austria collecting information on the social and economic conditions of those countries. Kay became a convinced free-trader and published the results of his observations in *The Education of the Poor in England and Europe* (1846), *The Social Condition and Education of the People in England and Europe* (2 vols., 1850), and other works, including *The Condition and Education of Poor Children in English and in German Towns* (1853). His first book led to a difference with William Whewell, master of Trinity.

Kay earned his living as a barrister while participating in Liberal politics, mostly at the local level. He became a judge of the Salford hundred court in June 1862 and in 1863 married Mary Elizabeth, daughter of Thomas *Drummond (1797–1840), civil servant in Ireland, and his wife, Maria. Kay became QC in 1869 and from February 1872 was solicitor-general to the county palatine of Durham. He contested Salford unsuccessfully as a Liberal in 1874 and 1877, but was ill during the 1877 campaign. He took part, with his brother James, in provision for teacher training when the first teacher-training college was established in Battersea. Kay wrote on free trade in land for the *Manchester Examiner* (his articles were posthumously edited by his widow with a preface by John Bright and published as *Free Trade in Land* in 1879; the volume went into many editions). Kay's *The Law Relating to Shipmasters and Seamen, their Appointment, Duties, Powers* (2 vols., 1875) was in its day a standard work, and was revised by J. W. Mansfield and G. W. Duncan (1894).

In London Kay lived at 18 Hyde Park Gardens; he died at his country house, Fredley, near Dorking, on 9 October 1878. His wife survived him. His obituarist remarked: 'he will perhaps be remembered rather as a philosophical thinker than as an ardent partisan' (*Manchester Examiner*).

H. C. G. MATTHEW

Sources *Manchester Examiner* (11 Oct 1878) · 'Memoir', J. Kay, *Free trade in land* (1879) · Venn, *Alum. Cant.* · Boase, *Mod. Eng. biog.* · *CGPLA Eng. & Wales* (1878)

Wealth at death under £5000: probate, 9 Nov 1878, *CGPLA Eng. & Wales*

Kay, Richard (1716–1751), medical practitioner and diarist, was born on 20 March 1716 in Baldingstone, near Bury, Lancashire, the eldest son and second child in the family of two sons and four daughters of Robert Kay (1684–1750), doctor, of Baldingstone, and his wife, Elisabeth (1684–1751), daughter of Samuel Taylor, nonconformist minister, of Moston, near Manchester. John *Kay (1704–1780/81) of Bury, the inventor of the flying shuttle, was his second cousin. The family were nonconformists, attending the Presbyterian chapel in Silver Street, Bury. He was educated locally, leaving school in December 1730 to help his father in the running of his practice. His father saw no need for any further training, intending his son to learn his medical skills from him, but in August 1743, encouraged by a cousin who was in practice in Manchester, Kay

enrolled for one year's training as one of the three pupils of Benjamin Steade, house apothecary at Guy's Hospital, London. On his return to 'Balderstone' with a new box of 'chirurgic instruments', he took over most of the responsibility for the practice.

Kay began to keep a diary on 11 April 1737, shortly after his twenty-first birthday, and extracts were first published anonymously as *A Lancashire Doctor's Diary* (1895) by Robert Kay of Southport. The diary is of particular interest because of the picture it gives both of medical practice in the first half of the eighteenth century, and of the life of nonconformists in the half century after the 1689 Toleration Act gave congregations the right to open their own chapels.

Although Kay does not go into much detail about his year at Guy's Hospital, what information he does give is a unique record of medical education in the eighteenth century. He attended lectures, studied midwifery with the famous man-midwife William Smellie (1697–1763), and watched operations and amputations. After his return the diary records more medical information, although he does not usually give full details of his daily rounds, because he thinks it would be tedious. Nevertheless, a picture is built up of the cases that a provincial doctor had to deal with, and how they were treated, including the man who cracked his skull when the cow he was bleeding threw him, the man who broke his neck falling off a load of hay, and the woman who murdered her illegitimate baby and left him in a ditch. Most ailments were treated by blistering, bleeding, or sweating, and amputations without anaesthetics were common. He goes into detail about the case of a Mrs Driver, whose cancerous breast he amputated, and from whom six months later he removed 500 new tumours: 'she was sick and very poorly after the operation' (*Diary*, 142, 7 June 1749) and died the following year. He delivered many stillborn babies, and attended numerous funerals, many of them of children. He had to travel many miles on horseback to see his patients, often staying to drink a 'dish of tea' with them, or overnight.

About half of the diary is concerned with his religious faith. Kay was a deeply religious man, who worked every day for three years on his 'little manuscript', *Entrance upon the World, or, Self-Employment in Secret*, spiritual exercises in which he tried to improve his mind and qualify himself for what God would call him to do in life. He presented this to his parents in 1740. He attended chapel every Sunday, and went to monthly lectures and prayer meetings as well as his daily prayers and meditation. He ends each diary entry with a short prayer, usually relevant to the events of the day; after delivering his cousin's wife of stillborn twins, he prays: 'Lord, Bless Child-bearing Women; support them under the Severe pain and extream peril of Childbearing' (*Diary*, 134, 24 Dec 1748). Sometimes his prayer was practical; after being out on a wet evening: 'Lord, Preserve me from catching Cold' (*Diary*, 127, 4 March 1748). Every 5 November he attended a service of thanksgiving for deliverance from the 'popish plot' of 1605. As a young man he sometimes indulged in more frivolous pursuits, such as a trip to Kersal Moor races, although he ended that day's diary entry: 'Lord … give Grace and Strength to watch and guard against mad Frolicks, foolish sports, unseasonable and dishonourable Diversions, and wicked and sinful irregularities' (*Diary*, 23, 26 May 1738). He was shocked when he heard the new organ played in the old church in Manchester: music in a religious service seemed 'a merry way of getting to heaven' (*Diary*, 123, 25 Nov 1747).

Kay mentions events of national importance, as when in London he heard war against France declared in the City (31 March 1744), but the most exciting was the 1745 Jacobite rising. He notes the advance of the rebels, bent on putting a 'Popish Pretender' on the English throne. When the Jacobite army reached Carlisle in its march southwards Kay's Manchester relatives hid their valuables and fled to Baldingstone for safety, and when it was in retreat Kay travelled to Manchester to see them, 'having never seen the rebells, or any in Highland Dress' (*Diary*, 103, 10 Dec 1745). On 27 April 1746 he attended a service of thanksgiving for the defeat of the rebels at Culloden. His account brings home the loyalty of the nonconformists to the Hanoverian succession, which preserved the country from 'Popish slavery'.

In 1750 Kay begins to record an outbreak of 'spotted fever' (probably typhus), which carried off several members of his family, including his brother-in-law. His final entry, on 19 July 1750, breaks off in mid-sentence, and the family tree records that his father died on 20 October 1750, and his sister Rachel on 1 January 1751. As Kay, his sister Elizabeth, and his mother all died within a few weeks of each other in October, it is probable that they too were victims of spotted fever. Richard Kay died, unmarried, in Baldingstone on 2 October 1751 and was buried in the chapel graveyard in Bury.　　ANNE PIMLOTT BAKER

Sources *The diary of Richard Kay, 1716–51, of Baldingstone, near Bury, a Lancashire doctor*, ed. W. Brockbank and F. Kenworthy, Chetham Society, 3rd ser., 16 (1968) · J. J. Bagley, *Lancashire diaries* (1975), 102–23

Archives Chetham's Library, Manchester, diary · Man. CL

Kay, Robert (1728–1802). *See under* Kay, John (1704–1780/81).

Kay, William (1820–1886), biblical scholar, the youngest of nine children of Thomas and Ann Kay of Knaresborough, was born on 8 April 1820 at Pickering in the North Riding of Yorkshire. He passed two years at Giggleswick School before winning an open scholarship to Lincoln College, Oxford, on 15 March 1836. He graduated BA in 1839 with a first class in classics and a second in mathematics. He was elected a fellow of Lincoln College on 22 October 1840, where he was appointed a tutor in 1842. After proceeding to an MA, he was elected Pusey and Ellerton Hebrew scholar. He took holy orders in 1843, and in 1844 published a translation of one volume of Fleury's ecclesiastical history, which he edited under the supervision of J. H. Newman.

In 1849, after proceeding to a BD, Kay went to India to take up the job of principal of Bishop's College, Calcutta.

Here he became a figure of some importance in ecclesiastical circles and published several works at the college press, including *The Influence of Christianity on the Position and Character of Women* (1859). The most important of these works was his translation of the Psalms (published 1864; 3rd edn, enlarged and improved, London, 1877). The editorial notes, chiefly critical and exegetical, although somewhat dry in form, seemed suggestive and thoughtful in matter. In 1855 he returned to England for the first time in six years and was awarded a DD from the University of Oxford. In 1864 he resigned his post at Calcutta and returned to Oxford. In 1865 he was made select preacher for the university and in 1869 was appointed Grinfield lecturer on the Septuagint. In 1866 he was presented by Lincoln College to the rectory of Great Leighs, near Chelmsford, Essex, where he remained for the rest of his life, dividing his time between his pastoral work and some writings. *A Sermon on the Unity of the Church* was published in 1866 and *Commentary on the Two Epistles of St. Paul to the Corinthians* was edited and published after his death by fellow clergyman John Slatter.

In 1870 Kay was invited to join the committee to revise the Authorized Version of the Old Testament for the edition subsequently known as the Revised Version (1885). Although he contributed conscientiously to the work, his scholarly conservatism created tensions; his dislike of the historical critical method was clearly reflected in his commentaries on Isaiah and Hebrews (Speaker's Bible, 1875, 1881) and in his contribution of notes on Ezekiel in the commentary published by the Christian Knowledge Society. He also challenged the textual critical work of H. Hupfield and the controversial writings of J. W. Colenso in his *Crisis Hupfeldiana; being an examination of Hupfield's criticism on Genesis as recently set forth in Bishop Colenso's fifth part* (1865), a polemical work of conservative biblical scholarship. Kay was also an honorary canon of St Albans from 1877, and one of the bishop's chaplains. He died, unmarried, on 16 January 1886 at Great Leighs near Chelmsford, after a painful illness.

W. A. GREENHILL, *rev.* JOANNA HAWKE

Sources J. W. Burgon, preface, *Lives of twelve good men*, new edn (1891) · *Foreign Church Chronicle and Review*, 10/37 (March 1886) · personal knowledge (1891) · P. Schaff and S. M. Jackson, *Encyclopedia of living divines and Christian workers of all denominations in Europe and America: being a supplement to Schaff-Herzog encyclopedia of religious knowledge* (1887) · Boase, *Mod. Eng. biog.* · J. Slatter, preface, in W. Kay, *A commentary on the two epistles of St. Paul to the Corinthians*, ed. J. Slatter (1887), v–vii

Wealth at death £2451 1s.: probate, 11 Nov 1887, *CGPLA Eng. & Wales*

Kay, William Kilbourne (1856–1929), mail-order retailer, was born on 11 September 1856 at Market Harborough, Leicestershire, the son of Richard Kay, a doctor. Nothing else is known about his education or early life. However, on 15 February 1883, when he married Jessie Farenden (b. 1857/8), daughter of Charles Farenden, telegraph engineer, in Southampton, he was described on the marriage certificate as a jeweller's assistant. By 1886 Kay was selling goods via mail-order catalogue from premises in Foregate Street, Worcester. He was not the founder of British mail-order retailing; Pryce Jones has a greater claim, and the Bradford-based Fattorini family was ahead of him in selling to customers organized into clubs. Yet he was the first mail-order retailer to devote himself exclusively to the mail-order club business. By 1894 he had embraced the club system in a big way, supplying watches and jewellery to members of 'Kay's Universal Clubs'. Each club member paid a weekly instalment, in total sufficient to purchase an item from the catalogue, and then drew lots to decide whose turn it was to take it home. This boosted the purchasing power of individual customers who might otherwise not have bought at all.

Kay's business flourished and in 1896 he bought Skarratt & Co., long established as watchmakers in Worcester. This allowed him to claim that his firm dated from 1794. It also enabled him to manufacture a range of English Lever watches; these sold in thousands to railwaymen requiring a reliable timepiece. By 1900 Kay was employing fifty packers and clerks at his extensive Shrub Hill premises and he was able to claim that his 6000 spare-time agents were servicing 250,000 customers annually. Kay's catalogue was by then offering a vast range of goods, including clothing, boots and shoes, and household furniture. By 1919, when the company cheekily published a brochure to celebrate 125 years in business, its customers numbered about 500,000.

Kay was a ruthless competitor, not averse to denigrating rival firms, some of which, he claimed, 'were under the thumb of unscrupulous Jews' (Kay & Co. *Catalogue*). As an employer he was a stern disciplinarian, though proud that his modern offices made 'every reasonable provision for the health and comfort of those engaged' (Kay & Co., *125 Years*, 13). He did not neglect civic duties, and served the city of Worcester as high sheriff in 1898–9, councillor from 1896 to 1902, and magistrate from 1900. Kay died at his Worcester home, The Elms, Battenhall, on 2 May 1929, having been ill for three years, and was buried in the churchyard at Hallow, just outside the city. Little is known about his personal life, but he was survived by his wife and by three sons and three daughters. The family retained control of the firm until 1937, when it was absorbed into Isaac Wolfson's Great Universal Stores group.

DILWYN PORTER

Sources Notes and papers useful in compiling a history of Kays, Worcs. RO, BA 5946/3 · R. Coopey, S. O'Connell, and D. Porter, 'Mail order in the United Kingdom, *c.*1880–1960: how mail order competed with other forms of retailing', *International Review of Retailing, Distribution and Consumer Research*, 9/3 (1999), 261–73 · S. O'Connell and D. Porter, 'Cataloguing mail order's archives', *Business Archives*, 80 (2000), 44–54 · *The history of 125 years*, Kay & Co. (1919) · *Catalogue*, Kay & Co. (1894) · private information (2004) · *Worcestershire Echo* (13 June 1898) · *Worcestershire Herald* (11 May 1929) · B. Mills, *Towards a history of Kay & Co Ltd* (2002) · m. cert. · d. cert.
Archives Worcs. RO, business MSS | Reality plc, Worcester, minute books relating to Kay & Co.
Likenesses photograph, repro. in Kay & Co., *History of 125 years*, 1

Kaye [Quaye], **Cab** [real name Augustus Nii-Lante Kwamlah Quaye] (**1921–2000**), musician, singer, and entertainer, was born at 53 Torrington Square, Bloomsbury, London,

on 3 September 1921, the only son and elder of the two children of Caleb Jonas Quaye (Ga name Kobla Quaye), (*c.*1895–1922), a pianist whose stage name was Mope Desmond, and his wife, Doris, *née* Balderson, a music-hall artist. His father was a Ga from the Gold Coast, his mother was English. He was descended from a dynasty of musicians. His paternal grandfather was minister and organist of the Methodist church in Accra, and a great-grandfather played drums with a company of *asafo* warriors (the *asafo* being semi-military bodies organized outside the traditional ruling hierarchies of the Fanti and Ga). His father was killed in a railway accident when Quaye was four months old and the family moved to Portsmouth, where he grew up with his mother and sister.

On leaving school Quaye sold newspapers and sang and danced in local cafés for small change. He won a local talent contest, then at the age of fourteen auditioned successfully for the bandleader Billy Cotton, whom he joined as a band boy before graduating to singer and touring with the band; their recording in 1936 of *Shoe Shine Boy* launched his career. At after-hours clubs in London, Quaye encountered prominent African American musicians, including Fats Waller, on whom he modelled his later piano style. He sang with dance bands in the capital and at the seaside, then in 1939 spent five months in the merchant navy as a galley-boy, using the name Caleb Quaye. He travelled to Siberia and Montreal, where he took lessons from a Canadian drummer. On his return to England in 1940, he was employed by the bandleader Ivor Kirchin and, known as Young Cab, he began playing drums in addition to singing. He replaced Don Johnson as Ken 'Snake Hips' Johnson's vocalist at the Café de Paris and broadcast with his orchestra, but his call-up saved him from the bomb that fell on the café in March 1941, killing the orchestra's leader. During his merchant navy service he travelled again to Canada and to South America and also sustained an extraordinary series of injuries that necessitated an operation performed in New York; while recuperating there, he met and performed with several distinguished jazz musicians. On 5 March 1940 he married Theresa Edna (*b.* 1919), a tailoress from London's East End whose father, Cyril Austin, was a Barbadian seaman. As Theresa Desmond, she sang with Quaye's later bands and was involved with him also in operating a theatrical booking agency. They had three children, Theresa (Terri; *b.* 1940), a singer, drummer, and pianist, Caleb (*b.* 1948), a guitarist who became a minister of religion, and Tanya Elizabeth (*b.* 1952), a community worker and historian.

In 1945 Quaye travelled to India to entertain the forces in a stage act that included the Bermudan actor Earl Cameron. On his return he became the host of Joseph Feldman's popular Sunday afternoon jazz sessions at 100 Oxford Street; there, with an audience eager for radical ideas, he was closely associated with the new wave of jazz modernists, introducing them alongside Caribbean and African instrumentalists, singers, and dancers. About this time he changed his surname to Kaye, and it is by this name that he appeared in later published sources, although he continued to use Quaye intermittently and in his private life.

Working with the bands of Leslie 'Jiver' Hutchinson and Tito Burns, Kaye developed a reputation for energetic singing in the rhythmic African American tradition. He played guitar and in 1948 formed his own Ministers of Swing, which included the leading jazz modernists Ronnie Scott and John Dankworth. In 1950 he assembled an 'all-coloured' band, the first British unit to play before civilian audiences in post-war Germany. Following a long stay in the Netherlands with this group, he established himself as a solo artist in Paris, where he demonstrated an ability to fashion emotive ballads in the manner of Billie Holiday, as well as excite in the wordless scat-singing idiom. After this he performed more usually by accompanying himself at the piano, veering between progressive modern jazz and the more populist rhythm and blues exemplified by Louis Jordan. He reached his largest audience in 1958 through the prototype pop television programme 6–5 *Special*, and on tour with its road show.

Despite his jazz associations with musicians such as the trumpeter Humphrey Lyttelton, Kaye had a strong sense of cultural nationalism and worked often with fellow black Britons. It was through increasing contact with the post-war wave of black settlers that his confidence and sense of himself as an African developed. He established contact with members of his Ghanaian family, and, although he never used it professionally, revived his Ga name, Nii-lante. When Ghana achieved independence in 1960 he was employed as entertainments officer by the Ghana high commission, then in August 1961 he went to Accra as entertainments manager of the Industrial Development Corporation. In 1962 he appeared at the Ghana jazz festival, but his official job ended in 1966 when President Kwame Nkrumah was deposed. He moved to Lagos, Nigeria, and remained there, apart from a visit in 1964 to New York, until 1970. In that year, following his divorce, he married a woman named Evelyn (*c*.1943–1982), an Igbo Nigerian, and returned to Britain.

In London Kaye attempted to rekindle the excitement of an earlier era, but found changes. A particular kind of refined cabaret milieu inspired him, and he discovered this in Amsterdam, where he reverted to the name Quaye. In 1979 he opened a piano bar there and on 21 March, following his divorce, married Jeanette van Rooy, formerly van der Brink (*b*. 1938), a dress designer, becoming stepfather to her children: Norbert (*b*. 1961), Nicole (*b*. 1962), and Barbera (*b*. 1967). He was also the father of Finley Quaye McGowan (born Finley McGowan in Edinburgh in 1975), the singer known as Finley Quaye.

Quaye was a dedicated and exciting musical performer whose significance went further than the ability to deliver an effervescent song while playing capable stride piano. Although he travelled widely during an extraordinary life, he never lost his place in the British jazz psyche. He was an inspirational figure to expatriate Africans and jazz modernists alike, and his presence in British jazz circles served as a link between that community and the music's African past. He died from cancer in Amsterdam on 13 March 2000, survived by his wife, Jeanette, his four children, and his three stepchildren. He was buried in Amsterdam.

VAL WILMER

Sources J. Marshall, 'Torpedoed … shipwrecked … injured, but he met all the swing stars', *Melody Maker* (26 Dec 1942), 6 · B. Okonedo, 'Like father, like son', *Melody Maker* (26 May 1973), 6 · V. Wilmer, *The Guardian* (21 March 2000) · S. Voce, *The Independent* (17 March 2000) · *The Times* (21 March 2000) · *Daily Telegraph* (20 April 2000) · personal knowledge (2004) · private information (2004) · b. cert. · m. cert. · seamen's papers
Likenesses J. Marshall, photograph, 1942, repro. in *Melody Maker* (26 Dec 1942) · V. Wilmer, photograph, 1961 (with Ronnie Scott), repro. in *The Guardian* (21 March 2000) · photographs, before 1961, priv. coll. · V. Wilmer, photographs, 1961–71, priv. coll. · V. Wilmer, photographs, 1973, priv. coll. · photograph, 1977, repro. in *The Times* · photograph, repro. in *Daily Telegraph*

Kaye, Sir Cecil (1868–1935), intelligence officer in India, was born on 27 May 1868, at Rosevale, Madron, near Penzance, Cornwall, the son of William Kaye, an officer of the Bengal civil service, and his wife, Jane Margaret, *née* Beckett. He entered Winchester School in March 1881. In March 1889 he joined the 2nd battalion, the Derbyshire regiment, as an officer. In 1892 he transferred to the Indian army and saw active service in the fierce campaigns of 1897 to 1898 against the tribes of the north-west frontier. He was awarded a medal with clasp for his services. From 1900 to 1901 he was a member of the British contingent of the international expeditionary force sent to suppress the Boxer uprising in northern China. At Tientsin he met Margaret Sarah, the daughter of the Revd T. Bryson, of the London Missionary Society; they married in 1905, and had one son and two daughters. In 1908 Kaye was appointed to the general staff at Indian army headquarters, Simla, where he served as deputy adjutant to the quartermaster-general in the intelligence branch.

Upon the outbreak of the First World War in August 1914 Kaye was appointed deputy chief censor, India. In this capacity he worked closely with the government of India's political intelligence office, the department of criminal intelligence (DCI), which was then under the distinguished leadership of Sir Charles Cleveland. Kaye made a reputation in India for his ability to cipher and decipher secret messages. At the end of the war he visited London, where he studied the home government's facilities for signals intelligence; the experience made him conscious, as he admitted to close friends, that he was only a beginner in the field. Kaye was made CSI in 1917 and CBE in 1919.

In 1919 Kaye was seeking retirement from the Indian army when, to his surprise, he was offered the directorship of the department of central intelligence (as the DCI was named after March 1918), following Cleveland's resignation. The government of India had initially offered the post to David Petrie of the Indian police, who was too exhausted to take it. On accepting, Kaye was placed on special duty under the home department on 29 September 1919. His appointment was initially temporary, but on 7 May 1920 he was confirmed in this office. Though he never acquired Cleveland's high reputation, Kaye was an efficient head of intelligence and was popular with his colleagues. He played a significant role in shaping the government of India's restrained response to Russian Bolshevism. As early as February 1923 he wrote that there were few Bolshevik agents in India of whom the DCI did not know. All the available evidence indicates that his conclusion was accurate.

In 1924 Kaye retired as director of central intelligence and was knighted for his work. He was succeeded by David Petrie. At the beginning of 1925 he began work on *Communism in India*, which appeared the following year as a secret publication of the government of India. In this volume he summarized the conclusions of his department about its work against the Bolsheviks and their Indian agents for the period 1919 to 1924. He retired from the army in 1925 and, after a short period in England, took service as a minister of the small Indian princely state of Tonk. On retiring from service there, he settled at Srinagar in the foothills of the Himalayas. He wrote weekly letters to the journal *Near East and India*. Kaye and his wife continued to be popular figures in the social life of the British government at its twin centres of New Delhi and Simla. On 5 March 1935, a few days after his daughter's wedding, he died of a heart attack at New Delhi. At his request the funeral took place at Sanawar in the Simla hills. An obituarist noted his 'peculiar faculty of putting his ear to the ground and ascertaining the trend of opinion and movements, whether open or subterranean', going on to observe that his 'small neat handwriting was an index of his precision' (*The Times*, 6 March 1935). His daughter Mary Margaret Kaye (*b*. 1909) gained repute as a popular novelist and wrote an autobiography, *The Sun in the Morning* (1990), which covers the period of her father's active career.

RICHARD POPPLEWELL

Sources *Proceedings of the Home Department of the Government of India*, A ser. (1919–24) · C. Kaye, *Communism in India*, ed. M. Saha (1971) · *The Times* (6 March 1935) · R. J. Popplewell, *Intelligence and imperial defence* (1995) · WWW · b. cert.

Kaye, Sir Emmanuel (1914–1999), industrialist, was born on 29 November 1914 in Russia, the eldest child in the family of two sons and one daughter of Zelman Kaye, a wheat merchant, and his wife, a botanist who had trained in Paris at the Sorbonne. He grew up near Kew Gardens, in Kew, Surrey, and was educated at Richmond Hill School, leaving at the age of fifteen after the death of his father. He took a job with a small engineering firm in Mortlake, and studied engineering in the evenings at Twickenham Technical College.

In 1940 Kaye and a colleague, John Sharp (*d*. 1965), left the firm and pooled their savings to buy two lathes and set up their own engineering business in rented rooms at Mortlake railway station. J. E. Shay Ltd (a combination of E. Kaye and J. Sharp) made precision gauges, tools, and instruments for large companies, including Ford and Hoover. Looking ahead to the future of the company once the Second World War ended and government orders dried up, in 1943 they bought Lansing Bagnall & Co., a small company in Isleworth making electric platform trucks and Imp tractors, which was about to go bankrupt, and

founded Lansing Bagnall Ltd. For the rest of the war employees of both factories were occupied in making parts of radio control mechanisms for bomber aircraft, but at the same time the firm began to develop prototypes for post-war production, among them a new industrial tractor, the Model A, introduced in 1945, which remained in production until 1965. On 25 August 1946 Kaye married Elizabeth (*b*. 1925/6), the daughter of Mark Cutler, a sub-postmaster: they had one son and two daughters.

In 1946 Kaye and Sharp toured the United States and became sole agents importing Baker electric fork-lift trucks: fork-lift trucks were hardly known in England, although they had been used by American forces during the war. At the same time they developed the Model P truck, the first powered pallet truck made in Britain. A few months before Kaye's marriage, he and Sharp had bought a 40 acre site in Basingstoke, Hampshire, which had been earmarked by the government for new town development after the war, and in 1949 they opened a factory employing a workforce of fifty, making Model P fork-lift trucks, which proved so popular that by 1951 they were building 350 a year. They also won the concession to import and sell heavy steel mill and die-handling trucks from the Automatic Transportation Company of Chicago, and they supplied twenty-five of these to the south Wales steel industry between 1949 and 1956. In 1961 they opened a new factory and introduced the very successful Rapide electric fork-lift truck. Kaye displayed his new models to the public at the biennial Mechanical Handling Exhibition at Olympia, and later at Earl's Court, and other publicity ventures included 'Express Productivity' in 1955, when he chartered a train which travelled round the country for six weeks, demonstrating the potential of mechanical handling equipment. After Lansing Bagnall lent three fork-lift trucks to Shepperton film studios in 1958 for the making of *I'm All Right Jack*, released in 1960, the name Lansing Bagnall became familiar all over the world, and the firm took advantage of this to mount displays in the foyers of cinemas where the film was showing. Meanwhile, they established overseas subsidiary companies, starting in Switzerland in 1957, and in 1961 they set up Lansing Bagnall International Ltd.

In 1966 a new holding company, Lansing Bagnall Group Ltd, was incorporated, and Kaye became chairman in 1970. The company expanded to become the biggest employer in Basingstoke, with a workforce of 3500 at its peak, and the largest manufacturer of electric fork-lift trucks in Europe, with nine overseas companies, and forty worldwide distributors. By 1969, 60 per cent of all electric trucks exported from the United Kingdom were built by Lansing Bagnall at Basingstoke. Winner of five queen's awards for export achievement between 1969 and 1980, in 1972 Lansing Bagnall became the first company to win queen's awards for both export achievement and technological innovation. The company made other materials handling equipment, and also diversified for a time into lawnmowers and industrial robots.

In 1989 Kaye sold Lansing Bagnall to the German manufacturing firm of Linde, and became honorary president of what became Lansing Linde Ltd. He went on to found Kaye Enterprises Ltd, developing a scheme he had started in 1977 to provide capital for young entrepreneurs setting up in business, enterprises including retirement homes and computer software. Among his other business interests were chairmanships of the Elvetham Hall conference centre (1965–98), Pool & Sons (Hartley Wintney) Ltd (1967–90), Kaye Steel Stockholders (1978–95), and Kaye Office Supplies Ltd (1983–9). He also bought a stake in the consortium which bought the Coventry Climax fork-lift truck business from British Leyland in the early 1980s.

Kaye played an active part in dealings between business and the government, and in 1968 he founded the Unquoted Companies Group, an alliance of large private firms opposed to the industrial policies of the Labour governments of the 1960s and 1970s. He was a member of the council of the Confederation of British Industry from 1976 to 1989, and from 1985 to 1992 he was on the organization's economic and financial policy committee. He was also a member of the Council of Industry for Management Education from 1970 to 1987, and of the Reviewing Committee on the Export of Works of Art from 1977 to 1980. Strongly opposed to British membership of the single European currency, he was a founder member of Business for Sterling in 1998.

A believer in alternative medicine, Kaye was a patron of the British Homeopathic Association from 1987, vice-president of the Natural Medicines Society from 1986 and of the National Pure Water Association, and from 1977 a fellow of the Psionic Medical Society, which promoted alternative treatments for incurable diseases. Chairman of the Thrombosis Research Trust from 1985, he donated the money to found the Thrombosis Research Institute in London, opened a building named after him in 1990, and served as its first chairman, while other beneficiaries of his generosity included the National Portrait Gallery in London, where he funded a new room, and charities in Israel. His interests extended to chess and opera, and he went to the Salzburg Festival every year for thirty-three years. He was a trustee of Glyndebourne from 1977 to 1984.

Kaye was knighted in 1974. He died on 28 February 1999 in the Hampshire Clinic, Basing Road, Basingstoke, survived by his wife and their three children.

ANNE PIMLOTT BAKER

Sources L. T. C. Rolt, *Lansing Bagnall: the first twenty-one years at Basingstoke* (1970) · *Daily Telegraph* (3 March 1999) · *The Times* (15 March 1999) · private information (2004) [David Kaye, son] · *WWW* · m. cert. · d. cert.
Archives CAC Cam., archives of Lansing Bagnall
Likenesses P. Brason, ink drawing, 1990, priv. coll.; repro. in www.paulbrason.co.uk/Drawings/SirEmmanuelKaye.htm, accessed 31 Oct 2002 · P. Brason, oils, 1991, NPG · photograph, repro. in *Daily Telegraph*
Wealth at death £46,346,189—gross; £31,149,107—net: probate, 30 July 1999, *CGPLA Eng. & Wales*

Kaye, John (1783–1853), bishop of Lincoln, was born on 27 December 1783 at his parents' home in Angel Street, Hammersmith, the only son of Abraham Kaye (1728/9–1823), linen draper, and his wife, Susan Bracken (1739/40–1829).

John Kaye (1783–1853), by Samuel Lane, *c.*1840

Abraham moved to 17 Friday Street, Cheapside, about 1789, trading there as an importer of French cambric until about 1799.

Educated by the Greek scholar Charles Burney (whose school was at Hammersmith and then at Greenwich), Kaye matriculated at Christ's College, Cambridge, on 6 February 1800, and became a foundation scholar on 17 December 1800. At Cambridge he studied under Richard Porson, forming a close lifetime association with C. J. Blomfield, afterwards bishop of London, and J. H. Monk, afterwards bishop of Gloucester. In 1804 he achieved the rare distinction of graduating BA as both senior wrangler and senior chancellor's medallist, also taking the second Smith's prize, and on 5 December 1804 was elected to a Christ's fellowship. He graduated MA in 1807, BD in 1814, and DD in 1815. He served as college tutor from 1804 until, on 5 September 1814, when still aged only thirty, he was elected master of Christ's. During 1815–16 he was vice-chancellor of Cambridge University. On 18 July 1815 he married Eliza (d. 1864), eldest daughter of the Cambridge banker John Mortlock; they had one son and three daughters.

Considered for the regius professorship of Greek on Porson's death in 1808, Kaye withdrew in favour of Monk. The July 1816 vacancy in the regius professorship of divinity placed Kaye in a delicate position. As vice-chancellor he was ineligible for any professorship; he was an elector and moreover responsible for convening the electoral body, and he was known to be the preferred candidate. After taking legal advice, the other electors deferred appointing until November, when Kaye ceased to be vice-chancellor.

Kaye's strength of candidacy and known personal probity averted any scandal.

Although the Norrisian and Lady Margaret professors of divinity at Cambridge regularly delivered courses of lectures, the regius professor's public lectures had been suspended for over a century. Kaye reinstated them, observing that while his predecessors had no need to lecture, the spread of printing giving ready access to the latest work in divinity, his own day attributed the absence of lectures to indolence. For subject he chose the fathers, fostering the general revival in patristic studies which helped incubate Tractarianism. Kaye published lectures on Tertullian and the ecclesiastical history of the second and third centuries (1825), Justin Martyr (1829), Clement of Alexandria (1835), and Athanasius and the Council of Nicaea (posthumous, 1853). These won lasting esteem; his Justin Martyr was still in print, unaltered, in 1917.

In 1820 Lord Liverpool made Kaye bishop of Bristol. The see's low revenues necessitated retaining his chair and mastership. Consecrated at Lambeth on 30 July 1820, Kaye continued to reside in Cambridge, Liverpool's valued adviser on university affairs. He took a leading part in Cambridge curriculum reform, particularly the 'ten-year' degree scheme for non-graduate clergymen. He became president of the Philosophical Society in 1827 and a fellow of the Royal Society in 1848.

Kaye established himself as an active diocesan, aligning himself with the high-church reforming group known as the Hackney Phalanx. He denounced baptism in private homes, sloppy enactment of the Lord's Supper, and irregular conducting of marriages without banns, and reinstated the historic office of rural dean. As bishop of Bristol he concerned himself with the slave trade, urging proper recognition of slaves as fellow human beings with spiritual needs, and hailing the eventual liberation of slaves throughout the British empire as 'an act of national ... justice' (J. Kaye, Sermons and Addresses, ed. W. F. J. Kaye, 1856, 441).

In February 1827 Liverpool translated Kaye to the diocese of Lincoln, then comprising 1273 benefices. Kaye resigned his professorship, remaining master of Christ's until 1830, and moved to the episcopal palace at Buckden, Huntingdonshire. Concerned at the strength of dissent in his vast diocese, he set about reinvigorating parochial life. He promoted church extension and parsonage building, enforced the holding of two Sunday services, and combated non-residence and pluralism. Ably supported by his archdeacons, particularly Charles Goddard of Lincoln and the Hackney Phalanx associate Henry Bayley of Stow, he again reinstituted rural deans. Kaye welcomed the 1839 innovation of diocesan boards of education, and in 1844 commissioned a thoroughgoing diocesan overhaul of church schools. He supported the National Society, the SPCK, and the Society for the Propagation of the Gospel, but refused to endorse the evangelical Bible Society because it included dissenters. Kaye detested evangelicals, urging Liverpool in 1821 to avoid their preferment as 'in general most unfit to be trusted with Power' (Knight, 20).

Kaye had strong views on ordination training. In 1819 he argued that all ordinands should undertake examined postgraduate study in divinity. At Lincoln he refused to ordain or license non-graduates, and was the first bishop to insist all his Cambridge ordinands sit the postgraduate voluntary theological examination introduced in 1843. He was asked in 1838 to examine Princess Victoria on her progress in general studies prior to her coronation. As bishop of Lincoln, and hence visitor to Lincoln and Brasenose colleges, he won the respect of Oxford: Balliol elected him its visitor in 1848, and he was a key mediator during the 1851 disputed Lincoln rectorship election involving Mark Pattison.

The troubled years of reform in church and state which followed Kaye's translation marked a watershed in his episcopal career. His maiden speech in the House of Lords, in 1828, supported repeal of the Test Acts. He voted with his conservative Hackney Phalanx colleagues against Catholic relief in 1829 and against the 1831 Parliamentary Reform Bill, but parted decisively from them during the ensuing crisis. Kaye, with Blomfield and Monk, voted for the 1832 bill, declaring unambiguous support for the principle of reform. Their reformist credentials proven under fire, in 1835 Blomfield, Kaye, and Monk formed the episcopal nucleus of Peel's revolutionary ecclesiastical commission.

As a commissioner Kaye learned for the first time how dire was the church's situation in the new urban manufacturing centres. His 1838 Letter to the Archbishop of Canterbury made a personal apologia for the radical measures the commissioners felt compelled to propose. Kaye saw the need for sacrifice: the Established Church Act of 1836 cut the Lincoln episcopal revenues by around half, and the transfer of Huntingdonshire to the Ely diocese cost Kaye his palace. The commissioners remodelled Riseholme, 2 miles outside Lincoln, for his new residence; the expenditure caused scandal and was censured by an 1848 parliamentary report.

Kaye was initially sympathetic to Tractarianism; Newman reckoned his 1837 charge to the clergy of his diocese supportive. In 1841 he forbade one of his clergy, Bernard Smith (1815–1903), rector of Leadenham, to keep a cross and candlesticks on the communion table. Smith, influenced by Wiseman, converted to Roman Catholicism at Christmas 1842. The Morning Herald accused Newman of counselling him to retain his rectory after conversion. Kaye used hard words about Newman's role in the affair. Following a pacific intervention by Pusey, Kaye accepted Newman's explanations and apologized, but remained deeply unhappy; Newman's secession to Rome he thought 'an action which he should have taken far sooner' (3 Nov 1845, Kaye correspondence). Kaye's 1846 charge contained a bitter attack on the Tractarians as betraying the English Reformation. He was a co-founder of the shortlived 1844 English Review, intended to replace the Tractarian British Critic, and resigned from the Camden Society over the 1845 Round Church controversy.

Kaye wrote for the British Magazine under the pseudonym Philalethes Cantabrigiensis, attacking Wiseman's Letters on the Rule of Faith and Thomas Moore's Travels of an

Irish Gentleman in Search of a Religion. An uncompromising opponent of Catholic 'errors', Kaye was kind to R. W. Sibthorp following his 1843 return to Anglicanism, after ordination and ministry as a Roman Catholic priest. Sibthorp reconverted to Rome in 1865.

Kaye died on 18 February 1853 at his palace at Riseholme, and was buried in the churchyard there. A memorial effigy by Westmacott at Lincoln Cathedral, echoing a medieval chantry tomb, caused acrimonious controversy as too naturalistic: 'exhibiting … not the triumph of the Christian over death, but of death over the Christian' (*Report of the Lincoln Diocesan Architectural Society*, 1858). The Kaye prize, endowed in 1861 from the balance of the memorial fund, continued to be awarded into the twenty-first century.   E. A. VARLEY

Sources R. Foskett, 'John Kaye and the diocese of Lincoln', PhD diss., U. Nott., 1957 · F. M. R. Knight, 'Bishop, clergy and people: John Kaye and the diocese of Lincoln, 1827–1853', PhD diss., U. Cam., 1990 · *Lincolnshire Chronicle, and Northampton, Rutland, and Nottingham Advertiser* (25 Feb 1853), 4e–f · *Lincoln, Rutland, and Stamford Mercury* (25 Feb 1853), 3d · J. A. Jeremie, *The Times* (22 Feb 1853); repr. with slight abridgment in J. Kaye, *Nine charges, with other works*, ed. W. F. J. Kaye (1854); and with minor changes in *Works of Bishop Kaye*, 8 (1888) · *DNB* · O. Chadwick, *The Victorian church*, 2 vols. (1966–70) · G. F. A. Best, *Temporal pillars: Queen Anne's bounty, the ecclesiastical commissioners, and the Church of England* (1964) · J. Peile, *Biographical register of Christ's College, 1505–1905, and of the earlier foundation, God's House, 1448–1505*, ed. [J. A. Venn], 2 (1913) · Venn, *Alum. Cant.* · Lincoln College, Oxford, Kaye correspondence · *Lincolnshire Chronicle* (4 March 1853)
Archives Lincoln College, Oxford, corresp. · Lincs. Arch., corresp.; corresp. relating to the Quadring estate | BL, corresp. with Liverpool, the bishop of Moray, the third and fourth earls of Hardwicke, John Hobhouse, and the duchess of Kent · BL, corresp. with Sir Robert Peel, Add. MSS 40303-40573, *passim* · LPL, letters to Charles Golightly
Likenesses T. Lawrence, oils, *c.*1828 (finished by F. R. Say), Old Palace, Lincoln · J. Ternouth, marble bust, 1834, Brasenose College, Oxford · S. Lane, portrait, *c.*1840, bishop's palace, Lincoln [*see illus.*] · R. Westmacott junior, memorial effigy, 1857, Lincoln Cathedral · oils, Christ's College, Cambridge

Kaye, Sir John William (1814–1876), military historian, born in London, and baptized on 30 June 1814, was the second son of Charles Kaye of Acton, Middlesex, sometime solicitor to the Bank of England, and his wife, Eliza, daughter of Hugh Atkins. He was educated at Salisbury, at Eton College (*c.*1826), and Addiscombe College (1831–2), which he later remembered with affection, and praised as 'a great nursery of Indian captains' (Kaye, 1.147). In 1832 he went to India as a Bengal artillery cadet (commissioned 14 December 1833). He married in 1839 Mary Catherine (1813–1893), daughter of Thomas Puckle, chairman of quarter sessions for Surrey. Following ill health, he resigned from the army on 1 April 1841, and devoted himself to writing. He at first remained in India, and in April 1841 joined the staff of the *Bengal Harkaru* ('The atlas'). He started the *Calcutta Review* in 1844, editing it and contributing nearly fifty articles on political, military, and social subjects. He also wrote a novel, *Long Engagements: a Tale of the Affghan Rebellion* (1846). However, about 1845 Kaye returned to England for a professional literary career. In 1856 he entered the home civil service of the East India

Company, and on the transfer of the government of India to the crown in 1858, he succeeded John Stuart Mill as secretary of the foreign department of the India Office; he was made a KCSI on 20 May 1871. Failing health obliged him to retire in 1874, and he was awarded a generous pension by the India Office. His country residence was Cliff House, Laugharne, Carmarthenshire.

Kaye was a prolific writer and frequent contributor to periodicals. In 1851 he published his two-volume *History of the War in Afghanistan*, in 1852 he edited Buckle's *Memoirs of the Services of the Bengal Artillery*, and in 1853 he edited Tucker's *Memorials of Indian Government*. He published a history of the *Administration of the East India Company* (1853), *The Life and Correspondence of Charles, Lord Metcalfe* (2 vols., 1854), *The Life and Correspondence of Henry St. George Tucker* (1854), *Selections from the Papers of Baron Metcalfe* (1855), *Life and Correspondence of Sir John Malcolm* (2 vols., 1856), and *Christianity in India* (1859). In 1861 he edited *The Autobiography of Miss Cornelia Knight*.

Kaye's best-known work, *The History of the Sepoy War in India, 1857–8* (3 vols., 1864–76), is 'a well-ordered and comprehensive narrative'. In the last volume he commented on the conduct of the 52nd (Oxfordshire light infantry) and the third column of assault at the siege of Delhi, and a controversy followed. Major J. A. Bayley's *Assault of Delhi* (1876) defended the regiment, and Henry Durand in 1876 vindicated his father in a pamphlet entitled *Central India in 1857*. *The History of the Sepoy War* was revised and continued by Colonel G. B. Malleson, and the whole work, entitled *Kaye and Malleson's History of the Indian Mutiny*, was completed in six volumes in 1890. In 1867 Kaye published *Lives of Indian Officers*, originally a series of articles called 'Indian Heroes' in *Good Words* (1866). In 1867 he supplied the text to a series of illustrations from drawings by W. Simpson, entitled *India Ancient and Modern*, and in 1868, with J. F. Watson, edited Taylor's *People of India*. In 1870 he published *Essays of an Optimist*, articles reprinted from the *Cornhill Magazine*. Kaye died at his residence, Rose Hill, Forest Hill, London, on 24 July 1876. His works are still used by historians, and his *Sepoy War* is still considered a standard work.   E. J. RAPSON, *rev.* ROGER T. STEARN

Sources *The Times* (27 July 1876) · *The Athenaeum* (29 July 1876), 146 · F. J. Goldsmid, *The Academy* (5 Aug 1876), 136 · *Pioneer Mail* (9 Aug 1876) · H. M. Vibart, *Addiscombe: its heroes and men of note* (1894) · *Dod's Peerage* (1875) · J. W. Kaye, *Lives of Indian officers*, 1 (1867) · C. Hibbert, *The great mutiny, India, 1857* (1978) · S. Wolpert, *A new history of India* (1993) · E. Stokes, *The peasant armed: the Indian revolt of 1857* (1986) · Boase, *Mod. Eng. biog.* · H. E. C. Stapylton, *The Eton school lists, from 1791 to 1850*, 2nd edn (1864) · P. J. O. Taylor, ed., *A companion to the 'Indian mutiny' of 1857* (1996) · J. M. Brown, *Modern India: the origins of an Asian democracy*, 2nd edn (1994) · CGPLA Eng. & Wales (1877)
Archives BL, corresp. with Sir Austen Layard, Add. MSS 38991, 39103–39118 *passim* · NL Scot., letters to Alexander Campbell Fraser · SOAS, letters to Sir William Mackinnon
Likenesses A. Brodie, plaster bust, BL OIOC
Wealth at death £1500: administration with will, 9 March 1877, *CGPLA Eng. & Wales*

Kayode, Oluwarotimi Adebiyi Wahab [Rotimi] **Fani-** (1955–1989), photographer, was born in Lagos, Nigeria, on 20 April 1955, the son of Chief Remi Fani-Kayode (1921–

1995), balogun of Ife and politician. The Kayode family traditionally held the title of Akire, keepers of the shrine of Ifa, the oracle, in Ile-Ife, the cradle of Yoruba culture. Fani-Kayode moved to Britain with his family in 1966, when his father was ousted from his position as deputy prime minister of the western region by the military coup which ended Nigeria's first republic. After education at Millfield School Fani-Kayode travelled to the United States to study economics and fine art at Georgetown University (c.1976–80) before taking an MA in fine art (specializing in photography) at the Pratt Institute in Brooklyn, New York. His degree work included surrealistic colour portraits of black men in Yoruba attire.

In 1983 Fani-Kayode returned to Britain, where he settled in Brixton, London, and pursued his career as a photographer. He was a founder member of and was the first to chair Autograph (the association of black photographers) in 1987; he was also active in the Brixton Artists' Collective. His photographic work explored Yoruba traditions, especially of spirituality. His work also explored black sexuality and its relationship to homosexuality. His photographs, such as *Bronze Head* (1987) and the last series of photographs he made with his partner, Alex Hirst, were often compared with the images of Robert Mapplethorpe, though he frequently acknowledged other influences, including Henri Cartier-Bresson, George Platt Lynes, and Alfred Stieglitz, as well as west African traditions of visual representation. Alex Hirst described Fani-Kayode's photographs as 'complex, sometimes disturbing, but always honest and elegant' (*The Independent*, 28 Dec 1989).

Fani-Kayode's photographs were included in exhibitions at the Art Show Gallery, London, in 1984, Brixton Art Gallery in 1985, the Oval House Gallery, London, in 1986 and 1987, and in 'Bodies of Experience: Stories about Living with HIV' at the Camerawork Gallery, London, in 1989; he also held solo exhibitions at 181 Gallery, London, in 1988, and the Submarine Gallery, London, in 1989. In 1988 he published a book of photographs, *Black Male/White Male*. He died of AIDS-related illness at Coppetts Wood Hospital, Muswell Hill, London, on 21 December 1989, and was survived by his partner, Alex Hirst. Posthumous retrospectives of his work were held at the 198 Gallery, London, in 1990, and at the Black Art Gallery, London, in 1991; his photographs were also included in the 'Ecstatic Antibodies' exhibition at Battersea Arts Centre, London, in 1989, and in the 'Retro-Spective' exhibition at the Impressions Gallery, York, and the Chapter Gallery, Cardiff, in 1995. In 1996 Editions Revue Noire of Paris published his last, collaborative, work as *Rotimi Fani-Kayode and Alex Hirst, photographs*. PAULINE DE SOUZA

Sources M. Sealey and J. L. Pivin, *Rotimi Fani-Kayode and Alex Hirst, photographs* (Paris, 1996) · *Rotimi Fani-Kayode, 1955–1989: communion* (1995) · D. Bright, *The passionate camera: photography and bodies of desire* (1998) · D. A. Bailey, 'Photographic animateur: the photographs of Rotimi Fani-Kayode in relation to black photographic practice', *Third Text*, 13 (winter 1990–91), 57–63 · A. Hirst, *The last supper: a creative farewell to Rotimi Fani-Kayode* (1992) · K. Mercer, 'Mortal coil: eros and diaspora in the photographs of Rotimi Fani-Kayode', *Over Exposed: essays on contemporary photography*, ed. C. Squiers (1999), 183–210 · *The Independent* (28 Dec 1989) · d. cert.

Keach, Benjamin (1640–1704), Particular Baptist minister, was born on 29 February 1640 in Stoke Hammond, Buckinghamshire, the son of John and Fedora Keach. He was baptized at Stoke Hammond on 6 March of that year. His parents could not afford formal education, and Keach was therefore apprenticed to trade, apparently as a tailor.

Described as a 'precocious youth' (Whiting, 84), Keach nevertheless seems to have been rigorously self-educated. Questioning the validity of infant baptism at an early age, he devoted himself to scriptural study and presented himself for believer's baptism by immersion in 1655. Three years later, aged eighteen, he entered the General Baptist ministry at a church in Winslow, Buckinghamshire; he had not, however, been ordained. In 1660 Keach married Jane Grove (c.1640–1670) of Winslow; they went on to have four daughters and a son. After the Restoration in 1660 Keach—a 'Bold and zealous preacher' (Ivimey, 1.339)—was frequently harassed and arrested for his unlicensed activities. In 1664 he narrowly escaped trampling when troops interrupted a meeting; saved by an officer's intervention, he was nevertheless prosecuted and briefly imprisoned.

Later in 1664 Keach published anonymously *The Child's Instructor*. Beyond basic instruction in reading, writing, and arithmetic, this primer attacked paedobaptism, advocated lay preaching, and expressed explicitly millenarian sentiments. Intercepted by a local Anglican rector, this overtly educational exposition of Baptist doctrine was deemed 'schismatic and heretical' (*CSP dom.*, 1663–4, 595), and Keach was arrested for sedition. He was indicted at the Aylesbury assizes on 8 October and tried the following day. Keach refused to renounce the book's tenets under pressure. He was imprisoned for a fortnight and pilloried at Aylesbury, where he transformed his public humiliation into an opportunity to preach before a supportive crowd. His pillorying at Winslow the following week was executed more strictly, and on this occasion copies of his book were burnt by the hangman. Of the 1500-copy imprint of this book, not one survived. Keach was finally fined £20 and bound upon surety to good behaviour.

Following this episode, Keach and his family were apparently unable to settle in Buckinghamshire. For the next four years Keach preached on an itinerant basis, and was imprisoned again at least once before moving to London in 1668. He quickly became ordained, and was appointed elder of a General Baptist congregation based in Tooley Street, Southwark. Meeting in private houses, this congregation nevertheless failed to escape prosecution by parochial and state authorities. Throughout this period Keach was inclining spiritually towards Calvinism, a process catalysed by contact with William Kiffin and Hanserd Knollys.

In 1670 Keach's beloved wife died aged thirty. In 1672 Keach declared himself a Calvinist and, presumably on the basis of a split in his church, founded a Particular Baptist church in Horselydown, Southwark. The declaration

Benjamin Keach (1640–1704), by Michael Vandergucht, pubd 1701 (after J. Surmans)

of indulgence that year facilitated erection of a meeting-house in Goat Street, Horselydown, and the congregation and building expanded rapidly over subsequent decades. Also in 1672, under the officiation of Knollys, Keach married Susanna Partridge (*née* Skidmore) (d. 1727), a widow from Hertfordshire; the couple subsequently had five daughters. Around this time, Keach rewrote *The Child's Instructor* from memory and was fined £20; the book went on to enjoy extensive reprinting in Pennsylvania.

Keach's subsequent career as a Particular Baptist minister was controversial, influential, and remarkably active. Over the next three decades he engaged unwaveringly in public and printed controversy with opponents of all denominations. In the mid-1670s he published an attack on Quakerism and began an extended polemic with the proponents of infant baptism. In 1674 Keach published a brief, but by all accounts pointed, polemic—of which no copy survives—against the paedobaptist arguments of Richard Baxter. Seeking to expose perceived contradictions in Baxter's theology, Keach criticized in particular his bias towards conditional justification; Baxter retorted in print the following year. Keach was still publishing against paedobaptists the year before his death, and while Crosby emphasizes Keach's own adherence to the rules of disputation (Crosby, 4.286) he did occasionally elicit harsh *ad hominem* retorts. Similarly, he disputed Henry

Danvers's opposition to the laying on of hands on baptized believers in 1675, and published a further defence of the controversial practice as late as 1698.

Keach was also involved in heated disputes with his own church. First and foremost, he withstood opposition within his congregation to establish congregational hymn singing as an intrinsic element of worship. Hymns, indeed, had been incorporated into the notorious *Child's Instructor*. In the mid-1670s Keach introduced hymn singing in the Horselydown church at the end of the Lord's supper. Over the next two decades, the practice was extended to include, firstly, public thanksgiving days and, finally, regular Sunday worship. Keach's initiative elicited vociferous opposition both among and outside his congregation. In 1691 a number of objectors within the church seceded to form a new congregation in Tooley Street; meanwhile, Keach was obliged to defend the practice in print against other Baptist leaders. While not a pioneer of congregational hymn singing, Keach was hugely influential in its establishment within Baptist churches. He published a number of hymn collections, including *Spiritual Melody* (1691); no copy survives of his earliest collection (c.1674). A further dispute centred upon a minority promulgation of the seventh-day sabbath within his congregation; Keach's quashing of the disturbance was attended by the publication in 1700 of *The Jewish Sabbath Abrogated*, a work which received the approbation of Archbishop Tillotson.

In 1688–9 Keach published two key works, *Distressed Sion Relieved* and *Antichrist Stormed*, which clearly declared his whig sympathies. Having advocated the payment of ministers in a controversial treatise of 1688, he was among the conveners of a general assembly of Particular Baptist elders and ministers the following year. The assembly endorsed Keach's recommendations for a paid ministry, and sent him on a preaching mission throughout East Anglia; Keach proceeded to establish a church at Lavenham, Suffolk, prompting a printed dispute with a local rector, and secured the erection of meeting-houses in south-east London and Essex.

In addition to his polemical writing, Keach produced an exegetical and didactic *œuvre* of exceptional generic diversity, ranging from allegory (*War with the Devil*, 1673; *The Progress of Sin*, 1684) to quasi-epic poetry (*The Glorious Lover*, 1679). In 1682 he published an ambitious key to scripture metaphors, which constituted the greater part of Thomas Delaune's *Tropologia*. A collection of sermons, *A Golden Mine Opened*, appeared in 1694, and an exposition of the parables, *Gospel Mysteries Unveil'd*, was published in folio in 1701. From the late 1680s, moreover, Keach ran a printing and bookselling business from his home in Horselydown.

Keach died in London on 18 July 1704, and was buried in Southwark Park, London. Outlived by his second wife and at least six daughters, he left a thriving ministry in which he was succeeded by his son-in-law Benjamin Stinton. If his other son-in-law is to be believed, Keach was affectionate towards his family, loyal to his friends, and generally 'pleasant and cheerful', though prone to inexplicable and disturbing outbursts of temper (Crosby, 4.306–7); Ivimey and Wilson emphasize his capacity for charity and forgiveness. He was also, however, intolerant of alternative viewpoints to his own, and was isolated by his unwelcome attempts to interfere with other Baptist churches. Keach's uncompromising nature, however, was his strength: his remarkable career was fuelled by the single-mindedness with which he consolidated and promulgated his convictions against perpetual opposition, firstly from the Restoration state and then from within nonconformist and Baptist communities themselves. The numerous debates and practical initiatives in which Keach so prominently participated had fundamental influence on the subsequent development of the Baptist movement.

BETH LYNCH

Sources T. Crosby, *The history of the English Baptists, from the Reformation to the beginning of the reign of King George I*, 4 vols. (1738–40) · W. Wilson, *The history and antiquities of the dissenting churches and meeting houses in London, Westminster and Southwark*, 4 vols. (1808–14) · J. Ivimey, *A history of the English Baptists*, 4 vols. (1811–30) · B. Keach, *The travels of true godliness*, 2nd edn (1831) · J. B. Vaughn, 'Public worship and practical theology in the work of Benjamin Keach (1640–1704)', DPhil diss., U. St Andr., 1989 · Greaves & Zaller, *BDBR* · M. A. G. Haykin, *Kiffin, Knollys and Keach* (1996) · Wing, *STC* · *CSP dom.*, 1663–7 · 'The trial of Mr. Benjamin Keach, at the assizes at Aylesbury, in Buckinghamshire, for a libel: 17 Charles II. AD 1665', *State trials*, 6.701–10 · W. T. Whitley, *A history of British Baptists* (1923) · C. E. Whiting, *Studies in English puritanism* (1931); repr. (1968) · *A biographical history of England, from the revolution to the end of George I's reign: being a continuation of the Rev. J. Granger's work*, ed. M. Noble, 1 (1806) · A. C. Underwood, *A history of the English Baptists* (1947) · B. Keach, *A golden mine opened* (1694) · K. Dix, *Benjamin Keach and a monument to liberty* (1985) · G. H. Pike, *The Metropolitan Tabernacle* (1870) · *Baptist Quarterly*, 2–26 (1924–76) · N. H. Keeble, *The literary culture of nonconformity in later seventeenth-century England* (1987) · J. Smith, *Bibliotheca anti-Quakeriana, or, A catalogue of books adverse to the Society of Friends* (1873) · J. Julian, ed., *A dictionary of hymnology*, rev. edn (1907) · *DNB*
Likenesses J. Drapentier, engraving, *c*.1697, repro. in B. Keach, *The display of glorious grace* (1698), frontispiece · J. Drapentier, line engraving (aged fifty-seven), BM, NPG; repro. in B. Keach, *A trumpet blown in Zion* (1694) · J. Drapentier (aged fifty-four), repro. in Keach, *Golden mine opened*, frontispiece · M. Vandergucht, line engraving (after J. Surmans), NPG; repro. in B. Keach, *Gospel mysteries unveil'd* (1701), frontispiece [*see illus.*] · copper-plate engraving?, repro. in Keach, *Travels of true godliness*, frontispiece · engraving (in young age), repro. in B. Keach, *The Baptist-catechism*, 16th edn (1764), frontispiece · oils, Metropolitan Tabernacle, Elephant and Castle, London · woodcut, repro. in B. Keach, *The progress of sin*, 4th edn (1724), frontispiece

Keal, Minna (1909–1999), composer, was born Minnie Nerenstein on 22 March 1909 at 81 Wentworth Street, Spitalfields, east London, into a Yiddish-speaking family from Grodno, Russian Poland, the eldest daughter of Jacob Nerenstein (*d.* 1926), a Jewish prayer-book publisher and seller, and his wife, Fanny. Though none of her family had any formal musical training, her mother sang Hebrew folksongs and her uncle Leibel was an accomplished self-taught violinist; Minnie herself was much influenced by the singing of the cantors at her local synagogue. She began composing her own music at the age of twelve, later describing her early works as 'English with a Jewish overlay' (*http://www.musicweb.uk.net/keal*). She was educated at Commercial Street School and Clapton county

school, Hackney, before entering the Royal Academy of Music (1928). During her year there she studied composition under William Alwyn and changed her name to Minna. Several of her works were performed at academy concerts and in the East End, at Whitechapel Gallery and the People's Palace.

From the time of her father's death in 1926, Minnie Nerenstein had helped her mother run the family business, dividing her time between school or the academy and work behind the counter. As the business expanded her mother continued to support her musical ambitions, but other relatives accused her of letting her mother work long hours while she mainly 'scribbled notes'. Eventually she left the academy. 'I figured that if I'd been a genius, everyone would have insisted that I carry on, but the only person who did was William Alwyn' (*Daily Telegraph*, 1 Dec 1999). She married Barnett Samuel (1906–1971), a lawyer, the son of Jacob Samuel, a draper, on 28 July 1931, though she later said that 'In my heart of hearts I knew it wasn't going to work' (ibid.); they had one son, Raphael Elkan *Samuel (1934–1996), historian. Active in left-wing causes, including bringing refugee children to England, Minna renounced Judaism and converted to Stalinism, joining the Communist Party of Great Britain (CPGB) in 1939. In 1941 she left her husband (who disliked her political activities; they divorced in 1946) and moved with her son and piano to Slough, where she worked in a factory making parts for Spitfires and was, as she later put it, 'as political as could be' (*The Times*, 15 Nov 1999). After the war she returned to London and worked as a secretary at the *Daily Worker* and then in various mundane clerical jobs. From 1953 she lived with William Bernard (Bill) Keal (*d.* 1995), a fellow communist who had worked at the same factory in wartime, and whom (now also divorced, and working as a script writer) she had met again through the Workers' Musical Association. They married on 14 February 1959. They had by then left the CPGB over the Soviet invasion of Hungary: it was, Minna later said, 'shattering … far worse than giving up Judaism' (*Daily Telegraph*, 1 Dec 1999).

After retiring in 1969 Minna Keal attended the Guildhall School of Music, took her LRAM diploma (qualifying her as a music teacher), and gave piano lessons. Encouraged by the composer Justin Connolly (who had come to her house to examine one of her pupils, and had been much impressed by the early compositions which she had pulled from a cupboard to show him) she resumed composing, and studied first under Connolly himself and then under Oliver Knussen. Her earlier compositions had been romantic and melodic, but her later works were uncompromisingly modernist, influenced by her study of Bartók, Shostakovich, and Schoenberg. A *Lament* (1978) and a wind quintet (1980) were followed by her symphony (1987), five years in the making, which was, she said, 'about the turmoil of human existence and the spiritual search for serenity and permanence' (*The Independent*, 16 Nov 1999). It was performed at the BBC Proms in 1989, conducted by Knussen in the same concert as the première of John Tavener's *The protecting veil*, and received a standing ovation. Her *Cantillation* (1988) for violin and orchestra, drawing inspiration from the chanting she had heard in synagogues as a girl, was first performed in 1991, by Odaline de la Martinez and the European Women's Orchestra. Another major work, her cello concerto (1994), in three continuous movements, was premièred at the Snape Proms, Aldeburgh, in 1994. Various shorter pieces followed. In March 1999 Minna Keal was honoured with a ninetieth birthday concert at the Royal Academy of Music. Two CDs of her music were issued in her lifetime. She died at her home, Acres Plough, Shootacre Lane, Princes Risborough, Buckinghamshire, on 14 November 1999, having been predeceased by both her husband and her son.

ALEX MAY

Sources *The Times* (15 Nov 1999) · *The Independent* (16 Nov 1999) · *Daily Telegraph* (1 Dec 1999) · www.musicweb.uk.net/keal, Sept 2002 · b. cert. · m. certs. · d. cert.
Archives FILM Channel 4, documentary
Likenesses photograph, 1984, repro. in *Daily Telegraph* · photograph, 1989, repro. in *The Times* · photograph, 1998, repro. in *The Independent*

Kean, Charles John (1811–1868), actor and theatre manager, born on 18 January 1811 in or near Waterford, Ireland, was the second and only son to survive childhood of the actor Edmund *Kean (1787–1833) and his wife, Mary Chambers (1779–1849). On his father's historic success at Drury Lane in 1814, his future seemed assured. He attended Mr Styles's school at Worplesdon, Surrey, and the Revd Polehampton's school at Greenford, near Harrow. In 1824 he entered Eton College as an oppidan, and rose to the fifth form in his first year. When his father's fortunes plummeted in 1827, he had to leave the school.

Early career, early failure When Edmund Kean refused to settle £400 a year on his wife, from whom he was separated, Charles declined the cadetship in the East India Company which his father had arranged, whereupon Edmund angrily cut him off. With his name his only asset, Charles turned to the stage, where Stephen Price, the Drury Lane manager, offered him an engagement for three seasons, beginning at £10 weekly. Curiosity and publicity brought a packed house for the début of the youth, who was sixteen years old and totally inexperienced, on the opening of the season, on 1 October 1827. As Young Norval in John Home's *Douglas*, he was mercilessly condemned by the critics and soon faded from attention, and acted for only twelve nights in seven months: Young Norval in *Douglas* six times, Achmet in *Barbarossa* three times, Frederick in *Lovers' Vows* twice, and Lothair in *Adelgitha* once. In the provinces during the summer he gained experience and expanded his repertory. He first acted with his father, with whom he was reconciled, in Glasgow on the anniversary of his début and first tasted success in an Edinburgh engagement. After returning to Drury Lane in December 1828 he played Romeo twice, to contemptuous reviews. He first acted with Ellen Tree, whom he was eventually to marry, in *Lovers' Vows*, on 26 December. In 1829 he returned to the provinces with meagre success (except in Edinburgh), and with his father played a few nights at Dublin and Cork. On 6 October 1829, as Reuben Glenroy in *Town and Country*, he began at the

Charles John Kean (1811–1868), by Samuel John Stump, *c.*1830 [as Sir Edward Mortimer in *The Iron Chest* by George Colman]

Haymarket at £20 for six nights, and the last two nights in *The Iron Chest* gained him mixed but generally favourable notices, his first in London. After a brief, mismanaged tour in the Netherlands he went to America in 1830, and played with some success in major cities. Back in London in January 1833 he was engaged at Covent Garden, where on 25 March he played Iago to his father's Othello, with Ellen Tree as Desdemona. In Act III Edmund collapsed on stage into Charles's arms; it was his final performance. On 25 February young Kean first played Hamlet in London and on 4 March acted his first original role, in *Reputation, or, The State Secret*. On 24 April he appeared in Sheridan Knowles's new play, *The Wife*, with Ellen Tree. When the season ended he went to the provinces, having declared he would never again act in London until he could command £50 nightly, the highest salary previously known there. Later that year (1833) Kean and Ellen Tree joined a company to tour Germany, which again proved an abortive venture. During the tour the couple became engaged, but the opposition of both of their mothers soon ended the engagement; there appears to have been no further association between them until their careers again coincided at the Haymarket in 1840.

London successes Appearances at Dublin, Brighton, Liverpool, Birmingham, and especially Edinburgh drew increasingly enthusiastic reviews and crowded houses, and Kean became a favourite of fashionable society, notably at Brighton under the patronage of the duke and duchess of St Albans. He sought out men of critical acuity and influence for advice, focusing on *Hamlet* to build his reputation. Reports in the London press of his provincial success created a demand for his engagement there: 'The Liverpool critics seem quite Kean mad', reported the *Theatrical Observer* in 1835. That year his account book totalled gross income as £2573 for 193 performances; for 1837 the total was £3455 for 183 nights.

In 1837 Kean had two offers from London managers. W. C. Macready had often followed his engagements in the provinces and knew first-hand of his successes. Whether to capitalize on Kean's growing popularity or to ameliorate the threat to his own eminence, Macready offered him an engagement in his forthcoming management at Covent Garden, but Kean was uneasy about placing himself under Macready. When he later accepted Alfred Bunn's offer for January 1838 at Drury Lane (at the £50 a night he had demanded), which put him in competition with Macready, and then won astounding success in *Hamlet*, Macready's enmity was ensured. It was to shadow the rest of Kean's career and colour historical evaluations of his life.

Kean's Hamlet on 8 January 1838 was a theatrical landmark; a brilliant success, it drew packed houses and enthusiastic reviews, establishing the actor, until the arrival of Charles Fechter and then Henry Irving, as England's pre-eminent Hamlet, acknowledged as such even by unfriendly critics, and confirming him as a star in the first rank. By it he won the favour of the young Queen Victoria and of fashionable society, which lionized him. He acted for forty-four nights in the engagement: twenty-one in *Hamlet*, seventeen in *Richard III*, five in *A New Way to Pay Old Debts*, and once as Shylock. Negative reviews began to appear where Macready's influence existed, and a re-engagement in May was unsuccessful. In July 1838 Kean's account book cited £4567 8s. for 140 performances the previous year.

Kean's Hamlet of 1838 drew unanimous praise. *The Times* of 10 January deemed him 'an accomplished, elegant, and when the scene requires it, an energetic actor without bombast'. His approach was described as philosophical and melancholic with flashes of passion. Soliloquies were strong in feeling, and scenes with Ophelia and Gertrude were marked with variety of emotion and intensity, but lengthy pauses and some tearful sentimentality were criticized. The *Morning Post* reported it to be an apt combination of the classical and romantic styles. In later years, as Kean's acting style moved towards realism, so did his Hamlet, but it remained his most classical role, never so realistic as his later Shakespearian characters.

Success in the provinces and a Haymarket engagement of seven weeks at £50 nightly in 1839 brought Kean £7242 7s. 5d. He then went to America, but illness and other misfortunes tempered his success. At the Haymarket on 1 June 1840, he followed *Hamlet* with *Richard III* and *Macbeth*, both with new scenery, and *Macbeth* played for fifteen nights. Macready was concurrently engaged, but Kean performed all the Shakespeare.

Kean returned to the provinces, playing often with Ellen Tree, particularly in *Romeo and Juliet*, in anticipation of his own staging of the play at the Haymarket in 1841, which was the first documented instance of Kean as a director.

The production was praised, but his Romeo was poorly received as being a role unsuited to his talents. He recorded £6474 11s. for the year.

Marriage and changing repertory On 29 January 1842 Kean married Ellen Tree (1805–1880) [*see* Kean, Eleanora] at St Thomas's Church, Dublin, and that night played *The Gamester* and *The Honeymoon* with her. In his account book he wrote 'The day I was married' and entered 'Recd £480'. For more than financial reasons it was a fortuitous event in Kean's life. Ellen's devotion shed the one undimmed lustre on a life which was harried by controversy, criticism, misadventures, and disappointments. In a singularly happy marriage, he enjoyed the unfailing love and support of a great and lovely woman whose career merged with and influenced his own. On 27 February at Glasgow, his mother having finally accepted the marriage, they first, and always thereafter, appeared together as Mr and Mrs Charles Kean.

Changes in Kean's repertory followed as he acted with Ellen in her pieces, notably domestic drama, and moved away from major dependence on the conventional roles of tragedians. The new direction proved more suited to his abilities, diminishing excesses of the romantic style and increasing realism and restraint as he succeeded in such plays as *The Lady of Lyons*, *The Gamester*, and *The Stranger*. At the Haymarket in 1842 they gave the première of Knowles's *The Rose of Aragon* under Kean's supervision. (Their only child, Mary, was born on 18 September 1843.) *Richard III* at Drury Lane on 20 January 1844 was Kean's first production of Shakespeare in the 'Macready manner'—unified, specifically designed staging with historical accuracy. To provincial theatres for two years Kean brought a supply of costumes for supporting actors and supernumeraries, scene designs, and accessories, and he personally superintended historical productions of *Richard III* and *Macbeth*, thus introducing the 'Macready manner' to the provinces. He also took it to America, where the Keans acted for nearly two years, beginning in September 1845. At the Park Theatre in New York in January 1846 he produced *Richard III* and followed it with a spectacular *King John*, using Macready's promptbook and designs, but neither production was profitable, and he abandoned plans for others. The other major event at the Park was the première of George Lovell's *The Wife's Secret*, commissioned by Kean, on 12 October 1845; it was also a great hit at London's Haymarket in January 1848. Its staging was highly praised, and Kean's acting drew notices equalling those of his wife. The play ran for thirty-seven consecutive nights at the Haymarket and remained in the Keans' repertory to the end of their careers; during their Princess's Theatre management it was acted forty times.

Management and social aspiration In 1848 Kean was appointed director of royal theatricals at Windsor Castle, a new project to give royal support to the stage, and the Keans acted the first season in *Hamlet*, *The Stranger*, and *The Merchant of Venice* for three of the five nights. It was a singular honour, and Kean held the position, through recurring contention with jealous actors and rival managers, until

1857, when Ellen's solicitation by letter of a knighthood for her husband cost him the position. However, in 1848 the appointment was a turning point, for it changed his plans to retire early. Royal patronage gave him the opportunity to lead Victorian theatre into new vigour and levels of excellence through management.

Under Kean's management (1850–59) the Princess's was London's leading theatre. He began as co-manager with Robert Keeley, but assumed sole authority before staging *King John* on 9 February 1852, his first great historical production, a repetition of his New York production of 1846. On 24 February *The Corsican Brothers*, a new play by Dion Boucicault that gradually replaced *King John*, was one of Kean's major successes, both as actor and director; revived several times, it reached 243 performances. *Anne Blake* in 1852 had forty-one performances, with *Much Ado about Nothing* and *The Merry Wives of Windsor* staged the same season. On 14 February 1853 a splendid *Macbeth* began a run of eighty-nine performances, and Byron's *Sardanapalus* followed in June for ninety performances. *Faust and Marguerite*, a spectacular melodrama, opened on 19 April 1854 for ninety-six performances, and *The Courier of Lyons* ran for fifty nights beginning on 26 June.

In 1854 Kean leased the theatre until 1859 and contracted his company for the same time. The best of his management followed. On 13 January 1855 *Louis XI*, generally considered Kean's finest role, received unanimous praise; it was acted ninety-one times by the end of his management and remained in his repertory to the end of his career. *Henry VIII* followed on 16 May; with new roles for both Keans, it was a major triumph, playing successively for a hundred nights, for fifty the next season, and for thirteen in the final season. Kean's Wolsey was his first new Shakespearian role at the Princess's; notable for 'restrained force' and realistic detail, it was highly praised. *The Winter's Tale* opened on 28 April 1856 for 102 performances. On 1 September *Pizarro* was historically and spectacularly staged to open the season and played for sixty-nine nights; from 15 October it was combined with *A Midsummer Night's Dream*, without the Keans, which played for 184 performances. On 14 March 1857 *Richard II* opened and ran for 112 nights, followed by *The Tempest* on 1 July, which had eighty-seven showings. On 17 April 1858 *King Lear*, which Kean had acted in 1836 in the provinces, was played for only thirty-two nights; although lauded in the press, the play and Kean's aptly dark and barbaric staging proved unattractive to audiences. It was followed on 12 June by a sumptuous and colourful *The Merchant of Venice*, using scenic replications of the city's landmarks, most notably the Rialto, with the canal waters actually reflecting passing gondolas, the bridge, and crowds crossing it. It was performed for seventy-two consecutive nights to end the season, and then for the first thirteen nights of Kean's last season of management. After *The Merchant*, Kean turned to revivals of major productions to fill out the season, the only new production being *Henry V*, his most spectacular effort. It opened on 28 March 1859 and was performed successively eighty-four times, sixty-one as the sole play for the night. *Henry VIII* was given on the final

night of his management, 29 August 1859, when Kean's curtain speech lengthily defended the aims, practices, and achievements of his management.

Failure of his hopes for knighthood and the loss of the directorship of the Windsor theatricals in 1857 had been a psychological turning point for Kean. Idealistic visions for his profession faded, but his contracts of 1854 had held him to management for two more seasons. He became increasingly irritable and contentious. Cheating by his box-office staff led to a public rumpus when he dismissed Massingham, the manager, and there were other asperities within the company. In July 1858 Kean chaired the public meeting for establishing a dramatic college for ageing actors, but matters went awry and his participation faded. With his will gone and his health failing, his public and private statements were pervaded with resigned defeat.

Touring, at home and abroad Management having depleted his means for the lifestyle the Keans desired, on leaving the Princess's, Kean's goal became pursuit of income. With three supporting players to act, superintend rehearsals, and relieve Kean of onerous details, the Keans turned to the provinces, where they drew crowded houses despite increased prices. For the first three seasons Kean reported an average gross of £8000, but his entourage made expenses heavy. They played engagements at Drury Lane in 1861 and 1862 and were back at the Princess's from 10 July to 16 October 1862. At a testimonial dinner at St James's Hall on 22 March 1862, with W. E. Gladstone in the chair, Kean was presented with a set of silver valued at £2000. With their attraction waning in the provinces, Kean looked abroad, but civil war in America obviated their going there. Before their departure to Australia, the Keans gave a platform reading on 26 June 1863 at St James's Hall. Stripped of scenery and stage business, Kean's performance drew no cavilling about faculty articulation or vocal harshness, and reviewers, notably that of *The Times*, gave fulsome praise. The Keans acted for nine months in Australia, beginning on 10 October 1863 in Melbourne, before going to California and Vancouver and, via Panama and Jamaica, where they gave readings, to New York. The civil war over, their opening was delayed by Lincoln's assassination until 26 April 1865, and after New York they toured widely in the United States, ending with a farewell performance at New York's Broadway Theatre on 16 April 1866. Illness, bad teeth, and problems with tour managers plagued Kean during both the American and the Australian tours.

After returning to England the Keans acted at the Princess's in *Henry VIII* for fifteen nights, *Louis XI* for eleven, and *Hamlet* for three, and for their benefit on 2 June they gave *The Merchant of Venice* and *The Jealous Wife*. On 28 May Kean appeared before the 1866 parliamentary committee on theatre regulation, giving pessimistic but perceptive testimony, and in June he was elected a fellow of the Royal Geographical Society. In September the Keans returned to the provinces, where they drew crowded houses. They were at their new home, 47 Queensborough Terrace, London, for the Christmas season. Engagements in January

1867 took them to Bristol and then Bath, where they celebrated their silver wedding anniversary; Edinburgh and other towns followed.

On 28 May 1867 at Liverpool, Kean acted *Louis XI*, and suffered a heart attack after the performance. He died on 22 January 1868, four days after his fifty-seventh birthday, at the couple's London residence, 47 Queensborough Terrace, and was buried beside his mother at St Catherington, Horndean, Hampshire.

Personal characteristics Kean's personality was influenced by the separation of his parents before he was ten and his upbringing by a doting but emotionally unstable and dependent mother. A spoiled and indulged child, rudely deprived of affluence, exploited and then unmercifully damned publicly in his effort to find means of support for himself and his mother, it is not surprising he was childishly hypersensitive and almost pathological in his hunger for praise, traits that led to many squabbles and subjected him to ridicule, notably in *Punch*. But he was socially convivial and moved easily in fashionable circles. He had high standards of personal morality, was truly a Victorian gentleman, and his industry, will, and resolution under recurring adversity earned him success. Very popular at Eton, he formed friendships with many men of later note, and those ties served his career well. Also at Eton he acquired a scholarly bent and developed his athletic ability, particularly in fencing, and these traits were put to good use in his professional life. He stood 5 feet 7 inches at maturity, without advantage in physique on stage. Slight of build as a youth, rather stout after forty, he later shrivelled with premature ageing. From his mid-thirties he suffered from gout, and he had Bright's disease in his final years. He had flashing eyes, an odd nose, dark hair, and a rather immobile face. Reports by hostile critics, notably in *Punch*, of his speech being denasalized (that is, *n*, *m*, and *ng* sounds changed to *d*, *b*, and *g*) have been repeated in subsequent evaluations of his acting, but that criticism is questionable in view of contradictory testimony from contemporaries, most notably by Ellen Terry. While his voice was harsh at high volume, it was excellent in normal and quiet passages.

Acting style Kean's feeble first efforts on stage should be overlooked. He applied himself assiduously, and, with encouragement and advice from many, he soon improved. Early on he played his father's roles in his father's style, which, with his name and resemblance in appearance and mannerism, drew harsh criticism for imitativeness, a charge that persisted long after his father's death and his own departure from his father's style and repertory. Despite his physique, he was notably athletic on stage, fenced expertly, and was graceful and agile, even in later years, when gout permitted. In voice, figure, and temperament he was by nature unsuited to the Romantic style, and he was late in coming to realize the qualities he did possess. Under the influence of his wife he diminished reliance on his father's roles and moved toward realism; for his Wolsey, Richard II, Leontes, Lear, and Louis XI, imitation disappeared as a criticism. Even in the 1830s he had

begun to temper externality and exaggeration, vocal and physical. He had studied the role of Hamlet closely and developed new business and line readings. In the 1840s he further developed restraint, and new roles at the Princess's were marked by subtlety, realistic detail, and a quiet 'restrained force'. This style reached its maturity in Louis XI, which Westland Marston identified as the role that 'set the seal upon what I have called his second manner in tragedy', after which Kean 'never went back entirely to his old style' (*Our Recent Actors*, 1.190). Other contemporaries described Kean's acting in much the same vein, and modern studies agree that his later characters were uniquely individualized, complex, and multi-dimensional, researched for realism, and physically detailed. The identity of the actor was submerged, and his performances were subtle and polished, without artifice, staginess, or conventionality. Having learned the value of repose, he often used, by repression of externals, a deadly quiet that chilled and awed audiences; even emotionally charged scenes retained a subdued intensity, giving, in Dutton Cook's words, 'a sort of drawing room air little known upon the British stage' (*Hours with the Players*, 2.254).

Kean was the leading actor of mid-Victorian England, with a wide range of successful roles to bear witness to his versatility. Not only did he succeed in tragedy, he was without peer in gentlemanly melodrama; in comedy, notably as Benedict and Ford, he drew warm praise, even from hostile critics.

Managerial style While Kean reached his zenith as an actor at the Princess's, his contributions as manager there were more significant. In early seasons he sought new plays and had notable successes, particularly with 'gentlemanly melodrama', but he increasingly turned to historical productions of Shakespeare. During his management, seventeen Shakespearian plays were performed for 1264 nights, fifteen three- or five-act new plays were performed for 823 nights, his spectacular staging of two 'standard' plays had 154 performances, and ordinary staging of standard plays accounted for the remainder.

Kean's personal dedication, financial and artistic, at the Princess's was remarkable. The Keans took no salaries, and extant evidence, with expenditures from the box office or personal accounts unknown, suggests little more than 1 per cent profit from the nine seasons. His theatre was not large, and his production methods expensive. In his retirement speech he reported that he had spent 'a little short of £50,000 for one season', that for some productions he employed more than five hundred persons, and that he had spent about £10,000 for stage improvements and scenery to be left at the theatre. He personally researched scenery, costumes, and properties, for which he was elected a fellow of the Royal Society of Antiquarians in 1857. Actors and scenic artists were employed under lengthy contracts, leading to unity of conception and ensemble in execution. Most historical productions were planned for more than a year and then carefully rehearsed under Kean's personal supervision. His specially conceived and researched productions for given plays, his development of realism through spectacular antiquarianism, his emphasis on intensive rehearsals, and his personal supervision of all elements, from conception to execution, to secure integrated unity of production markedly advanced Macready's methods. Moreover, this mode of production was developed in a sustained programme for nine years. Added to the development of the director's function were Kean's change from the repertory system to long runs of productions and his advances in lighting and scenic methods. He brought the electric arc spotlight to England, and his use of limelight for special effects was notable. Asymmetrical settings, large expanses of scenery placed diagonally in full stage scenes, and extensive use of bridges, steps, ramps, and levels allowed increased use of stage space, particularly vertically, to facilitate variety in groupings, new means of picturization, and greater three dimensionality of scenery—hence greater realism. All this must have required an early use of the 'plantation' system to mount and change scenery, with traditional wing-and-drop forestage settings to mask the massive scene shifts.

Assessment First as an actor and then as a manager, Kean drew hyperbole from detractors and admirers in the press. His historical revivals drew charges of 'upholstery', the smothering of actors and plays in spectacle, from a persistent faction, a criticism that may seem apt by modern standards. In the context of Kean's times and his aims, its validity diminishes. Kean's intention was not spectacle but historical accuracy, a kind of realism that when conscientiously executed was inevitably spectacular, given the plays he produced. He was staging history lessons as well as revitalizing Shakespeare for audiences of his time. That this suited his audiences' tastes was proven by large attendances and warm praise from a very great majority of the reviewers, who described productions in lengthy columns. While he cut texts severely, omissions were judicious, very like those of his contemporaries, notably Phelps and Macready, and much like late twentieth-century practice. He seldom modified Shakespeare's scene sequence, and language was unchanged except for references to the deity. He did interpolate huge spectacular episodes, as in *Richard II*, *Henry V*, and *Henry VIII*, based on textual possibilities, to exhibit historical events with archaeological detail and a cross-section of the society of a play's time. To facilitate his educational purpose, he sold at the theatre his editions of the plays with extensive notes on the text and his staging, and large playbills provided audiences with notes and antiquarian sources.

Kean's view of theatre as a potentially educational institution, rather than a commercial source of entertainment, and his intent for it to become socially relevant foreshadowed the independent theatre movement at the end of the century. At the Princess's, Kean also moved the theatre towards social respectability, and fashionable audiences began returning to it. Henry Irving of the Lyceum was influenced by Kean's management and Beerbohm Tree copied Kean's productions in his Shakespearian programme at Her Majesty's Theatre at the turn of the century. More important was Kean's influence on the duke of Saxe-Meiningen, who advanced Kean's concepts

and methods with a higher aesthetic intention and then spread them throughout Europe. Kean's forty years on the stage rather neatly spanned the middle of the century; he had been a major figure in the transition from Romanticism to realism in stage production.

M. GLEN WILSON

Sources J. W. Cole, *The life and theatrical times of Charles Kean … including a summary of the English stage for the last fifty years*, 2 vols. (1859) • M. G. Wilson, *Charles Kean: a chronicle of his career* (1998) • V. Francesco, 'Charles Kean's acting career, 1829–1867', PhD diss., Indiana University, 1974 • M. G. Wilson, 'Charles Kean: a study in nineteenth century production of Shakespearean tragedy', PhD diss., Ohio State University, 1957 • B. Threlkeld, 'A study of the management of Charles Kean at the Princess's Theatre, 1850–1859', PhD diss., Ohio State University, 1955 • W. G. B. Carson, *Letters of Mr and Mrs Charles Kean relating to their American tours* (1945) • J. M. D. Hardwick, *Emigrants in motley: the journal of Charles and Ellen Kean in quest of a theatrical fortune in Australia and America* (1954) • J. W. Marston, *Our recent actors*, 2 vols. (1888) • D. Cook, *Hours with the players*, 2 vols. (1881) • A. Bagot, *Coppin the Great* (1965)
Archives Boston PL, letters • Dickinson College Library, Carlisle, Pennsylvania, corresp. • Garr. Club • Harvard TC • Harvard U., Houghton L., touring accounts • Hunt. L., letters • Ohio State University, Columbus, Theatre Research Institute • Theatre Museum, London • U. Texas • University of Rochester, New York | NL Scot., corresp. with James Halliwell-Phillipps • Pomona College, Claremont, Norman Philbuck collection • Royal Arch., letters from members of royal household
Likenesses portrait, c.1828, Harvard TC • S. J. Stump, oils, c.1830, NPG [*see illus.*] • W. Daniels, oils, c.1838, V&A, Enthoven collection • attrib. R. M. Drummond, chalk drawing, c.1838, NPG • S. J. Stump, oils, c.1838, NPG • A. E. Chalon, watercolour drawing, 1840, Athenaeum, London • R. Dadd, double portrait, oils, c.1840 (with Mrs Kean), Yale U. CBA • photographs, 1855–9, Garr. Club • photographs, 1855–9, V&A, Enthoven collection • photographs, 1855–9, NPG • photograph, 1856, NPG • double portrait, watercolour drawing, c.1858 (with Mrs Kean), V&A • W. Etty, oils, 1860, University of Bristol • E. G. Lewis, chalk drawing, NPG • P. M. B., miniature (as Richard III), Royal Shakespeare Theatre, Stratford upon Avon, Warwickshire • H. W. Phillips, oils (as Louis XI), Garr. Club • S. J. Stump, miniature, Guildhall Art Gallery, London • J. Wedderburn, two pencil and watercolour drawings, NPG • stipple and line engraving (as Gloucester in *Richard III*), BM • theatrical prints, BM, Harvard TC, NPG
Wealth at death under £35,000: probate, 25 March 1868, *CGPLA Eng. & Wales*

Kean, Edmund (1787–1833), actor, was born on 4 November 1787 in the Gray's Inn chambers of his maternal grandfather, George Saville *Carey, who lived in shabby gentility on his earnings as a lecturer and entertainer. Kean's date of birth and parentage have both been disputed. His mother, Ann Carey (*d*. 1833), divided her time between acting and prostitution. Her grandfather, the playwright Henry Carey, was an illegitimate son of George Savile, marquess of Halifax, after whom her father was named. The likelihood is that Kean's father was Edmund Kean (*d*. 1793), at that time articled to a surveyor. This Edmund was the youngest of three brothers. Little is known of Aaron, the eldest, beyond the fact that he was frequently drunk. The second, Moses, a moderately successful entertainer, was the unmarried partner of a Drury Lane actress, Charlotte Tidswell. Edmund, who shared Aaron's dependence on alcohol, committed suicide in 1793, and the evidence

Edmund Kean (1787–1833), by James Northcote, 1819 [standing; as Brutus in *Brutus* by Howard Payne]

suggests that Ann Carey, who had two other children by a man named Darnley, found her new son burdensome.

A loveless childhood Kean's childhood, particularly after the death in 1792 of his uncle Moses, was loveless. He was shipped between the homes of Mrs Price, his mother's widowed sister, and Charlotte Tidswell, without being welcome in either. When possible they farmed him out with strangers, and their attempts to educate him were half-hearted. It was, nevertheless, Charlotte ('Aunt Tid') who most strongly influenced him during his migratory childhood. The duke of Norfolk may have interceded to procure her initial engagement at Drury Lane, and it was on rumours of her liaison with him that Kean would later build the fiction of his aristocratic parentage. Charlotte was sufficiently competent to sustain her place at Drury Lane until 1822, when she retired at the age of sixty. It was with her that Kean first observed the backstage life of London's leading theatre.

The smatterings of information about Kean's childhood rarely rise above the anecdotal level. Aunt Tid may well have listened to, and even refined, his early recitations from Shakespeare; she may have licensed his occasional appearances, from infancy through boyhood, on the Drury Lane stage. The problem is that Kean's first three biographers shared with their subject a talent for embroidery that enforces scepticism. Bryan Waller Procter (Barry Cornwall), the first to produce a systematic life of Kean (1835), shrewdly observes in the records of his boyhood a tendency to run away when the going became tough. This was an unattractive characteristic that would remain with him. But Procter, although more circumspect than Hawkins and Molloy, had also to rely on the sort of stories that friends had heard from a friend of Kean's, and Kean in his cups was capable of wild inventiveness. It may, then, be doubted that he ever walked from Southwark to Portsmouth, where he embarked as a cabin-boy on a Madeira-bound ship, or that, at the age of four, he had to wear leg-irons because of the brutality of his acrobatic training at Drury Lane (if he ever did wear irons, incipient rickets is a likelier cause). It is, however, quite plausible that he exhibited his precocious talents anywhere from middle-class drawing-rooms to East End taverns. Ann Carey made money however she could, and there was obviously something captivating about the small, dark-eyed, and athletic boy. Perhaps with the agreement of Aunt Tid, he was marketed as an infant prodigy. A surviving playbill, dating from 1801, advertises the appearance at the Great Room, no. 8, Store Street, Bedford Square, of 'The Celebrated Theatrical Child, Edmund Carey, not eleven years old'. Kean, like the Infant Phenomenon in *Nicholas Nickleby*, was small enough to pass as some years younger than his true age. His later contempt for Master Betty, the sensation of the London season of 1804, may hark back to this period in the life of 'Master Carey'.

Early struggles Kean may have made a few undistinguished appearances on the Drury Lane stage before the end of the eighteenth century. He had certainly experienced the seedier life of a strolling player, perhaps with his mother as a member of the Saunders company, perhaps with John Richardson, who had pitched his first portable booth-theatre at Bartholomew fair in 1798. It was as a tumbler that Kean was featured at such fairs, one among the crowd:

Pimps, pawnbrokers, strollers, fat landladies, sailors,
Bawds, bailies, jilts, jockies, thieves, tumblers and tailors.
(G. A. Stevens, 'Sports of the City jubilee')

The story persists that Kean, rehearsing or performing a tumbling trick, fractured a leg so badly that it never fully mended. Versatility was an asset among strollers, and Kean would later credit Richardson with giving him his first acting opportunity in a major part, that of Young Norval in John Home's *Douglas*. More consistently, though, he tumbled and danced, developing the talents that would make him an outstanding Harlequin on provincial circuits.

Kean's first 'adult' engagement, no longer as 'Master Carey', was with Samuel Jerrold's company at Sheerness in spring 1804. He was ambitious to play leading roles in tragedy, but the taste of the time was against him. The model tragedian was the tall and stately John Philip Kemble. Kean was volatile, even fidgety, and less than 5 feet 7 inches tall. He had penetrating, dark eyes—many people remembered them as black—and dark hair. Until alcohol lamed and bloated him, he was light on his feet and thin-faced. Above all, there was a fierceness bordering on malevolence about the way he presented himself on stage and, all too often, off it. Jerrold gave him secondary roles. After a year Kean had had enough. He returned to London and further disappointment. He was reduced to playing in a fit-up theatre in Wivell's Billiard Room, Camden Town. A Belfast engagement in the summer of 1805 led nowhere, though it enabled him, from a secondary position, to observe the acting of Sarah Siddons. Perhaps because his determination to make something memorable of even a minor role marked him out, Kean drew the unfavourable notice of Mrs Siddons. He would later claim that she patted him on the head after a performance, saying, 'You have played very well, sir, *very* well. It's a pity, but there's too little of you to do any thing' (Cornwall, 3rd edn, 59). Mrs Siddons could certainly be cutting. At the height of Bettymania, she referred to Betty as 'the baby with a woman's name' (R. Manvell, *Sarah Siddons*, 1970, 284). More surprisingly, but no less typically, Kean, in the depths of his provincial doldrums, refused to act with Betty.

That outburst of professional pique occurred in Stroud in 1808. There would be much more reprehensible refusals to brook rivalry during Kean's years of fame. The years between Belfast and Stroud were inglorious. In minor roles at the Haymarket in 1806 he was scarcely noticed, and, after a spell with Sarah Baker's company on the Canterbury circuit, he rejoined Samuel Jerrold in September 1807. There was little kudos to be gained from acting in Sheerness, but it gave Kean a brief first chance in leading roles. Amid rumours that he had offended a local dignitary, Kean found his Sheerness engagement suddenly terminated. He was liable, throughout his life, to express his fear of neglect through attacks on those in authority. The significant outcome this time was a relegation to secondary roles in William Beverley's company on the Gloucester circuit. Another new member of the company, Columbine to Kean's Harlequin in *Harlequin Mother Goose*, was an Irishwoman eight years his senior. Mary Chambers (1779–1849) had left Waterford for Cheltenham with the intention of working as a governess. Acting was a stage-struck afterthought. She was temperamentally unsuited to the morally lax world of the theatre, but she was under its spell in the spring of 1808. In the long run regrettably, she was also under the spell of the wildly ambitious and sexually charismatic Kean. They were married in Stroud on 17 July 1808. On her side at least, it was a love match. Kean, beguiled by Mary's gentility, may have hoped for a substantial dowry, or, frustrated by her modesty, may have seen its only antidote in marriage. The aftermath was greater hardship than either had ever known.

Their first move was from the Gloucester circuit to Cheltenham, whose manager, John Boles Watson, had a theatrical empire stretching from Wales to Leicester. Kean was allowed his share of leading roles until the company reached the important theatre town of Birmingham, where he responded to his relegation to secondary parts by getting drunk—repeatedly. It was probably in Birmingham, and perversely linked to his married state, that a pattern of prolonged drinking bouts was established. These 'benders' lasted anything from three days to a week. The immediate result in Birmingham was debt. When, in June 1809, the Keans were offered an engagement with Andrew Cherry's company in Swansea, they had to leave Birmingham secretly and walk the 180 miles to Swansea. If Mary, six months pregnant, had dreamed of stability, she had ample time to reflect on her choice of husband. Their first son was born on 13 September 1809 and christened Howard, the family name of the dukes of Norfolk.

Trying to curb his impulsiveness in view of his new responsibilities, Kean remained with Cherry for two years. The company toured Ireland as well as Wales, and it was in or near Mary's home town of Waterford that their second son, Charles John *Kean, was born on 18 January 1811. It was, after all, Charles Howard whom Kean liked to claim as his father. Also in Waterford, Kean's swordsmanship as Hamlet excited the admiration of Thomas Colley Grattan, stationed there as a subaltern. Grattan was the most loyal of the many men of distinction who befriended Kean over the years. Kean was sorely in need of friends in the months that followed his rash decision to leave Cherry's company when his demand for an increased salary was denied. The Keans arrived in England jobless and made a poverty-stricken tour of Scotland and the north of England, during which they were sometimes reduced to begging. It was a relief when, in January 1812, Richard Hughes engaged Kean to play leading roles on the Exeter circuit. His pride was both restored by the chance to act Macbeth, Richard III, Hamlet, and Othello, and dented by the greater demand for his Harlequin. Kean's now habitual dissipation was both symptom and cause of the failure of his marriage. His letters to London managers made no impression, and his behaviour became almost predictably irrational. Never at ease in comedy, he acted carelessly opposite Dorothy Jordan when the great comic actress joined the company for its Weymouth season in October 1812, and in Guernsey the following April he was so consistently drunk that the audience turned against him. Knowing that the money he earned should go towards supporting his sickly wife and sons, he spent it on prostitutes and drink. Self-belief vied with self-hatred to produce his explosive versions of both Richard III and Edmund Kean.

It was the chance attendance of Dr Joseph Drury, retired headmaster of Harrow School, at a playhouse in Teignmouth that initiated the change in Kean's fortunes. Drury commended the young provincial actor to the amateur gentlemen then in control of Drury Lane, with whom he had some influence. After a delay, during which the Keans' elder son sickened with the after-effects of measles, the Drury Lane gentlemen dispatched their acting manager, Samuel Arnold, to Dorchester, where he watched Kean as Octavian in Richard Cumberland's *The*

Mountaineers on 15 November 1813. Octavian, monumentally dignified in adversity, was in John Kemble's repertory and certainly not a gift for the demonic Kean. But Arnold, knowing the desperate financial state of Drury Lane in 1813, was sufficiently impressed to make Kean an offer, and even to allow him the choice of part for his début at England's premier theatre. It was unfortunate that the offer came just after the impecunious Kean had accepted a less attractive one from Robert William Elliston, new lessee of London's Olympic Theatre. While Kean haggled to extricate himself from the Olympic contract, Howard's condition worsened. He died on 22 November 1813, a month after his fourth birthday. Penniless and distraught, Kean arrived in London early in December 1813 with the dispute between Elliston and Drury Lane unresolved. It seemed to him a choice between Harlequin at the Olympic and Shakespeare at Drury Lane.

Triumph at Drury Lane In the new year of 1814 Kean languished, unpaid and fearful, until an agreement was reached between Arnold and Elliston. It involved a reduction from £8 to £6 in his promised salary, with the £2 going towards compensating Elliston. It was not until 26 January 1814 that Kean made his legendary début as Shylock, thereby recovering at a stroke the sinking fortunes of Drury Lane. In a famous retrospect, written over two years later, William Hazlitt recorded the impact: 'We wish we had never seen Mr. Kean. He has destroyed the Kemble religion and it is the religion in which we were brought up' (*The Examiner*, 27 Oct 1816). Hazlitt's perception that, in taking on Shylock, Kean was also taking on John Kemble, is informative. Even in adversity, Kean was naturally adversarial. Acting for himself, he was also acting against a society that had scorned him. Inner fury, amounting frequently to paranoia, fuelled his finest performances and made them dangerous to a degree unrivalled on the English stage. He found points of identity with Shylock, and it was at these points that his intensity thrilled regency audiences. 'The character never stands still', wrote Hazlitt after the second night on 1 February 1814. 'There is no vacant pause in the action; the eye is never silent' (*Morning Chronicle*, 2 Feb 1814). For the critics close up in the pit, Kean's eyes were always a dominating feature, but he was a people's actor too, celebrated in the upper gallery as Kemble rarely was. His voice, reputedly weak in the upper register, resonated in the vastness of Drury Lane. He would continue to abuse it. In later years, it would crack under the strain, forcing him to hold back for most of a performance to preserve the energy for its peaks. The famous transitions from the rhetoric of high passion to the startlingly conversational may have owed as much to necessity as to art. He was envious of the vocal richness of Kemble's heir, Charles Mayne Young. Sober, he acknowledged the quality of Young's musical voice; drunk, as he generally was by 1823, he would rant to James Winston about having to act with 'that bloody thundering bugger'. Drury Lane was sparsely patronized for Kean's first performance, but full for his second and for almost all the sixty-eight nights he played before the season ended in

July 1814. On 12 February 1814 he gave his first London performance of Richard III, the part that best accommodated his genius. G. H. Lewes's memory held a boyhood image of the exquisite grace with which Kean would lean against the side scene while Anne railed at him: 'It was thoroughly feline—terrible yet beautiful' (Lewes, 10). If his Shylock was, in Douglas Jerrold's eyes, like a chapter of Genesis, his Richard was Mephistophelean. It can be partially recovered in the detailed record of his movements and vocal inflections made a decade later by the American actor James Hackett. Lord Byron compared Kean with his own corsair:

> There was a laughing devil in his sneer,
> That raised emotions of both rage and fear;
> And where his frown of hatred darkly fell,
> Hope withering fled, and Mercy sigh'd farewell!
> (Byron, 'The Corsair', ll. 223–6)

There is more than coincidence in the contemporaneous vogues for Kean and Byron's heroes. On 5 May 1814 Kean, one of the few actors to have overwhelmed his Iagos, played Othello. Surprisingly perhaps, he preferred it to Iago, which he played two days later, and would intermittently perform throughout his career. Othello's singularity among complacent Venetians, like Shylock's, activated Kean's own sense of isolation. He had the capacity, as well as the need, to make distinctive any character he impersonated, but his intuitive reading of the texts proposed to him enabled him to select parts that met him half-way. Luke, in Sir John Burgess's adaptation of Massinger's *The City Madam*, fitted the mould; it was the last new role in his triumphant first season at Drury Lane. He was doubtful only about his Hamlet, first performed on 12 March 1814, despite critical acclaim. He knew he was not at his best when required to burn slowly, and Hamlet, though a compulsory part of a tragic actor's repertory, was never his favourite.

Kean became the victim of his success, as he had been the victim of his failures. Welcomed in society, he often made a fool of himself, not least by his misguided sprinkling into conversation of half-understood Latin and Greek tags. His wife relished polite company, and for a while Kean indulged her with dinner parties. His salary was increased to £20 per week in March 1814, and in the provincial tour that followed he commanded £50 per night. There were gifts from admirers and a benefit that brought him over £1000. In October 1815 he leased a large house in Clarges Street, Piccadilly. Although some neighbours took offence at an upstart actor's presumptuousness in moving to a fashionable area, Mary had a fine setting for her dinner parties. Kean had completed a second season at Drury Lane, adding to his previous parts Macbeth (5 November 1814), Romeo (2 January 1815), and Richard II (9 March 1815). He was a competent Macbeth, too energetic as Richard, and ineffective as Romeo. His enemies were ready with unfavourable comparisons. Eliza O'Neill's Juliet at Covent Garden was the talk of the town. Kean's Drury Lane Romeo lacked her appealing innocence. The burden of being the theatre's only effective draw was heavy, and

Romeo was one of several dubious choices during this second season. Thomas Morton's *Town and Country*, in which Kean played Reuben Glenroy, is a dull play, and Cumberland's *The Wheel of Fortune*, even with Kean as Penruddock, a gloomy one. Mrs Wilmot's *Ina* lasted only one night, with Kean in the main part. The committee's control of the repertory was dangerously biased. Outside Shakespeare, Kean's best opportunities came in the vengeful role of Zanga in Edward Young's *The Revenge* and as Abel Drugger in *The Tobacconist*, an afterpiece carved out of Ben Jonson's *The Alchemist*. This latter role gave rise to an unresolved debate about Kean's quality in comedy. He would have liked to emulate Garrick's versatility, but Lewes is probably right that 'he had no playfulness that was not as the playfulness of a panther, showing her claws every moment' (Lewes, 10).

The move to respectability in Clarges Street concealed a counter-move to depravity in the streets around Covent Garden. In summer 1815 Kean founded the Wolves Club, a drinking society largely composed of theatrical professionals dedicated to debauchery. Rightly or wrongly, its members were regularly accused of forming a claque in support of Kean or against any actor who threatened his supremacy. They bolstered Kean's emerging megalomania. The major creation of his third season was Sir Giles Overreach in Massinger's *A New Way to Pay Old Debts*. Overreach was, with the arguable exception of King Lear, the last of Kean's great parts. Byron was not the only person to be convulsed by his mad ravings in the final act. For Hazlitt, Kean's faultless playing of the role simply confirmed his greatness. But on 26 March 1816, when he should have been performing Sforza in Massinger's *The Duke of Milan*, Kean was drunk in a Deptford tavern. It was his first betrayal of the Drury Lane audience. By 9 May, when he created the title role in Charles Maturin's *Bertram*, he had been forgiven. Bertram was his second successful new role of the 1815–16 season. Kean had been unimpressed by the play at first reading, but he cut and rewrote it to make his own role paramount. Maturin was not consulted. Few living writers had the status to challenge the judgement of a leading actor.

Early in his fourth season, on 28 October 1816, Kean played Shakespeare's Timon. The performance was admired, but houses were moderate. Drury Lane was losing the contest with its perennial rival, Covent Garden. William Charles Macready made his début at Covent Garden on 16 September 1816, audiences crowded to see Kemble there in his farewell season, and, on 12 February 1817, the young Junius Brutus Booth made his well-publicized first appearance in London. Booth had openly modelled himself on Kean, who found the imitation disconcerting. When Booth quarrelled with the Covent Garden management, Kean plotted to have him contracted to Drury Lane, where, on 20 February 1817, Kean as Othello obliterated Booth's Iago. The mortified Booth returned to Covent Garden, soon to emigrate to America where he founded a famous theatrical dynasty. It was not the last time Kean set about destroying a rival, and the retirement of Kemble on 23 June 1817 left him unchallenged as king of tragedy.

The middle years Kean was thirty in 1817, and discerning critics feared that he was already past his prime. Drink-sodden and suffering from venereal disease, he lived like a cautionary tale on the perils of fame. He employed a private secretary, ran a fleet of Thames wherries, and paraded his pet lion in London's streets. His income, unprecedented for an actor, was matched by his expenditure, and he no longer bothered to conceal his philandering. The number of missed performances increased and, although reliable in his old parts, he found new ones difficult to master. The four false starts in the 1817–18 season included Barabas in Marlowe's *The Jew of Malta* (24 April 1818) and Shakespeare's King John (1 June 1818). Kean was now claiming the right to veto new plays. If overruled, he could always destroy them with a lacklustre performance, as he did Jane Porter's *Switzerland* on 15 February 1819. The probable truth is that, for the first time, he was experiencing the actor's overwhelming fear of failure. Kean was temperamentally bound to camouflage fear with bluster, as he did notoriously in the case of Charles Bucke's *The Italians*. This play was submitted to Drury Lane in November 1817, when Kean endorsed the committee's recommendation that it be staged. But Kean had second thoughts about his intended role as Albanio. The delaying tactics he employed were, at best, undignified, and Bucke's patience wore out. Early in 1819 he published the play with a tell-tale preface on the conduct of Drury Lane, concluding that, 'though Mr. Kean is saving that establishment with his right hand, he is ruining it with his left'. In the ensuing pamphlet debate, public opinion was predominantly on Bucke's side. The Drury Lane audience forced from Kean a perfunctory apology that satisfied no one.

The dispute was the last straw for Drury Lane's amateur committee. In summer 1819 they put the theatre up for rent, and Kean was one of the bidders. To his chagrin he was outbid by Elliston. To make things worse, Elliston held him to his contract, thus postponing plans for a lucrative visit to America. Kean made his first appearance under Elliston, in this his seventh season at Drury Lane, on 8 November 1819. His choice of Richard III was given a new piquancy by the fact that Covent Garden's new star, Macready, was currently playing it there. The rivalry served both theatres, but Kean made the mistake of extending it by tackling Coriolanus, in which Macready had recently made an impression, on 25 January 1820. Kemble had specialized in muscular Roman roles. They fitted Kean no better than the cerebral Hamlet or even Romeo. Much more notable was his London début, on 24 April 1820, as King Lear. The version was Nahum Tate's, and Kean's performance, as dictated by his stamina, was one of fits and starts. But the vivid transitions were there, together with the hair-raising pathos. Audiences rallied to him for his pre-American farewell performances in the summer of 1820. The contradictory relationship with Elliston continued. They were drinking and whoring companions at the same time as they were professional contenders. The diary of Elliston's waspish acting manager, James Winston, records their debauchery with suspicious relish. If Winston is to be trusted, Kean would copulate with actresses or prostitutes before and after a play, and during its intervals as well. Such excess is more than mere self-indulgence. Kean's first visit to America was an image of his flight from himself. In the spring of 1820 he had begun what was to be a fateful affair with Charlotte Cox, with the apparent collusion of her eminently respectable husband, a London alderman and member of Drury Lane's general committee. This was the most obsessed and obsessive relationship Kean ever had. It would reach a savage conclusion in 1825. Meanwhile, during his last week in London, two paternity suits were brought against him. He set sail from Liverpool on 7 October 1820 and, on 29 November, opened as Richard III at the Anthony Street Theatre, New York.

Kean was the first major English actor to tour America since George Frederick Cooke in 1810. His behaviour was exemplary and his reception enthusiastic. Able to select only his favourite parts and unthreatened by competition, he was more stable than he had ever been. From December to May, in New York, Philadelphia, Boston, and Baltimore, he scarcely put a foot wrong. But then, ignoring advice, he resolved on a return visit to Boston. Bostonians did not attend the theatre in summer. Kean opened to a poor house on 23 May 1821, and when even fewer were present at curtain-up on 25 May he declined to perform. Press reaction converted a tantrum into an international insult. Warned that his appearance in any American theatre would precipitate a riot, Kean embarked for England on 7 June 1821. Having made £6000 in six months, he would have liked to stay longer.

Led back to Drury Lane at the head of a triumphal procession cannily staged by Elliston, Kean opened as Richard III on 23 July 1821. Before the end of the week he had also played Shylock and Othello. There followed a break until November. Charlotte Cox was uppermost in his mind. Her once prosperous husband had toppled into bankruptcy, and she was pressing Kean to leave his wife. Kean found himself in the unusual position of advising caution. Despite the warmth of his initial welcome, the fickle audience was disappointed by him. His eighth season at Drury Lane was a financial and artistic failure. None of his new characters, which included Wolsey in *Henry VIII* (20 May 1822), held the stage, and the season brought Elliston to the brink of ruin. As usual, Kean ran away, this time to the Isle of Bute, where, in October 1822, he acquired a house and 20 acres. It was there that he heard of Elliston's emergency plan to enliven the 1822–3 season by pitting three dissatisfied Covent Garden stars against three of his Drury Lane regulars. Kean's opposition was to be the dignified tragedian, Charles Mayne Young. Resentful and anxious, Kean skulked in Scotland until November 1822. To public delight, he then engaged with Young in *Othello* on 27 November, and once the press had awarded him a narrow victory entered into more confident battle in *Venice Preserv'd* (Jaffeir to Young's Pierre) and *Cymbeline* (Posthumus to Young's Iachimo). Despite the inflated salaries he was paying, Elliston had recovered some ground by the end of the season. Kean and his manager, though, were at loggerheads over the future. Kean's contract had a year to

run, and he was desperate to establish a position of strength from which to negotiate. But Elliston was notoriously slippery, and matters were unresolved in the summer of 1823. The affair with Charlotte Cox was unresolved too, and the strain was telling on Kean. He was shocked to hear of Elliston's decision to engage Macready for the coming season. It was one thing to take on an ageing star like Young, another to confront a rising star. Kean remained in his Scottish retreat until Macready's initial run was over, and there was little of note in his four months of performance from December 1823 to April 1824. For the first time at Drury Lane, he was almost unobtrusive.

Trial and decline Kean's affair with Charlotte Cox finally exploded in mutual recrimination early in 1824. Almost at once Charlotte left home to live with her husband's clerk. In her abandoned bedroom, tied together by a ribbon, were the letters Kean had written to her. They would furnish the incriminating evidence at the trial a year later. On 9 April 1824 Cox took out a writ against Kean for criminal conversation with his wife. Kean's apparent unconcern may have been a pretence. Once his Drury Lane commitments were over, he ran away, initially to Brighton and then, with his wife, to France. He was making a sad attempt to keep his family together. He had arranged for Charles to go to Eton College in June, with an annual allowance of £300. It would not be easy for an actor's son to survive at Eton, even though his father had a house in Clarges Street and an estate in Scotland. In July 1824 Kean signed a new contract with Elliston. He was to receive an unprecedented £50 per night for twenty-three performances in the new year.

The case of *Cox v. Kean* was heard on 17 January 1825 in an atmosphere of prurient public interest. The court found for the plaintiff, awarding him damages of £800. Neither marriage survived the trial. Acceding to her wish to separate, Kean settled on Mary £504 per year, out of which she was to pay for Charles's education. The allowance of £50 per year, which he had been paying to his importunate mother since his first success in 1814, continued until his death. It was an act of bravado, in the fraught atmosphere following the trial, for Kean to return to Drury Lane on 24 January 1825. His Richard III, though played right through, was drowned out by conflicting voices in the auditorium. The same was true of *Othello* on 28 January. *The Times* led a press campaign against 'that obscene little personage' (28 Jan 1825), castigating this 'obscene mimic' (29 Jan 1825) for his failure to abase himself before the audience. After playing Sir Giles Overreach in front of a clamorous audience on 31 January, Kean claimed in a curtain speech to have 'made as much concession to an English audience as an English actor ought' (Hawkins, 2.243). For the remaining twenty nights of his engagement, he was generally allowed to perform without significant interruption, but there was uproar again at most of the venues on his subsequent provincial tour. In the long run, this hostility destroyed him. After the Cox trial, Kean was rarely again a great actor and never a self-sufficient man.

When Kean sailed for America in September 1825, it was

with the hope of escaping to make a new home there; but he opened to the now familiar pandemonium at the Park Theatre, New York, on 14 November 1825. There was a generous response to the statement he then published in the *National Advocate*, and the rest of his New York performances passed off peacefully. Albany audiences were also tolerant, but in Boston on 19 December 1825 Kean was driven from the stage and there was a serious riot. Much shaken, Kean continued his tour for a further year, ranging from Charleston in the south to Montreal, where he was rapturously received by Canadian audiences, for whom an English star was a rarity. His decision to return to England may have been the result of a cruel deception. Kean was given to understand that the owners of Drury Lane wished him to succeed the bankrupt Elliston as lessee. He sailed for England on 6 December 1826, not knowing that the lesseeship had already been purchased by the American Stephen Price.

The American tour had restored Kean's fortunes and improved his health, but it had stretched him to the limit. Bitter about the lesseeship of Drury Lane, he took rooms in Hummums Hotel, near Covent Garden, and resumed his dissipated habits. The chronic gastritis and gallstones discovered at his autopsy began at this time to affect him, and his leg was often too painful to bear his weight; Raymund FitzSimons questions the contemporary diagnosis of gout, suspecting that a syphilitic lesion was a likelier cause. The slow poison of mercury treatment may have contributed to his inability to memorize new parts and his increasing difficulty in sustaining familiar ones. His fumbling forgetfulness on the night of 21 May 1827 turned into an embarrassing fiasco the production of his friend Colley Grattan's *Ben Nazir*. The remorseful Kean began to talk of retirement, but he had one resentful trick to play first. Because Stephen Price had refused him a share in Drury Lane, Kean elected to play his farewell season at Covent Garden. Price countered by announcing as his new star Kean's son Charles. Father and son had made some attempts at reconciliation, though Charles had taken his mother's side in the separation and defied his father by turning actor. The prospect of rivalry threatened their tenuous alliance, and it was probably fortunate that Charles inherited so little of Edmund's charisma. Price's ruse proved ineffective.

Though needing to nurse his health, Kean was more effective at Covent Garden than he had been of late at Drury Lane. His private life, though, was in disarray. He was living with a formidable Irish prostitute called Ophelia Benjamin, whom he feared and needed. In the early summer of 1828 he was fit enough to fulfil an engagement in Paris, but his reception was lukewarm and he retreated to his Scottish property, returning refreshed to Covent Garden in October 1828. In January 1829 his health collapsed and he had to take three months' rest. A tour of Irish theatres with his son had to be abandoned in Cork in April 1829, when he collapsed again. It was restarted a month later, and again interrupted for reasons of Kean's health. After recuperating in Scotland, he returned to London, only to quarrel with Charles Kemble, the manager of

Covent Garden. From December 1829 to March 1830 Kean was back at Drury Lane, where he found his reception encouraging. Foolishly, he attempted another new part, Shakespeare's Henry V, but at its opening on 8 March 1830 his memory failed again. In despair, he announced his retirement for a second time and played a second round of farewells in the summer of 1830. The problem was that he could not afford to retire so early. He had squandered money, not least in fits of drunken generosity, so that, too ill to make the intended trip to America, he was forced to return to Drury Lane in January 1831. The newspapers mocked him in anticipation of a third retirement.

In the spring of 1831 Kean made his final bid for independence when he leased the King's Theatre in Richmond, Surrey, setting up home in the adjacent cottage. When strong enough, he acted there as well as at the Haymarket. He was living now under the care of the seventy-year-old Charlotte Tidswell, who had driven Ophelia Benjamin away. Illness had so tamed Kean that he agreed to play opposite Macready at Drury Lane during the 1832–3 season. Honours were even when they appeared in *Othello* on 26 November 1832, and they repeated it intermittently until Kean's health failed again. Captain Polhill, Drury Lane's new lessee, refused the ailing actor a loan in the new year of 1833. Kean took the only revenge available to him by crossing to Covent Garden to play Othello opposite his son's Iago. The performance on 25 March 1833 was his last. Unable to complete it, he was carried back to Richmond, where, after languishing for several weeks, he died on 15 May 1833. An application to bury him next to Garrick in Westminster Abbey was denied, and on 25 May he was buried at the Old Church in Richmond. Six years later Charles Kean had a memorial tablet placed in the church. Long before then Kean's widow, with whom he had been reconciled shortly before his death, had sold most of his possessions at auction to pay off his debts.

Kean's repertory of great roles was small and his range narrow, but he remains the English theatre's supreme example of the charismatic actor. Three years after his death, Alexandre Dumas *père* chose him as the subject of a play, *Kean* (later reworked by Jean-Paul Sartre), seeing in Kean an embodiment of the rebellious spirit of Romanticism. The image has been historically persuasive.

PETER THOMSON

Sources R. FitzSimons, *Edmund Kean* (1976) • B. Cornwall [B. W. Procter], *The life of Edmund Kean*, 3rd edn, 2 vols. (1847) • F. W. Hawkins, *The life of Edmund Kean*, 2 vols. (1869) • H. N. Hillebrand, *Edmund Kean* (1933) • G. H. Lewes, *On actors and the art of acting* (1875) • J. F. Molloy, *The life and adventures of Edmund Kean*, 2 vols. (1888) • *Drury Lane journal: selections from James Winston's diaries, 1819–1827*, ed. A. L. Nelson and G. B. Cross (1974) • W. Hazlitt, *A view of the English stage* (1818) • W. Shakespeare, *Oxberry's 1822 edition of King Richard III: with the descriptive notes recording Edmund Kean's performance*, ed. A. S. Downer, facs. edn (1959) [with additional notes and introduction] • post-mortem report

Archives Harvard U., Houghton L., corresp. • Theatre Museum, London • V&A NAL, commonplace books, letters, and draft of a speech

Likenesses S. Cousins, pencil drawing, 1814, NPG • G. Cruikshank, cartoon, 1814, BM • J. J. Halls, oils, 1814, Theatre Museum, London • H. H. Meyer, mezzotint, pubd 1814 (after W. H. Watts),

BM · S. Joseph, bust, 1815, Drury Lane Theatre, London · J. North-cote, oils, 1819, NPG [*see illus.*] · G. Clint, group portrait, oils, 1820, Garr. Club · G. Clint, oils, 1820, Theatre Museum, London · J. E. Carew, marble statue, 1833, Drury Lane Theatre, London · G. Clint, oils (as Richard III), Garr. Club · S. De Wilde, pencil and watercolour drawing (as Richard III), Garr. Club · T. Jones, etching, NPG · attrib. D. Maclise, oils (as Hamlet), NG Ire. · H. Meyer, oils (as chief of the Huron Indians), Garr. Club · J. Prynn, etching and stipple, NPG · attrib. T. Wageman, pencil drawing, NPG · theatrical prints, BM, NPG · three portraits, oils (probably as Richard III), Garr. Club

Kean [*née* Tree], **Eleanora** [Ellen] (**1805–1880**), actress, was born on 12 December 1805, probably in London, the third of the four daughters of Cornelius Tree, an East India House official. Ellen Tree's sisters, who included (Anna) Maria *Tree, all went on the stage but retired on marriage. Ellen Tree first acted as Olivia to her sister Maria's Viola in an operatic version of *Twelfth Night* at a private theatre in Berwick Street, and her official début at the age of seventeen was in the same role for Maria's benefit at Covent Garden in 1822. After touring with Maria she was engaged at Bath, where she opened as Lydia Languish in *The Rivals* on 7 February 1824 and played leading comedy roles for two seasons with scant success. Charles Kemble acted for her benefit on 6 March 1826, and in the following May she played in W. C. Macready's benefit. After spending that summer in Birmingham, she was engaged at Drury Lane to play twelve leading roles at 10 guineas weekly, where she remained for three seasons while acting at the Haymarket in the summers. She saw Charles Kean's début at Drury Lane on 1 October 1827 and acted with him in *Lovers' Vows* on Boxing day 1828. The turning point of her career came in 1829 at Covent Garden, where she began an engagement as Lady Townly in *The Provoked Husband*. Other successes followed, and for her benefit she played Romeo to Fanny Kemble's Juliet. It was a stunning success, but she declined to play it thereafter. Fanny Kemble deemed her the only Romeo with whom she acted who really looked the part. In the summer of 1830 Ellen played in Dublin, Glasgow, and Edinburgh and acted Julia in *The Hunchback* with its author, Sheridan Knowles, who later wrote, to suit her talents, *The Wife*, *Love*, *John of Procida*, and *The Rose of Aragon*. At Covent Garden on 25 March 1833 she played Desdemona with Edmund and Charles Kean when Edmund collapsed during *Othello*, his last performance. On 24 April she acted with Knowles and young Kean in *The Wife*, and, having declined an engagement at Drury Lane and withdrawn from playing Cleopatra with Macready, she joined Kean for an abortive tour of Germany. There they became engaged, but parental disapproval resulted in termination of the arrangement. In 1834 her Myrrha with Macready in *Sardanapalus* at Drury Lane was poorly received, but Rachel in *The Jewess* ran for more than a hundred nights. *The Red Mask* and *The Ransom* (as did *The Jewess*) suited her femininity and evocation of sympathy for suffering virtue. After resigning from playing opposite Macready in *Ion* in June 1836, she took the title role in October as a breeches part and, despite some controversy, was a success.

Ellen Tree then went to America, and opened on 12

Eleanora Kean (1805–1880), by unknown artist

December 1836 at the Park Theatre, New York, as Rosalind, which she followed by Viola, Beatrice, and other established roles. She acted nightly at the Park and toured major cities, from Boston to New Orleans, drawing crowded houses and enthusiastic reviews. She returned to England in 1839 with £12,000 profit. On 3 September she played both Viola (in *Twelfth Night*) and Pauline (in *The Ransom*) at the Haymarket. At Covent Garden on 4 November, in Knowles's new comedy, *Love*, she was a great success, and Leigh Hunt's *A Legend of Florence* was equally successful. In 1840 at the Haymarket she acted with Charles Kean, now an established star, and then played with him in the provinces, most frequently in *Romeo and Juliet*, in preparation for Kean's staging of the play at the Haymarket in 1841. In Dublin on 29 January 1842 she married Kean (1811–1868) [*see* Kean, Charles John], and they acted together that night in *The Gamester* and *The Honeymoon*. They first appeared as Mr and Mrs Charles Kean in Glasgow on 27 February. Truly a Victorian, Ellen Tree was thereafter known professionally as Mrs Charles Kean and acted only with her husband. The couple lived in mutual devotion for twenty-six years, with Ellen unfailingly supporting, defending, and protecting her husband in matters personal and professional.

In 1842 at the Haymarket, the Keans brought out Knowles's new play, *The Rose of Aragon*, as their main attraction. Ellen's repertory contrasted with her husband's previous dependence on established tragic roles, and under her influence his acting style moved towards restraint and realism. For the next two seasons her acting was interrupted by pregnancy difficulties, and on 18 September 1843 their only daughter, Mary (*d.* 1898), was born. In 1845 they went to America, and acted at the Park Theatre in New York between tours to major cities, again from Boston to New Orleans. Ellen was Constance in Kean's great historical staging of *King John*, and Evaline in the première of Lovell's *The Wife's Secret*, both at the Park. On the couple's return to England they produced Lovell's play with great success at the Haymarket, on 17 January 1848; it remained in their repertory thereafter. The Keans were favourites of Queen Victoria and Prince Albert, and when the royal theatricals at Windsor Castle were initiated in 1848 with Kean as director, Ellen played with him as Ophelia, Portia, and Mrs Haller in *The Stranger*. She appeared in all Kean's productions at Windsor Castle, except for two seasons when she was ill. In 1857 she indiscreetly importuned the queen in a letter to knight her husband and he was dropped as director.

In 1849 Ellen Kean was well received in the première of *Strathmore* by Westland Marston. In 1850 Kean became manager of the Princess's Theatre, where Mrs Kean played three to five times weekly in such roles as Ophelia, Viola, Portia, Beatrice, Lady Macbeth, Gertrude, Hermione in *The Winter's Tale*, Constance in *King John*, the title role in *Anne Blake*, the Chorus in *Henry V*, Mistress Ford in *The Merry Wives of Windsor*, Katherine in *Henry VIII*, Elvira in *Pizarro*, Mrs Oakley in *The Jealous Wife*, Evaline in *The Wife's Secret*, and lesser roles, many of them in light comedy as main or second pieces. Illness kept her from acting from January 1854 to May 1855, but as often as she was able she assisted in stage direction, supervised costuming, and coached young actresses, notably Ellen Terry, Carlotta Leclercq, and Agnes Robertson. Most importantly, she supported her husband during the vicissitudes of his management and furthered his development of 'repressed force', realistic detail, and greater subtlety, in old as well as new roles, both in Shakespeare and in 'gentlemanly melodrama'.

Early portraits show that Ellen Kean was not conventionally pretty, but she was generally considered beautiful. From the stage her features were strong and expressive. Her aquiline nose was offset by large flashing eyes, abundant brown hair, full lips, and a dazzling smile. She stood 5 feet 4 inches tall, was slender and graceful, with a resonant, musical, and emotively expressive voice. Her unique laugh could set audiences into gales, even from offstage in *Much Ado about Nothing*. Westland Marston reported she projected gaiety as easily as feminine tenderness and pathos. She was less effective in roles which contravened her staunchly Victorian moral code, such as Lady Macbeth and Gertrude, but as Portia, Viola, Hermione and Queen Catherine she excelled. She was well suited to contemporary comedy, domestic drama, and 'gentlemanly melodrama', with a special strength in noble suffering portrayed ideally in a 'new quiet style' with 'sympathetic truth', according to Marston, although she lacked the physical and imaginative powers for great tragic roles. In early years she dressed plainly off stage, but as a matron her wardrobe tended to be eccentric. On stage she persisted with hoop skirts and flowing robes, an obvious anachronism in Kean's antiquarianism, for which she did extensive costume supervision. Photographs during and after the Princess's years show her to be matronly and plain, sometimes even homely. While she still drew warm reviews for her fine voice, excellent diction, and line reading, as well as consummate command of character in established roles, it was in new mature roles that she was later most successful. In private life she was reported to be as engaging as she was on stage.

The Keans left management in 1859 and undertook to recoup losses at the Princess's by provincial tours and limited London engagements in established roles. In 1863 they went to Australia, where they toured for nine months before going to California, Vancouver, and New York. They then toured the American east, the mid-west, and the war-ravaged south before returning to England in July 1866, exhausted, old before their time, their great financial goals unrealized. After a London engagement they played in the provinces until Kean's heart attack at Liverpool in May 1867. After his death the following January, Ellen lived on at 47 Queensborough Terrace in relative seclusion and professional retirement until her own death there, on 20 August 1880. Following a private funeral she was buried beside Charles in the churchyard at St Catherington, Horndean, Hampshire.

Ellen Kean's career spanned forty-five years. In her time she rivalled Helen Faucit as the country's leading actress, the range of her talents perhaps being more suited than Faucit's to the dramatic tastes of the age.

M. GLEN WILSON

Sources J. Reilly, 'Miss Ellen Tree (1805–1880), actress and wife to Charles Kean', MA thesis, Ohio State U., 1979 · J. W. Cole, *The life and theatrical times of Charles Kean … including a summary of the English stage for the last fifty years*, 2 vols. (1859) · M. G. Wilson, *Charles Kean: a chronicle of his career* (1998) · V. Francisco, 'Charles Kean's acting career, 1827–1867', PhD diss. Indiana U., 1974 · W. G. B. Carson, *Letters of Charles and Ellen Kean relating to their American tours* (1945) · J. M. D. Hardwick, *Emigrants in motley: the journal of Charles and Ellen Kean in quest of a theatrical fortune in Australia and America* (1954) · J. W. Marston, *Our recent actors*, 2 vols. (1888) · J. Coleman, *Players and playwrights I have known: a review of the English stage from 1840 to 1880*, 2nd edn, 2 vols. (1890) · C. Morris, *Life on the stage* (1902) · E. Terry, *The story of my life* (1908) · d. cert.
Archives Folger · Hunt. L., letters | NL Scot., letters to Elizabeth Rutherford · Royal Arch., letters from members of the royal household
Likenesses R. J. Lane, lithograph, 1836, Trinity College of Music, London, Mander and Mitchenson theatre collection · R. J. Lane, lithograph, pubd 1838, NPG · R. Dadd, double portrait, oils, *c.*1840 (with C. Kean as Hamlet), Yale U. CBA · LaRoche, photographs, 1855–9, Garr. Club · LaRoche, photographs, 1855–9, Theatre Museum, London, Enthoven collection · C. R. Leslie, oils, 1856, Royal Shakespeare Theatre, Stratford upon Avon, Warwickshire · watercolour drawing, *c.*1858 (with C. Kean), V&A · J. C. Armitage, engraving (after W. C. Ross, 1844), Trinity College of Music, London, Mander and Mitchenson theatre collection · W. H. Nightingale, pencil drawing, NPG · Southwell Bros, photograph, NPG · theatrical prints, BM, Harvard TC, NPG · three photographs, NPG · watercolour drawing, Garr. Club [*see illus.*]
Wealth at death under £3000: probate, 8 Jan 1881, *CGPLA Eng. & Wales*

Kean, Michael (1761–1823), miniature painter and owner of the Derby porcelain factory, was born in Dublin, possibly on 16 October 1761. He entered the Dublin Society's drawing schools on 7 February 1771 and there studied ornament, landscape, and figure drawing. He was a pupil of Francis Robert West, who had been appointed master of the figure drawing school in January of that year. The school aimed to give its pupils a grounding in art and to provide them with drawing skills for manufacturing industry. Kean would have found this approach extremely useful throughout his varied career.

On leaving the school Kean set out to become a sculptor and was apprenticed to the distinguished Irish sculptor Edward Smyth. On 2 December 1779 he was awarded the silver medal of the Dublin Society for his drawings of sculpture. During this early part of his career, both in Dublin and later in London, he earned his living as a miniature portrait painter working in watercolour on ivory. He also did some portraits in pastel. Signed work by Kean is rare and his reputation as a competent miniaturist rests on a small number of signed miniatures such as *A Portrait of an Unknown Man* (Victoria and Albert Museum, London). He settled in London, where he entered the Royal Academy Schools on 29 October 1784. He exhibited work at the Royal Academy each year from 1786 to 1790 and also at the exhibitions of the Free Society of Artists.

Kean may have worked as a decorator of porcelain: in 1795 he entered into a partnership with William *Duesbury (1763–1796) [see under Duesbury, William (bap. 1725, d. 1786)], the owner of the porcelain factory in Nottingham Road, Derby. After Duesbury's death in 1796 he took over the management of the factory. In 1798 he married Duesbury's widow, Elizabeth, née Edwards (d. 1840); they had one son. He built a new factory at Calver's Close and expanded the range of work. During his period of ownership the standard of porcelain decoration was very good and his artistic input increased the reputation of the factory. A hot-tempered man, Kean separated from his wife, quarrelling both with her and with his stepchildren over the running of the business, which resulted in a series of lawsuits. In 1811 he withdrew from the business and it was taken over by his clerk, Robert Bloor. The disputes continued and Kean returned to London, where he died in November 1823.

L. H. Cust, rev. Paul Caffrey

Sources W. G. Strickland, *A dictionary of Irish artists*, 1 (1913), 567–8 · B. S. Long, *British miniaturists* (1923), 248–9 · J. Twitchett, *Derby porcelain* (1980) · D. Foskett, *Miniatures: dictionary and guide* (1987), 580 · H. Blättel, *International dictionary miniature painters / Internationales Lexikon Miniatur-Maler* (1992), 516–17 · P. Caffrey, 'Irish portrait miniatures, c. 1700–1830', PhD diss., Southampton Institute, 1995 · *Proceedings of the Dublin Society*, 7 (1770–71), 80 · *Proceedings of the Dublin Society*, 16 (1779–80), 23 · A. Pasquin [J. Williams], *An authentic history of the professors of painting, sculpture, and architecture who have practiced in Ireland … to which are added, Memoirs of the royal academicians* [1796], 15 · G. Hall and others, *Summary catalogue of miniatures in the Victoria and Albert Museum* (1981), 34 · G. Savage, *English ceramics* (1961) · W. B. Howey, *English pottery and porcelain* (1960) · L. F. W. Jewitt, *The ceramic art of Great Britain, from pre-historic times*, 1 (1878), 56–114 · J. Murdoch and J. Twitchett, *Painters of the Derby china works* (1987) · Derby Local Studies Library, Duesbury MSS, ref. no. DL 82, files 1–21

Archives V&A

Keane, Ellsworth McGranahan [Shake] (1927–1997), jazz musician and poet, was born on 30 May 1927 in Kingstown, St Vincent, the third son and sixth child among the seven children of Charles E. Keane (d. c.1940/41), a policeman and waterworks mechanic, and his wife, Dorcas, née Edwards (d. 1961). Both parents were Vincentian. His father, who taught him the trumpet, also instilled in him a love of literature, and he started writing poetry while still a youngster. He joined brass bands at six, playing for dances and carnival parades, and by the age of eleven was travelling throughout the island with a leading dance band; he formed his own group three years later. He attended Kingstown Methodist school and St Vincent boys' grammar school, where he was dubbed 'Shakespeare' by his schoolfellows. In 1946 he joined the civil service and worked at the magistrates' court as a clerk. In the following year he returned to St Vincent boys' grammar school as a teaching assistant, then joined the staff and taught English language and literature, French, Latin, and history. He published two books of poetry, *L'Oubili* (1950) and *Ixion* (1952), while still in St Vincent, and continued to write poetry throughout his adult life.

Keane arrived in Britain in 1952. At the BBC he became a regular contributor to *Caribbean Voices*, a ground-breaking radio programme that launched many literary careers, reading poetry and interviewing fellow writers and musicians. He also began playing music in nightclubs, appearing as a flamboyant trumpeter in cabaret, and switching easily between the Latin-American idiom, calypso, and jazz. He worked with the guitarist Lauderic Caton and with the Guyanese pianist Mike McKenzie in his Harlem All-Stars before making his jazz club début in 1954. He did not then regard himself as a jazz musician and was indifferent towards his working environment, earning a living playing for dancers with the Nigerian percussionist Folorunṣọ ('Ginger') Johnson and others and singing bass with a vocal quartet.

An association with the alto saxophonist Joe Harriott altered Keane's view. Their working relationship had begun in McKenzie's band and at highlife and calypso recording sessions, and Keane, who was reading for a BA honours degree in English literature at University College, London, found an affinity with Harriott and his progressive musical ideas. He abandoned his studies in 1960 to play with the saxophonist's quintet. This was the group that introduced 'free-form' playing to England and with which Keane, now playing the wider-bore flugelhorn as well as the trumpet, achieved prominence. He left Harriott in November 1960 to pursue his studies, but did not complete his degree and soon returned. Through the attention he received with Harriott, he diversified. He played with the group led by the pianist Michael Garrick, accompanying poetry readings and in sacred settings, and worked also in the theatre as an actor, musician, and poet. He also secured session work at a time when black musicians were seldom admitted to the closed shop of commercial recording, being hired both as featured soloist

Ellsworth McGranahan Keane (1927–1997), by Val Wilmer, 1963 [right, playing the flugelhorn and trumpet, with Joe Harriott]

and section player for these and contemporary 'classical' record dates.

On 3 March 1954 Keane married Christiane Theresa Marie Joseph Richard (*b.* 1931), a librarian, and daughter of George Richard, branch manager for the Shell Mex oil company; they had two sons, Alan Daniel Keane (*b.* 1954) and Noel Julian Keane (*b.* 1962), who became a producer in the BBC World Service. Before 1965 he also began long relationships with Elizabeth Uma Ramanan (*b.* 1932), a secretary—their son Roland Ramanan (*b.* 1966) became a teacher and trumpeter—and with Muriel (Lou) Pick, with whom he lived in Germany and St Vincent and whom he married after his divorce.

In 1967 Keane left Britain to settle in Germany. He became featured soloist with Kurt Edelhagen's radio orchestra at Westdeutscher Rundfunk in Cologne and was at the peak of his jazz career when he returned to St Vincent in 1972 to become director of culture. His tenure in the post was short-lived (1973–4). He reverted to teaching and became principal of Bishop's College High School, Georgetown (1975–8), then taught French and English at Intermediate High School, Kingstown (1978–81). He continued to write poetry and received new impetus for this from the success of further publications: *One a Week with Water* (1979), which won the Cuban Casa de las Americas prize for poetry, and *The Volcano Suite* (1979).

In 1981 Keane travelled to Barbados to participate in Carifesta, then moved to New York and settled in the predominantly Caribbean part of the Bedford-Stuyvesant section of Brooklyn. There he occasionally played for dances

with calypso and soca bands but primarily wrote their musical arrangements, remaining in semi-retirement as a trumpet player until 1989, when friends in Europe persuaded him that his musical voice was still of significance. In that year he joined Michael Garrick in England for a recreation of the Harriott Quintet. He continued to travel to London and in 1991 made a BBC television film with the poet Linton Kwesi Johnson; he was also heard for the first time in public playing and reciting poetry in a reggae context.

Keane, 6 feet 4 inches tall, powerfully built and full-bearded, was an impressive figure. In his heyday he was regarded as the foremost jazz trumpeter of his generation in Europe, a resourceful and inventive improviser who matched a natural ferocity with introspection, reflecting strands of a personality he described as 'partly gentle and partly … vulgar and violent' (Wilmer, 45). His spare, witty verse, suggestive of an exasperated love affair with the Caribbean, was anthologized in *Contemporary Poets* (1970), the *Penguin Book of Caribbean Verse in English* (1986), and *You Better Believe It: Black Verse in English from Africa, the West Indies and the United States* (1973); another collection, *Palm and Octopus*, was published in 1994.

In the 1990s, following divorce from his wife Lou, Keane married for a third time. He remained based in Brooklyn, but visits to Norway revived his trumpet career. There he became well known through his television work for the singer and producer Erik Bye, playing music, but also featuring in *The Search for Mangas Coloradas* (1992–3), a television series about a slave ship that sank off the Norwegian coast. He gave concerts at unusual locations—on oil rigs, for fishermen, and in churches—and was in Norway when he became ill. He died from stomach cancer on 11 November 1997 in the Norske Radiumhospital, Oslo, and was cremated in the city; his ashes were returned to St Vincent. He was survived by his third wife and by the children of his earlier relationships.   VAL WILMER

Sources V. Wilmer, 'Burning 'Speare', *Wire*, 68 (Oct 1989), 44–5 • *The Guardian* (13 Nov 1997) • K. Grime, 'Star sideman: Shake Keane', *Jazz News* (31 Jan 1962), 8–9 • P. Nanton, 'In memoriam: Ellsworth McGranahan "Shake" Keane, 1927–1997', *Wasafari* (spring 1998), 40–44 • personal knowledge (2004) • private information (2004) • m. cert. [Christiane Theresa Marie Joseph Richard]

Likenesses V. Wilmer, photographs, 1960, priv. coll. • V. Wilmer, photographs, 1963, priv. coll. [*see illus.*] • V. Wilmer, photographs, 1989, priv. coll.

Keane, John, first Baron Keane (1781–1844), army officer, was born on 6 February 1781, second of the three sons of Sir John Keane (1757–1829) of Belmont, co. Waterford (who was made first baronet, of Belmont, in August 1801 and was MP for Bangor and Youghal until 1806), and his first wife, Sarah, daughter of Richard Keily of Lismore, co. Waterford. On 12 November 1794 he was appointed captain in a new regiment just raised on the Beresford estates (124th foot?), which was broken up immediately afterwards, when Keane was put on half pay. In November 1799 he was brought on full pay in the 44th foot, which he joined at Gibraltar and accompanied to Egypt, where he served as aide-de-camp to Lord Cavan. Keane obtained a majority in the 60th Royal Americans in May 1802, but continued on the staff in Egypt and Malta until 1803. On 20 August 1803 he became lieutenant-colonel 13th foot, joined the regiment at Gibraltar early in 1804, and returned home with it in 1805. He married, on 10 August 1806, Grace (d. 14 Jan 1838), second daughter of General Sir John Smith, Royal Artillery; they had four sons and two daughters.

After serving several years in Ireland, Keane accompanied his regiment to Bermuda as junior lieutenant-colonel, and commanded it at the taking of Martinique in 1809. He became a brevet colonel on 1 January 1812, and the same year was transferred to the 5th or Jäger battalion 60th foot. In April 1813 he joined Wellington's army in the Peninsula, and was at the head of a brigade of the 3rd division at Vitoria, the Pyrenees, Nivelle, the Nive, Vic Bigorre, and Toulouse. He became a major-general on 4 June 1814, was made KCB on 2 January 1815, and received a gold cross with two clasps for Martinique, Vitoria, the Pyrenees, Nivelle, the Nive, and Toulouse. Keane, whom Gleig described as 'a young and dashing officer', was selected for the expeditionary force going from the Garonne to America, but remained unemployed (*Supplementary Despatches*, 9.136). Later he was sent out to Jamaica with some reinforcements. In command of these and the troops which had been employed under General Ross at Bladensburg and Washington he embarked the fleet under the command of Admiral Sir Alexander Cochrane for an attack on New Orleans. Keane's force landed about 9 miles from New Orleans in December 1814, and repulsed an American attack on his position. On 25 December he was superseded by the arrival of generals Sir Edward Pakenham and Samuel Gibbs with additional troops. Keane commanded a brigade in the subsequent operations, and was severely wounded in two places while leading the left column in the unsuccessful attempt on New Orleans on 8 January 1815. His private journal of the operations, which he forwarded to Wellington, together with a letter from General Andrew Jackson to the American secretary at war, were published in Wellington's *Supplementary Despatches* (10.394–400). At the peace Keane returned home with the troops which had been employed under Sir John Lambert at Fort Bowyer (or Boya), Louisiana, and in July 1815 joined Wellington in Paris. In November 1815 he was appointed to command the 9th British infantry brigade of the army of occupation in France (ibid., 11.250), from which Wellington removed him early in 1817 (ibid., 11.663). Keane commanded the troops in Jamaica from 1823 to 1830, and during that time administered the civil government as well for the space of a year and a half. He became a lieutenant-general on 22 July 1830, and was made colonel of the 68th light infantry in 1831.

In 1833 Keane was appointed commander-in-chief at Bombay in succession to Sir Colin Halkett. He took up the command on 2 July 1834, and held it until October 1839. In 1838, as a result of the Persian siege of Herat, a large force of European and Indian troops had been collected on the north-west frontier, designated the 'army of the Indus', with Sir Henry Fane, then commander-in-chief in India, in command. In October 1838 the Bombay government was ordered to send a division under Keane into Sind to coerce the amirs and to co-operate with Fane. The division landed at Vikkur on the coast of Sind, where it was delayed until the end of December owing to a shortage of camels and boats. After many difficulties it advanced up the River Indus to Hyderabad and thence towards Rohri, near Shikarpur, to meet the Bengal column prior to marching to Kandahar via the Bolan Pass and Quetta. The situation at Herat having changed, the army of the Indus was reduced in strength and, to the regret of the whole force, Fane was replaced by Keane, who assumed command of the Bengal and Bombay columns advancing into Afghanistan, at Quetta, on 6 April 1839. At Kandahar, on 8 May, in the presence of Macnaghten, the British envoy, Keane, and the British force, Shah Shuja was placed on the throne with extraordinary pomp and state. From Kandahar the army advanced towards Kabul, arriving on 20 July before Ghazni (Ghuznee). Keane, whose operations had been marked by a reckless expenditure of transport animals, had left his battering-train behind at Kandahar, and when it became necessary to take Ghazni at all costs, recourse was had to blowing open one of the gates. The fortress was captured on 23 July 1839. The operations concluded with the occupation of Kabul on 7 August. In October 1839 the army of the Indus was broken up and, part of the force being left in Afghanistan under Major-General Elphinstone, the others marched for their respective presidencies, Keane leading back the Bengal column by way of Lahore. On 12 August 1839 he was made GCB, and on 19 December 1839 was made Baron Keane of Ghuznee and of Cappoquin, co. Waterford, with a pension of £2000 a year for his own and two succeeding lives, and was granted an augmentation to his family arms. He also received the thanks of parliament and of the court of directors of the East India Company. His first wife had died in 1838, and on 20 August 1840 he married Charlotte Maria (d. 1884), youngest daughter of Colonel Boland; there were no children of the marriage.

Keane was a man of violent temper who used the language of the barrack room. This cost him the appointment of commander-in-chief India, both Auckland and Wellington being opposed to him, although acknowledging his military qualities. As a commander in India and Afghanistan he was much criticized, and possibly misrepresented. He has been censured for his high-handed treatment of the amirs of Sind, and was called 'the fortunate youth', as having owed more to good luck than to ability: he was accused of undervaluing the company's troops, and of having failed to do justice to distinguished subordinates. He had an open row with Major-General William Nott, who accused Keane of unfairly favouring officers of the royal army as against those in the service of the East India Company.

Keane, who was a lieutenant-general, GCH, colonel 43rd light infantry, died at Burton Lodge, Hampshire, of dropsy, on 26 August 1844. He was succeeded by his son Edward Arthur Wellington Keane, second Baron Keane (1815–1882), who was succeeded by his younger brother

John Manly Arbuthnot Keane (1816–1901), on whose death on 27 November 1901 the peerage become extinct. Keane's widow married in 1847 William Pigott JP DL, of Dullingham, Cambridgeshire. She died on 8 September 1884.

H. M. Chichester, rev. James Lunt

Sources J. Foster, *The peerage, baronetage, and knightage of the British empire for 1883*, 2 [1883] · J. Foster, 'Keane of Derriheen House, Cappoquin', *The peerage, baronetage, and knightage of the British empire for 1882*, 1 [1882] [see also 'Pigott, Sir Robert'] · J. W. Kaye, *History of the First Afghan War*, 1–2 (1884) · *The Times* (1844) · H. Havelock, *Narrative of the war in Affghanistan in 1838–39*, 2 vols. (1840) · H. Everett, *The history of the Somerset light infantry* (1934) · Fortescue, *Brit. army*, vols. 10, 12 · G. R. Gleig, *The campaigns of the British army at Washington and New Orleans, in the years 1814–1815*, 4th edn (1836) · W. H. Dennie, *Personal narrative of campaigns in Affghanistan, Sinde, Beloochistan*, ed. W. E. Steele (1843) · W. Hough, *A narrative of the march and operations of the army of the Indus* (1840) · J. H. Stocqueler, *Memoirs and correspondence of Major-General Sir William Nott*, 2 vols. (1854) · *GM*, 2nd ser., 22 (1844), 426–8, 658–9 · P. Macrory, *Signal catastrophe: the story of a disastrous retreat from Kabul, 1842* (1966) · HoP, *Commons* · GEC, *Peerage*

Archives NRA, priv. coll., family corresp. | BL OIOC, letters from Sir Henry Fane and Lord Auckland, MS Eur. B 255 · Derbys. RO, letters to Sir Robert Wilmot-Horton, WH 2825 · PRO NIre., corresp. with Earl Belmore

Wealth at death under £45,000: *GM*, 659

Keane, John B. [Joseph] (*d.* 1859), architect, received his education as architect in the office of works at Dublin, and worked for the architect Sir Richard Morrison in the 1820s. He may have been the John Kane of co. Fermanagh who applied for a job with Morrison in 1809. In 1832 he designed the Roman Catholic church of St Francis Xavier, Dublin, and in 1858 that of St Lorcan Ua Tuathal, which he did not live to complete. In the 1830s and 1840s Keane designed the court houses at Tullamore, Nenagh, and Waterford. In the 1840s he added a large Doric portico to St Mary's Roman Catholic Pro-Cathedral in Dublin. He also worked on the cathedral of St Mel at Longford (1840–93). A leading figure in setting up the Royal Institute of Architects in Ireland in 1839, Keane appears to have been expelled when he was imprisoned for debt in 1850. As a result, perhaps, the building of the Queen's College, Galway (1846–50), from his designs was taken over by the board of works. Keane died in Dublin on 7 October 1859.

L. H. Cust, rev. Kaye Bagshaw

Sources J. Williams, *A companion guide to architecture in Ireland, 1837–1921* (1994) · [J. Graby], ed., *150 years of architecture in Ireland* (1989) · *Bulletin of the Irish Georgian Society* (1991) · P. Harbison, H. Potterton, and J. Sheehy, *Irish art and architecture from prehistory to the present* (1978) · private information (2004)

Keane [née Skrine], **Mary Nesta** [Molly; *pseud.* M. J. Farrell] (**1904–1996**), novelist and playwright, was born on 20 July 1904 at Kilnamora, co. Kildare, Ireland, into an Anglo-Irish family, the third of the five children of Walter Clarmont Skrine, governor of Mauritius, originally from a Somerset family, and his wife, the poet **(Agnes) Nesta Shakespear Skrine** [née Higginson; *pseud.* Moira O'Neill] (1865–1955). Nesta was born in Cushendun, co. Antrim, the daughter of Charles Henry Higginson and his wife, Mary. Her first published work was *An Easter Vacation* (1893), a seaside romance ponderously jocular in tone, which was followed

by a fairy story for children, *The Elf-Errant* (1893). In 1895 she married Walter Skrine. The work with which her name is principally associated, *Songs of the Glens of Antrim*, appeared in 1901 and became one of the most popular books of Irish regional verse. She was technically very skilled in the use of varied and complicated rhyming patterns. The poems, attempting the use of the Hiberno-English of the Glens of Antrim, run the gamut from sadness at lost love to mild comedy, and are all pervaded by love for the Irish homeland. Some were frequently anthologized (such as 'Corrymeela'). O'Neill lived for a time in Alberta, Canada, where her husband farmed extensively, and she included a section entitled 'Songs from North-West Canada' in *More Songs of the Glens of Antrim* (1921). Canada figures also as a location in her novel *From Two Points of View* (1924), an ambitious but rather contrived love story. The *Collected Poems of Moira O'Neill* appeared in 1933. She died in co. Wexford on 22 January 1955.

Mary Nesta Skrine, always known as Molly, spent her first five years in co. Kildare. The family then moved to Ballyrankin, co. Wexford, where she had a lonely and unhappy childhood. She was educated privately and patchily, briefly attending the French School in Bray, co. Wicklow. While she was at school, members of the IRA set fire to the family home. In the main she was left to the dubious care of a string of somewhat eccentric governesses, but she made splendid use of some of the more memorable oddities of these ladies in her later fiction. Her first fictional work, a light-hearted novel amusingly entitled *The Knight of the Cheerful Countenance*, was started when she was seventeen 'for pin money' to increase her meagre dress allowance, and she was surprised and gratified when it was published by Mills and Boon in 1926. She wrote it under the pseudonym M. J. Farrell, a name she selected from above a country public house as she was riding home from hunting. She used a pseudonym to avoid the scorn of her Anglo-Irish gentry friends, who, she believed, would have despised such arty pretensions in one of their own class. She retained the name for all her novels and plays until the surprise appearance of her most celebrated novel, *Good Behaviour*, in 1981.

In the 1920s and 1930s M. J. Farrell published a succession of novels, including *Young Entry* (1928), *Taking Chances* (1929), *Mad Puppetstown* (1931), *Conversation Piece* (1932), and *Full House* (1935). They were warmly received, and Hugh Walpole called her 'one of the best half-dozen younger women writers now writing in England' (Devlin, *The Rising Tide*, vi), not realizing that her literary labours were being conducted on John Bull's other island. *Devoted Ladies* (1934), about a lesbian relationship, and one of the most powerful and sexually potent of the M. J. Farrell works, moved Compton Mackenzie to dub it 'infernally good … a worldly wise, witty and remorselessly cruel book … certainly one of the most brilliant novels I have read in the last two years' (Devlin, *Devoted Ladies*, viii).

As a novelist Farrell belongs in the long and distinguished line of 'big house' Anglo-Irish ascendancy writers, which dates from Maria Edgeworth and Lady Morgan, and includes among its modern exponents George Moore and Elizabeth Bowen (her contemporary and close friend) and, latterly, Caroline Blackwood, John Banville, and William Trevor. Like these writers, she sets her fiction in the large gentry houses which are just beginning to crumble, as their owners' prestige and finances dwindle in an emerging, bourgeois, Catholic Ireland. An important respect in which she differs from most of these other writers is her avoidance of political themes, as in *The Rising Tide* (1937), which was set in 1900 during a period of home rule agitation.

Farrell concentrates instead on the claustrophobia of personal relationships within closely knit family groups. She meticulously observes the well-furnished interiors of her chosen mansions, delighting in details of carpets, curtains, bedrooms, fireplaces, chandeliers, and also the ruinously dangerous intimacies of family life. Occasionally, as in early chapters of *Devoted Ladies*, she moved her scene to London's gossipy literary milieu, but the fiction comes into its own once she has transferred her characters, both the lusty and the effete, to an Irish gentry dwelling, and the windswept acres over which their horses and hounds pursue the fox with a vigour unparalleled outside the works of Somerville and Ross. Riding and hunting were Farrell's favourite pastimes, and her prose comes vividly to life when she describes a day's gallop. She is equally good, however, at describing the terror felt by small ascendancy children when they are first forced to mount their troublesome ponies. (Her brother, Walter Skrine, despite having been seriously injured in the First World War, rode in the Grand National.)

On 20 October 1938 Molly Skrine married Robert Lumley (Bobby) Keane (1909/10–1946), a gentleman farmer, with whom she lived for five years before their marriage—unconventional in this as in much else. They had two daughters, Sally and Virginia. In the same year as her marriage she had a great success with her first play, *Spring Meeting* (1938); she was assisted by her close friend John Perry, whom she had met while staying at Woodrooff, his parents' house. The play was staged at the Ambassadors Theatre, and was directed, as were her other stage works, by John Gielgud. It gave the actress Margaret Rutherford her first starring role, as Bijou Furze, a formidable and eccentric elderly spinster who has a secret gambling habit. Sybil Thorndike and Lewis Casson had leading roles in another successful comedy, *Treasure Hunt*, at the Apollo in 1949. Molly's light-hearted plays won popular and critical approval, and James Agate said he 'would back this impish writer to hold her own against Noel Coward himself' (Devlin, *The Rising Tide*, i).

Bobby Keane's early death in 1946 meant that the family had to abandon their beautiful home, Belleville, in the Blackwater valley. The failure of her play *Dazzling Prospects* (1961) was another blow. It was put on at the Globe Theatre with Margaret Rutherford in the lead, and under the aegis of Molly's great friend the impresario Binkie Beaumont. But the play was wrong for the time, with very different, realistic works such as John Osborne's *Look Back in Anger*

taking over from frivolous comedy. M. J. Farrell fell silent for the subsequent two decades.

Molly Keane set about the difficult business of bringing up her two daughters in reduced circumstances, but never lost touch with either her Anglo-Irish friends or her large circle of literary acquaintances in London. She moved to England for five years but returned to Ireland when she bought a house at Ardmore, co. Waterford. Here she entertained the actress Peggy Ashcroft who, bedridden with influenza and needing something to read, asked her hostess whether she had written anything interesting lately. Keane had in fact submitted *Good Behaviour* to her old friend William Collins, who had published many of her M. J. Farrell novels, but Collins thought it far too dark and rejected it. Ashcroft thought the book a triumph, however, and sent it to her friend Ian Parsons of Chatto and Windus, who liked it but could not persuade Chatto to take it. *Good Behaviour* was eventually published by André Deutsch in 1981. It was a wickedly funny book in which Keane came into her own as a brilliant observer of family relationships and sexual conduct. Its finest achievement is its gawky and overgrown heroine, Aroon St Charles, who is far too dim to understand her cruel mother, homosexual brother, or lecherous father, but nevertheless triumphs over them all in the end, becoming in Keane's skilful depiction a terrifying epitome of menacing, unloved ugliness. It was shortlisted for the Booker prize and televised by the BBC in 1982, and a new readership acclaimed this 'unknown' Irish writer. All of the M. J. Farrell novels were reissued by Virago. Inspired by the novel's great success, Keane went on to publish two more lively novels, *Time after Time* (1983) and *Loving and Giving* (1988). Her cookery book, *Nursery Cooking*, was published in 1985. With an attractive pointed face and clear blue eyes, she had a sharp sense of humour. In her final years she was incapacitated by heart trouble, and she died on 22 April 1996 after a fall in her home at Ardmore.   JOHN CRONIN

Sources R. Welch, ed., *The Oxford companion to Irish literature* (1996) • R. Hogan and others, eds., *The Macmillan dictionary of Irish literature* (1980) • S. Guppy, *Looking back* (1992), 107–41 • C. Boylan, *Irish Times* (23 April 1996) • P. Devlin, introduction, in M. J. Farrell, *The rising tide* (1984) • P. Devlin, introduction, in M. J. Farrell, *Devoted ladies* (1984) • J. Quinn, ed., *A portrait of the artist as a young girl* (1990) • m. cert. • d. cert. [Agnes Nesta Shakespear Skrine]
Likenesses R. Gemmell, photograph, repro. in M. Keane, *Time after time* (1983), back of dust-jacket
Wealth at death £94,196—gross: probate, 1 Oct 1996, *CGPLA Eng. & Wales*

Kearley, Hudson Ewbanke, first Viscount Devonport (1856–1934), grocer and politician, was born on 1 September 1856, at Uxbridge, Middlesex, the youngest of ten children of George Ewbanke Kearley (1814–1876), plumber and later building contractor, and his wife, Mary Ann Hudson. Educated at Surrey county school, Cranleigh, from 1867 to 1871, in 1872 he joined Tetley & Sons, tea merchants.

In 1876 Kearley founded a wholesaling firm, known from 1887 as Kearley and Tonge, supplying tea and after 1880 other imported provisions to grocers. He thought the rigid separation of wholesale and retail distribution was nonsensical, and decided that the only way for a wholesaler to ensure an absolutely steady outlet for his goods was to retail them himself. Kearley therefore opened a shop at Brentford in 1878, and by 1890 had 200 branches known as International Stores. This choice of name was a master-stroke, for the word 'international' then had little commercial currency and connoted an ambitious, expansive modernity. International Stores sold a large selection of goods at competitive prices, unlike other national retail chains which distributed a limited range in large quantities. Kearley bought direct from importers and producers, and instituted both manufacturing and processing of own brands. In 1895 the combined businesses were floated to the public as International Tea Company's Stores Ltd. Kearley was an assertive, brusque man whom Osborne O'Hagan at this time found very difficult. Kearley withdrew from commerce after accepting public office, and sold his shares in International Stores for £4 million in 1927.

In 1888 Kearley married Selina (1851–1931), daughter of Edward Chester; they had two sons and one daughter. Kearley described his wife as 'the most loving, unselfish and warm-hearted and kindest darling that God ever gave to man' (Kearley, 231). She also proved a persuasive political canvasser.

Kearley was converted to advanced Liberalism by Gladstone's home-rule declaration, and was elected for the dockyard constituency of Devonport in 1892. Though a poor speaker, he made himself the spokesman in the Commons for the lower deck and dock employees. His special interests were working-class housing, the purity of food, and the maladministration of the Royal Patriotic Fund. In 1905 Kearley was appointed parliamentary secretary to Lloyd George at the Board of Trade, and hoped for cabinet preferment in the government reconstruction of 1908. Kearley believed that Asquith 'would willingly have had me at the Treasury' but was dissuaded by his permanent officials (Kearley, 146). Kearley was instead offered a baronetcy in 1908, in which year he also played a key role in the passage of the Port of London Bill through the Commons.

Kearley abandoned his cabinet hopes to become first (unpaid) chairman of the new Port of London Authority (1909–25). Sworn of the privy council in 1909, he retired from the Commons in January 1910 and was created Baron Devonport in July (his ennoblement provoking a poetic squib by Hilaire Belloc). Although his dock reorganization and investment programme were constructive achievements, he became notorious as an exponent of the invincibility of employers. His tactics during the dock strike of 1912 led Ben Tillett to shout on Tower Hill, 'May God strike Lord Devonport dead,' at which the crowd chanted, 'he shall die, he shall die' (Schneer, 160). He broke the strike, thus terminating two years of industrial ferment in Britain, but caused so much distress in east London that even Conservatives were squeamish.

In December 1916 Lloyd George appointed Devonport as food controller, mistaking, as Arthur Steel-Maitland noted, his 'bad manners … for strength of character'

(A. Steel-Maitland to J. Willoughby, 7 March 1917, Steel-Maitland MSS, 174/484). At the Ministry of Food Devonport was fussy, dilatory, and a poor delegator. He became estranged from his most able officials, and seemed so anxious to protect retailing interests that he waited until May 1917 before submitting a proposal for compulsory rationing. His ineptitude destroyed his authority with parliament and the public and he resigned on 30 May. As consolation he was advanced to a viscountcy in June 1917. Predeceased by his wife, Devonport died on 5 September 1934 at his Scottish estate, Kinloch, Dunkeld, Perthshire, and was buried at Hambleden, near Marlow, in Buckinghamshire on 10 September. His privately printed memoirs are vivid, zestful, and intelligent.

RICHARD DAVENPORT-HINES

Sources H. E. Kearley [Lord Devonport], *The travelled road: some memories of a busy life* (privately printed, Rochester, 1935?), 146, 231 · *The Times* (6 Sept 1934) · H. O. O'Hagan, *Leaves from my life*, 1 (1929), 397 · J. Schneer, *Ben Tillett: portrait of a labour leader* (1982), 160 · NA Scot., Steel-Maitland MSS, 174/484 · S. Tallents, *Man and boy* (1943), 235 · W. Beveridge, *British food control* (1928) · H. Belloc, *Complete verse* (1981), 232 · J. Harris, 'Bureaucrats and businessmen in British food control, 1916–1919', *War and the state: the transformation of British government, 1914–1919*, ed. K. Burk (1982), 135–56 · T. Healy, *Leaders and letters of my day*, 2 vols. (1928) · GEC, *Peerage* · A. C. Fox-Davies, ed., *Armorial families: a directory of gentlemen of coat-armour*, 7th edn, 2 (1929), 1080 · *The Times* (11 Sept 1934)
Archives HLRO, corresp. with David Lloyd George · NA Scot., letters to Philip Kerr, eleventh marquess of Lothian · NRA, priv. coll., Sir Alan Anderson MSS · PRO, corresp. as food controller, PRO 30/68
Likenesses F. Sargent, pencil drawing, 1893, NPG · G. C. Beresford, two photographs, 1903, NPG · P. A. de Laszlo, oils, Port of London Authority · J. Russell & Sons, photograph, NPG · B. Stone, two prints, NPG · photographs, Hult. Arch.
Wealth at death £1,897,818 15s. 3d.: probate, 31 Oct 1934, CGPLA Eng. & Wales

Kearne, Andreas (*fl.* 1627–1641), sculptor, was probably German and may have been related to the Swabian sculptor Leonhard Kern (1588–1662). He was, however, also said to be a Dutchman and this may imply that he emigrated to England via the Netherlands and spent some time there. By June 1627 he was in London, where, on the fifth of that month, he married Grace Lyppincott at the church of St Martin-in-the-Fields, Westminster, and in November of the same year he became a naturalized English subject. His name appears intermittently in the ratebooks of St Martin's parish from 1628–9 until 1637–8, indicating that he was a householder there for at least part of this time, and three children of his were baptized in the church, in 1628, 1632, and 1635 respectively.

Kearne's wife came from a Devon family well known to the eminent mason–sculptor Nicholas Stone the elder, who was also a native of that county. Stone was a cohabitant of St Martin's parish and, for at least the first two years of their residence there, the newly-wed couple lived close by him. The two men are said to have each carved a figure for the water stairs at Somerset House, London, and Stone's influence may have helped secure Kearne a commission for a statue of the king, Charles I, for the Royal Exchange. 'One Andreas' was paid for the work in April

1629 (CLRO, repertory of the court of aldermen, no. 43, fol. 152). It had a short life for in 1650 the council of state gave orders that it be defaced and it was taken down soon afterwards.

The eighteenth-century antiquary George Vertue has more to say about Kearne's connections with Stone, not all of it accurate. He was wrong to suppose that the two men were brothers-in-law, but right, perhaps, to believe that they collaborated on another London water-gate, that of York House, for which he says Kearne made a figure of a lioness. Vertue further states that Andreas was paid for 'working' stone figures of Venus and Apollo for the countess of Mulgrave and that he 'carved many statues' for Sir Justinian Isham 'about 4 miles beyond Northampton' at Lamport Hall (Vertue, *Note books*, 1.98). None of this information can be corroborated and in the case of Lamport this gives grounds for suspicion since some of the sculpture there is independently documented as the work of another sculptor, Peter Besnier. Isham, moreover, did not inherit the estate until 1651 by which time Kearne may have been dead. Far more credence can be given to the testimony of the famous Yorkshire royalist Sir Henry Slingsby, bt, who wrote in his diary for 1638 that Kearne had made two figures for him for the Red House at Moor Monkton, near York. One was a 'blackamore' in lead which held candles to light the great staircase and the other a memorial stone statue of a racehorse for the garden. Both survive, though in poor condition, and the lead statue of a black putto shows Kearne to have been an artist of some talent. The date and place of Kearne's death are not known. Stone's will, drawn up in January 1641, mentions 'Grace, the nowe wife of Andrew Qerne', implying that they were both alive at that time; however, a reference to a 'Mrs Carne' in the St Martin's ratebook for 1644 suggests that he had died by that time and that his widow had survived him.

ADAM WHITE

Sources *The diary of Sir Henry Slingsby of Scriven, bart.*, ed. D. Parsons (1836), 6, 7, 186–7 • Vertue, *Note books*, 1.92, 98 • J. Havill, 'Nicholas Stone, statuary, mason and architect (1586–1647)', typescript, 15–16 [circulated privately] • K. Gibson, '"The kingdom's marble chronicle": the embellishment of the first and second buildings, 1600 to 1690', *The Royal Exchange*, ed. A. Saunders (1997), 138–73, 142, 144 • 'The note-book and account book of Nicholas Stone', ed. W. L. Spiers, *Walpole Society*, 7 (1918–19), esp. 31, 34, 87, 136, 144 • MS ratebooks of the parish of St Martin-in-the-Fields, Westminster RO, F355ff. • M. Baker, 'Kern-Addenda: eine signierte Kain und Abel-Gruppe und ein Putto mit Dudelsack', *Sonderdruck aus Leonhard Kern, 1588–1662*, 2 (1990), 80 n. 1 [exhibition catalogue, Hällisch-Fränkische Museum, Schwäbisch Hall, Germany]

Kearney, Barnabas. *See* O'Kearney, Barnaby (1567–1640).

Kearney [Carney], **John** [Seán Ó Cearnaigh] (*b. c.*1545, *d.* after 1572), Church of Ireland clergyman, is said to have been a native of the barony of Leyney in co. Sligo and there is evidence that a branch of the Ó Cearnaigh family of Connaught were settled in Leyney in medieval times. Kearney went to Magdalene College, Cambridge, where he matriculated in November 1561 and took the degree of BA in February 1565. In Cambridge he was a contemporary of Nicholas Walsh, the future bishop of Ossory. Of Kearney's education before he went to Cambridge nothing is known; the short section on the Irish alphabet in his *Aibidil Gaoidheilge* suggests that he may have attended an Irish bardic school. Like a number of his coevals who were also members of the Irish literary class he was probably brought up as a protestant.

Little is known of Kearney's career between his graduation in Cambridge in 1565 and 1571. It is likely that he settled in Dublin and practised his calling as a cleric of the established church. The Scot John Carswell published the first book ever printed in Irish, *Foirm na nUrrnuidheadh*, in Edinburgh in 1567, a translation of John Knox's presbyterian Book of Common Order. In 1571 Kearney published the first book ever printed in Irish in Ireland, *Aibidil Gaoidheilge & caiticiosma* ('Irish alphabet and catechism'). Unlike Carswell's book, which was printed in Roman characters, Kearney's work was printed in a Gaelic typeface specially cut for the purpose. It was Kearney himself and Nicholas Walsh who obtained the type but the English administration in Ireland paid for it. The printing was done at the expense of Alderman John Ussher. The printer of *Aibidil Gaoidheilge* is not mentioned in the work itself. He may have been William Kearney, a kinsman of John's who was later involved in printing the New Testament in Irish. The date 1571 is perhaps a little early for William Kearney to have done the printing, however. Two hundred copies were printed, of which only four survive.

Aibidil Gaoidheilge is in five parts: (i) the author's epistle to the reader; (ii) an account of the Irish alphabet and some orthographical rules; (iii) an Irish translation of the catechism from the Book of Common Prayer of 1559; (iv) miscellaneous prayers for private use; (v) twelve articles of religion—a translation of *A Brief Declaration of Certain Principal Articles of Religion* published in Dublin in 1566–7 at the command of the deputy, Sir Henry Sidney. The prayers for private use include morning and evening prayer and a grace before meals, all taken from Carswell's Scottish book of 1567, although Kearney corrects Carswell's language in a number of places. After these prayers Kearney inserted his own translation of the prayer for the church militant from the Book of Common Prayer. This is a congregational prayer, not a private devotion, and it mentions both the queen and her bishops. It is likely that Kearney included it to give his collection of prayers a distinctively Anglican flavour. It has been suggested that a first edition of *Aibidil Gaoidheilge* appeared in 1563. This is highly unlikely since Carswell's book from which some of the prayers were taken did not appear until 1567.

At the time of publication Kearney was treasurer of St Patrick's Cathedral in Dublin. In 1572 the deputy, Fitzwilliam, suggested to the English privy council that Kearney should be appointed to the see of Tuam. But Kearney declined the offer because of the turbulent state of Connaught.

In 1602–3 William Daniel published an Irish translation of the New Testament, printed in the same fount as Kearney's *Aibidil Gaoidheilge*. In his epistle to the king, Daniel referred to all those who had been involved in the work of translating the book into Irish and he mentioned Nicholas

Walsh, Nehemiah Donellan and John Kearney. Under the year 1571 James Ware says,

> This year the Irish Characters for Printing were first brought into this Kingdom by Nicholas Walsh, Chancellor of Saint Patrick's in Dublin, and John Kerne, then Treasurer of the same; and it was ordered that the prayers of the Church should be printed in that Character and Language and a Church set apart in the chief Town of every Diocese, where they were to be Read, and a Sermon Preached to the common People, which was instrumental to Convert many of the Ignorant sort in those Days.

No further printing was done by Kearney and the Book of Common Prayer in Irish did not appear until 1608, when the work was seen through the press by William Daniel.

Nothing is known of Kearney's private life. Ware states that Kearney died *c*.1600 and was buried in St Patrick's. This statement is contradicted by an official document of 1587 which asserts that Kearney was already deceased at that time.   N. J. A. WILLIAMS

Sources B. Ó Cuív, ed., *Aibidil Gaoidheilge & caiticiosma* (1994) • N. J. A. Williams, *I bprionta i leabhar* (1987) • *The whole works of Sir James Ware concerning Ireland*, ed. and trans. W. Harris, 1 (1739)

Kearney, John (1744–1813). *See under* Kearney, Michael (1734–1814).

Kearney, Michael (1734–1814), scholar, was the elder of two sons of Michael Kearney, barber–surgeon of Dublin. After being educated at Ballitore School he entered Trinity College, Dublin, in 1748. Elected to a scholarship in 1750, he graduated BA in 1752 and was elected to a fellowship in 1757. He held the posts of professor of modern history (1769–78), regius professor of law (1776–8), and Archbishop King's lecturer (1774, 1777). In 1778 he resigned the former two on being presented to the college living of Tullyaughnish, in the diocese of Raphoe. In 1798 he was appointed archdeacon of Raphoe.

Kearney published *Lectures Concerning History* (1776), a slender work but clear and stimulating, and contributed two papers to the *Transactions of the Royal Irish Academy*, the first on the origins of the alphabet, the second on Sir Joshua Reynolds's *Discourses*. He also contributed some notes to Edmond Malone's edition of Boswell's *Life of Johnson*. He died in Dublin on 11 January 1814, and was buried in St Ann's, Dublin. His obituary notice in the *Gentleman's Magazine* unusually suggests that he was a very talented man who had failed to fulfil expectations. Kearney, the notice stated, was 'deeply read in divinity, versed in all the subtleties of metaphysical disquisition, unequalled as a historian, skilled alike in the learned and modern languages and critically acquainted with English literature', but for thirty-six years this profound scholar resided on his benefice 'in a remote country where his talents and learning were lost to the world' (*GM*, 84/1).

Kearney's younger brother was **John Kearney** (1744–1813), provost of Trinity College, Dublin, and bishop of Ossory. He was educated at the Revd Thomas Benson's school in Dublin and entered Trinity College in 1757. Elected a scholar in 1760, he graduated BA in 1762 and was elected to a fellowship in 1764. He was professor of oratory (1781–99) and Archbishop King's lecturer in divinity in

1782 and 1787. In 1782 he was co-opted a senior fellow. Three years later he played a leading role in what seemed to be a significant moment in college history. After hearing that the duke of Gloucester, chancellor of the university, had died he vigorously urged that Lord Charlemont should be elected his successor, arguing that an Englishman, especially one of 'high connections' would neglect the 'petty objects' that concerned Trinity. In fact the report of the duke's death was premature, and he survived until 1805.

A conscientious and popular don, Kearney was happy to see in the student body 'a rising spirit of literary ambition, of decent and respectful subordination and of polished and manly manners' (J. Kearney, *Sermon*, 1789). He encouraged Thomas Moore, then a student, to publish his translation of *Anacreon*, though warning him that the college board was unlikely to subsidize 'so amatory and convivial' a work. According to Moore, Kearney's house was 'the resort of the best society in Dublin', his wife being 'lively, literary and musical' and Kearney himself having a fund of 'dry drollery'. His wife's identity is unknown, but the marriage produced at least two children, John and Thomas Henry. Kearney published two sermons that he preached before the college, the second in May 1798, when 'the rage of democracy and the zeal of fanaticism' were threatening society. He also published anonymously in 1798 a poem that called on Henry Grattan to play 'a patriot's noblest part' by firmly opposing rebellion (BL, Add. MS 22976).

In 1799 Kearney, by then the senior of the Trinity fellows, was appointed provost, and in 1806 he was placed on the episcopal bench as bishop of Ossory. A cultured Dublin barrister was surprised to hear that he intended to reside continuously in his diocese, though he 'would find the want of suitable society' (Nichols, *Illustrations*, 8.64). His two aforementioned sons served in the diocese: John was chancellor of Ossory from 1809 until his death in 1838, and Thomas Henry was prebendary of Ossory from 1810 to 1812. Bishop John Kearney died at his palace at Kilkenny on 22 May 1813. He was buried in the cathedral, where the epitaph on his tombstone states that 'the duties of the episcopate he piously discharged, and in the studies of things divine and human he trained his mind with diligence and refinement'.

WILLIAM REYNELL, *rev.* R. B. McDOWELL

Sources Burtchaell & Sadleir, *Alum. Dubl.* • *GM*, 1st ser., 83/1 (1813), 592 • *GM*, 1st ser., 84/1 (1814), 201 • H. Cotton, *Fasti ecclesiae Hibernicae*, 2 (1848), 2.290 • J. B. Leslie, *Raphoe clergy and parishes* (1940) • *The manuscripts and correspondence of James, first earl of Charlemont*, 2 vols., HMC, 28 (1891–4) • *Memoirs, journal and correspondence of Thomas Moore*, ed. J. Russell, 8 vols. (1853–6)
Archives Bodl. Oxf., letters to Edmund Malone
Likenesses W. Cuming, portrait, TCD

Kearney, Theresa [*name in religion* Mary Kevin] (1875–1957), medical missionary, was born on 28 April 1875 on a small farm in Knockenrahan, Arklow, co. Wicklow, the posthumous child of Michael Kearney (*d.* 1875), and youngest daughter of his wife, Theresa Grennell. Her mother died when she was aged only nine. The family was left too poor to enable her to train to be a teacher as she wished, so at fifteen she went out to work as a children's carer and nursery governess at various charity schools in Dublin. When twenty she entered the Franciscan order in St Mary's Abbey, London, as a novice and in 1898 she made her vows as Sister Mary Kevin. Her hope was to serve her order's mission in Baltimore, USA. Instead, however, she was sent to Uganda in 1903 to join the first contingent of missionary sisters there.

Sister Kevin, as she was known, found a people suffering in the aftermath of civil war from famine and the killer diseases of malaria, sleeping sickness, and plague—as well as yaws and leprosy. Her dispensary under a mango tree was pitifully inadequate. Nevertheless, she and the other sisters learned to speak Luganda and tended the sick and dying. They erected their first primitive clinic and school and taught writing with a stick in the sand. They introduced the cultivation of new vegetables and fruit and taught the rules of basic hygiene in order to reduce the terrible rate of infant mortality from gastroenteritis. As soon as she had started one convent settlement, Sister Kevin was ordered to leave it to start another, even in dangerous 'lion country'; there the local tribal medicine men were hostile and she was stoned and the convent crops were laid waste by locusts. In 1910 she was made mother superior, but she felt increasingly frustrated by still having only half a dozen sisters. 'It was utterly heartbreaking to have to send sick people away because we could not take them in; to know that babies were dying in the villages when we might have been able to save them' (Louis, *Love is the Answer*, 80).

In 1919, on furlough in Europe, Mother Kevin tried to persuade the church to allow her to study gynaecology and obstetrics. Not only did she want to save lives: she was also aware that the protestant women missionaries in Uganda were both medically well trained and willing to train African women and so the Catholic church was losing converts to them. However, canon law forbade nuns to be midwives and her petition was refused. She was allowed only to study obstetrics for six months but might neither qualify nor practise. '"Believe me", she said, "that legislation will soon be changed"' (Louis, *Love is the Answer*, 101), and it was, in 1936. On her return to Uganda in 1921 Mother Kevin founded the first Catholic training school for Catholic nurses in Africa. She recognized that European nurses alone could never answer African needs. Similarly, and in the teeth of white racist scepticism, in 1923 she founded the new African congregation of the Little Sisters of St Francis. By 1939 she had founded nineteen convents, each with clinics, dispensaries, and schools. She founded a secondary school for girls, in 1940; and this institution produced Africa's first Catholic woman legislator, its first woman bachelor of science, and its first woman doctor.

Mother Kevin was formidable in her apparently tireless energy and she made commensurate demands on her sisters. She stacked brick-kilns before firing, she planted out saplings for new forests, and she worked in the laundry, in the bakery, and in the garden—as well as in the dispensary and on the wards. She started the first leprosarium in Uganda, where lepers could work and study and nurse one another, and the first blind school. After fifty years in Africa, in 1952 Mother Kevin became the first superior-general of a new order, the Franciscan Missionary Sisters for Africa. Almost fifty years later there were seven hundred African sisters in Africa—in Uganda, Kenya, Zambia, Zimbabwe, Transkei, and Ethiopia—many of them helping AIDS sufferers and AIDS orphans. In 1919 she had been appointed MBE and in 1955 CBE.

In her last years Mother Kevin was based in Baltimore and begged for the mission in Africa at church doors in the United States and Canada. After she died on 17 October 1957 in Boston, Massachusetts, at the age of eighty-two, her body was flown in state to be buried at the convent of her order in Dundalk, Éire. However the Ganda would not accept that 'Kevina' should be buried there. By public subscription her body was flown out again, this time to Africa, to rest finally in the ground of one of her first foundations, Nkokonjeru. Her cortège was saluted by all races and creeds.

SYBIL OLDFIELD

Sources M. Louis, *Love is the answer: the story of Mother Kevin* (Dublin, [1964]) • S. O'Hara, *Dare to live! A portrait of Mother Kevin* (1979) • S. M. Louis, *The unconventional nun* (1968) • *Sunday Review* [Dublin] (10 Nov 1957) • *Sunday Review* [Dublin] (24 Nov 1957) • *Sunday Review* [Dublin] (8 Dec 1957) • *The Times* (19 Oct 1957) • *The Times* (24 Oct 1957) • *Catholic Citizen* (15 Nov 1957) • E. A. Isichei, *A history of Christianity in Africa* (1995) • C. Oliver, *Western women in colonial Africa* (Westport, Massachusetts, 1982)
Likenesses photograph, c.1895, repro. in O'Hara, *Dare to live!* • photograph, c.1950, repro. in Louis, *Love is the answer*

Kearney, William Henry (1800/01–1858), watercolour painter, was probably the individual of that name, son of John and Eleanor Kerney, who was baptized at St Mary's, Rotherhithe, London, on 3 May 1801. He was admitted to the Royal Academy Schools on 18 November 1823 at the age of twenty-two. He was a founder member, and later vice-president, of the New Society of Painters in Water Colours (later the Institute of Painters in Water Colours), exhibiting 170 pictures there; he also exhibited nine times at the Royal Academy between 1823 and 1850. He mainly painted landscapes in a rather old-fashioned style: among his works are *Love's Young Dream*, *Ruins of the Sallyport, Framlingham* (National Gallery of Ireland, Dublin), *The Courtship of Quintin Matsys*, and *The Fatal Picture*. Two of his landscapes, views in Wales, are in the British Museum, London, and two are in the collections of the Victoria and Albert Museum, London. He published *Illustrations of the Surrey Zoological Gardens* (3 pts, 1832). Kearney died at his home, 114 High Holborn, London, on 25 June 1858. His wife, whose name may have been Hester, survived him.

ANNE PIMLOTT BAKER

Sources *Art Journal*, 20 (1858), 253 • *DNB* • Mallalieu, *Watercolour artists*, vol. 1 • S. C. Hutchison, 'The Royal Academy Schools, 1768–1830', *Walpole Society*, 38 (1960–62), 123–91, esp. 176 • J. Johnson, ed., *Works exhibited at the Royal Society of British Artists, 1824–1893, and the New English Art Club, 1888–1917*, 2 vols. (1975), 265 • Wood, *Vic. painters*, 3rd edn, 289 • Graves, *RA exhibitors* • Boase, *Mod. Eng. biog.* • *IGI* •

L. Lambourne and J. Hamilton, eds., *British watercolours in the Victoria and Albert Museum* (1980)

Kearns, William Henry (1794–1846), violinist and composer, was born at Dublin. He went to London in 1817, and for thirty years was a member of the orchestras of Her Majesty's and Covent Garden theatres. He played the violin at the Ancient Concerts in 1832 and the viola in the same orchestra from 1833 to 1846, appearing as principal on many occasions. He was a member of the Philharmonic Society, the organist of the Verulam Episcopal Chapel, Lambeth, and a highly regarded teacher, both of violin and singing; among his instrumental pupils was the prominent violinist Henry Smart.

Kearns perhaps achieved greater success as a composer than as a performer. He wrote music for *Bachelors' Wives, or, The British at Brussels*, an operetta performed on 16 July 1817 and published the same year, which was frequently repeated at the English Opera House (Lyceum Theatre) under S. J. Arnold. Kearns soon became musical adviser to Arnold and William Hawes, the directors of the theatre. He also directed Weber's *Der Freischütz*, Spohr's *Zemire und Azor*, Meyerbeer's *Robert le diable*, and many other foreign operas, including works by Marschner, at Covent Garden. His *Cantata, with Accompaniment for Pianoforte* (1823) attracted some attention, and a critic of the day found it 'as wild and as original as anything we have met for a very long time', and commented on 'an accompaniment as various as the passion intended to be represented, and [having] as much to do with it as the voice part itself' (*Quarterly Musical Magazine and Review*, 233). Kearns's *Three Songs of Early Piety* were published about 1840 and the first series of *The Comprehensive Tune-Book* (compiled by Kearns and H. J. Gauntlett) appeared in 1846; the latter contains only one original hymn by Kearns. Other works include piano accompaniments for A. F. Haeser's *The Triumph of Faith* (1837) and Haydn's *The Seasons* (with a new arrangement of the words by Edward Taylor), and *Songs of Christmas* (1847), consisting of 'elegant melodies of Handel, Haydn, Mozart, etc., selected and arranged'. Kearns was also successful in his revision of and additions to wind accompaniments for Handel's oratorios, including *Messiah* and *Israel in Egypt*, for the festival at Westminster Abbey in 1834 and for provincial festivals.

Kearns died at Princes Place, Kennington, London, on 28 December 1846, leaving a large family. An obituary in the *Musical World* (16 January 1847) praised his 'intimate knowledge of the properties of instruments in the orchestra' and his talents as both a teacher of singing and 'a very superior violinist'.

L. M. MIDDLETON, rev. DAVID J. GOLBY

Sources *Musical World* (16 Jan 1847), 41 · review of a cantata, *Quarterly Musical Magazine and Review*, 5 (1823), 233 · G. Grove, 'Kearns, William Henry', *New Grove* · *The Athenaeum* (9 Jan 1847), 52 · *The Athenaeum* (23 Jan 1847), 105

Kearsley, George (*c*.1739–1790), bookseller, was the son of John Kearsly, a Dublin currier; no other information on his parentage is recorded. He was apprenticed on 6 February 1753 to his great-uncle Jacob Robinson, a London bookseller, whose shop at 1 Ludgate Street Kearsley inherited at Robinson's death on 27 October 1759. From there he traded as G. Kearsly or G. Kearsley, settling upon the latter variant after 1783. His business enjoyed initial success, its output reaching as high as sixty imprints a year, yet this was soon to be checked by the first of several set-backs that marked his tumultuous career.

The original publisher of John Wilkes's periodical the *North Briton* (1762–3), Kearsley was among those arrested on 30 April 1763 for issuing the notorious no. 45. He was sent to the Tower and shortly thereafter released, having implicated Wilkes and his collaborators. Wilkes wrote:

> A panick seiz'd poor Kearsley, he gave up the printer, who was unknown, and to save himself invented a variety of particulars to colour his treachery to his friends. He had solemnly engag'd *never* to discover the printer, nor name any author till the last extremity. He very seldom saw any MSS. All his share in the transaction was paying the printer, receiving his own profits, and suffering his name to be at the bottom of the page as Publisher! (*BDMBR*, vol. 1)

Kearsley remained subject to prosecution, however, and in July 1764 he was declared guilty at trial, although his sentence was deferred. In the interim Kearsley, burdened with legal expenses, went bankrupt in August 1764 and fled to France to avoid imprisonment for debt. His creditors, having sold off his effects and copyrights, allowed him to return to England in late November 1764. A month later his creditors met again to consider how to recover their losses, at which gathering the playwright Samuel Foote is reported to have placated the company by exclaiming, 'Gentlemen, it is a common case for a bookseller to be seen among the creditors of an author; but for once! strange to tell! you see an author among the creditors of a bookseller' ('Chronicle', 1764, 113–14). On 25 January 1765 Kearsley was formally discharged after he presented evidence that he had been promised immunity in return for his having informed against Wilkes.

Permitted to re-establish himself in his former premises, Kearsley undertook a number of ventures aimed at regaining his former success, notably the launch of a popular series of pocket ledgers, court and city registers, and annual tax tables. He also tried his hand at literary magazines, including the *Sentimental Magazine* (1773–7) and the *Young Gentleman's Magazine* (1777). In 1773 he relocated to 46 Fleet Street, identified in later imprints as Johnson's Head. The following year he again ran afoul of the authorities when he published a version of the elder William Pitt's speech on taxation in the American colonies; threatened with prosecution Kearsley made a public retraction, which he promptly contravened by reissuing his pamphlet in a new edition. Among Kearsley's most lucrative enterprises was the publication, beginning in 1780, of a series of 'beauties' of various authors, including Shakespeare, Sterne, and Fielding. Among the most popular of these collections was *The Beauties of Johnson* (1781), editions of which continued to appear for the next seventy years, yet whose indiscriminate selection of essays from *The Rambler* evidently displeased Johnson himself (Boswell, *Life*, 214 n. 1). Despite this success Kearsley took bankruptcy on two occasions in 1784; by the end of that year he was not only back in business but attracting notoriety for coming out with a biography of Johnson only two weeks after the subject's death. In later years financial stability came with the huge popularity of John Wolcot's early Peter Pindar satires. At his death, in London on 6 December 1790, Kearsley's business passed to Catharine Kearsley (d. 1796?), probably his widow, and to his son George, who remained in the trade until 1813.   TREVOR ROSS

Sources ESTC · I. Maxted, *The London book trades, 1775–1800: a preliminary checklist of members* (1977) · D. F. McKenzie, ed., *Stationers' Company apprentices*, [3]: 1701–1800 (1978) · chronicle, *Annual Register* (1764) · chronicle, *Annual Register* (1765) · *European Magazine and London Review*, 18 (1790), 480 · C. H. Timperley, *Encyclopaedia of literary and typographical anecdote*, 2nd edn (1842) · R. R. Rea, *The English press in politics, 1760–1774* (1963) · Boswell, *Life*, vol. 1 · R. R. Rea, 'Anglo-American parliamentary reporting: a case study in historical bibliography', *Papers of the Bibliographical Society of America*, 49 (1955), 212–29 · 'Monthly chronologer for February 1765', *London Magazine*, 34 (1765), 109 · A. T. Hazen, 'The *Beauties of Johnson*', *Modern Philology*, 35 (1937–8), 289–95 · M. Treadwell, 'London trade publishers, 1675–1750', *The Library*, 6th ser., 4 (1982), 99–134 · J. J. Gold, 'Kearsley, George', *BDMBR*, vol. 1

Kearton, (Christopher) Frank, Baron Kearton (1911–1992), scientist and industrialist, was born on 17 February 1911 at Congleton in Cheshire, the only child of Christopher John Kearton and his wife, Lilian, *née* Hancock. Shortly afterwards the family moved to Tunstall in the Potteries. His father, a bricklayer, was one of five brothers all of whom, at the insistence of their father, became skilled craftsmen. It is believed that the family came originally from Yorkshire where they farmed at the remote end of Swaledale; there is a village 15 miles west of Richmond named Kearton. Kearton attended Hanley high school, from where he went to St John's College, Oxford, as an open exhibitioner in 1929. He read chemistry and graduated with first-class honours in natural science (chemistry) in 1933. He was one of many who was fortunate in having H. W. (Tommy) Thompson as tutor. It is of interest that he did not in fact present himself for the conferment of his BA and MA until 1959—perhaps an early example of his impatience to move to the next task. On 16 April 1936 he married Agnes Kathleen (Kay; d. 1997), the daughter of Samuel Pratt Brander, schoolmaster, who, after taking an honours degree in French at Bedford College, London, taught at Morecambe grammar school. They met while they were both at school through a common interest in tennis. They had two sons and two daughters.

Kearton was tall and well built; he was energetic, extrovert, articulate, and forceful. His restless energy and ambition frequently led him into controversy, but he invariably acted in what he saw to be the national interest. He had a lively, if sometimes sarcastic, sense of humour. He did not smoke, and drank but little, but had a healthy appetite. His leisure was taken up with his family which, whatever the pressures, was an overriding priority—he rejoiced in their successes and shared their problems and disappointments. He was devoted to his wife, and she, and his whole family and their doings, sustained and refreshed him—he was not immune to disappointment and frustration. He was a voracious reader. His business

(**Christopher) Frank Kearton, Baron Kearton** (1911–1992), by unknown photographer, 1969

life was austere but he delighted to entertain at his beautiful old home in Whitchurch, and to conduct his guests on an exhaustive and exhausting tour of his garden, in which he spent so much time.

Early career Upon graduation in 1933 Kearton joined the Billingham division of Imperial Chemical Industries Ltd (ICI). Thus began a career in which he played a major part in a wide range of industries—chemicals, nuclear, man-made fibres, textiles, and oil—and also, through the Industrial Reorganization Corporation (IRC), contributed to industrial development in Britain over an even wider front. He simultaneously took on a succession of diverse public appointments, concerned, *inter alia*, with the reorganization of the railways, the Atomic Energy Authority, the generation and supply of electricity, the development of scientific and technical policy, and the promotion of trade and investment between Britain and central and eastern Europe.

Kearton was a scientist, but the nature of his contribution over much of his career was typified by the job he took on his second day with ICI; he started at 6 a.m. as a shift operative on chemical plants working a fifty-six hour week, soon becoming shift manager and later refinery manager. Perhaps the most significant event in these early years was his inclusion as one of seven members of a newly formed unit to carry out chemical engineering research. It was one of the first of its kind in Britain and Kearton acquired familiarity with the multidisciplinary skills which he was to apply with such success in many fields.

The atomic bomb project Kearton's growing reputation in technical development work led to his being chosen to join a team formed by Wallace Akers who had himself been seconded from ICI in 1941 to lead, under Sir John Anderson, the British atomic bomb project, known by the code name Directorate of Tube Alloys. Although the phenomenon of nuclear fission had been confirmed in 1939, official scientific opinion throughout the world remained sceptical of its practical utility, and work to harness fission proceeded with little urgency. The theoretical work of R. E. Peierls and O. R. Frisch at Birmingham led to their memorandum of March 1940 in which they showed that it should be possible to make a bomb using as little as 5 kilogrammes of uranium 235, a naturally occurring isotope of uranium; they also outlined a possible means of separating this isotope and of constructing an explosive device. The impact of this memorandum was immediate and led to the rapid expansion of work in Britain and in the USA. Kearton worked on liaison with academics and on co-ordination of the work within ICI. Eventually he was responsible for the experimental station in north Wales which established the design features for an isotope separation plant.

The August 1943 Quebec agreement re-established a degree of collaboration with the United States' atomic bomb programme—the Manhattan project. The massive US effort had created a substantial lead over progress in Britain. The British government decided to transfer key scientists and engineers to the USA. Kearton went both to pass on unique British know-how, and to liaise between the scientists on both sides of the Atlantic. The work which he did is contained in 132 formal reports and in numerous letters. There is no doubt that in addition to his direct contribution he was able to make much use of his experience in the British post-war work on atomic energy. He also saw at first hand what could be achieved when a country harnessed its total resources to a clear objective; even today it is difficult to appreciate the huge physical and intellectual achievements of the Manhattan project in such a short time. This, and the construction of sophisticated manufacturing plants in a fraction of the time commonly accepted as normal in Britain, made a lasting impression. He also suffered two disappointments. He was one of many who did not think that the atomic bomb would be used and was dismayed when it was. His other, personal, regret came later. He worked with Klaus Fuchs in the USA; indeed they shared an office. Their friendship continued when both returned to Britain and Fuchs was a frequent visitor to Kearton's home. When suspicion of his espionage was aroused in 1949 it also fell on Kearton, who later described the period as 'the worst time in my life'.

The Courtaulds years Kearton returned to ICI in 1945 but found the lack of challenge not to his taste. He joined Courtaulds, prompted by a speech made by A. H. Wilson,

their newly appointed research director, describing a programme of reconstruction and investment. During the war Courtaulds had lost its American business (sold under pressure as a *quid pro quo* for the passage of the Lend Lease legislation) which in the 1930s had contributed more than half the total trading profits of the group. This created an urgent need to modernize existing, ageing, factories, to expand capacity, and to increase spending on research and development, in order to regain its position in the man-made fibre industry and to rebuild earnings. This was the company which Kearton joined.

Kearton spent twenty-nine years with Courtaulds, the first six years in research and development, with an ever widening remit, which led to his appointment to the board in 1952. The following ten years saw his influence grow throughout all the areas of the business, accompanied by both organic growth and acquisition, in which he was in the van; later, having led the opposition which defeated the bid made by ICI at the end of 1961, in 1962 he became chairman, retiring in 1975. The ICI bid brought him to public notice. While he was certainly not alone on the board in opposing the ICI proposal he led the opposition, and his quick thinking, confidence, and ability to articulate the arguments, often in colourful language, made him the man of the hour.

In 1946 Kearton joined a medium-sized company which was technically innovative, poorly managed, short of management potential, and severely weakened by the war. When he retired Courtaulds was a major international company in its chosen fields of forest products, fibres, chemicals, plastics, packaging, textiles, and marine and industrial coatings; highly profitable and with a strong balance sheet. The management which achieved this was led by a new team, forged by Kearton. His vision, drive, energy, and leadership were an inspiration. Of course he made mistakes: anyone who set out to do what he did, in the industrial and social climate of the time, inevitably did so, but they were dwarfed by his achievements.

Kearton's management methods and style were less admired. His authoritarian manner was fed by his undoubted success. His relationships with his board colleagues were often strained. His criticisms of what he saw as inadequate performance were delivered harshly and were often intensely personal. He believed that continued pressure could bring results, and that those who could not withstand such pressure were fundamentally unsuited to manage. This outlook damaged some careers irretrievably. He believed that softness at the top had a malign influence throughout the organization. He could be extremely kind on a personal basis to those who suffered private misfortune or family illness—but he did not parade these kindnesses.

Kearton has been described, deliberately, as an industrialist. He was less successful as a businessman. He had little feeling for the market place, and was often cavalier in his dealings with customers. His relations with the City were uneasy; he was often impulsive and was over-influenced by personalities, which sometimes led to errors of judgement. His relations with Whitehall and with the trade unions were ambivalent. On the one hand he took full advantage of tax and other government incentives for new investment, but he made no effort to cultivate relations with officials, whom he sometimes treated with contempt. With the unions he maintained a duality of approach. On the one hand he treated them as an obstacle to his drive for increased efficiency and profits, while on the other he strove to build personal relationships with the union leaders of the day.

Public appointments Kearton was appointed a member of the special advisory group of the British Transport Commission in 1960 by Ernest Marples, minister of transport. The total lack of any objectives or strategic aims for the management of the railways upon nationalization in 1948, and the absence of any guidance on the balance between the social needs of a public service and commercial viability, led to mounting losses and complete muddle in management. The group was charged with advising the minister on the resolution of this dilemma. Appointed in April, it reported in October. Its report was confidential but clearly formed the core of the white paper presented to parliament in December. The group, chaired by Sir Ivan Stedeford, comprised Henry Benson, Richard Beeching, Kearton, and two civil servants. Their achievement in six months was remarkable. They probed deeply into the facts and into management organization and practice and brought out into the open the dire situation. Their work led to the fundamental restructuring of the railways in which Beeching played such a central role and, in spite of much criticism, it saved the railways.

Not surprisingly Kearton's wartime experiences made him in great demand in the British nuclear programme. Indeed, from 1946 onwards repeated attempts were made to recruit him into the Atomic Energy Authority (AEA) in various capacities. None was successful but he nevertheless played an important part-time role in special technical tasks, and as a member of the Fleck inquiry into the 1957 Windscale fire, the worst known nuclear accident at that time. He was a part-time member of the AEA from 1955 to 1981. He was also a member of the Electricity Supply Research Council, 1954–77 (chairman 1960–77), a member of the Central Electricity Generating Board, 1974–80, and a member of the committee of inquiry into the structure of the electricity supply industry, 1974–5. His contributions across the whole gamut of nuclear issues centred upon his belief that a unified national policy was necessary—an issue still unresolved.

Perhaps the most direct involvement by Kearton in national industrial policy was his appointment as chairman of the Industrial Reorganization Corporation (IRC). This body was formed by the 1964 Wilson government, which believed that to achieve the full impact of modern technology intervention was necessary. There was a widespread view, not only among politicians, that British management was inadequate to bring about the changes needed to achieve international competitiveness. The IRC was set up to be an instrument of industrial policy and not a political tool as some had hoped. The choice of Kearton, known for his personal drive and his intolerance of bureaucratic interference, as chairman, and a board largely composed of successful industrialists, ensured its independence. In its short existence (it was formed at the end of 1966 and did its final deal in 1971) it had a remarkable impact; and it did so with small resources. Its staff never exceeded thirty in total, with some ten executives at any one time, and a total of only twenty-two throughout its existence. The executives came mainly from the private sector, with no formal contracts and on the understanding that they would serve for about two years.

The IRC had a crucial impact upon the motor industry, and upon the steps which led to the formation of the General Electric Company (GEC); and it was involved in some fifty mergers embracing, *inter alia*, textiles, instrumentation, paper, and engineering. The success of what it set out to do was not based upon coercion. On the contrary, the board determined that it should act only upon industrial and commercial logic, but with an eye to international strength. It did not have, or use, huge sums of money. In fact it used only about one-third of the £150 million made available. Its success rested upon three factors. What it sought to do went with the grain of prevailing industrial opinion; it was small and able to move quickly—the responsible executive, the managing director, and the chairman, met daily; and the executives were outstanding—young, ambitious, idealistic, and able. It was not by chance that many of them later became some of the most successful business leaders of their generation.

All of these tasks, and others not described here, were part-time. None lessened Kearton's hands-on management and direction of Courtaulds; indeed, they seemed to act as a further stimulus to action. His usual practice was to devote a set part of the day, often up to mid-morning, solely to the current public task, and then to spend the rest of the day on Courtaulds' affairs.

The British National Oil Corporation On 21 July 1975, the day before he was to retire from Courtaulds, Kearton met Tony Benn, the secretary of state for energy. They knew and respected each other. Within days Kearton had been appointed chairman designate of the British National Oil Corporation (BNOC). There were major differences of opinion between ministers as to the role of BNOC. Some were anxious to do nothing without the concurrence of the major oil companies. Others, including Benn, wanted BNOC to have a major commercial role. Kearton soon decided that the company must, in the national interest, have a direct involvement in the development of the North Sea. The arguments within government and between government and the oil companies dragged on, and Kearton became even more convinced of the role that BNOC should have, and increasingly frustrated by the lack of decision. It was one of the most active and turbulent periods of his career. Eventually BNOC was given participation rights and involvement in bidding for exploration licences, in spite of the continued protests of the oil companies. In 1979, its fourth year of operation, BNOC had a turnover of £3245 million and made a pre-tax profit of £75 million. In that same year it was involved in the drilling of nearly half the exploration wells on the continental shelf. By the end of the year it held agreements which gave it options on up to 51 per cent of the petroleum produced on the UK continental shelf. This, from a standing start, and against bitter opposition, was almost unbelievable. Kearton's successor as chairman, R. E. Utiger, wrote in 1980: 'I do not think that any other man could have created this Corporation in such a short time.'

Honours, awards, and assessment Kearton was made OBE in 1945 for his war work, knighted in 1966, and created a life peer, as Baron Kearton of Whitchurch, in 1970. Among many honours and appointments he was made a fellow of the Royal Society in 1971, and received ten honorary degrees and four honorary fellowships. He particularly treasured his appointment as chancellor of the University of Bath, from 1980 to 1992, in which he was notably proactive; Professor J. R. Quayle, the vice-chancellor, wrote a generous and moving tribute to his chancellorship in the *Bath Report* of 3 July 1992 on the day following his death.

When Kearton was made a life peer in 1970 he was deeply involved in industrial and academic affairs and played little part in the house. Once he did begin to attend regularly 'there was no stopping him', as a friend and fellow peer recalled (Wooding, 238). He was much respected and had a wide circle of friends. He served on several select committees, covering a wide range of issues, especially those concerned with European affairs; energy and manufacturing; science, technology, and innovation; and overseas trade. His participation was characterized by his penetrating insight, his direct style of speech which, as another peer wrote, 'could verge on the picturesque' (ibid., 238), and his unfailing courtesy to witnesses. He continued to attend the house and to take a full part even when he was desperately ill. His death from cancer at Stoke Mandeville Hospital, Buckinghamshire, on 2 July 1992 was seen as a tremendous loss. He was buried at Whitchurch.

Kearton had boundless energy, and was impatient and sometimes intolerant, unable to resist a challenge, whether concerned with national industrial affairs, *The Times* crossword, a popular radio quiz, or the village vegetable competition. His capacity for sustained effort and digestion of papers was legendary, as was his practice of communication with anyone at any level in the organizations with which he worked—frequently by hastily written cards, almost indecipherable, and usually containing cryptic messages which were stimulating or demoralizing, or both. His management style was not to everyone's taste. In dealing with people he sought to stiffen resolve and to test reaction to pressure; and thereby to convey the urgency and importance of the issue. He respected a robust response and could be both critical and inspiring. Some saw his many activities as driven by personal ambition. But this was only part of it. He had a deeply held belief in the future of his country. He believed in social justice, but had no time for the mere redistribution of wealth. Rather, he believed in the creation of wealth by the application of efficient management and modern technology. He believed in the importance of manufacturing industry and in individual enterprise; but he also believed that it was right to harness the country's total resources for the national good. He was a patriot.

NORMAN WOODING

Sources N. S. Wooding, *Memoirs FRS*, 41 (1995), 219–41 • D. C. Coleman, *Courtaulds: an economic and social history*, 3 (1980) • *Bath Report*, 29 (3 July 1992) [Lord Kearton issue] • Lord Dainton, 'Obituary of Christopher Frank Kearton', *St John's College Notes* (1992) • M. Gowing and L. Arnold, *Independence and deterrence: Britain and atomic energy, 1945–1952*, 2 vols. (1974) • L. Arnold, *Windscale, 1957: anatomy of a nuclear accident* (1992) • D. Hague and G. Wilkinson, *The IRC: an experiment in industrial intervention* (1983) • R. H. N. Hardy, *Beeching: champion of the railway?* (1989) • C. Kennedy, *ICI: the company that changed our lives* (1986) • A. W. Knight, *Private enterprise and public intervention: the Courtaulds experience* (1974) • C. Villiers, *Start again, Britain* (1984) • *The Times* (6 July 1992) • *The Independent* (29 July 1992) • *WW* • Burke, *Peerage* • private information (2004) • A. Sillery and V. Sillery, *St John's College biographical register, 1919–1975* (1978)
Likenesses photograph, 1969, repro. in Wooding, *Memoirs FRS*, 220 • photograph, 1969, News International Syndication, London [*see illus.*] • photograph, repro. in *The Times* (17 July 1992) • photograph, repro. in *The Independent*
Wealth at death £337,670: probate, 14 Aug 1992, *CGPLA Eng. & Wales*

Keary, Anna Maria [Annie] (1825–1879), novelist, was born at Bilton rectory, near Wetherby, West Riding of Yorkshire, on 3 March 1825, the sixth of eight children and the second daughter (there were five sons and three daughters). Her father, William Keary (d. 1856), was the only son of an ascendancy Irish family in co. Galway; her mother, Lucy (d. 1869), was the daughter of Hall Plumer of Bilton Hall. William Keary had joined the army early in life, and had fought in the Peninsular War, but on the loss of the Irish property had been obliged to sell his commission. He entered the church and was appointed to the living of Bilton, and then to the perpetual curacy of Sculcoates, a district of Hull, together with the small living of Nunnington in the North Riding of Yorkshire. There was an especial affinity between the father and his second daughter, and from him Annie heard much about Ireland that she was later to use in novels. Her childhood seems to have been lonely, worsened no doubt by poor health and lifelong slight deafness. The home life was of a puritanical austerity, but Annie and her sister Eliza Harriott *Keary (bap. 1827, d. 1914) amused themselves with imaginative games, many of which feature in her books for children.

In 1845 William Keary, whose health had long been precarious, finally had to give up the living and the family moved to Clifton, near Bristol. The surroundings were far more congenial, but Annie left in 1848 to take charge of the three children of a widowed elder brother in Staffordshire. She had a natural affinity with children and the six years that she spent in Trent Vale were perhaps the happiest of her life. But the brother remarried, and there followed a desolate period, in which her much-loved brothers Henry and Arthur both died, and a long-standing engagement was broken off.

Annie Keary's first children's book, *Mia and Charlie*, appeared in 1856 (the year of her father's death), and the following year saw *Sidney Grey* and *The Heroes of Asgard*; the latter retold Norse legends, and was a volume upon which her sister Eliza collaborated. In 1858 *The Rival Kings* appeared, a powerful story about gang warfare and children's hatred—a subject that few children's writers then chose to tackle. Her first adult novel, *Through the Shadows*, was published in 1859. During the ten years that followed she was preoccupied first with nursing her mother (who died in 1869), then with looking after four small cousins whose parents were in India, but she still managed to complete two further adult novels—*Janet's Home* (1863) and *Oldbury* (1869), both unremarkable domestic sagas—and three children's books.

During the eight years that Annie Keary was free of domestic ties she wrote *Castle Daly* (1875)—the first book to attract notice—*A York and a Lancaster Rose* (1876), *A Doubting Heart* (1879), and some children's stories. Although as always she had difficulty controlling the plot, *Castle Daly* is a remarkable and sympathetic account of the apparently irreconcilable differences between Celt and Saxon in Ireland, whose scenery and people she vividly evoked. She did the same in a children's book, *Father Phim* (1879). *A Doubting Heart* is the story of a young woman torn between making a worldly marriage and one for love. (The final pages were finished by a friend, Mrs K. Macquoid.) Like all her adult novels it suffers from being stretched to fill three volumes, but is strong on place and character. Some of it is set in Pégomas, near Cannes, in the south of France, where latterly she stayed for her health. Annie Keary died of breast cancer at 9 Lismore Road, Eastbourne, on 3 March 1879.

Annie Keary was gentle and warm-hearted. Despite strong religious faith she never felt entirely happy in any of the branches of the church that she tried. She invariably put family duties before her own interests, but she had many friends, from Charles Kingsley and his family to the girls at a home for unemployed young servants in Bessborough Gardens, Pimlico, London, which she and her sister had at one time helped to run.

GILLIAN AVERY

Sources [E. Keary], *Memoir of Annie Keary*, 2nd edn (1883) • *Macmillan's Magazine*, 42 (1880), 259–67 • *Letters of Annie Keary*, ed. E. Keary (1883) • Boase, *Mod. Eng. biog.* • d. cert. • *CGPLA Eng. & Wales* (1879)
Archives BL, corresp. with Macmillans, Add. MS 54922
Likenesses photograph, repro. in Keary, *Memoir*
Wealth at death under £4000: resworn probate, April 1881, *CGPLA Eng. & Wales* (1879)

Keary, Charles Francis (1848–1917), numismatist and writer, was born on 29 March 1848 at The Hollies, Trent Vale, Stoke upon Trent, Staffordshire, the second in the family of two sons and two daughters of William Keary (*b.* 1817?), solicitor, and his wife, Ann Archer, *née* Mee. He went to Marlborough College in 1862 and left two years later. In 1867 he went to Trinity College, Cambridge, from which he graduated BA in mathematics in 1871.

Keary started work in the department of medals and coins at the British Museum on 6 March 1872. He was elected to the Saville Club in 1874, edited *The Dawn of History: an Introduction to Pre-Historic Study* in 1878, and was made a fellow of the Royal Society of Antiquaries in June 1880. A contributor to the *Numismatic Chronicle*, Keary was one of the first to take a scholarly interest in Italian medals, publishing a British Museum guide in 1881. He also published *The Morphology of Coins* (1882) and contributed the Anglo-Saxon sections to *A Catalogue of English Coins in the British Museum* (1887). Having become a first-class assistant at the British Museum in 1886, Keary gave up his post in May 1887. At some time he was on the staff of the *Saturday Review*.

Keary's interests were diverse. Apart from his scholastic writings, he published on spiritualism, wrote poetry and rather mundane and dull novels influenced by French naturalism, including *A Mariage de Convenance* (1890), *The Two Lancrofts* (1893), and *Herbert Vanlennert* (1895). He was awarded the medal of the Royal Numismatic Society in 1894 but resigned as a fellow of the Royal Society of Antiquaries in 1896. He published the semi-autobiographical novel *The Journalist* in 1898 and wrote the libretto for Delius's opera *Koanga*, first performed in 1899. W. E. Henley had suggested Keary for *Thackeray* in Blackwood's Modern English Writers series but Charles Whibley did the book. Having travelled widely in Europe, Afghanistan, and India after leaving the British Museum, Keary had much material for his travel books, the main being *India: Impressions* (1903).

In 1912 Keary was awarded a civil-list pension of £70 'in recognition of the merits of his writing' (*The Times*, 6 July 1912). He began doing voluntary work in his old department at the British Museum in 1917 but failing health forced him to give it up. Keary did not marry. In late life he suffered from asthma and bronchitis and died on 25 October 1917 at his home, 5 Cambridge Terrace, Hyde Park. He was buried at Kensal Green cemetery.

DAMIAN ATKINSON

Sources [C. Whibley], 'Musings without method', *Blackwood*, 202 (1917), 835–6 • b. cert. • will • *WWW*, 1916–28 • private information (2004) [archivist, BM] • J. Sutherland, *The Longman companion to Victorian fiction* (1971) • E. Kilmurray, *Dictionary of British portraiture*, 3 (1981) • Venn, *Alum. Cant.*, 2/2 • H. A. Luard, *Graduati Cantabrigienses* (1884) • *The Times* (27 Oct 1917) • *New York Times* (29 Oct 1917) • *Numismatic Chronicle*, 4th ser., 18 (1918) • D. Sutton, 'Biographical study R. A. M. Stevenson: art critic', in R. A. M. Stevenson, *Velazquez* (1962) • civil list pensions, *The Times* (6 July 1912) • census returns, 1881 • *Synopsis of the contents of the British Museum, department of coins and medals: a guide to the Italian medals exhibited in the King's Library* (1881)
Archives NL Scot., 4553 HUT–K, vol. 2, fols. 274ff. • NL Scot., 4573 HOU–KEL, vol. 2, fols. 285ff. • NL Scot., corresp. • NYPL, corresp. | NYPL, Berg collection
Wealth at death £2139 16s. 3d.: probate, 25 Jan 1918, *CGPLA Eng. & Wales*

Keary, Eliza Harriott (*bap.* 1827, *d.* 1914), poet and children's writer, was born in Bilton rectory, near Wetherby, Yorkshire, and baptized at Sculcoates, Yorkshire, on 22 April 1827, one of the six surviving children of the five sons and three daughters born to William Keary (*d.* 1856), rector of the parish, and his wife, Lucy (*d.* 1869), daughter of Plumer Hall, of Bilton Hall. Her father originally hailed from Clough in co. Galway, Ireland, and emigrated to England after a loss of property. Eliza Keary lived in Nunnington, North Riding, and from 1845 to 1848 in Clifton, near Bristol. In her lifetime she was known chiefly for her collaborations with her older sister, novelist Anna Maria (Annie) *Keary (1825–1879). Together they published popular children's literature such as *The Heroes of Asgard* (1857), *Early Egyptian History for the Young* (1861), and *Little Wanderlin and other Fairy Tales* (1865). In 1882 Eliza Keary published a *Memoir of Annie Keary* and in 1883 she edited Annie Keary's letters. The memoir suggests that Eliza accompanied her sister on sojourns to Egypt and Pégomas, near Cannes, to do research and care for the chronically ill Annie. For a time the two sisters were also involved in running a home for unemployed young female servants in Bessborough Gardens, Pimlico.

In the late twentieth and early twenty-first centuries Eliza Keary's poetry has received increasing critical attention from feminist scholars and cultural historians interested in Victorian women poets. Her collection *Little Seal-Skin and other Poems* (1874) contains work in a multitude of forms ranging from the sonnet to verse drama to dramatic monologue. Isobel Armstrong and Joseph Bristow consider her breadth the mark of an iconoclast; they write: 'Most unusual for a woman writer of this period, many of the poems in *Little Seal-Skin* approach free verse. Both rhyme and metrical scheme are unorthodox'. Keary's three volumes of Bible selections, *Rays of Light: a Textbook* (1884), *The River of God* (1884), and *A Casket of Pearls* (1884), and poems such as 'Christine and Mary: a Correspondence' from *Little Seal-Skin* have rightly marked her religious fervour; however, the bulk of her work for adults and children addresses a wider range of subject matter. Her literature for children includes *The Magic Valley, or, Patient Antoine* (1877), *At Home Again* (1886), and *Pets and Playmates* (1887). *Enchanted Tulips and other Verses for Children*, a collaboration by Eliza, Annie, and their niece Maud Keary, who also served as editor, was published in 1914. In 1901 Eliza Keary edited *The Francis Letters by Sir Phillip Francis and other Members of the Family* with Beata Francis; her brother Charles F. Keary, also an author, provided a note to the edition. Keary died the widow of George Keary, a railway engine driver, on 3 November 1914 at her home, 46 Abbey Road in Enfield, Middlesex.   JODI LUSTIG

Sources [E. Keary], *Memoir of Annie Keary* (1882) · I. Armstrong, J. Bristow, and C. Sharrock, eds., *Nineteenth-century women poets* (1996), 458–9 · 'Keary, Annie', *DNB* · d. cert. · *IGI* · *The letters of Annie Keary*, ed. E. Keary (1883)

Keary, (Hall) William (b. **1815**, d. in or after **1879**), farm manager and land agent, was born in Farlington, Yorkshire, but nothing is known of his early history. Some time between 1841 and 1843, possibly as a new appointee when the second earl of Leicester inherited in 1842, he came to Longlands, the prestigious 'home farm' at Holkham, Norfolk, as farm steward. The farm had long been a centre of farming improvement and it must have been a challenging appointment for a young man of under thirty.

Until then the emphasis had been very much on experimentation, and like many other home farms Longlands had not made a profit. With the arrival of Keary it began making money, though this never amounted to more than a few hundred pounds a year.

By 1845 Keary was a member of the Royal Agricultural Society, and he wrote an essay on the management of cattle for the *Journal of the Royal Agricultural Society of England* in 1848, in which he demonstrated his interest in and understanding of the various breeds. Keary always ensured that Longlands was at the forefront of public attention. When James Caird visited the farm in 1850, he noted that 'the usual details of good farming were practiced' (Caird, 166–7). Keary continued the tradition of the previous steward of taking in farm students, and no doubt Longlands was a much sought-after destination for pupils. In 1851 Mr Baker, the agent, retired from the Holkham estate and William Keary took his place, combining the job with that of farm steward. The 1851 census describes Keary as 'land agent managing 1800 acres of land, employing 50 men, 14 boys and 12 women'. By this time Keary had married Anna D'Urban (b. 1812), who came from a well-known farming family in Sculthorpe, Norfolk. Between 1850 and 1861 eight of their children were baptized at Holkham; two of them died as infants.

The Holkham estate was now being run by a practical farmer. On taking charge Keary personally reviewed the seventy or so estate farms, noting the soil types, systems of cultivation, and state of the farm houses and buildings. In his 'Estate survey of 1851' he also described over 300 estate cottages, their state of repair, and the number of occupants (Holkham MS). He found much that needed doing and embarked on an expensive building programme, which included the erection of an ornate and extensive estate workshop at Longlands and the planned model farms at Egmere and in Holkham Park. All three projects were designed by the agricultural engineer G. A. Dean.

Between 1850 and 1858 expenditure on buildings and repairs rose dramatically, to well over £10,000 a year in most years. Keary soon gained a reputation for expensive building schemes, and he passed on his ideas to his pupils (Martins, 71–2). When Henry Parr Jones, a student of Keary's, went to Longleat from Holkham in 1859, he was said to have gained his extravagant ideas from his teacher (Thompson, 152). In the office Keary modernized the system of accounting, beginning the ledgers and general payment books. He also abandoned the laborious copying of letters into letter books and introduced copybooks containing an early version of carbon paper.

Keary's reputation as a man who could assess the problems and potential of an estate soon spread, and in 1862 he was asked by the duke of Norfolk to undertake a survey of his very run-down possessions in the south of the county. Keary was critical of what he found and was convinced that the holding back of expenditure would not pay in the long run; in his 'Report on the estate of the duke of Norfolk' (1863), he concluded his survey by saying that 'The time has come when a considerable outlay must be made if this property is to be raised to a condition worthy of its hereditary owner' (Norfolk RO, 2251520).

Keary left Holkham in 1863 and moved to Shropshire, where he was still living, at Aldenham, Bridgenorth, in 1879. He was an active member of the Royal Agricultural Society and he was a judge of the farm prize competition for the Oxford meeting of the society in 1870. Little is known of his later life, however, and it is not known when he died.

Keary's main achievement during his lifetime was to ensure that the Holkham estate's high reputation for encouraging agricultural improvement continued; his influence as an efficient, but high-spending, estate agent was felt beyond Holkham, and it came through his work with and writings for the Royal Agricultural Society and through his training of land stewards on the well-known Holkham estate. SUSANNA WADE MARTINS

Sources S. Wade Martins, *A great estate at work: the Holkham estate and its inhabitants in the nineteenth century* (1980), 71–2 · J. Caird, *English agriculture in 1850–51* (1852), 166–7 · H. W. Keary, 'Management of cattle', *Journal of the Royal Agricultural Society of England*, 9 (1849) · 'Report of the farm prize competition, 1870', *Journal of the Royal Agricultural Society of England*, 2nd ser., 6 (1870), 251–75 · report on the estates of the duke of Norfolk, 1863, Norfolk RO, Smiths Gore, 26/10/78, no. 22 · F. M. L. Thompson, *English landed society in the nineteenth century* (1963), 152 · estate survey of 1851, Holkham Hall, Norfolk, Holkham MS, H. W. Keary · census returns, 1851

Keate, George (1729–1797), writer and painter, the son and heir of George Keate of Isleworth, Middlesex, and his wife, Rachel, daughter of Count Christian Kawolski, was born in Trowbridge, Wiltshire, on 30 November 1729. Having been educated at Kingston free grammar school, he was articled as a clerk to Robert Palmer, steward to the duke of Bedford. Keate entered the Inner Temple in 1751 and was called to the bar in 1753. Although he never practised law, finding the work tedious, he retained his chambers and attended regularly there throughout his life, becoming bencher in 1791 and reader (an honorific title) in 1794.

Despite this loyalty to his professional background, Keate felt a keen longing from early manhood for the life of letters and art, as can be seen in six poems composed in 1751–3; they include 'A Pastoral Ode to Echo' in the tradition of Milton's 'L'allegro'. He undertook the grand tour in 1754, and travelled extensively through France and Italy to, ultimately, Geneva and Switzerland. His stay in Rome (December 1754–January 1755) inspired the poem *Ancient and Modern Rome* (1760). In it, as a devout member of the Church of England, he denounces Catholic superstition but praises religion as a great inspirer of art, sculpture, music, and architecture in Rome. The poem was praised by Voltaire, who admiringly quoted back to Keate some of the verses on the ephemerality of fame. The French *philosophe* became a close friend when Keate made his acquaintance in Geneva in 1756 and entertained him at his home, Les Délices. Keate's stay afforded him the opportunity to write *A Short Account of the Ancient History, Present Government and Laws of the Republic of Geneva* (1761), running to over a hundred pages, which was to attract much attention from the *Monthly Review*, the *Critical Review*, the *London Magazine*, and the *Scots Magazine*. Geneva is idealized as the home of liberty and a model of republican government. The work received encomiums from Voltaire, its dedicatee, who saw it as 'excellent en son genre, sage, vrai' and congratulated the city on being the object of such admiration (*Voltaire Correspondence*, letter 9723). It was eventually translated into French as the *Abrégé de l'histoire de Genève* (1774).

Keate was also a friend of the naturalist Charles Bonnet, whom he met during his visit to Geneva and who opened up to Keate the Bibliothèque de la Ville, of which he was librarian, thereby enabling the Englishman to obtain the documentation for his *Short Account of … Geneva*. But the most memorable relationship of Keate's life was with Voltaire. After Keate returned to England, Voltaire was never to see him again, but he was to write Keate at least twenty-five letters over a score of years (Voltaire's only regular English correspondent in this period) right up to the last year of his life. (A half-dozen letters from Keate to Voltaire have also survived.) Keate had shown Voltaire in Geneva the first canto of an epic poem about medieval Geneva entitled *The Helvetiad*, thereby acknowledging homage to Voltaire's epic *La Henriade*. But Voltaire was not enthusiastic about the work, which Keate thereafter abandoned. The work by Keate, however, which attracted Voltaire's greatest interest was a poem entitled *Ferney: an Epistle to Monsr de Voltaire* (1768). It begins with an extended eulogy of this 'calm Retreat' as a sort of earthly paradise, worthy of its illustrious denizen, the author of so many great works—Horace Walpole acidly commented that Keate 'gives M. de Voltaire an account of his own tragedies' (Keate, *Ferney*, iv). But then comes a tactful change of attitude. Keate, a strong supporter of Shakespeare, dares to insert a brief panegyric of the bard, whose works Voltaire had come to deplore. But despite this audacious initiative Voltaire responded amicably, praising once more Keate's poetic talents and adding that he would not fall out with Keate over Shakespeare. The poem, possibly because of its mildly scandalous nature, was reviewed favourably by the *Gentleman's Magazine* and the *Monthly Review*, while the *Annual Register* reprinted it in full.

Among Keate's other verse (he produced twelve volumes in all) one should note an *Epistle from Lady Jane Grey to Lord Guildford Dudley* (1762), an amatory piece in the style of Pope's 'Eloisa to Abelard', purporting to have been written by Keate's ancestor to her husband a few days before her execution; *The Ruins of Netley Abbey: an Elegy* (1764), which was much reprinted; and *The Alps* (1763), the earliest poetic celebration of these mountains in English, which received favourable notices from the *Monthly Review* and the *Critical Review*, as well as enthusiastic comments from Edward Young, to whom it was dedicated, and from Voltaire, who applauded its Miltonic tone. Keate also wrote prologues and epilogues for Shakespeare plays performed by the schoolboys of the academy at Hackney, and adapted Voltaire's *Sémiramis* for the English stage (though it was never performed).

After returning to England from Geneva in 1757, Keate befriended David Garrick, who thought him a 'very agreeable man … No man starts a laugh better' (*Letters*, letter 387). In May 1769 Keate accompanied Francis Wheler, steward of the court of records, to Garrick's house in the Adelphi to present him with the freedom of Stratford upon Avon, in recognition of the Shakespeare jubilee which Garrick had recently organized in the bard's birthplace. For his own part in the jubilee arrangements, Keate was given a mulberry standish but (contrary to what has been thought) he did not himself receive the freedom of Stratford, as a letter from Garrick (ibid., no. 551) makes clear.

On 7 February 1769 at St Luke's, Chelsea, Keate married Jane Catherine (1729/30–1800), daughter of Joseph Hudson and sister of Sir Charles Grave Hudson, bt. They later moved from the Inner Temple to a house in Charlotte Street, Bloomsbury, where Keate's friend Robert Adam undertook some improvements for him. Keate was a founder member of the Society of Artists (1761), and contributed eight paintings to its exhibitions as well as nearly thirty to the Royal Academy. Although never an academician, he joined those who seceded from the society in 1768 to found the academy, of which he was an honorary exhibitioner. His interests respectively in natural history and in antiquarian studies led to his being elected to fellowships of the Royal Society and of the Society of Antiquaries, both in 1766. Keate died at his Bloomsbury home on 28 June 1797, and was buried on 6 July at Isleworth, where a white marble monument with a bust by Nollekens was erected in his memory. Jane Keate died on 18 March 1800, aged seventy, and was also buried there.

Keate's gift for friendship ensured good relations with Samuel Johnson, Nollekens, and Angelica Kauffmann, in addition to those already mentioned. By contrast, Fanny Burney thought him to be a conceited dilettante. Although Keate is now remembered, if at all, as a minor artist, this seems a somewhat harsh judgement on one whose wide-ranging intellectual curiosity about literary, artistic, and scientific fields was genuine and deeply committed.

The Keates' daughter, **Georgiana Jane Henderson** [*née* Keate] (1770–1850), painter, exhibited four pictures at the Society of Artists in 1791. She married on 9 June 1796 John Henderson BCL (1764–1843), also an amateur artist and a patron of J. M. W. Turner. They had two sons, Charles Cooper *Henderson (1803–1877), equestrian painter, and John *Henderson (1797–1878), art collector, and three unmarried daughters. Their mother died on 8 January 1850 and was buried with her husband at Kensal Green.

HAYDN MASON

Sources A. M. Rousseau, *L'Angleterre et Voltaire* (1976) · K. G. Dapp, *George Keate esquire* (Philadelphia, 1939) · *Voltaire correspondence*, ed. T. Besterman (Geneva, 1968–77) · *The poetical works of George Keate, esq.* (1981) · *The letters of David Garrick*, ed. D. M. Little and G. M. Kahrl, 3 vols. (1963) · G. Keate, *Ferney*, ed. P. G. Tudor (1967) · G. Keate, *Abrégé de l'histoire de Genève* (1774) · M. W. England, *Garrick's jubilee* (Ohio State University Press, 1964) · P. M. Horsley, 'George Keate and the Voltaire–Shakespeare controversy', *Comparative Literature Studies*, 16 (1945) · *DNB* · *IGI*
Archives Bibliothèque Publique et Universitaire, Geneva, corresp. with Charles Bonnet · priv. coll., letters to Sir Adam Fergusson
Likenesses J. Nollekens, marble bust, 1797?, Isleworth parish church · J. K. Sherwin, line engraving (after J. Plott), BM, NPG; repro. in G. Keate, *Poems* (1781)

Keate, John (1773–1852), headmaster, was born at Wells, Somerset, on 30 March 1773. **William Keate** (1739–1795), his father, was educated as a scholar at Eton College and then entered King's College, Cambridge, where he held a fellowship from 1762 to 1768 and proceeded MA in 1767. He became master of Stamford grammar school, and was rector of Laverton, Somerset, from 1768 to 1795. In 1769 he married Anne, daughter of John Burland of Wells. He became a canon of Wells Cathedral in 1773, before dying at Chelsea Hospital, London, on 14 March 1795.

John Keate, who was the elder brother of Robert *Keate and nephew of Thomas *Keate, was placed on the foundation at Eton in 1784, and proceeded to King's College, Cambridge, in 1791. He was a brilliant writer of Latin verse, and throughout his life remained a fine classical scholar. He graduated BA in 1796, MA in 1799, and DD in 1810, and was elected a fellow of his college in 1795. About 1797 he became an assistant master at Eton, and took orders. In 1802 he became lower master and married in the following year Frances, daughter of Charles Brown MD; they had a son and six daughters. In 1809 he was elected headmaster. There were only seven assistants for some 500 boys, and Keate had to control about 170 boys in one room. Discipline was extremely bad; Keate himself was subjected to such indignities as the smashing of his desk. From the first he set himself to repress such turbulence and disorder, and by rough methods he gained the upper hand. Innumerable stories are told of his apparent ferocity, for instance of one occasion (30 June 1832) when he flogged more than eighty boys at night to suppress what appeared to be threatened rebellion. Undoubtedly he flogged too often, but he did so to support inadequate assistants; he seldom used the punishment on his own account. Nor were individual punishments excessive. Keate was not unduly harsh by the standards of the times—indeed boys often treated his punishments with levity, and he should have realized they were largely ineffective. Other criticisms are justified. The school rules were restrictive but had no force: for example, boating was tolerated and common, though the river was out of bounds. The pretence of observance was all that was required, and boys came to think that lying about misdemeanours was almost expected of them. Religious and moral instruction was very limited. The provost controlled chapel, where the services had little merit, but on Sundays Keate would take the whole upper school for a supposedly edifying hour of 'prayers'; yet this, known to the boys as 'prose', was in practice deplorable. His nickname, 'the Baffin', derived from his awkward cough.

Occasionally, Keate would speak to the boys with real eloquence and effect, notably after the death of Anthony Ashley-Cooper in a fight. Too often he preferred a line of

John Keate (1773–1852), by Richard Dighton, c.1815–16 [*A View Taken at Eaton*]

ill-tempered condemnation, which may have been something of a charade. The greatest neglected need was to increase the staff, to provide better supervision of the boys and smaller classes. But the fewer the masters, the more income each received. The curriculum was also culpably narrow; only Latin and Greek were taught, from a limited range of authors, with much time spent on learning by heart and composing verses. Other subjects such as French were offered as voluntary extra studies, but boys who chose to be idle could readily pass easy, dissolute lives. There was scope for those who were motivated—Keate permitted debating and acting, and literary publications. The group of boys around W. E. Gladstone were the most impressive of those who came out of Keate's Eton. His own skill as a teacher is proved by the success of his pupils at Oxford and Cambridge, and he took some measures to improve the competence of his weakest assistants. That he could not achieve more reform was partly because of the restraints imposed by Provost Goodall, a Bourbon even in that conservative office.

Kinglake describes Keate thus:

He was little more (if more at all) than five feet in height, and was not very great in girth, but in this space was concentrated the pluck of ten battalions. He had a really noble voice, and this he could moderate with great skill, but he had also the power of quacking like an angry duck, and he almost always adopted this mode of communication in order to inspire respect.   (A. W. Kinglake, *Eöthen*, 1859, 250)

His courage and real kindness of heart made him popular; the boys cheered him after the great flogging, and subscribed a large sum as a leaving present.

When Keate retired from the headmastership in 1834, Thomas Arnold had been seven years at Rugby, and an altogether more earnest conception of education was taking hold; the liberal anarchy of Keate's Eton was appearing increasingly outdated. Yet there is much in Sir Francis Doyle's judgement, that Keate knew, as Arnold did not, 'that there should exist for a certain time, between childhood and manhood, the natural production known as a boy' (F. Doyle, *Reminiscences and Opinions*, 1886, 48). Keate was not anxious to be provost when Goodall died in 1840. In 1820 he had been appointed canon of Windsor, and in the same year accepted the living of Nether Stowey, Somerset, which he exchanged in 1824 for the rectory of Hartley Westpall, Hampshire. There he lived after his resignation until his death on 5 March 1852 and there he was buried. His son, John Charles, succeeded him in his rectory. His sister-in-law, who often resided with the Keates, kept a diary which presents a gentler picture of Dr Keate than the caricature that has gained general acceptance.

W. A. J. ARCHBOLD, *rev.* TIM CARD

Sources H. C. Maxwell Lyte, *A history of Eton College, 1440–1910*, 4th edn (1911) · Venn, *Alum. Cant.* · M. Brown, diary, Eton, SR/22 · [W. H. Tucker], *Eton of old, or, Eighty years since 1811–1822* (1892) · C. A. Wilkinson, *Reminiscences of Eton* (1888) · Etoniana of various sorts, Eton · J. Chandos, *Boys together: English public schools, 1800–1864* (1984) · D. Newsome, *Godliness and good learning* (1961) · *GM*, 1st ser., 73 (1803), 788

Archives Eton

Likenesses R. Dighton, caricature, etching, c.1815–1816, BM, NPG [*see illus.*] · A. Edouart, silhouette, 1828, NPG · cartoons, Eton

Keate, Robert (1777–1857), surgeon, the fourth son of William *Keate (1739–1795) [*see under* Keate, John], rector of Laverton, Somerset, and Anne, daughter of John Burland of Wells, was born at Laverton on 14 March 1777. John *Keate, headmaster of Eton, was his elder brother. Keate was educated at Bath grammar school until 1792, when he was apprenticed to his uncle, Thomas *Keate. He entered St George's Hospital, London, in April 1793, and was made 'hospital mate' at Chelsea Hospital in 1794. In May 1798 he became a member of the Company of Surgeons and was appointed staff surgeon in the army.

Keate held appointments to George III and George IV, and later became sergeant-surgeon-extraordinary to William IV, and in 1841 sergeant-surgeon to Queen Victoria. In later life he said: 'I have attended four sovereigns, and have been badly paid for my services. One of them, now deceased, owed me nine thousand guineas.' William IV always paid him and showed great confidence in him, but his frequent journeys to Windsor badly affected his practice.

In 1800 Keate was appointed assistant surgeon to his uncle at St George's, and thereafter did nearly all his work. He retired from the army in 1810 with the rank of inspector-general of hospitals. He succeeded his uncle in 1813, as full surgeon at St George's, and held the post until 1853, by which time his powers had declined and he was finally removed by the governors. He was a member of the court of assistants of the Royal College of Surgeons from 1822 to 1857, examiner from 1827 to 1855, and president in 1831 and 1839. He married the youngest daughter of

H. Ramus, an Indian civil servant; they had two sons and four daughters. Keate died on 2 October 1857 in Hertford Street, Mayfair, London, aged eighty. He published nothing except some papers in the *Medico-Chirurgical Transactions* (vols. 10 and 32).

One son was **Robert William Keate** (1814–1873), educated at Eton College and at Christ Church, Oxford. He graduated BA in 1836 and MA in 1842. He was civil commissioner of the Seychelles from 1850 to 1852, lieutenant-governor of Grenada from 1853 to 1857, and governor of Trinidad from 1857 to 1864; afterwards he was governor of Natal from 1867 to 1872, and of the west African settlements in 1873. He died in April 1873. During his governorship of Natal he was the subject of a satire, *The Four Books of the Prophet Ignoramus* (1872).

G. T. BETTANY, *rev.* CHRISTIAN KERSLAKE

Sources *The Lancet* (17 Oct 1857) · *Medical Times and Gazette* (17 Oct 1857), 410–11 · J. F. Clarke, *Autobiographical recollections of the medical profession* (1874), 378, 387, 511 · *Autobiography of the late Sir Benjamin C. Brodie*, ed. B. C. B. [B. C. Brodie], 2nd edn (1865) · V. G. Plarr, *Plarr's Lives of the fellows of the Royal College of Surgeons of England*, rev. D'A. Power, 2 vols. (1930) · Z. Cope, *The Royal College of Surgeons of England: a history* (1959) · S. C. Lawrence, *Charitable knowledge: hospital pupils and practitioners in eighteenth-century London* (1996) · Foster, *Alum. Oxon.*
Likenesses J. P. Knight, oils, exh. RA 1850, St George's Hospital, London · J. Richardson-Jackson, mezzotint (after J. P. Knight), Wellcome L.

Keate, Robert William (1814–1873). *See under* Keate, Robert (1777–1857).

Keate, Thomas (1745–1821), surgeon, the son of William Keate, became a pupil at St George's Hospital, London, and from 1787 was assistant to John Gunning, surgeon to the hospital. He became regimental surgeon of the foot guards in 1778 and served as inspector of regimental infirmaries until 1798. On a vacancy arising as surgeon in succession to Charles Hawkins, there was a sharp contest in 1792 between Keate and Everard Home, whom John Hunter favoured. Keate was elected. He succeeded Gunning in 1798 as surgeon-general to the army, and the next year was elected a fellow of the Royal Society. He also became inspector of the National Cow-Pox Establishment. Keate was an examiner at the Royal College of Surgeons from 1800, and master in 1802, 1809, and 1818. He was an excellent surgeon, and was the first to tie the subclavian artery for aneurysm. But he was unpunctual and negligent of his hospital duties, and in 1813 he resigned from St George's. Keate was surgeon to the prince of Wales, afterwards George IV, and to Chelsea Hospital. At one time he was the owner of George Romney's *Wood Nymph*.

Keate wrote little on surgery. He published *Cases of Hydrocele and Hernia* (1788), and several controversial papers, the chief being *Observations on the Fifth Report of the Commissioners of Military Enquiry*; the report censured the medical board for showing a lack of proper control, for irregularities in promotion, for making new and unnecessary appointments, for waste and extravagance, and for

opening general hospitals unnecessarily. Keate had carried out his duties with success but blame had nevertheless fallen upon him. The board was dissolved in 1809 and Keate was retired with a small allowance. He then complained of how his public duties had interfered with his private practice. He was the uncle of the surgeon Robert Keate (1777–1857) and of John Keate (1773–1852), headmaster of Eton. Keate died in Chelsea Hospital, London, on 5 July 1821.

G. T. BETTANY, *rev.* MICHAEL BEVAN

Sources Venn, *Alum. Cant.* [William Keate] · Z. Cope, *The Royal College of Surgeons of England: a history* (1959) · S. C. Lawrence, *Charitable knowledge: hospital pupils and practitioners in eighteenth-century London* (1996) · *The record of the Royal Society of London*, 4th edn (1940) · N. Cantlie, *A history of the army medical department*, 1 (1974) · T. Keate, *Observations on the fifth report of the commissioners of military enquiry* (1808) · R. Jackson, *Letter to Mr Keate* (1808) · R. Jackson, *A letter to the commissioners of military enquiry … with a refutation of … a letter by Dr Bancroft* (1808) · *GM*, 1st ser., 91/2 (1821) · *Autobiography of the late Sir Benjamin C. Brodie*, ed. B. C. B. [B. C. Brodie], 2nd edn (1865) · W. G. Page, 'Account of St George's Hospital', *St George's Hospital Reports*, 1 (1866)
Archives NA Scot., papers relating to the dismissal of George Ernst from the service of the king
Likenesses T. Rowlandson, coloured etching, 1810 (*The Walcheren inquiry into the misconduct of the army medical board of three, resulting in its abolition*), Wellcome L.

Keate, William (1739–1795). *See under* Keate, John (1773–1852).

Keating [Keting], **Geoffrey** [Seathrún Céitinn] (*b. c.*1580, *d.* in or before 1644), Roman Catholic priest and historian, was born in the vicinity of Cahir, co. Tipperary, of parents whose names are not certain, but who were 'of good reputation and in warm circumstances' ('Preface', *Memoirs*). The Keatings, of Anglo-Norman descent, occupied significant amounts of land in the barony of Iffa and Offa, a region under the influence of the Butlers, barons of Cahir, in the sixteenth and seventeenth centuries. It is probable that those of the surname Keating in the parish of Derrygrath noted as pre-1641 landowners in the *Civil Survey* were Geoffrey Keating's immediate kinsmen. It is possible that he was the third son of James Fitz Edmund Keating of Moorestown (chancery bills, MS G 351). His early association with the MacGrath keepers of Seanchas, principal proprietors of the townland of Burgess, who conducted a school in the neighbourhood, may have arisen from a link between the MacGraths and his mother's family.

Travelling to mainland Europe for his university education, Keating was associated with the universities of Rheims and of Bordeaux. A chance reference in Philip O'Sullivan Beare's *Zoilomastix* suggests that Keating's doctorate in theology was obtained at Rheims, and his name also appears on a list compiled in 1619 of people associated with the Irish college at Bordeaux since its foundation in 1603 (*CSP Ire.*, 1615–25, 318).

Keating was ordained in the Roman Catholic church as a secular priest and had returned to work in his native diocese of Lismore before 1613. In that year he was named among sundry priests and friars active in co. Tipperary, and in 1615 he was described as 'a preacher and Jesuit resorting to all parts of the diocese' of Lismore (BL, Add. MS 19836, p. 281). In later life he was more specifically associated with the parish of Tubbrid, in the diocese of Lismore. Much of the anecdotal folklore evidence about his life can be traced to the comments published anonymously by Thomas O'Sullevane in the 1722 preface to the *Memoirs of the Rt. Hon. the Marquis of Clanricarde*. The stories of the difficulties he created for himself by his fearless expression of Tridentine Catholic doctrine, forcing him into hiding in the Glen of Aherlow, cannot be verified from contemporary sources. However, he appears to have had a considerable reputation as a preacher, and the evidence of his theological writings suggests that he would have been quite prepared publicly to name adulterers and other sinners in the course of his sermons.

Keating's earliest writings, all of which are in Irish, were theological. His tract on the mass, *Eochair sgiath an Aifrinn*, was probably written while he was still on the continent. His *Trí bhior ghaoithe an bháis*, a lengthy tract on death and repentance, drew on contemporary French sermon literature, tailoring it to the social and cultural circumstances of his Irish audiences.

Keating is best remembered for his narrative history of Ireland, from the creation of the world to the late twelfth century, entitled *Foras feasa ar Éirinn*, which went into circulation in manuscript about 1634. The work is drawn from earlier Irish manuscript sources, and could only have been compiled with the assistance of those who had the custody of important Irish manuscript compilations. Much of the time Keating spent away from his south Tipperary home was probably spent in the company of the families of hereditary historians and scribes. Links with the Mac Aodhagáin and Ó Maolchonaire families of scholars were probably particularly important. His *Foras feasa ar Éirinn* proved immediately popular, both for the story of the Irish people that it told and for the language and style in which it was presented. It was translated into both English and Latin in the seventeenth century, but the majority of its readers used the Irish-language versions that circulated very widely in manuscript. An adapted translation into English, published by Dermod O'Connor in London and Dublin in 1723, made Keating's history available to new groups of readers and was reissued periodically thereafter. The Celtic revival of the late nineteenth century generated renewed interest in Geoffrey Keating's writings and the full Irish language text was published for the first time, with an English translation, early in the twentieth century.

A significant number of poems attributed to Keating are extant in Irish manuscripts, particularly from the eighteenth and nineteenth centuries. In many instances the authorship of these compositions is uncertain. The edition of his poems published in 1900 over-represents the corpus of verse that can confidently be attributed to Keating. The attributions, however, are testimony to the high regard in which he has long been held by scholars and students of Irish language and literature. Although the date of Keating's death is uncertain, a dated inscription on a plaque above the west door of the chapel of St Kieran in Tubbrid, co. Tipperary, where he was probably buried, indicates that he was dead by 1644. The plaque is testimony also to the perception of his own parishioners that Geoffrey Keating was an exceptional pastor.

BERNADETTE CUNNINGHAM

Sources [T. O'Sullevane], preface, *Memoirs of the Rt. Hon. the marquis of Clanricarde* (1722) · B. Cunningham, *The world of Geoffrey Keating: history, myth and religion in seventeenth-century Ireland* (2000) · B. Cunningham, 'Seventeenth-century interpretations of the past: the case of Geoffrey Keating', *Irish Historical Studies*, 25 (1986–7), 116–28 · *CSP Ire.*, 1615–25, 318 [list of clergy associated with Bordeaux] · P. O'Sullivan Beare, *Zoilomastix*, ed. T. J. O'Donnell (1960) · G. Keating, *Foras feasa ar Éirinn / The history of Ireland*, ed. D. Comyn and P. S. Dinneen, 4 vols., ITS, 4, 8–9, 15 (1902–14) · G. Keating, *Trí bhior-ghaoithe an bháis / The three shafts of death*, ed. O. Bergin, 2nd edn (1931) · R. C. Simington, *The civil survey*, 10 vols. (1931–61), vol. 1 · chancery bills, NA Ire., MS G 351
Archives BL, works on history, theology, and poetry, Eg. MSS 107–109, 112, 181, 184, 188–189; Add. MSS 18749, 18954, 26704, 31875, 39665, 40766, 43789 · BL, copies of his history of Ireland, Sl. MSS 3806–3807: Add. MSS 4779, 4818, 18745, 27910, 31872–31873 · Bodl. Oxf., copies of his history of Ireland, MS Fairfax 29, MS Ir. d 1 · CUL, eighteenth-century copies of his history of Ireland · Franciscan Library, Killiney, Dublin, earliest transcripts of *Foras feasa ar Éirinn*, MSS A 14, A 15 · NA Ire., chancery bills, MS G 351 · Royal Irish Acad., transcripts of *Foras feasa ar Éirinn*, MSS 23 O 19, 24 P 43 · Royal Irish Acad., translations of *Foras feasa ar Éirinn* with biog. info., MSS 24 G 16, 24 I 5 · TCD, religious miscellany and transcripts, MSS 567, 1397, 1403

Keating, George (1762–1842), engraver and bookseller, was the son of the Roman Catholic bookseller Patrick Keating (1723/4–1816) and his wife, Julia Golightly (d. 1812). He was apprenticed to the engraver William Dickinson, and between 1775 and 1776 exhibited three chalk drawings with the Free Society of Artists. Between 1784 and 1799 he produced plates in mezzotint and stipple, predominantly after artists such as Reynolds, Gainsborough, and George Morland, and 'attained fair proficiency in the art' (Smith, 2.778). His best-known mezzotints are *Kemble as Richard III*, after Gilbert Stuart, and *Georgiana, Duchess of Devonshire*, after Reynolds. He had a shop in London at Air Street, Piccadilly, but in 1790 went on to join his father's business in Warwick Street, Golden Square. In 1800, following the death of James Peter Coghlan, the leading Catholic bookseller of the day, the Keatings took over Coghlan's firm. Under the title Keating, Brown, and Keating they continued to do business from Coghlan's premises in Duke Street, Grosvenor Square. After the death of Patrick Keating in 1816, the firm became known as Keating and Brown. Richard Brown died in 1837, and his widow continued to work with Keating until 1840, when differences arose and the partnership was dissolved. Keating then opened a shop in South Street, Manchester Square, but was unsuccessful, and in September 1840 a public subscription was opened for him in *The Tablet*.

Keating published many Catholic books, and edited the *Laity's Directory* from 1801 to 1839, the *Catholicon, or, Christian Spectator*, from 1815 to 1818, and the *Catholic Speaker* from 1824 to 1826. He died in Crawford Street, Marylebone, on 5 September 1842, having outlived his wife, Alicia (1782/3–1816), with whom he had two sons.

H. R. Tedder, rev. Asia Haut

Sources Gillow, *Lit. biog. hist.* · W. G. Strickland, *A dictionary of Irish artists*, 2 vols. (1913) · Redgrave, *Artists* · Bryan, *Painters* (1886–9) · J. H. Slater, *Engravings and their value*, rev. F. W. Maxwell-Barbour, 6th edn (1929) · I. Maxted, *The London book trades, 1775–1800: a preliminary checklist of members* (1977) · J. C. Smith, *British mezzotinto portraits*, 2 (1879), 778

Keating, Sir Henry Singer (1804–1888), judge, was born in Dublin on 13 January 1804, the third son of Lieutenant-General Sir Henry Sheehy Keating KCB and his wife, Mary Anne, the eldest daughter of James Singer of Annandale, co. Dublin. Educated at Trinity College, Dublin, where he graduated MA, he was admitted to the bar from the Inner Temple on 4 May 1832, and practised on the Oxford circuit, at the Oxford and Gloucester sessions. On 17 June 1843 he married Gertrude Marianne, third daughter of Major-General Robert Evans of the Royal Artillery. In 1849 he became QC, and was co-editor, with James Shaw Willes (1814–1872), of the third edition of the classic *Smith's Leading Cases*. In 1854 he was a member of the royal commission on legal education. In the same year he appeared for the unsuccessful plaintiff in *Hadley v. Baxendale* (1854), and in 1856 the extensive treatment of the case in the fourth edition of *Smith's Leading Cases* (again co-edited with Willes, who had appeared for the defendants) did much to secure the case's enduring status as a notable statement of the law.

In 1852 Keating was returned as MP for Reading, a seat which he held as a Liberal until promoted to the bench. In 1854 he was responsible for the passage through the Commons of the Bills of Exchange Act. In May 1857 he was appointed solicitor-general, and knighted; he lost the post on Palmerston's resignation in the following February, but regained it in June 1859 when Palmerston again became prime minister. On 14 December 1859 he was appointed judge of the common pleas.

Assessments of Keating's performance on the bench differ wildly, and often reveal more about the prejudices of the writers than the behaviour of the man. He had no major case-law pronouncements to his name. He seems to have been relatively liberal on penal matters, being the only judge to oppose adult flogging at the height of the public outcry which led to the Garrotters' Act of 1863 (though he remained in favour of flogging juvenile offenders), and wishing to narrow the scope of the offence of murder. He was generally agreed to have been quiet and courteous, though views differed on whether his modesty concealed a powerful legal brain or something less creditable. The *Law Journal* (6 February 1875) said of him that 'he was a true disciple of the law. He was not on the alert for the just, the moral, the fair, the equitable, the conscientious, and the expedient, those dangerous will-o'-the-wisps which lead judges astray from the beaten track of the law'. Much of the praise heaped on him was mere sycophancy, but other comments, not obviously intended for

public distribution, often contained high praise for his personal and legal characteristics.

On his retirement in 1875, much marked in the legal press, Keating was sworn of the privy council. He died on 1 October 1888 at 72 Marina, St Leonards, Sussex.

Steve Hedley

Sources *Law Journal* (6 Feb 1875) · *Law Times* (6 Feb 1875) · *The Times* (6 Oct 1888) · Boase, *Mod. Eng. biog.* · E. Foss, *Biographia juridica: a biographical dictionary of the judges of England … 1066–1870* (1870) · L. Radzinowicz and R. Hood, *A history of English criminal law and its administration from 1750*, rev. edn, 5: *The emergence of penal policy in Victorian and Edwardian England* (1990) · R. Danzig, 'Hadley v. Baxendale', *Journal of Legal Studies*, 4 (1975), 249 · E. Coleridge, *Life of Lord Coleridge*, 2 vols. (1904) · *GM*, 2nd ser., 20 (1843), 199 · DNB
Archives CUL, travel journals · Squire Law Library, Cambridge, notebooks
Likenesses D. J. Pound, stipple and line engraving (after photograph by Mayall), NPG; repro. in D. J. Pound, ed., *The drawing room gallery of eminent personages*, 3rd ser. (1860) · painting, NPG · portrait, repro. in *ILN*, 66 (1875), 183 · portrait, repro. in D. J. Pound, *The statesmen of England: comprising fifty portraits* [1862], 34 · wood-engraving (after photograph by London Stereoscopic Co.), NPG; repro. in *ILN* (20 Feb 1876)
Wealth at death £84,101 3s. 3d.: probate, 9 Nov 1888, CGPLA Eng. & Wales

Keating, John (d. 1691), judge, was the second son of Edmund Keating (d. 1683) of Dublin and Narraghmore, co. Kildare, and his second wife, Elinor, daughter of John Eustace of Harristown, co. Kildare, and sister of Sir Maurice Eustace (d. 1665), Irish lord chancellor. He graduated BA from Trinity College, Dublin, in 1655, entering Lincoln's Inn two years later. His legal education 'had been but slender', having been 'interrupted by the task of wooing and marrying a baronet's widow' (Ball, *Judges*, 2.289)—Grace (d. 1677), the daughter of Sir Thomas Holt of Aston in Warwickshire and the widow of Sir Robert Shuckburgh. The two married on 27 October 1659 at St Peter Paul's Wharf, London.

At the Restoration, Keating obtained the post of clerk of the crown and peace in Ulster, a post he contrived to retain despite his later elevation to the bench, under a special arrangement then negotiated. Appointed deputy clerk to the Irish parliament in 1661, Keating acquired celebrity by making a journey to London and back in the depths of winter in record time. Three lords justices governed Ireland in late 1661. Mountrath died on 18 December. By 1 January 1662, Keating had returned to Dublin with a fresh patent for Eustace and Orrery. Admitted to the King's Inns, Dublin, in 1662 Keating was soon in London again, offering advice on the measure that became the Irish Act of Explanation of 1665. In this fashion, and as counsel pressing the claims of the '49 officers, Keating became embroiled in the politics of securing a final settlement of the land question. Keating's prominence brought him the patronage of the duke of Ormond: in 1675 he became a judge in Ormond's palatinate of Tipperary, and in the following year attorney in Ireland for the duke of York. That same year Keating was made king's counsel, serving as an adviser on revenue matters. In 1677 Keating's wife died; he did not remarry.

In April 1679, at the insistence of Charles II, Keating was

appointed chief justice of common pleas in place of Booth, who had moved to be chief justice of king's bench on Povey's death. Ormond had demurred, sensing that the promotion would cause envy, but bowed to the inevitable and the king's determination when Domville, the attorney-general, the first choice, refused an offer. When Booth died two years later Keating declined a switch to king's bench. Keating's tenure of office coincided with a deterioration in the political climate, dominated first by the Popish Plot and its aftermath and secondly, following the accession of the duke of York as James II, the Catholicization of the administration, including the judiciary. Henry Hyde, second earl of Clarendon, who served as Irish lord lieutenant from 1685 to 1687, spoke highly of Keating, attributing to him 'as general a good reputation for worth and uprightness as any man in the kingdom' (Clarendon to Rochester, 30 May 1686, *Correspondence of Henry Hyde*, 1.414). Ó Bruadair's poem 'Searc na suadh an chrobhaing chumhra' ('Love of sages in the fragrant cluster'; 1682) is similarly adulatory. But it was impossible at the time to give universal satisfaction, and this was to prove Keating's eventual undoing.

As chief justice Keating faced other less transparent difficulties. For eighteen months, straddling the years 1681 and 1682, he presided over a one-man court. One puisne (Johnson) remained absent in England, and there had been delay in appointing a successor on the death of the second (Cusack), his own brother-in-law. Retrenchment on the circuit expenses of the judges in 1682 prompted objections to Ormond, but to no avail. Friendship with Ormond survived. That with Arran, Ormond's second son, blossomed. In letters to both, Keating furnished insight into the work of the Irish judge in the early 1680s. The conduct of jurors, the hazards of the ride into co. Kerry for the assizes, his frequent attacks of gout: all are recorded. An early supporter of offering pardons to prospective informers, by 1686 Keating had had a complete change of heart: 'a most dangerous course [that] hath brought many honest men to untimely death, without any fault in juror or judge' (letter to Arran, 3 Aug 1686, *Ormonde MSS*, new ser., 7.437). Rural poverty was highlighted, too, when he referred to officers of the revenue being obliged to distrain 'pots, dishes, kettles and blankets' (letter to Ormond, 17 Sept 1680, *Ormonde MSS*, new ser., 7.425). As a member of the Irish privy council Keating worked well with Clarendon. They agreed on the momentous question as to whether the injustices in the land settlement were best resolved by a commission of grace or a repeal of the 1662 Act of Settlement; Keating argued for the former.

With Tyrconnell in the saddle, following Clarendon's recall, Keating became increasingly isolated. Sensing the way the wind was blowing, he had already signalled his abandonment of support for a commission of grace. On changes to the corporate towns, and over the disciplinary charges brought against Sheridan, the secretary whom James had foisted on Tyrconnell, Keating cuts a lonely figure. The day after James arrived in person in Dublin in March 1689 Keating was removed from the privy council. He remained on the bench, the sole protestant. In July he vainly argued against the Jacobite parliament's legislation to drastically alter the land settlement. This won him no credit, however, when following William III's victory at the Boyne the next year he yet sought to retain office. Southwell, William's Irish secretary, and Porter, the lord chancellor, were sympathetic, but Keating's failure to break with James told against him, and he had proved no Macchiavelli. Early in 1691 Pine was named to succeed Keating in common pleas. Several months later, in October, Keating shot himself. Luttrell records that in November 1690 Keating was indicted for high treason in continuing to hold office under James. Whether this inspired Keating's suicide is problematic. He left no children.

W. N. OSBOROUGH

Sources F. E. Ball, *The judges in Ireland, 1221–1921*, 1 (1926) • F. E. Ball, 'Some notes on the Irish judiciary in the reign of Charles II [pt 1]', *Journal of the Cork Historical and Archaeological Society*, 2nd ser., 7 (1901), 26–42, vii–ix • *Calendar of the manuscripts of the marquess of Ormonde*, new ser., 8 vols., HMC, 36 (1902–20), vols. 5–7 • *CSP dom.*, *1679–91* • *The correspondence of Henry Hyde, earl of Clarendon, and of his brother, Laurence Hyde, earl of Rochester*, ed. S. W. Singer, 1 (1828) • J. Miller, 'The earl of Tyrconnell and James II's Irish policy, 1685–1688', *HJ*, 20 (1977), 803–23 • R. Bagwell, *Ireland under the Stuarts*, 3 (1916) • W. King, *The state of the protestants of Ireland* (1691) • *Duanaire Dháibhidh Uí Bhruadair / The poems of David Ó Bruadair*, ed. J. C. MacErlean, 3 vols., ITS, 11, 13, 18 (1910–17), vol. 2 • *State trials*, vol. 12 • *Calendar of the Stuart papers belonging to his majesty the king, preserved at Windsor Castle*, 7 vols., HMC, 56 (1902–23), vol. 6 • *The diary of William King, D.D.*, ed. H. J. Lawlor (1903) • E. Keane, P. Beryl Phair, and T. U. Sadleir, eds., *King's Inns admission papers, 1607–1867*, IMC (1982) • N. Luttrell, *A brief historical relation of state affairs from September 1678 to April 1714*, 2 (1857) • IGI

Keating, Maurice Bagenal St Leger (*d.* 1835), army officer and writer, entered the 3rd dragoons as cornet on 14 May 1778, but obtained a lieutenancy in the 22nd light dragoons on 16 December 1779, became captain on 20 June 1781, and major on 13 December 1782. In 1783 his regiment was disbanded, and he was put on half pay. He was MP for co. Kildare in 1790 and 1801. While still on half pay he was promoted lieutenant-colonel on 12 October 1793. On 8 April 1794 he was placed in command of the 107th foot, and when that regiment was disbanded in 1795 he was kept on full pay. He left the army in 1796.

Keating married Martha, second daughter of Anthony Brabazon, eighth earl of Meath. In 1784 he accompanied Consul-General George Payne on a tour through France and Spain to Morocco, of which he published an account entitled *Travels in Europe and Africa* (1816), reissued and retitled in 1817. He also published *Eidometria, or, Optic Mensuration* (1812), and a translation from the Spanish of a work by Bernal Diaz del Castillo as *The True History of the Conquest of Mexico* (1800). Keating died in 1835.

W. A. J. ARCHBOLD, *rev.* ROGER T. STEARN

Sources *Army List* • Burke, *Peerage* • E. Brydges, *Censura literaria: containing titles, abstracts, and opinions of old English books*, 2nd edn, 4 (1815) • [J. Watkins and F. Shoberl], *A biographical dictionary of the living authors of Great Britain and Ireland* (1816)

Keating, Thomas (*c.*1787–1870), chemist and druggist, was born in Homerton, Middlesex, the son of William Keating, attorney. Little is known of his early life but the court minute-book of the Wheelwrights' Company records that he was admitted to the company by redemption on 3 July 1812 and admitted to the livery on 20 October 1815. It was probably in the former year that he took over the retail chemist's business of Richard Battley at 79 St Paul's Churchyard, in the City of London, at first in tandem with various partners. The Post Office London directory for 1813 names the business as Keating and Murley, whereas the directory for 1834 gives Keating, Langford, & Co.; from 1839, however, Keating appears under his own name.

It was Keating's proprietary preparations that brought his name before the public, even earning him an entry in the *Oxford English Dictionary*. His patented cough lozenges were introduced about 1820, but his famous flea powder came later, and as Keating's Persian Insect-Destroying Powder was awarded a medal at the International Exhibition of 1862. The powder was registered under this name in the *Trade Marks Journal* of 11 October 1876, while handbills advertising it mention testimonials of 1859 and 1867. Somewhat earlier, a document dated 19 April 1856 records an assignment to Keating of an invention or secret for making cough lozenges, as security for a loan of £1200. The exact constitution of the lozenges at this time is uncertain, but they continued to be sold long after Keating's death and in 1909 were shown under analysis to contain morphine, alkaloids of ipecacuanha, extract of liquorice, sugar (partly as invert sugar), and gum. Keating's Pectoral Lozenges are listed in *Martindale: the Extra Pharmacopoeia* from 1910 to 1943, and Keating's Insect Powders continued to be produced until 1981 by LRC Products Ltd. Another line was Keating's Bonbons, first recorded as a type of worm tablet in the pharmaceutical supplier's catalogue of 1879 produced by Sangers. The issue of the *British and Colonial Druggist* for 7 April 1888 notes that the manufacturing process of the insect powder necessitated the employment of 'three pairs of edge runners [a type of crushing machine] and a number of hands'.

Keating was a founder member of the Royal Pharmaceutical Society of Great Britain in 1841 and was elected a member of the society's council that year. A report of a meeting of chemists and druggists on 15 February 1841 to discuss the encroachment on their profession by general practitioners sheds some light on Keating's attitude to his work by noting his comments that whereas the apothecary's pursuits 'led him from home a great portion of his time', the chemist 'was there constantly at home to attend the wants of the poor' (Holloway, 89).

Details of Keating's marriage and family are sketchy, but the returns of the 1851 census show him resident at the St Paul's address together with his fifty-two-year-old wife, Mary Anne Catherine, born in Pall Mall, London, and three daughters, all apparently unmarried: Mary Anne Lucy, aged twenty-nine, Catherine, aged twenty-seven, and Georgina Maria, aged twenty-two. The two eldest sisters are shown as having been born in the City of London, presumably at the family residence; the youngest was born in Brixton, Surrey. Keating's own age at this time is given as sixty-two. The Post Office London directory for 1848 also lists Thomas Keating jun. as a solicitor at this address. The younger Thomas Keating had presumably

married and moved elsewhere by the time of the census; he died in 1855 and his will is recorded as having been proved in the consistory court of London on 14 March 1855. His father's own will, made on 30 April 1868, further mentions a fourth daughter, Emma Frederica, as being married to Edmund Kirby.

Thomas Keating the elder died of 'decay of nature' at his home, 2 Princes Terrace, Bayswater, London, on 23 February 1870, said to be eighty-four. His wife died in 1877. The register of the Pharmaceutical Society for 1875 listed Catherine Keating and Georgina Keating as registered at 1 London House Yard, City of London, the premises close by St Paul's Churchyard at which Keating had registered his Persian Insect-Destroying Powder and where his preparations were manufactured. They were almost certainly the daughters already mentioned, the younger of whom died in 1902.   ADRIAN ROOM

Sources *British and Colonial Druggist* (7 April 1888) · *Chemist and Druggist* (26 July 1913) · S. W. F. Holloway, *Royal Pharmaceutical Society of Great Britain, 1841–1991: a political and social history* (1991) · *Secret remedies, what they cost and what they contain* (1909) · T. Keating, 'Keating's Persian Insect-Destroying Powder', *Trade Marks Journal* (11 Oct 1876)
Archives Wellcome L., family MSS
Wealth at death under £5000: probate, 27 June 1870, *CGPLA Eng. & Wales*

Keating, Thomas Patrick (1917–1984), artist and faker, was born on 1 March 1917 in Forest Hill, London, the fourth child in the family of four sons and three daughters of Herbert Josiah Patrick O'Brian Keating, a house painter, and his wife, Louisa DeLieu, a charwoman. He attended the local infants' school in Dalmain Road, where he learned to draw, and at the age of seven ran away to stay with his maternal grandmother in Eltham, Kent. There he attended Roper Street School. Three years later he returned to Forest Hill and Dalmain Road School where he won a paintbox for swimming a width of the local baths underwater. Painting and drawing became his obsession.

Leaving school at fourteen Tom Keating took a variety of jobs, including working as a latherboy and as a lift boy at the Capitol cinema in the Haymarket, before joining his father as a decorator. It was there he learned decorative skills and how to mix paint. In the evenings he attended art school in Croydon and Camberwell.

During the Second World War Keating served as a stoker in the Royal Navy and saw service in the Far East and on Russian and Atlantic convoys. After his ship was torpedoed he was invalided out of the navy and, at the age of thirty, he became a full-time art student at Goldsmiths' College, south London, on an ex-serviceman's grant. He failed his exams twice. He had wanted to teach and without a diploma that career was closed to him. It was the start of his bitterness towards an establishment he always viewed as hostile. In 1943 Keating married Ellen, daughter of James Graveney, printer. They had a son, Douglas, and a daughter, Linda.

Keating joined a restoration studio in London and while there was asked to make copies of a number of paintings.

Thomas Patrick Keating (1917–1984), by unknown photographer

He was later horrified to discover them being sold as genuine. It was then that he decided to flood the market with fakes (or 'Sexton Blakes' as he called them in his own variant of cockney rhyming slang) as a way of striking a blow for impoverished artists against rich dealers and collectors and of getting back at a world which he felt was both shunning and using him.

During the next twenty-five years Keating worked as a freelance restorer, his most important commission being the two years he spent restoring the Laguerre murals at Marlborough House. But all the time he was painting both in his own style and in that of other artists including Rembrandt, Constable, Krieghoff, Degas, Renoir, and Turner. He later admitted to putting more than two thousand fakes in the style of more than 130 artists into circulation. He released them on to the market gradually either by giving them away, selling them to recover the cost of his materials, or putting them into small auctions where they would not arouse suspicion.

Keating's faking became public knowledge in 1976 when it was revealed that thirteen watercolours attributed to Samuel Palmer were not by Palmer. Keating wrote to *The Times* and admitted he had done them. The newspaper hunt to find him (he was touring the west country on his motor cycle) and subsequent revelations turned him into a folk hero. His trial at the Old Bailey in 1979 was stopped because of his ill health, and he returned home to Dedham to continue painting. It was important, he said, that his faking should be discovered in order that the

'joke' should become public knowledge. 'If I had wanted to be a real faker', he later said, 'you would never have heard of me'. He also said that fooling the experts was his greatest joy in life; the thought of it made him helpless with laughter. Keating's object was never to make money. He was generous to a fault and remained poor throughout his life.

In 1982 Keating found new fame as presenter of Channel 4's *Tom Keating on Painters*, a series in which he talked about his favourite artists and demonstrated their style. This won him the Broadcasting Press Guild award for the best on-screen performance in a non-acting role. He followed this with a further series on the impressionists. In 1983, 135 of his paintings were sold at Christies for £72,000 and, for the first time in his life, he had real money. However, his health, which had never been good since the war, was declining rapidly. Keating died in Essex County Hospital, Colchester, on 12 February 1984.

RICHARD FAWKES, *rev.*

Sources *The Times* (13 Feb 1984) · T. Keating, G. Norman, and F. Norman, *The fake's progress* (1977) · personal knowledge (1990) · *CGPLA Eng. & Wales* (1984)
Likenesses J. Lewinski, photograph, 1977, NPG · T. P. Keating, oils (*Self-portrait as Rembrandt*), repro. in *The Times* (3 Nov 1989); Bonhams, Dec 1989 · photograph, repro. in *The Times* · photograph; Christies, 12 Dec 1983 [*see illus.*]
Wealth at death £102,021: administration, 7 Aug 1984, *CGPLA Eng. & Wales*

Keats, John (1795–1821), poet, was born in London, the eldest of the five children of Thomas Keats (*c.*1773–1804), inn manager, and his wife, Frances, later Frances Rawlings (1775–1810), daughter of John and Alice Jennings. Keats was baptized at St Botolph without Bishopsgate on 18 December 1795. He and his family seem to have regarded 29 October as his birthday, although the baptismal entry gives 31 October. An important factor in the development of Keats's reputation, during his life and in the decades following his death, was the belief that he was born in a coaching inn, the Swan and Hoop at 24 The Pavement, Moorgate, and that his father, Thomas, was an 'ostler' in the inn. This supposed humble origin, reinforced in the public mind by Leigh Hunt's ill-informed account in *Lord Byron and some of his Contemporaries* (1828), played its part in the notoriously savage politically inspired attacks made on Keats by tory reviewers during his lifetime, and it deeply coloured the nineteenth-century biographical tradition. But there is no evidence about Keats's place of birth, and his family background, for all its obscurities, was far from impoverished. Little is known of Keats's father, described as a man of common sense and respectability, whom Keats resembled in a short, stocky build, and an attractively alert bearing. The family name appears to originate in Devon or Cornwall, and there is evidence that Thomas Keats may have come from Reading. His marriage on 9 October 1794 at St George's, Hanover Square, was apparently a rushed affair; the couple were young and there were no family witnesses. Frances Jennings, the poet's mother, was recalled as excitable and attractive, and there is much to suggest also a reckless

John Keats (1795–1821), by Joseph Severn, 1816

impetuosity. Her father was a man of property who purchased the leasehold of the Swan and Hoop in 1774, adding the next-door property in 1785. Keats's brother George was born on 28 February 1797. The family moved to Craven Street, off the City Road, at Christmas 1798. Thomas Keats was born on 28 November 1799, and a fourth son, Edward, on 28 April 1801. George, Tom, and Edward were baptized at St Leonard, Shoreditch, on 24 September 1801, but Edward died before the end of the following year and was buried in Bunhill Fields on 9 December 1802. George and Tom played a significant part in Keats's short, intense life—George in the role of hard-headed realist, while Tom enjoyed a special empathy with the poet.

Later in December 1802 the family moved again, to the Swan and Hoop, where Mr Jennings had installed his son-in-law as manager. Keats's sister Fanny was born on 3 June 1803 and baptized at St Botolph's.

Schooldays In August 1803 Keats went to Clarke's School in Enfield. The headmaster was John Clarke, whose son Charles Cowden Clarke was an usher at the school. But Keats had barely begun his school life when his family was overtaken by catastrophe. On 16 April 1804 his father was killed in a fall from his horse. Keats's newly widowed mother almost immediately married William Rawlings, on 27 June at St George's, Hanover Square. The startling haste of this remarriage has fuelled speculation that Rawlings was an adventurer interested in Frances Keats's inheritance of some £2000. The couple took up residence in the Swan and Hoop, with Rawlings as manager.

Family relations now deteriorated badly, with consequences which cast a shadow over all Keats's subsequent

experience. His grandfather John Jennings died on 8 March, leaving a substantial estate which made generous provision for the various members of his family. As well as Keats himself, these included Jennings's widow Alice; Keats's mother, brothers, and sister, and his uncle the naval officer Midgley Jennings and his family; and John Jennings's sister Mary Sweetinburgh. But the terms of the will proved ambivalent and were challenged in chancery by Keats's mother, thus complicating and delaying any actual payment, to her brother, herself, or Keats. The action ultimately failed completely, following judgment by the master of the rolls on 29 July 1806. Frances parted from Rawlings about this time, and her whereabouts in the following three years are a mystery.

Keats's maternal grandmother, Alice Jennings, had after her husband's death lived in a rented house in Ponder's End north of London. Soon after her daughter's challenge to the will, the Keats children left their mother and stepfather at the Swan and Hoop and went to live with their grandmother at a new address in Church Street, Edmonton, near to Clarke's School. This arrangement apparently consolidated a serious split in the family, whereby Keats found himself caught up in bitter alienating enmity between his mother, his grandmother, and also his uncle Midgley, whose supposed military heroics Keats idolized as a boy. The situation perhaps goes some way to explain the extraordinary fact of the subsequent total absence of any reference by Keats to either of his parents. When Midgley died of a 'decline' on 21 November 1808, at thirty-one ominously young, Frances revived her original bill of complaint, but her failure to pursue it supports the possibility that she was reconciled with the family by the summer of 1809. Midgley's stock was divided equally between his widow and Alice Jennings. This meant that under the terms of his grandfather's will Keats could apply to chancery at any time after his twenty-first birthday for a quarter share of the estate, about £800.

The period of his mother's reconciliation with the family coincided with a change of attitude by Keats at school. Charles Cowden Clarke became a firm friend of Keats, and his *Recollections of Writers* includes a vivid account of the young poet. Clarke remembered him as the 'favourite of all' for his 'high-mindedness, his utter unconsciousness of a mean motive, his placability, his generosity' (Cowden Clarke and Cowden Clarke, 123). He had from an early age a striking physical presence that was remarked by observers throughout his life. At school he was conspicuous for extremes of passion, with a determination and physical courage belying his small stature. Another close friend of Keats at school was Edward Holmes, the future biographer of Mozart, who remembered Keats in childhood as attached not to books but to 'all active exercises', with a special relish for fighting (Rollins, 2.163–5). However, after January 1809 Keats surprised everyone with a resolve to 'carry off all the first prizes in literature' (Milnes, 13), a determination in which he succeeded. Keats's education at Clarke's was probably better than at the typical public school of the day. He covered scientific and practical subjects, Latin, and French, and although he never learned

Greek he imbibed from such works as Lemprière's *Classical Dictionary* an 'intimacy with the Greek mythology' (Cowden Clarke and Cowden Clarke, 124). The school's liberal principles were especially significant. Keats's first acquaintance with Leigh Hunt's *Examiner* dates from this time, and it was at Clarke's that Keats's politically radical sympathies, and his youthful enthusiasm for Hunt, began to develop. Keats's schoolboy friends, and particularly Cowden Clarke, strongly influenced his early reading and literary tastes, notably for Spenser. Keats and Clarke seem however to have drifted out of contact after 1817.

Keats's new commitment to his studies in 1809 no doubt owed much to renewed intimacy with his mother, which also brought new responsibilities as she was clearly unwell. Keats had already demonstrated a strong sense of family responsibility in his watchful solicitude for his little sister Fanny, and his younger brothers, which would continue throughout his life. But all sense of domestic security was destroyed by the death of his mother in March 1810, like Midgley from a 'decline'. Keats, who had always been markedly protective of his mother, gave himself up to 'a long agony of grief', hiding under an alcove beneath a master's desk at school (Milnes, 12). Keats's grandmother Alice Jennings now had a substantial estate to dispose of, having seen all other claimants die. On 30 July 1810 she executed a deed making the property over to John Nowland Sandell, a merchant, and Richard Abbey, a friend from her native village of Colne in Lancashire, to administer for her grandchildren. After Sandell's death in 1816 Abbey became sole guardian.

Apprenticeship and medical training Keats left Clarke's School in the summer of 1810, and at fourteen was apprenticed to the surgeon and apothecary Thomas Hammond, neighbour and doctor of the Jennings family. Keats moved in above his surgery at 7 Church Street, Edmonton. There seems no basis for the surmise of various biographers that Keats was forced into medical training, but the apprenticeship was expensive and began immediately to eat into the inheritance held in trust by Abbey. He made excellent progress, while his friendship with Cowden Clarke blossomed and his literary interests broadened and developed quickly. He kept up his school contacts and continued to receive informal tuition, completing a prose translation of the *Aeneid*. Some time probably in 1813 Keats quarrelled with Hammond and moved out, perhaps to live with his brothers in St Pancras. George had been removed from school early to work in Abbey's counting-house as a clerk, where he would shortly be joined by Tom. Keats's great-aunt Mary Sweetinburgh died in November 1813, and his grandmother Alice in December 1814. Keats told Richard Woodhouse that his early sonnet 'As from the darkening gloom a silver dove', as nearly Christian in sentiment as anything he wrote, was composed on her death. Fanny went to live with Abbey, who made it difficult for the brothers to visit, and discouraged correspondence. She remained with the Abbeys until her twenty-first birthday. Keats now had two sets of property in trust: £800 from John Jennings's will, and his share of the property held by Sandell and Abbey, which amounted to a quarter share in

some £8000. Keats never applied for the £800, and probably knew nothing of it. Although Abbey has often been blamed, he probably knew no more of it than Keats. William Walton, solicitor for Keats's mother and grandmother, certainly did know of it and should have informed Keats. George Keats was also ignorant of this money. On the death of Tom the surviving brothers' share was further augmented. This money could have made a very great difference to Keats, particularly as he struggled for funds in the last two years of his life.

According to Charles Brown, Keats did not think of writing verse until he had turned eighteen. His earliest known work, an 'Imitation of Spenser' eventually published in 1817, dates probably from early 1814. This, like most of the poetry surviving from his student days, is markedly derivative. Obvious models for the early work include Byron, Hunt, and popular writers of the day such as Chatterton and Moore. But even the 'Imitation of Spenser' has a quality of self-reflection which foreshadows Keats's genius in working through literary models to an idiom entirely his own. His verse over the next eighteen months demonstrates a persistent preoccupation with the idea of his own literary vocation and destined fame. There is also a clear affinity with liberal political ideals and heroes. The sonnet 'Written on the Day that Mr Leigh Hunt Left Prison' dates from February 1815, some eighteen months before Keats's first meeting with Hunt but explicitly acknowledging his influence. By the middle of 1815 Keats had been introduced through his brother George to George Felton Mathew, an aspiring young poet and member of a poetical set consisting mainly of young ladies, including Mathew's own cousins. Keats wrote some thinly mannered verses to members of this group, typified by the lines 'To some Ladies' in the tripping quatrains of Tom Moore. This set was soon outgrown, and Mathew was to prove ungenerous. But he stimulated Keats to new reading, in Fairfax's Tasso for example, and helped to focus Keats's youthful sense of literary ambition.

On 1 October 1815 Keats entered Guy's Hospital as a student, and followed a career implying some powerful patronage, as well as a genuine determination to qualify as a doctor. The distinguished surgeon Astley Cooper placed Keats under his own dresser, George Cooper, with whom he took lodgings close to the hospital at 28 St Thomas's Street in Southwark, with other medical students. The costs of this expensive new stage in his medical education further depleted the capital in Abbey's care, particularly after Keats was accepted as a dresser on 29 October, two days before his twentieth birthday. This was quick promotion and heralded a promising career, although Keats's medical notebook from the period survives and suggests an unmethodical approach. Throughout the later months of 1815 Keats continued to write poems, exploring sonnet forms especially, but also giving expression to evidently quickening mental powers in work which shows the new influence of Wordsworth, such as the 'Epistle to George Felton Mathew' of November 1815, or the sonnet 'O solitude!', also composed about this time. This was to become

Keats's first published poem when it appeared in *The Examiner* on 5 May 1816.

Keats made friends easily. He was popular among his fellow students, and enjoyed a constantly widening circle of acquaintance. Among new friendships at this time those with William Haslam and Joseph *Severn (1793–1879), introduced through George Keats in the spring of 1816, were of particular importance. Haslam, who was about Keats's age and became a solicitor, was deeply attached to Keats and greatly admired his abilities. He remained a dependable friend and ally, often helping with financial problems. Severn, two years Keats's senior, was apprenticed as an engraver when they first became acquainted, but had already begun to work as a painter. Their friendship grew steadily, until in Keats's final months Severn's devoted care earned him a special place in English literary history. Keats continued his medical studies, clearly to good effect. On 25 July 1816 he passed his exams to become a licentiate of the Society of Apothecaries. This was a serious test of his medical knowledge, and made him eligible to practise as an apothecary, physician, and surgeon. Following this success Keats took a holiday from his studies and visited Margate with his brother Tom. They left in August, Keats continuing to write and completing three verse epistles in Margate, which further develop the themes of poetic vocation and, with a sharpening focus, the projection of his own poetic achievement. They returned to London in September, and by 9 October Keats had taken new lodgings at 8 Dean Street, Southwark, with Tom and George, who had left Abbey's after quarrelling with a junior partner. Keats now faced a further period of study for his membership of the Royal College of Surgeons.

Poetic vocation: *Poems* (1817)   Immediately on his return to London Keats's life took a decisive turn as he was caught up in the excitement of powerful new literary friendships. By the middle of October he had been introduced by Cowden Clarke to his hero Leigh Hunt, after Clarke had shown Hunt some of his work. He expressed warm admiration, as did others such as Horace Smith, and a period of close intimacy with the Hunt circle began, matched by a newly dominant stylistic influence from Hunt in Keats's writing. Through Hunt Keats met the painter Benjamin Robert Haydon, already long launched on his picture 'Christ's Entry into Jerusalem' and in the midst of public controversy over the authenticity of the Elgin marbles. Keats was attracted to Haydon's artistic commitment and appetite for experience and argument, and Haydon, like many others at this time, was captivated by Keats's genial gusto and contagious sense of humour, and impressed by his passionate sense of poetic vocation. Another new friend, encountered through Haydon on 20 October, was John Hamilton Reynolds, a young writer with a promise which appeared to match Keats's own, and an easy-going quickness of wit which suited Keats's penchant for punning talk and artistic debate. The new intensity in Keats's literary life produced a burst of creativity. One evening in October Clarke introduced Keats to Chapman's translation of Homer, and after returning late to his lodgings

Keats wrote the sonnet 'On First Looking into Chapman's Homer', which he contrived to have delivered to Clarke by 10 o'clock next morning. The poem is an astonishing achievement, with a confident formal assurance and metaphoric complexity which make it one of the finest English sonnets. As Hunt generously acknowledged, it 'completely announced the new poet taking possession' (Hunt, *Lord Byron*, 249). Through November and December Keats's writing developed rapidly. He took on more directly the myth of his own personal and artistic growth, particularly in two long and ambitious poems, 'Sleep and Poetry' and 'I stood tip-toe upon a little hill'. These are experimental works, strongly influenced by Hunt and structurally unresolved, but most thoughtfully engaged with questions of literary history and Keats's place in it. Keats also began, with Hunt and others, to write poetry in timed competitions on agreed themes in prescribed forms, repeatedly demonstrating an exceptional facility in verse. George Felton Mathew had recently published 'To a Poetical Friend', on Keats, in the *European Magazine*, and on 1 December 1816 Hunt published the first of his 'Young poets' articles in *The Examiner*, quoting the sonnet on Chapman's Homer in full, and representing Keats along with Shelley and Reynolds as the new generation in English poetry. Keats and Shelley met for the first time in mid-December. It was at this time that Haydon took his famous life mask of Keats.

Early in December Keats was listed as a certified apothecary in the *London Medical Repository*, but the sense of poetic vocation now challenged his commitment to his studies, and he decided to give up medicine. Abbey was furious. According to his brother George's later account Keats had by his twenty-first birthday in October 1816 sold two thirds of his inheritance in trust with Abbey to meet the costs of his medical training, and was probably left with a legacy of little more than £500, giving an income of about £55 per year. Over the next eighteen months Keats must have spent more than his income from interest on the trust fund, and he also made a series of ill-advisedly generous loans, for example to Haydon. Relations with Abbey worsened progressively over this period. In mid-November Keats and his brothers had moved to new lodgings at 76 Cheapside. Among Keats's many new literary friends was the bookseller and publisher Charles Ollier, introduced by Clarke, who was already publishing Shelley and declared himself anxious to publish this new rising young star. Keats began to think of making up a volume of his poems. He also continued to develop ideas for an ambitious long poem on the myth of Endymion, which had been touched on in 'I stood tip-toe'.

Through Christmas 1816 and into the new year further important contacts were established and strengthened. Keats dined regularly with Hunt, Horace Smith, Haydon, and Reynolds. In February Hunt showed his work to the Shelleys, William Godwin, Basil Montagu, and William Hazlitt. Keats was soon afterwards visiting and dining with the Shelleys. Keats and Hazlitt may already have become acquainted by now, probably meeting first through Haydon. Hazlitt was an established figure in literary London, and a regular contributor to *The Examiner*. His conversation, lectures, and published criticism were to prove a powerful influence. Early in 1817 Keats's thinking about art deepened in dialogue with Hazlitt and Haydon concerning the achievement of Greek sculpture in the Elgin marbles, and the relation of reality to aesthetic ideals.

Keats continued to write poetry, still concentrating on the sonnet, the preferred form of his poetic apprenticeship. In February two sonnets appeared in *The Examiner*, where he now began to publish regularly. Many others were produced in the autumn and winter of 1816 and in the first months of 1817—mostly occasional in character, written to and about friends, often extemporized or produced feverishly overnight after an evening of excited talk. According to Clarke, one evening late in February, when the last batch of proofs of his first volume of poetry was brought for correction, Keats rapidly extemporized a dedicatory sonnet to Hunt, at 'a side-table, and in the buzz of a mixed conversation' (Cowden Clarke and Cowden Clarke, 138). *Poems* was published on 3 March 1817 by Charles and James Ollier, the first of the three books that Keats published in his lifetime. It contained nearly all the poems Keats is known to have written up to that date. Reynolds reviewed it favourably in *The Champion* for 9 March, but no one outside Keats's immediate circle showed any interest. As Clarke bluntly remarked, the book 'might have emerged in Timbuctoo' (ibid., 140). Little more than a month later a disappointed Charles Ollier wrote indignantly to George Keats of his regret at having published the volume, which one dissatisfied purchaser had characterized as 'no better than a take-in' (*The Athenaeum*, 7 June 1873, 725). Ollier's irritation was no doubt heightened by Keats's surprising decision, almost immediately after the appearance of his first book, to change publishers. He probably met John Taylor about March 1817 through Reynolds, whose *The Naiads* had been published in 1816 by the well-established firm run by Taylor and his partner James Hessey in Fleet Street. Taylor was particularly interested in Keats's projected long poem on Endymion. It was doubtless through Taylor that Keats also first met Richard Woodhouse, a lawyer who acted as an informal adviser to Taylor and Hessey in matters legal and literary. Woodhouse quickly came to the settled view that Keats was a poet of genius who would one day be ranked with the greatest English writers. He set about accordingly to record for posterity, during the period of his friendship with Keats, and after his death, as much material as he could find relating to Keats's poetry. This material mostly survives and has become a principal source of knowledge about Keats.

Probably at about this time, in March 1817, as Woodhouse recalled, one day when 'Keats and Leigh Hunt were taking their wine together … the whim seized them … to crown themselves with laurel after the fashion of the elder bards.' This light-hearted affectation was then discovered by visiting young ladies, on whose arrival Keats 'vowed that he would not take off his crown for any human being: and … wore it … as long as the visit lasted' (*Poems, Transcripts, Letters &c: Facsimiles of Richard Woodhouse's Scrapbook Materials*, ed. J. Stillinger, 1985, 4). The episode, which produced a series of weak sonnets, hints at what Keats came to regard as a mannered, trivializing, and frankly embarrassing quality in Hunt's influence.

Endymion Once Keats had definitely given up his medical career there was nothing to keep him near Guy's Hospital south of the river. Towards the end of March he moved north with his brothers to lodgings on the first floor of a house at 1 Well Walk in Hampstead, near to Hunt and his friends. The house belonged to Benjamin Bentley, the local postman. Keats was soon introduced by Reynolds to one of his Hampstead neighbours, Charles Wentworth Dilke. Dilke, six years older than Keats, was a tidy-minded civil servant in the navy pay office, with educated literary tastes which included a great enthusiasm for Shakespeare. He had published an edition of *Old English Plays*, and from the beginnings of this friendship Keats himself began to read Shakespeare and his contemporaries with a new concentration. Keats also seems to have met James Rice and Benjamin Bailey about this time, again through Reynolds. Bailey had matriculated at Oxford in 1816 and was reading for holy orders. Rice was a young man in poor health, but the wit and fortitude with which he bore his illness earned Keats's admiration. The intimacy with Hunt and his friends continued, but other literary contacts were beginning to influence Keats. Shelley, just three years Keats's senior, had already published a good deal. His reputation was not high, but the *Alastor* volume had appeared a year earlier, with a title poem of a quality and ambition that placed Keats's own poetic achievements in a fresh light. Keats now determined to test his abilities. He wrote to George that *Endymion* would be 'a trial of my Powers of Imagination and … invention … I must make 4000 Lines of one bare circumstance and fill them with Poetry' (*Letters of John Keats*, 1.169–70). The task was perhaps conceived in direct rivalry with Shelley, whose *Laon and Cythna* was written over an almost identical period of time in the middle six months of 1817. Keats decided to leave London to attempt his project in solitude, and left for the Isle of Wight, perhaps at Dilke's suggestion, on 14 April, spending the night at Southampton before crossing to Newport. He visited Shanklin, then took lodgings at Carisbrooke. The sonnet 'On the Sea' was probably written on 17 April, but this was Keats's last sonnet for many months. Work on *Endymion* began immediately. Keats left the Isle of Wight to visit Tom in Margate towards the end of April. The 'Hymn to Pan' was written at this time, amid worries about money which led to a loan of £20 from Taylor and Hessey.

In mid-May Keats sought a change of scene in Canterbury, remarking in a letter to his publishers that 'the remembrance of Chaucer will set me forward like a Billiard-Ball' (*Letters of John Keats*, 1.146). This strikes the authentic tone of Keats's correspondence. Few letters survive from Keats's first twenty years, but thereafter, and particularly from spring 1817, there is abundant record of Keats's brilliance as a letter writer. These letters articulate a personality of extraordinary critical intelligence, generous sympathies, and richly engaging tactful good humour, and are justly regarded as an achievement ranking almost with the poetry itself. Haydon noted Keats's 'exquisite taste for humour' (*Diary*, ed. Pope, 2.316), a quality which shines through his correspondence.

At the end of May Keats visited the village of Bo Peep near Hastings, where he met Isabella Jones. Keats's relations with women were never entirely comfortable. Woodhouse remarked that he had the 'idea that the diminutiveness of his size makes him contemptible, and that no woman can like a man of a small stature' (*Poems (1817): a Facsimile of Richard Woodhouse's Annotated Copy*, ed. J. Stillinger, 1985, 153), but he seems also to have found it difficult to take women seriously in intellectual terms, and to square the ordinary friendliness of social relations with his sexual drive. He admitted to Bailey that 'I have not a right feeling towards women' (*Letters of John Keats*, 1.341). The extent of his actual experience of sex is a matter for conjecture, although there seems to have been some kind of sexual liaison with Isabella Jones at this time, and the opening of book 2 of *Endymion* perhaps shows its influence. Some short lyrics from this period, such as 'Unfelt, Unheard, Unseen', also suggest recent sexual experience.

Keats returned to Well Walk on 10 June, and promptly borrowed a further £30 from Taylor and Hessey. Work on *Endymion* continued throughout the summer months. He read extracts to Clark and Severn in August. A draft of the first two books was complete by the end of the month. Late in the summer Keats met Charles Brown, a former schoolfellow of Dilke's. Brown had a comfortable competence inherited from his brother, and had already composed a libretto for the comic opera *Narensky* which had run for ten nights at Drury Lane in 1814. With Dilke he had built a double house in John Street, Hampstead, called Wentworth Place (later Lawn Bank, now Keats House). This was a significant new friendship, and over the next two years Brown became perhaps Keats's most intimate confidant and supporter. On 3 September, while his brothers were visiting Paris, Keats travelled to Oxford to stay with Bailey at Magdalen Hall, where he read Milton and Wordsworth, regularly took a boat on the Isis, and composed *Endymion* book 3 at a steady fifty lines a day. The third book was finished before the end of the month, and after visiting Stratford upon Avon with Bailey on 2 October Keats returned to Well Walk and began work on the fourth and final book of his poem. He also resumed his metropolitan social life, with frequent calls on Hunt, Haydon, Reynolds, Brown, Rice, and the Shelleys, among others. In the second half of October he was confined at Hampstead with an infection developed at Oxford. He treated himself with mercury, conceivably for syphilis, but probably for gonorrhoea. More seriously, his brother Tom was very unwell by the end of the month. And Keats's public reputation took an ominous turn with the publication in October of the first of the *Blackwood's* articles on the 'Cockney school', in which 'Z' launched a virulent attack on Hunt. Keats was not mentioned in the article, but his name appeared in capitals in the epigraph. A review by George Felton Mathew of the 1817 *Poems* had appeared in the *European Magazine* in May, followed in June by a series of much more positive notices by Hunt in *The Examiner*. Verse by Keats had also been appearing regularly over the summer, in *The Champion*, the *Monthly Repository*, and *The Examiner*. The association with Hunt, who had famously been imprisoned for a libel on the prince regent, now began to draw genuinely hostile fire from the tory reviewers. In the aggressive literary politics of the day, the 'cockney' epithet denoted a metropolitan upstart and vulgar pretension. It was aimed especially at Hunt, whose mannered style sorted awkwardly with a professed enthusiasm for Wordsworth. Keats was an obvious target as a well-known admirer and friend of Hunt, but the jibe also connected unfortunately with his supposed low social origins.

By the end of October Keats was planning to finish *Endymion* within three weeks, and after making further good progress he travelled on 22 November to Burford Bridge in Surrey, where at the Fox and Hounds inn he finished the poem on 28 November after a final burst of sustained writing at eighty lines a day. It was from this inn that Keats wrote a letter to Bailey exploring 'the authenticity of the Imagination'; 'The Imagination may be compared to Adam's dream—he awoke and found it truth' (*Letters of John Keats*, 1.185). This was the earliest of a series of critical reflections, articulated informally in the letters and in the midst of other preoccupations, which was to earn for Keats a special influence and prestige in twentieth-century literary criticism.

Late 1817 to early 1818: 'Isabella' Keats returned from Burford Bridge to Hampstead about 5 December, and entered on an increasingly busy social life, with new friendships and frequent visits to galleries, lectures, and the theatre. On 14 December he saw his brothers off on the coach to Teignmouth in Devon, where Tom was going for the sake of his health. Over the next few days Keats saw the actor Edmund Kean, whom he greatly admired and was said to resemble, in several roles including Richard III. He began to produce a series of miscellaneous shorter poems, and fell into regular and friendly intercourse with James and Horace Smith, Lamb, Hazlitt, William Godwin, and Thomas Noon Talfourd. He attended the Royal Academy exhibition on 20 December. The next day his review of Kean's acting appeared in *The Champion*. This heady mix of experience produced one of his greatest letters, when after a visit to the pantomime probably on 26 December with Brown and Dilke a discussion on the way home led to Keats's exposition in a letter to his brothers of 'negative capability', the quality that 'went to form a Man of Achievement especially in Literature and which Shakespeare possessed so enormously' (*Letters of John Keats*, 1.193).

It was probably at the same time, late in December, that Keats was stung by Wordsworth's response to his recitation of the 'Hymn to Pan' from *Endymion*, when according to Haydon 'Wordsworth drily said "a Very pretty piece of Paganism"' (Rollins, 2.144). In Haydon's account Keats never forgave Wordsworth for this slight, although the circumstances and date of the incident are unclear. Another celebrated event involving both Keats and Wordsworth certainly took place on 28 December, when Haydon gave his 'immortal dinner' for Keats, Wordsworth, Lamb, and Wordsworth's cousin Thomas Monkhouse. After several hours of inspired talk the company moved to take tea, where they were joined by some invited friends. The evening reached a memorable comic climax in an exchange between Wordsworth and the deputy comptroller of the stamp office, who spoke to the great poet in such ludicrously inappropriate terms that Lamb was moved to a pitch of drollery at their expense which reduced Keats and the company to helpless laughter.

This busy social life continued into January and February. Keats attended 'a sort of a Club every Saturday evening' and was invited by Haydon to dine 'every Sunday at three' (*Letters of John Keats*, 1.202, 204). He regularly attended Hazlitt's lectures. There were introductions to Henry Crabb Robinson, and, through the Shelleys, to Thomas Love Peacock, Thomas Jefferson Hogg, and Claire Clairmont. Freed from the discipline of his long poem, Keats now entered a freshly productive period. He had been seeing Wordsworth a good deal, and was reading the Elizabethans, under the influence of Hazlitt's lectures on the English poets. He now experimented confidently, and also returned to writing sonnets, in an assured and practised manner; 'On Seeing a Lock of Milton's Hair', 'On Sitting Down to Read King Lear', and 'When I have fears' were all written at this time. On 4 February his sonnet 'To the Nile' was composed in a timed competition with Hunt and Shelley. Later in the month, on 27 February, he wrote to John Taylor of his 'Axioms' in poetry, that it should 'surprise by a fine excess', and that if poetry 'comes not as naturally as the Leaves to a tree it had better not come at all' (ibid., 1.238). Keats was correcting *Endymion* and preparing it for the press throughout this period. Book 1 was delivered to the publishers on 20 January, and book 2 on 6 February. He finished the fair copy of book 3 before the end of the month, and began on book 4 while reading proofs for the first three books. He had also begun 'Isabella, or, The Pot of Basil', a narrative poem in *ottava rima* which was conceived in a project with Reynolds to produce verse tales from Boccaccio. Keats's own subject was probably suggested by Hazlitt. The poem represented a significant new departure, reaching for a sustained and studied complexity of texture he had not previously attempted.

But, as happened often in Keats's short life, this determined commitment to his maturing literary career was interrupted by personal problems. Tom had been spitting blood, but in spite of this George returned to London from Devon at the end of February, leaving Tom alone. George, whose behaviour now began to chime less perfectly with Keats's own best interests, had decided to marry and emigrate to America. Keats had little option at this short notice but to leave the preparation of *Endymion* to his publishers, asking Cowden Clarke to check proofs, and join Tom in Teignmouth. He left London by coach in a violent storm on 4 March, reaching Exeter on 6 March and arriving in Teignmouth the next day. He stayed at 20 Strand (now Northumberland Place). The Keats brothers had been spending time in flirtatious friendship with the three daughters of a Mrs Jeffrey, 'the Girls over at the Bonnet shop' (*Letters of John Keats*, 1.246) at 35 Strand, and Keats fell in with this routine. It rained continuously for six days after his arrival. Keats was insulted at the theatre in Teignmouth on about 10 March, in obscure circumstances. Tom had a haemorrhage on 13 March. Money was short, and George sent £20 in the middle of March. In spite of these worries Keats managed to finish copying *Endymion* book 4 by 14 March, and on 19 March he wrote and dated a first preface to *Endymion*, sending it with the remaining copy to his publishers on 21 March. He learned on 9 April that his preface had been rejected by Reynolds and his publishers, who feared that its apologetically defensive tone might expose him to public ridicule and attack. The next day he wrote and sent a new preface. This was still defensive, but struck a valedictory note in bidding farewell to his own period of poetic apprenticeship.

Keats's poetic career had reached a new level with the completion of 'Isabella' about the end of April. The poem has a tighter sense of narrative control, a more distinctive and independent stylistic identity, and a defter interweaving of symbol and story, than anything Keats had hitherto written. On 1 May, with *Endymion* and 'Isabella' completed, Keats wrote an 'Ode to May' in fourteen irregular lines, hinting at achievements which still lay a year ahead. Over the next two days he wrote one of his most important letters, to Reynolds, expounding his notion of life as a 'large Mansion of Many Apartments' (*Letters of John Keats*, 1.280), which sketched a model of personal and poetic maturity which gives powerful expression to Keats's gathering sense of human suffering and its relation to great art.

An advance copy of *Endymion* arrived on 24 April. Within a month the poem was published in London by Taylor and Hessey, dedicated 'to the memory of Thomas Chatterton'. At first it prompted little reaction beyond Keats's immediate circle, and even here responses were guarded. It seemed oddly constructed, and was not always easy to follow in its adaptation of classical narrative. More worrying, for instance to Taylor, was the poem's sometimes fervid sensuality and its Hunt-like mannerisms of style. The volume sold poorly and was ultimately remaindered. It is nevertheless a major achievement in the rich suggestivity of its symbolism, and in the extravagantly abundant detail of its poetic effects. Its reputation has grown since the mid-nineteenth century.

Life in Teignmouth had its attractions, including female admirers, a trip to Dawlish fair, and apparently a visit from Keats's friend Rice. But everything was overshadowed by Tom's failing health. In spite of continued blood-spitting, Tom was determined to return to London. The brothers set off on 4 or 5 May, apparently accompanied by Sarah Jeffrey, one of the Teignmouth girls, as far as Honiton. At Bridport Tom suffered a serious haemorrhage, and the remainder of the journey proved slow and difficult. They were back in Well Walk by 11 May.

Summer 1818: the walking tour Throughout May Keats was 'very much engaged with his friends' (*Letters of John Keats*, 1.286) in London. The idea of a walking tour in Scotland with Brown had been under discussion for some time, and this now began to take shape. It was to provide materials for the further attempt at a long classical poem, which had been hinted in the published preface to *Endymion*. This was *Hyperion*, for which Keats had undertaken serious reading, at Bailey's prompting, in Milton, Wordsworth, and Cary's Dante. But once again concentration on literary projects proved difficult for Keats to sustain in the face of pressing distractions. George married Georgiana Wylie on 28 May. Keats signed the register as a witness, troubled and depressed by George's imminent departure, the continuing difficulty of contact with his sister Fanny, still living under Richard Abbey's disapproving guardianship, and Tom's serious illness. Keats was himself unwell in early June, and his doctor instructed him not to go out for several days. There were financial worries. Keats needed cash to cover the expenses of his walking tour. George had debts to clear and costs to meet before his voyage to America. Tom had hoped to travel to Italy for his health, but was clearly too weak for the journey, so money had to be found to pay Mrs Bentley at Well Walk to look after him in Keats's absence. All this put pressure on Abbey's trust fund, and on the mutual understanding of the three brothers. The financial arrangements surrounding George's departure for America became a matter of serious controversy after Keats's death. George himself stated later that when he left for America he left his brother with nearly £300. This was later hotly disputed by Brown, who took George to mean that he had given money to Keats, whereas George probably meant that Keats had at that time some £300 of his own left in trust with Abbey. George had cashed his trust on coming of age in February 1818, and by his own account left £500 of the £1600 cashed to clear debts and leave some means to his brothers. Keats lived on this money during and beyond Tom's illness. Although George's conduct, and his subsequent accounts of it, leave room for doubt as to his motives, it seems likely that Keats ended up owing George money, and that George, who had money problems of his own, did what he felt he could to assist his brother.

A different distraction loomed in the form of the reviews of *Endymion*. Keats and his friends were apprehensive that the tory *Blackwood's Edinburgh Magazine* might continue its assault on Hunt by turning attention to Keats's published work. There were positive responses to *Endymion* from friends, and a favourable notice probably by John Scott in *The Champion*. But for the tories Hunt's influence marked Keats out as fair game, and a critical storm was now gathering.

Keats left London for Liverpool with George and Georgiana Keats and Charles Brown on 22 June. They arrived in Liverpool on the late afternoon of 23 June, and Keats and Brown set off on their tour early the next morning, taking the coach to Lancaster and leaving George and Georgiana asleep in the inn. They sailed for America a few days later. Keats and Brown walked from Lancaster through the south lakes. Keats was disappointed to find Wordsworth out when they reached Rydal on 27 June, and disillusioned too when he learned that Wordsworth was on electioneering business for the tory Lord Lowther. He was also struck by the prominence of Wordsworth's house and its familiarity to tourists. He nevertheless left a note for the poet, propped up on what he took to be a portrait of Dorothy, and after proceeding along Rydal Water to Grasmere was comforted by the humbler aspect of Dove Cottage.

The walkers continued northwards, climbing Skiddaw on 29 June, then going on to Carlisle, and from there by coach through Gretna Green to Dumfries. Keats wrote his sonnet 'On Visiting the Tomb of Burns' on this part of the journey. From Dumfries they walked westwards, from 2 to 6 July, first to Glenluce and then on foot and by mail coach through Stranraer to Portpatrick. From there they took a boat to Donaghadee in Ireland, and walked to Belfast and back. Keats's letters to Tom and others recording all of this journey are wonderfully animated and graphic, including an extraordinary account of a squalid old woman, encountered on the way back from Belfast, carried in a filthy sedan chair:

> like an ape half starved … in its passage from Madagascar to the cape … looking out with a round-eyed skinny lidded, inanity—with a sort of horizontal idiotic movement of her head … What a thing would be a history of her Life and sensations. (*Letters of John Keats*, 1.321–2)

They returned to Portpatrick on 8 July, walked via Stranraer to Ballantrae, and on to Girvan by 10 July, Keats producing here his sonnet 'To Ailsa Rock', and also completing the lines beginning 'Ah, ken ye what I met the day', in the manner of Burns but also anticipating 'La belle dame sans merci'. On 11 July they walked to Ayr, Keats quickly producing a sonnet while being shown round Burns's cottage, then on to Glasgow by 17 July, and through Inveraray and up into the highlands by 19 July, Keats writing verse all the time. They had walked to Oban by 21 July, and next day caught the ferry to the Isle of Mull, where they took on a punishing 37-mile walk right across the island rather than meet the expense of sailing round it. On 24 July they visited Iona and Staffa by boat, viewing seascapes and landscapes which made an obvious impact on Keats's writing. They rested in Oban, but Keats had developed a heavy cold in the crossing of Mull, and by the time the weary travellers moved on to Fort William on 1 August, climbing Ben Nevis on the following day, Keats was exhausted and suffering from an ulcerated throat brought on by bad tonsillitis. In Inverness a doctor declared Keats feverish and advised an immediate return to London. He took a coach to Cromarty and sailed on the smack *George* on 8 August.

Death of Tom Keats: *Hyperion* Keats was back in Well Walk on 18 August. His doctor insisted that he be confined to the house. The sore throat was still bad, he was suffering from toothache, and Keats was also dosing himself with mercury, probably fearing that his ulcerated throat might have a venereal origin. Tom was now gravely ill. Brown's half of Wentworth Place was being rented by a young widow named Frances Brawne and her three children.

Keats probably met the family about this time, but he was doubtless too worried by Tom's health to take notice of the eldest girl, Fanny, who was just eighteen. He made a copy of 'Isabella', and saw such friends as he could. Tom's condition offered little hope, and Keats's spirits received a further heavy blow with the appearance on 1 September of J. G. Lockhart's devastatingly offensive attack on *Poems* and *Endymion* in the August issue of *Blackwood's Edinburgh Magazine*, which concluded 'so back to the shop, Mr John' and ruthlessly pursued the jeering 'cockney' epithet and all its associations (3, August 1818, 524). This was followed on 27 September by J. W. Croker's attack on *Endymion* in the delayed April issue of the *Quarterly Review*, and at the same time Keats's *Poems* was savaged anonymously in the delayed June issue of the *British Critic*, which notoriously indexed *Endymion* as 'a monstrously droll poem' (new ser., 9, June 1818, 649–54). These attacks were plainly political in motivation, and aimed chiefly at Hunt. But they succeeded in sustaining a vitriolic and cruelly personal savagery at Keats's expense which has become legendary in literary history. His supposed low social origins were derided. His medical training became a running joke. His poetic ambitions, and even his lack of height, were ridiculed.

Friends offered assistance. Taylor and Bailey had tried to head off Lockhart's attack. An anonymous defence appeared in the *Morning Chronicle*, and Reynolds published a supportive notice in the *West of England Journal* which Hunt reprinted in *The Examiner*. Keats himself, unwell as he was, and beset by personal difficulties and the imminent tragedy of his brother's death, made courageous efforts to maintain his composure in the face of this public onslaught. To an extent he succeeded. He was shaken and upset, but his literary ambition and self-belief survived the crisis. He wrote to the George Keatses in mid-October, with a calm certainty, 'I think I shall be among the English Poets after my death' (*Letters of John Keats*, 1.394). He was soon planning a new volume of poems with Taylor and Hessey, to include *Hyperion* as its corner-stone.

In the last week of September Keats was again confined to the house with a sore throat. Tom was weakening daily. Keats nursed him intensively, but also managed some socializing as October wore on, and continued to write verse. Haslam in particular proved an invaluable friend at this time. By mid-October he was working on *Hyperion*. On 24 October he met Isabella Jones again, and visited her apartment. Money worries continued to dog him. In the midst of all this he continued to write letters with an immense zest for life and intellectual subtlety. The letter to Woodhouse of 27 October concerning the poetical character and Wordsworth's 'egotistical sublime' is a *tour de force*. As Keats's emotional experience darkened, and his talent began its quick ripening into greatness, disenchantment with Hunt became suddenly obvious. With the growing consciousness of his own powers, Hunt's poetic stature was by comparison diminished, and his influence now seemed an embarrassment.

Tom died on 1 December, and was buried in St Stephen, Coleman Street, a week later. Keats, shattered by the trials of the past six months, gratefully accepted Brown's generous invitation to live in Wentworth Place. Regular social life could now begin to resume. On 5 December he attended the prize-fight between Jack Randall and Ned Turner at Crawley Hunt in Sussex. The friendships with Brown and Haslam grew still more intense, and Keats began to move in a wider circle once more. He also managed to see more of his sister Fanny. To most of his friends Keats appeared to possess comfortable independent means. They did not know he was living on money left behind by George, and that he was constantly importuning Abbey for advances. Nevertheless late in December Keats was offering to lend Haydon money. As Christmas approached he could not shake off his sore throat.

Keats was also seeing more of Fanny Brawne [*see* Brawne, Frances (1800–1865)]. He dined with the family on Christmas day, and the couple came to an 'understanding', disapproved of by her mother because of her youth and Keats's uncertain prospects. Many among Keats's friends also disapproved of the relationship. Fanny struck them as superficial, vain, and flirtatious; and, although Keats clearly found her attractive and fascinating, he himself recognized a wilful affectation in her social manner. His doubts about the sincerity of her attachment often shaded into jealousy, and as his health began to fail these uncertainties led to sometimes unbalancing extremes of emotion. But Fanny was without question the great passion of Keats's life. The authenticity of her own feelings for Keats was long obscured after his death by the absence of documentary evidence, and the prejudices of nineteenth-century biography, which associated her influence with Keats's illness and decline.

Immediately after Christmas Keats had to postpone a trip to Chichester because of his sore throat, and was again confined for several days. He was somewhat better in January, which found him writing, and visiting. In spite of further financial worries, Haydon got his loan. Keats had to get £20 from Abbey before he could pay for his visit to Chichester in mid-January. Once there, in the midst of card parties and a visit to the Snooks (Dilke's sister Laetitia and her husband John) at Bedhampton, Keats managed to write most of *The Eve of St Agnes*. This is one of his greatest poems. Its sensuality and rich medievalism, and the tonal subtlety of its brilliantly coloured Spenserians, stand comparison with the finest narrative poems in the language. The poem confirmed Keats's extraordinary development towards artistic maturity in the months following his return from Scotland. But his sore throat had come back. At the beginning of February he returned to Hampstead and joined Brown, who had moved back into Wentworth Place.

Spring 1819: the great odes By 2 February *The Eve of St Agnes* was finished. Keats went out little in the wintry weather. In the middle of the month he attempted a companion piece to *The Eve of St Agnes*, 'The Eve of St Mark', but gave it up unfinished. It was about now, in one of the remarkable long journal-letters that Keats wrote to George and his wife in 1818 and 1819, that he observed how 'A Man's life of any worth is a continual allegory', going on to assert that

'Shakespeare led a life of Allegory; his works are the comments on it' (*Letters of John Keats*, 2.67). His financial worries persisted and deepened. He borrowed from friends, and there were frequent meetings with Abbey between February and April. By March he was going out more, with visits to the theatre and the British Museum. The period from February to May produced many of his finest and most important letters, including the journal-letter to the George Keatses which speaks of the world as a 'Vale of Soul-making': 'Do you not see how necessary a World of Pains and troubles is to school an Intelligence and make it a soul?' (ibid., 2.102). He wrote sonnets, tried to continue with *Hyperion*, read Hazlitt and the Elizabethans, and indulged an indolence which occasionally kept him in bed until 10 in the morning. He spent time coaching his sister Fanny for her confirmation. The relationship with Fanny Brawne moved closer to the centre of his life when on 3 April the Dilkes moved out of their half of Wentworth Place, and the Brawnes moved in. Fanny now lived next door to Keats.

The pace and intensity of Keats's writing increased. The famous walk on Hampstead Heath with Coleridge took place on 11 April. In mid-April he finally abandoned *Hyperion*. Its Miltonic conception was oppressive, and had repeated a pattern in which Keats's poetic career moved forward by imitating the voices of others. But this time the emergence of a new style in the unfinished third book marked a new confidence and artistic daring. The poem broaches abiding themes of human experience by a completely distinctive blend of condensed abstraction with sensuality and strong feeling. There is too an intellectual ambition in *Hyperion*, engaged with questions of growth and maturity, in literary, psychological, and historical terms, which placed Keats on the very threshold of consummated genius.

After the abandonment of *Hyperion*, troubled by financial and personal worries, and by the dark undertones of his failing health, Keats managed a supreme effort of creative energy. There was a flurry of writing in verse, Spenserians, Shakespearian and Petrarchan sonnets, couplets, quatrains, and doggerel. Then, some time in the last week of April, Keats's preoccupations with love, death, and poetry fused to produce the strange enigmatic power of 'La belle dame sans merci'. Before the end of the month, he had written the 'Ode to Psyche'. This difficult poem adapted sonnet rhymes to produce a complicated irregular form. Its themes embrace the great paradoxes of art and life, permanence and mutability, beauty and death. Over a few days Keats further explored the possibilities of the sonnet, expressing his frustration with its limits in 'If by dull rhymes our English must be chained'. At the beginning of May the themes of the 'Ode to Psyche', and the formal experimentation of the preceding weeks, were brought to a beautifully poised focus in the first of the great odes: the 'Ode to a Nightingale'. In Brown's later account, a nightingale had nested near Wentworth Place, and Keats

felt a tranquil and continual joy in her song; and one morning he took his chair from the breakfast-table to the

grass-plot under a plum-tree, where he sat for two or three hours. When he came into the house, I perceived he had some scraps of paper in his hand, and these he was quietly thrusting behind the books. On inquiry, I found those scraps … contained his poetical feeling on the song of our nightingale.   (Rollins, 2.65)

The 'Ode on a Grecian Urn' and the 'Ode on Melancholy' were written probably in immediate succession to the nightingale ode, each in a stanza differently adapted from English sonnet forms, and each offering its own inflection of the individual human encounter with great archetypes of experience. The less successful 'Ode on Indolence' was also written about this time. Towards the end of May Keats was again unwell and obliged to stay at home. Money worries returned yet again. In April he had remarked to George that he 'was not worth a sixpence' (*Letters of John Keats*, 2.93). By the end of the month he was thinking of moving to Teignmouth, or of becoming a ship's surgeon.

Summer and autumn 1819: *Lamia* and the 'Ode to Autumn'   On 8 June Rice called and invited Keats to accompany him to the Isle of Wight. By mid-June Keats was speaking of himself as engaged, and broke. He saw little of the Dilkes from now on, as they openly disapproved of the relationship with Fanny. On 16 June he learned that Mrs Midgley Jennings was filing a bill in chancery against the Keats family, and asked Haydon and others for the return of loans. Haydon's refusal annoyed him. Keats and Rice left on the Portsmouth coach on 27 June in a violent storm. They crossed to the Isle of Wight and settled in Shanklin. He sent love letters to Fanny Brawne, and wrote verse constantly through late June and into the first week of July. Keats was in an irritable state of health, but had completed the first part of *Lamia* by mid-July. Brown joined them in Shanklin, and Keats worked with him on a drama, *Otho*. He also began to revise and rework *Hyperion* as *The Fall of Hyperion*. With Brown's arrival the party fell into a routine of late nights and cards, placing further strain on Keats's health. Rice left towards the end of August, and Keats was left alone for a while in Shanklin while Brown travelled about the island. Keats was now deeply immersed in several major poems simultaneously, and writing with the confident fluency of an artist at the height of his powers. On Brown's return, they decided to visit Winchester, primarily to gather materials for Keats's poetic projects. On 12 August, with *Lamia* half-finished, they left Shanklin, narrowly missing an accident in the crossing from Cowes.

The first four acts of *Otho* were completed by 14 August. Keats now broke off his friendship with Bailey, who after courting Reynolds's sister had married someone else. He wrote to him for the last time on 14 August, expressing his ambition to 'make as great a revolution in modern dramatic writing as Kean has done in acting' (*Letters of John Keats*, 2.139). In fact the psychological tensions and insights of *Lamia* and the complex self-interrogation of *The Fall of Hyperion* suggest an almost novelistic quality in Keats's still emerging powers. *Otho* was finished by 23 August. Keats was desperately short of money. He borrowed from Hessey, and Haslam. Late in August and early in September at Winchester Keats completed *Lamia*, continued with *The Fall of Hyperion*, and revised *The Eve of St Agnes*. Brown left for Chichester about 7 September. Keats was distracted from his writing by a letter from George and hurriedly returned to London by the night coach on 10 September. His visit was brief but busy, with trips to the theatre and meetings with Woodhouse, Hessey, and Abbey. He managed to see his sister on 13 September and on the same day witnessed 'Orator' Henry Hunt's triumphal entry into London. He returned to Winchester two days later. The 'Ode to Autumn' was written in Winchester on about 19 September. This was his last major poem. By 21 September he had given up his revision of *Hyperion* because of its excessive Miltonic inversions; 'English ought to be kept up' (*Letters of John Keats*, 2.167).

Keats was considering a career in journalism. Brown rejoined him in Winchester at the beginning of October from Chichester, where he had illegally married his housekeeper. Keats and Brown returned together to London after a week. Keats saw Fanny Brawne on 10 October for the first time since June. He took lodgings at 25 College Street, Westminster, in order to live cheaply, but also to avoid living next door to Fanny. An obsession with her was beginning to take hold, and the College Street plan collapsed. After only a few days he again visited the Brawnes, spent two days with the Dilkes, left his lodgings and returned to Wentworth Place with Brown by about 21 October. Severn called on him a few days later and found him 'well neither in mind nor in body' (Sharp, 41). It was possibly at this time that he wrote the sonnet 'Bright star! Would I were steadfast as thou art', probably inspired by Fanny Brawne. This was long considered his last poem, because he wrote it out in Severn's copy of Shakespeare on the voyage to Italy in September 1820.

Illness: 1819–1820 November found Keats struggling to borrow money. Haslam once again provided assistance. He got money from Abbey for the first time in ten months. On 5 November Keats missed a lecture in which he was quoted by Hazlitt. He visited friends in London, and dined out regularly. On the 17th he announced in a letter to Taylor his determination 'not to publish any thing I have now ready written'; he hoped to try for a few poems 'at home amongst Men and women', which would 'nerve me up to the writing of a few fine Plays' (*Letters of John Keats*, 2.234). He was reading Holinshed's *Chronicles*, and working on a new play *King Stephen*, perhaps with Kean in mind. This work continued into December, when he also began a Byronic poem entitled 'The Cap and Bells', and apparently attempted one last revision of *Hyperion*. Just before Christmas he learned that *Otho* had been accepted by Drury Lane for the following season. On 22 December he wrote that he had been, and continued, 'rather unwell' (ibid., 2.238). On Christmas day, the anniversary of his first 'understanding' with Fanny, their engagement was formalized. His attempt to 'wean' himself from her in the autumn had failed. From this time Keats's passion for Fanny ran increasingly out of control as his health and hopes fell into terminal collapse.

Keats's brother George arrived from America on 9 January. He believed himself to have been swindled by the American naturalist John James Audubon, and with a young family found himself in serious financial straits. Keats dined with him on his arrival, and embarked on a round of social and business visits which brought the brothers into contact with many old friends. George drew his remaining legacy from Abbey, together with most of the money remaining to Keats in the Abbey fund, as this too was owing to him as a result of the financial arrangements made before his departure for America in June 1818. This left Keats in an extremely difficult financial position. George set off once more for Liverpool on 28 January, after seeing his brother for the last time. On 3 February, a bitterly cold day, Keats returned home to Hampstead late from town, travelling outside on the stagecoach to save money. He was feverish, and Brown realized immediately that he was seriously ill. As Keats retired to bed he coughed slightly, and Brown heard him say:

> 'That is blood from my mouth.' … he was examining a single drop of blood upon the sheet. 'Bring me the candle, Brown; and let me see this blood.' After regarding it steadfastly, he … said,—'I know the colour of that blood;—it is arterial blood;—I cannot be deceived in that colour;—that drop of blood is my death-warrant;—I must die.' (Rollins, 2.73–4)

He suffered a massive haemorrhage later that night.

Keats was confined for the rest of the month. In the middle of February he offered in anguish to break his engagement to Fanny. Barry Cornwall kindly sent books. He tried to proceed with 'The Cap and Bells'. Fanny sent a ring at the end of February, and assured him that she still wished to marry him. By early March he was suffering violent heart palpitations, but his doctor was optimistic about his condition by 8 March, and he was declared out of danger on 10 March. He started to work again, revising *Lamia* for his planned new collection. He dined with Taylor on 14 March. But a week later he had suffered several further attacks of heart palpitation. He did manage to get out late in March and early in April, and attended a private view of Haydon's 'Christ's Entry into Jerusalem' on 25 March. In April he was even planning a visit to Scotland with Brown. Taylor and Hessey received the manuscript of Keats's new volume of poems on 27 April. By the beginning of May he had given up the idea of accompanying Brown to Scotland. Brown had let Wentworth Place for the summer, so Keats took lodgings at 2 Wesleyan Place, Kentish Town, near to Hunt. Brown settled some debts for Keats and lent him money. Keats moved in to his new lodgings on 6 May, and then travelled with Brown on the smack to Gravesend, where they parted for the last time.

In the first half of June Keats was correcting proofs, and was still making social visits. He had a serious attack of blood-spitting on 22 June and was obliged to move into Hunt's house in Mortimer Terrace. He continued to spit blood for several days. It was now obvious to everyone, and above all to Keats himself, with his medical training, that he was gravely ill, with the same 'consumption', or tuberculosis, that had killed his mother, uncle, and brother. During this period, in the last week of June, Taylor and Hessey published Keats's *Lamia, Isabella, The Eve of St Agnes, and other Poems*, including all of the major odes, and *Hyperion*. Keats defiantly identified himself on the titlepage as 'the author of Endymion'. This collection is now recognized as among the most important works of English poetry ever published. Over the following weeks the book was widely noticed, generally in favourable terms. Jeffrey reviewed it enthusiastically together with *Endymion* in the *Edinburgh*, and began to redress the shameful injustices of Keats's earlier critical reception.

Keats's time was now short. Shelley's friend Maria Gisborne saw him at Hunt's early in July 'under sentence of death' (*Maria Gisborne & Edward Williams: their Journals and Letters*, ed. F. Jones, 1951, 40). His doctors had ordered him to Italy. After mid-July he was too ill to write. His jealous passion for Fanny Brawne became a torture of frustrated desire and thwarted hopes. He fell out angrily with Hunt over some supposed slight, and moved out on 12 August to live with the Brawnes in Wentworth Place for the month leading up to his departure for Italy. On this same day he received a generous invitation from Shelley to stay with him in Italy. Keats courteously declined. It was not clear who would accompany him to Italy, or where he would live, and he waited in vain for news on this matter from Brown. Abbey refused Keats money towards the end of August. By 30 August, after another haemorrhage, he lay in a dangerous state. On 11 September he dictated to Fanny Brawne his last letter to his sister, as he was unable to see her to say goodbye. Haslam was ready to go with Keats to Italy, but circumstances made this impossible, and he took on himself instead to arrange for Severn to go. Keats saw Fanny Brawne for the last time on 13 September 1821. He could not bring himself thereafter to write to her, or read her letters. Keats raised cash by assigning his copyrights to Taylor and Hessey, assisted by Haslam and Woodhouse. This was the closest he came to making a will. He boarded the *Mary Crowther* in London docks on 17 September with Severn and sailed to Gravesend, accompanied by the faithful Haslam.

Italy: death Keats and Severn parted with Haslam and sailed from Gravesend on the night of 18 September. They were repeatedly delayed, first by storms, then by calms. On 28 September they landed at Portsmouth and visited the Snooks at Bedhampton. After further false starts the voyage finally began about 2 October. It proved a dreadful ordeal. Keats repeatedly coughed until he spat blood. He sank into a deep depression. Severn was astonished at his survival. They reached Naples on 21 October but were held in quarantine for ten days, Keats's condition constantly deteriorating. In spite of this he forced himself to the appearance of gaiety, summoning up puns for Severn and somehow finding the strength to write to Mrs Brawne. 31 October was Keats's twenty-fifth birthday. Passport formalities were not completed until well into November, and he did not reach Rome until 15 November. They took lodgings on the piazza di Spagna, living on money cashed from his publishers' draft. Keats's last known letter, written to Brown on 30 November, speaks of his 'habitual feeling of my real life having past, and that I am leading a posthumous existence'. It ends 'I can scarcely bid you good bye even in a letter. I always made an awkward bow' (*Letters of John Keats*, 2.359). The final relapse came on 10 December. After much suffering, borne sometimes with great courage and fortitude, and sometimes with a terrible railing against his fate, Keats died at 11 p.m. on 23 February 1821. He was buried three days later in the protestant cemetery in Rome. Severn, who cared for him faithfully to the last, carried out his request that his gravestone be inscribed 'Here lies one whose name was writ in water'.

Posthumous fame News of Keats's death reached London a month later. Dilke took charge of the arrangements with Keats's family, and with Fanny Brawne. His trust in George led to a quarrel with Brown and Haslam, who deplored what they took George's conduct to have been towards Keats. Brown travelled to Italy in 1822, meeting Byron and others and settling there some years later. There were further serious fallings-out between Brown, Taylor, and Reynolds. These quarrels prevented an early biography by anyone who had been close to Keats. His financial affairs continued to present the family with problems which were not resolved until after his sister came of age in 1824. In 1826 Fanny Keats married a man named Llanos who had reputedly talked to Keats three days before his death. They left England for Spain in 1833 and never returned. George's finances recovered and prospered in America and he eventually paid all Keats's debts. He died suddenly in 1841. Fanny Brawne married Louis Lindo in 1833. She was vilified by Keats's circle for her apparent heartlessness, and this judgement was reinforced when the relationship with Keats became publicly known after the love letters were published in 1878. It was not until the publication in 1936 of her correspondence with Fanny Keats that the injustice of this view became clear.

Keats's death was widely attributed at the time to illness brought on as a direct result of the critical attacks on his work in 1818. Byron alluded to this with cruel flippancy in *Don Juan*:

'Tis strange the mind, that very fiery particle
Should let itself be snuffed out by an article.
(canto 2, stanza 60)

Shelley's magnificent elegy for Keats, *Adonais* (1821), gave further currency to this misconception. The first published biographical account was in Leigh Hunt's *Lord Byron and some of his Contemporaries* in 1828. Hunt was warm and sincere in his admiration for Keats, and just in his estimate of the poetry, but misleadingly lent credence to the view that Keats was embarrassed by humble social origins. After a period in which it seemed that Keats might sink into obscurity, his fame was finally secured by Richard Monckton Milnes's *Life, Letters, and Literary Remains of John Keats* in 1848. This drew extensively on the papers and reminiscences of Keats's friends, notably Woodhouse, Brown, Dilke, and Cowden Clarke. Its influence, among the Pre-Raphaelites and others, established Keats as a major poet. His early death, and the obscurity in which he died, nourished a tendency to idealize Keats once his fame was established. The absence of reliable contemporary likenesses supported this tendency. Like his fame, the familiar portraits of Keats are mainly posthumous, many of them deriving from Severn. Those who knew Keats agree that no likeness adequately catches his combination of a dauntless expression with animated features and a large, expressive mouth. Keats was quick to betray emotion. His height, 5 feet and three-quarters of an inch, was short but not unusually so for the age, and his attractive figure was compact and energetic until overtaken by illness. Descriptions of his hair vary, but it appears to have been a rich, curly reddish-brown. Witnesses disagree also about the colour of his eyes, but are at one in recalling the intensity of their gaze. Those who knew him comment repeatedly on his strikingly intense and handsome physical presence, which would cause passers-by to turn and look at him in the street.

Keats's reputation continued to rise throughout the Victorian period. Matthew Arnold in 1880 placed his achievement on a plane with Shakespeare. The tragic circumstances of Keats's early death, and the intense brevity of his poetic career, proved favourite subjects for twentieth-century biographers. His life has been researched and rewritten probably more than that of any other English poet. For many, Keats has epitomized a popular conception of the Romantic poet, yearning for escape from the pain and banality of everyday life into a sensuous dream world of the imagination. This underestimates Keats's intellectual toughness, literary professionalism, and humorous good nature. The generosity of his spirit, the influence of the letters, and the significance of his achievement for readers of poetry, have confirmed his stature as one of the greatest English poets.

KELVIN EVEREST

Sources The letters of John Keats, 1814–1821, ed. H. E. Rollins, 2 vols. (1958) • H. E. Rollins, ed., The Keats circle: letters and papers and more letters and poems of the Keats circle, 2 vols. (1965) • R. Gittings, John Keats (1968) • G. M. Matthews, ed., Keats: the critical heritage (1971) • W. J. Bate, John Keats (1963) • A. Motion, Keats (1997) • R. M. Milnes, Life, letters, and literary remains of John Keats, 2 vols. (1848) • C. Cowden Clarke and M. Cowden Clarke, Recollections of writers (1878) • W. Sharp, ed., Life and letters of Joseph Severn (1892) • L. Hunt, Lord Byron and some of his contemporaries (1828) • L. Hunt, Autobiography, 3 vols. (1850) • A. Ward, John Keats: the making of a poet (1963) • C. Ricks, Keats and embarrassment (1974) • S. Colvin, Keats: his life and poetry, his friends, critics, and after-fame (1920) • J. Barnard, John Keats (1987) • N. Roe, John Keats and the culture of dissent (1997) • E. Cook, ed., John Keats (1990) • The diary of Benjamin Robert Haydon, ed. W. B. Pope, 5 vols. (1960–63) • The complete works of William Hazlitt, ed. P. P. Howe, 21 vols. (1930–34) • T. Chilcott, A publisher and his circle: the life and work of John Taylor, Keats's publisher (1972) • D. Hewlett, Adonais: a life of John Keats, 2nd edn (1949) • G. H. Ford, Keats and the Victorians (1945) • A. Lowell, John Keats, 2 vols. (1925) • J. Wallace, ed., Lives of the great Romantics: Keats (1997) • W. H. Marquess, Lives of the poet: the first century of Keats biography (1985)

Archives BL, poems and papers, Egerton MS 2780 • CAC Cam., papers • Free Library of Philadelphia, papers • Harvard U., Houghton L., letters, literary MSS, and papers • Hunt. L., papers • Keats House, Hampstead, London, letters; notebook kept as a medical student • Morgan L., letters and literary MSS • NL Scot., letters and verses • NYPL, papers • Princeton University Library, papers • Ransom HRC, papers • Yale U., Beinecke L., papers | BL, letters to his sister Fanny, Add. MS 34019 • BL, corresp. with Benjamin Robert Haydon, MS Facs 337 • BL, journal letter to Thomas Keats, Add. MS 45510 • U. Leeds, Brotherton L., letters to C. Cowden Clarke • V&A NAL, letters to his publishers with MS of 'Sonnet on the grasshopper and the cricket'

Likenesses B. R. Haydon, pen and ink sketches, 1816 (for Christ's entry into Jerusalem), NPG; repro. in Pope, ed., Diaries of … Haydon, vol. 2 • B. R. Haydon, plaster cast of life-mask, 1816 (after matrix by Haydon), NPG; copy, Keats House, London • J. Severn, charcoal, 1816, V&A [see illus.] • C. A. Brown, silhouette, 1818, Keats House, London • C. A. Brown, pencil drawing, 1819, NPG • J. Severn, miniature, 1819, NPG • B. R. Haydon, oils, detail, 1820 (for Christ's entry into Jerusalem), Athenaeum of Ohio / Mount St Mary's Seminary of the West, Cincinnati, Ohio • G. Girometti, plaster medallion, 1821, Keats House, London • J. Severn, oils, 1821, NPG • J. Severn, pencil sketch, 1821, Keats–Shelley Memorial House, Rome; copy, Keats House, London • W. Hilton, oils, c.1822 (after miniature by J. Severn), NPG; on loan to Keats House, London • P. MacDowell, plaster bust, 1828, Keats House, London • C. W. Wass, stipple, pubd 1841 (after W. Hilton), BM, NPG • J. Severn, oils, c.1850, Keats House, London • A. Whitney, marble bust, 1873, Keats House, London • C. Smith, c.1880 (after death-mask by Gherardi, 1821), Keats House, London • plaster cast of death mask, priv. coll.; formerly on loan to NPG

Wealth at death effectively penniless; £800 in chancery, unknown to him: Gittings, John Keats; Motion, Keats; Bate, John Keats; R. Gittings, The Keats Inheritance (1964)

Keats, Sir Richard Goodwin

Keats, Sir Richard Goodwin (1757–1834), naval officer, was born at the vicarage at Chalton in Hampshire on 16 January 1757, the elder son of Richard Keats, curate of Chalton, headmaster of the free grammar school, Tiverton, rector of Bideford, and domestic chaplain to the duke of Clarence, and of his wife, Elizabeth. He entered New College School at Oxford in 1766 and was admitted to Winchester College in 1768 but lacked scholastic aptitude and was glad to enter the Royal Navy as a protégé of the earl of Halifax.

Early career Keats joined the Bellona (74 guns) on 25 November 1770 under Captain John Montague, and accompanied him to the Captain (74 guns) in 1771 when Montague was promoted rear-admiral and appointed commander-in-chief of the North American station. There he sent Keats to the sloop Kingfisher, commanded by his son James, who took the youth on with him to the Mercury (20 guns). They participated in several small boat actions, and, after the conquest of Rhode Island in December 1776, Keats returned to Admiral Montague, his flag then in the Romney (50 guns) as commander-in-chief at Newfoundland, which Keats was to govern in the next century. After his return to England he was promoted lieutenant (7 April 1777) into the Ramillies (74 guns) under Captain Robert Digby and was present at Augustus Keppel's inconclusive action with D'Orvilliers off Ushant a year later, the only major engagement in home waters during the American War of Independence. In 1779 he went with Digby to the Prince George (98 guns) where Prince William (later duke of Clarence and then William IV) was a midshipman in his watch for well over two years. Keats and Thomas Foley, another lieutenant who as a captain was also to be of Nelson's brotherhood, saw to the prince's professional education, and, in the words of Rear-Admiral

Sir Thomas Byam Martin, 'but for them his youthful spirits and propensities might not have been checked with such good judgement' (Kennedy, 47). They were present at the relief of Gibraltar in 1780 and 1781, when Keats followed Digby to the *Lion* (64 guns) and was promoted commander (18 June 1782) into the sloop *Rhinoceros*, which had been fitted out as a floating battery for the defence of New York. He went on to command the *Bonetta*, another sloop which took a leading part in taking the French frigate *Aigle* in the Delaware on 15 September 1782. She returned to England in 1785 and paid off. Unemployed, Keats went to live in France for four years; he returned to be made post (24 June 1789) into the *Southampton* (32 guns) at the request of the duke of Clarence who aspired—unrealistically—to foreign service as war approached.

In French and Spanish waters In 1793 Keats was appointed to the *London* (98 guns) in command but the ducal flag failed to materialize and in 1794 she was paid off, Keats going to command the *Galatea* (36 guns) in the frigate squadron led by Sir John Borlase Warren and then by Sir Edward Pellew off the west coast of France. In 1795 he saw the sadly mismanaged landing by French royalists at Quiberon, and off that coast he had the satisfaction of emulating, if on a smaller scale, Lord Hawke's successful disregard of a pilot's advice when on his own initiative he chased the larger French *Andromaque* into the shoals near Arcachon until she struck the ground and her colours on 23 August 1796. His return to home waters in 1797 was marred by his being turned out of his ship when the naval mutiny spread from Portsmouth to Plymouth, where Keats was ill-supported by Warren. He was appointed to the faster *Boadicea* (38 guns) and returned to French waters, firmly putting down an incipient mutiny. Keats's transit of the Brest roads by night, his capture of three large privateers and merchant ships, and his sagacious retreat on discovering Bompart's force (about which he warned Warren in time for him to defeat the threatened invasion of Ireland), were much to his credit. In April 1800 when Earl St Vincent came out to command the Channel Fleet his benevolent detachment of Keats put him in the way of several more prizes, until 22 February 1801 when he was given command of the *Superb* (74 guns) with which his name will always be associated.

In July 1801 Keats's detachment on blockade isolated him from Rear-Admiral Sir James Saumarez's first engagement with the Spaniards. He made up for it a week later when, after heroic repair work at Gibraltar, Saumarez got to sea on 12 July with five of the line, including the *Superb*, and two frigates to pursue a Franco-Spanish squadron twice its size. Following it into the Mediterranean, the admiral lost touch and told Keats to harass the enemy rear. This he instantly did, outsailing the fleet by the minute at over eleven knots until 'I found myself abreast of a Spanish three deck ship which, having been brought with two other ships, in nearly line abreast, I opened my fire upon them' at not more than 300 yards of the unsuspecting *Real Carlos* (112 guns), into which he fired three broadsides before she responded.

This evidently produced a good effect, as well in this ship as the others abreast of her, which soon began firing at each other, and, at times, on the *Superb*. In about a quarter of an hour, I perceived the ship which I was engaging, and which had lost her fore-top-mast, to be on fire; upon which we ceased to molest her, and I proceeded on to the ship next to hand, which proved to be the *San Antonio* of 74 guns … wearing a broad pennant and manned nearly equally by 730 French and Spanish seamen … which after some action struck her colours … I learn that in the confusion of the action the *Hermenegildo*, a first rate ship, mistaking the *Real Carlos* for an enemy, ran on board of her and shared her melancholy fate.   (Keats papers, Som., ARS)

Superb's surgeon thought the explosion of the two Spanish ships 'sublime and appalling'; Saumarez, who had seen *L'Orient* go up in Abu Qir Bay, said 'so awful a scene I have never yet witnessed' (Kennedy, 255). It may have been only an incident in the long French wars but it is still a memorable event and probably the best-known in Keats's career. Saumarez was made KB: for far less effort and gain Sir John Duckworth was at the same time similarly honoured, with General Trigge, for snapping up with no casualties the Danish and Swedish islands in the Caribbean. Keats received the thanks of parliament and saw his first lieutenant promoted. He remained in the Mediterranean under Sir Richard Hussey Bickerton through the brief peace, and was blockading Toulon when Nelson arrived to take the command in July 1803.

With Nelson—but not at Trafalgar Nelson was quick to perceive Keats's merits. Given fourteen days sick leave, he returned, still unwell, after nine rather than deprive the squadron of his ship. In October Nelson told the duke of Clarence that his mentor was 'a most valuable officer and does honour to your friendship. Every day increases my esteem for him as an officer and as a man' (16 Oct 1803, *Dispatches and Letters*, 5.248); in December he was described as 'a treasure to the service' (7 Dec 1803, ibid., 5.302). Nelson's mercurial temperament was such that he often exaggerated his expressions of praise or blame; his regard for Keats was constant and considerable. In January 1804 Keats achieved what Nelson saw as the complete diplomatic defeat of the dey of Algiers over the British consul. Nelson wrote to express his 'full and entire approbation' of his conduct (19 Jan 1804, ibid., 5.380), and told Lord Hobart that there had been 'nothing but rage and violence on the part of the dey and firmness on the part of Captain Keats, the stamp of whose character, if it was not so well known by his actions, is correctly marked by his sensible, clear letters' (20 Jan 1804, ibid., 5.381).

But in 1805 came professional dismay. Renowned for her sailing qualities—she had romped away from the flag off Algeciras—the *Superb* was now foul and needed careening; she had become Nelson's slowest ship, and the West Indian dash in March 1805 after the fruitless search up the Mediterranean made her captain apprehensive of being left behind. Nelson reassured him that he should 'have neighbour's fare in everything', and expressed his concern 'that you may think that the *Superb* does not go as fast as I could wish … I desire that you will not fret upon the occasion' (Nelson to Keats, 8 and 19 May 1805, *Dispatches and Letters*, 6.429, 442). Keats kept his studding sails perpetually set, sailing on when the squadron paused; there is no evidence that his ship hindered any of Nelson's intentions. She and her captain were remembered a century later in Sir Henry Newbolt's *The Old Superb*, set to music by Sir Charles Stanford. When the squadron returned to Plymouth, *Victory* and *Superb* pressed on to Portsmouth, Keats dining with Nelson, and discussing sympathetically Sir Robert Calder's action. Since joining the *Superb* (19 March 1801) and putting her into dockyard hands (22 August 1805), Keats had spent only one night out of her, and that because of the dey of Algiers, in those four years and five months. He met his admiral once more at Merton; it was to Keats that Nelson propounded his Trafalgar tactics, intended to bring about 'a pell mell battle which is what I want' (C. Oman, *Nelson*, 1951, 589).

But Keats was to miss Trafalgar, and it rankled. Having recommissioned *Superb*, he was detained at Plymouth while the Admiralty decided in which ship Sir John Duckworth should hoist his flag as third in command to Nelson. Lord Barham and his board procrastinated, Duckworth seemed keener to wait for his band—an Italian quartet—and for some of his old protégés, than to get to sea. All this was anathema to Keats, whose diary suggests a belief that he was simply giving Duckworth passage to his new command where a flagship awaited him, and who found that it was no longer Nelson to whom they reported on 15 November off Cadiz, which they blockaded for two weeks. There followed another Atlantic dash, the second within a year for Keats, when Duckworth lifted the blockade in pursuit of a French squadron with which he failed to deal, though Keats's opinion of that abandoned chase on Christmas eve is a corrective to William James's early nineteenth-century account. Yet again the diary conveys a note of resignation—Duckworth's flag 'being still in the Superb'—until the victory off San Domingo lightened the tone. But admiral and flag captain were temperamentally so much at loggerheads that they seldom spoke, occasionally even communicating in writing, though this did not prevent them from winning a neat little victory which, after Richard Strachan's action on 4 November 1805, virtually ended the power of the French battle fleet. Duckworth went into action making the seldom quoted signal 'This is glorious'; Keats silently hung a portrait of Nelson on the mizzen stay. Each received the appropriate gold medal. They rejoined the fleet in Cawsand Bay (13 May) when Duckworth went on compassionate leave. Keats, glad to be commanding a private ship once more, pleased to find himself a colonel in the Royal Marines and grateful for further parliamentary thanks, a 100-guinea sword from the patriotic fund, and a tribute from Duckworth for his 'firm and manly support' on 6 February, rejoined St Vincent and was sent to watch Rochefort as a commodore with a captain under him. Tucker was told that Keats rose in the estimation of the earl upon every report that he received on or from him, and that a baronetcy seemed appropriate; Keats was apparently consulted, but nothing came of the notion, although St Vincent rated him 'the most promising Officer on this side

the Atlantic [*sic*] … who must soon be at the head of our fleets' and told him that he had 'done everything becoming the character of a great Officer' (*Memoirs of Earl St Vincent*, 316–17, 319).

Expeditions and governorships Keats was relieved in April to command a secret expedition; its cancellation enabled him to take some sick leave from which he was recalled to hoist his pennant in *Ganges* (74 guns) and sent to reinforce Admiral James Gambier in the Baltic. Detached to safeguard the Great Belt, Keats welcomed the advent of the *Superb*, to which he shifted his pennant and in which, promoted rear-admiral on 2 October 1807, he hoisted his flag—an additional compliment from their lordships. He helped escort the Danish fleet to England in November and recuperated until appointed in April 1808 to convoy General Sir John Moore's expeditionary force to Göteborg. Saumarez sent him again to the Great Belt, where again he flew his flag in the old *Superb*. He was instrumental in rescuing the Spanish marqués de La Romana and his force, deployed by Napoleon and then garrisoning Danish territory, and anxious to return to Spain to support the rebellion against French occupation. The masterly evacuation of over 9000 troops and all their artillery and stores brought Keats a well earned KB; he took for his arms the motto on the Spanish commemorative medal—*Mi patria es mi forte*. Lord Mulgrave observed to Saumarez that his second had 'conducted his service with his customary talent, zeal and judgement' (25 May 1808, *Memoirs and Correspondence*, 1.114). Keats remained in the Baltic, assuming the overall command while Saumarez wintered in England and he and a reduced squadron were frozen into Winga Sound for Christmas 1808. In July 1809 he brought home a convoy of more than 400 ships. Within days of this he was off on the abortive campaign to the Scheldt, second in command to Richard Strachan; they were safely back by 8 September and in November the *Superb*, which had been Keats's virtual home for nine years as captain, commodore, and admiral, was taken out of commission. He went on leave to recruit his health and in 1809 was appointed governor of Malta 'which appointment however he soon afterwards resigned' on grounds unknown. He was recalled in July 1810, to hoist his flag in the *Implacable* (74 guns; Captain Cockburn), 'in a manner that could not be declined and that made health a secondary consideration', and to command off Cadiz, under French threat (Keats papers, Som., ARS). He supported several expeditions, including one from Algeciras which occasioned the battle of Barossa (5 March 1811). Having been advanced to vice-admiral on 1 August, and given the choice of joining the Mediterranean Fleet or remaining in command off Cadiz, he opted to become second in command to Sir Charles Cotton, who had succeeded Lord Collingwood in command of the Mediterranean station. But Keats's health continued to decline and he was invalided home in 1812. In 1813 he succeeded Duckworth as governor and commander-in-chief at Newfoundland, his flag in the *Bellerophon* (74 guns); the Anglo-American War (1812) did not concern him, and there was no activity to justify his recall to European waters. Peace offered no further employment and he hauled down his flag in 1816, having been advanced to GCB on the reconstitution of the Order of the Bath in 1815. He was promoted major-general in the Royal Marines on 17 May 1818, and admiral on 27 May 1825.

Final years and assessment In 1821 Keats was appointed governor of the Royal Naval Hospital, Greenwich, 'an appointment which was the more acceptable and agreeable as it was unsought on his part, but most graciously bestowed by His Majesty at the recommendation of the First Lord [Melville], as a remuneration for his long years of toil and warfare in the defence and support of his country' (Keats papers, Som., ARS). He became a member of the board of longitude until its demise in 1828 and in 1832 *ex officio* a director of the new Royal Sailingmen's Society which maintained a floating hospital in the *Chanticleer* off Millbank for Thames watermen.

Keats had been followed into the service by his nephew William, who entered as a volunteer on 30 September 1805. With his uncle, he missed Trafalgar but was present in the *Superb* at San Domingo and in the Baltic and, as his flag-lieutenant, at Newfoundland. He was promoted captain in 1826 but never employed. Admiral Keats did not marry until 27 June 1820 when, at the age of sixty-three, he wed Mary, eldest daughter of Francis Hurst of Alderwasley in Derbyshire; they had no children. He died, an admiral of the white, on 5 April 1834, his death hastened by the drowning of William's first wife a few weeks after her marriage. Keats was buried with full military honours at the express command of his old pupil, now William IV; the pall was carried by six full admirals in the presence of the full Board of Admiralty. His remains lie in a mausoleum in the grounds of his hospital, only a few miles upstream from Northfleet where his *Superb* had been built. For its chapel William IV commissioned a memorial, by Chantrey, to record their early naval service together, testifying to his 'esteem for the exemplary character of a friend, and his grateful sense of the valuable services rendered to his country by a highly distinguished and gallant officer' (*DNB*). Keats was a short man, stout and rather portly. He was neither taciturn nor loquacious, but urbane, and throve under difficulties. John Laughton's conclusion that Keats's fame rests on 'countless minor excellencies rather than any achievement of transcendental brilliance' is correct, but though he had no Trafalgar those 'who knew him well have no scruple in placing him at the very head of our naval phalanx, having shown himself second to none in gallantry, genius or talent' (*DNB*).

A. B. SAINSBURY

Sources DNB · NMM, Keats papers · Som. ARS, Keats papers · J. Ralfe, *Naval chronology of Great Britain*, 2 (1820), 81 · J. Marshall, *Royal naval biography*, 1 (1823), 342 · J. Ralfe, *The naval biography of Great Britain*, 2 (1828), 487 · *The dispatches and letters of Vice-Admiral Lord Viscount Nelson*, ed. N. H. Nicolas, 7 vols. (1844–6); repr. (1997–8) · W. James, *The naval history of Great Britain, from the declaration of war by France, in February 1793, to the accession of George IV in January 1820*, 5 vols. (1820–24); [4th edn] (1847) · E. P. Brenton, *The naval history of Great Britain, from the year 1783 to 1836*, 2 vols. (1837) · *GM*, 2nd ser., 1 (1834), 653 · L. Kennedy, *Nelson's band of brothers* (1951) · The memoirs of Earl St Vincent (1844) · Memoirs and correspondence of Admiral Lord de Saumarez, ed. J. Ross, 2 vols. (1838)
Archives NMM, letter-book · Som. ARS, corresp. and papers | BL, letters to Lord Nelson, Add. MSS 34919–34934 · BL, corresp. with William Windham, Add. MSS 37878–37879 · NL Scot., letters to Sir Thomas Graham · NMM, letters to Sir Thomas Foley · NMM, letters to Sir Thomas Graham · NMM, letters to Sir Samuel Hood · NMM, letters to Lord Melville · NMM, letters to Charles Yorke
Likenesses Ridley and Blood, stipple, pubd 1808 (after H. Matthews), BM; repro. in W. L. Clowes, *The Royal Navy: a history from earliest times to the present*, 7 vols. (1897–1903), vol. 5, p. 273 · J. Jackson, oils, 1822, NMM · W. Behnes, marble bust, 1831, Royal Collection · F. Chantrey, bust, 1835, Greenwich Palace Chapel · F. Chantrey, relief on memorial, Old Royal Naval College, Greenwich

Keay, John Seymour (1839–1909), politician, born at Bathgate, Linlithgowshire, on 30 March 1839, was the younger of the two sons of John Keay (*d.* 15 July 1841), Church of Scotland minister of Bathgate, and his wife, Agnes Straiton (*d.* 3 June 1864). Educated at Madras College in St Andrews, Keay was apprenticed in 1856 to the Commercial Bank of Scotland and in 1862 went to India to manage branches of the Government Bank of Bengal, which had recently been started to develop the cotton trade between India and England. He next entered the service of Sir Salar Jung, minister of Hyderabad, and had a successful public career. He then opened a private banking and mercantile business at Hyderabad and founded the cotton spinning and weaving mills later known as the Hyderabad (Deccan) Spinning and Weaving Co. Ltd; he remained a director of the company until his death. On 22 October 1878 he married Nina (*d.* 16 Jan 1885), second daughter of William Carne Vivian of Penzance. They had two daughters.

After twenty years in India Keay returned to Britain in 1882. His *Spoiling the Egyptians* (1882) and his articles for *The Echo*, reprinted as *Notes on Egypt* (1883), were a strong attack on the Gladstone government's occupation of Egypt and subsequent record there. He supported Indian demands for representation and was a member of the British committee of the Indian National Congress. In *The Great Imperial Danger: an Impossible War in the Near Future* (1887) he deprecated the fear of war with Russia and discussed with firsthand knowledge the Afghan frontier question. As an advanced Liberal, he unsuccessfully contested West Newington at the general election in 1885, but he won a seat at a by-election for Elginshire on 8 October 1889. He frequently intervened in the debates on the Irish Land Purchase Bill of 1890, about which he published *The Landlord, the Tenant, and the Taxpayer, an Exposure of the Irish Land Purchase Bill* (1890). His tenacious opposition infuriated the Unionist government. He was re-elected at the general election of 1892, but was defeated after a close contest in that of July 1895 and again in the Tamworth division of Warwickshire in January 1906, when he attacked tariff reformers in *The Fraud of the Protection Cry*. He had a country residence at Minchinhampton, Gloucestershire, and was president of the Stroud Liberal Club.

Keay died on 27 June 1909 at his London home, 44 Bassett Road, Kensington, and his remains were cremated at Golders Green crematorium.

CHARLES WELCH, *rev.* H. C. G. MATTHEW

Sources *The Times* (29 June 1909) • *The Times* (24 Aug 1909) • *India* (2 July 1909) • *Thacker's Indian directory* (1910) • *Gloucester Journal* (28 Aug 1909) • *Linlithgowshire Gazette* (2 July 1909) • WWW
Likenesses Spy [L. Ward], chromolithograph caricature, NPG; repro. in *VF* (8 Oct 1892)
Wealth at death £55,485 4s. 4d.: probate, 20 Aug 1909, *CGPLA Eng. & Wales*

Keayne, Robert (1595–1656), merchant, was born in Windsor, Berkshire, the son of John Keayne (*fl.* 1580–1594/5), a butcher. Nothing is known of his parents save his father's name and occupation. He was apprenticed at ten years of age to the London merchant John Heyfield. After eight years working in the Cornhill district he secured admission to the freedom of the Merchant Taylors' Company in 1615. In 1617 he married Anne Mansfield (*b.* 1598), with whom he had four sons, only one of whom, Benjamin, lived to adulthood. Earning the freedom of the city, he became a member of the Honourable Artillery Company of London in 1623.

Some time during the 1620s Keayne became attracted to the puritan movement. He subscribed as an adventurer behind Plymouth Colony. In 1634 he invested in the Massachusetts Bay Company and advised it on procuring armaments. On 17 July 1635 he, Anne, and Benjamin departed on the *Defence* for settlement in Boston. Arriving as a tailor, he soon established himself as a merchant of common goods and investor in land. He operated in the middle of Boston's merchant neighbourhood, building a house near the First Church and the central market. He also became a benefactor of town and church. He contributed money for military defences and for a schoolmaster. He bequeathed substantial sums to the poor fund operated by the First Church, to Harvard College, and to the town for building public meeting-rooms, a market-place, and a water conduit. A close associate of Governor John Winthrop and of the minister John Wilson, Keayne rose to civic prominence. He suggested the formation of the colony's artillery company (a voluntary militia), recruited its first members, became its first captain, and organized its initial operations. He also made substantial donations to the company. The people of Boston rewarded him with frequent election to the offices of selectman and deputy to the general court of the colony from 1639 to 1650.

Yet Keayne had come to Boston with a reputation for ambition; his aggressive business manner brought public censure as much as his success had brought him public prominence. In 1639 he was accused of violating the colony's prohibitions against excessive profit-making. In a much noted case, the occasion for a sermon by John Cotton against market-driven behaviours, he faced the charge that he had sold sixpenny nails for 10d. a pound. Although he successfully defended himself against that accusation, several citizens brought up other instances of his overpricing. The church censured him. The court fined him £200 (a large sum, eventually reduced to £80). In 1642 he suffered an equally humiliating affair. One Widow Sherman accused him of slaughtering her prize sow. Although Keayne was acquitted, the case became the occasion for further denunciations of the merchant as calculating and avaricious.

Keayne died from an illness, at Boston, on 23 March 1656. In his will he issued a self-defence which provides an intimate view of the puritan social conscience. He has accordingly come to symbolize the moral tensions within Massachusetts puritanism. His economic success allowed him to become a patron of the church and the town of Boston, yet his commercial tactics brought him a level of disrepute for which he became more widely, and perhaps unjustly, known.   MARK VALERI

Sources B. Bailyn, 'The *Apologia* of Robert Keayne', *William and Mary Quarterly*, 7 (1950), 568–87 • 'The *Apologia* of Robert Keayne', ed. B. Bailyn, *Publications of the Colonial Society of Massachusetts*, 42 (1964); pubd separately (1965) • O. A. Roberts, *History of the military company of the Massachusetts*, 1 (1895), 12–21 • S. Innes, *Creating the commonwealth: the economic culture of puritan New England* (1995), 160–91
Archives Mass. Hist. Soc., sermon notebooks • Rhode Island Historical Society, Providence, sermon notebook
Wealth at death £2569: Bailyn, '*Apologia* of Robert Keayne' (1950)

PICTURE CREDITS

Jenner, Edward (1749-1823)—© National Portrait Gallery, London

Jenner, Sir William, first baronet (1815-1898)—© National Portrait Gallery, London

Jennings, (Frank) Humphrey Sinkler (1907-1950)—© Lee Miller Archives; collection National Portrait Gallery, London

Jennings, Sir (William) Ivor (1903-1965)—© National Portrait Gallery, London

Jephcott, Sir Harry, first baronet (1891-1978)—© National Portrait Gallery, London

Jephson, Arthur Jermy Mounteney (1858-1908)—© National Portrait Gallery, London

Jerome, Jerome Klapka (1859-1927)—© National Portrait Gallery, London

Jerrold, (William) Blanchard (1826-1884)—© National Portrait Gallery, London

Jerrold, Douglas Francis (1893-1964)—© National Portrait Gallery, London

Jerrold, Douglas William (1803-1857)—© National Portrait Gallery, London

Jervis, John, earl of St Vincent (1735-1823)—© National Maritime Museum, London

Jervois, Sir William Francis Drummond (1821-1897)—© National Portrait Gallery, London

Jesse, Edward (1780-1868)—© National Portrait Gallery, London

Jessel, Sir George (1824-1883)—© National Portrait Gallery, London

Jessey, Henry (1601-1663)—© National Portrait Gallery, London

Jessop, Gilbert Laird (1874-1955)—Cheltenham Art Gallery and Museum

Jeune, Francis (1806-1868)—Ashmolean Museum, Oxford

Jevons, William Stanley (1835-1882)—© National Portrait Gallery, London

Jewel, Jimmy (1909-1995)—© Wolfgang Suschitzky / National Portrait Gallery, London

Jewel, John (1522-1571)—by permission of the President and Scholars, Corpus Christi College, Oxford. Photograph: The Paul Mellon Centre for Studies in British Art

Jewsbury, Maria Jane (1800-1833)—© National Portrait Gallery, London

Jinnah, Mohamed Ali (1876-1948)—Getty Images - Hulton Archive

Joachim, Joseph (1831-1907)—John Beatty; photograph National Portrait Gallery, London

Joad, Cyril Edwin Mitchinson (1891-1953)—© National Portrait Gallery, London

Joel, Solomon Barnato (1865-1931)—© National Portrait Gallery, London

John (1167-1216)—Worcester Cathedral, UK / Bridgeman Art Library

John [of Eltham], earl of Cornwall (1316-1336)—© Dean and Chapter of Westminster

John [of Gaunt], duke of Aquitaine and duke of Lancaster, styled king of Castile and León (1340-1399)—The British Library

John [of Lancaster], duke of Bedford (1389-1435)—The British Library

John of Bridlington [St John of Bridlington] (c.1320-1379)—The British Library

John, Augustus Edwin (1878-1961)—© National Museums and Galleries of Wales

John, Sir Caspar (1903-1984)—© courtesy the Artist's Estate / Bridgeman Art Library; collection Bradford Art Galleries and Museums

John, Griffith (1831-1912)—© National Portrait Gallery, London

John, Gwendolen Mary (1876-1939)—© Estate of Gwen John 2004. All rights reserved, DACS; collection National Portrait Gallery, London

Johns, Claude Hermann Walter (1857-1920)—© National Portrait Gallery, London

Johns, William Earl (1893-1968)—© reserved; collection Science & Society Picture Library; photograph National Portrait Gallery, London

Johnson, Amy (1903-1941)—© Capstack Portrait Archive; collection National Portrait Gallery, London

Johnson, Bryan Stanley William (1933-1973)—© Ian Yeomans; photograph National Portrait Gallery, London

Johnson, Dame Celia Elizabeth (1908-1982)—© John Springer Collection; Corbis

Johnson, Frances (1728-1812)—© Crown copyright in photograph: UK Government Art Collection

Johnson, Hewlett (1874-1966)—© National Portrait Gallery, London

Johnson, Isaac (1754-1835)—private collection, Suffolk Record Office, Bury St Edmunds

Johnson, John (1732-1814)—picture: Chelmsford Museums (photographer: Complete Photographic, Chelmsford)

Johnson, John de Monins (1882-1956)—© Bodleian Library, University of Oxford

Johnson, Joseph (1738-1809)—© National Portrait Gallery, London

Johnson, Kenrick Reginald Hijmans (1914-1941)—photographer unknown / Val Wilmer Collection

Johnson, Maurice (1688-1755)—© National Portrait Gallery, London

Johnson, Pamela Helen Hansford (1912-1981)—© Jorge Lewinski; collection National Portrait Gallery, London

Johnson, Samuel (1690/91-1773)—© Copyright The British Museum

Johnson, Samuel (1696-1772)—© Shelburne Museum, Shelburne, Vermont

Johnson, Samuel (1709-1784)—© National Portrait Gallery, London

Johnson, Thomas Ryder (1872-1963)—courtesy of the National Library of Ireland

Johnston, Sir Alexander (1775-1849)—© National Portrait Gallery, London

Johnston, Sir Archibald, Lord Wariston (bap. 1611, d. 1663)—Scottish National Portrait Gallery

Johnston, Arthur (c.1579-1641)—University of Aberdeen

Johnston, Brian Alexander (1912-1994)—Sten Rosenlund / Rex Features

Johnston, Edward (1872-1944)—© Estate of Arthur Henry Knighton-Hammond / National Portrait Gallery, London

Johnston, Francis (1760/61-1829)—© National Portrait Gallery, London

Johnston, George Lawson, first Baron Luke (1873-1943)—© National Portrait Gallery, London

Johnston, Sir Henry Hamilton (1858-1927)—© National Portrait Gallery, London

Johnston, James (1655-1737)—reproduced by kind permission of the Richmond Borough Art Collection, Orleans House Gallery

Johnston, John Lawson (1839-1900)—© National Portrait Gallery, London

Johnston, (Alexander) Keith, the elder (1804-1871)—The Royal Geographical Society, London

Johnston, (Alexander) Keith, the younger (1844-1879)—© National Portrait Gallery, London

Johnston, Thomas (1881-1965)—Estate of the Artist / Scottish National Portrait Gallery

Johnys, Sir Hugh (b. c.1410, d. in or after 1485)—reproduced by courtesy of H. M. Stutchfield, F.S.A., Hon. Secretary of the Monumental Brass Society

Joll, James Bysse (1918-1994)—© National Portrait Gallery, London

Joly, John (1857-1933)—© The Royal Society

Jones, Arnold Hugh Martin (1904-1970)—© National Portrait Gallery, London

Jones, Arthur Creech (1891-1964)—© National Portrait Gallery, London

Jones, (Lewis) Brian Hopkin (1942-1969)—photograph Jan Olofsson / Redferns

Jones, Claudia Vera (1915-1964)—© reserved; collection Claudia Jones Organisation, London; photograph National Portrait Gallery, London

Jones, (Emily Elizabeth) Constance (1848-1922)—by courtesy of Felix Rosenstiel's Widow & Son Ltd., London, on behalf of the Estate of Sir John Lavery; the Mistress and Fellows, Girton College, Cambridge

Jones, Daniel (1881-1967)—Historical Papers, University of Witwatersrand

Jones, Sir Edward Coley Burne-, first baronet (1833-1898)—© National Portrait Gallery, London

Jones, (Frederick) Elwyn, Baron Elwyn-Jones (1909-1989)—© National Portrait Gallery, London

Jones, (Alfred) Ernest (1879-1958)—courtesy of the British Psychoanalytical Society

Jones, Ernest Charles (1819-1869)—© National Portrait Gallery, London

Jones, Sir Harold Spencer (1890-1960)—© National Portrait Gallery, London

Jones, Inigo (1573-1652)—Devonshire Collection, Chatsworth. By permission of the Duke of Devonshire and the Chatsworth Settlement Trustees

Jones, John (c.1766-1827)—© National Portrait Gallery, London

Jones, John Gale (1769-1838)—© National Portrait Gallery, London

Jones, Sir John Morris- (1864-1929)—by courtesy of the National Library of Wales

Jones, John Paul (1747-1792)—courtesy of U.S. Naval Academy Museum

Jones, John Winter (1805-1881)—© National Portrait Gallery, London

Jones, Kathleen Letitia Lloyd (1898-1978)—private collection

Jones, (William) Kennedy (1865-1921)—© National Portrait Gallery, London

Jones, Leslie Grove (1779-1839)—© National Portrait Gallery, London

Jones, Sir Lewis Tobias (1797-1895)—© National Portrait Gallery, London

Jones, Noble Wimberly (c.1723-1805)—Collection of Telfair Museum of Art, Savannah, Georgia; Gift of the Wormsloe Foundation, 1981

Jones, Owen (1809-1874)—RIBA Library Photographs Collection

Jones, Philip, appointed Lord Jones under the protectorate (1617/18-1674)—private collection; © reserved in the photograph

Jones, Philip Mark (1928-2000)—© National Portrait Gallery, London

Jones, Richard Roberts (1780-1843)—© National Museums and Galleries of Wales

Jones, Thomas (1742-1803)—© National Museums and Galleries of Wales

Jones, Thomas (1870-1955)—© National Museums and Galleries of Wales

Jones, Thomas Gwynn (1871-1949)—private collection

Jones, William (1726-1800)—Ashmolean Museum, Oxford

Jones, Sir William (1746-1794)—The British Library

Jones, William West (1838-1908)—© National Portrait Gallery, London

Jonson, Benjamin (1572-1637)—© National Portrait Gallery, London

Jopling, Louise Jane (1843-1933)—© National Portrait Gallery, London

Jordan, Dorothy (1761-1816)—by courtesy of the Tate Gallery, London

Joseph, Keith Sinjohn, Baron Joseph (1918-1994)—© Nicholas Posner;